CHAMBERS
An imprint of Chambers Harrap Publishers Ltd
7 Hopetoun Crescent, Edinburgh, EH7 4AY

This edition published by Chambers Harrap Publishers Ltd 2005.
Hardback edition published 2004.
Previous edition published 1994.

© Chambers Harrap Publishers Ltd 2005

A CIP catalogue record for this book is available from the British Library.

ISBN 0550 10214 0

Designed and typeset by Chambers Harrap Publishers Ltd, Edinburgh
Printed and bound in Great Britain by Clays Ltd, St Ives plc

Contents

Contributors to this Edition   v

Contributors to the Previous Edition   vi

Introduction   vii

Essay Section:

     The Characters of Charles Dickens   ix

     Literary Sidekicks   xii

     The Characters of William Shakespeare   xiv

     Diarists in Literature   xvii

     The Angry Young Man   xix

     The Ghost in Fiction   xxii

     Serial Offenders – the Detective in Fiction   xxiv

     Literary Drinkers   xxvii

Dictionary of Literary Characters   1–726

Literary Awards   727

Index by Author   731

Contributors to this Edition

Managing Editor
Una McGovern

Compilers
Helen Bleck
Ian Brookes
Don Currie
Gary Dexter
Sheila Ferguson
Una McGovern
Sharon McTeir
Michael Munro
Hazel Norris
Elaine O'Donoghue
Mary O'Neill
Camilla Rockwood
Liam Rodger
Patrick White
Peter Whitebrook

Proofreaders
Helen Bleck
Gary Dexter
Dr Graham Frankland
Michael Munro

Specialist Consultants
Dr Paul Edmondson (Shakespeare)
Susan Shatto (Dickens)

Publishing Manager
Patrick White

Prepress Manager
Sharon McTeir

Prepress Controller
David Reid

The editors would like to acknowledge the contributions made to this book by the following people: Simon Hill, Mark MacKarel, Kate Nicholson, Tom Pinder, David Reid, Melissa Seddon and Anna Stevenson.

The editors would also like to thank the following authors for their comments and suggestions on the entries for their characters: Sebastian Faulks, Philip Pullman, Ian Rankin and Jacqueline Wilson.

Contributors to the Previous Edition

Editor
Rosemary Goring

Contributors
Dr Femi Abodunrin; Dr Colin Affleck; Diane Allison; Maxine Beahan; Jane Bonthron; Dr
Frances Bridger; Alan Campbell; Fran Cannon; Rachel Carroll; Pamela Cleasby; Anne Collett;
Dr Stephen Cramer; Angela Cran; Stuart Delves; Lucy Dolan; Dr I M Donaldson; Amanda
Farquhar; Donald Greig; Aaron Hicklin; Keith Hughes; Allan Hunter; P Jeremy Idle; Bryan
Jonson; Tina Lehmbeck; Cynthia Loudon; Kirstie McAlpine; Heidi Macpherson; Alan
McIntosh; Kenny Mathieson; Brian Morton; Michael Nash; Jim Orton; Alex Paulin; Greig
Proctor; Dr Mario Relich; Susan Rennie; Alexis Roberts; Chris Roberts; Gordon Roberts; Dr
Iain R Scott; Susan Seller; Gillean Somerville-Arjat; Joanna Swanson; Alan Taylor; Alison
Twaddle; Laurence Twaddle; Peter Whitebrook; Michelle Williams; Kristina Woolnough;
Cameron Wylie

Introduction

I believe that all novels ... deal with character, and that it is to express character – not to preach doctrines, sing songs, or celebrate the glories of the British Empire, that the form of the novel, so clumsy, verbose, and undramatic, so rich, elastic, and alive, has been evolved.

Virginia Woolf, 'Mr Bennett and Mrs Brown' 1924.

What is literature without characters? *Pride and Prejudice* without the proud Mr Darcy, *The Lord of the Rings* without the courageous Frodo Baggins, or *Nicholas Nickleby* without the brutal Wackford Squeers? For the reader, their favourite heroes, clowns, lovers, monsters, villains and supporting characters take on an existence far beyond the mere words on the page.

Literary characters are the vessels into which the ideas, aspirations, emotions and neuroses of the author can be poured and to which, through reading, we add our own. They can stand as memorable tokens of human character types, or be used as vehicles for social satire or commentary on the human condition; they can take us, the readers, with them to question our prejudices, reaffirm our beliefs, or simply to be entertained. We can identify with them, aspire to the qualities they embody, or rail against them, as we do with characters in the real world.

When we read, we share in the joy or despair of the author's players as they act out the scenes of their lives. We love with them, hate with them, and feel their fear and elation as the story unfolds. Who didn't shed a tear when Inspector Morse solved his last case, rejoice when Jane Eyre said of Rochester, 'Reader, I married him', or sleep a little more soundly when Count Dracula finally met his end?

Like a lepidopterist, this book pins down these many colourful creations in one accessible collection. In addition it offers eight essays from noted experts on various aspects of the character in literature, and adds at the end a comprehensive index of authors, including brief biographical information on these characters behind the characters.

The Characters of Charles Dickens

by Susan Shatto

Susan Shatto is General Editor of the Dickens Companions series, nine volumes to date (from 1986), and author of The Companion to 'Bleak House' (1986).

The Theatre

Dickens's approach to creating characters was theatrical. His daughter Mamie recalled lying on a sofa 'while my father wrote busily and rapidly at his desk, when he suddenly jumped from his chair and rushed to a mirror which hung near, and in which I could see the reflection of some extraordinary facial contortions which he was making. He returned rapidly to his desk, wrote furiously for a few moments, and then went back to the mirror. The facial pantomime was resumed, and then ... he began talking rapidly in a low voice.'

By delineating appearance, gesture and speech idiom, Dickens could invest his characters with individuality and the kind of vitality that actors have on the stage. While his contemporary novelists confined themselves to constructing characters within the conventions of 19th-century realism, Dickens drew on a range of literary and theatrical traditions: Jonsonian 'humours'; farce; pantomime; and caricatures inspired by those of his masters, Smollett and Fielding. In Dickens's fictional world, larger and more complicated than the worlds of other Victorian novelists, a grotesque like Sarah Gamp can rub shoulders with a Jonsonian 'humour' like Pecksniff and a strictly realistic character like John Westlock. Drawing on all these traditions, Dickens created nearly 1,000 characters. For autobiographical and artistic reasons, certain types of characters reappear throughout his fiction.

Orphans, Unloved Children and Bad Parents

Dickens's own miserable childhood inspired his most recurrent theme: the need of children to be loved. All his life, he blamed his parents for sending him to work, at the age of twelve, at Warren's Blacking Warehouse in London, and making him live alone in lodgings, while his father was imprisoned for debt in the Marshalsea Prison. 'No words can express the secret agony of my soul', he wrote of this time, and yet, 'my father and mother were quite satisfied'.

Again and again, Dickens represented his own feelings in the character of a child, either an orphan or the child of a bad parent, with profound moral sensibility. Oliver Twist, Little Nell (*The Old Curiosity Shop*), Florence Dombey (*Dombey and Son*), David Copperfield, Esther Summerson (*Bleak House*) and Little Dorrit are the most notable examples of children deprived of nurturing and left to fend for themselves. They illustrate, as well, the moral Dickens defined in his Preface to *Oliver Twist*: 'I wished to show, in little Oliver, the principle of Good surviving through every adverse circumstance, and triumphing at last'. Other characters of this type are the resourceful young servants: the Marchioness (*The Old Curiosity Shop*); Susan Nipper (*Dombey and Son*); and Charley Neckett (*Bleak House*).

In contrast to these characters are those whose loveless and traumatic childhoods cause them to become wayward, dissolute or delinquent. Notable examples are Little Nell's brother, Fred Trent; Louisa Gradgrind's brother, Tom (*Hard Times*); Little Dorrit's brother, 'Tip'; and Lizzie Hexam's brother, Charley (*Our Mutual Friend*). Some unloved children grow up to be merely unhappy – like Louisa Gradgrind and Estella (*Great Expectations*) – but others die, such as the two unfortunates, Smike (*Nicholas Nickleby*) and Jo (*Bleak House*). In the deaths of Little Nell (an orphan) and little Paul Dombey (who is motherless), Dickens was playing out his grief over the death of his beloved sister-in-law, Mary Hogarth, aged only 17.

Dickens felt that his own parents had rejected him and that his father was feckless and his mother distant. These are the traits he gives to the parents or foster parents of his numerous unloved child victims. Novels which include bad parents are: *Nicholas Nickleby* (Mrs Nickleby, a portrait of Dickens's mother); *The Old Curiosity Shop* (Little Nell's grandfather); *Barnaby Rudge* (Sir John Chester); *Dombey and Son* (Mr Dombey, Mrs Skewton); *David Copperfield* (Mr Micawber, a portrait of his father, and Mr Murdstone); *Bleak House* (Miss Barbary, Mrs Jellyby, Mrs Pardiggle, Mr Turveydrop); *Hard Times* (Mr and Mrs Gradgrind, Signor Jupe); *Little Dorrit* (William Dorrit, Mrs Clennam); and *Great Expectations* (Mrs Joe Gargery, Miss Havisham).

The Working Class

Socially, the majority of Dickens's characters are working class: actors, apprentices, clerks, landladies, musicians and servants, along with a host of unusual occupations, far outnumber the aristocrats and middle-class professionals. Dickens's own origins were lower middle class, but he was fascinated with humble occupations and with how people contrived to make their livings in an industrial era. He also had a profound belief in the Victorian 'gospel of work'. His interests and convictions are reflected in the scores of working-class characters who, despite their privations, exhibit happiness, generosity, honesty, resilience and innate intelligence.

He repeatedly created cheerful working-class families. The Crummles (*Nicholas Nickleby*), the Cratchits (*A Christmas Carol*), the Toodles (*Dombey and Son*), the Bagnets (*Bleak House*) and the Plornishes (*Little Dorrit*) all radiate kindness, unselfishness and good humour, and frequently at the centre of the family is a strong, capable woman such as Polly Toodle, Mrs Bagnet and Mrs Plornish. Then there are the surrogate parents who, despite having nothing themselves, adopt or befriend otherwise unloved children: these include Captain Cuttle and Solomon Gills (*Dombey and Son*); Clara and Daniel Peggotty (*David Copperfield*); Joe Gargery and Abel Magwitch (*Great Expectations*); and Betty Higden (*Our Mutual Friend*).

Resourcefulness, common sense and liveliness are other attributes Dickens used to characterize his honest working-class folk. The most notable of these are the Sancho Panza types of Sam Weller (*The Pickwick Papers*) and Mark Tapley (*Martin Chuzzlewit*), but 'Young Bailey' (*Martin Chuzzlewit*) and Cavalletto (*Little Dorrit*) share much of Sam and Mark's high spirits and quick-wittedness, even in the face of adversity.

The Grotesque, Satiric, Eccentric and Fantastic

The essence of Dickens's comic and bizarre characters is oddity. His sublime grotesques – Wackford Squeers (*Nicholas Nickleby*), Daniel Quilp (*The Old Curiosity Shop*) and Sarah Gamp (*Martin Chuzzlewit*) – are concoctions of incongruous appearance, ludicrous behaviour and ingeniously idiosyncratic language. Although they may perform a function in the plot, as extravagant distortions their main role is purely to energize and ornament it. Much of the energy of Squeers, Quilp and Gamp derives from their sadism and nastiness; freed by Dickens from the conventions of realism, their origins lie in the evil characters in fairy tales – Dickens's favourite reading as a child.

Many other characters are constructed from a combination of traditions – both realism and fantasy. Those who have something of the grotesque about them include the travelling chiropodist, Miss Mowcher (*David Copperfield*); Jeremiah Flintwinch (*Little Dorrit*) – whose neck is so twisted that he looks like he has hanged himself and been cut down with the rope still attached; Miss Havisham; and the dolls' dressmaker, Jenny Wren (*Our Mutual Friend*). The scenes in *Our Mutual Friend* featuring the one-legged ballad seller, Silas Wegg, and the sentimental taxidermist, Mr Venus – who meet when Wegg makes enquiries about the fate of his amputated limb – illustrate two of Dickens's most fantastic creations.

His cruellest characterizations are the larger-than-life satiric portraits intended to denounce vice and frailty. For example, the sleek, unctuous and hypocritical Seth Pecksniff (*Martin Chuzzlewit*) and the Rev Mr Chadband (*Bleak House*), like the pompous and self-satisfied Uncle Pumblechook (*Great Expectations*) and Mr Podsnap (*Our Mutual Friend*), all have their swollen egotism mercilessly deflated by the narrator.

Dickens uses comedy affectionately to characterize a host of his favourite types and eccentrics, such as Mr Pickwick and his friends; the amateur actors Vincent Crummles (*Nicholas Nickleby*) and Mr Wopsle (*Great Expectations*); the lisping circus owner, Mr Sleary (*Hard Times*); the old sea-dogs, Captain Cuttle and Captain Bunsby (*Dombey and Son*); and a score of elderly spinsters and widows. His greatest comic tool is his genius for verbal inventiveness. The idiosyncratic and extravagant speech traits of characters like Alfred Jingle, Sam Weller, Mrs Nickleby, Sarah Gamp, Mr Micawber, Flora Finching and Mr F's Aunt are verbal fireworks that constantly amaze and surprise.

Villainy, Violence, Passion and Repression

Dickens's aim in carefully constructing the externality of a character was to give the reader outward and visible signs of the inner personality. He could enhance complexity of characterization through an omniscient narrator, for a roving point-of-view can be used to illuminate a character's inner life. His ability to depict the inner recesses of the human heart and mind becomes apparent in the novels from *Dombey and Son* (1846) onwards. The loneliness, love and loss suffered by Florence Dombey and her father are evidence that Dickens had mastered the rendering of powerful emotions through character.

His lifelong interest in the criminal mind and mental abnormality, together with his reading of influential contemporary writings on the unconscious, made Dickens particularly interested in the darker emotions of guilt, fear, violence, passion and repression. His notable villains – Fagin, Monks and Bill Sykes (*Oliver Twist*), Ralph Nickleby, Jonas Chuzzlewit, James Carker (*Dombey and Son*), Rigaud (*Little Dorrit*) and Orlick (*Great Expectations*) – are deliberately characterized as stereotypes from Victorian popular theatre. Through such simplification, Dickens could achieve moral clarity. But at the same time he could dramatize a character's interior life. The terrors suffered by Fagin in the condemned cell and by Jonas Chuzzlewit after he viciously bludgeons to death Montague Tigg are powerful examinations of human psychology and moral degeneracy.

Although the Victorian moral code prevented Dickens from explicitly treating sexuality, he developed a variety of strategies to represent it. A recurrent type of character is the mythic 'Fatal Woman': the fascinating, dark beauty with a sexual energy which manifests itself in passion, violence and sometimes cruelty. His embittered and proud fatal women include Edith Dombey, Lady Dedlock

(*Bleak House*), Louisa Bounderby, Estella (*Great Expectations*), Bella Wilfer (*Our Mutual Friend*) and Helena Landless (*The Mystery of Edwin Drood*). His violent fatal women include criminals and women who have been seduced and abandoned: Alice Marwood (*Dombey and Son*), Rosa Dartle (*David Copperfield*), Mademoiselle Hortense (*Bleak House*), Miss Wade (*Little Dorrit*), Madame Defarge (*A Tale of Two Cities*), Estella (*Great Expectations*) and Estella's mother Molly, an acquitted murderess and the housekeeper held in thrall by Mr Jaggers. The beautiful fatal women in Dickens's last three novels – the petulant and passionate Bella Wilfer, Estella and Helena Landless – share names which sound so much like that of Dickens's mistress during these years, Ellen Lawless Ternan, that it seems likely that Ellen must have inspired not only their names but also something of their characterizations.

Autobiographical Characters

As his correspondence during his relationship with Ellen Ternan reveals, aspects of Dickens himself appear in the depictions of characters in his last two novels, *Our Mutual Friend* and *The Mystery of Edwin Drood*. The schoolmaster, Bradley Headstone, and the clergyman and choirmaster, John Jasper, are both outwardly respectable, but they are secretly obsessed with love and passionate jealousy. Headstone attempts to murder his rival, and there are suggestions that Jasper is the murderer of his rival and nephew, Edwin Drood. In the seduction scenes between Headstone and Lizzie Hexam and Jasper and Rosa Bud, Dickens orchestrates images of tempests, holocausts, evil spirits, struggles between wild beasts or between wild beasts and man, self-inflicted violence and escape from strong prisons to represent the power and terror in the men's repressed sexual impulses. There is little doubt that the characterizations of Headstone and Jasper are heavily informed by the fierce, submerged sensuality of Dickens's own character.

Literary Sidekicks

by Alan Taylor

Alan Taylor is Associate Editor of the Sunday Herald and co-editor with his wife Irene of The Assassin's Cloak: An Anthology of the World's Greatest Diarists and The Secret Annexe: An Anthology of the World's Greatest War Diarists. For the past eight years he has been fifty per cent of the Scottish team on Radio 4's Round Britain Quiz. In a previous existence he was a reference librarian.

Opposites Attract

When Margaret Thatcher said, 'Every prime minister needs a Willie', she was, of course, referring to her senior adviser, William Whitelaw. He was her crutch and her foil, loyal to a fault, candid and honest, always there when she needed him, someone to bounce ideas off and to take advice from. Much the same might be said of Sancho Panza, Don Quixote's faithful servant and sidekick. 'Sancho' is Spanish for 'paunch', which is apt, given Sancho Panza's preoccupation with filling his belly. But first appearances are deceptive and as Cervantes's novel progresses, both we and Don Quixote begin to warm to the rotund squire and, in particular, to his earthy common sense.

In many ways, the two are opposites, yin and yang. Throughout the book, they are rarely apart and their relationship is its core. Together they represent different, but complementary, facets of Spain. Quixote lives in the mind, oblivious to the various humiliations suffered by his country, master of the sprawling, out of control Spanish Empire whose wealth has drained away into foreign hands. Like Spain, he is impoverished, more concerned with his title to nobility than with putting food on the table. He is a melancholy dreamer, the Knight of the Sad Countenance, who becomes more and more lovable the longer the novel goes on. By the end of *Don Quixote* we are not laughing at him. Rather, we admire him. As Vladimir Nabokov wrote: 'He stands for everything that is gentle, forlorn, pure, unselfish and gallant'.

Sancha Panza, meanwhile, is a practical man, a shrewd peasant whose simplicity has forever been exploited and whose poverty has never diminished. Unlike Quixote, however, he does not have an iota of spirituality. His concern is with life's practicalities. He knows a windmill when he sees one. As he says, no one would mistake a windmill for a giant against which a deluded nobleman has no option but to tilt. Only someone such as Quixote, who has 'windmills on the brain', would think otherwise. Like Morecambe and Wise, Don Quixote and Sancho Panza are one of the great comic double acts: neither would be nearly as memorable, or as effective, without the other.

Sidekicks in Literature in English

Although Quixote and Panza are the archetypal literary sidekicks, there are many other examples. Dickens has Sam Weller and Samuel Pickwick, and Mark Tapley and Martin Chuzzlewit, while in James Fenimore Cooper's 'Leatherstocking' series (comprising five novels, including *The Last of the Mohicans*) Natty Bumppo, a white man who goes to live with the Delaware Indians, is befriended by Chingachgook, a Mohican chief. For Natty, the moral code of the Indians is preferable to the selfish exploitation of nature by the white settlers. The relationship between him and Chingachgook is echoed in Daniel Defoe's Robinson Crusoe and Man Friday, and in J M Barrie's Admirable Crichton, a butler who, when he is shipwrecked with his master, Lord Loam, assumes command of the situation. As the philosopher Anthony Quinton has noted, 'The clever servant or *servus dolosus* was standard equipment in the new comedy of the ancient world'.

Holmes and Watson

It was Don Quixote and Sancho Panza who were apparently uppermost in Arthur Conan Doyle's mind when he came to create Sherlock Holmes and Dr John Watson. There were, however, also living models for Holmes and Watson. The former was based on Dr Joseph Bell, a surgeon at the Edinburgh Infirmary, while the latter may owe a lot to Conan Doyle himself. Professor Wallace Robson has observed that 'the Holmes-Watson relationship is a magnificent example of friendship'. Moreover, it is one without any hint of homosexuality. Watson, who unlike Holmes is married, summed it up in *The Adventure of the Creeping Man*, 'I was a whetstone for his mind; I stimulated him; he liked to think aloud in my presence'.

Watson also performs the function of recording Holmes's cases. In that respect, he is Boswell to Holmes's Dr Johnson. Conan Doyle admired Boswell's biography but had some reservations about its subject. 'The book interests me – fascinates me – and yet I wish I could join heartily in that chorus of praise which the kind-hearted old bully has enjoyed ... If Boswell had not lived I wonder how much we should hear now of his old friend?'

Subsequently, Conan Doyle made Watson a romantic who is ruled by his heart, while Holmes is an empiricist who thinks things through methodically. Conan Doyle, implored by his readers to resurrect Holmes after he dumped him over the Reichenbach Falls, came to loathe the detective. However, he never lost his admiration of Dr Watson whose ability to listen never waned. For Holmes, he was the ideal sounding board.

The success of Holmes and Watson encouraged countless writers of detective fiction to imitate their partnership. Indeed, amongst the crime-writing fraternity 'Watson' is shorthand for a sidekick. Examples are legion, from Dashiell Hammett's Sam Spade – whose partner, Miles Archer, is shot dead in the opening pages of *The Maltese Falcon* – to contemporary duos such as Reginald Hill's Dalziel and Pascoe and Colin Dexter's Morse and Lewis. In the 1930s, Dorothy L Sayers gave Lord Peter Wimsey the services of Bunter who allows him to delve into areas beyond his upper-class bailiwick.

That is one function of the sidekick who is often a counterpoint to the boss or master. Like the straight man in a comedy act, they can ask the stupid questions which may lead to the intuitive or inspired deduction. In that regard, they stand in for the reader. They may also divert attention from the detective, allowing him to probe unhindered. Often, they provide a source of comedy by 'innocently' pricking their bosses' arrogance, pomposity or pretension with a well-timed intervention.

Jeeves and Wooster

Jeeves, however, Bertie Wooster's ever faithful, ever punctilious major-domo, would never be so presumptuous. Ostensibly, their relationship is that of master and servant but it is much more complicated than that. Jeeves may play the part of the traditional English butler to perfection but that is just one of the many roles he is called upon to play.

P G Wodehouse featured the odd couple in eight novels and thirty-four short stories, in all of which Jeeves comes to Bertie's rescue in one way or another, whether it involves concocting the perfect cure for a hangover or helping to extricate him from an unfortunate love match. Throughout the guiding principle is chivalric – one cannot be seen to let a chum down. This is a world in which small things matter, in which one ignores details at one's peril. The fate of civilization hangs in the balance if one does not toast a crumpet to perfection or one uses an incorrect form of address.

It can all be summed up in the following incident, which occurs in the middle of one of Bingo Little's matrimonial crises. Jeeves is attending to his master, who is so disturbed by Bingo's dilemma that when Jeeves says, 'The tie a little tighter, Sir, one aims at the perfect butterfly effect', Bertie so forgets himself as to cry out, 'Oh, Jeeves, what do ties matter at a time like this!' Whereupon a shocked Jeeves replies, 'There is no time, Sir, when ties do not matter'.

The Characters of William Shakespeare

by Dr Paul Edmondson

Dr Paul Edmondson is Head of Education at The Shakespeare Birthplace Trust in Stratford-upon-Avon.

'Why aren't they more human? ...'

... Imogen and Posthumus and Cymbeline – I find them beyond me – Is this my feminine weakness in the upper region? But really they might have been cut out with a pair of scissors – as far as mere humanity goes ... Of course, they talk divinely.

Although Virginia Woolf here misunderstands the deliberate fairy-tale elements of *Cymbeline* (she later came to appreciate them) during her rediscovery of the 'great William', the tone of her comments matches the thoughts of the many millions of readers and audience members, theatre practitioners and other creative artists who have sought to convey the immense *humanity* they perceive as present in Shakespeare's plays. For many, Shakespeare's most significant dramatic achievement is the great range of characters (the 'mere humanity') he depicted, including rulers and servants, argumentative lovers and precocious children, scorned women and reflective old men.

As early as 1623, with Leonard Digges's eulogistic verse at the front of the First Folio, people have appreciated Shakespeare's ability to draw striking, yet seemingly naturalistic, dramatic characters. Digges thought that Shakespeare's reputation would never die, or the stage be cleared of the 'Passions of Juliet, and her Romeo, / Or till I hear a scene more nobly take, / Than when thy half-sword parleying Romans spake.' Here Digges's observations go some way in attributing to Shakespeare's genius the ability to body forth memorable characters. Cultural history would go much further, and Virginia Woolf had a great deal of it on her side when she sat down to criticize Shakespeare's characterization in *Cymbeline*.

The Influence of the First Shakespearean Actors

It is possible to identify within the plays fleeting glimpses of the real actors for whom Shakespeare was writing his plays originally: his friends and his colleagues, for he probably knew exactly who would be speaking the parts, and how they would say them. Simply the idea of the theatrical ability of Richard Burbage, who was the first man ever to play Hamlet, King Lear and Othello, forms an impressive contrast to the now monumental cultural icons these roles have become. Clues are sometimes to be found in physical descriptions. For instance, it is possible that the same actor who played Dr Pinch in *The Comedy of Errors* ('a needy, hollow-eyed, sharp-looking wretch') also played Abraham Slender (with 'a little whey face') in *The Merry Wives of Windsor*, Cassius in *Julius Caesar* (with 'a lean and hungry look'), and Sir Andrew Aguecheek in *Twelfth Night* ('as tall a man as any's in Illyria'). In *Hamlet*, Polonius boasts that he once played Julius Caesar at university and was stabbed in the Capitol, just two scenes before being stabbed himself behind the arras. This comparison presumably meant more to Shakespeare's original audiences, for whom the casting of the same actor in both roles would have made a cruel irony even more powerful.

Imagine, too, the boy actor for whom Shakespeare might have written the comic and pathetic roles of Doll Tearsheet (or is it Tear-sheet) in *Henry IV Part 2*, Rosalind in *As You Like It*, and Ophelia in *Hamlet*. He was succeeded in ability, stature and emotional range by a boy with an altogether different emotional range and quality for whom Shakespeare wrote the voluptuous roles of Lady Macbeth (who has terrible nightmares), Cleopatra (whose crown slips just after she dies), and Volumnia in *Coriolanus* (who returns to Rome victoriously after ensuring the death of her beloved son): a fearsome triumvirate who destroy the men they love, but who also represent a creative progression in strength. Only the last of these three does not kill herself. It is worth remembering, then, that the stuff of which Shakespeare's characters are made is grounded to some extent in the personalities of the people who performed the roles first.

The Characters as Real People

The treatment of Shakespeare's characters as separate entities in their own right began early. *The Merry Conceited Humours of Bottom the Weaver* (1661) extracted and developed episodes from *A Midsummer Night's Dream*, and the now well-known frontispiece to a collection of comic pieces called *The Wits* (1662) shows an actor improvising the role of Falstaff standing near the front of a Renaissance-style stage. The appreciation of Shakespeare's characters as though they were real people deepened through the 18th century. William Hogarth's *Falstaff Examining His Recruits* appeared in 1730, and appears to be the first painting depicting characters by Shakespeare. Samuel Johnson's preface to his edition of Shakespeare (1765) did much to make popular the view that Shakespeare's characters are 'the genuine progeny of common humanity.' David Garrick's great Stratford Jubilee of 1769 was followed by a long-running show at the Drury Lane Theatre, which included a procession of characters. Appearing as abstract and brief chronicles of their own time (as actors dressed as Shakespeare's characters *always* do), these figures were no less than a powerful, if somewhat sentimental, expression of Shakespeare's increasing stature as an original dramatic genius – a point of origin, spawning many and varied selves. The imaginative impact of seeing major characters from different plays all at the same time is captured in Caroline Watson's engraving *Garrick Reading the Jubilee Ode* (1780), as well as in the Shakespeare Birthday celebrations held each year in Stratford-upon-Avon.

Maurice Morgann's landmark *Essay on the Dramatic Character of Sir John Falstaff* was published in 1777. Morgann's unlikely defence of Falstaff against the charge of cowardice re-imagines the fat knight's biography and sketches an impressionistic and honourable past for him. Falstaff had by now succeeded in not only dominating our overriding impression of *Henry IV Parts 1 and 2* and *The Merry Wives of Windsor*, but also in becoming a fully-fleshed person in his own right. In subsequent years, the great Romantic writers identified Hamlet as the character most representative of their own world-view. Self-absorbed and reflective, Hamlet, like Falstaff, became a real person through means of the then dominant and innovative cultural understanding: Shakespeare's 'characters are real beings of flesh and blood' (William Hazlitt); 'we love Hamlet even as we love ourselves' (Lord Byron). In 1851–2, Mary Cowden Clarke published the three-volume *Girlhood of Shakespeare's Heroines*, which presents imaginary biographies of 15 female characters, each ending with the first words that she speaks in the play. A C Bradley's influential *Shakespearean Tragedy* (1904) propagated detailed character analysis, and with the appearance of Sigmund Freud's theories of psychoanalysis, around the same time, new fields for character criticism were (re)created. At the end of the 20th century, American critic Harold Bloom's substantial book, *Shakespeare and the Invention of the Human*, reiterates long-familiar positions: the pre-eminence of Falstaff (and then Hamlet) among Shakespeare's altogether human creations.

Exuberant Gossips, both Major and Minor

Moreover, it is in Falstaff that one of the most important of Shakespeare's dramatic interests is perhaps most fully exemplified: inconsequentiality and a delight in exuberance. Shakespeare was consistently interested in gossip, and it is no coincidence that throughout his work there are characters (clowns often) who indulge themselves in verbosity (Polonius and Pandarus); who are comically loquacious (the Nurse in *Romeo and Juliet*, the Archbishop of Canterbury in *Henry V*); who are ready to talk and argue (the Clown or Gravedigger in *Hamlet*, Feste in *Twelfth Night*); and who help establish a background of human concern and discovery in the trivial (the three gentlemen who discuss court affairs in *The Winter's Tale*, and Autolycus who makes his living from fictions). And yet this technique of characterization can easily become a vehicle for subtle pathos. 'I have known thee these twenty-nine years come peascod-time, but an honester and truer-hearted man – well, fare thee well' muses Mistress Quickly as she sees Falstaff departing for the wars in *Henry IV Part 2*. Her broken sentence gestures towards secrets and half-remembered experiences, the associations of which are, perhaps at best, only vaguely intelligible to herself. It is through reflections such as these that Shakespeare crowns the commoner, and makes special the ordinariness of human life.

Minor characters often fulfil an important function. Mercadé in *Love's Labour's Lost* appears only to tell the Princess of France about the death of her father, but by so doing totally changes the dramatic climate and direction of the comedy; the Boy in *Henry V* glances at the barbarity of war with his longing for nothing more than 'a pot of ale and safety'; the drunk prisoner Barnadine in *Measure for Measure*, by simply refusing to die, becomes a central life-force amongst intrigue and austerity; and Crab the dog in *The Two Gentlemen of Verona*, with his master Launce, can come to represent the most honest and loyal relationship in the whole play.

It is impossible finally to identify Shakespeare's own points of views among those of his characters, but it is likely that it exists somewhere between the extremes of the irrational and inconsequential characters, on the one hand, and those who are logical and the rational, on the other. Although, as John Keats observed, Shakespeare seems to take equal delight in creating an Iago as in creating an Imogen, perhaps he does seem to take more delight in those characters who most allow him free rein to explore the irrational and inconsequential. Open any play which contains a high proportion of prose, and gossip and inconsequentiality will leap from the page to provide many examples of the sweat and magic that form the textual tissues of Shakespeare's characters.

The Annihilation of Self

In contrast to his relentless interest in completeness, saturation and totality, runs the equally consistent and parallel threat of an annihilation of self. It is curious that this seems to be most completely realized in *Richard II* which, together with *Henry VI Parts 1 and 3* and *King John*, is written entirely in verse. 'Thus play I in one person many people, / And none contented' reflects Richard just before his death, which leads him towards a meditative self-annihilation:

> But whate'er I be,
> Nor I, nor any man that but man is,
> With nothing shall be pleased till he be eased
> With being nothing.

This tension between being and not being (most concisely expressed by Hamlet's mysterious and world-famous 'To be, or not to be; that is the question') is explored repeatedly by Shakespeare. His enigmatic and haunting poem 'The Phoenix and Turtle' contains the lines:

> So they loved as love in twain
> Had the essence but in one,
> Two distincts, division none.
> Number there in love was slain.

which strive to convey something of indivisible selves. Often, the annihilation of self is related to theatrical imagery. Men and women are 'merely players' (for Jacques in *As You Like It*), life itself is 'but a walking shadow' (for Macbeth), and Coriolanus's sense of self breaks down in a tragic silence beyond the reach even of theatrical words, and he holds his mother by the hand.

The Characters' Lives beyond the Play

The afterlife of Shakespeare's characters is manifest in the works and approaches already mentioned here, but this dimension of his work goes far beyond the reaches of academic and cultural criticism. Shakespeare's characters are forever being reinvented in works of art – paintings, sculpture, music, ballet – to the extent that some of them seem to have achieved almost mythical status: Hamlet, Romeo and Juliet, Macbeth, and Falstaff. Related to their ongoing reputation is each and every theatre performance when an actor, a walking shadow, must irrationally make an audience believe that a particular set of circumstances is taking place for the very first time, among a believable group of people, who are somehow real. And then there are the issues raised by a play's ending. Audiences and readers will both have their own ideas about what might happen to each individual character once the stage has been cleared. Will Demetrius ever be released from the love potion in *A Midsummer Night's Dream*, and, if so, to what effect? Will the Lords of Navarre and the Ladies of France be able to marry in a year's time from the end of *Love's Labour's Lost*? Will Iago in *Othello* really remain silent through the cruel tortures that he is promised?

Three brief examples of how performances have helped to redefine Shakespearean characters will help to illustrate and deepen our understanding of an on-going process. John Barton's 1970 Royal Shakespeare Company (RSC) production of *Measure for Measure* ended with Isabella remaining on stage alone: the first time she had not accepted the Duke Vincentio's implied offer of marriage in close on four hundred years. Greg Doran's 1999 RSC production of *The Winter's Tale* took pains to show that Leontes was suffering from a condition known as morbid jealousy, to try and explain his terrible actions. In 2003 Doran's RSC production of *The Taming of the Shrew* similarly tried to explain Petruchio's treatment of Katharina through his grief for the death of his father.

Hamlet and Ophelia as Tea Companions

To return to Virginia Woolf and her misreading of *Cymbeline*: considerations of Shakespeare's characters have long sought to make them human, and re-forge them in new images, depending on the critic or artist, reader or audience member. Ever suspicious of academics who might try to claim Shakespeare's characters for their own, Woolf later advised readers everywhere to join in the exuberant, imaginative, and for Woolf class-conscious, process of understanding Shakespeare's human creations:

> All you have to do is to read [Shakespeare ...] If you find Hamlet difficult, ask him to tea. He is a highbrow. Ask Ophelia to meet him. She is a lowbrow. Talk to them, as you talk to me, and you will know more about Shakespeare than all the middlebrows in the world can teach you.

Diarists in Literature

by Alan Taylor

*Alan Taylor is Associate Editor of the Sunday Herald and co-editor with his wife Irene of The
Assassin's Cloak: An Anthology of the World's Greatest Diarists and The Secret Annexe: An
Anthology of the World's Greatest War Diarists. For the past eight years he has been fifty per
cent of the Scottish team on Radio 4's Round Britain Quiz. In a previous existence he was
a reference librarian.*

The Most Famous Diarist

Most of what we know about Elizabeth Pepys is contained in the diary of her husband, Samuel.
Throughout their often tempestuous marriage, he lusted after other women and had several affairs.
For her part, Elizabeth could be flighty, flirtatious, verbally abusive and physically violent. By his own
account, Samuel gave as good as he got. As Claire Tomalin, Pepys's biographer, notes, 'He was capable
of blacking her eye, or twisting or pulling her nose, thoroughly nasty behaviour though casual
violence, like a boy's angry lashing out, rather than calculated brutality.' For all that, Elizabeth and
Samuel were very much in love and when she died in 1669, at the age of 29, he was bereft.
Coincidentally, it was the same year he stopped writing his diary. He was to live another 34 years
without remarrying.

The Most Famous Diarist's Wife

Elizabeth knew Samuel kept a diary but did she keep one herself? Dale Spender, the feminist writer,
suggests she did. By Spender's account, published as *The Diary of Elizabeth Pepys* in 1991, Elizabeth
began keeping a diary on 13 October 1655, and did so until her death. However, the published version
concludes on 24 April 1661, constituting 'one third of the manuscript which has been recovered'.
Apparently, the manuscript was discovered in a house in Clapham, south London, where Pepys's
nephew and heir lived after the diarist passed away. According to Spender, Elizabeth did not write in
code, unlike her husband. Moreover, her writing was legible and decipherable. In an effort to give
credibility to her conceit, Spender supplies a scholarly introduction, a glossary and an index.

Elizabeth's diary, as it were ghosted by Spender, offers a stark and vivid portrayal of the life of women
in the 17th century, from the difficulties of dealing with a plague of pigeons – 'They did bat against
the walls and make most fearful sight which did have me quake' – to the 'unpleasantness of coupling'
with her husband. One of Elizabeth's most regular complaints concerns the emptying of chamber
pots, a noxious chore. 'Samuel filled a lot of them', explains Spender deadpan. 'Because they had
always been emptied for him – at home, in lodgings, at Cambridge – he wasn't aware of how often
they had to be cleaned and how awful the work could be. He simply expected chamber pots to be
washed without thinking much about the reality – that it was Elizabeth who would have to provide
the service. And she found this exceedingly galling.'

Spender's version of Elizabeth's diary is a skilful exercise in feminist revisionism, which may be read
as historical commentary to Samuel's real diary. It is the equivalent of a well-researched historical
novel, based on fact but also creative. Is this what Elizabeth Pepys was really like? Perhaps.

Those Who Did and Those Who Did Not

Interestingly, Spender's attempt to fill a gap is very rare. Though a huge number of prominent
historical figures kept diaries, many more did not. Thus we have Dorothy Wordsworth's diary but
not her brother William's. We know about James Boswell's bawdy life but how did his long-suffering
wife, Margaret, cope with his debauchery? Goebbels's diary, a copy of which was found buried in
woodland outside Berlin, survives but not Hitler's. Did he keep one? It would appear not, though in
1983 the *Sunday Times* published extracts from a diary said to have been written by the Nazi leader.
Alas, in its rush to print, the paper did not allow enough time to authenticate the documents which
were soon proved to be a crude forgery.

Diary Fashions

Diary-keeping came into vogue in the 19th century with the publication of the 17th-century diaries of
John Evelyn and Samuel Pepys. The latter's diary was a particular success and encouraged many
people to maintain a diary, from the Goncourt brothers in France (after whom the Prix Goncourt is
named) to Francis Kilvert, a rural curate who wanted to record just how 'curious and wonderful' a
thing life is.

The First Fictional Diarists

Towards the end of the 19th century came the first fictional diary of note, *The Diary of a Nobody*,
published by George and Weedon Grossmith in 1892. Their diarist was Charles Pooter of The
Laurels, Brickfield Terrace, Holloway. Pooter, whose diary covers 15 months in the early 1890s, lives

with his wife Carrie and their son. The bane of his life is his friend Lupin, though he is one among many who conspire to make Pooter's life a misery. He is a man easily slighted and suffers many minor humiliations, the overall effect of which is hilariously painful. The popularity of *The Diary of a Nobody* was immense, leading Hilaire Belloc to judge it 'one of the immortal achievements of our time'. 'Pooter' subsequently entered the lexicon. *The Chambers Dictionary* defines him as 'a petit bourgeois, conventional and unimaginative.'

The Diary of a Nobody offered a winning formula that has been followed on many occasions, both by real and fictional diarists. Into the former category fall diarists such as Alan Clark, the late Conservative Member of Parliament, whose indiscreet diaries offered much titillation in the 1990s; Chips Channon, an American socialite who was a fly-on-the-wall during the abdication crisis in the 1930s; and James Lees-Milne who, in diaries which span the second half of the 20th century, made a virtue of his inability to conceal his true feelings.

Further Fictions

Their fictional equivalents include E M Delafield's *Diary of a Provincial Lady*, Christopher Matthew's *Diary of a Somebody*, *The Secret Diary of Adrian Mole, Aged 13¾* by Sue Townsend and Helen Fielding's *Bridget Jones's Diary*. Delafield was the pen-name of Edmée Dashwood (1890–1943), a novelist, journalist and stalwart of the Women's Institute. The eponymous Provincial Lady copes with errant cooks, records her disappointment at the Book of the Month Club choice, and watches her husband, Robert, fall asleep over the *Sunday Pictorial*. Christopher Matthew drags Pooter into the 20th century in a diary featuring Simon Crisp, a young and eager marketing executive from a minor public school who, in his desperation to live the high life in London, ends up looking after a friend's budgerigar. Taking his lead from Bertrand Russell – 'The aristocratic rebel, since he has enough to eat, must have other causes of discontent' – Sue Townsend's Adrian Mole details with excruciating accuracy the travails of a teenager at the tail end of the last century. His Beatrice is called Pandora. Meanwhile, Bridget Jones's diaries document the life of a thirtysomething singleton in the 1990s. Her fear of being left on the shelf is manifest in her compulsive counting of calories consumed, units of alcohol imbibed and cigarettes smoked. The object of her desire is Mark Darcy. 'Would like to be like Tina Brown', she writes, 'though not, obviously, quite so hardworking'.

Modern Developments

On a more serious note, several modern novelists have adapted the diary form to their own ends. In 1937, George Bernanos, a French writer, published *The Diary of a Country Priest*, an account of a poor, weak, sick and disillusioned Catholic priest doing his daily duty in a hateful parish. In 1983 came *The Diary of a Good Neighbour*, which Doris Lessing offered to her usual publishers under the pseudonym Jane Somers only to have it rejected. It was reissued with its sequel, *If the Old Could*, under the title *The Diaries of Jane Somers*. The central character is the editor of a successful women's magazine. Carol Shields's *The Stone Diaries* is the fictionalized autobiography of Daisy Goodwill Flett – in the words of her memorial service, 'wife, mother, citizen of our century'. The diaries of 'Day's Eye' bear witness to the extraordinary lives of seemingly ordinary women. Most recently (2003), *A Box of Matches* by Nicholson Baker, a master miniaturist, unfolds day by uneventful day, the first event of which is the ritual lighting of the fire. There are 33 short chapters, one for each match in the box.

The Angry Young Man

by Peter Whitebrook

Peter Whitebrook was a drama critic and arts features writer for The Scotsman for many years. He has written and presented radio arts documentaries and is the biographer of the writer, critic and traveller William Archer. He was a consultant and a contributor to the Channel 4 Television documentary, John Osborne: Angry Man.

The First Angry Young Man

When, on 8 May 1956, *Look Back in Anger* opened at the unprepossessing Royal Court Theatre in London's Sloane Square, few people had heard of its author, a 26-year-old former repertory actor named John Osborne. Yet within days, London journalists were writing about him, and during the succeeding months almost everyone who went to the theatre, read newspapers or watched the bright new medium of television knew about the 'angry play' by the 'angry young author'. They also knew that Osborne and Jimmy Porter, his raging, self-pitying protagonist, were the pivotal figures of a new cultural trend upon which journalists, as journalists tend to do, had conferred a title. John Osborne was an Angry Young Man and Jimmy Porter was Anger's first spokesman in the theatre.

Exasperating and provocative, *Look Back in Anger* was startlingly different from any other play in London at that time. Jimmy and Alison Porter's dingy provincial attic flat with its gas meter, sink and ironing board, shabby table and fraying armchairs presented a stark contrast to the plumply-upholstered upper-middle-class Home Counties drawing rooms familiar from the plays of Noël Coward and Terence Rattigan. Neither had Coward nor Rattigan ever written so savage an account of marital discord or created a character whose passion burned with such vivid and sustained vitriol.

A lower-middle-class, 25-year-old graduate from a new university, Jimmy Porter has emerged into a Britain he derides as slumbering in post-war docility. Political and cultural power has shifted to the USA and, proclaiming that 'there aren't any good, brave causes left', Jimmy is left blistering with resentment. Between running a market stall selling sweets and distractedly improvising blues riffs on his trumpet, he unleashes venomous tirades 'against public apathy, *News of the World* morality, bishops who praise H-Bombs, English Sundays, J B Priestley, the entire English middle class and its prejudices, American evangelists, homosexuals, church bells and anything remotely posh or phoney.' His principal target, however, is Alison, his wife, the passive, upper-middle-class daughter of a retired government official, whom he attempts to goad into an anger as fervent as his own.

Origins

Although *Look Back in Anger* was thoroughly contemporary, the disenchanted young man was hardly an original figure, either in the theatre or elsewhere. Familiar as the melancholic of Jacobean drama, he had already appeared during the 20th century as the nihilistic Nicky Lancaster in Noël Coward's *The Vortex* (1924), while his post-war equivalent had materialized in the form of Freddie Page, the disaffected former fighter pilot in Terence Rattigan's *The Deep Blue Sea* (1952). But what was different about Jimmy Porter was that unlike the Jacobean melancholic, he stood centre stage and, unlike Freddie Page, revelled in his rage, which was both the driving force and, it seemed, the entire point of the play.

Jimmy Porter ignited fierce critical controversy. Some denounced him as a 'boorish oaf', 'an egomaniac', 'a spoilt neurotic bore who badly needed the attention of an analyst'. But he is 'like thousands of young Londoners today', countered the *Daily Express*, 'intense, angry, feverish, undisciplined'. The *New Statesman* agreed: 'If you are young, *Look Back in Anger* will speak for you'. Kenneth Tynan, the *Observer*'s flamboyant, campaigning drama critic, claimed that Jimmy Porter spoke on behalf of the '6,733,000 people' between the ages of 20 and 30 in Britain. And so began a summer of speculation as journalists, especially in the popular broadsheets, the *Daily Express* and the *Daily Mail*, debated what it was exactly that Jimmy Porter, and by extension John Osborne, were angry about.

Beginnings

The earliest whiff of post-war disquiet had been detected in *Hurry On Down* (1953), a first novel by John Wain, in which lower-middle-class Charles Lumley deliberately sidesteps the conventional graduate destiny of the civil service, BBC, journalism or academia to bury himself in provincial anonymity and become, by turn, a window cleaner, export delivery driver, hospital orderly, chauffeur, nightclub bouncer and finally comedy gag writer.

Three months later, along came *Lucky Jim*, Kingsley Amis's first novel, a farcical romance about Jim Dixon, an ineffectual history lecturer at a provincial university. Dixon attempts to rid himself of the neurotic Margaret while detaching the beautiful Christine from the dreadful Bertrand (the son of

Professor Welch, his madrigal-loving head of department) and simultaneously hang on to his job.

'A new hero has risen among us', pronounced the *New Statesman*. 'Is he the intellectual tough or the tough intellectual? ... He is at odds with his conventional university education ... he has seen through the university racket as he sees through all the others. A racket is phoneyness organized, and in contact with phoneyness he turns red, just as a litmus paper does in contact with an acid.'

In the theatre, however, the Angry Young Man had been noticably absent until the advent of *Look Back in Anger*.

A New Hero

Alert to the bitterness, confusion and sense of displacement felt by many of the immediate post-war generation, Wain, Amis and Osborne were chronicling a new kind of hero, one who recognized that during the decade since Britain had emerged victorious from World War II, the country had changed dramatically. The hopes invested in Clement Attlee's Labour government, which was swept into power in 1945, had failed to survive the crippling economic crisis and bitingly cold winter of 1947. Far-reaching social reforms had been offset by austerity measures and rationing, their severity in some cases exceeding those imposed during the war. In 1951, Labour had been ousted in favour of Churchill's Conservatives. Two years later, the dawning of a second Elizabethan Age, symbolized by the televised coronation of a new Queen, had coincided with a flurry of national achievements, including a British-led expedition conquering Everest and the English cricket team defeating Australia to win the Ashes. But by the end of 1956, the political and military humiliation of Suez and Britain's failure to intervene during the Soviet suppression of Hungary had all but annihilated the country's conception of itself as an influential world power. At the same time, highly educated young people were becoming increasingly vocal and increasingly critical. Jimmy Porter, reported the *Daily Mail*, represented a generation that had 'little belief in the church, in traditional moral values ... ' Jimmy Porter's 'is the genuine modern accent' confirmed the *New Statesman*, 'witty, relentless, pitiless ...'

Antecedents and Descendants

The Angry Young Man's closest literary antecedents were the impecunious Gordon Comstock, the forlorn bookshop assistant in George Orwell's *Keep the Aspidistra Flying* (1936) and John Kemp, the isolated northern scholarship boy in Philip Larkin's *Jill* (1946). He (and it was always a he) was more likely to be found in the provinces than in London, have a university education and, having rejected the moral code of his parents, live by one of his own devising. He drank beer rather than wine, liked jazz, dressed scruffily, did not own a car but possibly possessed a bicycle. A traditionalist who despised traditions, he valued high culture but detested those who made an affectation of doing so; he was a patriot who distrusted and even loathed the country's custodians and was intensely suspicious of 'abroad', especially of France, which was then culturally fashionable.

Meanwhile, commentators searched feverishly for further candidates to swell the ranks of Angry Young Men, the only qualifications being youth and the publication of a book or the production of a play. Seemingly on cue, Colin Wilson's first book, *The Outsider*, appeared on 28 May 1956, three weeks after the opening of *Look Back in Anger*.

As *The Outsider* was a quasi-philosophical treatise suggesting that the solution to the contemporary existentialist limbo of boredom, nausea and absurdity lay in Nietzschean transcendance, Wilson had no fictional protagonist to offer. Instead, journalists siezed upon Wilson himself, who looked like the popular conception of a young intellectual. He also had a satisfyingly bohemian history of various dishwashing jobs, and of sleeping under the stars on Hampstead Heath in order to save money while spending his days working on his book in the British Museum Reading Room. The result set critics rocking on their heels in astonishment.

'Extraordinary', gasped *The Sunday Times*; a 'luminous study of a representative theme of our time', cried the *Observer*. But who, journalists wanted to know, was Colin Wilson? He was described by some as a genius and was photographed hunched over a primus stove in his dilapidated Notting Hill flat: 'a classic rebel in a classic setting'.

Conservative Radicalism

But to cast the Angry Young Men, both creators and their creations, as rebellious, as some did, is an exaggeration and to see them as left-wing, as some did, is entirely erroneous. Anger was instinctive and sentimental and sprang from a sense of disenfranchisement that in Osborne's case was deeply felt, but if it was radical, then it was a conservative radicalism, perhaps not immediately apparent at the time but certainly so with hindsight. Neither Charles Lumley nor Jim Dixon want to change society, while Jimmy Porter harks back to the certainties of an Edwardian age represented by Colonel Redfern, Alison's father, the only onstage figure with whom he has no quarrel.

In 1957, a rather different Angry anti-hero appeared in John Braine's *Room at the Top*, a novel set largely in the fictional Yorkshire town of Warley during the early 1950s. Joe Lampton, a 25-year-old accountant, realizes he presents a dull figure in his 'light grey suit ... plain grey tie, plain grey socks and brown shoes', a 'badly wrinkled' trench coat and a hat 'discoloured with hair-oil'. Working class and overtly right-wing, he has no time for socialism; instead, convinced there is room at the top, he is determined to get there and clap his hands upon his share of material and sexual goodies. 'I wanted an

Aston Martin, I wanted a three-guinea linen shirt, I wanted a girl with a Riviera suntan – these were my rights, I felt, a signed and sealed legacy'.

Politics and Beer

Like other Angry fiction, *Room at the Top* portrays a young man in pursuit of a woman apparently socially beyond him. Yet Joe Lampton believes that his working-class disadvantages will be overcome simply by the acquisition of money. Susan Brown might not be sophisticated, but her father is a prominent and wealthy local industrialist and, moreover, a leading member of the Conservative Club. Having therefore ensured that Susan 'qualified for the grade financially as well as sexually', Joe sets her squarely in his sights. 'Joe will set a new fashion in heroes', declared the *Daily Express*, 'brash, innocent, cynical – wide and wide-eyed'.

If Joe Lampton has no time for a Labour government, then Arthur Seaton, the Midlands factory worker anti-hero of Alan Sillitoe's *Saturday Night and Sunday Morning* (1958), despises not only governments of all shades but authority in all its forms, which he believes is designed to suppress both him and those like him.

Sillitoe's evocations of grim housing, polluted canals and bleakly industrial townscapes give *Saturday Night and Sunday Morning* a documentary veracity. Like Jimmy Porter and Joe Lampton before him, Arthur Seaton is not particularly admirable or likeable. Opportunistic and amoral, his ethics are questionable, his outlook limited and his behaviour grotesque. Whereas *Lucky Jim* culminates in Jim's public drunkenness, *Saturday Night and Sunday Morning* opens as Arthur Seaton, with 'eleven pints of beer and seven small gins playing hide-and-seek in his stomach', crashes from the top to the bottom of the stairs at the White Horse pub. For Jim Dixon, drunkenness is a mortifying embarrassment, but for Arthur Seaton it is a weekly occurrence and not in the least shameful. Saturday night is 'the best and bingiest glad-time,' when 'the effect of a week's monotonous graft in the factory was swilled out of your system in a burst of goodwill' that might end either in a fight or in bed with someone else's wife, the one probably as satisfying as the other.

Yet despite his ostentatious parading of ill-informed prejudice as homespun wisdom and a buccaneering moral hypocrisy that allows him to bed a man's wife while cultivating a friendship with him, Arthur is not entirely without a roguish charm. He has a swaggering vigour that Lumley and Dixon lack and none of the rancour of Jimmy Porter. Unlike Joe Lampton, Seaton craves neither a life at the top, nor a sports car. Instead, his ambitions are confined to 'plenty of work, plenty of booze and a piece of skirt every month until I'm ninety', although only the second seems a reasonably safe bet.

Anger Fades

But the Angry Young Men were running out of bile. Theirs was never a coherent movement but mostly a journalistic invention. And yet Anger was an identifiable entity, symptomatic of the frustration of a generation coming of age at a time at which they expected both to contribute and receive much, but discovering instead that socially and politically, Britain and its executive of politics, the BBC, the law, the Church and journalism remained locked in the Establishment past.

As a literary form, Anger proved short-lived and its influence is debatable. Having pushed the door ajar for the anti-Establishment 1960s, the Angry Young Men found it increasingly difficult to be heard. Arguably, Anger's importance is not so much in what it was, whatever it was, than as a transition between the kinds of character presented in fiction and theatre before the war, and those that came later. Plays such as Arnold Wesker's *Chicken Soup with Barley* (1957) and novels such as David Storey's *This Sporting Life* (1960) began developing a seam of social realism that broadened during the 1960s to encompass women's voices: the rejected and disillusioned Jane Graham in Lynne Reid Banks's *The L-Shaped Room* (1960), for example, and the cautious, academically-distinguished Sarah Bennett in Margaret Drabble's *A Summer Bird-Cage* (1963).

Anger, perhaps, was not so much a new beginning as a crescendo in the symphony of disillusion that had begun several years previously, during the winter months of 1947, when, epitomized by appalling weather, everything seemed to begin going wrong.

The Ghost in Fiction

by Alan Taylor

Alan Taylor is Associate Editor of the Sunday Herald and co-editor with his wife Irene of The Assassin's Cloak: An Anthology of the World's Greatest Diarists and The Secret Annexe: An Anthology of the World's Greatest War Diarists. For the past eight years he has been fifty per cent of the Scottish team on Radio 4's Round Britain Quiz. In a previous existence he was a reference librarian.

Ghosts and their Effect

Like the poor, ghosts are always with us, usually frightening us out of our wits. Banquo, perhaps the most famous ghost in literature, is the archetype, the soul of a dead person making itself visible to the living. Banquo's ghost appears before Macbeth shortly after he has had his throat cut. Not surprisingly, Macbeth becomes unhinged when he sees it and cries in terror:

> Avaunt, and quit my sight! Let the earth hide thee.
> Thy bones are marrowless, thy blood is cold.
> Thou hast no speculation in those eyes
> Which thou dost glare with.

Typically, Banquo's ghost can only be seen by Macbeth, and he is accused by Lady Macbeth of ruining the post-assassination party. At first she tries to laugh it off, but as the blood drains from her husband's face and his attendants grow more perplexed, she calls a halt to proceedings: 'Stand not upon the order of your going,/ But go at once.'

Ghosts, then, and the effect they might have, were well known to the Elizabethans and were regularly referred to in their plays. However, it was not until the 19th century that the ghost story became a recognized genre and part of the literature of the supernatural. Usually, ghosts invoked horror but not always. They may be friendly as well as terrifying, comforting as well as shocking. In general, though, they are disturbing, inducing a state of acute paranoia. Fictional characters who see ghosts are rarely the same again.

The History of the Ghost Story

The history of the ghost story may be traced back to the Gothic romance, with its predilection for mists and mountains, cobwebbed castles, remote settings and an air of foreboding. Sir Walter Scott, who both influenced and was influenced by the Gothic, wrote several formative short stories which might be classified as ghost stories, including the blood-curdling 'The Two Drovers'.

The short story was the most comfortable form for ghost stories and they thrived in the 19th century in a plethora of magazines which revelled in jangling the nerves of their readers. In Britain the appeal of the ghost story was particularly strong. Among those who exploited the market most assiduously and brilliantly was Joseph Sheridan Le Fanu (1814–73), the Irish novelist and short-story writer perhaps best known for his mystery novel, *Uncle Silas*. After the early death of his wife, Le Fanu became a recluse, shunning all social life and shutting himself off in his house in Dublin, becoming known to his friends as The Invisible Prince. He was particularly fond of the village of Chapelizod on the outskirts of Dublin, a place familiar to him from his childhood. It became the setting for one his finest ghost stories, the novel, *The House by the Churchyard*. Le Fanu's first ghost story, written anonymously in 1839, was 'Schalken the Painter', about the seduction of a young woman by a living corpse. His work has been much anthologized and is highly influential. Like Edgar Allan Poe, with whom he has often been compared, his treatment of the supernatural is tinged with black humour. His first collection of ghost stories, *Ghost Stories and Tales of Mystery*, appeared in 1851 and is regarded as one of the genre's landmarks.

Charles Dickens

In the development of the ghost story, as elsewhere, it is hard to ignore the influence of Charles Dickens. He in turn was heavily influenced by his reading at Christmas 1847 of *The Night Side of Nature: or, Ghosts and Ghost-Seers* by Catherine Crowe, which became one of the most important books about ghosts and spiritualism published during the Victorian era. Not only did Dickens encourage many writers to try their hand at ghost stories through his editorship of such publications as *Household Words* and *All the Year Round*, he was himself a distinguished contributor to the genre. His short story, 'The Signal Man', is regularly anthologized.

Dickens's most famous ghost story is undoubtedly *A Christmas Carol*, which William Thackeray called a 'national benefit'. The novel, which contains Dickens's most eloquent protest against the conditions of the poor, details the reformation of the miserly Scrooge, the ghost of whose former partner, Jacob Marley, appears on Christmas Eve to inform him that he can expect three more phantom callers – the ghosts of Christmas Past, Present and Future. Wrapped in a chain made of 'cash-boxes, keys, padlocks, ledgers, deeds, and heavy purses wrought in steel', Marley's body is transparent, his eyes 'death-cold'. A *Christmas Carol* so pricked the conscience of one US factory owner that he gave his workers an extra day's holiday when he finished reading it. Dickens wrote several other ghost stories set at Christmas, thus initiating a tradition which continues to this day. As Jerome K Jerome said, 'the close muggy atmosphere of Christmas draws up ghosts like the dampness of the summer rain brings out the frogs and the snails'.

The Golden Age

What has been described as the Golden Age of the ghost story lasted from 1880 to approximately 1930, during which time the quality and quantity of stories soared. Among its notable practitioners were Robert Louis Stevenson (1850–94), who did not write many ghost stories, but those which he did write, including the *The Body-Snatcher* and *Thrawn Janet*, show his genius for creating supernatural terror; Lafcadio Hearn (1850–1904), whose intense interest in all things Oriental is never far from the surface; and Walter de la Mare (1873–1956), who is better known as a poet but whose stories still resonate spookily. Other names worth noting include Vernon Lee, Henry James, Algernon Blackwood and Oliver Onions.

Few of the above, however, could be classified primarily as writers of ghost stories. The same cannot be said of Montague Rhodes James (1862–1936), a scholar who, among other things, edited the work of Le Fanu, whom he admired hugely. James's stories were written for his own amusement and read out to his students at Cambridge on Sunday evenings in the winter term. His first collection, *Ghost Stories of an Antiquary*, remains a masterpiece of the genre. James, in common with many modern writers of ghost stories, locates his stories in a familiar setting – a university or a cathedral were often favoured – in which the extraordinary intrudes on the ordinary, the devil being in the juxtaposition. Three further collections followed. Carefully plotted and displaying considerable erudition, James's style was much copied but rarely matched.

Later Developments

The 20th century demonstrated no diminishing of appetite for the genre, though it remains an acquired taste. Nevertheless many writers appreciate how the introduction of a ghost may allow them to exploit conventions. Susan Hill (born 1942), for example, in her novel *The Woman in Black: A Ghost Story*, masterfully recreates the mood of the Victorian ghost story. Other modern writers have written notable ghost stories, including Elizabeth Bowen (1899–1973), L P Hartley (1895–1972) and Alison Lurie (born 1926). Another is Muriel Spark (born 1918), who is never shy or sentimental or squeamish about introducing the supernatural into her work. Her short story, 'The Portobello Road', is typical of her method: a dead woman, Needle, meets her killer, a childhood friend, at a street market in London. Nothing, it seems, could be more natural. In the world according to Spark, if you think you've seen a ghost the chances are you have.

Serial Offenders – the Detective in Fiction

by Natasha Cooper

Natasha Cooper worked in publishing for ten years before becoming a writer. Her first novels were historical, written under another name, but all of them included crime of one sort or another. She now concentrates on crime novels featuring Trish Maguire, a thirtysomething barrister, who lives and works in London. The novels are published in the UK by Simon & Schuster and in the USA by St Martin's Press.

In the Beginning

J I M Stewart (whose crime fiction was published under the name of Michael Innes) believed that the classic detective story could not succeed if it were peopled with realistic characters. This may seem odd to modern tastes, but Stewart belonged to the school that held the puzzle to be the most important aspect of the genre.

As he pointed out in the introduction to Penguin's 1966 edition of *The Moonstone* by Wilkie Collins, if readers were not to guess the identity of the murderer long before the end the story, they had to be able to suspect each member of the cast in turn. That would never be possible if the characters were truthfully and realistically portrayed.

This kind of puzzle-solving crime story is no longer fashionable. Indeed in many novels now, readers know the identity of the villain from the start, even though the detective may not. The interest lies in the accurately described psychology of the villains, the tension in watching the detective struggle to get to them before they kill again.

The Golden Age

Even in the Golden Age of classic British mystery fiction, one figure was allowed to have a credible personality. Readers had to be able to trust the series detective if they were to follow him or her through investigation after investigation, and so authors had to provide more fully developed characters.

Some sleuths have been considerably more credible than others. Wilkie Collins's Sergeant Cuff, although not himself a series character, is the paradigm of the realistic police detective. Like so many who came after him, including Inspector Morse, Sergeant Cuff is dour and much cleverer than his superiors, or the suspects and victim's relatives with whom he works. Cuff also belongs recognizably to the class from which most police officers would have been drawn at the time of his creation, which has not always been the case with the rest of his type. Writing in 1868, Wilkie Collins is said to have based Cuff on a real man: Inspector Whicher, who was one of the first specialist detectives to work within the London Police Force. Whether or not Whicher shared Cuff's unlikely hobby of breeding roses is not recorded, but that too became part of the pattern. Morse has his crosswords, classical music and real ale, Lew Archer found his recreation in reading, painting and natural history, while the gross but warm-hearted Detective Superintendent Andy Dalziel is devoted to his beloved single malt whiskies and shocking the bourgeoisie.

The Brilliant Amateur

While fictional police investigators like these have nearly always been more intelligent than anyone else in their environment, their colleagues in novels of amateur detection have usually been cloddish and stupid, which has the benefit of showing up the sparkling brilliance of their civilian counterparts.

The exemplar is, of course, Sherlock Holmes, whose dealings with Inspector Lestrade of Scotland Yard are typical. Inhumanly clever, detached from the emotional muddles of lesser men's lives, Holmes sees further and faster than anyone else. So elevated is he that he has to have Dr Watson to ask the awed questions that will elucidate the mysteries for readers who may not share the Baker Street sage's percipience. Their useful partnership has been copied in many series – both police and amateur – ever since.

By the time Arthur Conan Doyle died, there were distinct differences between the most popular strains of crime fiction in Britain and the USA. In Britain the so-called Golden Age was in full swing, with its aristocratic amateur sleuths, donnish puzzles, village settings and comfortable outcomes. Lord Peter Wimsey, for example, is quite as brilliant and well-informed as Sherlock Holmes, but he is also the younger son of a duke and fabulously rich. He lives in a perfect flat in Piccadilly, overlooking Green Park, and owns vast tracts of London.

Further up Piccadilly, in a side alley called Bottle Street, lives Margery Allingham's Albert Campion. That is not his real name, but it protects him from the embarrassment of being 'nearly royal'. One of the important differences between the two men is their attitude to the police. In *Whose Body?*

Wimsey's dealings with Inspector Sugg reflect Sherlock Holmes's disdain for Lestrade's limitations. Even in *Busman's Honeymoon*, when he rather likes Superintendent Kirk, Wimsey still feels infinitely superior. Campion, on the other hand, positively admires the police officers with whom he works most often: Stanislaus Oates and Charley Luke.

The Aristocratic Sleuth

Both Wimsey and Campion start their fictional lives as Woosterish silly-ass figures. Only as their series develop do they themselves become warm and rounded people. At first they are startlingly heroic in relation to physical pain and have little to do with ordinary emotions, although Wimsey does suffer from shellshock. The scenes in which memories of his past in World War I overwhelm him are among the most effective in Dorothy L Sayers's early novels. Much later, when both men have fallen in love – Wimsey with Harriet Vane, whom he saved from hanging for the murder of her lover, and Campion with the Lady Amanda Fitton, whose inheritance and title he rescued – they hurt as other men hurt and respond in ways that arouse the reader's genuine sympathy. Wimsey may propose to Harriet in Latin, but it is impossible not to know that he cares what her answer will be.

Even when such Golden Age heroes work within the police force, they tend to come from the upper classes. Ngaio Marsh's Detective Inspector Roderick Alleyn is constantly self-deprecating about his antecedents and is contemptuous of other people's surprise that the brother of a baronet should work at Scotland Yard. Yet he is often seen in white tie, looking 'like a grandee' beside his beautiful artist wife, Troy, and he tends to patronize his faithful Watson, Inspector Fox.

Josephine Tey's Inspector Alan Grant is a more realistic – as well as a much more likeable – figure, but even he has land-owning relatives in Scotland and a private income that means he can toy with the idea of resignation whenever his superiors become too intrusive.

These men have their descendants today, in characters such as P D James's Adam Dalgleish. While Dalgleish does not spring from the aristocracy and is not even particularly rich, he is nevertheless distinctly part of the privileged classes. A poet as well as a policeman, he inherits a second home from his aunt, and he is as far above the common herd as his predecessors. He is also as inhumanly detached from other people as Sherlock Holmes. There are occasions when Dalgleish appears to be on the brink of falling in love and remarrying (his wife died years ago in childbirth), but it never quite happens. Scholarly and self-sufficient, he is impossible to imagine in a nursery, a sweaty embrace or a marital row.

The American Loner

In the USA a different tradition developed after World War I, with the hard-boiled private eyes created by writers like Dashiell Hammet and Raymond Chandler. The settings of their novels are much grittier than those of the British Golden Age, and violence and corruption hide around every corner. Even at the end of a case, there is unlikely to be unalloyed joy for the survivors or the society they inhabit. Yet the private eyes themselves – men like Philip Marlowe and Sam Spade – fit into a long line of romantic heroes. Hard-drinking, world-weary and cynical though such men may often be, they act like knights errant, riding out to slay the dragons of injustice and cruelty, undeterred by any suffering of their own and driven by powerful, if sometimes eccentric, moral codes.

The Woman Investigator

Even though they are well-rooted in romantic traditions, these shabby heroes are considerably more credible than the all-too mockable figure of Hercule Poirot, with his dandified clothes and his conceit in the exercise of his 'little grey cells'. And yet Agatha Christie also created Jane Marple. Miss Marple's cases have all the unreality and neat puzzles so valued in the Golden Age and so derided by the mean-streets school of American writers, but she herself is a much more recognizable human being than Poirot. There were many middle-class women like Miss Marple left single in Britain after World War I.

However intelligent and warm-hearted such women might have been, they were also often despised, as the cruel contemporary term 'superfluous women' makes clear. Dorothy L Sayers's Miss Climpson is another, although she never takes the lead in any investigations, merely assisting Wimsey and Harriet. Usually poor, these women often had to exist on the margins of other people's lives, which is why – like Jane Marple – they saw and understood so much.

Miss Marple's successors have been more fortunate in fiction, as in real life. Even when poor, like Kinsey Milhone and V I Warshawski, they are their own women, and they are professionals in their own right. Heterosexual or gay, they take partners where they choose and live as they please. Deferring to no one, able to defend themselves verbally and physically, they not only represent a particular feminist ideal of the 1970s and 1980s but also fit into the traditions of the hard-boiled American private-eye novel.

Like so many fictional sleuths, both these women remain single. V I Warshawksi has plenty of lovers, but none stays beyond a book or two. It is as though a happy domestic life is inimical to success as a detective.

Love and Marriage

Throughout the canon there are only a few happily attached figures of either sex. One of the few is Commissario Guido Brunetti, Donna Leon's Venetian creation, who has a glorious home-life with an academic and aristocratic wife, Paola, who cooks for him, criticizes him when necessary, and introduces him into layers of society he could not have penetrated on his own.

Albert Campion made marriage work with Amanda – but they never lived together. Amanda Cross's character Kate Fansler and her husband have a similar relationship. In one novel he explained that he planned to give his wife so much space that she would come looking for him. Peter Wimsey and Harriet set off optimistically on married life in *Busman's Honeymoon*: he plans to leave her similar amounts of space in which to do her own creative work, untrammelled by his needs or desires. Interestingly that was the last of Sayers's full-length novels. Peter and Harriet feature, with their sons, in no more than a few short stories after that.

Much more typical of the whole genre is Kay Scarpetta, Patricia Cornwell's forensic pathologist, whose inability to manage any kind of relationship is contrasted by her invincibility in tracking down murderers. She is typical, too, of another recent development, in which crime writers have sought to give their lead characters professions that are connected with law enforcement and yet are independent of any police force. Scarpetta was the first of a crop of pathologists, but there are other careers that writers have found useful. Jonathan Kellerman has child psychologist Alex Delaware, and Val McDermid has Dr Tony Hill, a psychologist specializing in serial killers. Crime fiction also features journalists, lawyers, forensic dentists, archaeologists and many more.

The Gifted Maverick

This is not surprising when you consider the difficulties of reproducing a real police investigation of murder. There is so much routine to be carried out, so many door-to-door enquiries, statistical analyses, days of data processing, and fruitless interviews that no novel could contain them all. Film and television directors have the advantage over authors because they can set their detectives moving within incident rooms peopled by full teams of police and civilian staff.

Many novelists overcome the problem by making their police hero a maverick, who refuses to become a slave to routine. Ian Rankin's Inspector Rebus is such a character. Rebus is always breaking rules, going off on his own to work outside normal procedures, and avoiding all his colleagues except the appealing Siobhan Clarke, who protects him and defers to him and brings some much-needed warmth into his life. Like other fictional detectives, he has also been sent to work undercover and threatened with dismissal as a plot device to get him out of the police station.

Somewhat similar in outlook is the other great Venetian sleuth, Michael Dibdin's Aurelio Zen. He also shares the hard-boiled Americans' cynicism and mistrust of corruptible social institutions. And he, too, finds relationships hard to understand or manage.

Common Ground

What all these investigators have in common is an urge to uncover the truth – however uncomfortable it may be – and a determination to protect the vulnerable. Crime fiction will always change as society changes, and the characters within it will continue to reflect a mixture of reality and the fantasies and yearning of people for whom reality is too harsh. It is the most flexible genre, the most exciting, and the most popular; not least because its series characters are among the best-loved in the world.

Literary Drinkers

by James Quan Nicholls

James Quan Nicholls is Senior Lecturer in Media Communications at Bath Spa University College. He writes on the social history of drinking and its representation in the arts and is co-editor of A Babel of Bottles: Drink, Drinkers and Drinking Places in Literature.

Drinkers in Literature

Literary history is filled with literary drinkers. The novel in particular has often brought characters together around drink. Where better than the bar or pub to have people encounter one another outside of work or home? What better than drink to loosen their tongues, provoke their desires or reveal their hidden natures? Literary narrative needs the bar, the party and the nightclub just as it needs the tipsy revelation, the drunken disaster and the maudlin (or merry) monologue. Drink has always been one of the great alibis of the narrative twist.

Given drink's serendipitous role in story-telling, not to mention its historical ubiquity, an abundance of literary drinkers is only to be expected. The question is: where to begin? The Bible gives us Noah uncovered in his vineyard, the miracle at Cana and the Last Supper. Classical literature gives us Socrates sitting up all night drinking and philosophizing in Plato's *Symposium*. In Euripides's *The Bacchae*, by contrast, we see Pentheus ripped apart as punishment for denying the wine-god Dionysus his place in the social order. What these early examples show is that drinking, in fact, provides more than just the occasion for certain, unpredictable, forms of social interaction. It also stands in for bigger things: temptation, transcendence, community (usually all-male), and chaos.

While drinking can function symbolically in literature, it can also be the excuse for literature. *The Canterbury Tales*, after all, are instigated at the Tabard Inn, where 'strong was the win, and wel to drink us leste'. But drink is not just the occasion for any old story. Chaucer's Miller – one of English literature's first boozers – tells the bawdiest of the tales, one for which the narrator feels moved to apologize. Don't blame me if the story is rude, he says, the man was drunk when he told it. Perhaps more than anything else, drink provides a great excuse for the breaking of literary rules.

The Festive or Comic Drinker

In the medieval world, breaking rules, turning the world upside down, and laughing at convention were the domain of the great carnivals, and one of the central figures in medieval carnival was the 'lord of misrule'. If any literary character personifies this spirit, it is, of course, Sir John Falstaff. But Falstaff is not simply timeless, he is also a man out of time. He is a lord of misrule at the dawn of a new age and his downfall is that he lives at a time when political power was coming to rely increasingly on the public display of reason. The carnival spirit which Falstaff embodies is finally disavowed by Prince Hal because, however endearing, however vital, it represents all that kingly power does not.

Falstaff's roguish drunken irresponsibility is subject to fond indulgence but, ultimately, it is censured. Sarah Gamp, the bibulous nurse of Charles Dickens's *Martin Chuzzlewit*, clearly follows in this ambivalent comic tradition. The drunken mistreatment of her wards is indeed an affront to the serious responsibilities of her profession, and yet the sheer singularity of her character is irresistible. Her absurdly unconvincing efforts to maintain an appearance of sobriety, her constant references to the non-existent 'Mrs Harris', and her philosophic observations (all of which have the remarkable tendency to conclude on a reflection of Mrs Gamp's own saintly character) all defy any notion of rational propriety. And yet, old Martin Chuzzlewit's advice that she try 'a little less liquor, and a little more humanity' seems a recipe for a slightly duller, if eminently more sensible, world.

Comic drinkers of this kind are not merely humorous, they are anarchic. John Falstaff and Sarah Gamp are flies in the ointment of convention. In Kingsley Amis's *Lucky Jim*, Jim Dixon's drinking provides a riotous antidote to the world of well-ordered hypocrisy epitomized by Professor Welch and his family. Dixon's drinking is certainly the cause of pain and humiliation – to which the description of his hangover after a particularly embarrassing drunken evening at the home of the Welches is a memorable testimony. However, it also tears back the veneer of social status to reveal the unpleasantness it often disguises. Furthermore, while Dixon's drunken lecture on 'Merrie England' (an appropriately carnivalesque theme) appears at first to be yet another toe-curling disaster, it ultimately gives him the last laugh – and delivers a rare literary victory to the Falstaffian world view.

The Problem Drinker

Of course, the flipside of the comic drinker is the problem drinker: the addict. One of the first self-confessed literary alcoholics is the narrator of Charles Lamb's essay 'Confessions of a Drunkard'. 'Confessions of a Drunkard' predated, and doubtless influenced, Thomas De Qunicey's *Confessions of an English Opium-Eater*. It also influenced a young Walt Whitman when writing *Franklin Evans, or the Inebriate*, which was an early and successful temperance novel – albeit one which Whitman himself later dismissed as 'damned rot'.

Temperance and Victorian Fiction

Temperance fiction such as *Franklin Evans*, like the temperance movement itself, played a much more prominent role in Victorian society than is nowadays generally imagined. Indeed, the comic endearments of Sarah Gamp are unusual by comparison with much Victorian fiction, which tended to reflect temperance ideas in its depiction of drink and drinkers. Thomas Hardy's *The Mayor of Casterbridge* is more typical in this regard. Michael Henchard's sale of his wife while drunk reveals not just a weakness of character, but also a complete disregard of moral responsibility. His subsequent rise in social standing, by contrast, is reward for the self-mastery that is evidenced by his successful abstention from drinking. However, as the completion of his temperance pledge approaches it becomes clear that he has not altogether conquered his demons, and his tragic end is hastened by a return to the bottle. To the extent that his inner demons were not extinguished through abstinence, Michael Henchard challenges one influential strand of temperance thinking: that the self-destructive tendencies occasioned by alcohol were somehow contained in the drink itself. In every other sense, however, *The Mayor of Casterbridge* is in keeping with the orthodox temperance assertion that drink was the enemy of both private morality and social progress.

Conspicuous Sobriety

It is telling that the index of Michael Henchard's sober self-improvement is a swift rise through the ranks of middle-class society. In the latter half of the 19th century, conspicuous sobriety became an increasingly important sign of social respectability. Given this, a reaction to temperance ideology among the new, and burgeoning, world of bohemian artists and writers was almost inevitable. When Oscar Wilde said that 'a glass of absinthe is as poetical as anything in the world' he was, as ever, being more than facetious. In the late 19th and early 20th centuries, drink began to represent to many writers both a way of breaking open the sediment of literary tradition, and a way of positioning themselves and their work outside conventional bourgeois society. If sobriety became the mark of respectability, then drink became a badge of the avant-garde.

The Modernist Literary Drinker

It is, then, in literary Modernism, and especially the work produced by writers living in Paris between the wars, that the literary drinker acquires something approaching mythic status. One of the most famous literary drinkers of this period is Jake Barnes, hero of Ernest Hemingway's *The Sun Also Rises*. Barnes's determined stoicism is mirrored in his idiosyncratic approach to drinking. He is the first of a line of Hemingway heroes to play out the seemingly impossible discipline imposed by the author on his characters: that of being able to drink prodigiously while never succumbing to garrulousness, visible melancholy or plain stupidity. For Jake Barnes, controlled drinking acts as a rejection of the conventional morality exemplified by Prohibition, but also as both a defence against the chaos of the world in which he lives and, at the same time, the only way to make proper sense of that world.

Jake Barnes inhabits a Parisian café society teeming with would-be artists and writers (as well as feckless charlatans). Barnes, the perennial insider, moves in and out of this colourful scene with ease. In Jean Rhys's *Good Morning, Midnight*, Sasha Jensen experiences the same world very differently. For Jensen, the bars of Paris are not filled with bohemian bonhomie. Instead, the hostility she encounters at the hands of both the patrons and owners of the cafés she frequents is palpable; she is an older woman, drinking alone. Jensen's experiences contrast spectacularly with those of other Modernist literary drinkers. In F Scott Fitzgerald's *Tender is the Night*, Dick Diver may be doomed by drinking, but it is also at the heart of his glamorous social life. In James Joyce's *Ulysses*, Stephen Dedalus's drinking stands in the way of his writing, but it is also the lifeblood of his bohemian social circle. The contempt that Jensen's drinking repeatedly engenders suggests that, whatever else may have changed, the notion that female drinking was somehow shameful remained strong even in the most radical of social environments.

In many ways, Geoffrey Firmin – the 'Consul' of Malcolm Lowry's *Under the Volcano* – represents the culmination of the literary drinker as modern, and Modernist, hero. Brilliant, erudite and doomed, we know him only for one day – the Day of the Dead – in Quauhnahuac, Mexico, at the far edge of what Lowry calls this 'drunken revolving world'. While the Consul's drinking propels him headlong towards tragedy, it also represents a kind of spiritual defiance in the face of an apparently empty and amoral universe. For the Consul, drinking becomes a form of self-sacrifice: part compensation for the hollow brutality of a war-torn world, part deadly ritual privately echoing the ancient carnival of death in which his last day is spent.

Tragic Heroes

If only through the spectacle of its conclusion, *Under the Volcano* imbues the Consul with an aura of tragic heroism and spiritual significance. No such fortune awaits the heroine of Brian Moore's *The Lonely Passion of Judith Hearne*. Like the Consul, her drinking is associated with a collapse in religious faith. However, drunkenness provides her with no spiritual compensation – rather it simply precipitates a desperately mundane mental collapse. Where the drunken Consul wanders through exotic and darkly significant cantinas, the drunken Judith Hearne is evicted from a cheap guest house, pushed around by nuns, and callously ignored by a confessor priest with golf on his mind. Like Sasha Jensen, Judith Hearne punctures a very male myth of the grandiose and heroic drinker. Instead, she turns to drink as a source of solace and escape, the already limited pleasures of which are destroyed in no small measure by a society in which female drunkenness is treated with horrified indignation.

In much post-war fiction, the hyperbole of Modernist depictions of drinking is similarly punctured. In America, Charles Bukowski has Henry Chinaski drink his way through a decidedly unexotic world of barflies and bored housewives in novels such as *Factotum* and *Post Office*. Jim Dixon's significance is surely more comic than cosmic; and, a generation on, John Self's drinking in Martin Amis's *Money* is not a sign of spiritual compensation or artistic endeavour, but a mark of his own self-indulgence in a world of rampant consumption. Stripped of the aura of transgression bestowed on drink by a century of temperance campaigning and Prohibition, the post-war literary drinker returned to earth with a bump.

The Normalization of the Literary Drinker

Most recently, we can see this levelling out of literary drinking in Helen Fielding's *Bridget Jones's Diary*. Bridget Jones is neither a spectacular alcoholic, anarchic clown, philosopher manqué, nor exotic outsider. Her drinking is in every sense mundane – down to the listing of alcohol units drunk per day. Noticeably, it also takes place in a world where both men and women drink in equal measure. Bridget Jones, then, is less a 'literary drinker' than a literary character who drinks: arguably a more common figure in contemporary fiction than ever before. While this may signal a relaxation in cultural attitudes it certainly does not suggest a turn to sobriety; rather, it suggests that the book and the bottle look set to remain as closely entwined as ever.

A
Three Tall Women, 1991
Edward Albee

Based upon Albee's adoptive mother, A is 92 years old, 'thin, autocratic and proud, as together as the ravages of time will allow'. The other characters in the play, B and C, represent the same woman at different ages. Self-aggrandizing and domineering, A's memory is fading and her reminiscences descend frequently into rambling, revealing a life riddled with disappointment, grief and a sense of betrayal. 'The happiest moment of all? ... Coming to the end of it, when all the waves cause the greatest woes to subside ... '

Aaron, the Moor
Titus Andronicus, c.1589
William Shakespeare

An arch-villain, who plots rape and murder without qualms. He tells TITUS ANDRONICUS that he will have his sons returned alive if Titus cuts his own hand off; the severed heads of Titus's sons are then returned. He fathers QUEEN TAMORA's black baby; this too is supposed to be heinous. He boasts of digging up dead men and setting them at their friends' doors, and when finally captured by the forces of relative good, says how glad he is to have committed every crime.

Abbot, Caroline
Where Angels Fear to Tread, 1905
E M Forster

A tall, grave young woman with a strong sense of duty, she appears to be the kind of sound influence that maiden aunts welcome in a trusted travelling companion. However, her exposure to the sun-drenched beauty of Italy triggers a rebellion against the dead hand of conformity that she has previously experienced. Inspired to follow her heart rather than her social conditioning, she attempts to act with responsibility whilst torn between the dull morality of Christian England and the intoxicating liberty she has tasted abroad.

Abbot of Unreason, also known as Father Howeglas or the Monk of Misrule
The Abbot, 1820
Sir Walter Scott

A burlesque counterpart to FATHER AMBROSE and a folkloric figure associated with the Feast of Fools, he is a 'stout-made under-sized fellow, whose thick squab form had been rendered grotesque by a supplemental paunch, well stuffed. He wore a mitre of leather, with the front like a grenadier's cap, adorned with mock embroidery, and trinkets of tin.' He is killed by ROLAND GRAEME.

Abdiel
Paradise Lost, 1667
John Milton

'Among the faithless, faithful only he/Among innumerable false, unmov'd/Unshak'n, unseduc'd, unterrifi'd'. A blazing Seraph known for his zeal, he is the only one of Lucifer's band who refuses to break with heaven and turns his back on the destruction to come.

Abdul Alhazred
in the works of
H P Lovecraft, edited by August Derleth, 1945

An insane Arab who writes the *Necronomicon*, the sacred text of the cult of CTHULHU, only one copy of which – transliterated into Latin – exists in the university library at Arkham in New England.

Abel
House Made of Dawn, 1968
N Scott Momaday

Isolated in his native Jemez pueblo from childhood because of his 'outsider' father, Abel has returned home from service in World War II to face increasing loneliness. His attempt to re-enter the ceremonial life of the tribe ends in defeat and public humiliation at the hands of an albino who seems the epitome of the evil he has felt surrounding him from childhood, and whom he consequently kills. After inevitable imprisonment, he is sent to Los Angeles under the government Relocation programme and given a menial job. Reaching a physical and spiritual nadir, he experiences a healing vision of the 'runners after evil', from whom he learns a new approach. His second return to the pueblo begins his reintegration as, now mourning his grandfather's death, he joins the dawn runners of his vision and rediscovers his ability to sing.

Abessa
The Faerie Queene, 1590–6
Sir Edmund Spenser

She represents the Church of Rome. Unable to 'heare, nor speake, nor understand', she represents spiritual blindness. She is the daughter of Corceca, who symbolizes superstition, and she performs many Catholic rituals in the presence of UNA. She is kept healthy and fat from a feast of offerings stolen from various churches and is used as a whore by KIRKRAPINE.

Ablewhite, Godfrey
The Moonstone, 1868
Wilkie Collins

Judged to be the 'most accomplished philanthropist that England ever produced', Godfrey Ablewhite is a tall, suave barrister with a deep voice and charming manner, whose name is continually associated with the noblest Christian deeds of the day. His lavish double-life of reckless indulgence and financial embarrassment remains hidden from public view, but inevitably propels him into an increasingly desperate 'neck or nothing' situation that is to cost him his life.

Abou Ben Adhem
'Abou Ben Adhem', in *Book of Gems*, 1838
Leigh Hunt

He has lived an upright life without giving much thought to serving God. His cheerful love and care for his fellow men, however, earn him a leading place among those blessed for their love of God.

Absalom, in full Absalom Kumalo
Cry, the Beloved Country, 1948
Alan Paton

As lost as his biblical name suggests, REV STEPHEN KUMALO's son is a reformatory boy with a violent chip on his shoulder. He kills the white liberal ARTHUR JARVIS during a botched robbery and is sentenced to death. While in prison, he marries his pregnant girlfriend, thus leaving an ironic and ambiguous challenge to the new South African generation.

Absolom
Absolom and Achitophel, 1681
John Dryden

A satirical portrait of the Duke of Monmouth, the illegitimate son of Charles II. He is the young, handsome rival to his father King David in the Second Book of Samuel. Popular but naive, he succumbs to the political scheming of ACHITOPHEL. His military skills are to be put to use ('none so fit as warlike Absolom') and his illegitimacy is played on in order to oppose his father.

Absolute, Captain Jack
The Rivals, 1775
Richard Brinsley Sheridan

A soldier and the son of SIR ANTHONY ABSOLUTE, who adopts the identity of the poor Ensign Beverley in order to court LYDIA LANGUISH. He does not, in fact, share her romantic fancies, since he wants her money as well as her hand. The complications caused by his deceptions call on all his reserves of eloquence.

Absolute, Sir Anthony
The Rivals, 1775
Richard Brinsley Sheridan

A rich baronet who is 'hasty in everything', impatient and prone to fly into tempers (although he thinks he is self-controlled), he falls

out with his son CAPTAIN JACK ABSOLUTE over his peremptory plans for the latter's marriage. He believes that only harm comes from teaching girls to read.

Acasto
The Orphan, 1680
Thomas Otway

A nobleman and soldier retired from the court and living in the country, Acasto has two sons, CASTALIO and POLYDORE, and is the guardian of the orphan, MONIMIA. Benevolent, honest, a high-minded advocate of loyalist principles and politics, he is now a disillusioned man of peace who opposes his sons going to the wars. This may be the wisdom of age; on the other hand, he is full of contradictions. He recalls his dead wife with affection, but warns his sons against marriage, and proudly describes his own gallantry in war but prevents his sons from emulating him.

Achilles
Troilus and Cressida, 1601/2
William Shakespeare

The Greek leader with the reputation as the greatest warrior, Achilles is proud, lazy, egotistical and self-indulgent. He spends much of the time idling in his tent, being entertained by the spectacle of PATROCLUS mimicking his peers, despite the fact that they and the rest of the Greek army need his strength and example on the battlefield. He has no sense of honour or chivalry and brutally demonstrates this in his murder of the unarmed HECTOR.

Achitophel
Absalom and Achitophel, 1681
John Dryden

A satirical portrait of the Earl of Shaftesbury who, by virtue of the king's 'fatal mercy', has gone from 'pardoned rebel' to 'kinsman to the throne'. A staunch opponent of the Catholic succession, he is strong-minded, exceedingly able, 'sagacious, bold and turbulent of wit': a man prepared to take risks and enjoy danger. He is easily able to flatter and persuade ABSOLOM that his father David (ie Charles II) is unfit to rule and that Absolom has the right to rebel. His ambition is his downfall.

Achthar, Lord Anophel
Melincourt, or Sir Oran Haut-ton, 1817
Thomas Love Peacock

Wealth and status notwithstanding, Lord Anophel is a bubble-brain who excels at country pursuits. Impressed by education and intellectual interests, which he nonetheless finds incomprehensible, he foolishly relies upon the unsound, often unintelligible, advice of sycophantic, supposedly learned, employees. Coarse and brutish, he pursues his desires with no regard for anyone.

Acis
Back to Methuselah, 1921
George Bernard Shaw

Acis, a youth, appears during the final section (*As Far as Thought can Reach*) of this five-part play, set in a remote garden Utopia in 31,920AD. He is almost three years old but, as new-born children have the appearance of 16-year-olds, he seems to be almost 20. Acis is one of a band of young people destined for long life, devoting their early years to alfresco festivals of the arts and sport, on the threshold of discovering that he has creative power over himself but none over his friends.

Ackroyd, Roger
The Murder of Roger Ackroyd, 1926
Agatha Christie

'Possibly the most famous victim in the history of detective fiction.' Described as 'more impossibly like a country squire than any country squire could really be', he is considered the life and soul of King's Abbot village. A successful manufacturer of wagon wheels, he is almost 50 and is possessed of ruddy good health and a lively temper. A widower with a grown son, he had long been expected to marry one of his housekeepers, until the growing intimacy that develops with the widowed Mrs Ferrars. It is the latter's death and revelations that she was the victim of a cruel blackmailer that lead to Ackroyd's murder and the emergence of HERCULE POIROT from retirement.

Acrasia
The Faerie Queene, 1590–6
Sir Edmund Spenser

An enchantress whose name means 'without control'. She uses her wondrous looks and appearance of helplessness to captivate passing knights and ruin their earnest quests. A lewd seductress, she lives in a 'bowre of bliss' and her goals are pleasure and delight. Once she has taken a lover she then transforms him into an ugly monster and chains him up for eternity. She comes into conflict with SIR GUYON, KNIGHT OF TEMPERANCE, and their struggle is symbolic of the conflict between self-indulgence and self-restraint.

Acres, Bob
The Rivals, 1775
Richard Brinsley Sheridan

The rustic squire of Clod Hall, Devon, who pathetically attempts to be a figure of fashion in Bath. This 'silly boor' uses oaths that are supposed to be appropriate to each occasion. His candidacy for the hand of LYDIA LANGUISH leads him to challenge a rival to a duel, but his courage rapidly evaporates.

Acton, Robert
The Europeans, 1878
Henry James

On their first meeting, BARONESS EUGENIA feels instinctively that Robert Acton is the most important man in the room; her younger brother feels that he is 'the only person in the [Wentworths'] circle with no sense of oppression of any kind'. Harvard-educated, with experience of life overseas, he seems sophisticated and cosmopolitan alongside his Wentworth cousins, to whom he is something of a hero. Even so, 'he knew that he was by no means so much a man of the world as he was supposed to be in local circles'.

Ada (Adelaida)
Ada, or Ardor: A Family Chronicle 1969
Vladimir Nabokov

Black-haired Adelaida, a parody of Anna Karenina, is trapped by family and traditions. The strange invented society she inhabits is an amalgam of decadent moral cultures and tantalizing obscure references; her home, Ardis Manor, is set in an epic rural background. The recurring affair with her cousin VAN VEEN, revealed to be her brother, dominates her life. Their irresistable attraction is of one person halved: a tragic duality.

Adah
In the Ditch, 1972
Second-Class Citizen, 1974, collected as *Adah's Story*, 1983
Buchi Emecheta

A young Nigerian woman, bright, capable and warm, but brainwashed into believing that life in Britain offers greater freedom and independence than at home. She is, of course, a second-class citizen even within the confines of her own squalidly patriarchal home, where her husband FRANCIS dominates her utterly.

Adam
Back to Methuselah, 1921
George Bernard Shaw

The biblical character of the first man appears in the first section of this five-part play (and briefly in the last). *In the Beginning* is set partly in the Garden of Eden. Adam and EVE, who have been created immortal, discover a fawn which has broken its neck and thereby stumble upon the concept of death. With THE SERPENT, they embark upon a metaphysical debate on the cycle of death and birth, by which death is overcome. Adam becomes a peasant, digging the earth. He is burdened by fear and craves certainty in life.

Adam
Paradise Lost, 1667
John Milton

The first man and lord of Eden in 'naked Majesty', he is nonetheless conceived with the rugged simplicity of a Puritan. 'His fair large Front and Eye sublime declar'd/Absolute rule; and Hyacinthine Locks/Round from his parted Forelock manly hung/Clustering, but not beneath his shoulders broad.'

Adams, Alice
Alice Adams, 1921
Booth Tarkington

A respectable young woman who sees the key to her future success and security in the marriage market and sets out – unsuccessfully – to find herself a suitable husband.

Adams, Nick
In Our Time, 1925
Ernest Hemingway

The semi-autobiographical narrator-protagonist in a number of stories in this collection, he is an impressionable young boy-man drawn to the freedom, beauty and purity of the woods around the Michigan Lakes, and passionately fond of fishing and hunting. Through his father's work as a doctor, and his own friendship with the Indians, he is also exposed to the bitter, tragic dimension of life. He is wounded in World War I, and feels that 'everything was gone to hell inside of me', but in the story 'Big Two-Hearted River' is restored by the wilderness and the trout stream.

Adams, Parson (Abraham)
The History of the Adventures of Joseph Andrews and of his Friend Mr Abraham Adams, 1742
Henry Fielding

JOSEPH ANDREWS's comrade, he is a simple curate whose learning is not matched by even basic worldliness. 'He had applied many Years to the most severe Study, and had treasured up a Fund of Learning rarely to be met with in a University. He was besides a Man of good Sense, good Parts, and good Nature; but was at the same time as entirely ignorant of the Ways of this World as an Infant just entered into it could possibly be.' Often likened to Sancho Panza, he hijacks centre stage as Joseph's satirical function runs out of steam.

Adams, Roxy
Roxy, 1878
Edward Eggleston

A young woman from Ohio, she feels ill at ease in her environment, and is forced to compromise her more uplifting dreams and ambitions for the sake of survival.

Addams, Frankie
The Member of the Wedding, 1946
Carson McCullers

A twelve-year-old girl who, in the precarious state between childhood and adulthood, alternates between morbid fears and naive pretensions. She worries that her exceptional height is an omen of freakdom and affects the name of F Jasmine as an indication of her new maturity. In her desire to relieve the anxious sense of having no place in the world she becomes obsessed with her brother's marriage. However, her belief that she can become a 'member' of his wedding reveals her childish ignorance.

Addison, Joseph
The History of Henry Esmond, Esquire, 1852
W M Thackeray

An historical personage, the great essayist and poet is a relatively minor character in the novel. However, his confrontation with HENRY ESMOND following publication of *The Campaign*, his heroic poem about Blenheim, strongly underlines Thackeray's sense of the dangers inherent in glorifying men and deeds (and thus of believing Henry's own version of events).

Adenebi
A Dance of the Forests, 1960
Wole Soyinka

He is the village orator, a man governed by rhetoric and scripted attitudes rather than by genuine convictions. A materialist, he judges everything he does by a nice calculation of profit. Drawn back into the past like his friends, he becomes possessed by a spirit of destruction.

Adiewere
Idu, 1970
Flora Nwapa

IDU's husband, he is wealthy, reliable and hardworking, a respected member of his age group and the village society in which he lives. Content with his marriage, he is reluctant to marry a second wife despite intense social pressure to do so; his one attempt at polygamy ends when Idu becomes pregnant. Resigned to his duty as elder brother to the lazy Ishiodu, he continually attempts to help him improve his life.

Adizua
Efuru, 1966
Flora Nwapa

EFURU OGENE's first husband. An attractive but lazy man, he is not talented at farming or trading. He marries Efuru without paying the bride price and later leaves his wife for another woman. Adizua takes no responsibility for his mother, wife or child, and does not return home for his daughter's funeral.

Adkins, Celice
Being Dead, 1999
Jim Crace

A zoologist teaching at the university, married to JOSEPH ADKINS, Celice has a 'scientific passion' which defines and in the end betrays her. 'Tall, small-breasted, dressed like a man' with springy hair and a 'dizzy' face, her surprising affection for Joseph is gradually revealed despite her irritable comments about him and her disappointment with her own life. 'A warrior by nature, unafraid of battle, quick to raise her fists', to her alienated daughter her life looks dull, rigid and clerkish. Her coolly scientific outlook is undermined by her barely acknowledged human passion, the faint, but shocking, impression of which is the couple's true 'final legacy'.

Adkins, Joseph
Being Dead, 1999
Jim Crace

Joseph and his wife, CELICE ADKINS, are 'shoreline zoologists who never could resist the chance of poking about in the tides and shallows of the coast', a shared interest that brings and keeps them together. 'Noted for his coldness as much as for his brains' by his colleagues and seen as 'curmudgeonly, distracted, timid and thick-skulled' by Celice, he jokingly claims to be 'far too short' to do anything he doesn't want to do. Anxious, 'hesitant, quiet in conversation', eloquent only when singing in the 'mad, comic bass' which first charms her, he loves his wife and his attempt to resurrect their passion leads them to their fate.

Adletsky, Sigmund
The Actual, 1997
Saul Bellow

An enormously rich hotel magnate, Adletsky is 92 and 'a little guy, shrunken by his great age' and 'light enough to fly away into the everlasting'. Powerful and forthright, he is impervious to the opinions of others, and has little left in his life except leisure, reminiscence and spending money. Having suppressed his emotions while amassing his wealth, he employs HARRY TRELLMAN, a fellow 'oddball Jew', as an advisor, and engineers an encounter between Trellman and his long-lost love, AMY WUSTRIN.

Adonis
Venus and Adonis, 1593
William Shakespeare

Adonis is adored by VENUS, the goddess of sensual love, but whereas in Ovid's version of the story in *Metamorphoses* he returns her advances, in Shakespeare's account, he retreats. A teenager, he is awkward in her presence, uncertain of her motives and of the emotions she generates in him. To avoid her, he goes on a hunting expedition and is killed by a boar. When Venus discovers his body, it melts away, a purple-and-white flower growing in its place.

Adonis, Michael
A Walk in the Night, 1962
Alex La Guma

Angered at being sacked from his factory job for answering his white foreman back, he drinks to drown his sorrows and unintentionally kills an old Irish alcoholic who lives in the same run-down building as he does. Escaping from the police investigation he is blackmailed into joining a gang of small-time crooks.

Adriana
The Comedy of Errors, c.1594
William Shakespeare

The wife of ANTIPHOLUS OF EPHESUS, Adriana is concerned by his absence and rejects LUCIANA's advice that she should be patient. Instead, intrigued by DROMIO OF EPHESUS's report that her husband has apparently repudiated her and their home, she sets off in pursuit of him. Anger turns to jealousy when she mistakes ANTIPHOLUS OF SYRACUSE for her husband and learns that he has been pursuing her sister. Her assumptions result in Antipholus and Dromio of Syracuse taking refuge in an abbey, Adriana explaining to the abbess that the man she believes to be her husband is mad. Before the final reconciliations, Adriana is rebuked for her shrewishness.

Aegeon
The Comedy of Errors, c.1594
William Shakespeare

A merchant of Syracuse who travels to Ephesus in search of a lost son, Aegeon is condemned to death for coming ashore illegally. But by the end of the day he is reunited with both his twin sons, ANTIPHOLUS OF SYRACUSE and ANTIPHOLUS OF EPHESUS, and his long-lost wife, AEMILIA, and is reprieved. In one sense, therefore, the magic and mystery for which Ephesus was noted has cast a benevolent spell over grim reality; in another, love has triumphed and brought order to chaos.

Aemilia
The Comedy of Errors, c.1594
William Shakespeare

Believing that her husband, AEGEON, and her twin sons ANTIPHOLUS OF EPHESUS and ANTIPHOLUS OF SYRACUSE are dead, she has become an abbess at Ephesus. Although she does not recognize her son, she refuses to release Antipholus of Syracuse, who has taken refuge at the abbey. Later, she recognizes her husband and the family is reunited.

Aesop
The Battle of the Books, 1704
Jonathan Swift

A character in the most literal sense, in that he is not the historical Aesop but the works of the author of that name. Musing on a discussion overheard between a spider and a fly, Aesop draws a comparison between these creatures' relationship and that of the books around them. He exclaims that 'he has never known two cases so parallel and adapt to each other'. The spider with great pride 'feeding and engendering on itself', like the moderns, turns all into excrement and venom and eventually produces nothing but 'fly bane and cobweb', whereas the fly, with 'long search, much study … brings home honey and wax'. Thus the dispute concerning ancient and modern learning intensifies, as Aesop has now incited both sides to battle. When the battle breaks out Aesop is later found sleeping beneath a tree, his armour hanging in its branches.

Agamemnon
Troilus and Cressida, 1601/2
William Shakespeare

The commander of the Greek army, and brother to Menelaus, the Spartan king, whose wife HELEN is the cause of the war, Agamemnon is a respected leader who seeks a solution to a war which has been raging, on and off, for seven years. He is determined to win, but he shares and admires HECTOR's sense of honour and gallantry to his enemies.

Agape
The Faerie Queene, 1590–6
Sir Edmund Spenser

The mother of Priamond, Diamond and TRIAMOND. Her name is representative of Christian love. A fairy gifted with secret skills and powers of nature, she conceived in the wilderness with a handsome knight and then brought up her children in the forest. Concerned for their fates she sought out an evil enchantress, who told her that two of her sons would soon die.

Agar, Louise
Wise Virgin, 1982
A N Wilson

Assistant to the blind medieval scholar GILES FOX, whom she would like to marry, and not quite as amorphously sweet as her surname might suggest, she brings, via her mother, a certain vulgar energy into Fox's snobbishly cloistered life.

Agatha
The Family Reunion, 1939
T S Eliot

Youngest sister of AMY, DOWAGER LADY MONCHENSEY and the efficient principal of a women's college, she is the only member of the family invited to LORD HARRY MONCHENSEY's 'unsuitable' wedding. He calls her by her name, rather than 'Aunt Agatha', and considers her 'the completely strong' in her freedom from the family. She replies: 'I had to fight for many years to win my dispossession,/And many years to keep it'.

Agboreku
A Dance of the Forests, 1960
Wole Soyinka

An Elder of Sealed Lips and a shaman of Forest Head, it is he who maintains communication between the inhabitants of the physical and spirit worlds.

Agnes
A Delicate Balance, 1966
Edward Albee

A 'handsome' woman in her mid-fifties, content in her suburban life with her husband, Tobias, Agnes recognizes and accepts her own shortcomings and failures, but cannot exercise a similar tolerance in respect of her sister, the alcoholic CLAIRE. Striving fiercely to maintain a delicate balance within the family and her home, she finally concedes the merits of detachment, and retreats to a position of resignation, even regret: 'Everything becomes ... too late, finally; there's nothing there ... save rust; bones; and the wind'. Yet she still retains hope: after night, she observes, comes day, and 'when the daylight comes ... comes order with it'.

Agricola, Johannes
'Johannes Agricola in Meditation', in *Dramatic Romances*, 1845
Robert Browning

Browning's poetic re-creation of the 16th-century German reformer. He meditates on the inscrutable love of God, believing he has been chosen for salvation regardless of his life on earth. He is one of the elect and his salvation is sure even if he were to drink of all the sins in the world. His joy at the surety of heaven reveals his hypocrisy.

Agrippa, Menenius
Coriolanus, c.1607/8
William Shakespeare

He is a true blue-blooded patrician and politically quite astute. Although he really despises the plebeians, he makes the effort to make them see reason. He is unable to cope with the obstinacy of CORIOLANUS nor can he effectively outmanoeuvre the tribunes, JUNIUS BRUTUS and SICINIUS VELUTUS. His motives are usually good but he is overcome by forces which he cannot control.

Aguecheek, Sir Andrew
Twelfth Night, c.1601
William Shakespeare

A 'foolish knight' brought in by SIR TOBY BELCH to woo his niece OLIVIA. His comic appearance – tall, thin, with lank yellow hair – reflects his character. He confesses he has spent his time enjoying drinking, sport and dancing rather than in developing his intellectual capacity, which is reflected in his lack of ability in foreign languages and his ill-constructed letter of challenge to 'Cesario' (VIOLA). Taken in by Sir Toby's bonhomie, he fails to realize that he is being milked of his fortune. There is something

pathetic about his attempts to make an impression. Impetuous in his actions, he is a complete coward.

Ahab, Captain
Moby-Dick, 1851
Herman Melville

The 'ungodly, god-like captain' of the *Pequod*. He has been among colleges and cannibals, and has a livid white scar on his cheek, and a leg of whale-bone, a legacy of his earlier meeting with MOBY DICK. He has been a good sailor and family man, but is now a grim, fierce, unheeding figure who is consumed by his monomaniac obsession with exacting revenge on the whale. He would 'strike the sun if it offended' him, and drives his crew to enter an unholy pact to chase the whale.

Ahmed, Jimmy
Guerillas, 1975
V S Naipaul

Formerly a celebrated 'Black Power' revolutionary in London, Jimmy Ahmed sets up a commune in the West Indian island of his birth. He fantasizes about a young English visitor to the island, JANE, and becomes enraged by what he takes to be her superior attitudes. The novel he attempts to write about her reveals his great creative potential, hitherto hindered by his lack of self-knowledge.

Ahurole
The Concubine, 1966
Elechi Amadi

EKWUEME's first wife, Ahurole is betrothed to him when she is only eight days old. As a young woman she is irrational and moody, suffering from 'frequent unprovoked sobbing'. Caused mainly by the influence of a troublesome personal spirit, her difficulties as a young wife exacerbate Ahurole's behaviour. It is her insecurity which leads her to use a love potion, with disastrous results.

Aidallbery, Elizabeth
Elizabeth Alone, 1973
William Trevor

Admitted to hospital at the age of 41 for a hysterectomy, the compliant Elizabeth examines her untidily scattered life. Guilt has coloured it ever since, at the age of twelve, she was unable to cry at the funeral of her grim, disapproving father. Her unsatisfactory marriage to a man 13 years her senior, who became exactly like her father, has ended in divorce following her affair with a friend's husband, and her eldest daughter now barely speaks to her. Her time in hospital and fellow-patients, including the 'unnaturally compassionate' Miss Samson, help Elizabeth to discover how to be adequately alone.

Aimwell
The Beaux' Stratagem, 1707
George Farquhar

An impoverished younger son, Aimwell, with his fellow rake ARCHER, leaves the pleasures of London society to seek fortune and fame. Although severely financially reduced he is willing to spend what he has. Quick-witted and perceptive – he can spot an Irishman masquerading as a Frenchman! – he can be devious in pursuit of his own interests, but is also capable of falling in love at first sight with DORINDA, his intended victim. He reveals his true nobility when he saves her, and her mother, from three villainous highwaymen who break into their house.

Airman, the
'Journal of an Airman', in *The Orators: an English Study*, 1932
W H Auden
A disordered megalomaniac, epitomizing the Weak Strong Man of 1930s literature. Tortured by kleptomania (which may be a euphemism for something else) and by a paranoid belief in a 'universal conspiracy', he makes jottings which are superficially mad but may also convey shaman-like observations and insights gained when in a near-trance.

Ajax
Troilus and Cressida, 1601/2
William Shakespeare
A Greek leader of 'Trojan blood, nephew to HECTOR', Ajax commands little respect from his peers, who deride him for his stupidity and pride. 'Blockish' and 'self-willed', he is easily manipulated by flattery to accept Hector's challenge to the Greeks (really meant for ACHILLES). He is 'a man into whom nature hath so crowded humours that his valour is crushed into folly, his folly sauced with indiscretion'.

Akela
The Jungle Book, 1894
Rudyard Kipling
'The great gray Lone Wolf, who led all the Pack by strength and cunning'; Kipling said that the name means 'Alone'. He had already tangled with humankind when the man-cub MOWGLI came to the Pack, and he is justifiably wary of those who go on two legs. Thanks to Baden-Powell and the junior wing of the Scouting movement – once known as the Wolf Cubs – a whole generation of boys thinks of Akela as the archetypal authority figure.

Aku-Nna
The Bride Price, 1976
Buchi Emecheta
A young African woman, she slowly recognizes that her place in Nigerian society is determined by her value as a sexual commodity rather than by who she is as an individual.

Alan
Long Live Sandawara, 1979
Mudrooroo, formerly Colin Johnson
The teenage leader of an Aborigine resistance group in Perth, he is inspired by the exploits, recounted to him by NOORAK, of the legendary Sandawara and moves away from hopeless, unstructured violence to the centredness and moral sureness of full identification with his people and their homeland.

Albany, Duke of
The Fair Maid of Perth, or St Valentine's Day, in *Chronicles of the Canongate: Second Series*, 1828
Sir Walter Scott
Like his brother ROBERT III, KING OF SCOTLAND,

whom he resembles physically and whose throne he covets, Albany is not warlike by nature but has ample political skills to make up for this deficiency. 'He was experienced in the ways of court, calm, cool, and crafty, fixing upon the points which he desired to attain ... and never losing sight of them, though the winding path in which he trod might occasionally seem to point to a different direction.'

Albany, Duke of
King Lear, c.1607
William Shakespeare
GONERIL's husband, Albany represents in many ways the ordinary man who is stirred to do good by the evil of those around him. At first, he makes little impression on the action and is dismissed by his wife as a 'milk-liver'd man' and a 'moral fool', but eventually, outraged by the callous behaviour of his wife and her sister REGAN, his essentially good and honest nature comes to the fore and he takes charge of the kingdom.

Albertina
The Infernal Desire Machines of Doctor Hoffmann, 1972
Angela Carter
Albertina is the sexual being of DESIDERIO's dreams. The Empress of the Exotic, she is beautiful, surreal and mythically heroic in all her guises. She is a contradiction in being, and is maintained in appearance by the power of Desiderio's desire. She is strong-willed, brave, determined and believes in being amorous yet mysterious.

Albright, Mavis
Paradise, 1997
Toni Morrison
A timid, isolated young mother with an abusive husband, Mavis flees after the death of her baby twins. With the non-judgemental CONSOLATA she develops confidence in her abilities and discovers a resilient sense of self, becoming proud that 'the old Mavis was dead'. She happily believes that the dead children's spirits surround her at the Convent.

Alcibiades
Timon of Athens, 1607/8
William Shakespeare and perhaps Thomas Middleton
An Athenian captain, Alcibiades represents a clear-sighted, practical outlook upon life in contrast to TIMON OF ATHENS's myopic idealism. Less socially able than Timon, he has considerably more judgement of character. Yet, when his appeal to the Senate for the pardon of a friend is rejected, Alcibiades's subsequent defiance earns him a sentence of banishment. Later, he encounters Timon in his cave but Alcibiades's offer of help is refused. Instead, he accepts Timon's gold and marches on Athens in vengeance upon their mutual enemies.

Aldclyffe, Miss Cytherea
Desperate Remedies, 1871
Thomas Hardy
A bitter and complex old snob. As a girl she had been loved by the young CYTHEREA GRAYE's father, and she is full of regret about what her

life might have been. As true and fulfilling love has been denied her, she finds it difficult to show love and compassion for others, and she cruelly taunts Cytherea, whom she both envies and is attracted to. She claims that she longs to be 'artless and innocent', but although she is sad and lonely, she is also dark and mysterious.

Alden, Oliver
The Last Puritan: A Novel in the Form of a Memoir, 1936
George Santayana

The eponymous protagonist – not quite hero – he is fished out of Boston harbour much like a coelacanth, a surviving fossil from an older, more disciplined and strait-laced America based on duty and responsibility. While his dedicated rectitude is impressive, it is treated ironically, and his Harvard learning is seen as equally cold and lacking in passion.

Alden, Roberta
An American Tragedy, 1925
Theodore Dreiser

Roberta is a plain, working-class girl who is seduced by CLYDE GRIFFITHS and then abandoned when he switches his ambitions to the wealthy SONDRA FINCHLEY. Roberta's murder is based on the real-life killing of the pregnant Grace ('Billie') Brown in 1906 by her lover Chester Gillette.

Alen
The Pope's Wedding, 1962
Edward Bond

A 75-year-old recluse, he lives in a remote and disintegrating shack in East Anglia, becoming slowly engulfed by old newspapers and empty tins. He represents a richer social past, and the slow abandonment of the country and natural things by an increasingly technological society. He is mostly silent, perhaps resentful, perhaps suffering. He is looked after by PAT but in the eyes of SCOPEY he represents victorious independence, a successful revolution against convention. He becomes a figure of mystery, but in the end a scapegoat.

Alexander
Fire from Heaven, 1970
The Persian Boy, 1972
Funeral Games, 1981
Mary Renault

A deeply learned, enterprising, ambitious king, conscious of his own God-given status, boldly adventurous, but also utterly honest and true. He follows a stern, implacable moral code. Slightly-built, but possessed of legendary beauty, Alexander is the consummate soldier and Classical hero, leading his armies to ever more improbable feats of glory, but never losing his close identification with his own soldiers. His only true emotional ties are with his boyhood friend HEPHAISTION and the eunuch, BAGOAS. Alexander brings creativity to the art of war.

Alexandra
The Abbess of Crewe, 1974
Muriel Spark

The beautiful, aristocratic, dictatorial Lady Abbess of Crewe, who is both cynical and snobbish. While she strictly upholds the Rule of St Benedict in public, she privately encourages her supporters to use illegal methods, including electronic surveillance, to ensure the defeat of FELICITY, her rival for the position of Abbess. Her love of English poetry, grand self-assurance and outrageous hypocrisy are her saving graces.

Alexius Comnenus
Count Robert of Paris, 1831
Sir Walter Scott

A great Byzantine emperor, father of ANNA COMNENA, who wrote (and considerably magnified) his life story in the *Alexiad*. She was never able to win from him the title of emperor for her husband Nicephorus Briennius.

Alfie
Alfie, 1963
Alfie Darling, 1970
Bill Naughton

A sexually voracious lorry driver, with a love 'em and leave 'em philosophy. Emotionally independent, he keeps his feelings carefully measured, fearing that real engagement with others will make him vulnerable. His affairs, therefore, are based on quantity, not quality, and there is an edge of sadness and regret, an unfulfilled longing, in his bearing. He has not realized that by keeping those who might give him real love at arm's length, he is robbing himself of the possibility of happiness.

Alfieri
A View from the Bridge, 1955
Arthur Miller

A lawyer, the 'chorus' figure who presents the audience with his views as the play unwinds. A cautious, philosophical man, he is an adviser and friend to EDDIE CARBONE, knowing, however, that the legal sense he speaks will inevitably be rejected by Eddie's emotional involvement. His unusual dual role – as both a character in the play and a commentator on it – guides and structures the audience's reactions and sympathies.

Alfred, Mr
Mr Alfred M.A., 1972
George Friel

An alienated middle-aged schoolteacher and 'veteran pubcrawler', whose first name is not revealed. He is shy, timid, ineffectual, professionally marooned, and increasingly unable to communicate with the generation he must teach, taking refuge in drinking. His own poetic sensibility has never been fulfilled, and he is incapable of giving or receiving love. In the end, he loses his tenuous grip on reality and sinks into breakdown and madness in a graphically described urban wasteland.

Ali(x)
The.PowerBook, 2001
Jeanette Winterson

Ali ('Is that your real name?' 'Real enough.' 'Male or female?' 'Does it matter?') runs an e-mail service fashioning stories to order. An elusive, enigmatic fabulist and a plunderer of mythology,

Ali's stories deal equally with passion, sex and love. Alix (so named 'because x marks the spot') is the adopted child of a superstitious working-class couple. Curious and precocious, it is Alix's duty to 'cheat time', explore the world and 'find the buried treasure'. Ali and Ali(x) are perhaps the same person; frequently female, Ali finds herself disconcertingly ensnared by the love of which she writes: 'Thousands of miles away your tears tap tap on the board. If your make-up is run-proof, my heart isn't.'

Alice
Alice's Adventures in Wonderland, 1865
Through the Looking-Glass, and What Alice Found There, 1872
Lewis Carroll

Alice, a slightly prim seven-year-old, is an intelligent curious well-read little girl who pits her wits against the odd and often cross characters she meets, trying to make sense of them and their activities. She grows very small, then very large, but learns how to regulate her size. She tries to recite the improving poems written for middle-class Victorian children, but gets them confusingly wrong. The real Alice was Alice Liddell, daughter of the Dean of Christ Church Cathedral, Oxford.

Alice
The Good Terrorist, 1985
Doris Lessing

An angry middle-class girl, fighting against her background, Alice is full of self-conscious beliefs. She has principles, but becomes disappointed by the way that politics prove to be an unsatisfactory vehicle for them. Searching for inner peace, as well as outer contentment, she is full of guilt. She is a disenchanted 'good girl', who is loving, caring and anxious. Her rebellion comes from a crisis within her, but she is deeply sincere in her thoughts and feelings.

Alice
Magnificence, 1973
Howard Brenton

A homosexual Tory cabinet minister, with a background of Oxford and the army and a constituency 'the wrong side of Leicester', he is caustic, ambitious, ruthless and a favourite within the Conservative party. He is happy to adapt his image as necessary to maintain his popularity. His friend BABS, a former minister, is repelled by his compromises and accuses him of marketing himself as if he were a breakfast cereal. Babs clearly sees the steel beneath Alice's charm. 'You are a peculiarly modern, peculiarly English kind of fascist', he remarks.

Alice
Tiny Alice, 1965
Edward Albee

The richest woman in a world that clearly conforms to Lewis Carroll logic, she is another of Albee's violently destructive female figures. For obscurely symbolic motives, she is bent on the corruption of a lay Catholic brother, BROTHER JULIAN, whom she seduces and destroys.

Alison
The Owl Service, 1967
Alan Garner

Sickly and weak-willed, Alison is always rather too eager to please. She becomes the vessel for the strange force that is trapped in the claustrophobic Welsh valley where she lives with her mother and step-family, and which is mysteriously released through the owl-patterned dinner service she and GWYN find in the attic. Frightened by the strong emotions she feels within her, she is unable to express them properly. She would like to 'belong' to the valley in the way that Gwyn does, although ironically she does own the house, inherited from her father. She is torn between her affection for Gwyn and her sense of duty to her mother. She bends with the wind and has no real understanding of the force that possesses her.

Alisoun → Wife of Bath, the

Alithea
The Country Wife, 1675
William Wycherley

A young lady wooed by HARCOURT, Alithea delights in hoodwinking her other suitor, the fop SPARKISH. She tells Sparkish that the visiting clergyman (Harcourt in disguise) is out to marry her, and is highly amused when Sparkish mistakenly believes that she is suggesting the clergyman would marry *them*: 'Invincible stupidity! I tell you he would marry me as your rival, not your chaplain.'

Allbee, Kirby
The Victim, 1947
Saul Bellow

An anti-Semitic gentile who is sacked from his job and blames a Jewish acquaintance, ASA LEVENTHAL, for it. Initially a victim, he becomes a menacing victimizer, and a kind of repulsive, malicious 'double' to Leventhal, pursuing him into all corners of his life. He has no sense of his own guilt or deficiency, but blames a changing world, and feels like 'the Indian who sees a train running over the prairie where the buffalo used to roam'.

Allen, Arabella and Benjamin
Pickwick Papers, 1837
Charles Dickens

A friend of THE WARDLES, Arabella secretly marries NATHANIEL WINKLE, although her coarse, stout brother tries to marry her to BOB SAWYER, his friend, fellow medical student and drinking companion. The young men fail in the medical practice they set up and become surgeons for the East India Company.

Allen, Clara
Lonesome Dove, 1985
Larry McMurtry

GUS MCCRAE's former sweetheart, she is an almost archetypal image of frontier womanhood, indomitable but nurturing, independent but affectionate. With a disabled husband, she runs her Nebraska farm with fierce conviction and pride.

Allen, Esme
Amy's View, 1997
David Hare

A late middle-aged, well-known West End actress finding it increasingly difficult to secure suitable roles, Esme is domineering, manipulative, cruel, baleful and quick to take offence; but she is also sentimental, easy to please, and dedicated to the theatre. While enjoying a close if difficult relationship with her daughter AMY THOMAS, she is defiantly antagonistic towards her son-in-law, DOMINIC TYGHE, who stands for much that she despises.

Alleyn, Detective Inspector Roderick
A Man Lay Dead, 1934, et seq
Ngaio Marsh

The true gentleman of detectives, he has the right connections in society, and brings the elegance and gentility of his upbringing among the privileged echelons of society to the otherwise grimy world of crime-detection. Married to an artist, he shows a tenderness and capacity for sentiment unusual among those of his profession, but these softening qualities do not make him any less ruthless in his pursuit of the criminal, or any less tough in his defence of truth.

Allington, Margaret
The Return of the Soldier, 1918
Rebecca West

Margaret is dowdy and shabby, 'repulsively furred with neglect and poverty'. Her body has been scarred by hard work, but her simplicity and serene goodness remain intact. She is the woman whom CAPTAIN CHRIS BALDRY loved 15 years earlier, and although married to the dull Mr Grey, she has been a continuous presence in Chris's subconscious. It is her task to shatter Chris's innermost dreams and return him to mundane reality. She is an allegory of dignified altruism.

Allnut, Charlie
The African Queen, 1935
C S Forester

A man's man, with a fondness for gin, he is an easy-going, haphazard adventurer, who has learned the skills of his engineer's trade on the river deltas of Africa. He would prefer to be left to his own devices than be called to engagement with other people, but he is drawn into a relationship with the missionary ROSE SAYER which surprises him with its emotions, and draws from him deep resources of courage, imagination and warmth.

Allworthy, Miss Bridget, briefly Mrs Blifil
The History of Tom Jones, 1749
Henry Fielding

SQUIRE ALLWORTHY's only sister, she has reached an age at which she might be thought to have become an old maid, were it not for the fact that her maidenhood has been slightly compromised in the begetting of the foundling, TOM JONES. Despite, or because of, this, she is notably severe in morals, and it is this quality, rather than her pinched looks, which leavens the passion of her suitor and, more briefly, husband, CAPTAIN JOHN BLIFIL.

Allworthy, Squire
The History of Tom Jones, 1749
Henry Fielding

The foundling TOM JONES is found as an infant in the bed of this well-off and benevolent widower, giving rise to inevitable rumours of fatherhood (which prove to be reasonably close to home), but failing to disturb his equanimity, which is based on 'an agreeable person, a sound constitution, a solid understanding, and a benevolent heart'. He does, however, later turn Tom away, before it is discovered that the boy is his natural nephew.

Alma
The Faerie Queene, 1590–6
Sir Edmund Spenser

Alma is a fair and virginal maiden who dwells in a castle that represents Temperance (an allegory for the body, the mortal part of humankind). She is graceful and modest, with flowing golden hair and she dresses in a robe of lily white. Sober, liberal, wise and modest, she exists to 'nourish' her castle, and rules over the castle's other inhabitants, such as Appetite, Imagination, Judgement and Memory.

Alma
Mardi, 1849
Herman Melville

A god in Mardi. He is 'an illustrious prophet, and teacher divine' who appeared in past ages to the Mardians, and was known also as 'Brami' and 'Mannko'. He appears in 'dark and benighted times' as a Christ-like figure preaching 'the ways of truth, virtue and happiness', with 'promises of beatitude hereafter'.

Almond, Julia
A Pin to See the Peepshow, 1934
F Tennyson Jesse

The selfish, unfaithful, sharp-tongued, discontented protagonist, she is permanently someone 'for whom something lovely was about to happen'. She is the most dominant girl at her school, but has a face 'that needed everything to be just right'. She is wrapped up in dreams and fantasies of a life which her real situation denies, and she is finally destroyed by her inability to see beyond her dream to the truth of her evil lover's conduct, and is convicted of a crime she did not commit.

Aloetta, Moses
The Lonely Londoners, 1956
Moses Ascending, 1975
Samuel Selvon

A Trinidadian living in London, Moses has a job as a night-worker in a factory producing pot-scourers. He is competent and soft-hearted and acts as a beacon for all the new immigrants from the West Indies. Eager for news of home and full of comical stories about lively characters he has met in London, he makes his room a regular meeting place. Enjoying his position as 'old veteran' he teases the newcomers but, remembering his own fears on his arrival, shows compassion in helping them settle.

Alonso
The Tempest, 1611
William Shakespeare

The King of Naples, who was instrumental in the overthrow of PROSPERO, the Duke of Milan, by his brother, ANTONIO. Whereas his fellow conspirators suffer no pangs of remorse, indeed they even conspire to murder him, Alonso is so gnawed by guilt that he contemplates suicide. He is distraught at the apparent death of his son, but after they are reunited shows that he has learned from the experience.

Alphonso
The Gentleman Usher, 1602/3
George Chapman

A despotic duke who, despite his advanced years, pursues the hand of MARGARET, thus becoming the rival of his own son, PRINCE VINCENTIO. He attempts to woo Margaret with masques, but his artistic sense is somewhat lacking, as is, for a time at least, his paternal feeling.

Alpine, Frankie
The Assistant, 1957
Bernard Malamud

A bookish gentile who robs an old Jewish storekeeper, MORRIS BOBER, then returns to work for him. He is idealistic but lacking in direction and values. He falls in love with Bober's daughter, HELEN BOBER, and saves her from rape, but then forces himself on her. Frankie falls inextricably under Bober's influence, and after his death takes over his store, beginning to acquire Bober's virtues of honesty and forgiveness. His symbolic rebirth, begun when he falls into Bober's grave, is finalized when he is circumcised. 'The pain enraged and inspired him. After Passover he became a Jew'.

Alsemero
The Changeling, 1653
Thomas Middleton and William Rowley

The nobleman who usurps ALONZO DE PIRACQUO in BEATRICE-JOANNA's affections. Like Alonzo, he is at first blinded by love for her, seeing in her outward beauty an inner 'holiness'. He, however, is not as trusting as Alonzo and before marrying Beatrice uses a potion to test her virginity. Fooled at this point by her cunning, when he does discover her true nature he is horrified at the depths of her sin and at his own lack of judgement.

Altamont
The Fair Penitent, 1703
Nicholas Rowe

Altamont, a young gentleman, has been offered the hand in marriage of CALISTA by her father, SCIOLTO. But when he discovers that, contrary to her protestations, she is continuing her affair with LOTHARIO, he kills her lover in a duel. Despite this deed, he is not a natural man of action. In fact, he is rather an insipid character and appears to have few developed views on anything. His strongest friendship is not with Calista but with his brother-in-law, HORATIO, who warns him of her duplicity. It is this male comradeship which survives the play, strengthened by tragedy.

Altamont, Frederick → Bunce, Jack

Altamount, Col, also known as Armstrong
The History of Pendennis, 1848–50
W M Thackeray

An alias for BLANCHE AMORY's father, who has escaped from prison and is blackmailing SIR FRANCIS CLAVERING, who is now married to his ex-wife. Altamount has the ability to move unseen through society, and to be judged on his appearances and his shallow promises only.

Alter, Polly
The Truth about Lorin Jones, 1988
Alison Lurie

In her middle years Polly rebels against her reasonable but infuriating husband's idea of who she is. Confrontation becomes the keynote of her quest for truth and justice, but the gradual realization that emotions and relationships are complex and unpredictable forces her to rethink her rather fixed ideas. Given to feeling sorry for herself in times of difficulty, Polly has always felt herself abandoned by the men in her life, but her research into the life of LORIN JONES, with its conflicting perspectives and interpretations, alerts her to the disturbing fact that she has abandoned them.

Altofronto, Giovanni, Duke of Genoa → Malevole

Alu
The Swamp Dwellers, 1964
Wole Soyinka

The loyal wife of MAKURI and guardian of their precarious home in the swamps, where they eke out a thin existence in a treacherous land that stands in part for present-day Nigeria, but also as a metaphor for the human condition.

Alworth, Lady
A New Way to Pay Old Debts, 1633
Philip Massinger

A wealthy widow of high reputation and stepmother of TOM ALWORTH. She was deeply attached to her late husband and therefore assists his former benefactor, FRANK WELBORNE, in his strategy to regain his fortune. Her integrity is seen in her advice to LORD LOVELL not to marry the daughter of the rich SIR GILES OVERREACH because his gains are ill-gotten.

Alworth, Tom
A New Way to Pay Old Debts, 1633
Philip Massinger

An impecunious and romantic young gentleman, in love with MARGARET OVERREACH, daughter of the evil SIR GILES OVERREACH, who stole his father's lands. He is page to LORD LOVELL, who agrees to help him marry Margaret against her father's wishes, but he worries that Lovell will want her for himself. Among his virtues are loyalty and generosity.

Amanda
The Relapse, or Virtue in Danger, 1696
Sir John Vanbrugh

A woman with long experience of the failings of

LOVELESS, her husband, Amanda is alert for any signs of his relapsing into the rakishness which he promises he has abandoned for good. His proposed trip to London spells potential temptation, and she decides to accompany him. Yet it is she who becomes curious about the pleasures of metropolitan life and finds herself the object of WORTHY's attentions. A pragmatic judge of character, she is also rather provincial and emotionally self-deluding; her solution to her own temptation is to remain affectionate towards Worthy on the condition that he 'forbear to ask whatever is unfit for me to grant'.

Amar
The Spider's House, 1955
Paul Bowles

A young Arab who spins the ensnaring and toxic web of story which gradually draws in and paralyzes his outwardly sophisticated Western listeners. He is a disconcerting figure, similar in kind to the treacherous 'orientals' of 18th- and 19th-century Gothic novels.

Amaryllis
Back to Methuselah, 1921
George Bernard Shaw

Amaryllis appears during the final section of this five-part play. *As Far as Thought can Reach* is set in a remote garden Utopia in 31,920AD. She is a baby born from an egg on stage, but emerges, as children do in the future, aged about 16, with four years of childhood before her. She befriends STREPHON and is instructed by a SHE-ANCIENT that although she could live indefinitely, she will be killed one day by accident.

Amberley, Mary
Eyeless in Gaza, 1936
Aldous Huxley

A cultured older woman who initiates the young ANTHONY BEAVIS into sex, Mary Amberley reveals much about herself when she observes that 'People will insist on treating the *mons Veneris* as though it were Mount Everest. Too silly!' She descends to her lowest when she allows the cynical swindler Gerry Watchett to seduce her in the most degrading circumstances. She paradoxically finds 'this intolerable degradation' to be a revelation which 'was the Apocalypse, the whole Apocalypse at once, angel and beast, plague, lamb and whore in a single divine, revolting, overwhelming experience'. Her real Apocalypse, however, is still to come.

Amberson, Fanny
The Magnificent Ambersons, 1918
Booth Tarkington

It is ironic but telling that the last major bearer of the 'magnificent' name of Amberson should be a neurotic spinster, obsessively locked in the past.

Ambien II
The Sirian Experiments, 1980
Doris Lessing

An idealistic, honest and insightful 'snouted monster', Ambien is concerned with re-conciliation and unity. He enjoys full participation in the affairs of his cosmos. A great communicator between peoples, he is highly organized, and well respected. He has diplomatic tendencies, and is reflective rather than impulsive. His self-effacing style and candid admission of failure and regret endear him to the reader. Inspiring loyalty and establishing firm friendships, he injects a random, chaotic universe with a drop of hope.

Ambrose, Father, Abbot of Kennaquhair, formerly Edward Glendinning
The Monastery, 1820
The Abbot, 1820
Sir Walter Scott

The younger brother of SIR HALBERT GLENDINNING, he is 'light-haired, blue-eyed, and of fairer complexion, and not exhibiting that rosy hue which colours the sanguine cheek of robust health'. More suited to the cloister than to the open field, he takes holy orders.

Ambrose, Helen
The Voyage Out, 1915
Virginia Woolf

An open-minded woman, liberal and liberated, she is keen on progressive education and on promoting equality between the sexes. She feels, however, that women must behave in a manner worthy of equality. Caring and kind, with a lively sense of humour, she does not suffer fools gladly.

Ambrosio
The Monk, 1796
Matthew Gregory Lewis

This complex villain, swerving from chastity to sexual perversion and violence, and from supernatural power to satanic enslavement, brings chaos onto the heads of those around him. His repressed life and subsequent descent into spiritual and physical degradation exposes the concealed sickness of a church-dominated and politically corrupt system. He begets violence and is destroyed by it.

Amelia, Miss
The Ballad of the Sad Café, 1953
Carson McCullers

The solitary and eccentric storeowner whose life is transformed by the arrival of COUSIN LYMON. She is singular in both appearance and behaviour; over six feet tall with a masculine demeanour, she lives a simple life and is industrious despite her considerable wealth. Her love for Cousin Lymon reveals a capacity for selfless devotion, which is contrary to her reputation as a ruthless and formidable character.

Amelia Jane
Amelia Jane Again!, 1946
Enid Blyton

A clumsy big doll with black curly hair (of which she is rather proud) and a smart red dress, she has no manners at all; she never shakes hands, says how-do-you-do or offers her sweets to visitors to the nursery. She is forever teasing the other toys, playing pranks on them and interfering with their games, yet although she always does whatever she likes she is naughty, rather than wicked, and never means to harm anyone.

Amerigo, Prince
The Golden Bowl, 1904
Henry James

Naming him after the man who lent the New World its familiar name is a way of heightening James's old opposition between 'innocent' America and European 'experience'. Penniless, the prince woos and wins the heiress MAGGIE VERVER. All that comes between the glittering couple is a symbolic flawed bowl, bought by Maggie, but once viewed and coldly priced by CHARLOTTE STANT, Maggie's friend and the prince's former mistress.

Ames, Cathy, properly Cathy Ames Trask, also known as Kate Albey
East of Eden, 1952
John Steinbeck

A vicious and calculating ex-prostitute who marries the rancher ADAM TRASK and bears him twins, before deserting him and reverting to the brothel. 'There was a time when a girl like Cathy would have been called possessed by the devil ... [But] as though nature concealed a trap, [she] had from the first a face of innocence.'

Aminadab
'The Birthmark', 1843, in *Mosses from an Old Manse*, 1846
Nathaniel Hawthorne

An underworker in AYLMER's laboratory, he plays CALIBAN to the scientist's PROSPERO. 'With his vast strength, his shaggy hair, his smoky aspect, and the indescribable earthiness that encrusted him, he seemed to represent man's physical nature', and his name has been interpreted as a quasi-anagram of 'bad-in-man' (it is also a reversal of *bad anima*). Ironically, it is he who perceives the futility of Aylmer's search for physical perfection.

Amintor
The Maid's Tragedy, 1610
Francis Beaumont and John Fletcher

Because the king wants to conceal his relationship with his mistress Evadne, he forces Amintor, a courtier, to marry her. Amintor, who had hoped to marry ASPATIA, obeys the king's wishes. An honest and morally strict man, Amintor, it seems, is a virgin but discovers his new wife is not: 'A maidenhead Amintor at my years?' Having found out Evadne's secret, Amintor's honour is crushed, yet his personal humiliation is outweighed by his sense of loyalty and duty to the king, and he suffers in embittered and defeated silence. His refusal to act precipitates the final tragedy.

Amir, Karim
The Buddha of Suburbia, 1990
Hanif Kureishi

A young bisexual, Amir is the partly English and partly Indian son of Haroon (the 'Buddha' of the title). Having spent all his life in Britain, he regards himself as having 'emerged from two old histories', yet belonging wholly to neither. Leaving the suburbs for London, the former Imperial centre, he becomes an actor but is only offered 'ethnic' roles that require him to caricature his Asian origins. Solipsistic and apolitical, Amir is fascinated by the notion of success but frequently lacks confidence and motivation. However, he gains a deeper emotional understanding both of himself and others as a result of his complex relationship with Eleanor, an actress.

Amlet, Dick
The Confederacy, 1705
Sir John Vanbrugh

The son of MRS AMLET, Dick has inherited his mother's deviousness. In order to impress CORINNA GRIPE, he poses as a colonel, recruiting his mother's maid, FLIPPANTA, and his friend, Brass, to impersonate his staff. Dick is crafty, but not one of nature's great thinkers. In an attempt to make some quick money, he steals CLARISSA GRIPE's necklace, which is in his mother's possession, and tries to sell it. The plan is bungled, and Dick's fraudulence and foolishness exposed for all the world to see. By chance, though, Corinna loves him and all ends well.

Amlet, Mrs
The Confederacy, 1705
Sir John Vanbrugh

As a seller of cosmetics, Mrs Amlet is the kind of person in whom various women easily confide, but she is not averse to exploiting the occasional confidence. She acts, sometimes, as a pawnbroker, and is the current holder of CLARISSA GRIPE's necklace. Having observed the foibles of several ladies and their husbands, she concludes that 'everybody's for appearing to be more than they are, and that ruins all'.

Amoret
The Faerie Queene, 1590–6
Sir Edmund Spenser

The daughter of a wood nymph, and the twin sister of BELPHOEBE. The twins were separated at birth and Amoret was brought up in the paradise garden of fertility by Venus, the Goddess of Love, who bestowed many virtues upon her. She has a face of angelic beauty and a celestial soul.

Amory, Blanche
The History of Pendennis, 1848–50
W M Thackeray

A haughty and hard-hearted girl, thoroughly undeserving of her romantic-heroine name. She is a version of BECKY SHARP, stripped of the charm. When ARTHUR PENDENNIS falls in love with her, the match is cynically pursued by MAJOR PENDENNIS, who is all too well aware that Blanche is the daughter of the cynical and villainous Armstrong/COL ALTAMOUNT. Though Arthur feels obliged to honour his proposal, she decides in favour of HARRY FOKER, whose wealth is in beer.

Amphialus
The Countess of Pembroke's Arcadia, 1581–4, published 1590
Sir Philip Sidney

Son of CECROPIA, the sister-in-law of DUKE BASILIUS, he is the subject of his mother's plot to win him the throne. Regrettably, he lacks the courage for her murderous scheming.

Amritrao
A Passage to India, 1924
E M Forster

A 'fine-looking man, large and bony with gray closely cropped hair', he is a distinguished Calcutta barrister. A skilled courtroom tactician, who displays a cool head and logical mind, he is respected both professionally and personally but remains the scourge of the pukka English at the Chandrapore Club because of his 'notoriously' anti-British stance.

Amy
The Roaring Nineties, 1946
Golden Miles, 1948
Winged Seeds, 1950
Katharine Susannah Prichard

Pretty and vivacious, Amy is one of life's butterflies, attracted by the glitter of life. 'Amy was like a kitten that purred when it was well-fed and stroked caressingly'. Her main failing is a lack of moral backbone.

Ananias
The Alchemist, 1610
Ben Jonson

A deacon of the Brethren of Amsterdam (a strict sect of Anabaptists) and an associate of TRIBULATION WHOLESOME. He is one of several credulous people tricked by SUBTLE, FACE and DOL COMMON, a group of rogues posing as alchemists. Ananias believes that his consultations will result in wealth for his puritan sect. Later, his gullibility draws him into a plot to forge Dutch money.

Ananta
The Big Heart, 1945, revised edition 1980
Mulk Raj Anand

A politically enlightened Hindu artisan who attempts to organize his fellow coppersmiths against the encroachment of mechanization and proletarianization. Though generous in spirit and full of good-natured solidarity, he underestimates the power of progress and finally succumbs to it.

Ancients, He- and She-
Back to Methuselah, 1921
George Bernard Shaw

These long-lifers appear in the final section of this five-part play. *As Far as Thought can Reach* is set in a remote garden Utopia in 31,920AD. The Ancients are near naked, almost sexless and bald, and lead an ascetic, intellectual existence in contemplation of the relationship between the body, individual will and thought. 'The day will come when there will be no people, only thought', predicts one. 'And that will be life eternal', confirms another. They represent immortality, perpetual existence doomed to extinction by the flaw of inevitable accident.

Anderson
Professional Foul, 1977
Tom Stoppard

A Professor of Ethics at Cambridge, Anderson combines business (a congress) with pleasure (an international football match) on a visit to Prague. Although a man of the mind he is interested in the body, especially the unclothed female one. He is dismissive about his fellow theoreticians and their differing stances on the subject, yet he radically changes his own position on human rights after his meeting with, and the subsequent disappearance of, his ex-pupil HOLLAR, of whose plight he has been obtusely unaware. His supreme self-confidence, which allows him to lecture English international footballers on tactics, is briefly assailed but quickly retrieved.

Anderson, Bill
'Stiffner and Jim (Thirdly, Bill)', in *While the Billy Boils*, 1888
Henry Lawson

'Bill was mostly a quiet young chap, from Sydney, except when he got drunk – which was seldom – and then he was a lively customer from all around ... He held that the population of the world was divided into two classes – one was spielers, and the other was mugs. He reckoned that he wasn't a mug.'

Anderson, Charley
The 42nd Parallel, 1930
The Big Money, 1936, part of the *U.S.A.* trilogy, 1938
John Dos Passos

The good-looking North Dakota boy who makes a name for himself as a flying ace in World War I. Charley, on his return from Europe, finds himself sucked into the wheeling and dealing world of postwar, big-boom America. Seduced by the attraction of 'the big money', but simultaneously disillusioned when he finds it cannot buy him happiness, formerly reliable Charley starts to lead an increasingly dissipated lifestyle, his instability being paralleled by the great fluctuations in the stock market.

Anderson, Judith
The Devil's Disciple, 1897
George Bernard Shaw

Judith is the wife of PASTOR ANTHONY ANDERSON. Over 20 years his junior, she is a pretty, sentimental, proper woman; the admiration of others has given her a certain self-assurance. When the British army arrest RICHARD DUDGEON, mistaking him for the pastor, his parting kiss causes Judith to swoon. Representing the love motive in the Shavian scheme of things, she becomes infatuated with him, erroneously believing that he acted for her sake and not from his own motives. When sentence of death is pronounced, Judith desperately cries out that Dudgeon is not Anderson. After his reprieve, Dudgeon promises her that her confession will remain a secret.

Anderson, Pastor Anthony
The Devil's Disciple, 1897
George Bernard Shaw

Aged about 50, Pastor Anderson is a shrewd Presbyterian, 'a man capable of making the most of this world, and perhaps a little apologetically conscious of getting on better with it than a sound Presbyterian ought'. The play is set in New Hampshire during the American War of Independence. RICHARD DUDGEON's selflessness in allowing himself to be mistakenly arrested by the British army and tried as the rebel pastor transforms Anderson from a high-minded moralist into a man of action.

Andrews, John
Three Soldiers, 1921
John Dos Passos

A Harvard-educated composer, he enlists in the United States army in the hope of finding a decent, brave cause to give his life and art some grand significance. Disappointed and betrayed by the bureaucratic inertia and cruelty of the system, he deserts with the farm boy CHRISFIELD, and is arrested, leaving his precious score to be scattered by the wind.

Andrews, Joseph
The History of the Adventures of Joseph Andrews and of his Friend Mr Abraham Adams, 1742
Henry Fielding

He is the brother of Samuel Richardson's PAMELA ANDREWS, on whose trials and tribulations his life story is initially intended as a skit. As the only son of Gammer and Gaffar Andrews, he is placed in service under SIR THOMAS BOOBY, where repeated attempts are made on his chastity, and by and large are resisted. Notoriously, he rather fades from view as the novel progresses and the livelier PARSON ADAMS occupies the foreground.

Andrews, Neil and Pam
Just Between Ourselves, 1976
Alan Ayckbourn

Neil and Pam Andrews call at the home of DENNIS and VERA CROWTHORNE, to inspect the car which Dennis has for sale. Both couples are imprisoned in bleak marriages, yet the men cannot admit the anger and torment their wives are suffering. Good-natured, but sexually inadequate and emotionally myopic, Neil cannot understand why Pam, a former office supervisor and now a housewife, is so temperamentally unpredictable and emotionally and intellectually unfulfilled. She dreams of escape and romance, briefly, even with Dennis, while Neil, dithering and turning to the stronger Dennis for support, accepts investment advice that results in disaster.

Andrews, Pamela
Pamela, 1740–1
Samuel Richardson

Educated beyond her class position, the conspicuously beautiful and literate Pamela refuses to jettison her cherished belief in the sanctity of free will. She resists society's conception of woman as property and defiantly proclaims: 'Indeed I am PAMELA, HER OWN SELF'. Her employer, MR B, whom she eventually marries, subverts her putative independence with his tricks and disguises, and Pamela is reduced to considering suicide. Naively thinking that marriage will give her a place in society, Pamela is disabused of this notion by Mr B's 'polygamy and prerogative'. She discovers that marriage is a penance and a curse, a state of humiliating subordination.

Andrews, Polly
The Group, 1963
Mary McCarthy

Polly is that quiet type of girl who notices things and knows what is going on. She has the placid exterior to match her kindness and patience, but she is no stranger to emotional stress. Changed circumstances and family failings present practical problems; difficult decisions have to be made and responsibilities accepted. Genuinely interested in others and their problems, Polly is reserved about herself and shrinks from accepting sympathy. She copes and survives and is surprised to find, as if by accident, happiness with a man of similar strength and integrity.

Andrews, Todd
The Floating Opera, 1955, revised edition 1967
John Barth

A lawyer in his home town of Cambridge, Maryland, who is obsessed with his relationship with his late father, Thomas Andrews. He is haunted by their failures of communication, and writes a long letter to his dead father attempting to explain himself, but at the same time insisting on maintaining his freedom from him. He cannot acknowledge his love for Jane Mack, while his enquiries, and failed suicide-cum-mass-murder, lead him to an ultimately nihilistic conclusion.

Androcles
Androcles and the Lion, 1912
George Bernard Shaw

A Greek tailor and a Christian, Androcles is middle-aged, thin, apparently rather ridiculous, and cursed with a bickering wife. In the jungle, the sight of a lion terrifies him. But he loves animals, and the fact that the lion is incapacitated by a thorn in its paw inspires him to a torrent of baby talk as he extracts it. Later, when the captive Androcles is thrust into the Roman arena to be devoured by a lion, his adversary proves none other than his old friend. Their joyful embrace, a triumph of faith over fear, is sufficient to convert the Roman EMPEROR to Christianity.

Andromache
Troilus and Cressida, 1601/2
William Shakespeare

The dutiful wife of HECTOR. The night before her husband's final battle Andromache has ominous dreams of 'bloody turbulence' and 'shapes and forms of slaughter'. She begs and reasons with Hector not to fight that day, but to no avail.

Andronicus, Lucius
Titus Andronicus, c.1589
William Shakespeare

A son of TITUS ANDRONICUS, who shows disturbing willingness to sacrifice QUEEN TAMORA's son Alarbus. Lucius is later banished from Rome for trying to rescue two of his brothers from execution. He throws in his lot with the Goths, who wish to be revenged on Rome and its emperor, and returns at the head of an invading army.

Andronicus, Marcus
Titus Andronicus, c.1589
William Shakespeare

The brother of TITUS ANDRONICUS and Tribune of the Plebs. After attempting to disperse warring factions and make Titus emperor, he lets the latter cede authority to SATURNINUS. Upset by Titus's killing of his son Mutius Andronicus, he is further grieved when his brother goes mad, seeing the possibilities receding of knitting 'this scattered corn into one mutual sheaf'.

Andronicus, Quintus
Titus Andronicus, c.1589
William Shakespeare
One of the sons of TITUS ANDRONICUS. He is framed and executed alongside his brother Martius Andronicus for the murder of the emperor's brother BASSIANUS by AARON, THE MOOR and the evil sons of QUEEN TAMORA. They are out for revenge for the sacrificial murder of their brother, performed by the Andronicus family.

Andronicus, Titus
Titus Andronicus, c.1589
William Shakespeare
Apparently nobler and braver than all other warriors, Titus returns in triumph to Rome after years of war against the Goths. Unwisely, he both sacrifices a son of QUEEN TAMORA and lets the treacherous SATURNINUS become emperor. When he sees his family being destroyed by Tamora and her lover AARON, THE MOOR, he goes mad and raves almost touchingly, before baking his enemies' heads into a pie and charging headlong into a climactic bloodbath.

Andy
Moonlight, 1993
Harold Pinter
A foul-mouthed, raging former civil servant, Andy is first seen in the play bedridden and dying. Isolated from his sons (who occupy themselves with word games) and his daughter (who may be dead; she initially appears as a ghostly shadow), he blusters from his bed, insulting his wife, demanding contact with his children. He is also isolated from his younger self; a former lover recalls him as an elegant, romantic figure, but according to his wife, 'most people were ready to vomit after ten minutes in your company'. Yet behind his anger lies a profound fear of imminent death, a bitter awareness of his failures and the realization that he has long lost whatever faith he might have had. 'I don't believe it's going to be pitch black forever', he cries. 'There must be a loophole. The only trouble is, I can't find it.'

Angelica
Love for Love, 1695
William Congreve
A niece of FORESIGHT and in love with VALENTINE LEGEND, Angelica masterminds the plot to prevent SIR SAMPSON LEGEND disinheriting the high-spending Valentine in favour of his doltish younger son, BEN LEGEND. Her motives are based on love rather than money, for she is wealthy in her own right. Besides, she is spirited, determined and enjoys the fun. She also has an intuitive grasp of the vanities and foibles of men. Inducing Sir Sampson to propose marriage to her, she secures both the bond which Valentine foolishly signed, and his blessing on her marriage to his son. But as she sagely observes:

'the pleasure of a masquerade is done when we come to show our faces'.

Angelica, Princess
The Rose and the Ring, 1855
W M Thackeray
The only daughter of King Valoroso of Paflagonia, she is wooed by her cousin, PRINCE GIGLIO, who gives her a magic ring that makes the wearer beloved by all.

Angelo
Measure for Measure, c.1604
William Shakespeare
The lord who deputizes for DUKE VINCENTIO and is known throughout Vienna as 'a man of stricture and firm abstinence'. He seems to be devoid of human weaknesses and appetites, his pleasures being 'profits of the mind, study and fast'. The power he is given, however, has its corrupting effect on him, offering him temptation in the shape of ISABELLA begging for her brother's life. Despite (or perhaps because of) his repressive puritanism, he yields to this temptation, tyrannically abusing the power he has been given.

Angelo, Albert
Albert Angelo, 1964
B S Johnson
The central character in an experimental novel which ultimately undermines the concept of 'character'. He is a supply teacher who 'knew he was by vocation an architect and only by economic accident a teacher'. Ineffectual and out of place in school, he lacks curiosity about those around him, and is not 'sure enough of his own standards' to impose them on the children. He does architectural drawings and likes jazz, which first taught him 'what art meant'. He is an 'allornothinger' with women ('it's usually nothing'), and has had 'sexual problems, but not simple ones' since losing his girlfriend.

Angelo, Private
Private Angelo, 1946
Eric Linklater
An Italian soldier in World War II, who takes on universal significance as well as a vivid particularity. He lacks 'the great and splendid gift' of courage, and consequently makes a poor soldier, although he is especially assiduous in retreating, and ultimately deserts. He has great common sense and a generous and amorous nature which is exploited by his practical fiancée. He thoroughly masters 'the most useful of accomplishments, which is to survive'.

Angstrom, Harry → Rabbit

Angstrom, Janice
Rabbit, Run, 1960
Rabbit Redux, 1971
Rabbit is Rich, 1981
Rabbit at Rest, 1990
Rabbit Remembered, 2000
John Updike
RABBIT's wife, she first appears as a drab, slatternly girl, ill-equipped for motherhood. Tragically, the Angstroms' daughter is drowned

when Janice drunkenly drops her in the bath. After a period of separation, Janice and Rabbit are reconciled, and, although she tends to experience much of life through an alcoholic haze, she becomes stronger and more confident in middle age.

Angstrom, Nelson
Rabbit, Run, 1960
Rabbit Redux, 1971
Rabbit is Rich, 1981
Rabbit at Rest, 1990
Rabbit Remembered, 2000
John Updike

RABBIT and JANICE ANGSTROM'S son, he is a brash and intolerant product of a generation that fails to understand the underlying obsession with material success and moral rectitude that came with the 1950s. A permanent thorn in his father's flesh, he is an Angstrom who has dispensed with most of his legacy of anxiety and self-doubt. However, this liberation comes at a price when his cocaine addiction causes the ruin of the family business.

Angus
Butcher's Broom, 1934
Neil Gunn

Angus, one of the oldest inhabitants of Riasgan, is regarded by the villagers as their local bard who perpetuates the oral tradition of poems and legends. He lives with his son and his family in one of the more successful crofts. It is primarily through him that the history and traditions of the Gaelic culture, about to be obliterated by the Highland Clearances, are revealed.

Anna
The High Road, 1988
Edna O'Brien

Anna is a bitter and frustrated middle-aged woman, who is particularly disillusioned with men. She is in need of love, companionship and complicity. Gentle, sensitive and profound, she finds herself out of tune with the women of her age and class with whom she comes in contact. She finds a peculiar solace and excitement in her relationship with CATALINA, with whom she shares the feelings associated with male betrayal. Desperately depressed and horribly hurt, her story is a testimony to the plight of many bruised women.

Anna
The Snow Ball, 1964
Brigid Brophy

Adopted by her near-namesake Anne, whose white boudoir belies a decidedly unvirginal disposition, she is unsure whether her natural father is to be found among her stepmother's impressive collection of husbands. For the ball, she dresses as (and increasingly assumes the identity of) Donna Anna, the put-upon heroine of Mozart and Da Ponte's *Don Giovanni*.

Anna
Old Times, 1971
Harold Pinter

Anna is a mysterious, enigmatic presence, seeming at times as though she is less a real person than an aspect of KATE, although Kate alleges they are old friends. Anna agrees with this by recalling their carefree life sharing a flat in London 20 years previously. Cool, elegant and aloof, Anna becomes the subject of a contest of wills between Kate and her husband, DEELEY, who at first seems not to know Anna but then claims they met at a party. 'There are some things one remembers', declares Anna, 'even though they may never have happened. There are things I remember which may never have happened but even as I recall them so they take place.'

Annabel Lee
'Annabel Lee', 1849
Edgar Allan Poe

The speaker in the poem recalls his childhood love for the beautiful maiden Annabel Lee in a 'kingdom by the sea', and her reciprocated affection for him. Their love was 'the envy of the very angels', but was severed when she died. Their souls are reunited, however, as he lies by her in 'her tomb by the sounding sea'.

Annabella
'Tis Pity She's a Whore, c.1631
John Ford

Annabella is the sister of GIOVANNI, who considers her as perfect as a goddess and to whose advances she enthusiastically submits in an incestuous affair. She is a curious mixture of innocence, knowingness, cool-headed independence and emotional vulnerability. Not only is she enraptured by what she regards as a pure, untainted love, she is also terrorized by her father's authority and by the religious fervour of the Friar, who threatens damnation. For appearance's sake, she marries SORANZO. Her ruin results from his discovery that she is pregnant by Giovanni, whom she insists to the last is 'a noble creature ... in every part / So angel-like, so glorious'.

Anna Comnena
Count Robert of Paris, 1831
Sir Walter Scott

A Byzantine princess, daughter of the emperor ALEXIUS COMNENUS, wife of NICEPHORUS BRIENNIUS, and an important Classical historian. Her *Alexiad* is one of Scott's sources. In speech and manner she is insufferably prolix and pedestrian, rarely attaining a convincing solidity.

Annatoo
Mardi, 1849
Herman Melville

The ugly, shrewish wife of SAMOA, she has 'a lusty frame and a lustier soul'. She likes to 'coil herself away' in an empty cask in the hold, 'like a garter-snake under a stone'. She is given to stealing as if 'possessed by some scores of devils' which incite her to mischief as if on their own account.

Anne, Lady, formerly Anne Neville
Richard III, 1592–3
William Shakespeare

The widow of Edward, Prince of Wales, the son of HENRY VI. RICHARD, DUKE OF GLOUCESTER has murdered both her father-in-law and her husband, but claims he did so in order to be closer to her. Anne expresses her repugnance in some of the play's most colourful language: 'Thou dreadful minister of hell!', 'thou lump of foul deformity'. Nevertheless, Richard's presence is such that while she is repulsed, she is also hypnotized by his persuasiveness and more than a little convinced by his sentiments. It is a remarkable portrait of emotional distress being gradually turned into compliance under pressure. Anne indeed becomes his wife, but after the coronation dies in mysterious circumstances (on Richard's orders) and on the eve of the battle of Bosworth Field makes a brief reappearance as a ghost, cursing her husband.

Anne of Green Gables, properly Anne Shirley
Anne of Green Gables, 1908, et seq
L M Montgomery

A red-headed, hot-tempered, skinny orphan, adopted by mistake by Matthew Cuthbert and his sister Marilla, who had been hoping for a boy to help them run their Prince Edward Island farm. A sensitive, highly imaginative child with the soul of a poet and a tireless tongue, she describes her life as a 'perfect graveyard of buried hopes'. Exasperating, intriguing and loveable, she quickly wins her way into the hearts of the Avonlea community.

Annie
The Real Thing, 1982
Tom Stoppard

An actress and the second wife of HENRY, Annie is mercurial, passionate and capable of lasting affection although not necessarily of fidelity. Instinctive and liberal, her affair with an actor and her espousal of Brodie, a convicted left-wing arsonist, bewilder her husband but possibly make him both a better man and a finer writer.

Annixter
The Octopus: A Story of California, 1901
Frank Norris

A rancher of the San Joaquin Valley in California and one of those threatened by the encroachment of the railways. Toughly intellectual, 'his university course had hardened rather than polished him. He still remained one of the people, rough almost to insolence, direct in speech, intolerant in his opinions, relying upon absolutely no one but himself ... He was a ferocious worker, allowing himself no pleasures, and exacting the same degree of energy from all his subordinates. He was widely hated, and as widely trusted.'

Ann Veronica
Ann Veronica, 1909
H G Wells

Ann Veronica's story is that of proto-feminist rebellion against authority: cooped up at home by her father (aside from attending a secluded women's college) and called 'Little Vee' by him, she wants 'to live'. Showing a spirit developed on the hockey field and in theological debates, she runs away from suburbia to London, borrowing money and joining the suffragettes. She also

attends the Biology Lab at Imperial College, where she meets a man to whom she makes advances: scandalously, for the time.

anon (the editor)
The Aspern Papers, 1888
Henry James

An ambitious young editor with an interest in the works of JEFFREY ASPERN, a 19th-century poet. In order to win possession of the great man's love letters to his mistress, MISS BORDEREAU, who survives in Venice, he engages in a dangerous tactical game which presents him with a hard choice between professional advancement and personal liberty.

anon (the narrator)
Beautiful Losers, 1966
Leonard Cohen

An anthropologist and folklorist, he is a recognized authority on the unidentified A—s, 'a tribe I have no intention of disgracing by my interest'. He is locked in an ambiguous sexual triangle with his wife EDITH and the mysterious F, each of them perhaps representing aspects of a single fragmented consciousness.

anon (the assassin)
'Child's Play', in *Child's Play, with Eustace and the Prowler*, published in the USA as *Child's Play, The Bread of Time to Come: Two Novellas*, 1982
David Malouf

This 29-year-old male narrator has good reason to maintain his anonymity. 'I am what the newspapers call a terrorist.' His mission is to assassinate a well-known writer (ANON (THE WRITER)), whose works have largely defined the world he occupies and with whom he is obsessed.

anon (the writer)
'Child's Play', in *Child's Play, with Eustace and the Prowler*, published in the USA as *Child's Play, The Bread of Time to Come: Two Novellas*, 1982
David Malouf

'Essayist, philosopher, author of a dozen monuments to the art of narrative, he has created so much of our world that we scarcely know where history ends and his version of it begins ... His vision is epic' and even seems to anticipate his own assassination by the obsessive, nameless terrorist (ANON (THE ASSASSIN)) who recreates him so vividly in order to destroy him.

anon (the narrator)
Conference-ville, 1976
Frank Moorhouse

He is an Australian writer billed to deliver a paper at a prestigious literary conference. Among the other participants, and the object of his wry observations, are real figures from the Australian cultural scene.

anon (the corporal)
A Fable, 1954
William Faulkner

The leader of twelve pacifist 'disciples' in the French army of World War I, he is laden with more Christ imagery than any fictional character can be asked to bear convincingly. The natural son of a general, he is married to a woman called Magda (presumably from Magdalene), betrayed by one of his followers and executed along with two criminals. 'Resurrected' by a shell-burst on his grave, his remains are eventually taken to Paris and placed in the tomb of the Unknown Soldier.

anon (the narrator)
'The Figure in the Carpet', in *Embarrassments*, 1896
Henry James

He is a young literary critic obsessively concerned with uncovering the underlying significance of novelist HUGH VEREKER's work. Vereker has told him that there is a 'figure in the carpet' that he must discern. Though his friend CORVICK has apparently unravelled the secret (about which the young man had told him in the first place), the older critic dies before publishing his analysis and the young man remains in disappointed ignorance.

anon (the newspaperman)
The Great God Success, 1901
David Graham Phillips

A champion of the people against vested interests, he gradually loses the integrity of his vision as a muckraking journalist and begins to identify with the rich.

anon (the security technician)
1982, Janine, 1984
Alasdair Gray

He views humanity and its doings with the coldly prurient indifference of a surveillance camera. Alcoholic, misogynistic and menopausal, he is an inverted version of Hugh MacDiarmid's THE DRUNK MAN.

anon (the prowler)
'The Prowler', in *Child's Play, with Eustace and the Prowler*, published in the USA as *Child's Play, The Bread of Time to Come: Two Novellas*, 1982
David Malouf

A composite figure who haunts the women of an Australian suburb, he may be a night-time manifestation of almost any man in the neighbourhood. So archetypal a figure does he seem that his naked stalkings, spotted by neighbours or passers-by, are often not reported until after an attack. 'There are lines, it seems, that we are conditioned not to cross … His assurance comes from the very fact that he is a prowler: that is, one for whom the lines exist to be crossed.'

anon (the Captain)
The Secret Sharer, 1912
Joseph Conrad

The unnamed narrator, he is an inexperienced seaman who has taken charge of his first vessel (also unnamed) in the Gulf of Siam 'only a fortnight before'. He is 'like a stranger on board', anxious and self-doubting, until he picks up a sailor, LEGGATT, who has jumped ship, and appears in almost ghostly fashion. He helps this double or 'other self' to escape, and in doing so achieves a new self-possession, and the 'perfect communion of a seaman with his first command'.

anon (the jazz musician)
Strike the Father Dead, 1962
John Wain

The hero of the novel, he is a young jazz musician in open rebellion against his father's narrow academicism and bourgeois morality. Wartime London affords him considerable opportunity for a more dramatic self-definition.

anon (the narrator)
Surfacing, 1972
Margaret Atwood

Initially a concerned young woman searching desperately for her father, she becomes a provider of food for her companions and of information on survival. She is shown to be duplicitous, though not perhaps consciously, for she has lived with lies so long she half-believes them. Increasingly alienated from the human world and more attuned to the animal kingdom, in the end she discovers within herself the wisdom and power she needs to cope with the human realm, to which she must return.

anon (the governess)
The Turn of the Screw, 1898
Henry James

Thoroughly suspect as a narrator, the new governess at Bly may well be in the grip of an overwhelming sexual neurosis, partially directed at her employer, and largely expressed through her relationship to his nephew and niece (MILES and FLORA) and their supposed relation to the 'spirits' of her predecessor MISS JESSEL and PETER QUINT. There is in her voice a shrill edge of hysteria kept just under control.

anon (R H Dana jr)
Two Years Before the Mast, 1840
R H Dana jr, originally published anonymously

Dana's book was based on the journal that, as a former Harvard student, he wrote about his experiences during a voyage from Boston round Cape Horn to California. Though much of it has to be taken as fact, it is written with the vividness of fiction, and many of the characters (not least the clear-eyed, morally robust narrator) have to be seen as fictional, or at least composites. Dana's rage at the injustices he sees while onboard inspires him to take up the cause of the common seaman.

anon (the narrator)
The Unnamable, 1953
Samuel Beckett

A further incarnation of MOLLOY and MALONE, he is elderly, alone and dying. He occasionally sees them, or figures he believes might be them – and there is even an atmosphere that suggests the narrator may have already died and is awaiting their joining him. 'Where now? Who now? When now?' he asks. Like Molloy and Malone, the narrator is melancholy and impatient, yet in this novel there is the suggestion that love, or the hope of love, can be the only meaning for life. His final words are: 'I can't go on, I'll go on.'

anon (the central character)
Wild Cat Falling, 1965
Mudrooroo, formerly Colin Johnson

He is a part-Aboriginal, existing on the fringes of

Australian society. Having spent time in prison, his passive acceptance finally runs out and he reacts violently to a lifetime of rejection.

anon (the tall convict)
The Wild Palms, 1939, 'Old Man' section published separately in the *Viking Portable Faulkner*, 1954
William Faulkner

An instinctive stoic, he is freed from jail to assist in the rescue operation that follows the Mississippi floods of 1927. He refuses to capitalize on this unexpected freedom, sticking to his task indomitably and never questioning the system that imposes intangible constraints on his liberty.

Ansell, Stewart
The Longest Journey, 1907
E M Forster

The son of a provincial draper, Stewart Ansell possesses an unexpected academic prowess, which has taken him to Cambridge where he gains a First in the Moral Science Tripos. A lean, jaundiced young philosopher, whose favourite haunt is the reading room of the British Museum, he remains most at ease with the world of books and abstract ideas, disputing the work of Schopenhauer and eschewing the frivolities of life. Inclined to think that 'the impractical is its own reward', he still respects those who attempt to 'journey beyond it'.

Anselm
The Four Banks of the River of Space, 1990
Wilson Harris

A mysterious dreamer who shares essential biographical data with Wilson Harris, he hands over a book of spatio-temporal visions, 'live fossil stepping stones' within the dream of the 20th century, while on his way to a conference on the fate of the rainforests. Anselm is not his real name.

Anselm
The Recognitions, 1955
William Gaddis

A disgusting drunk and sexual pervert with acne-scarred cheeks (which he frequently sandpapers), he acts as a demonic tempter to the saintly STANLEY. In keeping with the book's obsessive tinkering with Christian imagery, he is named after the philosopher-saint who devised the Ontological Proof for the existence of God; it may be that Anselm is a nickname, for he is also addressed as Arthur.

Anthony, Dion
The Great God Brown, 1926
Eugene O'Neill

A tortured artist who represents the 'creative pagan acceptance of life' and is thus the antitype of the businessman WILLIAM A BROWN. Like the other characters in the play, his psychological self-division and role-playing are symbolized by the wearing of masks.

Antigonus
The Winter's Tale, 1611
William Shakespeare

Like CAMILLO, Antigonus is one of the lords at the Sicilian court of LEONTES. He refuses to believe that HERMIONE is unfaithful and advises the king to reconsider. Later, he obeys Leontes's order to take her newly-born child to some 'remote and desert place' and leave it to die. Arriving in Bohemia, he leaves the baby and runs, the subsequent stage direction being one of the most famous in Shakespeare: 'Exit, pursued by a bear'. A loyal, humane man, Antigonus does not, however, show any guilt at abandoning a child. He does so sadly, on pain of his own death, believing that even though helpless, the child has more chance of life there than at a cruel and irrational court.

Antiochus
Pericles, c.1608
William Shakespeare

Antiochus, the ruthless, defiant King of Antioch, proclaims that anyone hoping to marry his daughter must first solve the riddle he sets. Once PERICLES discovers its meaning, which is to describe the king's incestuous relationship with his daughter, Antiochus declares that he must be killed. Pericles escapes and Antiochus, who represents love perverted, receives heavenly retribution by being consumed by fire.

Antipholus of Ephesus
The Comedy of Errors, c.1594
William Shakespeare

In his mid-twenties, Antipholus is the twin brother of ANTIPHOLUS OF SYRACUSE and the son of AEGEON and AEMILIA. Since being shipwrecked in childhood, he has been separated from his parents and his brother. Since arriving in Ephesus, he has served as a soldier and married ADRIANA. During a series of adventures, he finds himself locked out of his house, arrested for debt and assumed to be a lunatic. Before the final reconciliation, Antipholus has discovered, through an intricate comedy of assumption and mistaken identity, more about his own nature and that of his wife.

Antipholus of Syracuse
The Comedy of Errors, c.1594
William Shakespeare

The twin brother of ANTIPHOLUS OF EPHESUS who, like him, has seen neither his brother nor his parents, AEGEON and AEMILIA, since their shipwreck when he was a child. Antipholus has settled in Syracuse and embarks on a quest for his brother. During his adventures, he finds himself accused by ADRIANA (unknown to him, his brother's wife) of having deserted her and, to their confusion, he woos her sister, LUCIANA, before taking refuge in an abbey. This is a comedy of prejudice and assumption within marriage, the family and sexual relationships, in which the characters, through mistaken identity, discover more about themselves and each other. In the end, everyone is reunited.

Antonio
The Changeling, 1653
Thomas Middleton and William Rowley

The 'Changeling' of the title, who epitomizes the premise that love makes fools of people, as he spends most of the action disguised as an idiot incarcerated in a madhouse in order to pay court to the doctor's beautiful wife. It is a disguise that becomes him all too well as his love for ISABELLA is based wholly on her outward beauty and is lacking in any sort of judgement on his part.

Antonio
The Merchant of Venice, 1594/5
William Shakespeare

The successful businessman of the title. Prone to depression, he allows his love for BASSANIO to let him fall foul of SHYLOCK, the Jewish money-lender whose business he threatens and whose religion he abhors. Alternately wise, vulnerable, noble and fatalistic, he ends the play as a father-figure to the young lovers in the plot.

Antonio
The Revenger's Tragedy, 1607
Thomas Middleton or Cyril Tourneur

An old, honourable and respected noble in THE DUKE's court, whose wife is raped by THE DUCHESS's youngest son. Consumed by grief and guilt, she poisons herself, leaving Antonio to mourn the passing of his 'Precedent for wives', and hopeless of finding justice. When the Duke and LUSSURIOSO die, one after the other, vic-tims of VENDICE's violent revenge, Antonio demonstrates a cynical sense of self-preservation when he condemns Vendice and his brother to death, reasoning that 'You that would murder him would murder me'.

Antonio
The Tempest, 1611
William Shakespeare

PROSPERO's brother, who usurped his throne and forced him, along with his baby daughter, to take to sea in a leaky boat. He is irredeemably evil, plotting with SEBASTIAN to murder their accomplice ALONSO. At no point does he repent, even when confronted with the evidence of his guilt. Where others learn about themselves Antonio, although forgiven by Prospero, remains the villain he always was.

Antonio
Twelfth Night, c.1601
William Shakespeare

A sea-captain who rescued SEBASTIAN from drowning, he shows his generosity by offering his purse to that unfortunate. Although he knows he will be unwelcome in Illyria because of his past action in sea battles, he is prepared to risk his own well-being by following Sebastian into the city. He shows his bravery by intervening in the duel between SIR ANDREW AGUECHEEK and VIOLA, whom he mistakes for Sebastian, and is upset when she appears to refuse to return the money he has loaned her. When arrested he accepts his fate, but is treated with respect by ORSINO.

Antonio
Two Gentlemen of Verona, c.1590
William Shakespeare

Antonio appears only in a single scene, and then to accept his servant's advice that he should send his son, PROTEUS, to the Imperial Court at Milan, to be in the company of his equals. He subsequently overrides his son's objections. Antonio, then, is by all brief appearances a conventional father and member of the nobility, and his concern that Proteus becomes 'a perfect man' underlines one of the play's themes as that of attaining maturity.

Antonio
Venice Preserv'd, or A Plot Discovered, 1682
Thomas Otway

In his early sixties, Antonio, 'a fine speaker in the Senate', is a cruelly satirical portrait of the philanthropist and reformer, the Earl of Shaftesbury. Lewd, devious, stupid and hypocritical, Antonio adores two things. One is the sound of his own voice; the other is being steadily whipped to sexual relief by the Greek courtesan, AQUILINA, whom he calls 'Nicky Nacky' and addresses in an excited torrent of juvenile endearments. Otway intends to emphasize political corruption, and measures it dramatically in terms of sexual unorthodoxy. Antonio's counterpart is the conspirator RENAULT.

Antonio Bologna
The Duchess of Malfi, 1623
John Webster

Steward and second husband of the DUCHESS OF MALFI, Antonio is a good horseman and an honest official, with interests in political reform and history. He wants a 'peaceful marriage' with the woman he loves, but their life together is disrupted by her scheming brothers.

Antonovna, Sophia
Under Western Eyes, 1911
Joseph Conrad

A leading member of the revolutionary group to which RAZUMOV ultimately confesses. She is a handsome woman with 'brilliant black eyes', and he sees her as 'the respectable enemy'. She is an ardent believer in her idealistic cause, and a woman of great dignity and integrity. She betrays a sympathy and understanding over Razumov's confession, recognizing that 'there's character in such a discovery', although such understanding seems misplaced in the context of the story.

Antony
All for Love, 1678
John Dryden

A man torn between his love for CLEOPATRA and his duty as a Roman husband and general, Antony is shown as capable of great loyalty to his friends and as a man of seriously conflicting emotions. He is eventually destroyed by his inner turmoil. Unlike Shakespeare's version of the character, he is more static, given to words rather than action. In the face of defeat he kills himself.

Antony, Marcus Antonius/Mark Antony
Julius Caesar, c.1599
Antony and Cleopatra, 1606/7
William Shakespeare

Initially Antony is presented as a young man 'given to sports, to wildness, and much company'. But this is a misjudgement by those conspiring against him, and in fact he is as much a political opportunist as they are. He knows exactly how to play on the emotions of the mob and proves to be a ruthless adversary, but is also able to recognize the essential nobility of MARCUS BRUTUS. In *Antony and Cleopatra* he is older but not wiser. His earlier emotional response to the death of JULIUS CAESAR leaves him governed by his emotions, and in Egypt his love for CLEOPATRA blinds him to his duty as a politician and a husband, resulting in defeat and death.

Antrobus, George
The Skin of Our Teeth, 1942
Thornton Wilder
A father figure, simultaneously a contemporary American, Adam, Noah and the inventor of the wheel. The source of human knowledge, he becomes President of the 'Ancient and Honourable Order of Mammals, Subdivision Humans'. He is always attracted by the 'other woman', LILY SABINA, but always returns to MRS ANTROBUS. His hopes of perfecting humanity are blighted by violence and evil, represented by his son HENRY ANTROBUS, but he puts his faith in philosophy.

Antrobus, Henry
The Skin of Our Teeth, 1942
Thornton Wilder
A 'clean-cut American boy', who has changed his name from Cain. Having killed his brother, Abel, he bears a scar on his forehead. Through the ages he spreads trouble and death, equating selfishness with freedom. He wants to murder his father, GEORGE ANTROBUS, who represents order, and to destroy his books, the foundation of civilization.

Antrobus, Mrs
The Skin of Our Teeth, 1942
Thornton Wilder
The quintessential wife and mother, a combination of Eve, Mrs Noah and a contemporary American matron. Maggie 'lives only for her children', believes in her husband, GEORGE ANTROBUS, makes a home, and holds her family together throughout history. As President of the 'Women's Auxiliary Bed and Board Society', she extols the institution of marriage.

Apemantus
Timon of Athens, 1607/8
William Shakespeare and perhaps Thomas Middleton
A 'churlish philosopher', Apemantus may appear sardonic and misanthropic, but he has dignity, insight and compassion, and lives by his principles. His cynical banter, for instance, shows him to be the intellectual superior of TIMON OF ATHENS and his entourage of flatterers, from whom he keeps himself at a studious distance. Reflecting upon the nature of human sincerity, he warns Timon that his friends are false and that he will be ruined. Later, when he visits Timon in his cave, he is pelted with stones. He leaves, bitterly threatening to tell those in Athens that Timon has gold.

Apley, George
The Late George Apley, 1937
John P Marquand
Born into a wealthy family, the descendant of the earliest colonists, he finds himself drifting in a

new America that he cannot quite come to terms with. He is sent abroad to cure him of a rebellious streak but then returns home to study law, and despite a fling with a lower middle-class Irish girl gradually settles into a life of dilettantish conservatism and the Puritanism of his ancestors.

Apollinax, Mr
'Mr Apollinax', in *Prufrock and Other Observations*, 1917
T S Eliot
Allegedly modelled on Bertrand Russell, Apollinax is charming, pointy-eared and controversial, appearing to shock his American hosts with a laugh 'like an irresponsible foetus … submarine and profound', that makes the teatime guests of Mrs Phlaccus and Professor Channing-Cheetah suspect that he is 'unbalanced'.

Apollodorus
Caesar and Cleopatra, 1898
George Bernard Shaw
Handsome and debonair, Apollodorus is a Sicilian, about 24 years old, who dresses 'with deliberate aestheticism'. Refusing to acknowledge the term 'carpet trader', he describes himself as a patrician; similarly, he does not keep a shop but 'a temple of the arts'. His belief is 'Art for Art's sake', yet carpet trader is what he is, and having brought carpets for CLEOPATRA's inspection, he rolls her up in one and secretly transports her from Alexandria, where the Egyptians are burning the harbour, to CAESAR in his stronghold in a lighthouse. Apollodorus subsequently stays in Egypt to serve Cleopatra.

Apollyon
The Pilgrim's Progress, Part I 1678, Part II 1684
John Bunyan
A scaly dragon who epitomizes the power of evil and its determination to overwhelm the Christian with the fiery darts of temptation, doubt and persecution. Fiercely opposed to Christ and embodying all the forces ranged against the pilgrim, he is only temporarily defeated by the word of truth with which CHRISTIAN is armed.

Appleby, Adam
The British Museum is Falling Down, 1965
David Lodge
Adam Appleby is in search of perfect happiness, but is pursued instead by his past mistakes and present worries. A 25-year-old practising Catholic and unsuccessful follower of the Rhythm Method, he is a third-year PhD student with only an abandoned chapter on an obscure Catholic belletrist to show for his labours. His dream is of unfettered sex, unrestricted by the fear of conception, but he soon discovers that this is not the only obstacle in his path to fulfilment. His is a foggy world of the imagination, where fact and fantasy interweave, and aspiring novelists self-consciously take notes at postgraduate sherry parties.

Appleby, John
Death at the President's Lodging, 1936, et seq
Michael Innes (J I M Stewart)
Originally from a modest rural background,

Appleby rises, over the course of some 30 books, from Scotland Yard inspector to Commissioner of the Metropolitan Police and a knighthood (despite mid-career retirement to marry into the gentry). Chiefly characterized by his dryly learned wit, he makes recondite literary allusions in a playful spirit, rather than to bludgeon the less erudite. His cases usually find him in donnish company, often in a country house setting, and are generally of a convoluted nature ideally suited to his logical but nimble mind. After retirement to his wife's family seat at Long Dream Manor, he continues to solve local crimes, in between pruning his roses.

Appleseed, Johnny
'In Praise of Johnny Appleseed', in *The Chinese Nightingale and Other Poems*, 1917
Vachel Lindsay

A semi-mythical character, loosely based on the pioneer John Chapman. He tramps the Appalachian fastnesses with bags of fruit seeds, sowing the wild places. His helmet is an old tin pan and 'Yankee Doodle' his marching song, as he moves through the woods 'priestly and free', dreaming that in heaven he will be rewarded with *two* wives.

Apsara, Vina
The Ground Beneath Her Feet, 1999
Salman Rushdie

Born Nissa Shetty into a fractured Greek-American-Indian family in Virginia, she fled to Bombay, transformed herself into Vina and, aided by ORMUS CAMA, becomes one of the greatest rock stars in the world, adored by millions and particularly famed for the anthem *The Ground Beneath Her Feet*, performed with her band, VTO. Independent, determined, unafraid, unruly and sexually inviting, she is possessed of a 'celestial voice' and a 'rage that drove her art and damaged her life'. She loves Ormus 'like a student', hungry for his opinions and his seriousness, in contrast to UMEED MERCHANT, whom she tolerates for his frivolity. A woman who lives life as a series of masquerades, she partly reflects the myth of Eurydice and vanishes in an earthquake.

Apthorpe
Sword of Honour, 1965
Evelyn Waugh

Apthorpe is a know-all, describing his alleged experience in Africa in stagey pseudo-army language. He and GUY CROUCHBACK, older than the other Halberdiers, are 'uncles' and treated as jokes. It is Guy who suffers most from Apthorpe's envy, touchiness, lies and his preposterous 'gear' which is transported from camp to camp, chiefly his 'Thunderbox', an antiquated chemical closet. But despite Apthorpe's idiocy he is promoted above Guy. When he is 'off colour', Guy visits him in hospital, but his gift of whisky proves fatal, and Guy is left to carry out Apthorpe's inconvenient instructions about the disposal of his gear.

Aquilina
Venice Preserv'd, or A Plot Discovered, 1682
Thomas Otway

A Greek courtesan, dispassionate, mercenary,

knowing and contemptuous, she plays the dominatrix over the senator, ANTONIO. She whips 'the eternal troublesome vexatious fool' to a frenzied sexual relief, and chases him out of her rooms while he pretends to be a dog. She is also a woman of great resolve: when she threatens Antonio with death, she means exactly what she says.

Arabanoo
The Timeless Land, 1941
Storm of Time, 1948
No Barrier, 1953
Eleanor Dark

JOHNNY PRENTICE's childhood friend, from the Australian convict settlement. His death is Johnny's first experience of loss, and leaves him consumed by a helpless fury of grief.

Arabella, later Angelica
The Female Quixote: or, The Adventures of Arabella, 1752, dramatized as *Angelica: or Quixote in Petticoats*, 1758
Charlotte Lennox

Like CATHERINE MORLAND in Jane Austen's *Northanger Abbey* (1818), her expectations of life are determined almost entirely by her reading of French romantic fiction. Real life, inevitably, turns out to be a compound of disillusioning surprises and dull routine.

Arabin, Rev Francis
Barchester Towers, 1857
Framley Parsonage, 1861
The Last Chronicle of Barset, 1867
Anthony Trollope

A High Church clergyman and Oxford fellow, appointed to the living of St Ewold by REV DR THEOPHILUS GRANTLY, so that he can assist in the ecclesiastical struggle against REV OBADIAH SLOPE. His search for truth almost took him into the Catholic Church, but he was saved for Anglicanism by REV JOSIAH CRAWLEY. Witty and celibate, he does not take women seriously nor value comforts, until belatedly realizing that he wants a wife, a home and professional advancement. His love for ELEANOR HARDING is beset by scruples about her money. As Dr Arabin, Dean of Barchester, he later helps Crawley.

Aragorn, known as Strider
The Lord of the Rings, 3 volumes, 1954–5
J R R Tolkien

Described by the wizard GANDALF as 'the greatest traveller and huntsman of this age of the world', on first sight he appears to FRODO BAGGINS as 'strange-looking, weather-beaten', a tall, stringy fellow with gleaming eyes and a wise expression. Knowledgeable about the ways of Middle Earth and well-versed in elven-lore, he is a sworn enemy of the evil Sauron the Great, and proves a staunch companion for Frodo and SAM GAMGEE. A charismatic, otherworldly figure, imbued with chivalric ethics, he is revealed as heir to the land of Gondor.

Arbaces
A King and No King, 1611
Francis Beaumont and John Fletcher

The King of Iberia, he falls in love with his

supposed sister, PANTHEA, whom he has not seen since childhood. He is young and handsome, a good professional soldier with a healthy sexual appetite. He is also 'vainglorious and humble, and joyful and sorrowful, in extremities, in an hour': a volatile mix of virtue and folly. His central conflict, though, is between reason (that it is a sin to love one's sister) and will (that he does indeed desire her). It is eventually revealed that Arbaces is a changeling and therefore 'no king'. At the same time, revelation of his true identity averts the spectre of incest, and the couple are free to marry.

Arbuthnot, Mrs Rachel
A Woman of No Importance, 1893
Oscar Wilde

Having been seduced and abandoned by Lord Illingworth, to whom she was 'a woman of no importance', Mrs Arbuthnot has since passed herself off as a widow, successfully raising their illegitimate son, Gerald. 20 years later, and still 'excessively handsome', she encounters Illingworth at a social gathering. Unaware of their relationship, he offers Gerald a job as his secretary, an eventuality the horrified Mrs Arbuthnot had not foreseen. Dignified and proud, she is still bitter at being wronged; arguably, she has a touch of martyrdom about her. Certainly, she does not shun the melodramatic gesture. However, her fierce moral principles dictate that she rejects Illingworth's belated offer of marriage, dismissing him as 'a man of no importance'.

Arbuthnot, Sandy
Greenmantle, 1916, et seq
John Buchan

One of those legendary figures allegedly thrown up by the British Empire, he has the protean skill to fit into almost any cultural environment, absorbing languages and customs as if by osmosis. On his first appearance this has a decidedly ambiguous outcome, when he finds himself in unwilling thrall to the cult of 'Greenmantle'. He is described as 'tallish, with a lean, high-boned face and a pair of brown eyes like a pretty girl's'.

Arbuton, Miles
A Chance Acquaintance, 1873
William Dean Howells

A wealthy young Bostonian who meets and seems to fall for KITTY ELLISON on a trip to Canada, apparently so little disturbed by their social differences that he proposes marriage. However, when he meets a friend from his own social circle, he snubs Kitty and she breaks off their engagement.

Arcati, Madame
Blithe Spirit, 1941
Noël Coward

A spiritualistic medium, Madame Arcati is a 'striking woman dressed not too extravagantly but with a decided bias towards the barbaric'. She is an avid bicyclist and enjoys a dry martini. Her spirit guide is a child called Daphne, and her fondness is for the music of Irving Berlin. Madame Arcati's slightly madcap appearance

and disparate enthusiasms, combined with the absolute seriousness with which she approaches her business and her blunt manner of shrugging off scepticism, mark her out as a true English eccentric. She is therefore at once reassuring and an implacable force of national identity. The seance itself, in which she invokes the spirit of ELVIRA CONDOMINE, borders upon high farce.

Archbald, Jenny Blair
The Sheltered Life, 1932
Ellen Glasgow

The fledgeling belle of a fallen age, with her 'warm mother-of-pearl vagueness', Jenny is a bundle of flirtatious innocence. The impulse which drives her is libidinal: 'I'm alive, alive and I'm Jenny Blair Archbald' she sings to the rhythm of life. Feeling an intense absence due to her father's death, she is susceptible to the power of older men and falls in love with the married GEORGE BIRDSONG. She convinces herself that she is not autonomous and spins subtle evasions of guilt. Her life demonstrates the pernicious use of illusions as a shelter from reality.

Archer
The Beaux' Stratagem, 1707
George Farquhar

Because of reduced circumstances Archer and his fellow rake AIMWELL alternate at being master and servant. Archer appears to adapt better to the part, being adept at gleaning information from servants and innkeepers. He is a handsome figure, catching the eye of several women, including Cherry, a simple country girl, and MRS SULLEN, but although he talks love to them, he refrains from actual seduction. His bravery is called upon when he has to defend Mrs Sullen, but he is not averse to using the wound he receives to gain more than medical attention.

Archer, Isabel
The Portrait of a Lady, 1881
Henry James

'Her errors and delusions were frequently such as a biographer interested in preserving the dignity of his subject must shrink from specifying.' Rescued from near-penury in Albany, New York, by her aunt Mrs Touchett, she is thrown up against the complex intrigues and attractions of European society. Essentially a fairy-tale princess, flawed and humanized by growing self-consciousness, she is expected to choose between the three men who desire her and find her own destiny, equipped at first only with native wit and beauty, but later reinforced by an independent fortune.

Archer, Lew
The Moving Target, 1949, and others
Ross MacDonald

A private detective, he is an ex-police officer who was fired for refusing to collude in the corruption in the police department, and whose wife left him because 'she didn't like the company I kept'. He is tough and determined, a 'not unwilling catalyst for trouble', but also intelligent and cultivated, with an interest in reading, painting and natural history, and a great curiosity about why people act as they do. He is sympathetic to the marginalized in society, and opposed to anyone threatening the environment.

Archer, Lind
Wild Geese, 1925
Martha Ostenso
Lind, a schoolteacher, is romantic, refined and sensitive to her new environment, but her character lacks depth and colour. Endowed with learning and beauty, the freedom and privilege of her class allows her to reflect upon the beauty and terror of nature as one might a painting – from a safe distance. That distance is threatened but remains intact. She is brushed by violence, touched by fear, but does not appear to suffer unduly.

Archer, Newland
The Age of Innocence, 1920
Edith Wharton
Newland Archer is the archetypal victim of the struggle between individual aspiration and the silent, forbidding authority of the social tribe. His life is a muffling of experience, vague and pallid. He may think he is more intelligent and better read than his friends, but he is conditioned to conform to repressive social codes: 'It was deeply distasteful to him to do anything melodramatic and conspicuous'. Attracted by the exotic foreignness of ELLEN OLENSKA, he is, however, constrained by the conventional, and learns instead to value the simplicity and tact of his wife, MAY WELLAND, showing how unheroic and limited in imagination he really is.

Archimago
The Faerie Queene, 1590–6
Sir Edmund Spenser
A powerful, wicked enchanter with a vast selection of spells. He exists to torment passing knights and to stop their quests. A master of the false image, he is the epitome of evil, whose weapons are deception and delusion. Malicious and cunning, he takes on many disguises, 'sometimes a fowle, sometimes a fish in a lake'.

Arcite
'The Knight's Tale' in *The Canterbury Tales*,
c.1387–1400
Geoffrey Chaucer
One of the two young knights who both fall in love with EMILY. Arcite shows more blatant self-interest than PALAMON, and on the eve of battle prays for victory over his erstwhile sworn brother. Although this will win him the bride, his primary concern is for martial and not marital success. Mars grants his prayer but Arcite's horse stumbles and he dies as a result of the fall.

Arden, Enoch
'Enoch Arden', 1864
Alfred, Lord Tennyson
The tragic hero of the poem. Determined to overcome early setbacks for the sake of his wife and children, he endures a forced separation of over ten years. On his eventual return to his village, he selflessly conceals his true identity so that his wife and children can continue to enjoy

their new-found prosperity from a second marriage.

Are, Lord
Restoration, 1981
Edward Bond
In 18th-century England, the aristocratic, privileged, foppish and unscrupulous Lord Are murders his wife, the daughter of a businessman, whom he has married solely for her money, and attempts to transfer the blame on to his footman, BOB HEDGES. Elegant, witty and tyrannical, Lord Are represents the ruling class of a corrupt social system. Implicit in his actions is the assumption that as long as moral values are shaped and enforced by his own class, with the compliance of others, he and his kind remain above the law.

Arethusa
Philaster, or Love Lies Bleeding, 1609
Francis Beaumont and John Fletcher
The virtuous, determined daughter of the King of Calabria, who has usurped the throne of Sicily, she is in love with PHILASTER, the rightful king, but is forced to communicate with him by means of his page, BELLARIO. Like Philaster, her heart rules her head, and having made her choice of lover in contradiction to the wishes of her father, she strives for emotional as much as political security.

Argante
The Faerie Queene, 1590–6
Sir Edmund Spenser
The incestuously begotten twin of Ollyphant, she is a child of the Titans. A cannibal with fiery eyes, she is immovably large, like a marble pillar. She carries off men on the front of her horse to satiate her desires, and sins against nature's law by performing unnatural sexual acts and having 'suffered beasts her body to deflower'. Both she and Ollyphant exist in contrast to BELPHOEBE and AMORET.

Argyle, Duke of (Archibald, Marquis of Argyle, Lord of Lorne, also known as McCallum More)
A Legend of Montrose, in *Tales of My Landlord: Third Series*, 1819
Sir Walter Scott
Leading supporter of the Convention of Estates and of Parliament in Scotland and the scourge of the Royalist Highland chiefs. 'Argyle was a man of more political enterprize than personal courage, and better calculated to manage an intrigue of state, than to controul the tribes of hostile mountaineers.' In person, he seems wrathful, suspicious and perfectly capable of treachery.

Ariel
The Tempest, 1611
William Shakespeare
A spirit of the air, Ariel was released by PROSPERO from the tree where he had been imprisoned for twelve years. However, because of the homage he owes he is not entirely free. Although desperate to return to the air, he cannot do so until Prospero allows him. He has the ability to enchant with his songs, and like PUCK he can

pass among mortals without being noticed. Although lacking emotions, he confesses that by living with humans he has almost developed feelings.

Arjillax
Back to Methuselah, 1921
George Bernard Shaw

A sculptor, Arjillax appears during the final section of this five-part play. *As Far as Thought can Reach* is set in a remote garden Utopia in 31,920AD. Instead of creating statues to resemble young, good-looking people, his new work is realist studies of HE- and SHE-ANCIENTS. He contends this to be a new and mature direction in his art, but his master, Martellus, denounces him, claiming that his disillusion with beauty is the beginning of disillusion with everything. Arjillax is on the brink of becoming an Ancient.

Armado, Don Adriano Del
Love's Labour's Lost, not later than 1594
William Shakespeare

'A man of great spirit', according to himself, or a mere 'plume of feathers' in the eyes of the PRINCESS OF FRANCE, Armado has no idea how to conduct himself with dignity at the Court of Navarre. Believing that ostentation in rhetoric and general behaviour is a great asset, he woos simple country wench JAQUENETTA by declaring 'I profane my lips on thy foot'. Frequently an object of ridicule, he receives his climactic comeuppance with BEROWNE's derision of his performance in the Pageant of the Nine Worthies.

Armitage, Mrs
The Pumpkin Eater, 1962
Penelope Mortimer

Having to cope with eight children and an unfaithful (third) husband pushes Mrs Armitage close to the edge of breakdown. Maintaining a precarious hold on her tense and fragile relationships amid the shifting moral sand of the Sixties, when all the old securities, if not under threat, were at least under close scrutiny, she is not helped in the quest to survive by the neuroses of her own complex and convoluted personality.

Armstrong, Grace
The Black Dwarf, 1816
Sir Walter Scott

Cousin to the young farmer HOBBIE ELLIOTT, who describes her (in a manner rather susceptible to misconstruction) as 'the best goer about the toun', by which he means to express admiration for her patent good sense and bustling energy. The Armstrongs are perhaps the most legend-heavy of the Border clans and Grace combines most of their positive virtues.

Armstrong, Johnnie
Armstrong's Last Goodnight, 1964
John Arden

Johnnie Armstrong, Laird of Gilnockie, boasts of effective independence from the Scottish king ('wha daur meddle wi' me?'), and makes illegal raids over the English border to prove it. His stammer makes him shy of negotiating politics with king's man David Lindsay himself, but he is otherwise fearless. His stripping naked in front of Lindsay's mistress wins her. He can be treacherous to others, but trusts his own clan and unwisely begins to trust Lindsay.

Armstrong, Kate
The Middle Ground, 1980
Margaret Drabble

A successful writer of lower-middle-class origins, she is particularly noted for depicting the lives of women. Now in middle-age, she is both tired of 'peddling opinions' and 'bloody sick of women'. She prefers instead 'emerging patterns, social shifts' and thinks of attempting to shape them into an explanation of the shifting, urban, frightening world about her. Kate also has an obsession with sewers and their odours. She is single and happy to be so. By others she is seen often as vain, credulous and rather foolish, and yet she is also receptive and, oddly, optimistic.

Arragon, Prince of
The Merchant of Venice, 1594/5
William Shakespeare

A 'deliberate fool' who carefully makes a decision about which of the three caskets he should choose in order to win PORTIA, and decides on the wrong one. His choice of the silver casket with its inscription 'Who chooseth me shall have as much as he deserves' is made with an ironic speech about the need for a meritocracy, and is rewarded by the 'portrait of a blinking idiot'.

Arrowby, Charles
The Sea, The Sea, 1978
Iris Murdoch

A retired theatre director, he is the self-deceiving and wholly unreliable narrator. A lifetime of enormous success and untrammelled egotism has left him haunted by grief, remorse and fear, and he has sought simplicity and moral redemption in hermetic isolation. Filling his narrative with protestations of his own repentance and humility, he believes he has at last abjured the magical powers of trickery and art, and sincerely wishes to be good. The manner in which he continues to tyrannize relatives, friends, and lovers, however, reveals him to be an enduringly cruel and Machiavellian manipulator.

Arrowsmith, Dr Martin
Arrowsmith, 1925
Sinclair Lewis

An idealistic young physician and biologist, he is disturbed by the crass commerciality and publicity-consciousness of most medical research. His discovery of the 'X-principle', a bacteriophage that promises enormous strides in the control of disease, loses him both his first wife and closest professional ally. Caught between the demands of professionalism and humanity, he retires from the social and professional treadmill.

Art, Young
Young Art and Old Hector, 1942
Neil Gunn

A young boy growing up in a small crofting community in the Scottish Highlands in the early part of the 20th century, he symbolizes the innocence and imagination of childhood. As he strives to find his place in the close-knit community, he is aided and befriended by OLD HECTOR, a crofter who treats him as the man he so desires to be. From their close relationship, Art learns the history and traditions of his people, and discovers the mysteries of courting and poaching, and the trials of growing up.

Artegall, the Knight of Justice
The Faerie Queene, 1590–6
Sir Edmund Spenser

Artegall was brought up by Astroea, a heavenly star maiden, the Goddess of Justice, who taught him 'equall balance with due recompense'. He represents temperance and justice, justice being the most desired virtue of a king. A rational man who is eternally faithful to his prophesied partner BRITOMART, he applies particular laws to particular places; he is also severe and uncompromising in meting out justice. His quest is to rescue IRENA from GRANTORTO.

Arthur
Early Morning, 1968
Edward Bond

The young, royal, siamese twin of GEORGE, he is surrounded by grotesque authoritarian adults, representatives of the Victorian ruling class. Well brought-up and educated, he later discovers this process to have disastrously limited his ability to act freely. Politically, he refuses to support Disraeli, but will not oppose him either. His indecisiveness and rebelliousness is at first seen as exasperating, but to the maturing Arthur it is more often the result of fear and puzzlement. He becomes mad, but transcends madness to achieve a new beginning. He accepts and learns from experience, and therefore is a symbol of hope.

Arthur
The Tenant of Wildfell Hall, 1848
Anne Brontë

Arthur, a happy, friendly child, is the little son of the mysterious MRS HELEN GRAHAM who has come to live at Wildfell Hall. His mother has courageously left her drunken profligate husband ARTHUR HUNTINGDON for fear that he will corrupt his son, and endeavours to make little Arthur detest wine to ensure that he will never share his father's vices. He likes GILBERT MARKHAM, who falls in love with his mother.

Arthur, Duke of Brittany
King John, 1590/1
William Shakespeare

Grandson of Henry II and nephew of KING JOHN, Arthur is the posthumous son of Geoffrey, Henry's second son, and although only a boy, has a legitimate claim to the throne. Yet John was bequeathed the crown by Richard I, Henry's third son, and considered by the English the rightful heir. However, John reigns not only over England and Ireland, but also four French provinces and, as the play begins, the French powers present Arthur's claims. A sensitive boy, Arthur becomes a pawn in political dispute: 'I

am not worth this coil that's made for me', he cries. Having jumped from a castle wall, he dies, but whether this is suicide or an accident is debatable.

Arthur, King
'Morte d'Arthur', 1842
Alfred, Lord Tennyson

The noble leader of the Knights of the Round Table, he fights his last battle in this poem. Although mortally wounded, he still musters sufficient power to force SIR BEDIVERE to return the enchanted sword Excalibur to the lake. In his final parting, Arthur offers devout words of comfort to the desolate Bedivere.

Arthur, Prince
The Faerie Queene, 1590–6
Sir Edmund Spenser

The same KING ARTHUR found in the Arthurian Legends. Symbolic of the perfect individual, he is virtuous, courageous, honest and eternal in his friendship. In *The Faerie Queene* he is presented as visiting Faerieland in order to do honour to the queen, GLORIANA, for whom he feels great love.

Arveragus
'The Franklin's Tale' in *The Canterbury Tales*, c.1387–1400
Geoffrey Chaucer

The husband of DORIGEN, he is a courtly man who regards marriage as a partnership and who wants to be the ideal husband. When he learns of his wife's dilemma he does not reproach her but insists that she must keep her word. His own sense of honour prompts that of others.

Arviragus/Cadwal
Cymbeline, 1609/10
William Shakespeare

The younger son of CYMBELINE, stolen from his royal parents, along with his elder brother, GUIDERIUS, when he was two years old, Arviragus is brought up in the idyllic surroundings of rural Wales instead of at the British court. With BELARIUS as a father and his old nurse for a mother, Arviragus, like his brother, grows up ignorant of his princely origins but still possessing all the noble virtues supposedly inherent in his royal blood. Like Guiderius, he is an enthusiastic and courageous soldier, though not always as forceful and savage as his brother.

Asch, Vida
Vida, 1980
Marge Piercy

Vida Asch has had many identities and political *noms de guerre*. A vigorous founder member of a radical underground subversive movement in America, her life since the Sixties has been structured by tense watchfulness, disguises which are also social commentaries and complex networks co-ordinating loosely like-minded activists. She makes use of relationships formed from intimate sexual or family experiences or the painfully evolving commune to create a convincing if paranoid purpose to her life.

Ash, Randolph Henry
Possession, 1990
A S Byatt

A 19th-century poet of note, over whom 20th-century scholars vie for pre-eminence in the study of his life and work. Ash emerges as a man interested not only in literature but also in science, natural history and philosophy. His writings reveal him as both romantic and domestic – a dutiful and caring husband who nevertheless enters quite deliberately upon a passionate adulterous affair with CHRISTABEL LAMOTTE. His legacy is an intriguing puzzle for rival 20th-century scholars, but their best efforts fail to uncover the whole story. That some things remain too precious and painful to be written of shows him to be a vulnerable and compassionate man.

Ashburnham, Edward
The Good Soldier, 1915
Ford Madox Ford

The apparent embodiment of the perfect English gentleman: 'an excellent magistrate, a first-rate soldier, one of the best landlords'. This blue-eyed eccentric is irresponsible with money, hopelessly sentimental, yet likeable, especially for his many overblown kindnesses to others. Less attractive is his inability to control his lust for all types of women, including his innocent ward NANCY RUFFORD, which causes his wife LEONORA ASHBURNHAM extreme anguish and eventually leads to his downfall.

Ashburnham, Leonora
The Good Soldier, 1915
Ford Madox Ford

A stately and beautiful woman who is married to the wayward EDWARD ASHBURNHAM. Possessing a 'purposeful efficiency', Leonora has seized control of her husband's chaotic finances and sorted them out. Similarly, she has worked tirelessly to perfect the impression that theirs is a model marriage, and appears devoted to their ward, NANCY RUFFORD. However, Leonora's desire for order is part of a larger lifelong obsession – to win back her husband's love. Highly passionate and jealous, she is utterly at the mercy of her feelings for Edward and will stop at nothing to achieve her goal, even going so far as to pimp for him.

Ashenden
Ashenden, 1928
W Somerset Maugham

Urbane, polyglot and sometimes flippant, Ashenden – a rising novelist and playwright – is recruited by British Intelligence during World War I and posted to Geneva. In this nest of spies, his lifelong study of human nature proves useful in the recognition and manipulation of agents on both sides. Though an 'amateur of the baroque', Ashenden is often struck by the tasteless melodrama of real life and retains for it a somewhat disturbing insouciance; ever the English gentleman, he is still capable of ruthlessness since 'only fools think war is fought with kid gloves on'.

Ashley, Ambrose
My Cousin Rachel, 1951
Daphne Du Maurier

Uncle of PHILIP ASHLEY, Ambrose is a rather sketchy, though crucial, figure. He is a much revered and, it would seem, morally aware gentleman. Our interpretation of his illness in Italy once he has married RACHEL ASHLEY determines our entire opinion of her. Whether he became neurotic because of a brain tumour, or really was being poisoned by Rachel, is pivotal to the story. He sends moving and beseeching letters to Philip, claiming that Rachel is his 'torment'. A very reasonable man who quite suddenly becomes irrational, he is a character who, although we never actually meet him, commands great sympathy.

Ashley, Lady Brett
The Sun Also Rises, 1926
Ernest Hemingway

A rootless British aristocrat in her mid-thirties who is wandering in Europe while awaiting a divorce. She is 'as charming when she is drunk as when she is sober', and wears her hair 'brushed back like a boy's', giving her a curiously androgynous quality. She is an inveterate socialite, sexually promiscuous, and avoids (or is incapable of) real emotional commitment. She gives up her young bull-fighter lover because she is 'not going to be one of those bitches that ruins children'.

Ashley, Philip
My Cousin Rachel, 1951
Daphne Du Maurier

The narrator and a very naive young man who, although in his early twenties, behaves more like a teenager. Easily influenced by those with stronger personalities and greater wisdom, he is loyal, persistent, mannerly and sincere, but lacks the ability to deal with adult problems and gets out of his depth with his cousin, RACHEL ASHLEY. At the point of writing the book, he clearly understands much more than he did at the time of the action.

Ashley, Rachel
My Cousin Rachel, 1951
Daphne Du Maurier

Rachel is portrayed as an extremely ambiguous woman. She has many endearing qualities and can win people over in an almost hypnotic fashion. Men in particular are intrigued by her worldliness and motherly control; women are annoyed by her. Highly sexual, she displays an array of feminine characteristics which, when combined, achieve startling effects. Though she is certainly fond of the good life, we are left in the dark as to whether or not she is wicked in her search for self-satisfaction.

Ashton, Lady
The Bride of Lammermoor, in *Tales of My Landlord: Third Series*, 1819
Sir Walter Scott

Modelled on the historical Lady Stair, she 'was of a family more distinguished than that of her lord, an advantage which she did not fail to use to the uttermost, in maintaining and extending her husband's influence over others ... Lady Ashton no more lost sight of her object than the falcon in his airy wheel turns his quick eyes from his destined quarry'. It is her object that her daughter, LUCY ASHTON, marry another suitor and not EDGAR RAVENSWOOD.

Ashton, Lucy
The Bride of Lammermoor, in *Tales of My Landlord: Third Series*, 1819
Sir Walter Scott

John Buchan considered her 'a green-sick girl, unfit to strive with destiny'. Scott is a little more fulsome and sympathetic: her 'exquisitely beautiful, yet somewhat girlish features, were formed to express peace of mind, serenity, and indifference to the tinsel of worldly pleasure ... The expression of the countenance was in the last degree gentle, soft, timid, and feminine ... something there was of a Madonna cast, perhaps the result of delicate health, and of residence in a family, where the dispositions of the inmates were fiercer, more active, and energetic, than her own.' The Ashton family is fierce enough, and her mother and father are implacably opposed to her love for EDGAR RAVENSWOOD; his appearance at the time of her arranged marriage drives her to insanity (an episode perhaps better known from Donizetti's operatic 'mad scene' than from the novel).

Ashton, Sir William, Lord Keeper
The Bride of Lammermoor, in *Tales of My Landlord: Third Series*, 1819
Sir Walter Scott

The new Lord of Ravenswood, he is a parvenu, having risen to wealth only during the civil wars, and is of far less impressive lineage than his lady, who thoroughly dominates him. He is, nonetheless, single-minded in defence of a title he has purchased and is determined to do everything in his power to prevent the marriage of his daughter LUCY ASHTON to the young EDGAR RAVENSWOOD.

Aslan
The Lion, the Witch and the Wardrobe, 1950, et seq
C S Lewis

A golden lion, huge and 'not tame', he is the lord of Narnia, an obvious Christ-figure, whose torture and death at the hands of the White Witch echo the biblical story, as does his resurrection. Serious, magisterial yet sometimes lighthearted and playful, he wins the hearts of his subjects, and, for the protection of Narnia, puts PETER, SUSAN, EDMUND and LUCY on the throne at Cair Paravel. A constant presence throughout the series, he inspires his people with courage and faith.

Aspatia
The Maid's Tragedy, 1610
Francis Beaumont and John Fletcher

Betrothed to AMINTOR and then deserted by him, she is arguably little more than a virtuous woman wronged. Amintor will not act against either the king's mistress Evadne or even the king himself after discovering he has been humiliated by them. Aspatia, therefore, abandoned, angry and impetuous, decides to take the law into her own hands. Disguising herself as her brother, she challenges Amintor to a duel. He kills her and, on discovering her identity, commits suicide.

Asper
Every Man out of his Humour, 1599
Ben Jonson

The presenter of the play, Asper is 'an ingenious and free spirit, eager and constant in reproof', who launches into a strong verbal attack upon the 'impious world' around him. When CORDATUS remonstrates with him, Asper retorts that the ensuing play will reflect 'time's deformity'.

Aspern, Jeffrey
The Aspern Papers, 1888
Henry James

A Romantic poet of the early 19th century, he lives on in a passionate correspondence with his mistress, MISS BORDEREAU, which is the target of the young narrator's machinations. Though he is long dead before the novella's action begins, it is his reputation and mystique that set events in motion.

Aspinall, Arvie
'Arvie Aspinall's Alarm Clock', in *While the Billy Boils*, 1888
Henry Lawson

A delicate little boy, obliged since the death of his father to earn his keep in the factory of Grinder & Bros. Rather than oversleep and miss his shift, he beds down on the factory steps, where a policeman finds him, thus beginning a local legend that culminates in the purchase (by subscription) of an alarm clock. Though ill with croup, Arvie determines to go to work, but when the alarm bell sounds, he is found to be dead in his cot.

Asterias, Mr
Nightmare Abbey, 1818
Thomas Love Peacock

An 'ichthyologist' and student of the oceanic underworld, Mr Asterias is fixated by mermaids and tritons.

Astley, Nancy, also known as **Nan King**
Tipping the Velvet, 1998
Sarah Waters

Nancy Astley, a young oyster seller in Whitstable, meets and falls in love with KITTY BUTLER and becomes her dresser. After a move to London the two become close although it is not until Nancy joins Kitty on the stage as a male impersonator, and changes her name to Nan King, that they become lovers. After the break-up of their relationship, Nan moves from rent 'boy' to wealthy woman's plaything before finally finding a place where she feels she belongs.

Aston
The Caretaker, 1960
Harold Pinter

A gentle and considerate man, he is revealed to have had electric shock therapy in a mental hospital, which has left him in a state where 'I couldn't ... get my thoughts ... together'. Abused by both his brother MICK and the querulous tramp, MAC DAVIES, whom he befriends, he spends much of the time on simple DIY tasks, eventually aiming to 'build that shed out in the garden'.

Atahuallpa
The Royal Hunt of the Sun, 1964
Peter Shaffer

Son of the Sun, Son of the Moon, Lord of the Four Quarters, Atahuallpa is the sovereign Inca of Peru. At 33 he is a magnificent warrior: tall, proud, honourable and distinguished by a 'serene arrogance'. Having killed his brother to gain absolute power, his 'spirit keeps an Empire sweet and still as corn in the field'. Captured and humbled by Spanish invaders who neither respect nor comprehend his authority, he is eventually garrotted.

Ate
The Faerie Queene, 1590–6
Sir Edmund Spenser

An ugly enchantress and friend to DUESSA, who brings discord wherever she travels. She has a squint that causes her eyes to look in different directions, a deformed mouth which spouts gall and venom, and a two-forked tongue in which both parts speak and neither agrees. She has odd feet and hands that point in opposite directions, and she sows the ground with the seeds of evil words and deeds, which then grow. She brings debate, dissension and malice to Faerieland.

Athelney, Sally
Of Human Bondage, 1915
W Somerset Maugham

It is she who frees PHILIP CAREY from the 'bondage' of his withdrawn sensitivity and aesthetic purism, wakening him to a realization that life is a matter of compromise, change and simple happiness. Significantly, perhaps, it is revealed that she is not, after all, pregnant; his offer of marriage is no longer one forced by convention, but neither is his life to be changed as dramatically as he had thought.

Athelstane of Coningsburgh
Ivanhoe, 1819
Sir Walter Scott

The intended husband of LADY ROWENA, by which match CEDRIC THE SAXON hopes to re-invigorate the Saxon line. Unfortunately, Athelstane is lumpish and pedestrian, by no means a match for the dashing courage of IVANHOE, his rival for Rowena's affections.

Atman, Weed
Vineland, 1990
Thomas Pynchon

A former lover of FRENESI GATES. Back in the 1960s, as a mathematics professor, he was 'neither charismatic nor personable'. He had been surrounded by a 'classically retrograde cult of personality' as a defender of the drug-taking, protesting young (he is perhaps modelled on the real-life literary critic Leslie A Fiedler). 'As a resident of the everyday world, Weed may have had his points, but as a Thanatoid [a bizarre Rotary of 1960s survivors] he rated consistently low on most scales, including those that measured dedication and community spirit.'

Attentive, Mr
The Life and Death of Mr. Badman, 1680
John Bunyan

The naive straight-man in the discussion of, and reflection upon, the life and death of MR BADMAN. His innocent questions allow the real interpreter, MR WISEMAN, to unravel the tragic story of a man who symbolizes all the arrogance of human nature rejecting God.

Atticus
Epistle to Dr Arbuthnot, 1735
Alexander Pope

Atticus was Pope's cant name for the critic and poet Joseph Addison. In this portrait he does not merely point out Addison's putative faults – suspicion in friendship and (most famously) 'Damn[ing] with faint praise' – but also mimics the elegant reversals and periphrastic evasions of his victim's own style.

Atwater, William
Afternoon Men, 1931
Anthony Powell

One of two listless characters (the other is called Pringle) who dominate the novel, he inhabits a seedily hedonistic demi-monde of London drinking clubs and late-night parties in the 1930s. Described as 'a weedy-looking young man with straw-coloured hair and rather long legs', he is a bespectacled Foreign Office reject who has found a job in a museum. The love of his life is Susan Nunnery; alas he is not the love of hers.

Aubery, Jean-Benoit
Frenchman's Creek, 1942
Daphne Du Maurier

A respectable gentleman, turned pirate, he needs great stimulus to get pleasure out of life. His ego waxes under the light of daring, but he is not totally self-absorbed, caring deeply for his fellow men, towards whom he is unswervingly loyal. Though wild, he is also a romantic and sensitive lover, as LADY DONA discovers.

Aubrey, Jack
Master and Commander, 1970, et seq
Patrick O'Brian

A tall, powerfully-built man, 'bold, sanguine, enterprising, with a face made for laughter', Aubrey is a Royal Navy Captain of the Napoleonic Wars, devoted to the service and an admirer of Nelson. Courageous and resourceful at sea, his daring and skill bring him great success against the enemy, and his prowess in taking prizes earns him the sobriquet of 'Lucky Jack Aubrey'. However, he is somewhat naive and even gullible when on land and often finds himself in financial difficulties. Surprisingly in such a man of action, he is an enthusiastic mathematician as well as a talented amateur violinist and often plays duets with his particular friend STEPHEN MATURIN.

Aubrey, Rose
The Fountain Overflows, 1956
Rebecca West

The child narrator, Rose intelligently evaluates what she sees and hears to assemble a picture of family life. An attractive child, with prematurely adult judgements and sensibilities, Rose is neither dogmatic nor self-assured about what is valuable in growing up. Her father is a source of instability and potential disruption, but her mother is a guardian angel who protects her from chaos and vulgarity. Rose affirms the attributes of eccentricity and is swept along by the flood of which she is a part.

Auclair, Euclide
Shadows on the Rock, 1931
Willa Cather
A middle-aged widower who has followed the great 17th-century Intendant, Comte Frontenac, to the river 'rock' of Quebec, where he gives his master medical and philosophical advice while looking after his twelve-year-old daughter Cécile in their notably ordinary and well-ordered household.

Audley, Lady
Lady Audley's Secret, 1862
Mary Elizabeth Braddon
Lucy Graham, beautiful fair-haired governess, captivates and marries the elderly Sir Michael Audley and reigns a happy singing presence in his mansion, luxuriating in fine rooms and silken magnificence. She has moments of fear and invents reasons for avoiding a stranger who comes with Sir Michael's nephew Robert. The stranger disappears. Robert, in seeking him, discovers many things about Lady Audley. She has deserted her child, she is bigamously married, she has attempted murder, but her true secret is that she suffers from intermittent inherited madness.

Audrey
As You Like It, c.1600
William Shakespeare
A simple country goatherd who is naïve enough to be flattered by TOUCHSTONE's nonsensical attentions and does not see through them to his desire merely to use her. She has enough country wisdom to realize that keeping clean and tidy is more important than beauty.

Aufidius, Tullus
Coriolanus, c.1607/8
William Shakespeare
The warrior leader of the Volscians is a fearless soldier but a treacherous one. His admiration for his arch-enemy CORIOLANUS is always tempered by his vow to destroy him, following the defeat of the Volscians at Corioli. He is a smooth-tongued political opportunist and seizes on Coriolanus's defection from Rome as a means to conquer it. He knows his enemy well enough to be able to manipulate him to such a pitch of anger as to ensure his death.

Aufsteig, Gen
Back to Methuselah, 1921
George Bernard Shaw
General Aufsteig appears during the fourth section of this five-part play. *Tragedy of an Elderly Gentleman* takes place on the shores of Galway Bay, Ireland, in 3000AD. He is alleged to be the Emperor of Turania, 'the greatest military genius of the age'. He himself claims to be

NAPOLEON, the Man of Destiny.

Augustus
Poetaster, 1602
Ben Jonson
An historical character appropriated by Jonson, Augustus, the grand-nephew of Julius Caesar, became Imperator Caesar Augustus. He was an educated, culturally sophisticated man, a patron of the arts and a close friend of OVID and VIRGIL. Jonson's Augustus is a rigidly authoritarian dictator, administering hard justice, yet at the same time a man of sensibility, wisdom and discrimination, able to distinguish true poetry from inferior versions.

Aunt Dot
The Towers of Trebizond, 1956
Rose Macaulay
The colourful woman who embarks on a journey to Turkey, where she is determined to establish an Anglican mission among the Muslims, and to pay particular attention to the women. She is a widow, her husband having been killed on a previous missionary trip, a fate which she herself escaped in dramatic fashion. She is small and plump, with a round, fair, smooth face and shrewd, merry blue eyes, and the disposition of a 'cheerful and romantic adventuress'.

Aunt Ruth (Ruth Gray)
Epitaph for George Dillon, 1954
John Osborne and Anthony Creighton
Aunt Ruth, the sister of Mrs Elliot, who has adopted GEORGE DILLON, is the family outsider. A divorcee, she has recently renounced communism and ended a tempestuous affair with a neurotic writer whose sole success was sustained self-pity. She is 'about forty, slim, smartly dressed, attractive', a naturally generous woman and the intellectual match of the volatile Dillon. The scene in which they confront each other, and almost give voice to their true feelings and fears, is the finest in the play. Ruth recognizes Dillon's sarcastic attacks upon others as frustration at his own failure as a writer, yet even her hard-won clarity of feeling cannot redeem him.

Aurelia
The Malcontent, 1604
John Marston
Duchess and consort to PIETRO JACOMO, usurper of the Duke of Genoa (MALEVOLE), Aurelia is caught by MENDOZA, 'a minion of the duchess', having an adulterous affair with Ferneze, a young courtier. Fearing her husband's wrath, she connives with Mendoza in his plot to oust Pietro. She later repents of what she describes as her 'brackish blood of beastly lust' and 'ravenous immodesty'.

Aurelius
'The Franklin's Tale' in *The Canterbury Tales*, c.1387–1400
Geoffrey Chaucer
A young, handsome paragon of the courtly graces. He is in love with DORIGEN, a married woman, and unscrupulously plays on her fears for her husband's safety to extract a promise that

she will be his. He resorts to magic to force her to keep her word but faced with her grief releases her.

Austin
True West, 1981
Sam Shepard

Following his university education, Austin has become a successful writer. He lives in the north of the USA with his wife and children, but has returned to Southern California to discuss a Hollywood deal. He meets his older brother, LEE, whose apparent freedom has always aroused his jealousy; suffering an outbreak of extreme sibling rivalry, he wants to escape from urban life to a Western wilderness.

Austria, Leopold, Grand Duke of
The Talisman: A Tale of the Crusaders, 1825
Sir Walter Scott

The vinous and slow-witted duke is contemptuously dismissed by RICHARD I as a possible leader of Christendom against the heathen, being believed to possess 'the peevishness of a wasp and the courage of a wren'. Weak rather than vain or tyrannical, he seems uneasy with his princely role, moving clumsily and with little awareness of his station.

Autolycus
The Winter's Tale, 1611
William Shakespeare

Autolycus is a volatile rogue. His principal dramatic function is to provide comic respite with his scandalous stories from the preceding bleak events at the court of LEONTES and, with his songs, to give added zest to the Bohemian sheep-shearing festivities. A fugitive from court, gambling and whoring have made him a ragged figure, but he scrapes a living as a petty thief and pedlar of ballads, and takes the view that if he can survive as a minor cheat and escape punishment in this world, then he will take his chance on divine retribution in the next. He is an endearing figure, who describes himself as 'a snapper-up of unconsidered trifles'.

Avellanos, Antonia
Nostromo, 1904
Joseph Conrad

The dutiful and devoted daughter of DON JOSÉ AVELLANOS, and later fiancée of MARTIN DECOUD. She is very independently minded by the standards of Sulaco (a city in the fictitious South American country Costaguana), having been born and educated in Europe, and does not accept the menial role assigned to women in that society. She is intelligent, and held to be 'terribly learned and serious'. A patriot, she assists her father in his political duties. After the death of Decoud, she continues her political career, but takes the opposite route to his, while apparently believing that this was 'poor Martin's intention' all along.

Avellanos, Don José
Nostromo, 1904
Joseph Conrad

An old-fashioned liberal idealist who 'is too old to descend personally into the centre of the

arena', but who is behind much of the political manoeuvring in the imaginary South American country Costaguana. Despite his advanced age, physical infirmity, and the ravages of imprisonment under the dictator Bento, he is eloquent (to the point of excess), energetic and skilful in political matters, and his powerful conviction remains undiminished. He earns the heroic inscription on his bust praising his 'lifelong struggle for Right and Justice'.

Avenel, Julian
The Monastery, 1820
Sir Walter Scott

The younger brother of Walter Avenel, he is 'a man of service', perfectly capable of loyalty when occasion demands, but not above usurping his dead brother's lands, ostensibly in the name of his niece MARY AVENEL, but with a ruthless assertion of descent by the male line only.

Avenel, Mary
The Monastery, 1820
The Abbot, 1820
Sir Walter Scott

First encountered as a pert child of five or six, when the ancestral WHITE LADY OF AVENEL first appears to her and her widowed, dispossessed mother. In later life she is the childless wife of SIR HALBERT GLENDINNING and ROLAND GRAEME's adopter. Kind, gentle and straightforward, she nonetheless carries the marks of a deep sorrow.

Avenel, White Lady of
The Monastery, 1820
Sir Walter Scott

A mysterious ancestral presence who appears to the AVENEL family in times of trouble or distress, she is (in the words of Scott's introduction) 'represented as connected with the family ... by one of those mystic ties, which in ancient times were supposed to exist ... between the creatures of the elements and the children of men'. Critics have found her an unconvincing contrivance.

Avery, Shug
The Color Purple, 1983
Alice Walker

A nightclub singer and 'The Queen Honeybee', Shug Avery is both flamboyant and vivacious. Attractive to CELIE because 'don't nothing seem to be troubling her mind', Shug is an important guiding force in her transformation. Relentlessly pursuing pleasure, she argues that 'them feelings ... some of the best stuff God did', but returns to Celie after 'she been where she been, seen what she seen, did what she did. And now she know.'

Avery, Tom
The Republic of Love, 1992
Carol Shields

The product of a pampered childhood, Tom Avery seems ill-equipped to sustain adult relationships and has been divorced three times before the age of 40. Although he is well-meaning, he comes across as a docile and slightly comical figure. Even after his life is transformed by his romance with FAY MCLEOD, he remains 'a man who is puzzled by life's offerings'.

Avril, Canon Hubert
The Tiger in the Smoke, 1952
Margery Allingham

Canon Hubert Avril, an elderly widower and uncle of ALBERT CAMPION, embodies the force of good in contrast to JACK HAVOC, the novel's principal force of evil. The canon represents Christian charity or 'disinterested love'. Wise, kind, tolerant and perceptive, he sees people as they really are and yet, believing in miracles, does not despair. Rather an eccentric figure in his familiar plaid coat with its two rows of bone buttons, reaching down to his boots, Canon Avril of St Peter of the Gate lives in amiable poverty in a small London square. 'His imagination was as wild as a small boy's and his faith ultimate.'

Aylmer
'The Birthmark', 1843, in *Mosses from an Old Manse*, 1846
Nathaniel Hawthorne

A version of PROFESSOR HENRY HIGGINS, he is a scientist, so immersed in science that he exchanges 'experience of a spiritual affinity' for the smoke and vapour of chemical experiment by marrying the beautiful Georgiana. She is marred in his eyes only by a single mark on her cheek, whose removal, once it is perceived as a flaw, becomes the consuming obsession of his life, and the source of his tragedy.

Azad, Krishan Chander
Seven Summers: The Story of an Indian Childhood, 1951, et seq
Mulk Raj Anand

The autobiographical hero of Anand's multi-volume account of a young Indian brought up in the casual brutality and intellectual narrowness of the colonial school system, who then travels to England to complete his education. Set apart from his fellow students by his colour and gifts, he nonetheless falls in love with a European woman. He has left India in the ferment caused by Mahatma Gandhi's earliest teachings, and returns anxious to study under him, and to write a novel that will embody his teachings.

Azaro
The Famished Road, 1991
Ben Okri

A spirit child who grows tired of 'coming and going' like Lazarus (after whom he was named; superstitious parents then dropped the initial letter) and chooses to inhabit the dream-like interspace between the spirit world and the living. There, his magical vision affords him a dramatic perspective on the tensions and contradictions of Nigeria as it stands on the brink of independence.

Aziz, Dr
A Passage to India, 1924
E M Forster

A small, athletic man with a modest moustache, he is a highly competent professional with a naive, romantic streak that expresses itself in his love of poetry, excitability and general passion for life. A vivacious, charming widower with three children, he is sensitive to his position in respect of India's English rulers and keen both to respect protocol and make a good impression. Touched by the sociability of MRS MOORE and ADELA QUESTED, he determines to show them the real India and is unwittingly involved in an incident that leaves him with a genuine hatred of his English masters.

B
Three Tall Women, 1991
Edward Albee

The three characters, A, B and C are portraits of Albee's adoptive mother at different ages. 52 years old and caring for A (her future self), B is a brittle but sympathetic woman, elegant, besieged by memories of family hypocrisy and a sexual encounter with a groom, and with a matter-of-fact understanding of marriage: 'men cheat; we cheat less, and we cheat because we're lonely; men cheat because they're men'. B thinks of herself as 'old enough to be a *little* wise, past being *really* dumb ... What I like most is being where I am – and fifty *is* a peak, in the sense of a mountain ... '

B, Mr
Pamela, 1740–1
Samuel Richardson

As cunning as Lucifer, this spindle-shanked young squire is absolute monarch over his servant PAMELA ANDREWS. Having abducted her, he assumes the right to label her as 'saucebox' and 'gewgaw', and strives to possess her inner being as well as her body. However, the 'very abandon'd Profligate' fumbles his chance to rape her. He undergoes a seemingly radical change of character and marries Pamela, but in fact only partially renounces his rumbustious persona; it remains lurking under the surface, competing with, and contradicting, his flimsy new virtuous self.

Baako Onipa
Fragments, 1969
Ayi Kwei Armah

As a scriptwriter for the television company Ghanavision Corporation, Baako wants both to reflect the culture and pride of his country and help fashion it into something resilient and honourable in the modern world. Yet Baako's disposition towards ethical deliberation is also his weakness. He is often too self-analysing for his own good. Unable to decide how much he should draw from the traditions of his people, how far he himself represents social hopes and anxieties, and whether his own creativity is itself spiritually redemptive or merely workmanlike, an already emotionally vulnerable personality teeters into madness. Baako sees himself as a persecuted artist. His struggle to reclaim his sanity is lonely, and largely sustained by his grandmother, NAANA.

Babbalanja
Mardi, 1849
Herman Melville

A long-winded old philosopher from Odo. He is 'a man of a mystical aspect, habited in a voluminous robe', is learned in Mardian lore, and much given to spouting quotations 'from ancient and obsolete authorities'. He is occasionally afflicted by a devilish spirit, Azzageddi, which seems to speak through him. He decides to stay in Serenia after seeing a vision of heaven there.

Babbitt, George Folansbee
Babbitt, 1922
Sinclair Lewis

Babbitt is middle-aged, middle-class, middle-brow, middle-everything. A pompous real-estate broker and 'booster' in Zenith – 'the Zip City' – he nonetheless shares his predecessor CAROL KENNICOTT's dream of a more dramatic and expansive life. Despite his radical and bohemian affectations, it is clear that he is instinct with Zenith and that it is, in the profoundest sense, his home – an expression of his essentially decent values.

Babbitt, Myra
Babbitt, 1922
Sinclair Lewis

The pompous banality of many of Lewis's men is matched by the cultural pretensions of his women. Like her husband GEORGE FOLANSBEE BABBITT, Myra is more three-dimensional than most, a complex figure from whom George attempts to win a personal independence but to whom he is inextricably and not at all tragically bound. She, too, is rather fine, and the illness that brings about their reconciliation is an ironic sign of her ability to change.

Babe
The Sheep-Pig, 1983
Dick King-Smith

Sheep farmer Hogget wins a piglet at a fair and takes him back to the farm, where the lonely little pig is adopted by the kindly sheepdog Fly and nicknamed Babe. Learning that he is intended for the farmer's dinner table, Babe decides to prove his worth by learning to herd sheep. But unlike the sheepdogs, who order the sheep about roughly, the polite 'sheep-pig' asks them nicely, a technique that wins him the affection of everyone on the farm and eventually makes him a hero.

Babs
Magnificence, 1973
Howard Brenton

A homosexual former cabinet minister and sometime friend of ALICE, Babs is now a Cambridge academic, and terminally ill. He is also, apparently, honest and emotionally vulnerable, loathing the new political image adopted by Alice in order to increase his standing within the Conservative Party. Babs sees through pretence and is intolerant of artifice. He is an old-style, one-nation Tory, and, therefore, implies Brenton, the modern Party has little sympathy for him.

Bachelor, The
The Old Curiosity Shop, 1841
Charles Dickens

A kind old gentleman who has always been called 'The Bachelor' by the simple folk in the remote village where he lives. The brother of MR GARLAND, he is the villagers' 'universal mediator, comforter and friend' and takes care of LITTLE NELL and her GRANDFATHER at the end of their wanderings.

Backbite, Sir Benjamin
The School for Scandal, 1777
Richard Brinsley Sheridan

A member of LADY SNEERWELL's gossiping coterie, who spreads slander about everyone. He devotes his malicious but not very pointed wit and his dubious poetic talents to writing satires on his contemporaries. MARIA is the object of his affections.

Baddun, Saul and Jasper
The Hundred and One Dalmatians, 1956
Dodie Smith

The brothers Baddun are as dissimilar as two brothers can be: Saul is heavy and dark, Jasper thin and fair. Both, however, are unwashed and unkempt and, above all, both are unloved. CRUELLA DE VIL's henchmen at the evil Hell Hall, their only interest in life is television, which they watch unceasingly; their ambition is to appear on 'What's my Crime?', a quiz show in which the contestants have to guess the crime committed by the guest. The dalmatians suspect that they are only half-human, but they cannot begin to imagine what foul species constitutes their other half.

Badger
The Wind in the Willows, 1908
Kenneth Grahame

A gruff grey animal of stern demeanour and great integrity, who 'simply hates Society'. He is held in enormous respect and some awe by the other animals, even the rascally inhabitants of the Wild Wood, where he lives. A kindly, paternal figure, whose motto is 'live and let live', he takes an active part in maintaining law and order and in trying to curb the worst excesses of TOAD's overheated ego.

Badger, Bayham
Bleak House, 1853
Charles Dickens

A doctor in Chelsea to whom RICHARD CARSTONE is apprenticed. He is the third husband of Mrs Bayham Badger, and admires her inordinately for having had two husbands already, a state of affairs which constitutes his favourite topic of conversation.

Badgery, Herbert
Illywhacker, 1985
Peter Carey

The con artist of Carey's title, he dreams of founding an aircraft industry in Australia, a plan thwarted by US expansionism and the ultimate redundancy of his conviction that lies and a brass neck are the only requisites for success.

Badman, Mr
The Life and Death of Mr. Badman, 1680
John Bunyan

Personifying every vice and sin imaginable, every abrogation of the image of God, he represents the unacceptable face of humanity, adrift from its roots in God. In relationships, in character and in actions, here is the worst and saddest a human can be: 'one massy body of sins'.

Baffin, Arnold
The Black Prince: A Celebration of Love, 1973
Iris Murdoch

A prolific popular novelist who in middle-age still has a raw, shy, boyish quality, Baffin was 'discovered' as a young graduate schoolmaster by an older writer, BRADLEY PEARSON. The solitary Pearson has subsequently become Baffin's spiritual father, and enjoys a special status in his family circle. But neither this long-standing friendship nor Baffin's marriage are as perfect as they seem.

Baggins, Bilbo
The Hobbit, 1937
The Lord of the Rings, 3 volumes, 1954–5
J R R Tolkien

An amiable member of the small, leathery-footed race called hobbits, he is the unlikely hero of *The Hobbit*, and a minor but significant character in *The Lord of the Rings*. Described by the wizard GANDALF as 'one of the best – as fierce as a dragon in a pinch', he is a comfort-loving creature from the dozy hamlet of Hobbiton in the Shire, who finds himself unwittingly embroiled in a series of heart-stopping adventures when he accepts the role of official 'burglar' to a posse of treasure-hunting dwarfs. In the ensuing events he discovers within himself unsuspected powers of bravery, cunning and a taste for the unknown, a revelation which is to influence the rest of his life.

Baggins, Frodo
The Lord of the Rings, 3 volumes, 1954–5
J R R Tolkien

The cousin and heir of BILBO BAGGINS, to whom Bilbo passes on his magic ring, a ring 'so powerful that in the end it would utterly overcome anyone of the mortal race who possessed it'. As its possessor he becomes embroiled, under GANDALF's direction, in a perilous journey to the Land of Mordor, where he hopes to crush the power of Sauron the Great, the Dark Lord. A courageous hobbit, endowed with greater strength and spirit than he would ever have credited, he undertakes this mission with the invaluable help of his fond and faithful ally SAM GAMGEE. In the process he grows much wiser, but sadder.

Bagheera
The Jungle Book, 1894
Rudyard Kipling
'Inky black all over, but with the panther markings showing up in certain lights like the pattern of watered silk. Everybody knew Bagheera, and nobody cared to cross his path; for he was as cunning as [the jackal] Tabaqui, as bold as the wild buffalo, and as reckless as the wounded elephant'.

Bagnet, Mr and Mrs
Bleak House, 1853
Charles Dickens
An ex-artilleryman and comrade of MR GEORGE ROUNCEWELL, Bagnet was called 'Lignum Vitae' in the army because of his solid features. The proprietor of a musical-instrument shop, he lives with his capable wife, 'the Old Girl', and their children, Malta, Quebec and Woolwich, named after the place of their birth in barracks. Bagnet is bankrupted through backing a bill for Mr George, and when Mr George is wrongly arrested for the murder of MR TULKINGHORN, Mrs Bagnet helps to re-unite him with his mother, MRS ROUNCEWELL, and, indirectly, to restore the family's savings.

Bagoas
The Persian Boy, 1972
Funeral Games, 1981
Mary Renault
When his noble family is murdered, Bagoas is captured and turned into a eunuch slave. Accepting his humiliating fate, he recovers his pride and achieves some status, first at the court of Darius and then at ALEXANDER's. There he gains the confidence and trust of the king and becomes his devoted servant and confidant. Vain and arrogant, but also fiercely protective of his master, Bagoas is the most sympathetic character of the trilogy – the feeling heart of the story. He loves, and is loved by, Alexander and when the great king dies, he alone is left to mourn while everyone else jockeys for political position at the funeral games.

Bagot, Bushy and Green
Richard II, not later than 1595
William Shakespeare
The 'caterpillars of the kingdom', three favourites of KING RICHARD II and, in the case of Bushy and Green, time-servers who desert him at the first hint of real danger. Bagot, however, remains loyal almost to the end. These sycophants advise the king badly, contribute to some extent to his downfall, and are accused of sexual misdemeanours with him: breaking 'possession of a royal bed'.

Bagstock, Major Joseph
Dombey and Son, 1848
Charles Dickens
A retired army officer, he hopes to benefit from

cultivating the friendship of MR PAUL DOMBEY, introducing him to THE HON MRS SKEWTON and her daughter, Edith Granger, who becomes EDITH DOMBEY. Vain and reactionary, he is a 'wooden-featured, blue-faced major, with his eyes starting out of his head'. Imagining that his neighbour, MISS LUCRETIA TOX, fancies him, he feels scorned on learning that she hopes to become the second Mrs Dombey. He treats with contempt his Indian servant, known as 'the Native'. Habitually referring to himself in the third person, his favourite refrain is 'Old Joe is tough, Sir, tough and devilish sly!'

Baguenault, Catherine
Seven Poor Men of Sydney, 1934
Christina Stead
The major female character in the novel, she is the half-sister of returning soldier MICHAEL BAGUENAULT and may also be his lover. She is intense, bright and life-affirming, but with an understanding of his dark side.

Baguenault, Joseph
Seven Poor Men of Sydney, 1934
Christina Stead
A printer in Sydney, he is the dull, plodding cousin of MICHAEL and CATHERINE BAGUENAULT. He seems to stand, in contrast to them, for a passive, second-hand view of life.

Baguenault, Michael
Seven Poor Men of Sydney, 1934
Christina Stead
CATHERINE BAGUENAULT's half-brother (and possibly her lover), he has returned from World War I deeply affected and introspective, brooding endlessly on the meaning of his existence.

Bailey, Benjamin (called **'Young Bailey'** and **'Bailey Junior'**)
Martin Chuzzlewit, 1844
Charles Dickens
A precocious, irrepressible, undersized boy who is the 'boots' at MRS TODGERS's Commercial Boarding House and the friend of POLL SWEEDLEPIPE. He leaves Mrs Todgers to become the liveried groom of MONTAGUE TIGG and is nearly killed when Tigg's carriage overturns. Recovering, he becomes Poll's business partner.

Bailey, Maud
Possession, 1990
A S Byatt
First impressions of Maud, an aggressive, power-dressed academic, are intimidating, but given an emotional rather than a rational context she becomes much less self-assured. Bewildered by her own feelings, she finds this uncertainty unsettling. She dare not let others get too close to her for fear of becoming their possession. Only the most diffident, undemanding offer of love is accepted and even then her response is 'I love you. I think I'd rather I didn't'.

Bailley, Harry
The Canterbury Tales, c.1387–1400
Geoffrey Chaucer
The host of the Tabard Inn where the pilgrims

assemble is handsome and strikingly manly. He keeps an excellent inn and is an astute businessman. He suggests the telling of the tales on the pilgrimage, and is revealed to be a man of great diplomacy, at home with both aristocrat and knave. His only lapse is his vicious but wholly justified rebuff to THE PARDONER, who tries to trick him.

Baines
'The Basement Room', in *The Basement Room and Other Stories*, 1935
Graham Greene
A butler, he is a good-hearted man trapped in a loveless marriage, and takes solace in a hopeless romance. He boosts his fading self-respect by telling PHILIP LANE fantastic tales of his colourful past in Africa. His wife MRS BAINES traps him into revealing his infidelity, and he kills her, but his attempt to make it appear a complete accident is foiled by Philip's inadvertent betrayal.

Baines, Constance
The Old Wives' Tale, 1908
Arnold Bennett
Reliable and conventional, Constance epitomizes all the virtues respected by the hardworking citizens of the Five Towns. Born into a significant merchant family, she is keenly aware of her place in the community and, unlike her sister, SOPHIA BAINES, does not seek to broaden her horizon. The two great adventures of her life are marriage and motherhood, in each of which she willingly plays a secondary role. Anxious to please everyone and incapable of deceit, she has an 'excellent, kind heart', but although open and artless she is not easily deceived. Others may take advantage or poke fun, but never without Constance being painfully aware of the fact.

Baines, Lila
Careful, He Might Hear You, 1963
Sumner Locke Elliott
The aunt and guardian of P S MARRIOTT, whom she has brought up in a loving but over-protective atmosphere. Beset by numerous worries and feelings of social inferiority, she is prone to asthmatic attacks and genteel sentimentality. She struggles to keep P S when her sister, VANESSA SCOTT, tries to obtain custody of him.

Baines, Mrs
'The Basement Room', in *The Basement Room and Other Stories*, 1935
Graham Greene
A housekeeper, the wife of the disaffected butler, BAINES, and a mean-spirited, disappointed woman who is seen, quite literally, as a witch by young PHILIP LANE. She bullies her husband, and is alternately brutal and fawning to Philip. She is killed when her husband knocks her downstairs when she confronts him over his lover.

Baines, Sophia
The Old Wives' Tale, 1908
Arnold Bennett
The good citizens of Bursley are convinced that beautiful Sophia is on the road to ruin when she

elopes with a travelling salesman. While it is true that his subsequent treatment of her bears out her family's worst fears, Sophia manages to survive and indeed prosper. It is her wilful, passionate nature which leads to her downfall but she is after all a Baines and it is the practical business-like attitude of a true Baines which enables her to endure. Sophia describes herself as 'criminally proud', but the pride is matched by a remarkable courage.

Bains, Guitar
Song of Solomon, 1978
Toni Morrison
Driven by the idea that 'everybody wants the life of a black man', Guitar's vision is distorted by bitter anger. A member of the vengeful Seven Days organization and MILKMAN DEAD's closest friend, he is, in Milkman's eyes, 'the one person left whose clarity never failed him'. Justifying his 'blood deep responsibilities' by asserting that his 'whole life is love', his murderous pursuit of Milkman is paradoxically resolved in a final leap where 'it did not matter which one of them would give up the ghost in the killing arms of his brother'.

Bajazeth
Tamburlaine the Great: Part I, 1587
Christopher Marlowe
Proud Emperor of the Turks, momentarily abandoned by 'sleepy Mahomet' and captured by the Scythian warrior TAMBURLAINE. Reduced to acting as his captor's mounting-block, and kept in a cage, he dashes his brains out.

Baker, Julius → Gunner

Baker, Nicole
The Executioner's Song, 1979
Norman Mailer
The girlfriend of executed murderer GARY GILMORE, and arguably the central character, she is a fragile but also resilient product of the same environment that produced Gary, in which family values and the success ethic have been turned on their heads.

Bakha
Untouchable, 1935
Mulk Raj Anand
An 18-year-old *Harijan* youth in India, considered untouchable by Hindus of higher caste. Despite this, he applies himself to his job of latrine cleaner with dedication and pride. The novel covers just 24 hours of his narrow but curiously capacious life.

Balaam, Sir
'Epistle III, To Allen, Lord Bathurst', in 'Moral Essays', 1732
Alexander Pope
A 'citizen of sober fame ... /A plain good man ... / Religious, punctual, frugal, and so forth', who is corrupted by unexpected good fortune (which he mistakes for his own skill and prescience). He falls victim to the ready temptations of St James's, a seat in Parliament, and the pleasures of the flesh, losing all when he is impeached and deserted by wife and friends.

Balchristie, Jenny
The Heart of Midlothian, in *Tales of My Landlord:*
Second Series, 1818
Sir Walter Scott

The housekeeper at Dumbiedikes, she is 'a good, buxom figure of a woman, betwixt forty and fifty', who has kept the laird's keys and generally managed matters with reliable good sense since his lady's death.

Balderston, Caleb
The Bride of Lammermoor, in *Tales of My Landlord:*
Third Series, 1819
Sir Walter Scott

The preposterous old butler of Ravenswood, still unswervingly loyal to the outlawed son of his former master, but for all that a caricature of the ancient family retainer, and a false note amid the tragic tones of the Ravenswoods' decline.

Baldry, Captain Chris
The Return of the Soldier, 1918
Rebecca West

A shell-shocked soldier, Captain Chris Baldry suffers a hiatus of memory, and can recall neither his marital status nor his experiences in the trenches. He would have been happy with MARGARET ALLINGTON, if he could have married her at the proper time in his life; the thought of her 'sent the blood running under his skin'. He is the epitome of English masculine decency, representing a tolerant liberal humanism. The truth of his position must be faced and Chris is 'cured' with Margaret's help. He returns to his wife, KITTY BALDRY, and a life of duty and obedience with 'a dreadful decent smile'.

Baldry, Kitty
The Return of the Soldier, 1918
Rebecca West

Kitty has been nurtured by the conditions of Edwardian society. She is deeply materialistic and has subordinated her soul to the pursuit of beauty. When CAPTAIN CHRIS BALDRY, the 'impregnable fortress of a gracious life', falls to MARGARET ALLINGTON, Kitty is wounded and baffled at her rejection by him and makes little effort to be patient or understanding of his problems. Dazed, she employs acrid irony instead of compassion. When Chris is finally 'cured', Kitty is delighted that uncertainty has been expelled.

Baldwin, George
Manhattan Transfer, 1925
John Dos Passos

A young, struggling lawyer in the Emery & Emery practice, George Baldwin shoots to prominence by successfully representing GUS MCNIEL. He is unhappily married to Cecily, who eventually consents to divorce. His professional diligence is always in conflict with his 'physical urgences', and his mistresses include ELLEN THATCHER, Nellie McNiel and Nevada Jones. Encouraged to go into politics, he wins the election as a Reform candidate for the post of District Attorney. Infatuated with Ellen, he seems finally to have worn down her resistance to marrying him.

Balfour, David
Kidnapped, 1886
Catriona, 1893
Robert Louis Stevenson

The young narrator. Plucked from obscurity to inherit an estate, he finds himself duped by his uncle and kidnapped. Wandering in the Highlands he sees the infamous murder of THE RED FOX. Throughout the tale he remains an innocent observer, a passive witness, rather than a man of action. This is a journey into adulthood, where he learns to take on responsibilities and become self-willed, discarding the blind obedience imposed by his stern Presbyterian upbringing. Through his encounter with the romantic, heroic figure of ALAN BRECK, he learns to loosen his emotions in a more spontaneous way. In *Catriona*, he is finally capable of expressing the love which might otherwise have remained repressed.

Balfour, Ebenezer
Kidnapped, 1886
Robert Louis Stevenson

A small, mean, stooping creature who is entirely sinister. His body seems wizened by a cheerless life spent without love being expressed or accepted. The unfinished, dilapidated House of Shaws is symbolic of the man's entire nature: a hollow existence with no warming soul at its heart. It is he who dupes his gullible nephew DAVID BALFOUR out of his inheritance of the House of Shaws by arranging his abduction. Ultimately, however, he elicits some sympathy because it is clear that he is only a pathetic, frightened old man, terrified of losing what little he holds dear.

Balfour, John, known as Burley
Old Mortality, in *Tales of My Landlord*, 1816
Sir Walter Scott

A dedicated Covenanter from Kinloch (not 'of Burley', as is sometimes thought) who is sheltered by young HENRY MORTON. John Buchan called him 'the eternal fanatic, inspired by a wild logic of his own, tortured and terrible but never base'. Red-haired, heavy-set and of an intense countenance, he is wanted for the murder of Archbishop Sharp of St Andrews.

Baliol, Mrs (Martha) Bethune
Chronicles of the Canongate: First Series, 1827
Sir Walter Scott

She comes from an ancient Scottish family and can remember back to the days before the '45 and to the time when Highland clans occupied the Scottish capital. In her age, she and her time-warped home have become an important social focus and such a conduit for historical and genealogical gossip that she becomes a valuable source for CHRYSTAL CROFTANGRY's story-collecting. 'A little woman, with ordinary features and an ordinary form, and hair which in youth had not decided colour, we may believe [her] when she said of herself that she was never remarkable for personal charms.' Experience has supplied what nature did not.

Balmawhapple, the Laird of (family name Falconer)
Waverley, 1814
Sir Walter Scott
Much given to field sports, he has an appetite and thirst to match. 'Young, stout, and active', he is also obstreperously open about his Jacobite sympathies when in his cups and inclined to let his sword do the talking for him.

Baloo
The Jungle Book, 1894
Rudyard Kipling
Seriously slandered by Walt Disney, 'the sleepy brown bear who teaches the wolf cubs the Law of the Jungle' is far from being the dozy hedonist of the animated film, but is rather a wise old vegetarian whose simple, uncompetitive needs grant him an honoured place among his fiercer comrades.

Balthazar B
The Beastly Beatitudes of Balthazar B, 1968
J P Donleavy
A funny yet infinitely sad character, haunted by a hollow sense of loss. A longing for acceptance dogs him through his days at a vile public school and at the University of Dublin. Rumbustious and spontaneous, he skirts on the edge of moral and emotional quagmires, squandering money, indulging to excess, flirting with anarchy. Yet through it all, he remains always in search of unconditional love.

Balthazar, Prince
The Spanish Tragedy, 1592
Thomas Kyd
The son of the Viceroy of Portugal, Balthazar has been captured by the Spanish. He courts BEL-IMPERIA and, for political reasons, has the support of her father, the DUKE OF CASTILE, and brother, DON LORENZO. She, though, loves DON HORATIO. Balthazar, his honour slighted and the political situation delicate, assisted by Don Lorenzo, stabs Horatio to death. In so doing he plunges himself into events over which he has no control. Neither perceptive nor likeable, he is eventually stabbed to death by Bel-Imperia.

Balthazar, S
Balthazar, 1958, and elsewhere in *The Alexandria Quartet*, 1968
Lawrence Durrell
An Alexandria psychiatrist and a friend of the tyro novelist L G DARLEY, who shows him the draft of his novel. Balthazar, who knows all the secrets of the heart, confides in Darley that JUSTINE has not loved Darley at all, a revelation delivered with his usual clinical calm.

Baltram, Edward
The Good Apprentice, 1985
Iris Murdoch
The handsome, charming and brilliant Edward, who always outshines his stepbrother, STUART DUNO, is the illegitimate son of famous painter JESSE BALTRAM. Not having known his mother or Jesse, 'any signal however faint from the dark lost planet of his parents' intrigues Edward. This concern inadvertently leads to his responsibility, at the age of 20, for his best friend's death and his subsequent persecution by the vengeful mother. His life destroyed by horror, grief and guilt, tortured by his wickedness and disgrace, when Edward receives a mysterious 'signal' from Jesse, he hopes he can perform some healing miracle, and becomes deeply involved with his father's strange household.

Baltram, Jesse
The Good Apprentice, 1985
Iris Murdoch
The reclusive Baltram is a painter, sculptor, architect, fiery socialist and charismatic Don Juan; a 'great man' whose work will be worth a fortune when he dies. But at his isolated, eerie fenland house his illegitimate son, EDWARD BALTRAM, whose pregnant mother Jesse callously 'dumped', finds him apparently senile and virtually imprisoned by his strange wife and two daughters. Apparently, Jesse has always been their hero, god and magician, the designer of their lives. But their present ambivalence about him makes Edward question the subsequent death – and the life – of this enigmatic man.

Balu
The Financial Expert, 1952
R K Narayan
As a mischievous child Balu was devoted to his father, MARGAYYA. But Margayya's mixture of over-indulgence and severity, combined with his relentless driving ambition for his son's academic success, turns Balu into a sullen, taciturn teenager whose idea of hell is a torturing God confronting him with his school record. For despite desperate paternal efforts Balu has no interest in or respect for learning and consistently remains bottom of his class. Yet another matriculation failure drives him to run away, but his intention never to return to his home town Malgudi is foiled.

Balue, Cardinal John of
Quentin Durward, 1822
Sir Walter Scott
At one time he was the favourite minister of LOUIS XI, KING OF FRANCE, a relationship Scott likens to that of Henry VIII and Wolsey. 'The cardinal, accordingly, had not escaped the error incidental to those who are suddenly raised to power from an obscure situation, for he entertained a strong persuasion, dazzled doubtless by the suddenness of his elevation, that his capacity was equal to intermeddling with affairs of every kind, even those most foreign to his profession and studies.'

Balwhidder, Rev Mr
Annals of the Parish, 1821
John Galt
Mr Balwhidder becomes minister of Dalmailing in Ayrshire when George III ascends the throne and ends his career when George III dies. In his Annals, he records in rambling and affectionate detail the events of his ministry and describes his flock and the changes he sees in customs and places, all of them reflecting events in the larger world – the loss of the colonies, the French revolution, the new factories. In everything he traces the hand of providence, moralizing

soberly on each year as it comes. He is not very clever and tells us more than he realizes about himself and his three very different wives.

Bamforth
The Long and the Short and the Tall, 1958
Willis Hall

Initially, he appears to be a stereotypical stage Cockney soldier. However, though he is crude, argumentative and superficially insensitive, he does, at the play's climax, show himself as the only one willing to defend the life of a Japanese prisoner – 'right here you stop and make a stand' – and establishes himself as a decent man who 'wasn't meant to be a hero' but who understands the theory and practice of war.

Bandello, Rico Cesare, known as **Little Caesar**
Little Caesar, 1929
W R Burnett

A ruthless Italo-American gangster, he established the basic matrix for many subsequent anti-heroes. Small and dark, apparently unaffected by any social constraints whatsoever, he achieves success by a mixture of physical violence and psychological intimidation.

Bandparts, Mr
Redheap, 1959, first published in the USA as *Every Mother's Son*, 1930
Norman Lindsay

A drunken 19th-century tutor in the town of Redheap, he represents a comically ambiguous role model for his young charges, but also a challenge to their cramped imaginations.

Banford
The Fox, 1923
D H Lawrence

Banford, 'a small, thin, delicate thing with spectacles' lives with her partner, MARCH, at Bailey Farm, which they are attempting to manage by themselves. Both women are known by their surnames and are 'the best of friends', although events prove Banford to be lacking in confidence and prone to jealousy. She is nervous and delicate, but generous and moderately well-off and therefore able to invest more heavily in the farm. Perhaps she also believes she is investing in March's loyalty. When HENRY GRENFEL arrives, she treats him initially as a brother, but when March's affections turn towards him, Banford begins to compete. Her story ends in tragedy.

Banford, Isabel
Pierre, 1852
Herman Melville

The illegitimate half-sister of PIERRE GLENDINNING, whose discovery precipitates a tragedy. She has a gaze of 'loveliness and loneliness', but her features reveal to Pierre 'the subtler expression of the portrait of his then youthful father, strangely translated'.

Banks, Christopher
When We Were Orphans, 2000
Kazuo Ishiguro

Christopher Banks claims to be a celebrated detective in 1930s London, but he is constantly haunted by the mystery of his parents' disappearance from Old Shanghai, when he was a boy of nine. From 1930 to 1958, Banks tells his story in flashbacks, travelling back to a now war-torn city to try to discover what happened to his parents, and trying to discover himself as fact and fantasy begin to blend, and as the memories of a troubled mind fail to make sense.

Bannon, Homer
Horseman, Pass By, 1961, reissued as *Hud*, 1963
Larry McMurtry

His name suggests both the literal and the mythological or symbolic aspects of his background. An Irish-American cattleman, he stands for the sort of heroic self-reliance that is disappearing in the face of increased government control. Unable to withstand the forces of change, he faces backwards into the past.

Banquo
Macbeth, c.1606
William Shakespeare

Fellow general and close friend of MACBETH, who is with him when he encounters THE THREE WEIRD SISTERS, who prophesy greatness for Banquo's children. A spiritually decent, brave man, he recognizes the witches as 'instruments of darkness' and, later, suspects that Macbeth 'play'dst most foully' in the killing of KING DUNCAN. Murdered by assassins who are to secure the lineage for Macbeth's own children, Banquo's loyalty and fatherly kindness contrast successfully with Macbeth's increasing alienation from humanity.

Bansi, Sizwe
Sizwe Bansi Is Dead, 1972
Athol Fugard et al

Sizwe Bansi is caught in the web of South Africa's apartheid system. His attempt to remain in Port Elizabeth and find a job that will ameliorate his family's poverty-stricken life runs counter to the 'Influx Control' policy of apartheid, and his only way out is to assume the persona of a dead man, Robert Zwelinzima, who, though dead, possesses a 'Native Identification Number'. Encouraged by the street-wise Buntu, Sizwe discovers that he has very few other options.

Baptista Minola
The Taming of the Shrew, early 1590s
William Shakespeare

A man of business, Baptista is prepared to sell his daughters to the highest bidder. He is desperate to marry off KATHARINA, agreeing to the first offer that comes along, although he does evince some concern about PETRUCHIO's odd behaviour and dress. At the same time, he fails to read LUCENTIO's intentions and to detect any of the many characters who appear in disguise at his house in pursuit of BIANCA. He appears to favour Bianca because of her docile obedience, but he comes to realize how badly he has misjudged his two daughters.

Barabas
The Jew of Malta, c.1592–4
Christopher Marlowe

A merchant of Malta, who gathers 'infinite

riches in a little room'. Fiercely anti-Christian –
'Rather had I, a Jew, be hated thus,/Than
pitied in a Christian poverty;/For I can see no
fruits in all their faith/But malice, falsehood,
and excessive pride' – he finds himself
fatally trapped between the cross and the
scimitar.

Barangaroo
The Timeless Land, 1941
Storm of Time, 1948
No Barrier, 1953
Eleanor Dark

The Aborigine wife of BENNILONG and mother of
DILBOONG, Barangaroo is a woman of fierce and
shrewish temperament. She dies soon after
Dilboong's birth.

Barban, Tommy
Tender is the Night, 1934
F Scott Fitzgerald

A tough French soldier of fortune who becomes
NICOLE DIVER's 'fierce lover'. He is proud of his
virile masculinity and his courage and physical
attributes (he fights a duel over an imagined – or
invented – slight), and is utterly determined to
conquer in his pursuit of Nicole. He is crude and
coarse in manner, unscrupulous in character, and
adopts a sceptical, scoffing attitude to almost
everything around him.

Barbara
The Old Curiosity Shop, 1841
Charles Dickens

The housemaid of MR and MRS GARLAND, she is
'very tidy, modest, and demure, but very pretty
too'. She meets KIT NUBBLES at the Garlands'
house and later becomes his wife. Her mother,
always referred to as 'Barbara's mother', attends a
dissenting chapel and is friendly with Mrs
Nubbles.

Barbary, Miss
Bleak House, 1853
Charles Dickens

The sister of LADY DEDLOCK and aunt of ESTHER
SUMMERSON, who lives with her until the age of
14. A grave, strict Calvinist whom Esther
believes to be her godmother, she is ashamed of
Esther's illegitimacy and, together with her
austere servant, MRS RACHAEL, makes Esther's
childhood grim and depressing.

Barbe, St → St Barbe

Bardell, Mrs Martha
Pickwick Papers, 1837
Charles Dickens

SAMUEL PICKWICK's comely but foolish widowed
landlady in Goswell Street. She misconstrues
his innocent remark as a marriage proposal and,
on the advice of the unscrupulous lawyers,
Dodson and Fogg, brings an action against
him for breach of promise. Unable to pay her
legal fees, she is sent to the Fleet Prison,
where she meets Mr Pickwick, imprisoned
for refusing to pay the costs of the lawsuit.
Pitying her, he pays both their costs and they are
released.

Bardolph
Henry IV Part I, 1596/7
Henry IV Part II, 1597/8
Henry V, 1599
William Shakespeare

Bardolph's dominant feature is his bulbous red
nose, which is the cause of much hilarity among
his associates. His cowardice, which is in
evidence during the robbery at Gad's Hill,
becomes clearer in the French wars, although he
shows some vocal bravery at Harfleur when he
encourages others to action. He is fond of his
master SIR JOHN FALSTAFF, for whom he often
acts as a messenger, and is affected by his death,
wishing that he could go with him. A thief from
beginning to end, he has his wish sooner than
expected, for he is hanged for stealing from a
French church.

Barfoot, Everard
The Odd Women, 1893
George Gissing

He acts as a sexual antagonist to the New Woman
RHODA NUNN, revealing to her the social realities
of a situation in which there are still simply too
many high-minded women to satisfy the more
basic needs of educated, cultured and essentially
sympathetic men like himself, forcing them to go
'down market' and search out working-class
wives and lovers.

Barkis, Mr
David Copperfield, 1850
Charles Dickens

A carrier who takes DAVID COPPERFIELD to
Yarmouth when he is first sent away to school, he
drives his horse as if asleep, prompting David to
imagine it would find its way as well without
him. A man of few words whose idea of
conversation is restricted to whistling, he
nonetheless declares his determination to marry
CLARA PEGGOTTY, asking David to convey to her
the words, 'Barkis is willin''. He eventually
marries her and on his death leaves her a good
sum of money.

Barklay, Catherine
A Farewell to Arms, 1929
Ernest Hemingway

A young and attractive British woman who
volunteered for nursing duties when her now-
dead fiancé joined up, with the 'silly idea he
might come to a hospital where I was'. Although
'a little crazy', she is really 'a simple girl'. She falls
in love with FREDERIC HENRY, and he with her. She
is prophetically 'afraid of the rain because I
sometimes see me dead in it'.

Barlow, Mr
The History of Sandford and Merton, 1783–9
Thomas Day

A Minister of the Gospel who is tutor to both
TOMMY MERTON and HARRY SANDFORD, and
would not exchange his position or 'the severe
duties it enjoins' for any other. He has led a
'retired manner of life' at a distance from the
'refinements of polite life', but is an astute judge
of his charges. He is rather long-winded in the
process, but reforms Merton by Christian
precepts and patient but firm example.

Barnabas, Dr Conrad
Back to Methuselah, 1921
George Bernard Shaw

One of two Barnabas brothers (the other being FRANKLYN BARNABAS), Conrad appears in the second section of this five-part play. *The Gospel of the Brothers Barnabas* is set in a Hampstead study during the early part of World War I. As Professor of Biology at Jarrowfields University, Conrad represents science, one component of the theory of Creative Evolution, for which he and Franklyn are spokesmen (Franklyn represents the religious aspect). As an advocate of the theory of longevity, Conrad suggests that by exercising subconscious will, human beings could live for 300 years.

Barnabas, Franklyn
Back to Methuselah, 1921
George Bernard Shaw

One of two Barnabas brothers (the other being CONRAD BARNABAS), Franklyn appears in the second section of this five-part play. *The Gospel of the Brothers Barnabas* is set in a Hampstead study during the early part of World War I. A former cleric, Franklyn, 'an impressive looking man of 50', represents the religious dimension of the theory of Creative Evolution, for which he and Conrad are spokesmen (Conrad represents the biological aspect). He is also a fellow advocate of his brother's longevity theory.

Barnabas, 'Savvy' (Cynthia)
Back to Methuselah, 1921
George Bernard Shaw

The 18-year-old daughter of FRANKLYN BARNABAS, 'Savvy' appears in the second section of this five-part play. *The Gospel of the Brothers Barnabas* is set in a Hampstead study during the early part of World War I. A modern young woman, she is socialist, impetuous, energetic and sceptical of the BARNABAS brothers' theories of long life.

Barnacles, Bill
The Magic Pudding, 1918
Norman Lindsay

He is gruffly dedicated to the protection of the (disconcertingly talkative) MAGIC PUDDING from the villainous WATKIN WOMBAT and POSSUM, who are trying to steal it.

Barnacles, the
Little Dorrit, 1857
Charles Dickens

'A very high family, and a very large family', they are 'dispersed all over the public offices' and administer the Circumlocution Office, the most important government department. Incompetent, inefficient and promoted through nepotism, if something needs to be done, they excel in the art of 'HOW NOT TO DO IT'. They obstruct ARTHUR CLENNAM in his enquiries about WILLIAM DORRIT and prevent DANIEL DOYCE from patenting his invention.

Barnes, Jake
The Sun Also Rises, 1926
Ernest Hemingway

An American newspaper correspondent who has attached himself to the rootless cosmopolitan set of LADY BRETT ASHLEY, with whom he is in love. Their relationship cannot be consummated, however, since he has been emasculated by a war wound. He adopts a stoical attitude to his injury, and looks for a way in which to live in the new, postwar world, hoping that 'maybe if you found out how to live in it you learned from that what it was all about'.

Barrow, Col Basil
Tunes of Glory, 1956
James Kennaway

Emotionally repressed and driven by a fierce commitment to traditional military values and standards, he cannot cope with the disruptive influence of a colleague, LT COL JOCK SINCLAIR, who seems to mock all the elements of life and morality that are so precious for him. To relax standards would be to entertain the Devil and to risk an avalanche of change and decline. This he will not permit, and it is this rigidity, and the ensuing conflict, which bring tragedy.

Barrow, G H
The 42nd Parallel, 1930
1919, 1932
The Big Money, 1936, forming the *U.S.A.* trilogy, 1938
John Dos Passos

A tall, stuttering Texan who is a Labour-man and aide to the president, Barrow promotes international peace and, on a personal level, espouses the benefits of free love to his various lady friends. However, despite his proclaimed affinity with the workforce and his apparently pagan tendencies, he is seen to be a bit of a phoney who, when it comes to a crisis, is more concerned about his own reputation and well-being than anything else.

Barry, Cornelius, also known as Chevalier de Balibari
The Luck of Barry Lyndon, 1844
W M Thackeray

The eldest brother of Barry's father, he gave up his estate on account of his obstinate adherence to papism. 'My uncle was a man of sixty years of age ... In height he was about my size, that is, six feet and half an inch; his cast of features singularly like mine, and extremely *distingué*. One of his eyes was closed with a black patch, however; he wore a little white and red paint ... and a pair of moustaches, which fell over his lip and hid a mouth that I afterwards found had rather a disagreeable expression.'

Barry, Gwyn
The Information, 1995
Martin Amis

An Oxford contemporary of RICHARD TULL (both men are now 40), Barry has become hugely famous as the author of *Amelior*, a mediocre but timely utopian novel. A man with 'greedy green eyes' and 'bright grey hair – the hair (Richard thought) of an obvious charlatan', Barry has an enviably young, rich wife, an expensive lifestyle, professional authority, social ease and the admiration of the media. To Tull's fury, these have made him invulnerable to criticism and, apparently, all of Tull's efforts to destroy him.

Bart, Lily
The House of Mirth, 1905
Edith Wharton
Brought up by her bitter, impoverished mother to be nothing but an exquisite ornament, the beautiful and vulnerable Lily has all the social graces and an ingrained love of luxury, but very little money. She is entirely dependent on the goodwill and largesse of wealthy New York society to maintain her precarious position within it. However, the different world she glimpses through the lawyer LAWRENCE SELDEN, and her own moral scruples and fastidiousness, dissuade her from acquiring the rich socialite husband essential to her survival. Her reputation unjustly ruined due to her innocence, she becomes a pathetic victim of the shallow society which moulded her.

Bartelby
The Piazza Tales, 1856
Herman Melville
A scrivener, or law-copyist. The narrator, his employer, says he is 'the strangest I ever saw, or heard of'. He is pale, cadaverous, respectable and 'incurably forlorn'. He is steady and honest, and at first is an assiduous copier, but abruptly determines that he 'would prefer not to' work in this way any more. He is respectful but unshakeable in his conviction, but continues to haunt the building in silence, and is eventually removed to prison by a new tenant, where he dies. The narrator links his morbid reaction to having worked in the Dead Letters office, and to the condition of all humanity.

Bartlett, Charlotte
A Room With a View, 1908
E M Forster
A cousin and chaperone to LUCY HONEYCHURCH, Charlotte Bartlett is a prim spinster with a long, narrow head, whose favourite role is that of the 'prematurely aged martyr'. She is a model of kindness and propriety, whose displays of self-deprecation and deference would try the patience of a saint and whose good intentions are often more of a hindrance than a help. However, she is neither as set in her ways nor as insensitive as others may think and is still capable of justifying the family saying that 'you never knew which way Charlotte Bartlett would turn'.

Bartlett, Hector
A Far Cry from Kensington, 1988
Muriel Spark
'*Pisseur de copie*', as he is branded by MRS HAWKINS, meaning a 'urinator of journalistic copy'. Pretentious in his social and intellectual poses and his appalling prose and conversational style, he lives 'mostly on his wits and a novelist called Emma Loy'. With his prickly red hair, gaudy clothes, stoop and fat face, he is cruel, vindictive and dangerous.

Barton, David
Strange Meeting, 1971
Susan Hill
A young, enthusiastic soldier, David is neither cynical, nor tarnished by suffering. He comes from a close, supportive and extremely loving family, which seems to act as a protective cushion around him, whatever predicament he finds himself in. He does not fear death, or life, and has a way of accepting his lot. Lively and irrepressibly honest, he greatly influences his friend JOHN HILLIARD. Fiercely loyal, David is open to new experiences and willing to learn.

Barton, John
Mary Barton, 1848
Elizabeth Gaskell
A sad, working-class man with a passionate desire for equality among the social classes, he becomes so embittered that he veers towards communist principles in an attempt to find a strategy to counter the injustices of his day. Disillusioned with what he sees around him, he would like Christian doctrines to govern the world, not capitalistic ones. He loves people in a broad, all-embracing way, and despairs of society.

Barton, Mary
Mary Barton, 1848
Elizabeth Gaskell
A working-class heroine who is passionate and impulsive and possesses an innate sense of justice. A capable girl with a skill for relating to others, she is influenced by her father, JOHN BARTON, who has a keen sense of the plight of their class. She can be haughty and even arrogant, but in the end she always chooses the morally sensible path.

Barton, Milly
'The Sad Fortunes of the Rev. Amos Barton', in
Scenes of Clerical Life, 1858
George Eliot
The beautiful, gentle, Madonna-like wife of nondescript REV AMOS BARTON, Milly is a perfect 'angel in the house', uncomplaining even in the face of complete exhaustion. Overburdened with children, and with another one on the way, Milly nonetheless never dreams of letting up in her wifely 'duties', and thinks only of Amos and the children when troubled times befall them. But such selflessness has a price, and Milly ultimately pays dearly for it.

Barton, Rev Amos
'The Sad Fortunes of the Rev. Amos Barton', in
Scenes of Clerical Life, 1858
George Eliot
The curate of Shepperton Church, bald-headed Amos Barton is the most ordinary of middle-aged men, undistinguished by either great virtue or tragic flaw. As father of six children, money-worries are never far from his mind, but he fails to appreciate, at least not until it is too late, the strain his wife MILLY BARTON is under to keep the house running smoothly. Falling foul, in his ignorance, of local gossip, worse is to follow, but in realizing the worth of what he loses, he lays a firm claim on our sympathies.

Barton, Susan
Foe, 1986
J M Coetzee
Mainly through letters, and for a fee, former

castaway Susan Barton tells her story to Mr Foe. She has rescued Cruso and Friday from their desert island by sighting an English ship, but Cruso does not survive the voyage to England. She and Friday, who is mute, barely eke out an existence in London. However, her own version of the Cruso story, and her concern for Friday, are important to her, hence her distress at Foe's male chauvinist distortions of the story in his own version, 'Robinson Crusoe'.

Bascombe, Frank
The Sportswriter, 1986
Independence Day, 1995
Richard Ford

Frank Bascombe is one of the great self-deceivers. In *The Sportswriter*, he is working as a journalist while struggling to come to terms with the death of his infant son and the break-up of his marriage. He reappears, six years older, in *Independence Day*, working as a real estate agent and attempting to deal with the disturbed behaviour of his surviving son. As the narrator of both novels, he retains a naive optimism as his life steadily falls apart.

Basdai
The Chip-Chip Gatherers, 1973
Shiva Naipaul

Sustained by 'medicinal' doses of rum from the local grog-shop, she matchmakes and plots, seeking to replace her own dead daughter with the beautiful but wayward SUSHILA. By whatever means, she has a rare insight into what makes EGBERT RAMSARAN tick, and she exploits it to the full.

Basho
Narrow Road to the Deep North, 1968
The Bundle, 1978
Edward Bond

The play is set in Japan in 'about the seventeenth, eighteenth or nineteenth centuries'. Basho, a poet-priest, is based upon the 17th-century poet, Matsuo Basho, who described the discovery of a child abandoned by its parents. In the play, the child turns out to be SHOGO. Basho, meanwhile, embarks upon 'a journey along the narrow road to the deep north'. A Buddhist believing in denial of the ego and the emotions, he appears to many as complacent and insular. His inactivity is in many ways morally culpable. On the other hand, he is so enraged by both Shogo's tyranny and his contempt for religious doctrine and belief, that he instigates a western coup. In *The Bundle* he again refuses to nurture an abandoned child, but this time the child grows up to be WANG, the leader of an insurrectionary army. The child is taken by THE FERRYMAN while Basho continues his journey. At the end of the play, the self-centred Basho appears in despair. Each time he has failed to learn from experience.

Bashville
The Admirable Bashville, 1901
George Bernard Shaw

Bashville is the footman to the high-class Lydia Carew, and secretly in love with her. When the boxer CASHEL BYRON, himself in love with Lydia, calls to see her, Bashville knocks him down. Later, he renounces his claim upon Lydia and

takes up boxing himself under the name of the Admirable Bashville.

Basilius, Duke
The Countess of Pembroke's Arcadia, 1581–4, published 1590
Sir Philip Sidney

The ruler of Arcadia, and father of PAMELA and PHILOCLEA, he is a mild and unworldly old duke, easily duped by more calculating characters, and now living in retirement in a rustic 'lodge'. 'He excels in nothing so much as in the zealous love of his people.' He appears to succumb to a potion administered by his wife GYNECIA (who believes it to be an aphrodisiac), but recovers in time for a general reconciliation.

Bassanio
The Merchant of Venice, 1594/5
William Shakespeare

Venetian nobleman. Charming if rather feckless, he begins the play by borrowing money from SHYLOCK, using his friend ANTONIO's name as credit, in order to pursue his courtship of the wealthy PORTIA, and hence is at the root of the play's major plot device. Handsome and essentially innocent, he is the object of love of both Portia and Antonio, and demonstrates fidelity and affection to them in return.

Bassianus
Titus Andronicus, c.1589
William Shakespeare

The brother of the Roman emperor SATURNINUS. With his brother he contests both the throne and the hand of TITUS ANDRONICUS's daughter Lavinia, which he obtains by force. He seals his own fate by finding QUEEN TAMORA consorting with AARON, THE MOOR and waxing indignant about this 'spotted, detested and abominable' foreigner: he is rapidly murdered by her two sons.

Bassington, Comus
The Unbearable Bassington, 1912
'Saki' (Hector Hugh Munro)

A handsome, faun-like youth with charm and humour but a lack of purpose. His extravagant tastes, especially in clothes, exceed his income and he perversely acts against his own interests, displaying cruelty, selfishness and greed when it would most benefit him to behave well. This strains his relationship with Francesca, his mother, who wants him to marry an heiress, and proves ultimately self-destructive.

Bassiolo
The Gentleman Usher, 1602/3
George Chapman

The gentleman usher to EARL LASSO, whose household he runs rather fussily. A slave to fashion, he is foolish, gullible, greedy for advancement and, because of his inflated opinion of himself, easily flattered. He is entirely unaware that he is a figure of ridicule to PRINCE VINCENTIO and MARGARET.

Bast, Edward
JR, 1975
William Gaddis

A sometime composer, and latterly schoolteacher, he is fired for remarks made about Mozart in an audio-visual teaching aid. Thereupon he is taken up by the youthful entrepreneur JR, but rejects economic success to return – like a secularized version of STANLEY in *The Recognitions* – to the purity of art.

Bast, Leonard
Howards End, 1910
E M Forster

A lowly clerk with lofty aspirations, Leonard Bast is a proud young Cockney who dreams of a more cultured life in which he can pronounce foreign names and converse with ease on any subject. Painfully aware of his social status and inadequacies, he is described as 'colourless, toneless ... [with] mournful eyes above a drooping moustache'. Loyal to his vulgar, older wife, Jacky, he is wary of the hand of friendship extended to him by the well-meaning HELEN SCHLEGEL, who regards him as 'such a muddle of a man and yet so worth pulling through'. His involvement with the Schlegel family is to bring only cruel misfortune upon him.

Bastables, the
The Treasure Seekers, 1899
The Wouldbegoods, 1901
The New Treasure Seekers, 1904
Oswald Bastable and Others, 1905
E Nesbit

Six motherless, middle-class children in Edwardian England – Dora, Oswald (the narrator), Dicky, the twins Alice and Noel, and Horace Octavius, known as H.O. Faced with grim realities of adult life – their father is in financial difficulties – they are cheerful, practical and brave in taking the initiative to better their lives collectively and individually. Using self-reliance rather than sentiment, they concoct schemes to make their fortune, befriending adults in the process in such a way as to highlight moral dilemmas of society. Kipling is their hero and 'good hunting' their motto.

Bas-Thornton, Edward
A High Wind in Jamaica, 1929
Richard Hughes

One of the younger Bas-Thornton children, who are kidnapped by pirates. He is entranced by the pirates' lifestyle and dreams of becoming their captain. From being a rather timid, respectful boy, he develops into an implacable teller of vivid, bloodthirsty tales. By his return home, he has lost much of his unaffected naturalness and has gained an acute awareness of what will please the general public. As a result, he wildly exaggerates stories of the pirates' cruelty and thus helps to ensure their eventual death sentence.

Bas-Thornton, Emily
A High Wind in Jamaica, 1929
Richard Hughes

Kidnapped by pirates along with her brothers and sisters, Emily is the central figure of this novel, which charts her development from being a happy, instinctive, adventurous child ('I have been in an Earthquake!') to her gradual emergence as a rational, self-aware, but morally suspect young woman. The principal catalyst for this transformation is her frenetic stabbing of a Dutch prisoner – a killing for which she allows others to be blamed. From believing herself to be 'a discrete person' capable of independent, even God-like action, Emily comes to know sin and the irrecoverable loss of innocence. Beneath her final, exterior 'ordinariness' lurks an awesome and terrifying moral ambiguity.

Bas-Thornton, John
A High Wind in Jamaica, 1929
Richard Hughes

The oldest of the Bas-Thornton children, who have been kidnapped by pirates, John is a daring, adventurous boy, noted for his 'general round energeticalness'. On the island of Santa Lucia, however, his over-enthusiastic spying causes him to fall and break his neck. His sisters and brothers do not witness his death, but seem strangely unconcerned anyway, much in the forgetful manner of small children. John, who had seemed destined to be the novel's hero, does indeed attain this status, posthumously, when later public opinion mistakenly assumes that he bravely sacrificed his life to protect his siblings from the 'cruel' pirates: a belief which ironically seals their fate.

Bas-Thornton, Laura
A High Wind in Jamaica, 1929
Richard Hughes

The youngest of the Bas-Thornton children, Laura is devoted to CAPTAIN JONSEN, the captain of the pirate ship on which she and her brothers and sisters are held captive. During the course of events she undergoes the transition from babyhood to childhood. Outwardly she seems a child, but inside, her child-mind coexists with the relics of her baby-mind, 'like a Fascist in Rome'. Yet, compared to her brothers and sisters, she is perhaps the only innocent on board ship.

Bas-Thornton, Rachel
A High Wind in Jamaica, 1929
Richard Hughes

An indomitable child who undergoes a religious phase as a captive on board a pirate ship. Viewing the world in terms of moral absolutes she displays 'a precocious ethical genius'. Her mission is to convert her 'deadly wicked' pirate kidnappers and, if she fails, she will call for the police! Her irrepressible nature remains undimmed by the vicissitudes of the voyage and she maintains her spirits by imaginatively converting every object on the ship into dolls – even pieces of oakum and marline-spikes become her 'babies' – much to the annoyance of the pirate crew.

Batchelor, Barbie (Barbara)
The Jewel in the Crown, 1966
The Day of the Scorpion, 1968
The Towers of Silence, 1971
A Division of the Spoils, 1975, forming *The Raj Quartet*
Paul Scott

The teacher who succeeded EDWINA CRANE at Muzzafirabad mission, Barbie lives in retirement with MABEL LAYTON, ministering to her in gratitude for being given a home. Although talkative and valiantly cheerful on the surface, she fears a lonely old age, and hides a 'secret sorrow': that God now seems to spurn her ardent faith and years of loyal service. With her working-class background she is held in contempt by the snobbish MILDRED LAYTON, who treats her abominably after Mabel's death.

Bateman, Patrick
American Psycho, 1991
Bret Easton Ellis

He is a handsome, sophisticated, charming and intelligent young man, who earns a huge income on Wall Street, wears designer clothes, and has an apartment in an exclusive building (the actor Tom Cruise lives in the penthouse). He is vain about his appearance, likes to party, listens to Genesis and Huey Lewis, and seems to be a sleazy version of 'the boy next door'. He is also, however, a cold-blooded psychopath, who likes to torture, mutilate and dismember his victims (men, women, children, dogs) for pleasure (erotic and otherwise), which he describes in horrifyingly dispassionate, first-person detail.

Bates, Charley
Oliver Twist, 1838
Charles Dickens

A member of FAGIN's den of child pickpockets. A sprightly lad who 'exhibited some very loose notions concerning the rights of property', which he appropriated into 'pockets which were so surprisingly capacious, that they seemed to undermine his whole suit of clothes in every direction'. Horrified by the murder of NANCY, he renounces the life he has led.

Bates, Miss
Emma, 1816
Jane Austen

'A woman neither young, handsome, rich, nor married', she is the kind-hearted daughter of an ageing mother who has fallen on hard times. 'A great talker upon little matters', she swaps innocent gossip and feels 'much obliged' to everyone for everything.

Bath, Major
Amelia, 1751
Henry Fielding

A man of ludicrous appearance and limited conversation, Major Bath exhibits an incongruous dignity when he is discovered in his transvestite garb. Nursing his pitiful sister, he is ashamed to have been caught doing good by CAPTAIN BILLY BOOTH as publicly he conforms to the behaviour society expects of him, an arrogant aggressiveness. His sole topics of discourse are war and his martial exploits, expressed in his usual hyperbole.

Bathgate, Billy
Billy Bathgate, 1989
E L Doctorow

A 'capable boy', attracted by the glamour of the gangsters. He places himself close to gang leader Dutch Schulz and becomes his protégé, part gofer, part apprentice hoodlum, part good-luck charm.

Bathies
The Kraken Wakes, 1953
John Wyndham

The name given to malign creatures from space which live in the depths of the ocean at enormous pressure. They emerge like the mythological sea-monster, the kraken, to prey on humans, firstly by taking boats at sea, then on land, where they are able to move in large, tank-like vehicles. They are some kind of gelatinous, protoplasmic mass with grasping ciliae or tendrils.

Battle, Mrs
Essays of Elia, 1823–33
Charles Lamb

For Mrs Battle, whist is like life: serious, not a mere pastime. Upright, her mind on her cards, she never interrupts a game. Quadrille, she thinks, suits the young; cribbage is vulgar; chess is boring. Whist with a good partner is like warfare in which you can glory in a clever stroke, and give no quarter. It takes skill and chance, as a good game should, and so to her delight – 'A clear fire, a clean hearth, and the rigour of the game'.

Baudricourt, Captain Robert de
Saint Joan, 1923
George Bernard Shaw

De Baudricourt is in command of the castle at Vaucouleurs, where the hens have stopped laying. A handsome, blustering but indecisive man, he agrees to see JOAN, who claims she is commanded by God to lead THE DAUPHIN to Rheims and see him crowned Charles VII. Against his better judgement, de Baudricourt agrees to give her a horse, armour and an escort. After she leaves, the hens begin laying again. This apparent miracle causes him to reflect that 'She did come from God'.

Baum family
The American Clock, 1983
Arthur Miller

The play recounts the effects of the Depression in America through a vast number of characters, the most important being the partly autobiographical Baums. Obliged by the loss of the family business to leave Manhattan and join poorer relatives in Brooklyn, the once-proud matriarch Rose deteriorates under the strain, while recalling the Broadway songs of the past that told of a better world. Moe, her husband, manages to cling to his dignity despite having to borrow subway fares from his son, Lee, who observes his parents' plight while philosophically adjusting to a new, harsher reality and yearning for 'the dream to come back from wherever it had gone to hide'.

Baumgartner, Hugo
Baumgartner's Bombay, 1988
Anita Desai

Shabby and physically unprepossessing, the solitary, timid and gentle Hugo is an elderly Berlin Jew who fled to India in the 1930s, shadowed forever by incomprehensible child-hood experiences. In one way, his story is that of the Jewish race itself: 'accepting, but not accepted'. Darkly Jewish in Aryan Germany, he is an obvious Westerner to the Indians, and was interned for the duration as an enemy alien. Relatively content living in noisome squalor with his many rescued cats and his only human friend, from happier pre-war days, the disreputable former dancer, Lotte, Hugo reluctantly helps a young German hippy, with tragic consequences.

Bawtry, Bessie
The Peppered Moth, 2000
Margaret Drabble

A gifted child of unaffectionate working-class parents in the early 1900s, Bessie 'always thought of herself as special'. Having grown up in a small town in the Yorkshire coalfields, she wins a scholarship to Cambridge. Although intelligent, good-looking, fastidious and hard-working, she is limited by her social unease, accent and precarious health; frequently anxious, she is sometimes 'overwhelmed by fear and apprehension'. Having graduated and married Joe Barron, her childhood sweetheart, Bessie becomes a full-time wife and mother. Burdened by disappointment and needled by self-pity and anger, she becomes increasingly harsh, dismissive and manipulative. Bessie is based upon the author's mother.

Baxter, Jody
The Yearling, 1938
Marjorie Kinnan Rawlings

Twelve-year-old Jody befriends an orphaned fawn in the Florida woods, but cannot prevent the animal from eating precious crops, and so it has to be destroyed. Loss forces the boy to grow up rapidly, to some extent souring his previously ideal and uncompromising relationship with the natural world.

Bayes
The Rehearsal, 1671
George Villiers, 2nd Duke of Buckingham

A fawning but self-admiring playwright (a parody of Dryden), he is the author of the dreadful heroic drama that is rehearsed within the play. A foolish plagiarist, he parades his nonsensical ideas on drama, including the beliefs that plot is insignificant and that stage effects are more important than words. He attributes the failure of his plays to his originality.

Baynes, Charlotte
The Adventures of Philip, 1861–2
W M Thackeray

GEN BAYNES's daughter, she is illuminated by the moral glow of incipient poverty. PHILIP FIRMIN loves her without hope of financial advantage, and so is loved in return. Together they stand outside society's cynical huckstering and manoeuvres.

Baynes, Gen
The Adventures of Philip, 1861–2
W M Thackeray

An old soldier of unsteady financial standing who has acted as co-trustee of PHILIP FIRMIN's inheritance. When the rascally DR GEORGE FIRMIN (Philip's father) decamps, Baynes is left liable and in imminent danger of bankruptcy and ruin.

Beach, Abner
The Copperhead, 1893
Harold Frederic

A New York farmer who sets his face against the rising tide of Abolitionist feeling (hence the novel's title) during the Civil War, thereby exposing himself to opprobrium and attack.

Beadle, Harriet, known as Tattycoram
Little Dorrit, 1857
Charles Dickens

A foundling from Thomas Coram's Hospital, she is taken in by MR and MRS MEAGLES as a maid for MINNIE MEAGLES and renamed Tattycoram. She is a sullen, passionate girl, and the Meagles kindly try to improve her temperament, but she runs off to become the companion of MISS WADE. She returns humble and penitent and brings with her documents, left with Miss Wade by RIGAUD, that reveal the legacy given to AMY DORRIT.

Beaker, Tracy
The Story of Tracy Beaker, 1991
The Dare Game, 2000
Jacqueline Wilson

Tracy Beaker is a ten-year-old with dark curly hair who lives in a children's home. Streetwise and sassy, but also deeply vulnerable, she shouts and stamps her feet at the unfairness of the world around her. She has 'a tendency to tell a few fibs now and again' but her fantasies involving her estranged mother hang on genuine dreams. She is funny, feisty and ultimately more understanding of her own needs and goals and of the world around her.

Beal, Major General Ira N
Guard of Honor, 1948
James Gould Cozzens

Beal is commander of a Florida airforce base which, despite his own naive and unaffected respect for the individual, still practises racial segregation and treats black airmen with brutal disregard. Beal is one of a line of well-intentioned but misfit liberals in US war fiction of the time, men who bring about disaster because they are insufficiently strong to combat evil effectively.

Bean Lean, Donald
Waverley, 1814
Sir Walter Scott

A Highland robber who removes a stand of cattle from the estate at Tully-Veolan while EDWARD WAVERLEY is visiting. Encountered in his stronghold, he appears 'thin in person and low in stature, with light sandy-coloured hair, and small pale features, from which he derived his agnomen of *Bean* or white … he appeared, on the whole, rather a diminutive and insignificant figure', not, in other words, the heroic bandit out of a painting by Salvator Rosa that Waverley romantically expects.

Beardsall, Lettie
The White Peacock, 1911
D H Lawrence

A middle-class young woman who, by rejecting the sensual GEORGE SAXTON, denies her innermost desires and, as she always has done, follows social convention. This might be interpreted as moral strength, and she sometimes wishes that it was so, but in fact, Lawrence suggests that it signifies a lack of emotional courage. Lettie's failure to realize her convictions represents her central, destructive weakness. Her dilemma is the choice between self-fulfilment on one hand and social position and success on the other. Like the white peacock, woman is presented as 'all vanity and screech and defilement'.

Beatrice
The Cenci, 1819
Percy Shelley

The daughter of COUNT FRANCESCO CENCI. Subjected from an early age to his cruelty and tyranny, she has nevertheless faced her life with forbearance and courage, providing a 'refuge and defence' for her mother and brother. She is a combination of 'loveliness and wisdom', whose courage and 'subtle mind' are blighted by the unnatural acts perpetrated on her by her father. These acts she feels can only be avenged by the count's death. Shelley called her 'a most gentle and amiable being', violently thwarted from her nature by the necessity of circumstance and opinion.

Beatrice
Much Ado About Nothing, 1598/1600
William Shakespeare

Niece to LEONATO, Beatrice is lively, kind, quick-witted and, at times, malicious. She has a sharp turn of phrase which she uses to torture her victim; most often this is BENEDICK, to whom she is drawn because he accepts and returns her teasing. When finally he declares himself, it is at her prompting, and she accepts in spite of her many declarations against marriage. Although she takes part in small deceptions, she can be duped herself. She is able to accept criticism and resolves to improve. She is, however, the only person prepared to believe in her cousin HERO, a belief for which she is willing to risk her love for Benedick.

Beatrice-Joanna
The Changeling, 1653
Thomas Middleton and William Rowley

The spoilt only child of an indulgent father, she is the central character in the tragedy, precipitating and orchestrating a tragedy which affects all those around her. Selfish and self-willed, she uses others to gain her own ends, but in doing so unwittingly places herself in the hands of someone more strong-willed than she is. Eventually she is forced to face facts to which she had previously blinded herself – that murder is a worse sin than adultery, and that actions can have undesirable consequences.

Beaty, Jack
The Thirteenth Night, 1981
Howard Brenton

The left-wing leader of a constituency Labour Party, Jack Beaty is struck over the head after a meeting one night. The remainder of the play, a contemporary re-working of *Macbeth*, unfolds in the form of Beaty's dream, in which he murders

the Labour prime minister, usurps power and evolves into a Stalinist figure, governing by tyranny and repression. Beaty is less a character than a device to allow Brenton to suggest that political power is inevitably corrupt and that revolutionary socialism has no more honourable a history than any other political doctrine.

Beauchamp, Lucas (Quintus Carothers McCaslin)
Go Down, Moses, 1942
Intruder in the Dust, 1948
William Faulkner

An old black sharecropper, descendant (on the wrong side of both blanket and colour line) of OLD CAROTHERS MCCASLIN, he is falsely accused of the murder of Vinson Gowrie, and becomes a 'tyrant over the whole county's white conscience'. He is defended by GAVIN STEVENS and befriended by Stevens's teenage nephew CHICK MALLISON (who learns the true circumstances of Lucas's innocence). Maintaining a quiet dignity throughout the trial, he pays Stevens (much against the lawyer's will) his full fee in small change.

Beauchamp, Nevil
Beauchamp's Career, 1876
George Meredith

An aristocratic young naval officer and hero of the Crimea, he contracts powerfully Radical views and contemplates a political career, before slowly recognizing that 'politics' is not just a matter of abstract ideological stances, but of quite specific acts and decisions that have relevance even in the bedroom. Perhaps inevitably, he falls in love with a woman of determinedly Conservative views.

Beauchamp, Sophonsiba
Go Down, Moses, 1942
William Faulkner

The wife of UNCLE BUCK MCCASLIN, who gets into her bed by mistake, then wins and loses her in a series of poker games. She is the mother of ISAAC MCCASLIN, hero of 'The Bear'.

Beau Geste
Beau Geste, 1924
P C Wren

Handsome, intelligent and debonair, he is driven by a family disgrace to join the French Foreign Legion with his two brothers. There he brings his genteel English upper-class values to the brutal world of Fort Zinderneuf, North Africa, where with his brothers he encounters the viciousness of camp discipline under the command of Sergeant Lejaune, and with ingenuity and courage takes justice into his own hands, sacrificing his life for the satisfaction of knowing that others will be spared the brutality he and his comrades have endured.

Beaumont, Ned
The Glass Key, 1931
Dashiell Hammett

The most enigmatic of the hard-boiled school of detectives. He is tall and slim, sports a neat moustache, and is a heavy drinker and compulsive gambler. In the past, he has suffered from tuberculosis. He has a highly cynical attitude, and keeps his emotions wholly hidden behind an imperturbable mask, but he is loyal to his friends, and something of an idealist.

Beaver, John
A Handful Of Dust, 1934
Evelyn Waugh

A 'rather pathetic' figure, not very popular, penniless, but always socially available, John Beaver lives in Sussex Gardens with his mother, an interior decorator and well-known society woman. Since leaving Oxford University, he has been fired by a struggling advertising agency and now sits indolently by the telephone, waiting for last-minute invitations. He travels down to Hetton for a weekend and is the focus of scandal when he becomes romantically involved with LADY BRENDA LAST, but he refuses to marry her 'unless she's properly provided for'.

Beavis, Anthony
Eyeless in Gaza, 1936
Aldous Huxley

Finding some old snapshots, Anthony Beavis, the central character of the novel, looks back over his life on his forty-second birthday. Through random flashbacks it emerges that his thirst for scientific knowledge, combined with a desire for absolute individual freedom, conflicts with his quest for spiritual enlightenment. Tormented by feelings of guilt over the suicide of a close friend, BRIAN FOXE, and his affair with HELEN LEDWIDGE, following a spell in war-torn Mexico with MARK STAITHES he finally adopts pacifism as his personal philosophy.

Bech, Henry
Bech: a Book, 1970
Bech is Back, 1983
John Updike

Updike's opposite in every sense, Bech is a blocked Jewish novelist, whose inability to write is symbolic of his failure to absorb himself in life, marriage, even in the possibility of success. Sourly detached from the literary world, with its market-obsessed compromises, he travels to Europe in pursuit of a grand theme and a sense of engagement.

Beck, Madame
Villette, 1853
Charlotte Brontë

The philanthropic, yet unaffectionate, headmistress of the girls' school in Villette, Madame Beck employs LUCY SNOWE as a teacher but does not hesitate to check her credentials by unscrupulously reading her personal letters. Well-organized and efficient, her benevolence seems to outweigh her capacity for sympathy, and it is only very rarely that she displays any passion at all, though her crafty machinations to prevent MONSIEUR PAUL EMMANUEL from liaising with Lucy perhaps hint at her own desire for a relationship.

Becker
The Americans, Baby, 1972
Frank Moorhouse

A brightly effective Coca Cola executive in Australia until his affair with T GEORGE MCDOWELL's daughter TERRI MCDOWELL lands him in disgrace and out of a job. As a consolation and to make ends meet, he becomes a jazz pianist.

Becket, Archbishop Thomas
Murder in the Cathedral, 1935
T S Eliot

Estranged from Henry II, to whom he was once 'arm' and 'better reason', Eliot's Archbishop is no otherworldly wraith, murdered for purely political ends, as history sometimes portrays him, but a sophisticated thinker who understands the ways of powerful men and the need for compromise, but cannot accept the values that guarantee violence and disorder. There is more than a little truth in the Knights' ironic suicide verdict after the assassination.

Beddows, Alderman
South Riding, 1936
Winifred Holtby

Seventy-two years old, plump, weatherbeaten and well schooled in the hardships of rural life, Mrs Beddows brings a frank and lively intelligence to her duties as alderman in the fictional South Riding of Yorkshire. Years of rich and difficult experience have taught her to be resigned to human failure, but she maintains her youthful vivacity and has a real gift for friendship. Capable and resourceful, she believes all problems can be solved by 'courage, good humour, and plain common sense'.

Bede, Adam
Adam Bede, 1859
George Eliot

Broad-chested, large-boned and muscular, Adam is a carpenter, estate manager and jack of most trades. His Christianity is healthy and moderate; he works industriously and has good judgement in most things except when it comes to dairymaid HETTY SORREL, with whom he is infatuated. Although he is ready to fight his employer ARTHUR DONNITHORNE to keep her pure, he is more suited in love to the Methodist preacher DINAH MORRIS.

Bede, Belinda
Some Tame Gazelle, 1980
Barbara Pym

The elder of two church-going spinster sisters in an English village, she has loved the ARCHDEACON HOCCLEVE since they were students 30 years before. She enjoys the abstruse literary quotations in his very peculiar sermons, and wonders if his wife Agatha really looks after him properly. The sisters' main pleasures are small supper parties and parish occasions. Very little makes Belinda happy; her love has mellowed over the years to a comfortable feeling like a cosy evening by the fire, but she cannot help secret delight when events suggest that it was Agatha who proposed to the archdeacon, not the archdeacon to Agatha.

Bede, Harriet
Some Tame Gazelle, 1980
Barbara Pym

The younger of two church-going spinster sisters

in an English village, she is outspoken and jolly, her main interest in life being to cherish young curates, making sure they have warm socks and plenty to eat. She organizes her quieter sister, BELINDA BEDE, into regular invitations to the curate of the moment for suppers of chicken smothered in white sauce. Clothes concern her also; she bullies Belinda into wearing what she considers proper. She herself likes close-fitting showy dresses over warm woollen underwear; since she is stout she is often found 'strengthening' corsets and having her dresses let out.

Bedivere, Sir
'Morte d'Arthur', 1842
Alfred, Lord Tennyson

The only surviving knight of KING ARTHUR's Round Table after the last great battle in Lyonness. Although beguiled twice by the jewelled hilt of Arthur's sword Excalibur, Bedivere finally succeeds in disposing of the sword according to his master's command. After helping the wounded king to his funeral barge, Bedivere is left to mourn alone.

Bedonebyasyoudid, Mrs
The Water Babies, 1863
Charles Kingsley

An awesome fairy, 'a very tremendous lady', who reads the news carefully every morning, especially the police cases. When the water children see her they all stand in a row 'very upright indeed'. She is spiky, ugly and dressed in black; she has green spectacles, a hooked nose and carries a great black rod. She doles out sea-candies to the water children, but pops a hard pebble into TOM's mouth in retribution for his tormenting. A karmic reckoner who rectifies Tom's behaviour, she says she is actually his best friend. She is the opposite of her sister, MRS DOASYOUWOULDBEDONEBY.

Beebe, Arthur
A Room With a View, 1908
E M Forster

A bald-headed clergyman with russet whiskers and a perennially cheerful disposition, Arthur Beebe is a vivacious, cultured man with a love of art history and a fascination with maiden ladies. Appointed to the rectory at Summer Street in Surrey, he continues an interest in the fate and character of LUCY HONEYCHURCH begun during his sojourn in Italy. A lively chatterbox who enjoys providing people with 'happy memories', he exults in Lucy's decision to abandon her marriage to CECIL VYSE. His confusion over her subsequent declaration of love for GEORGE EMERSON merely confirms his lack of true understanding.

Beeblebrox, Zaphod
The Hitch-Hiker's Guide to the Galaxy, 1979, et seq
Douglas Adams

Like FORD PREFECT, Zaphod is from the planet Betelgeuse. He is humanoid in appearance, although he does have an extra head and a third arm. An 'adventurer, ex-hippy, good-timer (Crook? Quite possibly), manic self-publicist, terribly bad at personal relationships, often

thought to be completely out to lunch', he uses his position as Imperial Galactic President to steal *Heart of Gold*, a state-of-the-art spaceship. He then sets out upon a quest, which he does not himself fully comprehend (for he has removed the relevant part of his brain), for the Ultimate Question, picking up Ford and ARTHUR DENT on the way.

Beech, Willie (William)
Goodnight Mister Tom, 1981
Michelle Magorian

When he is first evacuated from London, Willie Beech is 'thin and sickly-looking, pale with limp sandy hair and dull grey eyes'. At first a painfully shy and inhibited boy with a talent for art, away from the abuse of his mother Willie slowly learns about love and trust, helped by new friends and especially by TOM OAKLEY, the Mister Tom of the title. Willie faces many challenges in his new life and still has to undergo the horrors of his real home before he can look to his future with hope and love.

Beecham, Harold
My Brilliant Career, 1901
Miles Franklin

The handsome, wealthy, noble-minded suitor of SYBYLLA PENELOPE MELVYN. He is led on, then rebuffed in his advances, but is resolute in his determination to succeed. When he loses his fortune and she agrees to take him, however, his pride and ingrained sense of independence prevent him from complying – he is 'not a whimpering cur' to be accepted only out of pity. When his fortune is restored, however, she will no longer have him.

Beecham, Phoebe, née Tozer
Salem Chapel, 1863
Phoebe Junior, 1876
Margaret Oliphant

Daughter of a prosperous London Dissenting pastor, Phoebe goes to stay with her uneducated common grandparents, Mrs and MR TOZER, now retired. They come as a shock, but she finds friends by chance in the rector's family, and studies Church and Chapel, gentlemen and tradesmen, with interest, always her candid, curious self. She means to marry, and make a success of, foolish Clarence Copperhead, son of her father's rich leading member. Her choice is justified; he stands up to his philistine father and proves himself a man, though not a clever one.

Beechey, Douglas
Man of the Moment, 1988
Alan Ayckbourn

Middle-aged Douglas looks 'staggeringly unimpressive'. Yet, 17 years previously, he was the man of the moment when, as a bank clerk, he 'had a go' at VIC PARKS during a raid. Perhaps it was his fault that Vic's shotgun went off and Nerys, whom he subsequently married, was maimed. Briefly a national hero, Douglas has been forgotten while Vic has become a media personality. Reunited with Vic at the latter's Mediterranean retreat, Douglas is seemingly without rancour, accepting the loss of his career, a sad, childless marriage and a dismal home in

Purley. Yet beneath the docility simmer guilt, regret and possibly madness. He acts as an apparently unwitting agent of retribution.

Beelzebub
Paradise Lost, 1667
John Milton
Second only to SATAN in the legions of the damned, and a long way removed from his normal portrayal as the ignoble Lord of the Flies: 'deep on his Front engraven/Deliberation sat and public care;/And Princely counsel in his face yet shone/Majestic though in ruin'.

Beetle
Stalky & Co., 1899
Rudyard Kipling
A bespectacled public-schoolboy, one of the occupants, along with STALKY and M'TURK, of the notorious Number Five study. Like these comrades, he is not generally interested in such concepts as 'the honour of the house', preferring to fight for their gang. He reads Browning, composes verses lampooning the masters, and in later life becomes a writer.

Begbie, Francis
Trainspotting, 1993
Porno, 2002
Irvine Welsh
Francis Begbie (aka Franco or Beggar) is a lowering, humourless, boastful thug prone to outbursts of vicious violence at the least (if any) provocation. He is a graduate of 'approved school, prison 'n the casuals' networks, the freemasonaries that bams share'. He has outspoken contempt for the heroin-taking habits of friends such as RENTON and SICK-BOY ('ah nivir touch that shite'). They nevertheless tolerate (or endure) his company, partly from fear and partly simply because he is one of the people they grew up with. He in turn finds reassurance in their construction and maintenance of the legend that he is, quite literally, a psychopath.

Beggs, Alabama
Save me the Waltz, 1932
Zelda Fitzgerald
A quintessential Southern belle and judge's daughter, who epitomizes the Twenties flapper. Based largely on Zelda Fitzgerald, she grows through the materialism and male tradition that is the American Dream and seizes each possibility of hedonistic experience – clothes, parties, European travel. She finally dedicates herself to learning ballet, but her painful struggle, though successful, is too late for her physique and she has to return to America and subjugate her life to that of her artist husband and their daughter.

Beguildy, Jancis
Precious Bane, 1924
Mary Webb
Jancis is a slender little creature, with golden hair and a delicate face like a pale waterlily. She loves songs and old childish games and is easily made happy, saying 'O!' with lips like a red rose. Her father, WIZARD BEGUILDY, means to sell her to a gentleman, but when GIDEON SARN sees her

sitting by the window he must have her. She loves his strong body and masterful ways, but when he refuses refuge to her and their tiny doll-like son, she despairs utterly.

Beguildy, Wizard
Precious Bane, 1924
Mary Webb
Beguildy is no real wizard but a foolish man pretending to be mysterious. Too lazy to work, he lives on the impression he creates, boasting of having no God; but it is all talk. Clever enough to teach PRUE SARN book learning, he cannot see people laughing at him. He will 'raise Venus' for five pounds, but it is only Prue dangling naked in pink light, saving his daughter, JANCIS BEGUILDY, from this humiliating ordeal. When GIDEON SARN cheats him with Jancis, he fires his ricks in mean revenge.

Behrman, S
The Octopus: A Story of California, 1901
Frank Norris
A banker, real-estate agent, one of the political bosses of Bonneville and a representative of the new railroad. 'He was a large fat man with a great stomach; his cheek and the upper part of his thick neck ran together to form a great, tremulous jowl, shaven and blue-gray in color; a roll of fat, sprinkled with sparse hair, moist with perspiration, protruded over the back of his collar.' As greedy as an octopus, reaching in almost as many directions at once, he is a new type of man, as bland as his anonymous first initial; he is the polar opposite of MAGNUS DERRICK.

Belacqua, Lyra, later Lyra Silvertongue
Northern Lights, 1995
The Subtle Knife, 1997
The Amber Spyglass, 2000, forming the *His Dark Materials* trilogy
Philip Pullman
A rebellious, impulsive child, Lyra has been raised by scholars at Jordan College in the Oxford of her world. As she approaches adolescence she and her daemon are drawn into a conflict of epic proportions in which, although they do not fully understand it, they have an essential part to play. Tenacious, passionate, a natural leader and a skilful liar, Lyra is at first unaware that the fate of many worlds depends upon the choices she makes. As she matures, she becomes increasingly perceptive about the wider impact of her actions. Her meeting with WILL PARRY marks the beginning of a deep and heartfelt relationship that has great symbolic weight.

Belarius/Morgan
Cymbeline, 1609/10
William Shakespeare
A loyal lord who was wrongly accused of being a traitor and banished by CYMBELINE, Belarius took his revenge by kidnapping the king's two young sons, GUIDERIUS and ARVIRAGUS, and fleeing with them to Wales. Despite this vengeful act, Belarius is portrayed as a virtuous and kind man, living a healthy and honest life and bringing the two princes up as his own sons.

Twenty years after his crime, he atones for it and proves his loyalty by his part in the battle with the Roman army, and later by his revelation of his sons' true identity.

Belch, Sir Toby
Twelfth Night, c.1601
William Shakespeare

Although related to the countess OLIVIA, Sir Toby is not well regarded by her because of his fondness for drink, food and riotous company. His financial state is uncertain, so he has to live off SIR ANDREW AGUECHEEK. He enjoys practical jokes, especially those which bring humiliation to the victim, but he resents it when his fun is spoiled, often reacting angrily. He inspires devotion among his followers because of his humour, but he can behave callously to them.

Belford, John
Clarissa, 1748
Samuel Richardson

ROBERT LOVELACE's intimate confidant, Belford adheres to Lovelace's creed and is an integral member of his court. Initially, he participates in Lovelace's devilish plans to deflower the virtuous CLARISSA HARLOWE and confirms ANNA HOWE's assessment that all men are 'baboons'. However, unsettled by Lovelace's Hobbesian animality and disgusted by the way his Don Juanish body dominates his reason, he pleads with him to leave Clarissa pure. Moved by her suffering, Belford shifts his allegiance to Clarissa and is accused by Lovelace of being effeminate. He is transformed from a subordinated henchperson to a defender of virtue.

Belfounder, Hugo
Under the Net, 1954
Iris Murdoch

A pacifist, Hugo converts the armament factory inherited from his German immigrant father to the production of life-saving Very lights, rockets and fireworks. His gentle dark eyes reflect the innocence and beauty beneath his unkempt, shambling appearance. With a child's wonder he sees everything in life as uniquely astonishing, complicated and mysterious, and he is the nearest thing to a completely truthful person JAKE DONAGHUE has ever known.

Belial
Paradise Lost, 1667
John Milton

'A fairer person lost not Heav'n', yet his noble countenance and honeyed words conceal a mind industrious only in vice. In the great debate among the fallen angels, it is he who counsels a slippery caution.

Bel-Imperia
The Spanish Tragedy, 1592
Thomas Kyd

The sister of DON LORENZO and daughter of the DUKE OF CASTILE, Bel-Imperia is an independent, determined, sometimes aloof and impulsive woman who loves DON HORATIO. But because her father and brother support BALTHAZAR (whom she detests), Don Horatio is murdered (hanged by her brother and Balthazar). This might seem somewhat extreme; however, Bel-Imperia's affections have transferred quite easily in the past from one man to another, and perhaps Don Lorenzo was assuming they would do so again.

Belinda
The Rape of the Lock, 1712
Alexander Pope

A portrait of woman as a sexual commodity, more distinguished by the trinkets, furs and furbelows that surround her than by any physical or personal characteristics. She is consigned to the marriage game, with its shallow devices and indiscriminate pleasantries. Underneath the mock-heroic language and faery apparatus of the baron's courtship and her virginal defence, it is possible to glimpse a 'sprightly Mind' slowly succumbing to the conventional apotheosis of 18th-century Woman.

Bell, Laura
The History of Pendennis, 1848–50
W M Thackeray

The adopted daughter of HELEN PENDENNIS and the family saviour when she uses her money to rescue ARTHUR PENDENNIS from debts run up at 'Oxbridge' University. It is hoped that they will marry, but this ideal union is delayed by Arthur's Romeo-like susceptibilities. Like AMELIA SEDLEY in *Vanity Fair*, Laura is notably short-sighted when it comes to seeing the flaws in her lover.

Bell, Peter
Peter Bell, 1819
William Wordsworth

A potter by trade, he is a brutal ruffian, but it takes a pitiful ass, its drowned master and his mourning family to bring Peter Bell's wickedness home to him. His inadvertent involvement in their tragedy moves him to repent and reform his life.

Bellairs, Cecilia
Cousin From Fiji, 1945
Norman Lindsay

Coming from 'exotic' Fiji, she carries with her a certain cultural and erotic mystique. Her arrival and that of her daughter Ella among their outwardly straitlaced Australian kinfolk strips away the DOMKIN family's moral and social hypocrisies.

Bellario
Philaster, or Love Lies Bleeding, 1609
Francis Beaumont and John Fletcher

The young and handsome page to PHILASTER, the usurped King of Sicily who is in love with ARETHUSA, he enters Arethusa's service to become the means by which she and Philaster might communicate with each other. Later, he is accused of having an affair with her himself, but when he reveals himself to be Euphrasia, herself in love with Philaster and who disguised herself to be near him, all is forgiven. Bellario-Euphrasia symbolically represents the simple maxim that things are not always what they seem. She withdraws to lead a life of chastity, which seems rather hard luck.

Bellaston, Lady
The History of Tom Jones, 1749
Henry Fielding
One of TOM JONES's paramours, she is succinctly dismissed by SQUIRE WESTERN as 'that fat arse bitch'. Fashionable almost to the point of absurdity, she and her crinoline negotiate doorways in a species of three-point-turn, while her sexual charms are somewhat mitigated by halitosis that would do a spaniel proud.

Belle
Black Jack, 1968
Leon Garfield
A slight girl of 14, apparently mad, of a 'respectable' and well-connected family who believe they can ill afford the taint of insanity and strive to conceal it. Consigned to the madhouse so that her sister's marriage can go ahead unimpeded, but 'rescued' inadvertently by TOLLY and BLACK JACK, she has a sharp, teasing sense of humour, and increasingly long lucid moments as she spends time in the company of Tolly. She has a slightly dusty air, as of one who has long been consigned to the attic.

Bellefontaine, Benedict
Evangeline: A Tale of Acadie, 1847
Henry Wadsworth Longfellow
The father of EVANGELINE BELLEFONTAINE and friend of BASIL LAJEUNESSE, Benedict is the wealthiest farmer in the almost Utopian village of Grand-Pré, a French-Canadian settlement. At the age of 70 he is dignified, happy, hospitable and optimistic, 'at peace with God and the world', but he proves unable to cope with misfortune.

Bellefontaine, Evangeline
Evangeline: A Tale of Acadie, 1847
Henry Wadsworth Longfellow
The beautiful and saintly daughter of BENEDICT BELLEFONTAINE, Evangeline is betrothed to GABRIEL LAJEUNESSE in the idyllic community of Acadia (Nova Scotia). The lovers are separated after the expulsion of the Acadians by England, but in the long years of searching for Gabriel she continues to display her piety, serenity and spiritual strength, eventually devoting herself to the poor and sick.

Bellenden, Edith
Old Mortality, in *Tales of My Landlord*, 1816
Sir Walter Scott
'Generally allowed to be the prettiest lass in the Upper Ward [of Clydesdale]', she is the granddaughter of LADY MARGARET BELLENDEN. A certain vivacity and archness of manner redeems her from the charge of insipidity apparently levelled at blue-eyed blondes of the period. She is loved by and loves HENRY MORTON, but is separated from him for many years by her Royalist grandmother.

Bellenden, Lady Margaret, of Tillietudlem
Old Mortality, in *Tales of My Landlord*, 1816
Sir Walter Scott
A great lady of the Upper Ward of Clydesdale. Her form is described as 'erect and primitive', dressed

permanently in widow's weeds since her husband was executed for his allegiance to the rebel EARL OF MONTROSE. The high point and chief consolation of her life is that CHARLES II, en route to engage with Cromwell at Worcester, had taken breakfast at Tillietudlem.

Bellenden, Major Miles, of Charnwood
Old Mortality, in *Tales of My Landlord*, 1816
Sir Walter Scott
A gouty old soldier and brother-in-law to the widowed LADY MARGARET BELLENDEN. 'Although I had my share of the civil war, I cannot say I had ever so much real pleasure in that sort of service as when I was employed on the Continent and we were hacking at fellows with foreign faces and outlandish dialect.' He is the backbone of the nascent British Empire.

Bellinda
The Man of Mode, 1676
Sir George Etherege
Enthusiastic but weak-willed and stupid, Bellinda becomes a conspirator in DORIMANT's plan to drop his mistress, MRS LOVEIT. In so doing she allows herself to be seduced, and is in turn rejected.

Bellinda
The Provok'd Wife, 1696
Sir John Vanbrugh
The niece of LADY BRUTE, the eponymous provoked wife, Bellinda loves HEARTFREE and agrees to become his wife, though not without a good deal of soul-searching. She has observed the antagonism of her aunt's marriage, but although her faith in romantic love is shaken, it has not died. She marries cautiously but optimistically, hoping if not for love then for a deepening affection.

Bellingham, Henry
Ruth, 1853
Elizabeth Gaskell
A spoiled and self-indulgent young man, he is strong on flattery but weak in character. He likes to get his own way and, because of his privileged social position, he usually gets it. A superficial, cruel man, he admires RUTH HILTON's physical beauty, but cannot see beyond this. A victim of his upbringing, he deals with human situations mainly in terms of money.

Belphoebe
The Faerie Queene, 1590–6
Sir Edmund Spenser
The noble daughter of a wood nymph, and the twin sister to AMORET, with whom she shares a celestial soul. They were spontaneously conceived whilst their mother slept and sunbeams danced on her body. Belphoebe is the foster daughter of Diana and lives in the green forests of Faerieland, mixing herbal remedies and hunting wild animals. She is an idealized figure, free of sin, virtuous and kind, and is chastely loved by TIMIAS.

Belsize, Jack, the Honourable
The Newcomes, 1853–5
W M Thackeray
A one-time admirer of BARNES NEWCOME's wife,

he finds himself her refuge and protector when she is so shabbily treated by her husband that she runs away. The heir to substantial estates in Highgate, he cuts a swathe through the gaming rooms of Europe.

Belvidera
Venice Preserv'd, or A Plot Discovered, 1682
Thomas Otway

Belvidera has been disowned by her father, PRIULI, and is secretly married to JAFFIER, who has become involved in a plot to overthrow the Venetian state. After fighting off RENAULT, the conspirators' leader, who has attempted to rape her, Belvidera learns of the plot from Jaffier. Purposeful, manipulative, desperate, violent, she plays upon Jaffier's weakness of character by persuading him to reveal the plot to the Senate. Her flinty intelligence is matched, however, by an emotional vulnerability. When events spin beyond her control, she quickly disintegrates, eventually into madness.

Bem, Cardinal (Stephen)
The Colour of Blood, 1987
Brian Moore

Born the son of a stableman, Bem has become the Cardinal Primate of his Soviet-bloc country, and for years has managed to maintain peaceful relations between Church and State. But some within the Church regard him as a careerist and willing collaborator with a godless regime, and plan to incite an uprising. His life threatened, able to trust no one and stripped of his red robe, he draws upon his own physical and spiritual resources to avert the seemingly inevitable violence.

Ben
The Dumb Waiter, 1960
Harold Pinter

The 'senior partner' of two apparent assassins, waiting for their intended victim, he spends his time reading sensational newspaper articles and establishing authority over his subordinate, GUS. His urgent willingness to obey impossible requests from 'above', delivered through the dumb waiter, becomes a metaphor for his moral bankruptcy, reaching its height when he screams 'We've got nothing left! Nothing! Do you understand?'

Benbow, Horace (Horry)
Sartoris, 1929, full version published as *Flags in the Dust*, 1973
Sanctuary, 1931
William Faulkner

The son of an old Jefferson family and related to the SARTORISes. A lawyer by training, with a strong idealistic streak that comes out in his defence of the bootlegger LEE GOODWIN in *Sanctuary*, he marries the vulgar Belle Mitchell, a hopeless mismatch contracted in part to escape from his dominant sister NARCISSA BENBOW. A much more prominent figure in the original, uncut version of *Sartoris*, he largely disappears from Faulkner's work thereafter, and is restricted to bit parts in *Absalom, Absalom!* and *The Unvanquished*.

Benbow, Narcissa (Narcy)
Sartoris, 1929, full version published as *Flags in the Dust*, 1973
Sanctuary, 1931
William Faulkner

The selfish and possessive sister of HORACE BENBOW. In spinsterhood and later in widowhood, she attempts to dominate his life. Married to the buccaneering but ill-fated BAYARD SARTORIS, she becomes convinced that men are driven by shallow and selfish urges.

Bendrix, Maurice
The End of the Affair, 1951
Graham Greene

A somewhat cynical novelist of modest standing, he pretends an amorous interest in SARAH MILES in order to study her husband Henry, a senior civil servant, for a book he is writing, only to find himself falling genuinely in love for the first time. He is jealous and unwilling to trust her feelings for him, but is left desolate when she ends their relationship, hiring a private detective to follow her. His discovery that she still loves him comes too late.

Benedick
Much Ado About Nothing, 1598/1600
William Shakespeare

An avowed bachelor, Benedick enjoys participating in the 'merry war' with BEATRICE, although he appears to come off worse in most of the exchanges. A gentleman and a well-respected soldier, his reluctance to become involved in marriage encourages mockery on the part of his colleagues. Taken in by the deception aimed at him he declares himself to Beatrice immediately, suddenly aware of his true feelings. His love for Beatrice and a strong belief in right make him stand up for HERO to the extent of challenging his friend CLAUDIO to a duel. His relief when all are reconciled is genuine.

Ben Ezra, Rabbi
Dramatis Personae, 1864
Robert Browning

The Rabbi meditates on human life and death in his extreme old age. Only in age is it really possible to 'know'. Death is the crisis which perfects the soul, which is immortal. Man is a lump of clay fashioned on the potter's (God's) wheel, and whereas the wheel (of time) may run back or stop 'Potter and clay endure'. Rather than live for the moment only, the Rabbi believes that man should look 'up', for life on earth is but a passage to immortality in heaven.

Ben Hur
Ben Hur, 1880
Lew Wallace

A handsome young prince of Judea who grows up to be the friend of the noble Roman Messala. He finds he has to choose between the emotional ties of friendship and the moral bonds of his own Jewish faith when Roman rule over the province becomes more oppressive and Messala becomes the instrument of tyranny. Remaining true to his beliefs, Ben Hur loses his wealth and status, indirectly condemning his family to degradation and sorrow, but in the process he (and they) find strength in Christ.

Benjamin
Animal Farm, 1945
George Orwell

An angry, irritable and cynical donkey who expects little from life and is rarely disappointed. Much more perceptive than the other animals realize, he is one of the few to recognize that NAPOLEON and SQUEALER are creating a totalitarian regime and subverting the original principles of the revolution's Commandments. Only when his old friend BOXER is sacrificed does he rail against the gullibility and hypocrisy of his fellow animals.

Benjamin
The Waggoner, 1819
William Wordsworth

A Lakeland waggoner, mild and tender-hearted with his horses, he is a convivial figure in the neighbourhood. His fondness for drinking in the local inns and his natural kindness to a storm-bound family lead to his downfall and to a loss for all the people of the district.

Bennet, Elizabeth
Pride and Prejudice, 1813
Jane Austen

The lively, high-spirited heroine of the novel, Elizabeth, being honest, down-to-earth and unaffected, is greatly pained by the ill-bred crassness of her mother and younger sisters, and the irresponsibility of her father. Attractive and outgoing, she draws the attention of FITZWILLIAM DARCY, but, put off by his arrogance and pride, and blinded for a time by smooth-talking GEORGE WICKHAM, she rejects his first proposal of marriage. Eventually becoming enlightened, however, she puts aside her 'prejudice' against Darcy and acknowledges her deep love for him.

Bennet, Jane
Pride and Prejudice, 1813
Jane Austen

The eldest of the five Bennet daughters, Jane is also the most composed. Cheerful and mild-mannered, she likes to think the best of everyone, but is painfully forced to realize that people are not always quite as kind as she imagines them. In love with CHARLES BINGLEY, but hiding her passionate feelings beneath a veneer of serene complacency, she endures much needless suffering before being finally reunited with him.

Bennet, Lydia
Pride and Prejudice, 1813
Jane Austen

At 15, the youngest of the Bennet daughters, Lydia, unchecked by her father and encouraged by her mother, throws all her energies into her frivolous existence. Self-confident, volatile and empty-headed, she enjoys unbridled flirtations with the local soldiers, her peak of irresponsibility coming when she elopes with GEORGE WICKHAM.

Bennet, Mr
Pride and Prejudice, 1813
Jane Austen

The long-suffering husband of MRS BENNET, Mr Bennet is a mixture of 'sarcastic humour, reserve, and caprice'. Taking his pleasure in life from observing the absurdities of characters such as REV WILLIAM COLLINS, he keeps his sanity by seeming to humour his wife while really amusing himself, usually at her expense. He maintains a sometimes irresponsible distance from the constant marriage speculation in his household, and his favourite daughter is the unaffected ELIZABETH BENNET – who is well aware of his shortcomings as a husband and father.

Bennet, Mrs
Pride and Prejudice, 1813
Jane Austen

With five daughters to dispose of, Mrs Bennet's sole interest in life is in finding suitably wealthy gentlemen to marry them off to, regardless of any but her own feelings in the matter. Deficient in intelligence, tact and social skills, she is a source of embarrassment to ELIZABETH BENNET. The society whose gossip she feeds on has very limited horizons.

Bennett
How Many Miles to Babylon?, 1974
Jennifer Johnston

'In the great English tradition he has no Christian name.' Bennett is the English officer in the Irish regiment whom ALEX MOORE and JERRY CROW meet in Flanders. He leads them into some wild scrapes, but knows how to play the game and bend the rules where the others do not. He has a deadpan English exterior and the air of someone who has seen it all before. Bennett always pushes his luck; he can sleep anywhere, even in the trenches. He has a jaded attitude, caring about and fearing nothing. Inevitably he is the one who survives.

Bennett, Sarah and Louise
A Summer Bird-Cage, 1963
Margaret Drabble

Sarah and Louise are sisters; Sarah, the younger, is indecisive, cautious and academically distinguished. Just down from Oxford, she lives in a London bedsitter, while Louise, beautiful and assured, has recently married the wealthy but unlikeable novelist, Stephen Halifax. Sarah, the narrator, is intelligent, honest and intimate, but broods over 'the classlessness and social dislocation that girls of my age and lack of commitments feel'. The seeming vulnerability of women depresses her, as does the apparent marital and material security of Louise. For other marriages, she feels a mixture of envy and contempt. Louise, meanwhile, selfish and deceitful, exploits her marriage by spending Stephen's money while continuing an adulterous relationship.

Bennilong
The Timeless Land, 1941
Storm of Time, 1948
No Barrier, 1953
Eleanor Dark

DILBOONG's father, and the 'famous' Aborigine

protégé of GOVERNOR PHILLIP. As the leading exponent of the improvised tribal songs performed at *corroborees*, he is taken by the Governor to visit England. The English see him as naturally barbarous and ferocious, and try to 'civilize' and wean him into a liking for more refined living. But on his return to Australia Bennilong becomes increasingly overbearing and insolent, drunken, quarrelsome and menacing.

Benny the Blond Jew
Stories à la Carte, 1932
Damon Runyon

A St Louis mobster, he is entranced by a beautiful night-club hostess, DARK DOLORES, and discovers that she is the widow of one of his victims, and has vengeance in her heart. Besotted by her beauty, and short on brains, he is lured to a watery end by a combination of her seductive powers and her prowess as a cross-channel swimmer.

Benson, Miss
Ruth, 1853
Elizabeth Gaskell

A caring though bossy lady, she is opinionated and rather quick with her tongue. However, she is a character of depth, loyalty and true compassion, and even when initially unforgiving, she always 'comes round' in a truly Christian way. Sister of THURSTON BENSON, she is a capable woman, enjoying the feeling of being in charge of situations. Sensitive, kind and affectionate, she instils love and loyalty in those around her.

Benson, Thurston
Ruth, 1853
Elizabeth Gaskell

A compassionate dissenting minister, Mr Benson is understanding, tolerant, kind and mild-mannered. He reflects on any situation before he judges it, and is truly philanthropic in a completely un-self-congratulatory manner. He is a balance to his sister, MISS BENSON, and their relationship is a vital part of his character. He thinks deeply and logically, but his logic is often at odds with the society of which he finds himself a part. His heart is pure and untainted by social convention, yet he inadvertently misjudges people and situations because his mode of thinking is so far removed from the typical approach of his class and generation.

Bentley, Jack
'The Iron-Bark Chip', et seq, in *On the Track*, 1900
Joe Wilson and His Mates, 1901
Henry Lawson

The practised liar of the railroad gang and another of Lawson's roustabout outback types, forever moving from one 'spec' job to the next.

Bentley, Jesse
'Godliness: Part I/Part II', in *Winesburg, Ohio*, 1919
Sherwood Anderson

An Ohio farmer, he inherits the family land when his elder brothers are killed in the Civil War. The 'odd sheep' of the family, he once trained for the ministry. 'Small and very slender and womanish

of body', he is nonetheless powerfully resilient and has 'the trick of mastering the souls of his people'.

Bentley, Mrs
As For Me and My House, 1941
Sinclair Ross

Apparently suffocated and consumed by her marriage to PHILIP BENTLEY, 'Mrs Bentley', the diarist of their prairie life together, is not, however, what she seems. She paints herself in tones of grey, as trapped and frustrated, submitting and yielding, but also comments, 'the musician in me dies hard', and it is ultimately her music – her faith in her art – that brings release to both their lives. A woman who has 'reserved no retreat, no world of her own', she is forced to make a new life, she is the agent of change who both defines her and her husband's prison and contrives their escape from it.

Bentley, Philip
As For Me and My House, 1941
Sinclair Ross

A frustrated artist whose 'false front' as small-town minister is wearing thin. The ministry is a job not a faith, and prairie life cramps and stultifies his life and art. Grown in upon himself, Philip is trapped, but as MRS BENTLEY acutely observes, 'a man's tragedy is himself, not the events that overtake him'. Philip 'feels a situation better than he can think it through', but is saved by Mrs Bentley, who engineers both his crucifixion and his resurrection.

Benvolio
Romeo and Juliet, 1591–6
William Shakespeare

A kinsman of ROMEO, Benvolio attempts to act as peacemaker between the Montagues and the Capulets, but with little success. When the need arises he is prepared to become involved in the action. His good nature makes him a target for MERCUTIO's teasing, but he enjoys this, as he enjoys his gentle mockery of Romeo when the latter is deep in his infatuation with Rosaline. After the deaths of Mercutio and TYBALT he acts as apologist for Romeo, but fails to win a reprieve for him.

Beowulf
Beowulf, 7th/8th century, transcribed 10th century
anon, Old English

The 'battle-reckless' hero of the Geats, who rids Heorot, court of the Danish king Hrothgar, of the monster GRENDEL and then of Grendel's fearsome mother. In a later episode, the hero, in middle-age and now the Geat king, does battle with a dragon, and loses his own life in the struggle; his people mourn him as one of the world's gentlest men and rulers.

Berengaria, Queen
The Talisman: A Tale of the Crusaders, 1825
Sir Walter Scott

The daughter of Sanchez, King of Navarre, she is RICHARD I's queen and consort and a foil to his gruff simplicity of manner. Despite her undoubtedly queenly qualities, she is inclined to childish petulance and hypochondriac ailments, which are nonetheless easily beguiled.

Berenger, Eveline
The Betrothed, 1825
Sir Walter Scott

The beautiful daughter of Raymond Berenger, Norman lord of Garde Doloureuse Castle on the Welsh marches. She is only 16 when her father is killed, but takes over his responsibilities with considerable firmness of resolve, holding out against the importunity of Hugo de Lacy, Constable of Chester, who wants to wed and bed her before departing for the Crusades.

Bergmann, Friedrich
Prater Violet, 1945
Christopher Isherwood

Isherwood, the narrator of the novel, has been asked to write a screenplay for a film set in old Vienna, which Bergmann, a distinguished Austrian film-maker, will direct. They establish a close friendship, but Bergmann, intelligent, ironic, volatile and cultivated, despairs as he waits for news of his family, trapped inside an Austria torn by political troubles. Beside this, the progress of *Prater Violet*, the musical he is filming, appears rather absurd. His proud, anguished, bewildered face, his friend reflects, is 'the face of a political situation, an epoch. The face of central Europe.'

Bergson, Alexandra
O Pioneers!, 1913
Willa Cather

A Swedish immigrant girl in turn-of-the-century Nebraska. While her family battles unsuccessfully against the elements, her nature is marked by an unswerving devotion to the land. She was a tall, strong girl, and she walked rapidly and resolutely, as if she knew where she was going and what she was going to do next ... She had a serious, thoughtful face, and her clear, deep blue eyes were fixed intently on the distance, without seeming to see anything, as if she were in trouble.'

Berinthia
The Relapse, or Virtue in Danger, 1696
Sir John Vanbrugh

A scheming, intelligent and attractive young widow, Berinthia becomes an accomplice in WORTHY's plan to seduce her cousin, AMANDA, so that she might entice Amanda's husband, LOVELESS, into her own arms. It is she, rather than the gullible Loveless, who is in emotional and physical control of the situation. Having successfully engineered his relapse from honourable married man to seducer, Berinthia exultantly allows him to carry her into the bedchamber with only a whispered protest: 'Help, help, I'm ravished, ruined, undone. O Lord, I shall never be able to bear it.'

Bernstein, Baroness → Esmond, Beatrix

Berowne
Love's Labour's Lost, not later than 1594
William Shakespeare

Full of 'mirth-loving jest', Berowne is the sharpest and wittiest of the young men at the Court of Navarre who agree to abjure women to devote time to academic study. He has great patience in waiting to make fools of his peers when one by one they read out secret love poems. He too happens to be in love, having fallen for ROSALINE, the right-hand maid of the PRINCESS OF FRANCE. To begin to win her, however, he must lay aside his super-glibness, 'taffeta phrases, simple terms precise', and protest his simple love. Even then, there is more humbling to come.

Bertram
All's Well That Ends Well, 1602–3
William Shakespeare

The son of the COUNTESS OF ROUSILLON, Bertram is forced by the KING OF FRANCE to marry HELENA, whom he believes to be socially inferior. He promptly refuses to consummate the marriage and leaves for the Italian wars to escape 'the detested wife'. Eventually, Helena skilfully prevents his intended betrayal of her with another woman in Florence. Bertram returns a military hero. He and Helena are reconciled: they have proved themselves a match. Bertram is arrogant, graceless and snobbish, although having a wife so peremptorily thrust upon him by his king goes some way towards justifying his actions.

Bertram, Augusta
Travels With My Aunt, 1969
Graham Greene

HENRY PULLING's aunt – supposedly – although the true nature of their relationship is revealed as the story unfolds. A still vigorous 75-year-old, with flaming red hair and widely-spaced teeth, she is an extravagantly sensual, romantic woman with an incurable passion for love and adventure. She drags the highly reluctant Henry into a revelatory, exciting new life in the course of their travels.

Bertram, Edmund
Mansfield Park, 1814
Jane Austen

The younger son of SIR THOMAS BERTRAM and LADY BERTRAM and a man of humility and compassion. A friend and confidant to FANNY PRICE from the start, his treatment of her reveals him to be selfless and considerate at heart. Blinded by the charms of MARY CRAWFORD, however, his objectivity becomes blurred and he sacrifices integrity for misjudged gratification. Saved from an imprudent alliance by his impending ordination, his 'sincerity and steadiness' help to secure him the hand of Fanny.

Bertram, Harry, also known as Vanbeest Brown
Guy Mannering, 1816
Sir Walter Scott

The young heir to Ellangowan, he is kidnapped by pirates as a child and grows up in Holland unaware of his true parentage. He goes to India where (as Vanbeest Brown) he serves under COL GUY MANNERING, the astrologer who had prophesied hazard for the child on the morning of his birth. Brown is suspected of paying undue attention to Mannering's wife, but is actually in love with his daughter, JULIA MANNERING. The

Colonel is disinclined to approve the match, but reverses himself on a simple crux of social status. The 'heir of Ellangowan, whether possessed of the property of his ancestors or not, is a very different person from Vanbeest Brown, the son of nobody at all'.

Bertram, Julia
Mansfield Park, 1814
Jane Austen
The younger daughter of SIR THOMAS BERTRAM and LADY BERTRAM, and very much her mother's daughter in her selfish pursuit of her own ease and enjoyment. Petulant and with a 'warm temper and high spirit', she is given to 'unjust reflection' when denied her own way. Slighted by HENRY CRAWFORD, her subsequent elopement with MR YATES reveals a woman prone to jealousy, who lacks the self-knowledge to appreciate either the 'folly of her choice' or the impropriety of her actions.

Bertram, Lady
Mansfield Park, 1814
Jane Austen
The indolent and supine wife of SIR THOMAS BERTRAM and sister of MRS PRICE and MRS NORRIS. Selfish but not callous, she spends her days 'sitting nicely dressed on a sofa ... thinking more of her Pug than her children'. She relies on Sir Thomas for her opinions, speaks in a tone of 'calm languor – for she never took the trouble of raising her voice', and never thinks 'of being useful to anybody'. The most salient comment she utters is: 'I cannot think what the matter is with me ... I feel quite stupid.'

Bertram, Maria
Mansfield Park, 1814
Jane Austen
The elder daughter of SIR THOMAS BERTRAM and LADY BERTRAM, and a woman lacking self-denial, humility, shame and consideration. Duped by HENRY CRAWFORD, she marries MR RUSHWORTH, content in the knowledge of the estate and position such an alliance will secure, and determined not to give Crawford 'the triumph of governing her actions and destroying her prospects'. Poised, with 'a mind cool enough to seek all the comfort that pride and self-revenge could give', she throws herself into marriage, only to elope later with Crawford and thus compound vanity and pride with indiscretion.

Bertram, Sir Thomas
Mansfield Park, 1814
Jane Austen
The master of Mansfield Park, obliging husband of LADY BERTRAM and a stern but loving parent. His austerity and reserve render him to some 'unintelligibly moral and infamously tyrannical'. Announcing his intention to be 'happy and indulgent', he subsequently displays an uncharacteristic capacity for tenderness and compassion. He consents to the advantageous but ill-fated marriage of his daughter MARIA BERTRAM and MR RUSHWORTH, only to acknowledge later that he was 'governed by motives of selfishness and worldly wisdom'. Despite being the backbone of his family, the only time he unites them is in their horror

at his unexpected return from abroad.

Bertram, Tom
Mansfield Park, 1814
Jane Austen
The elder son of SIR THOMAS BERTRAM and LADY BERTRAM, and a man who from an early age 'feels born only for expense and enjoyment'. A charming rogue, he has a liking for the races and is 'gay, agreeable and gallant' as occasion serves. Despite his 'cheerful selfishness' and disrespect for both his father's reputation and brother EDMUND BERTRAM's future, he is redeemed by a bout of 'depressed nerves' and 'affected spirits', as a result of which he becomes 'what he ought to be – useful to his father, steady and quiet, and not living merely for himself'.

Bess
Porgy, 1925
DuBose Heyward
The pretty but weak-willed mistress of the murdering stevedore, Crown, she finds temporary happiness in her relationship with the crippled beggar, PORGY. Addicted to narcotics, she is unable to resist the insidious fascination which Crown exerts upon her. After Porgy is arrested, she leaves for the cotton plantations in despair, believing he will not return.

Beste-Chetwynde, Margot
Decline and Fall, 1928
Evelyn Waugh
'Fresh and exquisite as a seventeenth-century lyric', the Honourable Mrs Beste-Chetwynde is an eccentric millionairess with an unconfirmed reputation for having poisoned her husband. She falls in love with PAUL PENNYFEATHER at her idiosyncratic Hampshire country house, but involves him in her shady business of slave trafficking to South America, and he is arrested hours before their wedding. She marries instead Sir Humphrey Maltravers, the Minister for Transportation, who engineers Paul's premature release from prison, but she also enjoys an on-going affair with Paul's best man, Alastair Digby-Vane-Trumpington.

Beste-Chetwynde, Peter
Decline and Fall, 1928
Evelyn Waugh
Confident and expensively dressed, Peter Beste-Chetwynde is a pupil at DR AUGUSTUS FAGAN's Llanabba Castle School, where he receives half-hearted organ lessons from PAUL PENNYFEATHER, a new young master whom he befriends. He takes the credit for masterminding the romance between Pennyfeather and his mother MARGOT BESTE-CHETWYNDE when Paul is employed as his personal tutor during a vacation. On his uncle's death he inherits the title of Earl of Pastmaster and becomes a rowdy, sociable dipsomaniac at Scone College, Oxford, where he is a contemporary of Pennyfeather's.

Beti
The Far Journey of Oudin, 1961, part of *The Guyana Quartet*, 1985
Wilson Harris
An illiterate East Indian woman, bearing the

child of her dead husband OUDIN, which she must save from the diabolic moneylender Ram. She has vomited 'web or paper' (ie, the text itself) into the river, having eaten the fatal moneylender's bond at Oudin's death.

Betonie
Ceremony, 1977
Leslie Marmon Silko
An elderly Navajo medicine man, whose unconventional methods begin to cure TAYO of his sickness. He has chosen to remain living in his hogan despite the nearby growth of the squalid off-reservation town of Gallup, feeling that to do so keeps him in contact with the current lifestyle and ills of his own and other Native American people. Believing it necessary to adapt to meet the challenge of modern witchery, he is a committed modernizer, hoarding phone books and calendar photographs to use alongside his dried roots and tobacco; consequently he is distrusted by some traditionalists for changing what they see as immutable elements in healing ceremonies.

Betteridge, Gabriel
The Moonstone, 1868
Wilkie Collins
A loyal family retainer, widower Gabriel Betteridge has seen service as page boy, farm bailiff and steward in the house of Lady Julia Verinder. Now an old man with 'an active memory and legs to correspond', his devotion to the Verinders remains rock solid as he eagerly assists in unravelling the mystery of the missing Moonstone diamond. Stricken with 'detective fever', he becomes a kind of DR WATSON to the SHERLOCK HOLMES of SGT RICHARD CUFF, easing his own frustrations and worries with a pipeful of tobacco and recourse to his constant companion – a volume of *Robinson Crusoe.*

Beverley, Cecilia
Cecilia, or Memoirs of an Heiress, 1782
Fanny Burney
A young girl who is set to inherit a large fortune when she comes of age, but only on condition that any future husband must take her name. Until that time, she must run the gauntlet of her three unscrupulous guardians, each of whom reveals a different striking and incurable defect of character in their dealings with her. She is driven to despair and the brink of madness by her experiences, but is finally able to marry the man she loves.

Bevill, Thomas, later Lord Grampound
The New Men, 1954
Homecomings, 1956
C P Snow
Career politician, said to be have been modelled on Baron Hankey, who was Minister without Portfolio during World War II. 'He had the unusual gift of being both familiar and discreet; forty years before, when he began his career, he has set himself never to give away a secret, and never to allow himself the bright remark that makes a needless enemy'. Elsewhere, he is described as a 'cunning, tenacious, happy old man'.

Bevis
Bevis: the Story of a Boy, 1882
Richard Jefferies
An adventurous young boy, he and his friend MARK invent imaginative and secret worlds which transform everyday reality into something much grander. Buried in their fantasies, though, are deep recognitions about the power and sanctity of nature.

Bewethameer
The Orators: an English Study, 1932
W H Auden
A composite newspaper magnate, made up of the names of Beaverbrook and Rothermere, and a leading representative of the inner 'Enemy' that afflicts English cultural and political life.

Beynon, Butcher
Under Milk Wood, 1954
Dylan Thomas
The supremely physical fleshmonger of the village who, in his 'bloodied apron', wields his cleaver with threatening power and enjoyment. He dreams of cannibalism in the form of 'manchops', feeding catmeat to the cat and processing wildlife in general for human consumption. He terrifies his wife with his teasing, giving a literal meaning to pulling her leg.

Beynon, Gossamer
Under Milk Wood, 1954
Dylan Thomas
BUTCHER BEYNON's schoolteacher daughter represents, as her name suggests, the flighty female: visibly desirable but, because of her position, socially unattainable. She longs for refinement, but displays sensuality in shoes and red berries on her dresses. In her dream of a 'chintz curtained slaughterhouse', her two worlds merge. She is the object of Sinbad Sailor's secret love and she also feels his attraction, not caring if he is common as long as he is 'all cucumber and hooves'.

Bezuidenhout, Gladys
A Lesson from Aloes, 1980
Athol Fugard
Gladys reveals much about herself, and her bouts of nervous depression, when she rounds on her husband PIET BEZUIDENHOUT's 'Coloured' friend STEVE DANIELS: 'I accept, Steven, that I am just a white face on the outskirts of your terrible life, but I'm in the middle of mine and yours is just a brown face on the outskirts of that. Do you understand what I'm saying? I've got my own story. I don't need yours. I've discovered hell for myself.' Her bitterness is partly due to her harrowing interrogation by the security police because of her husband's political activities.

Bezuidenhout, Piet
A Lesson from Aloes, 1980
Athol Fugard
Formerly a political activist, Afrikaner Piet Bezuidenhout resigns himself to defeat in the struggle against apartheid, and spends his time tending to his plants. He must endure the suspicion of his 'Coloured' friend STEVE

DANIELS, who believes he may have acted as an informer, and his wife GLADYS BEZUIDENHOUT's flights into madness, but shows himself to be as resilient as his favourite plants, the aloes.

Bhaer, Dr
Good Wives, 1869
Little Men, 1871
Jo's Boys, 1886
Louisa M Alcott

Almost middle-aged, bearded and unkempt, the impoverished professor from Berlin is an unlikely hero. However, his generous heart and its innate sympathy with the child in everyone allows JO MARCH, left at home as maiden aunt, to learn to love and be loved, as he teaches her German with fairy tales. They find their happiness and vocation together establishing an ideal community for bringing up deserted children to follow truth, reverence and goodwill, which are his ideals.

Bharati
Waiting for the Mahatma, 1955
R K Narayan

When her father was killed in peaceful demonstrations against the British, Gandhi made the child Bharati his goddaughter, naming her 'daughter of India'. Now, lovely and vivacious, she is his devoted acolyte, and tours the country teaching his philosophy of truth, simplicity and non-violence. Visiting Malgudi with Gandhi she meets SRIRAM, who becomes a follower, and acting as his guru, falls in love with him. But when the Mahatma is imprisoned during the 1942 'Quit India' riots, Bharati is faithful to his plan and voluntarily surrenders to the police, spending years in custody, separated from Sriram.

Bholai, Julian
The Chip-Chip Gatherers, 1973
Shiva Naipaul

The apple of his parents' eyes, he is intended for greater things than the Settlement grocery store – medicine or dentistry, perhaps – but is nonetheless a powerful pawn in his father's attempts to inveigle some moral and social credit with EGBERT RAMSARAN. Julian and WILBERT RAMSARAN are schoolmates but refuse to be thrown together as friends, and it is only the arrival of SUSHILA and her daughter SITA that alters the picture.

Bholai, Vishnu
The Chip-Chip Gatherers, 1973
Shiva Naipaul

The Settlement grocer, he is the closest EGBERT RAMSARAN has ever come to having a friend. The second most powerful man in the area, Vishnu tries to gain leverage by getting his own son, JULIAN BHOLAI, to befriend WILBERT RAMSARAN.

Bianca
Othello, 1603/4
William Shakespeare

A woman of Cyprus, deeply attracted to the young lieutenant CASSIO. Her few appearances establish the contrast between the apparent shamelessness of her physical desire for Cassio (she is variously a 'strumpet', a 'fitchew' and 'trash') and her actual decency and loyalty. Innocently manipulated into IAGO's plot against OTHELLO, she stands by Cassio throughout.

Bianca
The Taming of the Shrew, early 1590s
William Shakespeare

Bianca, the younger daughter of BAPTISTA MINOLA and sister to KATHARINA, has the attributes desirable in a wife at that time. She is attractive and submissive, drawing men of all ages to her. Her sister treats her with physical cruelty, perhaps because Bianca is her father's favourite. Knowing that she will be able to control her father, she goes along with all the plans and schemes devised by LUCENTIO. While Kate is being tamed, Bianca is altering her attitude to her new husband: it is she who has become the dominant one.

Biddlebaum, Wing
'Hands', in *Winesburg, Ohio*, 1919
Sherwood Anderson

A figure of mystery in Winesburg. Largely silent, he 'talked much with his hands. The slender expressive fingers, forever active, forever striving to conceal themselves in his pockets or behind his back, came forth and became the piston-rods of his machinery of expression.' They are also the engines of his shame, for Wing, then called Adolph Myers, was run out of the Pennsylvanian town where he was schoolmaster, when his caresses were misread by a soft-witted boy.

Biddlecombe, Miss
Cousin From Fiji, 1945
Norman Lindsay

GRANDMA DOMKIN's closest friend and confidante who, despite her advanced age, still sees herself as a 'catch'. She passes her days in romantic fantasies.

Biddy
Great Expectations, 1861
Charles Dickens

MR WOPSLE's 'great-aunt's grand-daughter', she is a good and wise girl who teaches PIP to read and write and gradually falls in love with him, even though he patronizes her. She moves into the forge to look after JOE GARGERY and MRS JOE GARGERY, who is paralyzed following DOLGE ORLICK's assault. Pip finally comes to recognize her true worth, and on the death of Mrs Joe, she and Joe marry and have a son named after Pip.

Bidlake, John
Point Counter Point, 1928
Aldous Huxley

A painter and Gargantuan glutton and debauchee, whose paintings display exuberant excess. A compulsive seducer, his nemesis is brought about by an unexpectedly fatal illness. PHILIP QUARLES delivers the following verdict on him: 'Deplorable ... to see an Olympian reduced by a little tumor in his stomach to a state of sub-humanness. But perhaps ... he was always subhuman, even when he seemed most Olympian; perhaps being Olympian was just a symptom of sub-humanity.'

Biederman, Arnold, formerly Count of Geierstein
Anne of Geierstein, or The Maiden in the Mist, 1829
Sir Walter Scott

The willingly dispossessed Count of Geierstein, brother of COUNT ALBERT OF GEIERSTEIN, he is a Highland chieftain transplanted to the mountains of Switzerland. Dressed in skins, he appears wild and savage, 'but to such as looked rather at his countenance, the steady sagacious features, open front, large blue eyes, and deliberate resolution which it expressed, more resembled the character of the fabled King of Gods and Men'.

Biffen, Harold
New Grub Street, 1891
George Gissing

A gifted young writer, committed to contemporary realism, his aim is to write a novel of everyday life to be called *Mr Bailey, Grocer*. He is a curious mixture of idealism and almost obsessive practicality, falling hopelessly in love with AMY REARDON. Even his despair is marked by meticulous research, when he calculates the exact effects of the poison he will use to commit suicide.

Big Ears
Little Noddy goes to Toyland, 1949, et seq
Enid Blyton

Big Ears is a gruff, friendly old brownie, with white hair and beard and pointed ears. Already rather fat, he dresses in brightly striped clothes that make him look even rounder. He is very kind-hearted and patient, and takes little NODDY under his wing, teaching him all there is to know about life in Toyland. He lives in a jolly red toadstool house on the edge of the woods, and rides about on a bright red bicycle.

Big False Face
Take it Easy, 1938
Damon Runyon

So-called because of the fixed smile that decorates his face. After an early career picking pockets, he rises to considerable wealth as owner of several breweries. He is also something of a practical joker, whose attempt to dupe a rival with a well-tried ruse called the 'Brakeman's daughter' leads to his demise. He does, however, die with a smile on his lips.

Big Foot
Miguel Street, 1959
V S Naipaul

Big Foot is described by the young boy who narrates his story as 'really big and really black'. 'People were afraid of him because he was so silent and sulky; he *looked* dangerous, like those terrible dogs that never bark but just look at you from the corner of their eyes.' The narrator later discovers a hidden weakness in the big man, but does not, however, lose his fear of him: 'I felt like one of those small men in gangster films who know too much and get killed.'

Biggles
The Camels are Coming, 1932, et seq
Captain W E Johns

Having established himself as an air ace in World War I and fought with great bravery in World War II, Major James Bigglesworth ('Biggles' to his friends) enters the world of espionage. A typical British hero, strong, brave and a gentleman to all females no matter how villainous, his attitude to foreigners is at times rather jingoistic, although he respects a noble foe, especially his arch-enemy Von Stalhein. His loyalty to his country is unswerving, as it is to his close friends Ginger, Algy and Bertie. He is able to extricate himself from any danger using his ingenuity, his mastery of disguise and a penchant for innovative gadgets.

Bightit, Caesar
Capricornia, 1938
Xavier Herbert

Dubbed 'The Shouter', the flamboyant Bightit is an eminent big-city lawyer employed to defend first MARK SHILLINGSWORTH then NORMAN SHILLINGSWORTH in remote Port Zodiac. Ruddy and pop-eyed, tall, heavy and clumsy-looking, he is actually extremely nimble both physically and mentally. But while formidable in court, outside it he is comically dominated by his pretty little wife. Deeply in debt to him, Norman comes to see the wily Bightit as a huge, red and cunning spider, simultaneously his salvation and ruination.

Biglow, Hosea
The Biglow Papers, 1848
James Russell Lowell

A young New England farmer whose verse commentaries on contemporary society and issues are communicated in vigorous dialect. Though his diction is deceptively simple, his views are usually marked by robust commonsense.

Bigwig
Watership Down, 1972
Richard Adams

A rugged, heavily-built rabbit, with a thick growth of fur on his crown, like a cap – hence his name. A member of the Sandleford 'Owsla', the select band of rabbits surrounding the chief, Bigwig is the first to join HAZEL and FIVER when they decide to leave. Strong-willed, difficult and unwilling to comply with new rules, he is not a coward, but he dislikes uncertain outcomes. After an epic battle, it is he who proves to be the hardiest and wiliest fighter. He admits that this is his last fight, and, finally, agrees to accept Hazel as Chief Rabbit.

Bill
'That Summer', 1941, in *That Summer and Other Stories*, 1943–4
Frank Sargeson

One of Sargeson's archetypal working men, he is a rootless labourer, denied a settled role in society and constantly tempted to express his alienation in violence.

Billalong
The Timeless Land, 1941
Storm of Time, 1948
No Barrier, 1953
Eleanor Dark

The half-caste son of ANDREW PRENTICE and

half-brother of JOHNNY PRENTICE, Billalong is a carefree, light-hearted person who, unlike Johnny, in adulthood prefers to stay with the Aborigine tribe. But he understands and speaks English, and it is he who decoys Stephen and Patrick Manning away during Matthew Finn's attempt to free the convicts at Beltrasna. Although totally loyal to Johnny, Billalong is very reluctant to flout tribal customs and only does so when he no longer has any option.

Billickin, Mrs
The Mystery of Edwin Drood, 1870
Charles Dickens

A London landlady, and the widowed cousin of Mr Bazzard. She is characterized by candour and faintness ('I am as well … as I hever ham'). MR HIRAM GREWGIOUS takes ROSA BUD and her chaperone, MISS TWINKLETON, to lodge with Mrs Billickin, but she chooses to feud with Miss Twinkleton.

Billing, Mr
Smith, 1967
Leon Garfield

Mr Billing, the attorney, is both friend to MR MANSFIELD and the would-be husband of his daughter ROSE MANSFIELD. Rosy-cheeked, with a bushy black moustache, he is affable and talkative, witty and shrewd. Billing justifies his false betrayal of SMITH as a murderer by saying that, because he lives in the world, he must as a consequence adopt worldly ways. He truly believes that 'life's a race for rats and it's eat or be eaten'. He is openly a rogue, a cajoler and doer of favours, who is prepared even to condone murder and then to blame it on the world that he lives in. Finally he is discovered to have a heart as black as pitch, even though he has always kept his lawyer's hands an innocent white.

Billy the Kid, also known as William H Bonney
The Collected Works of Billy the Kid, 1970
Michael Ondaatje

Ondaatje's character is based on the legendary outlaw of the American West. Born in New York City, raised in Kansas City and Silver City, New Mexico, he took part in the Lincoln County cattle wars and was killed by his one-time friend, Sheriff Pat Garrett. He was simple-minded and outwardly affable, his ill-fitting dentures giving him a toothy smile even at moments of high stress.

Bingley, Charles
Pride and Prejudice, 1813
Jane Austen

The rich, good-looking young bachelor who takes up the tenancy of Netherfield, Bingley endears himself to all who meet him on account of his easy manners and lively good-humouredness. Developing a fondness for JANE BENNET which she reciprocates, he nevertheless allows his own feelings and judgement to be swayed by those of his sisters and FITZWILLIAM DARCY, and leaves Netherfield suddenly. But he remains constant to Jane, and eventually returns to her, slightly wiser.

Binks, Sir Bingo
St Ronan's Well, 1823
Sir Walter Scott

A preposterous English baronet who, having been manoeuvred into marriage with the glamorous but surly former Miss Bonnyrigg, is now too ashamed to return to his own country and passes the season at St Ronan's Well. He blusters unconvincingly.

Birdseye, Miss
The Bostonians, 1886
Henry James

Generally believed to be modelled on the educator Elizabeth Peabody, she is rather sourly recast as an old and cranky do-gooder, bearing a torch for lost causes. Her feminism – for all James's efforts to torpedo it – is clearly sincere, and she is a worthy propagandist.

Birdsong, Eva
The Sheltered Life, 1932
Ellen Glasgow

Suffering from a bungled hysterectomy, Eva fails to keep her reprobate husband, GEORGE BIRDSONG, from wandering. Her willed faith in the narrative of grand passion disintegrates and she falls from a state of false idealism into terror and violence, which leaves her hostile and vulnerable. She is engaged in a losing battle against the stresses of society and biology to preserve her sanity. Having murdered her husband in a jealous rage, she restores an artificial order to her disfigured life.

Birdsong, George
The Sheltered Life, 1932
Ellen Glasgow

Exceedingly handsome, generous to a fault and imperfectly faithful, George takes advantage of the misplaced trust of his wife, EVA BIRDSONG, and his own charm to seduce any attractive woman who comes his way. Less blind than Eva and JENNY ARCHBALD, he freely admits he lacks the strength of character to control his roving nature. He deceives himself when he chooses biology as his alibi and uses this to explain, if not excuse, his various flights from responsibility through the rituals of male bonding and illicit sex.

Birkin, Rupert
Women in Love, 1920
D H Lawrence

An idealized self-portrait of Lawrence, Birkin is a school inspector, and stands for a kind of Pantheism. There is a slight hostility, a slight reserve about him. While he would not seriously advocate the extinction of man, he suggests he is almost irrelevant to the great order of things: 'Let mankind pass away – time it did … There will be a new embodiment, in a new way.' Fundamental to Birkin's intellectual and spiritual reappraisal is that men and women must be freed from the shackles of conventional morality and social custom. An instinctive, impulsive man, he is the antithesis of GERALD CRICH. He meets his intellectual equal and soul mate in URSULA BRANGWEN.

Bishop, the
'The Bishop Orders His Tomb in St Praxed's Church',
in *Men and Women*, 1855
Robert Browning

The dying bishop acknowledges his illegitimate
sons, and gives orders for an opulent tomb to be
built for him to outshine all his rivals, especially
'old Gandolph'. He is more concerned with his
passion for luxuries and his rivals than he is with
the state of his soul. But as life draws to a close he
realizes that all is in vain; his sons will keep as
much as they can, having learned their greed
from him. With petulant disappointment he
dismisses them, resigned to the inevitable.

Biswas, Mohun
A House for Mister Biswas, 1961
V S Naipaul

Mohun Biswas's overriding ambition is to die in
his own house. He struggles on many fronts
within a society just emerging from colonialism
and one still struggling with a local feudal
oligarchy, and marries into one such feudal
family, the Tulsis, who are always willing to
assimilate son-in-laws into an expanding army
of cheap labourers. To liberate himself and his
only son Anand, Mister Biswas degenerates on
many occasions to a figure of fun, but one with a
resolute and rebellious instinct against all forms
of rituals or religious and cultural superstitions.

Bitzer
Hard Times, 1854
Charles Dickens

A pupil at THOMAS GRADGRIND's model school,
he is an unhappy product of Utilitarian
educational principles. Crammed full of hard
facts but lacking sentiment, imagination and
affection, he becomes an inveterate sneak and
opportunist. As a porter and clerk at JOSIAH
BOUNDERBY's bank, he holds 'the respectable
office of general spy and informer in the
establishment'. When he pursues TOM
GRADGRIND after Tom steals from the bank, he is
prevented from apprehending him by MR
SLEARY's trained horse and dog, and Tom is
allowed to escape.

Black, Lorimer
Armadillo, 1998
William Boyd

Lorimer Black is a young, good-looking and
mild-mannered loss adjuster, who also happens
to collect ancient bronze helmets and has
changed his name from Milomre Blocj. The
novel begins as Black arrives at an appointment
to find a hanged man waiting for him, and his
life spins out of control. Subsequently involved
in an apparent conspiracy, his life becomes
increasingly entangled as we discover his
personal history and he is forced to remove the
armour (hence the title) that he has donned.

Black Beauty
Black Beauty, 1877
Anna Sewell

As a young horse, Beauty is impulsive, spirited
and alert; with time he grows wise and
perceptive. Morally aware and with an inherent
sense of justice, he makes an excellent raconteur

and narrator. His lack of control over his own
destiny influences his outlook; he accepts his lot
and makes the best of it. Immensely loyal, gentle
and appreciative, he is extremely sentimental,
lamenting his separation from his family.

Black Dwarf, also known as Elshender the Recluse, or Elshie of the Mucklestanes, or the Wise Wight of Mucklestane Moor, but more properly Sir Edward Manley
The Black Dwarf, in *Tales of My Landlord*, 1816
Sir Walter Scott

'His head was of uncommon size, covered with a
fell of shaggy hair, partly grizzled with age; his
eye-brows, shaggy and prominent, overhung a
pair of small, dark, piercing eyes, set far back in
their sockets, that rolled with a portentous
wildness, indicative of partial insanity. The rest
of his features were of the coarse, rough-hewn
stamp with which a painter would equip a giant
in romance'. Predictably, the hermit is thought to
be in league with the Devil and to have an
attendant 'shadow' that moves between him and
the sun. He is later revealed to be Sir Edward
Manley, long believed dead.

Black George, properly George Seagrim
The History of Tom Jones, 1749
Henry Fielding

The gamekeeper on SQUIRE ALLWORTHY's estate
and father of MOLLY SEAGRIM. He is universally
disliked by the other servants and his downfall is
greeted with enthusiasm.

Black Jack
Black Jack, 1968
Leon Garfield

A seven-foot-tall murderous brute, who has
managed by cunning to cheat the gallows, but still
bears the hangman's red 'signature' around his
neck. Of terrifying aspect, with bristling black
beard and hair, he is prepared to kill anyone he
meets, but TOLLY, his saviour, gradually softens
his black heart. His thieving habits, however,
remain unreformed and he does not demur from
betraying the trust of those who have sheltered
him. His Achilles' heel is his fear of madness.

Blackacre, Jerry
The Plain Dealer, 1676/7
William Wycherley

Completely subservient to his litigious mother,
THE WIDOW BLACKACRE, but chafing at the bit,
Jerry Blackacre, 'A true Squire under Age',
attempts to turn the tables against her by plotting
with Freeman, MANLY's impecunious lieutenant,
to exploit inheritance law in his favour. When his
mother informs him that he is illegitimate,
Freeman reassures him, saying: 'I understand no
Law: especially that against Bastards, since I'm
sure the Custom is against that Law; and more
people get Estates by being so, than lose 'em.'

Blackburn
'Of This Time, Of That Place', 1943, in *Of This Time, Of That Place and Other Stories*, 1970
Lionel Trilling

Ruthless and insensitive, the antitype of the
waywardly gifted TERTAN. As a manipulator of

ideas and expert player of the system, he is heir to the intellectual future feared by his teacher JOSEPH HOWE.

Blackett, Mrs
The Country of the Pointed Firs, 1896
Sarah Orne Jewett

The herbalist ALMIRA TODD's mother, she lives with her son on Green Island, some way offshore from Dunnett Landing, where she and the unsophisticated William maintain a fertile but unforgiving smallholding, supplemented with fish. The old lady is as slight as her daughter is tall and mannish, but there is a special bond between them. Like her son, she has a sweet, light singing voice.

Blackett, Nancy and Peggy
Swallows and Amazons, 1930, et seq
Arthur Ransome

The red-capped, fearsome 'pirate' owners of the *Amazon* sailing dinghy, and the sworn enemies of their uncle, CAPTAIN FLINT. Deadly accurate archers, superior in both their sailing skills and local knowledge, the Blackett girls are also older and bigger than most of the Swallows (the WALKER children); yet despite this and their huge reserves of pirate cunning, they turn out to be hopeless at capturing ships. Peggy is a chatterbox, always giving secrets away; Nancy is an indomitable tomboy, a true wildcat, after whom the island where the Swallows have their camp was named. They are both rather imperious in manner, and have a strong sense of justice, which they are both determined to see prevail.

Blackett, William
The Country of the Pointed Firs, 1896
Sarah Orne Jewett

The herbalist ALMIRA TODD's middle-aged brother, he has chosen to remain with his mother, MRS BLACKETT, on their tiny island steading, working patiently at farming and fishing. Shy and intellectually undeveloped, he takes the pleasure of an 'untravelled boy' in the homely surroundings of Green Island; singing, which he does with unaffected simplicity, is the 'silent man's real and only means of expression'.

Blackhouse, Tommy
Sword of Honour, 1965
Evelyn Waugh

Tommy Blackhouse and GUY CROUCHBACK remain friends, in spite of – or perhaps because of – VIRGINIA TROY's having divorced them both in turn. They belong to the same club, Bellamy's, and meet from time to time during their respective postings. Tommy's heart is in soldiering, and he seems always to be aware of what is going on despite the endless confusion and 'flaps', as he is in a position to see files and know movements in advance. Attached to the Coldstreams, he is later seconded to train the newfangled commandos.

Blackpool, Stephen
Hard Times, 1854
Charles Dickens

A power-loom weaver in JOSIAH BOUNDERBY's factory. He is a simple, honest man whose life is made miserable by the occasional reappearances of his drunken wife, who has left him. If he could afford a divorce, he would marry RACHAEL, another factory hand. When he refuses to join a union, SLACKBRIDGE, the union leader, urges his fellow workers to ostracize him. Leaving Coketown to look for work, he is suspected of the bank robbery committed by TOM GRADGRIND. Returning home to prove his innocence, he falls into a disused mineshaft and, although rescued alive, is fatally injured and dies in the arms of Rachael.

Blacksmith, Jimmie
The Chant of Jimmie Blacksmith, 1972
Thomas Keneally

Keneally tells the (true) story of this quiet Aboriginal worker who suddenly erupts into violence and slaughters the family of his employer. Jimmie's background and the pressures placed upon him are all discussed, but the final motivation for his violence is left controversially vague.

Blackstick, Fairy
The Rose and the Ring, 1855
W M Thackeray

A mysterious personage who lives between the kingdoms of Paflagonia and Crim Tartary, known by the ebony wand or crutch which she carries. 'When she was young, and had been first taught the art of conjuring ... she was always practising her skill ... She had scores of royal godchildren; turned numberless wicked people into beasts, birds, millstones, clocks, pumps, bootjacks, umbrellas, or other absurd shapes; and, in a word, was one of the most active and officious of the whole college of fairies.'

Blackwood, Elodie
Intimate Strangers, 1937
Katharine Susannah Prichard

'Poor old Elodie' is 'caught for life', her career as a pianist subsumed by marriage and motherhood; but her music remains the source of spiritual depth in her life, acting as confessional and absolution, redeeming her from an everyday drudgery. Her essential self, although battered, is fed by an intensity of sensual delight in music, sea and lover – all have regenerative power.

Blackwood, Greg
Intimate Strangers, 1937
Katharine Susannah Prichard

'Poor old Greg' is a frustrated artist who would be more than he is but lacks the necessary depth and intensity. A returned soldier, his war experience has depleted his inner resource. A boy playing the part of a man does not inspire sympathy, and yet the misery, defeat and ultimate despair of a man displaced and alienated from his own society demands pity. Greg is dogged by a sense of inferiority and frustration.

Blaine, Amory
This Side of Paradise, 1920
F Scott Fitzgerald

An emblematic figure of the 1920s. Pampered by his wealthy and doting mother, he is an indolent youth with aristocratic pretensions, but his athleticism earns him an eccentric popularity at school. At Princeton University he becomes 'a literary bird', but because of the war, the family wealth has dissipated, and he works as an advertising writer, then takes to drinking after a disappointment in love. His fall, however, makes him face his overwhelming selfishness, and opens the way to the possibility of inner peace and 'the faint stirring of old ambitions and unrealised dreams'.

Blair, Barley
The Spy Who Came in from the Cold, 1963
John Le Carré

A jazz-loving whisky-tippler and publisher, Blair is thrust without warning into spy intrigue when a Russian woman, Katya, supplies a package for him containing apparently secret documents. British intelligence wish to know why it should be him; he swears at them and is only half-cooperative. He does go to Russia to meet the documents' author, but he begins to hold Katya's safety and future in higher regard than the needs of his British employers.

Blair, Jackie
The Montforts, 1928, revised edition 1963
Martin Boyd

Jackie is a tormented soul, his 'twisted nature' repellent to his younger brother RAOUL BLAIR. Difficult to love, impossible to understand, Jackie is seen only through Raoul's eyes. When World War I breaks out, Jackie has left his native Melbourne to study art in London. Living in self-imposed squalor, he appears 'more insane than ever' to the uncomprehending Raoul. He is totally preoccupied with his equally incomprehensible art and filled with rage at the war. Refusing to serve as a soldier, he dies in prison shortly before the Armistice, and is apparently little mourned. With his rage and torment seen only through the eyes of others, Jackie's inner self remains elusive, his main interest as a character stemming from his obvious foreshadowing of DOMINIC LANGTON.

Blair, Raoul
The Montforts, 1928, revised edition 1963
Martin Boyd

An obvious forerunner of GUY LANGTON, and an early Boyd self-portrait, young Raoul scorns his Melbourne society background and steeps himself in 'Shavianism, Post-Impressionism and Socialism'. World War I brings disillusionment. 'Upper middle-class patriotism' briefly replaces Fabianism, only to be weakened by the realities of service on the Western Front. But, unlike Guy, Raoul eventually achieves 'liberation of the spirit' in his relationship with his cousin. In a family chronicle that spans five generations, Raoul appears late, and the chronicle ends on the eve of his marriage; nevertheless, he is the most intensely drawn character of this crowded family history. Boyd's quest for 'the past within us' is concentrated in Raoul's search for identity against a backdrop of five generations of human inheritance.

Blake, Franklin
The Moonstone, 1868
Wilkie Collins

The nephew of Lady Julia Verinder, Franklin Blake becomes the unwitting courier of disaster when he agrees to transport the Moonstone diamond to the Verinder household. Well-travelled, romantic and impetuous, he has fallen in love with RACHEL VERINDER and is wounded to the core by her treatment of him after the diamond has disappeared. Determined to clear his name, he displays a terrier-like tenacity in unravelling the Moonstone mystery and consequently recapturing Rachel's affections.

Blake, Henry, also known as Henrico Blacus, Gilbert Hopewell, Henry Holland
Blake, or The Huts of America, 1859
Martin R Delany

An early proponent of Black Nationalism and Afro-American cultural pride, he rejects the meek pietism of Beecher Stowe's UNCLE TOM and becomes leader of a Cuban insurrection against white oppression. Powerful, intelligent and charismatic, he became a literary and political model for radical black writers in the 1960s.

Blake, Laura
Offshore, 1979
Penelope Fitzgerald

The depressed and confused wife of RICHARD BLAKE, Laura is a desperately unhappy woman. Beautiful and refined, she is a source of great pride to her husband, but his unwillingness to put her first makes her miserable. Although she exudes class and style, inwardly she is aching.

Blake, Nat
Little Men, 1871
Jo's Boys, 1886
Louisa M Alcott

A ragged orphan, one of the original twelve boys attending Plumfield, JO MARCH and DR BHAER's progressive home, who grows from street musician to orchestral violinist. Made strong and healthy in body and spirit in a school where pillow-fights are as important as lessons, Nat's one weakness of lying stems from a desperate desire to please.

Blake, Rachel
Sapphira and the Slave Girl, 1938
Willa Cather

SAPPHIRA COLBERT's daughter has more markedly modern views than her Southern patrician mother and is horrified by the inhumanity of slavery. A widow, her only reward for her pursuit of justice is conflict with Sapphira and the loss to diphtheria of one of her children.

Blake, Richard
Offshore, 1979
Penelope Fitzgerald

An ex-navy gent with a bit of money behind him, Richard lives with his wife LAURA BLAKE in a boat which he loves and she does not. Stubborn and self-engrossed, he likes to have the best of things in life, so he can feel a bit superior to those around him. Although he appears rational and level-headed, he is in fact deeply emotional, allowing arguments and decisions to rest upon feelings and impressions, rather than on facts. A sentimental romantic, he imagines his life and the people in it to be much more interesting than they really are.

Blakeney, Sir Percy
The Scarlet Pimpernel, 1905
Baroness Orczy (Mrs Montague Barstow)
Sir Percy, affected, self-satisfied dandy of the Prince Regent's set, in secret leads a band of gallant Englishmen who rescue innocent French aristocrats from the Terror. His many disguises are so clever that they fool Chauvelin, the French representative in London, and even Lady Blakeney, his French wife. They are estranged; she despises his foppishness; he, loving her deeply, thinks that she has in the past denounced someone and sent him to the guillotine. The truth emerges, and they are reconciled.

Blanche
King John, 1590/1
William Shakespeare
The daughter of the King of Castile and niece of KING JOHN. Her marriage to LEWIS THE DAUPHIN results in an alliance between England and France, but one which is broken when John is excommunicated.

Blanche, Anthony
Brideshead Revisited, 1945
Evelyn Waugh
An effeminate old Etonian with a pronounced stutter, Anthony Blanche is 'tall, slim, rather swarthy, with large saucy eyes' and a 'high peacock tread'. A nomad of uncertain descent, he joins his mother in Argentina and travels the world with her entourage, mixing in bohemian and exalted literary circles. Clever, audacious and blessed with the gift of insight, he leaves Oxford and takes a flat in Munich, then a tumbledown house in Constantinople. He travels with SEBASTIAN FLYTE and MR SAMGRASS from Constantinople to Beirut and later accompanies Sebastian from Marseille to Tangier, eventually showing up at CHARLES RYDER's private exhibition in London.

Blandamour
The Faerie Queene, 1590–6
Sir Edmund Spenser
A jolly, youthful and flirtatious knight with a fickle nature. He rides with DUESSA and ATE. His name refers to the blandishments and artful caresses of love. His 'fancie light' is 'always flitting as the waves wind' after each beautiful maiden that catches his eye.

Blatant Beast, the
The Faerie Queene, 1590–6
Sir Edmund Spenser
The son of ECHIDNA. He is a babbling monster of a thousand flapping tongues, who brings ill-will against all that is good; he defames noble knights and no honest lady can escape his reproach or shameful voice. He exists as the enemy to courtesy. He spreads slander and breeds malice;

it is the task of SIR CALIDORE, THE KNIGHT OF COURTESY to overcome him.

Blattergowl, Mr
The Antiquary, 1816
Sir Walter Scott
The portly minister of Trotcosey, he is mainly remarkable for a singularly unusual wig on top of which sits an equilateral cocked hat. He is 'a dreadful proser, particularly on the subject of augmentations, localities, teinds and overtures in that session of the General Assembly, to which, unfortunately for his auditors, he chanced one year to act as moderator'.

Bledsoe, Dr
Invisible Man, 1952
Ralph Ellison
A self-made black man who has risen from humble poverty to be head of a negro college in the South, and is known as a great educator, and a statesman among his people. He is looked upon by his pupils as an example, a man of influence, power and authority. But behind the bland façade and kow-towing manner towards wealthy whites, he is a strong, purposeful, cynical, self-serving manipulator who does not believe any of the idealistic principles he preaches, but is concerned only with maintaining his own controlling position.

Bleistein
'Burbank with a Baedeker: Bleistein with a Cigar', in *Poems*, 1920
T S Eliot
A 'Chicago Semite Viennese' who made his money in the fur trade, he gazes at the art in Venice with a 'lustreless protrusive eye', made watery with a mixture of greed and cigar smoke.

Blenkinsop, Dr
The Doctor's Dilemma, 1906
George Bernard Shaw
A general practitioner in a poor district of London, Blenkinsop is impoverished because his patients, mostly clerks and shop assistants, can neither afford to be ill very often nor to pay him highly for treatment. Blenkinsop's remedy for disease is usually the daily eating of a pound of greengages. He would have made a good doctor, but the capitalist medical system has dealt him the lowest cards and drained his confidence. He also suffers from tuberculosis. After much deliberation, SIR COLENSO RIDGEON treats the plodding, decent Blenkinsop rather than the unprincipled genius, LOUIS DUBEDAT.

Blenkiron, John Scantlebury
Greenmantle, 1916, et seq
John Buchan
A large-framed American, born and raised in Indiana, but latterly from Boston, he is a martyr to dyspepsia, no longer able to do justice to meals of 'oyster-crabs and devilled bones' and reduced to boiled fish, dry toast and milk. On his reappearance in *Mr Standfast* (1918), where he is again called upon to play a *provocateur*'s part, his appetite and constitution have been restored, but within a frame as lean and spare as Abraham Lincoln's.

Blick, Calvin
The Flight from the Enchanter, 1956
Iris Murdoch

Aide to MISCHA FOX, Blick has been morally 'killed' by his employer. Among other duties, he obtains the blackmail material used in Fox's manipulative schemes. Blick derives a vicarious excitement from these ventures, which include forcibly buying the magazine *Artemis*, published by ROSA KEEPE and HUNTER KEEPE. Blick is sardonically amused by the couple's loathing for him. Tall, with pale nondescript eyes and freckled hands that he adorns with rings, he likes women, 'if at all', who are long-legged, fine-boned and the same pale colour 'all over', like Rosa's lodger, ANNETTE COCKEYNE.

Blifil, Captain John
The History of Tom Jones, 1749
Henry Fielding

A handsome and well-educated half-pay officer who, with his brother Dr Blifil, is a welcome guest of SQUIRE ALLWORTHY (and doubly welcome to MISS BRIDGET ALLWORTHY). 'He was of a middle size and what is called well built. He had a scar on his forehead which did not so much injure his beauty, as it denoted his valour.' Age has lent him a more serious air and the ability to cover up his natural roughness. He dies suddenly of an apoplexy, an unseasonably short time after his marriage to Miss Bridget.

Blifil, Master
The History of Tom Jones, 1749
Henry Fielding

SQUIRE ALLWORTHY's nephew and son of CAPTAIN BLIFIL and BRIDGET ALLWORTHY, he is in every respect a foil to his childhood companion TOM JONES. Where Jones is incorrigible, Blifil displays a mature seriousness of manner, 'sober, discreet and pious beyond his age'. It is a contrast that Blifil learns to exploit when they grow up and enter into rivalry for the love of SOPHIA WESTERN, in which he proves to be a plotter of some subtlety. (It has been suggested that the odd name, which exists nowhere else and is unaccompanied by a Christian name, is an anagram of 'ill fib'.)

Blimber, Doctor
Dombey and Son, 1848
Charles Dickens

Proprietor of the expensive Brighton boarding school attended by the six-year-old PAUL DOMBEY, who is accompanied by his sister, FLORENCE. His establishment is 'a great hot-house, in which there was a forcing apparatus incessantly at work'. He is assisted by Mrs Blimber, who 'was not learned herself, but pretended to be', and his daughter Cornelia, 'dry and sandy with working in the graves of deceased languages'. On his retirement, she takes charge of the school and marries his assistant, Mr Feeder BA.

Bliss family
Hay Fever, 1925
Noël Coward

Judith Bliss, a retired actress, and her husband, David, a novelist, have two children, Simon, a painter, and Sorel. The family is self-contained,

mercenary, artistic and highly-strung, believing themselves above conventional manners, trading upon their questionable talent, hugging the idea that they are not like other people: 'We see things differently', observes Simon. Yet in abandoning one set of social rules they are putting another in place; the constant, desperate desire to be interesting and loved means that certain appearances and effects must be observed, even if they seem hysterical and abusive to others.

Blofeld, Ernst
Thunderball, 1961
Ian Fleming

A super-villain and JAMES BOND's most dangerous adversary. All his muscle has turned to fat, but his hands and feet are still surprisingly delicate and are large and doll-like – 'as Mussolini's were'. He has a gaze like a 'microscope, the window on the world of a superbly clear brain'.

Blood, Col Thomas
Peveril of the Peak, 1823
Sir Walter Scott

A bold revolutionary, remembered by history for his attempt to steal the Crown Jewels from the Tower of London. Scott describes him as 'tall, strongly built, and past the middle period of life … his countenance, but for the heavy cloud that dwelt upon it, might have been pronounced a handsome one'.

Blood, Lydia
The Lady of the Aroostook, 1879
William Dean Howells

In uncertain health, this beautiful young American schoolteacher boards the *Aroostook* to visit relatives in Europe and regain her strength. The only woman on board, she becomes the amorous target of two male passengers, one of whom gradually exposes the aristocratic nature ('blood') disguised by her simple, unformed manners.

Bloom, Leopold
Ulysses, 1922
James Joyce

A common man of ordinary actions, he is the true hero of the story. The son of a Hungarian Jew, he is cautious and meticulous, pedantic, honest and a sensible drinker. Bloom's love for his wife MOLLY BLOOM is true, but since the death of his son he has been unable to have sex with her. Instead they sleep head to toe and he kisses her bottom goodnight.

Bloom, Molly
Ulysses, 1922
James Joyce

Molly plays Penelope to her husband LEOPOLD BLOOM's Odysseus. Born of a Spanish mother, she can be fierily passionate and has a quick, theatrical temper. A mature woman who knows her own mind and desires, she puts her personal philosophy into practice. In her triumphant monologue, all of her earthiness spills onto the page as she muses on past loves and the difference between the physicality of her lover and the soul of her husband to whom she said yes after she made him propose all those years ago out at Howth Head.

Blott

Blott on the Landscape, 1975
Tom Sharpe

A secretive German gardener widely taken for an Italian, Blott is fixated on Englishness – particularly that of a bygone age. So he is in his element in South Worfordshire, ruled by an eccentric squirearchy in which his employers, a kinky MP and his formidable wife, play a pivotal role. Blott prizes 'certainty above all else' and the brick walls of the kitchen garden recall the security of his time as a prisoner of war. But a scheme to build a motorway through his beloved landscape forces him to lay down his history books and take up arms.

Blougram, Bishop

'Bishop Blougram's Apology', in *Men and Women*, 1855
Robert Browning

In the poem Blougram talks to a free-thinking journalist, Gigadibs, an atheist who maintains that the bishop should believe everything or nothing. Blougram is a hypocrite in that he has his doubts but does not care to express them, although he maintains that doubt is an essential ingredient for faith. Skilfully manipulating his opponent's arguments with dazzling casuistry, he converts Gigadibs but leaves his own sincerity open to question.

Blount, Jake

The Heart is a Lonely Hunter, 1940
Carson McCullers

An itinerant socialist whose unscheduled sojourn in the town ends abruptly in violence and flight. Once an evangelist, he now preaches his political enlightenment with a similar zeal but responds to defeat with alcoholic binges. Restless and irritable, he feels that he is bursting with words and anger: his volatile temper is always anticipating scorn and hostility and is rarely disappointed.

Blount, Kol

Seven Poor Men of Sydney, 1934
Christina Stead

In a post-World War I Sydney full of war-damaged men, this young cripple also has a more profound psychological disability, which turns into poetry, most notably a moving 'In Memoriam' for those who have been lost to history.

Blouzelinda

The Shepherd's Week, 1714
John Gay

Adept with butter, cream and curds, Blouzelinda is the object of Cuddy's and Lobbin Clout's affections. Sweet turnips are reported to be her favourite food: this has no explicit connection with her death at a tragically young age. The ravens and crickets cry for her, and in an oral will she determines who receives her straw hat and her leather bottle.

Blue

'Mr Butterfry', in *Mr Butterfry and Other Stories*, 1970
Hal Porter

An habitué of an Australian exiles bar in Tokyo (where the narrator met him during the postwar Occupation), he is now a travelling salesman – 'an ageing terrier of a spiv' – who still treats the Japanese as if he were a colonizer. In an ironic echo of Puccini and with a characteristically uncertain consonant, the bar-girls call him 'Mr Butterfry'.

Bluegum, Bunyip

The Magic Pudding, 1918
Norman Lindsay

A central character in the story and leader of the group of friends who strive to protect THE MAGIC PUDDING from the depredations of WATKIN WOMBAT and POSSUM.

Blunt, Anthony

A Question of Attribution, 1988
Alan Bennett

An historical figure appropriated by Bennett, Anthony Blunt was the 'fourth man' in the Cambridge spy-ring which included Kim Philby, Donald Maclean and GUY BURGESS. The play is set in Blunt's office at the Courtauld Institute during the 1960s, when he was its director and also the Keeper of the Queen's Pictures. Blunt is socially awkward and, as a result of his covert political and sexual activities, even more reticent than he is naturally. A proud man of political and academic convictions, he appears icy, disdainful, even arrogant and opinionated. Before CHUBB, his interrogator, Blunt's political ideals are shown to be never-ending illusions; perhaps, it is suggested, all ideals are.

Blunt, Sir Walter

Henry IV Part I, 1596/7
William Shakespeare

A loyal and trustworthy knight who believes in the legitimacy of an anointed king and who, for this reason, is used by King HENRY IV to act as an interlocutor with the rebels. He is held in great esteem by HOTSPUR who tries, unsuccessfully, to win him over. At the battle of Shrewsbury Sir Walter dies as he has lived, representing his monarch.

Bluntschli

Arms and the Man, 1894
George Bernard Shaw

A Swiss hotelkeeper's son and mercenary soldier fighting for the Serbs in the Serbo-Bulgarian war of 1885, Bluntschli is discovered by RAINA PETKOFF in her bedroom, hiding from Bulgarian troops. She also discovers that his revolver is empty and that, instead of ammunition, Bluntschli carries chocolate creams, prompting her to call him 'the chocolate cream soldier'. His unaffected pragmatism contrasts with her romantic view of the war. For him, the romantic view is farcical. Yet because he is the victim of an inferiority complex, he cannot see that Raina has fallen in love with him until, paradoxically, his true nature as a romantic is revealed.

Boanerges

The Holy War, 1682
John Bunyan

A key fighter in the army of God engaged in the struggle to retrieve the town of Mansoul, he finds himself unable, even with the support of his loyal comrades, to overwhelm the force of Diabolus. In the end it is only the intervention of Emmanuel that brings the final victory. His name has its roots in the Aramaic for 'sons of thunder', and he symbolizes the struggle of the faithful believer against the forces of sin and rebellion.

Boanerges, Bill
The Apple Cart, 1929
George Bernard Shaw

Boanerges is a man of 50, a heavily-built and aggressively left-wing Member of Parliament. Having first created a stir when contesting Northampton 25 years earlier, Boanerges has recently been appointed President of the Board of Trade and therefore gained a seat in JOE PROTEUS's Labour Cabinet. Arriving for an audience with KING MAGNUS dressed in a Russian blouse and peaked cap, his brusqueness melts beneath the king's quietly flattering courtesy. A republican, Boanerges supports the king's decision to abdicate and stand for election to Parliament, partly because he sees himself as a potential leader. Magnus outwits him, but they part with respect.

Bob, Captain
Omoo, 1847
Herman Melville

A fat, hearty Tahitian who is the relaxed guard of the sailors in the prison compound at Calabooza, where he 'bustles around like an old woman seeing the children to bed'. He has 'been to sea in his day', and is frank, cordial and jovial by temperament. He is a 'corpulent giant' who is 'literally as big and round as a hogshead', with an appetite to match, and his larder-depleting social visits are much feared on the poverty-stricken island.

Bobadill, Captain
Every Man in his Humour, 1598
Ben Jonson

In the Jonsonian sense, a 'humour' indicates an egotistical foible, and, in Bobadill's case, his is unrelenting bullying and boastfulness. A soldier who claims to have survived great battles and be something of an expert on fighting and weaponry, he is in fact a coward. He considers himself a fashionable man of the world, but in reality is a snob and a drinker. He is set up to be duped and at the end of the play is duly humiliated.

Bobby
In a Free State, 1971
V S Naipaul

An English civil servant working in a former African colony, Bobby drives with LINDA to a distant expatriate compound through territory riven by civil war. Alienated and disturbed in many ways, partly because he is a homosexual, Bobby tries to be positive about African society, yet to Africans he never appears to be anything other than patronizing, and occasionally even authoritarian. During the dangerous drive the couple undertake, the personal freedom and the opportunity to serve which Bobby seeks so desperately in Africa are exposed as egotistic illusions.

Bober, Helen
The Assistant, 1957
Bernard Malamud

The daughter of MORRIS BOBER, she is 'a good-looking girl' with a boring day job, who studies literature at night school. She is an idealist, and something of a dreamer, unable to give up her vision and accept reality. Under the influence of a story FRANKIE ALPINE tells her, she sees herself as a kind of snow-maiden protecting her chastity, until she loses it when he forces himself upon her. As the novel ends, she recognizes that Frankie, who loves her, has changed, and it seems that his hope that she will love him again may be realized.

Bober, Morris
The Assistant, 1957
Bernard Malamud

An old Jewish storekeeper. He is kind, scrupulously honest, virtuous to a fault, and suffers badly in business as a result of his inability to deny credit to the poor or cheat his customers. His compassion and forgiveness are almost Christ-like, but he sees himself as a failure. FRANKIE ALPINE becomes a kind of son to him, but he sets his heart against him after catching him 'stealing' (he is actually returning money from an earlier theft, which Bober knows about). He dies believing himself useless, but his goodness touches and alters the lives of those around him.

Bobwirridirridi
Poor Fellow My Country, 1975
Xavier Herbert

Known as 'Cock-Eye Bob' to the white settlers, Bobwirridirridi is an Aboriginal witch doctor with the Rainbow cult, a wise man who adopts JEREMY DELACY's grandson, PRINDY, as a tribal protégé. The representative of a proud and profound culture, Bobwirridirridi is a complex man. He is magisterial, mystical, independent. He is gracious, but authoritative and capable of great rage. He appreciates beauty, yet his moral code is harsh and simple.

Bodice and Fontanelle
Lear, 1973
Edward Bond

The daughters of LEAR, Bodice and her sister Fontanelle share a lust for power, a sharp if cynical political acumen and contempt for their husbands, of whom they dispose. Terrified of their father since they were young, they turn him out of office and out of doors. They are implacable women of great, if twisted conviction, of overriding arrogance and of a cruel, resolute intelligence. They are brutal metaphors of their family and environment. With the country plunged into civil war, they lead a Royalist army but are opposed by CORDELIA.

Boesman
Boesman and Lena, 1968
Athol Fugard

The bullying husband of LENA, his belief in South Africa's racial hierarchy is complete. As a brown-skinned 'Hotnot', he sees himself as different from the 'black kaffers' whom he considers the real downtrodden. However, Boesman's long experience of displacement by the White *Baas*'s Slum Clearance policy meets with a new understanding when his wife Lena insists on recounting the saga of their lives before an elderly African, whom she 'affectionately' calls 'Outa or Uncle – a condescending term towards Africans'.

Boffin, Mr and Mrs Nicodemus
Our Mutual Friend, 1865
Charles Dickens
A kind-hearted, 'ignorant and unpolished' couple, they become wealthy when Nicodemus (called 'Noddy') is made rich by the bequest of his late employer, the miserly dust-contractor, John Harmon. Earning the nickname 'the Golden Dustman', Boffin hires as his private secretary Harmon's son, JOHN HARMON, who has adopted the alias 'John Rokesmith'. Hoping to become educated, he also hires the unscrupulous SILAS WEGG to read literature aloud to himself and his wife 'Henrietty', whom he considers 'a high-flyer at Fashion', an opinion contradicted by her costumes. He learns of Wegg's plot to blackmail him from MR VENUS and humiliates Wegg. They take in the mercenary BELLA WILFER, the girl Harmon is required to marry to claim his inheritance, and to help Harmon test her character, Boffin pretends to become a miser in order to show her the disadvantages of wealth. With their help, Bella marries Harmon for love, not money. They propose to adopt the orphan Johnny, grandson of BETTY HIGDEN, but he dies prematurely. They care for the foundling, Sloppy, when Betty goes away, and train him as a cabinet-maker.

Bogart
Miguel Street, 1959
V S Naipaul
A denizen of Miguel Street in 1940s Port of Spain, Trinidad, Bogart's real name is unknown, and he is very secretive about himself. He is called 'Bogart' by everyone, particularly his friend HAT, because he likes to emulate the 'tough guy' image of the Hollywood star. His most hidden secret, namely that he married two women in different parts of Trinidad, leads to his downfall.

Bohr, Niels
Copenhagen, 1998
Michael Frayn
The play deals with the real-life meeting between Bohr, Europe's leading quantum physicist, and WERNER HEISENBERG, the German physicist, in Copenhagen in 1941, for which no definitive account exists. In the play, Bohr, who is half-Jewish, now lives in a country occupied by the Nazis. Heisenberg's former mentor, Bohr is authoritative and demanding, and a man for whom physics and the scientific community appear more important than even his children, whose names sometimes elude him. He is nevertheless not without sensitivity and compassion.

Bohun, Miss Ethel
School for Love, 1951
Olivia Manning
Miss Bohun hovers mantis-like over the household at Herod's gate in Jerusalem, thin and colourless, her hair girlishly braided around her head in an attempt to give herself an innocent appeal. She ruthlessly acquires the possessions of others, from houses and furniture to cats and potted plants, and thinks nothing of treating high-born Polish exiles as servants. She soon makes FELIX LATIMER her confidant, though she never initiates him into the mysteries of her religious group, the Ever-Ready Wise Virgins, who have arrived in the city to await the Second Coming, in anticipation of which she keeps her front room free. Firmly believing in the intrinsic value of vegetables ('the best Indian sages eat nothing else'), she serves little else to her unfortunate guests. She thinks the worst of people whilst trying to do her best for them and make a profit at the same time. Her avarice and her hypocrisy know no bounds.

Bohun QC
You Never Can Tell, 1897
George Bernard Shaw
Tall, stout and middle-aged, Bohun is the brilliant lawyer son of the head waiter of the Marine Hotel. Physically and spiritually coarse but ruthlessly cunning and logical, Bohun's 'terrifying power of intensely critical listening' has resulted in an acutely sharp intelligence and an ability to foresee and head off calamity. At the end of this comedy of manners with its farcical twists and turns, he pronounces a judgement of reconciliation between the perplexed members of the CLANDON family and FERGUS CRAMPTON.

Bois-Guilbert, Sir Brian de
Ivanhoe, 1819
Sir Walter Scott
A bellicose Knight Templar, he is 'a man past forty, thin, strong, tall, and muscular; an athletic figure, which long fatigue and constant exercise seemed to have left none of the softer part on the human form'. Burnt nearly black by the sun, he has a fierce aspect, made more prominent by a scar that damages one of his eyes. Having dishonoured Rebecca with his advances, he dies mysteriously in single combat with IVANHOE, though untouched by his antagonist's sword.

Bok, Yakov
The Fixer, 1966
Bernard Malamud
A middle-aged and disillusioned Jew grinding out a meagre existence as a handyman. He is an 'elongated, nervous man' who, after his wife leaves him, renounces his Jewishness even in his appearance, and departs the relative shelter of the ghetto to live illegally among gentiles. He is arrested and made a scapegoat (bok means goat) for the alleged ritual murder of a Christian child, but can confess only his misery and sense of worthlessness. His experiences in jail while awaiting trial lead him to the understanding that 'there is no such thing as an unpolitical man, especially a Jew'.

Bokonon, properly Lionel Boyd Johnson
Cat's Cradle, 1963
Kurt Vonnegut, Jr
An elderly black guru figure, the author of *The*

Book of Bokonon and mentor of the absurdist, fatalistic religion of Bokononism. He was born in Tobago, educated in London, and served as a soldier before setting out on the accidental-but-other-directed wanderings which brought him to San Lorenzo. He believes that a 'good society could be built only by pitting good against evil, and keeping the tension high', and plays his part in the charade of religion versus government on the island.

Bold, John
The Warden, 1855
Anthony Trollope

A young doctor with inherited properties in Barchester, where he becomes a reformer and town councillor, rather than developing a medical practice. He supports the reorganization of the charitable Hiram's Hospital, in opposition to the interests of his friend, REV SEPTIMUS HARDING, whose daughter ELEANOR HARDING he loves, thus leading to a conflict between his principles and personal feelings. He is handsome, enthusiastic, good and possibly a little conceited.

Bolden, Buddy
Coming Through Slaughter, 1976
Michael Ondaatje

Bolden is based on the semi-legendary jazz cornetist who lived from 1877 to 1931, but was never captured on record. He went insane at a street parade in 1905 and remained institutionalized for the rest of his life.

Boldwig, Captain
Pickwick Papers, 1837
Charles Dickens

The fierce and self-important landowner on whose property SAMUEL PICKWICK and his friends have trespassed while shooting. He finds Pickwick in a drunken stupor, abandoned by his friends, and has him removed to the pound in a wheelbarrow.

Boldwood, William
Far from the Madding Crowd, 1874
Thomas Hardy

Outwardly handsome, stern-looking and rich, Boldwood is a sensitive and reserved man who has arrived at middle age having learnt to repress his emotions. However, once BATHSHEBA EVERDENE offers him the prospect of romance, the equilibrium of his character is disturbed and he shows himself capable of an obsessive and self-destructive passion.

Boles, Meg
The Birthday Party, 1958
Harold Pinter

A woman of 60, she runs the 'boarding house' in which the action of the play occurs. Stupid and sentimental, she has entered into a mock-maternal relationship – with sexual overtones – with her long-term 'guest', STANLEY WEBBER. After the horrific events of the 'birthday party', she returns to the meaningless and repetitive chatter which forms the basis of her relationship with her husband, PETEY BOLES.

Boles, Petey
The Birthday Party, 1958
Harold Pinter

A decent man in his sixties, he is a deckchair attendant and husband to MEG BOLES, with whom he lives in their 'boarding house'. Despite his quiet, simple routine and limited speech, he is the only character who makes an attempt – albeit ineffectual – to save STANLEY WEBBER from NAT GOLDBERG and DERMOT MCCANN.

Boleyn, or Bullen, Anne
Henry VIII (All is True), c.1613
William Shakespeare and John Fletcher

Anne is a maid-of-honour to KATHERINE, QUEEN OF ENGLAND, whose beauty attracts King HENRY VIII at an entertainment given by CARDINAL THOMAS WOLSEY. Vivacious and charming, she declares to an old lady that 'I would not be a queen/For all the world', to which the woman replies that 'for little England', Anne would. Yet, even when created Marchioness of Pembroke, she appears less ambitious to become queen than to comply with Henry's wishes. Her principal role in the play is therefore as a dramatic foil to Katherine, and a means by which Wolsey becomes 'a poor fall'n man'.

Bolter, the
The Pursuit of Love, 1945
Nancy Mitford

The Bolter, one of the older RADLETTS, (FANNY's mother), perpetually 'bolts' with one husband after another, leaving Fanny to be brought up by her sister. When war breaks out, the Bolter arrives at Alconleigh with a Spanish lover, to Uncle Matthew's rage, which is mollified when he proves a splendid cook. The Bolter thinks LINDA and she are the same, but Fanny disagrees. Linda's wholehearted romantic need for love is quite different.

Bolton, Fanny
The History of Pendennis, 1848–50
W M Thackeray

A warm-hearted working-class girl with whom ARTHUR PENDENNIS has a notably non-sexual and amiable relationship. His mother inevitably jumps to the wrong conclusion, particularly after Fanny has nursed Arthur through a serious illness, and rejects her cruelly (and uncharacteristically). Later, Fanny finds security with the medical student SAM HUXTER.

Bolton, Harry
Redburn, 1849
Herman Melville

An English sailor, known as 'Bury' after his home town of Bury St Edmonds. He is 'one of those small, but perfectly formed beings, with curly hair and silken muscles, who seem to have been born in cocoons'. He is dapper, handsome in girlish way, a little mysterious, can 'sing like a bird', and is liable 'to yield to the most sudden, crazy, and contrary impulses'. He gambled away an inheritance in his dissolute youth and, although claiming experience at sea, is unable to face climbing into the rigging.

Bon, Charles
Absalom, Absalom!, 1936
William Faulkner

The natural child of THOMAS SUTPEN, his mother is a Haitian black woman. He grows up in New Orleans, where he meets his half-brother Henry at the University of Mississippi. Though the two fight together for the South in the Civil War, Henry kills him when he learns of Charles's black blood; Charles's own line, significantly renamed Bond, sinks into a degeneracy that matches that of the Sutpens.

Bonaparte, Detective Inspector Napoleon, also known as 'Bony'
The Barrakee Mystery, 1931, et seq
Arthur Upfield

Upfield's durable detective, he has an ambivalent relationship with the Queensland police force, frequently resigning from normal service to follow his own leads and hunches. Ambivalence ran deep in his creator, too. Originally portrayed as a white man, Bony was refashioned as a half-caste. An MA of Brisbane University, he keeps his tribally-scarred back and chest hidden under impeccable 'Western' clothes and his Aboriginal sensibilities hidden behind eyes of a reassuring blue. His forensic skills are those of a tracker, allowing him to follow microscopic clues missed by his heavily-shod colleagues.

Boncassen, Ezekiel
The Duke's Children, 1880
Anthony Trollope

An American scholar visiting England to study the English way of life. He is 'a man of wealth and a man of letters', but has no interest in business or politics. He has 'the reputation of being the most learned man in the States, and reputation itself often suffices to give a man dignity of manner'. He has been spoken about as a presidential candidate in some circles.

Boncassen, Isabel
The Duke's Children, 1880
Anthony Trollope

The daughter of the American scholar EZEKIEL BONCASSEN, accompanying him on his visit to London. She is said to be 'the prettiest young woman either in Europe or America at the present time', and seems so to LORD SILVERBRIDGE, who falls in love with her. She has inherited her father's intellect, and has a lively temperament, and a brilliant complexion which brings an unusual vitality to her countenance.

Bond, James, also known as '007'
Casino Royale, 1954, et seq
Ian Fleming

Bond has been a member of the British Secret Service since 1938, with a cover rank of Commander and 'business' credentials in the name of Universal Import and Export. He is licensed to kill, and was awarded the CMG in 1953 as a mark of his quality as an agent. A handsome man with a scarred cheek and hair 'carelessly brushed so that a thick black comma fell down over the right eyebrow', he has 'a wide and finely drawn but cruel mouth', and is fussy about martinis – 'stirred, not shaken' – and

cigarettes (special brand, three gold bands). He is less discriminating in his enthusiasm for women.

Bond, Sukey
The True Heart, 1929
Sylvia Townsend Warner

An 'odd little crow, all eyes and bones', Sukey Bond is a credit to the Warburton Memorial Female Orphanage, her one salient gift being a 'knack for obedience'. Shy and naive, she is judged to be 'no more able to look out for herself than the babe unborn'. During a new life in service, she wins the love of the gentle Eric Seaborn and is inspired with great boldness when that romance is denied her by Eric's rich mother. Unexpectedly possessed of a resolution that can move mountains, she even secures an audience with Queen Victoria in her successful quest to find everlasting happiness as Mrs Seaborn.

Bonduca
Bonduca, 1613–14
Francis Beaumont and John Fletcher

Bonduca is derived from the historical figure of the same name, more usually known as Boadicea or, properly, Boudicca. She is the 'Queen of the Iceni, a brave Virago', a forceful, determined, patriotic, brave and visionary if headstrong leader. Her vigour more than hints at fanaticism. At the opening of the play, she is furiously exhorting her troops into battle against the Romans. The more measured words of her cousin CARATACH, General of the Britons, appear to be a moderating influence.

Bones, Brom
'The Legend of Sleepy Hollow', 1820
Washington Irving

A 'rantipole hero' who has every physical advantage, from horsemanship to double-jointedness. His Herculean feats of strength are matched by his spirited practical jokes, 'frolics' and brawls. He boasts of outriding the local ghost, the Headless Horseman. His rival for KATRINE VAN TASSEL's affections, ICHABOD CRANE, is obsessed with the supernatural and is easily duped by Brom's impersonation of the ethereal rider, complete with pumpkin for a head.

Bones, Mr
Timbuktu, 1999
Paul Auster

Sancho Panza to the Don Quixote of WILLY G CHRISTMAS, Mr Bones is unconditonally faithful to and eternally protective of his unpredictable master. In outward appearance, he may be 'a mutt of no particular worth or distinction', a scruffy mongrel, 'part collie, part Labrador, part spaniel, part canine puzzle', with 'a perpetual bloodshot sadness lurking in his eyes'; yet he is a sympathetic, discerning observer of life, with an acute comprehension of the nuances of human language and psychology. Forever loyal, he resolves that after Willy dies, he will join him in Timbuktu, which he interprets as 'an oasis of the spirit' beyond the recognizable world.

Boniface, Abbot, later Blinkhoolie
The Monastery, 1820
The Abbot, 1820
Sir Walter Scott

He is not a man who lets spiritual urgency interrupt his dinner, but nor is he prodigal with forgiveness when confronted by heretics. At MARY, QUEEN OF SCOTS' fall, he leaves the monastery at Kennaquhair to FATHER AMBROSE and sets out to wander the earth as the peasant Blinkhoolie.

Bonington, Sir Ralph Bloomfield
The Doctor's Dilemma, 1906
George Bernard Shaw

In his fifties, 'BB' is a doctor of enormous and overbearing self-satisfaction and highly dangerous ignorance. He persists in the belief that any 'really stiff anti-toxin' will 'stimulate the phagocytes' sufficiently to kill all manner of germs, and having accidentally cured a prince, he has become a royal physician. Having agreed to treat the tubercular LOUIS DUBEDAT, BB mistimes the treatment and instead of curing, kills. His genuine distress at Dubedat's death is expressed by his heroic misquoting of Macbeth.

Bonnivard, François de
The Prisoner of Chillon, 1816
George Gordon, 6th Lord Byron

A patriot, imprisoned with others in the grim dungeons of the Castle of Chillon on Lake Geneva, his crime being love of liberty. He defies fetters and the cold lightless vault, believing man's soul to be immortal. Year after year he endures, seeing his companions die one by one until he is alone and near madness, but the song of a bird penetrates his dungeon and saves him. He longs for the lake and the mountains, but when he is at last set free, he has grown so used to prison that he leaves it with reluctance, and greets freedom 'with a sigh'.

Bonteen, Mr
Phineas Finn, The Irish Member, 1869
Phineas Redux, 1874
Anthony Trollope

A Member of Parliament and mediocre career politician. He has 'been a hack among the hacks', and 'a junior Lord, a Vice-President, Deputy Controller, a Chief Commissioner, and a Joint Secretary', but has risen 'as far as the ladder was accessible to him'. He is involved in exposing LADY LIZZIE EUSTACE's bigamous marriage. He is mysteriously murdered, and PHINEAS FINN is accused of the crime.

Bony → Bonaparte, Detective Inspector Napoleon

Booby, Lady
The History of the Adventures of Joseph Andrews and of his Friend Mr Abraham Adams, 1742
Henry Fielding

Unexpectedly widowed, and little troubled by the loss, JOSEPH ANDREWS's mistress (or employer) gives every sign of wishing to alter his terms of employment. Discomfited by his refusal, she sends him away, but continues to pursue him until eventually her attention is captured by a young dragoon.

Booby, Mr
An Apology for the Life of Mrs Shamela Andrews, 1741
Henry Fielding

A rich, dashing, but foolish young man, MR BOOBY is tricked by PAMELA into marriage. After his unsuccessful efforts to coerce Pamela into consummation outside wedlock, he admits defeat and acquiesces to her demands. But his ecstasy at possessing her soon turns to disaffection when Pamela wheedles money out of him. In time, he becomes a cuckold heading for impoverishment, disciplined for elevating lust above reason.

Booby, Sir Thomas
The History of the Adventures of Joseph Andrews and of his Friend Mr Abraham Adams, 1742
Henry Fielding

Fielding first used the name for Squire B—, PAMELA's attempted seducer, in his skit *Shamela* (1741). This, though, is not the same man. The name reflects the general contempt in which country squires were held by London society. JOSEPH ANDREWS's protector and first employer, he is apparently little missed by his widow, LADY BOOBY, on his unexpected demise.

Boone, Christopher
The Curious Incident of the Dog in the Night-Time, 2003
Mark Haddon

A 15-year-old with Asperger's syndrome, Christopher is methodical, observant and always truthful. Because he cannot interpret facial expressions or body language, he has difficulty dealing with other people, who tend to 'do a lot of talking without using any words'. He avoids all contact with strangers, and if anyone touches him, he usually screams. Against his father's wishes, he begins investigating the murder of a neighbour's dog, and uncovers a secret about his own family which leads him in an unexpected direction.

Boot, William
Scoop, 1938
Evelyn Waugh

The writer of a nature column 'Lush Places' in Lord Copper's newspaper *The Beast*, William is mistaken for his cousin John Courteney Boot and despatched to cover the civil war in Ishmaelia. Well-meaning but innocent, he finds himself lost and bewildered among the hardened war correspondents. He does not understand the jargon of the angry telegrams he receives from London; he does not understand that places marked on the map *must* exist even if they do not; and does not understand that if Lord Copper wants a war he must have a war, regardless of truth.

Booth, Amelia
Amelia, 1751
Henry Fielding

Fainting, swooning and weeping, Amelia is a paragon of 18th-century femininity. The virtuous and innocent wife of CAPTAIN BILLY

BOOTH, she defends unfashionable things like marriage, motherhood, goodness and love. Frail enough to be vulnerable to predatory libertines, she is strong enough physically and mentally to resist their dastardly attentions. But for all her sweetness she lacks judgement, as demonstrated by her marriage to the unreliable Booth.

Booth, Captain Billy
Amelia, 1751
Henry Fielding

Always in debt, Captain Billy Booth is constantly confronted with the cruelties of a brutal legal system. However, he deceives himself when he blames Fortune for his continual suffering. He is married to AMELIA BOOTH, but, enslaved by lust, makes love to his deviant old flame, MISS MATTHEWS. Insolent and adulterous, Booth is neither evil nor vicious but lacking in virtue, an example of unrestrained pragmatism.

Booth, Liz (Elizabeth)
Carpenter's Gothic, 1985
William Gaddis

The wife of PAUL BOOTH, she has inherited a mining concern in Africa, which she shares with her feckless, reckless brother Billy. Her money comes from an insurance swindle and her venal nature leaves her vulnerable to the diabolic MR MCCANDLESS.

Booth, Paul
Carpenter's Gothic, 1985
William Gaddis

A young Vietnam veteran turned media consultant, he manipulates the career of the charismatic preacher Elton Ude to his own ends. In a book much concerned with the failings of Christianity, he is the one character who still depends on the illusion of faith.

Borachio
Much Ado About Nothing, 1598/1600
William Shakespeare

Borachio instigates the plot against HERO, his only motives being the desire to please DON JOHN and the possibility of pecuniary reward. Having cultivated a relationship with Margaret, Hero's waiting-woman, he uses her as part of his plot; but when he has been apprehended and he realizes the game is up, he confesses that she was an unwitting party to deception. His repentance at the end, although out of character, appears genuine.

Bordereau, Miss
The Aspern Papers, 1888
Henry James

A decaying spinster in a Venetian *palazzo*, she is considerably glamorized by her youthful association with the Romantic poet JEFFREY ASPERN, who apostrophized her as 'Juliana'. Frail, but proudly defensive of her privacy, she passes on to her niece a recognition of the bargaining power that possession of the poet's surviving correspondence gives them.

Bordereau, Miss Tina
The Aspern Papers, 1888
Henry James

A plain, rather withdrawn girl, living with her aunt, MISS BORDEREAU, in a crumbling *palazzo* in Venice. The unnamed narrator (ANON) confesses to her his desire to publish the correspondence that passed between the poet JEFFREY ASPERN and the older Miss Bordereau in her youth. Displaying unsuspected subtlety, she makes marriage the price for her, by then dead, aunt's papers.

Borstal Boy
The Loneliness of the Long Distance Runner, 1959
Alan Sillitoe

Humiliated and crushed by the Borstal experience, he finds escape in the fact that he can achieve success and self-expression through his running. Given the deprivation of his background and the grim experiences of his upbringing, it is little wonder that he finds himself a cog in the machinery of law and order and a pathetic victim of its punishment. His greatest moment of defiance comes when he deliberately loses a crucial race, thus causing the brutal governor of his prison to lose face. A little triumph, it expresses the freedom of his spirit in the face of attempts by the 'system' to smother individuality.

Bosinney, Philip
The Forsyte Saga, 1922
John Galsworthy

An architect, he first encounters the powerful Forsyte clan at the beginning of the saga in 1886, at a party to celebrate his engagement to June, a daughter of JOLYON ('YOUNG JOLYON') FORSYTE. Most of the Forsytes are unsure of Bosinney. He is not rich, and once wore a battered soft hat on a social call, leaving the family to wonder whether he is socially ignorant or recklessly buccaneering. Uncertain and well-meaning, Bosinney is a moth to the Forsyte flame, burned when he destroys his chance of marrying June by falling in love with IRENE FORSYTE. He remains something of an enigma, and his death after falling beneath the wheels of a cab in thick fog might be either accidental or suicidal.

Bosola, Daniel de
The Duchess of Malfi, 1623
John Webster

A poor, valiant soldier who has gone unrewarded for violent services rendered and is prepared to do evil in order to advance. Bitter and witty, he spies on the DUCHESS OF MALFI at the behest of her brother FERDINAND, DUKE OF CALABRIA, to whom he is not afraid to speak frankly. He pities the duchess, but nevertheless supervises her brutal murder. Unrewarded once more, he changes sides, with fatal consequences.

Boswell
Boswell, 1964
Stanley Elkin

A professional wrestler, he has much of his illustrious namesake's obsession with greatness and its limits, exploring the boundaries of pain and self in ways that constantly nudge at the limits imposed by 'the rules'.

Bothwell, Sgt, more properly Francis Stewart
Old Mortality, in *Tales of My Landlord*, 1816
Sir Walter Scott

The son of Francis Stewart, Earl of Bothwell, who had frequently disturbed the reign of James VI. Young Bothwell joins the Life-Guards as a non-commissioned officer and is, for good and ill, the archetypal career soldier: brave and resourceful, but also cruel, opportunistic and licentious.

Bottom
A Midsummer Night's Dream, c.1594
William Shakespeare

Pushy and garrulous, he is nevertheless endearingly funny and un-self-critical. He is a common man, a weaver, confident enough of his melodramatic talents to lack the awe his peers feel in the presence of the duke THESEUS. His romance with TITANIA presents him both as a ridiculous 'ass' and as a warm and generous-spirited individual, a friend to fairy and peasant alike, an image further suggested by the genuine grief his fellow actors feel when he is 'transformed' and given an ass's head.

Boulderstone, Simon
The Levant Trilogy, 1977–80
Olivia Manning

At 20, newly married to a wife he hardly knows, Simon is drafted into the army, a raw recruit to the desert war. Following in his older brother Hugo's footsteps, he is much overshadowed by him. He is shy and unassuming, ready to accept advice from his senior officers and the men who serve him. As World War II progresses he becomes more wary of showing affection. His wounding and his recovery from paralysis leave him with a new vitality and self-confidence, and a maturity that enables him to come out from Hugo's shadow. He becomes less uncomplicated, less unassuming, less considerate of the feelings of others, and finally leaves his youth and his memories of Hugo behind him.

Bounderby, Josiah
Hard Times, 1854
Charles Dickens

A wealthy banker, merchant and manufacturer and close friend of THOMAS GRADGRIND, he marries the much younger LOUISA GRADGRIND. Coarse, big, loud and self-important, he boasts of having dragged himself up from the gutter to become a self-made man, but was actually helped by his respectable mother, MRS PEGLER, whom he pays to stay away. He rebukes his employee, STEPHEN BLACKPOOL, for wanting to divorce his wife when he cannot afford to and later readily believes TOM GRADGRIND's false accusations that Blackpool is guilty of robbery. After Louisa leaves him, he is publicly exposed as a liar when MRS SPARSIT turns up with his mother, who reveals the truth about his origins.

Bourbon, Sir
The Faerie Queene, 1590–6
Sir Edmund Spenser

A knight whose gallantry and glory are tarnished when his lover Flourdelis, or Fleur de lis, is enticed away by the tyrant GRANTORTO. Distressed at her blatant disregard for him, Bourbon throws away his shield in battle, but since this carries his coat of arms he loses his identity and pride. He is an allegory for French history, and the abandonment of the shield represents submission to the Catholic Church. He is later knighted by REDCROSSE, THE KNIGHT OF HOLINESS, which represents his return to the Protestant Church.

Bourne, Reuben
'Roger Malvin's Burial', 1832, in *Mosses from an Old Manse*, 1846
Nathaniel Hawthorne

A young veteran of the famous Lovell's Fight, fiercest of battles in the Indian wars of the 1720s, who is haunted by the memory of having been persuaded by his older companion ROGER MALVIN to leave him to die of his wounds. Reuben later marries Roger's daughter Dorcas and loses his son in expiation of his guilt.

Bow, Irving
The Everlasting Secret Family, 1980
Frank Moorhouse

The shifty and melancholic cinema owner in Pacific City, he is a paedophile, acting out his sexual predilections in an environment that is wholly given over to illusion and fantasy.

Bowen, Alix
The Radiant Way, 1987
A Natural Curiosity, 1989
The Gates of Ivory, 1991
Margaret Drabble

Alix, ESTHER BREUER and LIZ HEADLEAND have been friends since they were students together at Cambridge in the 1950s. Alix teaches English to young offenders and, later, moves with her family to the north and becomes counsellor to a notorious murderer locked in a high-security prison. Having an unassuming confidence, and being somewhat fatalistic, she has 'the illusion of moving in a small patch of light, her own small pocket of clarity'. The trilogy spans the 1980s; Alix, like the other women, is as much a marker as a character, her hopes, losses and dilemmas shaping and shaped by a decade.

Bowen, Evelina
Indian Summer, 1886
William Dean Howells

An American widow, travelling in Florence, where she renews acquaintance with the failed journalist Theodore Colville. 'She was ... in that moment of life when, to the middle-aged observer at least, a woman's looks have a charm which is wanting to her earlier bloom'. Described as 'almost Bernhardtesque', she is not above a little self-dramatization, but is essentially too honest to stand in the way of the mismatch she fears between her daughter and Colville, with whom she had had a youthful liaison.

Bowles, Sally
'Sally Bowles', 1937, in *Goodbye to Berlin*, 1939
Christopher Isherwood

A young, ebullient expatriate Englishwoman in the Berlin of the early 1930s, Sally Bowles sings at a seedy club. 'Her face was long and thin, powdered dead white. She had very large brown eyes, which should have been darker, to match her hair and the pencil she used for eyebrows.' Sally dresses gaudily and paints her nails green. Gullible and anxious about work, money and men, she has ambitions of glamorous notoriety. But as she is essentially a perfunctory talent, her efforts are poured into affectation and creating what she imagines is a suitably bohemian style. She is a tragic, lost figure.

Bowley, Sir Joseph
The Chimes, 1844
Charles Dickens

A fatuous, self-important Member of Parliament. Pretending to be the 'Poor Man's Friend and Father', he is actually a paternalist tyrant who considers the poor man 'his business' and discourages self-help as a kind of 'black-hearted ingratitude'.

Bowling, George
Coming Up for Air, 1939
George Orwell

An insurance salesman, locked in a perfunctory marriage, whose life is respectable but largely joyless. He is increasingly depressed by the imminence of another war, and feels that civilization is dying and that the whole world will be destroyed. Escaping the semi-genteel, dismal atmosphere of his family home, he returns to the small country town of his birth, only to find that his nostalgic dream of childhood cannot be sustained in the face of the apocalyptic future he foresees. His remembrance and preservation of the past is the only positive part of his disillusioning experience.

Bowling, Lt Tom
The Adventures of Roderick Random, 1748
Tobias Smollett

RODERICK RANDOM's maternal uncle and protector, he is a rough-hewn seaman who speaks with the staccato profanity typical of all Smollett's sailors. He bears rank on the man-o'-war *Thunder*, where Roderick later sees duty as a pressed man.

Bowman, Brenda
Happenstance, 1980
Carol Shields

After spending years bringing up her children and looking after her much-loved house, Brenda is surprised to discover that she has a talent for quilting. She is asked to attend a national quilting conference and spends the first week away from her husband, JACK BOWMAN, in 20 years of marriage. Over the course of her week away she thinks about the emotional investment she has made in her family and what it would take for her to risk it all.

Bowman, Jack
Happenstance, 1980
Carol Shields

The husband of BRENDA BOWMAN is, for the first time in his married life, left to look after his adolescent children for a week while his wife is away at a conference. Jack, a historian who has

been working on a book about Native Americans for a number of years, is suddenly faced with the alarming fact that his ex-lover has published an almost identical book. During the week of his wife's absence he not only has to try and come to terms with what this book meant to him, he also has to deal with a number of crises faced by some of his neighbours. These events lead him to re-evaluate his own life with regard to both his work and his family life.

Bowzybeus
The Shepherd's Week, 1714
John Gay

A yokel of consummate talent at playing the reed, who in the reaping season is found asleep in a field by a group of swains and lasses. They kiss him and tickle him with straw. He then sings a mixture of folk songs and psalms before falling over, red-faced and drunk.

Boxer
Animal Farm, 1945
George Orwell

A loveable, kindly horse who fearlessly supports the revolution on Manor Farm. Of limited intelligence, he is wise in heart and spirit, and believes implicitly, and naturally, in freedom. He is the hardest and most reliable worker, who devotes himself completely to the success of the farm. Through his friendship with the exiled scapegoat SNOWBALL, this honest, true labourer is viewed suspiciously by the ruling pigs. His health collapses through overwork and he is sent to the knacker's – the graveyard of the workers' revolution.

Boy, the
The Painted Bird, 1965
Jerzy Kosinski

A mute gypsy child trapped between the thundering languages of Stalinism and Nazism in wartime Poland. Brutalized by the invaders and by superstitious peasants, the Boy fantasizes a release from his 'vegetable' state in a multiplicity of bird-forms.

Boyet
Love's Labour's Lost, not later than 1594
William Shakespeare

The attending lord to the PRINCESS OF FRANCE, Boyet is a most persuasive negotiator in dealing with the Kingdom of Navarre. He is a shameless flatterer of the princess and is highly amused by the antics of KING FERDINAND and his friends when they try to woo the women he is looking after.

Boyle, 'Captain' Jack
Juno and the Paycock, 1924
Sean O'Casey

A work-shy Dubliner, he is known as 'Captain' to his equally feckless drinking pal, 'JOXER' DALY, although he has only been to sea once, and then on a coal boat to Liverpool. Boyle is the paycock (peacock) of the title. He struts, preens and postures, painting himself as the hero of many adventures. The husband of JUNO BOYLE, he is about 60, stout, grey-haired, stocky and bullish. Theirs is a loveless marriage and their brief social rise as a result of a supposed inheritance exposes their differences as much as Boyle's ludicrous boasting and pretensions expose their poverty. At the end, he is left drunkenly observing that 'th' whole worl's ... in a terr ... ible state o' ... chassis!'

Boyle, Juno
Juno and the Paycock, 1924
Sean O'Casey

The wife of 'CAPTAIN' JACK BOYLE, Juno is 45, 'and twenty years ago she must have been a pretty woman'. But now, after years of worry and strain, prettiness has been replaced by 'a look of listless monotony and harrassed anxiety'. She and her family live in a crumbling Dublin tenement. Intelligent, sometimes despairing, a realist, emotionally resilient and essentially a pacifist, she is named, not after the Roman goddess of the hearth but, according to Boyle, because the important events of her life happened in June. She is courageous and eventually triumphant, demonstrating the superiority of women over the vanities, weaknesses and slothfulness of men.

Boythorn, Lawrence
Bleak House, 1853
Charles Dickens

Schoolfellow and friend of JOHN JARNDYCE and litigious neighbour of SIR LEICESTER DEDLOCK, with whom he is in dispute over a right of way. Although tender-hearted and gentle, he is also impetuous and noisy, 'always in extremes, always in the superlative degree'.

Bozzle, Samuel
He Knew He Was Right, 1869
Anthony Trollope

A rather seedy former policeman who 'had not lived without a certain reputation in the police courts'. He now works as a private investigator and is rarely seen at home. He is engaged by LOUIS TREVELYAN to spy on his wife in discreet fashion 'for a consideration', and later assists Trevelyan in the abduction of his son from his mother.

Brabazon, Julia, later Lady Ongar
The Claverings, 1867
Anthony Trollope

A beautiful and ambitious young woman who passes over her impecunious childhood sweetheart, HARRY CLAVERING, for the wealthy but dissolute Lord Ongar. She has a cruel and remorseless streak in her nature, and when her husband, who mistreats her, quickly drinks himself to death, she attempts to reassert her hold over Harry, and lure him away from his new fiancée, but without success.

Brachiano, Duke of
The White Devil, 1612
John Webster

Also known as Paulo Giordano Ursini, Brachiano has apparently been a learned and respectable ruler, although with a reputation for meanness. His love for VITTORIA COROMBONA corrupts him and leads him first to reject his devoted wife ISABELLA and then to have her and Vittoria's

husband CAMILLO murdered. He rages jealously on suspecting that Vittoria is having an affair with a rival, then, after running away with her, marries her, regardless of his excommunication.

Bracknell, Lady
The Importance of Being Earnest, 1895
Oscar Wilde

An imperious and autocratic snob who, even more than the other characters, is concerned entirely with appearances. As GWENDOLINE's mother she sees it as her maternal duty to prevent her only daughter from becoming engaged to JOHN WORTHING and thus 'marrying into a cloak-room, and forming an alliance with a parcel'. She is uncompromising in her views and dictatorial in her attempts to foist them on to others.

Bradshaw, Mr
Ruth, 1853
Elizabeth Gaskell

A vicar who is quick to judge, he likes to think of himself as philanthropic, but he has no real conception of the complexity of delicate human situations. He is most comfortable with those who conform in a social and moral sense, even if underneath they are lacking in compassion. Less forgiving than a faithful Christian might be and narrow-minded in the extreme, he nevertheless shows remorse and learns that external actions do not always reflect the inner soul. Eventually he comes to a state of awareness befitting a man of his profession, and is humble enough to seek to make amends, even though it is too late.

Bradstreet, Anne
Homage to Mistress Bradstreet, 1956
John Berryman

A portrait based on the brilliant early American poet. The narrator depicts her genius, her passionate devotion to her husband (the Simon of the poem), her longing for children, her sense of losing her religious faith and her difficulty in being a poet in a pragmatic society. He then moves beyond historical fact by imagining her keeping sexual tryst with him.

Bradwardine, Baron of (Cosmo Comyne Bradwardine of Bradwardine and Tully-Veolan)
Waverley, 1814
Sir Walter Scott

An old hunting friend and co-religionist of SIR EVERARD WAVERLEY, who gives his nephew EDWARD WAVERLEY an introduction. Though good-hearted he is insufferably orotund and legalistically latinate in speech, a tendency that sits rather oddly with his tall, athletic figure and Frenchified clothes. Constant country sport and endless forensic argument seem to be no more than sublimations of his undying urge to do battle for the Good Old Cause.

Bradwardine, Rose, also known as 'the Rose of Tully-Veolan'
Waverley, 1814
Sir Walter Scott

The BARON OF BRADWARDINE's daughter, 'a very

pretty girl of the Scotch cast of beauty, that is, with a profusion of hair of paley gold, and a skin like the snow of her own mountains in whiteness. Yet she had not a pallid or pensive cast of countenance; her features, as well as her temper, had a lively expression.'

Brady, Brian
The Doubleman, 1985
C J Koch

In physique and in spirit he is the opposite of his crippled, insular cousin RICHARD MILLER. A tough, athletic character, with the sunlit temperament conventionally associated with Australians, he is also a 'double', a fantasy projection of the life Richard has been denied.

Brady, Francie
The Butcher Boy, 1992
Patrick McCabe

Obsessed with westerns and comics, Francie Brady or 'Pig Boy' lives in small-town Ireland. But when his mother takes her own life, he gradually becomes more alienated from society and unhinged from reality. Francie's delinquency leads to estrangement from his 'blood brother' Joe Purcell, and his growing obsession with the snobbish Mrs Nugent and her bookish son Philip becomes more sinister, culminating in a nightmarish dénouement. His unique and often hilarious world-view and childlike innocence only serve to counterpoint the horror of his actions.

Brady, Kate (Caithleen)
The Country Girls, 1960
Edna O'Brien

When such a sensitive young girl loses the mother she adores and is left with a father who terrifies and embarrasses her, the results are inevitably painful. Kate is gentle, sweet and principled, and is heavily dominated by her friend BABA BRENNAN. She grows up accepting humiliation regarding her family, her home and herself, but she is a bright girl and, though meek and kind, has a way of attracting people to her. She has a quiet but determined spirit that propels her into exciting situations.

Braggadochio
The Faerie Queene, 1590–6
Sir Edmund Spenser

As his name suggests, he is a braggart warrior. He is a narcissistic scoundrel uninterested in valour, virtue or honour but only concerned with himself and the way he looks. Vainly dressed in golden armour, he is as proud as a peacock. Boastful of his deeds, in reality he is foolish, cowardly, mean and lustful. He is described as having 'lofty looks hiding in a humble mind'.

Braid, Miss Hetty
The Finishing Touch, 1963
Brigid Brophy

She speaks in a booming baritone that lends her an aura of mannish authority in her role as co-proprietrix of a Riviera finishing school. She is adored by her beautiful partner MISS ANTONIA MOUNT, but everything about the relationship suggests that it is Miss Braid who

takes the conventional wifely role.

Brain, the
More Than Somewhat, 1938
Damon Runyon

A major gambling power in New York, and a man of many loves, the Brain prides himself on his appeal to the opposite sex, as a result of which he has gathered a collection of houses in which to keep his women. But when he falls victim to a hitman's bullet, he finds that the love offered him is shallow or non-existent, and only one woman, the recipient of a random act of generosity, shows him any real care.

Brainworm
Every Man in his Humour, 1598
Ben Jonson

The devious and cunning servant of KNOWELL, SENIOR, he plays on the egotistical foibles of the other characters to engineer a great deal of fun for himself. He is an astute observer and an effective mimic, disguising himself as a begging soldier in an attempt to prevent Knowell pursuing his son, Edward Knowell, to London. For pure amusement, he sells a sword at a hugely inflated price to the foolish STEPHEN. He ends the play as the feted guest of JUSTICE CLEMENT.

Braithwaite, Geoffrey
Flaubert's Parrot, 1984
Julian Barnes

The narrator, he is a retired doctor, melancholic by nature, with a taste for good food, travel and books. A passionate devotee of the great French novelist Gustave Flaubert, he dedicates himself to the obsessive pursuit of arcane facts about his life. His search to recover the writer's past is paralleled by his attempts to understand his own life. Both, however, remain ultimately elusive.

Bra' Man, also known as John Power
Brother Man, 1954
Roger Mais

Bra' Man is a shoemaker in a slum area of Kingston, Jamaica. Wise and cautious, he is convinced that beyond the poverty of his surroundings exists a more spiritually rewarding life. A Rastafarian, he tries to attain this not so much by political protest as by religious teaching. Outwardly an ordinary man, yet compassionate and generous in spirit, Bra' Man is at once commonplace and unique. The parallels with Christ are clearly evident: preaching a gospel of love and peace and offering the hope of redemption, Bra' Man is finally betrayed and killed by a mob. His body is rescued by MINETTE.

Bramble, Matthew (Matt)
The Expedition of Humphry Clinker, 1771
Tobias Smollett

The squire of Brambleton Hall, he is a grouchy hypochondriac, touring the country in search of cures and palliatives for a bewildering array of complaints. His selfish misanthropy is largely a front, though, camouflaging a gruff generosity and the disappointments of an unfulfilled life.

Bramble, Tabitha
The Expedition of Humphry Clinker, 1771
Tobias Smollett

Tabitha's nephew JERY MELFORD describes her as 'a maiden of forty-five, exceedingly starched, vain and ridiculous', heavily reliant on a rainbow wardrobe and a repertoire of grotesque simpers to sustain her reputation as a coquette. Her epistolary style is hampered by a profound dyslexia.

Brand, Ethan
'Ethan Brand', 1850, in *The Snow Image and Other Twice-Told Tales*, 1851
Nathaniel Hawthorne

A two-dimensional Faust, who sets out in pursuit of the Unpardonable Sin, only to discover it in the chambers of his own heart. To his companions in the lime-kiln, his cruel destruction of a young woman's soul represents 'the sin of an intellect that triumphed over the sense of brotherhood with man and reverence for God, and sacrificed everything to its own mighty claims!'

Brand, Mr
The Europeans, 1878
Henry James

A Unitarian minister, and the rather diffident suitor of GERTRUDE WENTWORTH. Despite the imperfections of his face and figure, which incline to fat, he is 'a young man of striking appearance. The expression of his little clean-coloured blue eyes was irresistibly gentle and serious; he looked, as the phrase is, as good as gold.'

Brandon, Col
Sense and Sensibility, 1811
Jane Austen

An old friend of the DASHWOOD family, Colonel Brandon is a solemn but very well-liked man, whose quiet disposition owes a lot to a great disappointment in love. Deeply attracted to the much younger MARIANNE DASHWOOD, he is unswerving in his loyalty to her and her family, and his sensible, unassuming manner and patient understanding are eventually rewarded with Marianne's hand in marriage.

Brandon, George → Firmin, Dr George

Brandon, Mrs → Gann, Caroline

Brandon, Tony
For the Rest of Our Lives, 1947
Dan Davin

An officer in the New Zealand Division in Egypt during World War II. An associate of FRANK FAHEY and TOM O'DWYER, he is 'a man who always went to meet his experiences, an enjoyer. But an enjoyer who was able to see that joy, like peace, is indivisible.' And so whatever Brandon does, he does with absolute conviction. He is sometimes a hedonist, sometimes anarchic, sometimes revolutionary. He is even suspected of being a Trotskyist. He is 28 and handsome, but his restlessness points to the central flaw in his character: he is an idealist, and wants the best for everyone, but his impatience means that he cannot be bothered with the self-discipline and

the slow struggle necessary to attain it.

Brandt, Margaret
The Cloister and the Hearth, 1861
Charles Reade

The beautiful, auburn-haired daughter of a poor scholar. She is a sweet, gentle, highly moral and rather reserved girl who falls in love with GERARD. They are separated by interfering family, and she is forced into a life of defiant but wretched misery with his child. Her soul is 'full of bitterness and grief' when he refuses to resume their life together, but she wrings an admission of love from him on her deathbed. Their son will grow up to be the philosopher Erasmus.

Brandt, Willy
Democracy, 2003
Michael Frayn

Based on real-life characters, the play deals with the association between Brandt, West German Chancellor from 1969 to 1974, and GUNTER GUILLAUME, a close aide. An idealist and womanizer, Brandt is an intelligent, clear-minded but indecisive politician dreaming of German reunification. A contradictory combination of vision and caution, pride and humility, he becomes increasingly introspective and isolated, and his misguided reliance upon Guillaume results in his resignation and downfall.

Brandysnap, Benjamin
The Magic Pudding, 1918
Norman Lindsay

Working as a market gardener has instilled in this large dog a practical home-grown wisdom that makes him a valued ally to the friends who protect THE MAGIC PUDDING.

Brangwen, Gudrun
The Rainbow, 1915
Women in Love, 1920
D H Lawrence

A daughter of WILL BRANGWEN and ANNA LENSKY, Gudrun is the younger sister of URSULA BRANGWEN. She too aspires to a new spiritual and moral beginning but, unlike her sister, sees herself as being part of the sophisticated, fashionable group led by people such as HERMIONE RODDICE. An artist, Gudrun has lived in the London studio world, but her work has not attracted particular notice. She can be cold, harsh, often watchful, has no maternal instincts, and does not know what she should be feeling: '*Nothing materialises!* Everything withers in the bud.' Yet her affair with GERALD CRICH, though ultimately tragic, is tempestuous and passionate.

Brangwen, Tom
The Rainbow, 1915
D H Lawrence

Tom Brangwen is born into a large family of Nottinghamshire farmers, a community in which the men look towards their own and the earth and the women towards broader society. His ambitious mother dispatches him to a grammar school, and later a love of poetry and things romantic draws him to LYDIA LENSKY, a Polish widow. She, like him, is an outsider, and it is this, together with their shared and instinctive quest for knowledge and intimacy, which unites them. Their marriage has its difficulties, but they are essentially happy, she finding stability in his way of life, he discovering that she fulfils his sense of the exotic.

Brangwen, Ursula
The Rainbow, 1915
Women in Love, 1920
D H Lawrence

The eldest child of WILL BRANGWEN and ANNA LENSKY, Ursula appears the most likely of the Brangwen sisters (the other being GUDRUN BRANGWEN) to discover a new, free spirituality once envisaged by her parents. An intellectual, sexual woman, she thinks of herself as being on a journey, 'a traveller on the face of the earth ... seeking the goal she knew she did draw nearer to'. In the hope of establishing a new consciousness based upon a deeper understanding of human nature, she becomes a teacher. 'Her spirit was active, her life like a shoot that is growing steadily'. She finds her union with RUPERT BIRKIN.

Brangwen, Will
The Rainbow, 1915
D H Lawrence

The nephew of TOM BRANGWEN, Will marries his cousin, ANNA LENSKY, Tom's step-daughter and LYDIA LENSKY's daughter. A reserved, even shy man, sensual and artistic, who can fashion beautiful objects from wood, he is 'a dark enriching influence' upon Anna. But he finds little emotional response from her, retreats into himself and becomes a disappointed man.

Brannon, Biff
The Heart is a Lonely Hunter, 1940
Carson McCullers

The owner of the New York Café, who observes the interactions of his customers with ceaseless curiosity. Although able to perceive the illusory nature of the relationships which are projected on to JOHN SINGER, he is himself perplexed by his own thoughts and feelings, particularly his tenderness for MICK KELLY. He is always questioning the world around him and after the death of his wife becomes preoccupied with contemplation and memory.

Brant, Captain Adam
Mourning Becomes Electra, 1931
Eugene O'Neill

The son of GEN EZRA MANNON's brother David, he is a family servant who plans to take revenge on the family by seducing the general's wife CHRISTINE MANNON. In the event, he falls in love with her and is implicated in her plot to kill her stricken husband. He is in turn killed by ORIN MANNON.

Bras-Coupé
The Grandissimes, 1880
George Washington Cable

A proud and indomitable African prince, brought to Louisiana as a slave but impossible to break in for plantation work. After assaulting his master during a bizarre double wedding ceremony in which he is 'given' the *voudou* PALMYRE DE PHILOSOPHE, he escapes into the swamps. An acquired appetite for liquor overcomes his huge physical and moral strength, and he is recaptured, to be tortured, mutilated and hamstrung.

Brass, Sally
The Old Curiosity Shop, 1841
Charles Dickens

The sister and business partner of SAMPSON BRASS, she is repulsive and manly in appearance. Her cruelty is depicted in her treatment of THE MARCHIONESS, her little servant. Although she is her brother's 'clerk, assistant, housekeeper, secretary, confidential plotter, adviser, intriguer, and bill of cost increaser', she refuses to join in his betrayal of DANIEL QUILP and warns Quilp of impending danger before escaping herself. Ultimately, she and Sampson are reduced to living wretched, homeless lives on the streets of London.

Brass, Sampson
The Old Curiosity Shop, 1841
Charles Dickens

A villainous 'attorney of no very good repute', he is DANIEL QUILP's sycophantic lawyer and the employer of DICK SWIVELLER. Full of cunning and intrigue, like his sister, SALLY BRASS, he engineers the false arrest of KIT NUBBLES and betrays Quilp. After years of hard labour in prison, he is reduced to being a vagrant in London with his sister.

Brassbound, Captain
Captain Brassbound's Conversion, 1899
George Bernard Shaw

Captain Brassbound, a trader in his mid-thirties and 'a man of few words, fewer gestures, and much significance', leads SIR HOWARD HALLAM, LADY CECILY WAYNEFLETE and an eccentric band of villains and wanderers to the Moroccan interior. There, Brassbound declares he is Hallam's nephew and accuses him of destroying his mother and appropriating the family estate. When revenge is denied him, Brassbound is robbed of purpose and dignity. He dedicates himself to love instead, proposing marriage to Lady Cecily. Yet he is denied this too as gunfire from his ship calls him back to sea.

Brathwaite, Edward Kamau
The Arrivants: A New World Trilogy, 1973
Edward Brathwaite

The masked persona of this New World trilogy, he moves through history on a voyage of racial and tribal discovery and recovery. The Black Man of the New World, he takes on the mask of slave and king, prostitute and prophet. He is Old and New World god – Ananse, Ogun, Legba and Shango. He is Uncle Tom and Rastaman, corrupt politician and violent revolutionary, inhabitant of Africa's jungle, Harlem's hustle and Britain's Brixton basement. He is Caribbean fisherman, carpenter and carnival CALIBAN, jazz singer, black rights leader and Mother. Ultimately he is the poet-drummer, singing Africa, singing hope into an embittered and embattled new world.

Brattle, Carry
The Vicar of Bullhampton, 1870
Anthony Trollope

A young fallen woman, in exile from the Wiltshire village of Bullhampton since being disowned by her formerly loving father. Now 'a poor, sickly-looking thing', she still retains some of her beauty. She feels shame and contrition, but is repelled by the dullness of respectability, needing the security of her home environment, to which REV FRANK FENWICK endeavours to return her.

Brattle, Sam
The Vicar of Bullhampton, 1870
Anthony Trollope

Son of the Bullhampton miller and brother of CARRY BRATTLE, whom he helps and defends. Independent and sometimes hard-working, his tendency towards defiance and idleness apparently derives from the imprudent favouritism shown to him in his boyhood by REV FRANK FENWICK. He has some dubious associates and is suspected of involvement in the murder of FARMER TRUMBULL.

Bray, Col James
A Guest of Honour, 1970
Nadine Gordimer

A white African, formerly a District Commissioner, he has been banished from the unnamed colony for alleged complicity with the now successful revolutionary independence movement. He is invited back as a guest of honour and offered a government post by his old friend PRESIDENT MWETA, but becomes embroiled in a new internecine class struggle.

Bray, Madeline
Nicholas Nickleby, 1839
Charles Dickens

The beautiful daughter of the selfish, debauched bankrupt, WALTER BRAY, she endures poverty and degradation while supporting her invalid father as an artist. She is unaware that under the terms of a deed stolen by the old moneylender, ARTHUR GRIDE, she will become an heiress on the day she marries. Her father tries to force her to marry Gride in order to secure his own release as a bankrupt, but Bray dies on the morning of the wedding and the plot collapses. NICHOLAS NICKLEBY, who has long loved her, abducts her from Gride, takes her to his mother's house, and eventually marries her.

Bray, Walter
Nicholas Nickleby, 1839
Charles Dickens

The broken-down, bankrupt father of MADELINE BRAY. An unscrupulous and selfish invalid, he forces her to endure poverty and degradation while supporting him. Learning that Madeline will become an heiress on the day she marries, according to a deed stolen by the old moneylender, ARTHUR GRIDE, he agrees with Gride and RALPH NICKLEBY to marry her off to Gride in order to secure his own release as a bankrupt. On the morning of the wedding, he dies, and the plan falls through.

Brayford, Hugo
Lucinda Brayford, 1946
Martin Boyd

Shallow and pleasure-seeking, he is the youngest son of the 11th Viscount Crittenden, and has no intention of allowing his marriage to a wealthy antipodean, LUCINDA BRAYFORD, to change his life; but World War I achieves what the quickly-disillusioned Lucinda could not. Wounded and horribly disfigured on the eve of Lucinda's planned elopement with her lover, Hugo wrings from her a promise to stay with him, in return for her 'discreet' extra-marital freedom. Although the remainder of his life is spent in passive self-imprisonment on the Crittenden estate, the moral compromise he has imposed on Lucinda continues to influence the direction of her life – even to the final cruel irony provided by the timing of his death.

Brayford, Lucinda, née Vane
Lucinda Brayford, 1946
Martin Boyd

A daughter of the wealthy Australian squatocracy, beautiful Lucinda delights her socially ambitious mother when she marries into the English aristocracy. But her bright glow of youth is soon to be extinguished. Her husband HUGO BRAYFORD's character and the events of two world wars darken her world; she loses husband, lover and son (STEPHEN BRAYFORD), and is left, alone, with a handful of dust. The ironies of her life are all too clear to Lucinda, one of whose greatest charms is her ready wit. But she has a moral fibre stronger than her ironic attitude might indicate, and hardier than that of those with whom she co-exists. Her values are those of Boyd's 'natural aristocrat', the outward futility of her life transcended by her personal integrity.

Brayford, Paul, later 13th Viscount Crittenden
Lucinda Brayford, 1946
Martin Boyd

'Paul took the best men of the past and compared them with the worst of the present.' HUGO BRAYFORD's half-brother, he is an anachronism, waspishly witty and obsessed with ancestry. Disgusted by the mores of contemporary society, he devotes his life to an 'enthusiastic pursuit of culture' and beautiful young men. A sustaining force in LUCINDA BRAYFORD's life, he eventually becomes the 13th Viscount Crittenden. Alas, his concept of aristocratic life is idealized. No longer able to indulge his Bohemian tastes and disdaining the society of his fox-hunting neighbours, the increasingly embittered Paul lives a life of lonely state.

Brayford, Stephen
Lucinda Brayford, 1946
Martin Boyd

The only child of HUGO and LUCINDA BRAYFORD and heir to an ancient viscountcy, he begins life with glorious prospects and impossibly high ideals. Both endearing and exasperating, he is deserted by his pretentious antipodean bride, and imprisoned for his refusal to fight. On Stephen's return home, 'his spirit seemed to be consuming his body'. He dies, but with his spiritual integrity intact.

Brazen
The Recruiting Officer, 1706
George Farquhar

A rival recruiting officer to CAPTAIN PLUME, Brazen is incompetent and lazy. He tries to impress with his boastful claims about his many supposed female conquests, and about his exemplary military career. However, he proves to be mostly talk, except when he is provoking duels with fellow-officers over ladies or recruits. His garrulousness and frequent verbal misunderstandings and malapropisms make him appear a ridiculous figure, yet there is something likeable about him, as is shown by Plume's willingness, after his decision to resign his commission, to hand over his new recruits to Brazen.

Breaux, Amy
'Old Mortality', in *Pale Horse, Pale Rider*, 1939
Katherine Anne Porter

Dead Aunt Amy is now a photograph and a memory in her Southern American family. High-spirited and reckless, she danced, broke engagements, laughed infectiously and married GABRIEL BREAUX, whom she did not love, after he was disinherited. Her early death is perhaps mysterious.

Breaux, Gabriel
'Old Mortality', in *Pale Horse, Pale Rider*, 1939
Katherine Anne Porter

Uncle Gabriel loved AMY BREAUX; her refusal to marry him perhaps prompted his wild behaviour, which led to his being disinherited. She then married him, but soon died. He marries again, but Amy remains the love of his life. The shabby, obese, drunken reality of the older Gabriel contrasts shockingly with the romantic image of him held by his young relatives MARIA and MIRANDA.

Breck, Alan
Kidnapped, 1886
Catriona, 1893
Robert Louis Stevenson

He has an open, honest expression, but eyes which 'had a kind of dancing madness in them, that was both engaging and alarming'. Although he has elegant manners and a well-educated mind, he is also the consummate man of action. He has all the nimble, physical charm of the Highlander and an easy-going approach to life's vicissitudes. But there is also a dangerous sense of moral ambivalence surrounding him, and his role in the Appin murder mystery is never fully resolved. The fraternal relationship between Alan and DAVID BALFOUR is based on their opposite qualities, which are nevertheless interdependent.

Breckinridge, Myra
Myra Breckinridge, 1968
Gore Vidal

Formerly film critic Myron Breckinridge, Myra is now the most disturbingly perfect example of womankind that modern science has been able to create. Taking her behavioural cues from the stars of Hollywood's golden era, she is now aggressively intent on living out all her myriad fantasies and shattering the conventions of acceptable sexual behaviour. An Amazonian warrior of unyielding purpose, she is as willing to violate old-fashioned stereotypes as she is to rape hapless stud Rusty Godowski.

Breedlove, Pecola
The Bluest Eye, 1970
Toni Morrison

'A little black girl who wanted to rise up out of the pit of her blackness and see the world with blue eyes', Pecola is trapped by the expectations of her society. Epitomising blackness, her anonymity encourages the prejudices of the community to be projected onto her: 'we were so beautiful when we stood astride her ugliness'. Thoroughly degraded, she is ultimately released by a descent into insanity and the conviction that she has 'the bluest eyes in the whole world'.

Brenda
The Bottle Factory Outing, 1974
Beryl Bainbridge

The room-mate of FREDA, Brenda is a small, timid woman, afraid of the world. Previously married, she is now frightened of all men, who for some reason always seem to want to touch her. Thus, she dresses strangely, wearing a large string vest and several layers of protective newspaper under her clothes. She is, as Freda says, 'a born victim', placed on this earth merely to accommodate others.

Brenhilda, Countess of Paris
Count Robert of Paris, 1831
Sir Walter Scott

The wife of ROBERT, COUNT OF PARIS, the countess is 'one of those stalwart dames who willingly hazarded themselves in the front of battle'. Despising the usual pursuits of her sex, she has become an Amazon of fearsome aspect and pitiless rigour. She is also not quite believable.

Brennan, Baba (Bridget)
The Country Girls, 1960
Edna O'Brien

A seemingly confident but deeply insecure young girl, Baba is not academically successful, but has developed a sharp, acerbic verbal wit. From a very unconventional home, she is unsure of her parents' love for each other and for her. Baba is deeply jealous of her friend KATE BRADY, but this is manifested as contempt. She has a lack of regard for her health and moral well-being, but is nonetheless a very sad and likeable person.

Brennan, Joseph
Wild Decembers, 1999
Edna O'Brien

As the Brennan family has farmed the same land in the west of Ireland for generations, Joseph feels as if he is the rightful custodian of much of the countryside thereabouts. When MICK BUGLER arrives to take possession of nearby family land, Brennan is intensely suspicious. Brennan is fundamentally a decent man, but, as 'the warring sons of warring sons', he and Bugler are soon in dispute. According to Brennan, the land, 'the storehouse of our past', is as vital as life itself and one has a duty to be as true to the land as to one's family. But when it appears that his younger sister, Breege, has broken this code by falling in love with his adversary, Brennan's resentment of Bugler and outrage against Breege's treachery result in his savagely beating her. Thus, it is Brennan, and not the newcomer Bugler, who eventually feels 'outside everyone and everything'.

Brer Fox
Uncle Remus, 1880
Joel Chandler Harris

A selfish, greedy and wholly malicious animal. Naturally, these traits help to get him deeper into trouble than he could have imagined. Most of the time, the trouble is a result of his desire to 'git' BRER RABBIT for any number of offences, most of which have to do with being made to look a fool.

Brer Rabbit
Uncle Remus, 1880
Joel Chandler Harris

Brer Rabbit delights in helping his fellow 'creeturs' make fools of themselves. He is not malicious in his actions, but can be cruel in driving home his point. He never sets out to harm someone deliberately; if their greed or selfishness gets them into a mess, it is not his fault.

Bretton, Dr John
Villette, 1853
Charlotte Brontë

The tall, handsome doctor at MADAME BECK's school, Dr John is also the son of LUCY SNOWE's godmother. Kind, generous, and even-tempered, he is, however, not the most intuitive of people, and for a long time fails to see GINEVRA FANSHAWE – the object of his infatuation – for the selfish, unpleasant person she is. Once enlightened as to her real nature, however, he finds loving respite for his gentle sensitivity in his childhood friend, PAULINE HOME.

Breuer, Esther
The Radiant Way, 1987
A Natural Curiosity, 1989
The Gates of Ivory, 1991
Margaret Drabble

Esther, ALIX BOWEN and LIZ HEADLEAND are old friends, having been students together at Cambridge during the 1950s. Esther has arguably taken the most risks, eschewing the security of possessions and family. Still single, she lives 'just off the wrong end of Ladbroke Grove' and bumps precariously along, making a living from occasional articles and lectures on art history. She, like the other women, is open to the gales and calms of the 1980s. She is cautious, perhaps timid, yet she is not dismayed by finding that things do not become clearer with middle-age, but derives sustenance from the fact that new prospects continually seem to beckon.

Brewster-Wright, Ronald and **Marion**
Absurd Person Singular, 1972
Alan Ayckbourn

Ronald, a bank manager, is remote and condescending, and Marion, supercilious and patronizing. Apparently secure at the summit of the provincial social and professional pyramid, they look upon the dreadful SIDNEY and JANE HOPCROFT with amused boredom and watch the emotional disaster of GEOFFREY and EVA JACKSON with indifference and incomprehension. Yet, underneath, their own marriage is decrepit.

Brewton, Brock
The Sea of Grass, 1937
Conrad Richter

The son of COL BREWTON and LUTIE CAMERON BREWTON. His startling blonde hair links him inextricably to his absent mother but the burning eyes are his father's and his wildness and eventual death as an outlaw make a pointed comment on his parents' widely diverging attitudes to the land and the life of the American south-west.

Brewton, Col
The Sea of Grass, 1937
Conrad Richter

The uncle of the book's narrator Hal, he is like 'some rude territorial czar', a figure of tremendous power and determination. He marries and loses the elegant LUTIE CAMERON BREWTON and fathers the wild and irrepressible BROCK BREWTON.

Brewton, Lutie Cameron
The Sea of Grass, 1937
Conrad Richter

A Missourian girl, thrown into the 'rude and uncongenial realities' of life in the American south-west, where she marries COL BREWTON. Delicate but full of spirit, she is presented as the quintessential civilizer, a bringer of culture to the rough frontier. She keeps her eyes averted from the endless sea of grass and shutters her garden off from the outstretched plain with climbing plants.

Bri
A Day in the Death of Joe Egg, 1967
Peter Nichols

The husband of SHEILA and father of JOE, a mentally handicapped girl, Bri is 33 and a teacher at a secondary modern school. Restless, prone to self-pity and inertia, anxious for attention, he treats the ten-year-old Joe as a two-year-old when the family is together, and as an adult unable to reply when alone with her. He lives from one day to the next ('I can't sustain a passion to the end of the sentence'), and because he has little idea of how Sheila feels about anything, guesses which responses might appeal to her and makes them. Marriage, Joe and teaching have stultified him. As he says, 'I just go through the motions now.'

Briana
The Faerie Queene, 1590–6
Sir Edmund Spenser

A strong, forward and determined lady, she is the prospective lover of Crudor, a cruel, disdainful and proud knight. He will only love her if she weaves him a mantle that is lined with the beards of Lords and the locks of Ladies. She has employed Maleffort, or 'evil attempt', a man of great strength, to cut off the locks of passing gentry.

Bridehead, Sue (Susannah)
Jude the Obscure, 1895
Thomas Hardy

A 19th-century 'new-woman', Sue is a complex, contradictory character whose masochistic and narcissistic tendencies conspire to make her life, and consequently those of her lovers, miserable. Hardy himself described her as an 'intellectualized, emancipated bundle of nerves'. She marries schoolteacher RICHARD PHILLOTSON out of a sense of duty but leaves to be with her cousin JUDE FAWLEY, to whom she is as much an unobtainable ideal as his dream of becoming a university man. She refuses to make their illicit relationship legal, seemingly because if married she would feel obliged to yield to sex with Jude; while unmarried, she can withhold as often as she wishes. The deaths of her children affect her deeply, extinguishing her rebellious ardour and leading her to return to Phillotson.

Brideshead, Lord ('Bridey')
Brideshead Revisited, 1945
Evelyn Waugh

The devoutly Catholic son of LORD MARCHMAIN, he is educated at Stonyhurst and Oxford. Despite talk of entering Parliament, the army and monastic life, he is 'completely without action in all his years of adult life' and leads a feudal, introspective existence at Brideshead, where he is Joint-Master of the local hunt and dreads social events. Prematurely heavy and bald, he speaks with gravity, indifference and restraint and seems older than his years. He becomes a renowned collector of matchboxes and marries Mrs Beryl Muspratt, the widow of a fellow collector. Disinherited by Lord Marchmain, who detests Beryl, he ends up in Palestine fighting in the Yeomanry.

Bridge, Mr
Mrs Bridge, 1959
Mr Bridge, 1969
Evan S Connell

Staid, humourless attorney Walter Bridge conceals inarticulate passion, but gives shares as Christmas gifts. He finds his troubling family a mystery, although he works himself into the grave for them. His values are 'financial security, independence and self-respect' and emotion does not enter his world. Quick to assess matters on immediate evidence, his power is such that he can stop a hold-up or his wife's fainting by force of will – 'don't be ridiculous'.

Bridge, Mrs
Mrs Bridge, 1959
Mr Bridge, 1969
Evan S Connell

Despite her unusual name, India Bridge is a typical Kansas City matron in the period before World War II. Acutely aware of awkward issues such as colour, poverty and her children's puberty, she meticulously avoids conflict: for her, etiquette is supreme. She judges people by their shoes and table manners and is puzzled by the gulf she feels between others' behaviour and her own. Finally widowed and alone, she is trapped by her inability to manoeuvre her car.

Bridgenorth, Alfred → Chelsea, Bishop of

Bridgenorth, Alice
Peveril of the Peak, 1823
Sir Walter Scott

Her birth is clouded by the death of her mother, as a result of which MAJOR BRIDGENORTH finds it impossible to accept her. She is taken in by Lady Peveril and becomes a playmate for young JULIAN PEVERIL until her father is reconciled to her existence.

Bridgenorth, Edith
Getting Married, 1908
George Bernard Shaw

A daughter of the BISHOP OF CHELSEA, Edith is outspoken and dogmatic, 'an ethical snob of the first water'. As guests arrive at the Bishop's Palace for her wedding to CECIL SYKES, she refuses to go to the church, having read that should her husband turn out to be a madman, murderer, forger or thief, she cannot be released from her vows. But while ST JOHN HOTCHKISS proposes drawing up a partnership deed instead, and the guests bicker, Edith and Cecil slip away and marry in an empty church, resolving to let the future take care of itself.

Bridgenorth, Gen 'Boxer'
Getting Married, 1908
George Bernard Shaw

A brother of the BISHOP OF CHELSEA and an uncle of EDITH BRIDGENORTH, the general is a distinguished, much decorated military man of 50 with a firm jaw. He is also 'ignorant, stupid and prejudiced, having been carefully trained to be so'. For years he has been hopelessly in love with LESBIA GRANTHAM, his sister-in-law, who repeatedly refuses his proposals of marriage. His is the crusty, cantankerous voice of conventional values.

Bridgenorth, Leo
Getting Married, 1908
George Bernard Shaw

Young, pretty, fussing, selfish and vain, Leo has persuaded her husband, REGINALD BRIDGENORTH, to grant her a divorce so that she might marry ST JOHN HOTCHKISS, a man nearer her own age, who amuses her. She imagines herself a thinker, although her thought is shallow. During the debate over whether EDITH BRIDGENORTH and CECIL SYKES should enter into a partnership deed, Leo announces that she would be willing to enter into an alliance with both Reginald and Hotchkiss. Later, she returns to Reginald.

Bridgenorth, Major
Peveril of the Peak, 1823
Sir Walter Scott

Though raised as a schoolfellow of SIR GEOFFREY PEVERIL, he is unable to embrace the Royalist cause and lends his support to Parliament during the Civil War. He is wounded bitterly by his wife's death in childbirth and finds it impossible to accept his baby daughter, ALICE BRIDGENORTH, an attitude that contrasts sharply with the warm paternalism of Sir Geoffrey.

Bridgenorth, Reginald
Getting Married, 1908
George Bernard Shaw

The eldest brother of Alfred Bridgenorth, the BISHOP OF CHELSEA, Reginald is 'hardened and tough physically', but 'hasty and boyish in manner and speech'. Essentially, he is a man who needs mothering, but LEO BRIDGENORTH, the young woman he marries, is not prepared to do so. Instead, she falls in love with ST JOHN HOTCHKISS and Reginald, muddled, forgetful, untidy and ill at ease with both women and marriage, submits with some relief to a divorce. They are later reconciled.

Bridget
Plagued by the Nightingale, 1931
Kay Boyle

A nondescript young American woman who has married NICOLAS, a Frenchman. They are staying with his generally dreadful and clinging family in Brittany, because of his illness. She cannot speak much French, but she is glad to be part of this clannish group, her own relatives having seen each other as free individuals. She loves Nicolas and wants to have his child, but his behaviour alienates her.

Bridie
'The Ballroom of Romance', in *The Ballroom of Romance and Other Stories*, 1972
William Trevor

An Irish spinster of 36, who looks after her one-legged farmer father following her mother's death. Tall, strong and weather-beaten, she escapes from the farm each Saturday night to a dance-hall, the Ballroom of Romance. The man she loved married another and the decent road-mender she wants for a husband is about to do the same, so, suppressing her emotions as usual, she reconciles herself to marrying eventually a shiftless, drunken, middle-aged bachelor, Bowser Egan.

Briennius, Nicephorus
Count Robert of Paris, 1831
Sir Walter Scott

The husband of ANNA COMNENA, much admired by the historian Gibbon, but who never managed to attain the imperial throne which Anna tried to manoeuvre for him. In the novel, he seems ill-disposed toward his frailties, which lead him to treason and a sentence of death, from which he is eventually pardoned.

Brierly, Henry (Harry)
The Gilded Age, 1873
Mark Twain and Charles Dudley Warner

Infected by the feverish get-rich-quick ethos of the post-Civil War boom, happy-go-lucky Brierly naively embarks on a career in land and railroad speculation, seeing it as an easy road to the acquisition of a fortune. Instead, he receives a sobering lesson in the corrupt politics of the Reconstruction and begins his pained, slavish

devotion to the captivating but unobtainable LAURA HAWKINS.

Briggs
The Virgin Soldiers, 1966
Leslie Thomas

Briggs is innocent and a little scared as he is swallowed up by the experience of National Service. He finds it cruel and terrifying, yet in the camaraderie of shared experience, he develops friendships that are deeper than those that he would otherwise have encountered. His youthful exploration of sex and his wide-eyed innocence as he meets the exotic world of the mysterious East place him in hilarious tight spots and steamy relationships, in which he learns about his sexuality and the pain of loving. Thus, he matures from nervous youth to full manhood.

Briggs, Miss
Hotel de Dream, 1976
Emma Tennant

The alcoholic Miss Briggs spent her childhood in India, homesick for an England hardly ever seen, and now longs for 'power and tropics to control'. She escapes the harsh reality of her life in the seedy Westringham hotel in sleep, and has a recurring dream of being singled out by the Queen to be her personal aide in a 'Silent Revolution' that will restore traditional values and worship of God to an England where 'defeat, poverty and apathy' reign.

Brigstock, Mona
The Spoils of Poynton, 1897
Henry James

The fiancée of OWEN GERETH, much to the chagrin of his mother, MRS GERETH, who dislikes the girl (and of Owen himself, who falls in love with FLEDA VETCH). The heiress to Waterbath, she is coarse and lacking in aesthetic judgement; the critic Gorley Putt describes her as 'hockey-mistressy'. When Mrs Gereth moves out of Poynton to make way for the young couple, taking all the house's treasures with her, Mona shows an unsuspected acquisitive and tough-minded side.

Brill, Miss
Miss Brill, 1922
Katherine Mansfield

A spinster and teacher of English abroad, whose absorbing occupation is to visit the Jardins Publiques every Sunday. One of life's watchers, she thinks herself an active participant. As witness to cameo relationships, she makes quick, superficial judgements by analysing external behaviour and constructing imaginary lives. When she overhears a similar conversation referring to herself, her little joy is extinguished.

Briscoe, Lily
To the Lighthouse, 1927
Virginia Woolf

She is an artistic and sensitive girl, unpretentious, caring and well-liked, but described by MRS RAMSAY as being of a rather odd appearance. She is set apart by her independence of spirit but above all by her clear-sightedness; whereas others around her are caught up in their own worlds, Lily has the ability to observe, and to analyse what she sees.

Brisk, Fastidious
Every Man out of his Humour, 1599
Ben Jonson

A fussy courtier and flamboyantly-dressed man of fashion, his appearance impresses FUNGOSO and FALLACE, who falls in love with him. A man of astonishing appearance but little substance, Brisk is eventually thrust into prison on account of his debts, from where he admits the foolishness of slavishly following fashion.

Britain, Benjamin
The Battle of Life, 1846
Charles Dickens

The manservant of DR ANTHONY JEDDLER, he is bemused by Jeddler's cheerful cynicism and has developed an 'uncommonly sour and discontented face'. He is rescued from desolation by CLEMENCY NEWCOME, whom he marries, and they become owners of The Nutmeg Grater Inn, where he is known as 'Little Britain'.

Britannus
Caesar and Cleopatra, 1898
George Bernard Shaw

Aged about 40, tall, solemn and slightly balding, Britannus is a Briton acting as secretary to CAESAR, who often calls him Britannicus as a little joke. Britannus's seriousness and almost overwhelming sense of the historical importance of the events about him are, however, impervious to comedy. He is, though, a thoroughly modern Englishman, and by maintaining the audience's awareness of the present, his behaviour suggests that no discernible progress in human affairs has been made in the world since ancient times.

Britling, Mr
Mr Britling Sees It Through, 1916
H G Wells

A small, casually-dressed intellectual Essex man, Britling has progressed from Pembroke and prize poems to writing third leaders for *The Times*. Vigorous at womanizing, hockey and, above all, talking politics, he fails to predict World War I. He tries to make up for this by allowing his son to go, fight and die and by theorizing total war in place of what has been the gentleman's pastime of the previous century.

Britomart
The Faerie Queene, 1590–6
Sir Edmund Spenser

Her name is taken from a union of the words Britain and Mars (or 'martial'). She represents chastity. Pure from blame, lust and sin, she dresses as a knight, having been brought up in the ways of a male warrior. Her quest is to seek the lover she has seen in a magic looking-glass (ARTEGALL, THE KNIGHT OF JUSTICE). Her destiny is to secure the future for her children. She has a constant, dedicated mind and does not stray from her chosen path.

Broadbent, Tom (Thomas)
John Bull's Other Island, 1904
George Bernard Shaw

An energetic, ebullient Englishman 'in the prime of life', Broadbent is confident, credulous, 'buoyant and irresistible'. An unimaginative man, he reduces everything to its most mundane and severely practical level. He is a man of action for whom the world is divided into the efficient and inefficient. In Shaw's terms, Broadbent is the essential philistine. A civil engineer in partnership with LARRY DOYLE, he travels to Ireland intending to build a hotel. Romantically in love with everything Irish, he is soon engaged to NORA REILLY, and asked to contest the next general election. Despite the forebodings of PETER KEEGAN he proceeds with his development plans.

Brobdingnagians
Gulliver's Travels, 1726
Jonathan Swift

This is the second race that LEMUEL GULLIVER comes into contact with. The Brobdingnagians exist in contrast to the LILLIPUTIANS. Whereas the Lilliputians are small, the Brobdingnagians are huge. A race of wise and noble giants, they are ignorant of and opposed to the ways of war, and pronounce human beings 'the most pernicious Race of little odious Vermin that Nature ever suffered to crawl on the Surface of the Earth'.

Brocklehurst, Mr
Jane Eyre, 1847
Charlotte Brontë

The grim-faced, fanatically puritanical head of Lowood school, clergyman Mr Brocklehurst rules it with an iron fist, maintaining that privation and hardship are essential to the edification of the girls in residence – but not apparently to that of his own daughters, whose lavish habits he seems to indulge. He is particularly unkind to JANE EYRE, but being little-liked at Lowood, his accusations are scarcely heeded, and a severe outbreak of typhus at the school forces the relaxation of his severest rules.

Brodie, James
Hatter's Castle, 1931
A J Cronin

A brutal, arrogant hat retailer who lives in an absurd castle-like house. He is a domestic tyrant, and is feared in the town. He is physically strong and hot-tempered, and lacks any redeeming conscience or sense of moral responsibility, being interested only in domination and self-gratification. He deludes himself about his invulnerable supremacy, but his overweening pride and self-destructive behaviour plunge him into a futile and ignominious decline, and ultimate abandonment.

Brodie, Miss Jean
The Prime of Miss Jean Brodie, 1961
Muriel Spark

An inspiring but morally flawed Edinburgh schoolmistress, in her prime from 1930 to 1939. Believing that teachers should 'lead out' what is in their pupils, she dispenses with most normal school subjects. She disapproves of the team spirit, yet establishes her own 'Brodie set' of six girls. She claims they are her vocation, but is so self-centred that she tries to use them to solve her personal problems. Although devoted to Beauty and Art, she admires Hitler and Mussolini. She has a 'dark Roman profile' and a taste for grandiloquence. Open-minded in some ways, she is convinced of her own rectitude; SANDY STRANGER thinks she has 'elected herself to grace'.

Bromden, Chief
One Flew Over the Cuckoo's Nest, 1962
Ken Kesey

The narrator, an Indian whose father was the last chief of their tribe. He is a massive, physically powerful man who has chosen to be a quiescent inmate of a mental institution, rather than face the world outside. He pretends to be dumb, again by choice, and sees the institution as being like a cartoon, which might 'be real funny if it weren't for the cartoon figures being real guys'. RANDLE PATRICK MCMURPHY's example gives him the strength (metaphorical and physical) to escape.

Bronowsky, Count (Dmitri)
The Jewel in the Crown, 1966
The Day of the Scorpion, 1968
The Towers of Silence, 1971
A Division of the Spoils, 1975, forming *The Raj Quartet*
Paul Scott

The influential and devoted vizier to the Nawab of Mirat. A Russian emigré brought from Monte Carlo in the 1920s to modernize Mirat, the charmingly urbane and dandyish homosexual, poetry-loving Count claims that an anarchist's bomb in St Petersburg was responsible for his lame leg and blind eye, over which he wears a rakish black patch. To British approval, he has successfully transformed what was a feudal autocracy into a semi-democratic state. At 70, he shrewdly plans to train his protégé, AHMED KASIM, to succeed him, seeing him also as a suitable husband for the Nawab's daughter.

Bronzomarte
The Life and Adventures of Sir Launcelot Greaves, 1760–1
Tobias Smollett

SIR LAUNCELOT GREAVES's horse, a heroic and noble creature, likened to Orlando's magical horses in Torquato Tasso's epic *Gerusalemme Liberata*.

Brook, Rhoda
'The Withered Arm', in *Wessex Tales: Strange, Lively and Commonplace*, 1888
Thomas Hardy

A tormented 'woman scorned', Rhoda seems to have a supernatural ability to bring harm to her rival, Gertrude Lodge, but finds this power disconcerting and becomes sympathetic to the woman who ought to be her enemy. A complex and sad figure, she remains respectable and dignified in spite of losing everything she ever loves.

Brooke, Celia
Middlemarch, 1871–2
George Eliot

The more conventional, in looks and manner, of the two Brooke sisters, Celia, unlike DOROTHEA BROOKE, is content to accept unquestioningly her untroubled, financially privileged existence and is secretly concerned about her sister's ardent religiosity. Governed by her practicality and material concerns, she marries SIR JAMES CHETTAM and, while remaining a kind and loving sister to Dorothea, is largely preoccupied by her status in society.

Brooke, Dorothea
Middlemarch, 1871–2
George Eliot

Puritanically devout, Dorothea, despite being rich and very beautiful, rejects fine clothes and material wealth. Initially naive, short-sighted and idealistic, she believes that her marriage to REV EDWARD CASAUBON will fulfil her intellectual and spiritual aspirations but, disillusioned by the realities of her situation, she finds herself increasingly drawn towards Casaubon's cousin, WILL LADISLAW. Generous, caring and almost saint-like in her social awareness, her most important achievement is her repudiation of egoism in recognition of the 'equivalent centre of self' in others.

Brooke, John
Little Women, 1868
Good Wives, 1869
Little Men, 1871
Jo's Boys, 1886
Louisa M Alcott

Tutor to LAURIE, his quiet grave manners win him the respect and love of the whole March family. His gentlemanly assistance to Mrs March (MARMEE), his admiration for MEG MARCH's independence and hard work and his almost feminine patience and generosity mean as much as his handsome brown eyes. Declared 'only good' on his sudden early death, his honourable ideals continue in his children, DEMI-JOHN and DAISY, as well as in their influence on his friends.

Brooke, Mr
Middlemarch, 1871–2
George Eliot

The penny-pinching, land-owning uncle and guardian of DOROTHEA and CELIA BROOKE. Though to a certain extent harmless in his ill-informed ramblings, he is nevertheless most definitely at fault in setting himself up as a Liberal reformer while remaining pitifully blind to the poverty in which his tenants are forced to live. Unable to think clearly for any length of time, this and his general lack of perception combine to ruin both his ownership of the *Pioneer* newspaper and his political ambitions.

Brookenham, Nanda
The Awkward Age, 1899
Henry James

A young woman who has just been 'brought out' of childhood and into the marriage market, where she immediately finds herself her own mother's rival for the attentions of a young civil servant, Vanderbank. Precociously sophisticated, she resists the proposals of her friend Mitchett and eventually accepts the uncondescending patronage of Mr Longdon, who sees her as a reincarnation of her grandmother, brought up to date. If the title refers to Nanda's position between childhood and adulthood, it also refers to a society poised between treating her as a commodity and recognizing her impressive individuality.

Brooks, Sgt
Rusty Bugles, 1948
Sumner Locke Elliott

An unfriendly and humourless soldier at a wartime ordnance depot in the Australian Northern Territory. He is interested only in his work, spending his leisure time conversing about the regimental accounting system. Regarded as a 'crawler' because of his conformism, he is a petty tyrant to lower ranks.

Browdie, John
Nicholas Nickleby, 1839
Charles Dickens

An honest Yorkshire corn-factor, he is betrothed to Matilda Price and is initially jealous of NICHOLAS NICKLEBY, with whom she flirts. But he and Nicholas become good friends, and he helps SMIKE to escape after he has been captured by WACKFORD SQUEERS. Later, he gallantly prevents the pupils at Dotheboys Hall from taking revenge on Mrs Squeers and her children after Squeers has been arrested. He eventually marries Matilda.

Brown
The Comedians, 1966
Graham Greene

The narrator, he is a lapsed Catholic and con artist, who sees life as a cynical comedy, not the tragedy which he had once expected. It is only his sense of humour which enables him sometimes still to believe in a god. As one of life's 'comedians', he is an accomplished dissembler and mercenary, able to suppress his real thoughts, while uncovering those of others: he is the ideal confessor and informer. His one true love affair has left him sceptical and disillusioned, believing in the necessity of evil. His life is now dedicated to self-preservation, but beneath his hard exterior lurks a frightening hurt.

Brown, Arthur
The Solid Mandala, 1966
Patrick White

The twin brother of the embittered clerk, WALDO BROWN, Arthur is mentally retarded. Yet whereas Waldo represses his emotions, Arthur responds to other people and the world about him with an intuitive, almost child-like candour. Certainly, he has a greater capacity for love. To people such as their neighbour, MRS POULTER, the brothers appear an eccentric couple, Waldo uncommunicative, Arthur spontaneous. Arthur becomes the dominant twin, invading his brother's life and unconsciously usurping his dreams. Arthur's four glass marbles, his most treasured possessions, represent to him the

divine secret of life. But even his imagination cannot save him: maddened by Waldo's hatred, he is eventually taken to an institution.

Brown, Berenice Sadie
The Member of the Wedding, 1946
Carson McCullers

A black cook employed by the Addams household, whose appearance is given a curious dimension by her blue glass eye. A wise and generous character, she is the strongest adult presence in FRANKIE ADDAMS's life and provides her with both love and scolding. Her personal history is marked by misfortune and injustice; she is preoccupied with the subject of the past and its themes of lost love, domestic violence and racial oppression.

Brown, Father
The Innocence of Father Brown, 1911
G K Chesterton

A Roman Catholic priest whose deep knowledge of the human soul makes him an outstanding amateur detective. In contrast to another great fictional sleuth, SHERLOCK HOLMES, he proceeds primarily by insight and intuition rather than logical deduction, and is an unflamboyant man. With a face 'as dull as a Norfolk dumpling' and eyes 'empty as the North Sea', he has such an unassuming, almost comical, appearance that he is invariably underestimated by the guilty – to their cost.

Brown, Goodman
'Young Goodman Brown', 1835, in *Mosses From an Old Manse*, 1846
Nathaniel Hawthorne

A young man of Salem who communes with dark forces and repents too late to save himself from losing Faith, his symbolically named wife. His name is really no more specific than 'Mr So-and-So', but there was controversy in Puritan circles as to whether 'goodman' could be applied to the unregenerate; in Brown's case, it is clearly intended to be ironic and ambiguous.

Brown, Ingrid → Rothwell, Ingrid

Brown, Jenny
Ship of Fools, 1962
Katherine Anne Porter

Aboard a liner to Europe in 1931 with lover, DAVID SCOTT, Jenny, a young American book-illustrator, considers leaving him and their cruel, almost continuous verbal warfare. The insular David grimly refuses to share anything at all with her or anyone else. This is a wounding affront to her joyous, extrovert friendliness and warm interest in people. But worse, he has gradually destroyed her confidence by belittling her, and leading her to change her colourful art and personal appearance. For Jenny, 'love' is tenderness, faithfulness, gaiety and goodness of heart to the beloved, with sex a natural part of it, but David forbids even the use of the word.

Brown, Johnnie
Johnnie Sahib, 1952
Paul Scott

A Cockney former office-boy who as a World War

II captain in Bengal works to establish the first ever air-supply units. Unconventional and charismatic, he provides his fellow-officers with excitement, and seems god-like to his Indian troops. But to his superiors he is a 'one-man awkward squad': a misfit impossible to control, constantly baulking at new orders and arrangements. The war is Johnnie's big chance to shine, but only the peculiar, relatively lax circumstances of this pioneering project make him seem a commanding figure. He is actually a bad leader – arrogant, reckless, selfish and immature, pathetically unable to accept necessary change as the war nears its end.

Brown, Kate
The Summer Before the Dark, 1973
Doris Lessing

After a stagnant family life, Kate experiments with ideas in an attempt to fill a void deep within her. She is extremely vulnerable, afraid of life, and confrontation. Overly accommodating, she achieves pleasure vicariously. Intelligent and sensitive, Kate rejects stereotypes of femininity, and on a journey of self-discovery she loses her inhibitions and begins to understand herself.

Brown, Laura
The Hours, 1998
Michael Cunningham

A pregnant young housewife in 1949 Los Angeles, married to a man she doesn't love, mother to a three-year-old boy whose devotion she cannot return, she feels trapped. Always a bookworm and solitary by nature, she seeks escape in immersing herself in Virginia Woolf's *Mrs Dalloway*. Struggling to connect with her ordinary life, she decides 'she will not mourn her lost possibilities, her unexplored talents', but her longing to be free leads her to flirt with suicide.

Brown, Mrs
Dombey and Son, 1848
Charles Dickens

Called by herself 'Good Mrs Brown', she is an ugly old beggar and thief who robs FLORENCE DOMBEY of her clothes and turns her into the street in rags. As a young woman, she was seduced by the uncle of EDITH DOMBEY and gave birth to ALICE MARWOOD, Edith's cousin. With Alice, she takes revenge on Alice's seducer, JAMES CARKER, by using ROBIN TOODLE to reveal to MR DOMBEY that his wife and Carker are eloping to Dijon.

Brown, Recktall
The Recognitions, 1955
William Gaddis

An art collector and not quite legitimate dealer who markets WYATT GWYON's forgeries as if they were the genuine article. His name has been linked (by Gaddis's leading critic Steven Moore) to the anal-retentiveness Freud associated with acquisitive types and collectors; it may also suggest a hint of pederasty in Brown's make-up. Like Goethe's Mephistopheles, he is followed by a small black poodle.

Brown, Tom
Tom Brown's Schooldays, 1857
Tom Brown at Oxford, 1861
Thomas Hughes

Tom Brown's adventures at Rugby public school take place during the 1830s, when the author was himself at Rugby and Dr Thomas Arnold was the revered, reforming headmaster. Tom, a squire's son, comes from 'a fighting family', competitive and quixotic. He epitomizes a code of living – tough, compassionate, patriotic, loyal, clean, fair-minded, liberal – that came to be known as 'muscular Christianity', and which Hughes believed the public schools could exemplify. Tom's enemy is the tyrannical HARRY FLASHMAN, over whom he eventually triumphs.

Brown, Velvet
National Velvet, 1935
Enid Bagnold

The youngest daughter of a rural Sussex butcher, Velvet is 14, with 'short pale hair, large protruding teeth, a sweet smile and a mouthful of metal'. She and the Browns represent an ideal English middle class; Mr Brown is rather retiring while Mrs Brown is a tower of vigour and efficiency around which the family rallies. Velvet is cast in her image. In a raffle she wins a horse, which turns out to be a natural jumper. Disguised as a jockey, she rides to victory in the Grand National steeplechase. Only when she collapses with exhaustion after the race is it discovered that she is a girl. Her win is declared void, but for Velvet, the achievement is all, and her conviction that life must go on is enough to smother any fleeting disappointment.

Brown, Vic (Victor)
A Kind of Loving, 1960
Stan Barstow

The novel's first-person narrator, he bares his soul with candour. A conventional upbringing within a family he deeply respects has instilled in him a set of moral absolutes which conflict with what he perceives as his own hedonistic inclinations. As a consequence he is constantly left feeling appalled by his own double standards. A voracious reader, music-lover and day-dreamer, he desperately wants to 'better' himself, but without denying the principles he sees in honest working folk. Ironically, it is his unimaginative wife INGRID ROTHWELL who describes him most accurately, referring to him as 'an upside-down snob'.

Brown, Waldo
The Solid Mandala, 1966
Patrick White

The twin brother of ARTHUR BROWN, Waldo is fastidious, studious and, in marked contrast to his almost child-like brother, intensely self-conscious. He has literary ambitions and believes that marriage to DULCIE FEINSTEIN will not only liberate him from Arthur, but also create the necessary conditions for authorship to flourish. But Dulcie turns him down and he fails to publish. Neither does he ever discover the 'intellectual companions with whom to exchange the Everyman classics and play Schubert after tea'. Resentful of his mounting failures, and of the backward Arthur who dogs his life at every turn, Waldo bitterly resigns himself to a career as a clerk and an interior life of seedy fantasy and self-disgust.

Brown, William A
The Great God Brown, 1926
Eugene O'Neill

A successful businessman, portrayed as the 'visionless demigod of our new materialistic myth', lacking any inner depth or emotional substance. Like the other characters, he adopts a series of masks to suggest his protean, almost amoebic nature.

Browne, Coral
An Englishman Abroad, television version 1983, stage version 1988
Alan Bennett

An historical figure appropriated by Bennett, the actress Coral Browne met GUY BURGESS while she was appearing in Moscow in 1956. Their encounter forms the basis for the play. Coral is presented as engaging, good-humoured, wry, someone not easily fooled, especially not by such a charmer (albeit seedy) as Burgess. Her Australian birth has resulted in a detachment that might not be shared by someone English.

Browne, Morgan
A Fairly Honourable Defeat, 1970
Iris Murdoch

She is a philologist, who has left her husband, TALLIS BROWNE, to teach in America. An affair there with JULIUS KING and a subsequent abortion have exacerbated her mental and emotional instability and, in despair, she counts on her elder sister, HILDA FOSTER, to make her feel 'brave' and 'safe' again as she always has done. Hilda contends that her sister has a compulsive desire to give up the world as there is a 'fanatical nun tied up inside her'. But manipulated by Julius, Morgan disrupts the lives of Peter, SIMON, Hilda and RUPERT FOSTER.

Browne, Tallis
A Fairly Honourable Defeat, 1970
Iris Murdoch

Deserted by his wife, MORGAN BROWNE, Tallis meekly accepts her infidelity and hopes for her return. He lives in appalling squalor with his irascible, domineering father, and, having abandoned his book on Marx and de Tocqueville, lectures on trade unions and works unremittingly for the under-privileged. Although 'feeble', 'a spiritless muddler' and 'hopelessly incompetent', he shows aggressive courage in defending the victim of a violent racial attack. He also exerts a mysterious power over Morgan even when they are apart; and calmly turns the other cheek to her destructive lover, JULIUS KING.

Brownlow, Mr
Oliver Twist, 1838
Charles Dickens

A good-hearted gentleman who befriends OLIVER TWIST after his wrongful arrest as a pickpocket and continues to have faith in him despite his suspicious disappearance. His housekeeper, Mrs

Bedwin, nurses Oliver through his fever, but his irascible though kind friend, Mr Grimwig, has less confidence in the boy's integrity. After MRS MAYLIE helps to reunite them, he discovers that Oliver is the son and beneficiary of an old friend. He recovers the inheritance from Oliver's half-brother, EDWARD LEEFORD (known as 'Monks') and adopts Oliver as his son.

Bruno, Charles Anthony
Strangers on a Train, 1950
Patricia Highsmith

A spoilt, rich psychopath, neither young nor old, who is the Mephistophelean heart of this wicked story. With his degenerate face and vulgar dress, he exudes the heavy scent of decadence, and intuitively lures GUY HAINES, his innocent victim, into complicity in murder – the killing of Guy's wife in exchange for that of his own father. Bruno is a gross, slothful character, dangerously juvenile, and unpleasantly memorable: an archetypal mummy's boy, whose interest in Guy is also implicitly sexual. Although his code of conduct is inverted, Bruno is, ironically, the only truly honest character in the novel.

Brute, Lady
The Provok'd Wife, 1696
Sir John Vanbrugh

The provoked wife of the title, Lady Brute is unhappily married to the blundering SIR JOHN BRUTE. Admittedly, she is not entirely blameless, as she married him not for love but for his estate, thinking that money would bring her contentment. She was wrong, and the relationship has deteriorated into mutual hostility. Disgruntled and further humiliated by her husband, Lady Brute considers an adulterous affair with CONSTANT, who has long been making overtures to her. But, after pondering and speculating, she draws back, wary of defying convention.

Brute, Sir John
The Provok'd Wife, 1696
Sir John Vanbrugh

Sir John has married LADY BRUTE, the title's provoked wife, mainly for erotic pleasure; she, on the other hand, has married him for his money. Frustrated, and disliking his wife more and more, Sir John does his best to humiliate her and her niece, BELLINDA, and seeks respite with the rakes of the town. He drinks, he carouses, he gets into scrapes, once stealing a set of clothes from a tailor. Boorish and misogynistic, he finally turns a rather improbable new leaf, promising to lead a better life.

Brutus, Decius
Julius Caesar, c.1599
William Shakespeare

A cynical character aware of JULIUS CAESAR's weaknesses: superstition and love of flattery. He manages by his cunning to 'interpret' CALPURNIA's dream on the eve of the Ides of March and ensures that Caesar will be present at the Capitol by tempting him with the offer of the crown and suggesting that his absence would reveal him as unfit for high office.

Brutus, Junius
Coriolanus, c.1607/8
William Shakespeare

He and SICINIUS VELUTUS are the two Tribunes of the People firmly opposed to the election of CORIOLANUS as consul. A skilful manipulator of the mob, Brutus astutely reads Coriolanus's character and engineers his trial. But he is a coward, and faced with the necessity for real action to save Rome he panics and relies on the patricians he despises to act for him.

Brutus, Marcus
Julius Caesar, c.1599
William Shakespeare

A political idealist who believes that all men are as honourable as he is. His republicanism and hatred of tyranny persuade him, after much searching of his conscience, that although JULIUS CAESAR poses no immediate threat the only way to save Rome is to assassinate him. His honesty blinds him to the wiles of the other conspirators – he is no match for the politically more practical CAIUS CASSIUS and later seriously underestimates the ability of ANTONY. Faced with defeat he dies honourably by his own sword, respected by his enemies: 'This was the noblest Roman of them all'.

Bryant, Beatie
Roots, 1959
Arnold Wesker

The daughter of East Anglian agricultural labourers, she returns home after living in London. Vital, intelligent but uneducated, she has rejected popular culture and brims with artistic and political ideas learned from RONNIE KAHN, her lover. Her vocabulary and passion meet parental bewilderment. Jilted by Ronnie, she turns upon her family with a blistering tirade, attacking their conservatism and their timidity. She then realizes these emotions are not Ronnie's but her own, and that she has stumbled upon her intellectual and emotional independence. 'I'm beginning', she cries jubilantly. *'I'm beginning!'*

Bryant, Jill
The Year of Living Dangerously, 1978
C J Koch

A tough-minded but ultimately naive American journalist, working in Jakarta during the final days of the Sukarno regime. She becomes involved with GUY HAMILTON, but her life is also observed obsessively by the dwarfish photographer BILLY KWAN, who is also at least half in love with her.

Brydon, Spencer
'The Jolly Corner', 1908
Henry James

Returning to America after many years in Europe, he experiences 'the differences, the newnesses, the queernesses, above all the bignesses' of the place, the piquant things he had once snobbishly dismissed as vulgar. He also encounters his own ghostly double: himself as he would have been had he never left. He is thus a salutary reminder of the perils of a life lived according to acquired rather than 'natural' principles.

Buchanan, Daisy
The Great Gatsby, 1925
F Scott Fitzgerald

A Southern belle who was loved by JAY GATSBY when he was a younger man, but who has married TOM BUCHANAN for his wealth. Beautiful, with 'an excitement in her voice that men who had cared for her found difficult to forget', she is embittered by her husband's infidelities, but remains fun-loving and flirtatious despite her disillusion. She allows herself to enter into Gatsby's dream, but is quick to retreat into the shelter of Tom's wealth and their shared indifference after his death.

Buchanan, Tom
The Great Gatsby, 1925
F Scott Fitzgerald

A wealthy, 'sturdy, straw-haired man of thirty, with a rather hard mouth and a supercilious manner'. He is married to DAISY BUCHANAN, but is a womanizer and a drunkard, with a mistress, MYRTLE WILSON. He is arrogant, vain, racist and a snob, but coarsely handsome and physically powerful. He is unscrupulous and dishonest, but, perhaps as a result, sees through JAY GATSBY's polished veneer. A liar and hypocrite, he is subject to violent moods swings, but is also shrewd and cunning.

Buck
The Call of the Wild, 1903
Jack London

A St Bernard for whom existence in the harsh, unforgiving climate of the Klondike is savage and brutal, both man and environment conspiring to make his life miserable. Each new owner is as violent as the last and life as a sled-dog is shot through with small cruelties and deprivations. When John Thornton, the one human to show him kindness, is killed, Buck makes his bid for freedom, turning his back on humans to live in the wild, free at last from petty tyrants and undeserved beatings.

Bucket, Charlie → Charlie

Bucket, Mr
Bleak House, 1853
Charles Dickens

A persevering, affable and imperturbable detective officer, he is hired by MR TULKINGHORN to make enquiries about LADY DEDLOCK and then investigates Tulkinghorn's murder. Circumstances lead him to arrest MR GEORGE ROUNCEWELL, but with the help of his sagacious wife, he identifies MADEMOISELLE HORTENSE as the murderer. He is hired by SIR LEICESTER DEDLOCK to investigate the disappearance of Lady Dedlock and, with ESTHER SUMMERSON, he finds her body. Finally, he discovers GRANDFATHER SMALLWEED to be holding the will that settles the case of *Jarndyce* v *Jarndyce*.

Buckingham, Duke of
Richard III, 1592/3
William Shakespeare

Buckingham becomes RICHARD, DUKE OF GLOUCESTER's chief advocate, secretly at first, while apparently maintaining loyalty to Edward IV (EDWARD, EARL OF MARCH). If Buckingham shows a lack of moral judgement in supporting Richard, he does, arguably, demonstrate a measure of political perspicacity, although his tactlessness sometimes lets him down. He is wrong in believing he might be able to manipulate Richard, who seems always to have a clear sense of Buckingham's usefulness and limitations. Buckingham has influence and successfully engineers Richard's accession to the throne, but while he has colluded in the king's butchery, conscience causes him to hesitate when Richard declares that the princes must be killed. Conscience is Buckingham's downfall. He is executed and later makes a ghostly appearance, cursing Richard on the eve of the battle of Bosworth Field.

Buckingham, George Villiers, Duke of
The Fortunes of Nigel, 1822
Peveril of the Peak, 1823
Sir Walter Scott

A portrait of the historical duke, in *The Fortunes of Nigel* he is the quintessential courtier, adapting his manner and mood to the temperament of those he serves: to JAMES I OF ENGLAND's light-hearted foolishness and his son PRINCE CHARLES's melancholy. He is described as both 'commanding' and 'graceful', and there is no hint in his make-up of the unnatural vice with which history has charged him. Scott heads his second portrayal of Buckingham with eight damning lines by John Dryden and is himself notably stiffer on Villiers than in the first. 'Amid the gay and the licentious of the laughing court of Charles, the duke was the most licentious and most gay'; yet despite his apparent dedication to pleasure, he never deviates from his pursuit of political power and influence.

Bud, Rosa
The Mystery of Edwin Drood, 1870
Charles Dickens

A pretty, coquettish orphan and a pupil at MISS TWINKLETON's seminary. When she and EDWIN DROOD were children, they were betrothed to each other by their fathers. But as she approaches 18, Rosa and Drood realize they are not in love; they agree to break off their match and remain friends. MR JOHN JASPER, Drood's uncle, forces his attentions on Rosa, apparently exerting a mesmeric or hypnotic power over her. When Drood disappears, Rosa's terror of Jasper increases, and she flees to her guardian, MR HIRAM GREWGIOUS, in London.

Budd, Alfie
One for My Baby, 2001
Tony Parsons

After losing his wife in a diving accident in Hong Kong, lonely, insecure Alfie returns to his native England. Struggling to come to terms with his bereavement, his grandmother's terminal illness, and the shock of his father leaving to live with a younger woman, he seeks comfort in brief relationships with the girls he teaches at a language school. He derives deeper satisfaction and self-awareness from his friendship with the Chinese man who teaches him Tai Chi, and from

teaching a divorced single mother eager to resume her education.

Budd, Billy
Billy Budd, Foretopman, 1924
Herman Melville

A tall, handsome, 21-year-old sailor who is willingly pressed into service on a British warship. Known as 'Baby Budd', he is straightforward and amiable, with a 'genial happy-go-lucky air'. He is strong and athletic, but detests confrontations. He is naive as well as innocent, and an unconscious fatalist. When JOHN CLAGGART falsely accuses him, his nervous stammer prevents him from answering, and he strikes out, killing him. He is condemned to hang, but goes to his death crying 'God Bless Captain Vere'.

Budd, Lanny
World's End, 1940, et seq
Upton Sinclair

The bright and almost infinitely adaptable bastard son of a munitions magnate, he becomes a world traveller, drawn into almost every international event and movement of any significance from the eve of World War I to the end of World War II. Blessed with his mother's good looks, wherever he goes he has admirers and friends in high places (including Franklin Roosevelt).

Buffone, Carlo
Every Man out of his Humour, 1599
Ben Jonson

A clown, an 'impudent, common jester', Buffone briefly introduces the play and dispenses advice when called upon to do so. He is part buffoon, part satirist, informing SOGLIARDO that he must wear gaudily fashionable clothes and run up debts in order to be properly accepted into society, and ridiculing PUNTARVOLO over the death of a beloved dog. Puntarvolo exacts his revenge and that of several others by taping up Buffone's mouth.

Bufo
Epistle to Dr Arbuthnot, 1735
Alexander Pope

Puffed with self-importance like the toad after whom he is named, he is representative of the wealthy *littérateur* who gathers a clique of eager hacks and would-be poets round himself, sustaining some 'with Port, and some with Praise'.

Bugler, Mick
Wild Decembers, 1999
Edna O'Brien

When Mick Bugler arrives in the west of Ireland from Australia to take possession of family land, he quickly falls into dispute with JOSEPH BRENNAN, who has farmed nearby for many years and regards himself as the true custodian of the surrounding country. With eyes 'the colour of treacle' and his 'scarlet shirt, leather gaiters over his trousers, and a belt with studs that looked lethal', Bugler cuts a dashingly romantic figure and, indeed, he is attractive to women, especially Brennan's younger sister, Breege. Despite having a fiancée in Australia who plans to join him in Ireland, Bugler encourages Breege's interest and become the catalyst of Brennan's violence towards her.

Bulbo, Prince
The Rose and the Ring, 1855
W M Thackeray

His Royal Highness, Crown Prince of Crim Tartary, Duke of Acroceraunia, Marquis of Poluphloisboio, and Knight Grand Cross of the Order of the Pumpkin. Credited with slaying the King of Ograria and 211 of the 218 giants in the Ograrian royal bodyguard, he knows all languages perfectly, plays every instrument in the orchestra, writes operas, and dances in the royal ballet. He is, perhaps, too good to be true.

Bull
Wind From An Enemy Sky, 1978
D'Arcy McNickle

The elderly chief of the Little Elk people who has fiercely maintained a traditional lifestyle for himself and his people despite the incursions of white settlers and the proddings of successive BIA (Bureau of Indian Affairs) agents. Although the younger of two sons, he was elected chief over his brother because of his outspoken opposition to assimilation and co-operation with the incomers. Proud for many years of having 'never learned how to talk to a white man', he has upheld the bitter rift with his assimilationist elder brother, HENRY JIM. Nevertheless, he recognizes the sincerity and urgency of the latter's plea for reconciliation, and responds in favour of unity, putting the interests of his people before his personal pride. Greatly respected and loved by his grandson and the young men of the tribe, he is strong-willed with great but quiet inner strength – a 'man who lives inside'.

Bullingdon, Viscount
The Luck of Barry Lyndon, 1844
W M Thackeray

The first son of HONORIA, COUNTESS OF LYNDON, 'a melancholy, deserted little boy, about whom his father was more than indifferent, and whom his mother never saw, except for two minutes at her levee'. He is much abused by his mother's new husband, BARRY LYNDON, who considers him transformed into a 'wild, savage and insubordinate' nature as he grows up.

Bullivant, Sir Walter
The Thirty-Nine Steps, 1915, et seq
John Buchan

A senior man at the Foreign Office, he initiates RICHARD HANNAY's most secret and desperate missions. He reappears in *Greenmantle* (1916), somewhat worn down by the pressures of command and by the loss of his son Harry, who has bravely brought out first news of the mysterious 'sign from the East'. Kindly but fixed in purpose and sternly fatalistic, he is a father-figure of the oldest, almost Hebraic sort.

Bullock, John
A Patriot's Progress, 1930
Henry Williamson

A young Everyman, he is catapulted from the mild routine of a clerkship in the city into the horrors of World War I. Bullock is the nearest an English writer ever got to the god-given obtuseness of Hašek's Good Soldier Svejk, except that Williamson's suffering innocent lacks Svejk's resourcefulness and wit.

Bulstrode, Mr
Middlemarch, 1871–2
George Eliot

A pale, sickly-looking man, he is the brother-in-law of Mr Vincy, the mayor. Although he has risen in Middlemarch society to the eminent position of wealthy banker, he is not very popular on account of his judgemental religious moralizing. When JOHN RAFFLES, a figure from his past, suddenly reappears in his life, he submits to blackmail in an attempt to protect his position in society, but is eventually publicly disgraced. Forced, however, to confront his guilt and shame about his unscrupulous past, he does try to make amends for his actions.

Bulstrode, Mrs
Middlemarch, 1871–2
George Eliot

Well-bred, well-off and proud of her unblemished past and immaculate appearance, honest Mrs Bulstrode prefers to leave undisturbed the finer details of her husband, MR BULSTRODE's history. When finally confronted with his dubious misdemeanours, however, she symbolically casts off her finery and shows nothing but loyalty, strength and compassion in staying to support him in the face of public scandal.

Bumble, Mr
Oliver Twist, 1838
Charles Dickens

The beadle of the parish workhouse where OLIVER TWIST is born, he first farms out the baby to the cruel Mrs Mann, then mistreats and neglects the boy, feigning concern when he runs away. To become workhouse master, he marries the matron, MRS CORNEY, whose few possessions and 'twenty pounds in ready money' he covets. Her shrewish temper makes his life miserable, and they both lose their posts through her involvement in the plot to defraud Oliver of his inheritance. They end up as paupers in the workhouse which they once tyrannized.

Bumppo, Natty
The Pioneers, 1823
The Last of the Mohicans, 1826
The Prairie, 1827
The Pathfinder, 1840
The Deerslayer, 1841, forming the *'Leatherstocking'
series*
James Fenimore Cooper

A woodsman and adventurer, also known as Leatherstocking, Deerslayer, Hawkeye and Pathfinder. The archetypal loner, he is a rough but highly moral and virtuous man, who embodies the best principles of natural man in his conduct and character, in contrast to the savages with whom he battles. He hates the restrictive life and wanton waste of civilization, but loves and knows the ways of the forest and wilds. He is generous and brave.

Bunce, Jack, adopts the name of **Frederick Altamont**
The Pirate, 1821
Sir Walter Scott

A dandyish pirate, dressed in a style which 'exhibited more extravagance than judgement', and whose manner is a mixture of arrogant self-confidence and cynical calculation. He contrasts sharply with the moody introspection of CLEMENT CLEVELAND.

Bundren, Addie
As I Lay Dying, 1930
William Faulkner

A woman of indomitable passion, trapped in a loveless and stultifying marriage with ANSE BUNDREN. She dies before the novel is completely under way, but her coffined body, transported to Jefferson for burial in accordance with her wishes, becomes the central focus of the story. Life with the mean-spirited Anse convinces her that 'words don't ever fit even what they are trying to say at'. She has had a brief, silent affair with the preacher Whitfield, which teaches her the relationship between action, words and silence, and which results in her third child, JEWEL BUNDREN.

Bundren, Anse
As I Lay Dying, 1930
William Faulkner

Tall and prematurely hunched, Anse has a mean, 'hangdog' expression and a greedily self-serving manner. He brings nothing to marriage with ADDIE BUNDREN but unwanted children and empty words; he considers her wishes only once, when she is lying on her deathbed.

Bundren, Cash
As I Lay Dying, 1930
William Faulkner

ADDIE BUNDREN's eldest child and the hard-working carpenter who shapes her coffin. Unlike his introspective younger brother DARL BUNDREN and impulsive half-brother JEWEL BUNDREN, he is primarily concerned with balance (an often-repeated word) and with precise measurement. Crippled during a disastrous river crossing, he spends the remainder of the journey to his mother's grave lying on her casket.

Bundren, Darl
As I Lay Dying, 1930
William Faulkner

The second of ADDIE BUNDREN's sons, he is an intense, inward-looking boy; 'he just thinks by himself too much'. Just beginning to experience the pangs of adolescence, it is he who feels the loss of his mother most intensely. In the course of her bizarre, protracted funeral procession, he twice attempts to submit her decaying corpse to the alien but cleansing elements of water and fire. Increasingly obsessive and withdrawn, he is ultimately committed to the state asylum.

Bundren, Dewey Dell
As I Lay Dying, 1930
William Faulkner

ADDIE BUNDREN's only daughter, she is pregnant by her boyfriend Lafe. Sexually precocious (as her name is perhaps intended to suggest), she holds a bleak view of human life as nothing more than a 'tub of guts', and sees sex as a fleeting consolation for being alone.

Bundren, Jewel
As I Lay Dying, 1930
William Faulkner

Silent and impulsive, with 'pale eyes like wood set into his wooden face', his characteristic motion is all straight lines and right angles, a geometry which is one of the novel's main symbolic strands. ADDIE BUNDREN's son (and posthumous guardian), he is the product of an adulterous affair with the preacher Whitfield (which may explain his dramatic apartness from his legal father ANSE BUNDREN, and from the other Bundren children) and is foredoomed to be her salvation as well as her punishment. His name may recall PEARL PRYNNE in Hawthorne's *The Scarlet Letter*; she also is the product of an adulterous affair with a clergyman.

Bundren, Vardaman
As I Lay Dying, 1930
William Faulkner

ADDIE BUNDREN's youngest son, he is a silent, intense little boy. Often presented as disturbed, he carries the small child's metaphoric literalism to abnormal lengths, confusing his dead mother with a large fish that has just been landed, a surreal detail that is in keeping with the book's underlying Christian symbolism and which yields one of the most memorable lines in American literature: 'My mother is a fish'. Unable to accept that she is truly dead in her coffin, he bores air-holes for her to breathe, mutilating her face in the process.

Bunny
The Amateur Cracksman, 1899
The Black Mask, 1901
The Thief in the Night, 1905
E W Hornung

Bunny Manners, RAFFLES's fag at their public school, discovers his secret double life only when, in desperation, he tries to borrow money from him and is told they are equally impecunious. Always nervous, he aids Raffles in his daring exploits, keeping watch as he breaks into mansions; he serves Raffles loyally, believing that he might have shone in whatever career he chose, admiring him and proud to be his accomplice, even though many a time he shivers with fear.

Bunsby, Captain Jack
Dombey and Son, 1848
Charles Dickens

An old sea-dog and master of the ship, the 'Cautious Clara', he is a friend and advisor of CAPTAIN EDWARD CUTTLE, but his advice is laconic and often unintelligible. He saves Cuttle from marrying MRS MACSTINGER but fails to prevent being captured himself, and she marries him.

Bunter, Bessie
Bessie Bunter of Cliff House School, 1949, et seq
Frank Richards

BILLY BUNTER's roly-poly sister, she is his image in

every respect, from her squeaky voice to her large, owl-like spectacles and lust for sticky toffee. The Fatima of the Fourth Form, she has a capacious mouth and a rapacious concern for other people's business. Those who displease her are labelled 'cats'. She indulges her curious sense of humour with petty schoolgirl pranks, but her misdeeds are always betrayed by her sticky-toffee handprints and her atrocious spelling.

Bunter, Billy (William George)
Billy Bunter of Greyfriars School, 1949, et seq
Frank Richards

The fat owl of the Remove, he is never far away when a study tea is being set out, and his greedy eyes are ever on the lookout for tuck parcels, no matter whose. His cries of 'Crikey!' and 'Yaroooh!' echo around the chalk-dusted corridors of Greyfriars. Eternally awaiting a postal order that never arrives, he is idle, untruthful, greedy and obtuse, but is not entirely without redeeming features, and has even been known to show a small measure of pluck in the face of danger. Sarcasm is wasted on him, and he agrees with MR QUELCH that caning does him no good at all.

Buonaventure, Father, alias of Prince Charles Edward Stuart
Redgauntlet, 1824
Sir Walter Scott

Not the spry young hero of the '45, but a heavy-set, melancholic man, already vitiated by drink and frustrated ambition. His priestly disguise is somewhat transparent, and he exudes an air of almost poignant dignity as he holds court in attic rooms in isolated houses on the Solway, plotting a final and equally doomed bid for the throne.

Burbank
'Burbank With a Baedeker; Bleistein With a Cigar', in *Poems*, 1920
T S Eliot

A latter-day and much watered-down MARK ANTONY, who falls for PRINCESS VOLUPINE, an even more unlikely Cleopatra, at a small hotel in Venice and is left to meditate on 'Time's ruins, and the seven laws'.

Burch, Lucas, also known as Joe Brown
Light in August, 1932
William Faulkner

A white bootlegger and associate of the half-caste JOE CHRISTMAS. When Joe murders his lover JOANNA BURDEN, Burch is the prime suspect, but informs the police that Joe is 'passing' for white. A later and more sophisticated version of LEE GOODWIN in *Sanctuary*, he poses interesting questions about the nature of identity, and not just racial identity, in the modern South.

Burchill, Mr, or Sir William Thornhill
The Vicar of Wakefield, 1766
Oliver Goldsmith

A shabby but respectable man who befriends DR PRIMROSE AND FAMILY. He appears to be a man of culture: his ideas on poetry certainly impress Sophia, and the vicar admits that he is becoming a wiser man through knowing him. It later

transpires that the persistent, amiable, if rather eccentric Burchill is in reality Sir William Thornhill, whose nephew, the Squire, has been the cause of so many of the Primroses' misfortunes. His appearance as benevolence disguised is crucial to the central theme of the book, that of learning compassion by experience.

Burde, Hilary
A Word Child, 1975
Iris Murdoch

The sardonic narrator of the novel. His 'small mean nasty flat' symbolizes his life of hopeless expiation for accidentally killing the woman he loved, destroying his own and his adored half-sister Crystal's happiness. A civil servant, his recreation is riding the underground, travelling endlessly on the Inner Circle, just killing time. Branded thoroughly bad and unlovable, Hilary was 'incurably maimed by injustice', but, discovering words, for a time found his salvation in languages. Now lost again, he despotically imposes rigid rules of contact upon everyone in his compartmentalized life in an attempt to abolish the possibility of accident. But his history nevertheless proves disastrously repetitive.

Burden, Jack
All the King's Men, 1946
Robert Penn Warren

Historical researcher and ex-journalist, Jack Burden, the novel's narrator, is well named, being oppressed by his own history: his alienation from his parents and unconsummated love for ANNE STANTON. A youthful idealist, he has become a world-weary cynic and lost his sense of purpose. As intellectual aide to politician WILLIE STARK, he at first ignores the corruption and double-dealing of Stark's administration. But he is later forced to recognize his own involvement, and that to have any future he must accept the past as an inevitable part of it.

Burden, Jim
My Ántonia, 1918
Willa Cather

Now a legal counsel for one of the great Western railroads, the narrator of ANTONIA SHIMERDA's story grew up with the girl in Nebraska, shared with her the 'incommunicable past', and is a sympathetic observer of her quest for a broader and more capacious life than is available on the great plains.

Burden, Joanna
Light in August, 1932
William Faulkner

A New Englander living in the American South, she holds obsessively apocalyptic beliefs about the race question. She becomes the lover of JOE CHRISTMAS and tries to use him as a living exemplar of the white race's historic curse. When she tries to force him to assert his supposed blackness more forcefully, he murders her.

Burge, Joyce
Back to Methuselah, 1921
George Bernard Shaw

Burge appears during the second section of this

five-part play. *The Gospel of the Brothers Barnabas* is set in a Hampstead study during the early part of World War I. Burge is one of two Liberal party grandees (HENRY HOPKINS LUBIN is the other) who call upon the BARNABAS brothers. He is mesmerically self-assertive, materialistic, opportunist, unimaginative and destructive.

Burge-Lubin
Back to Methuselah, 1921
George Bernard Shaw

Burge-Lubin appears during the third section of this five-part play. *The Thing Happens* is set in the parlour of the President of the British Islands in 2170AD. Burge-Lubin, the president, is a descendant of both JOYCE BURGE and HENRY HOPKINS LUBIN, from the second section of the play. He is middle-aged, handsome and genial. As most matters of state are administered by CONFUCIUS, he does little work, and is enjoying an affair with his black Minister of Health. He represents, therefore, the essentially unchanging nature of politicians and political power.

Burger, Rosa
Burger's Daughter, 1979
Nadine Gordimer

Rosa, 'named for Rosa Luxemburg', the German revolutionary, is the daughter of radical communists committed to fighting the apartheid system in South Africa. She is stubborn but courageous, and these qualities enable her, after her father's death in prison, to reject for a time the life of political responsibility for which she has been trained from childhood. Vulnerable and spotty as a schoolgirl, she grows into a sensual young woman and finally, and inevitably, becomes a committed activist and political prisoner as her father before her.

Burgess, Bessie
The Plough and the Stars, 1926
Sean O'Casey

A street fruit-seller and resident of a Dublin tenement, Bessie Burgess is a vigorous woman of about 40, with a strong, almost messianic sense of religious duty. 'Her face is a dogged one, hardened by toil, and a little coarsened by drink.' The play is set partly during the Easter Rising of 1916, but Bessie's son is fighting in France, a source of both pride and grief to her. Angry that others attach more importance to political events in Dublin, she appears to them puritanical, domineering and interfering: 'never content unless ... standin' senthry over other people's doin'!'

Burgess, Guy
An Englishman Abroad, television version 1983, stage version 1988
Alan Bennett

An historical character appropriated by Bennett, he was one of the Cambridge spy ring which included Kim Philby, Donald Maclean and ANTHONY BLUNT. Burgess, who meets the actress CORAL BROWNE at a theatre in Moscow, is presented as a seedy, vulgar, essentially tragic figure. Like Blunt, he has stepped aside from conventional ideas of patriotism, but like HILARY in an earlier Bennett play, he retains an

absorbing, though selective, affection for England. Wry and ironic, his ability both to discriminate and to preserve an intellectual fog, and his striking of postures, make him a likeable but exasperating figure.

Burgess, Ted
The Go-Between, 1953
L P Hartley

A 'working farmer' and neighbour of the Maudsleys, he is also the secret lover of the daughter of the family, MARION MAUDSLEY. The 'Water-carrier' of the narrator LEO COLSTON's imaginary zodiac, Ted has a strong and at times frightening physical presence – there is much intensity in all he does, but little finesse. He has a reputation as a ladykiller, but Marion describes him as weak; and he is weakened by his passion for her, sublimating his own wishes and will to hers.

Burglar, the (the Honourable Aubrey Bagot)
Too True to be Good, 1932
George Bernard Shaw

The son of an atheist father and Christian mother, his gift for preaching made him become a clergyman until his infatuation with a female petty criminal, THE NURSE, inspired him to become a burglar. As Bright Young Things, they plan to steal a necklace belonging to THE PATIENT. Caught in the act, they persuade her to travel with them on the proceeds, the Burglar adopting the alias of the Hon Aubrey Bagot. Later, he is reunited with his father, THE ELDER, and the fantasy ends as the reformed Burglar preaches an impromptu sermon on civilization.

Burgoyne, Gen John
The Devil's Disciple, 1897
George Bernard Shaw

Burgoyne is based on a real character, who was a minor dramatist and commander of British forces defeated at Saratoga in 1777, during the American War of Independence. (Shaw appears to have invented Burgoyne's nickname of 'Gentlemanly Johnny'.) In the play, he is 55, sleek and quick-witted, 'a born high comedian' whom Shaw makes the mouthpiece of his own satirical comedy. Consequently, Burgoyne observes that apart from the Americans, Britain has other enemies in the form of 'jobbery and snobbery, incompetence and Red Tape' in London.

Burgundy, Charles the Bold, Duke of
Quentin Durward, 1823
Sir Walter Scott

A portrait of the historical duke, he is 'the most hasty and impatient, nay, the most imprudent prince of his time'. He stands in hostile and suspicious relation to LOUIS XI, KING OF FRANCE, bound to him by feudal duty, but itching to be rid of such constraints. He is stern, brooding and inflexible, barely able to contain his real feelings during the parley at Péronne.

Burgundy, Duke of
Henry V, 1599
William Shakespeare

Deeply concerned about the effect the war against

the English has had on the country and people of France, the Duke of Burgundy is responsible for bringing the two sides together after Agincourt. He speaks eloquently and movingly about the benefits of peace and reconciliation, and his nobility is recognized and accepted by Henry V (HENRY, PRINCE OF WALES), who later seeks advice on how best to woo and win KATHARINE, PRINCESS OF FRANCE.

Burke, Agent
The Absentee, in *Tales of Fashionable Life*, 1812
Maria Edgeworth

LORD CLONBRONY's agent in Ireland and a perpetual disappointment to his master for his weak stomach regarding rents, foreclosures and profits. He is as honest as the day is long, but Lord Clonbrony intends to replace him with the immoral NICHOLAS GARRAGHTY.

Burke, Dan and Nora
In the Shadow of the Glen, 1903
J M Synge

Dan, a farmer and herder, and his younger wife Nora, live in 'the last cottage at the head of a long glen in County Wicklow', a lonely district made even more isolated by frequent storms. Theirs was the customary arranged marriage and it is both loveless and childless; their world is their unending, unrewarding work. Dan, gruff, conventional and embittered, feigns death one stormy night in order to trap his 'bad' wife with her lover, MICHAEL DARA. Nora, whose loneliness and despair have not yet extinguished her passion, responds, not to her lover who duly arrives, but to the poetry of THE TRAMP, who turns up unexpectedly at the cottage.

Burke, Edmond
Edmond, 1982
David Mamet

A white New York businessman, Burke is in his mid-thirties and happily married. But after visiting a clairvoyant, he becomes convinced that his world is disintegrating. Leaving his wife, he begins a terrifying descent into the urban underworld, a journey into Hades ending in his imprisonment for murder. Burke represents the kind of man who has been reduced by the almost superhuman demands of commerce and modern marriage to a state where hustling aggression masks a fearful, defenceless vulnerability. By extension, Burke also symbolizes the current state of life in New York City. Apparently a free man blessed with all of life's advantages, he is, in mythical terms, a soul in such desperate need of redemption that he undergoes an appalling purgatory to arrive at the truth about himself. Eventually, he makes an alliance with a black homosexual.

Burke, Mark
Cliffs of Fall, 1945
Dan Davin

From a family of New Zealand farmers, Burke returns from his studies at university during the vacation, increasingly aware that he is becoming divided from his family, not only by education, but by temperament and ambition. Being naturally a secretive man, he is loathe to confide

in anyone. Although his girlfriend is pregnant, he believes that real personal and professional fulfilment are possible only if all personal ties are broken. Yet at the same time, he admits that there is something natural, and certainly symmetrical, in a complete physical and spiritual union with another person. Burke is an understanding, compassionate man, but one who is equally a dreamer and a realistic planner.

Burke, Mat
Anna Christie, 1922
Eugene O'Neill

An uncouth but romantic Irish sailor shipwrecked at the mouth of the Hudson and rescued by CHRIS CHRISTOPHERSON and his daughter ANNA CHRISTOPHERSON, with whom he falls in love. Emerging as he does intact from the 'ole davil' of the sea, he appears to offer a hope of redemption to Anna, but, horrified by her past, he goes off to drown himself in drink. He and Chris enlist on the same ship but later return to be reunited with Anna.

Burke, Red
Working Bullocks, 1926
Katharine Susannah Prichard

Red neither intellectualizes nor articulates, he reacts. He is primal man: 'He was a man like one of his bullocks, rooted in his deep natural instincts, powerful and intent, with a capacity for dumb and obstinate endurance.'

Burkett, Dinah
The Echoing Grove, 1953
Rosamond Lehmann

Articulate and sexually liberated, volatile and offbeat, Dinah is a rootless representative of the avant-garde. No longer certain of stable moral parameters, her psyche is fractured and her thoughts are ridiculously melodramatic: 'Darkness, close up this fissure'. She has squandered her talent and her shabby flat is a token of her dissipated, haphazard life. Ruined by a doomed love affair with RICKY MASTERS – her sister's husband – the precariousness of life has eroded Dinah's rationality.

Burlap, Denis
Point Counter Point, 1928
Aldous Huxley

A canting hypocrite and sly seducer, he is the complete antithesis of MARK RAMPION, who comes across as a visionary in search of wholeness. Burlap's intellectual shallowness is revealed in one of his favourite maxims: 'Fascinatur nugacitatus'. The narrator signals Burlap's utter nullity with this description of the character on the way to a party: 'He had been ruminating on the fascination of nugacity all the way from Piccadilly Circus'.

Burley, Augusta
The Antiphon, 1958
Djuna Barnes

This play, written in verse which is often dense to the point of obscurity, dramatizes the tensions and feuds within a discordant family and, in particular, the relationship between Augusta and her daughter Miranda, who are psychologically and emotionally interdependent, sharing a love for and bitter resentment of each other. Both fearful of her daughter and domineering, Augusta is passionate, proud, brittle, uncomprehending, furious and vengeful.

Burnaby, Frankie
Hetty Dorval, 1947
Ethel Wilson
The narrator of HETTY DORVAL's story, Frankie grows up and gains wisdom over the course of the novel. Initially infatuated by beautiful, older, self-possessed Hetty, the young, curious and impressionable Frankie, 'incandescent with the devotion and distress of youth', is later precipitated into a vehement assertion of adulthood as she is forced to recognize the narcissistic and dangerous nature of Hetty's charm.

Burnet of Barns, John
John Burnet of Barns, 1898
John Buchan
A Borders landowner, whose residence by the Tweed, upstream from Peebles, is precisely the kind of 'storied' location beloved of Sir Walter Scott, a place which, like Burnet himself, seems to concentrate and focus several centuries of legend and heroic activity, as well as a profound identification with an ancestral home. He is moved by 'the impulses of high passion [and] the stirring of the heart'.

Burnham, Jerry
The 42nd Parallel, 1930
1919, 1932
The Big Money, 1936, forming the *U.S.A.* trilogy, 1938
John Dos Passos
A cameo-like figure, red-faced Burnham starts out as a technical adviser working in the same Washington office as JANEY WILLIAMS, with whom he strikes up a friendship. However, his main role is as the alcoholic war correspondent who reappears at various junctures to philosophize boozily, but quite acutely, on the events in hand.

Burns, Helen
Jane Eyre, 1847
Charlotte Brontë
JANE EYRE's friend at Lowood school, Helen is an eloquent and very knowledgeable young girl who is nevertheless victimized by one of the teachers. Christ-like in her endurance of evil and wrongdoing, she is the special friend of MISS TEMPLE and an example to Jane in her composure and self-control. She is of delicate constitution, and her life is soon claimed by consumption, but her religious beliefs make even her death a positive occurrence.

Burr, Aaron
Burr, 1973
Gore Vidal
The 'sprightly skeleton in many a celebrated closet', he is a hero of the American Revolution who has lived to a vigorous old age in which he has accumulated notoriety in the way that other people collect stamps. A charming, charismatic figure of short stature and unexpected wit, he

might have been the third President of America or the first Emperor of Mexico, had circumstances been different. A colourful adventurer to some, a treacherous blackguard to others, he remains the subject of myriad speculations that he chooses neither to confirm nor deny.

Burton, Florence
The Claverings, 1867
Anthony Trollope
The fiancée of HARRY CLAVERING, who lodges with her family. She is a short, rather plain, cautious but pleasant girl who compares badly in Harry's eyes with his beloved JULIA BRABAZON, but he falls in love with her nonetheless, and comes to regard her charms in a more favourable light. She insists on a long engagement, but his inheritance persuades her into an early marriage.

Burton, Sarah
South Riding, 1936
Winifred Holtby
The young headmistress whose appointment comes to epitomize the changing social and political face of the South Riding, Sarah Burton is the child of a poor and feckless Yorkshire family, returned from London to impose her reforming zeal upon a conservative and already anachronistic community. Vivid, independent and courageous, she lives by a creed of intellectual endeavour and individual achievement, but finds her crude rationale tempered and humanized by the influence of those she has been prepared to despise.

Bushy → Bagot, Bushy and Green

Busirane
The Faerie Queene, 1590–6
Sir Edmund Spenser
An evil enchanter who has incarcerated the fair AMORET in the deep dungeons of his castle. He keeps her in a state of fear and tortures her night and day, because she refuses to yield to him. His castle is surrounded by an evil-smelling sulphurous fire, and he uses black magic to fulfil his aims. Inside the castle the walls are covered with an aesthetic tapestry of gold and silk that illustrates evil and wickedness. At night a strange music blows and odd creatures and winged gods play. He sits scrawling his spells, writing in blood squeezed from the pure heart of the still-living virgin.

Buster
The Shiralee, 1955
D'Arcy Niland
The four-year-old daughter of Macauley, an Aussie swagman. She tramps alongside him as he wanders around the 'outback' in disgust with life after finding his wife in bed with a lover. He has taken Buster to punish his wife, and he nags her to be quiet when he wants to think, to stop complaining, to walk faster. But, as the miles pass, Macauley finds that he depends on her loyal companionship. In the end, faced with losing her after a car accident, he realizes that he loves his daughter, and that a shiralee is not

merely a burden or responsibility, but sometimes also a necessity.

Busy, Zeal-of-the-Land
Bartholomew Fair, 1614
Ben Jonson

A zealous Puritan, Busy is one of DAME PURECRAFT's hopeful suitors, and intends to appeal to her moral values by preaching to her at great length about the corruption and roguery of Bartholomew Fair. As punishment for his inordinate sermonizing, and because he loses a debate with a puppet, he is put in the stocks. TOM QUARLOUS engages him in conversation and reveals his puritanism to be fraudulent: in reality, Busy is materialistic and vain.

Butch
Furthermore, 1938
Damon Runyon

Not many safe-breakers are secure enough in their profession to take their squalling child with them, but when Butch is persuaded to take part in a criminal exploit while he is babysitting, in his simple-hearted way he can see no alternative. This complication is a challenge to his ingenuity and that of his companions, HARRY THE HORSE, SPANISH JOHN and LITTLE ISADORE.

Butler, Kitty
Tipping the Velvet, 1998
Sarah Waters

Kitty Butler is a male impersonator on the stage touring second-rate theatres when she meets NANCY ASTLEY. When Nancy joins the act Kitty finally achieves the celebrity status she has been searching for. Ashamed of her relationship with Nancy, she feels that if it were to come out that they were lovers their lives would be ruined. She opts for a conventional marriage, and the loss of Nancy from her life results in both her career and happiness dwindling.

Butler, Reuben
The Heart of Midlothian, in *Tales of My Landlord: Second Series*, 1818
Sir Walter Scott

A young Presbyterian minister and deputy schoolmaster of a parish near Edinburgh, he is the childhood sweetheart of JEANIE DEANS, concerned at the outset of the story about the fate of her sister EFFIE DEANS. He is 'weak in constitution and, though not timid in temper might be safely pronounced anxious, doubtful and apprehensive'. He links the book's two main plots when he becomes – by force of circumstance – chaplain to CAPTAIN JOHN PORTEOUS as the lynch mob prepares to execute him.

Butler, Rhett
Gone with the Wind, 1936
Margaret Mitchell

Like SCARLETT O'HARA, Rhett Butler shows real sexual magnetism. He is forthright to the point of rudeness and cares not at all for others' opinions. He is elemental and animalistic, but possesses the beguiling, reckless daring of a pirate. A man who has had a long, tough experience of life, far from the pampered society

of the plantations, he views the world with cynical humour. His scandalous reputation proves irresistibly tempting for most women, but Scarlett's adolescent, quixotic behaviour merely alienates the more worldly Rhett.

Butley, Ben
Butley, 1971
Simon Gray

Ben Butley, a lecturer in English at London University, is confronted by the breakdown of his marriage to Anne and by his homosexual relationship with Joey, a colleague. He is inquisitional, fretful, flippant, selfish and scathing; desperate to love and be loved and frightened of being abandoned. The savagery and cleverness of his language make him offensive, but reveal his vulnerability. 'You spread futility', declares Joey. This Butley finally admits: 'We're all pitiful ... The thing is to be pitiful with the right person, keep it from everybody else. And from yourselves whenever you can.'

Butterthwaite, Charlie
The Workhouse Donkey, 1964
John Arden

Ex-pauper, alderman and former Labour Mayor of an unnamed northern town, 'everyone's Uncle Charlie' displays a breezy confidence in all he does, whether laying a foundation stone, chatting up strippers in a nightclub, or telling a policeman that 'I'd ha' took twelve o' you bluebottles on' back at the time of the General Strike' – which he 'conducted and ruined single-handed' according to the town's leading Conservative. Now older but no wiser, he commits the rashest acts of his career due to gambling-inspired insolvency.

Buzfuz, Serjeant
Pickwick Papers, 1837
Charles Dickens

Counsel for MRS MARTHA BARDELL in *Bardell* vs *Pickwick*. He bullies the witnesses who appear for SAMUEL PICKWICK and creates a great impression, defeating Pickwick's barrister, SERJEANT SNUBBIN.

Byars, Master
And the Cock Crew, 1945
Fionn Mac Colla

Known to the people of Gleann Luachrach as the Black Foreigner, he is the greedy and cynical factor charged with clearing the glen for the coming of the sheep. He has none of MAIGHSTIR SACHAIRI's twisted idealism and stands entirely for naked commerce.

Byrne, Michael and Mary
The Tinker's Wedding, 1907
J M Synge

Michael Byrne, a tinker, Mary, his elderly mother, and SARAH CASEY are encamped on the edge of a village. Sarah has suddenly determined to marry Michael. Naturally a man of action, he is puzzled by this decision and views the threatened wedding with a stoical gloom. Mary, who dominates the play, is a kind of minor female SIR JOHN FALSTAFF: a friendly, worldly, Rabelaisian woman, especially when drunk. An imaginative conversationalist, she is capable of sly irony and, under the guise of disarming innocence, of knowing innuendo.

Byron, Cashel
The Admirable Bashville, 1901
George Bernard Shaw
The play, a blank-verse comedy, derives from Shaw's early novel, *Cashel Byron's Profession*. Boxer Cashel Byron falls for the high-class Lydia Carew, but cannot confess that he is a fighter. When Lydia discovers his identity, Byron defends the supposed barbarities of boxing against the iniquities of supposedly polite society. Because his mother was an actress, his speech is a Shakespearean and Marlovian caricature. Later, his mother reveals that he is really as highly-born as Lydia.

Byron, Harriet
Sir Charles Grandison, 1754
Samuel Richardson
A sprightly and satirical woman, Harriet copes admirably with the pedants, fops and pestering suitors who constitute London manhood. She is spirited enough to resist the evil attentions of SIR HARGRAVE POLLEXFEN and, although muffled, gagged and blindfolded, she manages to call out for help. Harbouring anxieties about her burgeoning sexuality, she dreams of hiding in subterranean caverns. However, after an elaborate wedding, she enters the public domain as SIR CHARLES GRANDISON's wife, and on her triumphal possession of the paradisical Grandison estate, she exclaims: 'What a happy lot is mine!'

BZ
Play It As It Lays, 1970
Joan Didion
A film producer and minor Beelzebub. He is the occasional lover of MARIA WYETH and eventually commits suicide lying by her side in a squalid motel room.

C
Three Tall Women, 1991
Edward Albee

The three characters, A, B and C, are portraits of Albee's adoptive mother at different ages. A young attorney, C is 26 years old and attempting to put 92-year-old A's personal affairs in order. A sensitive, optimistic, discriminating if somewhat naive woman, C has strict moral sensibilities, expecting both herself and a husband to be monogamous. 'I imagine I'll marry and be very happy', she declares. She imagines too, that whatever the obstacles before her, life will somehow come right in the end, and that: 'there *is* a lot of happiness along the way. *Isn't* there?'

Cabot, Abbie → Putnam, Abbie

Cabot, Eben
Desire Under the Elms, 1924
Eugene O'Neill

The youngest son of EPHRAIM CABOT and the last to remain on the farm, which he is now due to inherit. When his hated father brings home a new wife, Eben allows her to seduce him, failing to understand that she merely requires him as a breeding stud to take the place of his impotent father.

Cabot, Ephraim
Desire Under the Elms, 1924
Eugene O'Neill

A greedy New England farmer who has worked his second wife to death in order to gain control of her land. His sons hate him and only one now remains at home. To deny EBEN CABOT his inheritance, he marries ABBIE PUTNAM, by whom he hopes to father another heir.

Cade, Jack
Henry VI Part I, early 1590s
William Shakespeare

A people's revolt under Jack Cade forms an interlude to the main action of the play. A mercenary in the pay of RICHARD PLANTAGENET, DUKE OF YORK, Cade claims to be Lord Mortimer, descended from the Duke of Clarence, and leads a ragged band of Kentish hinds and peasants, the illiterate and politically betrayed, upon London. A headstrong, bullish, quick-witted, persuasive opportunist, Cade represents a dangerous English spirit of vicious, foolhardy and heroic anarchy.

Cadfael, Brother
A Morbid Taste for Bones, 1977, et seq
Ellis Peters

After a lifetime of soldiering in Europe, Cadfael became a Benedictine monk at the abbey of St Peter and St Paul in 13th-century Shrewsbury. While developing his knowledge of herbal remedies he has become an acute assessor of the character of those within the abbey and of its many visitors. His medicinal skills, his knowledge of Welsh, his horsemanship and his reliability mean that he is called on frequently to travel around the vicinity. He has developed a close, trusting friendship with the town's sheriff, Hugh Beringar, and although he keeps out of politics he is eager for peace in the country. His kindly nature encourages youngsters to use him as a confidante and allows him access to vital information that helps him to solve the many murders that occur round about him.

Cadmore, Margaret, Jr
Maru, 1971
Bessie Head

The adopted daughter of a White missionary in Botswana, whose names she inherited. Margaret's real mother is a 'Masarwa', Botswana's race of untouchables, also known as Bushmen. Margaret's Western education, her enigmatic composure and regal looks win for her the affection and love of the chieftains, MARU and Moleka. At a time when the entire village is roused in righteous indignation against a 'Masarwa' becoming a teacher to children of parents from a 'higher caste', the love triangle between Margaret, Maru and Moleka, and Maru's manoeuvring (which ends in marriage between Moleka and Maru's favourite sister Dikeledi), bring to an end a lifetime of societal prejudice.

Cadwal → Arviragus

Cadwallader, Mrs
Middlemarch, 1871–2
George Eliot

A minor but colourful character, Mrs Cadwallader, the wife of the rector, is assured of her own importance and skill in ordering the affairs of her neighbours. Looking down her nose at the rising merchant class, she embodies the traditional values of the landed aristocracy, believing that to be 'well-born' is of the utmost significance; though a terrible gossip she is partially redeemed by the precision of her sharp wit.

Caelia

The Faerie Queene, 1590–6
Sir Edmund Spenser

Gifted with grace, honour and wisdom, she is renowned in Faerieland for her purity and her sacred knowledge. Her purpose is to 'relieve the needes of wretched soules, and helpe the helplesse pore'. Her name means 'heavenly', and she spends all of her nights in prayer and her days doing good. She is the mother of three daughters: Faith, Hope and Charity.

Caesar, Caius Julius

Caesar and Cleopatra, 1898
George Bernard Shaw

Caesar was appropriated by Shaw to counter Shakespeare, who 'made a mess of Caesar under the influence of Plutarch'. Shaw's Caesar is therefore not a man of war, but a pragmatic politician and a man of words; not CLEOPATRA's lover but her tutor, instructing her in logical thought and the affairs of state. At 54, he is 'rather thin and stringy', but nimble of mind and light of heart. Vain, and prone to interpret military defeat as conquest, he is Shaw's first superman, a fantastic self-portrait of the author and an attempt to dramatize the Shavian philosophy.

Caesar, Caius Julius

The Ides of March, 1948
Thornton Wilder

Bald and ageing but charismatic, Caesar is a 'benevolent' despot. He is a reformer worshipped by the common people, but his absolute power inspires hatred among the intelligentsia and he foresees his death by 'tyrannicide' as inevitable. As a rationalist he abhors superstitious auguries, but nevertheless believes he was chosen by destiny. Although unimaginative and unreflective himself, he envies, above all, great poets. Epileptic and 'passionless', he seems neither to love nor inspire love; yet the women in his life remain wholly devoted to him.

Caesar, Julius

Julius Caesar, c.1599
William Shakespeare

He is seen by the conspirators as a threat to the republicanism of Rome, and it is the idea of Caesar as power which dominates the play. Superstitious and physically marred by deafness and epilepsy, as a private individual he is in many ways weak, but as ruler he sees himself as superior to all around him. He is inflexible in political decisions, 'constant as the Northern star'. Highly susceptible to flattery, he commits a fatal error in heeding the blandishments of the conspirators over the warnings of his wife CALPURNIA. The supreme ruler of Rome, after his death power is masterless until the resultant chaos is controlled by ANTONY and OCTAVIUS CAESAR.

Caesar, Octavius

Julius Caesar, c.1599
Antony and Cleopatra, 1606/7
William Shakespeare

JULIUS CAESAR's adopted heir. He swiftly takes command from the much older ANTONY in *Julius Caesar* and wields the real power in *Antony and Cleopatra*. A passionless, cold man, his sole motivation seems to be the desire to avenge Caesar's death and later to unite the whole Roman world under one efficient ruler. The only real emotion he displays is his genuine grief at the news of ANTONY's death and his realization of what the world has lost by it.

Cain

Back to Methuselah, 1921
George Bernard Shaw

A biblical character, appearing in the first section of this five-part play (and briefly in the last). *In the Beginning* is set partly in the Garden of Eden. Cain, a son of ADAM and EVE, has rebelled against parental authority. Although he has killed his brother Abel and become the first murderer, he protests he copied Abel, 'the discoverer of blood', to become, like him, 'a man of ideas, of spirit: a true Progressive'. This is in contrast to his father, a farmer and Conservative, whom he sees as a failure. Cain has will, but no imagination.

Caius, Dr

The Merry Wives of Windsor, c.1597
William Shakespeare

A highly-strung, ill-tempered French physician, Dr Caius is in love with ANNE PAGE. Believing SIR HUGH EVANS to be his rival, he challenges him to a duel which, thanks to THE HOST OF THE GARTER INN, fails to take place. MISTRESS FORD, however, approves of Caius as a husband for Anne, but Anne herself loves FENTON. During the masquerade and humiliation of SIR JOHN FALSTAFF in Windsor Great Park, Caius is married to someone he assumes to be Anne, but discovers to be a boy in disguise. Again he plans revenge: 'I'll raise all Windsor'. Yet his anger is impotent, for his own vanity has been his downfall.

Cal

Cal, 1983
Bernard MacLaverty

An unemployed Catholic youth who lives with his father in a loyalist housing estate in Northern Ireland. He is a loner who spends most of his time locked in his bedroom smoking and playing the guitar. Likeable and sensitive, frequently performing acts of kindness for others, he feels no religious hatred. However, he does not have the strength of character to stop himself becoming involved in terrorist activities. Desperately attracted to Marcella, a librarian, he fantasizes about a future with her, despite knowing that this is impossible.

Calchas

Troilus and Cressida, 1601/2
William Shakespeare

CRESSIDA's father, a Trojan who has betrayed his countrymen and defected to the Greek camp, leaving his daughter to fend for herself. He requires payment for his treachery, his first demand being that the Greeks offer the Trojan leader Antenor in exchange for Cressida so that she might join him.

Calcott, Jack
Kangaroo, 1923
D H Lawrence

An Australian and a former soldier, Jack Calcott is the deputy leader of the Diggers, a political group under the control of BEN COLLEY. He is a big, heavy and apparently indifferent man but with a latent, possibly dangerous energy that occasionally bursts out in reckless action. He is brave, watchful, patriotic and magnetic.

Caldicott, Maurice
The Vivisector, 1970
Patrick White

An art-dealer, he is one of several androgynous figures who slip in and out of the life of the painter HURTLE DUFFIELD. Inadequate and incomplete in themselves, they nevertheless have something to offer the exploitative Duffield. Caldicott is involved with the painter in two ways. He deals in art, and he is guiltily in love with him. Although Caldicott is an unsympathetic figure, his feelings have a regenerative and creative effect on Duffield, leading to a series of important paintings.

Caldwell, George
The Centaur, 1963
John Updike

He is Updike's latter-day equivalent of the wise, tutelary centaur Chiron, who in classical mythology gives up his gift of immortality for the sake of his son Prometheus. George is a high-school teacher in a small Pennsylvania town, a man who offers small certainties rather than grand heroism and a patient forbearance in place of vaulting ambition.

Caldwell, Peter
The Centaur, 1963
John Updike

GEORGE CALDWELL's son and pupil, he is a latter-day version of Prometheus, a driven and artistically ambitious boy whose dreams and nightmares stem from a single source. He fails to understand and at first attempts to reject his father's gift, but gradually comes to realize its worth.

Calepine, Sir
The Faerie Queene, 1590–6
Sir Edmund Spenser

An errant knight, related in name and attributes to SIR CALIDORE, THE KNIGHT OF COURTESY. He is beautiful, careful, gentle and of a soothing nature. Discourtesy enrages him, yet he controls his anger, irrespective of whether others think him cowardly. He treats maidens with great respect, leading them through torrential rivers and even telling little white lies in order to save their honour.

Caliban
'Caliban upon Setebos', in *Dramatis Personae*, 1864
Robert Browning

Browning's recreation of the monster of Shakespeare's play *The Tempest* meditates on the nature of his god Setebos, but can only think of him in terms of his own responses to the world. Caliban is callous and inhuman, yet wryly amusing; a primitive thinker with a crude urge for power, he reflects disrespectfully on his god until a thunderstorm sends him cowering and begging forgiveness.

Caliban
The Tempest, 1611
William Shakespeare

The fish-like offspring of a devil and the witch Sycorax, Caliban is only one step above the animals because, although able to talk, he lacks moral judgement and is incapable of learning good. A creature of nature he takes delight in the magical island he lives on, with its strange sights and sounds. He is also appreciative of the human beauty of MIRANDA. Because he has been PROSPERO's slave for so long he is resentful of him – yet he is prepared to become the servant of STEPHANO and TRINCULO, who offer him freedom in return.

Calidore, Sir, the Knight of Courtesy
The Faerie Queene, 1590–6
Sir Edmund Spenser

A mild man, beloved by his people, whose name means 'beautiful gift'. Handsome and gentle, he is a great orator who can steal the hearts of stony men with his speech. He loves truth and honesty, and is wise, loathing flattery and lying. His quest is to seek out and overcome all crudities and discourtesy.

Calista
The Fair Penitent, 1703
Nicholas Rowe

Impetuous, passionate and the fair penitent of the title, Calista has been promised in marriage by her father, SCIOLTO, to ALTAMONT, without being consulted. She is, however, already the lover of LOTHARIO, and continues seeing him until they are discovered by her prospective husband, who kills Lothario in a duel. Despite her barefaced denial that she was having an affair, Calista cannot wholly be blamed for what has happened. 'Why didst thou turn to folly … ?' asks Sciolto. 'It was because I loved', she replies.

Call, Woodrow F
Lonesome Dove, 1985
Larry McMurtry

A retired Texas Ranger in the post-bellum South, he is the driven, active partner in contrast to GUS MCCRAE, who represents rootedness and acceptance. Call is a dreamer, haunted by a vision of a more heroic past.

Callar, Morvern
Morvern Callar, 1995
Alan Warner

Morvern Callar works as a supermarket assistant in The Port, the remote Scottish fishing village where she grew up. When she discovers her nameless boyfriend's dead body on the kitchen floor just before Christmas, her clinical, determined response to his suicide is at once chilling and powerful. Left with her boyfriend's savings and a completed manuscript of his first novel, Morvern is presented with an opportunity to escape her job and surroundings; relocating to Spain she discovers 'that happiness that I never even dared dream I had the right'.

Callaway, Lew
The Passage, 1930
Vance Palmer

He is a rugged Australian fisherman, whose relationship to the natural environment is one of respectful antagonism, far removed from the bland nature mysticism of those in the cities who romanticize his job. He is ruggedly self-possessed, but not without sensitivity.

Calpurnia
Julius Caesar, c.1599
William Shakespeare

JULIUS CAESAR's wife, whose love for him nearly undoes the plot to assassinate him. She is aware that the portents and her dreams indicate danger to her husband: 'when beggars die there are no comets seen/The heavens themselves blaze forth the death of princes'. However, Caesar's susceptibility to flattery dissuades him from heeding the one voice that might have saved him.

Calum
The Cone-Gatherers, 1955
Robin Jenkins

A gentle, almost saintly, hunchback of limited mental capacity, he is employed with his brother Neil to reseed Lady Runcie-Campbell's pine woods which have been devastated by the war effort. The opposite to DUROR's Calvinistic grimness, he reverses the mythic archetype by bringing goodness into a fallen Eden.

Calvert, Bell
The Private Memoirs and Confessions of a Justified Sinner, 1824
James Hogg

The much maligned, unfortunate prostitute who, in return for MISS ARABELLA LOGAN's refusal to testify against her in court, relates to her an eye-witness account of the murder of GEORGE COLWAN. A minor figure who adds colour and intrigue to the plot, her main role is to assist Miss Logan in tracking down and identifying the murderer of George.

Calvert, Harold
Late Call, 1964
Angus Wilson

A recently widowed schoolmaster whose educational and social theories are optimistically geared to life in a 'new town'. For all his rather mannered affection, he is condescending towards his retired parents, treating them as representatives of a past long gone; despite all of which, he seems unable to respond to or even control his own children.

Calvert, Roy
Strangers and Brothers, 1940, et seq
C P Snow

A Cambridge don, and 'the most gifted man the College had produced in years', he cultivates a kind of eccentric picturesqueness in his life and tastes that leaves those who meet and work with him not entirely sure where they stand. As with all of Snow's characters, he has a real-life model: the brilliant sinologist Charles Allbery, a fellow

of Christ's College who was killed over Germany in 1943.

Calvert, Sylvia
Late Call, 1964
Angus Wilson

She has retired to a Midlands town called Carshall, having spent her life running a small hotel. In her naive, bland way, and from the marginal position that retirement affords her, she sees through the thin pretensions of the new town and the 'advanced' ideas of her son, HAROLD CALVERT.

Calvo, Baldassarre
Romola, 1863
George Eliot

A scholar and the adoptive father of TITO MELEMA, who suffers shipwreck and enslavement late in life. He survives to appear in Florence, thickset, heavy and bald, and to escape his captors. Once he realizes that Tito, at ease in that city, has been utterly ungrateful and not lifted a finger to help him, his life becomes dedicated to revenge. Old age and a fading memory are against him but his feelings remain passionate.

Calypha and Thelea
The Old Wives' Tale, 1595
George Peele

The brothers of the abducted DELIA, they are revealed as loyal and dedicated in their search, and generous in their giving of alms, but are otherwise largely a plot convenience. They 'courageously enter' the lair of the conjurer SACRAPANT, but are captured and put to work as slaves, while the bewitched Delia cannot recognize them, and cruelly berates them.

Cama, Ormus
The Ground Beneath Her Feet, 1999
Salman Rushdie

Born in Bombay the son of Parsi Anglophiles and haunted throughout his life by the fate of his brothers, one a silent mystic, the other a killer, Ormus becomes a popular composer of genius. With his partner VINA APSARA, with whom he enjoys a tumultuously hectic love affair, he emerges as one of the greatest artists in rock history. Handsome, adventurous and philosophical, following a near fatal car crash he has the ability of double vision, which enables him to see through the fissures in the visible universe and into a parallel one in which the everyday world and its history is refracted. His story reflects in part the myth of Orpheus.

Cambell, or Cambello
The Faerie Queene, 1590–6
Sir Edmund Spenser

The courageous brother of CANACEE and a friend to TRIAMOND. In order to stop the knights fighting for the hand of his sister he offers to wage battle against any one for her hand, but has a magic ring that stops all mortal wounds from bleeding and therefore, not unnaturally, most are afraid to confront him. Triamond fights him, but they are reunited in perfect friendship by the intervention of Cambina, Cambell's wife.

Cambina
The Faerie Queene, 1590–6
Sir Edmund Spenser

The sister of TRIAMOND and daughter of the fairy AGAPE. A peacemaker and bringer of harmony, she drives a chariot of wondrous design, which is pulled by two passive lions. She carries the rod of peace and, excelling in magic, she brews 'Nepente', a potion that instantly extinguishes grief and brings love and forgiveness.

Cameron, Rachel
A Jest of God, 1966
Margaret Laurence

Vividly inhabiting her own internal life, Rachel traps herself into what is expected of her – 'I dramatise myself. I always did. No-one would ever know it from the outside, where I'm too quiet.' A 34-year-old schoolteacher, she undergoes a profound series of psychological and physical discoveries as she finds her own voice. Living in a small town, she realizes that she must leave before the identity she possesses ossifies and traps her completely. Finally aware that her escape need not be sanctioned by anyone other than herself, she emerges, aware that 'I am the mother now'.

Camillo
The White Devil, 1612
John Webster

The stupid husband of the immoral VITTORIA COROMBONA, who has failed to give her satisfaction. Despite not sleeping with his wife, the DUKE OF BRACHIANO's attentions to her make him jealous. Having been sent on a mission by FRANCISCO DE MEDICIS to see how Brachiano behaves in his absence, he is murdered on the latter's orders.

Camillo
The Winter's Tale, 1611
William Shakespeare

Camillo, like ANTIGONUS a lord at the Sicilian court of LEONTES, is a man of courtesy, integrity and humanity. Leontes has looked upon him as his wisest and closest adviser: 'priestlike, thou/ Hast cleansed my bosom'. Leontes confesses to Camillo his suspicions of HERMIONE's infidelity, but while loyal, Camillo is independent and refuses to indulge the king. He is politically shrewd, and a peacemaker without personal interest other than seeing justice done. Early on he advises POLIXENES, the victim of Leontes's rages and, ironically, later performs a similar service for FLORIZEL, who has incurred Polixenes's anger. He helps to bring about the various reconciliations.

Camish, Simon
The Needle's Eye, 1972
Margaret Drabble

Like ROSE VASSILOU, Camish has tried to detach himself from his upbringing and make a new start. Shaking the dust of the north from his feet, he has become a successful lawyer and has manufactured an upper-middle-class life for himself. Yet he is unable to escape the old sensibilities. He comes to see the fixtures and fittings of his life as 'an act of misrepresentation'.

Intelligent and idealistic, he has worked for the common good; yet his own vaulting ambition and the rewards it brings make him rancorous, self-pitying and self-disgusted.

Campaspe
Alexander and Campaspe, 1584
John Lyly

Transfixed by her beauty, Alexander the Great captures Campaspe and bears her off. However his priorities are military rather than erotic and he soon abandons her in favour of the rougher company of his men. To console herself, she begins a long and remarkably coy flirtation with the court artist Apelles.

Campbell, Colin → Red Fox, the

Campbell, Dr Jeff
'Melanctha', in *Three Lives*, 1909
Gertrude Stein

A half-caste doctor in a small Southern town, who attracts but fails to return the love of MELANCTHA HERBERT. His detachment is the uncomfortable antithesis of her father's violence.

Campion, Albert
The Crime at Black Dudley, et seq, 1929–68
Margery Allingham

Albert Campion, amateur detective, appears in 21 of Allingham's 30 novels. In the early books Campion hides his astuteness beneath a mask of private-income indolence. Well-bred, pale-eyed, bespectacled, he is a 'silly ass' managed by his valet, the subversive but kindly Magersfontein Lugg. But he matures, wryly humorous but sometimes disillusioned, until at the end of World War II 'his old misleading vacancy of expression had vanished. But nothing had altered the upward drift of his mouth nor the engaging astonishment which so often and so falsely appeared in his eyes.'

Campo-Basso, Count of
Quentin Durward, 1823
Sir Walter Scott

A wily Italian nobleman who has brought his native wit to assist in the counsels of CHARLES THE BOLD, DUKE OF BURGUNDY. Machiavellian to the last, he shapes his advice in the fable of the traveller, the adder and the fox, recommending that the enemy be crushed with no mercy.

Canacee
The Faerie Queene, 1590–6
Sir Edmund Spenser

The sister of CAMBELL. Wise and learned in every science known to her day, she knows all the secrets of riddles and soothsaying. A herbalist who understands the speech of animals, she is modest, chaste and has many suitors. She is not moved by affection but has a well-governed mind.

Candlemass, Alfie (Aelfrieda)
Poor Fellow My Country, 1975
Xavier Herbert

A white authoress and reformer, Alfie Candlemass has arrived in the Northern Territory of Australia full of enthusiasm and idealism, only to grow disillusioned by government corruption and insensitivity. She falls in love with the liberal JEREMY DELACY, but even though he rejects her, he inspires her in her work for social change. Together, they attempt to transform Australia First into a political party sympathetic to the Aborigine cause. When Jeremy responds to her affection and she becomes pregnant by him, it seems that Alfie's romantic and political dreams are coming true. Yet when they are assaulted during a political meeting and she loses her baby, her dreams turn to tatters.

Candour, Mrs
The School for Scandal, 1777
Richard Brinsley Sheridan
A particularly talkative member of LADY SNEERWELL's group of slanderous gossips. She pretends virtuously to defend the maligned and to deplore scandal, while actually enthusiastically denigrating them and broadcasting it.

Cannon, George Edwin
The Roll Call, 1918
Arnold Bennett
HILDA LESSWAYS's son. A rising young public architect, he wants success and is susceptible to vice. Fascinated by women and their mystique, it is the affection and faith of one which inspires him and a chance remark from another which spurs him to an important step in the pursuit of his career. His treatment of women is sometimes callous, but he is capable of real devotion. When he enlists he sees it as his destiny as an Englishman, but one suspects he may be looking for escape from a life that has become disappointingly conventional.

Canterbury, Archbishop of
Henry V, 1599
William Shakespeare
Canterbury is cynical, ruthless, a manipulator and an opportunist. In order to divert anti-clerical feeling and prevent the threatened confiscation of Church property, he vigorously advises King Henry (HENRY, PRINCE OF WALES) to invade France and assert his claim to the French throne. He also promises financial support for the campaign from the Church. Seen from another angle, however, Canterbury is merely a man of his time. The Church was an enormously strong political lobby and Canterbury, as its head, brings his influence to bear upon the king in order best to defend the institution he serves.

Canty, Tom
The Prince and the Pauper, 1881
Mark Twain
A beggar whose dreams become reality when an exchange of clothes with his look-alike, PRINCE EDWARD, leads, unintentionally, to an exchange of identities. Although he becomes somewhat intoxicated with the fawning and flattery given to him in his new position, his kind and gentle nature endures. He does not abuse his power even when Henry VIII dies and he is proclaimed king. He learns that governing can be a dreary, wearisome business and that even a prince can feel lonely and isolated.

Capello, Bianca
Women Beware Women, c.1621
Thomas Middleton
A young and beautiful Venetian woman who disobeys her parents' wishes by eloping with LEANTIO, a Florentine merchant. She quickly becomes bored with the material poverty of her marriage and the social confinement her husband enforces on her. Her seduction by the DUKE OF FLORENCE provides the catalyst that changes her earlier infatuation with her husband into arrogant and selfish discontent.

Capodistria
Justine, 1957, and throughout *The Alexandria Quartet*, 1968
Lawrence Durrell
A wealthy goblin, obscurely related to JUSTINE, he spends his days sitting on his club terrace watching women pass by, 'with the restless eye of someone endlessly shuffling an old soiled pack of cards'. He is nicknamed 'Da Capo' on account of his sexual prowess.

Caponsacchi, Guiseppe
The Ring and the Book, 1868–9
Robert Browning
A nobly born, refined and cultivated young priest who is at first somewhat worldly and careless. However, when he sees POMPILIA and receives her pleas for help he realizes that as a priest he cannot abandon her to her fate and agrees to help her; it is his duty to God as well as to her. He is possessed of real courage and acts fearlessly to protect the woman who has given him a glimpse of true, pure and unselfish love.

Captain, the
Androcles and the Lion, 1912
George Bernard Shaw
A Roman patrician, the Captain is a handsome man of about 35, 'very cold and distinguished, very superior and authoritative'. Attracted by LAVINIA, a Christian Roman prisoner about to be martyred, the Captain debates the nature of faith and spiritual belief with her, and even proposes marriage in a vain effort to persuade her to recant and save herself. According to him, 'truth, if there be any truth, needs no martyrs'.

Captain Cat
Under Milk Wood, 1954
Dylan Thomas
A blind retired sea captain, he oversees all the goings on in the village. He pulls the 'loud get-out-of-bed bell', commanding action; he hears the children's rhymes as a timepiece; and he follows everyday routines, knowing people by their footsteps. His dreams are all sea memories of his voyages, dead shipmates and especially his love ROSIE PROBERT, over whom he cries like a child.

Capulet
Romeo and Juliet, 1591–6
William Shakespeare
JULIET's father, Lord Capulet, has maintained the feud with the MONTAGUES, although he is beginning to find it difficult to control some of his followers. At times lavish in his parties, he

can be generous, and even finds it in him to speak well of ROMEO. His marriage is unhappy, perhaps because of unfaithfulness on his part, yet he is eager to see his daughter settled in an alliance based on wealth and position rather than love. When she refuses he is furious, resorting to threats to achieve his desires rather than trying to find the reason for her behaviour.

Capulet, Lady
Romeo and Juliet, 1591–6
William Shakespeare

Lady Capulet expects her daughter, JULIET, to follow her example by marrying young and becoming a mother immediately. She is a cold, unfeeling woman, perhaps because of her husband's infidelity, perhaps because of her lost youth. There is no mother-daughter bond between Juliet and her, indeed NURSE holds more maternal sway than she does. Expecting the same obedience from her child that she shows her husband, she offers no love in return.

Carabas, Marquis of
Vivian Grey, 1826–7
Benjamin Disraeli

A powerful but largely unsuccessful politician, he becomes the centre of a new parliamentary cabal created by the ambitious VIVIAN GREY. It is clear that Carabas, a little like Disraeli himself, is disqualified from an automatic entrée into British political life by his foreign blood, but he lacks the enterprise and principle of later outsider figures in Disraeli's fiction.

Caratach
Bonduca, 1613–14
Francis Beaumont and John Fletcher

Caratach is derived from the historical figure of Caractacus (or Caradoc), the King of the Silures in western Britain during the reign of Claudius. He is the cousin of BONDUCA, and, in the play, the General of the Britons. Although noble, chivalrous and wise, he is also brusque, independent, and not one to forgive or forget easily. When Hengo, 'a brave boy', is murdered by the Romans, Caratach immediately kills in revenge. It has been suggested that Caratach is partly a portrait of Sir Walter Raleigh, a political malcontent languishing at that time in the Tower of London.

Carbone, Beatrice
A View from the Bridge, 1955
Arthur Miller

A direct, human woman with strong family values, she finds herself confused by the actions and attitudes of her doomed husband, EDDIE CARBONE. She fights to maintain her position as his wife, and is willing to bring her true fears about her relationship with their adopted niece, CATHERINE CARBONE, to the surface. Her practical advice and ability to cope make her an ideal partner for the flawed, idealistic Eddie, and he dies with her name on his lips.

Carbone, Catherine
A View from the Bridge, 1955
Arthur Miller

An innocent, sheltered girl, brought up by her aunt, BEATRICE CARBONE, and stifled with affection by her uncle, EDDIE CARBONE, she finds herself the focal point of a perplexing psychological struggle between her surrogate father and RODOLPHO, the handsome young Italian who falls in love with. A sweet, perhaps even coy, girl, her secure world is rudely shattered by sexual desire, family disunity and betrayal.

Carbone, Eddie
A View from the Bridge, 1955
Arthur Miller

A longshoreman with simple values, he is a good, decent man, haunted by the stifling affection and – perhaps unconscious – lust he feels for his niece CATHERINE CARBONE, whom he has brought up as his own child. Pushed by the fates, he is alienated by his family and community on betraying his illegal immigrant cousins to the authorities. Though his crime and its consequences are abhorrent, the audience cannot be without sympathy for this 'perversely pure' man.

Carbury, Lady Matilda
The Way We Live Now, 1875
Anthony Trollope

The mother of SIR FELIX CARBURY. She is a rather superficial, dilettantish lady, who adores her wicked son and is largely oblivious to his malpractices. She aspires to literary fame without the talent to achieve it, although she 'could write after a glib, commonplace, sprightly fashion, and had already acquired the knack of spreading all she knew very thin, so that it might cover a vast surface'.

Carbury, Roger
The Way We Live Now, 1875
Anthony Trollope

A second cousin of SIR FELIX CARBURY, but quite the opposite in character. He is about 40, with the 'appearance of great strength and perfect health. A more manly man to the eye was never seen'. He is good, kindly, honest, and sees through the corrupt commercialism around him, but his suit for the hand of Felix's sister Henrietta is unsuccessful.

Carbury, Sir Felix
The Way We Live Now, 1875
Anthony Trollope

The unscrupulous, corrupt son of LADY MATILDA CARBURY. He is 'beautiful to look at, ready-witted, and intelligent', but has a stony, unfeeling heart, and is a dishonest, conniving rogue beneath his pleasant exterior. He is supposed to elope with MARIE MELMOTTE, but instead takes her money and squanders it gambling, just as he has squandered his doting mother's fortune. His mother's friends dispatch him into exile on the Continent.

Cardew, Cecily
The Importance of Being Earnest, 1895
Oscar Wilde

JOHN WORTHING's ward, and the granddaughter of his adoptive father, Cecily is a very pretty, silly and ingenuous young girl who falls in love with her guardian's wayward younger brother without ever meeting him, largely because his name is Ernest. Impatient and impulsive, she is at the same time charming and irritating.

Cardinal, the
The Duchess of Malfi, 1623
John Webster

Brother of the DUCHESS OF MALFI and FERDINAND, DUKE OF CALABRIA, he is an extremely worldly but melancholic prelate, who tried to become pope by bribery. Unpleasantly cynical, he keeps a mistress but does not believe that his widowed sister should remarry. Although proud of his royal blood, he remains murderously calm on learning that his sister has married a commoner.

Cardinal, the
Women Beware Women, c.1621
Thomas Middleton

The brother of the DUKE OF FLORENCE, he plays an important role in highlighting the corruption and moral turpitude of the duke (and, by implication, many of the other characters). He is a pious man of 'spotless honour' who seeks to point out to his brother the error of his ways in order to save him from eternal damnation.

Carella, Gino
Where Angels Fear to Tread, 1905
E M Forster

Fresh from military service, he is a handsome, well-built young man of 21. The son of a provincial Italian dentist, he has the unconscious arrogance of someone raised to believe in the superiority of his sex. Amiable, indolent and happy to marry for money, he remains insensitive to the way his need for compliance distresses his English wife, LILIA HERRITON. Aggressively masculine at times, he also shows himself to be a devoted and loving father.

Carew, Poppy
The Vacillations of Poppy Carew, 1986
Mary Wesley

Though mousy-haired and sensible-looking, she does not conform to her strait-laced image. She switches between yearning for the lost and for the dead: her lover Edmund, who has run off with a richer prize, and her father Bob, whose death she precipitates by making him laugh when she tells him the news about Edmund. Her father, who made a fortune out of gambling and dallying with women, advised her to back outsiders, and she proceeds to apply this advice to her love life; only she is not sure who the outsiders are, so she hedges her bets. Hiding her emotions behind a mask of sunglasses or feigned sleep, she puts up the shutters completely on incidents she prefers to forget.

Carey, Philip
Of Human Bondage, 1915
W Somerset Maugham

His mother's death leaves him lonely and hypersensitive and his withdrawn nature is compounded by a club foot, which is a kind of Oedipal mark that, in a work as obviously autobiographical as this, symbolizes Maugham's restless self-questing and his nascent homosexuality. Raised by uncultured and narrow-minded relations, Philip turns to art and ideas with the same all-consuming hunger he later brings to adult relationships, like that with Mildred Rogers. He finds freedom through his relationship with SALLY ATHELNEY.

Carker, Harriet
Dombey and Son, 1848
Charles Dickens

The sister of JAMES and JOHN CARKER, she goes to live with John after his embezzlement of Dombey and Son is discovered. Her devotion to him is despised by James. She befriends ALICE MARWOOD and marries John's friend, the firm's head clerk, Mr Morfin.

Carker, James
Dombey and Son, 1848
Charles Dickens

The odious manager of Dombey and Son whom MR DOMBEY relies on implicitly. He despises both his brother, JOHN CARKER, and sister, HARRIET CARKER. His prominent features are 'two unbroken rows of glistening teeth, whose regularity and whiteness were quite distressing' and a smile 'like the snarl of a cat'. Resenting his subordinate position, he takes revenge by over-extending the firm's credit and eloping with EDITH DOMBEY to Dijon. Through ALICE MARWOOD, the mistress whom Carker has spurned, Dombey learns of his treachery and pursues him. Fleeing, he dies under the wheels of a train.

Carker, John
Dombey and Son, 1848
Charles Dickens

The elder brother of JAMES CARKER, he embezzled money from Dombey and Son when young, but is retained by the firm as a lowly junior clerk. Now a chastened and faithful employee, he befriends WALTER GAY, lives quietly with his sister, HARRIET CARKER, and is despised by James. He loses his post when James elopes with EDITH DOMBEY, but on inheriting James's fortune, he secretly makes over the annual interest to the bankrupt MR DOMBEY.

Carmichael, Augustus
To the Lighthouse, 1927
Virginia Woolf

A solitary, intellectual and rather eccentric old man. He is slovenly and unkempt – such trivialities as appearance do not bother him. Unhinged by suffering, an overpowering wife and a sense of his own irrelevance, he is a sad and pathetic character.

Carmody, Dr
Black Jack, 1968
Leon Garfield

The doctor makes his living by selling his remarkable Elixir of Youth, a potent formula that serves equally well as cough medicine or furniture polish. He conveys a natural authority and inspires great confidence both in his customers and in his companions in the travelling fair. Possessed of a powerful humanity and intelligence, he is convinced that he has the power to restore BELLE to good health. He claims to be a student of the human mind, and although on one level he is a fraud, he has the wisdom and perception to see into the true nature of others.

Carmody, Paddy, Ida and Sean
The Sundowners, 1952
Jon Cleary

A weak, apparently directionless man, Paddy is a wandering drover, driving small herds of cattle from place to place in the Australia of the 1920s. In contrast to him, his wife Ida is temperamentally unsuited to an itinerant life and longs to settle down. A determined and disciplined woman, she is also one of astonishing patience, with a great capacity for love. When Paddy throws away their chances of buying a farm by gambling away all their savings, Ida is bitterly disappointed but soldiers on at his side. Their young son, Sean, resilient and watchful, observes the relationship and the strength and weakness of his parents as he follows them from place to place.

Carne, Robert
South Riding, 1936
Winifred Holtby

A gentleman farmer whose family have farmed Maythorpe in the South Riding for 500 years, he commands his inheritance with easy authority. Gentle, melancholy and inarticulate, his way of life is grounded in centuries of tradition and in a deep reverence for the land, the seasons and the hierarchical order of creation. Generous and kindly towards his tenants, reactionary and obstructive in his politics, Carne has depleted his farm to maintain a disastrous marriage, and must make his stand against encroaching social change in the knowledge that he is already ruined.

Caro, Avice
The Well-Beloved, 1892
Thomas Hardy

Grandmother, mother and granddaughter, she is the 'three-in-one'. The cousin of JOCELYN PIERSTON, she is an extension of femininity who moves with him throughout his lifetime. An imaginary creature who taunts the sculptor throughout the tale, she, like all the others, proves ultimately unsatisfactory. She is too close to reality to constitute fully the impossible ideal.

Carol
Carol, originally titled *The Price of Salt*, 1952
Patricia Highsmith

An elegant, enigmatic sophisticate who becomes an object of affection and obsession for THERESE. Outwardly commanding, poised and even formidable, she begins to reveal a more tranquil sadness and vulnerability as their relationship develops. At first regarding Therese with amused detachment, Carol falls for her young friend's innocence and honest affection. Travelling across the USA, she breaks the bonds with her husband and family and becomes the catalyst for Therese's

journey into mature emotions and artistic integrity.

Carol
Oleanna, 1992
David Mamet

A student anxious to avoid failing her course, she appeals to JOHN, her professor, about what she should do. John's suggestion that she might gain a higher grade if she were to visit his office regularly, disturbs and bewilders her; later, having gained the support of a women's group, she chooses to interpret the invitation as a sexual advance, even though there has been no hint of previous flirtation between them. Her charges of sexual harassment culminate in a crisis during which she is the victim of John's physical assault. However, her precise motives, and whether she is even correct in her assumption of John's sexual interest in her, are left for the play's audience to decide.

Caroline
The Comfort of Strangers, 1981
Ian McEwan

Caroline, the daughter of a Canadian ambassador, grew up in a dull, happy home and knew nothing about sex until her marriage at 20. Now pale and crippled, she is the masochistic half of an unholy alliance that has developed between herself and her sadistic, hate-filled husband, ROBERT. During their sojourn in Venice, she is a willing accomplice in his depraved scheme to carry their sexually perverted 'pleasures' to their vicious conclusion, with COLIN as their victim.

Carpenter, Pete
Moving On, 1970
Larry McMurtry

To some extent, he must be regarded as a projection of McMurtry's awareness of his own role as an observer rather than a participant in the life of the old West. Pete tries to compile a book of rodeo photographs and to make a heroic film about a bronco rider. Almost unconsciously, the choices he makes in his own life – for freedom, rather than for respectability and success – align him with his ideals.

Carpenter, the → Five Guildsmen, the

Carpenter, the → Walrus and the Carpenter, the

Carr, Bernard, also given as Bernard Clare/Clayre
Bernard Clare, 1946, also published as *Bernard Clayre*, 1948, et seq
James T Farrell

A young writer who shakes himself free of his – and Farrell's – working-class Chicago-Irish background and establishes a career in the left-wing New York literary world. Rejecting the Catholic Church and espousing a peculiar brand of Nietzschean communism, he is a study in detached self-reliance and his rootlessness contrasts sharply with the backgrounds of earlier characters such as STUDS LONIGAN and

DANNY O'NEILL, who were all cut from the same loosely autobiographical cloth.

Carr, David
How to be Good, 2001
Nick Hornby

Cynical, embittered and lazy, married to KATIE CARR, who threatens to divorce him, David vents his frustrations in a column he writes under the heading of *The Angriest Man in Holloway* for a local London newspaper. Although intensely exasperating, he is also likeable and, after a fashion, reasonable. When DJ GoodNews, a faith healer, relieves his back pain, David is transformed into a zealously 'good' person: patient, loving, open-hearted, alarmingly generous, and proposing that every household in his street take in a homeless person. David represents some of the pretensions and many of the foibles of contemporary middle-class urban liberalism.

Carr, Henry
Travesties, 1975
Tom Stoppard

Largely portrayed through the faltering memories of Carr, a British Consular official, the play, a comedy, assembles several figures including Lenin, James Joyce and Tristan Tzara, all of whom happened to be in Zurich during World War I, and revolves around Carr's involvement in an amateur production of *The Importance of Being Earnest*. The older Carr relishes his former association with such luminaries while proving an unreliable narrator; the younger Carr presents a dandyish figure, easily ruffled, both bemused by and jealous of the artistic spirit, who likes to assert his authority over such figures as Joyce.

Carr, Katie
How to be Good, 2001
Nick Hornby

A north London General Practitioner, Katie astounds both herself and her husband DAVID CARR by telephoning him from Leeds, where he is attending a conference, and announcing that she wants a divorce. A hard-working doctor, wife and mother, she sublimates her anger and despair and, as a result, tends towards the neurotic. Although she considers herself a 'good person', her husband's transformation under the influence of faith healer DJ GoodNews, causes her to question her own moral principles.

Carr, Katy
What Katy Did, 1872, et seq
Susan Coolidge

The eldest of Dr Carr's six motherless children in a small New England town, careless Katy Carr leads her siblings and friends in boisterous escapades, until she suffers a serious spinal injury falling from a forbidden swing. Bedridden for two years, she learns the virtues of patience and making the best of things as well as other lessons in the 'School of Pain'. The morality of small things is enlivened by her ingenuous spirit. As her life studies continue she masters housekeeping, ladylike conduct at her boarding school and education of Americans abroad.

Carraway, Nick
The Great Gatsby, 1925
F Scott Fitzgerald

The narrator, he is a young mid-westerner who has come east to work, and is sucked into JAY GATSBY's seductive orbit because DAISY BUCHANAN is his cousin. He is sensitive, intelligent and cultured, and rejects the immoral blandishments around him, and the superficial values of the Long Island set. We see Gatsby through his eyes, and his rectitude sets the tone for the novel, but he is tolerant and non-judgemental in his assessment of him.

Carricker, Lt Col Benny
Guard of Honor, 1948
James Gould Cozzens

A brave and resourceful USAF pilot officer, he is also impulsive and prejudiced. When MAJOR GENERAL IRA N BEAL's plane, which Carricker is flying, is almost struck by another aircraft, Carricker angrily beats the young black pilot, sparking off a scandal about racial discrimination in the forces.

Carrie
Carrie, 1974
Stephen King

She lives with her fanatically religious mother and is the butt of endless persecution by schoolmates. When her periods begin, she suddenly acquires the power of psychokinesis, and when she is further humiliated at a high-school prom, she wreaks a terrible revenge on family, friends, and town.

Carrington, Lou
'St Mawr', in *St Mawr together with A Princess*, 1925
D H Lawrence

The daughter of a rich American, Lou has married Rico Witt, a struggling portrait painter. They live in London. Young, uprooted from her culture and rather a dreamer, Lou has a quiet aplomb and a quality of 'gamine knowingness' about her. But when her marriage disintegrates into mere acquaintanceship at close quarters, only intermittently punctuated by passionate love-making, her determination to renew herself and begin again takes precedence above all else. With the horse, ST MAWR, and her mother, she journeys to Texas, where they settle to a new life.

Carroll
Palace of the Peacock, 1960, part of *The Guyana Quartet*, 1985
Wilson Harris

The mysterious musician whose music on the Carib bone-flute animates the search for the paradise in which nothing has changed 'save for the "second death" that re-opens or re-visits every blind deed in the past'.

Carroll, Eva
The Book of Eve, 1975
Constance Beresford-Howe

After 40 years of marriage, 65-year-old Eva Carroll leaves her demanding husband and her comfortable home. Clutching her pension book, she begins a new life on the other side of Montreal. Respectable, middle-class mores have constrained her in the past; certainly nothing Eva has done can match the audacity of this. She surprises even herself. Although she soon acquires mannerisms that others might see as eccentric – wearing men's running shoes in winter, for instance – she plunges into her new life with vigour, radiating high spirits, bohemianism and anarchy. She even takes a lover, a 48-year-old Hungarian, who cooks marvellously.

Carruthers, Lord George de Bruce
The Eustace Diamonds, 1873
Anthony Trollope

A rather rootless, peripatetic gentleman who 'always had horses, but never had a home'. He was a colonel of the 'roughest regiment of Volunteers in all England', and was thought to like a wager, but is now said to be scrupulous in his financial transactions. He has occasional dealings in stocks and shares in the City. He is suspected by some of stealing LADY LIZZIE EUSTACE's diamonds, but later marries her after her bigamous union is dissolved.

Carson, Henry
Mary Barton, 1848
Elizabeth Gaskell

The mill-owner's son, he is a deliberately contrasting character to JEM WILSON. Rich, flash and perhaps superficial, he is portrayed as a victim of birth; he can never be popular or respected because of his father's position of power and thus suffers through his privilege.

Carson, Rod
Rusty Bugles, 1948
Sumner Locke Elliott

A newcomer to a hut of soldiers in a wartime ordnance depot in the Northern Territory of Australia. An educated and optimistic young man who has worked as a reporter, he sometimes expresses poetic thoughts about his surroundings. He feels sympathetic to the hostile VIC RICHARDS, seeing him as a tragic figure, and he encourages him to read intelligent books. As he becomes part of the group, he adopts its expressively free language.

Carstone, Richard
Bleak House, 1853
Charles Dickens

A ward of the Court of Chancery and a suitor in the case of *Jarndyce v Jarndyce*. With his cousin, ADA CLARE, he goes to live with JOHN JARNDYCE and ESTHER SUMMERSON. He restlessly tries one career after another but becomes obsessed with the lawsuit. Marrying Ada in secret, he devotes all his energies to the case, eventually falling ill. When the case ends with all the costs absorbed by lawyers, he dies of shock and disappointment.

Carter, Hal
Picnic, 1953
William Inge

He is 'an exceedingly handsome, husky youth' dressed in a worn T-shirt and dungarees, who is clearly down on his luck. Although he is a 'bum', he is fiercely proud, but also boastful, impatient and self-deceiving. A former college football hero from a dissolute family, he is obsessed with his innate badness, but believes that 'if I just had the chance, I could set the world on fire'. He risks everything to try to win MADGE OWENS.

Carter, Lt Col John
Miss Ravenel's Conversion from Secession to Loyalty, 1867
J W De Forest

A debonair Virginian (who nonetheless fights for the North in the American Civil War), he combines the aristocratic/chivalric ideal of Southern manhood with a ruthless sensuality. Briefly won over to the straight and narrow, he marries LILLIE RAVENEL, but his baser instincts prove too strong and he backslides into dissipation.

Carter, Rain
The Sandcastle, 1957
Iris Murdoch

The shy and naive daughter of a recently deceased painter, Rain spent a lonely childhood in the south of France. Moulded by her father's strong personality and powerful talent, she is only just beginning to discover herself and her own artistic form when she meets and falls in love with an older married man, WILLIAM MOR, and painfully grows up in the process.

Carter, Susan
The Witch of Edmonton, c.1621
Thomas Dekker, William Rowley and John Ford

A woman of elegance and charm, Susan is selected by FRANK THORNEY's father as a suitable bride for his son, and she duly marries him. But, innocent and optimistic, she is the hapless victim of Frank's hunger for position and money, for he has married her only to secure her dowry. Once he believes it to be in his grasp, he murders her, blaming the deed on her rejected suitors.

Carton, Sydney
A Tale of Two Cities, 1859
Charles Dickens

An intellectually gifted barrister, but dissolute and lacking willpower and self-discipline. While incapable of helping himself, he uses his legal mind to advance the career of his old school friend, MR STRYVER. In a treason trial, he saves the life of Stryver's client, CHARLES DARNAY, whom he closely resembles, and then falls in love with a witness, LUCIE MANETTE. Knowing himself unworthy, he declares his love and bids her farewell forever. Later in Paris, after Lucie and Darnay have married and had a child, he sacrifices his own life by changing places with Darnay in prison. His thoughts as he is taken to the guillotine are the closing words of the novel: 'It is a far, far better thing that I do, than I have ever done; it is a far, far better rest that I go to than I have ever known.'

Carver, Betsy and Jo
A Summons to Memphis, 1986
Peter Taylor

The daughters of GEORGE CARVER and elder sisters of PHILLIP CARVER, they embark on life as fresh-spirited débutantes but, under the controlling hand of their father, graduate into ungainly spinsterhood, dressing outrageously, boasting about invisible suitors and asserting a fierce independence in the form of a successful real-estate business. Seemingly loving daughters they remain deeply bitter about their thwarted early romances and, behind highly lipsticked smiles, are determined to even the score with their ageing parent.

Carver, George
A Summons to Memphis, 1986
Peter Taylor

A man of unwavering resolve, in both career and personal terms, who binds his family to him with threads of steel, George Carver elevated himself from the small-time ranks of a cautious legal family to become the youngest member elected to the Nashville state legislature. A distinguished athlete as well as lawyer, he is seen by his son, PHILLIP CARVER, as a 'man of iron will and courage and perfect skill and limitless intelligence'. His first brush with bad luck, in the form of Lewis Shackleford, threatens to ruin his career; but in retrospect, it is his wife and children's lives that are irreparably damaged by his insistence that the family move to Memphis and cut off all contact with their previous Nashville existence. His subsequent actions in blighting each of his children's marriage prospects foments smouldering but well-concealed resentment.

Carver, Phillip
A Summons to Memphis, 1986
Peter Taylor

A middle-aged rare-book collector and editor in a New York publishing company. The narrator of the story, he appears as a mild, dull character, introspective and emotionally repressed. This he attributes to the blighting effect of his father's dramatic career change when, after financial disaster inflicted by his erstwhile best friend Lewis Shackleford, GEORGE CARVER uprooted his family from Nashville to Memphis, thus, Phillip believes, inflicting permanent damage on himself, his mother and his sisters, BETSY and JO CARVER. Even when George Carver is in his eighties, Phillip remains dingily in his shadow, beginning to make sense of his justified resentment towards this manipulative, charismatic man, yet sickened by the unspoken warfare he witnesses between his siblings and their now vulnerable father.

Carwin, Francis
Wieland, 1798
Charles Brockden Brown

Carwin is, above all else, a trickster. His ability to impersonate and to throw voices is, in part, the cause of unhappiness, wrecked relationships, murder and madness. Carwin stands directly against notions of ultimate truth and knowledge, his art being used to obscure fact and to diminish human control over events. His enigmatic personality is the chief part of his attraction for others, 'the uncertainty whether his fellowship tended to good or evil'; it is this attraction that constitutes the danger.

Casamassima, Princess, formerly Christina Light
The Princess Casamassima, 1886
Roderick Hudson, 1876
Henry James

The one-time beacon of the sculptor RODERICK HUDSON's life, she is now separated from her husband Prince Casamassima and has become obsessed with the plight of the poor and down-trodden. Fiery-spirited and with the same aristocratic instincts as HYACINTH ROBINSON, she becomes the bellwether of the anarcho-utopian movement in London.

Casaubon, Rev Edward
Middlemarch, 1871–2
George Eliot

A pitiable figure, Casaubon is the ugly, elderly pedant who singles out DOROTHEA BROOKE to be his wife, motivated not by love but by his selfish belief that she will satisfy the requirements of his twilight years. Pompous and egotistic in his assurance of his superior intellect, he fails to recognize the outdated mediocrity of his unfinished work, *Key to All Mythologies*, and increasingly alienates himself from Dorothea because of his jealousy of her friendship with WILL LADISLAW. 'Spiritually a-hungered like the rest of us', he remains sadly self-obsessed to the end.

Casby, Christopher
Little Dorrit, 1857
Charles Dickens

Father of FLORA FINCHING and the hard, avaricious landlord of Bleeding Heart Yard. Called 'the Patriarch' because of his benevolent appearance, he conceals his extortionate practices by using his agent, MR PANCKS, to collect his rents. He is finally publicly exposed and humiliated by Pancks.

Casca
Julius Caesar, c.1599
William Shakespeare

A cynic and a back-stabber both metaphorically and literally. He strikes the first blow in the assassination of JULIUS CAESAR. He also, earlier, reports the offer of the laurel crown at the games by ANTONY, giving a lively but sarcastic account of the event. His lack of courage during the storm reveals his essential cowardice.

Case
The Beach of Falesá, 1892
Robert Louis Stevenson

An enigmatic villain, whose origins are obscure, but who clearly comes from an educated background. At times he can be sophisticated, talented company; at others he is the worst blasphemer of the islands. He is redeemed from total evil by the love he feels for his Samoan wife. A cynical, mercenary man, Case treats MR WILTSHIRE with charming kindness, intending to engineer his downfall.

Casey, Sarah
The Tinker's Wedding, 1907
J M Synge

A strong, good-looking, bright and talkative

tinker, Sarah Casey, 'the Beauty of Ballinacree', has determined to marry her lover, MICHAEL BYRNE. Her decision is less to do with love than with her realization that it is spring and that another year has gone by. She appears worried that her celebrated beauty might fade and old age overtake her while the chance of some kind of security passes her by.

Caspar, Billy
A Kestrel for a Knave, 1968
Barry Hines

An undersized adolescent who treats his kestrel with the love and care he has never known in his own family. His isolation is compounded by a semi-comic inability to communicate with adults, either at home or in school. He comes fully alive only with his kestrel, which manifests the strength, pride and independence he longs for but lacks. Some of the bird's indomitable spirit is left in him, however, even after it is cruelly killed.

Cass, Dunstan
Silas Marner, 1861
George Eliot

Dunstan, or 'Dunsey' to his few friends, is 'a spiteful jeering fellow, who seemed to enjoy his drink the more when other people went dry'. He blackmails his poor brother GODFREY CASS – and enjoys it – over the latter's secret and unwise marriage, and steals SILAS MARNER's gold when financially pressed. His main hobby aside from stealing and cheating is holding horsewhips in an action pose.

Cass, Godfrey
Silas Marner, 1861
George Eliot

Open-faced and good-natured, Godfrey finds himself in trouble over his secret marriage (exploited by his brother, DUNSTAN CASS) to a drunken wife. Consciousness of this hampers his wooing of NANCY LAMMETER, whom he eventually marries. By his first wife, however, he is the natural father of the foundling EPPIE. A sense of responsibility eventually makes him confront this fact when Eppie is a young woman, but he is too stubborn to realize that he is too late in declaring himself to become her father.

Cassandra
Troilus and Cressida, 1601/2
William Shakespeare

The daughter of King PRIAM and 'mad sister' of HECTOR and PARIS, Cassandra is a prophetess whose visions and doom-laden warnings are ignored by the Trojans. Dismissed by TROILUS as a 'foolish, dreaming, superstitious girl', she prophesies the downfall of Hector and of Troy.

Cassidy, Aldo
The Naive and Sentimental Lover, 1971
John Le Carré

A privately-educated middle-class Englishman who makes accessories for prams, such as the pram disc brake, which he invented. Consequently rich, Cassidy has a house, wife, kids and car. He finds a further dimension to life, however, in his love affair with the anti-

bourgeois, uninhibited Shamus and Helen, a couple that oscillate between clichéd hippiedom and an assumed aristocratic outlook. Offbeat experiences involving travel, football and sex follow, but it is Shamus who makes the rules, which Cassidy never understands. He is better suited to bourgeois family life.

Cassidy, Maggie
Maggie Cassidy, 1959
Jack Kerouac

A high school dropout in Lowell, she is in love with JACK DULUOZ, but finds his new lifestyle among the Beat writers inimical. Despite a rebellious adolescent streak, she wants to be married in accordance with Lowell values, and tells him: 'if you want to marry me ever don't try to have me come to this New York'. They are left, literally and metaphorically, 'miles apart'.

Cassio
Othello, 1603/4
William Shakespeare

'Honourable lieutenant' to OTHELLO, he is a loyal, physically attractive individual who becomes a pawn in IAGO's wicked plan to destroy the Moor. His anguish when alienated from the general he adores and his flippant nonchalance in dealing with BIANCA, who adores him, suggest the youthful naivety necessary to Iago's success. Left as ruler of Cyprus at the play's conclusion, he has learnt the virtues of leadership through a cruel apprenticeship.

Cassius, Caius
Julius Caesar, c.1599
William Shakespeare

Politically astute and envious of the power of JULIUS CAESAR, his ability to manipulate those less able than he is allows him to persuade MARCUS BRUTUS to join the plot to kill Caesar. Caesar alone sees him for what he is: 'he thinks too much, such men are dangerous' – one shrewd politician's recognition of another. However, after the assassination he reveals his weakness of character; unable to influence Brutus, he defers to decisions he knows to be calamitously impolitic, leading to defeat and death.

Cassy
Uncle Tom's Cabin, or, Life Among the Lowly, 1851–2
Harriet Beecher Stowe

A mulatto woman, sold to SIMON LEGREE in the New Orleans slave market to be his concubine. Proud and self-reliant, with none of UNCLE TOM's acceptance of his lowly status, she plots her escape, and is eventually revealed to be the mother of ELIZA, who shares her resilient self-awareness.

Castabella
The Atheist's Tragedy, c.1611
Cyril Tourneur

The daughter of Belforest, a rich baron, she promises herself in marriage to CHARLEMONT before he leaves for war. In his absence, however, she is forced by the evil manipulations of D'AMVILLE and her own dutiful and obedient nature to marry Rousard, D'Amville's son. The marriage remains unconsummated due to sickness on the husband's part (as well as disinclination on the wife's), and Castabella retains her chastity and innocence throughout. She is a faithful and virtuous woman who, together with her beloved Charlemont, faces the possibility of almost certain death with Christian fortitude and acceptance.

Castalio
The Orphan, 1680
Thomas Otway
One of the two sons of ACASTO, Castalio is the elder brother of POLYDORE and, like him, in love with MONIMIA, the orphan with whom they have been raised. A man of uncertain temper, he is evasive, often foolish, sentimental and ineffectual. Nevertheless, he possesses some psychological perception and deviousness, judging that he will win Monimia if he feigns indifference to her. Alternatively, this pretence might be caused by his recognizing a conflict between love and family loyalty. His secret wedding to Monimia suggests the charade is designed to deceive society, which would oppose a marriage between a wealthy man and a dowerless orphan.

Castile, Duke of
The Spanish Tragedy, 1592
Thomas Kyd
The Duke of Castile has two children, the evil DON LORENZO, and the virtuous BEL-IMPERIA. Together with his son, he supports PRINCE BALTHAZAR as a suitor for his daughter, not because he believes him a particularly good man, merely that the political situation seems to call for it.

Castilla, Cesar
The Mambo Kings Play Songs of Love, 1990
Oscar Hijuelos
A Cuban exile in New York, the Mambo King is a sentimental priapist who covers up his sense of loss and estrangement with a veneer of poised self-confidence and charm. Only as age overtakes him, and his physical prowess diminishes, does he succumb to the bitter melancholy that afflicts his brother, NESTOR CASTILLA.

Castilla, Nestor
The Mambo Kings Play Songs of Love, 1990
Oscar Hijuelos
CESAR CASTILLA's younger brother, he is the trumpeter with the band, an artist rather than a showman, whose feelings of loss are sublimated in the passionate 'Beautiful Maria of My Soul', a love-song dedicated to a girl he has left behind in Cuba. New York is agony to Nestor, and he slides helplessly into nostalgia.

Castiza
The Revenger's Tragedy, 1607
Thomas Middleton or Cyril Tourneur
The sister of VENDICE, and seemingly the only character whose virtue is unaffected by the corruption around her. Honourable and pure, she is untempted by LUSSURIOSO's promises of wealth and advancement in return for her becoming his mistress, and her chastity remains impenetrable even in the face of the persuasive 'Piato' and the arguments of her mother, GRATIANA.

Castle, Jan
The One Day of the Year, 1960 (play), 1967 (novel)
Alan Seymour
A middle-class Sydney girl and a college friend of HUGHIE COOK. They collaborate – and their relationship eventually founders – on an anti-war skit aimed at ANZAC Day, a date Hughie's father regards as sacrosanct.

Castle, Maurice
The Human Factor, 1978
Graham Greene
A secret agent with 30 years of service in the British intelligence forces. He is also a double agent, passing information on South Africa to the Russians, a betrayal based on personal allegiance to his communist contact rather than on political conviction. He longs for a quiet retirement in a place he calls 'Peace of Mind', but is caught passing one last (worthless) secret and has to escape to a life of estrangement and loneliness in Moscow.

Castlewood, Frank
The History of Henry Esmond, Esquire, 1852
W M Thackeray
As a child, the young heir of Castlewood is worried over and spoiled by his parents LADY RACHEL CASTLEWOOD and VISCOUNT FRANCIS CASTLEWOOD. 'He took their caresses as men do, and as if they were his right.' In later years, he is handsome and generous-hearted, untouched by false pride. An ardent Jacobite like his sister BEATRIX ESMOND, he becomes involved in a plot to restore the Old Pretender, JAMES EDWARD STUART.

Castlewood, Lady Rachel
The History of Henry Esmond, Esquire, 1852
W M Thackeray
Her much older husband, VISCOUNT FRANCIS CASTLEWOOD, considers her excessively possessive, but emotionally unresponsive. To young HENRY ESMOND, she seems like an angel of mercy, and it is the divide in her nature and the rapid exchange of emotions that is the most intriguing thing about her. It is tantalizingly unclear whether she really is a paragon who suffers unfairly at her husband's hands, or a cold shrew who lacks a basic spark of humanity and hides behind a display of extravagant sentimentality.

Castlewood, Viscount Francis
The History of Henry Esmond, Esquire, 1852
W M Thackeray
Presumptive heir to the estate, when his father dies at the battle of the Boyne. He is crusty and sarcastic, bluntly dismissive of his wife, LADY RACHEL CASTLEWOOD (particularly after she is scarred by smallpox), and of all her sex, whom he regards as smothering and passionless. A philanderer, with a powerful thirst and a love of gaming, he remains essentially amiable. When Lady Rachel responds to the attentions of LORD

MOHUN, Castlewood challenges his rival to a duel and is killed.

Casy, Jim
The Grapes of Wrath, 1939
John Steinbeck

A one-time preacher turned labour activist whom the JOADs meet on the road to California. He espouses a kind of countrified socialism, matched by great personal strength. He is jailed and later killed by vigilantes while leading a fruit pickers' strike.

Catalina
The High Road, 1988
Edna O'Brien

A tragic young woman subdued by her repressive family life, she is yearning for love and affection. She accepts her world and her place within it, but her soul is severely undernourished. A working-class Catholic who works constantly and is married to a brutal husband, she is a victim and a pawn. ANNA unwittingly uses her as well, but for the first time she feels someone is relating to her as a person. Ironically, it is this 'real' relationship which leads to her tragic end.

Catchprice, Benny
The Tax Inspector, 1991
Peter Carey

The nephew of CATHY MCPHERSON and grandson of GRANNY CATCHPRICE, 16-year-old Benny worked on a bench at the Spare Parts Department at Catchprice Motors, the family business, until his aunt sacked him. This is a crisis, for despite the fact that business is ailing, Benny had dreams of describing himself portentously as a car dealer. A languid, stringy youth, his ears apparently permanently shrouded by the headphones of a portable cassette-player, Benny is not bright but has a natural resilience. Like a vigorous weed, it seems that although he might be trampled down, he will stubbornly reassert himself. Perhaps it is this combination which others think of when they describe him as peacockish, even 'creepy'.

Catchprice, Granny
The Tax Inspector, 1991
Peter Carey

As the mother of CATHY MCPHERSON and the grandmother of BENNY CATCHPRICE, Granny is head of the Catchprice family. In her mid-eighties, she gives the appearance at first glance of being a tough old character. She is at times assertive to the point of outright aggression. She smokes strong cigarettes, and likes thick-cut chops with plenty of fat. She seems tall and dominant but is actually quite short and is often lonely and frightened. 'She ducked, she dodged, she avoided', is how Granny's reactions to each new family and business crisis are described. She lives on affectionately combative terms with her relations, yet strikes up a relationship with MARIA TAKIS that is almost motherly.

Catherick, Anne
The Woman in White, 1860
Wilkie Collins

The daughter of MRS JANE ANNE CATHERICK and Philip Fairlie, she bears a striking resemblance to LAURA FAIRLIE that makes her central to the diabolical plans of SIR PERCIVAL GLYDE and COUNT ISIDOR OTTAVIO BALDASSARE FOSCO. Unaware of her father's identity, she has coincidentally spent her happiest days in the company of Laura's mother and retains an affection for her benefactress that supersedes all other concerns. The 'woman in white' of the title, she is an innocent, bewildered young woman who has been confined to an asylum. Distressed, weary and suffering from a serious heart condition, she is prepared to risk every fibre of her being in Laura's service.

Catherick, Mrs Jane Anne
The Woman in White, 1860
Wilkie Collins

The mother of ANNE CATHERICK, she is a former maid, 'born with the tastes of a lady' and 'fond of foolish admiration and fine clothes'. Having sullied her reputation as a single woman, she married in haste but was abandoned when her husband discovered the extent of her deception. Now a strong-willed woman of mystery who receives an annual allowance from SIR PERCIVAL GLYDE, she has grown obsessed with her social position and is determined that those members of the small community in Welmingham who once ostracized her will one day attest to her respectability and wealth.

Catherine, or Cat, properly Catherine Hall
Catherine: a Story, 1839–40
W M Thackeray

She is based on the historical Catherine Hayes, who was burned at Tyburn in 1726 for the particularly horrible murder of her husband. Though a slattern and a minx, she is a great beauty, which earns her a certain leeway with her employer, the landlord of the Bugle Inn.

Catilina, Lucius Sergius
Catiline, his Conspiracy, 1611
Ben Jonson

An inhabitant of Rome in the 1st century BC, Catilina fails to win a consulship by election and consequently plans a military coup to overthrow the Republic and have himself installed as head of state. The insurrection is eventually quashed by Cicero. A ruthless man (he murdered his first wife and their son in order to marry his second), he is driven by insatiable ambition and lust for power. He is clever and manipulative and has the confidence of one who believes in his own invincibility. This, and his anger, are instrumental in his downfall.

Catrine
The Silver Darlings, 1941
Neil Gunn

Clinging to the crofting way of life to which she was brought up in Kildonan, Catrine's hatred of the sea can only be reinforced by the loss at its hands of first her uncle, then her beloved husband, TORMAD. Tragically left a pregnant widow at the age of 19, she leaves Dale for Dunster and in the ensuing years learns to control her extreme over-protectiveness of her son, FINN, as well as finally accepting that she must let go of the past in order to fulfil the potential of her own life.

Catriona → Drummond, Catriona

Cattistock, Dogberry (Dog)
Weymouth Sands, 1934
John Cowper Powys
A wealthy brewer in Weymouth, where he is the richest man in the town, but leads 'a wretched life' with his wife and 'idiot' son. He is a vigorous and unscrupulous man of action, and no lover of humanity. Aged about 40, but prematurely grey, he possesses 'immense reserves of massive, stubborn power'.

Cattleman, Katherine
The Nowhere City, 1965
Alison Lurie
A cool, conventional New Englander moved to California because of her husband's work, Katherine finds Los Angeles baffling, irritating and rather frightening. Described once as one of those people who 'thinks of the whole world as a small classroom they can't get out of', she gradually learns to make sense of the strange customs, costumes and language of her new surroundings, eventually finding a way out of the classroom and discovering a new self in the process. When her husband's enthusiasm for the West Coast wanes and he suggests that a return to the East will restore Katherine to her old self, her response is, 'That's what I'm afraid of'.

Cattleman, Paul
The Nowhere City, 1965
Alison Lurie
An unforeseen hiccup in his academic career plan takes Paul Cattleman from New England to Los Angeles, a move he embraces with his characteristic 'readiness for small adventures'. Some of these adventures, involving exotic Californian women, are almost too much for him to handle, while his assignment proves to be a disappointment and his wife a revelation. Paul's bewildered reaction to these events exposes as naive his attempt to lead a neatly compartmentalized life in which he is so 'squeezed up between the past and the future' that he is not really living at all.

Cauchon, Peter (Bishop of Beauvais)
Saint Joan, 1923
George Bernard Shaw
Cauchon is aged about 60, and presides at the trial of JOAN on a charge of heresy at Rouen. After she insists that the 'voices' that guided her were correct and that the counsel of the court represents the Devil, Cauchon reluctantly pronounces the sentence of excommunication. In the Epilogue to the play, he admits that the subsequent rehabilitation of Joan has resulted in his own disgrace, but declares that he acted faithfully and could have adopted no other course.

Cauldhame, Frank
The Wasp Factory, 1984
Iain Banks
A 16-year-old from a disturbingly dysfunctional family on a small Scottish island. His father has not registered his birth, and the reason for this becomes apparent in a late, shocking discovery. In the meantime, Frank derives gory entertainment from decapitating dead animals and trapping wasps in a sadistic device of his own invention, activities for which he offers no explanation or excuse. Occasional phone calls from his brother Eric, an asylum escapee, are received with the same disconcerting detachment.

Caulfield, Holden
The Catcher in the Rye, 1951
J D Salinger
A rebellious 16-year-old, so sickened by the 'phoniness' of life around him that he is unable to fit into the conventional mould. Those in authority consider him disruptive and wild, yet he is fresh, interesting and stimulating. With a sharp, critical eye and a strong set of opinions, he breezes his profane way through the relationships and connections of school and family, loathing hypocrisy and humbug. Capable of intense gentleness and sensitivity, his real problem is that other people are neither so honest nor so searching. Funny, raunchy and alive, he distrusts the world of adults, riddled as it is with insincerity.

Cavalletto, John Baptist
Little Dorrit, 1857
Charles Dickens
The fellow prisoner of RIGAUD in Marseilles, he later turns up in London and is employed by ARTHUR CLENNAM. Cheerful and good-hearted, he resides with MR and MRS PLORNISH, nurses Clennam when he is in the Marshalsea prison and helps to find Rigaud.

Cavan, Sir Paddy
The Roaring Nineties, 1946
Golden Miles, 1948
Winged Seeds, 1950
Katharine Susannah Prichard
A man with an eye on the main chance, he is a talker, a manipulator and a dissembler. Shrewd and tough and not above a little dirt and dishonesty, he stages his own career from nobody to man of considerable means. A 'greedy, unscrupulous egoist', his character blackens from book to book of the trilogy.

Cavidge, Anne
Nuns and Soldiers, 1980
Iris Murdoch
The clever, beautiful best friend of GERTRUDE OPENSHAW while at Cambridge, Anne converted to Roman Catholicism there and became a nun. Fifteen years later, feeling compelled to return to the world, she leaves her closed order. Although she has not lost her faith it has changed, and cultivating 'the metaphysics of waiting' she seeks to define the nature of a personal Christ. Gertrude, painfully bereaved, and possessive, hopes her friend will now stay with her forever. But the ascetic Anne dreams of a future with THE 'COUNT', whom she loves passionately, believing him to hold something of the 'failed' Christ she has discovered.

Cawdor, Alistair
Visitants, 1979
Randolph Stow

The coroner concluded in his report that 'It could perhaps be said that he came on the scene a little too early in the Territory's history.' However gifted a diplomat and tireless a worker, it becomes clear that Cawdor (with his fateful surname) is too tightly wrapped for his job as Patrol Officer to the outlying islands of Papua. While his colonial colleagues investigate a UFO sighting and encounter, it is clear that Cawdor has a 'visitant' inside him, a sort of violent historical taint. His ghastly suicide is a bloody echo of *Macbeth*: who would have thought the young man would have had so much blood in him?

Cayhill, Ephie
Maurice Guest, 1908
Henry Handel Richardson

The American princess abroad, she looks on Europe as the source of all that is glamorous and exotic and is inevitably drawn to the charismatic but untrustworthy figure of SCHILSKY.

Cecropia
The Countess of Pembroke's Arcadia, 1581–4, published 1590
Sir Philip Sidney

DUKE BASILIUS's sister-in-law, she is the mother of AMPHIALUS, for whom she has powerful ambitions. She has the fierce single-mindedness one associates with Shakespeare's LADY MACBETH and clearly would rather have dashed her son from her breast as an infant than have him grow into such a milksop.

Cedarfair, Proude
Darkness in St Louis Bearheart, 1978
Gerald Vizenor

He is a fourth-generation celebrant and protector of the sacred cedar circus, a circular sovereign nation on the shores of the *misisibi* within the Red Cedar Reservation. Disdaining relations with corrupt tribal officials, he has sought instead diplomatic links with outside governments, built a thriving export business in sacred cedar incense, and maintained peace for a decade until a national energy crisis leads government and reservation officials to covet his timber resources. Forced to abandon the circus, he begins a journey south through a country visibly decaying from the dominance of the philosophy of evil. Assuming the mythological role of the Good Gambler, he successfully confronts his wicked, gasoline-hoarding counterpart, and is able to complete his pilgrimage to the sacred ruins of Chaco Canyon, there to realize his visionary winter-solstice flight into the 'fourth world', whose creation follows the defeat of evil. He has shamanic powers and a trickster nature, and is trailed by loyal clown crows who attack perceived enemies.

Cedric the Saxon, also known as Cedric of Rotherwood
Ivanhoe, 1819
Sir Walter Scott

His name stems from his own obsessive pride in a descent all the way from Hereward: 'he was not above the middle stature, but broad-shouldered, long-armed and powerfully made, like one accustomed to endure the fatigue of war or of the chase ... Pride and jealousy there was in his eye, for his life had been spent in asserting rights which were constantly liable to invasion'. He is the father of IVANHOE.

Celia
As You Like It, c.1600
William Shakespeare

Daughter of DUKE FREDERICK and cousin of ROSALIND, Celia has wit, charm, a sense of humour, common sense and a strong sense of duty. She leaves her father's court to stay with the banished Rosalind, and eagerly engages in the deceptions practised on ORLANDO. She falls in love with OLIVER at first sight. She is an excellent foil to Rosalind.

Celie
The Color Purple, 1982
Alice Walker

Beginning as an abused 14-year-old, unable to take responsibility for her life, Celie comes to know happiness. Having lost both her children and her sister, NETTIE, she survives by telling herself 'I don't fight, I stay where I'm told. But I'm alive'. A pattern of abusive relationships is broken by the appearance of SHUG AVERY, and with Celie's developing sexuality comes an awareness of herself and her position in the world.

Celinda
The Adventures of Ferdinand, Count Fathom, 1753
Tobias Smollett

Aged about 15 (which is the age of maximum sexual allure for a Smollett hero-villain), the girl known as Celinda is the 'niece' (ie natural child) of a country gentleman of FERDINAND, COUNT FATHOM's acquaintance. Universally loved, except by her jealous aunt-cum-stepmother, she is also profoundly credulous and superstitious as a result of her sheltered education. With that in mind, Fathom resolves to 'undermine her innocence, that he might banquet his vicious appetite with the spoils of her beauty'.

Cenci, Count Francesco
The Cenci, 1819
Percy Shelley

An unnaturally cruel and sadistic old man, he delights in the pain and suffering of others, especially that of his own family, to whom he is a cruel tyrant. He has passed through 'a desperate and remorseless manhood' to reach a 'dishonoured age'; he prays for and rejoices in the death of two of his sons; he is a man with 'no remorse and little fear'. His senses dulled in old age by over-indulgence and corrupt sensuality, he finally turns to incest to excite his jaded palate.

Cereno, Captain Benito
The Piazza Tales, 1856
Herman Melville

The Spanish captain of the *San Dominick*, who is involved in a slave revolt on his ship. He is about 30, tall but not robust, his voice reduced to a whisper by a lung complaint. He is 'prey to settled dejection', and seems strangely reserved with all but his 'personal attendant', Babo, but is in fact a captive of that mutineer. He has 'a distempered spirit … in as distempered a frame', and is an incompetent sailor.

Chadband, the Rev Mr
Bleak House, 1853
Charles Dickens

A pompous and hypocritical Dissenting clergyman, he is 'a large yellow man, with a fat smile' who regularly uses pseudo-biblical language to 'edify' his listeners. He is unsympathetic to the plight of JO and, with his wife, the former MRS RACHAEL, becomes involved in a scheme to blackmail SIR LEICESTER DEDLOCK. They are found out by MR BUCKET.

Chaffanbrass, Mr
Phineas Redux, 1874
Anthony Trollope

A barrister whose speciality lies in defending criminals. He is a 'very dirty little man' with a range of irritating and unpleasant personal habits, and 'all manner of nasty tricks about him'. In court, he looks cruel, sharp and intolerable, and is in his element when faced with defending a case in which 'he has all the world against him'.

Chainmail, Mr
Crotchet Castle, 1831
Thomas Love Peacock

An adherent to the values of 12th-century chivalry, Mr Chainmail stands for 'beef and ale, lodging and raiment, wife and children, courage to fight for them all, and armour wherewith to do so'. He argues that modern civilization is corrupt, and that the 12th century, unfairly maligned by historians as the Dark Ages, was infinitely preferable – more moral and closer to the happy state of 'natural' man. Old-fashioned and kind-hearted, he is in essence a knight wandering around overgrown ruins, looking for a lady.

Challenger, Professor George Edward
The Lost World, 1912, et seq
Arthur Conan Doyle

A distinguished anthropologist and zoologist, Professor Challenger is a maverick. Demanding, independent, visionary, academically domineering, short-tempered and frequently violent, he is 'a homicidal megalomaniac with a turn for science', according to the news editor at the *Gazette*, and 'perfectly impossible', if his wife is to be believed. Although he is short, everything else about him is big, even outsize: an impressively well-built man, his eyes are piercing and his brows menacing, yet when he wishes, he adopts 'an enormously massive genial manner'.

Chamberlain, Eric
Ends and Means, 1977
Stanley Middleton

A bestselling writer, whose cold detachment from the human realities of family life brings misery to his lover and son, driving both of them to take their lives.

Chamberlain, Gregory
Seven Poor Men of Sydney, 1934
Christina Stead

A printmaster of Sydney and the employer of JOSEPH BAGUENAULT, TOM WITHERS and BARUCH MENDELSSOHN. He is a man who lives vicariously, dealing with life at arm's length, and refusing direct engagement with the contradictions of his nature.

Chamberlayne, Edward
The Cocktail Party, 1950
T S Eliot

A middle-aged barrister, apparently abandoned by his wife. He feels increasingly oppressed, almost to the point of madness, by the unreality of his role and the sense that 'she has made the world a place I cannot live in/Except on her terms'. No longer master of his fate, he discovers that only the mysterious SIR HENRY HARCOURT-REILLY offers an ambiguous salvation.

Chamberlayne, Lavinia
The Cocktail Party, 1950
T S Eliot

EDWARD CHAMBERLAYNE's wife, who also suffers from nervous prostration, allegedly brought on by the revelation of his affair with CELIA COPLESTONE, but actually caused by the defection of her lover PETER QUILPE. The Chamberlaynes are locked in a marriage of almost surgically precise cruelty and formidable lack of understanding.

Chambers, properly Valet de Chambre
The Tragedy of Pudd'nhead Wilson, 1894
Mark Twain

The white-skinned slave child who grows up with the identity of a white boy, TOM DRISCOLL, after a secret cradle swap by Chambers's mother. 'Petted, indulged and spoiled', the spiteful, vicious Chambers grows into a cowardly, thieving, dissolute egotist. Though shocked when his mother privately reveals to him his true identity, it enables him to shift the blame for his many shortcomings from himself to the $\frac{1}{32}$nd part of his blood that is negroid. However, his character remains unaltered and he continues to perform a series of ever more despicable deeds. He is the heir of JUDGE DRISCOLL, who remains unaware of his real identity.

Chambers, Frank
The Postman Always Rings Twice, 1934
James M Cain

Tall, light-haired and toughened by a hand-to-mouth existence, 24-year-old Frank Chambers has drifted aimlessly through life until his explosive encounter with the sultry CORA PAPADAKIS. Possessed by a passion that could melt the thickest iceberg, his sense of right and wrong quickly becomes subordinate to the possibility of being in the arms of a woman 'I wanted so bad I couldn't even keep anything on my stomach'.

Chambers, Ronnie
Hidden Laughter, 1990
Simon Gray

The local vicar in the country village where

Harry Pertwee, a literary agent, and his wife, LOUISE PERTWEE, own a weekend cottage, Ronnie is a man of doubt rather than conviction. He is indecisive, out of his depth with the modern domestic crises afflicting the Pertwees and their children, but well-meaning. A kind, tolerant and loving man, he is tormented by guilt. Instead of loving his wife, a permanent patient at a mental hospital, he silently loves his widowed housekeeper. At the heart of his distress is the fact that divine goodness appears so inexplicably rationed. Even the good-natured Louise does not realize how lonely and how decent Ronnie is.

Chamcha, Saladin
The Satanic Verses, 1988
Salman Rushdie

The 'man of a thousand voices', heard on countless advertisements, he is GIBREEL FARISHTA's travelling companion on the ill-fated India-London flight. As he falls towards the sea from the aircraft's explosion, Chamcha the Indian Anglophile sings 'Rule Britannia' ('Chamcha' being Urdu for 'toady'). While Gibreel starts looking angelic on surviving his fall, Chamcha grows demonic, with shiny, cloven hoofs and a large, erect penis. He becomes humanized, however, by hating Gibreel for leaving him in the lurch when racist police turn him over to British Immigration Authorities.

Chamont
The Orphan, 1680
Thomas Otway

A tough, blustery, penniless soldier of fortune, he is the brother of MONIMIA. Suspecting that his sister has been wronged by one of the brothers, he questions her about it remorselessly. This might seem bullying, domineering and at the least interfering, yet in the context of his society, his motives would be seen as entirely honourable.

Chan, Charlie
The House Without a Key, 1925, et seq
Earl Derr Biggers

A Chinese detective, based upon the real-life oriental sleuth, Chang Apana. An urbane family man, Chan is a classic of detective fiction: methodical, analytical, usually aided in his investigations by his impulsive elder sons. He has a philosophical streak and an aphorism for every occasion. His cool, logical deductive process usually results in him assembling all the suspects into one room before revealing the identity of the murderer. Chan also became the hero of several films.

Chance (the Gardener)
Being There, 1971
Jerzy Kosinski

Illiterate, orphaned and virtually mute, Chance is symbolically bound to the Old Man's garden by the umbilical hose he uses to water the plants. When the Old Man dies he is cast adrift in the world. When his name is misheard as 'Chauncey Gardiner' and his naive pronouncements mistaken for profound political and economic wisdom, he becomes an unwitting adviser to industrialists and presidents.

Chance, Jack
A Fringe of Leaves, 1976
Patrick White

A former professional birdcatcher in London, Chance killed his mistress and hid in the city sewers, scavenging for a living until he was arrested and deported to an Australian penal colony. Having escaped, he is hiding out in the bush when he encounters ELLEN ROXBURGH, a white woman captured by an Aborigine tribe. He escorts her back to a white settlement but, wary of his reception, returns to the outback. Believing the modern world to be weighed against a man of his class and background, the rough, tough Jack Chance represents the 'natural', arcadian man; the hunter and forager and man the survivor.

Chance, Nora and Dora
Wise Children, 1991
Angela Carter

Identical twin sisters now in their mid-seventies, Nora (Leonora) and Dora Chance ('Chance by name, Chance by nature') are the illegitimate daughters of SIR MELCHIOR HAZARD, the greatest Shakespearean actor of his day. Once dancers in the dying days of variety and known as the 'Lucky Chances', Nora and Dora now live in chaotic obscurity in south London. Sceptical, earthy, and swept along since youth by a tremendous optimism and, despite all their disappointments, an unquenchable love of the theatre and of romance, the sisters are as full of zest for life as ever. 'What a joy it is to dance and sing!' is the final line of the novel and the emotion which wells up most often in the sister's hearts.

Chancellor, Olive
The Bostonians, 1886
Henry James

The younger of BASIL RANSOM's Boston cousins, she is a dogmatic, even slightly strident, feminist, with a grimly opportunistic streak in her relationships. Unlike her sister Mrs Luna, she has learned to sublimate all outward sexual and romantic feelings, and her eventual defeat is clearly signalled in her inability to recognize that other lives are and must be lived in circumstances very different from her own.

Chandran
The Bachelor of Arts, 1937
R K Narayan

A history student, the only child of a retired district judge, he lives with his family in Malgudi's affluent Lawley Extension and completes his BA at Albert Mission College. After graduation, intending to study for a doctorate in England but bitterly disappointed in love, he becomes a *sanyasi*, a shaven-headed, loin-clothed holy man who lives by begging. Months later, he is shamed by poor villagers into realizing that his motives for renouncing the world are not spiritual but vengeful, and he returns to Malgudi to establish a new life there.

Chandran, Willie Somerset
Half a Life, 2001
V S Naipaul

Born of mixed-caste parentage in India in the

1930s and named after Somerset Maugham, Willie seems destined both to write and to never feel a strong sense of identity. Exchanging his parochial Indian life for a bohemian lifestyle in London, where he reinvents details of his past and has a book published, results in no more stability. Hasty marriage to a Portuguese-African woman leads him to move to colonial Africa, but even after 18 years there he is conscious of 'another self inside him', and remains unable to connect his internal and external lives.

Channing, Ryder
Run, River, 1963
Joan Didion
A social climber who inveigles his way into Sacramento Valley society. He is identified by LILY KNIGHT as a 'papier-mache Mephistopheles', but he is clearly the harbinger of a mechanistic and materialist future. He pays court to Martha McClellan but eventually jilts her and subsequently has an affair with Lily; it remains unclear whether Martha's suicide is really caused by her rejection, but Channing is murdered by Everett McClellan (Martha's brother and Lily's husband), whose exact motivation is equally uncertain.

Chantry-Pigg, Hon Father Hugh
The Towers of Trebizond, 1956
Rose Macaulay
A retired Anglican priest who accompanies AUNT DOT on her trip to Turkey. He is an unshakeable, wholly literal fundamentalist who has no truck with any other view point, an 'ancient bigot' who ran a modest church in London, and is now devoting his retirement to hunting for relics of saints, which he collects for his Dorset mansion house.

Chapin, Joe
Ten North Frederick, 1955
John O'Hara
A resident of Gibbsville, he trades on a well-known family name and a scroll from Yale Law School to build up a substantial business. His real ambition, however, is to enter politics, but he is hoist by his own petard attempting to buy his way into office. He spends his final days drinking morosely but with a certain refined dignity.

Charlemont
The Atheist's Tragedy, c.1611
Cyril Tourneur
The son of Montferrers and nephew to D'AMVILLE, he is injured most by his uncle's evil machinations. Determined to go to war to win honour and glory for himself and his family name, he leaves behind CASTABELLA, his intended wife. His return finds his father murdered, Castabella married to another and himself supposed dead. At first he is determined to avenge his wrongs, but the ghost of his father urges him to show patience and forbearance, which he does.

Charles
Chilly Scenes of Winter, 1976
Ann Beattie
He is a child of the sixties, attempting to come to

terms with a world in which neither the imagination nor 'love' (in whatever form it comes) seems to have the validity it had in those halcyon days. Haunted by paralysis and death, he is unable even to take a significant initiative to win back the girlfriend who has returned to her husband and to a life bereft of the very values he treasures.

Charles, Helena
Look Back in Anger, 1956
John Osborne
In her twenties, Helena is principally a friend of ALISON PORTER, and is an honest, independent, middle-class woman both in her upbringing and beliefs. JIMMY PORTER is therefore antagonistic towards her, yet she seduces him simply because she desires him. She feels no need to try to convert him. Her loyalty to convention, her moral sense of right and wrong are too strong to allow anything other than a temporary disruption.

Charles, Nick
The Thin Man, 1934
Dashiell Hammett
An interesting variation on the hard-boiled detective. He is a sophisticated playboy who has once been an agent, but has retired with his equally fast-living millionaire wife, Nora, who partners him in solving the case she persuades him to take. A hard-drinking wisecracker with a taste for the good things in life, he was a tough guy in his younger days, but now wants to concentrate on having fun drinking his wife's money.

Charles, Prince, later Charles I
The Fortunes of Nigel, 1822
Sir Walter Scott
JAMES I OF ENGLAND's son, 'afterwards the most unfortunate of British monarchs', he has the long auburn curls which Van Dyke later made famous. Even in early youth his face 'bore a shade of anticipated melancholy', which contrasts sharply with the light-hearted demeanour of the king and their shared favourite, GEORGE VILLIERS, DUKE OF BUCKINGHAM.

Charles II
Woodstock, or The Cavalier, 1826
Sir Walter Scott
Travelling his kingdom in search of loyal support during the Cromwellian interregnum, the Stewart king first appears in female disguise. Perhaps inevitably, he is a far less well-defined character than his antagonist OLIVER CROMWELL and limits his appearances to a series of regal *coups de théâtre*.

Charles II, King of England and Scotland
Peveril of the Peak, 1823
Sir Walter Scott
The middle-aged king's features are 'strongly lined, even to harshness, [but] had yet an expression of dignified good humour; he was well and strongly built, walked upright and yet easily, and had upon the whole the air of a person of the highest consideration'.

Charles VI, King of France
Henry V, 1599
William Shakespeare
Although well aware of the ability of Henry V (HENRY, PRINCE OF WALES) and his English troops, the ageing Charles VI is unable to organize his own forces because of the bickering between his nobles. He tries to buy Henry off with the twin offer of his daughter in marriage and several minor dukedoms. His subsequent demands for the surrender and ransom of the English king are ill-conceived and have the opposite effect. He does, however, accept defeat with dignity, meeting all Henry's terms in the hope that they will ensure a lasting peace for both countries.

Charles VIII
Romola, 1863
George Eliot
Dubbed the 'New Charlemagne' by the fanciful, the French King Charles's ambition is to show strength and statesmanship and 'march through Italy [among] … a grateful and admiring people'. When he enters Florence, however, he looks 'like a hastily-modelled grotesque'. His mouth is a slit, and one leg is not what it might be. He finally moves off from the city, unsure, after inconclusive bargaining.

Charles the Bold, Duke of Burgundy
Anne of Geierstein, or The Maiden in the Mist, 1829
Sir Walter Scott
Already presented in *Quentin Durward* (1823), Scott's later portrayal of the Duke of Burgundy is even more mixed as to character, combining 'cruelty with justice, magnanimity with meanness of spirit, economy with extravagance, and liberality with avarice'.

Charley
Death of a Salesman, 1949
Arthur Miller
Neighbour and friend to WILLY LOMAN, he represents many of the qualities Willy lacks: modesty, success in business, sensible parenting values. Willy derides him as 'disgusting' and an 'ignoramus' but, by the end of the play, he is giving Willy both money and vital advice – 'Nobody's worth nothin' dead'. His restraint and humanity eventually cause the desperate salesman to admit, 'Charley, you're the only friend I got'.

Charlie
The Little Drummer Girl, 1984
John Le Carré
'I'm subversive, for God's sake' protests Charlie, a pot-smoking, guitar-playing actress with a history of flirtations with the extreme left. Somehow, though, she is recruited by Israelis to pose as a dead terrorist's lover in order to capture his brother, another PLO member. Playing her most convincing role, she understandably suffers enormous stage fright. The 'central meekness … that seemed to attract her fatally to bullies' is in danger of taking her too far as she desperately answers the suspicious terrorists' questions.

Charlie, properly Charlie Bucket
Charlie and the Chocolate Factory, 1964
Charlie and the Great Glass Elevator, 1973
Roald Dahl
The only child of extremely poor parents, who wins the fifth and final Golden Ticket for a guided tour of WILLY WONKA's fabulous chocolate factory. The other winners are greedy, spoilt children addicted to watching television or chewing gum, and only Charlie survives the tour. His sensible goodness and genuine interest in all he sees so impress Mr Wonka that he makes Charlie his sole heir and successor. In *Charlie and the Great Glass Elevator,* Charlie becomes a resourceful hero who travels through space, his deeds earning recognition from the President of the USA.

Charlotte
Charlotte's Web, 1952
E B White
Charlotte is an eloquent spider who spins webs of wonder for the benefit of Wilbur, a much-loved pig. Sprinkling her web with epithets such as 'some pig', 'terrific', and 'humble', Charlotte saves her friend's life. Loyal and kind throughout, she bolsters Wilbur's confidence and enthrals him with stories. Clever, comforting, and supportive, she possesses all the ingredients essential for a best friend.

Charlotte
Plagued by the Nightingale, 1931
Kay Boyle
The oldest sister of NICOLAS, whom she tries to help. Married to her rich and almost half-witted cousin Jean, she becomes pregnant for the sixth time at the age of 32. She is tall and strong, but wishes she were graceful. She loves being part of a closely-knit family, and is genuinely maternal and sympathetic.

Charmian
Antony and Cleopatra, 1606/7
William Shakespeare
One of CLEOPATRA's closest attendants. Loyal and deferential, she is also independent, self-willed and unafraid to speak her mind. Advising Cleopatra in her relations with ANTONY, she urges her 'In each thing give him way'. However, teasing Cleopatra that she loved Caesar as deeply earns her a sharp rebuke. A soothsayer tells Charmian that she will outlive Cleopatra, and indeed she does, though only by moments. As soon as Cleopatra dies, Charmian speaks her tribute: 'Now boast thee, death, in thy possession lies/A lass unparallel'd'. She then applies an asp to her own breast and dies.

Charmond, Felice
The Woodlanders, 1887
Thomas Hardy
'If one word could have expressed Felice Charmond it would have been Inconsequence.' She has the superficial attractions of wealth and looks, but she is lazy, self-absorbed and capricious, and has earned the reputation of being 'a body who has smiled where she has not loved, and loved where she has not married'. Her use of a wig made from the hair of MARTY SOUTH

symbolizes her parasitic relationship with the woodlanders of Little Hintock.

Charrington, Mr
1984, 1949
George Orwell

Mr Charrington owns the shop above which WINSTON and JULIA rent a room where they can meet in secret and make love. He lives a troglodyte existence in his tiny shop and back kitchen, a relic of the past who remembers vaguely how life used to be before it became dominated by the Party. Yet even this seemingly harmless old man proves to be duplicitous and heartless. Not even the elderly, with their lingering affection for traditional ways, can be trusted.

Charteris, Leonard
The Philanderer, 1893
George Bernard Shaw

The philanderer of the title, Charteris is in his mid-thirties, a chattering socialist with tawny hair and beard and progressive views on the liberation of women. (In other words, he is a Shavian self-portrait.) His simultaneous relationships with JULIA CRAVEN and GRACE TANFIELD allow him to disparage conventional morality, but although frank with others, Charteris recoils from frankness himself. The version of the play most frequently performed ends with Julia marrying Dr Paramore and Charteris rejected but still fervent in his beliefs. The longer text shows the Paramore marriage to have failed and Charteris demanding the law be changed to make amicable divorce possible.

Charwell → Cherrell

Chase, Elyot, and Prynne, Amanda
Private Lives, 1930
Noël Coward

A divorced couple, Amanda and Elyot meet on adjacent hotel balconies five years after the split, while on honeymoon with their new partners, respectively VICTOR PRYNNE and SYBIL CHASE. Elyot is 'slim and pleasant looking'; Amanda is 'exquisite'. They are brittle, selfish and egotistical; the comedy arises from their conversation, which is guarded, evasive, probing and revealing. They believe they love each other. Yet although not entirely without feeling, they are unable to feel and communicate love, and are well matched because they can only cope with the appearance of love. They are actually more at home with flippancy, spite and mutual recrimination.

Chase, Gideon
An Insular Possession, 1986
Timothy Mo

A New Englander orphaned young and sent to China at the age of twelve to work for the Meridian trading company, Gideon at 20 is still naive, shy and rather priggish. His friend, WALTER EASTMAN, declares that he will always have a certain 'moral angularity'. Apart from his chaste devotion to ALICE REMINGTON, Gideon is not interested in girls, but, while disapproving of his colleague's brothel visits, he remains

uncritically devoted to Eastman and becomes assistant editor on his newspaper. Through FATHER RIBEIRO, Gideon secretly learns Chinese (forbidden to foreigners) and later acts as an interpreter for the British during the Opium Wars.

Chase, Jack
White-Jacket, 1850
Herman Melville

A British sailor in the US navy. 'No man ever had a better heart or a bolder' than the tall, handsome, bearded Captain of the Top on the warship *Neversink*. He is frank, polite, and much loved by his men. He has a 'high conceit of his profession as a seaman', and is devoted to duty. Well-read, he loves to sing and tell tales. He is 'a little bit of a dictator' in shaping the men to his liking, but a charming one. He has lost a finger in battle, and once deserted to the Peruvian navy, where he was known as 'Don John'.

Chase, Sybil → Prynne, Victor and Chase, Sybil

Chastitie
Ane Pleasant Satyre of the Thrie Estaitis, 1540
Sir David Lindsay

As physically attractive as her counterpart DAME SENSUALITIE, but an embodiment of chastity rather than sensual pleasure, Chastitie is adrift in the kingdom of REX HUMANITAS. Lamenting her banishment by all factions of society, she is incarcerated in the stocks at Sensualitie's bidding but, released by DIVYNE CORRECTIOUN, she successfully pleads her case to the king's parliament, thus inducing the reformation of the state's spirituality.

Chatterley, Lady Constance
Lady Chatterley's Lover, 1928 published privately in Florence, bowdlerized edition England 1932, full edition England 1960
D H Lawrence

The wife of SIR CLIFFORD CHATTERLEY, she is in her thirties, 'a ruddy-country-looking girl ... full of unusual energy ... not the least daunted by art or ideal politics'. Yet her vibrancy and intellectual energy is running to waste as her life at Wragby Hall deteriorates to a point where she feels 'spectral, not really existing'. It is not merely the sexual aspect of her affair with the gamekeeper, OLIVER MELLORS, which liberates her, but the tenderness and natural sensibilities he represents and for which she yearns.

Chatterley, Sir Clifford
Lady Chatterley's Lover, 1928 published privately in Florence, bowdlerized edition England 1932, full edition England 1960
D H Lawrence

The Chatterleys have 'stood for England and St George' for generations; Sir Clifford is a man of inherited wealth and privilege. The physical incapacity he sustained during the war represents an atrophied spirit, which Lawrence saw as corroding the English soul. He is authoritarian, boorish, insensitive (especially to the processes and forces of nature, which damns him in Lawrence's eyes), intellectually myopic and physically impotent. Although married to LADY CONSTANCE CHATTERLEY, he does not think sex 'really necessary'. He likes order and regimentation, and prefers Wragby Hall and the industrialized midlands to anywhere else, country which, like him, has 'a grim will of its own'.

Chaunticleer
'The Nun's Priest's Tale' in *The Canterbury Tales*
c.1387–1400
Geoffrey Chaucer
A rooster belonging to a poor widow, he lives in her yard with 'Seven hennes for to doon al his pleasaunce', of which his favourite is PERTELOTE. Vain and superstitious, he believes dreams to be portents and learnedly quotes classical and biblical authorities to prove his point. His vanity is almost his downfall but his quick wit enables him to escape from the fox who has tricked him.

Chavel, Jean-Louis
The Tenth Man, 1985
Graham Greene
A prosperous lawyer in France before World War II, he is 'a lonely fellow who made awkward attemps from time to time to prove himself human'. He is imprisoned as a hostage by the Germans, and draws a lot to die, but gives another man his fortune to take his place. He survives and adopts the name Charlot, but is haunted by guilt over his actions, and is unsuccessful in building a new life. He returns to his old home and seizes the chance of a fatal but liberating act of self-sacrificial atonement.

Cheeryble, Charles and Edwin
Nicholas Nickleby, 1839
Charles Dickens
Twins, and partners in the firm of Cheeryble Brothers, they are wealthy merchants and genial philanthropists. Noble and kind-hearted, they give NICHOLAS NICKLEBY a job as a clerk assisting their loyal employee, TIM LINKINWATER. They become concerned with the plight of MADELINE BRAY and help to expose the evil schemes of RALPH NICKLEBY. Their nephew, Frank, is a partner in the firm. They help to bring about the marriages of Nicholas to Madeline and Frank to KATE NICKLEBY. When they retire, Frank inherits the business and Nicholas becomes a partner.

Cheevy, Miniver
The Town Down the River, 1907
Edwin Arlington Robinson
This 'child of scorn' represents those who waste their lives believing that they were born 'after their time'. Miniver, mourning romance and art, curses the 'commonplace', and, in so doing, misses his place in war, in the creation of wealth and in life. Robinson's light tone encourages little sympathy for this character, who forgets his dreams through drinking.

Chelsea, Bishop of, originally Alfred Bridgenorth
Getting Married, 1908
George Bernard Shaw
Bridgenorth, the Bishop of Chelsea, is the father of six daughters, the youngest of whom, EDITH

BRIDGENORTH, is about to be married. Slim, active and genial, he is also a liberal of sometimes shockingly progressive views. At present, he is writing a history of marriage and expects that because the divorce laws in England are so punitive, marriage will become an outmoded institution, principally among the propertied classes. When Edith refuses to go to the church, he enthusiastically supports the idea of drawing up a mutually agreed deed of partnership between her and her fiancé, CECIL SYKES.

Chen, Ah
Sour Sweet, 1982
Timothy Mo
LILY CHEN's husband, whom she teasingly calls 'Fat Boy', is a stolid unambitious waiter in a Soho restaurant until (unbeknownst to Lily) he is forced to hide from a vengeful Triad group, and takes refuge in the suburban takeaway shop he and Lily open. Placid and equable, and a good, kind, if unexciting husband, Chen is always outwitted by his strong, manipulative wife, and cannot imagine any man finding her even remotely attractive, though Westerners appear to. He shares a silent rapport and love of gardening with his little boy, and is less impassive than usual when alone with Lily's understanding sister, MUI TANG.

Chen, Lily (Moon Lily)
Sour Sweet, 1982
Timothy Mo
Seemingly a traditional, subservient wife to her husband, AH CHEN, the brisk, mercurial Lily is exceedingly strong-minded, wilfully clever, and shrewdly ambitious for her small son. Her own life has been cruelly hard: motherless, she was raised as a boy by her Kwangsi boxing-champion father who mercilessly trained her in his savage martial art. Tall, slim and supple, stoical and energetic, she is physically stronger than her husband, and bosses her 'inferior' sister, MUI TANG. Lily is a dynamic homemaker, and instigates the opening of a takeaway shop, largely financed from painfully-saved house-keeping money. She regards the English, the 'foreign devil', as barbarians whose laws she can cheerfully break.

Cherrell, Adrian
The End of the Chapter, 1935
John Galsworthy
A nephew of REV CUTHBERT CHERRELL, and an uncle of DINNY CHERRELL, Adrian is a man whose instincts tell him that he should live in the country. However, because of his work (he presides as curator over a collection of anthropological remains), he lives in London on a government salary, which means he is perpetually poor. Aged just over 50, he is conservative, reserved and somewhat superstitious; 'trained to a coherent view of human history', Adrian accepted life with a half-humorous fatalism'.

Cherrell, Dinny (Elizabeth)
The End of the Chapter, 1935
John Galsworthy
The grandniece of REV CUTHBERT CHERRELL and

niece of ADRIAN CHERRELL, Dinny is Galsworthy's last portrait of an ideal woman. She is tall, dark-haired, intelligent, a good judge of character and shares her family's faith in her own capabilities. She encourages her diffident brother HUBERT CHERRELL to defend himself against a charge of conduct unbecoming to an officer, but troubles crowd upon her when she falls for Wilfred Desert, a man who has lost faith in himself and with whom FLEUR FORSYTE once contemplated an affair. His leaving her causes her own faith to crumble, and she is left 'wondering for whose inscrutable delight she was thus suffering'.

Cherrell, Hubert
The End of the Chapter, 1935
John Galsworthy

Having 'missed the expanding influence of the 'Varsity and London' by graduating directly from public school to the army (where he rose to the rank of captain and was awarded the DSO), Hubert finds himself adrift in England after eight years' service in Mesopotamia, Egypt and India. The brother of the more forceful DINNY CHERRELL, his last adventure was as a transport officer for an American professor leading an expedition into the interior of Bolivia. During a brawl, Hubert kills one of their half-caste porters in self-defence, and then stands accused of conduct unbecoming to an officer. A 'man of action forced into a state of thought' when his behaviour raises questions in the House of Commons, the sensitive, emotionally repressed Hubert relies on his sister for support.

Cherrell, Rev Cuthbert
The End of the Chapter, 1935
John Galsworthy

The Rev Cuthbert Cherrell is 88 years old and has represented God on earth for 55 of these, rising to become Bishop of Porthminster. At the opening of the work, he is on his deathbed, attended by his nephews, including ADRIAN CHERRELL. He never married and throughout his life buried his natural instincts beneath an expression of repressed dignity. Distinguished, grey-haired and quietly maintaining the old established order of things, he nevertheless verged at times towards the dandyish and was a very well-dressed bishop indeed.

Cherrington, Eustace
The Shrimp and the Anemone, 1944
The Sixth Heaven, 1946
Eustace and Hilda, 1947
L P Hartley

The 'shrimp' of the title, Eustace begins the trilogy as a gentle, sociable but physically weak child who is dependent upon others' approval. Bound to his family by ties of duty, guilt and affection, his few attempts at rebellion or escape end in disaster. He has a special attachment to his sister, HILDA CHERRINGTON, but embodied in that attachment is something which he recognizes as dependence and subjugation. He attempts, during his years at Oxford, to engineer a love affair between his sister and the dashing Dick Stavely – not only to ensure (albeit subconsciously) his own freedom, but also for

the sake of his sister's happiness, for which he feels himself responsible. However, Hilda's abandonment by Dick and subsequent nervous paralysis induce in him sufficient guilt to prevent his escape from her for ever.

Cherrington, Hilda
The Shrimp and the Anemone, 1944
The Sixth Heaven, 1946
Eustace and Hilda, 1947
L P Hartley

The puritanical and uncompromising elder sister of EUSTACE CHERRINGTON, Hilda is a manipulative and domineering personality. From childhood, she sees herself as Eustace's mentor and director, responsible for his moral and professional development and well-being, and she devotes herself to this cause with energy and determination. Unfortunately for Eustace, she has no understanding or sympathy for human nature or for people themselves – she is incapable of interacting with others on a normal, human level, seeing them as things to be manipulated and moulded as she thinks fit. As a young woman she embarks on a love affair with Dick Stavely, a friend of her brother's, but her need to control affects that also, and Dick, unable to comply with her demands, ends their relationship, leaving Hilda in such a shocked state that she is rendered temporarily paralysed.

Cheshire Cat, the
Alice's Adventures in Wonderland, 1865
Lewis Carroll

The Cheshire Cat appears up a tree, grinning amiably. It tells Alice that if she does not know where she wants to go, direction does not matter. Everyone here is mad, it says, including Alice. It disappears, then appears again to ask about the Duchess's baby. Alice complains of its suddenness, so it obligingly disappears slowly, tail first, leaving only its grin. At the croquet match it confounds the Queen by having no body from which its head (or grin) can be cut off.

Chester, Edward
Barnaby Rudge, 1841
Charles Dickens

The son of SIR JOHN CHESTER, but opposite in character. Honourable and gallant, he is in love with EMMA HAREDALE, the niece of his father's bitter enemy, MR GEOFFREY HAREDALE. When his father disowns him for refusing to find a rich heiress who can bring money to the family through marriage, he goes abroad to seek his fortune. Returning to England, he helps to rescue Emma and DOLLY VARDEN from abduction during the Gordon Riots. After his father's death, he marries Emma with her uncle's blessing, and they go to live abroad.

Chester, Sir John, formerly **Mr**
Barnaby Rudge, 1841
Charles Dickens

A suave, utterly selfish and unprincipled gentleman, he contrives to become an MP and gains a knighthood. His bitter enmity toward MR GEOFFREY HAREDALE, a Catholic, causes him to disown his son, EDWARD CHESTER, because of his attachment to Haredale's niece, EMMA

HAREDALE, and he refuses to try to save his illegitimate son, HUGH, from the gallows. He helps to foment the anti-Catholic Gordon Riots and dies in a duel with Haredale.

Chettam, Sir James
Middlemarch, 1871–2
George Eliot

More forward-looking than MR BROOKE in his land-ownership, red-whiskered Sir James is still to a degree motivated by self-interest, his enthusiasm for DOROTHEA BROOKE's scheme of providing new cottages for the tenants stemming as much from his personal desire to marry her as it does from his genuine kind-heartedness. Thwarted in his desire by her marriage to REV EDWARD CASAUBON, Sir James, in his realistic simplicity, instead marries CELIA BROOKE, and while he never ceases to disapprove of both of Dorothea's marriages, he swallows his prejudices in recognition of the value of her friendship.

Cheyne, Harvey
'Captains Courageous': A Tale of the Grand Banks, 1897
Rudyard Kipling

The spoilt, effete son of an American millionaire, he is literally and symbolically thrust into the stormy waters of experience when he is thrown overboard in the Grand Banks. His subsequent growth to maturity is painful, but ultimately satisfyingly complete.

Chichester, Captain Thomas
The Romans in Britain, 1980
Howard Brenton

A Special Air Services Regiment officer in contemporary Northern Ireland, Chichester is disguised as a farm-worker and Irish nationalist, labouring on a farm near the Irish border while plotting the assassination of O'Rourke, a Republican. Chichester is a maverick, a romantic intellectual, pondering the history of England and empires, driven perhaps a little mad by war, and now gaping at what he perceives to be the truth: that 'the dead in any war would vote for peace'. An assassin humanized by his trade, Brenton suggests, is either a very brave or a very lost man.

Chick, Mrs Louisa
Dombey and Son, 1848
Charles Dickens

Sister of MR DOMBEY, she is 'a lady rather past the middle age than otherwise, but dressed in a very juvenile manner'. Proud and unforgiving of weakness, she maintains that her first sister-in-law need not have died in childbirth, nor Dombey have become bankrupt, if they had only 'made an effort'. She rejects FLORENCE as not a true Dombey and her friend, MISS LUCRETIA TOX, for aspiring to become the second Mrs Dombey.

Chickenstalker, Mrs Anne
The Chimes, 1844
Charles Dickens

A stout old lady who keeps a shop 'in the general line' and to whom TROTTY VECK is in debt in a small way. In Trotty's dream on Christmas Eve, she marries Tugby, porter to SIR JOSEPH BOWLEY.

Chickerel, Ethelberta
The Hand of Ethelberta, 1876
Thomas Hardy

Sensitive and creative, Ethelberta is caught between two worlds, and so develops two personalities. Stifled and over-awed by the circles she is suddenly moving in, she is deeply ashamed of her working-class background. She sacrifices true love in favour of position, and becomes so adept at acting a part that she loses touch with her innermost self.

Chicks
Owls Do Cry, 1957
Janet Frame

A bland suburbanite, he tries to keep a threatening reality at bay and under control with a system of carefully neutralized clichés and aphorisms which have no meaning except as protective incantations.

Chiffinch, also known as **Smith**
Peveril of the Peak, 1823
Sir Walter Scott

The pander of CHARLES II, KING OF ENGLAND AND SCOTLAND, he is himself much addicted to wine and good living and travels around with his French cook Chaubert. It is only his declining capacity for drink that induces him to give away the machinations of the supposed Popish Plot to JULIAN PEVERIL.

Child, the
An Imaginary Life, 1978
David Malouf

A mysterious eleven-year-old boy, brought up by wolves, who haunts the life of the Roman poet OVID. Though strongly built, he is scrawny and calloused. His 'limbs are lightly haired, the chest hairless; but all along the spine there is a hairline, reddish in color like a fox, and it is that that terrifies the women and has made them unwilling to touch him'.

Childe, Joanna
The Girls of Slender Means, 1963
Muriel Spark

A resident of the May of Teck Club for young ladies of 'slender means', Joanna is training to be an elocution teacher. She loves English poetry, which she sonorously recites; NICHOLAS FARRINGDON realizes that poetry has replaced sex for her. Her first love having come to nothing, she decided, under the influence of poetic ideals, that it would be her last. Well-built and fair, with blue eyes and pink cheeks, this daughter of a rural clergyman has the ability to escape from individuality, which is demonstrated at the moment of disaster.

Childs, Jadine
Tar Baby, 1981
Toni Morrison

A hugely ambitious woman, Jadine is obsessed with 'how to make it in this world'. An orphaned child, she projects herself eternally into the apparent safety of the future, becoming a 'culture-bearing black woman', paradoxically unaware of whose culture she is bearing. Attractive to SON because of their similar position as outsiders, she alienates herself further by her worship of education and culture. Aware of the strictures of origins, Jadine abandons them 'to get out of my skin and be only the person inside – not American – not black – just me'.

Chillingworth, Roger
The Scarlet Letter, 1850
Nathaniel Hawthorne

The very type of harsh New England Puritan, with a hint of the diabolic, he is portrayed in angular blacks, with no softening detail but for the fact that he was once the wronged husband of HESTER PRYNNE. Returning, he becomes Hester's and ARTHUR DIMMESDALE's obdurate nemesis.

Chiltern, Lord Oswald Standish
Phineas Finn, The Irish Member, 1869
The Eustace Diamonds, 1873
Phineas Redux, 1874
The Prime Minister, 1876
Anthony Trollope

A nobleman, the brother of LAURA KENNEDY. He has a rough, even violent personality, a trait accentuated by his physical appearance and fiery red colouring, which 'imparted a certain look of ferocity to him, which was apt to make men afraid of him at first sight'. Despite that, and his reputation for hard-living, he possesses considerable depths of character, and successfully courts and marries VIOLET EFFINGHAM, albeit after fighting PHINEAS FINN in a duel over her.

Chiltern, Sir Robert
An Ideal Husband, 1895
Oscar Wilde

An Under Secretary for Foreign Affairs, 'intensely admired by the few, and deeply respected by the many', Sir Robert is 40, handsome, happily married, rather nervous, and proud of his success and his reputation for representing the highest moral principles. However, he is now confronted with blackmail; if he does not speak in favour of a fraudulent canal scheme supported by Mrs Cheveley, she threatens to release documents proving that his wealth resulted from passing privileged information to a European financier. 'I did not sell myself for money', he protests. 'I bought success at a price.' Determined to preseve his reputation, career and marriage, he turns for advice to his friend, LORD GORING.

Chinaski, Henry
Post Office, 1971, et seq
Charles Bukowski

He is a pugnacious, resilient character who takes a job as a postman and tries not to let the work interfere too much with his lifestyle based on heavy drinking, casual sexual encounters and racetrack gambling. His disreputable activities aside, a kind of dogged drive to do a good job keeps him going while colleagues fall by the wayside, until the idea dawns that writing about his life might prove a less arduous way of making a living.

Chingachgook
The Pioneers, 1823
The Last of the Mohicans, 1826
The Prairie, 1827
The Pathfinder, 1840
The Deerslayer, 1841, forming the
'Leatherstocking' series
James Fenimore Cooper

The occasional companion of NATTY BUMPPO, he becomes the last surviving Mohican chieftain after the death of his friend Uncas. He exemplifies all the qualities of the noble savage, being brave, resourceful, loyal and duly subservient to Bumppo. An idealized character, he stands in opposition to the evil savages, usually the Iroquois.

Chips, Mr
Goodbye, Mr Chips, 1934
James Hilton

Mr Chipping, known as Mr Chips to the boys and staff of Brookfield School, has lodged with Mrs Wickett, just opposite the school, for over a decade, ever since he retired as housemaster of School House. Brookfield, a public school, is only of 'the second-rank', and so, as a teacher of classics, was Mr Chips. Never a first-rate scholar, he has always preferred English detective stories to heavier literature, but now dreams his days away imagining that he was indispensable; which, in a way, he was. Good-natured, with a 'jerky, high-pitched voice that still [has] a good deal of sprightliness in it', Chips represents a Victorian England of kindness, sentiment, cricket, chapel and bumbling inefficiency.

Chivery, Young John
Little Dorrit, 1857
Charles Dickens

Son of the kindly turnkey at the Marshalsea, he is a sentimental youth, inclined to poetry and hopelessly in love with AMY DORRIT. Selflessly, he helps MR PANCKS investigate WILLIAM DORRIT's right to his inheritance and later tells ARTHUR CLENNAM that Amy loves him.

Chloe
Back to Methuselah, 1921
George Bernard Shaw

Chloe appears in the final section of this five-part play. *As Far as Thought can Reach* is set in a remote garden Utopia in 31,920AD. She is four years old which, in the future, represents a youthful maturity. To the despair of her romantic friend STREPHON, she has tired of dancing and prefers solitary contemplation of mathematics.

Chorus, the
Henry V, 1599
William Shakespeare

The Chorus appears on stage alone, linking one act of the play to the next. He apologizes for the deficiencies of playwriting and the theatre, and asks the audience to imagine that they are now at the English court, now in France, and now being transported to France with King Henry (HENRY, PRINCE OF WALES) and the English army. The Chorus, who speaks some of the most stirring verse in the canon, is frequently used to set the tone of the play in production. His speeches can be interpreted in many shades, from the extremes of fervent patriotism or offensive jingoism, thereby reflecting the pro- or anti-war sentiment of the times.

Chowder
The Expedition of Humphry Clinker, 1771
Tobias Smollett

TABITHA BRAMBLE's beloved dog, he is usually bested in encounters with larger members of his species, and takes a ferocious revenge on the ankles of the Bramble family. Prone to constipation while travelling, he gets relief from the administration of a 'lacksitif'.

Chris; Christopher; Christopher's Father
White Chameleon, 1991
Christopher Hampton

White Chameleon is a partly autobiographical play, drawing upon the experiences of the young Hampton and his family in Alexandria between the Egyptian Revolution of 1952 and the Suez Crisis of 1956. Chris, an impressionable and innocent outsider, is an evocation of the ten-year-old Hampton and part of the naturalistic action of the play, while Christopher, wry and reflective, is the same character in middle age and a chorus figure, commenting upon the action. Christopher's father, convinced that Egypt must be restored to the Egyptians, is not intended to be an accurate portrayal of the author's own father who, nevertheless, was a cable-and-wireless engineer as is the character in the play.

Chrisfield
Three Soldiers, 1921
John Dos Passos

A gentle farm boy from Indiana, enlisted in the United States army of 1917. Dragged down by the petty violence and aimless stupidity of the system, he kills an officer and deserts with JOHN ANDREWS.

Christabel
'Christabel', 1797–1801
Samuel Taylor Coleridge

Christabel, the lovely, virtuous daughter of SIR LEOLINE, offers comfort and lodging to the beautiful but distressed lady (GERALDINE) whom she finds while praying for her lover in the wood at midnight. Recognizing too late Geraldine's malevolent nature, Christabel is put under a spell by her which not only prevents her from speaking of Geraldine's taint, but also causes *her* to start exhibiting serpent-like characteristics. Managing, however, to appeal to her father to send Geraldine away, Christabel is mistakenly thought to be showing jealous inhospitableness and is consequently rebuffed by him in her efforts to dispel evil.

Christian
The Pilgrim's Progress, Part I 1678, Part II 1684
John Bunyan

Burdened by terrible guilt and driven by a need for forgiveness, he finds peace in responding to the Christian gospel and journeys in obedience and faith through a series of harrowing and challenging experiences that are typical of any who embark on the Christian way. His struggles, failures, triumphs and final glory are symbolic of the nature of faith.

Christian, Edward, also known as Richard Ganlesse
Peveril of the Peak, 1823
Sir Walter Scott

Scott expended some effort in later years to convince readers that Christian was a fabrication, a 'moral monster', and was not intended to portray the brother of the William Christian who died after being imprisoned on the Countess of Derby's orders. Christian/Ganlesse makes a smoothly insidious villain, brave and resolute but morally slippery and inflexible in his hatred of papists.

Christiana
The Pilgrim's Progress, Part I 1678, Part II 1684
John Bunyan

The wife of CHRISTIAN, she initially deplores his decision to set out on the journey of faith, only to come to faith herself and begin the pilgrim way in her own right. She encounters the same kinds of distractions, pressures and dangers as her husband but, in the supportive company of MR GREAT-HEART and MR READY-TO-HALT, she faces the challenges of the Christian life with courage and steadiness; her virtue is rewarded by her glorious reunion with Christian in the Celestial City.

Christmas, Joe
Light in August, 1932
William Faulkner

It is impossible to miss the symbolic significance of his initials, or of his adoptive surname (given to him by a brutal and racist grandfather, who dumps the half-caste child in an all-white orphanage on Christmas Eve). A more complex version of POPEYE in *Sanctuary*, whose colour is always a matter of some doubt, Joe is continually forced into stereotyped 'black' behaviour by his environment and by those close to him. When his lover JOANNA BURDEN is murdered, Joe is not initially suspected, but after the chief suspect – a white associate of Joe's – tells the police that Joe is black, he becomes the quarry of a lynch mob, rightly persuaded of his guilt but for the wrong reason. In a highly charged crucifixion scene, they shoot and castrate him.

Christmas, Willy G
Timbuktu, 1999
Paul Auster

The son of Polish war refugees, William Gurevitch suffered a breakdown during the 1960s and, inspired by Santa Claus, changed his name to Christmas. Now an unpublished vagabond poet, a 'genuine dyed-in-the-wool logomaniac', Willy is stubborn, rambling and tubercular: 'the smell of death had settled upon him'. Nevertheless, he journeys with his dog, MR BONES, from Brooklyn to Baltimore to find his former high-school teacher and bestow upon her the key to a left-luggage locker, where he has deposited his 74 notebooks of writings. Frequently muddled, he remains bent both upon saving his work and advising Mr Bones on the techniques of survival.

Christopher/Christopher's Father → Chris

Christopher, Annabel
The Public Image, 1968
Muriel Spark
An unprepossessing girl from Wakefield, Annabel played small film roles until an Italian director turned her into a beautiful star as 'the English Lady-Tiger'. A public image has been constructed for her and her husband, Frederick: the perfect couple, cool and respectable in public and sexually adventurous in private. However, Frederick resents her success so much that he tries to destroy her. She demonstrates determination and ingenuity in attempting to preserve her image, partly for the sake of her baby, the only real thing in her life.

Christopherson, Anna
Anna Christie, 1922
Eugene O'Neill
Though sent away by her father, CHRIS CHRISTOPHERSON, to live with relatives on the prairies, far from that 'ole davil sea', she was seduced by her cousin and fell into a life of prostitution and disease, which has given her a lasting hatred and suspicion of men. Ironically, it is a voyage on her father's barge that proves to be her ultimate redemption.

Christopherson, Chris
Anna Christie, 1922
Eugene O'Neill
ANNA CHRISTOPHERSON's Swedish-American father is a cantankerous old bargee, whose coal-blackened exterior masks the complex resonances of his name, which suggests both Christ and Columbus, and was used as the title of an earlier, unsuccessful version of the play. His barge is called the *Simeon Winthrop*, recalling the purer and more rigid ideals of the early American settlers. Chris wants to save his straying daughter from the 'ole davil' (another early title) of the sea, and cannot see her as anything but a pure-hearted virgin.

Chrysalids
The Chrysalids, 1955
John Wyndham
The Chrysalids are a group of children who are able to communicate in a telepathic fashion (they can 'talk in thought shapes'), and thereby form a collective entity as well as individual selves. Where Wyndham's other telepathic children, the MIDWICH CUCKOOS, are presented as malign, the Chrysalids are devoid of cruelty, and offer the hope of a new and better world emerging from the savage post-holocaust one they inhabit.

Chubb
A Question of Attribution, 1988
Alan Bennett
The Intelligence Service interrogator of the suspected Russian spy, ANTHONY BLUNT, he is an apparently amiable, even vague man, hardly the social equal of Blunt, who is cool and metropolitan; Chubb, 'while not naive, is definitely suburban'. As well as trying to penetrate the secret world of Blunt, he attempts to pierce the equally mysterious world of art. 'What am I supposed to think? What am I supposed to feel?' Chubb fruitlessly searches for absolutes; but in art, replies Blunt (and, it is suggested, in everything else as well), there are none.

Chuffey, Mr
Martin Chuzzlewit, 1844
Charles Dickens
ANTHONY CHUZZLEWIT's faithful but almost senile old clerk. When Anthony dies, he lives with his son, JONAS CHUZZLEWIT, who asks MRS GAMP to care for him and treat him as a lunatic. Despite his infirmity, he reveals Jonas's plan to poison Anthony.

Churchill (Joby Peake)
The Churchill Play, 1974
Howard Brenton
A gruff midlands journalist and prisoner in the Churchill Camp, somewhere in England at some time in the future, Joby Peake writes and plays the role of Winston Churchill in 'The Churchill Play', which the inmates perform for a visiting delegation of parliamentarians. Churchill is shown as arguably a great man, but one not fit to lead the country when he did. A victim of both his class and education, he is haunted by his father's death, prone to depression, blundering, and ignorant of the conditions in which many British people, especially the working class, live. Brenton has revised the entire piece several times.

Churchill, Frank
Emma, 1816
Jane Austen
A likeable young coxcomb who displays worrying signs of 'foppery and nonsense'. The son of MR WESTON's first marriage, he is the apple of his father's eye and can do no wrong until his conduct proves otherwise. In his deception of Highbury society he shows a natural talent for insincerity and expediency, but as the victim of his own deceit is redeemed by the heartfelt anguish of young love.

Chuzzlewit, Anthony
Martin Chuzzlewit, 1844
Charles Dickens
The younger brother of OLD MARTIN CHUZZLEWIT and father of JONAS CHUZZLEWIT, he is a warehouseman in Manchester. He has a faithful old clerk, MR CHUFFEY. With a face 'sharpened by the wariness and cunning of his life', he trains Jonas to be as mean and unscrupulous as himself. He has a fatal stroke on learning that Jonas has been trying to poison him to get hold of his money.

Chuzzlewit, Jonas
Martin Chuzzlewit, 1844
Charles Dickens
The son of ANTHONY CHUZZLEWIT, he is an uncouth, scheming villain taught by his father to 'do other men; for they would do you'. He marries MERCY PECKSNIFF, but his ill-treatment makes her miserable. To gain his inheritance early, he tries to

poison Anthony and believes he has murdered him when Anthony dies of a stroke. MONTAGUE TIGG exploits his belief to involve him in his fraudulent insurance company and hires MR NADGETT to investigate him. Driven desperate, he savagely murders Tigg, but Nadgett uncovers his crime. His nephew, CHEVY SLYME, helps to arrest him, but he bribes Slyme to let him poison himself in the coach on the way to prison.

Chuzzlewit, Martin
Martin Chuzzlewit, 1844
Charles Dickens

The selfish but likeable grandson of OLD MARTIN CHUZZLEWIT and the pupil of SETH PECKSNIFF, who takes him on in an attempt to ingratiate himself with Old Martin. After a quarrel with Pecksniff, initiated by Old Martin to test his character and separate him from MARY GRAHAM, with whom he is in love, he goes to America with MARK TAPLEY to seek his fortune. After he loses money in the fraudulent Eden Land Corporation, suffers hardship, disappointment and a severe fever, he returns morally reformed and, with his grandfather's blessing, marries Mary.

Chuzzlewit, Martin (Old Martin)
Martin Chuzzlewit, 1844
Charles Dickens

The rich, miserly head of the family, brother of ANTHONY CHUZZLEWIT and grandfather of MARTIN CHUZZLEWIT. Despite illness, he is 'a strong and vigorous old man, with a will of iron' who rightly suspects all his relatives of having designs on his wealth but wrongly believes that all mankind is selfish and grasping. He goes to live with his cousin, SETH PECKSNIFF, whose hypocrisy and avarice he immediately detects. He adopts as his paid companion MARY GRAHAM, telling her she will inherit no money from him. He tests young Martin, his favourite grandson, by making him seek his fortune in America and, when he returns as a reformed character, he gives his blessing to Martin's marriage to Mary. Finally, he exposes and denounces Pecksniff as a scheming hypocrite.

Cicio, properly **Francesco Marasca**
The Lost Girl, 1920
D H Lawrence

An inarticulate vaudeville artist and the lover of ALVINA HOUGHTON, Cicio is dark, mysterious, exotic and inscrutable. His relationship with Alvina in England is passionate and trans-forming, yet when they return to Italy, he is absorbed immediately into his own culture. This is one of close family ties and male comradeship, an exclusive society into which outsiders do not easily fit. Cicio is perhaps more of a dominating presence in the book rather than a real character; ultimately he is rather enigmatic.

Cipriano, Don
The Plumed Serpent, 1926
D H Lawrence

Together with Don Ramon, Don Cipriano is the leading advocate of the Mexican Quetzalcoatl revival, and as such he adopts the personality of the God of War, Huitzilopochtli. Strong,

vigorous, confident and exotic, Don Cipriano represents the deeply-entrenched spirit of savagery, nobility, and the culture of blood and male supremacy. When he marries KATE LESLIE, their wedding ceremony becomes a symbolic affirmation of his belief in the subjugation of woman to man.

Citrine, Charlie
Humboldt's Gift, 1975
Saul Bellow

The narrator, he is a young writer who receives ambiguous gifts, both physical and metaphysical, from his former mentor, VON HUMBOLDT FLEISHER. He is a successful novelist, but is caught up in a web of financial and contractual constraints which dictate his relations with other people, and with his art. Drawn into this cash-driven world (and underworld), he is at the same time 'other-worldly', intent on finding a new way to squeeze an inchoate US reality 'into art's garments', and into a transcendent vision of life appropriate to the combined tedium and terror of contemporary existence.

Claggart, John
Billy Budd, Foretopman, 1924
Herman Melville

The Master at Arms on a British warship, he is known as 'Jemmy Legs'. He is about 55, 'somewhat spare and tall, yet of no ill figure upon the whole', but with a complexion which 'seemed to hint of something defective or abnormal in the constitution and blood'. He is sober and deferential to his superiors, but has a kind of innate depravity which combines with his jealousy to turn him against BILLY BUDD. He has 'no power to annul the elemental evil in him, though readily enough he could hide it'.

Claiborne, Thomas
The Malefactors, 1956
Caroline Gordon

A 48-year-old poet who has once been gifted with poetic vision, but now simply pretends to write while carrying on a 'conversation' with a critical voice in his mind. He is learned, superior, morally corrupt, detached from those around him, and has retreated into a sterile world of the intellect, 'that circle that long ago you described and then of your own free will stepped inside'. His physical and mental decline into suffering is arrested only by religious conversion.

Claire
A Delicate Balance, 1966
Edward Albee

Lazy, self-indulgent and a spectacularly heavy drinker, Claire imposes herself upon her elder suburban sister, AGNES, and brother-in-law Tobias, feeling no compunction about living off them, while at the same time mocking them. A woman who tells the truth as she sees it, she is no respecter of delicacy and provides a malicious commentary upon everything around her. 'We love each other', she observes of the family, 'to the depths of our self-pity and greed. What else but love?'

Clancy of the Overflow
The Man from Snowy River and Other Verses, 1895
Andrew Barton ('Banjo') Paterson

An itinerant stockman, he is an Australian folk-hero, generally held to typify the hard-living, hard-driving men of the bush in the 1880s. Clancy's city friend, addressing a letter to him as 'Clancy, of the Overflow', receives a reply in an unfamiliar hand: 'Clancy's gone to Queensland, droving, and we don't know where he are'. The friend sits in his dingy, dusty office and pictures Clancy's carefree life, following herds of cattle over the plains and by the rivers, and at night camping under the stars. The friend dreams of changing places with Clancy, but realizes that Clancy would never suit office life.

Clandon, Dolly
You Never Can Tell, 1897
George Bernard Shaw

A 'very pretty woman in miniature', Dolly is the impetuous, 18-year-old twin sister of PHILIP CLANDON. Talkative and inquisitive, Dolly and Philip know they are the children of MRS LANFREY CLANDON by whom Dolly is spoiled, but have no idea as to the identity of their father. Their quest to find out constitutes one strand of this farcical play.

Clandon, Gloria
You Never Can Tell, 1897
George Bernard Shaw

At 20, Gloria is the elder sister of the twins, DOLLY CLANDON and PHILIP CLANDON, and like them, is unaware of the identity of her father. Their mother is MRS LANFREY CLANDON, a formidable feminist author, and Gloria is similarly idealistic. In her case, though, high-mindedness is diluted by youthful impatience, and her natural dominance tempered by inexperience. She is an emotional woman and the conflict between her passion and pride often results in an unfortunate coldness in her manner. Gloria is courted by VALENTINE, but their future together, as inheritors of the failures of the previous generation, will be uncertain.

Clandon, Mrs Lanfrey
You Never Can Tell, 1897
George Bernard Shaw

The estranged wife of FERGUS CRAMPTON and veteran woman's rights campaigner, she is now known as Mrs Clandon. She has single-handedly brought up three children (GLORIA, PHILIP and DOLLY CLANDON). Her dress is businesslike, 'ruling out all attempt at sex attraction, and imposing respect on frivolous mankind and fashionable womankind'. She is a militant author of great repute – in Madeira – and her radically instructive works on cooking, creeds, clothing and conduct are published as 'Twentieth Century Treatises'. Her passion is vested in principles and social issues rather than people, but although personal sentiment embarrasses her, she makes occasional overtures of fondness towards her children.

Clandon, Philip
You Never Can Tell, 1897
George Bernard Shaw

Philip is the 18-year-old twin brother of DOLLY CLANDON and younger brother of GLORIA CLANDON. The twins, unaware of the identity of their father, are rather like a comic chorus to the main events of the play. Philip, is a 'handsome young man in miniature', eager, decisive and graced with perfect manners, to whom suavity and self-possession are points of personal honour. Consequently, his regular shushing of Dolly when her conversational exuberance is in danger of resulting in indiscretion, seems like 'cutting a sheet of silk in two with a flash of lightning'.

Clane, Jester
Clock Without Hands, 1961
Carson McCullers

The grandson of JUDGE FOX CLANE. Emerging from a childhood sheltered and indulged by his grandfather's affection, he tentatively seeks to assert his own separate identity. A naive and romantic young man, the idealism of his new-found belief in civil rights is transformed into an unrequited love for SHERMAN PEW. It is the revelation of the circumstances of his father's suicide which enables him to leave youthful uncertainty behind and take his place in the world.

Clane, Judge Fox
Clock Without Hands, 1961
Carson McCullers

An elderly ex-congressman who dotes on his grandson, JESTER CLANE, and is amiably at ease with his old-fashioned bigotry. A self-appointed defender of the white South against the liberalism of the Federal Government, he is as unable to acknowledge the views of others as he is unwilling to recognize his role in his son's suicide and SHERMAN PEW's orphanhood. Approaching 90 years of age and suffering the after-effects of a stroke, the fanaticism of his opinions begins to take on the appearance of senility.

Clare, Ada
Bleak House, 1853
Charles Dickens

A ward of the Court of Chancery and a suitor in the case of *Jarndyce* v *Jarndyce*. With her cousin, RICHARD CARSTONE, she goes to live with JOHN JARNDYCE and ESTHER SUMMERSON, her friend and companion. She stands by Richard when he devotes himself to the lawsuit and marries him secretly, knowing that Mr Jarndyce would disapprove. When Richard dies, she and their baby go to live with Esther and ALLAN WOODCOURT.

Clare, Angel
Tess of the D'Urbervilles, 1891
Thomas Hardy

Angel is a romantic idealist with a liberal approach to intellectual matters, who has refused to follow his clergyman father's wishes that he become a minister. He perceives TESS DURBEYFIELD as 'a fresh and virginal daughter of Nature', but this idealized vision of her does not survive her revelation that she was seduced by ALEC D'URBERVILLE and bore him a child. 'You were one person; now you are another', is his bleak summary of his disillusioned reaction. This is despite Tess's instinctive and sincere forgiveness of his own past affair – a hypocrisy which reveals the limitations of his 'enlightened' cast of mind.

Clare, John
The Fool, 1974
Edward Bond

An historical figure appropriated by Bond, John Clare was an early 19th-century poet of great originality and evocative power, a Northamptonshire farm labourer lionized by literary London and several times certified as insane. Although Bond presents him as a man of understanding, intelligence and perception, Clare is also cautious, divided in love, and a man to whom circumstances occur rather than one who consciously shapes his own destiny. He does not initiate the debate on pay between DARKIE and LORD MILTON, for instance, but acts as arbiter. His dilemma is that he can neither change the world by understanding it, nor by force. 'Can't help what I am.'

Clarence, George, Duke of → George, Duke of Clarence

Claret, Captain
White-Jacket, 1850
Herman Melville

The large, portly captain of the warship *Neversink*. He is the son of a naval veteran, and has the service in his blood. He rules the ship in capricious fashion, handing out unjust punishments on the one hand, and allowing the men liberties on the other, but is not a cruel man at heart, and is even considered 'a lenient officer'. 'What he was, the usages of the navy had made him.'

Clarinda, Lady
Crotchet Castle, 1831
Thomas Love Peacock

Attractive, educated, challenging and spirited, Lady Clarinda teases and toys with her suitors, devising witty forms of gentle torment for them. Honest and astute, she is nonetheless neither judgemental nor cruel about the quirks of those around her.

Clarke, Mary Anne
Mary Anne, 1954
Daphne Du Maurier

A woman ahead of her time, this feisty lady is determined to get what she wants out of life – the good things which have eluded her for so long. Impulsive, passionate, yet desperately selfish, she has no real sense of the consequences of her actions and tends to live in the present, eager for thrills. Though unscrupulous in her quest for self-satisfaction, she is not entirely unlikeable. Determined to shake off the poverty of her upbringing and the ruins of her marriage, she is never happier than when she is plotting and scheming.

Clarke, Micah
Micah Clarke, 1889
Arthur Conan Doyle

The son of one of Oliver Cromwell's most loyal soldiers, he is a Puritan, brought up near Portsmouth and recruited to fight for a rebel army led by Monmouth against James II. After many adventures, Clarke joins Monmouth at Taunton in 1685 and eventually escapes death. He is humble, sometimes gullible, politically and emotionally idealistic, a brave man of action with considerable powers of persuasion.

Clarke, Paddy
Paddy Clarke Ha Ha Ha, 1993
Roddy Doyle

A typical ten-year-old from Dublin, he has many friends with whom he has high-spirited escapades, and an ambivalent but ultimately loving attitude towards his little brother Sinbad. Mischievous but not malicious, his boyish imaginings, miseries and triumphs make him an engaging character, especially in the innocence of his response to the imminent break-up of his parents' marriage.

Clarke, St John
A Dance to the Music of Time, 12 volumes, 1951–75
Anthony Powell

A bestselling and prolific novelist of the Edwardian era, he is a near contemporary of J M Barrie and H G Wells, and was at the height of his fame before the outbreak of World War I. He still believes he will be awarded the Nobel prize. His head resembles Blake's, 'the folds and crannies of his face' suggesting 'a self-applauding interior'. Despite such books as *Fields of Amaranth* and *The Heart is Highland*, when he dies in 1937 an obituarist mischievously reckons that he is more likely to be remembered for his love of the Peter Pan statue in Kensington Gardens than for his novels. To KENNETH WIDMERPOOL, however, he is what literature ought to be. The author denied that he is modelled on John Galsworthy.

Clarke, Thomas
The Life and Adventures of Sir Launcelot Greaves, 1760–1
Tobias Smollett

Nephew to CAPTAIN SAMUEL CROWE and an attorney at law 'whose goodness of heart even the exercise of his profession had not been able to corrupt'. Warmly passionate and somewhat given to libertinism, he is nonetheless painfully orotund in legal matters.

Claude, Sir
What Maisie Knew, 1897
Henry James

A wealthy Englishman, he has an affair with IDA FARANGE and, following her desertion, falls for MISS OVERMORE, who has married BEALE FARANGE. Ultimately, though, his only abiding affection and loyalty is reserved for young MAISIE FARANGE, whom he protects and supports in her new home with MRS WIX.

Claudio
Measure for Measure, c.1604
William Shakespeare

The brother of ISABELLA, he is condemned to death for seducing his intended wife, Juliette. He is a high-spirited and well-meaning young man caught up in and caught out by a repressive system. Not surprisingly, when he learns that Isabella could save his life by becoming ANGELO's mistress, he begs his sister to comply, but is filled with guilt and despair when she angrily and viciously rebukes him.

Claudio
Much Ado About Nothing, 1598/1600
William Shakespeare

A young gentleman who has excelled as a soldier, Claudio seeks a financially rewarding marriage rather than one based on love. Although he participates eagerly in the plot to bring BEATRICE and BENEDICK together, he is unable to recognize deception when he is affected by it, taking HERO's apparent guilt at face value. His repentance on learning the truth appears genuine, as does his agreement to marry LEONATO's 'niece'. He is treated leniently by his friends – and by Hero – who teach him the value of forgiveness.

Claudius
Hamlet, 1601/2
William Shakespeare

He has become King of Denmark after murdering his brother and marrying his sister-in-law GERTRUDE. Claudius is a very capable politician who can outmanoeuvre HAMLET at almost every turn. He sees through Hamlet's 'antic disposition' and realizes that his guilt is known. His callous attempts to engineer Hamlet's death result ultimately in his own.

Claudius
I, Claudius, 1934
Claudius the God, 1934
Robert Graves

A seemingly minor member of the Roman Imperial Family, who is neglected and despised by his power hungry relatives. Physically unprepossessing, Claudius the stammerer is regarded as a laughing stock, an ineffectual but kindly man, apparently destined to view history from the safety of the sidelines. In a tale of murder, corruption and sexual perversion, however, Claudius's very insignificance is his saviour and he, alone, survives unscathed the tortured reigns of his relatives to become emperor himself – much against his will and better judgement.

Clavering, Harry
The Claverings, 1867
Anthony Trollope

The childhood sweetheart of JULIA BRABAZON, he is jilted in favour of the wealthy Lord Ongar. He is 'six feet high, with handsome face and person, and with plenty to say for himself on all subjects', and has an agreeable and open disposition, although he is apt to be 'fickle, vain, and easily led'. He is engaged to FLORENCE BURTON, but is sorely tempted by the widowed Julia's offer of marriage, since he still loves her. His sense of duty prevails, however, and he inherits the family estate and marries Florence.

Clavering, Lady
The History of Pendennis, 1848–50
W M Thackeray

BLANCHE AMORY's mother, she is a cynical vulgarian, who uses her second husband's basic decency as a stepladder to social prominence. Her first husband, COL ALTAMOUNT, far from having perished, is still working behind the scenes.

Clavering, Sir Francis
The History of Pendennis, 1848–50
W M Thackeray

The second husband of BLANCHE AMORY's vulgar and acquisitive mother, he is a weak and rather susceptible man, easy prey for COL ALTAMOUNT's blackmail plot. He has, nonetheless, a certain dignity and self-awareness that sets him apart from a world in which sham and greed are paramount.

Clay, Martin
Headlong, 1999
Michael Frayn

Rather than focus on the book he is supposed to be writing, amiable philosopher Martin Clay develops an obsession with what he believes to be a priceless unrecognized painting on his neighbour's crumbling estate. He hurls himself into a complicated scheme to obtain the picture illegitimately, but is continually distracted from the practical aspects of his plan by pressing questions of iconography and attribution. Disorganized, selfish and demonstrating a tremendous capacity for self-deception, he is swiftly overtaken by the events he has set in motion.

Clay, Mrs
Persuasion, 1818
Jane Austen

Moving to Bath as companion to ELIZABETH ELLIOT and SIR WALTER ELLIOT, Mrs Clay is viewed with much suspicion by ANNE ELLIOT. Humorously unattractive, she nevertheless uses her persistent flattery and attentiveness to play up to Sir Walter, hoping to land herself a fortune by marrying him. However, rather unexpectedly, her gold-digging duplicity is finally revealed to him when she takes up with WILLIAM ELLIOT.

Clay, Sam
The Amazing Adventures of Kavalier & Clay, 2000
Michael Chabon

A Jewish youth in 1930s New York, Sam is underdeveloped and undereducated but has dauntless ambition and an eye for the main chance. He is astute enough to see that comics are going to be the next big thing but his efforts to cash in on the trend are unpromising until he teams up (as scriptwriter and ideas man) with the gifted artist JOE KAVALIER, his cousin. Success does not bring him happiness, particularly in terms of his rather confused sexuality, but he is devoted to his more glamorous and talented cousin.

Clayhanger, Darius
Clayhanger, 1910
Hilda Lessways, 1911
Arnold Bennett

The grim exterior Darius Clayhanger presents to the world is the product of terrible suffering in his early life. These experiences have left bitter memories which he chooses not to share, thereby perhaps depriving himself of sympathy and understanding. The gulf between him and his son EDWIN CLAYHANGER is not bridged when Edwin sees sense and continues in the family business, despite his ambitions elswhere. The real tragedy of Darius's decline into senility is that he dies still neither understanding nor understood.

Clayhanger, Edwin
Clayhanger, 1910
Hilda Lessways, 1911
These Twain, 1916
Arnold Bennett

From a slim schoolboy, he grows into a sensitive, hardworking youth who likes to read and longs for something more elegant and artistic than life in the Five Towns; somehow, though, he lacks the strength of will to stand up to his father DARIUS CLAYHANGER's commonsense view of life. Although resentful, Edwin gradually reconciles himself to this disappointment and to others, most notably HILDA LESSWAYS's inexplicable abandonment of him. His reaction to Hilda's return and explanation reveal a kindness and generosity of spirit which deserve more than the life of compromise and adjustment that their long-delayed marriage involves.

Claypole, Noah
Oliver Twist, 1838
Charles Dickens

MR SOWERBERRY's apprentice and a persecutor of OLIVER TWIST, he robs his master then joins FAGIN's gang under the name of 'Morris Bolter'. He spies on NANCY for Fagin, and his report to BILL SIKES that she has met ROSE MAYLIE and MR BROWNLOW leads to Bill's murder of Nancy. He eventually gives evidence against Fagin to gain his own freedom and sets up as an informer.

Clea, properly Clea Montis
Clea, 1960, and elsewhere in *The Alexandria Quartet*, 1968
Lawrence Durrell

An artist in Alexandria, struggling to make sense of the shifting patterns of light and shade, of emotions and relationships that make up the city's fabric. Her 'point of view' is, arguably, the most abstract and ornate of the separate narratives.

Clearwater, Hope
Brazzaville Beach, 1990
William Boyd

A British scientist living at Brazzaville Beach 'on the edge of Africa', she reflects upon her work observing chimpanzees in the wild, her marriage to a scientist in England and her relationship with a colleague in Africa. Highly intelligent and educated, she is nevertheless worried about doing the wrong thing emotionally, and searches for a similar order and stability in her personal life that is demanded in her approach to her profession. Yet her questions and doubts remain, turbulent and unanswered. Eventually, she resolves 'not to seek tranquility in certainty, but in permanently suspended judgement'.

Cleaver, Fanny → Jenny Wren

Cleishbotham, Jedediah
The Black Dwarf, in *Tales of My Landlord: First Series*, 1816, et seq
Sir Walter Scott

Parish clerk and school-master of Gandercleugh – 'the navel (*si fas sit dicere*) of this our native realm of Scotland', who acts as 'editor' of a series of tales gathered at the Wallace Inn. Scott's title is, as he admitted, misleading, for the tales are not the landlord's at all, but come to Cleishbotham via his assistant schoolmaster PETER PATTIESON, since deceased.

Clement, Father, or Clement Blair
The Fair Maid of Perth, or St Valentine's Day, in *Chronicles of the Canongate: Second Series*, 1828
Sir Walter Scott

CATHARINE GLOVER's confidant, he is a Lollard priest, much loved and respected by the citizenry of Perth, but hated and despised by the Dominicans as a heretic. A follower of Wycliffe (who, appalled by the venality of the Church, attacked its ruling structure and preached a democracy of grace), he has to flee Perth for the hills.

Clement, Justice
Every Man in his Humour, 1598
Ben Jonson

A lover of poetry and a 'merry old magistrate', Clement dispenses justice as he thinks fit, as much as by strict adherence to the law. A good man, it is in him that everyone confides after being fooled and frustrated by BRAINWORM. Typically, Clement rewards Brainworm by making him the honoured guest at a dinner at his home.

Clennam, Arthur
Little Dorrit, 1857
Charles Dickens

Reputedly the son of MRS CLENNAM, he turns out to be the child of his late father's first wife. He returns to London after 20 years in China working with his father. In Mrs Clennam's house he meets AMY DORRIT and becomes the means of releasing her father from the Marshalsea by discovering his inheritance. While Amy secretly loves him, he thinks of her as a child and falls in love with MINNIE MEAGLES, but she marries HENRY GOWAN. Naturally melancholy, he is further disappointed on meeting his childhood sweetheart, the fat and silly FLORA FINCHING. MISS WADE gives him her autobiography to read when he and MR MEAGLES visit her about Tattycoram (HARRIET BEADLE). Entering into partnership with DANIEL DOYCE, he ruins the firm by investing in a scheme of MR MERDLE and is imprisoned for debt in the Marshalsea. CAVALLETTO and Amy care for him, YOUNG JOHN CHIVERY confides that Amy loves him, and on his release he finally marries her.

Clennam, Mrs
Little Dorrit, 1857
Charles Dickens

An austere Calvinist, she has lost the use of her limbs and is confined to a wheelchair in her gloomy London house. She employs AMY DORRIT to do needlework and is attended by AFFERY and JEREMIAH FLINTWINCH. Moved by revenge and self-righteousness, she conceals from her supposed son, ARTHUR CLENNAM, that he is the son of her husband's previous wife, and she suppresses a codicil in her husband's will that leaves a legacy to Amy Dorrit, whose uncle helped Arthur's mother. When Flintwinch steals the papers containing the codicil, RIGAUD gets ahold of them and tries to blackmail her. Aware that her guilt has been discovered, she reveals the truth to Amy and begs forgiveness. When her house collapses, she is paralysed and struck dumb and dies three years later.

Cleon
Pericles, c.1608
William Shakespeare

The governor of Tarsus, a country threatened by famine, Cleon hears of the arrival of PERICLES's fleet with foreboding. But when he learns that Pericles comes in peace and brings grain, Cleon is quick to declare his friendship and agrees, with his wife DIONYZA, to look after Pericles's infant daughter, MARINA. Cleon is essentially an honest man, but weak-willed and easily swayed. When Marina is assumed murdered at Dionyza's orders, Cleon is dumbfounded. His wife scorns his cowardice, and he attempts to conceal the supposed crime.

Cleopatra
All for Love, 1678
John Dryden

Less fickle and scheming than Shakespeare's CLEOPATRA, her love for ANTONY is genuine and more noble. Face to face with Octavia, Antony's wife, she remains regally dignified and is more than a match for the Roman matron. She has lost reputation, honour and fame for love but she would sacrifice all: 'There wants but life, and that too would I lose/For him I love.'

Cleopatra
Caesar and Cleopatra, 1898
George Bernard Shaw

Cleopatra, together with her brother PTOLEMY DIONYSUS, should have succeeded to the Egyptian throne after the death of their father, but Ptolemy's guardians have turned her away. Although physically mature at 16, Cleopatra's attraction for CAESAR is not at all sexual – that, wrote Shaw, 'would be disgusting'. Her charm is that of a child. She is fearful, especially of the Roman invaders, timid towards the palace servants and impulsive and egocentric. Caesar tutors her in majesty, but she proves an imperfect student, learning only to conceal her feelings. Once she becomes queen, she reverts to conspiratorial politics.

Cleopatra, Queen of Egypt
Antony and Cleopatra, 1606/7
William Shakespeare

Cleopatra is vain, impulsive, flirtatious, cruel, and both politically shrewd and enormously naive. A middle-aged, vital woman, she throws herself into her love affair with ANTONY. They revel in each other: 'We are peerless', he

confirms. Yet she realizes their time and their world are slipping from them, and this, as much as the heady sense of romance and sexual passion, accounts for her sudden, unpredictable and sometimes apparently perverse switches of mood and temper. One moment she is playful, the next tempestuous, but always she is deeply sensual, and this might be the seedbed of her downfall.

Clerimont, Ned
Epicoene, or The Silent Woman, 1609
Ben Jonson

A gentleman and a close friend of SIR DAUPHINE EUGENIE, Clerimont agrees to help him in his attempt to become the heir of his uncle, MOROSE. Together they also plot to make SIR JOHN DAW and SIR AMOROUS LA-FOOLE look foolish. Clerimont is a friend of TRUEWIT, with whom he likes to discuss women and the ways of the world. He is a good-hearted man, but easily bored.

Clerk of Oxenfoord, the
'The General Prologue', in *The Canterbury Tales*, c.1387–1400
Geoffrey Chaucer

An advanced student reading for his master's degree, he eschews worldly acquisitiveness, preferring learning to material goods. His friends pay for his education, and this lean, soberly-dressed minor cleric prays for their souls. But his single-mindedness may be as self-interested as the materialism of those around him in a world where, after the Black Death, there was a serious shortage of parish priests. Quiet and sober, he seems always to be pondering some deep philosophical argument: 'not o word spak he more than was need'.

Clerval, Henry
Frankenstein, or, The Modern Prometheus, 1818
Mary Shelley

The best friend of VICTOR FRANKENSTEIN. He is a serious-minded, scholarly, literary man, but is capable of flights of charming and improving invention. His 'eyes and feelings were always quick in discerning the sensations of others', and he has a kind and unselfish nature, as he demonstrates by nursing his friend back to health.

Cleveland
Vivian Grey, 1826–7
Benjamin Disraeli

The designated leader of the new party managed by VIVIAN GREY, who nonetheless finds himself marginalized by Grey's obsessive factionalism. In a duel, Grey kills Cleveland, a moment that underlines the impetuosity of the one as much as the impotence of the other.

Cleveland, Clement
The Pirate, 1821
Sir Walter Scott

A Shetland pirate saved from shipwreck by MORDAUNT MERTOUN and transformed by the experience; he is a man of some principle and learning and inclined to nobility and honour rather than vice. This, and the restlessness of his spirit, are explained by his being the son of BASIL MERTOUN and ULLA TROIL.

Clickett ('the Orfling')
David Copperfield, 1850
Charles Dickens

An orphan girl from St Luke's Workhouse, she is the maid-of-all-work for MR and MRS MICAWBER and quickly informs DAVID COPPERFIELD that she is an 'orfling'. She has a strange habit of snorting and a vivid repertoire of lurid tales about the Tower of London.

Clinker, Humphry
The Expedition of Humphry Clinker, 1771
Tobias Smollett

'He seemed to be about twenty years of age, of a middling size, with bandy legs, stooping shoulders, high forehead, sandy locks, pinking eyes, flat nose, and long chin – but his complexion was of a sickly yellow; his looks denoted famine'; indeed his name may be derived from the cant expression 'to dine with Duke Humphry', which means to fast, and from a slang word for stools. Though unprepossessing in the extreme, this poor lad of Wiltshire makes himself indispensable to the Brambles (and even attractive to their maid WINIFRED JENKINS) before he is eventually discovered to be a sprig of MATTHEW BRAMBLE's own planting in the far-off days of youth and hot blood.

Clissold, William
The World of William Clissold, 1925
H G Wells

At the age of 59, William Clissold sits down to write three volumes of his impressions of life. After starting as a young research physicist he has sailed into deeper waters and begun to direct companies. A social mixer with strong opinions, he has met Jung and Nansen and passes judgement on Ramsay MacDonald and other politicians. His early socialism has given way to belief in an 'Open Conspiracy' of go-getting businessmen sorting the world out by rational planning. Alongside this public material he also discusses his failed marriage and the nature of women.

Clitheroe, Jack
The Plough and the Stars, 1926
Sean O'Casey

A bricklayer and a commandant in the Irish Citizen army, Jack is 25 and lives with his wife, NORA CLITHEROE, in a Dublin tenement. He is tall and well-built but lacks Nora's moral strength. He has 'a face in which is the desire for authority, without the power to attain it'. Clitheroe is committed to the Republican cause but, according to BESSIE BURGESS, would 'rather be unlacin' his wife's bodice than standin' at a barricade'. Weak-willed and easily swayed, he is bludgeoned by his companions into rejecting Nora and going to fight on the streets as part of the 1916 Easter Rising.

Clitheroe, Nora
The Plough and the Stars, 1926
Sean O'Casey

The wife of JACK CLITHEROE, Nora is 22, sharp,

full of nervous energy and anxious to get on in the world. 'The firm lines of her face are considerably opposed by a soft, amorous mouth and gentle eyes.' She is emotionally stronger than Jack, and his cruel rejection of her before he goes out to fight as part of the 1916 Easter Rising in Dublin, appals her. Affectionate, possessive and idealistic, she is nevertheless destroyed by the political fanaticism of others.

Cloddipole
The Shepherd's Week, 1714
John Gay

The 'wisest lout of all the neighbouring plain', Cloddipole knows how to predict the weather from various signs in nature and is also considered capable of judging the songs of fellow-rustics Cuddy and Lobbin Clout. After hearing them for a while, though, he says how weary he is of them and that they should get back to thatching and herding.

Clonbrony, Lady
The Absentee, in *Tales of Fashionable Life*, 1812
Maria Edgeworth

LORD CLONBRONY's wife, she is a massive snob, intent on buying and manoeuvring her way into London society. She is contemptuous of her Irish background and longs to see her son, LORD COLAMBRE, married into English money.

Clonbrony, Lord
The Absentee, in *Tales of Fashionable Life*, 1812
Maria Edgeworth

The eponymous absentee landlord, living off the profits of his Irish estates. He inhabits London society, where he relies on the smoothly Machiavellian Sir Terence O'Fay to handle his arm's-length business dealings.

Clotelle
Clotelle, or, the President's Daughter, 1853
William Wells Brown

The daughter of a mulatto slave and a white US Senator (by implication Abraham Lincoln). Her complexion is 'even fairer than that of her mother', and grows lighter as she ages. She is bold and intelligent, has been illicitly taught to read, and grows 'every day more beautiful', despite harsh treatment. A new mistress refines her education and manners, and she becomes 'open, frank, free and generous to a fault'. She is heroic in helping her lover escape, then marries a Frenchman and travels to Europe, where she is widowed, and is reunited with her former lover.

Cloten
Cymbeline, 1609/10
William Shakespeare

The son of the QUEEN, and stepson of CYMBELINE, Cloten has been earmarked by his mother first to marry IMOGEN, and then to take over the kingdom on the death of Cymbeline. Unfortunately for the Queen's plans, Cloten himself is a posturing and ridiculous clown, an 'arrogant piece of flesh', whose malicious plans for IMOGEN and POSTHUMUS LEONATUS (he means to rape the former and murder the latter) come to nothing because of his own ineptitude.

Clout, Collyn
Collyn Clout, 1521
John Skelton

The learned vagabond who narrates the poem, and proposes to 'shake out/All my cunning bag/ Like a clerkly hag' in a rhyme which 'hath in it some pith'. He vents his spleen against the abuses and failings of both laymen and ecclesiastics, notably the church hierarchy, including Cardinal Wolsey. Their fruitless contentions make him shudder.

Clov
Endgame, 1958
Samuel Beckett

Mercilessly cloven to HAMM, Clov is suitably named, though he is nevertheless contemptuous of his charge, and cannot decide whether to leave or serve him. 'Let's stop playing' he implores at one point. 'Never', rebukes Hamm. Generally considered to be incarnations of ESTRAGON and VLADIMIR at a later stage, Clov and Hamm are similarly interdependent, Clov's constantly repeated 'I'll leave you' echoing Estragon's 'I'm going'. Limping around the stage (Estragon also has problems with his feet), Clov maintains a grim sense of humour, and is clearly without any illusions. As he shuffles around Hamm, his speech and movement are suffused with rhythm and pattern, yet his personality is never negated.

Clove
Every Man out of his Humour, 1599
Ben Jonson

A fop who, with his friend Orange, appears briefly in the play. He speaks in a long-winded and rather boring fashion, and in this Jonson may be satirizing the style of the playwright John Marston.

Clover
Animal Farm, 1945
George Orwell

A mare and a friend of BOXER, with whom she shares several characteristics, being honest, conscientious and true. She believes in the central tenets of the revolution and is a caring friend to the other animals. Although she can remember the original Commandments, she remains loyal to the concept of an Animal Farm even after it has been taken over by tyrants. Clover still hopes that one day her ideal will be realized, but lives long enough to see the pigs transformed into men and the revolution turned on its head.

Clown, or Gravedigger
Hamlet, 1601/2
William Shakespeare

Known in the Quarto and Folio texts as Clown and commonly as the Gravedigger, despite the tumultuous political events taking place around him he is preoccupied only by his profession. It is he who turns up Yorick's skull for HAMLET to examine. Having taken up his job on the day of Hamlet's birth, he has been a sexton for 30 years. He treats the job and death itself as a matter of fact, without any undue emotion, speaking in riddles and aphorisms, and with a macabre wit.

He represents the idea that time defeats us all; he also provides an interlude of humour before the final scenes of slaughter.

Clumsey, Sir Tunbelly
The Relapse, or Virtue in Danger, 1696
Sir John Vanbrugh

A country squire and justice of the peace, Sir Clumsey is the father of MISS HOYDEN, whom he has promised in marriage to LORD FOPPINGTON. Slippery, pompous and foolish, Sir Tunbelly is also an enormous snob, virtually grovelling before Foppington, imagining that by marrying his daughter into the peerage he will himself gain distinction in metropolitan society.

Cly, Roger
A Tale of Two Cities, 1859
Charles Dickens

The partner of SOLOMON PROSS and an Old Bailey spy, he becomes a servant to CHARLES DARNAY in order to betray him, testifying against him at his London trial. To escape from danger, he arranges a fake funeral for himself, but when JERRY CRUNCHER comes to dig up the body, the coffin is empty. In Revolutionary Paris, he spies for both the old regime and the government.

Clytie (Clytemnestra)
Absalom, Absalom!, 1936
William Faulkner

A black slave on Sutpen's Hundred, she is also her owner's natural daughter. She represents resilience and endurance, hanging on to the old estate to the bitter end, when it is occupied only by herself, the aged HENRY SUTPEN, and the idiot Jim Bond.

Cockeyne, Annette
The Flight from the Enchanter, 1956
Iris Murdoch

The cosmopolitan daughter of a Swiss socialite mother and foreign diplomat father, Annette is ROSA KEEPE's charge. At 19, she leaves her London finishing school in the middle of a lesson for the 'School of Life'. Rather selfish, romantic and immature, she is devoted to her even more selfish brother, and at his instigation (to demystify her expectations of love), has already been deflowered by one of his friends. She pathetically dreams of living a quiet, slow-paced life in her own kind of world, one she has only 'glimpsed from trains'. Falling under MISCHA FOX's casually lethal spell she attempts suicide, then, ironically, sets off for Italy, knowing he is there.

Codlin, Thomas and Harris ('Short')
The Old Curiosity Shop, 1841
Charles Dickens

Partners known as 'Codlin and Short' in the Punch-and-Judy show which LITTLE NELL and her GRANDFATHER briefly join. While Codlin is surly and misanthropic, Short (also called 'Trotters') is kind and cheerful. Hoping for a reward for finding the runaways, Codlin tries to betray Little Nell and her Grandfather to the authorities, but they manage to escape.

Cody, Martin
Not Here, Not Now, 1970
Dan Davin

A university student in New Zealand, fresh from a small working-class community. Relishing the escape from his family, Cody looks forward to acquiring the freedom to live as he chooses and hopefully to fall in love. But there are difficulties. Having come from a sheltered home, Cody is shy, self-conscious and sometimes rather awkward. Because his family never express what they feel, Cody discovers that he too is unable to express his emotions coherently. He is also frightened of falling behind with his work. Eventually, he finds that love is only partly to do with the dreams of romance and that society as a whole is not something different from his own family, but is a family writ large.

Coe, Jane
A Charmed Life, 1955
Mary McCarthy

A 'big, tawny, ruminative girl' from a rich background, she is one of the best-liked people in the small community of New Leeds, being generous with hospitality and gossip. Gently controlling her husband WARREN COE, she detests domesticity and would rather buy a new set of wine glasses for a dinner party than dust down the ones in the attic. Affable and anxious to be seen to be scrupulously fair, she is not above indulging in small deceits, cleverly justifying her motives to herself in case she is ever found out.

Coe, Warren
A Charmed Life, 1955
Mary McCarthy

A pleasant 50-year-old artist, with 'an eager, boyish face, rather like a bird's' and a slight, thin build, he allows himself to be managed by his wealthy wife, JANE COE, believing that she knows best. Modest and uncertain about his work, he rates everybody else as a greater intellect than himself, but loves nothing better than to sit at the feet of his friends and peck at the crumbs of their lofty conversation. A mild man, yet capable of passion, he emerges as the most sympathetic, yet pathetic, character in the tale.

Coffey, Ginger (James Francis)
The Luck of Ginger Coffey, 1960
Brian Moore

Emigrating to Canada with his wife and daughter, the hearty, ever-hopeful Ginger – failed BA and lapsed Catholic – anticipates great things. But he is as unsuccessful there as he was in Ireland, although, as always, he does not see this as his fault; he is a master of self-deception, and bad luck or other people are always to blame for his misfortunes. A gambler at heart, irresponsible, selfish and spendthrift – the perennial boy still dreaming of exotic adventures and conquests – he is baffled by his family's alienation, and only when his wife leaves him does he begin to come to terms with reality.

Cogewea
Cogewea, the Half-Blood, 1927
Mourning Dove/Hum-ishu-ma

An 'own-headed' young woman of the American West with an equal love of, and aptitude for, range-riding and 'book learning'. Of mixed blood and educated both by her Okanogan grandmother and in white schools, she is frustrated at being one of 'a go-between people', dismissed in both white and Okanogan worlds despite her abilities. Spirited, independent and intelligent, with a fondness for practical joking, she attracts the devotion of her tongue-tied fellow ranch hands. But her undented belief in romance coupled with a lack of suspicion towards whites blinds her to all attentions but those of a duplicitous Eastern 'tenderfoot' until, beaten, robbed and deserted after their elopement, she comes to echo her grandmother's cynicism towards whites and disenchantment with interracial marriage.

Cohn, Calvin
God's Grace, 1982
Bernard Malamud

A short man in his late thirties, he is a palaeontologist who finds himself the last man alive on earth after God has visited a second flood upon humanity. His own survival, God tells him, is the result of a 'minuscule error'. His loneliness aboard ship is lightened by a baby chimpanzee called Buz, but when they land on an island they fall in with a community of chimps and gorillas. Cohn, agonizing over the meaning of existence and God's intentions, tries to shape them into human social relations, but goes to a Christlike fate at their hands.

Cokane, William de Burgh
Widowers' Houses, 1892
George Bernard Shaw

In his late forties and a friend of the young DR HARRY TRENCH, Cokane, with his affected manners and nervousness, cuts a rather ridiculous figure. His is the voice of conventional society. He is deferential, snobbish, Conservative, slippery and hypocritical, becoming, with apparent equanimity, secretary to LICKCHEESE, the former rent collector and now slum property speculator.

Cokes, Bartholomew
Bartholomew Fair, 1614
Ben Jonson

A foolish young man from Harrow, Cokes arrives in London to procure a licence to marry GRACE WELLBORN. But to his dismay, and that of his guardian, HUMPHREY WASPE, he is diverted by the attractions of the fair, where his gullibility is mercilessly exploited and he loses an enormous amount of money. He is particularly impressed by JOHN LITTLEWIT's puppet show, commenting loudly during the performance. Upset by his conduct, Grace leaves him.

Colambre, Lord, also known as Evans
The Absentee, in *Tales of Fashionable Life*, 1812
Maria Edgeworth

The son of LORD and LADY CLONBRONY, he increasingly chafes under his mother's attempts to marry him off and at rumours of the evils of his father's absentee landlordism. He travels incognito to Ireland to inspect the estates at first hand, a visit that confirms his high opinion of GRACE NUGENT, an Irish girl living – a little wistfully – in London society.

Colbert, Henry
Sapphira and the Slave Girl, 1938
Willa Cather

Because SAPPHIRA DODDRIDGE COLBERT has married very much below herself, Henry lives a virtually separate life in his mill, while his proud, intransient wife runs the farm. It is clear that he is drawn – sexually, sentimentally, or merely as to the sharpest possible contrast with the invalid Sapphira – to the slave girl NANCY TILL, but he is not yet ready to overturn Southern values by actively participating in her emancipation.

Colbert, Sapphira Doddridge
Sapphira and the Slave Girl, 1938
Willa Cather

A proud patrician Southerner whose life has been constrained by illness and by marriage to the unimaginative miller HENRY COLBERT, she is a powerful avatar of the 'Old South' in the years before the Civil War.

Colbourne, Edward, later Captain
Miss Ravenel's Conversion from Secession to Loyalty, 1867
J W De Forest

An intelligent but faintly dull young lawyer in New Boston (a town allegedly based on New Haven, Connecticut), he is a fervent Abolitionist. Though he originally fails to win the hand of LILLIE RAVENEL, his stolid virtue (an unexpected physical courage) eventually wins the day over the 'Southern' unreliability and vice of her first husband, LT COL JOHN CARTER.

Colburn, Deb
Working Bullocks, 1926
Katharine Susannah Prichard

Unconscious of the possibilities of intellectual life, Deb bases her being on feelings, not thought. As one with the forest, she is primal woman: 'She might have been a tree growing, or a spring welling, deeply, quietly, underground.'

Coldfield, Rosa
Absalom, Absalom!, 1936
William Faulkner

Sister-in-law to THOMAS SUTPEN, and briefly the object of his affections after the death of her sister Ellen, she survives on Sutpen's Hundred until 1910, when she passes on the story of the Sutpens to QUENTIN COMPSON, just before he leaves Mississippi for Harvard.

Cole, John Grady
All the Pretty Horses, 1992
Cities of the Plain, 1998
Cormac McCarthy

He is a 16-year-old youth living in the Texas of the 1950s, where the oil industry has replaced ranching as the main economic activity. His journey to Mexico in search of a chance to live the traditional cowboy lifestyle forces him to confront a darker reality and find heroism within himself. His innate romanticism is undimmed and reaches its apotheosis in his love for a Mexican prostitute and the violence this brings him.

Cole, Walter → Teach

Coleman
Antic Hay, 1923
Aldous Huxley

A complete nihilist, who wears a beard in mocking imitation of the Saviour, Coleman likes nothing better than to reduce all lofty ideas to the basest physiological level. It is characteristic of him to relate with some relish that as a schoolboy he eviscerated frogs: 'crucified with pins they were, like little green Christs'. Even when his exasperated mistress, Zoe, throws a piece of bread at him in public, he reacts merely with laughter, 'till the tears rolled down his face'.

Colin
Butcher's Broom, 1934
Neil Gunn

Colin is a young man fired by tales of his ancestors as told by ANGUS, his grandfather. He is gullible enough to believe the laird's promise of land to everyone who enlists in the army, clinging to the old belief in the laird's integrity and loyalty to his people. On his return from the wars many years later, wounded and disillusioned, he finds Riasgan destroyed and witnesses the savage death of DARK MAIRI and the culture he fought to preserve.

Colin
The Comfort of Strangers, 1981
Ian McEwan

The gentle, dreamy, marijuana-smoking Colin, an actor holidaying in Venice with his long-standing lover, MARY, becomes fatally sorry for the housebound CAROLINE. Caroline's husband, ROBERT, describes Colin as 'like an angel', for he is delicately made, with an almost feminine beauty and grace. However, unknown to Colin, for this very reason Robert has chosen him to complete his and Caroline's sexual fantasies. Colin's belief that it is class, not male dominance, which has been the most powerful single principle in shaping individual lives is horrendously contradicted.

Collatinus (Collatine)
The Rape of Lucrece, 1594
William Shakespeare

The husband of LUCRETIA. One of a group of noblemen boasting of their wives' virtue, Collatinus discovers that Lucretia, having rebuffed the advances of SEXTUS TARQUINIUS, has been raped by him. She commits suicide. Collatinus's initial response is one of both anger and shame: 'This windy tempest, till it blow up rain,/ Held back his sorrow's tide to make it more'.

Collector, the
The Collector, 1963
John Fowles

This psychologically warped young man is a

pathetic and frightening creation. The victim of a disturbed childhood, he feels rejected by his mother, an emotion that lies at the root of his psychopathic tendencies. His perception of femininity is peculiar: he sees women as traitors, fit for punishment, yet he is intrigued by images of those that are gentle, submissive, pretty and delicate. Basically he craves love and affection, but now he also craves power, control. He substitutes reality with fantasy, but unlike the average person, he wants to turn that fantasy into reality.

Collector, The, properly Mr Hopkins
The Siege of Krishnapur, 1973
J G Farrell

The chief administrator of Krishnapur (a fictionalized Lucknow), the Collector is a 'large and handsome man' with 'low side-whiskers [that] sprouted out stiffly like the ruff of a cat'. He favours high stiff collars and is a 'man of considerable dignity' who is admired by fellow members of the British community and is determined to bring civilization to what he sees as an uncivilized country. It is to his 'Residency', full of mementoes of the Great Exhibition, that the British retreat when the Indian troops rebel (the historical India Mutiny of 1857), an event humorously presaged by the appearance of chapatis in unexpected places. He tries to hold the commmunity together during the four-month siege but in its aftermath finds that the experience has given him a fuller understanding of India and, like the British Empire itself, led him to question the old certainties, to such an extent that years later, back in England, he concludes that 'culture is a sham'.

Colley, Ben ('Kangaroo')
Kangaroo, 1923
D H Lawrence

A Jewish lawyer and leader of the Diggers, a quasi-Fascist political group, whom RICHARD and HARRIET SOMERS encounter in Australia. The 'Kangaroo' of the title, he is an outwardly benevolent man, preaching an optimistic message of love and social change. Yet the message is really a threat. He is an extremist, a dangerous mix of culture and will, intellect and passion, willing to listen to nobody else's views, and a monomaniac intent on imposing order upon nature.

Colley, Cameron
Complicity, 1993
Iain Banks

A cynical, chain-smoking, drug-taking journalist with an Edinburgh newspaper. He finds his world turned upside-down when a series of gruesome assaults takes place, each one reflecting the social injustice for which the unknown attacker is seeking retribution. Having criticized all the victims in an article, he is implicated. As events unfold he is forced to think about his own ethics and morality, and a deeper, more vulnerable side of his personality is revealed.

Colley, Robert James
Rites of Passage, 1980
Close Quarters, 1987

Fire Down Below, 1989, collectively *To the Ends of the Earth*, 1991
William Golding

A young parson onboard a ship for Australia, he is a shy, ineffectual, querulous creature, who spends the early part of the voyage being violently sick. He impresses EDMUND TALBOT as being an easily intimidated, obsequious man who is easily dominated by the captain. He is regarded with barely-concealed contempt as 'five feet nothing of parson ... with a mingled air of diffidence, piety, triumph and complacency'. But Colley is a tragic, complex, much misunderstood figure who meets a violent end and is the object of a remorse which transforms the life of Talbot.

Collins, Bill (William)
Getting Married, 1908
George Bernard Shaw

An elderly greengrocer with 'a rather youthful waist', Collins is the brother-in-law of MRS GEORGE COLLINS. Gallant and reassuring, he has assisted at the wedding receptions of five of the Bridgenorth sisters, and arrives to do the same for the sixth, EDITH BRIDGENORTH. In the general discussion over the plausibility of the institution of marriage, Collins's view is that it does not bear thinking about too much. His philosophy is that one commits oneself first and thinks about it afterwards.

Collins, Mrs George (Zenobia)
Getting Married, 1908
George Bernard Shaw

Mrs George Collins is the Mayoress of the borough, a coal merchant's wife, a spiritualist medium and, it is revealed, the author of vivid love letters to the BISHOP OF CHELSEA under the name of Incognita Appassionata. She is aged somewhere between 40 and 50, a vital, resilient figure, although 'her beauty is wrecked' and her face is 'a battle-field of the passions'. Yet in his stage directions, Shaw calls her 'triumphant' and describes her company as 'irresistible'. Indeed, she radiates sexual power, and ST JOHN HOTCHKISS falls for her.

Collins, Rev William
Pride and Prejudice, 1813
Jane Austen

The cousin of the BENNET family who is set, by entail, to inherit their home, Longbourn. Mr Collins is a pompous, foolish young clergyman who, through the patronage of LADY CATHERINE DE BOURGH, has secured a parish for himself. Self-conceited but simultaneously obsequious, he is primarily a humorous figure whose formal solemnity is offset by his often ridiculous behaviour and grovelling manners.

Collins, Tom
Such is Life: Being Certain Extracts from the Diary of Tom Collins, 1903, and others
Joseph Furphy

His name comes from an Australian term meaning rumour-monger. As deputy-assistant-sub-inspector in the New South Wales public service, Collins has many adventures in the bush and is often himself the hapless butt of the joke. He prides himself on his directness, yet he is enormously long-winded: he believes himself to be intuitive and never lacking in insight, but in fact he is devoid of both. His philosophy is that life is a series of random events over which the individual has only haphazard influence.

Collis
The Emigrants, 1954
George Lamming

The novel follows the fortunes of a group of emigrants travelling from the Caribbean to England. Collis, the narrator, is an aspiring writer, emigrating mostly for economic reasons ('a better break'), but speculating occasionally as to whether there is not a more profound, maybe even mystical reason for their journey. Perhaps they are sailing in search of an identity and purpose. Yet however much he yearns to become an artist, Collis has one tragic failing: he can account for and recount his experiences but he cannot synthesize them into a new whole – he cannot make sense of what he sees and feels. Because of this, he becomes lonely and disillusioned.

Collyer, Hester
The Deep Blue Sea, 1952
Terence Rattigan

In her mid-thirties, Hester is unhappily married to a prominent High Court judge. Suddenly she is overcome by passion for FREDDIE PAGE, a former wartime RAF pilot; she leaves with him, but the love that Hester believes will be liberating is, in fact, destructive. Yet she is her own worst enemy. She is irrational, over-dramatic, imperious, obsessive, demanding, overbearing – on the other hand, she is desperately trying to clamber on to the ladder of a new life. Finally, she is reduced to living in a crumbling London rooming house, her dreams in ruins, and here the play begins, as she attempts to gas herself.

Colquhoun, Robert
Sunset Song, 1932
Cloud Howe, 1933, part of the trilogy *A Scots Quair*, 1946
Lewis Grassic Gibbon

The second husband of CHRIS GUTHRIE and socialist minister of first Kinraddie then Segget, tall, fair-haired Robert is kind-hearted, lively, and very loving to both Chris and her son EWAN TAVENDALE. Gassed during the war, however, he is prone to sudden black and impenetrable depressions, and his violent mood swings and idealistic belief in his 'dream' of redemption slowly come between him and Chris, effectively destroying their intimacy. Worn down by the tragedies of life, his increasing instability of mind is paralleled by his physical deterioration, and his end is a disturbing and dramatic one.

Colston, Dame Lettie
Memento Mori, 1959
Muriel Spark

A fat and selfish woman of 79. Wealthy and snobbish, she tries to manipulate people by threatening to cut them out of her will. She formerly did charity work as a prison visitor, but she has no sympathy for the vulnerable and

unfortunate. She is the first of her circle of old people to receive telephone calls stating 'Remember you must die', which eventually drive her to the verge of derangement.

Colston, Leo
The Go-Between, 1953
L P Hartley

The book's narrator, who recounts the childhood events from 50 years earlier which shaped his arid life. He spent the summer of 1900 visiting a school-friend at Brandham Hall. He begins the summer full of optimism and hope – he is the 'Mercury' of the zodiac, messenger to the beautiful god-like creatures who inhabit the adult world of the hall. When these 'gods' move out of their designated orbits and a tragedy results, Leo takes on himself the burden for destroying them, and from then on shuns the worlds of the imagination, emotion and experience, afraid of being hurt by them and of hurting others.

Colville, Theodore
Indian Summer, 1886
William Dean Howells

An American journalist travelling in Europe, where he meets his former acquaintance Mrs Lina Bowen, now widowed, and her ward Imogene. He proposes to the young girl but quickly loses her to a much younger man and only gradually recognizes that his future is with Mrs Bowen.

Colwan, George
The Private Memoirs and Confessions of a Justified Sinner, 1824
James Hogg

The first son and heir of the LAIRD and LADY OF DALCASTLE, George is a fine, handsome young man of moderate intelligence whose charm, generosity and good humour endear him to many. However, his popularity suffers, and his easy, outgoing nature becomes a troubled one, when he is haunted continually by the ominous presence of his estranged brother ROBERT WRINGHIM.

Cominius
Coriolanus, c.1607/8
William Shakespeare

The general in charge of the Roman forces against the Volscians, he is noble and big-hearted. His account of CORIOLANUS's bravery is no mere hero-worship but a generous tribute from one soldier to another. He is nonetheless the first to try to save Rome from Coriolanus, but in spite of his arguments is refused. He is representative of true patrician values.

Commandant, the
Natives of my Person, 1971
George Lamming

National hero of the Kingdom of Limestone, the Commandant is vain and ambitious. His greed for the acclaim of a corrupt, materialistic society leads him to practise self-deception and to rationalize the brutal actions of his naval endeavours as 'a duty that the future would purify'. However, his conscience is awakened by his mistress, the Lady of the House, and he embarks upon a mission with a more visionary aim, 'to set up a new world and a new order'.

Common Thift
Ane Pleasant Satyre of the Thrie Estaitis, 1540
Sir David Lindsay

A minor character in Part Two of the play, Common Thift is at once a tragic and a humorous figure. Unable to escape from the life of theft and petty crime to which he was born, his lot is an unenviable one and in his final betrayal by his master OPPRESSIOUN it becomes even more apparent that Common Thift is himself no more than another victim of corrupt society. His overriding concern with his bodily functions when faced with the gallows is laughable but also inspires pathos, in light of the fact that Oppressioun – the real villain of the piece – has escaped scot-free.

Compeyson
Great Expectations, 1861
Charles Dickens

A swindler and forger who passes for a gentleman, he is revealed to be the man who jilted MISS HAVISHAM on her wedding day, having failed to cheat her out of a small fortune. When he and his partner, ABEL MAGWITCH, are convicted, he ensures that Magwitch gets a heavier sentence. Many years later, he helps the police to arrest Magwitch during his escape down the Thames, but he is drowned when they both fall overboard in a struggle.

Compson, Benjy (Benjamin), originally christened **Maury**
The Sound and the Fury, 1929
William Faulkner

The idiot whose jumbled tale in the novel's opening section signifies the collapse of the Compson line. He is rechristened Benjamin – the lastborn, 'sold into Egypt' – by his brother QUENTIN COMPSON. At 33, he also bears unmistakable overtones of Christ and is eventually crucified/castrated on the orders of his other brother JASON COMPSON, after making confused sexual advances towards him. Obsessed with the stretch of pasture sold as a golf course to pay for CANDACE COMPSON's wedding, he is characteristically found clinging to the fence there, listening to the players calling 'Caddie', which sounds like his sister's pet name.

Compson, Candace (Caddy)
The Sound and the Fury, 1929
William Faulkner

The Compson daughter, she is obsessively loved by her brother QUENTIN COMPSON. Pregnant by another man when she married an eligible Indianian in 1910 (a stretch of pasture was sold off to pay for the wedding), her action broke Quentin's heart and he committed suicide. In a 1946 Appendix written for the *Viking Portable Faulkner*, Faulkner says she divorced, remarried a Hollywood magnate, divorced again, and sank from sight during the Nazi occupation of Paris.

Compson, Jason, IV
The Sound and the Fury, 1929
William Faulkner

'The first sane Compson since before Culloden and [a childless bachelor] hence the last.' Faulkner described him as 'logical rational contained'. With a strong calculating ego and an instinct for profit, he is the modernizing, forward-looking Compson, which renders his childless state and his summary castration of his retarded brother, BENJY COMPSON, doubly ironic.

Compson, Quentin
The Sound and the Fury, 1929
William Faulkner

Confusingly, the second Quentin Compson in *The Sound and the Fury* is a girl, CANDACE COMPSON's child: 'Fatherless nine months before her birth, nameless at birth and already doomed to be unwed from the instant the dividing egg determined its sex'. At 17, she steals the money cheated from her by Uncle JASON COMPSON and absconds with a bigamous 'pitchman'.

Compson, Quentin, III
The Sound and the Fury, 1929
Absalom, Absalom!, 1932
William Faulkner

If the three Compson brothers represent a single, composite 'mind of the South', Quentin is the superego: guilty, fussy, hypersensitive and haunted by the past. An able Harvard undergraduate, he is obsessed with his sister CADDY COMPSON and eventually commits suicide because of her disastrous marriage. In a 1946 Appendix written for the *Viking Portable Faulkner*, the novelist deals with the question of incest by characterizing Quentin as a man 'who loved not his sister's body but some concept of Compson honor precariously ... supported by the minute fragile membrane of her maidenhead ... Who loved not the idea of the incest which he would not commit, but some presbyterian concept of its eternal punishment ... Who loved death most of all.' Quentin is also the historically aware narrator of *Absalom, Absalom!*

Compton, Ben
1919, 1932
The Big Money, 1936, part of the *U.S.A.* trilogy, 1938
John Dos Passos

A young, studious Jewish-American, Ben commits himself uncompromisingly to Marx's class struggle, making use of his oratorical skills to spread the radical message. Physically weak, he nonetheless displays great mental fortitude in refusing to surrender his beliefs as a pacifist and conscientious objector, despite being treated with violence and contempt by the patriotic American police, and becomes something of a folk hero to the working class.

Comstock, Gordon
Keep the Aspidistra Flying, 1936
George Orwell

Gordon Comstock, 'aged twenty-nine and rather moth-eaten already', is bored by his humdrum existence working in a bookshop. He lives a lonely, dingy, depressed life in a small bedsit, from which there seems no escape. He despises the capitalist ethos and has forfeited a succession of better jobs because he prefers honest poverty to the selfish profiteering characteristic of society. Gordon's life is relieved by his efforts to be a poet, but his lonely, poverty-stricken state has smothered his creativity. In love, however, he finds a new maturity in outlook and artistry.

Comte de Gue, Jean → John/Comte de Gue, Jean

Conachar, later known as Eachin or Hector Maclan
The Fair Maid of Perth, or St Valentine's Day, in *Chronicles of the Canongate: Second Series*, 1828
Sir Walter Scott

Foster son of TORQUIL OF THE OAK, this young Highlander acts the part of attendant or minder to the elderly SIMON GLOVER, though it is Simon's daughter CATHARINE GLOVER who commands the major part of his loyalty. Tall and handsome, he is mettlesome to a fault, but has 'drunk the milk of the white doe' and lacks the moral courage to temper his recklessness. His adopted name of Hector reflects his mixture of virtues and vices.

Conchis, Maurice
The Magus, 1966, revised edition 1977
John Fowles

A rich and psychologically warped 'recluse' who enjoys playing games with people. His past life holds many secrets, and he only relates versions of his history which suit him. His world is that of the surreal, and the elaborate charade surrounding him might not be a charade at all. Mysterious, complex and devoid of sincere sentiment, he is a man whose life experiences have led him to a position of power: a power which simultaneously traps and liberates him.

Condomine, Elvira
Blithe Spirit, 1941
Noël Coward

Elvira, the first wife of the charming, self-centred Charles Condomine, died after just five years of marriage. 'I remember her physical attractiveness, which was tremendous', admits Charles to his second wife, Ruth, 'and her spiritual integrity which was nil'. Her spirit is invoked by the medium, MADAME ARCATI. Elvira – visible and audible only to Charles – is volatile, sometimes playful, sometimes wilful; relaxed one moment and ruthless the next, taunting, criticizing, bantering. She represents a grand, almost secret innermost desire which Charles can neither live with nor without.

Condorex, Arnold
Harriet Hume, 1929
Rebecca West

A young man on his way up through the worlds of government and high society, Arnold blusters through life, a parody of pompous absurdity. He is a mendacious hypocrite who will utter anything to facilitate advancement. He is fatuous enough to deny to HARRIET HUME that his life has been stained by shame, guilt or treachery. Repudiating the obligations of honour, he has lost touch with his inner life and his feelings have atrophied.

Confidence Man
The Confidence Man, 1857
Herman Melville

A metamorphosing trickster figure who appears in a variety of manifestations on board the river steamer *Fidele*. His personae include 'Black Guinea', 'John Ringman', 'John Truman', 'Frank Goodman' and a herb doctor, and his deceptions include extorting small donations, selling false stocks and pedalling quack remedies. His financial gains seem beside the point, since instilling trust and then tricking the gullible and greedy are sufficient reward in themselves.

Confucius
Back to Methuselah, 1921
George Bernard Shaw

Confucius appears in the third section of this five-part play. *The Thing Happens* is set in the parlour of the President of the British Islands in 2170AD. Dressed in a yellow gown and 'presenting the general appearance of a Chinese sage', Confucius is conceited, detached and logical, and presently employed as Chief Secretary to the president, BURGE-LUBIN. As such, he virtually controls state affairs.

Coningsby, Harry
Coningsby, or The New Generation, 1844
Benjamin Disraeli

Raised by his aristocratic grandfather and educated at Eton, Harry seems ready to take his place in the continuum of old Toryism. However, travelling through England to LORD MONMOUTH's estate, he awakens to the reality of the country and to the need for a new, enlightened politics. Though uncertain of his values, he is focused by a visit to his friend OSWALD MILLBANK's home in industrial Lancashire. He comes to believe that his future is in politics, espousing the progressive Young Englandism of the historical George Smythe (on whom he is supposedly modelled) and of Disraeli himself.

Conrad
The Castle of Otranto, 1764
Horace Walpole

Conrad is the sickly, puny, adored 15-year-old son of MANFRED, PRINCE OF OTRANTO. Manfred is on the point of marrying him to Princess ISABELLA OF VICENZA to ensure that he has an heir when a huge helmet with a mountain of black plumes crashes down and renders Conrad a mass of mangled flesh, thus beginning the series of calamities which afflict Otranto.

Conrad
The Corsair: A Tale, 1814
Byron, George Gordon, 6th Lord Byron

Chief of the pirates whom the Pacha Seyd has sworn to destroy, Conrad will not listen to the entreaties of Medora, his beloved, but goes to Seyd's court in disguise. When he is recognized, he calls his pirates to attack but gallantly saves Gulnare, Seyd's favourite. He calmly awaits his doom in prison, and although Gulnare brings him a knife to kill Seyd, he cannot do so treacherous a deed. However, Gulnare kills Seyd herself and Conrad escapes with her to his island retreat. There he finds Medora dead with grief, believing him to have perished. His one weakness, chivalry, has ruined their happiness.

Conrade
Much Ado About Nothing, 1598/1600
William Shakespeare

A supporter of DON JOHN, Conrade swears to follow his master to death, although he never actually manages to achieve that end. A gentleman by birth but not by behaviour, he has no obvious motive for taking part in the plot against CLAUDIO and HERO other than a perverse love of mischief. His ultimate frustration is shown in his dealings with DOGBERRY, whose ignorance he finds infuriating.

Conradin
'Sredni Vashtar', in *The Chronicles of Clovis*, 1911
'Saki' (Hector Hugh Munro)

A ten-year-old boy, suffering from loneliness, boredom, lack of affection and illness. His hated guardian, 'the Woman', dominates him so that he accepts he has not long to live. Only his imagination keeps him going, and that prompts him to worship a polecat-ferret as a god. He appeals to it for help, chanting a violent hymn.

Conroy, Gabriel
'The Dead', in *Dubliners*, 1914
James Joyce

Believing that literature is above all politics, Gabriel writes a column for his local newspaper. He has a genuine and caring character, and loves his wife GRETTA CONROY to excess. As a sentimentalist his moods fluctuate through 'proud, joyful, tender, valorious' and he possesses a poetic soul that swoons with universal understanding. Gabriel likes 'nothing better than to find himself at the head of a well laden table', where he can voice his carefully chosen opinions.

Conroy, Gretta
'The Dead', in *Dubliners*, 1914
James Joyce

The affectionate wife of GABRIEL CONROY, she is a beautiful and proud woman, whom Gabriel claims takes 'three mortal hours to dress herself'. Her marriage has for years not 'quenched her soul'. She is pleasant and witty yet haunted by the ghost of her childhood sweetheart Michael Furey. For all that she is disappointed in love she still finds Gabriel a 'very generous person'.

Consolata, also known as Connie or Consolata Sosa
Paradise, 1997
Toni Morrison

She is the matriarch of the unorthodox community of women who gather at the Convent, an 'ideal parent, friend, companion'. Deeply religious Connie experiences a passionate love affair, but later devotes herself to caring for her surrogate mother, the nun who rescued her as a child. When she dies Connie falls into a 'slug life' of depression and alcoholism, but despite her mental absence is a sheltering, soothing protector in the eyes of the women who join her – eventually roused, she finds purpose in helping these 'broken girls' to heal. Physically almost blind, she possesses supernatural spiritual insight and can 'step in' to others' souls.

Constable of France, the
Henry V, 1599
William Shakespeare

Though nominally in charge of the French army, the constable appears as one of the many quarrelsome nobles who oppose Henry V's (HENRY, PRINCE OF WALES) invasion of their country. At first he is dismayed because of the apparent lack of courage in the French army, but like his fellow-countrymen he underestimates the foe, boasting before Agincourt about how many prisoners he is going to take. He is aware of LEWIS THE DAUPHIN's unsteady character. When he realizes he is on the losing side, he prefers to sacrifice himself on the battlefield.

Constance
'The Man of Law's Tale', in *The Canterbury Tales*, c.1387–1400
Geoffrey Chaucer

The daughter of a Christian Roman emperor, she is married twice to pagan husbands whom she converts to her faith by her devotion and essential goodness. She is twice betrayed by her mothers-in-law on false charges and put out to sea to whatever fate may befall her. Her devotion to God and the saints is her protection and her reward is restoration to her father and her second husband.

Constance, Duchess of Brittany
King John, 1590/1
William Shakespeare

The mother of ARTHUR, DUKE OF BRITTANY and widow of Geoffrey Plantagenet, Constance is a moral, upright but voluble woman. She loves her son and is intensely ambitious that he, rather than the ruling KING JOHN, should be King of England. As Arthur is still a child, such an event would mean that she, rather then he, would wield pre-eminent power. Both France and Austria support her claims, and she despairs when they make peace with John. Having been thwarted, she becomes by turns indignant, embittered and scornful. When John subsequently defeats France in battle, she disintegrates into madness and grief.

Constant
The Provok'd Wife, 1696
Sir John Vanbrugh

Having made amorous advances to LADY BRUTE for two years, Constant is finally rewarded when she appears to respond. Her emotions, however, are motivated less by genuine affection than by a desire to take her revenge upon her husband, SIR JOHN BRUTE, who cannot abide her. He is rare among the male characters of the play in neither distrusting nor disliking women, and it seems a pity that he is the one who, at the end, remains unattached. But, as he observes, 'marriage [is] a lottery'.

Constantia
The Daughters of the Late Colonel, 1922
Katherine Mansfield

The younger sister of JOSEPHINE, Con ('pale as a

lemon') is the dreamer, staring off into the distance as if seeing camels. Ideas come to her – she is attached to her little Buddha and is prone to strange behaviour in moonlight. As terrified of life as her sister, she says 'let's be weak', which they are: they postpone life, leaving their father's clothes like a presence in his bedroom. The sisters complement each other by making silences together, two negative halves of one diminished and underdeveloped personality.

Constantine, Lady Viviette
Two on a Tower, 1882
Thomas Hardy

A romantic woman, who is rejected by her husband, she craves love and affection. She is lonely, unappreciated and bored with the life which wealth and position have afforded her. There are many social confines on such a woman, and she is ultimately miserable, as she does not follow her instinct of allowing her heart to rule her head. A pawn to the end, she is a pitiful, beautiful creature, who loses her youth and looks, without ever finding lasting contentment.

Continental Op
Red Harvest, 1929
Dashiell Hammett

The unnamed hero of several stories and novels, he is one of the earliest tough-guy private detectives, and takes his title from his employers, the Continental Detective Agency of San Francisco. He is fat and middle-aged, but is very professional in his business, very tenacious once on a case and extremely loyal to the agency. Tough and fearless, he revels in physical violence.

Conway, Mrs
Time and the Conways, 1937
J B Priestley

A loving and devoted mother, Mrs Conway fusses and frets, interfering dreadfully in the lives of her children, desperately wanting each to succeed. She fears the breakdown of the family terribly, and likes to feel she yields some kind of omnipotent power over its members. She has a lively sense of humour, but often has to use it to mask a harsher reality, for as time passes it becomes clear that her well-intentioned hopes and aspirations have placed her children under intolerable pressure.

Conyers, Gen Aylmer
A Dance to the Music of Time, 12 volumes, 1951–75
Anthony Powell

First encountered in *At Lady Molly's* (1957), he is described as a fine figure of a man, though perhaps 'a bit too fond of dressing himself up to the nines'. Well-connected ('Peacetime or war, Conyers always knew the right people'), his high-flying career in the army took him around the world's trouble spots. In Soudan, he saved the ruler's life by arming the palace eunuchs with rifles. ('Fellow gave him a jewelled scimitar – semi-precious stones, of course.') Pro-Boer, he retires on the outbreak of war in the Transvaal. A bachelor until he was almost 50, he married a woman 20 years his junior. They have a daughter called Charlotte. He dies in his eighties during

World War II when, as an air-raid warden, he collapses while pursuing looters attempting to steal a refrigerator. 'He died, as he had lived, in active, dramatic, unusual circumstances.'

Cook, Alf
The One Day of the Year, 1960 (play), 1967 (novel)
Alan Seymour

A Sydney lift-driver and war veteran, he regards ANZAC Day as virtually sacred, a commemoration of the great moment of comradeship and male bonding that lifted him briefly out of the sorry routine of everyday life.

Cook, Captain
'Five Visions of Captain Cook', in *Trio*, 1931
Kenneth Slessor

Captain Cook chooses to 'live by the devil', voyaging 'over the brink' and into the unknown. He is a schoolboy's dream of adventure and romance, more warlock than man: 'Those captains drove their ships/By their own blood, no laws of schoolbook steam/.../Daimons in periwigs, doling magic out'.

Cook, Dot
The One Day of the Year, 1960 (play), 1967 (novel)
Alan Seymour

Wife of ALF COOK and mother of HUGHIE COOK, she stands rather on the sidelines in their conflict, able to see right in both points of view but unable to assent fully to either. She remains a still centre of caring amid a lot of high-flown and sometimes rancorous discussion.

Cook, Hughie
The One Day of the Year, 1960 (play), 1967 (novel)
Alan Seymour

ALF COOK's son, a student who considers himself possessed of all the answers. He rejects Alf's sentimental nationalism and regards ANZAC Day as a celebration of bigotry and self-satisfaction. It is clear, though, that Hughie is a more isolated individual than his father and his relationship with JAN CASTLE is extremely brittle.

Cook, Nellie, née Ellen Cotter
Cotter's England, originally *Dark Places of the Heart*, 1966
Christina Stead

Nellie makes her living, improbably, as a journalist, with a particular gift for working-class stories in the English provinces. 'A strange thing, her shabby black hair [is] gathered into a sprout at the top of her small head, her back and backbone bent forward, her thin long legs stalking prudently, gingerly like a marsh-bird's', spearing the foibles of her friends and associates with a heron-sharp eye.

Cook, the
The Canterbury Tales, c.1387–1400
Geoffrey Chaucer

In the service of THE FIVE GUILDSMEN while they are on pilgrimage, he is a connoisseur of the strong ale of London and is given to selling reheated stale food in his fly-infested pastry shop. The open ulcer on his leg, a sign of bad personal hygiene, drunkenness and lechery, is no encouragement to eat his food.

Cooke, Ebenezer
The Sot-Weed Factor, 1960, revised edition 1966
John Barth

Based on the historical 18th-century 'poet laureate of Maryland'. The invented character struggles in vain to cope with the demands of a reality he never grasps. He is an idealistic innocent who decides to become a poet and remain a virgin, but succeeds only in the first aim. His inexperience and unwarranted idealism are continually undermined by his experiences in America, and his inability to choose appropriate responses. He accuses himself of 'the crime of innocence', but ultimately learns a certain pragmatism, and withdraws from the world.

Cookie (R J C)
The Year of Living Dangerously, 1978
C J Koch

The novel's narrator, he is a shadowy and rather mysterious figure whose casually revealed initials seem to suggest some complicity with the author himself, and who seems to have privileged access to documents that provide insights into the lives of the other characters.

Coomer, Harry → Kumar, Hari

Coonardoo
Coonardoo, 1929
Katharine Susannah Prichard

Aboriginal Coonardoo is the 'well in the shadows', the dark primal source of life. Sustained and devastated by a mute, long-suffering love for white station-owner, HUGH WATT, she is 'the dark mirror of his soul': 'Wherever Hugh went, Coonardoo followed'; when Coonardoo is banished the spirit of the land and its white 'owner' are blighted.

Cooper, Hiram Halsey
1919, 1932, part of the *U.S.A.* trilogy, 1938
John Dos Passos

A minor character, Cooper, as well as being a campaigner for Woodrow Wilson, is a lawyer and politician who acts as mentor and father-figure to the young DICK SAVAGE. Providing Dick with the money to attend Harvard University, he subsequently, in his rank of Major, smooths the way for Dick to be accepted into the army after being sent home from Italy.

Copeland, Brownfield
The Third Life of Grange Copeland, 1970
Alice Walker

Driven by the conviction that 'the white folks is the cause of everything', Brownfield divests himself of all responsibility for his actions. He is completely destroyed by having 'seen the nothingness himself' and the conviction that there is nothing he can do to change his circumstances. By submitting to the pattern of his father's life, he justifies his increasingly violent and vengeful nature by believing that it is somehow preordained. Despite finally realizing his own participation in events, he is unable to remove himself from a self-destructive cycle of actions.

Copeland, Dr Benedict
The Heart is a Lonely Hunter, 1940
Carson McCullers

A black doctor who tirelessly ministers to his impoverished community despite his own consumptive condition. His whole life is governed by a belief in the 'strong, true purpose' of the emancipation of his race; his private life is devoted to a programme of self-education and his public life to a zealous desire to convert others. He is regularly consumed with a rage of frustration when his personal creed of atheism and self-discipline is resisted by his family and his patients.

Copeland, Grange
The Third Life of Grange Copeland, 1970
Alice Walker

A man 'who learned to love hisself only after thirty years', Grange undergoes a profound series of changes. A violent drunk, he realizes that the winning of self respect is the first step to freedom and holds on to the philosophy that 'you got to hold tight a place in you where they can't come'. His experiences in the North and his relationship with RUTH bring him in touch with 'the *man* in him', allowing him to take ultimate responsibility for his own life and his son ('a beast Grange himself had created') and to free Ruth.

Coplestone, Celia
The Cocktail Party, 1950
T S Eliot

A bright society girl, once the lover of EDWARD CHAMBERLAYNE, and now desired by the novelist PETER QUILPE. Torn by a sense of sin and solitude, she comes to believe the world is all delusion. After escaping to 'Kinkanja' to work as a VAD she is murdered by the natives, 'crucified/ Very near an ant-hill'.

Copperfield, David
David Copperfield, 1850
Charles Dickens

The protagonist and narrator of Dickens's most autobiographical novel. The story is David's 'written memory' of his confrontation with life. A spoiled infant, his domestic idyll is cut short by his hated new stepfather, MR EDWARD MURDSTONE. His various hardships, from working in the warehouse of Murdstone and Grinby to attending Salem House school, to the death of his first wife, DORA SPENLOW, are followed by his happy second marriage to AGNES WICKFIELD. The events all play crucial roles in his passage from innocence to a painful apprehension of the world, and a comfortable but reflective middle age as a famous author.

Copperfield, Mrs Clara
David Copperfield, 1850
Charles Dickens

The mother of DAVID COPPERFIELD, she is pretty but weak-willed and an incompetent housekeeper. Widowed shortly before David's birth, she depends greatly on his nursemaid, CLARA PEGGOTTY, until her fatal remarriage to the stern MR EDWARD MURDSTONE. He and his sister, JANE MURDSTONE, dominate her and treat

David cruelly, and she dies of a broken heart when David is only six.

Copperfield, Frieda
Two Serious Ladies, 1943
Jane Bowles

An anxious wife who reluctantly accompanies her husband on a business trip to Panama. Her nervous disposition is initially aggravated by the prospect of alien surroundings but she finds contentment in the volatile company of a number of prostitutes and falls in love with one of them. On returning home, having left her husband for the company of this woman, she declares her satisfaction at having 'gone to pieces'.

Coram, Rob
The Merry-Go-Round in the Sea, 1965
Randolph Stow

At six years old, 'the boy was not aware of living in a young country ... He knew that he lived in an old, haunted land', messy with the everyday compromises of life. His only comfort is the image of the merry-go-round in the sea (it is actually the mast of a sunken barge), cyclical, eternal and safe.

Corbaccio
Volpone, or The Fox, 1606
Ben Jonson

A foolish, deaf and greedy old man in ailing health, he nevertheless hopes to outlive VOLPONE and inherit his considerable wealth. Like CORVINO and VOLTORE, he attempts to ingratiate himself by offering Volpone money. But Corbaccio is tricked by MOSCA into disinheriting his son, Bonario, to Volpone's advantage. He is later involved in a plot to save his own reputation and is duly punished for it.

Corbett, Cassandra
The Game, 1967
A S Byatt

An Oxford don, precise and self-contained, Cassandra Corbett cannot bear to be watched or discussed. She keeps contacts to a minimum, retreating from the practical emphasis of her Quaker background to the symbolism and authority of high Anglicanism. Symbols, whether religious or literary, are increasingly a refuge from the oppression of facts and objects. She applies the intricate rules of her childhood fantasy game to the imaginary life she inhabits, but the unexpected return of her lost first love and her sister JULIA CORBETT's need to re-examine their complex relationship, blurs the distinction between the real and the imagined on which her sanity depends.

Corbett, Julia
The Game, 1967
A S Byatt

'The guiding light of your life is this need to be liked', says Julia's lover. Unfortunately, she is a writer of domestic novels and given to recycling family and friends into her plots, a habit not likely to win her popularity. She has a great capacity for living and is curious about people, particularly the sister she loves but antagonizes (CASSANDRA CORBETT). Julia holds nothing back

of herself and desperately wants to make contact with the unyielding Cassandra. However, the legacy of the past makes every contact painful and Julia's final attempt at communication through her writing is most damaging of all.

Cordatus
Every Man out of his Humour, 1600
Ben Jonson

A friend of ASPER who, with his associate MITIS, watches the play and comments on the action. Cordatus has already seen it and so is able to advise Mitis on its general nature before it begins. His function is to present the author's point of view to Mitis and thus to the audience.

Corde, Albert
The Dean's December, 1982
Saul Bellow

A former journalist who has become a professor of journalism as an act of withdrawal, in an attempt to recover perspective and critical detachment. The violent external world will not be denied, however, and he is dragged back into an adversarial relationship with friends and family by events in Chicago and Romania. Although he feels himself to be 'inappropriate, incapable of learning the lessons of the twentieth century', he is man of real feeling, and is inexorably drawn 'to feel and to penetrate further' into the lives around him.

Cordelia
King Lear, c.1607
William Shakespeare

The youngest of KING LEAR's three daughters, Cordelia presents a vivid contrast to her sisters, GONERIL and REGAN. In response to her father's demands for avowals of love and affection, she refuses to pander to his destructive ego with false, futile flattery, instead insisting that she loves him 'according to my bond'. She is a compassionate but also a determined and strong-willed woman of integrity and intelligence, who is loyal and loving to her father even after being banished from his kingdom.

Cordelia
Lear, 1973
Edward Bond

This Cordelia is not, as in Shakespeare's play, LEAR's daughter, but the daughter of a priest and the leader of an insurrectionary peasant army against LEAR, BODICE and FONTANELLE. She has an acute, animal intelligence and instinct for self-preservation. However, she is as brutalized as her opponents are brutal, and therefore, after her victory, she sanctions the use of terror as a political weapon. She also continues the work on building the wall which Lear began, and which serves as both defence and prison. Cordelia sees pity for others essentially as self-pity and does her best to eradicate it. All this, it is suggested, derives from unhappiness and insecurity dating from childhood.

Corelli, Captain Antonio
Captain Corelli's Mandolin, 1994
Louis de Bernières

A captain in the Italian army during World War II,

Corelli is a sensitive man, uneasy in his role of occupier on the Greek island of Cephallonia. He is 'prone to dramatic exaggeration' with 'an ironic disregard for the truth', but inspires fierce loyalty in his men. Despite initial resistance, his natural exuberance, humour, inherent sense of justice and thoughtful intelligence gain the admiration of DR IANNIS, with whom he is billeted. The doctor's daughter, PELAGIA IANNIS, too is won over and the pair fall deeply in love. Firstly and foremost, however, he is a musician and everything in his life is coloured by his music.

Corey, Tom
The Rise of Silas Lapham, 1885
William Dean Howells

The son of a wealthy Boston family, his advances towards the bright but plain PENELOPE LAPHAM are misinterpreted by her family, who believe he is paying court to her prettier sister IRENE LAPHAM. In the event, Tom proves himself to be above petty considerations of class and status, marrying for love and rejecting the rigidly stratified city of his upbringing.

Corflambo
The Faerie Queene, 1590–6
Sir Edmund Spenser

The son of a huge giantess, he himself is also of great stature. His name means 'heart flame'. He rides a camel and from his eyes shoot two 'fierie beames', sharper than the points of needles, with which he can cause the death of his foes by 'casting secret flakes of lustfull fire' into their hearts from a distance. He has conquered many nations through the power of his 'infectious sight'.

Corin
As You Like It, c.1600
William Shakespeare

An old shepherd who is about to lose his living, he displays generosity and a genuine nobility of character in his dealings with others. His observations are sententious, unaffected and based on common sense, and his native wit allows him to challenge the court fool TOUCHSTONE.

Coriolanus (Gaius Martius)
Coriolanus, c.1607/8
William Shakespeare

The 'wonder boy' of the Roman army, almost suicidally brave in battle and as suicidally proud and intractable in the political arena. Always too much under the influence of his mother VOLUMNIA, he allows her to persuade him into situations where his temper will inevitably lead him into trouble. He makes no secret of his loathing of the plebeians and their tribunes, JUNIUS BRUTUS and SICINIUS VELUTUS, and walks straight into the trap they prepare for him. Blinded with anger at his treatment in Rome, he fails to see the danger of his alliance with his arch-enemy AUFIDIUS. A combination of pride and inability to refuse his mother's requests lead inevitably to his death.

Cormick, Edna
Dancing in the Dark, 1982
Joan Barfoot

Repressing her secret self in a desperate attempt to find happiness within a middle-class home and marriage, Edna becomes obsessed with perfecting her role as a housewife. Careful and quiet, she is 'afraid of changes and things that are not precise'. Sometimes, when her work is completed, Edna closes her eyes, listens to music and dreams of another self: dancing, singing, and laughing. Her true nature can only be revealed through 'madness' and the tragic end of her relationship.

Cornelia
The White Devil, 1612
John Webster

The mother of VITTORIA COROMBONA, FLAMINEO and MARCELLO. She is outraged by Flamineo's procuring his sister, by Vittoria's adultery, and by other manifestations of immorality. Despite being driven frantic when Flamineo murders Marcello, she lies to protect her surviving son. Her mental and physical state deteriorates further and it appears that her death is imminent.

Corney, Mrs
Oliver Twist, 1838
Charles Dickens

The cruel matron of the workhouse where OLIVER TWIST is born, she marries MR BUMBLE, the beadle, dominating and humiliating him. Learning the secret of Oliver's birth, she helps EDWARD LEEFORD (known as 'Monks') to defraud him of his inheritance. When the plot is discovered, she and Bumble are dismissed from their posts and end up as paupers in the workhouse which they once tyrannized.

Cornplow, Fred
The Prodigal Parents, 1938
Sinclair Lewis

The best indication of the shift and softening of Lewis's attitudes is the contrast between Cornplow and the earlier GEORGE FOLANSBEE BABBITT. Though Lewis clearly reserves a level of sympathy and liking for Babbitt, he is treated with satiric roughness. Cornplow, also a successful businessman, is antagonized by a family who have taken on radical communist ideas and who seek to undermine the family unit.

Cornwall, Duke of
King Lear, c.1607
William Shakespeare

REGAN's husband and KING LEAR's son-in-law, Cornwall is a perfect match for his callous and cruel wife. Similarly ambitious, he is also sadistic and vengeful in his treatment of the EARL OF GLOUCESTER and others. He is pitiless in his dealings with those over whom he yields power. He plucks out Gloucester's eyes.

Cortez, Francis
The Tree of the Sun, 1978
Wilson Harris

A novelist whose secret attempt to recount his wife JULIA CORTEZ's beauty and whose desire to create is a little more than a vague verbal correlative of the female characters' ability to bring something tangible out of themselves.

Cortez, Julia
The Tree of the Sun, 1978
Wilson Harris
The wife of FRANCIS CORTEZ, with whom she occupied the flat now taken by the painter DA SILVA DA SILVA and his wife JEN. Jen seems to have incarnated Julia's repressed and almost buried desire to have a child, while Julia's creativity has manifested itself as sickness.

Corthell, Sheldon
The Pit: A Story of Chicago, 1903
Frank Norris
A rich and successful artist, he offers LAURA DEARBORN a different, more aesthetically pleasing lifestyle than that offered by her husband CURTIS JADWIN. Though Laura has rejected Corthell she later has an affair with him, but ultimately refuses to abandon her sick and bankrupt husband.

Corvick
'The Figure in the Carpet', in *Embarrassments*, 1896
Henry James
A mature and learned literary critic, he is taken over by a quest for the mysterious 'figure in the carpet' running through the novelist HUGH VEREKER's work. Just before his sudden death, he claims to have discovered what the secret figure actually is. Though he divulges it to his new wife, GWENDOLYN ERME, he dies without publishing his findings and her subsequent demise guarantees that the secret is never exposed.

Corvino
Volpone, or The Fox, 1606
Ben Jonson
A merchant, Corvino is one of several men (CORBACCIO and VOLTORE being others) planning to worm their way into VOLPONE's confidence and thereby inherit his money. Corvino presents him with a pearl, but nothing happens. Later, when MOSCA describes the beauty and virtue of Celia, Corvino's wife, Volpone determines to see her. So great is the merchant's greed for money that, although he claims to be jealous of his wife's chastity, he enthusiastically attempts to prostitute her to Volpone, hoping that this might be the way to his fortune.

Cory, Richard
The Town Down the River, 1907
Edwin Arlington Robinson
The man with everything – good looks, style and money – who represents to the narrative voice the epitome of all his aspirations. Robinson is careful to establish Cory's warmth and humanity, as well as his apparent distance from the narrator and his fellows. His suicide brings home sharply the distinction between the superficial happiness of appearances – Cory is a 'gentleman from sole to crown' – and inner contentment.

Cosroe
Tamburlaine the Great: Part I, 1587
Christopher Marlowe
Brother and stronger right hand to the King of Persia, he makes TAMBURLAINE his regent and lieutenant-general to his armies, only to be cheated of crown and life in battle with his ambitious ally.

Costard
Love's Labour's Lost, not later than 1594
William Shakespeare
A clown arrested for wenching within KING FERDINAND's court following new and surprising restrictions. Costard proves verbally equal to Ferdinand's accusations, producing a string of puns and wordgames. He has been successful in chatting up JAQUENETTA, unlike his rival DON ADRIANO DEL ARMADO. Like Armado, though, he comes unstuck in the Pageant of the Nine Worthies, where he calls himself 'Pompey the Big' instead of 'Pompey the Great'.

Costello, Lefty
Waiting for Lefty, 1935
Clifford Odets
Committee-man in a taxicab drivers' union, he is eagerly awaited by the men as they decide whether or not to strike, and is not actually seen. In the event, he is murdered (again off-stage) before he can make his speech.

Costigan, Captain
The History of Pendennis, 1848–50
W M Thackeray
EMILY COSTIGAN's father, he is a disreputable old rogue, looking for nothing more than an easy passage through life. He thinks he may have found one in ARTHUR PENDENNIS, until MAJOR PENDENNIS convinces him that Arthur has no money.

Costigan, Emily, or Miss Fotheringay
The History of Pendennis, 1848–50
W M Thackeray
A pretty but flighty actress with a rather foreboding stage name, for whom ARTHUR PENDENNIS loses his head. A disastrous match is only narrowly averted when the Costigans are persuaded that Arthur is not the catch he seems.

Cosway, Antoinette → Rochester, Bertha

Cottar, the
'The Cottar's Saturday Night', 1786
Robert Burns
Representing an idealized portrait of an honest Scottish countryman, this saintly cottar, at home with his loving wife and respectful children, dispenses wholesome advice, hospitality, religion and virtue.

'Count', the (Wojciech 'Peter' Szczepanski)
Nuns and Soldiers, 1980
Iris Murdoch
Nicknamed by fellow-students who joked that all exiled Poles were counts, 'Peter', a civil servant, was actually born in England in 1939. He was ashamed of his Polish parents, only realizing after his grief-stricken, obsessively-patriotic father died how essentially Polish and alien he himself really was. In belated fealty he cultivates a stiff moral uprightness in Polish military tradition. His flat a 'citadel of loneliness', he has

only his books and radio for company until he develops a treasured friendship with Guy and GERTRUDE OPENSHAW. Silently worshipping Gertrude, after she is widowed he dares to hope she might return his love.

Courcy, Lady Alexandrina de
Dr Thorne, 1858
The Small House at Allington, 1864
Anthony Trollope

Introduced in *Dr Thorne* as one of Earl de Courcy's arrogant daughters, Lady Alexandrina is 30 in *The Small House at Allington* and eager to find a husband. She marries ADOLPHUS CROSBIE, whom she does not love, in the mistaken belief that her position in society will improve and that she could make him a good wife.

Courcy, Lady Amelia de
Dr Thorne, 1858
The Small House at Allington, 1864
Anthony Trollope

A daughter of Earl de Courcy, no member of the family is 'more wise, more solemn, more prudent, or more proud' than she is. Always mindful of the superiority of the aristocracy, she strongly opposes marriages with those lacking noble blood, until she herself marries Mortimer Gazebee, a high-class attorney. She continues to take a lofty view of her social position, but makes a good wife, partly because she is so economical.

Courtney, Alfreda
The Vivisector, 1970
Patrick White

The beautiful Alfreda is married to the wealthy Harry Courtney; they live at Sunningdale, an imposing and luxurious mansion. With his approval, Alfreda purchases young HURTLE DUFFIELD from his mother, the Courtneys' washerwoman, for £500. Duffield's apparent artistic talent confirms Alfreda's belief that she can recognize genius. As they have no child other than the crippled RHODA COURTNEY, their purchase also satisfies Harry's wish for a son. Alfreda whisks her adopted child off on a trip to Europe, demands that he address her as '*Maman*' and almost suffocates him with the overwhelming possessiveness of her love. An exquisite dilettante, she takes a casual interest in the anti-vivisection movement.

Courtney, Rhoda
The Vivisector, 1970
Patrick White

The adoptive sister of HURTLE DUFFIELD and the natural daughter of Harry and ALFREDA COURTNEY, Rhoda is hunchbacked and in delicate health. Nevertheless, she has an emotional strength and an unflinching insight into others for, as she observes, 'almost everybody carries a hump, not always visible, and not always of the same shape'. A realist, she is also compassionate, even sentimental, accusing Duffield of being too realistic and of seeing the truth 'too large'. Both his paintings and his own imagined invincibility, she warns, could fail him. Eventually, as an elderly woman reduced to near-poverty but with an undeviating

sympathy for local stray cats, she accepts accommodation in Duffield's home.

Cousin Sarah
The Cardboard Crown, 1952
A Difficult Young Man, 1955
Outbreak of Love, 1957
When Blackbirds Sing, 1962, collectively known as 'the Langton Tetralogy'
Martin Boyd

Cousin Sarah is Boyd's perpetual 'jinx'. This 'black, alpaca spinster' always has words that are 'gentle and righteous' and 'deeds always full of spite'. Possibly the most terrifying of Boyd's creations, she is a malicious presence whose deceptively kindly exterior does not fool, but who cannot be ousted, and wreaks on-going damage.

Coverdale, Miles
The Blithedale Romance, 1852
Nathaniel Hawthorne

A minor Transcendentalist poet who observes the utopian experiment at Blithedale and its participants with a happy capacity for self-deception. Aloof and ironic, he makes a thoroughly untrustworthy narrator.

Covett, Barbara
What Was She Thinking?: Notes on a Scandal, 2003
Zoë Heller

Barbara Covett, narrator of the story, is friend, colleague and confidante to SHEBA HART, a fellow teacher who is having an affair with a pupil. A solitary, judgemental individual, Barbara's ostensibly objective account of events reveals itself to be the recording of a devious, obsessive woman who lives vicariously through her friend. Sole person in whom Sheba can confide, Barbara manipulates the situation to make Sheba entirely dependent on her.

Cowardly Lion, also known as Zeke
The Wonderful Wizard of Oz, 1900
L Frank Baum

To some extent a more complex character than his two semi-human companions, his search is for a more abstract quality – courage – than the brains and heart the SCARECROW and TIN WOODMAN lack. As with the others, though, it becomes clear that the lion already has an impressive stock of bravery, which he uses to frighten away the evil spider that haunts the forest.

Cowley, Elmer
'Queer', in *Winesburg, Ohio*, 1919
Sherwood Anderson

The junior member of Cowley & Son, he is 'extraordinarily tall, and his arms long and powerful. His hair, his eyebrows and the downy beard that had begun to grow on his chin were pale almost to whiteness'. A newcomer to Winesburg, he is violent and inarticulate and obsessed with his supposed 'queerness'.

Cowper, Pamela
The Healing Art, 1980
A N Wilson

A youngish university lecturer stricken by breast

cancer. Unsupported by any confidence in the abilities of doctors, she 'trusted in luck, and the Virgin Mary and the power of prayer', but is haunted by an image of the martyred Saint Agatha, whose emblem is breasts on a dish.

Cowperwood, Frank Algernon
The Financier, 1912, revised edition 1927
The Titan, 1914
The Stoic, 1947
Theodore Dreiser

A self-made millionaire industrialist, closely modelled on the 'traction king' Charles Tyson Yerkes, whose career in America was tarnished by charges of embezzlement, but who went on to establish London's underground railway system. The younger Cowperwood of *The Financier* is described as having a head 'large, shapely, notably commercial in aspect ... already his eyes had the look that subtle years of thought bring. They were inscrutable.' His resistance to adversity and shock is soon to be tested to the full.

Cox, Stephen
A Natural Curiosity, 1989
The Gates of Ivory, 1991
Margaret Drabble

A novelist, an old friend of LIZ HEADLEAND and 'a traveller by nature. A political traveller'. He is the kind of man in whom people (especially women) confide – he is a free agent who obeys impulses. His latest impulse has been to travel to Cambodia to research a play about Pol Pot because 'he represented the apotheosis of the demented intellectual'. Sceptical and unfulfilled, Stephen follows his nose, watching and waiting for a story – for history. His ensuing plight awakens the world-awareness in Liz.

Coyle, Eddie
The Friends of Eddie Coyle, 1972
George V Higgins

Eddie is a loser. A small-time crook, he is unable to shake off the hold of the criminal fraternity, and his old connections lead him deeper and deeper into a trap. His life is cramped, seedy and sad, and he seems like a victim of forces beyond his control. His is a violent and chilling world, where betrayals are not forgiven, and where lying has cruel consequences.

Crabshaw, Timothy
The Life and Adventures of Sir Launcelot Greaves, 1760–1
Tobias Smollett

In stature (stocky) and in function (a kind of folksy wisdom, distilled out of repeated physical abuse), he unmistakably plays Sancho Panza to SIR LAUNCELOT GREAVES's Don Quixote. But he is also a grotesque representative of the common people, set in an often uneasy relationship to Greaves's rarefied and aristocratic knight errantry.

Crabtree
The School for Scandal, 1777
Richard Brinsley Sheridan

A malicious gossip who feeds on rumour. The 'odious uncle' of SIR BENJAMIN BACKBITE, he is,

like him, a member of LADY SNEERWELL's poisonous coterie. He slanders everyone, apart from his nephew, whose praises he sings and whose suit to MARIA he supports.

Crabtree, Cadwallader
The Adventures of Peregrine Pickle, 1751, bowdlerized edition 1758
Tobias Smollett

Crabtree is so profoundly deaf that it has become a sport among the wags at Bath to insult him in the roundest terms to his face: 'his disposition was altogether misanthropical; and ... he was admitted into company on account of the entertainment he afforded by his sarcastic observations, and the pleasant mistakes to which he was subject from his infirmity'. Having led a chequered and violent life, he is known among the ladies as the 'Scandalous Chronicle'.

Crake
Oryx and Crake, 2003
Margaret Atwood

Crake is the adopted name of SNOWMAN's former schoolfriend Glenn. Addicted to violent computer games and pornographic websites, Crake is immune to the sensitivities and sensibilities of others. Later, having become a eugenicist and heading the Paradice project, Crake designs the Crakers, a race with no concept of language, undisturbed by sexual desire or religious impulse. A misguided idealist, perhaps an agent of the chaos that ruins the landscape, he is both self-absorbed and destructive.

Crampton, Fergus
You Never Can Tell, 1897
George Bernard Shaw

The estranged and long-absent husband of MRS LANFREY CLANDON, Crampton is the father of GLORIA, PHILIP and DOLLY CLANDON and also VALENTINE's landlord. A man of about 60, he is an unprepossessing figure with 'an atrociously obstinate, ill-tempered, grasping mouth and a dogmatic voice'. He harbours a bitterness towards his wife and family, of whose whereabouts he is unaware. When their identities are revealed, Crampton resents their independence but is manipulated by FINCH MCCOMUS and BOHUN QC into a reconciliation of sorts.

Crane, Edwina
The Jewel in the Crown, 1966
The Day of the Scorpion, 1968
The Towers of Silence, 1971
A Division of the Spoils, 1975, forming
The Raj Quartet
Paul Scott

The district supervisor of Protestant mission schools in Mayapore, who in 1942 saved her first school, at Muzzafirabad, from being burned by an angry mob. She is outspokenly disapproving of the British Raj, but her compatriots find that this 'tough old bird' has intelligence and organizing abilities which outweigh her unacceptable agnosticism and pro-Indian sympathies. Faced with violence preceding Independence, she believes that her 35 years of good works and noble intentions have been an empty gesture. Wearing the white sari of widowhood and mourning she commits *suttee*, her funeral pyre symbolizing that of her beloved India.

Crane, Ichabod
'The Legend of Sleepy Hollow', 1820
Washington Irving

The village schoolmaster of Tarrytown is lank, dangling and loose-framed, with a nose 'like a snipe'. Nevertheless, he is a huge feeder, making the most of his weekly board with his pupils' parents. As singing master, he becomes enamoured of KATRINE VAN TASSEL's charms. His rival BROM BONES, however, takes advantage of his obsession with the supernatural and waylays him one witching time in the form of the Headless Horseman. Crane flees in utter terror but is felled by its pumpkin head; whether through fear or shame he is never seen again.

Cranmer, Thomas
Henry VIII (All is True), c.1613
William Shakespeare and John Fletcher

As Archbishop of Canterbury, Cranmer supports King HENRY VIII's contention that his marriage to KATHERINE, QUEEN OF ENGLAND is invalid. Not surprisingly, the king thinks of him as 'My learn'd and well-beloved servant', while CARDINAL THOMAS WOLSEY declares he is a 'heretic'. The authors present Cranmer as a good, even saintly figure who presides over ANNE BOLEYN's crowning. At the end of the play he prophesies a greater England under her daughter, Elizabeth, implying that although history appears chaotic, it is subject to a providential order. Yet Cranmer's support of an absolute ruler is not entirely altruistic, and the idea that he is a visionary is hardly substantiated in the play.

Cranstoun, Lord
The Lay of the Last Minstrel, 1805
Sir Walter Scott

MARGARET OF BRANKSOME's secret lover and her father's former enemy. After wounding SIR WILLIAM DELORAINE in single combat, he bravely substitutes himself for the incapacitated champion in the final duel with the English knight, SIR RICHARD MUSGRAVE. His victory frees the Branksome heir (who has been lured away and turned over to the English by Cranstoun's goblin page) and proves himself worthy of Margaret's hand in marriage, despite all her mother's fears and opposition.

Cratchit, Bob
A Christmas Carol, 1843
Charles Dickens

The ill-used and poorly-paid clerk to EBENEZER SCROOGE, he is unfailingly loyal and cheerful. With their six children, including TINY TIM, Bob and Mrs Cratchit provide one of Dickens's models of an impoverished but happy working-class family. When the GHOST OF CHRISTMAS PRESENT shows Scrooge the Cratchits at their jolly and affectionate Christmas dinner, Scrooge begins to regain his old 'good-hearted' self.

Cratchit, Tiny Tim → Tiny Tim

Cravat, Sabra
Cimarron, 1930
Edna Ferber

Unlike her lawyer husband YANCEY CRAVAT, who falls apart in a world of unrestricted opportunity, she is able to take the initiative and to confront the contradictions of a burgeoning society with great self-possession. While Yancey gradually sinks into decline, Sabra becomes a successful businesswoman and is eventually elected to Congress, spurred on by the same dogged practicality that has stood her in good stead from the outset.

Cravat, Yancey
Cimarron, 1930
Edna Ferber

Caught up in the hectic land rush of the Oklahoma Territory in the late 19th century, this gifted lawyer and writer is gradually destroyed by an aimless but avid *Wanderlust* that unbalances his moral centre and clouds his judgement. In contrast, his wife, SABRA CRAVAT, flourishes in their new environment.

Craven, Colin
The Secret Garden, 1911
Frances Hodgson Burnett

Bedridden since birth by the suffocating despair of his bereaved father, Colin has no disability except weakness. Like his dead mother's garden, locked away and seemingly lifeless, he is transformed by the healthy influence of his cousin MARY LENNOX, herself a difficult child. Gradually his strength grows, as does the garden, by force of the 'Magic' he understands as the mainspring of life, and which it is his future to discover.

Craven, Julia
The Philanderer, 1893
George Bernard Shaw

The 'beautiful, dark, tragic-looking' Julia is one of the two women (the other being GRACE TANFIELD) in love with LEONARD CHARTERIS. She, in her turn, is loved by the vivisector Dr Paramore, whom she finally marries. Unlike Grace, Julia uses her sexual allure as a weapon to make men seem foolish and to attract attention to herself. Grace is not jealous of Julia, but Julia is of Grace and this destroys her self-respect.

Crawford, Henry
Mansfield Park, 1814
Jane Austen

The nephew of Admiral Crawford, brother of MARY CRAWFORD, and a young man of fortune who has a great dislike for any 'permanence of abode or limitation of society'. Though not handsome, he has 'air and countenance' and a liking for the ladies which eventually proves his downfall. He toys alternately with the hearts of MARIA BERTRAM and JULIA BERTRAM as easily as he slips from malicious gossip to 'gentle gallantry'. Resolving to make FANNY PRICE love him, he catches himself out by falling in love with her. Failing to win her hand with emotional bribes and obsequious self-reformation, his inconstant character finds solace in a dishonourable and clandestine elopement with the recently-married Maria.

Crawford, Janie
Their Eyes Were Watching God, 1937
Zora Neale Hurston

Raised in 'the white folks' yard', Janie embarks on a quest for self-fulfilment and self-knowledge. Moulded into others' ideas of who she should be, she feels 'far away from things and lonely'. She survives by learning to maintain a façade of what is expected of her, husbands being 'just something she had grabbed up to drape her dreams over'. Kicking against her nanny's worship of objects and position, Janie finds 'a jewel down inside herself' and her vision of a fulfilled and fulfilling love is finally realized in her relationship with TEA CAKE.

Crawford, Mary
Mansfield Park, 1814
Jane Austen

The niece of Admiral Crawford, sister of HENRY CRAWFORD, and a young woman of fortune whose object in life is to marry well. Restless and flighty, and at times crass, insensitive and snobbish, she sets her sights on EDMUND BERTRAM, only to be struck aghast at his intention of entering the ministry, a profession to which she could never stoop, given her belief that 'obligation of attendance' at church is a 'formidable thing' which nobody enjoys, 'especially if the poor chaplain [is] not worth looking at'. Lacking delicacy of taste, mind and feeling, she believes that 'a large income is the best recipe for happiness', and holds that 'selfishness must always be forgiven ... because there is no hope of a cure'.

Crawfurd, David
Prester John, 1910
John Buchan

A young Fifer drawn out of the everyday world of Calvinist practicality and plunged into a netherworld of paganism, superstition and magic, haunted by the spectre of Prester John. It is, however, a world which shares his own culture's obsession with the mythic figure of the Lost Leader. David is sane and sceptical, brave but not reckless and loyal but instinctively suspicious of fatuous beguilements.

Crawley, Bute, Mr and Mrs
Vanity Fair, 1848
W M Thackeray

They are effectively a single personality. He is SIR PITT CRAWLEY's brother, a bland Laodicean clergyman, permanently in debt and addicted to hunting and fishing. She is ambitious and calculating, running his affairs and even writing his sermons.

Crawley, Grace
Framley Parsonage, 1861
The Last Chronicle of Barset, 1867
Anthony Trollope

First seen as a nine-year-old learning Classics from her father, REV JOSIAH CRAWLEY, Grace,

aged 19, plays an important role in *The Last Chronicle of Barset* as the beloved of MAJOR HENRY GRANTLY. She is poor, thin and shabbily dressed, but with a refined beauty. Clever and modest, meek and noble, she is selflessly concerned to save Henry, whom she loves, from the disgrace hanging over her family.

Crawley, Lady
Vanity Fair, 1848
W M Thackeray

SIR PITT CRAWLEY's wife, she is a sad, downtrodden creature whose refinement is of too fragile a sort to withstand her husband's brutal insensitivity. Sickly and insubstantial, she drifts off quietly.

Crawley, Miss
Vanity Fair, 1848
W M Thackeray

Enormously wealthy in her own right, SIR PITT CRAWLEY's spinster sister appears to elevate determined self-gratification over more sober virtues, and conspicuously favours her dissolute nephew RAWDON CRAWLEY and the governess BECKY SHARP, *until* they decide to run athwart class divisions and marry. At this, and at the prospect of her impending death, she adopts a narrow rectitude.

Crawley, Mrs
Framley Parsonage, 1861
The Last Chronicle of Barset, 1867
Anthony Trollope

Mary is the devoted wife of REV JOSIAH CRAWLEY and his comforter in his troubles. Although a lady, she brought no money to their marriage, and their poverty has physically harmed her. Unlike her husband, she is neither proud nor ashamed of being poor, and she heroically conceals from him her acceptance of charity for the benefit of him and their children. In *The Last Chronicle of Barset* she is convinced of his innocence and encourages him to fight the allegation against him.

Crawley, Pitt
Vanity Fair, 1848
W M Thackeray

SIR PITT CRAWLEY's elder son, he is a cold fish, both mean and ambitious. However, he is not so strait-laced as to be completely immune to his sister-in-law BECKY SHARP's vivacious personality, and he visibly grows in stature when she praises his abilities. He is also capable of great kindness to his heartbroken brother, RAWDON CRAWLEY.

Crawley, Rawdon
Vanity Fair, 1848
W M Thackeray

A brilliant but essentially shallow young officer who finds that society is increasingly less susceptible to his limited range of charms. For a time he is the perfect consort for BECKY SHARP, but she outgrows him rapidly and eventually rejects him altogether. Broken and disappointed, he leaves England for the tropics and a premature death.

Crawley, Rawdon jr
Vanity Fair, 1848
W M Thackeray

The son of BECKY SHARP and RAWDON CRAWLEY, he is a sad, insubstantial little boy through whom it is possible to see both his father's somewhat attenuated capacity for affection and his mother's chilly selfishness.

Crawley, Rev Josiah
Framley Parsonage, 1861
The Last Chronicle of Barset, 1867
Anthony Trollope

The cadaverous perpetual curate of Hogglestock, the husband of MRS CRAWLEY. As a gentleman and an accomplished scholar, he has been embittered by his poverty, which arouses both pride and shame in him; the former makes him resent and resist any attempt to help him. Stern, unsociable and with a pedantic mode of speech, his usual moroseness sometimes becomes deep depression, but he is forceful when asserting his religious beliefs. His hard work makes him respected by poor parishioners. In *The Last Chronicle of Barset*, accused of theft, he wallows in his sufferings. He realizes his faults, but is also too aware of his virtues.

Crawley, Sir Pitt
Vanity Fair, 1848
W M Thackeray

BECKY SHARP's employer, he is a cantankerous reprobate, whose lack of education and external marks of breeding contrast sharply with a sense of formidable but fading power. He is much attracted by Becky and, following the death of his downtrodden wife, LADY CRAWLEY, offers her his hand (and the prospect of a considerable fortune), unaware that she is already married to his son, RAWDON CRAWLEY. His decline into helpless senility and incontinence is slow and humiliating.

Crazy Jane
Words for Music Perhaps, 1933
Last Poems, 1939
W B Yeats

An earthy and fierce old Irishwoman, who loves Jack the Journeyman and hates the Bishop, the opponent of sensuality. She insists that human love must encompass both the body and the soul, and that in human life fair and foul are intimately related: 'Love has pitched his mansion in/The place of excrement'. Although anticlerical, she believes in God and the permanence of what exists: 'All things remain in God'. In 'Crazy Jane on the Mountain' she despairs at the inferiority of modern people compared with the greatness of the mythological past.

Creakle, Mr
David Copperfield, 1850
Charles Dickens

The sadistic and ignorant headmaster of DAVID COPPERFIELD's first school, Salem House, to which he is sent by MR MURDSTONE. Describing himself as 'a Tarter', he terrorizes his family and canes his pupils: 'He had a delight in cutting at the boys, which was like the satisfaction of a craving appetite'. Unable to speak above a whisper, he needs to have the surly, wooden-legged school lodge-keeper, Tungay, loudly repeat everything he says. Eventually, he becomes a Middlesex Magistrate in charge of a model prison in which LITTIMER and URIAH HEEP are prisoners.

Cresseid
The Testament of Cresseid, 1480–90
Robert Henryson

Deserted by Diomed for whom she has deserted Troilus, Cresseid curses Venus and Cupid. In a dream, the gods pass judgement on her for her promiscuity, and when she wakes she finds that she has leprosy, her beauty hideously disfigured. Living in a leper house she now has to beg in the street. Troilus passes, does not recognize her but is somehow reminded of the Cresseid he had known, and throws gold and jewels into her lap. When she is told who the man was she is distressed and warns other women to learn from her example and be faithful. She is a symbolic moral figure, rather than a full character in her own right, unlike Chaucer's CRISEYDE.

Cressida
Troilus and Cressida, 1601/2
William Shakespeare

The daughter of CALCHAS (a traitor to Troy who now resides in the Greek camp), Cressida is left to fend for herself in Troy with only her old and immoral uncle PANDARUS to oversee her. She manages fairly well, using a combination of wit and good sense. She becomes TROILUS's lover, but when she is taken to the Greek camp finds that circumstances and her sense of vulnerability prevent her from remaining faithful. Despising herself for her inconstancy, she, like her father, defects in spirit as well as in body to the Greek camp, finding a new protector in DIOMEDES.

Crewe, Flora
Indian Ink, 1995
Tom Stoppard

An exploration of cultural heritage and identity and the possibility of verifying the past, the play is set in India during the 1930s and in England 50 years later. Vivacious, flirtatious, independent and strong-willed, Flora is a young, well-known and much-travelled English poet who, while visiting India, embarks upon a romance with the painter and lover of literature, Nirad Das. During the mid-80s, an American biographer attempts to tease order from the happy chaos of Crewe's life, while her sister recalls that 'her weakness was always romance'.

Crewe, Mr
'Janet's Repentance', in *Scenes of Clerical Life*, 1858
George Eliot

Avaricious old Mr Crewe has been curate in Milby for half a century. A figure of fun to many of his parishioners on account of his ill-fitting wig and mumbled, inconsequential sermons, he is nevertheless accepted by most as being fundamental to life in Milby. With the arrival of the Protestant curate, REV EDGAR TRYAN, the religious order of the town is upset, and Mr Crewe, in being seized upon by the 'anti-Tryanites' as the embodiment of their threatened traditional values, temporarily enjoys the immoderate and inaccurate praise heaped upon his instructional capabilities.

Crewe, Sir Francis, Bart ('the Dog')
The Dog Beneath the Skin, 1935
W H Auden and Christopher Isherwood

The missing baronet of Honeypot Hall, he has actually been living among his villagers for years, sewn into a dog skin. From here, he gets a 'dog's-eye-view' of their shallowness and hypocrisy, a perception that ultimately leads to his destruction.

Crewler, Sophy
David Copperfield, 1850
Charles Dickens

The fourth of ten daughters of a poor Devonshire curate. She is the amiable sweetheart and later wife of DAVID COPPERFIELD's school-friend, THOMAS TRADDLES, who considers her to be 'the dearest girl in the world'. Once married and living in Traddles's cramped legal chambers, the couple cheerfully receive her many sisters for prolonged visits.

Crich, Gerald
Women in Love, 1920
D H Lawrence

Crich has something of a 'dual consciousness'; whatever else he might be doing, 'his eye ran over the surfaces of the life round him, and he missed nothing'. Like his friend and antithesis, RUPERT BIRKIN, he searches for a new beginning, but as the powerful, disciplined son of colliery owners, he sees salvation not in spiritual renewal, as do Birkin and URSULA BRANGWEN, nor in fashion, as does GUDRUN BRANGWEN, but in mechanization, industrial and human efficiency. As both he and Gudrun deny nature, indeed have no instinctive, sensitive inner spirit to free, Lawrence suggests they are doomed. Significantly, Crich dies on a glacier, crushed by the nature he seeks to control.

Crichton
The Admirable Crichton, 1902
J M Barrie

The perfect servant, he is so unobtrusive as to be undescribable. Having achieved the ambition of his life by becoming a butler at 30, he is conservatively dismissive of his master Lord Loam's 'Radical' insistence on making his servants equals for one day each month. Shipwreck on a desert island briefly turns his head, not in the direction of Radicalism, but toward the aristocratic conviction that in some past life he may have had royal blood. Recognized as a natural leader – 'the Gov', even – by his former employers, and passionately and reciprocally admired by Lady Mary Lasenby, he reverts to type on their return to 'the Other Island', ie London society.

Crick, Tom
Waterland, 1983
Graham Swift

'The history teacher', childless Tom Crick is 'a senior man who none the less wanted to remain in the classroom', distrusted by his Head Teacher while enthralling his pupils with his own disjointed, equivocal fairy-tale history. A mixture of phlegm and superstition, the product of his miraculous fenland childhood and haunted by the death of his half-brother Dick, he explains, immediately questions, sows doubt and forces the reiterated question 'why why why'? Insisting that man is a story-telling animal seeking meaning and explanation, he tries to impart the sense that insatiable curiosity is vital to life.

Crimond
The Book and the Brotherhood, 1987
Iris Murdoch

A self-obsessed theorist and political philosopher of the far left, he is abstract, cold and calculating and guns are his only hobby. He acts as the conscience of a group of university intellectuals through their maturation, remaining rigidly principled whilst the others shift ground. They continue to support him, however, in his lifetime's work of writing a book, yet even as he writes his masterpiece on socialism Crimond tramples on his friends and supporters and eventually destroys the group.

Crimsworth, William
The Professor, 1857
Charlotte Brontë

The narrator of the novel, he is an orphan and is estranged – through his own pride – from his maternal relations who might have helped him make his way in the world. Having to make his own way, and finding life as a tradesman in his brother's employment wholly unsuitable to his nature, he embarks on a career as a schoolteacher in Brussels. William is a young man gifted with considerable self-possession and self-control, and conscious of his own moral and intellectual superiority to the point of arrogance. He is cautious and prudent in everything he does, having a practical turn of mind combined with firm, even rigid opinions.

Criseyde
Troilus and Criseyde, c.1385–9
Geoffrey Chaucer

Widowed and held by the Trojans, Criseyde is motivated by her concern for her honour and her social position. Isolated from her father, she is willing to listen to whoever is advising her at the time and always does what society wants her to do. She wants to be loved by everyone but ends up loved by no one. She is cautious when PANDARUS approaches her on TROILUS's behalf but eventually yields. When she is restored to her father she is easy prey for Diomede and is effectively lost from the moment she allows him to be her friend.

Crisp, Simon
Diary of a Somebody, 1978, et seq
Christopher Matthew

A young and eager marketing executive from a minor public school who, through his unintentionally comic, sententious diary, tells of his desperation to live the high life in London, and how he ends up looking after a friend's budgerigar in Mitcham. An accident-prone late 20th-century POOTER, in later books he graduates to a weekly column in the *Mitcham and Tooting Times* and a twice-weekly stint on the local hospital radio.

Crisparkle, the Revd Septimus
The Mystery of Edwin Drood, 1870
Charles Dickens

One of the minor canons of Cloisterham Cathedral, he is a sociable bachelor and muscular Christian. He lives with his adoring mother, Mrs Crisparkle – a pretty, cheerful old lady whom the narrator refers to as 'the China Shepherdess'. He becomes the tutor of NEVILLE LANDLESS and begins falling in love with Neville's sister, HELENA LANDLESS. Crisparkle upholds Neville's innocence when he is suspected of having murdered EDWIN DROOD.

Crispinus, Rufus Laberius
Poetaster, 1602
Ben Jonson

One of the two poetasters in the play (the other being DEMETRIUS), he is self-aggrandizing and foolish, writing bad, affected poetry and plagiarizing what he cannot create himself. A proud man, he is descended from the nobility but is now in debt. His comparative poverty only inflames his pomposity and his propensity for forcing his attentions upon good writers, such as HORACE. He is a caricature of the playwright John Marston.

Cristo
The Whole Armour, 1962, part of *The Guyana Quartet*, 1985
Wilson Harris

The son of MAGDA, bound to her by a mystical umbilical cord, 'a simultaneous cord of peril, as of something stolen yet implicitly newly severed'. He wears the flayed skin of a jaguar as a costume and carnival mask.

Crittenden, Lord and Lady
Lucinda Brayford, 1946
Martin Boyd

When LUCINDA BRAYFORD marries HUGO BRAYFORD, Arthur Crittenden, 12th Viscount, becomes her brother-in-law. With his wife Marian he lives quietly in the country, dedicated to a life of noblesse oblige. Marian 'conveyed the impression that English gentlepeople did not live [beneath] ... gorgeous ceilings ... for pleasure, but only from a stern sense of duty to the lower orders'. Throughout the vicissitudes of Lucinda's life, only Arthur and Marian remain stable; Crittenden Hall (until Arthur's death) is an apparently constant backdrop to her adulthood, a place where she meets 'unchanging kindness'.

Crocker-Harris, Andrew
The Browning Version, 1948
Terence Rattigan

Once a brilliant Greek scholar, Crocker-Harris has been reduced to teaching classics to the Lower Fifth at a public school. Because of a weak heart, he is about to leave to teach at a crammer in Dorset. He is an ageing, unpopular, dry academic, an over-fastidious timetable planner and a disciplinarian apparently without feelings. His unfaithful younger wife claims that

'You can't hurt Andrew. He's dead.' To the good-natured schoolboy, Taplow, he seems 'shrivelled up inside like a nut', but when he gives the master a copy of Browning's translation of *Agamemnon*, Crocker-Harris helplessly breaks down. He is, it seems, an enormously sensitive man, but one destined to be derided and abandoned.

Croft, Admiral
Persuasion, 1818
Jane Austen

A minor but colourful character in the novel, Admiral Croft is the hale and hearty navy man who rents Kellynch Hall from SIR WALTER ELLIOT. Exceedingly good-humoured and pleasantly eccentric, he shows a comic naivety in his understanding of others' affairs of the heart, and his down-to-earth joviality runs in direct contrast to the inflated pride of Sir Walter.

Croft, Francis
The Bird of the Night, 1972
Susan Hill

A mad poet, searching for a sense of purpose in a world that regards his art as a self-indulgent hobby. Overly sensitive, mercurial, erratic and often self-absorbed, Francis devastates the life of his friend, HARVEY LAWSON, through his paranoia, depression and eventual suicide. A finely-tuned, creative spirit, he needs a buffer between himself and the world, but once word of his madness is out, he can endure no more.

Croft, Mrs
Persuasion, 1818
Jane Austen

The wife of ADMIRAL CROFT, and sister of CAPTAIN WENTWORTH, Mrs Croft is almost as ruddy-faced and well-travelled as her husband. Solid and full of energy, she is very open and demonstrative, and does not hide her affection for those she loves. Self-assured without being proud or arrogant, she is a lively, spirited, and very likeable woman.

Croft, Sgt Sam
The Naked and the Dead, 1948
Norman Mailer

The brutal NCO who is the secret hero of the book and the shadow side to the failed liberal, LT ROBERT HEARN. 'A lean man of medium height but he held himself so erectly he appeared tall. His narrow triangular face was utterly without expression ... His gelid eyes were very blue ... and his main cast of mind was a superior contempt toward nearly all other men.' He is both misogynistic and violent.

Croftangry, Chrystal
Chronicles of the Canongate: First Series, 1827
Sir Walter Scott

The narrator of the *Chronicles*, he is a man grown mature in experience and mellow disillusion. He is, of course, a portrait of Scott himself in only partially ironic disguise; like his creator he regrets the fading away of a more expansive and romantic past.

Crofts, Dr James
The Small House at Allington, 1864
The Last Chronicle of Barset, 1867
Anthony Trollope

A slightly-built country doctor, whose bright eyes balance the sternness of his face. Shy and unassuming, he is also quietly humorous and trustworthy. Lack of money holds him back from proposing to his beloved BELL DALE. He and his wife appear briefly in *The Last Chronicle of Barset*.

Crofts, Sir George
Mrs Warren's Profession, 1894
George Bernard Shaw

A powerfully-built man of 50, the bullish but shrewd Crofts is a 'combination of the most brutal types of city man, sporting man, and man about town'. As MRS KITTY WARREN's business partner, he has invested £40,000 in her 'profession' which turns out to be the management of an exclusive brothel in Brussels. Even though he may actually be the father of VIVIE WARREN, Mrs Warren's daughter, Crofts proposes marriage to her. Unable to accept rejection gracefully, he angrily spells out Vivie's dependence on the profits of sexual exploitation and insinuates she may be the half-sister of FRANK GARDNER, his rival for her love.

Croker, Charlie
A Man in Full, 1998
Tom Wolfe

A former Georgian Tech football star known as the 'Sixty Minute Man', Croker has transferred his wizardry on the pitch to the world of business. Acquisitive and vain, he has amassed a vast real-estate empire, a quail-shooting plantation and a young but demanding second wife. At 60, he is satisfied that he has retained 'the rude animal vitality of his youth'. Yet a new property development loses money and, faced with spectacular debts, Croker is shunned and belittled by many who had previously feted him, including the executives at PlannersBanc. Desperately laying off workers, including CONRAD HENSLEY, in an effort to staunch his losses, he is drawn into the political wheeler-dealing surrounding the lawyer, ROGER WHITE II.

Crombie, Dougal
Huntingtower, 1922
John Buchan

One of the 'Gorbals Diehards', the tough and unlettered youngsters (inspired by boys in a Sunday School class of Buchan's) who provide the craft and muscle in DICKSON MCCUNN's rather stiff-limbed struggle against evil. In fictional terms, he is a descendant of Conan Doyle's 'Baker Street Irregulars'.

Cromwell, Oliver
Woodstock, or The Cavalier, 1826
Sir Walter Scott

Following the received view of Cromwell's appearance to the letter, Scott presents the Lord Protector as a man of blunt and graceless capability, whose oratory is marred by a Puritan tendency to split hairs: 'though one of the most shrewd men in England, he was, perhaps, the most unintelligible speaker that ever perplexed an audience'.

Cromwell, Tacey
Tacey Cromwell, 1942
Conrad Richter

A prostitute on the Arizona frontier, she represents an unusually subtle and humane comment on the way women 'civilize' men in those places where normal social and cultural constraints do not apply.

Crosbie, Adolphus
The Small House at Allington, 1864
The Last Chronicle of Barset, 1867
Anthony Trollope

A tall, good-looking, articulate 'swell', whose income from his civil service post is sufficient to maintain his shining social position, so long as he remains a bachelor. He jilts his fiancée LILY DALE on finding that her uncle will not supply a dowry. Instead he marries LADY ALEXANDRINA DE COURCY, thinking that her connections will benefit his career. Selfish and with an inflated opinion of himself, he knowingly chooses the worse alternative, and immediately has many reasons to regret it.

Crossjay
The Egoist, 1879
George Meredith

The son of a poor relation of SIR WILLOUGHBY PATTERNE and a sub-lieutenant of marines, he lives as a dependent at Patterne, where he is tutored by VERNON WHITFORD. He is, though, by no means cowed and grateful for his position, and is instrumental in his kinsman's third great humiliation.

Crouchback, Guy
Sword of Honour, 1965
Evelyn Waugh

Divorced by his wife VIRGINIA TROY, Guy is left lonely and disillusioned, and, hoping to give his life dignity and purpose, enlists in 1939. But his companions in the Halberdiers think him an absurd old buffer, the drills are hard and pointless, his officer training bewildering, bleak and muddled. There is no place for courage, no sense of a just cause, merely 'general flaps', culminating for him in the withdrawal from Crete. His subsequent private life is equally confused, although acquaintances remark that he has come rather well out of the war – the final irony.

Crow, Jerry
How Many Miles to Babylon?, 1974
Jennifer Johnston

Tough and wiry, a working-class lad, he teaches ALEX MOORE to fight, and Alex teaches him how to ride. Jerry becomes the 'best horseman' and he and Alex dream of breeding and training horses. World War I interferes, however, and he joins up to be close to his friend, and, unbeknown to Alex, to learn tactics for the Republican cause. Jerry is knowing and driven by emotion, and represents something exciting and forbidden for Alex. He, in turn, is dependent on Alex. His tender-heartedness is their eventual undoing.

Crow, John
A Glastonbury Romance, 1932
John Cowper Powys

He is 'a frail, thin, loosely-built man of thirty-five' who was 'a penniless orphan at twenty', and has led an irregular and even squalid life in Paris. He returns to England in the hope that his formidable capitalist cousin Philip will give him 'a berth at Glastonbury', and becomes involved in Philip's plans to exploit the Grail legend. His life is engaged in 'making the whole Glastonbury legend into a mockery and a popular farce', and he remains sceptical about 'the dogmas of pseudo-scientific materialism' attached to the legend, even though he has a 'supernatural visitation' when he sees King Arthur's sword. He feels himself to be 'a hard, round stone defying the whole universe'.

Crow, Jonathan
For Love Alone, 1944
Christina Stead

He coached TESSA HAWKINS at the Tutorial College and later became her lover. On their first encounter, 'he had a gentle, plain manner when teaching, a thin face and dark eyes, and seemed to be about twenty-eight', but he gradually assumes an almost Mephistophelean character.

Crowe, Captain Samuel
The Life and Adventures of Sir Launcelot Greaves, 1760–1
Tobias Smollett

The Captain had commanded a merchantman on the Mediterranean run for many years, which explains his addiction to extended nautical metaphor and a manner of speaking that suggests he is standing in a high wind. He was considered to be a good, cautious skipper, 'brave, active, friendly in his way, and scrupulously honest; but as little acquainted with the world as a sucking child'. In Smollett's apparent attempt to modernize *Don Quixote*, he represents the more ridiculous side of SIR LAUNCELOT GREAVES's knight-errantry.

Crown, Alistair
A Solitary Grief, 1991
Bernice Rubens

As 'a psychiatrist who knew everything about everything', he is a punctilious, confident man professionally transforming chaos into order and darkness into clarity. Alistair has become the father of a baby girl, and although he wanted a boy, he gallantly takes flowers to his wife in hospital, albeit roses stolen from a nearby cemetery. But baby Doris has Down's Syndrome and threatens to become a 'lifelong albatross' to the appalled, outraged Alistair. Doris makes him feel vulnerable and guilty. Although he deals professionally with both emotions almost daily, he is unable to confront them in himself and becomes caught in a vortex of evasion and loathing.

Crowther, Ashley
Fly Away Peter, 1982
David Malouf

JIM SADDLER's employer and friend, he is as intellectually and culturally sophisticated as Jim is heaven-taught and naive. A graduate of Cambridge, he completes his education in Imperial Germany, but is no more prepared than Jim for the man-made horrors of the trenches.

Crowthorne, Dennis and Vera
Just Between Ourselves, 1976
Alan Ayckbourn

In this biting tragi-comedy, Dennis and Vera are visited by NEIL and PAM ANDREWS, interested in the old car which Dennis, a frenzied do-it-yourself fanatic, has for sale. It does not start. Dennis's response to this, as to everything else, especially his wife Vera, who is visibly suffering a breakdown, is a hearty, rallying laugh. Having once believed himself sensitive and thoughtful, Dennis has discovered he is deficient in both qualities. His relentless cheeriness and obsessive tinkering in the garage is partly a mask. Vera, who previously worked at Safeway's, but now cares for her poisonous mother-in-law as well as coping with Dennis, slides tragically from embarrassing, crockery-smashing nervousness into catatonia.

Croy, Kate
The Wings of the Dove, 1902
Henry James

The daughter of a once handsome adventurer in London society, a man now fading in charm and down on his luck, 'Kate had ... the extraordinary and attaching property of appearing at a given moment to show as a beautiful stranger, to cut her connexions and lose her identity, letting the imagination for the time make what it would of them – make her merely a person striking from afar, more and more pleasing as one watched, but who was above all a subject for curiosity.' What distinguishes her from MILLIE THEALE is her absolute firmness, even ruthlessness, of purpose in her desire to separate herself from an unpromising destiny.

Cruella de Vil
The Hundred and One Dalmatians, 1956
Dodie Smith

A tall, thin nightmare of a woman, her black eyes flash with red, her hair hangs down half black, half white from a razor-sharp parting. Expelled from school for drinking ink, she now favours tight-fitting dresses topped with fur. She feels the cold so much that she has to sleep on ermine sheets, and she eats so much pepper that she even tastes hot. Devilishly cruel, she drowns all 44 of her cat's kittens because they are not white. Her ambition is to have a black-and-white Dalmatian-fur coat to go with her black-and-white hair and her black-and-white car, which has the loudest horn in England.

Crummles, Mr and Mrs Vincent
Nicholas Nickleby, 1839
Charles Dickens

They run a touring theatrical company, with Crummles as the manager and his wife, a plump former actress, playing heavy dramatic roles or skipping rope and dancing the hornpipe between acts. Their daughter, Ninetta, called 'the Infant Phenomenon', has been ten years old for the last five years, and their two sons have also acted since childhood. The company's leading lady is MISS SNEVELLICCI. Crummles hires NICHOLAS NICKLEBY and SMIKE for a brief period before he and his family emigrate to America.

Cruncher, Jerry (Jeremiah)
A Tale of Two Cities, 1859
Charles Dickens

An odd-job-man and messenger at Tellson's Bank by day and, by night, a secret resurrection man. His macabre fascination with death is deplored by his pious wife, whom he bullies and calls the 'Aggerawayter'. His son, Young Jerry, is at first unaware of his nightly occupation but later becomes his father's assistant. Visiting Revolutionary Paris on business for the bank, he is struck by the uncertainty of human life amid the violence, and he resolves to give up his night job. After the rescue of Charles Darnay, he helps him and the MANETTES, and later MISS PROSS, escape from Paris.

Crusoe, Robinson
Robinson Crusoe, 1719
The Farther Adventures of Robinson Crusoe, 1720
The Serious Reflections … of Robinson Crusoe, 1720
Daniel Defoe

Impetuous and stubborn, his angry split with his parents leads him to a troubled life at sea and ultimately to shipwreck on a desert island where his resourcefulness and religious faith are stretched to the limit. Epitomizing all the virtues of the doughty Englishman, he demonstrates ingenuity and courage in overcoming the haunting loneliness of his island and in making a little England of the unprepossessing circumstances of his enforced exile. Throughout the struggle he develops a maturity and a deepened religious awareness unexpected in one of his previously testy temperament.

Cthulhu
'The Call of Cthulhu', and elsewhere
H P Lovecraft, edited by August Derleth, 1945

Worshipped by the OLD ONES, Cthulhu is a vast, amorphous life-form which embodies both the primeval origins of life and its entropic, undifferentiated end. Insofar as it has substance, Cthulhu resembles a jellyfish or giant amoeba.

Cuchulain
'Cuchulain's Fight with the Sea', in *The Rose*, 1893
The Death of Cuchulain, 1939, and others, 1939
W B Yeats

The mythological King of Muirthemne, taken by Yeats from an Irish epic, the *Táin Bó Cuálnge*, to be the central figure of poems and a sequence of plays. An idealized heroic warrior, the proud, wild Cuchulain (pronounced 'Cuhoolin') boasts of his luck, but he fails to drink at the well of eternal life and his amorous adventures (in which he neglects his wife, Emer) lead to tragedy. Described by Yeats as 'creative joy separated from fear', Cuchulain loses his individuality after death, although 'The Statues' and *The Death of Cuchulain* refer to his statue in the Dublin General Post Office, whither Patrick Pearse summoned his spirit during the 1916 Rebellion.

Cuff, Sgt Richard
The Moonstone, 1868
Wilkie Collins

A 'miserably lean' man with razor-sharp features, steely grey eyes, a melancholy voice and claw-like fingers, Richard Cuff is a shrewd and discreet detective with 20 years' experience of investigating family scandals. A figure of almost Holmesian renown who hums 'The Last Rose Of Summer' during his moments of deepest contemplation, even he is unable satisfactorily to resolve the disappearance of the Moonstone diamond. Subsequently in retirement, he enthusiastically embraces the life of a Dorking country gentleman and attends to his lifelong passion of growing roses.

Cullen, Sir Patrick
The Doctor's Dilemma, 1906
George Bernard Shaw

A veteran Irish doctor, Sir Patrick is modelled upon Sir Robert Christison, the Scottish toxicologist who became physician to Queen Victoria. The sceptical voice among the other doctors in the play, he is in his seventies and 'not quite at the end of his tether, but near it and resigned to it'. His attitude towards SIR COLENSO RIDGEON is almost fatherly, but towards others he can be gruff and uninviting, having neither the energy nor the inclination to make much of an effort socially. It is Sir Patrick who discusses with Ridgeon the dilemma of whether the latter should treat DR BLENKINSOP or LOUIS DUBEDAT, and implies that Dubedat might be treated by SIR RALPH BLOOMFIELD BONINGTON.

Cummings, Gen Edward
The Naked and the Dead, 1948
Norman Mailer

A chess player, inspired for life by the gigantic game-board of the Western Front in World War I. In the Pacific War, he treats men as if they were passive counters, to be manipulated abstractly. A latent homosexual, who receives profound sexual excitement from the loading and firing of an artillery shell, he contrives a double degradation of the weakly liberal and untouchable LT ROBERT HEARN.

Cunningham, Nurse
The Ante-Room, 1934
Kate O'Brien

TERESA MULQUEEN's pretty day-nurse. The daughter of a hard-drinking doctor, she was left friendless and penniless at 17 but by determined and gallant effort has become one of the best nurses in Ireland. However, her careful flirtations with doctors have led nowhere and, in 1880, as a woman alone at the age of 30 the future looms bleak and threatening. Realizing that REGGIE MULQUEEN will inherit all his family's wealth, reflecting that he is 'manageable', and also pitying him, Nurse Cunningham weighs her natural feelings and sensuality against the security she desperately desires.

Cunningham, Pearl
Summer of the Seventeenth Doll, 1955
Ray Lawler

'A biggish woman, well corseted, with dyed hair',

her priority is to attain a respectability which her status in society as a widowed working-class barmaid will always prevent. She desires a form of security from her relationship with BARNEY IBBOT which he can neither provide nor understand. Her attempt at 'a fling at the gay life', symbolized by her donning of red dresses in the second act, makes her, in Barney's eyes, a pale imitation of NANCY, his absent former lover. She finally departs, moralistically condemning the goings-on at OLIVE's home, and hoping to bring up her teenage daughter in better circumstances than those which she has experienced.

Curdie
The Princess and the Goblin, 1871
The Princess and Curdie, 1882
George MacDonald

The son of a miner, he works alongside him in the king's mines, digging for silver ore and composing aggravating verses to chase away goblins who infest the mountain roots. At first a seeming paragon of Christian virtue, he is a good-looking young man, strong, respectful and brave, whose head is not turned by the prospect of wealth or personal status. With time, however, he appears to be growing more coarse and ordinary, until the intervention of his beloved PRINCESS IRENE's great-great-grandmother, who not only makes him ashamed of his behaviour but shows him the danger the kingdom lies in, and bestows on him magical gifts to help him rescue both king and daughter.

Curran, Doctor (William)
The Ante-Room, 1934
Kate O'Brien

Returning from Europe to take over the provincial practice of his muddle-headed, well-liked father, Curran is confidently dynamic, brilliant, and unpopular. Most patients find him unsympathetic, though not TERESA MULQUEEN, whose courage touches him. Conventional and rather puritanical, his life meticulously mapped out, he intends to marry, but only in order to acquire a housekeeper and children. He will not choose a beautiful woman, as beauty is 'a troublesome thing'. However, all his plans go suddenly awry when the lovely but unattainable AGNES MULQUEEN becomes the 'mighty hunger' of his life, bringing out the best in him.

Curryfin, Lord Richard
Gryll Grange, 1860–1
Thomas Love Peacock

Despite his ridiculous position as 'a lecturing lord', who speaks on fish to fishermen and follows every fashionable philosophical treatise with his grasshopper mind, the young, handsome Lord Curryfin is nonetheless amiable and willing to please. Because of his fondness for scientific experiments, he is very accident-prone. Frequently embroiled in tangles, he cuts a slightly ludicrous but very likeable figure.

Curtis, Olivia
Invitation to the Waltz, 1932
The Weather in the Streets, 1936
Rosamond Lehmann

Invitation to the Waltz introduces us to Olivia as a gauche adolescent. A girl of delicate and refined sensibilities, she feels excluded from male values: 'Men are much, much queerer than I imagined.' In *The Weather in the Streets* her life is full of alarm and confusion. Reeling from a torrid affair and an abortion, her romantic beliefs splinter under the pressures of a social system that does not shield vulnerable women from the realities of illicit love.

Cusins, Adolphus
Major Barbara, 1905
George Bernard Shaw

An impoverished professor of Greek, Cusins is based upon the academic, Gilbert Murray. Seemingly mild, he is in reality determined, tenacious, even intolerant. His plight is that of the liberal scholar and political idealist confronted by the barbarism of the modern world. Determined to marry the energetic Salvationist, BARBARA UNDERSHAFT, he wins her and succeeds ANDREW UNDERSHAFT, her father, as head of his armaments factory. But his conversion does not wholly mean the defeat of idealism by the material power of the industrialist. It is an attempt by the former to absorb the latter with the hope of transforming it into a benevolent force.

Custance, Christian
Ralph Roister Doister, 1552/3
Nicholas Udall

A virtuous and rich widow, who is constant to her betrothed, Gawyn Goodlucke, and inclined to scold her servants. Angered by the advances of RALPH ROISTER DOISTER, whom she considers a 'dolt and lout', she eventually joins in MATHEWE MERYGREEKE's scheme to show him up.

Cutbeard
Epicoene, or The Silent Woman, 1609
Ben Jonson

A barber, Cutbeard is acting under orders to find a wife for MOROSE, and entices him to marry EPICOENE. Later, when Morose considers divorce, Cutbeard disguises himself as a doctor and, in a welter of halting Latin, describes the conditions necessary for the marriage to be annulled. He finally pronounces that there are no grounds for divorce at all.

Cute, Alderman
The Chimes, 1844
Charles Dickens

A pompous, sly, self-satisfied magistrate in the City of London who campaigns to 'put down' any 'nonsense' on the part of the poor, including want, starvation, sickness, young mothers and children and, above all, suicide. His hypocritical attitudes are exposed when his friend DEEDLES shoots himself. He is a crony of SIR JOSEPH BOWLEY.

Cuticle, Dr Cadwallader
White-Jacket, 1850
Herman Melville

The surgeon of the fleet on the *Neversink*. He is about 60, and a 'scrawny, bewigged, fake-toothed, glass-eyed butcher' with a love of morbid anatomy and deformities, which makes him the butt of practical jokers. His 'corporeal vitality' seems 'in a good degree to have dried out of him', but his mind appears 'undebilitated as in youth; it shone out of his remaining eye with basilisk brilliancy'. His 'apparent heartlessness' is really professional enthusiasm.

Cuttle, Captain Edward (Ned)
Dombey and Son, 1848
Charles Dickens

A retired seaman, he is a friend of WALTER GAY and his uncle, SOLOMON GILLS, whose partner in *The Wooden Midshipman* he becomes. With 'a hook instead of a hand attached to his right wrist', a large shirt collar which 'looked like a small sail', and a hard glazed hat, he is childlike and unworldly and has a stock of quaint sayings. When FLORENCE DOMBEY flees from home, he protects her until Walter Gay returns and marries her.

Cutty Sark, or Nannie
'Tam O'Shanter', 1793
Robert Burns

Nicknamed 'Cutty Sark' because of her short shift, Nannie is a comely young witch noted for much mischief in Ayrshire. Among the old hags prancing in their underskirts at a satanic revel, Nannie proudly displays a childhood slip which affords scant covering for her fetching womanly frame.

Cymbeline
Cymbeline, 1609/10
William Shakespeare

The King of Britain and strangely marginalized in the play, Cymbeline is himself 'govern'd' by his QUEEN. Taken in by his wife's beauty and flattery,

he is dominated and misguided by her. An ineffectual monarch and an unjust and unwise father, he alienates those closest to him.

Cymochles
The Faerie Queene, 1590–6
Sir Edmund Spenser

The brother of PYROCHLES, the son of a discordant god; together they represent a danger to Christianity. Cymochles is a dissolute character who is unable to remain constant. He continually fluctuates between violent and furious wrath and depraved indulgence in lascivious passions. He is without control and is prone to forget his quest to snatch one moment of sensual delight.

Cymodoce, also known as Cymoent
The Faerie Queene, 1590–6
Sir Edmund Spenser

A Nereid or sea-nymph, she is MARINELL's mother and the daughter of the sea-god Nereus. She loves her son immensely and is overtly over-protective, continually watching over him, and warning him each day never to have any doings with women, after a prophesy that 'a virgin strange and stout' may kill him.

Cypress, Mr
Nightmare Abbey, 1818
Thomas Love Peacock

Poet and purveyor of 'a lacerated spirit', Mr Cypress (a caricature of Byron and a satire on Byron's 'black bile') is a depressive who 'has no hope for myself or others'. His posture of despair – decay, degeneration and ruin are his themes – is mitigated by wine and by his imminent emigration to the Mediterranean.

Dabrowski, Anastasia, or Stacey Stevens
Her Mother's Daughter, 1987
Marilyn French

A sloppy, unfeminine woman whose forced cheerfulness masks the depression and anger that threaten to disrupt her seemingly calm existence. In her reluctance to become a woman and her inability to remain a girl, Anastasia fosters the masculine side of her personality. Revelling in her sexual encounters, she dismisses the day-to-day as inconsequential. As Stacèy Stevens, the famous photographer, she hides behind a camera lens in order to avoid focusing on herself, blind to the consequences of her actions.

Daggoo
Moby-Dick, 1851
Herman Melville

FLASK's harpooner. He is a 'gigantic, coal-black negro-savage, with a lion-like tread', and wears two golden hoops in his ears. He shipped on a whaler from Africa, and knows only 'the bold life of the fishery'. He has retained 'all his barbaric virtues', and moves around the ship 'in all the pomp of six feet five in his socks'.

Dahlia, Aunt
Carry On, Jeeves, 1925, et seq
P G Wodehouse

Large, exuberant, once a terror on the hunting field, Mrs Tom Travers, Brinkley Court, Worcestershire, is BERTIE WOOSTER's Aunt Dahlia. Always seeking finance for her magazine 'Milady's Boudoir' and losing money at baccarat, she works hard to keep her husband's dyspepsia at bay, even making Bertie help her steal silver cow-creamers for him from rival collectors. Aware of Bertie's limited intelligence and deploring it, she often leaps to his defence; she remains his 'good and deserving aunt', regarding him with mingled exasperation and fondness.

Dai Bread
Under Milk Wood, 1954
Dylan Thomas

The Donkey Street baker. Despite, or perhaps because of, having two wives, he is always in a rush; he sometimes forgets the bread for his own home. A small, hairy man with big pink lips and a wall eye, he looks an unlikely candidate for bigamy. Nevertheless, his feather bed has three pillows and his daytime and night-time wives, MRS DAI BREAD ONE and MRS DAI BREAD TWO,

seem to complement each other very satisfactorily.

Dai Bread One, Mrs
Under Milk Wood, 1954
Dylan Thomas

One of DAI BREAD the baker's wives, she is homely, immensely fat and corsetless – 'nice to be comfy, nice to be nice'. This easy-going attitude exemplifies her good nature: she likes to sit down to gossip and sees no irony in having to borrow bread when her husband forgets theirs. She wears a cap, clogs and a shawl and is the daytime wife. Both wives spend much of their time together and she is as enchanted as her husband with the other's glamour.

Dai Bread Two, Mrs
Under Milk Wood, 1954
Dylan Thomas

The 'other' wife of DAI BREAD the baker, she is really a brown-skinned, dark-haired gypsy in disguise. She wears scarlet and yellow petticoats and 'only a dab of scent else'; one heel of her shoe is missing and her dirty pretty knees are always showing. The night-time wife, she smokes a pipe to enhance the exotic image and tells fortunes in the tea leaves and a crystal ball, teasing her rival MRS DAI BREAD ONE.

Daisy
Good Wives, 1869
Little Men, 1871
Jo's Boys, 1886
Louisa M Alcott

MEG MARCH's twin daughter is good-natured, a 'round chubby sunshiny soul' as a child and as a little woman, sweet and domestic, like her mother and grandmother. Enamoured of NAT BLAKE's musical ability, she is devoted to him.

Daisy
The Painter of Signs, 1976
R K Narayan

Rejecting the traditional role of an Indian woman, at 13 Daisy ran away from her large, suffocating rural family, and was educated in Madras by a missionary organization, then trained in family planning and birth control. Opening a free advice centre in Malgudi, with evangelical zeal she spreads her new-age women's gospel throughout the surrounding area. Despite her discouraging, calculated coldness, she is pursued by the bedazzled RAMAN and succumbs. However, as Raman painfully discovers, she is 'a tight-lipped monomaniac', largely indifferent to everything but her work, who is prepared to sacrifice all to her crusade.

Daisy, Solomon
Barnaby Rudge, 1841
Charles Dickens

The parish clerk and bell-ringer in Chigwell, and one of JOHN WILLET's cronies at the Maypole Inn. As the only man to hear the alarm bell rung by Reuben Haredale on the night he is murdered by MR RUDGE, he gains self-importance from telling the story.

Dalcastle, Lady of
The Private Memoirs and Confessions of a Justified Sinner, 1824
James Hogg

The young wife of the hearty LAIRD OF DALCASTLE, she is a grim, unsmiling religious zealot who takes as her mentor the fervent predestinarian minister, ROBERT WRINGHIM. A joyless, grasping woman, she cannot bear to see others enjoying themselves, and shuts herself off from society, interesting herself only in pedantic debates about points of Calvinism and in the religious education of her second son.

Dalcastle, Laird of
The Private Memoirs and Confessions of a Justified Sinner, 1824
James Hogg

A minor but important character, the ageing Laird's carefree, fun-loving disposition receives a severe blow when he marries the pious young daughter of Baillie Orde. Largely a humorous figure, the Laird is nonetheless significant in his outspoken irreverence for the Reformed Church, and most notably in his refusal to acknowledge fatherhood of his estranged wife's second son, while he takes responsibility for and dotes wholeheartedly on the first child GEORGE COLWAN, whom he accepts as his own.

Dale, Bell (Isabella)
The Small House at Allington, 1864
The Last Chronicle of Barset, 1867
Anthony Trollope

Elder sister of LILY DALE, she is very fair, pretty and slender. She has an independent mind and is neither concerned about superficialities nor impressed by social status. Her uncle wants her to marry her cousin Bernard, but she loves DR JAMES CROFTS. She and her husband briefly appear in *The Last Chronicle of Barset*.

Dale, Laetitia
The Egoist, 1879
George Meredith

Though not quite 'on the shelf', she is certainly past the first bloom of beauty. Intelligent and perceptive, she is prepared to overlook SIR WILLOUGHBY PATTERNE's selfish egoism and marry him, even though he is involved with another woman. Unprepared, though, to marry him at *any* price, she eventually makes terms of her own choosing when he comes back to her after his various rebuffs.

Dale, Lily (Lilian)
The Small House at Allington, 1864
The Last Chronicle of Barset, 1867
Anthony Trollope

Lily is pretty, playful and vivacious. She loves ADOLPHUS CROSBIE, but is jilted by him. Courageously bearing her crushing disappointment, she then carries forgiveness to mawkish extremes. She rejects her faithful suitor JOHN EAMES on the grounds that, loving Crosbie, she can never love another. When Crosbie becomes a widower, she will not marry him, believing that he would despise her. She proclaims herself an 'Old Maid'.

Dalgarno, Lord
The Fortunes of Nigel, 1822
Sir Walter Scott

A buckish young nobleman aged about 25, whose ancestral home is only a few miles from NIGEL OLIFAUNT's, he is free and easy in manner, 'unencumbered either by pride or ceremony'. He does, though, have a streak of dishonourable profligacy which throws him into conflict with Nigel.

Dalgetty, Captain Dugald, of Drumthwacket
A Legend of Montrose, in *Tales of My Landlord: Third Series*, 1819
Sir Walter Scott

A loquacious soldier of fortune, who has seen service under virtually every prince and power of Europe, before throwing in his lot with the EARL OF MONTROSE. He takes particular pride in having been educated at the Mareschal College, Aberdeen, and having fought under the Lion of the North, Gustavus Adolphus, after whom his war-horse is named. Unembarrassed by principle, he makes a loyal friend once the terms of service have been clearly drawn up.

Dalgliesh, Adam
Cover her Face, 1962, et seq
P D James

Adam Dalgliesh first appears as a Detective Inspector at New Scotland Yard in 1962 in *Cover her Face*, but by 1986 and *A Taste for Death*, he has become Commander of a new squad investigating cases which, perhaps for political reasons, require a special sensitivity. He is a widower (his wife and baby having died during childbirth), and a poet with a quietly flourishing reputation. A wise man and a methodical, patient detective, Dalgliesh solves mysteries by a combination of imagination, sympathetic understanding, and a detachment which at times might border upon the callous. Occasionally, idly, he thinks of remarrying, but essentially he is self-sufficient and private.

Dalila
Samson Agonistes, 1671
John Milton

A beautiful young women of Sorek, the Biblical Delilah of Judges 16, she is made SAMSON's wife, not mistress, by the Puritan Milton. She is, though, not a whit less treacherous, cutting off his strength-giving hair and betraying him to the Philistines.

Dallas, Lloyd
Noises Off, 1982
Michael Frayn

The harassed director of *Nothing On*, a second-rate sex comedy, Dallas attempts to impose order upon a spiral of chaos; Frayn's play being a farce about the production of a farce. Patronizing, cajoling, angry and desperate, Dallas becomes ever more exasperated by the petty jealousies, rows and love affairs between his increasingly disruptive actors, including the tipsy Selsdon, the frantic Lejeune, deluded star Dotty and the forlorn Frederick. 'Getting on, getting off', cries Dallas. 'That's farce. That's theatre. That's life.'

Dalloway, Clarissa
The Voyage Out, 1915
Mrs Dalloway, 1925
Virginia Woolf

A fragile, gracious and fashionable lady, she examines life in depth. Although she claims to like the idea of equality, she is enveloped in a very conventional relationship with her husband. Garrulous, emotional, impulsive and in certain ways very astute, although she suffers inwardly she glitters to the outside world.

Dalloway, Richard
The Voyage Out, 1915
Mrs Dalloway, 1925
Virginia Woolf

A traditionally masculine man, Richard is interested in politics, warfare and women. He has little time for refined, cultural pursuits, though he seeks these things in a half-hearted way. His high opinion of himself and his wife's unstinting and puppyish devotion combine to make him a rather pompous figure. However, he does have some endearing qualities, such as his interest in justice and his concern about the disadvantaged in society.

Daly, 'Joxer'
Juno and the Paycock, 1924
Sean O'Casey

Indolent, deceitful, cunning, mercenary and hypocritical, he is the Dublin drinking pal of the unemployed 'CAPTAIN' JACK BOYLE. Aged about 60, he wears a perpetual ingratiating grin and has 'a face like crinkled paper'. As far as Republican politics are concerned, his view is that: 'It's better to be a coward than a corpse'. His usual response to the world is a nervous shrug of the shoulders. Most people treat him with contempt, yet he derives protection from the swaggering Boyle and, in return, flatters him outrageously to retain his patronage, praising his absurd stories and his drunken singing: 'Ah, that's a darlin' song, a daaarlin' song!'

Dalziel, Andy
A Clubbable Woman, 1970, et seq
Reginald Hill

Detective Superintendent Andy Dalziel is an overweight, uncouth, unreconstructed Yorkshireman with a tendency to scratch himself in public and a fondness for single malt whiskies. He always speaks his mind, often rather bigotedly and crudely, but is nevertheless a warm-hearted man who has the respect of his colleagues, notably his long-suffering, more liberal-minded partner Detective Sergeant (and later Detective Inspector) Peter Pascoe.

D'Ambois, Bussy
Bussy D'Ambois, 1604
The Revenge of Bussy D'Ambois, c.1610
George Chapman

Bussy D'Ambois is based upon the historical figure of Louis de Clermont Bussy, D'Amboise, a courtier of the French king Henri III and one-time governor of Anjou. Chapman's creation takes several fictional departures; for example, he is not a rich man. He is one of great courage but also considerable conceit, both noble and impetuous, a bit of a philosopher and a man of the world. Fiery, adventurous and amorous, he sees himself as an almost Herculean idealist. Killing off his hero did not prevent Chapman from writing a sequel. In *The Revenge of Bussy D'Ambois*, he reappears as a ghost, urging his brother, CLERMONT D'AMBOIS, to avenge his murder.

D'Ambois, Clermont
The Revenge of Bussy D'Ambois, c.1610
George Chapman

The scholarly brother of BUSSY D'AMBOIS. Instructed by the ghost of his brother to avenge his murder by the cuckolded Montsurry, he agrees to do so, but (unlike most revenge tragedies) only by the means of a formal duel. He is a fastidious, even pedantic man, and one much given to dispensing little homilies on the nature and joy of knowledge. Although he duly kills Montsurry, the social corruption surrounding him causes Clermont to become so despondent that he kills himself.

Dametas
The Countess of Pembroke's Arcadia, 1581–4, published 1590
Sir Philip Sidney

An uncouth herdsman who is made guardian of DUKE BASILIUS's daughter PAMELA; 'the most arrant, doltish clown that I think ever was … his behaviour such that he is beyond the degree of ridiculous'. Far from blessed in natural gifts, he has been unlucky, too, in his wife and daughter, MISO and MOPSA.

Damien
'The Merchant's Tale', in *The Canterbury Tales*, c.1387–1400
Geoffrey Chaucer

A courtly lover and adulterer, humble to his master JANUARY, courteous and apparently devoted to his lover MAY, but in the last resort treacherous. His rough lovemaking reveals that his own pleasure comes first.

D'Amville
The Atheist's Tragedy, c.1611
Cyril Tourneur

The brother of Montferrers, a baron, and the self-confessed atheist of the title, D'Amville is the orchestrator of his own tragedy. He rejects the Christian concept of God and the afterlife, seeing death as the final end and Nature as the ultimate power. It is these beliefs that motivate his actions, which are aimed at increasing his wealth, both for his own pleasure and to pass on to his two sons. Operating on an intellectual rather than an emotional level, he is proud of his faculties of reasoning. He dissembles to the other characters, but before the audience and Borachio, his servant, he reveals himself to be a single-minded and ruthless manipulator.

Dan
Little Men, 1871
Jo's Boys, 1886
Louisa M Alcott

At first glance this wild boy is a bad lot. Fighting, drinking, smoking and gambling, he literally sets alight Plumfield, the model school where he lives. Repeatedly forgiven and given chances by JO MARCH and DR BHAER, he gradually learns the lessons of rewards and, more importantly, personal satisfaction. He later wanders the world, following his natural bent for pursuing life rather than cultivating it.

Dan
Puck of Pook's Hill, 1906
Rudyard Kipling

A little boy growing up in rural Sussex, introduced to the magical progress of English history by PUCK. He is in every way an ordinary little boy, as his sister UNA is an ordinary girl; he struggles with Latin, is blessed with an uncertain temper, and, above all, has secrets.

Danger
Ane Pleasant Satyre of the Thrie Estaitis, 1540
Sir David Lindsay

As well as being one of DAME SENSUALITIE's ladies, Danger's name hints at her representation of the arrogant aloofness of women, common in the realm of 'courtly love'. Coarse and crude, her main role is in assisting the spread of 'sensuality' throughout the court, which she achieves through the simultaneous seduction of PLACEBO and SOLACE.

Dangerfield, Sebastian
The Ginger Man, 1955
J P Donleavy

Larger-than-life, with a rollicking approach to drink, women and good times, he comes to Ireland from America ostensibly to be a student, but in practice to have fun. He shows a refreshing passion for living, but his energy explodes amid the propriety and repression of postwar Ireland and Britain like a grenade.

Dangle
The Critic, 1779
Richard Brinsley Sheridan

To the disapproval of his wife, Dangle has become mixed up in the theatrical world, promoting plays and leading a pack of critics (although his opinions are not taken seriously by the most prominent theatre managers and playwrights). He is interested only in 'theatrical politics', not in the dangers facing the nation.

Daniels, Steve
A Lesson from Aloes, 1980
Athol Fugard

Defined as 'Coloured' by the apartheid regulations, Steve Daniels visits his old Afrikaner friend PIET BEZUIDENHOUT before leaving South Africa as a political exile. He suspects, however, that Piet betrayed him to the authorities when they were both political activists. Piet's highly disturbed wife, GLADYS BEZUIDENHOUT, encourages him in this suspicion. As a result, his relationship with the couple is full of dramatic tensions, awkward moments and disturbing revelations.

Danny
Tortilla Flat, 1935
John Steinbeck

Danny is the leading light of the Monterey paisanos, a King Arthur to their Round Table. A mule-skinner by trade, he inherits his grandfather's house up in Tortilla Flat on his return from World War I. 'He was related to nearly everyone in the Flat by blood or romance … Danny was small and dark and intent. At twenty-five his legs were bent to the exact curves of a horse's sides.'

'Dante'
Johnno, 1975
David Malouf

The narrator, and friend of JOHNNO, whom he observes with a certain ironic reserve. It is never clear to what extent he is drawn to Johnno's reckless self-reliance – some critics have linked it to the fashionable existentialism of the postwar setting – and how much he is fussily repelled by it. Equally, it is not clear how much weight to put on the literary resonance of his name.

Danvers, Mrs
Rebecca, 1938
Daphne Du Maurier

The housekeeper at Manderley. She is a sinister, cold, lifeless woman, showing emotion only over the deceased REBECCA DE WINTER, of whom she was passionately fond. She respects those who take control, and is irritated by the subservience of the second MRS DE WINTER, who describes her as having the 'face of an exulting devil'. Mrs Danvers is intent on the destruction of anyone who tries to replace her former mistress, and, twisted and tortured in her grief, turns Manderley into a shrine to the glorious Rebecca.

Daphne
Owls Do Cry, 1957
Janet Frame

Threatened by a repressive and emotionally stultified environment, she is forced to retreat, like almost all of Frame's heroines, into the tiny space behind the eyes. For her, reality becomes a verbal construct in which the 'innocence' of words is brutally violated by unwanted associations.

Dapper
The Alchemist, 1610
Ben Jonson

A gullible lawyer's clerk, he arrives at the house where SUBTLE, FACE and DOL COMMON have set up their fraudulent alchemy practice, and requests that they conjure him a familiar to help him win at gambling. Dapper is so credulous and greedy that not only does he believe Subtle's story that he is a favourite of the Queen of Fairy, but is willing to undergo ridiculous bathing rituals in order to prepare himself for meeting her. He is even convinced by Dol Common's impersonation of the fairy.

Dara, Michael
In the Shadow of the Glen, 1903
J M Synge

Michael Dara, a young herder and the lover of NORA BURKE, is a hesitant, indecisive young man, a shadow of Patch Darcy, Nora's former lover, now dead, whose presence as a mystical, heroic figure pervades this short play. At the end of the piece, Nora leaves with THE TRAMP while Michael stays drinking with her husband DAN. The 'quiet man' is therefore reprieved, his heart being not with Nora but with the community of men.

Darbishire, (Charles Edwin Jeremy)
Jennings Goes to School, 1950, et seq
Anthony Buckeridge

Darbishire's is a far less adventurous spirit than that of his great friend, JENNINGS, with whom he is one of the 79 boarders at Linbury Court Preparatory School in Sussex. Like Jennings, he is eleven years old, but although nature has not created him a man of action, loyalty to his friend often demands that he does his best to try and become one. He is fair-haired, wears spectacles and is no good at games. His studiousness is offset by a wry humour and his sense of logic by forgetfulness. He has an engaging tendency towards fantasy, in which he might picture himself as a world-famous scientist, inventor or explorer. The son of a country vicar, he has a maxim for most occasions, usually beginning his pronouncements with the phrase: 'My father says …'

Darcy, Dolour
Harp in the South, 1948
Poor Man's Orange, 1949
Ruth Park

The imaginative, intelligent, slum-born daughter of HUGHIE and MARGARET DARCY, Dolour believes that one day she will escape from the squalor of Sydney's Surry Hills. But the influences of poverty are stronger than Dolour's will. Her education is interrupted by illness, her sister's death in childbirth ties Dolour even more firmly to home, and the happy escape that she has so confidently relied on God to provide recedes even further, while the escape that does present itself exacts its own ironic toll. 'She knew the poor man's orange was hers, with its bitter rind, its paler flesh, and its stinging, exultant, unforgettable tang.'

Darcy, Hughie
Harp in the South, 1948
Poor Man's Orange, 1949
Missus, 1985
Ruth Park

'All his life he had been sixth-rate, failing in crises, sickening in emergencies, flying to the bottle when he was needed.' From his Irish

peasant forebears Hughie has inherited a maddening medley of characteristics. By turns belligerent and remorseful, hard-working and idle, he sees the squalor that he has brought his family to in Sydney's slums, but will never change. 'It ain't been much of a life for you', he tells his long-suffering wife, MARGARET DARCY, in a moment of penitent insight. But in the same breath he adds, 'We ain't licked yet.'

Darcy, Margaret
Harp in the South, 1948
Poor Man's Orange, 1949
Missus, 1985
Ruth Park

Reduced to a life of poverty in the slums of Sydney's Surry Hills, this hopeful Irish-Australian girl sinks resignedly into a life of loss and squalor, yet is sustained by Irish-Catholic faith and good humour and a fierce love for her feckless husband, HUGHIE DARCY, that nothing can destroy. 'There was no bitterness in her heart, no resentment, nothing at all but a trembling hope.' Known as 'Mumma', she has always understood that her earthly destiny is beyond her control; the faceless 'Them' of authority are the almighty ones on earth. Her faith in a kindlier world after death, however, comforts her through all her tragedies.

Darcy, Mr Fitzwilliam
Pride and Prejudice, 1813
Jane Austen

Tall, handsome, noble and rich, Darcy's disdainful pride makes him unpopular with the Bennet family and their friends. 'Continually giving offence', and defamed by GEORGE WICKHAM, he is initially viewed with particular dislike by ELIZABETH BENNET. However, he is eventually forced to swallow his proud and snobbish attitudes in his recognition of his love for her, and emerges as a kind, thoughtful and caring man prepared to protect and provide for those he loves, whatever the consequences.

Darcy Dancer → Kildare, Darcy Dancer

Daring Young Man on the Flying Trapeze
'The Daring Young Man on the Flying Trapeze', in *The Daring Young Man on the Flying Trapeze and Other Stories*, 1934
William Saroyan

An impoverished young writer in New York City during the Depression, his life seems to be identified with a circus performer whose dizzy swoops and swings mimic the vertigo of hunger and of rapidly alternating moods. When he returns to his apartment, the young man dies suddenly, drifting away in a swoon anaesthetized by hunger.

Dark Dolores
Stories à la Carte, 1932
Damon Runyon

A woman of terrible coldness of heart, she plans the destruction of her husband's killers with meticulous thought. Her hapless victims, among them BENNY THE BLOND JEW, are so overwhelmed by her beauty that they allow themselves to be lured out to sea by this latter-day Lorelei, who is also a skilled cross-channel swimmer.

Dark Mairi
Butcher's Broom, 1934
Neil Gunn

Dark Mairi is the central character in the novel and in the lives of the villagers of Riasgan. With her knowledge of the healing powers of plants and herbs, and chants and charms from the olden days, she symbolizes the land and the culture of the Gaels. She survives the many changes in her own life, comforts and gives strength to others by her presence, and yet is eventually regarded as a witch by the community she has so faithfully served. Her eventual brutal death symbolizes the murder of the Highland culture she epitomized.

Dark Man, the
The Woman, 1978
Edward Bond

A crippled former worker at the Athenian silver mines, the Dark Man becomes HECUBA's ally in the murder of HEROS and, by doing so, frees the island on which they have taken refuge from Athenian occupation.

Darke, Charles
The Child in Time, 1987
Ian McEwan

Charles, STEPHEN LEWIS's former publisher, is highly successful at everything he has ever undertaken. A careerist who tossed a coin to decide which party to join when he took up politics, he is now a junior-minister favourite of the Prime Minister, earmarked for rapid advancement. But after appointing Stephen to his Official Commission on Childcare sub-committee, Charles absconds, disappearing into the country with his wife, twelve years his senior. As Stephen discovers, Charles is a seriously disturbed, ambivalent person who ironically takes refuge in regressing to pre-pubescent boyhood once out of public life.

Darkie
The Fool, 1974
Edward Bond

Darkie is one of a group of farm labourers who, along with JOHN CLARE, knock on the door of the local manor house at Christmas, hoping to perform a song and a play in return for a meal. Resentful and embittered, Darkie considers the festive exchanges a charade and provokes LORD MILTON into debate. Darkie is an instinctive and sometimes expressive man, but has little sophistication or foresight, and only vaguely understands the gigantic forces of the industrial revolution in which he is being swept along.

Darley, L G
Justine, 1957, and throughout *The Alexandria Quartet*, 1968
Lawrence Durrell

The narrator of *Justine*, he feels that he is walking, like Dante's Virgil, in a city of the dead. He is a developing writer in Alexandria, observing and gathering experience, patently a projection of Durrell himself, who keeps Darley's name under wraps for some considerable time.

Darling, John, Michael and Wendy →
John, Michael and Wendy

Darnay, Charles
A Tale of Two Cities, 1859
Charles Dickens

Assumed English identity of the exiled French aristocrat, Charles D'Aulnais, the heir of the MARQUIS DE ST EVREMONDE, he has relinquished his inheritance in disgust at the cruel and inequitable system in France. In London, his corrupt servant, ROGER CLY, falsely accuses him of treason, but he is acquitted through the intervention of SYDNEY CARTON. After his marriage to LUCIE MANETTE and the birth of their child, he returns to Paris but is arrested and condemned to death because of the vengefulness of MADAME DEFARGE. In prison, he is visited by Sydney Carton, whom he closely resembles. Carton drugs him to prevent his protesting, exchanges clothing and ensures that he is safely rescued. Carton goes to the guillotine in his place in order that Darnay can enjoy a peaceful life with his family in England.

Darnel, Anthony
The Life and Adventures of Sir Launcelot Greaves, 1760–1
Tobias Smollett

Brother and heir to Squire Darnel, with whom SIR LAUNCELOT GREAVES's father, Sir Everhard Greaves, had agreed to alternate the parliamentary representation of Ashenton. But Anthony is harsh and stands for a new brand of politics which is only one step removed from mob rule.

Darnel, Aurelia
The Life and Adventures of Sir Launcelot Greaves, 1760–1
Tobias Smollett

A girl of astounding beauty, she comes from the family that had traditionally and hitherto politely opposed the Greaveses, but which is now under the control of her brutal uncle, ANTHONY DARNEL. It is widely accepted that she and SIR LAUNCELOT GREAVES are made for one another.

Darrelhyde, Professor Clement
Hackenfeller's Ape, 1953
Brigid Brophy

An eminent zoologist, whose intended study of rare East African apes in London Zoo leads him to an unexpected and unintended solidarity with his subjects in their moment of degradation. What he recognizes in them is instinct fettered but unsubdued by a life of convention.

Darrell, Dr Edmund
Strange Interlude, 1928
Eugene O'Neill

An admirer of NINA LEEDS, who sets aside his love for her in the interests of his scientific researches on Darwinism. However, they later have an affair, from which he has a child. Nina, however, will not divorce her husband, despite her growing love for Darrell, and they move apart.

Darrell, Larry
The Razor's Edge, 1944
W Somerset Maugham
An American traveller, marked by the Americans' clichéd superficiality about other cultures, he is steered away from materialism and self-obsession by a visit to India and a sojourn in a Hindu ashram.

Darroch, Rev George
The Awakening of George Darroch, 1985
Robin Jenkins
A gentle, pious man whose passionate evening prayers offer an audible hint of the seething desires that fuel his evangelical fervour (and which have led to a family of 15 children). Confronted with the Disruption of 1843 (which led to the secession of the evangelical Free Church from the Church of Scotland), he follows his heart. His fellow-ministers 'could not make up their minds whether they were dealing with a booby or with someone who, through Christ's favour, knew things that they, for all their erudition, never would'.

Dartie, Imogen, later Imogen Cardigan
A Modern Comedy, 1929
John Galsworthy
The daughter of WINIFRED and MONTAGUE DARTIE, and the sister of VAL DARTIE, Imogen rather resembles her father in her good looks and sensuousness. She takes after her mother, though, in her shrewdness and her understanding of others. Like the FORSYTEs, she is self-willed, competitive and inclined to selfishness, yet at heart she has grace and compassion.

Dartie, Montague
The Forsyte Saga, 1922
A Modern Comedy, 1929
On Forsyte Change, 1931
John Galsworthy
The husband of WINIFRED DARTIE, Monty is hardly in the same social class as his wife's family. A 'square and oiled' man, 'with a "handsome" look on his sallow face, and a big diamond stud in his shining shirt front', Dartie is ostentatious and clearly nouveau-riche. He has charm, but it is the charm of the rogue. A womanizer and a gambler, his debts are paid for first by his father-in-law JAMES FORSYTE, and then by his wife, for the Forsytes will do almost anything to avoid public scandal. In this Dartie outwits them, for he later absconds with a dancer and his wife's jewels.

Dartie, Val, properly Publius Valerius
A Modern Comedy, 1929
John Galsworthy
The grandson of JAMES FORSYTE, and the son of WINIFRED and MONTAGUE DARTIE, Val is christened Publius Valerius. He likes a flutter (a Dartie trait), but as he generally does quite well at it, he is known begrudgingly as the only one of the family who 'knows a horse from a donkey'. Rather ashamed of his roguish father, he makes a determined effort to be thought of as honourable. Wounded in the Boer War, he marries HOLLY FORSYTE and breeds racehorses.

Dartie, Winifred
The Forsyte Saga, 1922
A Modern Comedy, 1929
On Forsyte Change, 1931
John Galsworthy
The daughter of JAMES FORSYTE, the sister of SOAMES FORSYTE and the aunt of MICHAEL MONT, Winifred marries the rogue MONTAGUE DARTIE. Swept away by his glamour and charm, she is gradually disillusioned by his gambling and womanizing, and eventually only stays with him, paying his debts, for the sake of their children. She is emotionally brave, fashionable, self-contained and deeply unhappy.

Dartie, Rosa
David Copperfield, 1850
Charles Dickens
The companion of Mrs Steerforth, she is obsessively in love with her mistress's dashing son, MR JAMES STEERFORTH, the schoolmate and friend of DAVID COPPERFIELD. Aged 30, and with a scarred lip caused by the young Steerforth throwing a hammer at her, she is described by David as looking 'a little dilapidated – like a house – with having been so long to let'. Her passionate hopes are dashed when Steerforth elopes with LITTLE EM'LY, and she pursues a vindictive revenge on the girl.

Das, Bim (Bimla)
Clear Light of Day, 1980
Anita Desai
The ageing spinster Bim, a shabby, ironic, sharp-tongued teacher, still lives in the faded and enclosed Old Delhi house where as a popular, energetic and vivacious young girl she grew up with her odd family, declaring she would be a heroine. But, an independent-minded realist, who even in adolescence preferred history books to romances, Bim assumed responsibility for her three siblings and alcoholic aunt when her indifferent parents died. She still looks after her retarded younger brother, and with unspectacular heroism has made the life she wanted without ever leaving home.

Dashwood, Elinor
Sense and Sensibility, 1811
Jane Austen
The elder daughter of MRS HENRY DASHWOOD, artistic Elinor represents the 'sense' of the novel's title, being level-headed, rational and self-controlled. Trying to make sure that her mother and sister, MARIANNE DASHWOOD, do not let their emotions run to excess, she threatens to do violence to her own soul in suppressing her real feelings for EDWARD FERRARS. However, her natural generosity of spirit and affectionate nature eventually get their chance to flourish.

Dashwood, Fanny
Sense and Sensibility, 1811
Jane Austen
Daughter of MRS FERRARS and wife of JOHN DASHWOOD, Fanny's main purpose in life is in preventing her husband from spending any of his inheritance on his stepmother, MRS HENRY DASHWOOD, and her daughters, ELINOR DASHWOOD and MARIANNE DASHWOOD.

Resembling her mother in her selfishness and cold-hearted meanness, she is governed completely by her greed and superficiality, and remains blind to the real worth in people.

Dashwood, John
Sense and Sensibility, 1811
Jane Austen

Stepson of the widowed MRS HENRY DASHWOOD, John is entirely preoccupied with money matters and maintaining his own fortune and status in society. Instead of complying with his father's last request that he provide for his stepmother and half-sisters, ELINOR DASHWOOD and MARIANNE DASHWOOD, from his inheritance, John allows his already substantial selfishness and lack of compassion to be compounded by that of his wife, FANNY DASHWOOD, while simultaneously deceiving himself that he *is* doing his best by his relatives.

Dashwood, Marianne
Sense and Sensibility, 1811
Jane Austen

Quite the opposite of her sister, ELINOR DASHWOOD, Marianne is vivacious, open and demonstrative, and makes no attempt to conceal her feelings or 'sensibility'. Although clever, interesting and musically gifted, she initially lacks prudence, and when she falls hopelessly in love with JOHN WILLOUGHBY, the lessons she has to learn are painful and sobering ones. However, when she eventually recovers her vitality, her newly acquired 'sense' enables her to find fulfilment in her life.

Dashwood, Mrs Henry
Sense and Sensibility, 1811
Jane Austen

The widowed mother of ELINOR DASHWOOD, MARIANNE DASHWOOD and Margaret Dashwood, Mrs Dashwood is a generous, indulgent woman who finds herself in financially difficult circumstances following the death of her husband. Adapting to her change in lifestyle with good grace, however, she turns her well-meaning attentions to promoting the love interests of her two oldest daughters. Rather like Marianne she is overly romantic and prone to a lack of caution in life.

da Silva, Da Silva
Da Silva da Silva's Cultivated Wilderness, 1977
Wilson Harris

A Brazilian-born painter living and working in London. He was adopted by the British ambassador Sir Giles Marsden-Prince when his orphanage collapsed in a typhoon. 'He came to England in an aeroplane, a child with a long shadow born of mixed blood, mixed elements, dark blue oceanic sky, silver and apple moons, drowned stars and suns as he confessed in every self-portrait.'

Datchery, Dick
The Mystery of Edwin Drood, 1870
Charles Dickens

A mysterious 'white-haired personage with black eyebrows' who settles in Cloisterham after EDWIN DROOD's disappearance. His lodgings with MR and MRS TOPE overlook the rooms of MR JOHN JASPER, in whom he takes a great interest. Because there are many hints that Datchery is in disguise (is he Edwin Drood?), critics have suggested that, had Dickens lived to complete the novel, Datchery would have played an important role.

Datchet, Mary
Night and Day, 1919
Virginia Woolf

She has a broadly intellectual approach to life, reflecting on herself and her world in some detail. A self-assured 'guardian of solitude and passion', she controls her space and her destiny, unlike most women of her time. Yet she is jealous of KATHARINE HILBERY for securing RALPH DENHAM's affections.

Daubeny, Mr
Phineas Finn, The Irish Member, 1869
Phineas Redux, 1874
The Prime Minister, 1876
Anthony Trollope

A Member of Parliament who has been a Tory Prime Minister; he has been taken as representing Benjamin Disraeli. His distinction derives not so much from his intellect and depth of insight as from his ability to express himself with eloquence, grace and apparent profundity. His outward brilliance makes an especially striking impression in his country constituency of East Barsetshire.

Daughter
1919, 1932
John Dos Passos

Brought up, along with her two brothers, by her widowed father in Dallas, Texas, Daughter – Anne Elizabeth Trent – runs a little out of control at times. Vivacious and highly excitable, she is often let down when her romantic encounters fail to live up to her idealized expectations, and this is unhappily the case in her liaison with DICK SAVAGE. Finding herself pregnant and rejected, she is propelled desperately onwards in a frenzy of self-destruction which ends, inevitably, in tragedy.

Daunt, Jessica
Tiburon, 1935
Kylie Tennant

Jessica Daunt is 'long and slim and fastidious ... of the type that would like to be considered regal', and comes from Sydney to Warning Hill for her first job as a schoolteacher. Although she enjoys teaching, she finds it difficult to fit into the local community. She misses being the centre of attention as she was in Sydney, where there were scores of young men to 'adore her from afar and admire her quick wit and her gaiety'. Although Tiburon women find Jessica 'stuck up' and 'condescending to the lower classes', men recognize that 'there's good stuff in 'er if she 'adn't been brought up all wrong'. Through her friendship with PAUL WHITE she comes to understand more of herself and the lives of those around her, but eventually gives in to her frustration and returns to Sydney.

Dauphin, the (later **King Charles VII of France**)
Saint Joan, 1923
George Bernard Shaw
The Dauphin is a son of the mad King Charles VI, but as a result of the Treaty of Troyes recognizing Henry VI of England as King of France, he has not been crowned. Shaw presents him in his mid-twenties, 'a poor creature physically' with a servile expression. However, he is neither vulgar nor stupid but just prefers to keep out of trouble. Therefore, after JOAN defeats the English and crowns him at Rheims, he shows little gratitude, more a hope that she will now go home and leave him to make peace treaties instead of war.

Davers, Lady
Pamela, 1740–1
Samuel Richardson
An inveterate snob, the haughty Lady Davers is both proud and vain. She torments PAMELA ANDREWS with her constant goading about class, social precedence and the inviolable nature of hierarchy. She expects respect and humility from Pamela, and when this is not forthcoming, suffers a bout of colic; her disordered passions have led to hysteria and paranoia regarding the dismantling of rigid class boundaries.

Davey, Francis
Jamaica Inn, 1936
Daphne Du Maurier
The vicar of Altarnum, he is an albino, a self-confessed 'freak in nature and a freak in time'. Bearing a grudge against the age he was born into, he has apparently spent a lifetime finding different ways of coping with his various psychological problems. Joining the church was a last-ditch attempt which failed miserably. However, he leads a double life quite successfully for a time. He is a man at war with God or nature, with who or whatever has dealt him such an unfortunate blow. A warped and pathetic man, his function seems to be to prove to MARY YELLAN that social roles are no indication of a person's integrity.

David
Giovanni's Room, 1956
James Baldwin
A young American expatriate in postwar Paris, he is torn between his deeply-felt homoeroticism, as represented by his love for GIOVANNI, and his need to conform sexually, as in all else, to the demands of society.

David, Earl of Huntingdon → **Kenneth, Sir**

David, King
God Knows, 1984
Joseph Heller
A modernized version of the biblical psalmist and King of the Jews, he is presented here as a kind of archetypal Jewish comic, looking with wit and massive irony on his relationship with God, and with the machinations of power. He was 'always a vigorous, courageous, and enterprising soul', and a lusty progenitor of children, but is now grown old, and seeks to find peace with God – he awaits an apology from his maker – as he is about to die. His deathbed review of his life ranges across past and future, and reveals a vivid, cantankerous, outraged, compelling and extremely funny storyteller.

Davidson
'Rain', in *The Trembling of a Leaf*, 1921
W Somerset Maugham
A neurotically repressed Scottish missionary, marked by the life-denying obsessions of his race and religion, he is driven to a fatal re-examination of his principles in monsoon-soaked Samoa by his confrontation with the prostitute SADIE THOMPSON.

Davie
Butcher's Broom, 1934
Neil Gunn
The grandson of DARK MAIRI, he has always been divided by his love for the land and its people and his pride in their culture and traditions. He finds it hard to accept the acquiescence of the villagers to the proposed clearance, but equally hard to leave the village for a new life in America. The final shame of being forced to scrape an existence on the coast is more than he can bear and after the first winter he leaves with Kirsteen, thus in some way taking part of the old life with him.

Davies, Mac
The Caretaker, 1960
Harold Pinter
An old tramp, working as a dishwasher, and saved from violence by ASTON, who offers him a bed and a job as a 'caretaker'. Whingeing and pathetic, Davies attempts to play his mentally disturbed benefactor, and his brother, MICK, off against one another, to win their approval and the security of a home. Destined to return to his life of lonely and meaningless wandering, he is best characterized by his constant desire to get to Sidcup where his 'papers' – and hence his identity – are, supposedly, stored.

Davis
The Ebb Tide, 1894
Robert Louis Stevenson
One of a trio of Pacific-island treasure hunters. He is a sea captain who has followed a more rigidly moralistic path than his companions HERRICK and HYISH, but as a result his life has proceeded along well-defined tramlines which have left him blinkered. He elicits little emotion and expresses less. Yet although he is an essentially cold and ungiving man, he recognizes in others the humanity which he himself lacks.

Davison, Helena
The Group, 1963
Mary McCarthy
'All her life she had submitted to being talked *about* first and foremost by her mother.' Mrs Davison had set out to make her daughter 'the compleat girl' and had largely succeeded. Helena is intelligent, accomplished, witty and famously rich. She does not, however, enjoy this notoriety and becomes self-conscious when made the

centre of attention. A clear, logical thinker, to whom truth is important, she is impatient with any attempt to fudge issues or distort facts.

Davitch, Rebecca
Back When We Were Grownups, 2001
Anne Tyler

At the age of 53 Rebecca wakes up to a sense of having 'turned into the wrong person' and starts to fantasize about her 'true real life' rather than this, 'her fake real life'. Once 'the most serene and dignified of young women' but now the unregarded mainstay of the Davitch family, she is alienated by her current cornflake-hair and 'ramshackle face', and by the unrelenting jollity her role entails. Exploring her past and her present, musing on her relationship with her daughter and three stepdaughters (gained when she jilted her long-time boyfriend Will to marry Joe Davitch), she finally accepts that instant motherhood defined who she would become: 'a joyous, outgoing person', who as Joe said when he first saw her 'really had been having a wonderful time'.

Davoren, Donal
The Shadow of a Gunman, 1923
Sean O'Casey

Aged about 30, Davoren is an aspiring but bad poet, given to quoting Shelley and driven on by the conviction that everything forms a part in some grand design and that beauty might redeem everything. 'There is in his face an expression that seems to indicate an eternal war between weakness and strength ... a desire for activity ... an unquenchable tendency towards rest.' He shares a Dublin tenement room with SEUMAS SHIELDS. A vain man with neither humour nor scruples, Davoren exploits MINNIE POWELL's assumption that he is a gunman on the run. His character, therefore, gives an ironic slant to the title of the play.

Daw, Sir John
Epicoene, or The Silent Woman, 1609
Ben Jonson

The servant of EPICOENE, Daw appears unaware that his employer is really a boy in disguise. He also has in abundance the characteristics which, in Jonsonian terms, mark a fool: he is vainglorious and can neither distinguish bad poetry from good, nor tell why bad poetry is bad. Daw denounces several great authors while boasting of his own literary skills. He also claims to be a great success with women and lets it be known, falsely, that his conquests include Epicoene. He and his friend, the equally foolish SIR AMOROUS LA-FOOLE, are ridiculed and exposed by TRUEWIT.

Dawes, Clara and Baxter
Sons and Lovers, 1913
D H Lawrence

PAUL MOREL plunges into an affair with the sensual, serious and independent Clara Dawes, who has quarrelled with her husband, Baxter. As Paul's parents WALTER and GERTRUDE MOREL are characterized by their sharply differing temperaments, so Clara's spiritual strength and determination contrast with the weakness of Baxter's. MIRIAM LEIVERS, his former love, was emotionally possessive but Clara is not, and therefore her relationship with Paul is unopposed by his mother. According to Paul, sex is 'the culmination of everything' in love between man and woman, yet Clara feels differently, and returns to Baxter. His ensuing fight with Paul represents his own enlightenment and a turning-point of the novel.

Dawes, Rufus → Devine, Richard

Dawes, Selina
Affinity, 1999
Sarah Waters

A 'kept' woman used as a medium to entertain bored, working-class housewives, Selina finds herself imprisoned for assault and fraud after one of her séances. The beautiful and enigmatic object of MARGARET PRIOR's love, Selina encourages Margaret and eventually persuades her of her innocence. Through her diaries we find out the true nature of the events that lead to her imprisonment.

Dawkins, Jack (the Artful Dodger)
Oliver Twist, 1838
Charles Dickens

A leading member of FAGIN's den of child pickpockets, he is 'as roystering and swaggering a young gentleman as ever stood four feet six, or something less'. He introduces OLIVER TWIST to Fagin but is later convicted of theft and sentenced to transportation.

Dawson, Phoebe
The Parish Register, 1807
George Crabbe

Phoebe is the belle of the village, a rustic beauty with many admirers, but she is deceived by flattery and genteel manners. The squire's valet, once a tailor, seduces her; she is shamed, her clothing tattered and her infant in her arms. He marries her, but her sparkling eyes turn to reproach. Her husband turns out to be a bully, abusing her at home and spending their money on drunken pleasures.

Dawson, Wacka
The One Day of the Year, 1960 (play), 1967 (novel)
Alan Seymour

An old ANZAC comrade of ALF COOK, he is no less proud than his friend of the achievement celebrated in the Gallipoli parade, but takes a more moderate and reasoned line on patriotism and the remembrance of war, conscious that life has to be lived in the present, not the past.

Day, Fancy
Under the Greenwood Tree, 1872
Thomas Hardy

As her name suggests, this young school mistress is easily tempted to act on a whim. Bright, open and genuine, she is flirtatious and easily flattered, though she openly admits to her vanity. Although she is selfish, snobbish and, at times, thoughtless, Fancy's character seems to be in the making, rather than set this way for life. Capable of moments of insight and reflection, she chooses the dependable DICK DEWY over her other suitors.

She confesses to the vicar MAYBOLD: 'you praised me, and praise is life to me'.

Day, Geoffrey
Under the Greenwood Tree, 1872
Thomas Hardy

Devoted father of FANCY DAY, Geoffrey is a rather snobbish man who accepts the way things are, tolerating rather than enjoying many aspects of his life. Although he is keen on status, he is not unscrupulous in obtaining it. Putting his daughter's happiness before his own designs, he is a dreamer who copes reasonably well with harsh realities.

Dead, Milkman
Song of Solomon, 1978
Toni Morrison

Son of the prosperous Macon Dead, Milkman is obsessed by flight from childhood. Anchored to his family by a number of obsessive loves, he sets out to find what he is lacking. His quest strips him of both possessions and preconceptions, thus enabling him to discover a mythical past and to know that 'if you surrendered to the air, you could *ride* it'.

Dead, Pilate
Song of Solomon, 1978
Toni Morrison

Characterized by her absent navel, Pilate emerged from her dead mother's womb carrying her own afterbirth. A supernatural figure, she embodies wisdom and power. A primary force in MILKMAN DEAD's genesis, she is important to him because 'without ever leaving the ground, she could fly'.

Dead Man and Dead Woman
A Dance of the Forests, 1960
Wole Soyinka

In a former life, he was a captain in the army of MATA KHARIBU, and moves freely with Dead Woman between past and present. The couple are linked 'in violence and blood' with a whore, a historian, a carver and a shaman of the living generation.

Deadeye Dick, properly Rudolph Waltz
Deadeye Dick, 1982
Kurt Vonnegut, Jr

A pharmacist whose life is blighted by his having shot a pregnant mother of two as a child, thereby earning his nickname. He is a would-be writer who writes only one play, and thinks he may be a homosexual, but is not sure, since he has never had sex with anyone. He is wracked by guilt, and his chief objection to life is that 'it is too easy, when alive, to make perfectly horrible mistakes'.

Dean, Blanche
The Peach Groves, 1979
Barbara Hanrahan

On board ship to Australia in the 1880s, Blanche's brother, HARRY JONES, works to improve her speech and turn her into 'a different class of person'. Now married to an easily manipulated Adelaide lawyer, she has two young daughters, IDA and MAUDE DEAN, and lives in a villa in a fashionable watering-place. A self-interested, blue-eyed, silvery-haired 'Snow Queen', who

virtuously opines that 'God is good', Blanche secretly longs passionately for Harry. Visiting him in New Zealand, she undergoes a violent emotional crisis that deeply affects her daughters but leaves her selfishness and instinctive self-preservation relatively untouched.

Dean, Dixie
The Boys from the Blackstuff, 1984
Alan Bleasdale

A bitter man, with a strong line in sardonic humour, Dixie Dean has cut himself off from his former workmates because he believes they betrayed him. Riddled with guilt because of the way he has treated his eldest son, he abandons his belief in honest employment to 'moonlight', but is horrified at the bribery, graft and violence he is witness to. His fierce pride is gradually being whittled away but he is desperate to build a future for his four children, continually preaching the value of a good education to the two youngest and encouraging the older pair to go out and seek the work he hopes is waiting for them, if not for him.

Dean, Ellen
Wuthering Heights, 1848
Emily Brontë

Almost another member of the EARNSHAW family, loyal lifelong retainer Ellen Dean is a combination of nursemaid, friend, confidante and go-between and remains the sole witness to the tragic entanglement of the Earnshaw and LINTON households. A 'worthy woman' who continually tries to do her best by all parties concerned, her advice and wisdom are generally swept aside by the more powerful forces that oppose her good intentions.

Dean, Ida
The Peach Groves, 1979
Barbara Hanrahan

BLANCHE DEAN's perceptive younger daughter, the 'not quite so dear Ida', is pudgy, ginger-haired and freckled. Eclipsed by her sister, MAUDE DEAN, and hurt by maternal indifference, she 'sees, and remembers' everything in a Gothically-imaginative way. Having at last arrived in 'magic' New Zealand, she discovers that there are serpents in this Eden: AUGUSTUS MAUFE, 'dear old Mr Maufe', whose eyes belie his benevolence; the sinister TEMPE WIMPERIS; and even her uncle and lifelong hero, HARRY JONES. Aware of dark adult secrets, and resentful of them, she decides that dreams are dependable but reality is not. However, she is, finally, liberated from her mother's power to hurt.

Dean, Maude
The Peach Groves, 1979
Barbara Hanrahan

Almost 13, IDA DEAN's phlegmatic, ingratiating elder sister is a golden-haired 'peaches and cream' child. She is proud of being a shining model of all the Victorian virtues, and adores her mother, BLANCHE DEAN, whom she takes after. Maude apprehends as evil the strange new stirrings of her perfect body but demurely encourages AUGUSTUS MAUFE's lascivious attentions, until shockingly forced by TEMPE WIMPERIS to witness an incident involving Maude's uncle, HARRY

JONES, and her mother. Because of her likeness to Blanche, Tempe also uses Maude as a means of gaining revenge on Harry.

Dean, Sam (Samson)
Blood Rights, 1989, et seq
Mike Phillips

Having grown up in Manchester, this black freelance journalist and amateur sleuth, now based in London, knows intimately what life is like for poor black immigrants in an urban, predominantly white, society. He is both streetwise and university educated, and this diverse background, plus his quick wits, resourcefulness and investigative skills, gives him special advantages in obtaining inside information. Living alone, usually short of money, he has a broken marriage behind him. His estranged wife has custody of their young son, to whom he is devoted. Although toughened by circumstances, Sam Dean has a decidedly tender core.

Dean Jocelin
The Spire, 1964
William Golding

The dean believes that God has entrusted him with a mission to build the spire of the cathedral and bring it glory. He identifies himself with this vision, and its completion is central to his own destiny and sense of fulfilment. Although he is a good and kindly man, he is also flawed, for he finds anger and covetousness difficult to suppress, and sacrifices his love of others to his all-consuming drive to complete the spire. When he finally realizes his own selfishness, the spire of true self-knowledge is completed.

Deane, Drayton
'The Figure in the Carpet', in *Embarrassments*, 1896
Henry James

A literary critic and second husband of GWENDOLYN ERME. During Gwendolyn's first marriage she has been vouchsafed by CORVICK the secret of novelist HUGH VEREKER's work, and Deane is profoundly discomfited that she never saw fit to pass this career-making discovery on to him before her own death.

Deane, Lucy
The Mill on the Floss, 1860
George Eliot

The striking opposite to her cousin MAGGIE TULLIVER in appearance, petite, fair-haired Lucy is much admired for her accomplished manners and natural neatness, though her prettiness is, on the whole, of an unexceptional kind. Gentle, loving and generous, she is courted by handsome STEPHEN GUEST and adored by Maggie, but her guileless nature prevents her from seeing, until too late, the ardent feelings developing between those two. However, being naturally compassionate and forgiving, she eventually vindicates both of them.

Deans, Davie ('Douce Davie')
The Heart of Midlothian, in *Tales of My Landlord: Second Series*, 1818
Sir Walter Scott

A 'tough, true-blue Presbyterian ... of the most

rigid and unbending adherence to what he conceived to be the only possible straight line, as he was wont to express himself, between right-hand heats and extremes and left-hand defections'. He (precariously) rents land from the LAIRD OF DUMBIEDIKES at Woodend, where he lives with his second wife and two daughters.

Deans, Effie (Euphemia)
The Heart of Midlothian, in *Tales of My Landlord: Second Series*, 1818
Sir Walter Scott

The second child of DAVIE DEANS and half-sister of JEANIE DEANS. At the start of the narrative she is under jeopardy of a death sentence on a charge of 'murder presumptive'. This, as her sometime employer BARTOLINE SADDLETREE delightedly explains, is the legal construction put on her concealment of an illegitimate child by her lover SIR GEORGE STAUNTON. When the rioters, led by Staunton (alias 'Robertson'), break in, she refuses to escape, preferring to await her sentence.

Deans, Jeanie
The Heart of Midlothian, in *Tales of My Landlord: Second Series*, 1818
Sir Walter Scott

The elder daughter of DAVIE DEANS by his first wife, she is modelled on one Helen Walker of Irongray who, like Jeanie, walked to London to plead at court for the life of her sister. Jeanie is a model of constancy and moral vigour and her lone, single-minded journey and plain-spoken suit to Queen Caroline is one of the great set-pieces of literature. Though courted by the LAIRD OF DUMBIEDIKES, she loves the minister REUBEN BUTLER, but outshines the pair of them for sheer strength of character.

Dearborn, Laura
The Pit: A Story of Chicago, 1903
Frank Norris

A Massachusetts girl, brought to Chicago to live with her aunt. At first she seems little more than a convenient focus for the sharply contrasting needs and ambitions of three powerful men, but increasingly she asserts her own individuality, refusing to be excluded from experience but in the end refusing, too, to allow selfish motives to overcome her basic loyalty and affectionate nature.

Dearborn, Page
The Pit: A Story of Chicago, 1903
Frank Norris

The younger sister of LAURA DEARBORN, she eventually marries the young stockbroker Landry Court, who is on the rebound from her sister.

Death
The Colour of Magic, 1983, et seq
Terry Pratchett

An 'anthropomorphic personification' given real existence in the magical Discworld. Present in the background throughout the series, his speech always rendered in capital letters, Death takes centre stage in *Reaper Man*, when he loses his job and has to make his way in the world of mortals. Invisible to those who cannot believe what their eyes are telling them, and riding through the cosmos on a horse called Binky, Death appears to the dead to carry them to their own particular afterlife.

De Bero
Madmen and Specialists, 1970
Wole Soyinka

Trained in medicine, he becomes an intelligence agent in wartime, thereby seeming to betray a basic spiritual imperative and calling down on himself the influence of his father, who is an adept of the cult of As. He stands throughout as an example of idealism corrupted by pragmatic concerns.

de Beverley, Constance
Marmion, 1808
Sir Walter Scott

A renegade nun and the lover of LORD MARMION, who jilts her for LADY CLARE DE CLARE. In an effort to win him back, she follows him in the guise of a page. As revenge for having interceded in the dispute between SIR RALPH DE WILTON and Lord Marmion, she is betrayed to the convent in which she took her now perjured vows and is walled up alive.

Deborah
A Kind of Alaska, 1982
Harold Pinter

Having suffered from sleeping sickness for 29 years, Deborah awakens in hospital at the age of 45. Her speech is at times girlish and upper-middle-class, suggesting that her family were reasonably well-to-do. Yet the disjunction between her own imaginings and things as they actually are, frequently bewilders her. What often seems to her to be the present is in fact the past. A marriage, for example, imminent at the time of her falling ill, transpires not to have taken place. Hornby, her doctor, turns out to have married her sister, but: 'She is a widow', he tells Deborah. 'I have lived with you.'

de Bourgh, Lady Catherine
Pride and Prejudice, 1813
Jane Austen

The overbearing aunt of MR DARCY, and patron of REV WILLIAM COLLINS, Lady Catherine's formidable physical presence is reinforced by her authoritative, self-important manner. Arrogantly proud, conceited and snobbish, she loves nothing as much as the sound of her own voice. At first insolently trying to prevent her nephew from marrying, as she sees it, beneath him, she is eventually forced to reconcile herself to his choice of wife.

de Burgh, Hubert
King John, 1590/1
William Shakespeare

The chamberlain to KING JOHN. The king orders him to kill the child, ARTHUR, DUKE OF BRITTANY, by blinding him, but the boy pleads eloquently for mercy. Essentially a compassionate and cautious man, de Burgh relents: 'I will not touch thine eye/For all the treasure that thine uncle owes'. Instead, he hides

the boy but tells the king he is dead, humanity for once taking precedence over strict loyalty.

De Cintré, Claire
The American, 1877
Henry James

A nobly-born Parisienne of mixed French and English stock, with an impressive skeleton in the family closet, she both attracts and repels the wealthy American CHRISTOPHER NEWMAN with a smoky glamour. In the view of one character, less than convinced by the myth of her beauty, she is 'a great white doll of a woman, who cultivates quiet haughtiness ... [and] looks at you as if you were so much thin air'.

Deck, Danny
Moving On, 1970
All My Friends are Going to be Strangers, 1972
Larry McMurtry

A writer whose restless nature and rootless existence make him the focus for a generation of young intellectuals whose lives seem to be constrained by career structures and respectable ambitions. Even the act of finishing his novel fails to give structure to his life or substance to his dreams.

de Clare, Lady Clare
Marmion, 1808
Sir Walter Scott

A wealthy lady who, though betrothed to SIR RALPH DE WILTON, becomes the target of LORD MARMION's not altogether open-hearted attentions. She retires to a convent to escape him, thereby mimicking in reverse the career of CONSTANCE DE BEVERLEY, who abandoned the veil to follow Marmion.

Decoud, Martin
Nostromo, 1904
Joseph Conrad

A cosmopolitan intellectual from the imaginary South American country of Costaguana who effects a French insouciance, but is otherwise 'the very type of a fair Spanish Creole'. He has a sceptical outlook on life, and a cynical view of politics, and is initially dismissed as aimless and shallow by ANTONIA AVELLANOS, later his fiancée. His assumption of political responsibility brings a new seriousness and purpose to his character. He courageously aids NOSTROMO in fleeing with the silver from CHARLES GOULD's mine, but is unable to cope with the solitude of the island where he then guards the silver alone, which makes him 'doubt his own individuality', and eventually drives him into delirium and suicide.

de Coverley, Sir Roger
The Spectator, 1711–12
Joseph Addison and Richard Steele

An elderly Worcestershire baronet and landowner, and member of the Spectator Club, he rules his tenants with eccentric benevolence, choosing his clergyman for his willingness to preach sermons from a printed collection, and allowing nobody to sleep in church except himself. Crossed in love by a rich widow, he has never troubled to be fashionable since. His actions are those of a humorist, tinged with foibles but always tending to common sense. His servants have grown old in his service, but his oddities make him beloved rather than respected by his neighbours.

de Croye, Isabelle, first appears as Jacqueline
Quentin Durward, 1823
Sir Walter Scott

Seen by QUENTIN DURWARD at the inn, where she is serving incognito, she is the ward of CHARLES THE BOLD, DUKE OF BURGUNDY, and absconded from his lands, fearful of her position as a political pawn. Aged about 15, she has a grave beauty that reveals itself most tellingly in the voice Durward hears singing the ballad 'County Guy', unaware that it belongs to 'Jacqueline' in the inn.

Dedalus, Stephen
Stephen Hero, 1944
A Portrait of the Artist as a Young Man, 1916
Ulysses, 1922
James Joyce

The oldest son of a large Dublin family, Stephen is educated as exclusively as his father's increasingly precarious finances allow. He rejects his Catholic faith, the nationalism of his contemporaries and any prospect of a professional career. Though his masterpieces are as yet a mere twinkle in his eye, he cultivates a priestlike devotion to his chosen calling – the celebration of mortal beauty in literary art. His voluble scorn for the views of others leaves him isolated from his contemporaries. He is estranged from his family and has few close friends, while his sexual experiences have been limited to enthusiastic bouts of drunken debauchery in the seedier parts of Dublin.

Dedlock, Lady
Bleak House, 1853
Charles Dickens

The wife of SIR LEICESTER DEDLOCK and mother of ESTHER SUMMERSON by CAPTAIN HAWDON, to whom, as the young Honoria Barbary, she had once been engaged. Beautiful and dignified, she is at the centre of the fashionable world but is secretly haunted by her past. MR TULKINGHORN learns her secret, and his threats to reveal it cause her to run away. MR BUCKET helps Esther to find her, but they arrive too late, discovering her body at the gates of the paupers' graveyard where Hawdon is buried.

Dedlock, Sir Leicester
Bleak House, 1853
Charles Dickens

A proud, elderly baronet, fond of contemplating the inexhaustible subject of his family's greatness: he has 'a general opinion that the world might get on without hills, but would be done up without Dedlocks'. He deeply loves his wife, LADY DEDLOCK and, although he forgives her when he learns she had a child out of wedlock before their marriage, he suffers a stroke and never recovers. After her death, MR GEORGE ROUNCEWELL comes to care for him, and Volumnia Dedlock, an impoverished old maid cousin, becomes chatelaine of Chesney Wold.

Deedles
The Chimes, 1844
Charles Dickens

An apparently respectable banker and friend of SIR JOSEPH BOWLEY and ALDERMAN CUTE. He shocks the financial community by committing suicide in his banking house, thereby exposing Alderman Cute's hypocrisy in 'putting down' thoughts of suicide among the poor.

Deeley
Old Times, 1971
Harold Pinter

Married to KATE, with whom he lives in a remote converted farmhouse, Deeley questions her about ANNA, her old friend, whom she has not seen for 20 years but whose arrival is imminent. In a play dealing with the fallibility of memory and experience, the brusque, increasingly emotionally embattled Deeley later claims that he and Anna have already met. He also suggests that he is a film director, although undermines this by asserting that his name is Orson Welles. It is clear, however, as the play develops into a contest between Deeley and Kate over Anna, that the true bonds are those between the women, and that Deeley is the odd man out, the title of the film showing at the cinema at which he alleges he first met Kate.

Deever, Danny
'Danny Deever', in *Barrack-Room Ballads and Other Verses*, 1892
Rudyard Kipling

A non-commissioned officer in the British army, stripped of his rank and hanged in front of the regiment for murdering a sleeping comrade. Though described by the Colour Sergeant as 'a sneakin' shootin' hound', and by implication given to drink, there is no explicit indication of Deever's character, nor of his motive for the crime, nor the true degree of his guilt. Deever remains strangely unknown and unremarkable, the sad disgrace of his end and the implacability of military discipline emerging from the reactions of those forced to witness his execution.

Defarge, Ernest
A Tale of Two Cities, 1859
Charles Dickens

A Parisian wine shop owner, he is the husband of MADAME DEFARGE and leads the revolutionaries in the suburb of Saint Antoine. He looks after his old master, DR ALEXANDRE MANETTE, on his release from the Bastille, but on learning that Manette's son-in-law is the aristocratic CHARLES DARNAY, he renounces his loyalty to him and gains possession of the document which his wife ensures will condemn Darnay to death.

Defarge, Madame (Thérèse)
A Tale of Two Cities, 1859
Charles Dickens

The wife of ERNEST DEFARGE, and head of the Saint Antoine women in the Revolution, she is an eager spy and becomes the ringleader of the infamous knitting women who sit beside the guillotine. Having a watchful eye, 'a steady face, strong features, and great composure of manner', she 'was absolutely without pity'. She is intent on securing CHARLES DARNAY's death as revenge for the crimes against her brother and sister committed by his father and uncle, both the MARQUIS DE ST EVREMONDE. She is killed in a struggle with MISS PROSS, who wants to prevent her from learning that her mistress, LUCIE MANETTE, has already fled Paris. Her female assistant in the Reign of Terror, a grocer's wife known as 'the Vengeance', dies on the guillotine.

De Flores
The Changeling, 1653
Thomas Middleton and William Rowley
A servant in the house of Vermandero, he is variously described as 'good', 'kind' and 'honest'. Despite these recommendations, his actions throughout are motivated purely by his own sexual appetites and his pursuit of BEATRICE-JOANNA, his master's daughter. In a play which turns on its characters' self-deception, he is refreshingly clear-sighted and honest, at least with himself. Cynical and amoral, he is determined to have his 'will', not caring how he goes about getting it – even murder merely gives an edge to his sexual appetite.

de Grapion → Nancanou

Dehning, Julia
The Making of Americans, 1925
Gertrude Stein
Like her husband ALFRED HERSLAND, she comes from a wealthy middle-American background; their marriage establishes a powerful dynasty that unravels slowly in a dogmatic present tense. Julia is more a passive receptor than an active agent, a responsive antenna to changes in the surrounding environment rather than a rounded 'character'.

Deigh, Agnes
The Recognitions, 1955
William Gaddis
Introduced as resembling *la noyée de la Seine*, she is a prosperously suntanned version of this death-mask. She is an influential literary agent, and her name is a corrupt version of *Agnus Dei*, ('Lamb of God'), a symbol of Jesus Christ's sacrifice.

de Lacy, Damian
The Betrothed, 1825
Sir Walter Scott
HUGO DE LACY's nephew, he saves the Garde Doloureuse from the Welsh invaders, but then falls in love himself with his uncle's betrothed, EVELINE BERENGER. On first appearance he cuts a heroic figure, with 'a gallant countenance, coloured highly, but not inflamed, which looked out from a rich profusion of short chestnut curls'; he moves under his armour 'with such elasticity and ease, that it seemed a graceful attire, not a burden or encumbrance'.

Delacy, Danny
All That Swagger, 1936
Miles Franklin
A young Irishman who elopes with his beloved to Australia, and becomes the patriarch of his troubled family. He is 18 at the outset, with a

small pointed nose, ugly teeth, brilliant blue eyes and a 'meagre stature' with which 'to attack the wilds of the antipodes'. He proves to be a fearless if careless adventurer, and his 'courage was as inexhaustible as his energy', even after losing a leg. His determination to conquer the wild, though, costs him the love of his wife.

de Lacy, Hugo, Constable of Chester
The Betrothed, 1825
Sir Walter Scott
DAMIAN DE LACY's uncle, he makes a not altogether prepossessing suitor for EVELINE BERENGER. He 'scarce attained the middle size, and his limbs, though strongly built and well knit, were deficient in grace and ease of movement'. Bandy-legged, he limps from a jousting fall, and gives an impression of awkward power rather than the easy grace of his nephew.

Delacy, Jeremy
Poor Fellow My Country, 1975
Xavier Herbert
A fiercely independent and frequently acrimonious pioneer, Jeremy Delacy, the grandfather of PRINDY, is at odds with most of his fellow whites, many of whom he firmly believes to be bullies, thieves and hypocrites. For these reasons, he scorns the attentions of LYDIA LYNDBROOKE-ESK, who falls in love with him. A grim realist, he also rejects the idealism of ALFIE CANDLEMASS. At Lily Lagoons, where he farms, Delacy attempts to live in harmony with the environment and on good terms with the Aboriginal people. Eventually, though, he becomes more politically committed, and with Alfie joins a new party, Australia Free, and lobbies for Aboriginal rights. When he fails, he retreats further into himself and the country.

de Lacy, Randal
The Betrothed, 1825
Sir Walter Scott
HUGO DE LACY's kinsman, he has fallen from grace through youthful follies which have cost him his fortune and influence. His bravery and determination have not been affected by his decline, however, and he is still capable of resolute action. He appears at the Garde Doloureuse in the guise of a Lombard pedlar and hawk merchant, before regaining his chieftainship, a position that costs him his life.

Delafield, Curly
Knuckle, 1974
David Hare
Curly Delafield is the epigrammatic narrator-hero in this pastiche thriller. He is literate, his reading encompassing both George Moore's *Principia Ethica* and the works of Mickey Spillane, yet he is neither intellectual nor politically motivated. Although he makes his money as an arms dealer, his justification is that: 'I don't pick the fights. I just equip them.' By portraying himself as responsible only to himself and mapping his moral territory without regard to others, Delafield anticipates the get-rich-quick ethic which bloated England in the 1980s. Yet, as Hare himself observes, a 'crusade for

yourself is no crusade at all', and by failing to realize this, Delafield loses the love of Jenny Wilbur.

de la Marck, William, known as the Wild Boar of the Ardennes
Quentin Durward, 1823
Sir Walter Scott

LOUIS XI, KING OF FRANCE's agent, he is a curious mixture of wild nobility and almost animal savagery. Fiercely tusked and whiskered, with dim, reddened eyes, his expression is the perfect correlative of his violent nature, which with some corner of his personality he seems inclined to camouflage.

Delia
The Old Wives' Tale, 1595
George Peele

A fairy-tale beauty abducted by the conjurer SACRAPANT. She is 'the fairest for white and the purest for red, as the blood of the deer or the driven snow', but is also resilient, since she is fairer 'than running water, but harder far than steel'. She has been given a potion by her abductor which makes her 'forget herself', and unable to recognize her captive brothers, CALYPHA and THELEA. She is eventually saved by EUMENIDES.

Deliro
Every Man out of his Humour, 1599
Ben Jonson

A rich man, Deliro is so besotted with his wife, FALLACE, that he dotes on her relentlessly, insisting that he is unworthy of her and offering her expensive gifts. His delusion that she is virtuous, and loves him with the same single-minded devotion he shows her, evaporates when he catches her in the arms of FASTIDIOUS BRISK. Deliro ricochets from one extreme to the other, and condemns her as a lascivious strumpet.

Deloraine, Sir William
The Lay of the Last Minstrel, 1805
Sir Walter Scott

'A stout moss-trooping Scott was he,/As e'er couched Border lance by knee'. A faithful liegeman of the Lady of Branksome, 'steady of heart, and stout of hand', he is sent on the fateful mission to Melrose Abbey to collect Michael Scott's book of magic.

Del Sarto, Andrea
Men and Women, 1855
Robert Browning

A painter who has fallen short of his ideals and muses on what has, and might have, been. He has sacrificed his integrity to a woman who does not return his love, and sees that there is more artistry in a poor drawing by Raphael than in all his own cold technical perfection. He is resigned to the situation, and sitting in the twilight watches passively as his wife leaves to meet her lover.

Delt, Morgan
A Suitable Case for Treatment, 1962 (television); *Morgan – A Suitable Case for Treatment*, 1965 (film)
David Mercer

The son of working-class parents, a left-wing political idealist and an assistant in a café, Morgan Delt is a former Communist and failed writer on the brink of a nervous breakdown. Having been divorced by his wife and turned out of their home, he retreats to his car. Bitter, sullen and passionate, his behaviour becomes increasingly bizarre and anarchic as he discovers that 'there just doesn't seem to be anything ... that comes up to my best fantasies'. Morgan's increasing madness is seen as not only a response to, but a product of, an increasingly mad society.

de Melvil, Renaldo, later Count de Melvil
The Adventures of Ferdinand, Count Fathom, 1753
The Expedition of Humphry Clinker, 1771
Tobias Smollett

This young nobleman strikes MATTHEW BRAMBLE as 'sensible, easy and polite'. As a youth, his intelligence and moral substance are camouflaged by an unpromisingly awkward exterior, which makes him easy prey for FERDINAND, COUNT FATHOM's plausible cunning and he is somewhat unfairly used. In the later book, De Melvil and his lady turn out to be the long-lost parents of one Seraphina Melvilia.

Demetrius
A Midsummer Night's Dream, c.1594
William Shakespeare

Initially decried by his rival LYSANDER as a 'spotted and inconstant man', he is, in fact, a decent and straightforward young man, who genuinely loves his intended bride, HERMIA, and is prepared to fight both for her and for his later love (and eventual partner) HELENA. He throws himself unquestioningly into the many emergencies he encounters, combining passion with good manners in equal measure.

Demetrius
Poetaster, 1602
Ben Jonson

One of the two poetasters in the play (CRISPINUS being the other), he is an envious, inferior writer who presents himself as an excellent one. Described as 'a dresser of plays about town', he is Jonson's caricature of the playwright Thomas Dekker. When he and Crispinus are tried, they are both found guilty of bad and slanderous writing. He is sentenced to put his pomposity behind him and act honestly in the future.

Demetrius
The Robe, 1942
Lloyd C Douglas

A proud Greek slave whose conversion to Christianity while in Palestine leads him to seek, all the more eagerly, the liberty that he craves. His courage and dignity in the face of torture and, ultimately, martyrdom, are inspirational, his noble words of conviction and loyalty etching themselves deeply on friends and enemies alike.

Demi-John
Good Wives, 1869
Little Men, 1871
Jo's Boys, 1886
Louisa M Alcott

DAISY's twin, he becomes increasingly like his father, JOHN BROOKE, after the latter's death. He is a philosopher, questioning 'like a true Yankee', but also shows mechanical ability with his early 'sewin-sheen'. He loves reading and is a born teacher, serious, cheery and respected by the other boys. He becomes a journalist, not a minister as his mother, MEG MARCH, had hoped, but in running a publishing house and conventional marriage, he fulfils a manly ideal.

Demoke
A Dance of the Forests, 1960
Wole Soyinka
Creativity and destructiveness are equally balanced in this village woodcarver, a gifted artist with a tendency to viciousness and even overt violence, who has killed his apprentice. In a vision of the future, he speaks out about the violence to come.

Demolines, Madalina
The Last Chronicle of Barset, 1867
Anthony Trollope
A self-dramatizing intriguer, daughter of Lady Demolines and the late Sir Confucius, who, wanting a husband and money, sets her sights on JOHN EAMES. Her face is expressive, but not quite beautiful, and she possesses large eyes and tangled dark hair. Her 'ill-natured mischief' prompts her to cause trouble with anonymous letters.

Dempsey, Father
John Bull's Other Island, 1904
George Bernard Shaw
The parish priest in Roscullen, Ireland, Dempsey became a clergyman as a result of neither vocation nor ambition, but simply because the rural, reflective life suits him. He is parochial, a realist and, providing his authority is not contravened, an amiable and modest man. He is one of the deputation which asks LARRY DOYLE to stand for Parliament, but which transfers the offer to TOM BROADBENT.

Dempster, Janet
'Janet's Repentance', in *Scenes of Clerical Life*, 1858
George Eliot
The kind, noble-looking wife of ROBERT DEMPSTER, Janet's sweet good nature is eclipsed by the sadness and self-despair caused by long years of physical abuse at the hands of her alcoholic husband. Eventually thrown out by him, she finds an unexpected ally in REV EDGAR TRYAN and, in confessing her 'weakness' and self-loathing to him, paves the way for her own spiritual recovery, which gives her both the capacity for forgiveness and the strength to overcome her own alcohol dependence. She then, in her turn, ministers to others, remaining a devout and loving member of the parish for the rest of her days.

Dempster, Robert
'Janet's Repentance', in *Scenes of Clerical Life*, 1858
George Eliot
Dempster, the unscrupulous Milby lawyer, is a coarse, brutal man who leads the 'anti-Tryanites' in the town in a scathing and vindictive hate campaign against the REV EDGAR TRYAN. Years of alcohol abuse have turned the once loving Dempster into a bloated, monstrous tryannical figure who not only victimizes Rev Tryan but also makes a habit of drunkenly assaulting his long-suffering wife, JANET DEMPSTER, and he does little to recommend himself to our sympathies. But in the end, he is a character to be pitied, suffering weeks of tortured delusion and delirium before being finally released from his agony.

Denham, Ralph
Night and Day, 1919
Virginia Woolf
Ralph is self-conscious about his 'lowly', middle-class background, especially as the object of his affections, KATHARINE HILBERY, is of higher birth. He is insecure, craving respect and love, but is also deeply romantic and ultimately overcomes his pride in order to be true to himself.

Denner
Felix Holt the Radical, 1866
George Eliot
The personal servant of MRS TRANSOME, featuring as housekeeper and butler's wife, Denner is seemingly the one loyal and ever-present member of staff on the decaying Transome estate. She is her mistress's only real friend, ever obedient, and conceived of by Mrs Transome as being made of iron.

Dennis, Helen
Deephaven, 1877
Sarah Orne Jewett
Sophisticated but by no means arrogant or unsympathetic, she passes a summer with her friend KATE LANCASTER in the tiny New England seaside town of the title, observing the eccentricities of the inhabitants with a gentle detachment.

Dennis, Ned
Barnaby Rudge, 1841
Charles Dickens
Formerly a public hangman who took great pride in his job, which he refers to as 'working people off'. He becomes the ringleader of the Gordon Riots and wants to hang everyone opposed to them. He assists in the abduction of DOLLY VARDEN and EMMA HAREDALE. When he is arrested himself and condemned to hang, he is terrified by his fate. Dickens based the character on a real hangman of the same name.

Dennison, Charles
The Expedition of Humphry Clinker, 1771
Tobias Smollett
A fellow-reprobate of MATTHEW BRAMBLE's at Oxford, he has 'attained to that pitch of rural felicity' that Matt covets. With the support of a good wife, sound agricultural theory and modest tastes, he turns a decadent estate into the ideal of English country-house existence. Subsequent events reveal him to be the father of the disguised 'WILSON'.

Dennison, Jenny
Old Mortality, in *Tales of My Landlord*, 1816
Sir Walter Scott
The daughter and sole support of Niel Blane,

town piper and landlord of the Howff, she is marked by solid good sense and unflustered competence. As so often in Scott, this sets her against the somewhat aery and conventional breeding of the ennobled characters.

Densher, Merton
The Wings of the Dove, 1902
Henry James

A London journalist, quite without fortune, he is secretly engaged to KATE CROY, but is inveigled into courting the sickly MILLY THEALE, in the expectation that after her death he will inherit her money. With a wavering, uncertain nature, his spirit is so malleable as to allow him to be drawn into schemes with an easy rationalization of their more disreputable elements.

Dent, Arthur
The Hitch-Hiker's Guide to the Galaxy, 1979, et seq
Douglas Adams

A kind of English suburban everyman. Described as 'tall, dark haired and never quite at ease with himself', Arthur works in local radio in the West Country, and is entirely unaware, at the outset, of the interplanetary adventure which is about to befall him. This unpreparedness for his travels is central to the novel's humour, as he uncomprehendingly undergoes one intergalactic culture-shock after another. Arthur, it transpires, may, as the last survivor of the now-demolished Earth, hold some key to the question of life, the universe and everything, since the planet proves to have been a vast, organic computer which was demolished in error, moments before it was due to reveal the answer to the said question.

de Philosophe, Palmyre
The Grandissimes, 1880
George Washington Cable

A proud and tigerish *voudou* priestess, visited by AURORE NANCANOU and tended by JOSEPH FROWENFELD. She has been given in marriage to the slave BRAS-COUPÉ, and remains loyal to him, even when his condemnation might leave her free to pursue her love for HONORÉ GRANDISSIME.

de Piracquo, Alonzo
The Changeling, 1653
Thomas Middleton and William Rowley

Blinded by love, he is the first casualty of the tragedy. Betrothed to BEATRICE-JOANNA, he cannot see that she has transferred her affections to ALSEMERO and, oblivious to her faults, never suspects that she has hired her father's servant to kill him.

Deputy
The Mystery of Edwin Drood, 1870
Charles Dickens

A 'hideous small boy in rags' whom DURDLES pays to throw stones at him if he stays out at night, in order to drive him home. Also known as 'Winks', the urchin is employed at the lodging house in Cloisterham, where 'all us man-servants at Travellers' Lodgings is named Deputy'. Usually out at night, he is able to observe the comings and goings of MR JOHN JASPER.

Derek
Water with Berries, 1971
George Lamming

Derek, a West Indian exile, is an actor whose roles in London deteriorate from star part in *Othello* to that of a corpse. An orphan with a chapel education, his vulnerability shows itself in destructive tendencies, which bring about the break-up of a relationship between fellow West Indian ROGER and his girlfriend. His subsequent desperation leads to compulsive violence.

Deronda, Daniel
Daniel Deronda, 1876
George Eliot

Serious-minded, distinguished-looking and educated as a gentleman, Deronda is not sure who his parents are – none of his guardian Hugo's relatives look like him. He becomes interested in the Jews when he rescues a young Jewess, MIRAH LAPIDOTH, from a suicide attempt and then finds a long-lost brother. On later discovering his own Jewishness, he offers his 'soul and hand' to do 'any work' for his people. Adored by Mirah and loved by GWENDOLEN HARLETH for his compassion and understanding, he combines a 'feminine affectionateness' and a 'masculine independence' to continually beneficial effect.

Derrick, Harran
The Octopus: A Story of California, 1901
Frank Norris

MAGNUS DERRICK's youngest son and his assistant at Rancho de los Muertos. Blond and weathered, he is 'a very well-looking young fellow of twenty-three or twenty-five. He had the fine carriage that marked his father, and still further resembled him in that he had the Derrick nose – hawklike and prominent, such as one sees in the later portraits of the Duke of Wellington.'

Derrick, Magnus
The Octopus: A Story of California, 1901
Frank Norris

Known as 'the Governor', he is owner of the aptly named Rancho de los Muertos in the San Joaquin Valley and spokesman for the farmers in their struggle against the tentacular encroachment of the Pacific and Southwestern Railroad. Tall, 'and though now well toward his sixtieth year … as erect as an officer of cavalry … impressing one with a sense of gravity, of dignity and a certain pride of race'. An admirer of the statesman John Caldwell Calhoun, he once aspired to a political career. He had the gravitas to carry it off, but always seemed to miss his moment. In every sense, he belongs to an older America.

Derriman, Festus
The Trumpet Major, 1880
Thomas Hardy

A most unattractive creation, this overweight yeomanry cavalry officer is vain, greedy and cowardly. A petulant, insensitive and self-indulgent figure, he is also arrogant. He continues to pursue ANNE GARLAND, despite her deep contempt of him, which she tries to make apparent. His advances are pathetic, for he is no competitor in the battle of suitors.

Dersingham, Mr
Angel Pavement, 1930
J B Priestley

A weak-looking, middle-aged man, he is entrenched in the English public-school spirit. He is not a decision maker, and defers responsibility in a damaging way. Although he is immensely kind and upright, he is not astute in business. Part of a shallow middle-class social world, he shows integrity in personal relationships.

des Comines, Philip
Quentin Durward, 1823
Sir Walter Scott

A fictionalized version of Philippe des Commines, whose *Mémoires* provided the basic material for Scott's novel; the future historian is a sensible, politic man who alone seems to see the balance of destiny between his monarch and his liege lord CHARLES THE BOLD, DUKE OF BURGUNDY.

Desdemona
Othello, 1603/4
William Shakespeare

She overcomes racial prejudice, the intense disapproval of her father and the advances of RODERIGO to marry OTHELLO and become his 'soul's joy'. A paragon of goodness and love, both for her husband and for humanity, her faith and innocence are essential to IAGO's plot. While her human qualities are established in the domestic scenes with her servant EMILIA, even on her deathbed she shows no signs of fear or bitterness, rather of pity and compassion.

Desiderio
The Infernal Desire Machines of Dr Hoffmann, 1972
Angela Carter

Suspicious and courageous, Desiderio is a detective and an adventurer. He is the symbolic rational man in a time of total incapacitating chaos. Possessing an objective mind, he is one of only a handful of individuals who remain unaffected by Dr Hoffmann's machines. In his situation he feels only the 'dreadful boredom of long-term travellers at sea'.

De Spain, Manfred
The Town, 1957
The Mansion, 1959
William Faulkner

Mayor of Jefferson and president of Col Sartoris's bank. He is also the lover of EULA SNOPES, an association that continues with the knowledge of Eula's impotent husband FLEM SNOPES, who uses the situation as a lever to deprive de Spain of all his social and economic power and of his decaying mansion house.

Devaux, Andrée
A Compass Error, 1968
Sybille Bedford

Fortyish, elegant and with a classic cool beauty, Andrée is a rich, thoroughly worldly and unscrupulous woman. She deliberately entices the impressionable young FLAVIA HERBERT into falling in love with her, and into betraying the relationship between her mother, CONSTANZA

HERBERT and Michel Devaux, before revealing that she is not just Michel's cousin but also his estranged wife. Her manipulation of Flavia is inhumanly cold and cruel, and alters not just Flavia's happy relationship with Constanza and Michel, but the whole course of her future life.

Deven
In Custody, 1984
Anita Desai

A timid failed poet and born victim, Deven scrapes a living by working in the Hindi department of a small college in the arid province of Mirpore. The saving grace of his equally arid existence with his embittered wife is his passionate love for the classic poetry of his first language, Urdu, which he learned from his father. Bullied by MURAD into interviewing the great poet, NUR, he is overwhelmed equally by trepidation and exaltation. Absorbed into his hero's squalid but still sometimes magical world, Deven tragi-comically discovers that taking Nur's poetry into safe custody – and thus into his very soul – is both a 'shining honour' and an 'unendurable burden'.

Devine, Richard, also known as Rufus Dawes
His Natural Life, serialized 1870–2; as *For the Term of His Natural Life*, 1874
Marcus Clarke

Illegitimate son of Lady Devine and her lover Lord Bellassis, he is transported to Australia, having been innocently implicated in his natural father's murder. On the prison ship, he takes the name 'Rufus Dawes' and acquires a reputation as a 'man of mark', whose fine manners are laughed about behind his back, but who is treated with considerable respect by his fellow-convicts.

De Vionnet, Madame
The Ambassadors, 1903
Henry James

An elegantly cultured French lady, 'of a certain age', under whose very convincing spell young CHAD NEWSOME appears to have fallen. Not quite as *soignée* as some of James's earlier European great ladies, she commands the young American's admiration without the Machiavellian tricks of her predecessors.

de Wilton, Sir Ralph
Marmion, 1808
Sir Walter Scott

An English knight and the lover of LADY CLARE DE CLARE, he is the sworn enemy of LORD MARMION, who attempts to woo Clare away from him. When they meet in the lists, Marmion leaves him for dead but de Wilton survives and stalks his foe in the guise of a holy palmer.

de Winter, Max
Rebecca, 1938
Daphne Du Maurier

A man with much to hide, he is secretive and repressed, with a desire to control situations absolutely. But he is also capable of great loyalty and passion, and expects devotion from his partner in return. Unfulfilled in his first marriage, to REBECCA DE WINTER, he finds happiness with the second MRS DE WINTER. However, the memory of Rebecca is not easily erased.

de Winter, Mrs
Rebecca, 1938
Daphne Du Maurier

A shy and nervous woman, who has led a quiet, uneventful life until her marriage to MAX DE WINTER. A dreamy character, deeply in love with her husband, she becomes increasingly unhappy with life at Manderley, finding herself always in the shadow of Max's first wife REBECCA DE WINTER, and lacking the confidence with which to combat the difficulties of her new situation. Sensitive to the opinions of others, not least those of MRS DANVERS, she does not take easily to her new role as mistress of the house, but, as her awkwardness and naivety gradually diminish, she becomes a great source of strength to Max.

de Winter, Rebecca
Rebecca, 1938
Daphne Du Maurier

Though deceased when the novel begins, Rebecca is a powerful presence in the lives of the other characters. An exquisite creature, apparently adored by her husband MAX DE WINTER, she was a commanding figure at their home Manderley, and is still revered by its housekeeper, MRS DANVERS. An immensely appealing woman, amusing and astute, she was, however, marred by her inability to commit herself to a relationship, and this led to her untimely end.

Dewy, Dick (Richard)
Under the Greenwood Tree, 1872
Thomas Hardy

Dick is an ordinary young man: self-effacing, straightforward and lacking in complexities of thought. He is honest, trusting and although he sees faults in his beloved FANCY DAY, his heart is always willing to forgive. There is nothing exotic or particularly romantic about him, and at times his devotedness is almost comic. He has many lessons to learn, but will never intentionally hurt another living soul.

Dewy, Reuben
Under the Greenwood Tree, 1872
Thomas Hardy

Father of DICK DEWY, Reuben warns his son not to set his sights too high. He likes to hold on to the past, to a sense of order. He is not uncomfortable with social hierarchy, but will fight for what he believes in. Shrewd and perceptive, he is something of a leader, who enjoys influencing others, including his son. A lively imagination and a cynical view of the world he lives in make him an interesting man.

Dexter, Captain Richard
Devil-in-a-Fog, 1966
Leon Garfield

The brother of SIR JOHN DEXTER, who, we are told, abducted Sir John's only child and later attempted to kill Sir John himself. He is a slightly weak character, whose sensual nature

leads him to marry beneath him. The birth of his three sons triggers Sir John's fears that the Dexter estate, which is the subject of an entail, will pass into what he considers to be less worthy hands. Captain Dexter is made scruffy and shifty by his unfortunate circumstances, and he is the victim of much misplaced suspicion and contempt. In reality he is a loving father and a loyal husband, miserable in his exile from the heart of the Dexter family.

Dexter, Lady
Devil-in-a-Fog, 1966
Leon Garfield

A tall, cold, haughty woman, sharp in manner and guarded of her emotions. She is curt and slightly ironical in speech, never conforming to expectations. She dominates SIR JOHN DEXTER, and has a manipulative, capricious nature. 'A great lady', she is dignified in her movements and a graceful dancer. She comes to believe in and love GEORGE TREET, protecting herself all the while against possible disappointment, being nervous of giving love, in case she should not receive it back.

Dexter, Sir John
Devil-in-a-Fog, 1966
Leon Garfield

Sir John retains his austere good looks, in spite of his failing heart, his 'strange, profound eyes' being accentuated by a bony face. He presents a gentle, cheerful nature to the world, and is apparently proud of his 'son', GEORGE TREET. A perfect gentleman, he hides his steely self behind a calm reserve. Obsessed with the continuation of the Dexter family, and a much blacker character than is at first apparent, he is at his most peaceful when in the library, surrounded by pictures of Dexters past and present.

Dey, Annie
'The Ploughing Match', in *The Last Sister*, 1950
Fred Urquhart

The widow of a farmer in North-East Scotland, whose lifelong ambition to have a ploughing competition on her farm is achieved too late. Confined to her bed and speechless after a stroke, she is tormented by her helplessness and able to watch the proceedings only through binoculars. Nothing is as she had intended, just as the old ways that she maintained on the farm have been swept away. Angry, lonely and with her pride hurt, she dreams of the day as it should have been.

Diamond, Legs
Legs, 1975
William Kennedy

A fictionalized version of a notorious hoodlum who ran the rackets in upstate New York during the Prohibition period. Like F Scott Fitzgerald's JAY GATSBY, Diamond is portrayed as a man possessed by a dream of betterment so pure as to be corrupting.

Diaphanta
The Changeling, 1653
Thomas Middleton and William Rowley

BEATRICE-JOANNA's waiting woman, who is

apparently herself attracted to her mistress's husband, ALSEMERO. She agrees to Beatrice's request to take her mistress's place in the bridal bed on the wedding night, being motivated more by sexual desire than by the money she is offered. It is this that proves to be her undoing and she overstays her time in Alsemero's bed, thus incurring her mistress's jealousy and wrath.

Dick, Mr
David Copperfield, 1850
Charles Dickens

An amiable old eccentric whom MISS BETSEY TROTWOOD rescues from being sent to a lunatic asylum by his family. Lodging with her, he refuses to use his real name, Richard Babley, insisting on 'Mr Dick', while MR WILKINS MICAWBER always calls him Mr Dixon. He spends his time writing a Memorial of his wrongs for the Lord Chancellor but makes no progress because 'King Charles's head' – the execution of Charles I, which he associates with his own mental disturbance – keeps recurring in his writings. His pastime is to fly kites made from discarded pages of his writing.

Didi
The Madness of Didi, 1980
Obi Egbuna

Didi is in his fifties, and his hair is greying a little. When he arrives in a small Nigerian settlement, the villagers cannot decide who he is or what his purpose might be. He is certainly a commanding physical presence, fit and robust, yet there is something about him which is more than merely authoritative. His serenity and wisdom make Didi majestic, almost god-like. Evidently a man of piercing intelligence and worldly knowledge, he is also possessed of a firm, persuasive manner. It is as if he carries a vision within him from which he will not be deflected. He is an artist, a scholar, and something of a poet. Yet while some villagers see him as a hero and their natural leader, others detect a calculating, even subversive influence, and are watchful.

Diego de Zelos, Don
The Adventures of Ferdinand, Count Fathom, 1753
Tobias Smollett

A 'noble Castilian' who weaves in and out of the plot, sometimes in his own person, originally in the disguise of 'Hali', a Persian. Brought up as a warrior and head of one of the most distinguished families of his country, he is forced to give up fortune and honour and travel through Europe incognito, renouncing the cultured existence of his homeland.

Differ, Connie (Constance)
Capricornia, 1938
Xavier Herbert

The daughter of an Aborigine woman and OSCAR SHILLINGSWORTH's drunken but cultured English foreman. Having been placed under the care of the Protector of Aborigines, Humboldt Lace, Connie is first seduced by him then forced into marriage with another half-caste. Uneducated, frightened and isolated, the innocent victim of racism and spite, she descends helplessly into prostitution. The good Tim O'Cannon, a railway

fitter, attends to her as she dies of consumption and takes her daughter TOCKY O'CANNON into his own home. Connie embodies an Australian tragedy, that of a despised half-caste people, an embarrassment to the white European pioneers, driven to tragedy by prejudice and guilt.

Dilboong
The Timeless Land, 1941
Storm of Time, 1948
No Barrier, 1953
Eleanor Dark

Painfully ugly but gentle, tender and loving, Dilboong is the Mannions' Aborigine servant and nursemaid. She is unaware that she is BENNILONG's daughter, and the granddaughter of an even greater tribal singer, but has inherited their talent, and improvises songs on the small incidents of her pathetic life. Passionately devoted to her childhood playmate, MILES MANNION, she suffers during his long years in England, while meekly becoming PATRICK MANNION's mistress and bearing his child. She offers equal devotion to Miles's timid English bride who is, however, frightened and repelled by Dilboong's appearance. Facing permanent banishment from 'the daylight of her life', Dilboong feels she has nothing to live for.

Diligence
Ane Pleasant Satyre of the Thrie Estaitis, 1540
Sir David Lindsay

Diligence is at once a bona fide character and a theatrical device. As REX HUMANITAS's hard-working messenger his duties are many and his register varies from coarse to formal, according to the situation in hand. His main function, however, is as presenter of the play and mediator with the audience; in giving a brief synopsis of what is to follow he draws attention to the artifice of it all, the implication being that what is to be learnt from it should be transmitted into the real world.

Dillon, George
Epitaph for George Dillon, 1954
John Osborne and Anthony Creighton

A sensitive and apparently vital man, he is also an egomaniac being destroyed by a mercenary and small-minded society. An unsuccessful actor and playwright, he is 'a little over thirty, boyish, yet still every year his age'. Volatile, ironic, offensive and sincere, he is adopted by the Elliot family, who think of him as rather heroic. He meets his intellectual match in the feisty AUNT RUTH, but eventually a spicy version of one of his plays is taken up by the provincial circuit and he has no choice but to face the insignificance of his work and the instability of his marriage.

Dillon, Lilly
The Grifters, 1963
Jim Thompson

Her dangerous liaisons with organized crime clash with her profound love for her son, ROY DILLON, whom she is prepared to protect, yet at the same time is willing to trick. Long association with the underworld of crime has calloused her, and she is unable to deal with the complex emotions she feels for her son, including her ruthless, jealous concern for his future. Her dislike of his lover, MOIRA, and the complexities of their intricate deceptions, lead to tragic violence.

Dillon, Roy
The Grifters, 1963
Jim Thompson
A small-time con man, he drifts through the demi-monde of criminality, displaying a perverse kind of ingenuity and a ruthless optimism. Utterly shallow in his relationships, his self-interest is the determining principle in his life, and he will sacrifice everything to that. His relationships with his mother, LILLY DILLON, and his lover, MOIRA, are enigmatic and confused, and in the end the only person he believes in with any conviction is himself. This self-love spawns the treachery that brings about his final crisis.

Dilsey (Dilsey Gibson)
The Sound and the Fury, 1929
William Faulkner
The COMPSON family's cook, she appears to be the informing intelligence of the last section of the novel. She represents timeless values that seem to have been abandoned by the aristocratic whites. Faulkner later said that 'she held that family together for not the hope of reward but just because it was the decent and proper thing to do'.

Dilworthy, Senator Abner
The Gilded Age, 1873
Mark Twain and Charles Dudley Warner
Ostensibly a Christian statesman of humble origin and a paragon of political integrity, he is, in fact, a venal hypocrite, giving and receiving bribes in return for political favours, and abusing his privileges at the expense of the public purse. In mitigation, it must be said that the majority of his Washington colleagues behave in the same manner. Dilworthy invites the beautiful LAURA HAWKINS to Washington DC and involves her in mutually advantageous murky financial dealings and political intrigue.

Dimmesdale, Arthur
The Scarlet Letter, 1850
Nathaniel Hawthorne
Strangely passionless, the young minister has been HESTER PRYNNE's lover and unacknowledged father of her child. Torn by guilt, but unable to declare it publicly, he suffers the appearance on his chest (either psychosomatically or as the result of ROGER CHILLINGWORTH's 'potent necromanc[y]') of the same scarlet A stitched on Hester's clothing.

Dinmont, Dandie
Guy Mannering, 1816
Sir Walter Scott
A tough little Border farmer and huntsman, who befriends and assists Vanbeest Brown (HARRY BERTRAM) before his true identity has been revealed. Possessed of a hard head (literally and psychologically) and an unswerving disposition to 'call a spade a bluidy shovel', he is Scott's most unstinting and unsentimental portrait of sheer goodness.

Diomedes
Troilus and Cressida, 1601/2
William Shakespeare
A Greek leader who escorts CRESSIDA from Troy to the Greek camp where she is to join her traitorous father. Courageous in battle and impatient in love, he wins Cressida's favours within hours of meeting her. He shows a cynical but realistic attitude to the war and to HELEN's part in it, saying 'For every false drop in her bawdy veins/A Grecian's life hath sunk ... for every scruple/A Trojan hath been slain'.

Dionyza
Pericles, c.1608
William Shakespeare
The devious, jealous and politically naive Dionyza is the wife of CLEON, the governor of Tarsus. Having agreed to look after MARINA, the infant daughter of PERICLES, she becomes increasingly resentful that Marina, as she grows up, is more beautiful and intelligent than her own daughter, Philoten. Her resentment grows into demonic ruthlessness. Dionyza hires Leonine to murder Marina and then, supposing the crime has been done, poisons the assassin to ensure his silence. When Pericles returns, both she and Cleon pretend to mourn for his daughter.

Dissait
Ane Pleasant Satyre of the Thrie Estaitis, 1540
Sir David Lindsay
One of the three comic Vices who control the kingdom of REX HUMANITAS until the arrival of DIVYNE CORRECTIOUN, Dissait, as his name suggests, is particularly deceptive, it being he who suggests that he, FLATTERIE and FALSET should disguise themselves in order to beguile the king. Though closely in league with MERCHAND (the burgesses), he nevertheless places a curse on them and their offspring when he finally hangs for his sins.

Diver, Dick
Tender is the Night, 1934
F Scott Fitzgerald
A doctor, he is handsome and sympathetic, but in the course of the book he dives to the depths of despair and self-knowledge, and emerges emotionally scarred, but wiser. He is an intelligent, charming and romantic figure at the outset, and is thought likely to do great things, but his assumption of responsibility for his schizophrenic patient-turned-wife, NICOLE DIVER, sows the seeds of his destruction. He is jealous and possessive of her, but his marriage disintegrates as his confidence and self-esteem are eroded, and he comes to think of himself as 'the Black Death' as he descends into failure and obscurity.

Diver, Nicole
Tender is the Night, 1934
F Scott Fitzgerald
A wealthy, schizophrenic young American who is helped by a handsome young doctor, DICK DIVER. She falls in love with him, and finds in him the stability and sense of identity which she has lacked. She is attractive, but also fragile and vulnerable, and although their marriage and

lifestyle seem attractive to others, internal tensions are undermining the relationship. Nicole eventually becomes relatively independent, but at the expense of Dick's mental stability.

Divyne Correctioun
Ane Pleasant Satyre of the Thrie Estaitis, 1540
Sir David Lindsay

An allusively Protestant angel, representing the divine intervention of God, sent to reform both REX HUMANITAS and his kingdom, Divyne Correctioun is ruthless in his purification of the court. Causing the Vices (DISSAIT, FALSET and FLATTERIE) to take flight, he banishes DAME SENSUALITIE, releases VERITIE and CHASTITIE from the stocks and, by inspiring fear in him, induces the moral recovery of Rex Humanitas. While he shows leniency to the king's courtiers, Divyne Correctioun presides over the parliament of the Three Estates and fearsomely punishes all other offenders as a prerequisite to restoring harmony in the state.

Dixon, Jim
Lucky Jim, 1954
Kingsley Amis

Blundering his way from one social disaster to another in his efforts to impress his Head of Department, Dixon – the struggling university lecturer of the title – seems at first glance to be anything but 'lucky'. Accident-prone, outspoken and disinclined to work, he is ill-equipped to save his career, and he gives vent to his feelings of rage and loathing at academic life through hilarious facial contortions. But his luck lies in that, unlike most of the people he mixes with, he is capable of showing honesty, real affection and humour, and his strangely endearing character eventually finds its just rewards.

D J (Ranald Jethroe)
Why Are We In Vietnam?, 1967
Norman Mailer

A pre-draft sociopath, who tunes in to America's dark side with his friend and alter ego Tex Hyde, he attains a dubious manhood during a brutal hunting trip to Alaska with his father Rusty, a big corporate figure from Dallas. Obscene and hip, he has a turn of phrase like James Joyce on amphetamines.

Doane, Seneca
Babbitt, 1922
Sinclair Lewis

A socialist attorney in the city of Zenith, he impresses GEORGE FOLANSBEE BABBITT with visions of a socialist future and inspires him to turn away from his middle-class 'boosterism' and narrowly conventional insistence on respectability.

Doasyouwouldbedoneby, Mrs
The Water Babies, 1863
Charles Kingsley

She begins where MRS BEDONEBYASYOUDID ends and vice versa. Those who do not listen to the one must listen to the other. She visits the children on Sundays, and when she comes they dance and clap their hands. She has the 'sweetest,

kindest, tenderest, funniest, merriest face' the children have ever seen. She mothers them all, including TOM who adores her. Where her sister is the reckoner, she is the balm and reward for good behaviour.

Dobbin, Captain
'Captain Dobbin', in *Cuckooz Contrey*, 1932
Kenneth Slessor

A retired voyager of the South Sees, the Captain now 'spots boats', noting all significant and insignificant details in 'A ledger sticky with ink'. Still possessed by his beloved mistress the sea in mind and soul, he pores over atlases and maps, reading, writing, thinking and remembering. But he is oblivious to the darker side of his great love, and his romantic memories do not admit of death, fear, sweat and violence; cocooned in a 'little cemetery of sweet essences', he is forever locked in nostalgic innocence.

Dobbin, William
Vanity Fair, 1848
W M Thackeray

As his name, plodding nature, big feet and spluttering speech all suggest, he is the novel's willing horse. Often considered to be the only uncomplicatedly 'good' character in *Vanity Fair*, he subordinates his own love for AMELIA SEDLEY to that of his unreliable friend GEORGE OSBORNE. The price is very high. When Amelia eventually awakens to Osborne's shallowness and marries Dobbin, he is already broken by disappointment and hard use.

Dobie, Martha
The Children's Hour, 1934
Lillian Hellman

A highly-strung, nervous woman in her late twenties, she has worked hard to establish the financial viability and sound reputation of the Dobie School For Girls. Coping with a demanding relative, her emotional sustenance has been a deep and abiding friendship with KAREN WRIGHT. The intensity of her feelings for Karen does not go unnoticed but it is only a child's spiteful accusation of unnatural behaviour that forces her to confront the true implications of her affection, a moment of truth that shocks her to the core.

Dobson, Zuleika
Zuleika Dobson, 1911
Max Beerbohm

Niece of the Warden of Judas College, Oxford. When she visits her uncle during Eights Week, her fatal glamour drives the undergraduates mad with unrequited love and to lemming-like suicide in the Isis.

Doc (Doc Lee)
Cannery Row, 1945
John Steinbeck

Owner and proprietor of the Western Biological Laboratory, this lonely marine biologist is 'deceptively small, for he is wiry and very strong and when passionate anger comes on him he can be very fierce ... He wears a beard and his face is half Christ and half satyr and his face tells the truth.'

Doc Daneeka
Catch-22, 1961
Joseph Heller

A 'sad, birdlike man with the spatulate face and scrubbed, tapering features of a well-groomed rat'. He is the medical officer responsible for grounding airmen (or, given the self-negating nature of Catch-22, not grounding airmen), and is a 'very neat, clean man whose idea of a good time was to sulk'. He resents having been drafted 'just as the shop was starting to show a profit', and frets about his (excellent) health. He is a flight surgeon, but is afraid of flying; when the plane which he is supposed to be in (but is not) crashes, he is declared officially dead, and ends up 'padding through the shadows fruitlessly like a ubiquitous spook'.

Docherty, Tam
Docherty, 1975
William McIlvanney

An Ayrshire miner, he is small but physically powerful, and has a strong sense of independence in a world which conspires to deny it. His indomitable spirit and defiance of injustice are balanced by a bitter sense of his own futility and ultimate helplessness. He lives in a 'personal climate of squalls of sudden temper, spells of infectious pleasure that couldn't be forecast', and is given to periods of brooding introspection. He can be violent, but is never gratuitously so, and earns the highest respect of his tough community.

Doctor, the
The Adventures of Peregrine Pickle, 1751, bowdlerized edition 1758
Tobias Smollett

A young man, unseasonably dressed in black suit and tye-wig, he evinces 'all the uncouth gravity and supercilious self-conceit of a physician piping hot from his studies'. He is said to be modelled on Dr Mark Akenside, who had published *The Pleasures of the Imagination* in 1744, and who contributed greatly to the introduction of Enlightenment science into literature.

Doctor of Physic, the
The Canterbury Tales, c.1387–1400
Geoffrey Chaucer

Cautious of his own health, careful of his diet and very expensively dressed, he is in collusion with the apothecary at the expense of the patient. He revels in the money that is made during a plague and is indifferent to religion. Familiar with all the highest authorities on medicine and conversant with the treatment of all diseases, he is above all 'a verray parfit praktisour' at converting his skills into cash. He tells a tale of domestic pathos and daughterly self-sacrifice.

Dods, Meg
St Ronan's Well, 1823
Sir Walter Scott

The formidable landlady and resident harpy of the Cleikum Inn, Aultoun, which has been bypassed by the modish new spa at St Ronan's Well. 'She had hair of a brindled colour ... which was apt to escape in elf-locks ... long skinny hands, terminated by stout talons – grey eyes, thin lips ... and a voice that could match a choir of fish-women'. She is unmarried.

Dodsworth, Samuel
Dodsworth, 1929
Sinclair Lewis

A wealthy car manufacturer who, like his fellow Zenith inhabitant GEORGE FOLANSBEE BABBITT, turns his back on soulless business to pursue culture in Europe. His wife Fran has a different notion of what this means and cuckolds him with a series of men; Dodsworth's consolation is a high-minded relationship with an American widow, Mrs Cortright, who coaches him in the finer points of European civilization and inspires him with an altruistic, almost socialist, view of the new American city.

Dofu, Modin
Why Are We So Blest?, 1975
Ayi Kwei Armah

Modin Dofu arrives in America from his West African state with a comprehensive scholarship. He is one of those euphemistically described as 'these foreign students – Africans, Asians, Latins who talk all the time about what they'll do to overturn the system once they get out there'. Too late he realizes that once you become part of the 'American dream', the Promethean instinct must be quelled.

Dogberry
Much Ado About Nothing, 1598/1600
William Shakespeare

Because of his position as commander of the watch – an assortment of ignorant, aged or ramshackle misfits – Dogberry imagines himself a man of importance, but his attempted erudition results in a series of misunderstandings and mispronunciations. An essentially comic figure, he treats those of a higher social standing in an over-familiar manner. More by luck than good judgement, he and the watch uncover DON JOHN's plot; but he never realizes its importance, being more concerned with imagined slights to his character and verbal assaults on his dignity.

Dog-Woman, The
Sexing the Cherry, 1989
Jeanette Winterson

A truly Rabelaisian character (of mountainous size, dirty, with a flat nose, black rotten teeth and 'caves' in her face 'home enough for fleas'), she cannot remember her own name and so is called Dog-Woman because of the dozens of dogs she keeps in her shack beside the River Thames. Phenomenally strong (able to send an elephant flying into the air and stop a rifle bullet in her cleavage), it is her love for her son JORDAN, a love that she finds hard to show, that sustains her.

Dol Common
The Alchemist, 1610
Ben Jonson

A prostitute with a ready, bawdy wit, Dol Common is a co-conspirator with SUBTLE and FACE in setting up a fraudulent alchemy practice. Their plan is to make money by playing on the foolishness of others. Dol's part in the deception is to impersonate the Queen of Fairy and a mad noblewoman, which she does with zest and conviction.

Doll Tearsheet
Henry IV Part II, 1597/8
William Shakespeare

An ageing whore and companion to MISTRESS QUICKLY, Doll Tearsheet is abused for her diseased body by several male characters who appear to have intimate knowledge of her. While she may give her body to others, however, she saves her true affections for the substantial figure of SIR JOHN FALSTAFF, whose health she is concerned about because she fears that fighting by day and over-exertion by night may kill him. Her powers of invective are highly developed, especially towards PISTOL, for whom she saves her strongest epithets.

Dollar, Bob
That Old Ace in the Hole, 2002
Annie Proulx

Abandoned by his parents, Bob is brought up by his Uncle Tam whose nightly bedtime stories ensure that he becomes 'a sucker for stories told'. In the employ of Global Pork Rind, the 25-year-old Bob is dispatched as a hog farm scout to the Texas panhandle area where he soon becomes immersed in its folklore and way of life. Determined not to inherit his parents' irresponsibility, he strongly believes 'in following through on something he said he would do no matter how much he hated it' but his newfound feelings of belonging are at odds with fulfilling his assignment.

Dolon
The Faerie Queene, 1590–6
Sir Edmund Spenser

Dolon is an evil man of subtle wit and cunning mind, whose name refers to his treacherous nature. He was once a knight, but through his treachery and slyness he brought other knights to their downfall. He is the father of three sons, one of whom has been killed by ARTEGAL, THE KNIGHT OF JUSTICE, and he now seeks revenge.

Dombey, Edith, formerly Granger
Dombey and Son, 1848
Charles Dickens

The daughter of THE HON MRS SKEWTON, widow of Colonel Granger and second wife of MR DOMBEY, she is 'very handsome, very haughty, very wilful'. Pure at heart herself, she is persuaded by her scheming mother to marry Dombey for his money and position, and although it is a loveless marriage, she grows fond of FLORENCE DOMBEY, who calls her 'Mama'. To revenge herself on Dombey, she elopes to Dijon with JAMES CARKER, but she deserts him in the same hour they meet, revealing that she loathes him. She is unaware that she has a cousin who resembles her in beauty and pride, ALICE MARWOOD, who was previously seduced and abandoned by Carker and who has sought revenge by disclosing the elopement to Dombey. Years later, she meets Florence again, protesting her innocence and begging forgiveness for bringing shame on the family.

Dombey, Florence
Dombey and Son, 1848
Charles Dickens

The daughter of MR DOMBEY by his late wife, and the loving sister of PAUL DOMBEY, who calls her 'Floy'. Despising her for not being a boy, and jealous of Paul's love for her, her father rejects her, but she is loved by her stepmother, EDITH DOMBEY. The day after Edith elopes, she is driven from home by a blow from her father and takes refuge with CAPTAIN EDWARD CUTTLE, whom she met when WALTER GAY rescued her after her abduction by MRS BROWN. She is looked after by POLLY TOODLE and SUSAN NIPPER, and MR TOOTS falls in love with her and gives her the dog, Diogenes. After eventually marrying Walter, she goes to China with him. When they return to England, her broken, bankrupt and penitent father comes to live with them and their children, Paul and Florence, and she is reconciled with Edith.

Dombey, Mr Paul
Dombey and Son, 1848
Charles Dickens

A proud, wealthy merchant, head of the firm of Dombey and Son, he spurns his older child, FLORENCE DOMBEY, and her timid love for him, and focuses his affection and expectations on his son, PAUL DOMBEY, whose mother died giving birth to him and who dies himself aged only six. His loveless second marriage, to the proud EDITH DOMBEY, collapses when she elopes to Dijon with his firm's manager, JAMES CARKER. Having pursued Carker and seen him killed under a train, he feels disgraced, neglects his business and goes bankrupt. His junior clerk, JOHN CARKER, secretly makes over to him the annual interest on the fortune he has inherited from his brother, James. Penitent, wiser and humbled, he lives out his days cared for by Florence and WALTER GAY and their children.

Dombey, Paul
Dombey and Son, 1848
Charles Dickens

The frail son of MR DOMBEY, and heir to the firm of Dombey and Son, he is the focus of his father's love and expectations but reserves his own love for his sister, FLORENCE DOMBEY, whom he calls 'Floy'. Cosseted by his wet-nurse, POLLY TOODLE, and the servant, SUSAN NIPPER, he is wise beyond his years, with 'a strange, old-fashioned, thoughtful way'. Although he briefly withstands the rigours of DOCTOR BLIMBER's school, accompanied by his sister, he soon declines and dies aged only six, in the embrace of Florence. His death leaves his father distraught and disliking Florence more intensely.

Domkin, Grandma
Cousin From Fiji, 1945
Norman Lindsay

As matriarch of the family, she gives it its moral tone. Unfortunately for the other Domkins' social pretensions, she has lapsed into idiotic senility.

Domkin, Uncle George
Cousin From Fiji, 1945
Norman Lindsay

Though outwardly he is a model of middle-class

Australian rectitude, his private life is a tissue of deceit. Teetering on the verge of financial ruin and disgrace, he still manages to sustain two mistresses, unable to decide between them.

Domostroy, Patrick
Pinball, 1982
Jerzy Kosinski
A once-inventive and highly respected composer, reduced to playing an electronic organ in a Bronx nightclub-cum-pinball arcade, he is the opposite and apparent nemesis to the mysterious Goddard, a highly successful rock musician whose true identity is not known to the public.

Don
Don's Party, 1972
David Williamson
On Federal Election night, 1969, Don, a Melbourne schoolteacher, invites his friends to a party celebrating a Labour election victory which unexpectedly fails to materialize. A middle-aged and middle-class graduate, his radicalism proves something of a sham. His more financially successful friends bring out a boorishness in him which is manifested by insensitivity towards his wife, Kath. He treats the election like a football match, taking the opportunity to get drunk with his mates and forgetting the result by the end of the evening. Don is a study in political, sexual and financial frustration, learning nothing from a night of petty squabbles and over-indulgence.

Dona, Lady
Frenchman's Creek, 1942
Daphne Du Maurier
Dona is a mischievous and exciting rebel among her social class and family. She has a quest for passion and daring and is a confirmed risk-taker, traits that her wealth and position enable her to indulge. Although she appears shallow in a shallow society, she is capable of depth of feeling and true passion. An incurable romantic with a boring husband and few maternal feelings, it seems most natural to her to go off to sea with her exotic French pirate, JEAN-BENOIT AUBERY. A woman who has to push the boundaries out further and further for satisfaction, she can display profound loyalty, if she thinks it deserved.

Donaghue, Jake (James)
Under the Net, 1954
Iris Murdoch
Friend of HUGO BELFOUNDER and the breezy narrator of the novel, Jake is a footloose, charming Londoner, with beguiling Irish blarney and limited respect for the law. A self-professed 'literary hack', who translates French novels, he is really a talented writer. He hates to be alone and, often with faithful henchman FINN in tow, lives with various long-suffering friends, using MRS TINCKHAM's shop as his office. Rich in human frailty, Jake's saving grace is his unfailing ironic humour.

Donalbain
Macbeth, c.1606
William Shakespeare
The younger son of the assassinated KING DUNCAN, he speaks in only one scene of the play

and, perhaps surprisingly, does not reappear with the newly victorious MALCOLM, his brother, at the play's end. Though his contribution is essentially a reflection of his brother's thinking, he is at least Malcolm's equal in language and intellect, realizing immediately after his father's death, 'Where we are/There's daggers in men's smiles' and then making his escape, to Ireland.

Doña Maria → Marquesa de Montemayor, the

Donatello, Count of Monte Beni
The Marble Faun, 1860
Nathaniel Hawthorne
The aristocratic admirer of the art student MIRIAM and killer of her shadowy nemesis. He represents man in the state of nature, without knowledge of sin or guilt. He resembles the Faun of Praxiteles, and it is left unclear whether his ears, covered by long hair, are human or animal. His unthinking act of violence is seen as a 'happy fall' into the human condition, an induction into the moral and tragic.

Don Horatio
The Spanish Tragedy, 1592
Thomas Kyd
The son of HIERONIMO, Don Horatio is in love with, and is loved by, BEL-IMPERIA. He is as quick-witted and impetuous as she but, alas, does not live so long. His murder by PRINCE BALTHAZAR and DON LORENZO provides the mainspring of the plot: revenge by his father.

Don John
Much Ado About Nothing, 1598/1600
William Shakespeare
As he confesses he is a 'plain-dealing villain', enjoying causing trouble and seeking ways to harm those who are close to his brother DON PEDRO. The stigma of his illegitimacy, and the fact that he has no claim to any of his family's riches, rankle with him. Although he is of a melancholy nature he is treated civilly when with others, but prefers to keep his own company or that of his henchmen. There are few who actually like him, yet his charges against HERO are believed instantly.

Don Juan
Fifine at the Fair, 1872
Robert Browning
Although he is not named, it is convenient to call this speaker Don Juan. Conversing with his wife Elvira as they walk through a fair, he appears to be discoursing on philosophical questions about the reality of perception, using the dancer Fifine as an example of all that is ephemeral and his wife as all that is stable. But the entire argument proves to be merely a smoke-screen to cover up his infidelity with Fifine. He makes a feeble excuse to leave Elvira and visit Fifine again, callously giving his wife permission to leave him if he is more than five minutes.

Donkin
The Nigger of the Narcissus, 1897
Joseph Conrad
A troublemaking, anarchic young sailor who is

allied with JAMES WAIT against Captain Allistoun and SINGLETON on the *Narcissus*. He is an outcast with criminal tendencies, a confidence trickster who lacks a sense of duty and the courage and loyalty to join in for the common good on ship. He attempts to incite the crew to mutiny, but is eventually imprisoned after a violent confrontation with the captain.

Don Lorenzo
The Spanish Tragedy, 1599
Thomas Kyd

The son of the DUKE OF CASTILE and brother of BEL-IMPERIA, Lorenzo is almost the only person in the play who can be called truly malicious from the outset. He also has a developed streak of black humour: having just hanged DON HORATIO, he observes (in a reference to Horatio's relatively low birth): 'Yet he is at the highest now he is dead'.

Donn, Arabella
Jude the Obscure, 1895
Thomas Hardy

A ruthless country girl who has an astonishing sharpness of wit. Lively, resourceful and lustful, her morality is often dubious and her lack of analysis of base motives allows her to live exactly as she wants to. With few finer feelings, she despises JUDE FAWLEY's intellectual aspirations and survives on instinct alone.

Donne
Palace of the Peacock, 1960, part of *The Guyana Quartet*, 1985
Wilson Harris

A horseman who casts a cold eye on death, even as he is struck down. He bears the name of Mozart's promiscuous Don, but also of the English poet who declared victory over death. He tells his brother THE DREAMER, 'I'm the last landlord. I tell you I fight everything in nature ... I'm everything. Midwife, yes, doctor, yes, gaoler, judge, hangman, every blasted thing'. He is a latter-day Conquistador, brutal and idealistic, greedy but distinguished by the power of his imagination.

Donnel Dhu, the Black Prophet
The Black Prophet, 1847
William Carleton

A sinister seer in rural Ireland. He is 'provided with a set of prophetic declamations suited to particular occasions and circumstances', which he delivered 'in a voice of high and monotonous recitative, that caused them to fall with very impressive effect' on his simple listeners. He is strongly built, with features which are an 'indication of a two-fold character', and has a 'stern and inhuman' expression 'of great cruelty and extraordinary cunning'. He is convicted of murder, but 'neither admitted his guilt, not attempted to maintain his innocence, but passed out of existence like a man who was already wearied with its cares'.

Donnerhugel, Rudolph
Anne of Geierstein, or The Maiden in the Mist, 1829
Sir Walter Scott

The nephew of ARNOLD BIEDERMAN, he is fiercely committed to Swiss independence and has formed a league to defend it. Impressed but inflamed by ARTHUR PHILIPSON's skills as a bowman, he is eventually killed in the lists by the young Englishman.

Donners, Sir Magnus
A Dance to the Music of Time, 12 volumes, 1951–75
Anthony Powell

Known as 'the Chief', he is a rich industrialist and patron of the arts, the head of Donners-Brebner. Tallish, good-looking, with green eyes, he has a 'decidedly parsonic' air. Of Germanic or Scandinavian extraction, during World War I he is a member of the government. He employs KENNETH WIDMERPOOL, but sacks him for intriguing. A collector of paintings but with a low taste in literature, he has a firm grasp of cliché. Though he loses his parliamentary seat in 1924, during World War II he is a member of Churchill's War Cabinet. His voyeurism is the subject of much speculation, which Widmerpool belatedly acknowledges in *Hearing Secret Harmonies* (1975), referring euphemistically to his 'irregular practices'.

Donnithorne, Arthur
Adam Bede, 1859
George Eliot

A gentleman farmer, anxious to be loved by all, Arthur shows a patronizing disposition to those below him, wishing them to touch their caps to him. Though he is capable of kindness, his careless bad habits contrast with ADAM BEDE's uprightness; he seduces HETTY SORREL without serious regard for the consequences before riding off to do a spot of soldiering.

Donovan, Macy
Golconda, 1948, et seq
Vance Palmer

Donovan begins his career as a water carrier, but rapidly comes to espouse the cause of the Australian working man. He takes a job as a full-time union organizer and is inexorably drawn into politics, eventually being invited to stand as a Labour Party candidate.

Don Pedro
Much Ado About Nothing, 1598/1600
William Shakespeare

The Prince of Aragon, he is popular and good-humoured but, for his social position, he can be childishly frivolous, participating in small deceptions, such as attempting to bring BEATRICE and BENEDICK together, and wooing HERO for CLAUDIO. Yet he is easily deceived himself, accepting Hero's apparent un-faithfulness at face value. His behaviour towards her and her father, who has shown him great hospitality, is cold and callous, redolent of the soldier that he is. When he learns the truth he repents instantly, realizing that he must learn not to judge a person by outward appearance.

Donul
Young Art and Old Hector, 1942
Neil Gunn

Donul is YOUNG ART's teenage brother, who is plagued by his sibling's constant attention. While much more in tune with his place in the community, he can still at times sympathize with the youngster's desire to emulate his elders, but more often than not Art's attempts are met with contempt and rejection. Donul has grown beyond the imagination of childhood, and regards his young brother as a nuisance.

Doolittle, Alfred
Pygmalion, 1913
George Bernard Shaw

An elderly but vigorous dustman, with neither fear nor conscience, Doolittle is the father of ELIZA DOOLITTLE, a flower girl taken up by PROFESSOR HENRY HIGGINS. For five pounds, he jovially agrees to Higgins keeping her. Apart from drinking and mild swindling, Doolittle's preference is to do little and be 'one of the undeserving poor'. Yet Higgins's facetious remark that he is the most original moralist in England results in his being bequeathed £3,000 a year by an American moral reformist. Doolittle reappears transformed: dressed as a gentleman, about to marry his mistress, angrily accountable to 'middle class morality'.

Doolittle, Eliza
Pygmalion, 1913
George Bernard Shaw

The howling, prudish, tenacious Eliza is an 18-year-old flower girl whom the phoneticist PROFESSOR HENRY HIGGINS discovers one rainswept evening sheltering in the portico of St Paul's, Covent Garden. She wants to improve her speech to work in a florist's; he accepts a wager from COL PICKERING that he can thereby infiltrate her into polite society. Eliza later resents being remodelled into an automaton and having her feelings disregarded. She does not want Higgins's love but his respect. Her eventual rebellion is so devastating that by the end of the play she has asserted her right to live her own life and state the terms of any relationship.

Doone, Carver
Lorna Doone, 1869
R D Blackmore

Carver is the most feared of the Doones of Bagworthy, a lawless family that inspires 'the awe of all Devon and Somerset', and which holds LORNA DOONE captive. A giant of a man, Carver is courageous, cunning, vengeful and defiant. It is difficult to make a case for him as being anything other than an archetypal villain of Victorian romantic literature, but perhaps that is the reason for his on-going appeal.

Doone, Lorna
Lorna Doone, 1869
R D Blackmore

Kidnapped as a child by the Doones, a family of west-country outlaws and murderers, Lorna grows up into a beautiful young woman. Sensitive, chaste, pure in thought and complexion, she is the 'delight' of JOHN RIDD, who loves her, at first, from afar. For sentimental Victorians, Lorna epitomized the ideal woman, remaining virtuous despite being held captive by the wicked Doones. To a more modern and cynical age, Lorna might appear incredible, but

her sense of fun, her shrewdness and streak of recklessness make her an enduring romantic creation.

Dora (Dora Flood)
Cannery Row, 1945
John Steinbeck

The proprietress and madam of the Bear Flag 'Restaurant', she is 'a great big woman with flaming orange hair and a taste for Nile-green evening dresses ... through the exercise of special gifts of tact and honesty, charity and a certain realism [she has] made herself respected by the intelligent, the learned and the kind'.

Dores, Henderson
Stars and Bars, 1984
William Boyd

An Englishman in New York, Henderson Dores loves America but doubts whether America loves him. That people like him on first acquaintance is something he finds bewildering, as he does not like himself very much at all. He came to New York to effect a change of the spirit from something inhibitedly English to something more confidently worldly. He is almost 40, just under six feet tall and works at a fine art auctioneers. As he emerges from crippling shyness, he discovers that all he has to protect him is his native culture.

Dorigen
'The Franklin's Tale', in *The Canterbury Tales*,
c.1387–1400
Geoffrey Chaucer

She wishes to be the perfect wife to ARVERAGUS, but broken-hearted at his long absence and terrified that the rocks will wreck his ship she makes a foolish bargain with AURELIUS that she believes she will never have to keep. When the rocks disappear by magic she is faced with keeping the bargain and committing adultery, but being honest by nature tells her husband. Her love for Arveragus is revealed by her grief, persuading Aurelius to release her.

Dorimant
The Man of Mode, 1676
Sir George Etherege

A rake of bitingly dry wit, Dorimant begins to fall in love with HARRIET WOODVIL at the same time as discarding his mistress, MRS LOVEIT, with the help of BELLINDA, whom he seduces. At one stage, he has 'more Mistresses now depending than the most eminent Lawyer in England has Causes'. Yet beneath the surface of his flamboyance, and the undoubted entertainment of his roguishly amorous intrigues, there is something harsher in Dorimant than mere unscrupulousness. He derives pleasure not merely in collecting women, but in rejecting them. He is cynical and cruel, a misogynist enjoying the frisson of hurting women emotionally.

Dorinda
The Beaux' Stratagem, 1707
George Farquhar

At first Dorinda's personality is bland, her function being to act as a confidante to her sister-in-law, MRS SULLEN, whose side she takes against her dour brother. However, unlike that other lady she is not content or happy living in the country. It is ironic that her innocence and good nature overcome, then transform AIMWELL's plans from the mercenary to the marital. As she develops she reveals herself to be kind and considerate even to her supposed rival, Cherry.

Dormouse, the
Alice's Adventures in Wonderland, 1865
Lewis Carroll

The Dormouse, the third person at THE MAD HATTER's tea party, is half-asleep; the Hatter pours tea on its nose to waken it. It catches a word from the Hatter's song and repeats 'Twinkle, twinkle, twinkle, twinkle' so often that its companions have to pinch him to make him stop. It sleepily starts a tale about three little girls who lived in a treacle well and drew things beginning with M, and falls asleep again. Roused, it lists mousetrap, moon, memory, muchness … When ALICE leaves the tea party in disgust, the Hatter and THE MARCH HARE try to stuff the Dormouse into the teapot. It appears again at the trial of the Knave of Hearts, grumbling that Alice, sitting next to it, is squeezing it by growing too fast.

Dorothy
The Wonderful Wizard of Oz, 1900
L Frank Baum

A young Kansan girl whirled away from her home by a cyclone and deposited in the magical Land of Oz; there she is protected by a charmed cap and slippers. She is not particularly well-rounded, physically or psychologically, and her extra-ordinary journey is not intended to represent any transition into womanhood or to point up any moral more forcible than that childhood is precious and magically protective and should be preserved for as long as possible.

Dorrit, Amy, known as **Little Dorrit**
Little Dorrit, 1857
Charles Dickens

The daughter of WILLIAM DORRIT and niece of FREDERICK DORRIT, through whom she eventually gains a legacy from the father of ARTHUR CLENNAM. Though aged 22, she is diminutive and looks 'little more than half that age'. Born in the Marshalsea debtors' prison, she is called 'the Child of the Marshalsea' and cares for her widowed father and her selfish brother and sister, EDWARD and FANNY DORRIT. She looks after a simple-minded girl, Maggy, who calls her 'Little Mother'. MR PLORNISH finds her work as a needlewoman with MRS CLENNAM, and she meets ARTHUR CLENNAM and falls in love. FLORA FINCHING becomes another kind patron. When her father inherits his fortune, she accompanies the family on a Grand Tour, during which both her father and uncle die and their money is lost in the bankruptcy of MR MERDLE. Returning to London, she finds Clennam in the Marshalsea, and he at last recognizes her qualities. She learns of her legacy from Mrs Clennam and, on Clennam's release, they are married.

Dorrit, Edward, known as **Tip**
Little Dorrit, 1857
Charles Dickens

The son of WILLIAM DORRIT and brother of AMY and FANNY DORRIT. The influence of the Marshalsea prison has made him a selfish dissolute, unable to stick to any job and dependent on Amy for support. When the family's fortunes improve, he becomes more feckless, ruining his health by drinking.

Dorrit, Fanny
Little Dorrit, 1857
Charles Dickens

Elder sister of AMY DORRIT, she is as selfish as her brother, EDWARD DORRIT. She becomes a dancer and marries MRS MERDLE's rich but foolish son, EDMUND SPARKLER. She tyrannizes him and, being frivolous and heartless, neglects her children, leaving Amy to look after them.

Dorrit, Frederick
Little Dorrit, 1857
Charles Dickens

The gentle brother of WILLIAM DORRIT, he is ruined at the same time and supports himself by playing the clarinet in a grubby theatre orchestra. In his youth, he had helped the real mother of ARTHUR CLENNAM, and he is unaware that Clennam's father left a large legacy to his daughter or, if he has no daughter, to his youngest niece, who is AMY DORRIT. When William inherits his fortune, he travels with the family but dies in Rome within a few hours of his brother.

Dorrit, William
Little Dorrit, 1857
Charles Dickens

Father of AMY, FANNY and EDWARD DORRIT and brother of FREDERICK, he has been imprisoned for debt in the Marshalsea for 25 years. Amiable but irresolute, he accepts Amy's care and support and proudly enjoys the title of 'the Father of the Marshalsea', patronizingly requiring cash 'testimonials' from visitors. When ARTHUR CLENNAM's enquiries reveal his inheritance, he leaves prison a rich man and travels with his family on the Continent, hiring MRS GENERAL to 'polish' his daughters. His mind failing, he becomes ridiculous in his pride and grand airs and slowly declines. He dies in Rome, imagining himself to be back in the Marshalsea.

Dorval, Hetty
Hetty Dorval, 1947
Ethel Wilson

This beautiful and alluring 'woman of no reputation' is unconventional, self-possessed and mysterious. She can, and indeed wants to, inspire the devotion of others, but her inner self remains aloof – untouched and untouchable. Her worldliness is curiously innocent and she is revealed to be not so much evil as amoral – a wild, unfettered beauty, who ultimately lacks essential humanity and the capacity to love.

Doubloon, Maggie
Slouching Towards Kalamazoo, 1983
Peter DeVries

The teacher and lover of 15-year-old ANTHONY

THRASHER. Having 'rescued' him from an unstructured appetite for literature, she becomes herself a repository of satirical literary references. Pregnant with their child, she has to leave the child wearing a t-shirt marked 'A+', in recollection of HESTER PRYNNE's motif in Nathaniel Hawthorne's *The Scarlet Letter* (1850). Their child is called Ahab and Maggie's surname is an oblique reference to the coin that CAPTAIN AHAB pins to the mast in *Moby-Dick* (1851).

Douglas, Charlotte, formerly **Charlotte Bogart**
A Book of Common Prayer, 1977
Joan Didion
Her immigration form for Boca Grande defines her as 'Norteamericana, Turista, Madre', the last of which is profoundly ironic, since her daughter has run away to join a revolutionary faction and her second child, born to her and her dying second husband, is hydrocephalic and moribund. In Boca Grande she dreams of a fresh start, makes elaborate plans and writes 'impenetrably euphemistic' 'Letters from South America' for the US press. Her friend and chronicler GRACE STRASSER-MENDANA strives to make a convincing profile of Charlotte's character, but comes up with nothing but 'shimmer'.

Douglas, Dougal
The Ballad of Peckham Rye, 1960
Muriel Spark
A young Scotsman of 23 with an arts degree from Edinburgh University, hired by a textile factory in Peckham 'to bring vision into the lives of the workers'. He has a crooked shoulder, a wide smile, and bumps on his head, which he claims are the stumps of amputated devilish horns. Eager to hear the stories of people's lives, he adopts roles that will appeal to them, but he has an insuperable horror of illness. He spreads discord and emotional disruption in the course of his lucrative 'human research'.

Douglas, Marin
A Book of Common Prayer, 1977
Joan Didion
The daughter of CHARLOTTE DOUGLAS and her first husband, the junior college professor Warren Bogart, she absconds and becomes an outlaw after bombing the TransAmerica building.

Douglas, Mildred
The Hairy Ape, 1922
Eugene O'Neill
The daughter of a millionaire industrialist in the steel industry, she is shocked by an encounter with the stoker YANK while slumming below decks on a transatlantic liner. By calling him a 'filthy beast' she sets in motion Yank's steady questioning of his own humanity, and it is the iron bars made in her father's factories which rob him of his freedom and ultimately his life.

Douglas, Monica
The Prime of Miss Jean Brodie, 1961
Muriel Spark
An Edinburgh schoolgirl with a violent temper and an aptitude for mathematics, Monica is the

scientific member of the 'Brodie set', taught by MISS JEAN BRODIE. Physically unattractive, with a red nose and fat legs, she later marries a scientist.

Dousterswivel, Herman
The Antiquary, 1816
Sir Walter Scott
A practised charlatan who speaks of scientific subjects 'with more assurance than knowledge', and who in female company (which is presumed to be frailer and more susceptible) discourses broadly on things magical and cabalistic. He is a Low German, a lineage considered at the time to be sufficient guarantee of intellectual sharp practice.

Dove
Maurice Guest, 1908
Henry Handel Richardson
A slight and superficial personality, part of the artistic community at Leipzig, he stands for a view of creativity that sees it as a mere scaffolding for an insecure ego. Creatively stultified himself, he imposes undue value on the creations of others.

Dowd, Johnnie
Summer of the Seventeenth Doll, 1955
Ray Lawler
Young, virile and rather shy, he represents the generation which has supplanted that of ROO WEBBER, who regards him with competitive loathing. Ironically, he is compared to the young Roo by both BARNEY IBBOT and BUBBA RYAN. As the curtain falls, he has begun a relationship with Bubba which appears destined to the same fate as that of Roo and OLIVE.

Dowell, Florence
The Good Soldier, 1915
Ford Madox Ford
The wife of JOHN DOWELL, she is a pretty, coquettish American woman who chatters constantly. However, behind her apparently airy appearance lies a particularly cruel and calculating nature. Utterly selfish, she manipulates those around her to achieve her own ends. Her greatest victim is her husband, whom she married out of convenience, and whom she has turned into a ridiculous nursemaid figure by feigning a heart condition. This has left her free to carry on her affairs with other men. Her whole existence is stage-managed and when events overtake her she quits life in a suitably dramatic way, by committing suicide.

Dowell, John
The Good Soldier, 1915
Ford Madox Ford
The American narrator of a tale of hypocrisy and infidelity involving himself, his wife FLORENCE DOWELL, and the English couple, EDWARD and LEONORA ASHBURNHAM. Dowell appears unbelievably naive, allowing his wife to dupe him into taking her to live in Europe and turning him into a ridiculous nursemaid figure. A follower rather than a leader, Dowell grasps any stability he can and steers clear of emotions. The same is true of his story-telling; he adopts a friendly fireside tone and restricts himself to

sketching impressions. However, the horrors of the events are conveyed, showing that his innocence is not innate but adopted as a defence against reality.

Dowler, Mr
Pickwick Papers, 1837
Charles Dickens
A blustering ex-army officer who challenges NATHANIEL WINKLE to a duel in Bath in the mistaken belief that Mrs Dowler has been insulted. To avoid the duel, he absconds to Bristol, only to meet Winkle, who has done the same.

Dowling, Father
Such is My Beloved, 1934
Morley Callaghan
A Canadian priest, torn between his instinctive sympathy for the poor and downtrodden, notably two prostitutes he befriends, and his growing awareness of a social position which has taken him far away from his own working-class origins.

Dowling, Margo
The Big Money, 1936, part of the *U.S.A.* trilogy, 1938
John Dos Passos
Raised on the tawdry vaudeville circuit by her stepmother, beautiful Margo dreams of success and glory as a famous movie-star. Resilient and audacious, her ability to fabricate stories about herself works to her benefit, and despite being a terrible gold-digger, she remains humorously likeable, a born survivor whose sharp wits and good looks help her claw her way out of the gutter.

Downey, Ella
All God's Chillun Got Wings, 1924
Eugene O'Neill
A white woman, still mired in prejudice, who nonetheless accepts the offer of marriage with an intellectually superior black man, JIM HARRIS, whom she has previously rejected. Her first 'marriage', to the brutal Mickey, ends with the death of their child. Ella and Jim live for a time in France, traditional refuge for mixed relationships, but on their return to the USA her racism re-emerges and she goes mad, believing herself a child again.

Downright, George
Every Man in his Humour, 1598
Ben Jonson
The elder brother of WELLBRED, Downright is an irritable and straightlaced moralist, being especially put out by the behaviour of his brother and his friends, whom he sees as dissolute. He insults Wellbred and his friends, challenges CAPTAIN BOBADILL to a duel and defeats him because Bobadill, a coward, will not draw. Downright's 'humour' (or foolishness) is to accuse everyone of malicious or immoral behaviour without bothering to ascertain the facts.

Doyce, Daniel
Little Dorrit, 1857
Charles Dickens
An engineer and inventor, a friend of MR MEAGLES and ARTHUR CLENNAM's partner in an engineering firm in Bleeding Heart Yard. His attempts to patent his invention have been frustrated for years by the Circumlocution Office, and he goes abroad to gain recognition. Clennam invests the firm's money in a scheme of MR MERDLE, but on Merdle's collapse, Clennam is imprisoned for debt in the Marshalsea. Doyce returns, having been successful abroad and, with the help of Meagles, ensures Clennam's release.

Doyle, Larry (Laurence)
John Bull's Other Island, 1904
George Bernard Shaw
Doyle is a civil engineer in partnership with TOM BROADBENT. He is 36 and good-looking but, partly because he is an Irishman displaced in London, he has an air of restlessness and dissatisfaction in strong contrast to his partner's eupeptic jollity. After an 18-year absence, he reluctantly accompanies Broadbent to Ireland, realizing this will entail a confrontation with his former sweetheart NORA REILLY. If Broadbent represents action and improvement, Doyle represents intellect. He has rejected Ireland and smothered his capacity for dreams and emotional expression: 'He's as clever as be-blowed', Broadbent tells Nora, 'but ... he doesn't really care for anything or anybody'.

Doyle, Patrick
A Disaffection, 1989
James Kelman
A teacher who has 'become sickened by it', Doyle is an unmarried mid-twenties angst-ridden cynic. He frequently compares his life to that of the German poet Hölderlin, who went mad; he also muses on Cicero, Pythagoras and Socrates: 'these fucking ancient bastards hit the nail on the head'. He loves a fellow teacher, unrequited; she is disturbed by his anti-school anti-authoritarianism and would be more so if she heard him (involuntarily) vomiting in class or (deliberately) making his class say 'The present government, in suppressing the poor, is suppressing our parents'.

Dracula, Count
Dracula, 1897
Bram Stoker
A near-immortal Transylvanian vampire, who casts no reflection in the mirror, he is tall and gaunt, with a thin, aquiline nose, pale and 'extremely pointed' ears, and a mouth which is 'fixed and rather cruel-looking, with peculiarly sharp white teeth' which protrude over his lips. He feasts on the blood of young women, after which he 'looks as if his youth had been half-renewed'. He can metamorphose into animal shapes, and is relentlessly cruel, cold, immensely cunning, and wholly unforgiving. His cloaked figure is among the most famous of all manifestations of the horror genre.

Drake, Paul
The Case of the Velvet Claws, 1933, et seq
Erle Stanley Gardner
A brilliant detective, he is the aide-de-camp for the legendary lawyer PERRY MASON, his job being to untangle the knotty details of evidence, and

produce the case-winning rabbit out of the hat. This he can do because of his investigative vision and imagination. On more than a few occasions he arrives in the nick of time with the crucial missing piece of the jigsaw. Happy to be a back-room boy, he is unfailingly loyal and supportive.

Drake, Temple
Sanctuary, 1931, original text published 1981
Requiem for a Nun, 1951
William Faulkner

A teenage college student in Mississippi, she combines virginal allure with a knowing self-possession; as such, and as her curious name suggests, she is the repository of Faulkner's most complex feelings about Southern womanhood. Out on a necking date with the drunken GOWAN STEVENS, she is abducted by the animalistic but impotent POPEYE, who rapes her with perhaps the most notorious prop in American literature – the much-discussed bloody corncob – before placing her in a Memphis whorehouse. At the trial, she perjures herself to secure the conviction – and eventual lynching – of an innocent man. Last seen (in *Sanctuary*) on her father's arm in Paris, she is still protesting her 'innocence' and wronged honour in the sequel, *Requiem for a Nun*, where she is married to her former unreliable beau, Gowan Stevens.

Drawcansir
The Rehearsal, 1671
George Villiers, 2nd Duke of Buckingham

A character in the dreadful heroic drama by BAYES, which is rehearsed within the play. Described as 'a fierce Hero', he is a bombastic, bloodthirsty bully, who defeats entire armies and announces, 'I slay both friend and foe'.

Dreamer, the
Palace of the Peacock, 1960, part of *The Guyana Quartet*, 1985
Wilson Harris

The narrator, he is DONNE's brother, and is haunted by a dream of Donne's death. Afflicted with an incurable infection on one side, he has 'one dead seeing eye, and one living closed eye', a blindness that vouchsafes him a bitter vision of his brother's brutal idealism.

Dred
Dred: A Tale of the Great Dismal Swamp, 1856
Harriet Beecher Stowe

A runaway slave (bearing a name that is enshrined in the American Constitution through the Dred Scott Case) whose existence in the Great Dismal Swamp is a symbol of the degrading effects of life under the 'peculiar institution' that was shortly to come to an end, albeit by more violent and catastrophic means than Stowe suggests.

Dressler, Martin
Martin Dressler: The Tale of an American Dreamer, 1996
Steven Millhauser

A cigar maker's son in late 19th-century Manhattan, Martin is 14 years old when he enters the hotel business as a bellhop. Over the

years his vision and entrepreneurial skill lead him to ever greater heights of success, culminating in the building of the fabulous Grand Cosmo, a 'complete and self-sufficient world' that he imagines will render the city itself unnecessary. Driven by restlessness and a love of progress, he immerses himself so completely in the pursuit of his dreams that he loses his sense of proportion and becomes the agent of his own failure.

Driffield, Edward
Cakes and Ale, 1930
W Somerset Maugham

The archetypal Grand Old Man of letters, he was said (by everyone but Maugham, who routinely denied such associations) to be a portrait of the novelist Thomas Hardy. Gamy, cantankerous and averse to bathing, he is unmistakable and neatly debunks the idealized public image of the great writer.

Driffield, Rosie
Cakes and Ale, 1930
W Somerset Maugham

The first wife of the ageing writer EDWARD DRIFFIELD, she is recalled by the narrator in a series of flashbacks as a vivacious and attractive young woman. Her sexual promiscuity is an embarrassment to Driffield's second wife and friends, who attempt to remove all trace of her from the great man's literary legacy.

Drinkard, the Palm-Wine
The Palm-Wine Drinkard and His Dead Palm-Wine Tapster in the Deads' Town, 1952
Amos Tutuola

The eldest, and by far the laziest, of eight children, 'I had no other work more than to drink palm wine in my life'. This he does with heroic concentration, recounting his adventures in a drunken stream-of-consciousness.

Driscoll, Judge York Leicester
The Tragedy of Pudd'nhead Wilson, 1894
Mark Twain

Descended from the First Families of Old Virginia, the just, generous and kind-hearted judge is 'respected, esteemed and beloved' by the people of Dawson's Landing, Missouri. Although a 'freethinker', he has an anachronistic and unyielding reverence for his bloodline and the honour of the family name; a delightful irony given that his heir, the orphaned 'nephew' who lives under his roof and bears the name of Tom Driscoll, is unbeknown to the judge, the son of a slave (and actually called CHAMBERS).

Driscoll, Percy Northumberland
The Tragedy of Pudd'nhead Wilson, 1894
Mark Twain

Initially encountered as 'a prosperous man with a good head for speculations' and a growing fortune, Percy loses his wife shortly after the birth of his last, and only surviving child, TOM DRISCOLL. His white-skinned slave ROXY secretly substitutes his child for her own son, CHAMBERS. Unaware of the deception, Percy idolizes the boy for the remaining years of his life and deals harshly with his true son, whom he believes to be a slave child. Mercifully, the truth is still unknown to Percy when he dies a penniless and broken man.

Driscoll, Tom, properly **Thomas à Becket**
The Tragedy of Pudd'nhead Wilson, 1894
Mark Twain

The unfortunate Driscoll is secretly substituted in infancy for a white-skinned slave child with Negro blood called CHAMBERS. He therefore grows up speaking, thinking and behaving like a slave and spends a miserable childhood as the drudge and protector of 'Tom Driscoll', the true slave, at whose hands he suffers cruelty and humiliation. The real Tom endures stoically, repeatedly displaying the superiority of his strength, courage and moral rectitude over those of his tormentor.

Dr Jekyll/Mr Hyde
The Strange Case of Dr. Jekyll and Mr. Hyde, 1886
Robert Louis Stevenson

This is the most famous and succinct expression of Stevenson's views on the duality (and multeity) of the human personality. Dr Jekyll worships the ideal of perfectibility and attempts, in an exercise of free will, to create in himself a being from which all evil has been extracted. The result of this division of self is Mr Hyde, Jekyll's alter ego, who contains all the physical, emotional and sexual evil the doctor had hoped to expunge from his system. Jekyll contemplates his creature with terrified anxiety. His utopian experiment into the schizoid nature of man has led to a descent into chaos, for he has not been able to see that man is essentially ambiguous and ambivalent: that good and evil are mutually dependent.

Dromio of Ephesus
The Comedy of Errors, c.1594
William Shakespeare

The twin brother of DROMIO OF SYRACUSE, the servant of ANTIPHOLUS OF SYRACUSE, Dromio of Ephesus is the servant of ANTIPHOLUS OF EPHESUS. As the Antipholi are mistaken for each other, so are the Dromios, who also mistake their masters for each other, just as their masters mistake them. Like his master, Dromio is certified mad during the course of the play. He is, though, a more farcical character, suffering the traditional fate of clowns and servants by being beaten before taking part in the final reunions.

Dromio of Syracuse
The Comedy of Errors, c.1594
William Shakespeare

The twin brother of DROMIO OF EPHESUS, the servant of ANTIPHOLUS OF EPHESUS, Dromio of Syracuse is the servant of ANTIPHOLUS OF SYRACUSE. The Antipholi and the Dromios are mistaken for each other and share a series of adventures based upon false assumptions and mistaken identity. Dromio of Syracuse, as farcical a character as his brother, finds himself beaten for misdemeanours outside his control before discovering who is who in the reconciliations at the end of the play.

Drood, Edwin
The Mystery of Edwin Drood, 1870
Charles Dickens

A young engineer, an orphan and the nephew of MR JOHN JASPER. Drood was betrothed to ROSA BUD when they were children, but on Rosa's turning 18, they agree to break off their engagement and remain friends. At the home of Jasper, Drood meets NEVILLE LANDLESS, and the two instantly dislike each other. After drinking wine apparently spiked by Jasper, they quarrel violently. Soon afterwards, Drood disappears and, though his body is not found, suspicion falls upon Landless. Jasper vows to track down his nephew's murderer, but the novel breaks off with the mystery unsolved.

Droogs, the
A Clockwork Orange, 1962
Anthony Burgess

Speaking a language of their own and taking violent anarchy wherever they go in a futuristic Britain of grim desolation, they murder and rape at will. Lacking any moral sense and under the influence of hallucinogenic drugs, they practise their mindless violence within a society that responds by using science to change character. Horrifying though this violence is, it represents for the Droogs a statement about their individuality and the desire to challenge the unfair divisions between rich and poor. They remain, however, terrifying in their nihilism.

Drouet, Charles
Sister Carrie, 1900, suppressed; reissued 1907, complete text published 1983
Theodore Dreiser

A young 'drummer' or salesman in Chicago. He impresses the country girl CARRIE MEEBER with his worldliness and apparent sophistication and sets her up as his mistress, after which his shortcomings become ever more evident.

Drover's Wife, the
'The Drover's Wife', in *While the Billy Boils: Second Series*, 1892
Henry Lawson

Toughened by isolation (her husband is away with the herds much of the time) she nonetheless retains a surprising bloom of femininity and an affectionately protective stance towards her small but impressively foul-mouthed family. 'As a girl she built the usual castles in the air; but all her girlish hopes and aspirations have long been dead. She finds all the excitement and recreation she needs in the *Young Ladies' Journal*, and Heaven help her! takes a pleasure in the fashion plates … Her surroundings are not favourable to the development of the "womanly" or sentimental side of nature.'

Drugger
The Alchemist, 1610
Ben Jonson

One of several gullible people who seek advice at the so-called alchemy practice run by the cheats SUBTLE, FACE and DOL COMMON. The owner of a tobacco shop, he wants a means of establishing his success as quickly as possible; gratefully, he accepts the family crest which Subtle offers. He also accepts advice to remedy his faltering love life, putting on a flamboyant Spanish costume in a misguided attempt to impress DAME PLIANT.

Drummle, Bentley
Great Expectations, 1861
Charles Dickens

PIP's enemy and fellow boarder at MATTHEW POCKET's, he is an idle, proud young brute whom ESTELLA marries for money and position. He treats her cruelly and they separate. MR JAGGERS nicknames him 'The Spider' and believes him to be an intriguing study in criminality.

Drummond, Catriona
Catriona, 1893
Robert Louis Stevenson

A vibrant Highland heroine who takes over the role of ALAN BRECK in the second half of the tale, and completes the education of DAVID BALFOUR by introducing him to the emotional and sexual charms of women. Although, in some respects, she remains a shadowy figure, Catriona makes a palpable impression on David. She is a beautiful girl who has 'a kind of brightness in her like a coal of fire'. She has the capacity to challenge David's passivity and lift his spirits. In the contest between the Highlander (Catriona) and the Lowlander (David), it is clear that Stevenson habitually feels that the former, though flawed, has the most estimable spirit.

Drummond, Hugh 'Bull-dog'
Bull-dog Drummond, 1920
'Sapper' (Herman Cyril McNeile)

A larger-than-life hero of countless adventures, he meets his enemies with a very British kind of courage and disdain, a concentration on justice and fair play and a willingness to enter the lion's den with hardly a hair turned. He is an old-fashioned Buchanesque hero who stumbles on adventure and takes up the challenge with no-nonsense courage and a love of Britain. In his personal quest to see his arch enemy, Carl Petersen, brought to justice, he drives his adventures along at a headlong pace, much as he drives his prized Bentley along the country roads of England. He evidences all the 'bulldog' tenacity of the true Brit and symbolizes the archetypal hero's capacity for quick, ingenious thinking.

Drummond, James More
Catriona, 1893
Robert Louis Stevenson

The father of CATRIONA DRUMMOND. When DAVID BALFOUR first encounters him he feels a sense of pity for him, since the man seems 'a prey to a painful uneasiness'. However, on further inspection, James emerges as a mean-spirited, selfish man, with little sense of honour or personal respect, willing to do anything to escape the 'trumped-up' charge of which he is accused. James has little shame or pride in trying to seek help from whatever quarter. He is a low, despised creature.

Drunk Man, the
A Drunk Man Looks at the Thistle, 1925
Hugh MacDiarmid

Like TAM O'SHANTER, the Drunk Man goes

homeward and wifeward from the pub, under the gaze of the moon, and has disturbing visions while inebriated. Unlike Tam, however, he speculates on matters philosophical, musing over Dostoevsky, Spengler and Nietzsche and the cultural/political state of modern Scotland. Should readers be surprised at his erudition, 'You ha'ena' the respect you s'ud/For oor guid Scottish schoolin''.

Druse, Private Carter
'A Horseman in the Sky', in *Tales of Soldiers and Civilians*, 1891, published as *In the Midst of Life*, 1892
Ambrose Bierce

A young Virginian, 'the son of wealthy parents, an only child, [he] had known such ease and cultivation and high living as wealth and taste were able to command'. When the Civil War begins, he enlists with the Union army, an act that induces his father to disown him, albeit with grave courtesy. Selected for duty at an isolated outpost (as Bierce's heroes tend to be) he wakens to see a figure on horseback silhouetted against the sky. He fires, and man and horse plunge to the ground. Druse then blandly tells his sergeant that the man he has shot is his own father.

Dryfesdale
The Abbot, 1820
Sir Walter Scott

The steward at Lochleven, he is a fanatic, a regressive Anabaptist with a sourly prejudiced view of all other creeds. In an atmosphere of almost toxic hostility, it is he who actually tries to introduce poison into MARY, QUEEN OF SCOTS' food.

Dryfoos
A Hazard of New Fortunes, 1890
William Dean Howells

A wealthy farmer who has become rich through the discovery of natural gas on his land, he sets up the magazine *Every Other Week* as a worthy investment for his money and as a place to give his son CONRAD DRYFOOS an apparently risk-free training in business.

Dryfoos, Conrad
A Hazard of New Fortunes, 1890
William Dean Howells

The son of DRYFOOS, the wealthy proprietor of *Every Other Week*, a journal whose main purpose is to give Conrad a grounding in business. However, the young man becomes embroiled in socialist politics and is killed by a stray bullet during a strike demonstration.

Dubbo, Alf
Riders in the Chariot, 1961
Patrick White

One of the novel's four protagonists, the others being RUTH GODBOLD, MARY HARE and MORDECAI HIMMELFARB. Dubbo is the one most closely associated with the world of the imagination and mystery. A secret artist, he is an illegitimate, tubercular, half-caste Aboriginal who works alongside Himmelfarb at a bicycle-lamp factory. A compassionate man, he finds beauty and lyricism in the sleazier areas of

Sydney, where he shares a room with a prostitute. A natural outsider and a man apparently almost without moral sense, he recognizes in others something he has already recognized in himself: a need for spiritual freedom.

Dubedat, Jennifer
The Doctor's Dilemma, 1906
George Bernard Shaw

The beautiful wife of LOUIS DUBEDAT, Jennifer is a woman with 'the grace and romance of a wild creature, with a good deal of the elegance and dignity of a fine lady'. With her name derived from Guinevere, signalling Shaw's intention for his play partly to stand as a contemporary variation upon the Arthurian legend of heroism and chivalry, Jennifer romantically idealizes her husband, LOUIS DUBEDAT. After his death, her adoration of him is undimmed. But she marries again, happily, as he wished her to do, astounding the physician, SIR COLENSO RIDGEON, who erroneously believed she was attracted to him.

Dubedat, Louis
The Doctor's Dilemma, 1906
George Bernard Shaw

The 23-year-old Dubedat is a man without scruples or principles but an artist of considerable talent. (Shaw called the dishonourable man of genius 'the most tragic of all themes'.) Dubedat suffers from tuberculosis, and one of the dilemmas in the play is whether the physician SIR COLENSO RIDGEON should attempt to cure the gifted painter or the uninspiring DR BLENKINSOP. Dubedat is treated by SIR RALPH BLOOMFIELD BONINGTON and dies. Yet his tragedy is not in his death, but in his life, and the question remains whether Dubedat is a realist, or whether the effect of his unscrupulousness has been to corrupt the Life Force within him.

Dubin, William
Dubin's Lives, 1979
Bernard Malamud

A professional biographer in his late fifties, who wonders if his scrutiny of other lives has been at the expense of understanding and fully living his own. He is a moral, hard-working man, and struggles to fight off the ageing process through diet and exercise. He begins a study of the writer D H Lawrence which sparks off an examination of his own existence, and his relationship with his wife, Kitty, and their young housekeeper. In working out the dilemma, he learns to accept his own life.

DuBois, Blanche
A Streetcar Named Desire, 1947
Tennessee Williams

An intelligent but deeply confused and disturbed woman, who arrived in New Orleans to seek sanctuary at the home of her sister, STELLA KOWALSKI. Ridden with guilt over the death of her homosexual husband, Alan Grey, and sacked from her post as a teacher of English after an affair with a 17-year-old student, Blanche tries to escape from her past through literal cleansing and the prospect of marriage to the simple but

loving MITCH. However, her brother-in-law, STANLEY KOWALSKI, with 'honesty' as his defence, reveals her past, rapes her and destroys her already fragile mental state. Despite her snobbery, her promiscuity and her lying, she is a lonely woman who has 'always depended on the kindness of strangers', and may elicit considerable sympathy from the audience.

Dubrow, Donny
American Buffalo, 1975
David Mamet

The owner of a Chicago junk-shop, Donny offers friendship and employment to a young drug-addict named BOBBY GOULD. Donny imagines himself as a fairly straight sort of chap, humble and, within certain limits, reasonably honest, an anchor for others adrift upon the restless seas of life. But when the bombastic TEACH usurps their plan to steal a valuable coin collection, including an American buffalo nickel, Donny finds himself abandoning his somewhat muddled principles of friendship and honour to the extent that he finally rounds upon poor Bobby, beating him and ejecting him from the shop. Donny's delusion that he is an agent for good is ruthlessly exposed by Teach, who makes him reveal his vanity and greed.

Dubuque, the Lady from → Lady from Dubuque, the

Ducane, John
The Nice and the Good, 1968
Iris Murdoch

Silkily plausible in a way that suggests the paradox of the novel's title, he has round blue eyes and the hooked nose of a moral raptor. His hair is patchily grey; he is 43 and looks it.

Duchemin, Edith Ethel
Parade's End, 1924–8
Ford Madox Ford

A dark-haired, dark-clothed woman with an 'assured, tranquil manner'. Everything Edith Ethel thinks and does is absolutely 'in the tradition'. She suffers terrible abuse at the hands of her insane husband, yet she remains the most charming hostess. However, her 'silent heroism' masks a smug moral superiority and a deep hypocrisy. Sly and selfish, she will stop at nothing in order to maintain a smooth façade and improve her social standing.

Duchess, the
The Revenger's Tragedy, 1607
Thomas Middleton or Cyril Tourneur

THE DUKE's second wife, with three sons of her own, the youngest and 'dearest' of whom is charged with raping the wife of ANTONIO, an old nobleman. The Duchess is motivated largely by lust and apparently has an insatiable sexual appetite. She is determined to revenge herself on her husband for refusing to use his power to release her son and absolve him of his crime. She resolutely, and eventually successfully, pursues SPURIO, the Duke's illegitimate son, entering into a sexual liaison with him, not only to satisfy her lust but also to make a cuckold of her husband.

Dudgeon, Essie
The Devil's Disciple, 1897
George Bernard Shaw

The 16-year-old illegitimate child of the late Peter Dudgeon, Essie is 'a wild, timid looking creature with black hair and tanned skin', who lives with Peter's sister-in-law, RICHARD DUDGEON's mother. MRS DUDGEON resents Essie and bullies her, while JUDITH ANDERSON alternately patronizes and scolds her. Only Richard extends the hand of friendship and becomes her protector.

Dudgeon, Mrs
The Devil's Disciple, 1897
George Bernard Shaw

Mrs Dudgeon, the elderly, matronly mother of RICHARD DUDGEON, 'is not a prepossessing woman'. In fact, she is puritanical, fiercely proud, self-righteous and ill-tempered. Having worked hard all her life, she has little to show for it except an unquestioned reputation for piety and respectability among her neighbours, for whom alcohol and revelry are more tempting than religion and rectitude. Therefore, by being extremely disagreeable, Mrs Dudgeon is generally held to be extremely upright.

Dudgeon, Richard (Dick)
The Devil's Disciple, 1897
George Bernard Shaw

The 'Devil's Disciple' of the title and the family reprobate, Dudgeon's flamboyance and fanaticism almost conceal 'an extraordinary steadfastness'. He supports the American cause in the War of Independence, during which the play is set. He represents Shaw's own rebellion against British action in Ireland, but more importantly the Shavian war against false puritanism and the power of sexual attraction. He allows the British to arrest him erroneously as PASTOR ANTHONY ANDERSON, not, as Anderson's wife JUDITH ANDERSON supposes, for her sake, but because he has 'no motive' except that of acting objectively in the interests of the world.

Dudley, Constantia
Ormond, 1799
Charles Brockden Brown

A young woman who is a product of her upbringing. Educated by her father in rationalist philosophies, Constantia seeks out 'truth' (making her prey to ORMOND), and has a 'thirst for knowledge'. The imbalance in her character, a basic lack of imagination, puts her life at threat as she ventures into plague-ridden streets to do her 'duty' in paying her landlord. The strength of her character, however, outweighs her fallibilities, as evidenced by her opposition to marriage on the grounds that 'she herself would become the property of another'.

Dudley, Esther
Esther, 1884
Henry Adams

An independent and free-thinking young painter. She receives a commission to paint a church, despite her religious views, but finds herself falling in love with a young clergyman.

She comes to realize that she will never be able to reconcile their very different views on life, and breaks off the engagement, preferring to sacrifice her love rather than her beliefs.

Dud No-man
Maiden Castle, 1936
John Cowper Powys

A historical novelist, he writes in a state of trance-like inspiration, and is absorbed by the past. He has no name other than the self-adopted one he uses, 'talks' with his dead mother, and carries on a kind of cerebral love-making in his 'mental dalliance' with 'the spirit of his dead wife, who had died a virgin'. He is a 'lean, hook-nosed, clean-shaven individual' of about 40, who can be 'transported in a pleasurable glow of pride' by successfully carrying out any small physical task. He is the 'reverse of amorous', but first buys (from a circus) and then lives with WIZZIE RAVELSTON, until she denounces him as 'not a man', and rejects his sterile, 'etherealised sensuality'.

Duessa
The Faerie Queene, 1590–6
Sir Edmund Spenser

Her name means 'doubleness' and she is the epitome of duplicity. She is present throughout *The Faerie Queene* and represents the Scarlet Whore of Babylon and the faithless religion of Catholicism. She is the cruel and lecherous lover of many men, a wicked enchantress who delights in ruining the quests of passing knights. Although she appears to be beautiful, in reality she is hideously deformed, being half human and half monster, with scabbed skin, pustulating sores, a bald head and a fox's tail. She proclaims herself the daughter of deceit and shame and exists in opposition to FIDESSA, whom she claims to be.

Duffield, Hurtle
The Vivisector, 1970
Patrick White

The novel traces the life of the artist Hurtle Duffield from his childhood at the beginning of the century to his death during the 1960s. A romantic, Duffield longs to follow wherever events might lead him, yet simultaneously he yearns to impose his own will upon life and control his destiny. This results in him metaphorically treating others as a vivisector might an animal, liking to 'dissect on his drawing board down to the core, the nerves of the matter'. His experiences are shaped by several women, including a prostitute, NANCE LIGHTFOOT, a shipping magnate's wife, HERO PAVLOUSSI, and a pianist, KATHY VOLKOV. Eventually, despite his struggle to express the essence of his emotions, Duffield achieves a rather bland public fame.

Duffy, James
'A Painful Case', in *Dubliners*, 1914
James Joyce

A saturnine clerk with a harsh face, who hates both physical and mental disorder. He 'lives at a little distance from his body regarding his own acts with doubtful side glances'. Afraid of excesses he consumes the evening paper every night for dessert. He also has a habit of thinking of himself in the third person. Friendless, he sees his life as an 'adventureless tale'.

Duffy, Nicholas ('Nick')
Duffy, 1980, et seq
Dan Kavanagh

Short, stockily built, with powerful forearms and haunches, Nick Duffy is a former detective sergeant who was considered one of the 'best officers on the patch'. Incorruptible, he was put out of commission by a frame-up involving an under-age black youth. Forced to resign, he now operates as a security adviser and private investigator amidst a far from glamorous world of corruption and extortion. A promiscuous bisexual, he maintains a complex relationship with WPC Carol Lucas. Emotionally bruised and fearful of commitment, he is a stew of obsessions, from cleanliness and the ticking of clocks to the state of his health and his expanding waistline.

Dufrayer, Louise
Maurice Guest, 1908
Henry Handel Richardson

An older Australian woman living in Leipzig, where her aura of sexual experience has a strong impact on the musical community, attracting the young MAURICE GUEST, as well as the turbulent SCHILSKY.

Dufresnes, Harriet Cleve
The Little Friend, 2002
Donna Tartt

A baby when her nine-year-old brother Robin was murdered – the crime remains unsolved and has resulted in the children's mother benumbed with grief – Harriet is now twelve years old and determined both to assuage her guilt at being the surviving child and find Robin's killer to exact revenge. Living in Mississippi during the 1970s, Harriet has grown up a brooding, recalcitrant child with a vivid but fallible imagination, fuelled by voracious reading of adventure tales, particularly Captain Scott's diaries. Having decided that white-trash Danny Ratliff is the murderer, Harriet plans a series of reprisals that draw her deeper into her obsessions.

Duke, in full Harley Duke
The Battlers, 1941
Kylie Tennant

Known as 'the busker' to his fellow travellers, he has gone on the track with the naive hope of finding the road to success. A 'weedy youth with a mop of brown hair flopped over his forehead and an air of impudent self assurance', he survives by playing the odd tune and avoiding responsibility whenever possible. Generally optimistic, after months on the track Duke has spells of fear and disillusionment as he contemplates the downward spiral of his existence.

Duke, Stanley
Stanley and the Women, 1984
Kingsley Amis

Middle-aged, with a well-paid job, he lives in a comfortable part of north London, seemingly happily married to a wife who thinks of him as 'good old Stanley'. For Stanley is the sort of man who likes to please, who, although honest in his assessment of others, generally keeps his more contentious opinions to himself. Amiable, self-contained, he leads a pleasant, quiet life until Steve, his son by his first wife, begins to show signs of schizophrenia. His campaign to have him cured brings Stanley up against not only his former and present wives, but a female psychiatrist. The situation detonates all his prejudices against women, bureaucracy and modern life.

Duke, the
'My Last Duchess', in *Dramatic Lyrics*, 1842
Robert Browning

A collector and connoisseur of things beautiful who reveals himself to be an arrogant egoist of 'absurdly pretentious vanity' who has rid himself of his last wife because 'she had a heart ... How shall I say? ... too soon made glad,/ Too easily impressed'. All gifts, from a branch of cherries to his 900-year-old name, were the same to her. He could not accept this and she is now only a portrait in his gallery. All this he proudly relates to the ambassador who is negotiating on behalf of his next acquisition – a new bride!

Duke, the
The Revenger's Tragedy, 1607
Thomas Middleton or Cyril Tourneur

The pivotal character of the court, whose past influence is responsible for the pervading air of corruption. Although an old man, he is still prey to lustful desires and given to poisoning those women who resist his advances. A cunning, vicious and corrupt ruler, his lechery proves to be his downfall when he unwittingly asks VENDICE (in his guise as 'Piato') to procure a woman for him.

Dull
Love's Labour's Lost, not later than 1594
William Shakespeare

As his name suggests, Dull has little intelligence. His arrest of COSTARD for wenching and his subsequent report is farcical, Dull claiming to 'reprehend' (instead of 'represent') the person of KING FERDINAND, and then standing by while Costard puns his way through a defence against the charges brought. Later on he also stands silent while HOLOFERNES organizes the Pageant of the Nine Worthies.

Duluoz, Ti-Jean/Jack
Vanity of Duluoz, and others, 1968
Jack Kerouac

The split fictional persona adopted in several books by Kerouac (*duluoz* is Quebecois for 'louse'). He identifies with the saintly Gerard in *Visions of Gerard* (1963), and thereafter seeks an identity to fill the void of his death. He discovers his nascent creative powers in *Doctor Sax* (1959). *Vanity of Duluoz* offers a disillusioned perspective on the football hero of *The Town and the City* (1950). He is disgusted with 'new experiences of any kind' in *Desolation Angels* (1965), rejects small-town life in *Maggie Cassidy*

(1959), and has a mental breakdown in *Big Sur* (1962).

Dumaine
Love's Labour's Lost, not later than 1594
William Shakespeare

One of the attendant lords of KING FERDINAND, who agree to abjure women for the space of three years in order to devote time to academic study. As with the others, his oath breaks down. In his case, he falls in love with KATHARINE, one of the PRINCESS OF FRANCE's ladies, and writes appalling doggerel to her: 'On a day, alack the day/Love, whose month is ever May ... ' that is ridiculed by his friends.

Dumbello, Lord
Framley Parsonage, 1861
The Small House at Allington, 1864
Anthony Trollope

Gustavus, Viscount Dumbello is the taciturn heir of the Marquis of Hartletop; his 'muteness was his most eloquent mode of expression'. Immensely rich, he gives himself airs and becomes a Barsetshire MP. He proposes to GRISELDA GRANTLY, partly out of a spirit of competition with LORD LUFTON; although he then shows some reluctance to marry, he later turns out to be proud of his wife.

Dumbiedikes, Laird of (John Dumbie)
The Heart of Midlothian, in *Tales of My Landlord: Second Series*, 1818
Sir Walter Scott

Introduced at his father's deathbed as 'a tall, gawky, silly-looking boy of fourteen or fifteen', he grows very little in stature or substance, having seemingly inherited very few of his parent's tough genes. Though 'close and selfish enough, [he] wanted the grasping spirit and active mind of his father' and much of his day is spent mooning around his tenant's daughter JEANIE DEANS, with whom he is calfishly in love.

Dumbledore, Albus
Harry Potter and the Philosopher's Stone, 1997, et seq
J K Rowling

The headmaster of Hogwarts School of Witchcraft and Wizardry, he is thought to be 'the greatest wizard of modern times'. 'Tall, thin and very old', with flowing silver hair and beard, a crooked nose and sparkling eyes, Dumbledore is genial, benevolent and wise. He wields his authority fairly, and leavens it with not a little humour; he takes risks and encourages HARRY POTTER's independence. Yet his kindly exterior belies his strength. Reputed to be 'the only one ... Voldemort ... was frightened of', Dumbledore is an immensely powerful wizard, in whom LORD VOLDEMORT's supporters recognize a real threat to their ascendancy.

Duncan, King
Macbeth, c.1606
William Shakespeare

An old, much-loved ruler, softening as he ages, but still capable of making strong decisions when necessary. A jovial, generous family man, the tears he sheds early in the play serve to bring him closer to humanity despite various characters' insistence that he is a godly or saintly man. Even MACBETH, his eventual assassin, recognizes that Duncan's 'virtues, will plead like angels, trumpet-tongued, against the deep damnation of his taking-off'.

Dundreary, Lord
Our American Cousin, 1858
Tom Taylor

Our American Cousin is memorable for two reasons: one being that it was at a performance of the play in Washington in 1865 that an actor, J Wilkes Booth, shot President Lincoln, who died the following morning; the second is that it introduced the character of the slow-witted, bumbling, English eccentric, Lord Dundreary. E A Sothern, who created the role, developed and embellished what was originally a small part until it dominated the play, and in London in 1861, the lord's bushy side-whiskers set a new fashion, being known as 'dundrearies'.

Dunlap, Anna
The Good Mother, 1986
Sue Miller

A divorcee, who finds her relaxed modern approach to relationships and to openness about sexuality and physical frankness misunderstood by a fossilized legal system. Consequently, her lover's openness with her little daughter is sufficiently misunderstood to result in the child being taken from her mother and placed with her more traditional father. Anna Dunlap's pain is sharp and poignant, not least because what she has done has been misrepresented as perverted sexually abusive behaviour and not, as it was intended, as acceptance of sexuality and delight in the human experience of physical relationships.

Dunlavin
The Quare Fellow, 1954
Brendan Behan

Wry and crafty, the elderly Dunlavin has spent almost all his life in jail. Happily, laconically, he fulfils the role of sage and adviser to the inmates and several of the staff at the Dublin prison where he is serving his present term, and where THE QUARE FELLOW, a murderer, is shortly to be hanged. Philosophical, resourceful and, when necessary, defiant, he has not allowed prison to quash him: he sings, gossips, operates a trim domestic authority and tipples the methylated spirits a warder uses to massage into his rheumatic legs. He confronts the impending execution with a mixture of hard-nosed realism and mordant humour.

Dunn, Clarrie
The Boys Who Stole the Funeral, 1980
Les Murray

The body of Clarrie Dunn is stolen from a city funeral parlour by his great-nephew, KEVIN FORBUTT, and his friend, CAMERON REEBY. It is then transported north across Australia for burial in the remote New South Wales farming community in which he grew up. A World War I veteran, Dunn was always nostalgic for his birthplace. It was his dying wish that he be taken home, and the theft of his corpse and its burial brings the country community together in conspiracy. Later, his spirit, carrying the Common Dish, appears to Forbutt. Dunn represents the decent, hard-working soul of rural Australia.

Dunn, Ellie
Heartbreak House, 1916
George Bernard Shaw

Young and pretty, Ellie is the daughter of MAZZINI DUNN. Invited to CAPTAIN SHOTOVER's Sussex home by HESIONE HUSHABYE, she matures emotionally in a single day more than she might otherwise have done in years. Discovering her romantically idealized 'Marcus Darnley' is none other than HECTOR HUSHABYE, Hesione's husband, she becomes 'older and harder'. She remains determined to marry 'BOSS' MANGAN not, as before, to please her father, but to claw back the money she finds Mangan has swindled from him. Having tested her will power and defeated Mangan, Ellie finds emotional peace with Shotover, 'my spiritual husband and second father'.

Dunn, Mazzini
Heartbreak House, 1916
George Bernard Shaw

The father of ELLIE DUNN, Mazzini is earnest, unambitious and unsuccessful: a bit of a prig but likeable. Having been lent money by 'BOSS' MANGAN to start a business, Dunn watched it fail. He was so grateful when Mangan took it over, made it thrive and appointed him manager, that he unwaveringly supports the decision of the strong-willed Ellie to marry him. Sentimental and gullible, idealistic but resigned, he nonetheless maintains a steadfast, quiet dignity. HESIONE HUSHABYE recognizes his idealism and calls him her 'soldier of freedom'.

Duno, Stuart
The Good Apprentice, 1985
Iris Murdoch

Disliked by his stepmother while she was alive, and with a father who has always preferred his stepbrother, EDWARD BALTRAM, Stuart is clumsy, stolid and unimaginative. An atheist, he suddenly receives a spiritual 'call' and, withdrawing from academic life, takes a vow of celibacy and ponders how he can help others and achieve perfect goodness 'without the old supernatural scenery'. The unfortunate Stuart blunders around in other people's lives, self-absorbed, well-meaning and ineffectual. He is viewed as a corpse by JESSE BALTRAM, but as 'a negative presence, a sort of catalyst' unwittingly provokes a cathartic crisis for those around him, while prosaically resolving his own dilemma.

Dunois, Captain Jean ('Bastard of Orléans')
Saint Joan, 1923
George Bernard Shaw

Dunois becomes JOAN's principal ally in the struggle to have THE DAUPHIN crowned King of France, against the will of the English under Henry VI. In his mid-twenties, Dunois is a well-built man, good-natured, capable and free of affectations and foolish illusions. He attends the coronation, but warns Joan that should she go into battle with too few men in support, she will be captured and nobody will try to save her.

Dunstable, Miss Martha
Dr Thorne, 1858
Framley Parsonage, 1861
The Last Chronicle of Barset, 1867
Anthony Trollope

The humorous, generous and sympathetic possessor of an enormous inherited fortune, derived from an ointment, Oil of Lebanon. Her wealth causes FRANK GRESHAM's relatives to see her as a potential bride for him, but the two become friends. She values honesty highly. Being so rich, she does and says whatever she likes and is completely confident in society, but she finds it difficult to find a husband indifferent to her money; this problem is solved in *Framley Parsonage*, and the consequent alteration to her lifestyle saves her from the erosion of her goodness of which she was aware when she was in London society.

Dupin, C Auguste
'The Mystery of Marie Roget', 1842–3
'The Murders in the Rue Morgue', 1843
'The Purloined Letter', 1845
Edgar Allan Poe

An eccentric genius of extraordinary analytical and deductive powers who rarely leaves his shaded room by day, preferring to walk the night streets in search of the 'infinity of mental excitement' offered by observation. He solves mysteries by the power of ratiocination, and is never physically described, perhaps to emphasize his dominance by intellect rather than by emotion. He is poor but of good family, an avid reader, scholarly, romantic and arrogant.

D'Urberville, Alec
Tess of the D'Urbervilles, 1891
Thomas Hardy

Alec D'Urberville seems the very model of the moustache-twirling seducer of Victorian melodrama, right down to the 'my beauty' he uses to address TESS DURBEYFIELD. He is a verbal charmer and a fluent liar, with short-lived passions, and he ruthlessly exploits his social position and beguiling manner to satisfy his sexual appetites. However, his lustful and rapacious advances on Tess hide (initially even from himself) deeper feelings which later resurface to bring both of them to their doom.

Durbeyfield, Tess
Tess of the D'Urbervilles, 1891
Thomas Hardy

Tess is the loving and dutiful daughter of impoverished wastrel parents, and it is to please them that she sets out to reclaim her family's heritage, when her father is informed that they come of a noble, if much decayed, lineage. Initially naive and trusting, but sexually appealing beyond her years, she is valued by the men in her life not for herself, but as an ideal of womanliness, sensual or spiritual according to their own natures. A luminous, tragic creature, she remains, (in the words of Hardy's subtitle) 'a pure woman' in the sincerity of her passions and affections, through all the vicissitudes that fate and chance have in store for her.

Durden, Tyler
Fight Club, 1996
Chuck Palahniuk

A manic, anarchic force of mayhem, Tyler Durden bursts into the life of the unnamed narrator (a materialistic but disaffected employee of a car firm) after a chance meeting on a beach, and turns his unfulfilled and affectless existence upside down. Resentful of the drudgery imposed on modern man (sic) by contemporary society, Durden exploits every opportunity to commit acts of social sabotage against the established order and proprieties. With the narrator tagging along, he establishes a clandestine network of bareknuckle fighting clubs, ostensibly to give men back their self-respect. The true dimensions of his me-galomaniac ambitions only gradually become apparent.

Durdles
The Mystery of Edwin Drood, 1870
Charles Dickens

An alcoholic stonemason at Cloisterham Cathedral whom MR JOHN JASPER makes drunk in order to steal his keys and explore the crypt in secret. There are hints that Jasper has decided to murder EDWIN DROOD and is searching for a place to hide the body.

D'Urfe, Nicholas
The Magus, 1966, revised edition 1977
John Fowles

A middle-class Englishman with a degree in English Literature, d'Urfe curiously seems to lack real poetic imagination. He is, at times, pompous, selfish, brutish, while at others he can be childish and vulnerable in his quest for all things to have a simple explanation. Unable to express love towards women in a non-sexual way, his development of relationships is inhibited, as is his discovery of himself. Caught up in a world of pretence, he realizes that there are aspects of human consciousness that are not fathomable, but this seems to create more of a sense of confusion than of resolution.

Durgin, Jeff
The Landlord at Lion's Head, 1897
William Dean Howells

The go-getting proprietor of an increasingly fashionable country hotel which he has built up out of a run-down farm, he is irrepressibly confident and self-reliant, single-minded in his passions. His cultural purview is sharply contrasted to that of his friend, the painter Westover.

Durham, Clive
Maurice, 1914, published posthumously, 1971
E M Forster

Descended from a line of lawyers and landed gentry, Clive Durham is a 'very small man with simple manners and a fair face'. An outstanding classical scholar with a reputation for being somewhat aloof, his keen sense of right and wrong has convinced him that he is damned

because of his homsexuality. A platonic three-year relationship with MAURICE HALL affords him an idyll of happiness before he follows the path of respectability and least resistance; marrying, standing for Parliament and becoming 'quite the squire'.

Durham, Constantia
The Egoist, 1879
George Meredith

SIR WILLOUGHBY PATTERNE's second choice (somewhat on the rebound) in the marriage round and, on the face of it, a more immediately appealing and compliant beauty than LAETITIA DALE. She is, however, less willing to submit herself to his will and she elopes with a dashing young hussar.

Durie, Henry
The Master of Ballantrae, 1889
Robert Louis Stevenson

He is conventionally viewed as the 'good' brother, in contrast to his wicked sibling JAMES DURIE, the 'Master'. Sent by his family to fight for the government cause in the Jacobite Rising against his brother, Henry emerges the victor, and from this stems fraternal enmity. He is a dull, worthy man, a prisoner of his stern Calvinist beliefs. He is attracted to the ethos of a totally moral universe, while failing to acknowledge that this is not only an unattainable goal, but also a dangerous one. In attempting to kill his brother, he does not so much defeat evil as perpetuate it – in himself.

Durie, James
The Master of Ballantrae, 1889
Robert Louis Stevenson

The Master of Ballantrae. Assigned by his family to fight for the doomed Jacobite cause, he loses all in the conflict and becomes the enemy of his brother HENRY DURIE. He lives on his emotions rather than his reason and tends to act spontaneously, untrammelled by moral considerations. Although James is duplicitous, vain and wicked, he is also a very attractive character and Stevenson emphasizes how the roots of his misfortunes have been unfairly thrust upon him by his social circumstances. In Stevenson's morally ambiguous universe, James is another example of how evil is always leavened by good: indeed they are interdependent.

Duror
The Cone-Gatherers, 1955
Robin Jenkins

Lady Runcie-Campbell's gamekeeper, he embodies the evil of self-hatred in a story that reverses Genesis, with innocence penetrating the fallen garden of Calvinism in the form of the dwarf-like CALUM. The gamekeeper's twisted nature is echoed in his wife's physical disability and even in his name, with its hints of 'dourness'. His eventual suicide is a final denial of life.

Durward, Quentin
Quentin Durward, 1823
Sir Walter Scott

A jaunty Scottish youth of good family, he takes service with LOUIS XI, KING OF FRANCE's guard of

Scottish archers. 'His features, without being quite regular, were frank, open, and pleasing', and he proves to be loyal, trusting and quick to resent any evidence of injustice or cruelty.

Dusky Ruth
'Dusky Ruth', in *Adam and Eve and Pinch Me*, 1921
A E Coppard

The heroine of the story, Dusky Ruth is a completely mysterious barmaid whom the reader knows only by the name a stranger gives her. The secret sorrow that seems to weigh down her spirits prevents the stranger from seducing her though she offers herself to him.

Dutcher, Rose
Rose of Dutcher's Coolley, 1895
Hamlin Garland

A sensitive and self-cultured farm-girl who escapes the drudgery and spiritual vacuum of the rural mid-west. To college she brings not just a passionate love of literature and learning but a hard-won perspicacity and sensitivity to fact that stands her in good stead as a writer in Chicago.

Du Toit, Ben
A Dry White Season, 1979, originally published in Afrikaans as *'n Droë wit seisoen*, 1979
André Brink

An 'ordinary, good-natured, harmless, unremarkable' South African in the early 1950s, his life and expectations are suddenly overturned by the death of a man he has known. Ben's caring curiosity places him suddenly outside the pale of the familiar and the safe.

du Toit, Daphne
'The Go-Away Bird', in *The Go-Away Bird and Other Stories*, 1958
Muriel Spark

Daphne is one of the few people in a British colony in Africa who can hear the cry of the go-away bird, this symbolizing her understanding. The orphaned daughter of an Afrikaaner father and English mother, she becomes obsessed with England, but when she gets there her understanding fails.

Duval, Denis
Denis Duval, 1864, unfinished
W M Thackeray

The chastened but unbowed descendant of Huguenot refugees to Britain, he can discover no oppressions in ancestry more severe than those visited by 'her High Mightiness my wife, and his Serene Highness my son'. After schooldays, he enters His Majesty's Navy, but his story concluded abruptly with Thackeray's death, leaving only tantalizing notes and hints.

Duveen, Praxis
Praxis, 1978
Fay Weldon

Praxis is a person at odds with life. She has had a painful and confusing childhood, in which she endured an antagonistic relationship with her estranged parents and her successful sister. Challenging convention, she struggles to find a sense of deep contentment. She is not naturally maternal or submissive, but is capable of expressing love and compassion in her own way. It is herself whom she has trouble in accepting. Fighting notions which are deeply embedded in society regarding male/female relationships and relationships between women, she derives little comfort from observing other people's behaviour. Brave and unconventional, she ultimately is seen as an 'abnormal' woman. Judging herself in terms of wrongs and rights, not emotions, she reaches the point of self-awareness most people only dream about.

Dyar, Nelson
Let It Come Down, 1952
Paul Bowles

A sober and utterly conventional American bank clerk who gives up his job for a place in his friend's travel agency in Tangier. As he slowly realizes the agency is a front for illegal and immoral dealings, his civilized calm and equanimity are steadily eroded, until he is revealed in his 'true' instinctual nature as no less savage than those who surround him.

Dyer, Nicholas
Hawksmoor, 1985
Peter Ackroyd

In London in the early 18th century, he is planning the designs for several churches in the City and Westminster. Some of these churches, in the 20th century, are the scenes of murders investigated by NICHOLAS HAWKSMOOR, a character with whom Dyer is thematically linked. Working in the Age of Enlightenment, concerned with philosophical logic, scientific progress and reason, Dyer is secretly haunted by moral doubts, fears, metaphysical questions that defy reason, and by black spiritual beliefs: 'Thus was I taught by many Signes that Humane life was of no certain course'. Sceptical of the modern world, he methodically pours his Satanic understanding into his work.

Dyer, the → Five Guildsmen, the

Dymes, Felix
The Whirlpool, 1897
George Gissing

Unlike ALMA FROTHINGHAM, his sense of marriage is of a loosely structured, centrifugal relationship in which the parties are not bound to one another inwardly but remain part of a wider life and world. He is neither cynical nor uncaring, but is certainly unsentimental and rather solemn about it.

Dysart, Martin
Equus, 1973
Peter Shaffer

A weary, overworked psychiatrist in his mid-forties with an abiding love of Greece, Martin Dysart has reached a point of crisis that he has termed a 'professional menopause'. Married to a woman he no longer loves and serving a profession in which he scarcely believes, his many doubts and insecurities come into sharper focus as he treats the shocking case of ALAN STRANG. Admiring the passion with which the boy has pursued his obsessive love of horses,

Dysart is filled with self-loathing at having settled for being 'pallid and provincial'.

Dyson, John
Towards the End of the Morning, 1967
Michael Frayn

A journalist running the Nature Notes and Crossword section of a failing broadsheet newspaper, Dyson is 'dark and nervous and almost forty'. The owner of a delapidated car and a house in a district of London that refuses to be discovered by the intellectual and artistic middle-class of which he craves to be a part, Dyson has a growing conviction that life is inexorably passing him by. His despondency is offset, however, by a naturally buoyant optimism and a vigorous assessment of his worth as a journalist and his suitability as a pundit on television discussion programmes. Although boastful of his scraps of success and potential prospects, he is nevertheless an amiable, sympathetic figure.

Eames, John
The Small House at Allington, 1864
The Last Chronicle of Barset, 1867
Anthony Trollope

When first introduced, Johnny is a 'hobble-dehoy', awkwardly situated between boyhood and manhood. Good-hearted and reckless, he befriends LORD DE GUEST and rises in the civil service. His romantic and faithful love for LILY DALE is not returned, and to his regret he becomes entangled with Amelia Roper and other unsuitable companions in London. By the end of *The Small House at Allington* he has become a man, but in *The Last Chronicle of Barset* Johnny, now a figure of some note, again has an unfortunate involvement (with MADALINA DEMOLINES).

Earle, Judith
Dusty Answer, 1927
Rosamond Lehmann

Intellectually and socially emancipated, Judith is a Bright Young Thing with a sparkling personality. Narcissistic and sensual, she swims naked in the moonlight, revelling in anarchic jouissance. However, reality impinges and Judith's experience of alienation is embedded in her cry; '[I am] lost, lost, abandoned, alone, lost.' Expressing the breakdown of post-World War I heterosexual mores, Judith tentatively loves Jennifer, but is unsettled by the disturbance of gender roles. Rejected by the aloof and opaque homosexual Roddy, she muses, 'I am all uprooted and don't know what I shall do'.

Earlforward, Henry
Riceyman Steps, 1923
Arnold Bennett

A middle-aged, second-hand bookseller, Henry Earlforward is a martyr to his own avarice. This is a passion far beyond anything he feels for his new wife, VIOLET EARLFORWARD, one that is indeed powerful enough to draw her into his miserliness. Despite his meanness, though, there is something in Henry which arouses sympathy; he tries to act reasonably, but is a victim of his obsession.

Earlforward, Violet
Riceyman Steps, 1923
Arnold Bennett

Although merely prudent with her money before marrying HENRY EARLFORWARD, Violet soon becomes enmeshed in the miserly existence of the Earlforward household. She fights some battles over domestic economies – whether to have a fire lit or have eggs for tea – but she genuinely loves her husband and humours him by giving way more often than not. Silly and vulgar though she is, Violet retains sufficient objectivity to be aware of the folly of their life but she lacks the will to act. The consequences, tragically, are fatal.

Earnshaw, Catherine
Wuthering Heights, 1848
Emily Brontë

A haughty, headstrong girl whose spirits are 'always at high-water mark', she is deemed to have 'the bonniest eye, the sweetest smile and the lightest foot in the parish'. An untamed savage as a teenager, she discovers her perfect soul mate in the sullen, devoted HEATHCLIFF but finds her passion for him in conflict with the more ladylike qualities she acquires with maturity. Marriage to the kindly EDGAR LINTON does not refine her wild nature, however, and she remains wilful, selfish and inexorably drawn to the flame of Heathcliff's ardour.

Earnshaw, Hareton
Wuthering Heights, 1848
Emily Brontë

The son of HINDLEY EARNSHAW, and the last of the ancient Earnshaw stock, Hareton is a good-looking, athletic youth with thick brown curls and the coarse ways of a common labourer. Left penniless by the death of his father, he has been thrown on to the cold charity of HEATHCLIFF. Humiliated and humbled, he conceals his crushed pride and frustration beneath the unapproachable manner of a wild animal. Only the attentiveness of CATHERINE EARNSHAW ultimately permits him to realize his finer qualities.

Earnshaw, Hindley
Wuthering Heights, 1848
Emily Brontë

Displaced from the centre of his father's affections by the arrival of HEATHCLIFF in the Earnshaw household, Hindley develops a hatred that grows like a cancer. As master of Wuthering Heights, his bitterness finds expression in unfettered tyranny over the former favourite but fate intervenes to undermine his dominance and when his wife dies he is left a sullen, hopeless drunkard who squanders his inheritance at the gaming tables. Dead at the age of 27, his destruction has been Heathcliff's triumph.

Earwicker, Humphrey Chimpden, or Mr Porter
Finnegans Wake, 1939
James Joyce

The chief protagonist of *Finnegans Wake* and of all human history, he is publan of Chapelizod, Dublin. He is common, historical and legendary. As he dreams the entire course of human history, he is constantly transmuted; from bricklayer to general to giant, from loving father to father-lover. He dreams of history as man's perpetual fall and resurrection. His personal situation is underlain by an unconscious motive: the transfer of love from his wife ANNA LIVIA PLURABELLE to an incestuous longing for his daughter ISSY. His guilt is revealed in Freudian fashion by a stutter.

Easley, Grace
The Slave, 1964
Amiri Baraka

An archetypal white woman, who reinforces and upholds America's racial and sexual metaphors. Her first marriage to WALKER VESSELS, a black man, is a middle-class phenomenon, often regarded as the quintessential act of the liberated segment of the middle class. Grace gradually discovers that a whole range of cultural factors and mythological allusions have in fact determined her act.

Eastlake, Lakey (Elinor)
The Group, 1963
Mary McCarthy

An aloof, taciturn beauty and the leader of her set, Lakey has it all; she is a rich girl with a mind. She likes everything to be done the right way and expects others to see things as she does. Never short of admirers amongst her peers, she is cool and changeable in her relationships. Once she tires of people they are quickly dropped. It is only years later when she reveals her lesbianism and events disclose a fierce underlying loyalty in her, that her friends realize she is 'more human in many ways than they remembered'.

Eastman, Walter
An Insular Possession, 1986
Timothy Mo

A young American from Virginia, working for the Meridian trading company in Canton in 1833. Witty and volatile, headstrong and somewhat unstable emotionally, he is hero-worshipped by his younger compatriot, GIDEON CHASE. He loves ALICE REMINGTON, but is dismissed by her uncle, Meridian's senior partner, as a penniless adventurer and troublemaker, being bitterly and vociferously opposed to the opium trade, especially as practised by the British. Helped by FATHER RIBEIRO, he founds a liberal, irreverent newspaper in Macao, *The Lin Tin Bulletin and River Bee*, in opposition to the pro-establishment *Canton Monitor*, and becomes obsessed with the new science of photography.

Easy, John (Jack)
Mr Midshipman Easy, 1836
Captain Frederick Marryat

A naval midshipman. He inherits the philosophical bent of his father, and imbibes the egalitarian ideals which, as a child in the nursery,

earn him the nickname 'Equality Jack'. He is a strong, resourceful, well-made seaman, and an unshakably principled idealist, who stands up for sailors' rights against the worst abuses of the system.

Eaton, Alfred
From the Terrace, 1958
John O'Hara

Despite going from small-town Pennsylvania to big-city success in less than a generation, he is haunted by a prevailing sense of emptiness at the centre of his life. Neither wealth nor influence can mitigate this.

Echidna
The Faerie Queene, 1590–6
Sir Edmund Spenser

The mother of THE BLATANT BEAST. She looks like a beautiful and innocent maiden, but in reality is hideous, with the body of a dog, iron claws for ripping and tearing, a deadly stinging dragon's tail, and a great pair of eagle's wings to allow her to chase her prey. She is so hideous that she has to live amongst the caves and rocks, and even the gods are scared to look at her.

Eckdorf, Mrs Ivy
Mrs Eckdorf in O'Neill's Hotel, 1969
William Trevor

Brash and beautiful, Mrs Eckdorf photographs the sufferings of the poor in order to make expensive books for the rich. She believes that she exposes the truth, thus spreading understanding and love, and has no respect for privacy. Intuitively sensing a secret tragedy in a decayed Dublin hotel, she leaves her aridly tasteful Munich flat and becomes embroiled with an Irish family and its connections. Her unhappy past seems to give way to a new religious faith, but she exhibits signs of mental instability.

Eckhart, Miss
'June Recital' and 'The Wanderers', in *The Golden Apples*, 1949
Eudora Welty

A lonely, German-born piano teacher in the Delta town of Morgana, Mississippi. She tries to foster the talents of VIRGIE RAINEY, but is unable to divert her from sexual curiosity. As the girl makes love to a sailor, Miss Eckhart tries to set her 'free' in a sacrificial pyre of her music scores and of the metronome by which she had attempted to keep Virgie to a mechanical rhythm.

Ed
Entertaining Mr Sloane, 1964
Joe Orton

The lynchpin of a dysfunctional family that includes his reclusive father Kemp and his sister KATH, Ed paints himself as a pillar of respectability, having two bank accounts to his name and a position of responsibility. Deeply attracted to the clean-cut charms and athletic physique of the duplicitous SLOANE, he plots to make his desire a reality by first employing Sloane as a leather-clad chauffeur and then scheming to establish their relationship on a more permanent and gratifying basis.

Eddie
The Death of the Heart, 1938
Elizabeth Bowen

ANNA QUAYNE's occasional lover and an employee in her husband's advertising agency. A brash arriviste, he has a 'proletarian, animal quick grace', but is prone to 'cosmic black moods' when thwarted.

Eddie
Fool for Love, 1983
Sam Shepard

The play is set in familiar Shepard territory: a down-at-heel motel room on the edge of the Mojave Desert in California. Eddie, lean and fit, is a stuntman. He plans to take May, the woman he loves but has several times abandoned, with him across the plains of Wyoming. With equal intensity, Eddie desires May yet is vengeful towards her for rejecting him. A wanderer and a loner who has possessed several women, he has only now discovered the sensitivity of his passion and the nature of real love but is not sufficiently emotionally articulate to understand or express the force of his feelings. He wants to own May but she refuses to be owned; yet equally she needs to know that someone longs to possess her.

Edelman, Dr Talbot
Daughter Buffalo, 1972
Janet Frame

An obsessive and remote physician, he switches his academic specialism to Death Studies. Exploring the limits of moral understanding, he performs vivisection on his pet dog, in order to find out how it feels to hurt the one thing that he genuinely loves.

Eden, Martin
Martin Eden, 1909
Jack London

A sailor on the receiving end of a ruthless captain's savagery, his urgent need to campaign on behalf of the underdog leads to imprisonment on false charges, and subsequent adventures that turn his fortunes around. Champion of the weak and defenceless, he triumphs over unpromising circumstances, to find that true love is not measured in wealth but in integrity and class loyalty.

Edgar
King Lear, c.1607
William Shakespeare

The elder of the EARL OF GLOUCESTER's two sons, Edgar is honest and dutiful, though at first far too trusting. EDMUND describes him as 'a brother noble/Whose nature is so far from doing harm/That he suspects none'. This 'fault' leads him into exile from his father's house and into a disguise as a half-naked, mad beggar. Despite this, he remains a loyal and loving son who grows through his experiences and his suffering into a wiser and stronger character and eventually triumphs over the evil cynicism of his brother.

Edgeworth, Topaz
The Innocent Traveller, 1949
Ethel Wilson

Voluble, irrepressible, gaily flagrant or even unaware of social mores and conventions, 'Topaz was never to be tamed'. Innocent in the sense that her words and actions are unpremeditated, she is strangely untouched by 'the complicated fabric of living'. Concerned only with 'the veriest surface of material and psychic being', her irresponsibility is both endearing and irritating.

Edith
Beautiful Losers, 1966
Leonard Cohen

The wife of the unnamed narrator (ANON). Their triangular relationship with the mysterious F is compounded by her defection to South America with F, where they share a bath with the exiled Hitler, using human soap. She dies a suicide in the bottom of a lift shaft.

Edmund
King Lear, c.1607
William Shakespeare

The illegitimate son of the EARL OF GLOUCESTER and younger brother to EDGAR, Edmund is determined not to let either his own illegitimacy or his elder brother come between him and his father's fortune. He is a clever and manipulative personality who feels himself excluded from the natural bonds of family by his illegitimacy. Cruel and ruthless, he cynically exploits others' weaknesses and naivety to further his own ambitions.

Edmund
The Lion, the Witch and the Wardrobe, 1950, et seq
C S Lewis

Irritable, petulant and, at first, deceitful, Edmund betrays PETER, SUSAN and LUCY to the wicked White Witch before realizing the enormity of his treachery. Brought in time to his senses, he grows into a thoughtful, mature young king, worthy of ruling alongside his siblings.

Edny, Clithero
Edgar Huntly, 1799
Charles Brockden Brown

A curiously sympathetic murderer. Obsessed with his own sorrows, claiming that 'I deserve to be supreme in misery', Edny is the definitive outcast. Wandering and without friends, he takes to the wilderness to brood, walking out in his sleep. His confession to EDGAR HUNTLY appears frank and open, but it could just as well be deceitful and manipulative.

Edward, Earl of March, later Edward IV
Henry VI Parts II and III, early 1590s
Richard III, 1592/3
William Shakespeare

Edward Plantagenet, eldest son of RICHARD PLANTAGENET, DUKE OF YORK, appears briefly in *Henry VI Part II* and as Edward, Earl of March, in *Part III*, during which he is crowned Edward IV. He dies during the second act of *Richard III*. Proud, hedonistic, an effective and enthusiastic soldier, he is the antithesis of HENRY VI, whom he defeats in battle and whom his brother, RICHARD, DUKE OF GLOUCESTER, later stabs to death. He is, though, a killer when it is politically expedient: after the battle of Tewkesbury, he is the first to stab Henry's son,

Edward. But while he is both a magnetic and ruthless leader, he is not always an astute politician: his marriage to ELIZABETH WOODVILLE is based upon sexual attraction and loses him a good deal of popularity, especially with the nobility. Neither is he a perceptive judge of character, for while he is ambitious for the throne himself, he remains unaware of Gloucester's own intentions.

Edward, Prince, later Edward VI
The Prince and the Pauper, 1881
Mark Twain

The prince exchanges clothes with a pauper, TOM CANTY, 'for a jest', but is then alarmed to find himself unable to prove his true identity. Taken for a half-wit, he is an object of ridicule on his travels through London and Kent. Forced to undergo a series of hardships and humiliations, the prince witnesses the execution of the laws of the realm and learns the meaning of suffering and oppression. He develops a strong sense of justice, mercy and compassion which he vows to act upon once he has proved his true identity and ascended to the throne of England.

Edward II
Edward II, 1594
Christopher Marlowe

Plantagenet King of England, clouded in judgement by his passion for the disgraced PIERS GAVESTON. He is voluptuous and self-dramatizing, constantly aware that he is a character in a play with a tragic conclusion.

Edward IV → Edward, Earl of March

Edwards, Foxhall
You Can't Go Home Again, 1940
Thomas Wolfe

A literary associate of GEORGE WEBBER, he holds a much less sanguine view of the USA's future potential than does George, and represents a check to the young writer's vaulting optimism. Edwards is clearly modelled on Maxwell Perkins, the brilliant editor who shaped and trimmed Wolfe's massive manuscripts into publishable novels.

Edwards, Mog
Under Milk Wood, 1954
Dylan Thomas

The quiet village draper, 'mad with love' for MYFANWY PRICE, dressmaker and sweetshop-owner. They dream in unison, their expressive subject the small goods of their trades; but they will always be separated by love letters written on his headed notepaper as he conducts his passion at a distance from Manchester House with the imagined hope of tills for wedding bells. Always measuring people up for clothes, he values his love materially, considering her worth more than all the cloth in the world.

Eeyore
Winnie-the-Pooh, 1926
The House at Pooh Corner, 1928
A A Milne

One of Christopher Robin's companions, Eeyore is a gloomy donkey who lives in a Gloomy Place in the Hundred Acre Wood. He craves attention, but wallows in self-pity and pours cold water on the plans of others. Mishaps such as the loss of his tail do not help. 'After all one can't complain', Eeyore typically remarks, 'I have my friends. Somebody spoke to me only yesterday.'

Effingham, Violet
Phineas Finn, The Irish Member, 1869
Anthony Trollope

The intimate companion of LAURA KENNEDY, she is small, with delicate hands and feet. There is 'a softness about her whole person' which is misleading, since she is in fact determined and sharp-witted, and something of a covert manipulator of those around her. Men are greatly attracted by her, and she has several suitors, but eventually chooses LORD OSWALD STANDISH CHILTERN.

Egan, Captain Hugh
The Sullen Bell, 1956
Dan Davin

A New Zealander in his forties, he is revisiting his old London haunts from before World War II. Much has happened during the meantime, most notably his wife Alison's suicide. This has resulted in his sabbatical from university and his trip to England. A quiet, reserved man, Egan is not one to confide in others and generally shies away from intimacy. Ironically, the only person with whom he could have spoken about his wife was Alison herself. He finds sanctuary by himself, or in the company of former soldiers, people accustomed not to pry into the privacies of others. Through emotional pain, self-doubt and some self-pity, Egan comes to terms with his wife's death, and with himself.

Egbert
'England, My England', in *England, My England*, 1922
D H Lawrence

Tall, handsome, slim and agile, Egbert, a southerner, is independent, sensitive, generous, neither clever nor literary but passionate about things English. Winifred, his wife, a northerner, thinks of him not as a deeper but as a higher being. Egbert has no ambition other than avoiding the drudgery of earning three pounds a week in a profession. Instead, despite the fact that he is hopelessly impractical, he works the land around the cottage, pondering on the rustic English past, becoming 'a sort of epicurean hermit'. Yet Egbert, like England, is under threat and his dreams collide with reality. Sentimentality becomes bitterness, illusion becomes despair.

Egbo
The Interpreters, 1965
Wole Soyinka

The descendant of Nigerian warlords, alternately inspired and oppressed by the pressure of his ancestral past. His parents were drowned in the swamps and he feels strangely rootless, not quite connected to his own inheritance.

Egeus
A Midsummer Night's Dream, c.1594
William Shakespeare

A tiresome, old-fashioned but loyal man, his brief

appearances establish him as a doughty defender of a father's traditional rights at the expense of any paternal love or understanding. His desire to force HERMIA to marry DEMETRIUS, and his belief that THESEUS will make the right decision on the matter, contribute to his stuffy attacks on 'unhardened youth'.

Eglamour, Sir
Two Gentlemen of Verona, c.1590
William Shakespeare

There is marginal doubt as to whether 'Sir Eglamour' of Act 2 Scene, mentioned by JULIA as being 'fair' and by her waiting-woman as being 'a knight well-spoken, neat and fine' is, in fact, the 'Sir Eglamour' of Act IV Scene 3, to whom SILVIA appeals. In this scene, the first in which she appears, Silvia turns to him to escort her secretly to Mantua, knowing him to be a man who has loved, whose 'lady' has died and who now vows chastity. When they are beset by outlaws he, being 'nimble-footed', escapes and is pursued.

Eglantyne, Madame → Prioress, the

Egremont, Charles
Sybil, or The Two Nations, 1845
Benjamin Disraeli

A principled and passionate young Englishman who, dismayed at the country's deep social divisions and the uncaring attitudes of his brother LORD MARNEY, is attracted to the Chartist cause. He is also deeply attracted to the Chartist WALTER GERARD's daughter, SYBIL GERARD, whom he eventually marries. Like HARRY CONINGSBY in Disraeli's previous novel, Egremont is a living exponent of progressive Young Englandism. His marriage to Sybil promises a synthesis of enterprise with the more solid virtues of the old aristocracy.

Eisengrim, Magnus
Fifth Business, 1970
The Manticore, 1973
World of Wonders, 1975, published as *The Deptford Trilogy*, 1983
Robertson Davies

The premature child of a madwoman in rural Canada, Eisengrim was christened Paul Dempster. Befriended in childhood by DUNSTAN RAMSAY, hounded by the likes of PERCY BOYD STAUNTON, and eventually abducted, his often harsh life is an acknowledged process of escape and self-invention in which he develops qualities of ruthless will power and wolfish intensity of purpose. An awe-inspiring stage conjurer, the adult Eisengrim is pretentiously regal and a monster of vanity, but sensitive, aware and intuitive nevertheless. Ultimately he is a mystery, his inhuman egoism expressed as a continuous – endlessly interpretable – performance.

Eitel, Charles Francis
The Deer Park, 1957
The Deer Park: A Play, 1959, revised edition 1967
Norman Mailer

A film director who has sold out his art to commercialism, and shopped his political friends to the House Committee on Un-American Activities (his surname is pronounced 'I-tell'). Lover of ELENA ESPOSITO, but fatally detached from life, 'his manner has a way of offering some promise and then pulling it back ... If his sophistication is always evident, the facets of his nature are revealed by degrees – cynical, sly, idealistic, romantic, noble, corrupt, visionary, strong, weak, tortured, tender, a lover finally.'

Ekwueme
The Concubine, 1966
Elechi Amadi

Betrothed to IHUOMA, Ekwueme is destined to die through his attempts to marry the wife of the jealous Sea-King. A well respected and likeable young man, he becomes obsessed with love for the beautiful Ihuoma. His first marriage to AHUROLE fails, partly because of Ekwueme's immaturity and his need for a mother figure rather than a young wife.

Elder, Mr
Butcher's Broom, 1934
Neil Gunn

The partner of MR HELLER, he has little knowledge of and less regard for what he perceives as the savage Gael. While only a minor character, he epitomizes the ignorance and disinterest displayed by those in positions of power towards the people on the land they cleared, and embodies the callousness of self-interest and financial profit.

Elder, the
Too True to be Good, 1932
George Bernard Shaw

The Elder is THE BURGLAR's father. He is a tall, gaunt man who emerges from a cave. He is doubly despondent. Firstly, he had put his faith in scientific absolutes until Einstein's Theory of Relativity changed everything and left him bereft of a philosophy. Secondly, he is distressed that his son became a clergyman. The Elder proclaims his atheism and bemoans the appalling state of the world, but when he is reunited with the Burglar, he decides that he would prefer him to be a gifted preacher than an unsuccessful thief.

Elderly Gentleman, the
Back to Methuselah, 1921
George Bernard Shaw

The Elderly Gentleman appears in the fourth section of this five-part play. *Tragedy of the Elderly Gentleman* is set on the shore of Galway Bay, Ireland, in 3000AD. He is a conventional Edwardian, a representative of old-fashioned British moral standards and customs, and does not have long to live. He has come to Ireland on a sentimental journey and, although protesting to FUSIMA, ZOZIM and ZOO, he remains perplexed by long-lived people around him, who understand neither his colloquialisms nor his way of life. His death at the hands of THE ORACLE represents his faith in a spiritual future.

Eleanor
King John, 1590/1
William Shakespeare

The widow of Henry II, mother of KING JOHN,

and aunt to ARTHUR, DUKE OF BRITTANY. Greatly respected by the nobility, she was instrumental in establishing the acceptability in England of her son's claim to the throne. A manipulative, ambitious woman, she claims PHILIP FALCONBRIDGE as her grandson and warns John against CONSTANCE, DUCHESS OF BRITTANY, although she herself is hardly a more sympathetic character.

EleanorT
Slaves of New York, 1986
Tama Janowitz
A jewellery designer in her late twenties, with 'red, corkscrew curls', tiny blue eyes and 'buggy-whip' arms, Eleanor is plagued by chronic insecurity and a woeful lack of self-esteem. The kind of person who finds it 'traumatic even to make a decision on what to order from a restaurant menu', she wistfully yearns for a life blessed with a thriving career and a happy relationship, and frets that she is really just playing at being grown-up. Struggling to survive in New York, she tries prostitution and a servile relationship with moody artist Stash before striking out on her own for an uncertain future.

Elena
The Flute-Player, 1979
D M Thomas
A warm and promiscuous woman who reluctantly, in a country torn apart by revolution, turns to prostitution as a means of survival. She has an extraordinary ability to forget the past, even though she loses her baby and undergoes torture. She lives in the present, and is kind and generous, always helping the underdog. She is exceptionally tolerant and accepting of men. Elena is a nurturer, nursing many friends and supporting and cherishing artists she admires. Though damaged, she bears no grudges and ends up happy, her quick-wittedness having saved her life.

Elginbrod, David
David Elginbrod, 1863
George MacDonald
An old man who has tilled the land, but is now the 'general adviser and executor' to the local laird. He is an 'unusual old man', and although formally uneducated, he is uncommonly eager to learn from books, but already has the benefit of 'life intelligently met and honestly passed', which 'is the best education of all'. He is very devout, and has a childlike wisdom and innate goodness, and the 'true humility that comes of worshipping the Truth'. He is a moral and spiritual touchstone in the novel.

Elie
Butcher's Broom, 1934
Neil Gunn
Kind and generous, Elie's love for life is cruelly diminished when she has to leave the village of Riasgan to hide the shame of her bastard son. But the harshness of life drives her back home where, despite her shame, she finds warmth and shelter with DARK MAIRI. Her loveless marriage to ROB almost destroys her, but after his death she begins to regain some of her zest for life.

Elinor
The Adventures of Ferdinand, Count Fathom, 1753
Tobias Smollett
An 'innocent, unsuspecting country damsel', seduced and traduced by FERDINAND, COUNT FATHOM's calculating evil and driven mad by it. She is eventually delivered into the protection of the aptly named Mrs Clement.

Eliot, Irene
The New Men, 1954
C P Snow
The wife of MARTIN ELIOT, who marries her somewhat against the advice of his brother LEWIS ELIOT, who finds her shallow, if physically charming. 'She was a tall woman, full-breasted, with a stoop that made one feel that she was self-conscious about her figure; often when she laughed she made a bow which reduced her height still more, which made her seem to be acting like a little girl.'

Eliot, Lewis
Strangers and Brothers, 1940, et seq
C P Snow
Narrator of the *Strangers and Brothers* cycle, he rises from humble provincial origins in the Midlands to the Bar, thence to considerable influence in academia and government.

Eliot, Margaret
Homecomings, 1958, and others
C P Snow
Not untypical of Snow's female characters, she exerts a significant background influence, but rarely emerges as a fully-fledged character in her own right. Though initially she rejects LEWIS ELIOT, terminating their relationship to marry a children's doctor, they are later reunited after the suicide of Eliot's first wife. Margaret brings him a stability and commitment that he has not previously known.

Eliot, Martin
The New Men, 1954, et seq
C P Snow
The younger brother of LEWIS ELIOT and a scientist closely involved in early research into atomic fission at the Cavendish laboratory in Cambridge. He has an excellent, well-focused mind and an impressive dedication to duty.

Eliot, Meg
The Middle Age of Mrs Eliot, 1958
Angus Wilson
A bright, attractive woman in her early forties, devotedly married to a successful barrister, she is comfortably settled into the weave of upper-middle-class life in London, with its social round, charity work and closeness to the springs of power. Her life is torn apart when her husband is shot while they are on a celebratory tour to the East, and she has to rethink all her priorities.

Eliot, Sheila
Homecomings, 1958, and others
C P Snow
The complex, disturbed first wife of LEWIS ELIOT, she seems incapable of love, but addicted to tiny power struggles with her husband and friends.

She eventually commits suicide.

Elissa
The Faerie Queene, 1590–6
Sir Edmund Spenser
The discontented elder sister of PERISSA and MEDINA, she resents Perissa's appetite and Medina's reason. Furiously jealous, she is huffy, ungracious and wrathful. She is courted by HUDIBRAS.

Eliza (Eliza Harris)
Uncle Tom's Cabin, or, Life Among the Lowly, 1851–2
Harriet Beecher Stowe
A light-skinned slave on the Shelby plantation, whose desperate flight across the ice floes is intended to dramatize a stark contrast both with the forbearance of UNCLE TOM (who makes no attempt to resist being sold down river) and with the negative model of motherhood represented by Marie St Clare. As with many characters in the book, she has been found unconvincing by modern black critics, being perceived as an off-white fantasy figure.

Elizabeth
A Question of Power, 1974
Bessie Head
Elizabeth's mother was a white woman who was classified as insane because she was having a child by a 'native' stable boy. Elizabeth's attempts to find a place for herself in the strange world she inhabits lead to mental collapse and 'a journey to hell'. During her breakdown, her mind is invaded by the souls of SELLO and DAN MOLOMO. Disillusioned and insecure, Elizabeth becomes a victim of their manipulation. Her love for her son saves her from suicide and, with the help of TOM, she finally discovers a tentative sense of belonging.

Elizabeth, Queen → Woodville, Elizabeth

Elizabeth I, Queen of England
Kenilworth, 1821
Sir Walter Scott
Despite his romantic attachment to MARY, QUEEN OF SCOTS, Scott is too good a historian to weight his portrait of Elizabeth with undue prejudice. His stated intention is 'to describe her as at once a high-minded sovereign, and a female of passionate feelings', who hesitates between public duty and private attachments.

Ellen
The Way of all Flesh, 1903
Samuel Butler
The Pontifex's kitchen maid, Ellen is the first woman to attract the young ERNEST PONTIFEX's attention. She is beautiful, with a perfect figure 'erring if at all on the side of robustness'. But she has also fallen from grace. She is unmarried, pregnant and therefore instantly expelled from the uncharitable Pontifex vicarage. Much later, she marries Ernest and has two children by him, but when he discovers she is married already and is an alcoholic, she is promptly abandoned again and her children taken away. Ellen represents the idea of woman as a snare for the unwary male,

bringing with her a cargo of burdensome social conventions and responsibilities.

Ellicott, Miss Nancy
'Cousin Nancy', in *Prufrock and Other Observations*, 1917
T S Eliot
Her elders, whose manners were conditioned by Matthew Arnold and Ralph Waldo Emerson, were not sure quite what they felt about Nancy, who smoked, rode to hounds, hill-walked and 'danced all the modern dances'.

Ellie
The Water Babies, 1863
Charles Kingsley
The 'little lady in white' and daughter of Sir John, whom TOM first sets eyes upon when he lands in her room, black and sooty from the chimney. She meets him again in fairyland when, after her initial fear, she falls in love with him.

Ellieslaw, Vere, Laird of
The Black Dwarf, 1816
Sir Walter Scott
He 'kens naething about thae newfangled notions o' peace and quietness – he's a' for the auld-warld doings o' lifting and laying on'. He cynically allows his daughter to become a political pawn in his own power game, but is eventually thwarted and is obliged to live abroad, supported by her fortune.

Elliot, Anne
Persuasion, 1818
Jane Austen
Having been foolishly persuaded many years previously by her godmother LADY RUSSELL to break off her engagement to CAPTAIN WENTWORTH, Anne, 27 and the middle daughter of SIR WALTER ELLIOT, visibly shows the sadness this has brought her. Still attractive and pleasant, she has, however, lost her 'bloom', but soon starts to recover it when Captain Wentworth reappears. Kind, sensible and patient, her continuing devotion, and the realization that she was wrong to have let her good judgement be swayed by others less perceptive than herself, eventually bring her happiness.

Elliot, Elizabeth
Persuasion, 1818
Jane Austen
The elder sister of ANNE ELLIOT and MARY ELLIOT, Elizabeth has, since her mother's death 16 years previously, felt herself to be of prime importance in the running of the family home. She resembles her father, SIR WALTER ELLIOT, in her haughty self-conceit, which she continues to display after moving to Bath. Cold-hearted and snobbish, Elizabeth has few redeeming qualities.

Elliot, Mary
Persuasion, 1818
Jane Austen
The youngest of SIR WALTER ELLIOT's daughters, she is a fairly pathetic character who is whiningly self-indulgent to the point of irritation. Languid, feeble and almost constantly complaining about one thing or another, she is self-important, like her

father and her sister ELIZABETH ELLIOT, and makes a very demanding wife to CHARLES MUSGROVE, and an even more demanding sister to ANNE ELLIOT.

Elliot, Rickie
The Longest Journey, 1907
E M Forster

A lame, delicate and lonely child whose parents died when he was 15, Rickie Elliot grows into a naive, impressionable young man with an idealistic view of the world and the people in it. An enthusiastic student at Cambridge with no plans for the future, he is distracted from his philosophical ideals by a conventional desire to settle down and have a family. Marriage to the superficial AGNES PEMBROKE and employment as a housemaster at a minor public school continue his descent into rigid conformity, a process only challenged by the emotions unleashed on learning of the existence of his half-brother STEPHEN WONHAM.

Elliot, Sir Walter
Persuasion, 1818
Jane Austen

Forced to rent out his family home, as a result of his extravagant and careless overspending, widower Sir Walter still manages to find plenty of fodder for his puffed-up vanity. Foolishly superficial, and egotistically glorying in his title of Baronet, he cuts a ridiculous figure, inspiring nothing short of derision.

Elliot, William
Persuasion, 1818
Jane Austen

Cousin of the Elliot sisters and heir to Kellynch Hall, William, though handsome, discreet and in possession of polished manners is 'too generally agreeable' to everyone to be the genuine article. He hides a shady past and a marriage for money, and is revealed to be a selfish, double-dealing villain whose main concern is to prevent SIR WALTER ELLIOT from remarrying, so that he can be sure of inheriting the baronetcy.

Elliott, Christina
Weir of Hermiston, 1896
Robert Louis Stevenson

The daughter of CLEM ELLIOT of Cauldstaneslap. She has acquired a veneer of sophistication in Glasgow, dresses in the height of fashion and causes a considerable stir when she arrives at Hermiston. From her first sight of ARCHIE WEIR across a crowded church, she uses her coy but knowing innocence to attract his attention. She is a vain, contrary, flirtatious girl who retains something of the gypsy in her soul. Christina is not so much in love with Archie himself, as with the idea of being in love with him. Her self-absorption leaves her an easy prey to FRANK INNES's malevolent schemes.

Elliott, Clem (Clement)
Weir of Hermiston, 1896
Robert Louis Stevenson

The third of the Elliott brothers and the most successful in material terms. He is a sound, dependable businessman based in Glasgow, who has acquired a certain commercial acuity. Clem

has an air of expansive self-assurance and worldliness which his other brothers lack. He brings up his daughter CHRISTINA ELLIOTT to enjoy the high life of Glasgow and, in the process, creates the spoilt, self-centred girl who is to enter the country world of Hermiston with such fateful consequences.

Elliott, Dand (Andrew)
Weir of Hermiston, 1896
Robert Louis Stevenson

The youngest of the four Elliott brothers. He is a talented, courageous shepherd who works for his brother ROB ELLIOTT on the farm. His interest in the job is quixotic, however, and he deliberately only works the minimum hours to earn himself a living. Dand considers that he is above money and material things, and believes that true wealth resides in a free soul. Something of a ladies' man, he has an air of dreamy otherworldliness and sees his true vocation as a poet, albeit a minor one. He is a figure of fun, contrasting with the seriousness of the other characters.

Elliott, Gib (Gilbert)
Weir of Hermiston, 1896
Robert Louis Stevenson

The second of the Elliott brothers, he is a weaver. In contrast to his practical elder brother, ROB ELLIOTT, he has been something of an idealist, supporting the principles of the French Revolution. Thwarted in his radical impulses by the reaction of the legal system, he turns his attention to religious matters and becomes the leader of a Christian sect. He is shunned by his brothers for his extreme views, but represents the spirit of utopianism within the family.

Elliott, Hobbie, more properly Halbert, also known as Hobbie of the Cleugh-foot
The Black Dwarf, 1816
Sir Walter Scott

A 'substantial farmer, who boasted his descent from old Martin Elliott of the Preakin-tower, noted in Border story and song'. No man is better versed in such tales than the tough young huntsman. In speech, he is a virtual primer of Border Scots at the time of Queen Anne.

Elliott, Kirstie
Weir of Hermiston, 1896
Robert Louis Stevenson

The most purely sympathetic character in the novel. She is ADAM WEIR's housekeeper and manages 'a trim house and a good country table'. She is a generous-hearted, colourful character who, although past the prime of youth, is still a comely, handsome woman. Kirstie is a decent, dependable soul, fiercely loyal to the Weir family. She harbours a love for ARCHIE WEIR which she can barely express and, instead, must content herself by treating him as a nephew. Kirstie's yearning affection for the youth provides a counterpoint to the emotional coldness of her master and his son.

Elliott, Rob (Robert)
Weir of Hermiston, 1896
Robert Louis Stevenson

The eldest of the four Elliott brothers, he has

inherited the title of Laird of Cauldstaneslap. He is a decent man who is a church elder and is much respected in the parish. However, he is also an astute businessman in the affairs of his farm. He has hunted down and killed his father's murderer and is a symbol of honest, forthright retribution in a country too preoccupied with the niceties of civilized behaviour.

Ellis, Steve
Another Country, 1962
James Baldwin

IDA SCOTT's singing teacher, he is a pantingly eager and casually exploitative minor wheel in the music business. He babbles endless industry-speak, dispensing 'wet, hard' handshakes with forced sincerity. VIVALDO MOORE fears that he and Ida are having an affair.

Ellison, Kitty
A Chance Acquaintance, 1873
William Dean Howells

An unaffected New York girl, related in type to the LAPHAM sisters in a later book, she meets and falls in love with the upper-class Bostonian MILES ARBUTON during a trip up the St Lawrence into Canada. She is, however, acute enough to recognize the social gulf between them and breaks off their engagement.

Elmwood, Lady, previously **Miss Milner**
A Simple Story, 1791
Mrs Elizabeth Inchbald

As Miss Milner, she is a gay, flirtatious, worldly but rather silly girl who falls in love with a priest (LORD ELMWOOD), but agrees to keep their feelings secret. She is later able to marry him when he inherits a peerage. Her flighty nature and weak character are expressed in an affair with an old suitor, and she is expelled from the house by her outraged husband, along with her daughter, MATILDA ELMWOOD, to whom she has been a sorry moral example. She dies of remorse, leaving Matilda unprotected in a threatening world.

Elmwood, Lord
A Simple Story, 1791
Mrs Elizabeth Inchbald

He is a priest named Dorriforth, who falls in love with a flirtatious young beauty, Miss Milner (LADY ELMWOOD). They agree to conceal their love because of his position, but he is released from holy vows when he inherits a peerage and becomes Lord Elmwood. They marry, but he is incensed by her infidelity, and heartlessly banishes both her and their daughter, MATILDA ELMWOOD, quashing his own finer feelings in the process. His paternal instincts are rekindled when Matilda is threatened with abduction, and he returns her to the family home.

Elmwood, Matilda
A Simple Story, 1791
Mrs Elizabeth Inchbald

The daughter of LORD and LADY ELMWOOD. She is denied a 'proper education' by her flirtatious and unprincipled mother, and is eventually expelled from the house when her father discovers his wife's infidelities. Vulnerable and unprepared for life, she is left alone when her mother dies, and is threatened with abduction by a dangerous libertine, but is rescued and restored to honour by her repentant father.

Eloi
The Time Machine, 1895
H G Wells

Beautiful, graceful and only four feet tall, the Eloi welcome the Time Traveller as he arrives in the year 802,701 AD and ask him if he has come from the sun in a thunderstorm. Vegetarian and peacefully communistic, they sleep in huddles. They seem to be 'humanity on the wane', but this is only half the story: another post-human species exists below ground, the MORLOCKS, who use the Eloi in a controlled way as a food stock.

Elrigmore, Colin
John Splendid, 1898
Neil Munro

The narrator, who recalls the events of his youth from old age. He is a melancholy, philosophical dreamer, a peace-loving man who has forsaken his study of the Humanities and taken up arms. He has 'schooling and the wisdom of travel', but is careful, and indulges in 'a scrupulous balancing of chances' before venturing on any scheme. He loves the Highlands, his 'own countryside', and is ready to fight for it; he is drawn into the violent historical events of the novel alongside JOHN SPLENDID.

Elsmere, Robert
Robert Elsmere, 1888
Mrs Humphry Ward

A young clergyman recently graduated from Oxford, where he has been drawn into the passionate doctrinal debate stirred up by the Oxford Movement. Taking up a calling in Surrey with his wife, CATHERINE LEYBURN, he begins to read extensively, and to debate matters of theology with his devil's advocate, SQUIRE ROGER WENDOVER, a regime that gradually undermines a faith which was always more emotional than intellectual. Gradually, though, Robert rethinks his vocation and establishes the New Brotherhood of Christ, an evangelical mission in the East End of London. Though undoubtedly modelled on aspects of Mary Augusta Ward's own character, he is more a basis for the discussion of contemporary ideas about the Church than a fully convincing character.

Elton, Mr
Emma, 1816
Jane Austen

A vicar whose charm and good looks are a thin veneer in his prejudiced and mercenary quest to catch a wife. Despite winning the favour of EMMA WOODHOUSE, he lacks both the modesty to see the impropriety of an alliance with her, and the awareness to grasp her perception of him. Fearful of an imprudent alliance, in courting the wealthy Augusta Hawkins (the future MRS ELTON) he transforms eager sentiment and propriety into vanity and callousness.

Elton, Mrs
Emma, 1816
Jane Austen

Nouveau riche, crass, self-important and audaciously presumptuous, she is the spiteful, showpiece wife of MR ELTON, her '*caro sposo*'. Her 'airs of pert pretension and underbred finery' reveal a woman bereft of sense, sensibility and aesthetic judgement.

Em (Emily)
The Story of an African Farm, 1883
Olive Schreiner

Stepdaughter of Tant Sannie, owner of the South African farm where she grows up. Unlike her delicately high-minded cousin LYNDALL, Em grows up to be fat and placid. She falls in love with a new farm-hand, Gregory Rose, but he breaks off his engagement to her because of his infatuation with Lyndall. She is terribly upset by Lyndall's death, but it does result in Rose returning to marry her and life on the farm being restored to normal.

Eman
The Strong Breed, 1964
Wole Soyinka

A 'stranger' who maintains a tiny clinic in the bush with his daughter Sunma. Between them, they have lost all sense of mission, sustaining an uncertain existence with no informing philosophy or system of belief.

Emble
The Age of Anxiety, 1948
W H Auden

He enlisted in the navy during his sophomore year at college, but has now been cast ashore in a New York bar, where he comes up against others who have likewise been marooned by circumstance and disposition.

Emenike
The Concubine, 1966
Elechi Amadi

IHUOMA's first husband, Emenike is destined to die because of his marriage to the wife of the jealous Sea-King. 'Happy, optimistic and pushful', Emenike is respected by the village elders and is thought of as the ideal young man. A good wrestler, despite his light build, he is injured in a fight when 'his gods were not at home' to protect him.

Emerson, George
A Room With a View, 1908
E M Forster

A clerk in the general manager's office at one of the big railways, and the son of MR EMERSON, he is an intelligent, trustworthy young man whose preoccupation with the fate of the universe has lent him a somewhat melancholy air. Beguiled by LUCY HONEYCHURCH during a trip to Italy, he finds his ardour undiminished when they encounter each other once more as neighbours in Surrey. The prospect of romance alleviates his gravity, allowing lighter, more joyful spirits to assert themselves.

Emerson, Mr
A Room With a View, 1908
E M Forster

A bluff, friendly old widower of heavy build, and father of GEORGE EMERSON, he is the plain-speaking son of a labourer who advanced through the working classes and became a journalist for the socialist press. Now retired and in fading health, he retains a youthful spirit and a romantic streak, although his blunt honesty and lack of tact are more often misconstrued as rudeness than perceived as the actions of a kind-hearted man who refuses to stand on ceremony.

Emery, Stan (Stanwood)
Manhattan Transfer, 1925
John Dos Passos

The youthful son of the leading partner in Emery & Emery, GEORGE BALDWIN's law firm, Stan elects to eschew his privileged background in pursuit of the sublimity of failure. Sent down from Harvard University, he leads a carefree life of raffish, alcoholic abandon. A close friend of JIMMY HERF, he has an affair with the married actress ELLEN THATCHER, only to return from a drunken trip to Niagara Falls with a new wife, the actress Pearline. His wild dipsomania and subversive personal values lead him to commit spectacular suicide in an apartment blaze.

Emilia
The Man of Mode, 1676
Sir George Etherege

Young, virtuous and beautiful, Emilia loves and is loved by YOUNG BELLAIR, but disconcertingly finds herself the object of his father's attentions. Determined and intelligent, she outwits him with the help of the benevolent LADY TOWNELEY, and earns his blessing for her marriage to his son.

Emilia
Othello, 1603/4
William Shakespeare

A good, trusting woman who speaks her mind, her muscularity and bawdy humour present her as a neat foil to her mistress, DESDEMONA. Her loyalty to her husband, IAGO, makes her an unsuspecting link in his plot. The revelation of his true character, combined with her adoration of the dead Desdemona, make her cry, 'I'll kill myself for grief', entirely credible.

Emilius, Reverend Joseph
The Eustace Diamonds, 1873
Phineas Redux, 1874
Anthony Trollope

An eloquent, fashionable, but fraudulent preacher who 'was reputed by some to have reached such a standard of pulpit-oratory, as to have no equal within the memory of living hearers'. He is said to have been born in Hungary of Jewish extraction, but has hidden his past. His dishonesty becomes apparent when it is discovered that he has married LADY LIZZIE EUSTACE bigamously.

Emily
'The Knight's Tale', in *The Canterbury Tales*,
c.1387–1400
Geoffrey Chaucer

The prototype of the passive English heroine,

she really wants neither of the two knights ARCITE and PALAMON, and would rather remain chaste all her life and indulge her taste for hunting. She prays to Diana on the eve of battle that the knights may be reconciled and that she may be left in peace. Realizing that it is a woman's lot to submit, she asks that if she must marry one of them let it be the one who loves her most. Her prayer is granted when she agrees, after much persuasion, to marry Palamon.

Em'ly, Little
David Copperfield, 1850
Charles Dickens

The orphaned niece and adopted daughter of DANIEL PEGGOTTY and the object of DAVID COPPERFIELD's first love. She becomes an apprentice to MR OMER. A shy, pretty girl, she is betrothed to her cousin, HAM PEGGOTTY, but, having always wished to become a lady, she elopes with the dashing MR JAMES STEERFORTH on the eve of her wedding. Abandoned by him on the Continent some years later, she returns to London unmarried and humiliated. With the help of the prostitute, MARTHA ENDELL, she is reunited with her uncle, and the three emigrate to Australia. Long afterwards they learn that Ham has died attempting to save the life of a drowning man, who, when washed ashore, is revealed to be Steerforth.

Emma → Woodhouse, Emma

Emma
Betrayal, 1978
Harold Pinter

The wife of ROBERT, a publisher, Emma has recently concluded a seven-year-long affair with JERRY, her husband's great friend, and is currently enjoying a relationship with one of his clients. The owner of an art gallery, she is intelligent, discriminating, elegant and coolly in control of her feelings. Sharply observant, she recalls precise circumstances rather than emotions. Noting that to Robert and Jerry, their friendship is even more important than their marriages, she is able to manipulate the sensibilities of both. The play recounts Jerry and Emma's affair from beginning to end in reverse chronological order.

Emma
Summer of the Seventeenth Doll, 1955
Ray Lawler

OLIVE's mother, she is nearing 70, yet does not show her age until her climactic dismissal of ROO WEBBER and BARNEY IBBOT from their summer home of the last 17 years. Cynical and detached, she is able to provide a commentary on the events of the play, and on the past which dominates the other self-deluded characters. She holds no illusions about Barney, and acts quickly to remove Roo, perceiving his collapse despite her obvious affection for him. Ultimately she acts to protect her daughter, whom she recognizes as far too foolish to understand the nature of the changes which have taken place in Roo and Barney.

Emmanuel, Monsieur Paul
Villette, 1853
Charlotte Brontë

The unromantic anti-hero of the novel, Monsieur Paul is the fiery, little Professor of Literature at his cousin MADAME BECK's school. 'Dark, ascerbic, and caustic', only the very perceptive LUCY SNOWE can see through his veneer of crotchety irritability to the generous and passionate man beneath; and as Lucy grows more attached to him he likewise softens in his approach to her. Although he is rude and brusque when riled, it is his kind-heartedness which most distinguishes him.

Emmy
Soldier's Pay, 1926
William Faulkner

A plain, rather hopeless cousin of the wounded airman LT DONALD MAHON, with whom she fell in love before he went to war. Her constancy is severely tested by his appalling scar.

Emperor, the
Androcles and the Lion, 1912
George Bernard Shaw

A Roman Caesar, the Emperor is 'a divine personage' who uses his position of unassailable authority to behave like a martinet. A man with little sense of the value of human life, he pronounces sentences of death as easily as he confers crowns of honour. However, after the heroic exploits of FERROVIUS, and the astounding episode whereby ANDROCLES and the lion embrace in the arena, the Emperor hastily announces his conversion to Christianity.

Emsworth, Lord
Blandings Castle, 1935, et seq
P G Wodehouse

Clarence, ninth Earl of Emsworth, vague, amiable but absent-minded, is the owner of Blandings Castle and the father of Freddie Threepwood, a fact he would rather forget. Bullied by his sister Lady Constance, at odds always with his gardener Angus McAllister, all he wants is a quiet life in old clothes. His great joys are his prize pig, Empress of Blandings, and his yew avenue; he is fluffy-minded but cunning in his ability to wander off into the gardens and the distance where his sister and his secretary Baxter cannot find him or make him behave like a peer of the realm.

Endell, Martha
David Copperfield, 1850
Charles Dickens

An unfortunate young woman from Yarmouth who, with LITTLE EM'LY, becomes an apprentice of MR OMER. After being seduced, she escapes to London and becomes a prostitute. She redeems herself by helping DANIEL PEGGOTTY to be reunited with Little Em'ly. She emigrates to Australia with them and marries happily.

Enderby, F X
Inside Mr Enderby, 1963, et seq
Anthony Burgess, under the pseudonym Joseph Kell

A middle-aged poet who can now only write while sitting on the lavatory. Obsessed with his digestive system, and indeed often reduced to a crude phage, absorbing and expelling perceptions of his surroundings, after a course of psychotherapy he is renamed 'Piggy Hogg'. He has an honesty and courageous integrity lacking in most of those who surround him, and with his Catholic forenames and apocalyptic-sounding family name, he seems to represent the artist who persists heroically even beyond the end of his tether.

Endicott, John
'The Maypole of Merry Mount', 1836, 'Endicott and the Red Cross', 1837, in *Twice-Told Tales*, 1837, revised edition 1842
Nathaniel Hawthorne

Soldier-hero of the American Revolution, and 'Puritan of Puritans', who restores the 'moral gloom of the world' by hacking down the pagan maypole and who, in the later story, cuts the red cross from the English flag to demonstrate that he owes no allegiance either to the pope or King George.

English, Julian
Appointment in Samarra, 1934
John O'Hara

Outwardly successful, he runs a Cadillac dealership in a small but prosperous Pennsylvania town. Dissatisfied, though, with his existence, and conscious of the inherited weakness that comes down to him from his doctor father, he sets out on a self-destructive three-day bender that ends in his suicide.

English Patient, the
The English Patient, 1992
Michael Ondaatje

He lies, charred almost to death, in a remote Italian villa at the end of World War II, looked after by the devoted HANA. Speaking fitfully about his life before his plane crash in his beloved Libyan desert, he portrays himself as an English explorer, and is gradually revealed as a man of exceptional learning and intelligence, as well as humour, underlain by intense willpower, independence and pride. As he recalls a tortured love affair with a married American woman in Cairo, some doubt arises about his identity, leading Hana's friend Caravaggio to suspect that he is, in fact, a renowned Hungarian spy.

Enitharmon
Europe, A Prophecy, 1794
William Blake

The mother of ORC, Enitharmon is a symbol of society. She sleeps and dreams for 'eighteen hundred years', a sleep from which she awakes, unaware of the unfurling human history up to the French Revolution. She becomes selfish, concerned with her own comfort and the reverie of her own 'bliss', but is easily weakened by the presence of her passive 'sons & daughters', shown by the fact that she 'groans & cries in anguish and dismay' on witnessing Orc's revolutionary fury in France.

Enketei, Mira, also known as Miss Inkytie, etc
Amalgamemnon, 1984
Christine Brooke-Rose

A university teacher of humanities, we find her trapped in a nightmare world of subjunctives and conditionals, an eternal future tense. Could she be poised on the brink of intellectual as well as professional redundancy? Either way, she will play no part in a society governed by machine values, neat economic calculations, and a thorough-going denial of humanism.

Enobarbus, Domitius
Antony and Cleopatra, 1606/7
William Shakespeare

Enobarbus is a strong-minded, rugged Roman soldier and friend of ANTONY. Initially, he appears to think little of women: 'between them and a great cause they should be esteemed nothing', he advises Antony. Yet his cynicism seems only skin-deep, as some of the play's most lyrical verse includes his admiring description of CLEOPATRA's majestic power and womanliness: 'Age cannot wither her, nor custom stale/Her infinite variety'. When OCTAVIUS CAESAR declares war upon Antony and Cleopatra at Actium, Enobarbus, a shrewd military strategist, advises Antony to fight on land and not sea. His advice ignored, he defects to Octavius and, a 'master-leaver and a fugitive', dies of remorse.

Epicoene
Epicoene, or The Silent Woman, 1609
Ben Jonson

Epicoene is the silent 'woman' of the title. Because SIR DAUPHINE EUGENIE knows that his uncle, MOROSE, hopes to marry and thus disinherit him, he manipulates Morose into marrying Epicoene, a young boy disguised as a quietly-spoken, unobtrusive woman. Epicoene is happy to play along with the charade (which is revealed immediately the ceremony has taken place), because it exposes fools in high places.

Eppie
Silas Marner, 1861
George Eliot

The natural daughter of the squire's son GODFREY CASS, baby Eppie crawls away from her dying mother in the snow to find herself at the door of SILAS MARNER's cottage. Silas, miser and recluse, who has just had his gold stolen, sees a baby with 'soft yellow rings all over its head'. He brings her up with loving care and without punishments, and at the age of 18 she appears to retain childhood's innocence and spontaneous affection.

Erdman, Lisa
The White Hotel, 1981
D M Thomas

With crippling pains in her left side, thought to be caused by hysteria, Lisa Erdman becomes the subject of a psychoanalytical case-study by Sigmund Freud. She is an extraordinary and disturbing character – modest, yet a talented opera singer, reserved, yet highly sexed, selfless and loving to her adopted son, yet willing to lie to Freud. Her consciousness, which with her gift of second sight ranges over past, present and future, seems to represent humankind's troubled spirit attempting to escape the horrors of the modern world.

Erlynne, Mrs
Lady Windermere's Fan, 1892
Oscar Wilde

A woman with a 'dozen' pasts – none of them particularly respectable – she has nevertheless decided that she wishes to be accepted in society, and enlists the help of Lord Windermere in her endeavours. As a young woman, Mrs Erlynne deserted her husband and her baby daughter – LADY WINDERMERE – claiming never to have known a mother's feelings. Charming and considerably less heartless than she claims, she sacrifices her chance of social acceptance to prevent her daughter from leaving her husband and following her mother's path to shame and ignominy.

Erme, Gwendolyn
'The Figure in the Carpet', in *Embarrassments*, 1896
Henry James

The wife of the critic CORVICK, who claims to have discovered the secret 'figure in the carpet' that unifies the novelist HUGH VEREKER's work, and who has vouchsafed the secret to her. On Corvick's death, she marries another critic, DRAYTON DEANE, but dies herself without revealing the secret to him.

Erridge (Lord Warminster, known as Alf)
A Dance to the Music of Time, 12 volumes, 1951–75
Anthony Powell

Something of a misfit, tales of whose latest eccentric adventure fuel the gossip of London salons. Erratic in his behaviour, he is a high-minded revolutionary who throughout the 1930s supports a band of spongers and left-leaning hangers-on. Living in squalor and usually sporting an old corduroy jacket, he is given to tramping in the Midlands and other vaguely Orwellian exploits. In 1934 he is J G QUIGGIN's landlord and patron. When first met as a schoolboy by the narrator NICHOLAS JENKINS he is 'angular, sallow and spotty'. Later, at débutante dances, he appears bothered, bewildered and belligerent. With Quiggin, he sets sail for China but returns after only a month. Having inherited a small fortune from ST JOHN CLARKE, he decides to fund a literary magazine called *Fission*, but dies suddenly of a coronary thrombosis.

Errol, Cedric
Little Lord Fauntleroy, 1885
Frances Hodgson Burnett

Cedric Errol wears velvet and lace and calls his mother 'Dearest', but in fact embodies the innocent charm of the New World. His trusting naivety wins over his embittered English grandfather, the Earl of Dorincourt, to a 'grim smile'. Social problems of class, illness and poverty are patently soluble to him by simple redistribution of wealth in acts of impersonal charity. Loyal and fearless, he is a natural aristocrat.

Erzsberger, Matthias
Gossip from the Forest, 1975
Thomas Keneally

One of the German negotiators at the surrender which marks the end of World War I. A man of solid country stock, he is suspicious both of the cultured disdain of the British and French delegates and of Prussian militarism, which sweeps him under in 1919.

Escalus, Prince of Verona
Romeo and Juliet, 1591–6
William Shakespeare

The Prince of Verona, chagrined at the perpetual public brawling between Capulets and Montagues, tries desperately to keep the two families apart. A dispenser of justice, he is nevertheless partly responsible for the tragedy that ensues because he does not carry out his threat to execute the next person caught fighting on the street. He has difficulty finding the balance between severity and fairness, and it is his streak of generosity that causes him to banish ROMEO and hasten the impending tragedy.

Escot, Mr
Headlong Hall, 1816
Thomas Love Peacock

'Pale and saturnine', philosopher Mr Escot is dire and gloomy, a 'deteriorationist' and a depressed fatalist (drawn as a satirical portrait of the poet Shelley). He envisages corruption, disaster and decay everywhere. Scientific progress and civilization are for him retrogressive because they move further away from the ideal of pastoral man, 'the natural and original man', who was primitive but happy. A vegetarian who subscribes to a sackcloth theory – deprivation and self-denial will lead to pleasure – his romantic, sensitive turn of mind still allows that love offers hope for the future of humankind.

Esdras
Winterset, 1935
Maxwell Anderson

Father of the hoodlum GARTH, he represents the play's moral centre. Speaking like an Old Testament prophet, he provides a standpoint that is humane and compromising in place of the Mosaic violence of the main plot.

Esk, Sir Mark
Poor Fellow My Country, 1975
Xavier Herbert

The British-appointed Commander-in-Chief of the Australian army and father of LYDIA LYNDBROOKE-ESK. When, on the eve of World War II, he meets JEREMY DELACY, a white settler, Esk is impressed by his integrity and the conviction with which he holds his liberal beliefs. Something of a paradox, he represents an imperial power and is in many ways a natural colonialist, yet he does not make the mistake of underestimating the leadership potential of those theoretically opposed to his politics.

Esketh, Lady Edwina
The Rains Came, 1937
Louis Bromfield

Visiting Ranchipur with her rich and boorish older husband, the beautiful, bored and unhappy Edwina encounters TOM RANSOME, an old flame, and, seeking excitement, tries to revive their affair. But she is also attracted to the handsome Indian Army doctor MAJOR RAMA

SEFTI, and, caught up in the horrors of an earthquake, flooding and a cholera epidemic, volunteers for hospital work. A brittle, cynical aristocrat, she learns humility the hard way, and falling deeply in love with Sefti, is painfully transformed and redeemed by her experience of India.

Esmé

'For Esmé – with Love and Squalor', in *For Esmé – with Love and Squalor and Other Stories*, 1953
J D Salinger

'I'm quite communicative for my age', says Esmé, aged 13 and precociously articulate. Possessed of an unspecified title which she is reluctant to reveal in case it influences others' opinions of her, she is a recent orphan and acts as the protective guardian of her lively five-year-old brother Charles. Given to paraphrasing the critical statements made about her ('My aunt says I'm a terribly cold person'), she is at the same time acute and child-like, a contradictory figure who is both aloof and spontaneously warm.

Esme

The Recognitions, 1955
William Gaddis

WYATT GWYON's mistress, she serves as the model for many of his forged Old Masters. Of questionable mental balance, she puts a distinctive pause between the syllables of words. Gaunt after a (presumed) hysterectomy, 'her large eyes were exaggerated in their beauty by the hollows of her thin face', but are just too liquid to give her men the reflected image they desire from her. Some critics have suggested, rather bizarrely, that she is based on J D Salinger's character in the story 'For Esmé – With Love and Squalor' (see ESMÉ above); apart from the final part of that dedication, there seems no reason to make the connection.

Esmond, Beatrix

The History of Henry Esmond, Esquire, 1852, and as **Baroness Bernstein** in *The Virginians*, 1857–9
W M Thackeray

The beautiful and vivacious daughter of VISCOUNT FRANCIS CASTLEWOOD and LADY RACHEL CASTLEWOOD, who is nonetheless marred – or humanized – by a streak of arrogant pride, manifest in 'little imperial ways' that lift her above the run-of-the-mill romantic heroine. A passionate Jacobite, she is disdainful of HENRY ESMOND's apparently lowly birth, and rejects him, later becoming his stepdaughter when he marries her widowed mother. In *The Virginians* she has progressed into the kind of salty old age which, when combined with wealth, brings power but few real responsibilities. She takes as her favourite young HARRY ESMOND WARRINGTON, and leaves her money to him.

Esmond, Henry (Harry)

The History of Henry Esmond, Esquire, 1852
W M Thackeray

He grows up believing himself to be the illegitimate son of Thomas, Viscount Castlewood, and without a claim to a title that is, in fact, rightfully his. His lonely childhood is dramatically relieved when the new LADY CASTLEWOOD turns out to be the beautiful and (to Harry) angelically kind Rachel. Because of his constant self-aggrandisement, it is never clear how secure he is in his new self-image, or how constant are his attachments; he loves Lady Castlewood (and later marries her), either blind to her faults or prepared to accept them, but his attachment to the Jacobite cause is merely to impress her daughter BEATRIX ESMOND (who asserts that her parents' supposedly near-perfect marriage was in fact spoilt by Harry's overbearing nature).

Esposito, Elena

The Deer Park, 1957
The Deer Park: A Play, 1959, revised edition 1967
Norman Mailer

'Not so much beautiful as sexual. She moves in a vale of deep sexual musk', as open and stereotypically vulnerable as her lover, the film director CHARLES FRANCIS EITEL, and is sophisticatedly closed off to actual experience. A dancer, her steps are almost entirely dictated by men, but she is possessed of a quick shrewdness, instinctive loyalty, and an uncalculating honesty.

Espy, Rev Lionel

Racing Demon, 1990
David Hare

One of a group of south-London clergymen (the others include the REV TONY FERRIS and the REV HARRY HENDERSON), Lionel Espy is a humble, diffident man in his fifties whose family have been Church of England clergymen for generations. The social, moral and political disintegration he sees about him troubles him deeply and he is uncertain whether he, with his low-Church views, or the Church itself, can cope. The Church, he fears, has 'no connection with most people's lives'. He is a tragic figure, who loves his wife but cannot demonstrate love; whose commitment to God is absolute but who can no longer understand the nature of God or commitment itself.

Essrog, Lionel

Motherless Brooklyn, 1999
Jonathan Lethem

Lionel Essrog, nicknamed 'the human freakshow', has Tourette's syndrome. His condition manifests itself in verbal tics, shouting and compulsions to tap people's shoulders or touch objects. Food has a mellowing effect on these symptoms, as does sex, although he has few opportunities to take advantage of the latter. Good-natured, bright and somewhat diffident, he is one of the 'Minna Men' – four former residents of St Vincent's Home for Boys who work as a combined car service and detective agency in Brooklyn. When Frank Minna, their employer and father figure, is murdered, Lionel sets out to find the killer with little support from his colleagues.

Esteban

The Bridge of San Luis Rey, 1927
Thornton Wilder

Left as babies in the foundling basket at a Lima convent, Esteban and his twin brother, MANUEL, are so alike that no one can tell them apart. Having almost no need of words between them, when they do communicate verbally it is in a secret language devised when they were young. Having devotedly nursed Manuel, Esteban is torn apart by his death, and, deranged with grief, attempts suicide, but is rescued by the sympathetic Captain Alvarado. Esteban is on the bridge when it collapses.

Estella
Great Expectations, 1861
Charles Dickens
The beautiful daughter of ABEL MAGWITCH and MOLLY, the housekeeper of MR JAGGERS. Jaggers arranges for MISS HAVISHAM to adopt her and educate her as a lady, but she is taught to hate and torment all men, including PIP, who falls in love with her during their encounters at Miss Havisham's. She marries BENTLEY DRUMMLE for wealth and position but leaves him because of his brutality. The novel ends with the hint that, now chastened and softened in character, she eventually marries Pip.

Estragon
Waiting for Godot, 1955
Samuel Beckett
'Nothing to be done' intones the bowler-hatted tramp Estragon, thus summing up Beckett's guiding principle on life. Like his companion, the equally peripatetic VLADIMIR, Estragon comes to us with no history, deprived of possessions, lodging, food and health. He is a malcontent, seeking corporeal relief, less interested in why he is, as in how he is. Desperate to ward off silence, which surely spells death, he personifies the music-hall clown, constantly seeking amusements with which to fill in time.

Etherington, Earl of, formerly Lord Oakendale, also known as Francis Valentine BulmerTyrrel, known incognito by his middle names, FrankTyrrel
St Ronan's Well, 1823
Sir Walter Scott
A young English peer, approaching the age of 25. His half-brother and namesake is the elder Frank Tyrrel, who stands to inherit all if Etherington is not able to negotiate or cheat his way into an alliance with CLARA MOWBRAY of St Ronan's. Etherington is a cool and calculating young man, with a cynical disregard for others and a gambler's ability to dissemble.

Euarchus
The Countess of Pembroke's Arcadia, 1581–4, published 1590
Sir Philip Sidney
The just ruler of Macedon, father and uncle of PYROCLES and MUSIDORUS. He is the deus ex machina of the romance, condemning GYNECIA for the apparent murder of her husband, and the young princes for their moral derelictions. In this role, he is the model of impartial rectitude, tempered with mercy.

Eubulus
Euphues, orThe Anatomy of Wit, 1578
John Lyly
An old man of Naples, he takes it upon himself to complete EUPHUES's philosophically deficient education, wakening him to the pitfalls of a world in which nothing runs according to fixed rules.

Eugenia, Baroness Münster
The Europeans, 1878
Henry James
'She was not pretty; but even when it expressed perplexed irritation her face was most interesting and agreeable … Neither was she in her first youth … Her complexion was fatigued; her mouth was large, her lips too full, her teeth uneven, her chin rather commonly modelled.' Her title is a polite fiction, for at 33 her morganatic marriage to the Baron is at an end, and she has come across the Atlantic to Boston to seek a rich husband among her American kinsfolk.

Eugenides, Mr
The Waste Land, 1922
T S Eliot
A merchant of Smyrna, 'unshaven, with a pocket full of currants', he speaks French colloquially and has a taste for brief sexual encounters.

Eugenie, Sir Dauphine
Epicoene, orThe Silent Woman, 1609
Ben Jonson
A high-spirited, clever and cunning young knight, Eugenie is resentful of the disapproval of his uncle MOROSE, who can abide neither noise nor his nephew's way of life, and threatens to disinherit him. Knowing that he hopes to marry, Eugenie tricks him into marrying EPICOENE, supposedly a softly-spoken young woman, whom he knows to be a boy in disguise. Immediately the ceremony is performed, Epicoene becomes loud and talkative. In order to secure his inheritance, Eugenie promises to arrange a divorce; he then reveals Epicoene's true identity, making his uncle appear incredibly foolish.

Eumenides
The Old Wives' Tale, 1595
George Peele
A wandering knight, to whom the abducted DELIA is 'the lodestar of my life'. He generously gives his last money to help bury a stranger, thus unwittingly winning the ally, JACK'S GHOST, who will help him recover his love. He is valiant and determined in facing SACRAPANT, and is true to his word in being ready to kill Delia rather than break a promise to the Ghost.

Euphues
Euphues, orThe Anatomy of Wit, 1578
Euphues and His England, 1580
John Lyly
'A young gentleman … of more wit than wealth, and yet of more wealth than wisdom'. At the end of his student years in Athens, he travels to Naples where he gains a robuster education in the ways of the world, stealing his friend PHILAUTUS's lover LUCILLA, and finding himself jilted by her in turn before returning to a life of contemplation in Athens, his ability to overdo a simile quite unaffected.

Eustace → Cherrington, Eustace

'Eustace', known as the boy
'Eustace', in *Child's Play, with Eustace and the Prowler*, 1982
David Malouf

A mysterious red-headed boy who appears, semi-clad and carrying his boots, to a plain young girl, JANE, in a school dormitory, leading her away from her friends into an antiseptic, tiled bathroom. She names him after an illicit pet hamster secreted away amid odd smells in a dormitory wardrobe. Perceived by the girl as 'bare-legged, gangling, freckled, with a smell, a mixture of sweat and car-grease', the strongest associations he gives off are of death rather than sex, and it may be that his name carries an echo of L P Hartley's hero EUSTACE CHERRINGTON.

Eustace, Father
The Monastery, 1820
Sir Walter Scott

The polar opposite of the ABBOT OF UNREASON, 'he was a thin, sharp-faced, slight-made little man, whose keen grey eyes seemed almost to look through the person to whom he addressed himself. His body was emaciated not only with the fasts which he observed with rigid punctuality, but also by the active and unwearied exercise of his sharp and piercing intellect.'

Eustace, Lady Lizzie, originally Lizzie Greystock
The Eustace Diamonds, 1873
Anthony Trollope

An orphan, she marries SIR FLORIAN EUSTACE, and is quickly left a wealthy widow. Lured into a bigamous marriage with the REVEREND JOSEPH EMILIUS, she later marries LORD GEORGE DE BRUCE CARRUTHERS. She has clear, bright blue eyes which signal danger 'to those who know how to read a face'. Her soft, slim, lithe figure is constantly active, and she is 'almost snake-like in her rapid bendings and the almost too easy gestures of her body'. A shrewd and attentive listener with a ready understanding and native cunning, she is 'desirous to show not only as a beauty but as a wit'.

Eustace, Sir Florian
The Eustace Diamonds, 1873
Phineas Redux, 1874
The Prime Minister, 1876
Anthony Trollope

The husband of LADY LIZZIE EUSTACE, his appearance is brief. He is easily seduced into a proposal of marriage by her charm and astute manipulation. He is a wealthy young nobleman, but is known to be dying, and within a year of their marriage has died, leaving his fortune to his ambitious young widow.

Eva, or Little Eva, properly Eva St Clare
Uncle Tom's Cabin, or, Life Among the Lowly, 1851–2
Harriet Beecher Stowe

A child of unconvincingly angelic complexion and behaviour, her only possible fate is an early grave. Dressed in stainless white, blue-eyed and blonde, she is a sentimental idea of an uncorrupted nature that sees no divisions on the basis of class. The daughter of the kindly and cultured AUGUSTINE ST CLARE, she is rescued from certain death on the Mississippi steamship by UNCLE TOM.

Evandale, Lord
Old Mortality, in *Tales of My Landlord*, 1816
Sir Walter Scott

Handsome young suitor for the hand of EDITH BELLENDEN. He loses out to HENRY MORTON at the opening '*wappen-schaws*' and again, at the end, in love. Proud and rather sensitive, he is, like Morton, a moderate, though one that leans rather to the 'right' in matters political and doctrinal.

Evangelist
The Pilgrim's Progress, Part I 1678, Part II 1684
John Bunyan

His concern is for each man and woman to escape the destruction that befalls those who persist in sinful ways. His message is that the way of the cross is the only hope of salvation and he encourages CHRISTIAN throughout his journey with terse reminders of the basic message of the gospel that the sometimes toiling pilgrim has espoused.

Evans, Emma
The Garrick Year, 1964
Margaret Drabble

Married to David, an actor, and the mother of two children, Emma reluctantly agrees to renounce a television newsreading career in order to spend a year with her husband as part of a theatre company at Hereford. She seems to have a carefully ordered life and be a similarly ordered person, cool and, to some, even a little frightening. Instead of living real life, she attempts to construct an ordered artifice. This is partly a strength, but also her weakness since it is a device to mask her inhibitions. She is finally too sharp, observant and discerning to admit anything to herself other than the moral and emotional truth.

Evans, Joey
Pal Joey, 1940
John O'Hara

A nightclub master of ceremonies and raconteur, the roguish Joey has a line of patter that skirted standards of acceptability in 1940 and turned him into a minor cultural hero.

Evans, Lance-Bombardier
Events While Guarding the Bofors Gun, 1966
John McGrath

An 18-year-old soldier in command of his first guard, a six-strong detachment of Royal Artillery servicemen, in the British-occupied zone of Germany during the bitingly cold February of 1954. A grammar-school boy from Manchester who has won a mathematics scholarship to Cambridge, he is 'a nice boy, trying hard to be liked and not really succeeding: he lacks a basic level of humanity'. Unhappy and nervous, Evans tries to be both amenable and authoritative, yet the persistent contempt and taunting of O'Rourke, an embittered Irish gunner, provokes a frighteningly violent assault.

Evans, Sam
Strange Interlude, 1928
Eugene O'Neill
The loyal but simple-minded husband of NINA LEEDS. Nina is warned by Sam's mother that there is a strain of insanity in the family, and she chooses to abort their child, but Sam convinces himself that Gordon, the child from Nina's relationship with DR EDMUND DARRELL, is his own and the pride of fatherhood transforms him into a self-possessed and successful businessman before his sudden death.

Evans, Sir Hugh
The Merry Wives of Windsor, c.1597
William Shakespeare
A Welsh parson, Evans suggests ABRAHAM SLENDER to MISTRESS MARGARET PAGE as a suitor for her daughter, ANNE PAGE, but is later challenged to a duel by DR CAIUS, who loves Anne himself, and also believes that Evans adores her. He has such a thick Welsh accent that SIR JOHN FALSTAFF derides him for making 'fritters of English'. During the tormenting of Falstaff in Windsor Great Park, he disguises himself as a satyr and avenges himself upon Falstaff by burning him with a taper.

Eve
Back to Methuselah, 1921
George Bernard Shaw
A biblical character, Eve, the wife of ADAM, appears in the first section of this five-part play (and briefly in the last). *In the Beginning* is set partly in the Garden of Eden. THE SERPENT informs her that death may be overcome by birth, and reveals to her the secret of conception, to which she listens with 'overwhelming repugnance'. She and Adam later have a family, of whom CAIN is the only one to appear on stage. More curious and more optimistic than her husband, Eve maintains faith in the Life Force.

Eve
Paradise Lost, 1667
John Milton
If ADAM is formed for contemplation and valour, a spirit dedicated to God only, she is formed for 'softness and sweet attractive Grace' and for worship of the God in Adam. 'She as a veil down to the slender waist/Her unadorned golden tresses wore/Dishevell'd'.

Evelina
Evelina, 1778
Fanny Burney
A young girl who has been abandoned by her father, Lord Belmont, and brought up in seclusion by her guardian. She grows into a beautiful and intelligent young woman, but knows little of the ways of the world, and is taken in hand by an eminent society lady. The novel is the tale of her education in self-knowledge, responsible behaviour, and prudence as she is introduced into society, where she is mortified by her vulgar relatives, and ultimately acknowledged as an heiress by her father.

Evens
The Sea, 1973
Edward Bond
One of society's outsiders, the elderly, tramp-like Evens is a man uneasy with himself, conscious of his doubts and difficulties. 'I am a wreck, rotting on the beach', he reflects. He may be troubled, but in contrast to HATCH he is sane, and in contrast to MRS RAFI, who treats him with some deference, he is ultimately serene.

Everard, Col Markham
Woodstock, or The Cavalier, 1826
Sir Walter Scott
Nephew (and, when he marries ALICE LEE, son-in-law) of SIR HENRY LEE, who has taken a regiment in OLIVER CROMWELL's army, convinced that the Lord Protector is the only bulwark against political chaos. It is clear that sentiment plays a larger part in his nature than pure political calculation; an encounter with King Charles reconverts him to the Royalist cause and he is arrested by Cromwell in person. John Buchan stated that Everard was the model for Thackeray's HENRY ESMOND.

Everdene, Bathsheba
Far from the Madding Crowd, 1874
Thomas Hardy
Beautiful and possessing 'an impulsive spirit', Bathsheba exerts a powerful influence over the emotions of all the male characters in the novel. She is not without her faults, being vain, wilful and self-centred, yet she is a woman capable of deep feeling, and suffers greatly when events turn against her, as they are inclined to do. Over the course of the novel she comes to a richer understanding of her own character, and her impulsiveness is eventually tamed – to a degree.

Ewart, Nanty
Redgauntlet, 1824
Sir Walter Scott
A drunken Solway pirate charged with the task of taking off the Young Pretender from Scottish soil after his visit (disguised as FATHER BUONAVENTURE). Small, lean and intense, he is plagued by guilty memories of his family, and shows an unsuspected vein of honour when called upon to betray the prince to government troops.

Ewbank, James and Leonard
'The Brothers', 1800
William Wordsworth
Leonard is an adventurous seafarer who achieves his ambition to return to his boyhood home in the Lake District and cleverly discovers, from a talkative priest, the poignant fate of his younger brother James. Although bereft, Leonard is satisfied that James had enjoyed a happy and wholesome life.

Excellency, His
Anthills of the Savanna, 1987
Chinua Achebe
The increasingly despotic ruler of Karjan, who ruthlessly calls on old friends to maintain his corrupt mandate and secure for him the title of President-for-Life. There are clear signals in the

text that he is merely a degenerate latter-day form of the thrusting young optimists who peopled Achebe's earlier novels.

Eynsford Hill, Freddy
Pygmalion, 1913
George Bernard Shaw

A young man of 20, with no occupation, Freddy is shabby-genteel, idiotic, but well-meaning. He is the son of MRS EYNSFORD HILL and brother of Clara, and falls in love with ELIZA DOOLITTLE to whom PROFESSOR HENRY HIGGINS is teaching correct enunciation. Freddy is entranced by her laboured conversation and thrilled by her social blunder in blurting out 'Not bloody likely' at Higgins's mother's at-home. According to Shaw's postscript, he and Eliza later marry and open a flower shop near the Victoria and Albert Museum.

Eynsford Hill, Mrs
Pygmalion, 1913
George Bernard Shaw

The mother of Clara and FREDDY EYNSFORD HILL, who falls in love with ELIZA DOOLITTLE, Mrs Eynsford Hill has been brought up in Epsom and should therefore be of some social eminence. But she is apparently without her husband, and lack of money has forced her and the children to the shabby-genteel surroundings of Earl's Court. Her inability to recover her social well-being still distresses her, and she worries about the social and marital prospects for Clara and Freddy.

Eyre, Jane
Jane Eyre, 1847
Charlotte Brontë

Plain but fiercely passionate, orphan Jane suffers a cruel, loveless upbringing in the care of her aunt MRS REED, followed by a severe institutional education at Lowood school, but somehow manages to retain her optimism and fighting spirit throughout it all. As governess at Thornfield Hall, she experiences in her relationship with MR ROCHESTER all the agonies and ecstasies of love, but refusing to be swayed by passion she symbolically casts herself out into effectually a wilderness. However, eventually finding family and fortitude, she becomes mistress of her emotions and returns to Mr Rochester to consolidate their love.

Eyre, Simon
The Shoemaker's Holiday, 1599
Thomas Dekker

Simon Eyre is an historical figure, a draper and benefactor of the City of London, whom Dekker appropriated (among other sources) as the leading character for the play. For Dekker's purposes, Eyre becomes a shoemaker who supplies the LORD MAYOR OF LONDON with his footwear and eventually becomes Lord Mayor himself. Good-natured, cheerful and loyal, he is prone to rhetoric, yet his language is racy and idiomatic, suggesting a man with the common touch. He has a lively mind and his public-spiritedness, therefore, suggests not only a generosity towards his fellow Londoners but also a keen appreciation of the city's economic and mercantile potential.

Ezeulu
Arrow of God, 1964, revised edition 1974
Chinua Achebe

Ageing chief priest of Ulu, god of the Umuaro people, he falteringly upholds traditional ways against the modernizing trends of the colonial District Officers, Christian missionaries, and his own tribesmen. 'Away from Ulu, he felt like a child whose stern parent had gone on a journey.'

F
Beautiful Losers, 1966
Leonard Cohen

The mysterious and sinister lover of the unnamed narrator ANON and his wife, EDITH. It seems he has been an industrialist, using an unmanned factory as a private games room; a Member of Parliament; and a leading light in the Quebecois separatist movement. He is revealed to be in an institution, dying of tertiary syphilis.

Fabian
Passion Play, 1979
Jerzy Kosinski

A polo player and also a writer, Fabian travels America with his ponies in a self-contained VanHome, engaged on a 'voyage without destination'. Obsessed with his own ageing body, he is increasingly addicted to perverse sexual practices and to the formal but violent knight-errantry of his sport.

Fabian
Twelfth Night, c.1601
William Shakespeare

Fabian, who is a rather peripheral figure in OLIVIA's household, has found himself in trouble with her because of his fondness for bear-baiting. He instigates nothing himself, but is prepared to take an active part in other people's schemes, especially in the tricking of MALVOLIO and the setting-up of the comic duel between SIR ANDREW AGUECHEEK and 'Cesario' (VIOLA). However, when he realizes that matters are about to be revealed, he decides to confess his part in proceedings, perhaps fearing strong action on Olivia's part.

Face
The Alchemist, 1610
Ben Jonson

Housekeeper to LOVEWIT, and properly known as Jeremy, he adopts the nickname of Face when he takes SUBTLE and DOL COMMON into the house during his employer's absence, and becomes assistant to Subtle, who pretends to be an alchemist. Their plan is to cheat people out of money by playing upon their susceptibilities. Rascally, endearing, manipulative, quick-witted, cunning, energetic and ingenious, Face relishes deception. Even when Lovewit returns unexpectedly, Face has an answer: he merely expels his roguish companions and helps win DAME PLIANT for his master, thus earning Lovewit's admiration and gratitude.

Fagan, Dr Augustus
Decline and Fall, 1928
Evelyn Waugh

'Very tall and very old and very well-dressed', Dr Augustus Fagan is the supercilious, bombastic headmaster of Llanabba Castle School. Obsessed with such snobbish concepts as 'style' and gentlemanly 'tone', the well-meaning Fagan is thrifty, with an ostentatiously extravagant streak. He lives with his two daughters, Flossie and Dingy, who act as school housekeepers; PAUL PENNYFEATHER is offered a partnership in the school if he marries Flossie, but he declines and she enjoys a short-lived period of wedlock with the bigamous CAPTAIN GRIMES. Fagan finally takes charge of a struggling Nursing and Private Sanatorium in Worthing, where Pennyfeather's life is legally 'terminated' on a non-existent operating table.

Faggus, Tom
Lorna Doone, 1869
R D Blackmore

Short, 'strongly built and springy', Tom is in his mid-twenties and already something of an Exmoor legend. A great horseman and highwayman, he is essentially 'a jovial soul … not making bones of little things, nor caring to seek evil'. A good man and well-regarded, he is seen as an integral part of rural life, even a force of natural justice. Generous and celebrated, he is rough, tough and sympathetic. 'There was about him a genuine love of human nature.'

Fagin
Oliver Twist, 1838
Charles Dickens

The leader of a den of child pickpockets and receiver of stolen goods for BILL SIKES. He is 'a very old shrivelled Jew, whose villainous-looking and repulsive face was obscured by a quantity of matted red hair'. He is bribed by EDWARD LEEFORD (known as 'Monks') to make OLIVER TWIST a thief, but fails. He instigates the murder of NANCY by Sikes, but is betrayed by NOAH CLAYPOLE and convicted of complicity in her death. He spends a terrifying few days in the condemned cell before being hanged.

Fahey, Frank
For the Rest of Our Lives, 1947
Dan Davin

One of a group of officers and men, mostly attached to the New Zealand Division, stationed in Egypt during World War II, Fahey is an associate of TONY BRANDON and TOM O'DWYER.

He has just returned from a long period of sick leave, but is still mentally and physically exhausted. 'Illness had run dark tangents down from the corners of the eyes and cut the triangle above the mouth more deeply than age had had time to do.' Now an intelligence officer, he has become cynical, listless, a drinker, a man who looks 'like Baudelaire illustrated by Picasso. In his Absinthe Drinker phase.' A man whose convictions are in turmoil, Fahey finds his new job rather soothing.

Failing, Emily
The Longest Journey, 1907
E M Forster

The aunt and only near relative of RICKIE ELLIOT, Emily Failing is a widow in her late fifties with beautiful hair, a languid manner and an expression of 'slight but perpetual pain'. Unable to sell the Cadover estate after her husband's death, she has been forced to settle for life in Wiltshire among people that she openly despises. Increasingly lame, she derives a cruel pleasure from the vindictive manipulation of other people's lives and proudly declares herself to have been 'a dragon most of my life'.

Fainall, Mr and Mrs
The Way of the World, 1700
William Congreve

Like MIRABELL, Fainall is a man-about-town. A married man, he considers marriage a somewhat grim farce, and the knowledge that his wife was previously one of Mirabell's mistresses only serves to sour his rancour further. He does his best to preserve an outward display of cynical indifference, yet underneath he is a tumultuous mixture of cynicism, cruelty and envy. Mrs Fainall is desperately unhappy, a victim of events and emotions beyond her control, but is without bitterness, taking a philosophical view of the vanities of women: 'Female frailty!'

Fairchild, Battle
Delta Wedding, 1946
Eudora Welty

Father of DABNEY FAIRCHILD and owner of the Shellmound Plantation in Mississippi. He is the latest, and in many important regards the least heroic, in a long line of Fairchilds. The wedding of his daughter to his overseer TROY FLAVIN represents a significant moment in the family's changing fortunes.

Fairchild, Dabney
Delta Wedding, 1946
Eudora Welty

A fresh and beautiful 17-year-old girl who is about to marry the estate overseer, TROY FLAVIN, even though her family disapproves. She is aware of the burden of family expectations in all matters, but has experienced liberating 'moments of life when it did not matter who she was'. She defies her father over the marriage, and vows never to 'give up anything' in her joy of life.

Fairchild, Dawson
Mosquitoes, 1927
William Faulkner

A bumptious novelist who constitutes the senior literary figure in MRS PATRICIA MAURIER's floating salon, he 'resembles a benevolent walrus too recently out of bed to have made a toilet'.

Fairchild, Ellen
Delta Wedding, 1946
Eudora Welty

The mother of DABNEY FAIRCHILD. A 'slight, almost delicate lady, seeming exactly strong enough for what was needed of her life', she is more 'restful' than the other Fairchilds, and has a quiet, reflective, meditative presence amid the bustle of that never-still house. She seems able to focus her entire attention on whatever preoccupies her at any given moment.

Fairchild, George
Delta Wedding, 1946
Eudora Welty

DABNEY FAIRCHILD's uncle. The 'very heart of the family', he is also able to stand apart from it. He is strong, brave, humane, proud and independent, and is 'the kindest of them all', a man who would not 'say a deliberately wounding thing'.

Fairfax, Grace
A Note in Music, 1930
Rosamond Lehmann

A middle-aged frump, Grace is trapped in a stultifying marriage to a dull clerk in a bleak industrial town. She has allowed the passage of time to stifle her and has lapsed into inertia. But the immobility and stasis of her daily life is broken by her joyous summer holiday. Alone, she succeeds in fixing the perpetual drift of existence into 'forms absolute and eternal', stopping the flow of time by emotional disengagement. She cultivates a mask of impassivity and disavows the energies of life 'to be like stone before the world'.

Fairfax, Jane
Emma, 1816
Jane Austen

An endearing orphan, the niece of MISS BATES, reared from the age of three by her impecunious aunt and grandmother. Subsequently passed on to a military family 'of moderate fortune', she develops into a woman of 'decided superiority in both beauty and acquirements', whose naturally diffident nature assumes the cool air of cautious reserve when compromised by FRANK CHURCHILL's duplicity. Sincere and genuine, she is devoid of her fiancé's easy propensity for devious schemes.

Fairford, Alan
Redgauntlet, 1824
Sir Walter Scott

Alan is chained to his law books while his university friend DARSIE LATIMER goes in search of his destiny. His only diversion from the tough forensic regimen imposed by his father, SAUNDERS FAIRFORD, is the danger that befalls Darsie. He is widely thought to be Scott's closest self-portrait (they share poor health), and is a loyal, modest observer of the great rather than a man of action.

Fairford, Saunders (Alexander)
Redgauntlet, 1824
Sir Walter Scott

A stern but essentially kindly old Edinburgh lawyer (officially a Writer to the Signet), he seems to hold the secret of DARSIE LATIMER's parentage and inheritance. He is 'a man of business of the old school, moderate in his charges, economical and even niggardly in his expenditure, strictly honest in conducting his affairs and those of his clients, but taught by long experience to be wary and suspicious in observing the motions of others'.

Fairlie, Frederick
The Woman in White, 1860
Wilkie Collins

The uncle of LAURA FAIRLIE and master of Limmeridge House in Cumberland, he is a bachelor in his fifties who has a 'frail, languidly fretful, over-refined look'. An invalid for many years, he shows a devotion to his collection of coins and Rembrandt etchings far in excess of his concern for any living creature. Describing himself as a 'bundle of nerves dressed up to look like a man', he is upset by the slightest loud noise or the most minor of inconveniences; consequently his actions are dictated from the purely selfish motives of sparing himself any form of physical or emotional distress.

Fairlie, Laura
The Woman in White, 1860
Wilkie Collins

A fair, delicate young woman with the beauty and sweet grace of an angel, she has a generous nature and innocent trust in the world. Promised in marriage to SIR PERCIVAL GLYDE by her late father, she falls helplessly in love with her drawing teacher WALTER HARTRIGHT but feels that she must honour her commitment to Sir Percy when he refuses to release her from the marriage contract. Holding dear to her word causes her untold misery and hardship before her faith is rewarded by the ultimate triumph of good over evil.

Fairly, Fred
The Gate of Angels, 1990
Penelope Fitzgerald

A quiet academic, Fred is gullible and vulnerable, especially at the hands of worldly females, DAISY SAUNDERS in particular. A man distinguished by reason, rationality, precision and contemplation, he begins to behave quite out of character as his passion for Daisy develops. Fred has strong ties with his family and a high regard for them. He is confused and bruised by the new and complex world he enters, but somehow cannot help but be rather boring and predictable.

Fairservice, Andrew
Rob Roy, 1817
Sir Walter Scott

FRANK OSBALDISTONE's travelling companion and serving man; John Buchan likened him to Sancho Panza and considered him one of Scott's foremost comic creations: 'He is a real but low type of Scot, cunning, avaricious, indifferently loyal, venturesome in his own interest, but a craven in

the face of bodily peril, an incorrigible liar and braggart, and never more impudent than when his bluff is called.'

Faithful
The Pilgrim's Progress, Part I 1678, Part II 1684
John Bunyan

A Christian whose pilgrimage reaches its climax in the experiences of courageous martyrdom. His enthusiasm and encouragement sustain CHRISTIAN, and his example of patient suffering is sufficient to inspire HOPEFUL at least to journey along the way of faith.

Falcon, Ken
Rusty Bugles, 1948
Sumner Locke Elliott

A thin, not very well groomed, serious-looking Australian soldier. During his two years at an ordnance depot in the remote Northern Territory he has apparently been heard to speak only once, and hence has been nicknamed Dean Maitland (from an Australian silent film, *The Silence of Dean Maitland*). He has regularly called a telephone number at which there is never any answer. It is only belatedly realized that he is insane.

Falconbridge, Philip, the Bastard
King John, 1590/1
William Shakespeare

The illegitimate son of Sir Robert Falconbridge, Philip is a natural soldier, yet also the most sympathetic and humane character in a play dealing with political and religious confrontation. Although he has little innate respect for either people or hierarchy, Philip loyally serves KING JOHN as much because he is the ruling monarch as because he believes in his right to the throne. He also acts as a Chorus, commenting upon the action and bringing the audience up to date with events offstage. To him belong the final and most famous lines of the play, spoken at the end after John's death: 'This England never did, nor never shall,/Lie at the proud foot of a conqueror,/... Nought shall make us rue/If England to itself do rest but true!'

Falconbridge, Robert
King John, 1590/1
William Shakespeare

The younger son to Sir Robert Falconbridge (the elder being PHILIP FALCONBRIDGE). He appears briefly before KING JOHN to claim his inheritance from his late father on the grounds of his brother's illegitimacy. In doing so, apparently without scruple, he accuses his mother of adultery.

Falconer, Mr Algernon
Gryll Grange, 1860–1
Thomas Love Peacock

The owner of a restored tower, Mr Falconer lives with seven beautiful virginal sisters, an unorthodox arrangement derived from classical Greek social models. A romantic young man, he has an inclination towards despondency and disappointment. Where he finds pleasure and enjoyment, he anticipates greater disillusionment; reality, he believes, can only ever be a pale and unsuccessful imitation of the ideal. When he falls in love, after an internal tug-of-war he finally abandons the ideal for the real.

Faliero, Marino
Marino Faliero: An Historical Tragedy, 1821
Byron, George Gordon, 6th Lord Byron

A 14th-century Doge of Venice, fiery and passionate, intensely proud of his high office and its dignity. He is enraged when MICHEL STENO inscribes on the very throne of the Doge a gross insult, so gross that the Doge will not have it repeated when Steno is brought to trial. Instead of the harsh sentence Faliero thinks appropriate, Steno is merely condemned to one month in close arrest. Faliero cannot endure this and enters into a conspiracy with a mob of malcontents to overthrow Venice and its constitution. But the conspiracy fails, Faliero's part in it is revealed and he is executed.

Falkland
Caleb Williams, 1794
William Godwin

A nobleman who turns from being a figure of respect and honour, with a high status and reputation in his community, into a reclusive, devious schemer, who plots the downfall of a member of his household, CALEB WILLIAMS. In his anguished, remorseful decline, this complex character forsakes his natural chivalrous, benevolent personality and becomes increasingly obsessive. Godwin contends that his true, rational feelings have been poisoned by the corrupt, unjust society which traps us all. Deceiving himself, Falkland mistakes evil for truth.

Fallace
Every Man out of his Humour, 1599
Ben Jonson

Fallace is the unhappy and morally devious wife of DELIRO. She is so exasperated by his suffocating devotion and insistence that she is an ideal woman that she falls for the worthless but flamboyant FASTIDIOUS BRISK, stooping to attempted bribery in an effort to have him released from jail.

Fallow, Peter
The Bonfire of the Vanities, 1987
Tom Wolfe

A drunken and wholly unprincipled English journalist living on his befuddled wits and his fading ability to ingratiate himself socially in New York. His fortunes turn when he stumbles across the SHERMAN MCCOY case and scents a big break, but he is being manipulated in turn by vested interests. He becomes 'fervour personified' in chasing (and inventing) the story, and rises to a Pulitzer Prize for his efforts, in a counter-arc to McCoy's downfall.

Falset
Ane Pleasant Satyre of the Thrie Estaitis, 1540
Sir David Lindsay

Conspiring with FLATTERIE and DISSAIT in the deception of the king, REX HUMANITAS, Falset, like the other two Vices, is characterized by duplicity, and is the metaphorical master of the crooked craftsmen. Concealing his new identity under the guise of Sapience, he then forgets his 'new' name, the irony of this revealing only too clearly the counterfeit nature of his character. Quite prepared to double-deal even DISSAIT, his supposed ally, Falset is reunited with him in their final come-uppance.

Falstaff, Sir John
Henry IV Part I, 1596/7
Henry IV Part II, 1597/8
The Merry Wives of Windsor, 1597
William Shakespeare

Falstaff has a large appetite, not only for food and drink, but also for laughter and enjoyment. An enemy of all that is serious, he indulges in mockery and play-acting, lies for the sake of lying, acts the coward when the need arises and accepts praise for his bravery when he knows it is unwarranted. He recognizes that he is a figure of fun, and that many of his actions, such as enlisting the weak and the feeble as soldiers, are immoral; but he remains popular with his colleagues. He does misjudge his influence on Prince Hal (HENRY, PRINCE OF WALES), believing mistakenly to the end that he will become a leading figure in his new England, when he becomes king.

Famous Five, the
Five on a Treasure Island, et seq
Enid Blyton

A group of four children and a dog, who regularly find themselves embroiled in exciting, if improbable, adventures. Anne, Julian and Dick are the cousins of George (properly Georgina), a moody but courageous tomboy. Anne is stereotypically feminine, hating rough games and prone to tears, while the boys are jolly good sorts, even-tempered and fearless. Timmy, the dog, though prone to chewing things, is an exceptionally intelligent example of the species.

Fanciful, Lady
The Provok'd Wife, 1696
Sir John Vanbrugh

Proud, snobbish and affected, Lady Fanciful is flattered when HEARTFREE courts her, then aghast when he turns his attentions to BELLINDA. Her pride turns to spite, and, in revenge for what she sees as her own betrayal, she vindictively but unsuccessfully contrives to ruin the reputations of Heartfree and Bellinda.

Fane, Michael
Sinister Street, 1913
Compton Mackenzie

A thinly veiled version of the author himself, Fane grows up 'handicapped by a public school and university education', but maintains an outsider's perspective on Oxford, London and the demi-monde of pre-World War I England. His attitudes are open, frank and virtually unfettered by convention.

Fang, Mr
Oliver Twist, 1838
Charles Dickens

The violent and bullying magistrate who nearly sentences OLIVER TWIST for picking MR

BROWNLOW's pocket. His court is a travesty of justice, and he unwillingly has to acquit the boy when the bookseller who saw JACK DAWKINS commit the theft arrives in time to vindicate Oliver.

Fanny
The History of the Adventures of Joseph Andrews and of his Friend Mr Abraham Adams, 1742
Henry Fielding

A young girl in the service of SIR THOMAS BOOBY (and presumably not of his brother Sir John, as Fielding wrote in the first edition), who loves JOSEPH ANDREWS and is loved in return. Too simple-hearted and beautiful for MRS SLIPSLOP's taste, she has been set aside and lives with a farmer in the area. After many trials, the lovers are united and married.

Fanny
The Pursuit of Love, 1945
Nancy Mitford

Fanny spends holidays with her cousins, THE RADLETTS, discussing life and sex in the airing-cupboard. They are undisciplined and wild; she, formally educated, describes their life at Alconleigh with detached relish – fearsome Uncle Matthew 'hunting' the children like foxes for fun, childish campaigns against cruelty to animals, romantic LINDA with whom she later shares a London season. She marries an Oxford don, and is understanding of Linda, her two disastrous marriages and her true love Fabrice.

Fanshawe
Fanshawe, 1828
Nathaniel Hawthorne

A solitary scholar, fatally 'independent of the beings that surrounded him', and the prototype for several of Hawthorne's later cleric-romantics who are marked out by their detachment from everyday passions. Another character sees him standing atop a precipice and concludes 'there [was] something awful in the slight form that stood so far above him, like a being from another sphere, looking down upon his wickedness'.

Fanshawe, Ginevra
Villette, 1853
Charlotte Brontë

A well-to-do student at MADAME BECK's school whom LUCY SNOWE first encounters on the boat to Villette, Ginevra is a heartless, empty-headed beauty who toys shamelessly with the emotions of DR JOHN BRETTON while really her affections are engaged elsewhere. Selfish, narcissistic and flirtatious, she makes Lucy the unfortunate object of her incessant self-centred chatter, and spends her life doing exactly as she pleases, considering no one but herself.

Fansler, Kate
Sweet Death, Kind Death, 1984, et seq
Amanda Cross (Caroline Heilbrun)

A middle-aged American professor of English literature whose amateur detective work is based partly on intuition, partly on deductive reasoning. She is an ardent feminist, happily married to a New York lawyer. She smokes, and also drinks – a little too much she sometimes feels – but loathes sherry as the genteel tipple of her rich, feather-brained mother's social milieu. Disliking the reactionary and conservative, she is drawn towards the offbeat in terms of both the people she knows and the crimes she seeks to solve. Tall, attractive and elegantly dressed, she has a brisk manner and mode of speech, and is much given to literary quotation.

Farange, Beale
What Maisie Knew, 1897
Henry James

MAISIE FARANGE's father, he is feckless and prodigal; he has also been persistently unfaithful to his first wife. Divorced from IDA FARANGE when their daughter was six, he shares custody of her. He subsequently marries Maisie's former governess, MISS OVERMORE.

Farange, Ida
What Maisie Knew, 1897
Henry James

Dull, venal and no less spendthrift than her ex-husband (BEALE FARANGE), she is particularly adept at pouring venomous half-truths about him (most of which apply equally to herself) into her daughter MAISIE FARANGE's ear. Quickly tiring of her association with the wealthy SIR CLAUDE, she takes a succession of lovers.

Farange, Maisie
What Maisie Knew, 1897
Henry James

Her stolid air and long silences give her a reputation for stupidity, but twelve-year-old Maisie is perhaps the only person in the selfishly antagonistic Farange family with a clear grasp of what is going on, even if she does not always understand its significance. She spends alternate six-month periods with her divorced parents, and with successive governesses; from the second of these she gets at least a version of the affection she craves, while in SIR CLAUDE she finds a father figure of some reliability and substance.

Fardorough, the Miser
Fardorough, the Miser, 1839
William Carleton

A poor, miserly Irish farmer, he is 'a man of shrewd sense, and of strong, but not obvious or flexible feeling'. He is grave and cold in manner, with occasional outbursts of passion or temper. He is anxious over his impoverished farm, and is increasingly ruled by the 'devil of the avaricious – the famine-struck god of the miser'. The birth of a son arouses within him a 'conflict between avarice and affection'. He excuses parsimony as prudence or Christian duty, but has a 'defiled and perverted heart' and a 'close and gripping spirit' which prevent him from expressing his love for the child.

Farfrae, Donald
The Mayor of Casterbridge, 1886
Thomas Hardy

A Scotsman passing through Casterbridge on his way to seek his fortune in America, Donald Farfrae is persuaded by MICHAEL HENCHARD to stay and become the manager of his corn business. Farfrae's subsequent successful career acts as a contrast to the decline in Henchard's fortunes over the course of the novel, and represents the triumph of modern industry over traditional methods. Although admired by all in Casterbridge for his blend of 'the commercial and the romantic', readers are likely to find him a rather calculating and passionless figure.

Farintosh, Lord
The Newcomes, 1853–5
W M Thackeray

'Although [his] years were few, he had spent most of them in the habit of command; and from his childhood upwards, had been obeyed by all persons round about him.' Briefly the fiancé of ETHEL NEWCOME, the young marquis is of great rank but is notoriously dissipated. Ethel rejects him for reasons of her own.

Farishta, Gibreel
The Satanic Verses, 1988
Salman Rushdie

'Farishta' means archangel in Urdu; Gibreel is a variant of Gabriel. This dubious archangel has been the biggest star in the Indian movies before deciding to disappear from public life. He has also lost his faith in God, which becomes ironic when he dreams that he is the angel consulted by Mohammed about the possible worship of three idols. Occasionally hallucinating angelic status for himself outside of sleep, Gibreel charts an uncertain course through London and then India, his girlfriend's attempts to set him right proving unsuccessful. His story culminates in violence bred of cosmic arrogance and possible Satanic influences.

Farnon, Siegfried
If Only They Could Talk, 1970, et seq
James Herriot

When newly qualified vet JAMES HERRIOT arrives in the Yorkshire village of Darrowby, he joins the practice of experienced country vet Siegfried Farnon. Somewhat eccentric and with a volatile personality (repeatedly firing his younger brother TRISTAN FARNON, then forgetting about it), Siegfried is described as 'impossible'. He is kind-hearted and devoted to his work, yet remains unsentimental about his patients: 'Paint a black picture! If you say a case is going to recover, you could be in trouble if it doesn't.'

Farnon, Tristan
If Only They Could Talk, 1970, et seq
James Herriot

Tristan Farnon is the fun-loving younger brother of SIEGFRIED FARNON, JAMES HERRIOT's boss in a small Yorkshire veterinary practice. Initially a student, Tristan later qualifies and joins the practice. But even then, the likeable young vet would rather be out drinking than standing in a freezing farmyard, and his exploits often land him in trouble. Tristan's irresponsible attitude is an endless source of frustration for his elder brother, but their heated arguments make for amusing reading.

Farquar, Lois
The Last September, 1929
Elizabeth Bowen

A young Anglo-Irish girl, living on her family's estate at the tail end of the Ascendancy, and coming of age in an environment on which the strife-torn outside world simply does not impinge. She is engaged to GERALD LESWORTH, an attractive British officer who is little more than an abstract idealization of a good match and whom she does not love.

Farquhar, Peyton
'An Occurrence at Owl Creek Bridge', in *Tales of Soldiers and Civilians*, 1891, published as *In the Midst of Life*, 1892
Ambrose Bierce

Introduced just as he is about to be hanged from a railroad bridge in Northern Alabama, he is a well-to-do planter from an old Alabama family, a slave-owner and secessionist, but unable (for 'reasons of an imperious nature which it is unnecessary to relate') to fight for the Confederacy. Arrested and summarily condemned, he makes one final bid for freedom and appears to have shaken free both of the noose and his captors' bullets. But the end of the story reveals that he is already dead.

Farr, George
Soldier's Pay, 1926
William Faulkner

CECILY SAUNDERS's new lover, he marks the broadest possible contrast to the suffering LT DONALD MAHON, her former fiancé. Farr is selfish, venal and wholly dedicated to the gratification of his own wishes, incapable of even the smallest personal sacrifice.

Farrago, Captain John
Modern Chivalry, 1792–1815
H H Brackenridge

A bright Pennsylvania farmer who sets off with his servant TEAGUE O'REGAN to experience for himself the life and customs of his young country. A democrat of a Jeffersonian bent, but with a tinge of radicalism as well, he is too intelligently sceptical to be a Don Quixote, but there is nevertheless a touch of Quixote's idealism about him.

Farragut, Ezekiel
Falconer, 1977
John Cheever

An upper-class American academic and drug addict, imprisoned in Falconer jail for the murder of his brother, despite proclaiming his innocence. His eccentric family included a hostile father, and his relations with his wife have been difficult. His feelings of social and intellectual superiority include a belief that drugs heighten his consciousness. A sensitive man with a formal Christian faith, in this valley of dry bones Ezekiel weans himself off the visions induced by heroin and comes to terms with his own nature. This involves both a desire for redemption and the release of his homosexual instincts.

Farrant, Anthony
England Made Me, 1935
Graham Greene

The weak but plausible brother of KATE FARRANT. He has a deceiving charm and is a compulsive liar. He is a con-artist possessing the bravado of someone who is fundamentally fearful. Although he believes himself to be supremely cunning, he is in fact little more than a boy hopelessly foundering in a world of big business and much more astute men. Nevertheless, he holds firm to certain tenets of decency. These residual moral feelings are tested when he enters the employment of the megalomaniac ERIK KROGH, and it is the lonely, alienated Anthony who ultimately elicits our sympathy and respect as the centre of the novel's moral discourse.

Farrant, Kate
England Made Me, 1935
Graham Greene

Kate possesses many of the virtues which her feckless brother ANTHONY FARRANT lacks, such as reliability, efficiency and fearlessness. She has had the straightforward, successful life which Anthony had always yearned for, but in many respects Kate's character can only be defined when placed in contrast with that of her more colourful, errant brother. She is his mirror reflection, but like any reflection she is also less substantial. As the mistress of the great financier ERIK KROGH she has influence, but she is still his possession and only gains meaning through his status.

Farrar, Brat
Brat Farrar, 1949, published in USA as *Come and Kill Me*, 1951
Josephine Tey

Farrar adopts the identity of the young son of a wealthy horse-breeding family. The son is presumed to have killed himself but the impostor discovers that he is a near-perfect double and tries to insinuate himself into the family. The story is largely concerned with the problems of sustaining that identity in the face of strong sexual urges towards a cousin and his progressive discovery of a dark, murderous secret in the family.

Farrell, Spanky (George)
The Slab Boys Trilogy, 1982
John Byrne

Witty, but otherwise of unremarkable talent, Spanky Farrell's main driving force in life is 'Style', which takes in everything from a 1950s 'duck's-arse' hairdo to 1970s drugs, fringed jacket and cowboy boots. He works in the slab room, a paint mixing department, and as sparring partner to fellow Slab Boy PHIL MCCANN he sparkles, but his self-centred nature and lack of initiative indicate no real strength of character. Rather than trying to find practical ways to remedy his problems, he prefers to keep deluding himself as to the desirability of his lifestyle.

Farringdon, Nicholas
The Girls of Slender Means, 1963
Muriel Spark

Charming, shy and good-looking, this 'disappointing son of a good English family' expresses his confused political ideas in an unpublished book. Supposedly a poet and anarchist, he has doubts about his sexual and philosophical identity. He sees the May of Teck Club for young ladies of 'slender means' as a Utopian community, but his idealization of poverty is not shared by all of its inmates. A 'vision of evil' in the Club prompts his conversion to Roman Catholicism, and he is later martyred in Haiti.

Farrow, Jacy
The Last Picture Show, 1966
Larry McMurtry

A self-absorbed small-town girl, whose unassailable beauty and cool independence make her a point of yearning focus to her male contemporaries, and whose rejection of her stock, male-defined role is a symbol of changing times.

Fashion, Sir Novelty → Foppington, Lord

Father Time
Jude the Obscure, 1895
Thomas Hardy

A sober, 'too reflective' child, the only legitimate child of JUDE FAWLEY and ARABELLA DONN and named properly after his father. Old for his years (hence his nickname) and greatly disturbed, he is neither playful nor optimistic, his view of society and humanity having been blackened by early emotional suffering. The diverse combination of his parents, and the fact that he was conceived in lust, not love, have produced an outcast, a hybrid, and a loveless soul. His tragic suicide and the hanging of his half-brother and half-sister, 'done because we are too menny' are prompted by his stepmother SUE BRIDEHEAD telling him that she is to have another child, the family's circumstances already being straitened.

Fathom, Ferdinand, Count
The Adventures of Ferdinand, Count Fathom, 1753
The Expedition of Humphry Clinker, 1771
Tobias Smollett

The sprig of an English nobleman, he is born to a camp-following mother on the borders of Flanders and Holland. Weaned on gin and raised in the most sophisticated circles, he becomes a companion to the young RENALDO DE MELVIL. Sly, calculating and infinitely amoral, he is a master of the cunning stratagem and the bare-faced lie, having all the outward graces that his young companion and master so conspicuously lacks. He somewhat improbably reappears in *The Expedition of Humphry Clinker*, disguised as a country apothecary called Grieve.

Fatt, Harry
Waiting for Lefty, 1935
Clifford Odets

An agent of the bosses, who tries to persuade the militant taxi drivers that striking is against their interests. He is the antagonist of the unseen LEFTY COSTELLO.

Faulk, Maxine

The Night of the Iguana, 1961
Tennessee Williams

An 'affable and rapaciously lusty' woman in her middle forties, the recently widowed proprietress of a cheap hillside hotel in Mexico. Her difficult life has given her a 'realistically modest soul' and, in a play of philosophical and religious discussion, she is an earthy and honest presence, eventually gaining the object of her desires, LARRY SHANNON, as her companion.

Faulkland

The Rivals, 1775
Richard Brinsley Sheridan

Lover of JULIA MELVILLE, whose life he once saved. He is described as proud, noble, sincere and humble, but these qualities only strengthen the 'too exquisite nicety' that leads him to doubt Julia's love and to find continual cause for needless worry. He is, nevertheless, aware of his own folly.

Faustus, Dr John

Dr Faustus, 1594–1601
Christopher Marlowe

God-bothering scholar of Wittenberg, who makes a legendary compact with MEPHISTOPHILIS, and is granted unlimited powers for 24 years, at the expiry of which time his soul belongs to the Devil. A voluptuary and aesthete, his fondness for arcane knowledge is matched by a childish addiction to pranks. He is likened by Marlowe to the youthful Icarus, whose 'waxen wings did mount above his reach,/And melting, heavens conspir'd his overthrow'.

Fawley, Catherine

The Bell, 1958
Iris Murdoch

NICK FAWLEY's twin sister, she is secretive and palely beautiful, with heavy dark hair and large eyes of a cold sea-grey. She is known as 'our little saint' by the Imber community and is shortly to enter the abbey's Anglican-Benedictine closed order of nuns. Though timid and withdrawn, she seems somehow menacing to DORA GREENFIELD; and while MICHAEL MEAD feels her spirituality is an inspiration to all, it is also a 'centre of obscure emotional tension' among the others in the community. When the tension snaps in Catherine herself, she suffers a serious breakdown and reveals that she is desperately in love.

Fawley, Jude

Jude the Obscure, 1895
Thomas Hardy

A stonemason from the village of Marygreen, his marriage to the earthy ARABELLA DONN, born out of lust rather than love, deflects him from his path of becoming a scholar at Christminster (Hardy's Oxford). Despite assiduous reading of the Greek and Latin classics, his unconventional behaviour (children out of wedlock with his beloved muse and cousin SUE BRIDEHEAD) and lower social class result in repeated rejection and a downward spiral towards tragedy. Basically decent and with a strong sense of what is right, he is both a pessimist and a dreamy idealist, conflicting attitudes that conspire in his downfall.

Fawley, Nick

The Bell, 1958
Iris Murdoch

CATHERINE FAWLEY's cynical, dissolute and tormented twin. He lives alone in Imber Court's lodge until joined by young TOBY GASHE, and is attached to the lay community but not really of it. Sensing that he is a troublemaker, JAMES TAYPER PACE believes it was a mistake to take him in. His suspicions are well-founded as the now coarse, abrasive Nick was the beautiful, deviously clever pupil responsible for shattering MICHAEL MEAD's life. Consequently, for the indecisive Michael he is an 'appalling problem', one which is finally resolved in Nick's own appalling manner.

Fawn, Viscount Frederick

The Eustace Diamonds, 1873
Phineas Redux, 1874
Anthony Trollope

A government official, the only son of Lady Fawn, a highly virtuous lady who holds him in great awe, as do his eight sisters. In reality, however, he is an undistinguished gentleman of no great talents or strength of character. He is a hereditary peer, and progresses in public life as a result of prudence and diligence rather than ability. He is doomed to continual disappointment in love, and is rejected as a suitor by both VIOLET EFFINGHAM and MARIE GOESLER.

Fax, Mr

Melincourt, or Sir Oran Haut-ton, 1817
Thomas Love Peacock

The 'champion of calm reason' and 'the bearer of the torch of dispassionate truth', Mr Fax (based on Malthus) drily extols logic as the antidote to the chaos of emotion. Sometimes tedious in his pursuit of linguistic precision, his practical nature insists on the importance of money, and he acts as a foil to his friend, the romantic MR SYLVAN FORESTER.

Fay, Felix

Moon-Calf, 1920
The Briary-Bush, 1921
Floyd Dell

A representative figure of the 1920s, he leaves his small Illinoisan township to seek fame and fortune in literary Chicago, but in the sequel returns home (whether disappointed, sated or simply more mature and accommodating is not entirely clear) to marry the childhood sweetheart he had initially rejected.

Fayaway

Typee, 1846
Herman Melville

A native girl who is devoted to TOMMO. She is a 'beauteous nymph' who is the 'very perfection of female grace', with each feature 'as perfectly formed as the heart or imagination of man could desire'. She usually goes naked, or decked in flowers. She is unusually lightly tattooed, and likes to eat raw fish. She weeps 'convulsively' when Tommo departs.

Faye, Marion
The Deer Park, 1957
The Deer Park: A Play, 1959, revised edition 1967
Norman Mailer

A pimp, 'very special, slim, tight-knit, beautiful, as angelic in appearance as an animal and ... possessed of a fine voice, which is by turns rough-edged, musical, incisive, or sadistic as a whip'. An ambiguous character, Faye nurses an apocalyptic vision of a purgative nuclear holocaust.

Fearchar the Poet
And the Cock Crew, 1962
Fionn Mac Colla

If MAIGHSTIR SACHAIRI and the factor MASTER BYARS stand for the principles of destruction at work in Gleann Luachrach, the bard is a symbol of the lifestyle they threaten. A maker and a creator, he represents the pure essence of the Highland people, undiluted by doctrine or commercial imperatives.

Feathernest, Mr
Melincourt, or Sir Oran Haut-ton, 1817
Thomas Love Peacock

The 'parasite' of LORD ANOPHEL ACHTHAR, Mr Feathernest, as his name implies, assesses everything on the basis of profit and comfort to himself. Enthralled by money and by what it can buy, he occasionally admits to twinges of conscience, before brushing them aside in favour of expediency and the good life: 'If there be any man, who prefers a crust and water, to venison and sack, I am not of his mind ... Every man for himself, Sir, and God for all of us.'

Featherstone, Mr Peter
Middlemarch, 1871–2
George Eliot

A minor character, the 'old fox' Mr Featherstone, rich owner of Stone Court, is also the cantankerous, miserly uncle of FRED and ROSAMOND VINCY. Nursed in his ill-health by his other niece, MARY GARTH, his only concern is in outwitting his money-grabbing relatives, and while seeming to repent on his deathbed, he dies disinheriting them all, apart from his natural son, Joshua Rigg.

Fedallah
Moby-Dick, 1851
Herman Melville

CAPTAIN AHAB's harpooner. A Parsee, he is described as 'tall and swart, with one white tooth evilly protruding from its steel-like lips'. He wears a 'glistening white-plaited turban', and is smuggled on board with his crew. He remains 'a muffled mystery to the last', but his erratic prophecies about the white whale, MOBY DICK, have a dangerous influence on Ahab.

Federner, Anna
'The Good Anna', in *Three Lives*, 1909
Gertrude Stein

She is the faithful housekeeper of, successively, three households in Bridgepoint, a woman of stolid Bavarian virtues and an essential goodness. She is generous and self-effacing almost to a fault, losing all her boarding-house money because she can refuse nobody anything and eventually killing herself with overwork.

Feenix, Lord
Dombey and Son, 1848
Charles Dickens

An elderly nobleman and nephew of THE HON MRS SKEWTON, he is the cousin of EDITH DOMBEY and is always referred to as 'Cousin Feenix'. Kind and honourable, he gives support to Edith after she loses her reputation by deserting MR PAUL DOMBEY.

Feinstein, Dulcie
The Solid Mandala, 1966
Patrick White

A middle-class Jewish woman, Dulcie rejects a proposal of marriage from WALDO BROWN, but achieves a closer and more lasting friendship with Waldo's backward but more affectionate brother, ARTHUR BROWN. She eventually marries Leonard Saporta, through whom she rediscovers her religious faith, becoming in time a proud mother and grandmother. Set against the tragedy of Waldo and Arthur, Dulcie represents not only a vision of suburban fulfilment but also one of an almost divine family love.

Felden, Baron Julius Maria von
A Legacy, 1956
Sybille Bedford

A Francophile, Francophone South German aristocrat, whose secure old-fashioned background vanishes with the establishment of the Prussian-dominated German Empire. The associated changes give him a pessimistic outlook, and he escapes from Germany to idyllic idleness in France and later Spain, collecting antiques and eating good food. Jules, as he is usually called, loves animals, but is indifferent to human company. However, he becomes by marriage a member of an eccentric, rich Jewish family. Handsome and exquisitely dressed, he cuts himself off from others by his extreme refinement; this detachment involves an abandonment of responsibility. His second marriage is to CAROLINE TRAFFORD, whom he loves, and they have a daughter, FRANCESCA VON FELDEN.

Felden, Francesca von
A Legacy, 1956
Sybille Bedford

The narrator, who has inherited the family tales of her parents, BARON JULIUS MARIA VON FELDEN and CAROLINE TRAFFORD, and reconstructed the complete story. From her earliest years she is 'imprinted with the experiences of others', and she later contemplates the process of memory. In her multilingual and wealthy childhood (the first nine years of which are spent in Germany) she lacks the company of other children; she has a donkey, but it hates her.

Feldman
A Bad Man, 1967
Stanley Elkin

He runs a department store in a large American town, but like other Elkin characters has a fundamental problem in co-ordinating the disparate elements of his life and work, and lapses steadily into crime.

Felicia
Felicia's Journey, 1994
William Trevor

Felicia comes from a staunch Irish Republican family for whom she keeps house. At 17 she is 'not much to look at. Her nondescript hair grows in a widow's peak and is pulled straight back and held with hair clips. She is a small rabbity girl.' Desperate for love, she is easily seduced and becomes pregnant. Abandoned by her lover, she goes to England to try to find him, but her naivety and misplaced trust make her vulnerable in a world of which she has little experience. It is precisely this innocence that draws JOEY HILDITCH to her.

Felicity
The Abbess of Crewe, 1974
Muriel Spark

The tiny rival of ALEXANDRA in the election for Abbess of Crewe, Sister Felicity admires St Francis of Assisi and preaches love and liberty, but carries this too far by taking a Jesuit lover. She spends much of her time sewing and has a bourgeois image, despite her noble descent. The theft of her silver thimble by supporters of Alexandra starts a scandal.

Fell, Alice
'Alice Fell; or Poverty', 1807
William Wordsworth

A little orphan girl, she arouses pity when she weeps inconsolably for her ruined cloak on the coach to Durham. Her delight in a new one gives pleasure also to her benefactor.

Fellamar, Lord
The History of Tom Jones, 1749
Henry Fielding

A ganderish young nobleman who plots with LADY BELLASTON to bring about the downfall of SOPHIA WESTERN, and even attempts to force himself upon the girl, only to be rejected and then roundly rebuked by her foul-mouthed father.

Female Vagrant, the
'The Female Vagrant', 1798
'Guilt and Sorrow; or, Incidents upon Salisbury Plain', 1842
William Wordsworth

The subject of 'The Female Vagrant' and a principal character in 'Guilt and Sorrow; or Incidents upon Salisbury Plain', she is a sad victim of circumstances. While mourning the loss of her former spirit and optimism, she is instrumental in helping a wandering sailor come to terms with his own troubled past.

Fen, Gervase
The Case of the Gilded Fly, 1944, et seq
Edmund Crispin

Tall and lanky, with wild hair and a ruddy face, and occasionally sporting such accessories as an 'extraordinary hat' and an undrivable sports car, Fen is an irrepressible, irritating and farcical figure. He is an elaborate fictional game, often casting aspersions on the quality of Crispin's

writing, and even the credibility of the clues of the novels in which he appears. A professor of English language and literature at Oxford, he is more keen to investigate crime than to work on or converse about his subject.

Fenella
Peveril of the Peak, 1823
Sir Walter Scott

Allegedly modelled on Goethe's Mignon, she is actually EDWARD CHRISTIAN's daughter, planted in the guise of a deaf-mute to spy on her guardian, the Countess of Derby, who has named her after some ancient princess of the Britons. Dark-skinned and exquisitely formed, she has a sharp eye for detail and is 'mistress of many little accomplishments'.

Fenton
The Merry Wives of Windsor, c.1597
William Shakespeare

A young gentleman in love with ANNE PAGE, Fenton's relative poverty and his roistering have not endeared him to her father, although he is Anne's choice of husband. However, he admits that he was initially attracted by her father's money. That he now loves her not for her potential inheritance but for herself alone is a sign of his emotional maturity. Such a transformation distinguishes him from the provincial squabbling both of his rivals and the elder Pages and Fords. During the baiting of SIR JOHN FALSTAFF in Windsor Great Park, Fenton and Anne steal away to be married.

Fenwick, Rev Frank
The Vicar of Bullhampton, 1870
Anthony Trollope

The tall and balding vicar of the Wiltshire village of Bullhampton. Popular and good-humoured, he has an optimistic view of human nature and strongly believes in Christian forgiveness. He equally strongly opposes the tyranny of the MARQUIS OF TROWBRIDGE. These beliefs lead him to act imprudently, though always sincerely and honestly. His attempt to encourage the marriage of HARRY GILMORE and MARY LOWTHER has unfortunate consequences.

Fenwick, Russell
The Secret Ladder, 1964, part of *The Guyana Quartet*, 1985
Wilson Harris

Captain of a mutinous and sunstruck crew, he is engaged on a voyage of 'inquiry into the dramatic role of conscience in time and being, the dangers of mortal ascent and immortal descent'. He sails back and forth in time, navigating by dreams.

Ferdinand
The Tempest, 1611
William Shakespeare

Son of the King of Naples, Ferdinand believes himself the only survivor of the shipwreck that destroyed his father's ship. His mourning is short-lived, however, for he falls in love with MIRANDA at first sight and is prepared to undertake whatever tasks her father PROSPERO sets him to prove his affection is real. He becomes Prospero's willing slave, in contrast to ARIEL and CALIBAN who are unwilling subjects. His genuine devotion, uncomplaining subservience and compliancy win over his future father-in-law.

Ferdinand, Duke of Calabria
The Duchess of Malfi, 1623
John Webster

Brother of the DUCHESS OF MALFI and THE CARDINAL. Scheming and far from gullible, he rarely pays his debts but is quick to seek revenge. He threatens his sister to try to prevent her from marrying again, motivated by greed for her wealth and possibly, so extreme is his passion, by incestuous desire. He despises her husband ANTONIO BOLOGNA because he is a commoner. Immediately regretting the murder of his sister, he goes mad, developing lycanthropy.

Ferdinand, King
Love's Labour's Lost, not later than 1594
William Shakespeare

The King of Navarre. His inspired plan is to swear an oath, along with three reluctant friends, to do no wooing for three years, making the court 'a little academe' in the meantime. The plan goes wrong, however, when he falls for the PRINCESS OF FRANCE. In the course of his love, he loses most of whatever dignity he started with.

Fermor, Arabella
The History of Emily Montague, 1769
Frances Brooke

A spirited, vivacious woman of 22, who acknowledges that her favourite pastime is 'constantly flirting' with the numerous young men who surround her at Montreal's social events: 'if I can maintain my empire over hearts, I leave the men to quarrel for everything else'. Love is an amusement for Arabella, not the overriding concern of her life. Nonetheless she is a sensible young woman, and a good friend to EMILY MONTAGUE, although she cannot understand her friend's obsession with finding rapturous passion within a relationship. Arabella is the prime go-between in Emily's and COL EDWARD RIVERS' courtship, at the same time pursuing her own romance with CAPTAIN FITZGERALD.

Fermor, William
The History of Emily Montague, 1769
Frances Brooke

ARABELLA FERMOR's father, a senior officer in the army, stationed in Canada. William Fermor is entranced by the beauty and magnificence of nature in the New World. He is equally fascinated by the native people and settlers of the new colonies, and writes frequently to his patron in England detailing his observations. William believes that man is at his best when fully occupied, but not overstretched. A widower, he is a firm but loving parent to Arabella, concerned to check the 'certain excess of romance' in her temper, but otherwise allowing her to make her own mistakes under his watchful eye. A practical man, he feels a duty to ensure that his daughter and her friends marry appropriately and well.

Fern, Will
The Chimes, 1844
Charles Dickens

A poor but honest country labourer formerly employed by SIR JOSEPH BOWLEY, he comes to London to look for work, bringing with him his niece, Lilian. He is harshly dealt with by ALDERMAN CUTE, who wants him 'put down' as a vagrant. TROTTY VECK has a dream of what the future, as foretold by Alderman Cute and MR FILER, might hold for Will: he becomes a rick-burner and Lilian a prostitute. But the story ends by suggesting that they will lead happier lives.

Fernandez, Margaret
A High Wind in Jamaica, 1929
Richard Hughes

Margaret comes from one of the less-Europeanized, Creole families who live in Jamaica. She is the oldest of the children kidnapped by pirates, but claims no seniority. A loner through choice and circumstance, during the course of the voyage she passes into adolescence, leaves the company of the other children, and becomes the mistress of OTTO, the first mate. She is (wrongly) suspected of murder, but accepts her fate silently. Ostracized by the crew, as well as by the other children, she is treated and behaves like a neglected animal: a martyr with a disconcerting 'dull, meaningless stare'.

Ferrars, Edward
Sense and Sensibility, 1811
Jane Austen

The elder son of MRS FERRARS, mild-mannered Edward, in having no living of his own, finds himself at the mercy of his mother's whims, at least if he wants to inherit her fortune. Prolonging a youthfully foolish and secret engagement to LUCY STEELE only out of a sense of honour, he is unwittingly freed from his obligations to her by his brother, ROBERT FERRARS, leaving him in a position to consolidate his love for ELINOR DASHWOOD and satisfy his modest ambitions.

Ferrars, Mrs
Sense and Sensibility, 1811
Jane Austen

Mother to EDWARD FERRARS, ROBERT FERRARS, and FANNY DASHWOOD, Mrs Ferrars is a stubborn, haughty little woman who uses her financial hold over Edward to try to manipulate his life. Self-centred, arrogant and rude, she behaves like a spoilt child at every opportunity, and reacts in an extreme way when her son dares to go against her will.

Ferrars, Robert
Sense and Sensibility, 1811
Jane Austen

The younger brother of EDWARD FERRARS, Robert – a minor character in the novel – is completely unlike him in nature, being showy, conceited, and entirely assured of his own superiority. He ironically does his brother a great favour, while believing himself to be doing the opposite, when he supplants him in the affections of his fiancée, LUCY STEELE, who is the perfect foil to Robert's foppish emptiness and unscrupulousness.

Ferret, Mr
The Life and Adventures of Sir Launcelot Greaves, 1760–1
Tobias Smollett

This cynical quack is aptly named, having deep-set red eyes and the twitching nostrils of a polecat. 'He was never seen to smile: he was never heard to speak in praise of any person whatsoever: and he was never known to give a direct answer to any question that was asked: but seemed, on all occasions, to be actuated by the most perverse spirit of contradictions.' He is believed to be a composite satire on Smollett's foe, the self-styled 'Dr' John Shebbeare, who wrote *Letters to the People of England*, and on the writer of medical treatises, Dr Charles Lucas.

Ferrex and Porrex
Gorboduc, 1561
Thomas Norton and Thomas Sackville

Sons of GORBODUC and VIDENA. Though Ferrex, the elder, is favoured by his mother and treated unjustly by his father in having to halve his inheritance, both brothers are ambitious and treacherous and fall prey easily to flattery. Porrex is the more ruthless of the two, but it is suspicion of his brother that drives him to commit his murder. Both brothers assume power before they are mature enough, and so become the instruments for the disaster that their father's proud and unnatural decision has set in motion.

Ferris, Rev Tony
Racing Demon, 1990
David Hare

In his twenties, eager and fresh-faced, Tony Ferris is one of a group of south-London clergymen (the others include the REV LIONEL ESPY and the REV HARRY HENDERSON). Ferris is the racing demon of the title, a ruthless but charming young man, an ambitious clergyman and dangerous fundamentalist, determined to put Christ 'bang at the centre of things'. The gospel according to Ferris is that faith is a matter of irrevocable conviction and absolute logic. 'Respect for God means respect for life.'

Ferroll
Endymion, 1880
Benjamin Disraeli

In what is transparently a *roman à clef*, he is intended as a portrait of Count Otto Bismarck, the unifier of Germany. Disraeli cuts a rather monolithic figure down to size, humanizing him somewhat.

Ferrovius
Androcles and the Lion, 1912
George Bernard Shaw

Ferrovius is a powerful man in the prime of life, but one whose 'sensibilities are keen and violent to the verge of madness'. He is something of a legend to LAVINIA and their fellow Roman Christian prisoners as being responsible for several conversions. When struck by a Roman soldier, Ferrovius turns the other cheek, valiantly keeping a fiery temper under control. Later, in the arena, having initially refused to fight, he kills six gladiators. THE EMPEROR is so impressed that he proclaims that the persecution of Christians shall cease. Ferrovius resorting to a sword-of-God faith has thus saved others.

Ferryman, the
The Bundle, 1978
Edward Bond

Even though he cannot afford to feed an extra mouth, the Ferryman takes pity on the child whom BASHO has discovered but left abandoned on the banks of a river. (The child grows up to become WANG.) By taking the infant with him, the Ferryman acts selflessly and shows his humanity.

Feste
Twelfth Night, c.1601
William Shakespeare

The Fool, employed by OLIVIA, he enjoys his position, which allows him to indulge in badinage. Quick-witted and clever, he also has a serious side. Most people appreciate him, apart from MALVOLIO who denigrates him. As a result, Feste is prepared to take part in the revenge on the steward, showing his talent for mimicry by playing Sir Topas, the curate. He employs his skill with words to a more fruitful end by exacting payment from those who delight in his ability.

Fetch, Jeremy
Love for Love, 1695
William Congreve

The servant of VALENTINE LEGEND, he is a sharp thinker, a fast talker, a wit, and in many ways much wiser than his employer. 'Jeremy speaks like an oracle', observes Scandal, Valentine's friend; and indeed Jeremy has been warning him for a long time that his high living would land him one day in debt. Both Jeremy and Valentine scrupulously observe their station in life, but otherwise act as confederates; theirs is a secure alliance based upon mutual respect.

Feverel, Richard
The Ordeal of Richard Feverel, 1859
George Meredith

After his mother runs away with a poet, Richard falls under his father Sir Austin's grossly repressive 'System', an education based almost entirely on repressive discipline. Despite it, he falls in love with Lucy Desborough and secretly marries her. Susceptible as ever, Richard accepts their separation and passes his time reforming London prostitutes (briefly falling for one of them). His sense of honour is pricked by Lord Mountfalcon's designs on his wife. He is wounded in a duel but Lucy can no longer bear the shock and dies. Richard bears his 'ordeal' with maddening and perhaps unconvincing reserve.

Feversham, Harry
The Four Feathers, 1902
A E W Mason

Accused of cowardice by brother officers, and consequently rejected by Ethne Eustace, he is forced to undergo a complex rite of passage to prove that he is worthy after all of their society and her love. To modern tastes he may seem more convincing while still unregenerate.

Fevvers
Nights at the Circus, 1984
Angela Carter
A winged trapeze artist whose authenticity is subject to constant speculation. A young woman of statuesque figure and Cockney eloquence, she combines the fantastic and mythic qualities of a bird-woman with the bawdy humour of a turn-of-the-century music-hall entertainer. Outwardly characterized by her gargantuan appetites for food and money, she also betrays capacities for introspection and love.

Fezziwigs, the
A Christmas Carol, 1843
Charles Dickens
EBENEZER SCROOGE was formerly apprenticed to Mr Fezziwig, a kind-hearted and jovial merchant. The GHOST OF CHRISTMAS PAST presents to Scrooge the Fezziwig family – Mr and Mrs Fezziwig and their three 'beaming and lovable' daughters – while they are giving a Christmas ball for their workers at the warehouse. The vision helps Scrooge to recognize how lonely and selfish he has become.

Fibich, Thomas
Latecomers, 1988
Anita Brookner
The middle-aged business partner of THOMAS HARTMANN with whom he runs a greetings-card company, Fibich feels rather guilty that he has made a lot of money so apparently easily. In contrast to Hartmann, he behaves 'like a harassed salesman', suffering sometimes from neuralgia and nervously stirring tea with a pencil. A fellow German and wartime orphan, he has known Hartmann since their schooldays. They rely upon each other. Troubled and hesitant by nature, constantly self-assessing and almost painfully modest, Fibich is the antithesis of the charming Hartmann.

Fidelia
The Plain Dealer, 1676/7
William Wycherley
Disguised as MANLY's page, Fidelia is secretly in love with him. She therefore allows him to use her in a scheme to expose OLIVIA, who has betrayed him both romantically and financially. In the process, Manly, a self-confessed misanthrope, comes to realize that Fidelia's virtue is 'greater than [he] thought any was in the World'.

Fidelman, Arthur
Pictures of Fidelman: An Exhibition, 1969
Bernard Malamud
A naive and childlike Jewish-American art student and a 'self-confessed failure as painter' who goes to Italy to study art history. In the course of the six stories in the book, his growth in understanding is paralleled by his physical decline. A succession of events leads him into forgery, pimping and homosexuality, but at the same time he is moving from idealistic art student, then pretentious artist, to worthy artisan.

Fidessa
The Faerie Queene, 1590–6
Sir Edmund Spenser
The name under which the evil enchantress DUESSA goes in order to dupe REDCROSSE, THE KNIGHT OF HOLINESS. The name is meant to indicate her womanish frailty; she appears physically and mentally weak, yet uses her female charm and magical gifts to lull Redcrosse into a false sense of security.

Fielding, Cyril
A Passage to India, 1924
E M Forster
An intelligent, middle-aged man with 'sprawling limbs and blue eyes', he is the popular principal of the Government College at Chandrapore. Warm-hearted, with a natural sympathy for the underdog, he believes in the worth of the individual and treats all men as his equal, regardless of race, creed or colour. He is viewed as a disruptive force by the bastions of the English community, and their suspicions are confirmed when he stands alone to protest the innocence of DR AZIZ when he is accused in the wake of the incidents at the Marabar Caves.

Fielding, May
The Cricket on the Hearth, 1845
Charles Dickens
A friend of MRS MARY PEERYBINGLE and the former schoolmate of BERTHA PLUMMER, she is a pretty girl and in love with Bertha's brother, EDWARD PLUMMER. Believing him to be dead after his long absence in South America, she is persuaded by her mother to become betrothed to the unpleasant old MR TACKLETON. But on the day appointed for the marriage, Edward returns and she marries him instead.

Fielding, Sgt
Too True to be Good, 1932
George Bernard Shaw
Fielding, a well-built man in his late thirties, is a soldier in the expeditionary force nominally commanded by COL TALLBOYS, which has been sent to a nameless country to rescue Miss Mopply (THE PATIENT) from brigands. A rather puritanical man, he occupies a place called 'The Abode of Love', reading the Bible and *The Pilgrim's Progress*, and criticizing both. Subconscious instinct brings THE NURSE to Fielding's lair. During THE BURGLAR's final sermon, they sneak away together.

Filer, Mr
The Chimes, 1844
Charles Dickens
A friend of ALDERMAN CUTE, he is 'a low-spirited gentleman of middle age' with a disconsolate face. A political economist, he has an absolute faith in the value of statistics, particularly where they can be used to condemn the poor.

Finau, Tongan Chief
Between Two Tides, 1952
R D Fitzgerald
'Politic, subtle, dark', the Tongan chief is a fearless leader, afraid of neither man nor god and disregarding of custom and privilege. With a cool

head and burning will, he manoeuvres and manipulates both friends and enemies in the obsessive pursuit of his dream to unite and rule Tonga. 'Fighting, scheming, dissembling like very heartbreak', he is a man of enormous physical and mental energy. He treats WILL MARINER as though he were his son.

Fincastle, Ada
Vein of Iron, 1935
Ellen Glasgow
Descended from Scottish-Irish Presbyterians, Ada nonetheless does not allow moral dogma to erase her passions. She cannot transcend physical desire through rigid metaphysics and musters the courage to indulge her carnal appetite. As a single parent, then as the wife of a divorcee, she refuses to be broken by family pressures. She adjusts her dreams to a world plagued by war and economic depression with unyielding stoicism.

Finch, Alexander
'The Fat Man in History', in *The Fat Man in History*, 1974
Peter Carey
The kleptomaniac secretary of the Thirty-Second District, and – unofficially – of the clandestine 'Fat Men Against the Revolution', a committee established to protect the overweight from persecution by verbal association. He is sweat-stained and ungainly, his pockets stuffed with tins of shoplifted smoked oysters.

Finch, Atticus
To Kill A Mockingbird, 1960
Harper Lee
A widowed lawyer, and father of SCOUT and JEM FINCH. The novel's title derives from his assertion that 'it's a sin to kill a mockingbird', because, a neighbour explains, 'they don't do one thing but sing their hearts out for us'. Courageous, calm, honest and good-humoured, he tries to set a credible moral example to his children, although he often feels he has failed as a parent. His views are enlightened and humanitarian, and he displays great integrity as well as generosity of spirit. His common phrase, in difficult situations, is 'it isn't time to worry yet'.

Finch, Jem (Jeremy)
To Kill A Mockingbird, 1960
Harper Lee
An imaginative young boy with a questioning intelligence, he is a natural leader, and takes that role in his games with his little sister, SCOUT FINCH. He is occasionally impatient of her, but is generally protective. He feels he is a 'born hero', and has an exasperating sense of his superiority, but does possess true courage. Like Scout, he learns tolerance and understanding.

Finch, Scout (Jean Louise)
To Kill A Mockingbird, 1960
Harper Lee
The narrator, looking back on her childhood. Intelligent, somewhat precocious, sensitive and tomboyish, the young Scout has a quick temper. She can be aggressive and mischievous, but gradually learns tolerance and understanding. Bright and outgoing, she becomes vaguely aware of impending adolescence and the world which

lies beyond, and feels that she 'is getting more like a girl every day'.

Finching, Flora
Little Dorrit, 1857
Charles Dickens
The daughter of CHRISTOPHER CASBY and widow of Mr F, as she habitually calls him. Although affected and sentimental, her kind-heartedness shows in her giving work to AMY DORRIT. She is a crushing disappointment to her former sweetheart, ARTHUR CLENNAM who, after a 20-year absence, finds her fat, foolish and given to gushing, disjointed conversation. Despite having designs on him, she is genuinely delighted when he marries Amy. Her constant companion is Mr F's Aunt, a grim old eccentric whose 'deep warning voice' offers irrelevant remarks that 'confounded and terrified the mind'.

Finchley, Sondra
An American Tragedy, 1925
Theodore Dreiser
A wealthy industrialist's daughter in an upstate New York town (modelled on Cortland), she attracts the young CLYDE GRIFFITHS and leads him to plot the murder of his pregnant girlfriend, ROBERTA ALDEN. Sondra is everything Roberta is not and Clyde pays the ultimate price for his greedy passion.

Fink, Mike
The Robber Bridegroom, 1942
Eudora Welty
A legendary US bandit, he captures CLEMENT MUSGROVE and thus precipitates the meeting between ROSAMOND MUSGROVE and the robber bridegroom JAMIE LOCKHART, who rescues Clement from Fink's clutches.

Fink-Nottle, Gussie (Augustus)
Right Ho, Jeeves, 1934, et seq
P G Wodehouse
Augustus Fink-Nottle has spent his adult life in Lincolnshire studying newts, so is at a loss when moved by sudden passion for Madeline Bassett. His close friend BERTIE WOOSTER sends him to woo her at Brinkley Court, but he remains a wordless idiot, except on the subject of newts. Bertie and JEEVES discover that he is teetotal; they both, unknown to one another, lace his orange juice with gin, unaware that he has already consumed quantities of whisky. The result is the most memorable prize day ever known at Market Snodsbury Grammar School. Gussie continues to pursue the soulful Madeline, but in the end elopes with Emerald Stoker, daughter of a wealthy American and a splendid cook.

Finlay, Dr
Beyond This Place, 1953, et seq
A J Cronin
A young doctor who comes to the Scottish Highland town of Tannochbrae as a timid assistant to the local GP, Dr Cameron, and rises to become, as the latter jokingly tells him in a later story, 'a verra weel kent man in this part o' Scotland'. He is good-looking, physically active and an expert shot, but is unsuccessful in love.

Assertive to the point of being dictatorial, and somewhat smug and self-righteous, he can be rude and intemperate.

Finley, Boss
Sweet Bird of Youth, 1959
Tennessee Williams

Utterly corrupt, he believes that money and status can achieve any goal. A vulgar and cunning man, he has become the political 'boss' of St Cloud, ruthlessly manipulating his relations to conform to his moralistic and false stance on family values, based around bigotry and pseudo-Christianity. He is finally exposed by an anonymous 'heckler' at a political rally.

Finn
The Silver Darlings, 1941
Neil Gunn

Son of CATRINE and the late TORMAD, Finn grows up, to his mother's great distress, increasingly enthralled by sea-life. In his heroic exploits and gripping story-telling ability, he is reminiscent of the legendary Finn MacCoul, but the lessons Finn has to learn are nonetheless those of any young man crossing the threshold into adulthood. Overcoming his rivalry with skipper Roddie Sinclair for his mother's attention, Finn simultaneously reaches a heightened self-awareness, realizing that love, compassion and honesty are of far greater value than pride; in accepting, and declaring, his love for Una, his 'circle' of peace and wisdom is complete.

Finn (Peter O'Finney)
Under the Net, 1954
Iris Murdoch

Claiming to be a distant cousin of JAKE DONAGHUE, the humble, self-effacing and lugubrious Finn is Jake's trusty ally – sometimes servant, sometimes manager. His angular face and floppy brown hair make him quite handsome in a sad, lanky way, but he gives Jake's girlfriend the 'creeps'. He loves trouble, and is fond of breaking bad news, but Jake has faith in his intuition and unfailing support in a crisis.

Finn, Huck (Huckleberry)
The Adventures of Tom Sawyer, 1876
The Adventures of Huckleberry Finn, 1884, and others
Mark Twain

Son of the town drunkard in St Petersburg, Missouri, Huck is a streetwise and self-reliant youth, ill-suited to the discipline and regularity of family life. Unlike his friend TOM SAWYER, who has a love for showy but empty gestures, Huck puts his ingenuity and cunning to practical use in order to escape his brutal father. His decision to help JIM, a runaway slave, to escape his owner brings him some agonized and confused soul-searching, but loyalty, friendship and human feeling ultimately triumph over the misshapen conscience acquired in a slave-holding culture.

Finn, Phineas
Phineas Finn, The Irish Member, 1869
The Eustace Diamonds, 1873
Phineas Redux, 1874

The Prime Minister, 1876
Anthony Trollope

A young Irishman who is elected to the House of Commons, in part through the influence of Lady Standish (LAURA KENNEDY). He is 'six feet high, and very handsome, with bright blue eyes, and brown wavy hair, and a light silken beard', and is thought by some to be 'much too handsome to do any good'. His political career is secondary to romantic entanglements as he rises in society, but a combination of thwarted ambitions and innate decency eventually drives him back to his sweetheart in Ireland. He returns as a widower to make his mark in politics, but refuses higher office, and marries MARIE GOESLER.

Firmin, Dr George, also known as **George Brandon**
A Shabby Genteel Story, 1840
The Adventures of Philip, 1861–2
W M Thackeray

A fashionable and rather dashing doctor who, under the alias of George Brandon, exploits his status to seduce the impoverished CAROLINE GANN. He reappears in *The Adventures of Philip* as the hero PHILIP FIRMIN's father, pursued by his past and no more alive to his duties and responsibilities than he ever was.

Firmin, Geoffrey
Under the Volcano, 1947
Malcolm Lowry

An alcoholic British Consul, drowning his disappointment in a Mexican backwater. He is a 'poor lonely dispossessed trembling soul', who has lost his sense of his own worth, who will go without wearing socks, but will give his money to a beggar. He was a bashful child, but had been decorated in the war (although in dubious circumstances), and married a beautiful actress. His spiritual agonies and uncontrollable alcoholism produce an oddly demented, despairing lucidity, and he seems clearly doomed to the fate he meets on the Day of the Dead.

Firmin, Philip
The Adventures of Philip, 1861–2
W M Thackeray

The son of DR GEORGE FIRMIN, a society doctor and friend of Thackeray's regular narrator, ARTHUR PENDENNIS. Good-natured and un-selfish, but somewhat credulous, Philip has to suffer the repercussions of his father's indiscretions and evasions. Like other Thackeray heroes, he refuses to capitalize on the misfortunes of others. He is in love with CHARLOTTE BAYNES.

Fischelson, Dr Nahum
'The Spinoza of Market Street', in *The Spinoza of Market Street*, 1961
Isaac Bashevis Singer

A 'short, hunched', ageing man who has devoted his life to the study of the philosopher Spinoza in a lonely attic room, he is a mildly irritating yet amusing pedant who has applied so much logic to his life that it has gone quite stale and lost its meaning. His idea of escapism is to examine the stars through his telescope – until, that is, he falls ill and is tended by Black Dobbe, whom he marries. He takes an adolescent delight in rediscovering the ordinary pleasures of love and sex, suddenly seeing with dignity and humour what he had become.

Fischer, Carel
The Time of the Angels, 1966
Iris Murdoch

The deranged and godless Fischer is appointed rector of a non-existent City church destroyed in the Blitz. Believing that God's death has released his angels, the terrible principalities and powers of the Old Testament, into a world devoid of love, goodness and morality, he inspires dread in his daughter MURIEL FISCHER, in his younger brother MARCUS FISCHER and in PATTIE O'DRISCOLL, his slavishly devoted mistress. Increasingly isolated, obsessed by religious mania and his 'precious possession', ELIZABETH FISCHER, he moves inexorably towards retribution.

Fischer, Elizabeth
The Time of the Angels, 1966
Iris Murdoch

A 19-year-old invalid, niece and ward of CAREL FISCHER and MARCUS FISCHER. She has an otherworldly air and beauty with her pale complexion, long white-blonde hair and luminous grey eyes. She is housebound, and the darkly possessed – and possessive – Carel prevents even Marcus from seeing her. Ostensibly her only companion and confidante is her devoted cousin, MURIEL FISCHER; but Elizabeth shares an ugly secret with the mentally unbalanced Carel.

Fischer, Marcus
The Time of the Angels, 1966
Iris Murdoch

Returned from years in America, Marcus, a mild schoolmaster, is writing a treatise on morality in a secular age. He venerates but fears his elder brother, CAREL FISCHER, who at 16 took the place of their dead father. Appalled by rumours of Carel's madness, and denied all contact with him and their ward ELIZABETH FISCHER, Marcus, an unlikely knight errant, rather comically invades the embattled rectory. But confronted by Carel he again succumbs to his malevolent spell; and also to the different one cast by his former pupil, LEO PESHKOV.

Fischer, Muriel
The Time of the Angels, 1966
Iris Murdoch

CAREL FISCHER's 24-year-old daughter, an intelligent, self-assertive and ascetic woman. She is a devoted friend and adviser to ELIZABETH FISCHER, with whom she shares a theoretical 'sophisticated immoralism', and a very real animosity towards the servant PATTIE O'DRISCOLL. Terrified by her father, whose overbearing, sinister presence permeates the rectory, Muriel sees the kind caretaker, EUGENE PESHKOV, as the essential foil to her dark, malignant father. But she loves her father too, and with bitter irony eventually holds the power of life or death over him.

Fish, Oswald
Who Was Oswald Fish?, 1981
A N Wilson

The son of a wealthy Birmingham manufacturer of brackets and hinges, he capitalizes on the new vogue for ritualism in the church by adding communion rails and rood screens to Fish & Co's output. Disconcerted by the abject overcrowding of the 19th-century city, he recognizes he can do nothing about it and settles for a self-absorbed aestheticism which has a considerable impact on the lives of his present-day descendants and their associates. He is a mysterious figure, whose religious overtones cannot be overlooked.

Fisher, Mary
The Life and Loves of a She-Devil, 1983
Fay Weldon

Mary is the antithesis of her counterpart, RUTH. She is 'feminine' in the sense of being pretty, gentle, passionate yet passive, and is also rich and successful. Attractive to the opposite sex, she retains an independence and self-reliance envied by most women. When Mary falls in love, she is dedicated to her lover, despite the fact that he has a wife and children to leave behind. If she initially takes his separation from his wife rather lightly, the consequences come as an enormous shock. She does not consider much outside her own consciousness, and pays the price of being overly self-absorbed.

Fisher, Miss Naomi
The House in Paris, 1935
Elizabeth Bowen

Stiff, camphory, and with an air of translating everything she says uncertainly out of French before she utters it in English, she is designated to look after HENRIETTA (whose father's lover she has been) and LEOPOLD at the house in Paris while en route to their respective destinations.

Fisher, Sylvie
Housekeeping, 1980
Marilynne Robinson

An odd, drifting transient, Sylvie Fisher is a strange choice for guardian of two young girls (RUTH and LUCILLE STONE). Her refusal to adapt to society's norms makes her an outcast, a role she seems both to relish and ignore. Often silent and never predictable, Sylvie retains her transient mannerisms, preferring the company of nature to that of the community.

Fisker, Hamilton K
The Way We Live Now, 1875
Anthony Trollope

An American railroad proprietor who is associated with the Melmotte family, and marries MARIE MELMOTTE after her unfortunate experience with SIR FELIX CARBURY. A small man of about 40, with 'a well-twisted moustache', he is confident and forward in his manner, and is untroubled by scruples or doubts over his conduct. Shrewd rather than intelligent, his 'mind was not capacious, but such as it was it was his own, and he knew how to use it'.

Fitzdottrel, Fabian and Mrs Frances
The Devil is an Ass, 1616
Ben Jonson

A gullible and overbearing squire of Norfolk, Fabian Fitzdottrel is so jealous of his wife that he keeps her locked in her room; yet, when EUSTACE MANLY and WITTIPOOL offer him an expensive cloak if he will allow them to speak to her, he accepts. He likes to be admired for his clothes, and his vanity is even greater than his domestic tyranny. MEERCRAFT, a speculator, also preys on his vanity, offering him a bogus title if he will invest in a land deal. Fitzdottrel blunders into so many deceptions that he discovers he has lost both his lands and his wife, but when Manly assures him that the entire business has been a ruse to expose his foolishness and protect Mrs Fitzdottrel, he admits his errors.

Fitzfassenden, Epifania
The Millionairess, 1935
George Bernard Shaw

Handsome but quick-tempered, Epifania honoured her late father's wish that she marry a man who could turn £150 into £50,000 in six months. Alastair Fitzfassenden succeeded (by trickery), and she married him. She then falls for an Egyptian doctor who asks her to carry out a similar test: she succeeds by hard work. Epifania divorces and prepares to remarry. Powerful and arrogant, she appears a capitalist heroine: when her Egyptian doctor feels her pulse, he feels the beat of the Life Force. But her tragedy is that she diverts it merely into emotional dominance and material acquisition.

Fitzgerald, Burgo
Can You Forgive Her?, 1864–5
Anthony Trollope

A dissolute young man about town, said to be 'deep in every vice'. He is the nephew of LADY MONK, and has been disowned by his father over his behaviour. Although he is given to drinking heavily, squandering whatever money comes his way, and gambling recklessly, he is 'certainly among the handsomest of God's creatures', and is the subject of LADY GLENCORA PALLISER's troubled infatuation.

Fitzgerald, Captain
The History of Emily Montague, 1769
Frances Brooke

'A tall Irishman, with good eyes ... not handsome, but well made', he is the beau of ARABELLA FERMOR. The second son of an Irish baronet of good fortune, Fitzgerald has an income of about £500 a year, independent of his commission in the army, and is considered a fine match in Canadian social circles. His prospective father-in-law is suitably impressed: 'he is a man of excellent sense, and of honor, and has a very lively tenderness for my daughter'. Arabella, however, is attracted by his saucy, teasing ways. COL EDWARD RIVERS envies him those characteristics which make him appealing to women: 'you have a certain manly, spirited air, which promises them a protector; a look of understanding, which is the indication of a pleasing companion; a sensibility of countenance, which speaks a friend and a lover; to which I ought to add, an affectionate, constant attention to women, and a polite indifference to men, which above all things flatters the vanity of the sex.'

Fitzgerald, Morris
'The Wind at Your Door', 1958, in *Southmost Twelve*, 1962
R D Fitzgerald

One of the rebels of an Australian convict-led revolt, this Irishman would rather die under the lash than inform upon his fellows and his cause. Although born of poor stock, 'the breed of clod and dunce', he shows unflinching courage and intensity of faith.

Fitzpatrick, Francie
The Real Charlotte, 1894
E O Somerville and Martin Ross

Francie, with her wild-rose prettiness, has the impudence of the Dublin streets. She has always flirted; when CHARLOTTE MULLEN invites her to Tally Ho Lodge, she flirts with soldiers. She has no notion of marrying for money; it is all fun. But the practised Hawkins makes her love him, then leaves – he is engaged already and Francie marries RODDY LAMBERT as second-best. She is sorry for his ruin, and when she hears that Dysart has reversed his decision to dismiss him, she rides to tell him on a spirited horse he has given her, and is killed when it rears at a workhouse funeral of an old woman he and Charlotte had cheated.

Fitzpiers, Edred
The Woodlanders, 1887
Thomas Hardy

A young doctor who belongs to a noble but impoverished family, he is a social and intellectual snob. Self-indulgent and fickle, he flits from one thing to another, capable of being possessed by 'five distinct infatuations at the same time'. No sooner has he married GRACE MELBURY than he loses interest in her and becomes bewitched by the more cosmopolitan FELICE CHARMOND, but he is also unable to resist the hoydenish charms of the buxom Suke Damson.

Five Guildsmen, the (the Carpenter, the Dyer, the Haberdasher, the Tapestry Weaver, the Weaver)
The Canterbury Tales, c.1387–1400
Geoffrey Chaucer

Five indistinguishable members of the emergent middle class who ostentatiously display their new-found wealth. Pretentious social climbers, wearing the silver ornaments reserved solely for the nobility, all are anxious to attain status as civic dignitaries. They are accompanied by their equally pretentious wives and by THE COOK they have had the effrontery to employ.

Fiver
Watership Down, 1972
Richard Adams

HAZEL's nervous, twitchy brother, the runt of the litter, blessed with second sight. Incapable of concealing what he feels, he becomes trance-like or hysterical when in the grip of a vision. His terrifying forebodings of a blood-filled field set in motion the exodus from the Sandleford Warren. When the rabbits later hear from HOLLY the grim tale of the gassing of the warren, no one makes light of Fiver's 'feelings' again. Indeed, thereafter he is often consulted for advice by the other rabbits.

Fizkin, Horatio
Pickwick Papers, 1837
Charles Dickens
The parliamentary candidate for the Buff party in the Eatanswill election. He loses to THE HON SAMUEL SLUMKEY.

Flack, Mrs
Riders in the Chariot, 1961
Patrick White
Together with her friend, MRS JOLLEY, Mrs Flack is a broadly satirical portrait of the snobbish, bigoted, ostentatious and vulgar suburban matron, the type of woman caricatured by the comedian Barry Humphries, whom White much admired. At her home, which she calls her 'residence', Mrs Flack enjoys talking about hats and the various articles on her dressing table. After tea, she and Mrs Jolley like to sit listening to the rumblings and bubblings of their stomachs. Revelling in her own supposed normality and other people's apparent oddity, Mrs Flack is virulently xenophobic, and is partly responsible for the cruel taunting that leads to the death of MORDECAI HIMMELFARB.

Flamineo
The White Devil, 1612
John Webster
Although of distinguished Venetian ancestry, Flamineo is a poor graduate of the University of Padua. He seeks advancement as secretary to the DUKE OF BRACHIANO, on whose behalf he plots, procures his own sister VITTORIA COROMBONA, and even commits murder. Intelligent and witty, he comments bitterly on the action. He has some pangs of conscience when he drives his mother insane by murdering his brother in front of her, but he continues to scheme until the end.

Flanders, Jacob
Jacob's Room, 1922
Virginia Woolf
A character seen mainly through the eyes of others, Jacob is emotionally detached. He did not feel terribly valued as a child and has developed a self-sufficient approach to life. He likes to feel that he is in control of every situation and that he is composed, no matter what happens. Faintly contemptuous of others, his attitude borders on the arrogant, although he is not inwardly confident. He feels that he is immortal; he is young, male, intelligent, capable and unflappable. But it is this self-reliance which, ironically, is at the root of his vulnerability. A sad figure, he seems to have built a protective barrier around himself, which may keep trouble at bay for a while, but not forever.

Flanders, Moll
Moll Flanders, 1722
Daniel Defoe
Born in Newgate to a mother about to be transported for theft, she has a precarious start in life, being passed from the town mayoress to a kind gentlewoman whose son seduces her. Her continuing motivation is survival in a world where women have very little going for them, and her method is to spread her favours in the most rewarding manner. Forced to live on her wits and take opportunities when they arise, she is driven to theft, and has no compunction about using the men who cross her path for her own ends. Throughout a long and adventurous career she demonstrates a spirit and energy for life that is irrepressibly hopeful and calculatingly adaptable.

Flashman, Harry
Tom Brown's Schooldays, 1857, et seq
Thomas Hughes
A big, powerful 17-year-old, Flashman is leader of a group of bullies at Rugby School when TOM BROWN arrives as a new boy. Brutal, sneering and contemptuous, Flashman is a coward, but adept at maintaining the pretence of swaggering bravado. He can also be pleasant when it is in his interests, and has no scruples about toadying to others in exchange for their loyalty and approbation. Scorning the loyal, patriotic values of Brown and his friends, Flashman represents the tyrannical aspect of public school life, organizing beatings, and pinning Tom in front of a fire until his legs burn. England's bad apple, he is eventually expelled for drunkenness.

Flashman, Sir Harry
Flashman, 1969
George McDonald Fraser
A continuation of the character of HARRY FLASHMAN, he is the biggest coward and most shameless womanizer ever to have disgraced the uniform of the British army. He has had the good fortune – largely thanks to his natural talent as a linguist – to survive conflict in most of the major battlefields of his time. Driven by his appetite for vice of every type and wenches of every form, he stumbles his way through terrifying adventures across the globe, emerging with a quite undeserved reputation as a hero. Disarmingly frank in his memoirs, he reveals considerable charm in his honest self-assessment as a philanderer, cheat, coward and born survivor.

Flask
Moby-Dick, 1851
Herman Melville
The third mate on the *Pequod*, known as 'King-post' on account of his sturdy build. He is a 'short, stout, ruddy young fellow, very pugnacious concerning whales, who somehow seemed to think that the great leviathans had personally and hereditarily affronted him; and therefore it was a sort of point of honour with him, to destroy them wherever encountered'. He has an ignorant, unconscious fearlessness in the chase.

Flatterie
Ane Pleasant Satyre of the Thrie Estaitis, 1540
Sir David Lindsay
Clad in jester's clothes, Flatterie is associated with the sin of folly as well as flattery, and it is

his arrival which signals the chaos to follow. Glib, hypocritical and insincere, he is linked symbolically with SPIRITUALITIE and, fittingly disguised as a friar called Devotioun, he deceives – with significant ease – REX HUMANITAS himself. The most charming, and thus perhaps also the most dangerous of the three Vices, Flatterie gets off lightly, betraying FALSET and DISSAIT to escape the gallows though he has, as he himself declares, 'far ma falts nor my maits'.

Flavin, Troy
Delta Wedding, 1946
Eudora Welty

He is 'an overseer born and bred' who works on the Fairchild family plantation, and is engaged to be married to DABNEY FAIRCHILD. The family knows very little about his background, other than that he has 'a little mother in the hills'. He is twice Dabney's age, and a deliberate, cautious, slow-talking man with a kindly nature and a good heart.

Flavius
Timon of Athens, 1607/8
William Shakespeare and perhaps Thomas Middleton

The faithful steward of TIMON OF ATHENS, Flavius is a cautious, level-headed man, dismayed by Timon's rash generosity with money. He has, too, considerable insight into human nature, for when Timon is almost bankrupt, Flavius sadly advises that it will be useless for him to rely on his 'varnished friends' for help. Reflecting that 'riches point to misery and contempt', Flavius concludes that Timon has been 'undone by goodness'. He visits him in his self-imposed exile in his cave in the woods, where Timon accepts him as the one 'honest man', gives him gold and advises him to 'Hate all, curse all, show charity to none'.

Fleance
Macbeth, c.1606
William Shakespeare

An innocent boy who becomes one of MACBETH's main targets purely because he is BANQUO's son, and therefore destined – according to THE THREE WEIRD SISTERS' predictions – for future kingship. His brief, early appearance in the play, shortly before KING DUNCAN's murder, serves to establish economically the loving bond between father and son, adding a warm note to a chilling scene.

Fledgeby, 'Fascination Fledgeby'
Our Mutual Friend, 1865
Charles Dickens

A malicious money-lender who hides behind his fictitious firm, Pubsey & Co, and employs the elderly Jew, RIAH, as an agent for his extortionate practices. Dandified, boorish and 'the meanest cur existing', he bribes ALFRED LAMMLE and his wife to arrange a match with Georgiana Podsnap for her money, but when this falls through, he has Riah pressure them to pay their debts. When Fledgeby is revealed to be their true creditor, Lammle thrashes him and JENNY WREN puts pepper into his wounds.

Fleisher, Von Humboldt
Humboldt's Gift, 1975
Saul Bellow

A poet who is 'a great entertainer but going insane'. His intellectual and literary milieu is that of the 1950s, and he is obsessed with working out a grand, synthesizing conception of the role of the poet in a modern US society which is stripped of the old values and relationships, the old 'radiance' he wishes to foster. He has enjoyed some success, and is a mentor to CHARLIE CITRINE, but sinks into poverty, paranoia and neglect. Ironically, fame arrives posthumously.

Fleming, Henry
The Red Badge of Courage, 1895
Stephen Crane

A farm-boy, whose conception of military life and soldierly courage is based on romantic fiction rather than the brute fact of combat. Against his mother's wishes he enlists in the Union army, experiences violent doubts about his own appetite for battle and receives his ironic, bloody 'badge of courage' when he is struck by a comrade during an ignominious retreat. As narrator, Henry's is the only viewpoint on the campaign and the reader shares in his slow growth toward the quietly triumphant acclamation: 'He was a man.'

Fleming, Rhoda
Rhoda Fleming, 1865
George Meredith

A farmer's daughter, with little innate 'breeding', but nonetheless one of Meredith's exceptional women. She knows her mind and is ruthlessly intolerant of folly, in herself or in others. Marriage to Robert Armstrong only heightens her individuality.

Fleming, Rob
High Fidelity, 1995
Nick Hornby

The hapless owner of Championship Vinyl, a secondhand record shop in north London, and recently abandoned by his girlfriend, Fleming occupies his many aimless hours by rearranging his record collection, compiling his 'top five' lists of likes and dislikes, and wallowing in self-pity. Good-natured, fearful of being alone but equally wary of the responsibilities of intimacy and commitment, he is undecided as to whether he should be distraught or relieved by his girlfriend Laura leaving him. Essentially, at 35, he has failed to develop much beyond adolescent introspection, yet he eventually finds a sense of maturity and purpose.

Flesh, Ben
The Franchiser, 1976
Stanley Elkin

Ben's attempts to make a coherent whole of his scattered and piecemeal financial dealings are metaphorically linked to the multiple sclerosis from which he (like his author) suffers: messages fail to get through; connections are not made; there is a progressive loss of control.

Flett, Daisy Goodwill
The Stone Diaries, 1993
Carol Shields

Daisy tells her own story, documenting her fairly ordinary life: her unexpected birth, her marriage and widowhood, her children and even her own death. Although the details she relates, such as telling no-one about her husband's death, often give an impression of detachment, Daisy's claim that she is an unreliable narrator who is 'cursed with the lonely woman's romantic imagination and thus can support only happy endings' suggests deeper emotional feeling. Ultimately, the narrative layers create a complex character whose motives cannot be easily judged.

Flibbertigibbet → Sludge, Dickie

Flint, Captain, properly Jim Turner
Swallows and Amazons, 1930, et seq
Arthur Ransome

A plump, shy and rather lonely bachelor, the uncle of NANCY and PEGGY BLACKETT, he lives on a houseboat, with his green parrot Polly, a brass cannon and, it is rumoured, a hoard of treasure. Not surprisingly, the WALKER children are convinced he is a pirate, albeit a retired one, and they immediately christen him 'Captain Flint'. In reality he is a bad-tempered writer, holed up for the summer in an attempt to write a book about his extensive travels, and not keen on taking part in pirate games with the Blacketts. In time, however, he turns out to have a remarkably soft centre.

Flintwinch, Affery
Little Dorrit, 1857
Charles Dickens

Formerly the nurse of ARTHUR CLENNAM, she is MRS CLENNAM's servant and the wife of JEREMIAH FLINTWINCH. He and Mrs Clennam compelled her to marry him in an attempt to prevent her revealing the deception about the codicil and other schemes. She lives in terror, and her husband persuades her than she is merely sleepwalking or dreaming when she hears and sees secret comings and goings in the house. She is 'thankful to be quit of him' when he absconds to Holland after the death of Mrs Clennam.

Flintwinch, Jeremiah
Little Dorrit, 1857
Charles Dickens

MRS CLENNAM's cunning old clerk, and later business partner, his neck is so twisted that 'he had a weird appearance of having hanged himself'. Knowing that she has suppressed the codicil in her husband's will that leaves money to AMY DORRIT, he steals the documents, which fall into the hands of RIGAUD. He keeps his wife, AFFERY FLINTWINCH, in a state of terror and ignorance about his nefarious schemes. After Mrs Clennam's death, he escapes to Holland with some of her money, leaving Affery behind.

Flippanta
The Confederacy, 1705
Sir John Vanbrugh

The servant of MRS AMLET, Flippanta is recruited by her employer's son, DICK AMLET, to help him in his amorous pursuit of CORINNA GRIPE. She also becomes the go-between of CLARISSA GRIPE and ARAMINTA MONEYTRAP in their battle against their deceiving husbands. Observant and clever, Flippanta loyally serves the whims of others but is not for one moment deluded by them.

Flite, Miss
Bleak House, 1853
Charles Dickens

A frail, crazed elderly suitor in the case of *Jarndyce v Jarndyce*, she haunts the law courts and lives in constant expectation of a judgement. She is befriended by ESTHER SUMMERSON, ADA CLARE and RICHARD CARSTONE. She lodges with MR KROOK and keeps a number of caged birds with names such as 'Hope', 'Joy', 'Dust', 'Ashes' and 'Cunning'. When the lawsuit is settled, she gives the birds their freedom.

Flo, Vi, and Ru
Come and Go, 1965
Samuel Beckett

Three women of indeterminate age. Wearing full-length, tightly buttoned coats and hats whose brims shade their faces, they sit on a bench in half-light. Like many characters in Beckett's later plays, they have little texture and are hardly differentiated. They appear to be almost ghosts of their former selves. They speak, slowly and briefly, each asking another whether they detect any change in the other. A tragic memory seems to weigh over them about which they may not or cannot speak: perhaps they are the physical embodiment of memory itself.

Flood, Nora
Nightwood, 1936
Djuna Barnes

At the centre of a narrative set in the homosexual underworld of contemporary Paris, is the doomed lesbian love affair of Nora and ROBIN VOTE. Nora (based partly upon the author) is both protagonist and victim, a thoughtful, intelligent and caring woman who is helplessly in love with a destructive partner. Lurking outside the cafés where she suspects Robin to be spending too much time with too many people, Nora is, like many of the characters in the book, both introspective and lonely.

Flood-Jones, Mary
Phineas Finn, The Irish Member, 1869
Anthony Trollope

The simple Irish childhood sweetheart of PHINEAS FINN, to whom she is betrothed. She is 'one of those girls, so common in Ireland, whom men, with tastes that way given, feel inclined to take up and devour on the spur of the moment; and when she liked her lion, she had a look about her which seemed to ask to be devoured'. She marries Finn, but subsequently dies in pregnancy while still young.

Flora
Coningsby, or The New Generation, 1844
Benjamin Disraeli

The illegitimate daughter of LORD MONMOUTH,

she represents the degeneracy of the old aristocracy. Sickly and withdrawn, she works in a theatrical troupe until she inherits Monmouth's estate; at her death, she transfers her fortune to HARRY CONINGSBY, her natural nephew.

Flora
The Turn of the Screw, 1898
Henry James

A child of uncommon beauty, she is one of the unnamed (ANON) young governess's two charges at Bly, and one of the children she believes to be in communication with evil spirits, a charge Flora denies. In that regard, at least, she has a command that her brother, MILES, lacks and which allows her, for all her fear, to survive the governess's psychological assaults.

Florence, Duke of
Women Beware Women, c.1621
Thomas Middleton

Arrogant and ruthless, but possessed of a persuasive charm, he seduces BIANCA CAPELLO, knowing her to be married already to another man. His moral turpitude is highlighted by his belief that he can save his soul from hell by engineering the murder of LEANTIO, Bianca's husband, so that he can marry her himself and thereby wipe out his earlier sin of adultery.

Florimell
The Faerie Queene, 1590–6
Sir Edmund Spenser

A beautiful, virginal lady of 'steadfast chastity and virtue rare'. She is clad in a cloth of pure gold and rides a virginal white horse, although 'she her selfe is whiter manifold'. She has a great desire to become the wife of MARINELL and, ignorant of his predicament, pursues, and eventually wins him.

Florizel
The Winter's Tale, 1611
William Shakespeare

The son of POLIXENES and therefore Prince of Bohemia, he falls in love with PERDITA, whom he (and she) believe to be the daughter of a shepherd, but who is really the abandoned daughter of LEONTES. Florizel declares that the difference in their social status is no obstacle to their future together. Polixenes overhears and denounces him. Florizel, later reunited with Perdita and, through Camillo and Leontes, with his father, represents a natural vigour, innocence and idealism which his elders have lost. In Florizel, Shakespeare suggests, lies a new beginning.

Florizel, Prince of Bohemia
The Suicide Club, 1878
Robert Louis Stevenson

The hero of a series of interconnecting short stories. He is a young, charismatic prince of generous disposition and even temper, whose decadent, dilettante existence bores him and leads him to seek diversion in the deadly games of the Suicide Club. His secret life, masked behind a respectable façade, marks him out as a typical Stevenson character. Although his innate moral courage finally triumphs, he remains tainted by the cynicism of the Suicide Club.

Flosky, Mr Ferdinando
Nightmare Abbey, 1818
Thomas Love Peacock

'A very lachrymose and morbid gentleman' with a 'very fine sense of the grim and the tearful', Mr Flosky (a caricature of Coleridge) is a transcendentalist philosopher, a visionary and a poet. Arrogant and pompous, Mr Flosky continually twists conversation and comment into irony, paradox and philosophical conundrum. For him, nothing is simple; everything is complicated, mysterious and unfathomable: 'I never gave a plain answer to a question in my life.'

Flowers and Stone
The Music of Chance, 1990
Paul Auster

Two seemingly eccentric millionaires. JACK POZZI likens them to Laurel and Hardy: 'One's fat and the other's thin, just like Stan and Ollie. They're genuine peabrains, my friend, a pair of born chumps.' They have won a fortune on the lottery, and just keep on winning, as if 'God has singled us out from other men'. Behind that façade, however, they prove to be sinister figures who assume a malign but omniscient power over the lives of Pozzi and JAMES NASHE.

Flowers, Aunt Margaret
The Magic Toyshop, 1967
Angela Carter

Married to UNCLE PHILIP FLOWERS, Aunt Margaret is totally oppressed by his presence, so much so that from the day of her marriage she has been struck dumb. Her only 'verbal' means of communication is through her flute playing. She is pale, thin and moves in a bird-like fashion with either despair or a hungry smile upon her face. Dowdy and always in black, with a crippling silver necklace around her neck, she has uncontrollable long, red hair, which scatters pins wherever she goes. Desperate for children, she is affectionate and kind.

Flowers, Uncle Philip
The Magic Toyshop, 1967
Angela Carter

The cruel and tyrannical toy maker who owns the Magic Toyshop, he is a man of vast size, with a brooding sexual and oppressive air, and eyes that are colourless 'like a rainy day'. An ugly man, he has an irrational, violent and judgemental temper. His only joy is his puppets.

Fluellen; Gower; Jamy; Macmorris
Henry V, 1599
William Shakespeare

A nationalistic Welshman, while at the same time loyal to King Henry (HENRY, PRINCE OF WALES), Fluellen is a proud, quick-tempered soldier. He quarrels with Macmorris, believing that his Irish counterpart has little idea of the correct 'disciplines of war'. It usually falls to Gower, an English captain, to restrain Fluellen's more temperamental outbursts. A modest man, Gower has few illusions about himself or anyone else. Jamy, a Scots captain, represents the fourth member of a quartet revealing national similarities and differences, to which greater or lesser emphasis is given, depending on the production.

Flurry Knox (Florence McCarthy Knox)
Some Experiences of an Irish R.M., 1899
Further Experiences of an Irish R.M., 1908
In Mr Knox's Country, 1915
E O Somerville and Martin Ross

Flurry Knox looks like 'a gentleman among stable-boys and a stable-boy among gentlemen', which gives him considerable scope for his activities as horse-dealer, landlord and dedicated sportsman. He can see several sides to every question and expound them all in his engaging brogue and with convincing ingenuity. His conscience is slippery as an eel but under each dubious assertion there is a glimmer of mad consistency which for the moment silences argument. He is a charmer, a chancer and when things go wrong he concludes that 'it's nothing to signify'.

Flush
Flush, 1933
Virginia Woolf

Elizabeth Barrett Browning's spaniel, he knows that in her invalid company he must be quiet, but at other times he is lively, cunning and playful. He easily becomes jealous, and his life changes when he goes to Italy to live with his mistress and her new husband, the poet Robert Browning. Eventually he adapts to the fact that he is no longer the apple of his owner's eye, and he gradually becomes attached to her son 'Pen'. He is captured by dog thieves, a terrifying experience for a creature who is not brave, but Elizabeth pays the blackmail demand, and he lives a long and happy life of 13 years.

Flutter, Sir Fopling
The Man of Mode, 1676
Sir George Etherege

'Sir Fopling is a Fool so nicely writ,/The ladies wou'd mistake him for a Wit', cautions the epilogue to the play. The 'prince of fops', posturing, ostentatious, and with a love of the foibles of fashion, Sir Fopling Flutter is the eponymous man of mode, a showy acting role and butt to the comedy. Sir Fopling stands for folly; it is DORIMANT who represents wit, yet cannot help feeling jealous when Sir Fopling's advances upon MRS LOVEIT appear to be successful. But Sir Fopling is less a fool than a grotesque parody of Dorimant, and in the audience's eyes his character emphasizes Dorimant's shortcomings.

Flyte, Cordelia
Brideshead Revisited, 1945
Evelyn Waugh

The youngest child of LORD MARCHMAIN and LADY TERESA MARCHMAIN, Cordelia is 'bird-happy'; self-confident and loquacious, she is a fervent Catholic. She loyally loves her errant brother SEBASTIAN FLYTE more than anyone, visiting him in Tunisia when she is working for an ambulance unit in Spain. Although Cordelia grows up plain, her smile reveals 'all the family charm'. She is blessed with the frank insight of somebody poised between the world and the

monastic order, and continues her good work with her sister JULIA FLYTE in Palestine.

Flyte, Julia
Brideshead Revisited, 1945
Evelyn Waugh

'The most popular debutante' of her season, the enigmatic, leggy Julia Flyte has a face 'of flawless Florentine quattrocentro beauty'. Her greatest desire is to find a husband like the invented 'Eustace', a tragically widowed English diplomat, but she marries instead the materialistic, notorious MP divorcee, REX MOTTRAM. This union soon becomes loveless, however, and their child is still-born. Falling in love with CHARLES RYDER, who is bewitched by her 'haunting, magical sadness', she divorces Rex with the intention of marrying Charles, but his agnosticism clashes with her guilty, resurgent Catholicism and they part. She inherits Brideshead and ends up in Palestine, working for the Women's Service.

Flyte, Sebastian
Brideshead Revisited, 1945
Evelyn Waugh

The second son of LORD MARCHMAIN and brother of JULIA and CORDELIA FLYTE, Sebastian is a happy half-Catholic, 'in love with his own childhood'. An eccentric old Etonian possessing 'epicene beauty' and the family charm he so despises, his need to escape from reality is symbolized by his ubiquitous teddy bear Aloysius. As an Oxford undergraduate, his worsening introspective dipsomania gains media attention when he is arrested and imprisoned for drunken driving. Sent down from university, he is made to travel abroad but dishonestly evades his minders and tends a wounded German soldier in Tangier. Pale, weak, thin and unkempt, he unsuccessfully applies to be a missionary lay-brother in a monastery in Tunisia.

Fogg, Marco Stanley
Moon Palace, 1989
Paul Auster

An orphan and social misfit, he is a searcher after experience who 'did not believe there would ever be a future. I wanted to live dangerously, to push myself as far as I could go, and then see what happened to me when I got there.' His many strange adventures are a form of education, and he accepts his losses philosophically, since they enable him to arrive, at the end of the novel, at a beginning. 'This is where I start, I said to myself, this is where my life begins.'

Foible
The Way of the World, 1700
William Congreve

Married to WAITWELL, Foible is LADY WISHFORT's personal maid and also one of MIRABELL's accomplices in his various amorous intrigues. She has risen from poverty to the enviable position of a trusted confidante, partly by virtue of her sharp wits, her deftness in spotting the vanities and weaknesses of others and her ability to assume one mask one minute and another the next. From another point of view, of course, she is both infuriatingly meddlesome and unscrupulous.

Foker, Harry
The History of Pendennis, 1848–50
W M Thackeray
The heir to a substantial brewing fortune, he presents BLANCHE AMORY with the sort of economic future that ARTHUR PENDENNIS cannot possibly promise, together with a bland, passionless pragmatism that she utterly deserves. A basically decent man from the new aristocracy of trade, his virtues are essentially dull and practical.

Fola
Season of Adventure, 1960
George Lamming
The daughter of a West Indian policeman who embodies all the old values of colonialism, she is drawn to the ancestral magic of the old religion and a conception of herself uncompromised by white ways.

Foley, Rebecca
Pravda: A Fleet Street Comedy, 1985
Howard Brenton and David Hare
Rebecca is the daughter of Sir Stamford Foley, the owner of *The Leicester Bystander*, a newspaper on which ANDREW MAY works as a reporter. Her relationship with May develops as he climbs higher up the editorial ladder provided for him by LAMBERT LE ROUX, and she soon becomes his wife. She is stronger, subtler and more perceptive than her husband, making him promise not to tell the same lie more than three times a day. Although she represents the play's central force for moral good, even she cannot withstand the blazingly ruthless conviction of Le Roux.

Foley, Sylvia
The Impersonators, 1980
Jessica Anderson
Moon-faced and frizzy-haired, she bears a resemblance to 'the women painted by Hieronymous Bosch'. She returns to her native Australia after 20 years abroad, in a vague search for roots, stability and belonging of some kind. Thrown into the midst of a family crisis, she is torn by powerful and conflicting feelings about family, love and money. Unassuming and often distant, Sylvia's presence nonetheless makes a great impact on those around her.

Follet, Rufus
A Death in the Family, 1957
James Agee
A lonely but perceptive six-year-old, he is an innocent observer of his family. His father's death in a car accident, after an idyllic scene in which father and son share the laughter of a Chaplin film, becomes the basis of a symbolic exploration of the foundations of religion. Rufus, typically, manages to communicate directly with his father's ghost, and is vouchsafed a mystical vision by his cynically rational relative UNCLE ANDREW LYNCH.

Folliott, Rev Dr
Crotchet Castle, 1831
Thomas Love Peacock
A vigorous and convivial divine with 'a tolerable

stock of learning', the Reverend Doctor breathes commonsense and sometimes earthy perspective into the 'march of mind', the relentless intellectualizing and theorizing, that goes on around him. Not above a few risqué jokes, this bon viveur's great pleasures are good food, good wine and amiable conversation.

Fontanelle → Bodice

Fool, the
King Lear, c.1607
William Shakespeare
The constant loyal companion of KING LEAR during the first three acts, the Fool continually points out to his master the folly of his ways in allowing the fortunes of his old age to be dependent on his two elder daughters, GONERIL and REGAN.

Foppington, Lord, previously **Sir Novelty Fashion**
The Relapse, or Virtue in Danger, 1696
Sir John Vanbrugh
The former Sir Novelty Fashion, recently elevated to the peerage to become Lord Foppington, is probably the most famous dandy in drama. He is heartless, miserly, narcissistic and wildly extrovert in manner and dress, and, with his younger brother YOUNG FASHION, epitomizes the dashing, decadent society of St James's. Having inherited the greater proportion of their father's money, Foppington devotes himself to eluding his brother and planning his wedding to MISS HOYDEN, thereby increasing his fortune. One of the great comic roles, he is noted especially for his extravagance and his exclamation: 'Stap my vitals!'

Forbes, Cato
Henry and Cato, 1976
Iris Murdoch
Having outraged and alienated his atheist father by becoming not only a Roman Catholic but a priest, Cato, totally 'invaded by Christ', works at a near-derelict London mission. There he meets a beautiful delinquent youth, 'Handsome Joe', whom he hopes to save from criminality. Suffering an agonizing crisis of faith, and obsessively loving Joe, he gives up the priesthood, hoping they can make a new life together. But Joe cares only for Cato the priest, and resentfully inflicts a terrible physical and mental ordeal on him that ends tragically for both.

Forbutt, Kevin
The Boys Who Stole the Funeral, 1980
Les Murray
Together with his friend, CAMERON REEBY, Kevin Forbutt steals the body of his great uncle, CLARRIE DUNN, from a city funeral parlour, and takes it for burial back to the remote New South Wales community where Dunn was born. The corpse is buried, but the thieves are tracked down and Forbutt and Reeby escape into the bush. Angered by his father's infidelity to his mother and disillusioned by life in Sydney, Forbutt is looking for a new beginning. He discovers it after Reeby is killed. Having fallen

into a coma, he is visited by spirits from Aboriginal legend. On his recovery, he decides to devote himself to a simple, tough, rural life on a part of the farm that was once to have been Dunn's.

Ford, Frank
The Merry Wives of Windsor, c.1597
William Shakespeare

A rich man and one of Windsor's more influential citizens, Frank Ford is warned by PISTOL that SIR JOHN FALSTAFF is in love with his wife, MISTRESS ALICE FORD. Frank is immediately jealous and decides to avenge himself on Falstaff and expose his wife's infidelity. Disguising himself as 'Brook', he pays Falstaff to 'lay an amiable siege' to Alice Ford on his behalf. Ford is Shakespeare's most comically savage depiction of the depth to which irrational jealousy corrodes both reason and dignity. In the end, his jealousy is jolted out of him, but his dignity is so crushed in the process that he demands Falstaff returns his money.

Ford, Mistress Alice
The Merry Wives of Windsor, c.1597
William Shakespeare

Together with MISTRESS MARGARET PAGE, Alice Ford is one of the 'merry wives' and has, like her, received a love-letter from SIR JOHN FALSTAFF. Although she is faithful to FRANK FORD, her husband, he suspects otherwise, and the two wives plan to teach both men a lesson. They lure Falstaff into a succession of traps under the guise of assignations, two of which Ford disrupts, suspecting the worst and discovering nothing. The delighted Alice cannot decide which pleases her the most, deceiving Falstaff or fooling her husband. She succeeds in humiliating the former and curing the latter of his jealousy, and so claiming a new authority.

Foresight
Love for Love, 1695
William Congreve

The uncle of ANGELICA, Foresight is 'an illiterate old fellow, peevish and positive, superstitious'. A measure of his bumbling self-deception is his ludicrous portrayal of himself as something of a mystic, professing to understand astrology and palmistry, physiology and dreams.

Foresight, Miss Prue
Love for Love, 1695
William Congreve

The daughter of FORESIGHT by his first wife, Prue is 'a silly, awkward, country girl', and the intended bride of BEN LEGEND. However, she neither wishes to marry him, nor does he want to marry her. Yet she is not quite so innocent as she at first seems; the women in this play are often more devious, but more effective, than the men. Ben and Prue Foresight's adventures form the sub-plot to the main theme of VALENTINE LEGEND and ANGELICA.

Forest Father
A Dance of the Forests, 1960
Wole Soyinka

The creator of humankind, he acts as a kind of recording angel, questioning the three travellers

from the present about their lives, motives and actions. He exposes a world in which good and evil are evenly balanced and in which the dead claim no moral superiority over the living.

Forester, Mr Sylvan
Melincourt, or Sir Oran Haut-ton, 1817
Thomas Love Peacock

A believer in the virtues of 'savage man' and the corruptness of 'civilized life', Mr Forester is the guardian of SIR ORAN HAUT-TON, an ape whom he claims is the 'natural and original man'. Forester's obsessive but sincere attempts to prove the validity of his philosophical theories lead him to buy Sir Oran a baronetcy and a seat in Parliament and to introduce him, with some success, to society. Campaigner against the slave trade, he is worthy and virtuous, an unexciting hero but a perfect match for the paragon of perfection, ANTHELIA MELINCOURT.

Forrestal, Susan
The Waiting Room, 1967
Wilson Harris

When Susan and her husband die in an explosion, Wilson Harris finds a mysterious diary or log-book of their lives which appears to be a strange kind of fiction writing, documenting her obsession with a nameless and insubstantial lover who haunts her as if real. 'Susan suffered from an incurable complaint of the eyes and after three operations became almost totally blind at the age of forty.' Inevitably in Harris's fiction, blindness is a new form of vision.

Forrester, Marian
A Lost Lady, 1923
Willa Cather

The wife of a great railway pioneer, much older than herself, she is seen at first only through the eyes of a young boy, NIEL HERBERT, who adores her. Only slowly does it become clear that her confidently unconventional dishabille and the 'gay challenge' of her eyes represent the surfacing of a sluttish side, addicted to drink and working men, that is only kept in check as long as the Captain is alive.

Forrestier, Ray
The House in Paris, 1935
Elizabeth Bowen

He looks like 'any of these tall Englishmen who stand back in train corridors unobtrusively to let foreigners pass to meals or the lavatory'. He is 'the Englishman's age: thirty-six' and has 'exchanged the ambitions he once projected for business, which makes for a more private private life'.

Forsaken Merman, the
'The Forsaken Merman', in *The Strayed Reveller and Other Poems*, 1849
Matthew Arnold

A lovelorn amphibian, defined almost wholly by a sense of profound loss. Margaret, the mother of his children, who once sat beside him on the coral throne, has been lured away by church and 'humming town', leaving 'lonely for ever/The kings of the sea'.

Forsyte, 'Aunt Ann'
The Forsyte Saga, 1922
On Forsyte Change, 1931
John Galsworthy

The unmarried eldest daughter of Jolyon Forsyte, a builder, and the sister of JAMES, JOLYON ('OLD JOLYON'), SWITHIN and TIMOTHY FORSYTE. In 1886, at the opening of the saga, Aunt Ann is aged 87 and will die within the year. Upright, dignified, indulgent and severe, she personifies 'the rigid possessiveness of the family idea', that of unwavering loyalty to both the Forsyte clan and the idea of property as an instrument of social power and security. Ann's property (and she knows no other) is the family, 'their little secrets, illnesses, engagements, and marriages, how they were getting on, and whether they were making money'.

Forsyte, Fleur
The Forsyte Saga, 1922
A Modern Comedy, 1929
John Galsworthy

The daughter of SOAMES FORSYTE and ANNETTE LAMOTTE, Fleur meets and falls in love with her cousin JOLYON ('JON') FORSYTE in June Forsyte's art gallery. Both Soames and IRENE FORSYTE, his former wife and Jon's mother, are appalled at the affair. When Jon gives her up, the despondent Fleur marries MICHAEL MONT. Although she elicits sympathy, Fleur is too much a Forsyte not to crave social advancement and an emotional hold over others, and she uses her husband's political career to become a society hostess. During the General Strike, she works in a canteen, tries to entice Jon to return to her, and fails.

Forsyte, Holly
The Forsyte Saga, 1922
A Modern Comedy, 1929
On Forsyte Change, 1931
John Galsworthy

The granddaughter of JOLYON ('OLD JOLYON') FORSYTE and daughter of JOLYON ('YOUNG JOLYON') FORSYTE's second marriage, Holly, born in 1881, is the sister of JOLYON ('JOLLY') FORSYTE. A pretty woman, whose wistfulness is offset by her share of the Forsyte candour, she idealizes her brother and marries his dashing university friend, VAL DARTIE.

Forsyte, Irene
The Forsyte Saga, 1922
A Modern Comedy, 1929
On Forsyte Change, 1931
John Galsworthy

A complex and contradictory woman, Irene is at once a symbol of the beauty that destroys, and a woman bravely attempting to conceal the extent of her marital unhappiness. Her husband, SOAMES FORSYTE, battles to keep her, while she struggles to free herself of him. 'You may hunt me to the grave', she cries. 'I will not come.' When Soames plans a magnificent house to please her, Irene falls for PHILIP BOSINNEY, the architect, who dies in tragic circumstances. She finally divorces Soames when she takes up with JOLYON ('YOUNG JOLYON') FORSYTE, Soames's cousin, and becomes his wife. They have two sons, JOLYON ('JOLLY') and JOLYON ('JON') FORSYTE, and a daughter, HOLLY FORSYTE. Fussy, pragmatic, harsh, even cruel, Irene (like all true Forsytes) is also cold, possessive and determined.

Forsyte, James
The Forsyte Saga, 1922
On Forsyte Change, 1931
John Galsworthy

The brother of JOLYON ('OLD JOLYON'), SWITHIN, 'AUNT ANN' and TIMOTHY FORSYTE, James is the father of SOAMES FORSYTE and WINIFRED DARTIE. Tall and lean, he is the founder of the Park Lane legal firm of Forsyte, Bustard and Forsyte. James thinks purely in terms of money: 'money was now his light, his medium for seeing'. A liberal, he has brought up his children liberally. He sees the funeral procession of Queen Victoria and hears 'the groaning in his own heart at the sight of his Age passing'. Like all the Forsytes, he fears death.

Forsyte, Jolyon ('Jolly')
The Forsyte Saga, 1922
A Modern Comedy, 1929
On Forsyte Change, 1931
John Galsworthy

The grandson of JOLYON ('OLD JOLYON'), son of JOLYON ('YOUNG JOLYON') and brother of HOLLY FORSYTE, 'Jolly', like his father, has the competitive self-confidence of all the Forsytes. Well-built, upright and with a keen moral sense, he also has a natural lordliness which does not quite accord with changing times at the end of the Victorian era. He dies a soldier in the Boer War.

Forsyte, Jolyon ('Jon')
The Forsyte Saga, 1922
A Modern Comedy, 1929
John Galsworthy

The son of IRENE and JOLYON ('YOUNG JOLYON') FORSYTE, he is the much younger half-brother of HOLLY and JOLYON ('JOLLY') FORSYTE. Having been away from England for many years, he falls in love with FLEUR FORSYTE before realizing the closeness of their family relationship, and then giving her up and marrying Anne. Jon is moralistic, tall, upright, modern but by no means a modernist. He believes, for example, that public schools represent a symbol of stability and unchanging character in a confused and rapidly changing world.

Forsyte, Jolyon ('Old Jolyon')
The Forsyte Saga, 1922
On Forsyte Change, 1930
John Galsworthy

The brother of JAMES, SWITHIN, 'AUNT ANN' and TIMOTHY FORSYTE, and uncle to SOAMES FORSYTE, 'Old Jolyon' is a former tea merchant and the chairman of several companies. The head of the Forsytes, 'an upper middle-class family in full plumage', and aged over 80 when the saga opens in 1886, 'old Jolyon' is upright, alert and sentimental, and gives an impression of moral superiority. 'Having had his own way for innumerable years, he had earned a prescriptive right to it.' Shrewd and prudent, he is endowed with the virtues of an ideal father. This is hardly surprising as he is based upon Galsworthy's own father, a man whom he greatly respected.

Forsyte, Jolyon ('Young Jolyon')
The Forsyte Saga, 1922
A Modern Comedy, 1929
On Forsyte Change, 1931
John Galsworthy

The son of JOLYON ('OLD JOLYON') FORSYTE, he at first becomes a Lloyds underwriter, and then a painter. Of all the Forsytes, it is he who most dispassionately sees the family as symbols of their class and of rich, self-satisfied England. 'There are hundreds among the members of this club', he observes, notifying PHILIP BOSINNEY that they are identified by 'their sense of property'. They are 'half England', he adds, 'the three per cent half, the half that counts. It's their wealth and security that makes everything possible.' Independent, warm-hearted and comparatively modest, he marries IRENE FORSYTE, the former wife of his cousin SOAMES FORSYTE, and by whom he has two sons, JOLYON ('JOLLY') and JOLYON ('JON') FORSYTE, and a daughter, HOLLY FORSYTE.

Forsyte, Soames
The Forsyte Saga, 1922
A Modern Comedy, 1929
John Galsworthy

A solicitor and a connoisseur, Soames, the 'man of property', is the epitome of upper middle-class Edwardian England: proud, powerful, sentimental, emotionally ill-equipped and unforgiving when crossed. The son of JAMES FORSYTE and nephew of JOLYON ('OLD JOLYON') FORSYTE, he clings so tenaciously to the Forsyte creed of private ownership that he thinks of his unhappy wife, IRENE FORSYTE, upon whom he forced his love, as his possession. After their divorce, he marries his second wife, ANNETTE LAMOTTE, partly in the hope that she will bear him a son. Originally cast as the villain, Soames becomes something of a hero by the end of the six novels. He earns our sympathy not only because he is unlovable, but also because he realizes it and, tragically, can do little about it.

Forsyte, Swithin
The Forsyte Saga, 1922
On Forsyte Change, 1931
John Galsworthy

A former estate and land agent, and the brother of JAMES, JOLYON ('OLD JOLYON'), 'AUNT ANN' and TIMOTHY FORSYTE, Swithin has 'an impatience of simplicity'. His taste is reflected in his drawing room, facing Hyde Park, where the light from the candles in a cut-glass chandelier glint on gilt, marble and ormolu. He is a man of ostentatious wealth and comfort, a voluptuary, because for him and his kind, 'very little took place from morning till night'. Swithin frowns upon the land business even while he practises it, for he considers it vulgar. Essentially, he would like to be one of the aristocracy, and he consciously emulates their manners. To see his own family fall below the standard he has set for them socially rouses in him an almost inarticulate fury.

Forsyte, Timothy
The Forsyte Saga, 1922
A Modern Comedy, 1929
On Forsyte Change, 1931
John Galsworthy

The brother of 'AUNT ANN', JOLYON ('OLD JOLYON'), JAMES and SWITHIN FORSYTE, Timothy is a former publisher. Like the rest of the Victorian Forsytes, he is rich. In fact, he is 'a kind of incarnation of security haunting the background of the Forsyte universe', especially as he had never committed the imprudence of marrying, or encumbered himself in any way with children.

Fortinbras
Hamlet, 1601/2
William Shakespeare

This young nephew of the Norwegian king is a man of action, prepared to fight for his rights even for a plot of land too small to bury the dead after the battle. He recognizes those qualities in the dead HAMLET which would have made him a fitting king, but is nonetheless calmly able to take the Danish throne for himself.

Fortnum, Charley
The Honorary Consul, 1973
Graham Greene

The British Consul in a small Argentinian town. He is an alcoholic in his sixties, but is an amiable, generous man with an extraordinary capacity for selfless love. He marries a young Indian prostitute, and later forgives her affair with his friend DR EDOUARDO PLARR. He is kidnapped by a revolutionary group in a case of mistaken identity, but survives the ordeal.

Fortune, Timothy
Mr Fortune's Maggot, 1927
Sylvia Townsend Warner

'Tall, raw-boned and rather rummaged-looking', Timothy Fortune is a former bank clerk who has used his godmother's legacy to train as a deacon. A good man who is both humble and well-meaning, he spends ten years as a missionary in the South Seas before embarking for the remote island of Fanua where he naively hopes to gather souls as a 'child gathers daisies in the fields'. Easy-going and conscientious, he merely succeeds in misconstruing the love of a native boy, Lueli, as a genuine conversion to Christianity. The ultimate acknowledgement of this error rocks his faith and convinces him that 'the doom of love is always to be destroying the thing it looks upon'.

Foscari, Francis, Doge of Venice
The Two Foscari: An Historical Drama, 1821
Byron, George Gordon, 6th Lord Byron

The Doge of Venice, Francis Foscari, is anguished by the disgrace of his son JACOPO FOSCARI, twice banished from Venice for bribery and murder and now brought back from exile accused of plotting against the state. An old man, white-haired and distraught, he must face Jacopo's wife who begs for mercy, Venetians wronged by the Foscari who demand justice, his own feelings for his son as he is tortured upon the rack, and his duty as Doge. He signs the warrant for Jacopo's exile and bids him farewell but Jacopo, dreading another exile, dies. The Council of Ten decree that the Doge must abdicate. He leaves his palace for the last time and, hearing St Mark's bell ring for the election of his successor, dies.

Foscari, Jacopo
The Two Foscari: An Historical Drama, 1821
Byron, George Gordon, 6th Lord Byron

Twice banished from his beloved Venice for corruption and murder, Jacopo is brought back accused of plotting against the state. He is tortured upon the rack to make him confess but despite his agony refuses to do so. He is condemned to further exile from Venice and his wife's wish to go with him is denied. His father FRANCIS FOSCARI, DOGE OF VENICE, signs the warrant for his exile, but before the sentence of banishment can be carried out, Jacopo, remembering the blue sea around Venice, the city's beauty and the delight he feels in her, cannot face another exile. Already weak from his sufferings, he dies.

Fosco, Count Isidor Ottavio Baldassare
The Woman in White, 1860
Wilkie Collins

A man of 'monstrous corpulence' who bears a striking resemblance to Napoleon, Count Fosco is a highly-educated and cultured man whose villainy is all the more heinous because of the charm with which he cloaks his duplicity. Close to 60, with 'unfathomable grey eyes' and a sallow complexion, he is an experimental chemist with a fondness for opera, white mice and sweetmeats. Sly, resolute and fiendishly clever, he acts as a calming influence on the more aggressive impulses of his best friend and accomplice SIR PERCIVAL GLYDE. Married to LAURA FAIRLIE's aunt, he has only one apparent weakness, namely an admiration for MARIAN HALCOMBE.

Foster, Hilda
A Fairly Honourable Defeat, 1970
Iris Murdoch

The slightly overweight, 'angelic'-looking Hilda, one of the 'Socialist Old Guard', is a superb homemaker and formidable worker for worthy causes, believing efficiency to be an 'aspect of morals'. Intelligent, sensible and usually serene, she is seriously worried and upset about her dropout student son, and the chaotic, desperately unhappy life of her cherished younger sister, MORGAN BROWNE. At first disliking JULIUS KING as the cause of her sister's distress, Hilda is later charmed and duped by him, and together with her much-loved husband, RUPERT FOSTER, suffers the consequences of Julius's cruel actions.

Foster, Joan Delacourt
Lady Oracle, 1976
Margaret Atwood

Haunted by her obese childhood, she re-invents her past, becoming a different woman for each person with whom she comes in contact. She is an inept housewife, a closet writer of Gothic romances, the lover of an avant-garde artist, and a dazzlingly successful poetess. An 'escape artist' whose complicated life leads her to fake her own death, Joan is comic, clumsy and untidy. A romantic at heart, she longs to be rescued, even

as she runs further away from her husband, her life and her past.

Foster, Mr
Headlong Hall, 1816
Thomas Love Peacock

A thin, intense philosopher who analyses everything, draws import for humankind from all he sets eyes upon and delights in the achievements of science, Mr Foster is a 'perfectibilian'. The counterfoil to the gloomy MR ESCOT at the house party in Headlong Hall, Mr Foster holds that education and progress mean happiness and virtue for the human race.

Foster, Rupert
A Fairly Honourable Defeat, 1970
Iris Murdoch

Burly and boyish-looking, the blond and handsome Rupert is a civil servant and 'Sunday metaphysician' who is writing a book about 'real' virtue. He believes this is an instinctive thing connected with the heart and affections, the 'real' vice of the modern age being cynicism. Successful and popular, he is happily celebrating 20 years of model marriage to HILDA FOSTER, who thinks him 'incurably compassionate'. Altruistic but rather naive and self-satisfied, Rupert tends to see, hear and speak no evil. He misjudges his old friend, JULIUS KING, and falls victim to his all-too-real and vicious cynicism.

Foster, Simon
A Fairly Honourable Defeat, 1970
Iris Murdoch

Gay in every sense, Simon, the extravagant younger brother of RUPERT FOSTER, is loving, demonstrative and ingenuous, but insecure and very vulnerable. He is rather intimidated by, but adores, his austere older partner, AXEL NILSSON, and their relationship lends much-needed stability to his life. His happiness is undermined by Axel's old friend JULIUS KING, who forces him to witness a sardonically manipulated 'puppet show' involving the Foster family. Threatened by Julius and afraid to speak out, Simon feels responsible for the ensuing tragedy.

Fowler, Maudie
The Diaries of Jane Somers, 1984
Doris Lessing

An old lady who is filled with memories of how cruel the world can be and has become very bitter. A proud woman, she is afraid of losing control, of others deciding her destiny, and feels angry, confused and patronized. However, she gains much pleasure from JANE SOMERS's unexpected devotion.

Fowler, Thomas
The Quiet American, 1955
Graham Greene

A world-weary British foreign correspondent, Fowler is idly marking time in Saigon in 1952, as the war between the French and the Vietnamese rages around him. He is content simply to enjoy the pleasures of the opium pipe and his beautiful young mistress Phuong. He is forced into a more active involvement in the war, however, and to a degree of commitment, when the nature of his protective relationship with the American of the title (ALDEN PYLE) alters after he discovers that the latter is in love with Phuong and is not the innocent aid worker that he appeared to be.

Fox, Allie
The Mosquito Coast, 1981
Paul Theroux

An eccentric, cantankerous visionary, ingenious inventor and hatcher of madcap schemes, he sees himself as 'the last man' in a corrupt America of 'little men'. His idealistic, optimistic Yankee spirit drives him to take his family to the Mosquito Coast of Honduras, in search of the realization of his dream of an Edenic life, centring on his idea of creating an ice factory in the jungle. Their horrific experiences turn his vision into a nightmare, and he becomes increasingly unbalanced and tyrannical, leading to ultimate tragedy.

Fox, Giles
Wise Virgin, 1982
A N Wilson

A medieval scholar, his formal academic career has been as uncertain as his marital fortunes. Now, in the midst of his work on the hitherto undiscovered 13th-century 'Tretis of Loue Heuenliche', he has gone blind. He is snobbish, abrupt and intellectually as well as physically blinkered, but the surprising affection of his assistant LOUISE AGAR and the self-motivated actions of his daughter TIBBA FOX make a profound change in his life and ways.

Fox, Letty
Letty Fox: Her Luck, 1946
Christina Stead

A working-class girl in New York who becomes the lure and trap at the hub of her family's complex matrimonial web. With all the men out at work (and too weary otherwise for anything but food and sleep), she inhabits a conniving, calculating world that is wholly female.

Fox, Mischa
The Flight from the Enchanter, 1956
Iris Murdoch

A powerful and sinister press lord whose only striking physical feature is his eyes – one blue, one brown. No one knows his age, background or nationality and while people invariably respond to his extraordinary magnetism, they also fear him. He is sentimental about small creatures, claiming to love all living things, but when young killed animals out of 'pity'. His cold, cruel manipulation of the refugee NINA, and relentless pursuit of ROSA KEEPE demonstrate his inhuman patience in stalking his prey.

Fox, Tibba
Wise Virgin, 1982
A N Wilson

Named after a devout sixth-century Saxon princess, she is the daughter of the medieval scholar GILES FOX, turned into a domestic recluse by his blindness and sour absorption in the past. Adolescent to the core, she becomes the wise virgin of the title by tending the lamp of reality, taking her father's place in the real world.

Foxe, Brian
Eyeless in Gaza, 1936
Aldous Huxley

ANTHONY BEAVIS's best friend as a boy, Brian Foxe grows up into a very sensitive young man. He is particularly anxious to always do right in all circumstances, and whatever the personal cost. His moral sense, however, makes him too uneasy about his sexual desires, which affects his relationship with his fiancée, Joan. When Anthony seduces her, having been dared to do so by MARY AMBERLEY, it sets off a train of events which leads to Brian's tragic suicide.

Foxe, Mrs
Eyeless in Gaza, 1936
Aldous Huxley

A strong-minded character, Mrs Foxe is very possessive with her son BRIAN FOXE. Playing on his unselfish nature, she pressures him to renounce money he needs to secure a promising future with his fiancée, Joan. Mrs Foxe strikes everyone as a high-minded Christian but reveals herself to be ruthlessly manipulative.

Foy, Johnny
'The Idiot Boy', in *Lyrical Ballads*, 1798
William Wordsworth

The idiot child of the title, he is sent on the family pony to fetch a doctor for a sick neighbour. His delight in his aimless and fruitless moonlit ride causes acute distress to his doting mother, Betty Foy.

Fradubio
The Faerie Queene, 1590–6
Sir Edmund Spenser

Fradubio (Brother Doubt) was once a man but is now a tree. The true love of FRAELISSA, he stands groaning under the force of the harsh North Wind, and is tortured by the scorching rays of the sun. This is his punishment for being taken in by another woman's comely looks and doubting the nature of his own true and virtuous love.

Fraelissa
The Faerie Queene, 1590–6
Sir Edmund Spenser

Fraelissa's name means frailty. She is the spurned lover of FRADUBIO and has been transformed with him into a tree. Their love is truly spiritual and exists beyond the boundaries of base bodily desires, although Fradubio is tempted by another. Their relationship is representative of doubting individuals who abandon the Protestant Church and Queen Elizabeth I for the Catholic Mary, Queen of Scots.

Frail, Mrs
Love for Love, 1695
William Congreve

A sister of Mrs Foresight, Mrs Frail is a rather pathetic figure, an ageing woman, eager, almost desperate, for remarriage but no longer in the flower of youth. She sees marriage not so much as a union but as a kind of social corrective. According to her, manners are preferable to passion in a man, and the wedded state, she contends, is especially conducive to good manners: 'there is no creature perfectly civil but a husband. For in a little time he grows only rude to his wife, and that is the highest good breeding.'

France, King of
All's Well That Ends Well, 1602–3
William Shakespeare

The King of France is an old friend of the COUNTESS OF ROUSILLON's late husband, who makes their son, BERTRAM, his ward. Apparently fatally ill, he is cured by HELENA, the daughter of a physician, and as a reward he orders that she shall marry the man of her choice. The king is a benevolent despot, a man who remembers the old courtesies and ideals, and who speaks of them sometimes with irony and asperity. Over the court and the young people, he represents a fatherly, judicial presence, one of old-fashioned stability.

France, King of
King Lear, c.1607
William Shakespeare

A suitor to CORDELIA, KING LEAR's youngest daughter, and rival to the Duke of Burgundy for her hand, the King of France demonstrates his wisdom and his ability to distinguish and value a person at their true worth when he marries Cordelia despite her poor and cast-off state.

France, Princess of
Love's Labour's Lost, not later than 1594
William Shakespeare

Over in the Kingdom of Navarre on a diplomatic trip, the princess finds herself being wooed by KING FERDINAND. This affords great amusement to herself and her attendant ladies, who make fun of their lovers. Queenly responsibility finally comes to her with a jolt, though, when her father's death is announced. She dislikes flattery from Lord BOYET, saying that her beauty 'though but mean / Needs not the painted flourish of your praise'.

Franceschina
The Dutch Courtezan, 1605
John Marston

A courtesan who plans murderous revenge on her lover, YOUNG FREEVILL, for abandoning her in order to marry BEATRICE SUBBOYS. However, her foreign accent often makes her threats sound humorous: 'Now ick sall revange. Hay, begar, me sall tartar de whole generation! Mine brain vork it.'

Francis
In the Ditch, 1972, and *Second-Class Citizen*, 1974, collected as *Adah's Story*, 1983
Buchi Emecheta

The husband of ADAH, he is an arrogant wastrel, sexually hypercharged but emotionally blank and utterly insensitive to his young wife's needs and feelings.

Francisco de Medicis
The White Devil, 1612
John Webster

The Duke of Florence and brother of ISABELLA. Despite his high moral standards, he determines on revenge when his sister is murdered on the orders of her husband, the DUKE OF BRACHIANO. He has Brachiano's mistress VITTORIA COROMBONA prosecuted, and such is his passion that he personally takes a part in the working out of his plot against Brachiano, disguised as Mulinassar the Moor.

Frank
Educating Rita, 1979
Willy Russell

Frank is a disillusioned, dishevelled Open University tutor in his early fifties. A former poet with a broken marriage, and prone to binges of heavy drinking, his life is revitalized by RITA WHITE, a brash working-class woman who enrols for an English course. Rita wants to know 'everything', but to Frank, her raw sensibilities seem more vivid and valuable than his own extensive literary knowledge. But almost imperceptibly, he discovers that it is not his teaching but his emotional strengths and weaknesses which give Rita the confidence to make her own decisions in life, and, sadly, to break free of him. As she matures, he is left behind, drifting.

Frankenstein, Victor
Frankenstein, or, The Modern Prometheus, 1818
Mary Shelley

An idealistic young student of natural philosophy who conceives the grandiose notion of creating life from the inanimate. He pursues his aim 'with an ardour that far exceeded moderation; but now that it had finished, the beauty of the dream vanished, and breathless horror and disgust filled my heart.' His moment of over-reaching pride ruins his life, sparking off a catalogue of catastrophes, and he dies in pursuit of the monster he has created.

Frankenstein's Creature
Frankenstein, or, The Modern Prometheus, 1818
Mary Shelley

A misshapen and ugly creation galvanized into life by a young scientist, and endowed with supernatural strength. The creature is excluded forever from human society, but has very human needs and emotions, and acquires a lofty education from books. His creator's refusal to create him a mate turns him into a callous, vengeful murderer, conscious of his own fall ('the fallen angel becomes a malignant devil'), but unwilling or unable to restrain his monstrous impulses.

Frankford, Anne
A Woman Killed with Kindness, 1603
Thomas Heywood

The eponymous woman killed with kindness, Anne is married to JOHN FRANKFORD, seduced by WENDOLL, and turned out of her home, condemned by her husband to live in luxury elsewhere. She appears at first 'A perfect wife … meek and patient', and indeed her response to Wendoll's initial advance is to be incredulous, indignant and only a touch flattered. Yet she is impulsive, instinctive and sensual enough to be swept into overwhelming, liberating, thrilling passions: 'My soul is wand'ring and hath lost her way'. She is also a woman of conscience and moral orthodoxy, and her regret over the affair is genuine.

Frankford, John
A Woman Killed with Kindness, 1603
Thomas Heywood

A country gentleman, contented, magnanimous, perhaps rather complacent and priggish, Frankford is aghast to discover his wife, ANNE FRANKFORD, in the arms of his friend, WENDOLL. As astonishing as his wife's faithlessness is Wendoll's betrayal of their friendship. But instead of plotting a bloodthirsty revenge, Frankford plans to 'kill her even with kindness', banishing Anne from home and packing her off to a luxurious manor house, while depriving her of access to her children. Arguably, this public humiliation reveals Frankford's underlying cruelty; on the other hand, this is a domestic tragedy, and such melodramatic reproach appears more suited to the genre and to a distraught but kindly man.

Franklin, Lady
The Hireling, 1957
L P Hartley

A grief-stricken young widow who has spent the past two years mourning the loss of her husband, she has cut herself off from life, both socially and emotionally. Trusting and naive, she decides to use her chauffeur LEADBITTER in an experiment calculated to end her suffering by unburdening herself to him of the facts of her bereavement and her emotional devastation. This experiment works (as does Leadbitter's attempted seduction), awakening her to the possibilities of life; she becomes engaged to Hughie, a poor and opportunistic painter who plans to keep a mistress on his wife's money after they are married.

Franklin, the
The Canterbury Tales, c.1387–1400
Geoffrey Chaucer

A well-to-do landowner who has been a Member of Parliament for his county, a sheriff and an accountant. He is a sociable man and a generous host but appears to be too fond of the pleasures of food and drink; his public spiritedness and generosity are mentioned almost as afterthoughts to the description of his table. A generally likeable character, he tells a tale of true relationships in marriage.

Franz
King, Queen, Knave, 1968
Vladimir Nabokov

A pale, morbid youth in Twenties Berlin, he has a repellant sense of physicality, and plans avunculicide. He is seduced into ridiculous passion by his aunt, but both are outmanoeuvred by circumstances and by his benefactor uncle, a skilful entrepreneur and emporium-owner. His descent into madness is marked by absurd tableaux as all three become 'automannequins' manipulated by greed.

Franz, Victor
The Price, 1968
Arthur Miller

A police sergeant, Victor encounters his long-estranged brother, the materially successful WALTER FRANZ after 16 years, when they meet to clear family furniture after their father's death. By sacrificing his own chance of higher education and a scientific career to look after his father, who was ruined during the Depression, he freed his brother to study himself. Victor has long been hurt that his selflessness and sense of duty to others have gone unrecognized, both by his brother and his superiors in the police force. A decent man, with a perplexed wife, unable to appreciate Walter's success, Victor is corroded by resentment and desperately seeks redress.

Franz, Walter
The Price, 1968
Arthur Miller

A successful New York surgeon, Walter encounters his long-estranged brother, VICTOR FRANZ, for the first time in 16 years when disposing of the family furniture after their father's death. Walter had previously taken advantage of Victor's altruism to build his career, convinced that financial security would not only guarantee his being spared the fate of his father, ruined during the Depression, but bring emotional happiness as well. However, he is now bewildered and disappointed; material success, in which he had placed so much, has failed to immunize him against disappointment and guilt.

Frean, Harriet
The Life and Death of Harriet Frean, 1922
May Sinclair

Harriet lacks the necessary strength of character to rebel against the stifling and sterile values of her orthodox Victorian parents. She has been brought up to 'behave beautifully' and the narrow and starved life she leads reflects this socialization. Self-repressed and superficial, Harriet is a shadowy figure who lives her subdued life with sighing resignation. Too genteel to throw herself unreservedly at her lover – her friend's fiancé – Harriet is destroyed through her own weakness of will.

Fred
Saved, 1965
Edward Bond

Fred is 21 and physically powerful, part of a south-London community including LEN and PAM. His world is defined by work, money and women, each valued in an acquisitive and guarded sense. His closest relationships, though, are with other men, like Len, who speak his language, a combination of gangsterish, short sentences and mickey-taking remarks, and understand his priorities: that everything, including cigarettes and women, has its price and can be kept, exchanged or replaced by something more valuable. For him, life is a matter of negotiation.

Freda
The Bottle Factory Outing, 1974
Beryl Bainbridge

One of the two female protagonists in the story. Freda, the room-mate of BRENDA, is a singularly impressive woman of great stature, weighing in at 16 stone and with a personality just as awesome. Self-deluded, she believes herself to possess an artistic and sensitive soul, yet to others she appears to be a dominant and brash bully. Uninhibited and passionate, she wriggles her breasts with her hands whilst asleep, and when awake is determined, always, to have the last word.

Frederic of Vicenza
The Castle of Otranto, 1764
Horace Walpole

Frederic, believing himself nearest in blood to Alonso, comes to Otranto with a huge sabre bearing verses declaring that only the true line can rule there. MANFRED, PRINCE OF OTRANTO, still intending to marry Frederic's daughter, offers him MATILDA, his own daughter, in marriage. Frederic agrees, but a skeleton in monk's attire orders him 'to forget Matilda'. After the final apparition, when THEODORE, so like Alonso and so clearly the true heir, is proclaimed prince, Frederic suggests he marry ISABELLA OF VICENZA.

Frederick, Duke
As You Like It, c.1600
William Shakespeare

He has usurped the domain of his brother DUKE SENIOR. He is a churlish man capable of wilful behaviour, as demonstrated by his treatment of ORLANDO and ROSALIND. His sudden conversion at the end of the play, when he disbands his army and restores his brother's lands, is unexplained.

Frederick, Mr
Animal Farm, 1945
George Orwell

Mr Frederick owns one of the neighbouring farms to Animal Farm and is a born opportunist. His farm is smaller and better kept than MR PILKINGTON's and he is normally a tougher, shrewder operator. Initially he is sceptical about the animals' chances of running their land successfully, but soon he is willing to make deals with them. Hated and feared by the animals, he is, like his fellow humans, a shallow, unprincipled creature.

Freeman, Charles
In a Land of Plenty, 1997
Tim Pears

Charles Freeman, a businessman determined to better the lot of his future family, invests all his money in property and building up the small family-run engineering firm. He is single-minded in his approach to life and over a period of 40 years finds it more and more difficult to relate to the fact that his wife, MARY FREEMAN, and later his children, have different views on him on what makes life worthwhile.

Freeman, Mary
In a Land of Plenty, 1997
Tim Pears

CHARLES FREEMAN's wife initially falls in love with him because of his enthusiasm in trying to improve himself and his family. However, she suffers from bouts of serious depression and struggles to integrate her own creative interests, such as poetry and literature, with those of her husband.

Freeman, Will
About a Boy, 1998
Nick Hornby

Thirty-six and single, Freeman has no job, instead living comfortably off the £40,000 he receives each year in royalties from a Christmas hit written by his father. Although pursuing sexual adventures, he avoids the responsibility of commitment, striving instead to live, as his name indicates, as a free man. Charming, attractive, 'cool' and conversant with the latest fashions in music and clothes, Freeman is a likeable rogue. He invents a two-year-old son to gain entry to a single-parent group as part of his quest for young, lone mothers whom he reasons must be in need of sexual fulfilment. His encounter with Marcus, the twelve-year-old son of depressed single mother Fiona, begins a bewildering journey of self-discovery and growing maturity.

Freemantle, Alison
In the Place of Fallen Leaves, 1993
Tim Pears

Alison Freemantle is a 13-year-old girl living in Devon in the stiflingly hot summer of 1984. She is young enough still to believe that 'piskies' come and steal her things. She is always in the background, listening in to what is going on around her. Although she often does not understand what is being said, it is through her that we hear the goings-on in her village, including her own family's darker secrets.

Freeport, Sir Andrew
The Spectator, 1711–12
Joseph Addison and Richard Steele

Sir Andrew provides the commentary on trade and commerce for the Spectator Club. Rich, eminent and experienced, his outlook is far-seeing; he deplores war as barbarous; trade is an exchange and benefit to mankind far beyond conquest. His talk is plain and unaffected, the more valuable because his ships are working for him at the four corners of the world.

French, Marion
The Secret Rapture, 1988
David Hare

The elder sister of ISOBEL GLASS, Marion French is in her late thirties. Brittle, brisk and ambitious, she is already a junior minister in a right-wing Conservative government and destined for higher office. She is well-briefed and ruthless, and it is her profession – mission, even – to provide answers which ensure she is always at least one step ahead. Her father's death, though, which reunites her with Isobel, throws her into a quandary: 'I find it hard to strike the right attitude', she confesses. By the end of the play, though, she has learned a little from her sister about the value of love.

French, Mary
The Big Money, 1936, part of the *U.S.A.* trilogy, 1938
John Dos Passos

Brought up in Trinidad and Colorado Springs in an atmosphere of both racial snobbery and affinity with humankind, Mary takes her lead from her doctor-father and dedicates her life to helping those less fortunate than herself. Working tirelessly on behalf of the underprivileged, stout-hearted Mary refuses to compromise her principles, even when her emotional life repeatedly falls prey to 'the cause'. Practical and down-to-earth, she refuses to let herself be ensnared by empty society life, and even in the face of personal unhappiness continues to display great strength and generosity of spirit.

Frere, Lt Maurice, later Captain
His Natural Life, serialized 1870–2; as *For the Term of His Natural Life*, 1874
Marcus Clarke
Nephew of Sir Richard Devine and a guard on the prison ship taking Devine's son RICHARD DEVINE (now known as 'Rufus Dawes') to the Australian colonies. He reserves a special fury and cruelty for his disgraced kinsman.

Friar, the, also known as Brother Hubert
The Canterbury Tales, c.1387–1400
Geoffrey Chaucer
Brother Hubert, vowed to a life of poverty, chastity and obedience, is 'A wanton and a merry' ladies' man. When there is a profit to be made he is all things to all men, and he will even woo a poor widow's last farthing from her. A holy beggar by virtue of his calling, he has no time for the real beggars he is vowed to help. He uses and abuses his position for gain and to satisfy his sexual appetite. His tale is a bawdy rejoinder to that told against friars by THE SUMMONER.

Friar Bacon
Friar Bacon and Friar Bungay, 1587–9
Robert Greene
The master of Brasenose College, Oxford, a friend of FRIAR BUNGAY and a scholar and pyromancer, he is based very loosely upon Roger Bacon, the 13th-century scientist. His magic is intended to be benign, yet it invariably brings about grief and destruction. His magic glass causes the deaths of two young men who are provoked to a duel, and brings Lacy within a hair's breadth of execution at the hands of the Prince of Wales. Bacon's brazen head, upon which he has worked for seven years, is also a failure, bringing about the damnation of his student, Miles. Climactically, Bacon renounces his magic as trafficking with the Devil and embraces conventional Christianity.

Friar Bungay
Friar Bacon and Friar Bungay, 1587–9
Robert Greene
The friend and rival of FRIAR BACON, he serves to demonstrate the greater power of his colleague. When about to marry Lacy and Margaret, against the wishes of the Prince of Wales, he is struck dumb by the magic of Bacon, and conveyed to Oxford on the back of a devil. He comes off second best in a magic duel with the German magician, Vandermast, and is saved from humiliation by Bacon. Ultimately, he is of comfort to Bacon, providing him with support

and wise counsel at the great pyromancer's abandonment of magic.

Friar Jerome
The Castle of Otranto, 1764
Horace Walpole
Friar Jerome serves St Nicholas's Church beside the Castle of Otranto where stands the tomb of the first Alonso of Otranto. He constantly rebukes MANFRED, PRINCE OF OTRANTO, and defends the hapless princesses, forbidding HIPPOLITA to agree to an impious divorce. He sees, by a birthmark, that THEODORE is his long-lost son; he himself is the Count of Falconara, whose sorrows have led him to the religious life. Interpreting the portents, he can explain the mystery and show that Theodore is the true Prince of Otranto.

Friar Lawrence
Romeo and Juliet, 1591–6
William Shakespeare
At first the friar is a source of comfort to ROMEO and JULIET, calming their adolescent emotions. He agrees to perform their marriage, believing it to be the way to bring the Capulet and Montague families together, thus ending the feud. But, because he does not think about the possible outcomes, he finds himself drawn deeper into matters he cannot control. He uses his knowledge of plants to concoct the potion that he hopes will solve the problem. When finally he realizes that he has no check on events he runs away, leaving the youngsters to their fate.

Frietchie, Barbara
'Barbara Frietchie', 1864
John Greenleaf Whittier
A 90-year-old citizen of Frederick, Maryland, whose loyalty to the United States of America during the Civil War prompts her to wave aloft the Stars and Stripes, which has been shot down by Confederate soldiers. ' "Shoot, if you must, this old gray head,/But spare your country's flag", she said.' General Stonewall Jackson is shamed by her bravery into ordering his troops to march past without preventing her display of the 'Flag of Freedom and Union'.

Frisby, Maggie
Teeth 'n' Smiles, 1975
David Hare
The play is set at the Cambridge May Ball of 1969, where a rock band is due to play. Maggie, young, rebellious and selfish, is the singer. Raucous and intermittently energetic, she is, overall, second-rate, and while she would never admit this, probably knows it in her heart. She has, therefore, created a defiant personality, sousing herself in whisky and drugs, convincing herself that she is frightened of 'the thin filth of getting old, the thin filth that gets to cover everything'. Having almost destroyed herself, Maggie is also destructive towards others. Manipulated by her manager, she is simply expendable. She illustrates the futility of ill-thought-out anarchy.

Frisco

The Roaring Nineties, 1946
Golden Miles, 1948
Winged Seeds, 1950
Katharine Susannah Prichard

An opportunist, charming, gallant and dashing, 'Frisco was reckoned a good sort, despite his brag and bluster'. Steadfast in his passionate love for SALLY GOUGH but responsible only to himself, he is an inveterate Don Juan who moves ably across class barriers, playing the game of life for all it is worth.

Fritha

The Snow Goose, 1941
Paul Gallico

A strangely beautiful girl, in the big-boned Saxon mould, with long fair hair and haunting deep-set violet eyes, she is shy, grubby and only twelve years old when she first conquers her fear of PHILIP RHAYADER and takes a wounded snow goose to be healed by him. Enraptured by his skills as a storyteller, she almost believes that the goose is a lost princess, grounded in the marshes by a hunter's bullet. She becomes a hesitant visitor to Rhayader's lighthouse, but only when the bird is there, and from him learns the lore of wild birds. An unspoken love grows between them, but she turns away in fear, only later understanding what she has lost.

Frodo → Baggins, Frodo

Frome, Ethan

Ethan Frome, 1911
Edith Wharton

His 'lameness checking each step like the jerk of a chain', Ethan buckles under the crushing weight of a lifetime of humiliating failure and disappointment. His physical burden and sense of powerlessness constrict and silence him, making him seem 'a part of the mute landscape'. Trapped in Starkfield, in an emotionally sterile marriage, his mortal isolation and tendency to dissolution are relieved by MATTIE SILVER. Longing for the blissful rapture of escape with her, Ethan is, however, paralysed by economic circumstances. Emasculated by his wife, ZEENA FROME, he is a spectator at Mattie's banishment, a paradigm of manhood humbled by passivity and shame.

Frome, Zeena

Ethan Frome, 1911
Edith Wharton

The withered and censorious wife of ETHAN FROME, Zeena stagnates in a marriage resulting from the dictates of duty not passion. Her power over Ethan manifests itself in a critical silence, hinting at 'suspicions and resentments impossible to guess'. She chooses to look down on Starkfield, but is disinclined to accept any change. Requiring full-time care and fearing the poorhouse, she banishes MATTIE SILVER with whom she compares very poorly. Her joy at Mattie's departure turns to profound sorrow when she finds her prized pickle-dish, the one treasure of her miserable life, broken.

Front-de-Boeuf, Sir Reginald

Ivanhoe, 1819
Sir Walter Scott

The Lord of Torquilstone, he is the ambitious Norman knight to whom IVANHOE's castle and lands are assigned on the younger man's banishment from the realm. According to his master PRINCE JOHN, 'Front-de-Boeuf is a man more willing to swallow three manors such as Ivanhoe than to disgorge one of them'. He is, though, defeated by Ivanhoe in combat and his unearned gains are forfeit.

Frost, Mark

Mosquitoes, 1927
William Faulkner

'A tall, ghostly young man with a thin evaporation of fair hair and a pale prehensile mouth ... a poet who produced an occasional cerebral and obscure poem in four or seven lines reminding one somehow of evacuation excruciatingly and incompletely performed.'

Frothingham, Alma

The Whirlpool, 1897
George Gissing

Gissing's names are clearly intended to be symbolic. Alma's 'soul' is left swirling uncertainly in the wake of FELIX DYMES's deliberately unsentimental proposal. Whereas she expects a marriage to draw a couple ever closer, it is obvious that he takes a very different view of it, seeing it as a much looser and more anarchic contract.

Frowenfeld, Joseph

The Grandissimes, 1880
George Washington Cable

A first-generation American, this young apothecary loses his parents and sisters through fever almost as soon as they arrive in Louisiana. Himself recovering from illness, he becomes the novel's moral centre, expressing northern liberal objections to the 'peculiar institution' of slavery, but with an essentially Puritan vision that reflects a deep sexual squeamishness when confronted with people of mixed race.

Fruit-Norton, Elliot

Pravda: A Fleet Street Comedy, 1985
Howard Brenton and David Hare

A 'tall, stooping man in his mid-fifties, supercilious, with raddled boyish looks', he is the editor of *The Daily Victory*, a newspaper not too far removed from *The Times*. According to its new proprietor, LAMBERT LE ROUX, it is 'the only newspaper with England on its masthead'. Fond of quoting Latin maxims, Fruit-Norton considers himself a member of the intellectual first division and understands journalism to be primarily a vocation for the highly literate, the reflective, the thoughtful. *The Daily Victory*, in other words, should be written by gentlemen for gentlemen.

Ftatateeta

Caesar and Cleopatra, 1898
George Bernard Shaw

Ftatateeta is CLEOPATRA's chief nurse and she, not Cleopatra, is the sexual centre of the play. Likened to both a tiger and a crocodile, her presence is so predatory and her hold over her charge so great, that her power appears invincible. Yet POTHINUS bribes her to allow him to see Cleopatra, and later suggests to CAIUS JULIUS CAESAR that Cleopatra plans to reign alone and to murder him if necessary. On Cleopatra's orders, Ftatateeta kills Pothinus, but RUFIO kills her in revenge. Caesar feels no horror at her death, therefore symbolically neutralizing her power.

Fuchsia, Lady of Groan
Titus Groan, 1946
Gormenghast, 1950
Mervyn Peake

A passionate, moody, unpredictable girl, with wild black hair and a fondness for red velvet dresses. Initially jealous of TITUS GROAN, she is soon joined to him by fierce bonds of loyalty and love. Devoted to her father, only after his death does she feel herself to be truly 'of the blood', and part of Gormenghast. She dominates the feeble Nannie Slagg, though in a kindly way, and she can confide in DR ALFRED PRUNESQUALLOR. But for the most part she is surrounded by lovelessness, and grasps eagerly at the first straw of love treacherously held out by STEERPIKE.

Fulkerson
A Hazard of New Fortunes, 1890
William Dean Howells

A loquacious, self-confident acquaintance of BASIL MARCH, he is delegated to offer him the editorship of DRYFOOS's new journal, *Every Other Week*. He has no other substantial role in the story, but stands as a representative of all that is new and thrusting about New York City.

Fund-Jonet
Ane Pleasant Satyre of the Thrie Estaitis, 1552
Sir David Lindsay

In making only a fleeting appearance as the third of DAME SENSUALITIE's 'assistants', the principal purpose of Fund-Jonet – literally 'foundling Janet' – seems to be as sexual instructor to DANGER and HAMELINES. Having no direct bearing on the dramatic action, Fund-Jonet remains an insubstantial figure, but one whose apparently ambivalent sexual identity has been the cause of some speculation.

Fungoso
Every Man out of his Humour, 1599
Ben Jonson

The son of SORDIDO, he is a student deluded into thinking that appearances express substance. He is so impressed by the fop FASTIDIOUS BRISK that he persuades his father to lend him money, purportedly for law books but in reality for a new and fashionable wardrobe, which he hopes will denote him as a gentleman. He has exhausted all his funds before realizing the error of his ways.

Fuselli, Dan
Three Soldiers, 1921
John Dos Passos

An Italian-American factory worker from San Francisco, ground down by the impersonality and brutality of the army system. Does his name contain an echo of the nightmarish visions of the painter Henry Fuseli? Given that he, JOHN ANDREWS and CHRISFIELD all suggest different artistic means of capturing experience, it is possible.

Fusilier, Agricola
The Grandissimes, 1880
George Washington Cable

A courtly but garrulous old Louisianan, who has killed AURORE NANCANOU's young husband in a duel, and thus owes her a long-standing debt of responsibility that nonetheless barely tempers his inherited hedonistic self-satisfaction. He is stalked and eventually killed by HONORÉ GRANDISSIME, FMC, a ritual punishment for his refusal to accommodate modern values and contradictions.

Fusima
Back to Methuselah, 1921
George Bernard Shaw

Fusima appears in the fourth section of this five-part play. *Tragedy of an Elderly Gentleman* takes place partly on the shores of Galway Bay, Ireland, in 3000AD. She is a long-lifer and a guardian of the locality, who warns THE ELDERLY GENTLEMAN against the moral disease of 'discouragement'. She leaves him in the charge of ZOZIM.

G

G., 1972
John Berger

The bastard son of a wealthy Italian (whose initial – for Giovanni – he adopts) and an American socialist mother. His cryptic name also refers to Garibaldi, hero of Italian independence, and helps locate him as not so much a character in the conventional sense as an anti-heroic presence who inhabits history and makes it, though not in circumstances of his own choosing.

G

In the Castle of my Skin, 1953
George Lamming

G is the central character and first-person narrator of this autobiographical novel set in a village community in Barbados. His adolescent strivings for identity represent, in part, the island's struggle for independence from British colonialism. Curious and carefree as a child, he develops within the close-knit community into a sensitive and intelligent youth, identifying his own path in the labyrinth of conflicting influences of African ancestry and colonial power.

Gabbett

His Natural Life, serialized 1870–2; as For theTerm of His Natural Life, 1874
Marcus Clarke

An infamous cannibal convict, a giant of a man with wild, staring eyes. He escapes with the others from the penal colony and is sole survivor of the nightmare trek through the wilderness, by simple dint of outlasting and staying awake longer than his starving companions.

Gabelle, Theophile

A Tale ofTwo Cities, 1859
Charles Dickens

The postmaster and tax-collector on the estate of the MARQUIS DE ST EVREMONDE (THE YOUNGER), and a loyal servant of the family. He appeals to CHARLES DARNAY to come to Paris to save him when he is imprisoned by the revolutionaries, but then secures his freedom by denouncing his benefactor.

Gabriel

Paradise Lost, 1667
John Milton

'Chief of the angelic guards' of Eden, he takes his place on a towering outcrop of alabaster near the Eastern gate, watching tirelessly while his younger lieutenants disport carelessly below, their weapons thrown momentarily aside.

Gabriel-Ernest

'Gabriel-Ernest', in Reginald in Russia, 1910
'Saki' (Hector Hugh Munro)

A tanned, lycanthropic boy of about 16, found by the land-owner Van Cheele in his woods. His eyes have 'an almost tigerish gleam' and his laugh combines a chuckle and a snarl. With alarming honesty he announces that he only occasionally eats children. Van Cheele's aunt names him and has him clothed, but he reverts to his savage form.

Gadshill

Henry IV Part I, 1596/7
William Shakespeare

A minor figure, one of the band of robbers who follow SIR JOHN FALSTAFF, he takes his name from Gad's Hill, a notorious place for hold-ups. He is the 'setter', ie the person whose task it is to identify potential robbery victims and arrange for them to be waylaid. Adept at bribery, especially of petty officials, he is no braver than any of the others when set upon by Prince Hal (HENRY, PRINCE OF WALES) and POINS.

Gage, Adela

A House is Built, 1928
M Barnard Eldershaw

An attractive young Englishwoman who becomes engaged to WILLIAM HYDE at the age of 16 and, after five years of long-distance love, travels to Australia to marry him. 'Unacquisitive but intensely emotional', she finds herself at odds with the emotionally distant Hyde family, who are preoccupied with their social status and position. She eventually accepts the lack of intimacy in her life, but never really reconciles herself to it. Finding that she is not deeply loved by her husband undermines her confidence, and Adela remains unsure of herself: she 'would always be a little cautious, a little diffident'. She finds her greatest happiness in her son LIONEL HYDE: 'Always she took colour from the people she lived with, above all from the people she loved.'

Galant

A Chain ofVoices, 1982, originally published in Afrikaans as Houd-den-bek, 1982
André Brink

Aged 26, he is chief hand on NICOLAAS VAN DER MERWE's farm. He has been raised to consider himself part of the family, virtually a brother to the two sons, but is suddenly divided from them in a conflict over an orphan girl. He is accused of murdering van der Merwe as revenge for having been denied his liberty and equality.

Galbraith, Milly
Intensive Care, 1970
Janet Frame

In the aftermath of a highly technologized future war, her innocent sympathy for living things – trees in particular – appears as a sign of mental weakness. In a world where only 'the human' is accorded any value, she is the last representative of a romantic associationism between people and the rest of creation.

Galleotti, Martius, or Marti or Martivalle
Quentin Durward, 1823
Sir Walter Scott

A celebrated philosopher and poet, and the astrologer on whom the superstitious LOUIS XI, KING OF FRANCE depends, he is 'none of those ascetic, withered, pale professors of mystic learning, who bleared their eyes over the midnight furnace, and macerated their bodies by outwatching the polar bear. He indulged in all courtly pleasures, and, until he grew corpulent, had excelled in all martial sports and gymnastic exercises, as well as in the use of arms.'

Galore, Pussy
Goldfinger, 1959
Ian Fleming

Though movie versions have made a stock joke of the 'Bond girls', the original versions are no less stereotyped; they are merely more complex. A Southern girl, raped at twelve by her uncle, Pussy has turned an unsuccessful circus trapeze troupe into an all-female Harlem gang of cat burglars, a lesbian organization known as 'The Cement Mixers'. Needless to say, JAMES BOND regards it as a virtually holy mission to convert her to the joys of heterosexual passion.

Galt, Jaikie
Huntingtower, 1922
John Buchan

Like a rural version of the 'Baker Street Irregulars' in Sherlock Holmes stories, he is a streetwise urchin who puts the skills learned in the Glasgow slums to good use as a sidekick of DICKSON MCCUNN.

Gamgee, Sam
The Lord of the Rings, 3 volumes, 1954–5
J R R Tolkien

A simple rustic hobbit, the handyman of FRODO BAGGINS, he eavesdrops on his master's conversation with the wizard GANDALF, and consequently finds himself swept up in a highly dangerous adventure. Blunt, good-natured and utterly unselfish, he provides the support Frodo needs to carry out his almost impossible task.

Gamp, Mrs Sarah (Sairey)
Martin Chuzzlewit, 1844
Charles Dickens

A fat old nurse, midwife and layer-out of the dead, she is slatternly and ignorant of elementary nursing practice. She lodges with POLL SWEEDLEPIPE. Mr Mould, the undertaker, recommends her to SETH PECKSNIFF to lay out the body of ANTHONY CHUZZLEWIT, and she is hired to nurse MR LEWSOME and care for MR CHUFFEY. Although 'it was difficult to enjoy her society without becoming conscious of a smell of spirits', she pretends to be abstemious: 'Leave the bottle on the chimley-piece and don't ask me to take none, but let me put my lips to it when I am so dispoged'. She is characterized by idiosyncratic Cockney pronunciation and bizarre sayings, an ever-present umbrella and an imaginary friend named Mrs Harris, whom she uses as an authority for her own fabrications. She quarrels with her fellow nurse, BETSEY PRIG, when Betsey questions the existence of Mrs Harris.

Gandalf
The Hobbit, 1937
The Lord of the Rings, 3 volumes, 1954–5
J R R Tolkien

An inscrutable, beetle-browed wizard, who sets in motion the events of both stories. Combining the role of protector with conscience-pricker, he is a character of stern and uncompromising goodness, driven by his mission to pit his wits against the gathering forces of evil that threaten his country.

Ganlesse, Richard → Christian, Edward

Gann, Caroline, also known as Mrs Brandon
A Shabby Genteel Story, 1840
The Adventures of Philip, 1861–2
W M Thackeray

The daughter of an unsuccessful merchant, she is seduced by DR GEORGE FIRMIN, by whom she has a short-lived child. In the later sequel, she devotedly nurses Firmin's son, PHILIP FIRMIN, through a serious illness, and steadfastly refuses to expose her incorrigible former lover.

Gannet, Susan
Woman in Mind, 1985
Alan Ayckbourn

Susan is a middle-aged woman married to Gerald, a self-satisfied parson absorbed in writing a history of his parish, whom she no longer loves. Having suffered a knock to the head from a garden rake, she is comforted by an imagined family, both solicitous and appreciative of her, but interrupted, as she recovers, by her real family who scorn and take her for granted. As she has neither domestic influence, nor the physical or emotional strength to assert herself, she crumbles inevitably into neurosis.

Gant, Ben
Look Homeward, Angel, 1929
Thomas Wolfe

OLIVER and ELIZA GANT's son. As befits his biblical name, he is their favourite, the only person who can break through the barriers his family have erected around themselves. When he dies young of pneumonia, his brother EUGENE GANT is devastated. The watch Ben gives him, and which ticks on after Ben's death, becomes a permanent reminder of the dominance of time and a symbol of Eugene's growing distance in time and place from his childhood home.

Gant, Eliza
Look Homeward, Angel, 1929
Thomas Wolfe

EUGENE and BEN GANT's mother, she runs a small, intermittently solvent boarding house in their Southern home town. In contrast to her vast, dreaming hulk of a husband, OLIVER GANT, she is shrivelled inside with narrow acquisitiveness and an urge to dominate all those around her.

Gant, Eugene
Look Homeward, Angel, 1929
Of Time and the River, 1935
Thomas Wolfe

A famously autobiographical portrait. Like the classic *Bildungsroman* hero, he is defined almost entirely by his appetites (mostly for learning) and by vague and idealistic notions of personal grandeur. The son of OLIVER GANT, a monument salesman, and ELIZA GANT, a boarding-house keeper, and brother of BEN GANT, he desires nothing more than to swallow whole the world and all it offers. In the later book, he moves from his provincial Southern home to New York City, a university education, and a literary career. His idealism clashes with urban life and his life-affirming tolerance becomes somewhat compromised by a thread of anti-Semitism.

Gant, Oliver
Look Homeward, Angel, 1929
Thomas Wolfe

EUGENE and BEN GANT's father, he sells monumental statuary (such as the angel that haunts Eugene's youth) in a small Southern town. Monolithic himself, he is even more comprehensively illusioned than Eugene, his dreams fed by alcohol and disappointment. His nature, and the grotesque manner of his death, suggest a repressive Saturn figure, always on the brink of devouring his children.

Gantry, Elmer
Elmer Gantry, 1927
Sinclair Lewis

Gantry is a former professional football player, turned evangelical. Charismatically handsome, he establishes a mid-Western ministry by plagiarizing other preachers' sermons and playing on the susceptibilities of his female adherents. Another of Lewis's plausible 'boosters', he turns religion into a lucrative business.

Gardener, the
Richard II, c.1595
William Shakespeare

The gardener at the Duke of York's property at Langley, he is not only a groundsman but also something of a moral philosopher. Informing his assistant of Henry Bolingbroke's (HENRY IV) political and military ascendancy, he instructs him to deal with those plants in the garden which need cutting back, observing that KING RICHARD II should have (metaphorically) done the same in order to maintain the throne. In comparing a chaotic kingdom with an overgrown garden, he is both emphasizing the emblematic importance of the pastoral vision in contemporary thought, and expressing the central argument of the play, which is: who owns the garden of England, and is he fit to do so?

Gardiner, Col
Waverley, 1814
Sir Walter Scott

EDWARD WAVERLEY's commanding officer in the Hanoverian army, he is, like his young captain, 'a study for a romantic'. 'In person he was tall, handsome, and active, though somewhat advanced in life. In his early years he had been what is called... a very gay young man, and strange stories were circulated about his sudden conversion from doubt, if not infidelity to a serious and even enthusiastic turn of mind.' The historical Gardiner is known to have undergone a vision of Christ crucified that changed his personality utterly, and gave his mess a curious sedateness and solemnity.

Gardiner, Eunice
The Prime of Miss Jean Brodie, 1961
Muriel Spark

An Edinburgh schoolgirl. Small and neat, she is good at gymnastics and swimming, so she provides amusement for her fellow members of the 'Brodie set' and their teacher, MISS JEAN BRODIE, by performing somersaults and cartwheels. She goes through a religious phase and has a secret desire to be a Girl Guide leader, against Miss Brodie's precepts. In later life she becomes a nurse.

Gardner, Frank
Mrs Warren's Profession, 1894
George Bernard Shaw

Frank, 'pleasant, pretty, smartly dressed, cleverly good-for-nothing, not long turned 20', is the son of the REV SAMUEL GARDNER. He harbours an amiable and public disrespect for his father, perhaps because the Reverend pays his son's debts so unfailingly and so meekly. Frank falls romantically in love with Cambridge-educated VIVIE WARREN, but philosophically accepts her polite but insistent rejection of him and, for the meantime at least, life on a parental allowance of £400 a year.

Gardner, Rev Samuel
Mrs Warren's Profession, 1894
George Bernard Shaw

A former lover of the brothel-keeper MRS WARREN, Gardner is almost 60 and 'the fool of the family dumped on the Church by his father'. Superficially assertive, he is in reality apprehensive and perplexed, struggling to command respect as a father and as a man of principle and failing in both.

Gare, Caleb
Wild Geese, 1925
Martha Ostenso

JUDE GARE's father, he is a granite man, huge and immovable in body and mind, who believes himself to be omnipotent, and demands that all life and its working must advantage him. Intolerant, vindictive, avaricious and contorted by jealousy, he seems to have no redeeming traits. In a sense, he is inhuman, 'a spiritual counterpart of the land, as harsh, as demanding, as tyrannical as the very soil from which he [draws] existence'.

Gare, Jude (Judith)
Wild Geese, 1925
Martha Ostenso
Although her tyrannical father attempts to suppress the life in her, Jude remains passionate, sensual and instinctive. Embodying 'the embryonic ecstasy of life', she is a centauress of vivid and terrible beauty and strength.

Gargery, Joe
Great Expectations, 1861
Charles Dickens
A blacksmith, he is married to PIP's sister, MRS JOE GARGERY, who bullies him mercilessly. Being 'a mild, good-natured, sweet-tempered, easy-going, foolish, dear fellow', he protects Pip from her ill-treatment and takes him on as an apprentice. On becoming a gentleman, Pip grows ashamed of Joe's lack of cultivation, but through adversity comes to recognize his true worth. After Mrs Joe dies, he marries BIDDY and they have a son named after Pip.

Gargery, Mrs Joe
Great Expectations, 1861
Charles Dickens
PIP's sister and the first wife of JOE GARGERY, she was christened Georgiana Maria. She is a fearsome, shrewish woman who terrorizes both Joe and Pip, whom she brings up 'by hand' with the aid of her cane, Tickler. After she urges Joe to thrash his journeyman, DOLGE ORLICK, Orlick assaults her, leaving her paralyzed and speechless. She is cared for by BIDDY until her death.

Garland, Anne
The Trumpet Major, 1880
Thomas Hardy
A gentle, sweet-faced girl who is a curious mix of the conservative and the coquette. She knows exactly what and who she wants, and gets what she is after, breaking a heart in the process. Yet she is wholesome in her personal morals, and trusting of those around her. Feminine, intuitive, intelligent and sensitive, she appears to men to be the ideal woman of her day. The young BOB LOVEDAY finds her a bit too 'good', but the more mature JOHN LOVEDAY is only too happy to settle down with her.

Garland, Mr and Mrs, and Abel
The Old Curiosity Shop, 1841
Charles Dickens
The Garlands are a kindly, plump and placid old couple who become the employers and benefactors of KIT NUBBLES after he leaves the Old Curiosity Shop. Their gentle and devoted only son, Abel, is first an articled clerk and then a notary and partner of the lawyer, Mr Witherden. Mr Garland's brother, THE BACHELOR, takes care of LITTLE NELL and her GRANDFATHER in their last days.

Garnett, Prossy (Proserpine)
Candida, 1895
George Bernard Shaw
Known as 'Prossy', Miss Garnett, 'a brisk little woman of about 30, of the lower middle class, neatly but cheaply dressed ... notably pert and quick of speech', is employed secretary to the REVEREND JAMES MORELL. Although sensitive herself, she lacks the finer social graces and can be sharp and snobbish. Her rigid code of manners excludes any discussion of sentiment or emotion. Consequently, she is scandalized by EUGENE MARCHBANKS's forthrightness and shocked when he induces her to confess her secret infatuation with Morell. Prossy represents the subjugation of physical desire.

Garp, T S
The World According to Garp, 1978
John Irving
The initials are his given name, and derive from 'Technical Sergeant'. He is not especially intellectual, but is rigorously disciplined and brimming with serious purpose, with no real sense of fun. He loves wrestling, and becomes a writer immersed 'in a world of his own imagination'. He is 'an excessive man. He made everything baroque, he believed in exaggeration.' His life and marriage descend uncontrollably (but often darkly comically) into violence, horror and despair.

Garraghty, Nicholas and Dennis, also known as Old Nick and St Dennis
The Absentee, in *Tales of Fashionable Life*, 1812
Maria Edgeworth
Dubliners, and brothers, they are the grasping upper- and under-agents of LORD CLONBRONY. Appointed to squeeze every drop of profit out of one of his estates, they are slowly running it to ruin by bad husbandry and greed.

Garter, Polly
Under Milk Wood, 1954
Dylan Thomas
With her 'naughty mothering arms and body like a wardrobe', the fancy woman of Donkey Street is free with her love and dreams of babies – her neighbours think she should be arrested for having so many. Scrubbing floors and hanging out washing, she remembers her lovers, including Little Willy Wee, the unlikely captor of her heart. She expresses the sentiment at the heart of the play – 'Oh, isn't life a terrible thing, thank God?'

Garth
Winterset, 1935
Maxwell Anderson
Weak rather than irredeemably evil, he was TROCK's accomplice in the murder for which MIO's father was wrongfully executed. Unable to turn state's evidence against his powerful friend, he has to suffer the deferred horror of seeing his sister gunned down with Mio, who is her lover.

Garth, Caleb
Middlemarch, 1871–2
George Eliot
The father of MARY GARTH. Symbolically hopeless with money, but valuing the worth of

hard work above most other things, Caleb's contentment with the simplicity of his family life runs in obvious contrast to the miseries suffered by those around him whose sole motives are self-gain. Honesty being his greatest virtue, he is also kind and compassionate, and while not the most imaginative of men, his harmonious relationship with the land points to the inherent integrity of his nature.

Garth, Mary
Middlemarch, 1871–2
George Eliot

Unremarkable in looks but honest, generous and full of commonsense, Mary loves and is loved by FRED VINCY, but pointedly refuses to marry him until he has proved that he can be other than an idle gambler. Devoted to her family, Mary, though necessarily hard on him till he reforms himself, shows the same loyalty to Fred, and her frankness and lack of pretension endear her to everyone she meets.

Gascoigne, Mr
'Dr. Heidegger's Experiment', 1837, in *Twice-Told Tales*, 1837, revised edition 1842
Nathaniel Hawthorne

A 'ruined politician, a man of evil fame, or at least [who] had been so, till time had buried him from the knowledge of the present generation, and made him obscure instead of infamous'. He is an enthusiastic imbiber of DR HEIDEGGER's elixir of youth.

Gashe, Toby
The Bell, 1958
Iris Murdoch

Spending a month with the Imber community before going up to Oxford, the likeable, naive Toby is filled with energy, eagerness and hope. Keenly Christian, he is fascinated by the cloistered life, and as a town boy finds the country almost mystically significant. But he gets embroiled in the violent emotional undercurrents in the community, and experiencing his first confused sexual feelings, both homo- and heterosexual, towards MICHAEL MEAD and DORA GREENFIELD, is brutally manipulated by NICK FAWLEY. Accidentally discovering the abbey's 'drowned' medieval bell, at Dora's instigation Toby secretly recovers it, and emerges from his various ordeals chastened but relatively unscathed.

Gashford, Mr
Barnaby Rudge, 1841
Charles Dickens

The 'very sly and slinking' secretary of LORD GEORGE GORDON, he manipulates his employer for his own purposes. He organizes the abduction of EMMA HAREDALE and DOLLY VARDEN, but they are rescued by MR GEOFFREY HAREDALE, EDWARD CHESTER and JOE WILLET. After the Gordon Riots, he deserts Gordon to become a government spy. He eventually commits suicide by poisoning.

Gaspard
A Tale of Two Cities, 1859
Charles Dickens

A poor Parisian labourer who seeks revenge for the death of his child, killed by the recklessly driven coach of the MARQUIS DE ST EVREMONDE (THE YOUNGER). He clings on to the coach as it travels to the nobleman's chateau and, at night, stabs the Marquis to death as he sleeps. He is captured and hanged.

Gaster, Rev Dr
Headlong Hall, 1816
Thomas Love Peacock

As his name suggests, Gaster's fixation with food is all-consuming. His rush to get to any table and his absorption with his stomach and all matters culinary are an antidote to the philosophizing and high-thinking characters around him at the house party in Headlong Hall. His approach is prosaic: all human advances and the natural order of the world are for one thing only – to serve his stomach, his comfort, and appetites in general.

Gates, Frenesi
Vineland, 1990
Thomas Pynchon

ZOYD WHEELER's ex-wife and the mother of PRAIRIE WHEELER. For many years she has worked as a 'sting specialist' for the FBI, but has been left high and dry by Watergate, Reaganomics and recession, and is now the target of the nightmarish Federal Prosecutor BROCK VOND.

Gatsby, Jay
The Great Gatsby, 1925
F Scott Fitzgerald

The enigmatic central figure, he is a mid-western boy, born James Gatz, who was a poor drifter as a youth. As a young soldier he falls in love with DAISY BUCHANAN. After World War I he builds a fortune as a bootlegger, and tries not simply to win her back, but to eradicate the time between (and her marriage) as if it had never been. He is a romantic figure, but an egoist who is totally self-obsessed, unable to live outside the seductive dream-world he has created. At the same time, there is an odd kind of innocence about his delusion, and he is capable of acting with integrity and even a certain greatness.

Gaulden, Faro
The Peppered Moth, 2000
Margaret Drabble

Granddaughter of BESSIE BAWTRY, Faro is a glamorous, full-bodied, confident young woman, 'radiant with light. She dazzles.' A London-based science journalist, she is fascinated by the past (especially by the intricate network of her extended family), and both intrigued and fearful of the implications of genetic research. Her assertiveness, however, is undermined by her tenuous attachment (out of a sense of misplaced pity) for a morose, down-at-heel boyfriend. Passion and pity, she discovers, do not co-exist. A far better prospect is presented by the chivalrous, sympathetic archaeologist Steve Nieman, who releases the sensuous in Faro while drawing her back to her Yorkshire roots.

Gault, Lucy
The Story of Lucy Gault, 2002
William Trevor

In 1921, after her father, a modest Irish Protestant landowner, accidentally wounds a young nationalist intruder and announces the family must leave Ireland, eight-year-old Lucy hides in the woods. Believing her to have drowned, her parents depart. Secretive and solitary, Lucy grows up cared for by her parents' retainers. An introspective young woman nursing her guilt and awaiting her parents' foregiveness, she abandons her chance of happiness with Ralph, a young teacher ('I am not somebody to love'), devoting herself instead to beekeeping, reading 19th-century novels, and embroidery. Attractive ('a dimple made her smile mischievous'), she is a woman of great faith but a profound sense of martyrdom.

Gaunt, Griffith
Griffith Gaunt, or, Jealousy, 1866
Charles Reade

An impoverished young gentleman who gives up his inheritance for the woman he loves, but cannot come to terms with her sexual nature. He turns to drinking, and is consumed by mounting jealousy, which eventually erupts in an outpouring of demonic fury. He remarries bigamously, and his first wife is tried for his supposed murder, but they are finally reunited, and the good side of his nature triumphs in a life now dedicated to good deeds.

Gaunt, John of → John of Gaunt, Duke of Lancaster

Gauntlet, Emilia (Emily or Emy)
The Adventures of Peregrine Pickle, 1751, bowdlerized edition 1758
Tobias Smollett

The only daughter of a field-officer, who has passed a rather uncertain childhood in the care of a lascivious bachelor uncle. Her conventionally romantic beauty overcomes the oddity of her clothes, and PEREGRINE PICKLE is suffused with desire.

Gauntlet, Godfrey
The Adventures of Peregrine Pickle, 1751, bowdlerized edition 1758
Tobias Smollett

EMILIA GAUNTLET's older brother, he is about 20, 'of a middling size, vigorous make, remarkably well shaped, and the scars of the small pox, of which he bore a good number, added a peculiar manliness to the air of his countenance'. Though easy-going and open, his life and manners are wholly defined by the military career.

Gauri
The Old Woman and the Cow, 1960, republished as *Gauri*, 1976
Mulk Raj Anand

She is sold to an elderly moneylender to clear her mother's debt, but is then reunited with her husband, who rejects her in disgust. Gauri's story echoes that of the mythological Sita, but Anand provides a modern twist by having Gauri make a new, independent life for herself.

Gaveston, Piers
Edward II, 1594
Christopher Marlowe

Epicene favourite of EDWARD II and a 'night growne mushrump', whose sudden influence is much resented at court. A subtle manipulator, outlandishly dressed, he sees politics and war as a branch of aesthetics. He is unpromisingly betrothed to Lady Margaret de Clare.

Gavin
Party Time, 1991
Harold Pinter

The smoothly urbane host of an exclusive drinks party in an unspecified city (probably London), Gavin is evidently an influential, high-ranking government official, probably in the secret services, who has authorized (or at least approves of) the 'round-up' taking place in the streets below. Most of the guests approve of this, seeking to impress (and declare their allegiance to) Gavin by talking admiringly of the facilities of the 'health club' to which they belong, a place 'inspired' as one guest puts it, 'by a moral sense … unshakable, rigorous, fundamental constant'. The administration's 'aim', concurs Gavin, is 'normal service. We, if you like, insist on it.'

Gay, Walter
Dombey and Son, 1848
Charles Dickens

The nephew of SOLOMON GILLS and a junior clerk in Dombey and Son, he rescues FLORENCE DOMBEY after she has been abducted by MRS BROWN and falls in love with her. MR DOMBEY sends him to Barbados, where he is presumed drowned in a shipwreck. His uncle goes in search of him and he finally returns and marries Florence.

Gayheart, Lucy
Lucy Gayheart, 1935
Willa Cather

'A slight figure, always in motion, dancing or skating, or walking swiftly with intense direction, like a bird flying home.' She is haunted by music, but her name contains a single broad irony, for when the light of optimism goes out in her life, she is condemned to irretrievable misery.

Gaylord, Bernice
Gentlemen of Gyang Gyang, 1956
Miles Franklin

An artist of promise who comes to Australia from Paris to escape a traumatic love affair, which has also blocked her talent. She has a strange, unconventional beauty and a withdrawn, mysterious manner which attracts two suitors, one of whom she eventually marries. Her growing love for the wild territory re-awakens her sense of purpose in life, and frees her artistic longings.

Gaylord, Marcia
A Modern Instance, 1882
William Dean Howells

Intended as 'a modern instance' of the classical Medea, she is a passionate, rather fiery woman, whose love for her coolly philandering husband, the journalist BARTLEY HUBBARD, is gradually overborne by pride, leading her to take a satisfyingly modern financial revenge on his ill-gotten cash.

Gaylustre, Mrs Fanny
The Cabinet Minister, 1890
Arthur Wing Pinero
When Mrs Gaylustre calls at the home of SIR JULIAN and LADY KITTY TWOMBLEY in the morning, she is received as what she is: a dressmaker; in the afternoon she is received, reluctantly, as a lady. Not more than 30, she is an 'attractive, self-possessed, mischievous-looking woman'. She is also an unscrupulous opportunist, using her dressmaking abilities to gain social influence and exploiting her clients to help her succeed. She represents the threat perceived by the ruling class of a burgeoning, and possibly dangerously acquisitive, middle class.

Geard, John
A Glastonbury Romance, 1932
John Cowper Powys
The Mayor of Glastonbury, known as 'Bloody Johnny' from his constant references to the Blood of Christ. He is ugly and unkempt, with black, demonic eyes, and a strongly animal, instinctive nature. He is a self-styled prophet of a new religion, and is seen to have miracle-working powers. He has a lifelong 'hidden detachment' from human contact, and one of his 'deepest characteristics' is his 'deep secret of physical ease', an ability to give himself over to complete enjoyment of physical sensation.

Ged, or Sparrowhawk
A Wizard of Earthsea, 1967
The Tombs of Atuan, 1969
The Farthest Shore, 1972, forming the 'Earthsea' trilogy
Ursula Le Guin
A serious-minded, somewhat arrogant boy who desires to become a master wizard. Through his long and occasionally terrifying apprenticeship he gradually matures, coming to understand the nature of evil and good, and his own place in the magical scheme of things. In time he becomes one of the wisest and most powerful magicians in the land.

Geddes, Joshua
Redgauntlet, 1824
Sir Walter Scott
A Quaker encountered by DARSIE LATIMER during his sojourn in the western Borders. He has created a small Eden at Mount Sharon on the Solway, a garden where animals and birds wander around as pets, but he is in conflict with his neighbours, not just on matters of politics and doctrine but because of his illegal salmon-netting.

Gedge, Timothy
The Children of Dynmouth, 1976
William Trevor
Timothy's emotionally deprived background leads him to seek affection by trying to become a comedian. A solitary sharp-faced boy of 15, adept at petty theft, he makes a nuisance of himself by

chattering and joking to people. Conceiving the idea of a drag act combining comedy and death, he tries to bring it about by blackmailing the inhabitants of the Dorset resort of Dynmouth, whose behaviour he has observed closely. He lives essentially in a fantasy world and has no concern for those whose lives he disrupts.

Gee, Miss Edith
'Miss Gee: A Ballad', number XII of 'Songs and Other Musical Pieces', in *Collected Shorter Poems*, 1950
W H Auden
A thin-lipped, squinting spinster of Clevedon Terrace whose conventional religiosity and sexual squeamishness make her a perfect illustration of Georg Groddeck's belief that cancer is caused by 'foiled creative fire'. After her death, she is handed over to the morbid anatomy department for dissection. The whole sorry story is sung to the tune of 'St James Infirmary'.

Geierstein, Anne of
Anne of Geierstein, or The Maiden in the Mist, 1829
Sir Walter Scott
The eponymous heroine, she is the only child of the COUNT ALBERT OF GEIERSTEIN. More like her uncle ARNOLD BIEDERMAN than her father in temperament, she is utterly at home in the mountains and rescues Arthur de Vere (ARTHUR PHILIPSON), her eventual husband, when he falls into danger. Though there is a tinge of black magic in her ancestry, she bears a dignified simplicity of expression which implies 'at once a character of gentleness, and of the self-relying resolution of a mind too virtuous to suspect evil, and too noble to fear it'.

Geierstein, Count Albert of
Anne of Geierstein, or The Maiden in the Mist, 1829
Sir Walter Scott
The younger son of the old count, he has a far greater appetite for power and its trappings than his elder brother ARNOLD BIEDERMAN, who prefers the simple life of the mountains. He has thrown in his lot with the emperor and ostentatiously wears the peacock feather in public. Unlike his brother, he has but one child, the heroine ANNE OF GEIERSTEIN.

Gellatley, Davie
Waverley, 1814
Sir Walter Scott
One of those natural fools who were attached to great old houses, much like Shakespearean clowns. Davie has apparently rescued ROSE BRADWARDINE from a neighbour's bull and is now permitted to mooch around in fancy clothes, doing nothing more than puzzle visitors like EDWARD WAVERLEY with his antics and contortions. What sets Davie apart, though, is the gift of a beautiful singing voice.

Gellburg, Philip
Broken Glass, 1994
Arthur Miller
The play is set in Brooklyn in 1938. A 'slender, intense' man, the only Jew working at a traditional Wall Street bank, where he is employed mainly on business foreclosures,

Gellburg is hard-working, ambitious and determined to assimilate fully into surrounding society. Although he and SYLVIA have been married for several years, he has become too self-preoccupied a man to share his thoughts and feelings with her. It is only when she succumbs to a mysterious paralysis that he is forced to re-evaluate his marriage, his heritage and America.

Gellburg, Sylvia
Broken Glass, 1994
Arthur Miller

The play is set in Brooklyn in 1938. A quiet and, as it transpires, subdued and repressed housewife, Sylvia has for years been largely ignored by her husband, Wall Street banker PHILIP GELLBURG, and, as compensation, has retreated to living a vicarious life through reading books and magazines. Her reading of the events of *Kristallnacht*, however, has the dramatic and alarming effect of inducing a mysterious paralysis, so serious that she is confined to a wheelchair. The condition results in both her and Philip reflecting upon their origins, their marriage, tyranny and oppression, and hence to her decision that they must begin anew.

General, the, properly Francis Rupert Burnand Woolcot
Seven Little Australians, 1894
The Family at Misrule, 1895
Ethel Turner

The youngest of Captain Woolcot's seven children. Fat and dirty, he is loved by his sister JUDY WOOLCOT. By the age of six he is known, somewhat confusingly, as Peter, Jumbo or Billy, and he has a winsome lisp.

General, Mrs
Little Dorrit, 1857
Charles Dickens

An absurdly genteel widow whom WILLIAM DORRIT employs to chaperone and 'polish' AMY and FANNY DORRIT on their continental travels: 'Her way of forming a mind was to prevent it from forming opinions'. Anxious about impropriety, 'Mrs General's way of getting rid of it was to put it out of sight, and make believe that there was no such thing'. Nor was she to be told of anything shocking: 'passion was to go to sleep in the presence of Mrs General, and blood was to change to milk and water'. Her hope of marrying Dorrit is thwarted when he dies in Rome.

Genoa, Duke of → Malevole

George
Early Morning, 1968
Edward Bond

George is the young, royal, Siamese twin of ARTHUR and, according to Bond, 'the pure socialised version' of his brother. George is a conformist, does as he is told and follows the examples pointed out to him, in contrast to his restless, argumentative brother. Yet they cannot live without each other. Although George withers and dies, he reappears later as a ghost and reattaches himself to Arthur. The twins represent a social dialectic.

George
A Single Man, 1964
Christopher Isherwood

The bachelor narrator of the novel, he is an English literature lecturer at a Californian university. Superficially he is in an enviable position: successful, distinguished and popular. But the death of his homosexual lover in a car accident is a constantly painful memory. Outwardly happy, he is in reality tired and despairing. George's story is one of deep anguish: the predicament of a middle-aged, middle-class homosexual confronted by bereavement and appalling loneliness. His responses are by turns tragic, pathetic, wry and moving.

George
Who's Afraid of Virginia Woolf?, 1962
Edward Albee

A history professor on a small American campus, where the president happens to be George's hard-drinking wife, MARTHA. George stands – often rather querulously – for certain lasting values to which no absolutely fixed symbolic significance can be attached. However, the fact that he is willing to 'sacrifice' his and Martha's imaginary son is a clear reference to Abraham and Isaac and the Crucifixion; and the fact that the couple are, indeed, called George and Martha suggests they may also refer to the Founding Father and Mother of the United States, their child representing the principles of liberty and tolerance that are consistently violated in their viciously acrimonious domestic life.

George (George Harris)
Uncle Tom's Cabin, or, Life Among the Lowly, 1851–2
Harriet Beecher Stowe

ELIZA's husband, he is similarly light-skinned, so much so that he is able to 'pass' for white. Though critics have found this insultingly unconvincing, it is intended to illustrate the moral insignificance of colour. Like his wife, George is proud, resourceful and energetic in defence of his dignity and individuality.

George (George Milton)
Of Mice and Men, 1937
John Steinbeck

The friend and somewhat curmudgeonly protector of the giant LENNIE; both are itinerant labourers in Depression America. In contrast to Lennie, George is 'small and quick, dark of face, with restless eyes and sharp, strong features. Every part of him was defined.'

George III
The Madness of George III, 1991
Alan Bennett

By turns childlike, obscene, lucid, recalcitrant, sympathetic and pathetic, the king is believed by his doctors and family to be descending into insanity. A contemporary diagnosis would probably be porphyria, a metabolic malfunction. Affecting a hearty approach to royal duties, George's habit of appending 'What? What?' to the end of almost every remark reveals his desperate desire both to be liked and to stave off embarrassment, something he deeply fears.

Suffering various indignities at the hands of his doctors, he delights in domestic happiness with Queen Charlotte, and their private identities as 'Mr and Mrs King'.

George, Duke of Clarence
Henry VI Part III, early 1590s
Richard III, 1592/3
William Shakespeare

George is the second son of RICHARD PLANTAGENET, DUKE OF YORK. Witty and engaging, George is also soft-hearted, has flexible principles and is politically unreliable. He first joins the Wars of the Roses in the Yorkist cause in defiance of the House of Lancaster and Queen Margaret (MARGARET OF ANJOU), and is made Duke of Clarence for his prowess on the battlefield. Yet later, having observed his elder brother, Edward IV (EDWARD, EARL OF MARCH), wooing Lady Grey (ELIZABETH WOODVILLE), and voicing his opposition to the king's subsequent decision to marry her, Clarence defects to the opposing forces of the Earl of Warwick. Later still, he changes sides again, rejoining Edward. Margaret describes him accurately as 'a quicksand of deceit'.

George, Harris, and J
Three Men in a Boat, 1889
Three Men on the Bummel, 1900
Jerome K Jerome

Three bachelors who take a boating holiday on the Thames, and a cycling trip through the Black Forest. George is the cheerful optimist, while Harris is the practical one who cannot stop organizing things; although he assures the others he knows the secret of Hampton Court maze, this, as well as everything else, ends in his bemused embarrassment. J, based upon Jerome himself, is anecdotal, reflective and sentimental.

Georgina
Narrow Road to the Deep North, 1968
Edward Bond

A western Christian missionary and politician in Japan, sometime in the 17th, 18th or 19th centuries, Georgina and the Commodore assume power in the Japanese city once ruled by the dictator SHOGO. Georgina is articulate, honest, sexually repressed and lacking in guile. Guided by her religious convictions and, at a deeper level, by the inherited belief that her own social class will always wield power, the jolt of defeat and failure are so great that she is driven to mental distraction.

Geraldine
'Christabel', 1797–1801
Samuel Taylor Coleridge

A beautiful, fair maiden, clad all in white and found apparently abandoned in the woods by CHRISTABEL. Once she has been carried over the threshold of SIR LEOLINE's castle, she reveals the physical manifestation of the serpentine evil of her nature. Bewitching Christabel, she then engages the sympathies of Sir Leoline by presenting herself as the daughter of his estranged friend, Sir Roland de Vaux and, manipulative in her malevolence, she succeeds in blinding him to her true character while simultaneously turning him against his hitherto beloved daughter.

Gerard
The Cloister and the Hearth, 1861
Charles Reade

The son of a poor family, he is wrapped up in 'reading and penmanship', and becomes a skilled illuminator. He has a good heart and joyful humour, but his separation from MARGARET BRANDT and their son sends him off on a dissolute life of wandering, until a religious conversion takes him into the priesthood. He finds her again, but although still in love, he cannot break his vows; 'thy sweet body is dearer to me than my own; but a million times dearer to me are our immortal souls'.

Gerard, Brigadier Etienne
The Exploits of Brigadier Gerard, 1896, et seq
Arthur Conan Doyle

Etienne Gerard, who first appears as a 25-year-old lieutenant, is not a modest man. Soon after we meet him, he describes himself as 'the picked horseman and surest blade in the ten regiments of hussars', and informs us that 'everybody had heard of me since my duel with the six fencing masters'. Egocentric, dashing, romantic and, it is implied, possessing a healthy sexual appetite, Gerard is also excitable, bombastic, vain and mildly comic. He rises to become a brigadier and 'the friend and confident agent of the Emperor' Napoleon, but he is essentially a Victorian Briton's view of a Frenchman, rather than a fully rounded character.

Gerard, Sybil
Sybil, or The Two Nations, 1845
Benjamin Disraeli

The daughter of WALTER GERARD, a leading Chartist, she is later revealed to be the rightful heir of the Marney estate, left when CHARLES EGREMONT's cruel brother is killed in a riot. Her marriage to Egremont promises to heal the rift between 'the Two Nations'.

Gerard, Walter
Sybil, or The Two Nations, 1845
Benjamin Disraeli

A well-educated and highly principled man, he has taken up the cause of the new urban working class through the Chartist movement. It is clear, though, that for him, Chartism is too extreme; it is the next generation, his daughter SYBIL GERARD's and CHARLES EGREMONT's, that will begin the reconciliation of rich and poor.

Gereth, Mrs
The Spoils of Poynton, 1897
Henry James

The widowed chatelaine of Poynton, and guardian of its art and furniture. Refined in the extreme, 'she would rather have perished than looked *endimanchée*'. To some extent she seems to be defined by the precious objects that surround her and goes out of focus as a character when separated from them.

Gereth, Owen
The Spoils of Poynton, 1897
Henry James

MRS GERETH's son, he is rather more aesthetically minded than she is, less constrained by the material aspects of his inheritance. He falls in love with FLEDA VETCH, despite being betrothed to MONA BRIGSTOCK, and when he marries Mona, he owes the other girl a sentimental debt that, like their relationship, is caught up in the final catastrophe.

Gerhardt, Jennie
Jennie Gerhardt, 1911
Theodore Dreiser

A poor young girl from Ohio who has an affair (and subsequently a child) with the powerful Senator Brander. After his death, she has a relationship with the son of a rich industrialist, but terminates this when she discovers it will lead to his being disinherited. Affectionate, loyal and long-suffering, she is, one suspects, Dreiser's female ideal.

Gerontion
'Gerontion', in *Poems*, 1920
T S Eliot

The archetype of unheroic age, without passion and with fading senses, he sits amid the derelict promise of post-World War I Europe, 'an old man in a dry month/Being read to by a boy, waiting for rain'.

Gertrude
The Abbess of Crewe, 1974
Muriel Spark

A popular, moustached German nun, Sister Gertrude carries out religious negotiations in remote parts of the world on behalf of the Abbey of Crewe. FELICITY and ALEXANDRA, candidates in the election for Abbess, seek her advice via a special telephone link; her huskily-delivered remarks combine the cryptic and the cynical, and she diplomatically professes not to hear embarrassing details.

Gertrude, in full Gertrude Kumalo
Cry, the Beloved Country, 1948
Alan Paton

REV STEPHEN KUMALO's sister, she has been drawn out of their poverty-stricken rural background by the lure of the great city, Johannesburg. There she slides into prostitution, from which Kumalo cannot divert her, though he adopts her child, as he does his condemned son's. Their relationship symbolizes the way love has been tainted and perverted in a divided society.

Gertrude
Hamlet, 1601/2
William Shakespeare

The widow of HAMLET's father and wife of his murderer, CLAUDIUS, she is torn between her love for her son and her husband. This 'seeming virtuous queen' is the victim of circumstances, partly of her own making, which she cannot control. She is ruled by her emotions and dies by her own hand to save her son.

Geryoneo
The Faerie Queene, 1590–6
Sir Edmund Spenser

A 'strong Tyrant' with a triple body. Three torsos protrude from his waist, each with one arm and three legs. He uses his hideous physique to terrify the local population and utilizes his power to extort from them the sacrifice of cows. He is an allegory for Phillip II's control over Spain, Portugal and the Low Countries.

Getliffe, Francis
The Light and the Dark, 1947, et seq
C P Snow

A Cambridge colleague of LEWIS ELIOT and, like him, one of the young liberal-leftists who are nonetheless moved to support the existing 'government' against the incursion of radical but, they believe, inappropriate academic and organizational values.

Getliffe, Herbert
Time of Hope, 1949
C P Snow

Head of LEWIS ELIOT's first legal chambers (and the only man to address him by his initials, L S). He gives off an aura of contentment, as if in sight of the only things that life could ever grant him.

Ghost of Christmas Past, Ghost of Christmas Present and Ghost of Christmas Yet to Come
A Christmas Carol, 1843
Charles Dickens

The spirits which appear to EBENEZER SCROOGE in his dreams and teach him lessons about benevolence. The Ghost of Christmas Past shows Scrooge 'shadows of things that have been' in his past life. The jolly Ghost of Christmas Present conducts him to various scenes on Christmas Eve. The Ghost of Christmas Yet to Come shows him terrifying visions of the future, including Scrooge's burial in a neglected grave. Scrooge learns that he can prevent his own and others' misery by reforming his character.

Ghost, the
Hamlet, 1601/2
William Shakespeare

The spirit of HAMLET's dead father, a warrior king who was more at home on the battlefield, appears to reveal the truth of his murder by CLAUDIUS and to demand revenge from Hamlet. He is suffering the pains of Purgatory and only revenge can release him. He later returns to remind Hamlet that he has not yet obeyed him.

Ghote, Inspector Ganesh
The Perfect Murder, 1964, et seq
H R F Keating

The likeable, scooter-riding Inspector Ghote is with the plain-clothes Crime Branch of Bombay Police, but often fears being demoted and banished to some remote backwater with no school for his bright son, Ved, and where his wife, Protima, would miss the city. For although bribery is an accepted way of life, Ghote is incorruptible. He must therefore not only solve his cases but, because they frequently involve high-placed persons, also contend with extremely delicate situations. He nervously picks his way through these, under constant threat, harried by his superiors and domestic problems, but clinging to his principles and somehow winning through.

Gianni
The Bay of Noon, 1970
Shirley Hazzard

An Italian film producer and lover of the novelist GIOCONDA, he provides a flow of images which make it clear to the exiled JENNY that the only journeyings that are worthwhile are those that plumb the unconscious.

Giant Despair, the
The Pilgrim's Progress, Part I 1678, Part II 1684
John Bunyan

The keeper of Doubting Castle, a dangerous trap waiting for discouraged pilgrims on their way to the Celestial City, his chief pleasure is to gouge out their eyes and leave them to rot in the castle dungeons, or to lead them to wander to their death among the tombs around his keep. He meets his match at the courageous hands of MR GREAT-HEART.

Giaour, the
The Giaour: A Fragment of a Turkish Tale, 1813
Byron, George Gordon, 6th Lord Byron

Leila, the dark-eyed favourite of the Turkish lord Hassan, has been false to him with the Giaour – the Infidel. She has been recaptured, bound in a sack and plunged into the sea to drown. On his coal-black steed, the Giaour, his face pale with fury, avenges her by smiting off Hassan's head. But even an infidel Christian can feel remorse. He confesses his sin to a friar and ends his life in a monastery, penitent and silent.

Gibb, Judge Bob
Maximum Bob, 1991
Elmore Leonard

Long years on the Bench and a powerful intellect have honed Bob Gibb's ability to detect baloney at a thousand paces. Locked into a loveless marriage and attracted to a young female lawyer, driven by sexual hunger and armed with cynicism, he deals with the twin crises of his life – ridding himself of his crazed wife and avoiding murder by an outraged recipient of his off-beat sentencing policy. Many years of dealing with the low-life have had a coarsening effect upon him and his drift into amorality allows him to dispense with legal niceties.

Gibbs, George
Our Town, 1938
Thornton Wilder

A fundamentally good American boy, whose temporary faults of selfishness and conceit derive from his baseball expertise. A high-school romance leads to his marriage to EMILY WEBB, and he achieves his ambition to become a farmer.

Gibbs, Mrs
Our Town, 1938
Thornton Wilder

Born Julia Hersey, the wife of Dr Gibbs and mother of GEORGE GIBBS is a plump, pleasant pillar of the small community of Grover's Corners, New Hampshire. She sings in the church choir and dreams of visiting Paris. Believing that 'people are meant to go through life two by two', she is glad that her son marries EMILY WEBB. After her own death, in an unemotional, neutral state, she advises the recently deceased Emily to prepare for what is to come.

Gibson, Dick
The Dick Gibson Show, 1971
Stanley Elkin

Addicted to language, Dick is a late-night radio chat-show host, spinning fantastic variations on the problems of his phone-in guests, pushing even simple observations to the point of playful redundancy. In the process, he begins to expose the sheer oddity of the everyday world.

Gibson, Dilsey and Luster → Dilsey and Luster

Gibson, Molly
Wives and Daughters, 1866
Elizabeth Gáskell

Molly, the heroine of the novel, is charming, attractive and a loving daughter to MR GIBSON. She is a serene woman, rising above any display of raw emotion and avoiding confrontation at all costs. However, she lacks a certain independence and depth of character, possibly because she is motherless.

Gibson, Mr
Wives and Daughters, 1866
Elizabeth Gaskell

MOLLY GIBSON's father. He is a surgeon, respected by local people as an intelligent, reassuring, honourable and trustworthy man, and is much loved by Molly. However, he is not particularly perceptive and can misread people and situations.

Gibson Grey, Austin
The Accidental Man, 1971
Iris Murdoch

Comically hopeless at coping, the middle-aged but youthfully handsome, self-centred and asthmatic Austin is usually cosseted by crusading women friends. But he gives one of them the creeps with his 'soupy sort of emotions' and 'funny hand'. This was injured when he was ten, and causes him 'elder brother trouble', although, according to Austin, his brother (a knighted, highly-successful, retired diplomat) is now bent on reconciliation. With his fey, fragile young second wife, Austin shares an eerie, mutually obsessive love–fear relationship, which she has temporarily fled. Egotistical, jealous and destructive, his accident-rife existence creating havoc for others, Austin himself not only survives but flourishes.

Gicandi Player
Devil on the Cross, 1982, originally published in Gikuyu as *Caitaani Mutharaba-ini*, 1980
Ngugi waThiong'o

The mythical 'Prophet of Justice' who tells

Wariinga's story, he is a figure out of Gikuyu folklore, bringing a universal, almost philosophical dimension to an everyday story of deprivation and suffering.

Gid
Leaving Cheyenne, 1963
Larry McMurtry

A cattle rancher who has turned his back on the free life of the plains, where he worked as a freelance bronco-buster, in order to embrace an ethic of success and respectability. As such, he represents the psychological and moral antithesis of the free-spirited JOHNNY.

Giddens, Alexandra
The Little Foxes, 1939
Lillian Hellman

A pretty, delicate-looking girl of 17, she has a sense of virtue and decency that can only have been inherited from her ailing father Horace. Unsullied by the corruption at the heart of her family, she shows unexpected glimpses of her mother's fire as she asserts a growing independence that belies her 'sugar sweet' personality.

Giddens, Regina
The Little Foxes, 1939
Lillian Hellman

A handsome woman of 40, she is a venal, domineering matriarch with iced water in her veins. Stifled by the middle-class man's world of the American South at the turn of the century, she is projected by her social aspirations into a sophisticated life of refinement and luxury in Chicago. Her determination to make this dream a reality is chillingly relentless and, in a family akin to a nest of vipers, Regina proves to be the deadliest of them all.

Gigi→ Grace

Giglio, Prince
The Rose and the Ring, 1855
W M Thackeray

Heir to the throne of Paflagonia, but usurped by his uncle Valoroso XXIV, he is dismissed as a bit of a milksop, puling and crying for sugar plums. Intellectually, he is undoubtedly barren soil, but he proves to have a facility for sword-play and love-making. Though momentarily distracted by his cousin, PRINCESS ANGELICA, he is later reunited with his true love, PRINCESS ROSALBA.

Gikere
Ripples in the Pool, 1975
Rebeka Njau

SELINA's husband. A quiet, hardworking hospital assistant, he dreams of building a clinic in his home village. Criticized by his mother for marrying Selina, Gikere soon realizes that his wife is unwilling to help him. Weak and insecure, Gikere begins to drink heavily and destroys his relationship with Selina by beating her when she is pregnant.

Gikonyo
A Grain of Wheat, 1967
Ngugi wa Thiong'o

A revolutionary activist in the period before Kenyan independence, he is imprisoned by the authorities, an experience that nearly drives him insane and forces him to betray his comrades. When he is released, he discovers that his wife MUMBI is having a baby by his old rival KARANJA. After purging himself of guilt about his friends, he decides to accept the child as if it were his own.

Gilfil, Maynard
'Mr. Gilfil's Love-Story', in *Scenes of Clerical Life*, 1858
George Eliot

Respected by his parishioners as much for his dry-witted amiability as for his reassuringly repetitive sermons, Maynard Gilfil – the capricious old Vicar of Shepperton – harbours bittersweet memories of a past few would have dreamed possible for him. Experiencing, as a young man, all the pains and pleasures of unrequited love, he is finally rewarded for his unswerving loyalty and devotion to his childhood friend, CATERINA SARTI, with her hand in marriage. But his happiness is to be short-lived, snuffed out in a moment by her untimely death, wherein lies the key to the melancholic loneliness of his old-age.

Gilhaize, Ringan
Ringan Gilhaize, or The Covenanters, 1823
John Galt

As a young boy, Ringan has listened to his aged grandfather's first-hand tales of Cardinal Beaton, Mary Stuart and of the flashing fiery reflection in the Nor' Loch as Kirk o' Field blew up. In maturity he suffers grim persecution for his faith by the king's dragoons, clinging defiantly to Christ's covenanted Reformation. He describes the cruelty of the times and what he himself experiences in the loss of his wife and children, slaughtered by Claverhouse. Seized by a frenzy of despair, he vows vengeance and in the name of God kills Claverhouse in a kind of justified madness. He thus speaks vividly for three generations.

Gilian, the Dreamer
Gilian, the Dreamer, 1899
Neil Munro

A young boy with 'a timid and wandering eye', he is nice-looking, but a 'shy, frightened, dreamy child', who is considered odd in the village. He finds joy in books and nature, but is misunderstood and mocked, so that for a time 'his dreams, his fancies, his spectacles of the inner eye were things that he had grown ashamed of'. He fails to shine in practical matters, but his imagination flourishes. He falls in love with a local girl, but is bested by a dashing young man, and her broken promise to him is 'the herald of joy, the fool of illusion'.

Gillayley, Joe (Joseph)
The Bone People, 1983
Keri Hulme

Bereaved of his wife and baby son, and unable to cope with the special needs of his foster son SIMON P GILLAYLEY, Maori Joe's only outlet for his frustration and despair is in getting drunk and venting his anger on Simon. Caught between a desperate need for companionship and understanding and being too proud to ask for any real help, Joe can see no end to his problems and eventually takes his misguided love a step too far. But in subsequently finding inner peace in his previously neglected Maori customs and beliefs, the essential goodness and kindness of his nature re-emerge.

Gillayley, Simon P
The Bone People, 1983
Keri Hulme

Washed up on shore like a piece of jetsam, Simon, the opal-eyed autistic child at the heart of *The Bone People*, cannot help causing endless problems for his foster father JOE GILLAYLEY, and pays dearly for them. Unable to communicate in the normal manner, he compensates with increased sensitivity in other faculties and it is he who forges the link between Joe, KEREWIN HOLMES and himself, a bond he struggles indomitably to keep intact. Mischievous, but wise beyond his years, he offers only love and forgiveness – even in the face of physical violence – to those whom he strives to unite.

Gilligan, Joe
Soldier's Pay, 1926
William Faulkner

A demobbed soldier who comes to the aid of the appallingly wounded LT DONALD MAHON. He is awkward, unintelligent but genuinely kind. That he stays on at Mahon's side is partly due to humanity, but also to the fact that he has fallen in love with MARGARET POWERS, Mahon's other protector and eventual wife.

Gills, Solomon
Dombey and Son, 1848
Charles Dickens

A nautical instrument maker and proprietor of *The Wooden Midshipman*, he is the devoted uncle of WALTER GAY and old friend of CAPTAIN EDWARD CUTTLE, who becomes his partner. A 'slow, quiet-spoken, thoughtful old fellow' who is 'far from having a maritime appearance', he leaves Cuttle in charge of his shop and goes in search of Walter, presumed drowned in a shipwreck. Returning from abroad, he finds that Walter has reappeared and is to marry FLORENCE DOMBEY.

Gil-Martin
The Private Memoirs and Confessions of a Justified Sinner, 1824
James Hogg

The evil, satanic being who starts to haunt ROBERT WRINGHIM from the moment of his being assured that he is one of 'the elect'. Elusive and manipulative, Gil-Martin's chameleon-like ability to change his appearance to resemble others places him within the *doppelganger* tradition, but it remains deliberately inconclusive as to how far he should be identified as either a delusion or a manifestation of Wringhim's own disturbed consciousness.

Gilmore, Gary
The Executioner's Song, 1979
Norman Mailer

An historical murderer, executed by firing squad in Utah in 1978 at his own insistence. He is

presented by Mailer without his notoriously romantic glorification of criminality, but with a clear-sighted awareness both of his psychopathology and of the society which shaped him but failed adequately to provide him with a role.

Gilmore, Harry
The Vicar of Bullhampton, 1870
Anthony Trollope

The young squire of the Wiltshire parish of Bullhampton, who shoots, fishes and (having gone to Harrow and Oxford) sometimes reads. Liberal in his politics, generous, honest and good-looking, he has a high opinion of his own qualities. His life is disrupted by his passionate desire to marry MARY LOWTHER, who does not return his love.

Gimble, Peter
Saturdee, 1933
Norman Lindsay

A twelve-year-old scapegrace in the 19th-century town of Redheap, he leads a gang – Conkey Menders, Bullyo Peddlar, and Bufflehead – whose imaginative exploits constitute a rough-and-ready moral education, the only kind they are likely to receive in that environment.

Gimpel
'Gimpel the Fool', in *Gimpel the Fool*, 1957
Isaac Bashevis Singer

A baker who appears totally gullible and naive, even to the point of marrying a woman who sleeps with other men. A constant source of amusement in his village, Gimpel is exasperating in his acceptance of events. But his optimism, quiet faith and generous nature are admirable. His refusal to become like his companions, which he knows would be to court evil, is rewarded with kindness and peace of mind.

Gioconda
The Bay of Noon, 1970
Shirley Hazzard

A beautiful Italian novelist, who provides JENNY with the imaginative self-confidence to step outside the restrictive ties of family life and the limits ironically imposed by endless travel. She represents emotional self-possession.

Giovanelli, Mr
Daisy Miller: A Study, 1878, dramatized 1883
Henry James

When he first meets his rival for DAISY MILLER's attention, FREDERICK WINTERBOURNE regrets that she is not able to tell a 'spurious gentleman' from a real one. Giovanelli is all oleaginous charm and carefully practised English ('he had practised the idiom upon a great many American heiresses'), but with an unexpected dignity and sense of honour underneath.

Giovanni
Giovanni's Room, 1956
James Baldwin

The gay lover of the young American DAVID, he is no more clearly realized than any of Henry James's faintly exotic Europeans, as Baldwin himself recognized. Like those characters, he is catapulted into tragedy as much by the rather schematic nature of his presence in the novel as by any more profound moral or artistic necessity.

Giovanni
'Tis Pity She's a Whore, c.1631
John Ford
The son of a wealthy merchant, Giovanni is not so much an angry young man searching for a way to defy society, as some have suggested, as a vulnerable young scholar wondering how to maintain his aesthetic and moral convictions within a corrupt nation-state. He is an intelligent and discriminating man, albeit one that puts his own values above those of others, and in pursuing his love for his sister, ANNABELLA, he deliberately contravenes social and moral ethics. In consummating their love, though, he is swept along by force of fate rather than physical lust. His youth makes him compulsive and petulant, and his final act before his own death is to kill the one he loves, appearing at a banquet celebrating the wedding of Annabella and SORANZO brandishing his sister's still-bleeding heart on his dagger.

'Girl, the'
The Magus, 1966, revised edition 1977
John Fowles
More of an idea than a real person, she is an embodiment of femininity, the collective 'girl' being a muse for the mind of her wealthy 'employer' MAURICE CONCHIS. Ghostly, fragile, pale and ethereal, she is intelligent in the present but has no concept of her past. The world of nymphs, mermaids and muses combines in forming this creature into a being from Conchis's past. The question remains: is she simply a figment of his imagination?

Gismond, Count
'Count Gismond', in *Dramatic Romances*, 1845
Robert Browning
Gismond is the husband of the narrator, who is telling her friend Adela how he championed her when her honour was at stake. He slew the man who accused her of abusing her office of May Queen and married her. But when this 'Knight in shining armour' approaches she lies to him about the nature of the conversation, casting some doubts on her honesty.

Gitano
The Red Pony, 1937
John Steinbeck
An enigmatic paisano who befriends young JODY and introduces him to a darker, more brooding side of life in which life and death are not opposites but complementary forces.

Glace, Ed
Scented Gardens for the Blind, 1963
Janet Frame
Glace (or 'glass'?) is obsessed with the way language reflects unwelcome truths about personality and human nature. Researching the origins of names, he becomes convinced that people are merely bundles of linguistic information, loosely wrapped together by convention and by a polite fiction.

Gladney, Jack
White Noise, 1985
Don DeLillo
Chairman and head of Hitler Studies at the College-on-the-Hill, Blacksmith. Married, second time around, to the capable Babette, he is haunted by the toxic threat of a huge chemical spill and by his family's increasingly death-obsessed behaviour.

Glanvil
'The Scholar Gypsy', in *Poems: A New Edition*, 1853
Matthew Arnold
An impoverished but gifted Oxford scholar 'Who, tired of knocking at preferment's door,/ One summer morn forsook/His friends, and went to learn the gypsy-lore,/And roam'd the world with that wild brotherhood,/And came, as most men deem'd, to little good.'

Glascock, Charles, later Lord Peterborough
He Knew He Was Right, 1869
Anthony Trollope
A rather priggish, wealthy aristocrat, he is heir to the title of Lord Peterborough, which he eventually assumes. He is a suitor for the hand of NORA ROWLEY, but his position and wealth are not enough to overcome her love for his rival, HUGH STANSBURY. He rallies from this disappointment to marry a young American, CAROLINE SPALDING.

Glass, Buddy
'A Perfect Day for Bananafish', in *For Esmé – with Love and Squalor*, 1953
'Raise High the Roof Beam, Carpenters', 1955
'Seymour: An Introduction', 1959
J D Salinger
The second eldest of the unusual Glass progeny, the son of vaudevillians Les and Bessie and brother of SEYMOUR, ZOOEY and FRANNY GLASS. A tall young man when we first meet him, in whom some have seen autobiographical elements of Salinger, he is an aspiring author for whom writing is less a profession than a religion. Sensitive, intelligent and acutely perceptive, he shares an almost spiritual closeness with Seymour, whose death shadows the rest of his life.

Glass, Franny
Franny and Zooey, 1961
J D Salinger
An attractive 20-year-old with a gift for acting. The youngest of the eccentric but intellectually brilliant Glass family, she finds the apparently shallow materialism of modern life soul-destroying. Angry at the mediocrity and arrogance of her university lecturers and class-mates, demoralized by the ordinariness and greed of life, she hovers on the brink of nervous collapse, chain-smoking, weeping and refusing food. Only the astringent, astute intervention of her brother ZOOEY GLASS brings her to a more balanced appreciation of the world and an understanding of the need to strive for artistic perfection, no matter what the circumstances.

Glass, Isobel
The Secret Rapture, 1988
David Hare
Isobel Glass and her sister, MARION FRENCH, are

reunited after their father, an antiquarian bookseller, dies at his home in the country. In her early thirties, Isobel is a partner in a small design studio, has nursed her father through his last days and, according to Marion, 'can't resist being kind about people'. For Isobel, 'the great thing is to love. If you're loved back, that's a bonus.' A principled, good woman, her actions are sometimes interpreted by others as reproach or even a mute humiliation.

Glass, Robin Redbreast
The Infinite Rehearsal, 1987
Wilson Harris

The narrator – or perhaps *répétiteur* – of a fictional autobiography in which his character is never fully incarnated. He claims to be an adversary of Wilson Harris, 'but we share one thing in common, namely, an approach to the ruling concepts of civilization from the other side, from the rule or apparently eclipsed side of humanity'.

Glass, Seymour
'A Perfect Day for Bananafish', in *For Esmé – with Love and Squalor*, 1953
'Raise High the Roof Beam, Carpenters', 1955
'Seymour: An Introduction', 1959
J D Salinger

A child prodigy, star turn of the radio programme 'It's a Wise Child', and descended from 'an astonishingly long and motley double-file of professional entertainers', he goes to university at the age of 15, and becomes an English professor in his early twenties. The eldest of the Glass children, he describes himself as 'a kind of paranoic in reverse. I suspect people of plotting to make me happy.' Tall, with curly dark hair and an overly-prominent squint nose, he is an unusually sensitive, loving young man, who marries a woman clearly not his equal, emotionally or intellectually. Permanently fractured by the experience of war, he commits suicide at the age of 31. His death leaves permanent scars on his brothers BUDDY and ZOOEY, and his sister FRANNY GLASS; echoes of his personality continue to influence their lives.

Glass, Zooey
Franny and Zooey, 1961
J D Salinger

A slight, highly-strung, exceptionally bright 25-year-old, second youngest of the Glass family, who still harbours resentment over the attitudes imposed on him through childhood by his older brothers SEYMOUR and BUDDY GLASS. A talented actor who is making a name for himself, he is something of a loner, intensely dismissive of those whose intellect he does not rate, yet dominated by an awareness of the spiritual core of life. He has a particular affinity with his younger sister, FRANNY GLASS, whose vulnerability echoes some of his own experience.

Glaucé
The Faerie Queene, 1590–6
Sir Edmund Spenser

BRITOMART's caring, aged nurse. She has brought up Britomart since childhood and is deeply concerned for her well-being. She is an affectionate busybody, a comforter who is both wise and motherly. She understands sweet sighs and passions, yet does not understand Britomart's obsessive spirituality, for in her day it was youthful lust that drove individuals to distraction.

Glegg, Mrs
The Mill on the Floss, 1860
George Eliot

The oldest of the four Dodson sisters, Mrs Glegg never tires of upbraiding her sister MRS BESSY TULLIVER for her ill-judged marriage to MR TULLIVER, and her critical, quarrelsome nature riles not only the unfortunate Mr Tulliver but also her own husband, Mr Glegg. Domineering, tight-fisted and full of her own self-importance, it is nevertheless she, in her belief that one must stick by one's own kin, who emerges as an unexpected ally to MAGGIE TULLIVER, stoutly defending her niece's honour in the face of inconclusive evidence to the contrary.

Glendinning, Edward → Ambrose, Father

Glendinning, Mrs Mary
Pierre, 1852
Herman Melville

The mother of PIERRE GLENDINNING. She is an 'affluent and haughty widow' of 50, with a 'fine mind of medium culture' and a freedom from 'sordid cares'. She has retained her youthful beauty, and can still eclipse 'far younger charms'. Pierre often calls her 'sister Mary'. She is proud and righteous, leading to her estrangement from Pierre when he cannot reveal the true identity of ISABEL BANFORD (and thus his father's lapse from grace).

Glendinning, Pierre
Pierre, 1852
Herman Melville

A strong and athletic youth just emerging from his teens, 'well-developed in person and manners'. He is of good family and privileged upbringing, and is devoted to his mother, MRS MARY GLENDINNING, and his late father's memory, but longs for a sister. He is well-read, and a confirmed Christian with a strong sense of right and duty. He is engaged to LUCY TARTAN, but breaks this off when he discovers the true identity of ISABEL BANFORD. The consequent estrangement has tragic results for all, and he dies 'the fool of Truth, the fool of Virtue, the fool of Fate'.

Glendinning, Simon
The Monastery, 1820
Sir Walter Scott

The father of SIR HALBERT GLENDINNING and FATHER AMBROSE. The first lord of the Tower of Glendearg, he is one of those men who in happier times might have been content to remain in his castle and devote himself to his estate, but who is forced to take up arms in defence of land and liturgy, and dies for both at the battle of Pinkie-Cleugh.

Glendinning, Sir Halbert, later the Knight of Avenel
The Monastery, 1820
The Abbot, 1820
Sir Walter Scott

A sterner and more warlike child than his brother Edward (FATHER AMBROSE). He has 'hair as dark as the raven's plumage, black eyes, large, bold and sparkling, that glittered under eyebrows of the same complexion'. These same brows are lined and careworn in the sequel, when he is the husband of MARY AVENEL, but there is a stillness and calm about him to compensate for the passing of his turbulent youth.

Glendower, Owen
Henry IV Part I, 1596/7
William Shakespeare

The Welsh leader who joins the rebellion against HENRY IV, Glendower shows touches of Celtic mysticism, as well as a fondness for poetry and music. However, he is boastful, arrogant and easily angered, especially by HOTSPUR, who shows him none of the respect he believes he warrants. In spite of his promises, Glendower fails to turn up for the battle of Shrewsbury, thereby weakening the rebels sufficiently to bring about their defeat.

Gloriana
The Faerie Queene, 1590–6
Sir Edmund Spenser

Also known as TANAQUILL, she is the reigning Faerie Queene of the title. She is explicitly identified with Queen Elizabeth I, and her name, which means 'the glorious one', refers to her great power. She is the most honourable, virtuous, modest, wise and regal of all the characters who appear in the book, and all knights are in her service.

Glorvina, Lady
The Wild Irish Girl, 1806
Lady Morgan

She is a princess by birth, and 'like nothing on the face of God's creation but herself'. She is not so much wild as polite, patrician and diplomatic. She plays the harp and sings, is studious, hard-working, and something of a pedant when it comes to Ireland and its history. She is humane and tender-hearted, and is said to have healing powers, and to be a 'saint upon earth'. Her simple, artless looks belie her elegant manners.

Glossin, Gilbert, later briefly Laird of Ellangowan
Guy Mannering, 1816
Sir Walter Scott

Rascally factor of the Ellangowan estate, he engineers the kidnap of the heir HARRY BERTRAM, knowing that the title and land will fall cheaply, given the present laird's debts and obligations. Rather a cardboard villain, he is useful in setting the plot in motion.

Gloucester, Earl of
King Lear, c.1607
William Shakespeare

The father of two sons, and a loyal follower of KING LEAR, Gloucester is both coarse and rather foolish, but is also a well-meaning man and an affectionate and fair father – loving, he says, both his sons equally. He is naive and trusting in his dealings with EDMUND, his younger and illegitimate son, and proves himself to be compassionate in his attempts to help Lear at great risk to himself. Brutally blinded by the DUKE OF CORNWALL, betrayed by one son and estranged from the other, he at first becomes bitter and desperate, but eventually comes to accept, with fortitude and endurance, whatever the world has to offer him.

Glover, Barbara
A Dutiful Daughter, 1971
Thomas Keneally

Part fertility goddess, part sexual demon, she seems to come out of primitive religion and myth rather than from the pages of a modern novel. At the time of her menarche, her parents are transformed from the waist down into cattle. She is also incestuously involved with her brother DAMIAN GLOVER, and with a lover called Frederic (who may also be a projection of her brother).

Glover, Catharine
The Fair Maid of Perth, or St Valentine's Day, in *Chronicles of the Canongate: Second Series*, 1828
Sir Walter Scott

The Fair Maid of the title, she is esteemed the most beautiful girl in the royal city. Like any woman largely defined by good looks and compliance, she lacks colour. For St Valentine's Day, she chooses the blacksmith HENRY SMITH, which at least promises sensible cross-breeding of virtues.

Glover, Damian
A Dutiful Daughter, 1971
Thomas Keneally

The brother of BARBARA GLOVER and apparently also her lover, a relationship that has complicated his affair with Helen, a girl from the nearby town. It is not clear whether or not Damian (who carries a hint of demonism in his name) is also the 'Frederic' with whom Barbara makes love.

Glover, Simon
The Fair Maid of Perth, or St Valentine's Day, in *Chronicles of the Canongate: Second Series*, 1828
Sir Walter Scott

CATHARINE GLOVER's indulgent father, he is one of the senior citizens of Perth, combining affection with a querulous, Polonian rhetoric and a tendency to the mawkish. His surname is derived from his trade.

Glowry, Scythrop
Nightmare Abbey, 1818
Thomas Love Peacock

Disappointed in love, youthful philosopher Scythrop (based on Shelley) lounges around a gloomy tower in his father's abbey home reading romances and German tragedies. Prone to emotional extremes and to fashionable postures, his flighty mind turns to a sulky, self-indulgent melancholy, which is nurtured by the doom-and-gloom philosophers around him. Petulant, spoilt, huffy and torn between the love of two women, his predilection for melodrama and mystery tilt him towards the ridiculous.

Glumdalclitch
Gulliver's Travels, 1726
Jonathan Swift

A young female member of the BROBDINGNAGIANS who, fearing for LEMUEL GULLIVER's safety, takes care of him and treats him like a very precious plaything. Gentle and affectionate, she stands by her principles. She carries Gulliver about in a specially built box, teaches him the language and has a tendency to be overprotective.

Glyde, Sir Percival
The Woman in White, 1860
Wilkie Collins

A high-spirited, balding man of about 45 with a red scar across his right hand, he appears to be the most respected and gallant of gentlemen. Refined, tactful and considerate, his true nature is only revealed after his mercenary marriage to LAURA FAIRLIE. A merciless, ill-tempered bully with a mania for order, his claim to a baronetcy is as phony as his previous displays of good breeding and it is only his severe financial embarrassment that has prompted his lucrative union with Laura and the evil machinations that follow.

Goat-Boy, (George) Giles
Giles Goat-Boy, 1966
John Barth

A mythical creation within the novel's allegorical-parodic structure. He is the son by immaculate conception of WESCAC, a university computer, and Virginia Hector, daughter of the president of the university (which is also the universe). He completes the mythical ascent from the animal (his idyllic early life in the goat barn) to the human (he rises to be powerful grand-tutor of West Campus), and on to the heroic, as a modern-day Oedipus-cum-Christ figure whose purpose in living is usurped by his doctrine ('Gilesianism'). He must be driven out to die alone, so that his life-story, *The Revised New Syllabus*, can achieve the status of sacred text.

Gobble, Justice
The Life and Adventures of Sir Launcelot Greaves, 1760–1
Tobias Smollett

A preposterous magistrate, who has turned a haphazard and makeshift legal education into a source of advantage for himself and his equally unpleasant wife. His rule is as cruel as it is partial and inconsistent, and always motivated by personal gain. He also appears briefly in *Roderick Random* as a lovesick squire.

Gobbo, Launcelot
The Merchant of Venice, 1594/5
William Shakespeare

SHYLOCK's servant who, in the course of the play, runs from his master to go into service for BASSANIO. His slapstick comedy with his blind father and the rambling nonsense of his conversations with Shylock disguise a decent, witty and loyal young man, as testified by his

tearful parting from JESSICA and his barbed comments about his Jewish master.

God
The Adventures of God in His Search for the Black Girl, 1973
Brigid Brophy

If Brophy has long been concerned with justifying the ways of (wo)man to God, the deity here is more than content to accept his destiny as a fictitious extrapolation of our needs, doubts and fears. His aerially broadcast 'Godifesto' slowly flutters down over Rome like a thousand ragged paracletes, descending to peck up the crumbs man has left.

God
Paradise Lost, 1667
John Milton

His first words contain the recognition that all Creation is governed by free will and that the rebel angels are authors of their own tragic fall. Omniscient, 'High Thron'd above all highth' and surrounded by the 'Sanctities of Heaven ... thick as stars', he is nonetheless prone to irascibility, a sharp contrast to the overflowing love expressed by his only son.

Godbold, Ruth
Riders in the Chariot, 1961
Patrick White

One of the novel's four protagonists (the others being ALF DUBBO, MARY HARE and MORDECAI HIMMELFARB), Mrs Godbold arrived in Sydney from the fenlands of England many years previously. She now supports a large family and a violent, alcoholic husband by taking in washing. Somewhat hapless, but emotionally resilient, even saintly, Mrs Godbold has a limitless capacity for human love and warmth, once even retrieving her husband from a brothel. Pragmatic and stoical, she carries with her an air of simple human compassion, and befriends the ageing fellow immigrant, Mordecai Himmelfarb. Later, a widowed grandmother, she testifies to the majesty and power of a divine order.

Godbole, Professor Narayan
A Passage to India, 1924
E M Forster

An elderly Brahman with a grey moustache and a complexion 'as fair as a European's', he is an enigmatic Hindu poet and philosopher. Polite, attentive and courteous, he spends much of his time fussily consuming food and smiling benevolently at the world, offering offence to no one but refusing to be drawn on any matter of heated debate or general concern. Liked and respected by all, he remains as unfathomable as a bottomless pool.

Godden, Joanna
Joanna Godden, 1921
Sheila Kaye Smith

Stubborn and outspoken, Joanna runs the farm she has inherited on Romney and Walland marshes in spite of local criticism. She makes bad mistakes but will not be defeated, disregarding convention, comfortable in her simple religious beliefs, cheerfully loud in her clothes, 'a damn fine woman'. One lover dies, another proves too cheap and vulgar, but Joanna is not daunted; cherishing memories of the first and about to bear the child of the second, she confronts a new life in a new place with optimistic courage: 'the past and the future were still hers'.

Goëmagot or Gogmagot
The Faerie Queene, 1590–6
Sir Edmund Spenser

A fierce mythological giant who is slain by the great warrior Corineus and is thrown from the clifftops at Hoe. He was a general of Bute, the legendary first King of Britain. A vile creature, Goëmagot destroyed many warriors, fed upon their living flesh and 'drank mens vitall blood'.

Goering, Christina
Two Serious Ladies, 1943
Jane Bowles

A woman of wealth and privilege whose character is marked by religious fanaticism from an early age. In pursuit of 'sainthood' she allows her circumstances and relationships to be determined by chance despite her domineering personality; her personal creed of salvation involves the wilful embrace of social decline and so she renounces the comforts of property and allows herself to slip into the world of prostitution.

Goesler, Marie
Phineas Finn, The Irish Member, 1869
The Eustace Diamonds, 1873
Phineas Redux, 1874
The Prime Minister, 1876
The Duke's Children, 1880
Anthony Trollope

The widow of a Viennese banker, she has been left rich by her husband's death. She is a shrewd, intelligent woman of 'something over thirty years of age', who has considerable political influence, and is astute in her use of it. She has thick, black hair which disguises 'a certain thinness in her cheeks', and bright, dark blue eyes which 'seemed to intend that you should know that she employed them to conquer you, looking as a knight may have looked in olden days who entered a chamber with his sword drawn from the scabbard and in his hand'. She eventually marries PHINEAS FINN.

Goffe, William
'The Grey Champion', 1835, in *Twice-Told Tales*, 1837, revised edition 1842
Nathaniel Hawthorne

Never named as such, the mysterious 'Grey Champion' appears to be the Puritan regicide Judge Goffe, who fled to America at the Restoration. In Hawthorne's version of him, 'he wore the old Puritan dress, a dark cloak and a steeple-crowned hat, in the fashion of at least 50 years before, with a heavy sword upon his thigh, but a staff in his hand to assist the tremulous gait of age'.

Goldberg, Nat
The Birthday Party, 1958
Harold Pinter

A man in his fifties, he has reached a 'position' in the 'organisation'; with DERMOT MCCANN, he arrives at the BOLES's home, apparently to revenge himself on STANLEY WEBBER. His sentimental tales of a stereotypical Jewish upbringing, his seduction of MEG BOLES's blowsy young friend Lulu, and the implicit violence of his language and actions, make him a figure of sinister foreboding.

Goldfinger, Auric
Goldfinger, 1959
Ian Fleming

The most complex of JAMES BOND's adversaries. A British Jew, flame-haired, obsessively sunburnt, but violently agoraphobic, he carries a Nassau passport and underneath a front of respectability – a house at Reculver, membership of Blades and the Royal St Marks golf club at Sandwich – pours millions of dollars in bullion into the Soviet terror network SMERSH.

Goldweiser, Harry
Manhattan Transfer, 1925
John Dos Passos

Overweight, middle-aged and wealthy, 'gold teeth glittering in the sides of his mouth', Harry Goldweiser is a well-known theatrical stage-manager, responsible for ELLEN THATCHER and CASSANDRA WILKINS. He is infatuated with Ellen and employs his considerable gamut of rhetorical charms in promising to advance her career and shower riches upon her if she will agree to sleep with him.

Golightly, Holly
Breakfast at Tiffany's, 1958
Truman Capote

Her name suggests the independent, uninhibited, freewheeling nature of her character, but this fey, light-hearted, amoral young playgirl has an interesting past and 'a face beyond childhood, yet this side of belonging to a woman'. Although only 19, she made a mysterious transition from wife of an older veterinarian in Texas to New York high society, and disappears just as enigmatically to Brazil, leaving only her vivid, appealing memory.

Gollum
The Hobbit, 1937
The Lord of the Rings, 3 volumes, 1954–5
J R R Tolkien

A 'small slimy creature' who lives under the mountains, paddling his boat silently across the underground lake where he lives. He is 'as dark as darkness, except for two big round pale eyes in his thin face', and he talks disconcertingly to himself to ward off loneliness. Once a creature of the outside world, where he was called Smeagol, he became obsessed with a magical ring ('my precioussss') and, having killed to obtain it, has spent the rest of his life below ground. A pathetic, sly creation, he forges an uneasy relationship with BILBO BAGGINS and, later, with FRODO BAGGINS and SAM GAMGEE. Utterly untrustworthy, he nevertheless inspires a certain degree of pity.

Gondarino
The Woman Hater, 1605
Francis Beaumont, with some dialogue by John
Fletcher
An old soldier and the misogynist of the title,
Gondarino is so angered by the bawdy, frivolous
ORIANA that he has her incarcerated in a bordello
and invites the DUKE OF MILLAINE and the Count
Valore to witness her licentiousness for
themselves. Irascible, irrational, dyspeptic,
slanderous and especially sensitive to untoward
commotion, Gondarino cuts a perverse, comic
figure, railing against women in particular and
the world in general.

Goneril
King Lear, c.1607
William Shakespeare
KING LEAR's eldest daughter, who inherits half his
kingdom through flattery and guile, by pandering
to her father's vanity and pride. Driven by ruthless
ambition and selfish desire, she is both unnatural
and cruel in her treatment of her elderly father.
Callously calculating, she even poisons her own
sister REGAN in an attempt to secure the affections
of EDMUND. She is stabbed to death at the end of
play, possibly by Regan, but it might be suicide.

Gonzalo
The Tempest, 1611
William Shakespeare
An elderly councillor to the Duke of Naples,
Gonzalo had helped PROSPERO after his
overthrow. He behaves with courage and dignity
when the tempest threatens his life, and remains
optimistic, unlike the other survivors,
appreciating the wonders of the island they land
on rather than fearing them. His experience of life
has made him reasonably perceptive, and he
realizes that outward appearance and inner nature
are not necessarily connected; he fails, though, to
see the danger aimed at him. His ideas as to how he
would rule the island are Utopian and impractical.

Goodson, Barclay
The Man That Corrupted Hadleyburg, 1899
Mark Twain
The only truly honest and incorruptible man in
Hadleyburg, Mr Goodson falls victim to the
town's vindictiveness because he is too
contemptuous to defend himself. He fends off an
envoy from the town's Committee of Inquiry
with: 'Very well, then, tell them to go to hell – I
reckon that's general enough. And I'll give you
some advice, Sawlberry; when you come back for
the particulars, fetch a basket to carry the relics of
yourself home in.'

Goodwin, Lee
Sanctuary, 1931
William Faulkner
A member of POPEYE's bootlegging gang, he is
falsely accused of the rape of TEMPLE DRAKE, and
eventually hanged for the offence, largely as a
result of Temple's perjured testimony.

Goodwin, Morton
The Circuit Rider, 1874
Edward Eggleston
A young Methodist preacher (like his author), his

calling is a direct result of unhappiness in love; his
'circuit' along the advancing American frontier can
only be likened to conscription in the Foreign
Legion.

Goodwood, Casper
The Portrait of a Lady, 1881
Henry James
The most dogged and loyal of ISABEL ARCHER's
suitors, he is a self-made American of resolutely
independent beliefs, entirely devoid of artifice
or deceit.

Goole, Inspector
An Inspector Calls, 1947
J B Priestley
Shrouded in mystery, he is the typical, upright
policeman, commanding and artificially polite. At
times his role is that of the moral conscience of the
family he visits; hard on the family in a 'cruel to be
kind' manner, he acts as a catalyst, prompting self-
appraisal. The frightening aspect of his character
is his phenomenal knowledge of situations of
which he has been no part. He is never revealed
as an individual and we learn little of his own life.

Goosetrap, Melinda
The Adventures of Roderick Random, 1748
Tobias Smollett
A notorious coquette who fulfils the warning in
her surname by luring RODERICK RANDOM into
the circle of her admirers. Though wealthy, she is
of a 'cold, insensible disposition, dead to every
passion but vanity'.

Gorboduc
Gorboduc, 1561
Thomas Norton and Thomas Sackville
King of a mythical Britain, he is primarily a
morality figure who stands for the unity of the
commonwealth; when he is killed the
commonwealth falls into anarchy. Reaching old
age, Gorboduc worries about succession to the
throne, and takes advice from three counsellors.
He acts unwisely and decides to divide his realm
between his sons FERREX and PORREX. They fall
into dissension; Porrex kills Ferrex, and civil war
and anarchy break out. Gorboduc, by abnegating
responsibility and acting rashly and 'unnaturally',
releases destructive forces upon his life, his
family and his kingdom.

Gordeloup, Sophie
The Claverings, 1867
Anthony Trollope
The sister of COUNT EDOUARD PATEROFF, and
accomplice in their unsuccessful attempt to
convince JULIA BRABAZON that her late husband
wished her to remarry the count. She is a 'little,
dry, bright woman' of 50, with 'quick eyes, and
thin lips, and small nose, and mean forehead,
and scanty hair drawn back quite tightly from
her face and head'. She attaches herself in
parasitical fashion to Julia, hoping to indulge
her taste for good things through Julia's wealth.

Gordon
Mosquitoes, 1927
William Faulkner
A moody but gifted young sculptor, patronized

by MRS PATRICIA MAURIER, who makes a special exception for his dark beard and proletarian dishabille on the grounds that they represent the outward signs of genius at work.

Gordon, Lord George
Barnaby Rudge, 1841
Charles Dickens
Based on a real person, the youngest son of the third Duke of Gordon, and a fanatical Protestant who was the chief instigator of the violent Gordon Riots (1780). The novel depicts the riots and reports his subsequent career: his arrest for treason and then acquittal; his conversion to Judaism; his arrest for libelling the Queen of France and his death in Newgate Prison.

Gordon, Stephen
The Well of Loneliness, 1928
Radclyffe Hall
A lesbian who would have been happy if she had been a boy, for she was born into the landed gentry with the build and looks of an athletic male and given a masculine name. She passionately follows the pursuits of a country gentleman and displays a deep love for animals. When she falls in love with a local woman, she takes the male role, but the affair finishes and she is banished from her beloved countryside. Exiled in Paris she finds solace in writing and a sympathetic homosexual milieu, but sadly believes she can never be a 'true husband'.

Goring, Lord Arthur
An Ideal Husband, 1895
Oscar Wilde
The best friend of SIR ROBERT CHILTERN, and considered by some as 'the idlest man in London', Lord Goring is in many respects a portrait of Wilde himself. A bachelor, he is 34 ('but always says he is younger'), and appears to be merely a social butterfly given to delivering witty epigrams on literature, politics, fashion and society: 'Other people are quite dreadful. The only possible society is oneself.' Vigorously avoiding his father's attempts to pressurize him into marriage, he is nonetheless intelligent, incisive and wise. A compassionate and reliable friend, he is a good ally and a formidable foe. Being misunderstood as shallow, he reasons, 'gives him a post of vantage'.

Gorman, Marcus
Legs, 1975
William Kennedy
The novel's narrator, he plays NICK CARRAWAY to LEGS DIAMOND's JAY GATSBY. His memories of the gangster's inexorable rise are recorded in prose that seems objective enough, but Marcus is obviously in thrall to Diamond's myth. He is not an unreliable observer, but he gives away more than he realizes.

Gormann, Theo
The Sweets of Pimlico, 1977
A N Wilson
'A stout old man, with a puce complexion, and a white beard', as he first appears to EVELYN TRADESCANT in Kensington Gardens, scattering unposted letters before him in the wind, he

becomes a more mysterious, even threatening, figure. Apparently aristocratic, he seems to have worked as a drama critic and, despite his pacifism, to have been a friend of Goebbels.

Gostrey, Maria
The Ambassadors, 1903
Henry James
A quiet, middle-aged woman, one of life's observers, she seems to LAMBERT STRETHER to be 'the mistress of a hundred cases or categories, receptacles of the mind, subdivisions for convenience, in which, from a full experience, she pigeon-holed her fellow mortals with a hand as free as a compositor scattering type'.

Gotham, Harvey
The Only Problem, 1984
Muriel Spark
A rich, intelligent and cold Canadian, who displays 'perhaps a bit too much moral judgment'. Having left his wife on moral grounds, he is writing a monograph on the Book of Job, which he believes contains the 'only problem': why a good and omnipotent God permits and perhaps causes suffering. He adopts an ascetic life in a French cottage, but despairs when interruptions from outside disrupt his work. He is told by a comforter that he has experienced only distress, not actual suffering.

Gotobed, Elias
The American Senator, 1883
Anthony Trollope
Although he is the American senator of the title, he remains a background figure for most of the novel. He has travelled to England to study the manners and way of life of the English, and delivers his amusing conclusions in a public lecture which so infuriates his listeners that police are obliged to rescue him from injury.

Gough, Sally
The Roaring Nineties, 1946
Golden Miles, 1948
Winged Seeds, 1950
Katharine Susannah Prichard
Strong, compassionate and hardworking, Sally is the central character of the 'goldfields' trilogy. Uncomplaining, loyal and loving, but independent and assertive, she is a survivor: 'I am the daughter of a pioneer... and not ashamed to work: do whatever is necessary to earn a living'.

Gould, Bobby
Speed-the-Plow, 1975
David Mamet
A former mail-room worker in a film company, who has hustled his way to the top to become chief of production, Gould is far more concerned with winning psychological power battles than in making films, and in making films that sell rather than films of merit. Hugely confident, abrasive and jealous, he ostentatiously refers to himself as a whore. He is interested in nothing except the commercially viable. This applies even to his friendships and his love affairs. He plans to seduce his temporary secretary, but Karen has noticed what few others have: that Gould is an embittered idealist.

Instead of submitting to him, she presents him with his redemption: a book that might make a quality film. Gould finally admits that his professional and emotional life has largely been wasted.

Gould, Charles
Nostromo, 1904
Joseph Conrad

An Englishman who inherits the disused San Tome silver mine from his father. He sets out with an obsessive determination to make a success of it, and is not afraid to enter 'the mire of corruption' in order to do so. The early idealism he shares with his young wife, EMILIA GOULD, gives way to unsullied materialism, and he becomes the slave of the mine, steadily distanced from his wife, and from all human sympathies in the process. The other cost of his hard-won success is that he will be the last of the Goulds, since he and Emilia are childless, and the mine which has defined his life will pass into other hands.

Gould, Emilia
Nostromo, 1904
Joseph Conrad

The wife of the owner of the San Tome mine, CHARLES GOULD, and the 'only Englishwoman in Sulaco'. She was orphaned and brought up by a widowed aunt in Italy, and has retained a cosmopolitan sophistication and social command. She embarks on both marriage and running the mine with an idealistic 'air of adventure, of combat – a subtle thought of redress and conquest', but her life is slowly ruined by Charles's subjugation to the mine, 'as if the inspiration of her early years had left her heart to turn into a wall of silver bricks' amid the 'degradation of her young ideal of life'.

Gourlay, John
The House with the Green Shutters, 1901
George Douglas Brown

A wealthy but arrogant and mean-spirited businessman who has risen from humble origins to a position of influence in the town of Barbie, but has made many enemies, including his son, JOHN GOURLAY, JUNIOR. He is self-willed, excessively proud, tyrannical, unbending and intransigent, and is unable to adapt to change to save himself from ruin or from a final dramatic confrontation with his enraged son.

Gourlay, John, junior
The House with the Green Shutters, 1901
George Douglas Brown

The weak-willed, ineffectual, but nonetheless sensitive and intelligent son of JOHN GOURLAY. He has been brought up under his father's malign influence, partly spoiled and partly scorned, and further warped by the claustrophobic, narrow-minded attitudes of his home town.

Gow, Henry → Smith, Henry

Gowan, Henry
Little Dorrit, 1857
Charles Dickens

A dilettante artist who marries MINNIE MEAGLES against the wishes of MR and MRS MEAGLES. He treats his rival in love, ARTHUR CLENNAM, with disdain. With his equally snobbish mother, Mrs Gowan, distantly related to THE BARNACLES, he patronizes the Meagles but lives off their money because he is unsuccessful as a painter. Prior to his marriage, he had a relationship with MISS WADE but discarded her.

Gower → Fluellen; Gower; Jamy; Macmorris

Gowrie, Crawford
Intruder in the Dust, 1948
William Faulkner

A member of a violent family of Southern Montagnards, he is responsible for the death of his brother (from whom he has been stealing lumber) and for casting suspicion on the old black sharecropper LUCAS BEAUCHAMP. Brought to justice for the killing, he commits suicide in jail.

Grace, also known as Gigi
Paradise, 1997
Toni Morrison

Feisty, extrovert and uninhibited, Gigi remains with CONSOLATA at the Convent despite her frequently expressed desire for 'making tracks'. A strikingly attractive woman, her brashness hides her secret romantic idealism. Although outwardly confident, she lacks true commitment and realizes that 'she had not approved of herself in a long, long time'.

Grace-be-here, Corporal → Humgudgeon

Gradgrind, Louisa
Hard Times, 1854
Charles Dickens

The eldest daughter of THOMAS GRADGRIND, and later wife of JOSIAH BOUNDERBY. A pretty girl, she has assumed 'an air of jaded sullenness' as a consequence of her father's Utilitarian upbringing, but is suffused by 'a light with nothing to rest upon, a fire with nothing to burn, a starved imagination keeping life in itself somehow'. She sacrifices herself in an unhappy marriage to Bounderby to please her father and advance her brother TOM GRADGRIND's career. To escape her incompatible marriage and JAMES HARTHOUSE's proposal to elope with him, she returns to her father's house and, with the help of SISSY JUPE, finds reserves of courage and dignity in adversity.

Gradgrind, Thomas
Hard Times, 1854
Charles Dickens

A wealthy retired hardware merchant and MP for Coketown, he is a Utilitarian and the patron of a model school which teaches only facts and roots out all imagination and emotion. Inculcated with the same practical doctrines, his wife has become an invalid, his eldest son, TOM GRADGRIND, becomes a wastrel and a thief, and his devoted eldest daughter, LOUISA GRADGRIND, makes a loveless marriage, with disastrous results. Forced to admit that his own convictions have led to the misfortunes of his children, he is consoled by the circus people, MR SLEARY and SISSY JUPE, who help him to become humbler and wiser.

Gradgrind, Tom
Hard Times, 1854
Charles Dickens

THOMAS GRADGRIND's eldest son, known as 'The Whelp'. With his devoted sister, LOUISA GRADGRIND, he is brought up 'under one continuous system of unnatural restraint', and becomes a dishonest, selfish and dissipated youth who eventually robs from his employer, JOSIAH BOUNDERBY, while throwing suspicion onto the innocent STEPHEN BLACKPOOL. The circus manager, MR SLEARY, helps him to escape capture and he flees the country, eventually dying of a fever while proclaiming penitence and love for his sister.

Gradus
Pale Fire, 1962
Vladimir Nabokov

A revolutionary member of a Zemblan secret organization which plots to murder their exiled King Charles Xavier, now living in America under a pseudonym (CHARLES KINBOTE). Known variously as Jack Degree, Jacques de Gray or Vinogradus, the subversive agent of a detailed destiny tracks his prey in the best thriller tradition. He gains a literary dimension in his supposed appearances in the poem of the title, written by his quarry's reluctant mentor and his eventual accidental victim.

Graeme, Magdalen
The Abbot, 1820
Sir Walter Scott

ROLAND GRAEME's grandmother and single-minded protector, she is a staunch adherent to the old religion. Tall, rugged and plain-spoken, she is not above a tactical deception, and appears at Kinross as the fearsome and witch-like 'Mother Nicneven'.

Graeme, Roland
The Abbot, 1820
Sir Walter Scott

Less insipid than similar Scott heroes, Roland has much of his grandmother MAGDALEN GRAEME's fierce blood. Perpetually torn between free will and the force of circumstance, he seems at best impulsive and at worst inconstant or hypocritical; brought up in the AVENEL family's Protestant household, he remains essentially committed to the older religion, a tendency accentuated by his thrall to the cult of MARY, QUEEN OF SCOTS, and his love for her lady-in-waiting, CATHERINE SEYTON.

Graham, Jane
The L-Shaped Room, 1960
Lynne Reid Banks

A young woman, rejected by her family because of her unwanted pregnancy, and forced to cope alone. Coming into contact with a degree of human sadness and social deprivation new to her, Jane discovers a great deal about herself and the world she has come from. Through

encounters with a range of exotic and rather unsettling people in the grim lodgings in which she lives, she finds that her horizons are widened. She is gradually reconciled to her situation and, eventually, to her estranged father.

Graham, Mary
Martin Chuzzlewit, 1844
Charles Dickens

The young, charming paid companion to OLD MARTIN CHUZZLEWIT, she loves MARTIN CHUZZLEWIT, despite his grandfather's opposition, and waits for him to return from America. Meanwhile, SETH PECKSNIFF pesters her with lascivious attention. TOM PINCH secretly loves her from afar but selflessly rejoices in her eventual marriage to Martin.

Graham, Mrs Helen
The Tenant of Wildfell Hall, 1848
Anne Brontë

Mrs Graham and her little son, Arthur, come to live in the semi-ruinous Wildfell Hall; she is civil but chilly, and arouses much curiosity. She has married the profligate ARTHUR HUNTINGDON, convinced that she can reform him, and failing to do so, has flouted convention by leaving him, hoping to keep herself and her son by her painting. She gives GILBERT MARKHAM her diary to read to show that she is still tied to her loveless marriage, and unable to accept Markham's love. When her husband falls ill, she is drawn by her sense of duty to return and nurse him, wrestling with his soul to save him from damnation. After his death, her newfound wealth deters Markham, but in the end love conquers his scruples.

Grahame of Claverhouse, John, Viscount Dundee
Old Mortality, in *Tales of My Landlord*, 1816
Sir Walter Scott

The historical Graham was caricatured by his enemies as 'Bluidy Claver'se' for his cruelty in putting down the Covenanters, and by his supporters as 'Bonnie Dundee'. Scott is of the romanticizing party. 'Grahame of Claverhouse was in the prime of life, rather low of stature, and slightly, though elegantly, formed... The severity of his character, as well as the higher attributes of undaunted and enterprising valour which even his enemies were compelled to admit, lay concealed under an exterior which seemed adapted to the court or the saloon rather than the field. The same gentleness and gaiety of expression which reigned in his features seemed to inspire his actions and gestures... But under this soft exterior was hidden a spirit unbounded in daring.'

Grammarian, the
'A Grammarian's Funeral', in *Dramatic Romances*, 1845
Robert Browning

The scholar-master of a group of men who now carry his coffin to its resting place. He lived only for knowledge, eagerly pursuing his classical studies, down to the minutiae of Greek grammar, becoming in the end little more than 'an inanimate, mechanical gerund grinder'. The passion for learning that blinded him to all else in life has been passed on to his followers, one of whom comments: 'I wanted the grammarian... to spend his last breath on the biggest of the littlenesses'.

Grand Master of the Hospitallers of St John and Jerusalem, the Templars
The Talisman: A Tale of the Crusaders, 1825
Sir Walter Scott

A sinister and unpredictable figure whose personal morals are unimpeachable, but whose political sympathies seem to be dangerously fluid. He was 'a tall, thin, war-worn man, with a slow yet penetrating eye, and a brow on which a thousand dark intrigues had stamped a portion of their obscurity'.

Grandcourt, Henleigh
Daniel Deronda, 1876
George Eliot

A womanizer and ex-gambler, Grandcourt can talk in tones of drawling ennui or in a subdued manner indicating strong will. Rich enough not to worry about a dowry, and brazen enough to keep another woman on the side, he woos and wins GWENDOLEN HARLETH and, once married, shows the extent of his dominance and scorn. 'Oblige me in future by not showing whims like a mad woman at a play', he tells her after she has reacted disturbingly to his verbal cruelty. His insistence on making her behave 'properly' finds a counterpart in his assumption that the sea will let him yacht when he pleases: he is mistaken.

Grandfather
The Old Curiosity Shop, 1841
Charles Dickens

The proprietor of the Old Curiosity Shop, his name is never given, but as LITTLE NELL's maternal grandfather, it is not Trent, as is sometimes assumed. In his efforts to support his beloved granddaughter, he becomes addicted to gambling and loses repeatedly. He borrows from DANIEL QUILP, but after heavy losses, Quilp seizes the shop and all its contents, and Grandfather and Nell are made homeless beggars. Shattered in mind and body, he sets out with Nell to wander England in an attempt to escape the clutches of Quilp and Nell's dissolute brother, Fred Trent. They end up in a remote village where Nell dies. Her burial is kept secret from her grandfather, but he is found dead on her grave.

Grandison, Sir Charles
Sir Charles Grandison, 1754
Samuel Richardson

'A Rake in his address, and a saint in his heart.' Conscious of his duties as well as his rights, and social rather than individualistic, Sir Charles lacks the manly dash and brio of ROBERT LOVELACE, but is nonetheless a firm trustee of masculine superiority and hierarchy. Physically magnificent, he is an unswerving patriot and a resolutely incorruptible arbiter of truth and justice. With allusions to Adam and Christ, he is portrayed as the ideal man.

Grandissime, Honoré
The Grandissimes, 1880
George Washington Cable

Outwardly the proudest and most imposing of the dynasty, Honoré is haunted by the recognition of a world in which heroism is no longer possible, and by the threatening presence of his shadowy half-brother, HONORÉ GRANDISSIME, FMC. The Puritan JOSEPH FROWENFELD becomes his moral mouthpiece and conscience, leading him to resolve the feud with his NANCANOU rivals and acknowledge the mixed character of Southern society.

Grandissime, Honoré, fmc
The Grandissimes, 1880
George Washington Cable

HONORÉ GRANDISSIME's mulatto half-brother, he is a 'free man of color' (fmc) only as a matter of polite legal fiction. Landlord to the impoverished NANCANOU ladies, over whom he wields the threat of eviction and ruin, he is imprisoned by a profound self-hatred that eventually leads him to violence and suicide.

Grandmother, the
A Good Man is Hard to Find, 1948
Flannery O'Connor

An old-fashioned and genteel figure whose persistent wish is to be recognized as 'a lady'. Ignored by her son and scorned by her grandchildren, she struggles alone to assert her belief in propriety and 'good blood'. Her sentimental attitude to the Old South combines a nostalgia for the chivalry of her gentleman callers with a casual racism.

Granger, Hermione
Harry Potter and the Philosopher's Stone, 1997, et seq
J K Rowling

At first considered by HARRY POTTER and RON WEASLEY to be a 'bossy know-it-all', the studious and hardworking Hermione soon becomes firm friends with the pair. A voracious reader who loves learning and relishes homework, she is perceptive, thoughtful and determined. While often initially reluctant to break school rules, Hermione is nevertheless a staunch and brave ally, and her knowledge, intelligence and quick wits prove invaluable in the struggle against the evil LORD VOLDEMORT.

Grant, Alexandra
As If By Magic, 1973
Angus Wilson

HAMO LANGMUIR's goddaughter, she lives in search of some process of sexual and spiritual alchemy that will transform her narrow background and constrained hopes. As such, she is exceptionally vulnerable to charlatans and moral opportunists.

Grant, Inspector Alan
A Shilling for Candles: The Story of a Crime, 1936, et seq; he also appears as Gordon Daviot in *The Man in the Queue*, 1929
Josephine Tey

Polite, well-mannered CID man who continues police work despite a substantial inheritance simply because he enjoys the intellectual exercise. Although an active man, he is by no means an active detective, preferring to solve crimes in his head rather than on his feet. His most famous case (*The Daughter of Time*, 1951) is the murder of the Princes in the Tower, though Grant rarely favours a trail of evidence this cold. The suffocating atmosphere of that misdeed may have struck a chord, for Grant's one Achilles heel is incurable claustrophobia.

Grant, Robbie (Robert)
A Little Tea, A Little Chat, 1948
Christina Stead

A New York businessman, novelist and wholesale sexual opportunist in his fifties, he hides his predatory nature behind the unconvincingly cosy chat-up line which gives Stead her title.

Grantham, Lesbia
Getting Married, 1908
George Bernard Shaw

A sister-in-law of the BISHOP OF CHELSEA, Lesbia is a tall, slender, middle-aged woman, full of self-confidence and therefore somewhat unnerving to people younger than herself. She responds to others less with genuine sympathy than tolerant amusement. Defiantly avoiding the 'infinite dishonour' of marriage, she has refused several proposals, including ten from GEN 'BOXER' BRIDGENORTH. She wants to have children, but not a husband, apparently the reverse of LEO BRIDGENORTH who wants lovers, sometimes to mother, but seemingly no children. Lesbia remains throughout 'a glorious strong-minded old maid of old England!'

Grantly, Griselda
The Warden, 1855
Barchester Towers, 1857
Framley Parsonage, 1861
The Small House at Allington, 1864
The Last Chronicle of Barset, 1867
Anthony Trollope

First seen as Grizzel or Grisel, a 'bashful and timid' daughter of REV DR THEOPHILUS GRANTLY, she has become a cold and impassive beauty in *Framley Parsonage*. Humourless and socially ambitious, she enjoys dancing and is particularly interested in her dresses. After marrying LORD DUMBELLO she becomes a great figure in society, still silent, beautiful and lacking human feeling. By the time of *The Last Chronicle of Barset* her husband has succeeded his father and she is the Marchioness of Hartletop.

Grantly, Major Henry
The Warden, 1855
The Last Chronicle of Barset, 1867
Anthony Trollope

REV DR THEOPHILUS GRANTLY's brilliant, brave, but sometimes bullying second son, he grows up to be the gentlemanly young widower and former officer of *The Last Chronicle of Barset*. His hunting and farming existence is endangered by his father's threat to disown him if he insists on marrying the impoverished GRACE CRAWLEY. Although worried about the potential disgrace if Grace's father is convicted of theft, Henry stands by her, motivated mainly by love, but also by honour and obstinacy.

Grantly, Rev Dr Theophilus
The Warden, 1855
Barchester Towers, 1857
Framley Parsonage, 1861
The Small House at Allington, 1864
The Last Chronicle of Barset, 1867
Anthony Trollope

Archdeacon of Barchester, son of the bishop, and rector of Plumstead Episcopi. A very worldly and wealthy clergyman, who combines 'all the dignity of an ancient saint with the sleekness of a modern bishop'. Formidable and tactless, he supports too indiscriminately all the privileges of the established Church. There are elements of hypocrisy, ambition and snobbery in his character, but he is basically sincere, forgiving (except to DR THOMAS and MRS PROUDIE and their supporters) and gentlemanly.

Grantorto
The Faerie Queene, 1590–6
Sir Edmund Spenser

An allegory of injustice; he also represents the pope and the Catholic Church. He is a proud, lawless tyrant with a presumptuous gait, and his sturdy armour is rusted with blood. He stands armed like an Irish foot-soldier, a great pole-axe on his arm. He is of huge stature and is extremely ugly. Whether he is a man or a monster is difficult to discern.

Gratiana
The Revenger's Tragedy, 1607
Thomas Middleton or Cyril Tourneur

The mother of VENDICE, HIPPOLITO and CASTIZA, she has been left in relative poverty by her husband's death. Up to this point she has been a good and honourable woman but when her own son (disguised as 'Piato', a procurer of women for THE DUKE's son, LUSSURIOSO) tempts her with the prospect of an escape from her 'poor estate' she is prepared to sacrifice her daughter's honour and chastity – the prospect of an improvement in her circumstances blinding her for a while to the evil of her actions.

Gratiano
The Merchant of Venice, 1594/5
William Shakespeare

He is the most coarse, badly-mannered and foul-mouthed of BASSANIO's friends, but he is also the one who accompanies him to Belmont on his successful wooing of PORTIA and who most loudly appeals for ANTONIO's life – and SHYLOCK's demise – in the courtroom scene. This loud, honest man succeeds in winning the audience's affections to a much greater extent than his more affected companions, and is eventually rewarded through betrothal to NERISSA.

Gravedigger → Clown

Gray, Bill
Mao II, 1991
Don DeLillo

A reclusive writer, protected from the world by his assistant Scott Martineau and their shared lover Brita Nilsson. In a time when even literary personality is as mechanically reproducible as a

Warhol print, Gray finds it increasingly difficult to write and is drawn into the world of political violence.

Gray, Charlotte
Charlotte Gray, 1998
Sebastian Faulks

In 1942, Charlotte Gray joins British Intelligence and leaves Edinburgh for occupied France – ostensibly to work with the French Resistance, but also on a personal quest to find her lover, Peter Gregory. Disguised as a Frenchwoman, Charlotte uses her considerable intelligence and determination to penetrate the Resistance movement. Against the sinister backdrop of occupied France, she forms a close friendship with Jewish Resistance fighter Julien Levade. Though she appears cool, in control and sometimes aloof, Charlotte is revealed to be a passionate and complex character, struggling to come to terms with a painful childhood and to make sense of her feelings for the two men and for the country in which she is fighting.

Gray, Cordelia
An Unsuitable Job for a Woman, 1972
The Skull Beneath the Skin, 1982
P D James

At the beginning of *An Unsuitable Job for a Woman*, Bernie Pryde, a former policeman and proprietor of an unsuccessful London private detective agency, commits suicide. His partner, Cordelia Gray, inherits the business. 'Lonely, courageous and unprivileged', Cordelia is 22, slight, tough and grittily intelligent. Her mother had died soon after her birth and even now, 'belief in her mother's love was the one fantasy which she still could not entirely risk losing'. Perhaps this is partly the reason why Cordelia has an almost maternal sense of compassion. In *The Skull Beneath the Skin*, the agency is beginning to make a little headway.

Gray, Dorian
The Picture of Dorian Gray, 1891
Oscar Wilde

An immensely good-looking young man, who to begin with was 'very earnest, and had a beautiful nature'. Corrupted by his friendship with LORD HENRY WOOTON, who makes him aware for the first time of his own beauty, and of its transitory nature, Dorian becomes filled with 'a passion for sensations' and is made reckless and cynical by the knowledge that, however low he sinks in corruption and sensuality, a portrait of him painted by an artist friend will 'bear the burden of his shame', growing old and ugly whilst he retains eternal youth and beauty.

Gray, Jane
The Waterfall, 1969
Margaret Drabble

'It won't, of course, do: as an account, I mean, of what took place', confesses Jane, reflecting on her story. Jane is sometimes not entirely honest with herself, even though she surveys her circumstances and future hopes with something approaching honesty and detachment. A writer, deserted by her husband, with a child to support, she is suspicious, almost agoraphobic,

and vulnerable, and embarks upon a new relationship with James, the husband of her cousin Lucy. She is both romantic (the affair with James she finds in many ways liberating), yet cynical (she often mistrusts her feelings and finds romance and sex unpalatably competitive).

Gray, Jenny
The Prime of Miss Jean Brodie, 1961
Muriel Spark

An Edinburgh schoolgirl, Jenny is the best friend of SANDY STRANGER, a fellow member of the 'Brodie set'. Between them they produce an imaginary account of the sex life of their teacher, MISS JEAN BRODIE. Pretty, graceful and immune to boredom, Jenny sings well, takes elocution lessons, and after leaving school becomes an actress.

Gray, Menie
The Surgeon's Daughter, 1832
Sir Walter Scott

The eponymous daughter of Mr Gideon Gray, surgeon of Middlemass and the object of ADAM HARTLEY's and RICHARD MIDDLEMASS's affection. Her mother dies in childbirth and Menie seems disposed from the outset to a wandering, displaced life and to a fate that fails to promise the satisfactions of husband and family. She is a quiet, haunted girl.

Gray, Peterkin → Peterkin

Graye, Cytherea
Desperate Remedies, 1871
Thomas Hardy

A lady's maid to the intriguing MISS CYTHEREA ALDCLYFFE, her name is an epithet to the Goddess of Love. Fascinating, honest, educated and naive, she has a harrowing early life and finds herself alone in the world at a tender age. Described as being almost perfect physically, she is a sensitive and reflective young woman. Yet, despite her poise, grace and charm, true happiness eludes her for most of the novel.

Great-heart, Mr
The Pilgrim's Progress, Part I 1678, Part II 1684
John Bunyan

The courageous chaperone, adviser and spiritual director of CHRISTIANA and her family as they journey towards the Celestial City, he offers wise counsel, sound theology and brave action – not least as the slayer of THE GIANT DESPAIR. Using reasoned argument, scriptural proof and his long experience as an encourager of pilgrims, he is crucial for the survival and safety of the travelling band of vulnerable pilgrims.

Greaves, Sir Launcelot
The Life and Adventures of Sir Launcelot Greaves, 1760–1
Tobias Smollett

Smollett's hero is a Don Quixote stripped of his most ridiculous properties and equipped with some of the highest Tory virtues. Aged somewhere around 30, 'he was tall, and seemingly robust; his face long and oval, his nose aquiline, his mouth furnished with a set of elegant teeth white as the drifted snow'. His forename and purity mark him out as an Arthurian hero and he declares himself a novice of Knight Errantry, travelling around in full armour, redressing wrongs, combatting vice; his armour is lacquered black and his emblem is a quarter-moon embellished with the legend *IMPLEAT ORBEM* – 'let it fill the world'.

Grebe, Barbara
'Barbara of the House of Grebe', in *A Group of Noble Dames*, 1891
Thomas Hardy

A much indulged young girl, adored by her sensitive father and by her more down-to-earth mother, she is sweet-natured, her immaturity containing an element of superficiality. Realizing too late that beauty is only skin deep, in an act of self-sacrifice and personal persecution she resigns herself to a life which will never bear happiness. She is so wasted on an obnoxious husband that she physically wastes away.

Green → Bagot, Bushy and Green

Green, Florence
The Bookshop, 1978
Penelope Fitzgerald

A lonely and isolated figure, Florence is also pathetic, even tragic, losing everything, dignity included, through no fault of her own. Naive about the ways of the world, not to mention those of a small community, she is intelligent, opinionated and caring, yet she misjudges situations, seeing them as she would like them to be. She frightens people with her ideas of change, and her gentleness of character does not protect her once 'the knives are out'. She is a sad and vulnerable lady, who is shattered by her thwarted ambitions.

Green, Lesje (pronounced Lashia)
Life Before Man, 1979
Margaret Atwood

Lesje's Ukrainian-Jewish descent sets her apart from her Canadian surroundings, and her fondness for prehistoric times makes her unable to deal successfully with the present. A palaeontologist, she is practical and objective on the job, but fanciful and dreamy outside it. She is jumpy and often feels awkward. Cautious, apolitical, and afraid of divulging the personal, she is happier among things than people, whom she always feels she must appease.

Green Mantle → Redgauntlet, Lilias

Greener, Faye
The Day of the Locust, 1939
Nathanael West

A dull young actress who has come to Los Angeles with her downtrodden father. Determined to become this year's blonde, she is the point of focus for all the male characters in the book, an unattainable (but by no means untouchable) icon of tawdry success, whose own career seems to be limited to a small part in a film called *Waterloo*, which stands with TOD HACKETT's apocalyptic painting as one of the book's twin symbols.

Greenfield, Dora
The Bell, 1958
Iris Murdoch

As a Slade art student, the shallow and rather vulgar Dora met and married PAUL GREENFIELD, 13 years her senior, bedazzled by his sophisticated wooing, luxurious lifestyle and personal magnetism. Three years later, terrified by his wildly jealous and violent scenes, she leaves, but fearfully returns to him at Imber, a place she finds sinister. She submits to Paul's obsessional lovemaking although he otherwise openly despises her, and in the vain hope of liberation attempts a disastrously foolish 'magical act of shattering significance', aided by TOBY GASHE. However, she is a survivor, and proves unexpectedly heroic in saving CATHERINE FAWLEY's life.

Greenfield, Paul
The Bell, 1958
Iris Murdoch

A wealthy, snobbish art historian with exquisite tastes and violent passions. He is married to the highly unsuitable DORA GREENFIELD, for whom he claims to feel 'untiring and relentless love', although other than in bed he holds her in utter contempt and continually frightens and belittles her. Engaged in the study of medieval manuscripts at Imber, he orders Dora to join him there and relates a gruesome legend concerning the lost bell of Imber Abbey, sexually relishing her horror; but in so doing unintentionally shapes the events that free her from him.

Greenow, Mrs Arabella
Can You Forgive Her?, 1864–5
Anthony Trollope

She is reputedly a beauty, but has not been able to find a husband, and has acquired something of a reputation for flirting. She eventually marries an elderly, retired merchant of some means, and becomes 'quite a pattern wife' in her short but happy marriage, before settling into comfortable widowhood.

Greensleave, Bruno
Bruno's Dream, 1969
Iris Murdoch

Bruno, an elderly amateur zoologist, dreads his death by the terminal illness which has already disfigured him. In his shabby room he pursues his passion for spiders, and scrutinizes his father's stamp collection. Fearful, guilt-ridden and craving forgiveness, he grapples with the past: his marriage and infidelity, the nightmare circumstances surrounding his wife's death, and the reasons why his son, MILES GREENSLEAVE, rejected him. Miles's grudging reunion triggers Bruno's discovery of the meaning of the 'dream' that was his life, and its one enduring reality.

Greensleave, Diana
Bruno's Dream, 1969
Iris Murdoch

MILES GREENSLEAVE's beautiful second wife. She meekly accepts not coming first in his life, and dedicates herself entirely to caring for him in their safe domestic haven. Less uncompromising than Miles or her austere sister, LISA WATKIN,

Diana allows herself to respond to DANBY ODELL's raffish charm. But later Diana's and Lisa's roles are ironically reversed; during the harrowing last days of BRUNO GREENSLEAVE's life, the 'hedonist' Diana finds unexpected reserves of moral courage, compassion and understanding.

Greensleave, Miles
Bruno's Dream, 1969
Iris Murdoch

Miles is largely insulated against others, not least his dying father, BRUNO GREENSLEAVE, by his self-absorption. Devastated by the early death of his young first wife, throughout aimless years of despair Miles has remained convinced that he is a poet. Rescued from hopelessness by his second wife, DIANA GREENSLEAVE, and portentously preparing for visitations from the Muse, he faithfully records his intense examination of objects, while remaining peculiarly blind to people. When 'tall, cold angel' LISA WATKIN applies the painful spur of noble self-sacrifice, Miles, impervious to all else, is gripped by creativity.

Greenwald, Barney
The Caine Mutiny, 1951
Herman Wouk

A brilliant Jewish lawyer whose incisive and ruthless cross-examination of CAPTAIN QUEEG convinces the court-martial to acquit the 'mutineers' from the minesweeper *Caine*. A successful lawyer in civilian life, he uses his passion for justice to serve the cause of the accused underdog LT STEVE MARYK and saves his anger for the dilettante writer TOM KEEFER, whom he despises for his self-preserving and self-serving role in the affair.

Greenway, Aurora
Terms of Endearment, 1975
Larry McMurtry

A Texan widow who passes her time seeing off a selection of would-be second husbands, most of whom are entirely baffled by her off/on good humour, and frankly scared by her robust tongue. When her daughter, EMMA HORTON, announces that she is pregnant, Aurora experiences a crisis of identity, not yet feeling herself ready to be a grandmother. She is, in female, urban form, a version of the free-spirited cowboy figures who people McMurtry's Western novels.

Greenwood, Esther
The Bell Jar, 1963
Sylvia Plath

The bright young scholarship student from New England who, in her eagerness to experience life, discovers she is not always able to cope with the demands of reality. Recounting the events leading up to both her mental breakdown and her subsequent treatment in various psychiatric hospitals, Esther, rather uncomfortably, comes across as simultaneously vulnerable and off-putting: trapped within the limits of her own consciousness, her landscape is a bleak and suffocating one but she struggles, often torturingly, to free herself from it.

Gregory, Lucien
The Man Who Was Thursday: A Nightmare, 1908
G K Chesterton

A 'red-haired poet' and 'a man worth listening to, even if one laughed at the end of it', Lucien Gregory turns out to be the only real anarchist member of the Central Anarchist Council, which has been almost entirely infiltrated by police spies. Unmasked by GABRIEL SYME, he declares with Satanic hate: 'I am a destroyer. I would destroy the world if I could ... My red hair, like red flame, shall burn up the world.'

Greidinger, Aaron → Tsutsik

Grendel
Beowulf, 7th/8th century, transcribed 10th century
anon, Old English

A mythic man-eater, who terrorizes the Danish court of king Hrothgar, and who is destroyed by the Geat hero BEOWULF. His mother, more fearsome still, lives at the bottom of the mere. She seeks revenge for her offspring's death and is killed in turn by Beowulf. In the modern, first-person version, Grendel is 'humanized' and set in opposition to the bland civic ideals of the Danish court, achieving a kind of absurdist grandeur in the process.

Grenfel, Henry
The Fox, 1923
D H Lawrence

A young soldier, with blue eyes and a ruddy, rounded face, he calls unexpectedly at Bailey Farm, claiming he had once lived there. He has a similar effect upon the emotions of the women who run the farm – BANFORD and MARCH – as a fox upon chickens. March is spellbound, Banford slightly frightened. Grenfel is a man of the earth, a worker, sharp, practical, at ease with himself and eventually destructive; he is the catalyst of tragedy.

Grenville, Sir Richard
The King's General, 1946
Daphne Du Maurier

A fierce, even evil man, who is detested by many, but adored by some. He has marvellous powers of leadership, and is capable of inspiring others, but his wicked streak and his tendency to take everything too far, undo any good that he fosters. He is extremely proud of himself, and his family, but unfortunately for his faithful HONOR HARRIS, he is totally self-absorbed. He must lead a life filled with risks and excitement, and has a self-destructive streak. A great charmer, he can occasionally be thoughtful and loving, but his need to be heroic generally overcomes his more sensitive feelings.

Gresham, Frank
Dr Thorne, 1858
Framley Parsonage, 1861
The Last Chronicle of Barset, 1867
Anthony Trollope

Francis Newbold Gresham is the only son and heir of the identically named squire of Greshambury, to whom he is deeply attached. The young hero of *Dr Thorne*, he is handsome and strong. Because of his father's financial embarrassments he is told that he must 'marry money', but he loves the almost penniless MARY THORNE. In *Framley Parsonage* and *The Last Chronicle of Barset* he is a rich fox-hunting country gentleman.

Gresham, Mr
Phineas Finn, The Irish Member, 1869
The Eustace Diamonds, 1873
Phineas Redux, 1874
The Duke's Children, 1880
Anthony Trollope

The Prime Minister of England. The character is said to represent William Ewart Gladstone. He is a great orator, and is treated somewhat satirically as a 'man with no feelings for the past, void of historical association, hardly with memories – living altogether for the future which he is anxious to fashion anew out of the vigour of his own brain'.

Greta
The Sport of My Mad Mother, 1958
Ann Jellicoe

An Australian, the intermittently irritable 'mad mother' of the title. The critic Kenneth Tynan observed that this play 'stands in the same relationship to conventional play-making as jazz does to conventional music', and that an ideal production would have the atmosphere of spontaneous improvisation. Indeed, much of the dialogue is composed of cries, exclamations and repeated chantings; the characters dance, play and pretend to be musical instruments while acting out a celebration of teenage restlessness in which Greta behaves as supervisor.

Grewgious, Mr Hiram
The Mystery of Edwin Drood, 1870
Charles Dickens

A kindly bachelor lawyer and the guardian of ROSA BUD. When EDWIN DROOD disappears, he suspects MR JOHN JASPER of the murder. Rosa escapes the advances of Jasper by fleeing to her guardian for protection. His distrust of Jasper is further aroused, and he dedicates himself to solving the mystery of Drood's disappearance.

Grex, Lady Mabel
The Duke's Children, 1880
Anthony Trollope

An aristocratic lady who is the subject of an unsuccessful proposal of marriage from LORD SILVERBRIDGE. She is a pretty, clever woman with her finger firmly on the pulse of society gossip and scandal, a propensity which makes her seem 'a very interesting young lady'. She is in love with FRANK TREGEAR, but they agree that their respective lack of fortune forbids their marrying.

Grey
The Ancient Child, 1989
N Scott Momaday

A Kiowa woman who manages to rescue the artist SET from the contradictions that threaten to overwhelm his work, steering him back towards a nourishing accommodation with his people and their past.

Grey, Agnes
Agnes Grey, 1847
Anne Brontë

To ease her parents' misfortune, Agnes Grey becomes a governess in order to earn money. Her first post is a nightmare because of the cruel rowdy children. Her second, less dramatically unhappy but still lonely, makes her feel little better than a servant. Nonetheless, she remains there for two years, reasoning kindly but in vain with the worldliness of ROSALIE MURRAY and the rough tomboy habits of her sister, gently seeking to be an influence for good. Only REV MR WESTON, the curate, shows her friendship. After her father's death, she happily joins her mother in setting up a school, and meets Mr Weston again when is is appointed to the next parish.

Grey, John
Can You Forgive Her?, 1864–5
Phineas Finn, The Irish Member, 1869
The Eustace Diamonds, 1873
The Prime Minister, 1876
Anthony Trollope

A suitor for the hand of ALICE VAVASOR. He is a 'man of high character, of good though moderate means', and of good birth and education. He is talented and respectable, and 'noble, generous, clever, good – so good as to be almost perfect', but somewhat pompous and possessive, and a little dull. Although Alice initially chooses another, she eventually marries him.

Grey, Nanda, later Clara Batchelor
Frost in May, 1933
The Lost Traveller, 1950
The Sugar House, 1952
Beyond the Glass, 1954
Antonia White

A desperately sensitive and emotionally fragile girl, she is bound up in her parents' attitudes, both to her and to the world in general. Her father's Catholicism is a guiding force in her life, and her experiences at Convent school shape her character and destiny. Feeling constantly guilty and ashamed, particularly of her creativity, she wages an emotional struggle between what feels right and what is deemed right by those around her.

Grey, Sir Eustace
'Sir Eustace Grey', 1807
George Crabbe

Sir Eustace, rich, generous, happily married, never thanks God for the goodness shown him in his prosperity. His wife deceives him with his best friend, whom he pursues and kills in revenge. His wife subsequently pines and dies, and so do their two children. He suffers the deepest anguish, tormented by nightmares, and ends in a madhouse, where he is grateful for kindness and comes to know the grace of God.

Grey, Vivian
Vivian Grey, 1826–7
Benjamin Disraeli

Gifted but wayward, he learns that he can charm his way to success in society and politics. Aligning himself with the MARQUIS OF CARABAS, he builds a powerful parliamentary cabal, but becomes so addicted to factionalism that he conspires to form a new splinter party. When he kills his rival in a duel, he is forced to leave England, living out the rest of his days intriguing dispiritedly in the minor courts of Europe.

Greystock, Frank
The Eustace Diamonds, 1873
Anthony Trollope

The son of the Dean of Greystock, and cousin of Lizzie Greystock (LADY LIZZIE EUSTACE), he is a barrister by profession. He is 'quick, ready-witted, self-reliant, and not over scrupulous in the outward things of the world'. His political views are lightly held, and while he subscribes to the theory of the importance of duty, he prefers it when he is the recipient. He considers throwing over LUCY MORRIS for his cousin Lizzie, but eventually marries her.

Greystock, Lizzie → Eustace, Lady Lizzie

Gride, Arthur
Nicholas Nickleby, 1839
Charles Dickens

A lecherous and repulsive old moneylender, he is a partner of RALPH NICKLEBY in underhanded schemes and one of WALTER BRAY's main creditors. Possessing a deed showing that the beautiful MADELINE BRAY will inherit a fortune on her marriage, he plots to marry her himself, abetted by Ralph and her father. He is foiled on the morning of the wedding when Bray dies suddenly and Madeline is abducted by NICHOLAS NICKLEBY, whom she loves and later marries. His wizened, palsied and deaf housekeeper, Peg Sliderskew, steals the deed. Before Gride can be arrested for his duplicity, he is murdered in his bed by robbers. Peg is eventually transported.

Gridley, Mr
Bleak House, 1853
Charles Dickens

A ruined suitor in Chancery, he is referred to in court as 'the man from Shropshire'. In his efforts to obtain justice after 25 years, he is constantly arrested for contempt of court. MR GEORGE ROUNCEWELL gives him sanctuary from the law in his shooting gallery, but he collapses and dies as MR BUCKET comes to arrest him.

Griet
Girl With a Pearl Earring, 1999
Tracy Chevalier

Small and wide-eyed in appearance, 16-year-old Griet is employed to work as a maid in the household of the Dutch painter, VERMEER. She shows a natural instinct for colour and form which deepens when she begins to assist Vermeer by mixing his colours. Outwardly serene, she has passionate depths, hinted at by her untameable hair which she struggles to restrain within her cap. Her observant and astute nature illustrates her sensitivity and she and Vermeer are drawn to one another, but their closeness creates turmoil in the household, especially when she sits for the portrait of the title.

Griffen, Iris Chase
The Blind Assassin, 2000
Margaret Atwood

An 83-year-old widow, Iris Chase Griffen narrates her life story from a privileged childhood shared with her sister, Laura, to wealthy, brooding, isolated old age. Interwoven with her recollections is Laura's unpublished novel, *The Blind Assassin*, and documentary materials including the inquest into her suicide immediately after World War II. Laura's novel is a love story; Iris's marriage, to one of their industrialist father's business competitors, was predictably loveless and the romantic aspect of her nature is long buried. Reflective, analytical, sometimes secretive, perhaps manipulative, a woman whose misfortunes are largely of her own making, she assembles her memoirs in the hope that the granddaughter she has not seen for many years might one day read them.

Griffin → Invisible Man, the

Griffiths, Clyde
An American Tragedy, 1925
Theodore Dreiser

Brought up in Kansas City in a family of 'holy rollers', he is nonetheless obsessed with wealth and social position. His relationship with the working-class ROBERTA ALDEN is soured by his passion for the wealthy SONDRA FINCHLEY, and Clyde is driven to murder his pregnant girlfriend in a bid to clear the way for a social-climbing marriage to Sondra. Like most of Dreiser's characters, Clyde is modelled on a real person: in 1906, while working in his uncle's shirt factory in Cortland, New York, Chester Gillette drowned Grace ('Billie') Brown, a factory clerk, who was carrying his child.

Grille
The Faerie Queene, 1590–6
Sir Edmund Spenser

Once a man, he is now a pig, courtesy of an evil enchantress. When he is restored to human form by the virtuous sword of SIR GUYON, KNIGHT OF TEMPERANCE, he is distressed, because he had so enjoyed the 'delights of filth and foule incontinence'. Having lost the human gift of intelligence, he is returned once more to his base animalistic state. He represents the loss of human rationality.

Grimes, Captain
Decline and Fall, 1928
Evelyn Waugh

A very short man, with a red moustache and an artificial leg, Captain Grimes is a 'life-force', an old Harrovian who firmly believes that the Public School system will always save him when he is 'in the soup'. As a teacher at Llanabba Castle School, he is a walking-stick disciplinarian, given to making soul-searching personal confessions and frequent visits to Mrs Roberts's inn. In desperate trouble, he bigamously marries Flossie Fagan, only to fake his own death shortly afterwards. Arrested for undertaking a shady job for MARGOT BESTE-CHETWYNDE, he joins PAUL PENNYFEATHER at Egdon House Prison, from where he escapes by riding a horse mysteriously into the fog.

Grimes, John
Go Tell It On The Mountain, 1953
James Baldwin

A young teenage black boy, born illegitimately to his father's third wife and raised in the communion of the pentecostal Temple of the Fire Baptized in Harlem. His adolescent struggle with an awakening sexuality and with guilt and anxiety about his father allows Baldwin to 'flash back' into the early history of the family.

Grimes, Mr
The Water Babies, 1863
Charles Kingsley

The gruff and beastly master sweep who beats TOM, his pleasures are smoking his pipe and downing a pint in the pub. Deaf to all counsel to better his behaviour, he ends up in a hell-like labour camp. When Tom comes to the rescue, Grimes is touched, but it is only when he sees how cruel he has been, even to his mother, that his prison melts away. But he is then destined for purgatory, clearing the crater of Mount Etna.

Grimes, Peter
The Borough, 1810
George Crabbe

Stubborn, cruel and greedy, Peter Grimes the fisherman breaks his father's heart. He takes three boys in turn from the workhouse as apprentices, and beats, starves and neglects them. Neighbours hearing screams merely say 'Grimes is at his exercise'. In turn, each boy dies. Grimes has easy explanations, but he is shunned. He begins to see phantoms of his father and the boys, and stares helplessly at them for hours, as he leans on his oar. Urging suicide, they show him the horrors of punishment. Terrified, he dies.

Grimm, Percy
Light in August, 1932
William Faulkner

Sometimes Faulkner's names are almost too transparent. Grimm is the evil spirit who finally tracks down JOE CHRISTMAS for the lynch mob. A triple-distilled Southern Fascist, of the sort that filled the ranks of the Bund, he is also a figure out of fairy tale – the brothers Grimm? – being more goblin than real man.

Grip, the Raven
Barnaby Rudge, 1841
Charles Dickens

A raven (named after Dickens's own pet raven) which BARNABY RUDGE carries around the country in a basket, and is his constant companion, even when Barnaby is imprisoned. The bird amuses everyone by talking a great deal and likes to announce 'I'm a Devil!'.

Gripe
The Confederacy, 1705
Sir John Vanbrugh

An elderly, penny-pinching, gullible and devious man who, with his associate, MONEYTRAP, has become rich by their moneylending business. Although married to a woman of exasperatingly expensive tastes who has little time for him, he still has a weakness for the opposite sex, and avidly pursues his business partner's wife, ARAMINTA MONEYTRAP. Meanwhile, his own wife is being courted by Moneytrap.

Gripe, Clarissa
The Confederacy, 1705
Sir John Vanbrugh

The wife of the moneylender GRIPE, Clarissa finds herself pursued by his equally unscrupulous associate, MONEYTRAP. She is, though, a close friend of ARAMINTA MONEYTRAP, and the two women have no compunction in humiliating their husbands for their foolishness. Clarissa's view of men is dismissive: a husband, she informs her servant FLIPPANTA, is nothing but 'a growling animal'. However, believing herself to be something of a connoisseur of jewels, she has unfortunately expensive tastes, which her husband abhors, and which lead to numerous complications.

Gripe, Corinna
The Confederacy, 1705
Sir John Vanbrugh

The daughter of GRIPE and CLARISSA GRIPE, Corinna is being pursued by DICK AMLET. Despite the fact that he tries to lie his way into her affections, passing himself off as a colonel, Corinna loves him, believing she can see a man of substance beneath the masquerade. A modern audience might sympathize with a woman of little judgement taking on an unnecessary burden; alternatively, she might be seen as a person of considerable patience and not a little humour.

Griselda
'The Clerk's Tale' in *The Canterbury Tales*, c.1387–1400
Geoffrey Chaucer

She is a model of wifely, daughterly and motherly virtues. She endures without complaint all the distressing tests that her husband imposes on her, even that of leaving him and her child. Such is her meekness that she utters not one word of reproach when she is restored to him.

Groan, Titus, 77th Earl of Gormenghast
Titus Groan, 1946
Gormenghast, 1950
Titus Alone, 1959
Mervyn Peake

An unsmiling baby, with strange violet eyes, whose mother cares more for wild birds and her swarm of white cats than she cares for him, and whose father stands poised on the edge of madness, Titus grows into a lonely, restless child with a desperate longing for freedom. He is not good-looking, but he has a certain presence and authority. His characteristic scowl masks his deep hunger for love, and keeps him brooding on the ill-fate that has dealt him his burdensome legacy. He is caught in an agonizing dilemma – between his longing to escape his destiny and his deep pride in his lineage. His boyhood destroyed, his heart wounded and his courage tested by his bitterly fought victory over STEERPIKE, he sets off alone to face the world outside, his ears ringing with the countess's warning that all roads lead back to Gormenghast.

Grove, Lena
Light in August, 1932
William Faulkner

A repository of all the best human virtues, she is placed in the novel as a counterbalance to the thoroughgoing intolerance and violence of the other characters. At the end, she bears the child of an unknown father, an act of unthinking acceptance and compassion that balances the violent 'crucifixion' of JOE CHRISTMAS.

Grovelgrub, Rev Mr
Melincourt, or Sir Oran Haut-ton, 1817
Thomas Love Peacock

As unappealing as his name suggests, the plump Reverend Grovelgrub is a sycophant with one eye firmly fixed on pecuniary possibilities for himself. Vain and obsequious to the point of absurdity, he juggles self-interest with superficial and expedient service to his superiors. He plots and manipulates, an unsuccessful Machiavellian and a ridiculous villain.

Grubbinole
The Shepherd's Week, 1714
John Gay

The singer of a mock elegy in this mock pastoral, Grubbinole appears in the section entitled 'Friday, or the Dirge'. 'Woe is me', he begins, and sings of BLOUZELINDA's death. After this, however, he forgets his cares in 'ale and kisses' with a 'willing maid' and then starts proper drinking in an alehouse.

Grumio
The Taming of the Shrew, early 1590s
William Shakespeare

Although a faithful servant to PETRUCHIO, Grumio, who is small of stature, rarely carries out the tasks required of him without grumbling and complaining. He has the ability to irritate his master sufficiently to receive a blow but never enough to find himself dismissed, for he is well aware how far he can go. Much of his action verges on the farcical, especially when dealing with those under him, whilst his speech is lively, bawdy and peppered with asides. He enters enthusiastically into Petruchio's scheme to win KATHARINA over, although it costs him a few bruises.

Gruner, Elya
Mr Sammler's Planet, 1970
Saul Bellow

An elderly Jewish immigrant who has grown rich as a gynaecologist, and then in real estate. He is ARTHUR SAMMLER's nephew, and saved him from death in a concentration camp; he remains his generous mentor in the USA. He has 'Old World family feelings' and manners, and is sentimental about Poland. His vice is playing cards for high stakes, and he basks in the approval of those around him. Sammler feels he has met 'the terms of his contract with God'.

Gryll, Morgana
Gryll Grange, 1860–1
Thomas Love Peacock

Orphan and heiress, Morgana Gryll is a spirited lady, delighting in gently poking fun at the more preposterous conversations and postures of the men around her. Able to read Latin and Italian, she is educated and talented, singing ballads and commenting perceptively on those around her. She is also progressive, proposing marriage, in effect, to her shy, uncertain suitor.

Guasconti, Giovanni
'Rappaccini's Daughter', 1844, in *Mosses from an Old Manse*, 1846
Nathaniel Hawthorne

An impoverished young student at Padua, recently come out of the south, he casts himself in the romantic role of Dante to BEATRICE RAPPACCINI, unaware that her very touch is poison.

Gude Counsall
Ane Pleasant Satyre of the Thrie Estaitis, 1540
Sir David Lindsay

Representing both political sense and rational thought in general, Gude Counsall is initially prevented from exercising his good influence on REX HUMANITAS and his Scottish court by the presence of DAME SENSUALITIE and the Vices. Enabled, however, on the arrival of DIVYNE CORRECTIOUN, to assume his rightful position as political adviser to the king, Gude Counsall ensures that the reformation of the Three Estates is a just and morally sound one.

Guest, Lady Julia de
The Small House at Allington, 1864
The Last Chronicle of Barset, 1867
Anthony Trollope

The sister of LORD DE GUEST, she is 'a tedious, dull, virtuous old woman'. Although proud and sometimes snobbish, she has a strong sense of duty. She is very fond of JOHN EAMES and encourages his suit for the hand of LILY DALE.

Guest, Lord de
The Small House at Allington, 1864
Anthony Trollope

An unmarried Tory earl, who is proud of his ancient peerage but modest in his demeanour. Fat and sensible, he lives within his considerable means, concentrating on breeding cattle at Guestwick Manor. JOHN EAMES becomes the earl's protégé after rescuing him from a bull, and de Guest (whose Christian name is Theodore) helps and encourages his attentions to LILY DALE.

Guest, Maurice
Maurice Guest, 1908
Henry Handel Richardson

Escaping from a straitened and philistine middle-class background, this young Englishman has come to Leipzig as a music student, where he is captivated not just by art but by the exoticism of his companions, notably LOUISE DUFRAYER. He remains essentially innocent, only imperfectly aware of the motivations and impulses that govern others.

Guest, Stephen
The Mill on the Floss, 1860
George Eliot

Implicitly accepted as the fiancé of LUCY DEANE,

handsome young Stephen Guest finds himself increasingly attracted to her cousin MAGGIE TULLIVER. Although he is mildly conceited and patronizing, his passion for Maggie is nonetheless real enough and, moreover, reciprocated, but in his consuming desire to be with her he pushes her, and himself, into an irreversibly compromising position. However, in subsequently clearing Maggie of all blame, he simultaneously restores some modicum of respectability to his own character.

Guiderius/Polydore
Cymbeline, 1609/10
William Shakespeare
The elder of CYMBELINE's two sons, Guiderius was stolen from his parents when only three years old by BELARIUS, a lord banished by Cymbeline. Brought up in the wilds of Wales, believing Belarius to be his father and his nurse to be his mother, Guiderius nevertheless grows up with all the princely qualities appropriate to his birth. He murders CLOTEN, and cuts his head off.

Guido Franceschini, Count
The Ring and the Book, 1868–9
Robert Browning
Apparently noble but in reality greedy, cruel and vindictive, he savagely murders his wife POMPILIA and her supposed parents for deceiving him. On trial, he pleads the privilege of his social position, his code of honour, and his rights as a man in minor clerical orders, and insists that only POPE ANTONIO PIGNATELLI can judge him. He is nonetheless sentenced to death. Totally lacking in love and having no conscience for the evil he has done, he is a completely amoral man.

Guildenstern → Rosencrantz and Guildenstern

Guildenstern
Rosencrantz and Guildenstern Are Dead, 1967
Tom Stoppard
Like his companion ROSENCRANTZ, Guildenstern is a man with no past or future, whose present is uncertain. He is a figure defined only by the situation he is in and by the characters around him. Although an intellectual, he is an innocent trying to make sense of the world, hoping desperately that it is controlled by chance and not by predestination. Because he is slightly more aware of their predicament than Rosencrantz, he suffers more in his attempts to find meaning and order in life, his emotions spilling out in occasional violent acts.

Guillaume, Gunter
Democracy, 2003
Michael Frayn
Based on real-life characters, the play deals with the association between Guillaume and WILLY BRANDT, West German Chancellor from 1969 to 1974. A member of East Germany's secret service who became Brandt's close aide, Guillaume looks, according to Brandt, 'like the manager of a pornographic bookstore', neither intelligent nor ruthless enough to be a spy. Yet he is a dedicated agent who looks up to his employer and values his role as Brandt's confessor.

Guinea, properly Margaret ('Meg') Malone
Come in Spinner, 1951
Dymphna Cusack and Florence James
Golden-haired Meg is shrewd and tough. Known to all as Guinea after a painting of her titled *Guinea Gold*, she is the youngest of three young women working in the 'Marie Antoinette' Beauty Salon. It is 1941, and Sydney is seething with US servicemen, in town for 'rest and recreation'. Sex, silk stockings and abortion are rife. Guinea is pursued by Colonel Maddocks but finally, on the toss of a coin, settles for her long-time boyfriend Kim.

Guinevere (Guinevere McLeod)
Barbary Shore, 1951
Norman Mailer
Like her mythical namesake, Guinevere is the faithless consort of a fallen king. Nominal wife of the ageing Marxist ARTHUR MCLEOD and obsessed with the 'story that's worth a million bucks', which she hopes to sell to Hollywood, she represents the trashy corruption of postwar America. Sexually indiscriminate, she tries to bed MIKEY LOVETT and the deranged girl LANNIE MADISON, before absconding with the secret policeman LEROY HOLLINGSWORTH.

Gulliver, Lemuel
Gulliver's Travels, 1726
Jonathan Swift
An adventurer and gentleman traveller, whose goal is to discover unknown territories. Intelligent and scrupulous, he documents in minute detail each journey he makes. Although attempting to be objective in his journals, he only ends up being judgemental. He eventually succeeds in showing up the futility, corruption and irrationality of the human race.

Gumbril, Theodore
Antic Hay, 1923
Aldous Huxley
A restless intellectual, son of GUMBRIL SENIOR, Theodore Gumbril cultivates frivolous affairs, and indulges in witty conversations, notably with his tailor Bojanus, a Bolshevik sympathizer, and the capitalist Boldero. His one practical achievement is to invent 'pneumatic trousers' to make sitting more comfortable, successfully marketed as 'Patent Small-Clothes' by Boldero. Lacking self-confidence, Gumbril resorts to wearing a false beard in order to swagger as a 'Complete Man'.

Gumbril Senior
Antic Hay, 1923
Aldous Huxley
Father of THEODORE GUMBRIL, Gumbril Senior is altogether a more substantial Victorian figure, an architect with grandiose ambitions. He secretly makes a large model of Wren's London because he looks back on it as an ideal, utopian city. He says about Wren: 'He offered to build for the imagination and the ambitious spirit of man, so that even the most bestial, vaguely and remotely, as they walked those streets, might feel that they

were of the same race – or very nearly – as Michelangelo; that they too might feel themselves, in spirit at least, magnificent, strong and free.'

Gummidge, Mrs
David Copperfield, 1850
Charles Dickens

The poor widow of DANIEL PEGGOTTY's former partner, she becomes Mr Peggotty's house-keeper. Her constant complaint is that she is 'a lone, lorn creetur and everythink goes contrairy with me', but Mr Peggotty bears her self-pity with remarkable patience. She eventually emigrates to Australia with him and LITTLE EM'LY.

Gunga Dass
'The Strange Ride of Morrowbie Jukes', 1885
Rudyard Kipling

A former telegraphy operator, he has become de facto head of a bizarre community of cholera victims who are exiled to a large crater by the side of the Sutlej river. When MORROWBIE JUKES stumbles across them, it is Gunga Dass who demonstrates that the white man's supposed superiority means nothing in such a place.

Gunga Din
'Gunga Din', in *Barrack-Room Ballads and Other Verses*, 1892
Rudyard Kipling

The impoverished and much abused *bhisti* (native water-bearer) who served alongside a British regiment in Victorian India. Though unflatteringly recalled by one of those who used to beat and curse him, we nevertheless learn of Gunga Din's uncomplaining steadiness, his courage under fire and compassion for his thirsty tormentors; and of his self-sacrificing rescue of the wounded narrator. Cheerfully expecting one day to 'get a swig' from him in hell, Atkins, the narrator, concludes: 'Though I've belted you and flayed you,/By the livin' Gawd that made you,/You're a better man than I am, Gunga Din'.

Gunn, Ben
Treasure Island, 1883
Robert Louis Stevenson

The sole inhabitant of Treasure Island, marooned there by his fellow pirates three years before. First seen leaping through the forest, he resembles a monkey rather than a man and, indeed, his alienation from human companionship has caused him to become de-socialized, an offspring of nature. Ragged and lonely, he is a pathetic creature, craving only for a piece of cheese. He has regressed to a state of childhood in contrast to JIM HAWKINS, who is attaining a state of manhood. Through the help he gives in defeating LONG JOHN SILVER's pirates, Ben regains something of his old sense of worth and self-respect.

Gunn, Morag
The Diviners, 1974
Margaret Laurence

A writer who has carved with difficulty a successful career out of the mixed strands of her poor Scots immigrant childhood and the combined influences of her adoption by a garbage collector, marriage to an urbane English academic, and the mixed-race father of her troubled teenage daughter Pique. Always an outsider, she reaches a crisis of identity in her mid forties, seeing herself caught in 'the river of now and then': a stationary point buffeted by the currents of her past and future. Intermingling 'Memorybank movies' with events from her daily life, she is able to find a composite sense of herself, and concludes that she should continue to 'look ahead into the past, and back into the future, until the silence'.

Gunner, properly Julius Baker
Misalliance, 1910
George Bernard Shaw

'Gunner' is the name given by JOHN TARLETON to Julius Baker, a young clerk, 'cheaply dressed and strange in manner', who emerges from his hiding place in the portable Turkish bath at Tarleton's Hindhead home. He is armed with a pistol and threatens that he will shoot Tarleton and then himself as vengeance for Tarleton's seduction of his mother. He is disarmed by LINA SZCZEPANOWSKA. A socialist, Gunner first accuses capitalism of high-handed indecency and then ignorance. A regular visitor to his local Free Library, Gunner reads voraciously: 'Thats whats going to smash up your capitalism', he warns.

Guppy, William
Bleak House, 1853
Charles Dickens

A comic, vulgar cockney solicitor's clerk in the firm of Kenge and Carboy. He 'files a declaration' of marriage to ESTHER SUMMERSON, but is refused, and becomes obsessed with discovering her parentage. His investigations get him involved with LADY DEDLOCK and MR KROOK, and he discovers the remains of Krook on the night he dies. He withdraws his marriage proposal when Esther is disfigured by smallpox, but magnanimously renews it when he finds her looks recovered.

Gurth, the Swineherd
Ivanhoe, 1819
Sir Walter Scott

Born slave of CEDRIC THE SAXON, a contract that is sealed by the brass band that encircles his neck. He has a wild, unkempt appearance and a wardrobe made entirely from the skin of his former charges.

Gus
The Dumb Waiter, 1960
Harold Pinter

A simple, credulous man, he has, for years, worked with BEN as a hired assassin. The less detached of the two, it is, perhaps, his interest in their victims and the organization which employs him, which render inevitable his own killing.

Gustad Noble
Such a Long Journey, 1986
Rohinton Mistry

A mild, limping man who bears an injury from a

serious accident some years before but who is nonetheless in fine health for his 50-plus years. In youth, he imagined himself to be a Parsee St George, slaying injustice and evil. In adult life he has to watch from the sidelines while great events – specifically the Indo-Pakistani war – unfold at a distance from him.

Guster
Bleak House, 1853
Charles Dickens

Maid-of-all-work to MR SNAGSBY, she is a 'lean young woman from a workhouse (by some supposed to have been christened Augusta)'. Hard-working, she suffers from epilepsy and is harshly treated by Mrs Snagsby. She sympathizes with JO and is kindly treated by Mr Snagsby.

Guthrie, Chris
Sunset Song, 1932
Cloud Howe, 1933
Grey Granite, 1934, forming the trilogy *A Scots Quair*, 1946
Lewis Grassic Gibbon

The principal character in the trilogy, 'Chris Caledonia' survives two of her husbands (EWAN TAVENDALE and ROBERT COLQUHOUN) and separates from the third (CHAE STRACHAN) in a life that moves full circle from country to town to city, and finally back to the countryside of her birth. Acutely conscious of the very fact of her existence, and of her multiple 'selves', she remains throughout slightly removed from the realities of her life. A proud and, in some ways, solitary figure, her love/hate relationship with the land develops into an awareness that it, and change itself, are the only things that endure and she seems almost to become, in the end, part of the landscape itself.

Guy, Captain
Omoo, 1847
Herman Melville

The young cockney captain of the *Julia*, who 'by some favoritism or other, had procured the command of the vessel, though in no wise competent'. He is educated, but a landsman, and is 'no more meant to be at sea than a hair-dresser'. He leaves most of the work to his mate, JOHN JERMIN, and is the subject of much derision on board. Although sheepish and meek, he has 'a sort of still, timid cunning', but cannot retain control over his crew.

Guyon, Sir, Knight of Temperance
The Faerie Queene, 1590–6
Sir Edmund Spenser

A knight who is 'an Elfin born', and can trace his lineage in the lore of Faerieland. It is his duty to defend helpless maidens. His principal virtue is self-restraint. Able to withstand temptation, he has a heart of marble stone, although it proves to be somewhat flawed when he falls prey to intemperance for a time; however, he is redeemed by PRINCE ARTHUR. He is handsome, tall, intelligent and demure, yet also stern and fearsome.

Guzman, Don
Westward Ho!, 1855
Charles Kingsley

A Spanish sailor in the Armada, whose reckless seamanship is matched by a dashing romanticism which makes him a formidable contrast to his more plodding and earthbound rival in love and war, AMYAS LEIGH.

Gwendoline
The Importance of Being Earnest, 1895
Oscar Wilde

The object of JOHN WORTHING's affections, and, in his eyes at least, 'a sensible, intellectual girl', Gwendoline takes herself very seriously. Charming and sophisticated, she is nonetheless superficial and shallow. Unfortunately for Worthing, there are two obstacles in the way of their union – her mother LADY BRACKNELL's disapproval and the fact that her 'ideal has always been to love someone of the name of Ernest'.

Gwenwyn of Powys-land
The Betrothed, 1825
Sir Walter Scott

A fearsome Welsh chieftain in the wars with the Normans, and the slayer of Raymond Berenger, whose daughter, EVELINE BERENGER, he has pursued as more likely to provide him with heirs than his present barren consort. He perishes in the siege of Garde Doloureuse Castle.

Gwyllim, Mrs
The Expedition of Humphry Clinker, 1771
Tobias Smollett

Housekeeper at Brambleton Hall and recipient of TABITHA BRAMBLE's orthographically challenging letters. Very much an offstage presence in the book, she is presumed to maintain domestic order until the travellers' return.

Gwyn
The Owl Service, 1967
Alan Garner

An exile, returned to the Welsh valley of his childhood; his mother formerly acted as housekeeper to ALISON's father. He is bluff and joking in manner, down-to-earth and practical, in touch with his physical surroundings and also with the people and the past of the valley. Clever, but unlikely to rise above his background, he is destined instead to become one of the barrack-room lawyers of life, a big fish in a small sea. He has a determined nature and is prepared to endure discomfort. He is easily offended and often gruff and discourteous to those around him. It is Gwyn who comes to understand the workings of the force released from an owl-patterned dinner service. However, his pride, offended by a false belief that Alison has mockingly betrayed him, prevents him from being the one to save her from this force.

Gwyon, Wyatt, also known as Stephen
The Recognitions, 1955
William Gaddis

The novel's central character, he is a talented but disturbed artist. Under the residual impact of a New England Calvinist upbringing, he rejects any notion of art based on 'originality', in favour of faithful copy (ie forgery) of the Old Masters, all in pursuit of the aesthetic 'recognitions' buried therein. Torn as a child between the influence of his eccentric clergyman father, a sternly fundamentalist aunt and his maternal grandfather, he suffers a mysterious brain fever which leaves him with burning eyes and the recurrent nightmare that his hair is on fire. Towards the end of the novel, he is 'reborn' at the monastery of San Zwingli (where his mother's grave is) and is known henceforward as Stephen, after the first Christian martyr.

Gynecia

The Countess of Pembroke's Arcadia, 1581–4, published 1590
Sir Philip Sidney

The wife of DUKE BASILIUS. Very much younger than her husband, she is greatly taken with the beauty of the disguised PYROCLES and, while attempting to kickstart her marriage, appears to kill her elderly husband by administering what she believes to be an aphrodisiac. She is saved from burial alive only by his eventual wakening.

Haberdasher, the → Five Guildsmen, the

Hackett, Tod
The Day of the Locust, 1939
Nathanael West
A talented young artist and Yale graduate, he moves to Hollywood to make a living as a set designer. He gradually gives up on his art, though his huge unfinished canvas, *The Burning of Los Angeles*, is a surreal portent of the riot with which the novel ends, underlying the combustible flimsiness of the whole American spectacle.

Hackston of Rathillet, (David)
Old Mortality, in *Tales of My Landlord*, 1816
Sir Walter Scott
Described on the 'wanted' leaflet as 'tall, thin, black-haired', he is another of the gang pursued for the murder of Archbishop Sharp of St Andrews. It is known that Hackston stood back from the actual killing, but failed to prevent it.

Hagar
Song of Solomon, 1978
Toni Morrison
Obsessed with MILKMAN DEAD, Hagar destroys herself in pursuit of his attention. Asserting that 'he is my home in this world', she answers his rejections with a cyclic pattern of murderous attacks. A spoilt and indulged child, she is trapped by consumer ideas of beauty. Finally blaming herself for Milkman's inattention, she buys her way into a white myth of beauty that ultimately destroys her.

Hagenbach, Archibald von
Anne of Geierstein, or The Maiden in the Mist, 1829
Sir Walter Scott
A Swabian count who robs and imprisons SEIGNOR and ARTHUR PHILIPSON. He has lived so utterly by the harsh law of *Faustrecht* that he is obliged to leave his native land and enter the service of CHARLES THE BOLD, DUKE OF BURGUNDY, where his rugged talents can be put to new use.

Hagrid, Rubeus
Harry Potter and the Philosopher's Stone, 1997, et seq
J K Rowling
'Almost twice as tall as a normal man and at least five times as wide', bushy-haired, black-bearded Hagrid looks 'simply too big to be allowed'. Yet his outward wildness conceals a gentle, honest nature; he is huge but tender-hearted. Although sometimes overly trusting, with 'an unfortunate liking for large and monstrous creatures', he is a loyal and dependable ally of ALBUS DUMBLEDORE, for whom he works at the wizard school Hogwarts. He proves to be a fierce protector and warm friend to HARRY POTTER.

Haines, Guy
Strangers on a Train, 1950
Patricia Highsmith
Guy Haines's life of 'stillness and reserve' is transformed into a nightmare of guilt and implicit collusion in murder by a chance encounter, on a train, with the psychopathic CHARLES ANTHONY BRUNO. Guy's career as an architect is blossoming and the only restraint on his new life is his continuing marriage to his unfaithful wife Miriam. Bruno's offer to kill Miriam presents Guy with a horrifying, yet tantalizing, moral dilemma, whereby an idle wish can become actuality. He now has to confront the darker side of personality and social correctitude.

Hal, Prince → Henry, Prince of Wales

Hal of the Wynd → Smith, Henry

Halcombe, Marian
The Woman in White, 1860
Wilkie Collins
The half-sister of LAURA FAIRLIE, she is a tall, comely woman with a dark complexion, coal-black hair, a resolute jaw and piercing brown eyes. Intelligent, self-confident and loyal, the one flaw in her perfection is a marked lack of physical beauty. 'Never was the fair promise of a lovely figure more strangely and startlingly belied by the face and head that crowned it', notes WALTER HARTRIGHT. Fearless and forthright in her devotion to Laura, she is prepared to risk anything to substantiate her statement that 'my sister's future is my dearest care in life'.

Halcro, Claud
The Pirate, 1821
Sir Walter Scott
A Shetland bard, he is a little, slightly-built man, 'whose eye retained all the vivacity of spirit, which had supported him under the thousand vicissitudes of a changeful and precarious life'. He modestly demurs comparisons with John Dryden and the wits of London.

Halder, John
Good, 1981
C P Taylor

A professor of German literature at Frankfurt University, Halder is a man in his early forties, hard-working, sensitive and kind. A political sceptic, he watches the rise of Hitler's National Socialists during the early 1930s with some alarm. Yet Halder is emotionally restless and intellectually vulnerable. The Party presents him with not only an appealing agenda for the rebuilding of Germany but also an intellectually rigorous platform and a persuasive aesthetic. Moreover, the Party wants Halder, and he is seduced by being wanted. Gradually, he begins to make intellectual compromises. Eventually Halder joins the Party and becomes an SS officer attached to Auschwitz, charged with giving concentration camp practices a rational, humane explanation.

Haldin, Natalia
Under Western Eyes, 1911
Joseph Conrad

The sister of VICTOR HALDIN. She is a strong, healthy girl, with a determined walk and a brisk handshake. She is an idealistic (and somewhat idealized) revolutionary who would 'take liberty from any hand as a hungry man would snatch a piece of bread'. She is devoted to her brother, and transfers that devotion to RAZUMOV, believing him to be his benefactor. She is seen as a likely victim of the 'pestilential shadow' which hangs over Russian life, and which will 'devour her presently'.

Haldin, Victor
Under Western Eyes, 1911
Joseph Conrad

A revolutionary idealist who assassinates a government minister, flees to RAZUMOV for shelter, but is betrayed by him to the police. Pale-faced, he is 'tall and straight as an arrow', and has a 'lithe and martial figure'. He is a sincere, dedicated and courageous idealist, willing to sacrifice himself for the revolutionary cause, but also a moral nihilist and a dangerous fanatic who is guided by the demands of ideology, and is irrationally dedicated to the destruction of the established order.

Hale, Margaret
North and South, 1854
Elizabeth Gaskell

The heroine of the novel, a complicated young woman. Part realist and part idealist, she is capable of both great personal insight and self-deception. Having promised to live 'as brave and noble a life as any heroine she has read or heard of in Romance', she proves herself fit for the part. Spirited, educated, sensitive, confident and caring – what more could MR THORNTON ask for?

Half-Child, the
A Dance of the Forests, 1959
Wole Soyinka

A nightmarish vision of a future perpetually trapped in the limbo between the long ancestral sleep of pre-birth and the terrifying reality of birth, with its visions of violence and destruction.

Halifax, John
John Halifax, Gentleman, 1856
Mrs Craik

Halifax earns the title 'gentleman' by his merits, not from an accident of birth. Lowly born, but inherently honest and morally substantial, he is apprenticed to the tanner Abel Fletcher and rises to prominence via his friendship with Fletcher's invalid son and a lucky marriage to the wealthy Ursula March.

Hall, Maurice Christopher
Maurice, 1914, published posthumously, 1971
E M Forster

A deeply conventional chap destined for a predictable middle-class existence as a respectable stockbroker and family man, Maurice Hall finds his expectations of life shattered by the discovery of his homosexuality. A handsome, athletic young man, his devotion to fellow Cambridge graduate CLIVE DURHAM lights a fire that is 'never to be quenched again'. Tormented by his shame and loneliness, he struggles to find a cure for his 'affliction' but finds true peace of mind in accepting himself and bravely rebelling against the mores of the time.

Hallam, Sir Howard
Captain Brassbound's Conversion, 1899
George Bernard Shaw

A judge, and brother-in-law to LADY CECILY WAYNEFLETE, Hallam is 'more than elderly' and 'facing old age on compulsion, not resignedly'. Severely upright, he stands for justice as a form of institutionalized vengeance, representing the Fabian version of an inflexible, domineering, conquer-and-rule school of colonialism. Accused by CAPTAIN BRASSBOUND of appropriating the family estate, Hallam protests in his defence that he was unaware of the other's existence.

Halliday, Jack
The Man That Corrupted Hadleyburg, 1899
Mark Twain

Hadleyburg's resident cynic and shrewd observer of its vices. Positively revelling in misfortune, he is particularly prone to mocking his fellow citizens with theatrical gestures: 'Halliday carried a cigar-box around on a tripod, playing that it was a camera, and halted all passers and aimed the thing and said, "Ready! – now look pleasant, please", but not even this capital joke could surprise the dreary faces into any softening.'

Halliday, Vernon
Amsterdam, 1998
Ian McEwan

The editor of *The Judge*, a broadsheet newspaper with a falling circulation, Halliday meets his old friend CLIVE LINLEY at the funeral of MOLLY LANE, who has died at the age of 46. Both men are former lovers of Molly, and agree a pact that if either were diagnosed with a degenerative disease such as that which killed Molly, the other would help him die. A man 'without edges, without faults or virtues', 'revered' in his profession, Halliday is also shrewd, arrogant and perfidious. His decision to publish 'in the public interest' private photographs of right-wing Foreign Secretary Julian Garmony dressed in women's clothes and taken by Molly evidently with Garmony's consent, results in Linley accusing him of betraying Molly's privacy.

Hallijohn, Dr Cornelius
The Green Graves of Balgowrie, 1896
Jane Findlater

Minister of Eastermuir, he despises his calling and his congregation. Returning home drunk one night, he meets the MARJORYBANKS. The mother's malignant humour suggests that he take on her daughters' education. He watches them develop with delighted interest, shamed at times by their innocently sharp questions. He takes Lucie to London, but it is Henrietta whom he loves. When both sisters die, he sees in his sorrow the hand of God, and lives long, caring for his people, saving his soul, and believing he has not lost Henrietta for ever.

Halloran, Corporal Phelim
Bring Larks and Heroes, 1967
Thomas Keneally

An Irishman, pressed into the service of the British Empire as a guard in an Australian penal settlement. His loyalties are reawakened when he witnesses an Irish prisoner being punished and he switches his allegiance.

Hamelines
Ane Pleasant Satyre of the Thrie Estaitis, 1540
Sir David Lindsay

Along with DANGER and FUND-JONET, Hamelines – a name which had overtones of intimacy and familiarity – occupies a minor but significant role in the play as one of DAME SENSUALITIE's Venus-worshipping associates. Making her contribution to the seduction and moral disintegration of REX HUMANITAS's court in agreeing to the sexual gratification of WANTONNES, Hamelines is later implicitly banished from the kingdom, along with her mistress, by DIVYNE CORRECTIOUN.

Hamilton, Gavin
A Would-Be Saint, 1978
Robin Jenkins

Though unworldly to the point of masochistic self-denial, he is perceived by his girlfriend to be 'dangerously ambitious in a spiritual sense', addicted to good deeds. An adept in what he perceives as Scotland's new religion – football – he gives it up rather than be sanctified by it. An (extremely) conscientious objector in World War II, he exchanges a mining background for work in the forests of Argyll, another of Jenkins's innocents in a fallen Eden, surrounded by men of questionable conscience and motives.

Hamilton, Guy
The Year of Living Dangerously, 1978
C J Koch

An Australian journalist working in Jakarta in 1965, in the final days of the Sukarno regime.

With the dream of a strong, independent Indonesia destroyed, Hamilton becomes a conduit for the dreams and aspirations of his dwarf-like assistant and photographer BILLY KWAN, who also desires the same woman (JILL BRYANT). Out of their triangular association, he gradually learns the value of love.

Hamilton, Margaret
Looking for the Possible Dance, 1993
A L Kennedy

Born in Glasgow, Margaret Hamilton was brought up by her father, to whom she is strongly attached. She is a poor communicator, and seems 'to have been born set in her ways'. Attending university in England, Margaret meets fellow student COLIN MCCOAG, and they become lovers. When Colin abandons her, Margaret returns to Glasgow and becomes a community worker in a depressed area. Three years later, after the death of Margaret's father, Colin returns. They resume their relationship, but encounter difficulties. A traumatic experience at work and a shocking attack on Colin force Margaret to question what she wants from life.

Hamlet
Hamlet, 1601/2
William Shakespeare

Motivated and blinded by the desire to avenge his murdered father but plagued by doubts, Hamlet has a mind too analytic for his task. He is aware of the corruption of the world around him but cannot find a cure that will not corrupt him. His love for his mother, GERTRUDE, his revulsion at her second marriage to CLAUDIUS, his father's murderer, and his desire for vengeance plunge him into melancholy introspection one minute and frenzied activity the next, leaving him easily outwitted by Claudius. Of a basically noble nature, he is destroyed by a corrupt world.

Hamm
Endgame, 1958
Samuel Beckett

Asked by his attendant CLOV if he believes 'in the life to come', Hamm replies 'mine was always that'. Both pitiable and monstrous, he remains stranded in the centre of his room, isolated in his blindness, afflicted by a fear of the unknown. In a world seemingly devoid of human existence, it is only Clov's presence that guarantees his survival. Yet his autocracy implies a lack of humanity, exhibited in his cruelty to Nagg and Nell, whom he keeps imprisoned in dustbins. Only his wretchedness wins sympathy in a play which is structured as a chess game where all moves are carefully plotted despite the inevitability of failure.

Hammer, Paul
Bullet Park, 1969
John Cheever

A callous and deeply disturbed suburbanite who has wealth and success, but has found only bitterness in both, and becomes increasingly psychopathic. He was 'born out of wedlock' and neglected, and is melancholic, a heavy drinker, and an insomniac. He sees love as a 'heady distillate of nostalgia', and is taunted by his wife for being hen-pecked. He singles out his neighbour ELIOT NAILLES 'for attention', and attempts to crucify his son Tony in a crazed act of rebellion or revenge against the suburban ethos of Bullet Park and his own life.

Hammond, Muriel
The Crowded Street, 1924
Winifred Holtby
Entrapped within the narrow confines of Edwardian middle-class society, she has grown up prim, reserved, and properly submissive. Intelligent but credulous, her intense desire to conform has overrun her early intellectual aspirations and directed her towards a more respectable vocation: marriage. A failure in this, she considers herself an irrelevance and a nonentity. Alienated and withdrawn, utterly unmoved even by World War I, which has transformed the lives of her peers, Muriel's unlikely friendship with a stronger, more purposeful woman uncovers the resilience that will enable her to make one last pitch at happiness and fulfilment.

Hampton, Claudia
Moon Tiger, 1987
Penelope Lively
Good-looking, independent, intellectual, Claudia Hampton recalls her life and times from World War I until the present day, deliberating, with her usual mixture of curiosity and precision, how history bears upon individual destiny and vice versa. For Miss Hampton is a historian, and a popular one. A self-centred woman, she is considered by several people to be difficult. To many, including herself, she is 'someone'. She has travelled, she has suffered from typhoid and malaria; she has had one child and one miscarriage, and, among various minor loves, one great love. Her intellect and conversation have made her socially effective, but her greatest gift, friends and rivals agree, is being able to adapt and, if necessary, conceal.

Hana
The English Patient, 1992
Michael Ondaatje
A delicately beautiful 20-year-old Canadian nurse who, at the end of World War II, refuses to demobilize with the rest of her unit and chooses instead to remain in a crumbling villa near Florence with the severely burned pilot, THE ENGLISH PATIENT. Unseasonably matured by her experience of war, she combines an unusual degree of detachment from its atrocities with a natural warmth and child-like pleasure in the simple, sensual pleasures still left to her. In her relationship with the Sikh sapper Kip she tries to fuse the cultural breach she senses between the attitudes of east and west, but although their love for each other is true, neither is strong enough to counter wider world events.

Hanaud, Inspector
At the Villa Rose, 1910, et seq
A E W Mason
A stocky, broad-shouldered detective in the Sûreté, he considers himself and his colleagues to be the 'servants of chance', relying on patient application and blind luck, rather than intellectual gymnastics, to solve cases. Unusually, his 'Watson' is rather more colourful than himself; Ricardo enjoys his wine.

Hand, Laurel McKelva
The Optimist's Daughter, 1972
Eudora Welty
A slender, quiet, intelligent middle-class war-widow in her forties, she is the daughter of JUDGE MCKELVA. After her father's death, she discovers that she has not understood very much about him, but begins to come to terms with her feelings about both him and her late husband after a cathartic weeping 'for love and for the dead'. She is then free to leave the family house to the grasping WANDA FAY MCKELVA, and return to her independent life as a fashion designer in distant Chicago.

Hanema, Piet
Couples, 1968
John Updike
An architect and builder, he represents the four-square puritan virtues that his Dutch Protestant forebears brought to America. His surname, in which some have professed to detect both 'anima' and, less probably, 'enema', is a sign of his orderly personality. Married to Angela, who is indeed angelically beautiful, he has a passionate affair with FOXY WHITMAN.

Hannan, Will
'A Branch-Road', in *Main-Travelled Roads*, 1892, revised editions 1899, 1922, 1930
Hamlin Garland
A young farm-hand in the upper Mississippi valley. His muscular intelligence and simple pleasure in physical work are clouded by 'vague thoughts and great emotions' that lead him to ill-use his sweetheart Agnes, abandoning her to the tough disciplines of prairie life and marriage to another, while he pursues his fortune elsewhere.

Hannay, Richard, also known as Cornelis Brandt, Cornelius Brand, Richard Hanau; and at ranks from major to general
The Thirty-Nine Steps, 1915, et seq
John Buchan
He is first encountered at 'thirty-seven years old, sound in wind and limb, with enough money to have a good time, yawning my head off all day', and primed for adventure. A South African, more at home prospecting on the Veld than in English society, he is stoutly loyal to king and empire, better suited to action than to introspection, and marked by attitudes to class, race and gender which are not so much politically incorrect as downright prejudiced. He is a blunter and less amiable man than successive film versions have made him seem.

Happer, Hob → Hob the Miller

Happer, Mysie → Mysie of the Mill

Happy Prince, the
'The Happy Prince', 1888
Oscar Wilde
The Happy Prince is a beautiful, gem-encrusted,

gold-plated statue who occupies a place of honour high above the city. In reality, though, the prince is not happy, for, having lived a life of pure pleasure, he is only now, after his death, aware of 'all the ugliness and all the misery' of the city. Moved by compassion, he engages a swallow to help him alleviate some of the suffering he sees by giving away his jewels and gold to those who have nothing, until eventually he loses all his costly raiments but gains true immortality by his good deeds.

Harapha of Gath
Samson Agonistes, 1671
John Milton
A young man of giant size and strength, 'his look / Hauty as is his pile high-built and proud', he comes to mock the blinded SAMSON in prison at Gath, but disdains to take on the crippled man in single combat.

Harbans, Surujpat
The Suffrage of Elvira, 1958
V S Naipaul
A small-time politician thirsting to be elected for the constituency of Elvira in Trinidad's first post-independence election. He must, however, first propitiate the real powers in the area, Baksh and Chittarangan, leaders of the Muslim and Hindu communities respectively. In the process, he becomes a skilful manipulator of West Indian electoral politics (presented as richly comic) but proves to be no more authentically democratic than his sectarian mentors.

Harcombe, Timothy
English Music, 1992
Peter Ackroyd
The young son of the widowed Clement Harcombe, Timothy assists him after World War I in performing services of healing by invoking the spirits of the dead. Timothy appears to possess extraordinary gifts, but whether he is truly a visionary or merely a child of extraordinary imagination is unclear. Others think his upbringing unorthodox and Clement an unsuitable father. Trusting, but eventually discouraged by the real world, an optimist disappointed, Timothy relies increasingly upon his dreams. Transported back and forth through English culture, ever curious, he begins to understand the forces of history, the nature of art and culture and what it is to be English.

Harcourt
The Country Wife, 1675
William Wycherley
Friend of HORNER, and thereby privy to his sexual intrigues, Harcourt is a personable young man in love with ALITHEA. He has a rival for her favours in the foolish fop SPARKISH, but his disguise as a clergyman gives him many opportunities to declare his love for her in religious double-entendres.

Harcourt-Reilly, Sir Henry
The Cocktail Party, 1950
T S Eliot
The great psychiatrist first appears as the Unidentified Guest at LAVINIA CHAMBERLAYNE'S abortive party but later becomes an ambiguous guiding spirit to all the guests.

Hardcastle, Dorothy
She Stoops to Conquer, 1773
Oliver Goldsmith
Greedy, selfish, sarcastic and pretentious, the dreadful Mrs Hardcastle is the second wife of SQUIRE RICHARD HARDCASTLE. As the custodian of jewellery belonging to her niece, CONSTANCE NEVILLE, Mrs Hardcastle hopes she will marry her son, TONY LUMPKIN, so that the valuables stay in the family. Mrs Hardcastle's attitude towards Tony is divided. She spoils him, but vindictively calls him a 'viper'. Most of all, she is both vain and foolish. She lies about her age, and makes ridiculous attempts to appear highly fashionable in conversation and dress. Moreover, she is easily outwitted by the plans of the two pairs of lovers, MARLOW and KATE HARDCASTLE, and GEORGE HASTINGS and CONSTANCE NEVILLE.

Hardcastle, Kate
She Stoops to Conquer, 1773
Oliver Goldsmith
The daughter of SQUIRE RICHARD HARDCASTLE, step-daughter of DOROTHY HARDCASTLE and half-sister of TONY LUMPKIN, Kate is a dutiful daughter and, having 'spent a year or two in town', accomplished in the social graces. Yet she is far from dull, being also assured, independent, quick-witted and able to manipulate events to further her own interests, especially those in MARLOW.

Hardcastle, Squire Richard
She Stoops to Conquer, 1773
Oliver Goldsmith
Squire Hardcastle is married to his second wife, DOROTHY HARDCASTLE, and is the father of KATE HARDCASTLE and stepfather of TONY LUMPKIN. He owns a country mansion and likes 'old friends, old times, old manners, old books, old wine'. His name reflects his belief that the Englishman's home is an inviolable retreat, but nevertheless he is generously hospitable, declaring that his friends think of it as 'Liberty Hall'. He provides a large supper for his prospective son-in-law MARLOW, and is shocked by what he believes is his boorishness, although in other respects he is surprisingly tolerant. He indulges Dorothy's misguided attempts to be fashionable, and has an unusually liberal attitude towards his daughter, allowing her the final choice of husband.

Harding, Eleanor
The Warden, 1855
Barchester Towers, 1857
Framley Parsonage, 1861
The Last Chronicle of Barset, 1867
Anthony Trollope
Younger and loving daughter of REV SEPTIMUS HARDING; her romance with JOHN BOLD runs into difficulties when Bold supports reforms that would disadvantage her father. In *Barchester Towers* she is Mrs Bold, a rich widow, devoted to her baby. Trying to be fair to REV OBADIAH SLOPE, whom she dislikes, she is mistakenly believed to favour him as a husband. She actually marries

REV FRANCIS ARABIN, impressed by his burning desire for truth.

Harding, Rev Septimus
The Warden, 1855
Barchester Towers, 1857
Framley Parsonage, 1861
The Small House at Allington, 1864
The Last Chronicle of Barset, 1867
Anthony Trollope

Precentor of Barchester Cathedral, warden of the charitable Hiram's Hospital, and later holder of a living in the diocese. Kind, generous and humble to the point of saintliness, he is upset when JOHN BOLD calls for reforms in the organization of the hospital and it is implied that the warden receives money to which he is not entitled. Harding cannot bear public opprobrium and he must be sure that he is in the right; his modesty leads him repeatedly into self-doubt. His great love is music, and at moments of stress he mimes the playing of his cello.

Hardy, George
Master Georgie, 1998
Beryl Bainbridge

Surgeon, amateur photographer, alcoholic and repressed homosexual, Hardy is an enigmatic character presented through the eyes of various narrators linked by their experiences of an event that changed the course of their lives. He is adored by Myrtle, who was adopted by his family as a child, but more cynically viewed by his brother-in-law Dr Potter, and his former assistant and young lover Pompey Jones. Potter and Myrtle accompany him when, in his capacity as a surgeon, he leaves his dissolute life in Liverpool to serve in the Crimean War.

Hare, Dorothy
A Clergyman's Daughter, 1935
George Orwell

The only child of the Reverend Charles Hare. Her shabby-genteel life seems set in its conservative fashion, outlined in her daily 'Memo List', from the morning prayers she says in her aged flannelette night-gown to the prayers she repeats before she sleeps each night. Dorothy's sexless life is devoted to serving her father as though she were his housemaid, until the arrival of an elderly free-thinker, who completely alters the narrow path of her existence. She disappears from the East Anglian parish for a new life of hop-picking, poverty and private tuition but, in the process, she learns to live for herself.

Hare, Mary
Riders in the Chariot, 1961
Patrick White

As one of the novel's four protagonists (the others being ALF DUBBO, RUTH GODBOLD and MORDECAI HIMMELFARB), Mary Hare is a haughty, plain and awkward spinster. Her extravagant, self-indulgent, wealthy father built Xanadu, a pretentiously decorated but now crumbling mansion on the outskirts of Sydney, where she lives alone. A remnant of a disappearing social order, still anguished by memories of her father's violent death, she surveys all around her like a curious, imperious hawk. Spurned and

isolated as a child, she has learned to maintain a careful distance between herself and others, despite acquiring the garrulous MRS JOLLEY as her housekeeper. At heart, Miss Hare is an honest, instinctive, if possessive woman, with a capacity for love ignited by Himmelfarb, a vulnerable immigrant.

Haredale, Emma
Barnaby Rudge, 1841
Charles Dickens

The niece and ward of MR GEOFFREY HAREDALE and friend of DOLLY VARDEN. She is orphaned as an infant when her father, Reuben Haredale, is murdered by RUDGE. A Catholic, she loves EDWARD CHESTER, but his anti-Catholic father, SIR JOHN CHESTER, an enemy of her uncle, tries to prevent their marrying. Abducted with Dolly during the Gordon Riots, she is rescued by her uncle, Edward Chester and JOE WILLET. She and Edward eventually marry and live abroad.

Haredale, Mr Geoffrey
Barnaby Rudge, 1841
Charles Dickens

A Catholic squire and religious man, he is the great enemy of SIR JOHN CHESTER, and his opposite, being rough and abrupt but unselfish and honest. He is embittered by being suspected of murdering his brother, Reuben, 20 years ago, but he proves RUDGE to be the murderer. With EDWARD CHESTER and JOE WILLET, he rescues his niece, EMMA HAREDALE, and DOLLY VARDEN, who have been abducted during the Gordon Riots. At the ruins of his house, burnt down by the rioters, he meets Sir John Chester and kills him in a duel.

Hargenau, Ulrich
How German Is It, 1980, revised British edition 1982
Walter Abish

'Is it possible for anyone in Germany, nowadays, to raise his right hand, for whatever the reason, and not be flooded by the memory of a dream to end all dreams?' Returning 'from the edge of forgetfulness' after 18 months abroad, Ulrich is forced to re-examine his racial identity and loyalties. He compares his own betrayal of comrades in a left-wing terrorist group with his father's heroic role in the 1944 July Plot against Hitler.

Hari
The Village by the Sea, 1982
Anita Desai

The only son of a poor family living in a small fishing community on the west coast of India, Hari is the brother of LILA. With their mother seriously ill and their bewildered father often drunk, the children resolve that the family must somehow survive. Lila is more practical than her brother, an imaginative, lively boy who dreams of making his fortune in Bombay. Although he discovers city life to be cruel and often unreasoning, the experience of having to fend for himself strips Hari of his naivety and unquestioning trust. It also sharpens still further his sense of decency, compassion and justice.

Harker, Jonathan
Dracula, 1897
Bram Stoker

A young solicitor sent to the eerie Transylvanian castle of COUNT DRACULA, in connection with the latter's purchase of property in England. He is a sensible, upright, discreet, loyal young man who finds himself held prisoner by the count and his female Un-Dead, and witnesses appalling horrors. He succeeds in escaping the fate intended for him, and plays a hand in hunting down the count with ABRAHAM VAN HELSING.

Harkness, Gary
End Zone, 1972
Don DeLillo

The narrator, he is one of the most successful American football players of his generation. He grew up with a sign reading 'WHEN THE GOING GETS TOUGH, THE TOUGH GET GOING' pinned up by his father in his bedroom. Despite an almost self-destructive urge to fail, he seems destined for better and better things, constrained only by the limits of his language to conceive of anything different. He is prone, too, to bouts of apocalyptic fantasy.

Harland, Frank
Harland's Half Acre, 1984
David Malouf

A painter who, like all Malouf's central characters, has to confront a basic opposition between god-given nature and man-made society. Brought up on a stubbornly unyielding farm, he largely rejects the latter, preferring to live rough among the hobos and swagmen that haunt Queensland during the Depression, and painting in a deserted cinema that is symbolic of the emptiness of social dreams.

Harland, Joe
Manhattan Transfer, 1925
John Dos Passos

Once a brilliant and influential broker known as the 'Wizard of Wall Street', Joe Harland represents the downside of the American Dream. Ruined by drink and over-acquisitiveness, he deterministically blames 'the peculiar predominance of luck in human affairs' for his personal demise. Nursing a fondness for his cousin JIMMY HERF's deceased mother Lily, he vainly seeks family warmth at the Merivale household. Evicted for non-payment of rent, he spirals downwards from job to job until he finds employment as a night-watchman and becomes friends with JOE O'KEEFE.

Harleth, Gwendolen
Daniel Deronda, 1876
George Eliot

'The Spoiled Child', Gwendolen sees her family virtually ruined yet can still go gambling in fashionable resorts. Those in her household avoid offending her egotism. She plans to despise her wooer HENLEIGH GRANDCOURT, but fails, and in the unhappy marriage that follows, she faces the fact that she is 'selfish and ignorant' for the first time, with the help of the gentlemanly DANIEL DERONDA.

Harley
The Man of Feeling, 1771
Henry Mackenzie

An ironic model of the innocent and highly sensitive man, designed to appeal to the prevailing taste for the sentimental virtues. His own bashful sensitivity and innate goodness is of the type 'which the most delicate feelings produce, and the most extensive knowledge cannot always remove'. His rather unworldly and eccentric sensitivity, which leads him to regular bouts of tears at the harshness around him, is also manifest in his generosity toward the unfortunates he encounters.

Harlowe, Arabella
Clarissa, 1748
Samuel Richardson

An unpleasant, shrewish woman, Arabella is CLARISSA HARLOWE's pretentious sister. She subscribes wholeheartedly to her family's grasping capitalism, and is a firm believer in the merits of hierarchy and unfettered economic expansion. Her antipathy towards Clarissa is motivated by jealousy as she was rejected by ROBERT LOVELACE, who was not attracted by her transparent charms.

Harlowe, Clarissa
Clarissa, 1748
Samuel Richardson

A paragon of scrupulous moral judgement, Clarissa is the victim of her greedy and implacable family. Snatched from her omnipotent father by the debonair ROBERT LOVELACE, this 'angel of light' is transferred from one tyrannical regime to another, even more brutal. At the centre of a web of dishonesty and harassment, Clarissa resists Lovelace's attempts to efface her identity. Desiring the tranquility of an imagined Protestant nunnery, she would gladly abjure her fortune for 'empire o'er my mind'. Her death is an act of utopian transcendence, a longed-for escape from the oppression of bourgeois patriarchy.

Harman, Joe
A Town Like Alice, 1950
Nevil Shute

A ringer from Northern Australia, he encounters JEAN PAGET after his capture by the Japanese and during their forced march through the jungle. He is crucified for insubordination, and it is not at first clear that he has survived. After the war he goes in search of 'Mrs Boong' – Jean – unaware that she has inherited a fortune and is looking for him.

Harmon, John (alias John Rokesmith)
Our Mutual Friend, 1865
Charles Dickens

The son of old John Harmon, the rich, miserly dust-contractor. His father's will requires that he marry BELLA WILFER in order to receive his inheritance. He assumes the identity of a murdered man, Julius Handford, and then takes the name of 'John Rokesmith', in which guise he lodges with REGINALD WILFER in order to test Bella's character. He becomes secretary to MR and MRS BOFFIN, and with their help, Bella's mercenary nature is reformed and she marries him for love, unaware that he is heir to a fortune. After their marriage, MORTIMER LIGHTWOOD attempts to arrest him on suspicion of murdering John Harmon, but he reveals his true identity and finally enters into his inheritance.

Harold, Childe
Childe Harold's Pilgrimage: A Romaunt, 1812–18
Byron, George Gordon, 6th Lord Byron

Childe Harold, weary of life, sets out 'in joyless reverie' to travel over Europe, noting historic scenes and their significance. Portugal, Spain and the Greek islands, then Belgium, the Rhine and the Alps, and finally Italy, and her literature, are considered, in his poetic reflections on past sins and present sightseeing. Pride, gloom, bitter laughter, scorn, defiance and melancholy are evoked by the antique past or the more wild precipitous aspects of nature. He muses on tyranny, rebellion, ambition, vividly describing scenes like the ball in Brussels on the eve of Waterloo, and ends with a joyful apostrophe on the Ocean, which he finds most fully expressive of his own indomitable spirit.

Haroun
Haroun and the Sea of Stories, 1990
Salman Rushdie

An originally 'happy young fellow' who is suddenly confounded by his mother's adulterous desertion and his father's inability to tell stories professionally, brought on by Haroun's question 'What's the use of stories that aren't even true?' His encounter with an apparent burglar propels him into a fantastic other world, to which he is brought on the back of a mechanical flying bird. Adapting rapidly to new rules in the Walrus's Gup City, he battles on its behalf and for his father against the neighbouring Chup City's Cultmaster (read: Ayatolla Khomeini), who is against all good stories.

Harriet → Hatty

Harrington, Evan
Evan Harrington, 1860
George Meredith

The son of a tailor, he finds himself torn between family loyalty (and his mother's insistence that he carry on the hereditary trade) and his sisters' desire to see themselves as of finer social rank. In the event, he reaches an acceptable and individual compromise.

Harrington, J J
After a Fashion, 1987
Stanley Middleton

A brilliant academic, still in the upward half of his career curve. His wife has left him, however, tired of his inability or refusal to make real human contact, and Joe has to construct a compensatory world out of ideas and the recognition of his peers.

Harris → George, Harris, and J

Harris ('Short') → Codlin, Thomas and Harris ('Short')

Harris, Honor
The King's General, 1946
Daphne Du Maurier

A devoted, loving and meek girl, she is prone to bouts of lethargy and depression because her loved one, SIR RICHARD GRENVILLE, leads such a dangerous and erratic life. Brave and resourceful in the face of danger, she shows strength of character in the way that she copes with the overpowering family she marries into. She is astute in her observations and intelligent, and although her values are quite different from those of the man she loves, she cannot shake off her attraction to him. She is destined to lead a life of pain and suffering as she remains true to her heart but not to her perceptive head.

Harris, Jim
All God's Chillun Got Wings, 1924
Eugene O'Neill

Perhaps the most obvious reason why this play is no longer performed lies in the difficulties of portraying Jim for contemporary audiences. Intellectually gifted, but also clumsy and animalistic, he now seems a regressive portrayal of an American black man. His childhood love for ELLA DOWNEY comes to nothing until her brutal relationship with Mickey breaks down. He attempts to study law but her prejudice and incipient madness destroy him, exposing too much of the patient, unthinking loyalty associated with 'Uncle Tom-ism'.

Harris, Mrs Ada
Flowers for Mrs Harris, 1958, published in USA as *Mrs Harris goes to Paris*, et seq
Paul Gallico

A wiry widow, with work-worn hands, down-at-heel clothes and an indomitably cheerful air, Mrs Harris is the epitome of the London charlady. Her quietly forceful character is hinted at by her choice of headgear, a floppy green straw hat adorned with a flamboyant pink rose. She delights in her work, restoring order to the chaotic households of the select clientele she chooses to work for around Belgravia. Somehow she arouses in others all the virtues of courage and integrity; she can melt the icy heart of a salon manageress or charm an accountant with equal ease.

Harris, Natalie
The Heart of the Country, 1987
Fay Weldon

A prim and proper perfectionist housewife, Natalie is described as being surrounded by 'a female aura'. She has a neatness in her approach to life, a sense of propriety, but all this is thrown into disarray by her unfaithful husband, who leaves her with debts. In the wake of this she becomes much more aware of her own needs, takes greater risks, and is educated in the ways of the world. Growing in confidence, she realizes that she does find men attractive, but on her terms. She loses her husband, children and home, and yet in a sense she is only just beginning to live.

Harris, Tom
Two Years Before the Mast, 1840
R H Dana jr, originally published anonymously

He lacks the social and educational advantages of

his friend, the narrator Dana (ANON), but the young seaman has managed to attain a reasonable degree of learning by his own efforts. Of all the *Pilgrim* crew, he is the one closest to Dana's own point of view.

Harrison (Robert)
The Heat of the Day, 1949
Elizabeth Bowen

A shadowy and faintly sinister figure, who pursues STELLA RODNEY and lures her away from his namesake ROBERT KELWAY to whom he appears to be a kind of flesh-and-blood doppelgänger. He achieves this by a kind of sexual blackmail, offering in return his silence about Kelway's supposed espionage activities.

Harrison, Dr
Amelia, 1751
Henry Fielding

An exemplary man of unbending Christian principle, the pious Dr Harrison has a sententious homily for every occasion. His monumental morality is bombarded by the debaucheries of a decadent age, but he stands proud and erect. From his unassailable pinnacle as monarch of righteousness, he protects the hapless CAPTAIN BILLY BOOTH as well as he can.

Harry
The Snows of Kilimanjaro, 1936
Ernest Hemingway

An American sportsman and hunter who has never achieved his ambition to be a writer. He is dying of gangrene on safari, and feels 'a great tiredness and anger that this was the end of it'. He has killed his talent through lack of use, but instead has 'had his life and it was over and then he went on living it again', until he became something he despised, living off a succession of rich women. He had 'loved too much, demanded too much, and he wore it all out'.

Harry
Zigger Zagger, 1967
Peter Terson

A rejected boy with no father, a succession of 'uncles' and a sister married to the ultra-conservative Les, Harry Philpott's only escape from everyday life is on the football terraces. He is a failure at school, a failure at trying to find work and a failure with the opposite sex, losing his girlfriend Sandra to Vincent, centre-forward of the team he supports. At first he worships the anti-social ZIGGER ZAGGER, but gradually comes to realize that there is more to life than being part of the crowd.

Harry the Horse
Stories à la Carte, 1932
Furthermore, 1938
Damon Runyon

A hoodlum from Brooklyn, he is involved with his associates SPANISH JOHN and LITTLE ISADORE in a range of criminal activities, from gambling to bootlegging to murder: in short, they are 'very hard characters indeed'. With chilling ruthlessness, he swaggers his way through his community, invoking a healthy respect, and only occasionally allowing his hard-man image to be

modified by infatuation, most notably for Miss Maribel Marlo, whose enthusiasm for temperance is out of kilter with Harry's own underworld connections.

Hart, Sheba
What Was She Thinking?: Notes on a Scandal, 2003
Zoë Heller

Sheba Hart is a slightly absent-minded and bohemian pottery teacher, with high ideals but little ability to maintain discipline in class. Her feelings for her only pupil to display the slightest interest in art quickly turn from interest to desire, and this leads to an ill-fated affair which provides the excitement missing in her life. Only her devoted friend and colleague BARBARA COVETT stands by her after the affair becomes public, Sheba gradually becoming completely dependent on her as her world disintegrates.

Harthouse, James
Hard Times, 1854
Charles Dickens

A well-bred, good-looking idler who has tried a variety of occupations, 'got bored everywhere' and decided to become a potential parliamentary candidate. He attempts to alleviate his tedium by seducing LOUISA GRADGRIND, now married to JOSIAH BOUNDERBY, but SISSY JUPE berates and shames him for his scheming and he leaves Coketown.

Harting, Leo
A Small Town in Germany, 1968
John Le Carré

A lonely archivist with a brilliant memory, who has vanished from the British Embassy in Bonn along with secret files. His pursuer discovers that he has gone everywhere in the Embassy, combining a job that allows him access with the cold-blooded use of selected women to get keys to the normally out-of-bounds registry. Harting's extra-curricular activity turns out to be the pursuit of the past of a German war criminal turned charismatic right-wing politician. Since some of this past involves secret deals with the British, none of Harting's ex-colleagues wishes to know him.

Hartke, Lauren
The Body Artist, 2001
Don DeLillo

Lauren Hartke is a performance artist who uses her body as her medium. In her work, she 'tries to shake off the body' by dramatically altering her appearance. Aged 36, she has recently married Rey Robles, a much older film director, and they are living in a remote rented house on the east coast of America. After Rey commits suicide, Lauren continues to live in the house, where inexplicable experiences lead her to create her most ambitious piece, 'to become a blankness, a body slate erased of every past resemblance'. She also begins to accept Rey's death.

Hartley, Adam
The Surgeon's Daughter, 1832
Sir Walter Scott

He is apprenticed to MENIE GRAY's father, the surgeon Gideon Gray, and is a rival to RICHARD

MIDDLEMASS for Menie's affections. He meets her again in India, where she has gone in pursuit of Middlemass. Honest, sincere and direct, he is also somewhat naive in the ways of the world.

Hartman, Rev Curtis
'The Strength of God', in *Winesburg, Ohio*, 1919
Sherwood Anderson

Tall, bearded and reticent, the Presbyterian minister of Winesburg is unsure in his faith. 'He wondered if the flame of the spirit really burned in him and dreamed of a day when a strong, sweet new current of power would come like a great wind into his voice and his soul.'

Hartmann, Charles
The Girl at the Lion d'Or, 1989
Sebastian Faulks

In France of the 1930s, he is a wealthy man married to a woman he does not love, and is a member of a generation deeply affected by their experiences in World War I. Somewhat directionless, he seeks fulfilment in an affair with ANNE LOUVET, a spirited young waitress at the hotel of the title. His attempt to redeem her unhappiness ends in disaster. Also appears briefly in *Birdsong* and *Charlotte Gray*, uniting Faulks's French trilogy.

Hartmann, Thomas
Latecomers, 1988
Anita Brookner

A 'voluptuary' in late middle-age, Hartmann is a director of a greetings-card company in tandem with his partner THOMAS FIBICH. 'Of course the work was anathema to them both', but Hartmann sails through each day, dallying, enjoying lunch, aspiring to 'the sublime'. As a German brought to England to attend private school during World War II, he would have been an outsider but for Fibich, a fellow German and orphan at the same school. Now, Hartmann has 'charming' friends and has created a niche of bourgeois comfort and security. But when his daughter suffers a miscarriage, it appears that even he cannot control a naturally chaotic world.

Hartright, Walter
The Woman in White, 1860
Wilkie Collins

A 28-year-old teacher of drawing, devoted to his mother and sister Sarah, he is a modest professional man whose life is forever altered by his encounter with the 'woman in white' and his acceptance of employment at Limmeridge House in Cumberland, where he meets LAURA FAIRLIE. Beguiled by her beauty and grace, he shows a cat-like propensity for surviving the hazards of a dangerous foreign sojourn and displays dogged courage and determination as he later turns detective to seek justice and restore to Laura her name and rightful position.

Hartshorn, Priss
The Group, 1963
Mary McCarthy

Studious, nervous and solemn, Priss dislikes attracting attention to herself and has a horror of being a nuisance. Politically liberal and naturally idealistic, she 'could not imagine a more exciting time to come of age than right now in America'. This is a genuinely-held belief which is never quite shaken by the pressure of her domineering, strongly Republican husband. Despite the stress of her constant struggle to win Sloan's approval in every aspect of marriage and motherhood, Priss manages to see beyond the confines of her family and remains a crusader and a believer in progress.

Hartsook, Ralph
The Hoosier Schoolmaster, 1871
Edward Eggleston

Based on Eggleston's own brother, Ralph is a well-intentioned young man who takes over a village school in rural Indiana. As well as fending off the local sirens, he learns that he must adapt his methods to suit a robust, sleeves-rolled-up environment in which his blackboard training is of little use.

Harvey, Gabriel
Gabriel's Lament, 1986
Paul Bailey

Gabriel Harvey, the author of a study of itinerant preachers, is a lonely, tormented man. Looking back from the 1980s, he reflects upon a happy, though poor childhood spent during the 1940s and 1950s with OSWALD HARVEY, his father, and Amy, his mother, in an impoverished part of London. Everything changed, however, when Oswald inherited money. Amy mysteriously left and his father maintained she was on holiday: Gabriel recalls being bewildered and then distressed when he realized she would never return. Later in life, when he discovers the tragic secret of his mother and her suicide, Gabriel laments her, his impossible father and the lies and falsities of his youth.

Harvey, Oswald
Gabriel's Lament, 1986
Paul Bailey

A teller of tall tales and absurdly embellished memories of an impoverished childhood, Oswald Harvey, married to Amy, a woman 35 years his junior, is an ebullient, larger-than-life figure, dominating his young son, GABRIEL HARVEY. But when he inherits money, Oswald becomes a snob. Regulars at the local pub see a popular wag transformed into a bumptious bar-room philosopher. Amy leaves him, yet 'the Great Dissembler' as his son begins to call him, refuses to divulge the reason. Tormented by being abandoned and by the fact that his ideal of love has turned to ashes, Oswald becomes an exasperating, even heroically defiant figure, but one increasingly unable to confront grim reality.

Haskins, Timothy
'Under the Lion's Paw', in *Main-Travelled Roads*, 1892
revised editions 1899, 1922, 1930
Hamlin Garland

He is 'a tall man with a thin, gloomy face ... You would have felt that he had suffered much by the line of his mouth showing under the thin, yellow moustache'. Driven out of Kansas by successive plagues of grasshoppers, his spirit, if not his willingness to work, is almost broken.

Haslam, Rev Bill
Back to Methuselah, 1921
George Bernard Shaw

A young clergyman, Haslam appears in the second section of this five-part play. *The Gospel of the Brothers Barnabas* is set in a Hampstead study in the early years of World War I. A likeable but boyish personality, Haslam has 'nothing clerical about him except his collar'. He is engaged to 'SAVVY' BARNABAS and together they deride the BARNABAS brothers' theories that man might live for 300 years. 'It wont happen to me: thats jolly sure', remarks Haslam. Later, he reappears as the ARCHBISHOP OF YORK, aged 283.

Hastings, Captain Arthur
The Mysterious Affair at Styles, 1920, et seq
Agatha Christie

A bumbling but beloved DR WATSON to HERCULE POIROT's SHERLOCK HOLMES, he works as a secretary to an MP whilst sharing London rooms with the Belgian sleuth. An honest, trusting fellow who chronicles Poirot's celebrated cases, he leaves his companion's side to travel to Argentina with his new bride. In conversation, he is warmly recalled by Poirot as 'mon ami' despite his admission that he found Hastings 'occasionally of an imbecility to make one afraid'.

Hastings, George
She Stoops to Conquer, 1773
Oliver Goldsmith

Together with MARLOW, Hastings is one of the play's romantic heroes. He is in love with CONSTANCE NEVILLE, the niece of DOROTHY HARDCASTLE, and accompanies his friend to the Hardcastle home to see her and apprise her of his plan for their elopement. He flatters the appalling Mrs Hardcastle and is careful not to offend her husband, SQUIRE RICHARD HARDCASTLE. He has no compunction in using every ounce of his considerable social graces in order to be close to Constance, but although she has money, Hastings is not a fortune hunter.

Hat
Miguel Street, 1959
V S Naipaul

He has a 'passion for impossible bets', is 'like Rex Harrison' in appearance and is both friend and hero to the young boy who narrates these stories about Miguel Street in Port of Spain, Trinidad. He is popular with all the young boys on the street because of his playful sense of humour, but when one day he brings home a woman things turn sour for Hat and his friends: 'He had become a man with responsibility and obligations, and he could no longer give us all his time and attention.'

Hatch
Black Jack, 1968
Leon Garfield

The evil antithesis and mortal enemy of TOLLY, Hatch is DR CARMODY's mean-hearted and self-promoting apprentice, a vindictive blackmailer, made eloquent by greed. Sharp-witted, especially where there is a chance of financial gain, he might, in other circumstances, have

been a successful politician or judge.

Hatch
The Sea, 1973
Edward Bond

As the draper in a seaside village, fretting over his business, Hatch is, as MRS RAFI observes, 'over-imaginative'. In fact, his imagination has been both stunted and twisted by the oppressive society of the town and by his own fears and weaknesses. He appears an unhappy, sad, insecure, rather boyish figure, tramping wildly along the seashore, believing that visitors from outer space are stealthily plotting the subjugation of the human race. Yet he is distraught, a man driven mad by the cruelty of the world, the absurd and intolerable pressures of commerce and the position of servility and dependence from which he sees no escape for himself.

Hatchway, Mr Jack
The Adventures of Peregrine Pickle, 1751, bowdlerized edition 1758
Tobias Smollett

COMMODORE HAWSER TRUNNION's former lieutenant, in whose service he gave away one of his legs, and with whom he now lives as a half-pay companion, a more or less passive listening post for the commodore's endlessly re-run sea battles.

Hatteraick, Captain Dirk
Guy Mannering, 1816
Sir Walter Scott

The Dutch-accented leader of the smugglers who are induced to kidnap young HARRY BERTRAM. 'He was apparently a seafaring man, rather under the middle size and with a countenance bronzed by a thousand conflicts with the north-east wind. His frame was prodigiously muscular, strong and thick-set ... He was hard-favoured, and, which was worse, his face bore nothing of the *insouciance*, the careless frolicsome jollity and vacant curiosity of a sailor on shore.'

Hatterr, H
All About H. Hatterr, 1948
G V Desani

A 20th-century Everyman who has sucked up and personalized a polyglot dialect compounded of elements from popular fiction, philosophy, law, the movies and medicine. His own world-view is refreshingly simple: 'To be easy and comfortable appears to be the aim of all men: even at the expense of the other feller.'

Hatty, properly Harriet
Tom's Midnight Garden, 1958
Philippa Pearce

A 'tagger-on', the poor relation who runs along behind her cousins, trying to join in with their games. She alone of the cousins can see TOM, and becomes his playmate. In reality an orphan, she pretends to Tom to be a princess, a prisoner in exile. The tree-house she builds with him becomes a refuge from her cousins and aunt, a place where she can be herself. Hatty is a figure apart, both as a girl and as she grows up – 'a habit of solitude in early childhood is not easily broken'.

Hauksbee, Mrs
'The Rescue of Pluffles', in *PlainTales from the Hills*, 1890
Rudyard Kipling

'Mrs Hauksbee was sometimes nice to her own sex', but is more often 'honestly mischievous', with an irrepressible urge to meddle in the lives of younger colonials. She has seen them come and go, ripen and decay from promising buds straight out of Sandhurst into overblown old majors and colonels and she gives off a sense of understanding all humankind, but especially those of a class just above her own.

Hautia, Queen
Mardi, 1849
Herman Melville

The luscious, sensual Queen of Flozella a Nino, who holds men in her thrall, and has supernatural powers. She appears as an 'incognito' or phantom to TAJI in Odo, and spirits away YILLAH. She has a fathomless, 'mysterious, evil-boding gaze', but is radiant and 'lustrous as rainbows'. She transforms stolen maidens into her attending nymphs.

Haut-ton, Sir Oran
Melincourt, or Sir Oran Haut-ton, 1817
Thomas Love Peacock

Baron, Member of Parliament and, as his name suggests, an orangutan, Sir Oran is the satirical portrait of an evolutionary theory which held that apes were part of the human species and not vice versa. His guardian, MR SYLVAN FORESTER, asserts that Sir Oran is 'a specimen of the natural and original man', despite his silence, his ape-like gait and his 'ludicrous' face. He is also the vehicle for a satire upon the competence of politicians. Although he cannot speak, he nonetheless allies himself by his actions with the forces of good, and to an extent vindicates Sylvan Forester.

Havisham, Miss
Great Expectations, 1861
Charles Dickens

A beautiful heiress as a girl, she was jilted on her wedding day by COMPEYSON, and has lived ever since as an eccentric recluse, still dressed in her faded bridal gown. Now 'withered like the dress', she has adopted ESTELLA with the help of MR JAGGERS and educates her to steel herself against affection and break the hearts of young men. She leads PIP to believe she is his benefactor and encourages Estella to torment him. Contemptuous of her greedy, fawning relatives, she omits all except MATTHEW POCKET from her will. Her own heart is broken when Estella spurns her, and she seeks Pip's forgiveness at their last meeting, giving him money to help HERBERT POCKET. After Pip leaves, her dress catches fire and, despite his return and attempt to rescue her, she dies.

Havoc, Jack
The Tiger in the Smoke, 1952
Margery Allingham

If CANON HUBERT AVRIL represents Christian good, then Jack Havoc embodies brutal evil. A consistent villain and now a convicted murderer on the run, Havoc is tall, powerful, athletic, graceful, 'like an animal'. He is handsome, even though the prison pallor, the eyes that both attract and repel, the thin-lipped mouth and beautiful teeth make his face 'a design for a tragedy ... Grief and torture and the furies were all there naked'. Havoc has no compunction about cutting throats because, for him, life has little value. This absence of compassion and his almost religious sense of inevitable fate ('the Science of Luck'), make him both terrifying and pitiable.

Hawdon, Captain
Bleak House, 1853
Charles Dickens

A wretched law-writer who lodges with MR KROOK under the alias of Nemo (Latin for 'no one'). As a handsome young Army officer, he was the lover of LADY DEDLOCK before her marriage, and the father of her illegitimate child, ESTHER SUMMERSON. Now sunk into poverty and addicted to opium, his only friend is JO. When he dies in his squalid garret, he is buried in a paupers' graveyard at the gates of which Lady Dedlock's body is later found by Esther and MR BUCKET.

Hawk, Sir Mulberry
Nicholas Nickleby, 1839
Charles Dickens

A dissolute fashionable gambler, he tries to seduce KATE NICKLEBY but his grossness is punished by her brother, NICHOLAS. He dupes LORD FREDERICK VERISOPHT, then kills him in a duel and flees to France. On his return, he is arrested for debt and dies in prison.

Hawkins, Clay
The Gilded Age, 1873
Mark Twain and Charles Dudley Warner

The orphaned Clay displays the same unselfish devotion to his adoptive family in his adult life as he showed to his dying mother as a child. Enterprising, though practical and level-headed, he uncomplainingly takes on adult responsibilities at an early age and works to support the family while LAURA HAWKINS and Washington, her adoptive brother, continue to dream only of obtaining instant and fabulous wealth.

Hawkins, Jim
Treasure Island, 1883
Robert Louis Stevenson

Swept up on a treasure-hunting journey, he is an intrepid boy hero whose adventures take on the quality of a nightmare as he finds himself increasingly separated from calm domestic influences and social norms. Surrounded by the evil of LONG JOHN SILVER and his crew, Jim undergoes an education in maturity, learning to distinguish moral values, and he earns his place as a responsible individual in the company of adults. Although Jim conquers his childhood anxieties and wayward behaviour to become a fully socialized young man, it is cynically implied that this new life will inevitably be achieved at the cost of dullness and conventionality.

Hawkins, Laura
The Gilded Age, 1873
Mark Twain and Charles Dudley Warner

Shrewd, deep and exceptionally beautiful, she uses her charms, intelligence and cunning to pursue her dreams of attaining fabulous wealth and having men at her feet. A dangerous, unscrupulous schemer, she thrives in Washington DC where she lobbies for a project that she hopes will enrich her. She is impervious to the attentions of her legion of male admirers save one, the worthless scoundrel COL GEORGE SELBY.

Hawkins, Mrs Nancy
A Far Cry from Kensington, 1988
Muriel Spark

Although aged only 28, this fat, motherly war-widow is called Mrs Hawkins by everyone; only after she decides to be thin and has developed a more glamorous image is she known as Nancy. Always ready with advice – to the reader as well as to those about her – she eventually tires of being confided in and consulted. She loses jobs in publishing because of her insistence on calling HECTOR BARTLETT *'pisseur de copie'*. Kind, good and formidable, she enjoys her insomnia, which allows her to think and remember.

Hawkins, Nanny
Brideshead Revisited, 1945
Evelyn Waugh

A passionate Catholic with a 'lined and serene face', Nanny Hawkins is an omnipresent social and religious focus for the FLYTE family. Forever doing her needlework by the fire, with her radio for company, she continues to see adults as they were in childhood, and for years appears herself to be impervious to change. When CHARLES RYDER last visits her in the Brideshead nursery, however, she has suddenly aged greatly: her sight is failing, and her speech has reverted to the 'soft, peasant tones of its origin'.

Hawkins, Si ('Squire')
The Gilded Age, 1873
Mark Twain and Charles Dudley Warner

Described by his wife as 'a great, good, noble soul', he has a restless intellect and a thirst to make a fortune, characteristics which draw him and his family into the wake of the rainbow-chasing COL BERIAH SELLERS. Hawkins transmits his wild and fantastic hopes and ambitions to his son Washington and to his adopted daughter LAURA HAWKINS, firing their imaginations and causing them to grow up believing that great wealth will come easily and inevitably.

Hawkins, Tessa (Teresa)
For Love Alone, 1944
Christina Stead

Brought up in a huge, ramshackle family and an atmosphere of ruthless emotional laissez-faire, she becomes solitary and emotionally starved, obsessed with the conviction that love is her destiny. 'She smelled, heard, saw, guessed faster, loved more than others, it seemed to her.'

Hawks, Captain Andy
Show Boat, 1926
Edna Ferber

A riverboat captain on the Mississippi (the 'Old Man River' of Hammerstein's operetta), his growing inability to pilot his own life is signalled by his marriage to the apparently shore-bound and definitely strait-laced PARTHY ANN HAWKS, who takes over from him after his death.

Hawks, Parthy Ann
Show Boat, 1926
Edna Ferber

A rather proper schoolmarm from New England, she makes an unlikely bride for the showboat captain ANDY HAWKS. Nevertheless, she comes to understand the workings of the boat as well as Andy and takes over when he dies. Their daughter Magnolia has as much of her mother's primness as of her father's restless blood.

Hawksmoor, Nicholas
Hawksmoor, 1985
Peter Ackroyd

A senior police detective, he is investigating a series of murders which have been committed on the sites of various 18th-century churches in east London. His character is linked thematically in the novel with that of the 18th-century architect, NICHOLAS DYER. A blunt, methodical detective, a moralist troubled by life's tragedies, Hawksmoor is plagued by nervous stress, and prone to parodying remarks made by his colleagues. Yet he is also imaginative and speculative. A man who empathizes with the lineaments of history, pondering their nature and recognizing their resonances, he is a fatalist who believes the murderer and victim to be inclined to their own destruction.

Haxby, Gina
Haxby's Circus, 1930
Katharine Susannah Prichard

The focus of a small family circus – its crippled star, its energy, its future – Gina is a woman of great inner strength and courage, able to overcome the hardship of a disabled life: 'Oh, me, I'm tough!'

Haxby Palmer, Frieda
The Witch Of Exmoor, 1996
Margaret Drabble

Domineering, wilful and unpredictable, Haxby is a once-successful novelist and social sage whose career was ruined by the failure of her vast novel about Queen Christina of Sweden. Having retreated to a remote, abandoned and derelict hotel perching on the edge of a cliff, she evades her extended family who fearfully suspect her of writing vindictive memoirs. Impulsive (she abandons her car in the middle of a traffic jam) and headstrong (she conducts lengthy campaigns against various authorities), she is not wholly neglectful of the sensibilities of others but values independence and relishes the embarrassment and confusion her eccentricity causes among her mannered, cultivated children and their spouses.

Haydon, Bill
Tinker, Tailor, Soldier, Spy, 1974
John Le Carré

Right-wing in the Oxford Union, Haydon had been a linguist and hero before joining the Secret Service in 1939. In it he has become yet more legendary for his unorthodox charm and his leather jacket patches. Unfortunately, he is a Russian mole, found out by GEORGE SMILEY – whose wife Bill has had an affair with. Haydon's detection is unwelcome to everyone, especially those who suspected but preferred to stay ignorant.

Hazard, Sir Melchior
Wise Children, 1991
Angela Carter

Now aged 100 and frequently spoken of as the greatest Shakespearean actor of his day (an estimation with which he emphatically agrees), Sir Melchior is a rumbustious, feisty figure, an actor-laddie in the old, booming tradition. A good deal of his talent lies in his natural authority, charm, and the relentless and sometimes grating promotion of his own ego. A seducer and a rogue, he is a tall, handsome man with eyes 'as dark and sexy as the inside of a London cab in wartime'. He is the father of NORA and DORA CHANCE, illegitimate daughters whom he has professed to have forgotten about for many years while devoting himself to his glittering career.

Hazel
Watership Down, 1972
Richard Adams

A shrewd, sensible rabbit, Hazel accepts his brother FIVER's vision of the destruction of their warren, and convinces BIGWIG, Blackberry and a small band of followers that they must leave Sandleford in search of another home. Initially diffident, 'Hazel-rah' (Chief Rabbit) proves to be an adaptable, pragmatic leader, prepared to rely on the skills of others where his own are insufficient. Bold and tenacious, he leads from the front, shouldering risks for his companions.

Hazlett, Elsa
The Hothouse by the East River, 1973
Muriel Spark

From her overheated New York flat, 14 storeys up, Elsa stares out over the East River, while her shadow falls in the wrong direction. Her Montenegrin husband, Paul, thinks she is mad; yet, although she behaves strangely, acting just as she pleases and being subject to swings of mood, she seems no more insane than the people about her. She has changed since her early poverty in Sevenoaks and her time in British Intelligence during World War II, having become mysteriously rich. Paul also says that she is dead.

Headland, Liz
The Radiant Way, 1987
A Natural Curiosity, 1989
The Gates of Ivory, 1991
Margaret Drabble

Liz, ALIX BOWEN and ESTHER BREUER have been friends for many years, since graduating from Cambridge together in the 1950s. Liz is now a wife, mother and stepmother and, at the beginning of the 1980s (the decade the trilogy spans) is about to be divorced. She is a competent, confident and respected Harley Street psychotherapist who, by the third novel, is still practising but living spaciously in St John's Wood. She is independent, forthright, sometimes emotionally rash and often intellectually circumspect.

Headlong, Squire Harry
Headlong Hall, 1816
Thomas Love Peacock

A full-blooded, beefy man fond of country pursuits, good wine and with an aversion to drinking water, Squire Headlong also has a soft spot for intellectual and philosophical milieux. He is a bluff, occasionally domineering host, entertaining a motley band of philosophers, thinkers and scientists at Headlong Hall with ample amounts of burgundy. 'Pass the bottle' is his refrain; not a thinker himself, he gains prestige, he thinks, by association with intellectuals, whom he can, of course, 'buy' in with burgundy and venison.

Headmaster, the
Forty Years On, 1968
Alan Bennett

The head of Albion House, a minor English public school, he is a patrician of the old order, patriotic, pedantic but now also beleaguered and world-weary. On the day of his retirement, as he recalls having heard nightingales singing the evening before World War I was declared, world-weariness turns to anguish as he remembers a generation who never returned, and realizes that history is largely a matter of human fallibility and failure.

Headrigg, Cuddie
Old Mortality, in *Tales of My Landlord*, 1816
Sir Walter Scott

Recusant ploughman at Tillietudlem, kept back from the musters by his old mother, MAUSE HEADRIGG, on the slender grounds that he is ill. Less versed in matters doctrinal than Mause, he defines his position vis-à-vis the Established Church as 'non-enormity'.

Headrigg, Mause
Old Mortality, in *Tales of My Landlord*, 1816
Sir Walter Scott

The elderly mother of the ploughman CUDDIE HEADRIGG, she greets her betters with 'an expression of respect, mingled with obstinacy'. She is not above lecturing LADY MARGARET BELLENDEN on the niceties of Old Testament theology when her Presbyterian susceptibilities are engaged.

Headstone, Bradley
Our Mutual Friend, 1865
Charles Dickens

The schoolmaster of CHARLEY HEXAM, he seems 'a thoroughly decent young man' but has 'a manner that would be better described as one of lying in wait'. His fellow teacher, Miss Emma Peecher, loves him unrequitedly, while he is passionately obsessed with LIZZIE HEXAM, who is repelled by him. Jealous of his rival, EUGENE WRAYBURN, he disguises himself as ROGUE RIDERHOOD and attempts to murder Wrayburn. After being blackmailed by Riderhood, he tries to murder him but they drown together.

Hearn, Lt Robert
The Naked and the Dead, 1948
Norman Mailer

His college thesis is *The Cosmic Urge in Herman Melville*, but this is as far as he is able to go in search of ultimate truths and experiences. Cold and detached, he never gets below the surface of ideas or relationships. A lover tells him: 'you're nothing but a goddam shell ... a million miles away, aren't you, nothing ever hits you'. In the novel, he stands for flimsy liberalism, powerless in the face of the instinctual SGT SAM CROFT and GEN EDWARD CUMMINGS.

Hearn, Robert
Bring Larks and Heroes, 1967
Thomas Keneally

As a prisoner in an Australian penal settlement, he introduces his guard CORPORAL PHELIM HALLORAN to progressive and enlightened ideas, influencing Halloran's switch of loyalties.

Hearne, Judith
The Lonely Passion of Judith Hearne, 1955
Brian Moore

A lonely, neurotic spinster who has a tendency to drink. With no family and few friends, this pathetic soul flits from boarding house to boarding house, ever hopeful of a fresh start. She is a constant dreamer whose lifetime ambition has been to find happiness through marriage. Although she seems weak and silly, Miss Hearne's fragile resilience and her refusal to give in are incredible, and she evokes great pity and some anger when she is led on, then rejected, by the brash Mr Madden. Her loss of faith in God and eventual breakdown appear to be fully justified.

Heartfree
The Provok'd Wife, 1696
Sir John Vanbrugh

A dilettante, Heartfree astonishes himself by actually falling in love for the first time, not with the imperious LADY FANCIFUL, whom he is courting, but with BELLINDA, the niece of LADY BRUTE. At the outset of the play, Heartfree is a rake, boastful, critical of the apparent foibles of women; but love changes everything. Yet, while he is honest and open with his male friends, he is far more closely-guarded with the woman who is to become his wife.

Heartfree, Thomas
The Life of Jonathan Wild the Great, 1743
Henry Fielding

The head of an insipid and mediocre family, Heartfree is hopelessly outnumbered by mercenary and hostile men. His exemplary and honest life has brought him sentimental bliss, but his virtue is ineffectual in its determined passivity and is no counter to the dynamism of evil, as epitomized by the glamorous JONATHAN WILD. Ultimately, however, Providence intervenes and Heartfree prospers beyond his wildest dreams.

Heaslop, Ronny
A Passage to India, 1924
E M Forster

The City Magistrate of Chandrapore, he is a pleasant young man who has all too enthusiastically embraced the prejudices, snobbery and complacency of the English community in India. Although he was once unconventional and humanitarian, service in India has brought out the conformist in him and now he is content to dispense British justice, keep the peace and consort only with his own kind. Driven by work, duty and the herd instinct, he has acquired the sensitivity of a bull in a china shop and developed aspects of his character that his fiancée ADELA QUESTED 'had never admired'.

Heathcliff
Wuthering Heights, 1848
Emily Brontë

A proud, black-haired gypsy ragamuffin from the streets of Liverpool, he is brought into the Earnshaw household where his life is to be governed by a hatred for the tyrannical son HINDLEY EARNSHAW and an all-consuming passion for the daughter CATHERINE EARNSHAW. A lovestruck, uncultured and sullen teenager who determines to exact his revenge on the inhabitants of Wuthering Heights, he grows into a tall, handsome figure, 'rough as a saw edge and hard as whinstone'. He adopts the appearance of a country gentleman, but remains a solitary, morose schemer, lost in the maze of his grief after Catherine's death and unable to relish the triumph he has awaited all his adult life.

Heathcliff, Linton
Wuthering Heights, 1848
Emily Brontë

The son of HEATHCLIFF and ISABELLA LINTON, he is a delicate, snivelling child, prone to a succession of maladies. Raised in constant fear of attracting his father's thunderous ire, he becomes a petulant, self-centred young man capable of almost any deceitful act that will ensure his own comfort. Sickly and spineless, he lives long enough to endear himself to the good graces of his cousin CATHERINE LINTON and become her husband, thus serving Heathcliff's plan to unite the two families and be master of all their properties.

Heather
Palace Without Chairs, 1978
Brigid Brophy

The last daughter of the new king of Evarchia, she is a drunken lesbian, with a 'pachydermous' indifference to the vagaries of fortune as an historical anachronism. A character from opera uncomfortably transported into a too-real world, she is nonetheless a symbol of hope to set against the sterile 'fertility' of her family.

Heathfield, Alfred
The Battle of Life, 1846
Charles Dickens

The ward of DR ANTHONY JEDDLER, he is a

medical student and sweetheart of MARION JEDDLER. But after Marion's apparent elopement, he marries her sister, GRACE JEDDLER. He becomes a doctor who does 'useful, patient and unsung' work among the poor.

Hecate
Macbeth, c.1606
William Shakespeare

'The close contriver of all harms' who, as 'mistress' of THE THREE WEIRD SISTERS, appears to make one long speech in the middle of the play. She reveals herself as a shrewd and wicked leader – 'and you all know security/Is mortals' chiefest enemy' – though the patchy quality of her couplet speech, and its proximity to some untypical singing and dancing, suggests she may not be a Shakespearean creation.

Hector
Troilus and Cressida, 1601/2
William Shakespeare

The son of PRIAM, the Trojan king, and his 'crutch' during the war with the Greeks, Hector provides a model of valour and honour for the other Trojans. He is dignified and courageous in battle as well as being just and merciful – often when he has disarmed and beaten his enemies on the battlefield, he will 'bid them rise and live'. He is also an intelligent man, who can argue and reason eloquently.

Hector, Old
Young Art and Old Hector, 1942
Neil Gunn

Symbolizing the wisdom and knowledge of life, Hector has time on his hands and enjoys the company of YOUNG ART, who still sees the world with freshness and innocence. Hector realizes that the future of their culture depends on those such as Art and has the patience, understanding and humour to help guide the boy through the joys and pitfalls of life. He treats Art as an adult and an equal, and the two form a close relationship based on a love for the land and the community.

Hecuba
The Woman, 1978
Edward Bond

A character appropriated by Bond from Greek tragedy, she rules over a feudal Troy, defending the city against attack by the Greeks led by HEROS. Later, having withdrawn to an unnamed island, the wise, resilient, stoic, blind Hecuba cares for her mentally handicapped daughter, Ismene.

Hedges, Bob
Restoration, 1981
Edward Bond

The semi-literate footman of LORD ARE, he is expected to take the blame for his master's murder of his wife. Hedges is an honest man, yet despite the protestations of his wife, he is eventually hanged for a crime he did not commit. Although himself the victim of injustice, he nevertheless informs on a fellow footman who has stolen one of Lord Are's silver spoons, revealing that he is essentially compliant,

fulfilling the feudal role expected of him by the ruling class. Hedges has little education or spirit of moral or ethical enquiry; these, implies Bond, have been denied him by the social system he is part of.

Heep, Uriah
David Copperfield, 1850
Charles Dickens

The obsequious, hypocritical and scheming clerk in MR WICKFIELD's law firm and afterwards, his partner. Cadaverous, with 'hardly any eyebrows, and no eyelashes' and a bony hand 'like a fish', his constant claim is 'I'm a very umble person'. His mother, Mrs Heep, is equally ''umble' and his 'dead image, only short'. Jealous of DAVID COPPERFIELD, he connives to take control over Wickfield's business and has ambitions to marry his daughter, AGNES. His dishonesty is exposed by MR WILKINS MICAWBER, and Wickfield's property and reputation are restored. Heep is convicted of fraud, forgery and conspiracy and sentenced to MR CREAKLE's model prison.

Heidegger, Dr
'Dr. Heidegger's Experiment', 1837, in *Twice-Told Tales*, 1837, revised edition 1842
Nathaniel Hawthorne

'A very strange old gentleman, whose eccentricity had become the nucleus for a thousand fables.' He is the discoverer of Ponce de Leon's legendary Fountain of Youth, whose waters he administers to four aged friends, thereby demonstrating that time can only briefly be cheated.

Heidler, Hugh (H J)
Quartet, 1969, originally published as *Postures*, 1928
Jean Rhys

'Large, invulnerable, and perfectly respectable', he is known as a generous patron and an intellectual amongst the impoverished writers and artists of Montparnasse. Physically commanding, his cold eyes and fixed expression betray the brutality he brings to his relationships with women. Rumoured to have once suffered a nervous breakdown, he is now assured of his wealth and stature, and exerts tyrannical power over his wife, LOIS HEIDLER, and his lover, MARYA ZELLI.

Heidler, Lois
Quartet, 1969, originally published as *Postures*, 1928
Jean Rhys

The wife of HUGH (H J) HEIDLER, and MARYA ZELLI's chief antagonist, Lois is a compact and tidy woman, with the broad, coarse features of a peasant. 'An absolute primitive', she applies her limited intelligence solely to pleasing her husband and maintaining their joint respectability, even to the extent of colluding with him in his many extra-marital affairs.

Heisenberg, Werner
Copenhagen, 1998
Michael Frayn

The play deals with a real-life meeting in Copenhagen in 1941 between the German physicist Heisenberg and Europe's leading quantum physicist NIELS BOHR, for which no definitive account exists. In the play, Heisenberg, a pragmatist, may or may not have deliberately failed to make calculations that would have enabled the Nazis to build an atomic bomb. However, his exact moral position is unclear, and whether he is seeking information or absolution from his old friend, collaborator and mentor is debatable.

Held, Truman
Meridian, 1976
Alice Walker

Caught by the trends of black resistance, Truman vascillates among a series of truths. An artist and 'conquering prince', he pursues freedom by enforcing his own power and control. Realizing that he 'was always looking for Meridian, even when he didn't know it', he finally comes to terms with her need for solitude. Ceasing to search for the answers in political theories, he becomes aware that he must internalize this conflict before he can move on.

Helen
Down among the Women, 1971
Fay Weldon

Unbalanced, creative, with a sense of style, she is a complex character who comes to realize that because she is an equal to men, they cannot be content with her; she is too threatening. There is no possible solution for Helen, for though she has much to give, there is no one to give to.

Helen
Elidor, 1968
Alan Garner

The sister of NICHOLAS, DAVID and ROLAND, Helen is the peacemaker of the family, quietly prepared to go along with whatever her older brothers decide. She has no lack of courage, but is calm and cautious, and therefore provides a perfect foil for Roland's impetuousness. In the end she has a crucial role to play as the 'makeless maid' of the 'Lay of the Starved Fool'.

Helen
Troilus and Cressida, 1601/2
William Shakespeare

The wife of the Spartan king Menelaus. Her seduction by PARIS is the reason the Greeks and Trojans are at war. Whether or not she is worthy of the battle is argued by many – despite being charming and beautiful, she is described by one Greek as 'soiled' and 'false'.

Helen
White With Wire Wheels, 1970
Jack Hibberd

The beautiful, young, enigmatic and desirable Helen is a cool, calculating woman. Pitted against a trinity of 'Aussie male menaces', she plays them at their own game, shocking them with their own obscenities and, ultimately, with a vision of themselves 'frightened and unenlightened'.

Helena
All's Well That Ends Well, 1602–3
William Shakespeare

The orphaned daughter of a physician and ward of the COUNTESS OF ROUSILLON, Helena cures the KING OF FRANCE of an apparently fatal illness and, as her reward, claims the countess's son, BERTRAM, as her husband. Refusing to consummate the marriage with a commoner so peremptorily thrust upon him, Bertram leaves for the Italian wars. After Helena cleverly foils his intended betrayal of her with another woman, they are reconciled. Helena appears only sporadically during the play, yet its rhythm is measured by her evolution from a confused idealist and rebuffed lover into a ruthless woman of action, the equal of Bertram.

Helena
Helena, 1950
Evelyn Waugh

The mother of the Emperor Constantine and discoverer of the True Cross, she is first seen in her carefree youth, when she is described as being 'taller and lighter than the general taste required'. In maturity she is passionately devoted to the furtherance of the Christ cult.

Helena
A Midsummer Night's Dream, c.1594
William Shakespeare

She starts as the despondent victim of unrequited love, gazing longingly at her best friend's intended husband, DEMETRIUS; by the play's end, having encountered the many twists of the play's 'mortal' plot and been insulted as a 'canker-blossom' and 'painted maypole', she has him. She is a witty, reductive character, full of doubt and charm, an effective contrast to the more superficial HERMIA.

Helenus
Troilus and Cressida, 1601/2
William Shakespeare

The only son of King PRIAM who is not directly involved in the fighting between Greece and Troy, Helenus is a priest. He argues, unsuccessfully, for the cessation of the war, advising prudence and reason in his father's dealing with the Greeks.

Helicanus
Pericles, c.1608
William Shakespeare

'A figure of truth, of faith, of loyalty', Helicanus is a lord of Tyre who advises PERICLES to travel, and who governs Tyre in his place while he is away. He is absent for so long that the noblemen offer Helicanus the crown, but he refuses, deferring acceptance for a year. Subsequently, he is present at the reunion of father and daughter and is presented to THAISA. Helicanus is a rock of stability in a shifting world of deceptions and deceits.

Hella
Giovanni's Room, 1956
James Baldwin

The young woman who forces DAVID to rethink his homosexuality and his commitment to his young lover GIOVANNI. Like Giovanni, she is often little more than a bundle of characteristics, abstract options and focuses for David's floundering self-image.

Hellenore
The Faerie Queene, 1590–6
Sir Edmund Spenser

Spenser's degenerate version of Helen of Troy. She is the comely, graceful and youthful wife of MALBECCO, and has strong sexual desires which her husband cannot satisfy. Feeling trapped in her castle, she is easily taken in by romantic tale-tellers and her own fanciful day-dreams, and gladly succumbs to PARIDELL. She finds ultimate gratification with a band of satyrs, and refuses to return to her wealthy but feeble husband.

Heller, Mr
Butcher's Broom, 1934
Neil Gunn

An ambitious lawyer, driven by his desire for power and wealth. Knowing he has the complete backing of the landowners and thus the government itself, he systematically uses the laws of the land against the people, thus effectively forestalling all forms of resistance. He epitomizes the cunning and cruelty of those who abuse power for self-advancement while convinced of the justification of their actions.

Helstone, Caroline
Shirley, 1849
Charlotte Brontë

A young girl who has never known her own parents, she keeps house for her uncle, who shows her little attention and no affection. 'Modest and unassuming' by nature, she is beset by feelings of inadequacy and inferiority, and wishes she were a boy so that she might take up some sort of business or profession to gain meaning and control in her life. 'Docile yet quick', she is generous if passive; she is also unnaturally sensitive, and is reduced to complete despair by her unrequited love for her cousin.

Hench, Simon
Otherwise Engaged, 1975
Simon Gray

Sardonic to his acquaintances, publisher Simon Hench seduces young women without scruple, yet he is an ordered man, one of few words who prefers brevity in others. His detachment, provoking the rage and exposing the fears and weaknesses of those around him, appears to their eyes as cruel indifference or sneering contempt. 'Your sanity is of the kind that causes other people to go quietly mad around you', observes his unfaithful wife.

Henchard, Elizabeth-Jane → Newson, Elizabeth-Jane

Henchard, Michael
The Mayor of Casterbridge, 1886
Thomas Hardy

A tragic hero in the classical mould, Henchard is a man of forceful character, who achieves high social status only to be undone by the repercussions of an act of folly committed in his youth, when he sold his wife at a fair after a bout of drinking. Although he attempts to atone for this act in his later life, he remains haunted by it, and Fate conspires to punish him. His downfall is

accelerated by his stubborn pride and his poor judgement of character. Impulsive, moody and brutish, he is nevertheless capable of great sensitivity, generosity and nobility.

Henderson, Amy
Blaming, 1976
Elizabeth Taylor

During a trip to Istanbul she loses her husband (apparently from a heart attack after they have made love), and finds her life transformed. Blaming herself for his death, she becomes unfairly resentful of the kindness of strangers.

Henderson, Elias
The Abbot, 1820
Sir Walter Scott

The chaplain at Lochleven, he is a quiet, forebearing man, entirely free of the fanaticism that marks his more extreme Protestant brethren. 'He was a man in the prime of life, and possessed of good natural parts, carefully improved by the best education which those times afforded.'

Henderson, Eugene
Henderson the Rain King, 1959
Saul Bellow

A millionaire of Anglo-Saxon Protestant stock, he is both physically and emotionally overblown, obsessed by his own insatiable ego and need for self-gratification, driven by an inner voice demanding 'I want! I want!' He is powerful, violent, bursting with unfocused energy, disoriented, and 'displaced' in life, but also has a desperate hunger for spiritual discovery. His experiences in a mythicized Africa, where life is 'simplified and splendid', allow him to harness his initially destructive '*grun-to-molani*', or life-force, and discover a regenerative relationship with both humanity and nature.

Henderson, Miriam
Pointed Roofs, 1915, et seq
Dorothy Richardson

Amorphous, erratic and idiosyncratic, Miriam is primarily a creature of mind rather than body. Nonetheless, she pursues reality through sexuality and tries to discover freedom of action as well as thought. She defies masculine prerogatives, rejecting male hierarchies of value and rigid classifications. Sexually ambivalent, 'something between a man and a woman', she is attracted to the vivacious and radiant Amabel. Immersing herself in life, Miriam worships the moment.

Henderson, Rev Harry
Racing Demon, 1990
David Hare

Henderson is one of a group of south-London Church of England clergymen, the others including the REV LIONEL ESPY and the REV TONY FERRIS. Harry is middle-aged, thoughtful, quiet, benevolent, an excellent vicar. He is also homosexual, a fact he tries to keep secret, claiming that as the channel through which God's love passes, he, as an individual, is irrelevant. But 'if I upset my communicants in any way, then the focus is moved. From the Lord

Jesus. On to his minister.' Henderson's tragedy, or rather the Church's and his congregation's, is that his sexual affection and the Church's spiritual love are apparently incompatible.

Hendon, Miles
The Prince and the Pauper, 1881
Mark Twain

A fearless, swashbuckling, though somewhat down-at-heel adventurer, Hendon encounters PRINCE EDWARD in pauper's clothes and decides to 'cure' him by treating him like the royalty he claims to be. He has a strong sense of justice and fair play which makes him fiercely protective of the boy, who is the object of taunts and ridicule wherever he goes. Hendon's selfless and unwavering devotion wins him the prince's undying love and gratitude – and the prospect of ample rewards if ever he can prove his royal identity.

Henri
The Passion, 1987
Jeanette Winterson

A young Frenchman of peasant stock 'brought up by a priest and a pious mother' and sent to fight in the Napoleonic wars, Henri hero-worships Napoleon, for whom he works as a chicken chef. It is only when he meets VILLANELLE, however, that he discovers real passion in his unrequited and enduring love for her. He appears to lose his mind when imprisoned on a Venetian island but contents himself with the knowledge that 'being free is being able to love'.

Henri, Frances
The Professor, 1857
Charlotte Brontë

The half-English, half-Swiss seamstress who teaches lace-mending at ZORAIDE REUTER's school. Despite her poverty and her friendless state, she strives to better and educate herself, her ultimate goal being to become a teacher in England. When WILLIAM CRIMSWORTH first meets her, in her role of teacher/pupil, she is nervous and diffident, unable to control her charges; but he comes to see in her both 'judgement and imagination', and to view her feelings 'as susceptible as deep vibrating', 'her nature at once proud and shy'. He views her rather as a female version of himself – practical, reserved and intelligent, with firmly and passionately held convictions.

Henrietta
The House in Paris, 1935
Elizabeth Bowen

A young English girl despatched to her grandmother's in the Midi, and another of Bowen's displaced children, a pawn in the complex 'arrangements' of her family. When LEOPOLD first sees her in the house in Paris, she reminds him of 'a little girl he had once seen in a lithograph, bowling a hoop in a park with her hair tied on the top of her head in an old-fashioned way'.

Henry
The Dream Songs, 1969
John Berryman

A persona who embodies the poet's own constantly shifting and insecure emotional and intellectual states of mind in the long poems which make up *The Dream Songs*. He is 'a soul under stress', who has been 'pried/open for all the world to see'. He is a protean figure who cannot be pinned down to a series of encapsulated qualities, since he represents the abundant imagination and troubled consciousness of his creator.

Henry
The Real Thing, 1982
Tom Stoppard

'One of your intellectual playwrights', Henry has been married twice, first to Charlotte and currently to ANNIE. 'To marry one actress is unfortunate', he observes, 'to marry two is simply asking for it'. Politically conservative, phlegmatic, a lover of cricket and an admirer of pop rather than classical music, Henry equates affection with fidelity. Admitting that he cannot 'write love' because 'loving and being loved is unliterary', he learns through Annie's affairs that neither is as clear-cut as he once imagined and that compromises and adjustments must necessarily be made. He ends the play with a declaration of love and faith: 'Don't worry. I'm your chap.'

Henry, Frederic
A Farewell to Arms, 1929
Ernest Hemingway

An American, he is a volunteer ambulance driver in the Italian army in World War I. He is wounded, and, while recuperating, falls in love with a British nurse, CATHERINE BARKLAY. He becomes steadily disillusioned with the wanton slaughter and pointlessness of the war, and is 'embarrassed by the words sacred, glorious and sacrifice, and the expression in vain'. He deserts to make his own 'separate peace', but cannot finally evade tragedy.

Henry, Henry
Travelling People, 1963
B S Johnson

The elusive protagonist of this experimental novel, Henry Henry travels aimlessly, relating only tentatively to others, but absence of a storytelling focus is the point of his existence. A coherent story about him, in short, cannot emerge however much the reader instinctively hopes to get to know him.

Henry, Prince
King John, 1590/1
William Shakespeare

The son of KING JOHN, Henry makes a brief appearance at the end of the play. He procures a pardon on behalf of the rebellious noblemen and, present at his father's death, he supervises the arrangements for his burial. He appears a healing, sympathetic character, signifying a new beginning. Later, he will become Henry III.

Henry, Prince of Wales, also known as Prince Hal; afterwards Henry V
Henry IV Part I, 1596/7
Henry IV Part II, 1597/8
Henry V, 1599
William Shakespeare

There are three stages in his development, from

madcap Prince Hal to exemplary King Henry. As a youth under the tutelage of SIR JOHN FALSTAFF, while appearing to reject the values of the court he is, in fact, studying how to deal with persons from all walks of life. Then, as the reformed prince, he shows the strength of character and understanding he has been developing by his treatment of the defeated rebels. Finally, as the model king, he leads by example, putting into practice all he has learned, being merciful when need be, but demonstrating a capacity for ruthlessness and never losing either his courage or his wit.

Henry, Pug → Pug

Henry, Uncle
The Orators: an English Study, 1932
W H Auden

A homosexual uncle of THE AIRMAN, his suicide is apparently intended to reflect the inner rot and failure of self-belief that are the real source of the psychic 'Enemy' that haunts England.

Henry IV, Henry Bolingbroke
Richard II, not later than 1595
Henry IV Part I, 1596/7
Henry IV Part II, not later than 1597/8
William Shakespeare

Because he seizes the throne by force and has RICHARD II murdered, Henry is always seeking the approval of his subjects. Aware that he fails to meet the idea of a 'divine monarch', he conducts himself with dignity. A schemer by nature, he realizes that he must ensure peace at home while promising a pilgrimage to Jerusalem to keep rebellious subjects at bay. This would also help him to expiate the guilt he feels. He fails, however, to understand his apparently wayward son, Prince Hal (HENRY, PRINCE OF WALES), seeming at one time to prefer the more 'honourable' HOTSPUR. Father and son are reunited on his deathbed, but even then it takes a misunderstanding about the crown to bring them together.

Henry V → Henry, Prince of Wales

Henry VI
Henry VI Parts I, II, and III, early 1590s
Richard III, 1592/3
William Shakespeare

Shakespeare presents Henry as a good, even saintly man, an intellect who leaves affairs of state mostly in the hands of Queen Margaret (MARGARET OF ANJOU). He is sensitive and pious but politically naive, a man of peace overwhelmed by civil war. Having been 'chid from the battle', he soliloquizes that the happiness of the peasant's life is greater than that of the monarch. Having been stabbed to death in the Tower by RICHARD, DUKE OF GLOUCESTER, he makes a brief, ghostly appearance in *Richard III* during the night before the battle of Bosworth, tormenting Richard and blessing HENRY, EARL OF RICHMOND.

Henry VII → Richmond, Henry, Earl of

Henry VIII
Henry VIII (All is True), c.1613
William Shakespeare and John Fletcher

Henry VIII is in his early forties, impulsive, temperamental, with a lust both for life (he is a hunter, wrestler, musician, poet) and for women: particularly ANNE BOLEYN, a maid-in-waiting to KATHERINE, QUEEN OF ENGLAND. The authors' portrayal of the king addressing the divorce trial on his love for Katherine is given a dramatically ironic context by being placed close to his haste to marry Anne secretly before the ecclesiastical court has completed its deliberations and Katherine been announced as divorced. Central to the play is the relation between the Crown, the Church and State, over which, perhaps dangerously, the politically manipulative Henry emerges as a ruler of absolute power.

Henry XIII, King of Carpathia
His Majesty, 1927
Harley Granville-Barker

As the play opens, King Henry and Queen Rosamund of Carpathia shelter in exile in Zurich while their country disintegrates into political and economic shambles. (Carpathia, a fictional central European state, resembles both the Austro-Hungarian Empire and the struggling Weimar Republic.) In his forties, Henry is shrewd, ironic, quietly humorous, yet he will not fight to regain the throne. But neither is he a coward. Rather, he resolves to retain his decency and dignity in a cruel and humiliating world: his integrity and not his title proclaims his majesty. Yet he is also a fugitive, and must sadly accept that reality usually falls far short of ideals.

Henry Jim
Wind From An Enemy Sky, 1978
D'Arcy McNickle

The elder of two sons of a Little Elk chief, initially a ready convert to the assimilationist cause and considered a 'model Indian' by the government agents, he has gradually come to doubt the relevance of white values and to renounce the American ideal of self-reliance in favour of a more community-oriented outlook. His association with whites has sprung from a sincere belief in the importance of understanding them, and in this he has been as strong-minded and courageous as his traditionalist brother, BULL, doggedly going his own way and taking up 'progressive' farming, despite the deepening rift with the rest of his people. A prevision of his approaching death has led him to risk his brother's well-known anger by proposing a united effort to restore the tribe's sacred Feather Boy bundle and so re-establish a sense of wholeness and pride in the people that he feels his past actions have helped to destroy.

Henry Percy → Hotspur

Henshawe, Myra Driscoll
My Mortal Enemy, 1926
Willa Cather

Grandniece and heiress of the wealthy Irish Catholic immigrant John Driscoll who disowns her when she elopes with the son of an Ulster Protestant. Marriage brings her few satisfactions and much misery, and she is killed off rather bleakly and abruptly.

Hensley, Conrad
A Man in Full, 1998
Tom Wolfe
Conscientious, naive, 23 years old and with a family to support, Hensley loses his job at a Californian freezer plant when Atlanta real-estate tycoon CHARLIE CROKER closes down his ailing food division. Suburban and deferential, Hensley's values are 'order, moral rectitude, courtesy, cooperation, education, financial success, comfort, respectability, pride in one's offspring and, above all, domestic responsibility'. Yet unemployment and innocence undermine him. Directionless in a hostile world, he is eventually jailed for assault. In prison, and inspired by a book on the stoic philosophers, he begins to find redemption.

Hepburn, Philip
Sylvia's Lovers, 1863
Elizabeth Gaskell
A circumspect, upright man, ruled by his own peculiar moral code. He is tortured mentally, physically and spiritually by his obsessive love for his wife SYLVIA ROBSON, destroying himself through his passion, but dying happy in the knowledge that she has forgiven him his wrongs. Pathetic and needy, he suffers from trying to shape fate rather than allowing fate to shape him.

Hephaistion
Fire from Heaven, 1970
The Persian Boy, 1972
Mary Renault
The lifelong friend, and probable lover, of ALEXANDER. His life gains meaning through the exploits and achievements of Alexander and he matches him in bravery and judiciousness. Their symbiotic relationship is like that of brothers – Hephaistion being the older, supportive friend who is more cautious and conservative. He is capable of deep hurt when the king's strict code of honour demands that he is treated no differently from any of Alexander's other commanders in matters of politics and war. When Hephaistion finally dies, Alexander's own inner light is extinguished.

Herbert, Constanza
A Favourite of the Gods, 1963
A Compass Error, 1968
Sybille Bedford
Daughter of a wealthy expatriate American and an impoverished Italian prince, Constanza has courage, brilliance, social conscience and exquisite beauty. Adored by all, she seems favoured by the gods. But she is sacrificed to her difficult, demanding mother (who separates Constanza from her beloved father), and to the political ambitions of the opportunist Englishman she marries in London. Soon divorced, and later living unconventionally in Provence with her teenage daughter, FLAVIA HERBERT, Constanza finally meets her 'man of principle', Michel Devaux, but he is married to

the vindictive ANDRÉE DEVAUX.

Herbert, Flavia
A Favourite of the Gods, 1963
A Compass Error, 1968
Sybille Bedford
She spends her childhood and early teens in hotels and furnished houses in England, Italy and France, with her American grandmother and beautiful divorced mother, CONSTANZA HERBERT, constantly subjected to their emotional pressures and conflicts. At 17 she happily discovers her lesbianism, and, independent but naive, prepares for Oxford, dreaming of dedicating herself to writing on practical remedies for 'the curable ills of humanity'. But disconsolate after being tricked by ANDRÉE DEVAUX into betraying Constanza, she relinquishes Oxford, marries an ageing, homosexual 'established failure', and becomes a novelist.

Herbert, Melanctha
'Melanctha', in *Three Lives*, 1909
Gertrude Stein
The clever, 'subtle' daughter of a downtrodden half-caste woman and her violent black father in a Southern town. Her perspective on life is transformed by her relationships with two other, very different men, but she ends up deserted and abandoned, and dies of tuberculosis.

Herbert, Niel
A Lost Lady, 1923
Willa Cather
Cather once wrote that Niel wasn't really a character at all, but a 'peephole' into the world of MARIAN FORRESTER, something on which her charm could work. As a child, playing in the mid-west Arcadia of Sweet Water, he is entranced by her beauty and kindness, and her moral disintegration only slowly becomes evident to him in a series of disillusioning shocks.

Hereward
Count Robert of Paris, 1831
Sir Walter Scott
A young Varangian, he is the ideal blend of gentle beauty and warlike self-possession and ferocity. 'The young man's personal equipments exhibited a singular mixture of splendour and effeminacy, [and his] look of awakened attention and intelligence gave interest to the young barbarian.'

Hereward the Wake
Hereward the Wake, 1866
Charles Kingsley
Kingsley offers a romanticized, larger-than-life portrayal of the eleventh-century Lincolnshire outlaw that scarcely gains in credence from occasional, and often anachronistic, details of his domestic life with the redoubtable Torfrida.

Herf, Jimmy
Manhattan Transfer, 1925
John Dos Passos
A sensitive child, Jimmy Herf arrives in the USA on the Fourth of July. Sent away to school, he goes to live with his Uncle Jeff and Aunt Emily when his mother Lily dies. He turns down his uncle's offer of a business career and becomes a cub

reporter, moving in theatrical and intellectual circles. He passionately adores ELLEN THATCHER and they marry, have a son, but fail to achieve happiness and separate. Jimmy lacks ambition and direction, and as a reporter feels like 'a parasite on the drama of life'. Penniless, he ends up hitching a lift out of New York, going anywhere as long as it's 'pretty far'.

Heriot
To the Islands, 1958, revised edition 1982
Randolph Stow
An ageing Anglican missionary to the Aborigines, he suffers disillusion and self-doubt. Believing himself to have killed a man, he sets off on a journey in quest of the mythical Islands of Death, only to reach the final conclusion that 'my soul ... is a strange country'.

Heriot, George, known as Jinglin' Geordie
The Fortunes of Nigel, 1822
Sir Walter Scott
The wealthy Edinburgh goldsmith who followed JAMES I OF ENGLAND's court to London and later became one of his native city's greatest benefactors. He is quiet, respectable and obviously cultured, claiming the friendship of some of the age's greatest writers and artists. His value to the crown affords him significant access to the king and his opinion is highly valued.

Hermia
A Midsummer Night's Dream, c.1594
William Shakespeare
The pert and deceptively simple daughter of EGEUS, her love for LYSANDER – while bound by duty to marry DEMETRIUS – forms one of the play's many plot strands. Complacent in love, she shows fine primadonna qualities when rejected and is a very satisfactory contrast to the world-weary and pessimistic HELENA. By turns pushy and prim, she provides the play with some of its best comic moments.

Hermione
The Winter's Tale, 1611
William Shakespeare
Hermione, queen to LEONTES, makes a considerable impact, despite being offstage for so long and being reduced to a dramatic device at the end. At the outset, she appears a warm-hearted mother and wife and a convivial hostess to her husband's old friend, POLIXENES, flirtatious perhaps, but never venturing beyond the boundaries of close and comfortable association. Leontes's violent accusations of her infidelity come as a shock, not only to her but to everyone else at court, all of whom speak highly of her. Hermione knows she is innocent and remains spirited and collected. She spends several years in prison and in hiding before Leontes is taken to see a 'statue' of her: suddenly, the 'statue' comes to life and reconciliations ensue.

Hermsprong
Hermsprong, 1796
Robert Bage
Hermsprong is raised by American Indians in a supposedly 'primitive' society which, Bage suggests, has much to teach the decadent,

corrupt, de-natured world of 18th-century England. Returning to Europe, he visits France and appreciates the revolutionary changes there, before landing in Cornwall where the profligacy of English society and politics is viewed through the eyes of the innocent and untainted hero. His horrified reaction to the ridiculous, unnatural, but dangerous foibles of the English ruling class form the comic heart of this novel.

Hero
Much Ado About Nothing, 1598/1600
William Shakespeare
Being a dutiful daughter, Hero agrees to her father's wish that she should marry the wealthy young CLAUDIO, whom she knows but does not love. Normally quiet and demure she can bandy witticisms with a disguised DON PEDRO and participate enthusiastically in the plan to bring BEATRICE and BENEDICK together. However, when she is accused of unchastity by her future husband she is unable to defend herself verbally and faints. Her modest behaviour convinces the priest she is innocent. In spite of Claudio's treatment of her, when she is exonerated she is reconciled with him.

Heros
The Woman, 1978
Edward Bond
A character appropriated by Bond from Greek tragedy, he is the Athenian commander pursuing the Trojans ruled by HECUBA. He is a thoroughbred soldier, professional, vengeful, even fanatic. A prisoner of his religious fatalism, he harries the Trojans relentlessly, willing to take war to absurd lengths in order to win what might well become the most hollow of victories.

Herrick
The Ebb Tide, 1894
Robert Louis Stevenson
One of a trio of treasure-hunters on a Pacific island. More sympathetic and complex than either HYISH or DAVIS, he is interested in trying to discover the true purpose of man and the meaning of life itself. He does not find an answer in established religion, but he also rejects any atheistic solutions. Ultimately he adopts a more humanistic approach, which is both moral and tolerant. But this synthetic vision is swept aside by the deterministic system of Attwater, the lord of the island.

Herries, Rogue
Rogue Herries, 1930
Sir Hugh Walpole
He comes of indomitable Cumbrian stock, as if hewn out of the native stone. His determination and obduracy in defence of a traditional rural pastoral and a buoyantly progressive future cast him as a man poised between centuries and at the centre of an age-old dichotomy between town and city.

Herries of Birrenswork, Mr, more properly Mr Redgauntlet, or Mr Ingoldsby
Redgauntlet, 1824
Sir Walter Scott
DARSIE LATIMER's uncle, he is a passionate

Jacobite, deeply implicated in plans to restore the Young Pretender long after Culloden. His most cherished aim is to instil his nephew Darsie – who has hitherto evaded his clutches and lives at large in Scotland – with the same political ideals. Large and fierce, he bears on his forehead the strange ancestral mark of a hoof, which appears in moments of anger.

Herriot, James
If Only They Could Talk, 1970, et seq
James Herriot

James Herriot was a real-life vet (real name Alf Wight) who recorded his experiences in a small Yorkshire Dales practice in the 1940s. In a series of novels James manages to maintain his good humour and see the funny side of his work (even when delivering calves in the snow in the small hours) despite the tough conditions and his largely ungrateful patients. James encounters a wide range of human characters who are often no less challenging than their animals, from dour Yorkshire farmers to doting Pekinese owners, not forgetting his somewhat eccentric boss SIEGFRIED FARNON and Siegfried's brother TRISTAN FARNON.

Herriton, Harriet
Where Angels Fear to Tread, 1905
E M Forster

A pious and patriotic woman, she is noted for her bluntness and inability to see any side of an argument apart from her own. Deemed to have 'bolted all the cardinal virtues' without having been able to digest them, she disregards the feelings of others whilst indulging in all the insensitivity and self-righteousness one might expect from a god-fearing middle-class Edwardian matron whose experience of the wider world is limited.

Herriton, Lilia, née Theobald
Where Angels Fear to Tread, 1905
E M Forster

A woman of blowsy high spirits, 33-year-old Lilia is more of a merry widow than a properly grieving matron and mother following the death of her husband Charles. After twelve years of training and torture in the Herriton household, she makes a hasty lunge for freedom and happiness by marrying the handsome young Italian GINO CARELLA. However, whether chained to the rigid social proprieties of middle-class England or constrained by the more subtle dominance of patriarchal Italian life, she remains a restless spirit whom true happiness tragically eludes.

Herriton, Philip
Where Angels Fear to Tread, 1905
E M Forster

A tall, weakly-built young man of plain appearance with a respectable career at the Bar, he has decided that if he cannot reform the world then at least he can derive amusement from its more troublesome entanglements. Enchanted by his many trips to the continent, he has grown critical of the English society in which he dwells but remains the puppet of his mother's machinations. Italy, however, continues to

encourage the romantic within him and allows him to develop a fair-mindedness that enhances his innate decency.

Hersch, Jake
St Urbain's Horseman, 1971
Mordecai Richler

A Canadian Jew in London, forced to defend himself against criminal charges of which he is innocent. He dreams of a shadowy figure – the horseman of the title – who will set him free and bring the guilty to justice.

Hersland, Alfred
The Making of Americans, 1925
Gertrude Stein

The scion of a wealthy American family, whose marriage to JULIA DEHNING establishes a dynasty that takes 900 densely philosophical pages to unravel. Hersland is presented in a cubist and non-linear fashion, existing less as a full 'character' than as a set of abstract ideas about the persistence or non-continuity of personality through time.

Hervey, Mary
The Lovely Ship, 1927
Storm Jameson

The matriarch of a northern shipbuilding family, she is tough, self-possessed and utterly flexible in the face of changing times and circumstances. She is changed as little by success as she is smitten by failure.

Herzen, Alexander
The Coast of Utopia, 2003
Tom Stoppard

The 19th-century Russian political thinker and propagandist, sceptical of the universal political solutions propounded by his opponents. Herzen is a libertarian socialist advocating a process of gradual reform rather than revolutionary utopianism, believing that abstract ideals lead inevitably to confusion, exploitation and victimization. Moreover, the present, he declares, should not be subverted to the future: life is for living. Herzen appears in each of the plays that comprise the trilogy, which begins in Moscow in 1833 and ends 35 years later in Switzerland.

Herzog, Moses Elkanah
Herzog, 1964
Saul Bellow

An eccentric, despairing, world-weary Jewish-American scholar and intellectual, who is awaiting divorce from his second wife, and is apparently going mad. He briefly plans to murder his wife, their child, and her lover, but turns instead to an intellectual assault on life and history in an effort to make meaningful sense of his existence by writing a flood of unsent letters to friends, public figures and dead philosophers and thinkers. He reaches a perhaps temporary conciliation with the inexplicable ambiguities of the world, in which his life is 'not irrationally but incomprehensibly filled', and he has 'no messages for anyone'.

Hester

Hester: A Story of Contemporary Life, 1883
Margaret Oliphant

Wide-eyed young Hester studies society and genteel poverty; money is what matters. Her cousin, older, abler CATHERINE VERNON, supports many relatives and the family bank, but wins only malicious ingratitude, which she cynically accepts. Hester despises it, yet cannot like Catherine. She wants to be independent, but must conform and 'catch' a husband – without being acknowledged his equal. Edward Vernon steals the bank's money and demands that Hester elope, but she remains and watches Catherine save the bank once more. At last they appreciate one another, but too late. Catherine dies; Hester is left with two remaining suitors – what other hope has she?

Hester

The Mackerel Plaza, 1958
Peter DeVries

REV ANDREW MACKEREL's housekeeper, she is the sister of his dead wife. Bearing the same name as the fallen heroine of Nathaniel Hawthorne's *The Scarlet Letter* (1850), she represents a potential escape from the narrow constraints of Calvinism, but by the same token she also poses the threat of moral destruction.

Hewet, Terence

The Voyage Out, 1915
Virginia Woolf

A progressive young man, he is keen on ideas such as sexual equality, but in reality is easily annoyed by women. Refreshingly different from other young men in his elevated social station, he is intelligent, perceptive and astute, but likes to think he is much wiser than he actually is.

Hexam, Charley

Our Mutual Friend, 1865
Charles Dickens

The son of GAFFER HEXAM, the beloved brother of LIZZIE HEXAM and the ambitious pupil of BRADLEY HEADSTONE. Like his teacher, he is obsessed with becoming 'respectable'. Shunning his sister for rejecting Headstone's marriage proposal, he later shuns Headstone for bringing disrepute on his family through attempting to murder EUGENE WRAYBURN. He selfishly pursues his own career as a schoolmaster, intending to assume Headstone's post.

Hexam, Gaffer (Jesse)

Our Mutual Friend, 1865
Charles Dickens

A Thames waterman who recovers corpses from the river, robs them and turns them over to the police for a reward. His daughter, LIZZIE HEXAM, reluctantly assists him, but not his selfish son, CHARLEY HEXAM. One of the bodies they recover is wrongly identified as that of JOHN HARMON. Hexam's former partner, ROGUE RIDERHOOD, falsely accuses him of murdering Harmon, but he is found drowned before he can be arrested.

Hexam, Lizzie

Our Mutual Friend, 1865
Charles Dickens

Daughter of GAFFER HEXAM and sister of CHARLEY HEXAM, she reluctantly rows the boat while her father recovers corpses. She devotes herself to helping Charley become educated, but he spurns her when she refuses the proposal of his 'respectable' schoolmaster, BRADLEY HEADSTONE. She becomes a friend of JENNY WREN and falls in love with EUGENE WRAYBURN, allowing him to pay for her education while rejecting his love because of their difference in social class. After her father's death, she lives with Jenny Wren until RIAH helps find her a job by the Thames outside London in order to escape the attentions of Headstone and Wrayburn. By the river, she comforts the dying BETTY HIGDEN and rescues Wrayburn from drowning after Headstone tries to murder him. Despite the disapproval of 'Society', she finally agrees to marry Wrayburn.

Heyst, Axel

Victory, 1915
Joseph Conrad

A wanderer in the South Seas islands who has inherited a detached and even cynical (but nonetheless idealistic) view of life from his father. He believes that 'he who forms a tie is lost', and has been unable to come to terms with life and human attachment on any other basis. The 'germ of corruption' enters his soul when he helps a failing businessman and then a young girl, and although he learns the meaning of commitment to others, he does so too late.

Hiawatha

The Song of Hiawatha, 1855
Henry Wadsworth Longfellow

Sent by the Great Spirit, Gitche Manito, Hiawatha is the son of WENONAH and MUDJEKEEWIS, and is brought up by his grandmother, NOKOMIS. He learns about nature and proves expert at athletic pursuits. Tall, graceful and fearless, he sets out to improve the world for the benefit of its people. In his adventures he demonstrates his strength, generosity, nobility and knowledge. He grieves on the death of his wife, MINNEHAHA, then, after welcoming the white newcomers to America, he departs.

Hickey

The Iceman Cometh, 1946
Eugene O'Neill

A travelling salesman who visits the End of the Line Café every year and entertains the regulars with ribald tales of his wife and the iceman. This year, though, he has sworn to stay off drink and refuses to add to his stories, confessing instead that he has killed his wife. In order to preserve their dreams, the bar regulars conclude that he is insane.

Hicks, Shannon

Ride on Stranger, 1943
Kylie Tennant

The fourth daughter of a country family, she is sent off to her Aunt Edith's boarding house as a young girl to make something of herself. Never quite at ease, she resolves 'to find some place where I fit in ... some place meant for me'. A strong-willed young woman, with 'close-cut hair ... determined face, and neat insolent chin', she eventually goes to Sydney, where she progresses through an amazing assortment of jobs: from waitress to secretary; lecturer in Personal Magnetism to radio announcer; Proletarian Club organizer to union activist. Energetic, resourceful, quick-witted, with a gift for communication, she excels in all her jobs, but always grows dissatisfied and moves on. She finally finds peace back in her hometown, having married JOHN TERRILL and settled on his farm. Although their happiness is brief, Shannon carries on, coping, managing, surviving.

Hieronimo
The Spanish Tragedy, 1592
Thomas Kyd

The Marshal of Spain, Hieronimo discovers the dead body of his son, DON HORATIO, hanging in his garden and turns mad with grief. Discovering that DON LORENZO and PRINCE BALTHAZAR are the murderers, he plots a bloody revenge. Although he briefly reflects upon Romans 12:19 – 'Justice is mine, saith the Lord' – his grief and anger are too great to wait for divine retribution.

Higden, Betty
Our Mutual Friend, 1865
Charles Dickens

A poor but indomitable laundress who is haunted by the fear of ending her days in a workhouse. She keeps a 'minding-school' and also cares for her orphaned grandson, Johnny, and an 'adopted foundling, Sloppy. After MR and MRS BOFFIN arrange to care for Johnny and Sloppy, she sets out on a tramping life, but growing ill and weak, she dies in the arms of LIZZIE HEXAM.

Higginbotham, Mr
'Mr. Higginbotham's Catastrophe', 1834, in *Twice-Told Tales*, 1837, revised edition 1842
Nathaniel Hawthorne

Wealthy old man of Kimballton, rumours of whose murder by hanging come to the ears of one DOMINICUS PIKE. Anxious to discover the truth, Pike arrives just in time to prevent a real killing. In gratitude, Mr Higginbotham makes Pike his heir and offers the one-time tobacco pedlar his niece's hand.

Higgins, Professor Henry
Pygmalion, 1913
George Bernard Shaw

A Wimpole Street phoneticist, Higgins is 40, energetic and intellectually sharp. He has few social graces, and his manner is either genial, sullen or bullying. A bachelor, he is condescending towards women and it is hinted that his intentions are not always honourable. ELIZA DOOLITTLE, a flower girl whom he meets in Covent Garden, is eager that he teach her to speak correctly. He does so after accepting a wager from COL PICKERING that he can thereby launch her into polite society. Disregarding Eliza's sensibilities, he triumphantly turns her

into an automaton and is shaken, but not defeated, when she later rebels and abandons him.

Higgs, Dorothy
The Healing Art, 1980
A N Wilson

Though older than her friend and fellow cancer sufferer, PAMELA COWPER, she has been offered a good prognosis, and is sustained by an unreflective belief in the doctors' skills. Even so, her buoyant loquacity and practicality hide a profound fear of death.

Hight, Esther
The Country of the Pointed Firs, 1896
Sarah Orne Jewett

Esther is shepherdess of the most pampered sheep in Maine, where flocks do not traditionally require constant tending; 'she might have been Jeanne d'Arc ... touched with age and gray with the ashes of a great remembrance. She wore the simple look of sainthood and unfeigned devotion.'

Hightower, Rev Gail
Light in August, 1932
William Faulkner

Representative of the simultaneous collapse and persistence of the Christian story, he is a clergyman who has lost the urge to preach against evil and to protest the value of love. Instead, he obsessively recounts his grandfather's exploits in the Civil War.

Highway, Charles
The Rachel Papers, 1973
Martin Amis

The novel's narrator, he is an almost insolently intelligent, urgent, even arrogant, highly-sexed but virginal 19-year-old, determined to seduce an older woman before he is 20 and engulfed by university. The seduction has to be planned with daring, cunning, confidence and ingenuity, all of which qualities Highway possesses. This is just as well, as he does not have the tact, vision or poise of the usual Lothario. Quite the reverse, for his 'medium-length, arseless, waistless figure, corrugated ribcage and bandy legs gang up to dispel any hint of aplomb'.

Hilary
The Old Country, 1977
Alan Bennett

Hilary is in his early sixties, shabby and faded, a defector from the Foreign Office living in Russia. Surrounded by forest, he lives imaginatively in the England he left behind, painting a nostalgic landscape of the hedgerows and bookshops of the 1930s. This, and his carefully constructed façade of quiet amiability, provides cover for his constant re-evaluation of the political and emotional choices he has made in the past. Arguably, he has replaced one set of illusions by another, and it is the secret realization of this which makes him ever-watchful, restless unless everything is accounted for. Hilary is also a snob, and when not remote can be icily condescending.

Hilary, Mr
Nightmare Abbey, 1818
Thomas Love Peacock

'A very cheerful and elastic fellow' who finds pleasure and enjoyment everywhere, Mr Hilary is amiable and good-natured. His first inclination, no matter how unfortunate the circumstances, is to make a joke.

Hilbery, Katharine
Night and Day, 1919
Virginia Woolf

Katharine is caught between past and present worlds; attracted by the idea of independence, she wants to escape her prestigious family in the present, but she is also obsessed with her family's past. Sensitive, creative and imaginative, she proves above all to be true to herself.

Hilda
The Marble Faun, 1860
Nathaniel Hawthorne

A pale, untouchable virgin, symbolized by the doves she tends. A New Englander, she is studying art in Rome, and is a friend of MIRIAM and the sculptor KENYON. After the murder of Brother Antonio, she is drawn unwillingly into the orbit of the Roman Catholic Church.

Hilda → Cherrington, Hilda

Hilditch, Joey
Felicia's Journey, 1994
William Trevor

Joey is a 54-year-old single man, who weighs 19½ stone, wears thick glasses, and is fastidious about his appearance and habits. He works as a canteen manager, but his jovial and benevolent demeanour conceals his melancholic loneliness. He is in fact a psychopathic predator who befriends vulnerable young girls. His thrills derive from being mistaken for their lover and from their dependency on him, but when they try to break free he is unable to let them go. When the pattern is broken by Felicia's escape he begins to acknowledge his actions and descends into madness.

Hill, Avery
Maurice Guest, 1908
Henry Handel Richardson

HEINZ KRAFFT's much put-upon mistress, she has unmistakably masculine features and a masochistic nature, both of which play some part in her unhappy relationship with the young student. Her confusion and hurt are so great that she commits suicide.

Hill, Camilla
A Wreath of Roses, 1950
Elizabeth Taylor

Spending the summer with her old teacher and a close school-friend, as is their custom, she finds herself observing at close hand the sudden ageing of the one and the slow, painful disintegration of the other's marriage. At the same time, she is thrown into the company of a dark and obsessive ex-serviceman by the sight of a dramatic suicide at a country railway station.

Hill, Fanny
Memoirs of a Woman of Pleasure, 1748–9
John Cleland

Amateur 18th-century courtesan of boundless energy and undiscriminating submissiveness. Though positively verbose about the details of copulation, she has a surprisingly squeamish antipathy to calling a spade a spade (or any other instrument by its proper name).

Hill, Meridian
Meridian, 1976
Alice Walker

'Bearing the conflict in her own soul', Meridian inhabits her politics with a spiritual passion. Choosing to dissociate herself from the distancing of rhetoric, she occupies a vital position in the changing face of the black community. Unlike her contemporaries, she sees herself as 'held by something in the past', and someone who shall 'come forward and sing from memory songs they will need once more to hear'. Refusing to espouse the violent dogma of revolution, she undergoes a profound self-evaluation that, when echoed in the community, allows her to resurrect herself.

Hilliard, John
Strange Meeting, 1971
Susan Hill

The son of an ambitious and perfectionist mother, who believes she demonstrates love to her family, John is an emotionally repressed young man, with a deep love and respect for his sister, which is based more upon childhood memories than on any great rapport in the present. The horrors of war sharpen his senses and allow him to appreciate nature, friendship and beauty in a way which has never previously occurred to him. He is jealous of his friend DAVID BARTON's ability to relate to people and of the close-knit family he is a part of, but it is with David that for the first time he finds true human, mutual and respectful love.

Hilton, Ruth
Ruth, 1853
Elizabeth Gaskell

A sensitive and beautiful heroine, who comes to a tragic end through no greater sin than that of loving too much. Refined, gracious and naive, she is rejected in love, but carries on in noble style, with the affection and help of friends, and her own devotion to her son, Leonard. She inadvertently becomes entangled in a web of deceit, though she is not by nature a dishonest person. She loves deeply and sincerely, and is badly treated by the narrow-minded. Her background is a respectable one, and she is creative and dextrous, but her lack of self-respect and her need to feel worthy lead to an unhappy conclusion.

Himmelfarb, Mordecai
Riders in the Chariot, 1961
Patrick White

Together with ALF DUBBO, RUTH GODBOLD and MARY HARE, Mordecai Himmelfarb is one of four protagonists of the novel. A German Jew who becomes a university professor,

Himmelfarb is unable to prevent the arrest of his wife by the Nazis. He himself is detained in a concentration camp, from which he escapes. After World War II, he travels to Australia and becomes an assembly-line worker at a factory run by HARRY ROSETREE. Himmelfarb is the kind of person, his wife once said, to whom 'much will be made clear'. What is apparent is that his spirituality impresses some (such as the other three protagonists), but his orthodoxy outrages others, such as MRS FLACK. His faith, it seems, cannot give him the means to save himself, for he dies in a lynching, the victim of suburban xenophobia.

Hines, Doc (Eupheus Hines)
Light in August, 1932
William Faulkner

A sadistic self-styled nemesis of the black race, he murders his daughter's husband because he believes the man has Negro blood, and places his baby grandson JOE CHRISTMAS in a white orphanage, where he is bound to be mistreated by the other children. Later he leads the lynch mob that hunts down and crucifies Joe.

Hines, Rab
The Busconductor Hines, 1984
James Kelman

Employed as bus-conductor on what he describes as 'streetfaring vehicles of a public service nature', Hines is 'predisposed towards speculative musings' in order to cope with the boredom of his job. He has a 'wife and thirty-eight weans' to look after (one wean in reality) and shares with her an unfulfilled desire to get out (of Scotland, probably) and go somewhere else. 'A manic depressive bastard', he is known among the bus crews for his lateness, his humour and his outspokenness, having once been 'ejected from a branch meeting for applying the term shite to a chairman's summing up'.

Hinton, Frances
Look at Me, 1983
Anita Brookner

Frances works in the library of a medical research institute. She is sensitive and meticulous, attributes she brings to her job, where the main archival emphasis is upon dreams and madness. 'Problems of human behaviour still continue to baffle us,' she observes, 'but at least in the Library we have them properly filed.' Outside her working hours Frances spends a lot of time alone. Mainly as a result of laziness she has few friends, but as a good listener she finds herself in demand. Unattached, she falls cautiously in love. But the timid, it appears, are destined to be emotionally scalded.

Hipkiss, Bessie
The Ferret Was Abraham's Daughter, 1949
Jezebel's Dust, 1951
Fred Urquhart

Sandy-haired, snub-nosed, big-mouthed Bessie, nicknamed 'The Ferret', escapes from life in a poor Edinburgh tenement and her hated surname by fantasizing that she is a French princess. When her adored mother dies, her bullying father takes her away from school to look after him and her pestering siblings, and she later laments that she 'never had a chance'. After the outbreak of World War II she becomes somewhat too interested in men, under the influence of the flighty Lily McGillivray, but her naivety carries her through her misadventures.

Hippolita
The Castle of Otranto, 1764
Horace Walpole

Hippolita is the loving wife of MANFRED, PRINCE OF OTRANTO, mother of CONRAD and MATILDA. At first shocked by his decision to divorce her and marry Princess ISABELLA OF VICENZA after Conrad's death, she later agrees, thinking it her duty. Swooning as each calamity strikes Otranto, clinging to life only to prevent Matilda's forced marriage to Vicenza, she is overcome by Matilda's death and retires with the penitent Manfred to a religious life in the cloisters.

Hippolito
The Revenger's Tragedy, 1607
Thomas Middleton or Cyril Tourneur

The son of GRATIANA and brother of VENDICE. Lacking the aggressive and imaginative malice of his brother, he nevertheless plays a crucial role in helping Vendice carry out his plans for vengeance, though he is sometimes shocked by the violent malevolence behind them.

Hippolito
Women Beware Women, c.1621
Thomas Middleton

The uncle and lover of ISABELLA. Their relationship is consummated whilst she is under the misapprehension that he is not related to her. Hippolito's behaviour throughout suggests a muddled set of moral values: happy to indulge in an adulterous and incestuous relationship with his own niece, he is outraged at the suggestion that his sister LIVIA should also be enjoying an illicit liaison with LEANTIO, horrified at the effect such a scandalous affair would have on the family's honour.

Hippolyta
A Midsummer Night's Dream, c.1594
William Shakespeare

The 'bouncing Amazon' and 'warrior Love' to THESEUS, whose nuptial preparations provide the play's background. Although we are furnished with implicit details about her war-like past – including OBERON's admiration for her – she is a slight, rather passive character, though capable of humour, clearly contented with the future prospect of marriage to the noble duke Theseus.

Hirst
No Man's Land, 1975
Harold Pinter

A celebrated man of letters in his sixties, Hirst has one night either invited or been accompanied by SPOONER, a shabby poet, to his impressive home. Powerful, arrogant and frequently befuddled by drink, he is a man of uncertain temper and memory – his recollections of his wife, whom Spooner also appears to have known, and of bucolic summers, are distinctly dubious. He is, it appears, tormented, incapable of salvation and retreating, as Spooner observes, into a 'no man's land ... which remains forever, icy and silent'.

Hirst, St John
The Voyage Out, 1915
Virginia Woolf

Pompous and traditional, he is so full of chauvinism towards women as to render him comic. He would, however, like to be different. A victim of his class, upbringing and education, he is not cold, merely ignorant. Loyal to his friends, he will do anything to help of a practical nature, but he finds communication with women extremely tortuous. In need of female guidance, he finds an interesting companion in HELEN AMBROSE.

Hob the Miller, properly **Hob Happer**
The Monastery, 1820
Sir Walter Scott

The miller who services Glendearg, he is a man of some substance, his fortunes built on having a careful, calculating eye and a fine awareness of political economy, even on the small scale. His greatest treasure, though, is his daughter, MYSIE OF THE MILL.

Hobain, Felix, also known as **Makak**
Dream on Monkey Mountain, 1972
Derek Walcott

Makak-Macaque (or blue-arsed monkey) is the hallucinated hero of Walcott's illogical, derivative dream-play. In real life Makak is a 'sixty year old charcoal burner – ugly as sin'. In his dream, Makak leads a symbolic journey back to Africa, where, ably assisted by other characters who join his dream, he carries out the swift trial and occasional execution of those they call 'confounders of blackness'. Makak's ability to dream confirms his revolutionary potential, sapped and controlled by what he describes as 'the law and a Bible'.

Hobbs, Roy
The Natural, 1952
Bernard Malamud

The baseball player as heavily ironized mythical hero. His adventures parallel the myth of Parsifal redeeming the Wasteland in the Grail legend. He appears as a 19-year-old wonder pitcher, only to be shot by a mysterious woman for lacking any purpose, other than self-glory. He returns 15 years later as a batter to help an ailing team, complete with his highly-phallic bat 'Wonderboy', which droops when he has a form slump. He learns responsibility for others, but in a piece of poetic justice is himself struck out by a new young hero.

Hobby, Pat
The Pat Hobby Stories, 1939–41
F Scott Fitzgerald

A Hollywood hack scenario writer who had once been tipped for a great career, a prediction which has never been fulfilled. He is now a down-at-heel outsider on the fringes of the movie business, ready to seize any opportunity which might pull him back to the centre of the action, or simply bring him a few bucks or a screen credit. He is a resilient survivor, though, with a sardonic awareness of Hollywood's ways, in whom 'the gift of hope' has remained.

Hobden, the Hedger
Puck of Pook's Hill, 1906
Rudyard Kipling

Exponent of a lost country craft and 'particular friend' of the children DAN and UNA, he turns out to be lineally descended from a much earlier Hobden – or Hob of the Dene – and is the youngsters' most obvious physical link to a reality that existed before they were born. He is father of the Bee Boy.

Hobson, Maggie (Margaret)
Hobson's Choice, 1915
Harold Brighouse

Vivacious, energetic, intelligent and logical, Maggie is the daughter of a boot manufacturer and works as an assistant in the family shop. At 30, she is deemed to be past the marrying age, yet she is a forthright, determined woman and selects the timid bootmaker, WILLIE MOSSOP, as her husband. Having married him, she inaugurates her plan that they take over the family business, presenting her disapproving father with a 'Hobson's Choice'.

Hoccleve, Archdeacon
Some Tame Gazelle, 1980
Barbara Pym

The archdeacon, an irritable, trying man, makes unexpectedly tactless remarks and has to be humoured into good temper. He remembers with pleasure reading aloud to BELINDA BEDE when they were students – he may even prefer her company to that of his wife, who annoys him. He has little love for his clerical brethren and likes to make their visits uncomfortable. His sermons are long and recondite, with many quotations from minor authors whom only Belinda recognizes – only she really listens to them.

Hoenikker, Felix
Cat's Cradle, 1963
Kurt Vonnegut, Jr

One of the fathers of the atomic bomb, and the creator of the apocalyptic chemical 'ice-nine', which has the capacity to freeze the world solid, and which he leaves in the hands of his 'three strange kids'. He has a childlike curiosity about everything, and derives his most brilliant discoveries from playing around with ideas and objects, but he has no sense of responsibility for what he creates, and is not interested in people at all.

Hogan, John
Roads from Home, 1949
Dan Davin

The brother of NED HOGAN, John lives with his wife, Elsie, among the Irish Catholic community in a Presbyterian town in New Zealand. A strong, loyal man employed on the railways, he enjoys a game of rugby and a drink with his mates. He is brusque, but straightforward and trusting, with a respect for hard work and family values. He doggedly loves Elsie, knowing that she does not love him, yet he is too decent and too deferential to women, to release his disillusionment by anger and accusation. Elsie cannot help being unfaithful to him, yet because of his faith, John cannot leave her, nor is he able to contemplate divorce.

Hogan, Ned
Roads from Home, 1949
Dan Davin

The brother of JOHN HOGAN, Ned is trapped by the demands of an overbearing family. He lives among an Irish Catholic community in a Presbyterian town in New Zealand, and it is expected by his mother and her friends that he will become a priest. Ned is intellectual, but introspective and vulnerable. He concludes that Christianity is a delusion, that the world is an entirely natural phenomenon and that life is a process governed both by fate and chance and leading to inevitable death and darkness.

Hogg, Georgina
The Comforters, 1957
Muriel Spark

A bossy, hypocritical 'Catholic atrocity' and 'gargoyle', bane of the lives of CAROLINE ROSE and her boyfriend. She pries and spies, ready to 'do any evil under the guise of good'. She has an enormous bosom and no private life, which means that she vanishes when asleep.

Holborn, Jack
Jack Holborn, 1964
Leon Garfield

An orphan of about 14, he longs for two things above all else; to have a better life for himself and to discover the identity of his mother. In pursuit of the first goal he sails as a stowaway on the inappropriately-named *Charming Molly*, bound for Africa. Before he is found out, the ship is over-run with pirates, whose leader, CAPTAIN ROGERS, soon exercises a strange hold over Jack, convincing him that he knows his mother's name, which he will reveal only when Jack has fulfilled his triple obligations to him. On the long and arduous adventures that follow, Jack comes to know the depths of despair, and seems on occasion to be further away from his goals than ever. An impetuous, outspoken and even foolish young lad at times, he is usually moved by generous impulses, and acts nobly in extreme circumstances.

Holdenough, Rev Nehemiah
Woodstock, or The Cavalier, 1826
Sir Walter Scott

He is intended to represent the kind of straightforward, undogmatic Presbyterianism endangered by the zealotry and intolerance of English Civil War sectarians. 'He was a tall, thin man, and the vivacity of his eye indicated some irascibility of temperament ... His grizzled hair was cut as short as shears could perform the feat, and covered with a black skull-cap, which stuck so close to his head, that the two ears expanded from under it as if they had been intended as handles to lift the whole person.'

Holdsworth, Phillis
Cousin Phillis, 1864
Elizabeth Gaskell

Phillis is overly protected by her parents, and is so

indulged by them that she is rather pompous. She is intelligent, attractive, quick-witted and astute, yet she knows very few people and has seen nothing of life until she experiences love and a broken heart. Having learnt that life in the outside world can be hard, painful and uncontrollable, she shows deep strength of character when she resolves to put the experience behind her.

Holgrave
The House of the Seven Gables, 1851
Nathaniel Hawthorne

A young man of undisclosed but humble background and little formal education, he is successively a country schoolmaster, pedlar, journalist, dentist, ship's purser, Communard, lecturer on hypnotism and finally daguerrotypist. Representing the flexible energy and freedom from inherited constraints of Young America, he believes that 'the world owes all its onward impulses to men ill at ease'. He marries PHOEBE PYNCHEON, at which point he reveals himself to be a descendant of MATTHEW MAULE, whose curse hangs over the Pyncheons like the dead hand of the past.

Holiday, Mary/Stella
The Angel at the Gate, 1982
Wilson Harris

Secretary and patient of Father Joseph Marsden, she is profoundly self-divided, believing herself to be not one person, but two. Leaving instructions that her husband and 'Mary' look after their child, 'Stella' swallows a bottle of Valium. Father Ramsden calls in Wilson Harris to interpret her automatic writing.

Hollar
Professional Foul, 1977
Tom Stoppard

A young Czech living in Prague, who has been a student in England and who attempts to persuade his ex-professor, ANDERSON, to have his thesis on 'correct behaviour' translated. His stand on human rights puts him and his family under supervision and he is required to clean lavatories in spite of his intellectual ability. Although desperate, both frightened and frustrated by Anderson's lack of courage, he behaves with great politeness and accepts his refusal with good grace. His subsequent disappearance and the plight of his family help convince Anderson to change his attitudes.

Hollingrake, Boo, later Mrs Lopez and Olivia Davenport
The Vivisector, 1970
Patrick White

A friend of RHODA COURTNEY, she is a childhood acquaintance of the artist HURTLE DUFFIELD. Later, she becomes the mysterious Mrs Lopez, a patron of his work. Widowed, she remarries and becomes the determined party-goer and socialite, Olivia Davenport. It is while she is in this phase of her life that she comes closest to Duffield. Like him, her attitude to life is to take while she has the chance. She enjoys heterosexual relationships and the occasional lesbian flirtation. She even procures HERO

PAVLOUSSI to be Duffield's mistress. Her attitude to life verges upon the voyeuristic: she sees everything yet has little emotional response to anything. She observes, tantalizes and manipulates.

Hollingsworth
The Blithedale Romance, 1852
Nathaniel Hawthorne
A ruthlessly arrogant social reformer, whose belief in an appeal to the 'higher instincts' of criminals and other wrong-doers stems from his inability to find any flaw in his own character.

Hollingsworth, Leroy
Barbary Shore, 1951
Norman Mailer
A potent symbol of the totalitarian 'Barbary', he is a sadistic secret policeman sent to hunt down the old Bolshevik ARTHUR MCLEOD. A thuggish manipulator who worships sensation and believes that 'it's pointless to work for the future', he eventually absconds with Arthur's wife GUINEVERE, thus completing the mythological triangle hinted at in 'Leroy' (*le roi*).

Hollis, Kyra
Skylight, 1995
David Hare
The former lover of TOM SERGEANT, Kyra has found a new sense of purpose by becoming a dedicated although ill-paid teacher at a deprived inner-city school in London. When Sergeant visits her shoddy flat, she agrees that her surroundings might be better, but denies that she is wasting her talent. Clearly, though, she misses Sergeant's vitality and envies the energy he gains from working. Yet she too has a sense of worth and accomplishment. Independent, zealous, fiercely rejecting his right-wing views, she concedes that hers is a very personal political and social mission. 'I have', she admits, 'become my anger'.

Holly
Watership Down, 1972
Richard Adams
A captain of the Sandleford 'Owsla' (a coterie around the chief), he is reliable and courageous, always prepared to do his duty – but not to exceed it. He is a natural second-in-command, rather than a high-flier, perhaps even a trifle dull. After the destruction of the old warren, however, he seems to change radically, and proves briefly to be as skilled an adventurer as HAZEL or BIGWIG. But he does not relish the limelight, and soon returns to more comfortable ways.

Holmes, Kerewin
The Bone People, 1983
Keri Hulme
Tall, broad and bedecked in precious stones, New Zealander Kerewin has put her artistic talents to 'good' use and built a tower to live in and to keep other people at bay. Desperately saddened by a family feud, she keeps her contact with civilization to a minimum, but far from finding solace in her own company, she only feels

increasingly lonely and bitter. Startled out of her self-absorption by the intriguing JOE GILLAYLEY and his son SIMON P GILLAYLEY, however, she begins the long and often painful journey towards self-rediscovery, spiritual enlightenment and reintegration with humanity.

Holmes, Michael
An Equal Music, 1999
Vikram Seth
Michael is a violinist in the Maggiore quartet and shares an intense, almost familial, and often fraught relationship with the other members. From a modest background in Rochdale, he has disappointed and alienated his bewildered parents with his choice of career, having been inspired by his teacher Mrs Formby. Moody and volatile, he is involved in a lacklustre affair with Virginie, a much younger French student of his, but is still haunted by JULIA MCNICHOLL, a pianist whom he loved and abandoned inexplicably (even to himself) in Vienna ten years previously. The extent of this passion has rendered him 'irreparably imprinted with the die of someone else's being'.

Holmes, Sherlock
A Study in Scarlet, 1887, et seq
Arthur Conan Doyle
Probably the most famous fictional detective, Sherlock Holmes appears in four novels and 56 short stories. He both embodies Victorian conventions and flouts them: in the age of Nietzsche, his incisive mind and superior deductive logic mark him out as a superman. According to his associate, DR WATSON, he has made detection 'as near an exact science as it ever will be', praise which makes Holmes flush with pleasure, for he loves being flattered. Holmes is hyperactive, unemotional, a master of disguise, and possesses a sense of justice sometimes more sensitive than that of the law. He combats the intellectual 'stagnation' between cases by playing a Stradivarius violin or indulging in a 'seven-per-cent solution' of cocaine. In 2002 Holmes became the first fictional character to receive an Honorary Fellowship from the Royal Society of Chemistry.

Holofernes
Love's Labour's Lost, not later than 1594
William Shakespeare
A tedious schoolmaster. He is a pedantic walking Latin dictionary: 'The deer was as you know, *sanguis*, in blood.' His talents also extend to organizing the ill-fated Pageant of the Nine Worthies. His agreement that DON ADRIANO DEL ARMADO should act in it shows ham-headed judgement.

Holt, Father
The History of Henry Esmond, Esquire, 1852
W M Thackeray
The Catholic priest at Castlewood who acts as HENRY ESMOND's tutor, he is later forced to flee to the Continent when his Stuart sympathies place him in jeopardy. A marvellously acute portrait of the self-deluded, hermetic world of Jacobitism, he is the servant and representative of a class already overtaken by history. One

secret that he does possess is the true story of Henry Esmond's birth.

Holt, Felix
Felix Holt the Radical, 1866
George Eliot

The embarrassed heir to the quack medicine of his father, Felix vocally dissociates himself from parental follies. He worries his mother but heartens Lyon the minister with his independent speech. Though highly talented, he stays a humble watchmaker ('I mean to stick to the class I belong to'). Active in political discussion and left-wing oriented, he is suspicious of universal suffrage because of all the 'drunken and stupid votes' that would entail. Such radicalism earns him respect from some quarters but ridicule and enmity as well.

Holy Willie
'Holy Willie's Prayer', 1799
Robert Burns

A spiteful bachelor church elder in Mauchline, Ayrshire, he believes in the Calvinist doctrine of predestination. Although claiming to be one of God's elect, he unwittingly reveals his own hypocrisy, lust, drunkenness and greed.

Home, Captain Alexander
'Five Visions of Captain Cook', in *Trio*, 1931
Kenneth Slessor

A near-blind sailor who returns home to Scotland from the last voyage captained by Cook, but whose thoughts remain 'half-way round the earth' in the Pacific. The 'dim fog-shapes' that are home cannot match the vibrant colours and excitement of his inner journey into a magical, mysterious world. Memory and reminiscence are his life: 'Thus it had been/When Cook …'.

Home, Polly (Pauline)
Villette, 1853
Charlotte Brontë

A precocious but endearing child, devoted to her 'Papa', Polly grows up never forgetting her strong childhood attachment to DR JOHN BRETTON and, on becoming reacquainted with him ten years later, her affection for him blossoms into full-blown love. Delicately beautiful and, though a little bit proud, possessed of a charming and thoughtful nature, her almost spiritual qualities run in striking contrast to the wholly earthly concerns of her cousin, GINEVRA FANSHAWE.

Homos, Mr
A Traveller from Altruria, 1894
William Dean Howells

The eponymous traveller hails from an imaginary utopia which is founded on unselfish principles and in which civic responsibility is considered immeasurably superior to private satisfaction. During a holiday at a fashionable seaside resort, he tries out a brand of Christian socialism on a variety of contemporary types.

Honey
Who's Afraid of Virginia Woolf?, 1962
Edward Albee

The pallid, slim-hipped wife of the young instructor NICK, and as blandly innocuous as her name suggests. In a play obsessively concerned with birth and self-replication, it is revealed that Honey has undergone a phantom pregnancy; she is thus contrasted to the older MARTHA, who is presumably past child-bearing age, but who has had the courage to bring painfully into being an imaginary child.

Honey Barbara
Bliss, 1981
Peter Carey

In a world where everyone's exact social function is carefully delineated, she is something of a loose cannon. Half hippy and nature spirit, half urban prostitute, she has taken command of her life and destiny, controlling its wildly divergent extremes.

Honeychurch, Lucy
A Room With a View, 1908
E M Forster

The daughter of a prosperous solicitor who is fearful of being thought a snob, Lucy Honeychurch is a pretty, pale young girl with an unsullied and unformed view of the world and her place in it. A passionate piano player, her modest appetite for adventure is first satisfied by a trip to Italy. A single kiss from GEORGE EMERSON propels her on a homeward flight, fraught with confusion and remorse, but ultimately proves the key to romance and self-realization.

Honeycomb, Will
The Spectator, 1711–12
Joseph Addison and Richard Steele

Will Honeycomb stands in the Club for fashionable life. Full of gossip and anecdotes, he laughs easily and is rather a dandy, able to live on a comfortable fortune. He knows the history of hairdressing and clothes, topics of concern to the feminine world. He is spoken of as 'a well-bred fine gentleman', gallant though not young; time has made him wrinkled but not wise.

Honeythunder, Mr Luke
The Mystery of Edwin Drood, 1870
Charles Dickens

A belligerent and hypocritical philanthropist who bullies the ostensible beneficiaries of his charity. He is the guardian of HELENA and NEVILLE LANDLESS, but when Neville is suspected of murdering EDWIN DROOD, Honeythunder assumes that Neville is guilty and tries to break off relations with his wards.

Honoria, Countess of Lyndon, Viscountess Bullingdon
The Luck of Barry Lyndon, 1844
W M Thackeray

One of the great ladies of her time, a god-daughter of Lady Mary Wortley Montagu, and a woman of considerable personal accomplishment. 'Every adventurer who had a discovery in chemistry, a new antique bust, or a plan for discovering the philosopher's stone, was sure to find a patroness in her.' When her husband dies she marries BARRY LYNDON, who promptly sets about spending her considerable wealth.

Hood, Toby
A World of Strangers, 1958
Nadine Gordimer

A young Englishman who leaves his homeland for South Africa in the hope that he can lead a 'private life' there. His painful recognition is that in his new country history and politics are not abstract concepts but part of the fabric of everyday life.

Hook, Captain
Peter Pan: or The Boy Who Would Not Grow Up, 1904 (play), 1911 (book)
J M Barrie

An old Etonian pirate, he has already lost an arm to PETER PAN and the crocodile and now has an iron hook instead of a right hand. He is introduced as 'cadaverous and blackavised, his hair dressed in long curls which look like black candles about to melt, his eyes blue as the forget-me-not and of a profound insensibility, save when he claws, at which time a red spot appears in them'. At his most sinister when he is at his most polite, he is a man of fearless courage; 'the only thing at which he flinches is the sight of his own blood, which is thick and of an unusual colour'.

Hooligan, Mary
Night, 1972
Edna O'Brien

Mary has led a rich and varied life, and because of her colourful and active imagination, fantasy and reality are interwoven in her consciousness. Though somewhat bitter about the blows life has dealt her, she has a refreshing ability to laugh at herself and to value what she has achieved. Her mind is aglow with memories – sparks fly as she recalls events and experiences – but above all she is honest, probing, self-examining and candid. Alone rather than lonely, she has grown to be selective in the company she keeps. Having been through all the predictable, monotonous life experiences, she has now attained a state of heightened consciousness, and is lyrical in her expression.

Hooper, Edmund
I'm the King of the Castle, 1970
Susan Hill

A cold and emotionless boy, Edmund remains outside situations, unable to empathize in any way. This detachment enables him to be very astute and perceptive. He craves a feeling of power, desires control and success. His emotional repression seems to be connected to his mother: the fact that she is dead and that, when alive, she too was unfeeling. Quiet and solitary, he is unable to interact, unless it is to persecute CHARLES KINGSHAW. Either he has been psychologically tormented all his life, or Edmund is plain evil.

Hooper, Rev Mr
'The Minister's Black Veil', 1835, in *Twice-Told Tales*, 1837, revised edition 1842
Nathaniel Hawthorne

Parson of Milford, 'a gentlemanly person, of about thirty', he hides his face under a mask of crape, a mysterious gesture apparently intended to symbolize the hiddenness of all human nature, but one which loses him his fiancée and gains him nothing but the suspicion and fear of his parishioners.

Hoover, DeWayne
Breakfast of Champions, 1973
Deadeye Dick, 1982
Kurt Vonnegut, Jr

A Pontiac car dealer in 'Midland City'. A widower, he is 'fabulously well-to-do' and has 'oodles of charm', but is also on the edge of insanity as a result of a combination of chemical imbalance and bad ideas, supplied by the science-fiction guru KILGORE TROUT. Believing he is the only human with free will, while everyone else is really a robot, he turns into a homicidal maniac.

Hopcroft, Sidney and Jane
Absurd Person Singular, 1972
Alan Ayckbourn

Sidney, an appallingly vigorous and socially pushy shop-owner, develops his business using borrowed funds, and the Hopcrofts rise to the top of the social pile. They invite RONALD and MARION BREWSTER-WRIGHT and GEOFFREY and EVA JACKSON to a party, which Sidney runs like a military campaign and from which the bullied, accident-prone Jane finally takes refuge in the garden. Sidney's hatred of those who once sneered at him emerges when he forces them to play humiliating party games.

Hope
Two Years Before the Mast, 1840
R H Dana jr, originally published anonymously

A Kanaka seaman on the American brig *Pilgrim*, he contracts a blind devotion to the intelligent, passionate narrator Dana (ANON), who is both friendly and sympathetic. It may be that the portrayal of Hope had an impact on Herman Melville's QUEEQUEG in *Moby-Dick* (1851).

Hope, Alexandra (Alex)
Crossriggs, 1908
Mary and Jane Findlater

Alex, warm-hearted, proud, past her first youth, supports her family (which consists of an amiable, unpractical father, widowed sister and five young children) in middle-class shabby-genteel poverty. Her small jobs never pay enough. The unexpressed love between Alex and married Robert Maitland saddens her and leads to the wretched marriage and suicide of young wealthy Van, who also loves her. Bearing complex problems, sometimes impatient, restless, even bitter, her bright spirit is nevertheless loving, delighting in nature and her friends.

Hope, Edith
Hotel du Lac, 1984
Anita Brookner

Upper-middle-class, unprepossessing, middle-aged and reticent, Edith is staying, out of season, at a small hotel on the shores of Lake Geneva. As author of sunny romantic fictions, she has retired in disgrace from London after driving swiftly past the Registry Office only moments before her own wedding, having caught a glimpse, through the car window, of the appalling 'mouse-like seemliness' of her prospective husband. For Edith, yearning for the out-of-the-ordinary yet confronted by the humdrum, life appears full of emotional hurdles, resulting in her living in a state of nervous trepidation interspersed by periods of stoical calm.

Hope, Harry
The Iceman Cometh, 1946
Eugene O'Neill
Owner of the End of the Line Café, a run-down boarding house and bar where all the other characters congregate on Harry's birthday to listen to HICKEY's tales about his wife and the iceman. As his name suggests, he represents a refuge and slim possibility of transcendence for the low-life and no-hope drinkers.

Hopeful
The Pilgrim's Progress, Part I 1678, Part II 1684
John Bunyan
Powerfully moved by FAITHFUL's martyrdom at the hands of the cruel citizens of Vanity Fair, where Hopeful had lived for many years, he joins CHRISTIAN for the latter stages of his journey of discipleship and provides warmth, encouragement, conversation and companionship that make the journey tolerable. He epitomizes the spirit of brotherly affection and fellowship that marks the pilgrim's way.

Hopgood, Clara and Madge
Clara Hopgood, 1896
Mark Rutherford
The daughters of free-thinking and rationalist parents, they are convinced that women have the same educational and sexual rights as men. When Madge becomes pregnant by her boyfriend she refuses to marry him, believing that such a bond would be a cruel sham, and preferring the support and sympathy of her sister.

Hopkins, Mr → Collector, The

Hopkins, Oscar
Oscar and Lucinda, 1988
Peter Carey
With wild red hair, a long thin neck and a body that is 'light, airy, made from the quills of a bird', Oscar cuts a peculiar figure. He rebels against his strict Plymouth Brethren clergyman father, becomes an Anglican, and studies theology at Oxford before becoming a missionary in Australia. Driven simultaneously by religious zeal and the obsessional impulse to gamble, Oscar is a saintly figure in his guileless approach to life. These two driving forces combine with his love for LUCINDA LEPLASTRIER in an act of folly that has a tragic end.

Horace
Poetaster, 1602
Ben Jonson
A historical character appropriated by Jonson, Quintus Horatius Flacus was one of the greatest theorists of poetic form, succeeding in adapting Greek metres to Latin verse. Jonson thought highly of Horace, and in the play he presents himself through Horace as a noble man and a

masterly writer pestered by the inferior, plagiarizing talents of the bombastic CRISPINUS and DEMETRIUS, his caricatures of the playwrights John Marston and Thomas Dekker.

Horatio
The Fair Penitent, 1703
Nicholas Rowe
The brother-in-law of ALTAMONT, Horatio is also his friend and ally, who warns him that CALISTA, to whom Altamont is betrothed, is the lover of LOTHARIO. Because Altamont initially refuses to believe the accusation, their friendship is strained, but when he discovers it to be true, the breach is healed. Horatio acts in good faith, but he is not wholly without faults. He spies and pries, acting to preserve the family ties and the comradeship between his friend. To some, therefore, his motives might appear selfish and even suspect.

Horatio
Hamlet, 1601/2
William Shakespeare
Horatio is a scholar and a gentleman and the only true friend that HAMLET has. Trusted implicitly by the prince, he is clear-thinking and level-headed, a man 'that is not passion's slave'. It is fitting that it is he who survives to tell Hamlet's story.

Horatius
Lays of Ancient Rome, 1842
Thomas Babington Macaulay
When only the narrow wooden bridge across the Tiber stands between Rome and her attackers, Horatius calls for two friends to help him keep the foe at bay while the Romans destroy the bridge. If he dies, his death will be a worthy sacrifice for his country. His two friends fight well and leap back just as the bridge falls. Horatius, too late, has to leap into the strong currents of the river and swim. He commends himself to 'Father Tiber', to whom the Romans pray' and, though cumbered by heavy armour, manages to reach the landing-place, to cheers from friend and enemy alike.

Horman, Helene
Appointment in Samarra, 1934
John O'Hara
The girlfriend of a bootlegger, she becomes involved with JULIAN ENGLISH during his desperate flight from the restrictions of life in Gibbsville. A shop-soiled Helen, she leads Julian away from the beaten track of the everyday; it is not her fault that his end is so tragic.

Hornbeck, Mrs
The Adventures of Peregrine Pickle, 1751, bowdlerized edition 1758
Tobias Smollett
The lady with whom – depending on your edition – PEREGRINE PICKLE either 'enjoyed the luscious fruits of conquest' or was disappointed in his indiscriminate lust. Jealously neglected by a husband made impotent by years of dissipation, she is immediately drawn to Perry's debonair charms. Her distinctive phonetic orthography – 'coind sur', 'this lubbertea of latin you know' – suggests Irish extraction.

Hornblower, Horatio
The Happy Return, 1937, et seq
C S Forester

Insecure, intelligent, awkward in relationships, he reveals daring and imagination that explain his rapid promotion to the highest ranks in the British navy during the Napoleonic Wars. Unassuming, self-deprecating and tortured by guilt after a passionate love-affair, he is unaware of the devotion of his men and the admiration of his contemporaries. Great courage in the face of danger, and impressive seamanship and strategy skills make him an inspiring leader, yet he feels desperately the loneliness of command, and throughout his remarkable career remains uncomfortable with himself and with the trappings of success.

Horner
The Country Wife, 1675
William Wycherley

Horner, libertine hero of this comic drama, allows himself to be medically certified as impotent in order to prey on society ladies. He succeeds beyond his wildest dreams, when a succession of wives pretending to inspect his collection of fine china individually discover his actual virility. It quickly becomes evident that his connoisseur-like discussion of china with each one of them refers to something else entirely.

Hortense, Mademoiselle
Bleak House, 1853
Charles Dickens

The hot-tempered French lady's maid of LADY DEDLOCK, she seeks revenge on being dismissed from her post. When MR TULKINGHORN fails to reward her for helping to investigate Lady Dedlock's past, she murders him and throws suspicion on Lady Dedlock. Lodging with MR BUCKET and his wife, she is outwitted by them and arrested.

Horton, Emma
Terms of Endearment, 1975
Larry McMurtry

AURORA GREENWAY's daughter, she represents the settled suburban and academic values her mother instinctively rejects. Emma is married to a drab college lecturer, but when she announces that she is pregnant, her mother faces an identity crisis, unable to accept that she is old enough to be a grandmother.

Horvath, Odon von
Tales From Hollywood, 1983
Christopher Hampton

A historical character appropriated by Hampton. An Austro-Hungarian dramatist, he died in Paris in 1938. Hampton supposes that, instead, Horvath joined the European emigration of artists and writers to Los Angeles. His Horvath is 'a striking figure, fortyish, somewhat overweight ... his exophthalmia the most notable feature of his expressive face'. His presence emphasizes that events are not isolated nor history discontinuous. Imposing, stoical, curious, he discovers that in the film business money is all and art nothing, and that the

blacklisting and oppression which drove him from Europe are emerging in McCarthy's America, a country beset by a 'tragic innocence'.

Host of the Garter Inn, the
The Merry Wives of Windsor, c.1597
William Shakespeare

An amiable practical joker and lover of intrigue, the Host of the Garter Inn at Windsor hears most of the local gossip and agrees to help FRANK FORD in his confidence trick upon SIR JOHN FALSTAFF. In the matter of the rival suitors of ANNE PAGE, he supports the candidature of Fenton. Encouraging DR CAIUS to challenge SIR HUGH EVANS to a duel, he fools both by arranging a different rendezvous with each. Later, he helps to arrange Fenton's wedding to Anne.

Host of the Tabard Inn, the → Bailley, Harry

Hot Horse Herbie
Stories à la Carte, 1932
Furthermore, 1938
Damon Runyon

A man of eternal optimism, he haunts the race-courses of America, certain that he has figured out the winners, but never successful enough to fund that optimism out of his own pocket. A likeable loser, he lives in that demi-monde of the professional gambler, with its occasional highs, and its frequent need for belt-tightening and borrowing. His nickname evolves from his certainty that he has a 'hot horse' that is sure to beat the odds. Usually it doesn't.

Hotchkiss, St John
Getting Married, 1908
George Bernard Shaw

Hotchkiss is a smart and snobbish young man in his late twenties, 'correct in dress to the last thread of his collar, but much too preoccupied with his ideas to be embarrassed by any concern as to his appearance'. The intended new husband of LEO BRIDGENORTH, he talks to people as if implying a kindly consideration for their stupidity. This amuses some but profoundly irritates others. He suggests to guests assembled for the wedding of EDITH BRIDGENORTH to CECIL SYKES that 'England's first partnership deed' be drawn up between them.

Hotspur (Henry Percy)
Richard II, not later than 1595 ; *Henry IV Part I*, 1596/7
William Shakespeare

Chivalrous and brave, the epitome of honour, Hotspur is the kind of son that HENRY IV wishes he had sired. However, he is full of flaws, which eventually bring about his downfall. His impetuosity, while a benefit in his early battles, lands him in a situation on the battlefield of Shrewsbury that he cannot deal with; his quick temper is shown in his encounter with Henry; his rudeness to OWEN GLENDOWER almost causes a rift in the rebel forces; and his tendency to take people at face value is evident in his misjudgement of Prince Hal (HENRY, PRINCE OF WALES), whom he treats with scorn. He meets death with courage – but unnecessarily.

Houghton, Alvina
The Lost Girl, 1920
D H Lawrence
The lost girl of the title, Alvina, the daughter of a provincial draper, has been well brought up but longs for something other than commerce and marriage. Deciding to fathom her own spiritual, vocational and sexual nature, she becomes a nurse in London, a pianist at a cinema, and the lover of the enigmatic vaudeville artist, CICIO. The discovery and flowering of her sexuality becomes central to her being and to the novel. It becomes the means whereby she strives to cast off provincial England and become reborn; to lose one self and become another, more worldly, more sensuous and free.

Housman, A E
The Invention of Love, 1997
Tom Stoppard
The play opens in 1936, when Housman, the author of *A Shropshire Lad* among other poems, has just died. Nevertheless, he is a sprightly narrator, nostalgic, sometimes bitter, often sentimental, especially when recalling the great but unrequited love of his life, a university friend named Moses Jackson who, unfortunately for Housman, proved to be heterosexual but who inspired much of his later poetry. The younger Housman appears superficially full of energy and passionately interested in life around him but, obliged to suppress his love and conceal his homosexuality, retreats into anguish and loneliness, becoming an intensely private man denying himself true fulfilment.

Houston, Jack, also referred to as Zack Houston
The Hamlet, 1940
William Faulkner
A farmer in Yoknapatawpha County, whose dairy cow becomes the object of the idiot IKE SNOPES's affections. He is murdered by MINK SNOPES after demanding redress for a more conventional sort of trespass. Houston represents the quieter and more orderly type of traditional farmer against whom the Snopeses' flagrant modernism is largely directed.

Houyhnhnms
Gulliver's Travels, 1726
Jonathan Swift
A race of wise and noble creatures who have the physical shape of horses yet possess the gift of speech. Their grand maxim is to cultivate reason. Their behaviour is orderly and rational and the word *houyhnhnm* in their language not only means 'horse' but also symbolizes 'the perfection of nature'. They have no concept of lying, this being 'the thing which is not', nor any concept of war. They educate both males and females to the same level and in poetry excel above all other creatures. Truly virtuous, they represent ideal man.

Howe, Anna
Clarissa, 1748
Samuel Richardson
A prototype feminist who launches a caustic and debunking tirade against men, claiming that their rights are 'ostentatious nonsense' and that woman are cajoled and ensnared like birds. She despises the dehumanizing financial dependence of marriage and clings to the idea of going off to live with CLARISSA HARLOWE. She expresses this romantic notion in a paean to chastity and fidelity, an idealized spinsterhood. Anna's fundamental flaw is her levity, and she too glibly urges Clarissa to escape with ROBERT LOVELACE; blinded by his glittering wealth and rank, she ignores his base brutality.

Howe, Joseph
'Of This Time, Of That Place', 1943, in *Of This Time, Of That Place and Other Stories*, 1970
Lionel Trilling
A liberal university teacher, whose support for the brilliant but unstable TERTAN is defeated by the dominance of another student, the capable but soulless BLACKBURN.

Howe, Sir William
'Howe's Masquerade', in *Twice-Told Tales*, 1837, revised edition 1842
Nathaniel Hawthorne
A historical English general, he took over command of the army in America from Thomas Gage but failed to make an impression against Washington's men, resigned, and was summoned to Parliament to give an account of his actions. In Hawthorne's story, he gives a glittering ball in Boston at which an unplanned masque of ghostly figures representing the early settlers prophesies the end of royal rule in the colonies.

Howeglas, Father → Abbot of Unreason

Howler, Rev Melchisedech
Dombey and Son, 1848
Charles Dickens
A nonconformist preacher of 'the Ranting persuasion', he ministers to MRS MACSTINGER and marries her to CAPTAIN JACK BUNSBY.

Hoyden, Miss
The Relapse, or Virtue in Danger, 1696
Sir John Vanbrugh
Frustrated both by remaining a virgin and having been cooped up in the country for too long, the wealthy Miss Hoyden is eager to be married and enjoy metropolitan life. Her father, SIR TUNBELLY CLUMSEY, has promised her in marriage to LORD FOPPINGTON, but the pragmatic, determined and boisterous Miss Hoyden marries his younger brother, YOUNG FASHION, instead. She appears quite mercenary in this, for sex and bawdiness are her pleasure and as long as Fashion has access to her money, he rather enjoys the prospect that 'the whole kennel of beaux' will soon be 'at her tail'. After all, he declares admiringly, 'she'll show 'em sport'.

Hoyt, Rosemary
Tender is the Night, 1934
F Scott Fitzgerald
A naive but self-aware young film star who is seduced by DICK and NICOLE DIVER's opulent but morally empty lifestyle while she is in exile in Europe. She is young, wild, impressionable,

eager for experience, and rich, but also has a steely determination and discipline in seeking out what she wants, including Dick, who falls in love with her.

Hubbard, Bartley
A Modern Instance, 1882
The Rise of Silas Lapham, 1885
William Dean Howells

A clever but essentially unprincipled Boston journalist, whose lack of moral fibre and systematic infidelity alienate his wife MARCIA HUBBARD. Unshakably sure of himself, Hubbard (to whom SILAS LAPHAM describes his upbringing and aspirations in the later book) is eventually killed by a man into whose private affairs he has ruthlessly intruded.

Hubbard, Bill
Only Children, 1979
Alison Lurie

According to his wife, HONEY HUBBARD, Bill is someone who has 'forgotten how to play'. It is true that he is a serious man, keenly aware of his responsibilities to his family, to his job and to society. A decent, intelligent individual of liberal views, he enjoys being a father, happy to explain things with honesty and patience to his daughter. He feels less secure about his relationship with his wife, and his well-founded suspicions lead to increasingly obsessive behaviour which stifles the sense of fun and spontaneity that would make him more attractive to her.

Hubbard, Harry (Herrick), also known as ANCHOVY/BLUE, or AV/AILABLE, or 'Robert Charles', or 'Harry Field', or KU/CLOAKROOM, or KU/ROPES, or 'William Madden Libby', or 'Charley Sloate', or SM/ONION
Harlot's Ghost, 1991
Norman Mailer

A young CIA operative from a second-generation Agency family, he is initiated into the world of intelligence by HARLOT (HUGH FREMONT MONTAGUE), whose wife he later wins and marries. Posted to Berlin and Montevideo, he gains a purchase on the web of secrets that leads from the Cold War machinations of the early fifties to the assassination of John F Kennedy.

Hubbard, Honey
Only Children, 1979
Alison Lurie

A pretty Southern girl, wife of BILL HUBBARD, she is very worldly-wise about men and how to get them but, sheltered from other aspects of adult responsibility, she still has the self-centred attitude of a child. Although she has declined a college education in favour of a giddy social life, there is a surprisingly independent streak in her. She wants men to admire and desire her but is not prepared to be any man's doormat, nor is she happy to suffocate under any man's obsessive devotion, fearing that if she does not preserve some private life of her own she might 'just plain vanish'.

Hubbard, Marcia, née Gaylord
A Modern Instance, 1882
William Dean Howells

Howells considered calling the novel 'The New Medea' in recognition of Marcia's reincarnation of her Greek mythological counterpart's passionate and self-reliant nature. Repelled by her husband BARTLEY HUBBARD's amorality and constant philandering, she leaves him and strikes out on her own.

Hubert, Brother → Friar, the

Hud
Horseman, Pass By, 1961, reissued as *Hud*, 1963
Larry McMurtry

The stepson of cattle rancher HOMER BANNON, he represents a hardened and virtually amoral frontier mentality in which law and social forces are almost inoperative. In contrast to Homer's epic stoicism, with its backward-looking code, he anticipates a pragmatic future.

Hudibras
The Faerie Queene, 1590–6
Sir Edmund Spenser

A knight who courts ELISSA, to whom he is well suited. Hardy, tough and rash, he is a physically demonstrative man rather than an intelligent, reflective one. Foolish in his quests, he is prone to outbursts of unreason. He is not interested in the pursuit of good and virtuous deeds but rather in the fame and fortune that adventuring brings.

Hudibras, Sir
Hudibras, 1663, 1664, 1678
Samuel Butler

Sir Hudibras, a Presbyterian knight, is the main character of this three-part mock-heroic satire, which also features the sectarian Squire Ralpho. In the manner of Don Quixote and Sancho Panza, they set out on a journey by horseback and suffer several bizarre adventures. The pair having been imprisoned, a widow, whom Sir Hudibras intends marrying for her jointure, agrees to release them provided he undergoes a whipping. Grotesque, avaricious, lying and ruthless, Sir Hudibras later claims this has been done, but later still is forced to confess his misdemeanours.

Hudson, Roderick
Roderick Hudson, 1875, revised edition 1879
Henry James

A gifted young sculptor from Massachusetts who is taken to Europe by his patron Rowland Hallett to develop his precocious style under the influence of the classics. Though already engaged to Mary Garland, he falls under the spell of Christina Light (later PRINCESS CASAMASSIMA), and never quite regains his shaky moral equilibrium.

Hudson, Sir Geoffrey
Peveril of the Peak, 1823
Sir Walter Scott

Known to history as Henrietta Maria's dwarf, this tiny man enjoys an important place at court, where he is the queen's page, having been presented to her in a pie. Not above three feet six inches in height, he has a slightly preposterous dignity, imparted by rich clothes and a proud manner. He is imprisoned for his supposed part in the Popish Plot (which is where JULIAN PEVERIL encounters him), as a result of which his health is fatally undermined.

Huff, Walter
Double Indemnity, 1944
James M Cain

An honest, diligent insurance agent of lengthy experience and impeccable credentials, he finds his honesty turning to larcenous deceit when his overwhelming attraction to PHYLLIS NIRDLINGER leads him to plan murder. Fatalistic about the act and its consequences, he remains spellbound by a woman he grows to love 'like a rabbit loves a rattlesnake'.

Hugh
Barnaby Rudge, 1841
Charles Dickens

Wild, sullen and athletic, he is the ostler at the Maypole Inn and later a ringleader of the Gordon Riots. Although fond only of his dog and BARNABY RUDGE, he makes advances to DOLLY VARDEN and then assists in abducting her and EMMA HAREDALE. He is revealed to be the illegitimate son of SIR JOHN CHESTER and a wild gypsy woman, hanged at Tyburn, but when he himself is arrested and condemned to hang, his father refuses to intercede on his behalf, and he is executed.

Hugh
Morning Tide, 1930
Neil Gunn

The young hero and central consciousness of the novel, Hugh has much to think about as he grows up in his small fishing community. Shy and sensitive at first, his adolescent awkwardness diminishes as he approaches manhood and learns to deal with the various trials of life, comes to terms with his own, and his sisters', sexuality and becomes aware of his love for his mother when confronted with the very real possibility of her death.

Hughes, Stuart
Talking it Over, 1991
Love, etc, 2000
Julian Barnes

In his early thirties in the first novel, and an old school friend of OLIVER RUSSELL, whose air of superiority he sometimes only barely tolerates, Stuart is socially ill-at-ease and, as a result, frequently feels awkward and defensive. Working for a City clearing bank, he marries GILLIAN WYATT, only to discover, before much time has elapsed, that she is divorcing him for Oliver. Moving to the United States, Stuart again marries and divorces before returning to London, intent upon revenge. On the way, he has learned two maxims he holds vital: that 'you get what you pay for', and that 'real betrayal occurs among friends, among those you love'.

Hughes, Yosser
The Boys from the Blackstuff, 1984
Alan Bleasdale

Yosser is one of life's failures: he wants to work but has no skills or education. His frustration erupts frequently in acts of random violence, usually against authority or those he sees as representing authority. The only person he can rely on is GEORGE MALONE, but Malone's increasing ill-health means he has little real influence. Obsessed with the fear of losing his children after his wife has left him, Yosser becomes more and more manic. He is a pitiful and pitiable figure, although there are signs later that he is reaching a state of self-awareness.

Hulga
Good Country People, 1948
Flannery O'Connor

A frustrated adult daughter whose disability has confined her to her mother's household and thwarted her academic ambitions. Thirty-two years old, with a doctorate in philosophy, she is constantly infuriated by her mother's limited intellect and continuing presence in her life; she exaggerates the ungainliness of her artificial leg and changes her name from Joy to the deliberately ugly Hulga as a calculated affront.

Humanitas, Rex
Ane Pleasant Satyre of the Thrie Estaitis, 1540
Sir David Lindsay

Perhaps the most important figure in the play, Rex Humanitas is both a realistic and an allegorical character. At one and the same time the young, well-meaning but easily-led king of the country, and a representative of 'Everyman', or common human experience, his succumbing to temptation in the form of DAME SENSUALITIE serves as a warning to everyone. Blinded by over-indulgence in sexual pleasure, he is ignorant of the vice and corruption dominating his kingdom, but his personal reform through DIVYNE CORRECTIOUN paves the way for the public reform of the state.

Humbert, Humbert
Lolita, 1955
Vladimir Nabokov

A mentally troubled European intellectual adrift in America, he seduces and marries LOLITA's vulgar mother in order to keep close to her daughter, who reanimates his obsession with the undeveloped female body. Although he is 'horrible ... abject ... a shining example of moral leprosy', Humbert's witty, lively and lyrical prose makes him a compulsively engaging, though deeply disturbing, protagonist.

Hume, Harriet
Harriet Hume, 1929
Rebecca West

A concert pianist, Harriet displays intelligence and wit married to a genuine talent. Living on the edge of poverty, she recognizes her powerlessness, and accepts her marginal position. She is gloriously innocent, but knows that she cannot persuade the rest of the world to act on the basis of the harmony that she has found in her work. She realizes that 'humanity would be unbearably lackadaisical if there were none but my kind alive'. She is artistically febrile, but succeeds in imposing a contingent order on her frantic, diffuse existence by means of her art.

Humgudgeon, or Corporal Grace-be-here
Woodstock, or The Cavalier, 1826
Sir Walter Scott

With a verse of Holy Writ to suit every contingency (and especially those which present danger to himself), he is the human face of the New Model Army. For all his instinct for self-preservation, he is 'as determined a soldier as ever fought among the redoubted regiment of Ironsides, and possessed of no small a share of that exalted fanaticism which lent so keen an edge to the natural courage of those stern religionists'.

Humm, Anthony
Pickwick Papers, 1837
Charles Dickens

An itinerant preacher and President of the Brick Lane Branch of the United Grand Junction Ebenezer Temperance Association. SAM and TONY WELLER attend one of the meetings.

Humpty Dumpty
Through the Looking-Glass, and What Alice Found There, 1872
Lewis Carroll

Humpty Dumpty, the nursery-rhyme character, sits on a wall, his legs crossed, his face enormous. He is annoyed to be called an egg and cross when ALICE knows about all the King's horses and men. Nothing she says pleases him. He explains un-birthday presents and how he makes words mean what he wants them to mean. Alice asks him the meaning of the poem 'Jabberwocky', and he expounds on portmanteau-words, which have two meanings packed into one. He repeats an ill-tempered poem of his own in couplets that end abruptly without complete sense. He then says a sudden 'Goodbye'. As Alice goes she hears a crash – Humpty Dumpty has had his great fall.

Hunt, Alethea
A Woman of the Future, 1979
David Ireland

This absurdist novel tells the story of Alethea Hunt from conception until the age of 18 when she turns into a leopard. The novel is set in the future and Alethea, born into a rigidly divided social structure, observes surreal events in an ugly, desolate Australian landscape. Intelligent and sharp, convinced of her own magnificence and potential, she dreams of her power and fertility. Everything she does, she does better than others. Alethea delights in winning. In some senses, she is representative of a vision of Australia as an arcadia, a place of untapped riches, and it is this which is celebrated by her final transformation.

Hunt, Tufton
A Shabby Genteel Story, 1840
The Adventures of Philip, 1861–2
W M Thackeray

A rascally parson who performs the mock marriage ceremony between CAROLINE GANN and DR GEORGE FIRMIN. Later, this provides him with ideal ammunition for a blackmail plot.

Hunter, Elizabeth
The Eye of the Storm, 1973
Patrick White

In her eighties, bed-ridden and almost blind, the domineering and imperious Elizabeth Hunter is spending her last days in her imposing house in Sydney, looking back over her life. Because she manipulated rather than loved her family, her children, who return from Europe to be at her bedside, are themselves incapable of love. Mrs Hunter has, however, glimpsed a vision of redemption; 15 years earlier, during a cyclone on a tropical island, she experienced something of a spiritual rebirth. Although she remained hard-hearted, the experience led to her adopting a more sympathetic view of human vulnerability.

Hunter, Mrs Leo
Pickwick Papers, 1837
Charles Dickens

A celebrated Eatanswill literary lady and lion-hunting hostess, she entertains SAMUEL PICKWICK and his friends to a reading of her poem, 'Ode to an Expiring Frog'.

Huntingdon, Arthur
The Tenant of Wildfell Hall, 1848
Anne Brontë

Arthur Huntingdon, suave and charming, wins the heart of Helen (MRS HELEN GRAHAM); she thinks that her love will change his drunken profligacy, but he shows himself selfish and careless of her happiness. He becomes more dissipated, surrounds her with his worthless friends and is blatantly unfaithful. He torments her cruelly for five years but when he tries to corrupt his little son she flouts convention and leaves him. He grows worse. When she hears that he is dying, she returns, feeling it her duty to wrestle with his soul and try to save him from damnation. He curses and defies her, but in his last terrible days fear of God makes him beg her to pray for him.

Huntingdon, Mrs Helen → Graham, Mrs Helen

Huntly, Edgar
Edgar Huntly, 1799
Charles Brockden Brown

The bewildered protagonist of the novel, Edgar Huntly is a mine of contradiction. Believing himself to be rational he nevertheless undergoes psychological fragmentation under pressure; he egotistically assumes the centrality of his own consciousness yet imagines an outside, malignant power to be directing his fate. Unable to identify with either the expectations of the modern world, or the wilderness of the 'frontier', he is 'transformed' by experience (at one point of heightened fear of starvation, he considers eating part of himself), yet never achieves a settled sense of self. His contrary roles as fool and serious narrator make him intriguingly 'modern'.

Hurst, Mrs (Marion)
A Male Child, 1956
Paul Scott

In the bleak, debilitated time immediately after World War II, elderly Mrs Hurst, in her cheerless room in the family home, is succumbing to alcoholism. She is both pathetic and appalling, with her grotesque make-up, dyed red hair and vindictiveness towards her younger son, Alan, for having survived the war while his brother, Edward, a sensitive poet whom she idolized, was killed. When Alan brings home a wartime friend who is a writer, she tries to put him in Edward's place, while persuading him to undertake a biography of her novelist sister-in-law.

Hurstwood, George
Sister Carrie, 1900, suppressed; reissued 1907, complete text published 1983
Theodore Dreiser

An older, married man who runs a bar in Chicago. He attracts CARRIE MEEBER, who sees him as more intelligent and cultured than her lover CHARLES DROUET, and she elopes with him. But Hurstwood does not seem to function outside his native environment and declines rapidly into a pathetic dependency that drives Carrie away.

Hushabye, Hector
Heartbreak House, 1916
George Bernard Shaw

The husband of HESIONE HUSHABYE, Hector is a handsome, rather dandyish man of 50. A dreamer and philanderer, he has briefly convinced ELLIE DUNN that his name is Marcus Darnley and entranced her with spurious stories of dashing deeds. He appears both frivolous and ridiculous, but in reality he is a more tragic figure: a man of action whom aimlessness has rendered incapable of action. With a venomous mixture of disgust and self-loathing, he sees that the inhabitants of Heartbreak House, 'cultured, leisured Europe before the war', are 'useless futile creatures' who 'ought to be abolished'.

Hushabye, Hesione
Heartbreak House, 1916
George Bernard Shaw

A daughter of CAPTAIN SHOTOVER, (the other being LADY ARIADNE UTTERWORD), and married to HECTOR HUSHABYE, Hesione is one of the most vital characters in the play. Middle-aged, she has magnificent black hair and is 'uncorseted and dressed anyhow in a rich robe … that shews off her white skin and statuesque contour'. A woman of direct and sometimes shocking opinions, she is a romantic predator of powerful sexual magnetism. But her greatest days are over and at her heart lies a terrifying emptiness and fear. At the end of the play, she watches an air-raid exultantly, believing death offers a final 'glorious experience'.

Hutchins, Eveline
The 42nd Parallel, 1930
1919, 1932
The Big Money, 1936, forming the *U.S.A.* trilogy, 1938
John Dos Passos

Daughter of a rich Chicago minister, Eveline grows up with vastly different ideas on life from her strait-laced parents. Failing to make a great financial success of her interior design business with ELEANOR STODDARD, free-and-easy Eveline concentrates her energies on her frivolous society lifestyle, abandoning herself to a series of affairs which leave her, at the end of the war, feeling empty and directionless.

Hutley, Jem (called **Dismal Jemmy**)
Pickwick Papers, 1837
Charles Dickens

A down-at-heel actor and the brother of JOB TROTTER. ALFRED JINGLE introduces him to SAMUEL PICKWICK, to whom he narrates 'The Stroller's Tale'.

Huw 'Halfbacon'
The Owl Service, 1967
Alan Garner

Huw appears to ROGER to be no more than a simple-minded gardener/handyman, with a curious, roundabout way of speaking that might simply be put down to his Welshness. Unworldly and somewhat fey, he lives in squalor at the back of the stables of the Big House, with only a few planks for furniture. Despite his humble appearance, to the rest of the valley he is a Lord, and GWYN is his true son and heir. Moreover, Huw is in tune with the forces of the past and recognizes the signs that 'Blodeuwedd' is about to return and re-enact the eternal tragic legend of two young men who love the same girl and kill each other. Indeed, Huw's jealous nature earlier ensured that the same triangle of jilted love would perpetuate itself through another generation.

Huxter, Sam
The History of Pendennis, 1848–50
W M Thackeray

A kind and accommodating medical student with whom FANNY BOLTON finds consolation after being set aside by the Pendennises. Despite overtones of the word 'huckster' in his surname, he is far removed from the money-chasing ethos that prevails in the novel.

Hyde, Fanny
A House is Built, 1928
M Barnard Eldershaw

The unmarried eldest daughter of the quartermaster, JAMES HYDE, SENIOR, she is characterized by 'her common sense, her humour, her total lack of sentimentality'. Unconventionally attractive, her features have 'strong, definite lines'. The sensible, steady, and reliable older sister, she is completely humiliated by the rejection of her first love, and withdraws behind a barrier of silence and reserve. This rejection colours the rest of Fanny's life. Determined to find some meaningful occupation other than the pursuit of marriage, she finds a sense of purpose working in the family business, but this sole source of happiness is cruelly taken from her when it is deemed unsuitable to her social position. Thus, towards the end of her life, Fanny's 'inner core of bitterness remained untouched'.

Hyde, James, Junior
A House is Built, 1928
M Barnard Eldershaw

ADELA GAGE's and WILLIAM HYDE's eldest son, he is very much a Hyde: 'He had inherited the quartermaster's exceptional vitality, William's reserve, and Fanny's pride'. Heir apparent to the Hyde family fortunes, James is a boisterous and energetic child, much adored by his grandfather, father and aunt. He nonetheless grows up aware that he is not his mother's favourite: 'He was at odds with his mamma, he wanted her to love him, and still more, he wanted her to admire him, but he would not admit even to himself that he wanted these things'. Taken into the family business when he comes of age, he finds favour with his father and grandfather. The emotional distance from his mother continues to influence him, however, and a doomed love affair with a cousin ends in his tragic drowning while still a youth.

Hyde, James, Senior, known as 'the quartermaster'
A House is Built, 1928
M Barnard Eldershaw

He is 'a square, ruddy man, powerful and sanguine'. At the end of his sailing days, the English quartermaster decides to move his family to Australia. He sets up a store supplying ships, and his primary focus is to establish a secure business for his family: 'That he should set his shoulder to the wheel in this new country, and by his efforts build a house where his children's children might live in honour and security, seemed to him as good a thing as a man could do'. A character of 'unfailing good humour and boisterous generosity', he is happiest when facing new opportunities for expanding his empire. Family and business are inextricably linked for him, however, and he collapses on hearing of his grandson's death: 'His high courage, his iron will, and his magnificent vitality had blown out like a candle-flame'.

Hyde, Lionel
A House is Built, 1928
M Barnard Eldershaw

ADELA GAGE's and WILLIAM HYDE's second son. Two years younger than JAMES HYDE, JUNIOR, Lionel is from birth his mother's favourite. A small, sickly, delicate child, 'in his mother's eyes Lionel grew in beauty every day; for others he just grew and not very quickly'. Although his brother is favoured by their father's family, Lionel is content because he is truly loved by his mother: 'He was good-tempered, friendly, and quiet. He lived and let live. Only his mother loved passionately. She was necessary to him.' His brother's death throws Lionel's secluded world into upheaval, and he is forced to take James's place in the family business. Knowing he is a supplanter in his father's eyes, Lionel's confidence is undermined, and he does badly in the work, which does not suit him: 'He knew his attitude toward business was childish and absurd, and his diffidence hampered him as much as his ignorance'. Despite his inadequacies, Lionel perseveres, the links and power of the

family firm too strong to break.

Hyde, Maud
A House is Built, 1928
M Barnard Eldershaw

FANNY HYDE's younger sister, the youngest child of the quartermaster, JAMES HYDE, SENIOR. Maud is characterized by her cheerful nature: 'there were no creases in Maud, no sharp turnings, nothing irrational – a person who actually and without effort attained happiness'. As a young girl, Maud's primary concerns are romantic novels and new clothes; her 'brown curls, big brown eyes, and brilliant complexion' are the fashion of the day. Though Maud 'has an eye for every man she sees', her father notes that her head is 'screwed on the right way'. She eventually elopes with Humphrey Gillam, the son of her father's business rival, and has six children with him. Although this creates a rift between her and Fanny, Maud's cheery nature remains a focus of the family's social life.

Hyde, Mr → Dr Jekyll/Mr Hyde

Hyde, William
A House is Built, 1928
M Barnard Eldershaw

The only son of the quartermaster, JAMES HYDE, SENIOR, William is not eager to leave his 'quiet, clerkly, English life' and start up a new one in Australia, 'where he felt incompetent, ashamed, and ill at ease'. Aloof and supercilious, he resents having to associate with people he perceives as beneath him, and initially feels life at his father's store is 'vulgar and rough and a constant wound to [his] refinement'. In spite of this, he agrees to become a partner in Hyde and Son, where his cold formality is superseded by his finer qualities: 'justice, restraint, and an honourable but not impulsive generosity'. William's primary desire is to raise his family's social standing, yet although his wife and children are his main concern, he is an emotionally distant man, admiring and adoring them only from afar. He eventually achieves success in the family business, but never quite accepts living in the New World.

Hyish
The Ebb Tide, 1894
Robert Louis Stevenson

The most wicked of the trio of treasure hunters who vainly seek to outwit the owner of the Pacific island where they hope to make their fortune. He is more purely selfish than HERRICK or DAVIS, believing in a world where moral values are worthless and where man should be free to act as he likes. In most respects he is a despicable person, but his failings are weaknesses which can be found in everyone. Like all Stevenson villains he is not wholly evil.

Hymen
As You Like It, c.1600
William Shakespeare

The god of marriage, who appears suddenly at the end of the play to make possible its happy endings, and four weddings.

Hythloday, Raphael
Utopia, 1516
Thomas More

Cloaked, bearded and sunburnt, Hythloday is a Portugese-born wandering sailor introduced to Thomas More in Antwerp. He knows the laws and customs of diverse places, but will not put his knowledge at the service of kings, who prefer flatterers to approve of their militarism rather than real counsellors. Having dispensed, in argument, with the European social order, he says there is a country, called Utopia, which avoids such problems. 'Hythloday' is Greek for nonsense and 'utopia' Greek for nowhere; not all of his descriptions and proposals, however, should easily be discounted.

I

I
In Transit, 1969
Brigid Brophy

Unidentified, genderless and trapped in the between-state of an airport departure lounge, Brophy's 'character' speculates on the subjects that traditionally haunt the novel: identity, status, sexuality, physical and social mobility. In the end, (s)he is redeemed by the possibility of a 'You' who is lover, reader and second self.

Iachimo
Cymbeline, 1609/10
William Shakespeare

An Italian who, irritated by POSTHUMUS LEONATUS's claims of his wife IMOGEN's virtue and fidelity, wagers that he can bring back proof of her inconstancy by gaining access to her bed. An arrogant braggart who demonstrates much in the way of devious cunning, Iachimo is nevertheless a villain on the small scale, without the conviction of his evil actions, and, shortly after 'winning' the wager, is consumed by guilt and remorse.

Iago
Othello, 1603/4
William Shakespeare

OTHELLO's trusted ancient. Truly evil, he abuses the trust, loyalty and love he gains from others in his burning desire to destroy Othello, his motivation drawn from resentment (over CASSIO's promotion) and the entirely unsubstantiated belief that his general has committed adultery with his wife, EMILIA. His speeches, delivered in the prose of the common man, and full of fitting animal imagery, show him as a corrupt and Machiavellian manipulator in a play peopled with idealistic and noble characters. He is tortured at the end, but refuses ever to speak again.

Iannis, Dr
Captain Corelli's Mandolin, 1994
Louis de Bernières

Dr Iannis is the local doctor and central to the life of his village. An intelligent man, though mildly eccentric, he has a classical bent, but he does hold very progressive views on the education and role of women. A widower, he dotes on his daughter, PELAGIA IANNIS, whom he regards as equal to any male. He is employed in writing the definitive history of his Greek island home Cephallonia, but finds he is 'unable to write without passion', and considers all Greeks poets. His initial determination to 'resist occupation with dignity' is relaxed when he recognizes the humanity of the occupying Italians.

Iannis, Pelagia
Captain Corelli's Mandolin, 1994
Louis de Bernières

The daughter of the local doctor on the Greek island of Cephallonia, Pelagia has had the benefit of her father's education. Her liberal upbringing has made her a strong, independent young woman who hopes to become a doctor. Her awakening sexuality draws her into a betrothal with a handsome local fisherman, but prevents her from recognizing that he is not her intellectual equal. When Italian troops occupy her village, their captain, ANTONIO CORELLI, is billeted at her house. Only then, when matched against someone of similar spirit and intellectual curiosity, does she experience real love.

Ibbot, Barney
Summer of the Seventeenth Doll, 1955
Ray Lawler

A small and pugnacious Lothario and heavy drinker; because of a fundamental insensitivity and loquaciousness (as unfortunate, in its way, as ROO WEBBER's uncommunicativeness) he does much to break the bonds of friendship between himself, Roo and OLIVE. His womanizing has become an unpleasant mannerism and as his earlier roguish charm deserts him, he has, as EMMA points out, increasingly abandoned bragging in favour of outright lies about his conquests. His desire to avoid the consequences of change leads him to be disloyal to his mate Roo, in favour of JOHNNIE DOWD. His final gesture of support for the broken Roo demonstrates, too late, a fundamental warmth which has been all but buried beneath his pragmatism and childish irresponsibility.

Iden
Amaryllis at the Fair, 1887
Richard Jefferies

A Wiltshire farmer of solid rural virtue and unexpected psychological depths, he is a fictionalized version of Jefferies' own father, who deeply influenced his son's attitude to the natural world.

Idu
Idu, 1970
Flora Nwapa

Beautiful, calm and patient, she works hard and establishes a profitable business while efficiently continuing with her duties as wife and mother.

Idu is resigned to her duty to care for her troublesome sister, Anamadi, and her husband ADIEWERE's lazy brother, Ishiodu. An ideal wife, Idu is dedicated to her husband, and is tragically unable to live without him.

Ihuoma
The Concubine, 1966
Elechi Amadi

The reincarnated wife of the jealous Sea-King, and one of the most beautiful women in the village, Ihuoma avoids conflict and becomes known for her ability to settle quarrels among other women. Placing the needs of others before her own happiness, she hides her feelings for EKWUEME in order to conform to the expectations of her society. She is destined to sadness through the inevitable deaths of the men she loves.

Ikkemotubbe
The Sound and the Fury, 1929, and elsewhere
William Faulkner

'A dispossessed American King', also known as 'The Man' and 'Doom'. He is the Chickasaw chief who grants a square mile of his ancestral lands to the first American COMPSONS/SUTPENS, refugees who had themselves lost everything by throwing in their lot with a dispossessed Jacobite king.

Ilex, Miss
Gryll Grange, 1860–1
Thomas Love Peacock

An elderly, good-natured spinster, well-versed in art, music and literature, Miss Ilex proves gracious company, offering morsels of wisdom to confused young lovers. Regretting her own reserve in matters of the heart, she encourages others to risk their pride in the pursuit of love.

Imogen
Cymbeline, 1609/10
William Shakespeare

The daughter of CYMBELINE, she has married POSTHUMUS LEONATUS against her father's wishes. Apart from this filial disobedience (which in itself shows good judgement on her part), she is the ideal heroine. Many characters bear witness to her perfect beauty; she is virtuous and faithful to Posthumus throughout their lengthy separation despite temptations deliberately (if clumsily) laid in her path, and also despite the knowledge that her husband is actively seeking her death. She is described as 'tender', 'diligent' and 'true', but is also a practical and resourceful woman with a strong character, great vitality and a quick temper.

Imoinda
Oroonoko, or The History of the Royal Slave, c.1688
Aphra Behn, adapted for the stage by Thomas Southerne, 1695

The proud and beautiful daughter of a general to an African king, Imoinda loves OROONOKO. The king, in love with her himself, discovers the affair and orders that she be sold into slavery. A similar fate befalls Oroonoko. In Surinam, then an English colony, the couple are reunited but, after an unsuccessful rebellion by the slaves, Imoinda chooses to die at the hands of her lover,

thus representing the nobility of those degraded by slavery, and highlighting the hypocrisy of their so-called masters.

Inerarity, Raoul
The Grandissimes, 1880
George Washington Cable

JOSEPH FROWENFELD's assistant, he is a talkative and highly-strung young Creole, with auburn hair and an air of 'adolescent buoyancy'. He presents himself at the apothecary's with a passionately-felt but frightful painting of Louisiana, refusing to enter the Union that demonstrates a greater interest in bare flesh than in allegorical propriety.

Injun Joe
The Adventures of Tom Sawyer, 1876
Mark Twain

A chillingly ruthless villain lacking in any redeeming features, Injun Joe plans to mutilate an old woman on account of a long-held grudge against her late husband. Vengeful and wholly evil, he inspires fear not only by his presence but by his ominous absence. None are more afraid of him than TOM SAWYER and HUCK FINN, terrified witnesses to one of his black and foul deeds.

Inman
Cold Mountain, 1997
Charles Frazier

After he is severely wounded in a Civil War battle, Inman deserts from the Confederate Army to begin a long and perilous trek through the rural South to his home in North Carolina. He hopes to find ADA MONROE awaiting his return. Though exhausted and troubled by self-doubt, he is a courageous individual with a strong, instinctive moral sense and an abiding respect for the natural order of the world as he knew it before the war.

Innes, Frank
Weir of Hermiston, 1896
Robert Louis Stevenson

The handsome friend of ARCHIE WEIR, who follows him in the same course of study. Like Archie, he finds it difficult to inspire true friendship or intimacy. He is an irresponsible youth with a superficially charming, beguiling manner which fails to impress anyone. Pursued by the law for a gambling debt, he seeks sanctuary at the house of Archie and there he plots against his friend and his secret love for CHRISTINA ELLIOTT. This arch-manipulator is portrayed as a Mephisophelean figure, the catalyst of family tragedy.

Inquisitor, the (Brother John Lemaitre)
Saint Joan, 1923
George Bernard Shaw

Lemaitre is a 'mild, elderly' Dominican monk, representing the Inquisition at the trial of JOAN on a charge of heresy at Rouen. 'Joan was killed by the Inquisition', wrote Shaw, who saw her trial as 'a secret ... very terrible thing'. Ignoring the minor charges brought by JOHN DE STOGUMBER, the Inquisitor suggests that Joan is innocent by virtue of ignorance. Yet she is convicted and burned as a witch. He later admits a miscarriage of justice but, like PETER CAUCHON, protests that no other course could have been taken.

Interpreter
The Pilgrim's Progress, Part I 1678, Part II 1684
John Bunyan

The Interpreter's role is to inspire and encourage pilgrims such as CHRISTIAN by explaining some of the traditions, history and doctrines of the Christian Church. Patiently he explains to the inquiring pilgrim some of the blessings, opportunities and dangers he will encounter on the way. He offers the same service to Christian's wife, CHRISTIANA, when she too chooses the way of faith.

Invisible Man
Invisible Man, 1952
Ralph Ellison

The nameless black narrator, invisible 'simply because people refuse to see me' in his white-dominated society. He is a bright, intelligent high-school student, but is disoriented by his experiences in Negro College, and expelled. His search for identity takes him north and into left-wing politics, but it is the ultimate realization of his 'invisibility' which brings him fully to self-consciousness and the possibility of free action in the brightly-lit secret underground hole in which he is hibernating in 'a covert preparation for a more overt action' as he prepares to 'shake off the old skin and come up for breath'.

Invisible Man, the, previously Griffin
The Invisible Man, 1897
H G Wells

A large albino and former chemistry prizewinner named Griffin, who has discovered how to eliminate reflection and refraction from his body tissues and thus becomes known as 'the Invisible Man'. Poverty and the problems of nakedness incite him to robbery and murder; he does periodically make himself visible with a large coat, bandages, false nose and spectacles. Abrupt and bad-tempered, he is devoid of human sympathies and makes foolhardy plans to inaugurate a 'reign of terror' to give himself power and status.

Iqbal, Samad
White Teeth, 2000
Zadie Smith

Samad Iqbal, an educated Bengali, works as a waiter in a North London curry house. Tormented by his feisty young wife Alsana, who is bitter about moving to England, and their out-of-control twin sons, neither of whom are following the Muslim path he had intended for them, Samad laments his troubles with best friend ARCHIE, with whom he served in World War II. Samad's struggle to adapt to life in a foreign culture reflects the difficulties faced by many immigrant families: 'you begin to give up the very idea of belonging'. Though he considers himself a devout Muslim, British life is full of temptation for Samad. However, he compensates for the odd pint of Guinness by giving up masturbation, in 'a business proposition ... with God'.

Iras
Antony and Cleopatra, 1606/7
William Shakespeare

One of CLEOPATRA's closest attendants, Iras dies moments before Cleopatra, but whether from grief or the poison of an asp is not entirely clear. Like Charmian, Iras is loyal but sometimes contravenes Cleopatra's shifting boundaries of intimacy: what might be playfully respectful and teasing one moment is interpreted as impertinence the next.

Irena
The Faerie Queene, 1590–6
Sir Edmund Spenser

She represents the state of Ireland in Spenser's time, and her name indicates hope for an island of peace. As the country is Catholic it is seen as desirable to rescue it and put it in the hands of the rightful Protestant Church. ARTEGALL, THE KNIGHT OF JUSTICE, who is in the service of the Faerie Queene, is entrusted with her liberation. Her greatest enemy is GRANTORTO, by whom she is besieged. Her captivity and oppression break all the laws of nature.

Irene, Princess
The Princess and the Goblin, 1871
The Princess and Curdie, 1882
George MacDonald

The only daughter of a truly good and wise king, she is often left alone in his palace with her fond nurse Lootie while he is away on business of the realm. She is a beautiful, sweet-natured and inquisitive girl, whose courage and integrity aid young CURDIE's crusade to rid the realm of evil.

Ireson, Floyd
'Skipper Ireson's Ride', 1857
John Greenleaf Whittier

A hard-hearted fisherman who sailed past a sinking ship from his own town of Marblehead in New England, letting its crew drown. The outraged townswomen tar and feather him and jeeringly drag him along in a cart. He does not care what they do to him, since he is plagued by his conscience and the fear of posthumous justice.

Irish Airman, the
'An Irish Airman Foresees His Death', in *The Wild Swans at Coole*, 1919
W B Yeats

The Irish Airman is not legally obliged to fight in World War I, and he is neither pro-British nor anti-German, caring only for the Irish country people, whose interests are not affected by the conflict. He was motivated to join the British forces by an awareness of the pointlessness of his past and future life, preferring excitement and the heroic death that he knows awaits him.

Isaac of York
Ivanhoe, 1819
Sir Walter Scott

A wandering Jew, marked out by his yellow cap, and treated with instinctive discourtesy and dislike by Saxon and Norman alike. Only the mysterious pilgrim (KING RICHARD) and LADY ROWENA show him any kindness, but he is humanized by his love for his daughter REBECCA.

Isaacson, Rochelle and Paul
The Book of Daniel, 1971
E L Doctorow
They are modelled directly on Ethel and Julius Rosenberg, executed in the 1950s in the USA for supposedly selling atomic secrets to Russia. It is clear from their son DANIEL LEWIN's later recollections that the greatest dereliction of their lives has been not treason, but a failure of basic human priorities and a subordination of love to politics.

Isabel, Queen of France
Henry V, 1599
William Shakespeare
The Queen of France is present only at the peace treaty after the battle of Agincourt. She behaves with quiet dignity, hoping that her woman's voice will help effect a peace beneficial to both sides, and encouraging the marriage of her daughter KATHARINE, PRINCESS OF FRANCE to Henry V (HENRY, PRINCE OF WALES) as a means of bringing the two countries together permanently.

Isabella
The Changeling, 1653
Thomas Middleton and William Rowley
The young wife of Alibius, an old and jealous doctor, she is confined in a lunatic asylum for much of the time. A woman of good sense and a ready wit surrounded by fools and madmen, she is the target for the frustrated affections of Franciscus and ANTONIO. She explicitly illustrates the theme of the blind folly of love when she disguises herself as an old madwoman, throwing Antonio's disgust in his face when he rejects her advances on account of her changed appearance.

Isabella
'Isabella or the Pot of Basil', 1820
John Keats
The gentle heroine of the poem, her simple, tender love for Lorenzo is thwarted by her two brothers. Unhinged by her lover's murder, Isabella faithfully mourns him until her own tragic death.

Isabella
Measure for Measure, c.1604
William Shakespeare
About to enter a strict convent, but forced first to face the corruption of the outside world, Isabella is at times self-righteous and sanctimonious. Her brother CLAUDIO has been sentenced to death by ANGELO for seducing Juliette, and when Isabella is offered the chance to save her brother by submitting to Angelo's sexual demands, there is only one possible course of action for her. Her words 'More than our brother is our chastity' are chilling, illuminating her lack of sympathy for any sort of human frailty and her repressive and religiously obsessive attitude to life.

Isabella
The White Devil, 1612
John Webster
The virtuous and strongly maternal wife of the DUKE OF BRACHIANO. She pardons her husband's lust for VITTORIA COROMBONA and asks her brother FRANCISCO DE MEDICIS not to be strict with him. When Brachiano rejects her from his bed, to protect him from Francisco she pretends that her jealousy is the cause. For her pains, her husband has her murdered; ironically, his portrait, which she faithfully kisses every night, is poisoned.

Isabella
Women Beware Women, c.1621
Thomas Middleton
A young Florentine woman whose father has arranged a marriage for her to the imbecilic and unattractive 'Ward'. For some time she has enjoyed a close but innocent relationship with her uncle, HIPPOLITO (her 'best friend'), but her feelings of affection and compassion are shocked when he reveals that his love for her is not entirely platonic. In her naivety she is manipulated by her aunt, LIVIA, into a sexual relationship with Hippolito, believing him not to be her uncle after all.

Isabella, Queen
Edward II, 1594
Christopher Marlowe
Dispossessed of EDWARD II's affection by his 'minion' PIERS GAVESTON, she rebels against his feeble reign, and is driven into the arms of MORTIMER, THE YOUNGER. 'Subtill' and passionate, she takes on many of the 'male' characteristics her husband has abdicated.

Isabella of Vicenza
The Castle of Otranto, 1764
Horace Walpole
Isabella, reluctant to marry the sickly CONRAD, is even more reluctant to marry his father MANFRED, PRINCE OF OTRANTO, and pities his wife HIPPOLITA. Escaping through a subterranean passage to St Nicholas' Church with the help of a peasant, THEODORE, she is jealous of MATILDA whom he loves, but gradually grows more generous. Helped by FRIAR JEROME, she leaves Otranto and is rescued by Theodore from a Stranger Knight (her father in disguise). After the final terrifying apparition of Alonso ascending to heaven and the recognition of Theodore as the true prince, her father wishes her to marry Theodore.

Ishmael
Moby-Dick, 1851
Herman Melville
The name assumed by the narrator. He is 'tormented by an everlasting itch for things remote', and goes to sea at intervals 'as a way of warding off the spleen and regulating the circulation'. He ships on a whaler, the *Pequod*, inspired by 'the overwhelming idea of the great whale himself'. He recounts the entire tale of the chase after MOBY DICK, and is its only survivor.

Issy
Finnegans Wake, 1939
James Joyce
Daughter of HUMPHREY CHIMPDEN EARWICKER and ANNA LIVIA PLURABELLE and sister to SHAUN THE POST and SHEM THE PENMAN. She is

the object of her father's incestuous love, 'this bewitching blonde who dimples delightfully' being the Forbidden Fruit in the Eden of her father's dream. Her historical appearances in the Wake include the roles of Stella and Vanessa, who play two lover-daughters. Her ultimate role is to become her mother as history rolls through its Viconian cycle.

Ithuriel
Paradise Lost, 1667
John Milton

One of the junior angels appointed to guard ADAM and EVE in Eden, it is he who first encounters SATAN in the form of a toad, crouching by Eve's ear, and restores him to his usual shape with a touch of his spear.

Ivanhoe, in full **Wilfred of Ivanhoe**
Ivanhoe, 1819
Sir Walter Scott

Son and heir of CEDRIC THE SAXON, who nonetheless banishes him to prevent his love for LADY ROWENA blocking an advantageous marriage between her and ATHELSTANE OF CONINGSBURGH. In the Crusades Ivanhoe wins the admiration and gratitude of KING RICHARD and, like his liege, he returns to England incognito as the Disinherited Knight. When he removes his helmet to receive the winner's garland 'the well-formed yet sun-burnt features of a young man of twenty-five were seen, amidst

a profusion of short fair hair. His countenance was as pale as death and marked … with streaks of blood'.

Ivanovitch, Peter
Under Western Eyes, 1911
Joseph Conrad

A leading member of the revolutionary group to whom RAZUMOV confesses, he is treated satirically by Conrad. He has characterless features, is 'the most inconsiderate man alive', and was a dissolute youth before his revolutionary conversion. He was a political prisoner in Siberia, but escaped when a woman smuggled a file to him, and walked to safety carrying his chains. He is a 'feminist' thereafter, convinced of 'women's spiritual superiority', although he treats TEKLA badly. He returns to Russia and is united with a peasant girl.

Ivery, Moxon
Mr Standfast, 1918
John Buchan

One of GRAF VON SCHWABING's many manifestations, he disguises villainy (nothing less than the undermining of the British Empire's defences) under an aesthetic and intellectual exterior. A plump, middle-aged man, generally nondescript, he is disconcertingly silver-tongued, insinuating his point of view against the listener's will.

J → George, Harris, and **J**

Jabberwock
Through the Looking-Glass, and What Alice Found There, 1872
Lewis Carroll

ALICE finds a book containing a poem called 'Jabberwocky', only the letters are the wrong way round, as in a looking-glass. Many of its words are combinations of two other words, like 'slithy' (lithe and slimy) and 'mimsy' (flimsy and miserable). Others are vivid inventions. The Jabberwock is a beast with great claws and jaws; the hero takes his 'vorpal sword' and when the Jabberwock comes 'whiffling through the tulgey wood' promptly slays it and takes its head back to his admiring father. Several of the words in the poem are so convincing that they have become part of the English language, eg 'burbled', 'galumphing' and 'chortled'.

Jack
The Cement Garden, 1978
Ian McEwan

The solitary, spotty, adolescent narrator of the novel, Jack feels slight guilt over the death of his frail, irascible father, who had a fatal heart attack while cementing over his regimented garden. Far more traumatically, this is soon followed by his mother's death, which at his instigation he and his three siblings hide from the outside world. Tormented by sexual urges which are exacerbated by incestuous feelings for his elder sister, JULIE, in stifling heat Jack squalidly endures a somnambulistic period of both metaphorical and literal corruption, culminating in his seduction.

Jack
The Enigma of Arrival, 1987
V S Naipaul

A farm labourer whose well-ordered life as 'a man in tune with the seasons and his landscape' arouses the wonder, admiration and envy of the novel's WEST INDIAN NARRATOR. But Jack in reality suffers from a terminal illness. He is determined, however, to enjoy himself, through such humble pleasures as drinking with his friends in a local pub. Unwittingly, he helps the narrator to come to terms with his own sense of mortality, by inspiring him to write a valedictory book about Jack: 'faced with a real death, and with this new wonder about men, I laid aside my drafts and hesitations and began to write very fast about Jack and his garden'.

Jack
Lord of the Flies, 1954
William Golding

Jack displays an aggressive, hunting instinct which he feels should entitle him to leadership of the other boys with whom he is stranded on a desert island. He is a selfish, confident and dictatorial boy who shows little care or sense of responsibility, and constantly undermines the seriousness of RALPH's purpose with prankish acts. Although he considers himself manly, he remains essentially boyish and shallow, incapable of adult reactions or rational thought. He gleefully, and murderously, abandons civilized behaviour for a primitive life of 'fun' among his clan.

Jack, Colonel
Colonel Jack, 1722
Daniel Defoe

In spite of an earlier career as a common thief in London's underworld, through his travels and adventures he develops a genuine kindliness of spirit and a capacity for tender feelings. Although a hero with a rich experience of life (he has worked his way up from Virginia slave to freed man), he demonstrates vulnerabilities that make him attractive. This is no one-dimensional swashbuckler, but a man who makes mistakes, fails in his marriage, and acknowledges that the desire to get rich is his major motivation. Nervously feeling his way through the challenges that confront him, he is more anti-hero than hero.

Jack, Esther
Of Time and the River, 1935
The Web and the Rock, 1939
You Can't Go Home Again, 1940
Thomas Wolfe

An enterprising and successful set designer, she is the lover of GEORGE WEBBER, initiating him into a world of sex and fashion. She is believed to be modelled on Aline Bernstein, with whom Wolfe had an equally turbulent affair.

Jack's Ghost
The Old Wives' Tale, 1595
George Peele

The ghost of an importunate, handsome young lad who appears as a spirit to serve EUMENIDES (who has given money for his burial) on his quest to rescue DELIA, and becomes a 'copartner' in the venture, sharing half of everything. He cunningly stops Eumenides's ears with wool to avert the potency of SACRAPANT's enchantments, and then overcomes the conjurer while invisible. He claims half of Delia, but stops Eumenides from cleaving her in two when Eumenides proves himself ready to keep his vow.

Jackal, the
The Day of the Jackal, 1971
Frederick Forsyth

An assassin hired by the French underground movement, the Organisation de l'Armée Secrète, to kill General de Gaulle. Self-assured, ruthless, methodical, patient, detached and daring, he is a master of his craft. A private, discriminating man, he likes things of quality; an outsider from society, he is able to fit seamlessly into it. Because he insulates himself so completely from the moral implications of his profession, he is arguably the victim of a dangerous mental disorder.

Jackdaw of Rheims, the
The Ingoldsby Legends, 1840
R H Barham

The Jackdaw of Rheims, hopping impudently on the table, has stolen the cardinal's ring and flown off. The theft is discovered and a great curse invoked on the thief, whoever he may be. The Jackdaw appears, bald, limping and dim-eyed – clearly 'That's Him!' He reveals where the ring is hidden, the curse is taken off, and he becomes the most pious of birds, ultimately canonized as 'Jim Crow'.

Jackson, Duane
The Last Picture Show, 1966
Larry McMurtry

An average young man, caught up in the monochrome cycle that dominates life in the small Texan town of Anarene. His dreams, centred on the beautiful JACY FARROW, turn out to be slightly larger than his surroundings.

Jackson, Gen Thomas ('Stonewall')
Confederates, 1979
Thomas Keneally

A Southern hero of Bull Run, who serves as an example of a highly moral man fighting for an essentially immoral cause, in this case the preservation of slavery. For Jackson, war and its intimate mechanics are essential components of human existence and not deviations from it.

Jackson, Geoffrey and Eva
Absurd Person Singular, 1972
Alan Ayckbourn

Because of his philandering and her neurotic reliance on anti-depressant tablets, Geoffrey and Eva's marriage is collapsing. Because of his bungling, so is his reputation as an architect. At their Christmas Eve party, the second of three, at which RONALD and MARION BREWSTER-WRIGHT and SIDNEY and JANE HOPCROFT are present, Eva silently attempts and fails to commit suicide in the kitchen. Geoffrey bumbles in and out, while the others, celebrating, mistake her obsession for knives and the gas oven as a passion for domestic chores. By the third party, Geoffrey's career is ruined.

Jacob
The Slave, 1962
Isaac Bashevis Singer

An obstinate Jewish slave held by Polish peasants on an isolated hillside. Jacob is confused and full of doubts, and clings tightly to his faith with an exasperating attention to detail, believing this is the best way he can live under these conditions. Consumed by lust for the village girl Wanda, he submits after a terrible spiritual struggle. Once fallen, he is wracked with guilt, but feels he has little to lose and starts to see things in a new way. Growing less fearful, he takes control of his life, and through his love for Wanda reaches a new understanding of humankind. He sees the true spirit of faith – love for one's fellow man – and realizes that those who seem most pious are often the biggest hypocrites.

Jacomo, Pietro
The Malcontent, 1604
John Marston

Although he has succeeded in usurping the dukedom of Genoa at the expense of Giovanni Altofronto, Pietro is continually manipulated by others, including his wife AURELIA and the court fool MALEVOLE, who mocks and torments him as a cuckold. Pietro fails to realize that Malevole is actually Altofronto in disguise.

Jacqueline → de Croye, Isabelle

Jacques
As You Like It, c.1600
William Shakespeare

One of the exiled DUKE SENIOR's retinue. He is capable of rapid changes of mood, from foolish jester to the mourner of the dying stag. Once something of a libertine, he is still a cynic, and is personified by his own words: 'All the world's a stage' where 'one man in his time plays many parts'.

Jadwin, Curtis
The Pit: A Story of Chicago, 1903
Frank Norris

A powerful businessman, whose rugged self-reliance camouflages an unsuspected sense of isolation and vulnerability. He wins the heart of LAURA DEARBORN, but loses her when business begins to occupy too much of his time. His gambling on the wheat market, initially successful, eventually loses him his fortune and he ends as a broken convalescent, redeemed only by Laura's love and loyalty.

Jaffier
Venice Preserv'd, or A Plot Discovered, 1682
Thomas Otway

A noble Venetian youth, Jaffier has secretly married BELVIDERA, the daughter of PRIULI. They are contrasting figures. While she is purposeful, with a steely intelligence, he is pliable, volatile and essentially weak-willed. Theirs is a temperamental, perhaps even somewhat masochistic, love. Jaffier is penniless, but his appeals for help from Priuli are met with a hail of insults. Once involved in the plot against the state, his volatility and divided loyalties, his fear and propensity to panic, result in his betraying the conspirators and his friend, PIERRE. Eventually, in a perverted sense of atonement, he stabs Pierre to death on the scaffold and then kills himself.

Jagan

The Sweet Vendor, 1967
R K Narayan

A near-ascetic, wealthy widower, largely indifferent to money, he owns Malgudi's Sweet Mart. While overseeing his staff of cooks and stall-boy, he reads Hindu philosophy. As a Gandhi follower he was repeatedly imprisoned in his youth and he has now written a book, *Nature Care and Natural Diet.* A devout protector of life, he even wears 'non-violent footwear' (made from animals dead of old age). However, when his adored, spoilt only child, Mali, returns from America with an unheralded foreign 'wife' and, filled with big-business ideas, wants only his father's money, Jagan undergoes a sea change and dramatically rebels.

Jaggers, Mr

Great Expectations, 1861
Charles Dickens

A lawyer who advises MISS HAVISHAM and who is appointed by ABEL MAGWITCH, his former client, to serve as PIP's guardian and inform him of his 'great expectations'. He compels his housekeeper, MOLLY, the former mistress of Magwitch who has given birth to their daughter, ESTELLA, to allow Estella to be adopted by Miss Havisham. His clerk, JOHN WEMMICK, befriends Pip. He is held in awe by both Pip and his criminal clients and habitually washes his hands on returning from court. He is apparently stern, but Pip comes to recognize his humanity.

Jago, Dr Paul

The Masters, 1951
C P Snow

A colleague of LEWIS ELIOT at their unnamed Cambridge college and a defeated candidate for the post of Master. He is 'a man of fifty, and some, seeing that he had gone both bald and grey, thought he looked older. But the first physical impression was deceptive. He was tall and thick about the body, with something of a paunch, but he was also small-boned, active, light on his feet'. His eyes are bright and piercing, and give the disconcerting impression of belonging to a younger man.

Jagua Nana

Jagua Nana, 1961
Cyprian Ekwensi

A Lagos prostitute, she epitomizes sexual allure and ultimate availability, but strives at the same time to defer ageing by bringing some stability and order to a life that is by definition governed by the desires of others.

Jaime, Don

The Bridge of San Luis Rey, 1927
Thornton Wilder

LA PERICHOLE's son by the dissolute Viceroy of Peru, seven-year-old Jaime is a quiet, frail little boy with his mother's beauty and his father's tendency to convulsions. He bears his suffering with extraordinary patience and dignity, feeling mortal shame if any sign of it shows in public. Starved of affection, he silently follows his undemonstrative mother around, looking as though he has 'not yet learned the new language'

or 'found any friends', until taken in hand by UNCLE PIO.

Jake

Black Lightning, 1955
Roger Mais

A blacksmith-sculptor in Kingston, Jamaica, Jake is a proud, independently-minded man, so much so that he resents 'any thought of being dependent upon anyone for anything'. This results in his wife leaving him, after which he determines to be as self-sufficient as possible, modelling himself upon the biblical figure of Samson, whose statue he carves in his free time. But because he cannot decide whether life is governed by fate or will, Jake becomes gloomily introspective. Realizing at last that he is at odds with the world yet responsible for his own destiny, he destroys his carving in an act of self-disgust and attempted liberation.

Jake, Congo

Manhattan Transfer, 1925
John Dos Passos

As his name implies, Congo Jake is a happy-go-lucky character with a hint of the exotic about him. An able seaman with 'a deep gorilla chest', he has the simple philosophy of saving money when at sea to fund his binges when back on dry land. Dogged by ill-fortune – he loses a leg in Italy – he is always vivacious and remains a loyal friend of JIMMY HERF. He marries Nevada Jones and becomes involved in bootlegging, breaking his artificial leg in a dockyard struggle.

Jakins, Bob

The Mill on the Floss, 1860
George Eliot

A simple country boy, Bob, the red-haired, snub-nosed childhood friend of MAGGIE and TOM TULLIVER, grows up to be a canny packman with a keen eye for investment and, seldom lost for words, he manages to talk even miserly MRS GLEGG into purchasing some of his wares. Ever loyal to Maggie, he and his wife offer her lodgings when she is turned away by Tom, and his unswerving kindness and generosity to her confirm him, most definitely, as 'virtue in rags'.

James

James and the Giant Peach, 1961
Roald Dahl

A deprived orphan (his parents were eaten by a rhinoceros), he is exploited and verbally abused by his aunts, who give him neither toys nor books. He has no friends, and no pets. James is threatened with dreadful punishments if he dares to climb over the garden fence. He becomes fearful, lonely, silent and sad. However, help comes in the form of a magic, giant peach on a tree in the garden, and his fortunes change for the better. Befriended by the fantastic inhabitants of the peach, who help him survive, James joins them in an incredible adventure and escape. Saved from his past, he becomes a popular boy in a new country of friendly children.

James, Al

Guard of Honor, 1948
James Gould Cozzens

A crusading black journalist, it is he who

uncovers the story of racial discrimination at the Florida airbase where LT JG STANLEY WILLIS has been brutally beaten by a senior officer.

James, Clemency
The Catherine Wheel, 1960
Elizabeth Harrower

A 25-year-old Australian woman living alone in a London bedsit, studying for the bar by correspondence course and teaching French for a living. Feeling somewhat detached from 'real life', she enters into a doomed relationship with the volatile and erratic CHRISTIAN ROLAND, convinced she can save him from himself. Normally calm and cool, Clemency is drawn to the emotional turmoil in Christian, and although she denies it, she craves the intellectual and emotional challenges of her relationship with him.

James, Col
Amelia, 1751
Henry Fielding

The sceptical Colonel James laughs at both virtue and religion. He is apparently generous with money, and is the insolvent CAPTAIN BILLY BOOTH's companion. However, James's charity is a masquerade as he intends to violate the Captain's wife, the fragile AMELIA BOOTH. His public honour and chivalry conceal a violent and uncontrollable lascivious instinct.

James I of England
The Fortunes of Nigel, 1822
Sir Walter Scott

The king is a shapeless and paradoxical man, awry in nature as in dress. 'He was deeply learned, without possessing useful knowledge; sagacious in many individual cases without having real wisdom; fond of his power, and desirous to maintain and augment it, yet willing to resign the direction of that, and of himself, to the most unworthy favourites ... Even his timidity of temper was not uniform; and there were moments of his life ... in which he showed the spirit of his ancestors.'

James of the Glens, properly James Stewart
Kidnapped, 1886
Catriona, 1893
Robert Louis Stevenson

The man accused of committing the murder of THE RED FOX. Stevenson makes clear that he believes him to be innocent and, indeed, he is presented as showing real concern over the 'dreadful accident'. He is a wise, honourable man who understands that the murder will mean that the Stewarts will be blamed and he fears more for his family's safety than for his own. It is typical of his generous spirit, fine manners and infinite patience that, in the midst of all his anxieties, he takes time to talk to the young DAVID BALFOUR. He is portrayed as a man of probity and high stoicism: a martyr for the old Highland life of freedom.

Jamy → Fluellen; Gower; Jamy; Macmorris

Jan
Red Shift, 1973
Alan Garner

TOM's girlfriend, bright and middle-class, whose parents are psychologists and run a child guidance clinic, leaving them with little time for her. Although Tom gives her security, she knows that he cannot fulfil all her needs. Irreverent and unafraid of adult disapproval, she is more positive, sexually aware and pragmatic than Tom. She prefers to see their times apart as bringing closer their times together.

Jane
'Eustace', in *Child's Play, with Eustace and the Prowler*, 1982
David Malouf

A young girl in a boarding school for whom the hours of sleep and dreams 'were outside the rules. No bells governed them, they were free.' Her dormitory is visited at night by a mysterious red-haired boy ('EUSTACE'), whose interest in the plain, dumpy girl is not obviously sexual, but seems to prefigure the cessation of the senses, the absolute freedom of imagination and death.

Jane
Guerillas, 1975
V S Naipaul

Jane is very confused in her political attitudes, and rather prone to courting danger, both in her relationship to the emotionally burnt-out PETER ROCHE, and the mercurial JIMMY AHMED. Her privileged and sheltered English background blinds her to the complexities of West Indian racial politics. As a result, she comes to a tragic end at the hands of Jimmy Ahmed, and never succeeds in forging a solid identity for herself.

January
'The Merchant's Tale' in *The Canterbury Tales*, c.1387–1400
Geoffrey Chaucer

He is over 60, profligate, hypocritical and with a wife, MAY, 40 years younger than himself. His dependence on aphrodisiacs sends her into the arms of the younger DAMIEN. Prone to ignore good advice, he is a cynic who is easily tricked.

Jaquenetta
Love's Labour's Lost, not later than 1594
William Shakespeare

A lusty country wench who returns COSTARD's love but not that of DON ADRIANO DEL ARMADO. Jaquenetta generally enters and exits with Costard, and tends to greet Armado's remarks with sarcasm: the latter boasts 'I will tell thee wonders', to which she replies: 'With that face?'

Jardine, Sybil
The Ballad and the Source, 1944
A Sea-Grape Tree, 1976
Rosamond Lehmann

The Victorian beauty of an upstanding family, Sybil is a charismatic 'Enchantress Queen'. Having left her anaemic husband for a 'flesh and blood man', she longs obsessively for her daughter, but is denied access. Her rash action proves to be irredeemable, and she is ostracized by polite society for violating the implacable codes of patriarchal law. A militant feminist, Sybil is an embittered and manipulative woman, crushed by circumstances and punished for her resistance to society's conventions.

Jarl
Mardi, 1849
Herman Melville

An old sailor, also known as 'the Viking' and 'the Skyeman', who jumps ship with TAJI. He is a 'fine old seaman' of Viking extract from Skye, and exceedingly taciturn, although loyal and devoted to Taji. Until taking up with him, he is a 'lone, friendless mariner', illiterate and 'deplorably lacking in geography', but 'an honest, earnest wight; so free and simple'.

Jarley, Mrs
The Old Curiosity Shop, 1841
Charles Dickens

The kind-hearted proprietor of 'Jarley's Wax Works', she befriends and employs LITTLE NELL for a time to point out the figures to visitors. She claims that 'I won't go so far as to say I have seen waxworks quite like life, but I've certainly seen some life that was exactly like waxworks'.

Jarndyce, John
Bleak House, 1853
Charles Dickens

A kindly, generous and eccentric bachelor, and the owner of Bleak House, in St Albans, he is the guardian of RICHARD CARSTONE and ADA CLARE and protector of ESTHER SUMMERSON. Although a suitor in the case of *Jarndyce* v *Jarndyce*, he takes no part in it, having despaired of justice. Whenever in an ill temper, he declares that 'the wind is in the east' and retires to his 'Growlery'. He proposes marriage to Esther but, on learning that she loves ALLAN WOODCOURT, selflessly arranges her marriage to him and establishes them in a new Bleak House in Yorkshire.

Jarvie, Bailie Nicol
Rob Roy, 1817
Sir Walter Scott

A Glasgow merchant, with all the verbal skills and gift for fine calculation which that suggests. His Whiggish practicality and robust but kindly morality are the perfect foil to the vague romanticism and gentility of FRANK OSBALDISTONE, whom he accompanies into the Highlands; in John Buchan's view, 'he is the triumphant bourgeois, the type which endures when aristocracies and proletariats crumble'.

Jarvis, Arthur
Cry, the Beloved Country, 1948
Alan Paton

The son of a wealthy South African farmer, he holds markedly liberal views, including the belief that black 'crime' is a symptom not of innate evil but of specific social pressures. Ironically, just as he is finishing an essay on the question, he is murdered by REV STEPHEN KUMALO's son, ABSALOM. His own child provides the occasion for JAMES JARVIS's reconciliation with Rev Kumalo.

Jarvis, Hannah
Arcadia, 1993
Tom Stoppard

A best-selling author, Jarvis is researching the history of the gardens at Sidley Park, a large country house. A garden, she maintains, is a vibrant metaphor of intellectual and social change. Sharply intelligent, instinctive, confident and candid to the point of being blunt, she tends to distrust the motives of men, especially those of academic BERNARD NIGHTINGALE. Analysing the past to understand the present is more important, she declares, than proving theories. 'It is wanting to know that makes us matter.' The last word perhaps refers to the developments in both the 19th and 20th centuries, and the emergence of chaos theory, which form an important strand of the play.

Jarvis, James
Cry, the Beloved Country, 1948
Alan Paton

A well-off white farmer in the hills above Ndotsheni, in the Natal, South Africa. His son ARTHUR JARVIS is murdered by ABSALOM, but after his initial rage and grief die down, and he comes into contact with REV STEPHEN KUMALO, he gradually comes to understand and accept Arthur's conviction that the old South Africa must be swept away and a new humane order established in its place.

Jasper
The Knight of the Burning Pestle, 1607
Francis Beaumont

An apprentice to the merchant Venturewell, the 'prodigal' Jasper woos, and eventually wins LUCE, his employer's daughter. There is something slightly ridiculous about him, for the play is a freewheeling comedy of manners; he has bourgeois aspirations and can be both bullying and sentimental.

Jasper, Mr John
The Mystery of Edwin Drood, 1870
Charles Dickens

The uncle of EDWIN DROOD, who fondly calls him 'Jack', and the outwardly respectable choirmaster of Cloisterham Cathedral. But Jasper is a clandestine opium addict and regularly visits London's East End to smoke opium in the den of PRINCESS PUFFER. Dark, handsome but sombre, and only a few years older than his nephew, Jasper is passionately in love with Drood's fiancée, ROSA BUD. She is repulsed by his advances but somehow influenced by his strange mesmeric or hypnotic powers. When Drood disappears, Jasper helps to throw suspicion on NEVILLE LANDLESS as the murderer, but MR HIRAM GREWGIOUS and DICK DATCHERY suspect Jasper. Many hints in the unfinished novel suggest that Jasper murders his own nephew in an attempt to gain the hand of Rosa.

Javo
Monkey Grip, 1977
Helen Garner

A heroin addict, firmly in the grip of his 'monkey', Javo has only one focus in his life and is more than prepared to use any means at his disposal to feed his habit. His addiction, though, is little more than a symbol for a wider male compulsion to use love as a means of self-preservation and self-expansion rather than as an emotion sufficient in itself.

Jay, Francis
Dr Criminale, 1992
Malcolm Bradbury

As a former literary journalist for a defunct serious Sunday newspaper, Francis Jay is young (in his mid-twenties) but improbably naive, prone to dressing in a shell suit and trainers to catch the colourful spirit of the early 1990s. Commissioned by a television company to research the life of the eminent but frustratingly anonymous and elusive Dr Criminale, he is pitched into the glittering and mysterious new Europe of academic conferences, fluctuating political alliances and labyrinthine bureaucracy. An innocent abroad, sexually opportunistic and sometimes not entirely honest, Jay attains the age of reason while discovering something about the nature of man and his relationship to history.

Jeanette
Oranges are Not the Only Fruit, 1985
Jeanette Winterson

Brought up by evangelical Christians in the North of England in the 1960s, Jeanette is expected to follow her adoptive parents' example by becoming involved with the church and preaching the gospel. As a child this seems natural, but as a teenager who is more independent-minded than even she realizes at first, it is an expectation that she finds increasingly difficult to fulfil. When she falls in love with her friend Melanie and their affair is discovered, relations with church and family reach a nadir.

Jeavons, Lady Molly
A Dance to the Music of Time, 12 volumes, 1951–75
Anthony Powell

The fulcrum of *At Lady Molly's* (1955), she is a socialite in the mould of Lady Ottoline Morrell. The sister of Jumbo, Earl of Ardglass, and Katherine, Lady Warminster, she marries Lord Sleaford. 'She was only eighteen. Never seen a man before.' Widowed, she then marries 'a chap called Jeavons' whom she met at the Motor Show at Olympia. Though he plays a reasonable game of snooker he is 'no livewire'. 'Molly, on the other hand, is full of go.' Her house in South Kensington attracts a variety of strays, both animal and human. Handsome, extrovert, kindly and with a fallible judgement of people, she owns a menagerie of birds, cats and dogs, and a monkey named Maisky. She dies in London in 1941 when she is hit by a bomb.

Jed
Magnificence, 1973
Howard Brenton

One of a group of young people squatting in a derelict London house, Jed is the husband of MARY, who is pregnant. When the bailiffs evict them, Mary is assaulted and loses her baby. Jed is imprisoned and on his release announces

himself bent upon revenge. He is articulate, even intelligent, but innocent, and this, combined with an unrealistic, romantic notion of revolutionary politics, lures him into futile terrorism. He imagines that by one single, magnificent gesture (killing ALICE, a prominent politician) he will avenge his wife and unborn child. But even his attempt at heroism turns out to be a failure.

Jeddler, Dr Anthony
The Battle of Life, 1846
Charles Dickens

A widowed country doctor and the father of GRACE and MARION JEDDLER. He is 'a great philosopher' who looks 'upon the world as a gigantic practical joke: as something too absurd to be considered seriously, by any rational man'. But the disappearance and self-sacrifice of Marion convert him from cynicism and show him how serious the world is, and that 'love, deep-anchored, is the portion of all human creatures'.

Jeddler, Grace and Marion
The Battle of Life, 1846
Charles Dickens

The beautiful daughters of DR ANTHONY JEDDLER. Marion is betrothed to ALFRED HEATHFIELD but, realizing that her beloved sister also loves him, she disappears for six years. People believe that she has eloped with the spendthrift, MICHAEL WARDEN, but she conceals herself in her aunt's house until Grace and Alfred are married. In the final scenes of the improbable plot, Marion is lovingly reunited with her father and sister and marries a reformed Michael Warden.

Jeeves
The Inimitable Jeeves, 1924, et seq
P G Wodehouse

Jeeves, most gentlemanly of gentlemen's gentlemen, shimmers quietly in and out of rooms knowing unerringly what is required. He tends BERTIE WOOSTER like a guardian angel, adorning each passing moment with an apt quotation. His own speech is Augustan in its measured periods. He unbends in brief holidays at Ascot or the seaside, but returns to his post with dignity to avert whatever disaster may have threatened in his absence. He betrays no emotion, his most forcible protest being a grave 'Indeed, Sir?' He knows the complications of young love intimately, and always has a cure. Bertie attributes his massive brain to the eating of fish.

Jeffrey, Helen
John Ward, Preacher, 1888
Margaret Deland

Helen's unashamed commitment to freethinking values represents a discomfiting challenge to her preacher husband JOHN WARD's staunch Calvinism. She proves to be obdurate, however, and denies him even the deathbed comfort of knowing that she has turned to the Church.

Jekyll, Dr → Dr Jekyll/Mr Hyde

Jelkes, Hannah
The Night of the Iguana, 1961
Tennessee Williams

A watercolour artist who has travelled the world with her grandfather, the poet Jonathan Coffin (NONNO). Stranded in a seedy Mexican hotel, she befriends the defrocked priest, LARRY SHANNON, and reveals herself to be a thoughtful, perceptive and caring woman, who understands Shannon's mental problems, having herself recovered from a breakdown. Left with an uncertain future at the play's end, she is, as Shannon says, 'A lady, a *real* one, and a *great* one.'

Jellyby, Caroline (Caddy)
Bleak House, 1853
Charles Dickens

The eldest daughter of MRS JELLYBY, she marries PRINCE TURVEYDROP. A pretty but bitter and unhealthy-looking girl, she is exploited and overworked as an unpaid amanuensis to her mother in her charitable causes. ESTHER SUMMERSON becomes her devoted friend.

Jellyby, Mrs
Bleak House, 1853
Charles Dickens

A staunch devotee of charitable causes, she has 'handsome eyes, although they had a curious habit of seeming to look a long way off', as though always focused on Africa. Particularly devoted to the natives of Borrioboola-Gha, when that venture collapses, she takes up the cause of women's rights. Tirelessly campaigning and undeterred by failure, she neglects her appearance, her home and her family. Her meek husband becomes a bankrupt, and her exploited daughter, CAROLINE JELLYBY, grows embittered towards her mother.

Jen (Jen da Silva)
The Tree of the Sun, 1978
Wilson Harris

The wife of the painter DA SILVA DA SILVA, she has conceived a child by him which seems to represent a comment on his artistic creativity, her own racial and cultural antecedents, and, more bizarrely, on the lives and expectations of FRANCIS and JULIA CORTEZ who previously occupied their London flat.

Jenkins, Nicholas
A Dance to the Music of Time, 12 volumes, 1951–75
Anthony Powell

The son of a soldier, he is the self-effacing narrator of Powell's *roman fleuve*, whose career we pick up in the aftermath of World War I and follow to the early 1970s. Born in 1906 or 1907, he messes at school with CHARLES STRINGHAM and PETER TEMPLER, and discovers sex while dancing a foxtrot with Lady McReith. Encountering KENNETH WIDMERPOOL in France after both have left school, he tells him he wants to be a writer. On leaving university he moves to London and joins a small literary publisher. He tries his hand at screenwriting before the publication of his first novel at the beginning of the 1930s. He marries LADY ISOBEL TOLLAND. As war looms he is on his uppers and overcome by lethargy, but by the end of the war he is ranked captain. Postwar he lives in

a single room on the eighth floor of a Chelsea tenement, preoccupied with a biography of Robert Burton, the author of *The Anatomy of Melancholy*, and reading Proust. To make a living he gets a job 'doing the books' on a little magazine. As he grows older, he reflects that the reputation of his books increases the longer they have been out of print.

Jenkins, Rev Eli
Under Milk Wood, 1954
Dylan Thomas

An absent-minded poet and preacher, who carries religion out of Bethesda House into the realms of Welsh folk-literature and music. He dreams of eisteddfodau and writes the White Book of Llaregyb, a typical guidebook of the 'tiny dingle'. In ministerial black and bard-like white nightgown, he praises POLLY GARTER's sensuous singing for its musicality, not its morals. He clutches his brolly and his odes to himself and remembers his mother and his father, who died 'of drink and agriculture'.

Jenkins, Winifred
The Expedition of Humphry Clinker, 1771
Tobias Smollett

A maid at Brambleton Hall, she gives her letters home to fellow-domestic Mary Jones a pronounced Welsh slant that tends to compound her linguistic insufficiencies. She is eventually 'chined … in the holy bands of mattermoney' to HUMPHRY CLINKER, who is now revealed as her master's natural son. This elevation in rank 'to a higher spear' inevitably gives her great and condescending delight.

Jenkison, Mr
Headlong Hall, 1816
Thomas Love Peacock

Round-faced, buoyant and small, Mr Jenkison is a 'status-quo-ite', fence-sitting philosopher. Balancing pros and cons to a ridiculous extent, he argues that the human race neither advances nor deteriorates because of scientific developments. 'There is much to be said on both sides' is the sum of his opinions.

Jenkyns, Matty (Matilda)
Cranford, 1853
Elizabeth Gaskell

A meek and anxious younger sister, Matty is sweet-tempered, sensitive and well liked. She is very humble in attitude, and much of her character seems to have formed as a result of her older sister Deborah's domination. Fiercely scrupulous, she is too innocent in the ways of the world for her own good. She accepts that she will always be second best, but at times she longs to be different from everyone else.

Jennings, (John Christopher Timothy)
Jennings Goes to School, 1950, et seq
Anthony Buckeridge

One of the 79 boarders at Linbury Court Preparatory School in Sussex, where he and DARBISHIRE, his great friend and ally, are members of the third form. A lively eleven-year-old, Jennings is a natural leader, involving the hapless Darbishire in a series of schoolboy scrapes. Whereas Darbishire is the son of a rural clergyman, Jennings is from a Sussex market town; if Darbishire broadly represents the intellect, then Jennings stands for the practical. Dark-haired, inventive and impulsive, his overriding confidence sometimes results in boastfulness, and he can also be selfish and easily downcast. Yet he has an innate sense of right and wrong, and enormous compassion and resilience.

Jennings, Mrs
Sense and Sensibility, 1811
Jane Austen

A widowed friend of the DASHWOOD family, Mrs Jennings involves herself in everybody's business with neither tact nor subtlety. Far from being malicious gossip, however, her ceaseless chatter stems from a genuine concern for the well-being of her friends, and her demonstrative outbursts are suffered without complaint because of her good nature and kindness.

Jenny
The Bay of Noon, 1970
Shirley Hazzard

A bilingual secretary working at a NATO establishment in Naples, who finds herself trapped in an incestuous triangle with her brother and his wife. In order to free herself, she has to take a more imaginative journey, represented by her relationship with the beautiful Italian novelist GIOCONDA and her film-maker lover, GIANNI. Though vulnerable, she has an inner resilience and deep intellectual grasp.

Jenny (Genevieve Steinbauer)
Mosquitoes, 1927
William Faulkner

'A soft blonde girl in a slightly soiled green dress', she attaches herself to MRS PATRICIA MAURIER's niece on the sailing party and shows herself to be 'all cluttered up with men'.

Jenny
The Return of the Soldier, 1918
Rebecca West

The disturbingly complacent narrator of *The Return of the Soldier*, she does not concede the possibility that KITTY BALDRY is so blinded by class prejudice that it disqualifies her from the right to future happiness with a husband possessing egalitarian sympathies. Jenny initially hates MARGARET ALLINGTON, perceiving her as 'a spreading stain on the fabric of our life'. Secretly in love with CAPTAIN CHRIS BALDRY, she is 'stunned with jealousy' at his passion for Margaret. Gradually, however, she comprehends Margaret's innate goodness and celebrates it, and comes to see that Kitty is greedy and vacuous, 'the falsest thing on earth'.

Jenny, Miss (Virginia Sartoris Du Pré)
Sartoris, 1929, full version published as *Flags in the Dust*, 1973
William Faulkner

The widowed sister of COL JOHN SARTORIS, she is a patient and stoical observer of the violence that surrounds the family, a still centre in the midst of all the turbulence; 'a slender woman with a delicate replica of the Sartoris nose and that expression of indomitable and utter weariness which all Southern women had learned to wear'.

Jenny Wren, properly Fanny Cleaver
Our Mutual Friend, 1865
Charles Dickens

A doll's dressmaker, she is a crippled 'queer little figure', apparently a child but in fact a woman. Affectionate, but sharp-tongued and shrewd, she supports her alcoholic father, nicknamed 'Mr Dolls', scolding him like a naughty child. She calls the venerable RIAH her 'fairy godmother', and she befriends LIZZIE HEXAM, who lives with her after GAFFER HEXAM's death. She and Riah help Lizzie hide herself outside London to escape the attentions of BRADLEY HEADSTONE and EUGENE WRAYBURN. Eventually, Riah comes to live with her, and the end of the novel suggests that she marries Sloppy, the foundling adopted by BETTY HIGDEN and MR and MRS NICODEMUS BOFFIN.

Jenson, Sasha
Good Morning Midnight, 1939
Jean Rhys

The narrator of the novel, she has returned after nearly 20 years to Paris, intending to escape temporarily the stupefying loneliness of her life in London. Her looks marred by drink and poverty, she has become numbed and resigned to abject despair. In Paris, exposed to the cruel inquisitiveness of strangers and to the promptings of familiar streets and cafés, she is painfully reawoken to the past she has sought to obliterate. Sad and exhausted, but not without wit, Sasha is a character in control of nothing but the telling of her own story.

Jeremy
Black Dogs, 1992
Ian McEwan

Suddenly orphaned at eight, Jeremy, the novel's narrator, spent the rebellious 1960s 'like a six-foot cuckoo', seeking surrogate parents among those rejected by his friends, while living with his sister and observing the effects of domestic violence on his beloved little niece. Now a publisher in his forties, he enjoys the stability and contentment he craved, and has congenial parents-in-law, JUNE TREMAYNE and BERNARD TREMAYNE. While researching in France for June's biography he exorcizes and avenges his and his niece's unhappy childhoods, and uncovers facts which shake his rationalist beliefs.

Jermin, John
Omoo, 1847
Herman Melville

The mate, and virtual captain, of the *Julia*. He is short and thickset, with a 'heart as big as a bullock's', a face deeply marked by smallpox, and hair 'curled in little rings of iron gray all over his round, bullet head'. He has 'courage, seamanship, and a natural aptitude for keeping riotous spirits in subjection', but has a contempt for 'all weak infusions, and cleaved manfully to strong drink'. He is highly obstreperous when drunk, but has an 'irresistably good-natured way' of knocking men down which ensures no resentment. CAPTAIN GUY is in awe of him, but occasionally succeeds in using him for his own ends.

Jermyn, Matthew
Felix Holt the Radical, 1866
George Eliot

Low-born achiever and lawyer to the TRANSOMEs, Jermyn has helped make more wills in the local town, Treby Magna, than anyone else. He has fat hands and possesses conspicuous glibness, which he tries to limit by interjecting '– Ah –', every so often as if searching for a word. He is afraid of the heir, Harold Transome, discovering both his corrupt administration of the estate, and his affair with Harold's mother: Jermyn, therefore, is ironically at continual low-level warfare with his natural son.

Jero, Brother (Jeroboam)
The Trials of Brother Jero, 1960
Jero's Metamorphosis, 1974
Wole Soyinka

A fraudulent preacher from Lagos's notorious Bar Beach district, who keeps his congregation in thrall by admitting to his deceit, sustaining them in their dependence with a vision of a world which is fundamentally treacherous and unreliable. In the later play, he has gained a franchise to administer the last rites to political prisoners about to be executed by the government at Bar Beach.

Jerry
Betrayal, 1978
Harold Pinter

A successful literary agent, Jerry has recently concluded a seven-year-long affair with EMMA, the wife of his great friend ROBERT, a publisher. Yet Jerry has betrayed not only Robert, but also his own wife, Judith; moreover, he in his turn has been betrayed by Emma who, unknown to Jerry, told Robert of their affair after five years. Fastidious and circumspect, a man propelled by his emotions and given to dramatic gesture, Jerry appears to be condemned through his own actions to being hurt. The play recounts the affair from beginning to end in reverse chronological order.

Jerry
The Zoo Story, 1958
Edward Albee

A New York artist of the streets who engages in a bizarre confrontation – part narrative contest, part homosexual pick-up, part violent redemption – with the upper middle-class and successful PETER. The park bench on which they enact their respective dramas becomes alternately a psychoanalytic couch and the mechanism of Jerry's final, ironic 'crucifixion'.

Jervis, Mrs
Pamela, 1740–1
Samuel Richardson

Intrinsically good, Mrs Jervis is PAMELA ANDREWS's staunchest ally. However, she is incapable of seeing beyond surface appearances, which blinds her to the moral implications of Pamela's predicament. She naively puts her faith

in a metamorphosis of MR B's character, and tries to persuade Pamela to placate and appease him. With her intense concentration on the tangible and the practical, Mrs Jervis is a simple soul who lacks creativity and intelligence.

Jessel, Brian
A Landing on the Sun, 1991
Michael Frayn

A senior civil servant and a lone father with a wife in long-term hospital care, Jessel investigates the mysterious death of Summerchild, a colleague working on a secret government project. Conscientious and taciturn, a man of strict procedure and protocol, Jessel prides himself on being synonymous with the government buildings in which he works: 'A quiet facade, perhaps with a touch of distinction', and on his moustache and beard, behind which his 'whole personality is decently concealed'. But when he discovers that Summerchild was delving into the nature of happiness, not only is Jessel's punctilious sense of propriety undermined, but he also regains an understanding of the meaning of fulfilment, contentment and love.

Jessel, Miss
The Turn of the Screw, 1898
Henry James

Former governess at Bly, who left her job and subsequently died. The circumstances are unclear, but a relationship with the master's valet PETER QUINT is strongly hinted, and her successor, the narrator (ANON), 'sees' the dead couple as ghosts who are in communication with her two young charges, FLORA and MILES. Given the new governess's palpable sexual neuroses, it is clear that she has projected onto Miss Jessel many of her own complexes and obsessions.

Jessica
The Merchant of Venice, 1594/5
William Shakespeare

Daughter to Shylock, she confides to young LAUNCELOT GOBBO that 'our house is hell' and escapes from it, dressed as a page, to marry LORENZO, taking with her a considerable sum of her father's money and property. A slight character, lacking the humour of the other female leads in the play, she is essentially a romantic device in a play culminating in a multitude of marriages.

Jessup, Doremus
It Can't Happen Here, 1935
Sinclair Lewis

An idealistic newspaper editor in a small Vermont town, he opposes the presidential candidacy of a local man, BUZZ WINDRIP, who he fears will bring a form of Fascism to America. Silenced and imprisoned, he is gradually radicalized and is forced by circumstances to join in the revolutionary movement, which is organizing itself in Canada to overthrow the totalitarian regime that has taken control of the USA.

Jesus
Quarantine, 1997
Jim Crace

'Young and inexperienced', this Jesus in the days

and nights of his quest to discover 'what for, and why', lives a parable of the biblical Jesus's life. His absent presence leads those who are also 'in quarantine' to impose their hopes and dreams upon him, and in fact their instincts match his own 'smothered heart's desire' to be the chosen one and a healer, to encourage and support those like himself 'weak and blemished and imperfect'. The 'drama and … cruel romance' of his faith and his own stubbornness and fear triumph over all appeals to his vanity, and he does, ambiguously, achieve the glowing 'confidence of someone who was full of god at last'.

Jesus Christ
Paradise Regained, 1671
John Milton

The incarnated Son of God, born of a virgin mother as foretold, and baptized in glory by JOHN THE BAPTIST at the ford in Jordan. A 'Morning Star then in his rise', as Lucifer (see also SATAN) has fallen, he finds himself in a dark and pathless desert, where he has to endure the Temptation.

Jewel, or the Barbarian
Heroes and Villains, 1969
Angela Carter

Called Jewel because of the shining stones and feathers he wears in his hair, he is a tragic, illiterate, though not unintelligent savage. He is sensual and erotic with eyes like trick mirrors that 'can see out but can not be seen through'. Though violent, dominant and overtly masculine, he is prone to powerful romantic feeling. He, like MARRIANE, has no place in time, and seems to exist as an anachronism.

Jewkes, Mrs
Pamela, 1740–1
Samuel Richardson

A 'broad, squat, pursy, fat Thing, quite ugly', Mrs Jewkes colludes with the visceral MR B in the oppression of PAMELA ANDREWS. A 'bawdy London Prostitute', she presides over a tawdry bordello, and in her 'hoarse, man-like Voice' exhorts Mr B to deflower Pamela: 'What you do, Sir, do, don't stand dilly-dallying'. She is a wonderfully theatrical character who resembles an overheated pantomime dame.

Jim
The Adventures of Huckleberry Finn, 1884
Mark Twain

A runaway slave, he embarks on a raft journey down the Mississippi with HUCK FINN, a boy fleeing from his brutal father. During their subsequent adventures the two develop a remarkable bond of friendship and loyalty. Extremely superstitious, gullible and credulous, Jim is a comic figure who suffers many indignities. However, he is also a practical and resourceful man who loves and protects Huck and helps them both to survive.

Jimson, Gulley
The Horse's Mouth, 1944
Joyce Cary

Narrator and principal protagonist of the book. He is an impoverished and ageing painter whose amorality is matched only by his egocentricity. Although he lives solely for his art, he is the antithesis of the cultivated aesthete, and cares nothing for social conventions and manners or the normal modes of decent behaviour. A larger-than-life, brilliantly comic creation, he embodies the artistic temperament in memorably anarchic fashion.

Jingle, Alfred
Pickwick Papers, 1837
Charles Dickens

A loquacious, roguish strolling actor. An incessant talker and teller of tall stories, he speaks in a staccato style which uses disjointed phrases without verbs. His repeated embarrassments of SAMUEL PICKWICK and his friends include his thwarted elopement with Rachael Wardle (see THE WARDLES) for her money and his posing as a naval officer at MRS LEO HUNTER's party. Throughout, he sponges dinners and borrows money. He meets Pickwick for the last time in the Fleet Prison, where he and his servant, JOB TROTTER, are imprisoned. Released, he and Job emigrate to the West Indies.

Jinglin' Geordie → Heriot, George

Jiniwin, Mrs
The Old Curiosity Shop, 1841
Charles Dickens

The mother of BETSEY QUILP, she is 'known to be laudably shrewish in her disposition and inclined to resist male authority'. Living with her daughter and son-in-law, she is frightened of DANIEL QUILP but nevertheless tries to incite her timid daughter to rebel.

Jinny
The Waves, 1931
Virginia Woolf

Jinny is bright-eyed, wistful and ambitious. She wants, or needs, to stand out in a crowd, to matter to others and win their respect. But although she is keen to be noticed, she is also very afraid of life, wounded by reality, and deeply confused. She is thought to be based partly on the author herself.

Jip and Zab
Xorandor, 1986
Christine Brooke-Rose

The mutually correcting narrators are Blytonish – but computer-literate – twins whose father runs a nuclear-waste dump in Cornwall. While playing on the beach with their laptop computer, they begin to interface with a large rock which has the ability to communicate in computer language. The experience turns into an extended lesson in narrative technique.

Jo
Bleak House, 1853
Charles Dickens

An orphaned, illiterate young crossing-sweeper who lives in the slum of Tom-All-Alone's. Having known CAPTAIN HAWDON, he is a witness at the inquest and shows LADY DEDLOCK Hawdon's pauper grave. He is given shelter at Bleak House and transmits smallpox to ESTHER SUMMERSON's maid, CHARLOTTE NECKETT, who then gives it to Esther. Still on the run from the police, he is taken in by MR GEORGE ROUNCEWELL and dies in the Shooting Gallery, attended by ALLAN WOODCOURT.

Jo (Josephine)
A Taste of Honey, 1958
Shelagh Delaney

A passionate and bawdy working-class teenager, who moves with her slatternly mother, Helen, into a seedy flat in a slum area of Manchester. When Helen leaves with a man, Jo first invites her own boyfriend, a black naval rating, to spend Christmas with her and then, when he goes back to sea, asks a homosexual art student to take up lodgings. He too eventually leaves. Pregnant by the rating, Jo is resentful and defiant, but despite her youth and her impetuosity, she has a sense of authority and responsibility, declaring that: 'I really do live at the same time as myself, don't I?'

Joad, Ma
The Grapes of Wrath, 1939
John Steinbeck

The heart and motivating force of the Joad clan. Pa has largely ceded his authority to her and it is she who embodies Steinbeck's treasured view of 'the people' as stoical, resilient and courageous.

Joad, Rose of Sharon ('Rosasharn')
The Grapes of Wrath, 1939
John Steinbeck

Amid the hardships of Dustbowl America, she represents fertility and a sort of unthinking physical charity. Deeply loyal to her weak husband Connie (who eventually absconds) she is pregnant during the journey to California and in the novel's most controversial scene offers her breast to a starving hobo, having just been delivered of a stillborn child.

Joad, Tom
The Grapes of Wrath, 1939
John Steinbeck

The elder son of the Joad family, he has his mother's quiet resolve but can reveal a streak of violence when provoked. He joins the exodus for California having been released from a prison sentence for murder. Later on the journey he kills again, in retaliation for JIM CASY's murder, and ends the story a fugitive.

Joan (Jeanne d'Arc)
Saint Joan, 1923
George Bernard Shaw

Joan arrives at Vaucouleurs in early 1429, claiming that 'voices' from God command her to lead THE DAUPHIN to Rheims Cathedral to be crowned Charles VII of France. She is 'an able-bodied country girl of 17 or 18'. Resolute and imaginative, she has a 'hearty, coaxing voice, very confident, very appealing and very hard to resist'. Shaw, who believed Shakespeare had done Joan an 'infamous libel' in *Henry VI Part I*, transforms her from a religious fanatic into a practical, decisive force of change, a woman whose faith and instinct are handicapped by political naivety.

Joan of Arc
Blood Red, Sister Rose, 1974
Thomas Keneally

The historical Maid of Orléans is recast by Keneally as a 'potent maker of magic', a figure poised between everyday humanity and a wholly abstract historical resonance. Her attempt to awaken the French nobility to its historical role sets her at odds with every accepted division and exclusion in her society: those based on class, religion, and gender.

Joan of Arc (Joan la Pucelle)
Henry VI Part I, early 1590s
William Shakespeare

In *Henry VI* Joan is presented as 'a foul fiend of France', a witch, a political subversive, immoral, a cheat impertinently deriding the admirable English leader, Lord Talbot. Some commentators have described this portrayal as coarse English patriotic progaganda. Supporters of Shakespeare suggest the scene describing the trial was not written by him at all and therefore the blame cannot wholly be his, while still other apologists point out that the account is largely that given in Raphael Holinshed's *The Chronicles of England, Scotland and Ireland* (1577), then the orthodox view of Joan, and that from which Shakespeare was working.

Jobbry, Archibald
The Member, 1832
John Galt

A Nabob who returns to Scotland to settle. He finds many relatives hungry for assistance and thinks he can help them by entering Parliament and using influence. He becomes Member of Parliament for a rotten borough, finding himself adept at corrupt tricks. He even wins a contested election, outwitting by corruption his corrupt opponent. But he grows weary of this. When reform is talked of he is only a moderate Tory, and has had a taste of oppression by accidental arrest. He returns to his estate and thereafter remains a spectator.

Jobling, Tony
Bleak House, 1853
Charles Dickens

A friend of WILLIAM GUPPY and a penurious law-writer for MR SNAGSBY. Always hard-up, he uses the alias of Weevle. When CAPTAIN HAWDON dies, he moves into his room in MR KROOK's house, hoping to gain from discovering Hawdon's papers. With Guppy, he discovers Krook on the night he spontaneously combusts.

Jocelyn
Down among the Women, 1971
Fay Weldon

A perfectionist, she is stylish and extravagant. She tends to seek solace in the material world, though she suffers guilt as a result of this, blaming herself for appreciating objects of physical beauty. Hoping to find satisfaction in marriage, she can experience fulfilment only through others, either through their admiration of her, or through interaction with them. A conventional woman, afraid of 'deviance' in any form, she is as kind as she knows how to be.

Jocelyn, Canon
The Rector's Daughter, 1924
F M Mayor

The clergyman in a small village. He has a 'thin, stately figure, finely chiselled features, and eyes severe, satirical, and melancholy by turns'. He holds his emotions in strict check, and is unable to show his love for his children even in times of extremity. He loves books and scholarship, and has a boundless enthusiasm for learning, but despises the French.

Jocelyn, Mary
The Rector's Daughter, 1924
F M Mayor

The devoted daughter of CANON JOCELYN, she has dedicated her life to running his house. She is quiet, unassuming, dowdy, chooses a 'small dark chamber' for her bedroom, and has become attached to the dull, unchanging routine of village life. At the age of 35 she falls in love with a clergyman, and although unrequited, the emotional experience expands her heart, leaving her able 'to give more than dutiful gratitude to her friends; her natural tenderness found many outlets'.

Jody (Jody Tiflin)
The Red Pony, 1937
John Steinbeck

A young farm boy whose idyll is shattered by the loss of his much-loved pony, but who grows by the experience and by his contact with the mysterious GITANO.

Joe (Josephine)
A Day in the Death of Joe Egg, 1967
Peter Nichols

The daughter of BRI and SHEILA, she is ten years old, and apart from the stiffness of her legs and arms, physically normal. She is, though, mentally handicapped, and cannot support herself properly, needing to be propped wherever she is put. Much of the time she sits in a specially-built chair with a tray. 'Her face is pretty but vacant of expression.' Her closest approach to speech is 'A-aaah!' Her role in the play is that of a catalyst, exposing the strains she places upon the relationship of her parents.

Joe and Woman
Eh Joe, 1965
Samuel Beckett

The grey-haired, elderly Joe, sitting in his room, wearing carpet slippers and an old dressing-gown, responds to the voice of a woman, who neither he nor the audience can see. The voice emanates from the air around him. It appears that Joe and the woman may once have been lovers in Ireland (there are references to the Catholic liturgy and a feel of the Irish landscape), and that by abandoning her, Joe has spiritually condemned himself. Although the rhythm of her voice is even throughout, it seems that she is sometimes probing, sometimes taunting: 'Anyone living love you now, Joe ... Eh Joe ...?'

Joe (The Fat Boy)
Pickwick Papers, 1837
Charles Dickens

The obese and voracious servant of Mr Wardle (see THE WARDLES). He is always either asleep or eating, except when he tells of seeing TRACY TUPMAN and Rachael Wardle kissing in the garden.

Joe
The Time of Your Life, 1939
William Saroyan

A brooding drinker in Nick's Pacific Street Saloon, Restaurant and Entertainment Palace, he is haunted by the compromises demanded by a society based entirely on material values. To expiate his guilt, he performs nameless acts of kindness for strangers, befriending the down-trodden and neglected.

Joey
The Homecoming, 1965
Harold Pinter

A boxer and demolition man, the youngest of MAX's three sons. An athletic and sexually desirable man, the violence of his professional life is ironically contrasted with his intellectual innocence; alone among the characters in this bleak and unforgiving play he has genuine qualities of loyalty, fidelity and warmth.

John
Oleanna, 1992
David Mamet

A college professor, John is middle-aged and married. Apparently mild-mannered, he likes to impress and is capable of outmanoeuvring others in intellectual argument. His suggestion to failing student CAROL that she might receive a higher grade in return for her visiting his office, is foolish, but, although he finds her intriguing, he is not necessarily extending a sexual invitation. Carol, however, chooses to think otherwise and brings charges of sexual harassment, which astonish, anger and frighten John. The play ends with him physically assaulting her, although the truth of his intentions and the extent of his fault is left for the play's audience to decide.

John (John Darling)
Peter Pan: or The Boy Who Would Not Grow Up, 1904 (play), 1911 (book)
J M Barrie

Growing up in his father's shadow and very much his miniature, the older of the two Darling boys has a gruff adult manner quite out of keeping with his lack of experience and understanding. Although he is momentarily attracted by the notion of recruitment to the pirate ranks, he remains stalwart in his fealty to King and Country.

John/Comte de Gue, Jean
The Scapegoat, 1957
Daphne Du Maurier

John is a timid and reserved man, afraid of experimentation, lest it should lead to failure. His alter ego, Jean Comte de Gue, is quite the opposite: sharp, ruthless and selfish. He lacks John's acute conscience, and when John becomes his alter ego for a week, it is both frightening and cathartic for him. While John has played safe, Jean has led a desperately dangerous life. By becoming an impostor for his other self, John realizes how complex the world can be, seeing some of its moral ambiguities, and experiencing the excitement of emotions, especially love. After his time spent as Jean, John is confused about his identity. His beloved Béla tells him: 'Failure doesn't exist for you any more' – his journey through another world has exorcized his fears.

John, Annie
Annie John, 1983
Jamaica Kincaid

Annie's passage from pampered childhood to what she calls 'young ladyness' on her way to mature womanhood is like a pilgrim's progress. A brilliant and exuberant girl, her reciprocated love for her parents develops into hostile loathing for her mother and polite indifference to her ageing father. The sumptuous life of a village carpenter's daughter with washstand, shelf and bed made from pitch pine by an industrious father also changes with the cold embrace of colonial education. The story ends when Annie boards the jetty and sails for England, leaving behind her parents and native Antigua with the feeling 'I shall never see this again'.

John, King
King John, 1590/1
William Shakespeare

John is traditionally the most unpopular English king. Yet the characters of John (patriot, villain and fanatic) and the loyal PHILIP FALCONBRIDGE more than compensate for the work's undoubted dramatic weaknesses. When the French demand that he renounce the English throne in favour of ARTHUR, DUKE OF BRITTANY, John arranges the prince's death and marshals an army to invade France. A battle to assert English independence soon becomes a war against Roman Catholicism. John's struggles reflect contemporary Shakespearean concerns of nationhood and the power of religion.

John, Prince
Ivanhoe, 1819
Sir Walter Scott

The brother of KING RICHARD who is absent, a prisoner of the Turks at the Crusades, he has formed an alliance with Philip of France and with a group of ambitious and disaffected Norman nobles to depose Richard permanently and rule England for their own gain.

'John Macnab'
John Macnab, 1925
John Buchan

A fictional character within a fiction, he is the invention of a group of bored gentlemen who create him to enliven the Highlands with the sort of mythic outlawry the contemporary age lacks. More seriously, he fulfils Buchan's romantic attachment to the figure of the archetypal Lost Leader.

John of Gaunt, Duke of Lancaster
Richard II, not later than 1595
William Shakespeare

KING RICHARD II's uncle, a man of great wisdom

and patriotism who still hankers after the old days of warlike kings. He is a traditionalist who believes in the divine right of the king, and when his son Henry Bolingbroke (HENRY IV) is banished by Richard he even-handedly upholds the king's decision. His deathbed vision of his country and Richard's weakness as its ruler is prophetic, and his views represent the standards of good monarchy against which Richard will be judged.

John of Lancaster, Prince
Henry IV Part I, 1596/7
Henry IV Part II, 1597/8
William Shakespeare

The younger son of HENRY IV, from whom he appears to have inherited much of his nature, and brother to Prince Hal (HENRY, PRINCE OF WALES), John is a novice at warfare, bloodying his sword for the first time at the battle of Shrewsbury. When he is given the important task of dealing with a second group of rebel leaders he shows a streak of ruthlessness, ordering their execution even though they had agreed to his offer of peace. He is expedient rather than chivalrous. Like many others he misreads his brother's character, believing that he will favour his disreputable friends when he becomes king.

John the Baptist
Paradise Regained, 1671
John Milton

The great forerunner and harbinger of the Messiah, he baptizes souls at Bethabara. Despite initial doubts, he grants JESUS CHRIST the tribute of Jordan water.

John the Swede
Two Years Before the Mast, 1840
R H Dana jr, originally published anonymously

A fiery-tempered old salt on the brig *Pilgrim*. Though wholly unpredictable, he has a kind of savage nobility that is deliberately contrasted to the uncivilized – that is, black – members of the crew.

Johne the Common-weill
Ane Pleasant Satyre of the Thrie Estaitis, 1540
Sir David Lindsay

Emerging suddenly from the audience, Johne the Common-weill takes up the cause of the Pure Man and acts as champion for the common people of Scotland in general, in revealing to the Parliament the corruption afoot in the country under the existing auspices of the Three Estates (MERCHAND, SPIRITUALITIE and TEMPORALITIE). Eloquent and emotive, he successfully pleads the case for the country, and his vitriolic denunciation of Spiritualitie ensures their unfrocking and his own symbolic robing and seating in Parliament: John, the voice of 'the Common-weill', becomes the voice of democracy.

Johnno
Johnno, 1975
David Malouf

A young man growing up in Brisbane after the war, observed by his friend 'DANTE'. A free spirit, racked by profound doubts about himself, he is so unfettered as to be intensely self-destructive.

Johnny
Leaving Cheyenne, 1963
Larry McMurtry

One of the last of the old-style cowboys, his wild, frontier individualism clashes with the steadying hand of civilization, as represented by GID. He is desperately clinging on to a way of life which present-day economics and social pressures have made redundant.

Johnson, Evelyn→ Tashi

Johnson, Edward 'Coffin Ed' and Jones, Grave Digger
For Love of Imabelle, 1957, reissued as *A Rage in Harlem* et seq
Chester Himes

This pair of ruthless New York police detectives patrol the phantasmagoric urban jungle of Chester Himes's Harlem novels, imposing their own brand of law and order with 'identical big hard-shooting, head-whipping pistols'. Seldom seen apart, they are intensely loyal to each other. Grave Digger does most of the wisecracking while Coffin Ed says little, but the scars of an acid attack on his face turn livid when he becomes enraged. Their sardonic comments indicate they are perfectly aware of their social function in keeping the lid on the bubbling cauldron of the ghetto in the interests of the (white) powers that be.

Johnson, Hildy
The Front Page, 1928
Ben Hecht and Charles MacArthur

An idealistic but slightly naive young journalist who, through contact with a Machiavellian editor, is forced to reconsider the relationship between public and private values.

Johnson, Madam Alberta K
'Madam's Past History', 'Madam and the Rent Man' and others, collected in *One-Way Ticket*, 1949
Langston Hughes

Her entrepreneurial incursions destroyed by a no-good man and the Depression, Madam Alberta bears her losses bravely. Nothing and no one dominates this formidable woman, and she sees off hustlers and preachers with intimidating efficiency. Dispossessed and destitute, she retains her irreverent sense of fun and flippantly dismisses the census-taker, who denies her dignity and respect. Washed ashore by the African diaspora, Madam Alberta insists on her new identity: 'There's nothing foreign/To my pedigree:/Alberta K Johnson/American that's me.'

Johnson, Maggie
Maggie: A Girl of the Streets, 1893
Stephen Crane

A slum child from the lowest ranks of New York society. Rejected by her brutal, drunken mother and uncaring brother, she is successively seduced and rejected by representatives of the major institutions of American society, before she is finally admitted to the oldest profession of all, joining the city's 'painted cohorts' in a last desperate bid for survival.

Johnson, Mister
Mister Johnson, 1939
Joyce Cary

An African clerk, 'as black as a stone, almost a pure Negro', with a long, thin, loose-jointed frame and irrepressible energy. He is likeable, warm-hearted, outgoing and loquacious, and succeeds briefly in turning his life 'into a romance'. He is also vain, self-regarding, irresponsible and dishonest, traits which lead to his eventual sad downfall.

Johnson, Ned
The Rehearsal, 1671
George Villiers, 2nd Duke of Buckingham

A wit whose interests are food, drink, women, and the theatre. He dislikes nonsensical and bombastic new plays, such as the one by BAYES, a rehearsal of which he attends with FRANK SMITH. He pretends to praise the piece, while actually mocking it.

Johnson, Samuel
According to Queeney, 2001
Beryl Bainbridge

A fictionalized version of the writer, Samuel Johnson is an elderly academic who suffers from bad health, enhanced by his hypochondria. His appearance is ramshackle and shabby: he has scarred skin on his cheeks and neck, his large lips are forever champing and his charred wig is too small. He is prone to periods of depressive torment and is irascible and often boorish in behaviour. When he is accepted into the home of the Thrales, his fondness for their daughter QUEENEY THRALE gives him a sense of family, but his veneration of Mrs Thrale arouses the unwelcome sexual feelings he constantly struggles to repress.

Jolley, Mrs
Riders in the Chariot, 1961
Patrick White

Like her friend, MRS FLACK, Mrs Jolley is a caricatured portrait of the Australian suburban matron, small-minded, prejudiced and vindictive, while imagining herself to be rather sophisticated. She and Mrs Flack delight in domestic appliances and aids to personal grooming, revering them almost as religious artefacts, Mrs Jolley being profoundly moved by her friend's pastel-blue plastic dressing-table set. She works as housekeeper to MARY HARE and likes to sing hymns as she does her rounds. Like Mrs Flack, she is outraged when an orthodox Jew, MORDECAI HIMMELFARB, arrives to live among them.

Jollifant, Inigo
The Good Companions, 1929
J B Priestley

An unfulfilled schoolmaster, Jollifant is oozing with charm and despair. He is irresponsible and unprofessional, yet seems to be, above all, vulnerable. When he loses his job, he wanders out into the world, but his affable charm enables him to make contacts quickly, and to strike up a rapport with those he meets. He is imaginative and restless, yearning for emotional contentment, whilst appearing to be a 'jack-the-lad'. He achieves artistic and financial success, and never gives up hope of marrying his beloved Susie.

Jolter, Mr Jacob
The Adventures of Peregrine Pickle, 1751,
bowdlerized edition 1758
Tobias Smollett

A dull but pious man, appointed tutor to PEREGRINE PICKLE. His old-fashioned High Church zeal 'was so exceedingly fervent, as on some occasions, to get the better of his discretion', and to compound the sourness and severity of his manner.

Jonathan
The Magic Toyshop, 1967
Angela Carter

The brother of MELANIE. A typical snub-nosed, school-capped little boy, contentedly lost in model-making, he is totally unperturbed by change, enjoying an abstracted and absent-minded relationship with reality. His sister says that it is as though 'the real Jonathan has gone somewhere else and left a copy behind so that no one notices he is gone'.

Jones, Amos
On the Black Hill, 1982
Bruce Chatwin

The hot-blooded Welsh farmer who toils relentlessly to scratch a living for himself and his family from his hill-farm perched on the border of Wales and England. A strictly religious man who scorns education and the frivolities of the finer classes in favour of a very basic subsistence, he is a proud but dour figure who, far from mellowing with age, allows his resentment at his wife MARY JONES's more prosperous background and higher aspirations to damage the love between them.

Jones, Archie
White Teeth, 2000
Zadie Smith

An ordinary, white, working-class man living in North London, Archie Jones is something of a failure: even his suicide attempt (after a failed marriage) goes wrong when he is rescued. But the truth is, 'although he was not one of her better specimens, Life wanted Archie, and Archie, much to his own surprise, wanted Life'. His rescue sparks a chain of events in which he marries Clara, an exceptionally tall Jamaican teenager, and fathers a daughter, Irie. When not at work folding envelopes, Archie seeks solace in O'Connell's Café on the Finchley Road, where he and his wartime friend SAMAD IQBAL muse over the demands of modern family life.

Jones, Benjamin
On the Black Hill, 1982
Bruce Chatwin

Physically weakened by a childhood illness, Benjamin compensates for his lack of strength by greater brainpower than his brother LEWIS JONES, and in a natural aptitude for domestic tasks. Jealously possessive of his twin, he cannot bear to be parted from him, yet in other circumstances he shows a quiet dignity in the

face of persecution. Money-conscious to the point of avarice, he remains quaintly suspicious of 20th-century advancements, and finds his joy in life in his consuming love for his mother and brother.

Jones, Bridget
Bridget Jones's Diary, 1996
Bridget Jones: The Edge of Reason, 1999
Bridget Jones's Guide to Life, 2001
Helen Fielding

Single thirty-something Bridget intends to 'develop inner poise' as a 'woman of substance'. Yet her quest to be a better person is repeatedly thwarted as she wrestles with the temptations of alcohol, cigarettes and an energetic social life, while haphazardly pursuing Mr Right. Incurably late and incorrigibly addicted to self-help books, Bridget is lively, warm-hearted and loyal, if rather ditzy; her diaries document the ups and downs of singleton life in the 1990s with wit, warmth and often-unintentional humour.

Jones, Brutus
The Emperor Jones, 1920
Eugene O'Neill

A black American who has set himself up as emperor of a small Caribbean island, maintaining his power with the story that he can only be killed by a silver bullet. When the natives rebel, he takes refuge in the jungle, where he is assailed by ghostly images – 'Little Formless Fears' – from the folk memory of slave days, and then destroyed by bullets cast from silver dollars.

Jones, Eric
Another Country, 1962
James Baldwin

A bisexual actor, he lives with a handsome French boyfriend, over whom he exerts a powerful magnetism. He is the former lover of the jazz musician RUFUS SCOTT, who despises him because he comes from Alabama, and is nothing more than a Southern 'cracker' underneath his urbane, moneyed exterior.

Jones, Fiddler
The Spoon River Anthology, 1915
Edgar Lee Masters

He embodies the musician's spirit: fated to feel some 'vibration' constantly coming from the earth, he is thus required to neglect his work to play the fiddle, for, 'If the people find you can fiddle/why, fiddle you must, for all your life'. His whimsical and nostalgic monologue finds him, at the end, a poor man with only 40 acres of land and a broken fiddle, but without any regrets.

Jones, George
The Absence of War, 1993
David Hare

The third in a trilogy of plays dealing with British institutions (the first being *Racing Demon* (1990) and *Murmuring Judges* (1991) the second), *The Absence of War* looks at the plight of the Labour Party following a lengthy period in opposition and in the run-up to a general election. Party leader George Jones, a London bachelor, is a decent man of warmth, wit and liberal socialist ideals, but lacking in political ruthlessness. Stifled by his publicists, he is further impeded by an uncertain temper. Some commentators drew parallels between Jones and Labour Party leader (1983–1992) Neil Kinnock.

Jones, Grave Digger → Johnson, Edward

Jones, Jenny
The History of Tom Jones, 1749
Henry Fielding

She is assumed by MRS DEBORAH WILKINS and SQUIRE ALLWORTHY to be TOM JONES's mother, having been in attendance at the squire's house on the day before the baby Tom's discovery in Allworthy's bed. She 'was no very comely girl, either in her face or person; but Nature had somewhat compensated the want of beauty with what is generally more esteemed by those ladies, whose judgement is arrived at through years of perfect maturity'.

Jones, Lewis
On the Black Hill, 1982
Bruce Chatwin

The first-born, physically stronger son of AMOS and MARY JONES, gentle Lewis is also more outgoing than his twin brother, BENJAMIN JONES, harbouring a passion for aviation and a secret longing to be married and have a family. But, disappointed in his amorous endeavours and unwilling to hurt Benjamin by leaving him, he selflessly contents himself in the companionship of his brother and in the working of their farm.

Jones, Lorin, originally Lolly Zimmern
The Truth about Lorin Jones, 1988
Alison Lurie

The shy child Lolly, daughter of CELIA and DAN ZIMMERN, she dies in her forties, just as her paintings are gaining recognition within the Art establishment. Through the memories of others a confusing portrait emerges of a woman dedicated to her art and consequently unable to devote much energy to forming and sustaining relationships. Is the true picture that of a solitary, sensitive artist whose talent is exploited by others or of a ruthless self-centred woman obsessed by her work? Opinions differ as to her character but her talent is undeniable and her dedication to it remains the key to her life.

Jones, Major
The Comedians, 1966
Graham Greene

Emerging from a mysterious, ambiguous past, Major Jones is a small man with a rather small mind. He divides all people into 'toffs', who have a settled job and good income, and 'tarts', who pick up a living as best they can. Jones characterizes himself as a tart, surviving on his native wit. He is, however, an astute, perceptive man; a pragmatist who, through participation in battle, has learned to be cold-blooded and brutal. Jones is one of the novel's 'comedians' – a man adept at the art of dissembling. He is frightened only by the loss of inner meaning in his life.

Jones, 'Major' Harry
The Peach Groves, 1979
Barbara Hanrahan

After running away from his Liverpool slum home and bullying father to Australia together with his beloved sister, BLANCHE DEAN, Harry settled in New Zealand. He prospered there through hard, lonely work in the gum-fields, during which time he found a personal God. By adding 'Major' to his undistinguished name and acquiring a plain, wealthy wife, palatial home and stable of racehorses, the debonair Harry consolidated his success. But during an affair with his stepsister-in-law, TEMPE WIMPERIS, he begins to lose his God, and is doubly 'damned' when Blanche arrives, provoking a sexual and moral crisis.

Jones, Mary
On the Black Hill, 1982
Bruce Chatwin

The English wife of tenant-farmer AMOS JONES, Mary is chastised by her family for marrying beneath her. But being cheerful and immune to narrow-mindedness, she is initially enthusiastic about living on the land, and devotes her energies to the upbringing and education of her twin sons. However, the long hard years take their toll on her, and she dreams increasingly of her younger days in India while remaining, as always, a kind neighbour and a loving, if possessive, mother.

Jones, Millie
Absalom, Absalom!, 1936
William Faulkner

A poor-white girl, who lives with her grandfather on Sutpen's Hundred, she becomes the focus of THOMAS SUTPEN's last-ditch attempt to found a vigorous dynasty. When she delivers only a daughter, Sutpen rejects her.

Jones, Mr
Animal Farm, 1945
George Orwell

Mr Jones is a drunken farmer who has neglected the running of his premises and, after fleeing Manor Farm when the animals revolt, takes refuge in the Red Lion Inn. When he tries to return to the farm he is soundly defeated and thrown on to a pile of dung. His presence throughout the rest of the novel is that of a 'bogey man', a member of the old regime whose return is threatened if the animals do not obey their new dictators. Like all the humans in the novel, Jones is a very unsympathetic character, who amply merited the revolution against his rule.

Jones, Nancy
The Knack, 1961
Ann Jellicoe

Aged 17, Nancy's 'personality, like her appearance, is still blurred and unformed'. New to London, she looks distinctly provincial and is apparently utterly naive. Asking the way to the nearest YWCA hostel, she allows herself to be lured into a house by three young men, one of whom is the landlord, another of whom boasts of his sexual prowess. However gullible and ignorant Nancy appears, she nevertheless has a spiritual strength and an almost animal tenacity of will. Alleging that she was raped while she had fainted, she manages to disconcert and finally subdue her tormentors.

Jones, Rose
The Sea, 1973
Edward Bond

At the beginning of the play, Rose's lover, Colin, dies during a violent storm. Colin's friend WILLY is saved and, by a strange and delicate process of emotional inheritance, it is he that the perceptive, good Rose comes to love. Grieving and tragic, she is nonetheless a resilient, determined figure, sustained by a humanity which, suggests Bond, is integral to life. At the end of the play, she and Willy begin a new life together, thus representing hope for the future.

Jones, Tom
The History of Tom Jones, 1749
Henry Fielding

The classic flawed everyman of the English novel, he is a foundling, secreted by an unknown hand in the bed of SQUIRE ALLWORTHY. 'Born to be hanged' in the opinion of his adoptive family, he is easily overmastered by fleshly appetites, thus compromising or at least delaying his union with the beautiful (and, as it transpires, socially suitable) SOPHIA WESTERN.

Jones, Wash
Absalom, Absalom!, 1936
William Faulkner

A poor-white squatter on THOMAS SUTPEN's estate. When Sutpen seduces, then rejects, his granddaughter MILLIE JONES, Wash kills him with a scythe, thus bringing in a harvest of violence that has built up on the fated land for more than a generation.

Jonsen, Captain
A High Wind in Jamaica, 1929
Richard Hughes

The Danish captain of a pirate ship. 'A clumsy, great fellow, with a sad, silly face', he is a harmless rogue with a weak head for drink, and is dependent on the navigational skill of his great friend, the mate OTTO. Exasperated, at times, by the exuberant children whom he had never sought to kidnap, he mostly shows them great paternal affection. A tragic figure, he is damned by his own kindness in finally releasing the children, who have less notion of morality then himself.

Jordan
Sexing the Cherry, 1989
Jeanette Winterson

An orphan found wrapped in a sack in the slime by the River Thames, Jordan is brought up by the extraordinary THE DOG-WOMAN. A loner, he is at home on the sea and travels with John Tradescant (Charles I's gardener and the man who brought the first pineapple to Britain) on voyages of exploration. He is also travelling in 'an effort to catch up with my fleet-footed self, living another life in a different way' and in search of Fortunata, a dancer 'who may or may not exist'.

Jordan, Del
Lives of Girls and Women, 1971
Alice Munro

An intelligent and perceptive child, Del progresses through life in the small town of Jubilee with the conviction that 'there is no protection, unless it is in knowing'. Distrustful of the accounts of others, she submerges herself in experiences. Her bold confidence enables her to learn but distances her from the behaviour expected from a woman. Finally able to 'shuck off what [she] didn't want', her 'old devious, ironic, isolated self' re-emerges. Without the residues of others' expectations, she is able to embark on her 'real life' with a profound self-knowledge.

Jordan, Robert
For Whom the Bell Tolls, 1940
Ernest Hemingway

An idealistic American journalist fighting against the Fascists in Spain. He is a courageous and compassionate man, ready to die for the cause, which he sees as a universal one. He is intelligent and realistic, but also a man of action, although his conscience troubles him over the people he has to kill. He is frustrated and angered by operational deficiencies on his own side, but refuses to abandon his duties even when they are hopeless. His love for MARIA helps her emerge from her traumatic experiences.

Jorkins, Mr
David Copperfield, 1850
Charles Dickens

A proctor and partner in the firm of Spenlow and Jorkins, his place in the business 'was to keep himself in the background'. In reality 'a mild man of heavy temperament', he is constantly cited by MR FRANCIS SPENLOW as the most ruthless and obdurate of men, and used as the pretext for all of Spenlow's unpleasant decisions.

Jorrocks, Mr
Jorrocks' Jaunts and Jollities, 1838
R S Surtees

A Cockney grocer of irrepressible good humour, with an appetite for harmless diversion. Ancestor to a long line of diamond geezers, his adventures, if not his person, are believed to have provided the model for Charles Dickens's SAMUEL PICKWICK.

Joseph
Dangling Man, 1944
Saul Bellow

This irritable and suffering narrator-protagonist claims to have 'in a word, no character'. He is suspended between states of being (between resigning work and joining the army, and then his lost political commitment and rootless alienation), and is engaged in an inward-looking, existential search for meaning and self-discovery, one which 'unlocks the imprisoning self'. He is intelligent and highly sceptical, albeit with a somewhat romantic strain, at odds with the world in which he moves, but which he finally embraces in its most self-abnegating form.

Josephine
The Daughters of the Late Colonel, 1922
Katherine Mansfield
The elder Miss Pinner ('Jug') weeps, giggles and blushes and thus seems to be the more volubly decisive of the late Colonel's daughters. She remembers family, business and their mother, who has been dead since their Anglo-Indian childhood. However, she has strange ideas, such as running the household without servants, even though she is able to cook only eggs. Inclined to go off on tangents, her grasp of reality and communication is as shaky and fearful as that of her equally deprived sister, CONSTANTIA.

Jowles, Finn
The Magic Toyshop, 1981
Angela Carter
A wild, eccentric 19-year-old with an eloquent and romantic mind and a serene yet lively way of moving. Like his sister, AUNT MARGARET FLOWERS, he is pale-skinned and has bright red hair. Insolent, menacing and courageous, he is hard to communicate with. Although strangely beautiful he is also slovenly, giving off a faint, distasteful sexual smell.

Jowles, Francie
The Magic Toyshop, 1967
Angela Carter
Brother of AUNT MARGARET FLOWERS and FINN JOWLES, he is an ordinary man with a kind and loving heart, whose voice cracks through lack of use. He is ungainly and antique with a silent archaic smile. His passion is his violin music, which he plays to Aunt Margaret's flute and with which he also earns his living.

Joy
Poor Cow, 1963
Nell Dunn
Living in London with a small baby, little money and a husband who haunts the edges of the criminal underworld, Joy finds life full of pain and disappointment. Unable to function well in relationships with men, and supported only by the well-meaning affection of a feckless friend, she stumbles from miserable situation to crisis and feels control slipping through her fingers as she finds herself wading through the shabbiness of a lifestyle that has few moments of happiness or hope.

Joy, Harry
Bliss, 1981
Peter Carey
A middle-aged advertising executive, he succumbs to a heart attack, but after a bizarre out-of-body experience is revived to a radical perception of life and death, and of their ultimate rewards and punishments. This new world is one of absolute control and bee-like division of responsibilities.

JR
JR, 1975
William Gaddis
JR is not to be confused with J R Ewing, villain of the popular television soap opera *Dallas*, though Gaddis's character has the same instinct for

profit. A scruffy, ineducable sixth-grader in a high-tech Long Island school for problem and delinquent children, he amasses a (strictly notional) fortune by playing the stock market, replacing real economic understanding with a genius for linguistic mimicry.

Juan, Don
Don Juan, 1819–24
Byron, George Gordon, 6th Lord Byron
Don Juan, when only 16, so disgraces himself in Seville that his mother banishes him. Shipwrecked, he escapes from his companions, who have taken to cannibalism, and is washed up on a Greek island, where he falls into the arms of Haydee. Her pirate father punishes the lovers by selling Juan in Constantinople as a slave to a young countess. However, Juan later joins the Russian army, and so impresses the Empress Catherine that she sends him on an embassy to London, where he encounters fashionable London society and has more love affairs.

Judge, the
Winterset, 1935
Maxwell Anderson
He has wrongly condemned MIO's father for a murder actually committed by the evil TROCK. No longer of sound mind, he is forced to contemplate new evidence that underlines the error of his original judgement. The case in question was modelled on the judicial murder of the Italo-American anarchists Sacco and Vanzetti in 1927.

Judique, Mrs Tanis
Babbitt, 1922
Sinclair Lewis
An intriguing and beautiful widow with whom GEORGE FOLANSBEE BABBITT has a fairy-tale affair during his escape from life in Zenith City. It becomes clear, though, that her self-conscious bohemianism and artiness are superficial and unsustaining. Her name has fascinated some critics, who suspect that a telling anagram is buried in it.

Jukes, Morrowbie
'The Strange Ride of Morrowbie Jukes', 1885
Rudyard Kipling
While working as a civil engineer at the height of the Raj, he goes down with an attack of fever and is disturbed by the baying of dogs. When he attempts to kill the last and loudest of the pack by charging it down on his horse, he finds himself in a nightmarish place peopled by cholera victims. His race and status mean nothing here and he is gradually taken over by the unpredictable GUNGA DASS.

Julia
1984, 1949
George Orwell
In a cold, futuristic society, Julia works for the Ministry of Truth and operates novel-writing machines. She is a more optimistic, practical person than the rather cerebral WINSTON SMITH. Their friendship begins when Winston helps her after a fall in the corridor – a simple act of honest

kindness in a world of duplicity. In the love affair which develops, Julia is the more dominant partner. She also despises the Party, but is not ready for the more open rebellion of Winston. She too is tortured by the Party, and all the natural emotions which she felt for Winston, and her appetite for life, are destroyed.

Julia
Two Gentlemen of Verona, c.1590
William Shakespeare

Julia is described by PROTEUS, who loves her, as 'a swarthy Ethiope', in other words, one of dark colouring in contrast to the fair SILVIA. When he becomes infatuated with Silvia, Julia disguises herself as 'Sebastian' and enters his service as his page. She is clever, determined, clear-sighted and occasionally hot-headed; her ruse appears to work until she hears VALENTINE, who loves Silvia, declare that he will defer to Proteus. Julia then faints: her male disguise has failed to camouflage her feminine sensibility.

Julian
Everything That Rises Must Converge, 1956
Flannery O'Connor

An unemployed, college-educated young man who grudgingly fulfils his duty towards his mother (JULIAN'S MOTHER). Gloomy and resentful, he believes that his intellectual superiority renders him unemployable and is contemptuous of his self-sacrificing parent. He adopts a progressive attitude towards racial integration and knowingly provokes his mother's racist sentiments in order to vent his malice against her.

Julian
'Julian and Maddalo', 1818
Percy Shelley

The narrator of the poem and 'an Englishman of good birth', Julian is also 'a complete infidel and a scoffer at all things reputed holy', believing religion to be evil superstition. He has many good qualities and is moved to compassion when his friend COUNT MADDALO introduces him to a man driven mad by love, but any ideas he has of helping the man, he admits, are merely 'dreams of baseless good'.

Julian, Brother
Tiny Alice, 1965
Edward Albee

A young Catholic lay brother who is seduced and eventually killed by ALICE, the richest woman in the world, for reasons which are never made entirely explicit.

Julian, Emperor
Julian, 1964
Gore Vidal

The 'young and handsome' Roman emperor whose journey from Christianity to Mithraism, and from the consolations of philosophy to the fields of war, are traced in his own elegantly stylish 'memoirs', and the 'reminiscences' of two old philosophers 17 years after his death. The most successful general of the period, he is erudite, loves learning, and is something of a prig. He is indiscreet and impulsive by nature, but has learned to dissemble and disguise his thoughts amid the intrigues of court, without which skill he would not 'have lived past [his] twentieth year'.

Julian's Mother
Everything That Rises Must Converge, 1956
Flannery O'Connor

A widow whose considerable pride is invested in her college-educated adult son (JULIAN) as both the source of her social status and the vindication of her self-sacrificing struggle to raise him alone. Despite her reduced circumstances she lives a fantasy of social and racial superiority sustained by the memory of her grandfather's land- and slave-ownership. Her genteel affectation of condescending graciousness does not conceal her snobbery and racism.

Julie
The Cement Garden, 1978
Ian McEwan

Aspiring to be a famous athlete, the exceptionally beautiful Julie, aged 16, shy, reserved and with a quiet strength, rather intimidates her younger sister and two brothers, JACK and Tom. But after the death of their parents, and their macabre internment of their mother's body, she grotesquely plays head of the family, particularly with five-year-old Tom who regresses to babyhood. The older boyfriend she acquires is responsible for ending the children's nightmarish travesty of family life.

Juliet
Romeo and Juliet, 1591–6
William Shakespeare

The 13-year-old daughter of the Capulets has had little experience of life. After falling in love with ROMEO at first sight she reveals her youth by emotional outbursts when setbacks occur. As these increase she shows her growing maturity by dealing with them in a more practical manner than Romeo. After his banishment she stands on her own, rejecting NURSE's advice and turning against her parents whom she has always obeyed dutifully. Her inner strength is made clear by the courage she shows in going along with FRIAR LAWRENCE's plan and in facing death, alone, in the family vault.

Julius, Uncle
The Conjure Woman, 1899
Charles W Chesnutt

An old gardener, who tells spellbinding stories about plantation life in the American South. He is revealingly described by one of his white listeners: 'He was not entirely black, and this fact, together with the quality of his hair, which was about six inches long and very bushy, except on the top of his head, where he was quite bald, suggested a slight strain of other than negro blood. There was a shrewdness in his eyes, too, which was not altogether African, and which, as we afterwards learned from experience, is indicative of a corresponding shrewdness of character.'

July (Mwawate)
July's People, 1981
Nadine Gordimer
The talkative, loyal house-servant of MAUREEN SMALES and BAMFORD SMALES, he becomes their 'saviour' by rescuing them and their children from the revolution and hiding them in his village. The responsible, sometimes domineering, head of an extended family, he has become accustomed to the necessity of maintaining two lives – one of servitude in wealthy white society and one of authority amidst the basic poverty of village life.

Juniper, Brother
The Bridge of San Luis Rey, 1927
Thornton Wilder
A hard-working and devout little red-haired Franciscan from Northern Italy, Brother Juniper ministers to the Indians in 18th-century Peru. After witnessing the collapse of the bridge, he compiles a painstaking study to discover whether the five people who were killed died by accident or design. Trying to put theology among the exact sciences, he aims to convince those who sneered at faith. But the victims seem to be both good and bad, and ecclesiastical judges declare the Devil has made use of him.

Jupe, Signor
Hard Times, 1854
Charles Dickens
A clown in MR SLEARY's circus and the owner of the 'highly-trained performing dog Merrylegs'. Believing his career to be failing, he disappears with his dog, leaving behind his daughter, SISSY JUPE, to be cared for by Mr Sleary.

Jupe, Sissy
Hard Times, 1854
Charles Dickens
The daughter of the clown, SIGNOR JUPE, and a pupil at THOMAS GRADGRIND's model school, where her notions of fancy are abhorrent to his Utilitarian doctrine. Deserted by her father, she is cared for by MR SLEARY, the circus owner, before being taken into Gradgrind's household, where she proves kind and companionable, especially to LOUISA GRADGRIND, and a softening influence on the family's unrelenting regime of hard facts. She denounces JAMES HARTHOUSE for his attempt to seduce Louisa and later helps TOM GRADGRIND to escape arrest by sending him to Mr Sleary. With RACHAEL, she discovers STEPHEN BLACKPOOL after he falls into an abandoned mine shaft.

Jurgen
Jurgen, 1919
James Branch Cabell
A middle-aged pawnbroker (his wife has a worse name for him) in the mythical medieval kingdom of Poictesme. When his wife mysteriously disappears, he sets off to rediscover his lost youth and is magically restored to young manhood, visiting heaven and hell and enjoying a fling with a former sweetheart.

Justice Balance
The Recruiting Officer, 1706
George Farquhar
Although Justice Balance, SYLVIA's father, approves of CAPTAIN PLUME as a man, he cannot accept his marrying Sylvia, because he believes she is worthy of someone of a higher social standing. Though not naturally an authoritarian father, he attempts to send her away, but she reneges against him and takes matters into her own hands. When he realizes that his daughter has tricked him, he behaves with dignity and accepts the match. Although basically a decent gentleman and a fair judge, his conduct is at times improper because of his determination to provide recruits for the army.

Justin
To the Islands, 1958, revised edition 1982
Randolph Stow
A brave, resourceful and almost saintly Aborigine who shares HERIOT's physical and spiritual sojourn in the outback. It is his character, rather than the niceties of Anglicanism, that saves the missionary and brings him back, duly chastened, to reality.

Justine, properly Justine Hosnani
Justine, 1957, and elsewhere in *The Alexandria Quartet*, 1968
Lawrence Durrell
The fatefully beautiful Jewish wife of NESSIM and the focus of all the characters' desires and dreams. Though marred by pettiness and vanity, she is disconcertingly perceptive and enjoys 'the free vertical independence of the masculine life'. She also, of course, echoes the name of de Sade's heroine.

K, Michael
Life and Times of Michael K, 1983
J M Coetzee

With a cleft palate, low intelligence, and employed as a parks gardener in Cape Town, Michael K, like Kafka's Joseph K, cannot understand why the authorities continually harass him. He endures, however, attempting to take his aged mother to the country, in the midst of civil war, but after her death finds himself in a concentration camp. His only desire is to plant seeds everywhere he goes, but he is thwarted even by the misplaced charity of fugitives from the war.

Kaa
The Jungle Book, 1894
Rudyard Kipling

A magnificent rock-python, nearly 30 feet in length, he is inclined to deafness (like all his kind) and is rather short-sighted when he has just sloughed his old skin. At such times it is best to approach him with care. He despises his venomous brethren as cowards and is a doughty fighter, using his blunt head as a battering ram. The sound of his name, Kipling suggests, should resemble the open-mouthed hiss-spit of a large snake.

Kahn, Ada, Harry, Ronnie, and Sarah
Chicken Soup with Barley, 1957
I'm Talking About Jerusalem, 1958–9
Arnold Wesker

The first and last plays in the 'Wesker trilogy' (the second being *Roots*) deal with the fortunes and trials of the East End Jewish Kahn family from 1936 to 1959. Despite her nitpicking and tactlessness, Sarah is a proud mother and communist idealist who looks to the future with optimism. Harry, her shiftless husband whose political fervour rapidly cools in the face of potential violence, is reduced by two strokes to the state of a permanent invalid. Ronnie, their son, an aspiring socialist poet, is appalled by the Soviet suppression of the Hungarian uprising. Only Sarah, elderly but unbowed, still fights on: 'If you don't care, you'll die!' In *I'm Talking About Jerusalem*, the Kahns' daughter, Ada, and her husband Dave Simmonds, move to East Anglia and, by making furniture, attempt to build a socialist Jerusalem in the tradition of William Morris. Despite Ada's passionate, gritty determination, they fail. Each character, therefore, represents differing aspects of idealistic and spiritual strength and defeat in the face of political disillusion.

Kaplan, Hyman
The Education of Hyman Kaplan, 1937
The Return of Hyman Kaplan, 1959
Leo Rosten

An enthusiastic immigrant pupil of long-suffering Mr 'Pockheel' (Parkhill)'s beginners grade of the American Night Preparatory School for Adults. Possessed of an endearing phonetic humour and an everlasting beaming smile, he is 'cotter mens cloths' by day, and signs his name with a flourish in red crayon outlined in blue with green stars between each capital letter. His mispronunciation and grammatical errors reveal the rich variety of the cultural melting pot, as he attempts to grasp the vagaries of the standard English language and thence the nature of the New World.

Karanja
A Grain of Wheat, 1967
Ngugi wa Thiong'o

GIKONYO's rival for MUMBI, he is a totally compromised man who defines himself entirely in terms of white approval. Throwing in his lot with the British forces who still govern Kenya, he becomes the executioner of his one-time friends.

Karen (Karen Forrestier, née Michaelis)
The House in Paris, 1935
Elizabeth Bowen

At 19 she agrees to marry RAY FORRESTIER, but is briefly drawn in by the more dramatic, fuller life offered by MAX, with whom she has an affair and a child. The birth and existence of LEOPOLD, who is taken from her in infancy, is the 'shark's fin' that shows through the quiet surface of her life.

Karla
Tinker, Tailor, Soldier, Spy, 1974
The Honourable Schoolboy, 1977
Smiley's People, 1980
John Le Carré

A Russian spymaster, he is GEORGE SMILEY's eternal adversary. He has recruited moles from the English higher bourgeoisie before the war and imprisonment in Siberia. He met Smiley in Delhi when he was about to go back to Russia and face apparent death; he still returns and instead receives promotion. He shows human corruption (after working for years in a barren room at a bare wooden desk) and breaks rules to get his disturbed daughter to the West for treatment; this is discovered and ruthlessly exploited by Smiley.

Karlovich, Herman
Despair, 1965
Vladimir Nabokov
A fastidious half-Russian, half-German manufacturer of chocolate who becomes obsessed with creating his doppelganger out of a tramp. With precise flair and relish, he mounts an insurance swindle by murdering this double. His plan does not work, however, and his incredulous rage that others do not concur with his view of events is matched by the despair of the title – that his future struggle is to counter his insecurity and paranoia.

Kasim, Ahmed
The Jewel in the Crown, 1966
The Day of the Scorpion, 1968
The Towers of Silence, 1971
A Division of the Spoils, 1975, forming
The Raj Quartet
Paul Scott
MOHAMMED ALI KASIM's unhappy younger son. He is monumentally indifferent to almost everything and everyone, due to a crippling sense of failure and of having disappointed his distinguished father. Brought to Mirat by COUNT BRONOWSKY, who admires Ahmed's objectivity and social graces, he indulges his only real interest, hawking, while forcing himself to acquire a taste for drink, gloomily feeling that all he is capable of becoming in his own right is an alcoholic. With tragic irony it is the apolitical and religiously indifferent Ahmed who falls victim to political and sectarian reprisals by the Hindus.

Kasim, Mohammed Ali
The Jewel in the Crown, 1966
The Day of the Scorpion, 1968
The Towers of Silence, 1971
A Division of the Spoils, 1975, forming
The Raj Quartet
Paul Scott
An elderly Muslim politician, he was chief minister of the province of Ranpur from 1937 to 1939 but then, deferring to his unwise colleagues, resigned in the mass protest against the British Viceroy's declaring war on India's behalf without consultation. Still a leading member of the All-India Congress Party, opposed to violence and partition, Kasim is arrested in 1942 following the 'Quit India' riots, refusing the offer of freedom if he will resign and become a British puppet. He is devastated when during his imprisonment his eldest son joins the rebel Indian National Army raised by the Japanese to march on Delhi.

Kasson, Byron
Nigger Heaven, 1926
Carl Van Vechten
A writer convinced that his colour is a major bar to success, he slides into bitterness and self-doubt, failings that sour his relationship with MARY LOVE and lead him inexorably to an act of pointless violence.

Kastril
The Alchemist, 1610
Ben Jonson
Foolish, impetuous and often ill-tempered, Kastril

is DAME PLIANT's protective brother. He does not see hot-headedness as a fault, and approaches SUBTLE for advanced lessons in quarrelling. Subtle, hoping to marry Pliant to PERTINAX SURLY, advises him to relax his guard over her, but once he discovers the ruse, Kastril becomes argumentative and is only pacified when his sister marries LOVEWIT, a match engineered by FACE.

Kate
Old Times, 1971
Harold Pinter
Married to DEELEY, with whom she lives in a remote converted farmhouse, cool and elegant Kate reminisces upon her life in London 20 years previously, before she met her husband and when she shared a flat with ANNA, a woman whose arrival is imminent. Yet while being specific upon such details as the cafés they frequented and that Anna sometimes borrowed her underwear, Kate also claims to have 'almost totally forgotten' her. In a play dealing with the fallibility of memory and experience, a contest emerges between Kate and her husband over Anna, from which Kate emerges serenely but decisively victorious.

Kath
Entertaining Mr Sloane, 1964
Joe Orton
Starved of affection, the rapacious Kath finds all her maternal instincts aroused by the arrival of the attractive SLOANE as her new lodger. Now aged 41 and convinced that she has managed to retain her good looks, she desperately yearns for the physical comfort and affection provided by a young man who reminds her of the son she was forced to give up for adoption many years ago. Unsubtle in her overtures and possessive by nature, she welcomes her subsequent pregnancy.

Katharina (Kate)
The Taming of the Shrew, early 1590s
William Shakespeare
Kate, the elder daughter of BAPTISTA MINOLA of Padua, has a vicious temper. She reveals this in her aggressive language and her sometimes physical cruelty to her sister BIANCA, finding release in violence when she cannot deal with situations or people. Taken aback by PETRUCHIO and his rough behaviour, she is denied necessities such as food and sleep, and is forced into submission, becoming quiet, biddable and pliant. Yet underneath there lies real love for her tamer.

Katharine
Love's Labour's Lost, not later than 1594
William Shakespeare
A lady attendant to the PRINCESS OF FRANCE. Loved by DUMAINE, she claims that her lips 'belong to fortunes and to me' and refers to his love-verses as 'A huge translation of hypocrisy/ Vilely compiled, profound simplicity'. Like her companions, she gives her lover a year and a day to wait before he can woo her again.

Katharine, Princess of France
Henry V, 1599
William Shakespeare
Because her father seeks to make peace with

England by marrying her off to Henry V (HENRY, PRINCE OF WALES), Katharine decides to take a lesson in her future tongue. Although she is a princess of impeccable breeding she recognizes several apparent French obscenities in the words she has to learn. As a dutiful daughter she agrees to the marriage; however, there are indications that she may come to love the king eventually.

Katherine, Queen of England
Henry VIII (All is True), c.1613
William Shakespeare and John Fletcher

Queen to HENRY VIII, she is abandoned in favour of ANNE BOLEYN. Her fall is matched by that of CARDINAL THOMAS WOLSEY, as Anne's rise is reflected by that of THOMAS CRANMER, the play being less about the loves of a king than the relation between the monarch and the Church. Katherine is presented as a woman with a strong belief in herself, a noble, tragic figure. More than any other character, she represents opposition to absolute monarchial power. She voices Henry's doubts about the legality of their marriage, Wolsey's advice that she should renounce her title, and the judgement of an ecclesiastical court. Increasingly isolated, yet sustained by a vision of benevolent eternity, she nonetheless maintains a fiery spirit to the end.

Kathleen
Shadows on Our Skin, 1977
Jennifer Johnston

A teacher from Wicklow who has come via England to Derry. She is lonely and a misfit, but to JOE LOGAN she represents a delicious easiness and freedom. Kathleen recognizes that BRENDAN LOGAN is also an outsider, and though attracted to him she never lets this threaten her friendship with his brother Joe. She is beaten up on account of Joe, but, knowing his innocence, forgives him.

Kaul, Nanda
Fire on the Mountain, 1977
Anita Desai

A strong-minded elderly woman who desires peace and solitude in her old age. In Carignano, the house upon the hill, Nanda Kaul lives alone with her servant Ram Lal and seems to have achieved the life she has longed for. The arrival of her great-grandchild, RAKA, changes everything. At first Nanda Kaul resents the intrusion, but Raka defies all expectations and forces the old woman to reconsider her past and present life; in so doing she discovers new needs and is forced to face new truths.

Kavalier, Joe
The Amazing Adventures of Kavalier & Clay, 2000
Michael Chabon

He is a Jewish youth, native of Prague, who escapes to New York from Nazi-threatened Europe. While he is a talented amateur escapologist, it is his skill as an artist that earns him success in creating a popular comic called *The Escapist*, in partnership with his American cousin SAM CLAY. Together they enjoy fame and fortune in the golden era of American comics, but the always rather unworldly and melancholic Kavalier is haunted by the thought of his family in Europe suffering under Nazi persecution and he

is obsessed by the idea of aiding their escape to the USA.

Kear, Alroy
Cakes and Ale, 1930
W Somerset Maugham

A young artist on the make, who stands in the shadow of the great EDWARD DRIFFIELD. Just as Driffield is modelled on Hardy, Kear is unmistakably a version of Hugh Walpole; despite Maugham's dogged denials (which he sustained until Walpole's death), the original had no difficulty identifying himself.

Keating, Anthony
The Ice Age, 1977
Margaret Drabble

'A huge icy fist, with large cold fingers, was squeezing and chilling the people of Britain'. Written when it appeared inevitable that Britain would undergo a profound political shift to the right, *The Ice Age* shows a representative group of people engulfed in metaphorical ice. Anthony Keating, the son of a clergyman who became a television journalist, finds himself underemployed, bored and, angered by the general acceptance of mediocrity and low expectation, 'ripe for conversion, to some creed'. Swept along by the prospect of financial good times, he becomes a property speculator and 'at one with the spirit of the age', only to find himself tempest-tossed and marooned.

Keefer, Tom
The Caine Mutiny, 1951
Herman Wouk

An aspiring writer, he is a communications officer, whose articulate criticisms of CAPTAIN QUEEG steer LT STEVE MARYK towards the conclusion that the captain is unfit to hold command. Keefer is urbane and observant, but fundamentally self-interested, and he is forced to question himself at the deepest levels, both by the uncompromising condemnation of defence lawyer BARNEY GREENWALD and by his own failure of nerve under fire. An influential catalyst, he stands aloof from the explosive situation his observations have precipitated.

Keegan, Peter
John Bull's Other Island, 1904
George Bernard Shaw

White-haired but looking younger than his 50 years, Keegan is a solitary and self-sufficient former Irish priest. He loves the land, speaks to grasshoppers, is believed by some people in Roscullen to be mad and is persecuted by FATHER DEMPSEY, his successor. Yet the visionary Keegan anticipates the day when a country might live by the quality of its people rather than its material wealth, which he denounces TOM BROADBENT, the man of action, and LARRY DOYLE, the intellectual, for exploiting. Keegan represents dreams and mysteries and forms part of a conflicting trinity of dramatic forces.

Keeldar, Shirley
Shirley, 1849
Charlotte Brontë

A young heiress, and a 'brilliant, happy, youthful

creature', Shirley is blessed with most gifts that can be bestowed on a woman; she has wealth, beauty, intelligence and considerable charm. She has an acute sense of her own worth, without being arrogant, is fully aware of the advantages life has given her, and is determined to use them not just to profit herself, but to help others also. She is a spirited and independent woman who values her own freedom far above the conventions of society.

Keepe, Hunter
The Flight from the Enchanter, 1956
Iris Murdoch

ROSA KEEPE's younger brother. He edits the moribund *Artemis*, a women's rights magazine owned by his sister and a 'lot of old women'. With his long blond hair, smooth face and self-deprecating smile he is seen by some as a 'pretty boy'. Gentle and basically kind, but weak, he is both fascinated and frightened by MISCHA FOX, who wants to buy *Artemis*. To this end Hunter is blackmailed by CALVIN BLICK with compromising photographs of Rosa with JAN LUSIEWICZ and STEFAN LUSIEWICZ. Terrified by all the predatory men in his sister's life, Hunter does his ineffectual best to protect her.

Keepe, Rosa
The Flight from the Enchanter, 1956
Iris Murdoch

Named after the revolutionary Rosa Luxemburg by her Fabian mother, Rosa is robust and generous, darkly attractive and 'of a certain age'. Working as a history teacher then a journalist has disillusioned her, and in a final self-critical attempt to keep in touch with 'the People', she takes a job as a factory hand. She becomes sexually involved with the strange Polish immigrants, JAN LUSIEWICZ and STEFAN LUSIEWICZ, and when MISCHA FOX re-enters her life, helplessly succumbs to his deadly enchantment.

Kehaar
Watership Down, 1972
Richard Adams

A black-headed gull, rescued by the rabbits, who proves to be an invaluable ally, acting both as look-out and secret battle weapon. A gregarious, aggressive creature, he is soon befriended by BIGWIG, who relishes his tales of life on the 'Big Water'. His voice is harsh and raucous, his strange, distorted language not always easily understood by the rabbits. Despite his strong instincts to return to 'Peeg Vater' he remains loyal. He can be curt and condescending to those rabbits whom he perceives as 'land-lubbers', but he is indispensable for his detailed knowledge of the ways of men.

Keith, Willie
The Caine Mutiny, 1951
Herman Wouk

Privileged, dominated by his mother and easily influenced by the views of others, Lieutenant Keith matures through the experience of war and the nightmare of CAPTAIN QUEEG's command of the minesweeper *Caine*. Fundamentally well-meaning, he has to search his soul to find who he

is and what he values, and discovers that the love he has for MAY WYNN overrides all other considerations. His courage under fire and his capacity to command emerge in the crisis of war.

Keller, Joe
All My Sons, 1947
Arthur Miller

A 'heavy man of stolid mind and build', who has made a successful business from nothing, in the process sending his partner to jail for a ghastly crime which he himself committed. Aged 60, Keller loves his wife and children, and has a superficial respect for his neighbours, but his eventual suicide is a fitting end for one who has come to recognize the terrible consequences of his own profiteering.

Kellerman, Leo
In Search of Love and Beauty, 1983
Ruth Prawer Jhabvala

A German Jew living in New York, in whom the search for 'love and beauty' seems to have been perverted into something altogether darkly physical and power-obsessed, reflecting not just the evil presences left behind in 1930s Europe but the contradictions of the Jews' main country of refuge.

Kelly, Mick
The Heart is a Lonely Hunter, 1940
Carson McCullers

An independent and fearless young girl who, on the threshold between childhood and adulthood, is consumed with excitement about the future. She scorns the 'primping' of her older sisters, and her thoughts are occupied with inventions, adventures and, above all, music; music is the constant presence in the 'inner room' of her private thoughts and the possession of a piano is her most precious desire. However, the premature intervention of adult responsibilities gradually suffocates the unique freedom of her youth.

Kelly, Ned
Ned Kelly, 1942
Douglas Stewart

Heroic defendant of freedom, Ned Kelly, mythic Australian bushranger, is 'One man against all the world in the bush at Glenrowan'. The bush is Kelly country – an Australia that 'burns in the mind' – and the Irish convict in Kelly would burn his name, his blood and his fire into the heart of Australian complacency and small-mindedness: 'I've struck a few sparks already from this rock of a country;/Before I'm done, it'll blaze.'

Kelway, Robert
The Heat of the Day, 1949
Elizabeth Bowen

The lover of STELLA RODNEY, exposed as a spy by the shadowy HARRISON. He is rather unformed and carries a sufficient freight of ambiguity to make the charge of treasonous behaviour stick.

Kemp, John
Jill, 1946
Philip Larkin

'An undersized boy' from a working-class

background in the Lancashire town of Huddlesford, John Kemp becomes the protégé of his English teacher Joseph Crouch. He wins a scholarship to Oxford, where he shares rooms with Christopher Warner, a public-school socialite. Feeling lonely and inadequate, he invents the diary of Jill, 'a hallucination of innocence'. He is jolted by an air-raid on Huddlesford and by the eager working-class diligence of his friend Whitbread. Catching sight of 'Jill' in a bookshop, he is captivated. He eventually kisses her drunkenly at a party, is thrown into a fountain and causes his parents to pay a premature, anxious visit to Oxford when he contracts pneumonia.

Kenge, Mr
Bleak House, 1853
Charles Dickens
A partner in the firm of Kenge and Carboy, Solicitors, which acts for JOHN JARNDYCE, and to which RICHARD CARSTONE is articled. Because he 'appeared to enjoy beyond everything the sound of his own voice', he is known as Conversation Kenge.

Kenn
Highland River, 1937
Neil Gunn
Young Kenn is growing up in a small community in the Highlands, surrounded by friends and family. Despite the harsh way of life he feels safe and well-integrated, and sees life very much through shared experiences as he gradually explores further up river and into the hills surrounding his home. For him, the river of his childhood remains the source of the community and life. It is only when he looks back on his youth after leaving the community and surviving the Great War that he interprets his childhood very differently.

Kenn, Dr
The Mill on the Floss, 1860
George Eliot
A minor character, Dr Kenn is the kind, middle-aged parish priest in St Ogg's who befriends MAGGIE TULLIVER when she is ostracized by the rest of the townsfolk after her perceived 'elopement' with STEPHEN GUEST. Generous, charitable and recently widowed, he employs Maggie as governess to his now motherless children, but is forced to let her go when his name, and therefore his respectability as a clergyman, is slandered by his narrow-minded congregation.

Kennaston, Felix
The Cream of the Jest, 1917, revised edition 1920
James Branch Cabell
A writer who, by means of a strange runic talisman, is able to travel into the world of dreams. There he pursues a fleeting image of his erotic ideal, only to discover that she is in fact his wife.

Kennedy, Laura, née **Standish**
Phineas Finn, The Irish Member, 1869
Phineas Redux, 1874
Anthony Trollope
The daughter of the Earl of Brentford, and sister

of LORD OSWALD STANDISH CHILTERN. She is tall, with striking red hair and a noble bearing. She seems 'to despise that soft quiescence of her sex in which are generally found so many charms'. She loves PHINEAS FINN, but marries ROBERT KENNEDY for his fortune. After her husband's death, her love for Finn is rekindled, but her desperate hope that they will marry is extinguished when he chooses another, and she retires into the life of an embittered recluse.

Kennedy, Robert
Phineas Finn, The Irish Member, 1869
Phineas Redux, 1874
Anthony Trollope
A Member of Parliament for several Scottish boroughs, whom Lady Standish (LAURA KENNEDY) marries for his fortune, which he has inherited from his father's business, but is 'mistaken enough to suppose he had made himself'. He is a dry, dull, sanctimonious man who says very little to anyone and does nothing very much, his behaviour eventually driving his wife away. He blames PHINEAS FINN for her defection, tries to shoot him, and is afterwards removed to his Scottish estate, where he dies insane.

Kenneth, Sir, properly **David, Earl of Huntingdon, Prince Royal of Scotland**
The Talisman: A Tale of the Crusaders, 1825
Sir Walter Scott
A powerful and courageous young Knight of the Leopard, he is Scott's most complete and unswerving portrayal of the chivalric ideal. It is Kenneth who is inflamed by EDITH PLANTAGENET's beauty during her sojourn with the nuns at Engaddi, and it is he who pursues the magical banner through deserts which seem more convincing settings for his scarcely human heroism than aristocratic courts or halls.

Kennicott, Carol, née **Milford**
Main Street, 1920
Sinclair Lewis
A representative figure of the postwar American 'flight from the village', she despairs of bringing a touch of culture to Gopher Prairie in Minnesota, her husband's home, and absconds to Washington with the appealingly open-minded Erik Valborg. She is also an example of the saying that you can take the girl out of the small town, but not the small town out of the girl. Her sophistication is largely superficial and Gopher Prairie is revealed to be her ideal milieu.

Kennicott, Dr Will
Main Street, 1920
Sinclair Lewis
CAROL KENNICOTT's physician husband, he is the epitome of solid, pipe-smoking mid-west virtues. Obtuse and slightly plodding, he is by no means the partner of Carol's rather grandiose dreams, but his patience and essential kindliness win her back when she finally awakes from her dream of a broader and more exciting existence.

Kent, Earl of
King Lear, c.1607
William Shakespeare
A trustworthy follower of KING LEAR, Kent is a

vivid example of faithfulness and loyalty. He risks his position and good standing with the king in an attempt to point out to him the folly of his ways and to save him from eventual suffering. When he is banished from the kingdom, he disguises himself and continues to serve Lear to the best of his abilities despite danger to himself and the unlikelihood of any reward.

Kenwigs, Mr and Mrs
Nicholas Nickleby, 1839
Charles Dickens

Kenwigs is 'a turner in ivory', and the couple and their five children are fellow lodgers in the same house as NEWMAN NOGGS. They have pretensions to gentility because Mrs Kenwigs' uncle, MR LILLYVICK, is a collector of the water rate and their eldest daughters attend dancing classes twice a week. Noggs introduces them to NICHOLAS NICKLEBY, who teaches the girls French.

Kenyon
The Marble Faun, 1860
Nathaniel Hawthorne

An American sculptor resident in Rome. He has a 'quick sensibility' but may ultimately be, as MIRIAM finds him, no warmer than the idealized marble figures he carves.

Kepesh, David
The Breast, 1972
The Professor of Desire, 1977
The Dying Animal, 2001
Philip Roth

An academic and cultural commentator, preoccupied by his Jewishness and what it means to be a Jew in contemporary America, Kepesh is also enslaved by sexual desire. He lusts especially for female breasts, and indeed in *The Breast* he turns into one, only to discover that friends and lovers see him no longer as who but as what he is, valuing and judging him accordingly. Restored to human form in *The Professor of Desire*, Kepesh contemplates whether sexual desire necessarily results in happiness and concludes not. By the time of *The Dying Animal*, he is 70, has no ties and lives as he pleases. The object of his tumultuous sexual desires is now Consuela Castillo, an obliging student almost two-thirds his age. Naturally, Kepesh targets her monumental breasts, yet when Consuela is diagnosed as suffering from breast cancer, the self-absorbed, feckless Kepesh must choose between the guilt of freedom or the responsibility and possible tragedy of attachment.

Kestrel
Tourmaline, 1963
Randolph Stow

The rapacious hotelier of Tourmaline, whose ability to quench the spiritual as well as physical thirst of the drought-ridden wasteland is contrasted with that of MICHAEL RANDOM, the supposed water-diviner.

Kettledrummle, Rev Gabriel
Old Mortality, in *Tales of My Landlord*, 1816
Sir Walter Scott

A non-conformist clergyman, who shares the captivity of HENRY MORTON. Though a firebrand in the pulpit, when the enemy is far off and abstract, he shows poor stomach for the actual fray. 'The Reverend Gabriel was advanced in years, somewhat corpulent, with a loud voice, a square face, and a set of stupid and unanimated features, in which the body seemed more to predominate over the spirit than was seemly in a sound divine.'

Kew, Lady
The Newcomes, 1853–5
W M Thackeray

SIR BRIAN NEWCOME's mother-in-law and ETHEL and BARNES NEWCOME's grandmother, she is a cynical plotter who regards human happiness as a dispensable luxury when in the pursuit of successful matches. Jaded with London, she prefers to live in the clearer air of Brighton. She is considered by JACK BELSIZE to be 'an old dear, and the wickedest old woman in all England'; few disagree with the latter part of his assessment.

Kew, Lord
The Newcomes, 1853–5
W M Thackeray

ETHEL NEWCOME's cousin and suitor, he is a kindly but somewhat irresponsible young hedonist, whose resolutely indiscreet behaviour is the secret delight of old LADY KEW. His relationship with Ethel is abruptly terminated when he is killed in a duel.

Kezia
Prelude, 1920
Katherine Mansfield

A relatively solitary child, the sister of LOTTIE, and the youngest in a large exuberant family. Vivid details of her physical surroundings – the rented houses, night-time travel, the garden – are noticed by her fresh young mind. A natural explorer, 'Kezia could not open her eyes wide enough', she isolates small experiences so they become significant. Although aware of her fears and feeling horrors acutely, she dares to touch adult life as closely as possible.

Kihika
A Grain of Wheat, 1967
Ngugi waThiong'o

A revolutionary activist who becomes a martyr to the cause of Kenyan independence, and is executed by the British. He is arrogant and absolutist, and his unwillingness to compromise eventually leads to his betrayal by a former comrade. To some extent he serves as a mirror for the other characters.

Kildare, Darcy Dancer
The Destinies of Darcy Dancer, Gentleman, 1977
J P Donleavy

An Anglo-Irish aristocrat, fallen on hard times, who overturns all convention with his unorthodox approach to life and his rumbustious enthusiasm for fulfilling, in every way, his massive appetite for pleasure. He searches through a whole menu of women for one who will give him the true love he once found in the servant girl Leila, and is only saved from despair, and personal disintegration, by her return to him from a past he thought was forever lost.

Killigrew, Col
'Dr. Heidegger's Experiment', 1837, in *Twice-Told Tales*, 1837, revised edition 1842
Nathaniel Hawthorne

A white-bearded gentleman, 'who had wasted his best years, and his health and substance, in the pursuit of sinful pleasures', one of which was the WIDOW WYCHERLEY. With her and two other elderly friends, he is invited to drink of DR HEIDEGGER's Fountain of Youth.

Kinbote, Charles
Pale Fire, 1962
Vladimir Nabokov

'A remarkably disagreeable person', the crass and insensitive commentator on JOHN SHADE's posthumous poem seems to display the worst aspects of literary criticism. Convinced of his intimate relationship with Shade and resultant special insights, he perversely reads into the poem his own obsession with his native country, made to parallel Shade's lines. When a Zemblan assassin murders Shade with a bullet aimed at Kinbote, it is revealed that the latter is the exiled King Charles Xavier, whose life has been reduced to these footnotes.

King, Anna
Only Children, 1979
Alison Lurie

A spinster in her fifties, Anna King has all the qualities of a good teacher. She is a good listener, a clear thinker and she cares about her charges. Children trust her more than they do other grown-ups. She is practical, energetic, fun-loving and wise enough to see people as they are and not as they pretend to be. Although dedicated to her career, Anna has known real passion, but remains suspicious of a love which makes demands on every area of life, requiring the kind of sacrifices she is not prepared to make.

King, Julius
A Fairly Honourable Defeat, 1970
Iris Murdoch

A brilliant and distinguished biochemist who has given up research into biological warfare for humanitarian reasons, or so his friends believe. In fact Julius sees the human race as 'a loathsome crew' who 'don't deserve to survive'. Apparently 'all soul', 'straightforward – but sort of simple and very truthful' and 'morally attractive', Julius's real character is revealed in the cruel hoax he designs to demonstrate his contentions about human nature. His inhuman attitude may be partly explained by his past.

King, Nan → Astley, Nancy

King of England, the
The Shoemaker's Holiday, 1599
Thomas Dekker

As a soldier king, Dekker's model may well have been intended as a portrait of HENRY V. Certainly he seems to have several similar characteristics: a bluff, no-nonsense, patrician approach to

government but perhaps a susceptibility to a slightly begrudging sentimentality as well, especially when dashing noblemen, such as ROWLAND LACY, and pretty women, such as ROSE OTLEY, are involved.

Kingshaw, Charles
I'm the King of the Castle, 1970
Susan Hill

Charles is a boy destined to be controlled, rather than to control others. He is emotionally weak and not academically able, though far from stupid. An introspective child, he maturely faces up to his own personality, and is capable of enduring much, accepting suffering and anguish as though he deserves it. Intrinsically kind, he likes animals, and is sweet to EDMUND HOOPER during a storm, despite recognizing that the power balance will soon be reversed. Charles has experienced a childhood completely devoid of affection and direct attention. With a pessimistic and basically melancholic nature, he can see no way of escape from Edmund and his ultimate act of self-sacrifice is his suicide, a natural progression from his lonely, painful prison.

Kinraid, Charley
Sylvia's Lovers, 1863
Elizabeth Gaskell

He is self-made and opportunistic, in dramatic contrast to PHILIP HEPBURN. He steals SYLVIA ROBSON's heart, and achieves wealth and status, but remains lacking in self-knowledge and a sense of what is fundamental in life.

Kipps, Arthur
Kipps, 1904
H G Wells

A lowly assistant in a miserable draper's shop, Kipps finds his life transformed by a sizable inheritance. He looks for help from his former teacher Helen and a snob named Chester Coote, explaining 'I want to get with educated people who know 'ow to do things – in the regular proper way'. Despite or because of the consequent tuition about books, speaking and table-manners, Kipps never fits in with middle-class values and is happiest in the company of the working-class girl-next-door, Ann Pornick.

Kipps, Arthur
The Woman in Black: A Ghost Story, 1983
Susan Hill

A keen lawyer, he is a trusting, fresh young man, slightly bland in character, without much to set him apart from the crowd. Very eager to please – both his boss, and his fiancée – he has an eye for detail, and likes everything to be just so. He is not well-equipped to cope with events which are out of the ordinary, and it is only years after his agonizing encounter with 'the Woman in Black' that he is able to re-tell the story of how his wife and baby died. However, there is a sense in which he was very receptive to the ghostly goings-on, and he is portrayed as deceptively detached.

Kirk, Dr Howard
The History Man, 1975
Malcolm Bradbury

A lecturer in sociology at Watermouth University

in the year 1972, he is a product of the huge expansion of higher education of the previous decade. From humble northern beginnings, he has risen to become both idolized (by students and many women) and feared (by university authorities especially). He is brilliantly clever, radical and sexually promiscuous, a savagely incisive Marxist analyst. A 'citizen of the present', he embodies the 1970s: everything seems possible, everything is there for the taking for those sharp enough, hungry enough and nasty enough.

Kirkpatrick, Cynthia
Wives and Daughters, 1866
Elizabeth Gaskell

A fatherless child, whose mother certainly does not compensate emotionally for this loss in Cynthia's life. She is sent away to school, not even being allowed to return for holidays. When she eventually returns she proves to be astute, seeing through her mother's deviousness, and has a spirit of independence and a sparkle in her eye. With a strong conscience and an attractive personality, she outshines the novel's heroine, MOLLY GIBSON, in terms of strength of character.

Kirkpatrick, Mrs
Wives and Daughters, 1866
Elizabeth Gaskell

A cold and distant mother to OSBORNE, ROGER and CYNTHIA KIRKPATRICK, she is interested in her own well-being and little else. She is secretive and devious, turning on the charm when required, and although vulnerable in many ways, she is essentially a tiresome woman.

Kirkpatrick, Osborne
Wives and Daughters, 1866
Elizabeth Gaskell

He did well at school and fancies himself as a poet. But he is spoilt by his doting mother and does not have the moral conviction to succeed at Cambridge. A romantic, 'full of taste', he is nonetheless a rather unattractive man.

Kirkpatrick, Roger
Wives and Daughters, 1866
Elizabeth Gaskell

'A good steady fellow', he is scientific and logical, and has been likened to the English naturalist Charles Darwin in character. Roger is less dramatic than his brother, OSBORNE KIRKPATRICK, but actually achieves much more. He is shrewd, thoroughly wholesome and dependable, and very sensible – but dull.

Kirkrapine
The Faerie Queene, 1590–6
Sir Edmund Spenser

Kirkrapine is associated with church robbery, which represents both physical theft and spiritual abuses. He is a scurrilous thief who steals from the church and the poor boxes to feed his own desire for wealth. To him nothing is sacred. He also indulges in fornication with his whore ABESSA, whom he pays with his stolen trophies.

Kiro
Narrow Road to the Deep North, 1968
Edward Bond

The play is set in Japan sometime in the 17th, 18th or 19th centuries. Kiro is a gentle young priest, much given to reflection, equally eager to learn and to follow the path of his God. Yet he is also impressionable and his faith is stained by despair; so much so that he finally commits suicide. This, Bond suggests, is an appalling moral defeat.

Kirsteen
Kirsteen, 1890
Margaret Oliphant

Kirsteen's family, the Drumcarron Douglases, are proud but impoverished – their mother querulous and their father a brute. Red-headed Kirsteen scorns to marry for security and runs away to a mantua-maker's in London, where her skill earns her a partnership. Well-to-do, she does much for her family but gains small thanks; she has disgraced them by working and is a woman without a husband.

Kite, Sgt
The Recruiting Officer, 1706
George Farquhar

Realizing that, because of his low social standing, there is no chance of his rising to a higher position in the army, Sergeant Kite is prepared to use his wiles to gain as much as he can for himself. Adept at conning gullible country bumpkins into accepting the queen's money, he uses the disguise of 'Doctor Copernicus', the fortune-teller, to catch unwary tradesmen in the recruiting net. Nevertheless, he is an amiable figure, working relentlessly to help his captain WORTHY with his efforts to win MELINDA, and commenting sardonically on situations as he sees them.

Kitely
Every Man in his Humour, 1598
Ben Jonson

A rich merchant, Kitely is convinced that young gallants are plotting to seduce his wife and her younger sister. His foolishness (or 'humour') is his extreme gullibility. When the men whom he suspects accuse him of being jealous, he becomes almost insanely so and even more resolute in his suspicions. Misunderstanding follows misunderstanding until Kitely and his wife are eventually reconciled. His admission that he has learned the perils of jealousy shows that he is not without good grace.

Klebb, Rosa
From Russia With Love, 1957
Ian Fleming

Colonel in the Soviet terror network SMERSH and head of Otdyel II, the department of torture and death. Brutal, lesbian and disconcertingly coquettish, she wears shoes with poisoned spikes in the toes, one of which apparently kills JAMES BOND at the end of the first '007' story. She is a disappointingly negative feminist role model.

Klein, Honor
A Severed Head, 1961
Iris Murdoch

An American anthropologist and Cambridge don, the daughter of a German Jew. Her intellectual strength inspires nervousness in others, and her stocky build, heavy dour face, formidably stern mouth and narrow dark eyes at first rather repel MARTIN LYNCH-GIBBON, who sees her as a typically Germanic middle-aged spinster. But like the severed head believed by primitive tribes to be oracular, she becomes 'a terrible object of fascination' for Martin, partly because of her incestuous affair with her half-brother, Palmer Anderson.

Klesmer
Daniel Deronda, 1876
George Eliot

A first-rate musician and the happy combination of German, Slav and Semite, Klesmer is in demand at the best upper-middle-class English households. He shows honesty in telling GWENDOLEN HARLETH that she produces notes badly (though she has some acting talent) but encourages DANIEL DERONDA's protégée MIRAH LAPIDOTH whose voice, though not powerful, is superb for a drawing-room. Initially inhibited by social position from telling his rich pupil Catherine Arrowpoint his feelings for her, he later risks his job to marry her.

Klugman, Neil
Goodbye, Columbus, 1959
Philip Roth

A lower middle-class Jewish boy from Newark, who works in a library. He has a summer love affair with BRENDA PATIMKIN, a rich Jewish girl from a smart suburban neighbourhood. He poses as a detached observer, and affects a scornful disdain for her family's wealth, but at the same time is fascinated and seduced by it. The confusion of this ambivalent attraction and resentment extends to Brenda herself, and he is both aggressive and compliant towards her.

Knapp, John
Falling in Place, 1980
Ann Beattie

He is the head (nominally) of a family that seems determined to destroy itself, thereby reflecting his own failure to communicate either his love or his antagonisms and anxieties to them. Only when the disintegration becomes violently real do they begin to understand the true nature of their relationships.

Knarf
Tomorrow and Tomorrow and Tomorrow, 1947 (censored), 1983 (uncensored)
M Barnard Eldershaw

A distinguished writer whose second-millenium socialist country, once 20th-century Australia, is ruled by technocrats selected by lot. At 47, he is prey to doubts and disappointment, and estranged from his wife and son, REN. He is a romantic, fascinated by the lost civilization studied by his friend, ORD, at the archaeological site of Sydney. He sets his latest work there, in the 1920s to 1940s, and writes it in the appropriately 'antique' form of a novel, with HARRY MUNSTER as

its main character: an historical opus within the futuristic one inhabited by Knarf himself.

Knight, Henry
A Pair of Blue Eyes, 1873
Thomas Hardy

A powerful character, he is a man of words. Passionate about writing, he has a strong interest in nature, and is hopelessly idealistic. Inclined to be selfish, he becomes absorbed in his passions in order to remain detached from others.

Knight, Lady
The Tilted Cross, 1961
Hal Porter

The 40-year-old sexually driven Rose Knight despises her impotent husband, a colonial official in Van Diemen's Land (Tasmania), and hates his cousin, ASNETHA SLEEP. She is 'vain, malevolent and beautiful'; when her plan to gain revenge by seducing QUEELY SHEILL fails, she seeks vengeance more directly.

Knight, Lily (Lily Knight McClellan)
Run, River, 1963
Joan Didion

The daughter (and 'princess') of a defeated senator. She is, however, profoundly alienated from her environment, recognizing at her high-society wedding to the farmer EVERETT MCCLELLAN that 'there existed between her and other women a vacuum in which overtures faded out, voices became inaudible, connections broke'. She is obsessed with the courage of the ill-fated pioneer Donner-Reed party (which culminated in cannibalism) and neurotically divided between her search for a lost world and her passion for the parvenu RYDER CHANNING.

Knight, Sebastian
The Real Life of Sebastian Knight, 1941
Vladimir Nabokov

The dead Russian novelist son of an English mother, sought by his half-brother, who is attempting to write his correct biography. Glimpsed in the lives of his university tutor, his wife and other companions, Sebastian Knight is most present in his own writing. Trails over Europe are lost or mistaken, following a dense pattern of coincidence.

Knight, the
The Canterbury Tales, c.1387–1400
Geoffrey Chaucer

A 'verray, parfit, gentil knight', still clad in the stained clothes of his campaigning, and apparently a paragon of chivalric virtue. But the list of campaigns he has taken part in shows him to have been involved in some particularly bloody massacres. Generally regarded as an ideal figure against which to judge the other pilgrims, he is perhaps really one who has very humanly fallen short of his high ideals. His tale, as might be expected, is one of courtly love and chivalric pursuits.

Knight, Walter
Run, River, 1963
Joan Didion

LILY KNIGHT's father, he is a failed Southern

senator, living out his retirement in a grotesque parody of ante-bellum chivalry in an affair with Miss Rita Blanchard. He considers Lily to be an untouchable 'princess', but is unable to protect her from a wounding and hurtful world.

Knight of Avenel → Glendinning, Sir Halbert

Knightley, Mr
Emma, 1816
Jane Austen
The cornerstone of Highbury society and an upstanding figure of reliable mind and acute perception, he is a man of well-chosen words and hand-picked friends, whose emotions are kept in check by a firm rationale. As both a long-standing friend of the Woodhouse family and EMMA WOODHOUSE's brother-in-law, he is one of the few people able to perceive – and willing to criticize – her faults. Caught unawares by his love for her, the one spontaneous thing he does is to propose.

Knowell, senior
Every Man in his Humour, 1598
Ben Jonson
Knowell, senior is the father of Edward, a young gallant who accompanies his friend WELLBRED to London to mock CAPTAIN BOBADILL, MATTHEW and STEPHEN for their pretentiousness and foolishness. Knowell, a serious and orderly man, despairs of this and criticizes the way modern parents bring up their children (despite the fact that he too had an ill-spent youth). Yet, although he is disillusioned, he is far from foolish. He sees the good in people, especially his son, who returns not only with an extremely agreeable wife but intent on discussing poetry with his father.

Knox, Dr Robert
The Anatomist, 1930
James Bridie
Based on the 19th-century Scottish anatomy lecturer, Dr Robert Knox, endowed with eye-patch and a mistaken belief in his aptitude for the flute, becomes here a humorously larger-than-life figure. Conceited and contentious, he refuses to let human emotions interfere in his pioneering scientific work, even when it causes bitter argument between his friends. Not above making himself as well as them an object of his disparaging wit, he nonetheless defends with a new air of seriousness his right to be judged by his Maker and not 'the mob' when his name is finally linked with murderous body-snatchers, Burke and Hare.

Kochamma, Esthappen (Estha)
The God of Small Things, 1997
Arundhati Roy
'Estha occupied very little space in the world'. The twin brother of RAHEL KOCHAMMA, he is sent back to his estranged father after his mother's affair, and never sees his mother again. Deeply troubled by his part in the death in police custody of his mother's lover, he stops speaking, distracting himself with housework and constant walking. It is only his reunion with his sister 23 years after their separation that brings him a sudden new sense of life.

Kochamma, Rahel
The God of Small Things, 1997
Arundhati Roy
Rahel returns from a life of drifting to Ayumenem, India, when she hears of the return of her twin brother ESTHAPPEN KOCHAMMA. What should have been a comfortable middle-class childhood there was made tragic by the deaths of their cousin Sophie, their disgraced mother, and their 'untouchable' friend Velutha, with whom their mother was having an affair. Beautiful, introverted and troubled by grief and guilt, she finds emotional, then sexual, solace in her brother.

Kola
The Interpreters, 1965
Wole Soyinka
Where his friends want to modernize, legislate, write about or recapture the primitive energies of an older Nigeria, he is content to record it in endless sketchbooks, an obsession that sets him at one remove from the surrounding bustle.

Kongi
Kongi's Harvest, 1965
Wole Soyinka
President of Isma and the Spirit of Harvest, he regards meditation and passivity as the chief prerogatives and functions of his rule, rendering his ultimate harvest a highly uncertain one.

Koomson, Joseph
The Beautyful Ones Are Not Yet Born, 1970
Ayi Kwei Armah
The Honourable Joseph Koomson is an emergent politician in a newly independent African state. Fraudulent and ebullient, his sole qualifications are political sycophancy and the ability to mouth a few socialist phrases. As a minister in a government touting the latest fashion in political parlance, African Socialism is Koomson's pet topic. Even his proverbial flabby soft hands are described as 'idealogical hands' and the ironic understatement that belies the hands is further encapsulated by the story's lonely hero, THE MAN: 'should these hands not have become tougher than they were when their owner was hauling loads along the wharf?'

Korpenning, Bud
Manhattan Transfer, 1925
John Dos Passos
A rustic-looking boy from an upstate farm, Bud Korpenning optimistically comes to New York in search of employment. Having been beaten as a child, he has killed a man and subsequently suffers from a persecution mania that never allows him to settle. Always looking for the illusory 'centre of things' where he hopes to lose himself in the crowd, he flits restlessly from job to flophouse until finally, cowed and starving, he commits suicide by throwing himself off Brooklyn Bridge.

'Kosmonopolis, the Princess'
Sweet Bird of Youth, 1959
Tennessee Williams
The adopted name of Alexandra Del Lago, a Hollywood movie star who has fled to

anonymity following the première of her 'comeback' film which she erroneously believes has failed. Apparently vulnerable and dependent – on drink, drugs and the company of attractive young men – she is actually as she describes herself, a 'monster' who finally deserts CHANCE WAYNE when she realizes that her career can, in fact, successfully continue.

Kowalski, Stanley
A Streetcar Named Desire, 1947
Tennessee Williams

This 'gaudy seed-bearer' is the new American, a man of Polish stock who proclaims himself '100% American, born and raised in the greatest country on Earth'. Though poorly educated, his physicality and cunning make him more than a match for his sister-in-law, BLANCHE DUBOIS, whose sham 'reputation' and precarious mental state he systematically destroys, culminating in her rape while his wife, STELLA KOWALSKI, is giving birth in hospital.

Kowalski, Stella
A Streetcar Named Desire, 1947
Tennessee Williams

Younger sister to BLANCHE DUBOIS and persistently dominated by her, she has fled the home of her youth – 'Belle Reve' – to the very different world of New Orleans and the aggressive sexuality and further dominance of her husband, STANLEY KOWALSKI. Despite admitting that the 'Kowalskis and the DuBois have different notions', she never escapes from her deep physical desire for Stanley, and eventually commits her sister to a lunatic asylum after she has been raped by him. To a latter-day audience, her willingness to accept her brutish husband's world-view may make her culpable for the play's tragedy.

Krafft, Heinz
Maurice Guest, 1908
Henry Handel Richardson

An enigmatic, almost Mephistophelean figure, he moves among his fellow students at Leipzig according to motives of his own. Though he has a mistress, AVERY HILL, her masculine name gives away something of his own sexual ambiguity and it is possible that he is also involved with both LOUISE DUFRAYER and SCHILSKY.

Kramer, Larry
The Bonfire of the Vanities, 1987
Tom Wolfe

A struggling district attorney in the Bronx district of New York. He is Jewish, which makes him 'a rare thing' in the Homicide Bureau, and is rather pompous and vain about his unprepossessing physique. He dreams of escaping his present dull marriage and poverty. The SHERMAN MCCOY case, and his affair with a young juror, bring success and conquest within his grasp, but he lacks judgement, and deludes himself about his motives in pressing the case.

Krapp
Krapp's Last Tape, 1958
Samuel Beckett

Nostalgia is a consistent factor of Beckett's characters, but in Krapp it is the key theme. Now aged 69, Krapp listens to his voice as recorded at the age of 39, recalling his past follies and conquests (in particular a young lady in a punt) with disdain and delight. Between tapes, Krapp shuffles around the sparse stage, clowning with a banana or disappearing to find another drink. Having Krapp simultaneously present at both ages remains one of Beckett's masterstrokes.

Kravitz, Duddy
The Apprenticeship of Duddy Kravitz, 1959
Mordecai Richler

'Duddy Kravitz was a small, narrow-chested boy of fifteen with a thin face.' A determined self-improver, his obsessive ambition is to own land, and he minds very little what he has to do to escape the Montreal ghetto.

Krishna
The English Teacher, 1945
R K Narayan

Essentially a poet, Krishna always feels vaguely discontented in his job teaching English at Malgudi's Albert Mission College. When his adored young wife dies, only his infant daughter saves him from total despair. Through her he meets the eccentric headmaster of a nursery school who helps him to perceive his true vocation. He realizes he can no longer stuff students' heads with Western literary criticism and theories, recognizing that 'a century of wrong education' in India has produced 'cultural morons' – strangers to their own literary heritage and mere camp-followers of another – who provide nothing but efficient clerks for British administration.

Krogh, Erik
England Made Me, 1935
Graham Greene

A self-made, megalomaniac financier, the head of an international company. Never contradicted and constantly deferred to, he inhabits a universe dominated by his name and his fortune. But at its centre is a dull, conservative, rather ordinary man, who is socially gauche and lonely. Despite his haughty manner and cold-blooded treatment of employees, he is fundamentally unhappy, fearful of real human warmth and unable to respond spontaneously: his world is circumscribed by stultifying notions of correctness. Krogh is the ulitmate capitalist careerist, who has buried his miserable past in a pursuit of wealth and success which has only brought more misery.

Kronberg, Thea
The Song of the Lark, 1915
Willa Cather

Brought up in the desert town of Moonstone, she is set apart by the beauty of her singing voice. In her preface, Cather warns against thinking that Thea's voice is of the 'skylark order' as many readers have supposed. In fact, the title comes from an obscure French painting of a peasant girl looking up from her work in the fields to hear the lark's song, an image that applies equally to Thea's situation. In respect of Thea, Cather registers 'the interesting and important fact that, in an artist of the type I chose, personal life becomes paler as the imaginative life becomes richer … The story set out to tell of an artist's awakening and struggle; her floundering escape from a smug, domestic, self-satisfied provincial world of utter ignorance' into the world of opera.

Krook, Mr
Bleak House, 1853
Charles Dickens

The grotesque, illiterate and drunken proprietor of a rag-and-bone shop, he is known as the 'Lord Chancellor'. His tenants are MISS FLITE, CAPTAIN HAWDON and TONY JOBLING. He possesses papers which reveal Hawdon's past relationship with LADY DEDLOCK, but on the night arranged to give them to Jobling and WILLIAM GUPPY, he apparently spontaneously combusts, leaving only 'the cinder of a small, charred log of wood sprinkled with white ashes'. He is revealed to be related to the SMALLWEEDS, who inherit his papers containing documents which resolve the case of *Jarndyce v Jarndyce* and others with which the Smallweeds try to blackmail SIR LEICESTER DEDLOCK.

Kumalo, Absalom → Absalom

Kumalo, Rev Stephen
Cry, the Beloved Country, 1948
Alan Paton

The parish priest of the community of Ndotsheni in the Natal, a dry and impoverished place in the South African interior. He travels to Johannesburg to find his sister GERTRUDE and his son ABSALOM. A black man of quiet and indomitable courage, he helps his white counterpart JAMES JARVIS come to an understanding of their common cause in sweeping away the poisoned conventions of South African life.

Kumar, Hari (Harry Coomer)
The Jewel in the Crown, 1966
The Day of the Scorpion, 1968
The Towers of Silence, 1971
A Division of the Spoils, 1975, forming
The Raj Quartet
Paul Scott

Born into a middle-class orthodox Hindu family, Hari was taken to England at the age of two by his Anglophile father and given an exclusively English upbringing, including a public-school education. Left penniless at 18 when his father commits suicide, he returns to India, an unknown country whose languages he doesn't speak and where he is neither Indian nor English. Alienated and bitter, scraping an income and hating the squalor in which he is forced to live, during the 1942 riots he commits the heinous 'crime' of loving an English girl, DAPHNE MANNERS. She returns his love, but Kumar is victimized by the vengeful RONALD MERRICK.

Kurtz, Mr
Heart of Darkness, 1902
Joseph Conrad

A zealous European ivory agent who has a reputation for running the most efficient and profitable trading station, deep in the heart of the jungle. He is a cultivated, civilized, and perhaps even idealistic man, 'an emissary of pity, and science, and progress, and devil knows what else', but his experiences with the natives in this 'heart of darkness' turn him into something genuinely horrific. He uses his superior intelligence and weapons to subjugate the natives, and becomes a barbaric god to them, but at the cost of a plunge into an awful self-knowledge summed up in his dying words, 'The horror! The horror!'

Kwan, Billy
The Year of Living Dangerously, 1978
C J Koch

A strange, dwarf-like man, half-Australian, half-Chinese. He works in Jakarta as GUY HAMILTON's photographer, but builds up obsessive dossiers on Hamilton and on JILL BRYANT, the woman they both love. Personal relationships seem to have taken the place of his earlier political optimism and it is clear that Hamilton is a projection of Kwan's own desires.

Lace, Tocky → O'Cannon, Tocky

La Creevy, Miss
Nicholas Nickleby, 1839
Charles Dickens
A painter of miniatures and the landlady and loyal friend of the NICKLEBY family in London. A 'mincing young lady of fifty', kind and good-hearted, she eventually marries TIM LINKINWATER.

Lacy, Rowland
The Shoemaker's Holiday, 1599
Thomas Dekker
A young nobleman, Lacy is in love with ROSE OTLEY, whose father, the LORD MAYOR OF LONDON, opposes the match. A dashing, sharp, clever figure, he disguises himself as a Dutch shoemaker, is employed by SIMON EYRE and eventually marries Rose with the approbation of THE KING OF ENGLAND.

Ladislaw, Will
Middlemarch, 1871–2
George Eliot
The young second cousin of REV EDWARD CASAUBON, Will's cheerful, bright disposition is in marked contrast to the humourless sterility of his relation, and his friendship with DOROTHEA BROOKE quickly develops into infatuation. Discarding his artistic pretensions, he develops his political awareness while editor of MR BROOKE's *Pioneer*, and though an object of increasing suspicion in the town on account of his gypsy-like freedom and uncertain origins, he finds in Dorothea a sensitivity and generosity of spirit to complement his own.

Ladvenu, Brother Martin
Saint Joan, 1923
George Bernard Shaw
Ladvenu is a young Dominican monk who attends JOAN's trial for heresy at Rouen. Believing her to be innocent, he sympathetically tries to persuade her that her 'voices' were not from God but the Devil. Realizing that she might be burned as a witch, she agrees to recant and Ladvenu assists her in writing a confession. This, she retracts. After her death, Ladvenu becomes convinced of her saintliness as a martyr, and in the epilogue, informs King Charles (previously THE DAUPHIN) that he has worked for her rehabilitation.

Lady Bountiful
The Beaux' Stratagem, 1707
George Farquhar
A wealthy lady in the town of Litchfield, and mother to DORINDA and Sullen, Lady Bountiful is well-known for her generosity and advice in the curing of ailments. Her cures, of a homeopathic variety, are scorned by her daughter-in-law, MRS SULLEN. Well-meaning, if somewhat naive, she believes the best of everybody, even allowing ARCHER, after his feigned fit, access to her daughter.

Lady from Dubuque, the
The Lady from Dubuque, 1980
Edward Albee
A personification of death, for whom the three warring couples in the play are fearfully waiting. The Lady is also supposed to represent the Everywoman who is presumed no longer to understand Albee's drama and who is therefore also death to the process of dramatic creation and to the play itself.

Lady in Brown, also Lady in Yellow, Lady in Orange, Lady in Red, Lady in Green, Lady in Blue, Lady in Purple
for colored girls who have considered suicide/ when the rainbow is enuf, 1975
Ntozake Shange
The collective voice of black womanhood in the USA, these archetypal presences in Shange's 'choreopoem' speak in turn about the components of the Afro-American experience as it impinges on its mothers, sisters and daughters. The tone is angry but also joyous, proud even in despair, eternally affirmative.

Lady of Branksome, the
The Lay of the Last Minstrel, 1805
Sir Walter Scott
'Of noble race the Lady came;/Her father was a clerk of fame,/Of Bethune's line of Picardie'. Widowed in the Border war, she keeps to a secret bower that is guarded 'by word and by spell', nursing not grief but a deep desire for vengeance.

Laertes
Hamlet, 1601/2
William Shakespeare
POLONIUS's son and the brother of OPHELIA. He is as cynical in his view of the world as his father and automatically assumes that HAMLET's intentions towards OPHELIA are dishonourable. He is grief-stricken at the deaths of his father and sister and, believing Hamlet responsible for both, is easily manipulated by CLAUDIUS into a plot to kill him. However, Laertes finally shows his nobler side,

confessing the truth at the moment of death.

La-Foole, Sir Amorous
Epicoene, or The Silent Woman, 1609
Ben Jonson

Appropriately named, he is a snob and a boastful social climber who falsely claims to have made many sexual conquests, including EPICOENE, unaware that 'she' is really a boy. In an effort to ingratiate himself with society, La-Foole throws several parties, inviting as many guests as he can. He and his great and equally foolish friend, SIR JOHN DAW, are eventually ridiculed by TRUEWIT.

Laforgue, Father Paul
Black Robe, 1985
Brian Moore

A slight, pale, intellectual Jesuit from Rouen, Laforgue eagerly courts a martyr's death in 17th-century 'New France' (Canada), where Quebec is just a fort and a few wooden buildings. 'The Savages' he seeks to convert contemptuously regard the 'Black-robes' as a strange, inferior race of womanless men, obsessed with death and water sorcery (baptism). During a long winter journey through hostile territory, with a tribe of Algonquin, the violent culture-clash inflicts trials on Laforgue that cruelly test his vocation.

Lagadoans
Gulliver's Travels, 1726
Jonathan Swift

A race of frantic researchers, living in Lagado, the main city of the country governed by the LAPUTANS. So much emphasis has been placed on new ideas that the old tried and tested ways have fallen into disrepair, leaving the country in ruins. The city itself is populated with research colleges, which conduct impractical schemes and activities, such as producing sunbeams from cucumbers or converting human excrement to its original foodstuff. The professors, who are dirty, smelly and foolish, beg all those who enter the colleges to give more money for their research.

Laidlaw, Jack
Laidlaw, 1977
The Papers of Tony Veitch, 1983
Strange Loyalties, 1991
William McIlvanney

A streetwise but intellectually troubled detective inspector in the Glasgow police force, with a self-castigating penchant for 'doing penance for being him'. He has a sharply-honed guilt complex, a brooding dissatisfaction with his life, and an ambivalent attitude to his job, which he nonetheless does well. In his desk drawer he keeps books by philosophers like Kierkegaard, Camus and Unamuno, and feels his nature is a 'wrack of paradox'.

Laird, the, also known as **Sandy**, or the **Laird of Cockpen**
Trilby, 1894
George Du Maurier

A friend and admirer of TRILBY, this hirsute Dundonian shares a Paris studio with TAFFY and LITTLE BILLEE, and betrays every symptom of being something of a stage 'Scotchman'.

Lajeunesse, Basil
Evangeline: A Tale of Acadie, 1847
Henry Wadsworth Longfellow

The father of EVANGELINE BELLEFONTAINE's betrothed, GABRIEL LAJEUNESSE, and friend of her father, BENEDICT BELLEFONTAINE, Basil is the village blacksmith in the French-Canadian settlement of Grand-Pré and a respected member of the community. His realistic attitude helps him to prosper as a herdsman in Louisiana after the expulsion of the Acadians from Nova Scotia, although he always maintains his anger at England.

Lajeunesse, Gabriel
Evangeline: A Tale of Acadie, 1847
Henry Wadsworth Longfellow

The betrothed of EVANGELINE BELLEFONTAINE, the two having grown up together. The handsome Gabriel is grief-stricken when he and Evangeline are separated during the expulsion of the Acadians from Nova Scotia. His sadness prevents him from settling in Louisiana, despite the renewed prosperity of his father, BASIL LAJEUNESSE, and he heads into the wilderness, unaware that Evangeline is pursuing him across North America.

Lakota, Kyril
The Shoes of the Fisherman, 1963
Morris West

Twenty years in a Siberian prison camp did not break the spirit of this Roman Catholic priest who is now sent to Rome to promote the cause of the Soviet Union. A man of burning integrity, his unexpected and, to him, unwelcome elevation to the papacy in a time of global crisis requires of him vision and courage. This he demonstrates in the staggering decision to make the considerable wealth of the Church available to the famine-stricken people of the world.

Lakunle
The Lion and the Jewel, 1959
Wole Soyinka

Schoolmaster of Ilujinli, he dresses in the English style, wearing a clean but shabby suit, one size too small, that symbolizes how uncertainly his adopted values fit his actual station.

Lal, Kishori
Rich Like Us, 1983
Nayantara Sahgal

A shop owner and elderly idealist, Kashori Lal might once have become a researcher into Indian history had not the tide of political events in India swept him off in another direction. Although he is an atheist and a member of the Jan Sangh party, he attends religious and other parties' political rallies out of curiosity and sociological interest. This also gives him a feeling of political and intellectual rootedness and influence within a rapidly fluctuating country. He has something of the confidence trickster about him, and a political canniness for survival which makes him at times somewhat economical with the truth. Yet he remains staunchly on the side of individual free speech and independence.

Lal Singh
The Village, 1939
Across the Black Waters, 1940
The Sword and the Sickle, 1942, collectively *The Private Life of an Indian Prince*, 1953
Mulk Raj Anand

A young Sikh in the Punjabi countryside, he turns against his cultural roots by cutting off his hair and rejecting superstition. In the middle volume, his adolescent rebellion is tempered by experience, when he fights alongside the French on the Western Front. Later still, he becomes a revolutionary activist, bringing his resistance to political convention full circle.

Lamancha, Lord
John Macnab, 1925, et seq
John Buchan

A friend of SIR EDWARD LEITHEN, he is the Marquis of Liddesdale's son, a buccaneering MP and cabinet minister with a gift for 'pre-war grandiloquence' and an aura of adventure from before World War I. Despite his 'hidalgo-ish appearance', the title Lamancha 'had no connection with Don Quixote and Spain, but was the name of a shieling in a Border glen'.

Lamb, Mary
Everything You Need, 1999
A L Kennedy

After an unconventional upbringing in the care of her homosexual uncle and his partner, Mary is first introduced as a well-rounded young woman of 19. She leaves her home town on a scholarship arranged by author NATHAN STAPLES to the writers' colony on the island where he lives, unaware that he is the father she believes is dead. Their relationship is at first faltering, but develops into a strong bond of love and friendship. However, Nathan's failure to reveal that he is her father compromises Mary's understanding, and lends her an air of vulnerability.

Lamb, Michael
Lamb, 1980
Bernard MacLaverty

A teacher at an Irish borstal, where he is known as Brother Sebastian, Michael appears quiet and caring, and is able to win the trust of his pupils. An immense craving for love leads him to take one boy, Owen, on a trip away from the harsh environment of the borstal without permission. However, Michael's character has dangerous weaknesses, which result in tragedy, for he has never had the courage to face up to authority or confront his religious doubts, and is unable to deal with long-term responsibility.

Lambert, Gen
The Virginians, 1857–9
W M Thackeray

An impoverished old soldier with whose daughters, THEO and HETTY LAMBERT, the WARRINGTON brothers are entangled. Old, loving and kindly, he is also easily deceived, the result, it is suggested, of living in a household of women while he works in a world of paper battles.

Lambert, Hetty (Hester)
The Virginians, 1857–9
W M Thackeray

GEN LAMBERT's daughter, she is in love with HARRY ESMOND WARRINGTON, but he marries FANNY MOUNTAIN instead. She is sentimental and kind, but lacks something of the imperious glamour of her sister, THEO LAMBERT.

Lambert, Roddy
The Real Charlotte, 1894
E O Somerville and Martin Ross

Roddy is a great man in Lismoyle; his sickly wife brought him money, which he spends freely, and he is land-agent to the Dysarts. He has known FRANCIE FITZPATRICK since she was a child in Dublin; when she comes to stay with CHARLOTTE MULLEN at Tally Ho Lodge, he cannot keep away from her lively pert chatter. Charlotte is an ally in shady transactions, nothing more. When his wife dies, he thinks only of marrying Francie, but events do not go as planned.

Lambert, Theo (Theodosia)
The Virginians, 1857–9
W M Thackeray

The daughter of GEN LAMBERT and sister to HETTY LAMBERT. GEORGE ESMOND WARRINGTON falls in love with her, despite her family's poverty. She passes her time in 'lilliputian needlework', perhaps a symbol of the novel's intricate cross-stitching of lives.

Lambert Family, the
The Corrections, 2001
Jonathan Franzen

Matriarch Enid Lambert's main desire is to reunite her dysfunctional family for one perfect Christmas together. Her husband Alfred, a strict disciplinarian who spent his working life in the ordered environment of the railways, is now slipping into Parkinson's-induced dementia, a fact that Enid, in a permanent state of denial about her family, refuses to accept. Their oldest son, Gary, on the surface a stable banker and family man, is actually trapped in an unhappy marriage, clinically depressed and hiding his excessive drinking from his family. Gary's younger brother, Chip, is also floundering in life, having lost a teaching post after being seduced by a student and now finding himself in Lithuania engaged in fraudulent activities with a politician. Denise, sister of Gary and Chip, escapes a bad marriage only to re-evaluate her sexuality by having an affair with her boss's wife, thus sabotaging her promising career as a chef.

Lammeter, Nancy
Silas Marner, 1861
George Eliot

The object of GODFREY CASS's affections, Nancy refuses him more than once, but eventually accepts. 'Propriety and moderation' are the keynote to her thoughts. Though relatively well-born, she has not read much and mucks in with the making of butter and cheese. The narrator believes she has 'the essential attributes for a lady'. She forgives Godfrey for concealing his first marriage, acknowledging his goodness to her in their own marriage.

Lammle, Alfred
Our Mutual Friend, 1865
Charles Dickens

A friend of MR and MRS VENEERING and a fortune-hunter with 'too much sparkle in his studs, his eyes, his buttons, his talk, and his teeth'. A 'mature young gentleman', he marries a 'mature young lady', Sophronia Akersham, each having been told by the Veneerings that the other is rich. On honeymoon, they learn they have been deceived and set out to prey on their friends. After the failure of their mercenary schemes to arrange a match between FASCINATION FLEDGEBY and Georgiana Podsnap, and to ingratiate themselves with MR and MRS BOFFIN, they are forced to live abroad.

Lamont, Fergus
Fergus Lamont, 1979
Robin Jenkins

Ruthlessly self-reliant and egocentric, he is a latter-day version of James Hogg's 'Justified Sinner' (ROBERT WRINGHIM, THE YOUNGER), a soldier-poet of protean talents and identities, struggling to escape the narrow social and cultural confines of his native Gantock by means of aristocratic fantasies and a bizarre Celtic mysticism.

Lamotte, Annette
The Forsyte Saga, 1922
A Modern Comedy, 1929
John Galsworthy

The second wife of SOAMES FORSYTE and the mother of FLEUR FORSYTE, Annette is French, proud and generally dismissive of the English, whom she thinks cold, hypocritical and selfish. She and Soames are courteous to one another but live independent lives.

LaMotte, Christabel
Possession, 1990
A S Byatt

Although earlier commentators have concentrated on the domesticity and mysticism of this 19th-century poetess, feminists are now claiming her as a model of sturdy independence, who pursued her art in the context of a stable lesbian relationship. However, subsequent literary discoveries, linking her with RANDOLPH HENRY ASH, reveal a woman flattered by his attention, craving his approval as a poet and finally desiring him as a man. The giving of herself so utterly to Ash may disgust the feminists but it is Christabel's unrelenting determination to cope with her situation as she chooses that reveals the steel in her soul which they so admire.

Lampton, Joe
Room at the Top, 1957
Life at the Top, 1962
John Braine

Joe Lampton dominates both novels with his unswerving and aggressive desire for wealth and social recognition. These he puts above everything else. Happiness, he believes, if it

exists at all, comes about through money. He itches to be free of his dull job at the local town hall in a small Yorkshire town, and his ruthless opportunism results in his seduction of and later marriage to the rich young Susan Browne, despite his love for an unhappily married older woman. Success follows quickly, but gives way to disillusion, betrayal and bitterness.

Lanark/Duncan Thaw
Lanark: A Life in Four Books, 1981
Alasdair Gray

It is not altogether clear by what chronological and physical sleight the asthmatic dreamer Thaw, with his realistic working-class background in and around Glasgow, is transformed into the ageless Nietzschean quester Lanark in Unthank, with its dystopian landscape and constant darkness. However, the transformation does take place, and the corresponding characters of Thaw and Lanark are united by the desire for some level of imaginative understanding beyond the everyday.

Lancaster, Kate
Deephaven, 1877
Sarah Orne Jewett

Along with her friend HELEN DENNIS, she spends the summer in a tiny New England fishing port. With an amused tolerance and the most sympathetic irony, she and Helen observe the comings and goings of local worthies.

Lancaster, Nicky
The Vortex, 1924
Noël Coward

Well-groomed, witty and decadent, young Nicky Lancaster arrives home to England after a year in Paris studying the piano. He and his mother, Florence, are bound by a mutual self-deception that they are attractive, fashionable and loved. Nervous, prone to reclusive silences and moments of hysteria, Nicky is clearly unstable. In fact, he is addicted to drugs, and Florence is a nymphomaniac. They are caught in a vortex from which Nicky is the first to break out: 'It doesn't matter about death,' he cries, 'but it matters terribly about life.'

Landau, Nathan
Sophie's Choice, 1979
William Styron

Outwardly Nathan is witty, gifted and utterly attractive, but it becomes clear that SOPHIE ZAWISTOWSKA's lover is prey to deep manic-depressive swings and appalling bouts of unfounded jealousy. The young writer STINGO's innate unwillingness to see the darker side of things is nowhere clearer than in his initial encounters with Nathan.

Landless, Helena and Neville
The Mystery of Edwin Drood, 1870
Charles Dickens

Orphan twins, the children of English parents but born in Ceylon. They are handsome, 'very dark, and very rich in colour' and have 'something untamed about them both'. The wards of MR LUKE HONEYTHUNDER, they come to Cloisterham, where Helena becomes friends with

ROSA BUD at MISS TWINKLETON's school and Neville becomes the pupil of THE REVD SEPTIMUS CRISPARKLE. Neville begins to be attracted to Rosa and resents EDWIN DROOD's offhand manner towards her. When Drood disappears following a violent quarrel with Neville that has been orchestrated by MR JOHN JASPER, Jasper contrives to make Neville the chief suspect of Drood's murder.

Landlord, the
The Bundle, 1978
Edward Bond

An authoritarian, oppressive landlord, he uses the natural power of the river which flows through his land as a threat to keep the peasantry is check. When the river floods, the young WANG is forced to enter the landlord's service in order to buy places for himself and THE FERRYMAN's family in the rescue boat. Eventually the landlord's power is overthrown by Wang's guerilla army.

Landon, Rebecca
The Ballad and the Source, 1944
A Sea-Grape Tree, 1976
Rosamond Lehmann

A romantic girl, Rebecca is engrossed in a world evoked for her at second hand. Bewitched by the baroque SYBIL JARDINE, she enters a realm of intrigue and sexual machinations which she cannot fully comprehend, and has to negotiate both the poetic excess of Sybil's world and the banality of family life. In *A Sea-Grape Tree* Rebecca ceases to be dominated by Sybil's polemics and becomes a participant in life.

Lane, Harry
The Many Coloured Coat, 1960
Morley Callaghan

As a public relations man for a whisky company in Montreal, he enjoys a spectacular professional success. Clad in the 'many-coloured coat' of popularity, he is likened to the biblical Joseph and is virtually unhinged when a speculative business deal goes disastrously wrong, violating his feelings of cheerful invulnerability.

Lane, Molly
Amsterdam, 1998
Ian McEwan

Desirable, sophisticated, talented, a restaurant critic, photographer, 'daring gardener' and a woman with a private life of spectacular incident and diversity, Molly has died at the age of 46 from an unspecified degenerative disease. The novel opens at her funeral, at which her former lovers VERNON HALLIDAY and CLIVE LINLEY mourn their loss. The discovery of, and Halliday's decision to publish, photographs she has taken of Foreign Secretary Julian Garmony dressed in women's clothes, result in both men re-evaluating their principles of honour, loyalty and friendship.

Lane, Philip
'The Basement Room', in *The Basement Room and Other Stories*, 1935
Graham Greene

A young boy, 'between nurses' who is left with BAINES and his wife, MRS BAINES, during a two-week holiday. He idolizes Baines and his improbable stories, but is terrified of his shrewish wife. He witnesses her murder, and is the inadvertent cause of Baines being discovered. He suffers the traumatic effects of this premature exposure to a dark adult world in later life.

Langdon, Alison
Reflections in a Golden Eye, 1941
Carson McCullers

The fragile wife of MAJOR MORRIS LANGDON. Grief-stricken by the death of her baby daughter and neglected by her husband, she continues to suffer from a depression which reduces her to an act of self-mutilation. She finds transient consolation in her love of theatre and classical music but is troubled by a constant sense of imminent disaster.

Langdon, Major Morris
Reflections in a Golden Eye, 1941
Carson McCullers

The lover of LEONORA PENDERTON. His 'blunt, jovial and friendly expression' belies a nature which is both self-deceiving and lacking in sympathy; he chooses to believe that his wife, ALISON LANGDON, is ignorant of his infidelity and feels aversion for her illness and horror for their malformed dead baby. It requires Alison's death to shock him into a belated sense of responsibility.

Langley, Sir Frederick
The Black Dwarf, 1816
Sir Walter Scott

Described by Miss Vere as 'dark, stiff and stately', he is also scheming and ambitious, demanding Miss Vere's hand in marriage with little thought of her feelings or wishes. A conspirator to the last, he dies during the 1715 Jacobite insurrection.

Langmuir, Hamo
As If By Magic, 1973
Angus Wilson

A distinguished agronomist, who has developed a strain of rice which will revolutionize Third World food production, he appears to believe that his sexual hungers can be just as magically satisfied. He represents wrong-headed altruism erected over a shaky foundation of selfishness.

Langton, Alice
The Cardboard Crown, 1952
A Difficult Young Man, 1955
Outbreak of Love, 1957
When Blackbirds Sing, 1962, collectively known as 'the Langton Tetralogy'
Martin Boyd

Beautiful, decorous and romantic by nature, Alice brings wealth to THE LANGTON FAMILY, but receives little in return. Throughout her marriage to AUSTIN LANGTON, the family takes the fruits of her fortune for granted. The revelation of Austin's infidelity leads the stoical Alice to contemplate elopement with a sexually ambiguous admirer. But the admirer defects, a recession halves Alice's fortune, and her children disappoint her. When eventual freedom comes, she 'could not go back in time'. 'Too often we are given what we asked for when we no longer have the power to use the gift.'

Langton, Austin

The Cardboard Crown, 1952
A Difficult Young Man, 1955
Outbreak of Love, 1957
When Blackbirds Sing, 1962, collectively known as
'the Langton Tetralogy'
Martin Boyd

Son of the Chief Justice of Victoria, the English-born Sir William Langton, Austin has 'always liked the best of everything and naturally assumed that he should have it'. Scornful of convention and stuffy Toorak society, he is a 'very simple man and a very unhappy one, though he gave the appearance of being neither'. Outwardly a contented family man, he succumbs to the advances of an infatuated cousin almost immediately after his marriage to ALICE LANGTON. The resulting entanglement casts a long-term shadow over his relationship with his wife.

Langton, Baba, originally **Barbara Stanger**

The Cardboard Crown, 1952
A Difficult Young Man, 1955
Outbreak of Love, 1957
When Blackbirds Sing, 1962, collectively known as
'the Langton Tetralogy'
Martin Boyd

To THE LANGTON FAMILY, Miss Barbara Stanger of Moonee Ponds is a joke: a worldly vulgarian who knows the price of all and the value of nothing. But Baba foreshadows the rise of values that will submerge those of the aristocratic Anglo-Australian Langton tribe. Instinctively brutal, she uses her marriage to the gentle George Langton as her entrée to 'society'. She despises all that the Langtons care for, and worships all that they hold in contempt. 'The virtue which Baba most detested was pity', comments her nephew GUY LANGTON. But Baba knows instinctively that hers are the values for her era, and that she represents the wave of the future, beneath which the Langtons will ultimately drown.

Langton, Diana → von Flugel, Diana

Langton, Dominic

The Cardboard Crown, 1952
A Difficult Young Man, 1955
Outbreak of Love, 1957
When Blackbirds Sing, 1962, collectively known as
'the Langton Tetralogy'
Martin Boyd

The eldest surviving son of LAURA and AUSTIN LANGTON, Dominic is the eponymous 'difficult young man', first introduced to the reader as GUY LANGTON's 'poor dead, mad brother'. His 'very simple ideas of honour' are all too often seen as 'dumb insolence'. Handsome and compassionate but spiritually tormented, Dominic is unable to make any real contact with others, and his idealistic stand against World War I simply bewilders those who want to love him. Even his concept of romantic love is at odds with society's demands. According to Guy, Dominic was born with 'a darker knowledge which was denied us ... the awareness of evil combined with an obsession with the good'. Is Dominic sane? No, according to the world; yes, argues his brother.

Langton, Guy

The Cardboard Crown, 1952
A Difficult Young Man, 1955
Outbreak of Love, 1957
When Blackbirds Sing, 1962, collectively known as
'the Langton Tetralogy'
Martin Boyd

Sensitive and compassionate, Guy is both narrator and personifier of the sense of unease that underlies THE LANGTON FAMILY world. Met by the reader only in extremes of youth and old age, the apparently detached Guy is torn by the family conflicts that he is both investigating and chronicling. We learn little of his own outward adult life; however, as a family elder he tells a young cousin that he has always longed for 'the literary freedom of the outcast'. Because he is, to some extent, an autobiographical projection of Boyd, he does not allow himself to be fully formed in the reader's eye.

Langton, Mildred

The Cardboard Crown, 1952
A Difficult Young Man, 1955
Outbreak of Love, 1957
When Blackbirds Sing, 1962, collectively known as
'the Langton Tetralogy'
Martin Boyd

GUY LANGTON's Aunt Mildy, the daughter of ALICE and AUSTIN LANGTON, she is the antithesis of THE LANGTON FAMILY hope. Nicknamed 'Mildew' by her younger relations, she has been 'deprived all her life of an object of affection'. Left in the care of the puritanical COUSIN SARAH, nasally-accented Mildred grows up both inhibited and silly, 'the victim of her inordinate affection'. Mildred perhaps is the saddest result of the Langton upbringing. Unaccountably left behind in Australia, she becomes a pathetically mock-genteel hen-pheasant, ill at ease with her birds-of-paradise family. Longing to be coquettish, Mildred is simply embarrassing.

Langton, Steven and **Laura**

The Cardboard Crown, 1952
A Difficult Young Man, 1955
Outbreak of Love, 1957
When Blackbirds Sing, 1962, collectively known as
'the Langton Tetralogy'
Martin Boyd

Steven Langton and his wife Laura play no roles but those of glowingly-sketched parents. Artists both, they appear, through the eyes of their son GUY LANGTON, merely as somewhat detached figures. Whereas the inner lives of his more removed grandparents, ALICE and AUSTIN LANGTON, are laid bare, Steven and Laura remain behind closed doors. They serve only as conduits of heredity in Guy's chronicling; which, perhaps, is what they would most approve.

Langton family, the

The Cardboard Crown, 1952
A Difficult Young Man, 1955
Outbreak of Love, 1957
When Blackbirds Sing, 1962, collectively known as
'the Langton Tetralogy'
Martin Boyd

Torn by divided loyalties, the Anglo-Australian Langton family is well-established in 19th-century 'fashionable' Melbourne, but never cuts loose from its English gentry ancestry. Throughout the novels, three generations of Langtons constantly criss-cross between colonial Australia and Waterpark, the ancestral English estate. Drawn from Boyd's own family, the first 'Australian' Langtons are AUSTIN and his wife ALICE LANGTON. Their five children are STEVEN, George, Maysie, MILDRED and DIANA LANGTON. Grandchildren take prominence throughout the novels: primarily, two sons of Steven – DOMINIC and GUY LANGTON.

Languish, Lydia
The Rivals, 1775
Richard Brinsley Sheridan

A rich young lady of 17, who has gained romantic notions by reading novels. Because she is intent on achieving 'the prettiest distress imaginable', her lover, CAPTAIN JACK ABSOLUTE, pretends to her that he is an impoverished ensign; Lydia dreams of elopement and 'charming' poverty, in opposition to the wishes of her aunt, MRS MALAPROP.

Laodamia
'Laodamia', 1815
William Wordsworth

The faithful heroine of the poem, her prayers seem to be answered when the gods allow her dead husband to return to her briefly from the underworld. The despair that destroys her when she cannot be physically reunited with his spirit-form is symbolized in the trees which grow vigorously from his grave, but wither at the top.

Lapham, Irene
The Rise of Silas Lapham, 1885
William Dean Howells

Prettier than her older sister PENELOPE LAPHAM, and addled with romantic fiction, she believes that TOM COREY is wooing *her* instead of Penelope. It is Irene who swallows without question her father's conviction that the Laphams are as good as anyone in Brahmin Boston, and at the novel's conclusion she is the only character who is resentful of her lot.

Lapham, Mrs Persis
The Rise of Silas Lapham, 1885
William Dean Howells

SILAS LAPHAM's wife, she is no less a snob and parvenu than he is himself, but she alone remains haunted by the fate of his former partner MILTON K ROGERS. As such, she acts as Silas's conscience, a reminder of how far he has to fall.

Lapham, Penelope
The Rise of Silas Lapham, 1885
William Dean Howells

The older of SILAS LAPHAM's daughters, she hides a fine mind and a sharp wit behind a rather plain exterior. It is these qualities, rather than her sister IRENE LAPHAM's beauty, that attract the wealthy TOM COREY, though the Lapham parents are convinced that his eye is on the younger daughter. Penelope generously gives way to her sister, but the lovers are re-united, marry, and move to Mexico to escape the invidious

snobbery and status-consciousness that hold their families apart.

Lapham, Silas
The Rise of Silas Lapham, 1885
William Dean Howells

A Vermont farmer, husband of MRS PERSIS LAPHAM, he discovers that his land yields a mineral essential to the manufacture of paint. The find makes a rich man of him, but he lacks the social poise (or the head for wine) to make a go of Boston Brahmin society and he is humiliated, both socially and economically. His moral 'rise', as opposed to his more specious material ascent, occurs when he turns down the one dishonest act that could save his business and his prestige. Poor, but wiser, he returns to Vermont.

Lapidoth, Mirah
Daniel Deronda, 1876
George Eliot

A delicate and refined young Jewish woman, rescued from attempted suicide by DANIEL DERONDA. She has fled from Central Europe where her father, a dissolute actor, had been mistreating her. She takes to the Meyrick family instantly when Deronda settles her there, though she still wishes to find her real mother and brothers. The beginnings of a career are found when she sings professionally in drawing-rooms. She wishes to marry her idol Deronda, but does not understand his relationship to GWENDOLEN HARLETH.

Lapidoth, Mordecai
Daniel Deronda, 1876
George Eliot

A poor Jew, taken in by compatriots for charity, who works in a bookshop. He writes in Hebrew on Jewish questions and encourages debates among his gifted friends. Slowly dying of tuberculosis, and spiritually lonely, Mordecai is looking for some charismatic, intellectually gifted helper of the Jewish cause. Finding DANIEL DERONDA, he pleads 'You will be my life … you will take the inheritance'.

Laputa, Rev John
Prester John, 1910
John Buchan

He first appears to DAVID CRAWFURD in a Presbyterian pulpit and then (in a more telling apparition) on a Scottish foreshore, the ambiguous harbinger of a haunted African cult. His forename is suggestive of his role as a forerunner of Prester John, the mythical 'prêtre Jean' of African legend; his surname echoes Swift's floating island with its pseudo-scientific mumbo-jumbo and moral hair-splitting.

Laputans
Gulliver's Travels, 1726
Jonathan Swift

The inhabitants of the floating island of Laputa, they are scientific theorists, so immersed in intense speculation that they have lost the ability to communicate with others. Each inward-looking theorist employs a flapper to hit the mouth of the speaker and the ears of the listener thus creating a space for communication to take place. The theorists, however, are incompetent, and their ideas are of little use to the rest of society. Houses on the island are poorly built due to the contempt felt for the practical aspects of life, and aesthetic beauty is described in terms of rhombs, circles and parallelograms.

Larch, Richard
A Man from the North, 1898
Arnold Bennett

An efficient young provincial clerk with literary ambitions, he arrives confidently in London, but its wealth and glamour dazzle him, distorting his vision. Giving in to desire and impulse, he tastes every pleasure and the resulting moral weakness robs him of the will to make the decisions that might have made his dreams reality. His aspirations as a writer fail through lack of talent and application and a failure of nerve in his personal life leads to his settling for a safe but vaguely disappointing marriage.

Larkin, Martha
Blaming, 1976
Elizabeth Taylor

'Greatly taken up with her own language', which as an unknown writer she is much concerned with, she finds herself isolated from all but her fellow English speakers while on a tour to Istanbul. However, as an American she discovers herself more divided from than allied to the suddenly widowed AMY HENDERSON, unable to offer her comfort and fatally associated with her loss.

Larkins, the
The Darling Buds of May, 1958, et seq
H E Bates

A carefree family – Pop, Ma and numerous children – who live on a ramshackle farm deep in the Kent countryside. The young man who comes to investigate Pop's failure to pay income tax is intrigued by the Larkin lifestyle, Ma's table groaning with food and drink, and the eldest Larkin girl. He decides to stay on.

Larry
Such, 1966
Christine Brooke-Rose

Recovering from a heart attack, during which he briefly died, he is the novel's central consciousness, a Lazarus figure, brought back from the dead with new and dark perceptions about human relationships and the culture that attempts either to sustain or replace them.

Lars Porsena
Lays of Ancient Rome, 1842
Thomas Babington Macaulay

A proud and arrogant member of the Tarquin family, he swears to destroy Rome. He summons allies from all Italy and surveys with joy the havoc they wreak. They reach Rome; only the narrow wooden bridge across the Tiber stands in their way. HORATIUS and two friends keep the enemy from stepping onto the bridge while the Romans break it down. Just as it falls, the two friends leap back to land but Horatius is too late; he must swim the raging waters. Sextus curses him, but

Lars Porsena is generous enough to pray heaven to rescue so gallant an enemy.

Larsson, Elisabeth
An Instant in the Wind, 1976, originally published in Afrikaans as *'n Oomblik in die Wind*, 1975
André Brink

An 18th-century lady who, having lost her husband and their party, is set adrift in the South African interior. A fallen representative of a privileged race, she is rescued by the runaway slave ADAM MANTOOR, a sentimental attachment that never quite overcomes their differences of background and colour.

La Rue, Mrs
Miss Ravenel's Conversion from Secession to Loyalty, 1867
J W De Forest

LILLIE RAVENEL's rather worldly aunt, she becomes the seducer of her niece's already unreliable husband LT COL JOHN CARTER. This action takes place in Washington, a city poised uncomfortably between the values of North and South. Though fading in physical charms, she is a supreme manipulator and survivor.

Laskell, John
The Middle of the Journey, 1947
Lionel Trilling

Laskell's debilitating bout of scarlet fever is intended to echo Lenin's pamphlet *Left-Wing Communism: An Infantile Disorder*. His 'convalescence'-cum-mid-life-crisis confronts him with the opposing values of socialism and Christianity, as represented by his friends the Crooms and the renegade Marxist and born-again Christian GIFFORD MAXIM, and his ill-defined liberalism is tested when his mistress's child dies at the hands of her drunken husband.

Lasso, Earl
The Gentleman Usher, 1602/3
George Chapman

A nobleman owing allegiance to ALPHONSO, whose desire to marry MARGARET, Earl Lasso's daughter, he tries to further. He demonstrates his lack of principle by urging her to marry Alphonso on pragmatic grounds and even threatening her.

Last, Lady Brenda
A Handful of Dust, 1934
Evelyn Waugh

Lively and sociable, with a 'very fair, underwater look' of fragile beauty, Brenda is bored with her aristocratic, rural lifestyle at Hetton with her husband, TONY LAST. She initiates an affair with the feckless socialite JOHN BEAVER, whose mother sells her a small furnished flat near Belgrave Square. When her only son is unexpectedly killed in a riding accident, she realizes that she loves Beaver and that her marriage is doomed. She divorces Tony, but gains no lasting commitment from Beaver and becomes increasingly impoverished and slothful, finally marring Tony's friend, the MP Jock Grant-Menzies.

Last, Tony
A Handful Of Dust, 1934
Evelyn Waugh

'An upright, God-fearing gentleman of the old school', Tony Last enjoys a ritualistic, feudal life with LADY BRENDA LAST in the Victorian Gothic mansion of Hetton. When their son is killed, however, Brenda announces that she loves JOHN BEAVER and wants a divorce. Tony dutifully organizes a laughable weekend of 'infidelity', but turns against Brenda when she quadruples her alimony demands. He embarks upon a voyage of exploration to South America, where he contracts fever, and is rescued by MR TODD and nursed back to health, but is held against his will and forced to recite Dickens daily. He is presumed dead, and Edward Last inherits Hetton, resolving to restore it to 'the glory that it had enjoyed in the days of his cousin Tony'.

Lasunwon
The Interpreters, 1965
Wole Soyinka

A college-tied politician and lawyer who uncomplainingly dogs the company of his more vital friends, 'an eternal garbage can for their sporadic splurges'.

Latimer, Darsie, properly Sir Arthur Darsie Redgauntlet of that Ilk
Redgauntlet, 1824
Sir Walter Scott

Only his friend ALAN FAIRFORD's father SAUNDERS FAIRFORD seems to know the secret of Darsie Latimer's parentage. He has been raised in Scotland, protected from his uncle, MR HERRIES OF BIRRENSWORK, who wants to raise him as a Jacobite and who kidnaps his sister Lilias from their widowed mother. Throughout the story, he exhibits the passivity of a young man who, quite literally, does not know who he is.

Latimer, Felix
School for Love, 1951
Olivia Manning

An orphan and an exile, previously sheltered from the real world by his mother, Felix is stranded by the war and sent to live in Jerusalem with MISS ETHEL BOHUN, the adopted child of his father's parents. At first he can find little reason for living, but gradually he acquires new friends and allies. He seems always to disappoint those around him, from Miss Bohun to his tutor, and only the Siamese cat Faro gives him unqualified love. He begins to realize that truth and love and the real world are the things he needs to learn about, to escape from the story-book world of glib half-truths his mother inhabited.

Latour, Bishop Jean Marie
Death Comes for the Archbishop, 1927
Willa Cather

Closely modelled on the historical Bishop Jean Baptiste Lamy, the Vicar Apostolic of New Mexico: 'a priest in a thousand ... his bowed head was not that of an ordinary man – it was built for the seat of a fine intelligence. His brow was open, generous, reflective, his features handsome and somewhat severe ... Everything showed him to be a man of gentle birth – brave, sensitive, courteous' – and his mission is to bring the Christian message to his desolate diocese, where he feels much closer than in the city to the life and ways of his Master.

La Trobe, Miss
Between the Acts, 1941
Virginia Woolf

Described as 'bossy', Miss La Trobe is commanding, self-assured and aware of what she wants. She has a passionate zest and creativity, and has a vision which enables her to unify the fragmentary. Though she is a skilled artist, she is not successful, so any small glory is always tinged with a sense of failure. Because she is a perfectionist, her creativity will never be fulfilled. Satisfaction is an alien feeling for her, and she soon pulls herself up if she senses self-congratulation. However, her sense of vision never leaves her, and her spirit is indestructible.

Laughing Boy
Laughing Boy, 1929
Oliver La Farge

A young Navajo man, he elopes with SLIM GIRL but is shocked to discover that she already has a lover. His murder/suicide attempt fails, but he loses her anyway when she is murdered, leaving him to cope with the tangled emotions their relationship has conjured up.

Launce
Two Gentlemen of Verona, c.1590
William Shakespeare

A servant of PROTEUS, Launce is a clown who owns a dog, Crab. Because the dog cannot cry, Launce accuses him of not being a true friend, yet later goes to absurd lengths to prove his own loyalty to the animal, thereby parodying the play's principal theme of faith. Launce is droll, sometimes melancholic, but represents a hard reality, counterpointing the emotional follies and ideals of his employer and his friends. Sometimes, though, his (clownish) idealism is greater than that of Proteus.

Laura
The Garden Party, 1922
Katherine Mansfield

A young girl, newly awakened to life's possibilities, and her own vitality. Enthusiastically caught up in the delightful chaos of party preparations, she is sensitive to every mood and she changes accordingly. Confronted by the proximity of death, her extravagant initial reaction to stop the party of life is diverted by a hat. Later bravely visiting the mourning household, she tries to articulate the mystery 'Isn't life ...?'

Laura
Goblin Market, 1862
Christina Rossetti

Laura and her sister LIZZIE hear tiny goblin voices every morning and evening, calling alluringly to humans with offerings of luscious fruits of all kinds. Laura is the one who listens and goes to see the little men with their baskets and gold plates of grapes and pomegranates, peaches and mulberries. She has no money but gives them a curl from her golden hair. The fruits are delicious. But she can never hear the voices again, although her sister does. Laura grows listless, careworn, almost dying, and it is only when Lizzie braves the goblins for her sake that she is saved.

Laura
Lark Rise to Candleford, 1945
Flora Jane Thompson

A semi-autobiographical depiction of the author as a child growing up in an Oxfordshire hamlet in the late 19th century. A stonemason's daughter, Laura possesses a fine eye for detail and she vividly brings to life the ways and characters of a community on the brink of great change. Often found foraging in lanes and woods, she has an independent spirit and a strong curiosity which leads her further and further afield.

Laurie
Little Women, 1868
Good Wives, 1869
Little Men, 1871
Jo's Boys, 1886
Louisa M Alcott

A charming, talented, educated, rich heir, at risk of being spoilt by protective pampering before coming into the benevolent company of the March family. His high spirits match JO MARCH's, his heroes are his grandfather and Napoleon and his ambition is to be a musician rather than a businessman. Rejected by his first love (his best friend Jo), he is in danger of wasting his life until AMY MARCH takes charge of him, encouraging him to 'do something splendid'.

Lavender, Dr
Old Chester Tales, 1898
Margaret Deland

A wise and tolerant old minister in Old Chester, Pennsylvania, indulgently observing the lives and travails of his parishioners and of those who have so far escaped his attractively baited theological trap.

Lavenza, Elizabeth
Frankenstein, or, The Modern Prometheus, 1818
Mary Shelley

The cousin and fiancée of VICTOR FRANKENSTEIN. She is an innocent, intelligent, good-hearted and virtuous girl, who has been described as a young woman 'with loveliness surpassing the beauty of her childish years. There was the same candour, the same vivacity, but it was allied to an expression more full of sensibility and intellect'. She is murdered on their wedding night by her husband's creation, FRANKENSTEIN'S CREATURE.

Lavinia
Androcles and the Lion, 1912
George Bernard Shaw

A good-looking, resolute Roman patrician, Lavinia has been taken prisoner for her Christian beliefs and, despite the pleading of the handsome CAPTAIN, is about to become a martyr. They discuss the nature of faith, but she is unable to define its real essence other than to say that it is something greater and more mysterious than

even Christian teachings. She is a realist who has chosen death of her own free will, and her reprieve symbolizes the triumph of realists over idealists and philistines.

Lavinia
Titus Andronicus, c.1589
William Shakespeare

The daughter of TITUS ANDRONICUS. Initially passive, she sees herself squabbled over as a bride between the emperor SATURNINUS and his brother. She is soon raped by two Goth princes, who cut off her hands and tongue to keep her from informing on them. Resourcefully, she then opens Ovid at a rape scene to indicate what has happened to her and marks out the perpetrators' names in the sand. Her mutilated agony is ended when her father kills her out of pity.

Lavish, Eleanor
A Room With a View, 1908
E M Forster

'Short, fidgety and playful as a kitten, though without a kitten's grace', Eleanor Lavish is a clever, cheerful woman who has ventured to Italy in search of adventure and inspiration for her novel. A firm believer in the emancipation of women, who has flown in the face of convention all her adult life, she smokes cigarettes, refuses to follow the well-trod paths of less curious tourists and prides herself on her sense of originality.

Lawrence, Emily
The Long Prospect, 1958
Elizabeth Harrower

An unwanted and emotionally neglected child. Left with her grandmother Lilian when her parents split up, she searches for a sense of identity and a feeling of belonging. Lack of attention and affection create great insecurity in Emily: 'That crushing uncertainty had been … the most noticeable thing about her'. She blossoms under the attention of the lodger Max, who sees her as a victim of extreme deprivation. In spite of her uncertainty, Emily displays a sense of righteousness: 'under the ingratiating smile and puzzlement, was a basic, unshakeable belief in the rightness of a life that did not sin against intelligence and kindness'.

Lawrence, Frederick
The Tenant of Wildfell Hall, 1848
Anne Brontë

The squire and landlord of Wildfell Hall, and MRS HELEN GRAHAM's brother. He allows her to take refuge there with her son, ARTHUR, making part of the derelict house fit to live in and helping her sell her paintings. GILBERT MARKHAM misunderstands Lawrence's motives and out of jealousy attacks and wounds him. But Lawrence bears no lasting grudge, and keeps Markham informed of Helen's progress and her husband's death, generously showing him her letters.

Lawrence, Honor
'The Puzzle-Headed Girl', 1947
Christina Stead

'She had a chin dimple and a dimple upon her left cheek; and when the smile went, her face returned to its gravity, its almost sadness.' Employed by Augustus Debrett at the Farmers' Utilities Corporation, she becomes a kind of revenant or succubus, a grey-eyed survivor who haunts the men that have fallen under her spell. Her obsession with art reinforces the impression that she is an enigmatic Gioconda, but also her apparent belief that all life is contrivance.

Lawson, Harvey
The Bird of the Night, 1972
Susan Hill

A man with a desire to be a father figure and protector, Harvey Lawson lives his life through his friend FRANCIS CROFT, without wanting to exist fully in his own right. Patient, tolerant, cautious, perhaps even boring, he lives a life tortured by Francis's anguished existence. Lawson is a man of intense devotion and respect, yet in some vital way he appears to lack self-respect. He does not relate to others on an equal basis, remaining subservient and dominated; yet, although he can see in retrospect where he went wrong, he implies that he would do it all again given the chance, such was his love for and loyalty to Francis.

Lawton, Josh
Josh Lawton, 1972
Melvyn Bragg

A Cumbrian farm worker, he is a big, strong, silent man, 'so friendly and pleasant with everybody'. His bright, clear complexion (so clear that village girls embarrass him by asking what he uses for his skin) is apparently the outward sign of a spiritual pride and innocence. People like to be with him, his shyness making the more boisterous protective, his emotional vulnerability appealing to women. Yet his obstinacy and seeming ability neither to see nor hear anything that he would rather avoid, make him something of an enigma. Josh is a gentle man, but when sufficiently provoked has a swift, violent temper and he can be utterly unforgiving.

Layton, Mabel
The Jewel in the Crown, 1966
The Day of the Scorpion, 1968
The Towers of Silence, 1971
A Division of the Spoils, 1975, forming
The Raj Quartet
Paul Scott

MILDRED LAYTON's elderly mother-in-law who lives reclusively with the devoted BARBIE BATCHELOR at Rose Cottage in the hill station of Pankot. Twice widowed, Mabel is highly respected as a 'pukka memsahib' and matriarch of the English community, although there is faint disapproval of her withdrawal from public life, and a suspicion that she will welcome the end of British rule. No one realizes her contempt for British flag-waving and bitter condemnation of the treatment of Indians, or that since the slaughter of rioters at Amritsar she has contributed anonymously to funds for Indian widows and orphans.

Layton, Mildred
The Jewel in the Crown, 1966
The Day of the Scorpion, 1968

The Towers of Silence, 1971
A Division of the Spoils, 1975, forming
The Raj Quartet
Paul Scott

The mother of SARAH LAYTON and SUSAN LAYTON. She is the daughter of a general and wife of a colonel, both in the regular Indian army, and is an admired leader of her social circle even though, during the three years her husband has been a prisoner-of-war, she has become vague and distracted, drinks far too much and fails to pay her bridge debts. She is an essentially cold, hard and sour person who during her husband's absence has a joyless affair with one of his fellow-officers.

Layton, Sarah
The Jewel in the Crown, 1966
The Day of the Scorpion, 1968
The Towers of Silence, 1971
A Division of the Spoils, 1975, forming
The Raj Quartet
Paul Scott

Born into an Indian Army family, Sarah is a corporal at Pankot hill station during World War II. Her mother, MILDRED LAYTON, has always preferred her younger, prettier sister, SUSAN LAYTON, to whom Sarah loses her boyfriends. But the plainer, and more serious Sarah is the family's mainstay during her father's absence. She is quietly efficient, self-possessed and considerate, especially to the underprivileged. With her thoughtful open-mindedness, like GUY PERRON, to whom she is attracted, she perceives and is disturbed by the social and moral evils of British rule, exemplified in RONALD MERRICK's conduct.

Layton, Susan
The Jewel in the Crown, 1966
The Day of the Scorpion, 1968
The Towers of Silence, 1971
A Division of the Spoils, 1975, forming
The Raj Quartet
Paul Scott

SARAH LAYTON's younger sister. She is pretty and popular but is also a shallow social butterfly, seemingly intent only on being the centre of attention. She is irresistible to young men, among them Captain Teddie Bingham, who marries her but is killed in action shortly afterwards, leaving her pregnant. Pathetically unstable and frightened beneath her brittle exterior, Susan lacks a sense of identity, and is terrified by the feeling that she has no real existence. Suffering a nervous breakdown after the birth of her son, she then marries RONALD MERRICK, who served with Bingham and lost an arm trying to save him.

Leadbitter
The Hireling, 1957
L P Hartley

An ex-army man, who works as a chauffeur for anyone who cares to hire him. He has little or no emotional life, living only to work and remaining deliberately detached from all human contact. His appearance is 'smart, expensive and unapproachable', with 'a hint of menace'. He is a cynical and bitter man, but when he begins chauffeuring a new client, LADY FRANKLIN, a grieving young widow, his emotions and imagination are slowly awakened, and he loses his protective armour of pride and detachment with fatal consequences.

Leader, the
The Orators: an English Study, 1932
W H Auden
A quasi-mystical strongman, who will rise up and redeem English society from its sexual cravenness and intellectual disablement. At some points it is suggested that THE AIRMAN sees himself in the role, but in the fourth 'Ode', he is identified with Jonathan, the real-life infant son of the novelist and poet Rex Warner.

Leafy, Morgan
A Good Man in Africa, 1981
William Boyd
Morgan Leafy, the exasperated hero of this richly comic novel, is First Secretary at the British government Commission at Nkongsamba, the state capital of tropical, dusty, downtrodden Kinjanja, West Africa. The son of a catering manager at Heathrow airport and graduate of a new university in the Midlands, he is 34, fat, perpetually sweating, and has a rapidly receding hairline. Embittered by the inertia of his career and seethingly envious of his fellow diplomats, with their Oxbridge backgrounds and their wives, Morgan accosts the world with a mixture of misanthropy, resentment and guile. He is clearly offensive, yet his eternal, beleaguered optimism makes him strangely charming.

Leamas, Alec
The Spy Who Came in from the Cold, 1963
John Le Carré
Short and powerfully built, Leamas is an experienced British agent who sees his spy network in East Germany destroyed. He comes home and appears to deteriorate, unable to control his relationship to money or alcohol, though in reality a complex mission to destroy a German spy chief is being planned. While in England he becomes the lover of a librarian, Liz, who happens to be a communist. He then says goodbye to her and begins his mission, pretending to defect, but not everything is as it seems and he has little idea of the extent to which Control is manipulating him.

Leantio
Women Beware Women, c.1621
Thomas Middleton
The Florentine factor who persuades the beautiful BIANCA CAPELLO to marry him against her parents' wishes. He is infatuated by his beautiful bride, but regards her as a treasured possession rather than a beloved partner, hiding her away from other men's eyes so that she cannot be tempted to stray. When she does leave him, his well-meaning naivety changes at first to despair and then to bitterness and spite.

Leantio's Mother
Women Beware Women, c.1621
Thomas Middleton
A good-natured but ineffectual old widow who is

given the task of guarding her new daughter-in-law, BIANCA CAPELLO, by her son whilst he is away on business. Naive and easily manipulated, she fails in her task almost immediately, allowing Bianca to be seduced by the DUKE OF FLORENCE whilst she plays chess in a room just below.

Lear
Lear, 1973
Edward Bond
This modern Lear is a self-aggrandizing, brutal king, building a high wall about his kingdom. He has two daughters, BODICE and FONTANELLE, but the character of CORDELIA is no relation, unlike in Shakespeare's *King Lear*. Bond's Lear re-evaluates himself and his past; he accepts moral responsibility for his actions and tries to atone for them. Eventually, elderly and blind, he is shot while attempting to dismantle his own wall.

Lear, King
King Lear, c.1605–6
William Shakespeare
The egotistical and proud King of Britain, Lear, in his old age, seeks to relinquish the responsibilities of state to his daughters, GONERIL, REGAN and CORDELIA, whilst retaining his privileges and status. He is a foolish and rash old man, who mistakes flattery for affection and integrity for disloyalty. At first driven mad by the cruelty of his two elder daughters, eventually he develops a measure of humility and compassion, and despite his many faults, he is, as he says himself, 'a man/more sinn'd against than sinning'.

Learoyd, Private
'The Three Musketeers', in *Plain Tales from the Hills*, 1888
Soldiers Three, 1890
Rudyard Kipling
A private in B Company of a Line regiment (unspecified) and an example of 'genial blackguardism'. Judging by his elision of certain vocal sounds and general air of good-natured omniscience, he is a Yorkshireman.

Leary, Macon
The Accidental Tourist, 1985
Anne Tyler
Eccentric to a fault, Macon Leary is a travel writer who hates travel. Precise, pedantic and agoraphobic, he is at ease only with his own family. He detests change and chaos to such a degree that he is in danger of petrifying into old age without ever learning to love or to accept loss. Only through the intervention of another character is he able to recognize that the chaotic events which shape his life enable him to move forward, rather than stand still.

Leatherby, Marian
The Hearing Trumpet, 1976
Leonora Carrington
An eccentric, elderly woman who is unwillingly committed to a sinister retirement home. Ninety-two years old and profoundly deaf, she suffers the spite of her relatives with good-humoured resilience and leads an existence of quiet unconventionality. She may be powerless

within the structure of her family but in rebelling against the institution her particular combination of the practical and the fantastic comes into its own.

Lebanon, Joseph
The Cabinet Minister, 1890
Arthur Wing Pinero

An unscrupulous social climber, Joseph Lebanon, who is the brother of MRS FANNY GAYLUSTRE, is a social outsider represented in the then-familiar theatrical character of the sinister, money-grabbing Jew. A 'smartly-dressed, middle-aged person, of a most pronounced common Semitic type, with a bland manner and a contented smile', Mr Lebanon believes that by arranging to become moneylender to LADY KITTY TWOMBLEY, he and his sister can thereby enter society, apparently under her patronage. It is lower-class social vulgarity as much as his deceit which eventually betrays him.

Le Beau
As You Like It, c.1600
William Shakespeare

An affected, vain man and a courtier to the ruthless DUKE FREDERICK, Le Beau's pomposity provokes ROSALIND into putting her natural reserve to one side and expressing her true feelings in sympathizing with those who have lost their matches with Charles the Wrestler. Le Beau announces the wrestling match between Charles and ORLANDO and later advises Orlando to leave the palace.

Lecter, Dr Hannibal
Red Dragon, 1981
The Silence of the Lambs, 1988
Hannibal, 1999
Thomas Harris

Imprisoned for life for committing horrific cannibalistic murders, Lecter, a former psychiatrist of extraordinary intelligence, is first introduced in *Red Dragon*, when retired FBI agent Will Graham seeks his help in tracking down a killer. Again, in *The Silence of the Lambs* Lecter holds information, this time relating to serial killer 'Buffalo Bill', which the FBI is desperate to obtain. But as he finds his entertainment in 'playing with' and psychologically tormenting people, this information can only be had at a price. Seizing the chance to bolster his immense ego, 'Hannibal the Cannibal' begins his manipulation of Officer CLARICE STARLING and his captors in a manner which is terrifying in its subtlety, belying as it does his monstrous, highly dangerous nature. In *Hannibal*, Lecter is still at large, seven years after escaping from custody.

le Dain, Oliver, also known as Le Mauvais or Le Diable
Quentin Durward, 1823
Sir Walter Scott

Formerly the barber of LOUIS XI, KING OF FRANCE, he rose to become a favourite counsellor: 'a little, pale, meagre man ... his visage was penetrating and quick, although he endeavoured to banish such expression from his features, by keeping his eyes fixed on the ground, while, with the stealthy

and quiet pace of a cat, he seemed modestly rather to glide than to walk through the apartment'.

Le Diable → le Dain, Oliver

Ledwidge, Helen
Eyeless in Gaza, 1936
Aldous Huxley

Daughter of MARY AMBERLEY, but more sensible and vivacious, Helen is married to the pompous intellectual HUGH LEDWIDGE. Disillusioned with her husband, she has an affair with ANTHONY BEAVIS, which on his part is a purely opportunistic one. A bizarre incident in which a dead terrier inexplicably falls from an aeroplane and bespatters the sunbathing lovers horrifies Helen and leads her to transfer her affections to the communist militant Ekki Giesebrecht, but also, ironically, has the effect of forcing Anthony to realize that he really does love her.

Ledwidge, Hugh
Eyeless in Gaza, 1936
Aldous Huxley

'I won't inflict Kant on you ... But I think you'll have to read one of the modern Kantians.' This is how Hugh Ledwidge successfully woos Helen Amberley (HELEN LEDWIDGE) during a party. The marriage, however, turns out to be a disaster because his emotions do not match his intellectual eminence.

Lee
True West, 1981
Sam Shepard

An American failure, the uneducated, criminally inclined and scruffily dressed Lee has been living in the Californian desert. Returning to his mother's house, he meets his younger brother AUSTIN, whose success as a writer he envies. He has a chance to turn his sense of the American West to his advantage, but incompetence and intense sibling rivalry tell against him.

Lee, Alice
Woodstock, or The Cavalier, 1826
Sir Walter Scott

Said to be modelled on the novelist's daughter Anne, she is the ageing SIR HENRY LEE's chief support in the turbulent years of schism and civil war. She has undergone exactly the kind of change seen in Anne during Scott's own financial difficulties. 'A light joyous air, with something of a humorous expression, which seemed to be looking for amusement, had vanished before the touch of affliction, and a calm melancholy supplied its place, which seemed on the watch to administer comfort to others.'

Lee, Bill
The Naked Lunch, 1959
William S Burroughs

A writer who dares to loosen his mind with drugs, with a view to entering the world of hallucination, sexual nightmare and bizarre eroticism. Only by stretching his senses to the limit and beyond can he find in the maze of his drug-sensitized mind the full extent of its possibility. The result of his quest is a jumbled and sometimes terrifying plunge into the convoluted and bitter realm of the habitual drug-user, where creativity and craziness often overlap, and morality becomes meaningless.

Lee, Col
Woodstock, or The Cavalier, 1826
Sir Walter Scott

A brave but impetuous young Royalist, ALICE LEE's brother is almost killed by his own father as he enters Woodstock by a side window. He is trusted enough in the king's counsels to be allowed to protect CHARLES II by exchanging clothes with him, an act which brings him a death sentence from OLIVER CROMWELL himself. Like others of his class and sympathies, he is driven into exile and meets his death on the field at Dunkerque.

Lee, Lorelei
Gentlemen Prefer Blondes, 1925
Anita Loos

The original material girl, she had dabbled in a number of tiresomely demanding occupations before concluding that life was infinitely more bearable on a rich man's arm. Dinner at the Ritz, supper at the Trocadero or a twirl around a fashionable club were more than enough to fill a girl's day. Her journey from Little Rock, Arkansas, to the hoi polloi of Europe has left her with many fondly cherished souvenirs, among them a tiara and the practical philosophy that 'kissing your hand may make you feel very very good but a diamond and safire [sic] bracelet lasts forever'.

Lee, Madeleine
Democracy: An American Novel, 1880
Henry Adams

A bright, ambitious young New York widow who is drawn to Washington by the lure of 'the tremendous forces of government, and the machinery of society, at work. What she wanted was POWER.' She engineers a meeting with the powerful SENATOR SILAS P RATCLIFFE, and is initially dismissive of his coarseness and vanity, but finds herself attracted by his self-assurance and power. She rejects his advances when she discovers he is corrupt, and at the same time exhausts her fascination for the processes of power itself.

Lee, Simon
'Simon Lee, the Old Huntsman', in *Lyrical Ballads*, 1798
William Wordsworth

A retired Lakeland huntsman who still thrills to the baying of the hounds. Frail and destitute, he and his aged wife try to remain proudly independent, but Simon gratefully accepts help when it is given.

Lee, Sir Henry
Woodstock, or The Cavalier, 1826
Sir Walter Scott

An old Royalist, aged and weighed down by the troubled times in which he lives. Though his grasp of events is not always secure, he is still forthright, even impetuous, in action, and unswerving in his loyalties. These qualities he has passed on to his children, ALICE and COL LEE.

Lee Chong
Cannery Row, 1945
John Steinbeck

The Chinese grocer on Cannery Row and a curious combination of the kindly and the sinister; it is thought that he was wanted by the police during the Tong wars. 'Perhaps he is evil balanced and held suspended by good – an Asiatic planet held to its orbit by the pull of Lao Tze and held away from Lao Tze by the centrifugality of abacus and cash register.'

Leeds, Nina
Strange Interlude, 1928
Eugene O'Neill

The daughter of a college professor in New England. She secretly hates her father for having persuaded her fiancé not to marry her (though they were already lovers) before going off to fight in France, where he is killed. Her increasingly neurotic personality expresses itself in promiscuous relationships, underlining the theme that 'our lives are merely strange dark interludes in the electrical display of God the Father'.

Leeford, Edward ('Monks')
Oliver Twist, 1838
Charles Dickens

OLIVER TWIST's half-brother, he is a villainous rascal who uses FAGIN and the BUMBLEs as tools to help him defraud Oliver of his inheritance. NANCY discovers his plot and tells ROSE MAYLIE and MR BROWNLOW, who make him give Oliver £3,000, half the property remaining in his hands. Leaving the country, he is convicted of fraud in America and dies in prison.

Leete, Ann
The Marrying of Ann Leete, 1899
Harley Granville-Barker

Ann is the 20-year-old daughter of Carnaby Leete, a devious late 18th-century politician intending to marry her to the Whig, Lord John Carp, in order to effect his own political rehabilitation. But Carp's surprise kiss awakens not Ann's devotion but her rebelliousness, sensuality and sexual authority. Her choice is both emotional and political: she rejects Carp and marries the working-class gardener, John Abud. 'I was afraid to live', she admits, 'and now … I am content.' Ann is determined upon a new beginning, but her future is uncertain.

Leete, Dr
Looking Backward, 2000–1887, 1888
Edward Bellamy

A physician in a utopian Boston of the future, he describes to the time-traveller JULIAN WEST the progress that has been made in medicine, social welfare, education and civics since Julian's time. Leete is an old-fashioned progressive liberal, who is afforded the rare opportunity to demonstrate the validity of his position.

Leete, Edith
Looking Backward, 2000–1887, 1888
Edward Bellamy
DR LEETE's daughter, she is a descendant of the girl to whom JULIAN WEST was engaged back in 1887. They are thus fated to fall in love over again, suggesting that love is the one constant element that links the utopian future with the squalid and degraded past.

Le Fever, Lt
The Life and Opinions of Tristram Shandy, 9 volumes, 1759–67
Laurence Sterne
A dying soldier whose plight generates the warm sympathy and generosity of UNCLE TOBY SHANDY, who attends the stricken man and demonstrates true charity towards him. The ailing man's son is also caught up in the potential tragedy, and the whole situation presents an opportunity to understand the humanity of Toby and his sincerity of feeling. The son, in his turn, falls on hard times and Toby discovers that caring is open-ended.

Legend, Ben
Love for Love, 1695
William Congreve
The younger son of SIR SAMPSON LEGEND, Ben is 'half home-bred, and half sea-bred', and is intended by his father to marry MISS PRUE FORESIGHT. He is a ludicrous figure, hearty but hapless, yet, because of his father's displeasure with VALENTINE LEGEND, stands to come into an unexpected inheritance. The only thing is, neither Ben nor Prue want to marry each other. This sub-plot counterpoints the main intrigues of Valentine and ANGELICA, as Ben's rustic foolishness and gullible embarrassments contrast with the dashing romanticism of his brother.

Legend, Sir Sampson
Love for Love, 1695
William Congreve
The father of VALENTINE and BEN LEGEND, he is apparently so harsh, pompous and morally upright as to be unyielding. Because Valentine is in debt, he offers him £4,000 if he will sign a bond renouncing his inheritance in favour of his younger brother, Ben. Yet he is not so hard-hearted, nor so hard-headed, as to be immune to the wiles of a beautiful woman. ANGELICA so flatters his vanity that he melts and, preposterously, dreams of marriage. Through his example, Congreve makes a plea for common humanity.

Legend, Valentine
Love for Love, 1695
William Congreve
Valentine's expenditure has often been the subject of reproach by JEREMY FETCH, his servant and ally, but even he cannot help when Valentine's father, SIR SAMPSON LEGEND, forces him to sign a bond giving over his inheritance to his younger brother, BEN LEGEND. Valentine is dashing, handsome, even somewhat cultured, but he is no thinker. Fortunately, the beautiful ANGELICA with whom he is in love, is, and she devises a plot to make all end well.

Leggatt
The Secret Sharer, 1912
Joseph Conrad
A seaman who has killed another sailor and jumped ship. He is rescued by the unnamed captain (ANON), and sheltered in his cabin. He is almost a mysterious 'double' of his benefactor, and appears in ghostly fashion, taken at first for a 'headless corpse', and has a shadowy presence throughout. The captain helps him to escape, but he flees only to be 'hidden forever from all friendly faces, to be a fugitive and a vagabond on earth'.

Legree, Simon
Uncle Tom's Cabin, or, Life Among the Lowly, 1851–2
Harriet Beecher Stowe
By far the most complex character in the book, Legree is more than simply a sadistic drunk. It becomes clear that his ill-treatment of the slaves on his plantation (and in particular UNCLE TOM, whom he beats to death in an alcoholic rage) is largely explained, if by no means justified, by his own desperately loveless and crudely moralistic upbringing. Tom awakens in him a latent guilt and self-loathing that eventually explodes into violence.

Lehrer, Leo
The Genius, 1983
Howard Brenton
An American nuclear scientist specializing in unified field theory, Lehrer is in many respects a modern equivalent of Brecht's Galileo. Efficient, brilliant and sensual, he takes pleasure in knowledge for its own sake. Yet, as he realizes that science is being used as a political weapon, he finds himself unable to cope with the moral and political issues raised by his work.

Leicester, Robert Dudley, Earl of
Kenilworth, 1821
Sir Walter Scott
Secretly married to AMY ROBSART, the earl receives kinder treatment from Scott than from many earlier historians. 'A man of majestic mien', he is shown to be courtly, generous and loyal, his natural affections by no means corrupted by ambition. He can, however, be ruthless.

Leigh, Amyas
Westward Ho!, 1855
Charles Kingsley
A Devonshire seaman in Elizabethan times, he helps defend the South Coast against the Armada. His intense rivalry with the Spaniard DON GUZMAN is not just military, but also romantic, since both are in love with the same woman.

Leigh, Aurora
Aurora Leigh, 1857
Elizabeth Barrett Browning
The narrator, she is a spirited 'modern' woman, unafraid of flouting convention. Her early life is marred by the death of her parents, and she is in search of a surrogate mother. In Wordsworthian style, she channels her passion into Nature and ideas. This character, thought to be largely autobiographical, is unashamedly subjective,

concerned with her own inner experiences rather than objective reality. Aurora Leigh is a woman who does not shy from discussing sexuality, melancholy and the creative process. Although only the first half of her life is covered, it would appear that all her formative experiences are laid before us.

Leigh, Joanna
The Land of Green Ginger, 1927
Winifred Holtby

Tall, strong and golden-haired, she is the disorderly mistress of a desolate Yorkshire farm, where she attempts to care for two small daughters and her tubercular husband, TEDDY LEIGH. A woman of great vitality and unquenchable optimism, she finds release from the grinding monotony of her laborious and impoverished working life in the indulgence of her imagination. Fey, romantic and empathetic, by turns desolate and exalted, Joanna reaches continually beyond the restraints of reality to a world of intoxicating possibilities, vivid beauty and wild, strange enchantment.

Leigh, Teddy
The Land of Green Ginger, 1927
Winifred Holtby

Besotted with his own cerebral quest after aesthetic and intellectual perfection, and consumed by the desire to serve God and man, Teddy Leigh is slowly dying of tuberculosis on an isolated Yorkshire farm. Increasingly estranged from his wife JOANNA LEIGH, and unable to write his 'Life of Christ' or to support his family, he is wracked by self-pity, jealousy and impotent rage. Cruel, embittered, and egotistical, his is an essentially sensitive and imaginative nature, disfigured and transformed by poverty, futility and disease.

Leiter, Felix
Goldfinger, 1959, et seq
Ian Fleming

A CIA agent and friend and frequent associate of JAMES BOND. A rather prosaic, front-entrance type, he is useful for explaining the background or for mopping up the mess at the end, but is all at sea when it comes to the more subtle aspects of secret intelligence.

Leithen, Sir Edward
'Space', in *The Moon Endureth*, 1912, et seq, notably *Sick Heart River*, 1941
John Buchan

An Eton-educated Scot, he is a barrister and MP, who rises to become attorney-general. Closer in kind to Buchan than was RICHARD HANNAY, he is a man of principle and thoughtful intention rather than an adventurer, and there is, as he admits, a hint of 'ice in his heart', melted only when, facing death from tuberculosis, he sets off into the Canadian wilderness in search of some ultimate truth about himself and mankind.

Leivers, Miriam
Sons and Lovers, 1913
D H Lawrence

The lover of PAUL MOREL, Miriam is the reserved and serious daughter of a Nottinghamshire farmer. She is presented as an idealized woman, sexually alluring but morally virtuous, who gives herself physically to Paul in a spirit of martyrdom rather than of sexual partnership. (This contrasts sharply with the later relationship between Paul and CLARA DAWES.) In Lawrence's view, Miriam's denial of her desires and her sexuality dislocates her from nature and natural will; this is resented by Paul, who seeks a harmony with nature which, in Lawrence's estimation, is the most spiritually fulfilling state mankind can achieve.

Lem
The Emperor Jones, 1920
Eugene O'Neill

Leader of the natives on the emperor BRUTUS JONES's island, with perhaps just a hint of LEM(UEL) GULLIVER in his name. He refuses to accept his fellow black man's suzerainty and eventually kills him with bullets made out of silver dollars.

Le Mauvais → le Dain, Oliver

Len
Saved, 1965
Edward Bond

Len is in his early twenties, tall, slim, and part of a south-London community including FRED and PAM. In spite of his impoverished, brutal surroundings, he is a naturally good man. But his feelings are becoming deadened: his response to the murder of Pam's baby by his friends, for instance, is one partly of morbid fascination, partly moral indifference. He has no idea what his actions or feelings will be from one moment to the next, but as Bond himself writes: 'he lives with people at their worst and most hopeless ... and does not turn away from them. I cannot imagine an optimism more tenacious, disciplined or honest than his'.

Lena
Boesman and Lena, 1968
Athol Fugard

The wife of BOESMAN, she suffers a double oppression under apartheid. Apart from being displaced innumerable times under a cynical Slum Clearance policy, she escapes beating from her tyrannical husband only when he becomes aware that others, especially the White *Baas*, are laughing at his cowardice. When Lena finds an old African willing to listen to her story, she sits close to him with the conviction that 'Hotnot and Kaffer got no time for apartheid on a night like this'. The death of the old African terrifies Boesman and gives Lena the confidence she has always needed to confront her husband.

Lena
'The Gentle Lena', in *Three Lives*, 1909
Gertrude Stein

The epitome of female forbearance, she is a German serving-girl in Bridgepoint, married off by her calculating aunt to a dull and spiritless tailor, who views her as breeding stock rather than as a human being. She dies during her fourth childbirth.

Lennie (Lennie Small)
Of Mice and Men, 1939
John Steinbeck

'A huge man, shapeless of face, with large pale eyes, with wide, sloping shoulders', his shambling, bearish walk emphasizes his feeble-mindedness and he relies on the smaller, quicker GEORGE for protection. He is obsessed with animals, in particular a dead mouse that he carries with him.

Lennox, Mary
The Secret Garden, 1911
Frances Hodgson Burnett

From a thin, sour and self-confessedly disagreeable child orphaned by cholera in India, 'Mistress Mary' blossoms when she is deposited in deepest Yorkshire. At Misslethwaite Manor she discovers a walled, apparently dead garden and in it the secret of the reviving cycle of nature. The garden grows under her care and so does she. With the help of bluff, plain-speaking servants, she also rescues her sickly cousin COLIN CRAVEN from their shared neglect, replacing bad and sad thoughts with natural hope, strength and independence.

Lennox, Sandy → Orr, John/Lennox, Sandy

Lenny
The Homecoming, 1965
Harold Pinter

A psychopath, the middle of MAX's three sons, he is a multi-faceted and complex individual, capable on the one hand of an ironic examination of his elder brother TEDDY's academic credibility, and on the other of physical brutality and rape. He is a shady, mysterious figure and a moving force in his family's corrupt and corrupting circle.

Lenox, Susan
Susan Lenox: Her Fall and Rise, 1917
David Graham Phillips

The plaything of impersonal social forces, she drifts downward into a life of vice in the slums of Cincinnati. What is impressive about her is that, even in her moment of degradation, plunged into the world of white slavery, she is capable of rising above her circumstances with an unfeigned dignity that is far removed from melodrama.

Lensky, Anna
The Rainbow, 1915
D H Lawrence

The daughter of LYDIA LENSKY and stepdaughter of TOM BRANGWEN, Anna passes through a wilful, destructive childhood to inherit her mother's strength of spirit and mature into a self-sufficient woman. She has a certain toughness and resilience, mellowed by WILL BRANGWEN, her cousin, whom she marries. She is maternal and finds fulfilment in bringing up her children, yet she seems to have neither the determination nor the discrimination to fashion a better world: 'She would throw away the living fruit for the ostensible rind.'

Lensky, Lydia
The Rainbow, 1915
D H Lawrence

An impoverished Polish aristocrat, the widow of Paul, a failed political radical, Lydia marries TOM BRANGWEN, the son of Nottinghamshire farmers. She is proud and mysterious, sometimes aloof and often generous. In terms of society, religion and social attitudes, she is an outsider in the English midlands, and indeed, there is a distance and a sense of detachment about her which it seems that even Tom can seldom penetrate. Yet she is devoted to him; their marriage is a happy one because, suggests Lawrence, it is not dulled either by complete self- or mutual knowledge.

Leoline, Sir
'Christabel', 1797–1801
Samuel Taylor Coleridge

Baron of Langdale Hall, Sir Leoline, terminally saddened by the death in childbirth of his wife, devotes all his love to his daughter Christabel. When he is presented with GERALDINE, the supposed daughter of his long-estranged friend, Sir Roland de Vaux, he welcomes the chance to restore relations with him by returning Geraldine safely home. Blinded by her beauty and his own motives, he ignores his bard's forebodings and misinterprets Christabel's attempts to awaken him to Geraldine's inherent evil, rejecting her in the anger and shame he feels at having his attempts at rekindling friendship threatened in this manner.

Leon, Archilde
The Surrounded, 1936
D'Arcy McNickle

A young Salish man, the son of a Native American mother and Mexican rancher father, now earning a bare living off the reservation oddjobbing and playing his fiddle. He is seen by the resident priest as the bright hope of his missionized generation. But as his intended last visit home lengthens, reawakened feelings for his family and empathy for his people lead Archilde towards a realization of the interconnectedness of human life and history, coupled with a hastening agnosticism. Unable to follow his mother in returning to a tribal religion, he adopts a fatalistic philosophy, bitter at the deceptions of his former faith which has left him only with a superstitious fear of the Devil. Pushed through others' actions into outlawry, his eventual reintegration with his people is not spiritual, but a secular and philosophical acceptance of the impossibility of struggling against a communal fate.

Leona
Another Country, 1962
James Baldwin

A white woman from the South, who has run away from a violent background to search out some new configuration of love in New York City, where she becomes the lover of the black drummer RUFUS SCOTT. She is thin and rather pale, almost drab, the receptacle of Rufus's seething hatreds and needs.

Leonard, Ruth
Rabbit, Run, 1960
Rabbit is Rich, 1981
John Updike
Her affair with RABBIT is set up for them by a
friend and is clearly intended to offer each of
them comfort and pleasure without ties. Ruth is
attractive and approachable, but her ensuing
pregnancy is a cold reminder that actions in the
real world bring consequences. When she and
Rabbit meet again 20 years later, she refuses to
acknowledge that he is the father of her daughter.

Leonato
Much Ado About Nothing, 1598/1600
William Shakespeare
As governor of Messina, Leonato is deferential to
the powerful DON PEDRO and his followers,
offering them hospitality in his house. As
guardian of BEATRICE he is surprised when a
partner is found for her and as father of HERO he
is delighted at the prospect of her marrying a
gentleman as rich and successful as CLAUDIO.
When the damaging charges are made against
Hero he is more willing to believe the accusers
than his own daughter, displaying a rare show of
anger at her for the apparent staining of the
family name. When the truth is made known he
is brusque with Don Pedro and Claudio, but he is
prepared to forgive them when it is clear that they
did not act out of malice. He nevertheless enjoys
the small revenge he exacts at their expense.

Leontes
The Winter's Tale, 1611
William Shakespeare
The entire impetus of this play stems from the
violent and irrational accusation by Leontes, the
King of Sicilia, that his wife, POLIXENES, is having
an affair with his friend, POLIXENES, the King of
Bohemia. To everyone, this tirade comes as a bolt
from the blue. Leontes is clearly an obsessive
personality, and the cause of his jealousy may be
fear of being cuckolded by a false friend. Unable
to distinguish truth from fiction, he falls back on
pride, rejecting the advice of his concerned
courtiers, imprisoning his wife, banishing his
child, defying the oracle and by the very force of
his fixation turning himself and the world
around him into a bleak emotional winter.

Leopold (Leopold Grant Moody)
The House in Paris, 1935
Elizabeth Bowen
'A dark-eyed, very slight little boy who looked
either French or Jewish ... he had the stately
waxen impersonal air of a royal child in a picture
centuries old.' This is how HENRIETTA sees
Leopold when they meet at the house in Paris.
He has been brought up by an aunt (who
incidentally regards botany and mythology as
fair preparations for sex education) and cannot
remember the mother (KAREN) he was separated
from as an infant.

Lepidus, Marcus Aemilius
Julius Caesar, c.1599
Antony and Cleopatra, 1606/7
William Shakespeare
He is in name the third member of the triumvirate

ruling after the death of JULIUS CAESAR but, 'A
slight unmeritable man', he is actually little more
than the errand boy of both ANTONY and
OCTAVIUS CAESAR. He wields no power, and in
Antony and Cleopatra is an insignificant go-
between for the two opposing generals.

Leplastrier, Lucinda
Oscar and Lucinda, 1988
Peter Carey
A passionate young woman, 'charged with static
electricity', she shares an obsession with
gambling with OSCAR HOPKINS, whom she meets
on the ship travelling to Australia. She is
exceptional for her time, both in that she is a
female entrepreneur (she is the owner of a glass-
works in Sydney that she bought with her
inheritance and hence is known as the Glass
Lady), and in her fierce independence.

Le Roux, Lambert
Pravda: A Fleet Street Comedy, 1985
Howard Brenton and David Hare
A white South African 'in his early forties, heavily
built, muscular and dark', he is a newspaper
proprietor who has no compunction about
acquiring a British passport 'through normal
channels. Albeit at unusual speed', to acquire
Britain's most prestigious title, *The Daily Victory*.
Reptilian and frightening, Le Roux is a
manifestation of ruthless avarice, manipulative
unscrupulousness and glinting intelligence,
motivated by a single, dominating idea: 'To
succeed'. 'What I do is a natural thing. There is
nothing unnatural about making money.' He
epitomizes an international ethos of financial
greed and cultural and moral contempt.

Leslie, Faith
Hope Leslie, or Early Times in the Massachusetts,
1827
Catharine Maria Sedgwick
The daughter of Puritan settlers Alice and
Charles Leslie, she is more compliant and
accommodating than her sister HOPE LESLIE.
Perhaps ironically, then, she comes to accept the
ways of the Pequod tribe that capture her and
chooses to remain with them rather than be
'rescued'. At the end of the novel, as the wife of
ONECO, she is completely assimilated, joining the
Native Americans on their migration further into
the western frontier.

Leslie, Hope
Hope Leslie, or Early Times in the Massachusetts,
1827
Catharine Maria Sedgwick
One of the first truly independent heroines in
American literature, she rejects the constraints
imposed on women by Puritanism and prefers to
follow her own eminently practical and moral
instincts. In her search for her long-lost sister
FAITH LESLIE, she proves to be self-denying and
heroic.

Leslie, Kate
The Plumed Serpent, 1926
D H Lawrence
Forty years old and uncertain, Kate hovers at a
turning point in her life, wondering whether her

dormant spiritual and sexual self might still be reawakened, and if so, how. She is a thoughtful, questing woman, who has many ideals and has suffered many disappointments, but making important decisions has never been her strong point, and now she deliberates between abandoning England and settling abroad, or returning to her cultural roots and family community. She settles for Mexico, but does not wholly commit herself either to the country or to DON CIPRIANO, the tough, uncompromising man she marries. 'What a fraud I am!' she reflects.

Lesly, Ludovic (le Balafre)
Quentin Durward, 1823
Sir Walter Scott

Uncle to QUENTIN DURWARD and captain of LOUIS XI, KING OF FRANCE's personal guard of Scottish archers. He gets his nickname from a brutal, multi-coloured sabre scar that furrows one side of his face. Bold, honest and not averse to drink, he is unswervingly loyal and politic in his service of the French king.

Lesser, Harry
The Tenants, 1971
Bernard Malamud

An experienced writer who has been painstakingly working on his 'masterpiece' for nine years. He is white, middle-aged, friendless, totally self-absorbed, and obsessed by order and form, and as such is the polar opposite of his adversary, WILLIE SPEARMINT. They occupy the same crumbling tenement building, have a relationship with the same girl, and have a curious dependency on each other which they can never reconcile or accept. As a result, they become increasingly envious and adversarial.

Lessways, Hilda
Clayhanger, 1910
Hilda Lessways, 1911
These Twain, 1916
Arnold Bennett

Romantic and impulsive, Hilda declares her love for one man and immediately runs off with another. When this is explained she is revealed to be a woman of keen mind and insight who is, at the same time, wayward and illogical in her action. When she realizes the consequences of her disastrous infatuation she is filled with an overwhelming sense of guilt and shame, which makes her life a 'chill and stricken desolation of incommutable doom'. Reconciliation with EDWIN CLAYHANGER and their years together restore her to some kind of normality although she always remains something of a mystery.

Lester, Jeeter
Tobacco Road, 1932
Erskine Caldwell

A poor white man in Georgia, the rather vague and feckless father of 17 children. Scraping a living from the unforgiving soil proves a daunting task, and his natural optimism is eroded and finally overwhelmed by the sheer impossibility of his family's predicament. Hunger devastates and debilitates what small dreams he has, and he dies horribly with his wife as they try to make a fire to warm themselves.

Lestrade, Inspector
A Study in Scarlet, 1887, et seq
Arthur Conan Doyle

A 'sallow, rat-faced, dark-eyed fellow', is how DR WATSON describes Inspector Lestrade of Scotland Yard. He is an energetic, methodical and utterly unimaginative detective. According to SHERLOCK HOLMES, Lestrade is 'conventional – shockingly so'. Unlike Holmes, he cannot, for example, distinguish between the ashes left by different brands of cigar and tobacco. Neither does he have any affinity with footprints in dust or clay earth. He affects to deride Holmes's methods as madness, yet Holmes solves several of his cases while generously allowing the humbled Lestrade to take the credit for himself.

Le Sueur, Lucetta
The Mayor of Casterbridge, 1886
Thomas Hardy

Vivacious, ambitious and impulsive, Lucetta cuts an exotic figure in Casterbridge when she arrives from her native Jersey. After her marriage to DONALD FARFRAE, her overbearing manner causes her to become unpopular with the local people, who relish her humiliation when her earlier affair with MICHAEL HENCHARD comes to light.

Lesworth, Gerald
The Last September, 1929
Elizabeth Bowen

LOIS FARQUAR's fiancé, he is a handsome British officer who has seen action during World War I and is subsequently implicated in the Irish civil war. He is both an ideal suitor and a painful reminder of the violent world outside the protective walls of Danielstown, and when he dies there is a general sense of relief as well as shock.

Levanter, George
Blind Date, 1977
Jerzy Kosinski

Named after a westward-blowing Mediterranean wind, Levanter is a writer in pursuit of identities – in himself and others – that are not constrained by the totalitarian societies of 'the East' and the corrupt Europe of Nazism. In his author's words, Levanter 'is engaged in the Socratic quest – one's obligation to examine and assume responsibility for *one's own* actions'.

Leventhal, Asa
The Victim, 1947
Saul Bellow

A Jewish professional who is haunted by a malicious 'double' in the shape of an anti-Semitic colleague, KIRBY ALLBEE, who blames him for his dismissal. He has enough troubles and insecurities of his own, however, including emotional and sexual repression, touchiness about his racial identity, insecurity, a damaged sense of self and a slightly comic air of absurdity. He moves to a brink where 'illness, madness and death were forcing him to confront his fault', and ultimately emerges 'lucky' and reasonably successful, if still unfulfilled.

Leverett, Peter
Set This House on Fire, 1961
William Styron
Leverett is aptly named, for he is caught in the glare of Mason Flagg's charismatic evil like a hare caught in the beam of a flashlight. A young American in Italy after World War II, he finds himself enmeshed in the operatic tragedy that unfolds round Flagg's deadly game with the angst-ridden artist Cass Kinsolving (another name that invites closer inspection).

Levin, Sam
A New Life, 1961
Bernard Malamud
A New York-born college teacher living in a small-minded Midwestern town, where he is very much an outsider. He has come west to put his alcoholism behind him and start a new life, but is initially a figure of fun. He shirks responsibility in his battles with his arch-enemy on the faculty, Gilley, but has an affair with his wife which proves a turning point in his life. He grows towards a clearer moral understanding, and finds a new life with her, albeit not the one he had sought.

Levinsky, David
The Rise of David Levinsky, 1917
Abraham Cahan
The classic portrait of the Jewish-American *allrightnik*, David accepts the values of American life without question and, as his career thrives, quickly loses sight of his native standards and expectations. Closely based on William Dean Howells's SILAS LAPHAM, David entirely lacks Silas's moral growth and ability to weigh up his own experience.

Levov, Meredith ('Merry')
American Pastoral, 1997
Philip Roth
The daughter of wealthy glove manufacturer SEYMOUR LEVOV, Merry had a privileged childhood, yet in 1968, at the height of the Vietnam War and at the age of 16, she is transformed 'almost overnight' into a slovenly, contemptuous teenager immersed in extreme left-wing politics. Her political views, however, are more the product of adolescent resentment than any social analysis. For her father, being American means to love America; for Merry, it is the opposite. Implicated in a fatal explosion at the local general store, Merry goes into hiding, protected by the speech therapist who is attempting to cure her of a stammer. Having subsequently joined a Jainist sect in her search for a new equilibrium, she later emerges to work at an animal hospital.

Levov, Seymour ('the Swede')
American Pastoral, 1997
Philip Roth
'The Swede' is a wealthy glove manufacturer, having earned his nickname by virtue of his blue eyes, blonde hair and athletic prowess. Ridding himself of 'the old Jewish habits and attitudes' in order to further his integration and become an 'ideal' American, he abandons his largely immigrant community and aligns himself with American history by buying a house in a New Jersey village that was once a Civil War encampment. Socially and professionally, his successes come at a time, after World War II, when America was triumphant. Yet he is undermined by guilt that the passionate kiss he bestowed upon his daughter MEREDITH LEVOV when she was eleven, 'so alien to the emotional rules by which he was governed', precipitated her later rebellion. Rejected and isolated, his world collapses.

Lewin, Daniel
The Book of Daniel, 1971
E L Doctorow
In adult life, he reflects obsessively on the lives and execution of his parents ROCHELLE and PAUL ISAACSON (a fictionalized version of atomic 'spies' Ethel and Julius Rosenberg). It is clear that to Daniel they are guilty, but guilty first and foremost of a failure of love, rather than of treason against the USA.

Lewis, Cliff
Look Back in Anger, 1956
Déjàvu, 1991
John Osborne
In his mid-twenties in the first play, Cliff is a short, dark, big-boned man with 'the rather sad, natural intelligence of the self-taught', and the stoical target of a good deal of his friend JIMMY PORTER's invective: 'Well, you *are* ignorant, you're just a peasant'. On the contrary, Cliff is loyal, thoughtful, understanding and a necessary mediator in the tempestuous marriage between Jimmy and ALISON PORTER, absorbing the rage of one and administering comfort to the other. He returns in the later play, older, wiser and more detached but still loyally supporting his old friend.

Lewis, Louie
The Heat of the Day, 1949
Elizabeth Bowen
A young working-class woman with a baby son, fending for herself in wartime London and overwhelmed by it. 'Left to herself ... she looked about her in vain for someone to imitate.'

Lewis, Stephen
The Child in Time, 1987
Ian McEwan
Stephen, a children's author, lives at a time when Britain has officially-controlled, licensed beggars, and its government plans to regenerate the nation by reforming childcare practices. He is still devastated by the abduction of his three-year-old daughter two years earlier. His wife has left him, and having exhausted all practical methods of finding his child he lives in a kind of catatonic trance. His only activity is serving on a sub-committee of the Official Commission on Childcare. Experiencing strange visions of his own childhood, he becomes involved in CHARLES DARKE's bizarre problems, and in a government cover-up concerning childcare.

Lewis the Dauphin
King John, 1590/1
William Shakespeare
Lewis is the son of PHILIP, KING OF FRANCE.

Having married BLANCHE, the niece of KING JOHN, the Catholic Lewis disregards his wife and is persuaded by PANDULPH, the papal legate, to take up arms against John and invade England. He refuses to abandon the crusade even when he learns that John has made a submission to Rome. The ties of religion, like the ties of nationhood, are for Lewis stronger than mere ties of blood.

Lewis the Dauphin
Henry V, 1599
William Shakespeare

The son of CHARLES VI, Lewis the Dauphin makes a serious error of judgement by sending Henry V (HENRY, PRINCE OF WALES) an insulting gift of tennis balls. His contempt for the English army and its king is not matched by any noticeable military skill as he fails to relieve the siege of Harfleur and is defeated at Agincourt. His boastful and argumentative nature is ultimately responsible for the lack of organization among his own troops which brings disaster and death.

Lewisham, George
Love and Mr Lewisham, 1900
H G Wells

We first see Lewisham as a nervous 18-year-old teacher covered with 'scholastic chalk' and trying to look older by using glasses. He has ambitious plans for the future involving the acquisition of languages and science certificates. Some of these plans are realized and he becomes a defiant socialist, complete with red tie; he has to adapt, however, to the fact that his simple and conservative wife is dismayed by his intellectual and political side.

Lewsome, Mr
Martin Chuzzlewit, 1844
Charles Dickens

An assistant surgeon and friend of JOHN WESTLOCK. His poverty and indebtedness to JONAS CHUZZLEWIT lead him to sell Jonas the drugs he uses to try to poison ANTHONY CHUZZLEWIT. During an illness when he is brutally nursed by MRS GAMP and BETSEY PRIG, his guilty conscience causes him to reveal Jonas's attempt at poisoning.

Leyburn, Catherine
Robert Elsmere, 1888
Mrs Humphry Ward

ROBERT ELSMERE's wife, she is a devout northern girl, whose heart never quite leaves the Westmoreland hills. She is shocked by her husband's loss of faith, which leaves him with what she perceives as a barrenly rationalistic attitude. She is, however, intensely loyal, and though she doubts the value of what he is doing, agrees to join him in the East End of London with his New Brotherhood of Christ.

Liar, Billy, properly **Billy Fisher**
Billy Liar, 1959
Keith Waterhouse

A young working-class daydreamer who enlivens his dreary existence as an undertaker's clerk in a dull northern town with an elaborate fantasy life.

His existence becomes a series of comic misadventures sparked off by his propensity to tell lies, but his falsehoods are motivated by his need to 'reduce the monotony of living on the moon', which is how he sees the sterility of his public and private life. He is a mimic, and a comic character, but is ultimately strongly bound by his roots, and will never leave 'the moon'.

Lickcheese
Widowers' Houses, 1892
George Bernard Shaw

Employed as a rent collector by the slum landlord, SARTORIUS, the shabby Lickcheese, resentful of the other's wealth, resorts to shady dealing to acquire his own slum property. Lickcheese chooses property due for demolition, intending to make sufficient building improvements to guarantee the maximum compensation. A man of few scruples and incisive cunning, he represents the nature of capital at its most morally corrupt. Like a lurking spider, he draws Sartorius, the once upright DR HARRY TRENCH, and his friend WILLIAM DE BURGH COKANE, into his racket.

Liege, Bishop of (Louis of Bourbon)
Quentin Durward, 1823
Sir Walter Scott

A generous and kind-hearted ecclesiastical prince who, having abandoned the excesses of his youth, is inclined to ride only gently over the foibles of his brethren and subjects. He is a fast friend of the DUKE OF BURGUNDY. He is murdered by a follower of WILLIAM DE LA MARCK, presumably with the connivance of LOUIS XI, KING OF FRANCE, though Scott violates the chronology somewhat.

Lieutenant, the
The Power and the Glory, 1940
Graham Greene

The lieutenant has rejected Catholicism and is now more concerned with the practicalities of creating a better, fairer world in the present day. He tries to avoid questions of morality and, instead, acts in a pragmatic fashion. He is a lonely, isolated man, who has not known love, but who still follows a humane impulse to create a more joyous, richer life for the children on the Mexican settlement where he lives. Ultimately he is a sympathetic, tragic figure who, having lost his faith, has failed to find grace.

Liffey
Puffball, 1980
Fay Weldon

A pretty, feminine and accepting woman, Liffey is treated badly by those she trusts and cares for. She is vulnerable, gullible and meek, characteristics which seem to invite people to use her. After a traumatic childhood with an overbearing mother, she has grown used to concealing her thoughts and feelings. She has a childlike determination to get her own way, but learns from her mistakes. Motherhood creates a niche for her, offering a power she previously lacked, and she becomes stronger, determining to do things on her own terms.

Lightfoot, Nance
The Vivisector, 1970
Patrick White
The archetypal prostitute with a heart of gold. Uninhibited, sentimental (and rather sentimentalized by the author), Nance falls passionately in love with the artist, HURTLE DUFFIELD. An intuitive, straightforward woman, she is distraught when she discovers that Duffield exploits others for the sake of his art.

Lightwood, Mortimer
Our Mutual Friend, 1865
Charles Dickens
A young solicitor with a private income, he is the intimate friend of EUGENE WRAYBURN, with whom he indolently frequents the VENEERING dinner parties. Uninterested in the law, his only work is for MR and MRS BOFFIN, unravelling the Harmon inheritance. He is eventually inspired by the example of Boffin and JOHN HARMON to make something of himself and become a responsible character.

Lila
The Village by the Sea, 1982
Anita Desai
As the eldest daughter of an impoverished family living in a small fishing village in western India, it falls upon Lila and her brother, HARI, to try to help the family survive hard times. Hari wants to leave for Bombay and find success there, but Lila, while much more cautious than her brother, is arguably far more practical, at least in the short-term. She elects to work as a servant for a wealthy family of holiday-makers. By doing so she embraces the Indian woman's subservient role, but her actions are not merely forced upon her by necessity. Unlike her drunken father, Lila has a vibrant spirit and she refuses to be defeated by hardship. Not only is she determined, she is also emotionally mature and resilient.

Lilith
Back to Methuselah, 1921
George Bernard Shaw
Lilith, the Mother of Creation, is mentioned by THE SERPENT during the first section of this five-part play and appears in the final segment, *As Far as Thought can Reach*, which is set in a remote garden Utopia in 31,920AD. By imagination and force of will, Lilith originally divided herself to create both ADAM and EVE, because the burden of creation is such that two must share it. Lilith appears at the end of the play to deliver a long soliloquy on the nature and development of mankind: 'Of Life only there is no end'.

Lilliputians
Gulliver's Travels, 1726
Jonathan Swift
A race of small people who represent the moral and mental absurdity of humankind. Politically incompetent and petty-minded, they are governed by a king who gives ribbons to courtiers for jumping over sticks. They are mechanically naive and prone to much warmongering. They bury their dead with their 'heads directly downwards' because they believe that the earth is flat and, come judgement day, will turn upside down; thus when resurrected they will be found standing on their feet. As they mimic humans, it is shown that people are as contemptible as Lilliputians are small.

Lilly, Maud
Fingersmith, 2002
Sarah Waters
Orphaned at birth, Maud is brought up in near-total isolation at the crumbling house of her aged and deeply unpleasant uncle. Her chance to escape arrives when, at 17, she is persuaded into a secret marriage with a fortune-hunting acquaintance. Although her maid, SUE TRINDER, sees her as an innocent, Maud's eccentric upbringing has in fact made her unexpectedly hard-headed and 'as worldly as the grossest rakes of fiction'.

Lilly, Rawdon
Aaron's Rod, 1922
D H Lawrence
A charismatic but dangerous thinker who befriends AARON SISSON in London, nursing him when he falls ill. He is a dominating, powerful presence, although his philosophy of life borders upon the Fascist: 'there must be one who urges, and one who impels'. Lilly conceives of life as a competition in which only the strong and the quick survive; in which the weak are subjugated by the powerful. He is magnetic, even generous, but also bombastic and harsh. Aspects of his philosophy appeal to Aaron (there is an atmosphere of homoeroticism between them), but in general Lilly is undistinguished both as man and thinker.

Lillyvick, Mr
Nicholas Nickleby, 1839
Charles Dickens
A collector of the water rate, he is the well-off bachelor uncle on whom MRS KENWIGS bases her social standing and has expectations that her children will inherit his money. When he marries the actress, MISS HENRIETTA PETOWKER, the Kenwigs are devastated, but his new wife elopes and leaves him disconsolate. He is reconciled to the family and announces he will immediately settle money on all the children.

Lincoln, Abraham
'Abraham Lincoln Walks at Midnight', in *The Congo and Other Poems*, 1914
Vachel Lindsay
Lincoln is recreated by Lindsay as a 'mourning figure', pacing the darkened streets of Springfield, Illinois. 'A bronzed, lank man! His suit of ancient black,/A famous high top-hat and plain worn shawl,/Make him the quaint great figure that men love,/The prairie-lawyer, master of us all.'

Lincoln, Abraham
The Graysons, 1887
Edward Eggleston
Eggleston portrays the future president as a small-town lawyer who cleverly proves the innocence of a man falsely accused of murder. This version of Lincoln is an appealing balance of simple frontier practicality and idealism.

Lincoln, Abraham
Lincoln, 1984
Gore Vidal

A fictional portrait of the famous US president, from his inauguration at the beginning of the Civil War to his assassination at its end. The portrait is intimate rather than idealized. He is 'a successful lawyer and political failure' unexpectedly risen to power, and is a 'very complicated secretive sort of man', kindly, intelligent, sharp-witted, with a gift for flattery and story-telling, and a 'rustic western style'. He is a great orator, but needs 'a well-prepared brief', is 'strong as an ox', and a teetotaller who is 'averse to food in general'. He is not a religious man, but believes 'in fate — and necessity' to help guide him through 'so bloody and absolute a rebirth for his nation'.

Lind, Katharine
A Girl in Winter, 1947
Philip Larkin

Encouraged by her school, this young German girl starts up a correspondence with Robin Fennel, who invites her to stay with him in rural Oxfordshire. She soon becomes simultaneously infatuated and alienated by his stereotypically English formality, but discovers that the invitation was prompted by Robin's sister Jane. Years later, a series of personal disasters drives Katharine to wartime England, where she endures extreme despair and loneliness as an assistant in an urban Branch Library. A chance newspaper mention puts her back in contact with Robin, who visits her from his artillery camp, but he looks 'young and haggard', and fails to offer her the 'love, security, happiness and a British passport' which she desires.

Linda
In a Free State, 1971
V S Naipaul

Linda reduces her companion BOBBY to confessional self-exposure during their drive from an African capital to an expatriate colony in the hinterland. She is an Englishwoman sensitive to the violence and chaotic conditions resulting from the country's civil war, and is exasperated by Bobby's inability to face facts, telling him rather brutally: 'Every night in the compound you hear them raising the hue and cry, and you know they're beating someone to death outside. Every week there's this list of people who've been killed, and some of them don't even have names. You should either stay away, or you should go among them with the whip in your hand. Anything in between is ridiculous.'

Linda
The Pursuit of Love, 1945
Nancy Mitford

Linda longs for love but twice goes far astray seeking it. Her first husband is a man of commerce absorbed in making money, which Linda spends. Her second is a political activist; Linda is bored and leaves him. Alone in a Paris railway station during World War II, crying and penniless, she is picked up by the charming and understanding Fabrice who instals her in a luxurious flat. He is the Duc de Sauveterre, and becomes the love of her life, as she is of his, but the couple are tragically separated by the war.

Lindau, Henry
A Hazard of New Fortunes, 1890
William Dean Howells

A German socialist on the staff of BASIL MARCH's new journal *Every Other Week*, he rapidly falls foul of the paper's proprietor, DRYFOOS, who tries to have him dismissed. Lindau, however, resigns and subsequently dies of injuries sustained while trying to subdue a strike riot.

Lingard, Captain Tom
Almayer's Folly, 1895
An Outcast of the Islands, 1896
The Rescue, 1920
Joseph Conrad

Said to be based on a real seaman named William Lingard, he first appeared in Conrad's debut novel. He is known as 'the King of the Sea' in the Malay peninsula, where he has some shady associations. He is courageous, generous to the point of profligacy, and largely successful, but also dissipated and exploitative.

Linkinwater, Tim
Nicholas Nickleby, 1839
Charles Dickens

The elderly and loyal chief clerk of the CHEERYBLE brothers, who make NICHOLAS NICKLEBY his assistant. The Nicklebys become his good friends and introduce Linkinwater to his future wife, MISS LA CREEVY.

Linley, Clive
Amsterdam, 1998
Ian McEwan

A successful composer who views himself 'as Vaughan Williams's heir', Linley believes emphatically in the importance of traditional melody over contemporary experiment and innovation. Living in amiable bohemian chaos, self-absorbed and conservative, Linley is engaged on completing his Millennial Symphony. Having met his old friend VERNON HALLIDAY at the funeral of their former lover MOLLY LANE, who has died aged 46, he proposes that if either is diagnosed with a degenerative illness such as that which killed Molly, the other would help him die. Halliday's intention to publish compromising photographs offends Linley's sense of privacy and integrity; accusing Halliday of betrayal, he finds his own moral values being questioned in return.

Linton, Catherine
Wuthering Heights, 1848
Emily Brontë

The daughter of CATHERINE EARNSHAW and EDGAR LINTON, she is said to be a real beauty, combining the best features of both families and emerging as 'the most winning thing that ever brought sunshine into a desolate house'. Having inherited elements of the wilfulness in her mother's nature, she is inevitably drawn into the enduring conflict between Heathcliff and his neighbours but finds reserves of goodness and character within her to withstand his vilest machinations and find her own happiness.

Linton, Edgar
Wuthering Heights, 1848
Emily Brontë

A gentle, thoughtful man with large, serious eyes and a graceful figure, he is quietly but tenaciously devoted to his neighbour CATHERINE EARNSHAW, who eventually agrees to become his wife. At the time of her death, he retreats in grief from the world, living the life of a near-hermit as he waits to join her in the hereafter whilst immersed in concern for what fate may befall his daughter CATHERINE LINTON after his own death.

Linton, Isabella
Wuthering Heights, 1848
Emily Brontë

A year younger than CATHERINE EARNSHAW, Isabella is a striking contrast to her neighbour, her bright golden hair, porcelain skin and elegant manner proclaiming her a genteel young lady. However, there is also a recklessness in her nature for which she pays dearly. Blind to the faults of HEATHCLIFF, she marries him in haste and repents at leisure as she grows to regard him as a monster. Her one error casts a sinister shadow over the remainder of an unhappy life.

Lippi, Fra Lippo
Men and Women, 1855
Robert Browning

A painter-monk who has been caught by the Watch 'where sportive ladies leave their doors ajar'. As a starving eight-year-old he was put in a monastery. His only talent was for drawing but his portrayal of real human beings in religious art has offended his seniors, who demand that he should paint souls not bodies. But he can only paint the world as he sees it, for 'God made it all'. He has a tremendous zest for life.

Lippincote, Mrs
At Mrs Lippincote's, 1945
Elizabeth Taylor

After the death of her husband, she rents out her house to young people who find the association with mortality and Mrs Lippincote's own oddly Dickensian presence (topped off with a black straw hat on which a swan appears to have landed) decidedly off-putting.

Lise
The Driver's Seat, 1974
Muriel Spark

For more than 16 years, since she was 18, Lise has worked in an accountant's office, wearing a disapproving look until her hysterical outbursts began. She speaks four languages and lives in an obsessively neat one-room flat. As she sets off abroad, looking for a special man to solve the problems of her life, she wears lurid clothes to ensure that she is noticed as her appearance is generally nondescript. She pursues death, not sex (which makes her sad).

Lismahago, Lt Obadiah
The Expedition of Humphry Clinker, 1771
Tobias Smollett

Scalped by the Indians at Ticonderoga, this lantern-jawed old soldier presents a rather fearsome aspect to the world. 'He would have measured above six feet in height, had he stood upright; but he stooped very much; was very narrow in the shoulders, and very thick in the calves of the legs ... As for his thighs, they were long and slender, like those of a grasshopper.' Despite his natural and acquired disadvantages, he becomes the subject of TABITHA BRAMBLE's romantic interest.

Lister
Not To Disturb, 1971
Muriel Spark

The English butler of Baron Klopstock, given to philosophical remarks and quotations from English literature. He does not distinguish between the past, present and future, having already sold the story of the violent deaths of the baron and baroness and their 'secretary' before the event, declaring that they are 'within the realms of predestination'. On the fatal night he directs the activities of the servants in the Swiss mansion with his usual aplomb. Behind his respectable façade, he has been involved in extortion and pornography.

Listless, Mr
Nightmare Abbey, 1818
Thomas Love Peacock

Only female attentions raise any spark of life from Mr Listless, who spends his time in a supine position on a couch. Fashionable, foppish, and simultaneously lethargic and dispirited, he is a hypochondriac who is in fact bone idle. 'Laughter is pleasant, but the exertion is too much for me', he says, before returning to his 'favourite pursuit of doing nothing'.

Liszt, Franz
The Young Cosima, 1939
Henry Handel Richardson

The great composer is a later version of the wild Polish genius SCHILSKY (who in turn was probably based on Liszt). COSIMA VON BÜLOW's father, he is portrayed as temperamental, erratic and thoroughly egocentric.

Littimer
David Copperfield, 1850
Charles Dickens

The deferential manservant of MR JAMES STEERFORTH, his 'great claim to consideration was his respectability'. A detestable scoundrel, he arranges Steerforth's abduction of LITTLE EM'LY. When Steerforth decides to desert her, Steerforth insultingly suggests she should marry Littimer to gain respectability. His arrest is brought about by MISS MOWCHER and, with URIAH HEEP, he is last seen in MR CREAKLE's model prison.

Little, Vernon Gregory
Vernon God Little, 2003
D B C Pierre

Teenage white trash living in Martirio, Texas, Vernon has few friends, an absent father and an ineffectual mother who 'controls what you wear by keeping everything else damp in the laundry'. Regarded as a loner, he finds himself the prime suspect of the terrible crime that has taken place at his school. Betrayed by those around him and armed only with sardonic humour and total cynicism, Vernon seeks out the object of his lust: 'we nearly made out once … She was wasted, but conscious', and goes on the run. He receives help from some unlikely allies and, as we know, ugly ducklings can grow into beautiful swans.

Little Billee
Trilby, 1894
George Du Maurier

One of TRILBY's friends and admirers in Paris, he shares a studio with TAFFY and THE LAIRD. In Du Maurier's own etching, he looks younger than his companions, and he is described as being about 20 or 21, with 'a white, strong forehead veined with blue, large dark blue eyes, delicate regular features and coal-black hair'.

Little Caesar → Bandello, Rico Cesare

Little Isadore
Stories à la Carte, 1932
Furthermore, 1938
Damon Runyon

A minor New York gangster, he is forced to watch the downfall of his leader HARRY THE HORSE, brought about by his ill-considered attraction to a woman quite unsuited to someone of Harry's chosen profession. Dabbling in crime and vice with simple enthusiasm, he brings to his criminal activity and the violence that accompanies it, a total lack of moral focus.

Little Nell
The Old Curiosity Shop, 1841
Charles Dickens

The child companion and support of her feeble GRANDFATHER, she is 'nearly fourteen' and of angelic character. She is terrified by Grandfather's moneylender, DANIEL QUILP, who lusts after her. When the old man loses his shop and all his property through gambling, the pair leave London to escape from Quilp and Nell's dissolute elder brother, Fred Trent, who believes Grandfather is hoarding money to give to her. They wander the country, taking up employment from people they meet, and finally settle in the remote village where THE BACHELOR lives. She becomes the church caretaker and dies shortly before KIT NUBBLES, MR GARLAND and the Single Gentleman (the brother of Grandfather) arrive.

Littlepage, Captain
The Country of the Pointed Firs, 1896
Sarah Orne Jewett

A garrulous old shipmaster, much given to quoting Milton, and considered by the herbalist ALMIRA TODD to 'have overset his mind with too much reading'. In appearance, he resembles 'an aged grasshopper of some strange human variety'.

Littlepage, Virginius Curle
They Stooped to Folly, 1929
Ellen Glasgow

Too old, too timid and too complacent to move forward, Virginius is a 'caged hawk' who lives his life in a protracted panic. A sufferer of chronic dyspepsia, his philosophy of life is rooted in a hysterical dislike of women. He feels himself disenfranchised in a woman-dominated society; to him America is an 'oligarchy of maternal instincts'. Confined within a lifeless marriage, Virginius dreams of his feeble transgressions with Amy Dalrymple, the only time he abandoned himself to lust.

Littlewit, John and Win
Bartholomew Fair, 1614
Ben Jonson

As their name implies, they have little wit, although John imagines himself the wittiest and cleverest man alive. Against the wishes of his Puritan mother-in-law, DAME PURECRAFT, he takes his wife, Win, to Bartholomew Fair to see his puppet show. His greatest fault is his inability to judge character accurately. He leaves Win in the care of Knockem and Captain Whit, whom he believes to be 'very good men', but who are, in fact, drunks and cheats. Win is quite good-looking but as gullible as her husband, susceptible to flattery and, like DAME OVERDO, easily persuaded by her new companions to act like a prostitute.

Livia
Women Beware Women, c.1621
Thomas Middleton

The aunt of ISABELLA and sister of HIPPOLITO and Fabritio, Livia is treacherous and manipulative. She is cynical, corrupt and proud of her powers of persuasion and reasoning, using her strong will to manipulate people into awkward situations for her own entertainment, such as when she lies to Isabella about her parentage to encourage her to embark on an incestuous affair with her uncle.

Liza
Liza of Lambeth, 1897
W Somerset Maugham

Maugham's portrait of a poor London street-girl owes as much to Zola as to direct observation, but is nonetheless a convincing portrait of a figure over-determined and burdened by her environment.

Lizzie
Goblin Market, 1862
Christina Rossetti

Unlike her sister LAURA, Lizzie shuts her eyes and stops her ears to the tiny voices of the goblins offering their rich fruits. Laura has been beguiled by them, and is growing listless and weary, and is near to dying. Lizzie determines she must save her, and goes to the goblins with a silver penny. They ask her to feast with them but she refuses and will not open her lips to their fruit. She stands silently; they cannot persuade her, even with blows, and in the end give her back her coin and go away frustrated. She runs home, her clothes torn and wet with fruit juice, which, when Laura tastes it, is now bitter and scorching. Gradually the sisters return to the innocent happiness they enjoyed before encountering the goblins.

Lizzie, Aunt
Philadelphia, Here I Come!, 1965
Brian Friel

Aunt Lizzie is GAR O'DONNELL's aunt, the sister of his dead mother. A 'small energetic ... impulsive' woman, her physical demonstrativeness is disquieting to her only nephew. She has lived in America with her husband Con for 25 years and has 'come up in the world', now calling herself 'Elise' and bragging of her air-conditioned apartment with colour TV. Childless, she admits to resorting to a 'sorta bribery' in persuading Gar to start a new life with them in Philadelphia. Gar has his own reasons for accepting her offer.

Lochinvar
Marmion, 1808
Sir Walter Scott

'O, young Lochinvar is come out of the west'. One of the best-known characters in all literature (and a major source of the illusion that poetry should be recited in a rhythm like hoofbeats), he is actually the subject of an interpolated song which is played and sung by the lonely queen in Linlithgow Palace. Rather than be jilted by his love, who is about to be married off to a milksop, Lochinvar gatecrashes the wedding and bears her off on his steed.

Lochleven, Lady of
The Abbot, 1820
Sir Walter Scott

She is, in effect, the gaoler of MARY, QUEEN OF SCOTS, a role made easier by the lady's bitter resentment that James V did not marry her and legitimize her son, the regent, who can never ascend the throne. Her beauty and her nature have been soured by rejection and disappointment.

Locke, Alton
Alton Locke, Tailor and Poet: An Autobiography, 1850
Charles Kingsley

The eponymous hero and narrator, he is a child of the petite bourgeoisie, who is suddenly thrust into the turmoil and hardship of working-class life when he is apprenticed to a tailor. Armed only with his widowed mother's Baptist teachings, he gradually comes to an awareness of the divisions in English society, and is drawn into the Chartist movement.

Lockhart, Jamie
The Robber Bridegroom, 1942
Eudora Welty

The good-hearted robber bridegroom of the title, he is tall, handsome and brawny, with 'heavy yellow-locks'. He is a shrewd, cunning and ruthless bandit leader when in the woods with his followers, but a gentleman in town, and has 'nothing less than a dream of true love' in his heart. After various misunderstandings and travails, he marries ROSAMOND MUSGROVE and becomes a prosperous merchant, shedding all his wild ways 'like a skin', a transformation which was 'almost too easy to count as a change at all'.

Lockit, Lucy
The Beggar's Opera, 1728
John Gay

The daughter of LOCKIT, THE JAILER. She loves CAPTAIN MACHEATH, who sweet-talks her into believing marriage to be a possibility. She lets him free from her father's jail and tries to drug her rival POLLY PEACHUM ('that enveigling harlot') into revealing how her relationship with MacHeath stands.

Lockit, the Jailer
The Beggar's Opera, 1728
John Gay

A London jailer who sees CAPTAIN MACHEATH saunter in and out of his custody. He is father to LUCY LOCKIT, one of the captain's many lovers, and has a partnership in crime with THOMAS PEACHUM the lawyer, which sways unstably due to their vanities and rivalry. Like Peachum, he stands for corrupt authority, no better than the criminals it condemns.

Locksley
Ivanhoe, 1819
Sir Walter Scott

Better known to legend as Robin Hood, he is somewhat humanized in Scott's portrait, a sturdy yeoman with a proud independence and a dazzling ability with the bow. His forest lair is the centre of resistance to the usurping PRINCE JOHN.

Lockwood
Wuthering Heights, 1848
Emily Brontë

A painfully shy man who seeks no company but his own. The new tenant of Thrushcross Grove, he finds his curiosity piqued by his first encounter with HEATHCLIFF, a man he regards as 'more exaggeratedly reserved than myself'. He is drawn repeatedly to learn more of Heathcliff's life from ELLEN DEAN, but the satisfaction of his curiosity is enough to justify severing all further contact with Wuthering Heights and its ill-fated inhabitants.

Lockwood, George
The Lockwood Concern, 1965
John O'Hara

His family have lived in Gibbsville, Pennsylvania, for two generations before him, but like many of O'Hara's protagonists, he has become obsessed by the emptiness at the centre of his life and has pushed the self-destruct button. His final act of gratuitous defiance is to drive his criminal son to California; not able to break out of the mould himself, he has to do it vicariously.

Loftis, Peyton (Peyton Loftis Miller)
Lie Down in Darkness, 1951
William Styron

The second daughter of Helen and Milton Loftis. As her early life in Virginia is revealed in flashback, it is clear that her anguish and confusion are entirely explicable by reference to her parents' broken power-struggle of a marriage, her father's near-incestuous feelings for her, and the death of her elder sister. Peyton marries a struggling artist, but becomes increasingly promiscuous and finally takes her life by jumping from a skyscraper.

Logan, Brendan
Shadows on Our Skin, 1977
Jennifer Johnston

A Republican activist, and elder brother of JOE LOGAN. He is welcomed home by his father, but his mother calls his beliefs 'tripe'. However, she lets him have Joe's bed and he takes all that the home has to offer, keeping secret his own affairs. Brendan lacks Joe's grace and sensitivity, and insinuates his way into Joe's friendship with KATHLEEN. Always pulling rank on his brother, he is genuinely grateful when Joe saves his skin, but is finally devastated when Joe viciously discloses the identity of Kathleen's fiancé. Brendan then reveals his true nature as a coward and a thug.

Logan, Joe
Shadows on Our Skin, 1977
Jennifer Johnston

A likeable boy, a dreamer and would-be poet. He carries the burdens of his family which prevent him from doing his school work. He despises his weak and wasted father and his hollow memories of heroism, and pities rather than loves his over-protective and worn-down mother. He resents his brother BRENDAN LOGAN, who always spells trouble. Joe is watchful and thoughtful and finds real friendship with KATHLEEN who, like him, is a loner. Though courageous, he unwittingly betrays Kathleen, an act which opens his eyes to a world of secrecy and deceit.

Logan, Miss Arabella
The Private Memoirs and Confessions of a Justified Sinner, 1824
James Hogg

An old friend of the LAIRD OF DALCASTLE who, after his separation from his wife, comes to reside with him as his 'housekeeper' and substitute mother for GEORGE COLWAN. Greatly aggrieved by the murder of her beloved George and the subsequent death of the Laird, Miss Logan, with the help of BELL CALVERT, takes it upon herself to use all her intelligence to uncover the real perpetrators of the crime.

Logie, Maggie
'Maggie Logie and the National Health', in *The Dying Stallion*, 1967
Fred Urquhart

A poor widow in a Scottish village, where she is popular with the neighbours. She has a male friend for many years; he never gets round to proposing, but the two hurtle about on a motorbike. When she has to pay insurance stamps to finance the National Health Service, she decides that 'she must get her money's worth', and goes to bizarre lengths to ensure that she does.

Lolita (Dolores Haze)
Lolita, 1955
Vladimir Nabokov

Honey-hued, chestnut-haired, grey-eyed Lolita is 'a combination of naïveté and deception, of charm and vulgarity, of blue sulks and rosy mirth'. Her early teen years from twelve onwards are an awkward mix of conventional all-American kid ('gooey fudge sundaes, musicals, movie magazines') and sensual, sexualized 'nymphet'. Her initial apparent liking for HUMBERT HUMBERT gives way to boredom and despair, although the extent to which she is a willing and aware participant in their involvement is debatable. She escapes to a brief life of mundane normality.

Loman, Ben
Death of a Salesman, 1949
Arthur Miller

Elder brother to WILLY LOMAN, his death is announced in the course of the play, and his appearance in it is as a ghostly figure from Willy's memory. He represents both the spirit of opportunity – 'when I was twenty-one I walked out (of the jungle) and by God I was rich' – and the corruption of the American ideal ('Never fight fair with a stranger boy. You'll never get out of the jungle that way'). His final role is to aid and abet the suicide of his brother, who is a victim of the system Ben represents.

Loman, Biff
Death of a Salesman, 1949
Arthur Miller

The son of WILLY LOMAN, he is a lost soul who has wandered America in search of contentment, since his dreams and aspirations were shattered by the discovery of his idolized father's infidelity. Formerly a confident, handsome, popular sportsman, he has become a confused and unsuccessful adult, whose kleptomaniac tendencies and lack of moral backbone are symptomatic of his upbringing, filled with 'hot air' and unrealistic aspirations by his father, who believes in Biff's 'greatness' throughout.

Loman, Happy
Death of a Salesman, 1949
Arthur Miller

The younger son of WILLY LOMAN, he seeks his parents' approval and love through self-aggrandizement and bluster, both as a child and as an adult. His sexual duplicity, poor success as a businessman, and inability to face the truth are characteristics inherited from his father, rendering inevitable the saddening view he expresses at his father's graveside that Willy Loman 'had a good dream'.

Loman, Linda
Death of a Salesman, 1949
Arthur Miller

Loyal throughout to her husband, WILLY LOMAN, she 'more than loves him, she admires him', and is willing to sacrifice her relationship with her children to protect his fragile mental state. Essentially a peacemaker, she is capable of anger and strength, giving way to grief only in the play's requiem, when her long struggle to save Willy is over. Despite his abuse of Linda, he, like the audience, is aware that 'the woman has waited, and the woman has suffered'.

Loman, Willy
Death of a Salesman, 1949
Arthur Miller

The salesman of the title – a traveller dealing in lingerie – whose hopeless immersion in the many facets of the American Dream forms the play's essential theme and eventual tragedy. Desperate to be a 'well-liked' success in business and at home, he is, in fact, a limited and unpopular man, ridden with guilt at his infidelity and his failure as a salesman and as a father. An exhausted, pathetic figure by the time he kills himself, he still inspires love from his family and sympathy from the audience: he is a man created and crushed by a system, essentially just 'a little boat looking for a harbour'.

Lonelyhearts, Miss
Miss Lonelyhearts, 1933
Nathanael West

The anonymous hero, he is the (male) agony aunt of a New York newspaper, responding to the desperate pleas of the emotionally crippled or loveless. He sees this as a debased version of his father's Christian ministry. He is tempted into a sexual liaison with one of his correspondents, the wife of a disabled man, and achieves a kind of ironic martyrdom when the jilted husband shoots him at a moment of ambiguous reconciliation.

Long Rob Duncan
Sunset Song, 1932, part of the trilogy *A Scots Quair*, 1946
Lewis Grassic Gibbon

The miller at Kinraddie, and thus commonly known as 'Long Rob of the Mill', he is an independent thinker noted for his caustically-expressed anticlerical opinions, and sympathizes with the socialist views of his friend CHAE STRACHAN. He is popular with the people of the village, always willing to help any neighbour in difficulty, and has a fine singing voice. Unlike Chae, he argues against war with Germany and is imprisoned as a conscientious objector. Broken by the experience, and despairing at the changes wrought by war, he finally enlists, though not before a passionate sexual encounter with the widowed CHRIS GUTHRIE, whom he has long admired.

Long Ghost, Doctor
Omoo, 1847
Herman Melville

A ship's physician who shares the narrator's adventures. He is tall and bony, with a 'complexion absolutely colourless, fair hair, and light, unscrupulous grey eyes, twinkling occasionally with the very devil of mischief'. His past is 'enveloped in the profoundest obscurity', but he has 'spent money, drunk Burgundy, and associated with gentlemen', and possesses education and cultivation. He is a fine singer, has a quick temper, and a liking for practical jokes.

Longaville
Love's Labour's Lost, not later than 1594
William Shakespeare

An attendant lord to the King of Navarre, KING FERDINAND, who swears an oath alongside him temporarily to stay away from women. The object of Longaville's straying eye is MARIA, who describes her pursuer as possessing 'sovereign parts' and 'sharp wit matched with too blunt a

will'. He is frustrated at the end from winning her by having to wait for the space of a year and a day before she can be wooed.

Longleat, Honoria
Policy and Passion, 1881
Rosa Praed

The politician THOMAS LONGLEAT's daughter, she stands for passion, yet is required to make nice calculations of her own, confronted as she is by a choice between men who offer her dramatically different prospects in life. She is her father's daughter to the degree that she brooks no obstacle to the exercise of her will.

Longleat, Thomas
Policy and Passion, 1881
Rosa Praed

A self-made politician in Reichardt's Land (a fictional version of Queensland, Australia), he is tough and self-possessed but haunted by a convict past that stands in the way of an unobstructed path to power.

Longman, Mr
Pamela, 1740–1
Samuel Richardson

MR B's veteran steward, Mr Longman is a relic of a bygone age, representing fidelity, honesty and selflessness. His rusticity is reflected in his archaic diction, with his preference for obsolete phrases like 'Ads-bobbers' and 'Ads-heartlikins'. He loves PAMELA ANDREWS dearly and intercedes on her behalf when Mr B announces his intention to banish her. His heart melts at Pamela's plight and he accuses Mr B of being made of iron and steel.

Lonigan, Studs (William)
Young Lonigan: A Boyhood in Chicago Streets, 1932
The Young Manhood of Studs Lonigan, 1934
Judgement Day, 1935
James T Farrell

A bright young boy of Irish Catholic stock, he shows considerable imagination and promise when first encountered at 15, but is gradually overwhelmed by the stultifying atmosphere of the Chicago backstreets and a corrupt version of the 'American Dream'. Intellectually and sexually curious, he is too weak-willed to sustain a faintly ironic distance from his tough-guy companions and the compliant girls who surround them. Eventually he succumbs to what Farrell once described as the 'spiritual poverty' of his environment.

Lonoff, E I
The Ghost Writer, 1979
Philip Roth

A successful Yiddish writer who has turned to writing in English, and is revered as a great chronicler of the American-Jewish experience (the character has been seen as being based on I B Singer). His acolyte NATHAN ZUCKERMAN sees his work as having 'a celebrated blend of sympathy and politeness', but his wife Hope, who comes of old New England gentile stock, thinks he has been 'a model of literary patience', who has gone unrewarded.

Loop Garou
Yellow Back Radio Broke Down, 1969
Ishmael Reed
His name is a version of the French for werewolf and his is a similarly macaronic character, a black cowboy who is an adept of voodoo (or Neo-Hoodoo) and a conduit for a charged-up Afro-American language which expresses unfamiliar and unprecedented cultural configurations.

Lopez, Ferdinand
The Prime Minister, 1876
Anthony Trollope
A tall, handsome, self-possessed, but un-scrupulous young man. He has a good educa-tion, and is an accomplished linguist. Ambitious for power, he has 'a taste for being a master rather than a servant'. He marries EMILY WHARTON for her fortune, but his political ambitions are stunted when an attempted blackmail fails, and he is discredited. Realizing the extent of his ruin, he throws himself under a train.

Lord, My
Amelia, 1751
Henry Fielding
A benevolent philanthropist on the exterior, a scheming seducer at heart, this anonymous nobleman has a repertoire of bribery, blackmail and entrapment. Protected by his wealth and power, he lures virtuous women into com-promising positions to satisfy his sexual ambitions. He lives for the thrill of conquest.

Lord, Nancy
In the Year of Jubilee, 1894
George Gissing
Obliged to keep her marriage to LIONEL TARRANT secret, she thus appears to be an unmarried mother, a decidedly perilous position in Victorian society. Tarrant's refusal to put their relationship on an official footing is decidedly two-edged, leaving her 'free' but also socially isolated.

Lord Jim
Lord Jim, 1900
Joseph Conrad
A sailor who embodies the failure of the romantic hero. He is an idealist with an elusive and unattainable vision of conduct which he can never achieve, and 'an acute consciousness of lost honour'. In the crucial episodes, he abandons his ship in an impulsive moment, loses his Master's Certificate, but continues to punish himself in his own mind. He becomes a trading agent, and finds a degree of happiness, but makes a further serious misjudgement when confronted by a criminal, and concludes that a tainted, imperfect man can never act rightly.

Lord Mayor of London
The Shoemaker's Holiday, 1599
Thomas Dekker
Sir Roger Otley, Lord Mayor of London and the father of ROSE OTLEY, is an irascible character who disapproves heartily of his daughter's love for ROWLAND LACY. A time-serving local government official, the Mayor sees money as a means of self-aggrandisement.

Lorenzo
The Merchant of Venice, 1594/5
William Shakespeare
A young Venetian and friend to BASSANIO, his essential role is as the male partner in the 'young lover' subplot with JESSICA; their carefully planned elopement from the carnival triggers SHYLOCK's anger against ANTONIO. A romantic, occasionally witty figure, he ends the play at Belmont, happily united with Jessica.

Lorraine, Mrs
Vivian Grey, 1826–7
Benjamin Disraeli
Based on Lady Caroline Lamb, she is a larger-than-life figure on the London political stage, who exerts considerable influence through her salon. It is she who exposes VIVIAN GREY's plans to establish his own party, thus precipitating his duel with CLEVELAND and his eventual downfall.

Lorry, Mr Jarvis
A Tale of Two Cities, 1859
Charles Dickens
The confidential clerk at Tellson's Bank, he accompanies LUCIE MANETTE to Paris to be reunited with her father, DR ALEXANDRE MANETTE, after his release from the Bastille. 'Very orderly and methodical', diplomatic and kind, he befriends the Manettes when they arrive in London and later helps them and CHARLES DARNAY to escape from France after Darnay's rescue from prison.

Lost Leader, the
'The Lost Leader', in *Dramatic Lyrics*, 1842
Robert Browning
A loved and revered leader who has deserted his followers for money and position. Once a poet who taught a 'great language', he has broken from the freemen and sunk 'to the rear and the slaves'. He is generally thought to be based on the poet William Wordsworth who had become an establishment conservative in old age, betraying the radical liberalism of his youth in the eyes of his younger followers.

Lothario
The Fair Penitent, 1703
Nicholas Rowe
Rumbustious, proud and reckless, a libertine and deceiver, Lothario, although loyal to his male friends, is in many ways when it comes to women, thoroughly dishonourable. For an audience, though, he is eminently engaging. Gallant and carefree, he does not inspire love in women so much as blind infatuation. Having seduced CALISTA, who is betrothed to ALTAMONT, he dies when the aggrieved Altamont defeats him in a duel. He is the inspiration for, among others, ROBERT LOVELACE in Samuel Richardson's *Clarissa* (1748).

Lottie
Prelude, 1920
Katherine Mansfield
The middle child of an extended Edwardian family awaiting the arrival of another baby.

Sturdy and cheerful, she relishes being the centre of attention. Her tears at a change in the planned house removals dry immediately in the sunshine of sympathy; equally, her reaction to the physical shock of the decapitation of a duck is to laugh. She is a natural organizer, taking charge of her little sister KEZIA.

Lou
Bear, 1976
Marian Engel

A local history researcher, Lou is isolated and lonely, living 'like a mole, but buried deep ... among maps and manuscripts'. Her retreat into the past disengages her from human contact, leaving her trapped by introspective self-criticism and deeply dissatisfied with life. Assigned to catalogue the library of a 19th-century eccentric recluse on a remote island in Northern Ontario, she develops an affectionate friendship with the island's only other inhabitant, a bear. This intimacy reconciles her human and animal instincts and enables her to assert a new and confident individuality.

Louis
The Waves, 1931
Virginia Woolf

Although outwardly successful, Louis is not at peace with himself. Ashamed of his Australian roots, he is inhibited by his desire to become thoroughly English. He sees a divided world and is ambitious to bridge gaps, but, being part conformist and part rebel, is hindered by his own sense of confusion.

Louis XI, King of France, incognito as Maître Pierre
Quentin Durward, 1823
Sir Walter Scott

The French king is wily, brutally calculating, but also excessively pious, susceptible to each and every superstition and cult. He is first encountered by QUENTIN DURWARD while travelling in disguise as Maître Pierre, when he seems 'partly attractive and partly forbidding'. His strong features, sunk cheeks and hollow eyes had an expression of shrewdness and humour' which is nonetheless tempered by something sinister.

Louka
Arms and the Man, 1894
George Bernard Shaw

A servant, she is a good-looking girl undeterred by her supposed social inferiority to her employers, the Bulgarian Petkoff family. She is so defiant that her servility towards RAINA PETKOFF borders on the insolent. SERGIUS SARANOFF finds her enormously attractive.

Louvet, Anne
The Girl at the Lion d'Or, 1989
Sebastian Faulks

Anne Louvet is a passionate and beautiful young woman who has fled her home village because of disgrace brought upon her family by her father at the end of World War I. She is alone – in France in the 1930s – seeking happiness and some element of certainty in her life. She is content to work well beneath her capabilities as a waitress at the hotel

of the title until she has an affair with CHARLES HARTMANN who, although a married man, seems to her to offer stability and worldly experience.

Love, Mary
Nigger Heaven, 1926
Carl Van Vechten

A pretty young black girl, she works as a librarian in Harlem. Though she is in love with the writer BYRON KASSON, their relationship is soured by Byron's poverty and his bitter reaction to it. Even so, she refuses the advances of the gambler RANDOLPH PETTIJOHN.

Loveday, Bob (Robert)
The Trumpet Major, 1880
Thomas Hardy

A cocky, likeable young man, but a very poor judge of character, especially when it comes to women. Bob is a very stereotyped portrayal of a sailor, determined to sow his wild oats before settling down. His often selfish ends are usually met through a rakish charm. The fact that his straight and honest brother, JOHN LOVEDAY, fares less well, says much about Hardy's perception and portrayal of human nature.

Loveday, John
The Trumpet Major, 1880
Thomas Hardy

A reliable, gentle and noble man, who is perhaps too trusting and sincere for the society he lives in. He accepts defeat gracefully in the battle for ANNE GARLAND, the girl he loves, mainly because he understands what she wants. But somehow it is this very lack of spirit, selfishness and determination which Anne cannot admire. His loyalty is unending, and self-sacrifice is natural to him. His tragedy lies in his lack of aggression and his incompatibility with his age.

Loveit, Mrs
The Man of Mode, 1676
Sir George Etherege

Mrs Loveit is in the throes of utter and unreasonable infatuation. 'I know he is a Devil', she says of DORIMANT, 'but he has something of the Angel yet undefac'd in him'. She is unable to distinguish between appearance and reality and is prone to 'mistake Art for Nature'. Highly-sexed and a giddy fool, Mrs Loveit leaves herself open to being both deceived and patronized.

Lovel, actual name and rank Major Neville
The Antiquary, 1816
Sir Walter Scott

A young officer who, having fallen in love with Isabella Wardour, follows her to Scotland under the alias of Lovel (which the antiquary JONATHAN OLDBUCK thinks is the sort of name actors adopt) to avoid the notice of her father who disapproves of the match. He is later revealed to be not illegitimate at all, but the son and heir of Lord Glenallan and thus eminently weddable.

Lovel, Frederick
Lovel the Widower, 1860
W M Thackeray

A well-off city businessman with a companionable

manner and a house in Putney. To an extent his friends are bought by his easy ways and generous table. In later years, the only blot on his life is a nagging wife, who thoroughly and perhaps wisely disapproves of Lovel's friend, the narrator.

Lovelace, Robert
Clarissa, 1748
Samuel Richardson

Named after the heroic Cavalier poet, Robert Lovelace is a striking example of male hauteur. Posing as an enlightened Lockean liberal, he expresses indignant sympathy for CLARISSA HARLOWE's subjugation under the yoke of parental tyranny. However, this rhetoric is exposed as pap and piffle when he turns Clarissa into his slave and violently possesses her. A glamorous Satanic figure who spouts eloquent soliloquies, Lovelace is Beelzebub to a 'set of infernals'. A rampant misogynist, he perceives the world through a series of archaic military metaphors.

Loveless
The Relapse, or Virtue in Danger, 1696
Sir John Vanbrugh

An apparently reformed rake, having settled in the country and married AMANDA, Loveless returns once more to London, the scene of his old debaucheries. There, he succumbs to the provocative young widow, BERINTHIA, finding 'the pleasing fire of lawful love' with Amanda all but smothered by the 'raging flame of wild destructive lust'. Loveless is by no means an intellectual; in fact, his powers of reason are rather limited, but neither is he a particularly ruthless deceiver. He is weak-willed and furtive, but not calculating.

Lovell, Lord
A New Way to Pay Old Debts, 1633
Philip Massinger

A popular and gallant soldier and eminent peer. The rich SIR GILES OVERREACH wants him to marry his daughter, but Lovell declares that he could not marry a woman without aristocratic blood. He helps his page TOM ALWORTH to marry the girl by tricking Sir Giles, and himself marries LADY ALWORTH.

Lovett, Jack
Democracy, 1983
Joan Didion

A 'man for whom the accidental did not exist ... for whom information was an end in itself', he is an agent on the world stage, with none of the moral and imaginative limitations of INEZ VICTOR's husband. Jack is Inez's lover, an affair conducted across the fringes of the American empire, the charismatic Jack's 'sphere of influence'.

Lovett, Mikey
Barbary Shore, 1951
Norman Mailer

'Probably I was in the war ... 'An amnesiac writer with a reconstructed face, he boards in GUINEVERE's Brooklyn house. The novel's narrator, he becomes the inheritor of ARTHUR

MCLEOD's socialist legacy and of a mysterious 'little object', which is never identified.

Lovewit
The Alchemist, 1610
Ben Jonson

A city gentleman and the employer of Jeremy (FACE). When Lovewit hurriedly leaves town in fear of the plague, Face invites SUBTLE and DOL COMMON into his house to begin a fraudulent alchemist's practice. When Lovewit unexpectedly returns he is at first enraged to see the illegal use to which his house has been put, but is soon mollified when he discovers that by Face's roguery he has won a new wife, DAME PLIANT, and a good deal of money.

Lowder, Mrs
The Wings of the Dove, 1902
Henry James

KATE CROY's aunt, she is obsessed with her niece's marriage prospects and urges her to accept the proposal of the wealthy Lord Mark. Like many of James's older female characters, her slight detachment from the main drama only partially disguises her considerable influence.

Lowestoffe, Reginald
The Fortunes of Nigel, 1822
Sir Walter Scott

A Templar, he is 'a wild young gallant, indifferently well provided with money, who spent at the theatres and other gay places of public resort, time which his father supposed he was employing in the study of the law'. Nonetheless, he is 'shrewd, alert, and well acquainted with the town, through all its recesses, but in a sort of disrespectable way'.

Lowther, Mary
The Vicar of Bullhampton, 1870
Anthony Trollope

A beautiful, principled young lady of small means. Two men love her; trouble arises from her deeply considered decision to accept the proposal of HARRY GILMORE, whom she does not love, having released CAPTAIN WALTER MARRABLE, whom she does love, from their engagement because of his financial difficulties. These relationships involve her in unhappy conflicts of conscience and emotion.

Lubin, Henry Hopkins
Back to Methuselah, 1921
George Bernard Shaw

Lubin appears in the second section of this five-part play, *The Gospel of the Brothers Barnabas*, which is set in a Hampstead study during the early part of World War I. Lubin is one of two political candidates (JOYCE BURGE is the other), who call upon the BARNABAS brothers. In his late sixties, he is a Yorkshireman of quiet dignity and self-assurance but, like Burge, he is materialistic and unimaginative. He makes a partial reappearance in a later section as BURGE-LUBIN.

Lucas, Charlotte
Pride and Prejudice, 1813
Jane Austen

Neighbour and close friend of ELIZABETH

BENNET, Charlotte, with neither enthusiasm nor love, welcomes REV WILLIAM COLLINS's marriage proposal purely because of her 'disinterested desire of an establishment'. Having never been particularly good-looking, and having striven for so long to be married despite having little real interest in it, the fact that Collins originally proposed to Elizabeth is of little consequence to Charlotte – she can certainly not be accused of being proud.

Luce
The Knight of the Burning Pestle, 1607
Francis Beaumont
Daughter of the merchant Venturewell, she is betrothed by her father to the stupid Humphrey, but is loved by, and loves in return, the apprentice, JASPER. Her father is not an attractive character and she appears rather vapid, although her nature is harmless enough to win sympathy. But the grocer and his wife in the audience suspect an imminent satire upon London citizens and so thrust RAFE on stage to take over the action.

Lucentio
The Taming of the Shrew, early 1590s
William Shakespeare
Lucentio arrives in Padua from his home town of Pisa with the intention of studying but is quickly distracted by the sight of BIANCA. By resorting to deception and disguise he wins her heart. He is an attractive, likeable young man who earns forgiveness from his own father and future father-in-law by his open confession. He eventually discovers that he does not have the dominance over Bianca that he thinks he has.

Lucia, more properly Miss Emmeline Lucas, and subsequently Mrs Georgie Pillson
Queen Lucia, 1920, et seq
E F Benson
An amateur of music, Dante, yoga, calisthenics and the paranormal, she cultivates the absurd fantasy that she is Italian, for which her actual grasp of the language is painfully insufficient. Indeed, the only Italian with whom she appears in complete sympathy is Machiavelli. She maintains an obdurate rivalry with ELIZABETH MAPP.

Luciana
The Comedy of Errors, c.1594
William Shakespeare
The sister of ADRIANA, Luciana discovers to her astonishment that she is being courted by (she assumes) her brother-in-law, ANTIPHOLUS OF EPHESUS. The man is, in fact, his twin brother, ANTIPHOLUS OF SYRACUSE. Although Luciana is as quick to jump to false conclusions as her sister, she is more level-headed and has a greater tolerance of others. She does, though, defend Adriana against AEMILIA's accusation that much could have been avoided if it were not for her hot-headedness.

Lucifera
The Faerie Queene, 1590–6
Sir Edmund Spenser
The daughter of Proserpina, the Queen of Hell.

Vain and full of worldly pride, she lives in a beautiful but only superficially gilded palace, which represents the Catholic Church. She has taken it upon herself to make herself queen. Tyrannical, unjust and merciless towards her enemies, she sits in a golden carriage drawn by six unequal beasts and manned by her six counsellors: Gluttony, Idlenesse, Lechery, Avarice, Enuie and Wrath.

Lucilla
Euphues, or The Anatomy of Wit, 1578
John Lyly
The beautiful daughter of Don Fernando, she is betrothed to PHILAUTUS until the spurious charms of EUPHUES entice her away. Inevitably, perhaps, she tires of him in turn and jilts him. More than just a stock virgin-temptress, she contains the lineaments of a 'modern woman' who demands control of her own destiny.

Lucio
Measure for Measure, c.1604
William Shakespeare
A loyal friend of CLAUDIO, who accompanies and supports ISABELLA on her mission to beg for her brother's life, Lucio is very much a product of the licence and liberality of the past 14 years of misrule in Vienna. Lewd and lecherous, with a vivid imagination and a palpable disregard for the truth, he is nevertheless a compassionate and sympathetic personality, striking a vivid contrast to the main characters by his vitality, wit and zest for life.

Luck, Tommy
'The Luck of Roaring Camp', in *The Luck of Roaring Camp and Other Sketches*, 1870
Bret Harte
Tommy is the baby son of Cherokee Sal, a fallen woman in a rough Western mining camp. She dies giving birth to him, so the infant is adopted by the miners, on whom he has a remarkably uplifting effect. This child of nature, quiet, happy and grave, is known as 'The Luck', because Roaring Camp prospers after his arrival, but tragedy soon follows.

Luckett, Sayward
The Trees, 1940
Conrad Richter
A resilient pioneer girl, who raises a family of motherless brothers and sisters and leads them out of the Pennsylvania woods to the open country of Ohio. The story of the family is continued in *The Fields* (1946) and *The Town* (1950).

Lucky
Waiting for Godot, 1955
Samuel Beckett
POZZO's slave, he interrupts the play with lines delivered like artillery fire in a Joycean stream-of-consciousness manner which suggests, beyond pure nonsense, that mankind is in decline. That he arrives again the following day as a 'dumb' creature leading his now blind master merely underscores the point. 'He used to dance the farandole, the fling, the brawl, the jig, the fandango and even the hornpipe,' Pozzo informs

us. Now all he can manage are a few miserable steps of a dance he calls 'The Net'.

Lucretia
Coningsby, or The New Generation, 1844
Benjamin Disraeli

A minor member of the Italian aristocracy, she climbs ruthlessly in English society, setting traps for both HARRY CONINGSBY and the noble SIDONIA, before catching Harry's grandfather LORD MONMOUTH. Typically, she regards this marriage as a mere convenience in her ambitious rise and is unfaithful to him from the beginning.

Lucretia
The Rape of Lucrece, 1594
William Shakespeare

The central incident in this poem arises from a group of noblemen boasting of their wives' virtue; but only Lucretia, COLLATINUS's wife, is proved to live up to her husband's claims. SEXTUS TARQUINIUS, having failed to seduce her, rapes her at swordpoint. 'Mine enemy', she recalls 'was strong, my poor self weak,/And far the weaker with so strong a fear.' Having described the crime, she stabs herself.

Lucretius Brutus
The Rape of Lucrece, 1594
William Shakespeare

The father of LUCRETIA, Lucretius Brutus is clearly a benevolent and upright man. After his daughter's suicide, he pulls the knife from the 'purple fountain' of her breast and reflects that: 'If in the child the father's image lies,/Where shall I live now Lucrece is unlived?'

Lucy
The Country Wife, 1675
William Wycherley

Pert maid to ALITHEA, Lucy is crucial to the comedy's plot because she saves HORNER's elaborate stratagems from disaster. She also articulates some of the wittiest maxims, such as 'married women shew all their Modesty the first day, because married men shew all their love the first day'.

Lucy
The Lion, the Witch and the Wardrobe, 1950, et seq
C S Lewis

The youngest of four children, she is an impulsive, brave girl, warm-hearted and honest. It is she who discovers the secret of the magic wardrobe in the old professor's house, and leads her brothers and sister, PETER, EDMUND and SUSAN, into the land of Narnia. In time she becomes a delightful queen, the favourite of her Narnian subjects.

Ludens, Alfred
The Message to the Planet, 1989
Iris Murdoch

A kind, gentle and sometimes naive historian, Ludens tends to be jealously possessive of friends, his mother having vanished in his infancy. He is of Polish-Jewish descent, although, like MARCUS VALLAR, he has never felt Jewish. Falling in love with Marcus's daughter he is surprised to discover that Marcus wants her

to marry a Jew. A romantic, always fascinated by strong historical personalities, Alfred is unsettled, then obsessed by Marcus's personal and intellectual magnetism. Believing he holds the key to some deep, fundamental knowledge, he deserts his own work and suffers various emotional traumas in trying to discover the nature of this knowledge.

Lufton, Lady
Framley Parsonage, 1861
The Last Chronicle of Barset, 1867
Anthony Trollope

The widowed mother of LORD LUFTON, to whom she is devoted, and patron of REV MARK ROBARTS, whose sister LUCY ROBARTS she considers not good enough for her son. She likes getting her own way and approves of quiet, respectable people; she hates Whigs and the selling of family land. Affectionate to her own circle and generous to the poor, her strong High Church views lead her to oppose DR THOMAS and MRS PROUDIE and their party; she supports instead REV JOSIAH CRAWLEY.

Lufton, Lord
Framley Parsonage, 1861
The Last Chronicle of Barset, 1867
Anthony Trollope

Fine-featured and good-tempered, Ludovic, Baron Lufton of Lufton has been a friend of REV MARK ROBARTS since boyhood. Their friendship is strained by Lufton's financial dealings with NATHANIEL SOWERBY, and Lufton's relationship with his mother, LADY LUFTON, is affected by his love for LUCY ROBARTS; he always resents interference. As a magistrate in *The Last Chronicle of Barset* he sympathizes with REV JOSIAH CRAWLEY.

Luke, Walter
The New Men, 1954
C P Snow

Scientific colleague of MARTIN ELIOT in the atomic fission programme. 'Ever since [LEWIS ELIOT] had known him as a younger man – he was still not thirty – he had thrown the whole of his nature into everything he felt.' He is also capable of refreshing modesty.

Lula
Dutchman, 1964
Amiri Baraka

Lula describes herself as the child prodigy of a communist mother, 'the only person in my family ever to amount to anything'. Highly cynical, she perceives the mediocrity of American culture, and the hollowness of black middle-class families in their bid to fit into the mainstream of that mediocrity. She taunts CLAY CLAY WILLIAMS for trying to integrate himself in her white world, and boasts about her ability to control people like him in sociocultural and political terms.

Lumley, Charles
Hurry On Down, 1953
John Wain

After graduating, he rejects the straitened values of petit-bourgeois existence to become a kind of

English *picaro*, working in turn as a window cleaner, export delivery driver, hospital orderly, chauffeur, nightclub bouncer and finally comedy gag writer.

Lumpkin, Tony
She Stoops to Conquer, 1773
Oliver Goldsmith

The son of DOROTHY HARDCASTLE, stepson of SQUIRE RICHARD HARDCASTLE and half-brother of KATE HARDCASTLE, Tony Lumpkin is too quickly taken for a fool, and indulged by a foolish mother who keeps him in ignorance of the fact that he has come of age. A rustic clown with a healthy streak of natural intelligence and cunning, he is central to the farcical strand of the plot and finally integral to the romantic aspect as well. He misdirects MARLOW and GEORGE HASTINGS, initiates a vast and absurd charade of multiple mistaken identity, and finally leads his mother and CONSTANCE NEVILLE on a bizarre journey to the Hardcastles' house in order that Constance might rendezvous with Hastings.

Lunn, Joe
Scenes From Provincial Life, 1950
Scenes From Metropolitan Life, 1982
Scenes From Married Life, 1961
Scenes From Later Life, 1983
William Cooper

The narrator of the four novels, he begins his career in the first, set in 1939, as a science teacher at a school in an unnamed English provincial town. Restless, sceptical, ironic, with a strong sense of his own capabilities and the constraints that local society places upon him, Joe feels forced to act within certain conventions even while breaking others (such as sleeping with his girlfriend, Myrtle). She wants marriage; he longs for freedom and the novelist's life. His philosophy is to 'speak the truth, laughing. I'll do it or die in the attempt'. In subsequent novels, he becomes a civil servant in London and a novelist of some standing. In the last, he retires; spry but apprehensive, he still debates within himself the nature of emotional commitment.

Lupin, Mrs
Martin Chuzzlewit, 1844
Charles Dickens

The buxom and attractive widowed landlady of the Blue Dragon Inn in the Wiltshire village where SETH PECKSNIFF lives. Like TOM PINCH, she is at first taken in by Pecksniff but recognizes his rascality when she sees how he treats Tom and makes advances to MARY GRAHAM. She employed MARK TAPLEY as her ostler before he left for America, and on his return, they marry and run the inn together.

Luria, Alec
A Coat of Varnish, 1979
C P Snow

A scholar of intense intellectual penetration and considerable fleshly appetites ('When I've been to bed with one woman, I almost immediately want to have another'). Snow revealed that he was modelled on the Freudian scholar and critic Philip Rieff, husband of Susan Sontag.

Lurie, David
Disgrace, 1999
J M Coetzee

A professor of Romantic poetry in Cape Town, his 'magnetism' for women has formed 'the backbone of his life', but now his powers of attraction are waning. When an affair with a student sours and he loses his job because of his refusal to repent publicly, he flees to his daughter's smallholding in the Eastern Cape with plans of writing his opera on the life of Byron. His struggles to adapt to country life are compounded by a brutal attack, during which he is powerless to help his daughter, LUCY LURIE. His consequent guilt and his inability to understand her seeming acceptance of the assault result in a temporary estrangement. He finds a sort of redemption in his work with Bev Shaw at the animal sanctuary.

Lurie, Lucy
Disgrace, 1999
J M Coetzee

The daughter of DAVID LURIE, she lives alone on a smallholding in the Eastern Cape, making a living by keeping kennels and selling flowers and farm produce. Independent and different from her urban intellectual parents, she has become a 'solid countrywoman' – a transition which David, concerned for her safety, hopes is just 'a phase'. Her attitude to the assault, unwillingness to pursue her attackers (although they are known to her) and refusal to leave the land that she loves estrange her from her father temporarily. He eventually returns to tentatively rebuild their relationship, on her terms.

Lusiewicz, Jan
The Flight from the Enchanter, 1956
Iris Murdoch

The younger of the menacing Polish immigrant brothers befriended by ROSA KEEPE, who becomes their shared mistress. Jan is uncannily like his brother, STEFAN LUSIEWICZ, sharing his gaiety, slimness and freshness. Both have extraordinarily white flesh and deceptively crystal-blue eyes, and most women find their good looks and charm irresistible. But Jan tries to force himself on Rosa's lodger, ANNETTE COCKEYNE, and later, after stealing Annette's collection of unset gems, disappears.

Lusiewicz, Stefan
The Flight from the Enchanter, 1956
Iris Murdoch

JAN LUSIEWICZ's elder brother, Stefan more fully reveals the dark, primitive force underlying the brothers' superficial charm. He instigates their savage lovemaking with ROSA KEEPE, and after her submission becomes domineering, dictatorial and intimidating. Following Jan's disappearance he insists on moving in with Rosa and her brother, HUNTER KEEPE, and only the intervention of the more subtly threatening MISCHA FOX rids them of his frightening presence.

Lussurioso
The Revenger's Tragedy, 1607
Thomas Middleton or Cyril Tourneur

THE DUKE's son and heir, an immoral and

lecherous opportunist whose main motivation is the fulfilment of his own lascivious desires. He goes to great lengths in his attempts to seduce VENDICE's sister CASTIZA, securing the services of a 'pander' to persuade and pressurize her. 'Impudent and wicked', he is cynically and ruthlessly manipulative in his treatment of others, and is completely at home in the corrupt court of his father.

Luster (Luster Gibson)
The Sound and the Fury, 1929
William Faulkner

Faulkner described Luster as 'a man, aged 14', justifying adult status for DILSEY's son by his ability to look after and entertain BENJY COMPSON, 'twice his age and three times his size'.

Lutestring, Mrs
Back to Methuselah, 1921
George Bernard Shaw

Mrs Lutestring appears in the third section of this five-part play. *The Thing Happens* is set in the parlour of the President of the British Islands in 2170AD. A much younger version of Mrs Lutestring has already appeared as the Parlour Maid to the BARNABAS brothers. Now aged 275, she is 'apparently in the prime of life'. Elegant, decisive, she has 'the walk of a goddess', and is employed as Domestic Minister of the British Islands. She marries the ARCHBISHOP OF YORK, another long-lifer, to realize their mutual destiny of continuing the white race.

Luther, Martin
Luther, 1961
John Osborne

Osborne's Luther is a study of individual conscience defying authority in the form of the pope, and his age in the form of a prevailing religious convention in which genuine religious experience cannot be accommodated. But Luther, poetic and prophetic, is also struggling with his own conscience and imagination, uncertain of where either is leading him, resolved only to reject compromise. Fierce, neurotic, diseased, · humane, Luther is threatened and denounced by officialdom, yet stands firm.

Lycidas
Lycidas, 1637
John Milton

A mythological personification of Milton's friend Edward King who drowned in a flat calm in the Irish Sea, but also a projection of Milton's anxieties about his own poetic ambitions. Though there is no mistaking the genuineness and sincerity of the poet's grief, King remains a rather shadowy figure in the greatest of all English pastoral elegies.

Lydgate, Tertius
Middlemarch, 1871–2
George Eliot

The new doctor in Middlemarch, Lydgate is fundamentally a good man who falls victim to his pride and circumstances. Regarded with hostility by the other doctors on account of his arrogantly-held opinions and pioneering

methods, his desire to continue his research is further undermined by his foolish marriage to ROSAMOND VINCY. Finding himself enmeshed in a web of escalating debt, and suspected of bribery, he realizes too late how naively misguided had been his marriage, but in his compassionate treatment of MR BULSTRODE he reveals one of the strengths of his character.

Lyle, Annot
A Legend of Montrose, in *Tales of My Landlord: Third Series*, 1819
Sir Walter Scott

Rescued by the McAulays as a child from the bandit Children of the Mist, she was kept as a harpist in Darnlinvarach Castle. Her origins are wreathed in mystery, but it seems clear that she is of gentle birth: 'the lightest and most fairy figure that ever trod the turf by moonlight'. Her skill as a singer is the only remedy for the gloomy ALLAN MCAULAY's black tempers.

Lymoges, Duke of Austria
King John, 1590/1
William Shakespeare

Lymoges, the Duke of Austria, promises to support the claims of ARTHUR, DUKE OF BRITTANY as rightful King of England in place of the ruling KING JOHN, and emerges as the principal ally of PHILIP, KING OF FRANCE.

Lymon, Cousin
The Ballad of the Sad Café, 1953
Carson McCullers

A hunchbacked dwarf who arrives at MISS AMELIA's store to claim kin and whose residence sees its transformation into a thriving café. He is an uncanny figure of ageless appearance and mysterious origin but his instinctual sociability and mischief-making form the foundation of the café's popularity. He enjoys a pampered existence as Miss Amelia's beloved but the sudden transferral of his affections at the appearance of MARVIN MACY reveals a shrewd sense of loyalty.

Lynch, Joe
Five Bells, 1939
Kenneth Slessor

Joe, 'long dead', is gone from earth 'Yet something's there'. The unimportant, insignificant things of his life are remembered, 'slops of beer', his 'coat with buttons off', but also his 'raging tales of Irish kings and English perfidy,/And dirty perfidy of publicans'. He is an angry man, who rails against the injustices of the world, but whose vitality has been leeched away by lack of purpose.

Lynch, Uncle Andrew
A Death in the Family, 1957
James Agee

RUFUS FOLLET's uncle, he is harshly dismissive of religion and superstition, but on the day of his brother-in-law's funeral, as he tells Rufus, he sees a butterfly settle on the coffin and then soar up into the sky as the sun breaks through the clouds. It is the nearest thing he can imagine to a vision of God, and it acts as a counterbalance to the morbid religiosity of the Follets as they erect a mythology around the dead man.

Lynch-Gibbon, Martin
A Severed Head, 1961
Iris Murdoch

The novel's middle-aged narrator, a prosperous wine merchant who, while smugly married to a caring older wife he has no intention of leaving, enjoys a secret affair with a compliant young woman whom he treats callously. He is occasionally assailed by uneasy premonitions of punishment, and has assumed an air of resigned melancholy. When his wife falls in love with his close friend, psychiatrist Palmer Anderson, this feigned melancholy ironically becomes all too real. This is the first of several assaults on his massive selfishness and complacency, the most cataclysmic of which is the entry of HONOR KLEIN into his hollow, crumbling life.

Lyndall
The Story of an African Farm, 1883
Olive Schreiner

Lyndall, the heroine of the novel, grows up an orphan on a South African farm, together with WALDO, to whom she is close, and her cousin EM. A free spirit, and with advanced views on the social condition of women, she leaves the farm in order to live with her lover, an Englishman. Her death in childbirth, however, has a devastating effect on Waldo and Em. It is Gregory Rose, a farm hand engaged to Emily, but really in love with Lyndall, who discovers and narrates her 'hidden', and ultimately lonely, life away from the farm.

Lyndbrooke-Esk, Lydia
Poor Fellow My Country, 1975
Xavier Herbert

The daughter of SIR MARK ESK, the aristocratic Lydia is engaged to be married to Lord Vaisey, a landowner. But when she meets JEREMY DELACY at the Beatrice River races, the annual social event of the Australian Northern Territory, she falls in love with him. Lydia is a thoroughgoing representative of British colonial power: smart, predatory, possessive and ignorant of the damage that colonialism has done. Delacy, independent and liberal, presents a considerable challenge to a woman like Lydia, but her political philosophy is, in Delacy's eyes, bordering on the Fascist. Her affections are summarily rejected, yet she emerges from the encounter having seen for the first time the realities of life in the outback.

Lyndon, Barry, also known as Barry Redmond of Ballybarry
The Luck of Barry Lyndon, 1844
W M Thackeray

Obliged to flee from Ireland, believing that he has killed a man in a duel, he displays an impressive eye for the main chance, changing sides in the Seven Years War and spying on behalf of the Chevalier de Balibari (who turns out to be his uncle, CORNELIUS BARRY). The two become accomplices at the tables, until Barry finds an initially less taxing occupation as husband to HONORIA, COUNTESS OF LYNDON, after which his fortunes decline irrevocably.

Lyndon, Bryan
The Luck of Barry Lyndon, 1844
W M Thackeray

BARRY LYNDON's son by HONORIA, COUNTESS OF LYNDON; Barry dotes on the boy at the expense of young VISCOUNT BULLINGDON, whom he considers to be moody. Bryan, by contrast, 'was the most polite and engaging child ever seen; it was a pleasure to treat him with kindness and distinction; and before he was five years old, the little fellow was the pink of fashion, beauty and good breeding'.

Lyndon, Countess of → Honoria, Countess of Lyndon

Lyon, Esther
Felix Holt the Radical, 1866
George Eliot

The adoptive daughter of the minister Rufus Lyon, Esther is the offspring of French parents. This perhaps justifies her reading of the frivolous French novels for which the opinionated FELIX HOLT ticks her off, before falling in love with her when she shows her capacity for seriousness. The possibility of inheriting the TRANSOME estate through the French connection tempts her a little, but her wish to stay close to sober, working-class Felix means marriage to him and the rejection of the unhappiness of riches.

Lypiatt, Casimir
Antic Hay, 1923
Aldous Huxley

A flamboyant, opinionated egotist, who falls in love with MYRA VIVEASH, Lypiatt nevertheless has real and considerable artistic talent, perhaps even genius. That is why he can be so harsh in his judgement of the lightweight Mercaptan, a mediocre contributor to literary weeklies: 'You disgust me – you and your odious little sham 18th-century civilization; your piddling little poetry; your art for art's sake instead of for God's sake; your nauseating little copulations without love or passion; your hoggish materialism; your bestial indifference to all that's unhappy and your yelping hatred of all that's great'.

Lysander
A Midsummer Night's Dream, c.1594
William Shakespeare

One of the four mortal lovers involved in the play's complex romantic plot, he is an engaging mixture of youthful desire and inflammatory masculinity, willing to leave friends and reputation in order to be with his true love, and eventual wife, HERMIA. A true romantic, his language contrasts him neatly with the more straightforward DEMETRIUS.

Lysistrata
The Apple Cart, 1929
George Bernard Shaw

Lysistrata, the Powermistress General in JOE PROTEUS's Labour government, is the most intelligent member of the Cabinet. A grave, patriotic woman in academic robes, she possesses an almost obsessive sense of public duty: 'I love my department: I dream of nothing but its efficiency'. She administers the country's industrial power, yet she is consistently frustrated by the huge corporate strength of Breakages Ltd. Their economic success depends on repair contracts and they acquire and suppress all inventions designed to improve mechanical reliability. Lysistrata emerges, therefore, as the symbol of the Life Force contesting the reactionary power of capitalism.

M

Casino Royale, 1957, et seq
Ian Fleming

Head of the British Secret Service, he is JAMES BOND's immediate boss. Smoke-wreathed and laconic, he is inclined to be suspicious of his subordinate's methods and leisure-time pursuits. He is somewhat unsafely guarded in his lair by Miss Moneypenny, whose heart is Bond's.

Maas, Oedipa

The Crying of Lot 49, 1966
Thomas Pynchon

Californian hostess and wife of the disc jockey Mucho Maas. When she is named executrix of her former lover Pierce Inverarity's estate, she is launched on a quest that (as her forename suggests) probes the nature of the self in an information-glutted and interference-ridden society.

Mabs

Puffball, 1980
Fay Weldon

A large and fearsome woman, Mabs craves the state of pregnancy, ferociously jealous of her pregnant friend LIFFEY. An earth-mother figure, she is deeply insecure about her lack of femininity and harbours within the frailties of all women who are faced with low self-esteem and male infidelity, even though outwardly she appears confident and tough. A dabbler in witchcraft, she represents the dangerous, mysterious and mutable side of nature.

Mac

Rusty Bugles, 1948
Sumner Locke Elliott

A fat, lazy Australian soldier, adept at 'swy' (a gambling game played with coins). He tries to escape to hospital from the boredom of a wartime ordnance depot by means of self-induced dermatitis; he is distraught at the news that he is not the father of his wife's ninth child.

McAdam, Maureen

Dimboola, 1974
Jack Hibberd

The bride and minor participant at her own wedding reception, 'Reen' does little more than cry 'Watta weddin'' – outnumbered, out-vocalized and indeed upstaged by invited and uninvited 'guests'.

McAdam, Morrie

Dimboola, 1974
Jack Hibberd

The groom and minor participant at his own wedding reception, Morrie (properly, Morris) is no man of words, managing little more than a 'no worries' response. He is in fact the least important element in a drunken rite that is little more than an excuse for all-comers to air religious and sexual opinion and animosity.

MacAindra, Stacey

The Fire-Dwellers, 1969
Margaret Laurence

Profoundly dissatisfied with herself, Stacey begins a process of self-questioning that mirrors the magazine articles she reads. She sees herself trapped into the roles of mother and wife, taunted by memories of an earlier, more independent self. Rarely without a drink in her hand, she is aware that her children 'nourish me and they devour me too'. Criticizing herself for a tendency to use 'full technicolour and intense detail' to communicate, she concludes her internal debate with a reluctant but realistic acceptance of herself.

MacAlpin, Marian

The Edible Woman, 1969
Margaret Atwood

An 'ordinary' college graduate, Marian MacAlpin is restless in her dead-end job and ambivalent about her fiancé Peter. Inordinately influenced by society, she outwardly acquiesces in her limited role as a nice girl of the 1960s. However, her inability to eat betrays her inner turmoil. Repulsed by children, and regretting her decision to marry, Marian displays increasingly erratic behaviour. Only when she learns to use traditional symbols to indicate her feelings is she released from the constricted roles she has previously accepted.

McAlpine, Jim

The Loved and the Lost, 1951
Morley Callaghan

The novel's central consciousness, he is a young university lecturer who desperately tries to resist his growing attraction to PEGGY SANDERSON, disturbed by her apparent perversity and refusal to conform to 'normal' social standards.

Macapa, Maria (Miranda)

McTeague: A Story of San Francisco, 1899
Frank Norris

Housemaid and caretaker of the lodging house in which MCTEAGUE lives and runs his unlicensed practice. This little Mexican is notorious for her enigmatic catchphrase 'Had a flying squirrel an' let him go'. Like every other character in the book, her life is marked by an obsession with gold. Dismissed as 'a greaser and queer in the head', she believes that her forebears were wealthy enough to eat off gold plates.

McAulay, Allan
A Legend of Montrose, in *Tales of My Landlord: Third Series*, 1819
Sir Walter Scott

Lady McAulay's younger son, he was born to a mother driven half-mad by the murder of her brother by the Children of the Mist. His mother's own comfort and companion as a child, he becomes in adolescence a fierce avenger of his uncle's death, almost as wild as the men he pursues. Prone to violent fits of depression and suspicious temper, he is only soothed by the harp songs of ANNOT LYLE, whom he rescued from the bandits when she was a child.

MacAulay, Rev Aulay
The Ministers, 1979
Fionn Mac Colla

Minister of Strath, a neighbouring parish to REV EWEN MACRURY's Mellonudrigill, he is the effective leader of the local clergy, valued beyond his apparent deserts. 'He was … a dry, rusty, crusty man, a sarcastic bookish fellow who when he did move abroad never smiled.'

MacAusland, Libby
The Group, 1963
Mary McCarthy

Bright and optimistic, Libby sets out to make a glittering career and combines her considerable drive with enough talent to succeed. She is lively, gregarious and eager to be accepted by those she admires. Her vitality is initially attractive but her popularity is always short-lived. This puzzles her but she does not allow any hurt she feels to deflect her from her ambitions. If a relationship ceases to be fruitful Libby moves on, always looking forward, ready for the next step up the ladder.

Macavity
'Macavity: The Mystery Cat', in *Old Possum's Book of Practical Cats*, 1939
T S Eliot

Pursued by Scotland Yard and the Flying Squad with a charge sheet covering vandalism, larceny and the murder of lap-dogs, he is a master of the hair's-breadth escape. He is described as tall, thin, ginger-haired, with a domed head, serious expression, and a distinctive snake-like sway to his movements. Outwardly respectable and suave, he is considered by the law-and-order lobby to be 'a fiend in feline shape, a monster of depravity'.

Macbeth
Macbeth, c.1606
William Shakespeare

Scottish nobleman and a brave warrior. A loving husband and loyal friend, his flaw is ambition. Encouraged by his wife, LADY MACBETH, and by the supernatural machinations of THE THREE WEIRD SISTERS, he is transformed into a confused, anxious murderer, killing KING DUNCAN, and his best friend BANQUO, then many others, including women and children. For all this horror, the play's closing scenes demonstrate that some nobility and love remain, rendering too pat MALCOLM's final estimation of him as an 'evil butcher'.

Macbeth, Lady
Macbeth, c.1606
William Shakespeare

Wife of MACBETH. Though decried as a 'fiend-like queen' at the end of the play, she is infinitely more complex than this. Alternately a possessed fury, demanding that the spirits 'unsex me here/And fill me from the crown to the toe/top-full of direst cruelty', and an anxious, vulnerable woman, who cannot kill the king because he resembles her father; her eventual suicide is a product of her immense guilt. Strong, powerful and beautiful, she remains loyal to her husband throughout.

MacBriar, Ephraim
Old Mortality, in *Tales of My Landlord*, 1816
Sir Walter Scott

A young preacher, 'barely twenty years old; yet his thin features already indicated that a constitution, naturally hectic, was worn out by vigils, by fasts, by the rigours of imprisonment, and the fatigues incident to a fugitive life'.

McCaffrey, George
The Philosopher's Pupil, 1983
Iris Murdoch

The titular character, a wholly evil man who delights in his own extreme violence. His paranoia, chaotic excess and self-destructive fury are attributed by various characters within the novel to jealousy, academic failure, bereavement or loss. He is certainly a deeply wounded man, and is compellingly attractive to those, particularly women, who seek to understand and forgive him. His nature, however, is absolutely particular and un-accountable. Wildly aggressive, he is cowed in abject humiliation before JOHN ROBERT ROZANOV, a revered philosopher in whom he sees his only possibility for redemption.

McCandless, Archibald
Poor Things, 1992
Alasdair Gray

An earnest young public health officer in Glasgow, whose professional and private 'memoirs' form the basis of the novel. Whether or not he is an historical personage remains unclear, as is the exact nature of the woman he marries, Bella or Victoria Baxter.

McCandless, Mr
Carpenter's Gothic, 1985
William Gaddis

The presiding deity-cum-devil of the novel, who inhabits the ill-proportioned 'carpenter's gothic' house that is Gaddis's symbol of the failure of Christianity. A novelist and geologist (who claims to have discovered gold in Africa, where LIZ BOOTH and her brother Billy have inherited mining interests), he combines and conflates the creation of art and the alchemy of money.

McCann, Dermot
The Birthday Party, 1958
Harold Pinter

A young Irishman, he is the assistant to NAT GOLDBERG, chosen by him to work on the 'operation' to capture and destroy STANLEY WEBBER. The terseness of his language, combined with his sinister and repetitive paper-tearing ritual, provide a portrait of a violent psychopath only just under control.

McCann, Phil
The Slab Boys Trilogy, 1982
John Byrne

Slab Boy McCann's razor-sharp repartee with workmate SPANKY FARRELL only thinly veils a deep-rooted unhappiness stemming from a life of domestic mayhem in working-class Paisley. Master of the incisive one-liner, his often vicious tongue betrays the painful chip on his shoulder, but in the face of personal despair and frustrated ambition it is this ability to 'escape' through humour – however black – which allows him to retain not only his sensitivity and generosity but, above all, his optimism for life.

McCaslin, Isaac ('Ike')
'The Bear', 1935, in *Go Down, Moses*, 1942
William Faulkner

As a 16-year-old boy, already blooded for killing a buck, he embarks on the rite-of-passage bear hunt that is supposed to mark a transition to full manhood. He is, in fact, the last surviving male McCaslin, the son of UNCLE BUCK MCCASLIN and SOPHONSIBA BEAUCHAMP. The bear hunt is an expedition he has inherited as a birthright, but later in his life, with the 20th century dawning, the death of the bear acquires a different, still more complex significance.

McCaslin, Old Carothers (Lucas Quintus Carothers McCaslin)
Go Down, Moses, 1942
William Faulkner

Founding father (?1772–1837) of the McCaslin clan, he introduces the twin taints of miscegenation (by bedding his slave Eunice) and then incest (by seducing their child Tomey), thus guaranteeing the family's eventual degeneration and extinction.

McCaslin, Uncle Buck (Theophilus)
The Unvanquished, 1938
Go Down, Moses, 1942
William Faulkner

Twin son (with Uncle Buddy/Amodeus) of OLD CAROTHERS MCCASLIN, he wins and loses his wife SOPHONSIBA BEAUCHAMP in a poker game, and with her he fathers ISAAC MCCASLIN. He attempts to grant his slaves their freedom.

M'Choakumchild, Mr
Hard Times, 1854
Charles Dickens

The teacher employed at THOMAS GRADGRIND's model school to inculcate the virtues of hard facts. 'He and some one hundred and forty other schoolmasters, had been lately turned at the same time, in the same factory, on the same principles, like so many pianoforte legs'. An exponent of learning by rote, 'if he had only learnt a little less, how infinitely better he might have taught much more!'

McClellan, Everett
Run, River, 1963
Joan Didion

A gentleman farmer in the Sacramento Valley, California, he is a last representative of an old agrarian chivalry rapidly being overtaken by modern industry and mechanistic values. Married to LILY KNIGHT, he kills her lover (the man who also jilted his sister) before taking his own life, thus bringing a whole era to a not quite tragic end.

McCloud, King
Key Largo, 1939
Maxwell Anderson

A small-time American gangster, who has failed to rise to the moral challenge of the Spanish Civil War, and thereafter finds it impossible to commit himself to any but subjective and instantly gratifying causes. At the tail end of the 1930s, he represents Anderson's call for a solidarity based on personal courage.

McCoag, Colin
Looking for the Possible Dance, 1993
A L Kennedy

A native of Glasgow, Colin McCoag resembles 'nothing so much as a thin, plain-clothes policeman or a skinny Mormon out on a spree'. He is 'good at games' and has 'a competitive mind'. Colin becomes the lover of fellow student MARGARET HAMILTON, but leaves her. He spends three years working in London before returning to Glasgow and Margaret, but communication problems again jeopardize their relationship. A good deed Colin does for a stranger results in a horrifying act of retribution against him.

M'Combich, Robin Oig
The Two Drovers, in *The Chronicles of the Canongate: First Series*, 1827
Sir Walter Scott

Bright, able and physically slight, he is a young Highland drover who fatally ignores the warnings of his aunt, the sibyl Janet of Tomahourich. His ultimately murderous quarrel with the English herd HARRY WAKEFIELD is ostensibly about grazing, but also touches on political and cultural differences. His one act of violence has all the inevitability of true tragedy.

McComus, Finch
You Never Can Tell, 1897
George Bernard Shaw

Aged about 50, McComus is a long-standing friend of MRS LANFREY CLANDON. Once the firebrand of the Dialectical Society, he is now a solicitor, but insists that he is still a good student of Herbert Spencer and 'a Philosophic Radical standing for liberty and the rights of the individual'. Courteous, meticulous and inflexible (he warns against GLORIA CLANDON being swept into the flood tide of socialism), McComus is a man of imposing professional presence, and the agent who brings the Clandon clan together with FERGUS CRAMPTON.

McCoy, Frankie

You Can't See Round Corners, 1947
Jon Cleary

The 21-year-old Frankie McCoy is the product of an impoverished Sydney family. His background has sharpened him, teaching him to live by his wits, but has also nurtured a resentment against the social and economic system. As he is not particularly articulate, the grudge is largely unexpressed. Essentially he is a weak individual, ignorant of his own capabilities, a drifter and one of life's losers. Conscripted into the army during World War II, McCoy rebels against the discipline and deserts, resulting in his being rejected by his exasperated girlfriend. Having descended into gambling, he runs up debts which he attempts to pay by robbing a shop, and kills a woman in a fit of inarticulate rage.

McCoy, Sherman

The Bonfire of the Vanities, 1987
Tom Wolfe

The patrician, over-reachingly ambitious 'king of the bond market', he is tall, well-groomed, has a posture which is 'terrific to the point of imperious', and the arrogant confidence which comes from immense wealth and the social standing of original WASP stock. His lavish Park Avenue lifestyle is turned upside down when his mistress kills a young black man in his car, and the novel charts his gradual disintegration as he becomes 'a professional defendant' within the legal system, losing everything in the process.

McCracken, Jack

A Small Family Business, 1987
Alan Ayckbourn

A forceful man in his mid-forties, Jack McCracken inherits the directorship of Ayres and Graces, the family furniture business. At a celebratory party at which the extended family gathers, honest Jack demands a new beginning: even the appropriation of a few paper clips will no longer be tolerated. But he soon discovers that decency and integrity are outmoded in the ruthless world of the 1980s, where dishonesty and blackmail make more money than old ideals. Finally, he agrees that the Ayres and Graces distribution network be secretly made available to an Italian drug ring.

McCrae, Gus

Lonesome Dove, 1985
Larry McMurtry

A former Texas Ranger, who 'runs' a dilapidated ranch in South Texas just after the Civil War. In contrast to his driven and obsessive partner WOODROW F CALL, Gus is happy to spend his days playing cards and chastely romancing the town prostitute. Not far below the surface of Gus's relationship with Call is a sort of idealized marriage, in which he plays the gruffly domesticated wife.

McCreary, Fenian

The 42nd Parallel, 1930, part of the *U.S.A.* trilogy, 1938
John Dos Passos

The son of working-class Irish Catholic immigrants, uneducated 'Fainy' is forced, when his uncle's printing firm goes bankrupt, to bum his way across early 20th-century America in his search for work. Party, from an early age, to his uncle's Marxist outpourings, he becomes a half-hearted 'wobbly' in Nevada, and when his conscience subsequently prevents him from settling into a shallow, up-and-coming bourgeois existence, he rejoins the ranks of the radical travelling workforce.

McCullough, Glynnis

American Appetites, 1989
Joyce Carol Oates

A proud, self-satisfied woman, Glynnis McCullough cultivates and discards people at whim. A professional food writer, she spends much of her time in the kitchen, planning menus and orchestrating dinner parties. She has a careless attitude towards her husband, IAN MCCULLOUGH, until her position as his wife and lover is threatened, at which point she becomes angry, defensive and nasty.

McCullough, Ian

American Appetites, 1989
Joyce Carol Oates

A modest, yet successful man, Ian McCullough represents the American Dream. He is wealthy, respected and professional, and he has a charming hostess wife (GLYNNIS MCCULLOUGH). Yet he is frequently impotent, often abstracted, and poses questions to which there are no answers. At the age of 50 he finds himself dissatisfied with his suburban life. Increasingly preoccupied with a younger woman, he cannot foresee the result of his obsession.

McCunn, Dickson

Huntingtower, 1922, et seq
John Buchan

A retired Glasgow grocer, he has hung up his apron only to don the not altogether well-fitting mantle of heroism as he tackles the enemies of decency and good. Apart from his own sober instincts, his best weapons are the combined skills of the 'Gorbals Diehards', among them JAIKIE GALT and DOUGAL CROMBIE, who do his more dangerous work for him.

McDowell, T George

The Electrical Experience, 1975
Frank Moorhouse

A successful manufacturer of soft drinks in a small New South Wales town, George's earnest commitment to progress and the future is most obviously symbolized by his decision to convert his plant to electricity. Like Sinclair Lewis's GEORGE BABBITT, his American contemporary and counterpart, he is bourgeois solidity personified.

McDowell, Terri

The Americans, Baby, 1972
Frank Moorhouse

T GEORGE MCDOWELL's daughter, she grows up in a very different Australia from her father. Morals are looser in the 1960s and it is no longer possible to sustain an uncritical belief in progress. Father and daughter are largely estranged, no longer sharing basic values.

Macduff
Macbeth, c.1606
William Shakespeare

A thoughtful and courageous man, the Thane of Fife, he early suspects MACBETH of KING DUNCAN's murder and refuses to participate in the new regime. Loyal both to his country and to his family, his great grief on learning of the slaughter of his wife and children gives him depth and humanity. At the head of MALCOLM's army, he himself kills Macbeth, not merely as an act of politics or revenge, but as the duty of a decent man.

Macduff, Lady
Macbeth, c.1606
William Shakespeare

Wife of MACDUFF. Her brief appearance, in a scene of domestic tranquillity laced with tension, establishes her as a thoughtful and witty woman, anxious at her husband's sudden departure, but determined and brave in her protection of family and home. The contrast between her wistful conversation with her knowing son, and the random slaughter of mother and child, provides the play with its most shocking moments.

Macey
Red Shift, 1973
Alan Garner

A witness as a child to the destruction of his tribal home in occupied Roman Britain, he watched the burning thatches through the spokes of a turning chariot wheel, and the blue/silver/red visions triggered by this memory goad him on to murderous madness. Adopted by the mutinous Ninth legion, he is used by them like a weapon, harnessed and released when they desire. His madness is in reality a manifestation of a more ancient power; Macey sees it as another creature within himself, a separate entity. He uses the votive axe as a weapon, which gives him a holy authority for his massacres.

McFarg, Lloyd
You Can't Go Home Again, 1940
Thomas Wolfe

A literary friend of EUGENE GANT, he is believed to be modelled on the US novelist Sinclair Lewis. Though successful, he is bitter and pessimistic about US society, which he believes to be shallow and meretricious, a view that Gant at first resists.

MacFlecknoe
MacFlecknoe, 1682
John Dryden

MacFlecknoe is a satirical portrait of the playwright Thomas Shadwell, and is the imagined heir to a prolific but untalented Irish poet, Flecknoe. He is to adopt the poetic mantle because he 'never deviates into sense' and is capable of avoiding originality and of torturing 'one poor word ten thousand ways'. He is acclaimed by the uncritical mob and swears to maintain dullness until his death.

McGarrigle, Persse
Small World, 1984
David Lodge

A young lecturer and poet at the obscure University College, Limerick, McGarrigle has many of the qualities of the lovers of Romantic literature, the literary form upon which the novel draws. Having encountered and been enchanted by beautiful but elusive ANGELICA PABST, idealistic, naive McGarrigle recklessly casts his natural caution aside and dedicates much of his time and all his savings to pursuing his Holy Grail. When his dreams turn to dust, he transfers his ardour to another, almost as beautiful yet perhaps more attainable.

McGee, Travis
The Deep Blue Goodbye, 1964, et seq
John D McDonald

From the security of the 'Busted Flush' houseboat, won in a poker game, he moves with smoothness and ease to the rescue of innumerable damsels in distress. He has occasionally walked on the wrong side of the law, but finds performing 'salvage operations' for the return of stolen goods just as pleasing. Tall and handsome, this champion of the weak, and usually female, is an old-fashioned hero, rescuing maidens from dragons while retaining a thoughtful interest in the meaning of life.

Macgregor, Mary
The Prime of Miss Jean Brodie, 1961
Muriel Spark

This Edinburgh schoolgirl is treated unkindly by her fellow pupils and their teacher, MISS JEAN BRODIE, being regarded as a scapegoat, but she is nevertheless glad to be part of the 'Brodie set'. A stupid, clumsy, 'silent lump', she leaves school to become a shorthand typist, joins the Wrens during World War II, and dies in a fire at the age of 23.

Macgregor, Rob Roy
Rob Roy, 1817
Sir Walter Scott

Like FERGUS MACIVOR in *Waverley*, he is a confident balance of Highland and Lowland cultures, but has been driven from honest cattle droving into an outlaw existence by the unjust treatment meted out to him.

MacHeath, Captain
The Beggar's Opera, 1728
John Gay

A hero or villain according to taste, MacHeath is the leader of a gang of thieves. He compares the acquisition of women to that of money, always wanting more, to the extent of ordering prostitutes wholesale. This is detrimental to his safety. He promises to marry LUCY LOCKIT when he is already POLLY PEACHUM's husband, and is courteous to everyone's face. He drinks well in the condemned hold, preserving a bold front in desperate straits, being only temporarily at a loss when confronted by 'four wives more'. 'This is too much', he confides to LOCKIT, THE JAILER.

Machiavelli, Niccolo
Romola, 1863
George Eliot

The future writer of *The Prince*, he stays cynical and withdrawn, highly intelligent and excited by ideas but lacking TITO MELEMA's powers of personal persuasion. He correctly believes Tito to be too successful, hates Dolfo Spini's proto-Fascist thugs and despises the religious rhetoric of GIROLAMO SAVONAROLA. Among a number of cutting and to-the-point remarks, he says that it is a pity Savonarola's falsehoods 'were not all of a wise sort'.

Machin, Arthur
This Sporting Life, 1960
David Storey
A miner, unable to deal with his need for a wider spectrum of feelings because of a fundamentally flawed understanding of maleness. He takes a veneer of toughness from his mining world into the sporting world of rugby league. He enjoys the trappings of success – easy women and superficial popularity – but he never really finds peace of heart because his achievements remain hollow and strangely unfulfilling.

Machin, Denry (Edward Henry)
The Card, 1911
Arnold Bennett
Denry describes himself as 'a devil of a smart fellow', and few would disagree. Thrown back on his own resources, he seizes every opportunity to advance himself and does not let his conscience trouble him too much. Provincial society finds him outrageous but admires his ability to produce brilliant solutions in every crisis. He is the washerwoman's son who made the countess laugh, and is 'identified with the great cause of cheering us all up'. Denry finally becomes a popular and prosperous mayor of his home town, because he has the wit and the will to make his daydreams happen.

Machine, Frankie, properly Francis Majcinek
The Man with the Golden Arm, 1949
Nelson Algren
A dealer in a sleazy Chicago gaming house, who has a golden touch with cards (hence his nickname). He is also a morphine addict, having picked up the habit after being wounded in the war. He is coldly indifferent and afraid of commitment, while his capacity to love is 'caught inside'. He is riven by guilt of several kinds, but especially the 'special American guilt of owning nothing, nothing at all, in the one land where ownership and virtue are one'.

McHoan, Kenneth
The Crow Road, 1992
Iain Banks
'All the gods are false. Faith itself is idolatry', says vehement atheist and socialist Kenneth, shortly before being killed by lightning while climbing a church tower in a drunken attempt to prove the non-existence of God. The mildly eccentric, story-telling father of PRENTICE MCHOAN, the relationship between the two has deteriorated with the son's questioning of his black-and-white views. Although often 'genuinely altruistic', he is also opinionated and headstrong.

McHoan, Prentice
The Crow Road, 1992
Iain Banks
A family funeral brings Prentice back from

university to his rural Scottish roots. As well as youthful preoccupations with sex, drugs and the existence of God, he has other family concerns, not least his estrangement from his father KENNETH MCHOAN, and the disappearance some years earlier of his Uncle Rory. A sensitive, confused, and often unlucky young man, his quest to find answers about his family's history helps him gain maturity and, ultimately, a sense of perspective and acceptance.

Macilente
Every Man out of his Humour, 1599
Ben Jonson
Prone to rhetoric and long, musing speeches, Macilente likes everyone to know that he is both a scholar and a much-travelled man. He therefore feels entitled to dispense often uncalled-for advice. A gullible man, with a streak of cruel humour (he poisons one of PUNTARVOLO's dogs), his principal foible is envy, which he harbours until he has stored 'a world of malicious thoughts in his brain'. Eventually he is cured and admits that: 'I am empty of all envy now'.

McIntyre, Mrs
The Displaced Person, 1948
Flannery O'Connor
The thrifty farm owner whose employment of a Polish exile, Mr Guizac, is not an act of compassion but a business investment. Having married her first husband with a view to inheriting his property, she preserves his memory by adopting his self-justifying belief that wealth and responsibility are a thankless burden. She manages her employees with a shrewd self-interest and when Guizac's rigorous self-improvement appears to 'upset the balance' her approval is swiftly withdrawn.

MacIvor, Fergus, also known as Glennaquoich, Vich Ian Vohr, and Ian nan Chaistel
Waverley, 1814
Sir Walter Scott
A Highland chieftain who combines in EDWARD WAVERLEY's eyes his own uncertain mix of Jacobite romanticism and the more solid virtues associated with a Tory squire. 'His countenance was decidedly Scottish, with all the peculiarities of the northern physiognomy, but yet had so little of its harshness and exaggeration, that it would have been pronounced in any country extremely handsome ... [It] resembled a smiling summer's day, in which, notwithstanding, we are made sensible by certain, though slight signs, that it may thunder and lighten before the close of evening.' He lives by exacting 'black-mail' on the neighbouring landowners and farmers, a kind of protection money.

MacIvor, Flora
Waverley, 1814
Sir Walter Scott
Sister of the chieftain FERGUS MACIVOR, she immediately captures EDWARD WAVERLEY's heart with a nicely calculated mixture of romantic simplicity, the graces acquired from a polite education and upbringing and some outrageous *coups de théâtre*, as when she appears above him

on a dizzying crag. 'In Flora's bosom ... the zeal of loyalty burnt pure and unmixed with any selfish feeling; she would have as soon made religion the mask of ambitious and interested views, as have shrouded them under the opinions which she had been thought to think patriotism'.

Mack
Cannery Row, 1945
John Steinbeck

Leader of the gang of ruffians and layabouts who befriend the kindly biologist DOC; they represent, in equal parts, 'virtues and graces and laziness and zest', but their efforts to brighten up his lonely existence are beset by drunken misunderstanding.

Mackellar, Mr
The Master of Ballantrae, 1889
Robert Louis Stevenson

The factor of the Ballantrae estates and the friend and confidant of HENRY DURIE. As the narrator of the tale, he tends to give a biased account of the sibling rivalry within the Durie family, favouring Henry. They share the same righteous Presbyterian outlook and the same distaste for the adventures of his evil, romantically wayward brother JAMES DURIE. Mackellar is, himself, an unemotional man who has little time for love and, instead, affects a philosophic disposition. Nevertheless, he still possesses a certain stern charm.

McKelva, Judge
The Optimist's Daughter, 1972
Eudora Welty

The father of LAUREL MCKELVA HAND by his first wife, and husband of WANDA FAY MCKELVA, he is a respected and eminently respectable public figure who made what was generally seen as a rash second marriage. A tall, heavy man of 71, he is an 'optimist', but dies early in the book.

McKelva, Wanda Fay
The Optimist's Daughter, 1972
Eudora Welty

The second wife of JUDGE MCKELVA, she comes from a poor, uncultured Texas family far removed from his own social standing. Vulgar, brash, insensitive, selfish and self-serving, she proves to have lied about her family being dead when they arrive unexpectedly for the judge's funeral. She has no 'powers of passion or imagination', nor any feelings for the past, but belongs 'to the future'.

McKenzie, Hector
The Slab Boys Trilogy, 1982
John Byrne

Small in stature, hypersensitive Hector is an easy target for the verbal and physical lacerations of PHIL MCCANN and SPANKY FARRELL. Lacking in the essential 1950s style and confidence, 'mammy's-boy' Heck snivels his way through life, a pathetic, suicidal figure whose comic moment of glory is too fleeting and trivial to lend him anything other than our abject pity. A poor, sad scrap of humanity, the only constant factor in his life is a tendency towards mental instability.

Mackenzie, Mr
After Leaving Mr Mackenzie, 1930
Jean Rhys

An expatriate of independent means, who leads a life of uncomplicated hedonism in Paris. Respectable, conventional and unimaginative, he does not question the code which allows him to view women as commodities to be acquired and unceremoniously discarded by those who can pay. A cautious man, he remembers his excessive and imprudent sexual passion for JULIA MARTIN with embarrassment and distaste, and attempts to erase the affair from his orderly life.

Mackenzie, Mrs
The Newcomes, 1853–5
W M Thackeray

The mother of ROSEY MACKENZIE and mother-in-law of CLIVE NEWCOME, she is a domineering, manipulative snob, who regards all romantic feeling as a mere lubricant to social progress. When Clive's father loses his fortune and falls into her sphere of influence, she sees the perfect opportunity to take cynical revenge on her social and moral superior.

Mackenzie, Rosey
The Newcomes, 1853–5
W M Thackeray

She and CLIVE NEWCOME are manoeuvred into a marriage that he, for one, does not want, but which offers both a brief respite from the turmoil of society. Rosey is pretty but shallow and entirely dominated by her brutally hypocritical mother.

MacKercher, also known as **Mr M—**
The Adventures of Peregrine Pickle, 1751, bowdlerized edition 1758
Tobias Smollett

MacKercher is based on the historical Daniel MacKercher, once referred to by Smollett as the 'melting Scot'. He became embroiled in the famous 'Annesley Case', a dispute over a huge estate and its rival claimants, that became one of the *causes célèbres* of English inheritance law.

Mackerel, Rev Andrew
The Mackerel Plaza, 1958
Peter De Vries

Having lost his wife in a boating accident, Mackerel finds himself juggling with complicated urges in which his religious principles are at war with his basic human needs. Though he hears the siren call of another woman, it is his wife's sister HESTER (who is also his housekeeper) who subtly wins him over.

MacKilligut, Sir Ulic
The Expedition of Humphry Clinker, 1771
Tobias Smollett

A preposterous and loquacious Irish knight encountered at Bath, where he is planning a ball and taking dancing lessons. He seems 'to be about the age of three-score, stooped mortally ... tall, raw-boned, hard-favoured, with a woollen night-cap on his head'.

MacLain, King
'The Wanderers', in *The Golden Apples*, 1949
Eudora Welty
A small-town Zeus whose fierce grimace at the funeral of VIRGIE RAINEY's mother sparks off the girl's recognition that all human freedom is based on the sacrifice of others. Promiscuous as a young man, MacLain is an ambiguous version of the Fisher King who brings fertility to a barren place.

McLane, Howard
'Up the Coule', in *Main-Travelled Roads*, 1892, revised editions 1899, 1922, 1930
Hamlin Garland
Returning to rural Wisconsin from theatrical success in New York, he sees the blighted, unproductive landscape of his abandoned family as a series of brightly-lit dioramas that disguise the poverty and privation he has left behind. 'Portly, erect, handsomely dressed, and with something unusually winning in his brown moustache and blue eyes, something scholarly suggested by the pinch-nose glasses, something strong in the repose of the head'.

M'Laughlan, Peter
'Shall We Gather at the River?', et seq, in *The Romance of the Swag*, 1907
Henry Lawson
A bush missionary 'up-country and out back in Australia'. 'His past was a mystery, so, of course, there were all sorts of yarns about him. He was supposed to be a Scotchman from London, and some said that he had got into trouble in his young days and had had to clear out of the old country.' Some say he had studied for the law, some that he was a doctor. He is sombre, dark, bearded like Christ, and has a gift for holding impromptu congregations spellbound.

McLaughlin, Brad
The Star-Splitter, 1923
Robert Frost
Having failed at 'hugger-mugger farming', he burns down his house and uses the insurance money to buy a telescope with which to view the stars. Our perspective is gained through the narrative voice of McLaughlin's friend, who, at first scornful of his actions, becomes steadily more baffled and fascinated both by the telescope and its user. Brad represents those who give up 'real' work to pursue an ideal, though the poem's end suggests that this may be worthless: 'we've looked and we've looked, but, after all, where are we?'

McLeavy, Harold
Loot, 1966
Joe Orton
A delinquent youngster whose days have been happily spent in raiding slot machines and deflowering young women, Harold McLeavy is the kind of person who refuses to attend his mother's funeral because it might upset him. Having robbed a bank, he now dreams of starting a new life in Portugal with his best friend Dennis. However, a pathological inability to tell a lie would seem to place a life of crime in serious jeopardy, especially when he is confronted by a suspicious policeman.

McLeod, Arthur
Barbary Shore, 1951
Norman Mailer
His kingly name must be considered ironic, because Arthur is destined never to enter the Socialist kingdom to which his life has been dedicated. Nearing 50, and cuckolded by the ghastly GUINEVERE, he bestows on the amnesiac writer MIKEY LOVETT the remnants of his Socialist culture and an unidentified 'little object', which is all that remains of his utopian hopes.

McLeod, Fay
The Republic of Love, 1992
Carol Shields
Her name suggests an affinity with the fairy world, and her professional interest in mermaids contributes further to her ethereal persona. She is tall, attractive and gregarious, and has a supportive network of family, friends and colleagues, but she seems unable to commit herself to a successful romantic relationship until she falls in love with TOM AVERY.

Macleod, Vanessa
A Bird in the House, 1963
Margaret Laurence
Retrospectively narrating her past, Vanessa reveals herself as a lonely and isolated child. Relishing the imaginative space such solitude affords her, she is an outsider in the adult world of her family. Watching and recording familial dynamics from a number of different perspectives, she grows self-reliant from an early age and her resolve to escape the bleakness of her grandfather's house (either through literature or by breaking away) is strong.

McLour, Janet
Thrawn Janet, 1881
Robert Louis Stevenson
The housekeeper at the manse of Balweary. Many rumours surround her colourful past – superstitions suggesting that she is a witch, related to Satan himself. When she is forced to renounce the Devil by the folk of the parish, she suffers a stroke – her neck is thrawn – causing her head to hang to one side. Her body looks as though she has recently been hanged and she finds she cannot speak 'like a Christian woman'. In this preternatural state she becomes the catalyst for the minister MURDOCH SOULIS's transformation from an enthusiastic, gauche young minister into a severe, forbidding solitary.

McMahon, Phyllis Jean, alias **Fay**
Loot, 1966
Joe Orton
A devoutly Catholic nurse, 28-year-old Fay McMahon has a business-like approach to life, devoid of sentimentality or remorse. Widowed seven times in as many years, she finds a continuing attraction in any man with a healthy bank balance and can drive a hard bargain when pushed. Responsible for the recent death of Mrs Leavy, who generously recompensed her in a late change of will, she has, in the words of policeman JIM TRUSCOTT, 'practised her own form of genocide for a decade and called it nursing'.

McMann, Tom
Imaginary Friends, 1967
Alison Lurie

An impressive and respected sociology professor, Tom McMann uses his professional techniques and social skills to great effect in influencing and persuading others to his point of view. Aware of professional jealousy and unpopularity amongst colleagues, it is very important to him to maintain his pre-eminence and see his project successfully concluded. In pursuing his research he is not above distorting facts and influencing subjects in order to validate his theory. Reality can be rewritten and personality, particularly his own, changed with apparently convincing results. His sanity may be in question, but never his genius.

Macmaster, Vincent
Parade's End, 1924–8
Ford Madox Ford

Small, dark and immaculately groomed, Vincent exerts a powerful grip over every aspect of his life. Ruthless and passionless, he has mapped out a trajectory to which he unfailingly keeps, rising from lowly and embarrassing origins to the highest echelons of the establishment. To him the end justifies the means, and he sponges off his friend, CHRISTOPHER TIETJENS, takes the credit for his friend's genius and uses Christopher's wife to manipulate people in power.

Macmorris → Fluellen; Gower; Jamy; Macmorris

McMurphy, Randle Patrick
One Flew Over the Cuckoo's Nest, 1962
Ken Kesey

A persistent petty criminal who is hospitalized in a mental institution. His raucous personality, foul-mouthed, vulgar exuberance, an indomitable zest for life and mile-wide rebellious streak keep him in constant conflict with the system. He becomes the leader-hero of the inmates, and galvanizes them into positive rebellions of their own. Although he is lobotomized after a party goes tragically wrong, his example is not forgotten.

Macnab, John → 'John Macnab'

McNair, Siegmund
The Trespasser, 1912
D H Lawrence

McNair, who earns his living by playing in an orchestra, lives in London and, despairingly trapped within a loveless marriage, feels like 'a slow bullet winging into the heart of life'. He and the attractive but impossible Helena Verden escape for a brief holiday on the Isle of Wight but afterwards McNair discovers life to be unbearable both with his wife and without Helena. 'Humiliation at home, Helena forsaken, musical comedy night after night. That was insufferable – impossible.' It is so impossible that McNair hangs himself, the only one of Lawrence's principal protagonists to commit suicide, an act Lawrence presents as a defeat.

MacNamara, Mary
Down by the River, 1996
Edna O'Brien

When 13-year-old Mary becomes pregnant as a result of her widowed father's abuse, she initially tells no one but confides her feelings only to her diary. Living in Ireland where terminations are not available, Mary is presented as a grimly resilient victim not only of abuse, but of a judgemental society. However, when her pregnancy becomes public, she refuses to name the father and endures many hardships. Before she is able to visit England in order to have an abortion, Mary becomes the centre of a national debate and discovers that decision-making powers she believes should rightfully be hers have been usurped by various factions claiming to act in her interest.

McNicholl, Julia
An Equal Music, 1999
Vikram Seth

Julia McNicholl, a pianist, has been brought up in a cultured world 'unreachably different' from that of MICHAEL HOLMES – a world to which she introduces him when they meet and fall in love in Vienna as music students. Michael's abrupt departure from Vienna has caused her considerable distress. Ten years later, she is now married to James, an American banker, and is mother to Luke, who is 'six and ten twelfths'. Although she is slow to reveal her secret, she is led by her 'hunger' for someone to talk to about music to renew her relationship with Michael, causing her intense guilt and shame.

McNiel, Gus
Manhattan Transfer, 1925
John Dos Passos

Whilst working as a milkman for the Excelsior Dairy Company, Gus McNiel daydreams idly of going West and is run over by a freight train. Spurred on by the young lawyer GEORGE BALDWIN, who has an affair with his beautiful wife Nellie, he successfully sues the railroad company for damages. A 'rednecked snubnosed man', he recovers from the accident to become a powerful, limping Assemblyman. Having encouraged Baldwin to take political office, he feels personally betrayed when the latter announces that he will run on the Reform ticket.

Macomber, Francis
The Short Happy Life of Francis Macomber, 1936
Ernest Hemingway

A wealthy American on safari with his domineering wife, MARGOT MACOMBER. He is tall, well-built, considered to be handsome, and has 'just shown himself, very publicly, to be a coward' when faced with his first lion. In a subsequent encounter with buffalo, his fear turns to elation, and he is seen as 'a man coming of age', at last able to stand up not only to the animal, but also to his wife. His new-found confidence is shockingly short-lived.

Macomber, Margot
The Short Happy Life of Francis Macomber, 1936
Ernest Hemingway

An 'extremely handsome and well-kept woman of

the beauty and social position which had, five years before, commanded five thousand dollars as the price of endorsing, with photographs, a beauty product which she had never used'. She is 'cruel' and 'predatory', and gives up on her husband, FRANCIS MACOMBER, after he runs from a lion. Unable to accept his subsequent discovery of courage and independence, she precipitates a tragic ending.

McPherson, Cathy
The Tax Inspector, 1991
Peter Carey

The supervisor of the Spare Parts Department of Catchprice Motors, the dilapidated family firm near Sydney, she is the aunt of BENNY CATCHPRICE. In her mid-forties, she feels both unfulfilled and restless, exasperated by the family and business that tie her down and prevent her from realizing her dreams. A strident, confident woman, Cathy enjoys playing the guitar and singing in a folk-rock band. She wears cowboy boots and western clothes rather too young for her, creating a tough, abrasive image. In reality, she is terrified of bankruptcy and beneath her brusque exterior lies a rather conformist attitude.

McPherson, Sam
Windy McPherson's Son, 1916
Sherwood Anderson

Son of the drunken, blustering Windy, he grows up in bitter opposition to the narrow-minded philistine environment of Caxton, Iowa.

MacQuedy, Mr
Crotchet Castle, 1831
Thomas Love Peacock

A Scottish economist who talks in terms of 'rent, profit, wages, and currency' and 'production and consumption', MacQuedy advances the doctrine of logic and reason. A 'pound, shilling and pence' philosopher, he holds that everything has its market-place price, and nothing, not even a love-stricken heart, should be given away without consideration of economic values.

M'Quirk, Judy
Castle Rackrent, 1800
Maria Edgeworth

The pretty but unlettered Irish grand-niece of THADY QUIRK, retainer at Castle Rackrent; Sir Condy spins a ha'penny to determine whether he should marry her or ISABELLA MONEYGAWL, who isn't, by Thady's reckoning, worth half a tithe of Judy. She subsequently marries Captain Moneygawl's huntsman, loses her looks, and becomes somewhat 'smoke-dried' by drudgery.

MacRae, Neil
Barometer Rising, 1941
Hugh Maclennan

A chastened symbol of the 'new' Canada, he appears to return from the dead, after having apparently been discredited, imprisoned and then killed in the trenches because of the incompetence and self-protective malice of his uncle COL GEOFFREY WAIN, father of his sweetheart PENELOPE WAIN.

McRaven, Laura
Delta Wedding, 1946
Eudora Welty

A nine-year-old cousin of the FAIRCHILD family, who comes to live with them. She is a poor 'little motherless girl' who is fascinated by the sights and sounds around her, and feels an exciting conviction that 'at any moment she might expose her ignorance – and any moment she might learn everything'. She 'wanted so badly to be taken to their hearts', but also struggles against the feeling that the Fairchilds and their home 'is everything'.

MacRury, Rev Ewen
The Ministers, 1979
Fionn Mac Colla

He comes to the parish of Mellonudrigill as a modernizer, bringing English services in place of Gaelic, and an almost mystical spirituality that sits only uncomfortably alongside the time-serving pragmatism of his fellow clergy, such as REV AULAY MACAULAY. Amid accusations of unnatural vice, they try to hound him out.

MacStinger, Mrs
Dombey and Son, 1848
Charles Dickens

A formidable widow with three mischievous 'little MacStingers', she is the landlady of CAPTAIN EDWARD CUTTLE, whom she keeps in a state of terrified subjection. His friend, CAPTAIN JACK BUNSBY, saves him from having to marry her, but cannot prevent being captured himself.

MacTavish, Elspat (Elspeth)
The Highland Widow, in *Chronicles of the Canongate: First Series*, 1827
Sir Walter Scott

A figure so primeval in her grief, she almost seems a force of nature, combining fierce loyalty to her cateran husband and fierce maternal love for her son. Deranged by their loss, she lives on as an ambiguous relict before blending back into her wild surroundings.

McTeague
McTeague: A Story of San Francisco, 1899
Frank Norris

A San Francisco dentist, practising without a licence and frequently with a full belly of beer. His 'mind was as his body, heavy, slow to act, sluggish'. He is apparently harmless, but possesses a reservoir of pure sadism and greed, which emerges in his marriage to TRINA SIEPPE.

M'Turk, also known as Turkey
Stalky & Co., 1899
Rudyard Kipling

Boon companion of STALKY at the College. He is Irish, unprepossessing and invariably last to see the point of any new jape or wheeze devised to confound the authorities. He is, though, unshakeably loyal and forthright.

MacTurk, Captain Hector
St Ronan's Well, 1823
Sir Walter Scott

A superannuated Highland soldier, much addicted to toddy, who is called upon to act as peacemaker and referee at the Well despite his own bellicose and touchy nature. 'He always wore a blue coat and red collar, had a supercilious taciturnity of manner, ate sliced leeks with his cheese, and resembled in complexion a Dutch red-herring.'

McVey, Hugh
Poor White, 1920
Sherwood Anderson

A quiet, slightly withdrawn inventor who becomes the main vehicle for Anderson's portrayal of an Ohio farm community gradually being overtaken by the industrial spirit of the 20th century.

Macwheeble, Bailie Duncan
Waverley, 1814
Sir Walter Scott

There is some uncertainty whether the BARON OF BRADWARDINE's bailie is descended from a family known as Wheedle or as Quibble. He has a curious way of eating, which is to perch on the edge of a chair set some feet from the table and lean towards his plate so that a diner opposite can only see the crown of his wig. He also moves around in this odd position, resembling 'a turnspit walking upon its hind legs'.

McWhirr, Captain
Typhoon, 1903
Joseph Conrad

A sea-captain who must pilot his steamer through a dreadful storm. He is a stolid, four-square, reliable and dutiful officer with a single-minded obsession about order and his narrowly prescribed mission in life, but a very dull, unimaginative and ignorant man. His implacable character and imperturbable temperament enable him to save his ship, leaving his second mate to conclude that 'he got out of it very well for a stupid man'.

Macy, Marvin
The Ballad of the Sad Café, 1953
Carson McCullers

The husband of MISS AMELIA, whose marriage is unconsummated and short-lived. Described as 'bold and fearless and cruel', he combines handsome looks with a macabre criminal reputation – he is remembered, as a boy, for carrying with him the preserved ear of a man he had killed. When Miss Amelia's aversion to him persists beyond marriage, the reformation of his character effected by two years of unrequited love is dramatically reversed and a ruthless desire for revenge is born.

Mad Hatter, the
Alice's Adventures in Wonderland, 1865
Lewis Carroll

The Mad Hatter is having a tea party with THE MARCH HARE and THE DORMOUSE at one end of a table with places set all round it. They greet ALICE rudely; the Hatter says her hair wants cutting and asks a riddle to which there is no answer. He has quarrelled with Time ever since the Queen of Hearts said his song was murdering the time, and Time has taken his revenge by staying always at teatime, hence the number of places set. When the Hatter wants a clean cup, they all move on one

place, but only he benefits. Later he appears at the trial of the Knave of Hearts, where the Queen stares so hard at him that in fright he takes a bite out of his teacup.

Madame de S—
Under Western Eyes, 1911
Joseph Conrad

The companion of PETER IVANOVITCH, and a member of the revolutionary group with which RAZUMOV becomes entangled. She is 'a lady of advanced views, no longer very young, once upon a time the intriguing wife of a now dead and forgotten diplomat'. She is 'painted, bedizened, dead-faced, glassy-eyed, avaricious, greedy, unscrupulous'. She and Peter Ivanovitch are presented in slightly ridiculous, one-dimensional fashion, as 'the apes of a sinister jungle'. Razumov sees her as 'a wooden or plaster figure of a repulsive kind'.

Maddalo, Count
'Julian and Maddalo', 1818
Percy Shelley

A Venetian nobleman of ancient family and great fortune, he is a much-admired and respected friend of the narrator, JULIAN. He is also a 'genius', but this does not make him happy, only deeply and painfully aware of the inferiority of others and the nothingness of human life. Nevertheless, in the company of others he is invariably 'gentle, patient, and unassuming' as well as compassionate and generous – as evidenced by the practical kindness he shows the madman whom he introduces to Julian.

Maddison, Philip
A Chronicle of Ancient Sunlight, 15 volumes, 1951–69
Henry Williamson

A writer who reflects many of Williamson's own attitudes and aspirations, he experiences the slow decline of England up to the end of World War II. He remains a less than substantial presence during the sequence of novels, observing with some detachment the lives and destinies of his contemporaries while finding himself increasingly and instinctively drawn to older ways of life.

Madeleine
The Serpent and the Rope, 1960
Raja Rao

From an old-established French family, Madeleine is wealthy, contemplative, insular and melancholic. She studied at the University of Caen, where she met and married RAMA, attracted to him because his ascetic nature and his absorption in mythology strikes an echoing note in her. Yet in many ways she is his antithesis. Erotic and sensual, she represents the earthly, while he symbolizes the spiritual. In this way, the novel dramatizes the uneasy history forged between Asia and Europe.

Madeline
'The Eve of St. Agnes', 1820
John Keats

The pure young daughter of a savage family who are deadly enemies of her suitor, PORPHYRO. Her romantic prayers are answered daringly by her lover.

Madison, Lannie
Barbary Shore, 1951
Norman Mailer

A disturbed girl, living in the sleazy Brooklyn rooming house run by GUINEVERE. In keeping with the novel's underlying pastiche of Arthurian legend, her forename carries hints of 'Lancelot' and helps convey her sexual ambivalence. She is the lover successively of Guinevere, of the narrator MIKEY LOVETT, and, masochistically, of the secret policeman LEROY HOLLINGSWORTH.

Madras, Philip
The Madras House, 1910
Harley Granville-Barker

A partner in the Madras *haute couture* fashion house, Philip is in his mid-thirties and, being 'full up with moral precepts', intends to abandon business for the London County Council. The two most important aspects of a man's character, he declares, are 'his attitude towards money and his attitude towards women'. Encountering women either related to or working for him, he confronts issues of women's social, professional and sexual status. Anxiously he observes and reflects, his 'intellectual passion' for reform masking his practical limitations, for Philip is too cautious to change the world.

Madrigal, Anna
Tales of the City, 1978, et seq
Armistead Maupin

Dressing in flowing garb and evincing an air of mellow wisdom, Anna Madrigal owns 28 Barbary Lane, a 'crumbling, ivy-entwined relic' in San Francisco, where she houses an eclectic band of tenants. A compassionate, attractive woman who tapes joints to new inmates' doors as a welcome, she is tolerant of almost any eccentricity, perhaps because, as a transsexual (her name is an anagram of 'a girl and a man'), she knows the value of acceptance.

Maeve, Queen
The Old Age of Queen Maeve, 1903
W B Yeats

The High Queen of Cruachan and Magh Ai, wife of Ailell. In her youth she was beautiful and strong. Fierce and wise, but with 'a high heart', she has been advised by the Sidhe, the ancient gods of Ireland. In her old age the immortal Aengus asks for her assistance, which she courageously gives.

Magawisca
Hope Leslie, or Early Times in the Massachusetts, 1827
Catharine Maria Sedgwick

One of the first convincing portraits of a Native American woman in literature, she is the daughter of a Pequod chief, who has been defeated and reduced to semi-slavery. She is a female version of James Fenimore Cooper's CHINGACHGOOK, noble, resourceful and self-sacrificing, as when she saves the life of the white man who is later to become HOPE LESLIE's husband.

Magda
The Whole Armour, 1962, part of *The Guyana Quartet*, 1985
Wilson Harris

The terrible mother of CRISTO, bound to him by a mystical umbilical cord that expresses their connection and violent separation. There is a clear echo in their names and in their mythological function of Mary and Christ.

Magic Pudding, the
The Magic Pudding, 1918
Norman Lindsay

The eponymous dessert, it is a protean confection with an awesome power of attraction over its semi-human pursuers, POSSUM and WATKIN WOMBAT. Much amateur psychology has been deployed to explain the symbolism or emotional implications of a pudding that is possessed of the power of speech and the ability to change its flavour at will. In the circumstances, it is best to approach it as one would any other pudding: enjoy it now and worry about the consequences later.

Magiot, Dr
The Comedians, 1966
Graham Greene

A tall, striking negro doctor who is attending to the heart condition of BROWN's mother. He is a gentle, refined, literate man with the natural majesty, grace and bearing of a Roman emperor. The wisest and most admirable character in the novel, he is a reliable, comforting presence to all who know him. He possesses an acute moral sensibility, and it is perhaps inevitable that in 'Greeneland', Dr Magiot should also be a non-practising Catholic.

Magistrate, the
Waiting for the Barbarians, 1980
J M Coetzee

As nameless as the Empire he serves, this old magistrate is the subjective narrator of the novel. Legalistically fair-minded, he comes into conflict with the more ruthless Colonel Joll, who arrests the magistrate because of his affair with, and subsequent return of, a tortured prisoner to her nomadic people. Humiliated, tortured in turn and stripped of his power, the Magistrate grows to realize that he is really no better than his persecutor: 'I was the lie that Empire tells itself when times are easy, he the truth that Empire tells when harsh winds blow. Two sides of imperial rule, no more, no less.'

Magistretti, 'Maggie' (Maria)
The Italian Girl, 1964
Iris Murdoch

'Maggie' is the last of several young Italian nurserymaids employed to look after Edmund and Otto Narraway. She remains with the family, becoming a severe, nun-like general maid, all-knowing and indispensable, 'like a true house serf'. Dressed in black, her hair dragged back in a bun, the small familiar figure goes virtually unnoticed for years. But after Lydia Narraway's death, this Cinderella astonishingly becomes a beautiful woman, clad in red, her glossy black hair stylishly cut. Her air of assurance reveals someone other than patronized 'Maggie', and she begins to take a different place in Edmund's life.

Magnus, King
The Apple Cart, 1929
George Bernard Shaw

The King of England is a tall, studious-looking man, about 45 years old, intelligent, tactful and with considerable political skill. A realist, Magnus believes in 'the great abstractions … conscience and virtue'. In his debate with the idealist JOE PROTEUS, the Prime Minister, as to whether the monarchy should renounce the right of veto over Parliament, Magnus presents himself as standing for 'the future and the past, for the posterity that has no vote'. Kingship, he claims, represents the eternal rather than the expedient, and political security rather than the tyranny of popular ignorance.

Magnus, Peter
Pickwick Papers, 1837
Charles Dickens

The suitor of Miss Witherfield, the 'middle-aged lady, in yellow curl-papers', he challenges SAMUEL PICKWICK to a duel for mistakenly entering her bedroom at the Great White Horse, Ipswich. He absconds before the duel, but Pickwick and his second, TRACY TUPMAN, are arrested and taken before the Mayor, GEORGE NUPKINS.

Maguire, Mr
The Shadow of a Gunman, 1923
Sean O'Casey

Perhaps the gunman of the title, he is a member of the Irish Republican Army, 'a roarin' Republican' according to SEUMUS SHIELDS, and makes only a brief appearance in the play. He deposits a bag in a Dublin tenement (the room rented by Shields and DONAL DAVOREN), before going to an IRA job at Knocksedan. Unknown to Shields and Davoren, the bag contains explosives. Maguire and the violence he represents are perceived as a fact of Dublin life.

Maguire, Patrick
The Great Hunger, 1942
Patrick Kavanagh

Working a 14-hour day, his moustache 'clay-wattled', Patrick Maguire is the personification of the relentless harshness of rural Irish existence. Sexually frustrated, he lives with his mother and virgin sister until his mother dies at the age of 91. Labouring under the yoke of a repressive Protestant religion, he makes the field his bride, caring affectionately for his dog and cattle. His heart tells him, however, that 'God's truth is life', and although he remains kind and optimistic, he suffers a gnawing awareness of time passing and of the tragedy of what might have been.

Magwitch, Abel
Great Expectations, 1861
Charles Dickens

A rough and desperate convict to whom the young PIP brings food and a file to remove his fetters when he has escaped from a prison ship onto the Kent Marshes. He is re-captured and transported to Australia, where he becomes a wealthy sheep farmer, privately arranging with MR JAGGERS to become Pip's secret benefactor and author of his 'great expectations'. Meanwhile, ESTELLA, the daughter he has had with MOLLY, Jaggers' housekeeper, has been adopted by MISS HAVISHAM. Years later, under the alias of 'Provis', he illegally returns to England to enjoy Pip's having become a gentleman. With the help of HERBERT POCKET, Pip tries to smuggle him aboard a Thames steamer, but Magwitch is betrayed by his former partner, COMPEYSON, who drowns when they both fall overboard in a struggle. Arrested and condemned to hang, he escapes execution when he dies in prison, comforted by Pip's devoted care for him and the knowledge that Estella has become a beautiful lady.

Maharani of Ranchipur
The Rains Came, 1937
Louis Bromfield

Described by TOM RANSOME as 'the last queen', the shrewdly perceptive Maharani has immense dignity. Brought up in the harsher climate of the hills, where charity was considered weakness, she remarks that she learned tolerance and humanity only after her marriage, and a deeply ingrained toughness underlies her quiet manner. Following the earthquake and the Maharaja's death, she unhesitatingly takes control, declaring a state of emergency, and is ruthlessly prepared to rid Ranchipur of LADY EDWINA ESKETH, so that MAJOR RAMA SEFTI will not weaken in his duty to replace the Maharaja as ruler.

Mahon, Adam
Brides of Peace, 1979
Dan Davin

An anthropologist at Oxford University, Adam Mahon is a man of habits, whether they be orderly or disorderly. In fact, although he often appears punctilious to others, he has made rather a mess of his emotional life. He grieves over the death of a woman he wanted to marry, while confronting the rejection of the woman he has married. Later, he rediscovers the woman he should have married. The trouble with Mahon is his indecision. He is circumspect, apprehensive, evasive. He cannot take risks or accept responsibility easily, and lacks ambition. And although he prides himself on his tolerance and liberal principles, he sees and understands very little in the people around him.

Mahon, Christy
The Playboy of the Western World, 1907
J M Synge

Christy Mahon, 'very tired and frightened', arrives at a village in Mayo, claiming he has killed his tyrannical father. His vulnerability, his glinting way with words and daredevil personality combine to turn him from an object of perplexity and suspicion into a kind of rural Don Juan. In the warmth of PEGEEN MIKE's and WIDOW QUIN's admiration, he becomes a flamboyant, boastful local hero until his exposure as a rogue when the father himself arrives in pursuit of his wayward son. Christy then attempts, unsuccessfully, to kill his father, and leaves the village, apparently carefree, promising to continue 'romancing through a romping lifetime'.

Mahon, Lt Donald
Soldier's Pay, 1926
William Faulkner

An American volunteer in the Allied flying corps in World War I, he has been brutally, irreversibly wounded in the head. His family and friends prove unable to deal with the evil represented by his shocking scar, and the dying veteran's return to his home town in Georgia, with the war widow MARGARET POWERS in attendance, sets the small community against him, even after their marriage.

Mahon, Rev
Soldier's Pay, 1926
William Faulkner

LT DONALD MAHON's father, he is an Episcopal minister in a small Georgia community, constitutionally unable to deal with the evil reality represented by his son's terrible head wound. His faith is gradually eroded until he finally recognizes that heaven may simply be rest from suffering and not the bright garden party he had imagined.

Mahoney
The Dark, 1965
John McGahern

A widower eking out a basic existence for himself and an 'army of children' on a small farm in western Ireland. A starkly divided character, he harbours feelings of loneliness, failure and sexual frustration. These are taken out on the children he loves profoundly and possessively in the form of relentless verbal and occasional physical abuse. He possesses a tragicomic sense of drama – 'the beauty of energy' – but becomes increasingly drawn into 'tired introspection', playing endless games of patience, as his children turn him into an outsider in his own home.

Mahoney, son of
The Dark, 1965
John McGahern

The unnamed eldest son of the large Mahoney family, his early childhood is spent in fear of his violently confrontational father, his favourite refuge being the breezy dark of the outside lavatory. Whilst on a summer visit to his cousin Father Gerald, 'the red rose of life' beckons seductively, and he realizes he has no priestly vocation. Against his father's will, he throws himself into his studies at the Brothers' College, and wins a scholarship to Galway University. Within a week, his student dreams are shattered. Gnawed by a 'murderous feeling of defeat', he opts for the security of a desk job in Dublin.

Mahony, Cuffy, properly **Cuthbert Hamilton Townshend-Mahony**
The Fortunes of Richard Mahony, 1917–30
Henry Handel Richardson

The son of RICHARD and MARY MAHONY. Imaginative, precocious and musically gifted, he generally represses his emotions, except for occasional rages, and is regarded as a difficult

child. Like his father, he is beset by fears, often groundless. He asks innumerable questions and listens to adult conversations; he worries about his parents and wishes that people could be happy.

Mahony, Mary
The Fortunes of Richard Mahony, 1917–30
Henry Handel Richardson

The long-suffering and loyal wife of RICHARD MAHONY. When they marry she is called Polly, but she later uses her real Christian name. Modest, kind and refined, she always sees the good in people. She does not want to leave Australia and is too straightforward and friendly to understand the complexities of the English class system. As an obedient wife she does not believe in women's rights, but, being a very practical woman, she comes to realize that her husband is not always right. She distrusts the imagination and disapproves of books; her principal concern is her husband, and then their children.

Mahony, Richard, properly **Dr Richard Townshend-Mahony**
The Fortunes of Richard Mahony, 1917–30
Henry Handel Richardson

A poor Irish Protestant gentleman with an Edinburgh medical degree, who emigrated to Australia to seek his fortune. After marrying MARY MAHONY, concerned that he might develop a tradesman's soul, he gives up his unsuccessful shop to return to doctoring. In his ensuing career in Australia and England he displays a self-destructive and selfish urge to escape whenever he becomes bored with his life. In poverty self-pitying, in wealth extravagant and still unsatisfied, he is inconsistent in his attitude to class prejudice. Touchy and proud, he hates Australia, with which he can never come to terms, and demonstrates increasing insanity.

Mailer, Norman, also **Aquarius**, **the Reporter**, and **A-1**
Advertisements for Myself, 1959
The Armies of the Night, 1968, and others
Norman Mailer

The critic Al Alvarez considered Mailer's self-projections to be the most overdone characterization in US literature since MOBY DICK. In *The Armies of the Night*, Mailer becomes the protagonist of an anti-Vietnam rally in Washington, but also a living metaphor for the novelist trying to shape reality to his vision. Mailer has also appeared as a character in other people's books: libellously in Alan Lelchuk's *American Mischief* (1972) and as an army general in Richard Brautigan's *Sombrero Fallout* (1976).

Maitland, Bill
Inadmissible Evidence, 1964
John Osborne

Caustic, sensitive and despairingly aware of his own failures, Bill Maitland, a solicitor, imagines himself in a nightmare courtroom in which he must plead for his own life. Maitland is possibly prodigiously talented but blisters with self-loathing. Unable to cope with his caseload, sexually promiscuous and emotionally bankrupt, he is also the subject of an investigation by the Law Society in a matter of false evidence. Maitland has so far wasted his life and, although blazingly defiant, appears unable to change his direction and spirals into physical breakdown. His character has been understood to represent Osborne's metaphor for the ills of contemporary society.

Maitland, Margaret
Some Passages in the Life of Margaret Maitland, 1849
Margaret Oliphant

A Scots widow, living alone and known for good works, she is entrusted with the upbringing of an heiress. They agree well, but worldly relatives claim Grace, wanting her fortune. Margaret gathers courage to withstand these schemers. She watches with kindly prayer over Grace's love for her nephew, a minister. Grace's guardian turns out to be Margaret's old love, now reformed. The young laird is another nephew; having brought him to see his errors she can approve his love for her niece. All things work together for good, simultaneously with the Disruption in the Church of Scotland, to Margaret's pious satisfaction.

Maître Pierre → Louis XI, King of France

Major, (Sinclair Yeates), the
Some Experiences of an Irish R.M., 1899
Further Experiences of an Irish R.M., 1908
In Mr Knox's Country, 1915
E O Somerville and Martin Ross

Major Sinclair Yeates, an Englishman with Irish connections, leaves his regiment to become a Resident Magistrate in Ireland, administering the law in Petty Sessions Courts with a growing suspicion that perjury in witnesses is to be expected, that breaking laws is a human right and that assault and battery are honourable social customs. What seems simple grows more complicated the more it is explained to him. Only a sense of humour and fox-hunting maintain his sanity during this extraordinary widening of his horizons.

Makak → Hobain, Felix

Makely, Mrs
A Traveller from Altruria, 1894
William Dean Howells

A wealthy widow who sponsors MR HOMOS's speech about Altrurian principles of unselfishness and civic responsibility, but remains dilettantishly unaffected by anything she hears, content merely to espouse the latest intellectual fad.

Makuri
The Swamp Dwellers, 1964
Wole Soyinka

An old man of the swamps, where he lives with his wife ALU and their son Igwezu, representing a kind of stoical self-reliance in a shifting and unreliable environment.

Mal, Rod and Simon
White With Wire Wheels, 1970
Jack Hibberd

In this surreal play, the three men are collectively stereotypical of the 'Aussie male'; individually they are symbolized by the make, colour and part of their favourite car (Mal by the wire wheel of a white Valiant, Rod by the steering wheel of a 1962 Rover, Simon by the gearbox of a red Mustang). Boasting of exploits past, present and future, they are set up for a fall with the arrival of HELEN.

Malager
The Faerie Queene, 1590–6
Sir Edmund Spenser

Captain of the twelve troops who attack the Castle of Temperance. He rides a tiger, is very large and long-legged, yet is made up of such little substance that he seems like a ghost. He represents 'misrule', or the effect that sin has on the physical body. His skin is snake-like and has shrivelled. As a battle helmet he wears the skull of a dead man. He is followed by the two ragged hags of Impotence and Impatience.

Malagrowther, Sir Mungo
The Fortunes of Nigel, 1822
Sir Walter Scott

The lord of Girnigo Castle, he is an original, a gargoyle at Court. A former whipping-boy to James VI, he has borne a certain caustic resentment at humanity into his old age. Lacking three fingers of his sword hand, he has taken up the pen to write satirical verse, and spends much of his time away from St James's, mingling with the news-peddlers and impoverished artists of the city.

Malan, Joseph
Looking on Darkness, 1974, originally published in Afrikaans as *Kennis van die aand*, 1973
André Brink

A coloured man from the Cape, he serves his apprenticeship as an actor in London (where the role of OTHELLO remains the favoured ghetto for a black actor), before returning to South Africa to form an experimental troupe that constantly falls foul of the authorities. A relationship with a white woman leads inexorably towards a violent conclusion; Joseph reviews his life from the death cell.

Malaprop, Mrs
The Rivals, 1775
Richard Brinsley Sheridan

A cynical and superficial woman of almost 50, who believes that she is learned but is famous for misusing, through ignorance, long words that sound similar to the correct words. (Her 'nice derangement of epitaphs' has led to the word 'malapropism' entering the English language.) She is pursuing SIR LUCIUS O'TRIGGER, while trying to prevent the relationship between her niece, LYDIA LANGUISH, and a 'poor ensign' (actually CAPTAIN JACK ABSOLUTE).

Malbecco
The Faerie Queene, 1590–6
Sir Edmund Spenser

The husband of the fair HELLENORE. He is old, ugly, churlish and impatient, and lives in an impenetrable castle, in which his evil-gotten wealth is locked up. He has neither skills of court nor wit. He is secretive, jealous and distrusting towards his wife, with whom he is ill-matched. He cannot decide between his wife and his riches.

Malcolm
Little Malcolm and his Struggle against the Eunuchs, 1966
David Halliwell

As a result of his restless, boorish, embittered egotism, Malcolm earns the nickname of the 'Hitler for Huddersfield'. Expelled from art school, he plots the downfall of the principal, and encourages his fellow students to take up arms against eunuchry by helping to build the Party of Dynamic Erection. Written at a time when the student resentment and the youth counter-culture of the 1960s was gaining some notoriety, the play, and Malcolm, encapsulated some of that decade's anarchy-for-anarchy's-sake attitudes.

Malcolm
Macbeth, c.1606
William Shakespeare

The elder son of KING DUNCAN. His father's badly-timed announcement that he is to be Prince of Cumberland provides further fuel for MACBETH's ambitious plans. Alternately shrewd and rather naive, his lengthy conversation with MACDUFF in London reveals him to be a paragon of moral goodness, clearly to be contrasted with the evil Macbeth. By the end of the play, he has become a general of genuine ability, and a leader of diplomacy and conviction, bringing a new order to Scotland and re-establishing a 'civilized' monarchy in the wake of the tyrant's reign.

Maldon, Jack
David Copperfield, 1850
Charles Dickens

The idle, shiftless cousin of MRS ANNIE STRONG, he is set up in society through the efforts of DR STRONG, but remains ungrateful to his benefactor. His flirtation with Annie results in a brief estrangement between husband and wife.

Malebron
Elidor, 1968
Alan Garner

The King of Elidor, of noble bearing, with golden hair and clothes, who carries a golden spear before him. At first he appears to the children (ROLAND, NICHOLAS and DAVID, and HELEN) as a lame beggar, playing haunting tunes on a violin, which draw them to Elidor. Malebron has a questioning mind that has come to understand the links between the real world and Elidor, and the places where they can coincide: places of destruction, like a slum-clearance site, and places destroyed by war. He realizes that the 'Lay of the Starved Fool' must be the fragment of a dream that has turned the mind of its dreamer; the truth it contains is the secret that will win Elidor back from evil, and restore its lost treasures.

Malecasta
The Faerie Queene, 1590–6
Sir Edmund Spenser

The seductive and flirtatious Lady of the Castle

Joyous. She has no sense of sexual morality and happily takes the initiative in chasing her chosen partner. She dresses in sumptuous robes of gold, red and ermine and is surrounded by her knights Looking, Speaking, Joking, Kissing and Late Nights, who represent a scale of concupiscence.

Malengin
The Faerie Queene, 1590–6
Sir Edmund Spenser

He is representative of guile, and possesses a natural talent for evil. He lives in an underground cave, so deep that it has no end, but which may lead to the bowels of hell. It is riddled with winding passages that lead nowhere, and anyone who enters this cave will never return to the outside world. Malengin is a dishevelled man with hollow, dead eyes and long tangled hair. In one hand he carries a hooked staff for catching his human victims. In the other he carries a net, with which he 'fishes for fools' on the 'dry shores'.

Malevole, properly Giovanni Altofronto, Duke of Genoa
The Malcontent, 1604
John Marston

Disguised as a court fool, Malevole is actually Giovanni Altofronto, ousted Duke of Genoa, who aims to reclaim his dukedom from the usurper PIETRO JACOMO. His disguise, which deceives even his wife, MARIA, frees him to make caustic comments on courtly vice and corruption: 'Think this: this earth is the only ground and Golgotha wherein all things that live must rot; 'tis but the draught wherein the heavenly bodies discharge their corruption; the very muckhill on which the sublunary orbs cast their excrements.'

Malfi, Duchess of
The Duchess of Malfi, 1623
John Webster

A beautiful, virtuous and noble young widow, sister of FERDINAND, DUKE OF CALABRIA, and THE CARDINAL. She ignores the opposition of her brothers and the conventional requirements of her rank to marry the man she loves, ANTONIO BOLOGNA, who is a commoner. Although she despairs when she believes that Antonio and their children are dead, she retains her pride and faces death bravely.

Malfoy, Draco
Harry Potter and the Philosopher's Stone, 1997, et seq
J K Rowling

Sneering and smirking, boasting and gloating, Malfoy is a pale, spiteful boy who takes a nasty glee in others' misfortunes. He resembles his sinister, VOLDEMORT-supporting father, whose wealth and influence he uses unashamedly to get his own way. Malfoy is the arch-enemy of HARRY POTTER at the wizard school Hogwarts, where he is rarely found without his two thuggish henchmen, Crabbe and Goyle; caught alone, his bullying bravado crumbles to reveal cowardice and spiritual weakness.

Malheureux
The Dutch Courtezan, 1605
John Marston

Because of his passion for FRANCESCHINA, Malheureux finds himself employed as the instrument of her murderous revenge against his friend YOUNG FREEVILL. But having initially fallen for her, in due course his conscience forces him to confess all to Young Freevill, and to regret his lustful folly: 'That I, a man of sense, should conceive endless pleasure in a lady whose soul I know to be so hideously black!'

Malin
The Age of Anxiety, 1948
W H Auden

Formerly a Medical Intelligence Officer in the Canadian Air Force, he has come back to earth in a bleak postwar bar, where his almost clinical curiosity is fed by a group of case histories not so very different from his own.

Mallison, 'Chick' (Charles)
Intruder in the Dust, 1948
The Town, 1957
William Faulkner

The 16-year-old nephew of the lawyer GAVIN STEVENS, he visits the old black farmer LUCAS BEAUCHAMP in jail, partly in recognition of the old man's past generosity. Innocent himself, and largely unimplicated in the compromised system of justice, it is he who uncovers the circumstances of Beauchamp's innocence.

Mallory, Lee
The Flesheaters, 1972
David Ireland

In this surreal novel, Mallory writes from Merry Lands, a home for social outcasts, the difficult and the insane. The inmates spend much of their time playing games of obedience directed by O'Grady who, it turns out, is Mallory's father. Mallory suggests that he is the inmates' representative, and that he writes from a standpoint of objectivity. He contends that he has no beliefs and therefore no passion or guilt. Yet it becomes clear (or as clear as anything becomes in this novel) that what Mallory writes is partly a projection of his own inner turmoil. Eventually, he appears to accept that no man can entirely stand outside experience, or disavow responsibility for his own fate.

Malloy, Jimmy
Hope of Heaven, 1938, and others
John O'Hara

A newspaper reporter in Gibbsville, Pennsylvania, who goes on to modest success as a Hollywood scriptwriter, he acts as a catalyst for many of O'Hara's stories and a moral centre for the rest.

Malloy, Moose
Farewell, My Lovely, 1940
Raymond Chandler

When first spotted on a Los Angeles street, Malloy, an enormous gangster with outrageous dress sense, is 'about as inconspicuous as a tarantula on a slice of angel food'. Recently released from jail, he roams the city in search of his long-lost girlfriend, VELMA VALENTO.

Although he is essentially a gentle soul, his single-minded pursuit of the woman he loves leads him to kill more than once.

Malone
Malone Dies, 1951
Samuel Beckett

Elderly and ill, Malone inhabits a room that he identifies as apparently his own. Like MOLLOY before him, he is Irish and familiar with the feast days of the Roman Catholic church, for he speculates on how many more he might survive. Sceptical and melancholy, he waits for death with both resignation and hope, casting his mind begrudgingly over his past as he does so. 'I am content,' he reflects moodily, '... but not to the point of clapping my hands.' He seems to be attempting, but failing, to attain serenity and peace, wrestling for both an explanation of, and a release from, himself.

Malone, George
The Boys from the Blackstuff, 1984
Alan Bleasdale

George Malone, a universally respected character who values honesty, thrift and discipline, has believed in the work ethic for the 47 years he has been working; but, because of his strong political stance, he has been in continual conflict with management. He is so desperate to work that even in his final illness he leaves hospital in his pyjamas to seek employment. A father figure to the community, he tries to help and advise where he can, although his own life is rocked by the tragic death of his favourite son. His two other sons have moved away from him, both physically and spiritually. 'I can't believe there's no hope', he says shortly before he leaves a world that seems to reject much of what he has fought for.

Malone, Hector
Man and Superman, 1903
George Bernard Shaw

A 24-year-old American, Malone is secretly married to VIOLET ROBINSON. At heart a religious man, he has cultivated perfect manners and high moral sentiments, yet he is not without humour and is especially fond of long anecdotes. English people like him and quietly sympathize with his being American. His notion of England is at least 30 years out of date: when the English begin talking about Nietzsche and Anatole France, he devastates them by enthusing about Matthew Arnold and Macaulay.

Malone, J T
Clock Without Hands, 1961
Carson McCullers

The town pharmacist who is diagnosed as having leukemia. A man of common loyalties and prejudices, he resents his wife's independence and reveres the bigoted JUDGE FOX CLANE, whose friendship he values as a privilege. Assessing his life in the face of mortality, he is haunted by regrets and bitterness, but his growing disillusionment with his old props of belief enables him to make a moral act of defiance as he approaches death.

Malvin, Roger
'Roger Malvin's Burial', 1832, in *Mosses from an Old Manse*, 1846
Nathaniel Hawthorne

Grizzled veteran of the Indian wars, he persuades his young companion (and posthumous son-in-law) REUBEN BOURNE to leave him to die of his wounds in the forest, a decision that haunts Reuben's future life.

Malvolio
Twelfth Night, c.1601
William Shakespeare

The steward to OLIVIA, he has ideas above his station, which include marriage to his mistress. This self-deception is played upon by MARIA. A capable administrator, he lacks humour, as is shown by his attitude to FESTE, whom he describes with contempt, and the fact that he never smiles. He oversteps his position in his pompous behaviour to SIR TOBY BELCH and SIR ANDREW AGUECHEEK, who are his social superiors. Although he is treated cruelly, he refuses to make peace with his adversaries and ends up swearing revenge upon them.

Mammon
The Faerie Queene, 1590-6
Sir Edmund Spenser

A savage miser who hoards his wealth in a vast cave. His eyes are blurry, his face is uncouth and dirty and his hands have nails that look like massive claws. Underground in his cave he has more gold than could ever be spent, yet he passes the time feasting his eyes upon it and counting it compulsively. He represents the fact that God and riches cannot be simultaneously served.

Mammon
Paradise Lost, 1667
John Milton

The least elevated of the angels who shared SATAN's fall from heaven, 'for even in Heav'n his looks and thoughts/Were always downward bent, admiring more/The riches of Heav'n's pavement, trodden gold/Than aught divine or holy else enjoyed'. He is the despoiler of earth's riches.

Mammon, Sir Epicure
The Alchemist, 1610
Ben Jonson

The persuadable Sir Epicure approaches the alchemy business run by the rogues SUBTLE, FACE and DOL COMMON in the hope of procuring the philosopher's stone. He believes that, with this in his possession, he will realize his dreams of living in luxury, surrounded by beautiful and sexually adventurous women. He is not only materialistic and lewd but also hypocritical, telling Subtle, whom he foolishly believes to be a pious man, that he requires the stone only for the most respectable reasons. His meeting with Dol, in her disguise as a noblewoman, has disastrous consequences.

Man, the
The Beautyful Ones Are Not Yet Born, 1970
Ayi Kwei Armah

A lonely and agonized hero, who is pale and, for most of the time, passive. He wanders through a neo-colonial wasteland like a somnambulist. However, it is the desires of those described as 'the loved ones', symbolized by his wife and family, that threaten to push him to the depth of despair. The Man's inability and sheer unwillingness to take part in the corruption around him is derided by his family, just as the sterile affluence of less brilliant former schoolmates, like the Honourable JOSEPH KOOMSON, is flaunted in his face.

Man Friday
Robinson Crusoe, 1719
The Farther Adventures of Robinson Crusoe, 1720
Daniel Defoe

A 'savage' rescued by ROBINSON CRUSOE from becoming someone's lunch, he also provides the opportunity for Crusoe to demonstrate the imagined superiority of the educated white man over the credulous native. Notwithstanding the indignities he suffers at the hands of his tutor, a bond of common humanity binds the two desert-island dwellers together, though Friday is never in any doubt about who is master and who is servant.

Man from Ironbark, the
The Man from Snowy River and Other Verses, 1895
Andrew Barton ('Banjo') Paterson

Beards are fashionable in outback Ironbark, but when the Man from Ironbark comes to see the sights of Sydney he is impressed by the 'gilded youth' there and decides to ape city manners. He drops in to a barber's shop and tells the proprietor to shave his beard and whiskers clean off. The barber tricks him with a red-hot razor-back and makes him believe his throat is cut. While holding his throat 'to save his vital spark', he flattens the barber with one tremendous clout and then proceeds to wreck the shop. Eventually he returns to Ironbark, where 'flowing beards are all the go', and warns his fellow shearers of the tricks that city gents are likely to play on innocent country folk.

Man from Snowy River, the
The Man from Snowy River and Other Verses, 1895
Andrew Barton ('Banjo') Paterson

A young man of the high country in southern New South Wales. Though mounted only on a small, weedy horse, he joins a group of stockmen to recover three horses which have escaped and joined a herd of brumbies on the slopes of Mount Kosciusko. The herd stampedes, but the Man from Snowy River gives his horse its head, outrides his mates and races downhill over the scree and through the scrub, till he turns the fleeing horses and brings them safely back to camp.

'Man in Black, The'
The Citizen of the World, 1760-2
Oliver Goldsmith

A character encountered by Lien Chi Altangi, a mandarin from Peking, on his tour of London. 'The Man in Black' becomes the mandarin's friend and guide to life in London. Instinctive and sympathetic, a 'humorist in a nation of humorists', he is a part portrait of Goldsmith himself. Generous to the point of extravagance, he endows Zelis, his niece, and her husband, Hingpo, the mandarin's son, with 'a small estate in the country'. However, usually he pretends that he is mean and cynical.

Man of Ross, the
'Epistle III, To Allen, Lord Bathurst', in 'Moral Essays', 1732
Alexander Pope

A somewhat idealized version of the historical John Kyrle (1637–1724), who is buried in the chancel of the church of Ross in Herefordshire. Though his personal generosity is legendary, no permanent monument has been raised to his memory, and he is left with just the lisping gratitude of the babies he feeds and the sick to whom he ministers.

Man of the Hill
The History of Tom Jones, 1749
Henry Fielding

An elderly gentleman of Somerset, encountered by TOM JONES and MR PARTRIDGE on their travels. His interpolated story of raised expectations and fallen fortunes is intended as a salutary warning to Tom of the dangers of city life. Though a stock figure, he bears a quiet and moving dignity.

Man With The Hoe, the
The Man With The Hoe and Other Poems, 1899
Edwin Markham

'Bowed by the weight of centuries he leans / Upon his hoe and gazes on the ground, / The emptiness of ages in his face, / And on his back the burden of the world.' Markham's sentimentalized and slightly mawkish view of the downtrodden poor farmer was based on a painting by Jean François Millet (presumably *The Angelus*) and became one of the most popular poems ever published in the United States.

Manasseh, Joshua
The Adventures of Ferdinand, Count Fathom, 1753
Tobias Smollett

A kindly merchant of London, whose generous intervention helps to unravel the complexities of the story. He is considered to be highly significant as the first completely positive Jewish character in British fiction. His forename has obvious overtones of the Messiah, but his surname may well recall the Dutch rabbinical scholar Manasseh Ben Israel, who helped persuade Cromwell to allow the Jews back into England, an issue that was once again very much in the political eye in Smollett's time.

Manciple, the
The Canterbury Tales, c.1387–1400
Geoffrey Chaucer

A buyer of provisions at one of the Inns of Court, he is portrayed as greed incarnate. He is skilled at cheating even the most learned lawyers and an expert in making money through his 'creative accounting' and being always one step ahead of the law. His tale is a fable about talking birds, the moral of which is to beware of telling tales.

Manette, Dr Alexandre
A Tale of Two Cities, 1859
Charles Dickens

A physician in Paris who was imprisoned for 18 years in the Bastille because he had become acquainted with the crimes which CHARLES DARNAY's father and uncle, both the MARQUIS DE ST EVREMONDE, committed against MADAME DEFARGE's brother and sister. In prison, he makes shoes to prevent himself from becoming completely mad. On release, he is looked after by ERNEST DEFARGE and Madame Defarge. He recovers his sanity while living in London, but at times of stress reverts to being a cobbler. With his daughter, LUCIE MANETTE, and grandchild, he returns to France to save Darnay from the guillotine, but a written account of the crimes committed by the St Evremonde brothers is found in his old cell and used by Madame Defarge to condemn Darnay to the guillotine. After Darnay is saved, the doctor lives a peaceful life with his family in London.

Manette, Lucie
A Tale of Two Cities, 1859
Charles Dickens

The pretty, devoted daughter of DR ALEXANDRE MANETTE and later wife of CHARLES DARNAY. Before her marriage, SYDNEY CARTON declares his love for her but vows never to see her again because of his unworthiness. In Paris with her child, she shows great courage during the violence of the Revolution. Out of love for her, Carton sacrifices his life to save her husband. Her family's escape from Paris is partly indebted to the bravery of her devoted maid, MISS PROSS.

Manfred
Manfred: A Dramatic Poem, 1817
Byron, George Gordon, 6th Lord Byron

Manfred, a kind of Faustian superman, 'half dust, half deity', inhabits a castle high in the Alps, and is filled with guilt for an inexpiable crime: incestuous love of his now dead sister Astarte. He calls up spirits to grant him oblivion, but they cannot. He throws himself from a crag, but a hunter saves him. Finally, he invokes the Witch of the Alps to summon his dead sister and, descending to the Hall of Arimanes, sees her wraith, who tells him that his death is near. On his return to his castle a visiting abbot begs him to repent, but he cannot. When demons come to seize him, he defies their power and dies.

Manfred, Dorcas
Jazz, 1992
Toni Morrison

An orphan brought up by her puritanical aunt, 18-year-old Dorcas is outwardly dutiful but inwardly fiery, rebellious and hungry for excitement. 'Hardheaded as well as sly', she loves intrigue and 'liked to push people', although her boldness conceals the secret vulnerability of her tragic childhood. Sexually precocious, Dorcas soon tires of the sweet devotion offered by JOE TRACE. Although murdered by Joe, she refuses to betray his name as she lies bleeding, and dies wilfully by refusing help.

Manfred, Prince of Otranto
The Castle of Otranto, 1764
Horace Walpole

Usurper of the Princedom of Otranto, Manfred will stop at nothing to maintain his hold. When his son CONRAD is crushed by a supernatural helmet, he decides to divorce his wife HIPPOLITA and marry ISABELLA OF VICENZA himself. All go in terror of his maniac rages but he has the courage of the true Gothick villain, defying the prophesied portents that appear all too solidly in his castle and killing his daughter MATILDA in mistake for Isabella. He admits defeat only after the final thunderous apparition and retires to a religious life of atonement in the cloister.

Mangan, 'Boss' (Alfred)
Heartbreak House, 1916
George Bernard Shaw

In his mid-fifties, 'Boss' Mangan imagines himself to be a distinguished and dignified man. In reality, his features are commonplace and his manner pompous and vulgar. A fraud, who has the makings of a ruthless, philistine dictator, he is gradually humiliated, principally by ELLIE DUNN and HESIONE HUSHABYE.

Manly
The Plain Dealer, 1676/7
William Wycherley

'Of an honest, surly, nice humour', Manly is a sea-captain who trusts only OLIVIA, his betrothed, and VERNISH, an old friend. As he misanthropically puts it, 'I speak ill of most men, because they deserve it'. He does not realize that his page, the disguised FIDELIA, really loves him. Olivia, on the other hand, married none other than Vernish while Manly was absent in the Dutch wars and kept the fortune he had entrusted to her. His 'plain-dealing' with everyone, in short, ironically makes him a very bad judge of character.

Manly, Eustace
The Devil is an Ass, 1616
Ben Jonson

A young gallant and associate of WITTIPOOL, Manly conspires with his friend to rescue MRS FRANCES FITZDOTTREL from domestic imprisonment. He is clever, manipulative and has a good insight into the psychological weakness of others. He has possibly led rather a dissolute life, but is essentially a good man and acts only partly for fun. His main guide is his sense of honour and natural justice.

Mann, Hector
The Book of Illusions, 2002
Paul Auster

With his Spanish looks, trademark white suit and mischievously fluttering black moustache, Mann was an immensely watchable, if minor comedian of the silent film era, his character that of a little man striving to win social prestige and approval, overcome odds, get the girl and impress the boss. To Vermont professor David Zimmer, he seems a genius, yet nothing has been heard of Mann since he disappeared one day in 1928. The reason, Zimmer learns, was his implication in a murder. During the intervening years, pursued by guilt,

he has lived under many guises before retreating to an isolated home in New Mexico. There, he seeks redemption in art, making films that nobody will ever see.

Mannering, Col Guy
Guy Mannering, 1816
Sir Walter Scott

Coming down from Oxford, he takes the opportunity to travel in the Scottish Borders. As a guest of Godfrey Bertram at Ellangowan he casts a fateful horoscope for the new-born HARRY BERTRAM that vaguely predicts the young child's kidnap and disappearance. Mannering's astrological skills (learned of an old parson) are made no further use of than this one guilt-laden prognostication, which haunts him through his days in the Indian army, where he unwittingly encounters young Bertram in the form of Vanbeest Brown.

Mannering, Julia
Guy Mannering, 1816
Sir Walter Scott

COL GUY MANNERING's daughter, she is pursued by HARRY BERTRAM (in the person of Vanbeest Brown), who serenades her in secret with a little Indian melody played on a flageolet. In the opinion of her guardian Mr Mervyn, the girl 'has much of the romantic turn of [Mannering's own] disposition ... she has a lively and quick imagination, and keen feelings, which are apt to exaggerate both the good and evil they find in life'.

Manners, Daphne
The Jewel in the Crown, 1966
The Day of the Scorpion, 1968
The Towers of Silence, 1971
A Division of the Spoils, 1975, forming
The Raj Quartet
Paul Scott

The shy, clumsy and sweet-natured niece of a former liberal governor of Mayapore, Daphne is visiting India to work at the province's British hospital. She lives with her aunt's Indian friend, Lady Chatterjee, an arrangement disapproved of by the English community, particularly RONALD MERRICK. Merrick pursues Daphne, but she is instinctively repelled by him. Wholeheartedly loving India, she dangerously disregards its rigid taboos, and her fleeting, doomed love affair with HARI KUMAR during the violent riots of 1942 has tragic consequences for both of them.

Mannion, Conan
The Timeless Land, 1941
Storm of Time, 1948
No Barrier, 1953
Eleanor Dark

STEPHEN MANNION's young Irish second wife, widowed after eight years by his murder, is a quietly strong-minded sympathetic person. Of her uncongenial husband she says only 'he was not a kindly man', and when she discovers his long-standing affair with housekeeper ELLEN PRENTICE, she feels pity for Ellen, who was forced into the liaison. Conan prefers the more exciting life of Sydney to that at Beltrasna, and her strength of will and character are demonstrated when, refusing to return to Ireland, she serenely marries her stepsons' former tutor despite the social stigma incurred. She retains the affection and respect of MILES MANNION and PATRICK MANNION throughout, and is their trusted confidante.

Mannion, Miles
The Timeless Land, 1941
Storm of Time, 1948
No Barrier, 1953
Eleanor Dark

PATRICK MANNION's extrovert younger brother, who grows up to be a handsome, charming, cheerful and hearty man, with a tremendous zest for life, but who lacks sensitivity. His dream from childhood has been to discover a route over the mountains from Sydney to Australia's unknown interior. He nurtures this dream during the nine years he spends in London, ostensibly studying, and his aunt there describes him as 'thoroughly irresponsible'. He returns to Beltrasna with a highly unsuitable, pregnant wife, and, completely neglecting her, is helped by the outlaw JOHNNY PRENTICE to realize his dream.

Mannion, Patrick
The Timeless Land, 1941
Storm of Time, 1948
No Barrier, 1953
Eleanor Dark

STEPHEN MANNION's sensitive and reclusive eldest son, Patrick is devoted to philosophical thought and writing poetry and is regarded by his father's family as a pitiable eccentric. But he is conscientious and is, drilled to respect property, after his father's death he runs the family estate. He sleeps with his Aborigine servant-girl, DILBOONG, and to his shame fathers her child. Abhorring both public and private conflict and disorder, Patrick must nonetheless face up to the Bligh rebellion, and an agonizing dilemma concerning his childhood friend, JOHNNY PRENTICE. His life is further disrupted when he falls in love with the wife of his brother, MILES MANNION.

Mannion, Stephen
The Timeless Land, 1941
Storm of Time, 1948
No Barrier, 1953
Eleanor Dark

An early 'gentleman pioneer' of the Australian wilderness, Stephen, the father of MILES MANNION and PATRICK MANNION, is from an Irish landowning family, and has an estate outside Sydney, called Beltrasna after his home in Ireland. Wealthy, handsome and commanding, with a careless magnificence of dress and bearing, he can be very charming. But he is essentially cold, arrogant and cruel, and his harsh treatment drives away JOHNNY PRENTICE, the child of ELLEN PRENTICE, Stephen's housekeeper-mistress. When he is murdered, his young second wife, CONAN MANNION, does not mourn him.

Mannix
The Long March, 1956
William Styron

Survivor of a brutal forced march that leads to the death of several of his fellow-Marines. He is the archetypal bland liberal, chastened and humanized by an encounter with evil. His bleeding feet at the end are (perhaps) an echo of Jesus Christ's crucifixion wounds, but it is more important that he has become man incarnated in the most immediate and direct way.

Mannon, Christine
Mourning Becomes Electra, 1931
Eugene O'Neill

The sensual and faithless wife of GEN EZRA MANNON, and a later version of Clytemnestra in O'Neill's Freudian reworking of Aeschylus's *Oresteia*. She is having an affair with a kinsman, CAPTAIN ADAM BRANT. Fulfilling the inexorable logic of the Greek legend, she poisons her husband and subsequently, after learning of her lover's murder, commits suicide.

Mannon, Gen Ezra
Mourning Becomes Electra, 1931
Eugene O'Neill

A latter-day version of Agamemnon, he returns from the American Civil War to his family. His daughter LAVINIA MANNON (representing the Electra complex) loves him with a passion intermixed with the Puritan coldness she has inherited from him. He detests his son ORIN MANNON for commanding his mother's love. His wife CHRISTINE MANNON has cuckolded him with his nephew CAPTAIN ADAM BRANT; shocked into a heart attack at the discovery, he dies when Christine, pretending to give him medicine, administers poison.

Mannon, Lavinia
Mourning Becomes Electra, 1931
Eugene O'Neill

The daughter of GEN EZRA MANNON, who is rejected by her mother, CHRISTINE MANNON, in favour of her brother ORIN MANNON. Her passionate (Electra-like) love for her father gradually gives way, after their deaths, to a sensuous nature inherited from Christine and hitherto repressed. But this fails to protect her from her destiny. By the end, she is the last survivor of the dynasty, self-imprisoned behind the Puritan shutters of the Mannon house.

Mannon, Orin
Mourning Becomes Electra, 1931
Eugene O'Neill

The son of GEN EZRA MANNON, he is hated by his father for having consumed so much of his mother CHRISTINE MANNON's love. Cast as Orestes in the family tragedy, he kills his mother's lover, CAPTAIN ADAM BRANT, flees to the South Seas with his sister, LAVINIA MANNON, for whom he has incestuous longings, and commits suicide on his return to the USA.

Manoa
Samson Agonistes, 1671
John Milton

The aged father of SAMSON, he visits his blinded son in the prison at Gaza, prepared to make any sacrifice to secure his release from the Philistines.

Manolin
The Old Man and the Sea, 1952
Ernest Hemingway

A young boy who is the best friend and helper of the old fisherman SANTIAGO. His parents forbid him to go with the old man because he is 'unlucky' with fish, but the boy retains his faith and his loyalty. He is a baseball fanatic, and they spend much time discussing the distant exploits of Joe Di Maggio. He looks after the old man on land, and believes he still has much to learn from him about the sea and fishing.

Mansfield, Mr
Smith, 1967
Leon Garfield

A tall, stout elderly magistrate, straight-laced and somewhat dour. Having lost his sight twelve years earlier in a fire that also killed his wife, he now lives with his daughter, ROSE MANSFIELD, who refers to him as a saint. He confides in SMITH that he is in fact all too human and that it is Rose who is the saint. Wealthy but not contented, Mansfield guards his emotions carefully, never letting them show, since he cannot ever know how they will be received. His adventures with Smith teach him that his own heart has been all too neat and tidy, like the whole business of the law itself – obsessed with keeping to rules, but failing to administer true justice, concerned only with its own exclusive little patch.

Mansfield, Rose
Smith, 1967
Leon Garfield

The daughter of MR MANSFIELD the magistrate, she, like her father, tries to conceal her emotions. She seems amiable and kind, but is not above scowling at her blind parent when the need arises. However, she maintains her kindly tone, no matter what her demeanour betrays. Small and characterful, she is pleasant and peevish at the same time. Talkative and witty, she keeps her father well amused, and is utterly devoted to him. She grows to be very fond of SMITH, and although stunned by his apparent uncovering as a murderer, never loses faith in him, as befits her loyal nature and her perceptive judgement of character.

Man-Shy
Man-Shy, 1923–5
Frank Dalby Davison

A wild red heifer, who lives in the Australian bush. Having begun life as part of a domestic herd, she associates man with terror and pain, escapes, becomes homesick, is caught and escapes again. By this parable, Davison suggests that the unfettered animal (and perhaps human) spirit is resilient enough to withstand adversity and perhaps even become stronger by it. The heifer represents Heroic Will. However, expanding civilization, in the shape of managed farms, means the extinction of her kind and her way of life.

Manston, Aeneas
Desperate Remedies, 1871
Thomas Hardy

MISS CYTHEREA ALDCLYFFE's illegitimate son, Aeneas means a great deal to his mother, but she

is incapable of demonstrating love for him. He is emotionally needy and morally depraved, yet despite being a cunning villain, and a manipulator of people and events, he has a wicked charm, and is passionately in love with young CYTHEREA GRAYE. When he is revealed as a murderer, he has no option but to kill himself.

Mantalini, Mr Alfred and Madame
Nicholas Nickleby, 1839
Charles Dickens

Madame Mantalini is a fashionable dressmaker in Mayfair who employs KATE NICKLEBY. Mr Mantalini, whose real name is Muntle, is a likeable fop, idler and philanderer who had 'married on his whiskers; upon which property he had previously subsisted, in a genteel manner, for some years'. When his extravagance bankrupts her, she hands over the business to her assistant, Miss Knagg, and separates from her husband. After a spell in prison, his life is made miserable by an old washerwoman, for whom he turns the mangle.

Mantoor, Adam
An Instant in the Wind, 1976, originally published in Afrikaans as *'n Oomblik in die Wind*, 1975
André Brink

A runaway South African slave in the 18th century, he rescues ELISABETH LARSSON, a white lady who has lost her husband and their party in the interior. Adam is sentimental and tough by turns, in, but not of, the world that surrounds him.

Manuel
The Bridge of San Luis Rey, 1927
Thornton Wilder

Identical twins left as foundlings at the convent, Manuel and his brother ESTEBAN share dark good looks and a noble mien which suggest Castilian blood. They are uncannily close, but it is Manuel who makes all the decisions. His love for the actress LA PERICHOLE causes the first slight rift between the brothers. When he dies from an infected wound in his knee, Esteban is inconsolable.

Manuel, Dom
'The Biography of the Life of Manuel', in *The Works*, 1927–30
James Branch Cabell

The protean hero of Cabell's mythical Poictesme cycle (Poictesme is Cabell's mythical province of medieval southern France), he is the living embodiment of the tension between dream and reality. His life and that of his legitimate and bastard progeny stand as proof that this world is the only one we have and that the ability to value what it has to offer is the only categorical imperative.

Maplestead, Rick
The Merry-Go-Round in the Sea, 1965
Randolph Stow

The older cousin and idol of ROB CORAM. Significantly, whereas the younger boy dreams of fairground horses, spinning eternally on the merry-go-round, Rick looks after real animals, sharing their muscular physicality. He later goes off to war, an experience that vicariously but profoundly affects his young relative but also reveals his own ties to family, culture and a wider than personal history.

Mapp, Elizabeth, subsequently Mrs Benjamin Mapp-Flint
Mapp and Lucia, 1931, et seq
E F Benson

A substantial personage, with 'dimpled, well-nourished cheeks', who accounts herself first lady of Tilling until the arrival of her thereafter lifelong adversary, LUCIA. She is the owner (till misfortune delivers it into enemy hands) of 'Mallards', one of the foremost residences of Tilling. Later married to Major Flint, she enjoys a brief civic tenure as mayoress.

Mapple, Father
Moby-Dick, 1851
Herman Melville

The old preacher in the Whaleman's Chapel in Nantucket. A harpooner turned minister, he is known for his sincerity and sanctity. He still has 'a certain venerable robustness', and mounts to his pulpit by means of a ship's ladder, which he ascends with a 'truly sailor-like but reverential dexterity', despite his age. His sermon on Jonah and the whale greatly moves ISHMAEL.

Marasca, Francesco → Cicio

Marban
The Romans in Britain, 1980
Howard Brenton

A young Celt training to be a priest, he appears during the first part of the play, which is set north of the Thames in 54BC. He is a mystic: poetic, wise, pessimistic, watchful and, if he has to be, a killer. The victim of an attempted homosexual assault by two Roman soldiers, he represents the colonial conquered of all ages, as the soldiers represent imperial conquerors throughout history, and their contempt for those sometimes more noble than themselves who are abused, enslaved or exterminated.

Marcello
The White Devil, 1612
John Webster

A former soldier, attendant to FRANCISCO DE MEDICIS, Duke of Florence, and noted for his virtue. He is appalled that his brother FLAMINEO procures their sister VITTORIA COROMBONA for the DUKE OF BRACHIANO, and that she dallies with Brachiano. He defends their mother's honour and their family's name; as a result, he is murdered by Flamineo.

Marcellus
The Robe, 1942
Lloyd C Douglas

The Roman tribune whose infatuation with Diana, a ward of the emperor, leads to his enforced tour of duty in Palestine, where he encounters the newly-emerging Christian faith, and is impressed enough by it to be sympathetic towards its practitioners. Gambling in an idle moment for the robe of Christ, he finds himself haunted by its connection to his life. His struggle to cope with the appeal of Christianity is eventually settled by his conversion, a decision that costs him his life.

March
The Fox, 1923
D H Lawrence

The more robust of the two women partners running Bailey Farm (BANFORD is rather delicate), March is 'the man about the place'. She has learned carpentry at night school and does most of the outdoor work. Tough, practical and perhaps emotionally slightly reserved, she also has deeper, more tender qualities: she would like to take time to make a fire-screen, or to paint on porcelain. There is a suggestion that she is emotionally unfulfilled: 'she was a creature of odd whims and unsatisfied tendencies'. Her falling in love with a visiting soldier, HENRY GRENFEL, provokes Banford's jealousy.

March, Amy
Little Women, 1868
Good Wives, 1869
Little Men, 1871
Jo's Boys, 1886
Louisa M Alcott

Vanity in the youngest March sister gives her the ability to make herself agreeable by style and attractive refinement of natural good looks. From shame at petty embarrassments to a sensation of insignificance in the presence of Art on her European tour, she develops a sensibility to 'experiences and inconsistencies' in herself and others. Artistic and ambitious, she vows to 'polish up my talents and be an ornament to society'.

March, Augie
The Adventures of Augie March, 1953
Saul Bellow

A discontented American traveller, and adventurer in the realms of the mind and imagination, who determines to 'go at things as I have taught myself, free-style, and will make the record in my own way'. He battles against respectability and the deterministic influences of his Chicago-Depression youth in a welter of emotional, intellectual and moral extravagances, plunging into a world which offers too much 'hugeness, abundance, turbulence'. He looks vainly for a place where 'life can come together again and man be regenerated', but settles in the end for a 'mysterious adoration of what occurs'.

March, Basil
Their Wedding Journey, 1871
A Hazard of New Fortunes, 1890
An Open-Eyed Conspiracy, 1897
Their Silver Wedding Journey, 1899
William Dean Howells

Generally accepted to be an autobiographical portrait of the young journalist Howells, he is first seen with his wife, ISABEL MARCH, on a wide-eyed honeymoon trip through the not-quite-real landscape of modern America. He reappears after 18 drab years in insurance (during which he has nursed literary aspirations) when he is offered the editorship of a new journal, *Every Other Week*. The job throws him into contact with the new radical politics, and his polite equanimity is dramatically disturbed.

March, Beth
Little Women, 1868
Good Wives, 1869
Little Men, 1871
Jo's Boys, 1886
Louisa M Alcott

A shy kitten of a girl, whose gentle strength is an ideal held at the heart of her close-knit New England family. Musical, but unaware of her talents, and the confidante of blustering JO MARCH, her childlike happiness is found in being at home, safe with her parents. A real patient in suffering her debilitating illness, she shows true courage, when all hope is gone, in enjoying what time is left to her.

March, Charles
The Conscience of the Rich, 1958
C P Snow

The son and heir of a powerful Anglo-Jewish banking family, he encounters LEWIS ELIOT while they are training for the Bar and impresses him with his solitary struggle to come to terms with his Jewishness and with his father's expectations of him.

March, Isabel
Their Wedding Journey, 1871
A Hazard of New Fortunes, 1890
William Dean Howells

BASIL MARCH's bride, she is a clear-sighted and sympathetic foil to her husband's growing romanticization of the American landscape. In the later book, she becomes convinced that her husband's happiness, and that of the whole family, depends on his accepting the editorship of *Every Other Week*.

March, Jo
Little Women, 1868
Good Wives, 1869
Little Men, 1871
Jo's Boys, 1886
Louisa M Alcott

An ambitious free spirit, tamed by housekeeping, she is a rough colt-like tomboy who resents growing up, but eventually learns to curb her dreadful temper and find her literary voice. She plans 'romantic rubbish', resisting real emotion, reluctant to accept MEG MARCH's marriage or LAURIE's love. Fired by heroism and epic dreams of riches and fame, she stays at home to care for her parents, and is rescued from spinsterhood by her beloved DR BHAER.

March, Meg
Little Women, 1868
Good Wives, 1869
Little Men, 1871
Jo's Boys, 1886
Louisa M Alcott

The most domesticated of the March daughters, her envy of others' clothes and lifestyle stems from her dislike of being made to feel poor; but, when dressed up by so-called friends, her natural rejection of 'fuss and feathers', gossip and champagne, takes over. Basically serious and

dutiful, she finds marriage to JOHN BROOKE hard work rather than romantic.

March Hare, the
Alice's Adventures in Wonderland, 1865
Lewis Carroll

The March Hare, friend of THE MAD HATTER, is having tea with him and THE DORMOUSE when ALICE approaches. He invites her to have some wine when there is only tea. He begins a dispute about whether saying what you mean is the same as meaning what you say. He has damaged the Hatter's watch by treating it with butter; even though it was the best butter, he should not have put it in with the breadknife. He is a less aggressive personality than the Hatter but equally mad; all hares are traditionally mad in the spring.

Marchbanks, Eugene
Candida, 1895
George Bernard Shaw

An idealistic, dishevelled, 18-year-old poet of aristocratic birth, Marchbanks appears 'so uncommon as to be almost unearthly'. CANDIDA MORELL discovers him and brings him into the home she shares with her husband. Marchbanks is naturally apprehensive, but the very intensity and torment of his feelings results in a torrent of frank and forcefully expressed opinions. The REV JAMES MORELL is astounded to hear him proclaim that he loves Candida himself. Later, still chaste, but full of the moral strength and idealism of the writer, he rejects the security of Morellian domesticity and the lure of love, to fulfil his own higher and spiritual destiny as an artist.

Marcher, John
'The Beast in the Jungle', 1903
Henry James

In a reversal of the usual Puritan obsession with sin and guilt, he is haunted by all those things in his life that he has failed to do; indeed, by the life he has failed to live. He now regards experience as a beast, crouching in the jungle, waiting to destroy him.

Marchioness, the
The Old Curiosity Shop, 1841
Charles Dickens

The nickname given by DICK SWIVELLER to the small, shrewd, servant girl employed and badly treated by SAMPSON BRASS and SALLY BRASS. Swiveller secretly becomes her friend, and she runs away to nurse him when he falls ill. When the Brasses plot to have KIT NUBBLES arrested, she overhears them, and her revelations lead to their downfall and DANIEL QUILP's. Finally, Swiveller re-names her Sophronia Sphynx, pays for her to be educated as a lady, and marries her.

Marchmain, LadyTeresa
Brideshead Revisited, 1945
Evelyn Waugh

'Very, very beautiful, huge-eyed', with 'a voice as quiet as a prayer, and as powerful', Teresa Marchmain is married for 15 years to LORD MARCHMAIN before he goes abroad to the war, never to return to her. A pious Catholic, she is unable to divorce him, but is assiduously courted by the poet Sir Adrian Porson. She engages MR SAMGRASS, an Oxford don, to help her write a book about her brother Ned, whose death in the war left his abundant talent unfulfilled. A mysterious 'femme fatale' with an ironic sense of humour, she dies at Brideshead of a chronic illness she has kept secret for years.

Marchmain, Lord
Brideshead Revisited, 1945
Evelyn Waugh

The father of SEBASTIAN, JULIA and CORDELIA FLYTE. 'A tall and upright figure', with a noble, Byronic appearance, the Marquis of Marchmain leaves Brideshead to go to France with the Yeomanry and becomes a 'social leper' when he does not return. Instead, he takes up residence in Venice with his mistress Cara, a talented dancer, and remains 'a volcano of hate' towards his estranged wife, LADY TERESA MARCHMAIN. International turbulence drives him back to Brideshead to pass his declining years, and despite having renounced his Catholicism many years earlier, he makes the sign of the cross shortly before he dies.

Marchmill, Ella
'An Imaginative Woman', in *Wessex Tales: Strange, Lively and Commonplace*, 1896
Thomas Hardy

A romantic and a dreamer, Ella is born into an imaginative and literary family, and in her life with her uninspiring gun-dealer husband she craves some poetic intrigue. Her existence is not unsatisfactory, but she is unfulfilled and eager to explore life at a deeper level. The imaginary powers she possesses are capable of sending her into deep depression, over nothing tangible to the outside world. A fantasist who is no longer satisfied with her first love, she reckons she is ready for the true, second love of her life. Infatuated with the poet ROBERT TREWE, she comes to an inevitably tragic end.

Marco
A View from the Bridge, 1955
Arthur Miller

Cousin to BEATRICE CARBONE, his illegal immigration, with his brother RODOLPHO, to the United States, sets in motion the tragic chain of circumstances around which the play revolves. An immensely strong, quiet man, he has emigrated to support his wife and sick children in Italy. Eventually betrayed by EDDIE CARBONE, he kills him, demonstrating his belief that 'all the law is not in a book'.

Margaret
The Gentleman Usher, 1602/3
George Chapman

The daughter of EARL LASSO, Margaret rejects the advances of ALPHONSO, for whose son PRINCE VINCENTIO she has a noble love. She makes fun of BASSIOLO, but has some sympathy for him. Her courage and virtue are demonstrated by an act of self-sacrifice.

Margaret, Queen → Margaret of Anjou

Margaret, Sister
The Amen Corner, 1968
James Baldwin

A charismatic preacher who represents the contradiction and tension felt between religious belief of the most unreserved sort and the twin challenges of art and love. She is said to be based on the historical Mother Horn by whom Baldwin was saved as a child.

Margaret of Anjou
Anne of Geierstein, or The Maiden in the Mist, 1829
Sir Walter Scott

Wife of the lame-brained Henry IV, she effectively rules in his stead. After the defeat at Tewkesbury, she is ransomed by Louis XI and retires to France, where she lives out a lonely but still regal retirement.

Margaret of Anjou, later Queen Margaret
Henry VI Parts I, II and III, early 1590s
Richard III, 1592/3
William Shakespeare

In love with the Earl of Suffolk but married to HENRY VI and dealing with affairs of state on his behalf, Margaret becomes a leader of the House of Lancaster against that of York in the Wars of the Roses. Described by RICHARD PLANTAGENET, DUKE OF YORK as 'England's bloody scourge', she is furiously strong-willed, ambitious for power, a ruthless and sadistic military leader. Her appearance in *Richard III* is, from the point of view of history as well as characterization, wholly fictitious, for she left England before 1478, the date at which the play opens. Mad and vengeful, she curses Richard (RICHARD, DUKE OF GLOUCESTER) calling him, memorably, an 'abortive, rooting hog', and 'bottled spider'. She represents not only a continuum within the four plays, but also the part of the context of blood and lust for power that produced Richard himself.

Margaret of Branksome
The Lay of the Last Minstrel, 1805
Sir Walter Scott

The tears that she sheds on her father's bier are not just those of 'filial grief' but express her fears that her mother will forbid her marriage to the same LORD CRANSTOUN who had stood in arms against her father in the Border wars.

Margayya
The Financial Expert, 1952
R K Narayan

For this brilliant amateur financial adviser, interest is the greatest wonder of creation and rupees are mystically akin to ripening corn. He conducts his alfresco business under the nose of an enraged Cooperative Bank, until his accounts literally go down the drain at the hands of his wilful small son, BALU. Desperately looking for a livelihood, Margayya encounters the eccentric DR PAL, who miraculously provides the means to riches which, with his natural financial wizardry, Margayya is able to turn into a vast fortune. However, he never acknowledges his debt to Pal, who turns vengeful. There is poetic justice in the outcome.

Margo
The Dressmaker, 1973
Beryl Bainbridge
Margo is NELLIE's coarser younger sister. After working in the munitions factory she comes home, sits with her legs apart, drinks port, smokes cigarettes, and jokes with a dry, bitter sense of humour. Desperate for another life, she has a slightly hysterical appearance, wearing a cocktail dress several sizes too large. She is resentful that she has never had an opportunity to lose herself in love and sexual fulfilment and is jealous of anyone else's chance to grapple with romance.

Maria
'Clay', in *Dubliners*, 1914
James Joyce
Maria is a small, pathetic creature who dreams of simple things. She believes everyone is fond of her as she is affectionately named the 'veritable little peacemaker'. Never having had any true romance in her life, she lives as a spinster. A caring woman, she gives one of her carefully tended plants to all who visit her. She is quietly proud of her trim figure, and when she laughs or cries 'the tip of her nose nearly [meets] the tip of her chin'.

Maria
For Whom the Bell Tolls, 1940
Ernest Hemingway
A rather stereotypically depicted heroine who falls in love with ROBERT JORDAN. She is the traditionally dutiful, submissive female (in contrast with PILAR), and is sexually innocent, 'a girl of good morals', despite having suffered a traumatic rape at the hands of enemy soldiers. Jordan's rather embarrassing tenderness helps her overcome that trauma.

Maria
Love's Labour's Lost, not later than 1594
William Shakespeare
An attendant lady to the PRINCESS OF FRANCE. Loved by Lord LONGAVILLE of Navarre, she gives him a number of calculated backhanded compliments. She also exchanges sexual innuendos with the clown COSTARD. Finally, she makes Longaville wait a year and a day for her.

Maria
The Malcontent, 1604
John Marston
Wife of the ousted Duke of Genoa, Giovanni Altofronto, but unaware that he is disguised as the satirical court fool MALEVOLE, Maria remains steadfast in her love for her husband. When Malevole asks her to dance, she accepts but also declares her completely chaste and honourable intentions.

Maria
'Old Mortality', in *Pale Horse, Pale Rider*, 1939, 'The Old Order', in *The Collected Stories of Katherine Anne Porter*, 1964
Katherine Anne Porter
Sensible and serious Maria, who knows that she will never be beautiful, is brought up in the American South with her younger sister, MIRANDA. Surrounded by old people, she enjoys their memories of the dead, including the romantic AMY BREAUX, but she dislikes the dull convent school to which she and her sister are sent.

Maria
The School for Scandal, 1777
Richard Brinsley Sheridan
The young ward of SIR PETER TEAZLE. Her innocence and goodness enable her to see people's true qualities; she therefore loves CHARLES SURFACE and deplores the destruction of reputations by LADY SNEERWELL and her circle.

Maria
Twelfth Night, c.1601
William Shakespeare
Maria, the lady-in-waiting to OLIVIA, although witty and favoured by her mistress, has a devious side to her character for she is the one who concocts the idea of the letter to trick MALVOLIO, whom she resents because of his tactless behaviour towards the late-night revellers SIR ANDREW AGUECHEEK, SIR TOBY BELCH and FESTE. Her talent for forgery proves useful in this situation, as does her skill with words, which has already defeated Sir Andrew completely. She enjoys Malvolio's discomfort but realizes that, because of her love for Sir Toby, she has taken the matter too far.

Marianna
Measure for Measure, c.1604
William Shakespeare
Once engaged to be married to ANGELO, DUKE VINCENTIO's deputy, she is estranged from her intended husband. She remains loyal to him, however, even after five years' separation and despite the fact that he deserted her when her dowry was lost at sea, together with her brother. Loving and faithful, Marianna agrees to the duke's plan for her to replace ISABELLA in Angelo's bed, hoping it will lead, at last, to their marriage.

Mariella
Palace of the Peacock, 1960, part of *The Guyana Quartet*, 1985
Wilson Harris
DONNE's mistress, she is an *anima* figure, as insubstantial as sunlight or smoke or as brutally physical as a jaguar. She seems to haunt the jungle, a 'fleshly shadow ... a vulgar musing executioner'. Like all of Harris's 'characters', she is not a single self so much as a 'community of being'.

Marina
Pericles, c.1608
William Shakespeare
The daughter of PERICLES and THAISA, Marina is born at sea. As her mother is thought to have died, Pericles leaves her in the care of CLEON and DIONYZA. Later, Dionyza orders her to be killed because her beauty and intelligence outshine that of her own daughter. But instead, she is sold to a brothel, where her grace and principles of chastity not only protect her virtue but almost bankrupt the house. The proprietors agree she

should transfer to a respectable family and teach music. Marina is an idealized woman whose own ideals, despite all her trials, remain intact. Her eventual reunion with Pericles is one of the most moving of Shakespearean scenes.

Marinell
The Faerie Queene, 1590–6
Sir Edmund Spenser

The son of the sea-nymph CYMODOCE. He is excessively rich because of the treasures which the sea-god Nereus, father of Cymodoce, continually throws up on his beach. He is well known for his feats of strength and great deeds, and is famous for having battled against and killed more than 100 men. He never has any dealings with women because of a prophecy told in his childhood, which said that he would die at the hands of a virgin, but eventually he falls in love with FLORIMELL.

Mariner, Ancient
The Ancient Mariner, 1797–8
Samuel Taylor Coleridge

An old seafaring man who finds himself compelled to travel perpetually from one land to another, recounting his frightening supernatural experience of Death and Life-in-Death to strangers, in penance for his sin of shooting an albatross, the bird which brings good luck at sea. With his glinting, hypnotic eyes and long grey beard, he is a mysterious, almost other-worldly figure who inspires fear, but also wisdom, in the wedding guest he singles out to listen to, and learn from, his tale.

Mariner, Will
Between Two Tides, 1952
R D Fitzgerald

Tolerant and balanced, a man to whom duties are complex problems to be weighed and measured, Will chooses the way forward as 'the heart's hidden truth dictates'. The understudy of his ship's captain and then of TONGAN CHIEF FINAU, he would be great but lacks the necessary ruthlessness. A divided man at heart, he is caught between two worlds and two modes of being: Tonga and quest/England and security.

Maritana
The Roaring Nineties, 1946
Golden Miles, 1948
Winged Seeds, 1950
Katharine Susannah Prichard

A half-caste Aboriginal girl who moves uneasily between white and black worlds and is a tool of both. Naive and vulnerable, 'she had the same wild shy ways as the little rock wallaby'. Maritana is a victim, her life a tragedy.

Marius
Marius the Epicurean, 1885
Walter Pater

A sober young Roman scholar – allegedly based on the High Anglican bibliophile Richard Charles Jackson – he makes slow and ponderously idealistic progress towards Christianity and eventual martyrdom via most of the philosophies of the time.

Marjoribanks, Miss
Miss Marjoribanks, 1866
Margaret Oliphant

'A comfort to papa', she amuses him by her crowded 'Thursdays', her tireless manoeuvring, her floods of talk, her patronage of art, her ten-year-long managing of Carlingford society before she 'goes off'. But she finds no husband. Left without much money after papa's death, she sees her candidate win the election through her efforts, but is not content. Only when she marries Cousin Tom ('whom it was all the time') does she find her true vocation, managing and improving life for the poor tenants on their estate.

Marjorybanks, Henrietta
The Green Graves of Balgowrie, 1896
Jane Findlater

She is the plain, dark, forthright sister of LUCIE MARJORYBANKS and daughter of MRS MARJORYBANKS. As a child, she smashes DR CORNELIUS HALLIJOHN's decanter when she sees his drunkenness. Never commonplace in speech or action, she hungers for knowledge and understanding, showing herself to be strong where Lucie is childlike. Dr Hallijohn's teaching brings happiness and excitement; he loves her intelligence, she loves him as father, teacher and lover – but always second to her sister. Delaying marriage, she nurses Lucie faithfully to the end but falls ill herself. Looking forward passionately to the 'new life' with Cornelius Hallijohn, she is thwarted by her mother. The final Thursday charade in bitter cold results in her death.

Marjorybanks, Lucie
The Green Graves of Balgowrie, 1896
Jane Findlater

The younger sister of HENRIETTA MARJORYBANKS, she is fair, sweet and fresh, loving pigeons, music, sewing, flowers, simple domestic things. Weaker than Henrietta, she clings to her and fears her mother, MRS MARJORYBANKS, but she has a deep capacity for affection. Captain Dan Charteris visits Balgowrie and sees the sisters' extraordinary home-made dresses; out of amusement he makes love to Lucie. Desolate when he leaves, she gladly is taken to London, hoping to see him, but he avoids her. Her quaint nervous ways are so laughed at that she returns home broken-hearted and dies a slow, grieving death, nursed by Henrietta.

Marjorybanks, Mrs
The Green Graves of Balgowrie, 1896
Jane Findlater

Mrs Marjorybanks, strong-minded widow, brings up her two daughters (HENRIETTA and LUCIE MARJORYBANKS) very oddly, in the dark tower-house of Balgowrie. They run wild in childhood and in their teens perform a four-hour-long charade with tables and chairs like a soirée every Thursday. An atheist and radical even in the 1770s, she strides, tall and gaunt, like a grenadier, expounding her bleak views in letters to her late husband's first love in London. Harsh, domineering and a little mad, she shows no affection and as her daughters' lives are slowly destroyed she reads Voltaire and writes essays on education.

Mark
Bevis: the Story of a Boy, 1882
Richard Jefferies
Less intellectually aware than his playmate BEVIS, he is nonetheless a willing companion in their games and in their construction of elaborate historical fantasies.

Mark, Lord
The Wings of the Dove, 1902
Henry James
An impoverished English fortune-hunter who meets and woos MILLIE THEALE in Venice, eager for her money. Rejected, he spitefully reveals the relationship between KATE CROY and MERTON DENSHER to the dying girl, thus speeding her decline.

Markham, Gilbert
The Tenant of Wildfell Hall, 1848
Anne Brontë
Undeterred by spiteful neighbours, Markham determines to solve the mystery of the strange, unfriendly MRS HELEN GRAHAM now living with her little son, ARTHUR, at Wildfell Hall. He falls in love, and out of jealousy attacks her landlord, FREDERICK LAWRENCE, for visiting her. However, Mrs Graham gives Markham her diary recounting her wretched marriage to ARTHUR HUNTINGDON, a profligate drunkard, to show that she is not free to return his love. When she goes back to her dying husband out of duty, Markham is distraught, and when she becomes a widow, she is so wealthy that he despairs of approaching her, but their love overcomes these doubts.

Markheim
Markheim, 1886
Robert Louis Stevenson
Forced, through poverty, to pawn all his cherished possessions, he kills the pawnbroker whom he sees as a parasite on his own misfortunes. In this one existential moment, he becomes conscious of his true nature and confronts his conscience. Both repelled and fascinated by his deed, he is distraught with fear of retribution and is haunted by guilt. In the act of murder, Markheim achieves a type of liberation, only to discover that this freedom has merely released the evil within his own soul.

Marks, Grace
Alias Grace, 1996
Margaret Atwood
Based upon a true story of a servant imprisoned in 1843 for her involvement with a male colleague in the murder of their employer, the novel recounts Marks's meetings with a prison psychiatrist who encourages her to recall the gruesome events, committed 15 years earlier when she was 16, but which she claims are expunged by amnesia. Although lacking much formal education, she is intelligent, meticulous in her prison work and a protégé of the governor. Indeed, she may be more persecuted than perpetrator, yet she is both evasive and wily, and her professing amnesia may be the adroit use of the only weapon a powerless woman has at her disposal.

Marlborough, Duke of
The History of Henry Esmond, Esquire, 1852
W M Thackeray
Thackeray's portrayal of the historical victor at Blenheim is far from conventionally heroic. Indeed, Marlborough (who is encountered by HENRY ESMOND during the long European campaign) is presented as a warning against unthinking glorification of military heroes, who exhibit the same mixed nature as the rest of humanity.

Marley's Ghost
A Christmas Carol, 1843
Charles Dickens
The ghost of SCROOGE's former partner, Jacob Marley, which visits him on Christmas Eve to foretell three further ghostly visitors. Marley's Ghost, wrapped in a chain made of 'cash-boxes, keys, padlocks, ledgers, deeds, and heavy purses wrought in steel', warns Scrooge that the spirits will offer him the chance to escape his own fate of having to wander the world in chains forever as a consequence of his avarice and selfishness.

Marlow
She Stoops to Conquer, 1773
Oliver Goldsmith
Like GEORGE HASTINGS, Marlow is a romantic hero. His father, Sir Charles, has arranged a match for him with KATE HARDCASTLE, the daughter of SQUIRE RICHARD HARDCASTLE. Marlow travels to the country to meet her and creates a mixed impression. The squire believes him to be boorish, while Kate thinks he is bashful. Marlow is a man of some standing and takes himself very seriously; consequently, he is extremely easy to fool. Everyone except DOROTHY HARDCASTLE plays tricks upon him at some point in the play, whether it be the pranks of Kate and TONY LUMPKIN, or the deception of Sir Charles and Squire Hardcastle, hiding behind a screen to overhear his proposal to Kate.

Marlow, Charles
Heart of Darkness, 1902, and others
Joseph Conrad
The narrator-protagonist of several of Conrad's novels and stories. He has 'sunken cheeks, a yellow complexion, a straight back, an ascetic aspect, and, with his arms dropped, the palms of hands outward, resembled an idol'. He is a seafarer and a wanderer, with a great propensity for story-telling, and an insatiable curiosity for teasing out the complexities of meaning in his tales. As narrator, he mediates and often interprets the action, in which he usually has some involvement.

Marlowe, Philip
The Big Sleep, 1939, et seq
Raymond Chandler
A private detective who moves through a corrupt world without succumbing to that corruption. He is tough, streetwise and world-weary, but has

a curious nobility, a strong sense of natural justice, a desire to restore decency, and his cynicism about the 'mean streets' in which he moves is tempered by a streak of idealism. He is essentially an introspective loner, with a taste for classical music, poetry and art, and a sense of honour when it comes to women.

Marmee
Little Women, 1868
Good Wives, 1869
Little Men, 1871
Jo's Boys, 1886
Louisa M Alcott

Emphasizing the importance of pocket handkerchiefs, Mrs March, temporarily a single parent, brings up four very different daughters with gentle but firm advice. Aware of etiquette, the horrors of the Civil War and poverty, she sets examples by controlling her own temper, performing acts of charity and telling moral tales; she wisely withdraws to allow the girls to learn from their own mistakes.

Marmion, Lord
Marmion, 1808
Sir Walter Scott

Henry VIII's (fictitious) ambassador to the Scots, 'he was a stalworth knight, and keen,/And had in many a battle been;/The scar on his brown cheek reveal'd/A token true of Bosworth field'. Yet despite his grizzled and muscular nobility, he proves to be not above a little cynical manipulation, as when he abandons his lover CONSTANCE DE BEVERLEY in favour of the wealthy LADY CLARE DE CLARE. Having falsely accused SIR RALPH DE WILTON of treason and left him for dead at the joust, he himself meets his maker at Flodden.

Marmozet
The Adventures of Roderick Random, 1748
The Adventures of Peregrine Pickle, 1751,
bowdlerized edition 1758
Tobias Smollett

An unkind portrait, considerably toned down in later editions of *Peregrine Pickle*, of the actor David Garrick, whose over-the-top thespianism brought down all Smollett's scorn on the spurious emotionalism of the acting profession.

Marner, Silas
Silas Marner, 1861
George Eliot

A small, reclusive handloom weaver who sets up in Raveloe after being expelled from a harsh band of Methodists at a town in the North of England. Embittered and shy, he begins to be obsessed by a small but growing collection of gold coins. This habit is cured when he is robbed, and in their place comes a golden-haired baby he names EPPIE. Refusing to let her go, he brings her up – with assistance from some kind-hearted local women – and finds himself gradually humanized and integrated with the Raveloe community.

Marney, Lord
Sybil, or The Two Nations, 1845
Benjamin Disraeli

CHARLES EGREMONT's brother, he is a harsh and uncompromising landowner of the old style. He conceives of the new working class as his enemy and is unregenerate in his opposition to reform. Just as the radical Chartist STEPHEN MORLEY dies because of his extremism, so too does Marney, killed by rioters.

Marple, Miss Jane
Murder at the Vicarage, 1930, et seq
Agatha Christie

An elderly spinster who resides in the small village of St Mary Mead, Jane Marple is a tall, thin woman with fleecy white hair and china-blue eyes. She is thought to be around 80, and her main occupations appear to be those best suited to her years – knitting, gardening, healthy walks (arthritis permitting) and the odd treat of a sunshine holiday provided by her nephew Raymond. However, her love of tittle-tattle and her shrewd judgement of human nature have made her an amateur sleuth of great renown, whose investigations are more likely to unmask the guilty party than the concerted efforts of the proper authorities.

Marquesa de Montemayor, the (Doña Maria)
The Bridge of San Luis Rey, 1927
Thornton Wilder

The lonely child of a Peruvian cloth merchant, her ugliness and lisping speech are derided even by her family. When she is finally married off to a ruined Lima aristocrat, the Marquesa's appearance and behaviour become so grotesque that she is regarded as mad. The 'leprous affection' which physically mars her features is mirrored in her pathetic, voracious love for her beautiful but cold daughter. Paradoxically, this love is expressed in beautiful and elegant letters, 'a monument of Spanish literature'. She finds redemption through the orphaned PEPITA.

Marrable, Captain Walter
The Vicar of Bullhampton, 1870
Anthony Trollope

A dark and handsome soldier, of misleadingly ferocious appearance. His delinquent father having cheated him out of an inheritance, his romance with his second cousin MARY LOWTHER runs into difficulties, although they still love each other. He escapes from the dreaded prospect of returning to the army in India by staying with rich relatives.

Marriane
Heroes and Villains, 1969
Angela Carter

Marriane is privileged, having been brought up by her exceptionally learned father. As a result, unlike most of those around her in this post-apocalyptic world, she has a sense of time passing and of history. A haughty and naive child who feels she does not belong anywhere, she is continually searching for something else. Her ruling passion is anger rather than fear and she finds 'chaos even more boring than order'.

Marriott, Logan
Careful, He Might Hear You, 1963
Sumner Locke Elliott

A charming, handsome, irresponsible man from

Bacchus Marsh, an Australian country town. Five days after meeting SINDEN MARRIOTT, a twin spirit, they marry, but he goes off to prospect for gold before the birth of their son, P S MARRIOTT. She thus calls Logan her 'five-minute husband'. Life seems pointless after Sinden's death, so he does not return and takes no part in his son's upbringing.

Marriott, P S
Careful, He Might Hear You, 1963
Sumner Locke Elliott

His mother SINDEN MARRIOTT dies immediately after his birth. In a letter she describes him as 'a postscript to my ridiculous life', so he is always known as 'P S'. Brought up by his over-protective aunt LILA BAINES, since his father LOGAN MARRIOTT has no contact with him, he finds his life disrupted in his seventh year with the return to Australia of another aunt, VANESSA SCOTT. The two aunts struggle for custody of him; he finds the behaviour of adults difficult to understand, but the ensuing events enable him to discover his own identity.

Marriott, Sinden
Careful, He Might Hear You, 1963
Sumner Locke Elliott

A critically praised Australian novelist, who dies immediately after the birth of her son, P S MARRIOTT, and in the absence of her husband, LOGAN MARRIOTT. Impractical, impulsive and vivacious, she loves everyone indiscriminately; her sister VANESSA SCOTT says that she had 'a very happy and inaccurate life'.

Marsden, Charles
Strange Interlude, 1928
Eugene O'Neill

A quiet and shyly withdrawn novelist, in love with NINA LEEDS, but held back from any final commitment to her by his own bisexuality and by oedipal attractions parallel to, but not as antagonistic as, her own. He continues to observe her life and its dangerous deceptions, and after her husband dies, he offers her refuge in marriage.

Marsh, Mae
'Mae Marsh, Motion Picture Actress', in *Collected Poems*, 1923
Vachel Lindsay

A portrait of the historical actress Mae Marsh, 'she is madonna in an art/As wild and young as her sweet eyes:/A frail dew flower from this hot lamp/That is today's divine surprise.//Despite raw lights and gloating mobs/She is not seared: a picture still.'

Marshalson, Henry
Henry and Cato, 1976
Iris Murdoch

Born 'a bit unreal and second-rate' and always painfully belittled by his family, the young Henry prayed his hated elder brother would die. When he does, surprisingly young, Henry returns as heir to the family estate after eight years in America, where he had taken relatively happy refuge in teaching. Private, alienated and rather lost, Henry hates possessions, and astounds his domineering mother with his determination to

sell everything and give away the money. But wryly humorous surprises await him when he becomes involved in his brother's past, and the unnerving presence of old friends Colette and CATO FORBES.

Marston, Ben
Robbery Under Arms, 1888
Rolf Boldrewood

The father of DICK and JIM MARSTON, Ben is a big man in every way. He is authoritarian, obstinate and powerful, exercising an almost complete hold over his sons. It is he who lures them into a bushranging life, stealing and driving cattle with the enigmatic CAPTAIN STARLIGHT. Instinctive and bullish, Ben is in many ways the antithesis of the hardworking, respectable GEORGE STOREFIELD.

Marston, Dick
Robbery Under Arms, 1888
Rolf Boldrewood

Dick Marston tells the story of his bushranging life while in a prison cell awaiting execution. He and his brother, JIM MARSTON, strong but not well-educated men, are enticed into a life of crime by their father, BEN MARSTON, and join CAPTAIN STARLIGHT and his gang. Gullible, fickle, impetuous and reckless, Dick falls for KATE MORRISON, even though he also loves GRACEY STOREFIELD. After the intervention of GEORGE STOREFIELD, his death sentence is commuted to 15 years' imprisonment and, on his release, Dick marries Gracey. He is not a naturally evil man, but one shaped by the circumstances in which he finds himself. With his marriage, he achieves redemption and a more contemplative, fatalistic view of life.

Marston, Jim
Robbery Under Arms, 1888
Rolf Boldrewood

Like his brother, DICK MARSTON, Jim has been lured into a bushranging life by his father, BEN MARSTON, and together with him follows the mysterious outlaw, CAPTAIN STARLIGHT. During his adventures, Jim steals cattle, robs banks and falls in love with JEANIE MORRISON. The brothers are native-born colonial Australians, rough-and-ready and reckless. But while Jim is as easily influenced as his brother, he is a quieter, more chivalrous character.

Martha
Who's Afraid of Virginia Woolf?, 1962
Edward Albee

Loud, brassy and vicious-tongued, GEORGE's wife is one half of a tortured marriage which, despite its outward appearance of ruthless honesty, depends on one profound 'lie': the couple's imaginary son. Daughter of the college president, and thus the agent of George's success, she is presented as a *Walpurgisnacht* she-devil, with alcohol as her secret brew. In the end she is exposed as a helpless and vulnerable woman, as dependent on love as anyone else.

Marthy
Anna Christie, 1922
Eugene O'Neill

A elderly semi-prostitute who lives with CHRIS

CHRISTOPHERSON on his coal barge. When Chris's daughter, ANNA CHRISTOPHERSON, appears, it is Marthy, armed with her own experiences of low life, who sees through her deceptive exterior and recognizes her immorality.

Martin, Daniel
Daniel Martin, 1977
John Fowles
An emotionally repressed man, with a basic sense of human decency, Daniel has no means of expressing feelings, or even of recognizing them. His upbringing is crucial to understanding his character; he feels the loss of his mother acutely, but she is never talked about. His father's tense and undemonstrative personality did not help Daniel as a young boy to see the needs that were within him, let alone understand their roots. He spends his life chasing success, yet denying it also. Afraid of 'nakedness', of exposing his innermost soul to anyone, his relationships tend to be fraught with difficulties. A victim of his era, who is creative and sensitive, his psyche is bound up with his early exposure to religion and an eternal feeling of guilt.

Martin, Jack
The Coral Island, 1857
R M Ballantyne
One of three boys stranded on a desert island. Resourceful, charismatic and born to lead, he holds together the morale of his friends RALPH ROVER and PETERKIN after their shipwreck, when they are forced to make some sort of life from the bare bones of their desert-island home. Practical, courageous and enterprising, he is a real hero, coaxing and cajoling his companions into surviving.

Martin, Julia
After Leaving Mr Mackenzie, 1930
Jean Rhys
Set adrift from her penniless, middle-class family and confronted by the hostility of respectable society, she has for many years lived precariously in Paris on gifts and pay-offs from her various lovers. Hennaed and hollow-eyed, still beautiful, but 'too vulnerable ever to make a success of a career of chance', she is approaching middle age when MR MACKENZIE withdraws his support. Impecunious and disoriented, Julia musters the qualities which will enable her to survive: her desperate and unscrupulous cunning and the stoical indifference which masks both her courage and her withdrawal into psychosis.

Martin, Robert
Emma, 1816
Jane Austen
An unassuming, respectable young gentleman farmer, a victim of EMMA WOODHOUSE's 'unfair conjectures' due to his rank and social standing. His constancy of character and reliable integrity eventually secure him the hand of HARRIET SMITH.

Martinez, Corporal Julio
The Naked and the Dead, 1948
Norman Mailer
'Little Mexican boys also breathe the American fables ...'; he grows up driven by the success ethic and obsessed by the sexual inaccessibility of white Protestant girls. His reward is to 'go point' for LT ROBERT HEARN's platoon, acting as a reconnaissance man sent out ahead as 'Japbait'. Heroism is the back-door route to the American dream.

Martius, Gaius → Coriolanus

Maru
Maru, 1971
Bessie Head
The mythical hero of the novel. Destined to rule, Maru balances the forces of tradition against his affection for MARGARET CADMORE, JR, who belongs to the race of untouchables. His rival for her love is his bosom friend and fellow chieftain, Moleka. He contemptuously ignores the first enemy, tradition, but the second enemy is so powerful that he is left with no other choice than to appease Moleka with a sister who means so much to him.

Marvell, Ralph
The Custom of the Country, 1913
Edith Wharton
A gentle, mildly rebellious dilettante, Ralph belongs to the old New York élite, who he ironically describes as living on the 'reservation' around Washington Square. They are a cautious, middle-class and rigidly moralistic set, compared with the ascendent horde of nouveau riche 'invaders' with their vast wealth and energy. Cultured, ascetic and sensitive, he contentedly dabbles in law and poetry, dreaming of being a writer, but is himself defeated in the violent clash of values and personalities that constitutes his unhappy marriage to UNDINE SPRAGG, one of the 'invaders'.

Marwood, Alice
Dombey and Son, 1848
Charles Dickens
The illegitimate daughter of MRS BROWN, who was seduced by the uncle of EDITH DOMBEY, she strikingly resembles her cousin in beauty and pride. After being transported for crime, she returns to seek revenge on the seducer who abandoned her, JAMES CARKER. With the help of her mother and ROBIN TOODLE, who works for Carker, she arranges for MR PAUL DOMBEY to learn that Carker and Edith are eloping to Dijon. She is befriended by Carker's sister, HARRIET CARKER, to whom she relates her history before she dies.

Marwood, Mrs
The Way of the World, 1700
William Congreve
Ever since her rejection by MIRABELL, Mrs Marwood has harboured a grudge against him. Indeed, jealousy and a disposition to think the worst of everyone result in her disliking most people, including, to some extent, herself. She is having an affair with MR FAINALL, but suspects him of squandering her money. Hypocritical, subject to sudden and unpredictable shifts of emotion, she is her own worst enemy, and a consistent source of bitterness and ill-feeling.

Marx, Bernard
Brave New World, 1932
Aldous Huxley

An 'Alpha Plus' intellectual, who heretically longs for solitude, Bernard Marx and Lenina Crowne, his girlfriend, discover JOHN THE SAVAGE during a trip to an Indian reservation in New Mexico. Impressed by his vitality and individual eccentricities, they take him back to a futuristic London. Together with the Savage, Marx instigates a workers' rebellion by cutting off their supply of hallucinogenic 'soma' drugs. As a result, Marx is brought before MUSTAPHA MOND, the World Controller, for interrogation and punishment.

Mary
The Comfort of Strangers, 1981
Ian McEwan

A divorced feminist and erstwhile member of a women's theatre group, Mary has exhausting and frightening dreams about her children while on holiday in Venice with COLIN, her lover for the past seven years. Their relationship is now comfortable rather than exciting, but after their disturbing encounter with ROBERT and CAROLINE, Mary and Colin discover a new passion and depth of feeling for each other, more precious and profound for its maturity and their awareness of ageing. Despite misgivings, Mary, like Colin, is compulsively drawn back to Robert and Caroline, with terrible consequences.

Mary
The Death of the Hired Man, 1914
Robert Frost

A thoughtful and kind woman, who understands the needs and fears of both her husband, WARREN, and the old man, SILAS, who has come back to their farm to die. She is articulate and Christian in her concern for the farmhand and understands both her own domestic role (home is 'something you somehow haven't to deserve') and her place in the greater scheme of things, being grouped with the moon and 'the little silver cloud' at the poem's moving close.

Mary
Magnificence, 1973
Howard Brenton

The wife of JED, Mary is one of a group of squatters who install themselves in a derelict London house. She is a reserved, even naive woman, sewing revolutionary slogans on banners. Pregnant, she loses her baby when she is attacked by one of the bailiffs who come to evict them, an action which precipitates the main action of the play, Jed's quest for revenge.

Mary
Paradise Regained, 1671
John Milton

The virginal mother of JESUS CHRIST, she is not so consumed by her divine role as to set aside normal motherly cares about her only child. 'O what avails me now that honour high? To have conceiv'd of God, or that salute/Hale highly favour'd, among women blest;/While I to sorrows am no less advanc't,/And fears as eminent, above the lot of other women'.

Mary, Queen of Scots
The Abbot, 1820
Sir Walter Scott

This version of Mary is of the mourning-robed prisoner at Lochleven, serving out the days that will lead inexorably to the block at Fotheringay. Scott is aware that she is an almost mythic figure: 'Who is there, that, at the very mention of Mary Stewart's name, has not her countenance before him, familiar as that of the mistress of his youth, or the favourite daughter of his advanced age?'

Mary Rose (Mary Rose Blake, née Morland)
Mary Rose, 1920
J M Barrie

'If there is anything strange about this girl of eighteen ... it is an elusiveness of which she is unaware'. The 'tragic role' for which she has been prepared is long disappearance into fairyland on a mysterious Hebridean island.

Maryk, Lt Steve
The Caine Mutiny, 1951
Herman Wouk

The stolid, well-intentioned executive officer who feels it necessary to relieve CAPTAIN QUEEG of his command in order to save the ship, and who finds his career in the navy ruined by that decision. Observing the captain's increasingly bizarre actions, and encouraged to question his sanity by the younger officers, he is gradually convinced that something must be done. Reluctantly yet calmly, he takes charge of the ship, and proves himself a skilled and competent officer thereafter. His court-martial is an agony of hope against reason, though throughout it all he believes in the correctness of his actions.

Maskwell
The Double Dealer, 1693
William Congreve

The conniving double dealer of the title and former lover of the promiscuous LADY TOUCHWOOD, he enthusiastically joins her in a plot to ruin MELLEFONT who has rejected her amorous advances. Maskwell is essentially a confidence trickster, portraying himself as everyone's friend and ally, but he is much more than a mere rogue. He has the scheming malice of a Machiavelli and is motivated by both lust and greed.

Mason, Isley
'His Father's Mate', in *While the Billy Boils*, 1888
Henry Lawson

A favourite with the diggers and 'fossickers' of Golden Gully, 'he had fair hair, blue eyes, and a thin, old-fashioned face'. Motherless and beyond the reach of schools, he is being educated by a stern ageing father, whose close companion he is.

Mason, Martin
'The Wind at Your Door', 1958, in *Southmost Twelve*, 1962
R D Fitzgerald

The doctor and magistrate who, 'caught in the system', oversees the lashing of Australian convicts and looks aside, or even encourages further abuse. However, he cannot be daubed 'wholly black', for although in his official capacity he turns a blind eye to injustice and violence, in his own way he is a man of loyalty and some compassion. He is, in all, a weak man, unprepared to buck the system, always deferential, who in the end is as constrained as his convict prisoner, MORRIS FITZGERALD.

Mason, Perry
The Case of the Velvet Claws, 1933, et seq
Erle Stanley Gardner
A brilliant and tenacious lawyer, a paradigmatic figure of the court-room drama. With the support of his investigating partners and the encouragement of his close staff, he pushes and probes until the witness cracks or the case is saved at the last hour by the intervention of his team of detectives. In spite of his success rate, which might threaten to become boring, he keeps interest and enthusiasm alive through his verbal dexterity and unshakeable integrity.

Mastern, Cass
All the King's Men, 1946
Robert Penn Warren
JACK BURDEN's great-uncle and the subject of his abortive doctoral thesis in American history. Cass Mastern was a Confederate soldier who died in a military hospital in Atlanta in 1864, leaving letters and a journal telling of his 'darkness': the personal and public events that caused an acute moral and psychological crisis in his life. His testimony is central to Burden's disillusionment with the American dream and his attempts to escape his personal, more recent past.

Masters, Everyman
Carnival, 1985
Wilson Harris
He is the masked guide to carnival, the mythic exchange of masks which renders identity fluid. Like Dante's Virgil he is in the midst of life, but is not part of normal time or space. The narrator is his biographer (and may even be his creation).

Masters, Madeleine
The Echoing Grove, 1953
Rosamond Lehmann
Madeleine is the placid and conventional wife of RICKY MASTERS, a member of the landed gentry. Marriage provides her with a temporary haven from the terrors of modern life, but she soon learns that bourgeois respectability, social conservatism and elegant homes do not guarantee happiness. Feeling inferior to her sister, DINAH BURKETT, she views herself as a dowdy and discredited wife with suburban values; 'a bungler, a humiliated figure'.

Masters, Ricky
The Echoing Grove, 1953
Rosamond Lehmann
Consumed by guilt, frustration and unhappiness, Ricky is a character in disarray, a philanderer torn apart by unfulfilled passions. Displacing and sublimating his homosexual desires, he throws himself into heterosexual liaisons, crying 'I am not a pansy' in a most unconvincing manner,

a denial which causes him much mental and physical anguish.

Masterton, Sky
Stories à la Carte, 1932
Damon Runyon
A dedicated gambler, he is bowled over by the unlikely affection he feels for Salvation Army worker, Miss Sarah Brown. The confusion of feelings caused by this affection forces him to re-assess and ultimately renounce the life of the dice; compared with the prospect of life shared with Miss Brown, there is no contest.

Mata Kharibu
A Dance of the Forests, 1960
Wole Soyinka
A choleric king of the forests, reigning with his consort Madame Tortoise (ROLA). From appearing a noble and capable monarch, he is revealed to be petty and carping, susceptible to small jealousies and motiveless spite. The tribulations and spells of his court cast their spell forward in time to the haunted present day of the play's action.

Matfield, Miss
Angel Pavement, 1930
J B Priestley
An inflexible spinster, efficient and pedantic. Beneath this apparent rigidity, however, she is warm-hearted. Her uneventful life accounts for her small-minded attitude at work. Although devoutly middle-class, she is a hopelessly romantic, passionate creature.

Matheson, Alexander
'Alicky's Watch', in *The Last Sister*, 1950
Fred Urquhart
A nine-year-old boy whose mother has been dead for three days. So much has been going on that he has already got over this loss, and when his treasured watch stops on the day of her funeral, that seems a more distressing event than his bereavement. Although Alicky observes the adults closely, much of their behaviour goes over his head.

Mathilda, Miss
'The Good Anna', in *Three Lives*, 1909
Gertrude Stein
The third and last of ANNA FEDERNER's employers in Bridgepoint, she is large and lazy, somewhat fussy and penny-wise, and forever having to save Anna from the consequences of her own generosity. When she emigrates to Europe, she leaves Anna her house.

Matilda
The Castle of Otranto, 1764
Horace Walpole
Matilda, less loved by her father MANFRED, PRINCE OF OTRANTO than her brother CONRAD, hastens to comfort her mother HIPPOLITA when Conrad is crushed by a ghastly, supernatural helmet. Shocked by Manfred's intention to divorce Hippolita, she joins ISABELLA OF VICENZA to defend her. Courageous in freeing THEODORE, the prisoner in the black tower who falls in love with her, she is generous; when her

father stabs her in mistake for Isabella, she forgives him and begs others to forgive him too before she dies.

Matilda
Matilda, 1988
Roald Dahl
A child prodigy, unwanted and unloved by her parents, she finds solace and companionship in books. She has an extraordinary capacity for absorbing information. Discovering her ability at practical jokes, and making objects move by staring at them, she uses her powers to subdue the draconian regime of her new school, and its bizarre headmistress.

Matiwan
The Yemassee, 1835
William Gilmore Simms
The wife of the Yemassee chief SANUTEE, she takes the heartbreaking step of killing their son, OCCONESTOGA, rather than have him betray the tribe to the white colonists who are taking over Carolina.

Matlock, Lucinda
The Spoon River Anthology, 1915
Edgar Lee Masters
She represents contentment with her lot. Though she has known grief in the loss of eight children, her positive outlook and belief in simple values keep her going to the age of 96, when she has 'lived enough, that's all'. Her monologue is a reproof to 'degenerate sons and daughters' who lack the strength to love life in the way she has, and could be regarded as either inspirational or simplistic.

Matthew
Every Man in his Humour, 1598
Ben Jonson
Matthew is the typical vulgar poet. He thinks himself fashionable and worldly and puts on a show of erudition, but the poetry he claims as his own is plagiarized and palpably second-rate. He reads dreadful verses to a woman he hopes to impress, protesting that he wrote them that morning. He is caught out when JUSTICE CLEMENT, a lover of good poetry, challenges him to a verse-making contest. To pay for his pretensions and lies, Matthew is sentenced to do without, while everyone else joins Clement for dinner.

Matthews, Clara, also known as **the Countess**
No Laughing Matter, 1967
Angus Wilson
The mother of GLADYS, SUKEY, QUENTIN, RUPERT and MARCUS MATTHEWS, she has a certain cut-price chic that suggests greater sophistication than is the reality. She is sweet, tolerant and committed to thinking well of people.

Matthews, Gladys
No Laughing Matter, 1967
Angus Wilson
The eldest Matthews daughter, she is a rotund, unambitious spinster, known to the family as Podge, in whom is discovered an unexpected vein of courage when her lover runs foul of the law.

Matthews, Granny
No Laughing Matter, 1967
Angus Wilson
The dowager of the Matthews dynasty, she maintains a 'portwine, best plumcake solid affluence' in a 'shinyclean, pattern-neat, timetable-exact, great empty Italianate station of a house' in Ladbroke Grove in London. QUENTIN MATTHEWS prefers to live with her there than amid the turmoil of life with his brothers and sisters.

Matthews, Marcus
No Laughing Matter, 1967
Angus Wilson
The youngest of the Matthews children, he has a 'pear-shaped, altar boy's head and great dark Greco eyes'. In adult life he becomes a picture-dealer with a surprising aptitude for business.

Matthews, Margaret
No Laughing Matter, 1967
Angus Wilson
SUKEY MATTHEWS's twin sister, she is a successful novelist with a bitingly perceptive style and a public who admire her for her forthrightness and perspicacity.

Matthews, Miss
Amelia, 1751
Henry Fielding
'Very disagreeable in her Person, and immensely fat', the repellent and degenerate Miss Matthews is a most disreputable creature. Sexually rapacious, she lures the gullible CAPTAIN BILLY BOOTH from the security of monogamy and enjoys 'criminal Conversation' (sex) with him. She is a sturdy survivor, guilty of defiantly murdering a shiftless lover who subjected her to cynical exploitation. Cold and reserved, she is a counterpoint to the breathless and gushing AMELIA BOOTH.

Matthews, Quentin
No Laughing Matter, 1967
Angus Wilson
The eldest son of WILLIAM and CLARA MATTHEWS, he is a selfish womanizer of advanced socialist views, whose natural instinct for self-preservation gradually asserts itself over his more unselfish aspirations.

Matthews, Rupert
No Laughing Matter, 1967
Angus Wilson
The middle son of the family, he is a talented and sensitive actor whose success is only blighted by his refusal to compromise his personal vision to the vagaries of the new theatre. He is blessed from youth with good looks and an unshakeable sense of his own commanding appearance.

Matthews, Sukey
No Laughing Matter, 1967
Angus Wilson
MARGARET MATTHEWS's twin, she is quietly maternal and utterly domesticated, lavishing all

her personality on the task of motherhood; she stands as a complete contrast to her brittle, brilliant sister.

Matthews, William, also known as **Billy Pop**
No Laughing Matter, 1967
Angus Wilson

The improbable patriarch of the clan, caught up in his own imaginative vision of a more compelling reality and thus never quite at home in this one. The husband of CLARA MATTHEWS, he is a writer, enjoying modest success in various magazines.

Maturin, Stephen
Master and Commander, 1970, et seq
Patrick O'Brian

The illegitimate son of an Irish officer in the Spanish army and a Catalan lady of good family, Maturin is a skilled physician and an enthusiastic amateur naturalist. He serves as a Royal Navy ship's surgeon (and intelligence agent) with his particular friend JACK AUBREY primarily because of his deep-rooted opposition to Napoleon Bonaparte, whom he regards as a tyrant. He is a small, slight figure who describes himself as 'very far from being even tolerably good-looking', yet his romantic nature expresses itself in his lifelong love for the beautiful and dashing Diana Villiers. He is a man of science, a child of the Enlightenment, yet a devout Roman Catholic. A lover of music, he often duets with Aubrey on cello.

Mauberley, Hugh Selwyn
'Hugh Selwyn Mauberley', 1920
Ezra Pound

He is satirically representative of an epoch, the decadent, aesthetic 1890s; a minor versifier who leaves behind just one lapidary and soulless poem, 'Medallion' and whose epitaph, engraved on an oar, is: 'I was/And I no more exist;/Here drifted/An hedonist.'

Maud
'Maud; a Monodrama', 1855
Alfred, Lord Tennyson

A high-born young woman, she gives her love to her humbly-bred childhood friend, although thwarted by her brother and his lordly companions. Her sweetness and loyalty, which linger after her death, save her suitor from the morbid despair that threatens to destroy him.

Maudsley, Marcus
The Go-Between, 1953
L P Hartley

The youngest of the Maudsley children, with whom the narrator, LEO COLSTON, is invited to spend the summer holidays. From a higher social background than Leo, he is something of a snob, with a 'deep-seated conventionality'. His mother's favourite, he is precociously sophisticated – old for his age in most ways, and an 'arbiter of elegance and fashion' to the more naive Leo.

Maudsley, Marion
The Go-Between, 1953
L P Hartley

The sister of LEO COLSTON's school-friend MARCUS MAUDSLEY, Marion is the 'Virgin' of Leo's zodiac, and he idealizes her beauty and brightness – to him she is a goddess, gazing down on other mortals 'amused and a little mocking'. As well as being beautiful, however, she is formidable – 'almost as formidable as her mother', with whom there is a barely perceptible but almost constant clash of wills. She is a woman with an exceptionally strong will who ignores convention in her relationship with TED BURGESS, sublimating everything to her passion, a passion which is likened to the poisonous belladonna which grows in an outhouse: secretive, parasitic and overgrown.

Maudsley, Mrs
The Go-Between, 1953
L P Hartley

Young LEO COLSTON's hostess at Brandham Hall, she is a strong-willed woman who likes to organize everyone's social activities – and indeed their lives – to suit herself. In her presence, weaker characters are 'caught like a moth in the beam of her eye, that black searchlight, whose pressure and intensity never varied'. However, the effort of will needed to control the changing situation at Brandham Hall, and the growing knowledge that events are moving beyond her control, bring more pressure to bear than she can stand and she succumbs to her 'nerves' and eventually to a complete breakdown.

Maufe, Augustus
The Peach Groves, 1979
Barbara Hanrahan

Dressed as a girl until he was five, Maufe, the owner of the Peach Groves estate, then suffered the twin traumas of boarding school and his mother's death. This wealthy, seemingly benevolent and highly respectable 'old gentleman' in fact has a penchant for pornographic books, Auckland prostitutes, and little girls. Having been banished to New Zealand after 'a tot turned nasty in Hyde Park', he now lusts after 'poppet' MAUDE DEAN. Although sometimes comically pathetic, Maufe is a weak, cowardly and vicious man, who takes a slyly sadistic delight in publicly humiliating his timid son, OC MAUFE, and inspires fear in his wife, ZILLA MAUFE.

Maufe, Oc (Octavius)
The Peach Groves, 1979
Barbara Hanrahan

A sickly child nicknamed 'Melon' at school, the gentle, still childlike Oc who has a very large head and small body, and a nervous habit of flexing his thumb. Scared of his lecherous father, AUGUSTUS MAUFE, and neglected by his unbalanced mother, ZILLA MAUFE, whom he loves, Oc takes refuge in fairytale fantasies of being a handsome, heroic prince, and in bookbinding, to his horror having to deal with Augustus's pornographic collection. MAUDE DEAN is Oc's princess in real life and knowing she is in danger from his father he becomes her touchingly comic protector.

Maufe, Zilla
The Peach Groves, 1979
Barbara Hanrahan

AUGUSTUS MAUFE's 'Wifey', married for her inheritance, is big, heavy and so plain that he calls her 'Boiled Bull-dog'. She has a schizophrenic existence. As Zilla, she is inhabiting a world of increasingly frenetic 'inspirational' artistic activity with a spirit guide who, constantly reminding her of death, allows her no rest. But as 'Wifey', she is more like 'a standard Mama'. She is afraid of Augustus and her daughters, and, only feeling at ease with her delicate son, OC MAUFE, suffers her first breakdown when he goes away to school.

Maugham, Clara
Jerusalem the Golden, 1967
Margaret Drabble

From grimy, industrial Northam (a fictionalized version of Sheffield), Clara is naive, good-looking, clever, manipulative and sexually opportunistic. She aches to leave the north behind and enter the glittering, sophisticated, academic and professional world she had always imagined, the 'truly terrestrial paradise' conjured by the hymn *Jerusalem the Golden*. She longs to remake herself, cast off one being and assume another, more glamorous and assertive. 'Because she would live, she would survive.' But in order to survive, Clara puts will above human warmth and becomes increasingly detached from the ability to love.

Maugrabin, Hayraddin, also appears as the Disguised Herald
Quentin Durward, 1823
Sir Walter Scott

A rascally Bohemian or gypsy who repays QUENTIN DURWARD's rescue of his kinsman from the gallows with a sort of compromised and temporary loyalty that remains virtually intact almost to his own execution. 'He had a swarthy and sunburnt visage, with a thin beard, and piercing dark eyes, a well-formed mouth and nose, and ... the black elf-locks which hung around his face, and the air of wildness and emaciation ... rather seemed to indicate a savage than a civilized man.'

Maule, Gerard
Phineas Redux, 1874
The Duke's Children, 1880
Anthony Trollope

A suitor to ADELAIDE PALLISER, he is considered unsuitable (because of his lack of means) until Adelaide receives a bequest from MARIE GOESLER which enables them to marry. Although a strong and vigorous young man who enjoys physical pursuits, he likes to affect a lackadaisical air, and pretends 'that he never reads, and never thinks, and never does anything'.

Maule, Kitty
Providence, 1982
Anita Brookner

'Kitty Maule was very difficult to place.' In fact, her Christian name is really Thérèse, but she calls herself Kitty to assert the 'English side' of her Anglo-French ancestry, and her sense of place, her nationality and emotional inheritance are the questions which absorb her. Like DR RUTH WEISS, Kitty teaches literature (the Romantics) at a provincial university. Her lover, an historian, appears more interested in speculating on the nature of providence than in Romance, causing the anxious, sometimes melancholic Kitty even further consternation.

Maule, Matthew
The House of the Seven Gables, 1851
Nathaniel Hawthorne

A simple settler, ousted from his thatched homestead by the brutal COL PYNCHEON. Executed for 'witchcraft', he dies with a curse on his lips, and while the diligent but ill-starred Maules appear to die out, generations of Pyncheons drown in their own blood.

Maurice
Offshore, 1979
Penelope Fitzgerald

A prostitute, Maurice is creative and imaginative. He loves music, conversation and aesthetically pleasing people. Lonely despite having many acquaintances, he constantly hopes for a new life and for weeks at a time fantasizes that things are about to change. They do not.

Maurier, Mrs Patricia
Mosquitoes, 1927
William Faulkner

New Orleans hostess and patron of the arts, she transfers an informal salon to her boat, the *Nausikaa*. Large, loud and anxious, she is by no means possessed of as much good taste as she believes.

Maurya
Riders to the Sea, 1904
J M Synge

In this lament set on an island off the west coast of Ireland, where people are dependent upon the sea for their livelihood, the elderly Maurya and her two daughters mourn the drowning of her son and their brother, Michael. The play has echoes of the ritualistic qualities of Greek tragedy, and the women form a kind of dramatic chorus. The tough, stoical Maurya sees a vision of Michael riding a grey mare (a biblical image of death); this forms part of the mystical dimension of her acceptance that 'No man at all can be living for ever'.

Max
The Homecoming, 1965
Harold Pinter

A foul-mouthed, embittered, offensive man of 70, he is the 'father figure' to the family who people the play – TEDDY, LENNY and JOEY. His lack of love for the living and the dead, his pathetic whingeing and his know-all superiority on every human issue from racehorses to sex, make him a deeply repellent figure in a sinister environment.

Max (Max Ebhart)
The House in Paris, 1935
Elizabeth Bowen

A French-English-Jewish banker, originally engaged to MISS FISHER. He is 'not exactly mercenary', but it is clear that he is somewhat calculating, even dishonest. In the event, he jilts Naomi Fisher to have an affair with KAREN, which results in LEOPOLD's birth.

Maxim, Gifford
The Middle of the Journey, 1947
Lionel Trilling

A lapsed Marxist, whose career and attitudes anticipate those of the historical Whittaker Chambers. Maxim has embraced Christianity and attempts to convince JOHN LASKELL that its absolute moral truths have supplanted relativism, historicism and social determinism.

May
'The Merchant's Tale' in *The Canterbury Tales*,
c.1387–1400
Geoffrey Chaucer

Wife to the 60-year-old JANUARY, she is only 20 and is ready for seduction by DAMIEN. A stock figure in the courtly tradition – the wife who is also a willing mistress – May is quick-witted and callous, and easily talks her way out when she is caught *in flagrante delicto*.

May, Andrew
Pravda: A Fleet Street Comedy, 1985
Howard Brenton and David Hare

In his late twenties, he is a liberal reporter on *The Leicester Bystander* who is swept up by LAMBERT LE ROUX. 'You are … weak because you do not know what you believe', Le Roux tells him. This is true. As Le Roux buys more newspapers and puts him in successive editorial chairs, May begins to compromise his beliefs. With the help of his wife, REBECCA FOLEY, he attempts to extricate himself, but his uncertainty and impulsiveness are no match for Le Roux's ruthless, undeviating convictions. May represents the ill-thought liberalism of Britain being crushed by right-wing extremism, and the defeat of decency and truth by lies.

May, Joanna
The Cloning of Joanna May, 1989
Fay Weldon

The former wife of a dynamic nuclear energy entrepreneur, who divorced her after discovering her with a lover, Joanna May is 60, beautiful, an acute observer of the world around her, but bored. Believing herself to be unique and indivisible, her complacency is shattered by her discovery that, 30 years previously, her husband had cloned one of her eggs. An only child, and herself childless, she now realizes that she is the 'mother' to the four resulting 'clones': young women named Jane, Julie, Gina and Alice. Furthermore, each woman is involved in a crisis precipitated by a man, and through their various encounters, Joanna learns something of female solidarity and compassion.

Maybold
Under the Greenwood Tree, 1872
Thomas Hardy

A friendly and sincere young man, Maybold nonetheless treads on many toes in his quest for change in his new parish. However, he is capable of compromise and humility, and is not overly confident or arrogant. Having plucked up courage to ask FANCY DAY to marry him, he is gracious despite the treatment he receives from her. He strikes a healthy balance of being a man of ideals, principles and common sense. Something of a contradiction, he is described as having 'courageous eyes and a timid mouth'.

Maylie, Mrs
Oliver Twist, 1838
Charles Dickens

The kind-hearted widow who nurses OLIVER TWIST back to health after he is caught in the burglary of her house. She had adopted ROSE MAYLIE as a baby, and Rose is revealed to be Oliver's aunt. Her son, Harry, marries Rose and becomes a clergyman.

Maylie, Rose
Oliver Twist, 1838
Charles Dickens

An orphan, she is adopted as a baby by MRS MAYLIE and given her name. She is really Rose Fleming, the sister of OLIVER TWIST's mother, and has also been cheated by EDWARD LEEFORD (known as 'Monks'). When BILL SIKES learns from FAGIN that NANCY has met her, he murders Nancy. She marries Mrs Maylie's son, Harry.

Mayo, Andrew
Beyond the Horizon, 1920
Eugene O'Neill

The brother of ROBERT MAYO, he has a practicality and existential daring lacking in Robert. He is in love with the same woman as his brother, but in a bid for self-discovery, Andrew goes to sea, rejecting what he sees as the bondage of conventional relationships.

Mayo, Robert
Beyond the Horizon, 1920
Eugene O'Neill

The brother of ANDREW MAYO, but temperamentally his opposite, preferring introspection and dreams to action. Though he and his brother are in love with the same woman, only Robert is content to commit himself to marriage.

Mazeppa
Mazeppa, 1819
Byron, George Gordon, 6th Lord Byron

The aged Polish warrior Mazeppa, having fought alongside the Swedes in their defeat at Pultowa (1709), tells how, as a mere lad of 20, detected by an elderly Polish count as the seducer of his lovely young wife, he is stripped naked and bound with thongs to a wild Ukrainian horse. Terrified by its strange burden and lashed as it is set free, the horse gallops madly through forests and rivers, over rocks and precipices, by day and night, until it falls dead. Mazeppa, slipping in and out of consciousness, cannot free himself but lies, 'the dying on the dead', until he is rescued by Cossack peasants. No man, he says, should ever despair, however hopeless things seem.

Mazur, Yasha
The Magician of Lublin, 1960
Isaac Bashevis Singer

A travelling magician who can open any lock,

hypnotize people and perform amazing acrobatic stunts. 'A maze of personalities', Yasha is equally at home sparring with thieves or discussing philosophy. He is married to a respectable Jewish woman, Esther, yet he has several lovers in various towns. However, despite his apparent amorality he has a quickening conscience which leads him to question his actions. Ultimately, he returns to his faith and begins a period of the most severe penance.

Mead, Michael
The Bell, 1958
Iris Murdoch

A homosexual who, believing goodness and power to be incompatible, reluctantly leads Imber Court's lay religious community, a 'buffer state' between the 'closed' abbey and the outside world. Still 'disturbed and hunted by God', after years of striving to redeem himself Michael prepares to realize his early vocation for the priesthood, vindictively destroyed by his first genuine love, NICK FAWLEY. But Nick's re-appearance and the arrival of TOBY GASHE, who innocently provokes an indiscretion by the morally and spiritually frail Michael, together create a situation in which history is repeated.

Meagles, Minnie (Pet)
Little Dorrit, 1857
Charles Dickens

Also known as 'Pet', she is MR and MRS MEAGLES' pretty, spoilt daughter. ARTHUR CLENNAM secretly loves her, but she marries the dilettante but well-connected HENRY GOWAN against the wishes of her parents.

Meagles, Mr and Mrs
Little Dorrit, 1857
Charles Dickens

A wealthy, benevolent and simple couple, the doting parents of MINNIE MEAGLES and the benefactors of Tattycoram (HARRIET BEADLE). A retired banker, he prides himself on being 'practical' and supports DANIEL DOYCE and ARTHUR CLENNAM in their business affairs. Lamenting the childhood death of Minnie's twin sister, they are disappointed when Minnie marries HENRY GOWAN, although they are proud of his being well-connected. With Minnie married, they rejoice when the ungrateful Tattycoram, who ran away to MISS WADE, returns penitent and humble. With Doyce, Mr Meagles helps to get Clennam released from the Marshalsea.

Meany, Owen
A Prayer for Owen Meany, 1989
John Irving

His chief physical characteristics are that he is very small, and has a 'wrecked voice' which the narrator initially thought 'came from another planet', and later sees as somewhat otherworldly. He is a stoic martyr as a child, and is intelligent, imaginative, shrewd and a skilled manipulator of people. He believes that he is 'God's instrument', and has been 'assigned a role he was powerless to change'. He fulfils his own death prophecy, and becomes a hero, and 'a miracle, too'.

Meat Man
The Glass Canoe, 1976
David Ireland

Meat Man is so nicknamed because he is known to be sexually well-endowed. The narrator of the novel, he is also a writer, observing the various regular drinkers, the despairing, angry, bitter and uncomprehending refugees from modern life, at a pub on the outskirts of Sydney. A compassionate insider, Meat Man sees them as social victims whose only refuge is a schooner of beer (the eponymous glass canoe). He is compassionate and forgiving, but more often it seems that his stoicism is really a wilful refusal to recognize the destructiveness of the people around him. His point of view contrasts with that of SIBLEY.

Medbourne, Mr
'Dr. Heidegger's Experiment', 1837, in *Twice-Told Tales*, 1837, revised edition 1842
Nathaniel Hawthorne

Once a prosperous merchant, he 'lost his all by a frantic speculation, and was now little better than a mendicant'. With his friends and his former love, the WIDOW WYCHERLEY, he responds with unthinking enthusiasm to DR HEIDEGGER's promise of continual rejuvenation.

Media, King
Mardi, 1849
Herman Melville

The King of Odo, he is believed by some of his subjects to be semi-divine, but is hated by others, who are constantly trying to overthrow him. He has an 'endless pedigree', and is tall, strong and regal in manner. His 'simplicity of manners' and 'easy, frank demeanour' to the visitors are in contrast to his often harsh treatment of his subjects.

Medina
The Faerie Queene, 1590–6
Sir Edmund Spenser

The middle sister of ELISSA and PERISSA; together they represent the function of rational thought. As her name suggests, she is the 'golden Meane' between 'two Extremities', and excels her sisters in graces and appearance. She is of sober mind and is comely and courteous. Modest, honourable and wise, she is neither vain nor promiscuous. Appearing older than her age, she seeks peace and reason in all things.

Medina, Dominick
The Three Hostages, 1924
John Buchan

'As exotic as the young Disraeli and as English as the late Duke of Devonshire', he is a new and insidious kind of villain. Uncompromised by any of the usual vices – 'as aloof as Sir Galahad from any interest in sex' – he nonetheless pursues power ruthlessly.

Meeber, Carrie
Sister Carrie, 1900, suppressed; reissued 1907, complete text published 1983
Theodore Dreiser

A simple Wisconsin girl, 'full of the illusions of ignorance and youth', she comes to Chicago to find work, meeting the attractive but shallow salesman CHARLES DROUET on the way. As she grows less gullible, she becomes more positive in her actions, and she gradually takes command of her own life, leaving the shallow Drouet, by whom she has been kept, to start a relationship with GEORGE HURSTWOOD, thereafter keeping him. Her success in the theatre is an indication of her natural adaptability.

Meek, Private
Too True to be Good, 1932
George Bernard Shaw

Meek is Shaw's version of Lawrence of Arabia. He is part of the expeditionary force commanded by COL TALLBOYS, sent to a nameless country to rescue Miss Mopply (THE PATIENT) from brigands. Meek appears to be an insignificant, youthful figure, but is really an omnipresent military genius. Modest and obscure, Meek's vocation is his job.

Meercraft
The Devil is an Ass, 1616
Ben Jonson

Meercraft is a rogue, playing tricks on the susceptibilities of fools by promising he can make them rich. He interests FABIAN FITZDOTTREL in a bogus land-reclamation scheme, inducing him to contribute by offering to create him the Duke of Drown'd Land. Later, Meercraft advises him that he knows someone who could teach his wife polite manners. Like many confidence-tricksters, he lives on a knife-edge, surviving with some relief, from one day to the next.

Mehra, Lata
A Suitable Boy, 1993
Vikram Seth

The younger daughter of sentimental, well-to-do, widowed Mrs Rupa Mehra, Lata, a university student of English in the fictional Indian city of Brahmpur, initially resists her mother's campaign to find her a suitable boy to marry. A woman of 'erratic swings of mood', pragmatic, and able to pierce the artifice and pretensions of others and spot their foibles and fallibilities, she would like to be more rebellious and decisive; too often she is 'a mouse' when she would rather be 'a tigress'. However, her assertiveness is hampered by natural deference and a fear of passion, the latter causing her to reject the man she loves, the dashing Muslim cricketer, Kabir. Eventually, she submits.

Mehring
The Conservationist, 1974
Nadine Gordimer

A white South African who struggles for the soul of South Africa in the name of an abstract European heritage that is never precisely specified but which seems to be defined, conservatively, in opposition to the claims of his black compatriots. He is rich and powerful, but also curiously impotent.

Mehta, Victor
A Map of the World, 1983
David Hare

A expatriate Indian novelist whose conservatism has angered his critics, Mehta is invited to address a UN conference on poverty in Bombay and confronts the youthful idealism of British journalist Stephen Andrews. Additionally, both men find themselves contesting the affections of Peggy Whitton, a visiting American actress. Arrogant and erudite, Mehta is convinced that he holds the moral high ground, and indeed by the end of the play, Andrews concedes to his conviction that 'this feeling, finally, that we may change things, this is at the centre of everything we are. Lose that, lose everything'.

Melanie
The Magic Toyshop, 1967
Angela Carter

The sister of JONATHAN, she is a 15-year-old girl with romantic longings and a vivid imaginative streak. Emotional, sensitive and expressive, she feels uncomfortable with the FLOWERS family, finding them very different from the other people she knows. Nervous and desperately lonely, she prays 'Please God, let me get married or let me have sex'.

Melbury, George
The Woodlanders, 1887
Thomas Hardy

A hardworking and respectable businessman, he tends to be impressed by social rank and status. He dotes on his daughter, GRACE MELBURY, yet is not afraid of using her to advance his ambitions, and pays no heed to her reservations about marrying EDRED FITZPIERS. When the marriage turns out badly, he comes to realize the importance of soundness of character above social rank.

Melbury, Grace
The Woodlanders, 1887
Thomas Hardy

Grace has been transplanted from her rural home and given an expensive education by her timber-merchant father, which gives her ideas above her station. She is delicate and refined, but lacks maturity and assertiveness and has a tendency to float with the current of events. She is portrayed as an isolated figure, incapable of expressing powerful emotion, incapable of responding to the devotion of the socially inferior GILES WINTERBORNE.

Meldrum, Squire William
The Historie of Squyer Meldrum, c.1547
Sir David Lindsay

A contemporary of Sir David Lindsay, Fife-born Squire Meldrum is immortalized here as a romance-hero of the Middle Ages: well-built, handsome and honourable, he passes several glorious years fighting spectacular battles and rescuing, where necessary, fair damsels in distress. An exponent of 'courtly love' in his silver-tongued eloquence, he is nevertheless revealed, however allusively, as being something of a womanizer. Ending his days most un-romantically, however, in administering to the poor, his heroism becomes that of 'real' life rather than romance, but in his anxiety to ensure that his funeral highlights his career as knight and lover, he remains a gently ironic figure.

Melema, Tito

Romola, 1863
George Eliot

Strikingly handsome and wearing a red Levantine cap over long, dark-brown curls, Tito turns up shipwrecked in Florence in 1492. Cunning and multilingual, he starts charming his way to the top of the political tree, soon being used by Cardinal de Medici. On his way up he marries ROMOLA but betrays her and her father; never meaning to do wrong initially, his wish to get the 'utmost pleasure' means a wrecked marriage and a perpetually-worn mail coat to protect him from assassins and from his adoptive father BALDASSARRE CALVO, whom he has spurned.

Melford, Jery

The Expedition of Humphry Clinker, 1771
Tobias Smollett

The elder brother of LYDIA MELFORD, he is described by his uncle and guardian MATTHEW BRAMBLE as a 'pert jackanapes, full of college-petulance and self-conceit; proud as a German count, and as hot and hasty as a Welch mountaineer'. Quick to defend his sister's honour, it soon becomes apparent that he has been somewhat less respectful of his mistress Mrs Blackerby's.

Melford, Lydia

The Expedition of Humphry Clinker, 1771
Tobias Smollett

In the opinion of her brother JERY MELFORD, she is 'a fine, tall girl, of seventeen, with an agreeable person; but remarkably simple, and quite ignorant of the world'. Her uncle, rather more grouchily, considers her 'a poor, good-natured simpleton, as soft as butter, and as easily melted'. Either way, it is a disposition that leads her to contract a passion for the unsuitable 'WILSON', a travelling player.

Melincourt, Anthelia

Melincourt, or Sir Oran Haut-ton, 1817
Thomas Love Peacock

Twenty-one-year-old heiress and owner of Melincourt Castle, Anthelia is a paragon of virtue and a Romantic. With the grandeur of nature impressed upon her at an early age and armed with a considerable familiarity with Italian poetry, she clings to ideas of 'the age of chivalry'. Nothing but a husband who is 'a knight-errant in a brown coat' will do. Bookish and self-reliant by inclination rather than for social approbation, she fails to be impressed by the attentions of innumerable suitors, for she holds goodness, fairness and decency above all else.

Melinda

The Recruiting Officer, 1706
George Farquhar

Because she resents WORTHY's earlier rather cavalier behaviour in trying to make her his mistress, Melinda, having become an heiress, treats his overtures with scorn, even though she loves him. Her strong-willed, unsentimental, aggressive behaviour causes her to fall out with her best friend, SYLVIA, abuse her would-be lover, flirt with a rival and be duped by 'Doctor Copernicus' (SGT KITE). However, she knows all along that she will win over Worthy, once he has acknowledged her position and repented of his earlier treatment of her.

Melissa, properly **Melissa Artemis**

Justine, 1957, and elsewhere in *The Alexandria Quartet*, 1968
Lawrence Durrell

L G DARLEY's lover, she is pale, with 'blue-veined phthistic hands', and habitually wears a sealskin coat against the cold of an Alexandria winter. She 'penetrated my shabby defences not by any of the qualities one might enumerate in a lover ... but by the force of what I can only call her charity'.

Mellefont

The Double Dealer, 1693
William Congreve

The nephew and heir of Lord Touchwood, poor Mellefont finds himself relentlessly pursued by LADY TOUCHWOOD, whose advances he equally persistently rejects. Mellefont subsequently becomes the victim of MASKWELL's intrigues. That Maskwell almost succeeds in ruining him is a measure not so much of clever plotting as of Mellefont's supreme gullibility.

Mellors, Oliver

Lady Chatterley's Lover, 1928 published privately in Florence, bowdlerized edition England 1932, full edition England 1960
D H Lawrence

Gamekeeper to SIR CLIFFORD CHATTERLEY, Mellors enters upon a powerful and sustaining affair with his employer's oppressed wife, LADY CONSTANCE CHATTERLEY. A man who has chosen to live alone, Mellors does not instigate the relationship for sexual reasons; the affair begins slowly, once he has seen 'something so mute and forlorn in her'. Compassion and tenderness play equal parts to sexual desire. Mellors is an outsider, and in tune with the rhythms and processes of nature. He is free, one of the few resisting England's increasing mechanization. As far as Lawrence is concerned, Mellors's sensuality and instinctive intellectual vision represent the only hope for England and the English.

Melmoth

Melmoth the Wanderer, 1820
Charles Maturin

The villain of Maturin's claustrophobic anti-Catholic fantasy, he is a demonic figure who combines the roles of DR JOHN FAUSTUS and MEPHISTOPHILIS. An eternal outcast, he haunts the outer reaches of the tale, much as he haunts the fringes of 17th-century Europe, searching for a victim who will release him from his dreadful pact.

Melmotte, Augustus

The Way We Live Now, 1875
Anthony Trollope

A bogus financier who sets himself up in London, and through a series of cunningly duplicitous schemes is eventually elected to Parliament. He is 'a large man with bushy whiskers and rough thick hair, with heavy eyebrows, and a wonderful look of power about his mouth and chin'. He is skilled in playing upon the greed and weaknesses of his gullible dupes, but he is eventually disgraced, and kills himself.

Melmotte, Marie
The Way We Live Now, 1875
Anthony Trollope

The daughter of AUGUSTUS MELMOTTE, who plans to marry her off to a wealthy suitor lured by the prospect of an inheritance, rather than by her natural charms, which are few and unprepossessing – 'She was not beautiful, she was not clever, and she was not a saint'. A gullible girl, she falls in love with the wicked SIR FELIX CARBURY, who takes the money she has stolen for their elopement and abandons her. She later marries HAMILTON K FISKER and goes with him to the USA.

Melopoyn, Mr
The Adventures of Roderick Random, 1748
Tobias Smollett

His name is bastard-Greek for 'maker of songs' and he is by vocation a poet. His earliest productions are beset by misfortune and he is obliged to make his way in Grub Street as a common hack.

Melville, Ellen
The Judge, 1922
Rebecca West

A red-haired secretary in an Edinburgh law firm, Ellen reads intensely and has an independent mind. She is an autodidact, whose catholic literary tastes are revealed in her conversation which is studded with tags and proverbs. Those who patronize her are portrayed as lecherous or impotent philistines. She is married to the mentally-ill RICHARD YAVERLAND who confirms her adolescent assumption that people are not as 'nice as things'. Her character is tragically distorted and diminished by the couple's move to Essex.

Melville, Julia
The Rivals, 1775
Richard Brinsley Sheridan

The cousin of LYDIA LANGUISH, Julia is under the protection of SIR ANTHONY ABSOLUTE. A happy and musical woman, she faithfully loves FAULKLAND and is upset by his continual doubts about her feelings for him.

Melvyn, Sybylla Penelope
My Brilliant Career, 1901
My Career Goes Bung, 1946
Miles Franklin

An attractive, high-spirited, irrepressible young girl brought up in difficult circumstances on a poor, lonely farm. She is independent and self-confident, has a warm, compassionate, but blunder-prone nature, and a deep love of natural things. She dreams of a writing career, but is dismayed at the realization that 'only men could take the world by its ears and conquer their fate'. She is re-invented as a rather different character in the phony 'autobiography' *My Career Goes Bung*, which purports to 'refute' the earlier novel by altering her background and circumstances.

Mendelssohn, Baruch
Seven Poor Men of Sydney, 1934
Christina Stead

He is the intellectual among his fellow Sydney printers, a quiet, insightful man with the cultural resources of his European Jewish past at his fingertips. He holds a quietly philosophical perspective on injustice.

Mendoza
The Malcontent, 1604
John Marston

Apparently a cynical Machiavellian manipulator, Mendoza attempts to wrest the dukedom of Genoa from PIETRO JACOMO, himself a usurper. He makes a fatal mistake, however, trusting MALEVOLE the court fool (the rightful Duke of Genoa in disguise) to do his dirty work for him, and proves to be a comic dupe rather than a clever villain.

Mendoza (the Devil)
Man and Superman, 1903
George Bernard Shaw

A brigand chief in the Sierra Nevada, Mendoza is swaggering, idealist and sentimental, and between holding up passing motor cars is fond of regaling his followers with political speeches. His dark hair and upturned moustache are an appropriate Mephistophelean affectation because, in JOHN TANNER's dream, in which he finds himself a part of the Don Juan legend, Mendoza appears as the Devil. As such, he contests Don Juan's theory of the Life Force, maintaining that man has used his superior intelligence only to create the means of destruction. The power that governs the earth, he insists, is not that of Life, but Death.

Mendoza y de la Cerda, Ana de
That Lady, 1946
Kate O'Brien

A 16th-century Castilian aristocrat, Princess of Eboli and Duchess of Pastrana, who is the widow of the favourite minister of PHILIP II OF SPAIN. Tall and eccentrically beautiful, with only one eye, she arouses Philip's jealousy when she has a love affair with Antonio Perez, a younger minister. She is aware of her sin and worries about her soul, but she is too reasonable and innocent to realize the danger from the king, whom she has always admired. Despite cruel imprisonment, she forthrightly and proudly refuses to submit to his tyranny.

Menenhetet
Ancient Evenings, 1983
Norman Mailer

By dying at the moment of ejaculation, he is thrice reincarnated, successively as a charioteer, a high priest and a general in the Twentieth Dynasty (12th-century BC) court of Pharaoh Rameses IX and his queen Nefitiri.

Menteith, Lord (Earl of Menteith)
A Legend of Montrose, in *Tales of My Landlord: Third Series*, 1819
Sir Walter Scott

A young nobleman in the Royalist cause at the time of the Civil War. He shows greater regard for honour than for the niceties of rank and is not, perhaps, quite as bland as some of Scott's leading men, possessing a quickness of action and sharpness of tongue commensurate with his troubled times.

Mephistophilis
Dr Faustus, 1594–1601
Christopher Marlowe
Satan's emissary and representative upon earth, he signs the diabolic pact with DR JOHN FAUSTUS and accompanies him on his magical adventures. Remarkably humanized for a devil, he mourns his own loss of God: 'Why, this is hell, nor am I out of it./Thinkst thou that I who saw the face of God/ And tasted the eternal joys of heaven/Am not tormented with ten thousand hells/In being depriv'd of eternal bliss?'

Merchand
Ane Pleasant Satyre of theThrie Estaitis, 1540
Sir David Lindsay
Representing the burgesses and the merchants, Merchand is the third of the Three Estates who, under the corrupting influence of DISSAIT and FALSET, is badly in need of improvement. Accepting the truth of JOHNE THE COMMON-WEILL's complaints, Merchand readily agrees to its own reformation, and joins with TEMPORALITIE in condemning the greed and despotism of SPIRITUALITIE.

Merchant, the
'The General Prologue', in *The CanterburyTales*, c.1387–1400
Geoffrey Chaucer
A member of the emerging middle class of minor gentry, avarice and pride are his besetting sins. A cynical bore who never hesitates to tell of his wealth, he is well-dressed and well-horsed; everything about him shouts prosperity. However, he is, in fact, in debt. The narrator peers through the sham and delivers the ultimate snub to this pompous hypocrite: 'I noot how men him call'; he is destined to remain nameless.

Merchant, Umeed
The Ground Beneath Her Feet, 1999
Salman Rushdie
The narrator of the novel, Merchant is a Bombay photographer known as 'Rai'. An 'event junkie', he is close friends with ORMUS CAMA and VINA APSARA before they become rock stars recognized by millions. Rai likes and respects Ormus, while to Vina's mystique he pledges 'lifelong enslavement'. Expansive, light-hearted, wise and sceptical, a man of many stories, he feels privileged to be part of their inner circle, following and recording their success, for he appreciates the mercurial nature of chance and fate. But occasionally he allows himself to resent that 'from the start my place was in a corner of their lives, in the shadow of their achievements'.

Mercilla, Queen
The Faerie Queene, 1590–6
Sir Edmund Spenser
A virgin queen of great power and majesty. She is an allegory of Elizabeth I as a dispenser of mercy. Mercilla has many foes who wish to subvert both her dignity and the crown, as well as remove her from the throne. Her ambassadors are traitors who envy her sovereignty and good government. She nevertheless extends the hand of mercy to all.

Mercutio
Romeo andJuliet, 1591–6
William Shakespeare
Kinsman and close friend to ROMEO, Mercutio has contrasting sides to his nature. He can be humorous, enjoying a joke (usually obscene), and mocking Romeo's falling in love, which he believes is only sexual attraction. But there is a cynical, almost depressive side to him that is revealed in flights of fancy.When called upon to fight he can be brave, almost foolhardy, because he fatalistically believes that his death is preordained.

Merdle, Mr
Little Dorrit, 1857
Charles Dickens
An 'immensely rich' financier, MP and man of 'prodigious enterprise' who is finally exposed as 'simply the greatest Forger and the greatest Thief that ever cheated the gallows'. Although he and MRS MERDLE 'did everything for Society', he is dull and awkward at his own parties and despised by his butler. When he learns that his fraudulent schemes have been uncovered, he commits suicide in a Turkish bath. The collapse of his bank ruins thousands, including WILLIAM DORRIT, DANIEL DOYCE, MR PANCKS and ARTHUR CLENNAM.

Merdle, Mrs
Little Dorrit, 1857
Charles Dickens
MR MERDLE's wife and the mother of EDMUND SPARKLER by an earlier marriage. A Society hostess, she is 'not young and fresh from the hand of Nature, but was young and fresh from the hand of her maid'. She is referred to as 'the Bosom' because hers 'was a capital bosom to hang jewels upon' and Merdle 'bought it for the purpose'.When her fatuous son wants to marry FANNY DORRIT, a dancer, she bribes Fanny to stay away but promotes the marriage when WILLIAM DORRIT inherits his fortune.

Meredith, David
Closer to the Sun, 1960
The Far Road, 1962, and others
George H Johnston
A journalist and would-be 'great writer', obsessed with but never truly possessor of the beautiful CRESSIDA MORLEY. David's life is spent in search of 'real' life, 'real' love, the better life, the better love. Idealistic in the demands he makes of both his loves (writing and Cressida), he expects an impossible fidelity. The real world impinges upon the ideal world of his mind's creation, bringing him grief but, ultimately, sagacity.

Meredith, Jack
Closer to the Sun, 1960
The Far Road, 1962, and others
George H Johnston
Jack is delineated against and by his younger brother, DAVID MEREDITH. Jack accepts, even

glories in, the 'pot luck' quality of life, where David chafes and battles against it. Cocky, brash and self-assured, extravagant in word and gesture, and possessed of an enormous appetite for life, Jack's ruling philosophy is 'you got to have a go'.

Merion, Diana
Diana of the Crossways, 1885
George Meredith

A spirited young woman who rejects the passive and silent role assigned to Victorian brides and speaks out on public and emotional matters in a way that is inimical to her blunt, unimaginative husband Mr Warwick, who divorces her. She is based on the historical Caroline Norton who was apparently involved with Lord Melbourne (Lord Dannisburgh in the novel) and gave *The Times* information about the Corn Law repeal. Admired by more imaginative men than Warwick, she is nonetheless intensely loyal to her friends and unswayed by glamour or flattery.

Merivale, James
Manhattan Transfer, 1925
John Dos Passos

Although the same age as his cousin JIMMY HERF, the more formal James is 'perhaps a little more developed', a little adult, playing at being the banker he will inevitably one day become. He finishes World War I as Captain Merivale DSC. A well-known financier and society figure, he is 'the perfect wise virgin', a textbook success, prone to cliché-ridden, flatulent speeches. As a person he is image-conscious and self-obsessed, antagonistic towards his sister Maisie's marriage and perpetually harking back to his short-lived wartime glory.

Merivel, Robert
Restoration, 1989
Rose Tremain

A self-confessed 'very untidy man', son of a craftsman, Robert Merivel is a student of medicine at the restoration of the Stuart monarchy in 1660. Appointed by Charles II as physician to the Royal Dogs, he is drawn into the dissolute life of the court and gleefully wallows in self-indulgence. It is only after banishment from court that he is forced to experience the underside of Restoration England, re-assess what is truly of worth in life, rediscover his vocation as a doctor and aspire to a 'restoration' of his own.

Merle, Mme
The Portrait of a Lady, 1881
Henry James

The quintessence of 'European' sophistication and manipulative calculation. Living graciously in Florence, the mother of GILBERT OSMOND's illegitimate child, PANSY OSMOND, she match-makes tirelessly, spinning a self-serving web of profitable relationships around herself.

Merlin
The Sword in the Stone, 1937
T H White

The powerful wizard who teaches King Arthur. This famous version of the character, however, is a loveable eccentric (said to be based on the author) rather than a mighty manipulator of great destinies. He has the requisite wizard's cloak and beard, but 'some large bird seemed to have been nesting in his hair', so that he 'was streaked with droppings over his shoulders'. He still has wisdom, though, and oversees the young Arthur's bizarre education. A later unfinished book attempted to present him as a pacifist philosopher.

Merlin, Dorothy
The Unspeakable Skipton, 1959
Pamela Hansford Johnson

An Australian-born playwright with seven children, Dorothy writes esoteric verse-dramas which are all about motherhood on some exalted plane. An aggressive feminist, she repeatedly refers to herself as 'mother of men'. She is small and birdlike, loud, vulgar and pretentious, with an overbearing personality and an ego almost as big as DANIEL SKIPTON's. When he contrives to become her party's guide in Bruges, she manages to be still more overtly abrasive and unpleasant, and he meets his match, sometimes hilariously, in what he sneeringly thinks of as this 'educated Aboriginie'.

Merlyn, Jem
Jamaica Inn, 1936
Daphne Du Maurier

Brother of the unscrupulous JOSS MERLYN, he is a horse thief, yet is portrayed with a very endearing streak; in the world of criminals, he is far from being one of the worst. He has always been a wanderer, and has suffered the bruises of a fractured upbringing: his father was hanged and his mother, a religious freak, gave him little in the way of love. However, from somewhere he has picked up a sense of right and wrong and he abhors the unjust treatment of MARY YELLAN. A truthful character in a world of deceivers, his own form of deception is not one which would ever harm another. As his name suggests, this man is rare and precious in Mary's painful new life at Jamaica Inn.

Merlyn, Joss
Jamaica Inn, 1936
Daphne Du Maurier

A drunkard and a bully, Joss has a thirst for blood as well as brandy. Involved in a horrific smuggling scheme, he appears to be in charge of an entire ring of crime. In fact, he lacks real wit or cunning, and it emerges that someone else is in control of events. Incapable of experiencing guilt or shame, he is proud of his reputation as a terror, though his young niece perceives that it is only drink which gives him courage and that without it he is afraid of those who do not fear him.

Merrick, Ronald
The Jewel in the Crown, 1966
The Day of the Scorpion, 1968
The Towers of Silence, 1971
A Division of the Spoils, 1975, forming
The Raj Quartet
Paul Scott

Mayapore's district police superintendent during

the 1942 'Quit India' riots and Bibighar rape case, Merrick later transfers to the Indian army. He loses an arm in action, receives the DSO and marries SUSAN LAYTON. He is a hollow and self-made man; coldly calculating every correct word and gesture, he deliberately creates a public persona in the exact image of the British Raj. DAPHNE MANNERS and SARAH LAYTON both instinctively recoil from him for, although ostensibly kind and honourable, he is inhuman, bigoted and morally corrupt, particularly in his vicious personal vendetta against HARI KUMAR.

Merrilies, Meg
Guy Mannering, 1816
Sir Walter Scott

A gypsy, she is Scott's most dramatic and convincing representative of the dark side of human life. 'She was full six feet high, wore a man's great-coat over the rest of her dress, had in her hand a goodly sloe-thorn cudgel and in all points of equipment, except her petticoats, seemed rather masculine than feminine. Her dark elf-locks shot out like the snakes of the gorgon.' Her gift of prophecy is set against COL GUY MANNERING's more studied and rational approach.

Merrill, Neddy
'The Swimmer', in *The Brigadier and the Golf Widow*, 1964
John Cheever

A youthful-seeming upper-middle-class American who sees himself as 'a legendary figure' and decides one day to swim the eight miles to his house via the neighbourhood pools. This increasingly obsessive and uneasy journey takes him from energy to exhaustion and from an inspiring summer day to the cold and dark. He sees the falsity of his snobbish, prosperous life-style, the precariousness of his social status and, ultimately, the failure of his existence.

Merriman, Magnus
Magnus Merriman, 1934
Eric Linklater

An aspiring poet who has more good intentions than real talent. He is vain, self-serving, argumentative, pompous, fond of physical pleasures, over-pleased with himself, and ambitious beyond his capacities; as a consequence he is easily led into error. He is manipulated by an English newspaper as a political columnist, and manoeuvered into standing as a nationalist candidate in an unwinnable seat, where he is duly humiliated. His attempts to get back in touch with the land in his native Orkney as a wellspring for his poetry are fraught with disaster.

Merton, Tommy
The History of Sandford and Merton, 1783–9
Thomas Day

The son of a rich gentleman, he is 'naturally a good-natured boy, but unfortunately [has] been spoiled by too much indulgence', and as a result has become fretful and unhappy, not to say objectionable and ungrateful. He is weak, prone to illness, and has never been taught to read because it makes his head ache. The reforming

example of Sandford and the teachings of MR BARLOW eventually set him on 'a course which was very little concerned with his former habits'.

Mertoun, Basil, also known as Vaughan
The Pirate, 1821
Sir Walter Scott

The master of Yarlshof mansion in Zetland, with a character that suits the place exactly. 'The habits of Basil Mertoun were retired and gloomy. From loud mirth he instantly fled; and even the moderated cheerfulness of a friendly party had the invariable effect of throwing him into deeper dejection than even his usual demeanour indicated.' With NORNA OF THE FITFUL HEAD ('Ulla Troil') he is the natural parent of the buccaneer Captain Clement Cleveland.

Mertoun, Mordaunt
The Pirate, 1821
Sir Walter Scott

The son of BASIL MERTOUN. Little does Mordaunt know when he rescues the pirate CLEMENT CLEVELAND from the surf that he has saved the life of his own half-brother. His mother is a Spanish woman from Hispaniola, who was murdered by Basil. Dark-skinned and handsome, he is as blithe as his father is brooding.

Mervyn
People in Glass Houses, 1967
Shirley Hazzard

One of Hazzard's 'portraits from organization life', he is an Australian United Nations official, whose 'defensive scepticism' insulates him from any strong engagement with reality. Unlike the people he presumes to serve, he is protected from both joy and suffering by a gift for rationalization.

Mervyn, Arthur
Arthur Mervyn, 1799
Charles Brockden Brown

Rags-to-riches protagonist whose progress from rhapsodic, solitary country boy who 'sallied forth into the open air', to successful Philadelphian citizen is achieved as much by accident as by design. Although a loner, and lonely, Mervyn comprehends the interdependence of people, especially of city dwellers, although his attempts to do good often achieve opposite results to those intended.

Merygreeke, Mathewe
Ralph Roister Doister, 1552/3
Nicholas Udall

A mischief-making sponger, who amuses himself by merrily manipulating his patron, RALPH ROISTER DOISTER, encouraging him in his folly and openly mocking him. Anarchic and clever, he causes trouble for CHRISTIAN CUSTANCE, before recruiting her into his ploys.

Messenger, Ralph
Thinks ..., 2001
David Lodge

Messenger, as he is known to his family and friends, is 'something of a star' on radio and television discussion programmes and at the

University of Gloucester, where he is Professor and Director of the Holt Belling Centre for Cognitive Science. A powerfully built man in his late forties, with a 'fresh, lively conversational manner', he is confident, assertive and, according to the novelist HELEN REED, 'somewhat intimidating'. He is also manipulative and a compulsive philanderer, attractive to women, even, to her surprise, Helen herself. In private, he records his random thoughts and sexual reminiscences into a tape recorder, ostensibly in a scientific quest to probe deeper into the nature of thought.

Micawber, Mr Wilkins
David Copperfield, 1850
Charles Dickens

DAVID COPPERFIELD's improvident, shabby genteel landlord who tries to make a success of one type of work after another in order to support his wife, MRS MICAWBER, and five children. Unable to follow his own economic dictums, he is constantly beset by debtors, falling into despair at one moment and joyous optimism that 'something will turn up' the next. He delights in his own grandiloquent rhetoric, illustrated in his speech and even in the letters he writes to stave off creditors. Not even a spell in the Marshalsea debtors' prison can dim his unquenchable spirit. His exposure of URIAH HEEP's dishonesty leads to Heep's imprisonment and the restoration of MR WICKFIELD's reputation and property. Mr Micawber and his family emigrate to Australia, where he becomes a district magistrate and local celebrity.

Micawber, Mrs (Emma)
David Copperfield, 1850
Charles Dickens

The wife of MR WILKINS MICAWBER. A 'thin and faded lady, not at all young', she shares his extremes of optimism and despair, swooning one moment and enjoying a lamb chop the next. While acknowledging her husband's improvidence, she is wholly loyal to him. She has five children, and DAVID COPPERFIELD can never recall seeing her without one or other of the twins at her breast.

Michael
'Michael, A Pastoral Poem', in *Lyrical Ballads*, 1800
William Wordsworth

A strong and skilful shepherd, he dotes on Luke, the son of his old age, whom he hopes will make his fortune in the city and thus secure the family's Grasmere fields. Now, however, the sole reminder of the old man's broken dreams is an unfinished sheepfold in the Cumbrian hills.

Michael
Paradise Lost, 1667
John Milton

Prince of the Celestial Armies and SATAN's fiercest opponent. He is identified by a fiery sword forged in the Armoury of God. It is he who delivers a vision of the future course of mankind to ADAM, before accompanying him and EVE out of Eden, his sword standing at the gate as a reminder of their expulsion.

Michael (Michael Darling)
Peter Pan: or The Boy Who Would Not Grow Up, 1904 (play), 1911 (book)
J M Barrie

Instantly identified as 'obstreperous', the youngest Darling is a child in its purest form, without the cares and responsibilities enforced by Never-Never Land, and less inclined than his brother and sister (JOHN and WENDY) to mimic the deep-toned discussions of his parents.

Michaelis, Mrs
The House in Paris, 1935
Elizabeth Bowen

KAREN's mother, she is the mainstay of all the quiet, comfortable virtues associated with 'appropriate' marriage, which Karen implicitly rejects in her dramatic affair with MAX. Mrs Michaelis is effectively killed by the revelation of this affair and the child it brings about.

Michell, Roland
Possession, 1990
A S Byatt

His referees describe him as diligent, thorough and cautious and Roland is not deceived. He knows that people find him dull. Life is something that happens to him and he tries to fit in with it rather than take control. Confrontation and competition are threats against which he uses his 'natural defence of self-enfolded inattention'. Ultimately, though, it is his diligence and throroughness which are his salvation. His great literary discovery, involving RANDOLPH HENRY ASH and CHRISTABEL LAMOTTE, and its implications, breed a healthy selfishness and willingness to take responsibility for his own acts.

Mick
The Caretaker, 1960
Harold Pinter

A strange, detached figure, he is in the building trade 'with his own van' and is, apparently, the owner of the junk-filled house where the action of the play takes place. Alternately hospitable and sinister, he is a figure of implicit violence and dominates the addled and selfish tramp, MAC DAVIES, and his brother, ASTON.

Middlemass, Richard
The Surgeon's Daughter, 1832
Sir Walter Scott

Born in mysterious circumstances to a Catholic father, he takes the name of his birthplace and bears ever afterwards an air of pained disenchantment that does not, however, stop him forming a deep affection for MENIE GRAY. She follows him to India, but their love does not prosper. He is trampled to death at Bangalore.

Middleton, Clara
The Egoist, 1879
George Meredith

The daughter of an old scholar, who attracts SIR WILLOUGHBY PATTERNE after his rebuff by CONSTANTIA DURHAM, and becomes engaged to him. She is, though, unprepared to submit to his domineering personality and determinedly extricates herself from the relationship, drawing close to VERNON WHITFORD in the process.

Middleton, Gerald
Anglo-Saxon Attitudes, 1956
Angus Wilson

As a young man he has witnessed the excavation of a 7th-century Christian tomb which contained a gross pagan figure whose significance remains unknown. In later life, Gerald has become an expert on King Cnut; he also enjoys the status of Professor Emeritus, and marriage to the beautiful Inge. However, he is in some mysterious way unfulfilled, and the answer seems to lie in that puzzling discovery of his youth.

Middleton, Mr
The Egoist, 1879
George Meredith

An old scholar and wine-bibber, father of SIR WILLOUGHBY PATTERNE's fiancée CLARA MIDDLETON, he is said to be modelled on Meredith's own father-in-law, the novelist Thomas Love Peacock, and reflects the uneasy relationship the two men enjoyed. Middleton mirrors Peacock's conservatism in politics and liberality in fleshly pleasures, an exact reversal of Meredith's habitual stance.

Midnite, also known as Mr Daybrake
Midnite: The Story of a Wild Colonial Boy, 1967
Randolph Stow

A wily bushranger who travels the outback in the company of his cat – Khat – and cockatoo. Though played for laughs, he embodies profound truths about Australia's conception of itself, torn between shackles and the absolute freedom of uncharted space.

Midwich Cuckoos
The Midwich Cuckoos, 1957
John Wyndham

A group of children of non-terrestrial origin, born to host mothers in a small village who have been mysteriously impregnated during a 'dayout', much as a cuckoo will lay her eggs in another bird's nest. They look eerily alike, have piercing golden eyes, grow unnaturally quickly, and even as children, are highly gifted and intelligent, with the power to dominate and manipulate humans. They are able to merge telepathically to create a single group entity, and can also come together to compel actions in others. They have 'the *look* of genus homo, but not the nature', and eventually are recognized as a threat to the human race.

Miggs, Miss
Barnaby Rudge, 1841
Charles Dickens

The VARDENS' shrewish domestic servant, she is Mrs Varden's ally against her husband. She abandons them when the Gordon Riots break out in order to follow SIMON TAPPERTIT, whom she tries to attract. Rejected by the Vardens at the end of the riots, she becomes a turnkey at the local women's prison.

Miguel
The Day of the Locust, 1939
Nathanael West

A talentless young Mexican actor on the fringes of Hollywood. He is deliberately stereotyped and typecast: brutally sexual, macho, keeping fighting cocks and treating romance as if it were a bullfight.

Mikhulin, Gregory Matvieitch
Under Western Eyes, 1911
Joseph Conrad

The State Councillor who is representative of the narrow, autocratic and bureaucratic power of the Russian State, in opposition to the revolutionary group with which RAZUMOV becomes entangled. Sallow and unprepossessing in appearance, with 'nothing formidable about him', he is shrewd, persistent and coldly calculating in his manipulation of Razumov's hopeless plight, while succeeding in making him feel that he is 'the only man in the world able to understand his conduct'.

Milan, Duke of
Two Gentlemen of Verona, c.1590
William Shakespeare

The father of SILVIA, he presides over a court at which sons of noblemen congregate to complete their learning and to meet others of their social class. This contrasts with the lawless world of the Outlaws in the forest. While there is no evidence that the Duke is a political tyrant he is, arguably, a domestic one in that he has chosen THURIO as his prospective son-in-law, and champions his case over that of VALENTINE. However, in this he acts no differently from other men of his time and class.

Miles
The Turn of the Screw, 1898
Henry James

'He was incredibly beautiful', and his new governess, ANON (THE GOVERNESS), who has somehow been led to expect something different, is captivated by him. 'What I then and there took him to my heart for was something divine that I have never found to the same degree in any child – his indescribable little air of knowing nothing in the world but love. It would have been impossible to carry a bad name with a greater sweetness of innocence ... ': terms which suggest more about the governess's state of mind and moral being than the boy's, which remains the great enigma of the tale. It may be that he is a spoiled angel, in contact with demonic spirits. It may be that he is a simple child, partly good, partly bad.

Miles, Sarah
The End of the Affair, 1951
Graham Greene

The attractive wife of a dull civil servant. She begins an affair with MAURICE BENDRIX in casual fashion, but finds herself falling in love with him. That love, however, is only the prelude to a deeper religious experience when she makes a pact with God during a World War II bombing attack on London, in which she moves from unsatisfactory human affairs toward a commitment to God, and from loneliness and emotional emptiness to spiritual fulfilment. She becomes an almost saintly presence after her death.

Milestone, Mr Marmaduke
Headlong Hall, 1816
Thomas Love Peacock

Landscape gardener and improver (modelled on Humphry Repton), Mr Milestone joins the house party at Headlong Hall with his eye on getting a landscaping commission. A mouthpiece for the argument that landscapes can be improved by human intervention ('shaving and polishing', 'clumping and levelling'), Mr Milestone's preoccupation is human control over the chaos of nature via pagodas, Chinese bridges, gravel walks and bowling greens.

Milford, Ignez
Cockatoos, 1954
Miles Franklin

A young girl, whose name is pronounced 'Ee-nith'. She is responsible for 'adding spice to the daily round' of her small Australian town with her 'lively and unconventional ideas'. She is a free spirit who aspires to rise above her surroundings and enter a world of greater cultivation through studying music, and later writing, but is smothered by the small-minded attitudes around her. The loss of her vibrant singing voice is symbolic of the ultimate frustration of her hopes.

Milhone, Kinsey
A is for Alibi, 1986, et seq
Sue Grafton

A female detective, she was orphaned young but raised by an ideal role-model aunt. Living in streamlined perfection in a 'bachlerette', a neatly converted garage, she jogs, eats out and practises pistol shooting. Physically brave, she quickly assumes identities to gain confidences; acting intuitively, she is credulous enough to become involved in breathtaking finales.

Millaine, Duke of
The Woman Hater, 1605
Francis Beaumont, with some dialogue by John Fletcher

The duke is invited by GONDARINO to witness for himself the licentiousness of ORIANA. However, the plan fails dismally, thanks partly to the overwhelming misogyny of Gondarino, the winning spirit of Oriana and the duke's susceptibility to beauty, grace and effervescence. He astounds Gondarino by commending her virtue and asking for her hand in marriage. 'She tortures him admirably', he cries, watching his loved one taunt her furious accuser.

Millamant
The Way of the World, 1700
William Congreve

The heroine of the play, Millamant is witty, beautiful, rich and virtuous. She also does not appear to have ever been involved with a man before falling in love with MIRABELL and therefore, unlike the other characters, there is no whiff of scandal about her. However, she is never tedious, but intelligent, forthright and independent. She wants to marry, but on her own terms, under which she retains as much of her freedom as possible: hence the famous 'proviso' scene in which she spells out her conditions. She is vivacious but essentially serious: if she jokes about something it is usually a fair indication that it matters to her.

Millbank, Edith
Coningsby, or The New Generation, 1844
Benjamin Disraeli

OSWALD MILLBANK's sister, she is a pale, rather colourless creature, but put in the right setting (Italy rather than industrial Lancashire) she is sufficiently beguiling to win the heart of HARRY CONINGSBY. The couple offer the promise of a future England undivided by class antagonisms, balancing aristocratic breeding and industrial enterprise, and doing so with honesty and commitment.

Millbank, Mr
Coningsby, or The New Generation, 1844
Benjamin Disraeli

The father of HARRY CONINGSBY's friend, OSWALD MILLBANK, he is a successful Lancashire factory owner, who promotes an optimistic Whiggish vision of an England governed by self-made men of talent and enterprise. Not surprisingly, he and Harry's grandfather, the old Tory LORD MONMOUTH, are long-term enemies, and it later transpires that Monmouth prevented Millbank marrying Harry's mother.

Millbank, Oswald
Coningsby, or The New Generation, 1844
Benjamin Disraeli

The son of a Lancashire manufacturer, Oswald has been a friend of HARRY CONINGSBY since schooldays at Eton. Bright and sympathetic, he stands for the new meritocratic class that will gain its place in society on the basis of brains and effort rather than blood. The bond between the friends is reinforced when Harry saves his life.

Miller, Daisy (properly Annie P)
Daisy Miller: A Study, 1878, dramatized 1883
Henry James

The classic American 'princess' abroad in Europe, towed around in the wake of her *nouveau riche* mother. Pretty but unformed, she has the coquettishness that comes from a lack of experience, for 'in her bright, sweet, superficial little visage there was no mockery, no irony'. The 'Roman fever' to which she leaves herself fatally vulnerable is not just malaria, but also the spurious attraction of an exotic place.

Miller, Richard
The Doubleman, 1985
C J Koch

A shy, withdrawn man, somewhat in retreat from life, living in a world of fantasy and self-projection, best encapsulated in his vocation of radio actor and in his strong attraction to a vigorous, athletic cousin. Miller is a double man in that – like BILLY KWAN in *The Year of Living Dangerously* – his physical shape, compromised by polio, is not commensurate with the strength and extent of his desires.

Miller, the
The Canterbury Tales, c.1387–1400
Geoffrey Chaucer

'All brawn and very little brain', this thickset, red-bearded man is as strong as an ox, a champion wrestler and capable of breaking down any door by charging at it head down. He is also a cheat who keeps his thumb on the scales as he weighs the flour, a drunkard and a teller of bawdy tales. He leads the pilgrimage playing the bagpipes. Full of life, he is just the man to tell a tale about a dim carpenter, his pretty young wife and two Oxford students who vie for her affections.

Mills, George
George Mills, 1982
Stanley Elkin

A modest, uncomplicated Missourian whose daily grind as a furniture mover in St Louis is paralleled with the life of a medieval peasant. This raises the question of whose life has greater 'meaning', and whose is more strictly controlled by forces beyond his understanding.

Milner, Miss → Elmwood, Lady

Milton, John
Milton in America, 1996
Peter Ackroyd

Set in 1660, the novel's central character is loosely based upon the poet, already celebrated and stricken by blindness but not yet the author of *Paradise Lost*. Having fled England at the restoration of the monarchy for fear of arrest following his support of Cromwell and the Commonwealth, Milton arrives in New England to found the Puritan settlement of New Milton. Pious, but despotic and arrogant, Milton rejects beauty and the impulse of the senses and by doing so denies himself redemption. Briefly regaining his sight, he sleeps with a native American woman, but overwhelmed by self-disgust, is plunged once again into blindness.

Milton, Lord
The Fool, 1974
Edward Bond

The lord of the manor at which JOHN CLARE and DARKIE and the other farm labourers perform their Christmas song and play, he represents the hard-nosed capitalist ethics of the industrial revolution, exhorting them to behave in the national interest: 'Wages follow prices or civil institutions break down. Civilisation costs money like everything else.' Milton sees human ideals as irrelevant if not subjugated to the onward march of industry, politics and profit. However, as an elderly man he becomes bitter and self-pitying, beginning to understand too late that his own zest for mechanized efficiency has eroded love, human respect and dignity.

Milvain, Jasper
New Grub Street, 1891
George Gissing

Milvain represents the new gospel of literary art as a saleable commodity as he turns out work that deliberately panders to public taste. Cynical, egotistical and vain, he is, however, also genuinely appreciative of EDWIN REARDON's talents and friendship and is by no means an entirely unsympathetic character. Despite his stock villain's name, it is clear that he reflects

something of Gissing's own conviction that art must also be responsive to public demands.

Minafer, George
The Magnificent Ambersons, 1918
Booth Tarkington

The spoilt, snobbish son of a fading mid-western family, whose new, diminished name signals their contrast with the 'magnificence' of the ancestral Ambersons. He is a callous manipulator of the lives of others, but eventually receives his richly-deserved 'come-uppance'.

Minafer, Isabel Amberson
The Magnificent Ambersons, 1918
Booth Tarkington

The matriarch of the fading Amberson clan, she has a regal beauty and dignity of bearing that contrast sharply with the shallow breeding and vulgar mannerisms of her son, GEORGE MINAFER. In a society in rapid flux, she represents continuity and robust morality.

Minderbinder, Milo
Catch-22, 1961
Joseph Heller

A mess officer who becomes the most influential figure in the war zone through his syndicate, which becomes M & M Enterprises, standing for Milo & Minderbinder ('the & was inserted, Milo revealed candidly, to nullify any impression that the syndicate was a one-man operation'). He is the US entrepreneur gone mad, and is just trying to put the war 'on a businesslike basis'; he would like 'to see the government get out of the war altogether and leave the whole field to private industry'. He sets up a worldwide trading operation of phenomenal complexity which can deliver anything to anywhere. One deal involves having his own planes bomb his own base on behalf of the Germans at a huge profit.

Miner, Vinnie
Foreign Affairs, 1984
Alison Lurie

Through necessity Vinnie Miner has become a self-reliant woman, using her intelligence and resourcefulness to carve herself a reasonably happy life, only occasionally clouded by self pity. She is 'the sort of person that no-one ever notices' and so is free to observe and classify others, reworking them in the image of her own choosing. Her tastes and preferences are very decided and she seeks out only what is congenial, shunning all that offends. It is, however, the irritating, ill-educated CHUCK MUMPSON who forces her, through his disconcerting faith in her goodness, to an honest reappraisal of herself.

Minette
Brother Man, 1954
Roger Mais

A girl whom the compassionate BRA' MAN has rescued from the streets of Kingston, Jamaica, Minette becomes his faithful disciple, almost a Mary to his Christ. She may not be particularly articulate, but she is instinctive and possesses a clear sense of moral value and human dignity. Together with a fellow disciple, Jesmina, she rescues Bra' Man's body after he has been killed, and watches over him. When on the third day, he emerges from 'a deep sleep', the devoted Minette affirms that a new 'vision of certitude' lies before them.

Mingott, Mrs Manson
The Age of Innocence, 1920
Edith Wharton
Presiding over the 'tight little citadel' that is upper-class New York, this wealthy matriarch tartly observes that 'not one of them wants to be different; they're as scared of it as the smallpox'. Despite being heartier and more honest than most, her function is to screen family dishonour and police breaches of Good Form, ensuring that nothing disrupts the factitious harmony that is New York high society.

Minnehaha
The Song of Hiawatha, 1855
Henry Wadsworth Longfellow
HIAWATHA's beautiful and faithful wife, this daughter of an ancient arrow-maker is a member of the Dacotah tribe. Her changing moods make her as 'wayward as the Minnehaha', and she is named after that waterfall (the name means 'Laughing Water').

Minstrel, the
The Lay of the Last Minstrel, 1805
Sir Walter Scott
The last of his race, 'infirm and old;/His withered cheek and tresses gray,/Seemed to have known a better day'. He goes from door to door, begging for food, his harp carried by an orphan boy, but despite the fact that the Stuart throne has been usurped by a race of strangers he is still capable of song, and 'as he is supposed to have survived the [Glorious] Revolution [of 1688] might have caught somewhat of the refinement of modern poetry, without losing the simplicity of his original model'. He is, indeed, a most persuasive storyteller.

Minty
England Made Me, 1935
Graham Greene
A shabby, rather unsuccessful journalist. He is a cocky, ingratiating man, involved in a rat-race struggle for professional survival. Like his trapped spider, he too is a lowly, imprisoned creature and, like all the novel's main protagonists, he has cut himself off from his past. But the Catholic Minty retains a sense of guilt and morality; he hates himself and his parasitical behaviour. Although he is cynical about the worth of popular journalism, his idealism is not entirely extinguished. He understands fully the squalor of his existence and, through seeking belated atonement, attains a state of grace.

Mio
Winterset, 1935
Maxwell Anderson
The son of a man wrongly condemned and executed for a murder actually committed by the beastly TROCK. A HAMLET-figure, he is torn between revenge and his love for the sister of

Trock's accomplice GARTH. The young couple are swallowed up in the final tragedy.

Mirabell
The Way of the World, 1700
William Congreve
A dashing young rake, he is in love with MILLAMANT and hopes to induce her aunt, LADY WISHFORT, into approving their marriage. Clever, persuasive and a fine judge of character, he manages to impress almost everyone he meets. He and Millamant are well-matched, both in charm and intelligence. When she complains that he is too serious, and he protests she is frivolous, they are in fact testing each other. Although he has had other women, he is perfectly serious about wanting to marry her, promising that he opposes overindulgence in drink and would not ask her to paint her face or wear tightly-fitting corsets.

Miranda
'Old Mortality', in *Pale Horse, Pale Rider*, 1939
'The Old Order', in *The Collected Stories of Katherine Anne Porter*, 1964
Katherine Anne Porter
Romantic Miranda (whose surname is probably Rhea) believes, against the evidence, that she will grow up to be beautiful. Brought up with her older sister MARIA in the American South, she is bad-tempered but compassionate. Intelligent and interested in everything around her, she is also something of a tomboy. She elopes at the age of 17. Wanting to be independent and rejecting fictionalized family stories, such as those about AMY and GABRIEL BREAUX, she rather naively seeks the truth.

Miranda
'Pale Horse, Pale Rider', in *Pale Horse, Pale Rider*, 1939
Katherine Anne Porter
Presumably the adult version of MIRANDA in 'Old Mortality' and 'The Old Order', this character is 24 and writes for a newspaper. Her compassion, honesty and independence have got her into trouble, for instance, in opposing hypocritical patriotism. She dreams of death and broods on World War I, which is actually nearing its end. Amidst her feelings of malaise and fatigue, and surrounded by the funerals of influenza victims, she knows that her soldier lover will die. Finally she realizes that she must live.

Miranda
The Tempest, 1611
William Shakespeare
Because she has been brought up on a deserted island with only her father, PROSPERO, for human company, Miranda is a true innocent, untouched by the corruptness of the civilized world. Her inner goodness is reflected in her beauty, which even affects the monster CALIBAN. She has a tender nature, being genuinely upset by the shipwreck and the fate of those aboard. She falls in love with FERDINAND at first sight, initially taking him for a spirit, then agrees to marry him, although only with her father's blessing.

Miriam
The Marble Faun, 1860
Nathaniel Hawthorne
A dark opposite to her fellow art student HILDA, she represents sexual allure. Nothing is known of her origins, but she is stalked by a mysterious life model known as Brother Antonio, who is thrown off the Tarpeian Rock in Rome by her admirer, the COUNT DONATELLO.

Misfit, the
A Good Man is Hard to Find, 1948
Flannery O'Connor
A multiple killer who has escaped from the Federal Penitentiary. He has no memory of his crimes and no remorse but only a sense of injustice at his punishment and a conviction that Jesus has 'thrown everything off balance'. His manner is polite and even chivalrous and he dispatches his victims to their deaths without interruption of his pseudo-philosophical discourse.

Miso
The Countess of Pembroke's Arcadia, 1581–4, published 1590
Sir Philip Sidney
The shrewish wife of DAMETAS, 'so handsome a beldam that only her face and her splay-foot have made her accused for a witch'. Their only agreement is to disagree.

Missis
The Hundred and One Dalmatians, 1956
Dodie Smith
A pretty dalmatian, PONGO's not unintelligent wife, she is a natural mother who gladly 'adopts' the 82 puppies kept at Hell Hall by CRUELLA DE VIL. Although she understands less of the human language than Pongo, she is equally devoted to her human 'pets', the Dearlys. What she lacks in navigational skills (she cannot tell her left from her right) she makes up for in courage.

Mister Tom → Oakley, Tom

Mistress Quickly
The Merry Wives of Windsor, 1597
Henry IV Part I, 1596/7
Henry IV Part II, 1597/8
Henry V, 1599
William Shakespeare
The stout landlady of the Boar's Head Tavern, she enjoys SIR JOHN FALSTAFF's fooling but is easily taken in by him. Her attempts at trying to keep peace in her inn are mostly unsuccessful in spite of her claims that she keeps an orderly house. After the death of her first (unseen) husband she marries PISTOL, although she has been betrothed to NYM. Eventually she is forced to take action against Falstaff, but there is no chance that she will ever be paid what he owes her. Several of her speeches include unintended double entendres, but, in her description of Falstaff's death, there is genuine pathos.

Mitch, properly Harold Mitchell
A Streetcar Named Desire, 1947
Tennessee Williams
He at first appears 'different' from the rest of STANLEY KOWALSKI's friends – a gentle, sensitive, well-dressed man who goes home early to tend to his elderly, sick mother. His loneliness, and the fact that he too has suffered, mark him out as a potential partner and saviour for BLANCHE DUBOIS. By the end of the play, however, he has been warned off by Stanley, and his penultimate appearance, unshaven and in his work clothes, diminishes the perceived gap between himself and the brutish Stanley.

Mitchell, Harold → Mitch

Mitchell, Jack
'Enter Mitchell', et seq, in *While the Billy Boils*, 1888
Henry Lawson
A swagman in the Australian outback, 'he was short, and stout, and bow-legged, and freckled, and sandy. He had red hair and small, twinkling, grey eyes, and … the expression of a born comedian'. He is irrepressibly opportunistic, often leaving his victims not quite clear about what has happened to them.

Mitchem
The Long and the Short and the Tall, 1958
Willis Hall
The sergeant in charge of a group of six men, stranded behind Japanese lines in a hut in the Malayan jungle. Despite his claim that 'I can be the biggest bastard of them all', he is a reflective man, anxious to preserve the lives of his men but indecisive about how to do it. Ironically, his early decision to save the life of a Japanese prisoner costs the squad its existence.

Mitchens, Rummy
Major Barbara, 1905
George Bernard Shaw
A regular at BARBARA UNDERSHAFT's Salvation Army shelter, Mrs Mitchens is 'a commonplace old bundle of poverty and hard-worn humanity' who looks 60 but is probably about 45. Her habit is to spin spurious tales of woe with the intention of making Army workers feel all the more triumphant after apparently saving her soul. She is currently masquerading as a reformed prostitute.

Mitis
Every Man out of his Humour, 1599
Ben Jonson
An acquaintance of CORDATUS, Mitis joins him in watching the play and commenting on the action. Unlike Cordatus, Mitis has not seen the play before, and his function is to ask the kind of questions that an alert member of the audience might put to the author.

Mitty, Walter
The Secret Life of Walter Mitty, 1939
James Thurber
A timid and henpecked daydreamer who indulges in a rich and dramatic fantasy life (fuelled by proof-reading pulp fiction) while waiting for his wife to come out of the hairdresser's. In his fertile imagination, he transforms his mundane reality into a sequence of gaudy adventures in which he is the constant, admirable, brave, skilful and compassionate hero, culminating in his

unflinchingly facing a firing squad (as his wife returns), 'erect and motionless, proud and disdainful, Walter Mitty the Undefeated, inscrutable to the last'.

Moby Dick
Moby-Dick, 1851
Herman Melville

A white sperm whale of 'uncommon magnitude and malignity', which has removed CAPTAIN AHAB's leg in a previous encounter, and is said to have revealed a particular enmity in attacking other ships. Its identifying characteristics are a 'peculiar snow-white wrinkled forehead, and a high, pyramidial white hump', and a deformed lower jaw. Its colour is felt by ISHMAEL to hold particular metaphysical terrors, while its apparently intelligent maliciousness gives rise to half-baked rumours of its supernatural powers.

Mock Turtle, the
Alice's Adventures in Wonderland, 1865
Lewis Carroll

The Mock Turtle, the ingredient of mock turtle soup, is a melancholy creature with eyes full of tears, who once was a real turtle. When he and the Gryphon describe to ALICE their education, they use words which sound like but are not real subjects – Ambition, Distraction, Uglification and Derision, along with Laughing and Grief. They break off to tell her about the Lobster Quadrille, demand that she recite "Tis the Voice of the Sluggard' by Isaac Watts (which comes out as "Tis the Voice of the Lobster') and Alice and the Gryphon finally go off to the trial of the Knave of Hearts to the sound of the Turtle singing 'Beautiful Soup'.

Moffat, Elmer
The Custom of the Country, 1913
Edith Wharton

A common, thickset man, Moffat was once the swaggering young black sheep of UNDINE SPRAGG's home town. He 'always saw things big' and in New York becomes one of the wealthiest powers on Wall Street, through a combinaton of rough charm, shady deals, and what Undine's husband, RALPH MARVELL, at first admiringly sees as 'a kind of epic effrontery'. But for all his apparent geniality Moffat is extremely ruthless.

Moffitt, Simon
The Game, 1967
A S Byatt

As a scientist, Simon holds to facts and is wary of his own emotions, examining them rationally. He is afraid of whole-hearted commitment, except to his work, allowing himself to want only what he knows he cannot have. Attractive to women and loved by the two sisters (JULIA and CASSANDRA CORBETT), he is described by one as 'an emotional dabbler' and by the other, more seriously, as 'an emotional meddler', genuinely trying to make things turn out well without wholly involving himself. Thus accused of emotional cowardice, his own defence is that he 'wanted to be an ordinary man, not take on a destiny'.

Mohi ('Braid-Beard')
Mardi, 1849
Herman Melville

A historian from Odo, whose nickname comes from his beard, which 'is worn exceedingly long and grey'. He is a somewhat loquacious and 'venerable teller of stories and legends', and one of the keepers of the chronicles of the Kings of Mardi.

Mohun, Henry, Lord
The History of Henry Esmond, Esquire, 1852
W M Thackeray

A rakish and amoral figure in London society, he attempts to seduce LADY RACHEL CASTLEWOOD, thus tempting VISCOUNT FRANCIS CASTLEWOOD into a fatal duel at which young HENRY ESMOND acts as second. It has been suggested that the fact that 'hero' and villain share the same name is a subtle indication of Esmond's ambiguous character and of his own oedipal relationship with Lord and Lady Castlewood.

Moira
The Grifters, 1963
Jim Thompson

Attracted by the easy life of criminality, and enjoying a sexual amorality that lends itself to shameless opportunism, she finds herself out of her depth with ROY and LILLY DILLON, whose ruthlessness and cold-blooded violence reveal the inadequacies in her own thinking and criminal practice. Her shallow relationships and overweening greed result in cruel and deadly consequences.

Mole
The Wind in the Willows, 1908
Kenneth Grahame

An initially timid animal with little experience of life beyond the confines of Mole End and its ornate statuary, he is befriended by RAT and discovers the joys of life on the river. Somewhat impatient and occasionally foolish, he can also be a trifle petty, not to mention obtuse, yet is exceptionally kind, loyal and loveable.

Mole, Adrian
The Secret Diary of Adrian Mole, aged 13¾, 1982, et seq
Sue Townsend

The precocious son of constantly warring parents, Adrian first reveals his character through the diary he keeps for 15 months in 1980–2. He considers himself an intellectual and aspires to be a writer, but his use of clichés and repetitive adolescent phrases show him to be a stereotypical teenager with a gloomy attitude towards sport, sex, adults and family life. Embarrassed by the dissolute lifestyles and extramarital affairs of his parents, he is himself infatuated by a school classmate, Pandora Braithwaite. All of this is recorded with unconscious comic effect in the diary. Later volumes chart Adrian's continuing angst through adulthood, from his struggles with his first novel, *Lo! The Flat Hills of My Homeland*, to parenthood, divorce and an unusual career move to a television cookery show, *Offally Good*.

Moll → Yellowhammer, Moll

Mollie
Animal Farm, 1945
George Orwell

A pretty white mare who was the pampered pet of MR JONES, the farmer. The more spartan conditions of the post-revolutionary farm are not to her liking and she yearns for the comfort of her previous existence where, although she was not free, she was at least loved and spoilt with affection. Being a natural aristocrat, she has little sympathy for the tenets of Animal Farm and so decides to flee back to her human masters of the 'ancien régime'. For her, slavery is freedom.

Molloy
Molloy, 1951
Samuel Beckett

Old, crippled, but liberated from habit, he roams city, field and forest before collapsing in a ditch where the inevitability of death becomes merely another statement of being. Narrated by Molloy himself, the tale is told in the present even when relaying past events, thus contributing to a general sense of uncertainty. Few descriptions of Molloy better the literary critic Frank Kermode's: 'Molloy's life of falling, shambling, confusing, accepting, illustrates the true nature of all human life'.

Molly
Great Expectations, 1861
Charles Dickens

MR JAGGERS's housekeeper and the former mistress of ABEL MAGWITCH, by whom she has a child, ESTELLA. Supposed by JOHN WEMMICK to be part gypsy, she strangled another woman to death out of jealousy, but Jaggers succeeded in getting her acquitted. Having become 'a wild beast tamed' as his servant, she allows him to have MISS HAVISHAM adopt Estella and educate her as a lady.

Molly
Leaving Cheyenne, 1963
Larry McMurtry

A free-spirited and loving plainswoman, who evokes quite different reactions in JOHNNY and GID, who both love her. She possesses a gift of language and of consciousness that neither of them, for better or worse, can lay claim to. Given McMurtry's epic ambitions and frequent reference to a mythological past, it is quite possible that she is intended to echo aspects of Joyce's MOLLY BLOOM.

Moloch
Paradise Lost, 1667
John Milton

'The strongest and the fiercest Spirit/That fought in Heaven; now fiercer by despair', since the rebel angels were cast down into the pit. The epitome of brutal violence, he is characterized as a 'horrid King, besmeared with blood/Of human sacrifice and parents' tears'.

Molomo, Dan
A Question of Power, 1974
Bessie Head

A nightmarish figure, the soul of Dan Molomo invades ELIZABETH's mind, manipulating her thoughts and determined to destroy her. Dan's sexual appetite is insatiable, and he thrives on the emotional torture he inflicts on Elizabeth. The soul of Dan bears little resemblance to 'the living man', a 'short, black and handsome' cattle millionaire.

Mommy
The Sandbox, 1960
The American Dream, 1961
Edward Albee

The American matriarch reborn as a vicious torturer. In the earlier play, this surrealist-cum-absurdist figure abandons Grandma (who is still hale and hearty) to the personification of death. In the second, disappointed that her child does not conform to her clean-limbed and athletic ideal, she has him tortured and mutilated, before replacing him with a rather more macho son. It is not clear whether the two boys are intended to be identical, but they illustrate the same point; Daddy is of course also present in both plays.

Monchensey, Amy, Dowager Lady
The Family Reunion, 1939
T S Eliot

Too proud and 'country-bred' to take her chilled old bones south for the winter, she keeps the house at Wishwood alive 'To keep the family alive, to keep them together,/To keep me alive, and I live to keep them'. Even so, each birthday reminds her that her days are running out, while she waits fearfully for 'the clock to stop in the dark'.

Monchensey, Lord Harry
The Family Reunion, 1939
T S Eliot

AMY, DOWAGER LADY MONCHENSEY's son, he lost his wife in mysterious circumstances, when she disappeared overboard from a cruise liner. Absent from Wishwood for eight years, he returns to celebrate his mother's birthday, racked with paranoid delusions, and provides the focus of all the family's buried guilts.

Moncrieff, Algernon
The Importance of Being Earnest, 1895
Oscar Wilde

In the words of his aunt, Algernon is 'an extremely ... almost ostentatiously, eligible young man' who 'has nothing, but ... looks everything'. A spoilt sophisticate, he continually adopts a superior and flippant pose, displaying a consciously cynical and amoral attitude to life in general and marriage in particular. This changes when he meets CECILY CARDEW, his friend's ward, to whom he immediately becomes engaged and for whom he is willing to be re-christened, to become the 'Ernest' she has always dreamt of.

Mond, Mustapha
Brave New World, 1932
Aldous Huxley

Mustapha Mond is World Controller, the apex of a tiny élite allowed to read books in the negative utopia ruled by scientists in which he lives. During his interrogation of the rebellious JOHN THE SAVAGE and BERNARD MARX, he justifies the biological engineering which slots every human being into rigid categories as the only method to keep society stable and everyone happy. He hopes to 'civilize' the Savage but banishes Marx to an island full of like-minded misfits.

Moneygawl, Isabella
Castle Rackrent, 1800
Maria Edgeworth
The youngest daughter of Mr Moneygawl of Mount Juliet's Town, she is the rich bride of SIR CONDY RACKRENT and mistress of the castle in its last, bankrupt days. Condy chose her (over JUDY M'QUIRK) by a flip of the coin, and she repays this gallantry by fleeing the coop as soon as the bailiffs move in.

Moneytrap
The Confederacy, 1705
Sir John Vanbrugh
Like his associate GRIPE, the parsimonious Moneytrap has become wealthy through his activities as a loan shark. And just as Gripe falls for his wife ARAMINTA MONEYTRAP, so Moneytrap lusts after CLARISSA GRIPE. He imagines his money to be an inducement and himself to be something of a catch, but his unfettered sexual desire and his devious personality make him rather a pathetic figure, easily outmanoeuvred by the women.

Moneytrap, Araminta
The Confederacy, 1705
Sir John Vanbrugh
The wife of MONEYTRAP, Araminta finds herself the subject of amorous advances from GRIPE, her husband's devious associate. She is, though, a close friend of his wife CLARISSA GRIPE, and the two women join forces to exploit their husbands' sexual weaknesses. Like her friend, Araminta is a sharp schemer and adept at playing games of sexual politics, but, as FLIPPANTA observes, she has little else to fill her time.

Monimia
The Adventures of Ferdinand, Count Fathom, 1753
Tobias Smollett
Bearing an assumed name 'that implies her orphan situation' (because it was the name of the heroine in Thomas Otway's play *The Orphan*), she possesses a beauty so refined that even FERDINAND, COUNT FATHOM's sated senses are re-awakened, though in specifics – high forehead, smooth skin, snowy neck, fine black ringlets, moods vivacious and melancholy by turns – she seems straight off the production line of Smollett inamoratas. She is loved by RENALDO DE MELVIL.

Monimia
The Orphan, 1680
Thomas Otway
The orphan of the title, Monimia is the sister of CHAMONT, and raised alongside CASTALIO and POLYDORE, the sons of ACASTO. She is virtuous, idealistic but neither particularly intelligent nor perceptive, being easily fooled when Polydore one night takes the place of her husband. She is dowerless, and although she is in a position whereby a sexual relationship could be easily maintained, society would oppose her marrying Castalio or any other wealthy man. Her suicide is as much a result of her contravention of social manners as because her honour has been defiled.

Monina (Monina McLeod)
Barbary Shore, 1951
Norman Mailer
More of an idea than a real child, she is ostensibly the daughter of the old Marxist ARTHUR MCLEOD and his slatternly wife GUINEVERE. 'The child was completely naked … her body was extraordinary. She was virtually a miniature of a girl of eighteen, the limbs round, slender curves flowing from shoulder to hip, her luminous blonde hair lovely against the pale flesh.' Her name, with its echoes of 'monism', may suggest the reductive single-mindedness of the ideologies that Mailer is dissecting.

Moniplies, Richie, later Sir Richard Moniplies of Castle-collop
The Fortunes of Nigel, 1822
Sir Walter Scott
The son of an Edinburgh butcher (the name comes from the wrinkles in a piece of tripe), he is NIGEL OLIFAUNT's resourceful servant. By a mixture of chivalry and sordid cunning, violence and generosity, he attains wealth and rank of his own.

Monk, Colin
Intensive Care, 1970
Janet Frame
In a nightmarish future world, he initially accepts society's ruthless expunging of all that is not human; he himself has a mechanical shadow self called SANDY. Later, he comes to recognize the need for a protective and respectful attitude towards a world that is not merely a linguistic construct or a bureaucratic convenience.

Monk, Lady
Can You Forgive Her?, 1864–5
Anthony Trollope
The aunt of BURGO FITZGERALD. She is a tall, graceful, upright woman 'now about fifty years of age, who had been a great beauty, and who was still handsome in her advanced age'. She is rather indulgent of the wayward Burgo, although her husband, Sir Cosmo Monk, strongly disapproves of him.

Monk, the
The Canterbury Tales, c.1387–1400
Geoffrey Chaucer
A very worldly cleric, vowed to the contemplative life but openly revolting against it. His duty is to supervise the monastic lands, and, in the eyes of the naive narrator, he is 'a manly man' fond of outdoor pursuits. But his expensive clothes and excellent horse contradict his vow of poverty. He finds hunting and good food preferable to study or manual work, and is happy to leave God to look after the world. His tale is of such boring pomposity that THE KNIGHT eventually puts a stop to it.

Monk of Misrule, the → Abbot of Unreason

Monmouth, Lord
Coningsby, or The New Generation, 1844
Benjamin Disraeli

An unregenerate Tory of the old school, he is HARRY CONINGSBY's grandfather, and represents the selfish and socially partial style of the English aristocracy that is passing into history. He has claimed *droit de seigneur* over those whom his position demands he protect, and has interfered for his own ends in the lives of others. He is dismayed when the MILLBANK family, whose money comes from 'trade', buys an estate adjoining his own.

Monroe, Ada
Cold Mountain, 1997
Charles Frazier

Ada, a bookish, unconventional young woman from a wealthy background, finds herself struggling to manage a remote North Carolina farm after her father's death. Her nascent relationship with INMAN has been interrupted by his departure to fight in the Civil War, and while awaiting his possible return she wrestles with the demands of her new and difficult way of life. Initially dissatisfied and rather detached from her surroundings, she develops into a strong, pragmatic person, deeply engaged with the landscape in which she has chosen to settle.

Monsieur d'Olive
Monsieur D'Olive, 1604
George Chapman

Although lending his name to the title, D'Olive, a courtier, is a secondary character in a play revolving around different kinds of melancholy and reclusive obsession. By plunging him into romantic intrigue, however, Chapman transforms him into a magnificent comic creation reminiscent of MALVOLIO in *Twelfth Night*. Like him, D'Olive is extravagant, somewhat anarchic and self-aggrandizing, describing himself as 'the compound of a poet and lawyer'. Living by his wits, he is tormented by others practising their wit on him. A fool, he is finally gulled, although he gains our sympathy for in many ways he is far more humane than his tormentors.

Monster, the
Too True to be Good, 1932
George Bernard Shaw

The Monster, invisible to all but the audience, a microbe of 'luminous jelly with a visible skeleton of short black rods', sits in the sickroom of the wealthy young woman, THE PATIENT, who lies in bed asleep. Complaining that her sedentary way of life and rich diet are killing it, the Monster criticizes the stultifying over-protection to which the Patient is subjected by her mother, MRS MOPPLY, and the devotional attention of her doctor. The Patient's sudden exertion when she knocks down THE BURGLAR seems to cure the Monster, as it begins to leap about exultantly before jumping into the empty bed and falling asleep.

Mont, Michael
The Forsyte Saga, 1922
A Modern Comedy, 1929
John Galsworthy

A worthy, well-meaning man. The nephew of SOAMES FORSYTE, he marries FLEUR FORSYTE after her rejection by JOLYON ('JON') FORSYTE even though it is apparent that she does not love him. Mont is really no match for the Forsytes. A breezy individual who likes to be thought of as modern, he is not nearly as well-off as his wife, and his marriage elevates him socially. He abandons cigarettes for cigars, and publishing for Parliament.

Montag
Fahrenheit 451, 1953
Ray Bradbury

The idealistic hero of a dystopian nightmare. He is employed by the 'Fire Brigade', but his job is to burn banned books. Initially an obedient employee, he gradually begins to question the regime, and as his awareness of its iniquity grows, so does the battle within his own mind. His idealism and intelligence win out, and he ultimately rebels in a liberating act of revenge, throwing in his lot with a rural community dedicated to memorizing books for posterity.

Montague
Romeo and Juliet, 1591–6
William Shakespeare

ROMEO's father, he is supportive of his son, showing concern about his tendency to go out at night and stay at home during the day. He is unable to guess the reason, though it is evident that his own marriage is a happy one, unlike that of his deadly rival, CAPULET. Although ignorant of what has taken place he adroitly defends his son's killing of TYBALT. The death of his wife from grief, followed soon after by that of Romeo, comes as a body blow to him, yet he is prepared to settle his differences with Capulet and, magnanimously, to raise a golden statue to JULIET.

Montague, Emily
The History of Emily Montague, 1769
Frances Brooke

A young woman of 24, staying with her mother's relations in Montreal after the death of her uncle. A close friend of ARABELLA FERMOR, Emily is a 'prudent pretty sort of woman', beautiful but also of strong enough character to know her own mind. Orphaned at a young age and raised by relatives, Emily has learned to follow her heart in difficult decisions. Against all advice she decides to break her engagement to the wealthy Sir George, because she recognizes that her desire is not for affluence but for true friendship and affection. This 'melting sensibility' attracts her to her kindred spirit, COL EDWARD RIVERS, whom she eventually marries.

Montague, Hugh Fremont, also known as HARLOT, or 'Dr Taylor', or GALLSTONE, or GANTRY, or GHOUL
Harlot's Ghost, 1991
Norman Mailer

A senior CIA officer, and HARRY HUBBARD's *éminence grise*. A rock climber, he is crippled in a fall, after which his wife Kittredge defects to Hubbard's bed.

Montemayor, the Marquesa de → Marquesa de Montemayor, the

Monticue, Ethel
The Young Visiters, 1919
Daisy Ashford (Mrs George Norman), juvenilia

'Huffy', priggish and easily seduced by the joys of the moment, Ethel Monticue is a triumphantly self-possessed 17-year-old in search of a good marriage. Snobbishly rejecting the proposals of her social equal, MR SALTEENA, she prefers instead the material and physical advantages of Bernard Clark, whom she encourages to fall in love with her. After a few weeks' more or less innocent 'gaierty' together, they marry in Westminster Abbey. Her exciting life continues amid a happy abundance of offspring and new outfits.

Montoni
The Mysteries of Udolpho, 1794
Ann Radcliffe

A dissipated Italian quasi-nobleman in the circle around EMILY ST AUBERT's worldly aunt, he looks proud, intelligent and handsome, yet Emily views him with fear and distrust. His manners are insinuating but they hold a note of violence. He marries her aunt suddenly and takes her and Emily to his crumbling castle of Udolpho in the Apennines, where he starves his wife to death in the east turret. Emily and her maid, only secondary to his sinister purposes, are able to elude his carousing companions. Foiled, he dies in prison at Venice, possibly poisoned.

Montrose, Earl of (James Graham, Marquis of Montrose)
A Legend of Montrose, in *Tales of My Landlord: Third Series*, 1819
Sir Walter Scott

Co-author of the National Covenant, he later recanted and became a staunch Royalist. Eventually defeated in battle, he was executed on the High Street, Edinburgh, in the early summer of 1650. 'Montrose possessed that sort of form and face, in which the beholder, at the first glance, sees nothing extraordinary, but of which the interest becomes more impressive the longer we gaze upon them'. He is short and not conventionally handsome, but 'those who saw him when his soul looked through those eyes with all the energy and fire of genius – those who heard him speak with the authority of talent, and the eloquence of nature, were impressed with an opinion even of his external form, more enthusiastically favourable than the portraits which still survive would entitle us to ascribe to it'.

Montserrat, Conrade, Marquis of
The Talisman: A Tale of the Crusaders, 1825
Sir Walter Scott

'He was a handsome man ... bold in the field, sagacious in council, gay and gallant in times of festivity; but, on the other hand, he was generally accused of versatility, of a narrow and selfish ambition.' His loyalty to the Christian League is suspect after his contacts with Saladin and he earns the contempt and enmity of RICHARD I, who, Scott suggests, may well have been complicit in Montserrat's assassination.

Monygham, Dr
Nostromo, 1904
Joseph Conrad

An intelligent but psychologically wounded physician who is haunted both by his betrayal of comrades to the dictator Bento, and by the legacy of his physical sufferings at his hands, which have left him with a scarred face, prematurely grey hair, a deformed posture, and a limp. He is an outsider, and even a pariah, in society, and 'his short, hopeless laugh' suggests 'an immense distrust of mankind'. He has real integrity, however, and his brave defiance of the rebel general Sotillo, and his loyal but unexpressed love for EMILIA GOULD, help him to restore his self-respect and position.

Moody, Joss
Trumpet, 1998
Jackie Kay

Joss is a mixed-race jazz trumpeter (with an African father and a Scottish mother) who has made many records and played all round the world. As a young man he was 'well dressed, astonishingly handsome, [with] high cheekbones ... thick black curly hair ... neat nails, beautiful hands ... skin the colour of Highland toffee'. However, Joss was originally Josephine and since a teenager has bound his/her breasts and lived as a man, marrying Millie, a white Scottish woman, in the 1950s. Only on Joss's death, with which the novel begins, does this become known to the public and to his adopted son Colman. Joss's journey 'from girl to young woman to young man to old man to old woman' is an exploration of the theme of identity itself.

Moody, Judge Oscar
Losing Battles, 1970
Eudora Welty

The judge in Ludlow who sentences JACK RENFRO to two years in Parchman farm, and who finds himself at GRANNY VAUGHN's birthday celebration after a not wholly accidental mishap in his car. He is 55 years old, with high blood pressure and hay fever, and is pompous and overbearing in court, where his 'whole battle-cry is respect'.

Moon Blossom → Tang, Mui

Moon Lily → Chen, Lily

Moore, Alex (Alexander)
How Many Miles to Babylon?, 1974
Jennifer Johnston

The naive yet virtuous hero of the story. In the sheltered upbringing of the Irish gentry, Alex forms a private and secret friendship with JERRY CROW, made fast by their mutual love of horses. He despises his manipulative mother and is exasperated by his father's inability to stand up to her. She drives Alex to the trenches of World War I, where his passion for truth and fairness brings him no affection from his commanding officer and no respect from his troops. This, and his deep love for his rank-and-file friend Jerry, bring about his tragic downfall.

Moore, Dotty
Jumpers, 1972
Tom Stoppard
The wife of GEORGE MOORE, a distracted professor of moral philosophy, Dotty is an almost absurdly sentimental, unstable former musical comedy star who suffers a breakdown while watching the first moon landings on television: a distant, romantic sphere has been transformed for her into merely another, albeit remote, reality. Withdrawing from sexual relations with her husband, she engages in a series of charades, evading the question of the corpse in her bedroom and the enquiries of a farcical Inspector Bones.

Moore, George
Jumpers, 1972
Tom Stoppard
A professor of moral philosophy, Moore attempts to write a lecture proving the existence of God while his wife, DOTTY MOORE, is going not so quietly dotty in the bedroom. Chivvying away at elusive philosophic precision ('I don't claim to *know* that God exists, I only claim that he does without my knowing it') he fails to notice the domestic chaos under his own nose. Vain and self-absorbed, he is nevertheless aware of his frailty and desolation. Moore may be absurd, but he is never pathetic.

Moore, Louis
Shirley, 1849
Charlotte Brontë
The tutor to SHIRLEY KEELDAR's invalid cousin, and also in the past to Shirley herself, he is a grave and serious man, of superior taste and understanding, rendered passive and retiring by his position of tutor in the household. However, he makes a rewarding friend and an excellent companion. In love with Shirley, he is too proud and aware of his poverty to declare himself to her until he believes his love is thoroughly returned. Being a man of 'entire self-possession', he manages to hide his feelings well.

Moore, Mrs
A Passage to India, 1924
E M Forster
The mother of RONNY HEASLOP, she is an elderly woman with white hair and a ruddy complexion who has journeyed to India in the company of her intended daughter-in-law ADELA QUESTED. In rather low health, she is a fair and decent woman whose innate Christian tenderness gives way to weariness and cynicism as she experiences both the delights and dangers of India and intimations of her own mortality. Increasingly irritated by the world and its inhabitants, she plans a hasty retreat to England but dies at sea without regaining a sense of harmony.

Moore, Robert Gerard
Shirley, 1849
Charlotte Brontë
A half-English mill owner, he is an outcast amongst his Yorkshire neighbours, not just because of his foreign ancestry, but also because of his solitary, hard nature. His desire to clear his debts and forge his fortune in the world are his

consuming occupations, making him hard and careless of others, as well as unsympathetic and single-minded. A resolute and acute businessman, he is 'taciturn, phlegmatic and joyless', but is essentially good. Whilst 'stern in public', he is 'on the whole very kind in private' and comes sincerely to regret at least one of his less honourable attempts at advancing his fortunes.

Moore, Vivaldo
Another Country, 1962
James Baldwin
A white novelist of liberal tendencies, and a friend of the jazz musician RUFUS SCOTT. After Scott's death, Moore becomes the lover of his sister IDA SCOTT, but gets no closer to the mystery of his friend's life or his decision to end it.

Moorehouse, J Ward
The 42nd Parallel, 1930
1919, 1932
The Big Money, 1936, forming the *U.S.A.* trilogy, 1938
John Dos Passos
Brought up in Wilmington, Delaware, bright, blue-eyed Ward is forced, to his distress, to abandon his college education because of his father's enforced redundancy, and thereafter he sets his sights on bettering himself at any cost. Having his early romantic notions pummelled out of him by the sham of his first marriage, he transfers his youthful idealism to his career, and makes his way into the public spotlight as a publicity and public relations expert. But however well-meaning, Ward remains what he is frequently described as, 'a stuffed shirt'.

Mopply, Mrs
Too True to be Good, 1932
George Bernard Shaw
Mrs Mopply, an elderly but wealthy widow whose well-meaning but suffocating protectiveness has already killed her other children, is now nervously attending to her sick daughter, THE PATIENT. It is a neurosis that THE MONSTER, a microbe acting as a Chorus figure, despises. When Mrs Mopply employs a new attendant, THE NURSE, the play catapults into a fantasy of reversals at the end of which Mrs Mopply is hit on the head with an umbrella wielded by COL TALLBOYS. This knocks sense into her, and sets mother and daughter on a new course as independent women.

Mopsa
The Countess of Pembroke's Arcadia, 1581–4, published 1590
Sir Philip Sidney
DAMETAS's and MISO's daughter, she is beautiful but foolish; only alongside the divinely gifted PAMELA does she seem anything less than wonderful, 'a cuckoo to a nightingale'.

Mor, William
The Sandcastle, 1957
Iris Murdoch
Well-respected in the boys' boarding school where he teaches history, Mor suffers deeply from the constant nagging and ridicule of his

shrewish wife. When the Labour Party ask him to stand for Parliament, she claims that he lacks the personality for public life. Having always scrupulously observed the responsibilities of marriage, and believing that complete truthfulness is the basis for all virtue, Mor suddenly falls in love with young artist RAIN CARTER. He discovers a new sense of self, but also experiences a grave moral and psychological crisis.

Moran
Amongst Women, 1990
John McGahern

A tyrannical old widower who is compelled to dominate his family and have everything on his own terms or not at all. He is an old Republican and was once a guerrilla leader in the War of Independence. This glorious memory haunts him. Still handsome, he has become a recluse. Righteous and bitter, he cannot come to terms with his ultimate ordinariness. His relationships with Rose (his second wife) and his three daughters lie at the heart of his predicament: the complex challenge of love and fear, of self and other people.

Moran
Robbery Under Arms, 1888
Rolf Boldrewood

Moran is one of the bushranging gang led by the mysterious CAPTAIN STARLIGHT, which includes DICK and JIM MARSTON. He is arguably the only naturally evil character in the novel. He is modelled upon a real outlaw of the 1860s, 'Mad Dan' Morgan, a man of awesome ferocity and terrifying recklessness, who was probably insane. Moran has none of the innate honour of Captain Starlight or the Marstons. He is reptilian, churlish and motivated by an unrelenting rage.

Moran, Ira
Breathing Lessons, 1988
AnneTyler

A 'closed-in, isolated man' with a long, bony, olive face and narrow, dark eyes, he is seen by his wife MAGGIE MORAN as mysterious, restrained and silent, but also 'born competent', 'seamless and infallible'. Disappointed in his son, JESSE MORAN, and regularly irritated by Maggie, he escapes social occasions with his passion for solitaire. He feels his life has been a waste and a failure, having given up his dream to be a doctor in order to look after his father and disabled sisters, and then his own wife and family, though he does recognize that the true waste is 'his failure to notice how he loved them'.

Moran, Jesse
Breathing Lessons, 1988
AnneTyler

'Intensely, almost ridiculously social', good-looking Jesse is a singer in a rock band, fecklessly wandering from one job to the next. His mother, MAGGIE MORAN, sees him as endearingly generous and affectionate, while his critical father, IRA MORAN, finds him 'infuriating and pathetic', calling him 'Mr Moment-by-Moment'. Pride and lack of self-confidence make

him constantly at cross-purposes with his now-divorced wife, and his refusal to become 'one of those artificial fathers' has meant that he has lost touch with his daughter, despite Maggie's best efforts.

Moran, Maggie
Breathing Lessons, 1988
AnneTyler

Married to IRA MORAN, round-faced, constantly-dieting Maggie battles his image of her as an illogical 'whifflehead', and her own 'clownish, pratfalling' reputation. Emotional and impetuous, 'not a straight-line kind of person', she never gives up on those she loves or thinks need her help, leading her to meddle and 'start changing things around to suit her view', infuriating Ira and her adored son JESSE MORAN. Outsiders see them as a bickering couple, he 'forever so righteous' and she 'so willing to be wrong', yet they are each other's source of strength and joy, and together survive the disappointments of their 'ordinary' lives.

Morddure
The Faerie Queene, 1590–6
Sir Edmund Spenser

Spenser's name for 'Excalibur', the sword that belongs to PRINCE ARTHUR, which Merlin dipped in a magic potion and watched Arthur pull from the rock. A faithful, hard-biting weapon, it never fails and always brings victory. Neither steel nor stone can withstand its blows and it can only be used by its rightful owner.

Morden, Col
Clarissa, 1748
Samuel Richardson

CLARISSA HARLOWE's avenging cousin, Colonel Morden is a man of fortitude, generosity and courage. He vehemently worships Clarissa as a queen and an icon, and is revolted by her family's money-grabbing behaviour at the reading of her will. He challenges the abhorred ROBERT LOVELACE to a duel and displaying bravura swordsmanship mortally wounds him.

More, Sir Thomas
A Man for All Seasons, 1960
Robert Bolt

Bolt's version of this famous historical character focuses very directly on the internal emotional conflict generated by a clash between private and public imperatives. A brilliant, successful, just and loyal man who has achieved personal and political greatness, he is unable to reconcile the demands of the royal marriage with his conscience or beliefs, and sacrifices everything to his unshakeable principles. His example stands in contrast to the devious machinations around him.

More, Starky
Dead Men Running, 1969
D'Arcy Niland

Starky is based on the historical Douglas Starkie, who was described by Niland's wife Ruth Park as 'alien, impersonal, a talismanic force from a brutal history'. The most complex of Niland's characters, Starky is the outsider, carrying with him an uncompromising moral code. He radiates a natural power that might once have brought a crown, but instead forces upon others a moral choice that brings about his own inevitable end.

Moreau, Doctor
The Island of Doctor Moreau, 1896
H G Wells

A white-haired formerly great physiologist who left England after a vivisection scandal, Moreau works on a remote Pacific island. He tries to turn animals into men with a combination of biological wizardry and quasi-religious litanies involving threats against those who cannot behave like humans. Despite insisting on his own reasonableness and sanity to his visitor, Edward Prendick, he cannot control his experiment.

Morel, Paul
Sons and Lovers, 1913
D H Lawrence

The son of WALTER and GERTRUDE MOREL, who becomes his mother's ally against her husband, and whose maturing is the central theme of the novel. His sensitivity and secret ambitions to become a painter make him an outsider in the Nottinghamshire mining community in which he grows up. Ambitious, vain, emotional, questing, he learns to live a covert life, keeping his feelings to himself. With MIRIAM LEIVERS he has a loving but stifling relationship. He also enjoys a primarily sexual affair with CLARA DAWES. Thus the principal women in the book are cast as instruments of Paul attaining the age of reason, with all its doubts and decisions.

Morel, Walter and Gertrude
Sons and Lovers, 1913
D H Lawrence

Morel, a hard-drinking, irascible, tough Nottinghamshire miner and Gertrude, his wife, 'a rather small woman of delicate mould but resolute bearing', represent two strands of the English working-class character. Their clash of temperament and moral values lies at the heart of their tempestuous and ultimately pathetic and tragic marriage. Morel's bad temper masks a weak will and his male, public-house-oriented sociability contrasts sharply with Gertrude's strict nonconformist morality, her tendency to aloofness and her domineering possessiveness. She has a receptive, curious mind and is considered rather intellectual. Her achievements, though, are her children (who include PAUL MOREL); her ambition is to live vicariously through their successes.

Morell, Candida
Candida, 1895
George Bernard Shaw

The wife of the REV JAMES MORELL, Candida discovers the poet EUGENE MARCHBANKS and takes him under her wing, resulting in the emotional disruption of her household. While not a great intellect, her ability to manage people by engaging their affection and by making the most of her sexual allure (which Marchbanks rejects) is offset by dignity and an acute intelligence. Her most characteristic expression is one of amused maternal indulgence. Yet, for all

her bewitching of Marchbanks and the resulting opportunity to change the intellectual and emotional configuration of her life, she does not, in the end, do so.

Morell, Rev James
Candida, 1895
George Bernard Shaw

Morell is a Christian Socialist clergyman of the Church of England and husband to CANDIDA MORELL. Vigorous, enthusiastic and sympathetic, he is 'a first rate clergyman' but also, at 40, 'a great baby' who sees his Candida as a combination of wife, sister, mother and nurse. Condemned by EUGENE MARCHBANKS for being unappreciative of Candida and therefore unworthy of her, he nevertheless triumphs over his young rival as security and pragmatism defeat recklessness and idealism. Morell ends the play as he has begun, by worshipping his wife, the domestic angel incumbent at St Dominic's Parsonage.

Moresby, Kit
The Sheltering Sky, 1949
Paul Bowles

A neurasthenic New York society woman, who loses her husband, PORTER MORESBY, and then her mind while on a slumming trip to outlying parts of North Africa. She is taken into concubinage by desert Arabs and then 'rescued' by TUNNER, who has befriended the couple and fallen in love with Kit.

Moresby, Porter
The Sheltering Sky, 1949
Paul Bowles

A fashionable New Yorker, touring North Africa with his wife, KIT MORESBY, and his friend TUNNER. The downside of his intellectual sophistication is a bleakly experimental *nostalgie de la boue*, which reaches its logical climax when he dies of typhoid after a delirious vision of excrement and blood.

Morgan → Belarius

Morgan, Anna
Voyage in the Dark, 1934
Jean Rhys

Naive, hypersensitive and very young, Anna has left her Caribbean home for England, the promised land of her childhood. Unable to make sense of the cold, the dark and the unrelenting grey monotony of the seaside towns that she tours as a chorus girl, she withdraws into the sanctuary of her own vivid imagination, allowing the people and places she encounters to grow increasingly distant, distorted and unreal. Bewildered and compliant, she drifts passively towards moral destruction and essential oblivion.

Morgan, Eugene
The Magnificent Ambersons, 1918
Booth Tarkington

A leading representative of the 'new aristocracy' of industry and commerce in US life, this benign and cultured manufacturer of horseless carriages is a deliberate foil to the effete selfishness of GEORGE MINAFER.

Morgan, Harry
To Have and Have Not, 1937
Ernest Hemingway

A powerboat owner who hires his craft out for fishing trips, but is forced to turn to crime when business fails in order to maintain his family in their precarious position, a task he approaches with single-minded dedication. Tough and skilled, he is cynical of authority and offical injustice. He is increasingly aware that the odds are against him, an insight he finally articulates as 'one man alone ain't got no chance', a lesson that 'had taken him all his life to learn'.

Morgan, Mr
The Adventures of Roderick Random, 1748
Tobias Smollett

First mate of the *Thunder*, brimful of the noisy and sulphurous choler of stage Welshmen at the time. 'He was a short thick man, with a face garnished with pimples, a snub nose turned up at the end, an excessive wise mouth, and little fiery eyes, surrounded with skin puckered up in innumerable wrinkles.' Smollett mentions him again in *The Adventures of Peregrine Pickle* (1751), and makes a reference to a Widow Morgan, perhaps a relic of the old sailor, in *The Expedition of Humphry Clinker* (1771).

Morgan, Mrs Organ
Under Milk Wood, 1954
Dylan Thomas

The groceress and general shopkeeper of the village, who sells everything from custard to whistles. She is also a general purveyor of news, a gossip with a comment or an opinion on everyone, her mouth gobbling up items like a pelican. She sleeps curled up like an acquisitive mouse, her paws over her ears as she is a 'martyr to [her husband's] music', and she dreams of silence.

Morgan, Organ
Under Milk Wood, 1954
Dylan Thomas

The village organist, he thinks continually in musical terms, which is a great trial to everyone, especially his wife. He serenades Llaregyb from the chapel at early morning and nightfall. The only choice for him is between his heroes Palestrina and Bach, and he even thinks he sees the latter in the drunken form of CHERRY OWEN in the graveyard. Playing the organ with his fingers in his sleep, he snores mercifully quietly.

Moriarty, Dean
On The Road, 1957
Jack Kerouac

Based on Neal Cassady, who was a counterculture hero in the 1960s, he is a freewheeling, fast-living teenager, fresh from reform school and ready for anything. He 'actually was born on the road', and lives for movement, 'a fast car, a coast to reach, and a woman at the end of the road'. He is handsome and physically powerful, irresponsibly wild and eager for experiences of all kinds. He is entirely uninhibited, is open to experiment with drink, drugs and sex, and completely outrageous in his behaviour.

Moriarty, Professor
The Final Problem, in *The Memoirs of Sherlock Holmes*, et seq; magazine serialization 1892–3; book 1894
Arthur Conan Doyle

Professor Moriarty is SHERLOCK HOLMES's cleverest and deadliest enemy, a man equal in intelligence and cunning to the great detective himself. 'He is the Napoleon of crime', Holmes remarks to his associate, DR WATSON. Of good birth, Moriarty might have pursued a brilliant mathematical career, but 'a criminal strain ran in his blood'. He lurks like a spider, the mastermind at the heart of organized crime. Tall, thin, pale, ascetic-looking, his head moves slowly from side to side, lending him a sinister, reptilian air. It is Moriarty who grapples with Holmes above the Reichenbach Falls, after which Watson assumes that Holmes has plunged to his death.

Morland, Catherine
Northanger Abbey, 1818
Jane Austen

The naive, artless heroine, Catherine has an open, affectionate and demonstrative nature which endears her to HENRY TILNEY. Fuelled by the Gothic novels that she so avidly devours, her furtive imagination completely runs riot when she stays at Northanger Abbey but she learns, as a result, to see things, and people, as they really are. Moving from a state of ignorance to one of bliss, she recognizes that her reality offers her a lot more than her fanciful novels can.

Morland, James
Northanger Abbey, 1818
Jane Austen

A minor character in the novel, James is CATHERINE MORLAND's eldest brother who is, though very fond of her and a pleasant, kind man, unfortunately very unperceptive when it comes to choosing his friends. Unable to see that JOHN THORPE is not the most desirable of acquaintances, he is equally blind to the real nature of John's sister, ISABELLA THORPE, and as a result has to suffer the pain and indignity of a broken engagement to her.

Morley, Cressida
Closer to the Sun, 1960
The Far Road, 1962, and others
George H Johnston

A beautiful woman of unfathomable depth. A symbol of complete womanhood, she is pagan in her worship and her loyalty; she is a woman co-joined not to husband or lover, but to the natural world: to sea, sun and star. Her 'honesty' is not born of a human code but of an alliance with a pantheistic code.

Morley, Stephen
Sybil, or The Two Nations, 1845
Benjamin Disraeli

SYBIL GERARD's friend, he represents the hot-blooded, radical wing of the Chartist movement. His confrontational style dooms him to tragic failure and he is killed during a riot.

Morlocks

The Time Machine, 1895
H G Wells

Living underground in the year 802,701AD, the Morlocks are compared by the horrified Time Traveller to both apes and spiders. They look bleached, have large eyes, and come to the surface at night to feed off the childlike ELOI. It is surmised that humanity has split into these two species, descended from capitalists and labourers – the latter in 1895 being 'cut off from the natural surface of the earth'.

Morocco, Prince of

The Merchant of Venice, 1594/5
William Shakespeare

A noble and arrogant man, he has come to Belmont to attempt to win PORTIA's hand in marriage through choosing a casket, as outlined in her father's will. His choice of the gold casket with its inscription 'who chooseth me shall gain what many men desire' reflects his superior and domineering personality. In a play about racial prejudice, his presence adds another facet, particularly in view of Portia's comment, 'Let all of his complexion choose me so'.

Moroni, Fanny

The Lacquer Lady, 1929
F Tennyson Jesse

She is a naive, bold, impertinent, indolent, silly girl of part Italian, part Burmese and part English extraction, whose dreams 'were bolder, cruder, more rapacious, more vivid, but not more coherent than those of her schoolmates'. She grows into an attractive young woman, and becomes a favourite in the exotic but violent Burmese court, but is the agent of its destruction when she betrays a political secret for love. After the collapse of that world, she makes an undistinguished second marriage, but 'seemed to have ceased to exist ... even while her dimmed semblance had yet lingered there'.

Morose

Epicoene, or The Silent Woman, 1609
Ben Jonson

The reclusive, irritable, wealthy Morose has two ambitions: to marry and to live in a silent world. He abhors noise so much that he cannot bear to hear anyone talking, except himself, and prohibits any sound in or outside his home. Even his servants must communicate by hand signals. He also views the behaviour of his high-spirited nephew, SIR DAUPHINE EUGENIE, with severe disapproval. To teach him a lesson, Dauphine engineers a plot whereby Morose marries EPICOENE, apparently a quietly-spoken woman who, immediately after the ceremony, is revealed to be a boy in disguise.

Morrie (Morris)

The Blood Knot, 1961
Athol Fugard

Morrie fulfils his need to keep his darker-skinned brother ZACH emotionally subservient by involving him in various role-playing subterfuges which communicate racial op-pression in South Africa at that time. Highly self-disciplined, Morrie lives by his alarm clock

and his Bible, but is nonetheless able to identify strongly with his more feckless brother's existential pain.

Morris, Dinah

Adam Bede, 1859
George Eliot

Simply dressed, and wearing a Quaker cap, Dinah is a self-appointed Methodist preacher. Unlike many of her kind, however, she speaks honestly and directly from her own emotions, although she is over-disposed to biblical phrases: to her, HETTY SORREL is 'that poor wandering lamb'. A talent for comforting the unhappy and for considerate behaviour earns her the respect of many, especially Seth and ADAM BEDE.

Morris, Lucy

The Eustace Diamonds, 1873
Anthony Trollope

A friend of Lady Fawn, in whose house she is a governess. She has a winning way of putting both adults and children at their ease in conversation which makes her a 'treasure though no heroine. She was a sweetly social, genial little human being whose presence in the house was ever felt to be like sunshine.' She marries FRANK GREYSTOCK.

Morris, Margarite

The Newspaper of Claremont Street, 1981
Elizabeth Jolley

An ageing cleaning lady, Margarite is known in Claremont Street as 'Weekly' or 'Newspaper' because of her propensity to gossip. A British-born Australian emigrant who dreams of buying her own plot of land, Weekly is an isolated, eccentric and literal figure. As she sweeps and scrubs the houses of her employers, the untidy clutter of her own mind – long-suppressed memories and unsatisfied desires – resurfaces continually and disturbingly.

Morris, Mr

Jack Holborn, 1964
Leon Garfield

A slight man, his dapper appearance is spoiled by a faintly mildewy air, as if his clothes were always left to dry on his person. The ship's master-of-sailing, he is an excellent navigator both on sea and on dry land, leading the remnants of the crew through the jungle to the high ground and the river that will save them. He has a brisk, business-like manner, and is not easily scared by tales of murderous ghosts. He is steady and calm in a crisis, and it takes more than one squall to blow him off-course. Practical and patient, he trusts implicitly in his own skills. Although not physically strong, he is determined and self-willed. He is a man who knows the ways of the world and uses his knowledge in a wholly pragmatic way. His courage is without question or comparison.

Morrison, Cassie

'June Recital', in *The Golden Apples*, 1949
Eudora Welty

Hearing Beethoven's 'Für Elise' and watching with her brother as MISS ECKHART prepares a purgative fire of music scores for VIRGIE RAINEY and her sailor boyfriend, Cassie recalls the tense relationship between the elderly piano teacher and her favourite pupil.

Morrison, Jeanie
Robbery UnderArms, 1888
Rolf Boldrewood

The sister of KATE MORRISON, Jeanie meets JIM MARSTON, a bushranger, while he and his brother, DICK MARSTON, are in Melbourne spending the money they have earned herding stolen cattle from New South Wales. Less possessive, less impetuous and more patient than her sister, Jeanie is also more forgiving of others' foibles. Kate is in love with Dick, but in Jim, Jeanie meets a man more constant than his brother, and he eventually brings her to the Turon goldfields to be married. Kate's later betrayal of the brothers, though, results in Jim's death and Jeanie's despair.

Morrison, Kate
Robbery UnderArms, 1888
Rolf Boldrewood

The sister of JEANIE MORRISON, she meets the bushranger DICK MARSTON when he and his brother, JIM MARSTON, are in Melbourne spending the money they have earned herding stolen cattle from New South Wales. Quick-tempered and passionate, Kate is left behind when the brothers move on, and later marries a hotelier on the Turon goldfields. The marriage fails and when she discovers Dick is also at the goldfields, Kate plans to seduce him and win him back. When it emerges that Dick is in love with GRACEY STOREFIELD, the possessive, jealous, distraught Kate twice betrays the brothers and CAPTAIN STARLIGHT. From one point of view, she is coldly vindictive; from another, her actions arise from her rejection and unhappiness.

Morrison, Loch
'June Recital', in *The Golden Apples*, 1949
Eudora Welty

CASSIE MORRISON's brother, he is likened to the many-eyed Argus of mythology. If Cassie's reveries are triggered by sound and accompanied by passive immersion in the past, Loch is a more active presence, desperate to prevent the past overwhelming the present.

Morse, Inspector
Last Bus To Woodstock, 1975, et seq
Colin Dexter

A lover of classical music and an enthusiast for crosswords, Inspector Morse is a problem-solving detective, delving into the minutiae of a case rather than psychoanalysing his suspects. Always introduced as Morse, his student nickname, Pagan, is only revealed later in the series of novels, and his first name, Endeavour, is kept secret until the final book. Spiritually a loner, he has never married although he enjoys the company of women. He has a sound working relationship with his sergeant, Lewis, but finds his superiors unaccommodating and has been reprimanded for seeking to conduct matters his own way. He is very squeamish, a problem for a man who has to deal with corpses and attend autopsies. This, and his distaste for much of his

job, has meant that his need for alcohol has seriously affected his health, and Morse suffers a fatal heart attack in the final novel, *The Remorseful Day*.

Mortimer, Edmund
Henry IV Part I, 1596/7
William Shakespeare

One of the rebels in the alliance against HENRY IV, Edmund Mortimer tries to keep the peace between his father-in-law OWEN GLENDOWER and his irascible brother-in-law HOTSPUR; but he is essentially optimistic, treating both parties with respect. He has a passionate fondness for his wife, though he regrets the fact that he is unable to converse with her because she speaks only Welsh.

Mortimer, Julia
Losing Battles, 1970
Eudora Welty

A schoolteacher who is remembered by various members of the RENFRO family during the events surrounding GRANNY VAUGHN's birthday. Although she is already dead by the time of the action, she is an important figure in the book. She enforced strict discipline with her 'whistling switch', but was dedicated to learning and self-realization, and was ready to 'teach herself to death' in order that the children learn something. In her youth, 'every young blood in Ludlow was wild about her', but she never married.

Mortimer, Lady
Henry IV Part I, 1596/7
William Shakespeare

The wife of EDMUND MORTIMER and the daughter of OWEN GLENDOWER, she only speaks Welsh. Her devotion to her husband in spite of this barrier suggests their relationship is more than just a convenient political arrangement. Their closeness, and her willingness to sing for her husband, contrast with the more uneasy marriage of HOTSPUR and his wife.

Mortimer, the Younger
Edward II, 1594
Christopher Marlowe

Paramour of QUEEN ISABELLA and instigator of the barons' revolt against EDWARD II. Bluff and open, loved by the people, he becomes a Machiavellian schemer, but recognizes that even his 'virtue' is subordinate to Fortune's ever-turning wheel.

Morton, Henry
Old Mortality, in *Tales of My Landlord*, 1816
Sir Walter Scott

Son of the late Colonel Morton and nephew to the present proprietor of Milnwood (SILAS MORTON OF MILNWOOD), he is a moderate young man driven into the arms of the Covenanters by the cruelty and bigotry of the Crown troops. As a hero he is somewhat milk-and-waterish and his initial appearance in dramatic green armour at the *'wappen-schaws'* is never quite borne out by his subsequent actions, though he is steadfast in principle and in his love for EDITH BELLENDEN.

Morton of Milnwood, Silas

Old Mortality, in *Tales of My Landlord,* 1816
Sir Walter Scott

Uncle to HENRY MORTON and present incumbent of the seat of Milnwood. 'The old gentleman had been remarkably tall in his earlier days, an advantage which he now lost by stooping'; he has 'splay feet of unusual size, long thin hands, garnished with nails which seldom felt the steel, a wrinkled and puckered visage … together with a pair of little sharp bargain-making grey eyes'. As in face, so in nature: he is known to his tenants as 'Nippie'.

Mosca

Volpone, or The Fox, 1606
Ben Jonson

One of the most famous characters in the Jonsonian repertoire, Mosca is VOLPONE's parasite, his flattering, resourceful, devious servant, buzzing here and there like an angry little fly. By feigning illness, Volpone plans to add to his riches, capitalizing on the greed of others who offer him money in the hope of being named as his heir. Mosca appears to be the willing agent in this, luring corrupt men into Volpone's trap. Yet his own greed becomes too much for him, and the plans misfire when he attempts to betray Volpone and so · claim the accumulated wealth for himself.

Moseley, Hoke

Miami Blues, 1984, et seq
Charles Willeford

The antithesis of the glamorous Miami police detective of TV legend, Hoke Moseley seems plagued by all the ills of the middle-aged Anglo male. His dentures ('so patently false that they were the first thing people noticed … when they met him') are a constant reminder of the relentless ageing process (especially when stolen by a vindictive criminal). His pared-to-the-bone lifestyle is the consequence of a rash pre-divorce settlement, and he can barely keep up with his daughters' dentist bills. Despite his car-wreck of a personal life, Moseley is a tenacious and effective homicide detective, and does his best to build a new home life with his sometime police partner, Ellita Sanchez.

Moses

Animal Farm, 1945
George Orwell

The pet raven of MR JONES, the farmer, who escapes with him at the start of the novel. Years later it returns, an endless chatterer, talking of an animal heaven where all will find peace and solace. As the animals become more and more oppressed under the yoke of NAPOLEON, Moses fulfils the function of comforter; he makes their lot easier to bear by promising them a freer, more egalitarian life in the spiritual hereafter. Thus are the ideals of the revolution indefinitely postponed.

Moses

The Grass is Singing, 1950
Doris Lessing

A quiet, apparently gentle 'Mission boy' employed as a servant, who murders the mistress

(MARY TURNER) who almost trusted him. He is very methodical, careful and precise, and affects a caring demeanour, but his subservience masks an angry soul. He seems to embody the wounded pride and bitterness of his race.

Mossop, Willie

Hobson's Choice, 1915
Harold Brighouse

A man whose incapacitating shyness prevents him from reaping the full rewards of his prodigious talent as a bootmaker, he is employed by the Hobson family shoemaking firm, and selected by the affectionate but forthright MAGGIE HOBSON as her future husband. Mossop quails, but knows that once Maggie has spoken, he has no choice. With his craftsmanship allied to her financial expertise and grim determination, she plans to turn the business into a thriving success. Mossop complies because she provides him with equality, dignity and ambition, and he begins to fall in love with her. Because of Maggie, Mossop shines as highly as his boots.

Motley, Juan

Juan in America, 1931
Juan in China, 1937
Eric Linklater

An English descendant of Byron's *Don Juan,* he is 'vivid, darkly handsome, capable of irreverent laughter'. Wild and strong, he possesses great spirit and immense curiosity. With his British upper-class upbringing, he is launched as a kind of innocent on the seedy and wildly exotic new world of America. He has inherited his ancestor's fascination with women, but not his suave manner of dealing with them.

Moto, Mr

No Hero, 1935, published in Britain as *Mr Moto Takes a Hand,* 1940, et seq; he previously appears in *Ming Yellow,* 1935
John P Marquand

An omnicompetent Japanese secret agent, he is fit, agile and impressively polyglot, to a degree that makes JAMES BOND seem rather stuffy. Where they differ most profoundly is in ideology. In place of Bond's rather sceptical, very English pragmatism, Moto is fiercely loyal to the emperor.

Mottram, Rex

Brideshead Revisited, 1945
Evelyn Waugh

Having served with distinction in the Canadian army, Rex Mottram is 'the burlesque of power and prosperity' in London. Handsome and healthy, he inhabits a harsh, acquisitive world of politics, gambling and finance. He becomes an MP, reaching the fringes of government, and gains prestige and notoriety through his affair with the society figure Brenda Champion. A social-climbing divorcee, his grand wedding plans are thwarted by religion, and he has instead a low-profile marriage to JULIA FLYTE in the Savoy chapel. After his marriage he continues his affair, and is ashamed of Julia's failure to cut the required image. Their child is born dead, and Julia divorces him, hoping to marry CHARLES RYDER.

Mount, Miss Antonia
The Finishing Touch, 1963
Brigid Brophy

The joint head – with MISS HETTY BRAID – of a Firbankian finishing school on the Riviera, she hides a steely capability under a beautiful and elegant exterior. There is no doubt that she is the most effectual partner in the relationship.

Mountain, Fanny
The Virginians, 1857–9
W M Thackeray

The daughter of the former LADY RACHEL CASTLEWOOD's housekeeper, after whom she is named. She is the eventual choice of HARRY ESMOND WARRINGTON, who marries her rather than HETTY LAMBERT.

Mountford, Susan
A Woman Killed with Kindness, 1603
Thomas Heywood

Together with her brother, Sir Charles, Susan appears in the sub-plot of the play, counterpointing the main action of JOHN FRANKFORD, his wife ANNE FRANKFORD and her lover, WENDOLL. She has little of the moral complexity of Anne, being virtuous, sententious, rather a prig and sometimes a bore.

Mountjoy
Henry V, 1599
William Shakespeare

Because he behaves with dignity, even when delivering the most insulting message, Mountjoy, the French Herald, is treated with respect by Henry V (HENRY, PRINCE OF WALES). However, the Frenchman has to display true humility when he admits defeat after the battle of Agincourt. As a man of the upper classes, he is deeply shocked to discover that the blood of French nobles has been mingled in death with that of common French soldiers.

Mountolive, David
Mountolive, 1958, and elsewhere in *The Alexandria Quartet*, 1968
Lawrence Durrell

A crisp young diplomat, captivated by Alexandria, where he has been posted as a trainee to improve his Arabic. He finds himself acting secretary of legation, later ambassador, a focus for all the politicking that overlays the sexual and economic intrigues of the city.

Mountstuart, Logan Gonzago
Any Human Heart, 2002
William Boyd

An Everyman for the 20th century ('every life is both ordinary and extraordinary'), he was born in 1906 in Uruguay, educated at an English private school, and works variously as a writer, spy, New York art dealer and English lecturer in Nigeria. He mixes with famous people (including Picasso, Edward VIII and Wallis Simpson, Hemingway and the Baader-Meinhof Gang) in the course of a life of 'sporadic highs and appalling lows' lived over nine decades. A likable character despite having 'sometimes behaved less than well', his unflinchingly honest journal tells of his accepting attitude to his yo-yo life.

Mouse, properly Michael Tolliver
Tales of the City, 1978, et seq
Armistead Maupin

Gentle, self-deprecating, full of wisecracks, Mouse never gives up hope of meeting Mr Wonderful. A tenant of the renowned ANNA MADRIGAL at 28 Barbary Lane, and a close friend of MARY ANN SINGLETON, he throws himself wholeheartedly into the San Francisco gay scene, clutching a bundle of insecurities but buoyed up by an irrepressible optimism.

Mouth
Not I, 1972
Samuel Beckett

In this short play, the stage area is in darkness except for the actor's mouth, about eight feet above stage level. In a far corner, a dimly-lit figure in black appears to be listening. In a torrent of disjointed phrases, Mouth recalls shreds of memories: the anguish of birth, childhood, illnesses, moments of fear too appalling to recount. As in many of Beckett's shorter works, existence itself sometimes seems too painful to describe. There appears to be a longing for death and release, and a final acceptance of the love of God. Mouth, perhaps, represents the restless spirit as the body nears death.

Mouths, the
Prancing Nigger, 1924
Ronald Firbank

A black family in a tropical republic. Mr Ahmadou Mouth, religious and melancholic, does not want to leave their village, but his big, bored, social-climbing wife insists on moving to the capital, so they can enter Society. Their elder daughter, Miss Miami, enjoys the city's amusements, but is grief-stricken when her boyfriend dies. Her 13-year-old sister, Edna, with 'the sharp-soft eyes of a paroquet', becomes a harlot. Their 'delicate, charming, and squeamish' brother, Charlie, who used to hunt butterflies and dance with other village boys, becomes an habitué of a 'notorious Bar'. Such are the corruptions of civilization.

Mowbray, Clara
St Ronan's Well, 1823
Sir Walter Scott

JOHN MOWBRAY's younger sister, she is widely thought to be touched in the head. She shuns company and spends much of her time in riding habit, galloping distractedly around the country. Her secret guilt is that she was once cheated into an elopement by the young EARL OF ETHERINGTON, believing that she was actually running away with Etherington's elder half-brother Frank Tyrrel, whom she loves.

Mowbray, John, Laird of St Ronan's
St Ronan's Well, 1823
Sir Walter Scott

Shaws House has been considerably run down during his short tenure, its capital wasted by gambling and mismanagement. The Laird is even reduced to dipping into his sister CLARA MOWBRAY's tiny stock of capital to finance his debts from card games, before trying to marry her off to the calculating EARL OF ETHERINGTON.

Mowbray, Thomas, 1st Duke of Norfolk
Richard II, c.1595
William Shakespeare

At the beginning of the play, Mowbray stoutly denies the accusation levelled by Henry Bolingbroke (HENRY IV) that he has murdered the Duke of Gloucester, KING RICHARD II's uncle, but concedes that he might have mistreated him. An apparently loyal courtier, he covers up for Richard, on whose orders he has been acting. A duel follows and Mowbray is banished by the king. The question, though, is whether, in the unlikely event of his winning, Mowbray would have exercised the undoubted power he would have had over the monarch. He might well have blackmailed Richard, or have attempted to gain the throne himself.

Mowcher, Miss
David Copperfield, 1850
Charles Dickens

A dwarf chiropodist, hairdresser and dealer in cosmetics, with very short legs and 'a pair of roguish grey eyes', given to talkativeness and asking 'Ain't I volatile?'. Shrewd, observant, kind and honest, she makes herself useful to many people in various ways. She amuses MR JAMES STEERFORTH with gossip about her fashionable clients, but is implicated through foreknowledge in LITTLE EM'LY's elopement, and is much upset by it. Having high principles, she brings about the arrest of LITTIMER.

Mowgli
The Jungle Book, 1894
Rudyard Kipling

A 'man-cub' abducted – or possibly rescued – from civilization by the ferocious tiger SHERE KHAN but saved from slaughter by the wolf AKELA and coached in the Law of the Jungle by the wise bear BALOO. He lives his life in a state of nature; he 'grew and grew strong as a boy must grow who does not know that he is learning any lessons, and who has nothing in the world to think of except things to eat'.

Mozart, Wolfgang Amadeus
Amadeus, 1979
Peter Shaffer

A common vulgarian with a piercing, infantile giggle, an obsession with the scatological and the manners of a performing seal, Mozart would be an unwelcome guest at any gathering of distinction were it not for the fact that his music is touched by the hand of God. Broken in body and spirit during a lifetime of impoverishment and lack of critical appreciation, his sole comfort is the hope that posterity will have no choice but to acclaim his genius.

Mucklebackit, Saunders
The Antiquary, 1816
Sir Walter Scott

An east-coast fisherman, in his own estimation 'a dour carle battered by winds and foul weather at sea and land till I am maist as senseless' as his 'auld black bitch of a boat' in which his son is drowned.

He gives way to grief only once when the lad's coffin has left the house, but the next day is to be seen out, stoically mending the hull.

Mucklewrath, Habbakkuk
Old Mortality, in *Tales of My Landlord*, 1816
Sir Walter Scott

The most extreme and violent of the Covenanting preachers, he is possessed of a vision that he is Magor-Missabib, the wrath of God and scourge of the innocent. Mad as a hatter, he is also rather chilling.

Mudjekeewis
The Song of Hiawatha, 1855
Henry Wadsworth Longfellow

A brave warrior who steals the sacred Belt of Wampum from Mishe-Mokwa, the Great Bear, which he kills. The people make him 'Kabeyun, the West-Wind', 'Father of the Winds of Heaven'. He seduces WENONAH, who consequently gives birth to HIAWATHA. Later he welcomes his son, who fights him because he was responsible for Wenonah's death, but Mudjekeewis is immortal and invincible. He sends Hiawatha back to purify the world.

Mugo
A Grain of Wheat, 1967
Ngugi wa Thiong'o

Though held in reverence by his people as a hero of the Mau Mau, he has been so taken over by messianic visions that he betrays the leader of the rebellion to the British. Thereafter his life is torn apart by guilt.

Mulcahy, Henry
The Groves of Academe, 1952
Mary McCarthy

When college teacher Henry Mulcahy is threatened with loss of tenure, a serious blow for a family man, some see him as a victim of vindictive political interests; others are relieved to be rid of a lazy, self-opinionated bore who was never a team player. Having 'a gift for being his own sympathiser', Henry's own reaction is paranoid, seeing conspiracies and betrayals everywhere. His apparent helplessness belies relentless, calculating determination to protect his position as a 'superior individual'. Protesting that he seeks only justice, he forces others to choose whether they are with him or against him. It is not a choice anyone finds easy to make.

Mulcaster, Boy
Brideshead Revisited, 1945
Evelyn Waugh

An inveterate gambler with an 'ungainly frame', Lord Mulcaster has a penchant for cheap women and seedy nightclubs. He persuades SEBASTIAN FLYTE and CHARLES RYDER to leave a party for Ma Mayfield's Old Hundredth Club, and precipitates Sebastian's arrest for drunken driving by being heavy-handed and patronizing with the police. His sister Celia marries Charles, and Mulcaster becomes great friends with his young nephew 'Johnjohn'. His engagement is cancelled, and he is forced to make an out-of-court settlement with his fiancée.

Mulga Bill
Rio Grande's Last Race and Other Verses, 1892
Andrew Barton ('Banjo') Paterson
A tough old character from Eaglehawk in the far west of New South Wales. Fascinated by the new cycling craze, he turns out his old horse to pasture, buys himself a bicycle in town and sets off back home. But his new iron-framed steed also has a will of iron. The bicycle leaves the track and, with Bill white as chalk in the saddle, careers down the hill. Cycle and rider end up in Dead Man's Creek. Bill swims ashore, returns thoughtfully home and once more saddles up his faithful horse.

Mullen, Charlotte
The Real Charlotte, 1894
E O Somerville and Martin Ross
Unattractive but clever, Charlotte seems kindhearted but beneath her voluble public eccentricity she is sharp, cruel and greedy. A business crony of RODDY LAMBERT, the Dysart's land agent, she encourages his peculations, lends him money and expects him to marry her after she has deliberately let his wife die. Instead he marries FRANCIE FITZPATRICK, the flighty cousin she has imported to entrap the Dysart heir. Biding her time, Charlotte exacts revenge of a sort.

Müller, Kurt
Watch on the Rhine, 1941
Lillian Hellman
A large, powerful man in his late forties, he has devoted himself body and soul to the anti-Fascist struggle since witnessing the slaughter of 27 men in a Nazi street fight. Working undercover and fighting in Spain, he has been forced to let his family make many sacrifices on his behalf. The situation saddens him but he realizes nothing can be sacrosanct in an age when people are forced to take sides and fight for a world 'in which all men can die in bed'.

Müller, Sara
Watch on the Rhine, 1941
Lillian Hellman
A good-looking, well-bred woman in her early forties, she is now dowdy where once she would have been fashionably attired. Marriage to committed anti-Fascist KURT MÜLLER has taken her far from the comfort and security of her protected American life but she will wearily endure whatever sacrifice is necessary for the nobility of a just cause and for the man she loves.

Muller, Willy
Everything You Know, 2000
Zoë Heller
Willy Muller became estranged from his two daughters after his imprisonment for allegedly murdering his wife. After his release on appeal he wrote a lurid memoir of his marriage, earning him the disapproval of all and forcing him to flee to Los Angeles where, aware of his own physical decay, he spends his time venting his anger against the world on everyone around him. 'I am bad. A bad, bad man', he says of himself, but reading the diaries of his late daughter forces him to re-evaluate his life and come to terms with his past.

Mulligan, Buck
Ulysses, 1922
James Joyce
Stately, plump Buck Mulligan ascends into *Ulysses* with all the pomp and ridiculousness his medical-student mind can muster. His classical pretensions and loveable rogue charm wear as thin as the hair on his tonsured head, and he is neatly summed up in the conceited delight he displays in the foul epigrams which trip from his tongue.

Mulqueen, Agnes
The Ante-Room, 1934
Kate O'Brien
The beautiful, intelligent Agnes suffers quiet desperation in the Irish town of Mellick, running the wealthy, devoutly Catholic household of her dying mother, TERESA MULQUEEN, ineffectual father, DANNY MULQUEEN, and her brother, REGGIE MULQUEEN, all of whom are dependent upon her strength. Courted by DOCTOR CURRAN, she endures the 'mortal hurt' of her feelings for Vincent, the god-like husband of her much loved sister, MARIE-ROSE MULQUEEN, and tortured by her sinfulness has stopped attending Confession and Communion. However, during the fateful period of All Saints, various family crises come to a head, and Agnes discovers that Vincent returns her love.

Mulqueen, Danny
The Ante-Room, 1934
Kate O'Brien
TERESA MULQUEEN's wealthy but pathetic husband is a little chubby man full of platitudes, proverbs and feeble kindliness. He tries to cover the deep hurt, loneliness and desolation he feels over his wife's behaviour and terminal illness with cheerful, inconsequential chatter. Although jealous of the light that their son, REGGIE MULQUEEN, can bring to Teresa's ravaged face, Danny has never betrayed any resentment over her fierce devotion and dedication to her 'poor' Reggie, or the fact that she has almost forgotten her husband's existence.

Mulqueen, Marie-Rose
The Ante-Room, 1934
Kate O'Brien
AGNES MULQUEEN's adored elder sister. She is dependent on Agnes for support as her marriage to Vincent, the wealthy son of an upper-class Dublin family, becomes increasingly unhappy following the death of her baby and a subsequent miscarriage. Small and fragile-looking, golden-haired and pretty, she is enchanting to men and, being somewhat shallow and selfish in spirit, is confident of her power to charm. Her own kind of strength and courage are often mistaken for frivolity.

Mulqueen, Reggie
The Ante-Room, 1934
Kate O'Brien
TERESA MULQUEEN's son, a large wreck of a man aged 36. Infected by syphilis ten years earlier, after long hospitalization he now lives at home, still receiving mercury treatment, and barred

from marriage. Teresa, his 'only stay and light' has constructed a reclusive life for him, keeping him interested in various pursuits, one of which is playing Chopin pieces, but never in full. Once coarsely attractive, he is now wholly dependent, lazy, self-pitying and inept. He resolutely tries to deny his mother's imminent death and what this will mean, but finds eventual salvation in NURSE CUNNINGHAM.

Mulqueen, Teresa
The Ante-Room, 1934
Kate O'Brien

In her too-quiet house Teresa, devoutly Catholic mother-of-eight, is near death from cancer. In a morphine-induced dream in an attempt to find peace from her intolerable pain, she nevertheless fights determinedly to stay alive until her pathetically dependent son, REGGIE MULQUEEN, can somehow be fitted to life without her. For, although Teresa is naturally prudish, since Reggie contracted syphilis she has single-mindedly devoted her life to him, making his wasted, unhappily celibate existence tolerable, and neglecting her husband, DANNY MULQUEEN, and her other children in the process. She is terrified that Reggie will harm himself and others, but her prayers for a miracle 'shield' for him are answered in the form of NURSE CUNNINGHAM.

Mulvaney, Private
'The Three Musketeers', in *Plain Tales from the Hills*, 1888
Soldiers Three, 1890
Rudyard Kipling

The second of the 'Musketeers', he hails from Ireland. No less brashly self-confident than his comrades, he evinces an idiosyncratic philosophical stance that sets him slightly apart from them.

Mumbi
A Grain of Wheat, 1967
Ngugi wa Thiong'o

During her husband GIKONYO's incarceration for involvement in the anti-British uprising, she has a relationship with her former suitor KARANJA and has a baby by him. On Gikonyo's release she finds herself cast in a double isolation by her husband, who accepts the child but largely shuns her, only forgiving her later when he has expiated his own guilt.

Mumpson, Chuck
Foreign Affairs, 1984
Alison Lurie

A real-life caricature of an American tourist, Chuck Mumpson is big, brash and loud. The impression he gives is one of confidence, but in reality he is painfully aware of his shortcomings. Satisfaction at his successful struggle to overcome his miserable beginnings has been eroded by feelings of rejection: his company has retired him and his family are embarrassed by him. Despite these setbacks he remains optimistic, willing to see the best in others, and encouraging VINNIE MINER to do likewise. This generosity makes him vulnerable but his straightforward no-nonsense approach to people

and problems reveals a tough-minded individual who will not go down without a fight.

Munchkins
The Wonderful Wizard of Oz, 1900
L Frank Baum

Dwarf-like denizens of the Land of Oz, where they grudgingly serve THE GREAT OZ. They are neither good nor bad, and seem to underline the book's persistent parallelism between Oz and the condition of turn-of-the-century America.

Mundungus
A Sentimental Journey through France and Italy, 1768
Laurence Sterne

Based on the travel writer Dr Samuel Sharp, Mundungus is an example of those who bring to travel a very critical and demanding attitude, finding much to complain about and little to enjoy. As a contrast to PARSON YORICK's approach, this downbeat attitude is seen as very unsporting, and makes the travel experience largely pointless.

Mundy, Ted
Absolute Friends, 2003
John le Carré

A 'thoroughbred Englishman', veteran of boarding school, Oxford and Cold War espionage, Mundy first appears as a tour guide in Bavaria, a slightly comic figure seemingly 'all things to all men and nothing to himself, fifty in the shade, nice enough chap, wouldn't necessarily trust him with my daughter'. Introspective and haunted by his past, his political anger is fired once again by his old friend Sasha, and by Britain's participation in the war in Iraq and his conviction that 'the dismally ill-managed country he'd done a little of this and that for is being marched off to quell the natives on a bunch of lies'.

Mundy Family, the
Dancing at Lughnasa, 1990
Brian Friel

Times are hard – the play is set near fictional Ballybeg, County Donegal, at harvest time in 1936 – and the five adult Mundy sisters and one brother scrape by on very little money. The ages of the five range from 26 to 40. Kate, the eldest, is a schoolteacher and the only regular wage-earner. Maggie is the housekeeper, and Agnes and Rose, knitters. Chris, the youngest and the impudent mother of an illegitimate son, like Maggie has no income. Nevertheless, the family faces each day with enormous spirit. Kate is flinty, inhibited, domineering, and Maggie naturally rebellious, sceptical, generous, sometimes cynical, usually optimistic. Rose is 'simple' and protected by the others, especially Agnes, yet when they leave, eventually for England, both slide into despair and destitution. Their brother, Jack, a missionary priest repatriated from Africa after 25 years, is a reclusive, tragic, half-mad figure, sustained by his imagination and memories.

Munera
The Faerie Queene, 1590–6
Sir Edmund Spenser

The daughter of POLLENTE, she is an exploitative

lady with little regard for anything but wealth. She is fair, richly attired and, as a result of her father's exploits, very wealthy. She has golden hands and silver feet and many knights wish to take her for a wife. However, she refuses to marry anyone who cannot cross the bridge her father guards.

Muniment, Paul
The Princess Casamassima, 1886
Henry James
A social revolutionary in London, he has a notably persuasive tongue, but accepts the inevitability of violence. 'He moved in a dry statistical and scientific air in which it cost Hyacinth an effort of respiration to accompany him ... he sometimes emitted a short satiric gleam which showed that his esteem for the poor was small and that if he had no illusions about the people who had got everything into their hands he had as few about those who had egregiously failed to do so.' Despite the furiousness of his intellectual pace, he makes a profound impact on the young HYACINTH ROBINSON but leads him into the unresolvable contradictions that result in the young man's suicide.

Munoo
The Coolie, 1936, revised edition *Coolie*, 1972
Mulk Raj Anand
A downtrodden orphan who moves from one menial job to another until, worn out by poor working conditions and malnutrition, he dies of consumption. He is not despised because of his caste, but because he has failed to make it in a society increasingly geared to material success.

Munster, Ally
Tomorrow and Tomorrow and Tomorrow, 1947 (censored), 1983 (uncensored)
M Barnard Eldershaw
HARRY MUNSTER's shrewish wife. She is neglectful of the four children she has borne in five years of marriage, loathes country life and longs for the lights, entertainment and apparent riches of Sydney. Having achieved her aim of moving there, in a cramped apartment the shallow, selfish and greedy Ally, relatively unaffected by the death of one child, piles up debts through gambling and acquiring luxuries which she hides away for herself during the Depression. Growing increasingly slothful and slatternly, until even her children are shamed and revolted by her sleazy self-indulgence, Ally, as always, blames her long-suffering and estranged husband.

Munster, Harry
Tomorrow and Tomorrow and Tomorrow, 1947 (censored), 1983 (uncensored)
M Barnard Eldershaw
The central character of KNARF's 'historical novel', Harry is a World War I Anzac who is nagged by his wife, ALLY MUNSTER, into selling his small farm and moving to Sydney where, with a countryman's distrust of cities, he always feels alien. Believing in co-operative labour, he was sacked during the Depression for joining a union and feels some sympathy with communist SID WARREN. He is later rejected for service in World War II, and bitterly angered by

government lying to civilians. He is a decent man and a loving father with an intolerable marriage.

Murad
In Custody, 1984
Anita Desai
Son of a rich Delhi carpet-dealer, at school Murad bribed DEVEN, a poor widow's son, into doing his bidding. Later, as publisher of a literary magazine bought for him by his father, Murad fails to pay Deven for reviews and coerces him into approaching the poet NUR to obtain copy for a special edition of Urdu poetry, boasting of keeping alive its courtly idiom against 'that language of peasants, Hindi'. Shifty, untrustworthy, inconsistent and unscrupulous, Murad disclaims responsibility when the project ruins Deven.

Murdockson, Meg
The Heart of Midlothian, in *Tales of My Landlord: Second Series*, 1818
Sir Walter Scott
An 'old woman of the lower rank' and an associate of criminals, she expresses all emotion, even her affection for her deranged daughter MADGE WILDFIRE, with a 'strain of ferocity ... like that of the tigress'. It is she who attends EFFIE DEANS in her confinement and passes the newborn child on to the gypsies.

Murdstone, Mr Edward
David Copperfield, 1850
Charles Dickens
DAVID COPPERFIELD's cruel and tyrannical stepfather who is jealous of David's place in his mother's affections. Handsome, but gloomy and vindictively destructive, he dominates his weak wife, MRS CLARA COPPERFIELD, abetted by his equally callous sister, JANE MURDSTONE. On the death of Clara and their baby, he sends David to work in the hated warehouse of Murdstone and Grinby. He later marries a second wife, but he and his sister make her life miserable.

Murdstone, Jane
David Copperfield, 1850
Charles Dickens
MR EDWARD MURDSTONE's sister. Gloomy, hard and 'metallic', she resembles her brother in appearance and callousness. She assists in the process of breaking the spirit of MRS CLARA COPPERFIELD and persecuting young DAVID COPPERFIELD. Later, she and her brother make the life of his second wife equally miserable.

Murieta, Joaquin
Life & Adventures of Joaquin Murieta, 1854
John Rollin Ridge/Yellow Bird
The largely fictional character upon whom a Californian legend was built. Born with the requisite noble spirit and daring – as well as handsome features – of the romantic outlaw, Murieta has turned to a life of horse-stealing, robbery and murder after brutal first-hand experience of the racial hatred towards Mexicans after the Mexican War. Successfully maintaining the loyalty of an extensive and highly organized *banditti* network, he mounts

swift guerilla attacks on local rancheros and miners and enjoys the drama of hair's-breadth escapes. He insists on his followers respecting his code of honour, abhorring rape and never attacking those who have sheltered or otherwise helped him in the past. However, his plans to rerun the recent war and revenge his country's losses are cut short by government Rangers whose relentless pursuit ends in his shooting and humiliating decapitation.

Murphy
Murphy, 1938
Samuel Beckett

In a novel ripe with idiom, Murphy, above all, embodies Beckett's philosophy: the desire for constant retreat from the indignities of a world premised upon desires and rewards. Our first introduction finds him strapped into a rocking-chair, perversely enjoying the freedom of thought which this physical restraint makes possible. As an unemployed Irishman in London, Murphy's world is curiously recognizable, and the gallery of characters which surrounds him parodies those we can expect to pass in the street. That Murphy finds contentment working in an asylum where he views the patients as escapees from a 'colossal fiasco', sums up Murphy's attitude to life, which he sees as a troublesome prelude to death.

Murphy, Miles
A Charmed Life, 1955
Mary McCarthy

A 'fat, freckled fellow with a big frame, a reddish crest of curly hair, and small, pale-green eyes, like grapes about to burst', he is a great intellect, sharpening his ideas wherever he goes, much as he often sharpens his claws on those nearest to him. The first husband of MARTHA SINNOTT, he treated her cruelly, yet now, settled in a more placid marriage, feels a rekindling of fondness towards her. Magnetic and repulsive, he can generate tragedy with seemingly effortless ease.

Murray, Major Angus
Barometer Rising, 1941
Hugh Maclennan

PENELOPE WAIN's new suitor, he is a wounded army physician, whose strategy for healing himself is a dedicated application to alcohol. Outwardly shabby and disreputable, 'like a long-legged, alien dog in a strange place', he, like NEIL MACRAE, is ruined in COL GEOFFREY WAIN's ill-run regiment. Unlike MacRae, he resorts to a world-weary cynicism to get by.

Murray, Regent (more usually given historically as **Moray**)
The Monastery, 1820
The Abbot, 1820
Sir Walter Scott

Regent of Scotland from 1567 to 1570, the bastard son of James V and thus the half-brother of MARY, QUEEN OF SCOTS, to whom he extended a degree of religious tolerance despite his own conversion to Protestantism. To SIR HALBERT GLENDINNING's eye, 'the commanding form and the countenance to which high and important thoughts were familiar, the features which bore the resemblance of Scotland's long line of kings, were well calculated to impress awe and reverence'.

Murray, Rosalie
Agnes Grey, 1847
Anne Brontë

The charming but frivolous elder daughter of the Murrays, to whom AGNES GREY goes as a governess. Taken up with clothes and social position, she is thoughtless and wayward, and laughs at Miss Grey's attempts to instil higher values. Vanity rules; she even sets her cap at Miss Grey's friend the curate, REV MR WESTON, and expects Miss Grey to be amused by her flirtations. She is led by her desire for wealth to marry Sir Thomas Ashby but is fond enough of Miss Grey to invite her to Ashby Park where, in spite of her little daughter and her luxury, it is plain that there is little true happiness.

Murren, James
In a Strange Land, 1979
Stanley Middleton

His desire to make a success of his art as composer and organist leads him to turn his back on his native Midlands and move to London. Like many of Middleton's characters, he longs for some point of transcendence which will draw him out of everyday compromise and mess.

Musgrave, Sergeant
Sergeant Musgrave's Dance, 1960
John Arden

With three privates under his command, Jack Musgrave arrives in a northern town some time towards the end of the 19th century. His self-directed mission is to move the town to pacifism by showing it the skeleton of one of its own sons, killed in a colonial war. Despite possessing a stern inflexibility and a ready godfearing vocabulary of 'prayer', 'judgement', 'sin' and 'blood', he is unsure what to do next, but an unhealthy fascination with his Gatling gun suggests one option.

Musgrave, Sir Richard
The Lay of the Last Minstrel, 1805
Sir Walter Scott

The English champion, eager to avenge the murder of his brother by the Borderers and the despoliation of his lands by SIR WILLIAM DELORAINE. He is nonetheless killed when LORD CRANSTOUN substitutes himself for the wounded Deloraine in the final duel of honour.

Musgrove, Charles
Persuasion, 1818
Jane Austen

A minor character in the novel, Charles is the unfortunate husband of MARY ELLIOT, and brother to LOUISA MUSGROVE and HENRIETTA MUSGROVE. Good-natured and kind-hearted, but lacking in any great intelligence or strength of character, his only real interest outside his children is sport, and when not engaged in this pursuit he thoughtlessly fritters away his time.

Musgrove, Clement
The Robber Bridegroom, 1942
Eudora Welty

An 'innocent planter, with a bag of gold', who is the good but naive father in the fairy-tale context of the book. He is a 'man of peace', well-intentioned but gullible and superstitious, and given to 'trusting all listening people'. He is generous and kind, and 'would not cheat even a little midge of its pleasures'. He is a believer in the theory that 'all things are double'. His daughter is ROSAMOND MUSGROVE.

Musgrove, Henrietta
Persuasion, 1818
Jane Austen

Younger sister of LOUISA MUSGROVE and CHARLES MUSGROVE, Henrietta is a minor character whose interests are fairly trivial and commonplace. Fashionable, pretty and lively like her sister, she joins with her in making a great fuss over CAPTAIN WENTWORTH, but her pleasant though shallow nature does not make a lasting impression.

Musgrove, Louisa
Persuasion, 1818
Jane Austen

The sister of CHARLES MUSGROVE and HENRIETTA MUSGROVE, Louisa delights with her happy chatter and accomplished social graces. Taking the momentary fancy of CAPTAIN WENTWORTH, she suffers a nasty accident while with him in Lyme Regis, and during her convalescence is wooed and won by his quiet friend Captain Benwick. Pleasant enough, but inconsequential, she has no striking depth of character.

Musgrove, Rosamond
The Robber Bridegroom, 1942
Eudora Welty

The lovely, golden-haired daughter of CLEMENT MUSGROVE, she is 'so beautiful that she keeps the memory of [her father's] first wife alive and evergreen' in his heart. She is 'a great liar', and although she means to be truthful, 'the lies would simply fall out like diamonds or pearls'. She is maltreated by her wicked stepmother SALOME MUSGROVE, but accepts persecution uncomplainingly. She eventually succeeds in cunningly unmasking and marrying her robber-bridegroom, JAMIE LOCKHART.

Musgrove, Salome
The Robber Bridegroom, 1942
Eudora Welty

The second wife of CLEMENT MUSGROVE, and the evil stepmother in the fairy-tale context of the book. Her first husband was murdered by Indians, but she is 'an ugly woman they were all afraid of', and she survived the ordeal. She marries Musgrove, but there is 'no longer anything but ambition left in her destroyed heart'. She is heartless, inflexible and tireless in the pursuit of gratification of her selfish, greedy desires.

Musidorus
The Countess of Pembroke's Arcadia, 1581–4, published 1590
Sir Philip Sidney

A young prince, discovered naked in the sea following the burning of his ship and later revealed to be the nephew of EUARCHUS. By disguising himself as a shepherd, he gains access to the court-in-exile of DUKE BASILIUS, where he joins the family of the herdsman DAMETAS, and falls in love with the duke's daughter PAMELA.

Mutabilitie
The Faerie Queene, 1590–6
Sir Edmund Spenser

A goddess, whose name refers to the way that nothing in the universe is permanent – everything is subject to change. A descendant of the ancient lineage of Titans, she perverts nature by breaking its laws of justice. She confuses right and wrong and, like a curse, wields power over all mortal things.

Muzzlehatch
Titus Alone, 1959
Mervyn Peake

A brooding, bulky figure, with a massive chiselled jaw and a nose like a rudder. He contrives to appear both ragged and regal, with an air of monumental self-assurance and a curious detachment from the world. His manners are rough and ready; his voice imperiously echoing; his manner of speech chaffing and elliptical. He has no desire to be weighed down by anything, least of all an enigma such as TITUS GROAN, but he finds himself drawn to him, and frequently appears from nowhere to pluck him from danger. After the slaughter of his 'zoo', his abstraction turns into an all-encompassing lust for revenge, taking him over the brink of madness.

Mwawate → July

Mweta, President
A Guest of Honour, 1970
Nadine Gordimer

A former revolutionary, he is now president of his independent nation, but has to contend with a rapidly industrializing, western-style country in which his old principles no longer seem to carry any validity. He rapidly turns to the corrupt and violent practices of his colonial predecessors.

Mynhardt, Martin
Rumours of Rain, 1978, originally published in Afrikaans as *Gerugte van reën*, 1978
André Brink

A wealthy Afrikaner with a weak heart and an increasingly apathetic complacency regarding his social role, he is a member of a UN-sponsored mission in London, going glibly through the motions of planning the economic future of a continent in which he is ever more obviously in the minority.

Mysie of the Mill, properly Mysie Happer
The Monastery, 1820
Sir Walter Scott

The daughter of HOB THE MILLER, she is a 'dark-eyed laughter-loving wench, with cherry-cheeks, and a skin as white as her father's finest bolted flour'. Her not entirely refined beauty is refined by the prospect of a handsome dowry.

Mystic, Mr Moley

Melincourt, or Sir Oran Haut-ton, 1817
Thomas Love Peacock

'I am always poetical at breakfast, moral at luncheon, metaphysical at dinner and political at tea', says Mr Mystic. Owner of Cimmerian Lodge and a transcendentalist (based on Coleridge), Mr Mystic speaks in riddles and holds forth in gobbledygook jargon for hours on end. A ridiculous figure, with a veritable scramble of philosophical theories pouring from his mouth, he is described as a 'poeticopolitical, rhapsodicoproasaical, deisidaemoniao-paradoxographical, pseudolatreiological, transcendental meteorosophist'.

Naana
Fragments, 1969
Ayi Kwei Armah

The grandmother of BAAKO ONIPA, she represents strength and stability within a troubled and changing Ghana. It is as if she is the rock around which stormy seas swirl. At times Baako finds the political and cultural problems with which he is confronted overwhelming, and while Naana dreams of success for her grandson, she remains aloof from the daily intrigue and political manoeuvring that characterize modern life. She is essentially a woman of remarkable serenity and wisdom, virtues inherited from an older, tribal way of living. Her traditional piety, sense of community, and social and cultural continuity give her not merely a real emotional tenacity but also a profound symbolic importance.

Nadgett, Mr
Martin Chuzzlewit, 1844
Charles Dickens

The landlord of TOM and RUTH PINCH, he is a very secretive private enquiry agent whom MONTAGUE TIGG hires to investigate policyholders in his fraudulent company. He discovers that JONAS CHUZZLEWIT has tried to poison his father, ANTHONY CHUZZLEWIT, and later that Tigg has been murdered by Jonas.

Nailles, Eliot
Bullet Park, 1969
John Cheever

A chemist who is relatively content with the suburban mores of Bullet Park, and resents people 'always chopping at the suburbs' and their way of life. He is 'incurably' monogamous, sees his wife as the 'keystone of his love of the visible world', speaks to his old dog 'with a tenderness that could seem foolish', and travels to work every day on the train. He 'learns the obsessiveness of suffering' when his son takes ill, and relies increasingly on tranquillizers to carry him through the day. He is singled out as a victim by the psychopathic PAUL HAMMER.

Name, Elsie
Riceyman Steps, 1923
Arnold Bennett

Her existence is miserable, her work drudgery, her rewards minimal, but Elsie's heart overflows with kindness and generosity. General servant to the miserly HENRY and VIOLET EARLFORWARD, she suffers hardship and hunger, but her loyalty is such that she tortures herself with guilt when she yields to temptation and steals food from their meagre kitchen. She acts with instinctive kindness and patience towards those who depend on her, whether invalid lover or dying employer. Her unsophisticated goodness reaches heroic stature as circumstances place almost intolerable burdens on her willing shoulders.

Nan
Little Men, 1871
Jo's Boys, 1886
Louisa M Alcott

Brought to Plumfield as companion to docile DAISY and to provide female influence on the boys, tomboy Nan runs wild. Her huge imagination answers reckless dares: she swaps her necklace for kittens and harnesses the turkeycock. Accepting voluntary confinement of her high spirits, she curbs her frantic desire for entire liberty. Putting this energy to good use, she turns to medicine as a profession and grows into a brave, independent woman worthy of feminist admiration.

Nana
Peter Pan: or The Boy Who Would Not Grow Up, 1904 (play), 1911 (book)
J M Barrie

The DARLINGS' Newfoundland dog and nurse to the children; 'like all treasures she was born to it'. Chained up and unable to prevent the younger Darlings' departure for Never-Never Land, she maintains a vigil with their mother. Even so, 'she is the cynical one, and though custom has made her hang the children's night things on the fire-guard for an airing, she surveys them not hopefully but with some self-contempt'.

Nancanou, Aurore, or de Grapion
The Grandissimes, 1880
George Washington Cable

The impoverished, beautiful widow of a young planter killed in a gambling duel with the irascible AGRICOLA FUSILIER; 'no affair of honor in Louisiana ever left a braver'. She is a granddaughter of one of Louis Quinze's *filles à la cassette*, sent to America as marriage stock, but unwilling to accept her fate passively. Marriage to HONORÉ GRANDISSIME restores her to respectability.

Nancanou, Clotilde, or de Grapion
The Grandissimes, 1880
George Washington Cable

AURORE NANCANOU's daughter, she is no less beautiful than her mother. The two are often mistaken for sisters and, if anything, it is the mother who seems less mature and more coquettish, far more susceptible than the pragmatic Clotilde to the superstitious practices of *voudou*. Clotilde later marries the young Puritan apothecary JOSEPH FROWENFELD.

Nancy
Oliver Twist, 1838
Charles Dickens

A prostitute and thief who works for FAGIN, she is the mistress of BILL SIKES, to whom she remains loyal, despite his brutality. She befriends OLIVER TWIST, proving that 'there was something of the woman's original nature left in her still'. When she reveals to ROSE MAYLIE and MR BROWNLOW what she knows about the plot to defraud Oliver, Fagin tells Bill Sikes, and Sikes murders her.

Nancy
Summer of the Seventeenth Doll, 1955
Ray Lawler

Perhaps the most significant absence in Australian theatre, Nancy creates a sense of impending doom for her old associates by abandoning the group and marrying a local bookseller. In condemning Nancy's defection to the 'respectable' world, OLIVE serves only to hasten the collapse of her bonds with BARNEY IBBOT and ROO WEBBER, who are more prepared (if only slightly) to ˙compromise with the inevitable demands of middle age. Olive also alienates PEARL CUNNINGHAM, who is made to feel a substitute for Nancy, Barney's missing partner. Nancy is continually discussed by the other characters, but most tellingly by EMMA, whose egregious detachment allows her to comment that Nancy has simply been more perspicacious than Olive, having accepted the emotional and economic changes which age imposes.

Nanga, Chief, the Honourable Micah A, MP
A Man of the People, 1966
Chinua Achebe

'The most approachable politician in the country', whose bland populism masks a crudely opportunist nature. Formerly a teacher, he joins the People's Organization Party government on the coat-tails of a financial scandal, during which he assumes the ironic voice of moral outrage.

Nannie → Cutty Sark

Nanson, Phineas
The Biographer's Tale, 2000
A S Byatt

A postgraduate student of literature, small in stature but vast in vocabulary, he delights in rare words such as cryptogamy and Procrustean. But he becomes disenchanted with academic life and yearns for 'things'. Prone to self-doubt – 'I know what I think, I think' – he nevertheless embarks on a new life as a biographer. His subject – another biographer – proves difficult and Nanson is easily distracted.

Napoleon
Animal Farm, 1945
George Orwell

Unlike the other animals on the farm, this pig does not even pay lip-service to the revolutionary ideals of equality; instead he is largely indifferent to the others, concerned only to further his own rise to despotic power, using cruelty wherever necessary. The longer he remains in power, the more corrupt and hypocritical he becomes, luxuriating in his status and authoritarian control, degenerating ultimately into decadence and obsession. In him the revolution turns full circle and is reduced to an exercise in self-promotion.

Napoleon (General Aufsteig)
Back to Methuselah, 1921
George Bernard Shaw

Napoleon, 'the Man of Destiny', earlier reported to be GEN AUFSTEIG, really the Emperor of Turania and 'the greatest military genius of the age', appears in the fourth section of this five-part play. *Tragedy of an Elderly Gentleman* is set on the shore of Galway Bay, Ireland, in 3000AD. Napoleon arrives to consult THE ORACLE. Warfare has made him popular and powerful but in the end it will leave him reviled, weak, perhaps executed. What should he do? The Oracle recommends that he die before the tide turns. She shoots him; he falls, rises and protests vehemently before stalking off.

Narcissa
The Adventures of Roderick Random, 1748
Tobias Smollett

The object of RODERICK RANDOM's affections, she is a stock Smollett beauty in all particulars of white skin, dark ringlets and intelligent accomplishment. The social distance between them is only reduced by Roderick's skill as a poet and Narcissa remains essentially self-absorbed.

Nashe, James
The Music of Chance, 1990
Paul Auster

A fireman who takes to the road and falls in love with his 'new life of freedom and irresponsibility', feeling 'more and more at peace' with himself. His criss-cross driving is essentially an inner journey, until he meets JACK POZZI and fate begins to take a hand. He is trapped in a Kafkaesque nightmare by the eccentric millionaires FLOWERS and STONE, and initially enjoys the removal of all responsibility; gradually, though, he becomes aware that he has given up control of his life to chance, with tragic results.

Nataraj
The Man-Eater of Malgudi, 1961
R K Narayan

Nataraj's small printing works is a congenial rendezvous for friends, and anyone else needing to sit down. A mild, amiable man, brought up never to kill even flies, when the powerful stranger VASU appears he is half-fascinated, half-intimidated by him and agrees to give him 'temporary' accommodation, rent-free, in the attic. But to his horror Vasu, a taxidermist, turns the attic into a charnel-house, filling it with the animals he kills, among them Nataraj's cat. When Nataraj timidly protests, Vasu sardonically reports him to the rent authorities. Terrorized and tragi-comically distraught, Nataraj has his life laid waste by this 'terrible specimen of humanity'.

Nathanael, Sir
Love's Labour's Lost, not later than 1594
William Shakespeare

A curate and friend of the pedant HOLOFERNES. He plays Alexander the Great, rather inappropriately, in the Pageant of the Nine Worthies, which he helped to organize. He despises Constable DULL because the latter 'hath never fed of the dainties that are bred in a book'.

Nawab of Khatm, the
Heat and Dust, 1975
Ruth Prawer Jhabvala

The 35-year-old ruler of a tiny independent state, OLIVIA RIVERS's arrogant Indian lover lives apart from his wife, has a riotous, scandal-ridden past, and is reputedly not too particular about how he gets his money. Having disposed of the family jewels, he is apparently in league with dacoits (armed robbers), receiving a share of their spoils in return for his protection. He is handsome and forceful, but sometimes childish. Bored with palace life, and lacking self-restraint and discipline, he eventually incurs British displeasure and becomes ruler in name only.

Nawnim → Shillingsworth, Norman

Nawratt, Alexander
Capricornia, 1938
Xavier Herbert

One of Port Zodiac's two lawyers, the none-too-honest Nawratt is a powerful and eloquent advocate, but being lazy, vain and a drunkard loses more cases than he wins. Despite this he is still preferred to the feeble HANNIBAL NIBBLESOM, although both are eventually involved, on opposing sides, in the trials of MARK SHILLINGSWORTH and NORMAN SHILLINGSWORTH.

Nazneen
Brick Lane, 2003
Monica Ali

The quiet, passive Nazneen begins her life in Bangladesh before fatalistically entering into an arranged marriage and coming to live in London with her new husband Chanu. Simultaneously overwhelmed by the vibrant alien culture around her and bored by the routine of married life and the restrictions imposed on her as a Muslim woman, she gradually determines to break free of the life prescribed for her. Her subsequent affair with a charismatic younger man from the immigrant community is a transforming experience that makes her realize that she can control her own destiny.

Neckett
Bleak House, 1853
Charles Dickens

A sheriff's officer employed to arrest the debtor, HAROLD SKIMPOLE, who refers to him as 'Coavinses', the name of the sponging house that employs him. When he dies and leaves his three young children on their own, the eldest child, CHARLOTTE NECKETT, goes out to work in order to support her siblings.

Neckett, Charlotte
Bleak House, 1853
Charles Dickens

Called 'Charley', she is the eldest daughter of NECKETT and, although only 13 or 14 herself, supports her younger siblings by charring and washing after their father dies. Briefly a servant to the SMALLWEEDS, she becomes ESTHER SUMMERSON's devoted maid and, catching smallpox from JO, transmits it to Esther. She eventually marries a local miller.

Nectabanus
The Talisman: A Tale of the Crusaders, 1825
Sir Walter Scott

A dwarf of surpassing ugliness, who sweeps the chapel at Mount Carmel. He dresses in red samite with a white silk sash and a hat mounted with peacock feathers, but the richness of his clothes only serves to heighten his fearsome appearance. It is Nectabanus who brings news of Conrade, Marquis of Montserrat's assassination.

Needle
'The Portobello Road', in *The Go-Away Bird and Other Stories*, 1958
Muriel Spark

A ghost of Scottish origin, whose name derives from her literally finding a needle in a haystack in her youth. She always had a sense of being special and wanted to write about life, but was prevented by her perfectionism. She was thus irritated when people regarded her as lucky because of the ease with which she drifted along. A Catholic convert, she now haunts her murderer in the Portobello Road.

Nell, Little → Little Nell

Nellie
The Dressmaker, 1973
Beryl Bainbridge

An exceptionally pious yet giving elderly aunt who has taken on the role of mother for her demanding family. Inside her fragile and floundering body she struggles against a rising fear that no one can take care of things the way she does. She has strong moral convictions, yet never raises her voice. With baited breath she awaits the long journey of death. Her philosophy of life is 'Never sit down on someone else's lav and never eat a shop bought meat pie'.

Nenna
Offshore, 1979
Penelope Fitzgerald

Separated from her husband, with a family dependent on her, Nenna is confused and in need of support. A caring woman and committed mother, she is nevertheless rather offbeat, capable of mood swings and extreme rudeness. Part of her wants the conventional life to go well, and another part is rebellious, looking for excitement and thrills. At best, she is unpredictable, at worst, volatile.

Nerissa
The Merchant of Venice, 1594/5
William Shakespeare

Maid and personal attendant to PORTIA, she is also her friend, confidante and adviser, particularly in the matter of potential husbands. She replicates Portia's style and movements, assisting her in the court scene, falling in love with BASSANIO's ally, GRATIANO, and adding her own witty and lucid commentary throughout the play.

Neroni, Signora Madeline Vesey
Barchester Towers, 1857
Anthony Trollope

The beautiful daughter of Dr Stanhope, an absentee Barchester clergyman. Her romantic escapades in Italy culminate in an unfortunate marriage and her being crippled, after which she returns to Barchester with her family. 'A basilisk from whom an ardent lover of beauty could make no escape', she heartlessly lures men into her traps for her amusement. Although affected and cynical, she is also courageous, perceptive and sometimes on the side of good.

Nessim
Justine, 1957, and elsewhere in *The Alexandria Quartet*, 1968
Lawrence Durrell

Sarcastically nicknamed 'Prince', he is a wealthy Copt, unusually faithful to his wife JUSTINE, a fact that particularly puzzles the traders of Alexandria. He had been educated in Germany and England, his German experience encouraging his metaphysical interests, while 'Oxford had made him donnish and had only succeeded in developing his philosophic bent to the point where he was incapable of practising the art he most loved, painting'.

Nettie
The Color Purple, 1982
Alice Walker

A questioning and perceptive woman, the sister of CELIE, Nettie is representative of Celie's repressed freedom and becomes a second mother to her sister's lost children. Forced to abandon Celie, she embarks on a voyage of self-discovery. Realizing that 'the little I knew about my own self wouldn't have filled a thimble', she returns with a self-possession and knowledge of her origins that ironically match the changes in her sister.

Neville
The Waves, 1931
Virginia Woolf

He is uncomplicated, 'one and simple', an unpretentious man in a pretentious world. At ease with himself, he enjoys solitude but at the same time is not unaware of the needs and suffering of others.

Neville, Constance
She Stoops to Conquer, 1773
Oliver Goldsmith

The niece of DOROTHY HARDCASTLE, Constance has lived with her aunt's family since her father died. Her collection of jewellery means she is a rich woman, but the jewels are presently in Mrs Hardcastle's custody and, in order to maintain any peace at all, Constance has had to 'stoop to dissimulation' and allow her aunt to imagine that she loves her cousin, TONY LUMPKIN. In fact, she loves GEORGE HASTINGS. In comparison with KATE HARDCASTLE, Constance might seem rather a bland character, yet her courage and determination bring their rewards in the form of Hastings, her wealth and her independence from the Hardcastles.

Nevis, Ben (Hector MacDonald of Ben Nevis, Glenbogle, Glenbristle, Strathdiddle, Strathdun, Loch Hoch and Loch Hoo)
The Monarch of the Glen, 1941, et seq
Compton Mackenzie

As the title suggests, Mackenzie's comic Highland chieftain is treated with more irony and less respect than he obviously considers his due. Scottish only by a detail of genealogy, he was educated at an English public school and depends in his lairdship on a wealthy wife. His suzerainty is limited to passing judgement on nit-picking local issues and there is something of the tin-pot in his manner.

Newberry, Lizzy
'The Distracted Preacher', in *Wessex Tales: Strange, Lively and Commonplace*, 1888
Thomas Hardy

A young woman who enjoys excitement and adventure, Lizzy suffers from no moral scruples about being involved in the business of smuggling but rather relishes it as a welcome diversion from an otherwise humdrum existence. Although she has no regard for authority or legality, her spirit and self-possession in the face of danger make her an appealing character.

Newcome, Barnes
The Newcomes, 1853-5
W M Thackeray

ETHEL NEWCOME's brother, he is a mean-spirited and snobbish cynic, in every regard the true descendant of his grandmother LADY KEW. His marriage is a disaster, and his treatment of his wife borders on the criminal.

Newcome, Clemency
The Battle of Life, 1846
Charles Dickens

The cheerful but awkward servant to DR ANTHONY JEDDLER. Scrubbed, neat and infinitely loyal, she marries BENJAMIN BRITAIN and has three children.

Newcome, Clive
The Newcomes, 1853-5
W M Thackeray

The novel's central character, he is a likeable young man, his father's only son, who returns from India and falls in love with his cousin ETHEL NEWCOME. Social plotters surround them, however, and he sees too straight to withstand their machinations. Circumstances force him into an unsuitable marriage with the pretty but insubstantial ROSEY MACKENZIE, and they drift into poverty.

Newcome, Col Thomas
The Newcomes, 1853–5
W M Thackeray
The eldest son of the founding father of the dynasty, and half-brother of SIR BRIAN NEWCOME and HOBSON NEWCOME, he is an unassuming soldierly man of modest disposition and ambitions. He has lived most of his adult life in India but never quite gets the hang of English society on his return. Bankrupt, he is hounded into the Greyfriars almshouse by MRS MACKENZIE.

Newcome, Ethel
The Newcomes, 1853–5
W M Thackeray
SIR BRIAN NEWCOME's daughter and LADY KEW's granddaughter, she is turned into a pawn in the complex and cynical marriage-game of London society. Prevented from marrying CLIVE NEWCOME, she lurches from one unworkable relationship to another, before finally (and presumably, because Thackeray does not say so with any certainty) marrying the widowed Clive. Kind, imaginative and unworldly, she finds reality a bruising business.

Newcome, Hobson
The Newcomes, 1853–5
W M Thackeray
COL THOMAS NEWCOME's wealthy half-brother, he is a successful banker, along with his brother SIR BRIAN NEWCOME. He is, in the view of MAJOR PENDENNIS, 'a good fellow, but a vulgar fellow', with a wife to match. He votes with the Reformers, noisily unmasking traitors and thundering at aristocratic corruption.

Newcome, Sir Brian, Bart, MP
The Newcomes, 1853–5
W M Thackeray
'He looked like the "Portrait of a Gentleman at the Exhibition", as the worthy is represented; dignified in attitude, bland, unsmiling and statesmanlike.' COL THOMAS NEWCOME's half-brother, he sits in the House with the mild Conservatives, and at home follows High Church principles. He and his brother HOBSON NEWCOME are partners in Newcome Brothers merchant bank.

Newhouse, Michael
The Memoirs of a Peon, 1965
Frank Sargeson
A retired Lothario, 'stung by the snake of memory', and living almost exclusively in a past that for drama and emotional charge far outstrips the bland neutrality and sterility of the present.

Newman, Christopher
The American, 1877
Henry James
His name (with its allusion to Columbus) and the novel's title suggest that he is to be seen as an archetype of the self-made New World man,

open-minded but culturally unprofound, tangled in the deeper cultural roots of the aristocratic Europeans among whom he now lives.

Newsome, Chad
The Ambassadors, 1903
Henry James
The ne'er-do-well son of new Massachusetts money, he has fallen under the spell of a Parisian lady, an association that has led to him overstaying a 'finishing' tour of Europe and thus neglecting his responsibilities to the family firm. Europe has put a surprising polish on his rather raw American manners and his responses seem surprisingly mature and measured rather than boyish and spontaneous.

Newsome, Mrs
The Ambassadors, 1903
Henry James
A redoubtable Massachusetts widow, living off a fortune made on some unmentionable domestic object. Described by another character as a *'moral* swell', she is LAMBERT STRETHER's sponsor and de facto employer on his little magazine. Using that association, she sends him to Europe to track down her errant son. It is clear that marriage is also on the cards, though Strether's alacrity in accepting the mission would indicate that he is in flight from the suggestion.

Newson, Elizabeth-Jane
The Mayor of Casterbridge, 1886
Thomas Hardy
'A dumb, deep-feeling, grey-eyed creature', Elizabeth-Jane Newson accompanies her mother to Casterbridge where she is adopted by MICHAEL HENCHARD, who mistakenly believes her to be his natural daughter. She is motivated by high moral principles, and displays modesty, thrift and good sense in spite of having to cope with the death of her mother and rejection by her stepfather.

Ng, Adolph
The Redundancy of Courage, 1991
Timothy Mo
A young, homosexual, Chinese hotelier, he is the narrator of the novel. His homeland, a remote island north of Australia, has been invaded by right-wing neighbours. Likeable although unashamedly selfish and cowardly, Adolph is transformed under duress from an indolent, university-educated member of the leftist intelligentsia into a comically reluctant and inept guerilla-fighter, then, later, a servant to an enemy colonel. He is a born survivor, wryly able to accommodate these changes of heart as, for him, no fate is worse than death. He graphically relates the horrific events he encounters, but with a perky, insouciant black humour.

Ngotho
Weep Not, Child, 1964
Ngugi wa Thiong'o
A symbol of the disinheritance of the Gikuyu people, who have been robbed of their land and their cultural traditions by the colonizing powers. He claims an almost mystical connection to the land and ways of his ancestors.

Nibblesom, Hannibal
Capricornia, 1938
Xavier Herbert

A diligent man of strong moral character but so lacking in personality and so ineffective as an advocate that people who fail to secure the services of Port Zodiac's other lawyer, ALEXANDER NAWRATT, usually prefer to defend themselves. Nibblesom therefore works mainly as a solicitor, or as a last-resort counsel when Nawratt is too drunk to function. But he proves unexpectedly resourceful when MARK SHILLINGSWORTH, under his assumed name of Jack Ramble, is sued by the Labour Union's council.

Nicely Nicely Jones
Take it Easy, 1938
Damon Runyon

An unlucky marriage to a money-grabbing murderess may be responsible for his huge capacity for eating, but even that voracious appetite for food is overwhelmed by new-found love. Consequently, he can only stand by and offer advice when the whole of Broadway devotes its energies and cash to the great eating contest between Miss Violette Shumberger and Mr Joel Duffle. However, this role is crucial in determining the contest's outcome, and the experience teaches Nicely Nicely that combining love and food is to be preferred to being content with love only.

Nicholas and David
Elidor, 1968
Alan Garner

Nicholas, the eldest of the Watson children, takes his position very seriously. He and David bicker constantly, jostling for supremacy. They both tend to take a rational view of the events which lead them to the strange world of Elidor, and try to convince ROLAND that they are the victims of a mass hallucination. For unless Nicholas sees, he does not believe; he would rather describe unusually-linked events as 'coincidences'. David, however, has the grace to accept the possibility that Roland is right, and with his more practical mind provides a possible explanation for the unnerving effects of static electricity that pursue them wherever the Elidor Treasures are kept.

Nicolas
One for the Road, 1984
Harold Pinter

A high-ranking if heavy drinking State-employed interrogator, a man of discernment and erudition, Nicolas is also one of considerable brutality. Yet he argues that his deep love for family, state and country justifies the tortures and indignities he inflicts upon those he deems to have opposed the principles in which both he and the state believe. 'God', he declares, 'speaks through me', and his job, therefore, is simply 'to keep the world clean for God'. A cold-hearted tyrant, he nevertheless depends upon his victims for intellectual, and possibly sexual, gratification. Apparently lacking any life outside his job, he craves the respect, even love, of those he seeks to destroy.

Nick
Who's Afraid of Virginia Woolf?, 1962
Edward Albee

A young instructor at the same college as GEORGE, he appears to stand for all the 'modern' values – science, extreme rationalism, an escape from history – that George rejects. Flirting with MARTHA while his own wife HONEY lies upstairs sick and drunk, he is drawn into a violently cathartic confrontation that changes all their lives. Passive as he is, his name betrays the possibility that even he is a minor devil in this domestic purgatory.

Nickleby, Kate
Nicholas Nickleby, 1839
Charles Dickens

The beautiful sister of NICHOLAS NICKLEBY, she is apprenticed to MADAME MANTALINI by RALPH NICKLEBY. He introduces her to his dupe, LORD FREDERICK VERISOPHT, who falls in love, and to the lecherous SIR MULBERRY HAWK. She and her mother, MRS NICKLEBY, are rescued from Ralph's influence by Nicholas, and with the help of the CHEERYBLES, she eventually marries their nephew, Frank.

Nickleby, Mrs
Nicholas Nickleby, 1839
Charles Dickens

The foolish and loquacious widowed mother of NICHOLAS and KATE NICKLEBY, she is 'a well-meaning woman enough, but weak, withal'. She is characterized by her inaccurate memory and irrelevant and inconsequential conversation.

Nickleby, Nicholas
Nicholas Nickleby, 1839
Charles Dickens

With his sister, KATE, and his impoverished widowed mother, MRS NICKLEBY, he is forced to ask for assistance from his rich but evil uncle, RALPH NICKLEBY. Leaving his mother and sister under the apparent protection of Ralph, who hates him, he goes to Yorkshire to teach at WACKFORD SQUEERS's Dotheboys Hall, where he befriends poor SMIKE. After he thrashes Squeers in front of the boys, he travels with Smike to London, where he briefly teaches French to the daughters of MR and MRS KENWIGS. Meeting VINCENT CRUMMLES, he joins the company as an actor and playwright under the stage name of Mr Johnson, while Smike is made an actor. Returning to London to protect his sister from the unwanted attentions of two of Ralph's cronies, he confronts his uncle and punishes him. Accidentally meeting one of the CHEERYBLEs, he is given a job in their firm and falls in love with MADELINE BRAY. He rescues her on the day of her wedding to ARTHUR GRIDE and, with the patronage of the Cheerybles, eventually marries her and becomes a partner in the firm of Cheeryble Brothers.

Nickleby, Ralph
Nicholas Nickleby, 1839
Charles Dickens

The villainous uncle of NICHOLAS and KATE NICKLEBY, he is a rich but miserly moneylender with many debtors in his clutches, including WALTER BRAY. With ARTHUR GRIDE, he plots to have Gride marry MADELINE BRAY, but is thwarted when her father dies on the morning of the wedding. He refuses to help his sister-in-law and her children, making Kate and Nicholas work to support themselves and trying to exploit Kate's beauty by enticing his debauched cronies. He becomes a sworn enemy of Nicholas, who repeatedly defeats his illegal schemes. Exposed as a villain, and learning that the dead boy whom he long persecuted, SMIKE, is his own son, he hangs himself in despair.

Nicolas
Plagued by the Nightingale, 1931
Kay Boyle

Having returned with his American wife BRIDGET to his hated family in Brittany, because he is suffering from a hereditary bone disease, Nicolas is consumed by bitterness and self-pity. He spends his time being unpleasant to almost everyone and assuming that someone should supply him with money. His parents continually urge him to father a child, but he does not want to pass on the disease.

Nicole
Love Always, 1985
Ann Beattie

Nicole plays the part of a 14-year-old alcoholic in a television soap opera, a role that seems to sit comfortably alongside her aunt LUCY SPENSER's job of writing and replying to fictional letters for a magazine problem page. It turns out, though, that Nicole's fantasized alienation takes her closer to a real world than Lucy's imaginative detachment, and she acts as a powerful catalyst for change.

Nidderdale, Lord
The Way We Live Now, 1875
Anthony Trollope

A cousin of the DUKE OF OMNIUM, and AUGUSTUS MELMOTTE's preferred suitor for his daughter MARIE MELMOTTE. She, however, prefers SIR FELIX CARBURY, and attempts to elope rather than marry Nidderdale. 'He had a commonplace, rough face, with a turn-up nose, high cheek bones, no especial complexion, sandy-coloured whiskers, and bright laughing eyes.' He eventually marries another woman.

Nightingale, Bernard
Arcadia, 1993
Tom Stoppard

A clever, ambitious, self-seeking and querulous Sussex don, Nightingale is visiting Sidley Park, a large country house, intent upon proving his theory that Byron murdered the minor poet Ezra Chater during a duel in the grounds. 'Arrogant, greedy and reckless', according to HANNAH JARVIS, whose research into the gardens he condescendingly dismisses as 'trivial', he is bewildered that she resists his advances and mortified when his theory, which has been widely publicized and upon which he had built dreams of a glamorous future, proves unfounded.

Nikita (Nector)
Under Western Eyes, 1911
Joseph Conrad

A member of the revolutionary group to which RAZUMOV ultimately confesses. He is the most brutish and desperate of their number, and exacts arbitrary physical revenge on Razumov for the betrayal of VICTOR HALDIN by bursting his eardrums. This 'arch-slayer of gendarmes', however, proves to have killed in both camps, and is revealed as 'a traitor himself, a betrayer – a spy!'

Nilsson, Axel
A Fairly Honourable Defeat, 1970
Iris Murdoch

An old friend of JULIUS KING and a friend and Civil Service colleague of RUPERT FOSTER, Nilsson lives with Rupert's younger brother, SIMON FOSTER. Claiming that he is not ashamed of his homosexuality and would keep his relationships just as private if he were heterosexual, when accused of hypocrisy Axel confesses that he is afraid Whitehall will find him out. A clever, dry, rather silent man, undemonstrative and sometimes gloomy and morose, he tends to bully and nag the flamboyant, extrovert Simon, somewhat cruelly exposing his intellectual inadequacies in public, although he genuinely loves him.

Nina
The Flight from the Enchanter, 1956
Iris Murdoch

A Chelsea dressmaker financed by MISCHA FOX, and an 'incidental casualty' of his scheming, Nina is described contemptuously by ANNETTE COCKEYNE as 'some sort of refugee'. She is small and patient, good-tempered, humble and discreet. Her needlework is exquisite and she is ambitious to expand her business. But her hopeless devotion to Fox makes her his lonely, isolated slave. Finally realizing her position, she dreams of escape to Australia, whilst fearing deportation to Eastern Europe, and tries unsuccessfully to enlist ROSA KEEPE's aid.

Nioche, Noémie
The American, 1877
Henry James

A humbly-born copyist of paintings in Paris, where her father is CHRISTOPHER NEWMAN's French teacher. Cynical and manipulative, she stands both by profession and by instinct at one remove from things, attracting customers by her histrionic performances in the Louvre: 'The cultivation of the fine arts seemed to necessitate, to her mind, a great deal of by-play, a great standing off with folded arms and head drooping from side to side, stroking of a dimpled chin with a dimpled hand, fumbling in disordered tresses for wandering hair-pins'.

Niphet, Alice
Gryll Grange, 1860–1
Thomas Love Peacock

Pale, statuesque and athletic, Alice Niphet is an heiress for whom 'the artificial, the false, in any degree, is impossible'. Her accomplishments, her modesty, her unusual behaviour, her suppressed passion and generally mysterious personality make her a source of fascination for LORD RICHARD CURRYFIN, her suitor.

Nipper, Susan
Dombey and Son, 1848
Charles Dickens

FLORENCE DOMBEY's devoted maid, a 'short, brown, womanly girl of fourteen'. When she uses her sharp tongue to tell MR PAUL DOMBEY that he is mistreating his daughter, he dismisses her. She afterwards marries MR TOOTS, who considers her 'a most extraordinary woman'.

Nirdlinger, Phyllis
Double Indemnity, 1944
James M Cain

A former nurse specializing in pulmonary diseases, she is a mass killer who can discuss murder as 'casually as if it was a little trip to the mountains'. A blue-eyed blonde, her sweet face and reasonable manner disguise a cold, calculating mind that remains one step ahead of her enemies as she concludes a series of lucrative and seemingly perfect crimes.

Nixon, Cristal
Redgauntlet, 1824
Sir Walter Scott

Grizzled and muscular, with disconcertingly even white teeth, he is the villainous lieutenant and aide-de-camp of MR HERRIES OF BIRRENSWORK. He betrays the Jacobite plotters to the English garrison at Carlisle and pays with his life.

Nixon, Mr
'Hugh Selwyn Mauberley', 1920
Ezra Pound

A hard-headed writer of the 1890s, said to be based on Arnold Bennett, who dispenses solidly practical advice to tyro hacks from 'the cream gilded cabin of his steam yacht'. He suggests buttering up reviewers, constant self-promotion and always demanding an advance on royalties; 'And give up verse, my boy,/ There's nothing in it.'

Nnu Ego
The Joys of Motherhood, 1979
Buchi Emecheta

Predictably, perhaps, the 'joys' of her married life and motherhood are somewhat attenuated. A simple village girl, brought to Lagos with her new husband, she discovers that she has been reduced to the status of dispensable chattel, easily set aside when her man tires of her.

Noddy
Little Noddy Goes to Toyland, 1949, et seq
Enid Blyton

A little wooden man, with a funny nodding head and bright blue bead eyes. Soon after he is made he runs away, and meets BIG EARS the brownie who befriends him and takes him to Toyland. He soon chooses some smart new clothes: a red shirt and blue trousers, a yellow kerchief and belt, and a little blue hat with a bell on top. Noddy is not at all clever and knows almost nothing about life in Toyland, but he is funny and friendly, good at making up songs, and often quite brave. Big Ears tells him he must earn money to buy the things he likes, so he gets a yellow and red car with a loud horn and runs a taxi service for the other toys. He has only one enemy: Mr Plod, a grumpy old policeman.

Noggs, Newman
Nicholas Nickleby, 1839
Charles Dickens

A down-at-heels former gentleman, he is the confidential clerk of RALPH NICKLEBY, whom he despises. He befriends NICHOLAS NICKLEBY and helps him to expose Ralph's evil schemes by spying on him. With the CHEERYBLEs, he takes pleasure in finally confronting and denouncing Ralph, and he spends his last days happily in a country cottage near the home of Nicholas and his family.

Nokomis
The Song of Hiawatha, 1855
Henry Wadsworth Longfellow

A beautiful woman who falls to Earth from the moon in the form of a star. She gives birth to a daughter, WENONAH, whom she warns, in vain, to beware of MUDJEKEEWIS. Nokomis brings up the resulting grandson, HIAWATHA, in her old age, and tends to fuss about him.

Nolan, Des
Rusty Bugles, 1948
Sumner Locke Elliott

An Australian soldier, he is nicknamed 'the Gig Ape' (meaning a fool) because he has allegedly gone 'troppo' (ie mad) owing to prolonged boredom in a wartime ordnance depot in the remote Northern Territory. He seems no madder than most of his colleagues, and although he is the butt of some jokes, he also makes plenty himself. His interest in 'pervy' books and films starring glamorous actresses evidently derives from sexual deprivation; like his fellows, he has been waiting a long time to be relieved.

Nolan, Jim
In Dubious Battle, 1936
John Steinbeck

A young Californian who joins the Communist Party in California after the ruin of his family and makes common cause with the striking fruit pickers. When he is killed during a violent strike which he is leading, his corpse assumes an ironically Christ-like significance to his comrades.

Nolasco, Wallace
The Monkey King, 1979
Timothy Mo

Having been brought into an arranged marriage with May Ling, the daughter of MR POON's second concubine, he is initially seen as a victim of circumstances beyond his control. At Robinson Path, his new home, he enters into a subtle power struggle in order to better his standing in a household dominated by the tyrannical Mr Poon. Finally, he is set up as a scapegoat in a government corruption scandal and exiled to an obscure village. Here, he creates for himself a minor empire, utilizing a half-completed engineering degree to remove floodwater from the village's farmland and creating a viable tourist business from some remaining floodwater. Recalled to the city, he becomes Mr Poon's only viable successor, and takes over the family business on Poon's death. Although ostensibly Cantonese, Wallace is ever the outsider, beause of his Portuguese stock. Like the monkey king of the Chinese myth, he rises to power through sheer resourcefulness.

Nonno (Jonathan Coffin)
The Night of the Iguana, 1961
Tennessee Williams

A minor poet, travelling with his granddaughter in Mexico. At 92 he is a man of 'disgraceful longevity and temporary decrepitude' who, throughout the play, attempts to complete his last poem, declaiming fragments of it in counterpoint to the anguished conversations of the other characters. Finally, he achieves his goal and dies, leaving his granddaughter, HANNAH JELKES, alone.

Noongar
Wild Cat Falling, 1965
Mudrooroo, formerly Colin Johnson

He stands for the old way of the Aborigines, the rootedness and moral certainty that the nameless central character, ANON, has lost. Through their encounters Noongar infuses the young man with a new sense of purpose and of his place in the scheme of things.

Noorak
Long Live Sandawara, 1979
Mudrooroo, formerly Colin Johnson

The central opposition in this work is between a young, secularized and rather rootless man and an older figure who is steeped in Aboriginal ways. Noorak has witnessed the struggles of the legendary Sandawara and he uses these tales to inspire the young ALAN with a new sense of cultural purpose and personal wholeness.

Nora
Monkey Grip, 1977
Helen Garner

She contrasts sharply with her junkie boyfriend JAVO in that her love is unconditional and unstinted, and is involved in no computation of personal profit and loss. Only in the company of other women does she feel any substantial sense of individual self.

Norman
The Norman Conquests, 1973 (*Table Manners, Living Together, Round and Round the Garden*)
Alan Ayckbourn

Norman, an amiable but sardonic and immoral assistant librarian, is married to Ruth, an ambitious businesswoman. Having planned a weekend in East Grinstead with one sister-in-law, the untidy, desperately lonely Annie, he makes advances towards another, the manically-ordered, sexually-repressed Sarah. Norman provokes anger and desire in women, in-comprehension and irritation in men. Rico-cheting from one woman to another, he is eventually rejected by all of them. 'I only wanted to make you happy', he declares, genuinely hurt.

Norman, Alan
The Dog Beneath the Skin, 1935
W H Auden and Christopher Isherwood

A young man from the village of Pressan Ambo,

who is chosen by lots to search for and restore Iris Crewe's missing brother, the baronet SIR FRANCIS CREWE. In return, he is promised Iris's hand in marriage. If Honeypot Hall is the Grail, Alan is a bumpkinish Quester, a holy fool charged with the restoration of fertility to a barren land.

Norna of the Fitful Head, properly Ulla Troil
The Pirate, 1821
Sir Walter Scott

A mysterious kinswoman of BRENDA and MINNA TROIL, she is a wild visionary, driven to the point of madness by secret griefs. It is revealed that the pirate CLEMENT CLEVELAND is her natural son by BASIL MERTOUN.

Norris, Arthur
Mr Norris Changes Trains, 1935
Christopher Isherwood

William Bradshaw, a left-wing hopeful writer and the narrator of the novel, meets Mr Norris in a train to Berlin in the late 1920s. Arthur Norris is a gentleman by birth, but one who has been reduced to blackmail, theft and fraud to maintain the lifestyle to which he is accustomed. Sexually unorthodox and emotionally vulnerable, he conceals his baldness by a wig and proclaims himself to be a communist. But in fact he is a double agent, a shadowy figure in the political and criminal underworld. Yet, for all his corruption, there is an engaging, roguish quality about him.

Norris, Mrs
Mansfield Park, 1814
Jane Austen

The sister of LADY BERTRAM and MRS PRICE, Mrs Norris is a woman preoccupied with rank, status, money and gossip, whose snobbish allegiance to Lady Bertram belies the caring image she tries to nurture. She cloaks selfishness in epithets of generosity and patronizing benevolence, and enjoys nothing better than levelling her particularly virulent invective against anyone outside her immediate family.

North, Abe
Tender is the Night, 1934
F Scott Fitzgerald

An alcoholic composer who is part of DICK and NICOLE DIVER's fashionable set. He is physically awkward, but has a cutting if idiosyncratic sense of humour, and an ironic view of life. He is witty and sharp, and has a tendency to bait the people around him. His drinking takes its physical toll, and he is given up as a hopeless case by Dick.

North, Rev James
His Natural Life, serialized 1870–2; as *For the Term of His Natural Life*, 1874
Marcus Clarke

Alcoholic chaplain at Bathurst, said to be modelled on one Thomas Rogers. He recounts the conditions and fate of the convicts and later saves RICHARD DEVINE.

Northumberland, Lady

Henry IV Part II, 1597/8
William Shakespeare

Although she has lost her favourite son because of her husband's failure to take an active part in the rebellion against HENRY IV, Lady Northumberland is concerned in case she loses another loved member of her family. She therefore advises her husband, HENRY PERCY, EARL OF NORTHUMBERLAND, to go to Scotland until he has sufficient support to take part in another action against the king.

Nostromo (Fidanza, Gian' Battista)

Nostromo, 1904
Joseph Conrad

The captain of the dock workers in Sulaco. He is Italian by birth, and is a charismatic and courageous man who is likened to a magnificent animal, 'handsome, robust and supple'. He has a volatile temperament, and is subject to impulsive, unconsidered behaviour, although he can also be shrewd. He accepts no responsibility beyond gratification of his own immediate desires, and is totally obsessed with his image and reputation. He undertakes the 'most famous and desperate affair' of his life in fleeing with the silver, largely so that he will continue to be well thought of, but it is the cause of his undoing.

Nubbles, Kit (Christopher)

The Old Curiosity Shop, 1841
Charles Dickens

The 'shambling, awkward' shop-boy at the Old Curiosity Shop, and the devoted friend of LITTLE NELL. After GRANDFATHER and Little Nell set off on their wanderings, he is employed by MR and MRS GARLAND. Through the plotting of SALLY and SAMPSON BRASS and DANIEL QUILP, he is wrongly convicted of theft, but the testimony of THE MARCHIONESS proves his innocence and prevents his being transported. With Mr Garland and the Single Gentleman, he goes in search of Little Nell and her Grandfather, but Nell dies before they find her. He marries Mr and Mrs Garland's housemaid, BARBARA. His mother, Mrs Nubbles, is a devoted parishioner of the dissenting chapel, Little Bethel.

Nugent, Grace

The Absentee, in *Tales of Fashionable Life*, 1812
Maria Edgeworth

The cousin of young LORD COLAMBRE, who loves her in preference to the drab heiress his mother has chosen for him. She does not seem quite suited to London society. She is 'beautiful – in elegant and dignified simplicity – thoughtless of herself – yet with a look of thought, and with an air of melancholy, which accorded exactly with [Colambre's] own feelings'. There is an old ballad extolling the virtues of one Gracey or Gracee Nugent.

Nunn, Rhoda

The Odd Women, 1893
George Gissing

There is a none-too-subtle pun in her surname, for this representative of New Womanhood is implicitly forced to renounce her sexual needs and expectations in order to fulfil her feminist ideals. Her devil's advocate is EVERARD BARFOOT, who leaves her in no doubt about the political economy of contemporary marriage.

Nupkins, George

Pickwick Papers, 1837
Charles Dickens

The self-important Mayor of Ipswich. He first convicts SAMUEL PICKWICK, TRACY TUPMAN and SAM WELLER for breach of peace in the matter of PETER MAGNUS and Miss Witherfield's bedroom, but then quashes the convictions when Pickwick helps him to get rid of his unwanted houseguest, ALFRED JINGLE.

Nur

In Custody, 1984
Anita Desai

India's greatest Urdu poet, now white-bearded, dissolute and near-senile, lives in the noisy heart of New Delhi. He is surrounded by equally dissolute, quasi-literary 'clowns, jokers and jugglers', and is ruthlessly manipulated and browbeaten by his warring wife. Appalled, DEVEN, his fervent disciple, observes that the slovenly Nur is anything but dignified and impressive. But Nur nevertheless retains the power to dazzle and enchant him with his sometimes still resonant, authoritative voice and presence. Nur's sweeping efforts to reassert and financially exploit his illustrious reputation prove catastrophic for the luckless Deven.

Nurse

Romeo and Juliet, 1591–6
William Shakespeare

Before Juliet meets ROMEO, and in the early days of their relationship, Nurse is the most important person in her young mistress's life, taking over the mothering role that LADY CAPULET abandoned shortly after Juliet's birth. Her language is frequently bawdy, no matter what the company, and she cooperates in Juliet's plans to meet Romeo because she believes their friendship is harmless. However, after PARIS's offer, which she deems more suitable, she is quick to try to break up the lovers. As a result she loses her influence over Juliet, who rejects her interference.

Nurse, the (Susan 'Sweetie' Simpkins)

Too True to be Good, 1932
George Bernard Shaw

The Nurse is a petty criminal who, in association with THE BURGLAR, plans to rob THE PATIENT of a pearl necklace. When caught in the act, the three of them decide to sell the jewels and travel on the proceeds, the Nurse, whose name is Susan Simpkins, and is known as 'Sweetie', adopting the alias of the Countess Valbrioni. In this surrealist fantasy, the Nurse represents sex, the Burglar intellect and the Patient money.

Nym

The Merry Wives of Windsor, 1597
Henry V, 1599
William Shakespeare

An incorrigible rogue, Nym reluctantly takes to

soldiering in Henry V's (HENRY, PRINCE OF WALES) wars in France. A man of few words, he prefers to keep his own company, but when he does talk he is bad-tempered, foul-mouthed and aggressive, though his threats are empty for he is basically a coward. He loses his betrothed, MISTRESS QUICKLY, to PISTOL and, although there is a duel, Nym is largely apathetic about the matter. A thief throughout, he is hanged, perhaps for the same crime as BARDOLPH.

Oak, Gabriel
Far from the Madding Crowd, 1874
Thomas Hardy

Gabriel Oak occupies a unique social position in the novel between the land-owning classes and the unsophisticated rustics. A solid and reliable man, he is unruffled by disaster and gifted with the ability to overcome worldly problems, achieving a quiet dignity. Although he sees himself as 'only an every day sort of man', he proves himself to be brave, kind and utterly unselfish as he acts as BATHSHEBA EVERDENE's conscience and protector. His lack of self-worth comes close to excluding him from any personal happiness, but in the end his dependability wins the day.

Oakenshield, Thorin → Thorin Oakenshield

Oakhurst, John
'The Outcasts of Poker Flat', in *The Luck of Roaring Camp and Other Sketches*, 1870
Bret Harte

A calm, handsome gambler who is expelled from Poker Flat, a settlement in the American West, with three others who have incurred the disapproval of respectable citizens. Philosophical, generous and 'studiously neat' in his black clothes, he stands by the others when they are all trapped by snow, his self-possession and self-sacrifice setting them an example.

Oakley, Dorinda
Barren Ground, 1902
Ellen Glasgow

Through the land of the American South, Dorinda seeks to complete her all-consuming project: liberation from, and revenge against, male abuse of her body and emotions. Seduced, pregnant and abandoned, 'she could never be broken while the vein of iron held in her soul'. Her Presbyterian conscience, which foregrounds and privileges fortitude, endurance and self-reliance, leads her to purify her body and make money. But having achieved this, she sinks into a pattern of dreary habitual conduct and lacks happiness.

Oakley, Tom (MisterTom)
Goodnight MisterTom, 1981
Michelle Magorian

The Mister Tom of the title, Tom Oakley is a widower and is set in his ways until he starts to re-evaluate his life following the unexpected arrival of evacuee WILLIE BEECH. A man of average height, 'in Willie's eyes he was a towering giant with skin like coarse, wrinkled brown paper and a voice like thunder'. As he learns to care for Willie's physical and emotional needs he grows to understand what has been missing in his own life.

Oakroyd, Jess
The Good Companions, 1929
J B Priestley

An upright citizen, who is 'redundant' in the family home after his beloved daughter leaves for Canada. Unhappily married and depressed, he is searching for adventure, and he dramatically escapes his miserable existence. Full of spirit, he is not a selfish man, but he is driven to a selfish act. At times self-effacing and at others wildly confident, he has a decent streak which prevails when he decides to return to his responsibilities; he is only fulfilled, however, by travelling to join his daughter and her family in Canada.

Oates, Titus
Peveril of the Peak, 1823
Sir Walter Scott

Scott portrays the leading figure of the so-called Popish Plot as a vicious, braying ass with a crude fenland accent and a self-important air. Yet however absurd he appears, it is also clear that he is dangerous, possessing the power to send men to the dungeons or the block.

Obadiah
The Life and Opinions of Tristram Shandy, 9 volumes, 1759–67
Laurence Sterne

The faithful retainer of the strange Shandy household, his forgetfulness and blunderings simply add to the confusion and sense of dislocation within the family. It is he who has to fetch the crucial medical bag for DR SLOP to aid the birth of TRISTRAM SHANDY, and it is his clumsiness that precipitates the 'crisis of the crushed nose' that proves so emblematic for the whole untidy life of Tristram.

Oberon
A Midsummer Night's Dream, c.1594
William Shakespeare

The King of the Fairy Kingdom, he is all too human in his flaws: capable of great magic, he is also by turns pompous, angry and fickle, threatening his marriage – and the survival of the natural world – because of his desire to own TITANIA's 'changeling boy'. Though his trick on Titania is mean-spirited, he at least knows when to bring it to a halt, and his romantic nature, wisdom and capacity for poetry make his eventual reconciliation and contentment deserved.

Objeta
The Slave Girl, 1977
Buchi Emecheta

If there is a faint echo of 'object' in her name, then that is partly because, like many of her sisters in Emecheta's fiction, she has become a transferable commodity whose value as a human being is dependent on market forces.

O'Brien
1984, 1949
George Orwell

O'Brien is a loyal member of the Inner Party in Orwell's frightening vision of the future. At first, he appears to be a large, coarse man with a brutal aspect. Ironically, however, this torturer of WINSTON SMITH is shown to be a civilized, friendly, even charming man: the perfect inquisitor who can effortlessly dominate his victim by a mixture of aggression and love. In the latter part of the novel, he is Winston's only human contact and O'Brien, the victimizer, becomes his 'friend' in the Ministry of Love. Thus the agent of freedom and truth is seduced and traduced by this epitome of authoritarian rule – a man who smiles and smiles *because* he is a villain.

O'Brien, Robert
Across the Sea Wall, 1965, revised edition 1982
C J Koch

A journalist with an obsessive fear of being tied down. This leads him to take a fugue-like journey to India, a symbol of imaginative and erotic freedom which serves only to underline how essentially commonplace and second-hand his dreams actually are.

O'Cannon, Tocky, also known as **Tocky Lace** and **Tocky Pan**
Capricornia, 1938
Xavier Herbert

A white quadroon, Tocky is the daughter of Humboldt Lace, a superintendent of the Government Agricultural Experimental Station, and the half-caste CONNIE DIFFER. Rescued at the age of three from an Aborigine camp by the kind-hearted Tim O'Cannon, she is lovingly raised with his family until his death, when she is sent to a half-caste home, then to a Gospel Mission for delinquents. Running away, she meets NORMAN SHILLINGSWORTH in the outback and the two strike up a relationship based upon mutual sympathy as much as close affection. Tocky, who has no real conception of the ways of men, has had several lovers. A free spirit, a fighter and a hunter, she has few social graces, yet she has optimism, intuition and tenacity.

O'Carroll, Miss Marionetta Celestina
Nightmare Abbey, 1818
Thomas Love Peacock

'Blooming and accomplished', Marionetta (based on Shelley's first wife, Harriet Westbrook) is full of high spirits and delights in teasing her love-stricken cousin, SCYTHROP GLOWRY. An orphan without an inheritance, she is feisty, jolly and witty, a straight-talker who tackles the woolliest thinkers at Nightmare Abbey head-on, but a woman who is adept in the art of coquetry and who enjoys the mental stimulus of making men fall in love with her.

Occonestoga
The Yemassee, 1835
William Gilmore Simms

The son of SANUTEE and MATIWAN, he is killed by his mother for attempting to betray the Yemassee band to the white colonists. She destroys him rather than see him ostracized and condemned to eternal limbo by the laws of the tribe.

Ochiltree, Eddie
The Antiquary, 1816
Sir Walter Scott

One of the king's Bedes-men, or sturdy beggars, who roam Scotland, known colloquially after the blue gowns they wear as uniform, he seems to regard it as his duty to debunk JONATHAN OLDBUCK's more fanciful antiquarian notions, such as thinking that dykes and dirt-heaps but a few years old are actually Roman ramparts.

O'Connal, Brian
Who Has Seen the Wind, 1947
W O Mitchell

An inquisitive, sensitive child of a small prairie town, Brian searches for and begins to comprehend the mystery of life and death. The story of his prairie childhood tells of a spiritual progress towards human enlightenment. 'Life' is understood through sensation rather than intellect: 'the feeling' is his compass.

O'Connor, Clare
Act of Darkness, 1983
Francis King

An attractive 19-year-old governess, Clare despises the 'mess' of her Irish-Indian blood, and her disorderly home and family. She dislikes men and their 'sweatiness' and is only grudgingly fond of her ward, PETER THOMPSON. She is obsessively clean and neat, but her heavy make-up, gaudy clothing and general tendency to break rules are judged 'unsuitable' by Mrs Thompson. Bright, but indolent, restless and dissatisfied, Clare spends her time smoking, reading 'housemaid's trash' and dreaming of escape to classless Australia. A survivor, she ends up there – but not in the way envisaged.

O'Connor, Dr Matthew-Mighty-grain-of-salt-dante
Nightwood, 1936
Djuna Barnes

By the sheer, vivid force of his personality and the inordinate length of his rambling, metaphysical monologues, Dr O'Connor dominates the novel even though he is not its central character. He is loquacious, compassionate, poetic and self-searching, but appears lonely and adrift in the Parisian homosexual underworld. O'Connor is a disturbing character, magnificent, grotesque, self-deluding and pitiful. He is medically unqualified but earns a living as an illegal abortionist. While treating ROBIN VOTE he steals money from her room. He also admits to NORA FLOOD that he is a liar.

O'Connor, Jim
The Glass Menagerie, 1945
Tennessee Williams
A pleasant, well-mannered young man, he is the idealization of AMANDA WINGFIELD's wishes for her spinster daughter's future; a hardworking fellow employee of TOM WINGFIELD, his interest in public speaking and communications marks him out as a man destined to succeed. However, one evening of pleasant courtship passes, only to reveal his engagement to another girl, leaving the Wingfield women to their isolated life.

Octavia
Antony and Cleopatra, 1606/7
William Shakespeare
The sister of OCTAVIUS CAESAR. A friend of her brother suggests she be married to MARCUS ANTONIUS ANTONY as a political tactic to reconcile the two men. She duly becomes his wife but is, as ENOBARBUS observes, 'of a holy, cold, and still conversation'. Neither does she prove a match for CLEOPATRA, for Antony deserts Octavia to return to her. Torn between political expediency, loyalty and marriage to a reputed womanizer, Octavia is caught in a terrible dilemma. She is, as she admits, 'most wretched/ That have my heart parted betwixt two friends/ That does afflict each other!' Yet even though she is abandoned, she remains faithful to Antony.

Odd, Sgt Fred
Keep the Home Guard Turning, 1943
Whisky Galore, 1947
Compton Mackenzie
A Cockney soldier posted during World War II to the Hebridean island of Todday, where he falls (hopefully) in love with Peigi Macroon and battles (hopelessly) with the Gaelic tongue. His cock-sparrer common sense and resilience eventually win the day over profound cultural differences.

Oddjob
Goldfinger, 1959
Ian Fleming
AURIC GOLDFINGER's Korean manservant. He has hands so hardened by karate training that his skin and fingernails have been transformed into weapons almost as dangerous as his famous bowler hat, which is thrown like a frisbee. His linguistic embarrassments are compounded by a cleft palate – or 'creft parate', as he might say.

Odell, Danby
Bruno's Dream, 1969
Iris Murdoch
The widowed son-in-law of BRUNO GREENSLEAVE, Odell runs Bruno's printing works. He is rakishly attractive, flirtatious, light-hearted and hard-drinking. He cheerfully sleeps with his adoring maid, but remembers his wife and her love as a miracle, not quite understanding how such a thing could have happened to him, a 'shambler through pubs'. Despite his generosity and compassion in caring for Bruno during his terminal illness, Odell is viewed as a useless 'clown' by Bruno's supercilious son, MILES GREENSLEAVE.

Odili
A Man of the People, 1966
Chinua Achebe
A gifted young teacher and former pupil of CHIEF NANGA. As narrator, he sets his openly sensual, uncorrupted self against Nanga's blatant careerism.

O'Donnell, Gar
Philadelphia, Here I Come!, 1965
Brian Friel
We meet Gar O'Donnell, 'young, and strong and of average intelligence', on the eve of his emigration to America from the fictional Irish town of Ballybeg. There are two Gars: the gregarious, public Gar who is eager to leave; and the questioning, angry, private Gar. His father is cold and distant, his friends are thwarted and frustrated – despite all their bravado – and his beloved Kate Doogan has married someone else because of his cowardice. In the course of the evening and as he bids his various farewells, we see the conflicting truths behind his desire to emigrate to 'a vast restless place that doesn't give a damn about the past'.

O'Dowda, Fanny
Fanny's First Play, 1911
George Bernard Shaw
The 19-year-old daughter of the aesthetic Count O'Dowda, Fanny is a Cambridge student and a member of the university Fabian Society. She has written a play which her father has not read, but agrees to stage privately before an audience that includes four critics who are ignorant of the author's identity. This play is performed as a play-within-a-play. As a realistic, pro-suffrage comedy portraying young people rebelling against their parents and middle-class conventions, it naturally horrifies her father. Fanny represents the spirit of intellectual liberation.

O'Driscoll, Pattie
The Time of the Angels, 1966
Iris Murdoch
Irish-Jamaican Pattie is painfully sensitive about her colour and permanently scarred by her miserable childhood. A devout Christian, she was taken into CAREL FISCHER's home at 17 as a maid. At first blissfully happy, 'glorified' by his God-like kindness and affection, she later incurs his family's enmity by becoming his mistress. Frightened by his increasing strangeness and the rectory's fog-enshrouded isolation, she takes refuge in EUGENE PESHKOV's innocent love; but still in thrall to Carel, this promised happiness, too, eludes her.

O'Dwyer, Tom
For the Rest of Our Lives, 1947
Dan Davin
A New Zealander of Irish stock, O'Dwyer, together with TONY BRANDON and FRANK FAHEY, is one of a group of men, mostly attached to the New Zealand Division, stationed in Egypt

during World War II. O'Dwyer is a brusque, straightforward officer, thoughtful, sometimes fastidious, a compassionate man who likes reading Blake and is appalled by the lack of common decency in the world. His family impressed upon him what they understood to be the cruelty of the British in Ireland and are horrified when he chooses to join the forces. Yet O'Dwyer's political perspective is wider than theirs and, until now at least, largely theoretical. He is an idealist, but at the same time one whose feet are still on the ground. He responds quickly and easily to the common man as well as to the intellectual.

Offred
The Handmaid's Tale, 1986
Margaret Atwood

The product of a dystopic future, Offred is a woman whose only function is reproduction. She lives in Gilead, a patriarchal society which enforces a strict caste system. She is dressed entirely in red, except for her white hat, which acts as blinkers, and her name means literally 'Of Fred', to indicate to whom she belongs. Forbidden to read, write or communicate with others except in a highly formulaic manner, Offred dreams of escape. Experiencing apathy, complicity, anger and fear, she cultivates tiny forbidden pleasures, but the eyes that watch her every move make even these insubordinations highly dangerous.

O'Finney, Peter → Finn

O'Flaherty, Mrs
A World I Never Made, 1936, et seq
James T Farrell

DANNY O'NEILL's grandmother, she is the bedrock on which the family is grounded. Fiercely loyal to her Irish Catholic roots and wholly devoted to her grandson, she is sharply contrasted to the weak or compromised male characters and to the hysterical religiosity of her daughter LIZZ O'NEILL.

O'Flaherty, Tom
A World I Never Made, 1936, et seq, especially *The Face of Time*, 1953
James T Farrell

DANNY O'NEILL's grandfather and guardian, he is a tough but careworn teamster working in the Chicago stockyards. He embodies the books' often uneasy balance of self-reliance and solidarity, and represents for Danny the immigrant attempting to make good in a new country by submerging many of his native instincts under a pragmatic accommodation to 'the system'.

Ogedemgbe, Debbie
Destination Biafra, 1982
Buchi Emecheta

A young Biafran woman who finds herself thrown into the horrors of a murderous war in which her gender represents a double jeopardy.

Ogene, Efuru
Efuru, 1966
Flora Nwapa

Efuru is beautiful, hardworking and a talented business woman. Although she is faithful, trusting, understanding and willing to compromise, both her marriages to ADIZUA and Eneberi are unsuccessful. She suffers greatly when her only child, Ogonim, dies and Adizua, who has left her, refuses to return home for the funeral. Later, when Eneberi fails to trust her, Efuru chooses to live alone. Uhamiri, the goddess of the lake, chooses Efuru to be one of her worshippers.

Ogilvie, Ake
Cloud Howe, 1933
Grey Granite, 1934, part of the trilogy *A Scots Quair*, 1946
Lewis Grassic Gibbon

The third husband of CHRIS GUTHRIE. Typifying 'the folk of the Howe', workman Ake, in his basic outlook and crude desires, is an incongruous match for Chris. Though kind enough in his own way, he fails to engage more than her acquiescence in their marriage, but retaining something of the poet's perception, he realizes this and sets her, and himself, free.

Ogilvie, John (Juan Pendarves Ogilvie)
The Four Winds of Love, 6 volumes, 1937–45
Compton Mackenzie

Following the same public-school education as MICHAEL FANE in *Sinister Street*, Ogilvie becomes in turn a playwright, teacher, poet, philosopher, diplomat and indefatigable traveller, embracing every experience and political idea (and not a few of the women) that cross his path.

Oglethorpe, John
Manhattan Transfer, 1925
John Dos Passos

'A strange fish', he is a highly melodramatic actor with a carefully cultivated Oxford drawl and flamboyant homosexual tendencies. He marries ELLEN THATCHER and elevates her from a mere chorus girl, but in a ridiculous scene ends up by drunkenly denouncing her infidelity. He is 'a very complicated rather tragic person', too lazy to be a successful actor, and is genuinely in love with Ellen, the only woman he has ever loved.

Ogmore-Pritchard, Mrs
Under Milk Wood, 1954
Dylan Thomas

One of the 'tidy wives' of Llaregyb, she is a widow twice over, who controls her household with a mixture of obsessive hygiene and superstition. Mr Ogmore had been in the linoleum trade and Mr Pritchard was a failed bookmaker; one of them swallowed disinfectant to escape her. Still their ghosts return to list their daily tasks in her domestic battle against nature. For her, every object has its proper place, every function a correct method and people must behave accordingly.

O'Hara, Kimball, also known as Kim
Kim, 1901
Rudyard Kipling

The orphaned son of a British (or, rather, Irish) soldier of the Raj, he grows up on the streets of Lahore but is adopted by a Tibetan wise man. In the course of a journey to find a mystical river, he comes across his father's old regiment and becomes a kind of mascot, growing up to become a valued intelligence agent with an unparalleled understanding (for a white man) of the underside of Indian life.

O'Hara, Scarlett
Gone with the Wind, 1936
Margaret Mitchell

An impetuous, flirtatious and infuriating Southern belle, who delights in her powers of ensnarement. Scarlett is 'not beautiful, but men seldom realized it when caught by her charm'. Dreams of marriage with the aristocratic ASHLEY WILKES prove fruitless, and she realizes, too late, that the man most suited to match her fiery temperament is RHETT BUTLER. Her irresponsible behaviour is gradually subdued, but never conquered, through exposure to the horrors of the Civil War and the destruction of her beloved home, Tara. Symbolic of the Southern whites, Scarlett shows unsuspected reserves of courage and resilience as she restructures her broken plantation life.

Oisin
The Wanderings of Oisin, 1889
W B Yeats

In his old age this former heroic warrior and poet tells Saint Patrick the story of his adventures: he left his father Finn and the rest of the Fenians to go with his beloved Niamh to the land of the immortals. They spent a century on each of three islands, where Oisin successively experienced, as Yeats later put it in 'The Circus Animals' Desertion', 'Vain gaiety, vain battle, vain repose'. He opposes the Christianity that has taken over his world; now 'weak and poor and blind', he longs to be with the Fenians again.

O'Kane, Michen
In the Forest, 2002
Edna O'Brien

Set in the rural west of Ireland, the novel is based upon the real-life killing of a young mother, her daughter and a priest. Psychotic since childhood and further brutalized by his experiences in young offenders' institutions, where he is abused by priests and raped by inmates, O'Kane develops a dangerous obsession for Eily Ryan, a young mother who lives a bohemian life with her three-year-old daughter, Maddie. Having observed them through the windows of their cottage, O'Kane lures them to the woods, where he abuses and kills them. Disturbed and deeply disturbing, given to long, schizophrenic ranting, O'Kane is nevertheless as much a product of a harshly judgemental society and penal system as he is a man from whom innocence should be protected.

O'Keefe, Joe
Manhattan Transfer, 1925
John Dos Passos

Symbolic of a new order in US society, he is the ambitious, articulate and ardently committed representative of a local construction union. He becomes firm friends with JOE HARLAND after unsuccessfully attempting to recruit him. He

rises to the rank of sergeant-major during World War I, but also contracts syphilis despite claiming to have been careful. After the war, he returns to New York and becomes an outspoken union orator, acclaimed by the masses as 'a good guy' in his quest to fight for the rights of war veterans.

Okoh, Beatrice
Anthills of the Savanna, 1987
Chinua Achebe

A friend of CHRIS ORIKO and IKEM OSODI, Beatrice watches with a sort of calm despair the gradual degeneration of HIS EXCELLENCY's rule. Beautiful and wise, Beatrice seems to represent more stable values in a world constrained by venality and cynicism.

Okoko, or the Voice
The Voice, 1964
Gabriel Okara

Known to the villagers of Amatu as 'the Voice', he is arrogant, sceptical and self-opinionated, and inevitably falls foul of the chief and elders, who regard him as a troublemaker. He becomes a social and cultural outcast.

Okonkwo
Things Fall Apart, 1958
Chinua Achebe

A powerful man of the Obi in Eastern Nigeria, he 'was well known throughout the nine villages and even beyond'. He was tall and huge, and his bushy eyebrows and wide nose gave him a 'very severe look … When he walked, his heels hardly touched the ground and he seemed to walk on springs, as if he was going to pounce on somebody.' With a slight stammer, he finds his fists a more straightforward means of expression.

Okonkwo, Obi
No Longer At Ease, 1960
Chinua Achebe

Grandson of Okonkwo in *Things Fall Apart*. A bright maverick boy (who once embarrassed his village by writing to Adolf Hitler during the war) he is sent to Britain for an education, but reads English instead of law, as had been expected. On his return, he becomes a civil servant and falls victim to the corrupt atmosphere of Lagos.

O'Lan
The Good Earth, 1931
Pearl S Buck

A slave girl, whose marriage to WANG begins with great hopes and devotion but is challenged and threatened by his selfish and insensitive behaviour. Through the traumas of drought, famine and disaster, she holds together their fortunes, only to have her love dismissed and forgotten as her husband turns to another woman, and finds his goals shifting in the direction of social aggrandisement. Courage, hard work and great loyalty bring her nothing but disappointment and she derives only a little satisfaction from her husband's eventual realization that her love is the best thing he ever had.

Old Ben
'The Bear', 1935, in *Go Down, Moses*, 1942
William Faulkner

A huge, almost legendary grizzly that haunts the Yoknapatawpha woods, and is the target of an annual spring hunt by men and dogs. Lamed by a trap and uselessly peppered by buckshot and rifle balls, the bear is 'a phantom, epitome and apotheosis of the old wild life which the little puny humans swarmed and hacked at in a fury of abhorrence and fear'.

Old Major
Animal Farm, 1945
George Orwell

A visionary whose presence permeates the whole novel despite the fact he dies in the first chapter. Old Major dreams of a better world, where man has been exiled forever, and it is this ideal which inspires the other animals to revolt. It is his principles which form the basis of their Seven Commandments and which are eventually introduced by NAPOLEON and his followers. Old Major's association with the original, true spirit of the revolution soon becomes embarrassing for the new animal dictatorship and he is written out of history.

Old Mortality, more properly Robert Paterson
Old Mortality, in *Tales of My Landlord*, 1816
Sir Walter Scott

An old Cameronian, located midway between fact and legend, but remembered for having travelled around Scotland, repairing and re-inscribing the tombs of the Covenanting martyrs. It is he who passes on the violent tales that make up Scott's novel and though temperamentally and politically the novelist's opposite, he is also in a sense a symbol of Scott's own endeavour.

Old Ones
'The Whisperer in Darkness', and elsewhere
H P Lovecraft, edited by August Derleth, 1945

The worshippers of CTHULHU, they are ichthomorphic entities with designs on the human universe. They attempt to interbreed with people in order to take over the Earth, but the invasion is thwarted and they dissolve into a noxious goo which resembles sperm.

Oldbuck, Jonathan, strictly Jonathan Oldenbuck, or Oldinbuck of Monkbarns
The Antiquary, 1816
Sir Walter Scott

The Laird of Monkbarns, he is the dedicated antiquary of the title. Having proved himself an able but remarkably indolent law student, with no ambition to rise in the profession, this younger son had the good and unexpected fortune to succeed to his father's title when his elder brother died of a chill. He maintains Monkbarns frugally with his sister Grizel, a single house-servant and a gardener. Oldbuck's 'countenance was of the true Scottish cast, strongly marked, and rather harsh in features, with a shrewd and penetrating eye, and a countenance in which habitual gravity was enlivened by a cast of ironical humour'. (Though

it is said that the antiquary was modelled on Scott's old friend George Constable, there is some reason to think he incorporates some elements of his creator as well.) Hesketh Pearson called him 'the most entertaining bore in literature'.

Olenska, Ellen
The Age of Innocence, 1920
Edith Wharton

A glamorous woman, Ellen made a disastrous marriage to a Polish count. Fleeing him in dubious circumstances, her intrusion into New York society exposes it as a fortress of evasion. Like the Europe she has known intimately, she has produced a good deal more history than she can absorb, and certainly more than her staid relatives can tolerate. Her bohemian lifestyle alienates her family who perceive her as vulgar and self-parading – the embodiment of excess. She is vital, brave and more receptive to life than the narrow society she confronts and challenges.

Olifaunt, Nigel, Lord Glenvarloch
The Fortunes of Nigel, 1822
Sir Walter Scott

A young Scottish nobleman, he is threatened with the loss of his ancestral estates and attempts to recoup the money required to redeem his mortgage from JAMES I OF ENGLAND, who was in the debt of Nigel's father. The issue shows him to be a man of great *practical* honour, more concerned with the exactitudes of everyday life than with the abstract speculations beloved of his monarch. John Buchan thought he was no more than an example of 'embodied morality', but despite the impeccable propriety of his religion and sense of honour Nigel is more complex and rounded than many of Scott's male protagonists.

Olive
Summer of the Seventeenth Doll, 1955
Ray Lawler

'Despite a surface cynicism and thirty-nine years of age, there is something curiously unfinished about Olive, an eagerness that properly belongs to extreme youth.' Even more than ROO WEBBER, BARNEY IBBOT and BUBBA RYAN, she wishes to keep the conditions of her life exactly as they have been for the past 16 summers. PEARL CUNNINGHAM remarks that she is 'blind to everything outside this house and the lay-off season'. Her childishness is symbolized by her devotion to the 17 annually presented dolls of the title. She is destroyed by the alteration of circumstances which marriage to Roo would entail.

Oliver
As You Like It, c.1600
William Shakespeare

The eldest of the De Boys brothers, he despises his brother ORLANDO and plots his death with Charles the Wrestler. Proud, revengeful and overbearing to both his equals and his servants, he is redeemed when Orlando saves him from the serpent and the lion and he falls in love with CELIA.

Oliver, George

Getting On, 1971
Alan Bennett

A Labour MP for a northern constituency, he is about 40, 'rather glamorous once, now a bit florid, worn, running to fat'. He also used to be more radical, more passionate and more northern. Acerbic, sometimes angry and increasingly misanthropic, he is so self-absorbed that he fails to notice that his wife is having an affair, his mother-in-law is dying and his son is about to leave home. He fails to notice, in fact, that people tend to see him as a joke; often bored himself, he has become often rather boring.

Oliver, Parson

An Apology for the Life of Mrs Shamela Andrews, 1741
Henry Fielding

A stickler for moral and theological rectitude, Parson Oliver clings to the certainties afforded by scriptural authority. He is outraged by the scandalous behaviour of PARSON WILLIAMS and PAMELA. Warning young men to beware the dangers of sacrificing enduring comforts for transient passion, Parson Oliver proclaims his allegiance to the abstract codes of religion, virtue and honour, and scolds the wayward PARSON TICKLETEXTwith the firm injunction: 'Be the reverse of Williams.'

Oliver, Sir Quentin

Loitering with Intent, 1981
Muriel Spark

A subtly evil snob, the employer of FLEUR TALBOT and plagiarist of her novel. Obsessed with titles, he sets up the Autobiographical Association to encourage some faded members of the upper classes to write their memoirs, in which he takes a hand. White-haired and looking 'very slightly askew', he 'insists on complete frankness' while actually blending fiction and reality in a destructive manner.

Olivia

The Plain Dealer, 1676/7
William Wycherley

Though married to VERNISH, Olivia falls in love with MANLY's young page, FIDELIA, not realizing she is really a woman. Her declaration of love for Fidelia reveals her real attitude to Manly, to whom she was once betrothed: 'tho' my Husband were at the door, and the bloody Ruffian Manly here in the room, with all his awful insolence, I wou'd give myself to this dear hand, to be led away, to Heavens of joys, which none but thou canst give'.

Olivia

Twelfth Night, c.1601
William Shakespeare

Used to having her orders obeyed, the countess Olivia can only deal with ORSINO's persistent avowals of love by using the death of her brother as an excuse for avoiding him. Yet, when she falls in love with 'Cesario' (VIOLA) she reveals the same determination to capture her love as Orsino has shown towards her. The dignified behaviour she displays in her dealings with her servants, and even with her disreputable kinsman SIR TOBY BELCH, is replaced with flirtatiousness and stratagem. She takes pleasure in words, especially FESTE's wit and Cesario's poetry, but leaves unpleasant situations for others to clear up. Her offer of marriage being accepted, she rushes the ceremony through and is not at all discomfited to discover that her husband is not the same person she has been pursuing.

Olivier, Mary

Mary Olivier: A Life, 1919
May Sinclair

Circumscribed by environment and heredity, Mary describes her enforced limitations as inescapable. Her thoughts are choppy and disconnected, but never random or arbitrary; she is a talented and intelligent woman who lives a sad, empty life, sacrificing her true self and sublimating her desires. Thwarted by her inhibitions, Mary cannot isolate her essential self from the myriad 'persons that were called Mary Olivier'. Profoundly mystical, she glimpses 'secret happiness' in brief epiphanies, but nevertheless remains fundamentally excluded.

Ollamoor, Wat ('Mop')

'The Fiddler of the Reels', in *Life's Little Ironies: A Set of Tales with Some Colloquial Sketches Entitled a Few Crusted Characters*, 1894
Thomas Hardy

An itinerant fiddler of unknown foreign origin, sometime resident in Mellstock. Handsome and dark-skinned, he derives his nickname from his abundant hair, and his exquisite playing of dance tunes reduces musically sensitive children and even adults to tears. He exercises a particularly fatal effect upon the impressionable Caroline Aspent, who is unable to resist the witchcraft of his playing, and whom he seduces, later abducting their daughter.

Ollyphant

The Faerie Queene, 1590–6
Sir Edmund Spenser

The brother of ARGANTE, offspring of the giant race of Titans. He is born with an innate lust and through his life he 'sins against natures laws'. He roams the forests of faerieland in search of victims, irrespective of which sex. As an unpure creature he is terrified of virginity and chastity.

Omer, Mr

David Copperfield, 1850
Charles Dickens

Mr Omer is the fat and 'merry-looking' Yarmouth undertaker and draper who takes a kind interest in DAVID COPPERFIELD and measures him for mourning when his mother dies. He employs LITTLE EM'LY and MARTHA ENDELL as apprentices and after their seductions, he speaks sympathetically of them.

Omnium, Duchess of → Palliser, Lady Glencora

Omnium, Duke of
Can You Forgive Her?, 1864–5
Phineas Finn, The Irish Member, 1869
The Eustace Diamonds, 1873
Phineas Redux, 1874
Anthony Trollope

The 'old' Duke is PLANTAGENET PALLISER's uncle. He is a 'plain, thin man, tall, but undistinguished in appearance, except that there was a gleam of pride in his eye' which seemed constantly to proclaim his status. He is a bachelor, and is said to be a 'great debauchee', but a discreet one. Plantagenet Palliser becomes the Duke of Omnium on his uncle's death.

Oneco
Hope Leslie, or Early Times in the Massachusetts, 1827
Catharine Maria Sedgwick

The son of a defeated Pequod chief, his marriage to the white FAITH LESLIE is a rare example in 19th-century writing of a successful inter-racial relationship. Noble, devoted and unselfish, he stands in flat contradiction to the usual contemporary portrayal of Native Americans as either brutal savages or pantheistic innocents. Though the books are almost exactly contemporary, he may owe something to James Fenimore Cooper's Uncas in *The Last of the Mohicans* (1826).

O'Neill, Danny
A World I Never Made, 1936, et seq, and in nearly 50 short stories
James T Farrell

This character is acknowledged to be a more closely autobiographical version of Farrell's own Chicago-Irish background and steady politicization than was STUDS LONIGAN. Danny, though, is a less distinct figure, perhaps because he is much more conscious and driven in his ambition to be a writer and thus lacks something of Studs's ironic distance. Raised by his grandparents, he builds on TOM O'FLAHERTY's tradition-laden self-reliance with a thirsty course of reading at the University of Chicago.

O'Neill, Jim
A World I Never Made, 1936
James T Farrell

DANNY O'NEILL's father, he is a morally uncomplicated man, hardworking but without the essential fibre to protect him from the stultifying environment of working-class Chicago. The social aspirations which lift him up a rung from poorly-paid teamster to poorly-paid but 'respectable' shipping clerk are thwarted by a disabling thrombosis that renders him progressively weaker and more pessimistic, but also quietly courageous and forbearing.

O'Neill, Lizz
A World I Never Made, 1936, et seq
James T Farrell

The privations of working-class Chicago existence and the collapse of her dreams of social and spiritual improvement have somewhat unhinged DANNY O'NEILL's mother's already highly-charged nature. In contrast to her own mother's indomitable faith, she espouses a hysterical religiosity that increasingly represents a retreat from painful reality.

O'Neill, Monk
A Stretch of the Imagination, 1972
Jack Hibberd

Ably and articulately conversant with his inner self, his is no graceful submission to ageing, but a defiant last stand against death, symbolically figured in the visitant 'Mort Lazarus'. Monk ruminates and expostulates upon his past, present and doubtful future life and loves with a sardonic and caustic humour. He plays every line for all it is worth.

Ongar, Lady → Brabazon, Julia

Openshaw, Gertrude
Nuns and Soldiers, 1980
Iris Murdoch

In her thirties, Gertrude's clear-eyed 'look of happy authority' is dimmed by the terminal illness of her adored husband. She is certain that metaphorically she will die with him, but is devotedly helped through her agonizing bereavement by ANNE CAVIDGE and THE 'COUNT'. Amazingly soon, Gertrude falls helplessly (and to her friends shockingly) in love with her husband's protégé, artist Tim Reede, a scrounger and habitual liar, but his lack of morality clashes with her own cast-iron sense of duty and decency.

Ophelia
Hamlet, 1601/2
William Shakespeare

Ophelia is an obedient daughter to POLONIUS and although in love with HAMLET rejects his advances when ordered to do so by her worldly father. Her innocence is her undoing; rejection by Hamlet and the death of her father at his hands drive her to insanity and suicide. Her death is a source of great sorrow to her brother LAERTES.

Ophelia, Miss
Uncle Tom's Cabin, or, Life Among the Lowly, 1851–2
Harriet Beecher Stowe

AUGUSTINE ST CLARE's spinster cousin, brought south to look after EVA, she represents the neurotic repressions of extreme New England puritanism, with its deeply divided and ambivalent view of humanity. Not quite as mad as her Shakespearean name might suggest, Ophelia is hysterically disgusted by the laxity of Southern morals and by the 'dark' nature of the slave child TOPSY.

Opimian, Rev Dr Neophilus
Gryll Grange, 1860–1
Thomas Love Peacock

With a weakness for analysis, theorizing and discourse, Dr Opimian is a learned, well-meaning and well-rounded character, his interests ranging from good food and wine to walking and reading 12th-century verse. A classicist at heart, he describes himself as 'matter-of-fact', although he is kindly and concerned about the welfare of others.

Oppressioun
Ane Pleasant Satyre of the Thrie Estaitis, 1540
Sir David Lindsay
The vice governing the temporal state, and master – in both naturalistic and allegorical respects – of COMMON THIFT, Oppressioun's selfish, tyrannical nature is beautifully revealed in the symbolism of his final dirty trick. Cruelly betraying even his own assistant by conning him into taking his place in the stocks, Oppressioun makes good his escape, caring nothing for the unhappy fate of Common Thift, perhaps his most poignant victim.

Oracle, the (the Pythoness)
Back to Methuselah, 1921
George Bernard Shaw
The Oracle of the temple appears in the fourth section of this five-part play. *Tragedy of an Elderly Gentleman* is set on the shore of Galway Bay, Ireland, in 3000AD. Veiled, robed and majestic, the Oracle (or Pythoness) is a woman about 170 years old, who receives several seekers of wisdom, including NAPOLEON. Finally, she is approached by THE ELDERLY GENTLEMAN, who is distraught because he does not know whether to stay and die of discouragement or go home and die of despair. He touches her hands, and dies.

Orc
America, 1793
The First Book of Urizen, 1794
William Blake
A complex character in Blake's symbolic order, Orc is prey to the harmful designs of others, at times symbolizing repressed humanity, bound with 'the Chain of Jealousy' and resenting his own children. Yet, he is largely the very stuff of revolutionary fervour and liberation, denounced by imperial power as 'Blasphemous Demon, Antichrist, hater of Dignities,/Lover of wild rebellion, and transgressor of God's Law'. Orc has a great sense of his own power, his language confronting 'That stony law I stamp to dust', the law of church and empire, of repression and greed. He declares his main aim to be 'to renew the fiery joy' of life.

Ord
Tomorrow and Tomorrow and Tomorrow, 1947 (censored), 1983 (uncensored)
M Barnard Eldershaw
KNARF's sharp and sardonic archaeologist friend, he has discovered everything he can about the old Australian civilization. He tends to be combative and short-tempered and is sometimes exasperating, but Knarf finds something comforting about his strong, unsentimental and impersonal mind, knowing it is not devoid of imagination, 'the secret nourishment of the spirit'. For his part, Ord acknowledges that Knarf's fictional recreation of the ancient era and its people brings that world vividly alive for him in a way that the actual remains do not.

O'Regan, Teague
Modern Chivalry, 1792–1815
H H Brackenridge
CAPTAIN JOHN FARRAGO's servant, he has the fiery red hair of his ancestors and an arrogant self-possession that leads everyone he encounters to bestow honours and privileges on him. His social climb is only halted when he is tarred and feathered (an occupational hazard for an exciseman in the young USA) and shipped off to France as a specimen of a hitherto unknown species.

Orford, Ellen
The Borough, 1810
George Crabbe
Ellen suffers a multiplicity of woes; her stepfather ill-treats her, her lover marries another woman, she bears his child in disgrace and that child is mentally afflicted. Nevertheless she marries and has sons, but her husband joins a severe religious sect, turns against her and hangs himself. From the workhouse, Ellen sees misfortunes overtake all her children. Still faithful to God, in her 'winter-calm of life' she teaches young children in her small school, but loses her sight. She is resigned; she lives to pray, love God and mankind, and await death.

Orgoglio
The Faerie Queene, 1590–6
Sir Edmund Spenser
A 'hideous gyant all horrible and hye'. Three times taller than the average man, he causes the earth to groan under his feet. He is representative of the earthquakes that are expected to occur during the Last Judgement. He is puffed up with empty wind and full of 'sinful crime', as well as being evil, merciless, and matchless in battle.

Oriana
The Woman Hater, 1605
Francis Beaumont, with some dialogue by John Fletcher
Lively and witty, she attracts the hatred of GONDARINO and sometimes gleefully, sometimes angrily, probes the extent of that hatred, taunting and teasing him. Even though, after having been consigned to a bordello, she manages to remain *virgo intacta*, she is as knowing as she appears to be innocent. Coleridge once remarked that Beaumont's heroines are often virgins with the minds of strumpets, a description that neatly fits Oriana. There is an atmosphere of moral ambiguity about her.

Oriko, Chris
Anthills of the Savanna, 1987
Chinua Achebe
HIS EXCELLENCY's Minister of Information, he is blamed for the almost inevitable failure to secure a presidency-for-life for his old school-friend. He slowly recognizes that past loyalties will not stand in the way of present realpolitik.

Orinthia
The Apple Cart, 1929
George Bernard Shaw
The mistress of KING MAGNUS, proud, aristocratic Orinthia is 'romantically beautiful and beautifully dressed', but her nature is far from that suggested by her appearance. She is ambitious, devious and heartless, intending to win the king and become queen in place of Jemima. 'Oh, drown her: shoot her' she tells him.

The monarch's job, she reminds him, is 'to wipe your boots on common people'.

Orlando
As You Like It, c.1600
William Shakespeare

The youngest son of Sir Rowland de Boys. Courteous even in adversity, he has physical strength and a naturally noble character. Once he has fallen in love with ROSALIND and moved into the forest he becomes almost a figure of fun in his pathetic lovesickness, and is easily duped by her disguise as a boy. His better nature quickly conquers any desire for revenge on OLIVER when he rescues him from the serpent and the lion.

Orlando
Orlando, 1928
Virginia Woolf

A character designed to challenge preconceptions about sexuality, Orlando is an intriguing, likeable and positive figure. Inspired by Vita Sackville-West, Orlando is a man/woman who moves arbitrarily through time, his/her nature changing to suit the character role he or she assumes.

Orlick, Dolge
Great Expectations, 1861
Charles Dickens

JOE GARGERY's swarthy and resentful journeyman, he has a grudge against PIP and hates MRS JOE GARGERY. His secret assault on her eventually causes her death. He helps COMPEYSON to locate the hiding place of ABEL MAGWITCH and sets a trap to lure Pip, whose friends arrive just in time to save him from being killed.

Ormond
Ormond, 1799
Charles Brockden Brown

A definitive anti-hero. A mixture of political idealist and cynic, Ormond allows nothing and nobody to stand in the way of his desires. To him, murder is 'benevolent' if, for example, it removes the troublesome father of a desired woman. He paradoxically uses deception and impersonation in order to seek out 'truth'. Even a woman's death does not deter him from seeking sexual gratification: 'Living or dead, the prize that I have in view shall be mine.'

Oroonoko
Oroonoko, or The History of the Royal Slave, c.1688
Aphra Behn, adapted for the stage by Thomas Southerne, 1695

The grandson and heir of an African king, he loves and is loved by IMOINDA, the daughter of his grandfather's general. Yet the king also loves her, and on discovering their affair, orders that she be sold as a slave. For his part, Oroonoko is captured by English slave-traders and taken to Surinam, where the lovers are reunited. Given the slave-name of Caesar, Oroonoko leads an unsuccessful revolt. The proud Imoinda chooses to die at his hands; he is discovered beside her body and executed. Oroonoko represents both true royal nobility, faith in love, and a moral consistency which,

although ruthless, is higher than that of his so-called white superiors.

Orr, John/Lennox, Sandy (Alexander)
The Bridge, 1986
Iain Banks

As accident victim Sandy Lennox lies in a coma in hospital, his unconscious mind recreates his life as John Orr, rescued from the sea and onto a fantastic, city-like construct called the bridge. Suffering from amnesia, he struggles to lend detail to his vague memories of the 'real' world, and to make sense of his new situation, his frightening dreams, and his attraction to the chief engineer's daughter, Abberlaine.

Orsino
Twelfth Night, c.1601
William Shakespeare

Obsessed with the idea of being in love, Orsino pursues the countess OLIVIA, refusing to take no for an answer. He behaves like a conventional lover, delighting in melancholy songs and verses. His belief that men are more steadfast in love than women is given the lie when he turns his attention to VIOLA almost immediately when she reveals who she is and how she feels about him. Generous by nature and an appreciative participant in verbal sparring with FESTE, he has the dignity that his position demands of him. When he has ANTONIO arrested he orders that he be well treated because he acknowledges his bravery and seamanship.

Ortheris, Private
'The Three Musketeers', in *Plain Tales from the Hills*, 1888
Soldiers Three, 1890
Rudyard Kipling

The archetypal Cockney fighting man: no braver than he need be, no more honest than circumstances strictly demand, but utterly loyal and completely true to himself when not under the awful compulsion of self-preservation.

Orton, Daniel
The Virgin in the Garden, 1978
Still Life, 1985
A S Byatt

A large, dark, brooding man who cannot bear to be inactive, Daniel has taken Holy Orders out of a need to impose order and discipline on his world. His Christianity is energetically practical; he follows a no-nonsense, straight-talking Christ, taking more interest in work than in theology. The confusion he feels at his fierce passion for STEPHANIE POTTER quickly becomes a conviction that they must marry. In love, as in all things, Daniel 'can't do wi' half measures'.

Oryx
Oryx and Crake, 2003
Margaret Atwood

A child prostitute whom SNOWMAN first sees on a pornographic website, Oryx turns from performing a sexual act and looks at the camera with so piercing an expression that he instantly falls in love. A south-east Asian girl sold into prostitution by her parents, she turns up, many years later, in the Paradice Dome, where she is

CRAKE's lover and accomplice. Enigmatic, hypnotic, streetwise and fleeting, her mere glance is sufficient both to entrance and terrify Snowman. Yet this later Oryx may be an impostor or an illusion.

Osbaldistone, Frank (Francis)
Rob Roy, 1817
Sir Walter Scott

Estranged from his father as a result of his refusal to enter the family counting house, he is farmed out to his uncle SIR HILDEBRAND OSBALDISTONE. Osbaldistone Hall is not the place for progressive or forward-looking ideas and Frank is drawn into the intrigues (some pettily financial, some romantic) that surround the Jacobite rising of 1715. Critics have often missed the subtleties of his first-person narrative, in which he reveals more than he is aware, but, by common consent, he is the weakest of Scott's heroes.

Osbaldistone, Rashleigh
Rob Roy, 1817
Sir Walter Scott

Villainous son of SIR HILDEBRAND OSBALDISTONE and FRANK OSBALDISTONE's nominated replacement in the London counting house. Rashleigh stands for every effort to overturn the natural order. He is deeply involved in Jacobite plotting and has in addition set his sights on his cousin DIE VERNON. The insinuating softness of his voice is not matched by his looks, which are plain, though not vulgar, and marked by 'an expression of art and design, and, on provocation, a ferocity tempered by caution, which nature had made obvious to the most ordinary physiognomist, perhaps with the same intention that she has given the rattle to the poisonous snake'.

Osbaldistone, Sir Hildebrand
Rob Roy, 1817
Sir Walter Scott

FRANK OSBALDISTONE's uncle and probationary guardian, he is a positive Nimrod, whose exploits in the field are only matched by the amount of claret he drinks. He maintains an old-fashioned establishment at Osbaldistone Hall, coupled with attitudes and politics that go back at least a generation.

Osborne
Journey's End, 1928
R C Sherriff

Osborne is the second-in-command, after DENNIS STANHOPE, of a small contingent of soldiers including JIMMY RALEIGH, sharing a dugout defending the Western Front in the German spring offensive of 1918. A former schoolteacher, he is much older than the others and has not been so long in service. Consequently, in marked contrast to Stanhope, he is still breezily humorous, occupying himself with little domestic details, giving the air of making the best of a bad job. But he is not blind to Stanhope's deterioration, nor wholly immune from the realities of trench existence, and slowly all his optimism seeps away.

Osborne, Col Frederic
He Knew He Was Right, 1869
Anthony Trollope

A Member of Parliament, and old friend of the ROWLEY family. He is a pleasant and charming old gentleman with a liking for over-indulging in both hospitality and wine, who has earned a reputation for taking an undue interest in the wives of others. His frequent visits to the Trevelyan household to see Emily, while perfectly innocent, trigger LOUIS TREVELYAN's jealous over-reaction, with tragic consequences.

Osborne, George
Vanity Fair, 1848
W M Thackeray

A social climber and snob, despised by his brother officers for his pretensions, he nonetheless manages to charm almost everyone with his good looks and polished manner. Duplicitous to a degree, he wins the unquestioning devotion of AMELIA SEDLEY until, after his death at Waterloo, his true nature (suspected by BECKY SHARP) begins to emerge.

Osborne, John
Vanity Fair, 1848
W M Thackeray

Father of GEORGE OSBORNE and formerly a friend of JOHN SEDLEY whom, as his fortunes decline, he increasingly regards as a liability. Vain, snobbish and cold-hearted, he attempts to break up his son's relationship with AMELIA SEDLEY.

O'Shaugnessy, Sergius
The Deer Park, 1957
The Deer Park: A Play, 1959, revised edition 1967
'The Time of Her Time', in *Advertisements for Myself*, 1959
Norman Mailer

The narrator of Mailer's projected but unfulfilled nine-novel journey into the American psyche. An Air Force pilot and sometime bullfight instructor, he is marooned in the drinking and gambling haven of Desert D'Or at the end of the war. Blonde-haired, blue-eyed, Slavic-Irish, he is 'cocky with an undertone of sadness, and a constant hint of humor. Wry, tough, but always intelligent – which is to say he does his best to conceal the quality of his intelligence.'

Osmond, Gilbert
The Portrait of a Lady, 1881
Henry James

ISABEL ARCHER's eventual husband is a selfish dilettante, an expatriate widower living in questionable style in Italy with his young daughter. Cool and calculating, he is nonetheless highly attractive: 'he indulged in no striking deflection from common usage, he was an original without being an eccentric'.

Osmond, Pansy
The Portrait of a Lady, 1881
Henry James

The illegitimate daughter of GILBERT OSMOND and MME MERLE, she is a frail and sickly child and partly for that reason commands the self-denying loyalty of her stepmother ISABEL ARCHER. She is wooed by, but eventually rejects, one of Isabel's former suitors, the English LORD WARBURTON.

Osodi, Ikem
Anthills of the Savanna, 1987
Chinua Achebe

A poet and editor of the *National Gazette*, he marginalizes himself dangerously by writing fiercely principled editorials in opposition to the despotic and morally degenerate rule of his old friend, HIS EXCELLENCY.

Ossipon, Alexander
The Secret Agent, 1907
Joseph Conrad

A revolutionary, known as 'the Doctor' because he was once a medical student, although he did not finish his studies. He is robust, with a 'bush of crinkly yellow beard' and a 'red, freckled face, with a flattened nose and a prominent mouth'. He is wholly unscrupulous, and considers himself to be an intellectual, although he is more properly seen as obtuse and insensitive. Greedy and unemotional, he exploits all those around him, although he seems to suffer some remorse over his betrayal of WINNIE VERLOC.

Osterman
The Octopus: A Story of California, 1901
Frank Norris

A rancher in the San Joaquin Valley, he camouflages his abilities as a negotiator on the farmers' behalf behind a goatish sense of humour and motley dress. He has a 'comic actor's face, with ... brownish-red cheeks, protuberant ears and a horizontal slit of a mouth'.

Oswald
King Lear, c.1607
William Shakespeare

GONERIL's steward, a malicious and insolent character who takes pleasure in the licence he is given to insult KING LEAR and his followers. He is self-interested and sly – 'a serviceable villain' in EDGAR's words.

Oswald, Lee Harvey, also known as **'Leon'**, or **'O H Lee'**, or **'Hidell'**
Libra, 1988
Don DeLillo

Putative assassin of John F Kennedy (DeLillo identifies three others), subsequently shot dead by the nightclub owner JACK RUBY. If conspiracy theorists are to be believed, the historical Oswald's documented life in New York, New Orleans and Dallas and as a defector in the USSR was in intelligence parlance a 'legend'. DeLillo reconstructs a report by an educational psychologist characterizing Oswald as 'feeling almost as if there is a veil between him and other people through which they cannot reach him, but he prefers this veil to remain intact'.

Otford, Eric
Rusty Bugles, 1948
Sumner Locke Elliott

Nicknamed Ot, he is a tall, awkward, red-haired young soldier in the Australian Northern Territory. Not very intelligent, he keeps adopting new crazes, such as physical exercises

and gardening, and thinking up schemes to raise money for his engagement to 'the Rosebud', to whom he makes extremely frequent reference.

Othello
Othello, 1603/4
William Shakespeare

He is an unparalleled general, a diplomat, a poet and a lover; his dignity and nobility win him the heart of DESDEMONA; his human decency and desire for peace – 'Put up your bright swords for the dew will rust them' – win him the intense loyalty of his friends and soldiers. The unwitting victim of a warped manipulator, IAGO, he gives way to paranoia and jealousy, finally killing the thing he loves most, as a result of loving 'not wisely, but too well'. His crime is horrific and yet, at the tragedy's end, we can only agree with CASSIO that he was 'great of heart'.

Otley, Rose
The Shoemaker's Holiday, 1599
Thomas Dekker

The daughter of the LORD MAYOR OF LONDON, the determined, stubborn Rose is in love with ROWLAND LACY, but the match is opposed by her father. Nevertheless, Rose, an ideal woman, wins both her man and THE KING OF ENGLAND's approval.

O'Trigger, Sir Lucius
The Rivals, 1775
Richard Brinsley Sheridan

A tall Irish baronet, who is amorously corresponding with MRS MALAPROP under the impression that she is LYDIA LANGUISH. His poverty makes him particularly touchy about his honour and his quarrelsome nature leads him to duel and to encourage others to do so.

Otter, Captain Thomas and Mrs
Epicoene, or The Silent Woman, 1609
Ben Jonson

A retired sea-captain, poor Captain Otter is so thoroughly and constantly nagged by his wife that he retreats whenever possible into alcoholic befuddlement, contentedly naming his many drinking glasses after wild animals. An added respite comes when he is able to masquerade as a parson in order to advise MOROSE on the possibilities of divorce. Mrs Otter is a snob. Conscious of her social position and seeking any means by which to improve it, she regards her indolent husband as her main impediment to social progress. When she overhears him drunkenly mocking her, she almost bursts with rage.

Ottley, Edith
The Little Ottleys, 1962
Ada Leverson

A delightful, good-humoured, mild, accommodating, but quietly determined woman. She is 'young and pretty, but not obvious', cheerful and intelligent, and passionately devoted to her children. In the course of an unhappy marriage she learns to have the courage of her desires, and to seek the freedom to pursue her own happiness.

Otto
A High Wind in Jamaica, 1929
Richard Hughes
The Viennese mate of a pirate ship. A proud, dapper little man who is clever, multilingual and very resourceful, he possesses more common sense, intelligence and cunning than his old accomplice, CAPTAIN JONSEN. He has the foresight to know that, with the advent of the steamship, the heyday of piracy has passed and that, in the Victorian era, the high moral temper of the Church spells the end of the old freewheeling world he once knew. His interest in the child captives goes beyond mere friendliness and he adopts the oldest girl, MARGARET FERNANDEZ, as his mistress.

Otto (Otto Pivner)
The Recognitions, 1955
William Gaddis
A tyro dramatist, he is more proficient at dramatizing his own banal existence than at writing plays (he wears a sling to make himself more interesting). Like many other characters in the novel, he is in search of his missing father (MR PIVNER). He is also representative of the book's impressive roster of fake artists, being a comic version of the hero WYATT GWYON.

Oudin
The Far Journey of Oudin, 1961, part of *The Guyana Quartet*, 1985
Wilson Harris
BETI's husband, he has sold his soul to the moneylender Ram and after death travels backwards and forwards in time, chosen to 're-visit or re-play the deeds of the past in a new light of presences woven closely into the tapestry of past action'.

Outland, Tom
The Professor's House, 1925
Willa Cather
A gifted pupil of Professor GODFREY ST PETER, he discovers an ancient cliff city at Blue Mesa in the American south-west, a discovery that is met with frustrating official indifference. Doomed to die in World War I, he represents for the professor all the wasted promise of youth.

Overdo, Justice and Dame
Bartholomew Fair, 1614
Ben Jonson
A justice of the peace, Adam Overdo imagines himself to be wise, just and incorruptible. He tours Bartholomew Fair in disguise, searching for misdemeanours. His foolishness is exploited several times, most disastrously when he signs away his ward, GRACE WELLBORN, to the clever but manipulative WIN WIFE. Dame Overdo is fond of quoting her husband's little maxims, but once at the fair she drinks far too much and, like WIN LITTLEWIT, is persuaded by Knockem and Captain Whit to act like a prostitute.

Overend, Daisy
'Daisy Overend', in *The Go-Away Bird and Other Stories*, 1958
Muriel Spark
A small and charming but unsympathetic lady with literary and political pretensions in postwar London; her two lovers are a poet and a political exile. Her elegant clothes reflect her formative years in the Twenties. She employs the narrator (who claims to have forgotten Daisy's real name) as an assistant, but proves not to share her sense of humour.

Overmore, Miss, subsequently Mrs Beale Farange
What Maisie Knew, 1897
Henry James
A young, pretty governess employed by IDA FARANGE for her daughter, MAISIE FARANGE, and then discharged in favour of MRS WIX. She is loyal and even affectionate to Maisie, but when re-engaged by Ida's ex-husband, ostensibly as governess again, she begins to neglect the girl, devoting all her time to BEALE FARANGE, whom she eventually marries.

Overreach, Margaret
A New Way to Pay Old Debts, 1633
Philip Massinger
The beautiful, dark-haired daughter of SIR GILES OVERREACH, Margaret's modesty, compassion and virtue contrast with his arrogance and wickedness. She indignantly rejects her father's advice to sacrifice her honour in order to gain an aristocratic husband, and she considers her birth too lowly for her to marry a lord. She romantically loves the young TOM ALWORTH.

Overreach, Sir Giles
A New Way to Pay Old Debts, 1633
Philip Massinger
An utterly villainous London merchant who has acquired large estates by extortion and the corruption of the law, ruining numerous families in the process. He despises the aristocracy, using impoverished members of it as servants, but he wants to marry his daughter MARGARET OVERREACH to a lord. He uses her advancement as a justification for his crimes, while being prepared to sacrifice her honour to achieve her marriage. His contempt for the social order is matched by his arrogant atheism. The success of his opponents drives him mad.

Overton
The Way of All Flesh, 1903
Samuel Butler
The middle-aged narrator of the novel, who is ostensibly a friend of the family, he makes his living by writing for the theatre. A tolerant, forgiving man, clearly sympathetic towards ERNEST PONTIFEX, Overton's voice is sometimes more recognizably that of Butler himself, occasionally introducing some special pleading on Ernest's behalf.

Ovid
Poetaster, 1602
Ben Jonson
An historical character appropriated by Jonson, Publius Ovidius Naso was a colourful character who wrote erotic and mythological verse and, after his expulsion from Rome, poems of exile. Jonson approved of Ovid and draws a sympathetic portrait of a young man reluctantly

studying law, his poetic ambitions mocked by his father. But love gives Ovid courage and he resolves to dedicate himself to writing. Later, he devises an 'impious' court masque which provokes the wrath of AUGUSTUS and for which he is banished. A writer's life is especially hazardous, implies Jonson, when patronage is held in political hands.

Ovid (Publius Ovidius Naso)
An Imaginary Life, 1978
David Malouf

The great poet of *Metamorphoses* lived between 43BC and 17AD and wrote of love, mythology and exile. 'Called Naso because of the nose ... What I had a nose for was news – what was fashionable, what would go ... noses are political, even when all you are putting them into are the most private places.' Banished from his people and living on the edge of the known world in conditions of some privation, he is haunted by a mysterious wolf-boy (THE CHILD), who reappears to him throughout his life.

Owen, Cherry
Under Milk Wood, 1954
Dylan Thomas

This typical Welshman has revelry down to a fine art. His cheerful good nature shows in both drunken and sober behaviour: he wreaks limited damage to the house and there is always supper for breakfast. His wife delights in having virtually two husbands. His repertoire includes dancing on the table, crying, singing 'Bread of Heaven' and finally snoring like a brewery, all in a predictable sequence.

Owen, Frank
The Ragged Trousered Philanthropists, 1914
Robert Tressell

A builder and decorator in his early thirties, 'an exceptionally good workman', slightly built and with 'a suggestion of refinement in his clean-shaven face', Owen is considered a bemusing figure, even 'a crank', by his fellow workers. Interested in neither football nor racing, he is instead wholly absorbed by politics as applied to the common man, patiently explaining to his mates the cruelties of capitalism and the need to introduce socialism. However, he is less certain as to how this transition might be achieved. Principled and pragmatic, he has little faith in the winning of economic reforms through collective action, recognizing that first he must convince his co-workers that political debate is not beyond the province of the working class.

Owens, Flora
Picnic, 1953
William Inge

A 'widow lady of about forty', she has been 'both father and mother' to MADGE and MILLIE OWENS since her husband's death ten years before. She is a tidy, hardworking, stern, 'rather impatient little woman' who is greatly concerned with appearances. Underneath 'a certain hardness in her character', she loves her daughters deeply.

Owens, Madge
Picnic, 1953
William Inge

An 'unusually beautiful girl of eighteen', who seems to take her looks very much for granted in an unassuming rather than arrogant fashion, although no one else does. She is not sure what use being pretty is, and seems to envy her sister MILLIE OWEN's intelligence. She is being courted by a wealthy suitor, and a comfortable future beckons, but she falls in love with HAL CARTER, and sets aside her easy option to follow him into an unknown future.

Owens, Millie
Picnic, 1953
William Inge

The boisterous, assertive 16-year-old younger sister of MADGE OWENS, her belligerent manner hides a basic shyness. She is not blessed with her sister's beauty, and is envious of it, but is intelligent and academically gifted. Something of a tomboy, she has a sharp temper and a rebellious streak. She is determined to 'go to New York, and write novels that'll shock people right out of their senses'.

Owens, Tommy
The Shadow of a Gunman, 1923
Sean O'Casey

One of the residents in the Dublin tenement in which DONAL DAVOREN and SEUMUS SHIELDS share a room, Tommy is in his mid-twenties, tall and thin. His voice, thanks to too much drinking and smoking, is reduced to a husky drawl. A hero-worshipper, he is anxious to be on good terms with those, like Davoren, whom he thinks braver than himself, partly because he instinctively seeks protection but also because he hopes to be thought of as glamorous in some way. He is also loquacious, and will 'talk from morning till night when he has a few jars in him'.

Oxford, Harry
The Egoist, 1879
George Meredith

A dashing young hussar who offers CONSTANTIA DURHAM a more open and romantic match than does SIR WILLOUGHBY PATTERNE. Though superficially appealing, it is not clear that Oxford is anything more than a romantic second lead, straight out of stock. The younger couple nevertheless elope, leaving Sir Willoughby humiliated.

Oz, the Great
The Wonderful Wizard of Oz, 1900
L Frank Baum

Perhaps reflecting prevailing US attitudes to Eastern potentates and more directly to a sequence of ineffectual US presidents, the Great Oz is revealed to be a tawdry fake, ruling over a barren, sterile kingdom whose golden approach promises much and delivers nothing.

Ozongo
The Voice, 1964
Gabriel Okara

The chief of the village at Amatu, he sternly represents traditional values but also resists any drift to modernity that will weaken his position.

Ozymandias

'Ozymandias', 1820
Percy Shelley

The 'king of kings' who, in his arrogance and egotism, erected a statue to himself as a symbol of his power and majesty. Nothing now is left of him or of his 'mighty works' that he boasted of – just a 'shattered visage' and two 'trunkless legs of stone'. The scene provides an ironic commentary on the arrogance of a mere mortal who is as subject to time and decay as everything else is.

Pablo
For Whom the Bell Tolls, 1940
Ernest Hemingway
The head of the band of guerillas to which
ROBERT JORDAN is attached, he has been a
capable soldier, but is growing weak and
suspicious. He resents Jordan's presence both as
a soldier and as a rival for MARIA. Although he is
cunning and cannot be trusted, he is also a brave
man and a skilled leader, and is the only one able
to rescue the band after the operation goes wrong.

Pablo (Pablo Sanchez)
Tortilla Flat, 1935
John Steinbeck
One of Danny's Friends, the knights-errant of
Tortilla Flat, led by DANNY. Only Pablo's
preposterous appetite and determined recid-
ivism save him from a longer jail sentence. He is
paroled early to save the police from bankruptcy,
allowing him to continue a career of determined
drunkenness.

Pabst, Angelica
Small World, 1984
David Lodge
As the novel is modelled upon literary romance,
Pabst is an extraordinarily beautiful woman, 'tall
and graceful, with a full, womanly figure and a
dark, creamy complexion', who encounters and
enchants PERSSE MCGARRIGLE at an academic
conference. Claiming to have been a foundling
discovered on board a Dutch aircraft and
completing a doctoral dissertation on Romance,
she mysteriously disappears to be pursued across
the world by McGarrigle. She is further physically
distinguished (not that McGarrigle has evidence
of this) by a distinctive birthmark, 'like an inverted
comma', high on her left thigh. Is McGarrigle's Holy
Grail therefore merely a clever quotation?

Page, Andy
'The Iron-Bark Chip', et seq, in *On the Track*, 1900
Joe Wilson and His Mates, 1901
Children of the Bush, 1902
Henry Lawson
Nobody on the railroad gangs works any harder
or more innocently than Andy, and few are
embarrassed by so little basic brain power. Like
his comrades, he moves on to other 'spec' jobs as
the season demands.

Page, Anne
The Merry Wives of Windsor, c.1597
William Shakespeare
Anne, the daughter of GEORGE and MISTRESS
MARGARET PAGE, is a good-looking, spirited,
determined woman, yet one who 'speaks small'
and has 'seven hundred pounds and
possibilities'. These are the qualities that result
in three hopeful suitors, SLENDER (approved by
her father), DR CAIUS (approved by her mother)
and FENTON, approved only by herself. On
hearing her mother's choice, she replies that she
would 'rather be set quick i'th' earth/And
bowled to death with turnips'. During the
masquerade humiliating SIR JOHN FALSTAFF in
Windsor Great Park, Anne plays the Fairy Queen
and slips away to marry Fenton.

Page, Freddie
The Deep Blue Sea, 1952
Terence Rattigan
A former wartime RAF pilot, the shallow,
flirtatious Freddie discovers that he has
inadvertently released full-flooded passion in
HESTER COLLYER, the wife of a High Court
judge. Yet Freddie is not as glamorous, strong or
romantic as Hester thinks he is, or he would
wish. He drinks and is idle, restless and
thoughtless. He fails to secure a job as a test
pilot. 'I can't be a ruddy Romeo all the time', he
complains, although in his casual, anguished,
emotionally entangled way, he feels more for
Hester than he has felt for anyone else.

Page, George
The Merry Wives of Windsor, c.1597
William Shakespeare
A rich gentleman of Windsor, George Page is
married to MISTRESS MARGARET PAGE and is the
father of ANNE PAGE. Although warned by NYM
that SIR JOHN FALSTAFF has made advances to his
wife, George makes light of it, and when he
hears of a similar approach to ALICE FORD,
advises FRANK FORD to do the same. George
rather likes Falstaff. In fact, he rather likes
everyone except FENTON, one of his daughter's
suitors. According to George, Fenton is 'a
gentleman of no having'. Instead, he favours
SLENDER. He knows that Margaret will never
turn against him, but his attempts to impose his
will upon Anne meet implacable resistance.
Later, he accepts her marriage to Fenton with the
best grace he can muster.

Page, Mistress Margaret (Meg)
The Merry Wives of Windsor, c.1597
William Shakespeare
Like her friend ALICE FORD, Mistress Margaret,
or Meg, Page is one of the 'merry wives' and, like
Alice, has received a love letter from SIR JOHN

FALSTAFF. But unlike FRANK FORD, Margaret's husband, GEORGE makes light of Falstaff's advances. Margaret chides Ford for his jealousy, and with Alice plans to humiliate Falstaff while apparently setting a series of assignations. Later, she devises Falstaff's public tormenting in Windsor Great Park. At the same time, she supports DR CAIUS as the suitor of her daughter, ANNE PAGE. But, although she might predict the follies of men, Margaret does not predict her daughter's determined independence. She learns to accept Anne's marriage to FENTON, and encourages George to do likewise.

Paget, Jean, nicknamed **Mrs Boong**
A Town Like Alice, 1950
Nevil Shute

She has grown up in England and Malaya, and is caught up in the Japanese invasion of South-East Asia. Captured, she shows the same resilient nature that stands her in such good stead in business after the war, when she inherits a fortune. Her recollection of JOE HARMAN's heroism leads her to search for him when she discovers that he has survived.

Pal, Dr
The Financial Expert, 1952
R K Narayan

A sociologist, psychologist and odd 'scientific thinker', Pal believes that men think only of money and sex, and that God has made him to enlighten people about the latter, which is the key to universal happiness. Having capriciously given his manuscript, *Bed Life*, to the shocked, near-destitute MARGAYYA, he disappears for years. In his absence Margayya publishes the book under the more discreet title *Domestic Harmony*, and it proves to be a bestseller, the foundation of untold wealth. But when the poor, but still helpful, Pal returns to Malgudi he befriends – and influences – Margayya's son, BALU, with catastrophic results.

Palamon
'The Knight's Tale', in *The Canterbury Tales*,
c.1387–1400
Geoffrey Chaucer

Sworn friend to ARCITE, he sees EMILY first and, believing her to be the goddess Venus, falls in love with her. A more courtly character and much more devoted to the religion of Love than Arcite, he prays to Venus on the eve of battle that he might win Emily.

Palfrey, Mrs
Mrs Palfrey at the Claremont, 1971
Elizabeth Taylor

Having spent most of her life in the East, she retires to a genteel hotel on the Cromwell Road and begins to slide into a perpetual Sunday afternoon until she meets the would-be writer Ludo, whom she tries to pass off as her grandson, and who awakens her to possibilities she had not hitherto imagined.

Pallet, Layman
The Adventures of Peregrine Pickle, 1751,
bowdlerized edition 1758
Tobias Smollett

Some have argued that this is a satirical portrait of Hogarth (who used the artist's palette as a virtual trademark) but it may have been inspired by someone else. Certainly, Smollett's portrayal of a monoglot snob desperately trying to prove his superior artistic credentials amid the great works of France and Flanders does not seem to have caused Hogarth any offence. Already extravagantly dressed for the trip, Pallet's attire becomes increasingly exotic after he falls in with PEREGRINE PICKLE.

Palliser, Adelaide
Phineas Redux, 1874
The Duke's Children, 1880
Anthony Trollope

A cousin of PLANTAGENET PALLISER. She is a 'tall, fair girl, exquisitely made, with every feminine grace of motion, highly born, and carrying always the warranty of her birth in her appearance'. The 'gift of personal loveliness' has not been bestowed on her, but she takes pride in her health, strength and aristocratic bearing. She falls in love with GERARD MAULE, but his lack of fortune is a barrier to their marriage until her friend MARIE GOESLER passes a bequest from the old DUKE OF OMNIUM to her.

Palliser, Lady Glencora, later **Duchess of Omnium**
Can You Forgive Her?, 1864–5
Phineas Finn, The Irish Member, 1869
The Eustace Diamonds, 1873
Phineas Redux, 1874
The Prime Minister, 1876
Anthony Trollope

A Scottish heiress (her maiden name is MacCluskie) who marries PLANTAGENET PALLISER, becomes the Duchess of Omnium through his inheritance, and is the mother of three children by him. She is a woman of deep feelings and strong sensual needs, to whom love and intimacy are 'absolutely essential', but her husband's failure to understand her nature leads to a continued infatuation with her former lover, the handsome but dissolute BURGO FITZGERALD. Duty triumphs, though, and she remains with Plantagenet, concentrating her considerable energies and ambitions on advancing his political career, although she eventually over-reaches herself in her desire to wield power and influence.

Palliser, Lady Mary
The Duke's Children, 1880
Anthony Trollope

The only daughter of PLANTAGENET PALLISER. She has 'given no signs of extravagance or other juvenile misconduct', but worries her father by the simple fact of being 'beautiful and young', and requiring to be brought out into society. She has inherited her mother's quick manner of speech and sharp intelligence as well as her looks, but is taller and more graceful, and has an innate dignity. She is determined to marry FRANK TREGEAR, and ultimately succeeds in overcoming her father's objections.

Palliser, Lord Gerald
The Duke's Children, 1880
Anthony Trollope

The younger son of PLANTAGENET PALLISER. A

bright, likeable boy, he finds himself in trouble when he disobeys a college ruling forbidding attendance at the Derby, and is sent down from Cambridge, where he has been 'almost as popular at Trinity as his brother had been at Christ Church'. Investigation of the facts suggests 'that the lad should be allowed another chance', and he goes to Oxford, and thence into the diplomatic service, a convenient role for younger sons.

Palliser, Plantagenet
Can You Forgive Her?, 1864–5
Anthony Trollope

The politician who gives the Palliser series its name. He marries LADY GLENCORA PALLISER, and inherits the DUKE OF OMNIUM's title. As a young man, he has 'wealth, position, power, and the certainty of attaining the highest rank', but chooses to pursue a course of duty in dedicating himself to politics rather than pleasure, in which sphere 'he laboured with zeal and perseverance'. He has no real talent or ability, but rises in his plodding, respectable way to the highest office in the land. His sense of propriety is tried to the limit by his children's shortcomings and their wish to make unsuitable marriages.

Palliser-Yeates, John
John Macnab, 1925
John Buchan

Head of a banking firm, he is regarded as an authority on the 'aberrations of postwar finance'. He is also reputed to be something of an adventurer, bored with the civilities of city life and addicted to mountain exploits. Weary of inactivity, he joins with SIR EDWARD LEITHEN, SIR ARCHIBALD ROYLANCE and LORD LAMANCHA to plot the mythical exploits of 'JOHN MACNAB'.

Pam
Saved, 1965
Edward Bond

In her early twenties, Pam is part of a south-London community which includes FRED and LEN. Sexually promiscuous, she picks up Len one evening and takes him home with her. Later, she drops him for Fred, whom she claims to be the father of her child, but Len nevertheless moves in as a lodger to the house she shares with her parents. The family is at war with itself, and Pam is as frustrated, apathetic and dulled as the others. When her baby is murdered in the local park, the tragedy leaves her numb with horror, yet she can be indifferent to a child's cries. She has little to offer the brutal, urban society in which she lives.

Pamela
The Countess of Pembroke's Arcadia, 1581–4, published 1590
Sir Philip Sidney

The elder of DUKE BASILIUS's two daughters, her beauty is almost literally ravishing, capturing men's hearts with a destructive violence. Poised and self-confident, she 'avoids not pride with not knowing her excellencies'. Impressed by her qualities, Samuel Richardson took the name for his great fictional heroine, PAMELA ANDREWS.

Pamela, in full Pamela Andrews
The History of the Adventures of Joseph Andrews and of his Friend Mr Abraham Adams, 1742
Henry Fielding

JOSEPH ANDREWS's sister, she inevitably plays a smaller role in Fielding's novel than she does in Samuel Richardson's earlier account of her adventures. But she acts as her brother's sympathetic confidante and she is present to bless (a little condescendingly, one feels) his marriage to the unaffected FANNY.

Pamela
An Apology for the Life of Mrs Shamela Andrews, 1741
Henry Fielding

Pamela is a shameless gold-digger who marries the wealthy MR BOOBY for his money. The epitome of pretence and hypocrisy, Pamela is linguistically corrupted into the debased Shamela. Referred to as 'saucy chops', 'hussy' and 'slut', Shamela lives up to her reputation by counterfeiting virginity on her wedding night; the theatricality of her manufactured blush is the highlight of her performance. Callous and cynical, the sexually insatiable Shamela is an unedifying combination of prurient bawdiness and unchecked greed.

Pan, Tocky → O'Cannon, Tocky

Pancks, Mr
Little Dorrit, 1857
Charles Dickens

CHRISTOPHER CASBY's reluctant agent and rent collector among the poor tenants of Bleeding Heart Yard, he is a bustling man who 'snorted and sniffed and puffed and blew, like a little labouring steam-engine'. Despite his better nature, he takes the blame for Casby's ruthlessness but ultimately seeks revenge by exposing and humiliating him in front of his tenants. He helps ARTHUR CLENNAM discover WILLIAM DORRIT's right to his inheritance. Naively, he invests his money in MR MERDLE's fraudulent schemes and loses everything when Merdle goes bankrupt. Ultimately, he becomes chief clerk in the firm of DANIEL DOYCE and Clennam and afterwards their partner.

Pandarus
Troilus and Criseyde, c.1385–9
Geoffrey Chaucer

Uncle to CRISEYDE and the worldly go-between for her and TROILUS. He is her chief adviser in the absence of her father. His motives are not evil but he fails to read his niece's character accurately enough. A wily and cunning man he is known more for what he does in the poem than for what he really is.

Pandarus
Troilus and Cressida, 1601/2
William Shakespeare

CRESSIDA's loving and good-natured uncle, Pandarus is also a coarse and immoral bawd, actively seeking the consummation of TROILUS's love for Cressida, and taking a crude pleasure in overseeing as much of it as he can. He spends much of his time observing and commenting on others rather than joining in the action himself.

Pandulph
King John, 1590/1
William Shakespeare

A cardinal and papal legate, Pandulph is a devious tactician and religious fanatic. He pronounces the papal sentence of excommunication against KING JOHN and encourages France to declare war against him. When John reconciles himself to Rome, Pandulph intercedes with LEWIS THE DAUPHIN.

Panthea
A King and No King, 1611
Francis Beaumont and John Fletcher

The daughter of the Iberian Queen Mother, she is the supposed sister of ARBACES, the king, who loves her with an almost uncontrollable lust. Such intensity of feeling provokes a similar response in her. Arbaces sees her as an ideal, as, in many ways, she is, but it is the nature of ideals to have extreme effects. One moment, he cannot think of words eloquent enough to describe her, the next it seems she has bewitched him.'Alas, sir, am I venom?' she asks. 'Yes, to me', he replies. Love, though, triumphs: Arbaces is revealed to be a changeling and Panthea the true queen.

Pantier, Benjamin
The Spoon River Anthology, 1915
Edgar Lee Masters

An alcoholic attorney who, having known 'aspiration' and 'glory' in his early years, turns to despair and drink as a result of rejection by his wife, MRS BENJAMIN PANTIER, who 'snared my soul/with a snare which bled me to death'. Left deserted, in a dingy back room, his only comfort and companion is his dog, Nig, who eventually joins him in the grave.

Pantier, Mrs Benjamin
The Spoon River Anthology, 1915
Edgar Lee Masters

'A woman well endowed', she seeks in her monologue to explain her alienation from and desertion of her husband, BENJAMIN PANTIER. Having 'snared' him, she finds his literary pretensions and 'ladylike' attitudes offended by her husband's philistinism and by his smell 'of whisky and onions'. Implicit in her words is her knowledge that the community blames her for his eventual death.

Papadakis, Cora, (née Smith)
The Postman Always Rings Twice, 1934
James M Cain

A small woman with dark, soft, curly hair and sparkling teeth, Cora has the kind of looks that stop men in their tracks, and a scheming mind that knows how to make the most of them. A former beauty-contest winner from Iowa who once dreamt of Hollywood stardom, she finds her big-league aspirations unsatisfied by life as a hash-slinging waitress at a roadside tavern and marriage to NICK PAPADAKIS. When FRANK CHAMBERS drifts into her sights, she is seized upon as her passport to something better.

Papadakis, Nick
The Postman Always Rings Twice, 1934
James M Cain

A proud, patriotic, Greek-born American, Nick Papadakis considers himself something of a dandy – dressing snappily, oiling his black hair with bay rum and taking pleasure in a rich tenor voice. Attached to his wife CORA PAPADAKIS with dog-like devotion, he eagerly desires a child as confirmation of the bliss that he misguidedly believes himself to have secured.

Papen, Richard
The Secret History, 1992
Donna Tartt

Intellectual misfit Richard Papen leaves his poor white background in Plano, California, to study at Hampden College, Vermont. He joins a small group of intellectuals, under the tutelage of an eccentric classics professor, to study Ancient Greek. As Richard tries to fit in with his new 'friends' and situation, he learns of the secret they share, and becomes involved in the murder – of classmate Buddy – that this situation leads to. The guilt that consumes him sets the course of Richard's life, 'I suppose at one time in my life I might have had any number of stories, but now there is no other. This is the only story I will ever be able to tell.'

Paperstamp, Mr
Melincourt, or Sir Oran Haut-ton, 1817
Thomas Love Peacock

A sketchy character and poet (based on Wordsworth and named after Wordsworth's acceptance of a job distributing stamps), Mr Paperstamp is identified by only 'an affected infantine lisp' and his perennial grey waistcoats.

Paracelsus
Paracelsus, 1835
Robert Browning

He seeks at first knowledge in Nature that will benefit his fellow men but his search becomes that of the secret of life itself. Although urged to learn from the great men of the past, he rejects this because evil still haunts the earth. The death of the poet Aprile makes him realize that he must put his knowledge at the service of humanity. However, his success as a teacher masks the truth that he has become content with lower aims. He aspires again, but worn out and on his deathbed realizes that his striving for absolute knowledge is in vain and that man must be content and accept his limitations.

Paradise, Sal
On The Road, 1957
Jack Kerouac

The narrator, based on Kerouac himself. He has been ill, and has separated from his wife, but his meeting with DEAN MORIARTY begins 'the part of my life you could call my life on the road'. He leads a dual existence, the other part being spent at home writing, and he takes to the road when that becomes too depressing, drawing energy and vitality from Moriarty, whom he sees as a kind of primitive life-force. The trips usually end in disillusionment, and a dejected return to the sobriety of his 'white ambitions'.

Para Handy, properly Peter MacFarlane
Para Handy and Other Tales, 1931
Neil Munro

The captain of a coastal puffer, he likes a dram and a friendly conversation. He is 'a short, thick-set man, with a red beard, a hard round felt hat, ridiculously out of harmony with a blue pilot jacket and trousers and a seaman's jersey'. He has a curious gesture of seeming to be about to scratch his ear, then drawing back. He is un-justifiably proud of his leaky old boat, and is driven to paroxysms of indignation at any slight against it. He has 'a rather gallant way with women', but 'cannot be bothered' to get married. He is shrewd, but is a hatcher of elaborate schemes which he cannot pull off, although he is never deterred for long by failure.

Pardiggle, Mrs
Bleak House, 1853
Charles Dickens

A self-proclaimed philanthropist, she is an ac-quaintance of JOHN JARNDYCE, who detests her because she belongs to that class of charitable people 'who did a little and made a great deal of noise'. Formidable and voluble, she bullies her five resentful children into giving their pocket-money to charitable causes and displays her patronizing insensitivity on a visit to some un-employed brick makers.

Pardoner, the
The Canterbury Tales, c.1387–1400
Geoffrey Chaucer

A minor cleric who rides with THE SUMMONER, singing a duet with him. His thin treble voice, lanky blond hair and inability to grow a beard suggest a lack of virility. He shamelessly abuses the Church to which he belongs, selling pardons and false relics. His deceptions are highly skilled, and when he introduces his tale he reveals himself to the pilgrims as a confidence trickster of the highest calibre. His prologue and tale are a brilliant example of his own skills, but also demonstrate his spiritual bankruptcy.

Pargiter, Col
The Years, 1937
Virginia Woolf

Arrogant, wealthy and esteemed, the colonel makes good use of his privileged position in society to get what he wants in life. He is imperious and haughty to those 'beneath' him, but is in many ways a pathetic figure, craving respect, love and a sense of purpose. He is generous and capable of expressing some genuine affection for his children and mistress, and shows a distant concern for MRS PARGITER, his sick wife, but in reality remains somehow unable to reach the hearts of those he clearly loves.

Pargiter, Mrs
The Years, 1937
Virginia Woolf

A sickly and pathetic woman, hovering between life and death, she remains a distant figure throughout the novel. She spends much of her time asleep, and when she occasionally awakens is unable to arouse affection in others because her illness has made her seem selfish and demented.

Her family display great ambivalence towards her and her predicament; clearly, she has suffered greatly, but she has also lost her perspective on reality.

Parham, Billy
The Crossing, 1994
Cities of the Plain, 1998
Cormac McCarthy

He is a 16-year-old cowboy working on a ranch in New Mexico just before World War II. Drawn to animals and the wild, he undertakes a series of journeys into Mexico, in search of a wild wolf and, later, stolen horses. His experience of Mexico as a more cruel and savage land brings him a maturity and wisdom that to some extent allows him to counterbalance the romanticism of JOHN GRADY COLE, with whom he undertakes a later journey across the border.

Paridell
The Faerie Queene, 1590–6
Sir Edmund Spenser

Spenser's degenerate version of Paris, lover of Helen of Troy. He is a handsome and lusty but rather fickle knight, and his quest is to bring FLORIMELL back to the court of Maidenhead. He is a seductive and passionate young man, eager to possess the beautiful HELLENORE, whatever the consequences.

Paris
Romeo and Juliet, 1591–6
William Shakespeare

A young nobleman, the count Paris offers to marry JULIET. Handsome and rich, though considerably older than she, he is regarded as a suitable match by LORD and LADY CAPULET. His behaviour is impeccable, for he treats his bride-to-be with courtesy on the one occasion when he meets her. By visiting her tomb at night he shows that he must have had some feeling for her. It is his misfortune to be the inadvertent victim caught up in a family feud.

Paris
Troilus and Cressida, 1601/2
William Shakespeare

A son of PRIAM, King of Troy, it is Paris who has precipitated the war between his father's kingdom and the Greeks by seducing HELEN away from her rightful husband, Menelaus (King of Sparta and brother to AGAMEMNON, King of the Greeks). He shows little remorse for this, or for the amount of blood spilt, and, besotted, is determined to keep her.

Paris, Judith
Judith Paris, 1931
Sir Hugh Walpole

In the Herries dynasty, she stands as a civilizing influence, softening and reconciling the harshness of her male kinfolk. To them and to her suitors, she represents the unattainable ideal of absolute identification with place, something that is denied them by their sex.

Parker, Amy
The Tree of Man, 1955
Patrick White

The wife of STAN PARKER, Amy has dutifully

raised their children on their New South Wales farm, and now stands back, disappointed by his refusal of intimacy. His isolation is more apparent than ever after his return from World War I. While Stan embarks upon a private search for God, Amy, passionate, unfulfilled and restless, acquires a lover. She is a woman who needs to possess rather than to give; the failure of the marriage is as much her fault as Stan's and her subsequent love affair is selfish. Her actions set in motion a train of events which convince her that there is no ordered pattern to life. Existence, for Amy, is a series of random experiences.

Parker, Ma
Life of Ma Parker, 1922
Katherine Mansfield

The pathetic personification of a hard life of poverty, illness and death, this shabbily dressed charlady battles against other people's filth. She feels 'sorry for those who had no-one to care for them', and her life is spent in the service of others. When her beloved grandson dies of consumption, her terrible despair manifests itself. He was 'all she'd got from life', and she needs to cry, but, caught as she is in the grip of convention, there is nowhere for her proud little soul to go break its heart.

Parker, Stan
The Tree of Man, 1955
Patrick White

As a young man, Stan appears unassuming, stoical. 'He was nothing much. He was a man.' He searches for stability, clearing the land he inherits in the Australian outback and building a home for himself and AMY PARKER, his wife. Working on the farm and raising their children, he believes, will bring the 'contentment of absolute perfection'. Yet his love proves inadequate for the demanding Amy and, as the emotional bedrock for which he is searching eludes him, Stan withdraws into himself, distancing himself from the family and deliberating the existence of God. Finally, he accepts that the only certainty to be found is the mystical rhythm of nature, and that God, if he is anywhere, is within rather than beyond life.

Parks, Vic
Man of the Moment, 1988
Alan Ayckbourn

A powerful man in his forties, Vic served nine years' imprisonment after being convicted of an armed bank robbery, during which DOUGLAS BEECHEY 'had a go'. Reckoning that he has paid his debt to society, Vic has subsequently retreated to a luxury Mediterranean villa and become a television personality. Symbolizing 1980s Britain – a materially greedy, increasingly soulless nation – Vic is celebrated, but still callous and cruel, abusing his servants, his wife and his children's bovine nanny. She and Douglas prove unlikely agents of retribution.

Parmalee, Rees
Pursuit of the Prodigal, 1959
Louis Auchincloss

A wealthy New Yorker with a conventionally mandarin lifestyle and CV, he experiences a growing disenchantment and decides to kick over the traces and turn his back on his former way of life.

Parolles
All's Well That Ends Well, 1602–3
William Shakespeare

Parolles is a companion of BERTRAM during the Italian war. HELENA correctly describes him as a liar, fool and coward. His boasting, and his uproarious humiliation by his fellow officers (who pretend to be the enemy, capture and blindfold him, and listen while he betrays their military secrets) is a great set piece of the play. Parolles represents the moral antithesis of Helena. However, when she and he discuss virginity at the beginning, his advice to 'Keep it not; you cannot choose but lose it', appears to steel her determination to outwit Bertram and compromise him sexually.

Parrington, Eva
'Old Mortality', in *Pale Horse, Pale Rider*, 1939
Katherine Anne Porter

Cousin Eva, a shy and ugly spinster brought up in the shadow of her flighty mother, teaches Latin in a 'Female Seminary' and fights for votes for women. In later years she is fierce, bitter and fond of money, but she defends the memory of AMY BREAUX to her young relative MIRANDA. Her receding chin is the bane of her life.

Parry, Jed
Enduring Love, 1997
Ian McEwan

Ponytailed, with a big, open, boney face and clear, blue-grey eyes, Parry is 28 years old, unemployed and living in Hampstead on the proceeds of an inheritance. Developing an obsessive love for JOE ROSE, whom he encounters in the course of a tragic ballooning accident one summer's day on the Chiltern Hills, Parry stalks him and beseiges him with assurances that their love is both mutual and divinely inspired, and that his purpose is to 'bring' Rose 'to God'. A deeply disturbed and disturbing young man, Parry's deluded euphoria is curdled into vengeful hatred by Rose's rejection of him.

Parry, Will
The Subtle Knife, 1997
The Amber Spyglass, 2000, parts of the *His Dark Materials* trilogy
Philip Pullman

Will, an intelligent, serious and sensitive boy, conceals his mother's mental instability until circumstances force him to take drastic action in her defence, after which he goes on the run. He has great strength of mind and is 'good at not being noticed', qualities which he hopes will see him through a solitary journey in search of his missing father. Self-sufficient and intensely private, he is reluctant to let down his guard even when he urgently needs help and support. After meeting LYRA BELACQUA he learns that his life must take a path he could not have predicted, and that his fate is closely linked to hers.

Parson, the
The Canterbury Tales, c.1387–1400
Geoffrey Chaucer
The archetypal 'good shepherd' who puts the needs of his flock before his own, leads a holy and simple life and practises first what he will later preach. He is defined partly by his abstract virtues and partly in terms of what he does not do, ie seek preferment and neglect his parish duties. His tale is a lengthy sermon on the Seven Deadly Sins.

Partridge, Mr
The History of Tom Jones, 1749
Henry Fielding
A worthy and thoroughly unworldly school-master, initially accused of being TOM JONES's natural father, who becomes the young man's trusted companion, travelling with him as a barber-surgeon.

Passant, George
Strangers and Brothers, 1940, (also entitled *George Passant* in some editions)
C P Snow
A Midlands solicitor's clerk and lifelong mentor and friend of LEWIS ELIOT. Later, he is taken up by Eliot again and is found a job in Whitehall. He is supposed to be modelled on Snow's own childhood friend Herbert E Howard.

Passmore, Laurence ('Tubby')
Therapy, 1995
David Lodge
The highly successful writer of the television situation comedy series, *The People Next Door*, 'Tubby', as he is widely known, is in his late-fifties, 'more pear-shaped than barrel-shaped', bald, and, according to his therapist, a perfectionist impeded by low self-esteem. Although his therapeutic career embraces several methods of treatment, none cures the mysterious pain in his knee. Neither does his obsession for the life and works of Kierkegaard soothe his escalating doubts and sudden middle-aged *angst*. Beset by a collapsing marriage, Tubby embarks upon a search for lost contentment during which he finds himself on a pilgrimage with an old flame from his youth.

Pastorella
The Faerie Queene, 1590–6
Sir Edmund Spenser
A comely shepherdess of modest grace, who is also of noble birth, thus embodying rustic innocence and courtly sophistication. On seeing her beauty SIR CALIDORE, THE KNIGHT OF COURTESY falls in love with her graceful purity. Her beauty dims the beauty of other women like a bright lamp shining in the darkness.

Pat
The Pope's Wedding, 1962
Edward Bond
Pat is married to SCOPEY and lives in a small, dowdy flat. She has promised her mother that she would care for ALEN, a recluse, and does so until Scopey takes over from her. Because she and Scopey and many of their friends are poor, and live in tied farm cottages, Pat sees most things in financial terms, and copes with a life she believes will not change too much with a brave, defensive fatalism.

Pateroff, Count Edouard
The Claverings, 1867
Anthony Trollope
The brother of SOPHIE GORDELOUP, and unsuccessful suitor for the hand of the widowed JULIA BRABAZON. He has the same parasitical nature as his sister, and an easy, affable manner to accompany it. He is 'a fair man, with a broad, fair face, and very light blue eyes', and is 'well-made, active, and somewhat broad in the shoulders', although a little short in stature. His cultivated speech 'hardly betrayed that he was not English'.

Paterson
Paterson, 1946–58
William Carlos Williams
The semi-mythical protagonist of the long poem, who merges his identity with that of the author, and also with the town of Paterson, New Jersey, the subject of the poem. He is not a character in the conventional sense, but a consciousness through which the complex matrix of ideas in the poem can be reflected on a human level ('a man in himself is a city').

Patient, the (Miss Mopply)
Too True to be Good, 1932
George Bernard Shaw
At the outset of the play, the Patient lies ill in bed, asleep, while THE MONSTER, a disgruntled microbe, complains that her wealthy, unhealthy lifestyle is making it ill. When THE NURSE and THE BURGLAR arrive to steal a necklace, the Patient, in a sudden flurry of activity, knocks the Burglar down. The blow liberates them all. The Patient walks out of the world of money and her mother's (MRS MOPPLY's) neurotic over-protectiveness.

Patimkin, Brenda
Goodbye, Columbus, 1959
Philip Roth
A myopic upper-class teenage girl from a rich Jewish family, she has a summer affair with NEIL KLUGMAN, a lower middle-class Jewish boy. She has an idealized notion of love, but at the same time is sexually open, intelligent, witty and able to hold her own in the verbal infighting characteristic of her elegant but barbed social milieu. She has ambivalent feelings about her world, but is ready to accept its benefits, and grasp its opportunities. These do not ultimately include Neil.

Patroclus
Troilus and Cressida, 1601/2
William Shakespeare
ACHILLES's companion and, according to THERSITES, his 'masculine whore', Patroclus describes himself as having 'little stomach to the war'. He spends his time in Achilles's tent mocking and mimicking the Greek leaders for his friend's amusement, and keeping him from more serious matters of war. Later, he realizes that he is or may be seen to be a bad influence on Achilles and encourages him to take up arms

again, and it is his death that finally spurs Achilles into action.

Patterne, Sir Willoughby
The Egoist, 1879
George Meredith
The egoist of the title, he is a good-looking, wealthy and influential man, but one determined to shape life and individuals to his own selective pattern and requirements. The story recounts his successive humiliations as the women he selects as helpmeets come to recognize his true nature and reject him.

Pattieson, Peter
The Black Dwarf, in *Tales of My Landlord: First Series*, 1816, et seq
Sir Walter Scott
The usher and assistant – since deceased – to JEDEDIAH CLEISHBOTHAM, he is supposed to have collected and compiled the stories heard in the Wallace Inn, Gandercleugh, which are gathered together as *Tales of My Landlord*, a patent misnomer, since the publican narrates none of them.

Patullo, Duncan
The Gaudy, 1974
Young Patullo, 1975
A Memorial Service, 1976
The Madonna of the Astrolabe, 1977
Full Term, 1978, forming *A Staircase in Surrey*
J I M Stewart
The Scottish narrator of this 'Oxford Quintet', Patullo is a successful playwright in his forties, who returns to his old college, Surrey, as university Reader in Modern European Drama. Having had, by Edinburgh standards, 'a disreputably Bohemian childhood', and leading a solitary life since his brief, disastrous marriage, he needs to be part of a stable, close-knit community. But his undergraduate love for his college is now tempered by the more objective, ironic eye of the adult playwright, and he recognizes its cloistered eccentricities. Subsequent events are related with dryly humorous insight.

Paulina
The Winter's Tale, 1611
William Shakespeare
The wife of ANTIGONUS, one of the lords at the Sicilian court of LEONTES, the forthright and fair-minded Paulina believes that Leontes's denunciation of HERMIONE as unfaithful is evidence of mental illness. She reproaches him, attempting to prick his conscience and Leontes responds by patronizing and bullying her, and appealing to Antigonus: 'Can'st not rule her?' Later, she announces Hermione's death, appearing to believe the queen is dead when she is not. But if Paulina is deliberately deceiving Leontes, rather than being deceived herself, she is being cruel to be kind, forcing the king to consider his actions. Her husband having been killed by a bear, she later marries CAMILLO.

Pauper (The Pure Man)
Ane Pleasant Satyre of the Thrie Estaitis, 1540
Sir David Lindsay
Arriving on-stage during the Interlude, the Pauper is seemingly not part of the main action of the play. However, in his grievous complaints against the system of death duties and teinds operated by the Church and the landlords, it becomes clear that his plight is right at the heart of the *Satyre*. A naturalistic character straight out of the 'real' world, his part in the action and his ultimate fate are of the utmost significance.

Pavloussi, Hero
The Vivisector, 1970
Patrick White
The wife of Greek shipping-tycoon whom BOO HOLLINGRAKE procures as a mistress for HURTLE DUFFIELD, the intensely arrogant and egotistical Hero embarks on a pilgrimage to Greece, convinced that when she arrives she will experience a spiritual rebirth. Duffield accompanies her. The quest is a failure, as Hero is disgusted by the filth of the place. Impressed by her voracious sexual appetite, Duffield imagines her both as an ideal woman and his spiritual bride. But Hero is far too self-centred and brittle for such a fantastic arrangement.

Pawkie, Provost
The Provost, 1822
John Galt
Provost Pawkie describes his municipal career with satisfaction. He has never resorted to 'jookerie cookerie' but, more subtly, has insinuated ideas into one person's mind after another, privately, over wine or toddy, so that each goes away thinking them his own. By this means he has had himself elected councillor, bailie and three times provost; similarly he arranges for a suitable piece of silver plate to be presented to him on his resignation. Genial and pleased, he has supported progress, and if some small advantage has accrued to him, like the contract for volunteers' uniforms, why shouldn't it?

Peace, Sula
Sula, 1980
Toni Morrison
In spite of growing up in a chaotic household, Sula is driven by a desperate loneliness. Attracted to NEL WRIGHT because 'they found in each other's eyes the intimacy they were looking for', she endows the relationship with an emotional freedom. Her sexual and social independence earns her a role as scapegoat for the community, which paradoxically brings it unity.

Peachum, Polly
The Beggar's Opera, 1728
John Gay
The wife of CAPTAIN MACHEATH, whom she trusts because 'in the romance you lent me, none of the great heroes were ever false in love'. She fights her parents, who are horrified by the match – THOMAS PEACHUM fearing it will jeopardize his own position. She also fights LUCY LOCKIT for MacHeath's affections and pleads for her husband's life with the jailers.

Peachum, Thomas
The Beggar's Opera, 1728
John Gay
The least attractive of a bad bunch, Peachum is a

lawyer and receiver of stolen goods, who uses incriminating information to damn his associates when it suits him. He suggests his daughter POLLY PEACHUM betray her husband in order to become a rich widow. Often cynically aphoristic, he notes that gamesters and highwaymen treat their whores well but their wives badly, and explicitly likens his own sort to corrupt great statesmen. He and LOCKIT, THE JAILER are based on Sir Robert Walpole and his sidekick Lord Townsend.

Peak, Godwin
Born in Exile, 1893
George Gissing
In a novel very much concerned with male and female attitudes to the New Woman, it is Peak who sets out the types of women encountered in an age of partial emancipation. His is a lofty view, largely out of touch with the actual women one encounters in the book, and Peak's viewpoint is revealed as that of an authoritarian sentimentalist.

Peake, Joby → Churchill

Pearl (Pearl Prynne)
The Scarlet Letter, 1850
Nathaniel Hawthorne
The illegitimate child of HESTER PRYNNE and the unacknowledged child of ARTHUR DIMMESDALE. Dressed fantastically as a simulacrum of the embroidered A (for adulteress) on Hester's breast, she stands out amid the priestly black and 'sad-colored garments' of the townsfolk as a living symbol of the power of love and imagination. As such, she is not quite a fully rounded human character.

Pearson, Bradley
The Black Prince: A Celebration of Love, 1973
Iris Murdoch
The novel's narrator, an insular writer who has spent his working life as a tax inspector. After producing only three slim 'literary' books in 40 years, he intends to devote himself in glorious solitude exclusively to his magnum opus, and is disapproving of his book-a-year protégé, ARNOLD BAFFIN, for having sacrificed art to wealth and fame. Fussy and secretive, Pearson admits to being a nervous and conventional slave to habit. But his self-centred existence is severely threatened by the Baffins, his volatile ex-wife and his neurotic sister, and, when he falls deliriously in love with Baffin's student daughter, the ordeal he believes essential to great art arrives with a vengeance.

Pecksniff, Charity and Mercy
Martin Chuzzlewit, 1844
Charles Dickens
The daughters of SETH PECKSNIFF and as hypocritical as their father. Hoping to benefit financially, he marries off the younger and prettier Mercy to JONAS CHUZZLEWIT, but she is cruelly treated. MRS TODGERS comforts her, suffering improves her character, and after Jonas's suicide, she is cared for by OLD MARTIN CHUZZLEWIT. The sour and shrewish Charity becomes betrothed to a lodger of Mrs Todgers,

Augustus Moddle, but he deserts her on the morning of their wedding.

Pecksniff, Seth
Martin Chuzzlewit, 1844
Charles Dickens
The cousin of OLD MARTIN CHUZZLEWIT, he is a duplicitous hypocrite intent on unctuously persuading his cousin to leave his money to him rather than the other Chuzzlewit relatives. Posing as an architect and land surveyor, although 'he had never designed or built anything', he accepts pupils merely to gain their premiums. He takes on young MARTIN CHUZZLEWIT in an attempt to ingratiate himself with Old Martin, unaware that Old Martin has detected his true character from their first meeting. Believing he is currying favour with the grandfather, he quarrels with the grandson, who sets off for America. Hoping to gain power over Old Martin, he takes him into his home, to be cared for by his hypocritical daughters, CHARITY and MERCY PECKSNIFF. His exploited assistant, TOM PINCH, at first worships him but discovers his true nature and is dismissed. His lasciviousness and fondness for drink are revealed in his wooing of MARY GRAHAM, who repulses him, and his visit with his daughters to MRS TODGERS's Commercial Boarding House. He is ruined after JONAS CHUZZLEWIT dupes him into investing in MONTAGUE TIGG's fraudulent insurance company. After he is publicly exposed, denounced and struck down by Old Martin, all the while protesting that he is a 'moral man', he becomes an alcoholic begging-letter writer.

Peebles, (Poor) Peter
Redgauntlet, 1824
Sir Walter Scott
Plaintiff (and also apparently defendant) in a litigation of Dickensian complexity against his former drapery partner Paul Plainstanes. Impoverished, hungry, bibulous and quite mad, he stands as a reminder of the perils of law untempered by humanity and reason.

Peerybingle, John
The Cricket on the Hearth, 1845
Charles Dickens
A country carrier, and the husband of MRS MARY PEERYBINGLE. He is lumbering and slow, 'so heavy but so light of spirit; so rough upon the surface, but so gentle at the core; so dull without, so quick within; so stolid, but so good!' Doting upon his much younger wife, he grows jealous over a mysterious rival, blaming himself rather than condemning her, before his error is revealed.

Peerybingle, Mrs Mary (Dot)
The Cricket on the Hearth, 1845
Charles Dickens
The pretty and agreeable wife of JOHN PEERYBINGLE, she is called Dot on account of her dainty stature. Her role in secretly arranging the return of EDWARD PLUMMER on the day that MAY FIELDING is supposed to marry MR TACKLETON leads her husband to suspect her of infidelity.

Pegeen Mike, properly Margaret Flaherty
The Playboy of the Western World, 1907
J M Synge

The daughter of Michael Flaherty, a publican near a village in Mayo, she is 'a wild-looking but fine girl', aged about 20. Her spirit is magnificent, too great and too imaginative, perhaps, to be constrained by her environment. She falls for CHRISTY MAHON, a rural Don Juan, and wins him against fierce opposition. Yet Christy's heroism is founded on lies, and when he leaves, her spirit is crushed. She loses not merely 'the only Playboy of the Western World', but also her belief in the transforming power of love and the ideal of reckless, transcending romance.

Peggotty, Clara
David Copperfield, 1850
Charles Dickens

The plump and practical sister of DANIEL PEGGOTTY, servant of MRS CLARA COPPERFIELD and DAVID COPPERFIELD's adored nursemaid and friend. After Clara dies, she marries MR BARKIS, who has long wanted to marry her, and finally becomes housekeeper to the adult David.

Peggotty, Daniel
David Copperfield, 1850
Charles Dickens

The brother of CLARA PEGGOTTY, he is a kind-hearted Yarmouth fisherman who lives in a converted boat with his niece, LITTLE EM'LY, his nephew, HAM PEGGOTTY, and MRS GUMMIDGE. A rough but honest bachelor, he is delighted when Little Em'ly and Ham become engaged, but distraught when Little Em'ly elopes with MR JAMES STEERFORTH. He searches for her on the Continent and, with the help of the prostitute, MARTHA ENDELL, they are finally reunited in London, after which all three emigrate to Australia.

Peggotty, Ham
David Copperfield, 1850
Charles Dickens

A strapping, good-natured boat-builder and fisherman, he lives with his uncle, DANIEL PEGGOTTY, and Daniel's adopted niece, LITTLE EM'LY. They become engaged, but she runs away with MR JAMES STEERFORTH on the eve of the wedding, thus breaking his heart. Some years later, during a great storm on Yarmouth beach, he dies attempting to save the life of a drowning man. When the body is washed ashore, it is revealed to be that of Steerforth.

Pegler, Mrs
Hard Times, 1854
Charles Dickens

The mother of JOSIAH BOUNDERBY, she is a respectable countrywoman who worked hard in order to give her son a start in life. Ungrateful, he pays her £30 a year to stay away so that he can maintain the fiction that he has pulled himself up from the gutter. She is discovered by MRS SPARSIT, who makes her reveal in public that Bounderby has lied about his upbringing.

Pelet, Monsieur
The Professor, 1857
Charlotte Brontë

The master of the Brussels school where WILLIAM CRIMSWORTH embarks on his teaching career, Pelet is a Frenchman 'both by birth and parentage', and seems to the narrator to embody many attributes of that race, being immoral and capricious, as well as 'cold and blasé' in his attitude towards women. His appearance is 'gentleman-like' and the impression he gives is one of gentleness, but William quickly becomes aware of the 'existence of flint or steel under an external covering of velvet' and notes how Pelet treats those he considers inferior with insensitivity and disdain.

Pelham, David
Season in Purgatory, 1975
Thomas Keneally

A young British army surgeon, seconded to Tito's partisans in World War II. Though sympathetic to their cause, he recognizes that war is the province of cynical game-players who operate at a considerable distance from the blood of battle and that war itself is an irredeemable instinct.

Pembroke, Agnes
The Longest Journey, 1907
E M Forster

Described as a mixture of 'insight and obtuseness', Agnes Pembroke is a robust, canny woman, able to accept the death of a lover or a daughter with a surprising lack of emotion. Practical, devious, venal, she is 'content with the daily round, the common task, performed indifferently'. However, in the idealistic eyes of RICKIE ELLIOT she appears as someone altogether more heroic and becomes his wife. Essentially superficial, she seeks to provide him with loyal, steadfast encouragement but winds up moulding him to her desires. Ultimately, 'she loved to mislead others, and in the end her private view of false and true was obscured, and she misled herself'.

Pendennis, Arthur
The History of Pendennis, 1848–50
The Newcomes, 1853–5
W M Thackeray

A young man in whom decency, affection and noble intentions are compounded with venial weakness and a certain unfixity of resolve. His romantic interests, like his various career moves, are shakily if honestly contracted. Fleet Street seems, for a time, the only likely outlet for his talents. However, there is enough heroism dormant in him to guarantee a safe domestic and professional haven.

Pendennis, Helen
The History of Pendennis, 1848–50
W M Thackeray

ARTHUR PENDENNIS's widowed mother, she is good-hearted and unworldly, motivated almost exclusively by love for her rather flighty son. She is, however, one of Thackeray's downtrodden women, about whom it is only possible to feel ambivalent, uncertain to what extent she capitalizes on her misfortunes and to what degree she is the architect of them. She generously adopts LAURA BELL, but it is Laura who saves the family from ruin. The question is, was this a matter of luck or calculation?

Pendennis, Major
The History of Pendennis, 1848–50
W M Thackeray

ARTHUR PENDENNIS's uncle, he is an Irishman who hides his peccadillos behind army rank. Tactically he is rather subtle, easing Arthur out of an 'unsuitable' marriage to EMILY COSTIGAN and politicking quietly for BLANCHE AMORY, even though he knows that her father, the villainous COL ALTAMOUNT, is still alive.

Penderton, Captain
Reflections in a Golden Eye, 1941
Carson McCullers

The estranged husband of LEONORA PENDERTON. Humiliated by his wife's infidelity and isolated in leadership, he is also tormented by his repressed desires for other men. An insomniac who seeks diversion from unhappiness in hard work, he is in constant search of relief from his restlessness. Ultimately, his volatile and contradictory emotions become fixed on PRIVATE ELLGEE WILLIAMS.

Penderton, Leonora
Reflections in a Golden Eye, 1941
Carson McCullers

The handsome and independent wife of CAPTAIN PENDERTON and lover of MAJOR MORRIS LANGDON. A sensuous and impulsive woman, she is described as both fearless and 'a little feeble-minded'. Her reputation as an excellent horsewoman earns her the simple title of 'The Lady' while her sexual magnetism draws the obsession of PRIVATE ELLGEE WILLIAMS.

Pendleton, Virginia
Virginia, 1913
Ellen Glasgow

As a young lady, Virginia's loveliness and lightly-worn happiness dazzled all who knew her. She is a proper Southern lady who believes, as her education has prepared her, that marriage is the solution to all the questions of a woman's life. Unfortunately, her own marriage brings misery, suffering and the surrender of selfhood to a man whose personality is oppressive. Despite outbursts of petulance, snobbery and self-pity, Virginia retains her blind romantic enthusiasm and kindness. She occupies a world of deluded fantasies.

Penfeather, Lady Penelope
St Ronan's Well, 1823
Sir Walter Scott

She runs her own little salon at the Well, gathering her forces opposite those of Lady Binks. St Ronan's affords her ample opportunity for exercising her pretensions to culture and learning as she strives to keep her fading looks turned to the most flattering available light.

Penniless, Pierce
Pierce Penniless His Supplication to the Devil, 1592
Thomas Nashe

A poor scholar and tyro poet, who 'having spent many years in studying how to live, and lived a long time without money, having tired [his] youth with folly and surfeited his mind with vanity', repents of selfless devotion to learning and art and addresses himself to prosperity.

Pennyfeather, Paul
Decline and Fall, 1928
Evelyn Waugh

As an unassuming, unexceptional student of divinity at Scone College, Oxford, Paul Pennyfeather is stripped naked in the quadrangle by drunken revellers and is sent down 'for indecent behaviour'. He becomes a teacher at Llanabba Castle School, North Wales, and is offered a vacation job as a personal tutor in an eccentric country house, where he falls madly in love with his pupil's mother, the millionairess MARGOT BESTE-CHETWYNDE. She accepts his proposal of marriage, and through her he becomes involved in slave trafficking and is arrested hours before their highly public wedding. Sentenced to seven years' penal servitude, he is quickly released and his death faked; he diffidently continues his studies at Oxford.

Penrose, Robyn
Nice Work, 1988
David Lodge

A progressive, *Guardian*-reading young lecturer in PHILIP SWALLOW's English department at Rummidge University, Penrose contends that there is no 'essence' constituting anyone's identity, merely 'a subject position in an infinite web of discourses' such as 'power, sex, family, science, religion, poetry etc', a network within which she includes her partner, Charles. She encounters businessman VICTOR WILCOX as part of a project in which she is to view industry at work. Initially antagonistic towards his conservative orthodoxy, her inabilities to gauge the politics of the workplace result in her learning a new respect for Wilcox's world of free enterprise.

Pepita
The Bridge of San Luis Rey, 1927
Thornton Wilder

A 14-year-old orphan girl 'borrowed' from the convent to be companion to THE MARQUESA DE MONTEMAYOR. She is also singled out by the abbess as eminently suitable to continue her lifelong and selfless work among the needy. Patient, quiet, intelligent and industrious, she becomes a source of revelation and redeeming self-knowledge for the marquesa.

Percival
The Waves, 1931
Virginia Woolf

Based on the author's brother Thoby Stephen, who died of typhoid as a young man, Percival is the central character in the novel, though he does not appear in person. He is put on a pedestal by others, who see him as utterly heroic and loveable, and his tragic death proves devastating for them.

Percy and Edwina

Hackenfeller's Ape, 1953
Brigid Brophy

Rare captive specimens of *Anthropopithecus hirsutus Africans*, a species of apes named by and for a sober Dutch zoologist. They are held in London Zoo, where they are made the subjects of an intrusively detailed study of primate sexual behaviour. Percy refuses to comply, and is threatened with the hot seat on an early space probe until PROFESSOR CLEMENT DARRELHYDE comes to their defence.

Percy, Henry, Earl of Northumberland

Richard II, not later than 1595
Henry IV Part I, 1596/7
Henry IV Part II, not later than 1597/8
William Shakespeare

Northumberland agrees reluctantly to join his brother, THOMAS PERCY, EARL OF WORCESTER, and his son, HOTSPUR, in rebellion against HENRY IV, the man he helped put on the throne, because he feels he has not been amply rewarded. He proves unreliable, conveniently falling ill before the battle of Shrewsbury. Indeed many, including his daughter-in-law LADY PERCY, believe that this is a feigned illness. His unreliability is emphasized by his failing to join a second rebellion led by the Archbishop of York. Such is the power and influence of his name that his support of a cause can guarantee heavy involvement from other minor figures. When he does finally take up arms, it proves abortive and he is defeated and killed.

Percy, Lady

Henry IV Part I, 1596/7
Henry IV Part II, 1597/8
William Shakespeare

Almost entirely passive in the presence of her husband HOTSPUR, Lady Percy is concerned that his failure to take her into his confidence may indicate that he does not care for her. When asked by him to sing, she shows her stubbornness and refuses. After Hotspur's defeat and death, she blames her father-in-law, HENRY PERCY, EARL OF NORTHUMBERLAND, showing an uncommon burst of anger. In spite of this she is reluctant to see more family blood shed and urges him to flee.

Percy, Lewis

Lewis Percy, 1989
Anita Brookner

'He was, he thought, destined to become a ruminant, a haunter of libraries'. A studious man, still living with his elderly mother while completing his thesis (on fictional heroism) at the British Museum, he is tentative and methodical, but would like to acquire a heroic air himself. He imagines working for the British Council, 'representing England' and gaining an aura of experience and authority which women might find attractive. Inspired by literature, he marries but, neither happy nor unhappy, arrives only at a state of indifference which is broken only by external crisis.

Percy, Thomas, Earl of Worcester

Henry IV Part I, 1596/7
William Shakespeare

Worcester, along with his brother, HENRY PERCY,

EARL OF NORTHUMBERLAND, and his nephew HOTSPUR, rebels against the king they aided to the throne, arguing that they have been rewarded inadequately for the important part they played. His real grudge appears to be more personal as he fails, deliberately, to pass on HENRY IV's offer of peace to Hotspur in case it is accepted. He understands his nephew better than most, warning against his rash behaviour and trying to heal the harm his rudeness causes. When the alliance starts to fall apart, Worcester would rather fight against uneven odds than submit to his enemy.

Perdita

The Hundred and One Dalmatians, 1956
Dodie Smith

Perdita, or Spotty as she was originally called, is a pretty, delicate dalmatian, with unusual liver-coloured markings. Starved of love by the farmer who owns her, separated from both her husband and her litter of eight pups, she is the perfect foster mother for some of MISSIS's brood. She cares for the pups selflessly and unpossessively and is heartbroken when they are stolen. Her delicate state of health means she cannot take part herself in the search, but she has a vital role to play as comforter to the Dearlys, Nanny Cook and Nanny Butler.

Perdita

The Winter's Tale, 1611
William Shakespeare

The daughter of LEONTES and HERMIONE, Perdita is the infant whom Leontes orders ANTIGONUS to take from the court and leave to die; she appears as a 16-year-old shepherdess, a vivacious, natural spirit, suspicious of artifice. She has a long discussion with the disguised POLIXENES on the subject, in which she puts forward an argument for the supremacy of nature over art, and at the sheep-shearing festival, feels uncomfortable 'pranked up' in carnival dress. Her nobility of birth is revealed by the innate sophistication of her charm and manners, something to which FLORIZEL, the son of Polixenes and Prince of Bohemia, instinctively responds. She is both rustic and courtly, practical and idealistic and, as the heroine of a romance, discovers her true identity and her love for the prince.

Peregrine

Volpone, or The Fox, 1606
Ben Jonson

An English gentleman travelling in Venice, Peregrine encounters SIR POLITIC WOULD-BE, recognizes him as a gullible fool, and taunts him so thoroughly that Would-Be has to leave the city. Peregrine is a heartless, malicious snob, a meddler in other people's affairs and a bully who derives enjoyment from humiliating others.

Perez, Catalena

The Whole Armour, 1962, part of *The Guyana Quartet*, 1985
Wilson Harris

The Portuguese wife of one of RUSSELL FENWICK's crew, she narrowly escapes rape by a 'nameless presence above her who promises to save her'; she receives the vision vouchsafed to special individuals 'in times of singular ordeal or singular ecstasy'.

Perichole, La (Camila)
The Bridge of San Luis Rey, 1927
Thornton Wilder

A highly talented and bewitching actress, mother of three illegitimate children by the Viceroy of Peru, La Perichole began performing at the age of twelve, singing in cafés and sleeping locked in a wine bin until rescued by her 'Pygmalion', UNCLE PIO. She is incapable of expressing her own feelings, or of harmonizing the conflicting demands in her crowded life. Discontent driving her to seek some unknown fulfilment in 'respectability', she rejects the stage and faithful Uncle Pio. Later, disfigured by smallpox, she becomes a recluse, but eventually discovers the truth about love.

Pericles
Pericles, c.1608
William Shakespeare

The Prince of Tyre and the play's stoical hero, Pericles sets off on a journey in search for a wife. He sails first to Antioch, and then to Tarsus before being shipwrecked and eventually arriving at Pentapolis, governed by SIMONIDES. Pericles marries THAISA, Simonides' daughter, who gives birth to MARINA; but when his wife is thought to have died, he gives Marina into the care of CLEON and DIONYZA. Pericles, Thaisa and Marina are presented as an idealized family and the values of constancy embodied by each of them are celebrated by their eventual reunion.

Perissa
The Faerie Queene, 1590–6
Sir Edmund Spenser

The younger sister of ELISSA and MEDINA, she has a large appetite for life, enjoys herself intemperately and takes everything to excess, whether food, drink or sex. Possessed of no 'measure in her mood, no rule of right', she is exuberant and extravagant and takes SANSLOY as her lover.

Peronett, Hugh
An Unofficial Rose, 1962
Iris Murdoch

Recently widowed, this retired civil servant, a failed artist and incorrigible romantic, resents having long ago relinquished the 'peril' of a great love affair with bewitching, mysterious EMMA SANDS. Hoping to recapture the past with her, the conventional, correct Peronett engages in reckless and morally dubious behaviour. Both delighted and appalled by his 'crime', he discovers the impossibility of rewriting the past, but takes a wry satisfaction from having altered the face of his world.

Perrin, Mr Vincent
Mr Perrin and Mr Traill, 1911
Sir Hugh Walpole

A master at Moffatt's school for boys, he is nervous and obsessive about his work, and also convinced that the duty of education is the straightforward communication of ready-made truths, not a training in independent thought. 'He was long and

gaunt; his face might have been considered strong had it not been for the weak chin and a shaggy, unkempt moustache of a nondescript pale brown. His hands were long and bony, and the collar that he wore was too high, and propped his neck up, so that he had the effect of someone who strained to overlook something.'

Perron, Guy
The Jewel in the Crown, 1966
The Day of the Scorpion, 1968
The Towers of Silence, 1971
A Division of the Spoils, 1975, forming
The Raj Quartet
Paul Scott

The upper-class, wryly humorous and unconventional Perron stubbornly resists being commissioned during World War II, and in 1945 is a Field Security sergeant and has voted Labour in the postwar election. He has a Cambridge degree in British imperial history, but finds India unnervingly different from his academic knowledge of it. Attracted to SARAH LAYTON, he is drawn into her social circle, and meets RONALD MERRICK, whom he loathes. Despite his skill in self-preservation, Guy experiences personally some of the horrific realities attendant upon the partitioning of India.

Person, Hugh
Transparent Things, 1972
Vladimir Nabokov

This tall, sad, clumsy pun of a protagonist turns tricks for his author to show verbal dexterity and the storyteller's art. Revisiting Switzerland at various times, he encounters death, sex, love and murder, and filters each with detached passion. His story repeats itself with obsessive precise detail – names are nearly the same so that slight shifts of coincidence confuse reality. Human life, he says, can be compared to a person dancing in a variety of forms around the self: these merge into the hero, through whom all things are visible.

Pert, Mr
White-Jacket, 1850
Herman Melville

A midshipman on board the warship *Neversink*. He is known as 'milk-and-water', and is invariably to be found scurrying around on some errand for the superior officers. His congenital cockiness is heightened by his position, and he is disliked by the men under him.

Pertelote
'The Nun's Priest's Tale', in *The Canterbury Tales*
c.1387–1400
Geoffrey Chaucer

CHAUNTICLEER's favourite hen and as down-to-earth as he is pompous and sententious. She ascribes his dream of capture by a beast to a choleric superfluity and not to portentous warnings of his fate, and recommends a good purgative and laxative. Her beauty temporarily overcomes his fear. Hers is the voice of common sense.

Pertwee, Louise
Hidden Laughter, 1990
Simon Gray

Louise, a novelist, and Harry, a literary agent,

own a weekend cottage in Devon, although the only villager they trouble to get to know is the local vicar, RONNIE CHAMBERS. Louise has such a capacity for both love and fretfulness that she smothers Harry's love for her. Worrying about the present so much makes her dread the future. Like Ronnie she is absorbed by doubt, but unlike him Louise is also so self-obsessed that she ceases to realize how deep Ronnie's private fears really are. Harry is unfaithful to her and when he finally leaves, she does not know whether to be happy or grieved.

Peshkov, Eugene
The Time of the Angels, 1966
Iris Murdoch

A White Russian driven from St Petersburg when he was six, Eugene, the rectory caretaker, treasures his brief childhood happiness. After years in labour and refugee camps he sees the world itself as a 'transit camp'; his only possessions are his mother's icon of the Trinity, and a plant that, like himself, somehow survives in his dark concrete box of a room. Gentle, honest and kind, he is the father of the delinquent LEO PESHKOV, and loves PATTIE O'DRISCOLL, a 'fellow citizen' of his exiled life.

Peshkov, Leo
The Time of the Angels, 1966
Iris Murdoch

EUGENE PESHKOV's student son. He is a compulsive liar and cheat, described by his former teacher, MARCUS FISCHER, as a 'trouble-maker of genius'. Singularly beautiful, with strawberry-blonde hair, he hopes to seduce the indifferent MURIEL FISCHER. She attempts to introduce him to ELIZABETH FISCHER as a healthy diversion, but Leo more successfully charms Marcus.

Peter
The Lion, the Witch and the Wardrobe, 1950, et seq
C S Lewis

The oldest of four children, he is an upright, decent boy, anxious to be fair-minded, and slow to criticize. He is particularly close to his sister LUCY, and is the first to believe her fantastic tales of Narnia and its inhabitants. In time he becomes a model king, ruling Narnia with his siblings with a mixture of sternness and good humour.

Peter
The Zoo Story, 1958
Edward Albee

A successful advertising executive who meets with the unpredictable JERRY in a New York park and has his middle-class repressions gradually stripped away by the artist's provocative and ultimately violent behaviour. Stabbing Jerry in self-defence marks Peter's first properly con-summated relationship with another human being.

Peterborough, Lady → Spalding, Caroline

Peterborough, Lord → Glascock, Charles

Peterkin
The Coral Island, 1857
R M Ballantyne

The youngest and most vulnerable of the three boys forced to endure life on a desert island, he is tearful and hesitant, overwhelmed by the experience. Rather shy and weak, he is loyally supported by his friends JACK MARTIN and RALPH ROVER, and copes remarkably well with the adjustments that are forced on him, never once letting the side down.

Peter of Pomfret
King John, 1590/1
William Shakespeare

A hermit, living in Pontefract, Peter has created a reputation for himself by prophesying that 'ere the next Ascension-day at noon' KING JOHN will lose the English crown. Outraged, John orders him to be imprisoned and, on the day in question, to be hanged. Yet, when on that day John makes peace with Rome, he reflects that Peter was essentially correct: 'I did suppose it should be on constraint;/But, heaven be thank'd, it is but voluntary'.

Peter Pan
Peter Pan: or The Boy Who Would Not Grow Up, 1904 (play), 1911 (book)
J M Barrie

De facto leader of the Lost Boys, he first appears wearing little more than autumn leaves and cobwebs, searching with the fairy TINKERBELL for his shadow, which he lost when a window sash fell on his departing figure. Invisible to those who have passed beyond the age of innocence, he has the ability to fly, and exists in permanent flight from any reminder of passing time or pressing reality (mothers chiefly). An ally of Tiger Lily in the long conflict with CAPTAIN HOOK, he believes death will be an 'awfully big adventure'. His home directions are among the most famous in literature: 'Second to the right and then straight on till morning'.

Peters, Jeff
'Hostages to Momus', and others, in *The Gentle Grafter*, 1908
O Henry

A gentle grafter, who together with ANDY TUCKER delights in acts of 'bunco' that defraud the wealthy, arrogant or pretentious. Still, he has his scruples; 'in all my illegitimate inroads against the letter of the law the article sold must be existent, visible, producible'. Jeff's joy in the confidence game is in the game itself, although he never objects to its inevitably lucrative outcome.

Petersen, Harald
The Group, 1963
Mary McCarthy

Working in the theatre as a stage-manager or assistant director, this young man is confidently awaiting his breakthrough as a playwright. Convinced of his own genius and the rightness of his opinions, he is irritated by any opposition and does not hesitate to use his verbal skills to dominate and to wound. He pushes his admiring wife KAY STRONG's patience to the limit, repeatedly hurting her simply to evoke a response, and the marriage suffers from the combined effects of her devotion and his self-regard, as surely as it does from his drinking and womanizing.

Peterson, Stan
Down in the City, 1957
Elizabeth Harrower

A moody, erratic man, proud of the prestige his marriage to ESTHER PRESCOTT has brought him, yet resentful of his wife's privileged background. Involved in numerous illegal businesses, Stan 'was a man of grunts and nods and silences. If he could avoid an eye or a question, he did, his expression enigmatic'. He loves Esther deeply, but his feelings of insecurity in her presence, as well as his inherent disregard for women, lead to rows and violence. Esther eventually realizes that Stan's personality is 'one so precariously balanced on his desperate need for universal admiration, that criticism, however just, from anyone he deemed superior, plunged him from normality to a state where pride was burned and thought and feeling ran molten.'

Petit the Poet
The Spoon River Anthology, 1915
Edgar Lee Masters

His name symbolizes the 'littleness' of his life; in his monologue he satirizes his addiction to poetic form ('triolets, villanelles, rondels, rondeaus') and bemoans the amount of time he has wasted ('all my life long') before he became aware that great poetry exists in his natural surroundings and in the men and women of his village. The 'unnatural' way he has approached his art contrasts neatly with FIDDLER JONES.

Petkoff, Raina
Arms and the Man, 1894
George Bernard Shaw

Raina is the youthful, beautiful daughter of Catherine and Major Petkoff, a Bulgarian family of high social pretension. Her pervasive romanticism, it seems, has been learned in the nursery and now in adult life symbolizes her immaturity. She sees the Serbo-Bulgarian war from a child's point of view and as an opportunity for a display of dashing heroism by her adored SERGIUS SARANOFF. However, the practical capability of the mercenary soldier BLUNTSCHLI, whom she discovers taking refuge in her bedroom, convinces her that life is serious and he, not Sergius, becomes the object of her affections.

Peto
Henry IV Part I, 1596/7
William Shakespeare

A very minor member of SIR JOHN FALSTAFF's 'minions of the moon', who participates in the robbery on Gad's Hill, Peto emulates his master by leaving early and lying profusely when challenged. He is representative of the Elizabethan underclass who hoped that the advent of Prince Hal (HENRY, PRINCE OF WALES) to the throne would mean prosperity for those such as Falstaff and his followers.

Petowker, Miss Henrietta
Nicholas Nickleby, 1839
Charles Dickens

An actress at the Theatre Royal, Drury Lane, and then with VINCENT CRUMMLES's company. A friend of MR and MRS KENWIGS, where she meets NICHOLAS NICKLEBY, she marries Mrs Kenwigs' uncle, MR LILLYVICK, but soon elopes with a half-pay captain.

Petrie, Miss Wallachia
He Knew He Was Right, 1869
Anthony Trollope

A somewhat affected American poetess living in Florence, where she is captivated by the history and culture of European civilization. She is a friend of CAROLINE SPALDING, and is opposed to her marriage to CHARLES GLASCOCK. Caroline gently satirizes her friend as 'the American Browning'.

Petrie, William
'The Dying Stallion', in *Selected Stories*, 1946
'Elephants, Bairns and Old Men', in *The Laundry Girl and the Pole*, 1955
Fred Urquhart

An old farmer in North-East Scotland, who loves and understands horses. He is out of sympathy with his sons-in-law (who want him to introduce tractors), and with his nagging daughters and noisy grandchildren. He lives in the past with his memories, especially of his dead son, who shared his feelings for the old ways. His remaining relatives do not understand him, so he escapes from them to be with his favourite stallion.

Petruchio
The Taming of the Shrew, early 1590s
William Shakespeare

Having spent much of his life travelling the world, Petruchio comes to Padua with the express intention of finding himself a wealthy wife. He is self-possessed and assertive, treating his servants with the brusqueness they deserve. He agrees to marry KATHARINA without seeing her, apparently unconcerned by her reputation for violence because she is rich. To overcome her fiery nature he has to be the tamer, his tactic being to prove himself more contradictory and headstrong than she. He is cruel because he wants to break her spirit, but he takes pleasure in the wooing, especially the outcome, for he seems to be fond of her, and maybe even loves her.

Pettijohn, Randolph
Nigger Heaven, 1926
Carl Van Vechten

A Harlem gambler who pursues MARY LOVE and, more successfully, LASCA SARTORIS. He is successful and wealthy, but also irredeemably vulgar, and there is a whiff of violence around him that bodes a bad end.

Petworth, Dr Angus
Rates of Exchange, 1983
Malcolm Bradbury

Dr Petworth is 'not a character in the world historical sense'. He is 'a man who is styleless'. A linguist, he is expert in vowel shifts and phonemes, and teaches these in Bradford, where he lives with a small, sad and uncommunicative wife. In the summer of 1981, the dawn of the age of 'Sado-Monetarism', he is dispatched upon a lecture tour of Slaka (a fictional Eastern European country loosely modelled upon Bulgaria). Circumspect, provincial, watchful, groping for facts and finding them fiction or, at the most, fable, Petworth discovers everything to be subject to rates of exchange.

Peveril, Julian
Peveril of the Peak, 1823
Sir Walter Scott

Larger-minded than his father, SIR GEOFFREY PEVERIL, his role as page to the Countess of Derby throws him headlong into the intrigues and naked rivalries of Restoration politics and up against a plot that involves his childhood playmate ALICE BRIDGENORTH. Though conventional, Julian has a straightforwardness that sets him apart from other Scott heroes.

Peveril, Sir Geoffrey
Peveril of the Peak, 1823
Sir Walter Scott

A Derbyshire nobleman, the father of JULIAN PEVERIL, he is a committed Royalist who falls foul of the anti-Catholic smear campaign known as the Popish Plot. He is a man 'who had many of the ordinary attributes of an old-fashioned country gentleman, and very few individual traits to distinguish him from the general portrait of that worthy class of mankind. He was proud of small advantages, angry at small disappointments, incapable of forming any resolution or opinion abstracted from his own prejudices'.

Pew, Sherman
Clock Without Hands, 1961
Carson McCullers

A black orphan whose blue eyes indicate a mixed race parentage and who yearns to discover the identity of his mother. A proud and precocious young man with a volatile temper, he is driven by a desire for intellectual and social self-improvement. The traumatic revelation of his family history provokes him to an act of protest which is both selfless and reckless.

Phaedria
The Faerie Queene, 1590–6
Sir Edmund Spenser

A glittering, seductive temptress who entertains CYMOCHLES with fantastic tales and merry laughter. Beautiful in both her behaviour and her endearments, she appears to be the most pleasant of all womankind. She slowly and blissfully punts her ornate gondola on the 'Idle Lake'. She considers adulterous love more praiseworthy that the spoils of war.

Phaon
The Faerie Queene, 1590–6
Sir Edmund Spenser

The son of Proteus, a sea god who can assume any shape he wishes in order to beget children. His mother is a gentle nurse who knows 'skill in leaches craft'. Taking after his mother, Phaon learns the healing art and becomes the physician of the Gods.

Phebe
As You Like It, c.1600
William Shakespeare

A shepherdess loved by SILVIUS, she haughtily rejects his advances as she clearly has ideas above her station. She has her comeuppance when she falls in love with the disguised ROSALIND, who rejects her. But ultimately she is realist enough to see that marriage to Silvius is the best life for her.

Phelan, Billy
Billy Phelan's Greatest Game, 1978
William Kennedy

A high-rolling gambler in 1930s upstate New York, his 'greatest game' is a bid to free the kidnapped son of the McCalls, who run Democratic machine politics in Albany. It is clear that Billy's world is no more than a shadow of a brighter and more heroic past (an impression that is reinforced by the appearance of his father FRANCIS PHELAN in *Ironweed*).

Phelan, Francis
Ironweed, 1983
William Kennedy

BILLY PHELAN's father, he has been a major league baseball star, but is now a drunken derelict, sentimentally reliving his great days and gradually coming to terms with his past as he roams the streets of Albany.

Philaster
Philaster, or Love Lies Bleeding, 1609
Francis Beaumont and John Fletcher

The rightful King of Sicily, he has been usurped by the King of Calabria. Philaster is in love with Calabria's daughter, ARETHUSA, but is forced to communicate with her by means of his page, BELLARIO. When he understands Bellario to be having an affair with her himself, Philaster is plunged into despair. His personality is such that he veers from the heights of elation to the depths of melancholy. He is a man of emotional extremes, an idealist searching for absolutes. A sensual man, Philaster feels rather than reasons, and has little practical or political vision.

Philautus
Euphues, or The Anatomy of Wit, 1578
John Lyly

A young Italian gentleman, he is betrothed to LUCILLA, but loses her to his Athenian friend EUPHUES, a betrayal that affects their relationship somewhat materially. Philautus, though, has a more mature and reasonable attitude to the experience and seems likely to survive the disappointment.

Philip → Firmin, Philip

Philip
The Philanthropist, 1970
Christopher Hampton

Hampton's play is partly an inversion of Molière's *Le Misanthrope*. A bachelor don and specialist in philology with an obsession for anagrams, Philip is not a true philanthropist but a disappointed idealist. Intellectually honest but emotionally fumbling, his desire to please merely results in exasperating everyone. His painful efforts to avoid offence, his inability to say no and his lack of ambition only partially conceal a deep-seated fear of life. His dithering integrity extends even to admitting his fundamental shortcoming: 'My trouble is, I'm a man of no convictions. At least, I think I am.'

Philip, King of France
King John, 1590/1
William Shakespeare

Philip, along with LYMOGES, DUKE OF AUSTRIA, supports the claims of ARTHUR, DUKE OF BRITTANY to the English throne in place of the ruling KING JOHN. Treacherous and vacillating, he demands that John abdicate, and accuses him of being a usurper. A peace of sorts is brokered between them when Philip consents to the marriage of his son, LEWIS THE DAUPHIN, to BLANCHE, John's niece. Yet, although Philip might challenge constitutional authority, he defers to the Catholic Church and reneges on their alliance when PANDULPH threatens him with excommunication if he continues to support the English 'arch-heretic'. Later, he admits his defeat by John.

Philip II, King of France and Navarre, known as Philip Augustus, originally Denis Mountjoie
The Talisman: A Tale of the Crusaders, 1825
Sir Walter Scott

Constitutionally cautious and unwilling to compromise domestic concerns for the defence of Christendom, he is a politic rather than heroic figure. 'Philip might be termed the Ulysses, as Richard [I, Coeur-de-Lion] was indisputably the Achilles, of the Crusade. The King of France was sagacious, wise, deliberate in council, steady and calm in action.'

Philip II of Spain
That Lady, 1946
Kate O'Brien

An ascetic, pious and ruthless absolute monarch, who governs his empire with an obsessive and exhausting attention to detail. He has always had a flirtatious relationship of mutual admiration with ANA DE MENDOZA Y DE LA CERDA, now the widow of his favourite minister, and his vanity is hurt when she has an affair with a younger minister. Typically, his feelings of insecurity prompt him to act cruelly.

Philippa
Some Experiences of an Irish R.M., 1899
Further Experiences of an Irish R.M., 1908
In Mr Knox's Country, 1915
E O Somerville and Martin Ross

Philippa, the immediate reason for THE MAJOR's embarking upon his Resident Magistracy, finds rural Ireland even more bewildering than he does. Everything there is more violent and noisy. Conversations with the housekeeper are conducted in what seems a foreign tongue; supplies even of milk for a tea-party are late; football and athletics are like guerilla warfare, and when she follows the hunt on a bicycle she is saddened that the foxcub is dead when hauled out of a culvert. Even so, she gets on well with FLURRY KNOX and soon settles down cheerfully among the friendly savages.

Philipson, Arthur, actually De Vere
Anne of Geierstein, or The Maiden in the Mist, 1829
Sir Walter Scott

The son of the banished Earl of Oxford, SEIGNOR PHILIPSON, he is rescued in the Alps by ANNE OF GEIERSTEIN. His skills as a bowman are reminiscent of those of QUENTIN DURWARD, whose strong likeness he bears, but they win for him the rivalry of RUDOLPH DONNERHUGEL. Restored to his true estate, he marries Anne.

Philipson, Seignor, actually De Vere, Earl of Oxford
Anne of Geierstein, or The Maiden in the Mist, 1829
Sir Walter Scott

A banished English nobleman travelling incognito as a merchant in Europe, where he becomes embroiled in CHARLES THE BOLD, DUKE OF BURGUNDY's wars. He is accompanied by his son, ARTHUR PHILIPSON, and his reaction to the young man's apparent loss in the mountains is a measure of his reliance on him.

Phillip, Governor (Arthur)
The Timeless Land, 1941
Storm of Time, 1948
No Barrier, 1953
Eleanor Dark

The first governor of New South Wales, who captained the first fleet to Botany Bay in 1787, and founded the settlement at Sydney in 1788. He then steered the colony through times of great privation, perceiving its potential importance. Bent on 'civilizing' the natives, Phillip makes a favourite of the tribal singer, BENNILONG, and takes him on a visit to England trying, unsuccessfully, to convert his protégé to the English way of life.

Phillips, Sir Watkin, Bart
The Expedition of Humphry Clinker, 1771
Tobias Smollett

The chief recipient of JERY MELFORD's letters, he is said to be modelled on a Jacobite Member of Parliament called Sir Watkin Williams Wynn, who sat for Denbighshire in the early 18th century. Like Wynn, Phillips is a graduate of Jesus College, Oxford, and is obviously privy to Jery's affairs.

Phillotson, Richard
Jude the Obscure, 1895
Thomas Hardy

The anti-hero of the novel, a school-master whose conventionality, as opposed to JUDE FAWLEY's progressiveness, makes him unappealing. A man of rationality and principle, his passion for SUE BRIDEHEAD causes him to disgrace himself in an altogether irrational fashion. However, he is naive in affairs of the heart, and is deluded about himself and his unattractiveness to the youthful Sue. Passive rather than active, he is, above all, a sentimentalist.

Philly the Weeper
Stories à la Carte, 1932
Damon Runyon

Whoever claimed there was honour among thieves had not met Philly the Weeper, for, as a thoroughgoing opportunist and self-preserver, he is quite prepared to pull a fast one over others of his profession (small-time crooks and gamblers), and shamelessly takes his chances to get rich with the minimum of effort or legality whenever they arise. As such, he sometimes finds it necessary to hide from those who are disappointed at his venal and insensitive ways.

Philoclea
The Countess of Pembroke's Arcadia, 1581–4, published 1590
Sir Philip Sidney

The younger and milder of DUKE BASILIUS's daughters, 'so bashful as though her excellencies had stolen into her before she was aware'. She is seduced by the radiant PYROCLES.

Phipps, Miss Dora
The Battlers, 1941
Kylie Tennant

Known to most on the road as 'the fat madwoman', she is the parasite of the travelling community. Haughty, disapproving, with affected upper-class speech and manners, she latches on to any group that does not physically eject her. She manages to take from her companions even while abusing them, avoids any kind of work, and is first in the queue when food is on offer; yet she remains tenaciously oblivious to the concerted attempts of her companions to get rid of her.

Phlebas the Phoenician
'Death By Water', in *The Waste Land*, 1922
T S Eliot

A drowned sailor, once handsome, lulled into forgetfulness by the motion of the sea.

Pi (Piscine Molitor Patel)
Life of Pi, 2002
Yann Martel

Named after a swimming pool in Paris, Piscine, or 'Pi', is the son of a zookeeper in Pondicherry, India. A precocious child, he experiments with various religions to see which fits him best (following Hinduism, Christianity and Islam). When he is 16, his family leave their zoo and join a cargo ship to transport themselves and a number of their animals to a new life in Canada. When the ship sinks, Pi is apparently left in a lifeboat with a hyena, an injured zebra, an orang-utan and a Royal Bengal tiger called Richard Parker. His story relates the will to live and the nature of humanity, as Pi reveals his desire to survive and utilizes all his knowledge and all his faith in an attempt to reach dry land.

Pickering, Col
Pygmalion, 1913
George Bernard Shaw

Pickering is an elderly, amiable man of a military background, a student of Indian dialects. Having met a fellow scientist, PROFESSOR HENRY HIGGINS, in Covent Garden on the same night that they encounter ELIZA DOOLITTLE, Pickering lodges with him at Wimpole Street. He wagers Higgins that he cannot transform Eliza's speech sufficiently for her origins to pass undetected in polite society. At first as insensitive to her feelings as Higgins, he is jolted into a new awareness by Higgins's indignant mother after the experiment has ended.

Pickle, Gamaliel
The Adventures of Peregrine Pickle, 1751, bowdlerized edition 1758
Tobias Smollett

PEREGRINE PICKLE's father, the son of a London merchant, he suffers chronic anxiety about the state of his property and interests. Otherwise, he seems to be extremely difficult to arouse. 'The sallies of his youth, far from being inordinate or criminal, never exceeded the bounds of that decent jollity which an extraordinary pot, on extraordinary occasions, may be supposed to have produced in a club of sedate book-keepers … The passion of love never interrupted his tranquillity', and his life is managed by his maiden sister, Mrs Grizzle, who persuades him to remove to the country, and eventually arranges his marriage.

Pickle, Peregrine
The Adventures of Peregrine Pickle, 1751, bowdlerized edition 1758
Tobias Smollett

The complete moral opportunist, he has a nose for any situation that will serve to his aesthetic (including sexual) or monetary advantage. His credibility as a magician and as a parliamentary candidate suggests both the extent and the limitations of his resources. He is a not entirely amiable rogue.

Pickwick, Samuel
Pickwick Papers, 1837
Charles Dickens

A retired man of business and confirmed bachelor, 'the very personation of kindness and humanity', he is the genial founder and chairman of the Pickwick Club. With three other members, TRACY TUPMAN, AUGUSTUS SNODGRASS, NATHANIEL WINKLE and his servant, SAM WELLER, he sets out on two years of travel and adventures, intending to record his observations. They are initially involved in merely comic incidents, but the innocent Pickwick's encounters with the law and imprisonment for debt in the Fleet Prison introduce him to the darker side of life and 'scenes of which I had no previous conception'. On his discharge from the Fleet, he resigns from the club, it is dissolved, and he settles down in Dulwich, contented to see his young friends happily married, including Sam Weller, whose wife he makes his housekeeper.

Pictor Ignotus
'The Unknown Painter', in *Men and Women*, 1855
Robert Browning

'I could have painted pictures like that': the unknown painter claims that had he chosen he could have been famous, but then he would have had to sell his works and leave them at the mercy of buyers to love or hate. They would have become mere possessions. Instead, he prefers to work on church and cloister paintings, for the sake of Art. But is he really as talented as he thinks he is or is he just envious of real genius?

Pied Piper of Hamelin, the
'The Pied Piper of Hamelin', in *Dramatic Romances*, 1845
Robert Browning
An amusingly outlandish character, dressed in a coat of red and yellow, who agrees to rid Hamelin of its rats. When the Mayor refuses payment he pipes another tune, to which all the children except one lame boy follow him through a door in a mountain and disappear, leaving the town in mourning.

Pienaar, Peter
Greenmantle, 1916, et seq
John Buchan
The man from whom RICHARD HANNAY learnt all his 'veld-craft', he is 'about five foot ten, very thin and active, and as strong as a buffalo'. He has 'pale blue eyes, a face as gentle as a girl's, and a soft sleepy voice'. After the Greenmantle adventure, he enlists in the Royal Flying Corps where, despite his advanced age, he becomes a semi-legendary ace; *Mr Standfast* (1918) finds him sadly reduced, having been disabled in a crash, but still an actor in the drama.

Pierce, Joel
Of Time and the River, 1935
Thomas Wolfe
A young Northerner of wealthy family who befriends EUGENE GANT. At first Eugene considers him the epitome of all he aspires toward, but increasingly he comes to regard him as shallow and materialistic.

Pierce, Mildred
Mildred Pierce, 1941
James M Cain
A self-sacrificing pillar of maternal strength, she has known life on the wrong side of the tracks and is determined that her ungrateful daughter Veda will enjoy all the advantages she never had. Swallowing her pride to don a waitress's apron, she slaves tirelessly for the good of an upwardly-mobile child who grows to despise her common roots. For her, happiness always remains elusive.

Pierce of Exton, Sir
Richard II, not later than 1595
William Shakespeare
He presumes too much on Henry Bolingbroke's favour and wrongly assumes that KING RICHARD II's death will please him. Immediately the deed is done he regrets it. This impulsive rashness is rewarded with banishment. Shallow and changeable, he sees the enormity of his crime and accepts his punishment.

Pierre
Venice Preserv'd, or A Plot Discovered, 1682
Thomas Otway
A soldier, Pierre nurses a grievance against the Venetian Senate and, hearing that JAFFIER has been insulted by PRIULI, draws him into the plot against the state. Pierre is the one character in the play who approximates to the idea of a conventional hero. He is gallant and full of rhetoric, and although his conspiratorial motives are fuelled by revenge, he is at the same time a political idealist. Arguably, though, he is

a bad judge of men: his friendship with and loyalty to Jaffier precipitate catastrophe.

Piers the Plowman
Piers Plowman, 14th century (late)
William Langland
An honest English labourer, whilst wandering on the Malvern Hills Piers has a protracted vision of the world in microcosm. Summary of Piers's character is impossibly complicated by variant texts and the likelihood of multiple authorship, but his narrative is typified by the allegorical treatment of secular, ecclesiastical and spiritual notions, many of which are portrayed with telling contemporary detail. In one version, Piers's all-seeing eye makes him similar to, if not synonymous with, Jesus Christ.

Pierston, Jocelyn
The Well-Beloved, 1892
Thomas Hardy
An idealistic sculptor who seems unable to relate to women in any satisfactory way. He is vain in that his 'real' ideal is a woman who is the female equivalent of himself. He rationalizes his philandering with the notion that every woman he becomes involved with is in fact the same creation, femininity itself. He is a complex man who is ultimately self-indulgent, though he is attractive in the sense that he faces up to the dissatisfying nature of human relationships, striving to find the ultimate relationship, instead of enduring a stultifying existence.

Piggy
Lord of the Flies, 1954
William Golding
Of the schoolboys stranded on a desert island, Piggy is the outsider, alienated because of his different background, his asthmatic condition, his size and his sloth. He instantly becomes a figure of ridicule, but, to an extent, he masochistically colludes in this. Nevertheless he is a knowledgeable, rational boy who understands the situation more acutely than the others and attaches himself to RALPH, not just because he is desperate to be liked, but also because he recognizes that Ralph represents the group's one hope for civilized continuity. His ability to remind the boys of unwanted truths is repaid by his own death.

Piglet
Winnie-the-Pooh, 1926
The House at Pooh Corner, 1928
A A Milne
A small piglet with a stripey jumper, he lives in the Hundred Acre Wood with all his friends. His littleness, sensitivity and modesty are his most endearing features, although he can be truly brave when his adventures with WINNIE-THE-POOH demand it.

Pignatelli, Pope Antonio
The Ring and the Book, 1868-9
Robert Browning
A very old man, he has to review the case of the murder of POMPILIA and her parents before pronouncing sentence on COUNT GUIDO FRANCESCHINI. He seeks guidance from the

judgements of his predecessors, but finds they conflict with each other. He tries to judge the case as God would see it, but doubts that Divine Truth dwells in him even as pope. Finding in the end that he cannot trust his reason alone he turns to faith; totally convinced of Pompilia's innocence he can find no reason to free Guido and condemns him to death.

Pike, Dominicus
'Mr. Higginbotham's Catastrophe', 1834, in *Twice-Told Tales*, 1837, revised edition 1842
Nathaniel Hawthorne

A travelling tobacco pedlar. After hearing (and spreading) rumours and counter-rumours regarding the hanging of MR HIGGINBOTHAM, he travels to Kimballton and arrives just in time to save the old man from murder and, by way of reward, to marry his niece.

Pilar
For Whom the Bell Tolls, 1940
Ernest Hemingway

One of the more convincing female characters in Hemingway's fiction, perhaps because her qualities are essentially those of the typical male hero, she is tall and strongly-built, and dominates a band of guerillas by willpower and natural authority. She has a stinging tongue, and is both respected and feared. Sexually powerful, experienced, and self-aware, she can be brutally coarse, but is also capable of great tenderness and delicacy of feeling.

Pilgrim, Billy
Slaughterhouse 5, 1969
Kurt Vonnegut, Jr

A naive but prosperous optometrist who becomes 'unstuck in time', and is transported back and forth through his past and future in unpredictable fashion. He is 'a funny-looking child who became a funny-looking youth – tall and weak and shaped like a bottle of Coca-Cola'. His principal destinations are World War II (especially the firebombing of Dresden), an airplane crash, and the planet Tralfamadore, under the influence of which he comes to believe his mission on earth is to 'prescribe corrective lenses for Earthling souls'.

Pilkington, Mr
Animal Farm, 1945
George Orwell

Mr Pilkington owns one of the neighbouring farms to Animal Farm and is 'an easy-going gentleman farmer', quite content to spend most of his time in idle pursuits like fishing and hunting. He cares little for his run-down farm. Essentially selfish, he cannot even unite with his rival MR FREDERICK to defend their mutual interests. At first he scorns the idea of a farm run by animals and helps to mount an attack. Eventually, looking after his own interests, he learns to make deals with NAPOLEON and the other animals. For him, profit is more important than principle.

Pilon
Tortilla Flat, 1935
John Steinbeck

One of the paisanos of Tortilla Flat and a

drinking friend of the semi-legendary DANNY. He is, perhaps, a fraction more cautious and calculating than his comrades, but 'the curse of realism' lies on him only uneasily.

Pinch, Dr
The Comedy of Errors, c.1594
William Shakespeare

He is crucial to the comic catastrophe and appears in Act IV to 'exorcize' ANTIPHOLUS OF EPHESUS, who is believed to be mad. The thinness of his physical appearance is reiterated for comic effect and, in productions, his brief speech can often become an extended moment of high comedy.

Pinch, Tom and Ruth
Martin Chuzzlewit, 1844
Charles Dickens

A gentle and good-hearted brother and sister whose innocence initially leads others to take advantage of them. A former pupil and unpaid assistant of SETH PECKSNIFF, Tom first worships his employer, but on recognizing his true character, he is dismissed. He insists that Ruth leave her job as governess with a family who bully and humiliate her, and the two live together in London in genteel poverty with MR NADGETT as their landlord. Tom, who is ungainly and prematurely old in appearance, secretly but chivalrously adores MARY GRAHAM and, although patronized by young MARTIN CHUZZLEWIT, he watches over her while Martin is in America. He supports himself and Ruth through employment anonymously provided by OLD MARTIN CHUZZLEWIT, and she falls in love with his friend, JOHN WESTLOCK. When Martin marries Mary and John marries Ruth, he is unselfishly 'tranquil, calm and happy' and makes his home with Ruth and John.

Pincher Martin
Pincher Martin, 1956
William Golding

A sailor whose warship is sunk by a U-Boat. Shaking off his heavy seaboots, he is able to stay afloat and scramble on to a rock. As he waits in hope of rescue, snatches of his former life pass before him. His battle to scale the rock becomes a metaphor for the struggle of life itself: the questing after faith and meaning in the face of all adversity. The harrowing, dyspeptic ending, when the true nature of Martin's fate becomes clear, has the quality of nightmare and subverts the meaning of what had seemed an inspiring, if pitiable, tale of human endurance and self-belief.

Pinchwife, Margery
The Country Wife, 1675
William Wycherley

Married to the brutally coarse MR PINCHWIFE, Margery is a good-humoured, unspoiled country woman who learns how to take advantage of the pleasures and intrigues of London town life, particularly with the help of aristocratic rake HORNER. Unlike other high society ladies she is devoid of hypocrisy, and plots to outwit her husband only because he is too unreasonably possessive.

Pinchwife, Mr

The Country Wife, 1675
William Wycherley

A supposedly reformed libertine, who 'could never keep a whore' successfully, Pinchwife does not allow his young 'country wife' much freedom to enjoy herself. He even locks her up on occasion to save her from the depredations of other men, though he trusts her with the apparently impotent HORNER. Ironically, the more he restricts his wife, the more he incites her to cuckold him.

Pinfold, Gilbert

The Ordeal of Gilbert Pinfold, 1957
Evelyn Waugh

Transparently a version of the middle-aged Waugh, he is a successful novelist in his fifties, suddenly and devastatingly haunted by visual and auditory hallucinations which bring back the ridicule and disgust of his harsh Catholic upbringing.

Pinkie

Brighton Rock, 1938
Graham Greene

A frighteningly immature boy-psychopath who is the central character of the novel. He is an intelligent, calculating youth who has never known innocence and who hides his fear and uncertainty behind a façade of sadistic behaviour and bravado. In attempting to act like a big-time mobster, he only reveals the small-time origins from which he will never escape. Pinkie hates sex and has never known love. He has thus become socially and emotionally retarded and we sense his frustration and the tragic waste of his life. He has enough religious feeling to believe that he cannot escape damnation; this self-knowledge is his one redeeming feature.

Pio, Uncle

The Bridge of San Luis Rey, 1927
Thornton Wilder

The illegitimate son of a Castilian nobleman, Pio ran away from home at the age of ten and has since lived on his wits, amassing a vast and varied knowledge in the process. In Peru he meets the unschooled but talented twelve-year-old LA PERICHOLE and buys her from her exploiter. With selfless devotion, as both her mentor and servant, he turns her into a consummate actress, at the same time satisfying his own passion for great Spanish literature and theatre. An 'aged Harlequin', although he is 'disreputable' his witty company delights everyone.

Pip

Moby-Dick, 1851
Herman Melville

A little Alabama-negro cabin boy, also known as 'Pippin'. He is bright, tender-hearted, genial and cowardly until he falls from a boat, and is lost for a time in the 'heartless immensity' of the sea, an experience which 'drowned the infinite of his soul', and drives him mad. He develops a touching affinity with that other affected mind, CAPTAIN AHAB.

Pip, nickname of **Philip Pirrip**

Great Expectations, 1861
Charles Dickens

The novel's narrator and hero, known as Pip from his infant inability to pronounce his full name. Brought up by his sister, MRS JOE GARGERY, and JOE GARGERY and BIDDY, he expects to become a blacksmith. But when very young, he helps an escaped convict, ABEL MAGWITCH, who remembers his kindness years later, having made good in Australia. Told by MR JAGGERS that he has a secret benefactor, he ungratefully leaves Joe to go to London to be educated as a gentleman. He is horrified to learn that a convict is the author of his good fortune, not MISS HAVISHAM, whom he had supposed also intended him to marry ESTELLA. Growing to love Magwitch, he tries to smuggle him out of England to prevent his arrest, but the attempt is foiled and Magwitch condemned to hang. He comforts Magwitch as he dies before he can be executed. Now penniless, he is cared for by Joe during a long illness. When he recovers, he has learnt humility, pays his creditors and becomes a clerk and later a partner with HERBERT POCKET in the merchant house of Clarriker and Co. The novel ends with the hint that he eventually marries Estella.

Pipchin, Mrs

Dombey and Son, 1848
Charles Dickens

An elderly widow in Brighton with whom PAUL and FLORENCE DOMBEY lodge while Paul attends DOCTOR BLIMBER's school. Bitter and stern, she 'takes in' children to support herself and gives them 'everything that they didn't like, and nothing that they did'. She later becomes MR PAUL DOMBEY's housekeeper.

Piper, Ethel

Redheap, 1959, first published in the USA as *Every Mother's Son*, 1930
Norman Lindsay

Ethel is her brother ROBERT PIPER's senior by a year but more than one step ahead of him in her sexual experimentalism. There is a hint of incest between the brother and sister, resolved only when she enters into a relationship with the mild Dr Niven.

Piper, Robert

Redheap, 1959, first published in the USA as *Every Mother's Son*, 1930
Norman Lindsay

Youthful blood rises vigorously in the average 19-year-old, but rarely with such indiscriminate vigour as in this youngster from 19th-century Redheap. He is as potent and venturesome as his environment is dead and barren.

Pipes, Tom

The Adventures of Peregrine Pickle, 1751, bowdlerized edition 1758
Tobias Smollett

One-time bosun's mate to COMMODORE HAWSER TRUNNION and now the butt of his choleric nostalgia for past battles. A minor, seafaring Apollo, he can deflect and soothe the worst storms with tunes played on his bosun's whistle, 'a tone ... that seemed to be the joint issue of an

Irish bagpipe and a sow-gelder's horn'. He later acts as PEREGRINE PICKLE's footman and master of revels.

Pippa
Pippa Passes, 1841
Robert Browning

Innocently enjoying her only holiday of the year – New Year's Day – Pippa wanders through Asolo singing and dreaming of the 'four great ones of Asolo'. She imagines herself as each in turn: the adulterous Ottima, the sculptor's new bride; the patriot Luigi and his mother; and finally the Archbishop. She rejects the first three because 'God's love is best'. Each of these characters is changed by hearing Pippa's innocent singing, even the Archbishop who is plotting to abduct her and send her to a brothel because she is the unknowing heir to his brother's fortune.

Pirrip, Philip → Pip

Pisario
Cymbeline, 1609/10
William Shakespeare

A servant to POSTHUMUS LEONATUS who remains in the British court after his master is banished, it is largely Pisario's intervention that prevents a real tragedy from occurring. He is loyal and dutiful – a 'sly and constant knave' according to the QUEEN – but nevertheless disobeys his master's orders to murder IMOGEN, rightly sceptical of Posthumus's claims of her infidelity.

Pistol
The Merry Wives of Windsor, 1597
Henry IV Part II, 1597/8
Henry V, 1599
William Shakespeare

As his name suggests, Pistol is primed, ready to explode at any time and harm friends and foe. He is short-tempered, foul-mouthed and boastful, especially about his prowess in a fight, a trait that leads him into conflict with FLUELLEN, who makes his breath fouler by forcing him to eat a raw leek. A thief by nature, his main prizes are a cowardly Frenchman who surrenders to him on the battlefield, and MISTRESS QUICKLY whom he steals from NYM.

Pitkin, Lemuel
A Cool Million: The Dismantling of Lemuel Pitkin, 1934
Nathanael West

Pitkin borrows his forename (and his satiric distortion) from Swift (LEMUEL GULLIVER). An ironic reversal of the Horatio Alger success-myth, the breakdown of Lemuel's belief in the great American way is dramatized by his scalping (the archetypal villainy of the Red Indian), the loss of a leg (an echo of Melville's CAPTAIN AHAB), and steady physical dismantlement in a nightmarish vaudeville act.

Pitman, Sir Jack
England, England, 1998
Julian Barnes

'A big man in every sense of the word', Sir Jack is 'less a captain of industry than a very admiral', 'an entrepreneur, innovator, ideas man' who 'dazzles with his larger-than-life charm'; or so reads the tribute carved in stone in his immense offices. A patriot who affects large cigars and MCC braces although he is not a member of the MCC, he builds 'England, England' on the Isle of Wight, a vast tourist attraction, a replica assemblage of everything English, from Stonehenge to Buckingham Palace and from Dr Johnson to Manchester United. Cynical and manipulative, his feline sense of survival enables him to conduct a secret life in which he enacts the part of a baby at an expensive brothel.

Pivner, Mr
The Recognitions, 1955
William Gaddis

OTTO's missing father, with whom Otto never quite manages to organize a reunion; when they try to meet at Christmas, Mr Pivner lapses into a diabetic coma. An ardent self-educator, 'Mr Pivner's attention rarely came upon things at first hand'.

Pizarro, Francisco
The Royal Hunt of the Sun, 1964
Peter Shaffer

A ruthless Spanish soldier of fortune and veteran of two previous expeditions to the New World, the 63-year-old Francisco Pizarro embarks on a further journey to Peru in search of gold, glory and a renown that will live on in the pages of history. Troubled by an old wound and a melancholic preoccupation with death, he finds no solace in Christian faith but begins to think he could believe in the Inca warrior ATAHUALLPA. When the latter's mortality proves as inevitable as his own, the momentary call of faith passes.

Placebo
Ane Pleasant Satyre of the Thrie Estaitis, 1540
Sir David Lindsay

Fellow hedonistic courtier of WANTONNES and SOLACE, Placebo joins with them in recommending the delights of sensual pleasure to his master, REX HUMANITAS, and likewise partakes in the subsequent sexual activity at the court. Laying the blame for the example set him at the feet of the prelates, Placebo is himself forgiven by DIVYNE CORRECTIOUN for his misguided behaviour.

Plagiary, Sir Fretful
The Critic, 1779
Richard Brinsley Sheridan

A playwright, noted for plagiarism and bad writing. In his envy he attacks other writers (including Sheridan) and, although eager to solicit comments on his own works, he rejects even the mildest criticisms. He hates being adversely dealt with in the newspapers (although he affects unconcern), but even worse is not to be mentioned at all.

Plantagenet, Edith
The Talisman: A Tale of the Crusaders, 1825
Sir Walter Scott

She is not quite conventionally beautiful, but gives away her royal breeding by tiny gestures and a regal manner when SIR KENNETH (Prince David) sees her among the nuns at Engaddi. Though their initial contact is shrouded and silent, and Kenneth's real identity is still unknown, they fall in love and eventually marry.

Plantagenet, Richard → York, Richard Plantagenet, Duke of

Plarr, Dr Edouardo
The Honorary Consul, 1973
Graham Greene

A doctor in his mid-thirties, he is a friend of CHARLEY FORTNUM, and has an affair with Fortnum's young wife. He sees himself as both a racial and political outsider in Argentine society, and is connected to the group who kidnap Fortnum. He is strangely drawn to Fortnum's capacity for selfless love, and does all he can to help him, despite his feelings for his wife.

Platt, Irina
Murmuring Judges, 1991
David Hare

The second of a trilogy of plays dealing with British institutions (the first being *Racing Demon* (1990) and the third *The Absence of War* (1993)), *Murmuring Judges* deals with the criminal justice system. An idealistic young black lawyer, Platt is engaged upon a case in which a man has been imprisoned for his part in a robbery, and discovers that every aspect of the legal and penal system is male-dominated, inefficient and in places corrupt, causing her to re-evaluate her expectations and moral standpoint.

Pleydell, Paulus
Guy Mannering, 1816
Sir Walter Scott

Edinburgh attorney and bon viveur, who assists COL GUY MANNERING in the resolution and restitution of Ellangowan estate. He 'was a lively, sharp-looking gentleman, with a professional shrewdness in his eye, and, generally speaking, a professional formality in his manners' which is nonetheless allowed to slip as the company of 'learned' friends and claret begin to take hold.

Pleyel, Catherine
Wieland, 1798
Charles Brockden Brown

The best friend of the novel's narrator, CLARA WIELAND, Catherine Pleyel is more acted upon than acting. 'Endowed with an uncommon portion of good sense', she hardly interrupts the actions of the main protagonists but relays confusing information and impressions to Clara, saying 'I cannot tell', 'he permitted me merely to know', 'I gathered, from hints', and so on. Her compassion for THEODORE WIELAND is unable to save her from death at his hands, but to the end she is a repository of goodness, pleading with her husband to 'tell me thy cause of grief'.

Pleyel, Henry
Wieland, 1798
Charles Brockden Brown

'Guided by reason', this rational, realistic 'champion of intellectual liberty' is as fooled by the trickster FRANCIS CARWIN's ruinous games as anyone. Trusting only his senses and his intellect, Pleyel 'knows' he hears his beloved, CLARA

WIELAND, engaged in furtive and romantic conversation with Carwin; he trusts his own 'knowledge' over Clara's honesty, not recognizing that his interpretation of experience is as flawed as any. The most obvious adversary to Carwin, Pleyel is unable to counter him.

Pliant, Dame
The Alchemist, 1610
Ben Jonson

A beautiful, wealthy, foolish young widow, with no real feelings or opinions of her own, she is jealously protected by her brother, KASTRIL. Accompanying him when he visits SUBTLE for advice on improving his quarrelling technique, she is then pursued by Subtle and FACE, and confronted by the disguised PERTINAX SURLY, whom she considers marrying. When LOVEWIT returns to the house, she immediately agrees to transfer her affections to him instead.

Plornish, Mr and Mrs Thomas
Little Dorrit, 1857
Charles Dickens

A generous, good-hearted couple, tenants of CHRISTOPHER CASBY in Bleeding Heart Yard, he is a frequently unemployed plasterer and his wife affectionately cares for her children and her father, Old Nandy. Having been imprisoned in the Marshalsea, Plornish meets AMY DORRIT and they help her to find work with MRS CLENNAM. Through ARTHUR CLENNAM, CAVALLETTO becomes their lodger, and Mrs Plornish proudly converses with him in ludicrous pidgin Italian, considered in Bleeding Heart Yard to be 'but a very short remove indeed from speaking Italian'. When the DORRITs become rich, Plornish is found a share in a builder's business and his wife is able to open a grocery and general shop in Bleeding Heart Yard.

Plumdamas, Peter
The Heart of Midlothian, in *Tales of My Landlord*, 1818
Sir Walter Scott

A garrulous old shopkeeper of the Grassmarket in Edinburgh, whose chief occupations seem to be the viewing of executions with his female colleagues and neighbours, and inexpert forensic argument.

Plume, Captain
The Recruiting Officer, 1706
George Farquhar

A gentleman officer of reduced means, and the recruiting officer of the title, Captain Plume has fought with great bravery on the Continent, especially at the battle of Blenheim. Sent to Shrewsbury as a recruiting officer he hopes to renew his love affair with SYLVIA, but on discovering that as an heiress she is socially above him, he behaves honourably by withdrawing his claim. He is attractive to the opposite sex and a true friend to WORTHY, whose happiness he attempts to secure. While reluctant to fight over a woman he is prepared to engage in a duel with his rival, BRAZEN, over a recruit (Sylvia in disguise). He is not reluctant to give up his military career in the interests of love.

Plummer, Bertha

The Cricket on the Hearth, 1845
Charles Dickens

The blind daughter of CALEB PLUMMER and friend of MRS MARY PEERYBINGLE. Her father protects her from knowledge of how impoverished they are and how they suffer because of his heartless employer. She falls in love with her vision of MR TACKLETON, but when she finds she has been innocently deceived by her father, she cherishes him even more because of his pure and unselfish motives.

Plummer, Caleb

The Cricket on the Hearth, 1845
Charles Dickens

A poor toymaker, employed by MR TACKLETON. A 'spare, dejected, thoughtful, grey-haired old man', worn down by poverty, he is devoted to his blind daughter, BERTHA PLUMMER, and shields her from the harsh truths of their life by spinning a fairy-tale fantasy.

Plummer, Edward

The Cricket on the Hearth, 1845
Charles Dickens

The son of CALEB PLUMMER, he is engaged to MAY FIELDING. After many years' absence in South America, he is assumed dead and returns to find May engaged to marry old MR TACKLETON. With the help of MRS MARY PEERYBINGLE, and to the delight of everyone, he arrives in time to prevent the wedding and ends up marrying May himself.

Plurabelle, Anna Livia, or Mrs Porter

Finnegans Wake, 1939
James Joyce

Wife of HUMPHREY CHIMPDEN EARWICKER, mother of SHAUN THE POST, SHEM THE PENMAN and ISSY. To Joyce she is the River Liffey: she is the perpetual, patient current running through history. Fluid as well as solid and spatial, both renewer and renewed, her creativity is constantly contrasted with the thunderous rise and fall of her husband.

Plyant, Sir Paul, Lady and Cynthia

The Double Dealer, 1693
William Congreve

Sir Paul is a wealthy fool, excessively fond of his wife, who is as petulant and insolent to him as she is to everyone else. Their marriage is as rickety as that of Lord and LADY TOUCHWOOD. Cynthia, their daughter, is promised to MELLEFONT, but the double-dealing MASKWELL has his eyes on her fortune. The family represents a mire of emotional deceptions and posturing vanities, although Cynthia, a pleasant, straightforward woman, is one of the few characters to emerge with much credit at the end of the play.

Pnin, Professor Timofey

Pnin, 1957
Vladimir Nabokov

A perpetually displaced person who teaches Russian at an American college and also lectures to women's clubs. His hypersensitively European attention to details of dress, grammar and travel confuse him in the commonsense New World –

he cannot see the wood for the trees. From his highly developed cranium soaring above where his spindly and perfectly shod legs take him, he is both innocent and intensely cerebral: while analysing poetry linguistically, his chair plays slapstick with him.

Pocket, Herbert

Great Expectations, 1861
Charles Dickens

The amiable son of MATTHEW POCKET, he is PIP's closest friend and instructs him in etiquette when they share rooms in Barnard's Inn. He is secretly helped by Pip, acting on MISS HAVISHAM's instructions, to become a partner in the house of Clarriker and Co, and he and Pip try to smuggle ABEL MAGWITCH out of England to escape arrest. Eventually prospering as a merchant, he is joined in the firm by Pip and marries his sweetheart, Clara Barley.

Pocket, Matthew

Great Expectations, 1861
Charles Dickens

A relative of MISS HAVISHAM, he is the father of HERBERT POCKET and becomes PIP's tutor. Well-educated, an early marriage 'impaired his prospects', and he struggles to support his impractical wife and a family of eight children. Although other Pocket relatives toady to Miss Havisham in the hope of a legacy, he is the only one bequeathed anything, since he never sought any money from her.

Pocock, Sarah

The Ambassadors, 1903
Henry James

CHAD NEWSOME's married sister is very much a chip off her mother's block: vulgar, disapproving and relentlessly prim. Sent to Europe in LAMBERT STRETHER's wake in the hope of forwarding his stalled mission to remind Chad of his family responsibilities, she goes in with as much abrasive energy as Strether has shown sympathetic reserve.

Podsnap, Mr John

Our Mutual Friend, 1865
Charles Dickens

A wealthy marine insurance dealer and member of 'Society', he is pompous, opinionated and self-satisfied. He condemns everything that is 'Not English!', and in order to protect the innocence of his daughter, Georgiana, he refuses to hear of any topic that might 'bring a blush into the cheek of the young person'. Georgiana, crushed by 'the mere dead-weight of Podsnappery', falls prey to ALFRED LAMMLE's attempt to marry her to FASCINATION FLEDGEBY, but she is rescued in time when Mrs Lammle reveals the scheme.

Poins

Henry IV Part I, 1596/7
Henry IV Part II, 1597/8
William Shakespeare

Although he is one of those who drink at the tavern at Eastcheap along with SIR JOHN FALSTAFF, Poins becomes friendly with the young Prince Hal (HENRY, PRINCE OF WALES). He devises the plan to trick the fat knight on Gad's Hill, but tends to defer to his royal accomplice when it comes to the confrontation. Indeed, he admits, 'I am your shadow, my lord; I'll follow you' – and he does. He is the honest rogue who recognizes his superior, unlike the others who misjudge Prince Henry, imagining he will remain Hal forever.

Poirot, Hercule
The Mysterious Affair at Styles, 1920, et seq
Agatha Christie

A Belgian private detective who retired from his native police force in 1904, Hercule Poirot is of modest stature, with an egg-shaped head, green eyes, suspiciously dark hair for a man of his years and a luxuriant waxed moustache that is his pride and joy. Though prissy in manner, there is little that escapes his attention and he displays both a sense of the dramatic and a love of his own importance as he solves murder cases with an analytical manner that involves much exercising of his 'little grey cells'.

Poliport, Matilda
Jumping the Queue, 1983
Mary Wesley

Menopausal, maddening, full of life yet longing perversely for death, Matilda is a mass of contradictions. She is friendly yet friendless, loving yet unloved, kindly yet frequently horribly unkind. Her fondness for using coarse expressions precludes her from membership of the Women's Institute. Full-mouthed, weak-chinned, she has a white crest of hair that completes her bird-like appearance. Her plans for her death are meticulously thought out and involve not only sweeping the house but also sweeping away all remnants of her past life. She is fonder of animals than of her own four children, who obviously sense her preference, since they largely ignore her. Not naive, she is nevertheless adept at deluding herself and ignoring the unpleasant facts about those closest to her. Death will be for her a last new sensation, and she seeks it out with the same sensuality with which, in happier times, she once sought life.

Polixenes
The Winter's Tale, 1611
William Shakespeare

Polixenes, the King of Bohemia, is an old friend of LEONTES, the King of Sicilia, and a visitor to his court when Leontes accuses his own wife, HERMIONE, of infidelity with their guest. Therefore, Polixenes is cast in the traditional character of the wronged associate, an innocent forced to wait until his guiltlessness can be proved. Later, at the Bohemian sheep-shearing festival, where FLORIZEL, his son, dances with PERDITA, he is cast in the double role of the disguised king and the angered father, a traditional comedic device. He is a commanding, possibly benevolent ruler, and a passionate man capable of frightening anger. Yet his rages are short-lived and sometimes have a touch of the absurd in them.

Pollente
The Faerie Queene, 1590–6
Sir Edmund Spenser

A cruel, ugly and deceitful pagan, whose name

refers to his powerful stature. He guards a toll bridge across a river, and if the toll is not paid the traveller must die. He throws the offender over the bridge, robs the victim of their wealth, and takes his spoils to his daughter MUNERA.

Pollexfen, Sir Hargrave
Sir Charles Grandison, 1754
Samuel Richardson

The importunate Sir Hargrave is thwarted in his attempt to force HARRIET BYRON into marriage by her resilience and resourcefulness. A licentious persecutor of virtuous womanhood, he is portrayed as an ideal candidate for castration – the punishment that Charlotte Grandison prescribes for unreconstructed libertines. He is vastly inferior to the perfect SIR CHARLES GRANDISON.

Pollitt, Big Daddy
Cat on a Hot Tin Roof, 1955
Tennessee Williams

The play's action takes place on the day he is told that he is dying of cancer. An immensely wealthy landowner who started with nothing, he is by turns cruel and kind to those he loves and who love him. A larger-than-life figure, superficially vulgar and crude, he has nonetheless 'bred tolerance' over the years; his frankness with BRICK POLLITT when dealing with Skipper's death shows his potential for love. His humour and the sheer force of his personality make him a curiously attractive character.

Pollitt, Big Mama
Cat on a Hot Tin Roof, 1955
Tennessee Williams

The constant butt of her husband BIG DADDY POLLITT's humour and bad temper, she nonetheless unreservedly loves him. As the play progresses, she develops from a silly, gullible and talkative old woman into a figure of honesty and love. In a tale about corruption and lying she stands out as a simple exponent of decent, unpretentious values.

Pollitt, Brick
Cat on a Hot Tin Roof, 1955
Tennessee Williams

A former American football hero who becomes a sports commentator. At the play's beginning he has been crippled by an accident jumping hurdles when drunk. His invalid state takes on a symbolic value as he reveals his mistrust of the world's 'mendacity', which has caused both his drinking problem and his estrangement from his wife, MAGGIE 'THE CAT' POLLITT. The direct and brutal conversation he holds with his father, BIG DADDY POLLITT, in which Brick reveals the circumstances surrounding his friend Skipper's death, awakens him from his detached state, and in the rewritten Act Three, it appears he may be ready for a more normal life as plantation owner, husband and, possibly, father.

Pollitt, Gooper
Cat on a Hot Tin Roof, 1955
Tennessee Williams

A lawyer, the elder brother of BRICK POLLITT, who has persistently borne a grudge regarding his parents' greater affection for his attractive and diffident sibling. Aided by his repellent wife MAE POLLITT, by whom he has fathered a tribe of 'no-neck monsters', he pursues his dying father's wealth in an unemotional, legalistic manner; by the play's conclusion, when he has failed, he is revealing glimmers of a greater humanity and self-understanding.

Pollitt, Henny (Henrietta)
The Man Who Loved Children, 1940
Christina Stead

Well-born, cultured and vain, an old-fashioned Southern belle, she is unprepared for the drudgeries of motherhood-times-five. Her precariously maintained 'calm of frequentation' often spills over into hysterical near-violence, exacerbated by her biologist husband's manipulative joviality.

Pollitt, Louie (Louisa)
The Man Who Loved Children, 1940
Christina Stead

The product of SAM POLLITT's first marriage, she is the eldest of the Pollitt children and the only one immune to her father's buffoonery. 'Strict and anxious' around her younger step-siblings while her parents re-enact the American Civil War, when she is left in sole charge she treats them with vague benevolence, lost in wool-gathering dreams.

Pollitt, Mae
Cat on a Hot Tin Roof, 1955
Tennessee Williams

A 'monster of fertility' who has married into the wealthy Pollitt family and produced a litter of offensive and ugly children. Her grasping meanness, insincerity and vulgarity make her a suitable contrast to the attractive and vibrant MAGGIE 'THE CAT' POLLITT, though the object of their endeavours – BIG DADDY POLLITT's wealth – remains the same.

Pollitt, Maggie 'the Cat'
Cat on a Hot Tin Roof, 1955
Tennessee Williams

A bright, energetic and witty woman whose poor background makes her feverishly anxious to hold on to the wealthy lifestyle she has gained through her marriage into the Pollitt family. Throughout the play, she constantly reaffirms her love – particularly her physical love – for her husband BRICK POLLITT, who has drifted into a state of alcoholic diffidence. Though, in her way, just as selfish as the brother and sister-in-law with whom she is competing, her final victory is satisfying for those captivated by her charm and determination.

Pollitt, Sam (Samuel Clemens)
The Man Who Loved Children, 1940
Christina Stead

The indulgent father of the title, he is a good-looking and idealistic young biologist. His easy-going delight in parenthood and in childish jokes masks an appetite for control which is hypocritically out of tune with his Northern-liberal convictions. One suspects that his wife (with his pet names, 'Henny' and 'Moth') and his brood of five are just another animal experiment.

Pollock, Major David
Table Number Seven, the second of two plays under the general title *Separate Tables*, 1954
Terence Rattigan

In his fifties, with a clipped military moustache and neat clothes, he bores everyone at the Beauregard Private Hotel at Bournemouth with his reminiscences of service in the Black Watch. He is, in fact, a fraud. 'I don't like myself as I am … so I had to invent another person.' The self he dislikes has been convicted of a misdemeanour in a local cinema, yet the guests, including the timid, cosseted Sibyl, forgive him. He and Sibyl form a close bond of mutual understanding: 'we're both of us frightened of people', he admits, 'and yet we've somehow managed to forget our fright when we've been in each other's company'.

Polly
Up the Junction, 1963
Nell Dunn

Tired of the comfortable and sheltered life she has enjoyed so far, Polly wants to savour life on the wrong side of the tracks and, to this end, immerses herself in the drudgery and routine of factory life and the conditions of the working classes. Her experience is a rather idealized one, for the people she meets are generally accepting and friendly, able to cope with what some might consider a patronizing attempt to identify in a temporary and unreal way with people she is always in danger of treating as 'specimens' rather than as individuals.

Polly, Alfred
The History of Mr Polly, 1910
H G Wells

Badly educated but with intellectual cravings, Mr Polly pronounces words with his own distinctive flourishes: 'Bocashieu'; 'Rabooloose'; 'sesquippledan verboojuice'. His career progresses from apprentice outfitter to clothes-shop owner, but this improvement comes alongside an alienated wife and boredom. Attempts at arson and suicide do not go as planned but give Polly the sense that he can 'break through the paper walls of everyday circumstance' and change his life for the better.

Polly, Aunt
The Adventures of Tom Sawyer, 1876
Mark Twain

A grey-haired, bespectacled woman who is continually outwitted by her unruly orphaned nephew, TOM SAWYER, a calculating exploiter of her credulous nature. Her Calvinist faith urges her to be a strict and stern disciplinarian when dealing with her charge, but, more often than not, the tenets of her religion yield to the tender impulses of her gentle and forgiving heart.

Pollyanna
Pollyanna, 1913
Pollyanna Grows Up, 1915
Eleanor H Porter

A pretty, well-mannered and intelligent American orphan, whose natural kindliness and optimism overcome the grouchy ingratitude and soured world-view of the adults into whose lives she breezes. Spreading sunshine by the sheer attractiveness of her charm and personality, she wins the hearts and affection of almost everyone she comes into contact with.

Polonius
Hamlet, 1601/2
William Shakespeare

A courtier with a cynical and simplistic view of the world, and the father of LAERTES and OPHELIA. The corruption of the court is but expediency in his eyes. Once an idea has taken hold he cannot or will not change his mind. Pompous and tediously verbose, he pays for his meddling with his own life. 'Thou wretched, rash, intruding fool farewell.'

Polydore
The Orphan, 1680
Thomas Otway

One of the two sons of ACASTO, Polydore is the younger brother of Castalio and, like him, in love with MONIMIA, the orphan with whom they have been raised. Polydore is a rake with 'all the arts of fine persuasion'. He knows of his brother's feelings for Monimia but not of their secret marriage; brutally, he deceives both by taking Castalio's place in her bed. Having provoked a duel with his brother, he commits suicide by running on to Castalio's sword. Perhaps this is an admission of guilt, a final realization of honour and moral value; certainly it is poetic justice.

Polydore → Guiderius

Pomeray, Cody
Visions of Cody, 1973, and others
Jack Kerouac

Like DEAN MORIARTY, he is a fictional version of Neal Cassady, a 1960s counter-culture hero. He appears as Cody in more than one novel, including *Big Sur* (1962), but is the sustained focus of this book. JACK DULUOZ sees him as a vital life-force, and 'one of the most remarkable men I have ever seen', but also becomes aware of his evasiveness, his unfocused energy, and lack of direction. He comes to see him as 'my greatest enemy – because while I saw him as an angel, a god, etcetera, I also saw him as a devil, an old witch, even an old bitch from the start'; he is finally freed of his influence.

Pompeius, Sextus
Antony and Cleopatra, 1606/7
William Shakespeare

Pompeius (known usually as Pompey) is a hard-living, free-wheeling and independent soldier, apparently without friends. Frank and excessively confident, he nevertheless harbours enormous bitterness, stemming principally from his father's murder. His crusading puritanism makes him a serious potential threat to the stability of the Roman world.

Pompey Bum
Measure for Measure, c.1604
William Shakespeare

A roguish member of the low-life of a corrupt Vienna, Pompey is a bawd and a servant to the innkeeper Mistress Overdone. Really, he is a villainous little type and an open opportunist. After he is sent to prison he becomes assistant to Abhorson the hangman.

Pompilia
The Ring and the Book, 1868–9
Robert Browning

The almost saintly wife of COUNT GUIDO FRANCESCHINI. Faced with his unspeakable mental cruelty she turns to the Church for help. At first none is forthcoming, but then she meets the young priest GUISEPPE CAPONSACCHI and, anxious to save her unborn child, persuades him to engineer her escape. Relating her story on her deathbed, she reveals herself to be an uneducated innocent in a world of treachery, but capable of great courage to protect her child. As she dies, she is able to forgive even the husband who has murdered her.

Ponder, Daniel
The Ponder Heart, 1954
Eudora Welty

The eccentric uncle of EDNA EARLE PONDER, he wears a flamboyant grey stetson and white suit. He is rich, but is given to sprees of random generosity from the depths of his 'ponder-ous' heart, in which he freely gives his money away. He is polite and mannerly, and the 'sweetest, most unspoiled thing in the world', but lacks any real sense of moral or natural propriety, intelligence, or commonsense, and is tried for tickling his young wife to death.

Ponder, Edna Earle
The Ponder Heart, 1954
Eudora Welty

The narrator. The niece of DANIEL PONDER, who, 15 years earlier, gave her the hotel she now runs. She tells the story of his trial. A strong-willed woman who likes to 'size people up', she is alert and observant, but also highly comic and somewhat unreliable as a story-teller.

Ponderevo, Teddy (Edward)
Tono-Bungay, 1910
H G Wells

George Ponderevo meets his 26-year-old shopkeeper uncle 'Teddy' and diagnoses a 'teddiness or teddidity': 'nimbleness without grace' and 'alertness without intelligence'. After a failure and swindle or two, Teddy hits on inventing 'Tono-Bungay', the all-purpose restorative tonic, with which he makes his millions. He becomes extraordinarily ambitious, which he voices with his customary post-sentence 'whispering zest': 'Country gentleman. Freedom from grochery. Cuttin' canals ... makin' tunnels ... New countries ... new centres ... Zzzz.' Overextension, bankruptcy and illness see Teddy deludedly take his own worthless potion as medicine.

Pongo
The Hundred and One Dalmatians, 1956
Dodie Smith

A handsome, commanding dalmatian, with magnificent jet-black spots and black-rimmed eyes, Pongo wears his considerable intellect lightly, and still has a puppyish twinkle about him. He is the husband of MISSIS, and the proud and devoted father of 15 puppies. After they are stolen by CRUELLA DE VIL, he has both the skill and the knowledge to initiate a search and get them back to London again. His gentle words of encouragement carry Missis and the puppies through many a moment of despair.

Pontellier, Edna
The Awakening, 1899
Kate Chopin

The submissive but vaguely dissatisfied young wife of a stuffy businessman in New Orleans. She senses the possibility of new spiritual and sexual awareness as she experiences the romantic Creole culture of Grand Isle. She is left numbed and empty when rejected by the man she loves, and is unable to come to terms with the responsibility she feels to her children. In a desperate final attempt at independence, she swims out into the 'soft, close embrace' of the sea.

Pontifex, Alethea
The Way of all Flesh, 1903
Samuel Butler

An aunt of ERNEST PONTIFEX, the novel's central character, Alethea is modelled partly upon one of Butler's own aunts and partly on a close woman friend. A mild, benevolent woman, she discreetly encourages Ernest during his unhappy upbringing by a tyrannical father, THEOBOLD PONTIFEX, and his equally woeful schooldays. Later, after his release from prison, she bequeaths him enough money to be able to begin a literary career. As Ernest writes daring, emotionally honest books, Alethea is thus the agent of justice, enabling him to avenge himself upon his dreadful family.

Pontifex, Ernest
The Way of all Flesh, 1903
Samuel Butler

The son of THEOBOLD PONTIFEX, grandson of GEORGE PONTIFEX and great-grandson of JOHN PONTIFEX, Ernest is a part factual and later idealized portrait of the author. As the unhappy victim of fierce family oppression, his childhood is a matter of 'fear and shrinking'. Yearning for affection and kindness, he grows up inept, but his priggishness is offset by his being 'more inclinable to moderate vice than immoderate virtue', a quality which lands him in prison. After his release, he marries and abandons ELLEN and, receiving a legacy from his aunt ALETHEA PONTIFEX, becomes an author, writing books in which he says 'things no one else would say'. He also represents a Freudian idea of the subconscious will directing the subject forever onward in search of a new beginning.

Pontifex, George
The Way of all Flesh, 1903
Samuel Butler

A version of Butler's own grandfather, a headmaster of Shrewsbury School and Bishop of Lichfield, George Pontifex, father of THEOBOLD PONTIFEX and grandfather of ERNEST PONTIFEX, is a successful publisher of religious tracts. He is lucky with money, 'sitting still and letting money run, as it were, right up against him'. In the novel, he is painted as a tyrannical and canting man which, in fact, Butler later recognized to be rather a distortion of the truth. However, George represents part of the cycle of male domestic tyranny.

Pontifex, John
The Way of all Flesh, 1903
Samuel Butler

The father of GEORGE PONTIFEX, grandfather of THEOBOLD PONTIFEX and great-grandfather of ERNEST PONTIFEX, he is a village carpenter. He thus represents the kind of rural simplicity which Ernest (and Butler and several of his contemporaries) found highly admirable. Equally, he represents a genuine and instinctive humility, both in human and religious terms, which is markedly absent from his son and grandson.

Pontifex, Theobold
The Way of all Flesh, 1903
Samuel Butler

Theobold Pontifex is a recreation of (perhaps assault upon is a more accurate description) Butler's own father, an unyielding, authoritarian clergyman whom he detested. The grandson of JOHN PONTIFEX, son of GEORGE PONTIFEX and father of ERNEST PONTIFEX, Theobold is a middle-class, arrogant, self-righteous, intolerant and malevolent man. His milder wife, Christina, is a portrait of the author's mother. Yet Theobold represents not only merely a person or a class, but an oppressively Victorian social and moral system. His code of joylessness and duty, enforced by domestic tyranny and violence, is one of the central targets of the book.

Poole, Grace
Jane Eyre, 1847
Charlotte Brontë

The surly, mysterious seamstress at Thornfield Hall, Grace is a little too fond of her pint of porter, but not without good reason. Mistakenly believed by JANE EYRE to be the malevolent force threatening MR ROCHESTER, it transpires that Grace is simply a common and honest woman, who has been secretly charged by Mr Rochester with the unenviable task of guarding his insane Creole wife.

Poon, Mr
The Monkey King, 1979
Timothy Mo

'Compromise was at the centre of Mr Poon's political system, and in securing Wallace, he had achieved such a balance'; so begins the memorable struggle between Poon and his pragmatically-created son-in-law WALLACE NOLASCO. Small, pot-bellied and bald, Poon is said to have made his considerable fortune by secret trading with the Japanese during their occupation of Hong Kong from 1942 to 1945. A decade has passed, and Poon has become a miserly autocrat, controlling his family by subtle checks and balances. Having exiled Wallace, Poon is forced to recall him, realizing that his whoring and heavy-drinking son, Ah Lung, will never be fit to control the family's business interests, and that his own health is failing. At his funeral, three denominations of holy men preside, illustrating Poon's characteristic motto: 'You could be better safe than sorry.'

Pooter, Charles
The Diary of a Nobody, 1892
George and Weedon Grossmith

A genteel clerk, and an archetypal suburbanite. He is prone both to making social gaffes, of which he is preternaturally aware, and to physical accident, and lives in a state of heightened anxiety over his position in society. He is a snob, especially in petty matters, and obsequiously deferential to those he considers his superiors. Despite that, he is respectable and worthy, and has a curiously engaging integrity which survives the ridiculousness of his nature and actions.

Popeye
Sanctuary, 1931
William Faulkner

An expression of pure evil, described in chillingly mechanical terms, he is leader of the gang of bootleggers that kidnaps TEMPLE DRAKE. Impotent and sadistic, he rapes her with a corn-cob. He is eventually hanged for a murder he did not commit, though his unusable alibi is that at the time of the crime in question, he was killing another man.

Popper, Ruth
The Last Picture Show, 1966
Larry McMurtry

The neglected, love-starved wife of the sports coach in Anarene, Texas, she is the opposite of JACY FARROW's cool independence, remaining trapped in a role determined for her by generations of men.

Poppins, Mary
Mary Poppins, 1934
P L Travers

Mary Poppins arrives mysteriously with the East Wind, with only a large carpet bag and a parrot-headed umbrella for luggage. Plain rather than pretty, she resembles a thin wooden dutch doll, with large hands and feet, shiny black hair and piercing blue eyes. She smells comfortingly of toast and wears starchy white aprons. Terribly vain, she is never happier than when admiring her own reflection in a shop window. Gruff-mannered in the extreme, she does not waste time with being nice, and sniffs a great deal, mostly with displeasure. Yet she has an irresistible charm for the Banks children, and, indeed, for the entire animal kingdom, who treat her like a queen, and whose language she understands perfectly. Mary Poppins is capable of anything, even of levitating herself and a perfectly-set tea-table ten feet in the air – but then she is first cousin once removed (on her mother's side) to a Hamadryad.

Poppyseed, Miss Philomela
Headlong Hall, 1816
Thomas Love Peacock

Miss Poppyseed (a satirical portrait of novelist Amelia Opie) is the maiden aunt author of romantic novels who writes, reportedly, 'for the express purpose of supporting every species of superstition and prejudice'. Tedious and long-winded when talking about her novels, which are her only topic of conversation, she is pandered to by a coterie of sycophantic critics.

Porgy
Porgy, 1925
DuBose Heyward

A crippled beggar who is unable to get around other than in a small goat-cart, he is well known in the waterfront neighbourhood for his luck at throwing dice. He falls in love with BESS, and finds temporary happiness with her. In the opera *Porgy and Bess* (1935) which Heyward co-wrote with the Gershwins, his essential decency is given greater and more sentimental stress.

Porgy, Lt
The Partisan, 1835
William Gilmore Simms

He is a good-natured, cracker-barrel Carolinian, fighting with Generals Marion, Greene and Sumter in the guerrilla campaigns in the Carolina swamps during the War of Independence. It is Porgy who brings a touch of humour and humanity to a brutal and destructive campaign.

Porphyria's Lover
'Porphyria's Lover', in *Dramatic Romances*, 1845
Robert Browning

He has murdered the woman he loves but whom he has no right to love. She 'too weak ... to set [her heart's] struggling passion free' has left a ball to be with him. Happy at her confession of love he calmly strangles her to keep her forever, and in matter-of-fact tones tells how he has sat all night with the body 'And yet God has not said a word'.

Porphyro
'The Eve of St. Agnes', 1820
John Keats

Ardent lover of the young MADELINE, he braves the murderous hatred of Madeline's savage kinsfolk to win her for his bride on the enchanted Eve of St Agnes.

Porretta, Clementina della
Sir Charles Grandison, 1754
Samuel Richardson

Clementina is a devout Catholic who expresses a preference for the union of souls over a temporal alliance. She falls in love with the heretic SIR CHARLES GRANDISON, despite her belief that he is damned. Driven by the dichotomies of love and duty, and of mind and body, into a madness which is manifested in her rambling letters, Clementina is an irreparably fragmented character. Ophelia-like, she carries flowers and attempts suicide by drowning. She suffers a symbolic martyrdom, unable to reconcile fervent passion with idolatrous spirituality.

Porrex → Ferrex and Porrex

Porteous, Captain John
The Heart of Midlothian, in *Tales of My Landlord: Second Series*, 1818
Sir Walter Scott

'... a name memorable in the traditions of

Edinburgh, as well as in the records of criminal jurisprudence, [he] was the son of a citizen of Edinburgh, who endeavoured to breed him up to his own mechanical trade of a tailor. The youth, however, had a wild and irreclaimable propensity to dissipation', which led him into the armed forces, where his 'harsh and fierce habits rendered him formidable to rioters or disturbers of the public peace'. His violent misconduct while supervising the execution of Wilson leads to his own condemnation, a sentence pre-empted by the lynch mob.

Porteous, Nora Roche
Tirra Lirra by the River, 1978
Jessica Anderson

Returning in her late seventies to the oppressive Brisbane suburb she grew up in, the artistic, independent and rebellious Nora recalls Sir Lancelot's song, '"Tirra lirra" by the river', and she relives her youth and constant romantic longing for some Camelot and a plumed knight. Seeking them in Sydney she was driven to near-breakdown by a chauvinist, self-centred husband, but later achieved a more congenial life in England. Now, as she ponders alone, her memory finally yields up early events which, although repressed, have indelibly coloured the intervening years.

Porter, Alison
Look Back in Anger, 1956
John Osborne

The middle-class wife of JIMMY PORTER, tall, slim and dark, Alison is 'turned in a different key' to her husband, 'a key of well-bred malaise'. The butt of so much of Jimmy's invective, as she stands relentlessly ironing his clothes, she appears unsure whether he loves or loathes her. Yet at the same time she believes (even though she temporarily leaves him) that he is worth saving and that by knowing him, she will herself become a better person and discover her own direction. Through Jimmy, she discovers both love and enormous emotional pain, yet she values both as true feeling.

Porter, Jimmy
Look Back in Anger, 1956
Déjàvu, 1991
John Osborne

In his mid twenties in the first play, Jimmy is restless, malicious, proud, sensitive, puritan, patriotic, anarchic and defiant, a working-class graduate of a new university who finds that society has no place for him. For many, he encapsulated the sense of disappointment, even resentment, of educated, postwar youth who felt, with Jimmy, that: 'There aren't any good, brave causes left'. Married to ALISON PORTER, he lives with her in a dingy attic flat, and runs a market sweet stall with his friend CLIFF LEWIS. In the later play, he returns, older, divorced, the owner of a substantial farmhouse, but little wiser. Anger, he reflects, ' … comes into the world in grief not grievance. It is mourning the unknown, the loss of what went before you … '

Porter, Mr → Earwicker, Humphrey Chimpden

Porter, Mrs → Plurabelle, Anna Livia

Porter, the
Macbeth, c.1606
William Shakespeare

The Porter, when drunk, imagines himself to be the keeper of hell's gate, and provides, through his drunken ramblings, a moment of relief from the murderous intensity of the preceding scenes and those that follow. Though much of his humour has lost its topicality, he presents a miniature portrait of a bawdy and vulgar man, apparently unaware of the 'hell' that is about to be uncovered by the arrival of MACDUFF.

Portia
Julius Caesar, c.1599
William Shakespeare

Wife to MARCUS BRUTUS and the archetypal devoted and stoical Roman matron. She shows her love for Brutus in her passionate desire to share his troubles, and suffers a self-inflicted wound to demonstrate her constancy. Faced with defeat, like her husband she sees no alternative to suicide, and swallows hot coals.

Portia
The Merchant of Venice, 1594/5
William Shakespeare

A witty, attractive woman, she finds herself honour-bound to choose her husband through the system of caskets stipulated in her father's will. While submitting to this – and politely putting up with the blandishments of some awful suitors – she establishes her intelligence, humour and forcefulness in the courtroom scene where, disguised as Balthazar, a doctor of laws, she outwits SHYLOCK and (more gently) goes on to fool her husband, BASSANIO.

Portnoy, Alexander
Portnoy's Complaint, 1969
Philip Roth

The narrator, allegedly pouring out his hilarious past in confessional manner to a psychiatrist, DR SPIELVOGEL. He feels himself to be 'living in the middle of a Jewish joke'. His mother, Sophie, dominates his childhood, and although he is a good Jewish boy who gets good grades at school, he expresses his secret rebellion through compulsive masturbation. In later life he is a successful lawyer, but cannot throw off the legacy of his mother's influence, and continues to seek escape – albeit in vain – by frenzied sexual activity with non-Jewish women. The final irony arrives when he becomes impotent when faced with tough Jewish women in Israel.

Poseidon
The Whole Armour, 1962, part of *The Guyana Quartet*, 1985
Wilson Harris

The descendant of runaway African slaves, he is the dark, nameless presence (able, like his mythological namesake, to take on a multiplicity of forms) who sexually threatens CATALENA PEREZ. As such, he represents the jungle, history, the subconscious.

Posnet, Blanco
The Shewing-Up of Blanco Posnet, 1909
George Bernard Shaw

A somewhat dandyish drunkard, in his thirties, he lives in a small town in the USA. 'Evidently a blackguard', he is accused of stealing a horse. He denies the charge but later admits that he took the animal, believing it belonged to his brother, Elder Daniels, who owes him money. Posnet is about to be hanged when a woman claims that he gave her the horse, so she could take her dying child to a doctor. As a result, Posnet is freed and launches upon an impromptu sermon, reflecting on divine intervention.

Possum
The Magic Pudding, 1918
Norman Lindsay

Quick and lithe, with flexible morals, he is the ideal partner for WATKIN WOMBAT in the plot to steal THE MAGIC PUDDING, although he is not, perhaps, beyond rehabilitation.

Post, Laura
Of Men and Angels, 1985
Mary Gordon

Laura Post is dangerous. The perfect puritan, a psychopath programmed to lead 'a religious life', she becomes part of the household of Anne Foster, an art historian with two children. Her casual progress takes the nature of a Fate, as her internal life is revealed. Needy, unloved, abused as a child, her presence questions theories of mother-love, childcare and trust in human relationships.

Poste, Flora
Cold Comfort Farm, 1932
Stella Gibbons

Orphaned at 19, the well-educated, well-dressed and strong-willed Flora decides that, since she has little money and cannot earn a living, she will live off her relatives, THE STARKADDERS, who live at Cold Comfort Farm. She finds that their melodramatic and primitive way of life does not match her desire for 'everything to be tidy and pleasant and comfortable', so she sets out to civilize them, armed with the commonsense philosophy of her favourite writer, the Abbé Fausse-Maigre.

Posthumus Leonatus
Cymbeline, 1609/10
William Shakespeare

A 'poor but worthy gentleman' whose father (a valiant and renowned soldier) died before, and his mother as, he was born. From infancy he was brought up in the court as a member of the royal family and 'playmate' to IMOGEN, CYMBELINE's daughter. Posthumus is established from the outset as a man of considerable virtue and great worth, but is nevertheless banished by Cymbeline when he marries Imogen against the king's wishes. Later, driven to distraction by misguided jealousy, he plans the murder of his own wife, and, thinking his plan successful, is made rash and reckless by remorse, proving himself as valiant a soldier as his father in the ensuing battle with the Roman army.

Pothinus
Caesar and Cleopatra, 1898
George Bernard Shaw

Guardian to PTOLEMY DIONYSUS, the boy-king of Egypt, Pothinus is 50 and a eunuch. He is also energetic and quick-witted, but a vulgar, devious politician, impatient and unable to control his temper. Having suggested to CAIUS JULIUS CAESAR that CLEOPATRA might assassinate him in order to reign alone, Pothinus is murdered by Cleopatra's nurse, FTATATEETA.

Potter, Frederica
The Virgin in the Garden, 1978
Still Life, 1985
A S Byatt

Brilliant young Frederica Potter, sister of STEPHANIE POTTER, is a passionate explorer of every idea, but is singularly awkward and inexperienced in the world of adult relationships. Undaunted by her shortcomings she puts herself forward at every opportunity, going all out to get what she wants. Every disaster becomes a lesson learned, and subsequently applied, as she single-mindedly channels her considerable energy towards forcing entry into every sphere, personal or social, where she senses that access is being denied her. People, men particularly, are categorized and targeted. 'You only want everything', remarks one of those who finds her passion alarming.

Potter, Harry
Harry Potter and the Philosopher's Stone, 1997, et seq
J K Rowling

'Small and skinny, with brilliant green eyes and jet-black hair', he is famous as 'the boy who lived', having survived a lethal curse by LORD VOLDEMORT. Left an orphan and marked by a lightning-shaped scar, he grows up knowing nothing of his past, but at the wizard school, Hogwarts, must confront his celebrity; he wrestles with self-doubt and thirsts to prove himself on his own merits. A bright, resourceful and strong-willed boy, immensely loyal to his friends, his inquisitiveness and strong moral sense often lead him into danger as he realizes his continuing significance to Voldemort. Fighting against the sorcerer's revival with bravery and ingenuity, he demonstrates abilities beyond his years.

Potter, Isreal
Isreal Potter, 1855
Herman Melville

He is based on the hero of the anonymous *Life of Isreal Potter* (1824). A New England farm boy with an adventurous and rebellious spirit, he runs away to sea on a whaling ship after trying various jobs. His adventures take him into uniform, involve him in secret societies, and bring him into contact with great historical figures and events, before he returns to humble labour. Old, infirm, and in poverty, he returns to the USA for the first time in 45 years, hoping for a pension, but when refused, writes his colourful memoirs and dies.

Potter, Stephanie
The Virgin in the Garden, 1978
Still Life, 1985
A S Byatt

A brilliant academic future is predicted for Stephanie, sister of FREDERICA POTTER, but she refuses to follow her overbearing father's ambition for her and further confounds him by marrying a curate, DANIEL ORTON, whose work she admires, but whose faith she cannot share. Stephanie has never really wanted anything very much for herself, but as the demands of marriage, family and parish overtake her she realizes that even her modest private expectations are being frustrated; there is, quite simply, no time to read a book. She recognizes her disappointment, but lacks the will to break out of the cocoon of self-denial.

Potterson, Abbey
Our Mutual Friend, 1865
Charles Dickens

Proprietor of the Six Jolly Fellowship Porters, a respectable public house in the otherwise rough docklands of London. She befriends LIZZIE HEXAM, and her brother later helps to reveal that 'John Rokesmith' is, in fact, JOHN HARMON.

Potts, Helen
Picnic, 1953
William Inge

An older widow lady who lives next door to the OWENS family with her demanding invalid mother, and hires HAL CARTER to do odd jobs in the yard. She is a neat, hardworking, 'merry, dumpy little woman close to sixty' who is Mrs Potts in name only, since her mother had her runaway marriage annulled; she keeps the name to spite her.

Poulengy, Bertrand de
Saint Joan, 1923
George Bernard Shaw

De Poulengy, given the unlikely nickname of 'Polly', is a gentleman-at-arms at the castle of Vaucouleurs. In his thirties, he is a dreamy, deliberate man who nonetheless becomes one of JOAN's first supporters. He convinces CAPTAIN ROBERT DE BAUDRICOURT to equip her with a horse and armour, advising that her sincerity and faith might raise the morale of the French troops.

Poulter, Mrs
The Solid Mandala, 1966
Patrick White

A neighbour of ARTHUR and WALDO BROWN, Mrs Poulter has a somewhat sceptical view of religious faith, but nevertheless comes to believe, sometimes even hopefully, in Armageddon. Her fears that everything might come to a tragic end appear to be linked to her own sad emotional history, for although she has an abundant love to give, it has always been thwarted or rejected. For instance, Mrs Poulter is both compassionate and naturally maternal, yet her own daughter was stillborn and her husband retreats from her love. She later manages to find some comfort in a friendship with the backward and compassionate Arthur.

Povey, Samuel
The Old Wives' Tale, 1908
Arnold Bennett

When Samuel Povey marries CONSTANCE BAINES and becomes the owner of the Baines family business, his self-satisfaction is complete: he is now a shopkeeper with a position to maintain. A solid, excellent citizen, his worthiness is singularly uninspiring. Fatherhood adds to his self-esteem but his efforts to impose his will in that area are undermined by a mixture of stern discipline and over-indulgence. His occasional flashes of passion, resulting from jealousy and sensitivity to criticism, come as a surprise in one so generally stolid.

Powell, Fola
Season of Adventure, 1960
George Lamming

A former student of an exclusive college for girls, Fola is a beautiful, middle-class, light-skinned young woman who has led a sheltered, rather privileged life. As such, she is 'a stranger within her own gates' on the newly independent island of San Cristobal (Lamming's fictional West Indies). Some say her reserve is a sign of conceit, while to others it is a modest symptom of her self-assurance. Yet Fola is not as self-assured as some might think. She is both intelligent and observant and keenly feels herself being tugged in two cultural directions, towards both the British and the Caribbean. Gradually, she becomes obsessed by re-evaluating her own cultural history and identity in the light of her new experiences. She longs to discover a sense of purpose.

Powell, Minnie
The Shadow of a Gunman, 1923
Sean O'Casey

A resident in the Dublin tenement in which DONAL DAVOREN has a room, Minnie is 23 but, as a result of having to earn her own living, has an assurance beyond her years. She is not well-educated, but good-looking and well-dressed. She is ludicrously romantic and has a sense of fun, liking to dance, but no sense of fear and little judgement of character. This is both unfortunate and foolish, for she is at ease with most people, and many of those she meets are rogues or worse. In the end, it proves to be a fatal weakness.

Power, Paula
A Laodicean, 1881
Thomas Hardy

A character who is not fully fleshed out, Paula lacks psychological depth and an inner spirit. She is impressionable and, though she is a romantic with an obsession for medievalism, is much influenced by modern thinking. We learn about her behaviour from the dilemma of her suitors. High-minded and virtuous, like many of Hardy's heroines she is divided within herself by a desire for social promotion and the ideal of love with a kindred spirit.

Powers, Margaret
Soldier's Pay, 1926
William Faulkner

A young war widow who befriends and falls in

love with the hideously wounded veteran LT DONALD MAHON. Returning home with him, she represents a manifestation of love that his small Georgia community cannot countenance, even after the couple marries. Throughout, she consistently rejects the awkward advances of the soldier JOE GILLIGAN.

Poynter, Arthur
Hotel de Dream, 1976
Emma Tennant

Widower and ex-lieutenant-colonel, the elderly, thin and shaky Mr Poynter, only male guest at the Westringham hotel, builds in his sleep a regimented city – all white, all squares and rectangles – of which he is supreme dictator. The future tense is banned there and England's finest hour is recalled by loudspeakers blaring out Churchill's speeches, Vera Lynn and ITMA. But things fall apart when MISS JEANETTE SCRANTON invades his city with a horde of naked Amazons (her dreams having become entangled with his) and then pursues him into his waking hours.

Poyser, Martin
Adam Bede, 1859
George Eliot

Dairy-farmer and husband of the loquacious MRS POYSER, Martin is more laid-back than his wife, only being harsh in judgement about improvident farmers. His portly figure is matched by a jolly, round face. His good tenancy goes largely unrewarded by the squire, ARTHUR DONNITHORNE, who does not give him new gates when they are wanted. His desire to see dairymaid HETTY SORREL marry well is also frustrated.

Poyser, Mrs
Adam Bede, 1859
George Eliot

The aunt of DINAH MORRIS and employer of HETTY SORREL, Mrs Poyser is good-looking, with sandy hair and is often seen in a checkered apron. She is hard on dirty floors, laziness and Hetty's vanity and lets people know her opinions in a great many words. She is also an opponent of changes at her dairy, wishing to receive no further responsibilities from ARTHUR DONNITHORNE.

Pozzi, Jack ('Jackpot')
The Music of Chance, 1990
Paul Auster

A young poker player. He is first encountered in a cowed and battered state, but once out of danger 'he began to show his true colours, and it wasn't long before he was talking his head off'. Brash and self-confident, he is a good player, but has aspirations beyond his capabilities. He gets JAMES NASHE ensnared with FLOWERS and STONE by tempting him with a game that offers 'the chance of a lifetime', but loses.

Pozzo
Waiting for Godot, 1955
Samuel Beckett

A squire of the realm, a landowner and slave-driver. Both exasperated and exasperating, Pozzo commands total attention. He insists on

his own goodness and seeks pity, but his display is a charade. Treating his slave LUCKY with utter contempt, he keeps ESTRAGON and VLADIMIR simultaneously entertained and scandalized. Returning the following day he claims to be blind, professing never to have met the two tramps before. Some critics have seen Pozzo as Godot, representing an Old Testament God in the first act, and the New Testament in the second, when he is more of a victim, 'acquainted with sorrow'.

Praed
Mrs Warren's Profession, 1894
George Bernard Shaw

An old friend, but never a lover, of the brothel-keeper, MRS KITTY WARREN, Praed, or Praddy as she calls him, is a middle-aged architect with a strict, although unconventional, sense of propriety. He is a man of genuine consideration and dignity in a world which does not care much for either.

Prefect, Ford
The Hitch-Hiker's Guide to the Galaxy, 1979, et seq
Douglas Adams

On Earth, there was always 'something very slightly odd' about Ford Prefect, perhaps because he proves to have been an interplanetary hitch-hiker, sent to update the entry on Earth in *The Hitch-Hiker's Guide to the Galaxy*. He had, however, managed to disguise himself as an out-of-work actor and drunken wastrel. Once in space, he reverses his former relationship with ARTHUR DENT, becoming, as it were, the man-of-the-worlds to the latter's innocent. Much comedy is created by his inability to understand Arthur's sense of irony for, it is explained, 'they don't have sarcasm on Betelgeuse', Ford's planet of origin.

Prentice, Andrew
The Timeless Land, 1941
Storm of Time, 1948
No Barrier, 1953
Eleanor Dark

JOHNNY PRENTICE's father, and the convict husband of ELLEN PRENTICE. He abandons his family following his escape and spends the rest of his life hiding out in the bush. When he falls sick there, he is nursed back to health by Aborigines, and takes one of their women with him, later fathering a son, BILLALONG. Prentice is drowned saving Billalong and his mother from a flooded river, and because the eight-year-old Johnny appears there at that time, the tribe believe he is Andrew's spirit reincarnated.

Prentice, Ellen
The Timeless Land, 1941
Storm of Time, 1948
No Barrier, 1953
Eleanor Dark

A convict woman and mother of three children, the first conceived when she was raped by a fellow prisoner on the ship, the others after her marriage to another convict, ANDREW PRENTICE. After her husband deserts her she provides for her children by becoming STEPHEN MANNION's housekeeper and mistress. But Stephen is a harsh man, and, to Ellen's grief, one of her sons,

JOHNNY PRENTICE, runs away. She is a woman of turbulent, sometimes violent emotions, necessarily repressed, with a fierce sense of duty and protectiveness towards her family. She swears PATRICK MANNION to silence, with tragic consequences.

Prentice, Johnny
The Timeless Land, 1941
Storm of Time, 1948
No Barrier, 1953
Eleanor Dark

The eight-year-old son of ELLEN PRENTICE, he is long believed dead after running away from Beltransa and the cruel treatment of STEPHEN MANNION. But he is independent, resourceful and rebellious, and finds refuge with his dead father's Aborigine second family, which includes Johnny's half-brother, BILLALONG. Later, with Matthew Finn, an escaped convict who becomes his surrogate father and teacher, he establishes a remote mountain settlement to be populated by freed prisoners. Only Ellen and Johnny's childhood friend, PATRICK MANNION, know he is alive, rejecting the white man's world and raiding its riches. When Finn is killed by Stephen Mannion, Johnny's revenge has terrible consequences for Ellen.

Prescott, Esther
Down in the City, 1957
Elizabeth Harrower

STAN PETERSON's well-heeled wife, she has come from a life of seclusion, wealth and privilege, but one of emotional distance and, indeed, isolation: 'enthusiasm was alien to her, real warmth beyond her capacity'. 'Rather tall', with 'impersonal grey eyes [and a] narrow face', Esther is not beautiful, but is classically attractive. She marries Stan, at the age of 33, after having known him for two weeks, and despite the obsessive nature of their relationship, for the first time in her life Esther feels emotionally in touch with someone else. Despite and perhaps because of their rows, Esther perseveres in the marriage. She sees herself and Stan as 'unique, their union losing nothing for being dangerous and dark at times'.

Presley
The Octopus: A Story of California, 1901
Frank Norris

A poet from the East who has taken up the cause of the San Joaquin farmers. A complex character, his sympathies seem at first to be engaged on grounds of taste rather than high moral principle and he tends to regard the Far West as a suitable setting and subject for a tumultuous romance of heroic struggle. It is his unwritten 'Song of the West' that inspires him, rather than the farmers' dogged determination to work the land and fight off the railway interests. Under his swarthy exterior, he seems introspective, 'morbidly sensitive to changes in his physical surroundings', and faintly consumptive.

Pretty-man, Prince
The Rehearsal, 1671
George Villiers, 2nd Duke of Buckingham

A character in BAYES's appalling heroic drama, which is rehearsed within the play. Bayes has

given him would-be witty remarks. Despite his royal blood, he believes his father to be the old fisherman who brought him up. He loves Cloris and argues heroically with PRINCE VOLSCIUS about the merits of their respective lovers.

Prewitt, Robert E Lee
From Here to Eternity, 1951
James Jones

A private soldier, he is a 'very neat and deceptively slim young man' from the Southern mountains. He plays guitar, and loves to play bugle. He was a good boxer, but gave this up after blinding a man. He is set to be a 'thirty-year man' in the army, but constantly falls foul of the expectations of his officers, particularly over his refusal to box. Although strong-willed, with immense physical endurance, he finally cracks under the psychological and physical pressure.

Priam
Troilus and Cressida, 1601/2
William Shakespeare

The King of Troy, Priam is an old man who is dependent upon his six sons – and especially upon HECTOR, his 'crutch' – not only for their prowess on the battlefield, but also for their advice on matters of state. He himself seems unsure that the war with the Greeks is a worthy one, but fights on, persuaded by his sons that his own 'worth and honour' are bound up in it.

Price, Fanny
Mansfield Park, 1814
Jane Austen

The eldest daughter of Lieutenant and MRS PRICE and impecunious niece of SIR THOMAS BERTRAM and LADY BERTRAM. A shy child with no 'glow or complexion', 'afraid of everybody and ashamed of herself', she develops in the care of her cousins into a well-principled and religious woman of strict moral standing, but never ceases to be 'as fearful of notice and praise as other women [are] of neglect'. Her lucid mind and clear perception are compounded in 'all the heroism of principle' but, 'having also many of the feelings of youth and nature', she finds her judgement at times coloured by a yearning for romanticism, which is given expression by quoting Cowper.

Price, Gethin
Comedians, 1975
Trevor Griffiths

Gethin Price is one of six aspiring comics being trained in the tricks of the trade by EDDIE WATERS. A van driver, Price is in his mid-twenties, a talented, passionate, angry, emotionally wounded man, who 'argues like other people breathe'. During a club try-out and without warning, he abandons his clownish mime act to deliver a savage verbal attack upon two life-size dummies, howling his hatred at an exploitative and exploited society. Comedy, for Price, is a matter of political truth.

Price, Hyacinth
Mr Scobie's Riddle, 1983
Elizabeth Jolley

Matron and owner of the Hospital of St Christopher and St Columbus, Hyacinth Price, rotund and forever tripping over buckets, disguises her bullying nature with a veneer of management officiousness. Feared by inmates and laughed at by staff, she is a ridiculous figure whose connivances to get patients to sign over their worldly goods to her are doomed to failure. Her comical weaknesses include whisky, a sponging ex-husband, and the occasional rest upon the bosom of her long-suffering lesbian friend.

Price, Mrs
Mansfield Park, 1814
Jane Austen

The mother of FANNY PRICE and impecunious sister of LADY BERTRAM and MRS NORRIS. Burdened with a 'superfluity of children', she offloads Fanny, her eldest daughter, on her wealthy relatives. She is not unkind, but has 'neither leisure nor affection to bestow' on her daughters, and spends her days in 'a kind of slow bustle – always busy, without getting on'. Preoccupied with matters domestic, even the scandal of MARIA BERTRAM and HENRY CRAWFORD's elopement fails to distract her for more than a few minutes from dirty carpets and packing-cases.

Price, Myfanwy
Under Milk Wood, 1954
Dylan Thomas

The dressmaker and sweetshop-owner who is beloved at a distance by MOG EDWARDS the draper. She dreams of a muscular love, but in reality her idea of bliss is domestic, kept cosy by hot-water bottles and neatly sewn garments. Their long-term love letters are their only communication, where passionate declarations alternate with business exchanges. A light-weight, bird-like creature, she will never leave her world for love.

Price, 'Snobby'
Major Barbara, 1905
George Bernard Shaw

A regular at BARBARA UNDERSHAFT's Salvation Army shelter, Snobby is young, agile, sharp, lazy and dishonest. A skilled painter embittered by unemployment, his view is that as the working man provides the rich with meals, the poor are deserving of anything they can get. Like RUMMY MITCHENS, he is happy to fabricate past misdemeanours (even claiming to have beaten his mother), in order to provide himself with some amusement and convince his Salvationist saviours of the scale of their achievement.

Prig, Betsey
Martin Chuzzlewit, 1844
Charles Dickens

A nurse and bosom-friend of MRS SARAH GAMP, she is 'of the Gamp build, but not so fat; and her voice was deeper and more like a man'. She had also a beard. As ignorant of nursing practice as Mrs Gamp, and as brutal towards patients, she quarrels with her friend when she questions the existence of the imaginary Mrs Harris.

Prime, Guy
The Embezzler, 1966
Louis Auchincloss

As his name perhaps implies, his success and social standing are grounded on nothing more substantial than a set of narrowly codified ideas about what it means to be a man. Although highly sociable, he is morally derelict and less than secure in his self-image.

Primrose, Dr, and **family**
The Vicar of Wakefield, 1766
Oliver Goldsmith

Dr Primrose, the rich Vicar of Wakefield, lives comfortably with Deborah, his socially-bedazzled wife, and their six children, GEORGE PRIMROSE, Olivia, Sophia, Moses and two small boys. As a family they are generous, respectable, inoffensive, gullible and naive: George and Moses, for example, are easily duped at a fair, the latter induced into spending all his money on a gross of green spectacles. The romantic Olivia is seduced and deserted by the rogue, Squire Thornhill, the demure Sophia is abducted and mistakenly believed to be dead, and the often sententious Primrose loses his fortune. He endures this battering with fortitude, grace and optimism. Later, MR BURCHILL restores their fortunes.

Primrose, George
The Vicar of Wakefield, 1766
Oliver Goldsmith

The eldest son of DR PRIMROSE, he is about to marry ARABELLA WILMOT when her father cancels the wedding. George then leaves to seek his fortune in London. But instead of a fortune, the disappointed, provincial, gentlemanly but rather dreaming George discovers more of the harshness and sudden cruelties of life. He is as disaster-prone as the other members of his family: having challenged Squire Thornhill to a duel to avenge Olivia, his seduced and abandoned sister, George is beaten by thugs and bundled off to prison. Later, he is able to prove to Arabella that he loves her not for her fortune, but for herself.

Princess Puffer
The Mystery of Edwin Drood, 1870
Charles Dickens

An old hag and opium addict who runs the East End opium den frequented by MR JOHN JASPER. After EDWIN DROOD disappears, Jasper goes to smoke opium with her, and she follows him back to Cloisterham. DICK DATCHERY watches them and is interested to discover the connection between them.

Prindy
Poor Fellow My Country, 1975
Xavier Herbert

The grandson of JEREMY DELACY, he is of Irish, English and Aboriginal descent. His quest is to discover his true identity and cultural heritage. Prindy not only has great enterprise and a certain amount of self-reliance, he has considerable curiosity and responds to Jewish and Indian as well as Aboriginal culture. It might also be argued that he has all the gullibility of innocent youth. His death during an initiation ceremony held by BOBWIRRIDIRRIDI suggests that it may not after all be possible to unite Australia's cultural and ethnic diversity in a new and harmonious society.

Pringle, Dr
The Ayrshire Legatees, 1821
John Galt

Dr Pringle, minister of Garnock in Ayrshire, is left a fortune by his cousin, an Indian Nabob. He and his family procure mourning-garments to match this sad occasion and he, his wife, his sentimental daughter Rachel and his legal son Andrew travel to London to see that all is in order. Letters pass between them and their friends in Garnock, giving their impressions of London's worldly ways, wasteful grand houses, cold preachers and 'thin kirks'; it is clear that Dr Pringle will be glad to return to Scotland, grateful to providence for his prosperity.

Pringle, Guy
The Balkan Trilogy, 1960–5
The Levant Trilogy, 1977–80
Olivia Manning

Guy is a tall, gregarious figure, shabbily dressed, short-sighted and slightly clumsy, his pockets stuffed with papers and books. His apparent interest in anyone and everyone contrasts with a strange insensitivity to the needs of individuals, notably those of his wife, HARRIET PRINGLE. He is very sure of some things in life, and believes that 'freedom is the knowledge of necessity' and that 'there is no wealth but life'. He is forever giving, never expecting anything in return, and gives the impression of being either a saint or a fool. He is intellectually arrogant, with no time for metaphysics or for religions other than Marxism, and his charitableness and good nature leave him open to deceivers and the second-rate.

Pringle, Harriet
The Balkan Trilogy, 1960–5
The Levant Trilogy, 1977–80
Olivia Manning

Early on in their marriage, Harriet realizes how little she knows of GUY PRINGLE. After his whirlwind courtship, she had hoped to be united with him at the centre of a new and unfamiliar world, but instead she finds herself relegated to a fringe role in his major production. Her constant fear is that Guy will be taken into people's hearts, whereas she will always remain the stranger. Forthright, irritable and frequently mis-understood, she boasts that she never follows examples, and admits that her enjoyment of life is not spoilt by Guy's generosity but by her own lack of it. In her loneliness she turns to more readily loveable, though less reliable, companions.

Prior, Billy
Regeneration, 1991
The Eye in the Door, 1993
The Ghost Road, 1995, forming the *Regeneration* trilogy
Pat Barker

Prior, 'a thin, fair-haired young man' with 'a supercilious expression' has been rendered temporarily mute by his war experience. He has a combative relationship with DR WILLIAM RIVERS, although ultimately it is one of reciprocal affection. Prior is intensely curious about Rivers, and his 'constant *probing*' is discomfiting to the neurologist. Scathing about the class differences

which survive intact at the Front and bitterly disappointed with himself for 'breaking down', Prior is determined to return to duty, despite his chronic asthma. In Sarah Lumb, a munitions factory worker with whom he starts an affair, he finds a 'haven' from the terrors of war.

Prior, Margaret
Affinity, 1999
Sarah Waters

After a series of unhappy events and a failed suicide attempt, Margaret Prior, a 'spinster' about to turn 30, attempts to take her mind off the difficulties in her life by doing charitable work at a woman's prison. Here she meets inmate and spiritualist, SELINA DAWES, and Margaret's initial fascination with Selina soon develops into something much more powerful. Margaret, an educated woman of the upper classes, was born into a world where very few options were open to her and it is only through her passion for Selina that she is able to find a way to escape the prison of her own life.

Prioress, the, also known as **Madame Eglantyne**
The Canterbury Tales, c.1387–1400
Geoffrey Chaucer

She has delusions of grandeur. Her over-fastidious table manners, her expensive habit, her willingness to display her good looks, her jewellery, and her excellence in singing are all betrayals, albeit minor ones, of her vocation. Her charity appears not to extend beyond her compassion for small animals. She even travels in greater state than THE KNIGHT. Her pretensions betray a shallow character, and her tale of sentimental piety is marred by rampant anti-semitism.

Priscilla (Priscilla Moody)
The Blithedale Romance, 1852
Nathaniel Hawthorne

The pale but interesting younger sister of the exotic ZENOBIA. She falls under the spell of the mesmerist DR WESTERVELT, who violates the sanctity of her rather mysterious nature.

Prism, Miss
The Importance of Being Earnest, 1895
Oscar Wilde

The sententious spinster employed as CECILY CARDEW's governess, she spends much of her time pining after the local clergyman. In her younger days she was in the employ of LADY BRACKNELL and, through her absent-mindedness, was responsible for losing the infant JOHN WORTHING at Victoria station. Foolish and uncharitable, she is variously described as Cecily's 'esteemed governess and valued companion', 'the most cultivated of ladies, and the very picture of respectability', and (perhaps nearer the truth) 'a female of repellent aspect, remotely concerned with education'.

Priuli
Venice Preserv'd, or A Plot Discovered, 1682
Thomas Otway

A proud, intransigent senator, Priuli has disowned his daughter, BELVIDERA, who has secretly married JAFFIER. His domestic authoritarianism and tyranny represent the contemptuous political oppression of the Senate.

Probert, Rosie
Under Milk Wood, 1954
Dylan Thomas

'Come on up, boys, I'm dead' is the haunting call of CAPTAIN CAT's great love. Shared by other sailors, now ghostly voices themselves, 'lazy, early Rosie' of Thirty-Three Duck Lane has her name tattooed on his belly. He recalls her as a safe haven, a sure point in his sea life, but she is now fading into the margins of memory, which makes her more emotionally significant for him.

Proctor, Elizabeth
The Crucible, 1953
Arthur Miller

A restrained and quiet individual, willing to follow the religious codes of the time but not allowing them to interfere with her devotion to her husband, JOHN PROCTOR, and family. She stands up for herself both in speech and in spirit, but her hurt, her anger and a certain coldness of character make her more than a simple embodiment of goodness.

Proctor, John
The Crucible, 1953
Arthur Miller

He is a farmer, obstinate and straightforward, yet also a man of principle; it is his principles, and his temporary lapse in them, through adultery, which make him the central figure of this complex play. Not an archetypal countryman, he is capable of genuine sensitivity, particularly in his relationship with his wife, ELIZABETH PROCTOR, and the closing act reveals him also as a man of poetry and passion.

Proctor, Rev Morley
The Rector, 1863
The Perpetual Curate, 1864
Margaret Oliphant

Mr Proctor, for 15 years scholar of All Souls, accepts the living of Carlingford for the sake of a home for his mother, but fails in pastoral duties, especially toward the dying. He is shy, tongue-tied, a scholar, not a true pastor, and fears all women. His conscience makes him resign and return to All Souls, his mother happy in Oxford, but he cannot retreat to the academic life; Carlingford has made him see he must be a true Christian clergyman.

Profane, Benny
V, 1963
Thomas Pynchon

An aimless 'schlemiel', he is discharged from the USS *Scaffold* and joins another complement of half-alive bohemian mariners on the turbid sea of postwar America. Apart from drinking and womanizing with the 'Whole Sick Crew', his days are spent with a patrol searching the New York sewers for overgrown albino alligators, unwanted pets flushed away by their owners.

Prohack, Arthur Charles
Mr Prohack, 1922
Arnold Bennett

Wealth comes suddenly to Mr Prohack, disturbing the regular pattern of his life and forcing him to adjust to very different circumstances. He meets this challenge with an endearing mixture of innocence and shrewdness. He stands in awe of the splendour he now encounters and, though wise in his investments, he remains baffled by women. His lively wit and homespun wisdom rest on a foundation of real understanding and intellect and any mild deceptions he practises are outweighed by his basic decency.

Propter
After Many a Summer, 1939
Aldous Huxley

A voluble visionary, Propter is in favour of small communities, and advocates a philosophy of mystical detachment, believing that 'No iron necessity condemns the individual to the futile torment of being merely human'. His enlightened views, however, fall on stony ground in a satirically portrayed California, whose decadence and materialism he condemns.

Prospero
The Tempest, 1611
William Shakespeare

As Duke of Milan, Prospero was popular but ineffectual, spending his time in study. His interests being philosophical rather than material, he spends his time on the enchanted island developing magical powers which he uses to effect his revenge, although he aims to improve his enemies rather than punish them. A fond father, he has been tutor to his daughter MIRANDA. He approves of her falling in love with FERDINAND, but like many fathers he is suspicious of the young man's motives. He can be short-tempered and impatient, especially with CALIBAN, whose treachery he finds hard to forgive; but he is also kind and generous to those who have done him good service.

Pross, Miss
A Tale of Two Cities, 1859
Charles Dickens

The devoted maid of LUCIE MANETTE, her grim and eccentric manner disguise a noble, unselfish character. She inspires a kind of terror in MR JARVIS LORRY. Her brother, SOLOMON PROSS, has stripped her of all her money in order to gamble. When the Manettes escape from Paris with CHARLES DARNAY, she stays behind to conceal their flight and struggles with MADAME DEFARGE, who has come to find them. She accidentally kills Madame Defarge with her own pistol but becomes permanently deafened by the noise of the shot. With the help of JERRY CRUNCHER, she escapes safely back to England.

Pross, Solomon (John Barsad)
A Tale of Two Cities, 1859
Charles Dickens

The heartless brother of MISS PROSS, he robs her of all she possesses and abandons her. With his partner, ROGER CLY, he plots to get CHARLES DARNAY arrested for treason in England and testifies against him. In Paris, under the alias of John Barsad, he spies for both the old regime and the Revolutionary government but is recognized by Miss Pross and SYDNEY CARTON. Threatened with exposure, he is forced to help Carton rescue Darnay from prison.

Prosser, Gabriel
BlackThunder, 1935
Arna Bontemps
A powerful black slave, perhaps modelled on Toussaint L'Ouverture, who leads a rebellion in America at the time of the French Revolution. His forename, given to him by white men, is a triumphant expression of his power.

Proteus
Two Gentlemen of Verona, c.1590
William Shakespeare
Proteus is one of the 'two gentlemen', the other being VALENTINE, who describes him as: 'His years but young, but his experience old;/His head unmellowed, but his judgement ripe'. In fact, Proteus's heart rules his head and he is not quite such a friend as Valentine believes. He is, as his name suggests, variable, and he betrays both his friend and JULIA in an attempt to win Valentine's lover, SILVIA, for himself. This is after he has claimed that love for Julia has 'metamorphosed' him. He may, perhaps, feel rather inferior to Valentine's learning and envious of his success with Silvia. The play looks at the emotional maturing of two impossibly idealistic young men, and at the end, Proteus learns that immediate self-interest and treachery bring no reward.

Proteus, Joe
The Apple Cart, 1929
George Bernard Shaw
Joe Proteus, the Prime Minister of a Labour government and an astute, cunning politician, is Shaw's caricature of Ramsay MacDonald. A man seemingly qualified for nothing other than being prime minister, his sentimental oratory and apparent rages are tactics to spur his ineffectual, squabbling Cabinet into action. In his debate with KING MAGNUS as to whether Britain should seem to be governed by the monarchy or Parliament, the idealistic and ambitious Proteus represents himself as a democrat challenging the inherited tyranny of royalty.

Prothero, Pokey (Mary)
The Group, 1963
Mary McCarthy
A very rich society girl who is naturally passive, even lazy. That she has actually made the effort against her parents' wishes to attend college and pursue a professional goal is surprising and irritating to her family. Rather ignorant of any social setting different from her own and totally unabashed by her wealth, Pokey is unselfconsciously able to ask straight questions and pass blunt opinions. She can also, when it occurs to her, be generous in a practical way.

Proudfute, Oliver
The Fair Maid of Perth, or St Valentine's Day, in *Chronicles of the Canongate: Second Series*, 1828
Sir Walter Scott
A 'reasonably wealthy' bonnet-maker of Perth, he is well-intentioned but tactless, a shortcoming that scarcely justifies his sudden murder at the High Street corner.

Proudie, Dr Thomas
Barchester Towers, 1857
DrThorne, 1858
Framley Parsonage, 1861
The Last Chronicle of Barset, 1867
AnthonyTrollope
The Low Church Bishop of Barchester. Ambitious, somewhat superficial, and with a desire to live in fashionable society, his position is increasingly undermined by his dominating wife, MRS PROUDIE. After early attempts to escape her control, he submits for the sake of a comfortable life, but he eventually despairs at her interference in his episcopal duties.

Proudie, Mrs
Barchester Towers, 1857
DrThorne, 1858
Framley Parsonage, 1861
The Last Chronicle of Barset, 1867
AnthonyTrollope
The domineering wife of DR THOMAS PROUDIE, whose diocese she aspires to govern. Her worldly interests and ambitions are in conflict with both her religious enthusiasm, which focuses on Sabbatarianism, and her urge to economize. Energetic and overbearing, the 'she-bishop' genuinely believes that her opponents (including REV DR THEOPHILUS GRANTLY, LADY LUFTON, REV JOSIAH CRAWLEY and many others) represent the forces of evil. She is courageous and entertainingly larger than life, but her behaviour, prompted by ignorance and ambition, undoes her husband and herself.

Provincial Lady
The Diary of a Provincial Lady, 1930
E M Delafield
The unnamed heroine of ordinary rural life in Devonshire between the wars, she records various episodes for herself and readers of *Time and Tide* in a dry, clipped personal dialogue shaded with ironic humour. A pillar of the community, she observes with affectionate wit her family, the 'servant problem', Our Vicar's Wife and other local gentry as well as her own role in middle-class society. She conducts her long-suffering existence with style and understatement; while totally involved, she is able to detail social situations with amused and amusing detachment.

Prudence
Tumatumari, 1968
Wilson Harris
The wife of a prospector on a Guyanese river, she is suddenly widowed and left alone in an alien environment. Her grief sparks off recollections of her family's attempts to come to terms with and subdue its physical and psychological surroundings.

Prufrock, J Alfred
'The Love Song of J. Alfred Prufrock', in *Prufrock and Other Observations*, 1917
T S Eliot

'No! I am not Prince Hamlet, nor was meant to be.' The balding, middle-aged Prufrock is self-condemned to the fringes of things, a diffident observer – 'Politic, cautious, and meticulous' – rather than a participant. Instead of swimming in life's fullness, he paddles at its edges, his trousers carefully rolled, consumed with doubt.

Prunesquallor, Dr Alfred
Titus Groan, 1946
Gormenghast, 1950
Mervyn Peake

A commoner, elevated to artificial status by his profession as castle physician, and saddled with an unbearable sister, Irma, Prunesquallor is given to frequent outbursts of irritatingly high-pitched laughter, effeminate gestures and extravagant posturings. He is verbose to a degree, his trillings and warblings forming a mask to conceal the workings of a powerful brain. Tall, with elegant, crane-like legs, he has a delicate, fine-featured face, with a shock of white hair, marble-smooth skin and tombstone teeth. He loves FUCHSIA, LADY OF GROAN as if she were his own daughter, and shows true compassion in his dealings with TITUS GROAN's deranged father. He has a mind of his own, yet he is determinedly 'of the place'.

Prussian Officer, the
'The Prussian Officer', in *The Prussian Officer*, 1914
D H Lawrence

This captain is obsessed by his young orderly, so jealous of his physical energy and stamina that he humiliates him and eventually pays with his life. The traits in the captain's nature provide the themes of homo-eroticism, domination and humiliation, jealousy and sadism, and this short story distils several of Lawrence's main recurring themes, including the nature of emotional and intellectual honesty and man's relationship with nature.

Prynne, Amanda → Chase, Elyot and Prynne, Amanda

Prynne, Hester
The Scarlet Letter, 1850
Nathaniel Hawthorne

Once married to the grim nemesis who now calls himself ROGER CHILLINGWORTH, Hester falls in love with the minister ARTHUR DIMMESDALE and has a child by him. In punishment, she is required to wear the letter A in scarlet on her breast. Defiantly, she embroiders it in rich threads and elaborate stitchings, turning the shameful badge of an adulteress into a complex symbol of America, *amor* and art, each of which is echoed in the elaborate dress of her daughter PEARL.

Prynne, Victor, and Chase, Sybil
Private Lives, 1930
Noël Coward

Victor has been abandoned by Amanda Prynne on their honeymoon, as Sybil has been discarded by ELYOT CHASE on theirs. They are subsidiary characters; in fact, in Coward's words, 'little better than ninepins, lightly wooden, and only there at all to be repeatedly knocked down and stood up again'. Victor and Sybil are united in outrage: 'I'd no idea anyone behaved like that', cries Sybil. They are deliberately commonplace people and Elyot and Amanda's audacity provokes only a commonplace response. Victor is rather hearty, but fails to succeed in challenging Elyot to a fight, and Sybil is verbally dismissed by Amanda.

Pryor, Mrs
Shirley, 1849
Charlotte Brontë

SHIRLEY KEELDAR's governess and companion, Mrs Pryor is also CAROLINE HELSTONE's estranged mother, having deserted her cruel and violent husband when her daughter was in her infancy, and lacking the courage and confidence to claim her after his death. Diffident and reserved, she appears stiff, awkward and proud. She is uncertain and nervous, her habits retiring and solitary, those of a woman disillusioned by life. She finally finds a measure of the happiness that has eluded her all her life when she is reunited with her daughter.

Psmith
Psmith in the City, 1910
Psmith Journalist, 1915
Leave it to Psmith, 1923
P G Wodehouse

Ronald Psmith (the P is silent), once a reporter in New York, later a fugitive from the fish trade in London, advertises his services in a newspaper. Confident, tall, affable, well-dressed and with a brilliantly fluid conversational style, he is asked by Freddie Threepwood to help him steal Aunt Constance's necklace at Blandings Castle, where he is taken for a Canadian poet. Other guests are also jewel thieves. Through all these social embarrassments, Psmith emerges with absolute aplomb and enjoyment.

Ptolemy Dionysus
Caesar and Cleopatra, 1898
George Bernard Shaw

Ptolemy is the 10-year-old younger brother of CLEOPATRA, and King of Egypt, maintained on the throne by POTHINUS and a retinue of protectors. He is killed in the Alexandrine Wars.

Puck
A Midsummer Night's Dream, c.1594
William Shakespeare

A 'merry wanderer of the night', a miscreant fairy famed for his mischief, humour and trickery, and loyal favourite of OBERON, King of the Fairy Kingdom. Though he is a swaggering poseur among his peers, and, essentially, an errand-boy by trade, his reflections on human frailty, his acrobatic energy and the poetry of his whimsical closing speech justify the affection he engenders.

Puck
Puck of Pook's Hill, 1906
Rudyard Kipling

'A small, brown, broad-shouldered, pointy-eared person with a snub nose, slanting blue eyes, and a grin that ran right across his freckled face'. He is conjured up by performing *A Midsummer Night's Dream* three times on Midsummer Eve in the middle of a fairy ring, and becomes a channel for a magical pageant of English history from old times to the present.

Puff
The Critic, 1779
Richard Brinsley Sheridan
An 18th-century public relations man, who describes himself as 'a practitioner in panegyric' and 'a professor of the art of puffing'. He uses various techniques to promote plays, personal relationships, and other projects. He is the author of a ludicrous tragedy, 'The Spanish Armada', a rehearsal of which constitutes a play within the play.

Pug
The Devil is an Ass, 1616
Ben Jonson
A lesser devil who visits Earth in the guise of servant to FABIAN FITZDOTTREL, Pug marvels at the stupendous vanities of mankind and the tricks men play upon fools. He decides to join the action by attempting to seduce his master's wife, but the plan misfires. One by one, all his schemes for deception and seduction are thwarted. He is eventually imprisoned and concludes sadly that he, a devil, cannot hope to compete with the evil done by human beings.

Pug, properly **Victor Henry**
The Winds of War, 1971
War and Remembrance, 1975
Herman Wouk
A gifted naval officer, he finds himself rubbing shoulders and debating issues with influential policy-makers during the time of pre-war tensions, and then required to cope with the pressures of high command when hostilities break out. Being an uncomplicated man, he finds himself blown about by the inevitable fluctuations of fortune: the tension of relationships, the fear and the loss, the betrayals and the failures that are part of the experience of war. He subsequently emerges with greater strength of character.

Pugh, Mr
Under Milk Wood, 1954
Dylan Thomas
The wheedling, soft-soaping smile under the walrus moustache of the village schoolmaster masks a potentially malevolent personality: he longs to murder his dreadful wife. By extensive reading, such as 'Lives of Great Poisoners' – his hero is Dr Crippen – he plots imaginary ends for her. He commits dark deeds of domestic violence such as spitting in vases and encouraging the mice with cheese. All food could be a source of death, but he brings her not arsenic but 'your nice tea'.

Pugh, Mrs
Under Milk Wood, 1954
Dylan Thomas
The schoolmaster's wife, she is a cold, bitter individual, an object of wishful uxoricide. She

gets her complaint in before the event and, from her window, watches for human failings in her 'proper glasses'. To her, people are either 'persons' or pigs. Quite the opposite of POLLY GARTER, the target of her particular rage, she is 'sweet as a razor ... [a] nutcracker wife'.

Pulham, H M
H M Pulham Esq, 1941
John P Marquand
The pressures of a new age and changing social values set him slightly at odds with the Brahmin Puritanism of his Boston family. However, his rebellion is only token and he quickly reverts to ancestral ways.

Pullet, Mrs
The Mill on the Floss, 1860
George Eliot
The favourite sister of MRS BESSY TULLIVER, Mrs Pullet is preferred by the young TOM and MAGGIE TULLIVER only because she seems slightly less intolerant of them than their aunt, MRS GLEGG, does. House-proud, fastidious and attired in the most fashionable clothes, Mrs Pullet prides herself not only on her family's impeccability and advantageous marriage, but also on her ability to be effortlessly moved to tears by anything, from the death of a distant acquaintance to the showing of her best bonnet. Overly concerned by society's opinion of her and her relations, she remains a humorously pathetic figure.

Pulling, Henry
Travels With My Aunt, 1969
Graham Greene
The narrator, and seemingly the nephew of AUGUSTA BERTRAM. He is her opposite in every sense, a quiet, cautious retired bank manager who seeks only an uneventful bachelor routine amid his flowers. His adventures with his aunt reveal a capacity for pleasure which he did not realize he possessed, as well as the true nature of his blood tie to her.

Pumblechook, Uncle
Great Expectations, 1861
Charles Dickens
JOE GARGERY's uncle, he is a wealthy corn-chandler and seed merchant. Although respected by MRS JOE GARGERY, he is pompous, bullying and hypocritical, tormenting the young PIP but becoming obsequious when he suddenly comes into property. He changes to become spuriously compassionate and forgiving when Pip is left impoverished after the death of ABEL MAGWITCH.

Puntarvolo
Every Man out of his Humour, 1599
Ben Jonson
A self-possessed and inordinately boastful knight, Puntarvolo's arrival on stage is heralded by the sound of foxhounds. He finds himself outside a house and, seeing at a window a woman who turns out to be a servant, engineers a conversation which quickly becomes a eulogy of himself. He does exactly the same when his wife appears. If his obsessive vanity makes him

detestable, his equally excessive hospitality endears him to many. When MACILENTE poisons one of his dogs as a joke, he sees his folly ('humour') and in turn 'dishumours' the clown, CARLO BUFFONE, by taping up his mouth.

Pupin, Monsieur
The Princess Casamassima, 1886
Henry James
An émigré bookbinder and communist, he helps introduce HYACINTH ROBINSON to both vocations. Quiet, intense and convinced, he nonetheless maintains his beliefs between hard, dogmatic covers: 'a constructive democrat (instead of being a mere scoffer at effete things), and a theorist and an optimist and a visionary'.

Purecraft, Dame
Bartholomew Fair, 1614
Ben Jonson
A wealthy Puritan widow, Dame Purecraft is the mother of WIN LITTLEWIT. She is a mature, beautiful woman who attracts several suitors, among them WINWIFE and ZEAL-OF-THE-LAND BUSY. Her particular weak spot, though, is believing the pronouncements of fortune-tellers. As she has been told that she will only be happy with a gentleman, but one who also happens to be mad, she is on the lookout for such a man at Bartholomew Fair. She is flattered by TOM QUARLOUS, who gives her ample evidence that he is deranged, and marries him before she realizes that he is sane.

Purfoy, Sarah
His Natural Life, serialized 1870–2; as *For the Term of His Natural Life*, 1874
Marcus Clarke
Lady's maid and nurse to Sylvia Vickers, six-year-old child of a military officer on a prison ship going out to Australia. She is the lover of JOHN REX, an association that explains her puzzling willingness to travel to the colonies.

Pursewarden, Percy
Justine, 1957, and elsewhere in *The Alexandria Quartet*, 1968
Lawrence Durrell
An apparently minor character, he works for British intelligence, and is the key to the story's various searches. Despite the fact that he is a suicide, he speaks out for artistic wholeness and for the consistent application of vision, and his papers are referred to throughout the sequence.

Putnam, Abbie, later Abbie Cabot
Desire Under the Elms, 1924
Eugene O'Neill
Half his age, she is chosen by EPHRAIM CABOT to be his third wife and bear him the new son he requires. She seduces EBEN CABOT, the existing heir, merely in order to become pregnant, but falls for him and, to prove her love, smothers her new-born baby to death.

Pygmalion
Back to Methuselah, 1921
George Bernard Shaw
A scientist, Pygmalion appears in the final section of this five-part play. *As Far as Thought can Reach* is set in a remote garden Utopia in 31,920AD. He is a youth with a perpetual smile of eager benevolence, a bore with 'the eager confidence of the fanatical scientist'. ARJILLAX has sculpted two statues which Pygmalion has managed to infuse with life to create 'artificial human beings'. The young people are revolted by their robotic reflexes and their proclamations to be 'the children of Cause and Effect ... Determinists'.

Pyle, Alden
The Quiet American, 1955
Graham Greene
The American of the title. He is good-natured, innocent, and politically idealistic: dangerous qualities in the political minefield of Vietnam, where he is on an aid mission. He is gradually sucked into local affairs, and is ultimately murdered by the Communists, to whom he is betrayed by British journalist THOMAS FOWLER who is also a rival for the love of a Vietnamese girl Phuong.

Pym, Arthur Gordon
The Narrative of Arthur Gordon Pym, 1838
Edgar Allan Poe
His father was a 'respectable trader in sea stores' in Nantucket, and he conceives 'the greatest desire to go to sea', largely thanks to the stories of his school-friend Augustus. He has an 'enthusiastic temperament and somewhat gloomy though glowing imagination', and it is the visions of shipwrecks and death which make the biggest impression on him. These are given full rein in his account of his own wild adventures on a voyage as a stowaway, involving mutiny, shipwreck, capture by cannibals, rescue, and a final unresolved encounter with a mysterious, gigantic shroud-figure in the Antarctic.

Pym, Magnus
A Perfect Spy, 1986
John Le Carré
Powerful, stately and of the Anglo-Saxon administrative class, Magnus has been Deputy Head of (Spy) Station at the Washington British Embassy and is now Head in Vienna. He goes missing without warning, the result of a past that has got out of control. A series of inadequate mother-surrogates combined with a con-man father have prepared the way for his own individual duplicity and the 'bad habit of protesting loyalty to everyone he met'.

Pym, Rick
A Perfect Spy, 1986
John Le Carré
MAGNUS PYM's father. Since the 1930s, when he conned away a Baptist church's Appeal Money to pay for a non-existent motorcoach, Rick has been an imaginative and daring liar. He starts an insurance company, marries an MP's daughter and acquires an Ascot mansion on dubious credit. Occasional failure and police pursuit never daunt him. His relationship with Magnus is always more important than his relationships with women, and towards the end of his life he follows his son from country to country,

annoying and worrying him with demands for friendship and money.

Pyncheon, Clifford
The House of the Seven Gables, 1851
Nathaniel Hawthorne
False imprisonment for the supposed murder of his uncle has reduced this 'abortive lover of the beautiful' to the simplicity of a grizzled child. Delicately beautiful but also weak, venal and greedy, he represents the final decadence of the Pyncheons and, in his crazy desire to escape the past and plunge into 'the great centre of humanity', their last faint hope.

Pyncheon, Col
The House of the Seven Gables, 1851
Nathaniel Hawthorne
Brutal ancestor of CLIFFORD and HEPZIBAH PYNCHEON, identified by a descendant of the man he dispossesses as 'a model conservative, who, in that very character, rendered himself so long the evil destiny of his race'. He is responsible for the death of the settler MATTHEW MAULE and the recipient of Maule's curse: that 'God will give him blood to drink'.

Pyncheon, Hepzibah
The House of the Seven Gables, 1851
Nathaniel Hawthorne
The elderly sister of CLIFFORD PYNCHEON, as obsessively attached to the past as he is desperate to forget it. F O Matthiessen in *American Renaissance* sums her up perfectly as the 'embodiment of decayed gentility, sustained only by her delusion of family importance, lacking any revivifying touch with outward existence'.

Pyncheon, Jaffrey
The House of the Seven Gables, 1851
Nathaniel Hawthorne
The unscrupulous cousin of CLIFFORD and HEPZIBAH PYNCHEON, he gains the family inheritance by making it appear that their uncle's death by apoplexy was the result of an act of violence on Clifford's part. He subsequently rises to material wealth and the judgeship. Cold and obdurate, he is granite to Clifford's cracked porcelain.

Pyncheon, Phoebe
The House of the Seven Gables, 1851
Nathaniel Hawthorne
The niece of HEPZIBAH and CLIFFORD PYNCHEON, her moral energy – unwonted for a Pyncheon – is explained by the fact that her father married 'beneath' him. She marries the artist HOLGRAVE, thus redeeming the family curse.

Pynsent, Miss, known as 'Pinnie'
The Princess Casamassima, 1886
Henry James
A quiet, rather retiring dressmaker, she is the spinster guardian of HYACINTH ROBINSON, whom she also makes her heir. Her home is a haven of respectability and reserve amid the hectic bustle of lower-middle-class London; her characteristic manner, though kindly, is 'a certain stiff, quaint, polished politeness, of which she possessed the secret and which made her resemble a pair of old-fashioned sugar-tongs'.

Pyrochles
The Faerie Queene, 1590–6
Sir Edmund Spenser
The brother of CYMOCHLES. Together they are seen as the enemies of Christianity. Pyrochles is renowned for his fiery disposition, volatility, wrathfulness in battle, and his cruelty. Descended from immortal ancestors, he has an air of the supernatural about him. His red horse and suit of armour sparkle like fire and 'round his feet smouldring dust did him smoke'. Whilst in combat he takes no care for his own safety, but lashes out in rage.

Pyrocles
The Countess of Pembroke's Arcadia, 1581–4, published 1590
Sir Philip Sidney
A young noble, first seen astride the broken mast of a burning and wrecked ship, and only later revealed to be a prince of Macedon. He gains entry to DUKE BASILIUS's court dressed as an Amazon, a disguise that causes a certain sexual confusion; the duke and his wife GYNECIA both fall in love with him, affections which turn to fatal condemnation when he is discovered in bed with their daughter PHILOCLEA.

Quackleben, Dr Quentin
St Ronan's Well, 1823
Sir Walter Scott

A physician who owes his social and professional standing at St Ronan's Well to having been the first to declare its beneficial and therapeutic properties. This spurious expertise he has negotiated into a specialized understanding of whatever subject the conversation brings up.

Quaife, Roger, MP
Corridors of Power, 1964
C P Snow

A young Conservative Member of Parliament who is beginning to make an impact on the British political scene, though in person he seems large and shambling, in sharp contrast to the officer-class types who have entered Westminster with him. His wife Caroline (Caro) is the daughter of an earl and much of his social cachet comes from her.

Quant
The Age of Anxiety, 1948
W H Auden

A tired old widower 'who would never now be more than a clerk in a shipping office near the Battery'. He came to the USA at the age of six, and his mind is still full of highly coloured images from his youth, these days topped up by alcohol.

Quare Fellow, the
The Quare Fellow, 1954
Brendan Behan

Although he forms the constant subject of the play, he never appears on stage. The play is set in a Dublin prison, where 'the Quare Fellow' is to be executed within 24 hours. A pork butcher, he murdered his brother by hacking him with a meat cleaver, and the condemned man's fate occupies the thoughts of the staff and inmates, including DUNLAVIN, who describes the crime as 'a real bog-man act'.

Quarles, Philip
Point Counter Point, 1928
Aldous Huxley

A novelist, who comments: 'The chief defect of the novel of ideas is that you have to write about people who have ideas to express – which excludes all but .01 per cent of the human race. Hence the real, the congenital novelists don't write such books. But then I never pretended to be a congenital novelist.' Quarles, who has none of his wife RACHEL QUARLES's religious faith, becomes so disillusioned, particularly about how

the physical tends to overwhelm the spiritual, that he allows himself to be murdered by political thugs while listening to a Beethoven Quartet.

Quarles, Rachel
Point Counter Point, 1928
Aldous Huxley

Wife of the novelist PHILIP QUARLES, she is decribed as 'in a word … a Christian and not a humanitarian'. Her religious certainties contrast strongly with her husband's agonized scepticism. Summing up the generation represented by the ruthlessly hedonistic Lucy Tantamount, she states that 'Everybody strains after happiness, and the result is that nobody's happy'. She also observes that 'Happiness is like coke – something you get as a by-product in the process of making something else'.

Quarlous, Tom
Bartholomew Fair, 1614
Ben Jonson

A clever, sharp-witted man. With his friend WINWIFE he enjoys himself at Bartholomew Fair by exposing the foolishness, gullibility and corruption of others. He plots to have BARTHOLOMEW COKES's marriage licence stolen from HUMPHREY WASPE and, by disguising himself as a madman, succeeds in courting DAME PURECRAFT and having JUSTICE OVERDO sign the licence.

Quartermaine, St John
Quartermaine's Terms, 1981
Simon Gray

Quartermaine, a bachelor, vague, courteous and well-meaning, has taught with decreasing effectiveness at the Cull-Loomis School for English at Cambridge since it opened. His presence in the staffroom is reassuring if exasperating. His inability to say no is both his charm and his weakness. Always ready to baby-sit or make up numbers at a dinner party, his services are ceaselessly in demand while his amiability and generosity are seldom appreciated. Nobody sees the tragic loneliness behind the light-hearted exterior; yet Quartermaine similarly fails to recognize the pain in others.

quartermaster, the → Hyde, James, Senior

Quayle, Justin
The Constant Gardener, 2000
John Le Carré

The First Secretary at the British High Commission in Nairobi, whose wife, human rights activist Tessa, is discovered murdered in northern Kenya, Quayle is a handsome, diffident man, who under normal circumstances 'loves nothing more that toiling in the flowerbeds on a Saturday afternoon – a gentleman, whatever that means – the right sort of Etonian, courteous to a fault'. His quest to discover his wife's killers takes him to Germany, the Sudan and Canada, and deep into the hypocrisy and corruption of various governments and pharmaceutical companies, on whose activities Tessa had written a damning report. Increasingly, Quayle is forced to reconsider his relationship with the State and the institutions he serves, the nature of his love for his country and his duty to himself and those he loves.

Quayne, Anna
The Death of the Heart, 1938
Elizabeth Bowen

Ash-blonde Anna originally attracted her husband THOMAS QUAYNE with her air of 'smiling offhand melancholy'. Growing dumpy with incipient (and premature) middle age, she exercises her considerable aesthetic talents only in maintaining an elegant household, best characterized by its ubiquitous cut-glass lamps.

Quayne, Portia
The Death of the Heart, 1938
Elizabeth Bowen

A 16-year-old by-blow of her father's adulterous affair, she is 'left' to the care of her stepbrother and sister-in-law on his death. Acting with 'orphaned unostentation', she confronts the world, the flesh and the Devil with palpable unease. 'Her body was all concave and jerkily fluid lines; it moved with sensitive looseness, loosely threaded together: each movement had a touch of exaggeration, as though some secret power kept springing out.' Confused by the sophistications of the moneyed world into which she has been dropped, 'she could not believe there was not a plan of the whole set-up in every head but her own'.

Quayne, Thomas
The Death of the Heart, 1938
Elizabeth Bowen

A successful advertising executive, building on his mother's fortune with a partnership in his own agency, he gives off a strong sense of not wanting to be touched and seems unequal to the challenge of looking after his illegitimate step-sister PORTIA QUAYNE for the year specified in his father's will.

Queeg, Captain
The Caine Mutiny, 1951
Herman Wouk

The unstable captain of the minesweeper *Caine*, his brutal, unreasonable and excessively petty actions convince his crew that he is unfit for command, while his seeming cowardice under fire robs him of any respect they might have felt. Cross-examined by BARNEY GREENWALD during the court-martial of the 'mutineers' from his ship, his rambling discourse and self-justifying arrogance reveal him as dangerously insecure and stubborn. He is a man unable to admit mistakes, whose tendency to victimize vulnerable members of his crew explains their loathing for him.

Queen (wife to Cymbeline)
Cymbeline, 1609/10
William Shakespeare

Wife to Britain's monarch, CYMBELINE, the Queen married him late in life, when she herself was a widow. She is a scheming and devious woman who rules the king through flattery and guile, having married him for power and position and now seeking to pass that power on to her own son, CLOTEN. Malevolent and ruthless, she plans murder to further her ambitions, but fools few people, apart from the king, by her dissembling.

Queen, Ellery
The Roman Hat Mystery, 1929, et seq
Ellery Queen (Frederick Dannay and Manfred B Lee)

Teasingly, this sleuth's name is also the pseudonym of his creators, and he is ostensibly the author of the Ellery Queen œuvre. Tall, gangling and scholarly-looking, he has an endearingly breezy charm and wit. Although sometimes falling for women he remains a bachelor, sharing an apartment with his father, Inspector Richard Queen, a New York policeman. Like Sherlock Holmes he is in the classic Edgar Allan Poe tradition of 'ratiocination', his dazzling powers of deductive reasoning solving 'locked room'-type mysteries and other brainteasers.

Queen, the (Isabella)
Richard II, not later than 1595
William Shakespeare

In Isabella, Shakespeare apparently conflates the two historical wives, Anne of Bohemia and Isabella of France. The queen is gentle, kind and devoted to KING RICHARD II but capable of regal anger when he submits too readily to his deposition. However, she is too meek to have any influence over her headstrong husband and finally accepts with quiet dignity that all is ended.

Queequeg
Moby-Dick, 1851
Herman Melville

STARBUCK's harpooner. A Polynesian prince who has taken up whaling, he has a 'certain lofty bearing', and is 'a George Washington cannibalistically developed'. His skin is 'a dark purplish yellow colour', covered with tattoos. He has a 'simple, honest heart' and an 'innate sense of delicacy', and becomes fast friends with ISHMAEL. He both eats and shaves with his harpoon.

Quelch, Mr (Henry Samuel)
Billy Bunter of Greyfriars School, 1949, et seq
Frank Richards

The dour, gimlet-eyed form-master of the Remove, he is never without his pocket copy of the *Odes* of Horace, worn thin by 30-odd years of chafing against his bony chest. When not at his typewriter, tapping out the latest enthralling chapter of the history of Greyfriars School, he is to be found striding across the cliff-top paths, the other Greyfriars' 'beaks' trailing far behind him. The only things that disturb his calm are the misdeeds of BILLY BUNTER, or a finicky debate with Mr Prout about the intricacies of Latin grammar. Quelch is the applier of swift justice in the form of 'whops'; methodical and thorough in all his schoolmasterly duties, he is crusty but just.

Quentin
After the Fall, 1964
Arthur Miller

The history of Quentin's relationships, primarily with women, is presented in the play as an extended confession. A successful lawyer, preoccupied by thoughts of guilt and betrayal at the hands of parents, friends and partners, Quentin doubts whether emotional ties between two people are either possible or sustainable, and whether he is able to love again. His two wives, firstly Louise and secondly the naive, entrancing and ultimately tragic Maggie, accuse him of being emotionally distant. But: 'We are all separate people', he concludes regretfully. 'I tried not to be, but I have to survive too, honey … ' Several commentators have seen the play as a semi-autobiographical reflection upon Miller's marriage to Marilyn Monroe, who at the time of writing had recently died.

Querry
A Burnt Out Case, 1936
Graham Greene

A famous church architect in his mid-fifties, he is the 'burnt out case' of the title, devoid of desires or ambitions, and hardly able to feel emotions of any kind. He flees his outwardly successful but inwardly desolate existence for a simple life in the African jungle, where he seems about to grasp the hope of spiritual redemption, but with ultimately tragic consequences.

Quest, Martha
A Proper Marriage, 1964
A Ripple From the Storm, 1964
Landlocked, 1965
The Four-Gated City, 1969, forming *The Children of Violence* quintet
Doris Lessing

Martha has left behind an emotionally unsatisfying childhood, and through adult experiences is now trying to untangle her confused feelings and desires. Sadly, she often becomes more entangled in the process as she is such a deep thinker. However, she is also intelligent, astute and hardworking, and seems to realize that her efforts are not entirely in vain as they all lead to a greater understanding of self. As her name sugggests she is on a searching journey; she is restless and anxious to come to terms with the world, but wants to fight the evil she sees in it, and this dual purpose often tears her apart.

Quested, Adela
A Passage to India, 1924
E M Forster

A plain, fair-minded woman who journeys to India to join her fiancé RONNY HEASLOP, she is determined to break from the interminable civility and tedium of the English set and experience at least a taste of 'the real India'. Sensible, sincere and full of good intentions, she is to pay dearly for her curiosity. An in-built honesty and strength of character ultimately compel her to see that justice is done and she regards the ensuing derision offered by both sides of the Anglo-Indian divide as 'due punishment for her stupidity'.

Quick, James
For Love Alone, 1944
Christina Stead

An American businessman, working in London, who gives TESSA HAWKINS her first job in the city. He lives alone in a friend's vacant flat in Mayfair, 'abstemious by habit, neither drinking, eating, nor loving much', and conducts a one-sided correspondence with his American wife by which *he* sends her ready-written postcards addressed to himself which she need only sign, stamp and drop in the mail.

Quiggin, J G
A Dance to the Music of Time, 12 volumes, 1951–75
Anthony Powell

Part inspired by the critic Cyril Connolly, whose habit it was to mark his place in books with a bacon rasher, he is a full-time reviewer and Marxist. At undergraduate parties he appears as 'a fierce little animal, trapped by naturalists'. Thickset, balding and older-looking than his contemporaries, he has a grating North Country accent. Sent down without a degree he embarks on a career in the literary world. A book is always in the pipeline, publication of which is perennially imminent, but the years roll by without anything appearing until 1939 when he abandons the idea of authorship. He runs away with Mona Templer and sponges off ERRIDGE, for whom Mona eventually deserts him. He founds the publisher Quiggin & Craggs and the magazine *Fission*, which owes something to *Horizon*. Falling under the conservative influence of Ada Leintwardine, he drops his favoured military attire, fathers twins and publishes the successful memoirs of a Tory statesman.

Quilp, Betsey
The Old Curiosity Shop, 1841
Charles Dickens

The timid, ill-treated wife of DANIEL QUILP, she befriends LITTLE NELL. She is 'a pretty little, mild-spoken, blue-eyed woman, who having allied herself in wedlock to the dwarf, in one of those strange infatuations of which examples are by no means scarce, performed a sound practical penance for her folly, every day of her life'. After Quilp's death, she inherits his property, marries again and lives happily.

Quilp, Daniel
The Old Curiosity Shop, 1841
Charles Dickens

A villainous moneylender, rent-collector and ship-breaker, grotesque in appearance and 'so low in stature as to be quite a dwarf, though his head and face were large enough for the body of a giant'. Using practical jokes, he cruelly torments his wife, BETSEY QUILP, and her mother, MRS JINIWIN, as well as habitually beating his servant boy, Tom Scott. Having taken possession of the Old Curiosity Shop, forcing LITTLE NELL and her GRANDFATHER to flee, he tries to track them down, lusting after Little Nell and believing Grandfather to have a secret hoard of money. With SALLY BRASS and SAMPSON BRASS, he plots to have KIT NUBBLES arrested, but is ultimately betrayed by THE MARCHIONESS. Attempting to escape arrest, he falls into the Thames and drowns.

Quilpe, Peter
The Cocktail Party, 1950
T S Eliot

A young novelist with minimal talent and disposable morals, he has an affair with LAVINIA CHAMBERLAYNE but throws her over in pursuit of CELIA COPLESTONE. He decamps to America and the film industry, where illusion reigns, people are interchangeable and reality can be readily copied.

Quin, Auberon
The Napoleon of Notting Hill, 1904
G K Chesterton

A little, childlike man, Auberon Quin is elected King, a purely honorific title, of a whimsically futuristic London. Renowned for his quirky humour, and generally considered as 'a man who cares for nothing but a joke', he plays his kingly role with the expected frivolity, making every borough as colourfully medieval as possible, and reviving heraldry and long-forgotten pageantry. Notting Hill, however, rebels under the leadership of ADAM WAYNE.

Quin, Dinny
The Roaring Nineties, 1946
Golden Miles, 1948
Winged Seeds, 1950
Katharine Susannah Prichard

Ever ready with a yarn about the old days, Dinny is a pioneering prospector of the West Australian goldfields who bridges the generations of the trilogy. Warm, friendly, honest and an ardent and loyal supporter of workers' solidarity, Dinny is a good mate: 'Dinny Quin, now, he's one of nature's gentlemen. Never known him to do a mean thing … I'd trust Dinny with my life.'

Quince, Michael
Pravda: A Fleet Street Comedy, 1985
Howard Brenton and David Hare

From an old English patrician family and now a Member of Parliament, Quince is in his late thirties, fat, wan and pliable. Anxious for promotion but realizing he has no talent, he allows himself to be manipulated by LAMBERT LE ROUX into helping him acquire the *The Daily Victory*, Britain's most prestigious newspaper.

Quince, Peter
A Midsummer Night's Dream, c.1594
William Shakespeare

A carpenter and producer of amateur dramatics, he acts as a disciplinary force on the other 'mechanicals', giving structure and organization

to their rehearsals and preparation, and never losing their respect or affection. Though their eventual performance – including Quince's dreadful prologue – is risible, he never loses dignity, patiently rising above his fellow actors' innocent stupidity and anxiety.

Quinn, Victor
My Zinc Bed, 2000
David Hare

A millionaire and former Marxist, Quinn hires Paul Peploe, a young poet and reformed alcoholic, as a copywriter for his burgeoning Internet business. A theme running through the play is that the difference between conviction and compulsion is in many ways illusory, and that the former frequently becomes the latter. Quinn therefore emerges as a Mephistopheles undermining the faith of those around him and thereby asserting his power and authority.

Quint, Peter
The Turn of the Screw, 1898
Henry James

A former valet at Bly, who was intimately associated with the former governess, MISS JESSEL. He is now dead, but whether he appears as a demonic revenant or only as a manifestation of the new governess's sexual anxieties is left highly ambiguous. He is described as having had close-curling red hair and whiskers, with a pale face, thin lips and arched eyebrows, an outline that lends itself rather well to diabolic projections.

Quirk, Jason
Castle Rackrent, 1800
Maria Edgeworth

Attorney Quirk is the son of the RACKRENTs' retainer THADY QUIRK (though the old man views his offspring with less than paternal pride), and is one of the 'gripers' who seize control of the bankrupt castle when its debts and mortgages finally come home to roost.

Quirk, Thady
Castle Rackrent, 1800
Maria Edgeworth

An elderly retainer to three generations of RACKRENTs and narrator of their story, which he records from memory, but with the reassurance that 'there's nothing but truth in it from beginning to end … for where's the use of telling lies about the things which everybody knows as well as I do?'

Quiros, Captain
Captain Quiros, 1964
James McAuley

On the first voyage to Santa Cruz, Quiros acted as peacemaker and mediator. Now, with devout and pious intent, he envisages a new crusade, led 'with bloodless sword', and thus captains a voyage to the Great South Land. He is held up as 'the noblest and the last conquistador' and a 'prince of charity and valour', but his piety creates a division between himself and his crew; he lacks empathy, and asks 'too much of Honour and Fortitude'.

Quiverful, Mr

The Warden, 1855
Barchester Towers, 1857
Framley Parsonage, 1861
The Last Chronicle of Barset, 1867
Anthony Trollope

Mr Quiverful's main appearance is in *Barchester Towers*, where he is a poor clergyman who cannot afford to bring up his 14 children decently. He hopes to obtain the well-paid wardenship of Hiram's Hospital; although so desperate for money that he cannot care too much about his reputation, he is nevertheless concerned for REV SEPTIMUS HARDING, the other candidate for the post. In *The Last Chronicle of Barset* he is still worried about expense and bound up in his family's struggles.

Quiverful, Mrs

Barchester Towers, 1857
Framley Parsonage, 1861
The Last Chronicle of Barset, 1867
Anthony Trollope

Letitia, wife of MR QUIVERFUL, wants only to have herself and her 14 living children decently clothed and fed, and therefore she has no sympathy with her husband's scruples regarding his possible appointment to a well-paid post. A heavy woman, she has a good heart and her husband always discusses his problems with her. She remains grateful to their patron, MRS PROUDIE.

Quixote, Monsignor

Monsignor Quixote, 1982
Graham Greene

The village priest of El Toboso who believes himself to be a descendant of Cervantes's famous knight. He is a gentle, modest, good-humoured man who finds himself unexpectedly promoted to Monsignor. Before taking up the post, however, he sets off on an adventure-strewn journey across Spain in an antiquated Seat 600 called Rocinante and with a Communist mayor known as Sancho for a companion; like his famous 'ancestor', he is pronounced mad. His trip ends tragically.

Quoyle, R G

The Shipping News, 1993
Annie Proulx

His 'failure of normal appearance' combined with a savage brother and his father's relentless criticism ensure that Quoyle has no expectations from life. He takes a passive role and 'camouflages torment with smiles and silence'. The death of his worthless wife leaves him with two young children and no direction until his aunt enters his life and persuades him to set up home with her in Newfoundland. This move to his family's birthplace and a job on the local paper find Quoyle slowly becoming comfortable in his own skin and experiencing a sense of belonging for the first time in his life.

Rab
Rab and his Friends, 1859
Dr John Brown

'A sort of compressed Hercules of a dog', indeed 'a huge mastiff', Rab is renowned for his fighting prowess. He is also poignantly faithful to James Noble, a 'severe little man' working as a Howgate carrier in Edinburgh. The dog, because he has to be restrained, helps James through the agony of watching his wife, Aislie, being operated on without anaesthetic. Soon after, however, she dies, followed shortly by her heartbroken husband. Rab's aggressively inconsolable reaction falls foul of the new carrier, who makes this confession: 'Dead! What did he die of? Weel sir, ... he didna exactly dee; he was killed. I had to brain him wi' a rackin-pin; there was nae doin' wi' him.'

Rabbit, properly **Angstrom, Harry**
Rabbit, Run, 1960
Rabbit Redux, 1971
Rabbit is Rich, 1981
Rabbit at Rest, 1990
John Updike

The hint of 'angst' in his surname is not accidental. Updike's toothy anti-hero is a barometer of lower-middle-class American life between the late 1950s and 1980s. Starting out as a gadget salesman, married to his high-school sweetheart (JANICE ANGSTROM), he is economically and spiritually marginal, fondly looking back to his years as a school basketball hero. He experiences a sexual awakening (minus his wife) during the liberated 1960s; eases into an uncomfortable but accepting middle age; and enjoys the fruits of the USA's economic boom in the 1980s as a dealer of Japanese cars – albeit at the price of a dysfunctional family and a set of clogged arteries.

Rabbitte family, the
The Commitments, 1987
The Snapper, 1990
The Van, 1991, forming *The Barrytown Trilogy*
Roddy Doyle

The Rabbittes are a close-knit, working-class Dublin family. This warm, loving, but often obstreperous household consists of Jimmy Rabbitte, his wife Veronica, and their children, Les, Sharon, Jimmy Junior, Darren, and twins Tracy and Linda. In the trilogy, *The Commitments* focuses on Jimmy Junior and his efforts to establish a soul band; *The Snapper* centres around the pregnancy of unmarried Sharon; *The Van* describes the exploits of Jimmy (Senior) escaping the boredom and poverty of unemployment by going into partnership with his friend who has bought a clapped-out fish-and-chip van.

Rabinowitz, Lynne
Meridian, 1976
Alice Walker

Epitomizing her own comment 'I live for the moment, no looking back for me', Lynne cuts herself off completely from her parents and her own cultural heritage. Immersing herself in the Civil Rights Movement, she is rapidly made aware of the fact that 'by being white, [she] was guilty of whiteness' and by living with TRUMAN HELD she is divorced from any sense of belonging. Believing that the sacrifices she makes in order to enter the black community are enough, she rapidly descends into stereotype, becoming 'clear, dead water'.

Rachael
Hard Times, 1854
Charles Dickens

A Coketown factory worker and the devoted friend of STEPHEN BLACKPOOL, whom she would marry if he could afford to divorce his alcoholic wife. She defends Blackpool when he is wrongly accused of theft and joins in the search for him when he disappears. She and SISSY JUPE discover him after he falls into an abandoned mine shaft, and she comforts him as he dies.

Rachael, Mrs
Bleak House, 1853
Charles Dickens

The forbidding and austere servant to MISS BARBARY and nurse to ESTHER SUMMERSON, she shares Miss Barbary's grim Calvinism and helps to make Esther's childhood miserable. She becomes the wife of THE REV MR CHADBAND.

Rackrent, Sir Condy, properly **Sir Connolly**
Castle Rackrent, 1800
Maria Edgeworth

'By the grace of God heir-at-law to the Castle Rackrent estate', he comes of 'a remote branch of the family ... Born to little or no fortune of his own, he was bred to the bar, at which ... he doubtless would in process of time, if he could have borne the drudgery of that study, have been rapidly made King's Counsel'. He takes the easier route of marriage to ISABELLA MONEYGAWL (a choice dictated by spinning a coin) and a slow, luxurious decline into bankruptcy. For his amusement, he plays dead at his own wake.

Rackrent, Sir Kit
Castle Rackrent, 1800
Maria Edgeworth

The younger brother of SIR MURTAGH RACKRENT and inheritor of Castle Rackrent. He has 'lived away to the honour of his country abroad', little heeding the hardships at home, even when he returns with a (reputedly) wealthy wife. She is 'a *Jewess*', profoundly averse to sausages and Mass.

Rackrent, Sir Murtagh
Castle Rackrent, 1800
Maria Edgeworth

Heir and polar opposite to SIR PATRICK RACKRENT, the wellspring of the dynasty. He is 'a great lawyer', and uses professional skill to weasel out of paying his father's many debts. A stalwart guardian of his own purse, he marries into the Skinflint family, his bride a widow of advanced years whose resilience and equal dedication to thrift surprise and discomfit the old miser. She commits the ultimate sin of surviving him.

Rackrent, Sir Patrick, originally Patrick O'Shaughlin
Castle Rackrent, 1800
Maria Edgeworth

The founding father of this Irish dynasty and a notable host. Said to be the inventor of raspberry whiskey, he is carried off by an apoplexy just as his guests are about to toast him; they mourn him twice as much when they learn that SIR MURTAGH RACKRENT is his heir.

Radcliffe, Maggie
The Takeover, 1976
Muriel Spark

A self-centred American millionairess with an appearance 'absolutely imperious in its demands for attention'. Superstitious and with a tendency to hysteria, she turns against her associate Hubert Mallindaine following her marriage to the Marchese di Tullio-Friole. Her international lifestyle is threatened by financial difficulties, paralleling the world economic situation after the 1973 oil crisis.

Radigund
The Faerie Queene, 1590–6
Sir Edmund Spenser

The ruling queen of a female warrior tribe, she is an allegory for reason overcome by passion. Described as half man, and possessed of a raging heart, she is subversive and unnatural, and refuses to obey male law. She is lusty and sexually active, hotly pursuing the object of her desires. She appears irrational and unfit for leadership.

Radletts, the
The Pursuit of Love, 1945
Nancy Mitford

The Radletts are brought up at Alconleigh by an irascible eccentric father and an acquiescent mother, all 'Hons' since father is a peer of the realm. Used to dramatic rages, they accept them as normal. The sons go to Eton, the girls learn reading, writing, French and the piano since father thinks these all they require. They read,

form wild ideas, speculate about the facts of life and grown-ups, and indulge in elaborate 'teases', roaring with laughter. Consistency is irrelevant; they hunt, yet battle against cruelty to animals. Each strongly individualistic and undisciplined, they develop, inevitably, in differing – and at time disastrous – directions.

Radley, Boo (Arthur)
To Kill A Mockingbird, 1960
Harper Lee

Part of a group of troublemaking youths as a boy, he was released by the court into his parents' care. He has been a reclusive prisoner in their house ever since, and although harmless and even benevolent, he is the subject of much fearful speculation among the local children. He likes to watch their games, and surreptitiously leaves them presents. He is a 'big child' himself, but ultimately saves both SCOUT and JEM FINCH from murder, forcing them to revise their preconceptions.

Rafe
The Knight of the Burning Pestle, 1607
Francis Beaumont

An apprentice, Rafe is pushed on to the stage from the audience by his employer, a grocer and his wife, during a comedy of manners concerning JASPER's wooing of LUCE. Rafe carries on his shield the emblem of the burning pestle (used by shopkeepers) and therefore his function on stage, urged on by the overflowing pride and patriotism of the grocer and his wife, is to play the hero, and thereby spin the comedy into a grand and pantomimic satire of knight-errantry. Rafe is an innocent abroad who fights several battles and survives many adventures to endear himself to one and all.

Raffles
The Amateur Cracksman, 1899
The Black Mask, 1901
The Thief in the Night, 1905
E W Hornung

Raffles is a suave, elegant figure in top hat and tails, smiling mockingly as he sets out in the night to steal jewels, tiaras or cash from wealthy aristocrats or the vulgar rich. He adorns society with his urbane wit and perfect manners, savouring his double life with consummate amusement. He is an athlete, which helps him in burglaries and frustrates Inspector Mackenzie, but in the end expiates his life of crime by volunteering in the Boer War, in which he is killed.

Raffles, John
Middlemarch, 1871–2
George Eliot

The agent who brings about the public downfall of MR BULSTRODE. An unsavoury, unkempt character, motivated as much by the desire to torment people as to extort money from them, Raffles has a powerful hold over Bulstrode and uses it to blackmail him. Descending, however, into alcoholism, he dies while in Mr Bulstrode's care, a fact which only adds fuel to the suspicion surrounding Bulstrode's reputation.

Rafi, Mrs
The Sea, 1973
Edward Bond

The centre of power in a small seaside town, Mrs Rafi is a domineering, imperious woman with a taste for being seen to do things correctly. Money means little to her, because she has always been wealthy, and she rides roughshod over everyone's feelings because she believes they expect it of her. Her principal occupation is devising social events, while her principal enemy is HATCH, the local draper. But whereas he goes mad, Mrs Rafi, in a slow dawn of something like compassion, realizes that one day she will be elderly, possibly senile and treated by others as if she were mad.

Ragged Dick
Ragged Dick, or Street Life in New York, 1867
Horatio Alger, Jr

A ragged street waif who makes a precarious living as a bootblack. He is given to playing tricks, gambling, drinking, smoking and extravagance, but is inherently honest, virtuous in his own way, and generous to those as deprived as himself whenever he has a little money. He is wise to all the dodges, swindles and con-tricks of the day. His rise, though, is due to luck rather than virtue, and his story as the prosperous young man Richard Hunter is told in *Fame and Fortune* (1868).

Railway Children, the → Roberta, Peter and Phyllis

Rainborough, John
The Flight from the Enchanter, 1956
Iris Murdoch

An old friend of ROSA KEEPE, PETER SAWARD and MISCHA FOX, Rainborough is an executive with SELIB, the European refugee labour organization through which NINA, STEFAN LUSIEWICZ and JAN LUSIEWICZ have entered Britain. Languid, nostalgic and given to melancholy, he lives alone in his childhood home, never able to harness his energies to any single task, and respects and envies the scholarly, industrious Saward. He is defeatist about his work and life, believing that mediocrity is the inevitable outcome of all human effort, and makes a wryly humorous attempt to seduce ANNETTE COCKEYNE, although he regards her as 'appallingly juvenile'.

Rainey, Virgie
The Golden Apples, 1949
Eudora Welty

A character in several stories in *The Golden Apples*, she is a gifted but rebellious girl, living in the small town of Morgana, on the Mississippi Delta. Sexually aware (in contradiction of her forename), she turns her back on her loyal but lonely piano teacher MISS ECKHART, who has tried to foster her talent, and is almost destroyed in her tutor's sacrificial fire. Following her mother's death and her ritual immersion in the Big Black River, she comes to recognize the significance of the mythological print of Medusa and Perseus on Miss Eckhart's wall.

Rais, Gilles de
Saint Joan, 1923
George Bernard Shaw

De Rais is a dandyish, self-possessed young man who, at a fashionably clean-shaven court, wears a short curled beard dyed blue. This earns him the obvious nickname of Bluebeard. A patron of the arts, he specializes in devising pageants. At Chinon with THE DAUPHIN when JOAN arrives to persuade him to fight the English, de Rais attends the coronation at Rheims. His own self-interest causes him to be suspicious of Joan; he concludes her actions to be guided principally by obstinacy and pride.

Raju
The Guide, 1958
R K Narayan

A voluble, opportunist tourist guide in the fictional southern Indian town of Malgudi, who is imprisoned for corruption. Upon his release, he takes refuge in an abandoned temple and discovers that others, one by one, imagine his reticence to be the philosophical musing of a holy man. As Raju has always had 'a kind of water-diviner's instinct' and prison has further trained him to take advantage of any chance that fate throws in his path, he quickly emulates the part of a spiritual guide, growing a beard and long hair, assuming an air of dignified authority.

Raka
Fire on the Mountain, 1977
Anita Desai

NANDA KAUL's great-grandchild, she is 'a thin, fragile, secretive girl whose intrusion Nanda Kaul deeply resents'. Her name means 'the moon', but she is not 'round-faced, calm or radiant' and defies all Nanda Kaul's expectations. Raka's rejection of Nanda Kaul is 'natural, instinctive and effortless'. She is a natural recluse, closer to nature and the elements than she is to people.

Raleigh, Jimmy
Journey's End, 1928
R C Sherriff

Three years younger than DENNIS STANHOPE, Raleigh attended the same public school, where he hero-worshipped the older boy. Family connections have now secured him a posting to serve under Stanhope at the Western Front in the spring of 1918. Naive, optimistic and eager to impress, Raleigh represents the public-school values of honourable service and team spirit which he and Stanhope once shared.

Ralph
Lord of the Flies, 1954
William Golding

The natural leader of a group of boys stranded on a desert island. A responsible boy, he has a sense of the priorities of survival in an alien environment, and of the need to plan for rescue. He is a sensible, tolerant, well-behaved character whose democratic instincts lead him to establish assemblies where all can voice their opinions. Ralph displays great moral courage in the face of the more irrational, wilder behaviour of the other boys. Finally, he alone retains a sense of the civilized world they have lost.

Rama (Ramaswamy)
The Serpent and the Rope, 1960
Raja Rao

Rama's mother died when he was young and his father remarried. A Brahmin ('that is, devoted to Truth and all that'), he thinks of himself as an orphan. Highly-educated, anxious and drawn by an introspective nature to gloom, he has travelled throughout India and Europe, meeting and marrying MADELEINE on the way. Burdened by the weight of his cultural and spiritual inheritance, Rama embarks upon a philosophical and religious quest, attempting to discover whether and how history, and in particular Hindu myth, might still provide the mystical framework for modern life.

Raman
The Painter of Signs, 1976
R K Narayan

Malgudi's 'artist in lettering', an attractive, thoughtful confirmed bachelor proud of his logic and rationality, who enjoys a contented, orderly existence with the devoted aunt who has cared for him since childhood. Providing a sign-board for a new Family Planning centre, he meets DAISY and is afflicted by the 'true love sickness' he has previously derided. The self-sufficient, liberated Daisy is a complete enigma to him, but desperate for her love he accedes to all her imperious conditions, yet even then loses out to her fanatical sense of mission.

Ramble, Jack → Shillingsworth, Mark

Rambotham, Laura Tweedle
The Getting of Wisdom, 1910
Henry Handel Richardson

An impetuous Australian girl, sent by her genteelly impoverished widowed mother to a boarding school in Melbourne. Her 'natural buoyancy of spirit', tactlessness and naive desire to be liked lead to continual ups and downs in her scholastic career. She realizes that she should try to be like the other girls, but is always going to what are seen as unladylike extremes, being too perceptive and imaginative to be limited by convention.

Ramorny, Sir John
The Fair Maid of Perth, or St Valentine's Day, in
Chronicles of the Canongate: Second Series, 1828
Sir Walter Scott

A noble but violently reckless associate of the young Prince David (ROTHSAY, DUKE OF ROTHSAY). His hand is severed in the fight at Perth and, once its ring has been identified, he is banished from the royal service. He nonetheless retains the loyalty of the heir-apparent, to whom he confides his treachery with the DUKE OF ALBANY. Tortured by pain and opiate nightmares, he is a savage, tragic figure whose last vestiges of pride are stripped away before his ignominious hanging.

Ramos, Connie
Woman on the Edge of Time, 1979
Marge Piercy

A Mexican-American victim of urban domestic violence in bleakest 1970s Chicago, who transcends the horrors of incarceration in mental institutions. Her ability to send her mind forward to a comparatively ideal ruralized community in post-Armageddon Massachusetts opens up inspiring possibilities for individuals, in which parenthood is the responsibility of everybody. With help from her future friends, she sabotages the surgical treatment proposed for her, and her schizophrenia continues its successful self-preservation.

Ramotswe, Precious
The No.1 Ladies' Detective Agency, 1998, et seq
Alexander McCall Smith

An intelligent and engaging heroine, Mma Ramotswe is the founder of the No.1 Ladies' Detective agency, and the only lady private detective in Botswana. Having survived an abusive marriage and lost her only child, she sells the cattle she inherits from her father to set up her own business in the Botswanan capital Gaborone. 'Traditionally built', fond of bush tea and full of wisdom, Mma Ramotswe is a problem solver as much as a detective, gently dealing with the cases brought to her through a blend of common sense, instinct and observation.

Rampion, Mark
Point Counter Point, 1928
Aldous Huxley

Mark Rampion stands out because he is the only well-balanced character in the novel. He alone makes a case for a healthy balance between sexual passion and reason: 'A man's a creature on a tight-rope, walking delicately, equilibrated, with mind and consciousness and spirit at one end of his balancing pole and instinct and all that's unconscious and earthy and mysterious at the other.'

Ramsaran, Egbert, originally **Ashok**
The Chip-Chip Gatherers, 1973
Shiva Naipaul

The founder of the Ramsaran Transport Company, and husband of RANI RAMSARAN, he is a self-made man who has ruthlessly turned his back on the shacks of the Settlement to establish a personal autarchy marked by sadistic insensitivity to those around him. Hypochondriac, but an obsessive body builder, he is paranoically afraid of doctors and other professionals. Wiry and strong, with a high-pitched, whining voice, he tends a short moustache with fanatical care. He has no friends, only clients.

Ramsaran, Rani
The Chip-Chip Gatherers, 1973
Shiva Naipaul

EGBERT RAMSARAN's wife, she is an awkward, plain woman, swiftly abandoned after the birth of their son. She conveys the impression of being 'a bloodless, boneless creature on whom the sun had never shone'. She fills in her days indiscriminately collecting worthless stamps, and dies quietly and without fuss to make way for a new mistress.

Ramsaran, Wilbert
The Chip-Chip Gatherers, 1973
Shiva Naipaul
EGBERT RAMSARAN's son, he stands inevitably in his father's heavy shadow, fearful and withdrawn. The object of his father's obscure dynastic fantasies, he is virtually incapable of making relationships on his own terms, a situation that only changes after his mother's death and the arrival of the beautiful SUSHILA.

Ramsay, David
The Fortunes of Nigel, 1822
Sir Walter Scott
An 'ingenious, but whimsical and self-opinionated mechanic', Ramsay is a London clockmaker whose practical nature is sometimes overshadowed by his devotion to more abstract studies. He is representative of the novel's underlying struggle between learning and common sense, honour and fair dealing.

Ramsay, Dunstan
Fifth Business, 1970
The Manticore, 1973
World of Wonders, 1975, published as *The Deptford Trilogy*, 1983
Robertson Davies
Ramsay is a Canadian history teacher and academic of dour Scots descent: a man of 'Highland temper and granite determination'. Estranged from his mother, and both inspired and guilt-ridden by the crazed saintliness of Mary Dempster (MAGNUS EISENGRIM's mother), he recovers from World War I to study hagiography and the mysterious light and shade of the human soul. Unflinchingly acute and observant, his retrospective, partial account examines the sometimes terrifying mystery of life and spiritual self-discovery. Unlike his lifelong 'friends' Magnus Eisengrim and PERCY BOYD STAUNTON, whilst secretly longing for a place in posterity Ramsay remains an enabler rather than a doer.

Ramsay, Margaret
The Fortunes of Nigel, 1822
Sir Walter Scott
DAVID RAMSAY's daughter – and NIGEL OLIFAUNT's future wife – she is about 20 years old, 'very pretty, very demure, yet with lively black eyes, that ever and anon, contradicted the expression of sobriety, to which silence, reserve, a plain velvet hood, and a cambric ruff, had condemned [her].'

Ramsay, Mr
To the Lighthouse, 1927
Virginia Woolf
Mr Ramsay is a cold and distant father, a demanding idealist who is remote and careless in his everyday dealings with his family, yet he cares deeply about many things. An exacting man, whom MRS RAMSAY humours unashamedly, he is however not entirely devoid of endearing qualities and shows both sincerity and an acute sense of responsibility.

Ramsay, Mrs
To the Lighthouse, 1927
Virginia Woolf
Immensely sociable, and given to lavish exaggeration, Mrs Ramsay likes to have an intimate knowledge of everyone around her. She is content only if she is the centre of her world, and, with her own eight children and various hangers-on, strives to create one big happy family. She is dominant and egotistical but extremely kind and caring, a strong woman well able to deal with the somewhat difficult MR RAMSAY.

Ramsden, Roebuck
Man and Superman, 1903
George Bernard Shaw
A joint guardian of ANN WHITEFIELD, Ramsden is 'more than a highly respectable man: he is marked out as a President of highly respectable men'. He is one of life's corporate leaders. A Unitarian and Free Trader since boyhood and an Evolutionist since the publication of Darwin's *The Origin of Species*, he consequently views himself as an extremely advanced thinker and vigorous social reformer. Yet he is ignorant of the arts and thoroughly disapproves of JOHN TANNER. In Tanner's Don Juan dream, Ramsden the philistine becomes solidified into the Statue and represents conventional morality.

Ramsumair, Ganesh
The Mystic Masseur, 1957
V S Naipaul
According to the narrator of the novel, the history of Ganesh Ramsumair, 'masseur, mystic, and, since 1953, M.B.E.', is, 'in a way, the history of our times'. Posing as an expert on Hinduism, and a spiritual healer and doctor of sorts, Ganesh is of humble background but adept at taking advantage of the complex racial politics of his Caribbean island country. On reaching the pinnacle of success he coldly rounds on an admirer and informs him that his name is actually 'G. Ramsay Muir'.

Randall, Captain
The Beach of Falesá, 1892
Robert Louis Stevenson
One of the colonials who has stayed too long in the islands for his own well-being. He has grown fat and dissolute through indulgence in the easy lifestyle of the South Seas. Once the orderly, respected commander of a ship, he is now a wreck of a man, attended only by mosquitoes which hum around him, and by human parasites who suck his business interests dry, while he sits Buddha-like in a drunken stupor. He symbolizes the fate of so many westerners who have treated the colonies as a dustbin for their failure: a place of refuge from their own selves.

Randall, Rebecca
Rebecca of Sunnybrook Farm, 1903
Kate Douglas Wiggin
She is a slender, dark-haired girl with an 'air of being small for her age', who grows from childhood to late teens in the course of the book. She has remarkable eyes which glow 'like two stars', a sharp sense of humour, and is lively, eager, curious, quick-witted, intelligent, often wilful, and never satisfied. She is 'a thing of fire and spirit' who 'was plucky at two and dauntless at five', and turns into a dutiful, hardworking and cheerful young lady.

Random, Michael
Tourmaline, 1963
Randolph Stow

Dumped half-dead in the dry and desolate town of Tourmaline, he is taken to be a water-diviner who will rescue the town from drought. He takes on the role, however arbitrary it may seem, but is soon supplanted by another false prophet.

Random, Roderick
The Adventures of Roderick Random, 1748
Tobias Smollett

During her confinement, Roderick's mother dreams that she is delivered of a tennis ball. The devil-midwife whacks it away into space, but on its return it roots itself and produces a fragrant tree. How accurate this is as a prefiguring of Roderick's life is difficult to say, but it captures both his frequent submission to travel and the casual violence that seems to surround him. Raised by his grandfather and 'seasoned in adversity', he trains as a surgeon's mate in the Royal Navy. An unprincipled rogue, he reflects much of his creator's choleric nature but also something of his innate goodness and generosity. He is loosely based on Le Sage's eponymous *Gil Blas*.

Rankin, Leslie
Captain Brassbound's Conversion, 1899
George Bernard Shaw

A missionary at Mogodor in Morocco, he is 'an elderly Scotchman, spiritually a little weatherbeaten … with a faithful brown eye, and a peaceful soul'. Although he has never converted a Moor, Rankin nevertheless remains 'a convinced son of the Free Church and the North African Mission'.

Ransom, Basil
The Bostonians, 1886
Henry James

A young Mississippi lawyer, who comes to Boston to make his fortune and, through the rather passive offices of Verena Tarrant, who attracts him, finds himself enmeshed in the nascent suffragist movement that is supported by his cousin OLIVE CHANCELLOR. Blithe and slightly bland, his go-getting enterprise masks a comfortable acceptance of the sexual status quo.

Ransom, Elwin
Out of the Silent Planet, 1938
Perelandra, 1943
That Hideous Strength, 1945
C S Lewis

A linguist, he is an ordinary, decent, scholarly man thrown into great interplanetary affairs. An emblematic, almost allegorical figure rather than a rounded character, he stands for Christian moral values in a universe where the (often much distorted) evils of scientific humanism and greedy capitalism threaten the existence of the race.

Ransom, Michael Forsyth
The Ascent of F6, 1936–7
W H Auden and Christopher Isherwood

The archetypal flawed man of action of the 1930s, he is said to have been modelled on T E Lawrence ('Lawrence of Arabia'). Persuaded by his mother to lead a mountaineering expedition to F6, a peak in the disputed territory between British and Ostnian Sudoland (an area overseen by his twin brother Sir James at the Colonial Office), he loses his life and that of his fellow climbers in the Promethean ascent. His life is a parable of the artist who succumbs to the blandishments of the state and of popular success.

Ransome, Tom
The Rains Came, 1937
Louis Bromfield

The son of an English earl, Ransome, an artist, came to Ranchipur to paint the MAHARANI OF RANCHIPUR's portrait and has stayed on, increasingly disillusioned with his old life and the West generally. He has a reputation as a hard-drinking, womanizing 'bounder', but although his love, LADY EDWINA ESKETH, arrives eager to revive their youthful affair, he is drawn to the unsophisticated young daughter of the couple who run the American mission. After the earthquake, the Maharani demonstrates her faith in Ransome's essentially good qualities by appointing him her personal aide in dealing with the crisis.

Raphael
Paradise Lost, 1667
John Milton

A glorious six-winged angel sent down by GOD from heaven to admonish ADAM and EVE about their moral responsibilities, in the course of which he describes to them the war in heaven and Lucifer's fall.

Rappaccini, Beatrice
'Rappaccini's Daughter', 1844, in *Mosses from an Old Manse*, 1846
Nathaniel Hawthorne

The beautiful but fated daughter of the scientist DR GIACOMO RAPPACCINI, who turns her into a living poison by constant homoeopathic exposure to a living plant. At first sight, her admirer GIOVANNI GUASCONTI feels as if 'here were another flower, the human sister of those vegetable ones, as beautiful as they, more beautiful than the richest of them, but still to be touched only with a glove, nor to be approached without a mask'.

Rappaccini, Dr Giacomo
'Rappaccini's Daughter', 1844, in *Mosses from an Old Manse*, 1846
Nathaniel Hawthorne

The archetypal soulless scientist, who 'cares infinitely more for science than for mankind', and who 'would sacrifice human life, his among the rest, or whatever else was dearest to him, for the sake of adding so much as a grain of mustard to the great heap of his accumulated knowledge'. Nothing is dearer to him or more cynically manipulated than his daughter BEATRICE RAPPACCINI.

Rashid
Haroun and the Sea of Stories, 1990
Salman Rushdie

A storyteller 'whose cheerfulness was famous

throughout the sad city'. Known to his admirers as the 'Ocean of Notions' and to his detractors as the 'Shah of Blah', he suddenly dries up when trying to tell a story for one of the lying politicos who employ him. His wife also leaves him, and he smashes all the clocks. Thanks to his son HAROUN, however, he finds a chance in the fantastical Gup City to regain his abilities and perhaps his wife too.

Rasselas
The History of Rasselas, Prince of Abissinia, 1759
Samuel Johnson

Dissatisfied with the eventless drowsiness of life in Happy Valley, heedless of Imlac the philosopher and anxious to see the world, he breaks through the mountain to the outside world and, with Imlac, the princess and her maid, reaches the civilization of Egypt. Questioning all and sundry to find the secret of true happiness, they find that disillusion always follows its appearance; even the bright sea becomes boring. Sadly they go home, each planning a personal happiness which they know will be impossible, 'a conclusion in which nothing is concluded'.

Rassendyll, Rudolf
The Prisoner of Zenda, 1894
Anthony Hope

Rudolf Rassendyll, having Elphberg blood, resembles the King of Ruritania. When the king is drugged and imprisoned, Rassendyll is crowned in his stead to foil Black Michael. He must continue the deception, loving and being loved by Princess Flavia, until the king can be rescued from Zenda by Rassendyll, Colonel Sapt and friends. All enemies are killed, except RUPERT OF HENTZAU. Honour demands that Rassendyll leave Flavia to fulfil her destiny as Queen; his strength in doing this makes Sapt call him 'the finest Elphberg of them all'.

Rat
The Wind in the Willows, 1908
Kenneth Grahame

A water rat with a 'grave round face ... and thick silky hair', whose eyes twinkle with life, and who firmly believes that 'there is *nothing* – absolutely nothing – half so much worth doing as simply messing about in boats'. A friendly, warm-hearted creature fond of the comforts of life and known to scribble poetry in his spare time, he initiates the rather shy MOLE into the joys of the river, and with him finds himself embroiled in a series of adventures that take them from the security of the riverbank to the depths of the Wild Wood and the Wide World beyond.

Ratchkali
The Adventures of Ferdinand, Count Fathom, 1753
Tobias Smollett

A rascally Tyrolese with whom FERDINAND, COUNT FATHOM conspires to cheat his young master and friend at dice. Among his other skills, he is an 'exquisite lapidary', adept in the art of setting jewels.

Ratcliffe, James, also known as 'Daddy Rat'
The Heart of Midlothian, in *Tales of My Landlord: Second Series*, 1818
Sir Walter Scott

The 'father of a' the misdoers in Scotland' who, like EFFIE DEANS, refuses the opportunity of escape from the Tollbooth and seems inclined to go straight and give the authorities what assistance they need in the pursuit of 'Robertson' (SIR GEORGE STAUNTON).

Ratcliffe, Senator Silas P
Democracy: An American Novel, 1880
Henry Adams

A coarse, vain, highly manipulative but powerful and poised political broker who is able to manoeuvre the president elect to his own ends as a consequence of his extensive political machinations, and knowledge of the workings of Washington. He is corrupt in the use of his influence, allowing himself to be bought. He falls in love with MADELEINE LEE, but is rejected as a consequence of that dishonesty, and departs, wrathfully nursing his wounded pride.

Ratliff, V K
The Mansion, 1959
William Faulkner

An itinerant sewing-machine salesman, he may be seen to represent the same mechanized world as the SNOPESes and offers probably the most sympathetic viewpoint on their self-serving progress. He is perhaps the closest thing to an omniscient narrator in the trilogy.

Ravelstein, Abe
Ravelstein, 2000
Saul Bellow

An idiosyncratic professor of philosophy, Ravelstein, 'with his bald, powerful head was at ease with large statements, big issues and famous men, with decades, eras, centuries'. A controversial and newly-wealthy polemicist of conservative values, Ravelstein is now dying of AIDS and busy spending his money in Paris. The character is modelled upon the Chicago professor, Allan Bloom.

Ravelston, Wizzie
Maiden Castle, 1936
John Cowper Powys

A girl who has been brought up in a convent, and later in a circus, where DUD NO-MAN finds and buys her. She is initially pathetic, with her pinched, sharp, desperate face which is 'not in the remotest degree pretty', and her boyish frame, but the 'sensual attraction of her figure' has 'a deep and magical mystery'. She grows to possess a passionate, vital strength, and ultimately rejects the sterile Dud for a more masculine lover.

Raven, James
A Gun for Sale, 1936
Graham Greene

A lonely, physically ugly, emotionally tormented outsider. Alienated from society and his family after a brutal upbringing, he lives an isolated existence. He carries out a political assassination, but is betrayed by his employers, and becomes obsessed with revenge, which is achieved only at the cost of his life.

Raven, the
The Raven, 1845
Edgar Allan Poe

The speaker in the poem, he is a 'weak and weary' student who is sorrowing for the loss of his 'rare and radiant maiden', Lenore. His soul is burning within him as he sits in his lonely room, until he is visited by a raven, a 'grim, ungainly, ghastly, gaunt, and ominous bird of yore'. At first, the bird beguiles his 'sad soul into smiling', but its repeated 'Nevermore!' to all his questions leads him to the increasing certainty that Lenore is lost forever, and dashes his hope of remission from despair.

Ravenal, Gaylord
Show Boat, 1926
Edna Ferber

The archetypal matinee idol, he sweeps Magnolia Hawks (daughter of CAPTAIN ANDY HAWKS and PARTHY ANN HAWKS) off her feet. After their daughter is born, he sweeps Magnolia off to Chicago, but there the archetype is further confirmed when he proves to be faithless and abandons her.

Ravenal, Kim
Show Boat, 1926
Edna Ferber

The daughter of Magnolia Hawks and GAYLORD RAVENAL, and grand-daughter of CAPTAIN ANDY HAWKS, she is the third generation to go into show business. Born on the showboat, she aspires to higher things and after many travails makes it on the Broadway stage.

Ravenel, Lillie
Miss Ravenel's Conversion from Secession to Loyalty, 1867
J W De Forest

Brought up in New Boston (the original is apparently New Haven, Connecticut), this young New Englander is nonetheless drawn to the romance and dash of the antebellum South and thus to the more passionate suit of LT COL JOHN CARTER, who seems a more appealing beau than the reliable EDWARD COLBOURNE. Marriage to Carter is a tissue of deception and betrayal and Lillie gradually learns the error of her misplaced loyalty and the moral worth of the Unionist cause.

Ravenswood, Edgar, Master of Ravenswood
The Bride of Lammermoor, in *Tales of My Landlord: Third Series*, 1819
Sir Walter Scott

The son and heir of the deposed and indigent Lord Ravenswood, who has had to cede his ancestral home to the parvenu SIR WILLIAM ASHTON. Edgar is in love with LUCY ASHTON, but their marriage has been forbidden and circumvented, with tragic consequences. John Buchan called young Ravenswood 'a fully realized type of the aristocrat on whom the ends of the earth have fallen'.

Rawley, Walter
Mr Vertigo, 1994
Paul Auster

Transformed from 'a piece of human nothingness' into Walt the Wonder Boy by MASTER YEHUDI, nine-year-old Walter survives a harsh training with his 'vivid way with words' and pragmatic guts to become a famous performer, devoted to his taskmaster. A natural showman, he is happiest when pushing his talent as far as possible, and loses self-respect and hope when he can no longer perform. However, he remains at heart 'a street boy ... with jazz in his blood ... his eye on the main chance ... a quick tongue and a hundred angles', and after many setbacks, some self-inflicted, he eventually concludes that his gift is universal; to achieve it 'you must let yourself evaporate ... feel your soul pouring out of you', and in this he finds his redemption.

Rawlins, Lacey
All the Pretty Horses, 1992
Cormac McCarthy

A young cowboy, he is a friend of JOHN GRADY COLE, whom he accompanies, game for adventure, into Mexico. More grounded in reality and less inclined to introspection, he acts as a counterbalance to his friend's romanticism, and while steadfastly loyal, his lack of Cole's obsessive drive and mental toughness leads him to doubt the wisdom of the other youth's perseverance in the face of cruel misfortune.

Ray, Martha
'The Thorn', in *Lyrical Ballads*, 1798
William Wordsworth

A deranged woman, she nurses a doleful secret. Mystery surrounds the baby she was carrying when she was deserted by her lover, but for 20 years she has kept a mournful vigil, which no-one dares to disturb, beside a remote moss-covered mound of earth.

Razumov
Under Western Eyes, 1911
Joseph Conrad

A vulnerable student who is 'as lonely in the world as a man swimming in the deep sea'. His isolation and sense of intellectual superiority are shattered by the arrival of VICTOR HALDIN in his rooms, and his subsequent betrayal of the revolutionary pitches him into a nightmare of conflicting torments, in which he feels Haldin has 'stolen the truth of my life from me, who had nothing else in the world'. His mounting anguish and confusion over the betrayal is exacerbated when he falls in love with NATALIA HALDIN, and he finds relief in final confession, but also a retribution which leaves him deaf and crippled.

Ready, Masterman
Masterman Ready, 1842
Captain Frederick Marryat

A 'weather-beaten old seaman' who has been a sailor for over 50 years, but is still 'a hale and active man', and a brave and honest one. He is a skilful mariner, and lives up to his name, being 'seldom at a loss' when any problem arises. He is shipwrecked on a Pacific island with the surviving company of the vessel, and dies after being wounded by a savage.

Ready-to-Halt, Mr
The Pilgrim's Progress, Part I 1678 Part II 1684
John Bunyan

A crippled pilgrim, eager to share the journey with CHRISTIANA and the band of pilgrims, who drags his disabled body the whole length of the pilgrim way, with faith and inspirational courage. At the end he receives the healing and new life he has hoped for all his days. His example serves as a beacon of hope to all the faithful who bear the cross of illness.

Reardon, Amy
Grub Street, 1891
George Gissing

Gissing's women are inclined to be either supportive muses or economic and psychological leeches. Amy combines the two qualities. Though she is basically loyal to her husband EDWIN REARDON's idealized artistic vision, she is at heart materialistic and over-respectful of public opinion, and ultimately rejects his purism with some contempt.

Reardon, Edwin
New Grub Street, 1891
George Gissing

AMY REARDON's husband. As a writer, he is torn between the inward dictates of art and the outward requirements of success and social responsibility. Frustrated and essentially weak-willed, he succumbs to the conflict in his nature, never giving shape to the vision of greatness that possesses him.

Reba, Miss
Sanctuary, 1931
William Faulkner

Madam of the Memphis brothel where TEMPLE DRAKE is deposited by the evil but plausible POPEYE. She is something of a stock character, with an off-the-peg heart of gold which comes into play as she slowly recognizes Popeye's degeneracy.

Rebecca
Ivanhoe, 1819
Sir Walter Scott

The daughter of the old Jew ISAAC OF YORK, she is an exotic beauty, likened by her admirers to the Rose of Sharon and the Lily of the Valley. Her description implies, without ever clearly stating, a certain sexual self-awareness (as in the unbuttoned neck of her tunic). Though less vulnerable to anti-Semitic superstition than her father, she is suspected of witchcraft. She shows considerable courage in rescuing IVANHOE from peril and then in suppressing her love for him. (Thackeray satirized her in a skit called *Rebecca and Rowena*, 1850.)

Rebecca → de Winter, Rebecca

Rebus, John
Knots and Crosses, 1987 et seq
Ian Rankin

Detective Inspector Rebus is a natural outsider, having been brought up in a Fife mining town but now working in smart-but-sordid Edinburgh. Run-ins with his superiors, whom he sees as dishonest or self-serving, and a series of unsuccessful relationships with women, only encourage this perception. In later novels, his colleague Siobhan Clarke is one of the few people whom he trusts. As he ages (in real time over the course of the series of novels), his rebelliousness mellows but his inner anger still smoulders. A big drinker (a regular at the Oxford Bar) and smoker, he also has a fondness for classic rock, especially The Rolling Stones (the title of three books, *Let It Bleed*, *Black and Blue* and *Beggars Banquet* are all Stones albums).

Redburn, Wellingborough
Redburn, 1849
Herman Melville

He acquired a fascination for the sea and 'foreign things' as a boy, which bred in him a 'vague prophetic thought, that I was fated, one day or other, to be a great voyager'. He grows to be 'an erring and wilful boy' who determines to ship as a sailor, and signs up for 'my first voyage' (the subtitle of the book). He has a miserable time under the parsimonious CAPTAIN RIGA, sees much deprivation and depravity in Liverpool and London, and returns home sadder and wiser.

Redcrosse, the Knight of Holiness
The Faerie Queene, 1590–6
Sir Edmund Spenser

The main protagonist of Book One of *The Faerie Queene*. He represents Saint George, who kills a dragon. He is descended from the Saxon kings, and is 'the goodliest man in all that companie' at the court of the Faerie Queene, GLORIANA. He wears a 'bloudie crosse' upon his coat of arms and is worthy, strong and 'faithfull in deed and sword'. He is partner to UNA, who represents truth, and whom he loses and must seek out.

Red Fox, the, properly **Colin Campbell**
Kidnapped, 1886
Robert Louis Stevenson

Red-headed Colin of Glenure is a government agent in Scotland after the '45 Rising, charged with rooting out Jacobites and destroying old Highland customs. He is a clever, conniving man who uses his charm and friendship against his fellow Scots. Colin is attempting to displace the Stewarts of Appin from their land and replace them with Campbells. DAVID BALFOUR excuses his behaviour by saying he is only carrying out orders, but ALAN BRECK's argument that he is an evil Campbell who enjoys his job of emasculating his old clan rivals, the Stewarts, carries greater weight. Colin's mysterious murder is the engine of the entire plot thereafter.

Reddy, Kate
I Don't Know How She Does It, 2002
Allison Pearson

Married with two small children and working as a fund manager in the City, 35-year-old Kate Reddy epitomizes the woman who has it all. What she lacks, however, are enough hours in the day. Unable to concentrate on the moment because she must continuously plan what still needs to be done, she can never achieve the impossibly high standards she sets herself and is weighed down by her guilt at being a working mother. The hectic whirlwind of her life results in her conducting all her friendships (and an affair) via email, and failing to recognize her husband's growing despair.

Redgauntlet, Lilias, first appears as **Green Mantle**
Redgauntlet, 1824
Sir Walter Scott

DARSIE LATIMER's (as yet unrecognized) sister, she first appears to her brother's friend ALAN FAIRFORD wrapped in a mysterious green gown, which nonetheless fails to disguise her beauty. She and Darsie have been separated as children and consigned to wildly different backgrounds, he to Scotland, she to a life on the Jacobite fringes in England.

Redl, Alfred
A Patriot for Me, 1965
John Osborne

A young Galician without wealth or social influence, he began his career in the Austrian Imperial Army in the 1890s. He attempts to hide his Jewishness and his homosexuality in order to advance in Intelligence, but by the end of the first act he is seen in bed with a young man: 'Why did I wait – so long?' he cries. Later, he is blackmailed and forced to spy for Russia. Eventually, he commits suicide. Dedicated, hardworking, patriotic and lonely, he is an admirable man destroyed by a decadent system refusing to adapt to a changing world; he thus becomes a scapegoat for a disintegrating empire.

Redlaw, Mr
The Haunted Man, 1848
Charles Dickens

The haunted man of the title, he is a chemist and lecturer who conjures up a spectre on Christmas Eve. The spectre, his alter ego, agrees to cancel his remembrance of the wrongs and sorrows he has suffered. Unfortunately, he also loses his happy memories and compassion for humanity, as well as gaining the malign gift of passing the affliction on to others. He is eventually redeemed and his influence counteracted by the goodness of Milly Swidger, wife of the lodge-keeper at his college.

Redmond, Barry, of Ballybarry → Lyndon, Barry

Reeby, Cameron
The Boys Who Stole the Funeral, 1980
Les Murray

Reeby, a former university student, and his friend, KEVIN FORBUTT, steal the body of Forbutt's great-uncle, CLARRIE DUNN, from a city funeral parlour and take it for burial back to the remote farming community in New South Wales where he was born. The body is duly buried. An impetuous, quick-tempered man of strong opinions, Reeby escapes with his friend as the police arrive. Having taken a casual job driving a truck of beef for illegal sale, Reeby is later shot and killed trying to evade the police. He represents the reckless outlaw instinct.

Reed, Eliza
Jane Eyre, 1847
Charlotte Brontë

The elder daughter of MRS REED, and sister of JOHN REED and GEORGIANA REED, Eliza is a selfish, avaricious child who grows into a very pious young woman. Tall, thin, and pallid, and puritanical in both dress and outlook, on the death of her mother she takes herself off to a nunnery in France where, 'quiet and unmolested', she can live out her joyless existence in peace.

Reed, Georgiana
Jane Eyre, 1847
Charlotte Brontë

The younger daughter of MRS REED, and sister of JOHN REED and ELIZA REED, Georgiana's cherub-like appearance belies a selfish, spiteful, and acrid nature. 'Universally indulged' as a child on account of her beauty, she ends up a plump, lazy, society lady whose main interest lies in satisfying her vanity and superficiality by making an 'advantageous match'.

Reed, Helen
Thinks ... , 2001
David Lodge

A novelist in her forties, with 'nice eyes, very dark pupils, pretty face' but with a touch of 'something melancholy', she is 'calm, efficient, conscientious' and mourning the death of a beloved husband. A lapsed Catholic of high moral principles, and conscious that widowhood has frequently left her emotionally divided between her 'neurotic self and more rational, observing self', she becomes tutor in creative writing at the University of Gloucester, where she is bewildered to find herself entering into a relationship with the assertive RALPH MESSENGER, a scientist who disparages the writing of fiction. Apt to reflect upon and quote from the works of Henry James, she discovers a renewed strength and utilizes her experiences in a new novel.

Reed, John
Jane Eyre, 1847
Charlotte Brontë

MRS REED's only son, and the brother of ELIZA REED and GEORGIANA REED, John is an extremely ugly character, not only in looks but in nature. A spoilt, obese, unaffectionate child, he treats JANE EYRE with great hostility, often assaulting her viciously, but continues to be indulged by his mother nonetheless. As a young man he leads an extravagant lifestyle, and his untimely death, reputedly suicide, follows a rapid descent into debt, vice, and ill health.

Reed, Mrs
Jane Eyre, 1847
Charlotte Brontë

The mistress of Gateshead Hall, Mrs Reed is guardian to her niece JANE EYRE only at her late husband's request. A robust, formidable, stony-eyed woman, she treats young Jane with great aversion and cruelty, refusing to accept her as one of the family and encouraging her children, JOHN REED and GEORGIANA REED, to act accordingly. After sending Jane to Lowood school, she is haunted many years later by her harsh treatment of her, but dies still feeling great antipathy towards her.

Reefy, Dr
'Paper Pills', in *Winesburg, Ohio*, 1919
Sherwood Anderson
'He was an old man with a white beard and huge nose and hands.' All that he knows is written on scraps of paper which are then scrunched into hard, pill-like balls in his pockets. In mysterious circumstances he marries a beautiful, tall, dark girl who had come to him because she was pregnant. The girl dies a year later.

Reeve, the
The Canterbury Tales, c.1387–1400
Geoffrey Chaucer
He is a kind of general foreman on an estate, supervising the work done and collecting the monies due. An old man who has become expert in feathering his own nest, he keeps himself to himself. In earlier days he was a carpenter, hence his explosion of anger at THE MILLER's tale, and his retaliation with a story of a dishonest miller who is cheated and cuckolded by two students from Cambridge.

Regan
King Lear, c.1607
William Shakespeare
KING LEAR's second daughter and wife of the DUKE OF CORNWALL. Though younger than her sister GONERIL, she is equal to her in cunning and cruelty. Like Goneril, she is more than willing to flatter Lear's vanity in a bid to win a large portion of his kingdom, but when he can serve no further use, treats him with a ruthless and wicked disregard. Whilst appearing at times less forceful than her sister, she is if anything more sadistic. Goneril poisons her.

Regan, properly Henrietta Stoker
No Laughing Matter, 1967
Angus Wilson
The MATTHEWS family's Cockney cook, she is a loud, disreputable bawd; 'blowsy, randy, cowlike, cockney, [with] Marie Lloyd features', she is the unappreciated rock on which the family is grounded.

Regan, Dave
'The Iron-Bark Chip', et seq, in *On the Track*, 1900
Joe Wilson and His Mates, 1901
Henry Lawson
A ganger on the great railway-building projects of turn-of-the-century Australia, he has also been a 'bushy' and a drover and a digger. He started out rather soft, but toughened up dramatically, and is resilient and resourceful, not above cutting a few corners when the need arises, and certainly not above a little honest duplicity.

Reginald
Reginald, 1904, *'Reginald in Russia'*, in *Reginald in Russia*, 1910
'Saki' (Hector Hugh Munro)
A cynical, witty and insouciant young man who will not admit to being older than 22. 'To have reached thirty is to have failed in life', he

remarks. His main interest is in his appearance, particularly his fashionable clothes and exotic boutonnières, but he enjoys all luxuries. He moves in respectable society, doing his best to spread social disorder. He has not entirely serious ambitions as a writer, a patron referred to as 'the Other', and a friendly interest in servant boys.

Reilly, Harry
Appointment in Samarra, 1934
John O'Hara
The focus of JULIAN ENGLISH's obsessive snobbery. A well-heeled Irishman without a gleam of cultural sophistication, he has kept Julian's business afloat during hard times by propping it up with loans. For this reason, Julian hates and fears him.

Reilly, Ignatius J
A Confederacy of Dunces, 1980
John Kennedy Toole
Suspicious, fat and flatulent, Ignatius J Reilly of New Orleans is waging a one-man crusade against modern life. His restless girlfriend, Myrna Minkoff of the Bronx, is adamant that he is in far greater need of her sexual attention than he is willing to admit, but the full extent of Reilly's voracity is reserved for other things, food being one of them. He is an intellectual of sorts, an ideologue, even, but at each and every turn, the contemporary world threatens to outwit him.

Reilly, Nora
John Bull's Other Island, 1904
George Bernard Shaw
Nora, LARRY DOYLE's former sweetheart, is a slight, 'almost sexless' woman. Regarded as plain in Irish eyes, to the Englishman TOM BROADBENT, entranced by all things Irish, she is both attractive and ethereal. Perhaps her delicacy of manner and melodious voice make her all the more so. In Ireland for the purpose of developing land, Broadbent sees Nora as yet another development project: he proposes and is accepted. He plans to feed her, plump her up and transform her into a competent English housewife. The story of Broadbent and Nora is one interpretation of England's historical response to the Irish.

Reinhardt, Mrs
'Mrs. Reinhardt', in *Mrs. Reinhardt and Other Stories*, 1978, published in USA as *A Rose in the Heart*, 1979
Edna O'Brien
A bitter 'woman scorned', she is a pitiful creation. Intelligent, sophisticated, attractive and wealthy, all she lacks is youth. She laments the loss of the latter and also mourns the fact that she has no daughter, recognizing that women can support one another. A dreamy idealist, she finds reality unbearable. Afraid and insecure, she is ensnared in suffering by a thoughtless husband. A kind, sensitive and compassionate woman, she is refined, but not robust.

Remington, Alice (Barclay)
An Insular Possession, 1986
Timothy Mo
A 20-year-old American who comes to China

with her aunt, as her uncle is head of the Meridian trading company in Canton. It is the 19th century and no women are allowed there, so families are domiciled in the pleasant Portuguese territory of Macao, where the men spend their leave. Alice fears being an old maid and thinks life in Macao unnatural; she is filled with gaiety inspired by the presence of the men, and 'plunged in despond' and 'inanition' by their absence. She enchants WALTER EASTMAN and GIDEON CHASE, and falls in love with Eastman 'although he is not rich'. But she shows little determination when her uncle objects to the relationship.

Remus, Uncle
Uncle Remus, 1880
Joel Chandler Harris

A storyteller who regales his master's little boy with tales of BRER RABBIT and the other 'creeturs'. Most of the time his stories tell of Brer Rabbit's mockery of the greed, selfishness, and stupidity of the other animals. In telling his stories, Uncle Remus makes liberal use of his status as 'favourite' amongst the slaves on the plantation to correct gently – and without Brer Rabbit's more forthright mockery – the faults of a typically self-centred child.

Ren
Tomorrow and Tomorrow and Tomorrow, 1947 (censored), 1983 (uncensored)
M Barnard Eldershaw

At 19 the frank and guileless Ren is about to begin the eight years compulsory social service which, in his regimented 24th-century country, irrevocably decides each individual's future. Believing that this land of unprecedented peace and plenty lacks the vital element of freedom prized by their early Australian ancestors, though not sure what this is, he and his 'Union of Youth' challenge the technocratic government to 'bring back liberty' because without it life is impoverished. While painfully losing his romantic naiveté, Ren gains a greater intimacy with KNARF, the writer father he loves but has never really known.

Renault
Venice Preserv'd, or A Plot Discovered, 1682
Thomas Otway

The French leader of a group of conspirators planning the overthrow of the Venetian republic, Renault prefers virtue to wealth, but has nevertheless sacrificed virtue to ambition. He acts not so much from political conviction as from motives of opportunism and greed for power. In many ways, he is a variant of ANTONIO and a satirical version of the Earl of Shaftesbury. Renault has an unscrupulous lust for sex: finding that JAFFIER has left BELVIDERA in his charge, he promptly assaults her. Otway thus suggests that this political rebel is as corrupt as the senators he plans to overthrow.

Renfrew, Dottie
The Group, 1963
Mary McCarthy

Any girl who thinks of her mother as the nicest person in the world must have had a pretty good start in life. Dottie's background is financially and emotionally secure and this, together with her Christian faith, gives her confidence and maturity. All this is shaken by the pain of a passionate but doomed love affair. However, her training reasserts itself and Dottie's pragmatism dictates another course, which she has the wisdom and the will to follow.

Renfro, Beulah (Beecham)
Losing Battles, 1970
Eudora Welty

The mother of JACK RENFRO, she is in her late forties, and is tall, bony, and impatient in movement. She is the epitome of hospitality, but knows 'how to let fly' as well. Her principal characteristic is the loudness and stridency of her voice, and the degree to which she employs it.

Renfro, Jack
Losing Battles, 1970
Eudora Welty

The eldest son of BEULAH RENFRO, and favourite grandchild of GRANNY VAUGHN. He has been serving a two-year jail term for the pompously inflated charge of 'aggravated battery and theft' imposed by JUDGE OSCAR MOODY. He is 19, and a simple, strong, good-hearted boy with an open, friendly face and no real malice in him; but he is also stubborn, and has a predilection for getting himself into trouble.

Renton, Mark 'Rent-boy'
Trainspotting, 1993
Porno, 2002
Irvine Welsh

Intelligent and articulate, Mark Renton leads a life which veers from the extremes of 'self-centred smack apathy' when he is using heroin, to his 'frequent self-analytical phases', when he assesses life, his friends and his opportunities. He has tried and rejected both an apprenticeship as a joiner and a spell as a university student, and in his more nihilistic moods sees life as 'aw ugly compromise, an timid surrender, progressively until death'. Faced with this bleak prospect, he finds his heroin addiction a viable alternative, telling himself that 'trying to manage a junk problem is the ultimate challenge'.

Renzo, Frank
On Green Dolphin Street, 2001
Sebastian Faulks

A 'tall lean man, his cropped hair showing the first dust of grey', Frank Renzo comes to Washington at the time of Kennedy's 1960 election campaign determined to re-establish his position as a leading journalist. Blacklisted during the McCarthy era, he is a man of social and personal conscience but these honourable traits are put to the test when he meets and falls in love with MARY VAN DER LINDEN, the wife of a diplomat he first encountered during the conflict in French Indo-China.

Reuter, Zoraide
The Professor, 1857
Charlotte Brontë

The mistress of the girls' school which

neighbours the boys' school run by MONSIEUR PELET, Zoraide Reuter appears to be a cautious and prudent woman with a good business sense. Her charm lends her the appearance of attractiveness, and there is an air of tranquillity in all she does. This appearance is somewhat deceptive, however, masking as it does a cold, calculating and manipulative mind which searches for weaknesses in others so that she might gain power over them. She views 'pride, hardness, selfishness' as 'proofs of strength', and is a woman wholly motivated by self-interest.

Rex
To the Islands, 1958, revised edition 1982
Randolph Stow

A young Aborigine at the mission run by HERIOT, his subversive and alienated presence disturbs the old Anglican because it seems a close reflection of his 'civilized' values. They eventually come to blows and Heriot believes he has killed the man.

Rex, John
His Natural Life, serialized 1870–2; as *For the Term of His Natural Life*, 1874
Marcus Clarke

A mutinous convict who escapes and returns to England to impersonate RICHARD DEVINE, whose half-brother he turns out to be. It further transpires that Rex has been responsible for the murder of Lord Bellasis.

Rhayader, Philip
The Snow Goose, 1941
Paul Gallico

Rhayader is a young man of 27 when he turns his back on the world and moves to an abandoned lighthouse at the mouth of the Aelder, on the edge of the great Essex Marsh. A small but powerful figure, with a deformed back and a crippled left arm, he is a gifted artist, able to capture the salty loneliness of the wild marshland; he is also an expert sailor, and a healer of wild creatures. Rebuffed by the world, he has despaired of it. Instead, he creates a sanctuary for migrating birds, who return year after year. He loves FRITHA, but cannot adequately express his feelings, certain they will not be returned. His finest moment comes when he sacrifices his life to rescue a handful of men from the carnage of Dunkirk.

Rheims, Archbishop of
Saint Joan, 1923
George Bernard Shaw

The archbishop is presented as a resolute, pragmatic 'political prelate with nothing of the ecclesiastic about him except his imposing bearing'. He first encounters Joan when she arrives at Chinon to see THE DAUPHIN. Used to instructing and occasionally bullying the Dauphin, the archbishop is so impressed by Joan's sincerity that his own faith is reawakened. Later he officiates at the coronation of the Dauphin as Charles VII, but warns Joan that the Church will do nothing to prevent her inevitable fate in the battle between religion and politics.

Riah
Our Mutual Friend, 1865
Charles Dickens

A venerable Jew indebted to FASCINATION FLEDGEBY for releasing his father from debt, he serves as agent in Fledgeby's fictitious money-lending firm, Pubsey & Co, and takes the blame for his master's sharp practices. His hard life is uplifted by his friendship with JENNY WREN, who calls him her 'fairy godmother'. Gentle and noble, he helps LIZZIE HEXAM escape from BRADLEY HEADSTONE and EUGENE WRAYBURN by finding employment for her outside London. He finally leaves Fledgeby and goes to live with Jenny Wren.

Ribeiro, Father (Joaquim)
An Insular Possession, 1986
Timothy Mo

A Portuguese Jesuit missionary illegally residing in Macao in a squalid poor-Chinese quarter. To ALICE REMINGTON he is a rough-looking, swarthy, greasy man in a shabby, dusty habit, with filthy nails, brown and broken teeth and a high-pitched laugh, who reeks of garlic. But Ribeiro is also a brilliant scholar, speaking eight languages and writing a lengthy dissertation on Chinese nomenclature. 'A man of latitude in all respects', he is liberal and sympathetic, generously helping WALTER EASTMAN and GIDEON CHASE despite the dangers to himself.

Rice, Archie
The Entertainer, 1957
John Osborne

Archie Rice, the Music Hall entertainer of the title, is about 50, his grey hair brushed flat, his act a 'cheeky-chappie' routine. Working near the end of the Music Hall era, he is reduced to incidental appearances between tableaux of nearly-nude girls: the latest fashion. Brave and optimistic, he is now equally acerbic, sad and nostalgic, patronizing everyone, including his wife, Phoebe, whom he pities, and his father, Billy, whom he much admires. Real thought and deep, sincere feeling seem to Archie to be things of the past. Bitter and resentful, he despises both his meagre audience and himself: 'his face held open by a grin, dead behind the eyes'.

Rich, Brackenbury
The Suicide Club, 1878
Robert Louis Stevenson

A distinguished soldier of the Indian wars – gallant, courageous, but modest and retiring. He is an independent, resilient man who can be relied upon in a crisis. In London civilian life, Rich still searches for challenges and adventures, and is the obvious candidate to help FLORIZEL, PRINCE OF BOHEMIA, combat the sinister and deadly president of the Suicide Club. In this tale he represents the forces of justice and normality.

Richard I, known as Coeur-de-Lion
The Talisman: A Tale of the Crusaders, 1825
Sir Walter Scott

The bluff, warlike Richard is the second Plantagenet monarch, succeeding Henry II after his brother Henry's co-regency. To Scott, he seems 'wild and generous, a pattern of chivalry, with all its extravagant virtues and no less absurd errors'. Not the least of these last is a cruelty and intolerance that would sit better on a heathen potentate than on a defender of Christendom.

Richard II, King
Richard II, not later than 1595
William Shakespeare

A man of many parts; he is authoritative, avaricious, insensitive, capable of great self-dramatization, a philosopher of sorts but also childlike. Easily led by sycophants, in the eyes of his elders he lacks the judgement and more warlike virtues of his royal predecessors. His tragedy is his inability to equate his own vision of his role as king with what that position realistically demands of him. Faced with opposition which he cannot overcome, he adopts an attitude of Christ-like martyrdom and hands over the crown to his rival Bolingbroke (HENRY IV). Once stripped of all the trappings of monarchy he begins to see clearly: 'I wasted time and now doth time waste me'.

Richard III → Richard, Duke of Gloucester

Richard, Duke of Gloucester
Henry VI Parts II and III, early 1590s
Richard III, 1592/3
William Shakespeare

Shakespeare's controversial Richard is restless, lustful, envious, malicious, murderous and a master of dissimulation. Yet he is not at all a rag-bag of evil qualities; he may be memorably physically deformed, yet his mind is agile and sharp, his language quick and supple and full of the wit of the charnel-house. He claws his way to the throne, from the moment in *Henry VI Part II* when he urges his father, RICHARD PLANTAGENET, DUKE OF YORK, to 'tear the crown' from Henry's head, and achieving his goal not merely by butchery but because he understands and exploits the motives and weaknesses of those about him. Nurtured in a context of treachery and civil unrest, he is both a tyrant and a dark force of nature, but what makes Shakespeare's portrait so compulsive is that it is also a complex psychological study of political ambition and corruption.

Richard, King (Richard Coeur de Lion)
Ivanhoe, 1819
Sir Walter Scott

Second Plantagenet King of England, he reigned for a scant ten years from 1189 to 1199. Shipwrecked in the Adriatic on his way home from the Crusades, he was forced to continue his journey incognito, hampered by the efforts of his brother PRINCE JOHN and his brother's allies in Europe to prevent his re-assumption of the throne. In *Ivanhoe* he appears first as a mysterious pilgrim who shows marked kindness to the Jew ISAAC OF YORK, but later reveals himself to his champion LOCKSLEY, who sees him as the protector of Saxon rights.

Rechele
Satan in Goray, 1958
Isaac Bashevis Singer

Hailed as a prophetess by followers of the false Messiah SABBATAI ZEVI, Rechele is tormented by dreadful dreams and visions, and has strange magical powers. She is held in great awe, barely regarded as human, with a body 'like mother-of-pearl'. In reality, she is a sad, pathetic victim of others' evil ways. Scarred by ill-treatment in her childhood, she lives in a perpetual trance of fear and has not the will to resist marriage to one of the sect, or possession by the evil spirit.

Richards, Edward and Mary
The Man That Corrupted Hadleyburg, 1899
Mark Twain

Mr and Mrs Richards are a poor old couple but among the happiest and most honest citizens of Hadleyburg. Mr Richards, though, has a secret to hide: he saved the Rev Mr Burgess from the wrath of Hadleyburg, though at the expense of the innocent BARCLAY GOODSON, and is himself protected by the Rev Mr Burgess. Conscience-stricken, Mr and Mrs Richards fall ill and die, further damaging the reputation of Hadleyburg.

Richards, Jem
'Melanctha', in *Three Lives*, 1909
Gertrude Stein

A ne'er-do-well gambler, to whom MELANCTHA HERBERT becomes engaged on the rebound. He is plausible, charming, but profoundly ineligible and finally deserts her.

Richards, Vic
Rusty Bugles, 1948
Sumner Locke Elliott

An Australian soldier, bored with life at a wartime ordnance depot in the remote Northern Territory. Feeling that he did not have 'any chances' – he had to leave school at 13, because of his drunken father – he is full of resentment and sees everything as 'a racket'. At first hostile to the newcomer ROD CARSON, his growing friendship with him expands his intellectual horizons and increases his enthusiasm for life. Having been promoted to hut corporal, he stands up to the petty tyranny of SGT BROOKS.

Richardson, Jake
Jake's Thing, 1978
Kingsley Amis

An Oxford don, Jake Richardson is almost 60, round-faced, bespectacled and easy-going, has an ulcer and is married to the overweight Brenda, with whom he lives in north London. Although Jake has many years of lechery behind him and still contemplates sex, he finds himself unaccountably unable to perform it satisfactorily. In fact, a meal and a film on television seem a more enticing prospect. He has lost his libido (the 'thing' of the title), and visits various therapists in an effort to resuscitate it. Yet what really frightens Jake is discovering he has little capacity for genuine love and compassion. It is this which makes him view the modern world and his adventures in psychotherapy with both defiance and an appalled curiosity.

Richardson, John
The Daysman, 1984
Stanley Middleton

A school headmaster, tempted by his appetite for

the public forum into a self-centred and pompous role of being all things to all people. Only the stability and steadiness of his wife save him from destruction.

Richmond, Harry
The Adventures of Harry Richmond, 1871
George Meredith
A snob and egoist very much in the mould of EVAN HARRINGTON (and a first draft for SIR WILLOUGHBY PATTERNE). Life and marriage to Janet Ilchester knock off a few of his more elaborate affectations.

Richmond, Henry, Earl of, later Henry VII
Henry VI Part III, early 1590s
Richard III, 1592/3
William Shakespeare
Richmond is the son of Edmund Tudor, Earl of Richmond, and Margaret Beaufort, daughter of JOHN OF GAUNT. During the reign of Edward IV (EDWARD, EARL OF MARCH) he takes refuge in France but returns in 1485, two years after Richard III (RICHARD, DUKE OF GLOUCESTER) takes the throne. A few months later, he kills the king at the battle of Bosworth, the decisive battle in the Wars of the Roses, and by doing so unites the Houses of Lancaster and York and, as King Henry VII, inaugurates the Tudor era. Shakespeare presents him as England's youthful hope, a man of conscience, and of physical and moral courage; a providential force, a soldier bringing with him the calm that follows the storm. In the words of King HENRY VI, Richmond is the 'pretty lad' destined to become king and 'prove our country's bliss'.

Rickard, Miss ('Mouse')
No Laughing Matter, 1967
Angus Wilson
Great-aunt to the MATTHEWS family children, she is well-travelled and knowledgeable; 'she is herself their gazetteer and their medical dictionary rolled into one ... and all [this] she offered with a nonchalant gracious bend of her ageing, thin, pemmican-dry pioneer's body that disclaimed all praise'.

Ridcully, Mustrum
Reaper Man, 1991, et seq
Terry Pratchett
The larger-than-life Archchancellor of Unseen University, the university of magic in Ankh Morpork, attended by the wizards of the Discworld. With a gung-ho attitude and a distinct lack of tact, he leads a bumbling band of senior wizards through a series of magical adventures. His lack of interest in technical detail often renders him oblivious to the danger he is in, despite the protestations of those around him.

Ridd, John
Lorna Doone, 1869
R D Blackmore
The narrator of the novel, Ridd is the epitome of the English countryman as perceived by the Victorian romantic imagination. He is good-natured, reticent, honest, obstinate and emotionally vulnerable, with an unabashed love of natural beauty and a deep understanding of the countryside around him. In his own words, he is 'nothing more than a plain unlettered man', but once he sees LORNA DOONE he is 'touched by sudden delight' and transformed: 'I must forever love'.

Rider, Dr Edward
The Doctor's Family, 1863
Margaret Oliphant
Dr Rider, newcomer to Carlingford, works faithfully among the poor, but his wastrel brother FRED RIDER, back from Australia, rouses his helpless rage, which is exacerbated by the arrival of a wife and five unruly children. The children are shepherded by NETTIE UNDERWOOD, Fred's Australian sister-in-law, who is so pretty, capable and unselfish that Dr Rider falls in love with her, but she, devoted to the others, will not marry him. He works on with mingled anger and despair until a tragic turn of events works to his advantage.

Rider, Fred
The Doctor's Family, 1863
Margaret Oliphant
Fred is a fat, useless waster who fills his brother DR EDWARD RIDER's pleasant room with cigar smoke and novels. He expects the doctor to keep him and, when his family arrive, to keep them too. NETTIE UNDERWOOD, his sister-in-law, despises him but feels responsible for her sister and the children. Deaf to all appeals, continuing his self-indulgent drunken life, Fred one night, returning from an inn, falls into the canal and is drowned, thus removing at least one of the problems facing Nettie and the doctor.

Rider, Susan
The Doctor's Family, 1863
Margaret Oliphant
Susan, FRED RIDER's Australian wife, is the opposite of her sister NETTIE UNDERWOOD – faded, tearful, helpless, lamenting everyone's cruelty and injustice to her and Fred. Incapable of looking after her children, she leaves them to Nettie. By tears and complaints she has nagged Nettie into bringing them to England; after Fred's death she begins nagging her into returning to Australia when an Australian friend comes looking for her, wanting to marry her and take her home – which suits her lazy, vain selfishness much better.

Riderhood, Rogue (Roger)
Our Mutual Friend, 1865
Charles Dickens
A desperate 'waterside-man with a squinting leer', he tries to gain the reward offered by MR BOFFIN for the arrest of the murderer of JOHN HARMON by telling MORTIMER LIGHTWOOD that the guilty man is his former partner, GAFFER HEXAM. Becoming a lock-keeper, he learns of BRADLEY HEADSTONE's attempt to murder EUGENE WRAYBURN and blackmails him. But Headstone attacks him and they both drown. His daughter, Pleasant Riderhood, an un-licensed pawnbroker, eventually marries MR VENUS.

Ridgeon, Sir Colenso
The Doctor's Dilemma, 1906
George Bernard Shaw

An eminent physician, Ridgeon is modelled upon Sir Almroth Wright, respected for his work on vaccine therapy. Ridgeon has devised a cure for tuberculosis by inoculation. A youthful-looking man of 50, he is sensitive and diligent. He romantically idealizes JENNIFER DUBEDAT as much as she does her husband, LOUIS DUBEDAT, an unscrupulous but talented artist. Ridgeon's dilemma is whether to treat him or the worthy but dull DR BLENKINSOP. He chooses the latter. After Dubedat's death he discovers Jennifer to be happily remarried. The man of science has been so romantically deluded, therefore, as to have 'committed a purely disinterested murder'.

Riesling, Paul
Babbitt, 1922
Sinclair Lewis

A young artist-turned-businessman, he fills GEORGE BABBITT's head with the intoxicating idea of freedom and suggests to him for the first time that the known world stretches further than the town limits of Zenith City.

Riga, Captain
Redburn, 1849
Herman Melville

Russian by birth, he prefers to be thought American. He is a 'fine-looking man, about forty, splendidly dressed, with very blond whiskers, and very white teeth, and what I took to be a free, frank look out of a large hazel eye'. On shore, he is deceptively 'bland, benevolent and bewitchingly merry', but at sea is hypocritical, dishonest, and treats the men badly, including cheating them of pay. He is 'extravagant in his personal expenses, but a niggard to others'.

Rigaud
Little Dorrit, 1857
Charles Dickens

A villainous Frenchman with polished manners and a 'theatrical air', he uses the aliases Blandois and Lagnier. Awaiting trial for murdering his wife, he is the cell-mate of JOHN BAPTIST CAVALLETTO in Marseilles. Having escaped, he reappears in London and visits JEREMIAH FLINTWINCH. He deposits with MISS WADE documents obtained from Flintwinch that show how MRS CLENNAM has suppressed a codicil in her husband's will that leaves a legacy to AMY DORRIT. He accompanies HENRY GOWAN to Venice and returns to try to blackmail Mrs Clennam, but he is killed by the sudden collapse of her house.

Rigby, Mr
Coningsby, or The New Generation, 1844
Benjamin Disraeli

As a Tory Member of Parliament, he is effectively LORD MONMOUTH's placeman, an unprincipled and greedy manipulator who shares his sponsor's conviction that all lesser orders are mere stepping stones to financial and social success.

Rikki-Tikki-Tavi
The Jungle Book, 1894
Rudyard Kipling

'He was a mongoose, rather like a little cat in his fur and his tail, but quite like a weasel in his head and his habits. His eyes and the end of his restless nose were pink; he could scratch himself anywhere he pleased, with any leg, front or back, that he chose to use; he could fluff up his tail till it looked like a bottle-brush, and his war-cry, as he scuttled through the long grass, was: *Rikk-tikk-tikki-tikki-tchk!*' In his 'Chant' the tailor Darzee calls him 'valiant' and 'true'.

Rima
Lanark: A Life in Four Books, 1981
Alasdair Gray

The girlfriend of LANARK. Her humanity is ironically underlined by the strange disease of dragonhide and by her transformation, in the hell chapters, into a full- but still warm-blooded lizard.

Rincewind
The Colour of Magic, 1983, et seq
Terry Pratchett

An inept and awkward 'wizzard' (as it says on his hat) with a cowardly streak and an unerring sense of self-preservation, his only talent is for languages. In his regular brushes with DEATH he is often saved by 'the Luggage', a magical wooden chest on legs which follows him everywhere. Rincewind acquired the Luggage from Twoflower, the very first Discworld tourist.

Ringold, Ira
I Married a Communist, 1998
Philip Roth

Physically powerful, imposing, Jewish and sexually vigorous, Ringold is a Newark roughneck, a former hobo who discovered Communism while serving in the army during World War II. Later, he becomes an actor under the name of Iron Rinn, appearing in left-wing radio dramas. Achieving national prominence by becoming the fourth husband of Eve Frame, a famous actress, his political activities come under the scrutiny of government investigators. Blacklisted, his professional and domestic lives disintegrate, the final blow being his wife's publication of a damning memoir under the same title as the novel.

Rintherout, Jenny
The Antiquary, 1816
Sir Walter Scott

JONATHAN OLDBUCK's sole house-servant, she is as reliable and unobtrusive as her brother Tam, since gone for a soldier in Flanders, was a scapegrace. Jenny exemplifies the untranslatable Scottish virtue of 'sonsiness', but there is evidence that she is a more substantial person than the antiquary's rather patronizing summation might imply.

Ripley, Gran'ma
'Mrs Ripley's Trip', in *Main-Travelled Roads*, 1892, revised editions 1899, 1922, 1930
Hamlin Garland

After 23 years of marriage and bondage to prairie

farm life, Mrs Ripley, 'pathetically little, weazened and hopeless in her ill-fitting garments ... [but with] a peculiar sparkle in her little black eyes', resolves to kick over the traces and make a visit to her family back east. The jolt of separation rekindles a mutual affection with Ethan Ripley and on her return 'she took up her burden again, never more thinking to lay it down'.

Ripley, Tom
The Talented Mr. Ripley, 1956, et seq
Patricia Highsmith

An alarming creation: a charming, cultured, but deadly hero who is a totally amoral psychotic. Leaving a trail of corpses which stretches from America to Europe, Ripley tantalizingly evades police scrutiny using a mixture of phlegmatic coolness and reckless daring. Bewitching his friends, and the reader, he invites our collusion in his crimes. He possesses a constantly calculating mind which is at its most rational when dealing with the disposal of the corpses of his victims. His emotions are fully engaged only in the art and execution of murder: an act from which he then distances himself with the true psychopath's indifference.

Rip Van Winkle
'Rip Van Winkle', 1819
Washington Irving

The easy-going good nature of the Kaatskill village farmer is his downfall. He prefers odd jobs to regular work, will eat 'white bread or brown' and is continually nagged by his wife. Escaping to the mountains, he encounters a ghostly Hendrik Hudson and his crew playing bowls, and drinks of their 'old Hollands'. He wakes to find he has slept through 20 years of changes, including his wife's death and the whole Revolutionary War. Now he tells tales of 'before the war', the envy of henpecked husbands.

Risley, Elaine
Cat's Eye, 1988
Margaret Atwood

A successful visual artist, Elaine Risley is haunted by a childhood playmate whose cruel betrayals continue to hurt. She took to fainting as a child to forestall confrontations, and still feels unable to deal with most women. Instead, she makes cutting remarks and becomes known for her bitchiness. Only with men does she feel comfortable, choosing to think of herself as one of the guys. Yet as she grows older she finds it difficult to become emotionally involved, preferring to be the rejecter rather than the rejected.

Rita
The Dressmaker, 1973
Beryl Bainbridge

The niece of NELLIE and MARGO, she is 'damp behind the ears' and acts as though she has been 'wrapped up in tissue paper all her life'. Excluded from childhood friendships because of her withdrawn and sober character, she is desperate to escape the confining nature of her aunts' dry household. As a teenager she is self-conscious, awkward around boys and anxious for her own love story to begin.

Ritchie-Hook, Brigadier
Sword of Honour, 1965
Evelyn Waugh

A notorious Halberdier veteran from World War I, often wounded, twice court-martialled, Brigadier Ritchie-Hook delights in a new war in which to exercise his eccentricity. He glares through one monstrous eye and his black-gloved right hand has only two fingers. His type of training is 'biffing', as bloodily as possible, smashing imaginary enemies, with no thought of withdrawal. GUY CROUCHBACK is with him in a raid on Dakar, in which Ritchie-Hook defies orders, breaks rank and brings home the dripping head of an African sentry.

Rittenmeyer, Charlotte
The Wild Palms, 1939
William Faulkner

A married woman who joins her doctor lover in a long flight from the stultifying conventions of social existence, but fails to find anything other than a drastic and fatal confirmation of the essential sterility of her values.

Rivers, Col Edward
The History of Emily Montague, 1769
Frances Brooke

A 'tall handsome colonel of twenty seven ... five feet eleven inches, well made, with fine teeth, speaking eyes, a military air, and the look of a man of fashion'. Intelligent, kind and gentlemanly, he is a man of only small fortune, who has emigrated to Canada in order to improve his prospects. Much of the time, however, his mind is occupied with the opposite sex, being 'an immense favorite with the ladies'. Although he takes care to pay attention to all women in his company, he is in search of a deep, affectionate, lasting love, rather than endless flirtations. Preferring mature women to inexperienced young girls, he falls in love with EMILY MONTAGUE at their first meeting, seeing in her the soul mate for whom he has been searching.

Rivers, Diana
Jane Eyre, 1847
Charlotte Brontë

Darker and more striking than her sister MARY RIVERS, Diana is strong-willed and possessed of an instinctive understanding of people. Kind, compassionate, and intelligent, she views life with clear-sighted rationality, backing up JANE EYRE in her decision not to marry ST JOHN RIVERS, and applauding her eventual marriage to MR ROCHESTER.

Rivers, Dr William
Regeneration, 1991
The Eye in the Door, 1993
The Ghost Road, 1995, forming the *Regeneration* trilogy
Pat Barker

A neurologist and anthropologist, fictionalized by Barker, he has left his research at Cambridge to treat men with war-related psychological disorders at Craiglockhart War Hospital. He is devoted to his patients to the detriment of his own health and is aware that he is a father-figure or 'male mother' to almost all of them, including SIEGFRIED SASSOON and BILLY PRIOR. The task of 'curing' these broken men in order to return them to war creates great conflict for him, as does his knowledge that his method of encouraging patients to remember and allow themselves to feel the terror is at odds with his own lifelong 'rigorous repression of emotion and desire'.

Rivers, Mary
Jane Eyre, 1847
Charlotte Brontë

The more reserved, but equally graceful and gentle, of ST JOHN RIVERS's two sisters, Mary, like her sister, DIANA RIVERS, is a model of kindness and virtue. Like Diana, she becomes a close friend to JANE EYRE, a friendship which is deepened further by the discovery that they are in fact cousins, and one which remains unsullied by St John's differences with Jane.

Rivers, Olivia
Heat and Dust, 1975
Ruth Prawer Jhabvala

The pretty but rather shallow young wife of an official in the Indian Civil Service, Olivia is bored with colonial life, and despite loving her upright, stuffy husband, falls under the potent spell of an Indian prince, THE NAWAB OF KHATM. When she becomes pregnant she is uncertain who the father is, but flees to the Nawab following a backstreet abortion, the motive for which remains obscure.

Rivers, St John
Jane Eyre, 1847
Charlotte Brontë

JANE EYRE's cousin, a young parson, who takes her in when she is destitute, and the brother of DIANA RIVERS and MARY RIVERS. He is tall, fair, and blue-eyed, but his finely-chiselled features cannot hide his restless, inexorable nature. He is essentially a good man, but, repressing his earthly passions under his missionary zeal, he tries to use his implacable will and religious despotism to force Jane to marry him and accompany him to India. Shunning all enjoyment in a Calvinistic dedication to his ministerial duties, he drives himself to an early death for the sake of his creed.

Rob
Butcher's Broom, 1934
Neil Gunn

Rob is a kind and generous man but his overpowering lust for and jealousy of ELIE results in violence and shame, and despite knowing that his love is destructive he cannot resist his basic desires. Elie's further withdrawal into herself after their marriage only feeds Rob's anger, and his excessive drinking finally leads to his death. He is a simple man, torn between love and masculine pride in the face of the community.

Rob Roy → Macgregor, Rob Roy

Rob the Grinder → Toodle, Robin

Robarts, Lucy
Framley Parsonage, 1861
The Last Chronicle of Barset, 1867
Anthony Trollope

The youngest sister of REV MARK ROBARTS, with whom she lives at Framley Parsonage. Small and quiet, but clever and strong-minded, she pretends not to love LORD LUFTON because of her pride: she could not bear the disapproval of his mother, LADY LUFTON, or the adverse comments of the public. She then declares that she would only marry him if his mother asked her to. She selflessly helps the poor Crawleys, and in *The Last Chronicle of Barset* Lucy, now Lady Lufton, believes in REV JOSIAH CRAWLEY's innocence.

Robarts, Rev Mark
Framley Parsonage, 1861
The Last Chronicle of Barset, 1867
Anthony Trollope

As a boy Mark was friendly with LORD LUFTON and impressed LADY LUFTON; he later entered the Church on the understanding that they would give him the living of Framley. He seems to be always lucky, but his ambition leads him to become involved with people whose social eminence is not matched by the moral standards proper to a clergyman's companions, such as NATHANIEL SOWERBY. Foolishly allowing himself to be embroiled in Sowerby's financial collapse, he becomes aware of his sins, although it is difficult to extricate himself from worldly snares.

Robert
Betrayal, 1978
Harold Pinter

A publisher, Robert has long known that his wife, EMMA, has been having an affair with JERRY, his great friend. Despite having himself betrayed Emma for years, he is doubly affected by her infidelity; while he views the fact of her adultery with mocking indifference, contempt, and spite, he is more deeply affected by Jerry's betrayal of their old friendship. Having come to despise the petty jealousies and tyrannies of the book trade and the promotion of new novelists, one of whom is currently having an affair with Emma, Jerry's treachery and Emma's involvement with a novelist with whom he deals professionally, result in his decision to end the marriage. The play recounts Jerry and Emma's affair in reverse chronological order.

Robert
The Comfort of Strangers, 1981
Ian McEwan

The only son of a tyrannical, London-based diplomat who beat his children with a leather belt and used Robert as an unwitting male ally, setting him against his four sisters. Now obsessed with male dominance, the physically powerful but sexually sterile Robert, owner of a sinister male-only bar in Venice, befriends English tourists COLIN and MARY. Later, with the collusion of his crippled wife, CAROLINE, he vents his vicious sadism on Colin, with Mary a helpless, horrified witness.

Robert, Count of Paris
Count Robert of Paris, 1831
Sir Walter Scott

A bold Frank, who usurps the emperor's throne, but whose heroism at home and in the Crusades is eclipsed by that of his wife BRENHILDA, COUNTESS OF PARIS. Like many of Scott's later heroes, he has little independent substance and seems worked up out of the history books.

Robert III, King of Scotland
The Fair Maid of Perth, or St Valentine's Day, in *Chronicles of the Canongate: Second Series*, 1828
Sir Walter Scott

The second monarch of the House of Stewart, he is a man of many gifts but few that are suited to his station in life. 'The King of so fierce a people as the Scots then were, ought to have been warlike, prompt, and active, liberal in rewarding services, strict in punishing crimes'; failing in each of these, he weakly delegates unwelcome duties to members of his family and circle.

Roberta, Peter and Phyllis
The Railway Children, 1906
E Nesbit

Privileged middle-class children who are catapulted into a more trying, but exciting situation, they are little more than stereotypes. Roberta is a gentle, caring girl who tries so hard to be good she verges on the priggish – or so Peter tells her, being himself a more impetuous, down-to-earth type, while Phyllis is the dreamer of the trio, her laces always undone.

Robin
The Merry Wives of Windsor, c.1597
William Shakespeare

Robin is SIR JOHN FALSTAFF's page, and takes his love letters to MISTRESS ALICE FORD and MISTRESS MARGARET PAGE. His loyalty, though, is not entirely given over to Falstaff, as he connives with the 'merry wives' in their trickery; but neither does Robin wholly turn against his employer. He is a 'weathercock' and, as such, potentially dangerous.

Robin, Fanny
Far from the Madding Crowd, 1874
Thomas Hardy

A 'slight and fragile creature', Fanny is a natural victim. Her love for SGT FRANCIS TROY is sincere, but a confusion sends her to the wrong church on their wedding day, prompting his scorn and rejection. Abandoned and left to die during childbirth in the workhouse, it is only after her death that she is appreciated by Troy and is able to exercise power over the lives of others.

Robinson, Horse-Shoe
Horse-Shoe Robinson, 1835
John Pendleton Kennedy

Modelled on the novelist James Fenimore Cooper, he is a tough, talkative old Southern frontiersman, caught up in the controversy about revolution and loyalty in the period leading up to the American War of Independence.

Robinson, Hyacinth
The Princess Casamassima, 1886
Henry James

The illegitimate child of an English nobleman and a French lady, he is raised in London by MISS PYNSENT, indoctrinated into bookbinding and communism by MONSIEUR PUPIN and awakened to the contradictions both of European society and of his own lineage by the PRINCESS CASAMASSIMA. It is clear throughout that he will find these difficult to resolve, and his life ends in suicide.

Robinson, Mary
The Maid of Buttermere, 1987
Melvyn Bragg

Based upon a real character of the same name, she is the daughter of the owner of the Fish Inn at Buttermere in the English Lake District, an amiable young woman whose beauty inspires several 19th-century writers, including Wordsworth, Coleridge and de Quincey. She is innocent yet knowing, mysterious, chaste, elusive, and is known locally as the 'Buttermere Beauty', although her good looks have all but transformed her into a local curiosity. She rebels against her own image by submitting to the self-styled Colonel Hope, a dashing confidence trickster who pursues her.

Robinson, Miles Mary
Robinson, 1958
Muriel Spark

A member of a rich Catholic family, Robinson studied for the priesthood but left the Church, considering it to be steeped in heretical superstition, particularly with reference to the Virgin Mary (he has an antipathy to women). He bought a small island in the Atlantic, named it Robinson, and lived there as a recluse. Three survivors of an aeroplane crash on the island disrupt his ordered life and his detachment. His subsequent disappearance sets off quarrels and suspicions. The narrator, January Marlow, sums him up as a 'selfish but well-meaning eccentric'.

Robinson, Octavius ('Tavy')
Man and Superman, 1903
George Bernard Shaw

The brother of VIOLET ROBINSON, Octavius is the late Whitefield's adopted son and unsuccessful suitor of his daughter, ANN WHITEFIELD. He is a romantic, dapper and decorous man, 'the jeune premier; for it is not in reason to suppose that a second such attractive male figure should appear in one story'.

Robinson, Taft
End Zone, 1972
Don DeLillo

'The first black student to be enrolled at Logos College in West Texas. They got him for his speed.' He might have been one of the greatest players ever, 'his life story on the back of cereal boxes'.

Robinson, Violet
Man and Superman, 1903
George Bernard Shaw

OCTAVIUS ROBINSON's sister, as formidable as she

is good-looking, Violet is secretly married to the American, HECTOR MALONE. At the end of the play, when the truth is told, she promises Malone's father that she will try and effect a reconciliation between him and his son.

Robsart, Amy
Kenilworth, 1821
Sir Walter Scott
The beautiful daughter of SIR HUGH ROBSART. Secretly married to ROBERT DUDLEY, EARL OF LEICESTER, and kept not so much a prisoner as a recluse by the clandestine nature of their union, she is a figure whose 'milkmaid' charms have been leached by isolation and sorrow. Poised between listlessness and expectation, she is likened to an irregularly tended vine. She later perishes when Leicester believes the cunning RICHARD VARNEY's accusations of infidelity.

Robsart, Sir Hugh
Kenilworth, 1821
Sir Walter Scott
AMY ROBSART's father, he is 'a man of large size, which had been only kept within moderate compass by the constant use of violent exercise', and who is devastated by his daughter's secret marriage to ROBERT DUDLEY, EARL OF LEICESTER.

Robson, Daniel
Sylvia's Lovers, 1863
Elizabeth Gaskell
SYLVIA ROBSON's father. A strong, brave, but also stubborn and wilful man. He is persecuted for fighting for his own personal sense of justice rather than the justice of the legal world, but, finding himself enmeshed in affairs which are far beyond his control, proves ultimately to be his own worst enemy.

Robson, John
Anderby Wold, 1923
Winifred Holtby
Handsome, kindly, and slow-witted, John Robson is a middle-aged Yorkshire farmer, effortlessly dominated by his capable young wife, MARY ROBSON. Inarticulate and unwilling to assert himself, his deference and dogged devotion remain undiminished in the face of her irritation and contempt. A stoic and resilient character, he is wholeheartedly loyal both to his wife and to the traditional ideals he upholds against profound social and political disruption.

Robson, Mary
Anderby Wold, 1923
Winifred Holtby
The central character in *Anderby Wold*, she is a young Yorkshire woman who has endured hard work, heavy responsibility, and a joyless marriage in order to repay the mortgage on her farm. Her land secured, Mary pours her tremendous energies into acts of parochial philanthropy, but her benevolent interference is not always appreciated by those upon whom it is relentlessly lavished. Vigorous, domineering and complacent, she is awoken to a sense of youthful rebellion through her unlikely friendship with DAVID ROSSITER, the young socialist who threatens to destroy her local sovereignty.

Robson, Sylvia
Sylvia's Lovers, 1863
Elizabeth Gaskell
Hot-headed, impulsive and idealistic as a young girl, Sylvia grows up to be a sharp and cynical woman, forced to realize that life is not about absolutes but, rather, is full of suffering. She has a hard streak which makes her unforgiving and bitter, but comes to realize that this is not a bearable way of life. She softens towards PHILIP HEPBURN, the husband who has wronged her, but remains a wretched creature, wiser but riddled with regrets.

Robyn, Patricia
Mosquitoes, 1927
William Faulkner
Niece of MRS PATRICIA MAURIER, after whom she is named. At 18, she seems coltish rather than nubile. To the carefully attuned senses of MR ERNEST TALLIAFERRO, she has a 'clean young odour ... like that of young trees'.

Roca
Haxby's Circus, 1930
Katharine Susannah Prichard
A circus dwarf, sensitive and suffering, yet able to use and abuse his deformity. Playing to the crowd for laughs, he empowers that deformity, disabling an insensitive humanity.

Rochcliffe, Lady Eleanore
'Lady Eleanore's Mantle', 1838, in *Twice-Told Tales*, 1842 (revised edition)
Nathaniel Hawthorne
A proud and unapproachable beauty, she is constantly wrapped in a mysterious mantle. This seems to represent and protect her virginity but it also comes to be associated with a fatal outbreak of smallpox that sweeps through Boston, where she has come to live with her guardian.

Roche, Peter
Guerillas, 1975
V S Naipaul
An anti-apartheid Englishman who has been tortured by the South African security police, Peter Roche is completely disillusioned and ends up working for American bauxite interests in a Caribbean island. He becomes a kind of father-figure to the would-be revolutionary JIMMY AHMED, and has a desultory affair with the more idealistic JANE, who came with him to the island. His political indifference towards the inhabitants of the island is mercilessly exposed, to his great discomfort, as he literally sweats out a radio interview with the shrewd Meredith.

Rochester, Adèle
Jane Eyre, 1847
Charlotte Brontë
The precocious little ward of MR ROCHESTER, Adèle, though reputedly not his own child, is the illegitimate daughter of his former mistress, a Parisian dancer. Petite, pretty, and coquettish, and very fond of dressing herself up, she has no talents to speak of, but under JANE EYRE's tuition she at least starts to learn self-discipline. A highly excitable child, what she lacks in learning she more than makes up for in affection.

Rochester, Bertha (Antoinette), née Cosway
Wide Sargasso Sea, 1966
Jean Rhys

Known to the world as the 'mad wife in the attic', the first Mrs Rochester is portrayed by Rhys as a tragic heroine, a beautiful Creole heiress whose life is crushed by the prejudice and subsequent rejection of others. She leads a life of deep-rooted isolation and unhappiness until her marriage to Mr Rochester. 'I never wished to live before I knew you,' she says, but ultimately he too diminishes and rejects her, and she is driven to despair, both by her all-consuming longing for him, and by the overwhelming horror of his betrayal of her.

Rochester, Mr
Jane Eyre, 1847
Charlotte Brontë

The dark, swarthy master of Thornfield Hall, Mr Rochester's moods are not to be predicted. Often gruff and short-tempered, he is in fact a kind and intelligent man, who secretly loves JANE EYRE as much as she does him. Already worn down by a life of dissipation and the tragic burden of a foolish and youthful marriage, he is forced to endure loneliness and learn humility before, maimed and blinded but spiritually intact, he is reunited with Jane.

Rock, Mr
Concluding, 1948
Henry Green

A retired scientist, Rock lives in a cottage in the grounds of a school, somewhere in an England dominated by a form of welfare state, at some time in the future. He is in danger of losing his cottage if elected to a home for elderly scientists, something he strenuously tries to prevent. Vigorously opposed to being organized against his will, the hard-pressed, long-suffering, lonely and emotionally vulnerable Rock stands for the spirit of individuality and dogged opposition to bureaucratic control. But just in case he should win all the reader's sympathy, he is also truculent and self-pitying.

Rod → Mal, Rod and Simon

Roddice, Hermione
Women in Love, 1920
D H Lawrence

Tall, sophisticated, fashionable and exotic, Hermione Roddice is 'a medium for the culture of ideas'. She collects interesting people, but while lavishly generous is intensely manipulative. She has a strong religious faith, and is arguably beautiful, yet in her face paint and flamboyant gowns she often appears macabre. She is intelligent and well-read, but brittle, a snob, even a bore. 'All her life, she had sought to make herself invulnerable, unassailable, beyond reach of the world's judgement.' Yet the permanent chink in her armour is her utter lack of self-sufficiency, the appalling suspicion that she has no inner emotional life at all.

Rodemaker, Rob
'Among the Corn-Rows', in *Main-Travelled Roads*, 1892, revised editions 1899, 1922, 1930
Hamlin Garland

A young sod-buster of buoyantly self-reliant nature, striving to make fertile the dry plains of Wisconsin. 'He was of German parentage, a middle-sized, cheery, wide-awake, good-looking young fellow – a typical claim-holder. He was always confident, jovial, and full of plans for the future … "I come West, just like a thousand other fellers, to get a start where the cussed European aristocracy hadn't got a holt on the people".'

Roderigo
Othello, 1603/4
William Shakespeare

'A gull'd Venetian gentleman', in love with DESDEMONA, who becomes the devious IAGO's ally and source of money in his plot against OTHELLO. Easily manipulated, he is a foolish, superficial fop, sustained in the audience's sympathy only by his adoration of his chosen love. Eventually killed by CASSIO during a bungled attempted murder, he is a victim both of Iago and of unrequited love.

Rodgers, Mildred
Of Human Bondage, 1915
W Somerset Maugham

Emotionally and materially rapacious, she is PHILIP CAREY's mistress. She takes but does not return either his love or his generosity, thus confirming him in the bleak Oedipal isolation into which his mother's early death has plunged him.

Rodney, Stella
The Heat of the Day, 1949
Elizabeth Bowen

An upper-middle-class divorcee in her forties, pretty and cultured, living in wartime London. Her ex-husband has recently died and her son Roderick is in the army. The 'screaming cat' Luftwaffe raids of September 1940 bring her together with her lover ROBERT KELWAY, but the liaison exposes her to blackmail by the shadowy HARRISON, who declares Kelway to be a spy.

Rodney, William
Night and Day, 1919
Virginia Woolf

KATHARINE HILBERY's fiancé, a nervous man with a very odd appearance. He is pompous and pretentious, but also quite pathetic; hopelessly inarticulate, he becomes rather ridiculous in his inability to express his feelings. Nonetheless, he eventually manages to win his true love, Cassandra.

Rodolpho
A View from the Bridge, 1955
Arthur Miller

BEATRICE CARBONE's cousin, a fair-haired, handsome young man who illegally emigrates to the United States because of his admiration for American culture of the 1950s and his desire to be an American. He is initially attractive and exciting to the sheltered CATHERINE CARBONE, and they fall in love, precipitating the play's tragedy, where the perverse EDDIE CARBONE rejects Rodolpho, using the excuse that he is 'funny' and 'not right' (ie effeminate) and betrays him – and his brother, MARCO – to the authorities.

Rodriguez, Don
The Adventures of Roderick Random, 1748
Tobias Smollett
A wealthy Spanish nobleman who (evincing that race's apparently endless facility in Smollett's eyes for being something other than they appear) is revealed to be the long-lost father of RODERICK RANDOM.

Roehampton, Lord
Endymion, 1880
Benjamin Disraeli
Disraeli's version of Lord Palmerston, a prime minister usually considered to be unremittingly tough and uncompromising, is both sympathetic and surprisingly gentle, allowing his mild and humorous side to show through the bluff exterior.

Roger
The Owl Service, 1967
Alan Garner
ALISON's stepbrother, a prickly, insecure character. Initially he is prepared to attempt friendship with GWYN, but Gwyn's bluntness and Roger's sneering manner mean they soon fall out. His overbearing, mocking ways betray the unsureness of his position in the house of his stepsister, having a new stepmother (a mysteriously unseen figure) as well as supernatural forces to contend with. Despite this, it is Roger who is open-hearted and flexible enough to recognize how Alison can be released from the evil power of the owls into the gentle ways of the flowers: in other words, to see the alternative patterns contained within the owl-patterned dinner service.

Roger
Water with Berries, 1971
George Lamming
A musician of East Indian descent and fellow exile of DEREK and TEETON, Roger is confused and angry about his racial identity. He is vulnerable and introverted, traits which contribute to his mental collapse when he discovers his white girlfriend is pregnant. He is a secretive person in both his musical creativity and his relationships, and stress brings out a destructiveness in him which leads him to commit arson.

Rogers, Captain
Jack Holborn, 1964
Leon Garfield
LORD SHERINGHAM's twin brother, he has a 'wickedly wirtuous' air about him that makes his crew instantly deferential. Even when not physically present, he still wields a powerful influence over his men, rather as a wicked father continues to control his children. He has the fresh-faced, close-cropped air of a country gentleman, but the sinister character that lies within is betrayed by his cold 'fish-like' eyes. He cynically makes use of JACK HOLBORN's search

for his mother to secure his loyalty and provide him with a second pair of eyes about the ship, to warn against possible mutiny. He has a desperate dignity about him, but it is hollow, based on the false hope that he will be saved from the noose and from admitting the truth about himself.

Rogers, Major Robert
Northwest Passage, 1937
Kenneth Roberts
Based on a real character, he is an adventurer, Indian-fighter, traveller and explorer, who commands the famous Rogers' Rangers in the war against the French in colonial America of the 1750s. He is a 'hell-raiser and a caution', whose massive build gives the impression of 'a kind of physical unkillableness', but he is 'at heart, a good-natured man'. He is a strict disciplinarian, and absolutely tireless, with an 'intense and violent energy of mind and body', and 'something elemental about him'. He is an inspirational leader of men. He becomes obsessed with finding the Northwest Passage to Japan, but is cheated, and has 'fallen low' by the end, although something indestructible in his spirit still remains.

Rogers, Milton K
The Rise of Silas Lapham, 1885
William Dean Howells
A former partner and creditor of SILAS LAPHAM, edged out of the business just before its moment of success. Both the Laphams recognize the wrong-doing, but Silas prefers to keep it buried, while his wife, MRS PERSIS LAPHAM, worries about it more openly. Rogers's rejection is the flaw in Lapham's fabulous 'rise' that threatens to compromise it fatally.

Roister Doister, Ralph
Ralph Roister Doister, 1552/3
Nicholas Udall
A wealthy buffoon, who boasts of his martial prowess while actually being an inept coward. He is given to falling exaggeratedly in love with women and overreacting when they reject him. Conceited and susceptible to flattery, he is too stupid to realize that MATHEWE MERYGREEKE is manipulating and mocking him, especially in his wooing of CHRISTIAN CUSTANCE.

Rojack, Stephen Richards
An American Dream, 1965
Norman Mailer
Professor of existential psychology at a small university in New York and author of *The Psychology of the Hangman*, he was a near-contemporary of John F Kennedy at Harvard where he had been 'a humdrum athlete and, as a student, excessively bright'. Husband – and murderer – of Deborah Caughlin Mangaravidi Kelly, an Irish-Sicilian who 'would have been bored by a diamond as big as the Ritz'.

Rola, or Madame Tortoise
A Dance of the Forests, 1960
Wole Soyinka
The village prostitute in both her past and present lives, and the langorous consort of MATA KHARIBU, she is a beautiful but pitiless predator,

content to see men degrade and even destroy themselves for her favours. Transported back into the mythical past, she foretells a future plagued by exploitation and violence.

Roland
Elidor, 1968
Alan Garner
Although he is the youngest member of the Watson family, Roland is by far the strongest-willed. He is sensitive, 'too highly strung' as his father complains; 'always imagining things' as his brothers would have it, and always ready to take a risk. Roland is chosen by MALEBRON to help save Elidor from darkness and evil because only he has the vision and power to undertake the quest. His mental powers are so strong that he is able to conjure up a real, physical door into the Mound of Vandwy, through which Elidor can enter the real world and vice-versa. Roland is the catalyst for the supernatural events which follow, and he is fully aware of his powers to both create and destroy.

Roland, Childe
'Childe Roland to the Dark Tower Came', in *Dramatic Romances*, 1845
Robert Browning
Roland is on a quest through wasteland, and peoples the silence with horrors from his own imagination. He finds the tower he seeks amid hills on which other questors stand, but never reveals the object of his quest. He has survived, but for what?

Roland, Christian
The Catherine Wheel, 1960
Elizabeth Harrower
A 30-year-old unemployed actor living in London, he is a selfish, moody and volatile young man who craves attention. 'Fair, above middle-height, with a compelling eye ... [and] overweening self-confidence', Roland has a drink problem and is unable to hold down a job. He forms relationships with women through a combination of charm and an ability to elicit pity: 'he had a bitter, private, despairing intensity about him'. CLEMENCY JAMES is alternately entranced and sickened by him, taken in by his disarming honesty about his numerous problems – 'his faults and virtues were on a grand scale, equally'. She eventually recognizes his manipulative and abusive behaviour, seeing him to be 'weird and ruthless and a broken-up baby who loved no one but himself'.

Roma, Richard
Glengarry Glen Ross, 1983
David Mamet
Roma is one of four Chicago real-estate salesmen competing in an office contest, the one selling the most lucrative land being promised the prize of a Cadillac, the second a set of steak knives and the remaining two to be fired. Roma, a predatory rising star, is determined to win. At a Chinese restaurant, he induces James Lingk to buy land at Glengarry Glen Ross, partly by flattering him with homespun philosophy. Roma appears relaxed and confiding; in fact, he is watchful and calculating, edging Lingk into a position of

vulnerability while encouraging him to regard him as his new-found friend, even guide. He is tough, sharp, ruthless, but his later aggression while under pressure fails to conceal a moral cowardice.

Romeo
Romeo and Juliet, 1591–6
William Shakespeare
Romeo, the teenage son of the Montagues, is infatuated at first by the fair Rosaline – or at least with the idea of being in love with her. He behaves in the traditional way of the lover – not eating, not sleeping and writing poetry, yet his impulsive nature is evident from the fact that he changes his affection so quickly to JULIET. Because of his immaturity he finds it difficult to deal with reverses calmly, but is subject to emotional extremes. His friendships are deep and he is held in respect by some of his enemies, but his impetuosity and his scorning of fate conspire to bring about his downfall.

Romford, Mr Facey
Mr Facey Romford's Hounds, 1865
R S Surtees
A fox-hunting man who embodies the essential qualities of Surtees Man: common sense rather than intellectualism, loyalty, humour, and a unshakeable facility for extracting good from any situation, no matter how bleak.

Romola
Romola, 1863
George Eliot
A beautiful and proud heroine, Romola shows surprising humility by wishing to marry some great scholar and act as his secretary. Having done the latter for her blind father, her life has been 'self-repressing' and 'colourless' until love and marriage with TITO MELEMA. The subsequent break-up finds her unsure of purpose in life, but after flight and attempted suicide she finds her vocation in fellowship with those suffering from plague and hardship, and in affirmation that 'God's kingdom is something wider' than the zealot friar GIROLAMO SAVONAROLA's vision.

Rosalba, Princess, also known as **Betsinda**
The Rose and the Ring, 1855
W M Thackeray
The daughter of the King of Crim Tartary, she is lost and presumed dead, the apparent victim of a curse by FAIRY BLACKSTICK, but survives and is taken up as the serving-girl of the Paflagonian PRINCESS ANGELICA. She is quiet and accommodating, unthinkingly loyal. Her secret is inscribed in a (not very difficult) puzzle embroidered on the edge of her cloak: PRIN ROSAL. Predictably, things come right in the end and she is united with PRINCE GIGLIO.

Rosalind
As You Like It, c.1600
William Shakespeare
Daughter of DUKE SENIOR, Rosalind is witty, impulsive and a bit of a tomboy. Banished and disguised as a boy, she finds refuge in the forest. Having previously fallen instantly in love with

ORLANDO, in the forest she undertakes to teach him how to woo his Rosalind and thus reveals the depth of her own love. She 'organizes' the romances in the play and ensures a happy ending for all.

Rosaline

Love's Labour's Lost, not later than 1594
William Shakespeare

An attendant lady to the PRINCESS OF FRANCE, and the wittiest of her little group. This makes her the natural counterpart to BEROWNE, who falls in love with her. She takes the lead in defying KING FERDINAND and his companions when they approach dressed as Russians, and she organizes the swapping of ladies' masks to confuse them. She gives Berowne the harshest task at the end: he must, ironically, 'visit the speechless sick, and still converse/With groaning wretches'.

Rosalynde

Rosalynde, or Euphues' Golden Legacy, 1590
Thomas Lodge

A prose romance interspersed with lyrics, *Rosalynde, or Euphues' Golden Legacy* is most widely known today as the principal source of Shakespeare's *As You Like It*, Lodge's Rosalynde being the original of Shakespeare's ROSALIND. Lodge's narrative, though, is a true pastoral, taking place in a romanticized Ardennes area of France rather than the Forest of Arden in Warwickshire, but the story of the high-born woman is similar to that which appears in the later play. Rosalynde, mild yet spirited, is really little more than a conventional pastoral type, showing by her actions that: 'younger brethren, though inferior in years, yet may be superior to honours'.

Rose, Caroline

The Comforters, 1957
Muriel Spark

Having converted to Catholicism, due to intellectual conviction rather than emotional attraction, Caroline no longer lives with her inquisitive boyfriend, Laurence Manders. Neurotic by nature, she is frightened when she starts to hear a typewriter and voices, but eventually realizes that she is sensing the composition of the book in which she is a character. She is writing a work on the modern novel and, not surprisingly, 'having difficulty with the chapter on realism'. Prim, fastidious and eager for truth, she criticizes her creator's taste and plot construction.

Rose, George Arthur, subsequently Pope Hadrian VII

Hadrian VII, 1904
'Baron Corvo'

A transparent act of wish-fulfilment on the author's part, Rose is a poor literary scholar who is dramatically elected pope, a figure of cloying goodness and cartoon emotions.

Rose, Joe

Enduring Love, 1997
Ian McEwan

The narrator of the novel, Rose is an author of scientific articles who encounters JED PARRY in the course of a tragic ballooning accident one summer's day on the Chiltern Hills. A meticulous, rational man, deeply immersed in the history of science and content in his relationship with Clarissa, an academic specializing in the works of Keats, Rose discovers his faith in reason undermined by Parry's obsessive stalking, and his bombardment of him with messages declaring his love and claiming that Rose loves him in return. Emphatically rejecting Parry, he becomes the victim of a murder attempt by killers employed by his now vengeful nemesis. As his relationship with Clarissa collapses, Rose is forced to conclude that reason and reasonable behaviour are not fixed entities but open to a variety of motivations and interpretations.

Rose, Serafina delle

The Rose Tattoo, 1951
Tennessee Williams

A volatile, sensual, vigorous Sicilian seamstress, Rose had lost her customary lust for life after the premature death of her truck driver husband, since when she has dutifully watched over the chastity of her 15-year-old daughter. However, her hot-blooded flamboyance is aroused once again by Alvaro Mangiacavallo who, despite having 'the face of a clown' is physically similar to Rose's husband and, like him, a truck driver. Her sexuality and passion is fired all the more by the revelation of her husband's infidelity.

Rosen, Rifkah

Poor Fellow My Country, 1975
Xavier Herbert

A Jewish refugee, Rifkah visits Lily Lagoons, the Northern Territory farm run by the liberal JEREMY DELACY during the months before World War II. Her understanding of the land and its people is in marked contrast to that of the anthropologist, Fabian Cootes. Rifkah is running from the past; she is also searching for an identity and a stable future, and as such, she has much in common with PRINDY, Delacy's mixed-race grandson. A sensitive, spiritual woman who radiates compassion and sincerity, she finds temporary fulfilment in a relationship with a priest.

Rosencrantz

Rosencrantz and Guildenstern Are Dead, 1967
Tom Stoppard

Along with his companion GUILDENSTERN, Rosencrantz is a character with no apparent place in life. Lacking a history, and with no discernible future, he is adrift in the present. Unlike Guildenstern, who seeks out a meaning for events, Rosencrantz is prepared to accept his situation without question. Open, innocent, naive and uninterested in what is happening to them, he is protected at first by Guildenstern, but as matters become increasingly uncertain, the position is reversed because his lack of curiosity prevents him being emotionally involved. His attempts to make Guildenstern happy are doomed, since he is unable to understand the reason for his depression.

Rosencrantz and Guildenstern
Hamlet, 1601/2
William Shakespeare

Two sides of one coin, they are sent for by CLAUDIUS to spy on HAMLET. Undergraduate wits, they are easily duped by the king and seen through by the prince, who callously organizes their deaths in England.

Rosetree, Harry
Riders in the Chariot, 1961
Patrick White

Haim Rosenbaum has a 'gift of assimilation', having successfully shed his Jewish identity and religion to emerge as Harry Rosetree, completely fused with Christian Australia and a keen advocate of the self-made-man ethic. With his wife, Shirl, and the 'kids', he lives in a textured-brick house in suburban Sydney, travelling to work each day to manage his Brighta Bicycle Lamps factory. Here, the newly-arrived German Jewish refugee, MORDECAI HIMMELFARB, takes a menial job on the assembly line. Like MRS JOLLEY and MRS FLACK, Rosetree is disturbed by his employee's religious orthodoxy, but for rather different reasons. While Himmelfarb's Jewish-ness inflames the ladies' racial prejudice, it pricks Rosetree's conscience, forcing him to question his motives and actions.

Rosetta
The Age of Anxiety, 1948
W H Auden

A buyer for a large New York department store and an habitué of a claustrophobic bar. Jewish by birth, the single, driving force of her life is the fear of poverty and of displacement.

Rosewater, Eliot
God Bless You, Mr Rosewater, 1965
Kurt Vonnegut, Jr

The staggeringly wealthy President of the Rosewater Foundation, he is 'crazy as a loon', a 'drunkard, a Utopian dreamer, a tinhorn saint, an aimless fool'. He is an expert sailor and good skier, but decides to use his fortune for philanthropic purposes among the poorest and most unwanted dregs of society, driven by deep, repressed memories of earlier tragedies. He is a 'flamboyantly sick man', inspired by the wilder ideas of science-fiction writers.

Ross
Ross, 1960
Terence Rattigan

Rattigan's portrait of T E Lawrence in Arabia (Ross is a pseudonym Lawrence once used) is partly an adventure story, in which Lawrence is shown to be an intellectual, practical man of action. It is also a serious study of an enigmatic man with an aversion, almost a fear, of fame, and a compulsion for assuming different identities, enabling him to withdraw from and reappear in the company of others at will. The play discreetly intimates that his withdrawal into anonymity after his capture and release by the Turks was a consequence of his discovering that he enjoyed being the victim of the kind of brutality the regime administered.

Ross, Col
Guard of Honor, 1948
James Gould Cozzens

A wise and balanced senior officer at the scandal-torn USAF base in Florida, he recognizes that prejudice and hatred are inevitable components of human nature and that (in a straightforward expression of the novel's moral position) 'a man must stand up and do the best he can with what there is'.

Rossiter, David
Anderby Wold, 1923
Winifred Holtby

A man of great intelligence, erudition and political integrity, he introduces himself as a 'rabid socialist of the most dangerous and disreputable type'. Despite his ill health and crippling reticence, he has come to Anderby to preach cooperation and organization to the rural working class. He is hated and feared by them as a crude, violent and dangerous subversive, but his naive idealism, good humour and playful wit endear him to MARY ROBSON, the local landowner with whom he forms an affectionate and sexually-charged relationship.

Rotherwood, Cedric of → Cedric the Saxon

Rothsay, Duke of Rothsay, Prince David of Scotland
The Fair Maid of Perth, or St Valentine's Day, in *Chronicles of the Canongate: Second Series*, 1828
Sir Walter Scott

The son and heir of ROBERT III, KING OF SCOTLAND, he is a wild and licentious youth, granted his dukedom (only the second in Scottish history) to give his career some semblance of dignity. His hand has effectively been put up for auction by the DUKE OF ALBANY, and he is unsatisfactorily married to the Earl of Dunbar and March's daughter. Loyal and trusting, he is murdered, probably by the agency of his banished friend, SIR JOHN RAMORNY, whose pardon he has sought.

Rothwell, Ingrid
A Kind of Loving, 1960
Stan Barstow

Ingrid loves VIC BROWN because he has the very qualities she lacks: imagination, originality and insight. She seems sweet, but dull. However, although simple in her outlook, she is not always straightforward in her motives and is certainly more astute than she appears. The victim of a domineering mother, she gradually becomes more assertive as she matures. Apparently confused by Vic's rejection of her, she actually understands, but buries, the truth. She is a victim of his disillusionment – she shattered his dream of an ideal woman, simply by being real.

Rothwell, Mrs
A Kind of Loving, 1960
Stan Barstow

An unashamed social climber, 'Ma Rothwell' has more respect for wealth and status than for intellect and 'the Arts'. She is a Conservative and a passionate Royalist, and is unimpressed by new ideas. Her husband works away from home most of the time, so she has had sole charge of her now married daughter, INGRID ROTHWELL. She tends to speak and think on behalf of Ingrid as well as interfering directly in her life. Mrs Rothwell enjoys a good argument, especially with her son-in-law, VIC BROWN. He describes her as 'stupid, bigoted and ignorant', but in fact she shows signs of being cunning, even erudite.

Rougemont, Sukie
The Witches of Eastwick, 1984
John Updike
Less beautiful and gifted than her sister-witches, she has nonetheless a 'simian' charm and intensity that makes her a powerful conduit for the coven's spells. It is clear, too, that the warlock DARRYL VAN HORNE is not susceptible to conventional ideas of female beauty.

Rouncewell, Mr
Bleak House, 1853
Charles Dickens
The elder son of MRS ROUNCEWELL and brother of MR GEORGE ROUNCEWELL, he is a great ironmaster who owns a successful ironworks and treats his employees humanely. His son Watt marries LADY DEDLOCK's maid, Rosa. He is reunited with his long-lost brother when Mr George, released from false arrest, turns up at the ironworks.

Rouncewell, Mr George
Bleak House, 1853
Charles Dickens
Called 'Mr George', he is the younger son of MRS ROUNCEWELL and the brother of MR ROUNCEWELL. He lost touch with his family when he ran away as a boy to enlist in the army, where CAPTAIN HAWDON was his commanding officer and MR BAGNET his comrade. Decent and upright, he owns George's Shooting Gallery in London and kindly looks after his lame, disfigured employee, Phil Squod. He is wrongly arrested for the murder of MR TULKINGHORN, who has tried to blackmail him. Released, he is reunited with his mother and brother and moves to Chesney Wold to care for SIR LEICESTER DEDLOCK.

Rouncewell, Mrs
Bleak House, 1853
Charles Dickens
The handsome and neat old housekeeper of SIR LEICESTER and LADY DEDLOCK at Chesney Wold and the mother of MR ROUNCEWELL and MR GEORGE ROUNCEWELL. Her reunion with the long-lost Mr George is arranged by MRS BAGNET.

Rousillon, Countess of
All's Well That Ends Well, 1602–3
William Shakespeare
Elderly and recently widowed, the Countess of Rousillon is BERTRAM's mother and the guardian of HELENA. The countess embodies the house of Rousillon, the traditional values of honour and feudal benevolence. The elegiac, nostalgic spirit of Rousillon provides both the context and counterpoint to the actions of the younger generation. Yet the countess's authority is

limited: although she thinks of Helena as her daughter, she cannot alone convince her son or others that she is their social equal. A woman of great integrity, the countess is kindly, humanitarian, wise and resilient. Bernard Shaw called this 'the most beautiful old woman's part ever written'.

Routledge, Mrs Amanda
Hotel de Dream, 1976
Emma Tennant
The stout, untidy proprietress of the Westringham, a squalid residential hotel in a near-derelict part of Kensington, her comfortable home until she was widowed. Like the residents who, she notes, 'sleep a lot', Mrs Routledge dreams, but hers are conscious ones. She fabricates a mysterious past for herself with which to charm the property developer who has secretly bought the hotel – for demolition – and who will make her 'young and comfortable' elsewhere. Meanwhile, flavouring her fantasies with gin, she lives vicariously the glamour and excitement of her social life.

Rover, Ralph
The Coral Island, 1857
R M Ballantyne
One of three boys shipwrecked on a desert island, he is the natural second-in-command to JACK MARTIN. Gifted with initiative, and prepared to cope in fine spirit with the deprivations of their situation, he happily accepts the role of NCO to Jack's officer in a situation that demands real nerve and enterprise.

Rowan, Laura
The Bird Falls Down, 1966
Rebecca West
Laura is the 18-year-old daughter of an MP and a beautiful, unhappy Russian mother. Drawn into the pre-World War I atmosphere of terror that demoralized the Russian aristocracy, Laura displays both worldly-wise understanding and an incredible ingenuousness. However, her attitude to events is unclear and undefined; she is a vapid girl with a tenuous grip on reality.

Rowena, Lady
Ivanhoe, 1819
Sir Walter Scott
The young kinswoman and ward of CEDRIC THE SAXON, she is a lineal descendant of King Alfred and is thus the brightest jewel in Saxon England. She is fair and blue-eyed, and is loved by and loves in return Cedric's son IVANHOE; she is, however, intended as the consort of ATHELSTANE OF CONINGSBURGH, a match that Cedric considers advantageous. (She is ridiculed in Thackeray's satirical sequel, *Rebecca and Rowena*, 1850.)

Rowley, Emily
He Knew He Was Right, 1869
Anthony Trollope
The eldest of Sir Marmaduke Rowley's eight daughters, she marries LOUIS TREVELYAN. Her upbringing in the Mandarin Islands has ensured that she is strong enough 'to sit on her horse the whole day long, and would never be weary with dancing at the Government House balls'. Her

friendship with COL FREDERIC OSBORNE arouses her husband's insane jealousy, but she is too stubborn – and confident of her innocence – to respond as he wishes and forbid her friend to visit. The result is tragedy.

Rowley, Nora
He Knew He Was Right, 1869
Anthony Trollope
The sister of EMILY ROWLEY, and her companion after her marriage. She is courted by the wealthy CHARLES GLASCOCK, and is predisposed to accept him, having had an education and upbringing 'which teaches girls to believe that it is a crime to marry a man without an assured income'. After a lengthy struggle with her finer feelings, however, she chooses love over riches, and marries the impecunious HUGH STANSBURY.

Roxana
Roxana, 1724
Daniel Defoe
Once a high-class kept woman with an unhappy first marriage and several children behind her, she is now respectably married to a wealthy Dutch merchant, but finds her present life overshadowed by her fear of the past being disclosed. Driven by fierce greed and dangerous vanity, she uses her natural intelligence and cunning to protect her new-found status. She allows expediency to determine her morality, a decision which leads her to adultery and connivance at actions of terrifying ugliness. A strong, independent and rather frightening woman, her repentance late in life lacks conviction.

Roxburgh, Austin
A Fringe of Leaves, 1976
Patrick White
An English gentleman whose family had moved to Cheltenham in the hope that his health might benefit from the mild Gloucestershire climate, the sickly Austin Roxburgh marries ELLEN ROXBURGH, a lonely woman whom he meets in the West Country. Theirs is an inhibited, melancholy marriage. Austin's passion (and refuge) is reading; when he and his wife are shipwrecked off the coast of Australia, Austin takes care to save his precious copy of Virgil. Yet the experience converts an emotionally repressed and morally strict man into one with a tenacious instinct for survival. In the face of such adversity, Austin turns almost into a man of action: 'the trappings of wealth and station [were] stripped from him'.

Roxburgh, Ellen
A Fringe of Leaves, 1976
Patrick White
Born in Cornwall and raised on a near-derelict farm, Ellen is a lonely young woman in an isolated, desolate landscape. A little afraid of life, she marries the invalid, AUSTIN ROXBURGH. Although at heart a melancholy figure, she becomes a woman of enormous physical and emotional strength. Together with her husband, she visits Van Diemen's Land (Tasmania), where she encounters Austin's brother, Garnet. To her horror, she discovers her carefully repressed

sexuality aroused by a coarse, passionate man she intensely dislikes. Following a series of traumatic events, she undergoes a complex spiritual renewal which leads her to understand the essential brutality of life, and the nature of good, evil and divine love.

Roxy (Roxana)
The Tragedy of Pudd'nhead Wilson, 1894
Mark Twain
A 16th part of black blood makes her a Negro in law, though only her speech distinguishes her from 'white' people. Although she accepts the prevailing belief that it is blood, and not skin colour, that distinguishes the races, she is unable to face one consequence of this belief – separation from her son CHAMBERS through his sale as a Negro slave. She therefore substitutes him for her owner's son, TOM DRISCOLL, thereby creating the basis for the story's many ironies. Not the least of these is that her son becomes her cruel master and brings her only suffering and heartache.

Royall, Charity
Summer, 1917
Edith Wharton
The ward of Lawyer Royall, Charity is a waif from a squalid background. She is shy but covers it with bravado and diffidence. Contemptuously aloof from the parochial villagers of North Dormer, she throws herself into a blissful affair with the urbane Lucius Harney which leaves her exultant and ecstatic. Later, pregnant and abandoned, she apathetically marries the wicked Lawyer. Her world collapses and she submits in a daze to him, yet, paradoxically, feels protected and secure in her despair.

Roylance, Sir Archibald
John Macnab, 1925
John Buchan
A coltish youngster, whose enthusiasm is mostly directed towards his thoroughbred horses, he is the owner of the small Highland retreat where he and his co-conspirators invent the mythical 'JOHN MACNAB'.

Rozanov, John Robert
The Philosopher's Pupil, 1983
Iris Murdoch
Ageing, exhausted and physically repulsive, he is the magical redeemer figure at the centre of the book. A distinguished but disillusioned and wearied academic, the feelings of terror, awe and compulsive desire he arouses in those he encounters are utterly mysterious. His power to disrupt and transform the life of an entire community is similarly unaccountable and apparently unintentional.

Rozanov, Sergei
Ararat, 1983
D M Thomas
A 50-year-old Russian poet, Rozanov spends the night with a blind student of his poetry, and at her suggestion spins an impromptu tale on 'Improvisation'. He casts this tale as three stories with the common theme of Mount Ararat, told by people with Armenian connections, who have

been thrown together by chance: a drunken Russian poet, an American woman romantic novelist, and an Armenian storyteller who teaches Russian literature. A skilled extempore storyteller, like his Armenian grandfather, Rozanov presents a series of cunningly interwoven stories.

Ruarangi
The Golden Lover, 1943
Douglas Stewart
The fat, lazy Maori husband of the beautiful and provocative TAWHAI. His chief concern is his stomach, and his claim upon warrior status is a joke. 'Of the earth', his dreams do not move much beyond eating and sleeping. In the words of his wife, 'he is pleasant for a husband, a kind of walking joke'.

Ruby, Jack
Libra, 1988
Don DeLillo
Dallas nightclub owner and killer of LEE HARVEY OSWALD, alleged assassin of John F Kennedy. Sleazily patriotic, he mixes with gangsters and 'dancers'. Paunchy and balding but with an impressively positive self-image, 'he was a physical-culture nut when he had the time'.

Rudge, Barnaby
Barnaby Rudge, 1841
Charles Dickens
The son of MR and MRS RUDGE, he is simpleminded but good-natured, with a fantastic appearance. Always accompanied by his raven, GRIP, he wanders about the countryside and gets swept up with the Gordon Rioters in their destructive acts. Arrested and condemned, he is pardoned through the intervention of GABRIEL VARDEN and returns to live with his mother.

Rudge, Mr and Mrs (Mary)
Barnaby Rudge, 1841
Charles Dickens
Rudge is the former steward of Reuben Haredale. Twenty years before the events in the novel, Rudge murders Haredale and his gardener. When the disfigured body of the gardener is found, people believe it to be that of Rudge. He lives secretively, moving as a malign, ghostly presence, and occasionally visiting his wife and son, Mary and BARNABY RUDGE, to demand money. Mary pretends to be a widow, and GABRIEL VARDEN helps in her attempts to hide from her husband. MR GEOFFREY HAREDALE unmasks Rudge as the murderer of his brother, and Rudge is arrested and hanged. When the Gordon Riots end, Mary and Barnaby move to the farm at the Maypole Inn.

Rudkus, Jurgis
The Jungle, 1906
Upton Sinclair
A poor Lithuanian immigrant whose desperate sufferings in the Chicago stockyards are described in terms appropriate to a martyrdom. Downtrodden by his employers, short-time work and obscene conditions, he is brutalized and stripped of moral dignity until he recognizes that socialism offers a way out. Few fictional

characters have had so direct an influence on social conditions; as a result of Sinclair's novel, a Pure Food and Drug Bill went rapidly through Congress.

Rufford, Nancy
The Good Soldier, 1915
Ford Madox Ford
Often called simply 'the girl', Nancy is tall and thin with long black hair, an unfortunate victim in the corrupt and complicated world of the characters around her. Her guardians, EDWARD and LEONORA ASHBURNHAM, have ensured she is – at the age of 21 – the embodiment of purity and innocence. They have given her a convent education and protected her from all sources of evil. Their cruelty in this respect is disturbingly revealed when Nancy awakens to the realities of life. She is hopelessly ill-equipped to deal properly with any situation and eventually goes insane.

Rufio
Caesar and Cleopatra, 1898
George Bernard Shaw
A Roman officer, unshakably loyal to CAIUS JULIUS CAESAR, Rufio is middle-aged, 'very blunt, prompt and rough, with small clear eyes, and plump nose and cheeks'. He is also in excellent physical condition and kills CLEOPATRA's nurse, FTATATEETA, in revenge for her murder of POTHINUS.

Rugby, John
The Merry Wives of Windsor, c.1597
William Shakespeare
'An honest, willing, kind fellow', Rugby is the servant of DR CAIUS. His greatest fault is that 'he is given over to prayer; he is something peevish that way'. Although he appears only briefly in the play, it appears his loyalty is hardly appreciated by his employer.

Rummyng, Elynour
'The Tunnyng of Elynour Rummyng', 1517
John Skelton
A bawdy old alewife who brews 'noppy ale' for all and sundry who pass by her shop in Leatherhead, so long as they be 'good ale drynkers'. She is notably fond of her own brew, and the poem, which depicts the low life of the period with coarseness and vitality, is concerned with describing the gallery of rogues and rascals who pass through her alehouse.

Rumpole, Horace
Rumpole of the Bailey, 1978
The Trials of Rumpole, 1979, et seq
John Mortimer
An Old Bailey hack, who has no wish to take silk. After a mediocre start at a minor public school and armed with a third-class degree in law from Oxford, he made a dazzling entry to his legal career, achieving some astonishing acquittals, as in the case of the Great Brighton Benefit Club Forgery. Ever unlucky in love, he was proposed to by Hilda, daughter of his Head of Chambers, who took his silence for assent. Grubbily resplendent in his tattered court garb, endlessly puffing at small cigars, Rumpole stalks the

corridors of the Old Bailey and the cells of Brixton and make occasional forays to Pommeroy's Wine Bar. He is kept going by the faint hope that his actions will keep some young lad from following in his father's criminal footsteps.

Rupert of Hentzau
The Prisoner of Zenda, 1894
Rupert of Hentzau, 1898
Anthony Hope

Debonair, villainous, ambitious, Rupert plots to steal the red rose sent by the queen to RUDOLF RASSENDYLL, with a letter, and give them to the jealous king. Rassendyll returns, still the king's double. Forced by events to kill the king before he opens the box with the rose, Rupert confronts Rassendyll, impudently offering to serve him as king. Rassendyll tears the letter from him and bids him fight 'like a gentleman'. Smiling and merciless, Rupert cheats. He is killed, but his malice continues after death.

Rush, Ann
Bring Larks and Heroes, 1967
Thomas Keneally

As a trusty in an Australian penal settlement, she is close to both prisoners and guards. It seems that she has entered into a secret marriage with the guard CORPORAL PHELIM HALLORAN, whose loyalty to the system has been undermined.

Rushworth, Mr
Mansfield Park, 1814
Jane Austen

A wealthy friend of TOM BERTRAM, and a 'heavy young man, with not more than common sense' who is 'inclined to marry'. Although at times obliging, he can also be sullen and resentful. He enjoys a day's sport, boasts of his dogs, is jealous of his neighbours and zealous in pursuit of poachers, and likes the idea of acting in a 'blue dress and pink satin cloak'. As someone who, were it not for his 'twelve thousand a year … would be a very stupid fellow', he characteristically fails to perceive that his marriage to MARIA BERTRAM is ill-fated from the start.

Russell, Lady
Persuasion, 1818
Jane Austen

Long-term neighbour to SIR WALTER ELLIOT, and godmother and mentor to his daughter ANNE ELLIOT, widowed Lady Russell, while being a kind and good woman, is at the same time a little snobbish in her attitudes, allowing a person's rank and good fortune to unduly colour her opinion of them. She is a big influence on Anne, but the advice she offers, though well-meaning, is unfortunately not always sound.

Russell, Oliver
Talking it Over, 1991
Love, etc, 2000
Julian Barnes

In his early thirties in the first novel, and an old school-friend of STUART HUGHES, Oliver is charming, indolent, pedantic; a philanderer delighting in convoluted wordplay (and overuse

of the word 'crepuscular') and a cynicism he believes is playful irony. Having lost his ill-paid job as a language teacher, he turns to various odd jobs before laying siege to Stuart's wife, GILLIAN WYATT. His pleasure at usurping Stuart seems as intense as his love for and subsequent marriage to Gillian. Unreliable, irritating yet amiable, he allows Gillian to support him while he writes unsaleable screenplays.

Rustum
'Sohrab and Rustum', in *Poems: A New Edition*, 1853
Matthew Arnold

A giant warrior in the Persian camp, he meets and kills his son SOHRAB (whose existence he has not hitherto suspected) in single combat between the Persian and Tartar armies. Son of Zal and rider of the legendary warhorse Ruksh, his shield, sword and club are all of a heroic size.

Ruth
The Homecoming, 1965
Harold Pinter

Wife to TEDDY, she returns with him from the United States to visit his family, whom she has never met. Her own peculiar behaviour, sexual licentiousness and linguistic idiosyncracies meld her quickly into the sinister family at the play's centre. Her comment 'I was different … when I met Teddy … first' renders more understandable her eventual decision to stay with his family and desert him.

Ruth
The Life and Loves of a She-Devil, 1983
Fay Weldon

Rejection and betrayal by her husband bring out the wickedness in Ruth. She is physically unattractive, but has been a caring and loyal wife and mother. When her husband leaves her for a romantic novelist, her depression and frustration know no bounds. Gradually, though, as she makes her husband and his lover suffer for the pain they have caused her, she begins to experience an exhilarating sense of power, and she slowly realizes that sweet behaviour is completely ineffectual when trying to survive in a man's world.

Ruth
'Ruth', 1800
William Wordsworth

The ill-fated Ruth is changed from a carefree young girl to a mad, harmless vagrant when she is deserted by her dashing American lover. Her only solace now comes from her rustic flute and the beloved woodlands which have nurtured her since childhood.

Ruth
The Third Life of Grange Copeland, 1970
Alice Walker

Educated by her grandfather to believe that 'Each day must be past, present and future', Ruth represents regeneration and freedom. Possessing 'two big eyes that searched for the truth in everything', she does not suffer from the same sense of fragmentation as her forebears, but is in complete control of herself. Her sense of injustice is a motivating force and, unlike her father, her memories of poverty and violence empower her to move on.

Rutherford
Rutherford, 1962
Douglas Stewart
The discoverer of atomic structure, Rutherford is a driven man, a courageous explorer of mind, earth and universe. He has a clear view of his place in history, and his creative power is seen to some degree as 'the spirit of the race': 'not just his own ambition/But all mankind's'. His failing might be that he places too much faith in 'the rule of the strong and the just'.

Rutherford, Mark
The Autobiography of Mark Rutherford, 1881, et seq, Mark Rutherford (William Hale White)
Brought up in a small Midlands town and coming from a Nonconformist background, 'Rutherford' is a thinly disguised (but undoubtedly less well-starred) version of White himself as the autobiographical structure makes clear. Trained to the ministry, he is increasingly assailed by loneliness and doubt and eventually loses his faith.

Rutledge, Anne
The Spoon River Anthology, 1915
Edgar Lee Masters
A benevolent patriot, her brief monologue from the grave reveals her as the face of the 19th-century American ideal, 'beloved in life of Abraham Lincoln'. Her language and tone, 'shining with justice and truth', suggest the simplicity of vision which characterizes many of Masters's villagers, though the latter-day reader may find her sententious and unreal.

Ryan, Bubba
Summer of the Seventeenth Doll, 1955
Ray Lawler
'A shy-looking girl of twenty-two' who has lived next door to OLIVE and EMMA for her entire life, and has thereby become a party to the charmed circle of her neighbours' lay-off-season celebrations. She shares the ill-fated resistance to change of ROO WEBBER, BARNEY IBBOT and Olive. Her nickname (Bubba is colloquial Australian for baby) exemplifies the inability of her friends to recognize her as a grown woman who, as PEARL CUNNINGHAM puts it, 'knows more than her prayers'. We learn her real name, Kathie, when she is asked out by JOHNNIE DOWD, with whom she appears to emulate the tragedy of her elders.

Ryan, Eddie
The Silence of History, 1963, et seq, comprising the *A Universe of Time* series
James T Farrell
A Chicago writer, he becomes the repository for all of Farrell's autobiographical concerns (they share a birthdate and certain other conspicuous features), and his increasingly abstract and elegaic political and philosophical speculations. In a sense, Ryan himself represents the passage of time.

Ryder, Charles
Brideshead Revisited, 1945
Evelyn Waugh
The narrator, Charles Ryder is an Oxford undergraduate when SEBASTIAN FLYTE vomits into his rooms. Thus a relationship of 'nursery freshness' and anarchic dissipation is spawned and, with his new friend, he visits Brideshead and Venice. Helpless to prevent Sebastian's self-pitying slide into alcoholism, he leaves Oxford to study art in Paris. In time he becomes a famous architectural painter; he ends an unhappy marriage to be with JULIA FLYTE, but religious differences force them to separate. Revisiting Brideshead as a wartime infantry Captain – 'homeless, childless, middle-aged, loveless' – he nevertheless retains an uplifting sense of all-encompassing human tragedy.

Ryder, Japhy
The Dharma Bums, 1958
Jack Kerouac
A Buddhist poet and mountain climber, based on the Beat poet Gary Snyder. He has a vision of a new America which will free itself from the cycle of production and consumption, a 'great rucksack revolution, thousands or even millions of young Americans wandering around with rucksacks, going up to the mountains to pray'.

Ryecroft, Henry
The Private Papers of Henry Ryecroft, 1903
George Gissing
He is an author who has looked into the maelstrom of 'Grub Street' and reacted in horror to its seething forces and desperate survivalism. Retiring to a distance, he is able to observe his own ambitions and methods with a degree of objectivity he has not previously enjoyed. One observer sees Ryecroft as an example of 'autobiografiction', a projection of Gissing rather than a fully realized character.

Sabbath, Mickey
Sabbath's Theater, 1995
Philip Roth

A 64-year-old former puppeteer, Sabbath is a hulk of a man, a 'whoremonger, seducer, sodomist, abuser of women, destroyer of morals, ensnarer of youth'. Plagued by the death of his brother and his abandonment as a child by his mother, Sabbath has made lechery the sum of his existence in both his art and his life. Following the death of Drenka, his sexually voracious mistress, a bereft and grieving Sabbath flings himself into a monumental rage against life. He anguishes over his dwindling potency, ransacks a friend's daughter's underwear drawer ('how could I not?'), mocks his wife's alcohol recovery programmes and desecrates Drenka's grave.

Sabich, Rusty (Rožat K)
Presumed Innocent, 1987
The Burden of Proof, 1990
Scott Turow

An honest mid-Western state prosecutor, who resists political coercion. He grew up in a poor neighbourhood, in fear of his hard-drinking Serbian father. His embittered wife is a highly intellectual mathematician with abstruse interests he cannot share, and he succumbs to a 'grand obsession' with a seductive fellow-prosecutor, later being charged with her murder. 'The injured son of an angry man', Rusty still nurses his wounds, and, although understanding, fears he lacks some quality essential to helping others in need.

Sabina, Lily
The Skin of Our Teeth, 1942
Thornton Wilder

The 'other woman', who tries to seduce GEORGE ANTROBUS with sex and the idea that life is only 'pleasure and power', but always ends up back in the kitchen. At times she turns into an actress, Miss Somerset, who takes a dim view of Wilder's play.

Sachairi, Maighstir (Mr Zachary Wiseman)
And the Cock Crew, 1962
Fionn Mac Colla

The Presbyterian minister of Gleann Luachrach, he 'is a king, nae less, in his ain parish', but allows his inflexible Calvinism dominion over his common humanity and betrays his flock to the sheep-herders of the Clearances. He is Mac Colla's most powerful portrayal of the negative aspects of radical Protestantism, a man destroyed and destructive because of the very purity of his vision.

Sacrapant
The Old Wives' Tale, 1595
George Peele

A powerful and wicked conjurer who abducts DELIA. He is 'a cunning sorcerer' with the power to chant spells and make himself appear young, though he is really 'aged, crooked, weak', and wretched. He claims that Delia is the mistress of his heart, but he is outwitted by JACK'S GHOST, and is punished for his 'foul' activities by having his soul descend to hell.

Saddler, Jim
Fly Away Peter, 1982
David Malouf

A quiet, reserved young man who has sunk himself into the task of documenting the movement of migrating birds on a Queensland nature reserve. He stands for innocence and for the cyclical, carefully differentiated and individuated patterns of nature, and it is these that are overturned in the vast migration of men to the battlefields of the Western Front in 1914 and 1915.

Saddletree, Bartoline
The Heart of Midlothian, in *Tales of My Landlord: Second Series*, 1818
Sir Walter Scott

Edinburgh harness- and saddle-maker; 'his genius, however … lay towards the weightier matters of the law … [He] had a considerable gift of words, which he mistook for eloquence, and conferred more liberally upon the society in which he lived than was at all times gracious and acceptable'.

Sagoe
The Interpreters, 1965
Wole Soyinka

A young journalist in the emergent Nigeria, he has abandoned the abstract principles of his 'philosophising days' for a more pragmatic accommodation to the awkward tension between old and new. Born 'with an emotional stomach', he espouses a non-revolutionary philosophy of protest which he calls Voidancy.

Saint → St

Sakamoto Chiyo/Nitta Sayuri
Memoirs of a Geisha, 1997
Arthur Golden

Transformed from Chiyo the fishergirl into

Sayuri, 'a woman who has made a career of entertaining men', the narrator describes, with constant disclaimers, how she became one of the most famous geishas in Gion, Kyoto. Repeatedly told how pretty, charming and clever she is, even as a child, she attributes this to the water in her personality, revealed through her translucent grey eyes: 'Water never waits. It changes shape and flows around things, and finds the secret paths no one else has thought about'. Indeed, her resourceful versatility and determination help her survive her harsh training and keep her hopes for 'something better' alive. Her story shows how she achieves her dreams as surely 'as a stone must fall to the earth'.

Saladin
The Talisman: A Tale of the Crusaders, 1825
Sir Walter Scott

By no means the villain of the piece, or a stock Eastern potentate, the Saracen leader exhibits considerable courage, reserve and asceticism. His manners 'were grave, graceful, and decorous; indicating, however, in some particulars, the habitual restraint which men of warm and choleric tempers often set as a guard upon their native impetuosity of disposition'.

Salar
Salar the Salmon, 1935
Henry Williamson

It was considered ironic that Williamson should have followed up his most successful character, the otter TARKA, with the species that came just below him in the food chain. Less individualized and much more abstract than Tarka – perhaps because he interacts with man less obviously – Salar becomes the occasion for a philosophical dithyramb about the cycle of nature and the unconscious heroism of its participants.

Salieri, Antonio
Amadeus, 1979
Peter Shaffer

An old, guilt-wracked figure seeking absolution at the hour of his death, Salieri's apparently illustrious life has been blackened by a murderous, all-consuming jealousy for the gifts that God has bestowed on his musical contemporary WOLFGANG AMADEUS MOZART. The son of a Lombard merchant, with ambitions to 'blaze, like a comet, across the firmament of Europe', he has been a prolific and acclaimed Royal Kapellmeister at the Habsburg court for a body of work that he alone discerns will stand as mediocre and worthless alongside the enduring glories of Mozart's compositions.

Salim
A Bend in the River, 1979
V S Naipaul

A Muslim, though descended from 'the Hindus of north-western India', Salim journeys from his home in East Africa to set up business as a trader at a bend of a central African river. He remains detached from the many Africans he meets, but is adept at negotiating the prevalent corruption, not least from the country's dictator. An alienated outsider, but also a born survivor, Salim makes the tough-minded observation that: 'The world is what it is; men who are nothing, who allow themselves to become nothing, have no place in it'.

Sally
Ruth, 1853
Elizabeth Gaskell

A fine, upright woman, Sally is a sincere churchgoer. A blunt woman, whose words can be cutting, she has a heart of gold and is deeply faithful to those she serves. She is not easily swayed by the opinions of others, and is steadfast and reliable.

Salmon, Susie
The Lovely Bones, 2002
Alice Sebold

Susie Salmon introduces herself to us, already in Heaven, following her violent rape and murder. When she died she was just a normal 14-year-old from a normal family, and in her adolescent image of heaven school 'textbooks were *Seventeen* and *Glamour* and *Vogue*'. Over seven years she watches her family struggle to come to terms with her death; it is only when they accept the past and achieve peace that Susie is able to move on herself, relinquishing her close interest in Earth to find happiness in Heaven.

Saltbush Bill
'Saltbush Bill', in *The Man from Snowy River and Other Verses*, 1895; *Rio Grande's Last Race and Other Verses*, 1892
Saltbush Bill, J.P., and Other Verses, 1917
Andrew Barton ('Banjo') Paterson

The 'King of the Overland', he is head drover in charge of a herd of sheep grazing the 'long paddock' during the hard drought of 1880. Bill is a crafty character and, not surprisingly, his sheep often stray into the lusher pastures of the local squatters including the runs of Stingy Bill, who begrudges every blade of grass. Gifted with a talent for ingenuity and sharp practice, when he is appointed Justice of the Peace he discovers he can earn a pound for holding an inquest on a fire; within the week, 25 homes on the nearby Aboriginal camp mysteriously burn down, and Bill spends Christmas, and £25, with his sister in Sydney.

Salteena, Mr
The Young Visiters, 1919
Daisy Ashford (Mrs George Norman), juvenilia

Mr Salteena is 'an elderly man of 42', fond of digging in the garden and partial to nice ladies, among them his house-guest ETHEL MONTICUE. The dashing legs and manners of a high-born friend having eclipsed the charms of his own dark hair and twisty whiskers, Mr Salteena determines to become a gentleman, but is not wholly successful. He continues to be flabbergasted by etiquette and embarrassed by his low birth and limited means. Unable to win back Ethel's affections, his marriage to 'Another' – and the consequent ten children – makes him morose, though he finds relief in prayer.

Sam → Gamgee, Sam

Sam the Lion
The Last Picture Show, 1966
Larry McMurtry

An ageing pool-hall and cinema owner in the small Texan town of Anarene, whose 'last picture' is the Howard Hawks movie *Red River*, a celebration of the frontier past which Sam experienced at first hand as a cowboy. His resilience and wisdom are an inspiration to the young men of the town.

Samgrass, Mr
Brideshead Revisited, 1945
Evelyn Waugh

A young history don at All Souls, Oxford, Mr Samgrass is 'a short, plump man, dapper in dress', with a genial manner and idiosyncratic speech. An author of several stylish books, he becomes involved with the Flyte family when he is chosen to edit a war book for LADY TERESA MARCHMAIN. He gives evidence of good behaviour at SEBASTIAN FLYTE's trial for drunken driving, and later agrees to reform him by taking him on a tour of Levantine monasteries. Sebastian evades his clutches, however, and JULIA FLYTE finally exposes Samgrass before Lady Marchmain.

Samient
The Faerie Queene, 1590–6
Sir Edmund Spenser

A fair maiden who lives at the court and serves QUEEN MERCILLA, and whose name means 'togetherness'. She has been sent as a messenger to the tyrant called THE SOLDAN in an attempt to rectify his wrong-doings, but his wife Adicia has stopped her. Betrayed by Mercilla's ambassadors, she is later unjustly imprisoned.

Sammler, Arthur
Mr Sammler's Planet, 1970
Saul Bellow

An elderly, one-eyed Jewish intellectual and writer who is the narrator-protagonist of a bleak, apocalyptic, but heavily ironic and satirical account of the new barbarism of modern urban life, and the degeneration of the self. He has escaped the death camps (literally from the grave), and views the excesses of civilization with a mixture of outrage and disgust leavened with compassion and a distanced, clinical neutrality; he looks on in 'kindly detachment, in farewell-detachment, in earth-departure-objectivity'.

'Sammy' (Samuels)
How Late It Was, How Late, 1994
James Kelman

Sammy, a Glaswegian with a criminal record, has a fondness for drinking and smoking. However, his current girlfriend does provide a stabilizing influence, and he has an affectionate, if sporadic, relationship with his son. Waking in a police cell after being beaten up, he discovers he has lost his sight, but Sammy is a born survivor. His reaction is philosophical: new problems arise every day and blindness is just another one to be dealt with. Used to what life throws at him he shows remarkable resilience and when suspected of involvement in his girlfriend's disappearance he is streetwise enough to engineer his own departure.

Samoa
Mardi, 1849
Herman Melville

TAJI's companion on his adventures. A 'tall, dark Islander, a very devil to behold, theatrically arrayed in kilt and turban'. He has a 'mutilated arm' which is amputated by his wife, ANNATOO. He is a fine, frank fellow, but stands 'a little in awe of his bellicose spouse', although he proves himself to be a hero in other respects.

Sampath, Mr
Mr Sampath: the Printer of Malgudi, 1949
R K Narayan

Regarded with deference in Malgudi, the generous, affable Mr Sampath, printer and enthusiastic amateur Thespian, has the instincts of an entrepreneur without the business acumen and his family live in near penury. Whole-heartedly supporting SRINIVAS's new weekly newspaper, he neglects his own customers to print it, but, as Srinivas is no businessman either, the paper fails. Penniless but undaunted, Sampath contrives to become a movie mogul and embarks on an epic film, but he is carried away by the glamour of this enterprise and its beautiful star, and chaos and disaster ensue for all concerned.

Sampson, Dominie (Abel)
Guy Mannering, 1816
Sir Walter Scott

Tutor to the young heir of Ellangowan, HARRY BERTRAM. 'He was of low birth, but having evinced, even from his cradle, an uncommon seriousness of disposition, the poor parents were encouraged to hope that their *bairn*, as they expressed it, "might wag his pow in a pulpit yet".' Tall, ungainly, with windmilling arms and a tic-ridden face, he is a grotesque and much put-upon figure.

Samson
Samson Agonistes, 1671
John Milton

The powerful wrestler has been reduced to impotence and blindness in the Philistine prison at Gaza by the treachery of his wife DALILA; 'My self, my Sepulcher, a moving Grave,/ Buried, yet not exempt/By privilege of death and burial/From worst of other evils, pains and wrongs'. He is often taken to be a projection of the sightless Milton's own situation after the Restoration (with its whiff of crypto-Catholicism) and the betrayal of his political ideals.

Sanderson, Peggy
The Loved and the Lost, 1951
Morley Callaghan

The daughter of a minister who has lost his faith, her life has become a capricious flight from 'normality'. Because of an early friendship with a black family in Montreal, she prefers the company of coloured people and is exposed to the obloquy of her workmates and employers, who cannot believe that such friendships are anything but perverse. Edmund Wilson considered her 'a kind of saint'.

Sandford, Harry
The History of Sandford and Merton, 1783–9
Thomas Day

An improbably virtuous farmer's son who is a moral exemplar as well as a true friend to TOMMY MERTON. He is upright, robust, tender-hearted, 'active, strong, hardy and fresh-coloured', with an 'honest, good-natured countenance'. He is cheerful, hardworking, charitable, kind to animals, careful and considerate, and has been taught to read by MR BARLOW.

Sands, Bernard
Hemlock and After, 1952
Angus Wilson

A great liberal humanist, he has a mysteriously ailing wife and conducts homosexual affairs with almost clinical detachment. His ambivalent attitude towards the Establishment is a reflection of his own divided nature, public and private.

Sands, Emma
An Unofficial Rose, 1962
Iris Murdoch

A famous writer of detective stories and the object of HUGH PERONETT's undying affection. 'Dog face Emma' to a jealous mutual friend, she is a small, hunched woman with dark inquisitive eyes, a 'ferret' nose, wiry grey hair and nicotine-stained fingers, but who somehow still manages to wield an extraordinary power over men. A semi-recluse and self-professed 'dreadful old *malade imaginaire*', who tyrannizes her paid companions, Emma is slyly adept at manoeuvring people into web-like situations she has 'invented' for them – in real life, as well as in her fiction.

Sandy
Intensive Care, 1970
Janet Frame

COLIN MONK's nightmare shadow self, he is a technological homunculus made of scrap metal and transplanted organs. In the attempt to exclude all that is not human, society has only managed to create something dangerously sub-human.

Sanglier, Sir
The Faerie Queene, 1590–6
Sir Edmund Spenser

A knight who represents untoward violence, his name refers to blood. Upon his shield is the mark of a 'broken sword in a bloodie field'. He has no concept of human suffering and enjoys the sport of the kill. He has no respect for love, honour or people's lives, and contentedly decapitates unwanted lovers.

Sangrail, Clovis
The Chronicles of Clovis, 1911
Beasts and Super-Beasts, 1914
The Toys of Peace, 1923
The Square Egg, 1924
'Saki' (Hector Hugh Munro)

A cynical, sceptical and entirely self-assured young man of 19, who claims to be 18. He is always ready with an ingenious scheme to help his friends, get his own way, or take revenge on pretentious, pompous and boring people. Vain

and living beyond his means, he sports expensive waistcoats, but his chief love is good food. He is noted for his 'irrepressible waywardness', and one hostess says of him that it is 'no use growing older if you only learn new ways of misbehaving yourself'.

Sansfoy
The Faerie Queene, 1590–6
Sir Edmund Spenser

The elder brother of SANSLOY and SANSJOY, all three of whom are 'bred/of one bad sire'. They are Saracens, and are identified as the 'Nephewes' of Night and enemies to Christianity, and together represent the deterioration of the human soul resulting from spiritual blindness. Sansfoy is a proud warrior who spends his time fighting errant knights and catching maidens, whom he imprisons in his castle.

Sansjoy
The Faerie Queene, 1590–6
Sir Edmund Spenser

Brother to SANSFOY and SANSLOY, he represents joylessness. An angry, adversarial character, full of jealousy, mistrust, cruelty and burning rage, he does not feel pleasure or love, nor is he ever contented. He is large and strong and knows the magic spell of disappearing.

Sansloy
The Faerie Queene, 1590–6
Sir Edmund Spenser

Sansloy represents lawlessness and symbolizes England gone astray. Brother to SANSFOY and SANSJOY, his name is written proudly across his shield. A bold and unruly warrior, he takes sexual pleasure indiscriminately and insensitively.

Santiago
The Old Man and the Sea, 1952
Ernest Hemingway

An old Cuban fisherman, he is 'thin and gaunt with deep wrinkles in the back of his neck', but his eyes are 'cheerful and undefeated', and he retains a great spirit. He loves baseball, and has a grandfatherly relationship with the boy MANOLIN. He is said to have become unlucky in finding fish, but he knows 'many tricks', has great resolution, and likens the sea to a woman who gives or withholds 'great favours'. The sharks may defeat him, but not the great fish itself.

Santinio, Alejo
Our House in the Last World, 1983
Oscar Hijuelos

A young Cuban, he has moved to New York City with his wife, MARCEDES SANTINIO, in pursuit of insubstantial dreams of success and cultural betterment. He finds himself forced to shed many of his native values, but is unwilling to abandon his enthusiasm for his new environment.

Santinio, Marcedes
Our House in the Last World, 1983
Oscar Hijuelos

ALEJO SANTINIO's wife, she is less sanguine than

he about the transition to North America. Unable to accommodate its demands, she sinks increasingly into a nostalgic withdrawal, dreaming of the past without will or hope.

Sanutee
The Yemassee, 1835
William Gilmore Simms
The chief of the Yemassee band and husband of MATIWAN, he is a last representative of the old ways that persisted before the white man came to America. Dying, he attempts to protect his culture from the inroads of the colonists.

Sapsea, Mr Thomas
The Mystery of Edwin Drood, 1870
Charles Dickens
An auctioneer and later mayor, he is 'the type of self-sufficient stupidity and conceit ... the purest Jackass in Cloisterham'. He affects an ecclesiastical manner and composes an elaborate epitaph to his wife in which he pompously praises himself.

Saranoff, Sergius
Arms and the Man, 1894
George Bernard Shaw
Tall, handsome, assertive and high-spirited, Sergius is a major in the Bulgarian army during the Serbo-Bulgarian war of 1885. He implicitly accepts conventional ideals, especially those of chivalry and heroism, but sees all too clearly the failure of people (including himself) to live up to them. This he mocks as the vital flaw in the human condition. From being loved by RAINA PETKOFF, Sergius eventually finds happiness with the servant, LOUKA. Shaw intended that he be seen not as a ridiculous blusterer but as a tragicomic figure in whose troubled sensibilities lie the real themes to the play.

Sardanapalus
Sardanapalus: A Tragedy, 1821
Byron, George Gordon, 6th Lord Byron
The effeminate and sybaritic King of Nineveh and Assyria. Openly false to his queen Zarina with the beauteous Greek slave Myrrha, he seems easy prey to Beleses, a Chaldean soothsayer, and the Median Arabaces who covets his throne. They lead a revolt against him. He casts off his perfumed luxury and fights like a hero,'inspired by Myrrha's exhortations, but is defeated. Ensuring that Zarina will be taken to safety, he orders a funeral pyre to be prepared round his throne, as befits the obsequies of a king. Myrrha fearlessly elects to share his doom; he mounts the pyre and she, putting a torch to it, joins him for their last embrace.

Sargent, Margaret
The Company She Keeps, 1942
Mary McCarthy
'A troublemaker' is how one lover describes Margaret and her behaviour bears this out as she revolts against the middle-class life she finds hypocritical, mediocre and smug – the life of her emotionally detached childhood and stifling marriage. Convinced, even proud, of her own intelligence, Margaret eventually finds her self-confidence crumbling with the life of moral anarchy which follows her divorce. Her romantic rebelliousness passionately espouses unpopular political causes but she is unable to give a similar commitment to personal relationships. An escape route must always be available; where it may lead is of secondary importance.

Sarn, Gideon
Precious Bane, 1924
Mary Webb
Dogged and graceless, Gideon loves the land only for what he can get out of it. He is driven by greed to acquire more and more ploughed fields, more ways of making money, the 'precious bane'. He works his sister PRUE SARN like a sergeant; all must earn for him, even his frail mother and JANCIS BEGUILDY, his betrothed. Greedy also in love, he tricks WIZARD BEGUILDY and sleeps with Jancis before their wedding, but Beguildy's revenge leads him to precipitate disaster.

Sarn, Prue
Precious Bane, 1924
Mary Webb
Imaginative, acutely aware of growing things, wise in old beliefs and the Bible, shunned as a witch because of her 'hare-shotten' lip, Prue fears her brother GIDEON SARN's greed for money, the 'precious bane'. Able to read and write, she is thoughtful. Loving KESTER WOODSEAVES, she believes that no one can love her; she is shyly glad that her part in WIZARD BEGUILDY's spurious 'raising of Venus' has shown Kester that her body is perfect. Kester recognizes her fineness of soul and courage in adversity. When she is taken as a witch, he carries her off to safety under his banner of love.

Sarti, Caterina
'Mr. Gilfil's Love-Story', in *Scenes of Clerical Life*, 1858
George Eliot
Brought as an orphan from Italy to live in an English manor, Caterina is raised with slightly less attention to detail than is usual for a young lady of her station. A beautiful singer, she is adored by MAYNARD GILFIL, but her ardent nature responds more to the thoughtless wooing of handsome young CAPTAIN ANTHONY WYBROW. Rebuffed by him, however, her intense love escalates into jealousy and her habitual tenderness into anger and bitterness. Tragedy follows and, though she rediscovers some peace of mind with Gilfil, her frail disposition never fully recovers from the emotional violence done to it.

Sartoris, Bayard (Old Bayard)
Sartoris, 1929, full version published as *Flags in the Dust*, 1973
William Faulkner
Head of the family banking interests, he grows up in awe of his violent father COL JOHN SARTORIS, emulating the old man's brand of wild justice when his mother is murdered. He later mellows and becomes the conservative defender – 'bearded, hawklike' – of traditional values against the encroachment of mechanization and 'Northern' ideas. He dies of shock during a crazy automobile stunt with his grandson, 'Young' BAYARD SARTORIS.

Sartoris, Bayard (Young Bayard)

Sartoris, 1929, full version published as *Flags in the Dust*, 1973
William Faulkner

Reckless to the point of seeming suicidal, he represents the 'glamorous fatality' of family and Southern tradition brought hard up against the machine age. He has never come to terms with his twin brother's death, also as a flier on the Western Front. His barnstorming antics eventually lead to his own demise as a test pilot in Ohio, but not before he has effectively killed his grandfather, 'Old' BAYARD SARTORIS, frightening him to death in a wild automobile stunt. His first wife, Caroline White, dies in childbed with their unnamed son. Bayard subsequently marries NARCISSA BENBOW, by whom he has, posthumously, another boy, BENBOW SARTORIS.

Sartoris, Benbow

Sartoris, 1929, full version published as *Flags in the Dust*, 1973
Sanctuary, 1931
Knight's Gambit, 1949
The Mansion, 1959
William Faulkner

Born on the day of his father 'Young' BAYARD SARTORIS's death in a test-flight accident, he is named after his mother's family in a bid to lay the ghost of Sartoris violence for ever. He reappears as a boy in *Sanctuary* and as a crack shot in *The Mansion*. The last glimpse of him is as a soldier in World War II, perhaps fulfilling his genetic destiny after all.

Sartoris, Col John

Sartoris, 1929, full version published as *Flags in the Dust*, 1973
The Unvanquished, 1938
William Faulkner

One of the few Faulkner characters whose dates of birth and death can be given with absolute accuracy. Born some time after the Civil War in 1873, he died in 1924, shortly after another war that was to change the South dramatically. Said to be modelled on his creator's own grandfather, Colonel William Fa(u)lkner, he remains more present to his descendants even in death than are most of the living generation.

Sartoris, Lasca

Nigger Heaven, 1926
Carl Van Vechten

A coloured actress working in Harlem, she gives off an air of overcooked exoticism which is just enough to turn the writer BYRON KASSON's head. She later finds a more appropriate partner in the gambler RANDOLPH PETTIJOHN.

Sartorius

Widowers' Houses, 1892
George Bernard Shaw

A rich slum landlord, 'a self-made man, formidable to servants, not easily accessible to anyone', he lives with his daughter BLANCHE SARTORIUS in comfort in Surbiton, while his tenants scrape a living in East London rookeries. He defends his methods to DR HARRY TRENCH and WILLIAM DE BURGH COKANE by claiming that rather than being the instigator of a social evil, he is merely a businessman struggling for survival in an evil world. Sartorius has wealth but not the social status conferred by old money. He therefore approves his daughter's engagement to Trench because the young man's aristocratic family will bring both financial security and social advancement.

Sartorius, Blanche

Widowers' Houses, 1892
George Bernard Shaw

Blanche is the spoiled and tempestuous daughter of a rich slum landlord, SARTORIUS. She is well-dressed, good-looking, 'vital and energetic rather than delicate and refined', a sexual predator who nevertheless lacks the curiosity to discover the source of her father's wealth. During a tour of the Rhine she encounters a young Englishman, DR HARRY TRENCH, who promptly asks her to marry him. Riding roughshod over everyone, a stranger to sensitivity, Blanche becomes Trench's wife, but only after he himself becomes involved in a property swindle. For her, financial gain is more important than love.

Sassoon, Siegfried

Regeneration, 1991, part of the *Regeneration* trilogy
Pat Barker

In 1917, Sassoon publishes his declaration of protest at the continuation of World War I and is sent to Craiglockhart War Hospital for treatment under DR WILLIAM RIVERS. In this fictionalized account, a warm affectionate bond grows between the two men. Handsome, prone to introspection, and shy rather than arrogant, Sassoon is a man in whom courage is 'the *dominating* characteristic'. Having hitherto led a desultory life of hunting, cricket and writing poetry, he has found in the army the 'only place' he has 'ever really belonged' and is worshipped by his men. The conflicts of his stance lead to nightmares and hallucinations and the final decision to return.

Satan

Paradise Lost, 1667
Paradise Regained, 1671
John Milton

It is the great problem of *Paradise Lost*, first identified by William Blake, that the fallen archangel is a far more heroic and compelling figure than Milton's irascible GOD or watery JESUS CHRIST. Haunted by the recognition that 'I myself am Hell', the great 'Adversary' prefers to reign in his own infernal kingdom than to serve in heaven. He sits on his throne like a gorgeous Eastern potentate, raised 'beyond hope' by a defiant resistance to the superior forces of good. In *Paradise Regained*, a chastened and much reduced figure, he continues his campaign by tempting Christ in the desert.

Saturninus

Titus Andronicus, c.1589
William Shakespeare

The son of the late Emperor of Rome. His accession seems momentarily to end the faction-fighting, but in fact generates much more. He marries QUEEN TAMORA, ruler of the defeated Goths, who has a vendetta against the ANDRONICUS family, and is consequently violently ungrateful to TITUS ANDRONICUS for having given him the crown, detesting 'that proud brag of thine that saidst I begged the empire at thy hands'.

Satyrane, Sir
The Faerie Queene, 1590–6
Sir Edmund Spenser
A brave knight, who loves to fight for ladies. His father is a satyr and his mother a lady, and he was brought up in the forests of Faerieland. An unruly child of nature, he is able to subdue the animals around him, but he also has powerful human longings and a desire for virtue, and in his later years his mother has a civilizing influence on him. He has a violent temper, yet is faithful, true and the enemy of shame.

Saunders, Bridget
Poor Richard's Almanack, 1733–58
Benjamin Franklin, and others after 1748
The formidably garrulous wife of RICHARD SAUNDERS, compiler of the *Almanack*. It is her scolding of his pointless star-gazing that eventually motivates him to put into writing the accumulated wisdom of a lifetime of financial non-success.

Saunders, Cecily
Soldier's Pay, 1926
William Faulkner
A flighty, 'modern' girl, formerly the fiancée of LT DONALD MAHON, she is disgusted by his ruined face and switches her affections to the selfish GEORGE FARR, with whom she elopes. The fact that her dress is transparent against the light is another symptom of the collapse of older, more chivalric and romantic values.

Saunders, Daisy
The Gate of Angels, 1990
Penelope Fitzgerald
A rather clichéd portrayal of a nurse: part caring, part selfish and cruel, she is a confident working-class girl, in every way the opposite of FRED FAIRLY. Very attractive, she is neither likeable nor very admirable, although she does have courage. Guilt-ridden about her mother's death, she seems to be driven by some inner source of energy. Like Fred, he becomes mixed up in a world she does not fully understand, but being less scrupulous she copes rather better.

Saunders, Professor Gordon
Down the Long Table, 1955
Earle Birney
A Canadian academic, working at a college in the USA, when he is summoned before a panel investigating un-American activities. Down the long table, he sees a face from his radical past and is thrown into a reverie about his gradual and then more dramatic politicization, and about the tension between his political commitment and his private feelings.

Saunders, Richard
Poor Richard's Almanack, 1733–58
Benjamin Franklin, and others after 1748

Taking his name from the historical compiler of the English *Apollo Anglicanus*, Richard rapidly became a representative American, whose robust sanguinity and pragmatic common sense were a by-word. Without Franklin's approval, later editions were titled (ironically, given Richard's chronic financial standing) *The Way to Wealth*. Self-improvement apart, the real drama of the *Almanack* comes from Richard's comic battle with his wife BRIDGET SAUNDERS, who regards him as a dreamy under-achiever.

Savage, John the
Brave New World, 1932
Aldous Huxley
Familiar with Shakespeare, and from an Indian reservation in New Mexico, John the Savage finds himself at odds with the 'Brave New World' of a scientifically ordered society which is populated by humans 'decanted' from test tubes. Divided into castes, its citizens conform to rigidly specific social roles. Brought to a futuristic London by BERNARD MARX, a disaffected 'Alpha Plus', the Savage, adding to his other 'defects', becomes involved with another disaffected person, Lenina, and cares for his aged mother. Rather than allow himself to be 'civilized' into eliminating all strong emotions and attachments, he hangs himself.

Savage, Richard Ellsworth (Dick)
1919, 1932
The Big Money, 1936, part of the *U.S.A.* trilogy, 1938
John Dos Passos
Fancying himself as an aspiring poet, amiable Harvard student Dick nevertheless takes himself off to war in France and Italy as part of a volunteer ambulance crew, a role he feels does not interfere with his reputed pacifism. Steady and caring to a degree, but not without a selfish streak when it comes to the prospect of curtailing his own freedom, Dick eventually sells out, accepting the easy option as part of the J WARD MOOREHOUSE 'set'.

Savile, Lord Arthur
Lord Arthur Savile's Crime, 1891
Oscar Wilde
A 'young man of birth and fortune', he is engaged to a beautiful woman whom he loves and admires. Informed by a chiromancer that he will commit murder, he is horrified at the prospect of the shame and misery this will bring his bride. Having a practical nature and 'that rarest of all things, common sense', he decides that it is his duty to get the murder out of the way discreetly before his marriage. He thus embarks on a number of ingenious and murderous attempts on the lives of various distant relatives.

Saville, Colin
Saville, 1976
David Storey
An educated intellectual, torn between his upbringing as a collier's son and his new, cultured world. He cannot feel at home in his old background, yet is never quite able to accept the implications of his new life as a teacher, with its occasional preciousness and danger of snobbery. A man adrift, his life is shrouded by lack of context, leading him to view the world

through a yellow fog of disappointment and disillusion.

Savitri
The Dark Room, 1938
R K Narayan

A middle-class woman married to Ramani, a manager of the Engladia Insurance Company, Savitri has three children and lives a quiet, sheltered, orthodox life in Malgudi. She is good-looking and outwardly self-assured, but in reality she is trapped both by social orthodoxy and an overbearing, demanding husband. Long-suffering, often self-pitying, she devotes herself to their three children. Savitri's first response, when her husband takes on a female employee, is to withdraw into herself. In so doing, she discovers her assertiveness and tenacity.

Savonarola, Girolamo
Romola, 1863
George Eliot

A Dominican friar uninhibited by social rules from preaching against worldliness and vice among his peers. He predicts CHARLES VIII as a great cleansing force; this goes anticlimactically wrong. Despite such mistakes, his great oratorical power is capable of moving ROMOLA, among many others, to tears. Savonarola eventually becomes carried away by his own rhetoric and makes too many enemies. He cannot see this, believing that 'the cause of my party is the cause of God's kingdom'. It is this that alienates him from Romola, who has valued his counsel but cannot stomach such fanaticism.

Saward, Peter
The Flight from the Enchanter, 1956
Iris Murdoch

After near-fatal tuberculosis and the loss of one lung, Saward, a historian of pre-Babylonian empires, lives quietly in a cave-like room crammed with art reproductions, trying to decipher an obscure ancient script although he knows it to be 'a mug's game'. He is a friend of JOHN RAINBOROUGH, and his unrequited love for ROSA KEEPE remains constant. It is to the trustworthy Saward that MISCHA FOX sometimes reveals something of his childhood; Saward feels tenderness for Fox at these moments, but sees him as another puzzle he will never solve.

Sawin, Birdofredum
The Biglow Papers, 1848
James Russell Lowell

A private soldier in the Massachusetts Regiment and something of a rascal, he is even more forthright and unapologetically illiberal in his views than HOSEA BIGLOW himself, contributing his two cents' worth to Biglow's exchange of verse letters.

Sawyer, Bob
Pickwick Papers, 1837
Charles Dickens

A medical student whom his friend, BENJAMIN ALLEN, tries to marry to his sister, ARABELLA ALLEN. With Benjamin, he sets up an unsuccessful practice before the two become surgeons for the East India Company.

Sawyer, Elizabeth
The Witch of Edmonton, c.1621
Thomas Dekker, William Rowley and John Ford

Elderly, lonely, 'poor, deform'd and ignorant', Elizabeth is a natural outsider from society. As such, she is persecuted by her neighbours until, in desperation, she makes a pact with the Devil, who manifests himself in the shape of a dog. With his help, she avenges herself upon her tormentors, sending one woman mad and indirectly inducing FRANK THORNEY to murder his wife, SUSAN CARTER. The portrayal of Elizabeth Sawyer and her 'witchcraft' is unusual in drama of the era, as this is essentially a sympathetic portrait of a woman driven to the end of her tether by the cruelty of others.

Sawyer, Tom
The Adventures of Tom Sawyer, 1876
The Adventures of Huckleberry Finn, 1884, and others
Mark Twain

A mischievous boy, a natural showman with a love for theatrical gestures and a craving for adulation, he is notorious for his pranks and escapades in his home town of St Petersburg, Missouri, on the Mississippi. His insatiable appetite for diversion and adventure frequently leads him into dangerous and desperate situations, but he repeatedly turns these to his advantage and profit. He is more given to bravado than his close friend HUCK FINN, but lacks the latter's sensitivity.

Saxton, George
The White Peacock, 1911
D H Lawrence

A vigorous, sensual man, Saxton is as attracted to LETTIE BEARDSALL as her brother Cyril is to him (Cyril describing their male friendship as 'more perfect than any I have known'). Saxton represents one of the great Lawrentian themes, that of emotional and spiritual maturity being attained only through harmony between man and nature. Yet Saxton is not always aware of this himself, and is sometimes violently destructive. His essential weakness, though, is narcissism.

Sayer, Rose
The African Queen, 1935
C S Forester

A feisty missionary to darkest Africa, her patriotism drives her to heroism in the company of the disreputable CHARLIE ALLNUT. Behind her prim face lies a brave and wise woman, whose nerve holds in crisis and whose ingenuity and dry humour win out in the face of danger and near tragedy. Her steely resolve and passionate aversion to drink make her a dramatic foil to her partner in adventure who, although he initially annoys her intensely, finally wins her love and respect, feelings not easily acknowledged in one usually so emotionally reserved.

Scales, Gerald
The Old Wives' Tale, 1908
Arnold Bennett

To turn the head at first sight of the headstrong, but nonetheless intelligent SOPHIA BAINES, travelling salesman Gerald Scales must have been quite something to look at. Their secret courtship and subsequent elopement owed much to his facility for deception and his powers of persuasion. However, his failure to realize that Sophia would insist on a speedy marriage and would countenance no other arrangement reveals a surprising lack of understanding in one so quick and clever. He is soon revealed as a seeker after pleasure, excitement and self-gratification, whose underlying weakness will lead inevitably to a tragic end.

Scarecrow, also known as Hunk
The Wonderful Wizard of Oz, 1900
L Frank Baum
DOROTHY's companion on the journey to Oz, where he hopes to find the brains that are lacking in his straw-stuffed head. As with his other friends, it becomes clear that all along he has had the capacity he craves so poignantly. It is not too fanciful to see Scarecrow as the symbolic representative of a downtrodden rural working class, held in thrall by the tawdry wealth of Oz.

Scarlet
Down among the Women, 1971
Fay Weldon
Daughter of WANDA, she is an essentially kind person who has been dealt some harsh blows in life. Insecure and unlucky, she is desperately searching for love. Because she is not personally fulfilled, her relationships with others, of either sex, seem to be doomed. Despite her low self-esteem, however, she slowly begins to understand herself.

Scarpetta, Kay
Postmortem, 1990, et seq
Patricia Cornwell
The first time we meet Kay Scarpetta she answers a phone call in bed, which she intuitively knows will tell her that another woman has been strangled. It is such intuition, and her desire to be appreciated as a woman working in a man's world, that drives the chief medical examiner of Richmond, Virginia, to abandon her private life and devote herself to investigating homicide.

Scatcherd, Sir Louis Philippe
Dr Thorne, 1858
Anthony Trollope
The only child of SIR ROGER SCATCHERD, whose baronetcy and alcoholism he ·inherits. His mental and physical weakness may be due to his being taken from his mother so she could suckle FRANK GRESHAM. Despite being sent to Eton and Cambridge, he is not a gentleman but a dissipated and 'close-fisted reprobate'. His faults, including boasting, selfishness and cowardliness, are blamed on his upbringing, and his love for MARY THORNE is genuine.

Scatcherd, Sir Roger
Dr Thorne, 1858
Anthony Trollope
A semi-literate stonemason who, after going to prison for killing his sister's seducer, becomes, by hard work, an extremely rich railway contractor, baronet and Radical politician. Always a heavy drinker, his social isolation from both the workers and the gentry helps to turn him into an alcoholic, and he ignores warnings about his health from his only friend, DR THOMAS THORNE. Although he insists on getting his own way, he is essentially sympathetic and is not ashamed of his lack of social polish.

Schilsky
Maurice Guest, 1908
Henry Handel Richardson
Probably modelled on Franz Liszt, this exotic Pole is the stereotypical musical genius, dominating the artistic community at Leipzig with his electric, bullying charm and ambivalent sexual power. He has an affair with LOUISE DUFRAYER, but possibly also with HEINZ KRAFFT.

Schindler, Oskar
Schindler's Ark, 1982
Thomas Keneally
Schindler is based on a real-life German manufacturer who courageously rescued more than 1,000 Jews from certain death in the camps. Keneally portrays him as a reckless gambler whose methods are as suspect as his aims are noble. A womanizer and drinker, he makes for an unusual saint, ambiguously balanced between altruism and complete self-absorption.

Schlegel, Helen
Howards End, 1910
E M Forster
An independent, unconventional woman, Helen is the younger of the Schlegel girls and considered prettier, more amusing and more irresponsible than her sister MARGARET SCHLEGEL. A supporter of Votes For Women and a believer in equality of opportunity for all, she has an affectionate and generous nature that prompts her to take a well-intentioned interest in the affairs of LEONARD BAST and to resist the values of HENRY WILCOX, who represents a type of Englishman that she would prefer to see confined to the pages of history.

Schlegel, Margaret
Howards End, 1910
E M Forster
A more imposing and less charming figure than her younger sister HELEN SCHLEGEL, Margaret is a sincere, independent woman with a face that seems 'all teeth and eyes'. Blessed with a private income, she favours temperance, tolerance and sexual equality and determines to embrace a life of risk. Marriage to HENRY WILCOX, a man 20 years her senior, helps her to banish an encroaching sense of morbidity and she makes heroic efforts to cope with his stolid, unemotional nature; this union is to 'alter her fortunes more than her character'.

Schoenhof, Elizabeth
Life Before Man, 1979
Margaret Atwood
Mourning the loss of her lover Chris and emotionally estranged from her husband, NATE SCHOENHOF, Elizabeth dreams of escape. She is good at recording the reactions of others but is considered remote. She dislikes feeling that anyone is more powerful than her, having grown

up with an overbearing aunt as a guardian. Battling against apathy and ire, she refrains from suicide only because of her responsibilities as a mother. She sneers at people who need reflections to know who they are; consequently, she does not realize that she lost sight of herself a long time ago.

Schoenhof, Nate
Life Before Man, 1979
Margaret Atwood

The husband of ELIZABETH SCHOENHOF and the lover of LESJE GREEN, Nate is a man torn between duty and love. He gives up law practice to make toys but betrays his craft by making it into a business to satisfy his wife. He considers himself formed by the women in his life, whom he always tries to make happy. He no longer believes in the justness of the universe, though he continues to have idealistic moments. He frequently betrays his moral ethics, in part to force a reaction from his wife and in part because he is constantly swayed by emotion.

Schouler, Marcus
McTeague: A Story of San Francisco, 1899
Frank Norris

An assistant in a dogs' hospital, and MCTEAGUE's one intimate friend, he also is an unlicensed dentist. Like his veterinary skills, his political ideas are haphazard and half-baked. He introduces McTeague to his cousin TRINA SIEPPE, thus precipitating the tragic chain of events that turns Schouler into her avenger.

Schwabing, Graf von
The Thirty-Nine Steps, 1915, et seq
John Buchan

He is not so much a single individual as a protean principle of evil, reappearing throughout RICHARD HANNAY's wartime adventures. His first avatar is an effeminately voiced young nobleman, whose ability to change his appearance allows him to pass himself off as First Lord; his last the bland but sinister MOXON IVERY in *Mr Standfast* (1918).

Sciolto
The Fair Penitent, 1703
Nicholas Rowe

The father of CALISTA, whom he promises to his friend ALTAMONT in marriage, Sciolto is a man who lives by rule and convention. He is also a stoic of almost superhuman proportions. When he learns of his daughter's affair with LOTHARIO, and his eventual death after a duel, he encourages her to commit suicide, which she does after he himself dies, having been mortally wounded in the disturbances following the fatal duel.

Sclaunder
The Faerie Queene, 1590–6
Sir Edmund Spenser

A hideous old hag with dirty skin and bitten nails. Ill-willed, malevolent, bitter and malicious, she bursts into fearful streams of poison and gall, her besetting vice being calumny and slander. She abuses others' goodness, is full of spiteful words and castigates anyone who walks by.

Scobie
The Heart of the Matter, 1948
Graham Greene

A middle-aged, Catholic policeman in a West African colony. Outwardly he appears a dull, unremarkable man, content to live out his life performing his equally dull duties. However, he is proof that even ordinary people can have extraordinary qualities. Scobie is an excessively generous, fair and honourable man, who always places others first and believes that everyone, except himself, is capable of eventually achieving forgiveness and mercy. He feels that he is responsible for creating happiness for those he loves, but since this is impossible he is doomed to a sense of personal failure. He is a genuinely good man whose pity for those around him is universal and ultimately inspiring.

Scobie, Martin
Mr Scobie's Riddle, 1983
Elizabeth Jolley ·

Martin Scobie is a quiet but unwilling patient at the Hospital of St Christopher and St Columbus. A former piano teacher, he retreats from the indignities of the old people's home into unsettling daydreams about an attractive young female pupil. Torn between sensual desire and the finer planes of culture and religion, he is a force of benign resistance to the rules of the home and the avariciousness of its matron, HYACINTH PRICE.

Scopey
The Pope's Wedding, 1962
Edward Bond

A young East Anglian farm-labourer, Scopey is part of a gang of dispossessed and restless young people who have little to do apart from play games bordering upon the violent. Although he has known happiness, he does not have the emotional capacity to sustain it. Instead, he is intrigued by ALEN, an elderly recluse whom Scopey's wife PAT looks after, because Alen's independence represents both a victory over the drudgery of social conformity, and a stand against the creeping emptiness of life. Instinctive, but not particularly rational, Scopey becomes so absorbed by Alen that he suddenly kills him in order to discover and inherit his mystery.

Scorby
Tiburon, 1935
Kylie Tennant

The new constable in Tiburon, he is a man of 'habitual arrogance', with a 'calm dictatorial manner'. A self-sufficient man, who believes himself superior to most people, he despises the 'herd instincts' of those around him and finds humankind in general 'weak, rather stupid, and lacking in decision'. Scorby is attracted to JESSICA DAUNT, who initially finds him 'good-looking, handsome, and rather frightening', but is quickly put off by his patronizing attitude. Scorby hates his job, but displays no leniency, and becomes known for his 'unholy zeal for baiting travellers' – he feels it is his responsibility to rid the community of these 'lower' elements. The campers in turn have a 'wholesome dread' of him. Much of Scorby's arrogance is a front, however, covering up his great loneliness: having made no friends in the town, he spends his spare time studying to be an aviation engineer, and longs for the day he might escape Tiburon.

Scott, Captain
Fire on the Snow, 1941
Douglas Stewart
The tragic hero of this verse drama of the defeated Antarctic expedition to the Pole, his optimism and courage are unfailing. He dies sure of himself, the rightness of his quest and the glory of perpetuity, declaring at the last, 'there's nothing I would change'. Although beaten physically by the snow, his will to endure is unquenched – 'a fire on the snow'.

Scott, David
Ship of Fools, 1962
Katherine Anne Porter
David, an American artist, is psychologically one of the walking wounded, emotionally strait-jacketed by an unhappy childhood and Quaker conscience, which makes him both inhibited and guilt-ridden. He and his lover, JENNY BROWN, are almost wholly incompatible. The coldly secretive, repressed and prudish David is repeatedly appalled and repelled by her 'terrible gregariousness', and her warm sensuality clashes with his way of making love 'suddenly, violently, grimly' to have it over with. A compulsive spoiler, almost the only time he is happy is when scoring some petty victory over Jenny.

Scott, Ida
Another Country, 1962
James Baldwin
'Ages and ages ago, [she] had not been merely the descendant of slaves ... she had once been a monarch'. Jazz-man RUFUS SCOTT's younger sister, she has a sultry majesty which lifts her out of the violent mire in which he is trapped. After Rufus's death, she becomes the lover of the white novelist VIVALDO MOORE and is groomed for stardom as a singer by STEVE ELLIS; she reminds one white woman of 'the young Billie Holiday', a distinctly double-edged compliment.

Scott, Rufus
Another Country, 1962
James Baldwin
A defiant black jazz drummer, driven to suicide by the indifference of society to his art, and by the complexity of relationships in a multiracial society. A controversial portrait of a black artist, his death (by jumping off the George Washington Bridge) was once seen as deeply compromising to a more positive image for American blacks.

Scott, Vanessa
Careful, He Might Hear You, 1963
Sumner Locke Elliott
The tall, beautiful, emotionally repressed aunt of P S MARRIOTT. As a girl she felt rejected by her mother, and the men she has met, including LOGAN MARRIOTT, have not matched her sexless ideal. She achieved the social standing she craved by becoming companion to a wealthy

relative. Thoroughly Anglicized, with a 'slightly Mayfair accent', she despises the Australia to which she returns in order to gain custody of the six-year-old P S. She sees him as a malleable version of his father, Logan, to be moulded, with the help of emotional blackmail, into someone who can fill her empty life. Her tragedy is that she achieves self-understanding too late.

Scoular, Dan
The Big Man, 1985
William McIlvanney
An unemployed miner whose talent lies in his ability to 'knock people unconscious very quickly, frequently with one punch'. He is known as 'the big man', with more than physical implications, but he lives uncomfortably within the image which the people of Thornbank have wrought for him. Although a wild youth, he is a self-contained but impulsive adult capable of kind and gentle acts, and does not abuse his strength. He takes part in a bare-knuckle fight for cash, partly to try to save his marriage, but his integrity leads him to fall foul of dangerous men. His decision to stand against their power brings 'a sense of his own life given shape'.

Scranton, Miss Jeanette
Hotel de Dream, 1976
Emma Tennant
A sturdy, sensibly clad schoolteacher always accompanied by a large brown carpet bag containing unmarked exercise books, exotic makeup – seldom used – and letters from a man who once said he would marry her. Miss Scranton suffers from constant remorse, over her parents – whose marriage she unwittingly disrupted – and over everything else, including her uncharismatic teaching. While having strange dreams of a primeval sandy beach inhabited by naked Amazons, who ritualistically mate with men who are then left to die, she conceives a passion for fellow-resident, ARTHUR POYNTER, when her dreamlife encroaches on his.

Scratch, Mr
'*The Devil and Daniel Webster*', 1937
Stephen Vincent Benét
The New Hampshire identity of the Devil. Urbane and 'soft-spoken' in his dark clothes, he carries a black pocket-book full of mortgages on souls, including that of JABEZ STONE. He shows many white teeth when he gives his 'terrible smiles'. Insisting to DANIEL WEBSTER that he is an American, he proves a dangerous adversary in court.

Scrooge, Ebenezer
A Christmas Carol, 1843
Charles Dickens
The miserly, misanthropic moneylender and surviving partner in the firm of Scrooge and Marley (see MARLEY'S GHOST). Once a 'good-hearted lad', he has become 'a squeezing, wrenching, grasping, scraping, clutching, covetous old sinner', 'hard and sharp as flint', and 'as self-contained, and solitary as an oyster'. But after a vivid dream on Christmas Eve, in which he is visited by Marley's Ghost and the

GHOST OF CHRISTMAS PAST, GHOST OF CHRISTMAS PRESENT and GHOST OF CHRISTMAS YET TO COME, the pity and terror he feels teach him a lesson, and he becomes a kind and generous benefactor to BOB CRATCHIT and all the Cratchit family.

Scudamour, Sir
The Faerie Queene, 1590–6
Sir Edmund Spenser

A valiant knight with a struggling soul. He carries the winged 'shield of love' which depicts the god of love in all his glory. Scudamour is in love with the angelic AMORET but, unable to find her, he grieves in wretched, burning torment. His distress is so serious it almost costs him his life.

Scuddamore, Silas Q
The Suicide Club, 1878
Robert Louis Stevenson

A simple, innocent young American who is typically adolescent in being a braggart among his male friends, while being bashful in the company of women. Every inch the amateur detective, his natural timidity is increasingly set aside to satisfy his all-consuming curiosity. Through his association with the sinister Suicide Club, he loses the gaucheness of youth and attains a wiser, but more melancholic adulthood. The moral turpitude to which he is exposed prepares him for a career in politics.

Scudder, Alec
Maurice, 1914, published posthumously, 1971
E M Forster

A butcher's son, Alec Scudder is the intelligent, hardworking undergamekeeper at the Penge estate of CLIVE DURHAM. A proud, working-class lad determined to make his way in the world, he has plans to emigrate with his brother to Argentina until he encounters MAURICE CHRISTOPHER HALL, when the possibility of a loving homosexual relationship is offered to him. Shrewd and suspicious, he is eventually won over by his lover, who describes him as 'a treasure, a charmer, a find in a thousand, the longed-for dream'.

Seagrim, Molly
The History of Tom Jones, 1749
Henry Fielding

The daughter of the gamekeeper BLACK GEORGE, she is TOM JONES's mistress, her compliant sexuality tempting him against all resolution to deviate from his pursuit of SOPHIA WESTERN.

Searing, Lt Adrian
'One of the Missing', 1888, in *Tales of Soldiers and Civilians*, 1891, published as *In the Midst of Life*, 1892
Ambrose Bierce

The senior of the two Searings, he experiences his brother's death in a Civil War battlefield in Georgia, and the symbolically complex circumstances leading up to it, from a considerable distance. Though attentive to the details of the battlefield, as befits his rank, he is unable to see what is really happening, in sharp contrast to his eagle-eyed brother, PRIVATE JEROME SEARING, who is entangled in the action.

Searing, Private Jerome
'One of the Missing', 1888, in *Tales of Soldiers and Civilians*, 1891, published as *In the Midst of Life*, 1892
Ambrose Bierce

A Union army soldier in the same unit as his brother, LT ADRIAN SEARING. Clear-sighted and a superb marksman, he is dispatched to the front line to reconnoitre Confederate troop movements. A stray shell, perhaps fired by an artillery captain he is preparing to snipe at, destroys the house in which he is sheltering, and he finds himself lying with his own cocked rifle pointing at his head, its hair-trigger sensitive to the slightest movement. Terrified by his predicament, which Bierce gives a universal significance, he commits suicide. Because of the dust on the body, his brother believes it belongs to an enemy soldier in Confederate grey.

Seaton, Arthur
Saturday Night and Sunday Morning, 1958
Alan Sillitoe

A factory worker and quick-witted rebel, who kicks over the traces of respectability and still comes up grinning when circumstances go against him. He is a cocky, larger-than-life figure who goes all out for what he wants, even when this is someone else's wife. Even when he gets his nose bloodied for his efforts, he refuses to dull the edge of his liveliness or rein in his sexual hunger. Despite the suffocation of the mechanical world of factory and production line, he emerges as a symbol of life, enthusiasm and laughter.

Sebastian
The Tempest, 1611
William Shakespeare

Sebastian holds his brother ALONSO, the King of Naples, responsible for their being shipwrecked. His greed for power and his evil disposition are encouraged by ANTONIO to such an extent that he is prepared to murder his brother. His treachery is prevented once, but he is willing to try a second time. Only the knowledge that PROSPERO is aware of his intentions stays his hand; he is prevented by fear, not guilt.

Sebastian
Twelfth Night, c.1601
William Shakespeare

Although devastated by the apparent death of his twin sister VIOLA, Sebastian treats ANTONIO and his generosity with kindness, affirming their friendship and disdaining the idea of accepting Antonio as his makeshift servant. His nature is somewhat impetuous, for he responds to OLIVIA's offer of marriage with disbelief but is not slow to accept. Conversely, he is not able to believe that Viola is who she says she is; he must have proof positive.

Secret Seven, the
The Secret Seven, 1949, et seq
Enid Blyton

The Seven comprise Pam, George, Peter, Jack, Janet, Barbara, Colin and Scamper the dog (an honorary member). Like all the best secret societies, the Seven have passwords, badges, a good supply of lemonade and stale rock buns, and a cosy shed for a meeting place. All they lack is a purpose, so they resolve to solve mysteries. They turn out to be fine detectives, spotting tyre tracks and noting down the patterns, disguising themselves to get close to the scene of the crime, and using their amazing powers of deduction. The girls have to be kept out of danger, though, since they cry at all the wrong moments. The police may never get called in until the last minute, but they are always jolly grateful to the Seven, and the Inspector is their greatest fan.

Sedley, Amelia
Vanity Fair, 1848
W M Thackeray
A school-friend of BECKY SHARP at Miss Pinkerton's Academy, she is as weak-willed and accommodating, trusting and uncynical, as Becky is the opposite. Amelia even idealizes the patently untrustworthy GEORGE OSBORNE, unable to delve below appearances. For Thackeray, she is an example of 'negative virtue'.

Sedley, John
Vanity Fair, 1848
W M Thackeray
Father to AMELIA and JOS SEDLEY, he is a successful businessman who has raised the family from the ranks of the middle-class to rub shoulders with aristocracy. His tragedy is that he cannot countenance any shrinkage in his expectations, and begins to gamble on ill-judged business projects in the hope of bringing back the good old days.

Sedley, Jos (Joseph)
Vanity Fair, 1848
W M Thackeray
AMELIA SEDLEY's brother, he founds his considerable self-importance on his former post as 'Collector of Boggley Wallah', despite which he patently lacks any real confidence. Selfish, fat and lazy, he treats his family badly and responds naively to BECKY SHARP's calculating flattery.

Sedley, Mrs
Vanity Fair, 1848
W M Thackeray
The wife of JOHN SEDLEY and mother of AMELIA and JOS SEDLEY, she finds it difficult to accept the family's diminished circumstances and, though sweet-natured like her daughter, becomes increasingly bitter and shrewish.

Sefti, Major Rama
The Rains Came, 1937
Louis Bromfield
A high-caste Indian Army doctor, a dedicated surgeon and scientist adored by his poor patients, Sefti has been designated to succeed the Maharajah as ruler of Ranchipur. To LADY EDWINA ESKETH he is a 'pale copper Apollo' annoyingly impervious to her seductive charms. But when Edwina volunteers for menial hospital work after the earthquake, propinquity and her unsuspected qualities achieve what her wiles could not. Sefti returns the love Edwina now genuinely feels for him, but must deal with the irreconcilable demands of personal desire and public duty.

Sejanus, Aelius
Sejanus, His Fall, 1605
Ben Jonson
The favourite adviser of Tiberius Caesar, he is as corrupt as the man he serves, but ambitious and hungry for political power. His resourcefulness, and his ability to prey on the weaknesses of those around him, flattering and browbeating his way to a position of advantage, mark him out as a potential dictator. His great flaw, though, is his pride, which increases with his power and eventually accounts for his fall. Such is the hatred in which he is held that his body is dismembered by a mob of citizens.

Sekoni
The Interpreters, 1965
Wole Soyinka
A young engineer in the new Nigeria. He ascribes his furious stammer – which he calls 'hiccups' – to cobbles swallowed in childhood. He suffers a violent nervous collapse on his return home with unfulfillable dreams of building a 20th-century nation with the mud and straw of an old tribal society.

Selby, Col George
The Gilded Age, 1873
Mark Twain and Charles Dudley Warner
This handsome former Confederate officer abuses the infatuated, irrational love and trust of LAURA HAWKINS over several years. His cruel, initial seduction of her is crucial in forming her resolution to regard men merely as stepping stones to her own advancement. However, she remains obsessed with Selby. Afraid to break with her yet unwilling to give her up, he snares himself in lies and false promises. When he finally chooses between Laura and his wife and family, the decision opens the denouement of the story.

Selden, Lawrence
The House of Mirth, 1905
Edith Wharton
A New York lawyer with a love of books and a rather shabby apartment, Selden is a reflective, popular and personable man who is accepted in high society but who has neither the means nor the inclination to be part of it. As an observer he is ironically amused by the complex code and manoeuvrings of New York's upper class, and of LILY BART in particular. Falling in love with her despite himself, he is incapable of preventing the cruel fate that overtakes her.

Seldom Seen Kid, the
Stories à la Carte, 1932
Damon Runyon
As a result of his occasional economy with the truth, most usually around the racetrack or some gambling joint, the Seldom Seen Kid, a young man with a winning smile and personable character, earns his title from his capacity to be absent when things get hot. When those who are less than pleased with him are found looking (gun in hand) for an opportunity to discuss some difference of interpretation, the Seldom Seen Kid cannot be found; which, in the

interests of his good health and longevity, is no bad thing.

Self, John
Money, 1984
Martin Amis

The 35-year-old, respected director of advertising commercials, he is on the brink of making his first feature film. At the moment, stressed, fat and feeling terrible, he commutes between London and New York, negotiating, hoping, whining, despairing, spending and making money. This last is one of his main interests, the others being fast food, drink and pornography, all in copious quantities. He is self-loathing and self-centred, yet sharp and literate enough (despite never having read *Animal Farm*) to see himself as what he is: vulnerable, uncomprehending and gullible. He represents, with Jacobean intensity, the cruel urban capitalist madness of his decade.

Selim
The Bride of Abydos: A Turkish Tale, 1813
Byron, George Gordon, 6th Lord Byron

Young Selim, despised by his father, the Pacha Giaffir, as 'son of a slave', dearly loves ZULEIKA, his sister. When Giaffir dooms her to marry an elderly Turkish lord, Selim is aghast. He asks her to meet him, and when she does, throws off his robe to reveal the barbaric splendour of a pirate; he is not in fact her brother but her cousin, son of Giaffir's murdered brother. He begs her to flee with him and share his life, but Giaffir and his men appear. Selim tries to escape but is slain, and Zuleika dies broken-hearted.

Selina
Ripples in the Pool, 1975
Rebeka Njau

'Selina was no ordinary girl: she was arrogant, self-centred, highly expensive and feared no man'. In an attempt to avoid loneliness, Selina marries a quiet and respectable man, GIKERE, who later becomes a violent and disillusioned alcoholic. Unable to recover from her harsh experiences as a young girl or to cope with the changes in her life once she is married, she becomes obsessed with Gikere's sister, Gaciru. As Selina's attempts to manipulate and control Gaciru become increasingly desperate, her insane jealousy leads to inevitable tragedy.

Sellers, Col Beriah
The Gilded Age, 1873
Mark Twain and Charles Dudley Warner

An imaginative, silvery-tongued opportunist who epitomizes the feverish speculative spirit of the US Reconstruction. (He was originally called Colonel Eschol Sellers, but this was changed in the book's second edition to avoid possible libel action.) Generous and well-intentioned, he shares his money-making schemes with his friends though more often than not the result is failure and poverty for all. Any money he accumulates is lost in whatever new get-rich-quick scheme comes his way, but he continues to feign prosperity while his family dines on turnips and water. His irrepressible optimism and refusal to acknowledge defeat and failure are so pronounced and powerful that it sometimes seems he has only a tenuous hold on reality.

Sello
A Question of Power, 1974
Bessie Head

ELIZABETH's 'lever out of hell'. The soul of Sello, which inhabits Elizabeth's mind and joins her on her 'journey to hell', is a philosophical and monk-like figure, bearing little resemblance to 'the living man', a practical crop farmer and cattle breeder. A Jekyll and Hyde figure, satanic and yet god-like, Sello manipulates and dominates Elizabeth while educating and advising her.

'Semitic Man, the', also known as Julius
Mosquitoes, 1927
William Faulkner

With his bald head, 'pasty loose jowled … flaccid face and dark compassionate eyes', he is the sardonic philosopher of the floating salon. He is the brother of MRS EVA WISEMAN, also a member of the party.

Sempill, David
Witch Wood, 1927
John Buchan

Like DAVID CRAWFURD before him, he is a young Scot, raised in a tradition of empirical scepticism, who is plunged dramatically into a world of pagan superstition and magic where he is obliged to set aside his better instincts for a time.

Seneca
Paradise, 1997
Toni Morrison

Abandoned and abused as a child and later the sexual plaything of a rich woman, Seneca has concealed and repressed her anguish, but secretly cuts herself as 'it steadied her'. A peacemaker, she obediently tries to please everyone in her desperation to be loved. She finds some safety with CONSOLATA at the Convent.

Senior, Duke
As You Like It, c.1600
William Shakespeare

Banished by his younger brother DUKE FREDERICK, Duke Senior appears as a forester, finding 'sermons in stones and good in everything'. He is a kind and courteous man but not without a sense of humour, especially when it comes to teasing JACQUES. Restored to his lands and his daughter ROSALIND, he leaves the forest without regret to return to the real world.

Sensualitie, Dame
Ane Pleasant Satyre of the Thrie Estaitis, 1540
Sir David Lindsay

Self-proclaimed daughter of Venus, Sensualitie is the lusty dame who, lauding her own physical attributes, seduces REX HUMANITAS, leaving him, and consequently his kingdom, powerless against vice and deception. Although she signifies the moral breakdown in society, her expulsion from the court by DIVYNE CORRECTIOUN heralds the return of rationality – GUDE COUNSALL – and therefore the moral recovery of the king and his courtiers.

Sentry, Captain
The Spectator, 1711–12
Joseph Addison and Richard Steele
Captain Sentry represents the army in the Club. He has seen valiant service for many years but has resigned to settle on his own small estate, a wise decision since he is SIR ROGER DE COVERLEY's heir. In his opinion, promotion in the army is often won by impudence and flattery rather than by ability, though in this he remains modest, saying that he has left military life because he is not good enough. His comments on such matters are always interesting because of his experience and his frankness.

Seonaid
Butcher's Broom, 1934
Neil Gunn
Seonaid is essentially the matriarchal spirit of the Highland community. Proud and outspoken, she is unafraid of crossing wits or words with the people of Riasgan, as is proved by her support of ELIE and her defiance of the evictors. She is the true fighting spirit of the village, and although she realizes the futility of resistance she openly vents her anger at the injustice of it all.

Sergeant, Tom
Skylight, 1995
David Hare
A hard-working, successful restaurateur whose vigorous, brusque manner and obdurate conservative views belie a deep vulnerability and a desperate need for love. It is three years since his wife discovered his affair with KYRA HOLLIS and a year since her death from cancer left him a widower. Not having seen Kyra for three years, he arrives at her rundown flat, hoping both to receive atonement for his guilt and perhaps begin their relationship again. In this play of romance and ideas, he is more bewildered than angered by Kyra's newly gained independence and sense of purpose.

Sergeant of the Law, the
The Canterbury Tales, c.1387–1400
Geoffrey Chaucer
A man who is expert in his own profession and quick to turn that knowledge to his own advantage. He is particularly adept at land purchasing, a questionable practice which allows him to feather his own nest at the expense of his clients from whom he commands large fees. His bland appearance conceals his all-consuming self-interest, and his tale, a moralizing, Christian romance, is oddly at variance with his true character.

Serpent, the
Back to Methuselah, 1921
George Bernard Shaw
The Serpent appears in the first section of this five-part play. *In the Beginning* is set in the Garden of Eden. Coiled in a tree, the Serpent is female, wise and 'the most subtle of all the creatures'. She is able to speak and teaches Eve the principle of death being overcome by birth, and reveals to her the secret of the creation of life. The Serpent represents Shaw's theory that human desires and customs are a continually evolving matter of both nature and nurture.

Set
The Ancient Child, 1989
N Scott Momaday
Like his predecessor Abel, his name suggests the double-ness of his nature. A successful artist in the white world of modern California, it is clear that like the Egyptian god Set he is condemned to inhabit a dry and sterile desert in which even his hectic potency is wasted. Only gradually, with the help of GREY, does he come to recognize the need to re-establish relations with his ancestral past.

Sethe
Beloved, 1988
Toni Morrison
An amalgam of attitudes about motherhood, Sethe is a woman charting her own survival through slavery's horrifically impersonal regime. Her memories, intermingled with myth and poetry, become something that 'is not a story to pass on'. Obsessed with 'the serious work of beating back the past', she is unable to take possession of, or even acknowledge herself. It is only through a traumatic reliving of events that she slowly moves to the uncertain realization that 'You your best thing, Sethe. You are'.

Seton, Patrick
The Bachelors, 1960
Muriel Spark
A small, thin, very softly spoken spiritualist medium, police informer and criminal. Middle-aged and worried-looking, he has a profound effect on many women because of his spiritual air and poetry reciting. He sees his life as comprising a happy childhood followed by 'unfortunate occurrences'. His evil-doing derives from a failure to appreciate the reality of other people.

Seton, Sally
Mrs Dalloway, 1925
Virginia Woolf
As a young woman Sally lacks the social status of some of her contemporaries, but her assurance, intelligence and beauty, along with a polemic streak, make her part of the 'set'. Bohemian, exotic (part French) and passionate, she has a quick temper and idealistic beliefs, both of which land her in trouble. But this Sally is an act, which alters when she conforms by marrying well. She is softened by motherhood, which gives her an aura of serenity rather than aggression, and her quest for power seems to have been rooted in a sense of inferiority, which marriage eradicates.

Severance, Nell
Swamp Angel, 1954
Ethel Wilson
Sensually and intellectually vigorous, Nell is a woman of enormous energy and strength – a mover – the centre from which others are motivated, directed, manoeuvred. Both disillusioned and indulgent of humanity and the human condition, Nell is at once 'of the world' and yet outside it, an ironic observer and yet the most active of participants in the human drama.

Sewell, David
The Rise of Silas Lapham, 1885
William Dean Howells

The minister of the LAPHAM family, he functions as a ghostly confessor, mediating in the troubled matter of the daughters' rivalry for the hand of TOM COREY, and able to see SILAS LAPHAM transformed into a true Christian by his humiliation.

Seymour, Jean-Marc
Borderline, 1985
Janette Turner Hospital

The narrator of this fragmented story, Jean-Marc assumes the position of a piano tuner who 'untangle[s] the out-of-tune world. Note by note'. By inhabiting the memories of his principal characters, he is able to reconstruct his own passions within their actions, fully aware as he does so that 'we impose our own lives on the world: the self as template'. Initially using this creative role as a refuge, he comes to relish the power and control it represents. Moving from technician to artist, he is able to survive only by maintaining the present as 'an infinite number of fictions'.

Seyton, Catherine
The Abbot, 1820
Sir Walter Scott

The daughter of a great Catholic house, she is a lady-in-waiting to MARY, QUEEN OF SCOTS, and is loved by ROLAND GRAEME. She has a fine sense of the ridiculous, and is in no way overawed or smug about either situation. By general consent, she is one of Scott's most human and vital heroines.

Shade, John
Pale Fire, 1962
Vladimir Nabokov

A New England professor and poet whose ghost haunts the novel obliquely through his four cantos of rhyming couplets. Plainly auto-biographical in content, the poem examines fundamental truths, his world shaken by the apparent suicide of his only daughter, a beloved ugly duckling. Reviewing attempts to come to terms with death, he finally is 'reasonably sure' of a succession in life. However, his intellectual doubt – 'Life Everlasting – based on a misprint' – is ironically confirmed in the accompanying commentary of his nemesis, CHARLES KINBOTE.

Shafton, Sir Piercie
The Monastery, 1820
Sir Walter Scott

Scott confessed to having based Sir Piercie 'upon some forgotten and obsolete model of folly'. An Englishman of high birth and rather euphuistic pretensions to culture, he looks on his Scottish hosts with considerable condescension; the only person unequivocally impressed with him in turn is the miller's daughter, MYSIE OF THE MILL.

Shagpat
The Shaving of Shagpat, 1856
George Meredith

An old oriental clothier and tale-spinner, who acts as a channel for a series of mysterious allegorical fantasies. He is married to the more earth-bound Kadza.

Shakespeare
Bingo, 1973
Edward Bond

Shakespeare is living the last year of his life at New Place, Stratford. A man of property and reputation, he sits in his garden, pondering on the horrors of his age. Grieving, evasive, troubled, complacent, fearful and pained by a brutal and jarring world, he wonders whether his work has actually had any effect at all. 'Was anything done?' he cries as, miserable and tired, he commits suicide. Whether he has judged himself too harshly, or correctly, or made the judgement on false moral choices, is for the audience to decide.

Shallow, Justice (Robert)
Henry IV Part II, 1597/8
The Merry Wives of Windsor, c.1597
William Shakespeare

Formerly of Clement's Inn, London, Shallow is now a Justice of the Peace in Gloucestershire. In *Henry IV Part II* he assembles a band of recruits for SIR JOHN FALSTAFF, apparently an old friend from London days, and later lends him money. In *The Merry Wives of Windsor* he both turns against Falstaff, outraged at his behaviour, and attempts to match his cousin, ABRAHAM SLENDER, with ANNE PAGE. Shallow is a gentleman of breeding and decency, with a rather moralizing, even self-important streak. A little frail, he is sometimes too kind for his own good.

Shalott, the Lady of
'The Lady of Shalott', 1833
Alfred Lord Tennyson

The lovely victim of an evil curse, she is bound to stick to her enchanted weaving task night and day, without ever looking out of the window. When Sir Lancelot rides past on his way to Camelot, the mysterious lady's self-discipline snaps and she resigns herself to her doom.

Shandon, Captain
The History of Pendennis, 1848–50
W M Thackeray

An Irish wide-boy, he edits the *Pall-Mall Gazette* from a debtor's prison, irrepressibly enthusiastic about a new project even while suffering the repercussions of those that have failed. It is Shandon who introduces ARTHUR PENDENNIS to Grub Street.

Shandy, Mrs
The Life and Opinions of Tristram Shandy, 9 volumes, 1759–67
Laurence Sterne

The wife of WALTER SHANDY and mother of TRISTRAM SHANDY. An oasis of normality in the midst of the scarcely contained craziness around her, she presses on with her life, largely undisturbed by the wild theorizing and bizarre behaviour that feature in her home, and tries to impose some order on the chaos that would only worsen were she not there to impose a modicum of stability and common sense. For this she is roundly misunderstood, but she refuses to rise to the criticisms that she is boring or unintelligent.

Shandy, Tristram
The Life and Opinions of Tristram Shandy, 9 volumes, 1759–67
Laurence Sterne
The bawdy, luckless narrator of his own life-story, one that is beleaguered by birth into a family peopled with eccentrics, and by early disfigurement. Using his strong powers of intellect and warm sense of humour, he tries to make some sense of the strange world he inhabits, where obscure discussion mingles with searching characterization, to evoke a sense of the special world that has since come to be known as Shandeism.

Shandy, Uncle Toby
The Life and Opinions of Tristram Shandy, 9 volumes, 1759–67
Laurence Sterne
A delightful, unashamed eccentric, blessed with a gentleness of spirit and with a devoted servant, CORPORAL TRIM. Badly wounded in the groin during a siege, Toby now maintains an interest in all siege-related matters, engrossed with the subject to the point of obsession. He floats through the Shandy household, untroubled by its complications, content to pursue his hobby undisturbed. When love beckons in the comely form of the widow MRS WADMAN, he copes with his new feelings and the pressures these entail with an ingenuous charm.

Shandy, Walter
The Life and Opinions of Tristram Shandy, 9 volumes, 1759–67
Laurence Sterne
The father of TRISTRAM SHANDY, he builds a world around himself, his family life and social connections in which general philosophizing and strong opinions play an enormous role, and where no opinions are more important than his. He loves to explore the unknown world of the possible, to stretch ideas until sometimes they snap into the ridiculous, and he cannot understand why others cannot think at his pace or share his enthusiasms. Strong-willed and sometimes overbearing, he is salvaged by a pomposity that makes people grin.

Shane
Shane, 1949
Jack Schaefer
An enigmatic cowboy who rides into the life of a frontier family, rescues them from a crisis by his courage and skill at shooting, then leaves them just as surprisingly, without sharing more than he needs to of his story or personality. He becomes a hero figure for the son of the house, representing natural justice and unwavering bravery in the face of threat, but Shane will not be tied down, and refuses to be involved in any long-term friendship that will restrict his freedom to move on.

Shanghai Jim
Empire of the Sun, 1985
J G Ballard
An English schoolboy caught in the Japanese invasion. He is obsessed by a cyclical vision of unending war, and develops an enormous will to survive amid the horrors of war and prison camp, where his character emerges as a curious, memorable mix of child and premature adult. He has a fantasy of flying, and admires the courage of the Japanese pilots. He has a guilty belief that he is personally responsible for starting the war, but has a concomitant conviction that he can miraculously bring people back to life, and takes responsibility for the survival of a number of adults.

Shankland, Anne
Table by the Window, the first of two plays under the general title *Separate Tables*, 1954
Terence Rattigan
Mrs Shankland is about 40 and seems entirely out of place at the unpretentious Beauregard Private Hotel, near Bournemouth. Her clothes are too smart and her coiffure too stylish, and she has 'an air of Belgravia and the smarter London restaurants'. She bears down upon the Beauregard in order to reclaim John Malcolm, her former husband and former Labour Government minister, who served a prison sentence after assaulting her. Her own subsequent second marriage also ended in divorce, partly the result of her selfishness, social ambitions and fear. She is also failing professionally, and is unable to bear the thought of drifting into old age alone.

Shannon, Larry (Lawrence)
The Night of the Iguana, 1961
Tennessee Williams
A priest, defrocked for atheism and the seduction of young female charges, he is 'a man of God on vacation' who brings a tour group of Southern church ladies to MAXINE FAULK's Mexican hotel, and is abandoned by them there. The play focuses on his complex mental state – he doesn't 'have a dime left in his nervous emotional bank account'. However, the physical blandishments of Maxine, and the spiritual advice of HANNAH JELKES combine to save this 'Protestant black Irish looney' from himself.

Shapiro, Joseph
The Penitent, 1983
Isaac Bashevis Singer
A wealthy and successful Jewish immigrant living in New York who is troubled by a sense of guilt about his materialistic lifestyle. Joseph's character has two strands: one side is unshakeable in its desire to tread the path of righteousness, while the other is ready to succumb to temptation. A struggle is waged within him – a vociferous dialogue between The Good Spirit and The Evil Spirit. Joseph's determination is admirable, if a little idealistic and fanatical, and he is only satisfied once he is living the most orthodox life in Jerusalem.

Sharp, Becky (Rebecca)
Vanity Fair, 1848
W M Thackeray
She is one of the most vividly drawn characters in English literature. Despite the disadvantages of her birth (to a French dancer and a struggling artist), Becky succeeds, via marriage to manipulable

members of the nobility, in climbing the social ladder. She is the archetypal anti-heroine, pitting her wits against convention with a bluntness and effortless social adaptability that allows her to move into almost every level of society. She is cold, opportunistic and pitiless, but remains endlessly seductive.

Sharp, John
Wake Up, 2002
Tim Pears

John Sharp tells us about his life as he drives into work on a Monday morning. A trained biochemist, now co-owner of a potato farm, he has collaborated with a genetic engineering company where experiments have started to go wrong. He has had a poor upbringing resulting in him wanting, and fighting for, something better. However, he is also a compulsive liar, a trait in his character that compares unfavourably with those of the more honourable people in his life, in particular his brother and his wife.

Shaunn the Post
Finnegans Wake, 1939
James Joyce

The twin brother of SHEM THE PENMAN, he is the postman, never the creator but merely the deliverer. As fighter and politician Shaunn's domain is the temporal, his occasional embodiment as a stone signifying his permanence and solidity and the deadness of the letter of the law.

Shaw, Felix
The Watch Tower, 1966
Elizabeth Harrower

Whether his flaws of character are a direct result of his lonely background and repressed homosexuality is questionable. Whatever the reason, Felix Shaw is undoubtedly evil. A misogynist of the worst imaginable kind, he takes pleasure in manipulating the lives of his young wife, LAURA SHAW, and her sister, CLARE VAIZEY. Hiding behind schizophrenic behaviour induced by chronic alcoholism, he continually offers hope of a kinder and more generous nature. But his rage is more fearful than Bluebeard's, and the threat he wields of physical violence overshadows Laura's and Clare's lives.

Shaw, Laura, née Vaizey
The Watch Tower, 1966
Elizabeth Harrower

A talented schoolgirl who dreams of becoming a doctor or an opera singer and seems capable of both, Laura is manipulated by first her mother and then her husband, FELIX SHAW. As a young woman in her early thirties, she has lost all hope for her own future and dreams that her cruel husband will become the kind and generous man she is convinced he can be. Repressed herself, she attempts to retain control of her younger sister CLARE VAIZEY's life and manipulates her relentlessly, using every emotional weapon available to her.

Shay, Heather
Capricornia, 1938
Xavier Herbert

Good-looking and self-possessed, she is in love with MARK SHILLINGSWORTH. Although she possesses a developed streak of vanity, Heather is a frank, strong and courageous woman. She is also an excellent judge of character and, when Mark apparently abandons her and Capricornia, refuses to renounce him. Her tenacity and foresight are well founded, for, after many years, Heather redeems him.

Shearwater, James
Antic Hay, 1923
Aldous Huxley

A distinguished scientist, Shearwater places little value on human emotions, and claims that he 'hasn't the leisure' to be interested in people. Consequently, when he is asked his opinion about love by MYRA VIVEASH, he revealingly replies, 'That's one of the subjects ... like the Great Wall of China and the habits of Trematodes, I don't allow myself to be interested in'.

Sheila
A Day in the Death of Joe Egg, 1967
Peter Nichols

'A truly integrated person', according to her husband BRI, Sheila is the mother of JOE. Her assurance and pragmatism are merely superficial, masking, not altogether successfully, a deep-seated sense of guilt and unease. Having been sexually promiscuous before becoming pregnant with her daughter, Sheila subconsciously feels that Joe's disabilities represent her punishment. Nevertheless, in contrast to her sceptical, despondent husband, she tells herself Joe might improve as she gets older. It is, as she perhaps knows, a forlorn hope.

Sheill, Queely
The Tilted Cross, 1961
Hal Porter

Tall, golden-haired and extremely handsome, young Queely is the son of a dissipated actor in Hobart Town, Van Diemen's Land (Tasmania). Uneducated and with a Cockney accent, he devotes himself to the unhappy, including JUDAS GRIFFIN VANELEIGH and ASNETHA SLEEP: 'Everyone who wants, I give them what they want of me. *Hif* their 'earts are wretched and put-upon'. His excess of innocence leads him to a horrific fate as a sacrificial victim.

Shem the Penman
Finnegans Wake, 1939
James Joyce

The twin brother of SHAUNN THE POST, one half of HUMPHREY CHIMPDEN EARWICKER's warring personality. Shem is the creative artist who produces his art from within, literally using his excrement as ink and his skin as parchment. At times a tree, representing life and generation, his is the monopoly of spiritual power.

Shephard, Isaac
Of Age and Innocence, 1958
George Lamming

The novel is set on the fictional island of San Cristobal, which reflects the history and culture of the West Indies. Disgruntled by his experiences in England, Shephard returns to the island to help organize a multiracial independence movement. Full of idealism, he recruits East Indian and Chinese leaders but, although winning popular support, neither overcomes the profound distrust of some sections of the community, nor his own dilemma: his passion for freedom and his desire for the approval of all who are interested in the island's future. His commitment to independence is undermined by his begrudging admiration for England. Ultimately a tragic figure, Shephard is a symbol of the crisis afflicting both the colonizer and the colonized.

Sherbon, George/Johor
Shikasta, 1979
Doris Lessing

According to his sister Rachel, George was a deeply analytical child, who held a very powerful position in the family. Both his brother and sister craved his respect and love. Although courteous and kind, he had a complex and cynical view of the world, and his attitude to others was complicated. He tended to see humans as functional machines, and seems to have enjoyed the power which came naturally to him. With regard to his partner, Suzannah, he is described as a 'power-lover'. His alter ego, Johor, is difficult to assess, since we meet him through his own voice, and are told that he has been influenced by the Shikastans, whose land he is investigating. He displays a false modesty which borders on smugness, and is concerned with control. In either world, he is an unattractive figure.

Shere Khan, also known as Lungri
The Jungle Book, 1894
Rudyard Kipling

A tiger, occasionally given to man-eating, who lives over by the Waingunga River, at some distance from the other jungle dwellers. As with all autocrats, his fixation on the letter of the law is matched by a sort of lofty contempt for the law per se, and he is something of an outsider.

Sheringham, Lord
Jack Holborn, 1964
Leon Garfield

He possesses a quiet dignity and authority that is immediately recognized by all who meet him, even if they are unaware of his true identity as a judge. He is identical both in outward appearance and manner of speech to his black-hearted pirate twin, CAPTAIN ROGERS, and cannot find peace until the wicked Captain has met his rightful end on the gallows.

Sherston, George
Memoirs of a Fox-Hunting Man, 1928
Memoirs of an Infantry Officer, 1930
Sherston's Progress, 1936
Siegfried Sassoon

A privileged young man, immersing himself in all that was pleasant about English country life – cricket, the Hunt, friendships, good education – only to have the idyll disrupted by experience in the trenches during Word War I. Bringing a critical view to the situation, he suppresses his anger at the waste and folly, disguising his hatred

of war under a veneer of nonchalance. But brave deeds and searching critiques cannot spare him the anguish of watching the destruction of a generation.

Shields, Seumus
The Shadow of a Gunman, 1923
Sean O'Casey

A heavily built man of 35, Shields rents a room with DONAL DAVOREN in a Dublin tenement. He scrapes a living as a pedlar, selling odd pieces of cutlery and pairs of braces. 'In him is frequently manifested the superstition, the fear and the malignity of primitive man'. Disillusioned with Republican politics, he maintains a mocking, sometimes cynical commentary on the current state of political and cultural nationalism. 'Oh, this is a hopeless country! … I taught Irish six nights a week … I paid me rifle levy like a man … Now, after all me work … the only answer you can get from a roarin' Republican to a simple question is "goodbye…ee".'

Shillingsworth, Marigold
Capricornia, 1938
Xavier Herbert

OSCAR SHILLINGSWORTH's daughter. She was taken as a child to South Australia and brought up there as a virtual sister to NORMAN SHILLINGSWORTH. She has inherited her father's social ambition and when she discovers that Norman is half-Aborigine, a fact that constitutes a serious impediment to her social and marital aspirations, she shuns him despite their close relationship. After landing a suitable husband, she goes to live in Singapore.

Shillingsworth, Mark, alias Jack Ramble
Capricornia, 1938
Xavier Herbert

The brother of OSCAR SHILLINGSWORTH and uncle of MARIGOLD SHILLINGSWORTH, Mark arrives in Capricornia (the Northern Territory) in 1904. A restless, unfulfilled man, a natural drifter with a weakness for alcohol, he soon becomes part of the low life in Port Zodiac (Darwin). He fathers a son, NORMAN SHILLINGSWORTH, by an Aboriginal woman, both of whom he abandons, and having murdered a Chinese storekeeper, disappears. Almost 20 years later, he resurfaces as Jack Ramble, a railway construction boss. His former lover, HEATHER SHAY, knows his secret and becomes his passport to public redemption.

Shillingsworth, Norman ('Nawnim')
Capricornia, 1938
Xavier Herbert

The son of an Aboriginal woman and a white settler, MARK SHILLINGSWORTH, he is deserted by his father while still an infant. He acquires the name of 'Nawnim' (No Name), which is later transmuted into Norman when he is taken in by his uncle, OSCAR SHILLINGSWORTH. For many years Norman remains ignorant of his real mother and father, but once he finds out, he embarks upon a physical and spiritual journey in search of his true heritage. Although an instinctive, intelligent and resilient man, Norman has no status in a society divided so violently between white settlers and Aborigines.

Shillingsworth, Oscar
Capricornia, 1938
Xavier Herbert

The determined and self-disciplined brother of MARK SHILLINGSWORTH, he arrives in Capricornia (the Northern Territory) in 1904. Having married Jasmine, he works to establish the Red Ochre cattle station and raise his family, including his daughter, MARIGOLD SHILLINGSWORTH, and Mark's half-caste son NORMAN SHILLINGSWORTH. His wife having left him, the disillusioned Oscar departs for Batman (Melbourne). Some see him as unsympathetic, inflexible and authoritarian, while others judge him to be discriminating and compassionate.

Shimerda, Ántonia
My Ántonia, 1918
Willa Cather

Cather stated that she wanted her heroine to be presented 'like a rare object in the middle of a table – which one may examine from all sides'. The daughter of Bohemian immigrants to Nebraska, Ántonia is seen mainly through the eyes of her childhood friend JIM BURDEN. Proud, resourceful and an object of desire, she survives, 'battered but not diminished', into vital middle age, a living symbol of frontier resolution.

Shinza, Edward
A Guest of Honour, 1970
Nadine Gordimer

A former revolutionary hero who has nevertheless been overlooked for a place in his country's new but increasingly corrupt government. His labour socialism places him in opposition to old friends and he plots a coup to restore power to the working people.

Shipley, Hagar, née Currie
The Stone Angel, 1964
Margaret Laurence

A proud woman, 'rampant with memory', Hagar struggles to come to terms with her mortality by intermingling past and present. Arguing that 'beyond the changing shell that houses me, I see the eyes of Hagar Currie', she is simultaneously old and young. Irascibly independent, she exhibits a profound self-knowledge that makes her account acutely personal. She learns that 'pride was my wilderness, and the demon that led me there was fear', and is finally able both to accept responsibility for her actions and to forgive.

Shipman, the
The Canterbury Tales, c.1387–1400
Geoffrey Chaucer

The master of *The Magdalene*, an excellent navigator from Dartmouth who sits rather awkwardly on his horse. He is a ruthless privateer, always with a dagger at the ready, who is quite capable of making his enemies walk the plank. He makes his money from his expert knowledge of the sea routes to France and Spain, and probably from a little smuggling as well. Basically a brave man to venture so far in a small boat, he tells a tale of female cunning.

Shiralee, the → Buster

Shirley → Keeldar, Shirley

Shirley, Peter
Major Barbara, 1905
George Bernard Shaw

A newcomer at BARBARA UNDERSHAFT's Salvation Army shelter, Shirley is exhausted and weak with hunger. Forty-six years old, he looks more. Having just been made redundant from his job as a fitter because of his grey hair, Shirley's emotions are a tormented mix of self-pity and wounded pride. He is loath to accept 'the bread o charity' in the form of a slice of bread and treacle and a cup of tea, but finally does so on the condition the Army treats it as a loan.

Shockley, Billie
City of Women, 1981
David Ireland

A 62-year-old retired water engineer and lesbian separatist, Billie lives in a Sydney from which the men have been banished, although their presence still lurks around the city periphery. Grieving for her lost daughter, and reminiscing about Bobbie, her former lover, Billie longs to have someone share her solitude. Having had a vigorous sexual past, she regrets losing it. She has Bobbie with her in the form of a leopard, which is some compensation, for at least the animal does not accuse her of overeating chocolate. Drinking too much, she sees herself as 'inventor, engineer, creator, exploiter, failed lover, failed friend, voyeur'. Yet she is a woman of enormous strength and through pain achieves a new beginning.

Shogo
Narrow Road to the Deep North, 1968
Edward Bond

Living in Japan, sometime in the 17th, 18th or 19th centuries, Shogo (who turns out to have been the baby BASHO discovered abandoned) overthrows the emperor and sets himself up as a dictator. He builds a city, partly in order to create material evidence of his autocracy and partly in an attempt to harmonize the discord of his own experience and create a rational morality for his actions. He is in his turn overthrown by GEORGINA and a group of westerners. A cruel leader, without pride but with a twisted sense of dignity, he is willing to do whatever is politically expedient to save himself.

Shonjen, Dr
'The Good Anna', in *Three Lives*, 1909
Gertrude Stein

A physician of Bridgepoint who takes on ANNA FEDERNER as his patient and – later – housekeeper. He is 'cheery, jovial, hearty, full of jokes that made much fun and yet were full of simple common sense and reasoning courage'.

Shoop, Earle
The Day of the Locust, 1939
Nathanael West

A Hollywood hanger-on and sometime cowboy actor, he dresses entirely in stagey 'Western' gear, twirling a lasso and talking in the tough, side-of-mouth style demanded of hard-riding tough-guys.

Shortley, Mrs
The Displaced Person, 1948
Flannery O'Connor
An employee of MRS MCINTYRE, who becomes obsessed with the newly employed Polish exile, Mr Guizac. A sullen and recalcitrant worker, she regards him with a deeply irrational and xenophobic suspicion; unable to distinguish between the victims and perpetrators of the atrocities in Nazi Europe she fears that he may carry the infection of their 'murderous ways'.

Shorty
Omoo, 1847
Herman Melville
A planter at Martair, who employs the narrator and DOCTOR LONG GHOST. He is 'a short little Cockney', but a 'good-looking young fellow' of 25, with cheeks burned red from 'his roving life'. Like his partner, ZEKE, he is quite illiterate, but has imbibed the spirit of invincible industry from him, and dreams of making an unlikely fortune from their poor plantation.

Shotover, Captain
Heartbreak House, 1916
George Bernard Shaw
An elderly, white-bearded, overbearing and seemingly impossible man, Shotover is a retired sea captain and visionary who 'sold his soul to the Devil in Zanzibar', to adapt to real life. Muttering conspiratorially about attaining 'the seventh degree of concentration', he also stores high explosives in a gravel pit behind his Sussex home, part of which resembles the interior of a ship. ELLIE DUNN calls it Heartbreak House. Sage, mystic and madman, Shotover has made it a place of self-delusion and revelation.

Shylock
The Merchant of Venice, 1594/5
William Shakespeare
A Jewish moneylender, whom persecution has made bitter; his motivation for the infamous 'pound of flesh' trickery is that ANTONIO is 'a Christian [who] lends out money gratis', and there can be no doubt of his malevolence towards most of his fellow men. However, he has been ill-used in the past, is shown no sympathy by any character in the course of the play, and demonstrates qualities of family love and financial sense which might shame his anti-Semitic opponents.

Sibley
The Glass Canoe, 1976
David Ireland
Sibley is an old school-friend of MEAT MAN, and, like him, observes the group of regular drinkers in a small pub on the outskirts of Sydney. But while Meat Man's attitude is one of detachment, Sibley, a zealous outsider, earnestly documents their foibles and anti-social attitudes as part of his research for a thesis on social psychology. In comparison with Meat Man, Sibley is a realist, seeing the world as it really is; but there is also a ruthless quality in Sibley, a combined horror and delight in the failures of others. He is an intruder, a killjoy whose death is presented as grotesque comedy.

'Sick-Boy' Williamson, Simon David
Trainspotting, 1993
Porno, 2002
Irvine Welsh
Of partly Italian extraction, Sick-Boy is a hedonistic womanizer who lives by his guilt- and caution-free belief that 'the morn takes care ay itsel'. Capable of turning himself out 'looking like an advertising executive', he carefully cultivates his image of a 'lovable cavalier' (most effectively to his friends' parents), but he is essentially 'a born exploiter'. He looks on his friends as 'an extremely limited company' and is even becoming gradually estranged from his childhood friend and fellow heroin-user MARK RENTON, as their ritual sniping at one another, long a cornerstone of their friendship, has taken on a harder, more resentful edge.

Sidi
The Lion and the Jewel, 1959
Wole Soyinka
The 'village belle', she carries huge bundles and water jars on her head, 'like a spider', and stands as the exotic opposite of the shabby schoolmaster LAKUNLE.

Sidonia
Coningsby, or The New Generation, 1844
Benjamin Disraeli
A wise and cultured Jew, whose social prominence has been earned in the face of England's deep-seated anti-Semitism. He acts as HARRY CONINGSBY's role model and tutor in civic responsibility, but he is also a mouthpiece for Disraeli's pride about Jewry's contribution to European civilization.

Sieppe, Trina, subsequently Trina McTeague
McTeague: A Story of San Francisco, 1899
Frank Norris
The cousin of MARCUS SCHOULER, she marries the dentist MCTEAGUE shortly after winning $5,000 in a lottery. Small, pretty, anaemically pale, she is crowned by an astonishing mass of blue-black hair. 'All the vitality that should have given color to her face seemed to have been absorbed by this marvelous hair'. Obsessed with her winnings, she grows miserly and goads McTeague into loutish greed and violence.

Signal, Malfred
A State of Siege, 1966
Janet Frame
Driven inwards and outwards at the same time, to physical exile on a small island, and towards an obsessive examination of the way language consistently fails to explain reality or dissipate fear, she is herself a disturbed linguistic 'signal', a projection of personality rather than a straightforward 'character'.

Sikes, Bill
Oliver Twist, 1838
Charles Dickens
A villainous housebreaker with no redeeming qualities, he terrorizes everyone he meets, including his 'fence', FAGIN. He fails in helping Fagin to turn OLIVER TWIST into a thief and brutally murders NANCY when Fagin reveals she

has informed on them. Accompanied by his ill-treated dog, Bull's-eye, he makes a terrified dash to escape arrest but dies by accidentally hanging himself as he falls from a roof.

Silas
The Death of the Hired Man, 1914
Robert Frost
His character is revealed to us through the conversation between the farmer, WARREN, and his wife, MARY. An old, simple, rural farmhand, he has come to regard their place as 'home', and has returned there to die. His fierce pride is suggested by his unwillingness to accept any comforts or to seek help from his wealthy brother; his life has been dedicated to work. Eschewing the benefits of education represented by the college boy, Harold Wilson, he has sought and found skill with the pitchfork.

Silas, Uncle
Uncle Silas, 1864
J Sheridan Le Fanu
A strange mixture of Swedenborgian pieties and murderous villainy, he plans to marry his niece Maud to his son for the sake of her fortune. His thin, clear voice, persuasive, apparently reasonable, always evil, makes Maud doubt her sanity. He is fertile in devices and lies. His appearance – white hair like John Wesley, ivory-white face and black garments like a Rembrandt portrait – suggest kindly benevolence but his heart is as cold as marble.

Silence, Justice
Henry IV Part II, 1597/8
William Shakespeare
Like his cousin JUSTICE SHALLOW, Justice Silence is also a Justice of the Peace. Of extreme age, he is seeing out his days graciously in a Gloucestershire orchard. Although a man of few words, Silence can quite easily contribute to much of the humour in the play.

Silenski, Cass
Another Country, 1962
James Baldwin
A friend of VIVALDO MOORE and RUFUS SCOTT and the wife of RICHARD SILENSKI. Rufus 'could never quite place her in the white world to which she seemed to belong. She came from New England, of plain old American stock – so she put it; she was very fond of remembering that one of her ancestors had been burned as a witch'.

Silenski, Richard
Another Country, 1962
James Baldwin
A Polish expatriate in New York, where he works as a college instructor. He was the novelist VIVALDO MOORE's English teacher and seems locked in quiet domestic harmony with CASS SILENSKI until he achieves success as a writer, at which point his ambitions and needs begin to change.

Silk, Coleman
The Human Stain, 2000
Philip Roth
A distinguished professor, Silk suggests that two

absent African-American students are 'spooks', and as a result is charged with racism and sacked. The accusation is unjust, Silk having used the word in its original sense, but it is also ironic because Silk is himself something of a ghost. He too is African-American although, being exceptionally light-skinned, he has for over half a century chosen to pass himself off as a white Jew. Now in his seventies, he begins an affair with Faunia Farely, a 34-year-old janitor, allowing the 'brute' of his lust full rein. Scheming and driven, Silk discovers himself pursued by furies and in many ways responsible for his own torments.

Silver, Harry
Man and Boy, 1999
Man and Wife, 2002
Tony Parsons
A seemingly content but shallow TV executive, and the married father of a baby son, his life changes when he loses his job and his wife leaves him after he has an impetuous one-night stand. After he takes custody of his child, he becomes a more sympathetic character who gradually overcomes his fear of responsibility, and forms new attachments outside the comforting familiarity of his previous life.

Silver, Long John
Treasure Island, 1883
Robert Louis Stevenson
One of modern literature's greatest psychopathic creations. A clever, vicious, smiling villain, Silver is capable of enormous charm and extreme cruelty, his wooden leg symbolizing a crippled personality whose ambitions have been thwarted and whose soul is maimed and incomplete. Conveying a menacing physical and sexual charge, Silver's appallingly speedy athleticism and lightning mood swings are the stuff of nightmares. As the original title of the novel (*The Sea Cook*) suggests, he is the central character: a diabolic force which is implacable and brooks no rational understanding; a plausible demon who can never be assuaged and dare not be forgotten.

Silver, Mattie
Ethan Frome, 1911
Edith Wharton
A poor, friendless girl, Mattie is the daughter of ZEENA FROME's cousin, who has murdered his wife and abandoned Mattie. Her misfortune indentures her to the Fromes, and her youth and enthusiasm offer ETHAN FROME a pathway out of the nightmare of isolation. She intoxicates him with her delicious charms, her ease and freedom. But Mattie's 'liberation' turns into an imprisonment as she is left entirely dependent on Zeena, enclosed in a suffocating space and enduring an existence of death-in-life.

Silver, Miss Maude
Pilgrim's Rest, 1948, et seq
Patricia Wentworth
A professional private detective, Miss Silver was previously a governess, and has privileged entree into police investigations led by her former charges, who regard her small person and

powers of detection with respect and admiration. Severe but kind, neat and dowdy, she seems of an earlier age, with her mouse-brown curled Queen Alexandra fringe, her carved bog-oak jewellery, the riot of Victoriana in her London flat, and her apt quotations from 'dear Lord Tennyson'. Armed with her knitting-bag, Miss Silver listens and observes while briskly making garments for niece Ethel and her children.

Silverbridge, Lord
The Duke's Children, 1880
Anthony Trollope
The eldest son of PLANTAGENET PALLISER. He is intelligent and personable, but wayward and undisciplined, and is sent down from Oxford for a 'more than ordinary youthful folly' (he has painted the dean's house red). He becomes Conservative member for Silverbridge in defiance of his father's Liberal allegiance, but with no great conviction. He owns a racehorse, but is unsuccessful in winning with it. He is astute in getting his way, notably in persuading his father to accept his marriage to ISABEL BONCASSEN.

Silvertongue, Lyra → Belacqua, Lyra

Silvia
Two Gentlemen of Verona, c.1590
William Shakespeare
Silvia, 'holy, fair and wise', her virtues praised in the song 'Who is Silvia?', is perceived by VALENTINE and PROTEUS as the ideal woman; so much so that first Valentine, then Proteus, fall in love with her. By doing so, the latter betrays both his friend and JULIA, whom he himself loves. That she is seen as ideal reflects not only the impossible idealism of the two gentlemen, but also the quality in Valentine to which Silvia responds and which she believes worth pursuing, even recklessly.

Silvius
As You Like It, c.1600
William Shakespeare
A shepherd in love with PHEBE, who wants nothing to do with him. A rustic lovesick swain, to ROSALIND he is a 'tame snake' whose manhood has been sapped by his blind adoration for a girl who is unworthy of him.

Simcox, Rev Simeon
Paradise Postponed, 1985
Titmuss Regained, 1990
John Mortimer
Like an anxious, balding eagle, the Red Rector of Rapstone Fanner presides over the spiritual needs of the inhabitants of the Rapstone Valley. Conveniently cushioned by his shares in Simcox Ales, he takes his campaigning stance against social injustice throughout the world. The objects displayed on his study mantelpiece provide a map of his interests and concerns – a bust of Karl Marx, a clutch of lecture invitations, a Nigerian carving of a pregnant woman. His actions are eccentric and frequently open to misinterpretation; he is fond of impersonating elephants. He never gives straight answers to questions, preferring, like many clergymen and politicians, to reply in impenetrable aphorisms.

Ultimately he neither believes enough in socialism nor in God, and the inheritance he passes on to the RT HON LESLIE TITMUSS (and hence, he hopes, to his own grandchild) is materially worthless.

Simeon Stylites, St
'St. Simeon Stylites', 1842
Alfred Lord Tennyson
Through lifelong service to God, healing the sick and the lame, and through painful mortification of his own flesh, he intends to lead his admirers towards God, and also to ensure his own exalted place among the saints and in the records of lesser mortals.

Simon → Mal, Rod and Simon

Simon
Lord of the Flies, 1954
William Golding
One of a party of schoolboys stranded on a desert island, Simon becomes the martyred saint who understands all, but is rejected for his honesty. He is the most caring and compassionate of the boys, harbouring deep currents of emotion which he finds difficult to express. Simon represents the moral and Christian core of the novel, for he is the prophet who recognizes the evil which resides in all humans. His superior wisdom is wantonly ignored by the other boys.

Simonides
Pericles, c.1608
William Shakespeare
The King of Pentapolis and father of THAISA, Simonides is, in contrast to ANTIOCHUS, and to CLEON and DIONYZA, a benevolent ruler and a kindly father whose sense of love remains untainted either by perversity or jealousy. He tests Pericles' resilience by insulting him; but having found him to be a man of principle, allows the marriage between his daughter and a stranger to take place.

Simonides
The Praise Singer, 1978
Mary Renault
Simonides is a poet, or praise singer, who records the tyranny of sixth-century Athens. Cursed with great ugliness, he compensates, emotionally, with a life lived through imagination and creativity. Apprenticed to the bard Kleobus, he eventually attains even greater fame than his master and, in Athens, he witnesses the court intrigues and corruptions which are the raw material for this, his autobiography. Simonides resurrects, in verse, the inspiring deeds of the past, lest their moral force be forgotten. He sees the poet as the conscience and the conservator of society, for as he says, 'We die twice when men forget'.

Simple, David
The Adventures of David Simple, 1744
Familiar Letters between the Principal Characters in David Simple, 1747
Volume the Last, 1753
Sarah Fielding
A moral, trusting, innocent and honest man who

falls prey to deceit at the hands of his younger brother, to whom he is devoted, but who cheats him out of his inheritance. Disillusioned and despairing over this fraud, he sets out in search of an honest friend who will restore his faith, but meets with a catalogue of hypocrisy and dishonesty on the streets of London, before falling in with three fellow-victims, one of whom he marries. The first book ends in reconciliation, but the final volume (1753) portrays the further crushing of innocence, with no such happy outcome.

Simple, Jesse B
'Conversation at Midnight', in the *Chicago Defender*, 1943, and in many later stories and articles, including *The Best of Simple*, 1961
Langston Hughes

Larger than life, Jesse B Simple is an idealist and incurable romantic in the Don Quixote mould. He hangs out with his buddies in Paddy's Bar, a Harlem speakeasy, spinning his colourful anecdotes. Having escaped rural poverty in the racist South, he has migrated north to the ghetto and perishes in its narrow confines. Deserted by his wife and victimized by garish landladies, Jesse never loses his earthy folk humour.

Simple, Peter
Peter Simple, 1834
Captain Frederick Marryat

A simple fellow at the opening of the book, he is 'the fool of the family', but claims for himself 'the merit of zealous and persevering continuance' in his vocation as a naval officer. A man of resolute spirit, his rite of passage includes many colourful adventures, until a final deluge of good fortune sees him elevated to 'Viscount Privilege, no longer the fool, but the head of the family'.

Simple, Peter
The Merry Wives of Windsor, c.1597
William Shakespeare

The servant of ABRAHAM SLENDER, Peter Simple lives up to his surname, yet he is not afraid to stand up for himself before his employer. His greatest fault is tactlessness, as he blurts out to DR CAIUS that Slender is in love with ANNE PAGE.

Simpson, Homer
The Day of the Locust, 1939
Nathanael West

A retired book-keeper in Hollywood, he falls for the would-be actress FAYE GREENER, but in lieu of a proposal (or even a straightforward proposition) offers her a 'business arrangement'. At the end of the novel, this representative of American business is engulfed by a mob crazed by the Hollywood spectacle and cheated of real transcendence.

Sinai, Saleem
Midnight's Children, 1981
Salman Rushdie

Ludicrous elements in Saleem Sinai's story include his birth in 1947 in India at the very moment of the nation's independence, and his being swapped that night with a well-off baby by a nurse. Originally an Englishman's bastard born to a servant-girl, he ends up in a well-to-do Indian family. Like other children born around Independence midnight, he possesses supernatural gifts such as telepathy. He uses these for voyeurism rather than anything constructive. After going through family rejection, coups, memory loss and war he is sterilized alongside others by an Indian government deeply suspicious of the gifts of Midnight's Children.

Sinclair, Lt Col Jock
Tunes of Glory, 1956
James Kennaway

Hard drinking is only a symbol of the attitudes to life and discipline and relationships that are typical of Sinclair and that bring the inevitable clashes with a newcomer to the barracks, COL BASIL BARROW, who despises Sinclair's laxity. Sinclair believes there is more to life than strict adherence to army regulations, and he is quite prepared to move the boundaries of what is officially acceptable in the interests of a broader and richer experience. In the claustrophobic atmosphere of an officer's mess, this can only fuel tension, and in this climate a fierce drama unfolds.

Singer, John
The Heart is a Lonely Hunter, 1940
Carson McCullers

John Singer, who can neither hear nor speak, becomes the focus of the combined visions and hopes of MICK KELLY, JAKE BLOUNT and DR BENEDICT COPELAND. Deprived of communication through sign language by the loss of his companion, he takes on the role of sympathetic 'listener' for others who project their own image onto his gentle, unassuming features. His own despair and isolation remain unbearably private.

Singh
The Chip-Chip Gatherers, 1973
Shiva Naipaul

EGBERT RAMSARAN's illegitimate son by an African woman, he lives in poor and uncomfortable conditions on an inland plantation. Harsh but melancholy, he has a mistress and child for occasional comfort, but mainly passes the time in bitter thoughts about the unjustness of his position.

Singh, Ralph
The Mimic Men, 1967
V S Naipaul

Retired in London, Ralph Singh reflects on his disastrous career as a politician in newly independent Isabella. His overwhelming sense of failure leads him to conclude that too many politicians of his generation merely mimic the former colonial overlords, and are therefore incapable of bettering their societies, still less severing economic dependence on the West. As he puts it, 'We mistake words and the acclamation of words for power; as soon as our bluff is called we are lost'.

Singleton
The Nigger of the Narcissus, 1897
Joseph Conrad

The mate of the *Narcissus*, and the oldest and

most experienced seaman on board. There is an almost mythological resonance to his singleness of purpose and 'unconscious' devotion to duty, in which he stands 'colossal, very old, old as Father Time himself'. He is strong, aloof and enduring, and seems to understand the men under him with 'a sharper vision, a clearer understanding' than their own.

Singleton, Captain
Captain Singleton, 1720
Daniel Defoe

A man who, because of his upbringing, has no 'sense of virtue or religion'. Kidnapped as a young boy and packed off to sea, his life becomes a catalogue of piracy and opportunism, studded with exciting voyages of exploration and punctuated by moments of crisis and disaster. Operating by a moral code of his own, he is unconstrained by the normal mores of society. Throughout his nefarious career, however, he demonstrates courage and ingenuity as he pursues his aims with single-minded determination and considerable success. As he reflects on his turbulent life from the security of wealthy exile in Venice, the regrets he expresses appear suspiciously like crocodile tears.

Singleton, Major
The Partisan, 1835
Katharine Walton, 1851
William Gilmore Simms

The hero of the Carolinian guerrilla campaign during the War of Independence, he re-emerges in the later book as a courtly Southern gentleman, an early version of Margaret Mitchell's RHETT BUTLER, but without the cynicism.

Singleton, Mary Ann
Tales of the City, 1978, et seq
Armistead Maupin

A discontented secretary from Cleveland, Ohio, she arrives in San Francisco for a week's holiday, and never leaves. Twenty-five, pretty and naive, she takes a room at 28 Barbary Lane and, under the auspices of its eccentric inmates, is quickly initiated into the city's quirks. Developing a close friendship with MOUSE, she reveals the resilient and ambitious spirit which in time will take her to the top of the media ladder, though at considerable personal cost.

Sinisterra, Mr Frank
The Recognitions, 1955
William Gaddis

A master forger and jailbird, whose bible is the *Counterfeit Detector* and whose ageing face is itself a masterpiece of cosmetic contrivance. Where WYATT GWYON attempts to recreate Old Masters, Sinisterra goes straight to the heart of the matter, printing $20 bills.

Sinnott, John
A Charmed Life, 1955
Mary McCarthy

A man of military background, 'quite remarkable-looking' and 'often taken for English', he lives with his wife MARTHA SINNOTT in the small, claustrophobic community of New Leeds, a New England haven of artists and writers. A man of considerable reserve and dignity, able to focus his attention more single-mindedly than Martha, he cannot always fathom her moods, and is aggravated by her spells of artistic self-doubt. Without, at first, any reason for mistrust, he fears Martha ever encountering her first husband, MILES MURPHY. With some intuition, he senses the danger this man poses.

Sinnott, Martha
A Charmed Life, 1955
Mary McCarthy

A 'strange, poetical-looking being', a one-time actress and now an aspiring playwright. She is happily married to JOHN SINNOTT but, although intensely grateful to be rid of her first and miserable marriage to MILES MURPHY, is nagged by the suspicion that her current partnership is too easy. A quixotic, complex woman of sharp intellect and introspective insight, she can be élitist and a little pretentious. Once promiscuous, now avowedly monogamous, she views a one-off infidelity with Miles as a minor event, until she finds herself pregnant, unsure of whose baby she is carrying. The prospect of a life-long embodiment of doubt, in the form of a child, is anathema to her rigorous sense of honesty.

Sisson, Aaron
Aaron's Rod, 1922
D H Lawrence

Like SIEGMUND MCNAIR in *The Trespasser* Sisson makes his living by playing in an orchestra and is trapped within a despairing, loveless marriage. He leaves home for London, where he encounters the charismatic thinker, RAWDON LILLY. Entranced partly by the apparently simple infallibility of Lilly's near-Fascist philosophy, partly by the eroticism of his ideas and of Lilly himself, and also by his fashionable new acquaintances, Sisson follows Lilly across Europe to Italy. He is searching for a new beginning, but as a consequence of his gullibility and weakness, finds himself swirling instead in an emotional and intellectual whirlpool.

Sita
The Chip-Chip Gatherers, 1973
Shiva Naipaul

SUSHILA's daughter, she bears the embarrassment of her birth and of her mother's public brazenness with more shame than Sushila is ever willing to show. Lodged in the Settlement, she is ritually promised escape and the opportunity to make something of her life, a prospect improved when her mother becomes EGBERT RAMSARAN's mistress.

Skald, Jobber (Adam)
Weymouth Sands, 1934
John Cowper Powys

He is a huge, swarthy man with a 'corrugated brow' and a powerful build which resembles 'a classic figure on an archaic frieze'. He lives close to nature on both land and sea, and seems to have a vein of native rock 'in his disposition, that makes him so far-off from everybody and yet so familiar with everybody'. He is imaginative, fond of reading, skilful with his hands, and exerts the 'authority of his personality' in a natural, unforced way. He hates the capitalist brewer DOGBERRY CATTISTOCK, and is in love with PERDITA WANE.

Skelton, Dick (Richard)
The Black Arrow, 1888
Robert Louis Stevenson

The introspective hero of this adventure story set during the Wars of the Roses. In a tale of total moral ambiguity, where all sides in the contest are fundamentally flawed, Dick is a curiously inert hero – seemingly paralysed by the extent of the evil which surrounds him. Nevertheless he is one of the few distinctly worthy influences in the novel and is contrasted, for effect, with a diabolic 'doppelgänger' – the other 'Richard', Richard of Gloucester. Dick symbolizes both the futility, yet also the absolute necessity, of opposing evil.

Skewton, the Hon Mrs
Dombey and Son, 1848
Charles Dickens

The mother of EDITH DOMBEY and aunt of LORD FEENIX, she is called 'Cleopatra' from a portrait painted in her youth. Now 70 and once handsome, she wears false curls, eyebrows and teeth and dresses as a coquette. Heartless and scheming, she treats Edith as a commodity and persuades her to marry MR PAUL DOMBEY for his wealth and position. Soon afterwards, she suffers a stroke, becomes paralysed and dies.

Skimpole, Harold
Bleak House, 1853
Charles Dickens

A charming but unprincipled dilettante, he affects childlike simplicity in order to sponge off JOHN JARNDYCE and neglect responsibility for supporting his own family. When JO seeks refuge at Bleak House, he accepts a bribe from MR BUCKET to reveal Jo's presence. Jarndyce eventually recognizes the immorality of his selfishness.

Skink
Double Whammy, 1987, et seq
Carl Hiaasen

The former governor of Florida, Clinton Tyree, aka Skink or occasionally 'the Captain', disappeared at the height of his popularity to hide out in the Florida backwoods where he survives on roadkill, living in a lakeside shack and later in abandoned vehicles. He cuts a fantastic figure in his bizarre clothing (orange rainsuit, chihuahua-fur waistcoat) and trademark shower cap, which contrast with his 'perfect teeth ... the kind nobody is born with', but is an endearing and heroic character as he rails against the ecological devastation and corrupt government of the state and takes his own vigilante action.

Skionar, Mr
Crotchet Castle, 1831
Thomas Love Peacock

Transcendentalist poet and avid reader and disciple of German transcendentalist philosophers, Mr Skionar (based on Coleridge) speaks in riddles, using 50 words when three words would suffice. His views are permanently in flux, for he is swayed constantly by 'sentiment and intuition'.

Skipton, Daniel
The Unspeakable Skipton, 1959
Pamela Hansford Johnson

A seedy, thoroughly obnoxious and paranoid English writer living in Bruges, Skipton augments his meagre income by acting as glorified guide to rich tourists such as DOROTHY MERLIN's husband. He is engaged on what he calls 'the greatest novel of the century' but, venomously loathing everyone, his writing is merely a scurrilous outpouring against real people barely fictionalized. His unspeakable behaviour is on such a monumental scale that he becomes comically pitiful in his attempts to preserve some dignity and the fallacy that he is a gentleman. He often emerges the loser from his sordid and humiliating activities.

Skrebensky, Anton
The Rainbow, 1915
D H Lawrence

A Polish aristocrat with whom URSULA BRANGWEN has a brief relationship, Skrebensky, unlike her, is constrained by social class, culture and temperament. He 'did not consider the soul of the individual sufficiently important ... Duty is very plain – keep in mind the material, the immediate welfare of every man, that's all'. This philosophy terrifies Ursula, but marks a significant stage in her emotional and spiritual development.

Skullion
Porterhouse Blue, 1974
Tom Sharpe

Rugged-faced, pipe-smoking, bowler-hatted, the Head Porter of Porterhouse College, Cambridge, is the ultimate conservative – for him there is 'no such thing as change for the better'. An extreme snob, he views the privileged students with a degree of contempt and saves his full admiration only for those men 'out of the top drawer'. He is happy in the knowledge that the outside world is 'none of his affair' – but when progress threatens the status quo it is time for him to leave the Porter's Lodge and take action.

Skywonkie, Billie
'Billie Skywonkie', in *Bush Studies*, 1902
Barbara Baynton

An Australian roustabout, and bush 'weather prophet' – a laughable profession in the drought-stricken, sun-blasted plains – Billie is casual, rough and aggressively humorous. However, despite his propensity for loud bluster and abuse, he is revealed to be pitifully browbeaten by his missus, Lizer, and is in fact a much softer character than he at first appears.

Slackbridge
Hard Times, 1854
Charles Dickens

A demagogic trades-union agitator and orator, he publicly denounces STEPHEN BLACKPOOL for refusing to become a union member and persuades Blackpool's fellow workers to ostracize him.

Slammer, Doctor
Pickwick Papers, 1837
Charles Dickens

Surgeon of the 97th regiment who challenges NATHANIEL WINKLE to a duel for an offence of which he is innocent, since it was perpetrated by ALFRED JINGLE while wearing Winkle's coat.

Slatter, Charlie
The Grass is Singing, 1950
Doris Lessing

Formerly a grocer's boy, Charlie is a self-made business man. He is rich, flash and selfish, and can be crude and vulgar, but is not an out-and-out villain. Ever shrewd and watchful, there is very little that he misses, and all his actions have an ulterior motive.

Slawkenbergius
The Life and Opinions of Tristram Shandy, 9 volumes, 1759–67
Laurence Sterne

An author, much admired by WALTER SHANDY as an authority on most things, especially the issue of noses. He is seen as 'a rich treasury of inexhaustible knowledge' to Walter, who draws fearlessly on his insights and arguments during his own interminable and intolerant discussions. Slawkenbergius's famous autobiographical tale of one nasally well-endowed, and of his adventures with the citizens of Strasbourg, is seen as especially helpful, given the circumstances of TRISTRAM SHANDY's own status as one nasally impaired.

Sleary, Mr
Hard Times, 1854
Charles Dickens

The proprietor of Sleary's circus, he employs his daughter Josephine, noted for her graceful Tyrolean flower act, and the equestrian performer E W B Childers, who marries her. He is a stout, kind-hearted man with 'one fixed eye, and one loose eye', a lisp and 'a muddled head which was never sober and never drunk'. He looks after SISSY JUPE when her father disappears and, with his trained horse and dog, he prevents the arrest of TOM GRADGRIND and helps him to escape abroad. The lesson he repeatedly teaches THOMAS GRADGRIND is that 'People must be amuthed, Thquire, thomehow, they can't be alwayth a working, nor yet they can't be alwayth a learning. Make the betht of uth; not the wurtht'.

Sleep, Asnetha
The Tilted Cross, 1961
Hal Porter

The crippled and rich Miss Sleep dresses bizarrely in a vain attempt to make herself attractive and chatters nervously, often in fractured sentences. The effect is of 'false dottiness'. She hates her cousin's wife, LADY KNIGHT, gains pleasure from the body of her pageboy, TEAPOT, and has a disastrous sexual relationship with QUEELY SHEILL.

Slender, Abraham
The Merry Wives of Windsor, c.1597
William Shakespeare

According to PETER SIMPLE, his servant, Slender has 'a little whey face, with a little yellow beard'. The nephew of JUSTICE SHALLOW, Slender has all the pretensions of a middle-class country family and all the imbecility as well. He is in love with ANNE PAGE, and in fact has the support of her father; yet, he has absolutely nothing to say to her except that his uncle and her father could put his case better than he. During the masquerade humiliation of SIR JOHN FALSTAFF in Windsor Great Park, he elopes with a fairy dressed in white, only to discover that his supposed bride is a postmaster's boy.

Slightly
Peter Pan: or The Boy Who Would Not Grow Up, 1904 (play), 1911 (book)
J M Barrie

PETER PAN's lieutenant among the Lost Boys, he takes his name from a pinafore marked 'Slightly Soiled' in which he was found abandoned. 'Quite possibly a genius, [he has a] home-made penny-whistle to which he capers entrancingly, with no audience save a Never ostrich which is also musically inclined'.

Slim Girl
Laughing Boy, 1929
Oliver La Farge

LAUGHING BOY's lover, she is both a passionate muse and a fatal *anima* figure whose own death represents a significant stage in the Navajo boy's entry into maturity.

Slingsby, Miss Helen
'Aunt Helen', in *Prufrock and Other Observations*, 1917
T S Eliot

Based on T S Eliot's maiden aunt, she lives *near* rather than *in* a 'fashionable square', ruling her household staff of four with some apparent sternness. When she dies, soon to be followed by her parrot but leaving the dogs 'handsomely provided for', 'there was silence in heaven/And silence at the end of her street'.

Slipslop, Mrs
The History of the Adventures of Joseph Andrews and of his Friend Mr Abraham Adams, 1742
Henry Fielding

A waiting woman and chambermaid to LADY BOOBY and an intriguer of some subtlety. 'She was a Maiden Gentlewoman of about Forty-five Years of Age, who having made a small Slip in her Youth had continued a good Maid ever since. She was not at this time remarkably handsome; being very short, and rather too corpulent in Body, and somewhat red, with the Addition of Pimples in the Face'.

Sloane
Entertaining Mr Sloane, 1964
Joe Orton

Orphaned at the age of eight, Sloane is now an angelic-seeming man of 20 with a full chest, narrow hips and the delicate skin of a princess. Capable of murder and deceit to achieve personal gratification, he is troubled by neither guilt nor remorse. Desired by his landlady KATH and her brother ED, he happily exploits the situation until a further act of murder leaves him at the mercy of their leniency.

Slocum, Bob
Something Happened, 1974
Joseph Heller
An outwardly moderately successful and still-rising executive in New York, who is filled with disgust at the mean, narrow, unfulfilled life he leads, and the insensitive, unsympathetic, detached man he has become. He is lacking in confidence and courage, and has a 'positive dread of everything unknown that may occur'. His life is riven by mistrust and anxiety at work and at home, where he evades the problems of his unhappy wife and troubled children.

Slop, Dr
The Life and Opinions of Tristram Shandy, 9 volumes, 1759–67
Laurence Sterne
He is portrayed rather as the villain of the piece, since his clumsiness with the new technology of midwifery leads to TRISTRAM SHANDY's nose being disfigured at birth. He also enjoys the disadvantage, at least as far as the Shandy household is concerned, of being a Roman Catholic, with all criticisms of the Roman church being directed upon his head. He serves as the butt for many of WALTER SHANDY's less kindly critiques of religious philosophy.

Slope, Rev Obadiah
Barchester Towers, 1857
Anthony Trollope
The chaplain of the Bishop of Barchester, DR THOMAS PROUDIE, and competitor with MRS PROUDIE for control of the diocese. His false humility conceals ambition. Ugly, sweaty and physically awkward, he nevertheless impresses many women by his flattery and religious fervour. He believes in the uncharitable, Low Church, Sabbatarian religion that he preaches, but his actions, such as his desire to marry ELEANOR HARDING for her money and his entanglement with SIGNORA MADELINE VESEY NERONI, make him a hypocrite.

Sloper, Catherine
Washington Square, 1881
Henry James
A 1949 film version of the book was called *The Heiress* and that gives the gist of her charms. A plain, intellectually drab girl, she stands to inherit a fortune and one of New York City's most fashionable addresses.

Sloper, Dr Austin
Washington Square, 1881
Henry James
A wealthy and cultured New Yorker, with a notably sardonic view of life, he is embittered by the death of his wife and son, clearly finding his shy, spinsterish daughter CATHERINE SLOPER a poor substitute as helpmeet and heir.

Slothrop, Lt Tyrone
Gravity's Rainbow, 1973
Thomas Pynchon
A young American serviceman, stationed in London as part of a secret intelligence unit, which is monitoring and studying Nazi V2 attacks. Slothrop is himself under surveillance. When he comes to realize that the sites of his numerous priapic episodes across London seem to attract rocket strikes, he embarks on a quest to uncover a huge conspiracy that seems to run the war and all its offshoots, and to solve the mystery of the bizarre experiments inflicted on him as a child.

Slowboy, Tilly
The Cricket on the Hearth, 1845
Charles Dickens
A foundling, and the domestic servant of JOHN and MARY PEERYBINGLE. Clumsy and of limited intellect, she is treated with kindness by the Peerybingles, even though she has a habit of holding the baby upside down and getting into difficulties.

Sludden
Lanark: A Life in Four Books, 1981
Alasdair Gray
The arch-trickster of Unthank and a friend of LANARK, he is a young man with an infallible instinct for sexual opportunism, moral transvaluation, and a really profitable scam. His name is described as sounding like 'a mouthful of something nasty'.

Sludge, Dickie, known as Flibbertigibbet
Kenilworth, 1821
Sir Walter Scott
The gnomish boy who leads EDMUND TRESSILLIAN to WAYLAND SMITH, he is 'a queer, shambling, ill-made urchin, who, by his stunted growth, seemed about twelve or thirteen years old, though he was probably, in reality, a year or two older, with a carroty pate in huge disorder, a freckled sunburnt visage, with a snub nose, a long chin and two peery grey eyes, which had a droll obliquity of vision'.

Sludge, Mr, the Medium
Dramatis Personae, 1864
Robert Browning
Sludge has been caught cheating at a seance. Barely managing to disguise his contempt for his clients, he justifies himself firstly by maintaining that it is his wealthy patrons' foolish belief in spiritualism that is the cause of his deceptions: 'It's all your fault, you curious gentlefolk'. However, in a change of tack he argues that perhaps there is something in spiritualism: after all, we believe that there is a heaven peopled with those who have died, so maybe there is also a means of contacting them. But alone, having taken money to leave town, he sarcastically berates his benefactor, asking 'is he the only fool in the world?', before setting off to swindle others.

Slumkey, the Hon Samuel
Pickwick Papers, 1837
Charles Dickens
The parliamentary candidate for the Blue party

in the Eatanswill election. He defeats HORATIO
FIZKIN.

Sly, Christopher
The Taming of the Shrew, early 1590s
William Shakespeare

A coarse, foul-mouthed tinker with no means of
paying for the drink he consumes, Sly has the
amazingly conceited idea that his family has a
noble background. When he finds himself
'elevated' to the nobility he accepts the situation
with only a slight show of surprise. He agrees to
be provided with a wife, though 'she' is not what
she seems, and the marriage never takes place.

Slyme, Chevy
Martin Chuzzlewit, 1844
Charles Dickens

The shabby and disreputable nephew of OLD
MARTIN CHUZZLEWIT, he is eager for his share of
Old Martin's money and aggrieved that his own
'true genius' is not recognized by society. He
makes MONTAGUE TIGG his 'catspaw', but Tigg
deserts him to set up his own fraudulent
business. He later joins the police and helps to
arrest his uncle, JONAS CHUZZLEWIT, for the
murder of Tigg. He accepts Jonas's bribe to
allow him to poison himself in the coach on the
way to prison.

Smales, Bamford
July's People, 1981
Nadine Gordimer

Well-built, blond and slightly balding, Bamford,
or Bam, is the husband of MAUREEN SMALES and
father of three children. Of part-Boer origins, he
is a rich architect from the city who escapes
with his family to the village of their house-
servant, JULY, when revolution breaks out. His
accustomed role of white 'patron' slowly gives
way to an acceptance of his present insecurities.
He uses his practical skills, as an architect and a
hunter, to contribute to village life, care for his
children and work towards integration.

Smales, Maureen
July's People, 1981
Nadine Gordimer

Maureen, blonde, lean and approaching 40, is the
wife of BAMFORD SMALES and mother of three
children. An English-speaking member of a rich,
white, South African community, she has her
idealism tested when, to escape the horrors of
revolution, she and her family flee to the village
of her house-servant, JULY. She has been used to
a life of luxury since childhood and the role of
dependant and the privations of village life
reveal her capacity for 'meanness' and disloyalty,
and lead to her bid for 'lone survival'.

Smalley, Lucy
Staying On, 1977
Paul Scott

Lucy Smalley is the long-suffering wife of
'TUSKER' SMALLEY, whom she battles (and
deceives) to restrain from self-destruction in the
changed circumstances of post-imperial India.
Scrupulously polite and keen to maintain
appearances, her blue-rinse vagueness hides
qualities of stubbornness and intelligence. Too

humane, too poor and too late to be a typical
memsahib, she worries about lonely widowhood
in a foreign country, longs for a vanished
homeland, and retires within clichéd romantic
fantasies. In old age she thinks of her life as a sad
one, 'like a flower that has never really bloomed'.

Smalley, 'Tusker'
Staying On, 1977
Paul Scott

A cantankerous British colonel of the old school,
Tusker's bibulous retirement in an Indian hill-
station is spent fulminating on the state of his
lawn, the indignities of impoverished old age,
and the loss of Empire. A man who needs
irritants and often invents them, his volcanic
outbursts belie a more vulnerable, disappointed
nature. In the 1970s Tusker clings to an illusory
and compromised past of political, cultural and
social certainties in which his only ambition has
been to survive as comfortably as possible.
Though grown devious and self-absorbed, he
remains irascibly devoted to LUCY SMALLEY.

Smalls, Lily
Under Milk Wood, 1954
Dylan Thomas

Lily Smalls, the butcher's wife's treasure, is no
better than she should be, or would like to think
herself so. By night she dreams of royalty in the
washhouse and ends up there with Nogood
Boyo, who is as he sounds. She daydreams of
secret love to her reflection, perm and conk and
all. She has a nice line in dumb insolence, but
sensibly sees through BUTCHER BEYNON's teasing
and reassures his wife over her unfounded fears.

Smallweed, Grandfather (Joshua)
Bleak House, 1853
Charles Dickens

A paralysed moneylender, he is 'a leech in his
disposition, a screw and a vice in his actions, a
snake in his twisting, and a lobster in his claws'.
Working for MR TULKINGHORN, he tries to
blackmail MR GEORGE ROUNCEWELL and, when
he inherits the papers of his brother-in-law, MR
KROOK, he tries to blackmail SIR LEICESTER
DEDLOCK with documents revealing LADY
DEDLOCK's past. His favourite amusement is
throwing cushions at his senile wife, Grandmother Smallweed. Their twin grandchildren,
the grotesque Bartholomew and Judy, have
inherited the family's obsession with hard facts
and the rules of arithmetic. Judy ill-treats
their servant, CHARLOTTE NECKETT, before
Charlotte leaves to become the maid of ESTHER
SUMMERSON.

Smart, Henry
A Star Called Henry, 1999
Roddy Doyle

Despite his tender years and his impoverished
background, Dublin street urchin Henry Smart
does not look for sympathy, and he has a
charisma that weaves a magic spell over
everyone, especially the women, he meets. His
response to being enlisted into the Irish
Republican Army at the age of 14 and taking part
in the 1916 Easter Rising is similarly unorthodox,
first shooting at shop windows and 'all the

commerce and snobbery that had been mocking me and other hundreds of thousands' rather than at British troops.

Smart, Jane
The Witches of Eastwick, 1984
John Updike

Of all the witches in the Eastwick coven, she seems the most susceptible to DARRYL VAN HORNE's ambiguous magnetism. Like the others she is highly expressive, being a gifted cellist.

Smeagol → Gollum

Smee
Peter Pan: or The Boy Who Would Not Grow Up, 1904 (play), 1911 (book)
J M Barrie

A bespectacled bosun and 'the only Non-conformist in Hook's crew', he is possessor of a cutlass called Johnny Corkscrew and is perhaps CAPTAIN HOOK's only real confidant.

Smeeth, Mr
Angel Pavement, 1930
J B Priestley

A sad figure, who lives and breathes the soulless world of the City of London, and has little identity outside the workplace. Utterly decent, he is inclined to take himself too seriously. There is a pathetic, vulnerable aspect to him, so that although he is efficient and invaluable to his company, he actually achieves very little. A family man, he is obsessed with security and responsibility. Veering towards the pessimistic, he is intuitive rather than perceptive. Endearing in many ways, he is a little man who grows in stature in the reader's mind.

Smelfungus
A Sentimental Journey through France and Italy, 1768
Laurence Sterne

When the novelist Smollett pursued a similar journey around Europe to that described by Sterne, he complained and grumbled about most things. Smelfungus is Sterne's satire of that negative attitude to all things foreign, a ribald lampooning of this writer's xenophobic and jaundiced view.

Smike
Nicholas Nickleby, 1839
Charles Dickens

The only child and long-lost son of RALPH NICKLEBY, who had secretly married for money a woman who then deserted him. Unknown to Ralph, the boy is sent at an early age to Dotheboys Hall, where he is beaten and starved and used as a drudge by WACKFORD SQUEERS and his family. With his spirit broken and almost half-witted, he is pitied and befriended by NICHOLAS NICKLEBY. When he runs away and is recaptured, Nicholas prevents Squeers from thrashing him. Together they go to London and act for a time in VINCENT CRUMMLES's company, where Crummles assigns him the stage name of Digby and turns him into 'an actor for the starved business'. Re-captured by Squeers, he is rescued by JOHN BROWDIE and finds his way back to the protection of Nicholas. He is cared for by MRS NICKLEBY,

KATE NICKLEBY and MISS LA CREEVY, begins to recover his natural intelligence and falls secretly in love with Kate. But aware that he is being hunted down by Squeers and Ralph, he begins to decline and dies in the arms of Nicholas after revealing his hopeless love for Kate. Only after his death is it disclosed that he is Ralph's son and thus the cousin of Nicholas and Kate.

Smiley, George
Call for the Dead, 1961, et seq
Tinker, Tailor, Soldier, Spy, 1974
The Honourable Schoolboy, 1977
Smiley's People, 1980
The Secret Pilgrim, 1991
John Le Carré

Smiley is short, fattish and bespectacled. He was recruited in 1928 for the British Secret Service ('the Circus') after studying 17th-century German literature at Oxford, has been a brilliant agent in Germany during the war, and moved on to home-based counter-espionage. He has a beautiful wife, Ann, who tends to leave him, but occasionally wanders back. His interrogation technique: formal, patient, bored and sceptical, is unmatchable. A perpetually worried and humanly concerned figure ('a bit of the failed priest in him'), he views his greatest triumphs – the unmasking of BILL HAYDON as a traitor and the blackmail-driven capture of KARLA – with ambiguous feelings. He is enormously hurt for Haydon as a friend, and feels he has destroyed Karla 'with the weapons I abhorred'. He later appears as a grand old man of the Secret Service, giving genial advice to young agents.

Smiley, Jim
The Celebrated Jumping Frog of Calaveras County, 1865
Mark Twain

Jim Smiley, an inveterate gambler, is the subject of a tall story by Simon Wheeler, an old man from 'the decayed mining town of Angel's'. When a relieved Parson Walker tells him that his seriously ill wife is getting better, he replies 'Well, I'll resk two-and-a-half she don't anyway'. He is especially skilled in training animals to win bets for him, the most famous being his jumping frog, DAN'L WEBSTER.

Smit, Hester
Hello and Goodbye, 1969
Athol Fugard

Irrepressible Hester Smit breaks out of the monotonous pattern of existence of 'the second-hand Smits of Valley Road'. Her explicit belief that it was that pattern of life that sent her mother to an early grave has strengthened her determination not to succumb to the emotional blackmail of a patriarchal society. To Hester, 'Happy families is fat men crawling on to frightened women'.

Smit, Johnie
Hello and Goodbye, 1969
Athol Fugard

Johnie's overwhelming complacency exacerbates his sister, HESTER SMIT. When Hester walks into their family house in Port Elizabeth, where she has abandoned Johnie and their crippled father, she disrupts the dull monotony of Johnie's life. In the process, dominant attitudes that shape individual and collective lives for many generations are revealed.

Smith → Chiffinch

Smith
Smith, 1967
Leon Garfield

A 'dirty, weaselish, villainous-looking remnant' of twelve, a pipe-smoking gin-swigging survivor of the treacherously dark alleyways around St Paul's in 18th-century London. A deft pick-pocket, the 'dockiment' he steals in error will, he feels sure, become his passport to great wealth and happiness, if only he were able to read it. His tender-heartedness, determination and perceptiveness ensure that he eventually achieves his goal. The fact that 'Smith of the alleyways' does indeed finally become 'Smith the 10000-guinea man' is due entirely to his native intelligence, his unremitting courage and his powerful instinct for survival against the most desperate odds.

Smith, Bessie
The Death of Bessie Smith, 1960
Edward Albee

The historical blues singer who died after allegedly being refused admission to an all-white hospital in the American South, succumbing to injuries from which she might well have recovered. In the play, Bessie is no more than a suffering presence round whom various minor figures work out their own obsessions.

Smith, Dancy, known as **'the Stray'**
The Battlers, 1941
Kylie Tennant

A toothless, hard-bitten young woman with a fierce temper and a predilection for foul language and enormous lies, she has been deserted 'on the track'. Given her nickname by SNOW after she attaches herself to his camp, she proves to be a true 'battler': industrious, impudent, hardy, cool, yet able to take a "'knock-back" as though it didn't matter, and come up to meet the next blow, with perhaps a curse, but at least come up and meet it'. She becomes torn, however, between attachments to her mates and her desire to escape the weary struggle of the road.

Smith, Frank
The Rehearsal, 1671
George Villiers, 2nd Duke of Buckingham

In London from his usual residence in the country, the blunt Smith attends with his friend NED JOHNSON a rehearsal of a heroic drama by BAYES, the sheer ineptitude of which surprises him. He keeps interrupting the performance to complain, mock and question the author about the absurdities of his work.

Smith, George
A Singular Man, 1964
J P Donleavy

George is strange. Living in a cocoon of self-imposed isolation, he finds his independence

undermined by a disturbing, unknown individual, 'J J', whose sinister letters rob George of his peace of mind. So does the beautiful Miss Tomson with whom, to his great surprise and discomfiture, he falls in love, an experience so delightful that it challenges his insularity. Previous associations have so bruised him that he normally shuns emotional connections, but now this two-pronged assault on his chilly serenity summons him to a reassessment of where happiness might be located.

Smith, Hank
A Connecticut Yankee in King Arthur's Court, 1889
Mark Twain

A 'man of knowledge, brains, pluck and enterprise', the practical-minded Smith quickly adjusts to his situation when he awakens from a blow on the head to find himself in Camelot in 528AD. Smith has the characteristic US faith in capitalism, democratic ideology and technology to solve all ills and is intolerant of those who oppose his innovations and reforms. He recounts his experiences with a marvellous dry humour but, sadly, is corrupted by the exercise of colossal power and comes to personify the darker aspects of the 19th-century expansionist USA.

Smith, Harriet
Emma, 1816
Jane Austen

Self-effacing and artless, eager to please and ready to learn, she is the naive protégée of EMMA WOODHOUSE and Highbury society. 'Tempted by everything and swayed by half a word', she is 'unlikely to be very, very determined against any young man who told her he loved her'. Blighted by what she is led to perceive as the shame of her unknown parentage, yet swayed by Emma's prejudices, she rejects a fitting offer of marriage from ROBERT MARTIN in favour of what is subsequently revealed to be an unfounded and unrequited adoration of MR ELTON.

Smith, Henry, or **Henry Gow**, or **Hal of the Wynd**
The Fair Maid of Perth, or St Valentine's Day, in *Chronicles of the Canongate: Second Series*, 1828
Sir Walter Scott

A squat but powerfully built blacksmith of Perth, he is a curious mixture of impulsive strength and shyness. He is chosen as CATHARINE GLOVER's valentine, and they eventually marry. It is Hal who kills both the Hammerman and TORQUIL OF THE OAK at the battle of North Inch.

Smith, Janet Belle
Real People, 1969
Alison Lurie

This sensitive lady writer has a problem. Although people and situations often suggest ideas for stories, she is constantly editing her work to avoid offending family and friends. Retreating to an artistic haven to revive her creative powers, she is stunned when her romantic assumptions are challenged. The guilt she had assumed was the result of using those around her as material for her art is exposed as an elaborate self-deception. The self-imposed censorship of her writing has become a censorship of her life, protecting her status and lifestyle at the expense of her talent.

Smith, Janey
Blood and Guts in High School, 1978
Kathy Acker

Sexually abused, a 'slave' in a world of violent and 'fascist' men, Janey's is a voice that longs for compassion and demands understanding and freedom. Direct and explicit language is her main weapon, and she revels in removing façades of decorous behaviour to expose the 'material' reality of political and sexual violence. In the face of humiliation and hatred, she says 'I have a right to be happy'.

Smith, Mr
The Comedians, 1966
Graham Greene

A former US presidential candidate. He cuts an impressive figure and adopts a grand, self-important manner befitting his former status, but despite this, there is still the unmistakable air of the small-town American tourist surrounding him and his deeply loyal wife. He remains blinkered and unflappable in the face of the atrocities in Haiti and possesses a certain inextinguishable innocence. It emerges that Smith has journeyed to the island as a representative of the vegetarians of America.

Smith, Mrs
Persuasion, 1818
Jane Austen

An old school-friend of ANNE ELLIOT, Mrs Smith is, on Anne's reacquaintance with her, a poor, young widow who, despite being both physically and financially crippled, retains great cheerfulness of spirit. Formerly married to William Elliot, it is she who enlightens Anne as to his real character. Later, through the efforts of CAPTAIN WENTWORTH, Mrs Smith has her husband's property rightfully restored to her.

Smith, Stephen
A Pair of Blue Eyes, 1873
Thomas Hardy

A straightforward character, he is attractive and industrious. Youthful and suave, he is much more city-based than countrified, and there is a certain 'feminine' air about him.

Smith, Wayland
Kenilworth, 1821
Sir Walter Scott

Originally apprenticed to a quack, he proves to have a native genius for the farrier's trade, practising this with a strong residue of cabbalistic nonsense which helps sustain his reputation for adherence to the black arts.

Smith, Winston
1984, 1949
George Orwell

Representative of the ordinary man in a bleak futuristic society, whose discontent with the ruling Party finally erupts into revolution, Winston works for the Ministry and knows how it purveys lies and manipulates people. He

himself is involved in the rewriting of history to serve Big Brother. He develops from being an outwardly complacent worker to a man who passionately attempts to uncover the truth. Finally brought to confront his 'crimes' by his torturer O'BRIEN, Winston surrenders and learns to love his oppressor. Victim and victimizer have become dependent on each other.

Smithers, Henry
The Emperor Jones, 1920
Eugene O'Neill

A trader on BRUTUS JONES's Caribbean island empire, he stands as a representative of the white mercantile society that brought about the Jones's own racial oppression. Though he warns the 'emperor' that the natives of the island are hostile, it is with American silver dollars that the headman LEM and his followers eventually kill Jones.

Smithson, Charles
The French Lieutenant's Woman, 1969
John Fowles

An 'intelligent idler', he is searching for fulfilment in a society which he finds superficial and restrictive. The victim of etiquette – elegant, fastidious, amusing and extremely self-indulgent – 'he was to live all his life under the influence of the ideal'. His outward cynicism masks his romantic inclinations, and eventually he becomes the exotic creature he has always wanted to be. His entanglement with SARAH WOODRUFF results in behaviour which Victorian society finds irresponsible, but which could be considered the only 'real' behaviour he has ever displayed.

Smooth-It-Away, Mr
'The Celestial Railroad', 1843, in *Mosses from an Old Manse*, 1846
Nathaniel Hawthorne

Director and leading stockholder of the Celestial Railroad, and the narrator's guide on his dream-journey from the City of Destruction through the Valley of the Shadow of Death.

Smorltork, Count
Pickwick Papers, 1837
Charles Dickens

A 'well-whiskered individual in foreign uniform', he is a guest of MRS LEO HUNTER at Eatanswill. He is spending three weeks 'gathering materials for his great work on England' and, although his grasp of the language is slight and eccentric, he compensates with his 'exhuberant' fancy.

Snagsby, Mr
Bleak House, 1853
Charles Dickens

A law stationer and former employer of CAPTAIN HAWDON, he is 'a mild, bald, timid man' sorely tried by his ill-tempered wife. He is kind to their servant, GUSTER, and his befriending JO involves him in the DEDLOCK affairs.

Snailsfoot, Bryce
The Pirate, 1821
Sir Walter Scott

A 'stout, vulgar little man, who had indeed the

humble appearance of a pedlar', or what is called a 'yagger' in the Shetlands. Superstitious and greedy, he is always present at shipwrecks, not to aid the survivors, but to salvage whatever is of value.

Snake
The School for Scandal, 1777
Richard Brinsley Sheridan
LADY SNEERWELL's treacherous and toadying agent in the dissemination of slander and gossip; he 'hasn't virtue enough to be faithful even to his own villainy'. Having committed a good action, he wants it kept secret, to protect his professional reputation for infamy.

Snark
The Hunting of the Snark: an Agony, in Eight Fits, 1867
Lewis Carroll
A Snark is an inconceivable creature never seen by man. Nine ill-assorted men, their occupations beginning with B, and a lace-making Beaver, sail away to find it, led by the Bellman with a totally blank map. A Snark tastes hollow but crisp; it rises late and eats when it likes; it cannot see a joke; it carries bathing-machines around with it; and it is ambitious. There are different kinds, but the Baker says that if it is a Boojum, and he finds it, he will vanish for ever. It is and he does.

Snawley, Mr
Nicholas Nickleby, 1839
Charles Dickens
A sanctimonious hypocrite and rascal, he sends his two stepsons to WACKFORD SQUEERS's Dotheboys Hall on the tacit understanding that they will die from maltreatment, malnourishment and disease. As the tool of RALPH NICKLEBY, he claims to be the father of SMIKE in order to separate him from the influence of NICHOLAS NICKLEBY and return him to Squeers. But his impersonation is discovered, and he risks being charged with perjury. To save himself, he reveals the scheme, naming Ralph as his employer and implicating Squeers as their co-conspirator.

Sneer
The Critic, 1779
Richard Brinsley Sheridan
A theatrical promoter who is trying to put on moral (but dreadful-sounding) plays. Highly critical of inferior productions, he wittily ridicules the likes of SIR FRETFUL PLAGIARY and sarcastically comments on PUFF's play 'The Spanish Armada'.

Sneerwell, Lady
The School for Scandal, 1777
Richard Brinsley Sheridan
Having been hurt by gossip in her youth, Lady Sneerwell, now a rich widow, enjoys gaining her revenge by spreading scandal and destroying reputations, and is helped in this by her associates. She assists JOSEPH SURFACE in his attempt to woo MARIA, because she wants Maria's beloved, CHARLES SURFACE, for herself.

Snell, Balso
The Dream Life of Balso Snell, 1931
Nathanael West
An American dreamer who confronts the archetypes of civilization and literature in the bowels of the Wooden Horse of Troy. His bland Americanism subverts the very idea of imaginative culture, but is underpinned by a monstrous sexual inadequacy, and the story, a parable of erotic 'adjustment', has the dynamic of a psychoanalytic breakthrough.

Snevellicci, Miss
Nicholas Nickleby, 1839
Charles Dickens
The daughter of an actor and a dancer, she is the leading lady of VINCENT CRUMMLES's company. Able to 'do anything, from a medley dance to Lady Macbeth', although none of it very well, she flirts unsuccessfully with NICHOLAS NICKLEBY but eventually marries a tallow chandler.

Snitchey, Jonathan
The Battle of Life, 1846
Charles Dickens
Attorney-at-law and partner, with Thomas Craggs, in the law firm of Snitchey and Craggs, DR ANTHONY JEDDLER's lawyers. Kindly and sharp-witted, he is the spokesman for his partner, speaking always 'for self and Craggs', and later 'for self and Craggs, deceased'. For his part, Craggs seems conscious 'of little or no separate existence or personal individuality'.

Snodgrass, Augustus
Pickwick Papers, 1837
Charles Dickens
A former ward of SAMUEL PICKWICK, a member of the Pickwick Club and an aspiring poet, 'poetically enveloped in a mysterious blue cloak with a canine-skin collar'. He spends much of his time pining for Emily WARDLE and finally succeeds in marrying her.

Snopes, Ab (Abner)
The Unvanquished, 1938
'Barn Burning', in *Collected Stories*, 1950
The Hamlet, 1940
William Faulkner
The earliest of the infamous clan to be mentioned, and a relatively minor figure in the Yoknapatawpha County novels. Nonetheless, his footsteps have a 'clocklike finality' that signifies the beginning of the end for traditional Southern values. A ruthless and acquisitive man, his standard reaction to any slight or pressure from landlords is to burn their outbuildings.

Snopes, Bilbo
The Town, 1957
The Mansion, 1959
William Faulkner
A relatively minor member of the dynasty, he is the son of I O SNOPES by his bigamous marriage to an unidentified woman from Frenchman's Bend, and the twin brother of VARDAMAN SNOPES.

Snopes, Byron
Sartoris, 1929, full version published as *Flags in the Dust*, 1973
The Town, 1957
William Faulkner
Author of the anonymous letters sent to NARCISSA

BENBOW in *Sartoris*. He marries an Apache woman and confirms his own wild blood by robbing COL JOHN SARTORIS's old bank and fleeing the county for ever.

Snopes, Clarence
Sanctuary, 1931
The Town, 1957
William Faulkner

Brother of the twins BILBO and VARDAMAN SNOPES, he first appears as a perjurer in *Sanctuary*, and re-emerges as a corrupt Mississippi state senator in the later Snopes saga, still convinced that everything, even the truth, has its price.

Snopes, Eck (Eckrum)
The Hamlet, 1940
William Faulkner

One of those rare Snopeses who possess a single recessive gene of goodness and hard-working honesty. He works as a blacksmith and farrier, but later blows himself up.

Snopes, Eula (Eula Varner)
The Hamlet, 1940
The Town, 1957
William Faulkner

The sensual but slovenly daughter of WILL VARNER, in whose store at Frenchman's Bend FLEM SNOPES cut his business teeth; 'her entire appearance suggested some symbology out of the old Dionysic times – honey in sunlight and bursting grapes'. Flem marries her (for a dowry that includes an old Civil War mansion) when she is pregnant with Hoake McCarron's child. She has a long-standing love affair with MANFRED DE SPAIN and commits suicide when threatened with exposure and scandal.

Snopes, Flem
The Hamlet, 1940
The Town, 1957
The Mansion, 1959
William Faulkner

The most successful and calculating of the Snopeses, dominated by an obsessive desire for respectability. AB SNOPES's son, he starts life as a grocer's boy in WILL VARNER's store, working under JODY VARNER, but works his way up to the presidency of COL JOHN SARTORIS's long-established bank in Jefferson. He is described as having 'eyes the color of stagnant water, and projecting from among the other features in startling and sudden paradox, a tiny predatory nose like the beak of a small hawk'. Sexually impotent, he plays a 'crippled Vulcan' to EULA SNOPES's sloppy Venus, marrying the girl for a cash and real-estate pay-off. He comprehensively betrays kin and kind alike, thus storing up a vengeful enmity against himself that inevitably leads to his destruction.

Snopes, Ike
The Hamlet, 1940
William Faulkner

A pathetic idiot (apparently the victim of a cleft palate), he is the son of one of AB SNOPES's unidentified brothers and latterly a ward of his cousin FLEM SNOPES. He is remembered chiefly for having had a sentimental (but all too physical) love affair with JACK HOUSTON's cow.

Snopes, I O
The Hamlet, 1940
William Faulkner

Father of St Elmo and MONTGOMERY WARD SNOPES, and (by a bigamous marriage) of the twins BILBO and VARDAMAN SNOPES. A half-educated man who has worked as a country schoolmaster, his learning consists largely of stringing together half-remembered quotations and sayings in virtually meaningless combinations.

Snopes, Linda (Linda Snopes Kohl)
The Hamlet, 1940
The Mansion, 1959
William Faulkner

The illegitimate daughter of EULA SNOPES and Hoake McCarron, she is only nominally a Snopes and becomes an instrument of justice, directed against the greed and violence of her adoptive father FLEM SNOPES. She is supported by her ageing beau, the lawyer GAVIN STEVENS, who has also courted her mother.

Snopes, Lump (Launcelot)
The Hamlet, 1940
William Faulkner

Brother of ECK SNOPES and, like all the family, aptly named. He takes over from the ambitious FLEM SNOPES as grocery clerk in WILL and JODY VARNER's store, but later shows typical Snopes enterprise in selling tickets for secret viewings of his cousin IKE SNOPES's bizarre sexual encounters with JACK HOUSTON's cow.

Snopes, Mink
The Hamlet, 1940
The Mansion, 1959
William Faulkner

A dirt-poor sharecropper, he is as viciously predatory as his name suggests and perhaps the most brutal of the clan. He murders JACK HOUSTON in retaliation for a minor pasturing fine, and is betrayed by FLEM SNOPES. He is convinced of the impersonal justice of 'Them', a nemesis much more abstract and determined than the biblical 'Old Moster' of his country cousins. On his deathbed, having revenged himself on his treacherous cousin, he attains a touch of pathos, if not of tragedy.

Snopes, Montgomery Ward
The Town, 1957
The Mansion, 1959
William Faulkner

I O SNOPES's son, he is a pornographer by trade, running a peep-show behind a typically respectable front. When he is arrested, his kinsman FLEM SNOPES 'arranges' a more socially acceptable charge of running an illegal still and distributing moonshine whiskey.

Snopes, Sarty (Colonel Sartoris)
'Barn Burning', in *Collected Stories*, 1950
William Faulkner

Perhaps the only member of the family to be treated completely sympathetically, he is AB

SNOPES's son and thus FLEM SNOPES's brother. As a boy he is witness to his father's vicious retaliation to Major MANFRED DE SPAIN's insistence on recompense for a damaged rug and is divided between family loyalty and an instinctive sense of justice.

Snopes, Vardaman
The Town, 1957
William Faulkner

Twin brother of BILBO SNOPES and a minor figure in the Snopes trilogy. He should not be confused with the idiot VARDAMAN BUNDREN in *As I Lay Dying*.

Snopes, Wallstreet Panic
The Hamlet, 1940
The Town, 1957
William Faulkner

The son of ECK SNOPES and brother of the equally elaborately named Admiral Dewey. He inherits his father's un-Snopesian honesty and becomes a respectable trader.

Snopes, Wesley
The Town, 1957
William Faulkner

Nephew of AB SNOPES and father of the poetically named Virgil and Byron, he is caught consorting with a young girl and is tarred and feathered by the enraged citizenry.

Snow
The Battlers, 1941
Kylie Tennant

Large, blond, rangy, with an 'animal keenness' and sensitivity to his environment, 'Snow' Grimshaw is one of the drifters in Australia in the 1930s, whose home is the open road. Restless and unsettled, he is driven by a 'burning discontent' which keeps him moving on, 'looking for something bigger than a comfortable life or work to do'. Solitary by nature, he unwillingly finds himself leading a band of ill-assorted travellers in their struggle to survive on the track.

Snow White
Snow White, 1967
Donald Barthelme

A 'tall dark beauty containing a good many beauty spots', she is not a conventional character, but an allusive, comic, self-consciously updated version of the fairy-tale princess. Seemingly looking after seven men while waiting for her prince to come, she is growing 'tired of being just a horsewife'. She is college educated, writes poetry, and is a modern, sexually liberated woman, but with reminders of her fairy-tale self in her fear of mirrors, apples and poisonous combs.

Snowball
Animal Farm, 1945
George Orwell

Snowball is the boar who formulated the code of Animal Farm: 'Four legs good, two legs bad'. He epitomizes the true spirit of the revolution and is a pragmatic animal, determined that the farm should succeed and that the animals become self-sufficient. He helps to educate the others and proves to be of further worth in organizing the defence of the farm in the Battle of the Cowshed. As a result of his activities, he is viewed by NAPOLEON as a rival and is expelled. Accused of being a traitor he is, ironically, one of the few sincere revolutionary leaders.

Snowe, Lucy
Villette, 1853
Charlotte Brontë

The impoverished heroine and narrator of the novel, Lucy travels alone to Villette where, lonely and friendless, she is employed in a girls' school run by MADAME BECK. Plain, frail, but also intelligent, imaginative, and given to wild bursts of passion, she suffers the torments of unrequited love in her relationship with DR JOHN BRETTON, and is quite frequently morose and down-hearted. Eventually finding independence, and real love and friendship in the unlikely form of MONSIEUR PAUL EMMANUEL, however, she becomes, in the end, much more than just another survivor.

Snowman
Oryx and Crake, 2003
Margaret Atwood

The narrator of the novel, who, as a boy, used to be known as Jimmy. Now, many years later and in the aftermath of a biotechnological disaster that has ruined the landscape, he lives, almost naked, in a tree, reviewing his shredded memories and mourning the loss of CRAKE and ORYX. Absorbed since childhood by violence and pornography, Snowman later becomes mesmerized by Oryx. A foolish fantasist, jealous lover and perturbed spirit, he embodies something of the Orpheus myth.

Snubbin, Serjeant
Pickwick Papers, 1837
Charles Dickens

SAMUEL PICKWICK's barrister in the case of *Bardell* vs *Pickwick*. His reasoned arguments are no match for the aggressive eloquence of MRS MARTHA BARDELL's counsel, SERJEANT BUZFUZ.

Sofia
The Color Purple, 1982
Alice Walker

A strong and self-assured woman, Sofia has had to fight against subjugation all her life. Asserting that 'a girl ain't safe in a family of men', she maintains her resistance at the cost of her freedom. An inspiration to CELIE when free, Sofia learns to repress her strength by imitating Celie's subservience; 'Miss Celie, I act like you. I jump right up and do just what they say'. Finally reawakened after an apparent submission, Sofia asserts that 'I already had my bad luck, she say. I had enough to keep me laughing the rest of my life'.

Sogliardo
Every Man out of his Humour, 1600
Ben Jonson

The brother of SORDIDO, Sogliardo has money and land, but neither of these, he discovers, qualifies him to be thought of as a gentleman. Foolishly, he asks CARLO BUFFONE for his advice and is told that to be properly accepted into polite society he must wear flamboyant clothes and run up elaborate debts. Yet every effort he makes to become a gentleman only serves further to expose his gullibility.

Sohrab
'Sohrab and Rustum', in Poems: A New Edition, 1853
MatthewArnold

A Tartar warrior, 'like some young cypress, tall and dark and straight', but 'softly reared'. Among the opposing armies of Tartars and Persians, he searches for his long-lost father, RUSTUM, to whom he will be identifiable by a pin-prick tattoo on the shoulder. He is fatally wounded by his father in single combat before either man's true identity is known.

Solace
Ane Pleasant Satyre of theThrie Estaitis, 1540
Sir David Lindsay

The most endearing of the king's three courtiers, Sandie Solace, full of fun and fond of a drink, can hardly be blamed for his excessive interest in sex. Comically verbose in praising his mother who had 'four and twentie on ane nicht', it is not surprising that he should wax lyrical about DAME SENSUALITIE, causing REX HUMANITAS to be sufficiently moved to invite her to court. However, his merry, playful nature is, in the end, to be welcomed, in moderation, rather than completely wiped out.

Solanka, Malik
Fury, 2001
Salman Rushdie

An Anglo-Indian intellectual, formerly a Cambridge academic, Solanka renounced the 'narrowness' of academic life in order to manufacture dolls for television series, one of which spawned a remunerative franchise industry. Now a late-middle-aged 'historian of ideas', he is disillusioned and restive. He abandons his wife and child in London for independence in New York, where he goes for long walks, the memories of which are frequently blotted out by alcohol. When it transpires that these walks coincide with the murders of women, he wonders whether he might indeed be the killer. 'Fury', he concludes, ' – sexual, Oedipal, political, magical, brutal – drives us to our finest heights and coarsest depths'.

Soldan, the
The Faerie Queene, 1590–6
Sir Edmund Spenser

The Soldan signifies the Pope, or Philip II. He is perceived as supporting injustice since he is married to Adicia, whose name represents injustice. He has a furious temper and is prone to excessive blasphemy. Proud and insolent, he rides a chariot with iron spikes attached to its wheels. His horses are fed with the flesh of half-dead men and his coat of arms is spattered with blood.

Solent, Wolf
Wolf Solent, 1929
John Cowper Powys

A 35-year-old history teacher, working on a bawdy history begun by his late predecessor,

with whom he identifies. He is tall, lean, and 'not an ill-favoured man; but on the other hand … not a prepossessing one'. Solitary, priggish and obsessive, he believes that reality is multiple, like a series of Chinese boxes. He is dominated by his mother, and powerfully attracted to two very different women, but drives away both and ends up alone, a fate he determines to face with the 'stoical resolution' which 'he had learnt from the hard woman who had given him birth'.

Solmes, Roger
Clarissa, 1748
Samuel Richardson

Physically grotesque, Roger Solmes has a distinctly reptilian aura. He is 'squat like a Toad', a clear allusion to the demonic SATAN in Milton's *Paradise Lost*. He has been chosen as CLARISSA HARLOWE's husband and master because he is a member of the ruling élite and exudes privilege. He views marriage as a commercial transaction and thinks of Clarissa as a luxury object. Clarissa loathes the saurian Solmes and his 'diabolical parsimony'. His negligible intellect and coarseness of mind are worthy of her disdain.

Somers, Jane
The Diaries of Jane Somers, 1984
Doris Lessing

Summer is Jane's least favourite season. She finds the fullness of life depressing. She desperately needs loving affectionate people in her life, who accept her as she is, but has trouble relating to others in any meaningful way because they pose a threat to her controlled solitude. Outwardly perfect, she appears self-absorbed but is, inwardly, deeply insecure, having had an uneasy childhood, always feeling that her sister was her mother's favourite. However, eventually, through an unlikely friendship she manages to examine herself and life in general in more depth and with confrontational candour.

Somers, Richard and Harriet
Kangaroo, 1923
D H Lawrence

The aftermath of World War I finds Richard and Harriet Somers disillusioned with England and with Europe: 'No man who has really consciously lived through this can believe absolutely again in democracy'. So they leave for Australia, where Richard is initially taken in by, and then repudiates, the gospel of love and will preached by BEN COLLEY, while Harriet is briefly transfixed by the darkly erotic sensibilities of JACK CALCOTT. Richard distrusts love and the power of love, yet by the time he and Harriet decide to leave Australia, each has admitted the necessity of spiritually renewing themselves.

Son
Tar Baby, 1981
Toni Morrison

'A man without human rites', Son enters the enclosed, humid world of the island of L'Arbe de la Croixe and becomes a catalyst for mounting tensions. A metaphor for the absent black in American history, his position is one that challenges the stance of the people he watches. Anchored to his own past, a 'Mama-spoiled black man', his convictions are challenged by the rootless JADINE CHILDS. A compassionate and fabulous figure, he finally effects a resolution that merges both the island's mythical past and his own uncertain future.

Sonali
Rich Like Us, 1983
Nayantara Sahgal

A 38-year-old official in the Ministry of Industry, marginalized for political reasons, she confronts the rapid political changes in India. A close friend of ROSE SURYA, she was born into a Brahmin family from Kashmir, yet an Oxford education has distanced her from her childhood orthodoxies. A student flirtation with Marxism failed because Sonali loathes political, religious and emotional regimentation, although she envies in others the capacity for mental discipline and purpose. She is a romantic, but of the reflective, intellectual kind.

Sonia
The Heart of the Country, 1987
Fay Weldon

An emotionally disturbed woman, bruised by her experiences with men, Sonia is seeking affection in whatever form she can find it and, despite her aggressiveness, is capable of real kindness. Incapable of accepting love, though, she is essentially self-destructive, punishing herself and, inevitably, others as well.

Sonny
'Sonny's Blues', 1957
James Baldwin

He re-enters his elder brother's life as a tiny newspaper story, having been picked up for selling and using heroin. Even as a child, Sonny seems capable of depths of passion and suffering quite alien to his more rational brother. Only at the piano, playing the blues, does he rise above the degrading cycle of need and despair that marks his life.

Soothsayer
Julius Caesar, c.1599
William Shakespeare

In emerging from the crowd of citizens to advise JULIUS CAESAR to 'beware the Ides of March', the soothsayer utters one of the most famous lines in the canon. He later reappears to impart sombre warnings to PORTIA and, on the morning of the Ides itself, to remind the dismissive Caesar that the day is not yet over. The soothsayer partly caters to the 16th-century audience's love of prophecy and magic, but Shakespeare also presents him as a restraining, moderating influence. Whether he is heeded or ignored reflects the obstinacy of the characters to whom he speaks. A soothsayer also features in *Antony and Cleopatra* and *Cymbeline*.

Sophie
The Evening of the Holiday, 1966
Shirley Hazzard

She is half-Italian, half-English, drawn between instinct and cautious reason in a romantic relationship with TANCREDI, never feeling entirely at home in any environment.

Soranzo
'Tis Pity She's a Whore, c.1631
John Ford

A nobleman, whom ANNABELLA agrees to marry while simultaneously enjoying an incestuous affair with her brother, GIOVANNI. Soranzo, meanwhile, has interrupted his own adulterous relationship with Hippolita in order to court and marry Annabella. Although Giovanni contravenes conventional morality, he is at least consistent in his love for Annabella and convinced of its purity, while Soranzo reflects the moral corruption of Parma, enjoying erotic poetry and plotting the death of his lover's husband. Sensual, manipulative and ruthless, he is a man almost wholly lacking in compassion.

Sordello
Sordello, 1840
Robert Browning

His story is traced against the complex background of the history of medieval Italy. Seeking always for the best, he lives a solipsistic existence and peoples his imagination with those who understand him. He is forced to face reality when he is chosen as the poet of Mantua but reverts to his dreams when people fail to understand him. When he finally awakens to love and the chance to take action for the good of his fellow-men it is too late, the long inner struggle has defeated him and he dies.

Sordido
Every Man out of his Humour, 1599
Ben Jonson

The elder brother of SOGLIARDO, he is a successful man: a wealthy farmer with barns filled to capacity from an excellent harvest. Yet he is greedy for more and scrutinizes the almanac, hoping for rain, while devising schemes of conserving the crops he already has. Eventually, in despair over his high-spending son, FUNGOSO, he attempts to hang himself. Not realizing who he is, some locals cut him down, but when they discover his identity they curse him. The shock of this jolts Sordido into realizing that 'no life is blest that is not graced with love'.

Sorrel, Hetty
Adam Bede, 1859
George Eliot

The POYSERs' pouting, kitten-like dairymaid, her looks make her scarcely resistible to ARTHUR DONNITHORNE and ADAM BEDE. For the former she lets down her hair and puts on large earrings. She means no harm, but though Adam imagines her to be perfect, he does not realize her vanity, her inability to perceive his feelings, and her lack of 'a single Christian ideal or Christian feeling'.

Sosostris, Madame
'The Burial of the Dead', in *The Waste Land*, 1922
T S Eliot

A 'famous clairvoyante', she 'had a bad cold, nevertheless/Is known to be the wisest woman in Europe,/With a wicked pack of cards'.

Soulis, Murdoch
Thrawn Janet, 1881
Robert Louis Stevenson

A 'severe, bleak-faced old man' who lives a lonely, ascetic life in the manse at Balweary. He is outwardly stern and unforgiving, but his eyes betray uncertainty and fear. Sometimes he prowls his land at night, groaning aloud to himself. And yet, when he arrived in the parish 50 years before, he was young, innocent and feckless. It is his encounter with the housekeeper JANET MCLOUR which has split his personality and turned him into a haunted, desperate solitary, whose liberal, creative view of life is supplanted by a morally deterministic one.

South, Marty
The Woodlanders, 1887
Thomas Hardy

Solitary, self-reliant and constant in her affections, Marty is strongly identified with the woodland in which she lives. Economic necessity forces her to suppress her feminine nature and adopt an almost masculine lifestyle – a choice which is symbolized by her cutting off her long chestnut hair at the start of the novel. Faithful to her beloved GILES WINTERBORNE throughout, she finally finds consolation in tending his grave.

Sowerberry, Mr and Mrs
Oliver Twist, 1838
Charles Dickens

He is the undertaker to whom OLIVER TWIST is apprenticed, and she is his wife, 'a short, thin, squeezed up woman, with a vixenish countenance'. His liking Oliver for being a good child-mute is resented by his wife and the apprentice NOAH CLAYPOLE. When he punishes Oliver for knocking down Claypole, Oliver runs away to London.

Sowerby, Nathaniel
Framley Parsonage, 1861
Anthony Trollope

Despite owning his old family estate of Chaldicotes, Mr Sowerby is impoverished by politics (he is a Barsetshire MP), gambling and luxurious living. He financially exploits friends such as LORD LUFTON and REV MARK ROBARTS, but conscience sometimes limits his depredations. His only hope is marriage to the rich MISS MARTHA DUNSTABLE. Aged 50, he dresses like a young man and is an attractive, good-humoured but dangerous companion. Although 'born to be a gentleman', he has turned out to be a rogue.

Spade, Sam
The Maltese Falcon, 1930, et seq
Dashiell Hammett

Arguably *the* hard-boiled private eye, who moves among, and is respected by, both sides of the criminal culture in his 'burg', San Francisco. He is tough, but carries no gun, and is a shrewd, cunning, streetwise operator. He has sharp, almost demonic features, and a wild, unpredictable streak in his nature. He is a man of honour in his own way, and an idealist at heart, but is not averse to breaking rules, and even laws, to get results.

Spalding, Caroline, later **Lady Peterborough**
He Knew He Was Right, 1869
Anthony Trollope

The elder daughter of an American minister living in Florence, she meets CHARLES GLASCOCK during a fraught journey, and eventually marries him. She is a 'pretty, clever-looking' young woman, and her suitor 'has never met any lady who talked better'. Her sensible, pragmatic American upbringing and bold, level-headed personality leave her unimpressed by the idea of assuming a noble title, but she is thought to have made a good catch nonetheless.

Spandrell, Maurice
Point Counter Point, 1928
Aldous Huxley

A restless experimenter with vice at its most debased, Spandrell becomes so bored with himself that he resorts to 'the corruption of youth' as the only form of debauchery that can give him any 'active emotion'. He wallows in evil partly for aesthetic purposes, and his impulsive murder of Everard Webley, a fascistic agitator and 'tinpot Mussolini', leads to fatal consequences for the novelist PHILIP QUARLES.

Spanish John
Stories à la Carte, 1932
Furthermore, 1938
Damon Runyon

The constant companion of HARRY THE HORSE and LITTLE ISADORE, he shares with them a capacity for sudden violence, and a total disregard for law or morality. Operating by the code of the streets, he explores the twilight world of the determined criminal, prepared to try his hand at most forms of vice.

Sparkish
The Country Wife, 1675
William Wycherley

A shallow fop, Sparkish pursues ALITHEA apparently not out of passion, or even lust, but purely because he thinks it is the fashionable thing to do. He prides himself on his wit, commenting, 'I think wit as necessary at dinner as a glass of good wine, and that's the reason I never have any stomach when I eat alone'.

Sparkler, Edmund
Little Dorrit, 1857
Charles Dickens

MRS MERDLE's fatuous son by her first marriage, he proposes to unsuitable women, including the dancer, FANNY DORRIT. Although his mother bribes Fanny to drop him, once the Dorrits become rich, she encourages the marriage. His wife treats him with contempt and considers him 'almost an idiot', but he rises to a high position in the Circumlocution Office.

Sparrowhawk → Ged

Sparsit, Mrs
Hard Times, 1854
Charles Dickens

JOSIAH BOUNDERBY's elderly, widowed housekeeper who boasts of her aristocratic connections.

When Bounderby dashes her hopes of marrying him by marrying LOUISA GRADGRIND, she spies on Louisa and JAMES HARTHOUSE, hoping to reveal some misconduct. She later discovers Bounderby's mother, MRS PEGLER, and unwittingly forces her to reveal in public that Bounderby's stories of youthful hardship are all lies. She is dismissed for publicly humiliating him.

Spearman, Rosanna
The Moonstone, 1868
Wilkie Collins

A silent, solitary woman with a deformed shoulder, Rosanna Spearman is a former thief from a London Reformatory who has been given a chance at a better life as second housemaid to Lady Julia Verinder. Diligent, modest and uncomplaining, her manner wins her few friends among the fellow domestics who are suspicious of her aloofness. Besotted by FRANKLIN BLAKE (who is unaware of her feelings), she commits suicide in despair at unrequited love and a world that has constantly withheld her share of happiness.

Spearmint, Willie
The Tenants, 1971
Bernard Malamud

A young black would-be writer who becomes a squatter in the crumbling tenement occupied by HARRY LESSER. He is outgoing, vital, life-loving, intuitive and interested in capturing the substance rather than the form of experience. He becomes totally obsessed by his book, refusing even to make love to his girlfriend in case it drains his creative juices (she departs to Lesser instead). Although he and Lesser are linked by their driven need to write, they can find no means of reconciliation, and eventually destroy each other.

Speed
Two Gentlemen of Verona, c.1590
William Shakespeare

Speed is both a clown and a servant to VALENTINE, but is much younger than his counterpart, LAUNCE. His is the customary banter of the licensed clown who, by knowing the ways of the world and the habits and traits of the man he serves, often seems wiser than his employer. It is he, for instance, who suggests to Valentine that SILVIA is in love with him.

Speed, Dave
Tourmaline, 1963
Randolph Stow

A desert-dweller with a visionary grasp of events in Tourmaline that outstrips the more prosaic perception of the narrator (known as THE LAW OF TOURMALINE). In a broadly symbolic book, he is perhaps the most abstract and insubstantial character.

Spencer, Paula
The Woman Who Walked Into Doors, 1996
Roddy Doyle

Addicted to the bottle and trapped in an abusive marriage, Paula, a Dublin cleaner, is not someone to envy. She says of the drink: 'I don't remember when I stopped liking it and started needing it' – and finds clever ways to control her craving. But her self-esteem is crippled by husband Charlo, a charmer turned psychopath whose tyranny can only be defeated by drastic measures. Paula – 'queen of the Pledge and J-cloth' – keeps going through fear, heartbreak and poverty thanks to her black humour and devotion to her children.

Spencer, the Younger
Edward II, 1594
Christopher Marlowe

Alone of all the nobles, he remains almost sycophantically loyal to EDWARD II and his cause, and is notably distraught at the king's fall. He is created Earl of Wiltshire for his pains.

Spenlow, Dora
David Copperfield, 1850
Charles Dickens

The only daughter of MR FRANCIS SPENLOW, she becomes DAVID COPPERFIELD's first wife on the death of her father, who had opposed the marriage. Like David's mother, MRS CLARA COPPERFIELD, she is pretty and artless but immature. She refers to herself as David's 'child-wife' and, like Clara, proves to be an incompetent housekeeper. Following the birth of a stillborn child, she dies at the same moment as her beloved girlhood companion, her lapdog, Jip.

Spenlow, Mr Francis
David Copperfield, 1850
Charles Dickens

The father of DORA SPENLOW, and the senior partner in Spenlow and Jorkins, Proctors in Doctors' Commons, where DAVID COPPERFIELD is articled as a clerk. A stiff and unbending man, he uses his mild-mannered partner as an excuse for his own tyrannical professional behaviour. He refuses to consider David as a suitor for Dora, but on his death, they marry. Although respected in life, when he dies his business affairs are revealed to be in disarray.

Spenser
The Godwulf Manuscript, 1973, et seq
Robert B Parker

A tough but civilized Boston private investigator. Ex-boxer and ex-cop, he enjoys good relations with former colleagues in the Police Department, particularly Lieutenant Quirk and Sergeant Belson. He is an accomplished cook, quotes poetry, and is fashion-conscious, although he likes his old-style apartment and car. His aide is his black friend, and ex-training partner, soft-spoken and deadly Hawk. Something of a modern knight, Spenser remains faithful to the only woman in his life, psychotherapist Susan Silverman.

Spenser, Lucy
Love Always, 1985
Ann Beattie

As 'Cindi Coeur' she writes and replies to the letters received by an underground magazine. Living in isolation in rural Vermont, she is significantly detached from the anxieties and pressures that exist in the wider world, until her teenage niece, NICOLE, comes to stay.

Sphere, McClintic
V, 1963
Thomas Pynchon

A jazz saxophonist at the V-Note club in the Bowery, New York. References to his origins in Fort Worth, Texas, and to his solos being 'something else' help identify him as a version of the revolutionary jazz composer Ornette Coleman; but Sphere's surname is also the pianist Thelonious Monk's middle name, and that connection is confirmed by his having a girlfriend called Ruby (a reference to Monk's tune 'Ruby, My Dear'). Sphere's credo-cummotto is 'Keep cool, but care'.

Spielvogel, Dr
Portnoy's Complaint, 1969
Philip Roth

A caricature psychiatrist who hears ALEXANDER PORTNOY's long outpouring of guilt. He describes the disorder 'Portnoy's Complaint' at the start of the book, noting that 'acts of exhibitionism, voyeurism, fetishism, auto-eroticism and oral coitus' did not bring the patient satisfaction, but instead produced 'overriding feelings of shame and the dread of retribution, particularly in the form of castration'. At the end of Portnoy's anguished confession, he says 'Now vee may perhaps to begin. Yes?'

Spintho
Androcles and the Lion, 1912
George Bernard Shaw

Spintho, 'a debauchee, the wreck of a good-looking man gone hopelessly to the bad', is one of a trio of Christians including ANDROCLES and FERROVIUS who join LAVINIA and the other prisoners about to take their chance in the Roman arena. Spintho has no religious faith but has converted under the delusion that as every Christian martyr is guaranteed a place in heaven no matter what his sins, he can safely spend his time on earth in moral abandonment.

Spiritualitie
Ane Pleasant Satyre of the Thrie Estaitis, 1540
Sir David Lindsay

Representing the clergy, Spiritualitie, the first, and most corrupt, of the Three Estates is more concerned about his secular well-being than the edification of the people of Scotland, so much so that he boasts of not having even read the Bible, 'New Testament nor Auld'. Greedily oppressing the poor and, in alliance with the Vices, driving out VERITIE and CHASTITIE in favour of DAME SENSUALITIE, Spiritualitie remains averse to reformation and, along with the Abbot and the Persone, is finally expelled from the court after being unfrocked, a hilarious process which reveals fools' costumes to be their natural garb.

Splendid, John, properly **McIver of Barbeck**
John Splendid, 1898
Neil Munro

A strong, rugged adventurer who takes arms against Montrose's depredations in Argyll in 1644. He is practical, instinctual, good-humoured and loyal, a natural leader of men. He is brave and unflinching in the face of danger, but also shrewd and cunning, and knows how to use guile and flattery as weapons. A 'bold fellow' with 'little schooling, but some wit and gentlemanly parts', he is a 'decent soul' who is named 'not for his looks but for his style'. He is vain, but would 'sooner be liked and loved than only admired'.

Spofford, Alexandra
The Witches of Eastwick, 1984
John Updike

In the delicate democracy of the Eastwick coven, she emerges as the most powerful single figure. Blonde-haired and creative, she turns her skill as an artist to the more serious business of casting spells, both malign and gentle.

Spondy
The Adventures of Peregrine Pickle, 1751, bowdlerized edition 1758
Tobias Smollett

Originally a savage lampoon of Henry Fielding, this character was toned down after his death in 1754, though Smollett does retain a sarcastic reference to Fielding's supposedly heavy-handed moralizing on 'the instability of human affairs, the treachery of the world, and the treachery of youth'.

Sponge, Soapy
Mr Sponge's Sporting Tour, 1853
R S Surtees

A sportsman of cheerful adaptability and impressive resourcefulness. Like his descendant, Charles Dickens's SAMUEL PICKWICK, he remains innocent of the more duplicitous and self-serving aspects of his society, preferring to see everything reduced to the metaphor of the cricket match, the rod-and-line, rowing or hunting.

Spooner
No Man's Land, 1975
Harold Pinter

Having apparently met HIRST, a celebrated man of letters, one night on Hampstead Heath and either infiltrated himself or been invited into his home, Spooner announces himself as a poet, 'a man of intelligence and perception'. Both men are in their sixties, yet Spooner is as much of a literary failure as Hirst is a success, reduced to a world of obscure magazines and collecting the glasses at a pub in Chalk Farm. Shabby and self-interested, Spooner feels that becoming Hirst's secretary would provide him not only with much-needed money but a roof over his head. Yet while deferring to Hirst and exposing his vulnerabilities, in many ways Spooner also feels a considerable compassion for him.

Sporus
Epistle to Dr Arbuthnot, 1735
Alexander Pope

A savage satire on the professional courtier and modelled on Lord Hervey, Pope gives him the name of Nero's eunuch 'wife' and calls him a 'Thing of silk', a 'mere white Curd of Ass's milk', before breaking off with the famous, final rhetorical question: 'Who breaks a Butterfly upon a Wheel?'

Spragg, Undine
The Custom of the Country, 1913
Edith Wharton

A small-town girl, the beautiful but spoilt, selfish and empty-headed Undine is an obsessive and unscrupulous social climber. After moving to New York, she twice marries into old aristocracies – first in America, to RALPH MARVELL, then in France – but, caring only for opulent glitter and public adulation, is bored and frustrated by their genteel poverty and manners. Preferring the brash vulgarity and fast-living world of the American nouveau riche, Undine is prepared to sacrifice all for her empty ambitions.

Springrove, Edward
Desperate Remedies, 1871
Thomas Hardy

A fine and idealistic man, he has many qualities in common with CYTHEREA GRAYE's father. He is a talented architect, which suggests a certain vision, but he is not emotionally insightful. Although highly educated and intelligent, Edward is not schooled in the ways of the world. However, his gentle patience enables him to be reunited with his love after three years of waiting.

'Spud' Murphy, Daniel
Trainspotting, 1993
Porno, 2002
Irvine Welsh

An inoffensive, good-natured petty thief and 'classic acid-heid', Spud Murphy wants to think the best of people and is, in his friend MARK RENTON's assessment, 'incapable ay upsetting a spurned lover wi a bad hangover'. Voluble and gregarious, though not very articulate, he comes across as 'naturally spaced out and seems as if he's oan drugs, even when he's clean'. His laid-back and benign outlook on life does nothing, however, to protect him from his persistent bad luck.

Spurio
The Revenger's Tragedy, 1607
Thomas Middleton or Cyril Tourneur

The bastard son of THE DUKE, he wants to be revenged on the whole world for his illegitimacy. Full of hate and malice, he views everything with cynicism and loathing, hoping for the worst possible outcome in all situations – 'if a bastard's wish might stand in force/Would all the court were turn'd into a corse'. He cynically enters into a sexual relationship with THE DUCHESS, despite the fact that he hates her too, hoping to bring 'confusion,/Death and disgrace' on her and her family.

Square, Mr
The History of Tom Jones, 1749
Henry Fielding

MR THWACKUM's antagonist in the field of theological controversy, he holds 'human nature to be the perfection of all virtue, and vice [but] a deviation from our nature in the same way that deformity of the body is'. It is a useful philosophical disguise when one's own nature is calculatingly venal.

Squealer
Animal Farm, 1945
George Orwell

Perhaps the most unpleasant and disquieting of all the animals on Animal Farm. A pig who is a brilliantly persuasive orator and bureaucrat, he employs all his powers to serve evil. He is an arch-hypocrite who can endlessly obfuscate the truth and deliver unpalatable lies. He is ever-watchful, ready to expel or annihilate anyone who deviates from the official code. Lacking real courage in battle, devoid of principles, Squealer is the type of politician who will always flourish, no matter what the regime. It is highly appropriate that he is the first to adopt the human way of walking on two legs.

Squeers, Wackford
Nicholas Nickleby, 1839
Charles Dickens

The sadistic and illiterate proprietor of the Yorkshire school, Dotheboys Hall, he hires NICHOLAS NICKLEBY as an assistant master at the instigation of RALPH NICKLEBY. His appearance 'was not prepossessing. He had but one eye, and the popular prejudice runs in favour of two', and 'his expression bordered closely on the villainous'. He is thrashed by Nicholas in front of the boys for thrashing poor SMIKE. When Nicholas and Smike leave the school, he recaptures Smike in London. He conspires with Ralph to steal the deed stolen by Peg Sliderskew from ARTHUR GRIDE which shows that MADELINE BRAY will inherit a fortune on her marriage. Caught in the act and possessing a stolen will, he is sentenced to transportation for seven years, and Dotheboys Hall is closed down for ever. His wife matches him in cruelty; their ugly daughter becomes infatuated with Nicholas; and their son, Wackford Junior, has grown plump on the deprivation of the other boys and is exhibited in London as evidence of the good treatment in the school. After her husband's conviction, Mrs Squeers and her children have to be rescued when the unfortunate pupils take revenge on them.

Squeezum, Justice
Rape Upon Rape, 1730
Henry Fielding

A grotesquely depraved character, Justice Squeezum indulges in a range of sordid and illegitimate practices, from extorting protection money from madams and pimps to rigging juries. He sees every miscreant as nothing more than the potential payer of a bribe. Henpecked by his wife, he is frightened that she will expose his 'Train of Rogueries' and pays her large sums of money to keep her quiet. The antithesis of the dry Justice Worthy, Squeezum's manifesto is condensed in his utterance, 'Gravity is the best Cloak for Sin'.

Squire, the
The Canterbury Tales, c.1387–1400
Geoffrey Chaucer

The son of THE KNIGHT, this young man is a fashionable dandy. Although he has some military experience, his principal activities have been more courtly. An accomplished musician and versifier, he is very much a ladies' man and devotes most of his energy to the pursuit of love. Naturally, his incomplete tale is one of high romance and fabulous adventure.

Squire of Dames, the
The Faerie Queene, 1590–6
Sir Edmund Spenser

He represents the social abuse of love. He is first met whilst being carried off by the giantess ARGANTE. In order to gain his lady's hand, he accepts her challenge to 'serve' (or seduce) every gentlewoman he meets in a year (over 300 in all). She then demands that he should find as many chaste ladies as he has found unchaste, but he can only discover three. He is courtly in speech and name, but has no other virtues.

Srinivas
Mr Sampath: the Printer of Malgudi, 1949
R K Narayan

The editor (and sole copywriter) of the crusading *Banner*, which he runs from the garret of MR SAMPATH's printshop. He is a pugnacious enemy of the slum conditions brought about by the industrialization of Malgudi. Aged 37, he has tried marriage, agriculture, bank-apprenticeship, teaching and law, but has always felt that his time was slipping away in trivial action. When Sampath is made bankrupt and turns film-maker, Srinivas becomes his script-writer, reluctantly forced to include romance and song and drama in his classical epic.

Sriram
Waiting for the Mahatma, 1955
R K Narayan

Brought up by his sharp-tongued but indulgent grandmother, at 20 the solitary and reclusive Sriram is without a college education and spends his time in idle self-indulgence, convinced he understands everything in life. Twin events that shake his belief in his own prowess and understanding are Gandhi's visit to Malgudi and meeting the Mahatma's god-daughter and disciple, the independent, elusive BHARATI, who he loves at first sight. Leaving Malgudi with the Gandhi camp, mainly to be near Bharati, he is later actively involved in the 'Quit India' campaign, and becomes a wanted man.

Stacey, Rosamund
The Millstone, 1965
Margaret Drabble

'My career has always been marked by a strange mixture of confidence and cowardice', reflects Rosamund Stacey at the beginning of the novel. Indeed, part of the cargo which she carries through life is a 'well-established, traditional, English morality'. As a result, she is in-dependent, reticent to the point of inhibition, sophisticated, clever and somewhat fatalistic. Yet her diffidence and reserve do not prevent her from having an illegitimate child, and while caring for the baby (born with a heart defect), she completes higher education and steps into work. The child is the instrument of Rosamund's growing maturity, self-assertion and realization that great and mysterious forces of nature are at work in the world.

Stackpole, Henrietta
The Portrait of a Lady, 1881
Henry James

ISABEL ARCHER's friend, she is a quick-witted and independent American who is writing a series of European sketches for a New York newspaper. Self-reliant and resourceful, she is nonetheless too literal-minded to understand the tacit conventions and subtle machinations of Euro-pean society, which she interprets (negatively, in the main) according to unswerving US standards.

Staithes, Mark
Eyeless in Gaza, 1936
Aldous Huxley

A misanthropic Marxist, Staithes, together with his friend, ANTHONY BEAVIS, seeks adventure in revolutionary Mexico, but only ends up losing a leg. His 'fanatical hermit's face' is grotesque: 'Under the skin each strip of muscle in the cheek and jaw seemed to stand out distinct and separate like the muscles in those lime-wood statues of human beings that were made for Renaissance anatomy rooms'.

Stalky
Stalky & Co., 1899
Rudyard Kipling

A sarcastic and cunning public-schoolboy, whose real name is Artie Corkran. He is the freckled leader of a closely knit gang of three, also containing BEETLE and M'TURK, which tricks and overcomes teachers, prefects and bullies (although the boys are not themselves averse to a bit of sadistic fun). Opposed to the conventional morality of the school, he also hates the hypocritical patriotism of politicians, while admiring imperialistic military action. After leaving the College, he becomes a legendary soldier of the British Empire.

Standish, Eden
The Living and the Dead, 1941
Patrick White

The sister of ELYOT STANDISH, Eden is a restless woman in search of emotional and intellectual fulfilment, and who believes she has found it in the self-absorbed Norman Maynard and the political teachings of Marx. Yet these prove insufficient to enable to her to overcome 'a singular, feverish sense of waste'. With Joe Barnett, a subsequent lover, Eden shares not only a political sensitivity but a sexual passion, and attains a sense of purpose. Barnett's death in the Spanish Civil War results in her also leaving Australia for Spain. An idealist, Eden has a vigour for life: 'We were not', she observes, 'born to indifference'.

Standish, Elyot
The Living and the Dead, 1941
Patrick White

Compared with his restless sister, EDEN STANDISH, he has little intellectual or physical vitality. Emotionally inhibited, cerebral, indecisive, Elyot represents the plight of the well-meaning, liberal intellectual when con-fronted with momentous political and social events. He vacillates. Eden's commitment in following her lover to the Spanish Civil War is something clearly beyond her brother. Elyot, though, recognizes all too clearly his own failures and those of his sister and domineering mother. It is this recognition which finally enables him to confront life, and to feel at last 'like someone who had been asleep and who had only just woken'.

Standish, Lady → Kennedy, Laura

Standish, Miles
The Courtship of Miles Standish, 1858
Henry Wadsworth Longfellow

The Captain of Plymouth, commander of the Pilgrim Fathers' twelve-strong army against the Indians, Standish is an experienced soldier, strong but ageing. He reads Caesar, but is somewhat stupid. Despite declaring that to have a thing done well, you must do it yourself, he sends his young friend John Alden to woo the beautiful Priscilla on his behalf (he is a widower). Usually rough but kindly, he rages at Alden when his scheme goes wrong, but his basic nobility overcomes his anger.

Stanhope, Dennis
Journey's End, 1928
R C Sherriff

The play is set in a dugout in the British lines during the German spring offensive of 1918. Although Stanhope, a 21-year-old captain, has survived three years on the Western Front, he has become prematurely aged and cynical from the experience, the fear and the alcohol he drinks in an attempt to dampen his nerves. He is a good and caring man at heart, and a good and imaginative soldier, but the terrible stress of war has altered his nature and made him unpredictable, veering from cool self-control to near-hysteria, something he is anxious his girlfriend at home will never discover.

Stanley
The Recognitions, 1955
William Gaddis

A young composer, whose devout Catholicism and sincere artistry set him at an opposite pole to both WYATT GWYON and OTTO, the two very different false artists with whom he forms an absurd trinity. All his work, amid a world of unfinished and partial designs, is to be a grand, final summation, but also his tomb. Stanley is much assailed by the world, the flesh and the Devil, but eventually attains the final, apocalyptic diapason in a rickety Italian church.

Stanley, Rose
The Prime of Miss Jean Brodie, 1961
Muriel Spark

An Edinburgh schoolgirl and member of the 'Brodie set'. A tomboy at the age of ten, she is later tall, blonde and attractive to boys (helped by her knowledge of things that interest them, such as cars). Her teacher, MISS JEAN BRODIE, says that Rose has 'instinct'; it is this that leads to her being 'famous for sex', a subject in which she has no particular interest. Soon after leaving school she marries a successful businessman.

Stansbury, Hugh
He Knew He Was Right, 1869
Anthony Trollope

A journalist, the nephew of JEMIMA STANSBURY. He is 'reputed to be somewhat hot in spirit and manner', and has a forcible style of arguing his case on whatever subject is at hand. He is 'impressionable, demonstrative, eager', and possesses 'the sweetest temper that was ever given to a man for the blessing of women'. He is successful in wooing NORA ROWLEY from his wealthier rival, CHARLES GLASCOCK.

Stansbury, Jemima, known as **Aunt Stansbury**
He Knew He Was Right, 1869
Anthony Trollope

The spinster aunt of HUGH STANSBURY. She is a small woman of 60, with 'bright grey eyes, and a strong Roman nose, and thin lips, and a sharp-cut chin'. She always dresses in black silk, and reserves the newest of her dresses for church, since 'Nothing, she was wont to say, was too good for the Lord's house'. She has an unbending sense of social and moral propriety, and cuts off her nephew when he takes up the unacceptable career of journalism.

Stant, Charlotte
The Golden Bowl, 1904
Henry James

An impoverished young American who has a brief affair with the equally penniless PRINCE AMERIGO. Subsequently she marries the father of her friend MAGGIE VERVER, who marries Amerigo, a quadrille that is put severely out of step when her earlier association with the prince is revealed.

Stanton, Anne
All the King's Men, 1946
Robert Penn Warren

Small and graceful, dark-haired and blue-eyed, Anne is seen by her childhood friend and love, JACK BURDEN, as someone with a 'certitude of self which comes from being all of one piece'. The daughter of an ex-governor of a Southern state, she is devoted to charitable works and her brother's well-being and at almost 35 believes she will be an 'old maid'. Her affair with WILLIE STARK devastates Jack who still loves her.

Staples, Nathan
Everything You Need, 1999
A L Kennedy

An author who feels he has wasted his gifts writing popular thrillers. He is tortured by his feelings for his estranged wife and his daughter, MARY LAMB, whom he has not seen for 15 years and who believes he is dead. When she joins the writers' colony on the island where he lives, he is filled with renewed devotion and the hope of revealing his identity to her. However, the situation is complicated by his frequent weakness and his tendency to undermine his own chances of happiness, and he often yields to indecision and depression.

Starbuck
Moby-Dick, 1851
Herman Melville
Chief mate on the *Pequod*. He is a native of
Nantucket, and is of Quaker stock. He is an
elongated, earnest, careful man who is well
adapted 'to endure hot latitudes, his skin being
hard as a twice-baked biscuit'. A 'steady,
steadfast man', he has faced many perils without
qualms, and is uncommonly conscientious. He is
given to intelligent superstition, and will have no
man in his boat who is not afraid of whales. He
attempts to dissuade CAPTAIN AHAB from his
'blasphemous' quest for vengeance.

Starbuck, Walter F
Jailbird, 1979
Kurt Vonnegut, Jr
A minor conspirator in the Watergate Affair while
a member of staff at the the Nixon White House,
where he served as Minister for Youth, despite his
age. He is a Harvard graduate, and an ex-
communist who came to believe in US
democracy, only to find himself guilty of
embezzlement, perjury and obstruction of
justice in its name. He finds 'the past ... so
embarrassing and the future so terrifying'.

Stark, Willie
All the King's Men, 1946
Robert Penn Warren
A self-made lawyer from a poor cotton and
mining area of the American South, Willie Stark,
JACK BURDEN's 'boss' is a corrupt, ruthless, right-
wing politician. As governor of his home state he
becomes a hero to the common people, and is on
his way to the White House on a tide of popular
acclaim when he is assassinated. Despite the
author's denial, Stark is often regarded as
portraying a real-life governor of Louisiana,
Huey Long, gunned down in the Capitol
building in 1935.

Starkadders, the
Cold Comfort Farm, 1932
Stella Gibbons
A family of uncouth, primitive and melodramatic
farming folk, which benefits from the civilizing
mission of a sophisticated relative, FLORA POSTE.
Living at Cold Comfort Farm (where there have
'always been Starkadders') are mad old Ada
Doom, who once saw 'something nasty in the
woodshed' and dominates her kinfolk; Amos, a
large, bitter religious maniac; his wife Judith,
whose life consists of histrionic poses; their
sons, mean Reuben, who loves the land, and
handsome Seth, who loves the cinema and
radiates animal sexuality; and the fey Elfine.
More distant relatives include Micah, Urk, Ezra,
Caraway and Harkaway.

Starlight, Captain
Robbery Under Arms, 1888
Rolf Boldrewood
One of the most dashing characters in Australian
fiction, Captain Starlight is the aristocratic,
mysterious leader of the bushranging gang which
includes JIM and DICK MARSTON. The romantic,
indeed Byronic, hero-villain of the novel, he is
probably at least partly modelled on Thomas

Smith, a highly successful bushranger who
operated during the 1870s under the alias of
Captain Midnite. Enigmatic, elegant, sharp and
professional, Starlight is a man with 'a soft voice
and pleasant smile which no woman ... could
fight against long'. Although a criminal, he is at
heart a man of honour. Courageous and
authoritative, he is a natural leader, treating his
men 'as if he was their king'. They respond,
naturally, as his subjects.

Starling, Clarice
The Silence of the Lambs, 1988
Thomas Harris
A tough, intelligent young FBI trainee who
matches her wits against the brilliant but
depraved mind of DR HANNIBAL LECTER in an
attempt to secure vital information which
will bring her closer to finding serial killer
'Buffalo Bill'. Psychologically manipulated by
Lecter into confronting her own childhood
traumas, Starling nevertheless takes strength
from the experience, finding in herself and in
her memory of her parents the resilience and
courage with which to persevere in her terrifying
mission.

St Aubert, Emily
The Mysteries of Udolpho, 1794
Ann Radcliffe
Brought up on their country estate by parents
valuing love of nature and beauty above riches,
Emily is sweet, affectionate and modest,
delighting in the woodlands and the mountains.
She composes poetry, sings, plays the lute, and
gives thanks to the Creator for all these
blessings. Bereaved of father and mother, she
does not yield to weak despair even when her
mercenary aunt becomes her guardian.
Sensibility prevents her from sinking to the level
of her vulgar companions; pride gives her
courage, even at Udolpho, where her beloved
VALANCOURT is close at hand.

Staunton, Percy Boyd ('Boy')
Fifth Business, 1970, part of *The Deptford Trilogy*, 1983
Robertson Davies
'Boy' Staunton is a brilliant, arrogant and
opportunist tycoon in 20th-century Canada.
The lifelong 'friend' of DUNSTAN RAMSAY, his
glittering public career is motivated by the need
for others' love and admiration, and is made
possible by his own moral vacuum. Unwilling to
delve into himself or accept any measure of guilt
for the derangement of MAGNUS EISENGRIM's
mother, Staunton's lack of imagination, his
relentless ambition and sexual philandering
make him an unattractive marvel of worldly self-
creation. In old age, he cannot truly escape his
roots or the consequences of his conceit, and he
dies mysteriously.

Staunton, Sir George, also known as 'Robertson'
The Heart of Midlothian, in *Tales of My Landlord: Second Series*, 1818
Sir Walter Scott
The hot-headed lover of EFFIE DEANS and father
of her lost child, he is a well-bred young man
who has fallen among the most violent and

disaffected elements of society. As 'Wildfire' he leads the rioters who lynch CAPTAIN JOHN PORTEOUS, attempting in the process to free his lover from the Tollbooth. He is eventually killed by his own son, 'the Whistler'.

St Barbe
Endymion, 1880
Benjamin Disraeli

A character created in revenge for Thackeray's cruel spoof of *Coningsby*, the hilarious *Codlingsby*. Disraeli portrays his rival as a crude oaf of uncertain intellect and taste.

St Clare, Augustine
Uncle Tom's Cabin, or, Life Among the Lowly, 1851–2
Harriet Beecher Stowe

When UNCLE TOM is first 'sold down the river', it is his good fortune to come to the notice of the cultured Louisianian whose child, EVA, he rescues. St Clare in turn temporarily rescues Tom from the slave market, buying him as a house servant. It is, though, only a temporary respite, for both Eva and St Clare are fated to die, a conclusion that underlines St Clare's ineffectuality in the face of real evil.

St Clare, Marie
Uncle Tom's Cabin, or, Life Among the Lowly, 1851–2
Harriet Beecher Stowe

AUGUSTINE ST CLARE's wife, she is a self-obsessed hypochondriac, a distillation of all the worst aspects of Southern womanhood. Derelict in her duties as a mother, it is she who precipitates the final disaster by selling UNCLE TOM to SIMON LEGREE.

St Cleeve, Swithin
Two on a Tower, 1882
Thomas Hardy

A passionate, handsome and somewhat obsessive young man, for whom there are no half measures: one area of desire seems mutually exclusive of another, although in time he grows to see his work and his woman, LADY VIVIETTE CONSTANTINE, as mutually dependent. His love is profound, and even when his lover has lost her looks, he pledges to marry her.

Stead, Charles
Brazen Prison, 1971
Stanley Middleton

A successful novelist, whose sympathies are torn between his wife's desire for ever-upward mobility and the social arrest represented by the family of a woman he had a brief relationship with when much younger.

Steele, Lucy
Sense and Sensibility, 1811
Jane Austen

Physically attractive, but lacking in elegance, education and sincerity, Lucy's main interest in life is herself. Secretly engaged to EDWARD FERRARS for four years, her motives in remaining so are inspired by her desire for social recognition rather than by love, as is proved by her subsequent apparently sudden change of heart. Sly and hypocritical in her scheming self-promotion, she deceives only those who are

themselves too shallow to see through her selfishness and ignorance.

Steelman
'Steelman', in *While the Billy Boils*, 1888
Henry Lawson

An itinerant con-man, roving the Australian outback in search of 'old friends' on whom he can sponge ruthlessly. A 'hard case', he can be violent and urbane by turns, preferring a softer approach where possible, but not averse to using his fists when the need arises, and then making his victim feel that he, and not Steelman, is guilty of bad manners.

Steenson, Willie, known as **Wandering Willie**
Redgauntlet, 1824
Sir Walter Scott

The tale that Willie tells of Sir Robert Redgauntlet is one of the best known in all of Scott's works. Less is known of its teller. Steenson is a grizzled old fiddler with a flowing beard and a wild and adventurous bearing which communicates itself most readily in his music, which seems almost beyond human capability.

Steerforth, Mr James
David Copperfield, 1850
Charles Dickens

The schoolmate and close friend of DAVID COPPERFIELD, whom he fondly calls 'Daisy'. Handsome, engaging and rich, he is also selfish and domineering. His proud mother, Mrs Steerforth, dotes on him, and her companion, ROSA DARTLE, loves him obsessively, even though her face is permanently scarred by a hammer he threw at her when a boy. Doubts over his integrity are confirmed when he persuades the naive LITTLE EM'LY to elope with him on the eve of her wedding to HAM PEGGOTTY. Some years later, after he has abandoned Em'ly, there is a great storm on Yarmouth beach in which a ship founders, and Ham Peggotty dies attempting to save the life of a drowning man. When the body is washed ashore, it is revealed to be that of Steerforth.

Steerpike
Titus Groan, 1946
Gormenghast, 1950
Mervyn Peake

A pale, ascetic apprentice cook, whose cold nature is ill-suited to the sweltering kitchen from which he soon escapes. He is thin and high-shouldered, his eyes glow red from a mask-like face, and his bulbous forehead bulges with schemes for self-advancement. His ultimate goal is to be Lord of Gormenghast, but he is prepared to take things one step at a time. He scutters about, gathering intelligence for future use, and insinuating his presence into the very heart of Gormenghast. Finally, he rises to become Master of Ritual, from which position he is able to subvert the law to suit himself. Lacking all conscience and remorse, he becomes an evil monster, a 'dragon' that young TITUS GROAN must slay.

'Stella' (Celinda Toobad)
Nightmare Abbey, 1818
Thomas Love Peacock

Arriving mysteriously at Nightmare Abbey, the beautiful, raven-haired young woman (based on Mary Godwin, Shelley's second wife) offers the pseudonym 'Stella'. A well-read, democratic feminist, she dwells on the injustices and miseries of the world. Of a 'gloomy' disposition, she is overburdened with seriousness and never smiles.

Stencil, Herbert
V, 1963
Thomas Pynchon

Stencil's surname suggests his purpose: to provide a meaningful outline for the random facts and treacherous verbal clues from which the history and culture of modern civilization is compounded. The focus of his search is the protean v, an initial whose receding fugitive shape and complex associations mimic the hopelessness of his quest.

Steno, Michel
Marino Faliero: An Historical Tragedy, 1821
Byron, George Gordon, 6th Lord Byron

A young Venetian aristocrat, who maliciously writes on the Doge's throne a couplet so insulting that the Doge, MARINO FALIERO, will not allow it to be repeated when Steno is on trial for his offence. However, Steno is only sentenced to a month in close arrest. Faliero, enraged by so inadequate a punishment, conspires with a mob to overthrow Venice. The plot is foiled and he is arrested and executed, but before he dies Steno makes his apology.

Stephanie
Too Late the Phalarope, 1953
Alan Paton

PIETER VAN VLAANDEREN's aunt, she is a neurotic but essentially sympathetic observer of the profound contradiction between his public persona and the secret guilts and impulses that lead him into self-destructive scandal. Hers is the true voice of a white South Africa teetering on the brink of changes it cannot control.

Stephano
The Tempest, 1611
William Shakespeare

Stephano is butler to the King of Naples, and companion to TRINCULO. He is argumentative and greedy, with the drunkard's courage and the bully's bravado. He claims not to be frightened by anything on the island, least of all CALIBAN, whom he hopes to exploit as a potential source of revenue. His rather twisted imagination allows him to go along with Caliban's plan to murder PROSPERO, because he envisages himself as king with MIRANDA as his queen.

Stephen
Every Man in his Humour, 1598
Ben Jonson

A young gallant, Stephen is a nephew of KNOWELL, SENIOR. A blundering, ignorant snob, he insists that hunting and hawking are the most important accomplishments for a man of fashion

and enterprise. But although bombastic, he is also acutely sensitive and becomes convinced that his cousin, Edward Knowell, is laughing at him. Deciding that a show of melancholy would be the best response, he duly affects melancholia. But his real foible (or 'humour') is that he is enormously impressionable. Admiring CAPTAIN BOBADILL's colourful swearing, he too begins to swear extensively; encouraged to praise MATTHEW's verse, he does so effusively.

Stephens, Keghead
Rusty Bugles, 1948
Sumner Locke Elliott

An Australian sergeant at a wartime ordnance depot, who is so bored by life in the remote Northern Territory that he cannot be bothered doing anything in his spare time. An eternal pessimist, he complains continually about his health and much else.

Stephenson, Howard L
The Man That Corrupted Hadleyburg, 1899
Mark Twain

Howard L Stephenson is the assumed name of a 'passing stranger' who feels he has been unforgivably slighted by a citizen of Hadleyburg (which prides itself as the most uncorruptible town in America). The stranger (a 'bitter man and vengeful') concocts a fiendish scheme that exploits human vanity and cupidity, and which succeeds in showing up the town's leading citizens as dishonest and hypocritical.

Stern, Alejandro 'Sandy'
Presumed Innocent, 1987
The Burden of Proof, 1990
Scott Turow

A skilled defence attorney, he is of Jewish-Argentinian extraction, and is a permanent outsider who is forced to re-examine his own past by his involvement in a complex case. He struggles to reconcile his powerful sense of professional duty as a lawyer with the conflicting pull of family ties and personal obligations.

Stevens, Gavin
Light in August, 1932
Intruder in the Dust, 1948
'Knight's Gambit', in *Knight's Gambit*, 1949
Requiem for a Nun, 1951
The Town, 1957
The Mansion, 1959
William Faulkner

A young lawyer, later the county attorney, who recurs in Faulkner's fiction, usually as a relatively passive observer of the scene. Harvard-educated and principled (even 'meddlesome'), he sets his face against injustice and against the aggressive modernism of the SNOPESes, with whom he is nonetheless romantically involved.

Stevens, Gowan
Sanctuary, 1931
The Town, 1957
William Faulkner

Nephew of the lawyer and county attorney GAVIN STEVENS (in *The Town* they are described as cousins), he is TEMPLE DRAKE's drunken date on the evening she is kidnapped by bootleggers. A spineless, cowardly young man, he makes partial reparation by marrying her.

Stevens, Mr
The Remains of the Day, 1989
Kazuo Ishiguro

An ageing butler at Darlington Hall, Stevens reflects upon his life in service and the changes he has witnessed in an English country house between the wars. Through his memories we learn of the changing nature of life for the English nobility, as well as his own sense of duty and the neglect this has led to in his personal life. As Stevens says, 'The fact is, of course ... I gave my best to Lord Darlington. I gave him the very best I had to give, and now – well – I find I do not have a great deal more left to give'.

Stevens, Stacey → Dabrowski, Anastasia

Stevenson, Zechariah
Heartland, 1964
Wilson Harris

Manager of a riverside depot in the Guyanese jungle; 'his instinct was that of a born gambler, overinclined to be sceptical of a self-sufficient model of fortune, and ... disposed to explore every fleeting vein of unconditional attachment to privilege and servitude'. The image and namesake of his businessman father, he is devastated when his father's business collapses in fraud and the old man is washed up drowned.

Stevie
The Secret Agent, 1907
Joseph Conrad

The halfwit brother of WINNIE VERLOC. He is 'delicate and, in a frail way, good-looking, too, except for the vacant droop of his lower lip'. He has a 'marked horror and dread of physical pain', and is unsuited to life's rigours, but is totally devoted to both Winnie and VERLOC, and easily led astray by the latter. He is humane and honest, and cannot stand any sight or mention of cruelty, suffering or social injustice.

St Evremonde, Marquis de (the elder)
A Tale of Two Cities, 1859
Charles Dickens

The father of CHARLES DARNAY, and elder of the twin brothers. He has died before the novel opens, but his history as a brutal oppressor of the peasantry is revealed when a document is found in the former prison cell of DR ALEXANDRE MANETTE. It is the account of the brothers' abduction and murder of MADAME DEFARGE's sister and brother which she uses to ensure the imprisonment and execution of Darnay.

St Evremonde, Marquis de (the younger)
A Tale of Two Cities, 1859
Charles Dickens

The uncle of CHARLES DARNAY, and successor to his elder brother, he is as brutal as his brother and as contemptuous of the poor. He hates his nephew for his liberal principles and refusal to accept his inheritance. He is stabbed to death in

bed by GASPARD in revenge for the death of the peasant's child, killed by the reckless driving of the nobleman's coachman.

Stewart, Alan Breck → Breck, Alan

Stewart, James → James of the Glens

Steyne, Lord
Vanity Fair, 1848
W M Thackeray

A dissolute and enervated aristocrat with whom BECKY SHARP arrives at some mutually beneficial 'arrangement' (presumably sexual) on her return to London. He is scarred when RAWDON CRAWLEY throws a diamond brooch in his face in a fit of jealous fury.

Stiffner
'Stiffner and Jim (Thirdly, Bill)', in *While the Billy Boils*, 1888
Henry Lawson

A rascally landlord, whose hotel is located between Christchurch 'and that other place – I forget the name of it'. 'He'd been a spieler, fighting man, bush parson, temperance preacher, and a policeman, and a commercial traveller, and everything else that was damnable; he'd been a journalist, and an editor; he'd been a lawyer, too ... He was meaner than a goldfield Chinaman, and sharper than a sewer rat'.

Stiggins, the Rev Mr
Pickwick Papers, 1837
Charles Dickens

Called 'the Shepherd', he is a ranting Non-conformist with 'a semi-rattlesnake sort of eye' who ministers to a fanatical flock of women, including MRS TONY WELLER, at the Emmanuel Chapel in Dorking. Tony exposes him as a drunk and a hypocrite and later kicks him down the street to immerse his head in a horse trough.

Stile, Sir Stentor
The Adventures of Ferdinand, Count Fathom, 1753
Tobias Smollett

A bizarre figure, encountered by FERDINAND, COUNT FATHOM at Paris. For a bet, he has undertaken to spend a month in Paris wearing nothing but the uniform of a jockey. He speaks in an exaggerated manner, much punctuated with 'Ecod!', 'Bodikins!' and 'Waunds!'

Stillwood, Esmond
Esmond in India, 1958
Ruth Prawer Jhabvala

A disenchanted, bullying despot in his own home, secretly and passionately longing for England, the ostensibly charming Stillwood lives in post-Independence New Delhi, giving private tuition in Indian culture, and advice on interior decorating to admiring foreign-diplomat wives. Something of a joke to other Englishmen, this dandyish, handsome womanizer is goaded to violence by the placid sloth of his beautiful and languorous Indian wife. He hoped for a blue-eyed, golden-haired child, a replica of himself, so his dark Indian-looking little son is a disappointment, and he is prepared to leave his family without compunction.

Stingo
Sophie's Choice, 1979
William Styron

A thinly disguised version of his Southern-born creator, Stingo is a tyro novelist who has moved from Tidewater, Virginia, to a Bronx boarding house, where he has a life- and consciousness-altering encounter with SOPHIE ZAWISTOWSKA and NATHAN LANDAU. Through them he learns that the mortal horrors of 20th-century Europe have long been enacted in the American South. By the end, he is a chastened narrator, perhaps aware that his fears of missing a great story because of his misguided faith in outward appearances have almost been realized. His unwillingness or inability to recognize evil has been overturned.

St Ives, Vicomte de
St. Ives, 1897
Robert Louis Stevenson

As a French prisoner-of-war in Scotland during the Napoleonic Wars, he is incarcerated in Edinburgh Castle, falls in love with a Scottish lass called Flora and makes his escape south of the Border. He is a fantastical character: sophisticated, refined, intellectual; a dashing, romantic figure with all the insouciance of the born aristocrat. His brio and zest for life contrast with the dourness of 19th-century Calvinist Scotland.

St Lys, Rev Aubrey
Sybil, or The Two Nations, 1845
Benjamin Disraeli

The Vicar of Mowbray is an able but somewhat shallow churchman of a High Church persuasion, the clear embodiment of a later view of Anglicanism as 'the Tory Party at prayer'.

St Mawr
'St Mawr', in *St Mawr together with A Princess*, 1925
D H Lawrence

St Mawr is a splendid, red-gold horse owned by LOU CARRINGTON: 'Such a marvellous colour! Almost orange!' Wild, restless and untamable, he defies the efforts of men to break him, but is the catalyst that encourages Lou to leave London and discover her spiritual and cultural home. Together with Lou and her mother, the horse travels to Texas, where the magnificent creature finally settles. As he does so, his power seems to diminish and he appears to become ordinary as if, having found a home, he leaves it to Lou to fashion a new future.

Stock, Baron Willi
The Comforters, 1957
Muriel Spark

Born in the Belgian Congo and probably of partly African descent, Baron Stock is a naturalized Briton. He tries to be very English, but his pronunciation is unusual. He runs an intellectual bookshop and is accused of being a Satanist, although he says that he merely has a great interest in diabolism. Markedly credulous about such matters, he confides in CAROLINE ROSE because she does not regard them frivolously.

Stockdale, Richard
'The Distracted Preacher', in *Wessex Tales: Strange, Lively and Commonplace*, 1888
Thomas Hardy

Stockdale is an innocent and naive young clergyman who falls in love with his landlady, LIZZY NEWBERRY. When he discovers that she is involved in smuggling, he has to face a dilemma between following his moral principles and his desire to remain with her.

Stockton, John, also known as **Bruce Dudley**
Dark Laughter, 1925
Sherwood Anderson

A newspaper man who becomes disenchanted with the drab, parasitic nature of his work and embarks on a Twain-like journey down the Illinois and Mississippi rivers, taking on work as a factory hand and an affair with his employer's wife, Aline Grey.

Stoddard, Eleanor
The 42nd Parallel, 1930
1919, 1932
The Big Money, 1936, forming the *U.S.A.* trilogy, 1938
John Dos Passos

Nurturing her 'refined' nature, and conscious of her fashionable good looks, Eleanor works her way up through New York's 'arty' set, becoming companion and interior designer to J WARD MOOREHOUSE. She greets the declaration of America's entry into World War I with fervent patriotism, but this is probably the most emotion she ever registers, being primarily a chilly, too-controlled, self-centred society lady.

Stogumber, John de
Saint Joan, 1923
George Bernard Shaw

Narrow-minded and fiercely nationalistic, Stogumber is chaplain to the Cardinal of Winchester. He is also a wholehearted opponent of JOAN, whom he claims must be a witch, for otherwise she and the French could not possibly have defeated the English. Stogumber puts religious and political expediency before humanity, even before sense. Having attended Joan's trial as an assessor, he watches her being burned at the stake and is overwhelmed by remorse. In the epilogue, he reappears as a slightly dotty clergyman, confessing his guilt of cruelty because he was ignorant of the full nature of its terror.

Stone → Flowers and Stone

Stone, Jabez
'The Devil and Daniel Webster', 1937
Stephen Vincent Benét

A very unlucky New Hampshire farmer, who is driven by misfortune to declare that he would sell his soul to the Devil. Being a man of his word, he cannot withdraw from this. He later regrets his agreement with MR SCRATCH, partly for religious reasons, and appeals to DANIEL WEBSTER for help.

Stone, Lucille
Housekeeping, 1980
Marilynne Robinson

The younger of two orphaned children, Lucille

internalizes the rules society sets down regarding the behaviour of young women, and fills her diary not with personal thoughts, but with lists of etiquette. Yet her attempts to impose an order on her surroundings consistently fail. Restless, sullen and unable to cope with such disarray, she flees her adolescent home, preferring the rules and regulations society imposes to the lackadaisical attitudes of her kin.

Stone, Mr
Mr Stone and the Knights Companion, 1963
V S Naipaul
A librarian very much settled in his bachelor ways, Mr Stone deals with the onset of retirement, which he fears, by marrying the more outgoing Margaret and setting up a 'Knights Companion' scheme to help old-age pensioners. Disappointment dogs him, however, because his marriage is not quite ideal and the firm he works for hijacks his plans to use for its own trivial public relations purposes. But Mr Stone's equable resilience proves stronger than his disillusion, and he refuses to admit defeat.

Stone, Ruth
Housekeeping, 1980
Marilynne Robinson
The elder of two orphaned children, Ruth Stone is a sad, introverted girl who prefers to follow rather than lead. Unconcerned about her appearance and increasingly truant from school, she ignores society's dictates and comes under the sway of her aunt, SYLVIE FISHER, associating more and more with nature. With this association comes self-knowledge and a blossoming of her character.

Storefield, George
Robbery Under Arms, 1888
Rolf Boldrewood
The father of GRACEY STOREFIELD, he is a former neighbour of the bushranging MARSTON family. But while the reckless Marstons resort to crime, the respectable Storefield, by relentless hard work, progresses inexorably towards prosperity and property. A high-minded but compassionate man, his intervention after DICK MARSTON is condemned to death results in the sentence being commuted to 15 years' imprisonment. Neither does he prevent Gracey from marrying him on his release.

Storefield, Gracey (Grace)
Robbery Under Arms, 1888
Rolf Boldrewood
The daughter of GEORGE STOREFIELD and a former neighbour of the bushranging MARSTON family. Stalwart, respectable and, as it turns out, long-suffering, she falls in love with DICK MARSTON, only to be abandoned as he leaves on his adventures. She represents the constant spirit of redemption, for, after many years and after Dick has been released from a 15-year prison sentence, Gracey marries him and together they settle in Queensland.

St Peter, Godfrey
The Professor's House, 1925
Willa Cather
A middle-aged academic who finds himself

unable to face up to the future and to the loveless materialism he detects in his family. He becomes more and more obsessed with bygones, particularly the wasted promise of his gifted pupil TOM OUTLAND, killed in World War I. He dislikes the family's new home and keeps his old house, spending much of his time there, and nearly succumbing to fumes from an unvented gas stove, a symbolic moment with a clear bearing on his suffocating absorption in the past.

Strachan, Chae
Sunset Song, 1932, part of the trilogy *A Scots Quair*, 1946
Lewis Grassic Gibbon
Farmer on Peesie's Knapp and valued neighbour and friend of CHRIS GUTHRIE, Chae is well-liked in Kinraddie though a source of amusement to some on account of his fiercely-held socialist views that 'Rich and Poor should be Equal'. Feeling that the war will somehow further the cause of socialism, Chae enlists in the North Highlanders, but is disillusioned by the changes he sees wrought in the countryside, and people, by the war.

Strachan, Noel
A Town Like Alice, 1950
Nevil Shute
The novel's narrator, he is an elderly English lawyer, who administers the legacy that makes JEAN PAGET a wealthy woman. He recounts her story with a cool but sympathetic detachment, reflecting a life utterly divorced from the brutality and sacrifice Jean and JOE HARMAN have undergone.

Straker, Henry
Man and Superman, 1903
George Bernard Shaw
Straker is JOHN TANNER's chauffeur, a polytechnic graduate and scientific socialist whom Tanner, half in quiet amusement, half in admiration, calls the New Man. Yet instead of being deferential towards his employer or his friends, Straker is cool, reticent and often sardonic, while simultaneously protectively vigilant. Far more perceptive than Tanner, Straker convinces him that it is he and not OCTAVIUS ROBINSON whom ANN WHITEFIELD intends to marry.

Strang, Alan
Equus, 1973
Peter Shaffer
A lean boy of 17, Alan Strang is committed for psychiatric treatment after having blinded six horses with a metal spike. Raised in a household of religious conflict and repression, he has transformed his obsessive love of horses into his own religion, turning their stables into a temple and worshipping with secret midnight rides. It is the discovery of his father's fallibility and the confused awakening of his own sexuality that have led to the confrontation between obsession and reality that prompted his brutal actions.

Strang, Gillespie
Gillespie, 1914
John MacDougall Hay
A monstrous, unfeeling and entirely ruthless self-

made man who dominates and ill-treats not only his family, but the entire town of Brierton, which he holds in economic thrall. Greedy, cunning, malignant, overweaningly ambitious, fatally proud and wholly irredeemable, he reduces his unfortunate wife to a state of pitiful degradation. He meets a violent end in an apocalyptic retribution.

Stranger, Barbara → Langton, Baba

Stranger, Sandy
The Prime of Miss Jean Brodie, 1961
Muriel Spark
An Edinburgh schoolgirl and member of the 'Brodie set', Sandy has tiny eyes and, being half-English, interesting vowel sounds. She is imaginative and perceptive; she and her friend JENNY GRAY amusingly speculate about the sex life of their teacher, MISS JEAN BRODIE, but Sandy comes to have a more critical view of her activities, helped by the 'insight' that Miss Brodie sees in her. In reaction to her teacher she develops 'Christian morals' and later becomes a nun. She writes a famous psychological work about moral perception, but is not at peace.

Strap, Hugh
The Adventures of Roderick Random, 1748
Tobias Smollett
A childhood friend of RODERICK RANDOM's and his loyal companion in years to come. His name reflects both his origins as a shoemaker's son and his future profession of barber. He marries the rescued harlot, MISS NANCY WILLIAMS.

Strasser-Mendana, Grace
A Book of Common Prayer, 1977
Joan Didion
The narrator, she is the widow of a former president of Boca Grande, slowly dying herself of pancreatic cancer. An anthropologist by training, she has 'lost faith in her own method … stopped believing that observable activity defined anthropos'.

Street, Della
The Case of the Velvet Claws, 1933, et seq
Erle Stanley Gardner
An efficient and attractive secretary, whose admiration for her boss PERRY MASON is unreserved. When a case is taking an infinity to break, she is standing by with understanding, intelligent input and real devotion.

Strephon
Back to Methuselah, 1921
George Bernard Shaw
A youth aged two years (approximately equivalent to our 18 years), Strephon appears in the final section of this five-part play. *As Far as Thought can Reach* is set in a remote garden Utopia in 31,920AD. He is in love with CHLOE, a girl twice his age, and is desolated by her desertion.

Strether, Lambert
The Ambassadors, 1903
Henry James
At 55, widowed and with a dead child, he feels he has missed his own train in life. He now edits a literary and artistic journal funded by the redoubtable MRS NEWSOME, an arrangement that seemingly gives her licence to call on him for assistance in a sensitive family matter. As he picks his notably delicate way in Paris, a manner he sustains in his jocose flirtation with Maria Gostrey, he begins to realize how much of life is passing him by.

Strickland
'The Mark of the Beast', 1890, et al, in *Life's Handicap*, 1891, also in *Kim*, 1901
Rudyard Kipling
A police chief, he 'knows as much of natives of India as is good for any man'. Seemingly omni-competent, he inhabits a brusque, male, Anglo-Saxon world in which physical might is courteously right and women and natives are considered much inferior to a good dog; Strickland's is a deerhound called Tietjens.

Strickland, Charles
The Moon and Sixpence, 1919
W Somerset Maugham
Modelled on the French artist Gauguin, who rejected bourgeois life and retreated to the South Seas, Strickland is a strongly anglicized version of the tension between duty and art, economics and the imagination, too circumspect (or too English) ever to settle unambiguously for freedom over responsibility.

Strider → Aragorn

Stringham, Charles
A Dance to the Music of Time, 12 volumes, 1951–75
Anthony Powell
The only son of Boffles Stringham and Amy Fox, he is a formative influence on NICHOLAS JENKINS, the novel's narrator. Tall, dark, he looked 'a little like one of those stiff, sad young men in ruffs, whose long legs take up so much room in sixteenth-century portraits.' A prankster and brilliant mimic, he leaves school for a farm in Kenya ('where men are men'), where he cuckolds a coffee planter. He falls off a horse, missing most of his first year at university, and leaves after a term to become private secretary to SIR MAGNUS DONNERS. He marries Peggy Stepney but they divorce and he lives alone and takes to drink. Incarcerated in the flat of his sister's governess, he becomes teetotal, paints in gouache and reads Browning. In 1939 he enlists in the Ordnance Corps. Through the influence of KENNETH WIDMERPOOL he is transferred to the Mobile Laundry Unit and is captured at the Fall of Singapore; he dies in a Japanese POW camp leaving everything to his niece Pamela Flitton (later PAMELA WIDMERPOOL).

Stringham, Mrs
The Wings of the Dove, 1902
Henry James
A friend of the ailing MILLIE THEALE, she travels with her to Europe almost in the role of a medical chaperone and plays a small but rather ambiguous role in Millie's fateful involvement with KATE CROY and MERTON DENSHER. Though less obviously calculating than MRS LOWDER, she

fills the same role that James frequently assigns to older women, that of a manipulative enabler who is able to stand back from the consequences of her actions.

Strinivasan, Swaminathan
Swami and Friends, 1935
R K Narayan

The ten-year-old Swaminathan is an imaginative boy of forceful opinions: candid, often cruel. He is also rebellious and gullible. At the Albert Mission School in Malgudi, he particularly admires Rajam, the son of a police super-intendent and a former pupil of an English school in Madras. Rajam is 'like a European', and Swaminathan is so impressed that he becomes embarrassed by his own orthodox Hindu family and emulates his new friend so closely that his schoolfellows call him 'Rajam's Tail'. Swaminathan's response is to treat them with contempt. He represents the tensions within India between British rule and the indigenous culture.

Strong, Dr
David Copperfield, 1850
Charles Dickens

The kindly proprietor and headmaster of the second school DAVID COPPERFIELD attends, in Canterbury. Much loved by his pupils, he devotes his life to slowly compiling a Greek dictionary, a task which they calculate will take him 1,649 years to complete. Aged 62, he has recently married a beautiful young wife, MRS (ANNIE) STRONG, but is briefly estranged from her because of her supposed relationship with JACK MALDON. They are re-united through the intervention of MR DICK.

Strong, Kay
The Group, 1963
Mary McCarthy

A shy young girl from the West, she deliberately sets out to change herself, becoming dynamic and unconventional in her attempts to be noticed by those she admires. Kay disregards the social nuances of her set, often saying what others have been thinking, and is unaware of the hurt caused by her remarks. Marriage diverts her personal ambition for she is in love with HARALD PETERSEN, or with the genius she perceives him to be, and being married to a genius is what makes her a somebody at last. When this relationship fails there is more than a marriage at stake.

Strong, Mrs (Annie)
David Copperfield, 1850
Charles Dickens

The beautiful young wife of DR STRONG, the elderly headmaster of DAVID COPPERFIELD's school. The marriage was arranged by her mercenary mother, Mrs Markleham ('The Old Soldier') in order that Dr Strong could support her family. Her mother encourages Annie's cousin, JACK MALDON, to flirt with her, leading to gossip. Although Dr Strong's faith in her never falters, they are briefly estranged but finally brought together with the help of MR DICK.

Strowde, Evan
The Secret Life, 1919–22
Harley Granville-Barker

Evan Strowde is 50, a politician who left Parliament during the war because his 'beliefs proved unworkable'. He has, he claims, 'no new ones' to put in their place. Not only has Strowde lost his political faith, but his capacity to love appears frozen. He has had two long affairs and, at country house parties, he meets both women again and encounters his war-maimed son, Oliver. Filled with romantic yearnings and prone to making ironic, waspish contributions to political debates, Strowde is a complex, detached character, representing the struggle of integrity and idealism against despair and reality.

Struldbrugs
Gulliver's Travels, 1726
Jonathan Swift

A race of immortal beings that is easily recognized by a red spot in the middle of their foreheads. They exist like normal humans until the age of 30, whereupon they become melancholy and dejected. On reaching the age of 80, they become dead in the eyes of the law, losing their teeth, hair and growing riddled with disease. Envying others their deaths while they descend into eternal senility, they function for the rest of their long lives in the most morose, opinionated, vain and unaffectionate ways possible.

Stryver, Mr
A Tale of Two Cities, 1859
Charles Dickens

A young London barrister who is successfully 'shouldering his way up in life' by secretly relying on the efforts and legal intellect of his old school-friend, SYDNEY CARTON, to help him win cases. He is called the 'lion' who gains from Carton's role as 'jackal'. He is counsel for CHARLES DARNAY at his trial in London, but the case is won through the intervention of Carton. His intention to propose to LUCIE MANETTE is discouraged by MR JARVIS LORRY, and he marries instead 'a florid woman with property'.

Stuart, Donna
Braided Lives, 1982
Marge Piercy

The blonde counterpart to her cousin JILL STUART, she does not survive the changes demanded by women's liberation. Described in terms of her looks, clothes and makeup, Donna sees herself as defined by her relationships, especially with men – 'He is all I ever dreamed of being', she says of her future husband. A victim of middle-class material aspirations, she becomes a television personality, doomed by her superficiality.

Stuart, James Edward
The History of Henry Esmond, Esquire, 1852
W M Thackeray

The Old Pretender, on whose behalf the younger Castlewoods seek a Stuart restoration. However, it becomes clear that he is little more than a sensual opportunist, preferring a dalliance with BEATRIX ESMOND to pursuit of the throne.

Stuart, Jill
Braided Lives, 1982
Marge Piercy

A lower middle-class, part-Jewish college graduate of 1950s Detroit, she is a hardworking poet who shows deep sympathy in her complex and close friendships and for current social issues – personal is political. Brave, strong and practical, she cares especially about the abortion issue. A survivor, she creates herself unconsciously as her own role model; she is also a superb cook.

Stubb
Moby-Dick, 1851
Herman Melville

The second mate on the *Pequod*. A native of Cape Cod, his attitude to life is 'happy-go-lucky; neither craven nor valiant; taking perils as they [come] with an indifferent air'. He is easy-going, good-humoured and careless. His small, black pipe is 'one of the regular features of his face'.

Subboys, Beatrice
The Dutch Courtezan, 1605
John Marston

Daughter of the 'old knight' Sir Hubert Subboys, Beatrice is courted by the very worldly YOUNG FREEVILL. Honourably chaste and innocent, she rebukes her bawdy-minded sister Crispinella with the words: 'for truly, severe modesty is women's virtue'.

Subtle
The Alchemist, 1610
Ben Jonson

A charlatan, Subtle is invited by FACE into LOVEWIT's house during his absence. Once installed, he sets himself up as an alchemist and, with Face and DOL COMMON as his assistants, begins to make money by exploiting the susceptibilities of those turning to them for advice. Subtle has the quick wits of the born trickster, a shrewd insight into human gullibility, a well-rooted streak of selfish cruelty and an instinct for self-preservation. This last comes in handy when Lovewit returns unexpectedly, and he is forced to abandon the house and his winnings.

Suddlechop, Benjamin
The Fortunes of Nigel, 1822
Sir Walter Scott

Second only to Sweeney Todd as the most celebrated barber in Fleet Street. Like his wife URSULA SUDDLECHOP he has other competences, administering to the sick in his capacity as barber-surgeon and encouraging confidences over a draught of wine in his speakeasy back room.

Suddlechop, Ursula, known as **Dame Ursley**
The Fortunes of Nigel, 1822
Sir Walter Scott

A Fleet Street milliner, she is 'scarce past forty, and her full, but not overgrown form, and still comely features, although her person was plumped out, and her face somewhat coloured by good cheer, had a joyous expression of gaiety

and good-humour, which set off the remains of beauty in the wane'. Like her husband, BENJAMIN SUDDLECHOP, she also wears a second hat (so to speak), acting as confidante and confidential agent for whomsoever requires and pays for her services.

Sullen, Mrs
The Beaux' Stratagem, 1707
George Farquhar

Mrs Sullen has entered into a loveless marriage with the boorish son of LADY BOUNTIFUL. Mentally she is more than a match for her husband and longs to go to London because she believes 'a man dare not play the tyrant in London'. She confesses to her sister-in-law, DORINDA, that her marriage is a sham, but when she tries to make Sullen jealous all he requests is not to be cuckolded openly. In spite of all she has been through she is still a romantic, and falls in love with ARCHER at first sight.

Summers, Emmeline
To the North, 1932
Elizabeth Bowen

Orphaned young, she now lives with her brother's widow in St John's Wood, London. She is 'tall, with slight narrow figure and hands ... At twenty five, she looked very young, or perhaps rather ageless ... her air between serenity and preoccupation made her look rather like an angel. She was not quite angelic', despite which she is portrayed as without stain in contrast to the seducer Markie.

Summerson, Esther
Bleak House, 1853
Charles Dickens

Narrator of half of the novel, she is the illegitimate daughter of LADY DEDLOCK and CAPTAIN HAWDON. Raised by her strict aunt, MISS BARBARY, her history is known to JOHN JARNDYCE, who pays for her education and then makes her housekeeper of Bleak House and companion to his ward, ADA CLARE. Compassionate and self-sacrificing, she befriends numerous poor and needy characters because she wishes to 'do some good in the world and win some love'. As a result of helping JO, she contracts smallpox and suffers disfigurement. A shrewd judge of character, she sees through the selfishness of HAROLD SKIMPOLE, recognizes the malign influence of MR VOLES and anticipates the decline of RICHARD CARSTONE. With MR BUCKET, she discovers her mother's body outside the graveyard where her father is buried. Hiding her love for ALLAN WOODCOURT, she agrees to marry Jarndyce out of gratitude and devotion, but Jarndyce selflessly arranges her marriage to Woodcourt and establishes a new Bleak House for them in Yorkshire.

Summoner, the
The Canterbury Tales, c.1387–1400
Geoffrey Chaucer

He is the bearer of writs to appear before the ecclesiastical courts. Avaricious and lecherous, with his fiery complexion, scabby eyebrows, pimples and falling beard, he has all the symptoms of venereal disease, and his physical corruption reflects an inner spiritual corruption. He has access to information about those 'summoned' and uses it for his own purposes. His only friend is THE PARDONER, who is equally corrupt. He tells a bawdy story about friars.

Sunday
The Man Who Was Thursday: A Nightmare, 1908
G K Chesterton

Elusive President of the Central Anarchist Council, who is always one step ahead of the police and GABRIEL SYME. At the end of the novel he is finally cornered, but he turns out to be much larger than life; if not God, certainly the force of Nature personified.

Superannuated Man, the
Essays of Elia, 1823–33
Charles Lamb

Elia has drudged for 36 years in the counting-house, his few holidays spoiled by their brevity. He has grown neurotic about his ability and has bad dreams. But one day his employers give him a quite unexpected annuity and he is free. Dazed, he cannot at first realize this. He can come and go as he pleases, savour the delights of books, shops and London, unhurried and at ease, for the first time in his life. He has entered another world. 'I have worked task-work', he says, 'and have the rest of the day to myself'.

Supple, Mr
The History of Tom Jones, 1749
Henry Fielding

The curate of SQUIRE ALLWORTHY's parish, he is 'a good-natured worthy man; but chiefly remarkable for his great taciturnity at table, tho' his mouth was never shut at it'. His social position is assisted by a complacent elasticity of opinion.

Surface, Charles
The School for Scandal, 1777
Richard Brinsley Sheridan

Although dissipation and extravagance have landed him in extreme financial difficulties, Charles is a frank and good-natured young man. He loves MARIA and his gratitude and generosity endear him to his uncle, SIR OLIVER SURFACE.

Surface, Joseph
The School for Scandal, 1777
Richard Brinsley Sheridan

Presenting the appearance of 'a man of sentiment' (that is, possessing moral principles), Joseph is really an 'artful, selfish, and malicious' hypocrite. In his attempts to impress, he often adjusts the opinions he expresses to suit the hearer. He has designs on both MARIA and LADY TEAZLE.

Surface, Sir Oliver
The School for Scandal, 1777
Richard Brinsley Sheridan

The rich, good-natured bachelor uncle of CHARLES and JOSEPH SURFACE. On returning from the East Indies he decides to test the characters of his nephews by concealing his identity and pretending to be a moneylender and a poor relation.

Surjue
The Hills Were Joyful Together, 1953
Roger Mais

Big and healthy-looking, Surjue is anxious to leave the yard in a slum quarter of Kingston, Jamaica, where he lives among assorted hard-working, indolent, pious and lawless neighbours. Intensely proud, vain, understanding of the foibles and failings of others, Surjue is a perceptive man with a keen sense of social justice. Indeed, he appears to have the wits to transcend his surroundings, but is prevented from doing so by his conviction that life is largely a matter of luck and that the world is divided between winners and losers. He scrapes by, earning a living by selling tips for the horse races, until, having been imprisoned for burglary, he dies attempting to take his chance on escape.

Surly, Pertinax
The Alchemist, 1610
Ben Jonson

A friend of SIR EPICURE MAMMON, Surly is the only one to see through the spurious jargon of SUBTLE, FACE and DOL COMMON and expose the bogus alchemists. Disguising himself as a Spaniard, he attempts to reveal Subtle as a fraud, then tries unsuccessfully to prove to DAME PLIANT that the men are rogues. Jonson suggests that the desire to believe exactly what one wishes, even when all the evidence is to the contrary, is, for most people, far preferable to admitting their fallibility.

Surya, Rose
Rich Like Us, 1983
Nayantara Sahgal

The wife of Ram, an Indian entrepreneur, Rose is in her early sixties, yet neither age nor 40 years of being a memsahib in India has dimmed her vital, vulgar personality and Cockney accent. Her eyes are blue, yet she has dyed her hair a defiant, fiery scarlet. She moves, smokes and drinks heavily, and is inclined to talk too much after too many drinks. She is tough, knowing and worldly-wise, but becomes more dogged and embittered after the comparatively wealthy Ram suffers a stroke. Yet she has an enormous capacity for love. SONALI is not the only one to be surprised by her apparent youth and to reflect that as a young woman, she must have been irresistible.

Susan
King of a Rainy Country, 1956
Brigid Brophy

She works for a London bookseller whose interests are not purely literary. She enters into a platonic marriage, which starts to unravel when she finds a picture of a young woman and begins to fantasize an idealized affair with her.

Susan
The Lion, the Witch and the Wardrobe, 1950, et seq
C S Lewis

Occasionally patronizing and self-consciously grown-up for her age, she does not quite fit in with her brothers and sister, PETER, EDMUND and LUCY, although she makes a beautiful, much admired queen. Essentially good, she is portrayed as unsatisfactory because of her growing interest in 'adult' things, such as lipstick and stockings, a trait that alienates her from the more wholesome attitudes of the others, and eventually cuts her off from Narnia and the restoring spirit of ASLAN.

Susan
The Waves, 1931
Virginia Woolf

Thought to be based on the author's sister, the English painter and decorative designer Vanessa Bell, Susan is imaginative and artistic, with a strong sense of justice. She is the daughter of a clergyman, and is morally correct, but many of her feelings seem to be buried deep within her. Although resolute and determined, she seems somehow very vulnerable and defenceless.

Sushila
The Chip-Chip Gatherers, 1973
Shiva Naipaul

The scandal of the Settlement, she is a bright, assured woman, no longer in the first flush of beauty, defiantly trailing around her illegitimate daughter SITA whom she has had by the local grog-merchant. EGBERT RAMSARAN's mother-in-law suggests her as a replacement for his dead and forgotten wife, and Sushila brings a spark of something hitherto forgotten or suppressed to the Ramsaran household.

Sussman, Esther
The Fat Woman's Joke, 1967
Fay Weldon

Esther is an unhappily married woman, depressed because she feels she is viewed as an object rather than as a person. Her insensitive husband describes her as fat, leaving her distraught. Thereafter, dieting and binging are ways in which she cries for help. Until now, cooking has been something she really could be praised for; but when food becomes the root of her negative self-image, she becomes completely uncouth about it, gorging on the most disgusting concoctions. Esther is a woman in crisis, who, after years of marriage, questions just how much her husband cares for the soul inside the body.

Sutpen, Henry
Absalom, Absalom!, 1936
William Faulkner

Child of THOMAS SUTPEN and Ellen Coldfield, he meets and subsequently kills his natural brother CHARLES BON at the University of Mississippi, horrified at Charles's black blood and his desire to marry JUDITH SUTPEN. He occupies an intermediate position in the family tragedy, still capable of action, but no longer blinded by his father's wild dynastic fantasies.

Sutpen, Judith
Absalom, Absalom!, 1936
William Faulkner

Younger sister of HENRY SUTPEN and second child of THOMAS SUTPEN and Ellen Coldfield. She attracts her half-brother CHARLES BON and might have married him had Henry not violently

intervened. She eventually dies of yellow fever with Bon's son, thus confirming her passive role in the unfolding tragedy.

Sutpen, Thomas
Absalom, Absalom!, 1936
William Faulkner

Owner of Sutpen's Hundred in Yoknapatawpha County, his story filters down through the generations to QUENTIN COMPSON III, grandson of the only man to befriend him when he arrived in Mississippi with his entourage of black Haitians. Raised among the poor whites of the West Virginian hills, he runs off to the Caribbean where he marries a planter's daughter and has a child by her. Shocked by the revelation of her black blood, which cuts across his dreams of aristocracy, he puts her aside and moves to Yoknapatawpha, where he marries Ellen Coldfield and has two more children. Obsessed with his dynastic dreams, he tries to sire a son on his sister-in-law and then on the granddaughter of WASH JONES, a squatter on Sutpen's Hundred, who subsequently murders him. Proud, indomitable and tainted with impossible dreams, he is the most thoroughgoing obsessive in the whole Faulkner canon.

Svengali
Trilby, 1894
George Du Maurier

One of a small and exclusive class of fictional characters who have lent their names to distinctive human types. He is a morally indeterminate manipulator of the young model and singer TRILBY, raising her from mediocrity leavened with humanity to an ambiguous pitch of artistic perfection that leaves her a mere conduit for Svengali's own creative force.

Swallow, Chick
Comfort Me With Apples, 1956
Peter De Vries

He inherits from his father-in-law the job of agony columnist on a small southern newspaper, a position his own marriage renders him patently unsuitable to perform.

Swallow, Philip
Changing Places, 1975
Small World, 1984
Nice Work, 1988
David Lodge

A lecturer in English at Rummidge University, Swallow seems at first sight rather ascetic, living vicariously through literature. He is, though, capable and intelligent but unlike MORRIS J ZAPP lacks the political abilities and ruthlessness usually necessary for a high-flying academic career. Beyond the damp air of Rummidge, his passions prove susceptible to arousal: in the first novel, Swallow is transplanted to Zapp's American campus at Euphoric State, but despite his sexual tumbling and dabblings in student politics, he never quite sheds his inhibitions and returns, rather ruefully, to domestic life at home. By the second novel, Swallow has been elevated to Head of Department, returning as such in the third volume in the sequence, a tall, thin, stooped and rather disappointed figure, having been robbed of desirable travel grants by cuts in university funding.

Swancourt, Elfride
A Pair of Blue Eyes, 1873
Thomas Hardy

Based on Hardy's first wife, Emma Gifford, Elfride is a study of female identity and sexuality. Both free and unfree, she is unable to shape her own identity; she vacillates, and lacks volition. Poised, cultured and dreamy, she is endearingly naive, but her ineffectual nature is frustrating. She contrasts with the 'new woman' so often at the centre of the Victorian novel: instead of being assertive and assured, she is melancholic and tense.

Sweedlepipe, Poll (Paul)
Martin Chuzzlewit, 1844
Charles Dickens

An elderly fashionable hairdresser and bird-fancier who has 'something of the bird in his nature'. He is MRS SARAH GAMP's landlord and, good-hearted and talkative, the admiring friend of BENJAMIN BAILEY, whom he takes into partnership.

Sweeney
Sweeney Astray, 1983
Seamus Heaney

In Seamus Heaney's adaptation of the medieval Irish work *Buile Suibhne*, the bellicose Sweeney is a possibly real seventh-century king. Transformed into a bird by the cleric Ronan's curse, Sweeney is compelled to 'roam Ireland mad and bare', surviving on a diet of watercress and water. After years of restless existence, he is wounded by a swineherd's spear and receives confession before dying. Like Heaney, Sweeney is an internal exile, caught between pagan cults and Christianity, a symbol of the artist in a conflict between free imagination and political obligation.

Sweeney
'Sweeney Erect', 'Sweeney Among the Nightingales', 'Mr Eliot's Sunday Morning Service', in *Poems*, 1920, 'Sweeney Agonistes', in *Complete Poems and Plays*, 1969
T S Eliot

A catch-all symbol of unthinking sensate brutality, ape-necked Sweeney nonetheless claims an understanding of the 'female temperament', one largely founded on the belief that life boils down to 'Birth and copulation and death./ That's all the facts when you come to brass tacks'.

Swift, Kate
Winesburg, Ohio, 1919
Sherwood Anderson

A schoolteacher in Winesburg. Small and neat, she has a reputation for a sharp tongue and a cold nature, which nonetheless disguise an instinctive closeness to her pupils. Not known as a pretty woman, with a blotchy, unhealthy complexion, she is transformed by a walk in a storm into a figure whose romantic glow confirms that her past life has been 'adventurous'.

Swindon, Major
The Devil's Disciple, 1897
George Bernard Shaw

A pale, sandy-haired, conscientious man in his mid-forties, Major Swindon is a British officer serving under GEN JOHN BURGOYNE in the British forces in New Hampshire during the American War of Independence. More pertinently, he serves as the butt of General Burgoyne's sarcasm during the trial of RICHARD DUDGEON.

Swithin, Mrs
Between the Acts, 1941
Virginia Woolf

'Old Flimsy', as she is known, is a fragile religious lady, whose spirituality borders on superstition. She is intelligent, but so distracted and preoccupied that she does not fully absorb what is said to her, or what is going on around her. Constantly fretting and fussing, she annoys even those who adore her. Dreamy, imaginative and romantic, her feel for the past increases her dizziness in the present. She is acquisitive of facts and is caring and gentle. Her days of being in total control are in the past; now that she is a widow and her children are grown up, she can afford to be eccentric.

Swiveller, Dick (Richard)
The Old Curiosity Shop, 1841
Charles Dickens

A good-hearted, convivial and witty fellow who supposes himself to be in love with SOPHY WACKLES. But his friend, Fred Trent, the brother of LITTLE NELL, persuades him to conspire to marry Little Nell for her GRANDFATHER's supposed hidden hoard of money. His innate decency leads him to rebel against the scheme. DANIEL QUILP finds him a job as clerk to SAMPSON BRASS, and he gets unwittingly caught up in the plot to arrest KIT NUBBLES. He is nursed through a bad fever by THE MARCHIONESS, and once he comes into his inheritance, he educates and marries her.

Sydney, Rosemary
Picnic, 1953
William Inge

A lodger with the Owens family. She is a spinster schoolteacher who is 'probably' as old as FLORA OWENS, but 'would never admit it'. She preaches one set of moral standards to the girls, but practises another, and is full of frustration at her situation. She likes to pretend a haughty indifference to, and independence of, men, but is after a husband, and succeeds in snaring one. She is 'a peck of fun' who 'says the craziest things'.

Sykes, Cecil
Getting Married, 1908
George Bernard Shaw

The intended bridegroom of EDITH BRIDGENORTH, he is aware that she is an outspoken advocate of good causes and apt to make rash statements from public platforms. But it is only on their wedding day that he discovers that should a lawsuit be brought against her after their marriage, he would be responsible for her debts. As he has a dependent mother and sisters, he claims he is unable to go to the church. While the guests debate a possible deed of partnership, he and Edith slip away to be married, resolving to let the future take care of itself.

Sylvester, Eaton
Pravda: A Fleet Street Comedy, 1985
Howard Brenton and David Hare
The business manager for LAMBERT LE ROUX, Sylvester is 'subtly Australian'. Confident to the point of cockiness, he takes an immature delight in refusing to adopt the social graces of the English establishment. 'How's it hanging?' he enquires, when introduced to a bishop. This, for Sylvester, is a show of defiance, demonstrating that he is no mere colonial underling, but it is possibly also proof that this is exactly what he feels he is. He is the coward sheltering behind the bullying Le Roux, smirking from behind his employer's shoulder whenever he embarks upon one of his sprees of sacking his newspaper editors and reporters.

Sylvia
The Recruiting Officer, 1706
George Farquhar
Sylvia, the daughter of JUSTICE BALANCE of Shrewsbury, is that rare Restoration character, a woman who initiates action for her own benefit. She has become an heiress unexpectedly, which puts her socially above her lover, CAPTAIN PLUME. Because she is a dutiful daughter and does not wish openly to displease her father, she dresses up as a soldier in order to pursue Plume. She is not a jealous girl, accepting Plume's many earlier affairs as part of soldiering, but she does actively prevent him from sleeping with a country girl.

Syme, Gabriel
The Man Who Was Thursday: A Nightmare, 1908
G K Chesterton
Introduced to the reader as 'a very mild-looking mortal, with a fair, pointed beard and faint, yellow hair', Gabriel Syme is a young poet antagonistic to his rival, the anarchistic poet LUCIEN GREGORY. Syme, however, is actually a Scotland Yard detective who has infiltrated the Central Anarchist Council under the code-name 'Thursday'. His nightmare consists of his attempt to unmask the other six members of the Council, all named after the days of the week, with their elusive President SUNDAY the most mysterious.

Symons, Henrietta
The Third Miss Symons, 1913
F M Mayor
She reached 'her zenith' at eight, when she was a charming, gracious little girl, but then 'slipped back into insignificance', and grew lonely and forlorn. She is clever, but had 'settled down to bad temper as a habit' by 13. She is disappointed in love, and sinks into a miserable, dull and aimless life of 'doing absolutely nothing' as a spinster, but is devoted to her youngest sister. She is briefly engaged when 'quite middle-aged and decidedly cross', but is little affected by disappointment when her suitor withdraws, having discovered her fortune is less than he imagined. She settles in Bath, and there finds 'a happier and more useful course of life'.

Szczepanowska, Lina
Misalliance, 1910
George Bernard Shaw
A Polish acrobat, Lina Szczepanowska makes her entrance as the passenger in a light aircraft that crashes into JOHN TARLETON's greenhouse at his Hindhead home. Lina is 'remarkably good-looking' and declares herself to be 'a woman of the world', strong, skilful, brave: 'I am independent: I am unbought: I am everything that a woman ought to be'. She represents salvation for the Tarleton family.

Szczepanski, Wojciech 'Peter' → 'Count', the

Tackleton, Mr
The Cricket on the Hearth, 1845
Charles Dickens
The harsh and ill-natured owner of Gruff &
Tackleton, toy-makers, and employer of CALEB
PLUMMER and BERTHA PLUMMER. Having chosen
the wrong vocation, he is the 'implacable enemy'
of children and makes toys that frighten them.
Treating the adoring Bertha with contempt, he
becomes engaged to MAY FIELDING. When their
marriage is prevented by the return of EDWARD
PLUMMER, he has a change of heart and becomes
a kind, jovial and happy man.

Tadpole
Coningsby, or The New Generation, 1844, et seq
Benjamin Disraeli
A self-serving political opportunist, one of a
kind spawned in the ferment of early Victorian
politics. Morally and intellectually amphibi-
ous, he has a disconcerting facility for self-
transformation.

Taffy, properly **Clive Talbot Wynne**; also known as **the Man of Blood**
Trilby, 1894
George Du Maurier
Despite his name, he appears to be a Yorkshire-
man, with all the blunt directness commonly
associated with that county. Fierce in appearance
and manner, he is a veteran of Balaklava (the
Heavy Brigade, presumably).

Tagg, John
The Party, 1974
Trevor Griffiths
'Short, stocky, very powerful, about sixty', his
face is 'cragged, expressionless'. An experienced
agitator and intransigent Trotskyist, the
Glaswegian Tagg is National Organizer of the
Revolutionary Socialist Party. While others
speak, he sits impassively, and then unleashes a
long, virtuoso speech that is both a hardline
socialist polemic and an attack on non-purists.
He is dangerous, intelligent, erudite, urgent,
authoritative and without scepticism: 'Theory is
concrete. It's distilled practice ... felt, in the veins,
in the muscles, in the sweat on your forehead'.

Taji
Mardi, 1849
Herman Melville
The narrator. A sailor who jumps ship, journeys
to the invented region of Mardi, and becomes
involved in a fruitless search for a lost maiden,
YILLAH. He is educated beyond the usual for a
sailor, and is a cultivated observer of the strange
kingdoms in which he journeys. On ship he is
known as 'a nob', a fact betrayed by 'something in
me that could not be hidden; stealing out in an
occasional polysyllable; an otherwise incomprehensible deliberation in dining; remote,
unguarded allusions to Belles-Lettres affairs'.

Takis, Maria
The Tax Inspector, 1991
Peter Carey
The tax inspector of the title, she is in her mid-
thirties when she arrives for an audit at
Catchprice Motors, the ramshackle family
business operated by GRANNY CATCHPRICE. Yet
Maria joined the tax department for 'bigger,
grander, truer' things than investigating
Catchprice's sordid and amateurish little
evasions. Fourteen years previously, she ran away
from her home and her marriage, and sees the
empire of tax as a kind of haven, a citadel of
equity and care. Her emotional weaknesses
engender a sense of guilt, but even more strongly
she feels a sense of mission. Maria wants to do
good. Although sometimes defensive and
thoughtlessly forceful, she is genuinely wary of
misusing her bureaucratic powers, and can be
observant and compassionate.

Talbot, Edmund
Rites of Passage, 1980
Close Quarters, 1987
Fire Down Below, 1989, collectively *To the Ends of the
Earth*, 1991
William Golding
The inquisitive narrator, he is a passenger on
board a ship bound for Australia where he is to
be an assistant to the governor. He is an
enthusiastic, self-confident, rather irritating
young man who records the events of the voyage
with wonderment and ebullience. Intrigued by
life below deck, he regards his companions with
a mixture of arrogance and naivety. The journey
becomes an education in life itself as Talbot's
initial character judgements are proved false
and he learns that even the most ordinary people
are more complex than he could ever have
imagined. He emerges a wiser, more circumspect
character.

Talbot, Fleur
Loitering with Intent, 1981
Muriel Spark
A young woman writing her first novel, while
living in a London bedsit. She is employed by SIR
QUENTIN OLIVER to work on the memoirs of his

associates. Life excites her, because it provides material for her book, and her book, in turn, is enacted in real life. 'How wonderful it feels to be an artist and a woman in the twentieth century', she thinks. She tells the reader about her ideas on the writing of fiction, which are reminiscent of Muriel Spark's own methods. A Catholic and expert on Cardinal Newman, she admires his and Cellini's autobiographies.

Talent, Keith
London Fields, 1989
Martin Amis

In that part of West London which Keith calls his patch, he is known as a cheat, a racketeer; but racketeering frightens him. And so Keith, television-addict, temporary and intermittent mini-cab driver, stolen-perfume vendor, seducer, husband (to Kath) and father (to little Kim), devises an ambition, 'one of wealth, fame and a kind of spangled superlegitimacy'. He aims to become a darts champion, appear on television and enter the real world. Tormented, semi-literate, conning and conned, he represents not so much the antithesis of culture, but something more dangerous: a tabloid culture of instant, worthless, cheerless gratification, one of crafty knowingness and constant perplexity.

Tallboys, Col
Too True to be Good, 1932
George Bernard Shaw

Tallboys is in nominal charge of an expeditionary force sent to a nameless country to rescue Miss Mopply (THE PATIENT) from brigands. In reality, the force is led by PRIVATE MEEK, a military genius with no taste for high rank, which leaves Tallboys with time to devote himself to painting watercolours. But whereas Meek is able to follow his vocation as a military strategist, Tallboys is prevented from wholeheartedly pursuing his as a painter: his wife demands they return to England.

Tallentire, Emily
The Hired Man, 1969
Melvyn Bragg

The young wife of JOHN TALLENTIRE, Emily is a local girl from the Cumberland fells. She is 'broad-browed, strong-nosed, eyes firmly apart, a regular mouth neither thin- nor thick-lipped, and her complexion shaded from the cream of her forehead to that soft redness of cheek'. She is a beauty and, to John at least, an ideal. Yet she is also forceful, and not so ready as her husband to accept compromise. Like him, she has ambitions to rise above their station in life, to break away from a life of itinerant farm labouring. But while John demurs, the fresh, vigorous Emily urges him onward. Her death robs him of his closest friend and ally.

Tallentire, John
The Hired Man, 1969
Melvyn Bragg

Set in Cumberland, the novel traces the life of John Tallentire from the 1880s until the 1920s, from young farm labourer to coal miner, chronicling his struggle to break free from being a 'hired man'. Married to EMILY TALLENTIRE,

John is a determined, sensual, reserved, often gruff man, one whose natural instincts sense much more than might be apparent from his day-to-day conversation. He is ambitious, dreaming of a better life elsewhere, but wary of taking risks. Content with simple pleasures, he sees his fellow hired hands as something approaching heroes.

Talliaferro, Mr Ernest
Mosquitoes, 1927
William Faulkner

Talliaferro works for a ladies' outfitters in New Orleans and presents himself as a man of wide but fussy culture, though his knowledge of art and life stems from a single 41-day tour of European cities. Widowed young, he takes a professionally detached but erotic interest in young women, and acts as a kind of chamberlain to MRS PATRICIA MAURIER's artistic salon.

Tallis, Briony
Atonement, 2001
Ian McEwan

The novel opens in the summer of 1935, when Briony is 13 years old. The daughter of a wealthy family with a large country house in Surrey, she is precocious and observant, but also jealous and protective, longing to be a part of adult life but failing to understand the complexity of adult desires and deceits. When her cousin, Lola, is assaulted in the gardens, Briony falsely accuses ROBBIE TURNER as her attacker, as a result of which he is convicted and imprisoned. This causes a lifelong estrangement between Briony and her sister CECILIA TALLIS, who loves Robbie. The novel, which we discover to have been written by Briony, is in part reparation for over 60 years of guilt.

Tallis, Cecilia
Atonement, 2001
Ian McEwan

In the summer of 1935, when the novel opens, the elder sister of BRIONY TALLIS is in her early twenties and recently down from Cambridge. The daughter of a wealthy family with a large country house in Surrey, Cecilia likes to think of herself as sophisticated, and to some extent she is. More importantly, she is independent and far more progressive than many of her sex and class. Therefore, when her lover, ROBBIE TURNER, son of the family housekeeper, is convicted of assault, she does not disown him as does her family, but instead aligns herself with him, turning her back upon the Tallises and in particular upon Briony, Robbie's accuser. During the war, Cecilia becomes a nurse in London and remains true to both Robbie and her moral principles.

Talus
The Faerie Queene, 1590–6
Sir Edmund Spenser

An iron man, previously the groom of the star maiden Astroea, who brought up ARTEGALL, THE KNIGHT OF JUSTICE in the ways of justice, and with whom he is now in service. Representative of the immovable and resistant forms of justice, he is blind to all pleas. In his hand he carries an iron sword with which he threshes out falsehoods and exposes the truth.

Tam O'Shanter
'Tam O'Shanter', 1793
Robert Burns

A pleasure-loving Ayrshire farmer who never misses an opportunity for a daily drinking spree, whether with the miller, the blacksmith, the local harlot, or especially with his boozing pal Johnny the Cobbler.

Tamburlaine
Tamburlaine the Great: Parts I and II, 1587–90
Christopher Marlowe

Scythian shepherd and warrior, whose vaunting ambition and ruthless cruelty sweep the known world, softened only by his love for ZENOCRATE, captured daughter of the Soldan of Egypt. A self-appointed 'scourge of God', he asserts that heaven holds no prize greater than 'the sweet fruition of an earthly crown'.

Tammas
A Chancer, 1985
James Kelman

Tammas, the 'Chancer', is a compulsive gambler who drifts along finding difficulty settling into a particular job or household: partly because circumstances are against him and partly due to his own character. A couple of girlfriends float in and out of his life, both of whom he treats in a randomly aimless way. The reader is deliberately deprived of any internal glimpse into his consciousness, and has to assess him from sparse narrative and sparse spoken words.

Tamora, Queen
Titus Andronicus, c.1589
William Shakespeare

The Queen of the Goths, recently defeated by Rome under TITUS ANDRONICUS. Horrified by the sacrifice of one of her sons, she uses her influence with her new-found husband the emperor SATURNINUS to pursue a vendetta against Titus. Alongside this she takes AARON, THE MOOR as her lover. Her tormenting of Titus with the murder of his sons, however, does not go unavenged.

Tanaquill
The Faerie Queene, 1590–6
Sir Edmund Spenser

Also known as GLORIANA, she is the Queene of Faerieland. She is representative of Elizabeth I who was monarch at the time of writing, and to whom the book is dedicated. She is portrayed as the last of the line of 'Briton Kings' that grew from the days of Elfin Emperors until Elizabeth's rule. She has succeeded to the throne after Oberon, otherwise known as Henry VIII, and is fair, noble, great in grace and learning.

Tancredi
The Evening of the Holiday, 1966
Shirley Hazzard

An Italian architect, representative of male power and facility, but constrained by his marriage from offering SOPHIE more than a compromised relationship.

Tanfield, Grace
The Philanderer, 1893
George Bernard Shaw

One of the two women (the other being JULIA CRAVEN) romantically involved with LEONARD CHARTERIS, the philanderer of the title. Grace, a widow, is the representative New Woman of the 1890s, a woman to whom self-respect means as much as being respected by others. Having discovered that Charteris has succumbed to the more obviously sexual charms of Julia, she despises and rejects him.

Tang, Mui (Moon Blossom)
Sour Sweet, 1982
Timothy Mo

Cowering in the home of her younger sister, LILY CHEN, for months after arriving in England, the quiet, timid and thoughtful Mui amasses understanding of the West from constantly watching television. Subsequently more tolerant of its ways than Lily, she makes friends with lorry drivers to whom she takes meals from the shop. Self-effacing and lacking her sister's confident recklessness, Mui astonishes Lily by becoming a mother, and unintentionally causes her some jealousy over her son and her husband, AH CHEN.

Tanner, John
Man and Superman, 1903
George Bernard Shaw

A wealthy socialist, John Tanner is young, loquacious, 'possibly a little mad', and emotionally unaware. He is the author of 'The Revolutionists' Handbook' and, as a bachelor, rebels against marriage and conventional morality. Appointed joint-guardian with ROEBUCK RAMSDEN of ANN WHITEFIELD, Tanner flees to the Sierra Nevada when told that Ann intends to marry him. There, he dreams that he is the realist, Don Juan, arguing in hell with the idealist, the Devil. Contending that sexual procreation is insufficient to realize man's higher evolutionary destiny, Don Juan espouses the theory of creative evolution and the Life Force, the theory of the man of action being both artist and thinker.

Tanqueray, Aubrey
The Second Mrs Tanqueray, 1893
Arthur Wing Pinero

Aubrey Tanqueray, a widower, a youthful 42, 'handsome, winning in manner', marries for the second time. His first wife was an 'iceberg'; his second, PAULA TANQUERAY, has a scandalous reputation as a society escort. Aubrey loves her, yet he is not so resiliently open-minded, nor as confident of the future as he would like to think. In fact, he is conventional, even stuffy, lacking humour, and soon treats Paula with aggrieved patience, making judgements he promised himself he would not. Aubrey cannot escape the moral and philosophical attitudes of his sex and his class.

Tanqueray, Paula
The Second Mrs Tanqueray, 1893
Arthur Wing Pinero

Paula Ray, a former society escort with a

reputation for promiscuity, marries AUBREY TANQUERAY to become the second Mrs Tanqueray. Aged 'about twenty-seven: beautiful, fresh, innocent-looking', she is also restless and world-weary. Aubrey offers a future away from London, but her yearning for peace and real love makes her vulnerable. She is snubbed by their small rural community, and Aubrey proves so weak a support that Paula rebels. Her sarcasm, her disposition to shock, her jealousy and destructive wit make her, in one sense, her own worst enemy.

Taper
Coningsby, or The New Generation, 1844, et seq
Benjamin Disraeli

His political sympathies are as insubstantial and flickering as a candle flame. An opportunist to the last, he bends with whatever wind currently prevails.

Tapestry Weaver, the → Five Guildsmen, the

Tapley, Mark
Martin Chuzzlewit, 1844
Charles Dickens

Ostler at MRS LUPIN's Blue Dragon Inn, with 'a whimsical face and very merry pair of blue eyes', he is an irrepressible optimist and believes that the greatest challenge in life is to remain jolly in the most depressing circumstances. He goes to America as the servant of MARTIN CHUZZLEWIT, and his good spirits and common sense in the face of adversity support Martin through all his trials and disappointments. Falling dangerously ill himself and unable to speak, he reassures Martin by feebly writing 'jolly' on a slate. When they return to England, he helps to expose SETH PECKSNIFF and then marries Mrs Lupin.

Tappertit, Simon (Sim)
Barnaby Rudge, 1841
Charles Dickens

An apprentice locksmith to GABRIEL VARDEN, he is bombastic, vain and conceited. He fancies himself in love with DOLLY VARDEN, but despises his admirer, MISS MIGGS. Captain of the 'Prentice Knights', whose object is to wreak vengeance on their tyrannical masters, he plays a leading role in the Gordon Riots and assists in the abduction of EMMA HAREDALE and Dolly Varden. His legs are crushed in the riots and, after discharge from prison, he is helped by Varden to become a bootblack.

Tarden
Cockpit, 1975
Jerzy Kosinski

A former agent of the American intelligence network known as 'the Service', he has been targeted for elimination by 'the hummingbirds', fellow-members of an élite group so secret that none of the agents is known to one another. A man with no future and only the murkiest of pasts, Tarden is obsessed with control and with leaving no trace of his disturbingly amoral actions.

Tarka
Tarka the Otter, 1927
Henry Williamson

Though irrepressibly cute and anthropomorphized, this West Country otter is not merely a bundle of didactic moral traits, but one component of a ruthless but effectively symbiotic rural scene. More acted upon than acting, he provides a dramatic, low-level perspective on man's desire to control and subjugate nature.

Tarleton
The Beach of Falesá, 1892
Robert Louis Stevenson

A missionary who arrives on Falesá with little knowledge of its customs or beliefs. The initially unfavourable impression he gives recedes as it becomes clear that he has a genuine desire to do well for the islands. He is a civilized, decent man who is secure in his moral purpose, but a little timid when faced with real evil in the shape of CASE. He is the one totally trustworthy, dependable white man in the tale and proves scrupulous in his rooting out of injustice.

Tarleton, John
Misalliance, 1910
George Bernard Shaw

John Tarleton, 'an immense and genial veteran' of the garment industry, has become both rich and influential by steering Tarleton's Underwear to pre-eminence in the market. He has an imposing house at Hindhead, Surrey, which is invaded by LINA SZCZEPANOWSKA and GUNNER. A man of power, he nevertheless cannot change the world. 'I am essentially a man of ideas', he protests; 'no man sees the comic side of it more than I'.

Tarnopol, Peter
My Life as a Man, 1974
Philip Roth

Another casualty of the 'good Jewish son' syndrome. He has been successful with a novel as a young writer, but it has not prepared him for finding emotional, sexual, creative or intellectual satisfaction. He is obsessed with literature, and has a need to turn his life into a text. He is hostile to women, but refuses to accept complicity in the failure of his marriage. The combination of a Jewish upbringing and a literary education have ill-prepared him for life, and he is struggling in vain to find a way to move from 'nice Jewish boy' to 'real (American) man'.

Tarquinius, Sextus
The Rape of Lucrece, 1594
William Shakespeare

Having attempted to seduce LUCRETIA, the wife of COLLATINUS, and been rebuffed, 'lust-breathed' Tarquinius, 'madly tossed between desire and dread', between wounded pride and shame, makes his way to her room at night and rapes her at swordpoint. Later, after Lucretia's suicide, the Romans consent to his banishment.

Tarr, Frederick
Tarr, 1918
Wyndham Lewis

An unsympathetic English artist living in Paris. His nervous shyness and 'gingerly, shuffling' manner are rooted in a pampered childhood and 'a gauche puritanical ritual of self, the result of solitary habits', which is specifically contrasted with the strain of Teutonic romanticism in his German rival, Kreisler. He is a creature of the intellect, portentous when he is trying to be amiable, and is contemptuous of Kreisler's emotional art, seeing 'deadness as the first condition of art: the second is absence of soul, and the human or sentimental sense'.

Tarrant, Lionel
In the Year of Jubilee, 1894
George Gissing

NANCY LORD's secret husband, he is unwilling to give up the freedom he can claim as a single man in Victorian society and thus persuades her to keep their marriage a private affair; in this way he claims the rights of a husband with none of the responsibilities.

Tarrant, Verena
The Bostonians, 1886
Henry James

She is the battleground over which the feminist OLIVE CHANCELLOR and the courtly Mississippi lawyer BASIL RANSOM act out a struggle for the soul of 'modern woman'. Verena is young, attractive and impressionable, but she turns out to have instincts that are stronger than ideological principle.

Tartan, Lucy
Pierre, 1852
Herman Melville

The fiancée of PIERRE GLENDINNING, she follows him to New York after he 'marries' ISABEL BANFORD, and dies there after learning the true identity of her rival. She is a beautiful, charming, quiet, fair-haired, blue-eyed girl who has 'floated as stilly through this life, as thistle-down floats over meadows'.

Tartar, Mr
The Mystery of Edwin Drood, 1870
Charles Dickens

A former naval lieutenant who has come into his fortune and retired. He becomes a neighbour of HELENA and NEVILLE LANDLESS in Staple Inn, where he meets THE REVD SEPTIMUS CRISPARKLE, his old schoolmate, and also ROSA BUD. He is a 'handsome gentleman ... of eight-and-twenty, or at the utmost thirty', and Rosa is immediately attracted to him. There are hints that, had the novel been completed, he would have played an important role and might have married Rosa.

Tarzan
Tarzan of the Apes, 1914, et seq
Edgar Rice Burroughs

The son of an English nobleman who is lost in the African jungle as an infant and reared to manhood by an imaginary species of great ape. He grows to be an intelligent, physically strong and noble-minded hero, combining the best qualities of his genetic inheritance (he is a perfect gentleman at heart) with the wild physicality and untainted naturalness of his upbringing. He is of interest as a modern example of the mythic hero, but the many

sequels to his original appearance badly diluted the initial concept of the character in increasingly bizarre adventures.

Tashi, also known as Evelyn Johnson
The Color Purple, 1982
Possessing the Secret of Joy, 1992
Alice Walker

A passionate, intelligent young African woman with an 'honest and open spirit', Tashi decides in her teens to undergo ritual scarification and female circumcision, believing that it will demonstrate loyalty to her people and their threatened traditions. However, she finds the ceremony brings not empowerment but enduring physical and emotional pain; irrevocably changed, she spends her life struggling to understand what has happened to her and to millions of other women. A symbolic and yet intensely human figure, Tashi places her experience within patriarchal culture and religious myth, and explores women's complicity in these customs; her journey leads her to a violent, yet joyful, conclusion.

Tashtego
Moby-Dick, 1851
Herman Melville

STUBB's harpooner. He is of undiluted Indian blood from Gay Head, near the whaling centre of Nantucket, and is a bold and unerring harpooner. The 'tawny brawn of his lithe snaking limbs' and his 'long, lean, sable hair, his high cheek bones, and black rounding eyes' all mark him as a descendant 'of those proud warrior hunters' of his tribe. The 'Gay-Headers' are prized among the whaling fleet.

Tasman, Abel
Heemskerck Shoals, 1949
R D Fitzgerald

A practical man, Abel is also a dreamer, bent not on the discovery and acquisition of material wealth, but of knowledge. However, the inventive and imaginative side of his mind is constrained by his practical, sober rationality. He is not so much a man frustrated by authority, as a man frustrated by his own reluctance to act without the sanction of authority.

Tate, Brian
The War Between the Tates, 1974
Alison Lurie

With every reason to feel satisfied with life, Brian Tate is beginning to doubt his achievements. He wants to look good and is skilled at self-justification, but he is disappointed, seeing himself as not quite successful enough in just the same way that he is not quite tall enough. The radical politics of his students and the rebellious attitudes of his children perplex him. His adulterous affair and the collapse of his marriage bewilder him further, but he goes on writing his own script for the future, always taking care to give himself a sympathetic role in it.

Tate, Erica
The War Between the Tates, 1974
Alison Lurie

Erica wants to do a good job as a wife and mother,

but suddenly she seems to be failing. The lovely children have become, in her description, 'nasty, brutish and *tall*', and her husband, BRIAN TATE, is having an affair. Confused by the changes in what had been an ordered, happy life she recalls the calm days before the 1960s revolution: 'we knew all the rules for that world', and longs for the return of the conventional. However, in her reaction to her husband's adultery she casts aside conventions and inhibitions and begins to make a more comfortable place for herself.

Tattered Tom
Tattered Tom, 1871
Horatio Alger, Jr

A girl street-waif who has been stolen from her rightful parents, and is duly rescued as reward for maintaining honest and morally uncorrupted ways in her degraded circumstances. She does, however, develop the same kind of quick-witted, streetwise toughness and guile which characterizes her male counterpart, RAGGED DICK. The original tomboy, she is gradually able to adjust to the demands of civilized society.

Tattle
Love for Love, 1695
William Congreve

Tattle is essentially a fool, 'half-witted … vain of his amours', yet he imagines himself as a dashing man-about-town on the same level as VALENTINE LEGEND and his friend, Scandal, who think of him as a bore. He is particularly proud of what he thinks of as his ability to keep a secret, and therefore imagines himself a worthy and discreet confidant, but cannot help making 'proclamation that he holds private intelligence'. Tattle is amiable, but credulous.

Tattycoram → Beadle, Harriet

Tavendale, Ewan (father)
Sunset Song, 1932, part of the trilogy *A Scots Quair*, 1946
Lewis Grassic Gibbon

Foreman at Upperhill Farm, Highlander Ewan lays first claim to CHRIS GUTHRIE's heart and marries her. Simple, kind-hearted and hard-working, Ewan, in his devotion to Chris, initially fails to live up to his reputation as a 'coarse tink brute', but after enlisting in the army he undergoes a drastic change of character, becoming a rough, drunken womanizer. After a bitter parting with Chris, Ewan ultimately redeems himself in her eyes when he comes to his senses and attempts to return to Blawearie for her forgiveness.

Tavendale, Ewan (son)
Sunset Song, 1932
Cloud Howe, 1933
Grey Granite, 1934, forming the trilogy *A Scots Quair*, 1946
Lewis Grassic Gibbon

The only son of CHRIS GUTHRIE, Ewan's lifelong preoccupation with history is fully realized when, as a young apprentice working in a steel works, he sets up a Workers' League to fight for better conditions. Self-sufficient, cool and aloof, after being tortured in prison he commits himself

totally to communism, forsaking in the process his girlfriend, Ellen Johns. Seeing himself as yet another victim in a long history of oppression, in his determination to win justice for the workers he becomes as hard and cold as the 'grey granite' of the title.

Tawhai
The Golden Lover, 1943
Douglas Stewart

A beautiful, intelligent young Maori woman, who questions her earthly allotment of toil for husband and village. She attempts to throw off the ties that bind her to the natural cycle of earth, seeking and momentarily catching hold of a golden vision of something more. She would do 'as she pleases' but finds herself bound by the sadness and the humour of the human condition.

Taylor, Anne
Emma, 1816
Jane Austen

The long-standing governess and friend of EMMA WOODHOUSE, and a woman of mild temper and measured sentiment. Happy in the security of an unexceptional marriage, she strives to indulge the whims of those around her. In her reluctant uncertainty over the character of her stepson, FRANK CHURCHILL, she shows greater discernment than her husband, MR WESTON, but in her partiality to Emma, she reveals herself to be as susceptible to flights of fancy as the rest of Highbury society.

Tayo
Ceremony, 1977
Leslie Marmon Silko

A young Laguna man, whose experiences in the Pacific in World War II have left him spiritually and psychologically shattered. Feeling failure for surviving in place of his more talented and popular brother, killed alongside him in the war, and responsibility, from his cursing of the jungle rain, for the long drought on his native desert, Tayo lives in constant fear of self dissolution. However, a visit to the Navajo medicine-man, BETONIE, begins his reconstruction, and his encounter with TS'EH secures it. He comes to see that his earlier sense of dissolution was visionary, confirming the unification of all cultures by the nuclear threat created out of the New Mexican desert, and returns to pass on this under-standing to his people.

Tayper Pace, James
The Bell, 1958
Iris Murdoch

TOBY GASHE sees this big, gentle and amiable ex-Guards officer, with his open friendly manner and popularity, as having the right combination of masculine virility and Christian candour. In his forties, James has come to the Imber community for health reasons after working for years in a London mission. Having turned down the community leadership, as someone people naturally follow he unwittingly usurps MICHAEL MEAD's authority. His strong and simple Anglican faith is more orthodox, and his moral principles more rigid, than Michael's, leading him to summary, calamitous action when

Michael's homosexual transgressions come to light.

Tea Cake
Their Eyes Were Watching God, 1937
Zora Neale Hurston

A laughing man full of life, Tea Cake remains outside the conventions of society. Truly free, he represents knowledge and liberation. Genuinely interested in JANIE CRAWFORD, he challenges the expectations of those around them. Dynamic and gregarious, he is instrumental in expanding Janie's horizons and even after his death lives as 'pictures of love and light against the wall'.

Teach, properly Walter Cole
American Buffalo, 1975
David Mamet

A poker-playing friend of DONNY DUBROW, the owner of the Chicago junk-shop in which the play is set, Teach becomes involved in a misguided plan to rob a local householder of what is assumed to be a collection of coins, including a valuable American buffalo nickel. Belligerent, impulsive, perhaps violent, Teach appears to be one of those reckless people who are the driving force of any situation, propelling it, as often as not, to destruction. His is a dynamic star role, but, in reality, his character is more complex. He has a lyrical, even tender aspect to him. He is both brutal and obscene, yet he has something of a poet's sensibility in that he understands every shift of the atmosphere between the people around him and, like the shrewd card-player he is, can pit one against the other.

Teapot, properly Orfée Maka
The Tilted Cross, 1961
Hal Porter

The 13-year-old black pageboy of ASNETHA SLEEP. He speaks in an 'over-cultivated monotone', having been taught to behave like an English gentleman, and habitually repeats aloud whatever is said to him. His feelings are strongly instinctive, he enjoys being whipped and treated like a toy by his mistress, and he is jealous of her relationship with QUEELY SHEILL.

Teazle, Lady
The School for Scandal, 1777
Richard Brinsley Sheridan

Removed from her modest country background by marriage to the much older SIR PETER TEAZLE, young Lady Teazle's basic good sense is concealed beneath her extravagant following of fashion and spreading of gossip, encouraged by LADY SNEERWELL and her associates. This leads to her falling out with her husband, whose authority she rejects.

Teazle, Sir Peter
The School for Scandal, 1777
Richard Brinsley Sheridan

Sir Peter is the old husband of a young wife, from which fact his troubles arise. He loves LADY TEAZLE and wants her to love him, but they keep falling out. He opposes LADY SNEERWELL and her fellow scandalmongers.

Teddy
The Homecoming, 1965
Harold Pinter

The son of MAX. He has left the deeply disturbed family background which provides the play's setting to teach philosophy at an American university. Returning with his wife, RUTH, he finds his academic superiority of no value, as he is drawn back into the web of violence, implicit sexual abuse and degradation from which he has escaped.

Teeton
Water with Berries, 1971
George Lamming

A West Indian exile from the mythical island of San Cristobal, Teeton is an artist and revolutionary who seeks temporary refuge in Britain. A friend of ROGER and DEREK, he lodges with the Old Dowager and his sensitivity leads to the development of a complex mother/son relationship between them. Despite achieving relative success as a painter he rejects his art as 'the fruits of exile', and ashamed of his earlier escape from his homeland becomes violent in his fight for independence at both a personal and political level.

Tekakwitha, Catherine
Beautiful Losers, 1966
Leonard Cohen

A mythical 17th-century Mohawk virgin, 'Lily of the Shores of the Mohawk River', she was the daughter of an Iroquois father and an Algonquin Christian mother. Her holy masochism in the face of sexual and religious persecution obsesses the narrator, ANON, who associates her with both Mary and the recently martyred 'Lady Marilyn' [Monroe].

Tekla
Under Western Eyes, 1911
Joseph Conrad

A shabby, sexless, downtrodden woman who has 'no use for a name', since 'no one talks to me, no one writes to me'. She was MADAME DE S—'s 'lady companion', but is later made a virtual outcast in society, and exists on the fringes of the revolutionary group, where she gives aid to crushed and crippled spirits. She accepts her terrible isolation and inhuman treatment in slavish, unthinking fashion, but despite being ostracized herself, continues to try to help others, and tends the crippled RAZUMOV 'unweariedly with the pure joy of unselfish devotion'.

Tellwright, Anna
Anna of the Five Towns, 1902
Arnold Bennett

A woman of property at the age of 21, Anna Tellwright is a 'victim of gold'. Her fortune and her will are subject to the control of a tyrannical father to whom she generally defers out of apparent timidity. There is in Anna, however, a desire to do what is right and in the boldest act of her life she dares to oppose her father because this higher duty demands it.

Templar, Simon
The Saint, 1928, et seq
Leslie Charteris

A very British latter-day Robin Hood, who

undergoes a character change, from master criminal to rescuer of damsels in distress and upholder of gentlemanly conduct. Danger makes him feel alive, while his love of the finer things in life, like good beer, is an endearing trait that occasionally leads him to bend the rules.

Temple, Charlotte
Charlotte: A Tale of Truth, 1791
Susanna Rowson

An innocent young English girl, she finds it difficult to preserve the sanctity of her own 'temple' and is seduced by an army officer, by whom she has a child. Her later life is passed in extreme poverty in the young USA.

Temple, Lucy
Charlotte's Daughter, or, The Three Orphans, 1828, later reprinted as *Lucy Temple*
Susanna Rowson

CHARLOTTE TEMPLE's daughter, she makes basically the same mistakes as her mother, but in a slightly different order. With the benefit of experience and hindsight, she is able to take a somewhat surer hold on her own destiny than did Charlotte.

Temple, Miss
Jane Eyre, 1847
Charlotte Brontë

Superintendent of Lowood school, Miss Temple is an angelic creature who befriends JANE EYRE in her hour of need and continues to be her mentor and guiding force during her time there. Tall and attractive, she is as graceful as she is serene, and her physical elegance is matched by her inner beauty and kindness. Just and gentle in her treatment of the girls, she risks incurring the wrath of MR BROCKLEHURST in trying to apply a little humanity to the running of Lowood.

Templer, Peter
A Dance to the Music of Time, 12 volumes, 1951–75
Anthony Powell

A school-friend of NICHOLAS JENKINS, his most notable feature is his ears, which are pointed like a satyr's, 'a race amongst whom Templer would have found some interests in common'. He smokes, drinks and professes never to have read a book for pleasure in his life. While still at school he enjoys sex with a girl on the pretext of consulting an oculist in London. With CHARLES STRINGHAM he is an unfortunate formative influence on Jenkins. After school his libidinous lifestyle continues. He marries a model called Mona but she leaves him for J G QUIGGIN. However, he continues to wreak havoc with other people's relationships. During World War II he is employed at the Ministry of Economic Warfare, but his second marriage fails and, overcome by melancholy and impotence, he joins a secret-service outfit. He is liquidated in mysterious circumstances.

Temporalitie
Ane Pleasant Satyre of the Thrie Estaitis, 1540
Sir David Lindsay

The second of the Three Estates, Temporalitie is an allegorical representation of the nobility. Initially, under the dominion of OPPRESSIOUN and the Vices (DISSAIT, FALSET and FLATTERIE), he is seen to be abusing his authority and, like the other two Estates, 'gangand backwart' in all possible senses. However, faced with reformation, Temporalitie sees the error of his ways and agrees to serve the good of his tenants, demanding that he and not SPIRITUALITIE should be solely responsible for promoting the worldly concerns of the common people.

Tenby, Edward
Apple of the Eye, 1970
Stanley Middleton

A successful architect, whose desire to build rational and meaningful environments is undermined by the psychological uncertainties and needs of three young women who enter his life.

Teppis, Herman
The Deer Park, 1957
The Deer Park: A Play, 1959, revised edition 1967
Norman Mailer

Head of Supreme Pictures and the presiding deity of the gaming house, Desert D'Or, he is loud, brutish, 'a man utterly in love with his own voice', 'whose compulsion is to philosophize in every remark'.

Terrill, John
Ride on Stranger, 1943
Kylie Tennant

'Neither old nor forbidding, a rather big-boned, awkward fellow who looked slower than he was and older than his twenty-eight years', he is an unsuccessful chemist living in Aunt Edith's boarding house, where he first makes the acquaintance of SHANNON HICKS. A quiet, retiring man, Terrill is a lover of books, with a secret passion for experimental farming. Shannon describes him as 'mad about soil and morbidly interested in tombstones', which he paints as a hobby. He acquires his own farm, and eventually marries Shannon, who believes he is 'the only sane person' she knows. Their happiness is short-lived, however; when the war begins John feels compelled to enlist. Shannon knows he will die: 'There was something about the man that invited death. Joining the army was an expression of a secret vice in him, a peculiar will to die that she had sometimes sensed'.

Terry, Isabelle
The Thinking Reed, 1936
Rebecca West

A tiresome and unpleasant woman, Isabelle is a young, wealthy American recently widowed. Emotionally adrift, she resents the unfairness of her husband having left her bereft and unprotected. She despises the futility and indolence of Europeans and their dreary world of meaningless small talk. She has relationships with four men, all of whom are inadequate and concludes, 'All men are my enemies'. When she becomes pregnant and miscarries, she views the loss of the child as emblematic of the fractured society in which she lives. She lapses into solipsism and her world view remains partial.

Tertan

'Of This Time, Of That Place', 1943, in *Of This Time, Of That Place and Other Stories*, 1970
Lionel Trilling

A brilliant but unbalanced student, perhaps inspired by the poet Allen Ginsberg in his student days. Despite the best efforts of his teacher JOSEPH HOWE, Tertan fails, or is failed by, the system.

Tessa

Romola, 1863
George Eliot

Tessa is chatted up by TITO MELEMA on the first morning of his stay in Florence: he sees a 16-year-old girl with a red hood and baby-like blue eyes. Later he goes through a mock marriage with her which she takes for real; she secretly bears his children. She is kind to BALDASSARRE CALVO and grateful to ROMOLA (who looks after her); she loves anything that is 'pretty' and later on, still so naive, is amazed at the wisdom of her children.

Teufelsdröckh, Professor Diogenes

Sartor Resartus, 1833–4
Thomas Carlyle

The imaginary German philosopher (whose name means 'God sent Devil's-dung') whose papers and notes are allegedly the subject of the book. He is an idealistic thinker in the German romantic mode, and in many respects a thinly veiled version of the author. His manner is by turns speculative, satiric, bathetic, allegorical, crudely humorous, and even apocalyptic, expressed in wild outbursts and digressions. He endures, and emerges revitalized from, a spiritual crisis.

Thaisa

Pericles, c.1608
William Shakespeare

The daughter of SIMONIDES, Thaisa marries PERICLES and, having given birth to MARINA during a storm at sea, is thought to have died. Her body is placed in a casket and committed to the water; later, it is discovered to have come ashore at Ephesus. Convinced that her husband and child have drowned, she assumes 'a vestal livery' and becomes a votaress at Diana's temple. Like Pericles and Marina, Thaisa represents constancy in love and emphasizes the values of the family, qualities which are celebrated in their eventual reunion.

Thatcher, Becky

The Adventures of Tom Sawyer, 1876
Mark Twain

The daughter of a judge, she is 'a lovely little blue-eyed creature with yellow hair plaited into two long tails'. Upon seeing her for the first time, TOM SAWYER is instantly smitten. Although regarded by him as little less than an angel, she can equal him in jealousy, spitefulness and emotional cruelty. However, when the pair are trapped without food or light in an underground labyrinth she displays a pluck and self-composure beyond her years, conquering her fear and putting her faith in Tom's ability to find an exit.

Thatcher, Ellen

Manhattan Transfer, 1925
John Dos Passos

Possibly not the true daughter of Ed and Susie Thatcher after a hospital mix-up at birth, Ellen is irresistible to men – 'a porcelaine figure under a bellglass' with vivid auburn hair. She marries the melodramatic JOHN OGLETHORPE, who advances her rising career as an actress. She divorces him and falls in love with STAN EMERY, whose child she has aborted when he unexpectedly leaves her. Tolerating the middle-aged advances of her corpulent theatrical agent HARRY GOLDWEISER, she marries the adoring but tragic reporter JIMMY HERF. They have a son, Martin, and she leaves the stage to become the successful editor of a society magazine. She and Jimmy agree to part and she resigns herself to marrying the lovestruck lawyer GEORGE BALDWIN. Never truly self-fulfilled despite material success, she is an aloof and shifting figure known as Ellen, Elaine and Helena.

Thaw, Duncan → Lanark

Theale, Millie

The Wings of the Dove, 1902
Henry James

It is KATE CROY who thinks of Millie as a 'dove', and there is a kind of fragile beauty about the young heiress, who is dying of an unspecified disease, that makes the characterization particularly appropriate. Her guardian MRS STRINGHAM thinks of her rather as a 'princess', and *that* brings into account her other asset. It is Millie's wealth that attracts her cynical suitors. Dove or princess, she lives in a curiously cushioned environment, elevated but inexperienced and essentially vulnerable.

Thel

The Book of Thel, 1789
William Blake

A passive 'virgin' whose virginity is not only sexual. Thel's weakness, paleness, fear of death but refusal to partake of life, are negatives in the world of Blake's poetry. While sympathizing with flowers, clouds and clods of clay in their transience, she actually does nothing for them, admitting 'I feed not the little flowers; I hear the warbling birds,/But I feed not the warbling birds'. Grieving for her own mortality, Thel is self-pitying and unimaginative, petrified by thoughts of change and experience.

Thelea → Calypha and Thelea

Theodore

The Castle of Otranto, 1764
Horace Walpole

A peasant, he is unaware of his nobility until FRIAR JEROME, disguised Count of Falconara, recognizes his birthmark and claims him as long-lost son. Imprisoned by MANFRED, PRINCE OF OTRANTO, he is freed by Manfred's daughter MATILDA who wins his love. In turn, he frees ISABELLA OF VICENZA from the Stranger Prince. Aghast and despairing after Matilda's murder by her father, Theodore – always noted as resembling the first Alonso – is proved by

Alonso's apparition to be the true prince. He does not love Isabella, but decides after a while that his only comfort will be with one who has known and loved Matilda.

Therese
Carol, originally titled *The Price of Salt*, 1952
Patricia Highsmith
A young set designer in New York. She is a nervous, self-conscious girl, lacking confidence in her own talents. Locked in an unsatisfactory affair with her boyfriend, Therese's lonely life is transformed by meeting CAROL, a wealthy, sophisticated married woman. At first gauche and inarticulate, feeling an intensity of love she has never before experienced, Therese bravely frees herself from the prison of her former life and finds emotional fulfilment, and professional self-respect, through her stormy, mercurial relationship with the older woman.

Thersites
Troilus and Cressida, 1601/2
William Shakespeare
A slanderous 'slave' who seeks to 'weaken and discredit' his masters, the Greeks, Thersites is motivated by malice and envy. He is an untrustworthy and cowardly troublemaker who never joins in the action directly, but instead provides a cynical and satirical commentary on it, reducing all the actions, ideals and arguments of Trojan and Greek alike to 'a whore and a cuckold'; that there is some truth in his vitriolic speeches becomes more evident as the action unfolds.

Theseus
The King Must Die, 1958
The Bull from the Sea, 1962
Mary Renault
Chosen for the (normally fatal) Bull Dance at the palace of Knossos on Crete, he defies fate, sees the royal house of Knossos topple in the island eruption and then leaves to claim his destiny – the throne of Athens. Theseus is a slender but sinewy hero, highly sexed, recklessly brave, touched with arrogance, but also with comradely feeling for his countrymen and future subjects. He is a man people will unquestioningly follow.

Theseus
A Midsummer Night's Dream, c.1594
William Shakespeare
The Duke of Athens and fiancé of HIPPOLYTA, he has an easy style and sense of fair play which endear him to TITANIA, the mortal lovers and the common folk alike. Though a forceful decision-maker, he is a just and tactful man, epitomizing, in his brief appearances, the liberal spirit which dominates the play.

Thomas, properly **Thomas Rowley**
Red Shift, 1973
Alan Garner
Thomas comes from the time of the English Civil War, when the village near Mowcop changes allegiance from king to Parliament and has its thatches burned accordingly. It now awaits the vengeance of the Irish. Thomas, like MACEY, has a deep knowledge of the forces that underlie things, although he lacks a formal education and

appears simple to some. He is easy to mould and dominate. Like Macey he glimpses madness, although it is possible that when he is 'badly' he sees God. Thomas in these moments senses Macey's presence and shares in his fear and his troubling visions.

Thomas, Amy
Amy's View, 1997
David Hare
It is Amy's view that if people were to love unconditionally, then many of their troubles would be avoided. However, it is an ideal she finds almost impossible to put into practice. Selfless and sensitive, reserved, thoughtful and cautious, she finds herself torn between the violently opposing views, mostly to do with the theatre, the media and culture generally, of her mother, ESME ALLEN, and her husband, DOMINIC TYGHE. Her unenviable choice is either the betrayal of one or the other, or of herself.

Thomas, Biggar
Native Son, 1940
Richard Wright
A poor but proud black youth from the slums of Chicago, he accidentally kills the white daughter of the wealthy family which employs him, and in panic also murders his own girlfriend. In prison, he experiences a new sense of existential freedom from the realization that his act has been the consequence of the conditions in which he was forced to live. He is unable or unwilling to articulate those feelings in court, beyond his defiant claim that 'what I killed for, I am!'

Thompson, Captain
Two Years Before the Mast, 1840
R H Dana jr, originally published anonymously
Thompson is first in a long fictional line of paranoid and brutal American sea captains. A cruel martinet, he runs the *Pilgrim* without a trace of humanity and with a literal rod of iron, dispensing summary discipline with a handspike.

Thompson, Helen
Act of Darkness, 1983
Francis King
The cool, reserved daughter of TOBY THOMPSON and his first wife, 18-year-old Helen returns to India after ten years, and meets her young half-brother, PETER THOMPSON, for the first time. She dislikes him, thinking him a spoiled brat and a sneak. The only people she loves are her father, and her eccentric, selfless Aunt Sophie, the inspiration for her ambition to be a doctor and do good works. Self-contained and calm, Helen has a formidable inner strength and obstinacy. Like CLARE O'CONNOR, with whom she has an affair, she wants an existence that is 'clean and crisp'; but subsequent events dictate otherwise.

Thompson, Peter
Act of Darkness, 1983
Francis King
The five-year-old blond and winsome Peter is a solitary, precocious child, spoiled by his mother and the family's Indian servants. His fragile almost ethereal beauty makes him adorable to some, while others, particularly men, sense a certain

unwholesomeness. He eavesdrops and spies, witnessing things that both terrify and excite him, and tells on the servants and his governess CLARE O'CONNOR. His bewildered attempts to understand the adult world and earnest efforts to win the love of Clare and his half-sister, HELEN THOMPSON, are touching. However, he also displays an unpleasant arrogance, slyness and relish for physical squalor and corruption.

Thompson, Sadie
'Rain', in *The Trembling of a Leaf*, 1921
W Somerset Maugham
A plump, coarsely attractive prostitute of about 27, not noted for her delicacy of expression. Escaping from an outbreak of moral outrage in Honolulu, she is on her way to a South Seas island when she falls into the clutches of an obnoxiously self-righteous missionary, DAVIDSON. Her 'loud-voiced and garrulous' personality wilts under the threat of prison, but she has resources of sexuality with which to fight sanctimoniousness.

Thompson, Toby
Act of Darkness, 1983
Francis King
A successful financier in 1930s India, Toby Thompson owns farms, businesses and hotels: a personal empire founded on his first wife's money. Ruddy, muscular and hearty, in his fifties his appetite – for money, success, food and women – is undiminished, his sights being set on governess CLARE O'CONNOR. Ruthless and irascible, domineering with his Indian employees, he loves his children, daughter HELEN THOMPSON and son PETER THOMPSON, if in an absentee and rather absent-minded way. He is particularly fond of Helen; Peter, a fragile mother's boy, often irritates him.

Thorin Oakenshield
The Hobbit, 1937
J R R Tolkien
An 'enormously important dwarf' of noble lineage, he is the leader of a band of fellow dwarfs intent on recovering treasure stolen from his ancestors by the dragon Smaug. Haughty, proud and a little tainted by typical dwarfish greed, he is essentially decent and fair; after gaining an initially unfavourable impression of his appointed 'burglar', BILBO BAGGINS, he comes to respect his accomplice.

Thornberry, Job
Endymion, 1880
Benjamin Disraeli
Disraeli's satire of oafish radicalism led him to combine the more overdone and exaggerated characteristics of William Cobbett and Corn Law reformer Richard Cobden. It is a harsher than usual portrait of Disraeli's political opponents, but undeniably effective.

Thorne, Dr Thomas
Dr Thorne, 1858
Framley Parsonage, 1861
The Last Chronicle of Barset, 1867
Anthony Trollope
A 'middle-aged bachelor country doctor', proud

of his ancient family but pragmatic in the practice of his profession. Other doctors look down on him for preparing medicines and charging low fees, but he believes that no one is his social superior. Despite his brusque manner, he is kind to children and the really ill, and he loves his niece MARY THORNE. His honesty and good sense appeal to MISS MARTHA DUNSTABLE; after their marriage he becomes a generous and independently minded country gentleman.

Thorne, Mary
Dr Thorne, 1858
Framley Parsonage, 1861
Anthony Trollope
Born out of wedlock, Mary is brought up by her adoring and adored uncle, DR THOMAS THORNE. From associating with the family of the local squire she acquires ladylike accomplishments. Quiet and modest by nature, she is passionate about justice and always generous. She and the squire's son, FRANK GRESHAM, love each other, but Mary self-sacrificingly colludes in her banishment from his presence, believing that people should not marry beneath them and that she would be ruining Frank's prospects. In her anomalous position, she does not know what rank she is. Her matrimonial problems resolved, in *Framley Parsonage* she supports the idea of her uncle marrying.

Thorney, Frank
The Witch of Edmonton, c.1621
Thomas Dekker, William Rowley and John Ford
Frank is in love with a servant, WINNIFREDE, and marries her secretly. When his near-bankrupt father announces that he has chosen SUSAN CARTER as his son's prospective bride, Frank acquiesces and goes through with the wedding, being far too weak to confess that he is already married. Besides, Susan comes with an impressive dowry. Encouraged by the Devil, who is summoned by the 'witch' ELIZABETH SAWYER, he murders Susan and tries to pin the blame on her rejected suitors. An amiable, plausible character, Frank is a fool rather than a malicious man, but his crime is discovered.

Thornton, Mr
North and South, 1855
Elizabeth Gaskell
Described by his beloved MARGARET HALE as 'a person engaged in trade', Mr Thornton is in fact far more than this. A proud, ambitious man with intellectual, as well as financial aspirations, he expresses a passionate sense of justice, and is controlled by his own moral conscience. Impulsive, caring, quick-tempered and self-opinionated, he keeps his public and private selves separate; his self-confidence masks self-doubt, and beneath his outward strength lies a convincing vulnerability.

Thorpe, Isabella
Northanger Abbey, 1818
Jane Austen
Selfish, manipulative and shallow, Isabella continually professes never to be thinking of herself while constantly doing just that. Preying on the naive affections of CATHERINE MORLAND,

she becomes engaged to her brother JAMES MORLAND, but throwing herself into a self-gratifying flirtation with CAPTAIN TILNEY, loses both James's and Catherine's affection, as well as the short-lived flattery of the captain. Self-seeking and insufferable, she is a highly ironical figure.

Thorpe, John
Northanger Abbey, 1818
Jane Austen
The disagreeable brother of ISABELLA THORPE, and friend of JAMES MORLAND, John is a stout, ungraceful man whose physical inelegance is matched only by the vulgarity of his manners. Impossibly conceited and foolish, his actions and thoughtlessness cause CATHERINE MORLAND much annoyance and trouble, and he is unmistakably a selfish, bungling buffoon.

Thrale, Queeney (Hester)
According to Queeney, 2001
Beryl Bainbridge
Queeney, born Hester, is a baby when SAMUEL JOHNSON first resides with her family. She grows into a precocious child and her mother, although proud of her achievements, is intimidated by her. From her earliest years she displays a wilful, defiant nature and she has little regard for her mother. Her correspondence, when she is a grown woman, shows that she has become cynical and acerbic, and that she has little nostalgia for her childhood or the perceived self-indulgence of her mother.

Thrasher, Anthony
Slouching Towards Kalamazoo, 1983
Peter De Vries
A brilliant but misdirected schoolboy, he has an affair (at the age of 15) with the teacher, MAGGIE DOUBLOON, who is giving him 'extra lessons'. Anthony comes from a fanatically puritanical family, in which the father is suddenly converted to atheism. His affair with Maggie results in a child, called Ahab, but it is the teacher's pneumatic stepdaughter Bubbles Breedlove whom he eventually marries.

Thrasher, Justice
Amelia, 1751
Henry Fielding
Demonstrably corrupt and monstrously ignorant, Justice Thrasher indiscriminately condemns people, releases them, or commits them to Newgate prison according to their appearance or how much they can pay him. A morally bankrupt legal system, peppered with loopholes allows him to dispense his perverted justice even though he has 'never read one Syllable of the Matter'.

Thumscrough
Capricornia, 1938
Xavier Herbert
The misanthropic state attorney who prosecutes the cases brought against MARK SHILLINGSWORTH and NORMAN SHILLINGSWORTH. He rarely loses a case, and is willing to resort to using the gallows, although this has never yet happened in Port Zodiac. He lives up to his name, striking terror

into the hearts of wrongdoers throughout Australia's Northern Territory, but, to the delight of all, meets his match in the defence counsel, CAESAR BIGHTIT.

Thurio
Two Gentlemen of Verona, c.1590
William Shakespeare
Thurio is the DUKE OF MILAN's choice as husband for his daughter, SILVIA. Her preferences, though, are emphatically towards VALENTINE, who describes the rather foolish Thurio as 'a kind of chameleon' who has 'an exchequer of words and, I think, no other treasure'.

Thursday → Syme, Gabriel

Thwackum, Mr
The History of Tom Jones, 1749
Henry Fielding
A staunch believer in Original Sin, Thwackum reinforces abstract theological argument with a liberal use of the cane and the tawse, as he tries to instil some rudiments of learning into TOM JONES and his more receptive companion, MASTER BLIFIL.

Tibbs, 'Beau'
The Citizen of the World, 1760–2
Oliver Goldsmith
A shabby, pretentious man saddled with a boring wife, 'Beau' Tibbs, like 'THE MAN IN BLACK', is one of the characters encountered by the Chinese mandarin Lien Chi Altangi in his daily forays into London life. Tibbs is a hypocrite, wearing dishevelled clothes and professing to despise the rich and fashionable while simultaneously aspiring to hobnob with them. His enthusiasm for the impending coronation is hardly containable, and at the pleasure gardens he insists upon a 'genteel box'. According to Tibbs, this will ensure their being noticed and considered suitably worldly and metropolitan.

Tickletext, Parson
An Apology for the Life of Mrs Shamela Andrews, 1741
Henry Fielding
The frivolous and voyeuristic Parson Tickletext derives a vicarious thrill from the sexual exploits of the shameless PAMELA. His sermons are panegyrics to Pamela, whom he sees as a paragon of morality, and she appears in her naked majesty in his dreams. Under the pastoral guidance of PARSON OLIVER, however, Tickletext moves from credulity and self-deception to a knowledge of Pamela which is also self-knowledge.

Tietjens, Christopher
Parade's End, 1924–8
Ford Madox Ford
Born into an ancient landed family and with a genius for figures, this hulking 'grey mass' of a man is one of society's chosen few, and is destined to rise to the top of the city establishment. Tietjens is an old-fashioned, paternalistic Tory who lends money freely and is apt to make grand gestures. Being rather eccentric, he follows his own rules rather than society's petty whims. However, when his sense

of honour takes him to the trenches of World War I his cosy world is shattered for ever.

Tietjens, Sylvia
Parade's End, 1924–8
Ford Madox Ford

A stunningly beautiful woman with 'an air of scornful insolence'. Cruel and confusing, Sylvia professes to hate all men, yet is said by her friends to be man-mad. On a lifelong mission to wreak revenge on males, she exerts all manner of psychological and sexual torture. Yet, for all her apparent heartlessness, Sylvia is not hateful. The victim of a restrictive era, she rebels against her oppressors in the only way she knows, and her grievances and motives are there for all to see.

Tifto, Major
The Duke's Children, 1880
Anthony Trollope

LORD SILVERBRIDGE's partner in ownership of a racehorse, which they name 'Prime Minister'. He is a 'well-made little man' with a shifty and boastful manner. His military title is of dubious origin, but he is 'one of the best horsemen in England', and Master of the Runnymede hunt. He is eventually so enraged by the young aristocrat's condescending manner towards him that he causes the horse to go lame just before the St Leger, bringing a huge financial loss to Silverbridge.

Tiger
A Brighter Sun, 1952
Turn Again, Tiger, 1958
Samuel Selvon

A Trinidadian of Indian origins, the central character of both novels. He has had little education but his integrity and loyalty help him cope with his early, arranged marriage to Urmilla and the responsibilities of fatherhood, whilst his common sense and compassion ensure that he rejects authoritarian and racist role models. His pride in his peasant roots is diminished by his later experiences on the cane plantation and he chooses instead to live in the multicultural city.

Tiger
The Bundle, 1978
Edward Bond

Tiger is disabled, having only one hand which, in this case, is an outward symbol of defective intellectual logic. Although he is, like WANG, an opportunist and political idealist, he does not interpret experience intellectually and therefore fails to be fully effective in his daily struggles.

Tigg, Montague (alias Tigg Montague)
Martin Chuzzlewit, 1844
Charles Dickens

A confidence trickster and associate of OLD MARTIN CHUZZLEWIT's nephew, CHEVY SLYME. He is 'very dirty and very jaunty; very bold and very mean; very swaggering and very slinking', and after he falls out with Slyme, he sets up the fraudulent Anglo-Bengalee Disinterested Loan and Life Insurance Company. He cultivates a prosperous appearance and hires BENJAMIN BAILEY as his liveried groom. From MR NADGETT he learns of JONAS CHUZZLEWIT's attempt to

poison ANTHONY CHUZZLEWIT, then blackmails Jonas and makes him dupe SETH PECKSNIFF into investing all his money in the company. He is ambushed in a wood by Jonas and bludgeoned to death.

Tigger
The House at Pooh Corner, 1928
A A Milne

A very bouncy tiger, Tigger arrives unexpectedly in WINNIE-THE-POOH's bedroom one night, and when morning comes starts a fight with a tablecloth. A series of tests to see what Tiggers might eat reveal that he likes neither honey (Pooh's favourite), nor haycorns (PIGLET's favourite), nor thistles (EEYORE's favourite), but he is very fond of Extract of Malt (as given to Roo by Kanga as a strengthening medicine), 'Which explains why he always lived at Kanga's house ... and had Extract of Malt for breakfast, dinner and tea.'

Tilburina
The Critic, 1779
Richard Brinsley Sheridan

Parodic heroine of 'The Spanish Armada', the play performed within Sheridan's play. The daughter of the Governor of Tilbury Fort, she loves DON FEROLO WHISKERANDOS. Having chosen love before patriotism, she goes mad after her lover's death. The actress playing the part justifies to PUFF the hefty cuts in his appalling play.

Tilford, Mary
The Children's Hour, 1934
Lillian Hellman

A sullen, 14-year-old pupil at the Dobie School For Girls, she is the one bad apple whose evil nature poisons the entire barrel. Spoilt and spiteful, she has a childish need for everything to adhere to her personal agenda and will mercilessly lie, cheat or steal to achieve her ends. An adolescent tyrant, easily able to manipulate most of the adult world, her malicious and careless talk costs lives.

Till, Nancy
Sapphira and the Slave Girl, 1938
Willa Cather

The slave girl of the title, she is the half-caste product of a casual union between SAPPHIRA and HENRY COLBERT's housekeeper and an itinerant artist. All the conflict of the novel is over the question of Nancy's status as property (which is Sapphira's view as an old Southerner) or as an independent human being (which, in different degrees, is the view of Henry Colbert and his daughter RACHEL BLAKE). Pretty and vivacious, Nancy may have engaged Henry's sympathies more than casually.

Tilney, Captain
Northanger Abbey, 1818
Jane Austen

A minor character in the novel, Captain Tilney is the elder brother of HENRY TILNEY and ELEANOR TILNEY, but does not resemble them in nature. Very handsome and fashionable, he is, however, lacking in taste, and he flirts shamelessly with

ISABELLA THORPE despite knowing of her engagement to JAMES MORLAND. But knowing nothing of honour nor decency, he dispenses with her almost as quickly as he took interest in her.

Tilney, Eleanor
Northanger Abbey, 1818
Jane Austen

Elegantly attractive, well-bred and unaffected in both manners and nature, Eleanor proves to be a much more valuable friend to CATHERINE MORLAND than does ISABELLA THORPE. Matching her beloved brother HENRY TILNEY in honesty and openness, her affection for Catherine is genuine rather than contrived, and she remains loyal to her even in the face of the unreasonable commands of her father GEN TILNEY.

Tilney, Gen
Northanger Abbey, 1818
Jane Austen

The temperamental father of HENRY TILNEY, ELEANOR TILNEY and CAPTAIN TILNEY, General Tilney's lavishing of attention on CATHERINE MORLAND is later revealed to have been prompted by his believing her family to be phenomenally rich. Apparently handsome and charming, if a touch eccentric, in his subsequent rude treatment of Catherine he exposes himself as being narrow-minded and completely money-oriented. He rules his home, Northanger Abbey, like a tyrant.

Tilney, Henry
Northanger Abbey, 1818
Jane Austen

The clergyman son of GEN TILNEY, warm-hearted Henry is immediately attracted to CATHERINE MORLAND. Intelligent, spirited and teasing, he makes her a lively companion and his attachment to her is completely free from artifice. Down-to-earth and frank, he refuses to bow to his father's bigoted prejudices, and rebels against his tyranny in following his own instincts and asking Catherine to marry him.

Tim → Yellowhammer, Tim

Timias
The Faerie Queene, 1590–6
Sir Edmund Spenser

He appears as both a squire and a royal courtier. Gentle-hearted and chivalrous, he has fallen in love with the wood-nymph BELPHOEBE. Rather than dishonour her name, he chooses to remain quiet about the depth of his feeling, and thus spends his time engulfed in sorrow, since there can be no joy without her.

Timon of Athens
Timon of Athens, 1607/8
William Shakespeare and perhaps Thomas Middleton

An Athenian nobleman, Timon is rich and generous, freely distributing his money among his friends, ignoring the warnings of FLAVIUS and APEMANTUS that he will soon be bankrupt. When he discovers he is financially ruined, and that his friends were merely fawners and flatterers, his incomprehension, anger and bitterness result not in revenge but in his retreating to a cave in the woods, hurling misanthropic insults at whoever passes by. This is a portrait of a benevolent man, more wealthy than wise, turned sour by leeching and ingratitude. Yet irony as well as anger colours Timon's tirades from the cave; there is an element of self-mockery as if he privately realizes his foolishness.

Tin Woodman, also known as Hickory
The Wonderful Wizard of Oz, 1900
L Frank Baum

It has been suggested that DOROTHY's companions on the road to Oz are representatives of an oppressed working class. The Tin Woodman believes he has no heart and that THE GREAT OZ can supply him with one. As with the other characters, this is an illusion on both counts. When the wizard fobs him off with fakes, it becomes clear that the Woodman already has a heart, but simply has not known how to use it.

Tinckham, Mrs
Under the Net, 1954
Iris Murdoch

The chain-smoking owner of a seedy newsagent's in Soho which JAKE DONAGHUE sometimes uses as his office and emergency bar. No one buys anything there but ice-cream and the *Evening News*, and most of the shop's yellowing stock is read by Mrs Tinckham herself. She sits surrounded by her many cats, a small radio playing softly and Jake's whisky under the counter. She is kind, utterly reliable, honest and 'pathologically discreet'; she knows everything, but repeats nothing.

Tinkerbell
Peter Pan: or The Boy Who Would Not Grow Up, 1904 (play), 1911 (book)
J M Barrie

An irascible and sulky fairy, who plays ARIEL to PETER PAN. Visible only as a point of light, she speaks in a language like tiny bells, which Peter understands and translates. Courageously swallowing a poisonous draught prepared for Peter, she is revived only by the audience's belief in fairies.

Tiny Tim
A Christmas Carol, 1843
Charles Dickens

The crippled youngest son of BOB CRATCHIT and his wife, he 'bore a little crutch, and had his limbs supported by an iron frame', but does not allow his misfortune to dampen his spirits. He joins in the family's toast to Christmas with the words, 'God bless us, every one!' When EBENEZER SCROOGE is given a vision of the scene, he is particularly moved by the plight of Tiny Tim. The GHOST OF CHRISTMAS PRESENT foresees that Tiny Tim will die unless Scrooge learns the lessons of charity and benevolence.

Tiresias
'The Fire Sermon', etc, in *The Waste Land*, 1922
T S Eliot

The mythic presence who brings unity to *The*

Waste Land cycle, he is ancient and androgynous, an 'old man with wrinkled dugs', and exists 'throbbing between two lives', poised between a heroic past and a banal present.

Tiriel
Tiriel, 1789
William Blake

One of the more obviously destructive characters in Blake's poetry, Tiriel's selfish nature is shown in his endless lies, his 'dissembling' language of deceit and concealment. His blindness indicates his ignorance. Speaking violently and in curses, Tiriel calls his children 'serpents' and curses his youngest daughter with 'Let snakes rise from thy bedded locks and laugh among thy curls!' (and they do!). Unable to accept change and the waning of his patrimonial power as 'king', he annihilates his children.

Tissera, Anil
Anil's Ghost, 2000
Michael Ondaatje

She is a forensic anthropologist in her mid-thirties, born in Sri Lanka but educated and trained in the USA, who returns to her native island at the behest of a human rights organization to examine a series of bodies that are being discovered. She struggles to maintain her scientific objectivity in the face of romantic entanglement, powerful memories of her childhood on the island and her awakened sympathies for the nameless dead whose tragedies she must try to reconstruct.

Titania
A Midsummer Night's Dream, c.1594
William Shakespeare

The wit and poetry of her opening scene serve as a sharp contrast to her unequivocal and ridiculous love for BOTTOM while she is under her husband OBERON's spell. She is a loyal and forceful mistress, at ease and in charge in the Fairy Kingdom. Though not unattracted to others, she is essentially an equal partner with Oberon and her strength of character is demonstrated by her forgiveness of him when they are reconciled.

Tithonus
'Tithonus', 1860
Alfred Lord Tennyson

Weary of eternal life without eternal youth, which had been bestowed on him by Aurora, goddess of the dawn, Tithonus now has only distant memories of the pleasures of youth. Envying 'happy men that have the power to die', he begs the goddess to revoke the gift she granted so long ago.

Titmuss, Rt Hon Leslie
Paradise Postponed, 1985
Titmuss Regained, 1990
John Mortimer

A youthful grasper of nettles in the Rectory garden, with sagging socks and an endless thirst for ginger beer and awkward questions, Leslie Titmuss transforms moth-like into a pale, Machiavellian politician, with coldly calculating eyes and the fluttering aura of one eager to move

on to brighter lights. The main motive for his relentless upward spiralling is that of revenge; on his father for wishing to keep him within his social class, and on the members of the Hartscombe Young Conservatives for pushing him into the river and sneering at his ready-made bow tie. Money is his god, and it must be conserved and nurtured, not given away to 'scroungers'. His tendency to make social gaffes makes him appeal to various women, but their sympathy is wasted; he is no underdog, although he invariably bites the hand that feeds him.

Toad, of Toad Hall
The Wind in the Willows, 1908
Kenneth Grahame

A flamboyant, conceited, wily individual, he is the bumptious, rich owner of Toad Hall ('one of the nicest houses in these parts, though we never admit as much to Toad'). Described unconvincingly by RAT as 'the best of animals', he drives his long-suffering friends to distraction with his ridiculous and short-lived passions – boats one day, motor cars the next – and above all with his refusal to listen to good sense.

Tobermory
'Tobermory', in *The Chronicles of Clovis*, 1911
'Saki' (Hector Hugh Munro)

An unusually intelligent cat, ill-advisedly taught to speak by Cornelius Appin, an eccentric savant. Aloof, sardonic and witty, he proceeds to deliver devastating observations on the activities and characters of the human members of his mistress Lady Blemley's house party. He is endangered by both the embarrassment that he causes and his more normal feline impulses.

Toby
Typee, 1846
Herman Melville

A sailor who jumps ship with TOMMO on Typee. He has a 'remarkably prepossessing exterior' and athletic ability, but is also a 'strange, wayward being, moody, fitful and melancholy', and quick-tempered. He is 'one of that class of rovers you sometimes meet at sea, who never reveal their origin, never allude to home, and go rambling over the world as if possessed by some mysterious fate they cannot possibly elude'. He disappears mysteriously, but is accounted for in a subsequent appendix.

Todd, Almira
The Country of the Pointed Firs, 1896
Sarah Orne Jewett

The local herbalist-healer in the little Maine seaport town of Dunnett Landing, she rents the narrator lodgings for the summer. A widow, racked by the memory of an earlier love for a man far above her station, she gives her writer guest an insight into the 'absolute, archaic grief' that possesses the plain-spoken countrywoman's large frame and fuels her healing gift.

Todd, Chrissie
The Boys from the Blackstuff, 1984
Alan Bleasdale

A man at the end of his tether because of

unemployment, Chrissie is desperate to find legitimate work. Pursued by the 'dole sniffers' and beset by debt, he is prevented from sliding into apathy by his wife Angie, who tries to goad him into fighting against their deprived circumstances. Unfortunately this causes his marriage to falter. He has a sense of pride in the work ethic but is distraught as he sees it crumbling around him. This seething inner rage finds expression in occasional violence, but normally he is cheerful on the exterior.

Todd, Joanna, known as 'Poor Joanna'
The Country of the Pointed Firs, 1896
Sarah Orne Jewett

A reclusive jilt, cousin to the herbalist ALMIRA TODD's late husband, she lived alone on Shell-heap Island, sheltered from the winds by Indian mounds, living on clams and lobsters, the produce of her potato patch and shy gifts from disappointed suitors. The narrator makes a pilgrimage to her grave and ruined cottage.

Todd, John James
The New Confessions, 1987
William Boyd

Born in Edinburgh in 1899, John James Todd looks back over his life, over 70 years later, from his refuge at a Mediterranean villa. Restless, sentimental, angry, he recounts the triumphs and failures of his erratic life, through two world wars, the rise of the film industry and the McCarthy era in the USA. Although Todd is 'hunkered down in the mulch of the phenomenal world', he remains throughout something of an outsider, craving to find both his real place and a greater degree of control over events. Vain but honest, sometimes astute but often foolish, he struggles to reconcile himself to 'the Age of Uncertainty and Incompleteness'.

Todd, Mr
A Handful Of Dust, 1934
Evelyn Waugh

Of Indian and Barbadian descent, Mr Todd lives in a mud-and-wattle hut amongst the Pie-wie Indians in Amazonas, an area fought over by Brazil and Dutch Guiana. He possesses a dozen cattle, a cassava plantation and some fruit trees, and commands respect because he owns a shotgun. He nurses the fever-crazed TONY LAST back to health using jungle medicines. Once Tony is well, he holds him captive, forcing him to read Dickens novels aloud to him daily, just as he once did to a Barbadian until he died.

Todgers, Mrs
Martin Chuzzlewit, 1844
Charles Dickens

Proprietor of Todgers's Commercial Boarding House in London, where SETH PECKSNIFF stays with his daughters, CHARITY and MERCY PECKSNIFF. Not handsome, but kind-hearted, she employs BENJAMIN BAILEY as her 'boots' and is always anxious about 'the passion for gravy among commercial gentlemen'. She befriends Mercy after she has been ill-treated by her husband, JONAS CHUZZLEWIT.

Tolland, Lady Isobel
A Dance to the Music of Time, 12 volumes, 1951–75
Anthony Powell

One of Lord Warminster's ten children, her intelligence makes her a bit of an oddity. NICHOLAS JENKINS, the novel's narrator, is instinctively drawn to her because she is 'different'. When at last he sets eyes on her, he knows at once that they will marry. Long-legged, with blue eyes and dressed in a tweed suit, she is intimate with the works of ST JOHN CLARKE and is widely read in forgotten fiction. She miscarries in 1936 but is eventually blessed with two children.

Tolliver, Michael → Mouse

Tolly, properly Bartholomew Dorking
Black Jack, 1968
Leon Garfield

An eager-to-please, law-abiding 14-year-old, made an orphan by the sea, and apprenticed to a draper by his uncle. Despite his loss, he retains his deep longing for the ocean and for a more adventurous life. Patient and affectionate, he is determined always to see the best in people, even in ruffians like BLACK JACK. So virtuous is he, indeed, that he can often cause offence. Devoted to the supposedly mad BELLE, he is brave, bold and resourceful, driven by a perverse longing to win the respect of Black Jack, who despises him so utterly.

Tom
A Question of Power, 1974
Bessie Head

A young and idealistic Peace-Corps volunteer from America. 'A permanent fixture in her life since the day they'd first met', he is essential in helping ELIZABETH regain her sanity. Tom is stable and honest, offering genuine warmth and friendship. Strong and determined, he refuses to allow Elizabeth's breakdown to destroy their relationship. Elizabeth admires his philosophical nature and values their long and varied discussions.

Tom
Red Shift, 1973
Alan Garner

A clever boy, Tom is at a crossroads in life, about to break out from his background and take up an open scholarship to Cambridge University. He lives with his parents in a caravan on the edge of a nondescript town near Crewe. He has a quote from his beloved books for every occasion but lacks simple words of his own. His girlfriend, JAN, accuses him of experiencing feelings vicariously through the words of others. He always knows things before he feels them; but he is aware of his faults, and admits that he needs 'a red shift', away from the cerebral and towards the emotional.

Tom
The Roaring Nineties, 1946
Golden Miles, 1948
Winged Seeds, 1950
Katharine Susannah Prichard

A man of the people, a staunch socialist working doggedly and passionately towards the better day:

'A stubborn loyalty to the men he worked with had become fixed in him. He could not separate himself from them, and from the struggle of the working class for a better way of life'.

Tom
Tom's Midnight Garden, 1958
Philippa Pearce

The pyjama-clad explorer of the midnight garden, which appears only after the grandfather clock has struck the 13th hour, and where Time does not follow its usual steady course. Both the garden and the girl, HATTY, who plays there soon become all-important to him. Both children are 'loners', separated from the people and places they love, united in their passion for the garden. Tom is not a keen gardener; he simply loves to climb trees, to find and build secret places, and to create his own special world. He strives to determine the true nature of Time, because he believes that this knowledge will allow him to stay for ever in the garden.

Tom
The Water Babies, 1863
Charles Kingsley

A boy chimney-sweep from a grim West Riding mill town. He has had no religious education, and has never washed. He works for MR GRIMES, who beats him and makes his life miserable, though he finds moments of happiness with his friends. When he is taken away to fairyland, Tom becomes a water baby with a lace collar of gills. He gives vent to his natural mischievousness and torments the water creatures. However, he is on a journey of instruction, and his character is slowly transformed in this fable of purification.

Tom, Lord
Smith, 1967
Leon Garfield

A towering giant, dressed all in green, and with a beard like bracken, Lord Tom lives for the chase and danger of the highwayman's trade. The money and the jewels he thieves on Finchley Common are all too quickly spent – he gladly exchanges one diamond brooch for an evening's ale in Highgate. He seems to be a powerful ally and protector for SMITH, but his greed gets in the way. Romantic and melancholy, he is an avid teller of tales about his adventures, both real and imaginary, but is troubled by his visions of the gibbet that he fears will be his end.

Tomkins, Joseph
Woodstock, or The Cavalier, 1826
Sir Walter Scott

A Cromwellian Independent, who drags REV NEHEMIAH HOLDENOUGH out of his pulpit. 'He was a stout man of middle stature, with a quick eye, and a countenance, which, though plain, had yet an expression that fixed the attention'. He considers William Shakespeare to be the source of most, if not all, modern evils.

Tommo
Typee, 1846
Omoo, 1847
Herman Melville

The narrator, a sailor who jumps ship in the Marquesas Islands, having decided rather to 'risk my fortune among the savages of the island than endure another voyage' under the tyrannical captain, although desertion is 'a rather inglorious thing' for 'an honest man'. He lives with the native Typees for a time, and is infatuated by the lovely FAYAWAY. He is not the usual rough sailor type, but has culture and education, and is an intelligent observer of life on the island.

Toobad, Mr
Nightmare Abbey, 1818
Thomas Love Peacock

A 'Manichaean Millenarian', Mr Toobad believes in the general and unmitigated decline of humankind and the omnipresence of evil, both of which will be replaced by the new dawn of a golden age (but 'not in our time'). He finds evidence of 'the temporary supremacy of the devil' in everything.

Toodle, Polly
Dombey and Son, 1848
Charles Dickens

The 'plump, rosy-cheeked, wholesome, apple-faced' wet-nurse of PAUL DOMBEY, she has the name 'Richards' imposed upon her by MR DOMBEY and his family because her own surname is not dignified. With her cheerful husband, a railway worker, she has five children of her own, including the troublesome ROBIN TOODLE. Dismissed for taking Paul and his sister FLORENCE to visit her family, she looks after Florence when she stays at *The Wooden Midshipman* and later cares for Dombey when he becomes bankrupt.

Toodle, Robin (Rob the Grinder)
Dombey and Son, 1848
Charles Dickens

The eldest son of POLLY TOODLE, also known as 'Biler', after the steam engine his father drove. MR DOMBEY gains him a place at the charity school, the Charitable Grinders (hence his nickname), but he is bullied by the street children because of his uniform and runs away. He works for JAMES CARKER as a spy and makes arrangements for the elopement with EDITH DOMBEY. He is forced by MRS BROWN to reveal to Dombey the place in Dijon where Carker and Edith are to meet. Finally, MISS LUCRETIA TOX employs him with a view to his 'restoration to respectability'.

Toomai, of the Elephants
The Jungle Book, 1894
Rudyard Kipling

He takes on his grandfather's soubriquet when he observes 'what man had never seen before – the dance of the elephants at night and lone in the heart of the Garo hills'. The son and heir to the responsibilities of the government elephant driver Black Toomai, the boy seems unbiddable and prone to mischief, but he has an instinctive understanding of the great beasts, which confers on him a wisdom far beyond his years and apparent intellectual resources.

Toomey, Kenneth
Earthly Powers, 1980
Anthony Burgess

An octogenarian homosexual novelist and playwright, he has lived a life punctuated by personal contacts with stirring moments of history, and involvement with the characters who fill the pages of contemporary history. Now weary and cynical, he is haunted by shallow relationships and the frequent sexual humiliations and vulnerability of growing old. In spite of his wealth, comparative success and doubtless erudition, he is a sad personality: sensual, aesthetic, reflective, self-deprecating and, finally, alone.

Toots, Mr
Dombey and Son, 1848
Charles Dickens

DOCTOR BLIMBER's senior pupil who, 'when he began to have whiskers, left off having brains'. Dim but amiable, he becomes a friend of PAUL DOMBEY and a devoted slave to FLORENCE DOMBEY, through whom he meets CAPTAIN EDWARD CUTTLE and SUSAN NIPPER. When he inherits money, he proposes to Florence and gives her a dog, Diogenes. He philosophically accepts that she cannot love him and instead marries Susan Nipper, whom he considers 'a most extraordinary woman'.

Tope, Mr and Mrs
The Mystery of Edwin Drood, 1870
Charles Dickens

The chief verger of Cloisterham Cathedral, Mr Tope is the landlord of MR JOHN JASPER, and his wife is Jasper's housekeeper. After the disappearance of EDWIN DROOD, DICK DATCHERY comes to lodge with the Topes, apparently in order to observe Jasper.

Topsy
Uncle Tom's Cabin, or, Life Among the Lowly, 1851–2
Harriet Beecher Stowe

'Never was born, never had no father, nor mother, nor nothin'. I 'spect I growed'. Little EVA's mischievous black companion, far beyond the reach of her tutor MISS OPHELIA's pietism, her function is to act partly as moral shadow to AUGUSTINE ST CLARE's brightly lit domestic scene; but there is also a more serious intent in what she says, for she demonstrates in miniature that the most odious and insidious aspect of slavery is that it robs people of their past. It is also noticeable that Topsy is 'bad' because she has been conditioned to believe she cannot do good.

Tormad
The Silver Darlings, 1941
Neil Gunn

Forced, in the aftermath of the Highland Clearances, to try to eke a living from the sea around Helmsdale, Tormad, the stocky, dark-haired husband of CATRINE, rises to the challenge, taking his new boat and crew out to fish for herring. Although filled with the spirit of adventure, Tormad is alive to Catrine's suffering at his departure, but it is his love and compassion, and his need to provide for her,

which spur him onwards, out to sea. Young and inexperienced, however, he fails to recognize approaching danger, and his fiery temper incites a fatal blow from the feared press-gang.

Torp, Gerda
Wolf Solent, 1929
John Cowper Powys

The daughter of a stone-cutter and tombstone carver, she has 'a kind of innocent wantonness' which is also 'a sort of terrible passivity' underlying 'the mysterious simplicity of her special kind of loveliness'. She is very much an earth-girl, vital and physical, and conversant with earth-lore and the ways of nature. She can imitate bird-song with aching beauty, a faculty she loses when her relationship with WOLF SOLENT founders, but recaptures when she finds a new lover.

Torquil of the Oak
The Fair Maid of Perth, or St Valentine's Day, in *Chronicles of the Canongate: Second Series*, 1828
Sir Walter Scott

A huge, grizzled woodsman, the adopted father of CONACHAR, he is attended at all times by his eight giant sons and by an overbearing conviction that life is governed by dark and fateful forces. He meets his death at HENRY SMITH's hands during the battle of North Inch.

Touchandgo, Susannah
Crotchet Castle, 1831
Thomas Love Peacock

The daughter of an absconded banker, Susannah, when rejected by her fiancé, retreats to Wales to work as a governess in a hale and hearty environment. In harmony with the natural landscape, she blooms, becoming plump, wholesome, modest, well-read and completely free of social fripperies.

Touchett, Ralph
The Portrait of a Lady, 1881
Henry James

ISABEL ARCHER's ailing cousin, he is probably the only character who recognizes her needs as an independent individual. He arranges for his father secretly to split his inheritance with Isabel, but realizes before his death that it has been the cause of great unhappiness for her. Only on his deathbed does Isabel recognize the extent of his love and understanding.

Touchstone
As You Like It, c.1600
William Shakespeare

The fool at DUKE FREDERICK's court and the companion in exile of ROSALIND and CELIA. His ability to chop logic and his acerbic wit cloak an opportunist who will make use of those simpler than himself, such as AUDREY. He has a brilliant capacity to use and misuse language, rarely coming off worst in an argument. He is morally shallow and cares little for those who cannot advance him.

Touchwood, Lady
The Double Dealer, 1693
William Congreve

The vain, promiscuous Lady Touchwood is in love

with MELLEFONT, her husband's nephew, but when her advances are rejected, her pride is soured and turns to vengeance. Enlisting the help of her unscrupulous former lover MASKWELL, in a scheme to ruin Mellefont's reputation, she finds herself submitting once more to his sexual magnetism.

Touchwood, Peregrine Scrogie
St Ronan's Well, 1823
Sir Walter Scott
This wealthy old man is the novel's *deus ex machina*, bringing not just his money but news to the scheming JOHN MOWBRAY that the man Mowbray's sister is to marry is not the real Lord Etherington, but a younger son. Touchwood's expression radiates 'self-confidence, and something like a contempt for those who had neither seen nor endured so much as he had himself'.

Touchwood Senior
A Chaste Maid in Cheapside, 1611–13
Thomas Middleton
The brother to the chosen suitor of MOLL YELLOWHAMMER who, finding himself in reduced circumstances, is forced to live apart from his wife in order to prevent any further additions to a rapidly increasing family. An affectionate and loyal brother, he employs his wit and cunning to aid his brother's suit of Moll. He uses the same talents to improve his own economic circumstances, impregnating the previously barren Lady Oliver Rix and persuading her cuckolded husband to pay him for the trouble.

Tourmaline, the Law of
Tourmaline, 1963
Randolph Stow
The novel's narrator, he is an observer rather than a powerful adjudicator and there is a sharp irony in his self-adopted title since the town seems to work according to a violent logic beyond law. He acts, at best, as a kind of fortune-teller, slowly dealing out the cards of a predestined and universalized story.

Tower, Alwyn
The Grandmothers, 1927
Glenway Wescott
A young American living in Paris, where he is 'a little self-consciously a poet'. He has escaped his stifling mid-west background, but has 'ignored nothing and forgotten nothing' of his grandmother's stories, and begins to reconstruct the tales of the lives of his pioneer forebears in his imagination. He is educated and passionately curious, and feels the need to come to terms with the 'unearned inheritance' of his history.

Towneley, Lady
The Man of Mode, 1676
Sir George Etherege
Benevolent Lady Towneley is the hub of high society and her house is a kind of salon; she herself is a welcome exception to the excesses of amoral cynicism which pervade much of the play. Despite her brother, Old Bellair, having instructed his son to marry HARRIET WOODVIL,

Lady Towneley assists her nephew in his campaign to win EMILIA.

Townsend, Morris
Washington Square, 1881
Henry James
A slightly brash, self-possessed young New Yorker who woos the heiress CATHERINE SLOPER for her money. Less vulgar than he is often made to sound, he represents a richness and diversity of experience against which she has locked herself away.

Tow-Wouse, Mr and Mrs
The History of the Adventures of Joseph Andrews and of his Friend Mr Abraham Adams, 1742
Henry Fielding
The warring landlord and landlady of the inn to which JOSEPH ANDREWS is brought after being set upon by the footpads. He is unwilling to offend, she to miss an opportunity to turn a few pennies. Between them, they run a relatively successful house.

Tox, Miss Lucretia
Dombey and Son, 1848
Charles Dickens
The faded, middle-aged spinster friend of MRS LOUISA CHICK, who introduces her to the household of MR DOMBEY, and the neighbour of MAJOR JOSEPH BAGSTOCK. She finds a wet-nurse for PAUL DOMBEY and becomes his godmother, but her influence is destroyed when the jealous Bagstock reveals to Dombey her aspirations to become the second Mrs Dombey. She later offers to pay for the education of POLLY TOODLE's children and employs ROBIN TOODLE in the hope of reforming his character.

Tozer, Mr
Salem Chapel, 1863
Phoebe Junior, 1876
Margaret Oliphant
Mr Tozer is a 'butterman', a vendor of butter, cheese and ham, of which his house always seems to smell. An active deacon in Salem Chapel, bluff, genial and pleased with himself, he takes REV ARTHUR VINCENT under his wing, assuring him that if he does as the Tozers advise, he will pull through. He judges a pastor's quality by the number of seats let in Chapel, and rejoices in hot, noisy, crowded tea-meetings, as do his wife and daughter. Some of the 'connection' condemn Arthur outright, but Mr Tozer rises up in a tea-meeting and makes a rousing speech in his favour, which carries the day.

Trabb's boy
Great Expectations, 1861
Charles Dickens
The impudent shop-boy of Trabb, the tailor and undertaker, he habitually embarrasses PIP in public after he has come into his 'great expectations': 'Words cannot state the amount of aggravation and injury wreaked upon me by Trabb's boy'. Performing a variety of extravagant antics in the street as Pip passes by, he is fondest of yelling 'Don't know yah, don't know yah, 'pon my soul don't know yah!'

Trace, Joe

Jazz, 1992
Toni Morrison

Told as a child that his parents vanished 'without a trace', Joe believes that 'the "trace" they disappeared without was me', so naming himself. Stranded in a lonely marriage, with a wife 'who takes better care of her parrot than she does me', he still secretly yearns for the mother who deserted him. He draws comfort from DORCAS MANFRED with a 'deepdown, spooky love', but when she too abandons him he shoots her 'just to keep the feeling going'. A fundamentally decent, well-liked man, Joe eventually rekindles a gentle companionship with VIOLET TRACE which brings peace, allowing him to embrace life and move on.

Trace, Violet

Jazz, 1992
Toni Morrison

Ashamed of her 'public crazinesses' and 'renegade tongue' – momentary eccentricities and verbal lapses to which she is prone – 50-year old Violet has retreated into silence, talking mainly to her caged birds. Although still handsome, with a face 'you'd never get tired looking at', she mourns her lost youth and childlessness, and has become emotionally estranged from her husband JOE TRACE. Roused from her lethargy by his murderous affair, she earns notoriety by her initial violent reaction, but her subsequent response is more complex. Eventually finding the daughter-figure she craves, she becomes able to reach out again, rediscover Joe and begin 'putting their lives together'.

Traddles, Thomas

David Copperfield, 1850
Charles Dickens

A schoolmate of DAVID COPPERFIELD's at MR CREAKLE's school, Salem House. Friendly and honourable, he is given to extremes of merriment and despair, and is frequently caned. Years later, he lodges with MR and MRS MICAWBER while reading for the Bar and hoping eventually to marry 'the dearest girl in the world', SOPHY CREWLER. He gets involved with the Micawbers' tortured financial affairs, helps to expose URIAH HEEP and qualifies as a barrister. In time, he marries Sophy, gains a competence, becomes a judge and is widely respected. Throughout, he remains David's loyal and affectionate friend.

Tradescant, Evelyn

The Sweets of Pimlico, 1977
A N Wilson

Left vulnerable after the ending of a shaky love affair, she consoles herself with a lifelong enthusiasm for nature study. In Kensington Gardens she meets THEO GORMANN, who refuses to conform to any of the taxonomic pigeonholes she has created for men.

Trafford, Caroline

A Legacy, 1956
Sybille Bedford

A beautiful young Englishwoman who, following an affair with an older married man, takes refuge from the possible consequences in marriage with BARON JULIUS MARIA VON FELDEN, whose love she does not return. Bored by their life in Spain, she takes lovers. She has an 'expression of untouchable serenity', a conscience about the derivation of her money from a coal mine, and an intellectual rigour, which she tries to pass on to her daughter FRANCESCA VON FELDEN and which leads to her leaving her husband. She is once described as 'an English gentleman'.

Traherne, Susan

Plenty, 1978
David Hare

A courier with Special Operations Executive during World War II, Susan Traherne's subsequent mental disintegration is presented as a metaphor of the collapse of British ideals in a time of postwar plenty. Superficially, Susan is the familiar literary character who had a tough, but on the whole good, war and cannot find a suitable place in peace. More substantially, she is a fighter, a woman who 'wastes no energy'. Impatient, perhaps even intolerant, she refuses to compromise and fade into a life she regards as politically hypocritical and emotionally inert. Yet what the highly-strung Susan is fighting, observes Hare, 'is life itself'.

Traill, Mr

Mr Perrin and Mr Traill, 1911
Sir Hugh Walpole

The 'new man' at Moffatt's school, he is younger and more eager than MR VINCENT PERRIN, less knocked about by the teacher's life. 'His figure was square, his back broad, his legs rather short – he looked, beyond everything else, clean'. It transpires in time that he is also his own man, by no means as pliable as Perrin hopes.

Tramp, the

In the Shadow of the Glen, 1903
J M Synge

The tramp arrives unexpectedly looking for shelter one rainswept night at the lonely cottage of DAN and NORA BURKE. A happy wanderer, he represents simple freedom, a fantastic alternative to a fixed life of drudgery. When the tramp arrives, Dan is feigning death, intending to catch Nora with her lover, MICHAEL DARA. But Nora's spirit responds instead to the vitality of the tramp, his sensitivity, practicality and hint of heroism meaning release from her lonely Wicklow glen.

Trampas

The Virginian, 1902
Owen Wister

Confusingly for a generation brought up on a television series very loosely based on Wister's book, Trampas is actually the villain of the piece, a Wyoming cowpuncher and cardsharp who confronts THE VIRGINIAN in a final, violent duel.

Tranio

The Taming of the Shrew, early 1590s
William Shakespeare

Trusted servant to LUCENTIO, Tranio has an easy-going relationship with his master. There is much verbal banter between them about Lucentio's falling in love, which results in an exchange of identities. Tranio is comfortable in his adopted role and enjoys the chance to order others around. He is a descendant of the comic servant/clown of the *commedia dell'arte*, having many of his characteristics – disguise, verbal humour, knockabout farce – but lacking any strong character of his own.

Transome, Harold
Felix Holt the Radical, 1866
George Eliot

The long-awaited returning son of MRS TRANSOME and heir to her estate. A self-proclaimed 'Radical' against a long tradition of family Toryism, he clarifies his position: 'a Radical only in rooting out abuses'. Old-fashioned where women are concerned, he considers them to have static ideas only and regards them 'as slight things'. Good-natured when not pressed, he becomes testy when MATTHEW JERMYN attempts to manipulate him or FELIX HOLT draws attention to his election agents' abuses.

Transome, Mrs
Felix Holt the Radical, 1866
George Eliot

The mistress of Transome Court. Living in relative poverty with a feeble and reclusive husband, she spends the story depressed and caught in contradictory affection between a son, HAROLD TRANSOME, and an ex-lover, MATTHEW JERMYN, who hate each other. Looking in the mirror she tells herself 'I am a hag', and pathetically clings on to a few remaining signs of privilege, such as receiving curtsies from her underlings. Her one friend, DENNER, is the housekeeper.

Trant, Miss Elizabeth
The Good Companions, 1929
J B Priestley

A dutiful daughter who looked after her father for 15 years before his death. Naive, sincere and trusting, she is excited by her new-found freedom and takes to the road. Previously she has only lived vicariously through novels; now she begins to uncover unsuspected areas of her personality. Essentially, though, she craves a conformist, domesticated existence. After her 'fling', she marries and finds true contentment.

Trapbois
The Fortunes of Nigel, 1822
Sir Walter Scott

An elderly miser of Alsatia, into whose home NIGEL OLIFAUNT comes during his European sojourn. So obsessed is Trapbois with his fortune that the notion of theft has 'taken possession of the old man's pineal gland'; he regards any newcomer as a larcenous intruder, and coughs and splutters in a paranoid frenzy.

Trapbois, Martha
The Fortunes of Nigel, 1822
Sir Walter Scott

The miser TRAPBOIS's daughter, she is as physically wry-necked as her father is morally and spiritually. She dresses in antiquated clothes

that 'assorted well with the faded complexion, grey eyes, thin lips, and austere visage of the antiquated maiden ... Her figure was tall, thin, and flat, with skinny arms and hands, and feet of the larger size'.

Trask, Adam
East of Eden, 1952
John Steinbeck

A quiet, rather withdrawn Salinas Valley farmer, Connecticut-born, whose life is ripped apart when he marries the ex-prostitute CATHY AMES. 'He covered his life with a veil of vagueness, while behind his quiet eyes a rich full life went on. This did not protect him from assault but it allowed him an immunity'.

Trask, Caleb and Aron
East of Eden, 1952
John Steinbeck

In recognition of the tainted idyll of his marriage and the fallen paradise of Salinas Valley, ADAM TRASK originally intended to call his twin sons Cain and Abel. Yet the brothers seem foredoomed to act out the Bible story, whatever their names. Aron, his father's favourite, is generous, easy-going and loving, while Caleb is fiery and Faustian and sets in train the sequence of events that lead to the final tragedy but also to his own humanization.

Travis, Poopy
'May We Borrow Your Husband?', in *May We Borrow Your Husband?*, 1967
Graham Greene

A new bride on honeymoon, whose husband is 'borrowed' by two homosexuals. Unable to recognize her husband's homosexual leanings, she blames herself for his lack of interest in her. She is 'a very tall girl, perhaps five feet nine, very slim, very young, with hair the colour of conkers'. She is open and friendly, but naive and, sadly, doomed to be hurt.

Trebell, Henry
Waste, 1907
Harley Granville-Barker

A distinguished lawyer, Henry Trebell is confident, influential, 'grown-up enough to do without dogma'. At a political house party, he seduces Amy, a flirtatious young woman, who subsequently becomes pregnant. There is no love between them, but although he promises to support her materially, she has an illegal abortion and dies. Amy asserted her right to choose, yet Trebell claims the right to grieve: 'The man bears the child in his soul, as the woman bears the body'. Trebell is capable of compassion, yet it is tainted by self-pity. The climate of political self-interest, moral sacrifice and compromise crushes Trebell's spirit, and he commits suicide.

Tredwell, Jasmine
Woman in a Lampshade, 1979 (play), 'Woman in a Lampshade', in *Woman in a Lampshade*, 1983
Elizabeth Jolley

Wearing a lampshade on her head is the central part of Jasmine Tredwell's fantasy life: 'the lampshade ... made her feel pretty, softly so and feminine'. The middle-aged wife of an inattentive professor, Jasmine puts on her lampshade hat and writes short stories, in which female characters repeatedly scorn undesirable young men. Even when she has the chance of real sex and excitement, she opts for fantasy. The pattern is fixed: she slides out of her arid life into fantasy, before slipping towards a tinkling, shrill kind of madness.

Tree, Hilma
The Octopus: A Story of California, 1901
Frank Norris
Daughter of the man who runs ANNIXTER's small dairy farm, she is young but disconcertingly nubile and awakens long-suppressed desires in her employer Annixter. Her hair, a key indicator of sexual nature for Norris, 'seemed almost to have a life of its own, almost Medusa-like'. Even so, there is a simplicity and delicacy about her that suggests a potential for refinement one might not expect to find in the far West.

Treece, Professor Stuart
Eating People is Wrong, 1959
Malcolm Bradbury
The head of the English department at a new university, Professor Treece is in his forties and conscious of his own increasingly myopic provincialism, of history taking place somewhere else, without him. He is 'a liberal humanist who believes in original sin', a romantic whose time passed with the 1930s and is now reduced to offering poetry readings and theatre trips to students he often finds difficult to understand. Isolated and sometimes despairing, Treece peers out at the world with baffled resignation.

Treet, George
Devil-in-a-Fog, 1966
Leon Garfield
A travelling actor who, when off-stage, is soberly dressed and sensible, he discovers himself to be the apparent son and heir of SIR JOHN DEXTER, a country squire. Undaunted by this new role, he dresses strikingly for the part, trying to remember THOMAS TREET's advice: that gentlemen either know already, or else stay ignorant, with a smile. Capable of rich and fiery oratory without really understanding its underlying emotions, he is as much of a mystery to himself as he is to others. He remains loyal to his family throughout and is, ultimately, 'too coarse, too bright and too strong to be truly a Dexter'.

Treet, Thomas
Devil-in-a-Fog, 1966
Leon Garfield
An erstwhile showman, now turned actor. A portly, slightly comical, yet dignified figure, his noble spirit is only lowered by the twice-yearly appearances of the 'Stranger', whose identity is a mystery but whose guineas keep the family solvent, almost. Mr Treet's particular genius is for special effects, which often go dramatically out of control. Misfortune, and a talent for throwing money away, mean that the ignominy of the stocks is only ever a breath away. Reckless and improvident, he is totally charming.

Trefoil, Arabella
The American Senator, 1883
Anthony Trollope
A handsome English woman of 30 who is determined to be married, and calculatingly manipulates her suitors in an attempt to realize the best prospects. Although she does not care much for pleasure, 'she did care to be a great lady – one who would be allowed to swim out of rooms before others, one who would snub others, one who could show real diamonds when others wore paste, one who might be sure to be asked everywhere even by people who hated her'. She achieves only a partial, compromised success in her effort, but at some cost to her reputation.

Tregear, Frank (Francis Oliphant)
The Duke's Children, 1880
Anthony Trollope
A friend of LORD SILVERBRIDGE at Oxford. He 'had taught himself to regard himself as a young English gentleman of the first water, qualified by birth and position to live with all that was most noble and most elegant; and he could have lived in that sphere naturally and gracefully were it not that the part of the "sphere" which he specially affected requires wealth as well as birth and intellect'. His lack of means leads the Duke of Omnium (PLANTAGENET PALLISER) to reject his suit for the hand of LADY MARY PALLISER, but the old man later sees his request as courageous rather than opportunistic, and relents.

Trelawny, Rose
Trelawny of the 'Wells', 1898
Arthur Wing Pinero
Rose, a young actress in the 1860s, is charming, restless, extravagant and apt to dramatize life as though it were melodrama. About to leave the 'Wells' for marriage to Arthur Gower and drawing-room society, she abandons her theatrical lodgings to live with her fiancé's relations in Cavendish Square. Her audacity astounds them; unused to the filial obedience and self-effacement they expect, she withers; yet, like the playwright TOM WRENCH, she longs for a new beginning. This she discovers in her true womanly nature.

Trellis, Dermot
At Swim-Two-Birds, 1939
Flann O'Brien
A fictional novelist, the proprietor of the 'Red Swan Hotel', who is clever enough to produce a fully grown man from nothing; 'a very familiar phenomenon in literature'! He has arbitrary rules of good and evil regarding literature, such as the colour of the binding of a book: if it is not green then the book is the 'work of Satan'. Everything he writes is similarly a product of immaculate 'conception'.

Trellman, Harry
The Actual, 1997
Saul Bellow
Late middle-aged and semi-retired, with 'a somewhat Mongolian and tawny complexion', the product of a Chicago orphanage and many years as a businessman in the Far East, Trellman returns to Chicago to find himself employed as

an advisor to the elderly SIGMUND ADLETSKY. Composed, philosophical and solitary, Trellman is an observer and listener, out of step with American society and especially the society of financial power and romantic love. Yet when he encounters AMY WUSTRIN, with whom he has been in love since high school, he is once again irresistibly drawn by the magnetic power of 'the heart's ultimate need'.

Tremayne, Bernard
Black Dogs, 1992
Ian McEwan

JEREMY's father-in-law, a disillusioned ex-communist and former Labour MP, was the 'voice of reason' during the Suez crisis and author of a Nasser biography, and is still a lively, radical contributor to BBC discussion programmes. He loves his dying, estranged wife, JUNE TREMAYNE, but on the strength of his own rationalistic and materialistic views, dismisses as female fancifulness her mystical reaction to her 'black dogs' experience. Visiting Berlin with Jeremy soon after the Wall comes down, Bernard reveals his own interpretation of that experience, and what happened to his marriage as a result.

Tremayne, June
Black Dogs, 1992
Ian McEwan

Like her husband, BERNARD TREMAYNE, June was a young communist during World War II. But honeymooning in France in 1946, she had a near-fatal encounter with feral black dogs, and seeing them as the embodiment of evil discovered a belief in God and the Devil, incompatible with communism. This divided her from her husband and eventually, although still in love with him, June moved to France, promoting and writing about her peculiar brand of mysticism. Brought back terminally ill to an English nursing home, she tells her son-in-law, JEREMY, her version of the 'black dogs' manifestation, and her chilling theory about the existence and nature of evil.

Trench, Dr Harry
Widowers' Houses, 1892
George Bernard Shaw

An earnest, frank, boyish man in his mid-twenties, Trench is engaged to BLANCHE SARTORIUS. However, having discovered the source of her wealth to be the enormous profits her father makes as a slum landlord, the upright Trench calls the engagement off. When SARTORIUS protests that his disintegrating property is mortgaged and that Trench is one of those reaping the interest, he capitulates, admitting that 'we're all in the same swim'. Marrying Blanche, Trench compromises his principles further by joining an investment swindle dreamt up by LICKCHEESE, Sartorius's former rent collector.

Trenor, Gus
The House of Mirth, 1905
Edith Wharton

The rich speculator husband of LILY BART's closest friend, Gus is a small-eyed, dull, coarse man who eats and drinks too much; his heavy, 'carnivorous' head sinks between his shoulders

and his jewelled rings are embedded in the flesh of his fat red fingers. He tries to buy Lily's sexual favours by putting her literally in his debt, something she naively fails to understand until too late, and he plays a major part in her downfall.

Trent, Little Nell → Little Nell

Trent, Michael
End of the World, 1984
Arthur Kopit

The play's central character and narrator, Trent is a dramatist who accepts a commission from Philip Stone, a millionaire, to write a piece about nuclear warfare. Trent, who models himself upon Dashiell Hammett's detective character, SAM SPADE (the play has affinities with *The Maltese Falcon*), hopes to give the impression of being a hard-boiled, pithy opportunist. In fact, he is circumspect, even timid at times. He is based in Stamford, Connecticut, the sign on his office door reading: 'Michael Trent – Playwright – No Domestic Comedies'. He believes implicitly in himself, although the play, a black comedy, is so constructed that the audience can see him more objectively.

Tressillian, Edmund
Kenilworth, 1821
Sir Walter Scott

The worthy but disappointed suitor of AMY ROBSART, he is 'a man aged between twenty-five and thirty, rather above the middle size, dressed with plainness and decency, yet bearing an air of ease, which almost amounted to dignity, and which seemed to infer that his habit was rather beneath his rank'. He is a steady, thoughtful man, whose surface calm disguises an intro-spective nature.

Trevelyan, Laura
Voss, 1957
Patrick White

Laura is the niece of Mr Bonner, a wealthy Sydney draper and one of the patrons of JOHANN ULRICH VOSS's expedition across Australia. Although outwardly rather an awkward, reserved, even priggish bluestocking, Laura is intelligent, pragmatic, sensitive and sympathetic. In her letter accepting his proposal of marriage, Laura describes both herself and Voss as 'faulty beings'. When Voss duly sets out on his journey, Laura stays in Sydney, communicating with him by letter and telepathy, preferring their two idealized selves to imperfect reality. After his death, she becomes even more aware of the transience of life and of the nature of divinity and of spiritual failure, eventually becoming the headmistress of a ladies' academy and a Mother of Mercy.

Trevelyan, Louis
He Knew He Was Right, 1869
Anthony Trollope

The orphaned son of a wealthy barrister, he marries EMILY ROWLEY. He is a tall, handsome, manly fellow, and is regarded as being intelligent, generous and 'a man sure to be honoured and respected'. Emily is impressed by his many charms, but quickly finds that 'he liked to have his own way'. When she disregards his order to ban COL FREDERIC OSBORNE from their house, it sparks off a jealous rage which turns by degrees to an obsessive, monomaniac madness.

Trewe, Robert
'An Imaginative Woman', in *Wessex Tales: Strange, Lively and Commonplace*, 1896
Thomas Hardy

A depressive poet, Trewe is the archetypal creative soul, who finds no solace in this bleak world. He craves female attention in the form of a caring, loving and gentle companion, but never achieves this. Incapable of relating to others, apart from in his imagination, he inspires love in ELLA MARCHMILL who, ironically, does not know him.

Triamond
The Faerie Queene, 1590–6
Sir Edmund Spenser

One of three brothers, the other two being Priamond and Diamond, who are now dead. They were so close that they seemed to share a soul, and as a legacy they have left him their virtues and strengths as well as giving him the gift of a longer life. He is representative of true harmony and love, and wins the hand of CAMBELL's sister, CANACEE.

Triffids
The Day of the Triffids, 1951
John Wyndham

Ambulant plants which were created as a result of 'a series of ingenious biological meddlings – and very likely accidental at that' in the USSR. An aeroplane carrying stolen seeds explodes, propagating the plants over a wide area. They grow seven feet tall, and 'walk' like a man on crutches, 'both strenuous and clumsy – faintly reminiscent of young elephants at play'. They are named triffids for their three root-like 'legs'. Initially a novelty, they have a fatal sting, and come to be associated with 'pain, fear and misery' after most of the human population is suddenly blinded by a meteor shower.

Trilby, in full Trilby O'Ferrall
Trilby, 1894
George Du Maurier

An artist's model in Paris. She falls under the influence of the ambiguous SVENGALI, who exerts a hypnotic hold over her and turns her into a brilliant singer, a gift that evaporates as soon as he is dead. (She merits a footnote, too, for lending her name to a hat.)

Trim, Corporal
The Life and Opinions of Tristram Shandy, 9 volumes, 1759–67
Laurence Sterne

The loyal servant of UNCLE TOBY SHANDY, he copes with his serious leg wound with a typical soldier's courage, and brings to his relationship with Toby a soldier's respect for his commanding officer. He is a talkative man, and his delight in public speaking and his occasional sermonizing reveal his understanding and insight; as a lover, he is energetic and forward in a way his master

can never quite emulate. His servile loyalty towards Toby contrasts with Toby's lack of self-regard and inability to stand on his dignity.

Trimingham, Lord
The Go-Between, 1953
L P Hartley

The ninth Viscount, Lord Trimingham was invalided out of the Boer War with a badly disfigured face and spends the summer of 1900 as a guest in his own house, Brandham Hall. He is the 'Archer' of the narrator LEO COLSTON's zodiac. In love with MARION MAUDSLEY, his host's daughter, he behaves honourably, marrying her and 'standing by her' even after the discovery of her illicit relationship with TED BURGESS, a neighbouring farmer.

Trimmer
Sword of Honour, 1965
Evelyn Waugh

Trimmer, the one Halberdier whom GUY CROUCHBACK dislikes, has a refined Cockney accent and avoids duty whenever possible, lying low with his artillery unit for a considerable time calling himself Captain McTavish. He meets and beds VIRGINIA TROY, Crouchback's bored ex-wife, in a fog-bound Glasgow hotel; he has been a hairdresser on the *Aquitania* and she his favourite customer. Despite his behaviour he is declared good 'hero' material, because of his looks, and is sent to America to publicize the British war effort, and disappears for ever. To Virginia's horror, he is the father of her child, and thus indirectly brings about her remarriage to Guy.

Trinculo
The Tempest, 1611
William Shakespeare

Although nominally jester to ALONSO, King of Naples, Trinculo shows little evidence of a sense of humour. He is a typical bully; afraid, at first, of CALIBAN, when he realizes that he will do him no harm he chides, berates and beats him until the monster turns from him to STEPHANO.

Trinder, Sue
Fingersmith, 2002
Sarah Waters

Raised by an unscrupulous baby farmer in a house full of thieves, 17-year-old Sue is described as 'a bad girl, not too nice about the fine points of the law'. She is not, however, completely without a conscience, and when she agrees to take part in a cruel confidence trick devised by a family friend, there is a certain amount of reluctance mixed with her bravado. Her part in the scheme is to present herself as lady's maid to the intended victim, MAUD LILLY, whose apparent naiveté arouses Sue's protective instincts.

Trist, Eadith
The Twyborn Affair, 1979
Patrick White

A fashionable, bohemian and flamboyant London brothel-keeper, Eadith maintains a kind of disguise by living partly in a world of her own making. In her case, it is one of extravagant burlesque. Eadith is a version of EADIE TWYBORN, EDDIE TWYBORN and EUDOXIA

VATATZES. Like them, she emerges as a person uncertain of him/herself and of others, seemingly assertive but in reality self-deluding, part of her battle being confusion over her gender, sexuality and its emotional consequences. To Eadith, conventional morality is complex and baffling.

Tristan l'Hermite
Quentin Durward, 1823
Sir Walter Scott

LOUIS XI, KING OF FRANCE's provost and legal enforcer, he is a 'stout-formed, middle-sized man … with a down-looking visage and a very ominous smile, when by chance he gave way to that impulse'. He administers a kind of frontier justice, hanging supposed miscreants on the basis of an extremely prejudiced outlook.

Trock
Winterset, 1935
Maxwell Anderson

A vicious hoodlum, who creates an elaborate poetry out of violence, he has managed to evade punishment for murder, allowing MIO's father to be executed in his place. Now dying, he is confronted with new evidence that condemns him unambiguously.

Troil, Brenda
The Pirate, 1821
Sir Walter Scott

The daughter of MAGNUS TROIL, she is as light – in looks and nature – as her sister MINNA TROIL is dark. A fairy-like form, she is irrepressibly buoyant in spirit, in no way prone to the melancholy reflections that afflict her sister.

Troil, Magnus
The Pirate, 1821
Sir Walter Scott

An old Shetlander, the father of BRENDA and MINNA TROIL, he is a wise and indulgent landlord, and a parent in whom indulgence sometimes has the upper hand over wisdom. He has 'strong and masculine features, rendered ruddy and brown by frequent exposure to severe weather – a quantity of most venerable silver hair … expressed at once his advanced age, his hasty, yet well-conditioned temper, and his robust constitution'.

Troil, Minna
The Pirate, 1821
Sir Walter Scott

The daughter of MAGNUS TROIL and sister of BRENDA TROIL, she has inherited from her Scottish mother the stately form and dark hair of the mainlanders and a sympathetic nature that responds with strong emotion to any tale of injustice or woe; 'there was something in the serious beauty of her aspect … that seemed as if [she] belonged naturally to some higher and better sphere, and was only the chance visitant of a world that was not worthy of her'.

Troil, Ulla → Norna of the Fitful Head

Troilus
Troilus and Cressida, 1601/2
William Shakespeare

A son of PRIAM, the Trojan king, Troilus is a young and rather naive romantic whose love for CRESSIDA bears many of the characteristics of infatuation – he idealizes his beloved and the idea of love itself. He takes himself and his love for Cressida very seriously, apparently being more concerned with that than with his duties on the battlefield. When Cressida proves to be untrue, his bitter disillusionment and hatred of DIOMEDES (her new suitor) drive him to reckless acts of martial valour.

Troilus
Troilus and Criseyde, c.1385–9
Geoffrey Chaucer

A brave warrior of the Trojan court who falls in love with the young widow CRISEYDE. Too good and shy to seduce her, he suffers the agonies of love in his devotion to her, and eventually it is PANDARUS, acting as go-between, who, literally, puts the two lovers to bed. When Criseyde returns to her father in the Greek camp, Troilus is desolate. The knowledge of her subsequent infidelity breaks his heart and he dies at the hand of Achilles.

Trompart
The Faerie Queene, 1590–6
Sir Edmund Spenser

BRAGGADOCHIO's wily henchman, he is full of 'cunning sleights and practick knavery'. He is quick-witted and sly, taking up with his master in order to gain protection and possible wealth. An eloquent man, he swells his master's vanity with subtle flattery. Together they function well.

Trotter, James Henry → James

Trotter, Job
Pickwick Papers, 1837
Charles Dickens

ALFRED JINGLE's sly servant and crony, the brother of JEMMY HUTLEY and the only man to prove too sharp for SAM WELLER. He is imprisoned with Jingle in the Fleet and emigrates with him afterwards to the West Indies.

Trotwood, Miss Betsey
David Copperfield, 1850
Charles Dickens

DAVID COPPERFIELD's eccentric great-aunt and benefactor, she lives as a recluse in Dover and cares for an amiable lunatic, MR DICK, her lodger. In her youth she married a cruel husband, then left him, resumed her maiden name, and now pays him to stay away. When the ragged young David appears at her cottage, having escaped from Murdstone and Grinby's warehouse and begging for protection, she adopts him as her son, renaming him Trotwood Copperfield. At first austere and strong-minded, her temper softens as a result of their loving relationship. She finances his education and start in life, but is disappointed when he marries the childish DORA SPENLOW rather than AGNES WICKFIELD. She loses money through URIAH HEEP's fraud on MR WICKFIELD but regains it when Heep is exposed. She enjoys a contented old age, heartened by David's second marriage to Agnes and his success as an author.

Trout, Eva
Eva Trout, 1969
Elizabeth Bowen

In nature as in name, she is a fish out of water. The product of a disturbed and ultimately disastrous marriage (her mother absconds when her husband's homosexuality is revealed), Eva is neurotic, disorderly and self-destructively uncommunicative, with all the influences of her life out of place: 'To reassemble the picture was impossible; too many of the pieces were lost, lacking'.

Trout, Kilgore
Breakfast of Champions, 1973, and others
Kurt Vonnegut, Jr

The imaginary science-fiction writer who appears in several of Vonnegut's novels (he is the favourite writer of BILLY PILGRIM, and of the philanthropist ELIOT ROSEWATER in *God Bless You, Mr Rosewater* (1965)), but plays his most central role here, where he is depicted as a snaggle-toothed, white-haired old man with 'pale white broomsticks for legs'. He becomes a famous and venerated artist and scientist when his pulp novels turn out to contain crucial insights on 'the importance of ideas as causes and cures of diseases', just as his off-beam philosophical notions illuminate earlier books. Philip José Farmer contributed to the Trout cult by writing a novel under his name, *Venus on the Half-Shell* (1975).

Trowbridge, Marquis of
The Vicar of Bullhampton, 1870
Anthony Trollope

Among the lands of John Augustus Stowte, Marquis of Trowbridge, is the greater part of the Wiltshire parish of Bullhampton, the vicar of which, REV FRANK FENWICK, is detested by this 'arrogant old fool'. Although stupid, reactionary, conceited and pompous, he does not deliberately do anything that he believes to be wrong.

Troy, Sgt Francis
Far from the Madding Crowd, 1874
Thomas Hardy

A clever and dashing soldier, Troy is 'the erratic child of impulse' who lives in the present and takes no thought for the consequences of his actions. He is a flatterer and a womanizer, who proves himself utterly unreliable and feckless. He rejects FANNY ROBIN and after marrying BATHSHEBA EVERDENE taunts WILLIAM BOLDWOOD with cruel relish. It is only in his genuine grief at Fanny's death that he appears in a sympathetic light.

Troy, Virginia
Sword of Honour, 1965
Evelyn Waugh

Virginia is GUY CROUCHBACK's ex-wife, whom he has allowed to divorce him for TOMMY BLACKHOUSE, whom in turn she has divorced for Augustus whom she did not marry; she is now married to Mr Troy but thinks he is divorcing her in the USA. Bright, shallow, attractive, she lives for the moment with little thought of consequences and is horrified to find herself pregnant by the revolting TRIMMER. Disgusted

by Guy's whimsical statement that by canon law she is still his wife – she would have preferred enjoyable seduction – she is nonetheless pleased to marry him again when she cannot find an abortionist.

Truelove, Pallas
Paradise, 1997
Toni Morrison

Having run away from betrayal by her mother, 16-year-old Pallas escapes from a gang who raped her and recovers with CONSOLATA in the security of the Convent. Her innocence lost, she briefly attempts to resume her affluent, sheltered former life, but soon returns to give birth to her son.

Truewit
Epicoene, or The Silent Woman, 1616
Ben Jonson

A friend of SIR DAUPHINE EUGENIE (whom he assists in his plot to make MOROSE marry EPICOENE) and of NED CLERIMONT, with whom he likes to discuss women, Truewit is an energetic, optimistic man. Loyal to his friends, he enjoys an escapade and stands firmly on the side of gallantry; as his name implies, he is both quick-witted and true.

Trulliber, Parson
The History of the Adventures of Joseph Andrews and of his Friend Mr Abraham Adams, 1742
Henry Fielding

A part-time clergyman, who makes a substantial living as a pig-farmer. This odd calling for a divine is reflected in his name, which combines 'trullibub' (a contemporary version of 'fatso') and 'trolubber' or day-labourer. He is approached by PARSON ADAMS for a loan after the travellers have lost all their money on the road.

Trumbull, Farmer
The Vicar of Bullhampton, 1870
Anthony Trollope

A farmer in the Wiltshire village of Bullhampton, who leases his land from the MARQUIS OF TROWBRIDGE. He is angered by trespassers on his fields and to discourage them keeps a ferocious bulldog, Bone'm. A widower, he sleeps with the box containing his carefully saved money. He and his dog are murdered by robbers, causing suspicion to fall on SAM BRATTLE.

Trumbull, Thomas
Redgauntlet, 1824
Sir Walter Scott

A sanctimonious Solway smuggler, he is 'a tall, thin, bony figure, with white hair combed straight down on each side of his face, and an iron-grey hue of complexion; where the lines ... of his countenance were so sternly adapted to a devotional and even ascetic expression that they left no room for any indication of reckless daring, or sly dissimulation'.

Trumpet, Solomon
Jack Holborn, 1964
Leon Garfield

Cast off as a mutineer from the treasure ship, the *Esperance*, Trumpet is picked up by the pirate crew of the *Charming Molly*. He is a neat dresser, quite small, with dark wavy hair and shrewd, brown, hooded eyes, rather like an owl. A cunning, subtle negotiator, as befits his former trade as a swindler, his only motivation at first seems to be his lust for the 'White Lady', a huge egg-shaped diamond with a subtle inner glow and the reputation of a curse upon it. A good judge of both men and jewels, he has within him a spark of humanity that is kindled into compassion and honour by the proximity of JACK HOLBORN and LORD SHERINGHAM.

Trunnion, Commodore Hawser
The Adventures of Peregrine Pickle, 1751, bowdlerized edition 1758
Tobias Smollett

Boon companion of GAMALIEL PICKLE in his country retreat and a habitual user of the local inn, which he fills with gale-force yarns of battles against the French, punctuated by round abuse of his companions. He is said to be modelled on the eccentric Admiral Daniel Hore, who re-ordered his house and domestic routines in rigorously nautical fashion. 'His complexion was tawny, and his aspect rendered hideous by a large scar across his nose, and a patch that covered the place of one eye'.

Truscott, Jim
Loot, 1966
Joe Orton

The famed Truscott of the Yard, who once tracked down the limbless girl killer, he is a bumptious, blustering police officer with a manic devotion to duty. His unorthodox methods include posing as a member of the Metropolitan Water Board to gain entrance to private homes without the tedious necessity of acquiring a search warrant. Violent, unpredictable and happy to entertain the concept of bribery, his unofficial credo is: 'waste time on the truth and you'll be pounding the beat until the day you retire'.

Tryan, Rev Edgar
'Janet's Repentance', in *Scenes of Clerical Life*, 1858
George Eliot

The mild-mannered Protestant curate of the chapel situated on the outskirts of Milby, Tryan falls prey to the derision of ROBERT DEMPSTER and the anti-Evangelical members of the town, but in refusing to rise to their bait, he retains his quiet dignity and self-respect. Overworking himself to the point of exhaustion in tending to the edification of others, he finds in JANET DEMPSTER both a soul to be saved and a loving friend with whom he can share his own sadness. Compassionate and generous to the last, he fights bravely against consumption long enough to ensure the certainty of her spiritual well-being.

Ts'eh
Ceremony, 1977
Leslie Marmon Silko

A member, as she describes herself, of the Montaño family, Ts'eh embodies the spirit of Tse-pina (Mount Taylor), the sacred mountain of the Laguna people in New Mexico. By spreading her blanket patterned with cloud and lightning designs, she causes snowstorms in the desert, and gathers plants the colour of the sky after rain

to replant in areas of drought. Her part in TAYO's life and healing is both practical and personal: her storm blanket ensures the safe escape of Tayo's uncle's stolen cattle, and she continues Betonie's instruction, teaching Tayo about the threat from 'the destroyers', and his central part in the ceremony to combat their witchery. She replaces the wartime nightmares in Tayo's dreams as, through her, he experiences an unpossessive love that is both sexual and spiritual, and begins to reconstruct his shattered sense of self.

Tsotsi
Tsotsi, 1980
Athol Fugard

Leader of a gang of Johannesburg thugs, or 'tsotsis', Tsotsi redeems himself over the course of the novel by learning to question himself, and acquiring sympathy for others. Ironically, his regeneration begins when he beats up Boston, one of his followers, for daring to ask him questions about himself.

Tsutsik, properly **Aaron Greidinger**
Shosha, 1978
Isaac Bashevis Singer

An aspiring writer. Although a rabbi's son, brought up in a Jewish ghetto in Warsaw, he leads a largely secular life. He drifts aimlessly, carrying on several affairs, allowing himself to be manipulated and living off money he has not yet earned. However, his return to his old street brings about a subtle yet profound change within him. When he locates his childhood companion, the tiny, backward Shosha, and marries her, his capacity for tenderness, patience and faithfulness is revealed.

Tucca, Pantilius
Poetaster, 1602
Ben Jonson

A gullible, abrasive, self-centred military captain, Tucca is unable to differentiate good poetry from bad. A changeable man, he appears to enjoy presenting differing aspects of himself to various people. He agrees with OVID's father that poets are to be generally despised, borrows money from him but fails to repay him. On the other hand, he lobbies for CRISPINUS's release from arrest without even knowing his alleged offence. A typical Jonsonian target, he is duly punished for his foolishness.

Tuck, Friar
Ivanhoe, 1819
Sir Walter Scott

Legendary companion of Robin Hood (or, here, LOCKSLEY), he espouses a muscular Christianity that is not above a little venial self-interest. John Buchan described him as having 'the jolly freedom of the woods in him', which accurately sums up his bounding appeal.

Tucker, Andy
'Hostages to Momus', and others, in *The Gentle Grafter*, 1908
O Henry

JEFF PETERS's partner in the art of 'bunco', he can never be held to 'legitimate ethics of pure swindling'. Andy's imagination is forever in search of some means of double-crossing the world. 'Out of respect for that conscience' of Jeff's, Andy allows his partner to remain ignorant of his duplicity – at least until the duo need to effect a quick exit. Then, and only then, will Andy enlighten his partner.

Tuere
The Voice, 1964
Gabriel Okara
A witch in the jungle, with whom OKOKO dallies when he has turned his back on the ways of the village. She represents a life lived beyond the reach of conventional values.

Tufton, Rev Mr
Salem Chapel, 1863
Margaret Oliphant
Retired pastor of Salem Chapel, crippled by a stroke and unaware that his flock wanted rid of him even before he was stricken, he sits complacent in a small stuffy room, the light obscured by ivy outside and geraniums within. He proclaims that his successor REV ARTHUR VINCENT's audiences will 'fall off', warns him to 'keep well' with the deacons – do what they tell him – and blandly advises sermons to the children and popular lectures as ways of keeping interest up.

Tulkinghorn, Mr
Bleak House, 1853
Charles Dickens
Attorney-at-law and solicitor to the Court of Chancery, he is the lawyer to the DEDLOCK family. 'Rusty to look at' and reputedly rich from the secrets of aristocratic families, of which he 'is known to be the silent depository', he is secretive and sinister. He involves JO, MR SNAGSBY, MR GEORGE ROUNCEWELL and MADEMOISELLE HORTENSE to help him learn the mystery of Lady Dedlock's past, and when he visits her and threatens to reveal her secret, she flees Chesney Wold and eventually dies a wretched death. He is murdered in his chambers by Hortense, angry at his refusal to reward her for her assistance.

Tull, Richard
The Information, 1995
Martin Amis
An Oxford contemporary of GWYN BARRY (both men are now 40), Tull, who is shabby, balding and domestically burdened, is as reduced by literary failure as Barry is elevated by success. His novels are increasingly abstract and unpublishable, and while Barry becomes lionized by the media, Tull is forced to toil in obscurity, reviewing books for *The Little Magazine*, a low-circulation literary journal. Brooding obsessively, Tull plots Barry's social and professional destruction. In the process, he becomes increasingly disassociated from his family and drawn into a world of chaotic violence.

Tulla, Earl of
Phineas Finn, The Irish Member, 1869
Anthony Trollope
The elderly patron of PHINEAS FINN, whom

he helps to ensconce as the member for Loughshane, much of which he owns, although he prefers to rest his 'gouty feet' in County Clare. He is 'a passionate old man' who has been a friend of Finn's father for many years, and has grown rather crotchety, especially on the subject of politics.

Tulliver, Maggie
The Mill on the Floss, 1860
George Eliot
Passionate, romantic and inquisitively intelligent, dark-haired Maggie dotes on her brother TOM TULLIVER, but is continually put down by him in her quest for love and knowledge. Hemmed in, but unable to escape from the narrowness of her existence on Dorlcote Mill, she discovers emotional and intellectual stimulation in the company of PHILIP WAKEM. Forbidden to see him, however, her repressed ardency responds to the marked attentions of STEPHEN GUEST, but in the ensuing drama her anguished struggles to do right result in her ostracism from the community. Forgiven by those who matter, however, her last act is one of bravery and, above all, love.

Tulliver, Mr
The Mill on the Floss, 1860
George Eliot
Mortgage-holder on Dorlcote Mill, well-meaning but misguided Mr Tulliver dotes on his children TOM and MAGGIE TULLIVER and manages his affairs in a decidedly haphazard manner, a combination of pride, obstinacy and soft-hearted generosity resulting in his eventual bankruptcy. Crippled by debt and long illness, his former amiability is replaced by black depression, and his deep-rooted hatred of Lawyer Wakem becomes the driving force, and ultimately the destroyer, of his life, a hatred which also resonates, with disastrous results, in the following generation.

Tulliver, Mrs Bessy
The Mill on the Floss, 1860
George Eliot
Whereas her husband's affections lie more with his daughter MAGGIE TULLIVER than with TOM TULLIVER, mild Mrs Tulliver makes much of her son, despairing at the dark, unkempt appearance of Maggie. Dominated by her husband, she is yet capable of defending *her* family name when necessary, and when faced with bankruptcy her thoughts run more on the fate of her best linen and china than anything else. Constantly reminded by her sisters of her poverty and troublesome children, she still, in all her naive simplicity, possesses the motherly love which will not let her turn her back when Maggie needs her most.

Tulliver, Tom
The Mill on the Floss, 1860
George Eliot
The beloved elder brother of MAGGIE TULLIVER, Tom, like his father, is proud and stubborn, and full of his own self-righteousness. Too restricted in both intellect and imagination to appreciate that other people's natures are not necessarily

like his own, he exerts his dominating influence on Maggie, cruelly forbidding her to see PHILIP WAKEM, the son of their father's arch-enemy. Impelled by his hatred of disgrace and failure to make good his father's losses, Tom works hard to regain Dorlcote Mill, but in bearing such a prejudiced grudge against Philip, he alienates himself, almost until the end, from the warm-hearted love of his sister.

Tunner
The Sheltering Sky, 1949
Paul Bowles

A young American of good heart but strictly rational values, he falls in love with KIT MORESBY partly because he pities her and partly out of an earnest, liberal desire to 'save' her. When her husband, PORTER MORESBY, dies in the desert and she is taken into concubinage by a group of Arabs, he rescues her and brings her back to 'civilization'.

Tupman, Tracy
Pickwick Papers, 1837
Charles Dickens

A member of the Pickwick Club, he is a stout middle-aged bachelor who falls in love with every pretty girl he meets. His wooing of Rachael WARDLE is spied on by JOE (THE FAT BOY), and frustrated when ALFRED JINGLE elopes with her for her money. Tupman pays Jingle £120 to get her back but nevertheless remains a bachelor and retires to Richmond.

Turner, Dick
The Grass is Singing, 1950
Doris Lessing

Dick, a farmer, is an honourable man but never manages to make a success of his life, either professionally or emotionally. Initially delighted with his strange wife, MARY TURNER, he soon finds he cannot relate to her. He is tolerant and fair, but boring and lacking in the sensitivity which his very needy wife requires.

Turner, Emily Stockwell
Love and Friendship, 1962
Alison Lurie

A woman of strong moral principles, she is shocked and scandalized at her own seduction by the attractive but dissolute Will Thomas. The monotony of her life as an academic's wife gives way to the excitement and danger of an illicit affair and Emily is torn between her overwhelming desire and her deeply ingrained sense of responsibility. The behaviour patterns which have been bred into her ultimately prove too strong to be cast aside. Her simple statement that she is 'used to being married' characteristically downplays her desperate struggle to reconcile personal needs with a strong conviction that promises and com-mitments are sacred.

Turner, Fred
Foreign Affairs, 1984
Alison Lurie

A troubled marriage, a less than secure job and rotten weather all conspire to make this visitor to London miserable and self-absorbed. Setbacks in life surprise and irritate Fred and it is a painful experience for him to discover that everyone is vulnerable and that vulnerability can make even the charming and attractive person selfish and cruel. Finding no ultimate satisfaction in the cynical world of the rich and famous, he is saved from despair by a natural optimism which only needs a little encouragement to reassert itself.

Turner, Jim → Flint, Captain

Turner, Job
Recovery, 1988
Stanley Middleton

A cool-headed and pragmatic school headmaster, whose life has been cut in two by the tragic death of his wife. His biblical forename reflects a somewhat ironic stance on suffering, and he begins to experience an uneasy thaw in his cold detachment when he starts to tutor Susan, a brilliant young pianist.

Turner, Mary
The Grass is Singing, 1950
Doris Lessing

She is neurotic and deeply unhappy. Her childhood was marred by her mother's personal bitterness, and she has grown up afraid of men, and of adult life in general. She mourns a past that never was, and is full of hopes and dreams for what never will be. She is incapable of relating to others at a deep level, least of all to her husband, DICK TURNER. Unable to rid herself of her mother's influence or her own inner turmoil, she is doomed.

Turner, Nat
The Confessions of Nat Turner, 1967
William Styron

Historical leader of a slave rebellion in Southampton county, Virginia, in 1831, he has a powerful, almost biblical vision and rhetoric that only partially conceal his inadequacy as an individual. Embittered by a broken promise to set him free, Nat is also haunted by sexual fantasies (largely of miscegenation) that are only uncertainly converted into messianic liberationism. He is a controversial literary character, whose recreation by a white Southerner has long been a point of contention among American blacks.

Turner, Robbie
Atonement, 2001
Ian McEwan

The novel opens in 1934, when Robbie, the son of the housekeeper at the Tallises' large country home in Surrey, has recently graduated from Cambridge. Although his education has been funded by the Tallises, he is not entirely accepted by them socially; however, he succeeds in winning the love of CECILIA TALLIS. When her sister BRIONY TALLIS falsely accuses him of assaulting Lola, her cousin, in the gardens, he is deeply aggrieved yet accepts his fate of imprisonment and rejection by the family. Cecilia honours his integrity by standing by him. Having served his sentence, he joins the army and witnesses horrific events in France and at Dunkirk.

Turner, Sam
A Small Town in Germany, 1968
John Le Carré
With a Yorkshire voice and a policeman's walk, Turner is not easily identified as a Fellow of St Anthony's, Oxford, or a Foreign Office special operative. He is chasing a vanished archivist from the British Embassy in Bonn. In the course of this he (correctly) disbelieves everyone in sight. He is deliberately rude ('You make me puke') and is not put off by beatings-up. For that matter, he hits women gratuitously in pursuit of the secrets he eventually finds.

Turnlung
Daughter Buffalo, 1972
Janet Frame
A New Zealand writer, past the peak of his powers and exiled in New York City, which seems to him like a dream-like landscape of death that challenges the imagination in the most direct way. Through his contact with the young physician DR TALBOT EDELMAN, he comes to recognize that the power to create is in fact the only one left to him.

Turp, Ethel
My Wife Ethel, 1939
Damon Runyon
Dizzy and delightful, she is a feisty New Yorker who shamelessly winds her husband JOE TURP round her finger and manipulates the world with her feminine wiles. Her conversation is lively and topical, but peppered with non-sequiturs, and she interprets events through an amusing filter of her own illogicality.

Turp, Joe
My Wife Ethel, 1939
Damon Runyon
Joe is an archetypal young man about New York: a snappy dresser, with an interest in all things sporting, and a delight in all things female, especially his adored wife, ETHEL TURP. Eager to please, keen to keep the peace, he is gentle, considerate and rather old-fashioned, leading him to recoil at some of the more 'modern' attitudes expressed by his vivacious wife.

Turpine
The Faerie Queene, 1590–6
Sir Edmund Spenser
Malicious, cruel and savage, he is the enemy of SIR CALIDORE, THE KNIGHT OF COURTESY and SIR CALEPINE, Knights of Courtesy. He is a man of great strength and manhood, but rather than turn these to good use he mocks all errant knights. He is terrible and stern because he was once beaten in a battle by such a knight. He will not help a lady in distress, neither will he show common hospitality. He believes that if knights are spiritual and valiant, they do not need others to be courteous to them.

Turton, Mr
A Passage to India, 1924
E M Forster
A man who has spent 25 years enforcing British rule in India, he has been the Collector of the Chandrapore District for six years and is regarded as leader of the local English community. Part of the ruling élite, he displays a commendable degree of tact and discretion and may once have shown a more compassionate face to the native populace. Now, he dutifully pays service to the notion of fair play whilst firmly committed to maintaining the status quo and discouraging any form of fraternization that might bridge the gap between rulers and subjects.

Turvey
Turvey: a Military Picaresque, 1949, reprinted as *The Kootenay Highlander*, 1960
Earle Birney
A simple Canadian soldier, spiritually akin to PRIVATE ANGELO and Hašek's Good Soldier Svejk, but less calculating than either. He accepts the military machine and its absurd values at face value and in doing so carves a small area of independence for himself.

Turveydrop, Mr
Bleak House, 1853
Charles Dickens
Considered a 'model of deportment', he is a fat, conceited, elderly gentleman who models himself on George IV. He names his son 'Prince' in honour of the late king, patronizes everyone and, the epitome of selfishness, lives with his son and sponges off him.

Turveydrop, Prince
Bleak House, 1853
Charles Dickens
A poor but hard-working dancing-master, he is named after the Prince Regent, whom his father, MR TURVEYDROP, venerates. He marries CAROLINE JELLYBY, who helps to make his dancing-school successful.

Tusher, Mrs Thomas
The History of Henry Esmond, Esquire, 1852
W M Thackeray
The bishop's wife, she is a kinswoman of the CASTLEWOOD family and thus doubly convinced of her importance. 'She had been waiting-woman to her ladyship in the late lord's time, and, having her soul in that business, took naturally to it when the Viscountess of Castlewood returned to inhabit her father's house'. She is, in many respects, a later version of the domineering MRS BUTE CRAWLEY in *Vanity Fair*.

Tweedledum and Tweedledee
Through the Looking-Glass, and What Alice Found There, 1872
Lewis Carroll
Tweedledum and Tweedledee, two funny fat little men, live in the same house but have separate signposts to it. One has 'Dum' on his collar, the other 'Dee'. If one makes a statement, the other says 'Contrariwise', even if there is no disagreement. ALICE remembers the nursery rhyme about the two having a battle but they seem friendly enough and dance with her and sing, until Tweedledum sees his broken rattle and blames his twin. They put on armour – bolsters, coal-scuttles, dish-covers, blankets and hearthrugs – helped by Alice, but when the sky

grows dark at the approach of the crow, they take to their heels and run away.

Twelvemough, Mr
A Traveller from Altruria, 1894
William Dean Howells

A popular novelist who encounters the traveller MR HOMOS at a seaside resort. He quickly recognizes that Altrurian principles would put him out of a job by removing people's need for consolatory fictions and wish-fulfilments.

Twinkleton, Miss
The Mystery of Edwin Drood, 1870
Charles Dickens

Principal of the Nun's House, the Seminary for Young Ladies in Cloisterham where ROSA BUD and HELENA LANDLESS are pupils. By day a schoolmistress, she spends the evenings discussing her own youthful romances and 'the tenderer scandal of Cloisterham' with her companion and assistant, Mrs Tisher, 'a deferential widow with a weak back, a chronic sigh, and a suppressed voice'. When Rosa flees to London, Miss Twinkleton becomes her chaperone in the lodging house of MRS BILLICKIN.

Twist, Oliver
Oliver Twist, 1838
Charles Dickens

An orphan, born in the workhouse where his mother dies, he is farmed out to a branch workhouse and ill-treated by the cruel Mrs Mann. Aged nine, he is removed by MR BUMBLE to be apprenticed to MR SOWERBERRY, from whom he runs away and becomes enmeshed in FAGIN's den of child pickpockets. JACK DAWKINS (the Artful Dodger) teaches him the trade, NANCY treats him kindly and BILL SIKES tries to make him a criminal. Proved innocent after his false arrest for thieving, he is rescued from the world of crime and vice by MR BROWNLOW, MRS MAYLIE and ROSE MAYLIE. They discover that he is the nephew of Rose and the natural son of Brownlow's old friend, and that he has been cheated of his inheritance by the plotting of his half-brother, EDWARD LEEFORD (known as 'Monks'). His inheritance is restored with the help of Brownlow, who adopts him as his son, and he lives happily among his circle of new friends. Throughout his adventures, he remains innocent and uncorrupted.

Twitcher, Jemmy
The Beggar's Opera, 1728
John Gay

One of CAPTAIN MACHEATH's band of London low-lifers, alongside such names as 'Crook-fingered Jack'. We meet his crew of fellow-thieves enjoying brandy, wine and tobacco in a Newgate Tavern. Jemmy has no inhibitions about his trade, declaring: 'Are we more dishonest than the rest of mankind? What we win, gentlemen, is our own, by the law of arms and the right of conquest'.

Twombley, Lady Kitty
The Cabinet Minister, 1890
Arthur Wing Pinero

A country-girl when she married SIR JULIAN TWOMBLEY, Kitty Twombley is now a London society hostess and her husband a cabinet minister. She is 'handsome, bright, good-looking', a woman of wit and almost indomitable spirit. Socially ambitious for her husband and grown-up unmarried children, she is frivolous and ostentatious but nevertheless lacks snobbery. She does, though, owe several thousand pounds to MRS FANNY GAYLUSTRE and JOSEPH LEBANON, something she keeps secret from Sir Julian. She finally promises to reform and become 'a sober, wise, happy and contented woman!'

Twombley, Sir Julian
The Cabinet Minister, 1890
Arthur Wing Pinero

Aristocratic but indecisive and detesting the browbeating and heckling at the House, Sir Julian is hardly cabinet minister material, and has only attained such eminence through the ambition of his wife, LADY KITTY TWOMBLEY. In fact, the press calls him 'The Square Peg' and the Opposition regards him as a matador regards a bull in the arena. In his mid-fifties, he would prefer the peace of a gentlemanly life in the country: in the end, he achieves it.

Twyborn, Eadie
The Twyborn Affair, 1979
Patrick White

The wife of JUSTICE TWYBORN, and mother of EDDIE TWYBORN, Eadie is bisexual and turns, occasionally and thankfully, away from her husband and into 'that other life' with her dearest friend, Joan Golson. In later years, though, Eadie has become too frequently drunk and maudlin. She has been a contradictory mother to Eddie: sometimes enveloping him in an almost suffocating love but just as often ignoring him. Naturally possessive, she has, with age, become aggressive. Versions of Eadie reappear in the novel as EUDOXIA VATATZES, Eddie Twyborn and EADITH TRIST.

Twyborn, Eddie
The Twyborn Affair, 1979
Patrick White

Eddie appears during the course of the novel in various guises, one being EUDOXIA VATATZES, the others EADIE TWYBORN and EADITH TRIST. This device is partly an attempt by the author to allow his character, paradoxically loving and contemptuous, tender and cruel, to be seen from various perspectives, both by others and by him/herself. In the second part of the book, Lieutenant Eddie Twyborn returns to Australia from World War I, hoping to rediscover his family, Eadie and JUSTICE TWYBORN. Having found his own emotional uncertainties reflected in his parents, Eddie ventures into the bush. Like Eudoxia, he is self-evading, using his journey not so much to reclaim his past as to escape 'from himself into a landscape'. His imperative is to search for an emotional and spiritual home; his destiny is to fail to find it.

Twyborn, Justice
The Twyborn Affair, 1979
Patrick White

Married, for better and usually worse, to EADIE

TWYBORN, and the father of EDDIE TWYBORN, he is an eminent circuit judge. An austere, watchful, undemonstrative man, he is often unnerved by his unpredictable wife and awed by his son, so much so that he distances himself from them.

Twysden, Agnes
The Adventures of Philip, 1861–2
W M Thackeray

One of the standard rites of passage for a Thackeray hero is to be rejected by his fiancée when it is revealed that his fortune has evaporated. PHILIP FIRMIN's cousin Agnes fulfils that role, and does so with a squeamishness and delicate sensitivity all her own.

Tybalt
Romeo and Juliet, 1591–6
William Shakespeare

A swaggering bully who delights in violence and hates anything to do with the Montagues, Tybalt is controlled with extreme difficulty by CAPULET. He sees insults where none exist, and uses his excellent swordsmanship to spread fear among his enemies. Yet he is obviously held in great respect, even affection, by his kinsfolk.

Tyghe, Dominic
Amy's View, 1997
David Hare

The husband of AMY THOMAS and son-in-law of ageing actress ESME ALLEN, Dominic is ambitious, self-important, ruthless and practical, a man who considers the hurt he might inflict upon others only when the damage has been done. Disparaging the theatre, which Esme adores, as 'no longer relevant', he becomes a successful member of the modern media hierarchy, making a critically acclaimed action film, the violence of which Esme condemns as incomprehensibly destructive. The loss of Amy in the process causes momentary atonement.

Typist, the
'The Fire Sermon', in *The Waste Land*, 1922
T S Eliot

Less real, somehow, and no less passive than the piles of underthings – 'combinations .../ Stockings, slippers, camisoles, and stays' – scattered around the untidy room where she entertains 'the young man carbuncular' to tea and casual sex on the put-me-up divan.

Tyrold, Camilla
Camilla, or A Picture of Youth, 1796
Fanny Burney

A lively and beautiful young woman who is the daughter of a respectable but far from wealthy rector in Hampshire, in whose house she lives with her sisters, brother and cousins. The central interest in her story concerns her love for her rather cautious and calculating suitor, and the outcome is teasingly delayed over the length of the novel by myriad plots and misunderstandings, many of which are designed to reveal the small failings and manifest virtues of Camilla herself in her passage from youth to womanhood.

Tyrone, Edmund
Long Day's Journey Into Night, 1956
Eugene O'Neill

Consumptive son of MARY and JAMES TYRONE and younger brother of JAMIE TYRONE, Edmund has travelled 'all over the map as a sailor' and has immersed himself in the works of Nietzsche, Engels, Baudelaire, Swinburne and others in a forlorn effort to lose himself and escape from the grip of family tragedy. Sensitive and nervy, Edmund states pensively that he will 'always be a stranger who never feels at home, who does not really want and is not really wanted, who can never belong, who must always be a little in love with death!'

Tyrone, James
Long Day's Journey Into Night, 1956
Eugene O'Neill

Gifted actor, husband of MARY TYRONE and father of JAMIE and EDMUND TYRONE, James Tyrone's insurmountable fear of poverty causes him to make disastrous life decisions that bring immense suffering upon each member of his family. A good man at heart, he drinks in order to obliterate the torment of knowing that he cannot go back in time and prevent all the subsequent regret, remorse and anguish.

Tyrone, Jamie
Long Day's Journey Into Night, 1956
Eugene O'Neill

Wracked with guilt and self-loathing, and haunted by the death of his baby brother Eugene Tyrone, Jamie is the cynical and heartbroken first-born son of MARY and JAMES TYRONE. Seen as a failed student and as a failed Broadway actor by his father, Jamie sees himself as a failure as a brother and a son. He seeks solace and oblivion in 'booze and whores' but finds only that he cannot escape from the unmanageable thoughts that keep the past forever with him.

Tyrone, Mary
Long Day's Journey Into Night, 1956
Eugene O'Neill

Beautiful and coquettish, Mary supposedly plans to become a nun until her life is turned upside down by the talented young actor, JAMES TYRONE. Introduced to morphine after complications following the birth of their younger son, EDMUND TYRONE, Mary is transformed from child of innocence to lonely 'dope fiend' and can never quite retrieve her faith and find the strength to break free from her addiction.

Tyrrel
Caleb Williams, 1794
William Godwin

Tyrrel represents the legal power of the ruling class. He is a wealthy landlord who tyrannizes a tenant farmer, Hawkins, and his family. He uses the law to destroy Hawkins's property and send his son to jail, and then he maliciously prosecutes his own cousin – an act which eventually leads to her death. By the strict code of English law, nothing Tyrrel accomplishes is illegal and thus he symbolizes the complete moral bankruptcy and corruption of the existing legal system. Tyrrel can blamelessly declare 'I did nothing but what the law allows'.

Tyrrel, Frank, originally **Francis Martigny**
St Ronan's Well, 1823
Sir Walter Scott

The illegitimate son of Lord Etherington and a Frenchwoman, Marie de Martigny, and the half-brother and bitter rival of Valentine Bulmer, EARL OF ETHERINGTON, whose original name he has been given. This young hero maintains a rather gruff distance from the chattering classes at the Well, concentrating on his sketches (which are clearly the work of a trained eye and hand) and on his fated mission to CLARA MOWBRAY.

Tyson, 'Paper'
The Cut-Rate Kingdom, 1980
Thomas Keneally

A veteran of Gallipoli, he becomes a newspaper journalist in the postwar years and wins the confidence of the Australian prime minister. His understanding of the mechanics of war lends him an important perspective on the events of World War II, during which Australia appears constantly under threat of invasion by the Japanese.

Uberife, Eneberi, or Gilbert
Efuru, 1966
Flora Nwapa

EFURU OGENE's second husband, he is called Eneberi by Efuru and Gilbert by his former school-friends. Eneberi is 'a warm-hearted lively and jovial man' and, in many ways, a good husband to Efuru. He is, however, dishonest and secretive, not telling her when he has a son with another woman or that he has been to jail. It is Eneberi's failure to trust Efuru that finally ends their marriage.

Udomo, Michael
A Wreath for Udomo, 1956
Peter Abrahams

A clever young African, plucked from village life and educated first by missionaries and thereafter in London, where he appears 'haunted and lonely'. He acquires a new image of himself as the instrument of his people's freedom and returns to the fictional state of Panafrica to lead the powerful, populist Africa Freedom Party.

Ulalume, narrator of
'Ulalume – A Ballad', 1847
Edgar Allan Poe

The narrator wanders without recognizing the 'ghoul-haunted woodland of Weir', where once he had strolled with his beloved Ulalume, in 'days when my heart was volcanic'. Now his thoughts are 'palsied and sere' over the loss, which he remembers with tears of undiminished grief. He attempts to rally his wilting soul with thoughts of Hope and Beauty, but comes unwittingly upon his lost love's tomb where he had laid 'a dread burden' a year before, and his heart grows 'ashen and sober'.

Ulrica, also known as Urfried
Ivanhoe, 1819
Sir Walter Scott

The old crone of the turret at Torquilstone, she is the daughter of Torquil Wolfganger, CEDRIC THE SAXON's friend and comrade-in-arms. Brought low by abuse and neglect, and living under an assumed name, she has a soothsayer's gift that is almost submerged in bile and hatred of the Normans.

Ulrich, Crown Prince of Evarchia
Palace Without Chairs, 1978
Brigid Brophy

Heir to the throne of Evarchia, he is waiting for his father to drop off the perch, so that he and his bizarre family can take over his Ruritanian kingdom.

Ulysses
Troilus and Cressida, 1601/2
William Shakespeare

An old and respected leader of the Greek army, he is both practical and devious. He demonstrates a mixture of cunning and cynicism in his attempts to restore a measure of order and discipline among the Greek troops, which he believes is necessary for their success in war.

Ulysses
'Ulysses', 1842
Alfred Lord Tennyson

The Greek hero chafes at his idleness after the excitement of the Trojan War. Now advanced in years, he resolves to 'drink life to the lees' by setting off on new voyages with his former companions, still determined 'to strive, to seek, to find, and not to yield'.

Uma
The Beach of Falesá, 1892
Robert Louis Stevenson

A coy young inhabitant of Falesá, whose manner is 'quick and timid, like a child dodging a blow'. She is the subject of a superstitious island taboo and, as a result, no one dares trade with her husband, MR WILTSHIRE. At first depicted as no more than a stereotypical native girl – all simplicity and innocence – Uma soon shows enterprise in protecting her husband's interests, thus undermining the clichéd Western view of native peoples as 'noble savages'.

Una
The Faerie Queene, 1590–6
Sir Edmund Spenser

She represents truth in its purest and most virtuous form and embodies 'openness' in contrast to DUESSA. A beautiful virgin, descended from royal lineage, she is gentle, mild and not open to temptation. She rides a milk-white horse, is religiously faithful and can tame wild animals with her innocence. Her partner is REDCROSSE, THE KNIGHT OF HOLINESS.

Una
Puck of Pook's Hill, 1906
Rudyard Kipling

Sister of DAN, she is the fairy PUCK's other human confidante. She is given to scowls and to bouts of high-handed behaviour, but is otherwise good and kind and seems if anything quicker on the uptake than her more prosaic brother.

Uncle Tom

Uncle Tom's Cabin, or, Life Among the Lowly, 1851–2
Harriet Beecher Stowe

A middle-aged and very dark-skinned American slave, whose forbearance and mild manner earned him the respect of his masters and the contempt of later generations of Black American writers who turned his name into a by-word for passive accommodation. Believed to have been based on a real-life slave, Josiah Henson, Tom is nonetheless an idealized figure trapped by all too realistic circumstance as he is sold 'down the river' into ever harsher conditions. His piety and self-sacrifice, in particular his violent death, are unmistakably Christ-like. An uneducated man, he affects others by example rather than by any reasoned understanding of his own position.

Undershaft, Andrew

Major Barbara, 1905
George Bernard Shaw

A millionaire armaments manufacturer and father of BARBARA UNDERSHAFT, Undershaft sells weapons to anyone willing to pay his price. A pragmatic, elderly man, he is watchful, ruthless, powerful and benevolent to his workers. He also has formidable reserves of strength. Undershaft, who represents the Life Force, a vital, ex-hilarating power, understands that it can be used equally for good or evil, and that the one embodies some of the other. As a man who can build cannons but neither courage nor conviction, who can provide employment but cannot change society, Undershaft is a victim of his own success. Eventually, he lures ADOLPHUS CUSINS and his daughter into the business.

Undershaft, Barbara

Major Barbara, 1905
George Bernard Shaw

The energetic daughter of ANDREW UNDERSHAFT, Barbara is a major in the Salvation Army and works at the Army's West Ham shelter. Her inspiration comes from within herself and this tenacity, her father explains, is the Undershaft inheritance. Barbara represents evangelical Christianity in the trinity that includes the idealistic scepticism of ADOLPHUS CUSINS and the 'money and gunpowder' philosophy of her arms-manufacturer father. Having lost her religious faith, she finds another as a woman of action. She marries Cusins, who becomes Undershaft's successor, and together they resolve to convert the power of materialism into a force for social good.

Undershaft, Lady Britomart

Major Barbara, 1905
George Bernard Shaw

The estranged wife of ANDREW UNDERSHAFT, Lady Britomart summons her husband to her expensive Wilton Crescent home in order to discuss the future of their grown-up children, and so initiates the tactical contest of will between Undershaft and their daughter, BARBARA UNDERSHAFT. She is aged about 50, well-bred, well-mannered and amiable, but also reckless, outspoken and commandingly imperious: 'a very typical managing matron of the upper class'.

Underwood, Nettie

The Doctor's Family, 1863
Margaret Oliphant

Energetic, capable, with shining dark hair, Nettie captures the heart of DR EDWARD RIDER when she arrives at his home with her sister, SUSAN RIDER, brother-in-law FRED RIDER, and their troupe of children. Powerless to stir Susan and Fred, she can almost manage their noisy offspring to whom she is devoted. She likes the doctor but must look after the children, seeing herself as their only hope. She humours Susan by starting to pack for their return to Australia, but discovering that she is not needed, accepts the doctor's offer of marriage, so long as he will take Freddie, one of the children, also.

Uplandtowers, Earl of

'Barbara of the House of Grebe', in *A Group of Noble Dames*, 1891
Thomas Hardy

A selfish and repulsive character, he is none-theless devoted to his love, BARBARA GREBE, and never remarries after her death. A jealous and brutish man, with little sense of remorse, he has no broad vision of the world, being able to relate only to the needs of his own world. Basically insecure and afraid of facing up to reality, he believes he can will Barbara to love him. He has no concept of the complexity of human emotions, and no sympathy with those beyond his experiences. An ultimately sad figure, in typically Hardyesque fashion he is not without likeable qualities.

Uriel

Paradise Lost, 1667
John Milton

One of the seven archangels appointed to stand nearest GOD's throne. The 'Regent of the Sun', he is marked by a divine effulgence and acts as God's eyes throughout Creation; he is not so clear-sighted, though, as to see through SATAN's disguise.

Urizen

America, 1793
The First Book of Urizen, 1794
William Blake

The defender of 'law' and established power, promoter of 'Kings and Priests', Urizen is mad with the desire to control, to impose 'unity' upon creation. His is a 'pale religious lechery', divorced from imaginative life. Abstract and mysterious, Urizen employs his 'Net of Religion' to ensnare mankind because otherwise 'no flesh nor spirit could keep/His iron laws one moment'.

Ursley, Dame → Suddlechop, Ursula

Usher, Madeline

The Fall of the House of Usher, 1839
Edgar Allan Poe

The twin sister of RODERICK USHER, with whom she has always shared 'sympathies of a scarcely intelligible nature'. She is suffering from a strange apathy, a 'gradual wasting away of the person', and seems to be close to death. She falls into a cataleptic trance and is buried alive, but returns to fall upon Roderick and 'in her violent and now final death-agonies, bore him to the floor a corpse, and a victim to the terrors he had anticipated'.

Usher, Roderick
The Fall of the House of Usher, 1839
Edgar Allan Poe

The last male of the venerable Usher line. He has a pallid, cadaverous complexion, and suffers from excessive nervous agitation, acute bodily illness and mental disorder. He has long had an 'excessive and habitual' reserve, a 'peculiar sensibility of temperament' expressed in wild artistic creations, a 'morbid acuteness of the senses' which exaggerates all sensory impressions, and a 'want of moral energy'. After burying his seemingly dead sister, MADELINE USHER, his knowledge of her stirrings sets him on an ultimately fatal 'struggle with the grim phantasm, FEAR', and brings down the House of Usher.

Utterword, Lady Ariadne
Heartbreak House, 1916
George Bernard Shaw

Blonde and good-looking, Lady Ariadne is one of the daughters of CAPTAIN SHOTOVER (the other being HESIONE HUSHABYE). Married to Sir Hastings, a 'numskull' colonial governor of the British Empire, she has become a philistine accustomed to the trappings of imperial power. According to her, 'there are only two classes in good society in England: the equestrian classes and the neurotic classes'. She represents the antithesis of the tragic dreamers of Heartbreak House, the self-satisfied, snobbish, riding, hunting, church-going and Conservative inhabitants of Horseback Hall.

Utterword, Randall
Heartbreak House, 1916
George Bernard Shaw

Randall Utterword, a product of public school, university and the Foreign Office, has 'the engaging air of being young and unmarried, but on close inspection is found to be at least over forty'. He is petulant, jealous and childish. These miserable qualities are concentrated in his love for his sister-in-law, LADY ARIADNE UTTERWORD, a love as slavishly devotional as it is lacking in mature feeling.

Utz, Kaspar
Utz, 1988
Bruce Chatwin

As averse to museums as he is to the unstable political climate of 20th-century Prague, eccentric Utz guards with astonishing vehemence his huge collection of valuable Meissen porcelain. Disillusioned with the lifestyles of both eastern and western Europe, he instead finds his 'reality' within the world of his graceful figurines, but becomes obsessed to the point of melancholy by his 'porcelain-sickness' and passion for opera singers.

V

V, 1963
Thomas Pynchon

Though she is associated with the English imperialist aristocrat Victoria Wren and with the glass-eyed Vera Meroving, V is more of an abstract female principle than an actual character. She is mentioned in an obscure and cabbalistic 19th-century manuscript, but appears to turn up in a plethora of guises (all initialled V) at every significant cusp of European history. The impossibility of definitively tracking her down is encapsulated in the shape of the letter V itself, which expresses the convergence of parallel lines at infinity, and thus makes a point about the book's strange bifurcated plot.

Vag

The Big Money, 1936, part of the *U.S.A.* trilogy, 1938
John Dos Passos

Making only a very fleeting, but telling, appearance, the young vagrant hitching at the side of the road is a testimony to the forgotten by-products of the American Dream. Lonely, hungry, homeless and jobless, he stands in frighteningly stark contrast to the rich, gluttonous businessmen in the aeroplane overhead, and there is a distinct lack of hope for any brighter future for him at all.

Vaillant, Father Joseph

Death Comes for the Archbishop, 1927
Willa Cather

He is so closely modelled on his historical original, Father Joseph Machebeuf, Vicar-General of the diocese of New Mexico, as to be almost a documentary rendition. 'One of the first things a stranger decided upon meeting Father Joseph was that the Lord had made few uglier men. He was short, skinny, bow-legged from a life on horseback, and his countenance had little to recommend it but kindliness and vivacity'.

Vaizey, Clare

The Watch Tower, 1966
Elizabeth Harrower

Strong and rebellious, Clare fights against the oppressive circumstances in which she lives. Unable to withstand the emotional blackmail of her sister LAURA SHAW, she withdraws into an internal world of books and thoughts. Her early attempts at escape fail. Working in an office, Clare finds it difficult to relate to other people in spite of being popular. It is only by helping a young man escape from the manipulative control of her brother-in-law, FELIX SHAW, that she discovers a way to freedom.

Valancourt

The Mysteries of Udolpho, 1794
Ann Radcliffe

The manly grace of Valancourt, encountered by EMILY ST AUBERT and her father in the Pyrenees, is a measure of his mind. On leave from his regiment, he is dressed as a hunter but has no desire to kill for sport. Modest, he has loved Emily from afar and gladly aids the travellers. When she is taken to Toulouse, he follows and wins her aunt's favour when he is found to be rich as well as noble. He is in the background during Emily's terrors at Udolpho, ready to help, although the victim of cruel slanders.

Valentine

Two Gentlemen of Verona, c.1590
William Shakespeare

Valentine is one of the 'two gentlemen', the other being PROTEUS. A principal theme of the play is their emotional maturing. Both are idealists, and both fall in love with SILVIA. But while Proteus resorts to betrayal in a vigorous attempt to win her, treachery is not part of Valentine's nature. He is faithful, but hardly the romantic hero: he tends to stand about, transfixed by her beauty, and it is Silvia who initiates the affair. Even after their attempted elopement, his banishment and various adventures in the forest, he considers relinquishing Silvia to Proteus in order to maintain their own friendship. Only JULIA's fainting precipitates a happy ending.

Valentine

You Never Can Tell, 1897
George Bernard Shaw

An impoverished young dentist, aged about 30, Valentine is poised on the threshold of his career: at the beginning of the play he has just extracted his first tooth, belonging to DOLLY CLANDON. Although his prospects are good and he is not without gravity, Valentine is essentially a humorist. He has no surname and therefore he alone in the play has no past. His courting of GLORIA CLANDON, Dolly's elder sister, becomes a tactical assault upon the views of the New Woman by what he claims to be the 'thoroughly modern' method of confessing his emotions.

Valentine, Basil

The Recognitions, 1955
William Gaddis

A dilettante art critic and spoiled priest, he bears

the pseudonym of a famous alchemist and is much concerned with turning base daubs into marketable currency. 'There were moments when [he] looked sixteen, days when he looked sixty … a face strong, unsympathetic, bearing all of the force which sympathy lacks'.

Valentine, Shirley
Shirley Valentine, 1986
Willy Russell

Shirley is 42, a Liverpool housewife. Her children have left home and her husband, Joe, ignores her. She talks, therefore, to the kitchen walls and, in a burst of liberating energy, goes on holiday to Greece with a female friend. 'Most of us die before we're dead and what kills us is the weight of all this unused life', she observes. 'Who would miss me?' she reflects. 'Me'. Shirley is philosophical, angry, vivacious, volatile, repressed; hers is an almost wasted, provincial life; her holiday offers the possibility of fulfilment, or at least of a distraction from appalling domesticity.

Valento, Velma
Farewell, My Lovely, 1940
Raymond Chandler

Velma, a nightclub singer said to be 'cute as lace pants', has been missing for more than five years when her former lover, MOOSE MALLOY, emerges from jail and begins his search for her. When discovered, she is found to have reinvented herself completely, giving up her identity and betraying those who love her in order to reach a position of wealth and privilege. She is a classic femme fatale.

Vallar, Marcus
The Message to the Planet, 1989
Iris Murdoch

The enigmatic, egotistical object of ALFRED LUDENS's veneration and obsessive quest. He was a mathematical infant prodigy and teenage genius, and after being away for years and seemingly raises an old friend from the dead. He is so strange and charismatic, so complex in his metaphysical 'deep thought', that he appears to be pursuing something of planetary importance. However, he is described by a former friend as 'that fascist anti-Christ' and 'a Sphinx without a secret', and Ludens increasingly fears he may be insane.

Valmont, Le Vicomte de
Les Liaisons dangereuses, 1985
Christopher Hampton

Le Vicomte de Valmont is 'strikingly elegant', a late 18th-century nobleman with an enviable reputation of sexual conquest, choosing and winning only the most interesting and beautiful women. Sharply intelligent, cynical, devious, independent and idealistic, he has sexual ambition without the tiresome burden of moral scruple; until, that is, he falls in love with Madame de Tourvel, a young virgin he had intended simply to deflower. Genuine love is his downfall, vanity and happiness being incompatible.

Valsen, Private Red
The Naked and the Dead, 1948
Norman Mailer

'In silhouette his profile consisted almost entirely of a large blob of a nose and a long low-slung jaw, a combination which made his face seem boiled and angry'. His early life is bounded by the looming Montana hills and the Company mine. With the Depression, he enters the 'hobo jungle', wandering America. He stands as representative for much of the brutalized sentimentality of 1930s 'proletarian' literature.

Vanamee
The Octopus: A Story of California, 1901
Frank Norris

A shepherd, 'he lived his life in the unknown … in the desert, in the mountains, throughout all the vast and vague Southwest, solitary, strange. Three, four, five years passed … He had melted off into the surface shimmer of the desert, into the mirage', only to reappear unexpectedly, an enigmatic, almost visionary presence, college-educated and highly articulate, but marked by tragedy. Sixteen years before, Vanamee's lover had been attacked and raped by a mysterious stranger; the girl died and Vanamee's unassuaged anger turned inward.

Vance, Philo
The Benson Murder Case, 1926, et seq
S S Van Dine (Willard Huntington Wright)

Hyper-educated and super-sophisticated, art connoisseur and amateur sleuth Philo Vance has a seemingly inexhaustible fund of detailed knowledge about obscure specialisms (from numismatics and Egyptology to dog breeding) which he draws on in solving his cases. Combined with his languid and affected manner ('pon my word' and 'don't y'know' are characteristic verbal tics), this makes him a sort of parodic combination of SHERLOCK HOLMES and LORD PETER WIMSEY. Ogden Nash famously summed up the reaction of many readers in his epigram: 'Philo Vance / Needs a kick in the pance'.

Van Der Horst, Mabel
Turbott Wolfe, 1925
William Plomer

A very independent-minded white South African woman, particularly for her time, Mabel Van Der Horst boldly pursues her future husband, the Zulu Zachary Msomi. Appalled by racialist attitudes, she gives this answer to a narrow-minded parson: 'My good man, there is no native question. It isn't a question. It's an answer'.

van der Linden, Charlie
On Green Dolphin Street, 2001
Sebastian Faulks

Charlie first appears to his future wife as 'ebullient, clear-eyed, certain he could reinvent the world', but then the world disappoints him. Disillusioned, and the victim of blackmail, he seeks solace in alcohol, becoming increasingly dependent on his wife. An English diplomat working in Washington at the height of the Cold War, his continual absences from home, plus his wife's blossoming affair, mean he is 'in trouble, not just with his health, but with his life'.

van der Linden, Mary
On Green Dolphin Street, 2001
Sebastian Faulks

Having lost her fiancé in World War II, Mary believes passion is behind her but finds love and fulfilment in her marriage to CHARLIE VAN DER LINDEN, a diplomat. A doting wife and mother, the 40-year-old Englishwoman provides much-needed stability for her husband. However, the death of her mother and the arrival of journalist FRANK RENZO in Washington throw her life into turmoil. When her husband succumbs to a nervous collapse in Moscow, Mary has to travel behind the Iron Curtain to fetch him home and resolve the future of all three characters.

van der Merwe, Nicolaas
A Chain of Voices, 1982, originally published in Afrikaans as *Houd-den-bek*, 1982
André Brink

A wealthy 19th-century Afrikaner farmer in the Cape of Good Hope, he is murdered by his chief hand, GALANT, when his promises of freedom and equality are not honoured. Though outwardly liberal, he is guilty of a profound double standard.

Van Der Valk, Piet
Love in Amsterdam, 1962, et seq
Nicolas Freeling

Inspector and later Commisaris in the Amsterdam police, whose imaginative non-conformity solves edgy social crimes with irresoluble moral undertones. Married to the French Arlette, he brings a very European instinct to detection: his breadth of experience in food, culture and psychology involves him personally in his cases. Whether dealing with old Nazis, street gangs or bereaved families, his despairing sense of natural justice carries him through.

Vandover
Vandover and the Brute, 1914
Frank Norris

A brilliant young San Francisco artist and socialite, who is reduced to virtual beggary by a short career of heedless sensuality, drunkenness and gambling. For a time only, he remains in control of 'the brute'. 'He was its master, and only on rare occasions did he permit himself to gratify its demands, feeding its abominable hunger from that part of him which he knew to be the purest, the cleanest and the best'.

Vane, Harriet
Strong Poison, 1930, et seq
Dorothy L Sayers

Although lacking conventional beauty, Harriet Vane is said to possess a 'really remarkable face', a 'curious deep voice' and a 'steady gaze'. A writer of detective novels, she is first encountered when she stands accused of murdering her lover. She is acquitted, thanks to the efforts of LORD PETER WIMSEY, who then asks her to marry him. Emotionally scarred by the events that have taken place, she refuses, anxious that their union would be based on gratitude rather than love. Highly educated, she later proves herself Wimsey's intellectual equal and the couple are eventually married.

Vane, Lady (the Lady of Quality)
The Adventures of Peregrine Pickle, 1751, bowdlerized edition 1758
Tobias Smollett

A beautiful benefactress, based on Frances Anne Hawes, whose explanation of her own up-and-down existence is that 'I have been unhappy, *because I loved, and was a woman*'. There were rumours that Smollett, who interpolates her thinly disguised memoirs much as Fielding included the story of The Man on the Hill in *Tom Jones*, published Lady Vane's memoirs with Hawes's permission and at her dictation.

Vane, Lady Isobel
East Lynne, 1861
Mrs Henry Wood

The heroine of the most famous melodramatic novel of the 19th century, Lady Isobel's nature partly reflects her surname. She is vain, passionate, impetuous; everything of which Mrs Wood vigorously disapproved. Having married Carlyle, a morally high-minded lawyer, Lady Isobel overhears him conversing with another woman, leaps to the wrong conclusion and 'in a moment of passion' submits to the advances of Levison, a former lover. She pays the price. Carlyle divorces her, and she is disfigured in a train accident. Disguised as Madame Vine, she returns to East Lynne, the Carlyle home, as governess to her own children. One of them dies in her arms, but her anguished cry of 'Dead! Dead! And never called me mother!' comes not from the novel but from a hugely successful Victorian stage adaptation.

Vaneleigh, Judas Griffin
The Tilted Cross, 1961
Hal Porter

A formerly well-known artist and writer, transported to Van Diemen's Land (Tasmania) for forgery (and suspected of murder). After nine years in captivity he has been released; his emotions purged by suffering, he is now an 'elegant defiant husk', still talking in a high-flown 'rococo style'. He protects himself from the past and present by his detachment, but retains his high artistic standards. His warnings to QUEELY SHEILL of the dangers of humane feelings are in vain.

van Groenwegel, Hubertus
The Children of Kaywana, 1952, et seq
Edgar Mittelholzer

A cruel and amoral Dutch planter in Guyana, he establishes a minor dynasty based entirely on his aggressive personal authority and on his innate ability to guess the weaknesses in those who come up against him. Though contemptible, he has an impressive self-confidence.

Van Helsing, Abraham
Dracula, 1897
Bram Stoker

An eminent Dutch medical man, he is an expert vampire hunter, and knows the full horror of their activities intimately. He reveals 'true grit, and he improves under strain that would kill a weaker nature'. Despite his fear and revulsion at the fearsome deeds he is forced to commit in eradicating such evil, deeds contrary to his own nature and calling, he nerves himself to his 'wild work' of destruction by 'thoughts of other dead, and the living over whom hung such a pall of fear'.

van Horne, Darryl
The Witches of Eastwick, 1984
John Updike

The new tenant of the big house at Eastwick, he becomes the focus of the local coven's sexual fantasies and antagonisms. Handsome and potent, he is half-man, half-devil.

Van Swieten, Ghysbrecht
The Cloister and the Hearth, 1861
Charles Reade

The burgomaster of Tergou, he is one of the chief instigators of the plot which separates GERARD from MARGARET BRANDT. He is a thoroughly unpleasant old man who is 'a notorious miser, and looked one generally'. He is rich, but is 'wretched in his wealth', since he is haunted by remorse over having acquired his opulence through cheating the Brandts of their rightful inheritance many years before.

Van Tassel, Katrine
'The Legend of Sleepy Hollow', 1820
Washington Irving

Possessed of 'beauty and great expectations', this only daughter of a substantial Dutch farmer in the New York State hills is the cause of much puzzlement in her many admirers. She sings in the church choir and wears a combination of old and new fashions, all of which suit her. 'Plump as a partridge' and something of a coquette, she secretly encourages BROM BONES's uncouth gallantries, but flirts with the preposterous ICHABOD CRANE, which leads to the latter's downfall.

van Vlaanderen, Pieter
Too Late the Phalarope, 1953
Alan Paton

The novel's central character, he is an Afrikaner war hero who, as an enlightened policeman and rugby player, is idolized by both black and white communities. However, his life and marriage have been blighted by his father's cruel negativity and he enters into a relationship with a black woman that brings scandal down on the family.

Varden, Dolly
Barnaby Rudge, 1841
Charles Dickens

The daughter of GABRIEL VARDEN and his wife, Martha, she is 'the very impersonation of good-humour and blooming beauty'. She is devoted to her father and supports him in domestic disputes with Mrs Varden and MISS MIGGS. A coquette, she causes SIMON TAPPERTIT to fall in love with her, and her sweetheart, JOE WILLET, to enlist. On the instructions of MR GASHFORD, she and her friend, EMMA HAREDALE, are abducted during the Gordon Riots. The pair are rescued by MR GEOFFREY HAREDALE, EDWARD CHESTER and Joe Willet, and she and Joe later marry.

Varden, Gabriel
Barnaby Rudge, 1841
Charles Dickens

A locksmith, he is jolly and honest, and an upholder of law and order in the Gordon Riots. His daughter, DOLLY VARDEN, is devoted to him, but his home life is made miserable by the combined efforts of his contrary wife, Martha, a Protestant fanatic, and their servant, MISS MIGGS. He secretly helps BARNABY and MRS RUDGE, and intervenes to have Barnaby released from prison. He shows great courage against the mob at Newgate prison, actions which make his wife recognize his qualities, and, after the riots, domestic harmony is restored.

Vardoe/Lloyd, Maggie
Swamp Angel, 1954
Ethel Wilson

Undemonstrative and yet compassionate and caring, Maggie has great inner strength and resource. She is the 'still' complement of her equally strong but energetic friend NELL SEVERANCE. 'I know what I want. I've worked it all out and I know I can do it', she declares: her method is marked by a quiet confidence and a self-containment gained through the pain and humiliation of an early and inappropriate marriage.

Varek, Neda
Golconda, 1948, et seq
Vance Palmer

A gifted sculptress, she draws much of her inspiration from contact with the aboriginal inhabitants of the Queensland countryside. Her semi-mystical contact with the land stands in contrast to MACY DONOVAN's tough-minded, pragmatic materialism.

Varner, Jody
The Hamlet, 1940
William Faulkner

'About thirty, a prime bulging man, slightly thyroidic, who was not only unmarried but emanated a quality of invincible and inviolable bachelordom.' He manages all the family business for WILL VARNER, of whom he is the ninth of 16 children.

Varner, Will
The Hamlet, 1940
William Faulkner

The 'fountainhead if not of law at least of advice and suggestion to a countryside which would have repudiated the term constituency if they had ever heard it'. The owner of the Old Frenchman place, he is the chief financial power of the county, soon to be overtaken by the SNOPESes.

Varney, Richard
Kenilworth, 1821
Sir Walter Scott

A villainous cavalier, he is bold, plausible and exceptionally cunning. He is EDMUND TRESSILLIAN's enemy, and has played the part of a pander in arranging the secret contract that binds AMY ROBSART to ROBERT DUDLEY, EARL OF LEICESTER, raising the girl from a modest background to fortune and prominence.

Vasques
'Tis Pity She's a Whore, c.1631
John Ford

The faithful servant of SORANZO, Vasques is almost as ruthless as his employer. However, he is arguably more crafty, is a better judge of character and is, perhaps, morally superior to many of the characters on display. When Soranzo rejects his lover, Hippolita, in favour of ANNABELLA, Vasques protects his employer by foiling her revenge. Likewise, it is Vasques who discovers that Soranzo's intended bride is incestuously involved with her brother, GIOVANNI. When Giovanni kills Soranzo at the end of the play, the good servant performs his most faithful act by dispatching his master's murderer.

Vassilou, Rose
The Needle's Eye, 1972
Margaret Drabble

Both Rose and SIMON CAMISH have attempted to cut themselves off from their roots and remake themselves: in Rose's words, to 'arrest the course of nature'. While Camish has craved the material trappings of success, Rose opts for self-denial, believing that it is easier for a camel to pass through a needle's eye than for the rich to attain the kingdom of heaven. She withdraws from her husband and children to live in a poor area and gives herself to theatrical gestures of self-absorption and self-sacrifice. She is selfish and self-pitying but convinces herself she is compassionate. At the end, she compromises, returning to her husband.

Vasu
The Man-Eater of Malgudi, 1961
R K Narayan

A skilled taxidermist and NATARAJ's unwelcome guest. He has come to Malgudi because the Mempi Forest there has a plentiful supply of the animals, reptiles and birds which he illicitly shoots then stuffs and exports, claiming cynically that his methods of preserving wildlife are better than those of the conservationists. Huge, bull-necked and hammer-fisted, he was previously a strongman in a travelling show, and displays a tigerish manner and sublime indifference to everyone else's rights and opinions. As Nataraj sadly observes, accommodating him is like having 'a middle-aged man-eater' on his premises, with all its unpredictable savagery and strength.

Vatatzes, Eudoxia
The Twyborn Affair, 1979
Patrick White

The 'daughter, ward, wife, mistress – whatever' of Angelos Vatatzes, a man who believes himself to be descended from Byzantine emperors, the androgynous Eudoxia idles away the days with her companion in the unkempt garden of a cottage near St Meyeul. A version of EADIE TWYBORN, EDDIE TWYBORN and EADITH TRIST, who appear in other parts of the novel, Eudoxia is young, lithe, romantically mysterious and self-evading. Chafing at the constrictions which Vatatzes's all-encompassing adoration places upon her, she deliberates suicide, yet lacks the resolve to encounter such finality. It becomes apparent that she is maintaining a posture. Joan Golson, a rich and bisexual Australian on vacation, finds herself drawn to Eudoxia, yet it seems that she is really attracted not to her femininity but to her maleness.

Vathek, Caliph
Vathek: An Arabian Tale, 1786
William Beckford

The ten-minute egg of hard-boiled orientalism. The Caliph of Samarah, he can kill a man with a single glance; in his lust for ultimate experience, he sacrifices 50 children to the Devil and travels to Istakar with the beautiful Nouronihar before realizing, too late, that his sensual pride has only guaranteed him destruction and damnation.

Vaughan, Barbara
The Mandelbaum Gate, 1965
Muriel Spark

This English spinster and teacher is prim, neat and cool, but also dark and intense; the daughter of a Jewish mother and an Anglican father, she is a Catholic convert. She worries about sin and morality and applies high standards to her behaviour, but she is irritated when others assume that she is innocent. Her Jewish ancestry puts her in danger when she crosses into Jordan during a pilgrimage to the Holy Land, but she carries on, so that a British diplomat helping her will see her as a 'good sport'.

Vaughan, Clarissa
The Hours, 1998
Michael Cunningham

She is a 52-year-old New Yorker, nicknamed 'Mrs Dalloway' by her one-time lover, the poet Richard Brown. She lives a literary life, working as a publisher's editor, but sees herself as 'a meager spirit, too conventional'. She is busy organizing a party in Richard's honour, while balancing the demands of her live-in partner, Sally, and her daughter, Julia. She recognizes powerful disappointment with her life, and fear that everything in it is anticlimactic compared to the moment years ago when she and Richard were in love.

Vaughn, Granny (Elvira Jordan)
Losing Battles, 1970
Eudora Welty

A shrunken but still lively old lady who is the head of an immense family of subsistence farmers in a poor Mississippi backwater, and presides over the gathering to celebrate her birthday, which provides the action of the book. She is especially fond of her nephew, JACK RENFRO. She is sometimes forgetful, and inclined to slip back into the past, but still has a cocky look and a lot of spirit.

Vavasor, Alice
Can You Forgive Her?, 1864–5
The Eustace Diamonds, 1873
Anthony Trollope

A cousin and intimate confidante of LADY GLENCORA PALLISER. She is 'tall and well-made', with dark brown hair and dark eyes, and is 'a fine, handsome high-spirited young woman'.

Her personality is staid and self-possessed, with 'nothing that was girlish in her manner'. She is unable to decide on a husband, and is engaged twice-over to her two suitors, before finally choosing to marry the stolid JOHN GREY rather than her wayward cousin GEORGE VAVASOR.

Vavasor, George
The Palliser Novels, 1864–80
Anthony Trollope

A stockbroker, he is the cousin of ALICE VAVASOR, whom he hopes to marry, but who eventually rejects him after much vacillation. His face is marked by a large, ugly scar. As a youth, he was a wayward, unconventional, but nonetheless fascinating young man who 'lived in open defiance of decency', and was generally regarded as being 'on the high road to ruin'. He reforms and applies himself to work and politics, but eventually suffers the disappointment of losing his seat in Parliament, and after trying to kill his rival for Alice, JOHN GREY, emigrates to the USA.

Veck, Meg (Margaret)
The Chimes, 1844
Charles Dickens

The devoted daughter of TROTTY VECK, she remains patient and optimistic through all the indignities brought on by their poverty. She is engaged to marry the handsome blacksmith, Richard, but in her father's dream of the future, as foretold by ALDERMAN CUTE and MR FILER, the match is broken off. When Trotty awakens, however, he finds to his delight that everyone is about to celebrate both a happy wedding and a happy New Year.

Veck, Trotty (Toby)
The Chimes, 1844
Charles Dickens

A ticket-porter (or messenger) in the City of London, known as 'Trotty' from his peculiar pace. A 'weak, small, spare old man, he was a very Hercules, this Toby, in his good intentions'. Persuaded by SIR JOSEPH BOWLEY and ALDERMAN CUTE that the poor are 'born bad', he becomes melancholy. He has a great affection for the church bells near his station and, in a dream on Christmas Eve, the chimes call him to the church, where he sees unhappy visions of the future and of the life ahead for his daughter, MEG VECK. But the visions also point the moral, 'that we must trust and hope, and neither doubt ourselves, nor the good in one another'. He awakes from his dream to find the chimes ringing in the New Year and realizes that the suffering he has witnessed has been merely a baseless vision.

Veen, Van
Ada, or Ardor: A Family Chronicle, 1969
Vladimir Nabokov

A writer in his nineties, he is the literary scion of a hugely sprawling Victorian family. Set in a turn-of-the-century America colonized by Russians as well as English and French, Venn's passion finds its reciprocal background in pyrotechnical verbal inventions and literary contrivances, a conflation of all histories. He is drawn into a lifetime of intermittent affairs with his supposed

cousin ADA, who is really his sister. Her tragic half-sister Lucette is also involved in the incestuous triangle, a victim of illicit passion.

Velutus, Sicinius
Coriolanus, c.1607/8
William Shakespeare

One of the two Tribunes of the People. Despised by CORIOLANUS, he and JUNIUS BRUTUS determine to use the plebeians to destroy him. Sly and astute, he skilfully manipulates the mob and rouses Coriolanus to anger. But he has a streak of cowardice in him and ultimately works for his own ends and not the good of Rome.

Venable, Violet
Suddenly Last Summer, 1958
Tennessee Williams

A wealthy widow, fierce, proud and defiant, Violet Venable reveres the memory of her son, Sebastian, who died the previous summer. He was, she claims, a paragon of virtue, a potentially great poet. Seated in the overgrown conservatory of her southern home, she recalls him with the adoration of a bereft lover. When her niece, Catherine, threatens to shatter this myth (Sebastian was a predatory homosexual who died being devoured by Mexican beggars), Violet exacts a hideous revenge by hiring a psychiatrist to testify to Catherine's madness and arrange a lobotomy that will silence her, promising him funding if he will do her bidding.

Vendice
The Revenger's Tragedy, 1607
Thomas Middleton or Cyril Tourneur

The 'Revenger' of the title, and the embodiment of righteous vengeance. He is the son of GRATIANA, and is a 'poor malcontent', whose father died in poverty (disappointed of his expected advancement from THE DUKE), and whose mistress was poisoned by the same duke for the crime of resisting his lust. Vendice comes to the Duke's court full of bitter, righteous anger. In his determination to avenge the crimes against his loved ones, he immerses himself in the corruption of his enemies, conjuring up vile punishments, imaginatively appropriate to the crimes committed. Aggressive and cynical, he views everything he sees with a jaundiced eye.

Veneering, Mr and Mrs Hamilton
Our Mutual Friend, 1865
Charles Dickens

A wealthy self-made man who has bought himself a parliamentary seat in a rotten borough. He and his wife, Anastasia, are 'bran-new people in a bran-new house in a bran-new quarter of London', but as arrivistes, they are still 'a trifle sticky', like freshly applied veneer. Their dinner parties are the place for the gossip of 'Society'. Frequent guests are MORTIMER LIGHTWOOD, EUGENE WRAYBURN, the foolish Lady Tippins and the polite, old-fashioned Melvin Twemlow, the only guest to defend courageously Wrayburn's marriage to LIZZIE HEXAM.

Venice, Doge of → Foscari, Francis

Venn, Diggory
The Return of the Native, 1878
Thomas Hardy

Diggory's unusual occupation – a 'reddleman' who collects red ochre for sheep dye – marks him out from the rest of rural society (even literally, as he is permanently coloured red from head to foot). His nomadic life on Egdon Heath allows him to keep a shrewd eye on the other characters, and especially to watch over the fortunes of his beloved THOMASIN YEOBRIGHT. At one with nature, and seeming almost an emanation of the Heath, he is a mysterious figure to those around him, and to some extent remains so, even to the reader.

Venner, Elsie
Elsie Venner: A Romance of Destiny, 1861
Oliver Wendell Holmes

A peculiarly snake-like young woman, whose eyes glitter and whose wild behaviour, odd character traits and strange powers are ascribed to the prenatal influence of a snake bite inflicted on her mother. She falls in love with a young student teacher, who interests an eminent professor in her case. She uses her serpent-sense to save his life by killing a rattlesnake, but when her love is unrequited, she falls ill and, losing her unusual qualities, fades away.

Ventidius
Timon of Athens, 1607/8
William Shakespeare and perhaps Thomas Middleton

Ventidius has his debts paid by the extravagantly generous TIMON OF ATHENS, who thinks him 'a gentleman that well deserves a help'. Later, Timon assures him the money was not a loan, but a gift. But after Ventidius inherits money, he refuses to help when his former benefactor falls on hard times. Ventidius, therefore, represents the mercenary spirit of Timon's fair-weather friends.

Venus
Venus and Adonis, 1593
William Shakespeare

The goddess of sensual love, Venus is enamoured of the youthful ADONIS. However, she finds the strength of her feelings makes him bashful and 'flint-hearted' in her presence, unable as he is to distinguish between lust and love. Unused to rejection, she continues to pursue him compulsively and, later, laments over his dead body: 'The kiss I gave you is bestowed in vain'.

Venus, Mr
Our Mutual Friend, 1865
Charles Dickens

A taxidermist and articulator of human bones. He is drawn into SILAS WEGG's plan to defraud MR and MRS NICODEMUS BOFFIN but, as an honest man, quickly repents and discloses the plot to Boffin. Deeply sentimental, he uses poetic language and laments his unrequited love for Pleasant Riderhood, the daughter of ROGUE RIDERHOOD, and an unlicensed pawnbroker with 'a swivel eye', but 'not otherwise positively ill-looking'. He eventually marries her when she overcomes her objection to his trade.

Vere, Captain Edward Fairfax ('Starry Vere')
Billy Budd, Foretopman, 1924
Herman Melville

The captain of a British warship, whose nickname comes from a poem by Marvell. He is a bachelor of about 40, short, modest, courageous, rather grave, and a 'sailor of distinction'. He is concerned about his men, but is a strict disciplinarian. His love of books and intellectual pursuits is seen by others as 'a queer streak of the pedantic running through him'. His devotion to duty requires him to condemn BILLY BUDD, although it causes him 'the agony of the strong' to do so.

Vereker, Hugh
'The Figure in the Carpet', in *Embarrassments*, 1896
Henry James

A brilliant novelist, whose works have not yet proved susceptible to critical explanation. He explains to a young friend (the narrator, ANON) that there is a 'figure in the carpet', an underlying pattern of significance to his work, but dies without revealing the secret.

Verinder, Rachel
The Moonstone, 1868
Wilkie Collins

Described as 'the finest creature that ever walked the ways of this lower world', Rachel Verinder is the teenage daughter of Lady Julia Verinder, whose birthday gift of the Moonstone diamond brings a dark cloud over the family. Small and slim, with jet-black hair and a complexion 'as warm as the sun itself', she finds her character severely tested when the theft of the diamond throws suspicion on both her and her estranged lover FRANKLIN BLAKE. Stern as steel, honourable and generous to a fault, she proves the equal of the ordeal that follows.

Verisopht, Lord Frederick
Nicholas Nickleby, 1839
Charles Dickens

A silly young aristocrat whom SIR MULBERRY HAWK dupes with the help of RALPH NICKLEBY. He becomes infatuated with KATE NICKLEBY, who has been used as bait by her uncle in order to get Verisopht further into Ralph's debt. Essentially honourable, he quarrels with Hawk over Hawk's immoral conduct. A duel follows, and Hawk shoots him dead.

Veritie
Ane Pleasant Satyre of the Thrie Estaitis, 1540
Sir David Lindsay

Solemn and dignified, Veritie is an allegorical representation of 'the truth', who symbolically clutches the New Testament. She seeks out REX HUMANITAS to underline to him his duty in setting a moral example to his subjects. Temporarily thwarted in her mission by the Vices (DISSAIT, FALSET and FLATTERIE) and the corrupt spiritual state, her patient stoicism is rewarded by the arrival of DIVYNE CORRECTIOUN, who frees her from the stocks and allows her to give her well-informed advice on the reformation of Spirituality.

Verloc
The Secret Agent, 1907
Joseph Conrad

The agent of the title. He has a shadowy past, but may be French. He is over 40, with the shabby air of 'having wallowed, fully dressed, on an unmade bed'. He is inadequate as a husband, as a dealer in pornography in Soho, and as a secret agent, a calling he follows despite a total lack of political conviction or loyalty of any kind. He is generally treated with contempt, but harbours an unshakeable self-delusion about his standing in others' eyes. His long-suffering wife is finally driven to bloody vengeance after he causes the death of her halfwit brother, STEVIE.

Verloc, Winnie
The Secret Agent, 1907
Joseph Conrad

The wife of the agent VERLOC, and sister of the halfwit, STEVIE, she is an attractive, neat, tidy woman who married Verloc to help her brother. Remarkably reserved, not to say repressed, she is devoted to Stevie. She is not of a curious disposition, believing that 'things do not stand much looking into'. Various betrayals leave her at last 'clear-sighted', but beyond saving.

Vermeer, Johannes
Girl With a Pearl Earring, 1999
Tracy Chevalier

A fictionalized version of the 17th-century Dutch painter, Vermeer is reliant on the benevolence of his patron. He has 'a long and angular face' with 'eyes grey like the sea' and his hair is brick-red. His involvement with his art distances him from his young wife and their continuously growing brood of children, and he presents a remote figure. When he employs a maid, GRIET, to assist him in the studio he becomes drawn to her and her artistic sensibility, but ultimately he requires an untroubled environment in which to work.

Vernish
The Plain Dealer, 1676/7
William Wycherley

'Bosome, and onely Friende' to MANLY, Vernish acts in a two-faced manner by keeping his old friend in the dark about the fact that he has married Manly's former betrothed, OLIVIA. Vernish also discovers that FIDELIA, though disguised as Manly's page, is actually a woman. Consequently, he temporarily gains the upper hand over both Olivia, who loves Fidelia, and the misanthropic but naively trusting Manly.

Vernon, Catherine
Hester: A Story of Contemporary Life, 1883
Margaret Oliphant

Catherine's brains and fortune save the Vernon family bank when HESTER's father ruins it. Exceptionally able, she keeps everyone under control, amused by ingratitude. Even her nephew Edward, whom she loves like a son, resents her. Young Hester wants to work and be independent but Catherine does not recognize that there is something of herself in this. Hester knows nothing of the past, but when she will not elope with Edward, who has speculated with the bank's money, he taunts her with it. She sees

Catherine's splendid brain save the bank again. The two should have loved, not hated, but it is too late. Catherine dies, broken-hearted.

Vernon, Die (Diana)
Rob Roy, 1817
Sir Walter Scott

Niece of SIR HILDEBRAND OSBALDISTONE, who enshrines in her given name some of the family's appetite for the hunt. A blunt and slightly tomboyish figure, she is nonetheless as powerfully attractive to the romantic FRANK OSBALDISTONE as she is to the more rapacious and calculating RASHLEIGH OSBALDISTONE. Her function at Osbaldistone Hall is a civilizing one, but she is not above a little unconvincing mischief. Critical opinion is divided over how successful a creation she really is.

Vernon, Phil
Harland's Half Acre, 1984
David Malouf

FRANK HARLAND's lawyer and his symbolic opposite. Brought up in a respectable, aspirational family, he chooses a life of order and material comfort which is sharply opposed to the reckless self-reliance chosen by Harland, but imposed on the armies of unemployed who haunt Depression-era Australia.

Verver, Adam
The Golden Bowl, 1904
Henry James

A self-made American, with the spontaneity and moral instinct that goes with the better kind of self-made men. At Fawns, his home, he muses on the paradox of power and responsibility, privacy and openness, that lies near the heart of the book: 'Everyone had need of one's power, whereas one's own power, at the best, would have seemed to be but some trick for not communicating it'. He is later married to CHARLOTTE STANT.

Verver, Maggie
The Golden Bowl, 1904
Henry James

Innocent, but by no means gullible, ADAM VERVER's daughter is obliged to take a more realistic, less sanguine view of human nature than the sheltered and moneyed environment of Fawns has given her. The invisible crack in the symbolic bowl is as much a reminder of the fatal flaw lying athwart her own relationship with the fortune-hunting PRINCE AMERIGO, as it is of the prince's moral compromise.

Vessels, Walker
The Slave, 1964
Amiri Baraka

An imaginative and didactic black man, Walker goes through the lengthy process of America's informal sexual education. As a member of a middle class that considers itself liberated, he marries a white woman, and thus believes that he has overcome every racial inhibition. The marriage fails because this conviction is based both on false assumptions and on a consciousness that is equally false.

Vetch, Anastasius
The Princess Casamassima, 1886
Henry James
An anarchist musician in London and perhaps the most romantic and least hidebound of the revolutionaries in HYACINTH ROBINSON's circle. He seems to represent spontaneity and a generous accommodation of reality: 'he was fond of his cup of tea, and only wanted to see the British constitution a good deal simplified'.

Vetch, Fleda
The Spoils of Poynton, 1897
Henry James
An attractive young woman of good taste, her appreciation of fine things brings her to the attention of MRS GERETH of Poynton, and thus to the notice of OWEN GERETH, who falls in love with her, despite already being engaged to MONA BRIGSTOCK. As with the other female characters, it is never quite clear whether it is her emotions or her relish for material things that is more firmly engaged.

Vickers, Ann
Ann Vickers, 1933
Sinclair Lewis
The character of this idealistic young social reformer was largely based on Lewis's second wife, the journalist Dorothy Thompson, and is compounded of admiration at her energy and exasperation at her careerist single-mindedness.

Vickery, Nathanael
Son of Morning, 1978
Joyce Carol Oates
Called 'Master' by his closest associates, Nathanael Vickery is a man obsessed with God; he believes himself to be merely a vessel of God, not a person in his own right. When not preaching, he is silent, self-contained and ascetic. He seeks perfection of his soul while neglecting his body, often appearing unkempt and unwashed, in clothes which suggest poverty. While preaching he is fierce, intense and radiant, and his melodious voice draws people by the thousands. His sermons leave him physically exhausted, almost comatose, yet he seems to have the power to heal himself.

Victor
'Victor: a Ballad', number XXXV of 'Songs and Other Musical Pieces', in *Collected Shorter Poems*, 1950
W H Auden
A 'mousey' young bank clerk whose narrow religious upbringing and parroted morality have not fitted him for normal life and relationships. He marries Anna, but quickly comes to recognize her faithlessness. Maddened by whispering voices and a messianic vision, he stabs her to death (to the tune of 'Frankie and Johnny').

Victor, Inez Christian
Democracy, 1983
Joan Didion
The wife of a Democratic senator who narrowly missed a presidential nomination. Unlike Didion's previous heroines, she believes that the past has to be confronted as a moral given. As such, she resists the loss of memory and moral relativism that public life seems to entail. An affair with the charismatic JACK LOVETT gives her a purchase on the real sources of power and influence.

Videna
Gorboduc, 1561
Thomas Norton and Thomas Sackville
Queen and wife of GORBODUC. She loves FERREX, her eldest son, and finds her husband's desire to divide his kingdom unjust and unnatural. She is filled with foreboding. She is suspicious of her younger son PORREX's pride and ambition, and when later proved right is driven by grief and rage to kill him in revenge. Horrified by this unnatural act, the people rise in rebellion and kill both Videna and Gorboduc.

Vijh, Jasmine
Jasmine, 1989
Bharati Mukherjee
'Greedy with wants and reckless from hope', Jasmine is a survivor. Widowed in India at 17, she escapes the isolation of her village for the promise of America. There she experiences physical brutality, intellectual stimulation, stifling repression worse than that of her home, and the love and affection of strangers and friends. Jasmine accepts and endures all of these, seeing them as rites of passage to her new life. She embraces her adopted culture, welcoming the opportunity it provides for recreating herself in a number of guises: 'For every Jasmine the reliable caregiver, there is a Jase the prowling adventurer'.

Village Atheist, the
The Spoon River Anthology, 1915
Edgar Lee Masters
Speaking from the grave, he tells of his eventual conversion from the world of 'the Shadow' – atheism – into 'hope and intuition' as a result of reading religious texts during his long terminal illness. His message of rigour and hope – 'Only those who strive mightily will achieve [immortality]' – is phrased in the language of a prophet and addressed to the young.

Villanelle
The Passion, 1987
Jeanette Winterson
A cross-dressing Venetian woman who works in the casino, Villanelle can walk on water as she was born with webbed feet. She is bisexual and falls in love with a married woman who steals her heart and hides it in a jar. Tricked into marriage with a French soldier, she escapes and meets HENRI in Russia, escaping with him back to Venice where she is at home in the city of mazes.

Vimes, Samuel
Guards! Guards!, 1989, et seq
Terry Pratchett
The captain of the Ankh Morpork City Watch, who always gets his man. When he first appears in *Guards! Guards!* he is an alcoholic in charge of a ragged and dwindling band of watchmen.

Helped by new recruit Corporal Carrott and his future wife Lady Sybil, he pulls himself together and returns the watch to its former glory. With an old-fashioned sense of right and wrong, he never allows rules to stand in his way as he pursues justice, even if this brings him into conflict with the powers that be.

Vincent, Mrs
Salem Chapel, 1863
Margaret Oliphant

REV ARTHUR VINCENT's mother is a ladylike little woman, fussing about small things, overcome by great anxieties, but always trying to keep up appearances. A pastor's widow, she knows the problems her son will have with his critical 'flock'. She visits them and, to keep them guessing, drops hints about Arthur having been offered a much bigger charge in richer Liverpool and the danger of his 'throwing it all up'. Her daughter's illness almost unhinges her, but she finds hope in the least improvement. Busy, tidy, neat, it is right that her faith, in Arthur and Providence, should be rewarded.

Vincent, Rev Arthur
Salem Chapel, 1863
Margaret Oliphant

Arthur Vincent, idealistic pastor of Salem Chapel, resents the confident well-meaning tradesmen who are his deacons, and their over-dressed wives. Phoebe Tozer (PHOEBE BEECHAM), grossly out to flatter him, disgusts him: she is a cruel contrast to gracious LADY WESTERN, whom he foolishly loves from afar. His attentions to her bring censure from his 'flock'; they treat him as their servant and give him ignorant, patronizing advice. Anxiety for his sister calls him away, causing more offence. A crowded meeting calling for his resignation is won over, but he resigns all the same, disillusioned, and chooses, for the moment, a literary life.

Vincentio
The Taming of the Shrew, early 1590s
William Shakespeare

The rich, aged father of LUCENTIO, he has to face odd behaviour from several characters, including a man and his wife who treat him as a woman, two of his own servants who deny knowledge of him, and a man whom claims that *he* is Vincentio. Yet, through all this he maintains his composure because he is afraid that his son has been murdered. However, once reconciled with Lucentio, he is prepared to vent his wrath, especially on TRANIO. He never loses his dignity because he believes in the family and that children should always obey their parents.

Vincentio, Duke
Measure for Measure, c.1604
William Shakespeare

The Governor of Vienna, he abdicates his responsibilities to a deputy in an attempt to improve on the laxity of the city's laws, which have been allowed to slide during his rule. The Duke has a reputation for virtue and wisdom and this is justified by his skilful manipulation of the other characters (whilst in disguise) to bring about a happy ending. He is a 'gentleman of all temperance' who would rather see others enjoying themselves than make merry himself.

Vincentio, Prince
The Gentleman Usher, 1602/3
George Chapman

The son of ALPHONSO, who is his rival in seeking the hand of MARGARET. Vincentio's love for her is deep and noble, but he promotes it by manipulating (while really mocking) BASSIOLO, whom he even allows to call him 'Vince'. His virtue is shown by the steadfastness of his devotion.

Vincy, Fred
Middlemarch, 1871–2
George Eliot

Brother of ROSAMOND VINCY, though kind-hearted and good-natured, he has been frittering his life away in idle pursuits, assured that his future will be secure when he inherits his uncle's fortune. In love with MARY GARTH, but in serious debt to her father, CALEB GARTH, Fred is forced to learn the errors of his ways when his uncle disinherits him. He eventually redeems himself in Mary's eyes, through hard work and honesty.

Vincy, Rosamond
Middlemarch, 1871–2
George Eliot

Beautiful but empty-headed, Rosamond, daughter of the mayor of Middlemarch, seeks to satisfy her craving for social status by marrying the well-born doctor, TERTIUS LYDGATE. Completely preoccupied with herself, her clothes and other people's opinions of her, she stubbornly refuses to recognize either the stark reality of their financial situation or the fact that it has anything to do with her extravagance. A vivid contrast to DOROTHEA BROOKE, Rosamond remains throughout an almost wholly selfish character.

Vinrace, Rachel
The Voyage Out, 1915
Virginia Woolf

Having led a sheltered and privileged childhood and adolescence, Rachel seems young for her years. Eager to learn about life and people, her ignorance is astounding, though she is certainly not stupid and keenly feels her lack of worldliness. A young woman 'at the edge of wonder', she is impressionable, vulnerable and open-minded. Her illness and death are mysterious: perhaps she is simply too fragile and precious for the 'real' world.

Viola
Twelfth Night, c.1601
William Shakespeare

Forced by circumstances to pretend to be a man ('Cesario'), Viola falls in love with her 'master', ORSINO. Because she cannot address him openly she uses her position as envoy to OLIVIA to speak her longings, disguising them as Orsino's words. When she realizes the effect they have had on Olivia she feels regret, for she too knows an apparently impossible love. She is capable of matching wit with others, but is reluctant to enter into any physical conflict. Her disguise is so successful that she takes in everyone, including her twin brother SEBASTIAN, but there are times when she would willingly give it all up and reveal her true identity.

Viola, Giorgio
Nostromo, 1904
Joseph Conrad
An elderly Genoese who fought with Garibaldi in Italy and Uruguay 'for the love of all humanity', and who has retained his liberal convictions and hatred of royalty, choosing to live in Costaguana because he 'cannot live under a king'. He has a 'leonine head' of white hair and an 'austere contempt for personal advantage' and material gain, but his views are clearly seen as anachronistic. He regards NOSTROMO as his son and a hero, but is the cause of his death.

Virgil
Poetaster, 1602
Ben Jonson
A historical character appropriated by Jonson, Publius Vergilius Maro became one of the greatest pastoral poets. Jonson thought highly of him, especially of his ability to achieve both popularity and a complex poetic form, and thus presents a sympathetic portrait. He and his writing are praised by AUGUSTUS, and he helps to conduct the trial of the poetasters CRISPINUS and DEMETRIUS.

Virgilia
Coriolanus, c.1607/8
William Shakespeare
The wife of CORIOLANUS, she is a quiet, retiring figure during her husband's absence at war. Continually overshadowed by her mother-in-law VOLUMNIA, she is dignified and calm when the latter is arrogant and angry. She is the archetype of wifely obedience and virtue.

Virginian, the
The Virginian, 1902
Owen Wister
Wister later called his unnamed cowpuncher hero 'the best thing the Declaration of Independence ever turned out'. Courageous and quietly dangerous (he is the source of the famous response 'When you call me that, *smile*'), he is the epitome of control in a lawless land. Chivalrous as well as brave, he wins the heart and hand of MOLLY STARK WOOD.

Vittoria Corombona
The White Devil, 1612
John Webster
Sister of FLAMINEO; a beautiful Venetian lady of distinguished ancestry and bad reputation, who is the ambiguous cause of the evil-doing of her lover, the DUKE OF BRACHIANO. She enjoys life and demonstrates her spirit when opposed. After the murder of her husband CAMILLO, she is confined to a 'house of penitent whores'; she proves impenitent, marries Brachiano, and faces death bravely.

Viveash, Myra
Antic Hay, 1923
Aldous Huxley
An attractive 'femme fatale', who ironically

considers herself as one of 'We poor decayed gentlewomen', Mrs Viveash becomes THEODORE GUMBRIL's mistress, but has felt 'dead inside' ever since her lover was killed in World War I. CASIMIR LYPIATT paints her portrait, but when she rejects his advances out of boredom, he bitterly tells her, 'You like playing with the victim ... he must die slowly'.

Vladimir
Waiting for Godot, 1955
Samuel Beckett
In contrast to his fellow tramp ESTRAGON, Vladimir is contemplative, alert to his existential predicament. Where Estragon finds comedy in life, Vladimir finds poetry. Life is a constant trial, but suffering is a prelude to salvation. So he waits for the elusive Godot, yet not without doubts and misgivings of his own. Unlike Estragon, who is rooted to his rock, Vladimir belongs to the tree. 'Vladimir is light', Beckett has observed, 'he is oriented towards the sky'. Alternately squabbling, parting and embracing, Vladimir and Estragon are inseparable, articulating the scale of human emotion and the necessity of companionship. Characteristically, Vladimir sums it all up: 'At this place, at this moment of time, all mankind is us, whether we like it or not'.

Voice, the → Okoko

Voldemort, Lord
Harry Potter and the Philosopher's Stone, 1997, et seq
J K Rowling
The living incarnation of evil, with the 'most terrible face ... chalk white with glaring red eyes', Voldemort is cruel, cunning and steeped in powerful black magic. Once a likeable, engaging boy at the wizard school Hogwarts, he immersed himself in the Dark Arts and emerged transformed as the 'greatest dark sorcerer of all time' to establish a reign of terror with his sinister supporters, the Death Eaters. Now barely alive after a failed attack on the infant HARRY POTTER, he hungrily seeks to regain his lost strength in order to rise again and renew his malevolent dominion.

Voles, Mr
Bleak House, 1853
Charles Dickens
RICHARD CARSTONE's solicitor, he is a thin, sallow man always dressed 'in black, black-gloved, and buttoned to the chin, there was nothing so remarkable in him as a lifeless manner, and a slow fixed way he had of looking'. His malign influence on Richard leads to Richard's becoming obsessed with the law and finally dying from frustration and exhaustion. Obsessed with respectability, he continually refers to his being a widower and the sole support of his daughters and an aged father in the Vale of Taunton.

Volkbein, Baron Felix
Nightwood, 1936
Djuna Barnes
Tall, bulky, with a long, oval face and a solemn

expression, Volkbein is a Jew of Italian descent who tries to impress others by inventing noble Austrian forebears. This is a plausible story: he has a large and well-furnished home in the centre of Vienna, financed by money-changing and dealing in valuable paintings and rare, first-edition books. However, like many who aspire to the nobility, Volkbein is too much in awe of the genuinely rich and noble to be absolutely credible.

Volkov, Kathy
The Vivisector, 1970
Patrick White

A young pianist, she reminds her friend the painter HURTLE DUFFIELD of several other women who have figured in his life. In looks and manner, she resembles aspects of BOO HOLLINGRAKE and NANCE LIGHTFOOT and, in her liking for cats, she is reminiscent of RHODA COURTNEY. Although Duffield has his most serious sexual and emotional relationship with Kathy, she is in one essential way different from the others: she not only is his equal artistically, but is able to exploit others to the same degree and is therefore as much a metaphorical vivisector as he. Emotionally aggressive and sexually devouring, Kathy plays tantalizingly with Duffield's feelings.

Volpone
Volpone, or The Fox, 1606
Ben Jonson

A rich Venetian magnifico, Volpone has no children and therefore no apparent heir to his considerable wealth. As this is widely known, several greedy Venetians attempt to gain his confidence in the hope that Volpone will leave them his money when he dies. To exploit their greed, the sly Volpone invests his considerable zest for life into feigning a fatal illness. When CORBACCIO, CORVINO and VOLTORE bring him gifts, he simply adds them to his already handsome stockpile of riches. Eventually, the myriad plotting is discovered.

Volscius, Prince
The Rehearsal, 1671
George Villiers, 2nd Duke of Buckingham

One of the heroic martial characters in BAYES's dreadful drama, which is rehearsed within the play. Having suddenly fallen in love with Parthenope, he debates with PRINCE PRETTY-MAN her merits as compared with those of the latter's beloved.

Voltore
Volpone, or The Fox, 1606
Ben Jonson

An avaricious advocate who brings VOLPONE gifts in the hope that he will become his heir, his downfall comes as a result of his greed being greater than his cunning. His plans to deceive lead to disaster as he makes one tactical error after another, attempting to accuse others of corruption in order to portray himself as above reproach. When he is forced to change his story altogether, he claims that his behaviour is a result of having been possessed by a devil.

Volumnia
Coriolanus, c.1607/8
William Shakespeare

A proud and domineering patrician, she has trained her son CORIOLANUS to be a man for whom 'valiantness [is] honoured … above all other virtues'. She alone is able to control his temper, but her efforts to do so frequently go wrong. It is a moot point whether she loves him for what he really is or for the honour he can gain. Her plea for him to spare Rome is her last success but she fails to see that it has signed his death warrant.

Volupine, Princess
'Burbank with a Baedeker; Bleistein with a Cigar', in *Poems*, 1920
T S Eliot

As predatory as her name suggests, she plays Cleopatra to the tourist BURBANK's Mark Antony, her gondola a much-diminished version of the Egyptian queen's lambent barge, out of which she offers the boatman a 'meagre, blue-nailed, phthisic hand' as she disembarks en route to another assignation.

von Bülow, Cosima, formerly **Cosima Liszt**, later **Cosima Wagner**
The Young Cosima, 1939
Henry Handel Richardson

RICHARD WAGNER's (historical) mistress, she is the wife of the conductor Hans von Bülow, who magnanimously conducts the première of *Tristan und Isolde* two months after Cosima has given birth to Wagner's illegitimate daughter. Cosima, the daughter of Liszt, is portrayed as passionate and feeling, strongly committed to the composer's potency and creativity, rather than to her husband's more coldly analytical nature. She is a powerful representation of the artistic muse, but is never relegated to being a mere handmaiden to genius.

Vond, Brock
Vineland, 1990
Thomas Pynchon

A Federal Prosecutor who has emerged out of the past like a grim nemesis to fulfil his dark obsession with ZOYD WHEELER's ex-wife FRENESI GATES. He is a latter-day Lombroso, convinced he can identify criminality in any face but saddled, despite his own self-image and looks, by the reputation of being a thug. 'Though his defects of character were many, none was quite as annoying as th[e] naked itch to be a gentleman'.

von Einem, Hilda
Greenmantle, 1916
John Buchan

Though RICHARD HANNAY, by his own account, knows 'nothing about women', he also believes that 'every man has in his bones a consciousness of sex' and, with an instinct combining attraction and repulsion, he responds to the mysterious von Einem, who cleverly manipulates the cult of Greenmantle. Unquestionably beautiful and overtly sexual, she embodies the 'glamour of a wild dream'. At her death, she is transformed into a figure from myth. 'She might be a devil, but she was also a queen. I considered that there might be merits in the prospect of riding by her side into Jerusalem'.

von Flugel, Diana, née Langton
The Cardboard Crown, 1952
A Difficult Young Man, 1955
Outbreak of Love, 1957
When Blackbirds Sing, 1962, collectively known as 'the Langton Tetralogy'
Martin Boyd

The beautiful and elegant hope of ALICE LANGTON's life, this favoured daughter marries WOLFIE VON FLUGEL, a gently bred but impoverished German immigrant devoid of material assets. When she marries him, destroying her mother's social hopes for her, she embarks on the life of worldly disappointment to which all Boyd female protagonists are doomed. But her dual strengths of moral value and irony are too strong for the temptations that the world offers her when her marriage proves hollow. Instead, Diana buries pain beneath laughter.

von Flugel, Wolfie
The Cardboard Crown, 1952
A Difficult Young Man, 1955
Outbreak of Love, 1957
When Blackbirds Sing, 1962, collectively known as 'the Langton Tetralogy'
Martin Boyd

The gently mocked suitor of the beautiful DIANA VON FLUGEL, Wolfie lives only for his musical genius. Perceived by his wife as an 'exotic and amusing animal' – and genius – Wolfie has always casually charmed the family into which he marries. Personally complacent, socially unworldly, he needs the stimuli of his young female students and his full-blown, socially unacceptable mistress – and, when World War I breaks, the support of his suddenly indispensable wife Diana as society turns bewilderingly xenophobic.

von Igelfeld, Professor Dr Moritz-Maria
Portuguese Irregular Verbs, 2003, et seq
Alexander McCall Smith

Von Igelfeld is a professor at the Institute of Romance Philology at Regensberg, and is extremely proud of his 1,200-page *Portuguese Irregular Verbs*, 'a work of such majesty that it dwarfed all other books in the field'. A somewhat aloof academic with artistic sensibilities, his lack of common sense allows him to be drawn into a series of bizarre and hilarious situations. He stumbles from one comic disaster to the next, always awaiting further recognition and reward for his seminal work.

Voss, Johann Ulrich
Voss, 1957
Patrick White

A proud, vain, even megalomaniac explorer who sets out from Sydney in an attempt to travel by horseback across Australia some time during the 1840s. (White is drawing a parallel with the German explorer, Ludwig Leichart.) A gaunt, imposing man, Voss imagines his journey partly as a struggle against nature. In his attempt to conquer and possess the country in which he lives, he hopes symbolically to rival God. Even his proposal of marriage to LAURA TREVELYAN is not the result of love, but is a product of his own overweening vanity. It is only on the expedition itself, when Voss is surrounded and overwhelmed by nature, that he learns humility. But by then, it is too late.

Vote, Robin
Nightwood, 1936
Djuna Barnes

The novel is set in the Parisian demi-monde, and Robin's character is derived partly from that of Thelma Wood, a sculptress who became Barnes's lover. Robin has a feline, wayward quality that her love affair with NORA FLOOD accentuates. She is a bundle of paradoxes: although seeming to be searching for domesticity and security, she can renounce neither her promiscuity nor her independence. Destructive, manipulative, she is proud yet pathetic. Sadly, Nora watches her trawling the cafés, moving 'from table to table, from drink to drink, from person to person'.

Voysey, Edward
The Voysey Inheritance, 1905
Harley Granville-Barker

The only one of the four adult Voysey sons to enter the family legal practice, Edward is dismayed when his father confesses that both he and his father before him have used trust funds in their care for personal speculation. The Voyseys' professional and upper-middle-class social eminence is therefore sustained by fraud. When his father dies, the self-conscious, unimaginative Edward confronts his tainted inheritance. Attempting to recompense his clients without ruining the family, he evolves from an idealist to a realist, from a 'well-principled prig' to a man who ironically follows his father's advice to 'cultivate your own sense of right and wrong ... deal your own justice'.

Vye, Eustacia
The Return of the Native, 1878
Thomas Hardy

Exotic, passionate and ruthless, Eustacia's great desire is 'to be loved to madness'. Her relationship with DAMON WILDEVE lasts only as long as he seems the best catch on offer, and she throws him over when CLYM YEOBRIGHT returns to Egdon Heath from Paris. After marrying Clym, her dream of escape from the Heath is cruelly dashed when she finds her husband's desire to return to his roots is a permanent one. Her final lament sums up the doomed grandeur of the picture she has of herself and her fate: 'How I have tried and tried to be a splendid woman, and how destiny has been against me!'

Vyse, Cecil
A Room With a View, 1908
E M Forster

Rich, well-mannered and well-educated, Cecil Vyse is said to resemble 'those fastidious saints who guard the portals of a French cathedral'. A self-conscious ascetic with little patience for the bustle and spontaneity of the world around him, he is also an insufferable prig, whose approach to life is an unattractive mixture of stilted emotions and supercilious posturing. In the words of romantic rival GEORGE EMERSON, he is 'the type who's kept Europe back for a thousand years'.

Wackles, Sophy
The Old Curiosity Shop, 1841
Charles Dickens

A pretty, good-humoured girl, the middle of three sisters, and a teacher in her mother's school for young ladies, she is engaged to DICK SWIVELLER, but marries Cheggs instead when Swiveller turns his attentions to LITTLE NELL.

Wade, Miss
Little Dorrit, 1857
Charles Dickens

A bitter, self-contained woman with an ungovernable temper, she assumes everyone she meets patronizes and humiliates her because of her illegitimate birth. She has had a relationship with HENRY GOWAN, but he discarded her. An acquaintance of MR and MRS MEAGLES, she recognizes in Tattycoram (HARRIET BEADLE) a kindred spirit and persuades her to be her companion. When Meagles and ARTHUR CLENNAM visit her to recover Tattycoram, she gives Clennam her autobiography to read, 'The History of a Self-Tormentor'. Maliciously, she conceals for RIGAUD the documents stolen by JEREMIAH FLINTWINCH that show how MRS CLENNAM has suppressed a codicil in her husband's will that leaves a legacy to AMY DORRIT. Tattycoram brings the documents with her when she returns to the Meagles.

Wadman, Mrs
The Life and Opinions of Tristram Shandy, 9 volumes, 1759–67
Laurence Sterne

A widow, searching for love or marriage, she closes in on UNCLE TOBY SHANDY, and only her anxiety about the precise nature of his embarrassing war-wound in the groin restrains her enthusiasm for his hand in marriage. Forward, shameless and rather desperate, with the air of a weary and reckless beauty, she entices the fumbling Toby well out of his depth. Her courtship techniques make up in vigour what they lack in subtlety.

Wadsmith, Miss Mary
'The Good Anna', in *Three Lives*, 1909
Gertrude Stein

The first person to give ANNA FEDERNER a job when she arrives at Bridgepoint, she is 'a large, fair, helpless woman, burdened with the care of two young children', her orphaned nephew and niece.

Wagner, Richard
Night and Day, 1978
Tom Stoppard

A world-weary, cynical, self-serving, adulterous veteran reporter covering an African civil war, Wagner is also an unapologetic supporter of the newspaper unions' closed shop policy. Both in news reporting and politics, his views diametrically oppose those of the naively idealistic journalist Jacob Milne. Wagner's credo is simple: 'I don't file prose. I file facts'. However, a printing strike, unwittingly precipitated by Milne, prevents Wagner's newspaper from publishing his exclusive interview with the dictator-president. The play's themes – the independence of the press, the interests of owners and the powerful influence of the unions – were vibrant political issues at the time of its writing.

Wagner, Richard
The Young Cosima, 1939
Henry Handel Richardson

In this portrait Wagner is presented as the lover of COSIMA VON BÜLOW rather than as a great composer, and he comes across as a humane and individual character, though undoubtedly marked by emotional and intellectual arrogance and by a deep streak of eccentricity that borders on madness.

Wain, Col Geoffrey
Barometer Rising, 1941
Hugh Maclennan

A representative of a generation of Canadians that has lost the energy and forward-looking spirit of the first pioneers, he has proved to be a grossly incompetent officer on the Western Front. When his nephew NEIL MACRAE (who has been his daughter PENELOPE WAIN's sweetheart) questions his authority, he attempts to court-martial him, leading directly to Neil's presumed death in a dug-out explosion, the first of many such detonations that lead inexorably to the cataclysmic (and historical) Halifax explosion of 6 December 1917.

Wain, Penelope
Barometer Rising, 1941
Hugh Maclennan

COL GEOFFREY WAIN's daughter and the sweetheart of her cousin NEIL MACRAE, she is thrown into the 'man's world' of warship design, where she is shrewdly successful. 'There was something delicate, something extremely fragile in the appearance of the girl alone against that angular background of motionless machinery and silent engines.' Her youth is offset by a dramatic lock of white hair.

Wait, James
The Nigger of the Narcissus, 1897
Joseph Conrad

A black sailor who is the 'nigger' of the title. His name is symbolic of his propensity to avoid work, and to try to get away with doing nothing for his pay by pretending illness. He represents a dangerous malaise, and is identified with the death principle, as 'something cold and gloomy that floated out on all the faces like a mourning evil', and is increasingly estranged from the rest of the crew in his alliance with DONKIN. Unknown to him, his illness is real, making him the dupe of his own scheme.

Waitwell
The Way of the World, 1700
William Congreve

Waitwell is a good and faithful servant to MIRABELL, and husband of FOIBLE. The extent of his loyalty to his employer can be judged by the fact that he agrees to impersonate one of Mirabell's uncles and thereby embarrass LADY WISHFORT, thus allowing Mirabell to establish a hold over her and further his campaign to marry her niece, MILLAMANT. Waitwell's loyalty is matched by his sense of intrigue. Even though he finds Lady Wishfort a bore, he nevertheless enjoys a lark. Throughout their adventures, the alliance between master and servant never breaks.

Waiyaki
The River Between, 1965
Ngugi wa Thiong'o

The novel's central character, he is an idealistic young Kenyan, charged with the belief that he can free his Gikuyu people from colonial rule, not by violence but by appropriating the positive aspects of white culture. Though he remains loyal to the old gods, he himself loves the daughter of a Christian pastor, believing that their relationship will help unify society.

Wakefield, Harry
The Two Drovers, in *Chronicles of the Canongate: First Series*, 1827
Sir Walter Scott

An English drover, killed at the climax of the fateful quarrel with ROBIN OIG M'COMBICH. He is powerfully built and well-favoured; as Robin exposes his former friend's dead face, he does so with the laconic comment, 'He was a pretty man!'

Wakem, Philip
The Mill on the Floss, 1860
George Eliot

The humpback son of Lawyer Wakem, who, despite being very articulate and literary, allows his self-consciousness about his deformity to make him withdrawn and irritably defensive, though he is essentially kind-hearted. Deeply in love with MAGGIE TULLIVER from an early age, his intimate friendship with her is prevented from flourishing further by TOM TULLIVER's tyrannical hold over Maggie, and when they

meet again years later Philip is madly jealous to find in STEPHEN GUEST a rival for her affections. Pinning all his hopes of happiness on her he can only be disappointed, but he eventually overcomes his wounded pride to assure her of his continuing love.

Walden, Ty Ty
God's Little Acre, 1933
Erskine Caldwell

The tantalizing search for hidden treasure on his land is Ty Ty Walden's major preoccupation, for it represents a chance to break out of the suffocating poverty of life as a poor white Georgia farmer. His basic naivety and quiet faith are expressed in the reserving of a 'tithe' acre – God's little acre – with a symbolic cross at the centre. There is a simplicity and integrity within him that balances the strangeness of his quest.

Waldo
The Story of an African Farm, 1883
Olive Schreiner

Son of the gentle German overseer, Old Otto, Waldo grows up with the spirited LYNDALL and her more conventional cousin EM. Like Lyndall, Waldo is very sensitive to the desolate Karoo landscape, and the two children are very close. Later, when he discovers that Lyndall has died in childbirth, his grief is only assuaged by his strength of feeling for 'that vast land'.

Waldo, Mr
Under Milk Wood, 1954
Dylan Thomas

This jack-of-all-trades rabbit-catcher, barber, herbalist, cat-doctor and quack is the perpetual subject of village gossip. A widower with a drink problem – he sells the furniture for it – and a rampant sexual urge, he is often the recipient of a paternity summons. As he sings his dirty songs, or talks to lampposts in his cups, his gentle 17-stone bulk harbours an earthy, self-forgiving wisdom – 'no lady is a lady all over'.

Walker, Bill
Major Barbara, 1905
George Bernard Shaw

A cowardly bully, Walker is angry that the Salvation Army has converted and accommodated his girlfriend. Searching for her, he arrives at BARBARA UNDERSHAFT's Army shelter, strikes the Salvationist Jenny Hill and threatens SNOBBY PRICE and PETER SHIRLEY. Challenged to fight Todger Fairmile, who has stood up to professional wrestlers at music-hall contests, his bravado evaporates. When he discovers that Fairmile is not only a convert but his girl's new companion, Walker prepares to fight. Later, he reports that instead of hitting him, Fairmile prayed for him. But his indignation does not entirely conceal his relief, and he and Barbara part on equal terms.

Walker, Coalhouse, jr
Ragtime, 1975
E L Doctorow

A black man in turn-of-the-century New York City, he takes an elaborate revenge on the Fire Department for the damage of his proudly treasured car and for his own racial harassment. His campaign draws in the son of a wealthy Jewish family, and eventually escalates to the point where he attempts to take over the J P Morgan library, a symbol of the culture that degrades them both with meretricious promises and constant rebuffs.

Walker, John
Swallows and Amazons, 1930, et seq
Arthur Ransome

The eldest Walker child, brother of SUSAN, TITTY and ROGER WALKER, he is the captain of the *Swallow*, a 14-foot dinghy with a brown sail that the children have the use of for the summer. He has been taught sailing by his father, who is a navy man, and can also fish, track, swim and set up camp. Above all else he is responsible (mostly), reliable and loyal, even when it means taking blame on to himself. A determined fighter, he is a good strategist, and is always firmly in command of his ship.

Walker, Kelvin
The Fall of Kelvin Walker, 1985
Alasdair Gray

Possessed by an almost Promethean ambition, this young Scot abandons Glasgow to seek his fortune in London. He is thin and somewhat shabby, with a 'blank, nearly characterless face', over which his lank hair slopes in a style reminiscent of Adolf Hitler. London fills him with excitement and purpose.

Walker, Roger
Swallows and Amazons, 1930, et seq
Arthur Ransome

The brother of JOHN, SUSAN and TITTY WALKER, 'Boy' Roger is the youngest crew member. He longs to sail like the others, but first he must learn to swim. His role on the voyage is to act as look-out and errand boy, a job he fulfils admirably. He finds all their adventures vastly enjoyable, which must owe something to his protected position as the youngest. For him, as for his brother and sisters, the power of imagination is strong, and he changes from being a sailor one minute, tacking across a field, to an intrepid explorer the next, looking anxiously behind him for poisoned arrows.

Walker, Susan
Swallows and Amazons, 1930, et seq
Arthur Ransome

The sister of JOHN, TITTY and ROGER WALKER, she is the mate of the *Swallow*, in charge of cooking and the stores, and fortunately fond of making lists and reading cookery books. It is up to her to ensure that the crew does not get scurvy whilst camped on the island. She also has to sew on a lot of buttons, which Roger is good at losing. Sensible and practical, she fusses about her family in a rather 'grown-up' way.

Walker, Titty
Swallows and Amazons, 1930, et seq
Arthur Ransome

The sister of JOHN, SUSAN and ROGER WALKER, she is the able seaman, a stalwart adventurer who proves her worth when she is left in charge of

Wildcat Island whilst the other Swallows lead an ambush on their rivals, NANCY AND PEGGY BLACKETT. Like the other children, she lives in her imagination; one minute she is Robinson Crusoe, the next a cormorant trying to catch minnows under the water. She is the letter-writer and log-keeper of the family. A romantic with a strong practical streak, she is brave, but not entirely fearless, and sometimes seems unsure of the boundaries between fiction and truth.

Walkinshaw, Claude
The Entail, or The Lairds of Gripp, 1823
John Galt

A penniless orphan brought up by an old servant, Maudge, he hears so much about his family's lost estate of Kittlestoneheugh that he becomes obsessed with the idea of restoring it. Starting as a pedlar at the age of 11, he drives hard bargains, lets Maudge die in poverty, eventually prospers and buys Grippy farm – the first part of Kittlestoneheugh to be reclaimed. His marriage and children are all made part of his driving urge. The entail which is to hold all together becomes his god; fairness, kindness, paternal feeling, domestic harmony, peace, content are all sacrificed. Only approaching death shows Claude the horror of his crime.

Wallingford, Patrick
The Fourth Hand, 2001
John Irving

A television news reporter with a US channel specializing in disasters, Wallingford finds his life transformed when he loses a hand in a freak accident of the type that fills his bulletins. He has had an easy life – attractive, likeable and shallow, he sees himself as 'a nice guy' and others agree. But his accident and the pioneering hand transplant he undergoes prove Wallingford is 'capable of growing up'. His complacency is shattered by his love for the homely widow of the new hand's donor.

Walpole, Cutler
The Doctor's Dilemma, 1906
George Bernard Shaw

A fashionable and dangerously ignorant surgeon, Walpole is an energetic, decisive man of 40, and something of a dandy. Obsessed with the idea that 95 per cent of the human race suffers from blood poisoning, he is a keen advocate of the removal of the 'nunciform sac', supposedly an organ full of decaying undigested food and waste matter which pollutes the blood and hampers its circulation.

Walravens, Madame
Villette, 1853
Charlotte Brontë

A minor but mysterious character, Madame Walravens makes a fleeting, though arresting, appearance in connection with MONSIEUR PAUL EMMANUEL, her benefactor, and MADAME BECK. A tiny, old, hunchbacked dwarf, bedecked – 'like a barbarian queen' – in jewellery, courtesy of her dead son, she has malevolent eyes which add to the air of Gothic intrigue surrounding her character. However, her interests are, somewhat humorously, revealed to be entirely worldly ones.

Walrus and the Carpenter, the
Through the Looking-Glass, and What Alice Found There, 1872
Lewis Carroll

TWEEDLEDEE sings about the Walrus and the Carpenter to ALICE: the two creatures, the sun shining in the middle of the night, invite the oysters to come and walk with them. The oysters come hurrying for the treat and wait while the Walrus and the Carpenter seat themselves comfortably on a rock and discourse philosophically. The two lament the sorry trick they are about to play on the oysters, and proceed to eat them all. After the song, Alice tries to determine which of the two to blame more, but TWEEDLEDUM and Tweedledee point out that one was as bad as the other, if not worse, and Alice has to give up.

Walsh, Peter
Mrs Dalloway, 1925
Virginia Woolf

Described as 'charming, clever, and with ideas about everything', Peter is an intellectual with a heart of gold, who has a self-destructive streak. When he falls in love with CLARISSA DALLOWAY he becomes vulnerable, growing obsessive in his pursuit of her. His undying and unreturned love for Clarissa leads him to go abroad, but he returns after another romantic disaster. He is witty, astute and sincere, but lacks common sense and the assertiveness necessary for survival.

Walton, Katharine
Katharine Walton, 1851
William Gilmore Simms

She is, in some respects, an early version of Margaret Mitchell's SCARLETT O'HARA, a young woman of considerable energy and personal courage, but still living in a male world dominated by military and mercantile values.

Walton, Robert
Frankenstein, or, The Modern Prometheus, 1818
Mary Shelley

The narrator of the novel, who encounters VICTOR FRANKENSTEIN in the Arctic wastes, and recounts his tragic story in letters and journals to his sister. He is a seafaring explorer, and an obsessive, solitary man who is driven by his dream-like vision of the North Pole as a 'region of beauty and delight' beyond the ice. His experiences leave him despondent at first, but finally turn him again towards human society.

Wamba, the son of Witless
Ivanhoe, 1819
Sir Walter Scott

The licensed fool of CEDRIC THE SAXON's household, he wears full motley, right up to a belled cap. Rather than a sword or knife – 'being probably considered as belonging to a class whom it is esteemed dangerous to entrust with edge-tools' – he carries a harmless stick.

Wanda
Down among the Women, 1971
Fay Weldon

Wanda has tried to rid herself of most of the traditional trappings of 'femininity'. She is bitter, cynical, depressed, feeling redundant when her husband marries a younger woman. Her unhappiness manifests itself in a cultivated lack of compassion, an aura of self-absorption, and a sense of sexual liberation. Yet the image she has created seems to sit uncomfortably on her and she gives very confusing messages to her daughter, SCARLET, who is made as miserable as her mother.

Wandering Willie → Steenson, Willie

Wandrous, Gloria
Butterfield 8, 1935
John O'Hara

She is said to be based on the life of Starr Faithfull, a 1920s starlet who behaved more like a fictional character than Gloria does. Starr set off a media scandal when her body was found washed up on a beach near New York. In the novel, O'Hara explores the pressures and thwarted aspirations that may have led to her death.

Wane, Perdita
Weymouth Sands, 1934
John Cowper Powys

A young woman of 25 who has come from Guernsey to be a lady's companion in Weymouth, where she meets and falls in love with JOBBER SKALD. She has a 'shy and evasive personality' and a 'fixed conviction that fate had made her so totally undesirable'. She is neither plain nor pretty, and is reserved, proud, and inclined to be critical. She was orphaned as a child, and had 'never had anything approaching a love affair' until meeting Jobber.

Wang
The Bundle, 1978
Edward Bond

Wang was the child whom BASHO saw abandoned and refused to nurture. Unlike the tyrant SHOGO in *Narrow Road to the Deep North*, Wang represents humanitarian potential for the future. Having suffered injustice throughout his life, he becomes the leader of an insurrectionist army. According to Bond, he 'combines action with rational concepts and when that happens then things can become truly creative'. Yet when he in his turn discovers an abandoned child, he hurls it into the river, reasoning that he must kill one so as not to be diverted from possibly saving hundreds.

Wang
The Good Earth, 1931
Pearl S Buck

A hardworking Chinese peasant, who marries a woman of extraordinary loyalty and devotion. Coping with good times and bad, he triumphs over the bad (becoming a prosperous landowner), but is corrupted by the good, betraying the love of his wife for a dancing-girl, and losing his best self to the aspirations of social advancement. In the end, he realizes how strong his first wife, O'LAN, has been, but by then he has broken her heart.

Wannop, Valentine
Parade's End, 1924–8
Ford Madox Ford

An elfish, energetic young woman with an

independent spirit. Educated and self-assured, Valentine attempts to break down conventions in a constructive and dignified way, fighting for votes for women, and speaking out against World War I. She is prone to many human weaknesses and insecurities, but her strength in coming to terms with these only makes her more endearing.

Wantonnes
Ane Pleasant Satyre of the Thrie Estaitis, 1540
Sir David Lindsay

One of REX HUMANITAS's three courtiers, Wantonnes – as his name suggests – is sexually promiscuous and, along with PLACEBO and SOLACE, encourages his king to follow suit. Bawdy and vulgar, it is he who, at the king's request, invites DAME SENSUALITIE to the court. By revealing himself to be foolishly ignorant rather than wilfully malicious, with his plea that he had not realized the danger of lechery because of its pervasion in the kingdom, he escapes with only a reprimand from DIVYNE CORRECTIOUN.

Wapshot, Cousin Honora
The Wapshot Chronicle, 1957
The Wapshot Scandal, 1964
John Cheever

The intractable orphaned daughter of a missionary couple, Cousin Honora was brought up by her wealthy Uncle Lorenzo and is renowned for her eccentric benevolence. Her money often saves her relatives from disaster, although the young LEANDER WAPSHOT considers her a 'skinflint'. A short-tempered and indomitable septuagenarian, she loves fire, fireworks and the smell of gunpowder. She is threatened with disgrace when it becomes clear she has never paid any income tax because Uncle Lorenzo forbade her to give his money to the government. However, faced with the threat of the poor house and/or prison, she eschews suicide and adventurously absconds to Italy, feeling that to be thoroughly irresponsible is a privilege of age.

Wapshot, Coverly
The Wapshot Chronicle, 1957
The Wapshot Scandal, 1964
John Cheever

With his long neck and disagreeable habit of cracking his knuckles, Coverly is by far the less attractive of LEANDER WAPSHOT's two sons. Accustomed throughout his youth to hearing his aunts remark 'poor Coverly will never amount to anything', he now shares a turbulent existence with his neurotic wife and fractious child, working at a missile site where, due to computer error, he works in public relations instead of the programming for which he was trained. However, capriciously given to rearranging the facts of his life, he cheerfully ignores unpleasant happenings; in contrast to his brother, MOSES WAPSHOT, his self-esteem is easily shaken.

Wapshot, Leander
The Wapshot Chronicle, 1957
The Wapshot Scandal, 1964
John Cheever

At 19, Leander, scion of St Botolph's oldest family, is forced to work beneath his dignity as a hotel desk-clerk. Captivated by an actress guest, he joins her touring Shakespeare company as a bit-player and bouncer. He is later married to liberated, do-gooder Sarah, and the couple have two sons, MOSES WAPSHOT and COVERLY WAPSHOT. A licentious man, his fine blue eyes and high colour give him a permanently boyish look. He is drowned while swimming and is said to haunt the family house.

Wapshot, Moses
The Wapshot Chronicle, 1957
The Wapshot Scandal, 1964
John Cheever

With his blond good looks, exacting canons of decency and engaging but deceptive humility, everyone in St Botolph's loves Moses – including the dogs. His brother, COVERLY WAPSHOT, is less popular, however, and their relationship is charged with sibling rivalry. Having left his banking career for a shady brokerage house, Moses amasses formidable debts. His troubles are aggravated when his wife leaves with his son following an affair with the grocery store delivery boy. Facing ruin when his rich COUSIN HONORA WAPSHOT also abandons him, Moses, armed with his silver-headed cane, which holds a pint of vermouth, tries to raise money on the strength of his charm and hilariously drowns his sorrows with the widow Wilston.

Warburton, Lord
The Portrait of a Lady, 1881
Henry James

Aristocratic friend of the TOUCHETTs and a suitor first of ISABEL ARCHER and later of her stepdaughter PANSY OSMOND. He represents the solid but essentially static virtues of the European nobility; 'with his pleasant steady eyes, his bronzed complexion, fresh beneath its seasoning, his manly figure, his minimizing manner and his general air of being a gentleman and an explorer, he was such a representative of the British race as need not in any clime have been disavowed by those who have a kindness for it'.

Ward, John
John Ward, Preacher, 1888
Margaret Deland

A devout Calvinist minister whose faith is strongly challenged by his love for the agnostic HELEN JEFFREY. His all too public struggle becomes the subject of scandal in their small Pennsylvania town and he dies without reconciling the tension at the centre of his life.

Ward, Laura
Palomino, 1980
Elizabeth Jolley

Former obstetrician and gynaecologist, Laura is a lesbian in her sixties who has suppressed her sexuality almost all of her life. A ferociously strong woman who lives alone on a farm in rural Australia, she has countered the pain of unreciprocated love by becoming entirely self-contained and self-reliant. She finally finds love and the release for a torrent of affection with Andrea, a younger, emotionally damaged woman. More used to the habit of self-denial and repression than to the free-flow of passion, Laura turns the tap on, but intermittently struggles to turn it off again.

Ward, Mira
The Women's Room, 1977
Marilyn French

Trapped by society's expectations of the suburban housewife, Mira Ward feels unhappy, isolated and victimized. When her marriage disintegrates, she discovers the world of female friendship and support, yet she comes to realize that even this is not enough to keep out pain. Continuing to fear invisibility and the loneliness that accompanies it, she feels alternately dead or electrically alive, but never truly happy: happiness is a condition she cannot maintain, believe in, or trust.

Ward, Victor
Glamorama, 1998
Bret Easton Ellis

'27 and hip', Victor Ward is vain, self-centred and incredibly shallow. An 'It Boy' and model living off the family money, he drifts from party to party and will never make conversation when he can quote a song lyric. He is obsessed with his appearance and only capable of superficial relationships. 'Handsome and dissatisfied', he struggles to comprehend a world beyond the 'semi-famous'. Victor's desire for acceptance leads him unwittingly into international terrorism.

Warden, Henry, formerly **William Wellwood**
The Monastery, 1820
The Abbot, 1820
Sir Walter Scott

A fanatical Protestant preacher, once the college friend of the intellectual sub-prior, FATHER EUSTACE: 'with the animation proper to the enthusiastic reformers of the age, [he] transgressed, in the vehemence of his zeal, the bounds of the discretional liberty allowed to his sect', falling briefly into the hands of the Crown; in the sequel, he is sole guest at the Castle of Avenel, triumphant as its Protestant chaplain, but by no means sure of his safety in a still-divided nation.

Warden, Michael
The Battle of Life, 1846
Charles Dickens

The dissolute young client of Snitchey and Craggs and neighbour of DR ANTHONY JEDDLER. He is wrongly suspected of having eloped with MARION JEDDLER, whom he loves. After Snitchey and Craggs help him to recover his lost fortunes, he reforms and does eventually marry Marion.

Warden, Sgt Milton
From Here to Eternity, 1951
James Jones

Described as 'the meanest son of a bitch in Schofield Barracks', he is obsessed with work, and with making his company superior, and will go to any lengths to ensure this. He hates anything which disrupts its smooth running, including perceived troublemakers like ROBERT E LEE PREWITT. He is contemptuous of officers and their 'beef-eating middle-class assurance' and values, but finds himself sucked into that category through his love for his superior's wife; he acutely feels the loss of self-respect which his capitulation entails.

Wardles, the
Pickwick Papers, 1837
Charles Dickens

Mr Wardle, a bluff and gregarious friend of SAMUEL PICKWICK, plays host to Pickwick and his companions when they visit him at Manor Farm, Dingley Dell. His mother, Mrs Wardle, is very old and very deaf. His spinster sister, Rachael, falls in love with TRACY TUPMAN, but ALFRED JINGLE elopes with her for her money and only relinquishes her when bought off by Tupman for £120. One of Wardle's daughters, Emily, overcomes her father's objections and finally marries AUGUSTUS SNODGRASS.

Wardour, Sir Arthur
The Antiquary, 1816
Sir Walter Scott

The father of LOVEL's lover Isabella (he strongly disapproves of and has thwarted the match), he is a man of 'large but embarrassed fortune'. Of a long-standing Jacobite family, he once shared his father's imprisonment in the Tower of London, but has come to accept the de facto legitimacy of the Hanoverians, even though he still prays in private for the restoration of the defunct Stuarts. Like JONATHAN OLDBUCK, he is an amateur of Scottish history.

Ware, Madeleine
Maurice Guest, 1908
Henry Handel Richardson

A sensible, straightforward girl, she serves to keep MAURICE GUEST's feet firmly on the ground amid the siren songs of artistic Leipzig. It seems likely that she, rather than LOUISE DUFRAYER, is the (female) author's representative in the story.

Ware, Theron
The Damnation of Theron Ware, 1896
Harold Frederic

The aspirant minister of the First Methodist Episcopal Church of Tecumseh, he is a 'tall, slender young man with the broad white brow, thoughtful eyes, and features moulded into that regularity of strength which used to characterize the American Senatorial type in those far-away days of clean-shaven faces and moderate incomes before the [Civil] War'. Already shaky in his faith, the ex-farmboy is ill-equipped to meet the challenge of the go-getting, free-thinking 1890s. Rejection by Tecumseh and a less attractive call from the parish of Octavius further damage his resolve.

Warīinga
Devil on the Cross, 1982, originally published in Gikuyu as *Caitaani Mutharaba-ini*, 1980
Ngugi wa Thiong'o

A socially and sexually downtrodden young Gikuyu woman, trapped in a cycle of history that has no place for her. Her story is told in a mythic, timeless way that elevates it above the mundane and turns it into an archetype of suffering.

Warland, Owen
'The Artist of the Beautiful', 1844, in *Mosses from an Old Manse*, 1846
Nathaniel Hawthorne

A young watchmaker whose quest for the spiritualization of machinery attracts the derision of the townsfolk. He is set in direct contrast to the rugged, utilitarian blacksmith, who is all fire and iron to Owen's delicately filigreed experiments, which culminate in a mechanical butterfly with all the fragility and evanescence of both life and art.

Warren
The Death of the Hired Man, 1914
Robert Frost

Frost avoids the stereotype in this portrayal of a north-eastern American farmer, presenting him as an articulate and sensitive man; despite saying that SILAS, the dying hired man, is 'nothing to us', his reflective and warm conversation with his wife, MARY, suggests otherwise. By the poem's close he has come to represent the victory of decency and humanity over hard economic facts.

Warren, Mrs Kitty
Mrs Warren's Profession, 1894
George Bernard Shaw

A sturdy, showily-dressed, forthright and vulgar woman in her mid-forties, Mrs Warren escaped a background of appalling poverty by becoming the manager of a brothel in Brussels, financed partly by SIR GEORGE CROFTS. She has survived in a capitalist system which regards women as property, rewards vice while sneering at virtue and degrades sex into casual promiscuity. Sentimental but cunning, Mrs Warren now wants the best of everything: friends, money, and the respect of her adult daughter, VIVIE WARREN, who discovers her past. Rejection by Vivie crushes her domineering spirit, but her natural resilience enables her to retreat with some dignity.

Warren, Sid
Tomorrow and Tomorrow and Tomorrow, 1947 (censored), 1983 (uncensored)
M Barnard Eldershaw

A key character in KNARF's 'historical novel', he is a communist taxi-driver who, after serving with the International Brigade in Spain, returns to Australia a fanatical revolutionary. He is a lean, hard man with sardonic eyes and mouth, always observant, watchful and guarded. Popular with his neighbours and attractive to women, he eschews permanent relationships until he meets HARRY MUNSTER's daughter. In the aftermath of World War II, Knarf's fictive version of history has a rebellious Australia about to be occupied by a right-wing military force of 'International Police'. But, commanded by Warren, the citizens destroy Sydney and flee far inland seeking a new freedom.

Warren, Vivie
Mrs Warren's Profession, 1894
George Bernard Shaw

Attractive, confident and determined, Vivie, daughter of the brothel-keeper MRS WARREN, is a 22-year-old graduate of Newnham College, Cambridge, who remains ignorant of the source of her mother's wealth. When she does entice her into admitting her past, Vivie rejects her emotionally while admiring the tenacity that enabled her to survive. Shaw suggests, though, that because of her mother, sex is forever tainted for the pragmatic and emotionally cautious Vivie. She turns her back upon the corrupt world of Mrs Warren and SIR GEORGE CROFTS, and also upon marriage to FRANK GARDNER, in order to concentrate upon her accountancy and legal career.

Warrigal
Robbery Under Arms, 1888
Rolf Boldrewood

The name derives from the Aboriginal word for the dingo, or wild dog, and denotes anything untamed and cunning. In this novel, Warrigal is the half-caste follower of the enigmatic and dashing bushranger, CAPTAIN STARLIGHT. A man of shifting allegiances, Warrigal favours whoever appears to have the advantage at any one time. Along with fellow gang-member, JIM MARSTON, Warrigal effects the escape of Starlight and Jim's brother, DICK MARSTON, from jail. Yet later, when Starlight, Dick and Jim plan to leave Australia for the USA, they are betrayed both by Warrigal and KATE MORRISON. Unruly and anarchic, Warrigal is also selfish and resourceful.

Warrington, George Esmond
The History of Pendennis, 1848–50
The Virginians, 1857–9
W M Thackeray

ARTHUR PENDENNIS's friend and room-mate during his brief apprenticeship in the law, he is the twin grandson of HENRY ESMOND. Sober and serious, George is a good and loyal friend, perhaps a little too good to be entirely convincing. His one miscalculation is to introduce Arthur to the debt-bound Irish journalist CAPTAIN SHANDON. In *The Virginians*, he is lost on a sortie against the French in the Colonies and is presumed dead, but escapes and survives to marry THEO LAMBERT, buoyed up by a legacy from SIR MILES WARRINGTON.

Warrington, Harry Esmond
The Virginians, 1857–9
W M Thackeray

HENRY ESMOND's grandson, he is twin to GEORGE ESMOND WARRINGTON and heir after his brother's presumed death. Less circumspect than his brother, he drinks deeper of life and plunges into a rather dissolute episode, during which he is manoeuvred into an engagement with his cousin MARIA WARRINGTON, who rejects him when George is found still to be alive. Something of an adventurer, he is taken up by BARONESS BERNSTEIN. After being with Wolfe in Quebec, he joins Washington during the War of Independence, finding himself on a different side to his brother. He marries FANNY MOUNTAIN and, when his brother settles in England, takes over the Virginia properties.

Warrington, Maria
The Virginians, 1857–9
W M Thackeray

A calculating and slightly predatory female, she believes that the way to a man's heart is through his wallet. Love, for her, is strongly conditional on the availability of financial resources and can decline with disconcerting speed.

Warrington, Rachel Esmond
The History of Henry Esmond, Esquire, 1852
The Virginians, 1857–9
W M Thackeray

The daughter of HENRY ESMOND and LADY RACHEL CASTLEWOOD, she introduces her father's memoirs to the public with considerable affection, but also with some interesting side-lights on her parents' and stepsister's real natures. As the wife of SIR MILES WARRINGTON, she re-appears in *The Virginians*.

Warrington, Sir Miles
The Virginians, 1857–9
W M Thackeray

From the English branch of the family, he exerts some power in the story by assigning his fortune to GEORGE ESMOND WARRINGTON, who has been cut off by his mother in punishment for having married THEO LAMBERT. He is cordial, considerate, a gentleman at ease with himself.

Warshawski, V I (Victoria)
Indemnity Only, 1982, et seq
Sara Paretsky

Fiercely independent, resourceful and agile as a leopard, V I Warshawski is a Chicago-based private investigator whose unrepentant disregard for legal niceties is a by-word in the city's police department. A lawyer by training, she projects a hard-bitten persona, but has a softer side that makes her susceptible to the demands of a motley array of lame ducks. Still haunted by the premature and protracted death of her mother, she enjoys a number of relationships, but remains wary of committing herself to one man in particular, sensing that the slightest encroachment of her fiercely-earned liberty would drive her insane.

Warwick, Earl of
Saint Joan, 1923
George Bernard Shaw

Richard de Beauchamp, the Earl of Warwick and tutor of the boy king, Henry VI, is presented as the advocate of the feudal and baronial system. In his mid-forties, he supports the burning of JOAN not so much because of her heresy, but for political expediency.

Waspe, Humphrey
Bartholomew Fair, 1614
Ben Jonson

The irritable and complaining guardian-servant of BARTHOLOMEW COKES, Waspe is an upright, conservative man at heart, saddened by Cokes's continual squandering. He persists in giving him advice, and when this fails, he gives way to his natural irascibility and resorts to abusing Cokes and quarrelling with anyone who annoys him. What perplexes and angers Waspe is that everyone appears to ignore his counsel. His foolishness is exposed when he is tricked into handing over Cokes's marriage licence.

Waters, Eddie
Comedians, 1975
Trevor Griffiths

'The Lancashire Lad', 70 years old and a former music-hall comedian, he is acerbic but soft-hearted and is training six young working-class stand-up comics at a Manchester evening class. Eddie was once a political radical, like GETHIN PRICE, but whereas Price believes his own brand of radical comedy might force change for a 'caged, exploited, prodded and pulled at' working class, Eddie has clung to the maxim that: 'Not everything true is funny, and not everything funny is true'. He accuses Price of being full of hatred. Price retorts that the tragedy of Eddie, who mellowed and stayed close to his audiences, is that he lost his anger.

Waters, Esther
Esther Waters, 1894
George Moore

A religious girl who is driven into service by her drunken stepfather. She is innocent of the ways of the world, and is seduced and abandoned by a footman, Larch. She endures poverty and humiliation with great stoicism and courage, until she marries the repentant Larch for the child's sake. Although left penniless after his death, she finally finds the spiritual peace she has sought.

Watkin, Lisa
Bruno's Dream, 1969
Iris Murdoch

The grave, rather gaunt Lisa is the intellectual and ascetic younger sister of DIANA GREENSLEAVE. She takes a first in Greats at Oxford, and is a Communist then a Catholic, and a member of the Poor Clares order. Years later, returning from Paris with tuberculosis, she lives with Diana, and is secretly in love with MILES GREENSLEAVE. Sternly virtuous and ostensibly dedicated, Lisa actually lacks the wholehearted commitment shown by her sister, and there is a surprising change in her austere life.

Watkins, Jerome
Henceforward …, 1987
Alan Ayckbourn

A composer of electronic music, Jerome is in his early forties and lives in north London. His wife and daughter having left him, Jerome lives alone, his despair and creative block symbolized by domestic clutter, his sensitivity and dedication to work by the pristine condition of his musical equipment. Incapable of either giving or receiving love, he seduces a woman only to record raw material for his 'Love' composition. Offered the chance of reuniting with his family, Jerome discovers his greater loyalty is to his music.

Watkins, Mr Utah
Under Milk Wood, 1954
Dylan Thomas

The farmer of Salt Lake Farm in the hills above

the village, whose first name and that of his property imply a certain zealotry. His pastoral method is one of rage and curses, which seem perversely to work. He calls in his cows to milking as 'damned fairies' and one kisses him; he orders his deaf dog to gore the cow in question and gets devoted attention instead. In his dreams, as he counts himself wrongly to sleep, he sees his wife as being like the sheep.

Watkins, Mrs Utah
Under Milk Wood, 1954
Dylan Thomas
The inconspicuous wife of the bombastic farmer MR UTAH WATKINS, she is reduced to a single image – that of her sheep-like quality. Her presence in his territory is that of a voice bleating out a knitting pattern and he counts sheep with her face in his dreams. She trails after her husband and has no personality of her own.

Watkins, Professor Charles
Briefing for a Descent into Hell, 1971
Doris Lessing
Vulnerable, confused and deeply sensitive, he becomes withdrawn after horrendous war experiences, and goes through a period of denial, forgetting people, events and relationships from his earlier life. His outer self is seen through the eyes of others: his wife, friends and acquaintances. A man who is not overly ambitious, he sees the futility of many aspects of life. For him, life is about learning to 'play little games', while war is a long and tedious nightmare.

Watson, Dr John
A Study in Scarlet, 1887, et seq
Arthur Conan Doyle
A former British army surgeon, wounded at the battle of Maiwand, Watson is searching for rooms in London when a friend introduces him to SHERLOCK HOLMES, himself looking for accommodation. Watson thereby becomes Holmes's faithful and trusted associate, a companionship which never falters, even though Watson marries and temporarily leaves 221B Baker Street. He is stalwart, stoic, credulous; the narrator of all but two of the adventures (Holmes foolishly tried his own hand twice), and represents the reader. Watson though, is no fool, and reveals a mischievous humour, while living for the times when 'I found myself seated beside him in a hansom, my revolver in my pocket, and the thrill of adventure in my heart'.

Watt
Watt, 1953
Samuel Beckett
Pushed around, ill-treated and generally bad-mouthed throughout, Watt is Mr Knott's servant, his employment a catalogue of incident and anecdote which merely emphasizes life's disorder. Devoured by a fruitless compulsion to ascribe meaning to his world, his desperate struggle to find substance where none exists is demonstrated in his difficulty to identify a pot with the word 'pot', or himself with the word 'man'. 'The point to remember about poor Watt', says literary critic Vivian Mercier, 'is that he

wants to believe in whatever he has been taught, whatever is in front of his nose'.

Watt, Hugh
Coonardoo, 1929
Katharine Susannah Prichard
Obsessed and consumed by the demands of his drought-stricken cattle-station in the north-west of Australia, Hugh is at once aware and yet resentful of the unspoken bond between himself and the Aboriginal woman, COONARDOO. Irresistibly drawn into the spiritual whirlpool, he struggles against this drowning with the repressed uprightness of the white man who does not succumb to the sensual depravity of 'black velvet'.

Waverley, Edward
Waverley, 1814
Sir Walter Scott
The son of a Hanoverian nobleman. Responsibility for his upbringing is shared by a Jacobite uncle, and the two antagonistic tendencies war within him. Because of ill-health and lack of application, his education has been 'somewhat desultory ... the dainty, squeamish and fastidious taste acquired by a surfeit of idle reading, had not only rendered our hero unfit for serious and sober study, but had even disgusted him in some degree with that in which he had hitherto indulged'. By the time he is commissioned in the Hanoverian army and sent north to Scotland he is already well primed for seduction by the 'storied air' of the Scottish Highlands and the romantic cause of the Young Pretender.

Waverley, Sir Everard
Waverley, 1814
Sir Walter Scott
He 'had inherited from his sires the whole train of Tory or High-Church predilections and prejudices which had distinguished the house of Waverley since the Great Civil War', and his loyalty to the Stuarts divides him from his young brother Richard, the father of Scott's hero EDWARD WAVERLEY. Disappointment in a youthful romance has led Sir Everard to enter his seventies a bachelor, but he treats Edward with a mixture of avuncular tolerance and paternal concern.

Waymarsh
The Ambassadors, 1903
Henry James
An American friend of LAMBERT STRETHER, he clearly regards it as his duty to confront Strether's reserve with the truths of the case. As such, he rather too obviously acts as chorus and narrative convenience.

Wayne, Adam
The Napoleon of Notting Hill, 1904
G K Chesterton
Considered a madman because of his visionary single-mindedness, Adam Wayne is the Napoleonic hero of the novel. As Provost of Notting Hill, he clashes with AUBERON QUIN, King of London, who cannot take local patriotism seriously. Wayne's determination to

preserve the independence of Notting Hill residents results in an eccentrically medieval war against all the other boroughs.

Wayne, Chance
Sweet Bird of Youth, 1959
Tennessee Williams

A man who was 'crowned with laurel in the beginning', he has become a beach bum and gigolo, but has returned to St Cloud to re-establish his relationship with his former lover, Heavenly, whom he unknowingly left behind pregnant and infected with venereal disease; the corruption of their innocent youth is a symbol of the corruption of the American ideal. Eventually, deserted by his most recent 'client', and without further hope of fulfilling his dreams, Chance is castrated.

Wayneflete, Lady Cecily
Captain Brassbound's Conversion, 1899
George Bernard Shaw

Unorthodox, practical and in her mid-thirties, Lady Cecily is a fearless adventuress and a woman of sharp intelligence, vitality and humanity. She sets out on an excursion to the Atlas mountains, accompanied by SIR HOWARD HALLAM and escorted by CAPTAIN BRASSBOUND. Her power and appeal is asexual and rests on the fact that she treats men as she would children in a nursery. She is the only woman in the play, and the female equivalent of Shaw's CAIUS JULIUS CAESAR. Hallam and Brassbound have a score to settle, but Lady Cecily outwits them both. Providence saves her from marrying Brassbound.

Weasley, Ron
Harry Potter and the Philosopher's Stone, 1997, et seq
J K Rowling

The best friend of HARRY POTTER and HERMIONE GRANGER at the wizard school Hogwarts, 'freckle-faced, red-haired, long-nosed' Ron is a good-natured and enthusiastic boy. Fiercely loyal to his close-knit family, he sometimes secretly wishes he could escape from the shadow of his five overachieving older brothers, feeling that 'everyone expects me to do as well as the others, but if I do, it's no big deal, because they did it first'. He is a steadfast, sincere and courageous friend.

Weatherwax, Mistress, also known as
Granny or Esme
Equal Rites, 1986, et seq
Terry Pratchett

The most powerful of the witches of the Ramtop Mountains. Stern and with a sharp tongue, her pragmatic approach to 'headology' contrasts with the showy magical exploits of the wizards. She is an imposing and domineering presence when at home in the village of Bad Ass for 'It was known throughout the Ramtop Mountains that Miss Weatherwax did not approve of anything very much', and wherever her adventures take her, her feet are always firmly on the ground. She is accompanied in her adventures by the formidable and far from strait-laced Nanny Ogg.

Weaver, Alun
The Old Devils, 1986
Kingsley Amis

A minor literary figure who thinks of himself as a great, if overlooked one, Weaver is the author of sturdily Welsh poetry which goes down well with Americans but which is generally agreed to be derivative of Brydan, a famous Welsh poet whose work Weaver had edited. (Several reviewers of the novel assumed Brydan to be Amis's satirical portrait of Dylan Thomas.) Having lived in London for many years, Weaver has made a career of being a professional Welshman, a purveyor of Welsh culture, particularly on television. He is a charlatan: self-satisfied, ingratiating and vaultingly ambitious. Even his famous mane of snowy-white hair is tinted with artificial whitener. Yet at the same time he is lively and (for a short while) stimulating company. The novel traces his return to South Wales, where he intends to become an omniscient literary and cultural figure.

Weaver, the → Five Guildsmen, the

Webb, Emily
Our Town, 1938
Thornton Wilder

The intelligent, imaginative daughter of the editor of the local newspaper in Grover's Corners, New Hampshire. After her marriage to GEORGE GIBBS, she dies in childbirth. In a transitional state, she relives her twelfth birthday and realizes that people do not appreciate life while it is happening.

Webber, George
The Web and the Rock, 1939
You Can't Go Home Again, 1940
Thomas Wolfe

Like Wolfe's earlier and equally autobiographical hero EUGENE GANT, Webber comes to New York City after a straitened childhood, this time in North Carolina. The overwhelming relationship of his life is a stormy affair with ESTHER JACK. An aspiring author, he travels to Europe to soak up its culture but (in the later book) recognizes with horror that this same culture has bred Hitler. Returning to the USA, he takes up the cause of the downtrodden and oppressed.

Webber, Roo
Summer of the Seventeenth Doll, 1955
Ray Lawler

Tall, tanned and taciturn, he exemplifies the Australian male character in all its strengths and insensitivities. Having placed enormous emphasis on youth and physical strength, he cannot cope with life at 41. Having long since rejected a conventional nine-to-five city life, yet unable to cut cane any longer, his inarticulate rage and frustration causes him to brawl with BARNEY IBBOT, and fail to stabilize his relationship with OLIVE. At curtain-fall, he appears destined for an embittered and lonely old age.

Webber, Stanley
The Birthday Party, 1958
Harold Pinter

A long-term guest in the BOLES's 'boarding house',

he is a former pier pianist, in his late thirties. A depressive, pursuing an Oedipal relationship with his ageing landlady, he is reduced to a gibbering wreck by the arrival of NAT GOLDBERG and DERMOT MCCANN, of whose 'operation' he is the target. Their psychological and physical violence reaches its height at Stanley's 'birthday party'; the following morning he is removed by them, to an unknown future.

Webster, Daniel
'The Devil and Daniel Webster', 1937
Stephen Vincent Benét

An American lawyer, farmer and politician, legendary in his lifetime. 'A man with a mouth like a mastiff, a brow like a mountain and eyes like burning anthracite', he also has a kind heart, and helps his fellow New Hampshireman JABEZ STONE defend his soul against MR SCRATCH. This proves to be his hardest case, requiring all his power to appeal to the hearts of men.

Webster, Dan'l
The Celebrated Jumping Frog of Calaveras County, 1865
Mark Twain

'Monstrous proud' of his jumping frog, Dan'l Webster, compulsive gambler JIM SMILEY gets his comeuppance when it loses a jumping contest due to foul play. While Smiley catches another frog to set up a contest, his rival fills Dan'l Webster full of buckshot. As a result the other 'feller's' frog easily wins the jumping contest, though ironically he got it from Smiley. He mockingly repeats his initial challenge, 'Well, I don't see no p'ints about that frog that's any better'n any other frog'; at which point Smiley picks up his amphibian and realizes he weighs too much.

Wedderburn, Alexander
The Virgin in the Garden, 1978
Still Life, 1985
A S Byatt

Casually beautiful, sensitive and creative, Alexander Wedderburn is the kind of man who attracts the admiration, confidences and passion of young women. He responds to these attentions readily enough and experiences genuine desire, but he never takes the irrevocable step, holding back from the kind of commitment in love that he devotes to his art. Although afraid of becoming confined in too close a relationship, 'in flight from suburbs and teacups', Alexander is capable of being supportive when needed and of selflessly sharing in other people's joy.

Wegg, Silas
Our Mutual Friend, 1865
Charles Dickens

An unscrupulous ballad-monger and fruit-stallholder with a wooden leg. He is engaged to read literature aloud to MR and MRS BOFFIN, charging extra for poetry on account of its 'weakening effect on the mind'. With his accomplice, MR VENUS, he attempts to blackmail his employers but is thwarted when Venus tells them of the plot. Exposed and humiliated, he is forced to return to his old jobs on the street.

Weir, Adam, Lord Hermiston
Weir of Hermiston, 1896
Robert Louis Stevenson

The towering, complex figure lurking at the heart of this unfinished masterpiece. A gruff, formidable man whose 'growls were in the nature of pleasantry', the lord justice-clerk conceals a dual personality. He seems unemotional, sufficient to himself. He does not suffer fools gladly and follows his own personal code of conduct to which all, but particularly his neglected son ARCHIE WEIR, must subscribe. Beneath this awesome exterior, however, recondite feelings of attachment reside, as well as a surprising vulgarity, loosened by drink. The inner conflict between the two halves of his character provide the tragic impetus of the novel.

Weir, Archie
Weir of Hermiston, 1896
Robert Louis Stevenson

Educated in a strict moral system by his mother before her early death, Archie Weir despises his father ADAM WEIR's grossness and his reputation as a 'Hanging Judge'. A loner, Archie finds friendship and any form of intimacy very difficult to express. He combines a delicacy of behaviour with outbursts of indignant rage and violence when he feels an injustice has been committed. The main drama of the novel arises not so much from Archie's abortive love for CHRISTINA ELLIOTT, but through the conflict with his father. Archie believes this struggle springs from their very different characters, but in fact it is caused by their essential similarities.

weird sisters, the three
Macbeth, c.1606
William Shakespeare

The 'weird sisters' begin the play and are one of the moving forces in it. Though clearly possessing supernatural powers (clairvoyance, flying, conjuring of spirits, etc) their lengthy exchanges also reveal human qualities of jealousy, humour and sisterhood, as well as establishing them as individual characters working as a team. Their careful insinuation of false ideals, and their equivocal and paradoxical language, bring home the full horror of belief in witchcraft to a modern audience.

Weiss, Dr Ruth
A Start in Life, 1981
Anita Brookner

A university lecturer, she is the first of Anita Brookner's intelligent, discerning, lonely and financially independent heroines. Sadly, she reflects that 'at forty ... her life had been ruined by literature', or rather, by the supposition that classical romantic literature was a faithful reflection of the world. Although her 'pale face prompted no speculations whatever' from other people, she visits Paris and has a reckless affair with an eminent philologist. Yet soon after she returns to England her new confidence and zest for life buckle beneath the weight of daughterly duty as she cares for her elderly father.

Welborne, Frank
A New Way to Pay Old Debts, 1633
Philip Massinger

Having lost a large inheritance, due partly to his own extravagance and partly to the machinations of his evil uncle, SIR GILES OVERREACH, Frank has been reduced to begging in rags and bitterness. Sir Giles continues to persecute him, but Frank, who has retained his pride, manages to outwit him. His wealth regained, he intends to become a soldier, in order to retrieve his honour.

Welland, May
The Age of Innocence, 1920
Edith Wharton

A vision of innocence, May blushes furiously when MRS MANSON MINGOTT refers to naked gods and goddesses adorning a ceiling. Circumscribed by paternalistic and chauvinistic ideologies, this creature of 'abysmal purity' is a living and breathing male fantasy. As NEWLAND ARCHER's devoted wife she becomes one of the most handsome and popular married women in New York, a model of pathetic dependence.

Wellborn, Grace
Bartholomew Fair, 1614
Ben Jonson

Grace is JUSTICE OVERDO's good-looking, determined, independent and sensible ward. Having been promised in marriage to BARTHOLOMEW COKES she rejects him because of his boorish behaviour at Bartholomew Fair and transfers her allegiance to TOM QUARLOUS and his friend, WINWIFE, marrying the latter.

Wellbred
Every Man in his Humour, 1598
Ben Jonson

A brother of GEORGE DOWNRIGHT, he is a young gallant who, with Edward Knowell, travels to London to mock the three fools, CAPTAIN BOBADILL, MATTHEW and STEPHEN. He is a man who enjoys practical jokes, but his malice has its limits. Sensitive to Edward's feelings, he helps to arrange his marriage. Although he is trustworthy at heart, his boisterousness often prevents trust being placed in him.

Weller, Larry
Larry's Party, 1997
Carol Shields

Inward-looking Larry sees his life as a complex series of choices, accidents and coincidences, an attitude that is reflected in his fixation with mazes. Finally, after two failed marriages and a move back to Canada from the USA, he and his partner organize a party, bringing together the people significant in his life. His guests conclude that a maze mirrors the human search for identity, where at the centre there is 'an encounter with one's self'.

Weller, Mr and Mrs Tony
Pickwick Papers, 1837
Charles Dickens

A coachman, Tony Weller is the good-natured and convivial father of SAM WELLER. Considering himself a warning to all men on the evils of marriage, he regrets his second marriage to the widowed landlady of the Marquis of Granby because she is a devoted disciple of the hypocritical REV MR STIGGINS. Fond of his pipe and a drink, he uses the money he inherits on her death to buy a pub. After his son's marriage, he dotes on his grandson, Tony Jnr.

Weller, Sam
Pickwick Papers, 1837
Charles Dickens

The son of MR and MRS TONY WELLER, he is SAMUEL PICKWICK's devoted manservant, hired by Pickwick at the White Hart Inn in London, where he is the 'boots'. He accompanies Pickwick and his friends on their adventures, his resourcefulness contrasting with their innocence and conventional respectability. He is a fund of tall stories and bizarre comparisons, all spoken in Cockney dialect. Kind and protective, he pays to be allowed to accompany Pickwick during his imprisonment in the Fleet. He marries the pretty housemaid Mary, who becomes Pickwick's housekeeper, while their son, Tony Jnr, is doted on by his grandfather.

Wells, Homer
The Cider House Rules, 1985
John Irving

Gentle, determined and 'compulsively neat', Homer Wells absorbs much skill and wisdom from Dr Wilbur Larch, founder of the remote Maine orphanage where he grows up. He wants 'to be of use' – an urge that stays with him – but does not share the old man's belief in abortion and leaves to make his own way. He has never seen the sea or been in love, but when he arrives to work at a fruit farm he has his heart and eyes opened to the world until he can say 'I'm happy, sometimes'.

Wemmick, John
Great Expectations, 1861
Charles Dickens

MR JAGGERS's confidential clerk, and a friend to PIP, he is businesslike and unsentimental in the office, where his motto is to acquire 'portable property'. But he reveals his sentimental side at home, a cottage embellished with fantastic ornaments and playful devices, where he courts Miss Skiffins and cares for his father, whom he affectionately calls 'the Aged P'. He helps Pip try to smuggle ABEL MAGWITCH out of England and eventually marries Miss Skiffins.

Wendoll
A Woman Killed with Kindness, 1603
Thomas Heywood

An impoverished gentleman of some social standing, he admits that by seducing ANNE FRANKFORD he has become a 'villain and a traitor to his friend', her husband JOHN FRANKFORD. He has a high sense of moral transgression, but is weak-natured and also an opportunist, taking Frankford's offer of maintenance with some alacrity and pressurizing Anne into beginning an affair with such persistence that she pities him. Wendoll himself blames the winds of fate for blowing him into such emotional high seas.

Wendover, Squire Roger
Robert Elsmere, 1888
Mrs Humphry Ward
A wealthy Surrey landowner, passionately committed to the life of reason over superstition. He opens his library to the young clergyman ROBERT ELSMERE, who gradually discovers there that his faith is built on sand rather than any logical foundation.

Wendy (Wendy Moira Angela Darling)
Peter Pan: or The Boy Who Would Not Grow Up, 1904 (play), 1911 (book)
J M Barrie
Identified in a stage direction as 'the one of the family, for there is one in every family, who can be trusted to know or not to know', she is bright, rational, instinctively sympathetic, her mother in miniature. And so she becomes in Never-Never Land, her 'last words' before being prepared for the pirates' plank being 'We hope our sons will die like English gentlemen'.

Wenonah
The Song of Hiawatha, 1855
Henry Wadsworth Longfellow
The tall, slender and beautiful daughter of NOKOMIS. Seduced by MUDJEKEEWIS, despite her mother's warnings, she gives birth to HIAWATHA, then dies in anguish, deserted by her son's father.

Wentworth, Captain (Frederick)
Persuasion, 1818
Jane Austen
Now rich and confident, having made himself a successful career at sea, Captain Wentworth, the brother of MRS CROFT, is eager to marry. As the former fiancé of ANNE ELLIOT, he still bears her a grudge for breaking off their engagement many years before, but realizes, in spite of a fleeting attachment to LOUISA MUSGROVE, that the love he feels for her has never really left him. Perceptive and attentive, he gradually lets down the barriers he has built up against Anne, and allows his true feelings to come to the fore.

Wentworth, Charlotte
The Europeans, 1878
Henry James
Elder sister of GERTRUDE WENTWORTH. She has the family pallor and slightness of frame, but her eyes are bright and mobile and she proves to be the real centre of a motherless family. She marries the minister MR BRAND, even though he is somewhat on the rebound from her sister.

Wentworth, Clifford
The Europeans, 1878
Henry James
Rusticated from Harvard for drunkenness, he is youthfully susceptible to his exotic European cousins. Bright and clever, he is 'apt to have an averted, uncomfortable glance, and to edge away from you at times, in the manner of a person with a bad conscience'.

Wentworth, Earl of Strafford
Strafford, 1837
Robert Browning
Politician and leader of the King's Party prior to the Civil War, he is recalled from Ireland and persuaded to lead Charles I's expedition to subdue the Scots. Defeated, he returns to impeach the Parliamentary Party but is himself impeached and condemned to death by the king he so trusts. Devotion to Charles motivates all his actions, and foreseeing the inevitable death of the king, he rejoices 'I shall die first'.

Wentworth, Gertrude
The Europeans, 1878
Henry James
'You would not have pronounced this innocent Sabbath-breaker especially pretty. She was tall and pale, thin and a little awkward; her hair was fair and perfectly straight; her eyes were dark, and they had the singularity of seeming at once dull and restless', a characteristic that perfectly captures her nature. Although she is courted by the ponderous MR BRAND, it is her debonair kinsman FELIX YOUNG who 'wakes her up'.

Wentworth, Rev Francis
The Rector, 1863
The Perpetual Curate, 1864
Margaret Oliphant
Mr Wentworth of St Roque's in Carlingford – fastidious, handsome and a gentleman – has troubles. He cannot afford to marry LUCY WODEHOUSE; his aunts disapprove of his High Church views; so do the Rector and his wife; a mysterious 'other lodger' where he lives and a missing girl create gossip; his brother is going over to Rome; the success of his wharf-side mission arouses jealousy. He continues on his way as calmly as he can and when he is called publicly to account, is cleared of all suspicion.

West, John Henry
The Member of the Wedding, 1946
Carson McCullers
The six-year-old cousin of FRANKIE ADDAMS. A tiny figure with gold-rimmed glasses and a contemplative demeanour, he sometimes has the uncanny appearance of an elderly or miniature adult. A compliant and sensitive child, he is absorbed by the eccentric world of his imagination – which is much exercised by the memory of a freak show hermaphrodite – and punctuates the conversation of Frankie and BERENICE BROWN with wild and persistent questions.

West, Julian
Looking Backward, 2000–1887, 1888
Edward Bellamy
Sent into a hypnotic trance, this young Bostonian is transported forward in time by more than a century, waking to a changed city in which capitalism has been effectively abolished and poverty eliminated. Here he meets DR and EDITH LEETE. A good-natured young man, he is somewhat dilettantish and is profoundly shocked by his return to the squalor of 19th-century Boston.

Westerby, Jerry
The Honourable Schoolboy, 1977
John Le Carré
Newspaper reporter Jerry is the 'schoolboy' in

the code of a telegram to him, and is 'honourable' as a result of his nobleman father. Used by GEORGE SMILEY as an agent to investigate a Hong Kong businessman, Ko, he finds early success, but falls for Ko's mistress and wishes to treat her honourably, thus upsetting the British operation. A physically large, capable sportsman, breezy of manner (calling his paper a 'comic'), he is a schoolboy in international spy diplomacy; his individual gifts are not a match against his own side plus the Americans.

Western, Lady
Salem Chapel, 1863
The Rector, 1863
Margaret Oliphant
The highest of Carlingford society, Lady Western is quite unaware of her effect on REV ARTHUR VINCENT. Speaking casually from her carriage, she bewitches him innocently with her charm and beauty. Her idle interest in his preaching is no more than that; she is not clever and hardly listens. Her elegance, like that of a creature from another world, makes him recoil from his homespun deacons. Her connection with his sister's disappearance, not of her seeking, almost drives him mad.

Western, Sophia
The History of Tom Jones, 1749
Henry Fielding
The object of TOM JONES's most lasting and pure-minded love, SQUIRE WESTERN's daughter is the opposite of her father in every regard. Tall and beautiful, with an air of breeding that far outstrips her 18 years, she is the novel's one unchanging moral standard.

Western, Squire
The History of Tom Jones, 1749
Henry Fielding
SOPHIA WESTERN's father, he has generally had a bad press. A country Tory of the forthright, hanging sort, who probably achieves his apotheosis at the head of a hunt. V S Pritchett considered him 'a cantankerous, greedy, rampaging hog, snorting and snouting round all the graces of life', to which there is no defence except that he is also capable of startling outbreaks of sentimental feeling and humanity.

Westervelt, Dr
The Blithedale Romance, 1852
Nathaniel Hawthorne
A sinister mesmerist who uses his powers to gain control over the fey and rather insubstantial PRISCILLA.

West Indian Narrator, the
The Enigma of Arrival, 1987
V S Naipaul
The narrator of the novel is a Caribbean writer from Trinidad, and of Indian descent. Having achieved international renown, he settles down in a Wiltshire country cottage, and idealizes what he takes to be the immemorial country life of rural England, particularly as he observes it in the activities of JACK, farm labourer and gardener. He comes to realize, however, that ultimately what really dominates his

consciousness is his own deepening sense of mortality.

Westlake, Ned
The Story of a Country Town, 1883
E W Howe
He is little more than a passive observer, watching halfway between entrancement and repulsion as a small-town tragedy unfolds before him. His characteristic stance is feigned detachment, but he cannot separate himself from the story he tells.

Westlock, John
Martin Chuzzlewit, 1844
Charles Dickens
A former pupil of Seth Pecksniff, a close friend of Tom Pinch and a friend of Mr Lewsome. He arranges for Mrs Gamp and Betsey Prig to nurse Lewsome through an illness, thus instigating the revelation of Jonas Chuzzlewit's attempt to poison Anthony Chuzzlewit. He finally marries Ruth Pinch.

Weston, Joby (Joseph)
Joby, 1964
Stan Barstow
A sensitive and perceptive young lad, struggling to make sense of adult life. Leaving behind a well-balanced and secure childhood, he is nonplussed by illness, political ideologies and the irrational contempt held between people. He wants to inhabit a safe and straightforward world, but he begins to realize that moral predicaments in real life are not solved as easily as they are at the movies.

Weston, Mr
Emma, 1816
Jane Austen
A man of 'unexceptionable character, easy fortune … and pleasant manners', the head of a family of 'gentility and property', who is always ready for any social engagement. Although a man of some perception, his objectivity becomes blurred by his haste to think the best of everyone, most noticeably in his willing acceptance of his estranged son FRANK CHURCHILL's integrity.

Weston, Mr
Mr Weston's Good Wine, 1927
T F Powys
A quaintly anglicized God, who brings to the village of Folly Down (a cheerier version of Bunyan's Vanity Fair) the little van from which he peddles his two most potent vintages, Love and Death.

Weston, Rev Mr
Agnes Grey, 1847
Anne Brontë
The curate of the parish in which live the Murrays, the parents of AGNES GREY's two lively charges. Shrewd and observant, he sees clearly how they tease their governess, and shows interest in and sympathy for her position. When Miss Grey leaves the Murrays, he says farewell but hopes they may meet again and that she shares his hope. Later, he is appointed to his own parish, near where she and her mother set up their school, and seeks her out.

Weston, Vance
Hudson River Bracketed, 1927
The Gods Arrive, 1932
Edith Wharton

In *Hudson River Bracketed*, this budding writer is battered by shameful experiences in his personal, social and professional lives. He fears looking like a 'hayseed and ignoramus' in the cosmopolitan New York arts scene and reads voraciously to overcome his deficits. His directness and will to literary power overcome the limitations of his hick background, and he finally enters the world of beauty, poetry and knowledge in *The Gods Arrive*, moving from a self-centred and egotistical ignorance of emotion, art and society to a degree of sensitivity and awareness.

Wexford, Chief-Inspector Reginald
From Doon With Death, 1964, et seq
Ruth Rendell

Chief-Inspector Reg Wexford of Kingsmarkham CID is a local man who has risen through the ranks to become one of the most efficient crime-solvers in Sussex. Middle-aged, of large build, and with an inclination to dress shabbily, he is a student of character, using his psychological insight in the solving of cases, and refusing to dismiss what he does not understand. Sensitive in his dealings with victims or reluctant witnesses, he can show a ruthless streak when dealing with inefficiency or modern technology. He is an avuncular figure to his fellow officers, especially his subordinate Inspector Burden, with whom he has forged a close personal friendship.

Whalen, Jonathan James
The Devil Tree, 1973
Jerzy Kosinski

'My impulse is not to speak or write, but to remain elusive.' Heir on his majority to his father's steel business, Whalen is a would-be writer, obsessed with the controlling power of language, which he hopes will conceal both 'the manipulative, malevolent adult who deceives and destroys; and the child who craves acceptance and love'.

Whana
The Golden Lover, 1943
Douglas Stewart

'The golden lover of your dreams', Whana is the personification of an ideal – love, art, beauty. His 'mountain torrent of words' are a poetry that tempts but ultimately cannot woo the beautiful Maori girl TAWHAI away from the humour and pathos of her village life: 'You are all the world, but you cannot be my home.'

Wharton, Emily
The Prime Minister, 1876
Anthony Trollope

A 'tall, fair girl, with grey eyes, rather exceeding the average proportions as well as height of women'. She marries the unscrupulous but persuasive FERDINAND LOPEZ, but after his suicide is remarried to her childhood sweetheart, a decent, handsome man named Arthur Fletcher, who has gone into politics. She is a little plain, but just 'as we do not light up our houses with our brightest lamps for all comers, so neither did she emit from her eyes their lightest sparks till special occasion for such shining had arisen'.

Wheatley, Gladys
The Big Money, 1936, part of the *U.S.A.* trilogy, 1938
John Dos Passos

A minor character, Gladys is the beautiful 'southern belle' CHARLEY ANDERSON marries after only a short romance. Coming from a rich, very religious background, Gladys disapproves of Charley's lifestyle, rejects his sexual advances after the birth of their second child, and stays with him only for superficial, materialistic gain (and even then only until she can have him set up so that she can sue him for divorce).

Wheatley, Stephen
Spies, 2002
Michael Frayn

Set mostly in the London suburbs during World War II, Wheatley is an 'undersized boy with teapot ears', the willing disciple of his friend Keith Hayward, following him 'open-mouthed and credulous' as they investigate Keith's conviction that his mother is a German spy whose treachery must be exposed. Stephen defers to Keith's authority, partly because he recognizes that the Haywards are higher in the social scale than his own family, and partly because doing so earns him the privilege of apparently being Keith's only friend. However, he is not without intelligence, deductive skill and, when the situation demands, bravery. In the process he discovers much that he does not understand until later in life, and some not even then.

Wheeler, Prairie
Vineland, 1990
Thomas Pynchon

ZOYD WHEELER's daughter, she hangs out with a hugely overgrown case named Isaiah Two Four, who plays in the heavy-metal band Billy Barf and the Vomitones. A cool and unembarrassable Valley Girl, she works at the Bodhi Dharma Pizza Temple and uses 'rilly', 'fresh' and 'awesome' as verbal punctuation marks.

Wheeler, Zoyd
Vineland, 1990
Thomas Pynchon

A victim/survivor of the 1960s, he lives on a government disability allowance which is continued as long as he manifests signs of mental disturbance; the local TV station broadcasts his 'insane' annual leap through a plate-glass window dressed in a lurid print frock. Like a flashback, he finds himself pursued anew by the grim BROCK VOND and the narcotics agent, DETECTIVE HECTOR ZUNIGA.

Whiffle, Peter
Peter Whiffle, 1922
Carl Van Vechten

He is little more than a mouthpiece for his author's more self-consciously dilettantish ideas, an aesthete with a fine eye for fashionable life in pre-World War I New York and Paris.

Whiskerandos, Don Ferolo
The Critic, 1779
Richard Brinsley Sheridan

Hackneyed hero of 'The Spanish Armada', the parodic tragedy within Sheridan's play. The son of a Spanish admiral, he is imprisoned in Tilbury Fort. In love with TILBURINA and loved by her and other women, he dies in a duel with a rival.

Whisky Priest, the
The Power and the Glory, 1940
Graham Greene

The namelessness of the priest imbues him with a universality; he represents a faith sustained against the odds. Outwardly weak and tired, he still fulfils his spiritual duties and responsibilities. He is a lonely, introverted man with an ever-present sense of sin and guilt, which he is unable to communicate. Being a drunkard and the father of a child, he is, by conventional standards, a deeply flawed man. But, although he is ashamed of himself and conscious of his own unworthiness, his faith and compassion for humankind are still strong. He typifies man's brave, but faltering, steps to a spiritual wholeness just beyond reach.

Whitaker
The Long and the Short and the Tall, 1958
Willis Hall

A young radio-operator, stranded with his squad in the Malayan jungle during World War II. His innocence and seriousness make him a target for his more experienced, older colleagues. By the play's horrific ending, he has been established as a symbol of naive manhood, an image strengthened by his final poignant cry of 'Mother'.

White, Paul
Tiburon, 1935
Kylie Tennant

One of the elder brothers of a large, poor white family in Tiburon. Silent, moody, and something of a loner, he dislikes work, and is happiest when buried in a book. JESSICA DAUNT is surprised that this 'tall clodhopper of a boy' from an 'undesirable environment' reacts so strongly to fine poetry. He also writes poetry and songs of his own, and, through sharing books and ideas with Jessica, falls in love with her. Although Jessica sees Paul as different from those around him ('he was something dark and cruel and selfish and sweet'), Paul does not seek to escape Tiburon, finding meaning and contentment in the community there.

White, Rita, properly Susan
Educating Rita, 1979
Willy Russell

A forthright 26-year-old working-class hair-dresser from the north of England, Susan (who assumes what she believes to be the more glamorous name of Rita) enrols in an Open University course in English because, she tells FRANK her tutor, she wants to know 'everything'. Rita craves education, not to converse about literature but to become stronger emotionally, to break free from the drudgery of her work and her housing estate and perhaps the bewildered,

fearful, resentful husband who throws her newly-acquired books into the fire. Her education, she protests, is 'life itself'. Yet although she passes her examinations and gains the confidence to make her own decisions, all her pretensions and uncertainties remain to inhibit her.

White Fang
White Fang, 1906
Jack London

A sled-dog, possibly part wolf, who endures the viciousness of dog-fighting and the bitter cold of the extremities of North Canada in the pioneering era. When he finally experiences human kindness, he tentatively responds, gradually becoming loyal and loving.

White II, Roger
A Man in Full, 1998
Tom Wolfe

A sleek, successful, light-skinned black Atlanta attorney (who cannot think of himself as 'African-American'), with an aesthete's appreciation of Stravinsky and bespoke tailoring, White's values and attitudes have resulted in the unwelcome nickname of 'Roger Too White'. Called upon to defend Fareek 'the Canon' Fanon, a former ghetto-boy and now Georgian Tech footballer accused of date rape by the daughter of a wealthy white businessman, he finds himself confronted by a black city mayor anxious both to defuse the political tensions the case is expected to provoke and alleviate the financial crisis of tycoon CHARLIE CROKER.

Whitefield, Ann
Man and Superman, 1903
George Bernard Shaw

The ward of ROEBUCK RAMSDEN and JOHN TANNER, Ann is an independent, forthright woman and intends to marry Tanner. She foils his escape to Spain by organizing a motor tour with friends. Her power, though, is not primarily sexual: Ann is 'perfectly ladylike', while inspiring confidence as 'one of the vital geniuses' of life. In Tanner's dream, in which he appears as Don Juan, Ann becomes Donna Ana, the female philistine and, like Roebuck Ramsden, representing conventional morality. Her eventual ensnaring of Tanner suggests not a defeat for the intellectual but the marriage of the biological and intellectual forces, the latter being the superior. Their union implies the beginning of a new age which Shaw anticipated as that of the Superman.

White-Jacket
White-Jacket, 1850
Herman Melville

The narrator, a common seaman on the US warship *Neversink*, where he is part of the maintop crew under JACK CHASE, whom he greatly admires. He is named after his 'outlandish garment of his own devising'. He belongs 'up aloft' on the 'giddy yard-arm', but manages to fall off on one occasion, and nearly drowns, losing his jacket in the process. He clearly is educated, and describes life on board in great detail.

Whiteoak, Adeline, née Court
The Building of Jalna, 1945, et al
Mazo de la Roche

Born in 1815, the matriarch of Jalna is introduced in a 'prequel' as the bright, passionate and thoroughly impulsive bride of Captain Whiteoak, who plucks her out of County Mayo and takes her off to found a dynasty in Canada, where the bulk of the tales take place. Even in youth, the indomitable characteristics that mark her as a mature and elderly woman are clearly in place.

Whitford, Vernon
The Egoist, 1879
George Meredith

A poor and rather sober young scholar who lives at Patterne in SIR WILLOUGHBY PATTERNE's employ as tutor to young CROSSJAY. He is sympathetic toward CLARA MIDDLETON and eventually marries her after she breaks off her engagement with Sir Willoughby. Whitford is thought to be modelled on the critic Sir Leslie Stephen and is, by and large, an admiring portrait.

Whitla, Eugene
The 'Genius', 1915
Theodore Dreiser

A talented artist and writer who seeks his fortune in Chicago. He makes a success as a newspaper illustrator and moves on to New York, where the pressures of fame, coupled with a rather slipshod approach to sexual morality, lead to a disastrous breakdown. His conversion to 'family values' and representational art underlines his recovery.

Whitman, Foxy
Couples, 1968
John Updike

The wife of a scientist at Boston University, she has a passionate affair with PIET HANEMA. She bears the surname of the democratic poet who preached polymorphous perversity as the great American way; her first name is equally unambiguous.

Whitman, Walt
Leaves of Grass, 1891
Walt Whitman

'Bearded, sun-burnt, gray-neck'd, forbidding', 'Walt Whitman, a kosmos of Manhattan the son', is the USA's poet of democracy, his poems narrated in prosaic style, growing organically like a creation of Nature, which he views in overtly Pantheistic terms. Full of the optimistic, pioneering spirit of a New World that was still uncharted, he sounds his 'barbaric yawp over the roofs of the world', his real subject being the USA, 'the Nation of many nations'.

Wholesome, Tribulation
The Alchemist, 1610
Ben Jonson

A pastor of the Anabaptist Brethren of Amsterdam, Wholesome is an associate of ANANIAS. He accompanies him to see the alchemist SUBTLE and his assistants, FACE and DOL COMMON, believing their consultations will result in riches for their puritan sect. He is even more gullible than Ananias, silencing his

scepticism and giving Subtle an enormous sum of money. Later, when he tries to retrieve it, he is turned away.

Whorehound, Sir Walter
A Chaste Maid in Cheapside, 1611–13
Thomas Middleton

The possessor of a number of mistresses and a suitor to the 'chaste' MOLL YELLOWHAMMER. Avaricious as well as lecherous, he believes the prospective marriage will fulfil all his requirements, providing him with a woman who possesses both a maidenhead and a dowry. When wounded in a fight with Moll's chosen suitor, he is terrified at the prospect of burning in hell for his sins, but blames the objects of his sin – his mistress and her complaisant husband – rather than himself.

Whymper, Mr
Animal Farm, 1945
George Orwell

A devious solicitor who acts as go-between for the animals and their human neighbours. Although he runs a very small business, he is sufficiently astute to realize that Animal Farm will need a broker and that he stands to make a fortune from commissions. Being all things to all men (and all animals) he is willing to prostitute his legal professionalism in return for self-advancement. The law is revealed to be as morally fickle as the successive governments of Manor Farm.

Wicked Witch of the West
The Wonderful Wizard of Oz, 1900
L Frank Baum

Like her sister from the East, the Witch of the West represents evil, specifically the crazed desire for gold and material progress that characterized contemporary California. (By contrast, the Witches of North and South are both good and kindly.) DOROTHY confronts the witch and manages to destroy her by dousing her with water.

Wickfield, Agnes
David Copperfield, 1850
Charles Dickens

DAVID COPPERFIELD's childhood companion and dear 'sister' when he lodges with her family while attending DR STRONG's school in Canterbury, and later his second wife. She acts as housekeeper to her widowed and unhappy father, MR WICKFIELD, who loves her obsessively. When URIAH HEEP fraudulently obtains control over her father's affairs, David fears that she might marry Heep in order to save her father from ruin. She loves David, but unselfishly befriends DORA SPENLOW when he marries her instead. After Dora's death and David's sojourn abroad, she marries him.

Wickfield, Mr
David Copperfield, 1850
Charles Dickens

A Canterbury solicitor and MISS BETSEY TROTWOOD's legal adviser. A widower, he lives with his daughter, AGNES WICKFIELD, but his obsessive love for her and his heavy drinking cause him to neglect his business. He falls into the clutches of his clerk and later partner, URIAH HEEP, who fraudulently obtains control of everything he owns. Nearly ruined, he regains his reputation and property when Heep is exposed by MR WILKINS MICAWBER.

Wickham, George
Pride and Prejudice, 1813
Jane Austen

The son of a former employee of FITZWILLIAM DARCY's father, Wickham, on first appearance, is a very charming, handsome young officer who delights all the ladies in the neighbourhood with his flattery and gallantry. Revealed, however, to be an irresponsible and unscrupulous playboy, his elopement with LYDIA BENNET confirms all that Darcy has told ELIZABETH BENNET about him.

Widmerpool, Kenneth
A Dance to the Music of Time, 12 volumes, 1951–75
Anthony Powell

The invariably ridiculous, eventually somewhat sinister, figure, who dogs Powell's *roman fleuve*. He is described as 'fairly heavily built, thick lips and metal-rimmed spectacles giving his face as usual an aggrieved expression'. A figure of fun to his fellow pupils at boarding school, he commits the solecism of wearing 'the wrong kind of overcoat', hence the name 'a Widmerpool' for any obtrusive or inappropriate garment. His first love is Barbara Goring, whom he has adored since his father supplied hers with manure; Barbara reciprocates by pouring a bowl of sugar over him at a ball. He marries Pamela Flitton (PAMELA WIDMERPOOL), the niece of CHARLES STRINGHAM. Indefatigable in his pursuit of power and status, he overcomes dismissal from Donners-Brebner, sexual rejection and social embarrassment to become a Labour MP and ultimately Lord Widmerpool. He exits from the stage in *Hearing Secret Harmonies* (1975), dying in his sixties in bizarre circumstances, having late in life taken to indulging in pagan sexual rites which, for reasons that are not entirely clear, involve running naked through a wood in the early hours of the morning.

Widmerpool, Pamela
A Dance to the Music of Time, 12 volumes, 1951–75
Anthony Powell

Christened Pamela Flitter, she is thought to be 'comely'. During the war she is an ATS driver. Rumours abound of her 'goings-on' and her sex life is referred to as 'gladiatorial'. Much younger than her spouse KENNETH WIDMERPOOL, she is expected to make 'an admirable canvasser' for her husband in his position as a backbencher, but gives him the runaround, disappearing abruptly from funeral services and other social occasions. For Widmerpool, 'Anything was preferable to lack of information as to what Pamela might be doing.'

Widow Blackacre, the
The Plain Dealer, 1676/7
William Wycherley

Petulant and terribly litigious, the Widow Blackacre is given to talking in almost incomprehensible legal jargon. Her blazing temper is often directed at lawyers who fail to do her bidding: 'Gadsbodikins, you puny Upstart in the Law, to use me so, you Green Bag Carrier, you Murderer of unfortunate Causes, the Clerks Ink is scarce off your fingers, you that newly come from Lamblacking the Judges shoes, and are not fit to wipe mine; you call me impertinent and ignorant!'

Widow Quin
The Playboy of the Western World, 1907
J M Synge

A vigorous, spirited woman of about 30 with 'a great yearning to be wedded' for the second time, Widow Quin is PEGEEN MIKE's principal rival for the love of CHRISTY MAHON. Independent, determined, passionate and shrewd, she killed her man by striking him with a pick, which gives her an advantage over Christy, whose boasts of killing his own father are shown to be false. It also gives her a sense of emotional maturity over Pegeen Mike.

Wieland, Clara
Wieland, 1798
Charles Brockden Brown

The confused narrator of the novel, who attempts to understand the events going on around her (such as the spontaneous combustion of her father). Clara's resilience is notable, and she admits that FRANCIS CARWIN's 'evil' influence in her life only gained hold because of 'the errors of the sufferers'. Clara combines fear, anger, desire and hatred, her experiences leading her to say: 'To all that is to come I am perfectly indifferent … I am callous to misfortune'.

Wieland, Theodore
Wieland, 1798
Charles Brockden Brown

Theodore's unswerving belief in the attainability of perfect 'truth' through rational means (he reveres Cicero's oratory) and his enthusiastic nature are an explosive mixture, leaving him vulnerable to FRANCIS CARWIN's deceits. The 'moral necessity and Calvinistic inspiration' which his sister, CLARA WIELAND, calls his 'props' lead to his 'transformation' into a murderer and suicide. He wishes to be more than '*mere man*', and so the murder of his children is thus 'a sacrifice to duty', the duty of following the 'voice' in his head.

Wife of Bath, the, also known as Alisoun
The Canterbury Tales, c.1387–1400
Geoffrey Chaucer

Fond of seeing and being seen, she acknowledges no superior. Over 40, a little deaf from a blow to the head from one her husbands and with widely spaced teeth – thought to indicate (among other things) lasciviousness – she surpasses others in everything, from the size and ostentation of her hats to the number of pilgrimages she has made. A loud and cheerful individual, she has had five husbands and now is on the lookout for number six. She has always had the upper hand over her husbands, and tells a tale of female domination in marriage.

Wilbourne, Harry
The Wild Palms, 1939
William Faulkner
A young New Orleans doctor who is conducting an affair with the married CHARLOTTE RITTENMEYER, with whom he shares a profound distrust of contemporary social values. Their flight in search of a more authentic existence condemns him to an ultimate betrayal of his professional oaths, and a painful proof of the impossibility of evading everyday responsibilities.

Wilbur, Rev Homer
The Biglow Papers, 1848
James Russell Lowell
The pastor of the First Church of Jaalam, he has also taken on the responsibility of editing and providing a commentary to HOSEA BIGLOW's dialect verses on current affairs. This he does with a stolid and humourless precision, no *i* undotted, no *t* uncrossed.

Wilcox, Henry
Howards End, 1910
E M Forster
A man of 50 with a 'copper-coloured face', Henry Wilcox is a stuffy Church of England traditionalist who reads *The Times*, believes that a woman's place is by her husband's side and would rather conceal his emotions beneath an implacable exterior than attempt to understand them. Brusque, businesslike, unthinking and sometimes unfeeling, he expects obedience and virtue from those around him, even if his own past contains its share of indiscretion. His marriage to MARGARET SCHLEGEL is based on a desire for 'comradeship and affection', which she provides, taking care not to upset his equilibrium with 'emotional talk or a display of sympathy'.

Wilcox, Victor
Nice Work, 1988
David Lodge
The Managing Director of Pringle & Sons, an ailing engineering firm in Rummidge, in the British Midlands, Wilcox is in his late-forties, believes fervently in the work ethic but doubts the future of the firm as much as his marriage to the menopausal Marjorie. Attempting to compensate for both his feeling of being short-changed and his short stature by adopting a brusque, even aggressive manner, Wilcox finds himself at odds with the academic ROBYN PENROSE, to whose intelligence he begrudgingly defers but whose liberal politics he instinctively derides as unrealistic. As their relationship grows, however, he later finds himself developing feelings he never knew he possessed, and an interest in poetry in all its forms.

Wild Boar of the Ardennes, the → de la Marck, William

Wild, Jane
The Bad Sister, 1978
Emma Tennant
The natural daughter of a Scottish laird, whose legitimate 'bad sister', Ishbel, is the same age, Jane gets her name from a commune of strange,

left-wing women all called 'Wild', and led by the witchlike Meg whose malign influence has dominated Jane's life. Imbued with their violently militant beliefs, and radical by temperament, Jane nevertheless searches for peace and harmony and, deprived of her father, for some 'missing male principle' in herself. When he and Ishbel are brutally murdered, the question is whether Jane is responsible, and who is really the 'bad sister'.

Wild, Jonathan
The Life of Jonathan Wild the Great, 1743
Henry Fielding
Jonathan Wild is a classic example of 'Bombast Greatness'. With allusions to Alexander the Great and Julius Caesar, there is no doubt that he is a 'great' man. However, corruption and hypocrisy seethe under the façade of heroism. He is a master of fraud, and even his marriage to Laetitia is a ridiculous pretence. An unscrupulous criminal, this swaggering rogue lives by duplicity and bullying thuggery.

Wildeve, Damon
The Return of the Native, 1878
Thomas Hardy
With a failed career as an engineer behind him, he has returned to become an innkeeper on his native Egdon Heath, but he now finds himself a dissatisfied outsider. He rejects nature, gambles and flirts, but despite his ladykilling prowess, he is cast off by EUSTACIA VYE. It is at least partly out of revenge for this spurning that he is prepared to marry THOMASIN YEOBRIGHT – an indication of the selfish, rash and shallow nature of his motivation.

Wildfire, Madge, properly Magdalen Murdockson
The Heart of Midlothian, in *Tales of My Landlord: Second Series*, 1818
Sir Walter Scott
The daughter of MEG MURDOCKSON, she is 'a tall, strapping wench of eighteen or twenty, dressed fantastically in a sort of blue riding-jacket, with tarnished lace, her hair clubbed like that of a man, a Highland bonnet, and a bunch of broken feathers … Her features were coarse and masculine, yet at a little distance, by dint of very bright, wild-looking black eyes, an aquiline nose, and a commanding profile, appeared rather handsome'. She is, nonetheless, quite mad.

Wildrake, Roger
Woodstock, or The Cavalier, 1826
Sir Walter Scott
A gentleman of Squattlesea Mere, 'in the moist county of Lincoln', who is called upon by COL MARKHAM EVERARD to deliver a packet to OLIVER CROMWELL. His name gives him away. As John Buchan says, he is 'the rakehelly cavalier of all time, bibulous, blasphemous, heroic, and endearing', and it is Wildrake who eventually announces the Restoration to the king.

Wilfer, Bella
Our Mutual Friend, 1865
Charles Dickens
The favourite daughter of REGINALD WILFER,

whom she adores, she is 'exceedingly pretty' but spoiled and impatient with the family's poverty. Under the terms of old John Harmon's will, she is betrothed to marry JOHN HARMON in order for him to claim his inheritance but, believing him to be dead before they can marry, she goes to live with MR and MRS BOFFIN and enjoys their life of wealth. Her mercenary nature is observed by Harmon when he lodges with the Wilfers under the name of 'John Rokesmith' and works as Boffin's secretary. For her benefit and to show her the ugly side of wealth, Harmon and Boffin make her believe that Boffin has become a miser. Her character is reformed and she marries 'John Rokesmith' for love, not money. Eventually, her husband's true identity is disclosed and they enjoy his inheritance.

Wilfer, Reginald
Our Mutual Friend, 1865
Charles Dickens

A poor, downtrodden clerk with a large family, he has a childlike, affectionate nature but is henpecked by his formidable wife, who affects a gloomy, majestic manner. She addresses him as 'R.W.' and his colleagues call him Rumty. His favourite daughter, BELLA WILFER, brightens his life with her playfulness and entertainments. On the day she marries 'John Rokesmith', unaware that he is JOHN HARMON, the three celebrate by dining together at Greenwich. Already made happy by Bella's marriage and the birth of a grandchild, he is finally able to resign his job when Harmon comes into his inheritance.

Wilford, Rennie
Bodily Harm, 1981
Margaret Atwood

A journalist for a glossy magazine, Rennie Wilford is a woman whose recent struggle with breast cancer has left her emotionally scarred. She is afraid to feel and prefers to consider herself a tourist and a transient, avoiding commitments and politics. She flees her roots and courts invisibility. Her sinister Caribbean surroundings and her inscrutable companions, however, teach her that running away and remaining uninvolved are limited options. While incarcerated in a Caribbean prison, Rennie learns to touch, which in turn restores her ability to feel.

Wilhelm, Tommy
Seize the Day, 1956
Saul Bellow

A middle-aged ex-actor turned inept salesman, whose ventures and plans are constantly beset by failure. His marriage is also failing, and he feels himself to be 'drowning' in a deadening emotional and spiritual constriction, in which 'the spirit, the peculiar burden of his existence, lay on him like an accretion, a load, a lump'. He has not lost hope of discovering a larger spiritual life, however, and after touching the bottom in his material decline, finds release in confronting another man's death with tears which carry him 'towards the consummation of his heart's ultimate needs'.

Wilkes, Ashley
Gone with the Wind, 1936
Margaret Mitchell

The courteous, gentlemanly object of SCARLETT O'HARA's obsession. He has a quality of reserve which sets him apart from his more forthright, even vulgar, neighbours. Although he hunts, gambles and participates in the social scene, these pursuits are not his sole aim in life. He is a complex figure of liberal persuasion, interested in books, music and in writing poetry. There is an Englishness of the Old South about his nature. Ashley's marriage to Melanie Hamilton triggers Scarlett's jealousy and her own subsequent, hard-learned lesson in maturity.

Wilkins, Cassandra
Manhattan Transfer, 1925
John Dos Passos

An ex-dancer, she is a mysterious, 'funny-looking girl' with an affected 'tittering lisp'. Prone to hysterical emotional outbursts, she is amusingly and idealistically obsessed with the pursuit of aesthetic perfection in her career as one of HARRY GOLDWEISER's actresses. Desiring only 'spiwitual beauty' in her relationships with men, she is financially abused and then made pregnant by her unemployed fiancé Morris McAvoy. In disgusted desperation, she turns to her friend and role-model ELLEN THATCHER, who arranges an abortion for her.

Wilkins, Mrs Deborah
The History of Tom Jones, 1749
Henry Fielding

A maidservant in the home of SQUIRE ALLWORTHY who, 'though in the fifty-second year of her age, vowed she had never beheld a man without his coat'. She is charged with finding out who the foundling TOM JONES's mother is. Her march down the main street of the village has the same effect as a hawk hovering above pigeons.

Willard, Buddy
The Bell Jar, 1963
Sylvia Plath

A medical student and one-time boyfriend of ESTHER GREENWOOD, Buddy remains a hazy figure who is significant only in so far as Esther's perception of him is concerned. He is seen to be a shallow, fairly harmless character, incapable of understanding Esther and never thinking to question his motives in wishing to marry her. At the same time he is a source of vexation to her, an obstacle which has to be overcome in her efforts to be free from the things which would restrict her.

Willard, Elizabeth
Winesburg, Ohio, 1919
Sherwood Anderson

'Tall and gaunt ... her face marked with smallpox scars. Although she was but forty-five, some obscure disease had taken the fire out of her figure.' The mother of the young Winesburg reporter, GEORGE WILLARD, she had 'borne a somewhat shaky reputation' in her youth. Inclined to be stage-struck, she 'had paraded through the streets with travelling-men guests at her father's hotel, wearing loud clothes and urging them to tell her of life in the cities'.

Willard, George
Winesburg, Ohio, 1919
Sherwood Anderson
George is a reporter on the *Winesburg Eagle*, a position that affords him an ideal perspective on the lives and peccadilloes of the townsfolk. Sitting with his girl in the deserted fairground he 'felt very keenly his own insignificance in the scheme of existence' and as if the mutual but unapproved attachment to Helen White had effected a 'minute adjustment in the machinery of his life', instilling in him the 'sadness of sophistication'. Shortly afterwards, he leaves Winesburg forever.

Willard, Jim
The City and the Pillar, 1948
Gore Vidal
The eldest son of an embittered county clerk and a martyr-like mother, he is an ordinary, middle-class youth from Virginia. Handsome, golden-haired and athletic, only his homosexuality sets him apart from the traditional values and comfortable assumptions of his peers. Inspired by a cherished recollection of a sun-drenched idyll with an adolescent soul mate, he vainly searches for a romanticized notion of masculine love that is forever denied him.

Willet, Joe
Barnaby Rudge, 1841
Charles Dickens
The son of JOHN WILLET of the Maypole Inn. A strapping lad of 20, he resents his father's treating him as a child. He is in love with DOLLY VARDEN, but when she snubs him, he enlists in the army, fights in the American War of Independence, and loses an arm. Returning to England in time to help his friends during the Gordon Riots, and to rescue Dolly and EMMA HAREDALE from abduction, he earns the affectionate respect of his father and later marries Dolly.

Willet, John
Barnaby Rudge, 1841
Charles Dickens
The landlord of the Maypole Inn in Chigwell. A burly, obstinate character, he is encouraged in his errors and dogmatism by his sycophantic cronies. He browbeats his son, JOE WILLET, until the boy runs off to be a soldier. When the Inn is wrecked in the Gordon Riots, he never recovers from the shock, or from the remorse he feels over Joe's lost arm.

William
Just William, 1922, et seq
Richmal Crompton
When not engaged in experimental cookery (stunning combinations of Turkish delight, Worcester Sauce, sardines and blackberries) William and the Outlaws spend their time 'trackin'' and 'shootin'' bows and arrows at things'. An eloquent conversationalist and subtle schemer, he is much maligned and misunderstood by his parents, who seem to prefer reading the paper and darning socks to fathoming the depths of his mind. His father, although convinced of William's lunacy, nevertheless appreciates his knack of ridding the family of unwelcome relatives. William's strong dramatic sense enables him to slip effortlessly from one role to another; in the same afternoon he can be Red Indian Chief, love-lorn swain, or shifty gangster. His good intentions combined with an over-literal turn of mind mean that it is just when he is 'tryin' to do good all the time' that his most amusing disasters occur.

William, Father
Alice's Adventures in Wonderland, 1865
Lewis Carroll
The Caterpillar demands that ALICE recite 'You are old, Father William', an improving poem by Southey, but something goes wrong with it. In her version, Father William, far from being an exemplary parent, stands on his head, turns back-somersaults, exercises his jaws by arguing with his wife and balances an eel on the end of his nose, and, when questioned further, tells his son to go away or else be kicked downstairs.

Williams, Abigail
The Crucible, 1953
Arthur Miller
An adolescent girl, niece to the local minister and, briefly, the lover of JOHN PROCTOR, to whose wife she was, at the time, in service. Her lustful desire to continue her relationship with Proctor is the root cause of the hysteria which dominates the play. She is a disturbed and frightening girl whose accusations carry the weight of simplicity and (apparent) naivety.

Williams, Caleb
Caleb Williams, 1794
William Godwin
A flawed hero. Employed in the household of the landlord FALKLAND, he discovers the secret machinations of his master and torments him. He in turn, however, finds himself unjustly brought to trial and is persecuted by his employer and by a society which, too often, abets injustice and despotism. Caleb philosophizes that 'sound reasoning and truth, when adequately communicated, must be victorious over error'. Nevertheless, he also sadly acknowledges that reason does not always triumph, and truth is often difficult to recognize. In many respects Falkland and Caleb are mirror images of each other.

Williams, Clay Clay
Dutchman, 1964
Amiri Baraka
America's quintessential black middle-class stereotype of the Civil Rights era. Predictable, unimaginative and assuming, Clay's identity could be read like an open book. However, his revolutionary potential, contained and sapped by years of 'Uncle Tom-ism', surfaces when a white woman, LULA, reminds him of the historical, cultural, social and economic factors that have determined Clay's position on America's ladder of racial stratification.

Williams, Janey
The 42nd Parallel, 1930
1919, 1932
The Big Money, 1936, forming the *U.S.A.* trilogy, 1938
John Dos Passos
The plain, quiet, middle-class Washington girl

who longs for her own independence and, in 1916, starts to work in New York as private secretary to J WARD MOOREHOUSE. Intelligent, ambitious and more than a little in love with J Ward, Janey works hard, but her prim, self-important and upwardly mobile nature create an awkward gulf between her and her family, most notably her formerly beloved rough-and-tumble sailor brother, JOE WILLIAMS.

Williams, Joe
The 42nd Parallel, 1930
1919, 1932, part of the *U.S.A.* trilogy, 1938
John Dos Passos

Beaten by his father as a boy, kind-hearted Joe runs away to join the navy, and despite being homesick and eager to settle down, circumstances contrive against him, making it impossible for him to leave the sea for long. Sickened by life as a seaman, constantly drinking and going to brothels, Joe nevertheless feels more at home and less disillusioned with this than with the high-powered, patriotic environment inhabited by his now standoffish sister, JANEY WILLIAMS.

Williams, Leslie
The Hostage, 1957
Brendan Behan

The hostage of the title, he is a young Cockney soldier in Ireland. Having been kidnapped, he is brought to a Dublin lodging house and part-time brothel run by Patrick, a veteran of the Irish rebellion, and inhabited by a motley crew of eccentrics and wastrels. Some are sentimental, some fanatical and others even wryly cynical in their love for Ireland, but Williams has little political commitment. Instead, he falls in love with the young servant, Theresa, whom he misguidedly hopes might help him escape.

Williams, Miss Nancy
The Adventures of Roderick Random, 1748
Tobias Smollett

Reduced to prostitution in the streets of London, she was formerly a respectable lady, brought up in a strict Presbyterian household. Comprehensively ill-used, she has run away and is cheated of a happy reconciliation with her father by his death. At the Marshalsea prison she is briefly confused with a fellow prostitute, Bett Carey. Rescued from her plight, she eventually marries RODERICK RANDOM's man HUGH STRAP.

Williams, Mr
Pamela, 1740–1
Samuel Richardson

Dependent on the patronage of MR B, Mr Williams lacks autonomy and the means for an authentic existence. The morally correct clergyman pities PAMELA ANDREWS and strives to free her from Mr B's tyranny. He is punished for his 'seditious commotions' and is imprisoned and viciously assaulted for his rebellion.

Williams, Parson
An Apology for the Life of Mrs Shamela Andrews, 1741
Henry Fielding

Preaching a pernicious doctrine that offers a specious, conscience-salving absolution while at the same time encouraging immorality, Parson Williams is a sophisticated manipulator of spiritual truths. He propagates an idealogy which asserts that personally-held beliefs and not public actions are important: singing psalms and honouring the clergy count for more than vigorous do-gooding. Energetic in the pursuit of pleasure, principally derived from the 'saucy Baggage' PAMELA, Parson Williams sings the praises of the body and not the glory of God.

Williams, Private Ellgee
Reflections in a Golden Eye, 1941
Carson McCullers

An enigmatic young soldier who becomes obsessed with LEONORA PENDERTON. In his childlike self-absorption he has neither friends nor enemies; wary of women and uninterested in the smoking, drinking and gambling of his comrades, his only emotional attachment is his bond with horses. His thoughts are elusive even to himself and his actions are always impulsive and sometimes violent.

Willieboy
A Walk in the Night, 1962
Alex La Guma

A rootless, unemployed boy, with a deprived upbringing of beatings and a subsequent criminal record. Scorning work, he makes his living by menacing individuals for money or relying on a network of credit. Finding the Irishman killed by MICHAEL ADONIS, he runs away, but is betrayed by another black man. Easily identified by his conspicuous yellow T-shirt, he is chased and fatally shot by the police.

Willing, Mr
The Late George Apley, 1937
John P Marquand

He is asked by GEORGE APLEY's son and daughter to prepare a memoir of their father's life. It is clear that he shares virtually all of Apley's conservative and Puritan values, but his poise slips sufficiently often to reveal the more negative aspects of Bostonian Brahminism as it confronts the 20th century.

Willis, Laetitia ('Letty')
The Expedition of Humphry Clinker, 1771
Tobias Smollett

Boarding-school friend and confidante of LYDIA MELFORD, she follows the course of the expedition by means of Lydia's letters until contrivance draws her into the final tying of knots. JERY MELFORD proclaims her 'a charming girl ... gay, frank, a little giddy, and always good-humoured. She has, moreover, a genteel fortune, is well born, and remarkably handsome'.

Willis, Stanley, Lt jg
Guard of Honor, 1948
James Gould Cozzens

A young black flier, he is involved in a near-miss incident with his commanding officer, MAJOR GENERAL IRA N BEAL while coming in to land at their Florida airbase. He is impulsively thrashed by LT COL BENNY CARRICKER, and his injuries become the basis of a protest against racial discrimination.

Willmore
The Rover, 1677
Aphra Behn

The play is set in a 17th-century Spanish colony during carnival, when three sisters wander through the streets, looking for suitable husbands. They encounter four Englishmen, led by Willmore, the wild, dashing, philandering but impoverished rover of the title. The play is in part a high comedy of sexual manners, part romp, part morality tale, part revenge tragedy. Willmore represents fickle boyish charm. Enamoured by Angelica Bianca, a famous courtesan, he also flirts with another woman, yet he has neither deceived nor enticed Angelica with promises he has no intention of keeping. Sometimes petulant and tactless, his flamboyance makes teasing tempting, vice alluring and adventuring irresistible.

Willoughby, John
Sense and Sensibility, 1811
Jane Austen

Handsome, affectionate and extremely lively company, Willoughby is worshipped by MARIANNE DASHWOOD and seems to reciprocate her feelings. As lacking in principles as he is in money, however, he is revealed to be a thoughtless trifler with affections, a libertine of extravagant habits whose impetuosity causes much grief, and while not entirely without conscience, he seems virtually powerless to modify his behaviour.

Willowes, Edmund
'Barbara of the House of Grebe', in *A Group of Noble Dames*, 1891
Thomas Hardy

A young man with everything in his favour, Edmund is much more than a pretty face. Intelligent, refined, artistic, sensitive and caring, he feels a deep and sincere love for BARBARA GREBE, with whom he elopes. When he is disfigured, he is still the same beautiful person, but is not arrogant enough to force himself upon another. He has dignity and pride, and believes in periods of reflection as part of a healing process.

Willowes, Lolly (Laura Erminia)
Lolly Willowes, 1926
Sylvia Townsend Warner

A gentle creature with large grey eyes, she is of 'middle height, thin and rather pointed', with a skin tone inclined to sallowness. Following the death of her father, she moves to London and is welcomed into the bosom of her brother's family as a well-liked if somewhat diffident maiden aunt. During the ensuing 20 years of deadening domestic routine she is described as 'not wildly anxious either to die or to live'. Then, at the age of 47, her long suppressed self-assertiveness finally emerges and she moves to the Chilterns, where she becomes a witch.

Willy
The Sea, 1973
Edward Bond

Willy survives the storm at the beginning of the play during which Colin, his friend and ROSE JONES's lover, dies. An honest, open man, curious for knowledge, he turns to the mysterious EVENS for help. At the end of the play, he and Rose anticipate a new life together. He represents compassion and freedom from prejudice which Bond suggests are crucial for our survival.

Willy-Nilly
Under Milk Wood, 1954
Dylan Thomas

Bandy-legged from riding his bicycle, the postman passes on the news in Llaregyb. He announces the contents of the letters as he delivers them, noting reactions as further gossip. His wife steams open the envelopes, but in her dreams her guilty conscience gets its revenge: she thinks she is being punished for tardiness at school, as her husband knocks on her as a door during his comatose rounds.

Wilmot, Arabella
The Vicar of Wakefield, 1766
Oliver Goldsmith

The daughter of a rich clergyman, Arabella is about to marry GEORGE PRIMROSE, the eldest son of the equally wealthy DR PRIMROSE, the Vicar of Wakefield. Dr Primrose is morally outraged to discover that Arabella's father is considering marrying for the fourth time, while Arabella's father cancels the wedding when he finds that Dr Primrose has lost his fortune. George leaves, and after many adventures in which each learns more of the cruelties and ironies of life, Arabella meets him again. This time, she melodramatically declares that if she cannot marry George, she will never marry at all.

'Wilson'
The Expedition of Humphry Clinker, 1771
Tobias Smollett

Objecting to a match decided by his parents, he escapes from Cambridge and becomes a strolling player, the better to pursue LYDIA MELFORD on her family tour through England and Scotland. Though rejected as an acceptable suitor by Lydia's guardian, he is subsequently discovered to be of gentle birth (son of CHARLES DENNISON) and reveals himself to be, in the words of Lydia's brother, JERY MELFORD, 'one of the most accomplished young fellows in England. His person is at once elegant and manly, and his understanding highly cultivated. Tho' his spirit is lofty, his heart is kind; and his manner so engaging, as to command veneration and love'.

Wilson, Alison
Old Mortality, in *Tales of My Landlord*, 1816
Sir Walter Scott

Trusted housekeeper and servant of SILAS MORTON OF MILNWOOD, towards whom she behaves with a subtle blend of 'freedom and respect'; though garrulous, she is close and loyal. She initially fails to recognize her younger master, HENRY MORTON, when he returns, Odysseus-like, after a long absence.

Wilson, David 'Pudd'nhead'
The Tragedy of Pudd'nhead Wilson, 1894
Mark Twain

On the day he arrives from New York this young lawyer is nicknamed 'Pudd'nhead' by the boorish citizens of Dawson's Landing, Missouri, who take literally his ironic humour and snort dismissively at his enthusiasm for the latest scientific ideas. He is pleasant and well-liked, but counts for nothing in the eyes of the townsfolk, who take their legal problems elsewhere. Rather than lapse into apathy and despair, he patiently endures a 20-year 'fight against hard luck and prejudice', keeping his wits sharp and awaiting the opportunity to redeem his reputation and launch his legal career.

Wilson, Jem
Mary Barton, 1848
Elizabeth Gaskell

A solid and dependable working-class lad, Jem feels deeply and is sincere in his actions. He is of fine moral calibre, has nothing 'fancy' about him, and is passionate in his devotion to MARY BARTON. Although he is dealt an unjust blow, he has the strength of character to overcome his predicament. An upright citizen, he demonstrates the respectability of the working classes.

Wilson, Joe
'Joe Wilson's Courtship', 1901, et seq
Henry Lawson

Narrator of life in the Australian outback. 'I wasn't a healthy-minded, average boy; I reckon I was born for a poet by mistake, and grew up to be a bushman, and didn't know what was the matter with me – or the world.'

Wilson, M Jennifer
So I am Glad, 1995
A L Kennedy

A radio announcer but also a loner, who describes herself as calm, devoid of emotion, and 'unspontaneous'. However, a gradual transformation is effected by the appearance of a confused new flatmate who claims to be 17th-century satirist Savinien Cyrano de Bergerac. Jennifer begins to take emotional risks and, after becoming his lover, is forced to admit the untruth of her previous notions of herself.

Wilson, Mr
The History of the Adventures of Joseph Andrews and of his Friend Mr Abraham Adams, 1742
Henry Fielding

This gentleman unburdens himself to PARSON ADAMS, describing his life in London society, his hatred for and then ambivalence towards the female sex, and his redemption by a young woman who advances him money when his fortunes are at a low ebb. Married, he leads a life of gentle melancholy, passing his days by tending his garden.

Wilson, Myrtle
The Great Gatsby, 1925
F Scott Fitzgerald

The mistress of TOM BUCHANAN, she is trapped in a fruitless marriage to a garage owner. She is a wild, violent, impulsive creature, given to vulgar and obscene language. She is an earthy, physical, wholly unexceptional and rather unintelligent woman, but suits Buchanan's undemanding requirements in a mistress. It is she who precipitates the final drama.

Wilson, William
William Wilson, 1839
Edgar Allan Poe

There are two William Wilsons in the story, which takes the *Doppelgänger* or 'double' as its theme. The first is a wild, passionate schoolboy, the second a quiet and unremarkable youth of similar name and appearance, who protects him in ways known only to them. The first becomes arrogant, degenerate and vicious, but the second continues to enter his life in times of crisis, or to prevent his doing evil. The first finally slays his 'double', and in doing so is made to realize 'how utterly thou hast murdered thyself'.

Wilt, Henry
Wilt, 1976, et seq
Tom Sharpe

An unfulfilled Liberal Studies lecturer at a Fenland technical college, Wilt has for ten years 'sat in front of classes answering irrelevant questions'. But this turns him into 'the man with the grasshopper mind' and stands him in good stead when he is interrogated about an apparent murder – a crime about which this most passive of men has merely fantasized.

Wilton, Candida
The Seven Sisters, 2002
Margaret Drabble

Late middle-aged and newly divorced, cultivated, sensible, unimaginative Candida Wilton arrives in London from Suffolk, installs herself in a small flat in Ladbroke Grove and, despite being 'washed out', embarks upon the process of beginning again. Cautious and reserved, she nevertheless appears conversational (the novel is apparently her diary), even though hers is, as she observes, 'a mean, prim, self-righteous, self-pitying' voice. Yet although she is startled by contemporary urban life, the litter, the impatience and the anger, she is not without a spirit of adventure and joins an evening class on Virgil's *Aeneid*. Following a windfall she embarks upon a journey to Greece (with six women classmates and friends), during which she arrives at a clearer understanding both of herself and others.

Wilton, Jack
The Unfortunate Traveller, 1594
Thomas Nashe

'Appendix or page' to the Court of Henry VIII and self-appointed 'King of the Cans and Black-jacks, Prince of the Pigmies, County Palatine of Clean Straw and Provant, and, to conclude, Lord High Regent of Rashers of the Coals and Red-herring Cobs'. One critic claims that Jack has 'neither conscience nor character', and his most frequent stance is one of amused detachment as he observes the brutal religious conflicts and persecutions of 16th-century Europe.

Wiltshire, Mr
The Beach of Falesá, 1892
Robert Louis Stevenson

The narrator, he is a bored, idle trader who has spent years in the South Seas and has become softened by its decadent lifestyle. He arrives at Falesá, where his marriage to the native girl UMA is little more than a sham, to which Wiltshire hypocritically consents. It emerges, however, that the girl is subject to a taboo and Wiltshire has been 'set up' so that no one will trade with him. As he realizes this duplicity and as his genuine love for Uma grows, he learns to respect island culture and appreciate Western corruption.

Wimperis, Tempe
The Peach Groves, 1979
Barbara Hanrahan

The half-Maori stepsister of 'MAJOR' HARRY JONES's wife, Tempe is a seriously disturbed 18-year-old, plagued by imperfectly remembered folklore passed on by her beautiful Maori mother, who died many years before. Although given an English name and education, Tempe has never relinquished her sense of belonging to 'the old magic race'. A 'half-thing', she loves Tennyson's poetry, and enacts Camelot fantasies in the woods, but also seeks the Maori god, Tane, there. She is Harry's mistress, and when he tries to end their affair she takes revenge on his wife, and on BLANCHE DEAN and MAUDE DEAN.

Wimsey, Lord Peter (Death Bredon)
Whose Body?, 1923, et seq
Dorothy L Sayers

Once described as looking like a 'melancholic adjutant stork', he is fair-haired with a big nose and a nature that is 'passionate and un-sentimental'. A perfect gentleman, he earned first-class honours in modern history at Balliol college, Oxford, before receiving the DSO for bravery behind enemy lines during World War I. Buried alive during one explosion, he remains prone to bouts of depression and nightmares. Since the war, he has pursued his interests in history, rare books, music and criminology. Assisted by his loyal retainer Bunter, he gains a reputation for infallibility as an eccentric amateur sleuth. Initially something of a monocled silly-ass, he matures over the years, particularly during his relationship with fellow detective HARRIET VANE.

Windermere, Lady
Lady Windermere's Fan, 1892
Oscar Wilde

A young married woman who was taught early 'the difference that there is between what is right and what is wrong', Lady Windermere is uncompromising in her moral stance, admitting to having 'something of the Puritan' in her and believing that everyone should live by hard and fast rules. A misunderstanding between herself and her husband, and the discovery that she is not above human weakness after all, enables her to compromise her unyielding position somewhat, and to become more human and compassionate.

Windrip, Buzz (Berzelius)
It Can't Happen Here, 1935
Sinclair Lewis

Windrip is a powerful politician from Vermont who seizes the American presidency, dividing and conquering the country with repressive violence, censorship and extreme racial and social prejudice. He is sometimes thought to be a Northern version of the Louisiana 'Kingfish', Huey Long, who was assassinated in the year *It Can't Happen Here* was published.

Windzer, Chal
Sundown, 1934
John Joseph Mathews

The son of a mixed-blood Osage father, one of the leading 'progressives' on the tribal council, and a full-blood mother with a converse lack of faith in 'the gov'mint', Chal is doomed from birth to be always 'out of step' in whichever of the two worlds he tries to live in. Born in Indian Territory on the verge of oil exploitation and statehood, he is unable to embrace white society and values unreservedly, perceiving this as a fault in himself, a 'queerness' that sets him apart. Only when alone in nature does Chal experience a return to the self-peace of his childhood. A sidelines admirer of the American Dream and the work ethic, he is a man of 'two dignities, one tellin' him to do something, and one tellin' him not to do anything'; unable finally to reconcile the two, he longs for a sense of spiritual release, but can find it neither in the Peyotists' sweatlodge, whose sense of community and harmony he cannot sustain, nor in the temporary oblivion conferred by Prohibition homebrew parties.

Wingate, Frances
The Realms of Gold, 1975
Margaret Drabble

Frances appears to be in the enviable position of having everything: successfully managing her career as an archaeologist, content in love and happy with her children. She is enthusiastic, gregarious, optimistic and complacent. She enjoys living, imagining and discovering new things, searching for 'a possible if not an ideal society'. Frances believes that landscape influences character, and peers at her own northern past, her family and its community, with the same intensity as she peers at the past of long ago. Gradually, she learns of her own history, reconciling herself to her beginnings and to her place in the evolutionary process of her own family and people.

Wingfield, Amanda
The Glass Menagerie, 1945
Tennessee Williams

At first she seems a tiresome, domineering woman whose fastidious attention to good manners and constant recollection of her youth in Blue Mountain render her son TOM WINGFIELD's frustrations all too understandable. But her energy, her essential optimism, and the lyricism of her language – particularly the famous 'jonquils' speech – finally reveal her as a resolute survivor and champion of family love and values.

Wingfield, Laura
The Glass Menagerie, 1945
Tennessee Williams

A shy, retiring, slightly crippled girl, she finds comfort at home playing her absent father's phonograph and caring for her 'menagerie' of glass animals, a symbol of the vulnerable fragility of her life and her dreams. Dominated by her mother, she is given one night of possible escape in the form of the long-awaited arrival of a 'gentleman caller', JIM O'CONNOR; when he reveals himself to be already engaged, she returns to her lonely, candlelit world.

Wingfield, Tom
The Glass Menagerie, 1945
Tennessee Williams

The narrative voice, stage director and a central character of this gentle play, he is clearly an autobiographical figure, frustrated by his job at Continental Shoemakers, and depressed by his claustrophobic home life with his garrulous mother and crippled sister. Having tried the cinema, and alcohol, as a means of escape, he eventually joins the Merchant Navy, but cannot ever truly escape and remains 'more faithful than I intended to be' to the image of his sister, LAURA WINGFIELD.

Wingrave, Owen
'Owen Wingrave', 1893
Henry James

A brilliant young man of military background, he alienates himself from his family by turning down a guaranteed place at Sandhurst. Haunted by accusations of cowardice, he sleeps in a room where an ancestor killed his son. In the morning, Owen, too, is dead, apparently killed by shame.

Winkle, Nathaniel
Pickwick Papers, 1837
Charles Dickens

A member of the Pickwick Club, he claims to be a sportsman, but his ignorance, including whether to sit on a horse backwards or forwards, repeatedly gets him into scrapes. He elopes with ARABELLA ALLEN despite his father's objections, but Pickwick helps in the reconciliation.

Winner, Arthur, jr
By Love Possessed, 1957
James Gould Cozzens

Brought up in a wealthy and successful background, this conservative lawyer would seem to embody all the characteristics reflected in his triumphant surname. Over just two days, punctuated by the striking of an antique clock of his father's which bears the inscription *amor vincit omnia*, he is forced to take stock of himself and rethink his romantic and moral priorities.

Winnie
Happy Days, 1961
Samuel Beckett

Beckett's first major female character, she is consistent with his greatest paradox, desiring release from her mortal bonds while remaining trapped in the 'muck' of existence. Yet her cruel predicament – immobilized up to her waist in a mound of sand – seems not to trouble the chattering Winnie, whose speech is full of humour. She is accompanied by Willie, an ailing man who remains behind the mound, mostly unseen and unheard. As with all Beckett's characters, Winnie is profoundly aware of the function of words in her life as time-fillers, but words sometimes fail or, worse, remind her of past failures. She has been best summed up by literary critic Ruby Cohn, as 'a new stage metaphor for the old human condition – burial in a dying earth, exposure under a ruthless sun'.

Winnie-the-Pooh
Winnie-the-Pooh, 1926
The House at Pooh Corner, 1928
A A Milne

The ursine companion of young Christopher Robin, he is a childlike mixture of selfishness and altruism. Being a 'bear of very little brain' he frequently finds himself in situations from which he has to be rescued, yet he always remains cheerful and optimistic. He has a close relationship with the other animals in his world, especially PIGLET, who is his dearest friend. His real weakness is 'hunny', which he is incapable of resisting. He has a charming line in malapropisms and there is more than a touch of whimsy about his 'hums'.

Winnifrede
The Witch of Edmonton, c.1621
Thomas Dekker, William Rowley and John Ford

A servant, she is rather a happy-go-lucky woman, easily led. She is pregnant, but whether by FRANK THORNEY, the man she marries, or by her employer, is uncertain. Poor Winnifrede's lot is to be incidental to a tale of male deceit and vulnerability, and to be saddled with a husband found guilty of murder.

Winslow, Ronnie
The Winslow Boy, 1946
Terence Rattigan

The story of Ronnie Winslow, 'about fourteen', who has been expelled from the Royal Naval College, Osborne, accused of stealing a postal order from another cadet, is based upon a real case. Ronnie vehemently claims his innocence, and his father, a prosperous upper-middle-class man in whose South Kensington home the action takes place, similarly campaigns to clear his son's name. Ronnie, tense, timid, dejected but implacable, is the catalyst for a debate upon injustices in the British legal system and a study of a wealthy English family under threat of disgrace.

Winter, Tom
Seven Poor Men of Sydney, 1934
Christina Stead

Working as a librarian in Sydney has placed him close to grand ideas of human progress, but not close enough to real life to make him an effective reformer. He is seduced by simplistic ideologies and magical solutions which stand no chance of success in the real world.

Winterborne, Giles
The Woodlanders, 1887
Thomas Hardy

Passive, down-to-earth, and in tune with nature,

Giles possesses a 'chivalrous and undiluted manliness'. In spite of his enviable richness of spirit, he is powerless to change his destiny, and resigned to accept whatever Fate should offer. His pathetic death is central to the novel.

Winterbottom, CaptainT K
Arrow of God, 1964, revised edition 1974
Chinua Achebe

District Officer at the Okperi station, disconcertingly susceptible not just to the Nigerian climate, but also to the magic and fetishism his belief in rational reform is intended to dispel.

Winterbourne, Elizabeth
Death of a Hero, 1929, unexpurgated edition 1930
Richard Aldington

GEORGE WINTERBOURNE's shallow and venial wife is now understood to be an unfairly biased portrait of the poet Hilda Doolittle ('H D'), to whom Aldington was married. In the novel, she represents the valueless cynicism which is violently purged on the Western Front.

Winterbourne, Frederick
Daisy Miller: A Study, 1878, dramatized 1883
Henry James

An amiable young American expatriate who hangs around the vicinity of his former *alma mater*, Geneva, ostensibly 'studying' but actually to be close to a lady, slightly older than himself, with whom he is smitten. Staying at Vevey on the lakeside, he meets the 'American princess' DAISY MILLER.

Winterbourne, George
Death of a Hero, 1929, unexpurgated edition 1930
Richard Aldington

Winterbourne moves from the vacuous hedonism of Edwardian England and a 'modern' marriage to the horror of the trenches, where he meets his death. The indefinite article in the title only partially camouflages Aldington's conviction that heroism itself has come to a stop; Winterbourne has to be seen as an autobiographical projection of deep misgivings about the novelist's own generation.

Winters, Reta
Unless, 2002
Carol Shields

In the midst of her comfortable and fulfilling life as a successful author and mother, 'sort of married' Reta, 'that sunny woman', finds herself catapulted into a 'period of great unhappiness and loss' when her eldest daughter, Norah, suddenly withdraws from her life and into herself. In trying to understand and help her, Reta starts to reflect on her own situation, and the mysterious quality of 'goodness' that seems to preoccupy Norah. She discovers her own pain and anger, her need to nurture and to understand; a 'growing perplexity with the world and its arrangements' turns eventually into an acceptance that life is a combination of scientific and metaphysical truth.

Winters, Timothy
'Timothy Winters', in *Union Street*, 1957
Charles Causley

The despair of the new Welfare State and a

sticking-place for the Butler Education Act, this undernourished 'Blitz of a boy' – 'ears like bombs and teeth like splinters' – lives on Suez Street with a drunken father and gin-soaked grandmother, his mother having run off with a bombardier. 'His belly is white, his neck is dark,/ And his hair is an exclamation mark./ His clothes are enough to scare a crow,/And through his britches the cold winds blow.'

Winthrop, Dolly
Silas Marner, 1861
George Eliot

The mother of EPPIE's eventual husband Aaron, Dolly is a 'mild and patient woman' who looks out for sadder folk to comfort. SILAS MARNER is one of her successful social work projects: she helps him with clothes for Eppie, offers general child-rearing advice, and invites him along to the local church which is basically an easy-going social club rather than the Calvinist oppresssion club expected by Silas. Her faith is a simple one, and the story we read is, to her, 'The will o' them above … it's dark to you and me'.

Winwife
Bartholomew Fair, 1614
Ben Jonson

A clever, manipulative but arguably rather too mercenary gentleman, Winwife courts DAME PURECRAFT for her wealth. However, there is a good-natured side to his buccaneering and, with his friend TOM QUARLOUS, he enjoys himself exposing the follies of those at Bartholomew Fair. This sufficiently impresses GRACE WELLBORN to enable him to win her as his wife.

Wirrun
The Ice is Coming, 1977
The Dark Bright Water, 1979
Behind the Wind, 1981, forming *The Song of Wirrun* trilogy, 1987
Patricia Wrightson

Wirrun is an adventurous but rather grave Aboriginal boy. An avid reader of newspapers, he is particularly interested in stories concerning mysterious, apparently inexplicable natural phenomena, and sometimes these set him off on his many journeys of discovery. For Wirrun, armed with his maps, is a compulsive traveller. Bright-eyed, intuitive and intelligent, he has no real home. He is a boy of the people, and especially sensitive to the folk-spirits from Aboriginal legend.

Wiseman, Mr
The Life and Death of Mr. Badman, 1680
John Bunyan

Mr Wiseman has watched MR BADMAN wreck his life and bring pain to others and now wishes to draw lessons from this for the benefit of MR ATTENTIVE. He is a shrewd observer with measured insight, who can put into context all Badman's misdeeds and their significance, and point up the compelling message that his miserable life clearly presents.

Wiseman, Mrs Eva
Mosquitoes, 1927
William Faulkner

The married sister of 'THE SEMITIC MAN', she is a

poet who tends to declaim rather than converse and to speak only in capital letters, mainly about Art and Philosophy.

Wishfort, Lady
The Way of the World, 1700
William Congreve
Rich and imposing, LADY WISHFORT is also the aunt of MILLAMANT and custodian of her fortune. Rather an unattractive woman, she is a gossip, meddlesome, vain and hypocritical. A social snob, she is anxious to marry, although men generally find her a bore. Therefore MIRABELL's plan of forcing her to allow him to marry Millamant (by inducing her to fall in love with a man he can later reveal to be his servant WAITWELL in disguise) plays upon all her emotional vulnerabilities.

Wishrop
Palace of the Peacock, 1960, part of *The Guyana Quartet*, 1985
Wilson Harris
Steersman of DONNE's ship and his understudy and twin in the dream journey into the interior. Having killed his wife and her lover and the sniggering catechist, he shoots himself, but remains alive. At the end it is Wishrop who is drawn up into CARROLL's web of music.

witches, the three → weird sisters, the three

Withers, Toby
The Edge of the Alphabet, 1962
Janet Frame
A withdrawn epileptic, prone to sudden storms of random mental activity, he represents the ways in which disorders of language are related to the disorder of the external world.

Withers, Tom
Seven Poor Men of Sydney, 1934
Christina Stead
A printer in GREGORY CHAMBERLAIN's Sydney plant, he takes a bitter and often antagonistic view of his place in life, dissipating his considerable energy and talent in pointless feuding and confrontation.

Wititterly, Mr and Mrs Henry
Nicholas Nickleby, 1839
Charles Dickens
They are pretentious residents of fashionable Belgravia with whom KATE NICKLEBY lives for a time as the companion to Mrs Wititterly (Julia). Though middle-class, she apes the manners of the aristocracy, is a snob and a hypochondriac. Her devoted husband, 'of rather plebeian countenance', considers her 'a hothouse plant, an exotic'. She resents SIR MULBERRY HAWK's visits to Kate and ends up dismissing her.

Wittipool
The Devil is an Ass, 1616
Ben Jonson
A young gallant and friend of EUSTACE MANLY, Wittipool assists him in devising a plan by which MRS FRANCES FITZDOTTREL might escape her tyrannical husband. Though not above deception

(few of Jonson's characters are), Wittipool is an honest and honourable man. Neither he nor Manly hopes to claim Mrs Fitzdottrel for themselves; they act out of a sense of adventure and in the interests of natural justice.

Witwould, Sir Wilfull
The Way of the World, 1700
William Congreve
A would-be wit, he is morally upright, comes from the country, and has a smattering of culture. Indeed, it is his ambition to go off on a Grand Tour of Europe. But his ways are provincial ways. He is a practical man, uneasy in society, and has little light-hearted small talk. The fashionable, convivial ways of town, where he plans to learn French before travelling, merely bewilder him. He is unsure how to respond in company, especially to women. Naturally shy, he can also become embarrassingly boisterous. But one thing he is not is a wit.

Wix, Mrs
What Maisie Knew, 1897
Henry James
Garrulous and unreliable, MAISIE FARANGE's second governess at least offers the affection and mothering that she craves and Maisie opts to stay with her (supported by SIR CLAUDE's money) in preference to either of her cold and neglectful parents.

Wizard of Oz → Oz, the Great

Wodehouse, Lucy
The Rector, 1863
The Perpetual Curate, 1864
Margaret Oliphant
Lucy Wodehouse is young, pretty, with blue ribbons and laughing eyes. She admires REV FRANCIS WENTWORTH and helps in his charitable works, wearing a sister-of-mercy cloak in deference to his High Church ideals and standing godmother to a row of slum children when they are to be christened at the Mission. Jealous when he seems too attentive to LADY WESTERN, she finds it hard to believe what is said against him and stands by him throughout the scandals.

Wodehouse, Miss
The Rector, 1863
The Perpetual Curate, 1864
Margaret Oliphant
The elder of the two Miss Wodehouses by 20 years, she has been almost a mother to LUCY WODEHOUSE. Kindly, religious, a keen knitter and a confirmed spinster, she accompanies Lucy in her charitable works, wearing the same High Anglican sister-of-mercy cloak but always secondary, shy, tongue-tied in the background. Perhaps this is what attracts the rector REV MORLEY PROCTOR. When the sisters lose their father, he proposes to Mary and, at first taken aback – 'at my age!' – she diffidently but happily accepts.

Woffington, Peg (Margaret)
Masks and Faces, 1852
Peg Woffington, 1853
Charles Reade
Based on the historical Peg Woffington, she is a

famous actress, and 'one of the truest artists of her day'. A beautiful woman, she is venerated by a wealthy man, who fails to see the worldly woman behind his idealized dream. Her discovery that he is married leads her to renounce her conquest, and ultimately her 'long life of folly and wickedness', which she abandons for 'purity and piety' in her final years.

Wolf Larsen
The Sea-Wolf, 1904
Jack London

A strange and disturbing man whose violent and sadistic behaviour towards the people he rescues from a shipwreck is bizarre and terrifying. He seems to be locked into a world where normal values do not apply and where evil dominates. Mysterious and haunting, he loves wielding the power to frighten and control, and when he ends his life crippled by blindness and insanity, not many feel a morsel of pity for him, so total has been his dedication to the use of terror.

Wolfe, Nero
Fer-de-lance, 1934, et seq
Rex Stout

This gargantuan Montenegrin sleuth almost never moves from his New York brownstone mansion, and relies on the resourceful footwork (and muscle) of his assistant Archie Goodwin for fact-gathering. Professing to be 'merely a genius, not a god', he mulls over the data of his cases while communing with the huge orchid collection in his attic, which is where his breakthrough insights often occur. Extraordinarily particular about his food and drink (though with a preference for imported beer rather than wine), Wolfe may win the prize for combining the largest number of far-fetched quirks of any major fictional detective.

Wolfe, Turbott
Turbott Wolfe, 1925
William Plomer

Eponymous hero of the novel, Turbott Wolfe is an English painter friendly with Africans near a trading station in South Africa. He rebels against white racism and falls in love with the beautiful Nhliziyombi, a Zulu girl. For him she represents 'that intensity of the old wonderful unknown primitive African life outside history, outside time, outside science' and also 'a living image of what has been killed ... by our obscene civilization that conquers everything'.

Wolsey, Cardinal Thomas
Henry VIII (All is True), c.1613
William Shakespeare and John Fletcher

All the forces of oppression in *Henry VIII* surge through one character, that of Cardinal Wolsey. Icily manipulative, arrogant and self-seeking, Wolsey, the 'butcher's cur', imposes punitive taxes to finance the French war, puts himself before his country and his own career above all others. At the beginning, he has HENRY VIII securely under his influence: 'He dives into the king's soul, and there scatters/Dangers, doubts'. But apprehended letters to the pope and the discovery of Wolsey's vast wealth alert Henry to the extent of the cardinal's hypocrisy and

corruption. The conflict between monarchy and papacy is resolved in victory for the Crown; ambition, Wolsey admits to Cromwell, has been the cause of his ruin.

Wombat, Watkin
The Magic Pudding, 1918
Norman Lindsay

Though of a species not previously known for larceny (unlike his sidekick POSSUM), he is the villain of the piece, bent on taking possession of the talkative MAGIC PUDDING.

Wonham, Stephen ('Podge')
The Longest Journey, 1907
E M Forster

The illegitimate half-brother of RICKIE ELLIOT, he has grown into a muscular, weather-beaten young man with piercing blue eyes and a 'narrow but not uninteresting brain'. Raised by EMILY FAILING and the butt of her constant teasing, he has the coarse, bullying manner of an unthinking country boy but displays a childlike purity of spirit. A harmless pawn in the games of others, he emerges 'half blackguard, half martyr'.

Wonka, Willy
Charlie and the Chocolate Factory, 1964
Charlie and the Great Glass Elevator, 1973
Roald Dahl

The mysterious, magical, reclusive owner of an amazing chocolate factory staffed by unseen workers. Five children, ingeniously selected by newspaper advertisement, are given a guided tour of the factory by Mr Wonka, during which he reveals his eccentric brilliance. His generosity to CHARLIE is unsurpassed, but extravagantly apt punishments await the others, all designed by this weird autocratic genius.

Wood, Lorena
Lonesome Dove, 1985
Larry McMurtry

The archetypal golden-hearted whore of Western legend, she turns her back on the limited custom of Lonesome Dove to join WOODROW F CALL and GUS MCCRAE on their cattle drive northwards. Her only ambition is to reach San Francisco and make a new life for herself there.

Wood, Molly Stark
The Virginian, 1902
Owen Wister

A Vermont girl of aristocratic bearing who travels west to teach at a school in the wilds of Wyoming. Rescued by THE VIRGINIAN from a flood-threatened stagecoach, she falls in love with him. Their marriage is seen as a union of her civilizing influence and his unaffected democratic chivalry and quiet courage.

Woodcourt, Allan
Bleak House, 1853
Charles Dickens

A handsome young surgeon, he attends the death of CAPTAIN HAWDON and eventually marries Hawdon's· daughter, ESTHER SUMMERSON. Devoted to the poor, he assists MISS FLITE, helps JO find a place in hospital and is present at Jo's deathbed. Leaving for India before he proposes to Esther, he returns to find her engaged to JOHN JARNDYCE. But his marriage to Esther is arranged by the selfless Jarndyce, who establishes the couple in a new Bleak House in Yorkshire, where Woodcourt becomes a doctor to the poor.

Woodhouse, Emma
Emma, 1816
Jane Austen

The younger daughter of MR WOODHOUSE, she is the toast of Highbury society. 'Handsome, clever, and rich', she has a sprightly wit and a quick mind which, when allowed to go unchecked, is given to 'fanciful' and at times 'unfair' conjectures. As a compulsive matchmaker her judgement is coloured by emotion and she is apt to be blinded by the delight she takes in her own schemes, the folly of which she comes to understand only when she realizes that she is in love herself, with MR KNIGHTLEY, her sternest critic.

Woodhouse, Mr
Emma, 1816
Jane Austen

A widower, doting father and a man of gentle compassion, he recommends a 'nice basin of gruel' at bedtime and is the contented victim of a 'ceaseless flow of happy regrets and fearful affection'. A 'valetudinarian all his life, without activity of mind or body, he [is] a much older man in ways than in years', opposed to change of every kind and to matrimony in particular 'as the origin of change'.

Woodruff, Sarah
The French Lieutenant's Woman, 1969
John Fowles

An ambivalent portrayal of vulnerable femininity, Sarah is juxtaposed between the pitifully neurotic and the skilfully cunning. Her doctor maintains that 'her sadness becomes her happiness'. She thrives on the intensity of her emotional responses, and torments herself with the complexity of her thoughts. Somehow, she is at once fragile and independent. Circumstances have cast her down, and cast her out. Despite the excuse of ostracization, though, it is difficult to accept some of her more affected, manipulative behaviour. Naked with insecurity, she gradually appears to become more self-assured, and yet continues to inflict pain and suffering on those close to her.

Woodseaves, Kester
Precious Bane, 1924
Mary Webb

Kester is a travelling weaver, who sees more than most. He is gentle, learned in flowers and beasts, loving the goodness of PRUE SARN and caring nothing for her harelip. He talks to her as no one else does; her quietness matches his own. Letters written by them on behalf of others convey their love; he smiles at this and remembers Prue wherever he goes, as she remembers him. When she is being ducked as a witch, he comes from nowhere, lifts her up beside him and rides off, ignoring the angry mob.

Woodvil, Harriet
The Man of Mode, 1676
Sir George Etherege

Harriet's parents and Old Bellair expect her to marry YOUNG BELLAIR but, like him, she prefers to defy them and make her own decisions. She represents the novel idea that one might marry for love, instead of marrying for status and hoping some kind of mutual amicability might emerge. Young and wealthy, her ideals and moral values are high and she has as much instinctive wisdom as beauty. However much DORIMANT declares his love for her, she remains detached until he proposes marriage, and then she imposes the condition that he follow her to the country to hear her reply.

Woodville, Anthony, Earl Rivers
Henry VI Part III, early 1590s
Richard III, 1592/3
William Shakespeare

Anthony is the brother of ELIZABETH WOODVILLE, later queen to Edward IV (EDWARD, EARL OF MARCH). His most significant appearance is in *Richard III* when, as a loyal and honourable man, he proposes that, Edward IV having died, his son, Edward, the Prince of Wales, be crowned. He is later imprisoned and executed on Richard's orders and briefly appears as a ghost to Richard on the eve of the battle of Bosworth.

Woodville, Elizabeth (Lady Grey), later Queen Elizabeth
Henry VI Part III, early 1590s
Richard III, 1592/3
William Shakespeare

Elizabeth, the sister of ANTHONY WOODVILLE, appears in *Henry VI Part III* as Lady Grey, the widow of Sir John Grey, petitioning Edward IV (EDWARD, EARL OF MARCH) for lands seized by the crown at her husband's death. Reluctantly at first, she becomes Edward's mistress and then, injudiciously from a political point of view, his queen. The DUKE OF BUCKINGHAM thinks of her as 'subtle', and indeed an emotional deviousness rather than political perspicacity appears to be her stronger suit. The assessment of Richard III (RICHARD, DUKE OF GLOUCESTER) is that she is easily persuaded and short-sighted: 'Relenting, fool, and shallow changing woman!'

Woolcot, Francis → General, the

Woolcot, Judy
Seven Little Australians, 1894
Ethel Turner

A thin, eager-faced Australian girl of 13, whose cleverness and mischievousness make her the ringleader among her six siblings. Christened Helen and also nicknamed Fizz, because of her energy, she has a habit of jocularly adopting an Irish accent. Her 'fearless honesty' leads to conflicts with her father, and her 'indomitable spirit and pluck' find expression in self-sacrifice.

Woolf, Virginia
The Hours, 1998
Michael Cunningham

She is a fictionalized version of the writer, shown in the throes of creating her novel *Mrs Dalloway* in 1923. A woman in her forties, she struggles to cope with the demands of family and her duties as a wife in a middle-class household complete with difficult staff, constantly aware that her sanity is fragile. Only her writing is satisfying to her, and she longs to escape dull but safe Richmond for London, hub of literary life and symbolizing freedom.

Wooreddy
Doctor Wooreddy's Prescription for Enduring the Ending of the World, 1983
Mudrooroo, formerly Colin Johnson

An Aboriginal wise man in 19th-century Tasmania, he is confronted with a world that is changing too rapidly for his fixed and very absolute perspective. He learns slowly that in order to survive he must adopt new ways of thinking.

Wooster, Bertie
The Inimitable Jeeves, 1924, et seq
P G Wodehouse

A member of the Drones Club, rich, well-connected, of minimal IQ but infinite good nature, Bertie is a young-man-about-town, prone to purchase and wear garments fashionable for the moment but pronounced unsuitable, with pursed lips, by his manservant JEEVES. He has become engaged frequently but never permanently. His well-meaning attempts to assist friends are invariably inept but Jeeves always saves the day. Unsympathetic relatives have summoned psychiatric consultants to look into Bertie, but to no avail; he continues to enjoy life in his unique way in spite of them.

Wooton, Lord Henry
The Picture of Dorian Gray, 1891
Oscar Wilde

Cynical and amoral, Lord Henry is described by a friend as 'an extraordinary fellow' who 'never says a moral thing' and 'never does a wrong thing'. But he is cruel and egotistical and can cause much harm merely by what he says. His conversation is 'brilliant, fantastic, irresponsible' and it has a great effect on his impressionable young friend, DORIAN GRAY, as he sets out deliberately to corrupt him, seeking 'to make that wonderful spirit his own'.

Wopsle, Mr
Great Expectations, 1861
Charles Dickens

A friend of the GARGERYs, he is a parish clerk uncommonly proud of his deep voice. He goes to London to become an actor, adopting a theatrical personality and the stage name of Waldengarver. He is not particularly successful, and PIP and HERBERT POCKET attend one of his hilarious performances as Hamlet.

Worldly Wiseman, Mr
The Pilgrim's Progress, Part I 1678, Part II 1684
John Bunyan

His preference is for any alternative route to salvation that bypasses the Cross and allows morality to be the key to redemption. He cannot quite believe that anyone will embark on the hard way of the pilgrim when there is a much easier one

that leaves the ego intact and avoids the many terrors of the way of true discipleship.

Wormold, James
Our Man in Havana, 1958
Graham Greene

A middle-aged Englishman in Havana. He sells vacuum cleaners for a living, but his daughter spends most of his earnings, and, needing money, he accepts the offer to become a British secret agent. He has no aptitude for spying, but does have a vigorously vivid imagination, and files a series of increasingly grandiose, extravagant fabrications. They prove to have very real and dangerous consequences, but in the skewed logic of the book, they turn him into a great success.

Worth, John
Entry into Jerusalem, 1983
Stanley Middleton

Like many of Middleton's characters, he is an artist whose perfectionism is a symptom of separation from the actual suffering of the people round him. Worth's equanimity is scarcely disturbed when his best friend collapses and then commits suicide.

Worthing, John
The Importance of Being Earnest, 1895
Oscar Wilde

Better known as 'Ernest in the town, and Jack in the country', he is the determined and sensible suitor to GWENDOLINE, ALGERNON MONCRIEFF's cousin. Unfortunately, on declaring his love, despite its being returned, he finds that it is nevertheless hopeless, due to his own dubious origins. Having been found in a handbag in the cloakroom at Victoria station, he has no clue to his real identity. The adopted son of a wealthy philanthropist, he now takes his duty as guardian to that gentleman's granddaughter very seriously – though to escape this duty occasionally, he has invented a wayward younger brother, named Ernest.

Worthy
The Recruiting Officer, 1706
George Farquhar

A gentleman of Shropshire, whose pursuit of MELINDA parallels CAPTAIN PLUME's of SYLVIA, each lady having come into a fortune that puts her a rung higher on the social ladder. Because he has treated her, earlier, in a rather offhand way he is finding her difficult to win, and has become an 'obsequious thoughtful, romantic, constant coxcomb', so that it is only with plenty of assistance that he is able merit her forgiveness. Finally he condescends to cast away all his romantic ideals and 'begin upon a new score'.

Worthy
The Relapse, or Virtue in Danger, 1696
Sir John Vanbrugh

Worthy's name is ironic, for he is a seasoned rake, and hot in pursuit of AMANDA, his former lover, now married to LOVELESS. When she successfully eludes his advances, Worthy sceptically observes that she has made 'that common mistake of fond wives, who conclude themselves virtuous, because they can refuse a man they don't like, when they have got one they do'. Accustomed to a buccaneering approach to life and love, he is rather put out when Amanda offers him a circumscribed place in her affections.

Would-Be, Sir Politic and Lady
Volpone, or The Fox, 1606
Ben Jonson

An English knight travelling in Venice, Sir Politic is a gullible fool who pretends to be an experienced traveller and man-of-the-world. His vain and muddle-headed wife, Lady Would-Be, appears as ridiculously pompous as he. Sir Politic is relentlessly taunted by PEREGRINE, while Lady Would-Be considers ways of becoming heir to VOLPONE. Essentially they are a comic couple, the humour arising from their profound misunderstanding of Venetian society.

Woundwort, General
Watership Down, 1972
Richard Adams

A savage, ruthless leader, Woundwort battles his way through life. In combat he fights to kill, ignoring his own wounds. Satisfying his lust for power by enlarging his kingdom, he imposes on it a harsh military regime, originally designed to ensure the survival of the warren but ultimately followed for its own sake. He provides his subjects with a strong role model that he expects them to emulate. Single-minded, sometimes obsessive, as in his pursuit of BIGWIG and the fugitive, he sees himself as a leader of genius. In reality he is a tyrant, who rules by fear and cunning.

Wrayburn, Eugene
Our Mutual Friend, 1865
Charles Dickens

A young barrister who hates the law and has 'had no business at all' for seven years, he is the intimate friend of MORTIMER LIGHTWOOD, with whom he frequents the dinner parties of the VENEERINGS. Through his casual interest in the JOHN HARMON affair, he meets LIZZIE HEXAM and, despite the difference in social class, they fall in love. He pays for her education and becomes the hated rival of BRADLEY HEADSTONE, whose obsessive love she has rejected. He is savagely attacked by Headstone but rescued from drowning by Lizzie. After she nurses him through a near fatal illness, his character is transformed by her love and he resolves to work purposefully. Lizzie at last agrees to marry him despite her scruples and the criticism of 'Society'.

Wraysford, Stephen
Birdsong, 1993
Sebastian Faulks

Young Englishman Stephen Wraysford's experiences in northern France define his life: the passionate affair with a married woman in 1910 that ends suddenly and then the 'unlivable reality' of trench warfare. After the horror of the Somme he has 'lost all connection with any earthly happiness that might persist' and feels 'tired in the soul … cast adrift in a perpetual present'. Although a brooding figure who is often described as strange, he forms a bond with his fellow soldiers, who admire him as an officer, and is driven on by an inextinguishable will to survive.

Wrench, Tom
Trelawny of the 'Wells', 1898
Arthur Wing Pinero

Tom Wrench, an engaging, volatile, impoverished young 'general utility' actor, echoes the young Pinero, but is in fact Pinero's version of the playwright T W Robertson, who introduced a style of realistic social comedy, which Pinero developed. His theme in this play is the inevitability of change. Tom is hopelessly in love with ROSE TRELAWNY, but while she discovers her new beginning in marriage, Tom summons his faith in himself and finds his by writing 'Life', a naturalistic comedy.

Wright, Karen
The Children's Hour, 1934
Lillian Hellman

An attractive woman of 28, she is an ideal schoolteacher, whose caring manner has won her the affection of her pupils and the respect of her superiors. Planning to marry Dr Joseph Cardin, she sees a rosy future before her until a malicious lie circulated by MARY TILFORD destroys every prospect of happiness.

Wright, Nel
Sula, 1980
Toni Morrison

Nel, an only child, is subject to the manipulation of her mother. Taking possession of herself with the statement 'I'm not their daughter. I'm not Nel. I'm me', she effects a vicarious escape through her relationship with SULA PEACE. Apparently the more complex of the two women, Nel is unaware of both her complicity in Sula's actions and of the importance of the relationship to her survival. Realization of both these points catapults her from her previous emotional consistency into 'circles and circles of sorrow'.

Wright, Vera
Cabin Fever, 1990
Elizabeth Jolley

Vera Wright, fragile and tormented, is feverish with the tossing and turning of her memories and unfulfilled longings: 'Whether things are written down or not they dwell somewhere within and surface unbidden at any time', she writes. As a young nurse during World War II, she finds herself pregnant by a married hospital doctor. A vessel of guilt and shame for whom the memory of childhood innocence and peace of mind is still tantalizingly clear, Vera feels her life to be irreparably fractured: she exists as a cork afloat on an ocean of isolating emotions.

Wringhim, Robert (the Elder)
The Private Memoirs and Confessions of a Justified Sinner, 1824
James Hogg

The bigoted, predestinarian minister who embodies all that is most destructive and extreme in the tenets of rigorous Calvinism. Arch-enemy to the LAIRD OF DALCASTLE,

Wringhim is, however, worshipped by like-minded LADY OF DALCASTLE and he is principally responsible for indoctrinating her – and, allusively, *his* – son ROBERT WRINGHIM with the belief that he is one of 'the elect', or 'chosen few'.

Wringhim, Robert (the Younger)
The Private Memoirs and Confessions of a Justified Sinner, 1824
James Hogg

A mean and spiteful figure, studious Wringhim – the 'justified sinner' of the title – is indoctrinated from an early age into believing in his infallible claim to divine grace. Haunted by the mysterious figure of GIL-MARTIN, however, he commits atrocious crimes, and we witness the increasingly despairing struggles of his dark, tormented spirit as he tries to keep justifying these in respect to his supposed predestination.

Wulf, Anna
The Golden Notebook, 1962
Doris Lessing

A writer in the grip of profound emotional and literary block, driven to the point of breakdown by personal and political contradictions that she can no longer encompass. Her response is a series of experimental notebooks in which she tries to break through her barriers to a new self-awareness.

Wunderlick, Bucky
Great Jones Street, 1973
Don DeLillo

A rock musician, in whom some critics have identified elements of Bob Dylan and Mick Jagger, he is appalled by the 'murderous love' of the fans and retires to a drab apartment in his native New York City.

Wustrin, Amy
The Actual, 1997
Saul Bellow

Descended from German-speaking Jews from Odessa and the object of HARRY TRELLMAN's fervent love ever since they 'briefly dated' in high school, Wustrin in the intervening 40 years before their encounter in late middle-age has somewhat haphazardly navigated the sexual revolution, been twice married and careered from rich to broke. A discerning interior decorator, she may no longer be a beauty but to Trellman she remains 'the one actual Amy'.

Wyatt, Gillian
Talking it Over, 1991
Love, etc, 2000
Julian Barnes

In her early thirties in the first novel, Gillian is a half-English, half-French picture restorer, 'an ordinary, private person', she claims. Having married STUART HUGHES, she allows herself to be wooed by his friend OLIVER RUSSELL, whom she

subsequently marries. Defensive and often passive, she rarely asserts her independence, seeing herself as somehow defined by the men in her life, and yet this results in her appearing unfulfilled. She is probably right when she declares that 'I loved each of them truly', although in the second volume she is considerably less certain.

Wybrow, Captain Anthony
'Mr. Gilfil's Love-Story', in *Scenes of Clerical Life*, 1858
George Eliot

The young nephew and heir of Sir Christopher Cheverel, Captain Wybrow, though uncommonly handsome, is nonetheless not an attractive character. Consumed by his own vanity and hypochondria, he is incapable of any honest, emotional interaction with anyone, and instead toys unashamedly with the feelings of CATERINA SARTI and, by default, those of his fiancée, Miss Assher. Acting only in his own interest, he tries to manipulate the people around him to make his life easier, but the stress he takes on in doing so can lead only to a tragic, if not wholly undeserved, end.

Wycherley, Widow (Clara)
'Dr. Heidegger's Experiment', 1837, in *Twice-Told Tales*, 1837, revised edition 1842
Nathaniel Hawthorne

Once considered a great beauty and the amorous target of her three old friends, COL KILLIGREW, MR MEDBOURNE and MR GASCOIGNE, she now lives in some seclusion as a result of certain scandalous stories. A willing participant in DR HEIDEGGER's rejuvenation experiment, she provides the most grotesque proof of the impossibility of cheating time.

Wyeth, Maria (Maria Wyeth Lang)
Play It As It Lays, 1970
Joan Didion

Wife of the movie director Carter Lang and passive 'star' of his semi-documentary 'Maria', which sounds like a Warhol product, and of his sexploitation vehicle 'Angel Beach', whose raped heroine does ironically seem to have 'a definite knack for controlling her own destiny'. Maria has 'trouble with *as it was*' and tries desperately to cut free from the past and obey her gambler father's injunction to 'play it as it lays'.

Wynn, May
The Caine Mutiny, 1951
Herman Wouk

Born on the wrong side of the tracks for the nice WASP WILLIE KEITH, with whom she grows up, she is a talented singer. She almost slides into the seedy life of night clubs and sleazy relationships, but being a good Catholic girl she keeps her integrity and is there when Willie Keith grows up and is ready for real love.

Xorandor

Xorandor, 1986

Christine Brooke-Rose

Improbable as it sounds, this character is a large rock on a Cornish beach which has acquired the functional and communicative characteristics of a megacomputer. Discovered by the 'nuclear' twins, JIP and ZAB, it combines logical hyper-sophistication and near-infinite mnemonic capacity with a 'human' tendency to syntactic confusion. The name derives from its willingness to embrace both exclusive and non-exclusive logical alternatives – XOR and OR – and as such it provides the twins with a working education in narrative method.

Yaeger, Webb
'Hearts and Crosses', in *Heart of the West*, 1907
O Henry

Having lost his manhood, he can never be any more than 'prince-consort' to his wife, Santa, 'the cattle queen'. In a fit of pique at his powerlessness, Webb leaves her, 'to be a man again'. A year later, Santa's message – a cross inside a heart – calls him back. On his return, Webb finds that the queen has abdicated in favour of the new 'king' of the Napolito Ranch – his wife's infant son.

Yahoos
Gulliver's Travels, 1726
Jonathan Swift

These creatures exist in opposition to the HOUYHNHNMS. They will eat anything that happens along, even the carcass of a diseased cow. They are different from humans, but to LEMUEL GULLIVER's horror, observable in this abominable animal is a perfect human figure. They are disposed to nastiness, are dirty, frequently get drunk, are contemptuous of one another, and are prone to excessive promiscuity. Corrupt, violent and greedy, they represent the degeneration of morality through time.

Yajnavalkja, Mrs
Valmouth, 1919
Ronald Firbank

A manipulative and sexually predatory black masseuse who dominates the demi-monde of Valmouth, a fashionable but faintly tacky watering hole. Turbanned and swathed in wildly clashing colours and tartans, she speaks in broad pidgin English, replete with 'dat', 'dese' and 'dose'.

Yakimov, Prince
The Balkan Trilogy, 1960–5
Olivia Manning

At first the gauntly noble prince seems little more than a tattered pretender to an inheritance that has been squandered by the war, an irritating leech on the great fortunes of others. But soon Yakimov takes centre stage as Pandarus, the tragi-comic hero of GUY PRINGLE's self-indulgent production of *Troilus and Cressida*, staged amidst the crumbling splendours of Bucharest. His strongest emotion is self-pity, and 'Poor old Yaki' is his constant cry. Half Irish, half White Russian, belonging both nowhere and everywhere, he surveys the scenes of destruction around him with humility and fear.

Yank, properly Robert Smith
The Hairy Ape, 1922
Eugene O'Neill

A symbol of man who has lost contact with his true nature. Brutalized by technology, Yank works as a stoker in the belly of a huge liner. Released from jail, where he was imprisoned in a cage made by MILDRED DOUGLAS's father, he attempts to join the International Workers of the World, but is dismissed as a 'brainless ape'. Visiting the Bronx Zoo, he frees the gorilla but is crushed and dumped in the beast's cage, dying in a steel prison once again.

Yates, Mr
Mansfield Park, 1814
Jane Austen

A friend of TOM BERTRAM, and a man with 'not much to recommend him beyond habits of fashion and expense'. Lacking discernment, diffidence, delicacy and discretion, to SIR THOMAS BERTRAM he is 'trifling and confident, idle and expensive', and his presence at Mansfield Park is obtrusive, 'wearisome' and 'offensive'. Bland and unseemly from the start, he seals his fate by eloping with JULIA BERTRAM.

Yaverland, Marion
The Judge, 1922
Rebecca West

Marion personifies psychoneurosis. Through the surfeit of psychobabble, it is difficult to discern a motive for the nocturnal wandering which leads to her destruction. Like the environment she inhabits, she is a blend of disparate elements made into a mysterious and sublime whole.

Yaverland, Richard
The Judge, 1922
Rebecca West

The illegitimate child of the local squire, Richard has a tortured relationship with his mother. He is a divided character; in Edinburgh he is successful and powerful, a figure of romance worthy of ELLEN MELVILLE, but on his return to Essex he loses control and exhibits lineaments and passions never previously revealed. He becomes a child babbling for his mother, hotly and jealously possessive. As he slips his hand around his mother's waist, the full extent of this Oedipal crisis becomes clear. He is an unpalatable mixture of repulsive egotism and displaced love.

Yehudi, Master
Mr Vertigo, 1994
Paul Auster

Quick, deft and experienced, Master Yehudi is 'perfectly at home in the jungle' of life. Seen through the eyes of his protégé, WALTER RAWLEY, he is a powerful and uncanny presence, who with a mixture of brutality, kindness and sarcasm transforms the street urchin into 'Walt the Wonder Boy'. Prophetic insight guides him while moneymaking dreams drive him: 'His mouth was one of the great huckster machines of all time, and once he got it going full tilt, the dreams poured out of it like smoke rushing through a chimney'. He has the ability to make his companions love and respect him despite his mistakes, and when his dreams are destroyed he 'just wouldn't quit', acknowledging his debt to Walt and eventually sacrificing himself to save the boy.

Yekl, known as Jake
Yekl: A Tale of the New York Ghetto, 1896
Abraham Cahan

Formerly Yekele Beril, Jake works in the garment district of New York's Lower East Side. An early version of the Jewish-American *allrightnik*, he has swallowed whole the go-getting drive and unreflective hedonism of American life, but is forced to rethink his values when his wife Gitl and their child follow him to the USA.

Yellan, Mary
Jamaica Inn, 1936
Daphne Du Maurier

A spirited orphan who has the courage and intelligence to undertake amazing acts of bravery and decision-making. She is a wholesome girl thrown into a world of danger and deceit, yet she copes admirably with the situations which beset her. Vulnerable yet tough, she is inspirational, a woman who will not become a martyr just to suit the powerful men around her.

Yellowhammer, Moll
A Chaste Maid in Cheapside, 1611–13
Thomas Middleton

The daughter of an avaricious and ambitious goldsmith, she is promised in marriage by her parents to the lecherous knight, SIR WALTER WHOREHOUND. The 'Chaste Maid' of the title, she is in love with another man, Touchwood Junior. After many attempts, and with the help of TOUCHWOOD SENIOR, she succeeds in marrying the suitor of her choice.

Yellowhammer, Tim
A Chaste Maid in Cheapside, 1611–13
Thomas Middleton

The son of Yellowhammer, the goldsmith, and brother of MOLL YELLOWHAMMER, Tim has returned home from Cambridge University with his tutor, with whom he spends much time discoursing in Latin. Despite his intellectual pretensions and smug snobbery, he is an ignorant and incompetent fool whose main concern at the prospect of his sister's death is writing an appropriate epitaph for the occasion.

Yellowley, Barbara, also known as Miss Baby
The Pirate, 1821
Sir Walter Scott

The younger sister of TRIPTOLEMUS YELLOWLEY and chatelaine of Stourburgh. She is a fanatical housewife who 'might have realised, if any one could, the idea of the learned philosopher, who pronounced that sleeping was a fancy, and eating but a habit ... She was up early and down late and seemed, to her over-watched and over-tasked maidens, to be as *wakerife* as the cat herself'.

Yellowley, Triptolemus
The Pirate, 1821
Sir Walter Scott

The chosen missionary of the Chamberlain of Orkney and Zetland, he lives at Stourburgh (or Harfra) with his sister BARBARA YELLOWLEY. The name was given to him by a curate who liked the combination of classical allusion and agricultural reference, and Triptolemus has been an 'improver' from the cradle. In his zeal for progress in farming, he appears to have been born a century too soon.

Yeobright, Clym (Clement)
The Return of the Native, 1878
Thomas Hardy

Clym is the 'native' of the title, and has returned from Paris to his native Egdon Heath. He has known and rejected the material and cosmopolitan pleasures so hankered after by EUSTACIA VYE, and his marriage to her is doomed when she realizes he has no intention of leaving again. He has idealistic plans of becoming a teacher, but when his eyesight begins to weaken he takes up the menial job of furze-cutter, which brings him closer to his beloved heath but horrifies both his wife and his class-conscious mother MRS YEOBRIGHT. His consequent estrangement from both leaves him feeling guilt for their tragic fates.

Yeobright, Mrs
The Return of the Native, 1878
Thomas Hardy

A proud woman, she is aloof from those around her whom she neither understands nor trusts. She is maternal, but can be stern with her niece, THOMASIN YEOBRIGHT, and she objects both to Thomasin's marriage to DAMON WILDEVE and that of her son CLYM YEOBRIGHT to EUSTACIA VYE. Yet, although she is undemonstrative, her heart is full of love, and her desire to be reconciled with her son leads her, through a series of coincidences and misunderstandings typical of Hardy, to her tragic death, believing herself (falsely) to be a 'broken-hearted woman cast off by her son'.

Yeobright, Thomasin ('Tamsin')
The Return of the Native, 1878
Thomas Hardy

Uncharacteristically gentle and sensitive for her family, Thomasin is blessed with common sense, and has strong domestic and maternal inclinations. But however much she values the opinion of her aunt MRS YEOBRIGHT, she is strong-willed enough to marry DAMON WILDEVE against her wishes. Unlike EUSTACIA VYE and Damon himself, she feels at home on Egdon Heath, where she was born and raised. In contrast with Hardy's other young female characters, she is neither capricious nor narcissistic. Instead, she is wholesome, serene and sympathetic.

Yeoman, the
The Canterbury Tales, c.1387–1400
Geoffrey Chaucer
As attendant on THE KNIGHT and THE SQUIRE he combines the functions of gamekeeper, huntsman and body-servant. He is neatly attired and takes scrupulous care of his equipment, all of which is of the best. He bristles with weaponry and is a particularly fine archer. A minor pilgrim, he does not tell a tale.

Yillah
Mardi, 1849
Herman Melville
A beautiful, gentle, white-skinned, golden-haired, blue-eyed maiden, who tells a fantastic story of her 'more than mortal' origins, and is 'lovely enough to be really divine'. She is enshrined as a goddess, then rescued by TAJI, but after brief happiness she mysteriously vanishes, and is never seen again. Her ethereal nature and 'wild beauty was a vail to things still more strange', and she sometimes seems 'a being of the land of dreams'. She is haunted by a vision of her death in a whirlpool.

Yog-Sothoth
'The Whisperer in Darkness', and elsewhere
H P Lovecraft, edited by August Derleth, 1945
The immortal leader of the ichthyous OLD ONES who worship CTHULHU, it leads the retreat to the planet Yogguth, from where the Old Ones attempt to intervene in human affairs. Like the others of its kind it represents sexual force and, simultaneously, the negation of creative sexuality.

Yolland, Lt George
Translations, 1981
Brian Friel
In Baile Beag (Ballybeg), County Donegal, in 1833, two cultures collide as British Royal Engineers coax the Irish-speaking community into helping them carry out a survey in which place names will be translated into English. Lieutenant Yolland is in his late twenties, tall, blond and awkward, 'a soldier by accident', a sensitive, fundamentally decent man, disturbed that he may be presiding over 'an eviction of sorts'. Yet he is a man of reason rather than instinct, pragmatic rather than spiritual, and therefore fails to understand fully the symbolic significance of either his own actions, or deeper cultural impulses of the Irish or English.

Yonadab
The Rape of Tamar, 1970
Dan Jacobson
The characters and incidents in this novel are derived from the story of the rape of Tamar, only daughter of David, King of Judah and Israel, by her brother, Amnon, as told in the Bible, in the second book of Samuel. Yonadab, David's

nephew, is the narrator of the novel and in many ways the instigator of the act. Symbolically, he is the perpetrator of the act. Self-conscious, cynical, detached, voyeuristic, obsessive, yet an intelligent man not without humour, Yonadab is contemptuous of creed yet needs something in which to believe.

Yoomy ('the Warbler')
Mardi, 1849
Herman Melville
A poet from Odo, he is a 'youthful, long-haired, blue-eyed minstrel' who is 'all fits and starts', and often absent-minded. He is pale and wan, but always neatly dressed. He favours amorous melodies, but will occasionally 'burst forth with lively lays of arms and battle'. He is capricious, and often 'swayed by contrary moods'.

Yorick, Parson
The Life and Opinions of Tristram Shandy, 9 volumes, 1959–67
Laurence Sterne
A good-natured, worldly-wise vicar, whose enjoyment of intellectual pursuits and obvious learning have never dulled his delight in matters frivolous or scandalous. He appears as a well-rounded personality, and his death is acknowledged by two full black pages within the novel.

York, Archbishop of
Back to Methuselah, 1921
George Bernard Shaw
The archbishop, formerly the REVEREND BILL HASLAM, appears in the third section of this five-part play. *The Thing Happens* is set in the parlour of the President of the British Islands in 2170AD. Although he must be older, the archbishop appears to be only 50. He admits that after his wife died aged 68, he discovered he would live for 300 years; at the moment he is 283. Because his longevity has caused pension difficulties, he has staged several 'drownings' and afterwards begun a new career somewhere else. Eventually, he marries MRS LUTESTRING.

York, Richard Plantagenet, Duke of
Henry VI Parts I, II and III, early 1590s
William Shakespeare
Richard Plantagenet's quarrel with the Lancastrian John Beaufort (later Duke of Somerset) in the Temple Garden, during which he plucks the white rose while Beaufort takes the red, is a decisive event, culminating in the Wars of the Roses. During the conflict, Plantagenet and the Yorkists defeat HENRY VI and Queen Margaret (MARGARET OF ANJOU) at St Albans. Plantagenet, the father of three sons, including RICHARD, DUKE OF GLOUCESTER, is himself captured by Margaret at Wakefield and stabbed to death. Ruthless, cunning and ambitious, he is a formidable man and opponent, both a proud medieval baron and a highly-skilled professional soldier.

Yossarian, John
Catch-22, 1961
Joseph Heller
The cunning Assyrian-American anti-hero

whose only aim and increasing obsession is 'to live forever or die in the attempt'. Everywhere he looks amid the lunacy of the war, he sees 'a nut, and it was all a sensible young gentleman like himself could do to maintain his perspective amid so much madness'. His attempts to overcome Catch-22 and escape the flying missions grow increasingly desperate and complex, but less fruitful. He is nothing if not a survivor, however, and manages to hang on (but not to prosper) in his crazed illogical world.

Young, Bertha
Bliss, 1920
Katherine Mansfield
The electric energy which enraptures this not-so-young mother is her springlike joy at participation in life. Preparing for a sophisticated dinner party of clever conversation, she adjusts her decor like a stage set. She feels the reckless emotion of 'how idiotic civilisation is' and senses the closeness of danger and desire in the stealthily attractive woman who is revealed as her husband's mistress. Nevertheless, the innocence of the lovely pear tree she sees as symbolic of herself survives.

Young, Della
'The Gift of the Magi', in *The Four Million*, 1906
O Henry
Despite saving hard, Della, a young wife, has only $1.87 with which to buy a Christmas present for her beloved husband JIM YOUNG. Desperate to express her love in a material manner, despite their poverty, she sells her most treasured possession so she can afford an expensive gift.

Young, Felix
The Europeans, 1878
Henry James
A moderately talented portraitist, the younger brother by five years of the BARONESS EUGENIA. 'Though he bore a noticeable resemblance to his sister, he was a better-favoured person; fair-haired, clear-faced, witty-looking, with a delicate finish of feature and an expression at once urbane and not at all serious.'

Young, Jim
'The Gift of the Magi', in *The Four Million*, 1906
O Henry
Poor and young, Jim (or James Dillingham Young, as he called himself in better days) is quiet, thin, serious-looking and basically sensible. He sells his most treasured possession so he can buy an expensive Christmas present for his wife DELLA YOUNG, thus expressing his love for her.

Young Bellair
The Man of Mode, 1676
Sir George Etherege
Young Bellair is 'by much the most tolerable of all the young men who do not abound in wit'. Ordered by his father to marry HARRIET WOODVIL, he prefers to follow his own instincts and court EMILIA instead. He represents, therefore, a breaking away from the old values of

duty and obedience, and the striking out for a new world of self-determination. Indeed, he risks disinheritance in the process.

Young Fashion
The Relapse, or Virtue in Danger, 1696
Sir John Vanbrugh
The younger brother of LORD FOPPINGTON, Young Fashion is aggrieved that he has inherited only a small proportion of their father's estate. Rakish, but undoubtedly hard done by, Young Fashion decides to take revenge upon his brother by marrying MISS HOYDEN, already promised in marriage to Foppington. All Young Fashion wants is her money, but his ruthlessness is mitigated by equal hard-heartedness on the parts of Foppington and Miss Hoyden, as each is on the lookout for material and sexual advantage. Indeed, marriage between Fashion and Hoyden will apparently suit them both, for he does not propose to grudge his wife's sexual liaisons as long as 'she brings me an estate that will afford me a separate maintenance'.

Young Freevill
The Dutch Courtezan, 1605
John Marston
Although amoral and opportunistic, Young Freevill is the hero of this comedy, and provides moralistic observations on the other characters. He ditches his mistress, FRANCESCHINA, to marry the sexually innocent but aristocratic BEATRICE SUBBOYS, piously saying of Franceschina: 'Providence all wicked art o'ertops'!

Young Man, the
The Stone, 1976
Edward Bond
In this short Bunyanesque parable, the 'eager and relaxed' Young Man attains the Age of Reason. He appears full of optimism, armed with the seven golden talents with which his parents have endowed him: Prudence, Soberness, Courage, Justice, Honesty, Love and Hope. He embarks upon a journey to deliver a stone to the Mason's house, but various characters attempt to win the talents from him, or corrupt them into sins. As the stone, his burden, grows increasingly large, the Young Man learns that in order to live in freedom he must be rid of the one who exploits him. Finally, he kills the Mason.

Young Man Carbuncular, the
'The Fire Sermon', in *The Waste Land*, 1922
T S Eliot
Opportunist lover of THE TYPIST, he is clerk to a small house agent, 'one of the low on whom assurance sits/As a silk hat on a Bradford millionaire'.

Yule, Alfred
New Grub Street, 1891
George Gissing
Half-maddened by poverty and lack of literary recognition, he treats his working-class wife with fussy disdain, embarrassed by her poor grammar and limited vocabulary, and subjects his daughter, MARIAN YULE, to the pointless discipline of 'research' that is never going to lead

to anything substantial. His eventual blindness is a further cruel twist of fate.

Yule, Marian
New Grub Street, 1891
George Gissing

ALFRED YULE's daughter, she is maintained as a virtual slave, doing pointless research for her father in the British Museum Reading Room, a place she increasingly sees as an inverted jar or spider's web, trapping all its futile occupants. Sympathetic and genuinely bright, she is the novel's one reliable moral centre.

Zab → Jip and Zab

Zabina
Tamburlaine the Great: Part I, 1587
Christopher Marlowe
Wife of the Turkish emperor, forced to stand by helplessly as her husband is humiliated by the Scythian TAMBURLAINE. When BAJAZETH dashes out his brains on the bars of his cage, Zabina is crazed with grief and takes her own life in the same manner.

Zach (Zachariah)
The Blood Knot, 1961
Athol Fugard
Brother of the lighter-skinned, domineering MORRIE, Zach finds life in their dilapidated shack too claustrophobic. Morrie attempts to alleviate the situation with role-playing games, but these end in provoking a potentially violent confrontation between them. Their 'blood-knot' as brothers binds them together, but emotionally they are hindered by the consequences of apartheid.

Zapp, Morris J
Changing Places, 1975
Small World, 1984
Nice Work, 1988
David Lodge
An American university lecturer, Zapp's middle initial, as he delights in explaining to female enquirers, stands for Jehovah: 'all women', he elaborates, 'love to be screwed by a god'. Sexual metaphors pepper the abstruse theories of his lectures to various world conferences, although his amorous prowess is by now in decline, the result of age and the rise of assertive feminism. Affecting loud check jackets and zeppelin-shaped cigars, in the first novel he takes part in a transatlantic exchange with PHILIP SWALLOW, coming to Rummidge University partly to delay costly divorce proceedings against him. In the second and third volumes in the sequence, he is still travelling the world, attending conferences, keeping an ear to the ground for gossip and intrigue, and hoping to be appointed to the UNESCO Chair of Literary Criticism, a post offering immense status, unlimited travel and no teaching or administrative duties.

Zawistowska, Sophie
Sophie's Choice, 1979
William Styron
When STINGO first meets Sophie in their Bronx boarding house, she seems exotically beautiful, older than himself and intriguingly 'experienced', archetypally 'European', and caught up in a relationship of astonishing passion and complexity with the gifted NATHAN LANDAU. There is, though, a dark side beneath her beauty, for she is a Polish Catholic survivor of Auschwitz, the daughter of an anti-Semitic professor of law and Nazi apologist. The price of her survival has been collaboration as secretary to the camp commandant, and (the harrowing 'choice' of Styron's title) the sacrifice of one of her children.

Zeke
Omoo, 1847
Herman Melville
A planter at Martair, who employs the narrator and DR LONG GHOST. He is 'a tall, robust Yankee' from the backwoods of Maine, sallow, and with a long face and a 'twang like a cracked viol'. A 'strong, ugly man' well adapted for manual labour, he has 'an invincible industry'. He is grave and taciturn, but with 'a deal of good old humour bottled up in him', and is frank, good-hearted, shrewd, resolute and illiterate.

Zelli, Marya
Quartet, 1969, originally published as *Postures*, 1928
Jean Rhys
A self-styled vagabond in flight from a respectable family, she enjoys a reckless existence on the fringes of the artistic subculture in Montparnasse. Perceptive, witty and equipped with a keen sense of dismissive irony, she loves her disreputable husband, STEPHAN ZELLI, and the colourful, unpredictable vitality of their life together, but finds herself helpless when, suddenly isolated, she is drawn into the subtle hypocrisies of respectable society. By turns supremely knowing and utterly malleable, Marya's strength lies in her unconventionality, her weakness in a pragmatic desire to conform.

Zelli, Stephan
Quartet, 1969, originally published as *Postures*, 1928
Jean Rhys
Reticent, evasive, and a liar, he is the loving but wholly unreliable husband of MARYA ZELLI. A dealer in pictures 'and other things', his dubious business transactions have earned him a term in prison and a lifetime on the run from the police of Paris and Amsterdam. Prison has broken the

air of calm, self-contained assurance with which he captivated his wife and secured his living, and he appears in the novel as a wolf-like creature with sharpened features, given to sporadic fits of despair and wild outbursts of irrational optimism.

Zen, Aurelio
Ratking, 1988, et seq
Michael Dibdin
An Italian police inspector in his mid-fifties whose most striking features are 'a nose as sharply triangular as the jib of a sailing boat' and 'grey eyes with glints of blue and a slightly sinister stillness', Zen is cynical and world-weary from his encounters with corrupt politicians and policemen as well as the Mafia. A lover of strong Nazionali cigarettes, espresso and grappa, he is haunted by memories of his hometown of Venice and his father, who disappeared in World War II.

Zenobia (Zenobia Moody)
The Blithedale Romance, 1852
Nathaniel Hawthorne
Daughter of the cynically manipulative Moody and 'dark sister' to the bloodless PRISCILLA, she is a committed feminist with an exotic sexual allure, she is thought – because of rather than despite Hawthorne's passionate disclaimers – to be modelled on the Transcendentalist writer and social critic Margaret Fuller.

Zenocrate
Tamburlaine the Great: Parts I and II, 1587–90
Christopher Marlowe
Divinely beautiful daughter of the Soldan of Egypt, 'whose fortunes never mastered her griefs', she is captured by the Scythian warrior TAMBURLAINE, losing her suitor Alcidamus, King of Arabia, in the bloody battles that follow. She later marries Tamburlaine who, despite his cruelty, commands her unfailing love.

Zephon
Paradise Lost, 1667
John Milton
One of the minor angels who guard Eden and one of those who discover SATAN crouching by EVE's ear. He pours scorn on Satan's unhumbled pride.

Zerkow
McTeague: A Story of San Francisco, 1899
Frank Norris
A Polish Jew with improbable red hair, he runs a junk shop in San Francisco, near to MCTEAGUE's surgery. 'He had the thin, eager, cat-like lips of the covetous; eyes that had grown keen as those of a lynx from long searching amid much decay and debris; and claw-like prehensile fingers ...' Underneath the distastefully casual anti-Semitism, he is a powerful symbol of the story's dominant passion: greed.

Zero, Mr
The Adding Machine, 1923
Elmer Rice
A badly-paid white-collar worker, 'a regular guy', whose life is hedged by frustration with his talkative wife and dull job. He impulsively kills

his boss in a frenzy of anger at losing his job and being replaced by an adding machine. In the afterlife he is interrogated by an official, Charles, who reminds him: 'You can't change the rules – nobody can – they've got it all fixed. It's a rotten system – but what are you going to do about it?'

Zevi, Sabbatai
Satan in Goray, 1958
Isaac Bashevis Singer
Based on the historical character of the same name, he is a dream-like, distant figure whom certain Jews have proclaimed as the 'true Messiah'. Although never directly seen, he is the root of the anarchy and iniquity in the town of Goray. Those who have encountered him tell of his brilliant jewels, the blinding brightness of his face, and his holiness. Such is the hold he has over his followers that some of them refuse to believe he has failed them when he becomes a Muslim.

Zigger Zagger
Zigger Zagger, 1967
Peter Terson
Zigger fulfils a dual role: firstly he is the narrator, introducing, informing and commenting in a sardonic matter on the failure of HARRY to do anything meaningful with his life; then he is the football thug, an amoral figurehead who incites trouble wherever he goes but leaves others to be caught.

Zimmern, Celia
Only Children, 1979
The Truth about Lorin Jones, 1988
Alison Lurie
Married to the extrovert DAN ZIMMERN, Celia Zimmern is the sort of woman who becomes invisible in a crowd. The happiest years of her life have been those spent in college, immersed in books, but although academically bright, she is inexperienced in the feminine art of managing men. Her intense love for the philandering Dan makes her vulnerable, sapping what little vitality she has.

Zimmern, Dan
Only Children, 1979
Alison Lurie
Physically and emotionally powerful, Dan likes people to do as he tells them. The husband of CELIA ZIMMERN, he is attractive and enjoys life to the full, expecting everyone else to join in the fun. Women seem to be there to be hunted, collected and moulded to his needs. Para-doxically, ANNA KING, the one woman who has resisted his dominance in her life is the one he most respects and desires. He is similarly dissatisfied in his career, where his creative talents are used to bring material success at the expense of literary creativity.

Zimmern, Lolly → Jones, Lorin

Zimmern, Roger
Imaginary Friends, 1967
Alison Lurie
A keen young academic, anxious for success and

respect, but not at any price, Roger Zimmern tries to do his job with integrity and has a naive faith in the professional impartiality of others. Deception, even when necessary for his research, does not come easily to him. 'You're so scrupulous, Zimmern, you should have gone into statistics', says one colleague. For all his professional objectivity, Roger is susceptible to emotions and he ascribes these lapses of jealousy, pride and lust to 'Stupid Roger'. This contempt is tempered however, by the suspicion that clever Roger is missing out on the fun.

Zita, Aunt
Wild Nights, 1979
Emma Tennant

The child narrator's paternal aunt, whose autumn visits to the stark, chill northern valley estate owned by the family herald summer's end. To the child, the flamboyant, excitement-seeking unconventional Zita brings warmth, strangeness and fabulous delights: nightly rides on the north wind, on 'long journeys into memory', to balls and banquets worldwide accompanied by exotic imaginary companions. But when low-spirited, Zita pathetically searches the family house for love, and at Halloween she is made a scapegoat by estate tenants resentful of their cold, bare existence.

Zogoiby, Moraes
The Moor's Last Sigh, 1995
Salman Rushdie

The last surviving member of the Zogoiby family, known as 'the Moor', aged 36 but doomed to age at twice the usual rate, he therefore has the physique of a 72-year-old. Over six feet tall with a deformed right hand, the son of a Christian mother and a Jewish father, the Moor reviews his life, speaking from atop a Spanish tombstone and reflecting upon 'the fall from grace of a high-born cross breed' in a story reflecting the multiple identities of India. Having subscribed to various faiths and political creeds and finally coming to believe in the power of 'love as the blending of spirits', Zogoiby longs for a revelation.

Zoo
Back to Methuselah, 1921
George Bernard Shaw

As companion to THE ELDERLY GENTLEMAN, Zoo appears in the fourth section of this five-part play. *Tragedy of an Elderly Gentleman* is set on the shore of Galway Bay, Ireland, in AD3000. She is 50 years old, describes herself as a 'flapper', resembles 'SAVVY' BARNABAS in an earlier section of the play, but appears to be even younger than Savvy's 18 years. She debates life and learning with the Elderly Gentleman, who is astonished by her view that 'we are made wise not by the recollections of our past but by the responsibilities of our future'.

Zozim
Back to Methuselah, 1921
George Bernard Shaw

A male 'nurse' to the ELDERLY GENTLEMAN, Zozim appears in the fourth section of this five-part play. *Tragedy of an Elderly Gentleman* is set on the shore of Galway Bay, Ireland, in AD3000. A long-lifer, he is 94 and therefore, like FUSIMA, has difficulty in understanding much of what the Elderly Gentleman says. He gives up, and leaves him in the charge of ZOO.

Zuckerman, Nathan
My Life as a Man, 1974, et seq
Philip Roth

First appearing as PETER TARNOPOL's fictive persona, Zuckerman moves to centre stage in the following three novels, known collectively as the *Zuckerman Bound* trilogy. In *The Ghost Writer* (1979) he is an aspiring novelist in search of his identity both as an artist and an American Jew, perceiving E I LONOFF as a kind of spiritual father and seeking from him 'the magical protection of his advocacy and love'. Yet he realizes that he also needs the recognition of his real, estranged father. In *Zuckerman Unbound* (1981), he is the infamous author of a controversial novel widely disparaged as anti-Semitic. Desperate to prove otherwise, Zuckerman becomes increasingly paranoid and confused. By *The Anatomy Lesson* (1983), his angst is manifest as physical pain but the way is clear to at least a partial acceptance of himself. In a further three novels, known as the *American Trilogy*, Zuckerman appears as the narrator, older, no longer so libidinous and reflecting upon recent American history and the people he knew.

Zuleika
The Bride of Abydos: A Turkish Tale, 1813
Byron, George Gordon, 6th Lord Byron

Zuleika, daughter of the Pacha Giaffir, is condemned to marry an elderly Turkish lord. She pours out her grief to her beloved brother SELIM. He reveals that he is secretly a pirate, and that she is not his sister but his cousin, as he is actually the son of Giaffir's murdered brother. She is ready to flee with Selim but he is slain by Giaffir and his men, and she dies, inconsolable.

Zuniga, Detective Hector
Vineland, 1990
Thomas Pynchon

A narcotics agent with the Drug Enforcement Administration, he reappears out of ZOYD WHEELER's past, an 'erratic federal comet who brought ... new forms of bad luck and baleful influence'.

Zweck, Norman
The Elected Member, 1969
Bernice Rubens

A clever and ambitious lawyer, Zweck is the son of a general shopkeeper. The family is London-Jewish, closely-knit, and he appears to have fulfilled all their hopes and his. Yet his brilliance seems too great a burden for him to bear. Zweck becomes addicted to drugs and degenerates from a sensitive high-achiever into a vulgar and belligerent man. The glittering intellectual powers for which he is noted have betrayed him, exposing him as weak, anxious and vulnerable. He withdraws into himself, and suffers his greatest betrayal when the family commits him to a mental hospital.

Literary Awards

Nobel prize for literature

Nobel prizes were established by a bequest in the will of Alfred Nobel (1833–96) to honour 'those who, during the preceding year, shall have conferred the greatest benefit on mankind'. The Nobel prize for literature is awarded annually to a person who has 'produced in the field of literature the most outstanding work in an ideal direction'. It was first awarded in 1901.

1901	Sully Prudhomme	1952	François Mauriac
1902	Theodor Mommsen	1953	Winston Churchill
1903	Bjørnstjerne Bjørnson	1954	Ernest Hemingway
1904	Frédéric Mistral, José	1955	Halldór Kiljan Laxness
	Echegaray	1956	Juan Ramón Jiménez
1905	Henryk Sienkiewicz	1957	Albert Camus
1906	Giosuè Carducci	1958	Boris Pasternak
1907	Rudyard Kipling	1959	Salvatore Quasimodo
1908	Rudolf Eucken	1960	Saint-John Perse
1909	Selma Lagerlöf	1961	Ivo Andric
1910	Paul Heyse	1962	John Steinbeck
1911	Maurice Maeterlinck	1963	Giorgos Seferis
1912	Gerhart Hauptmann	1964	Jean-Paul Sartre
1913	Rabindranath Tagore	1965	Michail Sholokhov
1914	*no award*	1966	Samuel Agnon, Nelly Sachs
1915	Romain Rolland	1967	Miguel Angel Asturias
1916	Verner von Heidenstam	1968	Yasunari Kawabata
1917	Karl Gjellerup, Henrik	1969	Samuel Beckett
	Pontoppidan	1970	Alexander Solzhenitsyn
1918	*no award*	1971	Pablo Neruda
1919	Carl Spitteler	1972	Heinrich Böll
1920	Knut Hamsun	1973	Patrick White
1921	Anatole France	1974	Eyvind Johnson, Harry
1922	Jacinto Benavente		Martinson
1923	W B Yeats	1975	Eugenio Montale
1924	Wladyslaw Reymont	1976	Saul Bellow
1925	George Bernard Shaw	1977	Vicente Aleixandre
1926	Grazia Deledda	1978	Isaac Bashevis Singer
1927	Henri Bergson	1979	Odysseus Elytis
1928	Sigrid Undset	1980	Czeslaw Milosz
1929	Thomas Mann	1981	Elias Canetti
1930	Sinclair Lewis	1982	Gabriel García Márquez
1931	Erik Axel Karlfeldt	1983	William Golding
1932	John Galsworthy	1984	Jaroslav Seifert
1933	Ivan Bunin	1985	Claude Simon
1934	Luigi Pirandello	1986	Wole Soyinka
1935	*no award*	1987	Joseph Brodsky
1936	Eugene O'Neill	1988	Naguib Mahfouz
1937	Roger Martin du Gard	1989	Camilo José Cela
1938	Pearl S Buck	1990	Octavio Paz
1939	Frans Eemil Sillanpää	1991	Nadine Gordimer
1940	*no award*	1992	Derek Walcott
1941	*no award*	1993	Toni Morrison
1942	*no award*	1994	Kenzaburo Oe
1943	*no award*	1995	Seamus Heaney
1944	Johannes V Jensen	1996	Wislawa Szymborska
1945	Gabriela Mistral	1997	Dario Fo
1946	Hermann Hesse	1998	José Saramago
1947	André Gide	1999	Günter Grass
1948	T S Eliot	2000	Gao Xingjian
1949	William Faulkner	2001	V S Naipaul
1950	Bertrand Russell	2002	Imre Kertész
1951	Pär Lagerkvist	2003	J M Coetzee

Booker Prize

The Booker Prize is awarded for the year's best novel, and is open to all citizens of Commonwealth countries or the Republic of Ireland. It was established in 1968 in the UK, and has been known as the Man Booker Prize since 2002.

1969	P H Newby *Something to Answer For*
1970	Bernice Rubens *The Elected Member*
1971	V S Naipaul *In a Free State*
1972	John Berger *G*
1973	J G Farrell *The Siege of Krishnapur*
1974	Nadine Gordimer *The Conservationist* and Stanley Middleton *Holiday*
1975	Ruth Prawer Jhabvala *Heat and Dust*
1976	David Storey *Saville*
1977	Paul Scott *Staying On*
1978	Iris Murdoch *The Sea, The Sea*
1979	Penelope Fitzgerald *Offshore*
1980	William Golding *Rites of Passage*
1981	Salman Rushdie *Midnight's Children*
1982	Thomas Keneally *Schindler's Ark*
1983	J M Coetzee *Life and Times of Michael K*
1984	Anita Brookner *Hotel du Lac*
1985	Keri Hulme *The Bone People*
1986	Kingsley Amis *The Old Devils*
1987	Penelope Lively *Moon Tiger*
1988	Peter Carey *Oscar and Lucinda*
1989	Kazuo Ishiguro *The Remains of the Day*
1990	A S Byatt *Possession*
1991	Ben Okri *The Famished Road*
1992	Michael Ondaatje *The English Patient* and Barry Unsworth *Sacred Hunger*
1993	Roddy Doyle *Paddy Clarke, Ha Ha Ha*
1994	James Kelman *How Late It Was, How Late*
1995	Pat Barker *The Ghost Road*
1996	Graham Swift *Last Orders*
1997	Arundhati Roy *The God of Small Things*
1998	Ian McEwan *Amsterdam*
1999	J M Coetzee *Disgrace*
2000	Margaret Atwood *The Blind Assassin*
2001	Peter Carey *True History of the Kelly Gang*
2002	Yann Martel *Life of Pi*
2003	D B C Pierre *Vernon God Little*

Pulitzer Prize in Letters: Fiction

Pulitzer Prizes, first awarded in the USA in 1917, are given annually for literature, drama, music and journalism. They were established in the will of Joseph Pulitzer (1847–1911), and the first Prize for fiction was awarded in 1918. The Prize was known as the prize for a novel, rather than fiction, until 1948.

1917	*no award*
1918	Ernest Poole *His Family*
1919	Booth Tarkington *The Magnificent Ambersons*
1920	*no award*
1921	Edith Wharton *The Age of Innocence*
1922	Booth Tarkington *Alice Adams*
1923	Willa Cather *One of Ours*
1924	Margaret Wilson *The Able McLaughlins*
1925	Edna Ferber *So Big*
1926	Sinclair Lewis *Arrowsmith*
1927	Louis Bromfield *Early Autumn*
1928	Thornton Wilder *The Bridge of San Luis Rey*
1929	Julia Peterkin *Scarlet Sister Mary*
1930	Oliver La Farge *Laughing Boy*
1931	Margaret Ayer Barnes *Years of Grace*
1932	Pearl S Buck *The Good Earth*
1933	T S Stribling *The Store*
1934	Caroline Miller *Lamb in His Bosom*
1935	Josephine Winslow Johnson *Now in November*
1936	Harold L Davis *Honey in the Horn*
1937	Margaret Mitchell *Gone With the Wind*
1938	John Phillips Marquand *The Late George Apley*
1939	Marjorie Kinnan Rawlings *The Yearling*
1940	John Steinbeck *The Grapes of Wrath*
1941	*no award*
1942	Ellen Glasgow *In This Our Life*
1943	Upton Sinclair *Dragon's Teeth*
1944	Martin Flavin *Journey in the Dark*
1945	John Hersey *A Bell for Adano*
1946	*no award*
1947	Robert Penn Warren *All the King's Men*
1948	James A Michener *Tales of the South Pacific*
1949	James Gould Cozzens *Guard of Honor*
1950	A B Guthrie, Jnr *The Way West*
1951	Conrad Richter *The Town*
1952	Herman Wouk *The Caine Mutiny*
1953	Ernest Hemingway *The Old Man and the Sea*
1954	*no award*
1955	William Faulkner *A Fable*
1956	MacKinlay Kantor *Andersonville*
1957	*no award*
1958	James Agee *A Death in the Family*
1959	Robert Lewis Taylor *The Travels of Jaimie McPheeters*
1960	Allen Drury *Advise and Consent*
1961	Harper Lee *To Kill a Mockingbird*
1962	Edwin O'Connor *The Edge of Sadness*
1963	William Faulkner *The Reivers*
1964	*no award*
1965	Shirley Ann Grau *The Keepers of the House*
1966	Katherine Anne Porter *Collected Stories*
1967	Bernard Malamud *The Fixer*
1968	William Styron *The Confessions of Nat Turner*
1969	N Scott Momaday *House Made of Dawn*
1970	Jean Stafford *Collected Stories*
1971	*no award*
1972	Wallace Stegner *Angle of Repose*
1973	Eudora Welty *The Optimist's Daughter*
1974	*no award*

1975	Michael Shaara *The Killer Angels*
1976	Saul Bellow *Humboldt's Gift*
1977	*no award*
1978	James Alan McPherson *Elbow Room*
1979	John Cheever *The Stories of John Cheever*
1980	Norman Mailer *The Executioner's Song*
1981	John Kennedy Toole *A Confederacy of Dunces*
1982	John Updike *Rabbit is Rich*
1983	Alice Walker *The Color Purple*
1984	William Kennedy *Ironweed*
1985	Alison Lurie *Foreign Affairs*
1986	Larry McMurtry *Lonesome Dove*
1987	Peter Taylor *A Summons to Memphis*
1988	Toni Morrison *Beloved*
1989	Anne Tyler *Breathing Lessons*
1990	Oscar Hijuelos *The Mambo Kings Play Songs of Love*
1991	John Updike *Rabbit at Rest*
1992	Jane Smiley *A Thousand Acres*
1993	Robert Olen Butler *A Good Scent From a Strange Mountain*
1994	E Annie Proulx *The Shipping News*
1995	Carol Shields *The Stone Diaries*
1996	Richard Ford *Independence Day*
1997	Steven Millhauser *Martin Dressler: The Tale of an American Dreamer*
1998	Philip Roth *American Pastoral*
1999	Michael Cunningham *The Hours*
2000	Jhumpa Lahiri *Interpreter of Maladies*
2001	Michael Chabon *The Amazing Adventures of Kavalier & Clay*
2002	Richard Russo *Empire Falls*
2003	Jeffrey Eugenides *Middlesex*

Index by Author

Where a character appears in a long series of works (as indicated by 'et seq' at the character's entry) only the first work of the series is given in the Index. Where a character appears in a number of works (but not a series), the works are listed individually both at the character's entry and in the Index.

A

Abish, Walter
◎ (born 1931) US novelist, short-story writer and poet. He explores ideas about cultural identity in *How German Is It* (1980).
How German Is It
Hargenau, Ulrich

Abrahams, Peter
◎ (born 1919) South African novelist and essayist. Originally a protest poet, and subsequently a journalist.
A Wreath for Udomo
Udomo, Michael

Achebe, Chinua
◎ (born 1930) Nigerian novelist, poet and essayist, known for his overtly political writings. *Anthills of the Savanna* (1987) was shortlisted for the Booker Prize.
Anthills of the Savanna
Excellency, His
Okoh, Beatrice
Oriko, Chris
Osodi, Ikem
Arrow of God
Ezeulu
Winterbottom, Captain T K
A Man of the People
Nanga, Chief, the Honourable Micah A, MP
Odili
No Longer At Ease
Okonkwo, Obi
Things Fall Apart
Okonkwo

Acker, Kathy, also wrote as **Black Tarantula**
◎ (1944–97) US novelist, short-story writer and performance artist, her work is visceral in approach and influenced by the drug imagery of **William S Burroughs**.
Blood and Guts in High School
Smith, Janey

Ackroyd, Peter
◎ (born 1949) English novelist, biographer and critic, he was literary editor of *The Spectator* (1973–77), and later (from 1986) chief book reviewer of *The Times*.
English Music
Harcombe, Timothy
Hawksmoor
Dyer, Nicholas
Hawksmoor, Nicholas
Milton in America
Milton, John

Adams, Douglas
◎ (1952–2001) English novelist and scriptwriter best known for his humorous radio series (later adapted for television), *The Hitch-Hiker's Guide to the Galaxy*, which he also wrote as a sequence of novels.
The Hitch-Hiker's Guide to the Galaxy
Beeblebrox, Zaphod
Dent, Arthur
Prefect, Ford

Adams, Henry
◎ (1838–1918) US historian and novelist, the son of writer and diplomat Charles Francis Adams (1807–86) and grandson of President John Quincy Adams (1767–1848). His autobiography *The Education of Henry Adams* (1907) was awarded the Pulitzer Prize in 1919.
Democracy: An American Novel
Lee, Madeleine
Ratcliffe, Senator Silas P
Esther
Dudley, Esther

Adams, Richard
◎ (born 1920) English novelist who made his name as a writer with the bestselling *Watership Down* (1972), an epic tale of a community of rabbits.
Watership Down
Bigwig
Fiver
Hazel
Holly
Kehaar
Woundwort, General

Addison, Joseph and **Steele, Richard**
◎ (1672–1719 and 1672–1729) English poet, playwright, essayist and politician Joseph Addison was co-founder of the magazine *The Spectator* with Irish essayist, dramatist and politician Richard Steele.
The Spectator
de Coverley, Sir Roger
Freeport, Sir Andrew
Honeycomb, Will
Sentry, Captain

Agee, James
◎ (1909–55) US novelist, poet, film critic and screen writer, he wrote classic film scripts including *The African Queen* (1951). His only novel, the unfinished semi-autobiographical *A Death in the Family* (1957), was awarded a posthumous Pulitzer Prize (1958).
A Death in the Family
Follet, Rufus
Lynch, Uncle Andrew

Albee, Edward
◎ (born 1928) US dramatist whose plays address the moral ambiguities of US middle-class life. He has been awarded three Pulitzer Prizes.
The American Dream
Mommy
The Death of Bessie Smith
Bessie Smith
A Delicate Balance
Agnes
Claire
The Lady from Dubuque
Lady from Dubuque, the
The Sandbox
Mommy
Three Tall Women
A
B
C
Tiny Alice
Alice
Julian, Brother
Who's Afraid of Virginia Woolf?
George
Honey
Martha
Nick
The Zoo Story
Jerry
Peter

Alcott, Louisa M(ay)
◎ (1832–88) US writer best known for *Little Women* (1868), which drew on her own home experiences, and became a children's classic. *Good Wives* (1869) was a sequel.
Good Wives
Bhaer, Dr
Brooke, John
Daisy
Demi-John
Laurie
March, Amy
March, Beth
March, Jo
March, Meg
Marmee
Jo's Boys
Bhaer, Dr
Blake, Nat
Brooke, John
Daisy
Dan
Demi-John
Laurie
March, Amy
March, Beth
March, Jo
March, Meg
Marmee
Nan
Little Men
Bhaer, Dr
Blake, Nat
Brooke, John
Daisy
Dan
Demi-John
Laurie
March, Amy
March, Beth
March, Jo
March, Meg
Marmee
Nan

Little Women
Brooke, John
Laurie
March, Amy
March, Beth
March, Jo
March, Meg
Marmee

Aldington, Richard, pseudonym of **Edward Godfree**
◎ (1892–1962) English poet, novelist, editor and biographer, his experiences in World War I left him ill and bitter, and also led to his best-known novel *Death of a Hero* (1929).

Death of a Hero
Winterbourne, Elizabeth
Winterbourne, George

Alger, Horatio, Jr
◎ (1832–99) US writer and clergyman, he wrote boys' adventure stories on the 'poor boy makes good' theme.

Ragged Dick, or Street Life in New York
Ragged Dick

Tattered Tom
Tattered Tom

Algren, Nelson
◎ (1909–81) US novelist, he was a leading member of the 'Chicago school of realism', and produced a series of uncompromising novels.

The Man with the Golden Arm
Machine, Frankie, properly Francis Majcinek

Ali, Monica
◎ (born 1967) Bangladeshi-born British writer. She worked in publishing and design before her first novel *Brick Lane* (2003) was published to critical acclaim. It was shortlisted for the Booker Prize.

Brick Lane
Nazneen

Allingham, Margery
◎ (1904–66) English detective-story writer, the creator of the fictional detective Albert Campion. She wrote a series of elegant and witty novels.

The Crime at Black Dudley
Campion, Albert

The Tiger in the Smoke
Avril, Canon Hubert
Havoc, Jack

Amadi, Elechi
◎ (born 1934) Nigerian novelist and playwright, regarded as one of the leading African writers.

The Concubine
Ahurole
Ekwueme
Emenike
Ihuoma

Amis, Kingsley
◎ (1922–95) English novelist and poet. He achieved huge success

with his first novel, *Lucky Jim* (1954), and went on to write a substantial body of novels, poetry and non-fiction. His son is the writer **Martin Amis**.

Jake's Thing
Richardson, Jake

Lucky Jim
Dixon, Jim

The Old Devils
Weaver, Alun

Stanley and the Women
Duke, Stanley

Amis, Martin
◎ (born 1949) English novelist and journalist. He worked for the *Times Literary Supplement* and *New Statesman*, but has been a full-time writer since 1979. He is the son of the writer **Kingsley Amis**.

The Information
Barry, Gwyn
Tull, Richard

London Fields
Talent, Keith

Money
Self, John

The Rachel Papers
Highway, Charles

Anand, Mulk Raj
◎ (1905–2004) Indian novelist and critic. His humanist novels, such as *The Coolie* (1936) and *The Village* (1939), depict life in the poverty-stricken Punjab. He later began an ambitious seven-volume autobiographical work of fiction, *The Seven Ages of Man*, which began with *Seven Summers: The Story of an Indian Childhood* (1951).

Across the Black Waters
Lal Singh

The Big Heart
Ananta

The Coolie
Munoo

The Old Woman and the Cow
Gauri

Seven Summers: The Story of an Indian Childhood
Azad, Krishan Chander

The Sword and the Sickle
Lal Singh

Untouchable
Bakha

The Village
Lal Singh

Anderson, Jessica
◎ (born 1925) Australian novelist, short-story writer and playwright. Her novels *Tirra Lirra by the River* (1978) and *The Impersonators* (1980) were both winners of the Miles Franklin Award.

The Impersonators
Foley, Sylvia

Tirra Lirra by the River
Porteous, Nora Roche

Anderson, Maxwell
◎ (1888–1959) US historical dramatist known for his commercially successful plays and screenplays.

Key Largo
McCloud, King

Winterset
Esdras
Garth
Judge, the
Mio
Trock

Anderson, Sherwood
◎ (1876–1941) US fiction writer, his best-known work is *Winesburg, Ohio* (1919), a collection of interrelated short stories which portray the 'secret lives' of marginal characters and the sensibilities of the young artist who observes them.

Dark Laughter
Stockton, John, also known as Bruce Dudley

Poor White
McVey, Hugh

Windy McPherson's Son
McPherson, Sam

Winesburg, Ohio
Bentley, Jesse
Biddlebaum, Wing
Cowley, Elmer
Hartman, Rev Curtis
Reefy, Dr
Swift, Kate
Willard, Elizabeth
Willard, George

anon, Old English
Beowulf
Beowulf
Grendel

Arden, John
◎ (born 1930) English playwright and novelist who trained as an architect. He has continually experimented with dramatic form and technique, both in the plays he has written alone and in the many pieces in which he has collaborated with his wife, Margaretta D'Arcy (born 1934).

Armstrong's Last Goodnight
Armstrong, Johnnie

Sergeant Musgrave's Dance
Musgrave, Sergeant

The Workhouse Donkey
Butterthwaite, Charlie

Armah, Ayi Kwei
◎ (born 1939) Ghanaian novelist concerned with corruption and the lack of unity in contemporary Africa.

The Beautyful Ones Are Not Yet Born
Koomson, Joseph
Man, the

Fragments
Baako Onipa
Naana

Why Are We So Blest?
Dofu, Modin

Arnold, Matthew

◎ (1822–88) English poet and critic who attracted attention for his application of the methods of literary criticism to scripture. His poems are mainly elegiac in mood and on pastoral themes.

'The Forsaken Merman'
Forsaken Merman, the

'The Scholar Gypsy'
Glanvil

'Sohrab and Rustum'
Rustum
Sohrab

Ashford, Daisy (Mrs George Norman)

◎ (1881–1972) English juvenile novelist who wrote her only book, the small comic masterpiece *The Young Visiters*, when she was nine. A bestseller, it has been adapted for stage and as a musical.

The Young Visiters
Monticue, Ethel
Salteena, Mr

Atwood, Margaret

◎ (born 1939) Canadian novelist, poet and critic. She won the 2000 Booker Prize with *The Blind Assassin*, and her novels, some of which have a science-fiction theme and some of which are about women's issues, have been shortlisted on four other occasions.

Alias Grace
Marks, Grace

The Blind Assassin
Griffen, Iris Chase

Bodily Harm
Wilford, Rennie

Cat's Eye
Risley, Elaine

The Edible Woman
MacAlpin, Marian

The Handmaid's Tale
Offred

Lady Oracle
Foster, Joan Delacourt

Life Before Man
Green, Lesje
Schoenhof, Elizabeth
Schoenhof, Nate

Oryx and Crake
Crake
Oryx
Snowman

Surfacing
anon (the narrator)

Auchincloss, Louis

◎ (born 1917) US novelist, short-story writer and critic, who studied law. His works chronicle the life of New York City and its inhabitants, particularly the aristocracy.

The Embezzler
Prime, Guy

Pursuit of the Prodigal
Parmalee, Rees

Auden, W(ystan) H(ugh)

◎ (1907–73) US poet and essayist, born in England. His early work reflects his concern with the social problems of the 1930s and his left-wing commitment. His conversion from liberal humanism to Anglo-Catholicism informs his later works.

The Age of Anxiety
Emble
Malin
Quant
Rosetta

'Journal of an Airman'
Airman, the

'Miss Gee: A Ballad'
Gee, Miss Edith

The Orators: an English Study
Bewethameer
Henry, Uncle
Leader, the

'Songs and Other Musical Pieces'
Gee, Miss Edith
Victor

Auden, W H (*see above*) and Isherwood, Christopher (*see* Isherwood, Christopher)

The Ascent of F6
Ransom, Michael Forsyth

The Dog Beneath the Skin
Crewe, Sir Francis, Bart ('the Dog')
Norman, Alan

Austen, Jane

◎ (1775–1817) English novelist, particularly remembered for her closely observed and often ironic depictions of the morals and mores of country life. Her first four novels were published anonymously; *Persuasion* and *Northanger Abbey* were both published posthumously (1818).

Emma
Bates, Miss
Churchill, Frank
Elton, Mr
Elton, Mrs
Fairfax, Jane
Knightley, Mr
Martin, Robert
Smith, Harriet
Taylor, Anne
Weston, Mr
Woodhouse, Emma
Woodhouse, Mr

Mansfield Park
Bertram, Edmund
Bertram, Julia
Bertram, Lady
Bertram, Maria
Bertram, Sir Thomas
Bertram, Tom
Crawford, Henry
Crawford, Mary
Norris, Mrs
Price, Fanny
Price, Mrs
Rushworth, Mr
Yates, Mr

Northanger Abbey
Morland, Catherine
Morland, James
Thorpe, Isabella

Thorpe, John
Tilney, Captain
Tilney, Eleanor
Tilney, Gen
Tilney, Henry

Persuasion
Clay, Mrs
Croft, Admiral
Croft, Mrs
Elliot, Anne
Elliot, Elizabeth
Elliot, Mary
Elliot, Sir Walter
Elliot, William
Musgrove, Charles
Musgrove, Henrietta
Musgrove, Louisa
Russell, Lady
Smith, Mrs
Wentworth, Captain (Frederick)

Pride and Prejudice
Bennet, Elizabeth
Bennet, Jane
Bennet, Lydia
Bennet, Mr
Bennet, Mrs
Bingley, Charles
Collins, Rev William
Darcy, Mr Fitzwilliam
de Bourgh, Lady Catherine
Lucas, Charlotte
Wickham, George

Sense and Sensibility
Brandon, Col
Dashwood, Elinor
Dashwood, Fanny
Dashwood, John
Dashwood, Marianne
Dashwood, Mrs Henry
Ferrars, Edward
Ferrars, Mrs
Ferrars, Robert
Jennings, Mrs
Steele, Lucy
Willoughby, John

Auster, Paul

◎ (born 1947) US novelist, poet and essayist. His novels have been critically acclaimed, and are often bleak and written with a meticulous but sparse style.

The Book of Illusions
Mann, Hector

Moon Palace
Fogg, Marco Stanley

Mr Vertigo
Rawley, Walter
Yehudi, Master

The Music of Chance
Flowers and Stone
Nashe, James
Pozzi, Jack ('Jackpot')

Timbuktu
Bones, Mr
Christmas, Willy G

Ayckbourn, Alan

◎ (born 1939) English playwright and director. A master of farce, his plays often shrewdly observe the English class structure, and he also excels in sheer mechanical ingenuity, making considerable experiments with staging and dramatic structure.

Index

Absurd Person Singular
Brewster-Wright, Ronald and Marion
Hopcroft, Sidney and Jane
Jackson, Geoffrey and Eva
Henceforward ...
Watkins, Jerome
Just Between Ourselves
Andrews, Neil and Pam
Crowthorne, Dennis and Vera
Man of the Moment
Beechey, Douglas
Parks, Vic
The Norman Conquests
Norman
A Small Family Business
McCracken, Jack
Woman in Mind
Gannet, Susan

Bage, Robert

◎ (1728–1801) English papermaker and novelist. A member of the Derby Philosophical Society, a group of political radicals, the mixture of humour and polemic he combined in his novels made them an immediate success.

Hermsprong
Hermsprong

Bagnold, Enid

◎ (1889–1981) English novelist, playwright and children's writer.

National Velvet
Brown, Velvet

Bailey, Paul

◎ (born 1937) English actor turned novelist. *Gabriel's Lament* (1986) was shortlisted for the Booker Prize.

Gabriel's Lament
Harvey, Gabriel
Harvey, Oswald

Bainbridge, Beryl

◎ (born 1934) English novelist and playwright, who worked as an actress and publisher's clerk before turning to writing full-time. Her work is marked by a caustic wit and a finely turned prose style.

According to Queeney
Johnson, Samuel
Thrale, Queeney (Hester)
The Bottle Factory Outing
Brenda
Freda
The Dressmaker
Margo
Nellie
Rita
Master Georgie
Hardy, George

Baldwin, James

◎ (1924–87) US writer and civil rights activist. His novels are often strongly autobiographical but marked by a Flaubertian attention to form. His journalism has been extremely influential and controversial.

The Amen Corner
Margaret, Sister
Another Country
Ellis, Steve
Jones, Eric
Leona
Moore, Vivaldo
Scott, Ida
Scott, Rufus
Silenski, Cass
Silenski, Richard
Giovanni's Room
David
Giovanni
Hella
Go Tell It On The Mountain
Grimes, John
'Sonny's Blues'
Sonny

Ballantyne, R(obert) M(ichael)

◎ (1825–94) Scottish children's writer. He began his career working for the Hudson's Bay Company and subsequently became the successful writer of numerous adventure stories 'for boys'.

The Coral Island
Martin, Jack
Peterkin
Rover, Ralph

Ballard, J(ames) G(raham)

◎ (born 1930) British novelist and short-story writer, born in China and initially known for his science fiction. His novel the *Empire of the Sun* (1985), which draws on his childhood experiences in wartime Shanghai, was shortlisted for the Booker Prize.

Empire of the Sun
Shanghai Jim

Banks, Iain

◎ (born 1954) Scottish novelist and science-fiction writer. He made a major impact with his controversial first novel, *The Wasp Factory* (1984), a study of insanity which shifted between psychological acuity and grotesque fantasy. He writes science-fiction novels using the name Iain M Banks.

The Bridge
Orr, John/Lennox, Sandy (Alexander)
Complicity
Colley, Cameron
The Crow Road
McHoan, Kenneth
McHoan, Prentice
The Wasp Factory
Cauldhame, Frank

Banks, Lynne Reid

◎ (born 1929) English novelist and playwright, she worked as an actress, journalist and teacher before turning to writing full-time. In addition to many novels, she has also published plays, biographical fiction and children's books.

The L-Shaped Room
Graham, Jane

Baraka, Amiri

◎ (born 1934) US poet, playwright and prose writer. He removed himself from his bourgeois roots into black nationalism and later Marxism-Leninism. A prolific poet and dramatist with over 50 titles to his name, he is best known for work dating from the early 1960s.

Dutchman
Lula
Williams, Clay Clay
The Slave
Easley, Grace
Vessels, Walker

Barfoot, Joan

◎ (born 1946) Canadian novelist. Her general theme, explored in a variety of settings, is that of a woman's search for self-identity in a society which seems to offer no palatable role.

Dancing in the Dark
Cormick, Edna

Barham, R(ichard) H(arris)

◎ (1788–1845) English humorist and clergyman. After unsuccessful attempts at novel writing, he began a series of burlesque metrical tales. Written under the pen name 'Thomas Ingoldsby' and collected under the title *The Ingoldsby Legends* (1840), they were immediately popular.

The Ingoldsby Legends
Jackdaw of Rheims, the

Barker, Pat

◎ (born 1943) English author. Her works include the highly-acclaimed *Regeneration Trilogy* of World War I novels – *Regeneration* (1991), *The Eye in the Door* (1993) and *The Ghost Road* (1995), the last of which won the Booker Prize.

The Eye in the Door
Prior, Billy
Rivers, Dr William
The Ghost Road
Prior, Billy
Rivers, Dr William
Regeneration
Prior, Billy
Rivers, Dr William
Sassoon, Siegfried

Barnes, Djuna

◎ (1892–1982) US poet, novelist and illustrator. She began her career as a reporter or illustrator, then became a writer of one-act plays and short stories. Her literary style has been acclaimed by many critics.

The Antiphon
Burley, Augusta

Nightwood
Flood, Nora
O'Connor, Dr Matthew-Mighty-grain-of-salt-dante
Volkbein, Baron Felix
Vote, Robin

Barnes, Julian
◎ (born 1946) English novelist and short-story writer, formerly a journalist and lexicographer. He has also written as **Dan Kavanagh**.

England, England
Pitman, Sir Jack

Flaubert's Parrot
Braithwaite, Geoffrey

Love, etc
Hughes, Stuart
Russell, Oliver
Wyatt, Gillian

Talking it Over
Hughes, Stuart
Russell, Oliver
Wyatt, Gillian

'Baron Corvo', real name **Frederick William Rolfe**
◎ (1860–1913) English novelist and essayist. A convert to Roman Catholicism, he felt his life was shattered by his rejection from the novitiate for the Roman priesthood, but it prompted his most famous work, *Hadrian VII* (1904), in which a 'spoiled priest' is unexpectedly chosen for the papacy.

Hadrian VII
Rose, George Arthur, subsequently Pope Hadrian VII

Barrie, J M
◎ (1860–1937) Scottish novelist and dramatist. After journalism and several autobiographical works, he turned to playwriting in 1890.

The Admirable Crichton
Crichton

Mary Rose
Mary Rose (Mary Rose Blake, née Morland)

Peter Pan: or The Boy Who Would Not Grow Up
Hook, Captain
John (John Darling)
Michael (Michael Darling)
Nana
Peter Pan
Slightly
Smee
Tinkerbell
Wendy (Wendy Moira Angela Darling)

Barstow, Stan
◎ (born 1928) English novelist, short-story writer and playwright. The mining communities of his youth provided much material for his fiction, which is firmly based in

the entanglements and difficulties of everyday experience.

Joby
Weston, Joby (Joseph)

A Kind of Loving
Brown, Vic (Victor)
Rothwell, Ingrid
Rothwell, Mrs

Barth, John
◎ (born 1930) US novelist. His books are much concerned with the processes of storytelling and the making of myths, explored in a mix of realism, fantasy and formidable learning.

The Floating Opera
Andrews, Todd

Giles Goat-Boy
Goat-Boy, (George) Giles

The Sot-Weed Factor
Cooke, Ebenezer

Barthelme, Donald
◎ (1931–89) US novelist and short-story writer. An experimentalist who rejected the traditions of the conventional novel form and was inventive in his use of language, he was associated with the mid-1960s avant-garde.

Snow White
Snow White

Bates, H(erbert) E(rnest)
◎ (1905–74) English novelist, playwright and short-story writer. One of the greatest exponents of the short-story form, his essay in literary criticism, *The Modern Short Story* (1942), is regarded as a classic.

The Darling Buds of May
Larkins, the

Baum, L(yman) Frank
◎ (1859–1919) US writer. He worked as a magazine editor until the publication and tremendous success of his second children's book, *The Wonderful Wizard of Oz* (1900), which was staged as a musical in 1901 and later filmed (1939).

The Wonderful Wizard of Oz
Cowardly Lion, also known as Zeke
Dorothy
Munchkins
Oz, the Great
Scarecrow, also known as Hunk
Tin Woodman, also known as Hickory
Wicked Witch of the West

Baynton, Barbara
◎ (1857–1929) Australian writer and socialite. Her writing describes the grime and squalor of the real bush, as endured by women and the underprivileged.

'Billie Skywonkie'
Skywonkie, Billie

Beattie, Ann
◎ (born 1947) US writer. She has written several novels and

collections of short stories, many of which focus on disaffected families or individuals.

Chilly Scenes of Winter
Charles

Falling in Place
Knapp, John

Love Always
Nicole
Spenser, Lucy

Beaumont, Francis
◎ (c.1584–1616) English Elizabethan dramatist. A friend of **Ben Jonson** and his circle, he is particularly known for his collaboration with **John Fletcher**.

The Knight of the Burning Pestle
Jasper
Luce
Rafe

Beaumont, Francis (*see above*) and **Fletcher, John** (*see* **Fletcher, John**)

Bonduca
Bonduca
Caratach

A King and No King
Arbaces
Panthea

The Maid's Tragedy
Amintor
Aspatia

Philaster, or Love Lies Bleeding
Arethusa
Bellario
Philaster

The Woman Hater
Gondarino
Millaine, Duke of
Oriana

Beckett, Samuel
◎ (1906–89) Irish author and playwright who lived mostly in France. His best-known play, *Waiting for Godot* (1955), exemplifies his absurdist view of the human condition. He was awarded the Nobel prize for literature in 1969.

Come and Go
Flo, Vi and Ru

Eh Joe
Joe and Woman

Endgame
Clov
Hamm

Happy Days
Winnie

Krapp's Last Tape
Krapp

Malone Dies
Malone

Molloy
Molloy

Murphy
Murphy

Not I
Mouth

The Unnamable
anon (the narrator)

Waiting for Godot
Estragon

Index

Lucky
Pozzo
Vladimir
Watt
Watt

Beckford, William

◎ (1759–1844) English writer and
art collector whose *Vathek* (1786) is
an Arabian tale of gloomy
imaginative splendour modelled
on Voltaire's style.

Vathek: An Arabian Tale
Vathek, Caliph

Bedford, Sybille

◎ (born 1911) German-born British
novelist, biographer, journalist
and travel writer. Several of her
novels take up the themes of
political and emotional family
inheritance.

A Compass Error
Devaux, Andrée
Herbert, Constanza
Herbert, Flavia

A Favourite of the Gods
Herbert, Constanza
Herbert, Flavia

A Legacy
Felden, Baron Julius Maria von
Felden, Francesca von
Trafford, Caroline

Beerbohm, Max

◎ (1872–1956) English writer,
caricaturist and theatre critic. He
succeeded **George Bernard Shaw**
as drama critic of *The Saturday
Review*. His best-known work was
his only novel, *Zuleika Dobson*
(1911), an ironic romance of
Oxford undergraduate life.

Zuleika Dobson
Dobson, Zuleika

Behan, Brendan

◎ (1923–64) Irish playwright,
twice imprisoned for IRA
activities. His first play, *The Quare
Fellow* (1954), starkly dramatized
the prison atmosphere prior to a
hanging. Elsewhere, his exuberant
wit, spiced with balladry and
bawdry and a talent for fantastic
caricature, can be found.

The Hostage
Williams, Leslie

The Quare Fellow
Dunlavin
Quare Fellow, the

Behn, Aphra

◎ (1640–89) English writer. She
had an adventurous life, growing
up in Surinam and later acting as a
professional spy in Antwerp. She
was perhaps the first professional
woman author in Britain.

The Rover
Willmore

Behn, Aphra (*see above*) (adapted
for the stage by Thomas Southerne)

*Oroonoko, or the History of the Royal
Slave*
Imoinda
Oroonoko

Bellamy, Edward

◎ (1850–98) US novelist. *Looking
Backward, 2000–1887* (1888) was
an immensely popular Utopian
romance that predicted a new social
order and influenced economic
thinking in the USA and Europe.

Looking Backward, 2000–1887
Leete, Dr
Leete, Edith
West, Julian

Bellow, Saul

◎ (1915–2005) Canadian-born US
writer. His best novels examine
Jewish-American identity and the
dilemma of liberal humanist values
in a fast-changing world. He won
the Nobel prize for literature in
1976.

The Actual
Adletsky, Sigmund
Trellman, Harry
Wustrin, Amy

The Adventures of Augie March
March, Augie

Dangling Man
Joseph

The Dean's December
Corde, Albert

Henderson the Rain King
Henderson, Eugene

Herzog
Herzog, Moses Elkanah

Humboldt's Gift
Citrine, Charlie
Fleisher, Von Humboldt

Mr Sammler's Planet
Gruner, Elya
Sammler, Arthur

Seize the Day
Wilhelm, Tommy

Ravelstein
Ravelstein, Abe

The Victim
Allbee, Kirby
Leventhal, Asa

Benét, Stephen Vincent

◎ (1898–1943) US poet and
novelist. His work was often
inspired by American history and
folklore, and he is best known for
his long poems, novels and short
stories such as 'The Devil and
Daniel Webster'.

'The Devil and Daniel Webster'
Scratch, Mr
Stone, Jabez
Webster, Daniel

Bennett, Alan

◎ (born 1934) English writer. He
came to prominence as an actor and
writer in *Beyond the Fringe* (1960),
and went on to write wry, mordant
plays and monologues for stage and
screen.

An Englishman Abroad
Browne, Coral

Burgess, Guy

A Question of Attribution
Blunt, Anthony
Chubb

Forty Years On
Headmaster, the

Getting On
Oliver, George

The Madness of George III
George III

The Old Country
Hilary

Bennett, Arnold

◎ (1867–1931) English novelist,
journalist and critic. His best-
known books are those set in the
pottery-making heartland of the
Five Towns in the Midlands.

Anna of the Five Towns
Tellwright, Anna

The Card
Machin, Denry (Edward Henry)

Clayhanger
Clayhanger, Darius
Clayhanger, Edwin
Lessways, Hilda

Hilda Lessways
Clayhanger, Darius
Clayhanger, Edwin
Lessways, Hilda

A Man from the North
Larch, Richard

Mr Prohack
Prohack, Arthur Charles

The Old Wives' Tale
Baines, Constance
Baines, Sophia
Povey, Samuel
Scales, Gerald

Riceyman Steps
Earlforward, Henry
Earlforward, Violet
Name, Elsie

The Roll Call
Cannon, George Edwin

These Twain
Clayhanger, Edwin
Lessways, Hilda

Benson, E(dward) F(rederic)

◎ (1867–1940) English novelist. He
was a prolific and popular writer,
as were his brothers A C Benson
(1862–1925) and R H Benson
(1871–1914). His works include a
number of volumes of
reminiscences.

Mapp and Lucia
Mapp, Elizabeth, subsequently Mrs
  Benjamin Mapp-Flint

Queen Lucia
Lucia, more properly Miss Emmeline
  Lucas

Beresford-Howe, Constance

◎ (born 1922) Canadian novelist
and short-story writer. Her novels
generally deal with contemporary
women, and are compassionate,
witty and gently effective.

The Book of Eve
Carroll, Eva

Berger, John

◎ (born 1926) English novelist, playwright and art critic. His writing has been strongly influenced by Marxism, and when *G.* (1972) was awarded the Booker Prize, Berger denounced the sponsors during his acceptance speech.

G.
G

Berryman, John

◎ (1914–72) US poet, biographer, novelist and academic. Best known for his poetry, including *Homage to Mistress Bradstreet* (1956), which established his reputation, while his major work is *The Dream Songs*, begun in 1955.

The Dream Songs
Henry

Homage to Mistress Bradstreet
Bradstreet, Anne

Bierce, Ambrose

◎ (1842–c.1914) US short-story writer and journalist. His most celebrated story is 'An Occurrence at Owl Creek Bridge'. He also compiled the much-quoted *Cynic's Word Book* (1906), now better known as *The Devil's Dictionary*.

'A Horseman in the Sky'
Druse, Private Carter

'An Occurrence at Owl Creek Bridge'
Farquhar, Peyton

'One of the Missing'
Searing, Lt Adrian
Searing, Private Jerome

Biggers, Earl Derr

◎ (1884–1933) US novelist and short-story writer of detective fiction.

The House Without a Key
Chan, Charlie

Birney, Earle

◎ (1904–95) Canadian poet, novelist and academic. He was a professor at the universities of Toronto and, after World War II, British Colombia.

Down the Long Table
Saunders, Professor Gordon

Turvey: a Military Picaresque
Turvey

Blackmore, R(ichard) D(oddridge)

◎ (1825–1900) English novelist. He wrote 15 novels, mostly with a Devonshire background, of which *Lorna Doone* (1869) is his masterpiece and an accepted classic of the West Country.

Lorna Doone
Doone, Carver
Doone, Lorna
Faggus, Tom
Ridd, John

Blake, William

◎ (1757–1827) English poet, painter, engraver and mystic. He produced many 'illuminated books', in which the text is interwoven with his imaginative designs. These were printed from engraved copper plates and then either hand-coloured or printed in colour by himself or his wife, Catherine Boucher.

America
Orc
Urizen

The Book of the Thel
Thel

Europe, A Prophecy
Enitharmon

The First Book of Urizen
Orc
Urizen

Tiriel
Tiriel

Bleasdale, Alan

◎ (born 1946) English dramatist. *The Blackstuff* (1980), and *The Boys From the Blackstuff* (televised 1982; published 1984), about a group of unemployed Liverpudlians, were an enormous success, and established his reputation for hard-hitting social dramas.

The Boys from the Blackstuff
Dean, Dixie
Hughes, Yosser
Malone, George
Todd, Chrissie

Blyton, Enid

◎ (1897–1968) English children's writer. She published over 600 books, and is one of the most translated British authors. Although her work has been criticized for racism, sexism and snobbishness, many of her stories remain classics.

Amelia Jane Again!
Amelia Jane

Five on a Treasure Island
Famous Five, the

Little Noddy goes to Toyland
Big Ears
Noddy

The Secret Seven
Secret Seven, the

Boldrewood, Rolf

◎ (1826–1915) Australian novelist. After a series of misadventures and some years as an inspector of goldfields, he started writing serials for Australian periodicals to pay his debts.

Robbery Under Arms
Marston, Ben
Marston, Dick
Marston, Jim
Moran
Morrison, Jeanie
Morrison, Kate
Starlight, Captain
Storefield, George
Storefield, Gracey (Grace)
Warrigal

Bolt, Robert

◎ (1924–95) English playwright and screenwriter. His screenplays include *Lawrence of Arabia* (1962) and *Dr Zhivago* (1965).

A Man for All Seasons
More, Sir Thomas

Bond, Edward

◎ (born 1934) English dramatist and director. His work uses a variety of metaphors for the corruption of the capitalist society. He has also written for television and radio.

Bingo
Shakespeare

The Bundle
Basho
Ferryman, the
Landlord, the
Tiger
Wang

Early Morning
Arthur
George

The Fool
Clare, John
Darkie
Milton, Lord

Lear
Bodice and Fontanelle
Cordelia
Lear

Narrow Road to the Deep North
Basho
Georgina
Kiro
Shogo

The Pope's Wedding
Alen
Pat
Scopey

Restoration
Are, Lord
Hedges, Bob

Saved
Fred
Len
Pam

The Sea
Evens
Hatch
Jones, Rose
Rafi, Mrs
Willy

The Stone
Young Man, the

The Woman
Dark Man, the
Hecuba
Heros

Bontemps, Arna

◎ (1902–73) US writer. He was a leading figure in the Harlem Renaissance of the 1920s and 1930s. He published poetry, novels, non-fiction and anthologies of African-American verse and folklore.

Black Thunder
Prosser, Gabriel

Bowen, Elizabeth

◎ (1899–1973) Irish novelist, short-story writer and critic. She composed a number of delicately-written explorations of personal relationships, of which *The Death of the Heart* (1938) and *The Heat of the Day* (1949) are the best known.

The Death of the Heart
Eddie
Quayne, Anna
Quayne, Portia
Quayne, Thomas

Eva Trout
Trout, Eva

The Heat of the Day
Harrison (Robert)
Kelway, Robert
Lewis, Louie
Rodney, Stella

The House in Paris
Fisher, Miss Naomi
Forrestier, Ray
Henrietta
Karen (Karen Forrestier, née Michaelis)
Leopold (Leopold Grant Moody)
Max (Max Ebhart)
Michaelis, Mrs

The Last September
Farquar, Lois
Lesworth, Gerald

To the North
Summers, Emmeline

Bowles, Jane

◎ (1918–73) US fiction writer and playwright. Ill health led to a slim literary output, but she was an original writer, and has been linked with **Gertrude Stein** whose influence is apparent. She was married to **Paul Bowles**.

Two Serious Ladies
Copperfield, Frieda
Goering, Christina

Bowles, Paul

◎ (1910–99) US novelist, composer, poet, travel writer and translator. Initially a composer and music critic, he lived in Tangier from 1952, and much of his work is set there. He was married to **Jane Bowles**.

Let It Come Down
Dyar, Nelson

The Sheltering Sky
Moresby, Kit
Moresby, Porter
Tunner

The Spider's House
Amar

Boyd, Martin

◎ (1893–1972) Australian novelist and poet.

The Cardboard Crown
Cousin Sarah
Langton, Alice
Langton, Baba, originally Barbara Stanger
Langton, Dominic
Langton, Guy
Langton, Mildred
Langton, Steven and Laura
Langton family, the
von Flugel, Diana, née Langton

von Flugel, Wolfie

A Difficult Young Man
Cousin Sarah
Langton, Alice
Langton, Austin
Langton, Baba, originally Barbara Stanger
Langton, Dominic
Langton, Guy
Langton, Mildred
Langton, Steven and Laura
Langton family, the
von Flugel, Diana, née Langton
von Flugel, Wolfie

Lucinda Brayford
Brayford, Hugo
Brayford, Lucinda, née Vane
Brayford, Paul, later 13th Viscount Crittenden
Brayford, Stephen
Crittenden, Lord and Lady

The Montforts
Blair, Jackie
Blair, Raoul

Outbreak of Love
Cousin Sarah
Langton, Alice
Langton, Baba, originally Barbara Stanger
Langton, Dominic
Langton, Guy
Langton, Mildred
Langton, Steven and Laura
Langton family, the
von Flugel, Diana, née Langton
von Flugel, Wolfie

When Blackbirds Sing
Cousin Sarah
Langton, Alice
Langton, Austin
Langton, Baba, originally Barbara Stanger
Langton, Dominic
Langton, Guy
Langton, Mildred
Langton, Steven and Laura
Lagton family, the
von Flugel, Diana née Langton
von Flugel, Wolfie

Boyd, William

◎ (born 1952) British author, born in Ghana. His first novel, *A Good Man in Africa* (1981), won the Whitbread Prize. In addition to novels he has written screenplays and adaptations.

Any Human Heart
Mountstuart, Logan Gonzago

Armadillo
Black, Lorimer

Brazzaville Beach
Clearwater, Hope

A Good Man in Africa
Leafy, Morgan

The New Confessions
Todd, John James

Stars and Bars
Dores, Henderson

Boyle, Kay

◎ (1902–92) US novelist, short-story writer, poet and essayist. She lived in Europe for 30 years as part of the literary fraternity of Paris's Left Bank.

Plagued by the Nightingale
Bridget
Charlotte
Nicolas

Brackenridge, H(ugh) H(enry)

◎ (1748–1816) Scottish-born US novelist, poet and lawyer. His main literary achievement, *Modern Chivalry*, loosely based on *Don Quixote*, was originally published in four volumes between 1792 and 1815.

Modern Chivalry
Farrago, Captain John
O'Regan, Teague

Bradbury, Malcolm

◎ (1932–2000) English novelist and critic. He was the author of numerous critical works embracing Modernist and post-Modernist ideas, as well as novels (many of them inspired by academia), short stories and television plays.

Dr Criminale
Jay, Francis

Eating People is Wrong
Treece, Professor Stuart

The History Man
Kirk, Dr Howard

Rates of Exchange
Petworth, Dr Angus

Bradbury, Ray

◎ (born 1920) US science-fiction writer, one of the earliest writers in the genre to be recognized for his literary merits.

Fahrenheit 451
Montag

Braddon, Mary Elizabeth

◎ (1835–1915) English novelist who attained fame with the sensational Victorian thriller, *Lady Audley's Secret* (1862), the story of a golden-haired bigamist.

Lady Audley's Secret
Audley, Lady

Bragg, Melvyn

◎ (born 1939) English novelist and television arts presenter. He has written a number of novels in the realist tradition, often based in his native Cumbria, and has been an effective collaborator on film and television projects, as well as being well known as a presenter and broadcaster.

The Hired Man
Tallentire, Emily
Tallentire, John

Josh Lawton
Lawton, Josh

The Maid of Buttermere
Robinson, Mary

Braine, John

◎ (1922–86) English novelist. His first successful novel, *Room at the Top* (1957), and his themes of aggressive ambition and determination to break through rigid social barriers identified him with the 'angry young men' of the 1950s.

Life at the Top
Lampton, Joe

Room at the Top
Lampton, Joe

Brathwaite, Edward

◎ (born 1930) West Indian poet and historian who made his reputation with three long poems, reprinted together in 1973 as *The Arrivants: A New World Trilogy*, each of which analyses a different aspect of West Indian blacks' dispossession and search for identity.

The Arrivants: A New World Trilogy
Brathwaite, Edward Kamau

Brenton, Howard

◎ (born 1942) English dramatist. In addition to numerous plays, he has also written translations of the work of Brecht, Goethe and Büchner.

The Churchill Play
Churchill (Joby Peake)

The Genius
Lehrer, Leo

Magnificence
Alice
Babs
Jed
Mary

The Romans in Britain
Chichester, Captain Thomas
Marban

The Thirteenth Night
Beaty, Jack

Brenton, Howard (*see above*) and
Hare, David (*see* **Hare, David**)

Pravda: A Fleet Street Comedy
Foley, Rebecca
Fruit-Norton, Elliot
Le Roux, Lambert
May, Andrew
Quince, Michael
Sylvester, Eaton

Bridie, James

◎ (1888–1951) Scottish dramatist and doctor. One of the founders of the Citizens' Theatre in Glasgow (1943).

The Anatomist
Knox, Dr Robert

Brighouse, Harold

◎ (1882–1958) English playwright. Although he completed over 70 plays, many of them amiably folksy one-act comedies set in Lancashire, his reputation depends on *Hobson's Choice* (1915) alone.

Hobson's Choice
Hobson, Maggie (Margaret)
Mossop, Willie

Brink, André

◎ (born 1935) South African novelist, playwright, critic and translator. An Afrikaans writer, who also writes in English, his seventh novel *Looking on Darkness* (1974) was banned by the South African authorities until 1982.

A Chain of Voices
Galant
van der Merwe, Nicolaas

A Dry White Season
Du Toit, Ben

An Instant in the Wind
Larsson, Elisabeth
Mantoor, Adam

Looking on Darkness
Malan, Joseph

Rumours of Rain
Mynhardt, Martin

Bromfield, Louis

◎ (1896–1956) US novelist and short-story writer. He published a number of novels on US life.

The Rains Came
Esketh, Lady Edwina
Maharani of Ranchipur
Ransome, Tom
Sefti, Major Rama

Brontë, Anne

◎ (1820–49) English novelist and poet, younger sister of **Emily** and **Charlotte Brontë**. In 1846 the sisters published a volume of poems under three pseudonyms, Currer Bell (Charlotte), Ellis Bell (Emily) and Acton Bell (Anne). Anne's two novels were *Agnes Grey* (1847) and *The Tenant of Wildfell Hall* (1848).

Agnes Grey
Grey, Agnes
Murray, Rosalie
Weston, Rev Mr

The Tenant of Wildfell Hall
Arthur
Graham, Mrs Helen
Huntingdon, Arthur
Lawrence, Frederick
Markham, Gilbert

Brontë, Charlotte

◎ (1816–55) English novelist and poet, elder sister of **Emily** and **Anne Brontë**. Charlotte wrote four complete novels: the last, *The Professor*, was published posthumously in 1857.

Jane Eyre
Brocklehurst, Mr
Burns, Helen
Eyre, Jane
Poole, Grace
Reed, Eliza
Reed, Georgiana
Reed, John
Reed, Mrs
Rivers, Diana
Rivers, Mary
Rivers, St John
Rochester, Adèle
Rochester, Mr
Temple, Miss

The Professor
Crimsworth, William
Henri, Frances
Pelet, Monsieur

Reuter, Zoraide

Shirley
Helstone, Caroline
Keeldar, Shirley
Moore, Louis
Moore, Robert Gerard
Pryor, Mrs

Villette
Beck, Madame
Bretton, Dr John
Emmanuel, Monsieur Paul
Fanshawe, Ginevra
Home, Polly (Pauline)
Snowe, Lucy
Walravens, Madame

Brontë, Emily

◎ (1818–48) English novelist and poet, sister of **Charlotte** and **Anne Brontë**. Her single novel, *Wuthering Heights* (1848), is an intense and powerful tale of love and revenge set in the remote wilds of 18th-century Yorkshire.

Wuthering Heights
Dean, Ellen
Earnshaw, Catherine
Earnshaw, Hareton
Earnshaw, Hindley
Heathcliff
Heathcliff, Linton
Linton, Catherine
Linton, Edgar
Linton, Isabella
Lockwood

Brooke, Frances

◎ (1724–89) English novelist and playwright. In addition to three novels, she wrote and staged plays, edited her own periodical, *The Old Maid*, and worked on a number of translations.

The History of Emily Montague
Fermor, Arabella
Fermor, William
Fitzgerald, Captain
Montague, Emily
Rivers, Col Edward

Brooke-Rose, Christine

◎ (born 1926) Swiss-born British experimental novelist and literary critic. Her fiction draws heavily on the *nouveau roman*, but with a quirkiness that is quintessentially English.

Amalgamemnon
Enketei, Mira, also known as Miss Inkytie, etc

Such
Larry

Xorandor
Jip and Zab
Xorandor

Brookner, Anita

◎ (born 1928) English novelist and art historian. She has written a number of elegant and witty novels, imbued with cosmopolitan melancholy. Her main characters are often women who are self-sufficient in all but love. *Hotel du Lac* (1984) won the Booker Prize.

Hotel du Lac
Hope, Edith

Latecomers
Fibich, Thomas
Hartmann, Thomas

Lewis Percy
Percy, Lewis

Look at Me
Hinton, Frances

Providence
Maule, Kitty

A Start in Life
Weiss, Dr Ruth

Brophy, Brigid

◎ (1929–95) English writer and critic. Her novels deal with such themes as vivisection, lesbianism and transsexuality. In 1972 she began a successful campaign for the establishment of a Public Lending Right.

The Adventures of God in His Search for the Black Girl
God

The Finishing Touch
Braid, Miss Hetty
Mount, Miss Antonia

Hackenfeller's Ape
Darrelhyde, Professor Clement
Percy and Edwina

In Transit
I

King of a Rainy Country
Susan

Palace Without Chairs
Heather
Ulrich, Crown Prince of Evarchia

The Snow Ball
Anna

Brown, Charles Brockden

◎ (1771–1810) US writer, the first professional US novelist. He made use of the English style of Gothic romance, and his works are full of incident and subtle analysis, but are extravagant in style.

Arthur Mervyn
Mervyn, Arthur

Edgar Huntly
Edny, Clithero
Huntly, Edgar

Ormond
Dudley, Constantia
Ormond

Wieland
Carwin, Francis
Pleyel, Catherine
Pleyel, Henry
Wieland, Clara
Wieland, Theodore

Brown, Dr John

◎ (1810–82) Scottish physician and essayist. Humour and pathos are the chief features of his style, as exemplified in *Rab and his Friends* (1859), his essay on the human nature of dogs.

Rab and his Friends
Rab

Brown, George Douglas

◎ (1869–1902) Scottish writer. He made his name, under the pseudonym George Douglas, with *The House with the Green Shutters* (1901), a powerfully realistic novel. He died of pneumonia before he was able to complete two other novels.

The House with the Green Shutters
Gourlay, John
Gourlay, John, junior

Brown, William Wells

◎ (c.1816–1884) US writer. He was born into slavery but gained his freedom and went on to help runaway slaves.

Clotelle, or, the President's Daughter
Clotelle

Browning, Elizabeth Barrett

◎ (1806–61) English poet. In 1845 she met **Robert Browning**, and married him the following year. They settled in Florence where they became the centre of a literary circle.

Aurora Leigh
Leigh, Aurora

Browning, Robert

◎ (1812–89) English poet. His wife was the poet **Elizabeth Barrett Browning**. His poetry is distinguished by its spiritual insight and psychological analysis; and he invented new kinds of narrative structure to take the place of the epic and the pastoral.

'Bishop Blougram's Apology'
Blougram, Bishop

'The Bishop Orders His Tomb in St Praxed's Church'
Bishop, the

'Caliban upon Setebos'
Caliban

'Childe Roland to the Dark Tower Came'
Roland, Childe

'Count Gismond'
Gismond, Count

Dramatis Personae
Ben Ezra, Rabbi
Sludge, Mr, the Medium

Fifine at the Fair
Don Juan

'A Grammarian's Funeral'
Grammarian, the

'Johannes Agricola in Meditation'
Agricola, Johannes

'The Lost Leader'
Lost Leader, the

Men and Women
Del Sarto, Andrea
Lippi, Fra Lippo

'My Last Duchess'
Duke, the

Paracelsus
Paracelsus

'The Pied Piper of Hamelin'
Pied Piper of Hamelin, the

Pippa Passes
Pippa

'Porphyria's Lover'
Porphyria's Lover

The Ring and the Book
Caponsacchi, Guiseppe
Guido Franceschini, Count
Pignatelli, Pope Antonio
Pompilia

Sordello
Sordello

Strafford
Wentworth, Earl of Strafford

'The Unknown Painter'
Pictor Ignotus

Buchan, John

◎ (1875–1940) Scottish writer and statesman. His strength as a writer was for fast-moving adventure stories, such as *Huntingtower* (1922) and *Witch Wood* (1927). He became best known, however, for his spy thrillers featuring Richard Hannay, starting with *The Thirty-Nine Steps* (1915).

Greenmantle
Arbuthnot, Sandy
Blenkiron, John Scantlebury
Pienaar, Peter
von Einem, Hilda

Huntingtower
Crombie, Dougal
Galt, Jaikie
McCunn, Dickson

John Burnet of Barns
Burnet of Barns, John

John Macnab
'John Macnab'
Lamancha, Lord
Palliser-Yeates, John
Roylance, Sir Archibald

Mr Standfast
Ivery, Moxon

Prester John
Crawfurd, David
Luputa, Rev John

Sick Heart River
Leithen, Sir Edward

The Thirty-Nine Steps
Bullivant, Sir Walter
Hannay, Richard, also known as Cornelis Brandt, Cornelius Brand, Richard Hanau
Schwabing, Graf von

The Three Hostages
Medina, Dominick

Witch Wood
Sempill, David

Buck, Pearl S(ydenstricker)

◎ (1892–1973) US novelist. Her earliest novels are coloured by her experiences while living in China as a missionary. Her later works are concerned with contemporary US life. She was awarded the 1938 Nobel prize for literature.

The Good Earth
O'Lan
Wang

Buckeridge, Anthony

◎ (born 1912) English author of schoolboy fiction. He is best known for the character Jennings, who first appeared in *Jennings Goes to School* (1950) and subsequently starred in 23 further adventures.

Jennings Goes to School
Darbishire, (Charles Edwin Jeremy)
Jennings, (John ChristopherTimothy)

Bukowski, Charles

◎ (1920–94) US poet and fiction writer. Born in Germany, and taken to the USA at the age of two, he worked variously as a dishwasher and truck driver while learning to write. He published more than 40 works, including poetry, novels and short stories.

Post Office
Chinaski, Henry

Bunyan, John

◎ (1628–88) English writer and preacher. Initially a tinker, he joined a Christian fellowship and became a preacher. Perhaps his best-known work is *The Pilgrim's Progress* (1678), essentially a vision of life recounted allegorically as the narrative of a journey.

The Holy War
Boanerges

The Life and Death of Mr. Badman
Attentive, Mr
Badman, Mr
Wiseman, Mr

The Pilgrim's Progress
Apollyon
Christian
Christiana
Evangelist
Faithful
Giant Despair, the
Great-heart, Mr
Hopeful
Interpreter
Ready-to-Halt, Mr
Wordly Wiseman, Mr

Burgess, Anthony

◎ (1917–93) English novelist, critic and composer. Among his many novels is his dark and violent vision of the future, *A Clockwork Orange* (1962).

A Clockwork Orange
Droogs, the

Earthly Powers
Toomey, Kenneth

Inside Mr Enderby
Enderby, F X

Burnett, Frances Hodgson

◎ (1849–1924) US novelist. Born in England, she emigrated with her family to Knoxville, Tennessee, in 1865, and there turned to writing to help out the family finances. In her lifetime she was rated one of the USA's foremost writers, and was a friend of **Henry James**.

Little Lord Fauntleroy
Errol, Cedric

The Secret Garden
Craven, Colin
Lennox, Mary

Burnett, W(illiam) R(iley)

◎ (1899–1982) US novelist and screenwriter. The success of his first novel, *Little Caesar* (1929), based around a character similar to Al Capone, led him to Hollywood. Subsequent novels were also made into films.

Little Caesar
Bandello, Rico Cesare, known as Little Caesar

Burney, Fanny

◎ (1752–1840) English novelist and diarist. *Evelina*, her first and best novel, published anonymously in 1778, describes the entry of a country girl into the gaieties of London life. As a portrayer of the domestic scene she was a forerunner of **Jane Austen**, whom she influenced.

Camilla, or A Picture of Youth
Tyrold, Camilla

Cecilia, or Memoirs of an Heiress
Beverley, Cecilia

Evelina
Evelina

Burns, Robert

◎ (1759–96) Scottish poet and songwriter. His poems are acclaimed for their lyrical quality, especially those written in his native Scots, and for his championing of the common man. He also collected and wrote lyrics for many Scottish airs, such as 'Auld Lang Syne' and 'A Red Red Rose'.

'The Cottar's Saturday Night'
Cottar, the

'Holy Willie's Prayer'
Holy Willie

'Tam O'Shanter'
Cutty Sark, or Nannie
Tam O'Shanter

Burroughs, Edgar Rice

◎ (1875–1950) US popular author. When he took to writing, his aim was to improve on the average 'dime' novel. *Tarzan of the Apes* (1914) was his first book to feature the eponymous hero. It spawned many sequels, as well as films, radio programmes and comic strips, making Burroughs a millionaire.

Tarzan of the Apes
Tarzan

Burroughs, William S(eward)

◎ (1914–97) US writer. While in New York in 1944 he became a heroin addict and in 1953 he published *Junkie*, an account of this experience. Novels such as *The Naked Lunch* (1959) established him as a leading figure of the Beat movement, though one who stood somewhat apart.

The Naked Lunch
Lee, Bill

Butler, Samuel

◎ (1612–80) English satirist. He is best known as the author of the poem *Hudibras* (published in three parts: 1663, 1664, 1678). A burlesque satire on Puritanism, it was immediately popular, and was a special favourite of Charles II. However, despite the king's generosity, Butler died in penury.

Hudibras
Hudibras, Sir

Butler, Samuel

◎ (1835–1902) English author, painter and musician. He is best known for his autobiographical novel *The Way of All Flesh*, published posthumously in 1903, a work of moral realism on the causes of strife between different generations which left its mark on **George Bernard Shaw** and much 20th-century literature.

The Way of All Flesh
Ellen
Overton
Pontifex, Alethea
Pontifex, Ernest
Pontifex, George
Pontifex, John
Pontifex, Theobold

Byatt, A(ntonia) S(usan)

◎ (born 1936) English novelist and critic. A highly respected critic, she later made her reputation as a novelist, with works such as *Still Life* (1985) and *Possession* (1990), which won the Booker prize. She is the elder sister of the novelist **Margaret Drabble**.

The Biographer's Tale
Nanson, Phineas

The Game
Corbett, Cassandra
Corbett, Julia
Moffitt, Simon

Possession
Ash, Randolph Henry
Bailey, Maud
LaMotte, Christabel
Michell, Roland

Still Life
Orton, Daniel
Potter, Frederica
Potter, Stephanie
Wedderburn, Alexander

The Virgin in the Garden
Orton, Daniel
Potter, Frederica
Potter, Stephanie
Wedderburn, Alexander

Byrne, John

◎ (born 1940) Scottish dramatist and stage designer. *The Slab Boys* (1978), concerning the lives of employees at a carpet factory, developed into a trilogy with the addition of *Cuttin' A Rug* (1980) and *Still Life* (1982). He has also written successfully for television.

The Slab Boys Trilogy
Farrell, Spanky (George)

Index

McCann, Phil
McKenzie, Hector

Byron, George Gordon, 6th Lord Byron (of Rochdale)
◎ (1788–1824) English poet of Scottish antecedents. His literary output and championing of political liberty is often overshadowed by his dissipated lifestyle and romantic image.
The Bride of Abydos: A Turkish Tale
Selim
Zuleika
Childe Harold's Pilgrimage: A Romaunt
Harold, Childe
The Corsair: A Tale
Conrad
Don Juan
Juan, Don
The Giaour: A Fragment of a Turkish Tale
Giaour, the
Manfred: A Dramatic Poem
Manfred
Marino Faliero: An Historical Tragedy
Faliero, Marino
Steno, Michel
Mazeppa
Mazeppa
The Prisoner of Chillon
Bonnivard, François de
Sardanapalus: A Tragedy
Sardanapalus
The Two Foscari: An Historical Drama
Foscari, Francis, Doge of Venice
Foscari, Jacopo

Cabell, James Branch
◎ (1879–1958) US novelist and critic, best known for his sequence of 18 novels, collectively entitled 'The Biography of the Life of Manuel' and set in the imaginary medieval kingdom of Poictesme.
'The Biography of the Life of Manuel'
Manuel, Dom
The Cream of the Jest
Kennaston, Felix
Jurgen
Jurgen

Cable, George Washington
◎ (1844–1925) US writer. After fighting as a Confederate soldier in the American Civil War, he embarked on a literary career. His finest work is *The Grandissimes* (1880), a profound study of caste and colour in New Orleans at the time of the Louisiana Purchase.
The Grandissimes
Bras-Coupe
de Philosophe, Palmyre
Frowenfeld, Joseph

Fusilier, Agricola
Grandissime, Honoré
Grandissime, Honoré, fmc
Inerarity, Raoul
Nancanou, Aurore, or de Grapion
Nancanou, Clotilde, or de Grapion

Cahan, Abraham
◎ (1860-1951) US novelist. He emigrated to the USA from Russia and his treatment of the experience of Jewish immigrants established him as a leading exponent of Jewish American fiction.
The Rise of David Levinsky
Levinsky, David
Yekl: A Tale of the New York Ghetto
Yekl, known as Jake

Cain, James M(allahan)
◎ (1892–1977) US thriller writer. A journalist and screenwriter, he lived for many years in Hollywood. Some of his novels, such as *The Postman Always Rings Twice* (1934), *Mildred Pierce* (1941) and *Double Indemnity* (1944) have been filmed with great success.
Double Indemnity
Huff, Walter
Nirdlinger, Phyllis
Mildred Pierce
Pierce, Mildred
The Postman Always Rings Twice
Chambers, Frank
Papadakis, Cora (née Smith)
Papadakis, Nick

Caldwell, Erskine
◎ (1903–87) US novelist and short-story writer. His works portray the experience of poor whites and blacks in the deep South. His best-known work is *Tobacco Road* (1932), of which the dramatized version by Jack Kirkland (1933) had a record run in New York.
God's Little Acre
Walden, Ty Ty
Tobacco Road
Lester, Jeeter

Callaghan, Morley
◎ (1903–90) Canadian novelist, short-story writer and memoirist. He originally studied law, but was encouraged to pursue a writing career by **Ernest Hemingway**, whom he met while working as a reporter on the *Toronto Star*.
The Loved and the Lost
McAlpine, Jim
Sanderson, Peggy
The Many Coloured Coat
Lane, Harry
Such is My Beloved
Dowling, Father

Capote, Truman
◎ (1924–84) US novelist, journalist and short-story writer. His best-known work, *Breakfast at Tiffany's* (1958), was highly successful, though cleaned up and sentimentalized, as a film (1961).

Breakfast at Tiffany's
Golightly, Holly

Carey, Peter
◎ (born 1943) Australian novelist who came to prominence with his first book *The Fat Man in History* (1974), a collection of short stories. He won his first Booker Prize in 1988 with *Oscar and Lucinda* (filmed in 1996).
Bliss
Honey Barbara
Joy, Harry
'The Fat Man in History'
Finch, Alexander
Illywhacker
Badgery, Herbert
Oscar and Lucinda
Hopkins, Oscar
Leplastrier, Lucinda
The Tax Inspector
Catchprice, Benny
Catchprice, Granny
McPherson, Cathy
Takis, Maria

Carleton, William
◎ (1794–1869) Irish novelist. Of poor birth, he wrote novels and sketches which were acute portrayals of peasant life.
The Black Prophet
Donnel Dhu, the Black Prophet
Fardorough, the Miser
Fardorough, the Miser

Carlyle, Thomas
◎ (1795–1881) Scottish historian, essayist and critic considered by his contemporaries to be one of the leading thinkers of his day. His first major work on social philosophy, *Sartor Resartus*, was published in instalments in *Fraser's Magazine* (1833–34) and as a book in the USA (1836). He compiled a romantic history of *The French Revolution* (3 vols, 1837) and also wrote a six-volume *History of ... Frederick the Great* (1858–65).
Sartor Resartus
Teufelsdröckh, Professor Diogenes

Carrington, Leonara
◎ (born 1917) British-born Mexican Surrealist painter and writer. In 1940 she suffered a nervous breakdown. She subsequently moved to Mexico which provides much of the inspiration for her highly imaginative painting and books.
The Hearing Trumpet
Leatherby, Marian

Carroll, Lewis, pseudonym of Charles Lutwidge Dodgson
◎ (1832–98) English children's writer and mathematician. His most famous book, *Alice's Adventures in Wonderland* (1865), had its origin in a boat trip which he made with Alice Liddell and her sisters, the daughters of the Dean

of his college, Henry George Liddell.

Alice's Adventures in Wonderland
Alice
Cheshire Cat, the
Dormouse, the
Mad Hatter, the
March Hare, the
Mock Turtle, the
William, Father

The Hunting of the Snark: an Agony, in Eight Fits
Snark

Through the Looking-Glass, and What Alice Found There
Alice
Humpty Dumpty
Jabberwock
Tweedledum and Tweedledee
Walrus and the Carpenter, the

Carter, Angela
◎ (1940–92) English novelist and short-story writer whose fiction is characterized by imaginative use of fantasy, vibrant humour and psychological symbolism. She also wrote poetry, children's stories, and radio plays and, with Neil Jordan, wrote the screenplay for the film from her stories, *The Company of Wolves* (1984).

Heroes and Villains
Jewel, or the Barbarian
Marriane

The Infernal Desire Machines of Doctor Hoffmann
Albertina
Desiderio

The Magic Toyshop
Flowers, Aunt Margaret
Flowers, Uncle Philip
Jonathan
Jowles, Finn
Jowles, Francie
Melanie

Nights at the Circus
Fevvers

Wise Children
Chance, Nora and Dora
Hazard, Sir Melchior

Cary, Joyce
◎ (1888–1957) English novelist. He fought in a Nigerian regiment in World War I and several of his novels, such as *Mister Johnson* (1939), draw on his African experience.

The Horse's Mouth
Jimson, Gulley

Mister Johnson
Johnson, Mister

Cather, Willa
◎ (1873–1947) US fiction writer, poet and journalist. She is perhaps best known for her three novels dealing with immigrants to the USA: *O Pioneers!* (1913), *The Song of the Lark* (1915), and *My Antonia* (1918), which is generally regarded as her best book.

Death Comes for the Archbishop
Latour, Bishop Jean Marie

Vaillant, Father Joseph

A Lost Lady
Forrester, Marian
Herbert, Niel

Lucy Gayheart
Gayheart, Lucy

My Antonia
Burden, Jim
Shimerda, Antonia

My Mortal Enemy
Henshawe, Myra Driscoll

O Pioneers!
Bergson, Alexandra

The Professor's House
Outland, Tom
St Peter, Godfrey

Sapphira and the Slave Girl
Blake, Rachel
Colbert, Henry
Colbert, Sapphira Doddridge
Till, Nancy

Shadows on the Rock
Auclair, Euclide

The Song of the Lark
Kronberg, Thea

Causley, Charles
◎ (1917–2003) English poet and children's writer. His close ties with his home town of Launceston in Cornwall provided him with a unique, rooted point of view on the world. His poetry gradually became more conversational in style, yet his meditations on family memories, life, landscape and legend are far from simplistic.

'Timothy Winters'
Winters, Timothy

Chabon, Michael
◎ (born 1963) US novelist. He won the 2001 Pulitzer Prize for Fiction for *The Amazing Adventures of Kavalier & Clay*, a novel which celebrates the golden age of the comic.

The Amazing Adventures of Kavalier & Clay
Clay, Sam
Kavalier, Joe

Chandler, Raymond
◎ (1888–1959) US detective-story and thriller-writer. Many of his novels such as *The Big Sleep* (1939) were successfully filmed. Chandler did much to establish the conventions of his genre, particularly with his cynical, wise-cracking but honest anti-hero, Philip Marlowe.

The Big Sleep
Marlowe, Philip

Farewell, My Lovely
Malloy, Moose
Valento, Velma

Chapman, George
◎ (c.1559–1634) English dramatist. Although perhaps best known for his translations of Homer, he also wrote many Elizabethan masques and dramas, often in collaboration.

Bussy D'Ambois
D'Ambois, Bussy

The Gentleman Usher
Alphonso
Bassiolo
Lasso, Earl
Margaret
Vincentio, Prince

Monsieur D'Olive
Monsieur D'Olive

The Revenge of Bussy D'Ambois
D'Ambois, Bussy
D'Ambois, Clermont

Charteris, Leslie, pseudonym of **Leslie Charles Bowyer Yin**
◎ (1907–93) US crime-story writer.

The Saint
Templar, Simon

Chatwin, Bruce
◎ (1940–89) English writer and traveller. He originally worked at Sotheby's, but was converted to a life of nomadic asceticism and began writing beguiling books which defy classification, combining fiction, anthropology, philosophy and travel.

On the Black Hill
Jones, Amos
Jones, Benjamin
Jones, Lewis
Jones, Mary

Utz
Utz, Kaspar

Chaucer, Geoffrey
◎ (c.1345–1400) English poet. He had a career as a diplomat and his exposure to French and Italian literature, especially the works of Boccaccio, is evident in his work. His most influential work *The Canterbury Tales* (c.1343–1400) shows a profound understanding of human nature, ranging from the urbane to the bawdy, and is written in a variety of metres, principally the rhyming couplet.

The Canterbury Tales
Bailley, Harry
Cook, the
Doctor of Physic, the
Five Guildsmen, the (the Carpenter, the Dyer, the Haberdasher, the Tapestry Weaver, the Weaver)
Franklin, the
Friar, the, also known as Brother Hubert
Knight, the
Manciple, the
Miller, the
Monk, the
Pardoner, the
Parson, the
Prioress, the, also known as Madame Eglantyne
Reeve, the
Sergeant of the Law, the
Shipman, the
Squire, the
Summoner, the
Wife of Bath, the, also known as Alisoun
Yeoman, the

'The Clerk's Tale'
Griselda

Index

'The Franklin's Tale'
Arveragus
Aurelius
Dorigen
'The Knight's Tale'
Arcite
Emily
Palamon
'The Man of Law's Tale'
Constance
'The Merchant's Tale'
Damien
January
May
'The Nun's Priest's Tale'
Chaunticleer
Pertelote
'The General Prologue'
Clerk of Oxenford, the
Merchant, the
Troilus and Criseyde
Criseyde
Pandarus
Troilus

Cheever, John
◎ (1912–82) US short-story writer and novelist. A contributor to *The New Yorker* for a number of years, he wrote funny, ironic, sad and sophisticated novels and stories, many of them focusing on the isolation and discontent of contemporary US life.
Bullet Park
Hammer, Paul
Nailles, Eliot
Falconer
Farragut, Ezekiel
'The Swimmer'
Merrill, Neddy
The Wapshot Chronicle
Wapshot, Cousin Honora
Wapshot, Coverly
Wapshot, Leander
Wapshot, Moses
The Wapshot Scandal
Wapshot, Cousin Honora
Wapshot, Coverly
Wapshot, Leander
Wapshot, Moses

Chesnutt, Charles W(addell)
◎ (1858–1932) US short-story writer and novelist. He is viewed as a pioneer of Black fiction and his works focus on the problems of racial and class identity in a post-Civil War society.
The Conjure Woman
Julius, Uncle

Chesterton, G(ilbert) K(eith)
◎ (1874–1936) English critic, novelist and poet whose detective priest, Father Brown, brought him widespread popularity. He also wrote literary studies, biographies and poetry.
The Innocence of Father Brown
Brown, Father
The Man Who Was Thursday: A Nightmare
Gregory, Lucien
Sunday

Syme, Gabriel
The Napoleon of Notting Hill
Quin, Auberon
Wayne, Adam

Chevalier, Tracy
◎ (born 1962) US novelist. A graduate of the renowned Creative Writing course of the University of East Anglia, her novels reflect her fascination with art, history and the lives of women.
Girl with a Pearl Earring
Griet
Vermeer, Johannes

Chopin, Kate
◎ (1851–1904) US novelist, short-story writer and poet. Her most famous work, *The Awakening* (1899), a realistic novel of sexual passion, provoked public condemnation. She has since been embraced by feminists as a *fin de siècle* iconoclast.
The Awakening
Pontellier, Edna

Christie, Agatha, also wrote as **Mary Westmacott**
◎ (1890–1976) English writer. She wrote more than 70 classic detective novels, including those featuring the popular sleuths Hercule Poirot, a Belgian detective, and Miss Jane Marple, a village spinster.
Murder at the Vicarage
Marple, Miss Jane
The Murder of Roger Ackroyd
Ackroyd, Roger
The Mysterious Affair at Styles
Hastings, Captain Arthur
Poirot, Hercule

Clarke, Marcus
◎ (1846–81) Australian novelist. His best-known book, serialized as *His Natural Life* (1870–2, filmed as *For the Term of His Natural Life*, 1927) is a vivid portrayal of the penal settlement in Tasmania.
His Natural Life
Devine, Richard, also known as Rufus Dawes
Frere, Lt Maurice, later Captain Gabbett
North, Rev James
Purfoy, Sarah
Rex, John

Cleary, Jon
◎ (born 1917) Australian novelist. He had his first big success with *The Sundowners* (1952, filmed 1960), and followed this with over 40 novels.
The Sundowners
Carmody, Paddy, Ida and Sean
You Can't See Round Corners
McCoy, Frankie

Cleland, John
◎ (1709–89) English novelist whose *Memoirs of a Woman of*

Pleasure (1748–49, better known as *Fanny Hill*) was a bestseller in its time. It achieved a second *succès de scandale* on its revival in the 20th century.
Memoirs of a Woman of Pleasure
Hill, Fanny

Coetzee, J(ohn) M(ichael)
◎ (born 1940) South African novelist. The political situation in his native country provided him with the base from which to launch his allegories and fables, attacking colonialism and demythologizing historical and contemporary myths of imperialism. He has won the Booker Prize twice: in 1983 for *Life and Times of Michael K* and in 1999 for *Disgrace*.
Disgrace
Lurie, David
Lurie, Lucy
Foe
Barton, Susan
Life and Times of Michael K
K, Michael
Waiting for the Barbarians
Magistrate, the

Cohen, Leonard
◎ (born 1934) Canadian poet, novelist and singer. Although better known as a singer-songwriter, he has published important works of poetry and fiction exploring religion and contemporary mythologies.
Beautiful Losers
anon (the narrator)
Edith
F
Tekakwitha, Catherine

Coleridge, Samuel Taylor
◎ (1772–1834) English poet, critic and philosopher. He was an influential literary critic and a close friend of **William Wordsworth**, with whom he collaborated on *Lyrical Ballads* (1798) – a manifesto of English Romanticism.
The Ancient Mariner
Mariner, Ancient
'Christabel'
Christabel
Geraldine
Leoline, Sir

Collins, Wilkie
◎ (1824–89) English novelist. He was a close friend of **Charles Dickens** and wrote the first full-length detective stories in English.
The Moonstone
Ablewhite, Godfrey
Betteredge, Gabriel
Blake, Franklin
Cuff, Sgt Richard
Spearman, Rosanna
Verinder, Rachel
The Woman in White
Catherick, Anne
Catherick, Mrs Jane Anne

Fairlie, Frederick
Fairlie, Laura
Fosco, Count Isidor Ottavio Baldassare
Glyde, Sir Percival
Halcombe, Marian
Hartright, Walter

Congreve, William
◎ (1670–1729) English dramatist and poet. He is famed for his witty Restoration comedies of manners which satirize the sexual morals of his time.
The Double Dealer
Maskwell
Mellefont
Plyant, Sir Paul, Lady and Cynthia
Touchwood, Lady
Love for Love
Angelica
Fetch, Jeremy
Foresight
Foresight, Miss Prue
Frail, Mrs
Legend, Ben
Legend, Sir Sampson
Legend, Valentine
Tattle
The Way of the World
Fainall, Mr and Mrs
Foible
Marwood, Mrs
Millamant
Mirabell
Waitwell
Wishfort, Lady
Witwould, Sir Wilfull

Connell, Evan S(helby)
◎ (born 1924) American novelist, perhaps best known for *Mrs Bridge* (1959) and *Mr Bridge* (1969), a portrayal of a stifling middle-class marriage as seen from both sides (filmed as *Mr and Mrs Bridge* 1990).
Mr Bridge
Bridge, Mr
Bridge, Mrs
Mrs Bridge
Bridge, Mr
Bridge, Mrs

Conrad, Joseph
◎ (1857–1924) Polish-born British novelist. Despite writing in his third language, he is renowned as a literary innovator and Modernist. His short stories and novels focus on man's corruptibility and the ease with which the thin veneer of civilization can be removed.
Almayer's Folly
Lingard, Captain Tom
Heart of Darkness
Kurtz, Mr
Marlow, Charles
Lord Jim
Lord Jim
The Nigger of the Narcissus
Donkin
Singleton
Wait, James
Nostromo
Avellanos, Antonia
Avellanos, Don José
Decoud, Martin

Gould, Charles
Gould, Emilia
Monygham, Dr
Nostromo (Fidanza, Gian' Battista)
Viola, Giorgio
An Outcast of the Islands
Lingard, Captain Tom
The Rescue
Lingard, Captain Tom
The Secret Agent
Ossipon, Alexander
Stevie
Verloc
Verloc, Winnie
The Secret Sharer
anon (the Captain)
Leggatt
Typhoon
McWhirr, Captain
Under Western Eyes
Antonovna, Sophia
Haldin, Natalia
Haldin, Victor
Ivanovitch, Peter
Madame de S——
Mikhulin, Gregory Matvieitch
Nikita (Nector)
Razumov
Tekla
Victory
Heyst, Axel

Coolidge, Susan, pseudonym of **Sarah Chauncy Woolsey**
◎ (1835–1905) US children's writer and literary critic. She wrote the Katy books (*What Katy Did* (1872), and its sequels) and other stories for girls in an easy unsentimental style.
What Katy Did
Carr, Katy

Cooper, James Fenimore
◎ (1789–1851) US novelist whose most famous works are adventures of the frontier which portray pioneer and Native American life.
The Deerslayer
Bumppo, Natty
Chingachgook
The Last of the Mohicans
Bumppo, Natty
Chingachgook
The Pathfinder
Bumppo, Natty
Chingachgook
The Pioneers
Bumppo, Natty
Chingachgook
The Prairie
Bumppo, Natty
Chingachgook

Cooper, William, pseudonym of **Harry Summerfield Hoff**
◎ (born 1910) English satirical novelist.
Scenes From Later Life
Lunn, Joe
Scenes From Married Life
Lunn, Joe
Scenes From Metropolitan Life
Lunn, Joe

Scenes From Provincial Life
Lunn, Joe

Coppard, A(lfred) E(dgar)
◎ (1878–1957) English short-story writer and poet. His deceptively simple tales of country life are characterized by their detailed observation and poetic quality.
'Dusky Ruth'
Dusky Ruth

Cornwell, Patricia
◎ (born 1956) US crime writer. Her experience of working in the Virginia medical examiner's office lends a high degree of accuracy to her hugely successful series of novels featuring Kay Scarpetta.
Postmortem
Scarpetta, Kay

Coward, Noël
◎ (1899–1973) English actor, playwright and composer. He wrote many successful plays, still popular today, all showing his strong satiric humour and unique gift for witty dialogue. He also wrote the music for most of his works.
Blithe Spirit
Arcati, Madame
Condomine, Elvira
Hay Fever
Bliss family
Private Lives
Chase, Elyot, and Prynne, Amanda
Prynne, Victor, and Chase, Sybil
The Vortex
Lancaster, Nicky

Cozzens, James Gould
◎ (1903–78) US writer. A Pulitzer Prize-winner, his novels usually feature professional men entangled in moral dilemmas.
By Love Possessed
Winner, Arthur, jr
Guard of Honor
Beal, Major General Ira N
Carricker, Lt Col Benny
James, Al
Ross, Col
Willis, Stanley, Lt jg

Crabbe, George
◎ (1754–1832) English poet. With the patronage of Edmund Burke and Dr Johnson, he published skilled verse narratives detailing country life in heroic couplets.
The Borough
Grimes, Peter
Orford, Ellen
The Parish Register
Dawson, Phoebe
'Sir Eustace Grey'
Grey, Sir Eustace

Crace, Jim
◎ (born 1946) English novelist whose books often reflect his powerful ability to create

Index

imaginary worlds and landscapes. *Quarantine* (1997) was shortlisted for the Booker Prize, as was *Being Dead* (1999), which also won the Whitbread Novel Award.

Being Dead
Adkins, Celice
Adkins, Joseph

Quarantine
Jesus

Craik, Mrs (Dinah Maria)

◎ (1826–87) English novelist who also wrote essays, children's stories and fairytales.

John Halifax, Gentleman
Halifax, John

Crane, Stephen

◎ (1871–1900) US writer and war correspondent. His novel *The Red Badge of Courage* (1895), which relates vividly the experiences of a soldier in the American Civil War, was received with acclaim, in particular for its psychological realism.

Maggie: A Girl of the Streets
Johnson, Maggie

The Red Badge of Courage
Fleming, Henry

Crispin, Edmund, pseudonym of **Robert Bruce Montgomery**

◎ (1921–78) English detective-writer, critic and composer. He wrote witty, comedic mystery novels and, under his original name, composed choral and orchestral works, songs, and film scores.

The Case of the Gilded Fly
Fen, Gervase

Crompton, Richmal, originally **Richmal Lamburn**

◎ (1890–1969) English writer. She published 50 adult titles but is best known for her *Just William* books, 38 short-story collections and one novel, about a perpetual schoolboy, the eleven-year-old William Brown.

Just William
William

Cronin, A(rchibald) J(oseph)

◎ (1896–1981) Scottish novelist. He was originally a doctor, and the medical stories in his Scottish novels formed the basis of the popular radio and television series *Dr Finlay's Casebook*.

Beyond This Place
Finlay, Dr

Hatter's Castle
Brodie, James

Cross, Amanda, pseudonym of **Caroline Heilbrun**

◎ (1926–2003) US essayist and novelist. A feminist scholar and teacher, she wrote fiction under her pseudonym, notably erudite

mystery novels featuring Kate Fansler.

Sweet Death, Kind Death
Fansler, Kate

Cunningham, Michael

◎ (born 1952) US novelist. A teacher of creative writing at Columbia University, he has written several novels, but major recognition came with the Pulitzer Prize-winning novel *The Hours* (1998, filmed 2002), a study of three women linked by **Virginia Woolf**'s book *Mrs Dalloway*.

The Hours
Brown, Laura
Vaughan, Clarissa
Woolf, Virginia

Cusack, Dymphna and **James, Florence**

◎ (1902–81 and 1902–93) Australian and New Zealand writers. *Come in Spinner*'s outspoken handling of adultery and abortion delayed its publication until 1951, and the full text was not published until 1988.

Come in Spinner
Guinea, properly Margaret ('Meg')
  Malone

Dahl, Roald

◎ (1916–90) British children's author, short-story writer, playwright and versifier. As well as writing popular, but macabre, stories for adults, he is one of the best-known children's authors of all time.

Charlie and the Chocolate Factory
Charlie, properly Charlie Bucket
Wonka, Willy

Charlie and the Great Glass Elevator
Charlie, properly Charlie Bucket
Wonka, Willy

James and the Giant Peach
James

Matilda
Matilda

Dana, R H, jr

◎ (1815–82) US writer and lawyer. While on a break from his law studies at Harvard, he sailed around Cape Horn to California and back. He describes this voyage in *Two Years Before the Mast* (1840).

Two Years Before the Mast
anon (R H Dana jr)
Harris, Tom
Hope
John the Swede
Thompson, Captain

Dark, Eleanor

◎ (1901–85) Australian novelist. A skilled writer, and a committed socialist and feminist, she was awarded various prizes. Her trilogy *The Timeless Land* (1941), *Storm of Time* (1948) and *No Barrier* (1953) charts the early years of European settlement of New South Wales.

No Barrier
Arabanoo
Barangaroo
Bennilong
Billalong
Dilboong
Mannion, Conan
Mannion, Miles
Mannion, Patrick
Mannion, Stephen
Phillip, Governor (Arthur)
Prentice, Andrew
Prentice, Ellen
Prentice, Johnny

Storm of Time
Arabanoo
Barangaroo
Bennilong
Billalong
Dilboong
Mannion, Conan
Mannion, Miles
Mannion, Patrick
Mannion, Stephen
Phillip, Governor (Arthur)
Prentice, Andrew
Prentice, Ellen
Prentice, Johnny

The Timeless Land
Arabanoo
Barangaroo
Bennilong
Billalong
Dilboong
Mannion, Conan
Mannion, Miles
Mannion, Patrick
Mannion, Stephen
Phillip, Governor (Arthur)
Prentice, Andrew
Prentice, Ellen
Prentice, Johnny

Davies, Robertson

◎ (1913–95) Canadian novelist, playwright and essayist. He is best known for the 'Deptford trilogy' – beginning with *Fifth Business* (1970). This work evolved from his earlier books set in Salterton, an imagined Ontario city.

Fifth Business
Eisengrim, Magnus
Ramsay, Dunstan
Staunton, Percy Boyd ('Boy')

The Manticore
Eisengrim, Magnus
Ramsay, Duncan

World of Wonders
Eisengrim, Magnus
Ramsay, Duncan

Davin, Dan

◎ (1913–1990) New Zealand novelist and short-story writer. Much of his fiction draws on his Catholic childhood and on his wartime experiences. He also had a distinguished career as a publisher and wrote critical works and memoirs.

Brides of Peace
Mahon, Adam

Cliffs of Fall
Burke, Mark

For the Rest of Our Lives
Brandon, Tony
Fahey, Frank
O'Dwyer, Tom

Not Here, Not Now
Cody, Martin

Roads from Home
Hogan, John
Hogan, Ned

The Sullen Bell
Egan, Captain Hugh

Davison, Frank Dalby

◎ (1893–1970) Australian writer. Having served in World War I and tried farming, he began writing full-time during the Depression. His books are grounded in his concern for the environment and his belief in the power of literature to improve society.

Man-Shy
Man-Shy

Day, Thomas

◎ (1748–89) English writer and barrister. A disciple of Jean Jacques Rousseau, he was interested in educational theory. He wrote didactic, moral children's tales.

The History of Sandford and Merton
Barlow, Mr
Merton, Tommy
Sandford, Harry

de Bernières, Louis

◎ (born 1954) English novelist. His early experiences as a teacher of English in Columbia are reflected in the magic realist style of his first three novels. He is best known for his fourth novel, *Captain Corelli's Mandolin* (1994), a World War II love story, which was a worldwide bestseller and has also been adapted for film and theatre.

Captain Corelli's Mandolin
Corelli, Captain Antonio
Iannis, Dr
Iannis, Pelagia

Defoe, Daniel

◎ (1660–1731) English writer and adventurer. He led a colourful life, involving imprisonment for dissent and working as a secret agent. A writer of astonishing versatility, he published more than 250 works in all, and was almost 60 by the time he published his most famous work *Robinson Crusoe* (1719). He is regarded by many as the first English novelist.

Captain Singleton
Singleton, Captain

Colonel Jack
Jack, Colonel

The Farther Adventures of Robinson Crusoe
Crusoe, Robinson
Man Friday

Moll Flanders
Flanders, Moll

Robinson Crusoe
Crusoe, Robinson
Man Friday

Roxana
Roxana

*The Serious Reflections of …
Robinson Crusoe*
Crusoe, Robinson

De Forest, J(ohn) W(illiam)

◎ (1826–1906) US writer. He served in the American Civil War and his vivid accounts of this, published in *Harper's Weekly*, were renowned. He also wrote novels about the war.

Miss Ravenel's Conversion from Secession to Loyalty
Carter, Lt Col John
Colbourne, Edward, later Captain
La Rue, Mrs
Ravenel, Lillie

Dekker, Thomas

◎ (c.1570–1632) English dramatist and pamphleteer. Imprisoned for debt several times in his life, he wrote several collaborative works. He is known for his realistic portrayal of daily London life.

The Shoemaker's Holiday
Eyre, Simon
King of England, the
Lacy, Rowland
Lord Mayor of London
Otley, Rose

Dekker, Thomas (*see above*), Rowley, William (*see* Rowley, William) and Ford, John (*see* Ford, John)

The Witch of Edmonton
Carter, Susan
Sawyer, Elizabeth
Thorney, Frank
Winnifrede

Delafield, E M, pseudonym of Edmée Elizabeth Monica Dashwood

◎ (1890–1943) English novelist. A former nurse who became a civil servant and served as a magistrate, she was the prolific author of novels which took a mildly but affectionately satirical look at the mores of genteel provincial life.

The Diary of a Provincial Lady
Provincial Lady

Deland, Margaret

◎ (1857–1945) US novelist. Her works were usually set in her native Pennsylvania and dealt with moral questions and social issues.

John Ward, Preacher
Jeffrey, Helen
Ward, John

Old Chester Tales
Lavender, Dr

Delaney, Shelagh

◎ (born 1939) English playwright and screenwriter. She completed her first and best-known play at the age of 18. *A Taste of Honey*, produced in London in 1958, was immediately seen as part of a young, 'angry' movement dealing realistically with working-class, provincial life. She has also written screenplays.

A Taste of Honey
Jo (Josephine)

Delany, Martin R(obison)

◎ (1812–85) US novelist, abolitionist and political theorist. He has been called the 'Father of Black Nationalism' and his works addressed racial questions a century before their more vehement expression.

Blake, or The Huts of America
Blake, Henry

de la Roche, Mazo

◎ (1885–1961) Canadian novelist. Besides writing a series of novels about the Whiteoak family, she also wrote children's stories, history, travel books and an autobiography.

The Building of Jalna
Whiteoak, Adeline, née Court

DeLillo, Don

◎ (born 1936) US novelist. His novels are characterized by linguistic inventiveness and black comedy. He is a highly influential writer whose works usually embrace American themes such as immigrants' experiences, the media and consumerism.

The Body Artist
Hartke, Lauren

End Zone
Harkness, Gary
Robinson, Taft

Great Jones Street
Wunderlick, Bucky

Libra
Oswald, Lee Harvey, also known as 'Leon', or 'O H Lee', or 'Hidell'
Ruby, Jack

Mao II
Gray, Bill

White Noise
Gladney, Jack

Dell, Floyd

◎ (1887–1969) US novelist. He was a radical journalist but turned his attentions more to fiction after the success of his first novel *Moon-Calf* (1920), a semi-autobiographical work which dealt with the disillusionment which characterized America between the wars.

The Briary-Bush
Fay, Felix

Moon-Calf
Fay, Felix

Desai, Anita

◎ (born 1937) Indian novelist.
The daughter of a Bengali
father and a German mother,
she has written novels for adults
and children as well as short
stories.

Baumgartner's Bombay
Baumgartner, Hugo

Clear Light of Day
Das, Bim (Bimla)

Fire on the Mountain
Kaul, Nanda
Raka

In Custody
Deven
Murad
Nur

The Village by the Sea
Hari
Lila

Desani, G(ovindas) V(ishnoodas)

◎ (1909–2000) US novelist. His
claim to posterity is dependent on
his eccentric and linguistically
inventive novel *All About H.
Hatterr* (1948). It was reprinted the
week after publication, but was
then neglected for several decades
before being resurrected as a
modern classic comparable to the
work of **James Joyce** and **Flann
O'Brien**.

All About H. Hatterr
Hatterr, H.

De Vries, Peter

◎ (1910–93) US novelist. He was
encouraged by **James Thurber** to
write for *The New Yorker*. A satirist
in his mentor's mould, he favoured
word play and was an inveterate
(and inventive) punster and
epigrammatist. He wrote more
than 20 novels.

Comfort Me With Apples
Swallow, Chick

The Mackerel Plaza
Hester
Mackerel, Rev Andrew

Slouching Towards Kalamazoo
Doubloon, Maggie
Thrasher, Anthony

Dexter, Colin

◎ (born 1930) English detective-
story writer. He began publishing
crime fiction in the mid-1970s,
introducing readers to his most
famous character, Inspector
Morse.

Last Bus to Woodstock
Morse, Inspector

Dibdin, Michael

◎ (born 1947) English writer of
crime fiction. Having studied at
the University of Sussex and in
Canada, he taught for four years in
Italy, which provides the backdrop
for many of his novels.

Ratking
Zen, Aurelio

Dickens, Charles

◎ (1812–70) English novelist. His
novels are a vivid portrayal of social
life in Victorian England, much of
it derived from his own
experiences. The breadth,
perception and sympathy of his
writing, his ability to conjure up
memorable characters in a few
paragraphs and the comic genius
which permeates even his most
serious works, have all ensured
that he continues to find a
receptive audience, both for the
books themselves and in film and
stage adaptations of his work.

Barnaby Rudge
Chester, Edward
Chester, Sir John
Daisy, Solomon
Dennis, Ned
Gashford, Mr
Gordon, Lord George
Grip, the Raven
Hardale, Emma
Haredale, Mr Geoffrey
Hugh
Miggs, Miss
Rudge, Barnaby
Rudge, Mr and Mrs (Mary)
Tappertit, Simon (Sim)
Varden, Dolly
Varden, Gabriel
Willet, Joe
Willet, John

The Battle of Life
Britain, Benjamin
Heathfield, Alfred
Jeddler, Dr Anthony
Jeddler, Grace and Marion
Newcome, Clemency
Snitchey, Jonathan
Warden, Michael

Bleak House
Badger, Bayham
Bagnet, Mr and Mrs
Barbary, Miss
Boythorn, Lawrence
Bucket, Mr
Carstone, Richard
Chadband, the Rev Mr
Clare, Ada
Dedlock, Lady
Dedlock, Sir Leicester
Flite, Miss
Gridley, Mr
Guppy, William
Guster
Hawdon, Captain
Hortense, Mademoiselle
Jarndyce, John
Jellyby, Caroline (Caddy)
Jellyby, Mrs
Jo
Jobling, Tony
Kenge, Mr
Krook, Mr
Neckett
Neckett, Charlotte
Pardiggle, Mrs
Rachael, Mrs
Rouncewell, Mr
Rouncewell, Mr George
Rouncewell, Mrs
Skimpole, Harold
Smallweed, Grandfather (Joshua)
Snagsby, Mr
Summerson, Esther

Tulkinghorn, Mr
Turveydrop, Mr
Turveydrop, Prince
Voles, Mr
Woodcourt, Allan

The Chimes
Bowley, Sir Joseph
Chickenstalker, Mrs Anne
Cute, Alderman
Deedles
Fern, Will
Filer, Mr
Veck, Meg (Margaret)
Veck, Trotty (Toby)

A Christmas Carol
Cratchit, Bob
Fezziwigs, the
Ghost of Christmas Past, Ghost of
Christmas Present and Ghost of
Christmas Yet to Come
Marley's Ghost
Scrooge, Ebenezer
Tiny Tim

The Cricket on the Hearth
Fielding, May
Peerybingle, John
Peerybingle, Mrs Mary (Dot)
Plummer, Bertha
Plummer, Caleb
Plummer, Edward
Slowboy, Tilly
Tackleton, Mr

David Copperfield
Barkis, Mr
Clickett ('the Orfling')
Copperfield, David
Copperfield, Mrs Clara
Creakle, Mr
Crewler, Sophy
Dartle, Rosa
Dick, Mr
Em'ly, Little
Endell, Martha
Gummidge, Mrs
Heep, Uriah
Jorkins, Mr
Littimer
Maldon, Jack
Micawber, Mr Wilkins
Micawber, Mrs (Emma)
Mowcher, Miss
Murdstone, Mr Edward
Murdstone, Jane
Omer, Mr
Peggotty, Clara
Peggotty, Daniel
Peggotty, Ham
Spenlow, Dora
Spenlow, Mr Francis
Steerforth, Mr James
Strong, Mrs (Annie)
Strong, Dr
Traddles, Thomas
Trotwood, Miss Betsey
Wickfield, Agnes
Wickfield, Mr

Dombey and Son
Bagstock, Major Joseph
Blimber, Doctor
Brown, Mrs
Bunsby, Captain Jack
Carker, Harriet
Carker, James
Carker, John
Chick, Mrs Louisa
Cuttle, Captain Edward (Ned)
Dombey, Edith (formerly Granger)
Dombey, Florence

Dombey, Mr Paul
Dombey, Paul
Feenix, Lord
Gay, Walter
Gills, Solomon
Howler, Rev Melchisedech
MacStinger, Mrs
Marwood, Alice
Nipper, Susan
Pipchin, Mrs
Skewton, the Hon Mrs
Toodle, Polly
Toodle, Robin (Rob the Grinder)
Toots, Mr
Tox, Miss Lucretia

Great Expectations
Biddy
Compeyson
Drummle, Bentley
Estella
Gargery, Joe
Gargery, Mrs Joe
Havisham, Miss
Jaggers, Mr
Magwitch, Abel
Molly
Orlick, Dolge
Pip, nickname of Philip Pirrip
Pocket, Herbert
Pocket, Matthew
Pumblechook, Uncle
Trabb's boy
Wemmick, John
Wopsle, Mr

Hard Times
Bitzer
Blackpool, Stephen
Bounderby, Josiah
Gradgrind, Louisa
Gradgrind, Thomas
Gradgrind, Tom
Harthouse, James
Jupe, Signor
Jupe, Sissy
M'Choakumchild, Mr
Pegler, Mrs
Rachael
Slackbridge
Sleary, Mr
Sparsit, Mrs

The Haunted Man
Redlaw, Mr

Little Dorrit
Barnacles, the
Beadle, Harriet, known as Tattycoram
Casby, Christopher
Cavalletto, John Baptist
Chivery, Young John
Clennam, Arthur
Clennam, Mrs
Dorrit, Amy, known as Little Dorrit
Dorrit, Edward, known as Tip
Dorrit, Fanny
Dorrit, Frederick
Dorrit, William
Doyce, Daniel
Finching, Flora
Flintwinch, Affery
Flintwinch, Jeremiah
General, Mrs
Gowan, Henry
Meagles, Minnie (Pet)
Meagles, Mr and Mrs
Merdle, Mr
Merdle, Mrs
Pancks, Mr
Plornish, Mr and Mrs Thomas
Rigaud

Sparkler, Edmund
Wade, Miss

Martin Chuzzlewit
Bailey, Benjamin
Chuffey, Mr
Chuzzlewit, Anthony
Chuzzlewit, Jonas
Chuzzlewit, Martin
Chuzzlewit, Martin (Old Martin)
Gamp, Mrs Sarah
Graham, Mary
Lewsome, Mr
Lupin, Mrs
Nadgett, Mr
Pecksniff, Charity and Mercy
Pecksniff, Seth
Pinch, Tom and Ruth
Prig, Betsey
Slyme, Chevy
Sweedlepipe, Poll (Paul)
Tapley, Mark
Tigg, Montague (alias Tigg Montague)
Todgers, Mrs
Westlock, John

The Mystery of Edwin Drood
Billickin, Mrs
Bud, Rosa
Crisparkle, the Revd Septimus
Datchery, Dick
Deputy
Drood, Edwin
Durdles
Grewgious, Mr Hiram
Honeythunder, Mr Luke
Jasper, Mr John
Landless, Helena and Neville
Princess Puffer
Sapsea, Mr Thomas
Tartar, Mr
Tope, Mr and Mrs
Twinkleton, Miss

Nicholas Nickleby
Bray, Madeline
Bray, Walter
Browdie, John
Cheeryble, Charles and Edwin
Crummles, Mr and Mrs Vincent
Gride, Arthur
Hawk, Sir Mulberry
Kenwigs, Mr and Mrs
La Creevy, Miss
Lillyvick, Mr
Linkinwater, Tim
Mantalini, Mr Alfred and Madame
Nickleby, Kate
Nickleby, Mrs
Nickleby, Nicholas
Nickleby, Ralph
Noggs, Newman
Petowker, Miss Henrietta
Smike
Snawley, Mr
Snevellicci, Miss
Squeers, Wackford
Verisopht, Lord Frederick
Wititterly, Mr and Mrs Henry

The Old Curiosity Shop
Bachelor, The
Barbara
Brass, Sally
Brass, Sampson
Codlin, Thomas and Harris ('Short')
Garland, Mr and Mrs, and Abel
Grandfather
Jarley, Mrs
Jiniwin, Mrs
Little Nell
Marchioness, the

Nubbles, Kit (Christopher)
Quilp, Betsey
Quilp, Daniel
Swiveller, Dick (Richard)
Wackles, Sophy

Oliver Twist
Bates, Charley
Brownlow, Mr
Bumble, Mr
Claypole, Noah
Corney, Mrs
Dawkins, Jack (the Artful Dodger)
Fagin
Fang, Mr
Leeford, Edward ('Monks')
Maylie, Mrs
Maylie, Rose
Nancy
Sikes, Bill
Sowerberry, Mr and Mrs
Twist, Oliver

Our Mutual Friend
Boffin, Mr and Mrs Nicodemus
Fledgeby 'Fascination Fledgeby'
Harmon, John (alias John Rokesmith)
Headstone, Bradley
Hexam, Charley
Hexam, Gaffer (Jesse)
Hexam, Lizzie
Higden, Betty
Jenny Wren, properly Fanny Cleaver
Lammle, Alfred
Lightwood, Mortimer
Podsnap, Mr John
Potterson, Abbey
Riah
Riderhood, Rogue (Roger)
Veneering, Mr and Mrs Hamilton
Venus, Mr
Wegg, Silas
Wilfer, Bella
Wilfer, Reginald
Wrayburn, Eugene

Pickwick Papers
Allen, Arabella and Benjamin
Bardell, Mrs Martha
Boldwig, Captain
Buzfuz, Serjeant
Dowler, Mr
Fizkin, Horatio
Humm, Anthony
Hunter, Mrs Leo
Hutley, Jem (called Dismal Jemmy)
Jingle, Alfred
Joe (The Fat Boy)
Magnus, Peter
Nupkins, George
Pickwick, Samuel
Sawyer, Bob
Slammer, Doctor
Slumkey, the Hon Samuel
Smorltork, Count
Snodgrass, Augustus
Snubbin, Serjeant
Stiggins, the Rev Mr
Trotter, Job
Tupman, Tracy
Wardles, the
Weller, Mr and Mrs Tony
Weller, Sam
Winkle, Nathaniel

A Tale of Two Cities
Carton, Sydney
Cly, Roger
Cruncher, Jerry (Jeremiah)
Darnay, Charles
Defarge, Ernest
Defarge, Madame (Thérèse)

Gabelle, Theophile
Gaspard
Lorry, Mr Jarvis
Manette, Dr Alexandre
Manette, Lucie
Pross, Miss
Pross, Solomon (John Barsad)
St Evremonde, Marquis de (the elder)
St Evremonde, Marquis de (the younger)
Stryver, Mr

Didion, Joan

◎ (born 1934) US novelist, journalist and essayist. From 1956 to 1963 she was associate feature editor of *Vogue* in New York and has worked and written for such magazines as *Esquire* and *National Review*. Her novels portray contemporary social tensions in a laconic style.

A Book of Common Prayer
Douglas, Charlotte, formerly Charlotte Bogart
Douglas, Marin
Strasser-Mendana, Grace

Democracy
Lovett, Jack
Victor, Inez Christian

Play It As It Lays
BZ
Wyeth, Maria (Maria Wyeth Lang)

Run, River
Channing, Ryder
Knight, Lily (Lily Knight McClellan)
Knight, Walter
McClellan, Everett

Disraeli, Benjamin

◎ (1804–81) English statesman and novelist. He managed to combine a successful political career with his fiction writing. In 1826 he became the talk of the town with the first volumes of his first novel, *Vivian Grey*. *Coningsby* (1844) and *Sybil* (1845) are political novels in which Disraeli's respect for tradition is blended with 'Young England' radicalism. Many of his fictional characters are based on his contemporaries.

Coningsby, or The New Generation
Coningsby, Harry
Flora
Lucretia
Millbank, Edith
Millbank, Mr
Millbank, Oswald
Monmouth, Lord
Rigby, Mr
Tadpole
Taper
Sidonia

Endymion
Ferroll
Roehampton, Lord
St Barbe
Thornberry, Job

Sybil, or The Two Nations
Egremont, Charles
Gerard, Sybil
Gerard, Walter
Marney, Lord
Morley, Stephen
St Lys, Rev Aubrey

Vivian Grey

Carabas, Marquis of
Cleveland
Grey, Vivian
Lorraine, Mrs

Doctorow, E(dgar) L(awrence)

◎ (born 1931) US novelist and academic who has won several literary awards. *Ragtime* (1975, filmed 1981) is generally regarded as his tour de force, in which he recreates the atmosphere of New York in the decades before World War II with wit, accuracy and appealing nostalgia.

Billy Bathgate
Bathgate, Billy

The Book of Daniel
Isaacson, Rochelle and Paul
Lewin, Daniel

Ragtime
Walker, Coalhouse, jr

Donleavy, J(ames) P(atrick)

◎ (born 1926) Irish novelist and playwright. His picaresque first novel, *The Ginger Man* (1955) was hailed as a comic masterpiece. The novels, plays and stories that followed are on the same theme, that of his own 'dreams and inner desires', and have been described as paler versions of *The Ginger Man*.

The Beastly Beatitudes of Balthazar B
Balthazar B

The Destinies of Darcy Dancer, Gentleman
Kildare, Darcy Dancer

The Ginger Man
Dangerfield, Sebastian

A Singular Man
Smith, George

Dos Passos, John

◎ (1896–1970) US novelist, playwright and journalist who is perhaps best-known for his monumental *U.S.A.* trilogy: *The 42nd Parallel* (1930), *1919* (1932) and *The Big Money* (1936). A digressive, dynamic epic, it consists of a medley of newsreel footage, snatches of popular songs, brief but vivid sketches of public figures and prose-poetry.

The Big Money
Anderson, Charley
Barrow, G H
Burnham, Jerry
Compton, Ben
Dowling, Margo
French, Mary
Hutchins, Eveline
Moorehouse, J Ward
Savage, Richard Ellsworth (Dick)
Stoddard, Eleanor
Vag
Wheatley, Gladys
Williams, Janey

The 42nd Parallel
Anderson, Charley
Barrow, G H
Burnham, Jerry
Hutchins, Eveline
McCreary, Fenian

Moorehouse, J Ward
Stoddard, Eleanor
Williams, Janey
Williams, Joe

Manhattan Transfer
Baldwin, George
Emery, Stan (Stanwood)
Goldweiser, Harry
Harland, Frank
Harland, Joe
Herf, Jimmy
Jake, Congo
Korpenning, Bud
McNiel, Gus
Merivale, James
Oglethorpe, John
O'Keefe, Joe
Thatcher, Ellen
Wilkins, Cassandra

1919
Barrow, G H
Burnham, Jerry
Compton, Ben
Cooper, Hiram Halsey
Daughter
Hutchins, Eveline
Moorehouse, J Ward
Savage, Richard Ellsworth (Dick)
Stoddard, Eleanor
Williams, Janey
Williams, Joe

Three Soldiers
Andrews, John
Chrisfield
Fuselli, Dan

Douglas, Lloyd C(assel)

◎ (1877–1951) US novelist. A pastor for many years, he wrote novels about religious and moral issues. Many of his novels were filmed including *The Robe* (1942, filmed 1953) which was the first Technicolor film.

The Robe
Demetrius
Marcellus

Doyle, Arthur Conan

◎ (1859–1930) Scottish writer of detective stories and historical romances. He began writing as a penniless medical practitioner. His Sherlock Holmes detective stories were serialized in *The Strand Magazine* and became so popular that when Conan Doyle tried to kill off his hero, he was compelled in 1903 to revive him.

The Exploits of Brigadier Gerard
Gerard, Brigadier Etienne

The Final Problem
Moriarty, Professor

The Lost World
Challenger, Professor George Edward

Micah Clarke
Clarke, Micah

A Study in Scarlet
Holmes, Sherlock
Lestrade, Inspector
Watson, Dr John

Doyle, Roddy

◎ (born 1958) Irish novelist and screenwriter. He spent many years as a teacher in a North Dublin suburb, fictionalized as Barrytown in his early novels. He won the 1993 Booker Prize for *Paddy Clarke Ha Ha Ha*.

The Commitments
Rabbitte family, the

Paddy Clarke Ha Ha Ha
Clarke, Paddy

The Snapper
Rabbitte family, the

A Star Called Henry
Smart, Henry

The Van
Rabbitte family, the

The Woman Who Walked Into Doors
Spencer, Paula

Drabble, Margaret

◎ (born 1939) English novelist whose works frequently concentrate on the concerns of intelligent, often frustrated middle-class women. She has also written a number of literary biographies. Her elder sister is **A S Byatt**.

The Garrick Year
Evans, Emma

The Gates of Ivory
Bowen, Alix
Breuer, Esther
Cox, Stephen
Headland, Liz

The Ice Age
Keating, Anthony

Jerusalem the Golden
Maugham, Clara

The Middle Ground
Armstrong, Kate

The Millstone
Stacey, Rosamund

A Natural Curiosity
Bowen, Alix
Breuer, Esther
Cox, Stephen
Headland, Liz

The Needle's Eye
Camish, Simon
Vassilou, Rose

The Peppered Moth
Bawtry, Bessie
Gaulden, Faro

The Radiant Way
Bowen, Alix
Breuer, Esther
Headland, Liz

The Realms of Gold
Wingate, Frances

The Seven Sisters
Wilton, Candida

A Summer Bird-Cage
Bennett, Sarah and Louise

The Waterfall
Gray, Jane

The Witch Of Exmoor
Haxby Palmer, Frieda

Dreiser, Theodore

◎ (1871–1945) US novelist. His works naturalistically portrayed the harsh conditions of early 20th-century US life and often aroused controversy. *An American Tragedy* (1925), based on

a real-life murder case, has survived as a classic, despite its leaden prose.

An American Tragedy
Alden, Roberta
Finchley, Sondra
Griffiths, Clyde

The Financier
Cowperwood, Frank Algernon

The 'Genius'
Whitla, Eugene

Jennie Gerhardt
Gerhardt, Jennie

Sister Carrie
Drouet, Charles
Hurstwood, George
Meeber, Carrie

The Stoic
Cowperwood, Frank Algernon

The Titan
Cowperwood, Frank Algernon

Dryden, John

◎ (1631–1700) English poet, critic and translator who was Poet Laureate from 1668–88. In a lifetime of industry, he completed translations of the classics, wrote plays – the best of which is *All for Love* (1678), written in blank verse – and satirical and didactic poems.

Absolom and Achitophel
Absolom
Achitophel

All for Love
Antony
Cleopatra

MacFlecknoe
MacFlecknoe

Du Maurier, Daphne

◎ (1907–89) English novelist and short-story writer. The granddaughter of **George Du Maurier**, she wrote a number of highly successful period romances and adventure stories. Many of them were inspired by Cornwall, where she lived.

Frenchman's Creek
Aubery, Jean-Benoit
Dona, Lady

Jamaica Inn
Davey, Francis
Merlyn, Jem
Merlyn, Joss
Yellan, Mary

The King's General
Grenville, Sir Richard
Harris, Honor

Mary Anne
Clarke, Mary Anne

My Cousin Rachel
Ashley, Ambrose
Ashley, Philip
Ashley, Rachel

Rebecca
Danvers, Mrs
de Winter, Max
de Winter, Mrs
de Winter, Rebecca

The Scapegoat
John/Comte de Gue, Jean

Du Maurier, George

◎ (1834–96) French-born English artist, cartoonist and novelist. He made his name as an illustrator and joined the staff of *Punch* (1864–96). He also wrote and illustrated three novels, including the very successful *Trilby* (1894).

Trilby
Laird, the, also known as Sandy, or the Laird of Cockpen
Little Billee
Svengali
Taffy, properly Clive Talbot Wynne; also known as the Man of Blood
Trilby, in full Trilby O'Ferrall

Dunn, Nell

◎ (born 1936) English novelist and playwright. Her early works of fiction were powerful portrayals of working-class women, and demonstrated her keen ear for dialogue. *Poor Cow* (1963) was filmed to great effect by Ken Loach in 1968. She has also written plays.

Poor Cow
Joy

Up the Junction
Polly

Durrell, Lawrence

◎ (1912–90) English novelist, poet, travel writer and playwright. He took numerous odd jobs and once said he had been driven to writing 'by sheer ineptitude'. He travelled widely as a journalist and in the service of the Foreign Office. He made his name with *The Alexandria Quartet* – *Justine* (1957), *Balthazar* (1958), *Mountolive* (1958) and *Clea* (1960).

Balthazar
Balthazar, S

Clea
Clea, properly Clea Montis

Justine
Capodistria
Darley, L G
Justine, properly Justine Hosnani
Melissa, properly Melissa Artemis
Nessim
Pursewarden, Percy

Mountolive
Mountolive, David

E

Edgeworth, Maria

◎ (1767–1849) Irish novelist. Hugely influenced by her father and his ideas on education, she published her first novel in 1800, a historical novel about Irish life, *Castle Rackrent*, which was an immediate success. She is also remembered for her children's stories.

The Absentee
Burke, Agent
Clonbrony, Lady
Clonbrony, Lord
Colambre, Lord, also known as Evans
Garraghty, Nicholas and Dennis, also known as Old Nick and St Dennis
Nugent, Grace

Castle Rackrent
M'Quirk, Judy
Moneygawl, Isabella
Quirk, Jason
Quirk, Thady
Rackrent, Sir Condy, properly Sir Connolly
Rackrent, Sir Kit
Rackrent, Sir Murtagh
Rackrent, Sir Patrick, originally Patrick O'Shaughlin

Egbuna, Obi

◎ (born 1940) Nigerian novelist, playwright, and short-story writer. As a scholarship student Egbuna studied in Britain, where he became involved in the Black Power movement. Many of his early works focus on racial issues. He returned to Nigeria in the mid-1970s, but after a military coup, left for the US.

The Madness of Didi
Didi

Eggleston, Edward

◎ (1837–1902) US writer and pastor. He held a Methodist ministry in Minnesota, and was editor of various journals. He also wrote several classic novels, among them *The Hoosier Schoolmaster* (1871), which was based on his brother's experience as a small-town teacher.

The Circuit Rider
Goodwin, Morton

The Graysons
Lincoln, Abraham

The Hoosier Schoolmaster
Hartsook, Ralph

Roxy
Adams, Roxy

Ekwensi, Cyprian

◎ (born 1921) Nigerian novelist. While rarely receiving critical acclaim, his works are hugely popular. Many of them portray the lives of ordinary people adjusting to historical change. He has also written short stories and books for children.

Jagua Nana
Jagua Nana

Eldershaw, M Barnard, pseudonym of **Flora Sydney Eldershaw** and **Marjorie Faith Barnard**

◎ (1897–1956 and 1897–1987) Australian writers. Flora Eldershaw, a teacher at a girls' school, and Marjorie Barnard, a librarian, collaborated on various works including novels, histories, short stories and essays.

A House is Built
Gage, Adela
Hyde, Fanny
Hyde, James, Junior
Hyde, James, Senior, known as 'the quartermaster'
Hyde, Lionel
Hyde, Maud
Hyde, William

Tomorrow and Tomorrow and Tomorrow
Knarf
Munster, Ally
Munster, Harry
Ord
Ren
Warren, Sid

Eliot, George, pseudonym of **Mary Ann** or **Marian Evans**

◎ (1819–80) English novelist, critic and poet. A voracious reader, she was well-educated in music and languages and travelled on the Continent. Her first novel, *Adam Bede* (1859), had enormous success, while *Middlemarch* (1871–72) is generally considered her greatest work. Her portrayals of farmers, tradesmen, and the lower middle class, generally of the Midlands, are hardly surpassed in English literature.

Adam Bede
Bede, Adam
Donnithorne, Arthur
Morris, Dinah
Poyser, Martin
Poyser, Mrs
Sorrel, Hetty

Daniel Deronda
Deronda, Daniel
Grandcourt, Henleigh
Harleth, Gwendolen
Klesmer
Lapidoth, Mirah
Lapidoth, Mordecai

Felix Holt the Radical
Denner
Holt, Felix
Jermyn, Matthew
Lyon, Esther
Transome, Harold
Transome, Mrs

'*Janet's Repentance*'
Crewe, Mr
Dempster, Janet
Dempster, Robert
Tryan, Rev Edgar

Middlemarch
Brooke, Celia
Brooke, Dorothea
Brooke, Mr
Bulstrode, Mr
Bulstrode, Mrs
Cadwallader, Mrs
Casaubon, Rev Edward
Chettam, Sir James
Featherstone, Mr Peter
Garth, Caleb
Garth, Mary
Ladislaw, Will
Lydgate, Tertius
Raffles, John
Vincy, Fred
Vincy, Rosamond

The Mill on the Floss
Deane, Lucy
Glegg, Mrs
Guest, Stephen
Jakins, Bob
Kenn, Dr
Pullet, Mrs
Tulliver, Maggie
Tulliver, Mr
Tulliver, Mrs Bessy
Tulliver, Tom
Wakem, Philip

'Mr. Gilfil's Love-Story'
Gilfil, Maynard
Sarti, Caterina
Wybrow, Captain Anthony

Romola
Calvo, Baldassarre
Charles VIII
Machiavelli, Niccolo
Melema, Tito
Romola
Savonarola, Girolamo
Tessa

'The Sad Fortunes of the Rev. Amos Barton'
Barton, Milly
Barton, Rev Amos

Silas Marner
Cass, Dunstan
Cass, Godfrey
Eppie
Lammeter, Nancy
Marner, Silas
Winthrop, Dolly

Eliot, T(homas) S(tearns)

◎ (1888–1965) US-born British poet, critic and dramatist. He worked for many years at Faber & Faber where he built up a list of new poets, including **W H Auden** and **Ezra Pound**. Besides his major works such as the allusive *The Waste Land* (1922), he also wrote verse plays including *Murder in the Cathedral* (1935) and a collection of children's verse, *Old Possum's Book of Practical Cats* (1939), influenced by Edward Lear. His critical essays were hugely influential. He was awarded the Nobel prize for literature in 1948.

'Burbank With a Baedeker; Bleistein With a Cigar'
Bleistein
Burbank
Volupine, Princess

The Cocktail Party
Chamberlayne, Edward
Chamberlayne, Lavinia
Coplestone, Celia
Harcourt-Reilly, Sir Henry
Quilpe, Peter

The Family Reunion
Agatha
Monchensey, Amy, Dowager Lady
Monchensey, Lord Harry

'Gerontion'
Gerontion

'Macavity: The Mystery Cat'
Macavity

Murder in the Cathedral
Becket, Archbishop Thomas

Prufrock and Other Observations
Apollinax, Mr

Ellicott, Miss Nancy
Prufrock, J Alfred
Slingsby, Miss Helen
'Sweeney Erect'
Sweeney
The Waste Land
Eugenides, Mr
Phlebas the Phoenician
Sosostris, Madame
Tiresias
Typist, the
Young Man Carbuncular, the

Elkin, Stanley

◎ (born 1930) US novelist and short-story writer. Elkin's novels often centre on the nature of evil and are characterized by comedy and a meticulous attention to language and its multiple possibilities.

A Bad Man
Feldman
Boswell
Boswell
The Dick Gibson Show
Gibson, Dick
The Franchiser
Flesh, Ben
George Mills
Mills, George

Elliott, Sumner Locke

◎ (1917–1991) Australian-born US novelist and playwright. He became an actor and wrote several plays. He became a US citizen in 1955 and worked as a scriptwriter for NBC and CBS television. He is best known for his semi-autobiographical novel *Careful, He Might Hear You* (1963).

Careful, He Might Hear You
Baines, Lila
Marriott, Logan
Marriott, P S
Marriott, Sinden
Scott, Vanessa
Rusty Bugles
Brooks, Sgt
Carson, Rod
Falcon, Ken
Mac
Nolan, Des
Otford, Eric
Richards, Vic
Stephens, Keghead

Ellis, Bret Easton

◎ (born 1964) US novelist. Hailed as the voice of the 80s generation, *American Psycho* (1991, filmed 2000) brought him notoriety with its themes of vacuous consumerism and amoralism.

American Psycho
Bateman, Patrick
Glamorama
Ward, Victor

Ellison, Ralph

◎ (1914–94) US novelist. *Invisible Man* (1952), his only completed novel, is the quest of a nameless black man, travelling from South to North, in search of a personal and racial identity. It had a seminal influence on other black writers and won the National Book Award.

Invisible Man
Bledsoe, Dr
Invisible Man

Emecheta, Buchi

◎ (born 1944) Nigerian novelist. She has lived in Britain since 1960 and her works focus on sexual politics and racial issues. Many of her later novels are set in West Africa. She has also written children's books and television plays.

The Bride Price
Aku-Nna
Destination Biafra
Ogedemgbe, Debbie
In the Ditch
Adah
Francis
The Joys of Motherhood
Nnu Ego
Second-Class Citizen
Adah
Francis
The Slave Girl
Objeta

Engel, Marian

◎ (1933–85) Canadian novelist. Many of her novels focus on women in contemporary society. *Bear* (1976), her best-known work, is a controversial tale of erotic love between a librarian and a bear. The Marian Engel Prize, inaugurated in 1986 to honour her memory, is awarded each year to a female Canadian writer for her body of work.

Bear
Lou

Etherege, Sir George

◎ (c.1635–1691) English dramatist who is often viewed as the founder of the comedy of intrigue. He sought his inspiration in Molière, and out of him grew the legitimate comedy of manners.

The Man of Mode
Belinda
Dorimant
Emilia
Flutter, Sir Fopling
Loveit, Mrs
Towneley, Lady
Woodvil, Harriet
Young Bellair

Farquhar, George

◎ (c.1677–1707) Irish playwright. He wrote the best of his plays, *The Beaux' Stratagem* (1707), during an illness but died before he could enjoy its success.

The Beaux' Stratagem
Aimwell
Archer
Dorinda
Lady Bountiful
Sullen, Mrs
The Recruiting Officer
Brazen
Justice Balance
Kite, Sgt
Melinda
Plume, Captain
Sylvia
Worthy

Farrell, J(ames) G(ordon)

◎ (1935–79) British author. He published six novels during a short writing career, among them *The Siege of Krishnapur* (1973), the story of the Sepoy uprising of 1857, which won the Booker Prize.

The Siege of Krishnapur
Collector, The, properly Mr Hopkins

Farrell, James T(homas)

◎ (1904–79) US novelist, short-story writer, critic and essayist. His first novel *Young Lonigan* (1932), which began the Studs Lonigan trilogy of life on Chicago's South side, was a landmark in US fiction for its indictment of the American Dream. He published more than 50 novels.

Bernard Clare
Carr, Bernard, also given as Bernard Clare/Clayre
Judgement Day
Lonigan, Studs (William)
The Silence of History
Ryan, Eddie
A World I Never Made
O'Flaherty, Mrs
O'Flaherty, Tom
O'Neill, Danny
O'Neill, Jim
O'Neill, Lizz
Young Lonigan: A Boyhood in Chicago Streets
Lonigan, Studs (William)
The Young Manhood of Studs Lonigan
Lonigan, Studs (William)

Faulkner, William

◎ (1897–1962) US novelist. The lyrical style of novels like *The Sound and the Fury* (1929) and *Absalom, Absalom!* (1936) account for his reputation as one of the modern masters of the novel. He apparently wrote *As I Lay Dying* (1930) in just six weeks. He received the 1949 Nobel prize for literature.

Absalom, Absalom!
Bon, Charles
Clytie (Clytemnestra)
Coldfield, Rosa
Compson, Quentin, III
Jones, Millie
Jones, Wash
Sutpen, Henry
Sutpen, Judith

Sutpen, Thomas

As I Lay Dying
Bundren, Addie
Bundren, Anse
Bundren, Cash
Bundren, Darl
Bundren, Dewey Dell
Bundren, Jewel
Bundren, Vardaman

'Barn Burning'
Snopes, Sarty (Colonel Sartoris)
Snopes, Ab (Abner)

'The Bear'
McCaslin, Isaac ('Ike')
Old Ben

A Fable
anon (the corporal)

Go Down, Moses
Beauchamp, Lucas (Quintus Carothers McCaslin)
Beauchamp, Sophonsiba
McCaslin, Old Carothers (Lucas Quintus Carothers McCaslin)
McCaslin, Uncle Buck (Theophilus)

The Hamlet
Houston, Jack, also referred to as Zack Houston
Snopes, Ab (Abner)
Snopes, Eck (Eckrum)
Snopes, Eula (Eula Varner)
Snopes, Flem
Snopes, Ike
Snopes, I O
Snopes, Linda (Linda Snopes Kohl)
Snopes, Lump (Launcelot)
Snopes, Mink
Snopes, Wallstreet Panic
Varner, Jody
Varner, Will

Intruder in the Dust
Beauchamp, Lucas (Quintus Carothers McCaslin)
Gowrie, Crawford
Mallison, 'Chick' (Charles)
Stevens, Gavin

Knight's Gambit
Sartoris, Benbow
Stevens, Gavin

Light in August
Burch, Lucas, also known as Joe Brown
Burden, Joanna
Christmas, Joe
Grimm, Percy
Grove, Lena
Hightower, Rev Gail
Hines, Doc (Eupheus Hines)
Stevens, Gavin

The Mansion
De Spain, Manfred
Ratliff, V K
Sartoris, Benbow
Snopes, Bilbo
Snopes, Flem
Snopes, Linda (Linda Snopes Kohl)
Snopes, Mink
Snopes, Montgomery Ward
Stevens, Gavin

Mosquitoes
Fairchild, Dawson
Frost, Mark
Gordon
Jenny (Genevieve Steinbauer)
Maurier, Mrs Patricia
Robyn, Patricia
'Semitic Man, the', also known as Julius
Talliaferro, Mr Ernest
Wiseman, Mrs Eva

Requiem for a Nun
Stevens, Gavin

Sanctuary
Benbow, Horace (Horry)
Benbow, Narcissa (Narcy)
Drake, Temple
Goodwin, Lee
Popeye
Reba, Miss
Sartoris, Benbow
Snopes, Clarence
Stevens, Gowan

Sartoris
Benbow, Horace (Horry)
Benbow, Narcissa (Narcy)
Jenny, Miss (Virginia Sartoris Du Pré)
Sartoris, Bayard (Old Bayard)
Sartoris, Bayard (Young Bayard)
Sartoris, Benbow
Sartoris, Col John
Snopes, Byron

Soldier's Pay
Emmy
Farr, George
Gilligan, Joe
Mahon, Lt Donald
Mahon, Rev
Powers, Margaret
Saunders, Cecily

The Sound and the Fury
Compson, Benjy (Benjamin)
Compson, Candace (Caddy)
Compson, Jason, IV
Compson, Quentin
Compson, Quentin, III
Dilsey (Dilsey Gibson)
Ikkemotubbe
Luster (Luster Gibson)

The Town
De Spain, Manfred
Mallison, 'Chick' (Charles)
Snopes, Bilbo
Snopes, Byron
Snopes, Clarence
Snopes, Eula (Eula Varner)
Snopes, Flem
Snopes, Montgomery Ward
Snopes, Vardaman
Snopes, Wallstreet Panic
Snopes, Wesley
Stevens, Gavin
Stevens, Gowan

The Unvanquished
McCaslin, Uncle Buck (Theophilus)
Sartoris, Col John
Snopes, Ab (Abner)

The Wild Palms
anon (the tall convict)
Rittenmeyer, Charlotte
Wilbourne, Harry

Faulks, Sebastian
© (born 1953) English author and journalist. His novels include a loose trilogy about France: *The Girl at the Lion d'Or* (1989), the bestselling *Birdsong* (1993) and *Charlotte Gray* (1998).

Birdsong
Wraysford, Stephen

Charlotte Gray
Gray, Charlotte

The Girl at the Lion d'Or
Hartmann, Charles
Louvet, Anne

On Green Dolphin Street
Renzo, Frank
Van der Linden, Charlie
Van der Linden, Mary

Ferber, Edna
© (1885–1968) US writer. Her work gives a lively, though sometimes sentimental, account of 1920s and 1930s US life, and she is probably best remembered as the writer of *Show Boat* (1926), which inspired the musical play of that name.

Cimarron
Cravat, Sabra
Cravat, Yancey

Show Boat
Hawks, Captain Andy
Hawks, Parthy Ann
Ravenal, Gaylord
Ravenal, Kim

Fielding, Helen
© (born 1958) English author. She achieved fame as the creator of *Bridget Jones's Diary*, originally a humorous newspaper column parodying contemporary cosmopolitan society through the confusions and neuroses of a discontented single young woman.

Bridget Jones's Diary
Jones, Bridget

Bridget Jones: The Edge of Reason
Jones, Bridget

Bridget Jones's Guide to Life
Jones, Bridget

Fielding, Henry
© (1707–54) English novelist. After a failed career as a satirical playwright he turned to law. Incensed by the publication of **Samuel Richardson**'s prudish *Pamela*, he ridiculed it in a pseudonymous parody, *An Apology for the Life of Mrs Shamela Andrews* (1741). In 1749 *The History of Tom Jones* was published to public acclaim, and it has endured as one of the great comic and picaresque novels in the English language.

Amelia
Bath, Major
Booth, Amelia
Booth, Captain Billy
Harrison, Dr
James, Col
Lord, My
Matthews, Miss
Thrasher, Justice

An Apology for the Life of Mrs Shamela Andrews
Booby, Mr
Oliver, Parson
Pamela
Tickletext, Parson
Williams, Parson

The History of the Adventures of Joseph Andrews and of his Friend Mr Abraham Adams
Adams, Parson (Abraham)
Andrews, Joseph
Booby, Lady
Booby, Sir Thomas
Fanny

Pamela, in full Pamela Andrews
Slipslop, Mrs
Tow-Wouse, Mr and Mrs
Trulliber, Parson
Wilson, Mr

The History of Tom Jones
Allworthy, Miss Bridget, briefly Mrs Blifil
Allworthy, Squire
Bellaston, Lady
Black George, properly George Seagrim
Blifil, Captain John
Blifil, Master
Fellamar, Lord
Jones, Jenny
Jones, Tom
Man of the Hill
Partridge, Mr
Seagrim, Molly
Square, Mr
Supple, Mr
Thwackum, Mr
Western, Sophia
Western, Squire
Wilkins, Mrs Deborah

The Life of Jonathan Wild the Great
Heartfree, Thomas
Wild, Jonathan

Rape Upon Rape
Squeezum, Justice

Fielding, Sarah

◎ (1710–68) English writer and translator. She achieved fame with the publication of *The Adventures of David Simple* in 1744. Two more volumes appeared in 1747 and 1753. She was the sister of **Henry Fielding**.

The Adventures of David Simple
Simple, David

Familiar Letters between the Principal Characters in David Simple
Simple, David

Volume the Last
Simple, David

Findlater, Jane

◎ (1866–1946) Scottish novelist. She was born in Perthshire, the daughter of a Free Church minister. She wrote works of her own and also collaborated with her sister (*see below*).

The Green Graves of Balgowrie
Hallijohn, Dr Cornelius
Marjorybanks, Henrietta
Marjorybanks, Lucie
Marjorybanks, Mrs

Findlater, Jane (*see above*) and Findlater, Mary

◎ (1865–1963) Scottish novelist. She wrote several novels of her own, including *Betty Musgrave* (1899) and *The Rose of Joy* (1903), a volume of *Songs and Sonnets* (1895), and collaborated with her sister Jane Findlater on the novel *Crossriggs* (1908).

Crossriggs
Hope, Alexandra (Alex)

Firbank, Ronald

◎ (1886–1926) English novelist. He travelled extensively in Spain, Italy, the Middle East and North Africa

and was exotic and eccentric. His novels (written on piles of blue postcards) are slight, but witty and innovative, anticipating **Evelyn Waugh**, **Anthony Powell** and Ivy Compton-Burnett.

Prancing Nigger
Mouths, the

Valmouth
Yajnavalkja, Mrs

Fitzgerald, F(rancis) Scott

◎ (1896–1940) US novelist. He captured the spirit of the 1920s ('The Jazz Age'), especially in *The Great Gatsby* (1925), his best-known book. Much of his fiction revealed both a fascination with the rich and a moral dismay at the aridity of their lives. He led the strenuous life of a playboy in Europe and the USA, exhausting both his financial and emotional resources.

The Great Gatsby
Buchanan, Daisy
Buchanan, Tom
Carraway, Nick
Gatsby, Jay
Wilson, Myrtle

The Pat Hobby Stories
Hobby, Pat

Tender is the Night
Barban, Tommy
Diver, Dick
Diver, Nicole
Hoyt, Rosemary
North, Abe

This Side of Paradise
Blaine, Amory

Fitzgerald, Penelope

◎ (1916–2000) English novelist and biographer. She was almost 60 when her first novel was published. She won the 1979 Booker Prize for *Offshore* and several of her other books were shortlisted at different times.

The Bookshop
Green, Florence

The Gate of Angels
Fairly, Fred
Saunders, Daisy

Offshore
Blake, Laura
Blake, Richard
Maurice
Nenna

Fitzgerald, R(obert) D(avid)

◎ (1902–87) Australian poet. He worked for many years as a surveyor, and his years spent in Fiji have influenced much of his poetry. His work is concerned with topics such as Australian history and humanitarian issues, usually interspersed with philosophical meditations on art, time and the nature of existence.

Between Two Tides
Finau, Tongan Chief
Mariner, Will

Heemskerck Shoals
Tasman, Abel

'The Wind at Your Door'
Fitzgerald, Morris
Mason, Martin

Fitzgerald, Zelda

◎ (1900–48) US journalist, short-story writer and novelist. Renowned for her rebellion against convention, she married **F Scott Fitzgerald** in 1918. She wrote 'Girl' sketches and the autobiographical novel *Save me the Waltz* (1932). The Fitzgeralds led a strenuous social life which exacerbated Zelda's mental illness.

Save me the Waltz
Beggs, Alabama

Fleming, Ian

◎ (1908–64) English novelist. He worked as a foreign correspondent, as a banker and stockbroker and as a senior naval intelligence officer during World War II. This varied career gave him the background for a series of twelve novels and seven short stories featuring Commander James Bond, the archetypal, suave British Secret Service agent.

Casino Royale
Bond, James, also known as '007'
M

From Russia With Love
Klebb, Rosa

Goldfinger
Galore, Pussy
Goldfinger, Auric
Leiter, Felix
Oddjob

Thunderball
Blofeld, Ernst

Fletcher, John

◎ (1579–1625) English dramatist. Much of his writing was achieved in collaboration. (*See* **Beaumont, Francis** and **Fletcher, John**, and **Shakespeare, William** and **Fletcher, John** for works and characters.)

Ford, Ford Madox, originally **Ford Hermann Hueffer**

◎ (1873–1939) English novelist, editor and poet. Brought up in Pre-Raphaelite circles, he published his first book when he was only 18. In 1908 he founded *The English Review*, in which he published many major authors of the day, and in 1924, while living in Paris, he was founder-editor of *The Transatlantic Review*. He also wrote almost 80 books.

The Good Soldier
Ashburnham, Edward
Ashburnham, Leonora
Dowell, Florence
Dowell, John
Rufford, Nancy

Parade's End
Duchemin, Edith Ethel
Macmaster, Vincent

Tietjens, Christopher
Tietjens, Sylvia
Wannop, Valentine

Ford, John

◎ (c.1586–c.1640) English
dramatist. He was greatly
influenced by Robert Burton,
whose *Anatomy of Melancholy*
(1621) turned Ford's dramatic gifts
towards stage presentation of the
melancholy, the unnatural and the
horrible in plays such as *'Tis Pity
She's a Whore* (c.1631). He often
collaborated with **Thomas Dekker**,
William Rowley and **John Webster**.

'Tis Pity She's a Whore
Annabella
Giovanni
Soranzo
Vasques

Ford, Richard

◎ (born 1944) US novelist and
short-story writer. His best-known
works are *The Sportswriter* (1986)
and its sequel *Independence Day*
(which in 1996 was the first novel to
win both the Pulitzer Prize and the
PEN/Faulkner Award). He also
writes short stories and has edited
various anthologies.

Independence Day
Bascombe, Frank
The Sportswriter
Bascombe, Frank

Forester, C(ecil) S(cott)

◎ (1899–1966) British writer. He is
best known for his creation of
Horatio Hornblower, a British
naval officer in the Napoleonic era
whose career he chronicled in a
series of popular novels. His novel
The African Queen (1935) was
successfully filmed in 1951. He also
wrote biographical and travel
books.

The African Queen
Allnut, Charlie
Sayer, Rose
The Happy Return
Hornblower, Horatio

Forster, E(dward) M(organ)

◎ (1879–1970) English novelist and
critic. In his novels he examined
with subtle insight the pre-1914
English middle-class ethos and its
custodians the Civil Service, the
Church and the public schools. He
also wrote short stories, essays,
biographies, and collaborated on
the libretto of Benjamin Britten's
opera, *Billy Budd* (1951).

Howards End
Bast, Leonard
Schlegel, Helen
Schlegel, Margaret
Wilcox, Henry
The Longest Journey
Ansell, Stewart
Elliot, Rickie
Failing, Emily
Pembroke, Agnes
Wonham, Stephen ('Podge')

Maurice
Durham, Clive
Hall, Maurice Christopher
Scudder, Alec
A Passage to India
Amritrao
Aziz, Dr
Fielding, Cyril
Godbole, Professor Narayan
Heaslop, Ronny
Moore, Mrs
Quested, Adela
Turton, Mr
A Room With a View
Bartlett, Charlotte
Beebe, Arthur
Emerson, George
Emerson, Mr
Honeychurch, Lucy
Lavish, Eleanor
Vyse, Cecil
Where Angels Fear to Tread
Abbot, Caroline
Carella, Gino
Herriton, Harriet
Herriton, Lilia, née Theobald
Herriton, Philip

Forsyth, Frederick

◎ (born 1938) English writer. He
served in the RAF and later became
a journalist. His reputation rests
on taut suspense thrillers such as
The Day of the Jackal (1971, filmed
1973), meticulously researched and
precisely plotted.

The Day of the Jackal
Jackal, the

Fowles, John

◎ (born 1926) English novelist. An
allusive and richly descriptive
writer, he wrote his first novel *The
Collector*, still perhaps his most
sensational, in 1963.

The Collector
Collector, the
Daniel Martin
Martin, Daniel
The French Lieutenant's Woman
Smithson, Charles
Woodruff, Sarah
The Magus
Conchis, Maurice
D'Urfe, Nicholas
'Girl, the'

Frame, Janet

◎ (1924–2004) New Zealand
novelist and short-story writer. She
spent much time in psychiatric
hospitals after severe mental
breakdowns, and her novels describe
an existence in which the looming
threat of disorder both attracts and
frightens. She was applauded in her
homeland, but only belatedly
received international recognition.

Daughter Buffalo
Edelman, Dr Talbot
Turnlung
The Edge of the Alphabet
Withers, Toby
Intensive Care
Galbraith, Milly
Monk, Colin

Sandy
Owls Do Cry
Chicks
Daphne
Scented Gardens for the Blind
Glace, Ed
A State of Siege
Signal, Malfred

Franklin, Benjamin, pseudonym
Richard Saunders

◎ (1706–90) US statesman,
diplomat, printer, publisher,
inventor and scientist. His many
inventions include bifocal glasses,
and he was an important diplomat
and founding father. He
commenced the publication of
Poor Richard's Almanack in 1733; it
became popular for its witty
aphorisms and attained an
unprecedented circulation. It was
continued by others after 1748.

Poor Richard's Almanack
Saunders, Bridget
Saunders, Richard

**Franklin, (Stella Marian Sarah)
Miles**, also wrote as **Brent of Bin**

◎ (1879–1954) Australian novelist.
She was extremely active in the
feminist movement, and worked
both in the USA and England. Her
work includes autobiographical
novels and a series of pastoral
romances. The Miles Franklin
awards are among Australia's most
prestigious literary prizes.

All That Swagger
Delacy, Danny
Cockatoos
Milford, Ignez
Gentlemen of Gyang Gyang
Gaylord, Bernice
My Brilliant Career
Beecham, Harold
Melvyn, Sybylla Penelope
My Career Goes Bung
Melvyn, Sybylla Penelope

Franzen, Jonathan

◎ (born 1959) US novelist and
essayist. He was a Fulbright
scholar in Berlin and worked for a
time in a seismology lab at Harvard
University. He won the National
Book Award for *The Corrections* in
2001.

The Corrections
Lambert Family, the

Fraser, George McDonald

◎ (born 1925) Scottish historical
novelist. Trained as a journalist, he
was deputy editor of *The Glasgow
Herald* (1968–9), but following the
success of his first novel *Flashman*
(1969) he left to become a full-time
writer.

Flashman
Flashman, Sir Harry

Frayn, Michael

◎ (born 1933) English dramatist,
novelist and translator. A journalist

by training, he has published a number of comic novels about the newspaper business. *Headlong* (1999) was shortlisted for the Booker Prize for Fiction and his novel *Spies* (2002) won the 2002 Whitbread Novel Award. He is married to the biographer Claire Tomalin.

Copenhagen
Bohr, Niels
Heisenberg, Werner

Democracy
Brandt, Willy
Guillaume, Gunter

Headlong
Clay, Martin

A Landing on the Sun
Jessel, Brian

Noises Off
Dallas, Lloyd

Spies
Wheatley, Stephen

Towards the End of the Morning
Dyson, John

Frazier, Charles

◎ (born 1950) US novelist. He was a university literature professor before retiring to his ranch to concentrate on writing. His first novel, *Cold Mountain*, a Civil War romance based on the life of one of his ancestors, was a bestseller, won the National Book Award.

Cold Mountain
Inman
Monroe, Ada

Frederic, Harold

◎ (1856–98) US novelist. After a poverty-stricken youth, he became a journalist and was European correspondent of *The New York Times*. He wrote several novels depicting his own background, but his best work is *The Damnation of Theron Ware* (1896), about the intellectual awakening of a young minister.

The Copperhead
Beach, Abner

The Damnation of Theron Ware
Ware, Theron

Freeling, Nicolas

◎ (1927–2003) English novelist. He is best known for his series of novels featuring the Dutch detective Van Der Valk.

Love in Amsterdam
Van Der Valk, Piet

French, Marilyn

◎ (born 1929) US novelist and essayist. She is famous for her feminist novels. The most famous is *The Women's Room* (1977) – a grim indictment of suburban married life.

Her Mother's Daughter
Dabrowski, Anastasia, or Stacey Stevens

The Women's Room
Ward, Mira

Friel, Brian

◎ (born 1929) Northern Irish playwright and short-story writer. His first major success was the play *Philadelphia, Here I Come!* (1965). His work often concentrates on the relation between people, language, custom and the land.

Dancing at Lughnasa
Mundy Family, the

Philadelphia, Here I Come!
Lizzie, Aunt
O'Donnell, Gar

Translations
Yolland, Lt George

Friel, George

◎ (1910–75) Scottish novelist. His teaching experiences are at the heart of his popular novel *Mr Alfred M.A.* (1972), which describes the disillusionment and downfall of a teacher betrayed by one of his female pupils.

Mr Alfred M.A.
Alfred, Mr

Frost, Robert

◎ (1874–1963) US lyric poet. From 1912 to 1915 he lived in Great Britain, where, encouraged by the poet Rupert Brooke and others, he published his first works. Returning to the USA, he became Professor of English at Amherst (1916), and continued to write lyric and narrative poetry which draws its characters, background and imagery from New England.

The Death of the Hired Man
Mary
Silas
Warren

The Star-Splitter
McLaughlin, Brad

Fugard, Athol

◎ (born 1932) South African dramatist and theatre director. His plays are mostly set in contemporary South Africa, but have universal resonance. His work has met with official opposition and some of his work has only been published and produced abroad.

The Blood Knot
Morrie (Morris)
Zach (Zachariah)

Boesman and Lena
Boesman
Lena

Hello and Goodbye
Smit, Hester
Smit, Johnie

A Lesson from Aloes
Bezuidenhout, Gladys
Bezuidenhout, Piet
Daniels, Steve

Sizwe Bansi is Dead
Bansi, Sizwe

Tsotsi
Tsotsi

Furphy, Joseph, pseudonym Tom Collins

◎ (1843–1912) Australian writer. From 1883 he worked in an iron foundry in Victoria, and contributed, under the name 'Tom Collins', a series of articles about rural Australian life to *The Bulletin* magazine. He also wrote a 1,220-page manuscript, *Such is Life: Being Certain Extracts from the Diary of Tom Collins*, which was eventually published in 1903.

Such is Life: Being Certain Extracts from the Diary of Tom Collins
Collins, Tom

G

Gaddis, William

◎ (1922–98) US novelist. His works include *The Recognitions* (1955), an epic about art, forgery, money and magic. An ambitious satirist, he was one of the USA's most prominent contemporary novelists. He won the National Book Award in 1976 and 1994.

Carpenter's Gothic
Booth, Liz (Elizabeth)
Booth, Paul
McCandless, Mr

JR
Bast, Edward
JR

The Recognitions
Anselm
Brown, Recktall
Deigh, Agnes
Esme
Gwyon, Wyatt, also known as Stephen
Otto (Otto Pivner)
Pivner, Mr
Sinisterra, Mr Frank
Stanley
Valentine, Basil

Gallico, Paul

◎ (1897–1976) US writer. During the 1920s and 30s he was one of most well-known sportswriters in America. In 1936, he moved to Europe to concentrate on fiction. *The Snow Goose* (1941) was an international bestseller.

Flowers for Mrs Harris
Harris, Mrs Ada

The Snow Goose
Fritha
Rhayader, Philip

Galsworthy, John

◎ (1867–1933) English novelist and playwright. In 1906 he published the first in his celebrated 'Forsyte Saga' series. Also a prolific playwright, he produced more than 30 plays for the London stage. He won the Nobel prize for literature in 1932.

The End of the Chapter
Cherrell, Adrian
Cherrell, Dinny (Elizabeth)
Cherrell, Hubert
Cherrell, Rev Cuthbert

The Forstye Saga
Bosinney, Philip
Dartie, Montague
Dartie, Winifred
Forsyte, 'Aunt Ann'
Forsyte, Fleur
Forsyte, Holly
Forsyte, Irene
Forsyte, James
Forsyte, Jolyon ('Jolly')
Forsyte, Jolyon ('Jon')
Forsyte, Jolyon ('Old Jolyon')
Forsyte, Jolyon ('Young Jolyon')
Forsyte, Soames
Forsyte, Swithin
Forsyte, Timothy
Lamotte, Annette
Mont, Michael

A Modern Comedy
Dartie, Imogen, later Imogen Cardigan
Dartie, Montague
Dartie, Val, properly Publius Valerius
Dartie, Winifred
Forsyte, Fleur
Forsyte, Holly
Forsyte, Irene
Forsyte, Jolyon ('Jolly')
Forsyte, Jolyon ('Jon')
Forsyte, Jolyon ('Young Jolyon')
Forsyte, Soames
Forsyte, Timothy
Lamotte, Annette
Mont, Michael

On Forsyte Change
Dartie, Montague
Dartie, Winifred
Forsyte, Holly
Forsyte, Irene
Forsyte, James
Forsyte, Jolyon ('Jolly')
Forsyte, Jolyon ('Old Jolyon')
Forsyte, Jolyon ('Young Jolyon')
Forsyte, Swithin
Forsyte, Timothy
Forsyte, 'Aunt Ann'

Galt, John

◎ (1779–1839) Scottish novelist. From 1809 to 1811 he travelled in the Levant, where he met **Byron** and he later started to write for *Blackwood's Magazine*. *Annals of the Parish* (1821) is his masterpiece, and its description of events in the life of a parish minister throws interesting light on contemporary social history. In 1826 he went to Canada, where he founded the town of Guelph. He returned to England penniless in 1829.

Annals of the Parish
Balwhidder, Rev Mr

The Ayrshire Legatees
Pringle, Dr

The Entail, or The Lairds of Gripp
Walkinshaw, Claude

The Member
Jobbry, Archibald

The Provost
Pawkie, Provost

Ringan Gilhaize, or The Covenanters
Gilhaize, Ringan

Gardner, Erle Stanley

◎ (1889–1970) US crime novelist. He was a successful defence lawyer and a hugely prolific writer. His best-known creation is the lawyer-sleuth Perry Mason, hero of 82 courtroom dramas.

The Case of the Velvet Claws
Drake, Paul
Mason, Perry
Street, Della

Garfield, Leon

◎ (1921–96) English children's author. His historical novels of high adventure, piracy and highwaymen owe not a little to **Robert Louis Stevenson**. He won various awards including the Carnegie Medal.

Black Jack
Belle
Black Jack
Carmody, Dr
Hatch
Tolly, properly Bartholomew Dorking

Devil-in-a-Fog
Dexter, Captain Richard
Dexter, Lady
Dexter, Sir John
Treet, George
Treet, Thomas

Jack Holborn
Holborn, Jack
Morris, Mr
Rogers, Captain
Sheringham, Lord
Trumpet, Solomon

Smith
Billing, Mr
Mansfield, Mr
Mansfield, Rose
Smith
Tom, Lord

Garland, Hamlin

◎ (1860–1940) US novelist and short-story writer. He vividly, and often grimly, described the farming life of the Midwest in short stories such as those in the collection *Main-Travelled Roads* (1887), as well as in verse and in novels.

'Among the Corn-Rows'
Rodemaker, Rob

'A Branch-Road'
Hannan, Will

'Mrs Ripley's Trip'
Ripley, Gran'ma

Rose of Dutcher's Coolley
Dutcher, Rose

'Under the Lion's Paw'
Haskins, Timothy

'Up the Coule'
McLane, Howard

Garner, Alan

◎ (born 1934) English novelist. He is fascinated by history and archaeology and many of his works, such as the classic *The Owl Service* (1967) and *Red Shift* (1973), combine myth with modern settings. Although he has written widely for children, he has also published novels for adults.

Elidor
Helen
Malebron
Nicholas and David
Roland

The Owl Service
Alison
Gwyn
Huw 'Halfbacon'
Roger

Red Shift
Jan
Macey
Thomas, properly Thomas Rowley
Tom

Garner, Helen

◎ (born 1942) Australian novelist, short-story writer, translator and screenplay writer. She worked as a teacher and then journalist until the success of her first novel *Monkey Grip* (1977, filmed 1981). In 1995, *The First Stone*, her non-fiction study of a sexual harassment case at the University of Melbourne provoked some controversy.

Monkey Grip
Javo
Nora

Gaskell, Elizabeth

◎ (1810–65) English novelist and biographer. In 1832 she married William Gaskell (1805–84), a Unitarian minister in Manchester. There she studied working men and women, and made important contributions to what came to be known as the 'Condition of England' novel. She was friends with **Dickens** and **Charlotte Brontë**, whose biography she wrote.

Cousin Phillis
Holdsworth, Phillis

Cranford
Jenkyns, Matty (Matilda)

Mary Barton
Barton, John
Barton, Mary
Carson, Henry
Wilson, Jem

North and South
Hale, Margaret
Thornton, Mr

Ruth
Bellingham, Henry
Benson, Miss
Benson, Thurston
Bradshaw, Mr
Hilton, Ruth
Sally

Sylvia's Lovers
Hepburn, Philip
Kinraid, Charley
Robson, Daniel
Robson, Sylvia

Wives and Daughters
Gibson, Molly
Gibson, Mr

Kirkpatrick, Cynthia
Kirkpatrick, Mrs
Kirkpatrick, Osborne
Kirkpatrick, Roger

Gay, John
◎ (1685–1732) English poet. In 1727 he produced the first series of his popular *Fables*. His greatest success was *The Beggar's Opera* (1728), set to music by Johann Pepusch, the outcome of a suggestion made by **Jonathan Swift** in 1716. Running for 62 performances, it attained unprecedented popularity.

The Beggar's Opera
Lockit, Lucy
Lockit, the Jailer
MacHeath, Captain
Peachum, Polly
Peachum, Thomas
Twitcher, Jemmy

The Shepherd's Week
Blouzelinda
Bowzybeus
Cloddipole
Grubbinole

Gibbon, Lewis Grassic,
pseudonym of **James Leslie Mitchell**
◎ (1901–35) Scottish novelist. *Sunset Song* (1932), his greatest achievement, was the first in a trilogy of novels. He collaborated with the poet Hugh MacDiarmid and made an important contribution to the Scottish renaissance. He also wrote a biography of the Scottish explorer, Mungo Park (1934).

Cloud Howe
Colquhoun, Robert
Guthrie, Chris
Ogilvie, Ake
Tavendale, Ewan (son)

Grey Granite
Guthrie, Chris
Ogilvie, Ake
Tavendale, Ewan (son)

Sunset Song
Colquhoun, Robert
Guthrie, Chris
Long Rob Duncan
Strachan, Chae
Tavendale, Ewan (father)
Tavendale, Ewan (son)

Gibbons, Stella
◎ (1902–89) English writer. She worked as a journalist and later began a series of successful novels. She also wrote poetry and short stories, but her reputation rests on *Cold Comfort Farm* (1933), a light-hearted satire on melodramatic rural novels. It has established itself as a classic of parody.

Cold Comfort Farm
Poste, Flora
Starkadders, the

Gissing, George
◎ (1857–1903) English novelist. A classical scholar, he was a prolific

author who usually wrote of poverty and failure. As well as fiction, he also wrote a notable critical biography of **Dickens** (1898) and a travel book, *By the Ionian Sea* (1900).

Born in Exile
Peak, Godwin

In the Year of Jubilee
Lord, Nancy
Tarrant, Lionel

New Grub Street
Biffen, Harold
Milvain, Jasper
Reardon, Amy
Reardon, Edwin
Yule, Alfred
Yule, Marian

The Odd Women
Barfoot, Everard
Nunn, Rhoda

The Private Papers of Henry Ryecroft
Ryecroft, Henry

The Whirlpool
Dymes, Felix
Frothingham, Alma

Glasgow, Ellen
◎ (1874–1945) US novelist, essayist and short-story writer. Born in Richmond, Virginia, she spent most of her life there apart from various trips to Europe from 1896. She was best known for her stories of the South.

Barren Ground
Oakley, Dorinda

The Sheltered Life
Archbald, Jenny Blair
Birdsong, Eva
Birdsong, George

They Stooped to Folly
Littlepage, Virginius Curle

Vein of Iron
Fincastle, Ada

Virginia
Pendleton, Virginia

Godwin, William
◎ (1756–1836) English political writer and novelist. His masterpiece, *Caleb Williams* (1794), was designed to give 'a general review of the modes of domestic and unrecorded despotism'. His daughter was **Mary Wollstonecraft Shelley**.

Caleb Williams
Falkland
Tyrrel
Williams, Caleb

Golden, Arthur
◎ (born 1957) US author. After university, where he specialized in Japanese art and history, he worked in Tokyo from 1980 to 1982. His first novel, *Memoirs of a Geisha* (1997), is written in the form of an autobiography and achieved worldwide success.

Memoirs of a Geisha
Sakamoto Chiyo/Nitta Sayuri

Golding, William
◎ (1911–93) English novelist who gained international celebrity with *Lord of the Flies* (1954). A chronicle of the increasingly malevolent actions of a group of schoolboys shipwrecked on a desert island in the wake of a nuclear war, Golding said that it arose from his five years' war service, and ten years of teaching small boys. He was awarded the Nobel prize for literature in 1983.

Close Quarters
Colley, Robert James
Talbot, Edmund

Fire Down Below
Colley, Robert James
Talbot, Edmund

Lord of the Flies
Jack
Piggy
Ralph
Simon

Pincher Martin
Pincher Martin

Rites of Passage
Colley, Robert James
Talbot, Edmund

The Spire
Dean Jocelin

Goldsmith, Oliver
◎ (1730–74) Irish playwright, novelist and poet. After a medical education at Trinity College Dublin and Edinburgh, he practised as a physician in Southwark, and was proofreader to **Samuel Richardson**. *The Vicar of Wakefield* (1766) secured his reputation as a novelist, and as well as achieving acclaim for his poetry, he also achieved high regard as a playwright with *She Stoops to Conquer* (1773).

The Citizen of the World
'Tibbs, Beau'
'Man in Black, The'

She Stoops to Conquer
Hardcastle, Dorothy
Hardcastle, Kate
Hardcastle, Squire Richard
Hastings, George
Lumpkin, Tony
Marlow
Neville, Constance

The Vicar of Wakefield
Burchill, Mr, or Sir William Thornhill
Primrose, Dr, and family
Primrose, George
Wilmot, Arabella

Gordimer, Nadine
◎ (born 1923) South African novelist and short-story writer. Apartheid, and her characters' reaction to it, is ever present in her fiction, most powerfully in *The Conservationist* (1974), joint winner of the Booker Prize. She was awarded the Nobel prize for literature in 1991.

Burger's Daughter
Burger, Rosa

The Conservationist
Mehring

A Guest of Honour
Bray, Col James
Mweta, President
Shinza, Edward

July's People
July (Mwawate)
Smales, Bamford
Smales, Maureen

A World of Strangers
Hood, Toby

Gordon, Caroline

◎ (1895–1981) American novelist.
She grew up in the Deep South,
which features prominently in all
her works. Her novels often
depict the contrast between the
genteel civility of the pre-War
agrarian South and post-war
industrialism.

The Malefactors
Claiborne, Thomas

Gordon, Mary

◎ (born 1949) US novelist and
academic. Her novels about
women are often rooted in the
Catholic tradition. She has also
written a memoir of her father, as
well as essays, short stories and
novellas.

Of Men and Angels
Post, Laura

Grafton, Sue

◎ (born 1940) US novelist. Her
bestselling 'Alphabet' murder
mysteries feature the Californian
private detective, Kinsey Milhone
and have won her a loyal following.

A is for Alibi
Milhone, Kinsey

Grahame, Kenneth

◎ (1859–1932) Scottish children's
writer. He was not allowed to go to
university as he had wished, and
spent some years working in the
Bank of England. In 1908 he
published his best-known work,
The Wind in the Willows, originally
written in the form of letters to his
son Alastair. It did not at first win
acclaim, but within a few years of
Grahame's death it had become a
children's classic.

The Wind in the Willows
Badger
Mole
Rat
Toad, of Toad Hall

Granville-Barker, Harley

◎ (1877–1946) English actor,
playwright and producer. In 1904
he became co-manager of the
Court Theatre and there followed
a four-year season that was a
landmark in the history of the
British theatre, setting new
standards of acting and design. His
prefaces to Shakespeare plays (4
vols, 1927–45) are valuable for their

original criticism and ideas on
production.

His Majesty
Henry XIII, King of Carpathia

The Madras House
Madras, Philip

The Marrying of Ann Leete
Leete, Ann

The Secret Life
Strowde, Evan

The Voysey Inheritance
Voysey, Edward

Waste
Trebell, Henry

Graves, Robert

◎ (1895–1985) English poet,
novelist, essayist and critic. He was
Professor of English at Cairo and
Professor of Poetry at Oxford
(1961–66). His best known novels
are *I, Claudius* (1934). His interest
in myth prompted *Greek Myths*
(1955) and *Hebrew Myths* (1963).

Claudius the God
Claudius

I, Claudius
Claudius

Gray, Alasdair

◎ (born 1934) Scottish novelist,
painter and playwright. Painting
was his first vocation and he came
late to novel writing; *Lanark*, his
first novel, was published in 1981
and hailed as a classic.
Unconventional and inventive, it
shows much of his artistic skill. He
has also published volumes of
short stories, poetry, and was
editor of *The Book of Prefaces*
(2000).

The Fall of Kelvin Walker
Walker, Kelvin

Lanark: A Life in Four Books
Lanark/Duncan Thaw
Rima
Sludden

1982, Janine
anon (the security technician)

Poor Things
McCandless, Archibald

Gray, Simon

◎ (born 1936) English dramatist,
director and novelist. He was a
lecturer in English literature at
Queen Mary College, London
(1965–85), and many of his plays
are set in the world of publishers,
or academics who publish. He has
written novels and several
television plays, but is best known
as a stage dramatist.

Butley
Butley, Ben

Hidden Laughter
Chambers, Ronnie
Pertwee, Louise

Otherwise Engaged
Hench, Simon

Quartermaine's Terms
Quartermaine, St John

Green, Henry, pseudonym of Henry Vincent Yorke

◎ (1905–73) English novelist. He
became managing director in his
father's engineering company in
Birmingham, but pursued a
parallel career as a novelist. He is
partial to terse and sophisticated
titles, and is an elliptical and highly
stylized writer.

Concluding
Rock, Mr

Greene, Graham

◎ (1904–91) English writer.
Extremely prolific (he wrote a
great number of novels, stories,
plays and biographies as well as
film criticism), his career as a so-
called Catholic novelist began with
Brighton Rock (1938), a thriller
which asserts that human justice is
inadequate and irrelevant to the
real struggle against evil.

'The Basement Room'
Baines
Baines, Mrs
Lane, Philip

Brighton Rock
Pinkie

A Burnt Out Case
Querry

The Comedians
Brown
Jones, Major
Magiot, Dr
Smith, Mr

The End of the Affair
Bendrix, Maurice
Miles, Sarah

England Made Me
Farrant, Anthony
Farrant, Kate
Krogh, Erik
Minty

A Gun for Sale
Raven, James

The Heart of the Matter
Scobie

The Honorary Consul
Fortnum, Charley
Plarr, Dr Edouardo

The Human Factor
Castle, Maurice

'May We Borrow Your Husband?'
Travis, Poopy

Monsignor Quixote
Quixote, Monsignor

Our Man in Havana
Wormold, James

The Power and the Glory
Lieutenant, the
Whisky Priest, the

The Quiet American
Pyle, Alden

The Tenth Man
Chavel, Jean-Louis

Travels With My Aunt
Bertram, Augusta
Pulling, Henry

Greene, Robert

◎ (1558–92) English dramatist. He
wrote plays and romances. The

latter are often tedious and insipid, but they abound in beautiful poetry. The most popular of his plays was *Friar Bacon and Friar Bungay* (1587–9). Greene helped to lay the foundations of English drama, and even his worst plays are valuable historically.

Friar Bacon and Friar Bungay
Friar Bacon
Friar Bungay

Griffiths, Trevor

◎ (born 1935) English dramatist. His works are often angry political pieces, such as *The Party* (1974), which revolves around a discussion of left-wing politics, and which saw Laurence Olivier in his last stage role, playing an eloquent Glaswegian Trotskyist.

Comedians
Price, Gethin
Waters, Eddie
The Party
Tagg, John

Grossmith, George and Grossmith, Weedon

◎ (1847–1912 and 1854–1919) English writers. The brothers are best remembered for their collaboration on *The Diary of a Nobody*, serialized first in *Punch* and published in book form in 1892.

The Diary of a Nobody
Pooter, Charles

Gunn, Neil

◎ (1891–1973) Scottish novelist. At his best when describing the ordinary life and background of a Highland fishing or crofting community, he wrote a number of short stories and novels with Scottish settings.

Butcher's Broom
Angus
Colin
Dark Mairi
Davie
Elder, Mr
Elie
Heller, Mr
Rob
Seonaid
Highland River
Kenn
Morning Tide
Hugh
The Silver Darlings
Catrine
Finn
Tormad
Young Art and Old Hector
Art, Young
Donul
Hector, Old

Haddon, Mark

◎ (born 1962) English novelist, illustrator, dramatist and screenplay writer. He has had a varied career, including some time spent working with young adults with autism. *The Curious Incident of the Dog in the Night-Time* (2003) won the 2004 Whitbread Book of the Year Award.

The Curious Incident of the Dog in the Night-Time
Boone, Christopher

Hall, Radclyffe

◎ (1880–1943) English writer. She began as a lyric poet but turned to novel writing. *The Well of Loneliness* (1928), which deals openly with lesbianism, was prosecuted for obscenity, and was banned in Great Britain for many years.

The Well of Loneliness
Gordon, Stephen

Hall, Willis

◎ (born 1929) English dramatist. His first stage success was *The Long and the Short and the Tall* (1958), dealing with the members of a British military patrol lost in the Malayan jungle in 1942. He has since collaborated extensively with **Keith Waterhouse**.

The Long and the Short and the Tall
Bamforth
Mitchem
Whitaker

Halliwell, David

◎ (born 1936) English dramatist. His most successful work, *Little Malcolm and His Struggle Against the Eunuchs* was first performed in 1965, directed by Mike Leigh and with Halliwell in the title role. He has written many radio plays.

Little Malcolm and his Struggle against the Eunuchs
Malcolm

Hammett, Dashiell

◎ (1894–1961) US crime writer. He joined the Pinkerton Detective Agency in New York as an operator. He wrote stories for magazines and became the first US author of authentic 'private eye' crime novels. Original, unsentimental and an acute social observer, he was a prolific writer and many of his novels were filmed, notably *The Maltese Falcon*. He was a longtime companion of **Lillian Hellman**.

The Glass Key
Beaumont, Ned

The Maltese Falcon
Spade, Sam
Red Harvest
Continental Op
The Thin Man
Charles, Nick

Hampton, Christopher

◎ (born 1946) English dramatist. He was the first resident dramatist at the Royal Court Theatre, London. His most commercially successful work has been *Les Liaisons Dangereuses* (1985), a penetrating study of sexual manners, morality and responsibility, adapted from the novel by Pierre Choderlos de Laclos.

Les Liaisons dangereuses
Valmont, Le Vicomte de
The Philanthropist
Philip
Tales from Hollywood
Horvath, Odon von
White Chameleon
Chris; Christopher; Christopher's Father

Hanrahan, Barbara

◎ (1939–91) Australian artist, novelist and short-story writer. A renowned artist, her paintings and prints have been exhibited throughout Australia and Europe. She wrote 15 novels, some autobiographical, some historical and many featuring the use of a child's perspective. They are noted for their blending of fantasy, myth and realism.

The Peach Groves
Dean, Blanche
Dean, Ida
Dean, Maude
Jones, 'Major' Harry
Maufe, Augustus
Maufe, Oc (Octavius)
Maufe, Zilla
Wimperis, Tempe

Hardy, Thomas

◎ (1840–1928) English novelist, poet and dramatist. Although trained as an architect, he wrote fiction from the start of his career. His fourth published novel *Far from the Madding Crowd* (1874) was a huge success. A flood of novels continued to appear until 1895, with vibrant, brooding descriptive passages providing the backdrop to potent tragicomedies. Thereafter, Hardy turned his attention to poetry and produced several volumes of lyrics, many of which express his love of rural life.

'Barbara of the House of Grebe'
Grebe, Barbara
Uplandtowers, Earl of
Willowes, Edmund
Desperate Remedies
Aldclyffe, Miss Cytherea
Graye, Cytherea
Manston, Aeneas
Springrove, Edward

Index

'The Distracted Preacher'
Newberry, Lizzy
Stockdale, Richard

Far from the Madding Crowd
Boldwood, William
Everdene, Bathsheba
Oak, Gabriel
Robin, Fanny
Troy, Sgt Francis

'The Fiddler of the Reels'
Ollamoor, Wat ('Mop')

The Hand of Ethelberta
Chickerel, Ethelberta

'An Imaginative Woman'
Marchmill, Ella
Trewe, Robert

Jude the Obscure
Bridehead, Sue (Susannah)
Donn, Arabella
Father Time
Fawley, Jude
Phillotson, Richard

A Laodicean
Power, Paula

The Mayor of Casterbridge
Farfrae, Donald
Henchard, Michael
Newson, Elizabeth-Jane
Le Sueur, Lucetta

A Pair of Blue Eyes
Knight, Henry
Smith, Stephen
Swancourt, Elfride

The Return of the Native
Venn, Diggory
Vye, Eustacia
Wildeve, Damon
Yeobright, Clym (Clement)
Yeobright, Mrs
Yeobright, Thomasin ('Tamsin')

Tess of the D'Urbervilles
Clare, Angel
D'Urberville, Alec
Durbeyfield, Tess

The Trumpet Major
Derriman, Festus
Garland, Anne
Loveday, Bob (Robert)
Loveday, John

Two on a Tower
Constantine, Lady Viviette
St Cleeve, Swithin

Under the Greenwood Tree
Day, Fancy
Day, Geoffrey
Dewy, Dick (Richard)
Dewy, Reuben
Maybold

The Well-Beloved
Caro, Avice
Pierston, Jocelyn

'The Withered Arm'
Brook, Rhoda

The Woodlanders
Charmond, Felice
Fitzpiers, Edred
Melbury, George
Melbury, Grace
South, Marty
Winterborne, Giles

Hare, David

Ⓒ (born 1947) English dramatist, director and filmmaker. He was resident dramatist and literary manager of the Royal Court Theatre in London (1969–71), and at Nottingham Playhouse in 1973, before becoming associate director of the National Theatre, London (1984). The best of his early works is *Teeth 'n' Smiles* (1975), a commentary on the state of modern Britain.

The Absence of War
Jones, George

Amy's View
Allen, Esme
Thomas, Amy
Tyghe, Dominic

Knuckle
Delafield, Curly

A Map of the World
Mehta, Victor

Murmuring Judges
Platt, Irina

My Zinc Bed
Quinn, Victor

Plenty
Traherne, Susan

Racing Demon
Espy, Rev Lionel
Ferris, Rev Tony
Henderson, Rev Harry

The Secret Rapture
French, Marion
Glass, Isobel

Skylight
Hollis, Kyra
Sergeant, Tom

Teeth 'n' Smiles
Frisby, Maggie

Harris, Joel Chandler

Ⓒ (1848–1908) US writer. Having absorbed much Georgia black folklore and many sayings and stories, he began to publish his 'Uncle Remus' tales in the Atlanta *Constitution*. His eight volumes of *Uncle Remus*, in which he collected 184 African-American folk tales, made him internationally famous, both to children and to students of folklore.

Uncle Remus
Brer Fox
Brer Rabbit
Remus, Uncle

Harris, Thomas

Ⓒ (born 1940) US writer. He spent time travelling through Europe before working as a reporter for the Associated Press in New York and later becoming a full-time writer. He is known for the detail and research which go into each novel.

Hannibal
Lecter, Dr Hannibal

Red Dragon
Lecter, Dr Hannibal

The Silence of the Lambs
Lecter, Dr Hannibal
Starling, Clarice

Harris, Wilson

Ⓒ (born 1921) Guyana-born English novelist. His masterpiece is *The Guyana Quartet*: *Palace of the Peacock* (1960), *The Far Journey of Oudin* (1961), *The Whole Armour* (1962) and *The Secret Ladder* (1963), which begins with a complex poetic exploration, and evolves into a composite picture of the various landscapes and racial communities of Guyana.

The Angel at the Gate
Holiday, Mary/Stella

Carnival
Masters, Everyman

Da Silva da Silva's Cultivated Wilderness
da Silva, Da Silva

The Far Journey of Oudin
Beti
Oudin

The Four Banks of the River of Space
Anselm

Heartland
Stevenson, Zechariah

The Infinite Rehearsal
Glass, Robin Redbreast

Palace of the Peacock
Carroll
Donne
Dreamer, the
Mariella
Wishrop

The Secret Ladder
Fenwick, Russell

The Tree of the Sun
Cortez, Francis
Cortez, Julia
Jen (Jen da Silva)

Tumatumari
Prudence

The Waiting Room
Forrestal, Susan

The Whole Armour
Cristo
Magda
Perez, Catalena
Poseidon

Harrower, Elizabeth

Ⓒ (born 1928) Australian novelist. She lived in Britain from 1951 to 1959. She returned to Australian and has worked in broadcasting and publishing and as a reviewer for the *Sydney Morning Herald*. She has written four intense psychological novels about the condition of women.

The Catherine Wheel
James, Clemency
Roland, Christian

Down in the City
Peterson, Stan
Prescott, Esther

The Long Prospect
Lawrence, Emily

The Watch Tower
Shaw, Felix
Shaw, Laura, née Vaizey
Vaizey, Clare

Harte, Bret

Ⓒ (1836–1902) US short-story writer, novelist and poet. He was secretary of the US Mint, then became US consul in Germany and later in Glasgow and spent the rest of his life in London. He established and edited various journals to which he and other writers contributed, including his friend **Mark Twain**.

'The Luck of Roaring Camp'
Luck, Tommy

'The Outcasts of Poker Flat'
Oakhurst, John

Hartley, L(eslie) P(oles)
◎ (1895–1972) English novelist and short-story writer. His early short stories established his reputation as a master of the macabre. Later he transferred his Jamesian power of 'turning the screw' to psychological relationships and made a new success with such novels as *The Shrimp and the Anemone* (1944). His best-known novel is *The Go-Between* (1953), a masterly portrayal of Edwardian England.

Eustace and Hilda
Cherrington, Eustace
Cherrington, Hilda

The Go-Between
Burgess, Ted
Colston, Leo
Maudsley, Marcus
Maudsley, Marion
Maudsley, Mrs
Trimingham, Lord

The Hireling
Franklin, Lady
Leadbitter

The Shrimp and the Anemone
Cherrington, Eustace
Cherrington, Hilda

The Sixth Heaven
Cherrington, Eustace
Cherrington, Hilda

Hawthorne, Nathaniel
◎ (1804–64) US novelist and short-story writer. He was a descendant of one of the first Puritan settlers and this influenced his classics such as *The Scarlet Letter* (1850) and *The House of the Seven Gables* (1851). He wrote prolifically for years but was only belatedly recognized in his own country (although hugely admired by **Herman Melville**).

'The Artist of the Beautiful'
Warland, Owen

'The Birthmark'
Aminadab
Aylmer

The Blithedale Romance
Coverdale, Miles
Hollingsworth
Priscilla (Priscilla Moody)
Westervelt, Dr
Zenobia (Zenobia Moody)

'The Celestial Railroad'
Smooth-It-Away, Mr

'Dr. Heidegger's Experiment'
Gascoigne, Mr
Heidegger, Dr
Killigrew, Col
Medbourne, Mr
Wycherley, Widow (Clara)

'Endicott and the Red Cross'
Endicott, John

'Ethan Brand'
Brand, Ethan

Fanshawe
Fanshawe

'The Grey Champion'
Goffe, William

The House of the Seven Gables
Holgrave
Maule, Matthew
Pyncheon, Clifford
Pyncheon, Col
Pyncheon, Hepzibah
Pyncheon, Jaffrey
Pyncheon, Phoebe

'Howe's Masquerade'
Howe, Sir William

'Lady Eleanore's Mantle'
Rochcliffe, Lady Eleanore

The Marble Faun
Donatello, Count of Monte Beni
Hilda
Kenyon
Miriam

'The Maypole of Merry Mount'
Endicott, John

'The Minister's Black Veil'
Hooper, Rev Mr

'Mr. Higginbotham's Catastrophe'
Higginbotham, Mr
Pike, Dominicus

'Rappaccini's Daughter'
Guasconti, Giovanni
Rappaccini, Beatrice
Rappaccini, Dr Giacomo

'Roger Malvin's Burial'
Bourne, Reuben
Malvin, Roger

The Scarlet Letter
Chillingworth, Roger
Dimmesdale, Arthur
Pearl (Pearl Prynne)
Prynne, Hester

'Young Goodman Brown'
Brown, Goodman

Hay, John MacDougall
◎ (1880–1919) Scottish novelist. After the publication of his first novel, the brooding *Gillespie* in 1914, Hay considered leaving the ministry to take up a career in writing, but, a victim of poor health, he remained a parish minister until his death aged 39. His son George Campbell Hay (1915–84) was an acclaimed Gaelic poet.

Gillespie
Strang, Gillespie

Hazzard, Shirley
◎ (born 1931) Australian-born US novelist. She spent a decade working for the United Nations and resigned to take up writing full time. Her second novel, *People in Glass Houses* (1967), satirized the UN, and she later published a factual exposé of that organization. Many of her short stories have appeared in *The New Yorker*.

The Bay of Noon
Gianni

Gioconda
Jenny

The Evening of the Holiday
Sophie
Tancredi

People in Glass Houses
Mervyn

Head, Bessie
◎ (1937–86) South African novelist and short-story writer. The consequences of her mixed parentage under apartheid greatly influenced her work. She was concerned with creating an indigenous voice which is also hospitable to European influences. She also wrote essays, sketches and social history.

A Question of Power
Elizabeth
Molomo, Dan
Sello
Tom

Maru
Cadmore, Margaret, Jr
Maru

Heaney, Seamus
◎ (born 1939) Northern Irish poet. An Ulster Catholic, he was so disturbed by the violence in the North that he moved to the Republic in 1972. Redolent of the rural Ireland in which he grew up, his work seems nurtured by the landscape – lush, peaty and, to an extent, menacing. One of the greatest modern poets writing in English, he is regarded as a worthy successor to **W B Yeats**. He was awarded the Nobel prize for literature in 1995.

Sweeney Astray
Sweeney

Hecht, Ben and **MacArthur, Charles**
◎ (1894–1964 and 1895–1956) US writers. Both worked as journalists and are best known for their collaboration on *The Front Page*, a fast-paced comedy about the moral ambiguities of the newspaper business.

The Front Page
Johnson, Hildy

Heller, Joseph
◎ (1923–99) US novelist. He served in the US air force in World War II and drew on the experience for his black comedy, *Catch-22* (1961). After selling slowly for some years it became an international bestseller and a byword for war's absurdity.

Catch-22
Doc Daneeka
Minderbinder, Milo
Yossarian, John

God Knows
David, King

Something Happened
Slocum, Bob

Heller, Zoë

◎ (born 1965) English columnist and novelist. Her novel *What Was She Thinking?: Notes on a Scandal* (2003), was shortlisted for the Booker Prize.

Everything You Know
Muller, Willy

What Was She Thinking?: Notes on a Scandal
Covett, Barbara
Hart, Sheba

Hellman, Lillian

◎ (1907–84) US playwright. Her first stage success, *The Children's Hour* (1934), ran on Broadway for 86 weeks. A left-wing activist, and sensitive to social injustice and personal suffering, she was one of the most persuasive playwrights in US theatre. She lived for many years with the detective writer **Dashiell Hammett**.

The Children's Hour
Dobie, Martha
Tilford, Mary
Wright, Karen

The Little Foxes
Giddens, Alexandra
Giddens, Regina

Watch on the Rhine
Müller, Kurt
Müller, Sara

Hemingway, Ernest

◎ (1899–1961) US novelist and short-story writer. In World War I he was an ambulance driver on the Italian front, where he was badly wounded. After returning to the USA he began to write features for newspapers. He went to Europe as a roving correspondent and in Paris he moved among other émigré artists such as **Ezra Pound**, **James Joyce** and **F Scott Fitzgerald**. According to the myth, drinking, brawling, big-game hunting, deep-sea fishing and bullfighting all competed with writing. He won the Pulitzer Prize in 1953 and the Nobel prize for literature in 1954.

A Farewell to Arms
Barklay, Catherine
Henry, Frederic

For Whom the Bell Tolls
Jordan, Robert
Maria
Pablo
Pilar

In Our Time
Adams, Nick

The Old Man and the Sea
Manolin
Santiago

The Short Happy Life of Francis Macomber
Macomber, Francis
Macomber, Margot

The Snows of Kilimanjaro
Harry

The Sun Also Rises
Ashley, Lady Brett
Barnes, Jake

To Have and Have Not
Morgan, Harry

Henry, O, pseudonym of **William Sydney Porter**

◎ (1862–1910) US short-story writer. In 1898, he was found technically guilty of embezzlement, and spent three years in jail. There, he adopted his pseudonym and began to write short stories, using coincidence and trick endings in his bold comic writing.

'The Gift of the Magi'
Young, Della
Young, Jim

'Hearts and Crosses'
Yaeger, Webb

'Hostages to Momus'
Peters, Jeff
Tucker, Andy

Henryson, Robert

◎ (c.1425–c.1508) Scottish poet. He is usually designated 'schoolmaster of Dunfermline'. His best-known poem is the *The Testament of Cresseid* (1480–90), a sequel to **Chaucer**'s *Troilus and Criseyde*.

The Testament of Cresseid
Cresseid

Herbert, Xavier

◎ (1901–84) Australian novelist. He is known mainly for his first novel, *Capricornia* (1938), and his last, *Poor Fellow My Country* (1975). The intervening years were spent drifting round Australia, a period which reinforced his sympathy with the treatment of Australia's Aboriginal people.

Capricornia
Bightit, Caesar
Differ, Connie (Constance)
Nawratt, Alexander
Nibblesom, Hannibal
O'Cannon, Tocky, also known as Tocky Lace and Tocky Pan
Shay, Heather
Shillingsworth, Marigold
Shillingsworth, Mark, alias Jack Ramble
Shillingsworth, Norman ('Nawnim')
Shillingsworth, Oscar
Thumscrough

Poor Fellow My Country
Bobwirridirridi
Candlemass, Alfie (Aelfrieda)
Delacy, Jeremy
Esk, Sir Mark
Lyndbrooke-Esk, Lydia
Prindy
Rosen, Rifkah

Herriot, James, pseudonym of James Alfred Wight

◎ (1916–95) English novelist. He grew up in Glasgow, and after years spent as a practising veterinarian in the Yorkshire Dales, he began writing of his experiences. His first book *If Only They Could Talk* was published in 1970.

If Only They Could Talk
Farnon, Siegfried
Farnon, Tristan
Herriot, James

Heyward, DuBose

◎ (1885–1940) US poet, novelist and playwright. He grew up in South Carolina, which is the setting for his novel *Porgy* (1925). In 1927, he and his wife Dorothy adapted it for the stage, winning a Pulitzer Prize. It was adapted by George Gershwin for his renowned opera *Porgy and Bess* (1935).

Porgy
Bess
Porgy

Heywood, Thomas

◎ (c.1574–1641) English dramatist, poet and actor. He contributed to the composition of 220 plays up to 1633, and he also wrote poetry, a volume of rhymed translations from Lucian, Erasmus and Ovid, and various pageants, tracts and treatises. Twenty-four of his plays have survived.

A Woman Killed with Kindness
Frankford, Anne
Frankford, John
Mountford, Susan
Wendoll

Hiaasen, Carl

◎ (born 1953) US novelist. Since 1976 Hiaasen has worked for *The Miami Herald* as an investigative reporter and as a columnist – a background which has provided much material for his fiction. He has written several best-selling satirical novels, and also published collections of his newspaper columns.

Double Whammy
Skink

Hibberd, Jack

◎ (born 1940) Australian dramatist. He worked as a doctor before devoting himself full-time to writing. *Dimboola* (1974) is one of Australia's most performed plays, although *A Stretch of the Imagination* (1972), a monologue by a dying man, is considered to be his best work.

Dimboola
McAdam, Maureen
McAdam, Morrie

A Stretch of the Imagination
O'Neill, Monk

White With Wire Wheels
Helen
Mal, Rod and Simon

Higgins, George V(incent)

◎ (1939–99) US novelist. He worked in newspapers before becoming a successful attorney and used his experience and observations of criminals at close quarters to telling effect in a spate of acclaimed literary thrillers.

The Friends of Eddie Coyle
Coyle, Eddie

Highsmith, Patricia

◎ (1921–95) US novelist. She specialized in crime fiction and thrillers, and her first novel, *Strangers on a Train* (1950), was filmed by Alfred Hitchcock in 1951. Her best novels are generally thought to be those describing the criminal adventures of her amoral psychotic anti-hero, Tom Ripley.

Carol
Carol
Therese

Strangers on a Train
Bruno, Charles Anthony
Haines, Guy

The Talented Mr. Ripley
Ripley, Tom

Hijuelos, Oscar

◎ (born 1951) US novelist. His Cuban-American heritage features strongly in his novels, particularly *The Mambo Kings Play Songs of Love* (1990), for which he was awarded the Pulitzer Prize. He has become known for his rich, sensuous language.

The Mambo Kings Play Songs of Love
Castilla, Cesar
Castilla, Nestor

Our House in the Last World
Santinio, Alejo
Santinio, Marcedes

Hill, Reginald

◎ (born 1936) English detective-story writer, best known as the creator of Detective Inspector Andy Dalziel.

A Clubbable Woman
Dalziel, Andy

Hill, Susan

◎ (born 1942) English novelist and playwright. Her novels, which tend to be formally-structured deliberations on the nature of loss and grief, deal with a wide range of themes. *The Woman in Black: A Ghost Story* (1983) was adapted into a long-running West End stage play. She also writes plays, short stories and books for children.

The Bird of the Night
Croft, Francis
Lawson, Harvey

I'm the King of the Castle
Hooper, Edmund
Kingshaw, Charles

Strange Meeting
Barton, David
Hilliard, John

The Woman in Black: A Ghost Story
Kipps, Arthur

Hilton, James

◎ (1900–54) English novelist. Many of his successful novels were filmed, including the best known *Goodbye Mr Chips* (1934, filmed 1939). He went to Hollywood

during the 1940s to work as a scriptwriter, and died in California.

Goodbye, Mr Chips
Chips, Mr

Himes, Chester

◎ (1909–84) US novelist. He spent nearly nine years in prison for armed robbery and after his release worked on a writers' project. He emigrated to Europe, where his tough detective stories were welcomed as serious existential fiction.

For Love of Imabelle reissued as *A Rage in Harlem*
Johnson, Edward 'Coffin' Ed and Jones, Grave Digger

Hines, Barry

◎ (born 1939) His novels are all set in his native Yorkshire, and deal with working-class life. He is best known for *A Kestrel for a Knave* (1968), also known as *Kes* following a successful film adaptation from his own screenplay, one of a number of collaborations with the filmmaker Ken Loach.

A Kestrel for a Knave
Caspar, Billy

Hogg, James, also called the Ettrick Shepherd

◎ (1770–1835) Scottish poet and novelist. He was a regular contributor to *Blackwood's Magazine* and his poetry reflects the strong Scottish vernacular tradition and the influence of Robert Burns. Of Hogg's prose works, the most remarkable is *The Private Memoirs and Confessions of a Justified Sinner* (1824), a macabre novel which anticipates **Robert Louis Stevenson**'s *Dr Jekyll and Mr Hyde*.

The Private Memoirs and Confessions of a Justified Sinner
Calvert, Bell
Colwan, George
Dalcastle, Lady of
Dalcastle, Laird of
Gil-Martin
Logan, Miss Arabella
Wringhim, Robert (the Elder)
Wringhim, Robert (the Younger)

Holmes, Oliver Wendell

◎ (1809–94) US physician and writer. From 1847 to 1882 he was Professor of Anatomy at Harvard. He began writing verse while an undergraduate, and *Elsie Venner: A Romance of Destiny* (1861) was the first of three novels foreshadowing modern 'Freudian' fiction.

Elsie Venner: A Romance of Destiny
Venner, Elsie

Holtby, Winifred

◎ (1898–1935) English novelist. She served in France with the Women's Auxiliary Army Corps

and was a prolific journalist. She wrote a number of novels with strong-willed women as her heroines, including *The Land of Green Ginger* (1927), but is chiefly remembered for her last and most successful, *South Riding* (1936).

Anderby Wold
Robson, John
Robson, Mary
Rossiter, David

The Crowded Street
Hammond, Muriel

The Land of Green Ginger
Leigh, Joanna
Leigh, Teddy

South Riding
Beddows, Alderman
Burton, Sarah
Carne, Robert

Hope, Anthony, pseudonym of Sir Anthony Hope Hawkins

◎ (1863–1933) English novelist. He was called to the Bar in 1887. He wrote several plays and novels in his spare time, but he is chiefly remembered for his 'Ruritanian' romances, *The Prisoner of Zenda* (1894; dramatized 1896) and its sequel, *Rupert of Hentzau* (1898).

The Prisoner of Zenda
Rassendyll, Rudolf
Rupert of Hentzau

Rupert of Hentzau
Rupert of Hentzau

Hornby, Nick

◎ (born 1957) English novelist. He worked as an English teacher and journalist before becoming a writer full-time. His novels often explore aspects of masculinity.

About a Boy
Freeman, Will

High Fidelity
Fleming, Rob

How to be Good
Carr, David
Carr, Katie

Hornung, E(rnest) W(illiam)

◎ (1866–1921) English novelist. He was the brother-in-law of Sir **Arthur Conan Doyle**, but in his own right was the creator of 'Raffles' the gentleman burglar, hero of *The Amateur Cracksman* (1899) and many other adventure stories.

The Amateur Cracksman
Bunny
Raffles

The Black Mask
Bunny
Raffles

The Thief in the Night
Bunny
Raffles

Hospital, Janette Turner

◎ (born 1942) Australian-born Canadian novelist and short-story writer. She has lived in Canada, the USA, India and England, and a

Index

sense of dislocation, homelessness and nomadicity colours her work.
Borderline
Seymour, Jean-Marc

Howe, E(dgar) W(atson)
◎ (1853–1937) US novelist. He owned and edited a daily newspaper and published collections of aphorisms and of editorials from his journal *E. W. Howe's Monthly*. His most famous novel *The Story of a Country Town* (1883) was praised by **Mark Twain** for its naturalism.
The Story of a Country Town
Westlake, Ned

Howells, William Dean
◎ (1837–1920) US novelist and critic. His editorship at *Harper's Magazine* (1886–91) made him the king of critics in the USA. A champion of Realism in US literature, he wrote numerous novels. His theories of fiction influenced **Mark Twain**, **Henry James** and **Stephen Crane**.
A Chance Acquaintance
Arbuton, Miles
Ellison, Kitty
A Hazard of New Fortunes
Dryfoos
Dryfoos, Conrad
Fulkerson
Lindau, Henry
March, Basil
March, Isabel
Indian Summer
Bowen, Evelina
Colville, Theodore
The Lady of the Aroostook
Blood, Lydia
The Landlord at Lion's Head
Durgin, Jeff
A Modern Instance
Gaylord, Marcia
Hubbard, Bartley
Hubbard, Marcia, née Gaylord
An Open-Eyed Conspiracy
March, Basil
The Rise of Silas Lapham
Corey, Tom
Hubbard, Bartley
Lapham, Irene
Lapham, Mrs Persis
Lapham, Penelope
Lapham, Silas
Rogers, Milton K
Sewell, David
Their Silver Wedding Journey
March, Basil
Their Wedding Journey
March, Basil
March, Isabel
A Traveller from Altruria
Homos, Mr
Makely, Mrs
Twelvemough, Mr

Hughes, Langston
◎ (1902–67) US poet, fiction writer and dramatist. Though initially rejected by black critics, he was eventually recognized as a major figure in the Harlem Renaissance of the 1920s. His memorable character 'Jesse B Simple' first appeared in racy newspaper sketches and thereafter in several volumes.
'Conversation at Midnight'
Simple, Jesse B
'Madam and the Rent Man'
Johnson, Madam Alberta K
'Madam's Past History'
Johnson, Madam Alberta K

Hughes, Richard
◎ (1900–76) English novelist and dramatist. He travelled widely in Europe, the USA and the West Indies, and eventually settled in Wales. He is best known for *A High Wind in Jamaica* (1929, US title *The Innocent Voyage*), a superior adventure yarn about a family of children captured by pirates while sailing to England.
A High Wind in Jamaica
Bas-Thornton, Edward
Bas-Thornton, Emily
Bas-Thornton, John
Bas-Thornton, Laura
Bas-Thornton, Rachel
Fernandez, Margaret
Jonsen, Captain
Otto

Hughes, Thomas
◎ (1822–96) English novelist. He was a Liberal MP (1865–74), was closely associated with the Christian Socialists, supported trade unionism and helped to found a model settlement in Tennessee, USA. He is primarily remembered as the author of the semi-autobiographical public school classic, *Tom Brown's Schooldays* (1857).
Tom Brown at Oxford
Tom Brown
Tom Brown's Schooldays
Brown, Tom
Flashman, Harry

Hulme, Keri
◎ (born 1947) New Zealand novelist, poet and short-story writer. She came to international notice by winning the 1985 Booker Prize with her first novel, *The Bone People* (1983), a spell-binding mixing of Maori myth and Christian symbolism. It also won the New Zealand Book Award for Fiction.
The Bone People
Gillayley, Joe (Joseph)
Gillayley, Simon P
Holmes, Kerewin

Hunt, Leigh
◎ (1784–1859) English poet and essayist. With his brother, a printer, he edited (1808–21) *The Examiner*, which became a focus of liberal opinion and attracted leading men of letters, including **Byron** and **Charles Lamb**. Hunt published several volumes of poetry himself, but was most influential as a critic and editor.
'Abou Ben Adhem'
Abou Ben Adhem

Hurston, Zora Neale
◎ (c.1901–1960) US novelist. She became a prominent figure in the Harlem Renaissance. Her best-known novel is *Their Eyes Were Watching God* (1937). Her last years were plagued by ill health and she died in poverty.
Their Eyes Were Watching God
Crawford, Janie
Tea Cake

Huxley, Aldous
◎ (1894–1963) English novelist and essayist. In 1932, in his most famous novel, *Brave New World*, Huxley warned of the dangers of moral anarchy in a scientific age. Later works explore mysticism and the controversial short cut to it, the drug mescalin.
After Many a Summer
Propter
Antic Hay
Coleman
Gumbril, Theodore
Gumbril Senior
Lypiatt, Casimir
Shearwater, James
Viveash, Myra
Brave New World
Marx, Bernard
Mond, Mustapha
Savage, John the
Eyeless in Gaza
Amberley, Mary
Beavis, Anthony
Foxe, Brian
Foxe, Mrs
Ledwidge, Helen
Ledwidge, Hugh
Staithes, Mark
Point Counter Point
Bidlake, John
Burlap, Denis
Quarles, Philip
Quarles, Rachel
Rampion, Mark
Spandrell, Maurice

Inchbald, Mrs Elizabeth
◎ (1753–1821) English novelist, playwright and actress. She was the author of 19 sentimental comedies, and also wrote novels and edited the 24-volume *The British Theatre* (1806–09).
A Simple Story
Elmwood, Lady, previously Miss Milner

Elmwood, Lord
Elmwood, Matilda

Inge, William
◎ (1913–73) US playwright and
novelist. He taught and wrote art
criticism for the *St Louis Star-
Times*. Outside the mainstream of
US theatre, he is nevertheless
important for his plays including
Picnic (1953), which won a Pulitzer
Prize.

Picnic
Carter, Hal
Owens, Flora
Owens, Madge
Owens, Millie
Potts, Helen
Sydney, Rosemary

Innes, Michael, pseudonym of **J I M
Stewart** (*see* **Stewart, J I M**)

Death at the President's Lodging
Appleby, John

Ireland, David
◎ (born 1927) Australian novelist,
poet and playwright. He had
diverse occupations before
becoming a full-time writer in the
1970s. He uses a surrealist style to
challenge complacency and the
self-deception of national myths.
He has won the Miles Franklin
Award on three occasions.

City of Women
Shockley, Billie

The Flesheaters
Mallory, Lee

The Glass Canoe
Meat Man
Sibley

A Woman of the Future
Hunt, Alethea

Irving, John
◎ (born 1942) US novelist. He
originally taught in university until
becoming a full-time writer after
the international success of *The
World According to Garp* (1978).
His sprawling novels with
convoluted plots and long
epilogues have proved hugely
popular.

The Cider House Rules
Wells, Homer

The Fourth Hand
Wallingford, Patrick

A Prayer for Owen Meany
Meany, Owen

The World According to Garp
Garp, T S

Irving, Washington
◎ (1783–1859) US writer. He served
as an officer in the 1812 war, and
from 1815–32 lived largely in
Europe. Under the pseudonym
'Geoffrey Crayon' he wrote *The
Sketch Book* (1819–20), a
miscellany including the tales 'Rip
Van Winkle' and 'The Legend of
Sleepy Hollow'. He was the first US

author to gain international
recognition.

'The Legend of Sleepy Hollow'
Bones, Brom
Crane, Ichabod
Van Tassel, Katrine

'Rip Van Winkle'
Rip Van Winkle

Isherwood, Christopher
◎ (1904–86) English-born US
novelist. His best-known work, *Mr
Norris Changes Trains* (1935), was
based on his experiences in the
decadence of post-slump, pre-
Hitler Berlin. In 1939 he emigrated
to California to be a scriptwriter
for MGM and in 1946 took US
citizenship. The Broadway musical
Cabaret (1968) was based on his
earlier Berlin stories, especially
'Sally Bowles' (1937).

Mr Norris Changes Trains
Norris, Arthur

Prater Violet
Bergmann, Friedrich

'Sally Bowles'
Bowles, Sally

A Single Man
George

Ishiguro, Kazuo
◎ (born 1954) Japanese-born
British novelist. *The Remains of the
Day* (1989), an elegiac study of a
vanishing class told through the
eyes of a butler, won Ishiguro the
Booker Prize.

The Remains of the Day
Stevens, Mr

When We Were Orphans
Banks, Christopher

Jacobson, Dan
◎ (born 1929) South African
novelist. Many of his works are set
in South Africa or the fictional
Republic of Sarmeda, although he
has lived in England since the late
1950s. The Bible features strongly
in works such as *The Rape of Tamar*
(1970), perhaps reflecting
Jacobson's upbringing as the
grandson of a Lithuanian rabbi.

The Rape of Tamar
Yonadab

James, Florence *see* **Cusack,
Dymphna** and **James, Florence**

James, Henry
◎ (1843–1916) US novelist and
critic. After a roving youth in the
USA and Europe and desultory law
studies at Harvard, he began in

1865 to produce brilliant literary
reviews and short stories. He was
the first novelist to deal with the
clash between the old and the new:
the impact of US life on the older
European civilization. He is the
acknowledged master of the
psychological novel, which has
profoundly influenced the 20th-
century literary scene. In 1915 he
became a British subject.

The Ambassadors
De Vionnet, Madame
Gostrey, Maria
Newsome, Chad
Newsome, Mrs
Pocock, Sarah
Strether, Lambert
Waymarsh

The American
De Cintré, Claire
Newman, Christopher
Nioche, Noémie

The Aspern Papers
anon (the editor)
Aspern, Jeffrey
Bordereau, Miss
Bordereau, Miss Tina

The Awkward Age
Brookenham, Nanda

'The Beast in the Jungle'
Marcher, John

The Bostonians
Birdseye, Miss
Chancellor, Olive
Ransom, Basil
Tarrant, Verena

Daisy Miller: A Study
Giovanelli, Mr
Miller, Daisy (properly Annie P)
Winterbourne, Frederick

The Europeans
Acton, Robert
Brand, Mr
Eugenia, Baroness Münster
Wentworth, Charlotte
Wentworth, Clifford
Wentworth, Gertrude
Young, Felix

'The Figure in the Carpet'
anon (the narrator)
Corvick
Deane, Drayton
Erme, Gwendolyn
Vereker, Hugh

The Golden Bowl
Amerigo, Prince
Stant, Charlotte
Verver, Adam
Verver, Maggie

'The Jolly Corner'
Brydon, Spencer

'Owen Wingrave'
Wingrave, Owen

The Portrait of a Lady
Archer, Isabel
Goodwood, Casper
Merle, Mme
Osmond, Gilbert
Osmond, Pansy
Stackpole, Henrietta
Touchett, Ralph
Warburton, Lord

The Princess Casamassima
Casamassima, Princess, formerly
  Christina Light

Index

Muniment, Paul
Pupin, Monsieur
Pynsent, Miss, known as 'Pinnie'
Robinson, Hyacinth
Vetch, Anastasius

Roderick Hudson
Casamassima, Princess, formerly
  Christina Light
Hudson, Roderick

The Spoils of Poynton
Brigstock, Mona
Gereth, Mrs
Gereth, Owen
Vetch, Fleda

The Turn of the Screw
anon (the governess)
Flora
Jessel, Miss
Miles
Quint, Peter

Washington Square
Sloper, Catherine
Sloper, Dr Austin
Townsend, Morris

What Maisie Knew
Claude, Sir
Farange, Beale
Farange, Ida
Farange, Maisie
Overmore, Miss, subsequently Mrs Beale
  Farange
Wix, Mrs

The Wings of the Dove
Croy, Kate
Densher, Merton
Lowder, Mrs
Mark, Lord
Stringham, Mrs
Theale, Millie

James, P(hyllis) D(orothy)
◎ (born 1920) English detective-
story writer. She worked in the
Home Office, first in the police
department, where she was
involved with the forensic science
service, thereafter in the criminal
law department. Since 1979 she has
devoted herself to writing. P D
James was awarded the Crime
Writers Association Diamond
Dagger in 1987. She was made a life
peer in 1991.

Cover her Face
Dalgliesh, Adam

The Skull Beneath the Skin
Gray, Cordelia

An Unsuitable Job for a Woman
Gray, Cordelia

Jameson, Storm
◎ (1891–1986) English novelist.
Her first success was *The Lovely
Ship* (1927), which was followed by
more than 30 books that
maintained her reputation as a
storyteller and stylist. She also
wrote poems, essays, criticism and
biography, and several volumes of
autobiography.

The Lovely Ship
Hervey, Mary

Janowitz, Tama
◎ (born 1957) US novelist and
short-story writer. She became an
overnight sensation with her
collection of stories about single
life in the big city, *Slaves of New
York* (1986).

Slaves of New York
Eleanor T

Jefferies, Richard
◎ (1848–87) English naturalist and
novelist. The son of a Wiltshire
farmer, he started as a provincial
journalist. His works include the
autobiographical *Bevis: the Story of
a Boy* (1882), and his last and most
successful novel, *Amaryllis at the
Fair* (1887).

Amaryllis at the Fair
Iden

Bevis: the Story of a Boy
Bevis
Mark

Jellicoe, Ann
◎ (born 1927) English playwright
and director. She wrote for the
Royal Court Theatre and was
associated with the English Stage
Company. She established her
reputation with the innovative
drama *The Sport of My Mad Mother*
(1958).

The Knack
Jones, Nancy

The Sport of My Mad Mother
Greta

Jenkins, Robin
◎ (born 1912) Scottish novelist. At
various times an English teacher in
Scotland, Afghanistan, Spain and
Borneo, he has set many of his
stories in these countries. A
prolific writer, his works fall into
three main groups: those set in
Scotland, those set in 'Norania', his
fictional Afghanistan, and those
dealing with 'Kalewentan', a far
eastern sultanate.

The Cone-Gatherers
Calum
Duror

Fergus Lamont
Lamont, Fergus

The Awakening of George Darroch
Darroch, Rev George

A Would-Be Saint
Hamilton, Gavin

Jerome, Jerome K(lapka)
◎ (1859–1927) English humorous
writer, novelist and playwright.
Leaving school at the age of 14, he
was successively a clerk,
schoolmaster, reporter, actor and
journalist. His magnificently
ridiculous *Three Men in a Boat*
(1889), the account of a boat trip up
the Thames from Kingston to
Oxford, established itself as a
humorous classic.

Three Men in a Boat
George, Harris, and J

Three Men on the Bummel
George, Harris, and J

Jesse, F(riniwyd) Tennyson
◎ (1888–1958) English novelist and
dramatist. She was a great-niece of
Alfred Lord Tennyson, and
studied painting, but during World
War I took up journalism as one of
the few female war correspondents.
She is best known for her novels set
in Cornwall, as well as *The Lacquer
Lady* (1929), set in Burma, and *A
Pin to See the Peepshow* (1934),
based on a famous murder case.

The Lacquer Lady
Moroni, Fanny

A Pin to See the Peepshow
Almond, Julia

Jewett, Sarah Orne
◎ (1849–1909) US novelist and
short-story writer. *The Country of
the Pointed Firs* (1896) developed
her interest in the psychology of
small, remote communities. She
also wrote romantic novels and
stories based on the provincial life
of her state.

The Country of the Pointed Firs
Blackett, Mrs
Blackett, William
Hight, Esther
Littlepage, Captain
Todd, Almira
Todd, Joanna, known as 'Poor Joanna'

Deephaven
Dennis, Helen
Lancaster, Kate

Jhabvala, Ruth Prawer
◎ (born 1927) German-born
British novelist, and short-story
and screenplay writer. She lived in
Delhi from 1951 to 1975 and most of
her fiction relates to India, taking
the viewpoint of an outsider
looking in. She won the Booker
Prize for *Heat and Dust* (1975). In
association with the film makers
James Ivory and Ismail Merchant,
she has written several
accomplished screenplays.

Esmond in India
Stillwood, Esmond

Heat and Dust
Nawab of Khatm, the
Rivers, Olivia

In Search of Love and Beauty
Kellerman, Leo

Johns, Captain W(illiam) E(arl)
◎ (1893–1968) English aviator and
children's author. He served with
some distinction in the Royal
Flying Corps before being shot
down and sent to a prison camp.
After retirement from the Air Force
he served in the Ministry of
Information (1939–45). His stories
are strikingly good flying yarns,
mostly based on his experiences in
World War I.

The Camels are Coming
Biggles

Johnson, B(ryan) S(tanley)
◎ (1933–73) English novelist and
poet. He published seven novels,

all of which experimented with form (some are interactive) and novelistic convention using the models of writers such as **Joyce, Flann O' Brien** and **Sterne**. He also wrote poetry. He committed suicide at the age of 40.

Albert Angelo
Angelo, Albert

Travelling People
Henry, Henry

Johnson, Pamela Hansford

◎ (1912–81) English novelist, playwright and critic. Her many novels, such as the tragicomical *The Unspeakable Skipton* (1959), are observant of both the world of her youth and of society in the 1960s and 1970s, and range from the comic to the morally insightful.

The Unspeakable Skipton
Merlin, Dorothy
Skipton, Daniel

Johnson, Samuel, known as **Dr Johnson**

◎ (1709–84) English writer, critic and lexicographer. For much of his life he had to rely on literary hackwork to earn a living. His momentous *Dictionary of the English Language* (1755) took him eight years to complete. In 1764 he founded the Literary Club with a circle of friends including **Edmund Burke** and **Oliver Goldsmith**. In 1765 he published his critical edition of Shakespeare's plays (8 vols), with its classic Preface.

The History of Rasselas, Prince of Abissinia
Rasselas

Johnston, George H(enry)

◎ (1912–70) Australian author and journalist. During World War II his syndicated dispatches from New Guinea, India, Burma, Italy and the North Atlantic were widely read. He later moved to the Greek islands with his wife and fellow-author, Charmian Clift. With her he wrote three novels. Johnston wrote short stories, plays and many novels, several under the pseudonym 'Shane Martin'.

Closer to the Sun
Meredith, David
Meredith, Jack
Morley, Cressida

The Far Road
Meredith, David
Meredith, Jack
Morley, Cressida

Johnston, Jennifer

◎ (born 1930) Irish novelist. She was born into a theatrical family in Dublin. Many of her novels focus on the political and cultural history of Ireland, often using the trope of the 'Big House', focusing on the Anglo-Irish Ascendancy.

How Many Miles to Babylon?
Bennett

Crow, Jerry
Moore, Alex (Alexander)

Shadows on Our Skin
Kathleen
Logan, Brendan
Logan, Joe

Jolley, Elizabeth

◎ (born 1923) English-born Australian novelist. She often uses lesbianism as a major theme. Her works include *Palomino* (1980) and *Mr Scobie's Riddle* (Melbourne Age Book of the Year award in 1982). She also wrote a semi-autobiographical trilogy set in postwar England.

Cabin Fever
Wright, Vera

Mr Scobie's Riddle
Price, Hyacinth
Scobie, Martin

The Newspaper of Claremont Street
Morris, Margarite

Palomino
Ward, Laura

Woman in a Lampshade
Tredwell, Jasmine

Jones, James

◎ (1921–77) US novelist. He served in the US army as a sergeant (1939–44), boxed as a welterweight in Golden Gloves tournaments, and was awarded a Purple Heart. His wartime experience in Hawaii led to *From Here to Eternity* (1951), a classic novel dealing with the period before Pearl Harbor, for which he received a National Book Award.

From Here to Eternity
Prewitt, Robert E Lee
Warden, Sgt Milton

Jonson, Ben

◎ (1572–1637) English dramatist. His early plays were largely unsuccessful. By discarding romantic comedy and writing realistically (though his theory of 'humours' was hardly comparable with genuine realism) he produced his four masterpieces – *Volpone, or The Fox* (1606), *Epicoene, or The Silent Woman* (1609), *The Alchemist* (1610) and *Bartholomew Fair* (1614). His lyric genius was second only to Shakespeare's, and he was also a considerable critic.

The Alchemist
Ananias
Dapper
Dol Common
Drugger
Face
Kastril
Lovewit
Mammon, Sir Epicure
Pliant, Dame
Subtle
Surly, Pertinax
Wholesome, Tribulation

Bartholomew Fair
Busy, Zeal-of-the-Land
Cokes, Bartholomew
Littlewit, John and Win

Overdo, Justice and Dame
Purecraft, Dame
Quarlous, Tom
Waspe, Humphrey
Wellborn, Grace
Winwife

Catiline, his Conspiracy
Catilina, Lucius Sergius

The Devil is an Ass
Fitzdottrel, Fabian and Mrs Frances
Manly, Eustace
Meercraft
Pug
Wittipool

Epicoene, or The Silent Woman
Clerimont, Ned
Cutbeard
Daw, Sir John
Epicoene
Eugenie, Sir Dauphine
La-Foole, Sir Amorous
Morose
Otter, Captain Thomas and Mrs
Truewit

Every Man in his Humour
Bobadill, Captain
Brainworm
Clement, Justice
Downright, George
Kitely
Knowell, senior
Matthew
Stephen
Wellbred

Every Man out of his Humour
Asper
Brisk, Fastidious
Buffone, Carlo
Clove
Cordatus
Deliro
Fallace
Fungoso
Macilente
Mitis
Puntarvolo
Sogliardo
Sordido

Poetaster
Augustus
Crispinus, Rufus Laberius
Demetrius
Horace
Ovid
Tucca, Pantilius
Virgil

Sejanus, His Fall
Sejanus, Aelius

Volpone, or The Fox
Corbaccio
Corvino
Mosca
Peregrine
Volpone
Voltore
Would-Be, Sir Politic and Lady

Joyce, James

◎ (1882–1941) Irish writer and poet. Although he left Ireland for good in 1903 and spent the rest of his life on the continent, Dublin provides the setting for most of his work. The collection of stories published as *Dubliners* (1914) was greeted enthusiastically, and Joyce was championed by **WB Yeats** and

Ezra Pound, among others. In 1922 his seminal novel, *Ulysses*, was published in Paris. Its explicit stream-of-consciousness description of the thoughts and happenings of everyday life immediately provoked violent reactions, and it was not published in the UK until 1936, but it is now regarded as a major advance for fiction. He exercised a major influence on his contemporaries, and on later generations of writers.

'Clay'
Maria

'The Dead'
Conroy, Gabriel
Conroy, Gretta

Finnegans Wake
Earwicker, Humphrey Chimpden, or Mr Porter
Issy
Plurabelle, Anna Livia, or Mrs Porter
Shaunn the Post
Shem the Penman

'A Painful Case'
Duffy, James

A Portrait of the Artist as a Young Man
Dedalus, Stephen

Stephen Hero
Dedalus, Stephen

Ulysses
Bloom, Leopold
Bloom, Molly
Dedalus, Stephen
Mulligan, Buck

Kavanagh, Dan, pseudonym of **Julian Barnes** (*see* **Barnes, Julian**).

Duffy
Duffy, Nicholas ('Nick')

Kavanagh, Patrick

◎ (1905–67) Irish poet and novelist. He farmed before leaving for Dublin in 1939 to pursue a career as a writer and journalist. Perhaps his greatest achievement is *The Great Hunger* (1942), a passionate poem about the harsh reality of life for a frustrated Irish farmer and his elderly mother, which is in deliberate contrast to the romantic rural fantasy evoked by poets such as **Yeats**.

The Great Hunger
Maguire, Patrick

Kay, Jackie

◎ (born 1961) Scottish poet, dramatist and novelist. Born of a Nigerian father and Scottish mother, she was adopted by a white couple and this background informs much of her work. Her

first novel, *Trumpet* (1998), won the Guardian Fiction Prize.

Trumpet
Moody, Joss

Keating, H(enry) R(eymond) F(itzwalter)

◎ (born 1926) English crime-writer. He is perhaps best known for his Inspector Ghote books, and has won the Crime Writers Association Gold Dagger twice. In 1996 he was awarded the CWA Cartier Diamond Dagger for a lifetime's achievement.

The Perfect Murder
Ghote, Inspector Ganesh

Keats, John

◎ (1795–1821) English poet. He was a medical student in London hospitals, but took to writing poetry. **Leigh Hunt** introduced him to other young Romantics, including **Percy (Bysshe) Shelley**, and published his first sonnets in *The Examiner* (1816). *Lamia and Other Poems* (1820) was a landmark in English poetry.

'The Eve of St. Agnes'
Madeline
Porphyro

'Isabella or the Pot of Basil'
Isabella

Kelman, James

◎ (born 1946) Scottish novelist, short-story writer and playwright. *A Disaffection*, his third novel, was shortlisted for the Booker Prize in 1989. He has carved a niche as the spokesman for the disaffected, downtrodden and disenfranchised, and his fourth novel, *How Late It Was, How Late* (1994), won the Booker Prize.

The Busconductor Hines
Hines, Rab

A Chancer
Tammas

A Disaffection
Doyle, Patrick

How Late It Was, How Late
'Sammy' ('Samuels')

Keneally, Thomas

◎ (born 1935) Australian novelist. The publication of *The Chant of Jimmie Blacksmith* (1972) marked the beginning of his mature fiction. His reputation grew steadily until he published *Schindler's Ark* (1982). It was a controversial winner of the Booker Prize because it blurred the boundary between fact and fiction.

Blood Red, Sister Rose
Joan of Arc

Bring Larks and Heroes
Halloran, Corporal Phelim
Hearn, Robert
Rush, Ann

The Chant of Jimmie Blacksmith
Blacksmith, Jimmie

Confederates
Jackson, Gen Thomas ('Stonewall')

The Cut-Rate Kingdom
Tyson, 'Paper'

A Dutiful Daughter
Glover, Barbara
Glover, Damian

Gossip from the Forest
Erzsberger, Matthias

Schindler's Ark
Schindler, Oskar

Season in Purgatory
Pelham, David

Kennaway, James

◎ (1928–68) Scottish novelist. *Tunes of Glory* (1956) was his first novel and remains his best known. He also wrote the screenplay for the film version (1960).

Tunes of Glory
Barrow, Col Basil
Sinclair, Lt Col Jock

Kennedy, A(lison) L(ouise)

◎ (born 1965) Scottish novelist and short-story writer. She has published several award-winning novels and short-story collections. She also writes screenplays, reviews and is a lecturer in creative writing at St Andrew's University.

Everything You Need
Lamb, Mary
Staples, Nathan

Looking for the Possible Dance
Hamilton, Margaret
McCoag, Colin

So I am Glad
Wilson, M Jennifer

Kennedy, John Pendleton

◎ (1795–1870) US novelist and essayist. He practised law and had a political career while writing sketches, essays and poems. His best-known work is his novel *Horse-Shoe Robinson* (1835), a historical romance.

Horse-Shoe Robinson
Robinson, Horse-Shoe

Kennedy, William

◎ (born 1928) US novelist and screenwriter. He served in the US army (1950–2) before becoming a journalist and eventually a full-time writer. *Legs* (1975), which combines fact and fiction, is the first of the 'Albany novels'. He won a Pulitzer Prize for *Ironweed* (1983).

Billy Phelan's Greatest Game
Phelan, Billy

Ironweed
Phelan, Francis

Legs
Diamond, Legs
Gorman, Marcus

Kerouac, Jack

◎ (1922–69) US novelist. He worked at various careers including as a mechanic and sports journalist before enlisting in the

US navy (1943), from which he was quickly discharged. He was identified as leader and spokesman of the Beat Generation, a label he coined then came to regret and repudiate. On *The Road* (1957), his second novel, has been much imitated and has made Kerouac a cult hero.

The Dharma Bums
Ryder, Japhy

Maggie Cassidy
Cassidy, Maggie

On The Road
Moriarty, Dean
Paradise, Sal

Vanity of Duluoz
Duluoz, Ti-Jean/Jack

Visions of Cody
Pomeray, Cody

Kesey, Ken

◎ (1935–2001) US writer. Associated with the 1950s 'Beat' movement, he also worked as a ward attendant in a mental hospital, an experience he used to telling effect in *One Flew Over the Cuckoo's Nest* (1962). Filmed in 1975, it won five Academy Awards.

One Flew Over the Cuckoo's Nest
Bromden, Chief
McMurphy, Randle Patrick

Kincaid, Jamaica, originally Elaine Potter Richardson

◎ (born 1949) US novelist and journalist. Born in Antigua, she is known for her novels, although she has also published non-fiction works.

Annie John
John, Annie

King, Francis

◎ (born 1923) English novelist, short-story writer and critic. He spent a number of years working abroad for the British Council and his novels are set in many countries. He has also written short stories, travel books and a study of **E M Forster**.

Act of Darkness
O'Connor, Clare
Thompson, Helen
Thompson, Peter
Thompson, Toby

King, Stephen

◎ (born 1947) US author. He began his career as an English teacher. From the mid-1970s he produced a series of highly suspenseful horror novels, often with a supernatural twist, some of which have become classics.

Carrie
Carrie

Kingsley, Charles

◎ (1819–75) English writer. A Christian Socialist and a rector, he threw himself into various schemes

aimed at the improvement of the working classes. He was hugely prolific and his best-known works include the children's classic *The Water Babies* (1863).

Alton Locke, Tailor and Poet: An Autobiography
Locke, Alton

Hereward the Wake
Hereward the Wake

The Water Babies
Bedonebyasyoudid, Mrs
Doasyouwouldbedoneby, Mrs
Ellie
Grimes, Mr
Tom

Westward Ho!
Guzman, Don
Leigh, Amyas

King-Smith, Dick

◎ (born 1922) English author. He worked as a farmer and factory hand before becoming a primary school teacher and later a writer of children's fiction. His first book was published when he was 54. He remains best known, perhaps, for *The Sheep-Pig* (1983), which was filmed as *Babe* (1995).

The Sheep-Pig
Babe

Kipling, Rudyard

◎ (1865–1936) English writer. Born in India, he was educated in England before returning to work as a journalist in Lahore. He eventually settled permanently in England. His output is diverse. He was awarded the Nobel prize for literature in 1907.

'Captains Courageous': A Tale of the Grand Banks
Cheyne, Harvey

'Danny Deever'
Deever, Danny

'Gunga Din'
Gunga Din

The Jungle Book
Akela
Bagheera
Baloo
Kaa
Mowgli
Rikki-Tikki-Tavi
Shere Khan, also known as Lungri
Toomai, of the Elephants

Kim
O'Hara, Kimball, also known as Kim

'The Mark of the Beast'
Strickland

Puck of Pook's Hill
Dan
Hobden, the Hedger
Puck
Una

'The Rescue of Pluffles'
Hauksbee, Mrs

Soldiers Three
Learoyd, Private
Mulvaney, Private
Ortheris, Private

Stalky & Co.
Beetle

M'Turk, also known as Turkey
Stalky

'The Strange Ride of Morrowbie Jukes'
Gunga Dass
Jukes, Morrowbie

'The Three Musketeers'
Learoyd, Private
Mulvaney, Private
Ortheris, Private

Koch, C(hristopher) J(ohn)

◎ (born 1932) Australian novelist. Born in Tasmania, he spent some time in India, which inspired *Across the Sea Wall* (1965, rev edn 1982). Koch's exotic thriller *The Year of Living Dangerously* (1978) became immensely popular through Peter Weir's 1982 film.

Across the Sea Wall
O'Brien, Robert

The Doubleman
Brady, Brian
Miller, Richard

The Year of Living Dangerously
Bryant, Jill
Cookie (R J C)
Hamilton, Guy
Kwan, Billy

Kopit, Arthur

◎ (born 1937) US playwright. He writes satirical comic dramas on contemporary issues.

End of the World
Trent, Michael

Kosinski, Jerzy

◎ (1933–91) Polish-born US novelist. He emigrated to the US in 1957. The trauma of war had rendered him (literally) speechless and his quasi-autobiographical novel *The Painted Bird* (1965), is a classic of Holocaust literature.

Being There
Chance (the Gardener)

Blind Date
Levanter, George

Cockpit
Tarden

The Devil Tree
Whalen, Jonathan James

The Painted Bird
Boy, the

Passion Play
Fabian

Pinball
Domostroy, Patrick

Kureishi, Hanif

◎ (born 1954) English novelist and screenplay writer. Following several successful screenplays, he published the novel *The Buddha of Suburbia* (1990), for which he won the Whitbread First Novel prize. He also wrote the screenplay for the television version of the novel (1993).

The Buddha of Suburbia
Amir, Karim

Kyd, Thomas

◎ (1558–94) English dramatist.
Known for his tragedies, especially
The Spanish Tragedy (1592), he has
been credited with a share in other
plays, and some claim he wrote the
lost original *Hamlet*. Imprisoned in
1593 on a charge of atheism
(Unitarianism), which he tried to
shift on to **Christopher Marlowe**'s
shoulders, he died in poverty.

The Spanish Tragedy
Balthazar, Prince
Bel-Imperia
Castile, Duke of
Don Horatio
Don Lorenzo
Hieronimo

La Farge, Oliver

◎ (1901–63) US novelist and
anthropologist. He conducted
three archaeological expeditions to
Arizona and also expeditions to
Guatemala and Mexico. His
knowledge and experience is
reflected in *Laughing Boy* (1929), a
novel of Navajo life, for which he
won the Pulitzer Prize.

Laughing Boy
Laughing Boy
Slim Girl

La Guma, Alex

◎ (1925–85) South African
novelist. A journalist, he spent
some time in detention and under
house arrest before emigrating to
London in 1966. From 1978 to his
death, he was the ANC
representative in Havana. He is
considered one of South Africa's
major 20th-century writers.

A Walk in the Night
Adonis, Michael
Willieboy

Lamb, Charles

◎ (1775–1834) English essayist and
poet. He first achieved success
with the joint publication with his
sister Mary of *Tales from
Shakespeare* (1807). His first essay
for the new *London Magazine*,
'Recollections of the old South Sea
House', was signed 'Elia'. Collected
as the *Essays of Elia* (1823–33),
these became his best-known
works.

Essays of Elia
Battle, Mrs
Superannuated Man, the

Lamming, George

◎ (born 1927) Barbadian novelist.
He was a teacher in Trinidad and in
Venezuela before going to England
in 1950, where he worked as a
factory labourer and hosted a book
programme for the BBC West
Indian Service. Beginning with *In
the Castle of My Skin* (1953), he has
explored the West Indian
experience in a complex and highly
textured way.

The Emigrants
Collis

In the Castle of my Skin
G

Natives of my Person
Commandant, the

Of Age and Innocence
Shephard, Isaac

Season of Adventure
Fola
Powell, Fola

Water with Berries
Derek
Roger
Teeton

Langland, William

◎ (c.1332–c.1400) English poet.
Educated at the Benedictine school
at Malvern, he became a clerk and
may have earned a poor living in
London from 1362 by singing in a
chantry and by copying legal
documents. His famous work is
Piers Plowman, a medieval
alliterative poem on spiritual
pilgrimage.

Piers Plowman
Piers the Plowman

Larkin, Philip

◎ (1922–85) English poet. In 1955
he became librarian at the
University of Hull. His early poems
appeared in the anthology, *Poetry
from Oxford in Wartime* (1944), and
in a collection, *The North Ship*
(1945). His *Collected Poems* was
published posthumously in 1988
and became a bestseller. He wrote
two novels, *Jill* (1946) and *A Girl in
Winter* (1947), essays and many
articles on jazz.

A Girl in Winter
Lind, Katharine

Jill
Kemp, John

Laurence, Margaret

◎ (1926–87) Canadian novelist.
Her husband's job as a civil
engineer took them to England,
Somaliland and Ghana. In 1962 she
moved to England, where she wrote
her famous 'Manawaka series'
based on her home town.

A Bird in the House
Macleod, Vanessa

The Diviners
Gunn, Morag

The Fire-Dwellers
MacAindra, Stacey

A Jest of God
Cameron, Rachel

The Stone Angel
Shipley, Hagar, née Currie

Lawler, Ray

◎ (born 1921) Australian
playwright. It was not until his
ninth play *Summer of the
Seventeenth Doll* (1955) that he
achieved success. Lawler himself
played Barney in the original
production and in the London
première (1957) which won the
Evening Standard award.

Summer of the Seventeenth Doll
Cunningham, Pearl
Dowd, Johnnie
Emma
Ibbot, Barney
Nancy
Olive
Ryan, Bubba
Webber, Roo

Lawrence, D(avid) H(erbert)

◎ (1885–1930) English novelist,
poet and essayist. He became a
schoolmaster and after the success
of his first novel, *The White
Peacock*, he decided to write full-
time. He made his reputation with
the semi-autobiographical *Sons
and Lovers* (1913). He was shocked
by prosecutions for obscenity over
the private publication in Florence
of *Lady Chatterley's Lover* in 1928.
Opinion is still divided over his
literary worth but his effect on the
younger intellectuals of his period
is certain.

Aaron's Rod
Lilly, Rawdon
Sisson, Aaron

'England, My England'
Egbert

The Fox
Banford
Grenfel, Henry
March

Kangaroo
Calcott, Jack
Colley, Ben ('Kangaroo')
Somers, Richard and Harriet

Lady Chatterley's Lover
Chatterley, Lady Constance
Chatterley, Sir Clifford
Mellors, Oliver

The Lost Girl
Cicio, properly Francesco Marasca
Houghton, Alvina

The Plumed Serpent
Cipriano, Don
Leslie, Kate

'The Prussian Officer'
Prussian Officer, the

The Rainbow
Brangwen, Gudrun
Brangwen, Tom
Brangwen, Ursula
Brangwen, Will
Lensky, Anna
Lensky, Lydia
Skrebensky, Anton

Sons and Lovers
Dawes, Clara and Baxter
Leivers, Miriam
Morel, Paul
Morel, Walter and Gertrude

'St Mawr'
Carrington, Lou

St Mawr
The Trespasser
McNair, Siegmund

The White Peacock
Beardsall, Lettie
Saxton, George

Women in Love
Birkin, Rupert
Brangwen, Gudrun
Brangwen, Ursula
Crich, Gerald
Roddice, Hermione

Lawson, Henry
◎ (1867–1922) Australian poet and short-story writer. His mother, Louisa Lawson, was a founder of the movement for women's suffrage in New South Wales, and from her Henry acquired the radical opinions which coloured his own writing.

'Arvie Aspinall's Alarm Clock'
Aspinall, Arvie

Children of the Bush
Page, Andy

'The Drover's Wife'
Drover's Wife, the

'Enter Mitchell'
Mitchell, Jack

'His Father's Mate'
Mason, Isley

'The Iron-Bark Chip'
Bentley, Jack
Page, Andy
Regan, Dave

Joe Wilson and His Mates
Bentley, Jack
Page, Andy
Regan, Dave

'Joe Wilson's Courtship'
Wilson, Joe

'Shall We Gather at the River?'
M'Laughlan, Peter

'Steelman'
Steelman

'Stiffner and Jim (Thirdly, Bill)'
Anderson, Bill
Stiffner

Le Carré, John
◎ (born 1931) English novelist. He worked in the British Foreign Service but resigned in 1964 to become a full-time writer. His novels present the unglamorous side of diplomacy and espionage, a world of boredom, squalor and shabby deceit.

Absolute Friends
Mundy, Ted

Call for the Dead
Smiley, George

The Constant Gardener
Quayle, Justin

The Honourable Schoolboy
Karla
Smiley, George
Westerby, Jerry

The Little Drummer Girl
Charlie

The Naive and Sentimental Lover
Cassidy, Aldo

A Perfect Spy
Pym, Magnus
Pym, Rick

The Secret Pilgrim
Smiley, George

A Small Town in Germany
Harting, Leo
Turner, Sam

Smiley's People
Karla
Smiley, George

The Spy Who Came in from the Cold
Blair, Barley
Leamas, Alec

Tinker, Tailor, Soldier, Spy
Haydon, Bill
Karla
Smiley, George

Lee, Harper
◎ (born 1926) US novelist. The daughter of a lawyer, she was a descendant of Robert E Lee and a childhood friend of **Truman Capote**. She won a Pulitzer Prize for fiction (1961) for her only novel, *To Kill a Mockingbird* (1960).

To Kill A Mockingbird
Finch, Atticus
Finch, Jem (Jeremy)
Finch, Scout (Jean Louise)
Radley, Boo (Arthur)

Le Fanu, J(oseph) Sheridan
◎ (1814–73) Irish novelist and journalist. He was a grand-nephew of **Richard Sheridan**. He abandoned law for journalism and also wrote novels and short stories, and his works are remarkable for their preoccupation with the supernatural.

Uncle Silas
Silas, Uncle

Le Guin, Ursula
◎ (born 1929) US science-fiction writer. She is a prolific and skilled writer of science fiction and fantasy for children and adults. In her 'Earthsea' trilogy, she depicts a magical but threatening world, in which every village has its small-time sorcerer and the forces of evil are uncomfortably close.

The Farthest Shore
Ged, or Sparrowhawk

The Tombs of Atuan
Ged, or Sparrowhawk

A Wizard of Earthsea
Ged, or Sparrowhawk

Lehmann, Rosamond
◎ (1901–90) English novelist. She was educated at Girton College, Cambridge, which provided the background for her first novel, *Dusty Answer* (1927). Her novels show a fine sensitive insight into character and emotion and her women especially are brilliantly drawn.

The Ballad and the Source
Jardine, Sybil
Landon, Rebecca

Dusty Answer
Earle, Judith

The Echoing Grove
Burkett, Dinah
Masters, Madeleine
Masters, Ricky

Invitation to the Waltz
Curtis, Olivia

A Note in Music
Fairfax, Grace

A Sea-Grape Tree
Jardine, Sybil
Landon, Rebecca

The Weather in the Streets
Curtis, Olivia

Lennox, Charlotte
◎ (c.1729–1804) British novelist and playwright. Her most famous work, *The Female Quixote: or, The Adventures of Arabella* (1752), is a satirical romp through the life of Arabella, a young lady besotted with French romantic novels.

The Female Quixote: or, The Adventures of Arabella
Arabella, later Angelica

Leonard, Elmore
◎ (born 1925) US thriller writer. His screenplays and novels are remarkable for their relentless pace and vivid dialogue. In later years he has reached a new audience through high-profile cinematic adaptations of his novels.

Maximum Bob
Gibb, Judge Bob

Lessing, Doris
◎ (born 1919) Rhodesian writer. She became involved in politics and in 1949 moved to London. In 1956 Rhodesia declared her a 'prohibited immigrant'. Her works have dealt with such issues as the sterility of white civilization in Africa as well as feminist themes. Latterly, she has also attempted science fiction, but her commitment to exploring political and social undercurrents in contemporary society has never wavered.

Briefing for a Descent into Hell
Watkins, Professor Charles

The Diaries of Jane Somers
Fowler, Maudie
Somers, Jane

The Four-Gated City
Quest, Martha

The Golden Notebook
Wulf, Anna

The Good Terrorist
Alice

The Grass is Singing
Moses
Slatter, Charlie
Turner, Dick
Turner, Mary

Landlocked
Quest, Martha

A Proper Marriage
Quest, Martha

A Ripple From the Storm
Quest, Martha

Index

Shikasta
Sherbon, George/Johor
The Sirian Experiments
Ambien II
The Summer Before the Dark
Brown, Kate

Lethem, Jonathan
◎ (born 1964) US novelist. He has experimented in various genres and his novels include *Motherless Brooklyn* (1999). He has also published short stories and novellas.
Motherless Brooklyn
Essrog, Lionel

Leverson, Ada
◎ (1865–1936) English novelist and journalist. She bravely supported **Oscar Wilde** during his trial in 1895. Her six novels, often domestic stories of difficult marriages (not unlike her own), were republished in one volume as *The Little Ottleys* in 1962.
The Little Ottleys
Ottley, Edith

Lewis, C(live) S(taples)
◎ (1898–1963) British novelist, literary scholar and religious writer. He was a distinguished teacher at Cambridge and won a wide popular audience during World War II for his broadcast talks and his books on religious subjects. His series of seven books for children, *The Chronicles of Narnia*, is suffused with Christian allegory and ethics, and remains a children's classic.
The Lion, the Witch and the Wardrobe
Aslan
Edmund
Lucy
Peter
Susan
Out of the Silent Planet
Ransom, Elwin
Perelandra
Ransom, Elwin
That Hideous Strength
Ransom, Elwin

Lewis, Matthew Gregory, nicknamed **Monk Lewis**
◎ (1775–1818) English novelist. In 1794 he was an attaché to The Hague and it was there he wrote the hugely successful Gothic novel, *The Monk* (1796), which was influenced by his formative reading of tales of witchcraft and the supernatural.
The Monk
Ambrosio

Lewis, Sinclair
◎ (1885–1951) US novelist. He became a journalist and wrote several minor works before *Main Street* (1920), the first of a series of bestselling novels satirizing the arid materialism and intolerance of

US small-town life. He received the Nobel prize for literature in 1930, becoming its first US laureate.
Ann Vickers
Vickers, Ann
Arrowsmith
Arrowsmith, Dr Martin
Babbitt
Babbitt, George Folansbee
Babbitt, Myra
Doane, Seneca
Judique, Mrs Tanis
Riesling, Paul
Dodsworth
Dodsworth, Samuel
Elmer Gantry
Gantry, Elmer
It Can't Happen Here
Jessup, Doremus
Windrip, Buzz (Berzelius)
Main Street
Kennicott, Carol, née Milford
Kennicott, Dr Will
The Prodigal Parents
Cornplow, Fred

Lewis, Wyndham
◎ (1882–1957) English novelist, painter and critic. With **Ezra Pound** he instituted the Vorticist movement. His novels, including *Tarr* (1918), are powerful, vivid satires. He is also highly regarded as a painter.
Tarr
Tarr, Frederick

Lindsay, Norman
◎ (1879–1969) Australian artist and writer. He was born into a celebrated family of Australian artists. His diverse, controversial (and now dated) novels mostly portray aspects of a Rabelaisian Melbourne peopled by drunken but lovable artists and disapproving clergy. His children's book *The Magic Pudding* (1918) is a perennial favourite with adults too.
Cousin From Fiji
Bellairs, Cecilia
Biddlecombe, Miss
Domkin, Grandma
Domkin, Uncle George
The Magic Pudding
Barnacles, Bill
Bluegum, Bunyip
Brandysnap, Benjamin
Magic Pudding, the
Possum
Wombat, Watkin
Redheap
Bandparts, Mr
Piper, Ethel
Piper, Robert
Saturdee
Gimble, Peter

Lindsay, Sir David
◎ (c.1486–1555) Scottish poet. He was appointed 'usher' (1512) of the newborn prince who became James V and in 1538 he appears to have been Lyon King-of-Arms. *Ane*

Pleasant Satyre of the Thrie Estaitis, his most remarkable work, was performed at Linlithgow in 1540.
The Historie of Squyer Meldrum
Meldrum, Squire William
Ane Pleasant Satyre of the Thrie Estaitis
Chastitie
Common Thift
Danger
Diligence
Dissait
Divyne Correctioun
Falset
Flatterie
Fund-Jonet
Gude Counsall
Hamelines
Humanitas, Rex
Johne the Common-weill
Merchand
Oppressioun
Pauper (The Pure Man)
Placebo
Sensualitie, Dame
Solace
Spiritualitie
Temporalitie
Veritie
Wantonnes

Lindsay, Vachel
◎ (1879–1931) US poet. He studied painting in Chicago and New York, and from 1906 travelled the USA like a troubadour, reciting his poetry in exchange for hospitality. His poems are highly rhythmic and influenced by ragtime, band music and the cadences of evangelical preaching.
'Abraham Lincoln Walks at Midnight'
Lincoln, Abraham
'In Praise of Johnny Appleseed'
Appleseed, Johnny
'Mae Marsh, Motion Picture Actress'
Marsh, Mae

Linklater, Eric
◎ (1899–1974) Scottish novelist. He was a journalist and academic before embarking on a varied career as a broadcaster and a prolific writer of novels, popular histories, books for children, plays and memoirs. *Juan in America* (1931), a picaresque classic, is his most enduring novel.
Juan in America
Motley, Juan
Juan in China
Motley, Juan
Magnus Merriman
Merriman, Magnus
Private Angelo
Angelo, Private

Lively, Penelope
◎ (born 1933) English novelist and children's author. A preoccupation with the relationship between the present and the past and a vivid sense of time and place form the central thread of much of her writing. She won the Booker Prize with *Moon Tiger* (1987).

Moon Tiger
Hampton, Claudia

Lodge, David

◎ (born 1935) English novelist and
literary critic. He has spent most of
his career in academia and his
critical and theoretical writing
(most of which is concerned with
contemporary fiction) has been
influential. Several of his novels,
which are gently comic, have an
academic setting.

The British Museum is Falling Down
Appleby, Adam

Changing Places
Swallow, Philip
Zapp, Morris J

Nice Work
Penrose, Robyn
Swallow, Philip
Wilcox, Victor
Zapp, Morris J

Small World
McGarrigle, Persse
Pabst, Angelica
Swallow, Philip
Zapp, Morris J

Therapy
Passmore, Laurence ('Tubby')

Thinks …
Messenger, Ralph
Reed, Helen

Lodge, Thomas

◎ (c.1558–1625) English dramatist,
romance writer and poet. About
1588 he took part in a buccaneering
expedition to the Canaries, and
wrote his best-known work, the
romance *Rosalynde, or Euphues'
Golden Legacy* (1590), which
supplied Shakespeare with many of
the chief incidents in *As You Like It*.

*Rosalynde, or Euphues' Golden
Legacy*
Rosalynde

London, Jack, pseudonym of John
Griffith Chaney

◎ (1876–1916) US writer. He was
successively sailor, tramp and gold
miner before he began his career as
a writer. He used his knowledge of
the Klondike in his highly
successful novels, all of which
reflect his preoccupation with the
struggle for survival.

The Call of the Wild
Buck

Martin Eden
Eden, Martin

The Sea-Wolf
Wolf Larsen

White Fang
White Fang

Longfellow, Henry Wadsworth

◎ (1807–82) US poet. He made
numerous visits to Europe and was
Professor of Modern Languages
and Literature at Harvard
(1836–54). His most popular works
are *Evangeline: A Tale of Acadie*
(1847), a tale of the French exiles of

Acadia, and *The Song of Hiawatha*
(1855), which is based on the
legends of Native Americans.

The Courtship of Miles Standish
Standish, Miles

Evangeline: A Tale of Acadie
Bellefontaine, Benedict
Bellefontaine, Evangeline
Lajeunesse, Basil
Lajeunesse, Gabriel

The Song of Hiawatha
Hiawatha
Minnehaha
Mudjekeewis
Nokomis
Wenonah

Loos, Anita

◎ (1893–1981) US writer. She began
writing screenplays for D W
Griffith in 1912. Her comic novel
about Hollywood, *Gentlemen
Prefer Blondes* (1925), was
enormously popular and was made
into both a film and a musical,
though readers failed to recognize
it as a satire.

Gentlemen Prefer Blondes
Lee, Lorelei

Lovecraft, H(oward) P(hillips)

◎ (1890–1937) US science-fiction
writer and poet. From 1923 he
was a regular contributor to
Weird Tales, and his cult following
can be traced to the 60 or so stories
first published in that magazine.
The posthumous volumes of
stories were edited by August
Derleth.

'The Call of Cthulhu'
Cthulhu

'The Whisperer in Darkness'
Old Ones
Yog-Sothoth

Lowell, James Russell

◎ (1819–91) US poet, essayist and
diplomat. At the outbreak of war
with Mexico (1846), he wrote a
satiric poem in the Yankee dialect,
out of which grew *The Biglow
Papers* (1848). An ardent
abolitionist, he also wrote serious
poems, sketches and essays.

The Biglow Papers
Biglow, Hosea
Sawin, Birdofredum
Wilbur, Rev Homer

Lowry, Malcolm

◎ (1909–57) English novelist. He
left public school to become a deck
hand on a ship bound for China. In
later life a wanderer and alcoholic,
he lived in Mexico, then in British
Columbia, before returning to
England. He is best known for
Under the Volcano (1947).

Under the Volcano
Firmin, Geoffrey

Lurie, Alison

◎ (born 1926) US novelist. Since
1968 she has taught at Cornell

University and academic life forms
the backdrop to her first books,
such as the ironically titled *Love
and Friendship* (1962), and *Foreign
Affairs* (1984) which won her the
Pulitzer Prize.

Foreign Affairs
Miner, Vinnie
Mumpson, Chuck
Turner, Fred

Imaginary Friends
McMann, Tom
Zimmern, Roger

Love and Friendship
Turner, Emily Stockwell

The Nowhere City
Cattleman, Katherine
Cattleman, Paul

Only Children
Hubbard, Bill
Hubbard, Honey
King, Anna
Zimmern, Celia
Zimmern, Dan

Real People
Smith, Janet Belle

The Truth about Lorin Jones
Alter, Polly
Jones, Lorin, née Zimmern
Zimmern, Celia

The War Between the Tates
Tate, Brian
Tate, Erica

Lyly, John

◎ (c.1554–1606) English dramatist,
novelist and politician. His
Euphues, or The Anatomy of Wit
(1578), a romance in two parts, was
received with great applause. It
lead to the term 'euphuism',
referring to artificial and extremely
elegant language, with much use
made of complex similes and
antitheses.

Alexander and Campaspe
Campaspe

Euphues and His England
Euphues

Euphues, or The Anatomy of Wit
Eubulus
Euphues
Lucilla
Philautus

MacArthur, Charles see Hecht, Ben
and MacArthur, Charles

Macaulay, Rose

◎ (1881–1958) English novelist.
Her most famous novel *The Towers
of Trebizond* (1956) was awarded a
James Tait Black Memorial Prize.
She also wrote verse, travel books
and essays.

The Towers of Trebizond
Aunt Dot
Chantry-Pigg, Hon Father Hugh

Macaulay, Thomas Babington

◎ (1800–59) English writer and politician. For nearly 20 years, he was one of the most prolific and popular of the writers on the *Edinburgh Review*. He was legal adviser to the Supreme Council of India (1834–38) and on his return in 1839 became MP for Edinburgh, and later Secretary of War.

Lays of Ancient Rome
Horatius
Lars Porsena

McAuley, James

◎ (1917–76) Australian poet, critic and writer. He spent much time during and after World War II in Papua New Guinea, where he likened the destruction of traditional social structures there to the larger upheavals of the western world. His verse is of a classical and visionary style.

Captain Quiros
Quiros, Captain

McCabe, Patrick

◎ (born 1955) Irish novelist and playwright. Born in Monaghan, he worked as a teacher in London for a time. The novel *The Butcher Boy* (1992), a black comedy, won the Irish Times Irish Literature Prize for Fiction. Besides novels, he has also published children's fiction, plays and short stories.

The Butcher Boy
Brady, Francie

McCarthy, Cormac

◎ (born 1933) US novelist. He studied at the University of Tennessee, but left without graduating. His first novel, *The Orchard Keeper* (1965), was acclaimed as an exemplar of 'Southern Gothic'. His Western-inspired 'Border Trilogy', opening with *All the Pretty Horses* (1992), won him a wide international readership.

All the Pretty Horses
Cole, John Grady
Rawlins, Lacey

Cities of the Plain
Cole, John Grady
Parham, Billy

The Crossing
Parham, Billy

McCarthy, Mary

◎ (1912–89) US novelist and critic. She wrote book reviews and worked as an editor and theatre critic for the *Partisan Review* (1937–48). As well as novels, she also wrote documentary denunciations of US involvement in the Vietnam War.

A Charmed Life
Coe, Jane

Coe, Warren
Murphy, Miles
Sinnott, John
Sinnott, Martha

The Company She Keeps
Sargent, Margaret

The Group
Andrews, Polly
Davison, Helena
Eastlake, Lakey (Elinor)
Harshorn, Priss
MacAusland, Libby
Petersen, Harald
Prothero, Pokey (Mary)
Renfrew, Dottie
Strong, Kay

The Groves of Academe
Mulcahy, Henry

Mac Colla, Fionn, pseudonym of Thomas Douglas MacDonald

◎ (1906–75) Scottish novelist. He spent some time in Palestine and then returned to Scotland, where he spent many years teaching in the Western Isles. He is a major figure of the Scottish Renaissance.

And the Cock Crew
Byars, Master
Fearchar the Poet
Sachairi, Maighstir (Mr Zachary Wiseman)

The Ministers
MacAulay, Rev Aulay
MacRury, Rev Ewen

McCullers, Carson

◎ (1917–67) US novelist. *The Heart is a Lonely Hunter* (1940), her first book, distinguished her immediately as a novelist of note. Along with **William Faulkner**, **Tennessee Williams** and **Truman Capote** she is credited with fashioning a type of fiction labelled by critics as Southern Gothic.

The Ballad of the Sad Café
Amelia, Miss
Lymon, Cousin
Macy, Marvin

Clock Without Hands
Clane, Jester
Clane, Judge Fox
Malone, J T
Pew, Sherman

The Heart is a Lonely Hunter
Blount, Jake
Brannon, Biff
Copeland, Dr Benedict
Kelly, Mick
Singer, John

The Member of the Wedding
Addams, Frankie
Brown, Berenice Sadie
West, John Henry

Reflections in a Golden Eye
Langdon, Alison
Langdon, Major Morris
Penderton, Captain
Penderton, Leonora
Williams, Private Ellgee

MacDiarmid, Hugh, pseudonym of Christopher Murray Grieve

◎ (1892–1978) Scottish poet. He was a founder-member of the

National Party of Scotland (which became the Scottish National Party). He became the leader of the Scottish Renaissance and dedicated his life to the regeneration of Scots as a literary language.

A Drunk Man Looks at the Thistle
Drunk Man, the

MacDonald, George

◎ (1824–1905) Scottish novelist, lecturer and poet. He is best known for his children's books.

David Elginbrod
Elginbrod, David

The Princess and the Curdie
Curdie
Irene, Princess

The Princess and the Goblin
Curdie
Irene, Princess

McDonald, John D(ann)

◎ (1916–1986) US crime writer. He created his famous series character Travis McGee in his 44th novel *The Deep Blue Goodbye* in 1964, and went on to write 21 books featuring him – all having a colour in their title.

The Deep Blue Goodbye
McGee, Travis

MacDonald, Ross, pseudonym of Kenneth Millar

◎ (1915–83) US thriller writer. His 'Lew Archer' series is sustained by tough and witty dialogue and rare intelligence, and many of his novels have been adapted for Hollywood.

The Moving Target
Archer, Lew

McEwan, Ian

◎ (born 1948) English writer of novels, short stories and screenplays. His first collections of stories attracted notoriety for their preoccupation with the erotic and the macabre. Less obtrusive but equally consistent is the nature of romantic love, a theme explored in novels such as *Enduring Love* (1997) and *Amsterdam* (1998, Booker Prize).

Amsterdam
Halliday, Vernon
Lane, Molly
Linley, Clive

Atonement
Tallis, Briony
Tallis, Cecilia
Turner, Robbie

Black Dogs
Jeremy
Tremayne, Bernard
Tremayne, June

The Cement Garden
Jack
Julie

The Child in Time
Darke, Charles
Lewis, Stephen

The Comfort of Strangers
Caroline
Colin
Mary
Robert
Enduring Love
Parry, Jed
Rose, Joe

McGahern, John

◎ (born 1934) Irish novelist and short-story writer. He worked as a schoolteacher in Dublin until the publication of his second novel *The Dark* (1965), which was banned in Ireland for its treatment of religion and sexuality. *Amongst Women* (1990) was shortlisted for the Booker Prize. He is often considered Ireland's finest living author.

Amongst Women
Moran
The Dark
Mahoney
Mahoney, son of

McGrath, John

◎ (1935–2002) English writer, director and filmmaker. His first success was *Events While Guarding the Bofors Gun* (1966). As founder and artistic director of the 7:84 Scotland theatre company (1973–88) he also wrote many plays exploring the cultural and political struggles within Scotland.

Events While Guarding the Bofors Gun
Evans, Lance-Bombardier

McIlvanney, William

◎ (born 1936) Scottish novelist and poet. He taught from 1960 to 1975, when he took up writing full-time. His novel *Docherty* (1975) won the Whitbread Novel Award. He has also published thrillers, poetry, essays and journalism.

The Big Man
Scoular, Dan
Docherty
Docherty, Tam
Laidlaw
Laidlaw, Jack
The Papers of Tony Veitch
Laidlaw, Jack
Strange Loyalties
Laidlaw, Jack

Mackenzie, Compton

◎ (1883–1972) English writer. In World War I he served in the Dardanelles, and in 1917 became director of the Aegean Intelligence Service in Syria. His considerable output includes *Whisky Galore* (1947, filmed 1949).

The Four Winds of Love
Ogilvie, John (Juan Pendarves Ogilvie)
Keep the Home Guard Turning
Odd, Sgt Fred
The Monarch of the Glen
Nevis, Ben (Hector MacDonald of Ben Nevis, Glenbogle, Glenbristle,

Strathdiddle, Strathdun, Loch Hoch and Loch Hoo)
Sinister Street
Fane, Michael
Whisky Galore
Odd, Sgt Fred

Mackenzie, Henry

◎ (1745–1831) Scottish writer. He was a crown attorney in the Scottish Court of Exchequer (1765) and his sentimental, but highly influential, novel *The Man of Feeling* was published in 1771. He was one of the founders of the Royal Society of Edinburgh.

The Man of Feeling
Harley

MacLaverty, Bernard

◎ (born 1942) Irish novelist and short-story writer. Born in Belfast, he worked as a laboratory technician before studying at Queen's University. He subsequently moved to Scotland and became a teacher. As well as novels, he has also written screenplays and radio and television plays.

Cal
Cal
Lamb
Lamb, Michael

MacLennan, Hugh

◎ (1907–90) Canadian novelist and essayist. He lectured in classics and later became Professor of English at McGill University. His novel *Barometer Rising* (1941) is considered to be a Canadian classic. He won the Governor General's Literary Award five times.

Barometer Rising
MacRae, Neil
Murray, Major Angus
Wain, Col Geoffrey
Wain, Penelope

McMurtry, Larry

◎ (born 1936) US novelist. He helped to establish the Western as a serious contemporary genre through his vision of the history of his home state of Texas. Hollywood's interest in his work consolidated his reputation.

All My Friends are Going to be Strangers
Deck, Danny
Horseman, Pass By
Bannon, Homer
Hud
The Last Picture Show
Farrow, Jacy
Jackson, Duane
Popper, Ruth
Sam the Lion
Leaving Cheyenne
Gid
Johnny
Molly
Lonesome Dove
Allen, Clara

Call, Woodrow F
McCrae, Gus
Wood, Lorena
Moving On
Carpenter, Pete
Deck, Danny
Terms of Endearment
Greenway, Aurora
Horton, Emma

McNickle, D'Arcy

◎ (1904–77) US novelist. His mother was French Cree and she and her children were adopted to the Native American Flathead (or Saltish) tribe. His novels focus on crises of identity and the conflicts between cultures. His first novel *The Surrounded* (1936) is a Native American approach to the Western genre.

The Surrounded
Leon, Archilde
Wind From An Enemy Sky
Bull
Henry Jim

Magorian, Michelle

◎ (born 1948) English children's writer. She studied drama and spent many years working as an actress before publishing her first book *Goodnight Mister Tom* (1981), which won the Guardian Prize for Children's Fiction.

Goodnight Mister Tom
Beech, Willie
Oakley, Tom (Mister Tom)

Mailer, Norman

◎ (born 1923) US novelist and journalist. During World War II he served in the Pacific. His first novel *The Naked and the Dead* (1948), a social satire and anti-war commentary, became a bestseller, establishing him as a leading novelist of his generation. As a polemicist, campaigner and protester he was prominent throughout the 1960s and has won several Pulitzer Prizes.

Advertisements for Myself
Mailer, Norman, also Aquarius, the Reporter, and A-1
An American Dream
Rojack, Stephen Richards
Ancient Evenings
Menenhetet
The Armies of the Night
Mailer, Norman, also Aquarius, the Reporter, and A-1
Barbary Shore
Guinevere (Guinevere McLeod)
Hollingsworth, Leroy
Lovett, Mikey
McLeod, Arthur
Madison, Lannie
Monina (Monina McLeod)
The Deer Park
Eitel, Charles Francis
Esposito, Elena
Faye, Marion
O'Shaugnessy, Sergius
Teppis, Herman

Index

The Executioner's Song
Baker, Nicole
Gilmore, Gary

Harlot's Ghost
Hubbard, Harry (Herrick), also known as
ANCHOVY/BLUE, or AV/AILABLE, or
'Robert Charles', or 'Harry Field', or KU/
CLOAKROOM, or KU/ROPES, or
'William Madden Libby', or 'Charley
Sloate', or SM/ONION
Montague, Hugh Fremont, also known as
HARLOT, or 'DrTaylor', or GALLSTONE,
or GANTRY, or GHOUL

The Naked and the Dead
Croft, Sgt Sam
Cummings, Gen Edward
Hearn, Lt Robert
Martinez, Corporal Julio
Valsen, Private Red

'The Time of Her Time'
O'Shaugnessy, Sergius

Why Are We In Vietnam?
D J (Ranald Jethroe)

Mais, Roger
◎ (1905–55) Jamaican novelist.
Politically awakened by the
Kingston riots of 1938, he became
one of the first Jamaican writers to
depict the miserable conditions of
the working class in short stories
and novels such as *The Hills were
Joyful Together* (1953) and *Brother
Man* (1954).

Black Lightning
Jake

Brother Man
Bra' Man, also known as John Power
Minette

The Hills Were Joyful Together
Surjue

Malamud, Bernard
◎ (1914–86) US novelist and short-
story writer. One of the leading US
writers of the later 20th century, he
wrote fiction that mingled
mysticism, pessimism and gentle
humour, and drew on the idiom of
Jewish America. He won the
National Book Award twice and
the Pulitzer Prize in 1967.

The Assistant
Alpine, Frankie
Bober, Helen
Bober, Morris

Dubin's Lives
Dubin, William

The Fixer
Bok, Yakov

God's Grace
Cohn, Calvin

The Natural
Hobbs, Roy

A New Life
Levin, Sam

Pictures of Fidelman: An Exhibition
Fidelman, Arthur

The Tenants
Lesser, Harry
Spearmint, Willie

Malouf, David
◎ (born 1934) Australian novelist
and librettist. A full-time writer

since 1978, he has written some
verse, but is best known for his
novels. His second novel, *An
Imaginary Life*, received wide
acclaim when it was serialized by
The New Yorker in 1978. He has
written several librettos.

Fly Away Peter
Crowther, Ashley
Saddler, Jim

Harland's Half Acre
Harland, Frank
Vernon, Phil

An Imaginary Life
Child, the
Ovid (Publius Ovidius Naso)

'Child's Play'
anon (the assassin)
anon (the writer)

'Eustace'
Jane
'Eustace', known as the boy

Johnno
Johnno
'Dante'
'The Prowler'
anon (the prowler)

Mamet, David
◎ (born 1947) US dramatist, screen
writer and director. His best-
known plays address the
psychological and ethical issues
that confront modern, urban
society. He has translated works by
Chekhov and written various
screenplays. He has also directed
films and published essay
collections.

Oleanna
Carol
John

American Buffalo
Dubrow, Donny
Teach, properly Walter Cole

Edmond
Burke, Edmond

Glengarry Glen Ross
Roma, Richard

Speed-the-Plow
Gould, Bobby

Manning, Olivia
◎ (1908–80) English novelist. In
1939 she went abroad with her
husband, a British Council
lecturer, to Bucharest. Her
experiences there formed the basis
of *The Balkan Trilogy* (1960–5).

The Balkan Trilogy
Pringle, Guy
Pringle, Harriet
Yakimov, Prince

The Levant Trilogy
Boulderstone, Simon
Pringle, Guy
Pringle, Harriet

School for Love
Bohun, Miss Ethel
Latimer, Felix

Mansfield, Katherine, pseudonym
of **Kathleen Mansfield Beauchamp**
◎ (1888–1923) New Zealand short-
story writer. She went to London in

1908, determined to pursue a
literary career. *Bliss* (1920)
confirmed her standing as an
original and innovative writer.

Bliss
Young, Bertha

The Daughters of the Late Colonel
Constantia
Josephine

The Garden Party
Laura

Life of Ma Parker
Parker, Ma

Miss Brill
Brill, Miss

Prelude
Kezia
Lottie

Markham, Edwin
◎ (1852–1940) US poet. His most
famous poems, in *The Man With
The Hoe and Other Poems*, were a
protest against the exploitation of
labour and made Markham a
public figure. The title poem was
inspired by a Millet painting.

*The Man With The Hoe and Other
Poems*
Man With The Hoe, the

Marlowe, Christopher
◎ (1564–93) English dramatist who
influenced Shakespeare. His
Tamburlaine the Great (1587–90)
was, in spite of its bombast and
violence, infinitely superior to any
tragedy that had yet appeared on the
English stage. Earlier dramatists
had used blank verse, but Marlowe
was the first to discover its strength
and variety. Marlowe led an
irregular life, kept dubious
company, and was on the point of
being arrested when he was fatally
stabbed in a tavern brawl.

Dr Faustus
Faustus, Dr John
Mephistophilis

Edward II
Edward II
Gaveston, Piers
Isabella, Queen
Mortimer, the Younger
Spencer, the Younger

The Jew of Malta
Barabas

Tamburlaine the Great
Bajazeth
Cosroe
Tamburlaine
Zabina
Zenocrate

Marquand, John P(hillips)
◎ (1893–1960) US novelist. A war
correspondent and advertising
copywriter, he wrote popular
stories for magazines, featuring the
Japanese detective Mr Moto. He
went on to produce a series of
notable novels gently satirizing
affluent middle-class US life.

H M Pulham Esq
Pulham, H M

The Late George Apley
Apley, George
Willing, Mr

No Hero
Moto, Mr

Marryat, Captain Frederick

◎ (1792–1848) English naval officer and novelist. After a naval career in the West Indies and in Burma, he resigned in 1830 to lead the life of a writer. He was the author of a series of novels on sea life as well as stories for children.

Masterman Ready
Ready, Masterman

Mr Midshipman Easy
Easy, John (Jack)

Peter Simple
Simple, Peter

Marsh, Ngaio

◎ (1899–1982) New Zealand detective-story writer and theatre director. After a brief career on stage, she introduced her detective hero Detective Inspector Roderick Alleyn in her first novel *A Man Lay Dead* (1934), which was followed by 30 more stories. During the 1940s and 1950s she devoted much time to theatrical production in New Zealand.

A Man Lay Dead
Alleyn, Detective Inspector Roderick

Marston, John

◎ (1576–1634) English dramatist and satirist. He began to write tragedies and in 1604 published a comedy, *The Malcontent* (1604), dedicated to **Ben Jonson**, with whom he had many quarrels and reconciliations. He gave up play-writing and took holy orders in 1609.

The Dutch Courtezan
Franceschina
Malheureux
Subboys, Beatrice
Young Freevill

The Malcontent
Aurelia
Jacomo, Pietro
Malevole, properly Giovanni Altofronto, Duke of Genoa
Maria
Mendoza

Martel, Yann

◎ (born 1963) Canadian novelist. He grew up in places as diverse as Alaska, Costa Rica and France and has continued to travel. After a variety of occupations, he began to write. He received widespread acclaim with *Life of Pi* (2002), which won a number of awards, including the Booker Prize.

Life of Pi
Pi (Piscine Molitor Patel)

Mason, A(lfred) E(dward) W(oodley)

◎ (1865–1948) English novelist. He became a successful actor, and subsequently combined writing with politics. With *At the Villa Rose* (1910) he introduced his ingenious Inspector Hanaud. From then on he alternated historical adventure and detective fiction.

At the Villa Rose
Hanaud, Inspector

The Four Feathers
Feversham, Harry

Massinger, Philip

◎ (1583–1640) English dramatist. He became a playwright and although he wrote many plays on his own, much of his work was done in collaboration with others, particularly **John Fletcher** and **Francis Beaumont**. *A New Way to Pay Old Debts* (1633) is one of Massinger's most masterly comedies.

A New Way to Pay Old Debts
Alworth, Lady
Alworth, Tom
Lovell, Lord
Overreach, Margaret
Overreach, Sir Giles
Welborne, Frank

Masters, Edgar Lee

◎ (1869–1950) US writer. He was a successful lawyer in Chicago, then turned to writing poetry. He became famous with the satirical *The Spoon River Anthology* (1915), a book of epitaphs in free verse about the lives of people in Illinois. He published several more collections and some novels.

The Spoon River Anthology
Jones, Fiddler
Matlock, Lucinda
Pantier, Benjamin
Pantier, Mrs Benjamin
Petit the Poet
Rutledge, Anne
Village Atheist, the

Mathews, John Joseph

◎ (c.1894–1979) Native American novelist. Having studied at Oxford and Geneva, he travelled widely throughout Europe and North Africa before returning to the US. He was a widely respected leader of his tribe, serving on the Osage Tribal Council for eight years.

Sundown
Windzer, Chal

Matthew, Christopher

◎ (birthdate unknown) English writer and journalist. He has been a columnist for most of the major newspapers, and currently writes on books and TV for the *Daily Mail*, and is well known as a broadcaster.

Diary of a Somebody
Crisp, Simon

Maturin, Charles

◎ (1782–1824) Irish dramatist and novelist. He was a curate in Loughrea and Dublin, but made his name with a series of extravagant novels in a macabre vein that rivalled those of **Ann Radcliffe**. These include *Melmoth the Wanderer* (1820), which influenced Honoré de Balzac.

Melmoth the Wanderer
Melmoth

Maugham, W(illiam) Somerset

◎ (1874–1965) English writer. A year's medical practice in the London slums gave him the material for his first novel, the lurid *Liza of Lambeth* (1897), and the magnificent autobiographical novel, *Of Human Bondage*, eventually published in 1915. During World War I he served as a secret agent in Geneva and Russia. He also visited Tahiti and the Far East, visits which inspired *The Moon and Sixpence* (1919). He also wrote plays and published essays.

Ashenden
Ashenden

Cakes and Ale
Driffield, Edward
Driffield, Rosie
Kear, Alroy

Liza of Lambeth
Liza

The Moon and Sixpence
Strickland, Charles

Of Human Bondage
Athelney, Sally
Carey, Philip
Rodgers, Mildred

'Rain'
Davidson
Thompson, Sadie

The Razor's Edge
Darrell, Larry

Maupin, Armistead

◎ (born 1944) He is best known for *Tales of the City*, his comic novel set in San Francisco. Originally a serial in a daily newspaper, this book and its successors chronicle and celebrate a variety of alternative lifestyles.

Tales of the City
Madrigal, Anna
Mouse, properly Michael Tolliver
Singleton, Mary Ann

Mayor, F(lora) M(acDonald)

◎ (1872–1931) English novelist and short-story writer. Educated at Cambridge, she became an actress against the wishes of her parents, but ended her stage career on the death of her fiance. Her novels, such as *The Third Miss Symons* (1913), often focus on the theme of spinsterhood and are significant for their depiction of women at the turn of the century.

The Rector's Daughter
Jocelyn, Canon
Jocelyn, Mary

The Third Miss Symons
Symons, Henrietta

Melville, Herman

© (1819–91) US novelist, short-story writer and poet. He became a bank clerk but, in search of adventure, joined a whaling ship bound for the South Seas. His masterpiece is the novel *Moby-Dick* (1851), but he also wrote short stories. He is now regarded as one of the USA's greatest novelists. *Billy Budd, Foretopman*, an unfinished but brilliant novella, was published posthumously in 1924.

Billy Budd, Foretopman
Budd, Billy
Claggart, John
Vere, Captain Edward Fairfax ('Starry Vere')

The Confidence Man
Confidence Man

Isreal Potter
Potter, Isreal

Mardi
Alma
Annatoo
Babbalanja
Hautia, Queen
Jarl
Media, King
Mohi ('Braid-Beard')
Samoa
Taji
Yillah
Yoomy ('the Warbler')

Moby-Dick
Ahab, Captain
Daggoo
Fedallah
Flask
Ishmael
Mapple, Father
Moby Dick
Pip
Queequeg
Starbuck
Stubb
Tashtego

Omoo
Bob, Captain
Guy, Captain
Jermin, John
Long Ghost, Doctor
Shorty
Tommo
Zeke

The Piazza Tales
Bartelby
Cereno, Captain Benito

Pierre
Banford, Isabel
Glendinning, Mrs Mary
Glendinning, Pierre
Tartan, Lucy

Redburn
Bolton, Harry
Redburn, Wellingborough
Riga, Captain

Typee
Fayaway
Toby
Tommo

White-Jacket
Chase, Jack
Claret, Captain
Cuticle, Dr Cadwallader
Pert, Mr
White-Jacket

Mercer, David

© (1928–80) English dramatist. Television plays such as *A Suitable Case for Treatment* (1962) explored his fascination with mental health, psychiatry and his struggle to reconcile a belief in socialism with the repression he saw in Eastern Europe.

Morgan–A Suitable Case for Treatment
Delt, Morgan

A Suitable Case for Treatment
Delt, Morgan

Meredith, George

© (1828–1909) English novelist. His disastrous marriage gave him an insight into relations between the sexes, which appear as largely in his work as his other great interest – natural selection as Nature's way of perfecting man. He did not achieve general popularity as a novelist until *Diana of the Crossways* appeared in 1885.

The Adventures of Harry Richmond
Richmond, Harry

Beauchamp's Career
Beauchamp, Nevil

Diana of the Crossways
Merion, Diana

The Egoist
Crossjay
Dale, Laetitia
Durham, Constantia
Middleton, Clara
Middleton, Mr
Oxford, Harry
Patterne, Sir Willoughby
Whitford, Vernon

Evan Harrington
Harrington, Evan

The Ordeal of Richard Feverel
Feverel, Richard

Rhoda Fleming
Fleming, Rhoda

The Shaving of Shagpat
Shagpat

Middleton, Stanley

© (born 1919) English novelist. All his novels are set in his hometown of Nottingham (or its surrounds) and chronicle ordinary people and provincial life.

After a Fashion
Harrington, J J

Apple of the Eye
Tenby, Edward

Brazen Prison
Stead, Charles

The Daysman
Richardson, John

Ends and Means
Chamberlain, Eric

Entry into Jerusalem
Worth, John

In a Strange Land
Murren, James

Recovery
Turner, Job

Middleton, Thomas

© (c.1580–1627) English dramatist. A versatile writer, Middleton was repeatedly employed to write the Lord Mayor's pageant. *The Changeling* (written in conjunction with **William Rowley**) is one of his best works. He was also concerned in the authorship of some of the plays included in the works of **Francis Beaumont** and **John Fletcher** and is now widely thought to have written *The Revenger's Tragedy* (1607).

A Chaste Maid in Cheapside
Touchwood Senior
Whorehound, Sir Walter
Yellowhammer, Moll
Yellowhammer, Tim

Women Beware Women
Capello, Bianca
Cardinal, the
Florence, Duke of
Hippolito
Isabella
Leantio
Leantio's Mother
Livia

Middleton, Thomas (*see above*) and **Rowley, William** (*see* **Rowley, William**)

The Changeling
Alsemero
Antonio
Beatrice-Joanna
De Flores
de Piracquo, Alonzo
Diaphanta
Isabella

Middleton, Thomas (*see above*) or **Tourneur, Cyril** (*see* **Tourneur, Cyril**)

The Revenger's Tragedy
Antonio
Castiza
Duchess, the
Duke, the
Gratiana
Hippolito
Lussurioso
Spurio
Vendice

Miller, Arthur

© (born 1915) US playwright. His first successful play, *All My Sons* (1947), reflected the preoccupation with moral issues that was to characterize his work. His modern tragedy, *Death of a Salesman* (1949), won the Pulitzer Prize and brought him international recognition. One of the major playwrights of the 20th century, he has also published short stories and adaptations of Ibsen.

After the Fall
Quentin

All My Sons
Keller, Joe

The Crucible
Proctor, Elizabeth
Proctor, John
Williams, Abigail

The American Clock
Baum family

Broken Glass
Gellburg, Philip
Gellburg, Sylvia
Death of a Salesman
Charley
Loman, Ben
Loman, Biff
Loman, Happy
Loman, Linda
Loman, Willy
The Price
Franz, Victor
Franz, Walter
A View from the Bridge
Alfieri
Carbone, Beatrice
Carbone, Catherine
Carbone, Eddie
Marco
Rodolpho

Miller, Sue

◎ (born 1943) US novelist. Having married young and been a single mother for many years, she often takes relationships and the family as her theme. Her debut novel *The Good Mother* (1986) was an acclaimed bestseller.

The Good Mother
Dunlap, Anna

Millhauser, Steven

◎ (born 1943) US novelist and short-story writer. He won the Pulitzer Prize with *Martin Dressler: The Tale of an American Dreamer* (1996). He also writes novellas and short stories.

Martin Dressler: The Tale of an American Dreamer
Dressler, Martin

Milne, A(lan) A(lexander)

◎ (1882–1956) English writer. He joined the staff of *Punch* as assistant editor, and became well known for his light essays and his comedies. In 1924 he achieved world fame with his book of children's verse, *When We Were Very Young*, written for his own son, Christopher Robin Milne (1920–96). Further children's classics include the enchantingly whimsical *Winnie-the-Pooh* (1926) and *The House at Pooh Corner* (1928), memorably illustrated by E H Shepard.

The House at Pooh Corner
Eeyore
Piglet
Tigger
Winnie-the-Pooh
Winnie-the-Pooh
Winnie-the-Pooh
Eeyore
Piglet

Milton, John

◎ (1608–74) English poet. Early works include the pastoral elegy *Lycidas* (1637). The Civil War in England, into which he threw himself with revolutionary ardour, silenced his poetic output for 20

years except for some Latin and Italian pieces and occasional sonnets. After the Restoration Milton went into hiding for a short period, was arrested and subsequently released. Although blind from 1652 onwards, he went on to write his great works *Paradise Lost* (1667), *Paradise Regained* (1671) and *Samson Agonistes* (1671).

Lycidas
Lycidas
Paradise Lost
Abdiel
Adam
Beelzebub
Belial
Eve
Gabriel
God
Ithuriel
Mammon
Michael
Moloch
Raphael
Satan
Uriel
Zephon
Paradise Regained
Jesus Christ
John the Baptist
Mary
Satan
Samson Agonistes
Dalila
Harapha of Gath
Manoa
Samson

Mistry, Rohinton

◎ (born 1952) Indian-born Canadian novelist and short-story writer. His novels and short stories reflect his Parsi upbringing and usually involve a large cast of characters. He has been listed for the Booker Prize three times.

Such a Long Journey
Gustad Noble

Mitchell, Margaret

◎ (1900–49) US novelist. She studied for a medical career, but turned to journalism. After her marriage in 1925, she began the ten-year task of writing her only novel, *Gone with the Wind* (1936). It won the Pulitzer Prize, sold over 25 million copies, was translated into 30 languages and was the subject of a celebrated film in 1939.

Gone with the Wind
Butler, Rhett
O'Hara, Scarlett
Wilkes, Ashley

Mitchell, W(illiam) O(rmond)

◎ (1914–98) Canadian novelist and dramatist. He grew up in the prairies and travelled in Europe before returning to Canada to become a schoolteacher. His first novel, *Who Has Seen the Wind* (1947), was immediately hailed as a classic. He was fiction editor for a

magazine for many years as well as writing scripts for his popular radio serial 'Jake and the Kid'.

Who Has Seen the Wind
O'Connal, Brian

Mitford, Nancy

◎ (1904–73) English novelist and biographer. One of the famous Mitford sisters, she established a reputation with her witty novels such as *The Pursuit of Love* (1945). As one of the contributors to and editors of *Noblesse Oblige* (1956), she helped to originate the famous 'U', or upper-class, and 'non-U' classification of linguistic usage and behaviour.

The Pursuit of Love
Bolter, the
Fanny
Linda
Radletts, the

Mittelholzer, Edgar

◎ (1909–65) Guyanese novelist. Born in New Amsterdam, Mittelholzer helped to establish the foundations of Guyanese and West Indian literature in the 1940s. He emigrated to England where he died by committing suicide. He is best known for his monumental Kaywana trilogy, in which he presents the history of the Van Groenwegel family from the 17th century to agitation for independence in British Guiana in 1953.

The Children of Kaywana
van Groenwegel, Hubertus

Mo, Timothy

◎ (born 1950) Hong-Kong born English novelist. Born to a Cantonese father and an English mother, he worked as a journalist for a time. Three of his novels have been shortlisted for the Booker Prize.

An Insular Possession
Chase, Gideon
Eastman, Walter
Remington, Alice (Barclay)
Ribeiro, Father (Joaquim)
The Monkey King
Nolasco, Wallace
Poon, Mr
The Redundancy of Courage
Ng, Adolph
Sour Sweet
Chen, Ah
Chen, Lily (Moon Lily)
Tang, Mui (Moon Blossom)

Momaday, N(avarre) Scott

◎ (born 1934) Native American writer. Born on a Kiowa reservation, he became a literary scholar and won a Pulitzer Prize for his first novel, *House Made of Dawn* (1968). Besides novels, he has also published collections of poetry; an intricate collection of Kiowa tribal and family stories and Kiowa history; and the

Index

autobiographical book, *The Names* (1976).

The Ancient Child
Grey
Set

House Made of Dawn
Abel

Montgomery, L(ucy) M(aud)

ⓒ (1874–1942) Canadian novelist. She was born and brought up on Prince Edward Island. Her first book was the phenomenally successful *Anne of Green Gables* (1908). She followed it with several sequels, of which *Rilla of Ingleside* (1921) is an invaluable description of the impact of World War I on the island community.

Anne of Green Gables
Anne of Green Gables, properly Anne Shirley

Moore, Brian

ⓒ (1921–99) Irish-born Canadian novelist. After World War II he worked for the United Nations in Europe before emigrating to Canada in 1948, where he became a journalist and adopted Canadian citizenship. *The Lonely Passion of Judith Hearne* (1955) was particularly admired for its portrayal of women.

Black Robe
Laforgue, Father Paul

The Colour of Blood
Bem, Cardinal (Stephen)

The Lonely Passion of Judith Hearne
Hearne, Judith

The Luck of Ginger Coffey
Coffey, Ginger (James Francis)

Moore, George

ⓒ (1852–1933) Irish novelist. He lived a bohemian life in London and Paris, until turning to realist fiction with his novels of low life. He was involved with Lady Gregory and **W B Yeats** in setting up the Abbey Theatre in Dublin.

Esther Waters
Waters, Esther

Moorhouse, Frank

ⓒ (born 1938) Australian novelist and short-story writer. He worked as a journalist in Sydney and in various other locations throughout Australia before becoming a full-time writer. He is a master of discontinuous narrative.

The Americans, Baby
Becker
McDowell, Terri

Conference-ville
anon (the narrator)

The Electrical Experience
McDowell, T George

The Everlasting Secret Family
Bow, Irving

More, Thomas

ⓒ (1478–1535) English politician and scholar. In 1529, against his own strongest wish, he was appointed Lord Chancellor. In 1534 Henry VIII was declared head of the English Church and More's steadfast refusal to recognize anyone other than the pope as head of the Church led to his sentence for high treason. Refusing to recant, he was beheaded. With his *Utopia* (1516), More takes his place with the most eminent humanists of the Renaissance.

Utopia
Hythloday, Raphael

Morgan, Lady

ⓒ (1783–1859) Irish novelist. She supported her family, first as a governess, then as a writer of sentimental poems and novels. In 1812 she married a surgeon, Thomas Charles Morgan (1783–1843), who was later knighted. Her works were bestsellers of their day.

The Wild Irish Girl
Glorvina, Lady

Morrison, Toni, pen name of Chloe Anthony Morrison

ⓒ (born 1931) US novelist. She explores in rich vocabulary and cold-blooded detail the story of African-Americans in a white-dominated culture. She was awarded the Nobel prize for literature in 1993, which confirmed her as one of the most important contemporary US novelists.

Beloved
Sethe

The Bluest Eye
Breedlove, Pecola

Jazz
Manfred, Dorcas
Trace, Joe
Trace, Violet

Paradise
Albright, Mavis
Consolata
Grace, also known as Gigi
Seneca
Truelove, Pallas

Song of Solomon
Bains, Guitar
Dead, Milkman
Dead, Pilate
Hagar

Sula
Peace, Sula
Wright, Nel

Tar Baby
Childs, Jadine
Son

Mortimer, John

ⓒ (born 1923) Called to the Bar in 1948, he was a constant defender of liberal values. His series of novels featuring Horace Rumpole, an amiable defence barrister, has been adapted for television as *Rumpole of the Bailey*. He has written many plays and adaptations for the stage and has published autobiography, made notable translations, and

written several television screenplays.

Paradise Postponed
Simcox, Rev Simeon
Titmuss, Rt Hon Leslie

Rumpole of the Bailey
Rumpole, Horace

Titmuss Regained
Simcox, Rev Simeon
Titmuss, Rt Hon Leslie

The Trials of Rumpole
Rumpole, Horace

Mortimer, Penelope

ⓒ (1918–99) English novelist. Her detailed and precise works usually deal with women's experiences, particularly of relationships and marriage (she was married for a time to **Sir John Mortimer**). Her novel *The Pumpkin Eater* (1962) was adapted for the screen by **Harold Pinter**.

The Pumpkin Eater
Armitage, Mrs

Mourning Dove/Hum-ishu-ma

ⓒ (1888–1936) Native American novelist. *Cogewea, the Half-Blood* (1927) is one of the earliest novels to be written by a Native American woman. She was a migrant worker for much of her life and was one of the first women elected to her tribal council.

Cogewea, the Half-Blood
Cogewea

Mudrooroo, originally Colin Johnson

ⓒ (born 1938) Australian novelist. His first novel *Wild Cat Falling* (1965) was the first published novel by an Aboriginal writer. He is highly active in Aboriginal cultural affairs and has also written poetry and plays. In 1988 he changed his name to Mudrooroo.

Doctor Wooreddy's Prescription for Enduring the Ending of the World
Wooreddy

Long Live Sandawara
Alan
Noorak

Wild Cat Falling
anon (the central character)
Noongar

Mukherjee, Bharati

ⓒ (born 1940) Indian-born US novelist. Born in Calcutta, she was educated there and in the USA. She subsequently moved to Canada, where she lived before eventually returning to the USA. Her Bengali heritage and personal experience as an immigrant feature strongly in her works.

Jasmine
Vijh, Jasmine

Munro, Alice

ⓒ (born 1931) Canadian short-story writer and novelist. Her stories, published for many years without being collected, are recognized as among the finest of the day. They are often set in rural and semi-rural Ontario, the landscape of her childhood, or feature women who have escaped from such backgrounds. *Lives of Girls and Women* (1971) is her only novel to date.

Lives of Girls and Women
Jordan, Del

Munro, Neil

◎ (1864–1930) Scottish novelist and journalist. He was editor of the *Glasgow Evening News* from 1918 to 1927. He wrote romantic Celtic tales and humorous Highland novels but is best known for his humorous tales about a Clyde steamboat, collected as *Para Handy and Other Tales* (1931).

Gilian, the Dreamer
Gilian, the Dreamer

John Splendid
Elrigmore, Colin
Splendid, John, properly McIver of Barbeck

Para Handy and Other Tales
Para Handy, properly Peter MacFarlane

Murdoch, Iris

◎ (1919–99) Irish-born English novelist, playwright and philosopher. Her fiction mostly deals with the conflict of good and evil in the context of involved personal relationships, often attended by strange situations and incidents and written with a pervasive blend of realism and symbolism. *The Sea, The Sea* (1978) won the Booker Prize.

The Accidental Man
Gibson Grey, Austin

The Bell
Fawley, Catherine
Fawley, Nick
Gashe, Toby
Greenfield, Dora
Greenfield, Paul
Mead, Michael
Tayper Pace, James

The Black Prince: A Celebration of Love
Baffin, Arnold
Pearson, Bradley

The Book and the Brotherhood
Crimond

Bruno's Dream
Greensleave, Bruno
Greensleave, Diana
Greensleave, Miles
Odell, Danby
Watkin, Lisa

A Fairly Honourable Defeat
Browne, Morgan
Browne, Tallis
Foster, Hilda
Foster, Rupert
Foster, Simon
King, Julius
Nilsson, Axel

The Flight from the Enchanter
Blick, Calvin
Cockeyne, Annette

Fox, Mischa
Keepe, Hunter
Keepe, Rosa
Lusiewicz, Jan
Lusiewicz, Stefan
Nina
Rainborough, John
Saward, Peter

The Good Apprentice
Baltram, Edward
Baltram, Jesse
Duno, Stuart

Henry and Cato
Forbes, Cato
Marshalson, Henry

The Italian Girl
Magistretti, 'Maggie' (Maria)

The Message to the Planet
Ludens, Alfred
Vallar, Marcus

The Nice and the Good
Ducane, John

Nuns and Soldiers
Cavidge, Anne
'Count', the (Wojciech 'Peter' Szczepanski)
Openshaw, Gertrude

The Philosopher's Pupil
McCaffrey, George
Rozanov, John Robert

The Sandcastle
Carter, Rain
Mor, William

The Sea, The Sea
Arrowby, Charles

A Severed Head
Klein, Honor
Lynch-Gibbon, Martin

The Time of the Angels
Fischer, Carel
Fischer, Elizabeth
Fischer, Marcus
Fischer, Muriel
O'Driscoll, Pattie
Peshkov, Eugene
Peshkov, Leo

Under the Net
Belfounder, Hugo
Donaghue, Jake (James)
Finn (Peter O'Finney)
Tinckham, Mrs

An Unofficial Rose
Peronett, Hugh
Sands, Emma

A Word Child
Burde, Hilary

Murray, Les

◎ (born 1938) Australian poet, critic and editor. He has worked as a translator and a freelance writer and lived in England and Europe for a time. His poetry, which has made him one of Australia's leading literary figures, is revered for its perceptive evocation of rural life. *The Boys Who Stole the Funeral* (1980) is a verse-novel in 140 sonnets.

The Boys Who Stole the Funeral
Dunn, Clarrie
Forbutt, Kevin
Reeby, Cameron

Nabokov, Vladimir

◎ (1899–1977) Russian-born US novelist, poet and critic. Following the Bolshevik Revolution, he and his brother went to England to study. He subsequently lived in Berlin where he published his first novels (in Russian) and spent time in Paris before emigrating to the USA. He began to write in English and published many short stories and novels. *Lolita* (1955) was a *succès de scandale* and allowed him to abandon teaching and devote himself to writing full-time.

Ada, or Ardor: A Family Chronicle
Ada (Adelaida)
Veen, Van

Despair
Karlovich, Herman

King, Queen, Knave
Franz

Lolita
Humbert, Humbert
Lolita (Dolores Haze)

Pale Fire
Gradus
Kinbote, Charles
Shade, John

Pnin
Pnin, Professor Timofey

The Real Life of Sebastian Knight
Knight, Sebastian

Transparent Things
Person, Hugh

Naipaul, Shiva

◎ (1945–85) Trinidadian novelist and travel writer. The younger brother of **V S Naipaul**, he wrote fiction – including *The Chip-Chip Gatherers* – and non-fiction.

The Chip-Chip Gatherers
Basdai
Bholai, Julian
Bholai, Vishnu
Ramsaran, Egbert, originally Ashok
Ramsaran, Rani
Ramsaran, Wilbert
Singh
Sita
Sushila

Naipaul, V(idiadhar) S(urajprasad)

◎ (born 1932) Trinidadian novelist. He dabbled in journalism before his first novel, *The Mystic Masseur* (1957), was published. The book which made his name was *A House for Mr Biswas* (1961), a spicy satire spanning three Trinidadian generations but focusing on its eponymous six-fingered sign-writer. Thereafter the Caribbean figured less prominently in his work, which grew steadily darker

Index

and more complex. He was awarded the Nobel prize for literature in 2001.

A Bend in the River
Salim

The Enigma of Arrival
Jack
West Indian Narrator, the

Guerillas
Ahmed, Jimmy
Jane
Roche, Peter

Half a Life
Chandran, Willie Somerset

A House for Mister Biswas
Biswas, Mohun

In a Free State
Bobby
Linda

Miguel Street
Big Foot
Bogart
Hat

The Mimic Men
Singh, Ralph

Mr Stone and the Knights Companion
Stone, Mr

The Mystic Masseur
Ramsumair, Ganesh

The Suffrage of Elvira
Harbans, Surujpat

Narayan, R(asipuram) K(rishnaswami)

ⓒ (1906–2001) Indian novelist. His first novel, *Swami and Friends* (1935), and its successor *The Bachelor of Arts* (1937), are set in the enchanting fictional territory of 'Malgudi'. He also published stories, travel books, books for children, essays and a memoir.

The Bachelor of Arts
Chandran

The Dark Room
Savitri

The English Teacher
Krishna

The Financial Expert
Balu
Margayya
Pal, Dr

The Guide
Raju

The Man-Eater of Malgudi
Nataraj
Vasu

Mr Sampath: the Printer of Malgudi
Sampath, Mr
Srinivas

The Painter of Signs
Daisy
Raman

Swami and Friends
Strinivasan, Swaminathan

The Sweet Vendor
Jagan

Waiting for the Mahatma
Bharati
Sriram

Nashe, Thomas

ⓒ (1567–1601) English dramatist and satirist. He showed a talent for

vituperation which he expressed in such works as *Pierce Penniless His Supplication to the Devil* (1592). *The Isle of Dogs* (1597), now lost, drew such attention to abuses in the state that it was suppressed, the theatre closed, and the writer himself thrown into the Fleet prison.

Pierce Penniless His Supplication to the Devil
Penniless, Pierce

The Unfortunate Traveller
Wilton, Jack

Naughton, Bill

ⓒ (1910–92) English novelist and playwright. His family emigrated from Ireland to Bolton in Lancashire when he was young. He wrote plays for television, radio, stage and film. Many of his works examine northern working-class culture. The 1966 film version of his stage-play, *Alfie* (1963), for which he wrote the screenplay, caught the spirit of 1960s Britain.

Alfie
Alfie

Alfie Darling
Alfie

Nesbit, E(dith)

ⓒ (1858–1924) English writer. Educated at a French convent, she began her literary career by writing poetry. Financial difficulties forced her to turn to popular fiction and children's stories, including *The Treasure Seekers* (1899) and *The Railway Children* (1906).

The New Treasure Seekers
Bastables, the

Oswald Bastable and Others
Bastables, the

The Railway Children
Roberta, Peter and Phyllis

The Treasure Seekers
Bastables, the

The Wouldbegoods
Bastables, the

Ngugi wa Thiong'o, originally **James Ngugi**

ⓒ (born 1938) Kenyan novelist. One of East Africa's foremost novelists, Ngugi's literary targets have included governmental corruption, socioeconomic exploitation, and religious hypocrisy. He was imprisoned for a year without trial for his involvement with a community theatre in his home village. He has taught at universities in Africa, Europe and the USA.

A Grain of Wheat
Gikonyo
Karanja
Kihika
Mugo
Mumbi

Devil on the Cross
Gicandi Player
Wariinga

The River Between

Waiyaki

Weep Not, Child
Ngotho

Nichols, Peter

ⓒ (born 1927) English playwright. He worked as an actor and teacher before starting to write for television and stage. His first stage success was *A Day in the Death of Joe Egg* (1967), a black comedy about the burden of raising a handicapped child, based on his own family's experiences.

A Day in the Death of Joe Egg
Bri
Joe (Josephine)
Sheila

Niland, D'Arcy

ⓒ (1919–67) Australian writer. He won many prizes for short stories and novels, and in 1955 achieved international fame with his novel *The Shiralee*. *Dead Men Running* (1969, later an ABC serial) is perhaps his best novel. He also wrote radio and television plays and short stories.

Dead Men Running
More, Starky

The Shiralee
Buster

Njau, Rebeka

ⓒ (born 1932) Kenyan writer. She worked for many years as a teacher. She published her powerful novel *Ripples in the Pool* in 1975.

Ripples in the Pool
Gikere
Selina

Norris, Frank

ⓒ (1870–1902) US novelist. He first studied art but later turned to journalism. He was influenced by Émile Zola and was one of the first US naturalist writers, his major novel being *McTeague: A Story of San Francisco* (1899), a story of lower-class life in San Francisco.

McTeague: A Story of San Francisco
Macapa, Maria (Miranda)
McTeague
Schouler, Marcus
Sieppe, Trina, subsequently Trina McTeague
Zerkow

The Octopus: A Story of California
Annixter
Behrman, S
Derrick, Harran
Derrick, Magnus
Osterman
Presley
Tree, Hilma
Vanamee

The Pit: A Story of Chicago
Corthell, Sheldon
Dearborn, Laura
Dearborn, Page
Jadwin, Curtis

Vandover and the Brute
Vandover

Norton, Thomas and **Sackville, Thomas**

◎ (1532–84 and 1536–1608) English poets. A successful lawyer, Thomas Norton collaborated with the statesman Thomas Sackville on the tragedy *Gorboduc*, which was performed before Queen Elizabeth I (Sackville's second cousin) in 1562, and has some claim to be considered the first true English tragedy.

Gorboduc
Ferrex and Porrex
Gorboduc
Videna

Nwapa, Flora

◎ (1931–93) Nigerian short-story writer and novelist. She has been called the mother of modern African literature. She worked as a teacher, in various government posts and also established her own publishing press. Her fiction deals with contemporary Nigerian life, especially women's issues.

Efuru
Adizua
Ogene, Efuru
Uberife, Eneberi, or Gilbert

Idu
Adiewere
Idu

Oates, Joyce Carol

◎ (born 1938) US writer. A prolific fiction writer and essayist, her work is violent and impressive in its social scope, and her fiction challenges received ideas about the nature of human experience. She has taught at various universities, including Princeton, and has also published short stories, poetry, essays and critical writings.

American Appetites
McCullough, Glynnis
McCullough, Ian

Son of Morning
Vickery, Nathanael

O'Brian, Patrick, pseudonym of **Richard Patrick Russ**

◎ (1914–2000) English writer. He is best known as the author of 20 vivid and well-researched books detailing the naval and terrestrial exploits of Captain Jack Aubrey and Doctor Stephen Maturin, during the Napoleonic era.

Master and Commander
Aubrey, Jack
Maturin, Stephen

O'Brien, Edna

◎ (born 1932) Irish novelist, short-story writer and playwright. Her dominant themes are loneliness, guilt and loss, articulated in musical, sensuous prose. She caused a scandal in Ireland with her first novel *The Country Girls* (1960). She has also published short stories and non-fiction.

The Country Girls
Brady, Kate (Caithleen)
Brennan, Baba (Bridget)

Down by the River
MacNamara, Mary

The High Road
Anna
Catalina

'Mrs. Reinhardt'
Reinhardt, Mrs

In the Forest
O'Kane, Michen

Night
Hooligan, Mary

Wild Decembers
Brennan, Joseph
Bugler, Mick

O'Brien, Flann, pseudonym of **Brian O'Nolan**

◎ (1911–66) Irish writer. He studied German, Irish and English and worked in the Irish Civil Service until his premature retirement in 1953. The publication of the hilarious and narratively ambitious novel *At-Swim-Two-Birds* in 1939 owed much to **Graham Greene**'s enthusiasm.

At Swim-Two-Birds
Trellis, Dermot

O'Brien, Kate

◎ (1897–1974) Irish playwright and novelist. She worked as a governess in Spain after university and moved to London in 1930. A remarkable observer of life, she suffered a profoundly unhappy marriage, and her novels are best understood by appreciation of her consciousness of a lesbian sexual identity.

The Ante-Room
Cunningham, Nurse
Curran, Doctor (William)
Mulqueen, Agnes
Mulqueen, Danny
Mulqueen, Marie-Rose
Mulqueen, Reggie
Mulqueen, Teresa

That Lady
Mendoza y de la Cerda, Ana de
Philip II of Spain

O'Casey, Sean

◎ (1884–1964) Irish playwright. He worked as a labourer and for nationalist organizations before beginning his career as a dramatist. His early plays, dealing with low life in Dublin – *The Shadow of a Gunman* (1923) and *Juno and the Paycock* (1924) – were written for the Abbey Theatre, Dublin. Later he became more experimental and impressionistic.

Juno and the Paycock
Boyle, 'Captain' Jack
Boyle, Juno
Daly, 'Joxer'

The Plough and the Stars
Burgess, Bessie
Clitheroe, Jack
Clitheroe, Nora

The Shadow of a Gunman
Davoren, Donal
Maguire, Mr
Owens, Tommy
Powell, Minnie
Shields, Seumus

O'Connor, Flannery

◎ (1925–64) US novelist and short-story writer. She was brought up in the Bible belt of the Deep South, and in her work she homed in on the Protestant fundamentalists who dominated the region. Her characters seem almost grotesque and freakish, but she was describing her reality, and her heightened depiction of it is unforgettable.

The Displaced Person
McIntyre, Mrs
Shortley, Mrs

Everything That Rises Must Converge
Julian
Julian's Mother

Good Country People
Hulga

A Good Man is Hard to Find
Grandmother, the
Misfit, the

Odets, Clifford

◎ (1906–63) US playwright and actor. He helped found the Group Theatre, New York, in 1931, under whose auspices his early plays were produced. The most important US playwright of the 1930s, his works are marked by a strong social conscience and grow largely from the conditions of the Depression of that time.

Waiting for Lefty
Costello, Lefty
Fatt, Harry

O'Hara, John

◎ (1905–70) US novelist and short-story writer. He was born in Pottsville, Pennsylvania, which in his fiction becomes 'Gibbsville', the setting for *Appointment in Samarra* (1934). Two of his works, *Butterfield 8* (1935) and *Pal Joey* (1940), became film and stage successes and many of his stories were published in *The New Yorker*.

Appointment in Samarra
English, Julian
Horman, Helene
Reilly, Harry

Butterfield 8
Wandrous, Gloria

From the Terrace
Eaton, Alfred

Hope of Heaven
Malloy, Jimmy

The Lockwood Concern
Lockwood, George
Pal Joey
Evans, Joey
Ten North Frederick
Chapin, Joe

Okara, Gabriel

◎ (born 1921) Nigerian poet and novelist. The son of an Ijo chief, he was educated in Nigeria and the USA and worked in publishing and government posts. His poems are widely anthologized. His poetic novel *The Voice* (1964) has aroused much interest for its linguistic experimentalism. Okara has also published children's books.

The Voice
Okoko, or the Voice
Ozongo
Tuere

Okri, Ben

◎ (born 1959) Nigerian novelist, poet and short-story writer. Educated in Nigeria and England (where he now lives), he published his first novel in 1980. His third novel, *The Famished Road* (1991), won the Booker Prize.

The Famished Road
Azaro

Oliphant, Margaret

◎ (1828–97) Scottish novelist. Her first novel was written when she was just 16, but her first published work came in 1849. She was widowed in 1859, and found herself in debt with an extended family to support and educate. She went on to write almost a hundred novels.

The Doctor's Family
Rider, Dr Edward
Rider, Fred
Rider, Susan
Underwood, Nettie
Hester: A Story of Contemporary Life
Hester
Vernon, Catherine
Kirsteen
Kirsteen
Miss Marjoribanks
Marjoribanks, Miss
The Perpetual Curate
Proctor, Rev Morley
Wentworth, Rev Francis
Wodehouse, Lucy
Wodehouse, Miss
Phoebe Junior
Beecham, Phoebe, née Tozer
Tozer, Mr
The Rector
Proctor, Rev Morley
Wentworth, Rev Francis
Western, Lady
Wodehouse, Lucy
Wodehouse, Miss
Salem Chapel
Beecham, Phoebe, née Tozer
Tozer, Mr
Tufton, Rev Mr
Vincent, Mrs

Vincent, Rev Arthur
Western, Lady
Some Passages in the Life of Margaret Maitland
Maitland, Margaret

Ondaatje, Michael

◎ (born 1943) Canadian poet and novelist. Born in Sri Lanka, he emigrated to Canada in 1962. Two decades later, he portrayed his aristocratic and eccentric relatives in a beguiling memoir, *Running in the Family* (1982). His novel, *The English Patient* (1992), won the Booker Prize.

Anil's Ghost
Tissera, Anil
The Collected Works of Billy the Kid
Billy the Kid, also known as William H Bonney
Coming Through Slaughter
Bolden, Buddy
The English Patient
English Patient, the
Hana

O'Neill, Eugene

◎ (1888–1953) US playwright. Following a fragmentary education, he signed on as a sailor on voyages to Australia, South Africa and elsewhere. He spent six months in a TB sanatorium, where he began to write plays. *Beyond the Horizon* (1920) was awarded the Pulitzer Prize and followed by other plays. O'Neill then began experimenting in new dramatic techniques and wrote the trilogy *Mourning Becomes Electra* (1931), among others. *Long Day's Journey into Night* (first performed posthumously in 1956; Pulitzer Prize 1957) is probably O'Neill's masterpiece. He was awarded the Nobel prize for literature in 1936.

All God's Chillun Got Wings
Downey, Ella
Harris, Jim
Anna Christie
Burke, Mat
Christopherson, Anna
Christopherson, Chris
Marthy
Beyond the Horizon
Mayo, Andrew
Mayo, Robert
Desire Under the Elms
Cabot, Eben
Cabot, Ephraim
Putnam, Abbie, later Abbie Cabot
The Emperor Jones
Jones, Brutus
Lem
Smithers, Henry
The Great God Brown
Anthony, Dion
Brown, William A
The Hairy Ape
Douglas, Mildred
Yank, properly Robert Smith
The Iceman Cometh
Hickey
Hope, Harry

Long Day's Journey Into Night
Tyrone, Edmund
Tyrone, James
Tyrone, Jamie
Tyrone, Mary
Mourning Becomes Electra
Brant, Captain Adam
Mannon, Christine
Mannon, Gen Ezra
Mannon, Lavinia
Mannon, Orin
Strange Interlude
Darrell, Dr Edmund
Evans, Sam
Leeds, Nina
Marsden, Charles

Orczy, Baroness (Mrs Montague Barstow)

◎ (1865–1947) British novelist and playwright. Born in Hungary and educated in Paris and Brussels, she then studied art in London. *The Scarlet Pimpernel* (1905) was the first success in her long writing career. It was followed by many popular adventure romances, which never quite attained the success of her early work.

The Scarlet Pimpernel
Blakeney, Sir Percy

Orton, Joe, pseudonym of John Kingsley

◎ (1933–67) English dramatist. After training as an actor at RADA in London, he turned to writing vivid, outrageous farces. He was murdered by his lover, Kenneth Halliwell, who subsequently killed himself.

Entertaining Mr Sloane
Ed
Kath
Sloane
Loot
McLeavy, Harold
McMahon, Phyllis Jean, alias Fay
Truscott, Jim

Orwell, George, pseudonym of Eric Blair

◎ (1903–50) English novelist and essayist. He served in Burma in the Indian Imperial Police and then literally went *Down and Out in Paris and London* (1933). He fought and was wounded in the Spanish Civil War and he developed his own brand of socialism. During World War II, he was a war correspondent. His intellectual honesty motivated his biting satire of communist ideology in *Animal Farm* (1945). It also prompted his terrifying prophecy for mankind in *1984* (1949).

Animal Farm
Benjamin
Boxer
Clover
Frederick, Mr
Jones, Mr
Mollie
Moses
Napoleon

Old Major
Pilkington, Mr
Snowball
Squealer
Whymper, Mr

A Clergyman's Daughter
Hare, Dorothy

Coming Up for Air
Bowling, George

Keep the Aspidistra Flying
Comstock, Gordon

1984
Charrington, Mr
Julia
O'Brien
Smith, Winston

Osborne, John
◎ (1929–94) English playwright
and actor. His plays *Look Back in
Anger* (1956), and *The Entertainer*
(1957) established Osborne as the
leading young exponent of British
social drama. The 'hero' of the first,
Jimmy Porter, the prototype 'Angry
Young Man', and the pathetic,
mediocre music hall joker Archie
Rice, both echo the author's
uncompromising hatred of
outworn social and political
institutions and attitudes. He also
wrote screenplays and volumes of
autobiography.

Déjàvu
Lewis, Cliff

The Entertainer
Rice, Archie

Inadmissible Evidence
Maitland, Bill

Look Back in Anger
Charles, Helena
Lewis, Cliff
Porter, Alison
Porter, Jimmy

Luther
Luther, Martin

A Patriot for Me
Redl, Alfred

Osborne, John (*see above*) and
Creighton, Anthony

Epitaph for George Dillon
Aunt Ruth (Ruth Gray)
Dillon, George

Ostenso, Martha
◎ (1900–63) Norwegian-born
Canadian novelist. She worked as a
rural schoolteacher and newspaper
reporter. She became romantically
involved with novelist/teacher
Douglas Durkin, and they later
collaborated on novels. In 1925 she
published her masterpiece, *Wild
Geese*, hailed as a landmark in
Canadian realism.

Wild Geese
Archer, Lind
Gare, Caleb
Gare, Jude (Judith)

Otway, Thomas
◎ (1652–85) English dramatist. He
failed utterly as an actor, but had
greater successs as a playwright.

His greatest work, *Venice Preserv'd,
or A Plot Discovered* (1682), is a
masterpiece of tragic passion.

The Orphan
Acasto
Castalio
Chamont
Monimia
Polydore

Venice Preserv'd, or A Plot Discovered
Antonio
Aquilina
Belvidera
Jaffier
Pierre
Priuli
Renault

Palahniuk, Chuck
◎ (born 1961) US novelist. His first
novel was rejected, but he achieved
cult status with his novel *Fight Club*
(1996).

Fight Club
Durden, Tyler

Palmer, Vance
◎ (1885–1959) Australian novelist
and critic. He travelled widely in
England and Europe and returned
home with the aim of developing
and promoting a national
literature in Australia with his wife
Nettie. His works include novels,
poetry, essays and short stories.
The Vance Palmer Prizes (Fiction
and Non-Fiction) are awarded each
year to contemporary Australian
writers.

Golconda
Donovan, Macy
Varek, Neda

The Passage
Callaway, Lew

Paretsky, Sara
◎ (born 1947) US crime writer.
Born in Kansas, she worked for a
research firm and as a marketing
manager for an insurance company,
before becoming a full-time writer
in 1986. That same year she co-
founded Sisters in Crime, an
organization devoted to promoting
women crime writers.

Indemnity Only
Warshawski, V I (Victoria)

Park, Ruth
◎ (born c.1923) Australian writer.
Her first success was with the novel
Harp in the South (1948), which
won a newspaper competition.
This story of Sydney slum life has
been translated into ten languages
and forms a trilogy with *Poor Man's*

Orange (1949) and the
retrospective *Missus* (1985). She
also wrote some popular children's
books and novels for adolescent
readers.

Harp in the South
Darcy, Dolour
Darcy, Hughie
Darcy, Margaret

Missus
Darcy, Hughie
Darcy, Margaret

Poor Man's Orange
Darcy, Dolour
Darcy, Hughie
Darcy, Margaret

Parker, Robert B(rown)
◎ (born 1932) US crime writer. At
graduate school he studied the
works of **Raymond Chandler** and
Dashiell Hammett. He is best
known for his 'Spenser' series,
featuring a Boston-based ex-boxer
and ex-cop which began with *The
Godwulf Manuscript* (1973).

The Godwulf Manuscript
Spenser

Parsons, Tony
◎ (born 1955) English columnist
and novelist. During the 1970s, he
worked for the *NME* (*New Musical
Express*) as a journalist. He has
published collections of his
journalism as well as highly
successful novels.

Man and Boy
Silver, Harry

Man and Wife
Silver, Harry

One for My Baby
Budd, Alfie

Pater, Walter
◎ (1839–94) English critic and
essayist. His *Studies in the History
of the Renaissance* (1873) displays
the influence of the pre-
Raphaelites with whom he
associated. His philosophic
romance, *Marius the Epicurean*
(1885), appealed to a wider
audience. He was hugely
influential as a critic and theorist.

Marius the Epicurean
Marius

Paterson, Andrew Barton, also
called **Banjo**
◎ (1864–1941) Australian bush
poet and balladeer who is best
known for his verse 'Waltzing
Matilda', which he set to an old
Scottish melody. Under the
pseudonym 'The Banjo' (the name
of a bush racehorse) he contributed
verse to the Sydney periodical *The
Bulletin*. He also wrote two novels,
a collection of short stories and a
book of verse for children.

*The Man from Snowy River and Other
Verses*
Clancy of the Overflow
Man from Ironbark, the

Man from Snowy River, the
Saltbush Bill

Rio Grande's Last Race and Other Verses
Mulga Bill
Saltbush Bill

Saltbush Bill, J.P., and Other Verses
Saltbush Bill

Paton, Alan

◎ (1903–88) South African writer. He spent several years as a schoolteacher and from 1935 to 1948 he was principal of the Diepkloof Reformatory for young offenders. From his deep concern with the racial problem in South Africa sprang the novel *Cry, the Beloved Country* (1948). He was national president of the South African Liberal Party from 1953 to 1960.

Cry, the Beloved Country
Absalom, in full Absalom Kumalo
Gertrude, in full Gertrude Kumalo
Jarvis, Arthur
Jarvis, James
Kumalo, Rev Stephen

Too Late the Phalarope
Stephanie
van Vlaanderen, Pieter

Peacock, Thomas Love

◎ (1785–1866) English novelist and poet. He entered the service of the East India Company in 1819 after producing three satirical romances, *Headlong Hall* (1816), *Melincourt, or Sir Oran Haut-ton* (1817) and *Nightmare Abbey* (1818). *Crotchet Castle* (1831) concluded this series of satires. He also published two romances.

Crotchet Castle
Chainmail, Mr
Clarinda, Lady
Folliott, Rev Dr
MacQuedy, Mr
Skionar, Mr
Touchandgo, Susannah

Gryll Grange
Curryfin, Lord Richard
Falconer, Mr Algernon
Gryll, Morgana
Ilex, Miss
Niphet, Alice
Opimian, Rev Dr Neophilus

Headlong Hall
Escot, Mr
Foster, Mr
Gaster, Rev Dr
Headlong, Squire Harry
Jenkison, Mr
Milestone, Mr Marmaduke
Poppyseed, Miss Philomela

Melincourt, or Sir Oran Haut-ton
Achthar, Lord Anophel
Fax, Mr
Feathernest, Mr
Forester, Mr Sylvan
Grovelgrub, Rev Mr
Haut-ton, Sir Oran
Melincourt, Anthelia
Mystic, Mr Moley
Paperstamp, Mr

Nightmare Abbey
Asterias, Mr

Cypress, Mr
Flosky, Mr Ferdinando
Glowry, Scythrop
Hilary, Mr
Listless, Mr
O'Carroll, Miss Marionetta Celestina
'Stella' (Celinda Toobad)
Toobad, Mr

Peake, Mervyn

◎ (1911–68) English writer and artist. Born in China, where his father was a missionary, he was educated in England, where his reputation as an artist grew. His first novel, *Titus Groan* (1946), was the first part of a Gothic fantasy trilogy completed in *Gormenghast* (1950) and *Titus Alone* (1959). He published two volumes of verse and illustrated several classics, notably *Treasure Island*.

Gormenghast
Fuchsia, Lady of Groan
Groan, Titus, 77th Earl of Gormenghast
Prunesquallor, Dr Alfred
Steerpike

Titus Alone
Groan, Titus, 77th Earl of Gormenghast
Muzzlehatch

Titus Groan
Fuchsia, Lady of Groan
Groan, Titus, 77th Earl of Gormenghast
Prunesquallor, Dr Alfred
Steerpike

Pearce, Philippa

◎ (born 1920) English children's author. Educated at Cambridge, she worked for the BBC and in publishing. She made her name with the classic *Tom's Midnight Garden* (1958), which won the Carnegie medal. She has also written numerous short stories and edited anthologies.

Tom's Midnight Garden
Hatty, properly Harriet
Tom

Pears, Tim

◎ (born 1956) English novelist. His first novel, *In the Place of Fallen Leaves* (1993), a coming-of-age novel set in the English countryside during the 1984 drought, won numerous awards. His second novel, *In a Land of Plenty* (1997), a family saga, was filmed for BBC television.

In a Land of Plenty
Freeman, Charles
Freeman, Mary

In the Place of Fallen Leaves
Freemantle, Alison

Wake Up
Sharp, John

Pearson, Allison

◎ (birthdate unknown) English journalist, critic and novelist. She is an award-winning newspaper columnist and appears regularly on television and radio. Her first novel, *I Don't Know How She Does It* (2002), a social comedy about

working motherhood, has been highly successful on both sides of the Atlantic.

I Don't Know How She Does It
Reddy, Kate

Peele, George

◎ (c.1558–1596) English dramatist. He lived a bohemian life in London as actor, poet and playwright. *The Old Wives' Tale* (1595) probably gave **Milton** the subject for his *Comus*.

The Old Wives' Tale
Calypha and Thelea
Delia
Eumenides
Jack's Ghost
Sacrapant

Peters, Ellis, pseudonym of **Edith Mary Pargeter**

◎ (1913–95) English crime writer and novelist. She wrote a string of quietly successful detective novels under her pseudonym. Real success, however, came when she was in her sixties when she hit upon the idea of Brother Cadfael, a medieval detective. *A Morbid Taste for Bones* (1977) was an instant hit, and a series was born.

A Morbid Taste for Bones
Cadfael, Brother

Phillips, David Graham

◎ (1867–1911) US novelist and journalist who was involved in the movement of reform-minded journalism in the early 20th century. He also wrote powerfully in several novels in favour of the emancipation of women. He was assassinated by someone who thought his work encouraged female moral depravity.

The Great God Success
anon (the newspaperman)

Susan Lenox: Her Fall and Rise
Lenox, Susan

Phillips, Mike

◎ (born 1947) Guyanese-born English novelist. He came to England as a child and worked for the BBC and lectured before becoming a full-time writer. He is best known for his crime novels featuring black journalist Sam Dean. He has also written screenplays, other novels and a collection of essays and short stories.

Blood Rights
Dean, Sam (Samson)

Piercy, Marge

◎ (born 1936) US author. Her first collection of poetry was published in 1968. Over a dozen collections followed. Her novels merge feminism, science fiction and social concerns.

Braided Lives
Stuart, Donna

Stuart, Jill
Vida
Asch, Vida
Woman on the Edge of Time
Ramos, Connie

Pierre, D B C pseudonym of **Peter Finlay**
◎ (born 1961) Australian-born writer. He was brought up in Mexico and the UK and worked as a cartoonist and designer, and has had a colourful life involving gambling and drugs (D B C stands for Dirty But Clean). His first novel, *Vernon God Little* (2003), won the Booker Prize.
Vernon God Little
Little, Vernon Gregory

Pinero, Arthur Wing
◎ (1855–1934) English playwright. Many of his earlier plays were comedies. In 1893, with *The Second Mrs Tanqueray*, he began a period of realistic tragedies which were received with enthusiastic acclamation and made him the most successful playwright of his day. He was the author of some 50 plays.
The Cabinet Minister
Gaylustre, Mrs Fanny
Lebanon, Joseph
Twombley, Lady Kitty
Twombley, Sir Julian
The Second Mrs Tanqueray
Tanqueray, Aubrey
Tanqueray, Paula
Trelawney of the 'Wells'
Trelawny, Rose
Wrench, Tom

Pinter, Harold
◎ (born 1930) English dramatist. His first London production, *The Birthday Party* (1958), was trounced by critics unused to his highly personal dramatic idiom. A superb verbal acrobat, he exposes and utilizes the illogical and inconsequential in everyday talk to induce an atmosphere of menace or of claustrophobic isolation. Other plays deal with explicitly political themes.
Betrayal
Emma
Jerry
Robert
The Birthday Party
Boles, Meg
Boles, Petey
Goldberg, Nat
McCann, Dermot
Webber, Stanley
The Caretaker
Aston
Davies, Mac
Mick
The Dumb Waiter
Ben
Gus
The Homecoming
Joey
Lenny

Max
Ruth
Teddy
A Kind of Alaska
Deborah
Moonlight
Andy
No Man's Land
Hirst
Kate
Spooner
Old Times
Anna
Deeley
Kate
One for the Road
Nicolas
Party Time
Gavin

Plath, Sylvia
◎ (1932–63) US poet. She won a Fulbright Fellowship to Cambridge, where she studied English and married the poet Ted Hughes. Often termed a 'confessional' poet, she was influenced by Robert Lowell, amongst others. Her late poetry was published posthumously. Her only novel, *The Bell Jar* (1963), was published just before her suicide, under the pseudonym Victoria Lucas.
The Bell Jar
Greenwood, Esther
Willard, Buddy

Plomer, William
◎ (1903–73) South African-born British novelist. He was a farmer and trader in South Africa before becoming an author, and also lived for a while in Greece and Japan. Besides novels, short stories and poetry, he also wrote the librettos for several of Benjamin Britten's operas.
Turbott Wolfe
Van Der Horst, Mabel
Wolfe, Turbott

Poe, Edgar Allan
◎ (1809–49) US poet and short-story writer. Having been dishonourably discharged from the army, he turned to journalism and story-writing and published *Tales of the Grotesque and Arabesque* in 1840. His poem *The Raven* appeared first in the *New York Evening Mirror* and won him immediate fame. His short stories show genuine originality, and his poems were admired by **W B Yeats** and others.
'Annabel Lee'
Annabel Lee
The Fall of the House of Usher
Usher, Madeline
Usher, Roderick
'The Murders in the Rue Morgue'
Dupin, C Auguste
'The Mystery of Marie Roget'
Dupin, C Auguste

The Narrative of Arthur Gordon Pym
Pym, Arthur Gordon
'The Purloined Letter'
Dupin, C Auguste
The Raven
Raven, the
'Ulalume – A Ballad'
Ulalume, narrator of
William Wilson
Wilson, William

Pope, Alexander
◎ (1688–1744) English poet. As a child, he suffered from a tubercular infection of the spine and began writing at an early age. In 1711 he produced his seminal work, *An Essay on Criticism*, whose couplets caused a stir. *The Rape of the Lock* (1712) confirmed him as a poetic force.
'Epistle III, To Allen, Lord Bathurst'
Balaam, Sir
Man of Ross, the
Epistle to Dr Arbuthnot
Atticus
Bufo
Sporus
'Moral Essays'
Man of Ross, the
The Rape of the Lock
Belinda

Porter, Eleanor H(odgman)
◎ (1868–1920) US novelist. She studied music at the New England Conservatory. In 1913 she published *Pollyanna*, the story of an orphaned girl, which was an immediate success and has retained its popularity ever since. A sequel, about the 'glad child', *Pollyanna Grows Up*, was published in 1915.
Pollyanna
Pollyanna
Pollyanna Grows Up
Pollyanna

Porter, Hal
◎ (1911–84) Australian writer. He had a varied career, working as a journalist, as a teacher in Australia and Japan, as director of the National Theatre in Hobart and as a librarian. As well as novels and autobiography, he also wrote travel books, short stories, poetry and drama.
'Mr Butterfry'
Blue
The Tilted Cross
Knight, Lady
Sheill, Queely
Sleep, Asnetha
Teapot, properly Orfée Maka
Vaneleigh, Judas Griffin

Porter, Katherine Anne
◎ (1890–1980) US writer. She worked as a reporter and actress, moved to Greenwich Village, New York, and then went to Mexico (1920–2), where she took up

Index

Mexican causes. She published short stories, essays and novels.

'Old Mortality'
Breaux, Amy
Breaux, Gabriel
Maria
Miranda
Parrington, Eva

'The Old Order'
Maria
Miranda

'Pale Horse, Pale Rider'
Miranda

Ship of Fools
Brown, Jenny
Scott, David

Pound, Ezra

© (1885–1972) US poet, translator and critic. He travelled widely in Europe and published his first collection of poems in Venice. From 1924 he made his home in Italy, where he became involved with fascist ideas and created resentment by anti-democracy broadcasts in the early stages of World War II. In 1945 he was escorted back to the USA and indicted for treason. The trial did not proceed, however, as he was adjudged insane, and he was placed in an asylum until 1958. As a poet of the Imagist school at the outset of his career, he was a thoroughgoing experimenter and **T S Eliot** regarded him as the motivating force behind 'modern' poetry.

'Hugh Selwyn Mauberley'
Mauberley, Hugh Selwyn
Nixon, Mr

Powell, Anthony

© (1905–2000) English novelist. He worked in publishing and journalism before World War II, and by 1936 had published four satirical novels. After the war he returned to book reviewing and began the series of novels he called *A Dance to the Music of Time* – twelve volumes covering 50 years of British upper-middle-class life and attitudes.

A Dance to the Music of Time
Clarke, St John
Conyers, Gen Aylmer
Donners, Sir Magnus
Erridge (Lord Warminster, known as Alf)
Jeavons, Lady Molly
Jenkins, Nicholas
Quiggin, J G
Stringham, Charles
Templer, Peter
Tolland, Lady Isobel
Widmerpool, Kenneth
Widmerpool, Pamela

Afternoon Men
Atwater, William

Powys, John Cowper

© (1872–1963) English novelist, poet and essayist. Of some 50 books, his best known are his novels, particularly *Wolf Solent*

(1929), *A Glastonbury Romance* (1932) and *Weymouth Sands* (1934).

A Glastonbury Romance
Crow, John
Geard, John

Maiden Castle
Dud No-man
Ravelston, Wizzie

Weymouth Sands
Cattistock, Dogberry (Dog)
Skald, Jobber (Adam)
Wane, Perdita

Wolf Solent
Solent, Wolf
Torp, Gerda

Powys, T(heodore) F(rancis)

© (1875–1953) English novelist and short-story writer. He was the brother of **John Cowper Powys**.

Mr Weston's Good Wine
Weston, Mr

Praed, Rosa, also wrote as Mrs Campbell Praed

© (1851–1935) Australian novelist. She based her romantic novels on the privations of her early married life on outback Queensland stations. In 1875 she and her husband moved to London where she became a popular novelist, mixing in literary circles which included **Oscar Wilde**.

Policy and Passion
Longleat, Honoria
Longleat, Thomas

Pratchett, Terry

© (born 1948) English author. His early career was spent as a journalist and press officer for the Central Electricity Generating Board (1980–87). His first fantasy novel, *The Carpet People*, appeared in 1971, and the first in the Discworld series, *The Colour of Magic*, in 1983.

The Colour of Magic
Death
Rincewind

Equal Rites
Weatherwax, Mistress

Guards! Guards!
Vimes, Samuel

Reaper Man
Ridcully, Mustrum

Prichard, Katharine Susannah

© (1883–1969) Australian writer. She worked as a journalist in Melbourne and London. She became a founding member of the Australian Communist Party (1920), and her socialist convictions coloured much of her subsequent work.

Coonardoo
Coonardoo
Watt, Hugh

Golden Miles
Amy
Cavan, Sir Paddy
Frisco
Gough, Sally

Maritana
Quin, Dinny
Tom

Haxby's Circus
Haxby, Gina
Roca

Intimate Strangers
Blackwood, Elodie
Blackwood, Greg

The Roaring Nineties
Amy
Cavan, Sir Paddy
Frisco
Gough, Sally
Maritana
Quin, Dinny
Tom

Winged Seeds
Amy
Cavan, Sir Paddy
Frisco
Gough, Sally
Maritana
Quin, Dinny
Tom

Working Bullocks
Burke, Red
Colburn, Deb

Priestley, J(ohn) B(oynton)

© (1894–1984) English novelist, playwright and critic. He had already made a reputation with his critical writings when his novel *The Good Companions* (1929) gained him a wide popularity. As well as novels, he wrote plays and was also a master of the essay form.

Angel Pavement
Dersingham, Mr
Matfield, Miss
Smeeth, Mr

The Good Companions
Jollifant, Inigo
Oakroyd, Jess
Trant, Miss Elizabeth

An Inspector Calls
Goole, Inspector

Time and the Conways
Conway, Mrs

Proulx, Annie

© (born 1935) US writer. She began her career as a freelance journalist, publishing her first collection of short stories in 1988. *The Shipping News* (1993), an evocative novel set in Newfoundland, was a major success, winning a number of awards including the Pulitzer Prize in 1994.

The Shipping News
Quoyle, R G

That Old Ace in the Hole
Dollar, Bob

Pullman, Philip

© (born 1946) English writer. Having travelled widely as a child, he studied at Oxford, and eventually became a teacher and lecturer. He is best known for his fantasy trilogy *His Dark Materials*, comprising *Northern Lights* (1995) (winner of the Carnegie Medal), *The Subtle Knife* (1997) and *The*

Amber Spyglass (2000). *The Amber Spyglass* was the first 'children's book' to win the Whitbread prize.

Northern Lights
Belacqua, Lyra

The Subtle Knife
Belacqua, Lyra
Parry, Will

The Amber Spyglass
Belacqua, Lyra
Parry, Will

Pym, Barbara

◎ (1913–80) English novelist. For much of her adult life she worked at the International African Institute in London (1958–74). She published three novels in the 1950s, then lapsed into obscurity until, partly through the support of **Philip Larkin**, her works became more recognized.

Some Tame Gazelle
Bede, Belinda
Bede, Harriet
Hoccleve, Archdeacon

Pynchon, Thomas

◎ (born 1937) US novelist. He was born in Glen Cove, New York, and educated at Cornell University. Seen by some as wilfully obscure, by others as an experimentalist, he has a sprawling and loquacious style, and uses fabulous structures in which the normal conventions of the novel have been largely abandoned.

The Crying of Lot 49
Maas, Oedipa

Gravity's Rainbow
Slothrop, Lt Tyrone

V
Profane, Benny
Sphere, McClintic
Stencil, Herbert

V

Vineland
Atman, Weed
Gates, Frenesi
Vond, Brock
Wheeler, Prairie
Wheeler, Zoyd
Zuniga, Detective Hector

Queen, Ellery, pseudonym of **Frederick Dannay** and **Manfred B Lee**

◎ (1905–82 and 1905–71) US writers. The two authors were cousins, born in New York City. As businessmen they entered a detective-story competition, and won with *The Roman Hat Mystery* (1929). They used Ellery Queen

both as a pseudonym and as the name of their detective.

The Roman Hat Mystery
Queen, Ellery

Radcliffe, Ann

◎ (1764–1823) English romantic novelist. She published the first of her Gothic romances in 1789. She was praised by **Sir Walter Scott**, and influenced writers such as **Byron**, **Shelley** and **Charlotte Brontë**. Her particular brand of writing prompted **Jane Austen**'s satire *Northanger Abbey*.

The Mysteries of Udolpho
Montoni
St Aubert, Emily
Valancourt

Rankin, Ian

◎ (born 1960) Scottish crime writer. He was born in Fife, and educated at Edinburgh University. His first book was *The Flood* (1986), published under the pseudonym Jack Harvey, but it was the introduction of the cynical, impatient and emotionally repressed John Rebus that made his reputation.

Knots and Crosses
Rebus, John

Ransome, Arthur

◎ (1884–1967) English journalist and children's writer. He was widely travelled and, having learned Russian in 1913, was sent to cover the Revolution as a journalist. He had been a published author for a quarter of a century before the appearance of *Swallows and Amazons* (1930), the first of twelve perennially popular children's novels.

Swallows and Amazons
Blackett, Nancy and Peggy
Flint, Captain, properly Jim Turner
Walker, John
Walker, Roger
Walker, Susan
Walker, Titty

Rao, Raja

◎ (born 1908) Indian novelist. He studied in India and Europe, and travelled widely in India in search of his spiritual heritage. His works are deeply rooted in Brahmanism and Hinduism and spiritual quest.

The Serpent and the Rope
Madeleine
Rama (Ramaswamy)

Rattigan, Terence

◎ (1911–77) English playwright whose work displays not only a wide range of imagination but a deep psychological knowledge. He was responsible for several successful films made from his own and other works.

The Browning Version
Crocker-Harris, Andrew

The Deep Blue Sea
Collyer, Hester
Page, Freddie

Ross
Ross

Table by the Window
Shankland, Anne

Table Number Seven
Pollock, Major David

The Winslow Boy
Winslow, Ronnie

Rawlings, Marjorie Kinnan

◎ (1896–1953) US novelist and journalist. She was awarded the O Henry Memorial Award in 1933 for her short story 'Gal Young Un' and is best remembered for her Pulitzer Prize-winning novel *The Yearling* (1938).

The Yearling
Baxter, Jody

Reade, Charles

◎ (1814–84) English novelist and playwright. In 1843 he was called to the Bar, but never practised. He first wrote for the stage in 1850, and went on to produce 40 dramas. After 1852 he wrote a succession of unsuccessful plays and successful, usually profitable novels.

The Cloister and the Hearth
Brandt, Margaret
Gerard
Van Swieten, Ghysbrecht

Griffith Gaunt, or, Jealousy
Gaunt, Griffith

Masks and Faces
Woffington, Peg (Margaret)

Peg Woffington
Woffington, Peg (Margaret)

Reed, Ishmael

◎ (born 1938) US novelist, poet and critic. Born in Tennessee, he grew up in New York and has taught in various universities including Harvard, Yale and Berkeley. He uses parody, surrealism and satire to challenge literary and social conventions.

Yellow Back Radio Broke Down
Loop Garou

Renault, Mary

◎ (1905–83) English-born South African novelist. Born in London, she travelled extensively, particularly in Greece, and emigrated to South Africa in 1948. She is best known for her historical novels set in Ancient Greece.

The Bull from the Sea
Theseus
Fire from Heaven
Alexander
Hephaistion
Funeral Games
Alexander
Bagoas
The King Must Die
Theseus
The Persian Boy
Alexander
Bagoas
Hephaistion
The Praise Singer
Simonides

Rendell, Ruth, also writes as **Barbara Vine**

◎ (born 1932) English detective-story writer. She worked in journalism before the publication of her first novel, *From Doon With Death* (1964). She has written a series of novels featuring Chief-Inspector Wexford, as well as mystery thrillers. Since 1986, she has also written psychological thrillers under the pen name of Barbara Vine.

From Doon With Death
Wexford, Chief-Inspector Reginald

Rhys, Jean

◎ (1894–1979) British novelist. She was born in the West Indies, moving to England in 1910. At the end of World War I she went to live on the Continent, spending many years in Paris. In 1966 she published what was to become her best-known novel, *Wide Sargasso Sea*, which was based on the character of Rochester's mad wife in **Charlotte Brontë**'s *Jane Eyre*.

After Leaving Mr Mackenzie
Mackenzie, Mr
Martin, Julia
Good Morning Midnight
Jenson, Sasha
Quartet
Heidler, Hugh (H J)
Heidler, Lois
Zelli, Marya
Zelli, Stephan
Voyage in the Dark
Morgan, Anna
Wide Sargasso Sea
Rochester, Bertha (Antoinette), née
  Cosway

Rice, Elmer

◎ (1892–1967) US dramatist. Born in New York, he studied law, then turned to writing plays. His output was prolific.

The Adding Machine
Zero, Mr

Richards, Frank

◎ (1875–1961) English children's writer. Born in London, he began to write stories for magazines and comics while still a schoolboy. He wrote for boys' papers and produced many well-known school stories in book and play form.

Bessie Bunter of Cliff House School
Bunter, Bessie
Billy Bunter of Greyfriars School
Bunter, Billy (William George)
Quelch, Mr (Henry Samuel)

Richardson, Dorothy

◎ (1873–1957) English novelist. She became a Fabian and started her writing career with works about the Quakers and George Fox. She was the first exponent of the 'stream of consciousness' style later made famous by **Virginia Woolf**.

Pointed Roofs
Henderson, Miriam

Richardson, Henry Handel, pseudonym of **Ethel Florence Lindesay Robertson**

◎ (1870–1946) Australian novelist and short-story writer. She travelled widely with her mother, and studied music at the Leipzig Conservatory. Her musical interest is reflected in some of her novels.

The Fortunes of Richard Mahony
Mahony, Cuffy, properly Cuthbert
  Hamilton Townshend-Mahony
Mahony, Mary
Mahony, Richard, properly Dr Richard
  Townshend-Mahony
The Getting of Wisdom
Rambotham, Laura Tweedle
Maurice Guest
Cayhill, Ephie
Dove
Dufrayer, Louise
Guest, Maurice
Hill, Avery
Krafft, Heinz
Schilsky
Ware, Madeleine
The Young Cosima
Liszt, Franz
von Bülow, Cosima, formerly Cosima
  Liszt, later Cosima Wagner
Wagner, Richard

Richardson, Samuel

◎ (1689–1761) English novelist. His first novel, *Pamela* (1740–1), is 'a series of familiar letters ... published in order to cultivate the Principles of Virtue and Religion', and this was the aim of all his works. His second novel, *Clarissa* (7 vols, 1748), made him famous, and he became acquainted with **Dr Johnson** among others.

Clarissa
Belford, John
Harlowe, Arabella
Harlowe, Clarissa
Howe, Anna
Lovelace, Robert
Morden, Col
Solmes, Roger
Pamela
Andrews, Pamela
B, Mr
Davers, Lady
Jervis, Mrs
Jewkes, Mrs
Longman, Mr
Williams, Mr
Sir Charles Grandison
Byron, Harriet
Grandison, Sir Charles
Pollexfen, Sir Hargrave
Porretta, Clementina della

Richler, Mordecai

◎ (1931–2001) Canadian novelist. He travelled in Europe, and worked for the Canadian Broadcasting Corporation before moving to England in 1959. He achieved a breakthrough with *The Apprenticeship of Duddy Kravitz* (1959) and his works show both bawdy humour and vitriolic satire.

The Apprenticeship of Duddy Kravitz
Kravitz, Duddy
St Urbain's Horseman
Hersch, Jake

Richter, Conrad

◎ (1890–1968) US novelist and short-story writer. He moved to New Mexico after working variously as a farm hand, clerk and journalist, and he was profoundly affected by the landscape of the South West.

The Sea of Grass
Brewton, Brock
Brewton, Col
Brewton, Lutie Cameron
Tacey Cromwell
Cromwell, Tacey
The Trees
Luckett, Sayward

Ridge, John Rollin (Yellow Bird)

◎ (1827–67) Native American journalist, novelist and poet. He was born into an important Cherokee family and his father and grandfather were both assassinated while he was still a boy. In 1854 he published his only novel, *Life & Adventures of Joaquin Murieta*.

Life & Adventures of Joaquin Murieta
Murieta, Joaquin

Roberts, Kenneth

◎ (1885–1957) US novelist and essayist. Educated at Cornell University, he worked as a journalist before concentrating on writing historical novels.

Northwest Passage
Rogers, Major Robert

Robinson, Edwin Arlington

◎ (1869–1935) US poet. He was brought up in Gardiner, Maine, which provided the background for 'Tilbury Town', the fictional New England village of his best poetry. He won Pulitzer Prizes for three of his collections.

The Town Down the River
Cheevy, Miniver
Cory, Richard

Robinson, Marilynne

◎ (born 1943) US novelist and essayist. She began work on her first novel, *Housekeeping* (1980), while still at graduate school. Regarded by many as a classic, it won numerous awards.

Housekeeping
Fisher, Sylvie
Stone, Lucille
Stone, Ruth

Ross, Martin *see* Somerville, E O and Ross Martin

Ross, Sinclair

◎ (1908–96) Canadian novelist and short-story writer. Having worked in a bank for 40 years, he retired and went to live in Spain and Greece. He achieved fame with his first novel, *As For Me and My House* (1941).

As For Me and My House
Bentley, Mrs
Bentley, Philip

Rossetti, Christina

◎ (1830–94) English poet. A member of the famous artistic family, her grandfather published a pamphlet by her before she was in her teens. *Goblin Market* (1862) is her best-known work.

Goblin Market
Laura
Lizzie

Rosten, Leo, also wrote as Leonard Q Ross

◎ (1908–97) US writer. He went to the USA at the age of three as the son of Polish immigrants, and many of his humorous novels and short stories focus on the immigrant experience and its impact on language.

The Education of Hyman Kaplan
Kaplan, Hyman

The Return of Hyman Kaplan
Kaplan, Hyman

Roth, Philip

◎ (born 1933) US novelist. His first book was *Goodbye Columbus* (1959), a collection of short stories. There followed two novels, *Letting Go* (1962) and *When She Was Good* (1967), before publication of *Portnoy's Complaint* (1969) made him notorious. He has won numerous literary awards.

American Pastoral
Levov, Meredith ('Merry')
Levov, Seymour ('the Swede')

The Breast
Kepesh, David

The Dying Animal
Kepesh, David

The Ghost Writer
Lonoff, E I

Goodbye, Columbus
Klugman, Neil
Patimkin, Brenda

The Human Stain
Silk, Coleman

I Married a Communist
Ringold, Ira

My Life as a Man
Tarnopol, Peter
Zuckerman, Nathan

Portnoy's Complaint
Portnoy, Alexander
Spielvogel, Dr

Sabbath's Theater
Sabbath, Mickey

The Professor of Desire
Kepesh, David

Rowe, Nicholas

◎ (1674–1718) English poet and dramatist who produced eight plays. Lothario in *The Fair Penitent* (1703) was the prototype of Lovelace in **Samuel Richardson**'s *Clarissa* (1748), and the name is still the eponym for a fashionable rake. In 1715 Rowe was appointed Poet Laureate.

The Fair Penitent
Altamont
Calista
Horatio
Lothario
Sciolto

Rowley, William

◎ (c.1585–c.1626) English actor and playwright. Little is known about him, except that he collaborated with a number of other writers. (*see* **Dekker, Thomas, Rowley, William** and **Ford, John**, and **Middleton, Thomas** and **Rowley, William** for works and characters.)

Rowling, J(oanne) K(athleen)

◎ (born 1965) English children's writer. She began her career as a teacher of English and French. Her first children's book, *Harry Potter and the Philosopher's Stone* (1997) was an immediate success, and was followed by hugely successful sequels. Rowling won the British Book Awards Children's Book of the Year prize in 1999.

Harry Potter and the Philosopher's Stone
Dumbledore, Albus
Granger, Hermione
Hagrid, Rubeus
Malfoy, Draco
Potter, Harry
Voldemort, Lord
Weasley, Ron

Rowson, Susanna

◎ (c.1762–1824) English-born US novelist, poet and playwright. She went to the USA as a child and returned to England in 1777 where she produced several novels and books of verse. On the success of *Charlotte: A Tale of Truth* (1791) she returned to the USA where she worked in theatre.

Charlotte: A Tale of Truth
Temple, Charlotte

Charlotte's Daughter, or, The Three Orphans
Temple, Lucy

Roy, Arundhati

◎ (born 1961) Indian author. She trained at the Delhi School of Architecture and wrote two screenplays before producing her first novel, *The God of Small Things* (1997) which won the Booker Prize. She has written widely on environmental and nuclear issues.

The God of Small Things
Kochamma, Esthappen (Estha)
Kochamma, Rahel

Rubens, Bernice

◎ (1923–2004) Welsh novelist and short-story writer. She has worked as a teacher and freelance film director. Her Jewish background often features in her books, and her fourth novel, *The Elected Member* (1969), won the Booker Prize.

The Elected Member
Zweck, Norman

A Solitary Grief
Crown, Alistair

Runyon, Damon

◎ (1884–1946) US writer and journalist. After service in the Spanish–American War (1898) he turned to journalism. His first books were volumes of verse, but it was his racy short stories, written with liberal use of slang and depicting life in underworld New York and on Broadway, which won him popularity.

Furthermore
Butch
Harry the Horse
Hot Horse Herbie
Little Isadore
Spanish John

More Than Somewhat
Brain, the

My Wife Ethel
Turp, Ethel
Turp, Joe

Stories à la Carte
Benny the Blond Jew
Dark Dolores
Harry the Horse
Hot Horse Herbie
Little Isadore
Masterton, Sky
Philly the Weeper
Seldom Seen Kid, the
Spanish John

Take it Easy
Big False Face
Nicely Nicely Jones

Rushdie, Salman

◎ (born 1947) Indian-born British novelist. With his second novel, *Midnight's Children* (1981, Booker Prize), Rushdie emerged as a major international writer. His fourth book, *The Satanic Verses* (1988), was banned in India in 1988, and the orthodox Iranian leadership declared it blasphemous and issued a fatwa against him. Rushdie was forced into hiding for a time but continued to publish.

Fury
Solanka, Malik

The Ground Beneath Her Feet
Apsara, Vina
Cama, Ormus
Merchant, Umeed

Haroun and the Sea of Stories
Haroun
Rashid

Midnight's Children
Sinai, Saleem

The Moor's Last Sigh
Zogoiby, Moraes

The Satanic Verses
Chamcha, Saladin
Farishta, Gibreel

Russell, Willy

◎ (born 1947) English playwright. He is one of the most frequently performed of contemporary British dramatists, and is best known for the highly successful stage play and film *Educating Rita* (1979).

Educating Rita
Frank
White, Rita, properly Susan

Shirley Valentine
Valentine, Shirley

Rutherford, Mark, pseudonym of William Hale White

◎ (1831–1913) English novelist and journalist. Having abandoned his training as an independent religious minister, he entered the Civil Service. He continued writing journalism and during the 1850s began to publish novels and works of philosophy.

The Autobiography of Mark Rutherford
Rutherford, Mark

Clara Hopgood
Hopgood, Clara and Madge

Sackville, Thomas see Norton, Thomas and Sackville, Thomas

Sahgal, Nayantara

◎ (born 1927) Indian novelist and journalist. She was born into a prominent political family. As well as novels, she has written volumes of memoir, biography and essays.

Rich Like Us
Lal, Kishori
Sonali
Surya, Rose

'Saki', pseudonym of Hector Hugh Munro

◎ (1870–1916) English novelist and short-story writer. Born in Burma, he turned to journalism in England after a spell in the Burmese police force. Although he also wrote novels, he is best known for his short stories. He was killed on the Western Front during World War I.

Beasts and Super-Beasts
Sangrail, Clovis

The Chronicles of Clovis
Conradin
Sangrail, Clovis
Tobermory

'Gabriel-Ernest'
Gabriel-Ernest

Reginald
Reginald

'Reginald in Russia'
Reginald

The Square Egg
Sangrail, Clovis

The Toys of Peace
Sangrail, Clovis

The Unbearable Bassington
Bassington, Comus

Salinger, J(erome) D(avid)

◎ (born 1919) US novelist and short-story writer. His first and most famous novel was *The Catcher in the Rye* (1951). It was succeeded by four works about the Glass family, including *Franny and Zooey* (1961). Salinger lives in rural reclusion in New Hampshire.

The Catcher in the Rye
Caulfield, Holden

'For Esmé – with Love and Squalor'
Esmé

Franny and Zooey
Glass, Franny
Glass, Zooey

'A Perfect Day for Bananafish'
Glass, Buddy
Glass, Seymour

'Raise High the Roof Beam, Carpenters'
Glass, Buddy
Glass, Seymour

'Seymour: An Introduction'
Glass, Buddy
Glass, Seymour

Santayana, George

◎ (1863–1952) Spanish–US philosopher, poet and novelist. Born in Madrid, he taught at Harvard (1889–1912), but eventually settled in Rome. He began writing poetry, but he was also a successful novelist with *The Last Puritan: A Novel in the Form of a Memoir* (1936).

The Last Puritan: A Novel in the Form of a Memoir
Alden, Oliver

'Sapper', pseudonym of Herman Cyril McNeile

◎ (1888–1937) English novelist and short-story writer. He had a distinguished military career, but

is remembered chiefly for the invention of Captain Hugh 'Bull-dog' Drummond, introduced in 1920 in the novel *Bull-dog Drummond*, bearing the subtitle *The Adventures of a Demobilized Officer Who Found Peace Dull*.

Bull-dog Drummond
Drummond, Hugh 'Bull-dog'

Sargeson, Frank

◎ (1903–82) New Zealand short-story writer and novelist who made his name with collections of short stories in which he satirized the provincial attitudes of those around him.

The Memoirs of a Peon
Newhouse, Michael

'That Summer'
Bill

Saroyan, William

◎ (1908–81) US playwright and novelist. Largely self-educated, he won literary fame with his first work, *The Daring Young Man on the Flying Trapeze* (1934), a volume of short stories. Idealistic and opposed to commercialism, he refused the Pulitzer Prize awarded in 1940 for his play *The Time of Your Life* (1939).

'The Daring Young Man on the Flying Trapeze'
Daring Young Man on the Flying Trapeze

The Time of Your Life
Joe

Sassoon, Siegfried

◎ (1886–1967) English poet and novelist. He suffered experiences in World War I that made him detest war, and led to their fierce expression in several volumes of poetry. His later poems are predominantly spiritual.

Memoirs of a Fox-Hunting Man
Sherston, George

Memoirs of an Infantry Officer
Sherston, George

Sherston's Progress
Sherston, George

Sayers, Dorothy L(eigh)

◎ (1893–1957) English detective-story writer. Beginning with *Whose Body?* (1923), her novels tell the adventures of her hero Lord Peter Wimsey in various accurately observed milieux, such as advertising in *Murder Must Advertise* (1933) or campanology in *The Nine Tailors* (1934).

Strong Poison
Vane, Harriet

Whose Body?
Wimsey, Lord Peter (Death Bredon)

Schaefer, Jack

◎ (1907–91) American writer and journalist. He worked for over 20 years as a journalist and made his breakthrough as a writer with *Shane* (1949), a tale of a gunman's involvement with a homesteading family in Wyoming.

Shane
Shane

Schreiner, Olive

◎ (1855–1920) South African writer and feminist. At the age of 15 she became a governess to a Boer family. She later lived in England (1881–9), where her novel *The Story of an African Farm* (1883) was published under the pseudonym 'Ralph Iron'.

The Story of an African Farm
Em (Emily)
Lyndall
Waldo

Scott, Paul

◎ (1920–78) English novelist who served in the British and Indian armies in the 1940s. His best-known work is *The Raj Quartet* which provides a vivid portrait of India during the last years of the Raj. *Staying On* (1977), which can be seen as a coda to the Quartet, was awarded the Booker Prize.

The Day of the Scorpion
Batchelor, Barbie (Barbara)
Bronowsky, Count (Dmitri)
Crane, Edwina
Kasim, Ahmed
Kasim, Mohammed Ali
Kumar, Hari (Harry Coomer)
Layton, Mabel
Layton, Mildred
Layton, Sarah
Layton, Susan
Manners, Daphne
Merrick, Ronald
Perron, Guy

A Division of the Spoils
Batchelor, Barbie (Barbara)
Bronowsky, Count (Dmitri)
Crane, Edwina
Kasim, Ahmed
Kasim, Mohammed Ali
Kumar, Hari (Harry Coomer)
Layton, Mabel
Layton, Mildred
Layton, Sarah
Layton, Susan
Manners, Daphne
Merrick, Ronald
Perron, Guy

The Jewel in the Crown
Batchelor, Barbie (Barbara)
Bronowsky, Count (Dmitri)
Crane, Edwina
Kasim, Ahmed
Kasim, Mohammed Ali
Kumar, Hari (Harry Coomer)
Layton, Mabel
Layton, Mildred
Layton, Sarah
Layton, Susan
Manners, Daphne
Merrick, Ronald
Perron, Guy

Johnnie Sahib
Brown, Johnnie

A Male Child
Hurst, Mrs (Marion)

Staying On
Smalley, Lucy
Smalley, 'Tusker'

The Towers of Silence
Batchelor, Barbie (Barbara)
Bronowsky, Count (Dmitri)
Crane, Edwina
Kasim, Ahmed
Kasim, Mohammed Ali
Kumar, Hari (Harry Coomer)
Layton, Mabel
Layton, Mildred
Layton, Sarah
Layton, Susan
Manners, Daphne
Merrick, Ronald
Perron, Guy

Scott, Sir Walter

◎ (1771–1832) Scottish novelist and poet. Born in Edinburgh, he spent much time in the Borders, an area which features in many of his works. He translated Goethe and collected ballads before turning to novels. He is particularly remembered for his historical 'Waverley' novels.

The Abbot
Abbot of Unreason, also known as Father Howeglas or the Monk of Misrule
Ambrose, Father, Abbot of Kennaquhair, formerly Edward Glendinning
Avenel, Mary
Boniface, Abbot, later Blinkhoolie
Dryfesdale
Glendinning, Sir Halbert, later the Knight of Avenel
Graeme, Magdalen
Graeme, Roland
Henderson, Elias
Lochleven, Lady of
Mary, Queen of Scots
Murray, Regent
Seyton, Catherine
Warden, Henry, formerly William Wellwood

Anne of Geierstein, or The Maiden in the Mist
Biederman, Arnold, formerly Count of Geierstein
Charles the Bold, Duke of Burgundy
Donnerhugel, Rudolph
Geierstein, Anne of
Geierstein, Count Albert of
Hagenbach, Archibald von
Margaret of Anjou
Philipson, Arthur, actually De Vere
Philipson, Seignor, actually De Vere, Earl of Oxford

The Antiquary
Blattergowl, Mr
Dousterswivel, Herman
Lovel, actual name and rank Major Neville
Mucklebackit, Saunders
Ochiltree, Eddie
Oldbuck, Jonathan, strictly Jonathan Oldenbuck, or Oldinbuck of Monkbarns
Rintherout, Jenny
Wardour, Sir Arthur

The Betrothed
Berenger, Eveline
Gwenwyn of Powys-land
de Lacy, Damian
de Lacy, Hugo, Constable of Chester
de Lacy, Randal

The Black Dwarf
Armstrong, Grace
Black Dwarf
Cleishbotham, Jedediah
Ellieslaw, Vere, Laird of
Elliott, Hobbie, more properly Halbert, also known as Hobbie of the Cleugh-foot
Langley, Sir Frederick
Pattieson, Peter

The Bride of Lammermoor
Ashton, Lady
Ashton, Lucy
Ashton, Sir William, Lord Keeper
Balderston, Caleb
Ravenswood, Edgar, Master of Ravenswood

Chronicles of the Canongate: First Series
Baliol, Mrs (Martha) Bethune
Croftangry, Chrystal

Count Robert of Paris
Alexius Comnenus
Anna Comnena
Brenhilda, Countess of Paris
Briennius Nicephorus
Hereward
Robert, Count of Paris

The Fair Maid of Perth, or St Valentine's Day
Albany, Duke of
Clement, Father, or Clement Blair
Conachar, later known as Eachin or Hector Maclan
Glover, Catharine
Glover, Simon
Proudfute, Oliver
Ramorny, Sir John
Robert III, King of Scotland
Rothsay, Duke of Rothsay, Prince David of Scotland
Smith, Henry, or Henry Gow, or Hal of the Wynd
Torquil of the Oak

The Fortunes of Nigel
Buckingham, George Villiers, Duke of
Charles, Prince, later Charles I
Dalgarno, Lord
Heriot, George, known as Jinglin' Geordie
James I of England
Lowestoffe, Reginald
Malagrowther, Sir Mungo
Moniplies, Richie, later Sir Richard Moniplies of Castle-collop
Olifaunt, Nigel, Lord Glenvarloch
Ramsay, David
Ramsay, Margaret
Suddlechop, Benjamin
Suddlechop, Ursula, known as Dame Ursley
Trapbois
Trapbois, Martha

Guy Mannering
Bertram, Harry, also known as Vanbeest Brown
Dinmont, Dandie
Glossin, Gilbert, later briefly Laird of Ellangowan
Hatteraick, Captain Dirk
Mannering, Col Guy
Mannering, Julia
Merrilies, Meg
Pleydell, Paulus
Sampson, Dominie (Abel)

The Heart of Midlothian
Balchristie, Jenny

Butler, Reuben
Deans, Davie ('Douce Davie')
Deans, Effie (Euphemia)
Deans, Jeanie
Dumbiedikes, Laird of (John Dumbie)
Murdockson, Meg
Plumdamas, Peter
Porteous, Captain John
Ratcliffe, James, also known as 'Daddy
  Rat'
Saddletree, Bartoline
Staunton, Sir George, also known as
  'Robertson'
Wildfire, Madge, properly Magdalen
  Murdockson

The Highland Widow
MacTavish, Elspat (Elspeth)

Ivanhoe
Athelstane of Coningsburgh
Bois-Guilbert, Sir Brian de
Cedric the Saxon, also known as Cedric
  of Rotherwood
Front-de-Boeuf, Sir Reginald
Gurth, the Swineherd
Isaac of York
Ivanhoe, in full Wilfred of Ivanhoe
John, Prince
Locksley
Rebecca
Richard, King (Richard Coeur de Lion)
Rowena, Lady
Tuck, Friar
Ulrica, also known as Urfried
Wamba, the son of Witless

Kenilworth
Elizabeth I, Queen of England
Leicester, Robert Dudley, Earl of
Robsart, Amy
Robsart, Sir Hugh
Sludge, Dickie, known as Flibbertigibbet
Smith, Wayland
Tressillian, Edmund
Varney, Richard

The Lay of the Last Minstrel
Cranstoun, Lord
Deloraine, Sir William
Lady of Branksome, the
Margaret of Branksome
Minstrel, the
Musgrave, Sir Richard

A Legend of Montrose
Argyle, Duke of (Archibald, Marquis of
  Argyle, Lord of Lorne)
Dalgetty, Captain Dugald, of
  Drumthwacket
Lyle, Annot
McAulay, Allan
Menteith, Lord (Earl of Menteith)
Montrose, Earl of (James Graham,
  Marquis of Montrose)

Marmion
de Beverley, Constance
de Clare, Lady Clare
de Wilton, Sir Ralph
Lochinvar
Marmion, Lord

The Monastery
Ambrose, Father, Abbot of Kennaquhair,
  formerly Edward Glendinning
Avenel, Julian
Avenel, Mary
Avenel, White Lady of
Boniface, Abbot, later Blinkhoolie
Eustace, Father
Glendinning, Simon
Glendinning, Sir Halbert, later the Knight
  of Avenel

Hob the Miller, properly Hob Happer
Murray, Regent
Mysie of the Mill, properly Mysie Happer
Shafton, Sir Piercie
Warden, Henry, formerly William
  Wellwood

Old Mortality
Balfour, John, known as Burley
Bellenden, Edith
Bellenden, Lady Margaret, of
  Tillietudlem
Bellenden, Major Miles, of Charnwood
Bothwell, Sgt, more properly Francis
  Stewart
Dennison, Jenny
Evandale, Lord
Grahame of Claverhouse, John, Viscount
  Dundee
Hackston of Rathillet, (David)
Headrigg, Cuddie
Headrigg, Mause
Kettledrummle, Rev Gabriel
MacBriar, Ephraim
Morton, Henry
Morton of Milnwood, Silas
Mucklewrath, Habbakkuk
Old Mortality, more properly Robert
  Paterson
Wilson, Alison

Peveril of the Peak
Blood, Col Thomas
Bridgenorth, Alice
Bridgenorth, Major
Buckingham, George Villiers, Duke of
Charles II, King of England and Scotland
Chiffinch, also known as Smith
Christian, Edward, also known as
  Richard Ganlesse
Fenella
Hudson, Sir Geoffrey
Oates, Titus
Peveril, Julian
Peveril, Sir Geoffrey

The Pirate
Bunce, Jack, adopts the name of
  Frederick Altamont
Cleveland, Clement
Halcro, Claud
Mertoun, Basil, also known as Vaughan
Mertoun, Mordaunt
Norna of the Fitful Head, properly Ulla
  Troil
Snailsfoot, Bryce
Troil, Brenda
Troil, Magnus
Troil, Minna
Yellowley, Barbara, also known as Miss
  Baby
Yellowley, Triptolemus

Quentin Durward
Balue, Cardinal John of
Burgundy, Charles the Bold, Duke of
Campo-Basso, Count of
de Croye, Isabelle, first appears as
  Jacqueline
de la Marck, William, known as the Wild
  Boar of the Ardennes
des Comines, Philip
Durward, Quentin
Galleotti, Martius, or Marti or Martivalle
Lesly, Ludovic (le Balafre)
Liege, Bishop of (Louis of Bourbon)
Louis XI, King of France, incognito as
  Maître Pierre
Maugrabin, Hayraddin, also appears as
  the Disguised Herald
Tristan l'Hermite

le Dain, Oliver, also known as Le Mauvais
  or Le Diable

Redgauntlet
Buonaventure, Father, alias of Prince
  Charles Edward Stuart
Ewart, Nanty
Fairford, Alan
Fairford, Saunders (Alexander)
Geddes, Joshua
Herries of Birrenswork, Mr, more
  properly Mr Redgauntlet, or Mr
  Ingoldsby
Latimer, Darsie, properly Sir Arthur Darsie
  Redgauntlet of that Ilk
Nixon, Cristal
Peebles, (Poor) Peter
Redgauntlet, Lilias, first appears as
  Green Mantle
Steenson, Willie, known as Wandering
  Willie
Trumbull, Thomas

Rob Roy
Fairservice, Andrew
Jarvie, Bailie Nicol
Macgregor, Rob Roy
Osbaldistone, Frank (Francis)
Osbaldistone, Rashleigh
Osbaldistone, Sir Hildebrand
Vernon, Die (Diana)

St Ronan's Well
Binks, Sir Bingo
Dods, Meg
Etherington, Earl of, formerly Lord
  Oakendale, also known as Francis
  Valentine Bulmer Tyrrel, known
  incognito by his middle names, Frank
  Tyrel
MacTurk, Captain Hector
Mowbray, Clara
Mowbray, John, Laird of St Ronan's
Penfeather, Lady Penelope
Quackleben, Dr Quentin
Touchwood, Peregrine Scrogie
Tyrrel, Frank, originally Francis Martigny

The Surgeon's Daughter
Gray, Menie
Hartley, Adam
Middlemass, Richard

The Talisman: A Tale of the Crusaders
Austria, Leopold, Grand Duke of
Berengaria, Queen
Grand Master of the Hospitallers of St
  John and Jerusalem, the Templars
Kenneth, Sir, properly David, Earl of
  Huntingdon, Prince Royal of Scotland
Montserrat, Conrade, Marquis of
  Nectabanus
Philip II, King of France and Navarre,
  known as Philip Augustus, originally
  Denis Mountjoie
Plantagenet, Edith
Richard I, known as Coeur-de-Lion
Saladin

The Two Drovers
M'Combich, Robin Oig
Wakefield, Harry

Waverley
Balmawhapple, the Laird of
Bean Lean, Donald
Bradwardine, Baron of
Bradwardine, Rose, also known as 'the
  Rose of Tully-Veolan'
Gardiner, Col
Gellatley, Davie
MacIvor, Fergus, also known as
  Glennaquoich, Vich Ian Vohr, and Ian
  nan Chaistel

MacIvor, Flora
Macwheeble, Bailie Duncan
Waverley, Edward
Waverley, Sir Everard
Woodstock, or The Cavalier
Charles II
Cromwell, Oliver
Everard, Col Markham
Holdenough, Rev Nehemiah
Humgudgeon, or Corporal Grace-be-
here
Lee, Alice
Lee, Col
Lee, Sir Henry
Tomkins, Joseph
Wildrake, Roger

Sebold, Alice
◎ (born 1963) US novelist. Her first
publication was *Lucky* (1999), the
chilling memoir of her brutal rape
in her first year at Syracuse
University, New York. Her debut
novel, *The Lovely Bones* (2002),
received critical acclaim.

The Lovely Bones
Salmon, Susie

Sedgwick, Catharine Maria
◎ (1789–1867) US novelist. She was
born into a wealthy Massachusetts
family, and wrote a number of
popular novels, often focusing on
young women or orphans in native
settings.

*Hope Leslie, or Early Times in the
Massachusetts*
Leslie, Faith
Leslie, Hope
Magawisca
Oneco

Selvon, Samuel
◎ (1923–94) Trinidadian novelist,
playwright and short-story writer.
He served in the Royal Navy during
World War II and emigrated to
London in 1950. He moved to
Canada in 1978. He is perhaps best
known for his lyrical and witty
novels about the Caribbean
experience in London.

A Brighter Sun
Tiger
The Lonely Londoners
Aloetta, Moses
Moses Ascending
Aloetta, Moses
Turn Again, Tiger
Tiger

Seth, Vikram
◎ (born 1952) Indian poet, novelist
and travel writer. He was born in
Calcutta and educated at
universities in England, the USA
and China. His second novel, *A
Suitable Boy* (1993), is one of the
longest single-volume novels in
English and has won numerous
awards.

An Equal Music
Holmes, Michael
McNicholl, Julia
A Suitable Boy
Mehra, Lata

Sewell, Anna
◎ (1820–78) English novelist. She
was born in Great Yarmouth,
Norfolk, and was an invalid for
most of her life. Her only book is
Black Beauty (1877), written as a
plea for the more humane
treatment of animals.

Black Beauty
Black Beauty

Seymour, Alan
◎ (born 1927) Australian
dramatist. Seymour lived abroad
for many years, before eventually
returning to Australia in 1995. His
best-known play, *The One Day of
the Year* (1960), is regarded as a
classic of Australian theatre,
although it caused outrage when it
was first performed because of its
perceived anti-military stance.

The One Day of the Year
Castle, Jan
Cook, Alf
Cook, Dot
Cook, Hughie
Dawson, Wacka

Shaffer, Peter
◎ (born 1926) English playwright
and novelist. His plays are
variations on the themes of genius
and mediocrity, faith and reason,
and the question of whether God,
if he exists, is benevolent or not.

Amadeus
Mozart, Wolfgang Amadeus
Salieri, Antonio
Equus
Dysart, Martin
Strang, Alan
The Royal Hunt of the Sun
Atahuallpa
Pizarro, Francisco

Shakespeare, William
◎ (1564–1616) English playwright,
poet and actor, considered
England's greatest dramatist. Born
in Stratford, he spent much of his
working life in London, where he
helped to found the Globe Theatre.
His numerous plays were hugely
successful during his lifetime, and
he was given royal patronage by
James I.

All's Well That Ends Well
Bertram
France, King of
Helena
Parolles
Rousillon, Countess of
Antony and Cleopatra
Antony, Marcus Antonius/Mark Antony
Caesar, Octavius
Charmian
Cleopatra, Queen of Egypt
Enobarbus, Domitius
Iras
Lepidus, Marcus Aemilius
Octavia
Pompeius, Sextus
As You Like It
Audrey
Celia

Corin
Frederick, Duke
Hymen
Jacques
Le Beau
Oliver
Orlando
Phebe
Rosalind
Senior, Duke
Silvius
Touchstone
The Comedy of Errors
Adriana
Aegeon
Aemilia
Antipholus of Ephesus
Antipholus of Syracuse
Dromio of Ephesus
Dromio of Syracuse
Luciana
Pinch, Dr
Coriolanus
Agrippa, Menenius
Aufidius, Tullus
Brutus, Junius
Cominius
Coriolanus (Gaius Martius)
Velutus, Sicinius
Virgilia
Volumnia
Cymbeline
Arviragus/Cadwal
Belarius/Morgan
Cloten
Cymbeline
Guiderius/Polydore
Iachimo
Imogen
Pisario
Posthumus Leonatus
Queen (wife to Cymbeline)
Hamlet
Claudius
Clown, or Gravedigger
Fortinbras
Gertrude
Ghost, the
Hamlet
Horatio
Laertes
Ophelia
Polonius
Rosencrantz and Guildenstern
Henry IV Part I
Bardolph
Blunt, Sir Walter
Falstaff, Sir John
Gadshill
Glendower, Owen
Henry IV, Henry Bolingbroke
Henry, Prince of Wales, also known as
Prince Hal; afterwards Henry V
Hotspur (Henry Percy)
John of Lancaster, Prince
Mistress Quickly
Mortimer, Edmund
Mortimer, Lady
Percy, Henry, Earl of Northumberland
Percy, Lady
Percy, Thomas, Earl of Worcester
Peto
Poins
Henry IV Part II
Bardolph
Doll Tearsheet
Falstaff, Sir John
Henry IV, Henry Bolingbroke

Henry, Prince of Wales, also known as
  Prince Hal; afterwards Henry V
John of Lancaster, Prince
Mistress Quickly
Northumberland, Lady
Percy, Henry, Earl of Northumberland
Percy, Lady
Pistol
Poins
Shallow, Justice (Robert)
Silence, Justice

Henry V
Bardolph
Burgundy, Duke of
Canterbury, Archbishop of
Charles VI, King of France
Chorus, the
Constable of France, the
Fluellen; Gower; Jamy; Macmorris
Henry, Prince of Wales, also known as
  Prince Hal; afterwards Henry V
Isabel, Queen of France
Katharine, Princess of France
Lewis the Dauphin
Mistress Quickly
Mountjoy
Nym
Pistol

Henry VI Part I
Cade, Jack
Henry VI
Joan of Arc (Joan la Pucelle)
Margaret of Anjou, later Queen Margaret
York, Richard Plantagenet, Duke of

Henry VI Part II
Edward, Earl of March, later Edward IV
Henry VI
Margaret of Anjou, later Queen Margaret
Richard, Duke of Gloucester
York, Richard Plantagenet, Duke of

Henry VI Part III
Edward, Earl of March, later Edward IV
George, Duke of Clarence
Henry VI
Margaret of Anjou, later Queen Margaret
Richard, Duke of Gloucester
Richmond, Henry, Earl of, later Henry VII
Woodville, Anthony, Earl Rivers
Woodville, Elizabeth (Lady Grey), later
  Queen Elizabeth
York, Richard Plantagenet, Duke of

Julius Caesar
Antony, Marcus Antonius/Mark Antony
Brutus, Decius
Brutus, Marcus
Caesar, Julius
Caesar, Octavius
Calpurnia
Casca
Cassius, Caius
Lepidus, Marcus Aemilius
Portia
Soothsayer

King John
Arthur, Duke of Brittany
Blanche
Constance, Duchess of Brittany
de Burgh, Hubert
Eleanor
Falconbridge, Philip, the Bastard
Falconbridge, Robert
Henry, Prince
John, King
Lewis the Dauphin
Lymoges, Duke of Austria
Pandulph
Peter of Pomfret
Philip, King of France

King Lear
Albany, Duke of
Cordelia
Cornwall, Duke of
Edgar
Edmund
Fool, the
France, King of
Gloucester, Earl of
Goneril
Kent, Earl of
Lear, King
Oswald
Regan

Love's Labour's Lost
Armado, Don Adriano Del
Berowne
Boyet
Costard
Dull
Dumaine
Ferdinand, King
France, Princess of
Holofernes
Jaquenetta
Katharine
Longaville
Maria
Nathanael, Sir
Rosaline

Macbeth
Banquo
Donalbain
Duncan, King
Fleance
Hecate
Macbeth
Macbeth, Lady
Macduff
Macduff, Lady
Malcolm
Porter, the
weird sisters, the three

Measure for Measure
Angelo
Claudio
Isabella
Lucio
Marianna
Pompey Bum
Vincentio, Duke

The Merchant of Venice
Antonio
Arragon, Prince of
Bassanio
Gobbo, Launcelot
Gratiano
Jessica
Lorenzo
Morocco, Prince of
Nerissa
Portia
Shylock

The Merry Wives of Windsor
Caius, Dr
Evans, Sir Hugh
Falstaff, Sir John
Fenton
Ford, Frank
Ford, Mistress Alice
Host of the Garter Inn, the
Mistress Quickly
Nym
Page, Anne
Page, George
Page, Mistress Margaret (Meg)
Pistol
Robin

Rugby, John
Shallow, Justice (Robert)
Simple, Peter
Slender, Abraham

A Midsummer Night's Dream
Bottom
Demetrius
Egeus
Helena
Hermia
Hippolyta
Lysander
Oberon
Puck
Quince, Peter
Theseus
Titania

Much Ado About Nothing
Beatrice
Benedick
Borachio
Claudio
Conrade
Dogberry
Don John
Don Pedro
Hero
Leonato

Othello
Bianca
Cassio
Desdemona
Emilia
Iago
Othello
Roderigo

Pericles
Antiochus
Cleon
Dionyza
Helicanus
Marina
Pericles
Simonides
Thaisa

The Rape of Lucrece
Collatinus (Collatine)
Lucretia
Lucretius Brutus
Tarquinius, Sextus

Richard II
Bagot, Bushy and Green
Gardener, the
Henry IV, Henry Bolingbroke
Hotspur (Henry Percy)
John of Gaunt, Duke of Lancaster
Mowbray, Thomas, 1st Duke of Norfolk
Percy, Henry, Earl of Northumberland
Pierce of Exton, Sir
Queen, the (Isabella)
Richard II, King

Richard III
Anne, Lady, formerly Anne Neville
Buckingham, Duke of
Edward, Earl of March, later Edward IV
George, Duke of Clarence
Henry VI
Margaret of Anjou, later Queen Margaret
Richard, Duke of Gloucester
Richmond, Henry, Earl of, later Henry VII
Woodville, Anthony, Earl Rivers
Woodville, Elizabeth (Lady Grey), later
  Queen Elizabeth

Romeo and Juliet
Benvolio
Capulet
Capulet, Lady

Index

Escalus, Prince of Verona
Friar Lawrence
Juliet
Mercutio
Montague
Nurse
Paris
Romeo
Tybalt
The Taming of the Shrew
Baptista Minola
Bianca
Grumio
Katharina (Kate)
Lucentio
Petruchio
Sly, Christopher
Tranio
Vincentio
The Tempest
Alonso
Antonio
Ariel
Caliban
Ferdinand
Gonzalo
Miranda
Prospero
Sebastian
Stephano
Trinculo
Titus Andronicus
Aaron, the Moor
Andronicus, Lucius
Andronicus, Marcus
Andronicus, Quintus
Andronicus, Titus
Bassianus
Lavinia
Saturninus
Tamora, Queen
Troilus and Cressida
Achilles
Agamemnon
Ajax
Andromache
Calchas
Cassandra
Cressida
Diomedes
Hector
Helen
Helenus
Pandarus
Paris
Patroclus
Priam
Thersites
Troilus
Ulysses
Twelfth Night
Aguecheek, Sir Andrew
Antonio
Belch, Sir Toby
Fabian
Feste
Malvolio
Maria
Olivia
Orsino
Sebastian
Viola
Two Gentlemen of Verona
Antonio
Eglamour, Sir
Julia
Launce
Milan, Duke of

Proteus
Silvia
Speed
Thurio
Valentine
Venus and Adonis
Adonis
Venus
The Winter's Tale
Antigonus
Autolycus
Camillo
Florizel
Hermione
Leontes
Paulina
Perdita
Polixenes

Shakespeare, William (*see above*)
and Fletcher, John (*see* **Fletcher,
John**)

Henry VIII (All is True)
Boleyn, or Bullen, Anne
Cranmer, Thomas
Henry VIII
Katherine, Queen of England
Wolsey, Cardinal Thomas

Shakespeare, William (*see above*)
and Middleton, Thomas (*see*
Middleton, Thomas)

Timon of Athens
Alcibiades
Apemantus
Flavius
Timon of Athens
Ventidius

Shange, Ntozake
◎ (born 1948) US dramatist and
novelist. Her writing celebrates
African-American women and the
ability to survive. She earned
widespread recognition with her
drama, *for colored girls who have
considered suicide/when the
rainbow is enuf* (1975), which
innovatively combines music,
poetry and dance.

*for colored girls who have
considered suicide/when the
rainbow is enuf*
Lady in Brown, also Lady in Yellow, Lady
in Orange, Lady in Red, Lady in Green,
Lady in Blue, Lady in Purple

Sharpe, Tom
◎ (born 1928) English satirical
novelist. After graduating from
Cambridge, he served in the Royal
Marines and worked as a social
worker, teacher and photographer
before turning to full-time writing.

Blott on the Landscape
Blott
Porterhouse Blue
Skullion
Wilt
Wilt, Henry

Shaw, George Bernard
◎ (1856–1950) Irish dramatist and
critic. He left Ireland to follow his
mother and sister to London,
where he entered a long period of
struggle and poverty, and
developed a belief in socialism
which underlay all his future work.
As well as being an important
playwright, Shaw was also an
influential music and drama critic.
He was awarded the Nobel prize for
literature in 1925.

The Admirable Bashville
Bashville
Byron, Cashel
Androcles and the Lion
Androcles
Captain, the
Emperor, the
Ferrovius
Lavinia
Spintho
The Apple Cart
Boanerges, Bill
Lysistrata
Magnus, King
Orinthia
Proteus, Joe
Arms and the Man
Bluntschli
Louka
Petkoff, Raina
Saranoff, Sergius
Back to Methuselah
Acis
Adam
Amaryllis
Ancients, He- and She-
Arjillax
Aufsteig, Gen
Barnabas, Dr Conrad
Barnabas, Franklyn
Barnabas, 'Savvy' (Cynthia)
Burge, Joyce
Burge-Lubin
Cain
Chloe
Confucius
Elderly Gentleman, the
Eve
Fusima
Haslam, Rev Bill
Lilith
Lubin, Henry Hopkins
Lutestring, Mrs
Napoleon (General Aufsteig)
Oracle, the (the Pythoness)
Pygmalion
Serpent, the
Strephon
York, Archbishop of
Zoo
Zozim
Caesar and Cleopatra
Apollodorus
Britannus
Caesar, Caius Julius
Cleopatra
Ftatateeta
Pothinus
Ptolemy Dionysus
Rufio
Candida
Garnett, Prossy (Proserpine)
Marchbanks, Eugene
Morell, Candida
Morell, Rev James
Captain Brassbound's Conversion
Brassbound, Captain
Hallam, Sir Howard
Rankin, Leslie

Wayneflete, Lady Cecily
The Devil's Disciple
Anderson, Judith
Anderson, Pastor Anthony
Burgoyne, Gen John
Dudgeon, Essie
Dudgeon, Mrs
Dudgeon, Richard (Dick)
Swindon, Major
The Doctor's Dilemma
Blenkinsop, Dr
Bonington, Sir Ralph Bloomfield
Cullen, Sir Patrick
Dubedat, Jennifer
Dubedat, Louis
Ridgeon, Sir Colenso
Walpole, Cutler
Fanny's First Play
O'Dowda, Fanny
Getting Married
Bridgenorth, Edith
Bridgenorth, Gen 'Boxer'
Bridgenorth, Leo
Bridgenorth, Reginald
Chelsea, Bishop of, originally Alfred
    Bridgenorth
Collins, Bill (William)
Collins, Mrs George (Zenobia)
Grantham, Lesbia
Hotchkiss, St John
Sykes, Cecil
Heartbreak House
Dunn, Ellie
Dunn, Mazzini
Hushabye, Hector
Hushabye, Hesione
Mangan, 'Boss' (Alfred)
Shotover, Captain
Utterword, Lady Ariadne
Utterword, Randall
John Bull's Other Island
Broadbent, Tom (Thomas)
Dempsey, Father
Doyle, Larry (Laurence)
Keegan, Peter
Reilly, Nora
Major Barbara
Cusins, Adolphus
Mitchens, Rummy
Price, 'Snobby'
Shirley, Peter
Undershaft, Andrew
Undershaft, Barbara
Undershaft, Lady Britomart
Walker, Bill
Man and Superman
Malone, Hector
Mendoza (the Devil)
Ramsden, Roebuck
Robinson, Octavius ('Tavy')
Robinson, Violet
Straker, Henry
Tanner, John
Whitefield, Ann
The Millionairess
Fitzfassenden, Epifania
Misalliance
Gunner, properly Julius Baker
Szczepanowska, Lina
Tarleton, John
Mrs Warren's Profession
Crofts, Sir George
Gardner, Frank
Gardner, Rev Samuel
Praed
Warren, Mrs Kitty
Warren, Vivie

The Philanderer
Charteris, Leonard
Craven, Julia
Tanfield, Grace
Pygmalion
Doolittle, Alfred
Doolittle, Eliza
Eynsford Hill, Freddy
Eynsford Hill, Mrs
Higgins, Professor Henry
Pickering, Col
Saint Joan
Baudricourt, Captain Robert de
Cauchon, Peter (Bishop of Beauvais)
Dauphin, the (later King Charles VII of
    France)
Dunois, Captain Jean ('Bastard of
    Orléans')
Inquisitor, the (Brother John Lemaitre)
Joan (Jeanne d'Arc)
Ladvenu, Brother Martin
Poulengy, Bertrand de
Rais, Gilles de
Rheims, Archbishop of
Stogumber, John de
Warwick, Earl of
The Shewing-Up of Blanco Posnet
Posnet, Blanco
Too True to be Good
Burglar, the (the Honourable Aubrey
    Bagot)
Elder, the
Fielding, Sgt
Meek, Private
Monster, the
Mopply, Mrs
Nurse, the (Susan 'Sweetie' Simpkins)
Patient, the (Miss Mopply)
Tallboys, Col
Widowers' Houses
Cokane, William de Burgh
Lickcheese
Sartorius
Sartorius, Blanche
Trench, Dr Harry
You Never Can Tell
Bohun QC
Clandon, Dolly
Clandon, Gloria
Clandon, Mrs Lanfrey
Clandon, Philip
Crampton, Fergus
McComus, Finch
Valentine

Shelley, Mary

◎ (1797–1851) English writer. She
was the daughter of Mary
Wollestonecraft and William
Godwin. In 1814 she eloped with
Percy Shelley and they lived abroad
until his death. Her first and most
impressive novel was *Frankenstein,
or, The Modern Prometheus* (1818).
She also published verse, tales and
accounts of her travels in Europe.

*Frankenstein, or, The Modern
Prometheus*
Clerval, Henry
Frankenstein, Victor
Frankenstein's Creature
Lavenza, Elizabeth
Walton, Robert

Shelley, Percy (Bysshe)

◎ (1792–1822) English lyric poet
and writer. In 1814 he eloped with

his second wife, **Mary Shelley**, and
spent most of the remainder of his
life abroad, primarily in Italy,
where he eventually drowned. With
radical political and social views,
he was a leading figure in the
Romantic movement. He was a
friend of **Lord Byron** and
acquainted with **John Keats**.

The Cenci
Beatrice
Cenci, Count Francesco
'Julian and Maddalo'
Julian
Maddalo, Count
'Ozymandias'
Ozymandias

Shepard, Sam

◎ (born 1943) US dramatist and
actor. He worked in the avant-
garde theatre of New York in the
1960s. He has written over 40
plays, often dealing with American
mythologies. He has also appeared
in films and has written
screenplays.

Fool for Love
Eddie
True West
Austin
Lee

Sheridan, Richard Brinsley

◎ (1751–1816) Irish dramatist. The
son of an Irish actor, he became
proprietor and manager of Drury
Lane Theatre. Eventually a
Member of Parliament and a
renowned political orator, he is
best remembered for his witty
comedies of manners.

The Critic
Dangle
Plagiary, Sir Fretful
Puff
Sneer
Tilburina
Whiskerandos, Don Ferolo
The Rivals
Absolute, Captain Jack
Absolute, Sir Anthony
Acres, Bob
Faulkland
Languish, Lydia
Malaprop, Mrs
Melville, Julia
O'Trigger, Sir Lucius
The School for Scandal
Backbite, Sir Benjamin
Candour, Mrs
Crabtree
Maria
Snake
Sneerwell, Lady
Surface, Charles
Surface, Joseph
Surface, Sir Oliver
Teazle, Lady
Teazle, Sir Peter

Sherriff, R(obert) C(edric)

◎ (1896–1975) English playwright,
novelist and scriptwriter. He
achieved an international
reputation with his first play,

Journey's End (1928), which was based on his experiences in the trenches during World War I.

Journey's End
Osborne
Raleigh, Jimmy
Stanhope, Dennis

Shields, Carol

◎ (1935–2003) Canadian author and academic. Born in Illinois, she moved to Canada in 1957. She taught at various Canadian universities while writing award-winning novels dealing with the extraordinary sides of love and family life.

Happenstance
Bowman, Brenda
Bowman, Jack

Larry's Party
Weller, Larry

The Republic of Love
Avery, Tom
McLeod, Fay

The Stone Diaries
Flett, Daisy Goodwill

Unless
Winters, Reta

Shute, Nevil

◎ (1899–1960) English novelist. He served in World War I and immediately afterwards began an aeronautical career. He emigrated to Australia after World War II. His best-known work is *A Town Like Alice* (1950).

A Town Like Alice
Harman, Joe
Paget, Jean, nicknamed Mrs Boong
Strachan, Noel

Sidney, Sir Philip

◎ (1554–86) English poet and patron. He travelled widely in Europe. Returning to England, he was knighted in 1582 and appointed Governor of Flushing in 1585. He died from injuries sustained while leading an assault on a Spanish convoy in the Netherlands. None of his work was published in his lifetime.

The Countess of Pembroke's Arcadia
Amphialus
Basilius, Duke
Cecropia
Dametas
Euarchus
Gynecia
Miso
Mopsa
Musidorus
Pamela
Philoclea
Pyrocles

Silko, Leslie Marmon

◎ (born 1948) US poet, novelist and short-story writer. Born of mixed white, Native American and Mexican heritage, she was raised in a pueblo in New Mexico. Her best-known work is the novel *Ceremony* (1977).

Ceremony
Betonie
Tayo
Ts'eh

Sillitoe, Alan

◎ (born 1928) English novelist and short-story writer. He achieved fame with his first novel, *Saturday Night and Sunday Morning* (1958). He has also written plays and screenplays from his novels.

The Loneliness of the Long Distance Runner
Borstal Boy

Saturday Night and Sunday Morning
Seaton, Arthur

Simms, William Gilmore

◎ (1806–70) US novelist. He edited the *City Gazette* in his hometown of Charleston and also published poetry. *The Yemassee* (1835) is a sympathetic account of Native Americans, a subject he returned to in many of his short stories.

Katharine Walton
Singleton, Major
Walton, Katharine

The Partisan
Porgy, Lt
Singleton, Major

The Yemassee
Matiwan
Occonestoga
Sanutee

Sinclair, May

◎ (1863–1946) English novelist. She became an advocate of women's suffrage and also took an interest in psychoanalysis, as revealed in some of her 24 novels.

The Life and Death of Harriet Frean
Frean, Harriet

Mary Olivier: A Life
Olivier, Mary

Sinclair, Upton

◎ (1878–1968) US novelist and social reformer. He horrified the world with his exposure of meat-packing conditions in Chicago in his novel *The Jungle* (1906). Later novels were increasingly influenced by his socialist beliefs. He also wrote a monumental eleven-volume series about Lanny Budd, starting with *World's End* (1940).

The Jungle
Rudkus, Jurgis

World's End
Budd, Lanny

Singer, Isaac Bashevis

◎ (1904–91) US Yiddish writer. Born in Poland, the son of a rabbi, he emigrated to the USA in 1935. There he joined his brother, working as a journalist for the *Jewish Daily Forward*. He set his novels and short stories among the Jews of Poland, Germany and the USA, combining a deep

psychological insight with dramatic and visual impact. He was awarded the Nobel prize for literature in 1978.

'Gimpel the Fool'
Gimpel

The Magician of Lublin
Mazur, Yasha

The Penitent
Shapiro, Joseph

Satan in Goray
Rechele
Zevi, Sabbatai

Shosha
Tsutsik, properly Aaron Greidinger

The Slave
Jacob

'The Spinoza of Market Street'
Fischelson, Dr Nahum

Skelton, John

◎ (c.1460–1529) English satirical poet. He was tutor to Prince Henry (the future Henry VIII). He produced translations and elegies and became known for his satirical vernacular poetry.

Collyn Clout
Clout, Collyn

'The Tunnyng of Elynour Rummyng'
Rummyng, Elynour

Slessor, Kenneth

◎ (1901–71) Australian poet and journalist. As an official war correspondent he covered the Battle of Britain and then followed the Australian Imperial Forces through the Near East and North Africa. He contributed many poems to various periodicals and published several collections.

'Captain Dobbin'
Dobbin, Captain

Five Bells
Lynch, Joe

'Five Visions of Captain Cook'
Cook, Captain
Home, Captain Alexander

Smith, Alexander McCall

◎ (born 1948) Scottish novelist. Born in Zimbabwe, he is Professor of Medical Law at the University of Edinburgh and helped to establish a law school at the University of Botswana. He has published over 50 books, but achieved worldwide fame with *The No. 1 Ladies' Detective Agency* (1998), the first in a series of detective novels set in Botswana.

The No. 1 Ladies' Detective Agency
Ramotswe, Precious

Portuguese Irregular Verbs
von Igelfeld, Professor Dr Moritz-Maria

Smith, Dodie

◎ (1896–1990) English playwright, novelist and theatre producer. Although she wrote a number of very successful plays, she is, perhaps, best known for her children's book, *The Hundred and One Dalmatians* (1956).

The Hundred and One Dalmatians
Baddun, Saul and Jasper
Cruella de Vil
Missis
Perdita
Pongo

Smith, Sheila Kaye

© (1887–1956) English novelist.
She was born and spent most of her
life in Sussex and set all her novels
there, portraying the landscape
and rural life with great warmth.

Joanna Godden
Godden, Joanna

Smith, Zadie

© (born 1975) English novelist.
Born in London and educated at
Cambridge, her first novel was
White Teeth (2000). It was an
immediate bestseller and won
numerous awards.

White Teeth
Iqbal, Samad
Jones, Archie

Smollett, Tobias

© (1721–71) Scottish novelist. He
sailed as surgeon's mate in the
expedition to Carthagena against
the Spanish in 1741 and
subsequently settled in London. As
well as writing novels, he also
translated Cervantes's *Don Quixote*
and published his *History of
England* (3 vols, 1757–8) and *Travels
in France and Italy* (1766).

*The Adventures of Ferdinand, Count
Fathom*
Celinda
de Melvil, Renaldo, later Count de Melvil
Diego de Zelos, Don
Elinor
Fathom, Ferdinand, Count
Manasseh, Joshua
Monimia
Ratchkali
Stile, Sir Stentor

The Adventures of Peregrine Pickle
Crabtree, Cadwallader
Doctor, the
Gauntlet, Emilia (Emily or Emy)
Gauntlet, Godfrey
Hatchway, Mr Jack
Hornbeck, Mrs
Jolter, Mr Jacob
MacKercher, also known as Mr M—
Marmozet
Pallet, Layman
Pickle, Gamaliel
Pickle, Peregrine
Pipes, Tom
Spondy
Trunnion, Commodore Hawser
Vane, Lady (the Lady of Quality)

The Adventures of Roderick Random
Bowling, Lt Tom
Goosetrap, Melinda
Marmozet
Melopoyn, Mr
Morgan, Mr
Narcissa
Random, Roderick
Rodriguez, Don
Strap, Hugh
Williams, Miss Nancy

The Expedition of Humphry Clinker
Bramble, Matthew (Matt)
Bramble, Tabitha
Chowder
Clinker, Humphry
de Melvil, Renaldo, later Count de Melvil
Dennison, Charles
Fathom, Ferdinand, Count
Gwyllim, Mrs
Jenkins, Winifred
Lismahago, Lt Obadiah
MacKilligut, Sir Ulic
Melford, Jery
Melford, Lydia
Phillips, Sir Watkin, Bart
Willis, Laetitia ('Letty')
'Wilson'

*The Life and Adventures of Sir
Launcelot Greaves*
Bronzomarte
Clarke, Thomas
Crabshaw, Timothy
Crowe, Captain Samuel
Darnel, Anthony
Darnel, Aurelia
Ferret, Mr
Gobble, Justice
Greaves, Sir Launcelot

Snow, C(harles) P(ercy)

© (1905–80) English novelist and
physicist. Having studied science,
he worked in academia and in
government and his work shows a
keen appreciation of moral issues
in a science-dominated age.

A Coat of Varnish
Luria, Alec

The Conscience of the Rich
March, Charles

Corridors of Power
Quaife, Roger, MP

Homecomings
Bevill, Thomas, later Lord Grampound
Eliot, Margaret
Eliot, Sheila

The Light and the Dark
Getliffe, Francis

The Masters
Jago, Dr Paul

The New Men
Bevill, Thomas, later Lord Grampound
Eliot, Irene
Eliot, Martin
Luke, Walter

Strangers and Brothers
Calvert, Roy
Eliot, Lewis
Passant, George

Time of Hope
Getliffe, Herbert

Somerville, E(dith) O(enone) and
Ross, Martin, pseudonym of **Violet
Florence Martin**

© (1858–1949 and 1861–1915) Irish
novelists. Cousins, they are best
known for their literary
partnership as 'Somerville and
Ross'.

Further Experiences of an Irish R.M.
Flurry Knox (Florence McCarthy Knox)
Major, (Sinclair Yeates), the
Philippa

In Mr Knox's Country
Flurry Knox (Florence McCarthy Knox)

Major, (Sinclair Yeates), the
Philippa

The Real Charlotte
Fitzpatrick, Francie
Lambert, Roddy
Mullen, Charlotte

Some Experiences of an Irish R.M.
Flurry Knox (Florence McCarthy Knox)
Major, (Sinclair Yeates), the
Philippa

Soyinka, Wole

© (born 1934) Nigerian dramatist,
poet and novelist. After spending a
time in London, he returned to
Ibadan in 1959, and productions of
his plays immediately established
him in the forefront of Nigerian
literature. From 1967 to 1969 he
was a political prisoner, and he has
since held professorships at various
universities. He was awarded the
Nobel prize for literature in 1986.

A Dance of the Forests
Adenebi
Agboreku
Dead Man and Dead Woman
Demoke
Forest Father
Half-Child, the
Mata Kharibu
Rola, or Madame Tortoise

The Interpreters
Egbo
Kola
Lasunwon
Sagoe
Sekoni

Jero's Metamorphosis
Jero, Brother (Jeroboam)

Kongi's Harvest
Kongi

The Lion and the Jewel
Lakunle
Sidi

Madmen and Specialists
De Bero

The Strong Breed
Eman

The Swamp Dwellers
Alu
Makuri

The Trials of Brother Jero
Jero, Brother (Jeroboam)

Spark, Muriel

© (born 1918) Scottish novelist,
short-story writer, biographer and
poet. Born in Edinburgh, she spent
some years in Central Africa before
returning to Britain in 1944 where
she worked in the Foreign Office.
Since the early 1960s she has lived
mainly in New York and Italy. She
achieved public success with her
sixth novel, *The Prime of Miss Jean
Brodie* (1961).

The Abbess of Crewe
Alexandra
Felicity
Gertrude

The Bachelors
Seton, Patrick

The Ballad of Peckham Rye
Douglas, Dougal

The Comforters
Hogg, Georgina
Rose, Caroline
Stock, Baron Willi
'Daisy Overend'
Overend, Daisy
The Driver's Seat
Lise
A Far Cry from Kensington
Bartlett, Hector
Hawkins, Mrs Nancy
The Girls of Slender Means
Childe, Joanna
Farringdon, Nicholas
'The Go-Away Bird'
du Toit, Daphne
The Hothouse by the East River
Hazlett, Elsa
Loitering with Intent
Oliver, Sir Quentin
Talbot, Fleur
The Mandelbaum Gate
Vaughan, Barbara
Memento Mori
Colston, Dame Lettie
Not To Disturb
Lister
The Only Problem
Gotham, Harvey
'The Portobello Road'
Needle
The Prime of Miss Jean Brodie
Brodie, Miss Jean
Douglas, Monica
Gardiner, Eunice
Gray, Jenny
Macgregor, Mary
Stanley, Rose
Stranger, Sandy
The Public Image
Christopher, Annabel
Robinson
Robinson, Miles Mary
The Takeover
Radcliffe, Maggie

Spenser, Sir Edmund

◎ (c.1552–1599) English poet. His first original work, *The Shepheard's Calender* (1579), dedicated to **Sir Philip Sidney**, heralded the age of Elizabethan poetry. In 1580 he was appointed secretary to the Lord Deputy in Ireland. He acquired Kilcolman Castle in Cork (1586), where he lived until it was burned down in an insurrection, forcing him to flee to London. His most enduring work is *The Faerie Queene* (1590–6).

The Faerie Queene
Abessa
Acrasia
Agape
Alma
Amoret
Archimago
Argante
Artegall, the Knight of Justice
Arthur, Prince
Ate
Belphoebe
Blandamour
Blatant Beast, the
Bourbon, Sir

Braggadochio
Briana
Britomart
Busirane
Caelia
Calepine, Sir
Calidore, Sir, the Knight of Courtesy
Cambell, or Cambello
Cambina
Canacee
Corflambo
Cymochles
Cymodoce, also known as Cymoent
Dolon
Duessa
Echidna
Elissa
Fidessa
Florimell
Fradubio
Fraelissa
Geryoneo
Glaucé
Gloriana
Goëmagot or Gogmagot
Grantorto
Grille
Guyon, Sir, Knight of Temperance
Hellenore
Hudibras
Irena
Kirkrapine
Lucifera
Malager
Malbecco
Malecasta
Malengin
Mammon
Marinell
Medina
Mercilla, Queen
Morddure
Munera
Mutabilitie
Ollyphant
Orgoglio
Paridell
Pastorella
Perissa
Phaedria
Phaon
Pollente
Pyrochles
Radigund
Redcrosse, the Knight of Holiness
Samient
Sanglier, Sir
Sansfoy
Sansjoy
Sansloy
Satyrane, Sir
Sclaunder
Scudamour, Sir
Soldan, the
Squire of Dames, the
Talus
Tanaquill
Timias
Triamond
Trompart
Turpine
Una

Stead, Christina

◎ (1902–83) Australian novelist. She went to the USA at the outbreak of war, where she became a senior writer for MGM in Hollywood. She left the USA in 1947 and finally returned to her homeland in 1974, in which year she was the first winner of the Patrick White Literary Award.

Cotter's England
Cook, Nellie, née Ellen Cotter
For Love Alone
Crow, Jonathan
Hawkins, Tessa (Teresa)
Quick, James
Letty Fox: Her Luck
Fox, Letty
A Little Tea, A Little Chat
Grant, Robbie (Robert)
The Man Who Loved Children
Pollitt, Henny (Henrietta)
Pollitt, Louie (Louisa)
Pollitt, Sam (Samuel Clemens)
'The Puzzle-Headed Girl'
Lawrence, Honor
Seven Poor Men of Sydney
Baguenault, Catherine
Baguenault, Joseph
Baguenault, Michael
Blount, Kol
Chamberlain, Gregory
Mendelssohn, Baruch
Winter, Tom
Withers, Tom

Steele, Richard *see* **Addison, Joseph** and **Steele, Richard**

Stein, Gertrude

◎ (1874–1946) US writer. Born in Pennsylvania, she spent her early years in Europe. Having studied psychology and medicine in the USA, she then settled in Paris, where she came into contact with writers and artists including Picasso and Matisse.

'The Gentle Lena'
Lena
'The Good Anna'
Federner, Anna
Mathilda, Miss
Shonjen, Dr
Wadsmith, Miss Mary
The Making of Americans
Dehning, Julia
Hersland, Alfred
'Melanctha'
Campbell, Dr Jeff
Herbert, Melanctha
Richards, Jem

Steinbeck, John

◎ (1902–68) US novelist. He was born in California, studied at Stanford and worked as a reporter in New York and later as a war correspondent. His major work, *The Grapes of Wrath* (1939), won the 1940 Pulitzer Prize. He won the Nobel prize for literature in 1962.

Cannery Row
Doc (Doc Lee)
Dora (Dora Flood)
Lee Chong
Mack
East of Eden
Ames, Cathy, properly Cathy Ames Trask

Index

Trask, Adam
Trask, Caleb and Aron
The Grapes of Wrath
Casy, Jim
Joad, Ma
Joad, Rose of Sharon ('Rosasharn')
Joad, Tom
In Dubious Battle
Nolan, Jim
Of Mice and Men
George (George Milton)
Lennie (Lennie Small)
The Red Pony
Gitano
Jody (Jody Tiflin)
Tortilla Flat
Danny
Pablo (Pablo Sanchez)
Pilon

Sterne, Laurence
© (1713–68) Irish novelist. He was ordained in 1738, and was appointed to a living in Yorkshire and eventually made a prebendary of York, where, in 1759, the first two volumes of *The Life and Opinions of Tristram Shandy* were published. *A Sentimental Journey through France and Italy* appeared in 1768, shortly before he died in London.

The Life and Opinions of Tristram Shandy
Le Fever, Lt
Obadiah
Shandy, Mrs
Shandy, Tristram
Shandy, Uncle Toby
Shandy, Walter
Slawkenbergius
Slop, Dr
Trim, Corporal
Wadman, Mrs
Yorick, Parson

A Sentimental Journey through France and Italy
Mundungus
Smelfungus

Stevenson, Robert Louis
© (1850–94) Scottish writer. His childhood was afflicted by constant illness, and he suffered throughout his life from a chronic bronchial condition. His first major works describe travels in Belgium and northern France undertaken to improve his health. The romantic adventure story *Treasure Island* brought him fame in 1883. He spent his last years in the South Seas.

The Beach of Falesá
Case
Randall, Captain
Tarleton
Uma
Wiltshire, Mr

The Black Arrow
Skelton, Dick (Richard)

Catriona
Balfour, David
Breck, Alan
Drummond, Catriona
Drummond, James More

James of the Glens, properly James Stewart
The Ebb Tide
Davis
Herrick
Hyish
Kidnapped
Balfour, David
Balfour, Ebenezer
Breck, Alan
James of the Glens, properly James Stewart
Red Fox, the, properly Colin Campbell
Markheim
Markheim
The Master of Ballantrae
Durie, Henry
Durie, James
Mackellar, Mr
St. Ives
St Ives, Vicomte de
The Strange Case of Dr. Jekyll and Mr. Hyde
Dr Jekyll/Mr Hyde
The Suicide Club
Florizel, Prince of Bohemia
Rich, Brackenbury
Scuddamore, Silas Q
Thrawn Janet
McLour, Janet
Soulis, Murdoch
Treasure Island
Gunn, Ben
Hawkins, Jim
Silver, Long John
Weir of Hermiston
Elliott, Christina
Elliott, Clem (Clement)
Elliott, Dand (Andrew)
Elliott, Gib (Gilbert)
Elliott, Kirstie
Elliott, Rob (Robert)
Innes, Frank
Weir, Adam, Lord Hermiston
Weir, Archie

Stewart, Douglas
© (1913–85) Australian writer. Born in New Zealand, he moved to Sydney, where he became literary editor (1940–61) of *The Bulletin* magazine, and later worked for a publishing house. As well as poetry, he also wrote radio drama, biographies, and edited a number of anthologies and two collections of bush ballads.

Fire on the Snow
Scott, Captain
The Golden Lover
Ruarangi
Tawhai
Whana
Ned Kelly
Kelly, Ned
Rutherford
Rutherford

Stewart, J(ohn) I(nnes) M(ackintosh), pseudonym Michael Innes
© (1906–94) Scottish novelist, critic and detective-story writer. Born in Edinburgh and educated at Oxford, he subsequently taught at

universities in the UK and Australia. Under his own name he published critical studies and a quintet of novels about Oxford. As Michael Innes he wrote a series of popular and successful novels featuring the donnish, erudite John Appleby (*see* **Innes, Michael**).

Full Term
Patullo, Duncan
The Gaudy
Patullo, Duncan
The Madonna of the Astrolabe
Patullo, Duncan
A Memorial Service
Patullo, Duncan
Young Patullo
Patullo, Duncan

Stoker, Bram
© (1847–1912) Irish writer. Educated at Trinity College Dublin, he entered the Civil Service, but turned to literature, and joined Henry Irving in running the Lyceum Theatre in London from 1878 to 1905. He is best remembered for the classic vampire story *Dracula* (1897).

Dracula
Dracula, Count
Harker, Jonathan
Van Helsing, Abraham

Stoppard, Tom, originally **Thomas Straussler**
© (born 1937) British dramatist. Born in Czechoslovakia, he moved to England in 1946. After some time in Bristol, he worked as a journalist and theatre critic in London. He made his name with *Rosencrantz and Guildenstern Are Dead* (1967). He has also written short stories, screenplays and film scripts.

Arcadia
Jarvis, Hannah
Nightingale, Bernard
The Coast of Utopia
Herzen, Alexander
Indian Ink
Crewe, Flora
The Invention of Love
Housman, A E
Jumpers
Moore, Dotty
Moore, George
Night and Day
Wagner, Richard
Professional Foul
Anderson
Hollar
The Real Thing
Annie
Henry
Rosencrantz and Guildenstern Are Dead
Guildenstern
Rosencrantz
Travesties
Carr, Henry

Storey, David
© (born 1933) English dramatist and novelist. An art student and

professional Rugby League player, he became known for his novel, *This Sporting Life* (1960). He won the Booker Prize for *Saville* (1976).

Saville
Saville, Colin

This Sporting Life
Machin, Arthur

Stout, Rex

◎ (1886–1975) US detective-story writer. Before becoming a writer he invented a school banking system that was installed in 400 cities throughout the USA. His great creation is Nero Wolfe, the phenomenally fat private eye.

Fer-de-lance
Wolfe, Nero

Stow, Randolph

◎ (born 1935) Australian novelist, poet and librettist. He worked as an anthropologist and subsequently taught at universities in the UK and Australia. *Tourmaline* (1963) is an Australian version of **T S Eliot**'s *The Waste Land*.

The Merry-Go-Round in the Sea
Coram, Rob
Maplestead, Rick

Midnite: The Story of a Wild Colonial Boy
Midnite, also known as Mr Daybreak

To the Islands
Heriot
Justin
Rex

Tourmaline
Kestrel
Random, Michael
Speed, Dave
Tourmaline, the Law of

Visitants
Cawdor, Alistair

Stowe, Harriet Beecher

◎ (1811–96) US novelist. She became famous for her *Uncle Tom's Cabin, or, Life Among the Lowly* (1851–2), which immediately focused anti-slavery sentiment in the North. Her second anti-slavery novel, *Dred: A Tale of the Great Dismal Swamp* (1856), was praised by such contemporaries as **George Eliot**.

Dred: A Tale of the Great Dismal Swamp
Dred

Uncle Tom's Cabin, or, Life Among the Lowly
Cassy
Eliza (Eliza Harris)
Eva, or Little Eva, properly Eva St Clare
George (George Harris)
Legree, Simon
Ophelia, Miss
St Clare, Augustine
St Clare, Marie
Topsy
Uncle Tom

Styron, William

◎ (born 1925) US novelist. Unafraid of controversial topics, he

has tackled racism in *The Confessions of Nat Turner* (1967, Pulitzer Prize), and the fate of Holocaust survivors in *Sophie's Choice* (1979).

The Confessions of Nat Turner
Turner, Nat

Lie Down in Darkness
Loftis, Peyton (Peyton Loftis Miller)

The Long March
Mannix

Set This House on Fire
Leverett, Peter

Sophie's Choice
Landau, Nathan
Stingo
Zawistowska, Sophie

Surtees, R(obert) S(mith)

◎ (1803–64) English journalist and novelist. He practised as a lawyer and later became a Justice of the Peace and High Sheriff of Durham County. He founded the *New Sporting Magazine* in 1831 where he introduced John Jorrocks, a sporting Cockney, whose adventures were later contained in *Jorrocks' Jaunts and Jollities* (1838).

Jorrocks' Jaunts and Jollities
Jorrocks, Mr

Mr Facey Romford's Hounds
Romford, Mr Facey

Mr Sponge's Sporting Tour
Sponge, Soapy

Swift, Graham

◎ (born 1949) English novelist and short-story writer. International acclaim arrived on the publication of his third novel, *Waterland* (1983), which was shortlisted for the Booker Prize.

Waterland
Crick, Tom

Swift, Jonathan

◎ (1667–1745) Anglo-Irish satirist and clergyman. Family connections helped him become secretary to the diplomat, Sir William Temple. The death of Queen Anne in 1714 disappointed all his hopes and he accepted his 'exile' to the Deanery of St Patrick's Cathedral, Dublin. Despite his loathing for Ireland he threw himself into a strenuous campaign for Irish liberties. He was the author of the world-famous satire *Gulliver's Travels* (1726).

The Battle of the Books
Aesop

Gulliver's Travels
Brobdingnagians
Glumdalclitch
Gulliver, Lemuel
Houyhnhnms
Lagadoans
Laputans
Lilliputians
Struldbrugs
Yahoos

Synge, J(ohn) M(illington)

◎ (1871–1909) Irish dramatist. He attended Trinity College, Dublin, and spent several years in Germany and Paris until, on the advice of **W B Yeats**, he settled among the people of the Aran Islands (1899–1902), who provided the material for several of his plays. He had a profound influence on the next generation of Irish playwrights and was a director of the Abbey Theatre, Dublin from 1904.

In the Shadow of the Glen
Burke, Dan and Nora
Dara, Michael
Tramp, the

The Playboy of the Western World
Mahon, Christy
Pegeen Mike, properly Margaret Flaherty
Widow Quin

Riders to the Sea
Maurya

The Tinker's Wedding
Byrne, Michael and Mary
Casey, Sarah

Tarkington, Booth

◎ (1869–1946) US writer. Many of his novels are set in Indiana and the Midwest. *The Magnificent Ambersons* (1918) won the Pulitzer Prize.

Alice Adams
Adams, Alice

The Magnificent Ambersons
Amberson, Fanny
Minafer, George
Minafer, Isabel Amberson
Morgan, Eugene

Tartt, Donna

◎ (born 1963) US novelist and short-story writer. Born and educated in Mississippi, she became a literary sensation with her ambitious first novel *The Secret History* (1992). Her second novel *The Little Friend* (2002) appeared almost a decade later.

The Little Friend
Dufresnes, Harriet Cleve

The Secret History
Papen, Richard

Taylor, C(ecil) P(hilip)

◎ (1928–81) Scottish dramatist. His most famous work is *Good* (1981), a powerful play set in the Third Reich. He also adapted and wrote plays for television.

Good
Halder, John

Taylor, Elizabeth

◎ (1912–75) English novelist and short-story writer. She wrote her first novel, *At Mrs Lippincote's* (1945), while her husband was in the R.A.F. Her hallmark is quiet, shrewd observation of middle-class life in the south-east of England.

At Mrs Lippincote's
Lippincote, Mrs

Blaming
Henderson, Amy
Larkin, Martha

Mrs Palfrey at the Claremont
Palfrey, Mrs

A Wreath of Roses
Hill, Camilla

Taylor, Peter

◎ (1917–94) US short-story writer, novelist and playwright. Concerned with the smaller crises and conflicts of upper middle-class life in the Southern states of the USA, primarily Tennessee, his fiction often focused on the manners and mores of a vanishing society.

A Summons to Memphis
Carver, Betsy and Jo
Carver, George
Carver, Phillip

Taylor, Tom

◎ (1817–80) Scottish dramatist and editor. Called to the Bar in 1845, he also worked for the government. From 1846 he wrote or adapted over a hundred pieces for the stage. He edited autobiographies, translated *Ballads and Songs of Brittany* (1865), and in 1874 became editor of *Punch*. He was also *The Times* art critic.

Our American Cousin
Dundreary, Lord

Tennant, Emma

◎ (born 1937) English novelist. Of an aristocratic family, she spent her summers in Scotland and was presented at court as a debutante. She founded the innovative literary magazine *Bananas* in the 1970s. Her novels are often characterized by stream of consciousness and use of fantasy, while some are unconventional sequels to classics.

The Bad Sister
Wild, Jane

Hotel de Dream
Briggs, Miss
Poynter, Arthur
Routledge, Mrs Amanda
Scranton, Miss Jeanette

Wild Nights
Zita, Aunt

Tennant, Kylie

◎ (1912–88) Australian novelist, dramatist and short-story writer. Born in Manly, New South Wales, her works captured the broad canvas of Australian people, society and landscapes with irony and humour.

The Battlers
Duke, in full Harley Duke
Phipps, Miss Dora
Smith, Dancy, known as 'the Stray'
Snow

Ride on Stranger
Hicks, Shannon
Terrill, John

Tiburon
Daunt, Jessica
Scorby
White, Paul

Tennyson, Alfred, Lord

◎ (1809–92) English poet. His early ventures in verse were slighted by the critics of the day as being too sentimental, but the volume of *Poems* of 1842 established his fame. He was revered throughout Victorian England and in 1850 he succeeded **William Wordsworth** as Poet Laureate.

'Enoch Arden'
Arden, Enoch

'The Lady of Shalott'
Shalott, the Lady of

'Maud; a Monodrama'
Maud

'Morte d'Arthur'
Arthur, King
Bedivere, Sir

'St Simeon Stylites'
Simeon Stylites, St

'Tithonus'
Tithonus

'Ulysses'
Ulysses

Terson, Peter, pseudonym of Peter Patterson

◎ (born 1932) English dramatist. He worked as a teacher in his native Tyneside and is known for his work with the National Youth Theatre, beginning with *Zigger Zagger* (1967). He has also written for radio and television.

Zigger Zagger
Harry
Zigger Zagger

Tey, Josephine, pseudonym of Elizabeth Mackintosh, who also wrote as Gordon Daviot

◎ (1897–1952) Scottish crime and mystery writer. Her main invention was Inspector Alan Grant. She also wrote plays and a biography of Viscount Dundee.

Brat Farrar
Farrar, Brat

A Shilling for Candles: The Story of a Crime
Grant, Inspector Alan

Thackeray, W(illiam) M(akepeace)

◎ (1811–63) English novelist. Born in India and educated at Cambridge, he spent much time abroad, especially in Paris, returning to London in 1837.

Despite a troubled family life, he contributed reviews, parodies, sketches and serials to various publications, most famously to *Punch*, but is best remembered for the great novels which established his fame.

The Adventures of Philip
Baynes, Charlotte
Baynes, Gen
Firmin, Dr George, also known as George Brandon
Firmin, Philip
Gann, Caroline, also known as Mrs Brandon
Hunt, Tufton
Twysden, Agnes

Catherine: a Story
Catherine, or Cat, properly Catherine Hall

Denis Duval
Duval, Denis

The History of Henry Esmond, Esquire
Addison, Joseph
Castlewood, Frank
Castlewood, Lady Rachel
Castlewood, Viscount Francis
Esmond, Beatrix
Esmond, Henry (Harry)
Holt, Father
Marlborough, Duke of
Mohun, Henry, Lord
Stuart, James Edward
Tusher, Mrs Thomas
Warrington, George Esmond
Warrington, Rachel Esmond

The History of Pendennis
Altamount, Col, also known as Armstrong
Amory, Blanche
Bell, Laura
Bolton, Fanny
Clavering, Lady
Clavering, Sir Francis
Costigan, Captain
Costigan, Emily, or Miss Fotheringay
Foker, Harry
Huxter, Sam
Pendennis, Arthur
Pendennis, Helen
Pendennis, Major
Shandon, Captain
Warrington, George Esmond

Lovel the Widower
Lovel, Frederick

The Luck of Barry Lyndon
Barry, Cornelius, also known as Chevalier de Balibari
Bullingdon, Viscount
Honoria, Countess of Lyndon, Viscountess Bullingdon
Lyndon, Barry, also known as Barry Redmond of Ball
Lyndon, Bryan

The Newcomes
Belsize, Jack, the Honourable
Farintosh, Lord
Kew, Lady
Kew, Lord
Mackenzie, Mrs
Mackenzie, Rosey
Newcome, Barnes
Newcome, Clive
Newcome, Col Thomas
Newcome, Ethel
Newcome, Hobson
Newcome, Sir Brian, Bart, MP

Pendennis, Arthur

The Rose and the Ring
Angelica, Princess
Blackstick, Fairy
Bulbo, Prince
Giglio, Prince
Rosalba, Princess, also known as
  Betsinda

A Shabby Genteel Story
Firmin, Dr George, also known as George
  Brandon
Gann, Caroline, also known as Mrs
  Brandon
Hunt, Tufton

Vanity Fair
Crawley, Bute, Mr and Mrs
Crawley, Lady
Crawley, Miss
Crawley, Pitt
Crawley, Rawdon
Crawley, Rawdon jr
Crawley, Sir Pitt
Dobbin, William
Osborne, George
Osborne, John
Sedley, Amelia
Sedley, John
Sedley, Jos (Joseph)
Sedley, Mrs
Sharp, Becky (Rebecca)
Steyne, Lord

The Virginians
Esmond, Beatrix (as Baroness Bernstein)
Lambert, Gen
Lambert, Hetty (Hester)
Lambert, Theo (Theodosia)
Mountain, Fanny
Warrington, George Esmond
Warrington, Harry Esmond
Warrington, Maria
Warrington, Rachel Esmond
Warrington, Sir Miles

Theroux, Paul

◎ (born 1941) US writer. He has led
a footloose life that is reflected in
his literary output. His extended
travels are recounted in various
books. Of his novels *The Mosquito
Coast* (1981) won the James Tait
Black Memorial Prize.

The Mosquito Coast
Fox, Allie

Thomas, D(onald) M(itchell)

◎ (born 1935) English poet and
novelist. He learned Russian while
on National Service, and has
published numerous translations.
His early poems range across
science fiction, erotica, and
evocations of his native Cornwall.
He has also written novels and five
'improvisations' on Cold War
themes.

Ararat
Rozanov, Sergei

The Flute-Player
Elena

The White Hotel
Erdman, Lisa

Thomas, Dylan

◎ (1914–53) Welsh poet. He
worked for a time as a reporter and
established himself with the
publication of *Eighteen Poems* in
1934, in which year he moved to
London, later settling permanently
back in Wales. He spent the war
years working as scriptwriter and
broadcaster for the BBC. From
1944 he worked intermittently on a
radio 'play for voices' about a Welsh
seaside village. It eventually
became *Under Milk Wood* and
was published posthumously
in 1954.

Under Milk Wood
Beynon, Butcher
Beynon, Gossamer
Captain Cat
Dai Bread
Dai Bread One, Mrs
Dai Bread Two, Mrs
Edwards, Mog
Garter, Polly
Jenkins, Rev Eli
Morgan, Mrs Organ
Morgan, Organ
Ogmore-Pritchard, Mrs
Owen, Cherry
Price, Myfanwy
Probert, Rosie
Pugh, Mr
Pugh, Mrs
Smalls, Lily
Waldo, Mr
Watkins, Mr Utah
Watkins, Mrs Utah
Willy-Nilly

Thomas, Leslie

◎ (1931) Welsh writer. He worked
as a newspaper correspondent
until becoming a full-time writer
with the success of his first novel,
the bestselling *The Virgin Soldiers*
(1966).

The Virgin Soldiers
Briggs

Thompson, Flora Jane

◎ (1876–1947) English writer. She
left school at the age of 14, married
young and wrote mass-market
fiction to help support her
increasing family. During her
sixties she published a semi-
autobiographical trilogy, combined
as *Lark Rise to Candleford* (1945). It
is a remarkable feat of observation
and memory, showing the erosion
of rural society before modern
industrialism.

Lark Rise to Candleford
Laura

Thompson, Jim

◎ (1906–77) US pulp novelist. He
was born in Oklahoma and his
experiences of the hardship of the
Depression and the oilfields of
Texas inform his fiction.

The Grifters
Dillon, Lilly
Dillon, Roy
Moira

Thurber, James

◎ (1894–1961) US humorist and
cartoonist. He was editor of *The
New Yorker* from 1927 to 1933. He
then continued as a regular
contributor of humorous essays
and sketches. He is perhaps best
known for his short story, *The
Secret Life of Walter Mitty* (1939).

The Secret Life of Walter Mitty
Mitty, Walter

Tolkien, J(ohn) R(onald) R(euel)

◎ (1892–1973) British philologist
and writer. He was Professor of
Anglo-Saxon (1925–45), and of
English Language and Literature
(1945–59) at Oxford. His scholarly
publications include an edition of
Sir Gawain and the Green Knight
(1925), and studies on *Chaucer*
(1934) and *Beowulf* (1937). His
interest in language and saga and
his fascination for the land of
Faerie prompted him to write tales
of a world of his own invention.
These include *The Hobbit* (1937),
and the more complex sequel, *The
Lord of the Rings* (3 vols, 1954–5).

The Hobbit
Baggins, Bilbo
Gandalf
Gollum
Thorin Oakenshield

The Lord of the Rings
Aragorn, known as Strider
Baggins, Bilbo
Baggins, Frodo
Gamgee, Sam
Gandalf
Gollum

Toole, John Kennedy

◎ (1937–69) US novelist. Eleven
years after his suicide, Toole's
mother showed his only novel *A
Confederacy of Dunces* to the writer
Walker Percy. Widely acclaimed on
its publication in 1980, the novel
won the Pulitzer Prize of that year.

A Confederacy of Dunces
Reilly, Ignatius J

Tourneur, Cyril

◎ (c.1575–1626) English dramatist.
Little is known of his life. He
published several poems, but his
fame rests on two plays, *The
Revenger's Tragedy* (1607), which
many now believe was written by
Thomas Middleton, and the *The
Atheist's Tragedy* (c.1611).

The Atheist's Tragedy
Castabella
Charlemont
D'Amville

Townsend, Sue

◎ (born 1945) English dramatist
and novelist. She has written
several plays but is best known for
her series of books featuring
Adrian Mole, starting with *The
Secret Diary of Adrian Mole, aged
13¾* (1982).

*The Secret Diary of Adrian Mole, aged
13¾*
Mole, Adrian

Index

Travers, P(amela) L(yndon)

◎ (1899–1996) Australian-born writer. Born on a sugar plantation in Queensland, she spent time in Ireland and England as a young woman. She worked as a dancer, actress and journalist, but is best known for her stories about Mary Poppins, the first of which was written while she was recuperating from an illness.

Mary Poppins
Poppins, Mary

Tremain, Rose

◎ (born 1943) English author. Born in London, she studied at the Sorbonne, Paris, and at the University of East Anglia. She has written numerous short stories and several plays for radio but her best-known work is the novel *Restoration* (1989).

Restoration
Merivel, Robert

Tressell, Robert, pseudonym of **Robert Noonan**

◎ (1870–1911) Irish novelist. Born in Dublin, he emigrated to South Africa and settled in England after his wife's death. He is best remembered for his novel, *The Ragged Trousered Philanthropists*, which was eventually published posthumously (1914), and became a classic of the Labour movement.

The Ragged Trousered Philanthropists
Owen, Frank

Trevor, William

◎ (born 1928) Irish short-story writer, novelist and playwright. He taught, sculpted and wrote advertising copy before devoting himself to literature.

'The Ballroom of Romance'
Bridie

The Children of Dynmouth
Gedge, Timothy

Elizabeth Alone
Aidallbery, Elizabeth

Felicia's Journey
Felicia
Hilditch, Joey

Mrs Eckdorf in O'Neill's Hotel
Eckdorf, Mrs Ivy

The Story of Lucy Gault
Gault, Lucy

Trilling, Lionel

◎ (1905–75) US literary critic and author. He became Professor of English at Columbia University in 1948. A trenchant and influential writer, he held that culture was central to the human experience, and that art and literature cannot exist in a vacuum.

The Middle of the Journey
Laskell, John
Maxim, Gifford

'Of This Time, Of That Place'
Blackburn

Howe, Joseph
Tertan

Trollope, Anthony

◎ (1815–82) English novelist. He spent many years in the Civil Service. His first novels were not successful, but with *The Warden* (1855), the first of several Barchester novels, came an inkling of his genius. He also wrote a second, more ambitious sequence known collectively as the 'Palliser' novels.

The American Senator
Gotobed, Elias
Trefoil, Arabella

Barchester Towers
Arabin, Rev Francis
Grantly, Griselda
Grantly, Rev Dr Theophilus
Harding, Eleanor
Harding, Rev Septimus
Neroni, Signora Madeline Vesey
Proudie, Dr Thomas
Proudie, Mrs
Quiverful, Mr
Quiverful, Mrs
Slope, Rev Obadiah

Can You Forgive Her?
Fitzgerald, Burgo
Greenow, Mrs Arabella
Grey, John
Monk, Lady
Omnium, Duke of
Palliser, Lady Glencora, later Duchess of Omnium
Palliser, Plantagenet
Vavasor, Alice

The Claverings
Brabazon, Julia, later Lady Ongar
Burton, Florence
Clavering, Harry
Gordeloup, Sophie
Pateroff, Count Edouard

Dr Thorne
Courcy, Lady Alexandrina de
Courcy, Lady Amelia de
Dunstable, Miss Martha
Gresham, Frank
Proudie, Dr Thomas
Proudie, Mrs
Scatcherd, Sir Louis Philippe
Scatcherd, Sir Roger
Thorne, Dr Thomas
Thorne, Mary

The Duke's Children
Boncassen, Ezekiel
Boncassen, Isabel
Goesler, Marie
Gresham, Mr
Grex, Lady Mabel
Maule, Gerard
Palliser, Adelaide
Palliser, Lady Mary
Palliser, Lord Gerald
Silverbridge, Lord
Tifto, Major
Tregear, Frank (Francis Oliphant)

The Eustace Diamonds
Carruthers, Lord George de Bruce
Chiltern, Lord Oswald Standish
Emilius, Reverend Joseph
Eustace, Lady Lizzie, originally Lizzie Greystock
Eustace, Sir Florian
Fawn, Viscount Frederick
Finn, Phineas

Goesler, Marie
Gresham, Mr
Grey, John
Greystock, Frank
Morris, Lucy
Omnium, Duke of
Palliser, Lady Glencora, later Duchess of Omnium
Vavasor, Alice

Framley Parsonage
Arabin, Rev Francis
Crawley, Grace
Crawley, Mrs
Crawley, Rev Josiah
Dumbello, Lord
Dunstable, Miss Martha
Grantly, Griselda
Grantly, Rev Dr Theophilus
Gresham, Frank
Harding, Eleanor
Harding, Rev Septimus
Lufton, Lady
Lufton, Lord
Proudie, Dr Thomas
Proudie, Mrs
Quiverful, Mr
Quiverful, Mrs
Robarts, Lucy
Robarts, Rev Mark
Sowerby, Nathaniel
Thorne, Dr Thomas
Thorne, Mary

He Knew He Was Right
Bozzle, Samuel
Glascock, Charles, later Lord Peterborough
Osborne, Col Frederic
Petrie, Miss Wallachia
Rowley, Emily
Rowley, Nora
Spalding, Caroline, later Lady Peterborough
Stansbury, Hugh
Stansbury, Jemima, known as Aunt Stansbury
Trevelyan, Louis

The Last Chronicle of Barset
Arabin, Rev Francis
Crawley, Grace
Crawley, Mrs
Crawley, Rev Josiah
Crofts, Dr James
Crosbie, Adolphus
Dale, Bell (Isabella)
Dale, Lily (Lilian)
Demolines, Madalina
Dunstable, Miss Martha
Eames, John
Grantly, Griselda
Grantly, Major Henry
Grantly, Rev Dr Theophilus
Gresham, Frank
Guest, Lady Julia de
Harding, Eleanor
Harding, Rev Septimus
Lufton, Lady
Lufton, Lord
Proudie, Dr Thomas
Proudie, Mrs
Quiverful, Mr
Quiverful, Mrs
Robarts, Lucy
Robarts, Rev Mark
Thorne, Dr Thomas

The Palliser Novels
Vavasor, George

Phineas Finn, The Irish Member
Bonteen, Mr

Chiltern, Lord Oswald Standish
Daubeny, Mr
Effingham, Violet
Finn, Phineas
Flood-Jones, Mary
Goesler, Marie
Gresham, Mr
Grey, John
Kennedy, Laura, née Standish
Kennedy, Robert
Omnium, Duke of
Palliser, Lady Glencora, later Duchess of Omnium
Tulla, Earl of

Phineas Redux
Bonteen, Mr
Chaffanbrass, Mr
Chiltern, Lord Oswald Standish
Daubeny, Mr
Emilius, Reverend Joseph
Eustace, Sir Florian
Fawn, Viscount Frederick
Finn, Phineas
Goesler, Marie
Gresham, Mr
Kennedy, Laura, née Standish
Kennedy, Robert
Maule, Gerard
Omnium, Duke of
Palliser, Adelaide
Palliser, Lady Glencora, later Duchess of Omnium

The Prime Minister
Chiltern, Lord Oswald Standish
Daubeny, Mr
Eustace, Sir Florian
Finn, Phineas
Goesler, Marie
Grey, John
Lopez, Ferdinand
Palliser, Lady Glencora, later Duchess of Omnium
Wharton, Emily

The Small House at Allington
Courcy, Lady Alexandrina de
Courcy, Lady Amelia de
Crofts, Dr James
Crosbie, Adolphus
Dale, Bell (Isabella)
Dale, Lily (Lilian)
Dumbello, Lord
Eames, John
Grantly, Griselda
Grantly, Rev Dr Theophilus
Guest, Lady Julia de
Guest, Lord de
Harding, Rev Septimus

The Vicar of Bullhampton
Brattle, Carry
Brattle, Sam
Fenwick, Rev Frank
Gilmore, Harry
Lowther, Mary
Marrable, Captain Walter
Trowbridge, Marquis of
Trumbull, Farmer

The Warden
Bold, John
Grantly, Griselda
Grantly, Major Henry
Grantly, Rev Dr Theophilus
Harding, Eleanor
Harding, Rev Septimus
Quiverful, Mr

The Way We Live Now
Carbury, Lady Matilda
Carbury, Roger
Carbury, Sir Felix

Fisker, Hamilton K
Melmotte, Augustus
Melmotte, Marie
Nidderdale, Lord

Turner, Ethel

◎ (1872–1958) Australian novelist and children's author. She wrote the children's page for the *Illustrated Sydney News* and *The Bulletin*, under the name 'Dame Durden'. Her first book, *Seven Little Australians* (1894), is now a classic of Australian literature.

The Family at Misrule
General, the, properly Francis Rupert Burnand Woolcot

Seven Little Australians
General, the, properly Francis Rupert Burnand Woolcot
Woolcot, Judy

Turow, Scott

◎ (born 1949) US writer. Born in Chicago, he taught creative writing at Stanford before studying law at Harvard. He still combines a high-profile legal career with writing hugely successful novels which have been translated into over 20 languages.

The Burden of Proof
Sabich, Rusty (Rožat K)
Stern, Alejandro 'Sandy'

Presumed Innocent
Sabich, Rusty (Rožat K)
Stern, Alejandro 'Sandy'

Tutuola, Amos

◎ (1920–97) Nigerian novelist. He worked variously as a farmer, blacksmith, messenger and later for the Nigerian broadcasting company. *The Palm-Wine Drinkard and His Dead Palm-Wine Tapster in the Deads' Town* (1952) is his most popular book, written in a musical pidgin.

The Palm-Wine Drinkard and His Dead Palm-Wine Tapster in the Deads' Town
Drinkard, the Palm-Wine

Twain, Mark, pseudonym of Samuel Langhorne Clemens

◎ (1835–1910) US writer and journalist. He was first a printer, and later a Mississippi riverboat pilot. He edited a newspaper and in 1864 moved to San Francisco as a reporter. In 1867 he visited France, Italy and Palestine. His two greatest masterpieces, *The Adventures of Tom Sawyer* (1876) and *The Adventures of Huckleberry Finn* (1884), are drawn from his own boyhood experiences, and give vivid accounts of life on the Mississippi frontier.

The Adventures of Huckleberry Finn
Finn, Huck (Huckleberry)
Jim
Sawyer, Tom

The Adventures of Tom Sawyer
Finn, Huck (Huckleberry)
Injun Joe
Polly, Aunt

Sawyer, Tom
Thatcher, Becky

The Celebrated Jumping Frog of Calaveras County
Smiley, Jim
Webster, Dan'l

A Connecticut Yankee in King Arthur's Court
Smith, Hank

The Man That Corrupted Hadleyburg
Goodson, Barclay
Halliday, Jack
Richards, Edward and Mary
Stephenson, Howard L

The Prince and the Pauper
Canty, Tom
Edward, Prince, later Edward VI
Hendon, Miles

The Tragedy of Pudd'nhead Wilson
Chambers, properly Valet de Chambre
Driscoll, Judge York Leicester
Driscoll, Percy Northumberland
Driscoll, Tom, properly Thomas à Becket
Roxy (Roxana)
Wilson, David 'Pudd'nhead'

Twain, Mark (*see above*) and Warner, Charles Dudley (*see* Warner, Charles Dudley)

The Gilded Age
Brierly, Henry (Harry)
Dilworthy, Senator Abner
Hawkins, Clay
Hawkins, Laura
Hawkins, Si ('Squire')
Selby, Col George
Sellers, Col Beriah

Tyler, Anne

◎ (born 1941) US novelist and short-story writer. Raised in North Carolina, she has lived in Baltimore, Maryland since 1967. Writing mainly of life in Baltimore or in small Southern towns, and concerned with the themes of loneliness, isolation and human interactions, she has had a productive career and won several literary prizes.

The Accidental Tourist
Leary, Macon

Back When We Were Grownups
Davitch, Rebecca

Breathing Lessons
Moran, Ira
Moran, Jesse
Moran, Maggie

Udall, Nicholas

◎ (1504–56) English dramatist. Edward VI appointed him prebendary of Windsor. He translated Erasmus and selections from the Great Bible but is chiefly remembered as the author of the

Index

comedy *Ralph Roister Doister*, written 1552/3.

Ralph Roister Doister
Custance, Christian
Merygreeke, Mathewe
Roister Doister, Ralph

Updike, John

© (born 1932) US novelist, poet and critic. He worked for *The New Yorker* as a staff journalist and has continued to contribute short stories, poems and book reviews. A hugely prolific writer, he writes about themes that dominated the 20th century: sex, adultery, religion and materialism.

Bech: a Book
Bech, Henry

Bech is Back
Bech, Henry

The Centaur
Caldwell, George
Caldwell, Peter

Couples
Hanema, Piet
Whitman, Foxy

Rabbit at Rest
Angstrom, Janice
Angstrom, Nelson
Rabbit, properly Angstrom, Harry

Rabbit is Rich
Angstrom, Janice
Angstrom, Nelson
Leonard, Ruth
Rabbit, properly Angstrom, Harry

Rabbit Redux
Angstrom, Janice
Angstrom, Nelson
Rabbit, properly Angstrom, Harry

Rabbit Remembered
Angstrom, Janice
Angstrom, Nelson

Rabbit, Run
Angstrom, Janice
Angstrom, Nelson
Leonard, Ruth
Rabbit, properly Angstrom, Harry

The Witches of Eastwick
Rougemont, Sukie
Smart, Jane
Spofford, Alexandra
van Horne, Darryl

Upfield, Arthur

© (1888–1964) Australian writer of detective fiction. Brought up in England, he emigrated to Australia in 1911. He gained recognition with *The Barrakee Mystery* (1931) which introduced the character Detective Inspector Napoleon Bonaparte. He wrote 29 Bonaparte mysteries; an unfinished 30th was completed and published posthumously.

The Barrakee Mystery
Bonaparte, Detective Inspector Napoleon, also known as 'Bony'

Urquhart, Fred

© (1912–95) Scottish short-story writer and novelist. Born in Edinburgh, he worked as bookseller's assistant and

labourer, and later became a publisher's reader and literary editor. He published eleven collections of his short stories as well as novels.

'Alicky's Watch'
Matheson, Alexander

'The Dying Stallion'
Petrie, William

'Elephants, Bairns and Old Men'
Petrie, William

The Ferret Was Abraham's Daughter
Hipkiss, Bessie

Jezebel's Dust
Hipkiss, Bessie

'Maggie Logie and the National Health'
Logie, Maggie

'The Ploughing Match'
Dey, Annie

Vanbrugh, Sir John

© (1664–1726) English playwright and baroque architect. Born in London and educated in France, he suffered imprisonment in the Bastille as a suspected spy. He later became a leading spirit in society life and scored a success with his first comedy, *The Relapse, or Virtue in Danger* (1696). He was also the architect of Castle Howard and Blenheim Palace.

The Confederacy
Amlet, Dick
Amlet, Mrs
Flippanta
Gripe
Gripe, Clarissa
Gripe, Corinna
Moneytrap
Moneytrap, Araminta

The Provok'd Wife
Bellinda
Brute, Lady
Brute, Sir John
Constant
Fanciful, Lady
Heartfree

The Relapse, or Virtue in Danger
Amanda
Berinthia
Clumsey, Sir Tunbelly
Foppington, Lord, previously Sir Novelty Fashion
Hoyden, Miss
Loveless
Worthy
Young Fashion

Van Dine, S S, pseudonym of Willard Huntington Wright

© (1887–1939) US writer of detective fiction. He worked as a literary editor for the *Los Angeles Times* and also wrote for various

magazines and journals. During a long illness he began to write detective fiction under his pseudonym.

The Benson Murder Case
Vance, Philo

Van Vechten, Carl

© (1880–1966) US novelist. Born in Iowa, he was active as a music, dance and drama critic throughout his life. His best-known novels, such as *Nigger Heaven* (1926), deal with New York cultural life in the 1920s.

Nigger Heaven
Kasson, Byron
Love, Mary
Pettijohn, Randolph
Sartoris, Lasca

Peter Whiffle
Whiffle, Peter

Vidal, Gore

© (born 1925) US novelist, essayist and polemicist. He spent much of his childhood in Washington and in 1943 joined the United States Army Reserve Corps. After a period as a television commentator he returned to writing novels, essays and historical fiction.

Burr
Burr, Aaron

The City and the Pillar
Willard, Jim

Julian
Julian, Emperor

Lincoln
Lincoln, Abraham

Myra Breckinridge
Breckinridge, Myra

Villiers, George, 2nd Duke of Buckingham

© (1627–87) English politician and playwright. A Royalist during the Civil War, he went into exile after the Battle of Worcester – later returning secretly to England. At the Restoration he recovered his estates and became a Privy Councillor. He was the author and part-author of several comedies, including *The Rehearsal* (1671), a parody of Dryden's tragedies.

The Rehearsal
Bayes
Drawcansir
Johnson, Ned
Pretty-man, Prince
Smith, Frank
Volscius, Prince

Vizenor, Gerald

© (born 1934) Native American poet and novelist. A member of the Minnesota Chippewa Tribe, he was educated at the University of Minnesota and at Harvard and has held professorships at a number of universities.

Darkness in St Louis Bearheart
Cedarfair, Proude

Vonnegut, Kurt, Jr

◎ (born 1922) US novelist. He served in the US army infantry (1942–55) and was awarded the Purple Heart. During the 1960s he emerged as one of the USA's most influential, potent and provocative writers.

Breakfast of Champions
Hoover, DeWayne
Trout, Kilgore

Cat's Cradle
Bokonon, properly Lionel Boyd Johnson
Hoenikker, Felix

Deadeye Dick
Deadeye Dick, properly Rudolph Waltz
Hoover, DeWayne

God Bless You, Mr Rosewater
Rosewater, Eliot

Jailbird
Starbuck, Walter F

Slaughterhouse 5
Pilgrim, Billy

Wain, John

◎ (1925–94) English critic and novelist. He lectured in English literature at Reading University (1947–55) before becoming a freelance author. His works include novels, poetry, biography, children's books, plays and critical studies.

Hurry On Down
Lumley, Charles

Strike the Father Dead
anon (the jazz musician)

Walcott, Derek

◎ (born 1930) West Indian poet and dramatist. Born in St Lucia, he was educated there and in Jamaica, to both of which he subsequently returned as a teacher. His first poems were published in Trinidad in 1948. He founded the Trinidad Theatre Workshop in 1959, and has written and staged numerous plays. He was awarded the Nobel prize for literature in 1992.

Dream on Monkey Mountain
Hobain, Felix, also known as Makak

Walker, Alice

◎ (born 1944) US writer. Her essay *In Search of Our Mother's Gardens* (1983) is an important rediscovery of a black female literary and cultural tradition. An accomplished poet, she is, however, better known for her novels, especially *The Color Purple* (1982, Pulitzer Prize).

The Color Purple
Avery, Shug
Celie

Nettie
Sofia
Tashi, also known as Evelyn Johnson

Meridian
Held, Truman
Hill, Meridian
Rabinowitz, Lynne

Possessing the Secret of Joy
Tashi, also known as Evelyn Johnson

The Third Life of Grange Copeland
Copeland, Brownfield
Copeland, Grange
Ruth

Wallace, Lew

◎ (1827–1905) US writer and soldier. He served in the Mexican War (1846–8) and in the Federal army in the US Civil War (1861–5). He was the author of several novels, including the very succesful *Ben Hur* (1880).

Ben Hur
Ben Hur

Walpole, Horace

◎ (1717–97) English writer. Educated at Eton and Cambridge, he undertook the Grand Tour with the poet Thomas Gray. Returning to England in 1741, he became an MP. He wrote essays and verse. His Gothic novel *The Castle of Otranto* (1764) set the fashion for supernatural romance. He is also remembered for his letters, which deal with party politics, foreign affairs, art, literature and gossip.

The Castle of Otranto
Conrad
Frederic of Vicenza
Friar Jerome
Hippolita
Isabella of Vicenza
Manfred, Prince of Otranto
Matilda
Theodore

Walpole, Sir Hugh

◎ (1884–1941) English novelist. Born in New Zealand and educated at Cambridge, he became a teacher, then an author. He wrote prolifically and his books were enormously popular during his lifetime.

Judith Paris
Paris, Judith

Mr Perrin and Mr Traill
Perrin, Mr Vincent
Traill, Mr

Rogue Herries
Herries, Rogue

Ward, Mrs Humphry

◎ (1851–1920) English novelist. She was born in Hobart, Tasmania and became secretary to Somerville College, Oxford (1879), before moving to London in 1881, where she wrote for various periodicals. Her novels are all on social or religious issues.

Robert Elsmere
Elsmere, Robert
Leyburn, Catherine
Wendover, Squire Roger

Warner, Alan

◎ (born 1964) Scottish novelist. He has won various literary awards and has been nominated as one of 20 'Best of Young British Novelists' by *Granta* magazine. He now lives in Ireland. His works include *Morvern Callar* (1995).

Morvern Callar
Callar, Morvern

Warner, Charles Dudley

◎ (1829–1900) US writer. He practised law in Chicago and later settled as an editor in Hartford. In 1884 he became co-editor of *Harper's Magazine*. He is best known for his collaboration with **Mark Twain** (*see* **Twain, Mark** and **Warner, Charles Dudley**).

Warner, Sylvia Townsend

◎ (1893–1978) English novelist. She published novels, poetry, essays and eight volumes of short stories, many of which had previously appeared in *The New Yorker*.

Lolly Willowes
Willowes, Lolly (Laura Erminia)

Mr Fortune's Maggot
Fortune, Timothy

The True Heart
Bond, Sukey

Warren, Robert Penn

◎ (1905–89) US novelist and poet. A professor at various universities, including Yale, he established an international reputation with his Pulitzer Prize-winning political novel about the governor of a Southern state, *All the King's Men* (1946).

All the King's Men
Burden, Jack
Mastern, Cass
Stanton, Anne
Stark, Willie

Waterhouse, Keith

◎ (born 1929) English novelist, dramatist, humorist and journalist. Born in Leeds, he first came to critical and popular attention with *Billy Liar* (1959), a whimsical novel about a working-class dreamer. The following year it became the basis of a successful play.

Billy Liar
Liar, Billy, properly Billy Fisher

Waters, Sarah

◎ (born 1966) Welsh novelist. She was inspired to write her first novel, *Tipping the Velvet* (1998), while completing her PhD thesis on lesbian historical fiction. She has won numerous awards for her subsequent novels *Affinity* (1999) and *Fingersmith* (2002).

Affinity
Dawes, Selina
Prior, Margaret

Index

Fingersmith
Lilly, Maud
Trinder, Sue

Tipping the Velvet
Astley, Nancy
Butler, Kitty

Waugh, Evelyn

◎ (1903–66) English writer. *Decline and Fall* (1928) was his first and immoderately successful novel. During the war he published four books, including *Brideshead Revisited* (1945). He was revered as a wit and a stylist and one of the 20th century's greatest comic novelists.

Brideshead Revisited
Blanche, Anthony
Brideshead, Lord ('Bridey')
Flyte, Cordelia
Flyte, Julia
Flyte, Sebastian
Hawkins, Nanny
Marchmain, Lady Teresa
Marchmain, Lord
Mottram, Rex
Mulcaster, Boy
Ryder, Charles
Samgrass, Mr

Decline and Fall
Beste-Chetwynde, Margot
Beste-Chetwynde, Peter
Fagan, Dr Augustus
Grimes, Captain
Pennyfeather, Paul

A Handful Of Dust
Beaver, John
Last, Lady Brenda
Last, Tony
Todd, Mr

Helena
Helena

The Ordeal of Gilbert Pinfold
Pinfold, Gilbert

Scoop
Boot, William

Sword of Honour
Apthorpe
Blackhouse, Tommy
Crouchback, Guy
Ritchie-Hook, Brigadier
Trimmer
Troy, Virginia

Webb, Mary

◎ (1881–1927) English writer. She lived mostly in Shropshire, market-gardening and novel-writing. *Precious Bane* (1924) won her belated fame as a novelist of Shropshire country life.

Precious Bane
Beguildy, Jancis
Beguildy, Wizard
Sarn, Gideon
Sarn, Prue
Woodseaves, Kester

Webster, John

◎ (c.1580–c.1625) English dramatist. He was the collaborator of **Thomas Dekker**, **John Ford** and others, and in 1604 he made some additions to *The Malcontent* of **John Marston**. He is best known,

however, for his two tragedies, *The White Devil* (1612) and *The Duchess of Malfi* (1623).

The Duchess of Malfi
Antonio Bologna
Bosola, Daniel de
Cardinal, the
Ferdinand, Duke of Calabria
Malfi, Duchess of

The White Devil
Brachiano, Duke of
Camillo
Cornelia
Flamineo
Francisco de Medicis
Isabella
Marcello
Vittoria Corombona

Weldon, Fay

◎ (born 1931) English novelist, television screenplay writer and polemicist. Born in Worcestershire, she was brought up in New Zealand but returned to England as a child. She became a successful advertising copywriter before publishing her first novel, *The Fat Woman's Joke* (1967). Her recurring themes include the nature of women's sexuality and experience in a patriarchal world.

The Cloning of Joanna May
May, Joanna

Down among the Women
Helen
Jocelyn
Scarlet
Wanda

The Fat Woman's Joke
Sussman, Esther

The Heart of the Country
Harris, Natalie
Sonia

The Life and Loves of a She-Devil
Fisher, Mary
Ruth

Praxis
Duveen, Praxis

Puffball
Liffey
Mabs

Wells, H(erbert) G(eorge)

◎ (1866–1946) English novelist, short-story writer and popular historian. He studied biology and then lectured until eventually concentrating full-time on writing. He threw himself into contemporary issues and achieved fame as a novelist with *The Time Machine* (1895), which pioneered English science fiction. He also wrote comic novels.

Ann Veronica
Ann Veronica

The History of Mr Polly
Polly, Alfred

The Invisible Man
Invisible Man, the, previously Griffin

The Island of Doctor Moreau
Moreau, Doctor

Kipps
Kipps, Arthur

Love and Mr Lewisham
Lewisham, George

Mr Britling Sees It Through
Britling, Mr

The Time Machine
Eloi
Morlocks

Tono-Bungay
Ponderevo, Teddy (Edward)

The World of William Clissold
Clissold, William

Welsh, Irvine

◎ (born 1961) Scottish writer. Born in Leith, he spent several years in London exploring the drugs and punk rock scenes before returning to Scotland in the late 1980s and starting to write. He acquired cult status with the novel *Trainspotting* (1993).

Porno
Begbie, Francis
Renton, Mark (Rent Boy)
'Sick-Boy' Williamson, Simon David
'Spud' Murphy, Daniel

Trainspotting
Begbie, Francis
Renton, Mark (Rent Boy)
'Sick-Boy' Williamson, Simon David
'Spud' Murphy, Daniel

Welty, Eudora

◎ (1909–2001) US novelist and short-story writer. She was born in Mississippi. During World War II she was on the staff of *The New York Review of Books*. She started writing short stories and published several collections. She wrote five novels, mostly drawn from Mississippi life, and received many awards, including the Pulitzer Prize and the National Medal for Literature.

Delta Wedding
Fairchild, Battle
Fairchild, Dabney
Fairchild, Ellen
Fairchild, George
Flavin, Troy
McRaven, Laura

The Golden Apples
Rainey, Virgie

'June Recital'
Eckhart, Miss
Morrison, Cassie
Morrison, Loch

Losing Battles
Hand, Laurel McKelva
McKelva, Wanda Fay
Moody, Judge Oscar
Mortimer, Julia
Renfro, Beulah (Beecham)
Renfro, Jack
Vaughn, Granny (Elvira Jordan)

The Optimist's Daughter
McKelva, Judge

The Ponder Heart
Ponder, Daniel
Ponder, Edna Earle

The Robber Bridegroom
Fink, Mike
Lockhart, Jamie
Musgrove, Clement
Musgrove, Rosamond
Musgrove, Salome

'The Wanderers'
Eckhart, Miss
MacLain, King

Wentworth, Patricia, pseudonym of **Dora Amy Elles**
◎ (1878–1961) Indian-born English writer of detective fiction. She wrote over 70 crime novels, almost half of which feature her most famous heroine, spinster and amateur detective Miss Maude Silver.

Pilgrim's Rest
Silver, Miss Maude

Wescott, Glenway
◎ (1901–87) US novelist. He lived in France in the 1920s. His most successful novel, *The Grandmothers* (1927), is a portrait of frontier life in his home state of Wisconsin.

The Grandmothers
Tower, Alwyn

Wesker, Arnold
◎ (born 1932) English dramatist. He was born in London's East End, of Jewish immigrant parents, and his family background is an important ingredient of such plays as the Kahn family trilogy, beginning with *Chicken Soup with Barley* (1957).

Chicken Soup with Barley
Kahn, Ada, Harry, Ronnie, and Sarah
I'm Talking About Jerusalem
Kahn, Ada, Harry, Ronnie, and Sarah
Roots
Bryant, Beatie

Wesley, Mary, pseudonym of **Mary Aline Siepmann**
◎ (1912–2002) English novelist. She wrote two children's books before publishing her first adult novel at the age of 70. She subsequently produced a succession of popular books dealing with middle-class mores.

Jumping the Queue
Poliport, Matilda
The Vacillations of Poppy Carew
Carew, Poppy

West, Morris
◎ (1916–99) Australian novelist and playwright. He trained for the priesthood but left before taking vows. His works include such prize-winning novels as *The Shoes of the Fisherman* (1963). He also dramatized several of his works.

The Shoes of the Fisherman
Lakota, Kyril

West, Nathanael, pseudonym of **Nathan Wallenstein Weinstein**
◎ (1903–40) US novelist. He lived in Paris for a few years before returning to New York, where he worked in journalism. He went to Hollywood in 1935 to write scripts for a minor studio, using this experience for *The Day of the Locust* (1939).

A Cool Million: The Dismantling of Lemuel Pitkin
Pitkin, Lemuel
The Day of the Locust
Greener, Faye
Hackett, Tod
Miguel
Shoop, Earle
Simpson, Homer
The Dream Life of Balso Snell
Snell, Balso
Miss Lonelyhearts
Lonelyhearts, Miss

West, Rebecca, pseudonym of **Cecily Isabel Andrews**
◎ (1892–1983) Irish-born novelist, journalist and critic. She trained for the stage in London, where she became involved with the suffragettes and the left-wing press. She later worked in journalism in the US and made several trips to the Balkans. She published eight novels.

The Bird Falls Down
Rowan, Laura
The Fountain Overflows
Aubrey, Rose
Harriet Hume
Condorex, Arnold
Hume, Harriet
The Judge
Melville, Ellen
Yaverland, Marion
Yaverland, Richard
The Return of the Soldier
Allington, Margaret
Baldry, Captain Chris
Baldry, Kitty
Jenny
The Thinking Reed
Terry, Isabelle

Wharton, Edith
◎ (c.1861–1937). US novelist and short-story writer. She was educated at home and in Europe and settled in Paris in 1907. *The House of Mirth* (1905) established her as a major novelist. She published almost 50 works, including travel books and volumes of verse, but she is known principally as a novelist of manners.

The Age of Innocence
Archer, Newland
Mingott, Mrs Manson
Olenska, Ellen
Welland, May
The Custom of the Country
Marvell, Ralph
Moffat, Elmer
Spragg, Undine
Ethan Frome
Frome, Ethan
Frome, Zeena
Silver, Mattie
The Gods Arrive
Weston, Vance
The House of Mirth
Bart, Lily
Selden, Lawrence
Trenor, Gus
Hudson River Bracketed
Weston, Vance

Summer
Royall, Charity

White, Antonia
◎ (1899–1979) English novelist, journalist and translator. She spent much of her life struggling with religious faith, mental illness and her complex relationship with her father. Many of these themes are found in her novels.

Beyond the Glass
Grey, Nanda, later Clara Batchelor
Frost in May
Grey, Nanda, later Clara Batchelor
The Lost Traveller
Grey, Nanda, later Clara Batchelor
The Sugar House
Grey, Nanda, later Clara Batchelor

White, E(lwyn) B(rooks)
◎ (1899–1985) US essayist, children's novelist, poet and parodist. His long association with *The New Yorker* began in 1925. His reputation rests on his bestselling novels for children, in particular *Charlotte's Web* (1952).

Charlotte's Web
Charlotte

White, Patrick
◎ (1912–90) Australian novelist. He went to Cambridge and after war service in the RAF he wrote several novels before settling in Australia. He achieved international success with *The Tree of Man* (1955). He was awarded the Nobel prize for literature in 1973.

The Eye of the Storm
Hunter, Elizabeth
A Fringe of Leaves
Chance, Jack
Roxburgh, Austin
Roxburgh, Ellen
The Living and the Dead
Standish, Eden
Standish, Elyot
Riders in the Chariot
Dubbo, Alf
Flack, Mrs
Godbold, Ruth
Hare, Mary
Himmelfarb, Mordecai
Jolley, Mrs
Rosetree, Harry
The Solid Mandala
Brown, Arthur
Brown, Waldo
Feinstein, Dulcie
Poulter, Mrs
The Tree of Man
Parker, Amy
Parker, Stan
The Twyborn Affair
Trist, Eadith
Twyborn, Eadie
Twyborn, Eddie
Twyborn, Justice
Vatatzes, Eudoxia
The Vivisector
Caldicott, Maurice
Courtney, Alfreda
Courtney, Rhoda

Duffield, Hurtle
Hollingrake, Boo, later Mrs Lopez and
  Olivia Davenport
Lightfoot, Nance
Pavloussi, Hero
Volkov, Kathy

Voss
Trevelyan, Laura
Voss, Johann Ulrich

White, T(erence) H(anbury)

◎ (1906–64) English novelist. He
wrote more than 25 books,
including science fiction, but he is
best known for his interpretation
of the Arthurian legend, a
tetralogy known collectively as *The
Once and Future King* (1958), the
first part of which, *The Sword in the
Stone* (1937), is a children's classic.

The Sword in the Stone
Merlin

Whitman, Walt

◎ (1819–92) US poet. Born in Long
Island, he worked variously as an
itinerant teacher and in journalism
and also spent time working as a
volunteer nurse in the army
hospitals of the US Civil War. His
masterpiece *Leaves of Grass* was
originally a small, twelve-poem
volume, which grew in the eight
succeeding editions (until 1891) to
nearly 440 pages.

Leaves of Grass
Whitman, Walt

Whittier, John Greenleaf

◎ (1807–92) US Quaker poet and
abolitionist. Born in
Massachusetts, he was largely self-
educated. In 1829 he entered
journalism, and in 1831 published
Legends of New England, a
collection of poems and stories.

'Barbara Frietchie'
Frietchie, Barbara

'Skipper Ireson's Ride'
Ireson, Floyd

Wiggin, Kate Douglas

◎ (1856–1953) US novelist. Born in
Philadelphia, she moved to San
Francisco to organize the first free
kindergarten school in the West
(1878). She wrote novels for both
adults and children, but was more
successful with the latter.

Rebecca of Sunnybrook Farm
Randall, Rebecca

Wilde, Oscar

◎ (1854–1900) Irish playwright,
novelist, essayist, poet and wit. An
accomplished classicist at Oxford
University and a renowned dandy
and wit, he wrote the classic
children's fairy stories *The Happy
Prince and Other Tales* (1888) for his
children. He wrote one novel, *The
Picture of Dorian Gray* (1891) and
built his dramatic reputation with
plays such as *Lady Windermere's Fan*
(1892) and his masterpiece, *The
Importance of Being Earnest* (1895).

In 1895 he was imprisoned for
homosexuality. On his release he
travelled on the Continent and
died in Paris.

'The Happy Prince'
Happy Prince, the

An Ideal Husband
Chiltern, Sir Robert
Goring, Lord Arthur

The Importance of Being Earnest
Bracknell, Lady
Cardew, Cecily
Gwendoline
Moncrieff, Algernon
Prism, Miss
Worthing, John

Lady Windermere's Fan
Erlynne, Mrs
Windermere, Lady

Lord Arthur Savile's Crime
Savile, Lord Arthur

The Picture of Dorian Gray
Gray, Dorian
Wooton, Lord Henry

A Woman of No Importance
Arbuthnot, Mrs Rachel

Wilder, Thornton

◎ (1897–1975) US writer and
playwright. He was educated at
Yale, served in both wars and
taught at the University of Chicago.
His works include the novel *The
Bridge of San Luis Rey* (1927,
Pulitzer Prize) and the plays *Our
Town* (1938, Pulitzer Prize) and *The
Skin of Our Teeth* (1942, Pulitzer
Prize).

The Bridge of San Luis Rey
Esteban
Jaime, Don
Juniper, Brother
Manuel
Marquesa de Montemayor, the (Doña
  Maria)
Pepita
Perichole, La (Camila)
Pio, Uncle

The Ides of March
Caesar, Caius Julius

Our Town
Gibbs, George
Gibbs, Mrs
Webb, Emily

The Skin of Our Teeth
Antrobus, George
Antrobus, Henry
Antrobus, Mrs
Sabina, Lily

Willeford, Charles

◎ (1919–88) US crime-story writer.
He went on the road as a teenager
during the Depression. He had a
20-year military career and was
decorated for his service during
World War II. Although he had
written numerous novels and was
teaching at the University of
Miami, he did not achieve fame
until the publication of *Miami
Blues*, the first of the Hoke Moseley
novels, in 1984.

Miami Blues
Moseley, Hoke

Williams, Tennessee

◎ (1911–83) US playwright. Born in
Mississippi, he worked at various
menial jobs. *The Glass Menagerie*
(1945) earned him the New York
Drama Critics' Circle Award and
introduced him as an important US
playwright. He was awarded the
Pulitzer Prize in 1948 for *A Streetcar
Named Desire* (1947), and again in
1955 for *Cat on a Hot Tin Roof* (1955).

A Streetcar Named Desire
DuBois, Blanche
Kowalski, Stanley
Kowalski, Stella
Mitch, properly Harold Mitchell

Cat on a Hot Tin Roof
Pollitt, Big Daddy
Pollitt, Big Mama
Pollitt, Brick
Pollitt, Gooper
Pollitt, Mae
Pollitt, Maggie 'the Cat'

The Glass Menagerie
O'Connor, Jim
Wingfield, Amanda
Wingfield, Laura
Wingfield, Tom

The Night of the Iguana
Faulk, Maxine
Jelkes, Hannah
Nonno (Jonathan Coffin)
Shannon, Larry (Lawrence)

The Rose Tattoo
Rose, Serafina delle

Suddenly Last Summer
Venable, Violet

Sweet Bird of Youth
Finley, Boss
'Kosmonopolis, the Princess'
Wayne, Chance

Williams, William Carlos

◎ (1883–1963) US poet and novelist.
He was born in Connecticut and
educated in Europe. **Ezra Pound**
had a considerable impact on his
developing interest in poetry. His
early volumes steered him towards
the simple free-verse idiom, with its
focus on immediate physical detail,
which would characterize his work.

Paterson
Paterson

Williamson, David

◎ (born 1942) Australian
playwright and scriptwriter. Born
in Melbourne, he graduated in
mechanical engineering but turned
to writing plays and scripts for
films and television. Some of his
stage works have subsequently
been filmed, and he has also
written other film scripts,
including *Gallipoli* (1981).

Don's Party
Don

Williamson, Henry

◎ (1895–1977) English writer.
After service in World War I he
became a journalist, but turned to
farming in Norfolk and eventually
settled on Exmoor. He wrote
several semi-autobiographical

novels, but he is best known for his classic nature stories, especially *Tarka the Otter* (1927, Hawthornden Prize).

A Chronicle of Ancient Sunlight
Maddison, Philip

A Patriot's Progress
Bullock, John

Salar the Salmon
Salar

Tarka the Otter
Tarka

Wilson, A(ndrew) N(orman)
◎ (born 1950) English novelist, biographer, critic and journalist. He is a prolific writer and while many of his earlier novels were comedies of manners, works such as *The Healing Art* (1980) and *Wise Virgin* (1982) deal with specific moral issues.

The Healing Art
Cowper, Pamela
Higgs, Dorothy

The Sweets of Pimlico
Gormann, Theo
Tradescant, Evelyn

Who Was Oswald Fish?
Fish, Oswald

Wise Virgin
Agar, Louise
Fox, Giles
Fox, Tibba

Wilson, Angus
◎ (1913–91) English writer. He worked in the British Museum Library in London and began writing in 1946. The novels *Hemlock and After* (1952) and *Anglo-Saxon Attitudes* (1956) were both bestsellers, and his later novels also received critical acclaim.

Anglo-Saxon Attitudes
Middleton, Gerald

As If By Magic
Grant, Alexandra
Langmuir, Hamo

Hemlock and After
Sands, Bernard

Late Call
Calvert, Harold
Calvert, Sylvia

The Middle Age of Mrs Eliot
Eliot, Meg

No Laughing Matter
Matthews, Clara, also known as the Countess
Matthews, Gladys
Matthews, Granny
Matthews, Marcus
Matthews, Margaret
Matthews, Quentin
Matthews, Rupert
Matthews, Sukey
Matthews, William, also known as Billy Pop
Regan, properly Henrietta Stoker
Rickard, Miss ('Mouse')

Wilson, Ethel
◎ (1888–1980) Canadian novelist and short-story writer. Born in South Africa, she spent some time in England before moving to Canada, where she was educated.

Hetty Dorval
Burnaby, Frankie
Dorval, Hetty

The Innocent Traveller
Edgeworth, Topaz

Swamp Angel
Severance, Nell
Vardoe/Lloyd, Maggie

Wilson, Jacqueline
◎ (born 1945) English children's writer. Since her breakthrough novel *The Story of Tracy Beaker* (1991), she has written almost 70 hugely successful books for children, often dealing with gritty subjects such as death, divorce and bullying.

The Dare Game
Beaker, Tracy

The Story of Tracy Beaker
Beaker, Tracy

Winterson, Jeanette
◎ (born 1959) English writer. Her first novel, *Oranges Are Not the Only Fruit* (1985), drew heavily on her own upbringing as the adopted daughter of Pentecostal evangelist parents and won the Whitbread Prize. Further novels include *Sexing the Cherry* (1989) and *The.PowerBook* (2000). She has also published essays, short stories and a children's book.

Oranges are Not the Only Fruit
Jeanette

The Passion
Henri
Villanelle

The.PowerBook
Ali(x)

Sexing the Cherry
Dog-Woman, the
Jordan

Wister, Owen
◎ (1860–1938) US writer. He took a music degree at Harvard and intended to become a composer, but won fame with his novel of cowboy life in Wyoming, *The Virginian* (1902).

The Virginian
Trampas
Virginian, the
Wood, Molly Stark

Wodehouse, P(elham) G(renville)
◎ (1881–1975) English novelist. He worked for the Hong Kong and Shanghai Bank for two years before beginning to earn a living as a journalist and story writer. He became a US citizen in 1955. His many works include librettos and over 100 books, and he is best known as the creator of Bertie Wooster and his legendary valet, Jeeves.

Blandings Castle
Emsworth, Lord

Carry On, Jeeves
Dahlia, Aunt

The Inimitable Jeeves
Jeeves
Wooster, Bertie

Leave it to Psmith
Psmith

Psmith in the City
Psmith

Psmith Journalist
Psmith

Right Ho, Jeeves
Fink-Nottle, Gussie (Augustus)

Wolfe, Thomas
◎ (1900–38) US novelist. He was born in North Carolina. After an abortive start as a playwright, his first novel was *Look Homeward, Angel* (1929). *The Web and the Rock* (1939) and *You Can't Go Home Again* (1940) were published posthumously.

Look Homeward, Angel
Gant, Ben
Gant, Eliza
Gant, Eugene
Gant, Oliver

Of Time and the River
Gant, Eugene
Jack, Esther
Pierce, Joel

The Web and the Rock
Jack, Esther
Webber, George

You Can't Go Home Again
Edwards, Foxhall
Jack, Esther
McFarg, Lloyd
Webber, George

Wolfe, Tom
◎ (born 1931) US journalist, critic and novelist. He received his doctorate in American Studies from Yale University and later he worked as a reporter. Much of his work has appeared in periodicals such as *Rolling Stone*, as did his bestselling first novel, *The Bonfire of the Vanities* (1987).

The Bonfire of the Vanities
Fallow, Peter
Kramer, Larry
McCoy, Sherman

A Man in Full
Croker, Charlie
Hensley, Conrad
White II, Roger

Wood, Mrs Henry
◎ (1814–87) English novelist. She suffered a spinal disease which confined her to bed or a sofa for most of her life. Her second published novel, *East Lynne* (1861), was an immense success.

East Lynne
Vane, Lady Isobel

Woolf, Virginia
◎ (1882–1941) English novelist, critic and essayist. She was a member of the Bloomsbury Group of philosophers, writers and artists. In 1917 she and her husband Leonard Woolf formed the Hogarth

Index

Press. Regarded as a major figure in the Modernist movement, she made a significant contribution to the development of the novel.

Between the Acts
La Trobe, Miss
Swithin, Mrs

Flush
Flush

Jacob's Room
Flanders, Jacob

Mrs Dalloway
Dalloway, Clarissa
Dalloway, Richard
Seton, Sally
Walsh, Peter

Night and Day
Datchet, Mary
Denham, Ralph
Hilbery, Katharine
Rodney, William

Orlando
Orlando

To the Lighthouse
Briscoe, Lily
Carmichael, Augustus
Ramsay, Mr
Ramsay, Mrs

The Voyage Out
Ambrose, Helen
Dalloway, Clarissa
Dalloway, Richard
Hewet, Terence
Hirst, St John
Vinrace, Rachel

The Waves
Jinny
Louis
Neville
Percival
Susan

The Years
Pargiter, Col
Pargiter, Mrs

Wordsworth, William

◎ (1770–1850) English poet. After travelling on the Continent, he spent much of his life in the Lake District. With **Samuel Taylor Coleridge**, he published *Lyrical Ballads* (1798), the first manifesto of the new Romantic poetry. He became Poet Laureate in 1843.

'Alice Fell; or Poverty'
Fell, Alice

'The Brothers'
Ewbank, James and Leonard

'The Female Vagrant'
Female Vagrant, the

'Guilt and Sorrow; or, Incidents upon Salisbury Plain'
Female Vagrant, the

'The Idiot Boy'
Foy, Johnny

'Laodamia'
Laodamia

'Michael, A Pastoral Poem'
Michael

Peter Bell
Bell, Peter

'Ruth'
Ruth

'Simon Lee, the Old Huntsman'
Lee, Simon

'The Thorn'
Ray, Martha

The Waggoner
Benjamin

Wouk, Herman

◎ (born 1915) US novelist. Born in New York City, the son of Jewish immigrants, he served in the US navy in the South Pacific in World War II, the experience of which he drew on for his classic war novel, *The Caine Mutiny* (1951). It won the Pulitzer Prize and became a successful play and film.

The Caine Mutiny
Greenwald, Barney
Keefer, Tom
Keith, Willie
Maryk, Lt Steve
Queeg, Captain
Wynn, May

War and Remembrance
Pug, properly Victor Henry

The Winds of War
Pug, properly Victor Henry

Wren, P(ercival) C(hristopher)

◎ (1885–1941) English novelist. He was successively a teacher, journalist, explorer and soldier in the French Foreign Legion, which provided him with the background for *Beau Geste* (1924), the first and best of his romantic adventure novels.

Beau Geste
Beau Geste

Wright, Richard

◎ (1908–60) US novelist, short-story writer and critic. Born on a plantation in Mississippi, the grandson of slaves, he left the South during the Depression and became a journalist. *Native Son* (1940) became a central – albeit problematic – work in the development of a black literary sensibility.

Native Son
Thomas, Bigger

Wrightson, Patricia

◎ (born 1921) Australian children's writer. She was born in rural New South Wales and started writing for her own children. She has won numerous literary awards for her books which regularly feature Aboriginal culture and myth and her concern for the environment.

Behind the Wind
Wirrun

The Dark Bright Water
Wirrun

The Ice is Coming
Wirrun

Wycherley, William

◎ (c.1640–1716) English dramatist. *The Country Wife* (1675), Wycherley's coarsest but strongest play, and *The Plain Dealer* (1676/7), were both based on plays by Molière. They are unaffectionate portrayals of contemporary sexual mores and the conventions of marriage.

The Country Wife
Althea
Harcourt
Horner
Lucy
Pinchwife, Margery
Pinchwife, Mr
Sparkish

The Plain Dealer
Blackacre, Jerry
Fidelia
Manly
Olivia
Vernish
Widow Blackacre, the

Wyndham, John

◎ (1903–69) English science-fiction writer. As a child he was fascinated by the stories of **H G Wells**, and in the late 1920s began to write science-fiction tales for popular magazines. In 1951 he published his most successful novel, *The Day of the Triffids*.

The Chrysalids
Chrysalids

The Day of the Triffids
Triffids

The Kraken Wakes
Bathies

The Midwich Cuckoos
Midwich Cuckoos

Yeats, W(illiam) B(utler)

◎ (1865–1939) Irish poet. He was born in Dublin, the son of an artist, and was interested in mysticism, the occult and Irish myth, the latter of which is the source for much of his poetry. Having spent some time in England, he returned to Ireland and founded the Irish National Theatre with Lady Gregory. He became a member of the Irish senate in 1922, on the foundation of the Irish Free State. He was awarded the Nobel prize for literature in 1923.

'An Irish Airman Foresees His Death'
Irish Airman, the

'Cuchulain's Fight with the Sea'
Cuchulain

The Death of Cuchulain
Cuchulain

Last Poems
Crazy Jane

The Old Age of Queen Maeve
Maeve, Queen

The Wanderings of Oisin
Oisin

Words for Music Perhaps
Crazy Jane